Fine Hand Quilting

Diana Leone
&
Cindy Walter

Published by

Krause Publications
700 East State St., Iola, WI 54990-0001
Telephone 715-445-2214
www.krause.com

Please call or write for our free catalog of publications. Our toll-free number to place an order or obtain a free catalog is 800-258-0929 or please use our regular business telephone 715-445-2214 for editorial comment and further information.

Library of Congress Catalog Number 99-66142
ISBN 0-87341-835-2

Most photos in this book:
Richard Johns, San Jose, CA
Ross Hubbard and Kris Kandler, Krause Publications, Iola, WI

Table of Contents

From the Authors

Diana Leone (left) and Cindy Walter (right)

From Diana:

Cindy came to me excitedly one day and said, "I have a great idea... Krause is my new publisher for *Snippet Sensations* and they are interested in any other quilting-type books that I would write for their publishing company. How about you and I revising two of your older books, *Attic Windows* and *Fine Hand Quilting*?" I had recently retired from being a quilt shop owner and was really looking forward to "retirement." As a fabric designer, lecturer, judge, author, and until recently a shop-owner, I thought I was through with the writing stage of my life. But, Cindy had a good idea. No other book had been written to replace the original classic *Fine Hand Quilting* (shown below), so why not revise and update the book that had become the standard on hand quilting? So, I said, "yes," to Cindy, "as long as you do all of the work." So once again, with enjoyment, Cindy and I bring you another great book. My thanks to Cindy for "doing all the work" and to Krause for its professionalism on all accounts. *Fine Hand Quilting* remains the best book available for all quilters world-wide. Enjoy it and keep on quilting.

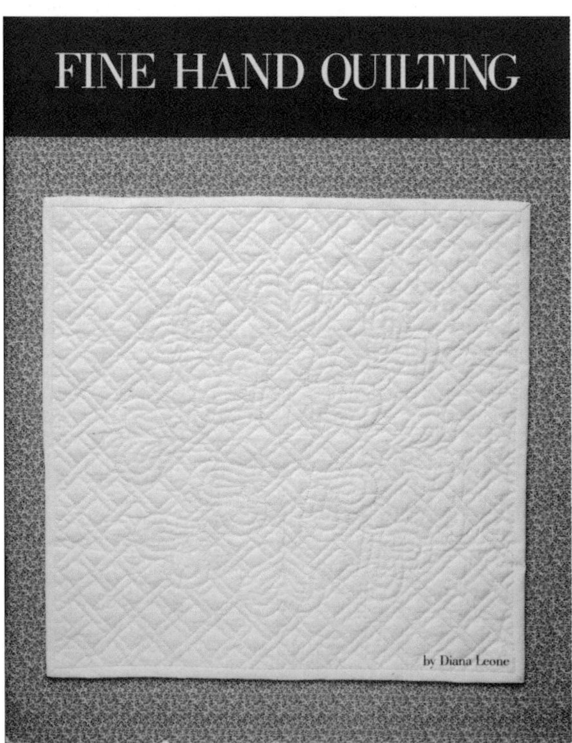

When Cindy and I began, we knew the first step would be to investigate and test all of the new products, notions, and materials available today. The manufacturers were most helpful in updating our information and were generous in providing us samples to test and photograph. We found the information in the original text was sound and true; the traditional techniques and tools have withstood the test of time. The second step was to add the new quilts and the section "How to Quilt This Quilt." "Tips from the Pros" is another exciting addition. As a final bonus, we provide three beginner projects.

My thanks to my family and friends who have contributed their time, patience, and the lending of their great quilts, all of which has made this new and colorful book become an important part of everyone's quilting library. I am proud to have been, and continue to be, an influence on your quilting heritage. Carry it on, share your work, and teach others to quilt, especially children.

Diana Leone

From Cindy:

When I first asked Diana if she was interested in rewriting *Fine Hand Quilting*, she answered "yes" so quickly that I thought she was joking. But, I certainly wasn't when I replied, "I'll do it." I knew, as did Diana, that the original book was the compendium on hand quilting and could not be replaced by anyone else. The book needed to become available again. Diana was very clear right from the beginning that she was "retired," and didn't plan to do "any" of the work. You have to understand that "retired" to Diana means designing fabric lines, creating quilt exhibits, teaching around the world, spending time with her family, and building a new home. I have always revered Diana as a "Matriarch of Quilting" in the United States, so it was an honor for me to be involved with her and this book, and I was willing to do any amount of work. We needed to rewrite and update the text to include the new tools on the market, refine techniques, and to include the addition of contemporary quilting techniques. Also, because the original photographs were black and white, it also meant shooting all new color photography.

As the author of *Snippet Sensations* (shown below), most people believe I am only interested in contemporary quilts, but this isn't the case. I come from a long line of quilters and truly love every aspect of the art. I have been teaching traditional quilting techniques, and hand quilting, for more than a decade. There are several good hand quilting books on the market, but none of these approach the topic as I do with my students and as thoroughly as Diana taught in the original *Fine Hand Quilting* book. What an exciting concept to combine the thoughts of two quilters from different generations. Not only will our readers learn from our book, it was a learning adventure for both of us. We are in agreement about the concept of the book: We do not want to preach to you about "right and wrong" tools or techniques; we want to tell you about the techniques and tools we have both discovered and used successfully for years.

I would like to thank my family and friends for their continued support. The manufacturers in our industry were wonderful and helpful; not only did they generously give us products to test, they supplied us with valuable and current information.

A huge hug and thank you to Diana for allowing me to be part of this adventure. We truly hope you have fun and enjoy this all-new edition of *Fine Hand Quilting*.

Cindy Walter

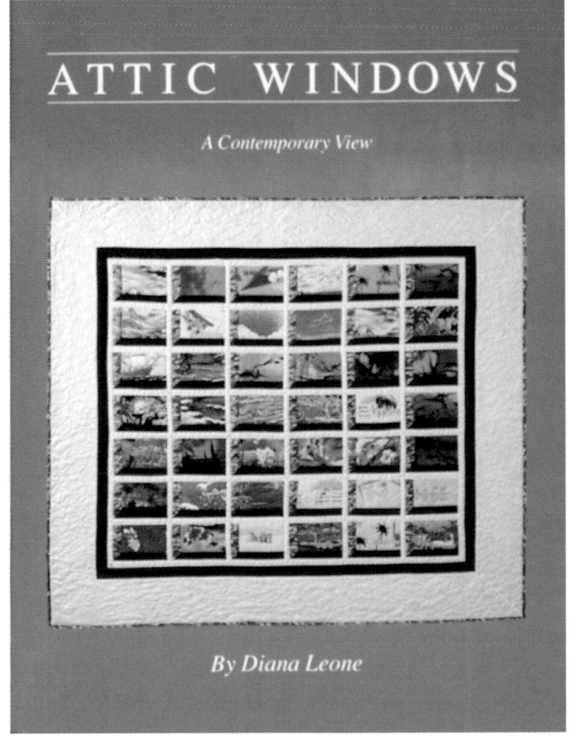

Diana and Cindy have also teamed up to revise Diana's Attic Windows *(shown here is the original). Watch for it in 2000!*

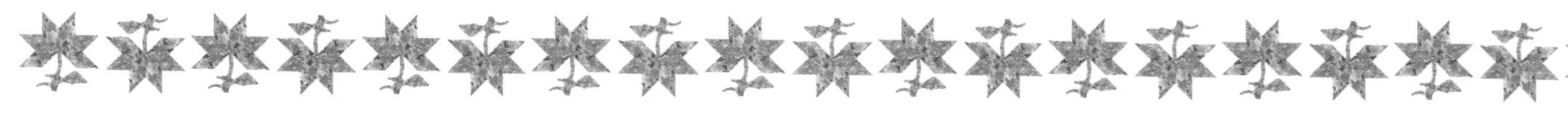

Chapter 1 Introduction to Quilting

Most people say that hand quilting is simply a running stitch used to hold the quilt's three layers together. Hand quilting is much more; it is a refined technique that becomes an art form which can give us a glimpse into history and document our lives. Your own quilting will parallel your life experiences. The practice and patience required to learn the technique of hand quilting will be rewarded with many hours of reflection and personal satisfaction.

The hand quilting techniques you will learn from practicing the exercises in this book basically consist of making straight, even, and short running stitches with your threaded needle, while following a quilting design line. The choice of the quilting design depends on your skill level and the quilt's intended use. Quilting may be used to outline pieced patchwork, a printed design on the fabric, or it may evolve into a very carefully thought-out artistic complement to the pieced, appliquéd, or whole-cloth top. Some of the quilts you make will be used and enjoyed, while others will be showcases of your work and should become family heirlooms. The one fact we realized while writing this book is that hand quilting is easy, fun, and it is here to stay. So, begin and enjoy the journey (for yourself and the generations to come).

Throughout this book you will notice boxes that contain "Tips from the Pros." Many famous quilters use traditional and innovative techniques and here they share their tips with you.

We bring to you our favorite of the tried and true, most universal, and the traditional, methods of hand quilting. It is a process of progressive steps:

- ★ Before hand quilting begins, the quilt top must be formed, which can be done by piecing or appliquéing, or by selecting a whole piece of fabric. A quilting design is chosen that will complement the design of the top. The quilting design is marked on the top. Because the function of the quilting stitch is to hold the quilt's three layers together—top, batting, and backing—the quilting lines are usually planned to be a minimum of 3 inches away from each other.
- ★ The top, batting, and backing are layered together on a large, flat surface and then basted using any of the methods included in this book.
- ★ This basted "sandwich" is then quilted by hand, with multiple running stitches using a frame or hoop (or in your lap with no hoop).

This book covers the supplies you will need ("tools of the trade"), how to prepare the quilt top, the actual quilting technique, and how to bind the quilt. The supplies used in quilting are very important; the selection of the best needle, thread, and thimble will make all the difference in the world. We suggest you read Chapter 2 before beginning the quilting technique.

Finally, we have included step-by-step instructions for three wall hanging quilts so you can practice on any of these easy projects before quilting a large quilt.

Welcome to the wonderful world of hand quilting.

Palamopore Wood Block, 45" x 65", late 1700s–early 1800s. The cotton fabric for this quilt was block printed by hand. The artist cut designs into 3- to 5-inch blocks of wood. Many different blocks were used to print this piece of fabric. The blocks are inked and stamped onto the cloth. The blocks were so well designed that you cannot see the join. Little is known about this particular piece, except that it represents one of the first hand-printed small quilts from the late 1700s. It was delicately hand quilted and is in excellent condition. It was sewn to a cotton backing fabric and framed for preservation. Collection of Diana Leone.

World's Fair Quilt, 90" x 108", 1940. The pattern was featured in the Sears Century of Progress in Quilt Making *book, 1937. This very popular Autumn Leaves pattern (formerly "Thousand Leaves") was possibly available as a widely circulated "Century of Progress" kit, and was made and exhibited during the time of the World's Fair in 1940. This top was made in the 1930s and was sent to the Philippines to be hand quilted in 1996. The hand quilting is perfect and showcases the quilter's tiny stitches. The designs complement and emphasize the fine hand appliqué. Collection of Diana Leone. Below: Quilting detail.*

Quote from the 1937 book,* Sears Century of Progress in Quilt Making*: "While the art of appliqué and patchwork comes to us from ancient Egypt and the Early Chinese, America is more concerned with the art as dating from our early Colonial days. Quilt making was originally classed among the fine arts, one of the luxuries enjoyed only by the nobility. But in the pioneer days of early America, quilt making became a necessity, unrestricted to class. And for the reason that blankets, 'the soft, fluffy blankets as we know them,' were mostly unknown, making quilts was an important part of every woman's home planning."

Quilt Designing

If you are a quilt maker and have designed a quilt, you have most likely spent a lot of time constructing your quilt top. Hand quilting will also require additional time and consideration, because it is as important as constructing the top. Besides holding the top, batting, and backing together, the hand quilting adds a surface design and gives the quilt its raised look. The hand quilting process enhances your quilt and is worthy of your best efforts. If you are new to the field of quilt making, you might wonder how to achieve any level of accomplishment. It is not as difficult as you may think. Follow along, begin to quilt, and enjoy the journey.

This book introduces you to all of the methods, tools, materials, and exercises you will need to learn to hand quilt. Of course, you will need a finished quilt top. If you plan to make the quilt top, and this is your first quilt, we suggest taking a basic quilt-making class at your local quilt shop. We also recommend *The New Sampler Quilt* book (C&T), by Diana Leone, to teach you the basics of quilt construction. A Sampler quilt includes great practice areas for hand quilting. Further, it allows you to try different quilting designs, marking tools, and threads, and you will gain the experience and confidence you need to continue into the world of hand quilting.

All elements of designing and executing the quilting design lines will come together with experience, after you have devoted some time and practice to the actual hand quilting. Eventually, you may want to learn how to design your own quilting lines. Study the work of traditional and contemporary quiltmakers, because they are creating some of the most beautiful quilts imaginable. If you study these artists' works, you will find they have spent a lot of time and creative energy deciding just where and how to quilt their quilts. In order for the work of a contemporary quiltmaker, or anyone, to withstand the test of time, the hand quilting must be well designed and integral to the piece.

Teal Sampler, 90" x 108", 1990, by Diana Leone, hand quilted by April Murphy. Diana designed this sampler to use all thirty blocks from her The New Sampler Quilt (C&T) *book; you may recognize it from the cover. The quilting is exceptional. If you want to showcase your fine hand quilting, use a solid fabric. The quilting becomes lost in a print.*

Recent Quilt History

When the few small quilt shop owners went to trade shows twenty-five years ago and explained to the fabric salesmen that they were going to purchase their fabrics, cut them up into small pieces, and sew them back together with someone else's fabrics, the manufacturers were appalled. That would be like cutting an oil painting in half and hanging it on the wall with half of someone else's painting! The quilters went on to say, "Then we are not only going to recreate a piece of yardage, we are going to make many small stitches, by hand, to hold the three layers of fabric and batting together forming a warm blanket called a quilt."

Today, quilt shops are abundant in the United States, even in the smallest communities. The combined voices of quilt shop owners have made themselves heard in a big way in the fabric business. The manufacturers have listened and, over the years, have made many tools and fabrics available to our industry, specially designed just for us.

Years ago, Diana asked manufacturers for a 24-inch round hoop on a stand, and for needle distributors to package size 12 between needles. Along with these and many other ideas she thought of, the manufacturers listened. Since that time, they have continued to listen and make improvements on the specific tools and fabrics necessary for the quilter. We have tested the old and new products for you (see Chapter 2). In the future, as new tools become available, write to us with your questions and requests, or ask your local quilt shop to supply them. Quilters want, and should use, the best products available. Your enthusiasm and curiosity has helped this industry learn, grow, and produce products to meet our needs. There has been significant improvement, in the past twenty years, in the quality of tools and materials we all use.

In 1975, Diana said, "Quilting is 'in' and here to stay." Well, not only was she correct then, but it is still alive now and growing. Quilting is a viable craft. Great quilts are being made for the home, and collectors are displaying quilts on corporate walls and in museums. The quilt business is stable and exciting because quilting has become a part of our lives again.

We are constantly amazed when we see quilts and realize the hundreds of hours that have been devoted to produce these works. It pleases us that we all can find the time for hand quilting in the twenty-first century. When everything around you is computerized and swirls at a fast pace, you will look forward to the times you set aside for hand quilting. Watch out—it is addictive. You will realize a sense of pride in knowing that you have made a quilt, possibly an heirloom, and you will thoroughly enjoy the process.

Laura in Redwork, 42" x 42", 1998, by Johanna Wilson, Redwork designs by Jan Boehm and Ruth McKinney, pieced by Shelly Hall, embroidered by Kathy Goral, quilted by the Yellowstone Trail Quilters. Johanna designed this quilt from an antique quilt hanging in the town of Walnut Grove, Minnesota's, museum. The pattern is available through Plum Creek Patchwork (see Sources and Suppliers). The hand quilting is diagonal, point-to-point, avoiding as many seams as possible.

Types of Quilts

Quilt tops are generally divided into four basic categories: counterpane (whole cloth), patchwork, appliqué, and innovative or contemporary. The variations are limitless within each category, and the categories can overlap. This book details how the quilting is accomplished after the top is completed.

Counterpane or Whole-cloth Tops

Marking a quilting design on a solid, whole piece of fabric creates a counterpane or whole-cloth quilt. A whole-cloth top may appear to be easier to quilt than a pieced top because there are no seams to contend with; however, these quilts are, as a rule, very elaborate and showcase the expertise of the quiltmaker. This quilting displays the best workmanship because every stitch shows. The central designs are usually curvilinear, pictorial motifs that may include trapunto, which is a stuffed design creating a bas-relief. The background has some style of straight-line quilting that emphasizes the central design and may include stippling, which is quilting stitches that are randomly and densely quilted to fill the background with texture. Make your first whole-cloth quilt following the directions in Project Two.

White on White Basket, 42" x 42", by Meryl Lehman-Tapungot. Mryl is a master quilter from the Philippines. Her perfect, tiny stitches are showcased on this miniature quilt. Collection of Diana Leone. Below: Quilting detail.

Patchwork Tops

Patchwork, where small pieces of material are sewn together by hand or machine, is the most popular method of forming a top. An endless selection of designs is available for you to use in making the top, from strip piecing to elaborately executed pictorial tops. Whether the piecing is simple or elaborate, you must contend with the bulky seam allowances that will occur. To make the hand quilting easier, learn to mark, cut, piece, press, and trim very accurately at each step along the way.

When piecing patchwork, whether by hand or machine, use a 1/4-inch seam allowance and press all of the seams to one side; this produces a stronger seam and the bulk is to one side. The hand quilting is done away from the seam's bulk. The most common practice is to quilt an outline, or echo, 1/4 inch away from the seams on each of the patchwork pieces. When pieced and plain blocks are set together, curvilinear quilting designs are usually used in the plain blocks to enhance them and complement the pieced blocks. Make an easy patchwork quilt following the directions in Project Three.

With the advantage of good-quality threads, fabric, and batting, and the use of a quality sewing machine to piece the top, Diana recommends that you press the seams open instead of to one side whenever possible. This technique is very helpful where many seams come together as in the center of a star block. Press the seams to one side or open as you wish. In the past, it was believed that batting may migrate through the seam if it is pressed opened. If you think the batting may beard, press the seams to one side.

A Rainbow Swirl, 49" x 49", 1998, fabric dyed by Stacy Michell, top designed by Marti Michell (using The Perfect Patchwork templates), top pieced by Toni Hearn, hand quilted by Cindy Walter. Cindy echoed the patchwork areas 1/4 inch from each seam and used template #348 from Quilting Creations for the border. Black thread was used to emphasize the quilting lines. This quilt was made by alternating a Rambler block and Martha Washington's Star. The blocks merge to form a strong pattern across the surface of the quilt. Collection of Stacy Michell.

Appliqué Tops

Appliqué means to cut a shape of fabric and to "lay it on" another piece of fabric. Appliqué designs can range from simple to very complex, and may take more time to complete than most pieced quilts. An appliquéd top is a great achievement by any quilt artist.

The quilting stitches usually follow around the perimeter or "echo" the appliquéd shape(s). You may quilt directly in the ditch, which is exactly where the appliqué touches the background, or 1/8 inch from the seam line, or "ditch." Appliqué quilts are enhanced by a lot of quilting in the plain areas. Quilting every inch or less to cover the background produces a quality quilt.

Hawaiian quilting consists of a central appliqué, or island, from which the quilting radiates in concentric rows from the center appliqué to the outer border or edge, which is called the lei. There is very little straight-line quilting used on these quilts. Instead of marking with a pencil, the width of a finger or narrow strip of paper is used as a guide for the distance between the rows of quilting.

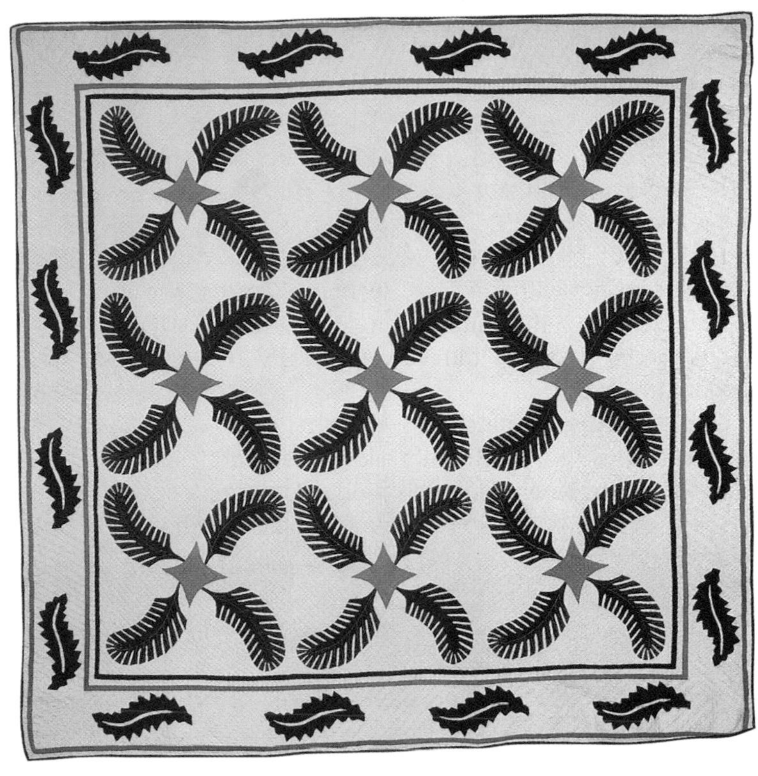

Princess Feather, 80" x 80", 1870. The workmanship of the maker features fine details in the appliqué area. Note the fine yellow embroidery stitched around the appliqué. The quilting is balanced to the weight of the appliqué. The border shows parallel lines of three rows stitched only 1/16 inch apart. The hand quilting in the blank areas next to the appliqué area appears behind the appliqué. The quilting helps emphasize the appliqué, and the straight lines complement the curvilinear line of the appliqué. Collection of Diana Leone. Left: Quilting detail.

Contemporary Quilts

In the recent past, quilters have begun to break the traditional rules for piecing and quilting a quilt. This is called "being innovative." If a quilter from the 1800s walked into a large quilt show today, she would probably think she was on a different planet. At a quilt exhibit you will see raw edges on appliqué, the use of fusible webs, seams sewn inside out, threads left hanging, and embellishments of all types. It is now common for the contemporary quilt artist to combine hand and machine techniques on the same quilt. Contemporary quilts are quilted with freedom and creativity; the quilt maker designs the quilting. This may sound intimidating, but it is actually easy and exciting. We have included Chapter 6 to introduce you to the possibilities. Experiment; the sky is the limit—the twenty-first century is here!

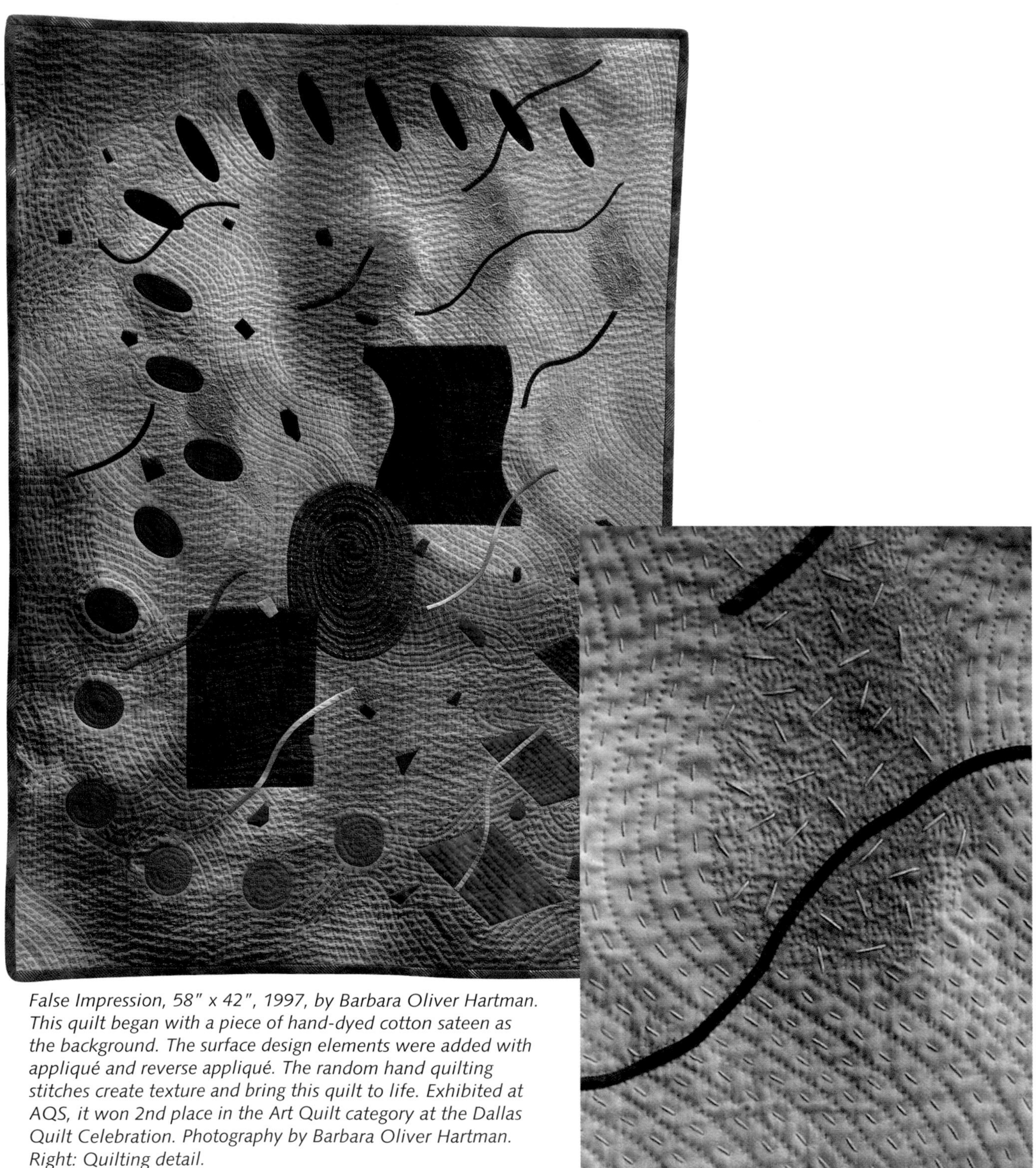

False Impression, 58" x 42", 1997, by Barbara Oliver Hartman. This quilt began with a piece of hand-dyed cotton sateen as the background. The surface design elements were added with appliqué and reverse appliqué. The random hand quilting stitches create texture and bring this quilt to life. Exhibited at AQS, it won 2nd place in the Art Quilt category at the Dallas Quilt Celebration. Photography by Barbara Oliver Hartman. Right: Quilting detail.

Chapter 2 Quilting Supplies and Materials

Your top is made. Now is the time to design the quilting lines, mark the top, and begin the hand quilting.

There are many great and useful tools made specifically for quilters. To find what works best for you, try several variations of each tool. The selection and availability will vary at your local quilt shops. If the shop nearest you doesn't carry the quality items you need, suggest the items to the shop owner. The tools we refer to in this book are ones that we have used and tested; they work well and are readily available to all shops in all areas. Having the correct and best tools is extremely important in the quality of work you produce and the enjoyment you receive from the process of hand quilting.

The materials that will comprise your quilt are batting and the fabrics used for the quilt's top, back, and binding. Use the best quality fabrics and batting you can afford (ask the advice of your local quilt shop owner). Using quality materials is very important and it will help your quilt withstand usage, washings, and the test of time.

After teaching hundreds of students how to quilt, Cindy says: "If you are already an experienced quilter and have trouble creating small and fine stitches, you are most likely using a lesser-quality needle, an ill-fitting thimble, or a thick batting. All of your materials should be the best available."

General Supply List

Here is a checklist of the basic quilting tools, fabrics, and materials you will need. The following sections give details about each item on the checklist to help you make choices.

- ★ Hoop or frame
- ★ Markers: pencils, pens, or other marking tools
- ★ Quilting line tool: stencils, templates, and measuring tools
- ★ Thimble
- ★ Between needles
- ★ Quilting thread
- ★ Scissors and thread snips
- ★ Basting needles and thread, safety pins, straight pins, quilt spray adhesive, or basting gun (all optional, depending on basting technique)
- ★ Batting
- ★ Quilt top
- ★ Fabric for quilt back and binding
- ★ Sewing machine

Hoops and Frames

Some quilters hold a quilt in their hands without a hoop or frame. Diana uses this method occasionally. We both highly recommend that everyone use a hoop or frame to learn to hand quilt. We have had students who have taken our quilting classes because they were having trouble creating even or straight stitches. Each time, we simply taught them how to use a hoop or frame and their problems were easily resolved. (Chapter 4 covers how to secure the quilt in the hoop or frame.)

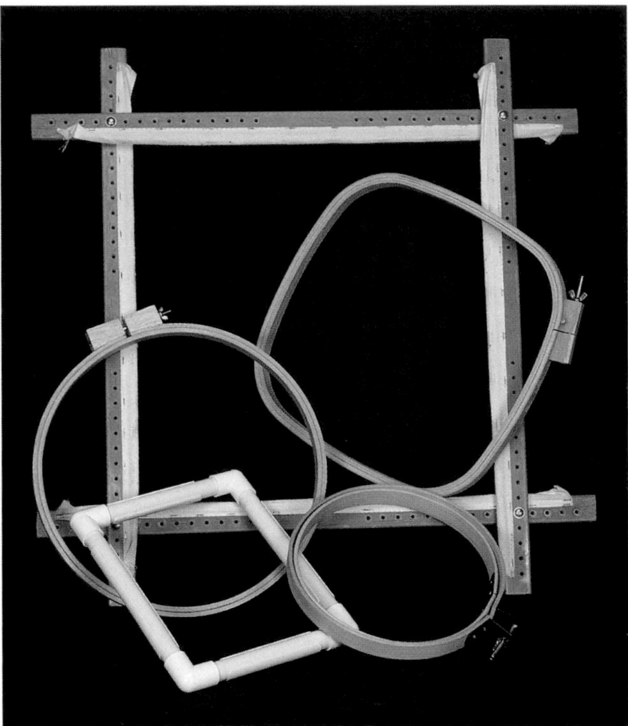

Various types of hoops and lap frames.

Hoop

A hoop consists of two round or oval pieces of wood, one fitting inside of the other. A portion of the quilt is held taut between the two rings. The newest shaped hoop is "almost square." Both of us like this new shape and recommend it. Hoops are wonderful because they can be put onto your quilt easily and make the project portable. The appropriate hoop for you is whatever size feels comfortable (a 14-inch round or oval is the minimum, with a 27-inch being about the largest you can easily handle). Make sure you can easily reach to the middle of the hoop with both hands. Purchase a well-made smooth hoop, so it will not harm your quilt.

A round or oval hoop cannot hold the quilt's edges, because there is not enough fabric to fill the dimensions of the hoop. To quilt the edges, use an "almost square" or a "D"-shaped hoop (half hoop with a straight muslin attachment side); or to use a round hoop, sew a long strip of fabric, 12 inches or so, to the edge of the quilt. This fabric extension will fill the hoop and allow tension at the edges to be maintained while quilting.

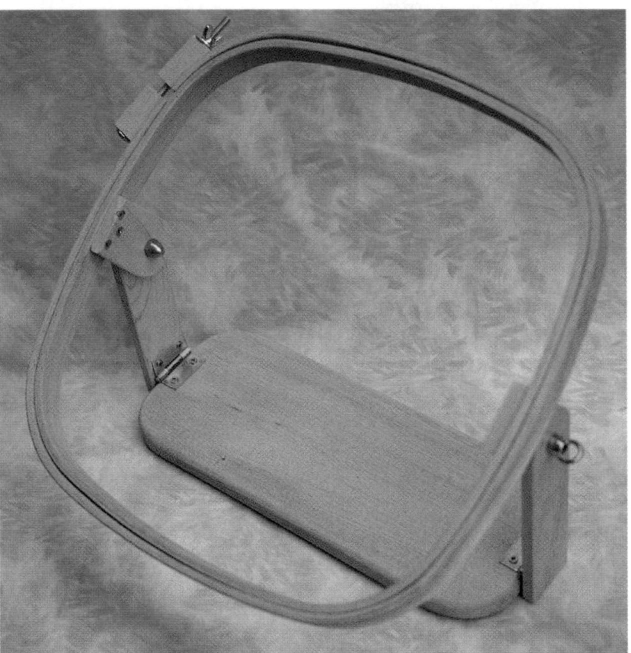

This new almost-square hoop, made by the Marie Company, allows you to quilt almost to the edge of your quilt. Roy Volk of Calgary, Canada, made the stand holding the hoop for Diana.

Floor Frame

Quilting floor frames hold the quilt taut while you quilt, and more than one person can work on a quilt at the same time. Frames come in many variations. The long wooden bars of the frames have fabric strips attached; the quilt is pinned to these fabric strips, and the quilt layers are rolled around the long bars until 36 inches, or so, are exposed, ready to hand quilt. Floor frames can be beautiful pieces of furniture, simply bars clamped together.

Because you will be sitting at the frame for quite some time, it should be comfortable at your sitting height. The frame should be strong enough to hold your leaning weight without bending the long bars. The frame's long bars should accommodate the width of the quilt.

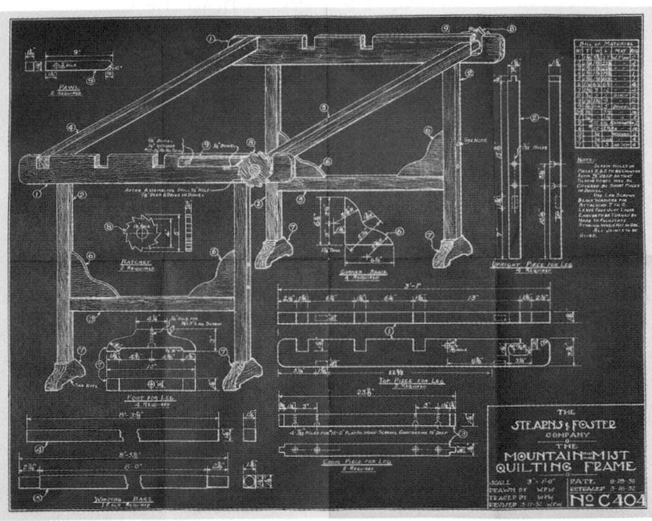

Diana has a beautiful frame that was made for her by her father-in-law. It is from the Stearns and Foster Mountain Mist Quilt Frame pattern #404 with one variation: he added a metal tongue and groove in the middle and extension boards so the frame can extend up to 120 inches long. (Order a pattern from Stearns and Foster, 100 Williams St., Cincinnati, OH 45215.)

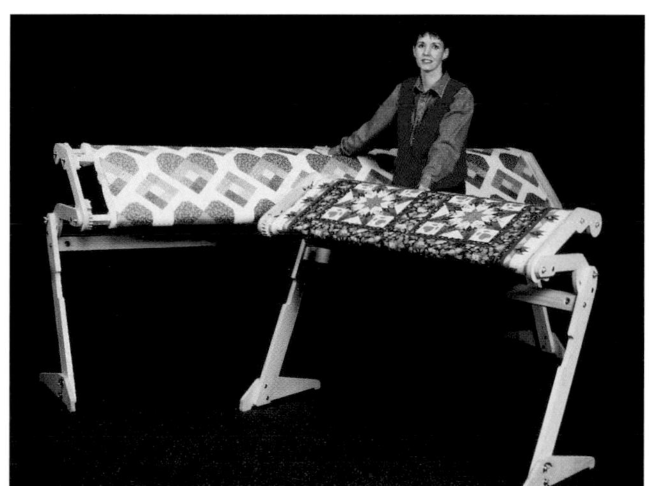

Floor frames by The Grace Company.

Lap Frame

Four wooden bars (about 24 inches long), with fabric strips attached, are screwed together with a nut and bolt to create a square or rectangular lap frame. As with the larger floor frame, the quilt layers are attached by pinning the quilt to the fabric strips. The lap frame is moved from area to area around the quilt, beginning in the center. An area is pinned and quilted, and then the frame is moved to an adjacent area. It may take a little more time to pin your quilt to a muslin attachment frame than snapping it in a hoop, but the results are worth the effort. Cindy prefers this type of small square frame because one can quilt right to the edge of the quilt and it keeps the layers taut and squared to the edges of the frame. She uses this frame for both small and large quilts.

Tip: Chairs

A comfortable straight-backed chair is important. Chairs on rollers, with adjustable height and back angle, are great. An ergonomic chair is worth every penny and will add comfort to the hours spent hand quilting.

PVC pipe frames, like the Q-Snap, are convenient to use, but you will need to continually tighten the quilt's tension.

Markers

One of the most frequently asked questions is "What tools should I use to mark my quilt?" Anything that transfers or marks the quilting design onto your quilt top qualifies as a marker. Whether it is good, comes out easily, and will last long enough to quilt the project is another story. A marker should last through the quilting process, yet wash out and not show after your work is done. It is difficult to find one tool that will do it all. Try the selection of markers we recommend and use what works for you.

We have tested all of the newer water-soluble and air-soluble (disappearing) pens especially made for fabric marking. For some types of craft projects, these pens work very well. You can easily see the markings and they disappear, or wash out, as claimed. But, we suggest you do not use them on an heirloom-quality quilt. The dyes may recede into the batting and reappear later, especially after being washed or ironed. More importantly, the pens might leave a chemical residue, which will cause future damage to the quilt top's fabric. In the past, holes appeared after the marking had disappeared. In two pens we tested, the ink was dried out when we opened the package. We also had problems using the disappearing ink pen; it would disappear instantly before we could finish marking our small quilt top. Only time will tell, but for now don't use a chemical pen on an heirloom-quality quilt.

Diana first discovered Berol Verithin, FaberCastell Col-erase pencils and other washable semi-hard pencils more than twenty-five years ago for quilt design marking. These pencils remain our first recommendation. The silver and white pencils are the most versatile because they show on medium to dark fabrics. They are also referred to as quilters' pencils and are easy to find in quilt shops.

Several books recommend not using a regular lead pencil because it doesn't wash out. Our ancestors used lead pencils to mark tops for decades, and you may see some marks remaining on antique quilts. In one of our tests, most regular pencils washed out, but in a different test (with different fabric) the pencil wouldn't wash out with any type of detergent. To be safe, we recommend that you use quilters' pencils. With any type of pencil, use a light hand, because a heavy hand could damage the fabric and leave permanent marks. Also, use caution when marking a top with a light box; you may not realize how dark you are marking the top because the light makes the lines look lighter. Hold the pencil at an angle for smoother marking.

Note that the dark pencil lines on this Amish Embroidered Anniversary Quilt will not wash out.

There are dozens of other marking tools that should be tried and may work for you. Try a chalk pencil or a bag of chalk, a Chalkoliner, a sliver of soap, or any of the variety of colored pencils. Quarter-inch seam tape works great as a guide to follow to "echo" seam lines. We use 1/4-inch tape often, especially when working on quilts that have a lot of patchwork. Your choice is personal. Remember to test the marker first, stay with the tried and true tools we recommend, and always test anything with chemicals. Keep a small pencil sharpener in your sewing box; dull pencils create fat, dark lines and are a nuisance.

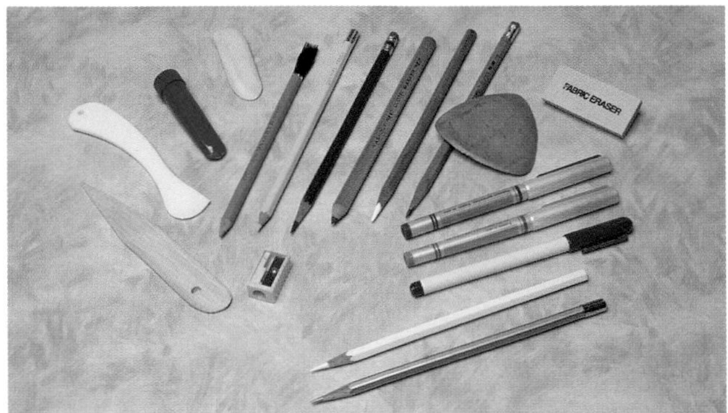

Selection of markers.

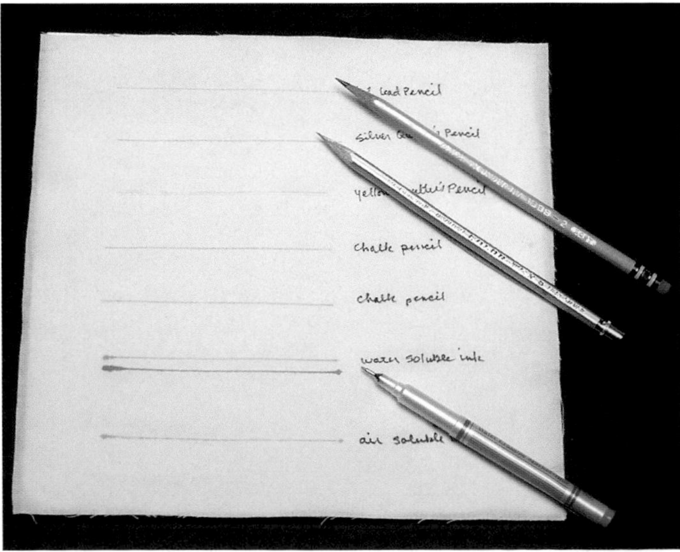

A test of different marking tools.

Quilting Line Stencils, Templates, and Marking Tools

Measuring and marking tools include any device that you can use to mark a line around, over, or through, the quilt top.

Stencils are made of a thin plastic-like material and have long, narrow slits to guide the marking tool. Quilt shops have hundreds of pre-cut stencils available. Ask to see catalogs and order what you like. Stencils are very convenient, especially for large-bordered areas, and are relatively inexpensive.

Templates are shapes that are traced around to mark a quilting line. Thin plastic is available for you to cut any shape and create a template to trace around.

Rulers are measuring devices used to calculate the placement of quilting design lines. Many innovative rulers have been devised by quilters and are available in your local quilt shop. Clear plastic rulers are especially useful for marking because you can see through them and align the quilting marks in rows. The perfect tools to mark 1/4-inch parallel echo lines along the seam line of patchwork areas are a 1/4-inch x 1/4-inch x 12-inch Plexiglas rod or a 1-inch x 6-inch clear ruler with 1/4-inch markings.

Many books and magazines contain printed quilting designs to be traced onto a quilt top. This tracing works especially well if the fabric is light enough to see through. Use a light box or window to trace lines on darker fabrics.

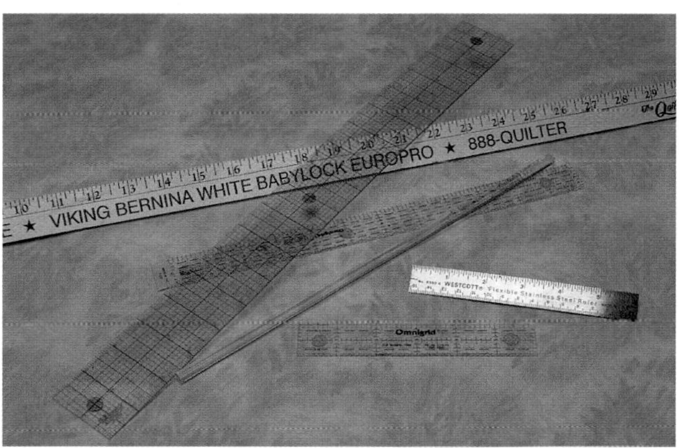

A variety of straight-edge marking tools.

Plastic stencils, coloring books, and other line drawings are good sources for quilting line ideas.

Using a straight-edge tool to trace lines onto light fabric. The 1/4-inch square Plexiglas rod is used to draw 1/4-inch echo lines around the seamlines.

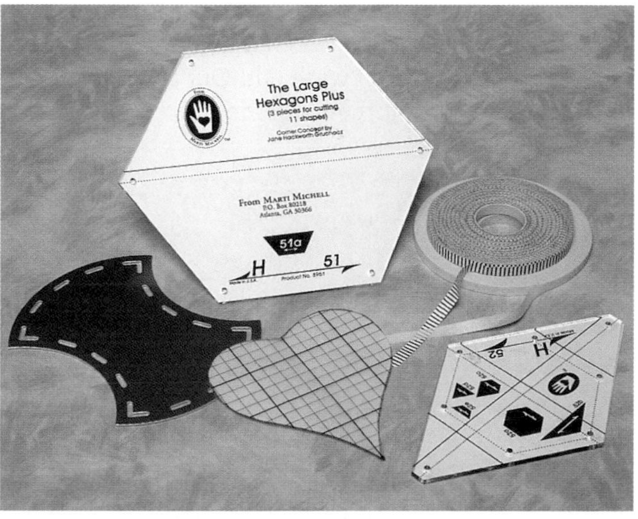

A variety of template shapes to trace around for quilting lines.

Quilting Thimbles

You must use a thimble. You may think that you can hand quilt without using one, but your fingertips will soon become so sore that you cannot continue quilting. You may be tempted to use the underside of your fingernail to push the needle, but do not do this because it will cause damage to your nail.

When you were given your first thimble, it probably did not fit correctly, got in the way, or fell off. Now is the time for you to learn how to use one correctly, and it might take some time to get use to it, but it is well worth the effort. Try different types of thimbles on different fingers and the different techniques until you find the best thimble and finger combination. Designed with the hand quilter in mind, there are flat-end, indented-end, raised-edge, and open-ended thimbles, shown here:

Quilting Finger Thimble

A thimble fits on the middle (or longest) finger of the hand you use to hold the needle on the top side of the quilt. The thimble is used to push the eye end of the needle through the quilt. The best thimble for this finger is a metal one. Use a quilting thimble, not a sewing thimble. Sewing thimbles are rounded (convex) on the end and have lots of small indentations, while quilting thimbles are flat with a lip (concave) at the end and have large indentations on the end and sides to hold the eye end of the needle.

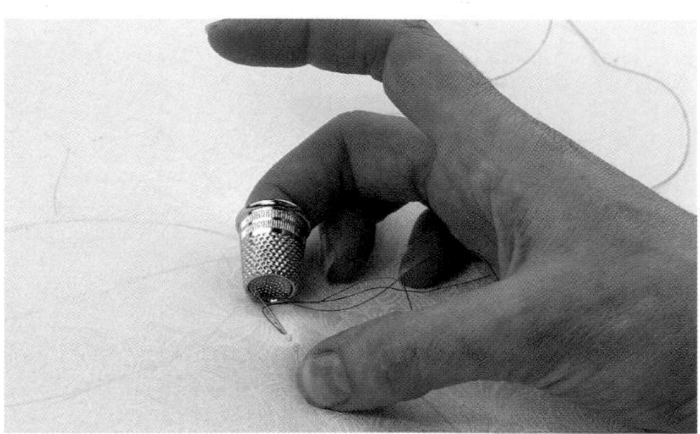

Quilting thimble for the middle finger.

The most important criteria for selecting a thimble is that it fits correctly on the longest finger of your quilting hand. It should be large enough for the tip of your finger to fit snugly into the tip of the thimble. If it is too small and the tip of your finger doesn't completely reach inside to the tip of the thimble, you will have less control of the needle. It is too large if it falls off your finger with any movement. You cannot buy a thimble by looking at it; you must try it on. Knowing your thimble size isn't good enough. Every country that manufactures thimbles uses a different size numbering system.

A metal thimble may be difficult to use at first, and you will say, "Oh, this is impossible." Keep trying; we know that once you learn how to use one you will be glad.

Some metal thimbles have a tiny lip inside the top rim (because of the concave tip). There is room for a small amount of fingernail in this lip (the Collins brand has a lip). Some brands of metal thimbles do not have any lip inside, so your fingernail must be kept very short. If you have long nails, try one of the thimbles made to allow for this, such as leather or shaped plastic. Diana has used the Nimble Thimble since its inception in the mid-1970s. She can use a metal one but prefers her leather one.

Underhand Thimble

Learn to quilt with nothing on your underneath finger. You must be able to feel the tip of the needle the instant it comes through the backing and touches this finger. This under finger is also used to return the needle to the top of the quilt. There are several varieties of thimbles on the market for the underhand; unfortunately, they do not allow you to feel the needle. The underneath fingers will occasionally become sore, and calluses will develop. We trade off fingers, alternating between the index and middle finger underneath. Place the pad of the under finger flat against the back of the quilt and use this area of the finger to return the needle through the back of the quilt.

In *The Quilter's Handbook*, Michael James describes how he uses two thimbles and a round hoop. A hammered-flat metal thimble on the underhand allows the needle to glance off its rim and return the needle quickly through the top.

Thimble Varieties

The above thimble methods are our favorites. We stress that there is not only one "way" to quilt. Experiment and find what works best for you. Remember, the goal is to finish your quilt with stitches that will hold the layers together as nicely as possible, and above all, enjoy yourself.

Thumb Thimble

The thumb on the top hand is very important; it pushes the fabric down and out of the way of the needle, so the needle can return up through the top. For most people, the needle will come up right in front of your thumbnail; these people will never need a thumb thimble (this is Diana's case). On the other hand, some people allow the tip of the needle to touch their thumb (this is Cindy's case); these people should consider a thumb thimble. Cindy uses light-weight leather, or a "Wrap-It" flexible thimble. It is impervious and protects her thumb.

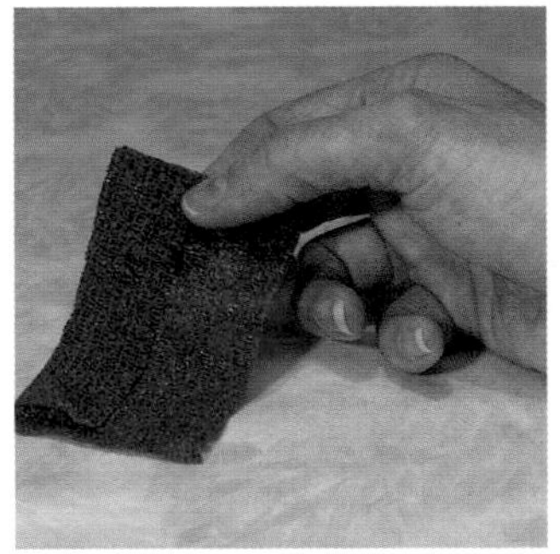

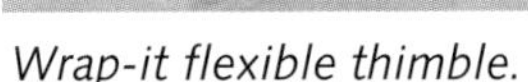

Wrap-it flexible thimble.

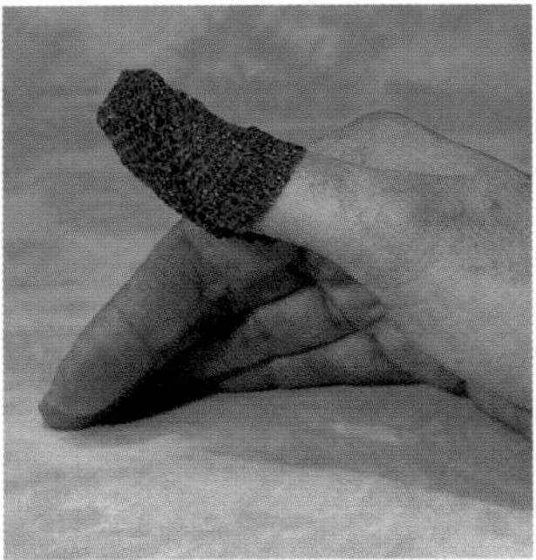

Wrap-it folded to fit thumb.

Alaskan Memories Via Colorado, 59" x 46", 1998, by Terri Wiley. This Single Irish Chain is embellished with floral appliqué on the border. It was machine pieced, hand appliquéd, and quilted with different shades of quilting thread. Terri created it for the book Time for a Chain *by Nancy Smith and Lynda Milligan (Possibilities Publications).*

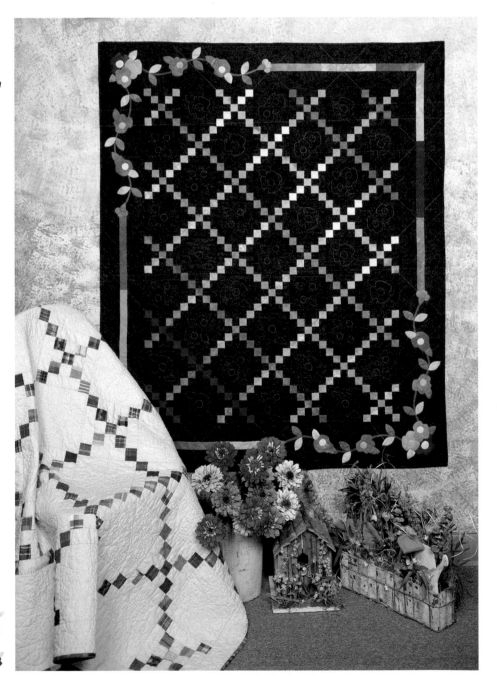

Diana relays a bit of history: "Carol Joy invented the Nimble Thimble in the mid-1970s. She was taking a class at my quilt shop, The Quilting Bee, and discovered she could not use conventional thimbles because of her long fingernails. She went home and within a week had designed and made her first leather thimble. It is made of flexible leather with a metal piece laminated at the tip and an opening at the end for users with long nails. Carol was one of the first entrepreneurs in the modern quilt world."

Quilting Needles

A quilting needle is called a between. It is very short with a thin, sturdy shaft. The smaller the needle's number, the longer the needle; for instance, a size 9 needle is longer than a size 12. Your local quilt shop will supply you with the best needles needed for fine hand quilting. Ask for quality needles; John James, Richard Hemming & Son (has a large eye), Clover, and Piecemakers are just a few of the quality brands that are readily available. The size and shape of needles vary by brand.

A variety of needles and needle threaders.

Contrary to what you may believe, large needles (size 8 and 9) are actually harder to use because the needles are thick. You have to push harder to get the larger needle through the layers; it is hard to stop pushing in time to form short stitches. Both of us start our students with a size 10 needle and graduate them to a size 11 or 12 as soon as possible.

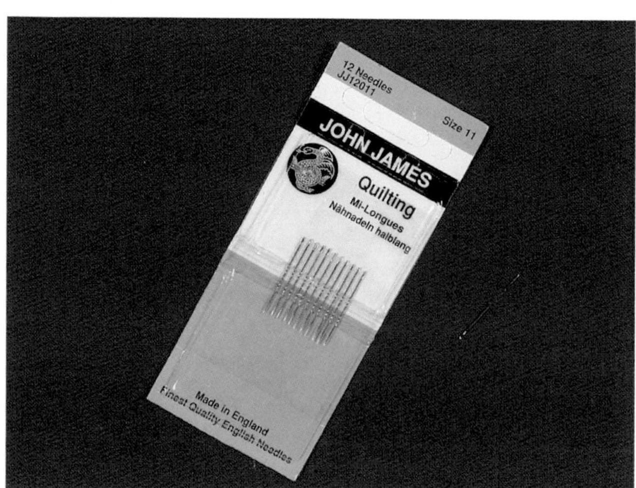

Size 11 between needles.

The old adage, "the shorter the needle the shorter the stitch," is very true. If the tiny size 12 needle is just too short for your fingers to handle, you'll do fine with a size 10. We both love the new size 11, which several companies are making.

A useful tool is a needle threader. The wire in an average needle threader is too thick to fit into the tiny eye of the between needle. Look for the better quality and thinner quilting needle threaders. If you are having difficulty threading your needle, turn the needle over. The way the eye is milled causes one side of the eye to be smoother and easier to thread. If it becomes dull or bent after a few hours of use, throw it away and use a new one.

A storage container for your special needles can be something as simple as a 35mm film container, a wooden needle holder, or even a sterling silver needle holder. Cindy uses a woolen needle purse, which her Grandma made more than fifty years ago. Emery-filled pincushions are best, and even a bar of soap is useful, but as a last resort, store your extra needles in a simple piece of paper. Some needles come in a small glass cylinder, with a stopper in the end. We have found them to be hazardous. Cindy recently had a "needle accident." While traveling, the stopper came off of a tube of needles in her suitcase. When unpacking her suitcase, needles scattered, causing a dangerous "needle disaster."

Diana began importing the size 12 between needles into the United States in 1976. While teaching in Japan in the mid-1970s, she found size 12 needles and small scissors in a tiny shop. She brought them home to her students in California. Because they were so popular, she started importing them and selling needles to shops across the country. Clover Needlecraft now supplies these needles to the United States.

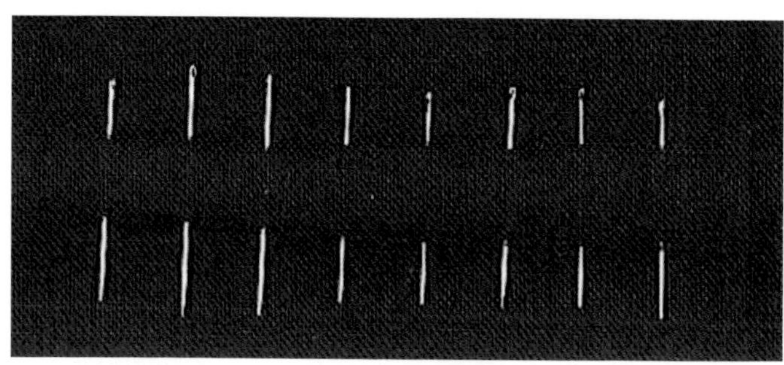

Different brands; a variety of lengths, all size 10.

Other Types of Needles

Each type of needle has a specific use. Use a long Milliner (size 5, 6, or 7) for thread basting the quilt. Some people prefer curved needles for basting. Sharps (size 9, 10, or 12) are long and very thin needles and are used to appliqué or embroider. A Crewel needle may be used for embroidery, hemming, and basic hand sewing.

Select the correct type of needle for each task. Start each project with a brand new needle. If it becomes dull after a few hours of use, throw it away and use a new one.

Tips from the Pros

Master hand quilter and instructor Nancyann Johanson Twelker says: "If I am going to quilt at a bee or demonstrate quilting, I place the quilting thread with needles in a large pill bottle and write the size of the needle on the lid of the bottle. It is a real asset to have the needles already threaded. Load them all onto the spool of thread. I hold onto the first needle on the spool with my thumb and first finger and pull thread through the eye of all the other threaded needles until I have a length of thread needed. Cut the thread and fasten it on the slot of the spool. My threaded needle is ready to go; all I have to do is knot the end of the thread to start quilting.

Quilting Needles Chart

Brand	Size 10	11	12	Ease of Needle	Breaks and Bends	Comments
Clover Gold Eye			x	***	***	Good needle
Clover Regular	x			****	***	Good needle
Clover Regular			x	****	***	Good needle, small eye
Collins Platinum	x			***	*	
Collins Platinum			x	**	***	
Colonial	x			**	***	
Colonial		x		***	**	
Colonial			x	****	**	
Dritz	x			*	***	Thick shaft
EZ	x			**	***	Thick shaft
EZ			x	**	***	
John James	x			****	****	Great needle
John James		x		****	****	Favorite
John James			x	****	***	Great needle
John James St. Steel	x			***	*	Eye snaps off
Piecemakers	x			****	***	Good needle
Piecemakers			x	****	***	Good needle
Richard Hemming	x			****	****	Great needle for students
Richard Hemming		x		****	***	Favorite
Richard Hemming			x	****	***	Great needle
Roxanne Int'l	x			***	****	

**** = Excellent *** = Great ** = Average * = Poor

Quilting Thread

High-quality thread is now available to all. Top brands are found in most quilt shops and department stores worldwide. Thread companies are continually improving the quality of their threads to meet the high standards of today's quilters. Any thread will hold the quilt's layers together, but yours should be of the same high quality as your fabric, batting, and workmanship, to last as long as the life of the quilt. Poorer quality thread looks like a length of spun lint and breaks easily; good thread is smooth when you run it between your fingers, it is tightly twisted, and is strong. Among others, the quality brands of hand quilting thread we use include Mettler, Gutermann, YLI, Coats & Clark, and Signature.

Tip: Make one of the three projects in the book. Use different threads to practice and see which one you like best.

We used to draw the strands of thread over the edge of a piece of beeswax to coat the thread. Today, most hand quilting threads are coated with wax or glaze. This coating not only helps prevent the thread from knotting and fraying, but it is also makes it easier to thread the needle. Do not use these coated threads in your sewing machine because the coating can build up in the tension guide. Cindy keeps beeswax in her quilting supplies to show her students (and it reminds her of her Grandma).

Use the correct type of thread for the task. For beginners, we recommend 100-percent cotton hand quilting thread for hand quilting. Once you are experienced, exercise your creative right to use any type of thread while quilting. You will notice that several quilts in this book use decorative thread, like metallic or even pearl cotton, to enhance the quilting lines. Whether by hand or by machine, most quitters use only 100-percent cotton thread, along with 100-percent cotton fabric to construct the quilt. One-hundred percent polyester thread is thin and strong and will thread easily; however, this thread is too strong to use with cotton fabrics and may eventually wear holes in the quilt. Some quilters like cotton/polyester blend thread because it doesn't fray.

Diana conducted an experiment with three different groups of hand quilting students. She gave each group a different quality brand of hand quilting thread and had them use only that thread for a twelve-week class. At the end of the class, she asked the students if they liked the thread. Half of each class liked their thread; half didn't feel the thread was adequate. What does that prove? Thread choice is a very personal one, so experiment. Try the variety that is available in your locale. And yes, it is okay to use different brands, types, and colors in one quilt.

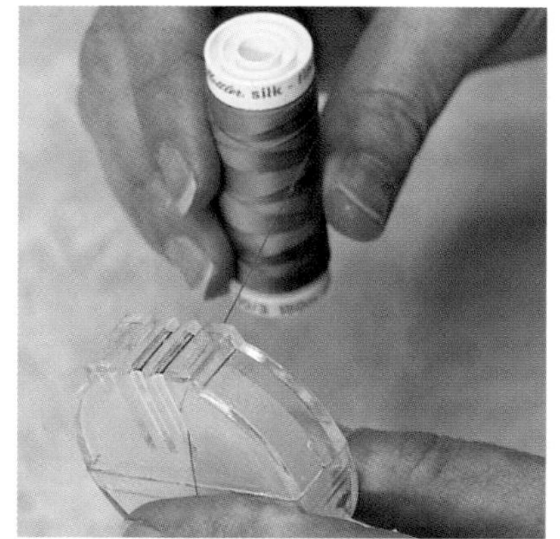

Pulling thread over beeswax.

Cindy and Diana have worked with the Mettler thread company to develop a high-quality natural hand quilting thread. The new thread is 100-percent cotton and comes in a large variety of colors. New threads from other manufacturers are available; check with your local quilt shop.

Tips from the Pros

Judy Pleiss, quilt designer for Kaye England: "I suggest beginning quilters use thread colors that match their projects, so uneven stitches are not so apparent. I encourage the use of a busy, multi-print for the backing fabric. It hides the uneven stitches and allows the quilter to change thread colors while still having an attractive back."

Variety of decorative quilting threads.

Amish Sampler, 90" x 108", 1985, designed by Diana Leone, hand quilted by Doris Olds. Diana collects Sampler quilts. Amish Samplers are very rare, and she didn't have one in her collection, so she decided to make one. She varied the thread colors throughout. A khaki green thread was used to quilt in the dark and black areas; it added color and emphasized the fine hand quilting. This quilt was featured on the cover of Diana's German-language book Das Grosse Buch vom Quilten (The Big Book of Quilting) *(Rosenheimer). The thirty-six block patterns are also found in the English version,* The New Sampler *(C&T). The Sampler quilt provides a great foundation on which to practice your hand quilting. Practice not only your stitches, but also try different techniques like different weights and colors of threads, different needles, and thimbles. Above: Quilting detail.*

Scissors and Thread Snips

In the day of rotary cutters, we both still love good scissors and use at least three different kinds during the quilt making process. We use 7- or 8-inch blades for cutting multiple layers of fabrics, 4-inch blades for cutting single layers of fabrics, and small, sharp embroidery scissors and thread snips to clip threads when hand quilting. Once the quilt top is constructed and we are ready to quilt, we only need to keep small embroidery scissors or thread snips nearby.

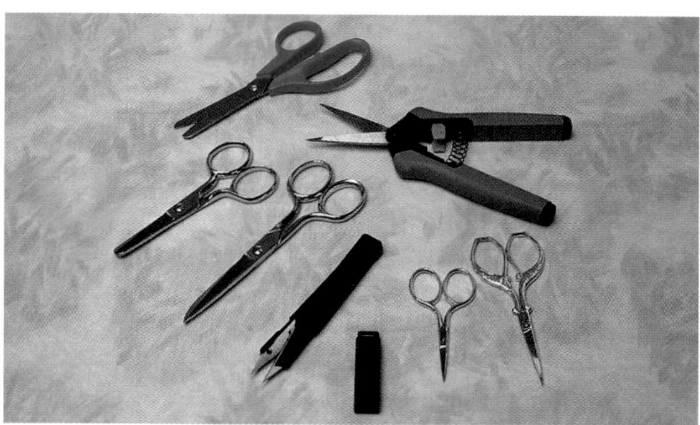

Various scissors and thread snips.

Basting Tools: Safety Pins, Straight Pins, Quilt Spray Basting Adhesive, and Basting Gun

In Chapter 3, we will talk about and demonstrate the different methods to baste a quilt. You will use needles and thread, safety pins, basting adhesive, or a tagger (basting gun) to baste. The tried and true method is needle and thread basting (with Milliner needles and white cotton thread). Diana primarily uses a basting gun and spray adhesive, and Cindy prefers size 1 nickel-plated safety pins. As you can see, it is a personal choice.

> ***Tip: Take a moment to put thread snips and small scissors on a thin, bright ribbon to wear around your neck.***

Batting

Batting is the filler sandwiched, or layered, between the quilt top and backing. Its function is to add an additional layer to the quilt, provide warmth, a thermal effect, and give the quilt a bas-relief once hand quilted. It is important to buy the right type of and the best quality batting you can find. It will reward you by being easy to quilt and last the lifetime of your quilt. Inexpensive battings can cause all sorts of disasters, including bearding or fiber migration through the weave of the fabric. Poor quality unbonded batting can separate and large clumps can form inside the quilt. We recommend premium "bonded and/or treated" batting, which is readily available at your local quilt shop. It is soft, pliable, uniform in thickness, and will not beard or come apart with use. The label will say bonded, premium-quality batting. This unseen layer is so important to your success. Make the extra effort to find the best, and you'll be happy in the long run. Quilt shop employees know which brands are the best and which are available in the area, so rely on their advice.

A variety of available quality battings.

Batting comes packaged in sheets that are cut to the most common dimensions used for quilts, from crib to king size. It can also be purchased by the yard, in various widths. Batting comes in a variety of thickness (loft), from very thin to thick. Thin-loft batting (1/8-inch to 1/2-inch thick) gives an old-fashioned flat look and is the easiest to needle (quilt through). Medium-loft batting (1/2-inch to 1-inch thick) is the most commonly used batting and is also easy to needle. Thick-loft batting (1-inch to 2-inch thick) gives you the effect of a comforter and is usually used in quilts, or comforters, that are tied.

Polyester, Cotton, Wool, and Silk Battings

If you are a beginning quilter, we strongly recommend you use a thin polyester batting. Polyester is the most common batting used for hand quilting. It is very easy to quilt small stitches through this batting, and it is lightweight, easy to find, and inexpensive.

Cotton batting is heavier because it is dense and therefore more difficult to "needle" and make small stitches. But, cotton is warm, drapes well, and some people want to say their quilt is made with 100 percent cotton (from fabric, to thread, to batting). Cotton batting is our choice for machine quilting.

Wool is easy to needle while hand quilting, meaning you can easily make small stitches, and it is warm. It has great recovery (creases will fall out easily), but it is more expensive than cotton or polyester.

Silk is wonderful to needle and is lightweight (the quilt floats on top of you). Silk is expensive, though, and requires dense quilting and hand washing.

Preparing the Batting

There is no need to pre-wash any of the battings currently on the market. Over the past several years, the major manufacturers have changed how they make batting. Not only are they pre-washing the cotton batting for you, they are removing the seeds and other natural fibers that used to make it difficult for us to work with these battings.

Most battings come vacuum-packed in a plastic bag. Take the batting out of the bag and unfold it a day before you intend to baste your quilt. This allows it to relax and removes the wrinkles caused by the packaging.

Tips from the Pros

Diana places batting (out of the bag) in the dryer for a few minutes, which allows it to relax and fluff. Also, a hair dryer on warm, not hot, held over the flat batting will quickly remove wrinkles.

A variety of thin battings.

Batting Chart

Manufacturer	Brand	Stitches needed per inch	Balling/Bearding	Comments
Fairfield	Soft touch cotton	2-4	None	NP, very thin, lightweight
Fairfield	Poly-fil Cotton Classic	3-5	None	NP, 20% poly, soft, drapable
Fairfield	Low-loft poly	2-4	Minimal	RB
Fairfield	Poly-fil Traditional poly	2-4	Minimal	NP, dense, drapable
Hobbs	Heirloom Cotton	4	None	NP, shrinks 3-5%, can pre-wash
Hobbs	Heirloom Cotton, 20% poly	4	None	NP, shrinks, 3-5%, can pre-wash
Hobbs	Washable Wool	3	Beards	RB, low loft
Hobbs	Thermore Poly	6-8	Minimal	RB, thinnest poly available
Hobbs	Polydown	4-6	Minimal	RB, NW
Kelsul	Dream Cotton, Request 3	8	None	NP, 1% shrinkage, low loft
Kelsul	Dream Cotton, Select 4	8	None	NP, 1% shrinkage, drapable
Morning Glory	Glory Bee II	2-4	Minimal	RB, comforter or tied
Morning Glory	Glory Bee I	2-4	Minimal	RB, NW
Morning Glory	Needle Punch Poly	2-4	Minimal	NP, dense
Morning Glory	Cotton Batting	10	None	NP, NW
St. Peter Mill	Nature's Comfort wool	3	Minimal	C, NW
Stearns	Mountain Mist B.R. Cotton	2	None	C, thin and soft
Stearns	Mountain Mist Poly	3	Beards	RB, NW
Stearns	Mountain Mist Quilt-lite P.	3	Beards	RB, NW
The Warm Co.	Warm n' Natural cotton	10	None	NP, very clean, lies flat
The Warm Co.	Warm n' White cotton	10	None	NP, bleached
The Warm Co.	Soft n' Bright poly	10	Minimal	NP, NW, lies flat

NW = Needles well
NP = Needle-punched
RB = Resin-based
C = Carded (not bound)

Orange/Cream Silky, 28" x 34", 1997, by Laverne Mathews. This whole-cloth quilt was made as an exercise for the artist to experience the feel of silk fabric and wool batting. Both are very easy to handle and enjoyable to "needle." Because one side of the quilt is orange fabric, and the other side is cream, she used purple thread so the quilting lines would show on both sides.

Fabric for Quilt Tops

Selecting Fabric

Quilt shops are very careful about providing the best of all worlds for you, the quilter. You will find the staff knowledgeable, and the fabrics are carefully selected for use in quilt making. Cotton fabric with a medium thread count of 68-78 is best for quilting. Fabrics with too low of a thread count will not hold up to the test of time in a quilt. This lower quality fabric is lighter in weight and may have fewer threads. It is limp, you can easily see through it, and it is made for garment makers and discount fabric chain stores. Fabrics with a high thread count such as 120-300 are difficult to needle (this is why you shouldn't use percale bed sheets when hand quilting). Quilters often fall into the trap of thinking they might use a sheet for the back of their quilt because of its large size and lower cost. Use the same quality fabric for the backing and binding as you use in the top.

It is fun to choose a fabric with a motif that you can actually quilt around (without drawing on quilting lines). We've included this idea in Project One (see page 88).

Quilting stitches are hidden in a print and show more on a solid fabric. Use a printed fabric if the quality of your stitches is a concern. Use a solid fabric when you want to showcase your work.

Diana designs fabric for several major manufacturers. Her recent designs for Northcott/ Monarch are printed on quality fabric with a silk-like feel. Cindy's new fabric designs for Spring Industries—For Quilters Only division—is also printed on a quality cloth suitable for all quilts.

Color on color solids by Diana Leone.

Storm Trail, 89" x 97", 1978, designed by Diana Leone, pieced by Doris Olds, hand quilted by Lillian Wofington. It is quilted 1/4 inch from the seam line (echoed). Even though the quilting doesn't show because of the printed fabric, it adds a wonderful low bas-relief and softness that is only found with hand quilting. Collection of Diana Leone.

Pre-washing and Testing Fabric for Shrinkage and Color Fastness

One of the most frequently asked questions is, "Do I have to pre-wash my fabrics?" Even though you may not want to hear it, the answer is, "you probably should." Pre-washing your fabric serves many important factors: it removes excess dye, shrinks it, removes the sizing (which softens the fabric), will make it easier to hand quilt, and is washable in the future.

To pre-wash fabrics, sort them into piles of lights and darks (wash red, navy, and blacks separately). Place fabrics in the machine with cool or warm water, never hot. You do not need to use soap, because the fabric is not dirty, but if you do choose to use soap, use Orvus quilt soap or a mild phosphate-free soap sold at quilt shops. Do not use regular laundry detergent, because the harsh chemicals will stay in the fabric and cause deterioration.

Place a large, dry towel in the dryer with the wet fabric. It will act as a buffer and absorb the water. Set the timer for eight to ten minutes on cool or warm. Remove the fabric while it is slightly damp and smooth it with your hands on a flat surface. Let the fabric finish drying at room temperature or press it dry with an iron.

The selvages are the woven edges of the fabric that contain double amounts of thread. It is best if this thicker area is not used in a quilt because it is very hard to quilt. Remove (cut off) all selvage edges after you have washed the fabric and before cutting it into quilt pieces.

Around the Twist, 58" x 58", 1998, by Diana Morrison, hand quilted by Cindy Walter. Diana was inspired to make this quilt because of a similar one she saw at the In the Beginning quilt shop in Seattle, Washington. Although the quilt is stunning because of her choice of fabrics, the quilting lines do not show in the prints. Cindy suggested that she combine hand and machine quilting on this quilt, but to Diana's desire, it was completely hand quilted. Most of the patchwork areas are echoed, with a stencil from Quilting Creations International used in the border.

Diana seldom pre-washes her fabrics. Her quilts are for the wall, and if they are ever washed, she feels the quilt will be handled as one piece and will be handled and washed carefully. She also feels that the fabrics she uses are pre-tested, color-fast, and the best quality. If you are a beginner and are still learning about fabrics, Diana recommends that you pre-wash all of your fabric.

Cindy forces herself to pre-wash for several reasons: the softened fabric is easier to needle, and if you are using a fusible web on the quilt, it adheres better to washed fabric. In an effort to convince students to pre-wash, Cindy conducted a pre-washing experiment in one of her classes. She took four quality fabrics from a quilt store and cut them 2 inches wide by 40 inches long. She then washed them in warm water and dried them in the dryer. The results were astounding. The amount that each piece of fabric shrunk was different, from 0 to 2 inches.

Fabric Collections: The Stash

Every quilter should have a complete fabric collection. Purchase 1/2 yard or more of any fabric. (Diana buys at least 1 yard.) It is your palette, without which you cannot paint. Artists in any field have to have all of the necessary tools and materials to create and complete projects at their disposal. You should never feel guilty if you have extra fabric; you should feel reassured. The more fabric you have, the better. We also like to buy the latest colors and designs; using current fabrics establishes the date of the quilt. New fabrics are a statement of our times. Future fabrics are waiting to be discovered by you.

Store fabric collections in clear plastic bins or on shelves. Fold the fabrics with the print side out so that you can easily see the colors when you are ready to select fabrics. If you can see your fabrics, you will use them more readily.

Fabric for Backing and Binding

Backing Fabric

It is best to choose the same quality fabric for the back as you used for the top. The color and design of the back should complement and enhance your work on top. If the quilt is more than 42 inches wide, you will need two lengths to "fill" the larger size. If the quilt is more than 84 inches wide, you will need three lengths of fabric for the backing. The backing strips can be placed horizontally or vertically. Vertical seams are best because they aid in the drape of the quilt on a bed or wall. Pieced or scrap backs are great, and we both make creative pieced backs for our quilts.

Binding Fabric

We suggest using bias cut binding for curved-edged quilts and straight-edged binding for straight-edged quilts. The width of the binding (single or double fold) and the perimeter of the quilt determine the amount of fabric you will need for the binding. We include instructions in Chapter 5 for a single- or double-fold straight-edge binding. Single or double binding is a matter of preference. We both use either method depending on the project. In general, use double-fold on quilts that may receive more wear, and single-fold on wall hangings with little wear intended.

Life's Memories (see whole quilt on the following page). Diana Leone created interesting quilt art on the back of this quilt. She added large pieces of tropical fabric around the Attic Window blocks.

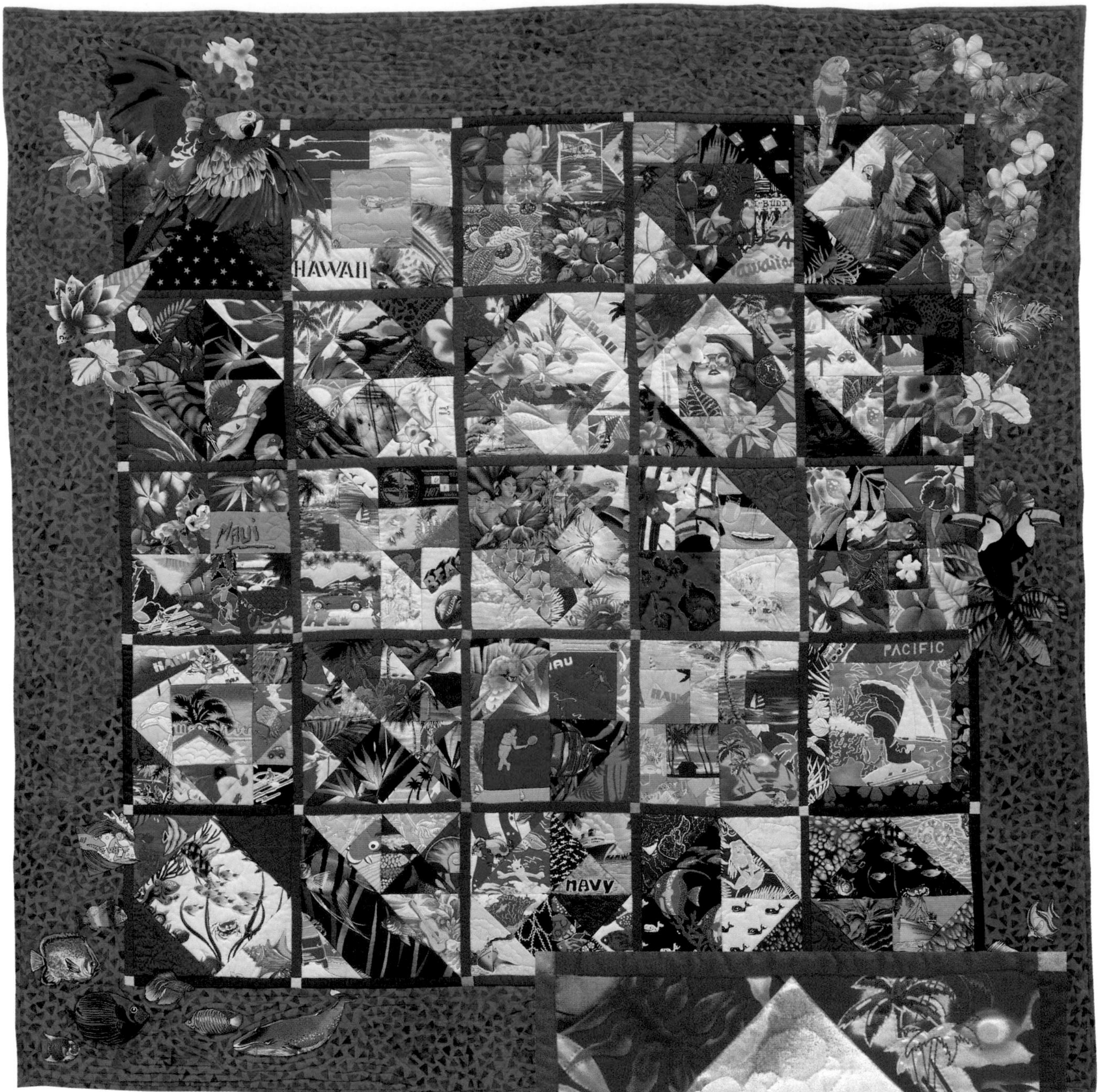

Life's Memories, 58" x 58", 1987, by Diana Leone, hand quilted by Doris Olds. Diana designed this quilt to use more than 250 fabrics. Each fabric is a meaningful part of her memory of the Hawaiian Islands. The flowers and parrots around the edges of the quilt and border were hand appliquéd. Even though the hand quilting lines are lost in the printed fabric, they are the desired soft-textured bas-relief. Right: Quilting detail.

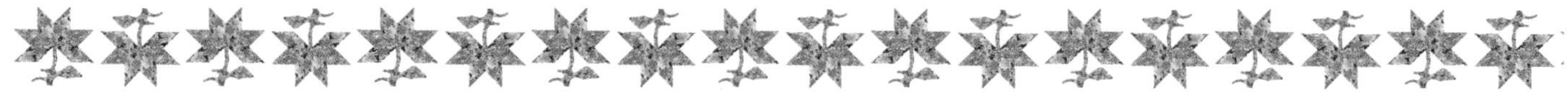

Chapter 3 Prepare for Hand Quilting

After selecting the materials for your quilt and gathering the necessary tools, there are several things you will need to do before the hand quilting can begin:

- ★ Select a quilting line design
- ★ Mark the top
- ★ Choose the thread color
- ★ Prepare the backing fabric
- ★ Layer the quilt
- ★ Baste the quilt

Sampler, 98" x 68", 1987, hand pieced and hand quilted by Cindy Walter. This was Cindy's first Sampler quilt. The blocks are from the book The Sampler Quilt, *by Diana Leone (rewritten and now published as* The New Sampler, *C&T). Cindy made the quilt in a class at her local quilt shop and can still remember the wonderful teacher, Carol, because she resparked her interest in quilting. Cindy used a square lap frame to quilt this quilt, as she does with almost all of her large quilts. She custom-fit the lavish feather and cable border pattern to fit her quilt, by first tracing it onto butcher paper, the exact size of the borders. A year later she felt the border needed more quilting, so she added the grid lines after the quilt had already been bound. Above: Quilting detail.*

Select a Quilting Line Design

When selecting the quilting design, you also need to think about how you are going to transfer the design lines onto the quilt top. Use a stencil with narrow slits to mark through, or trace a drawn design through light fabric (use a light box to trace through darker fabric). You can use rulers, or straight edges, to mark straight echo lines or grids. With more contemporary quilts, you can free-motion hand quilt without pre-marking any lines, similar to stippling. Because designing and cutting your own stencils will take hours, we recommend buying a pre-made stencil to hasten the process. Look for designs that are as continuous as possible. For the beginner, choose lines that are straight or only softly curved. Hand quilters look for the longest continuous lines so they can quilt as much as possible without turning or stopping.

Diana enjoys designing intricate quilting line patterns; maybe this comes from her artist background. Cindy is always in a hurry to start the actual hand quilting, so to speed up the process she either buys a pre-made stencil from her local quilt shop, echoes the patchwork, draws on grid lines, or free-motion quilts her tops. The three projects in this book offer this variety for your selection.

Through the Garden Wall, 52" x 52", 1998, designed, made, and hand quilted by Philomena Durcan. This beautiful Celtic design is made from strips of bias appliqué and regular appliqué on a whole cloth. Directions for this quilt, along with several of Philomena's other original projects, are featured in her book A Celtic Garden *(Celtic Design Company). The curvilinear designs in the blank areas and the grid lines throughout the quilt set off the floral appliqués. (Other Celtic design stencils are available through Celtic Design Company or Sten Source International.)*

White on White, 18" x 18", 1980, by Diana Leone. Diana designed this small quilt to become a "Sampler" of hand quilting. She used more than ten different Mettler threads. Use the colors of threads like paint to practice. You may recognize this quilt from the cover of the original Fine Hand Quilting *book. Below: Quilting detail.*

Tips from the Pros:

Diana says: "My best organizational tip is to have a separate bag for each hand-quilting project in progress. Include quilting needles, the right color quilting thread, and a pair of thread snips in each bag. I place the bags in the closet by the front door; when I leave the house, I take a project with me. I look forward to sitting at a sports game with my husband or the wait at a doctor's office."

The quilting design you select should complement the design of your quilt top. (Refer to Chapter 6 for additional quilting inspiration.) There are some basic rules of thumb about where you quilt what type of design. Consider the following:

- The pieces of a patchwork quilt top are usually quilted 1/4 inch away from the seams, which outlines, or "echoes," the shapes. This anchors all of the seam lines and echoes the design shape.

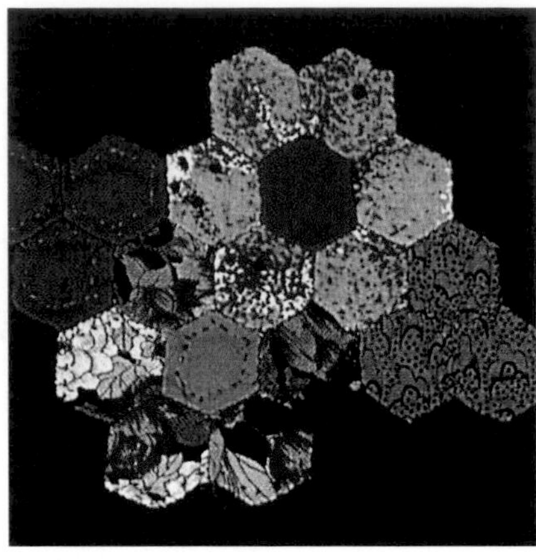

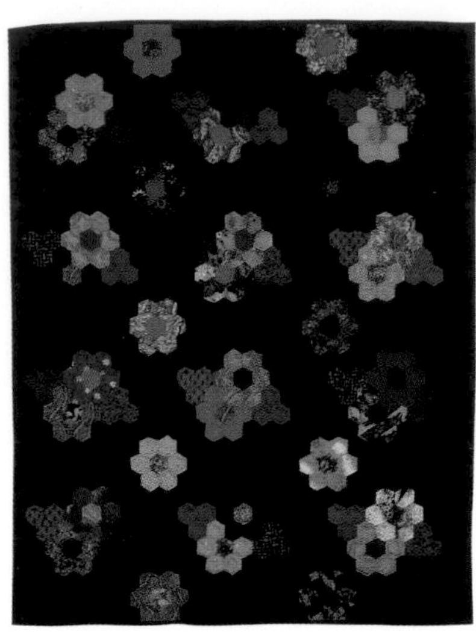

Miniature Hexagons, 14" x 19", 1989. The widest point on these petite pieces measures 3/4 inch. It was hand pieced English style and finely hand quilted with a very thin batting, in an echo style outlining each seam. Collection of Diana Leone.

- Curvilinear designs from stencils or traced drawings are used on blank blocks, borders, and lattices to complement the straight-line quilting in the patchwork area. Curvilinear designs are usually quilted in the blank blocks found between patchwork blocks.

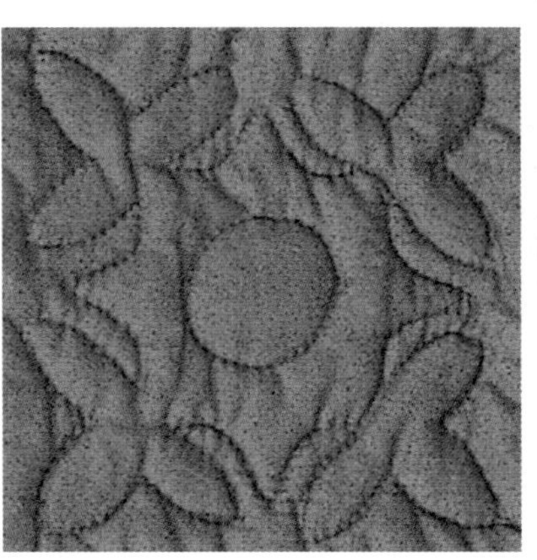

Bits and Pieces, 72" x 90", 1960, by Lucille Draper (Dorothy Jacques' mother and Cindy Walter's grandmother). Lucille used scraps of fabrics from the family's old clothing. Dorothy can recognize fabric in the quilt from several of her mother's dresses and aprons. Notice the decorative quilting motif in the plain areas between the patchwork. The quilting echoes the patchwork seams. Collection of Dorothy Jacques.

- Appliqué designs are normally outlined very close to the edge of the appliqué shape in the background fabric. This outline quilting raises the appliqué pieces, making them three-dimensional or bas-relief. The plain, or blank, areas are then quilted with designs that make the background recede. Straight lines, cross-hatching, and free-form stipple are appropriate designs as a background for appliqué.

Detail from Philomena Durcan's Through the Garden Wall (the whole quilt found on page 34). Notice the quilting around the appliquéd areas.

- The density and complexity of your quilting lines are up to you. For beginners, we recommend a design with straight lines and soft curves. Quilting every 3 inches is sufficient. Experienced quiltmakers will want to showcase their hand quilting with more complex designs and stitches every inch or less. A quilt will display flat and beautifully when it is quilted closely.

Focal Point, 36" x 26", 1997, by Deirdre Amsden. Deirdre is the creator and author of Watercolour Quilts *(TPP). Her inspiration for Focal Point was a poem about the contrast of seeing things from a distance when traveling on a train, when out walking, and again when examined closer up. The poem echoes how most people look at quilts. For the translation into cloth, she sorted prints by scale and value and then used these two elements to create an illusion of depth. The quilting reinforces the feeling of scale. She wanted to give viewers the feeling that they could step into the quilt and walk into the distance. Photography by James Austin.*

California Vintage, 1998, by Kathy Galos. Kathy designed and created this beautiful quilt (patterns available, see Sources and Suppliers). The packed freeform stipple quilting causes the background to recede and the appliqués to come alive.

Mark the Top

Marking the quilt's top is a major stage in the creation of the quilt. The process may take hours or days to complete successfully. By this time, you have selected or created the quilting designs and the top is pressed, trimmed, and ready to mark. In the course of transferring the quilting design onto the quilt top, you will probably use a variety of quilt marking tools, depending on the color and the print of the fabrics used in the top. Refer to the section on marking tools in Chapter 2 for the best tools to use.

Test the marking tool on scraps of the actual fabrics used in the top. Find out which marker shows best on which colors of fabric. Wash the test piece to make sure the lines wash out.

If you are using a chalk marker, you will have to mark small areas at a time, or re-mark areas, because the chalk will brush off as you work. The same is true with disappearing (air-soluble) ink pens; mark only the area you plan to quilt that day.

Try 1/4-inch wide masking tape for echoing patchwork areas.

When echoing patchwork areas, try 1/4-inch wide masking tape. There's no need to mark the quilting lines when you quilt next to the tape. It is definitely easy, fast, and worth a try, especially on dark fabrics where the markings may not show. Be careful not to let your quilting needle touch the edge of the tape, because the glue will affect the needling. Remove the tape when you are not quilting, because it may leave a residue on the quilt's surface.

When using a pencil to mark with rulers, templates, or stencils, hold it at a 45-degree angle so it will glide across the fabric smoothly. Make smooth, light strokes that are just dark enough to see. Keep your pencil sharpened because fine lines are easy to follow and will wash out. We have seen many quilts marked with such a heavy hand that the quilt was ruined because the markings wouldn't wash out. If you make a mistake while marking, leave it alone and wash it out later. Do not use colored erasers because they have dye in them, usually pink, that will rub into your fabric. There are white erasers made especially for quilters.

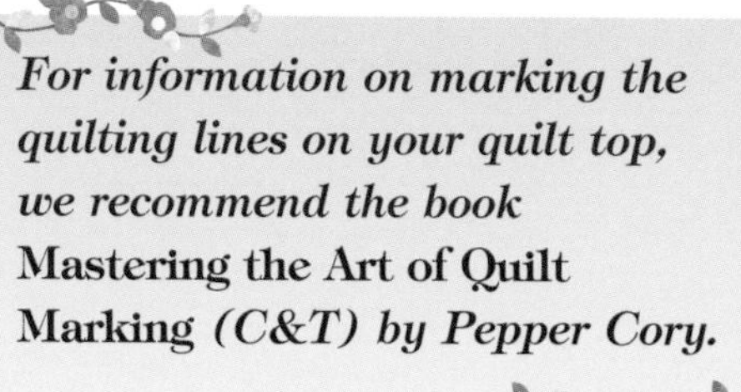

For information on marking the quilting lines on your quilt top, we recommend the book **Mastering the Art of Quilt Marking** ***(C&T) by Pepper Cory.***

Single Irish Chain, 48" x 56", 1990, by Cindy Walter. Cindy loves the look of a simple grid. She made this crib-sized quilt to show quilting line ideas to her quilting students. Cindy used a simple yardstick to mark the long parallel lines.

Trace a Printed Design

Tracing a design means to place the printed design under the fabric and trace the lines of the design onto the quilt top with a quilt-making tool. This technique is especially good when marking on light-colored fabric. To see through darker fabrics, use a light box. Use a light hand when using a light box, because the lines will be darker than they appear.

Your local quilt shop can supply you with books full of quilting lines to trace on your top. Mark over the lines first with a felt marker so they will be easier to trace. Coloring books are Diana's favorite source of designs for children's quilts.

Tracing lines is easy through light fabric.

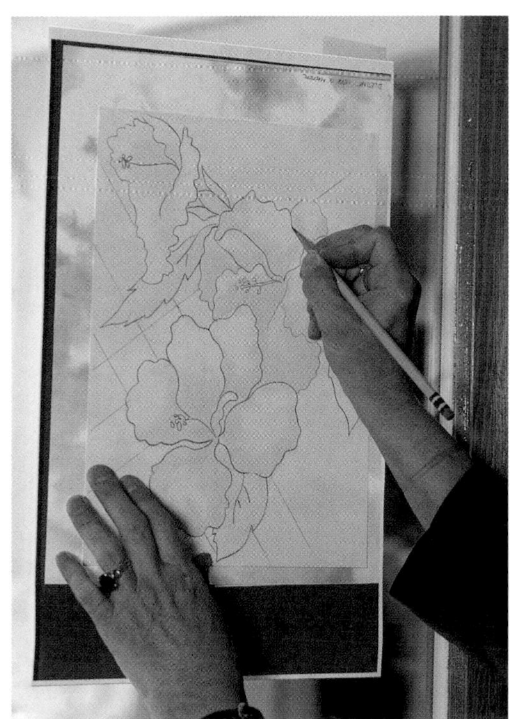

You can purchase a light box, or make one by opening the extension of a dining table and placing a sheet of glass over the opening, with a lamp underneath (the room needs to be dark). For small projects, hold the piece against a window (or the TV screen).

Favorite Flowers, 1998, by Sandra Miller. What a beautiful example of a Borderie Perse quilt. We recommend Barbara Barbers' Borderie Perse *(AQS) book for more information on the technique. Sandra quilted along the floral design in the border instead of drawing on a border pattern and hand quilted the background fabric in a free-motion stippled design.*

Using Stencils

Using a stencil is the easiest method of marking. Position it on top of the quilt and mark through the slits with a quilt-marking tool. Hundreds of quilting line stencils are available at your local quilt shop. If the shop doesn't have the exact one you want, ask to see a catalog and order a design. Make your own stencil by drawing or tracing the design on a piece of white paper with a black marker, then trace it onto a piece of Mylar (see-through plastic available at your local quilt shop). With a hot knife or an X-acto knife, cut 1- to 2-inch long slits on the lines. Leave "bridges" so the stencil doesn't fall apart. Making your own stencil is not easy and you must use the correct plastic; some plastics may melt and are toxic, so it is easier to buy ready-to-use pre-cut designs.

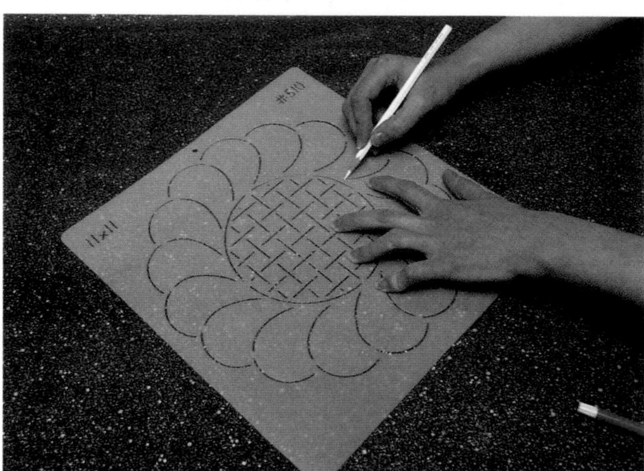

Using Templates

A template differs from a stencil in that you mark around the edges of a cut shape rather than through slits. To make a template, draw or trace any shape you want onto a sheet of plastic and cut out the shape with your non-fabric cutting scissors. Any ordinary object can double as a template. For example, a tin can or jar lids make perfect circles, and cookie cutters come in interesting shapes and are easy to mark around.

Choosing your quilting design is a personal decision and can be as traditional or innovative as you wish. At first, rely on traditional designs and develop your own inner resources and adapt them to your needs when you are ready. Anything that can be translated into a line drawing can be used. Look for design ideas and adapt them to your quilt.

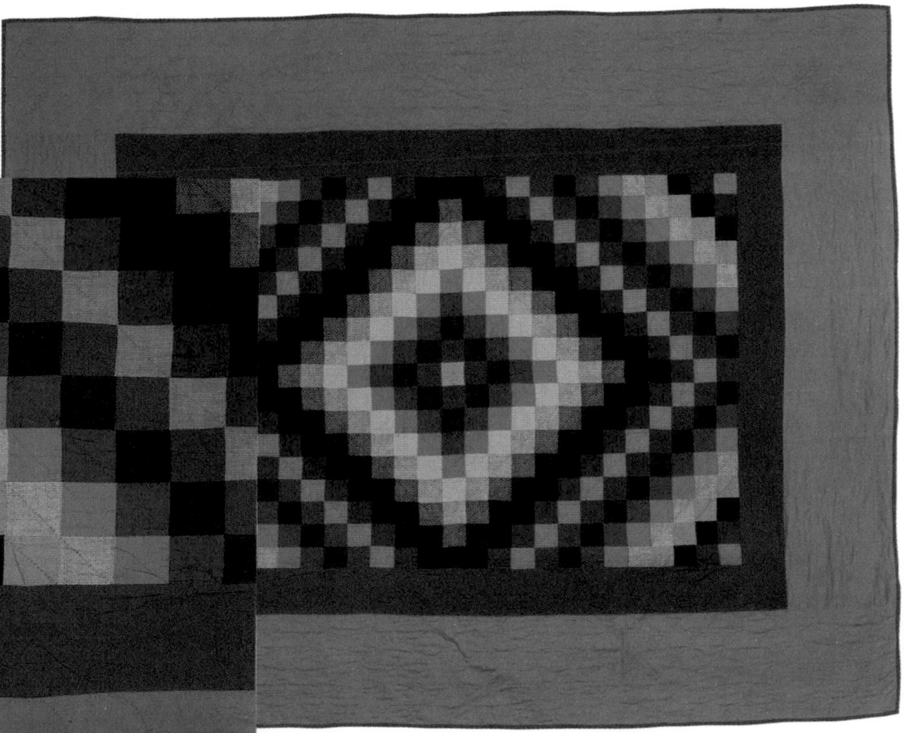

Amish Trip Around the World, 82" x 94", 1951. This quilt showcases typical Amish fabric colors. Notice the half circles (scallops) quilting line in the border. The diagonal quilting lines are easier because you can avoid some of the bulky seams. Collection of Diana Leone. Left: Quilting detail.

Choose Thread Color

Choosing thread color will take some planning. The thread's color should complement the colors of the quilt top and enhance the quilting design. It is common for traditional quilts to be quilted entirely with one thread, off-white for instance; Cindy loves the look of white thread on white fabric. Diana uses gray or green-gray on black fabric. She also uses any brand of quality thread to find the exact color she needs. She mixes color, brands, and types of thread in one quilt. Feel free to change the color of your thread throughout your project to match or contrast with the fabric. Remember the different colors will also show on the back.

Prepare the Backing Fabric

A traditional method for selecting the backing fabric is to use a fabric that coordinates with the top. Remember that the quilting stitches will show on the back. A beginner usually has a more difficult time making the backside stitches as even as the topside stitches, so select a backing fabric that will blend, or hide, the stitches on the back. Plan the backing fabric to be 2 inches larger in all dimensions than the quilt top. The top may slightly shift even though it is securely basted. Bring the extra backing fabric around to the front and pin, or baste, along the edges to protect them from fraying while quilting.

Pre-wash the backing fabric to prevent future shrinkage and to make it easier to quilt. If your quilt top is more than 42 inches wide, piece two lengths together. If your quilt is wider than 84 inches, piece three lengths together. If you need two panels, piece the back with a center panel and two half-side panels. The back will drape better and you will avoid a common problem of a puckered center seam.

Using only one fabric on the back is beautiful because it will showcase the quilting, but we both enjoy making scrap, or pieced, backs. Piece together large leftovers of the fabric used for the top. The back design can be as simple or elaborate as you wish. Remember the extra seams on the back may add to the difficulty of the hand quilting. Remove any selvage edges before sewing the backing fabric. Press seams to one side.

Colourwash Spillikins, 80" x 63", 1998, by Deirdre Amsden. When Deirdre was a child growing up in England, the game now known as pick-up-sticks was called Spillikins. It was one of her favorite indoor games. She used to play the game on the floor, which inspired the wood grain quilting design. She changed the thread color for each strip and used an assortment of printed fabrics and pure cotton wadding (batting) was used in the making of this masterpiece. Photography by James Austin. Right: Quilting detail.

Layer the Quilt to Prepare for Basting

A quilt "sandwich" consists of the top, batting, and backing fabric. You need a large surface to position the layers and create the quilt sandwich. A large table works best. Raise the table with 4- x 4-inch blocks placed under the legs to make the working surface high enough to be comfortable. As a last resort, if you don't have a large table, you can use a tile (not carpeted) floor (this will be hard on your body, but it works). Follow these steps:

- Find the centerlines of the table and backing fabric.
- Lay the backing fabric right side down on the table, matching centerlines. Tape the backing fabric to the table with masking tape, if desired.
- Center the batting over the backing fabric; carefully smooth any wrinkles.
- Tape the center of the backing's edges to the center of the table's edges.
- Center the quilt top right side up of the batting. Carefully smooth away wrinkles, working from the center outward, being careful not to stretch the quilt top out of shape.

Consider covering the table with either plastic sheets taped to the underside of the table or cutting mats. The plastic sheets or mats protect the table from needle marks, and you can hear the needle prick the plastic, which means it has gone through the layers of the quilt.

Baste the Quilt

Basting holds the three layers together during the hand quilting process. Basting is accomplished with one of several different methods. Different tools are used such as thread and needle, safety pins, a basting gun, or spray adhesive for the different techniques.

Thread Basting

This is a traditional method of basting. Diana perfected this method in 1975 and has used it ever since. You will need:

Large table (36 x 72 inches is perfect)
Two assorted sized packages of Milliners needles (or a large curved needle), sizes 3-9
White cotton thread
Thimble
Scissors
Books or wooden blocks to raise table height (optional)
Top layered with backing and batting

Thread basting with long lengths of white thread. Baste from the center out to the edges in a grid every 3 to 4 inches.

- Start in the center of the quilt, making two to three 2-inch long stitches, and then pull the length of the thread through the quilt. Baste vertically and horizontally about 3 inches apart, always from the center out.
- When you reach the part of the quilt that is hanging over the edge of the table, leave the threaded needle in the quilt's edge. Once the entire surface on the table is basted, pull the quilt to one side, moving the unbasted area onto the table. Baste the remaining areas.
- Check to make certain there are no wrinkles on the back. If so, clip the basting threads in that area and rebaste.

To thread baste:

- Raise the table's height by placing books or wooden blocks under each leg until its height is comfortable.
- Thread about a dozen Milliner needles (size 3-9) with long double strands of white thread.
- Cut the thread long enough to reach from the center of the quilt to its edges and back again.
- Tie a large "waste knot," or rolled knot, in the end of the thread. This knot is called a waste knot because it will be cut off, or wasted. Never use this knot for quilting or sewing. The large knot is easy to clip away when ready to remove the basting thread.

Safety Pin Basting

Cindy prefers safety pin basting and has used this technique on both small and large quilts for years.

- You will need nickel- or brass-plated safety pins, size 0 or 1, depending on the batting's thickness (the thinner the batting, the smaller the pin).
- Begin in the center and work your way out to the edges. Slide a safety pin into the top, batting, and backing, and then back up through all of the layers (without closing it) every 3 to 4 inches.
- Once all of the pins are in, go back and close them.

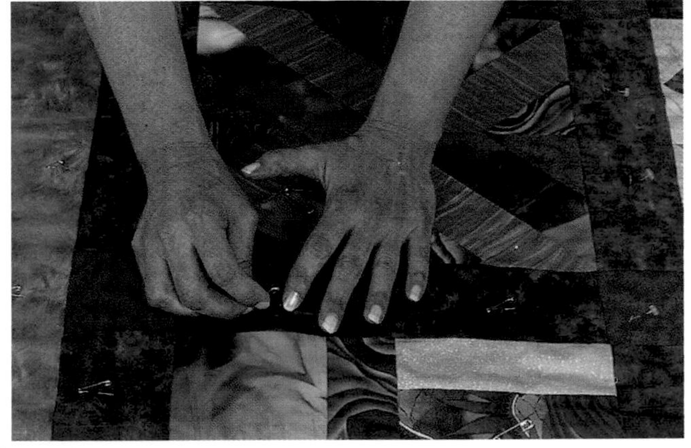

Basting With a "Tagging" Gun

This is Diana's tool of choice: a plastic gun with a thin needle on the end shoots a plastic anchoring string (tag) through all of the layers and back to the top. Look for a quality brand with a thin needle. Diana prefers the Dennsions brand because it is the only one she has found with a thin needle; other brands are inadequate for quilt basting and should not be used. We don't recommend a basting gun for heirloom-quality quilts because the needle may leave small holes that will show up on some fabrics. Use old scissors when it is time to remove the tags. Note: Diana feels that the hole made by the plastic tag is no larger than that made by a safety pin.

The trick of using a tagging gun is to push the plastic tag through the front to the back and out the front. The tag is very secure and holds the three layers together.

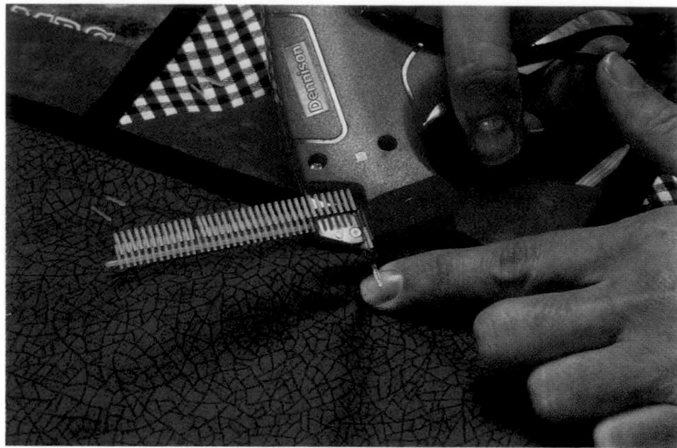

The forefinger of the underhand is firmly pushing the quilt against the end of the gun. This helps force the tag through all of the quilt's layers.

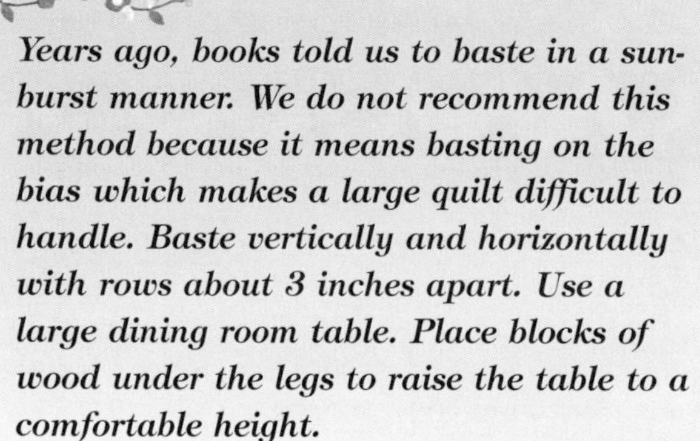

Years ago, books told us to baste in a sunburst manner. We do not recommend this method because it means basting on the bias which makes a large quilt difficult to handle. Baste vertically and horizontally with rows about 3 inches apart. Use a large dining room table. Place blocks of wood under the legs to raise the table to a comfortable height.

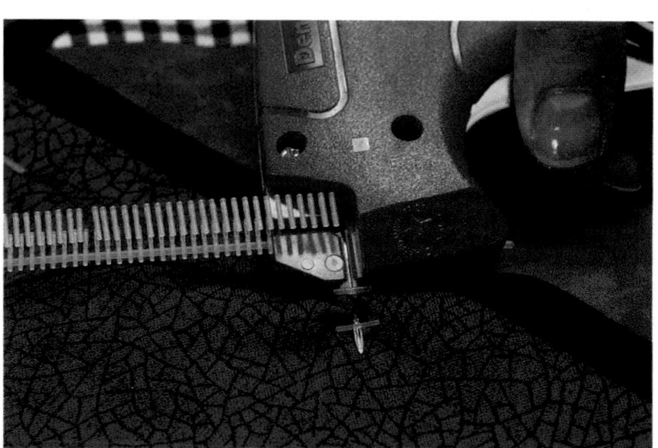

The needle is pulled back, leaving the tag in the quilt.

Fabric Spray Adhesives

We have used two different fabric spray adhesives, KK2000 and 505, to baste our quilts. We found the sprays to be fast and efficient when working with small quilts. The spray temporarily holds the quilt layers together and does not effect the needling. (We do not recommend using any chemicals with heirloom-quality quilts.) The spray is sprayed on one side of the batting, and the top is placed on top of the batting. The spray is sprayed on the other side of the batting, and placed over the wrong side of the backing.

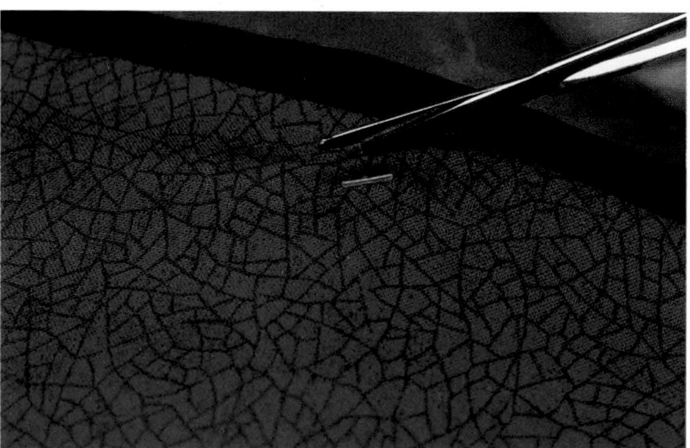

Once you are finished quilting, use curved tipped or old scissors to clip and remove the tags.

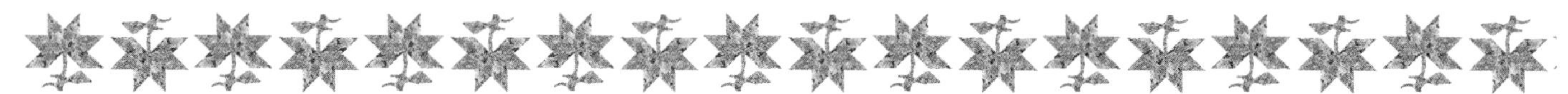

CHAPTER 4 Quilting

You've completed all of the careful preparation and are ready for the fun. The quilting method varies from person to person and from country to country. The variations involve using different finger and thimble combinations. We list a few of these variations for you to try at the end of this chapter. Many books will tell you their way is right, better, or best—but we both say that no particular technique is right or wrong. The important thing is that you are developing your hand quilting and enjoying the process. The method and results will change and develop as you progress. The two of us have traveled throughout the world teaching quilting, observing quilters, and attending quilting events. The technique we are going to teach you is the one we see used most often and the one we use.

Once your quilt is marked, layered, basted, and placed in a hoop or frame, you are ready to quilt. Gather your hand quilting supplies: quilting thread, size 10, 11, or 12 between needles, thimbles, and small scissors.

QUILT HOLDING METHODS

Learning to use a small, short needle, a thimble, and a hoop might be new to you. It may feel clumsy and impossible to use and manipulate these tools at the beginning. Let's start with one thing at a time; straight, even stitches are more important to the overall look of the quilt than short stitches. Our preferred technique includes using a hoop or lap frame. Always start quilting in the center of your quilt, working out from the center. Do not skip areas, leaving them for later, because this might cause a pucker on the back. Quilters differ in the amount of tautness they like the quilt to have while they stitch. We used to say make it tight enough "to bounce a quarter," but a little give makes it easier to manipulate the needle. Most importantly, it should be smooth in the frame or hoop, with some tautness and no puckers (and no waviness) on the front or the back of the quilt.

Hoop

Hoops are aids to help you quilt more evenly and easily. We recommend a 14-inch square, round, or oval to begin with and, when possible, use a larger hoop, up to 24 inches.

We really like the new "almost square" hoop. If the quilting line is at least 1½ inches from the edge of the quilt, this square frame will allow you to quilt all the way to the quilt's edge. This square hoop is our top pick of new products.

To use a hoop:

- Loosen the screw and take the two rings of the hoop apart.
- Place the center of the quilt on top of the smaller (inside) hoop.
- Place the larger outer hoop over the top. Push the outer ring and slide down around the inner hoop, trapping the quilt between the two rings.
- Make sure the layered quilt is pulled smooth (top and backing) in the hoop and tighten the hoop's screw to tighten the quilt into the hoop.
- When you have quilted the area in the hoop, unscrew the hoop and reposition it next to the area you have just quilted. Do not skip areas. It is all right to overlap areas by placing the hoop over an area that is half quilted and half waiting to be quilted. Remember to work from the center out.
- Loosen the hoop when you aren't working on the project.

Lap Frame

This frame has muslin strips attached to the four wooden bars. A quilt is secured in this frame with long quilting pins by pinning the quilt to the frame's muslin strips. Lap frames are very efficient because you can quilt to the quilt's edge (unlike a round hoop). Also, the pin-mounting procedure allows the seam lines of the quilt to be blocked square, which is especially helpful on quilts with a lattice or sashing. It does take more time to mount the quilt in a lap frame than in a hoop, but it is worth the effort. Cindy uses this type of frame for both small and large quilts that have predominately square lines, like a Sampler Quilt or an Irish Chain. She uses a hoop for all other types of quilts (because a hoop is fast to use), such as a Hawaiian appliqué or a Double Wedding Ring.

To use a lap frame:

- Place the center of the quilt over the frame.
- With one hand underneath and one on top, feel the frame's fabric strip. The frame is underneath the quilt. Begin to pin the side closest to your body. Pin the quilt to the fabric strips, from the top, using about six pins.
- Turn the project around 180 degrees and pin the quilt to the opposite side of the frame, slightly pulling it taut as you pin it. Pull the backing fabric first, then the batting and top.
- Pin the third and fourth sides, using about six pins in each side, to the sides of the frame.
- Check the back. Both the front and back of the quilt should be smooth and slightly taut.
- Just like the hoop, when you have quilted the framed area, unpin and move the frame to an adjacent area and repin the frame. Do not skip areas. Remember to begin the quilting in the center of the quilt.

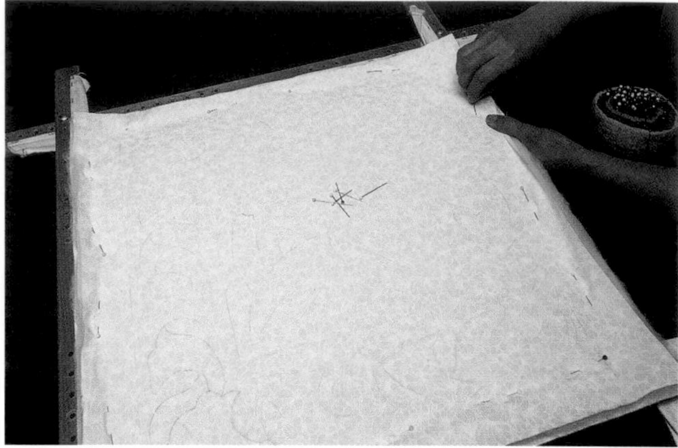

Pinning a small quilt to a lap frame.

Floor Frame

If you have room, you may want to try a floor frame (floor frames need a large dedicated space). Two ends of the quilt are attached to the frame's long fabric-covered bars with pins or thread basting. The entire quilt is stretched onto the large frame, or the quilt is rolled so that about 36 inches are exposed to be quilted. If it is rolled, quilt from the middle to the edge. When you quilt to an edge, leave the threaded needles in the quilt. Reroll the frame and continue quilting with the threaded needles. Floor frames have a wonderful nostalgic feeling and are perfect for a gathering of quilting friends; many people can sit around a frame, visit, and get the work done quickly.

Small Sampler, 68" x 83", 1991, hand pieced and hand quilted by Cindy Walter. This was the first quilt Cindy made to hang on a wall; she usually made bed quilts. The use of black fabric shocked her friends at the time, but now she thinks it makes the quilt interesting. The blocks are from The Sampler Quilt *(now called* The New Sampler Quilt, *C&T), by Diana Leone. Cindy echoed the patchwork seams and used a simple cable stencil in the lattice and border.*

Threading the Needle and Making the Starting Knot

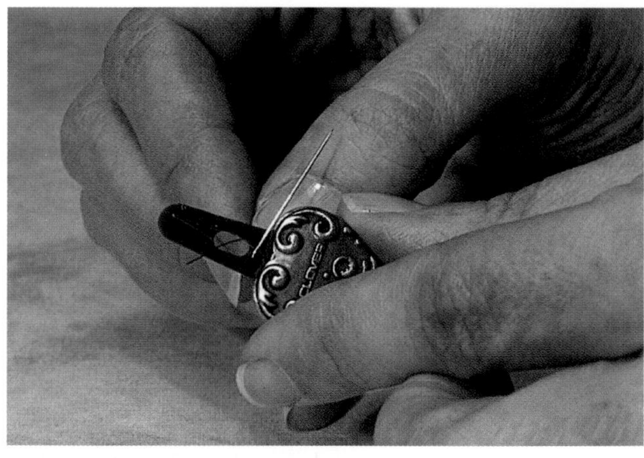

Believe it or not, there is a proper procedure for threading the needle. You will be threading a lot of needles in the course of quilting, and these tips will help:

- Holding the spool with the fingers of your left hand (if you are right-handed), pull off the length of thread with your right hand, about 18 inches. Let the spool roll between your fingers so the thread comes off the side, rather than off the top or bottom of the spool. Unwinding the thread from the spool in this manner helps to prevent further twisting and tangling of the thread.
- Make a clean cut at the end of the thread with sharp scissors or clippers. Insert this cut end through the needle's eye. Use a quilter's needle threader to help thread the small eye of the between needle as a helpful aid.
- Push 6 to 8 inches of thread through the needle's eye.
- Cut the thread off the spool about 12 inches from the needle. Knot the end you cut off the spool. The total length of thread should be about 18 inches.
- Tie a single or large double knot on the end of the thread. If you are using a very fine thread, the knot may pull through the surface of the quilt, and you may have to form a double knot.

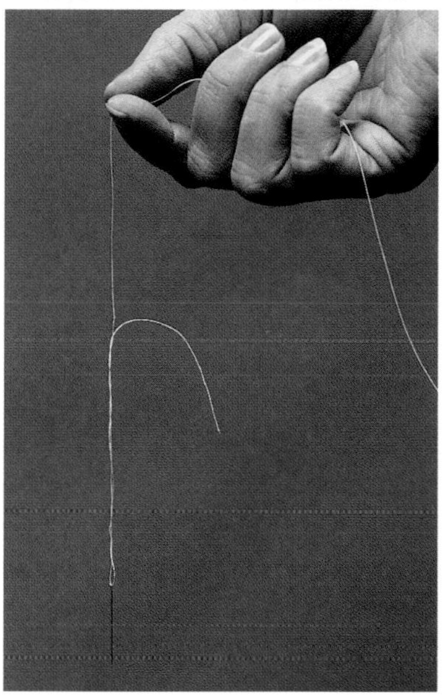

Drop the needle and let the thread unwind.

Tips from the Pros

Cindy's foolproof threading method: Most people hold the needle and try to slide the thread through its eye, but Cindy holds the thread and slides the eye onto the thread. Hold the thread so only the tip is exposed. Set the eye of the needle on the thread—easy.

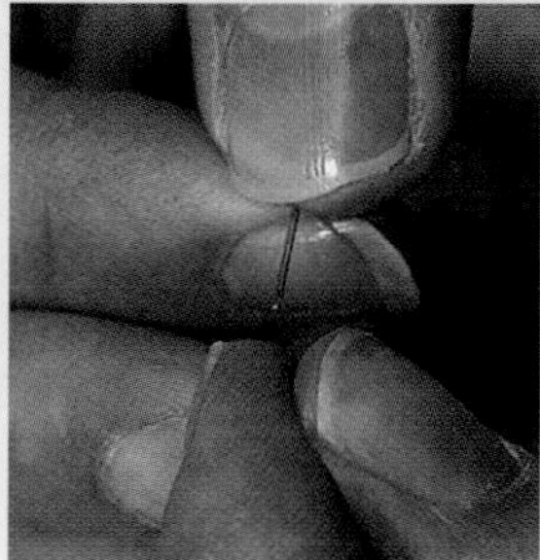

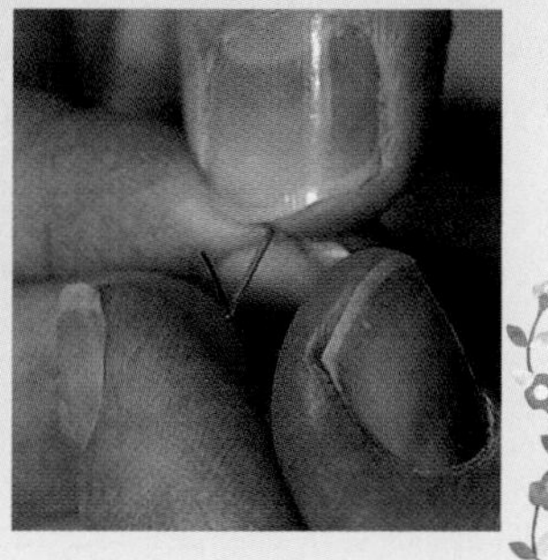

Tip: Diana threads eight to ten needles at a time. She then places them in a pincushion—they are ready to use. She always threads needles when she stops quilting. The needles are ready to use and she looks forward to starting again the next day.

Quilter's Knot

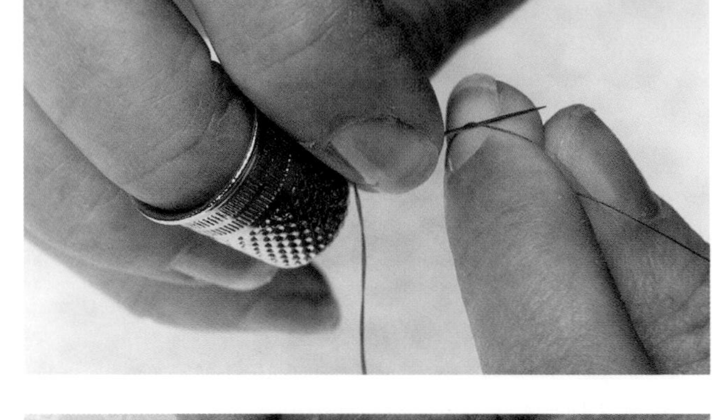

- **Diana's Knot:** To make a quilter's knot, hold the tail of the thread about 1 inch from the end between the thumb and forefinger of your left hand. Hold the needle with your right hand, pull the thread tight, and wrap the thread around the forefinger of your left hand. Holding the loop that has been formed around your finger, take the needle in your right hand and place the tip of the needle between the loop of thread and the fingernail from the knuckle direction, pointing it toward your body. Push the needle under the thread.

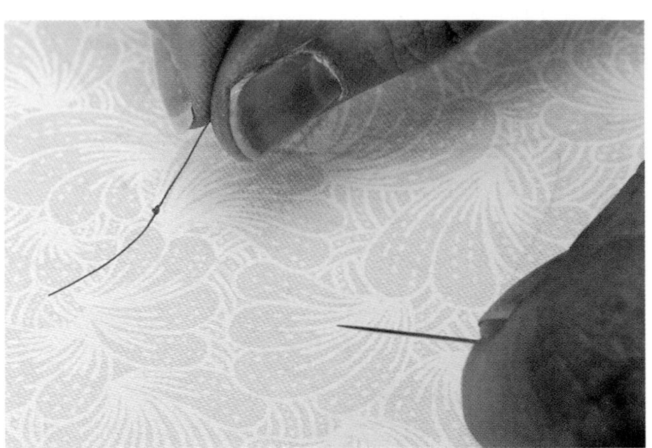

- Grasp the needle with your thumb and forefinger of the right hand, pulling the thread off your finger. A single knot will form about 1 inch from the end of the thread.

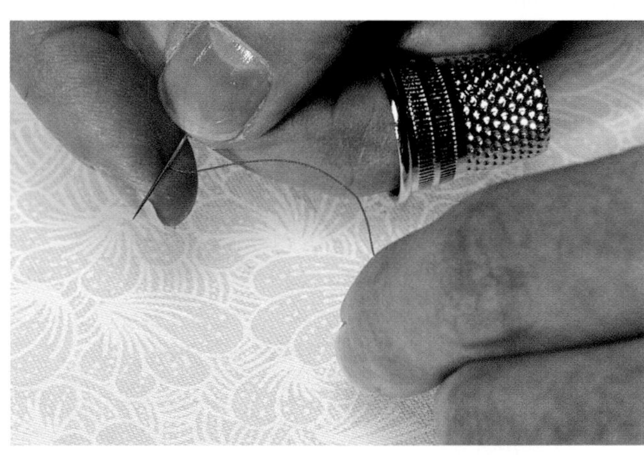

- **Cindy's Knot:** Place the tip of the thread on your left index finger. Place the tip of the needle on the thread. With your right hand, wrap the thread around the needle twice.

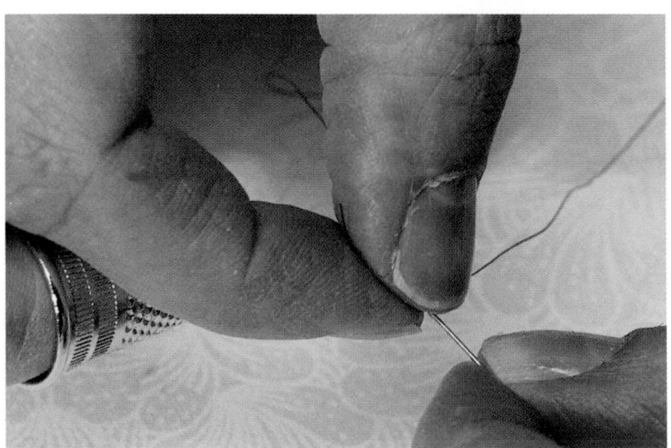

- With your left thumb and index finger, hold the knot area and pull the tip of the needle with your right hand. Keep pulling the needle all the way through until the knot is at the end of the thread.

The Quilting Stitch

Quilting is a fluid motion. The experienced quilter would not necessarily "start or stop pushing" during the process. He or she would have a continual and rhythmic movement. In these instructions, we tell you to do this because students usually push too hard. You will learn to control your needle without pushing, or by placing only slight pressure on it. Once you gain control, the rocking motion will become a rhythmic, constant movement.

When you come to a corner, turn your frame, hoop, or body so that you can once again quilt toward yourself. Practice at corners and sharp turns. Do not pull the thread to pucker the quilt. When you learn to quilt backwards, you will not have to rotate the hoop and you can quilt a longer continuous line. To travel to an adjacent quilting area, usually less than 1 inch, slip the needle between the layers into the batting and bring the tip of the needle back up to where you want to begin again. When you need to travel more than an inch, it is better to make a knot, cut the thread, and start over at the new place. Make sure these traveling stitches do not come out the back. It is best to not travel more than an inch. Note dark thread lines will show through light fabric and the quilt may pucker.

Now is the time to wear a thimble. Place it on the middle finger of your quilting hand. Position yourself so that you are sitting upright in front of the floor frame or hoop on a stand. If using a hoop or lap frame, sit upright and lean the edge of the hoop or lap frame on the edge of a table or on your knee. Your quilting forearm should be resting on top of the quilt with your hand reaching into the middle of the hoop. Your underhand is entirely under the quilt. If using a hoop or lap frame, it may be resting on the inside of the underhand wrist.

Our fast and efficient, tried and true, method of quilting is to place three or four stitches on the needle before pulling it through; this is called multiple stitches or "rock and roll." A rocking motion between the thumb and middle finger of the quilting hand creates a rhythm that will become easy and fast. The quilting hand will be on top of the quilt, with a thimble on your middle finger. The thimble cradles the needle, while pushing it through the layers and forcing it back up and out of the quilt top. The thumb on your quilting hand assists in the needle's return to the top by moving the fabric down and out of the way in front of the needle. The index finger of your underhand will help the needle to return up when the needle's tip grazes off the tip of this finger. Both hands work together. Please follow along with the detailed instructions next to the following photos to learn multiple-stitch quilting (and practice, practice, practice).

Hiding the Knot

To prevent knots from showing, we suggest popping, or sinking, the knots between the quilt's layers. Form a single knot and enter the quilt sandwich from the top (go through the batting but not the backing), about an inch from where you will begin quilting. Bring the needle up at the point where your quilting will begin and gently tug on the thread to "pop" the knot through the top fabric to bury it in the batting.

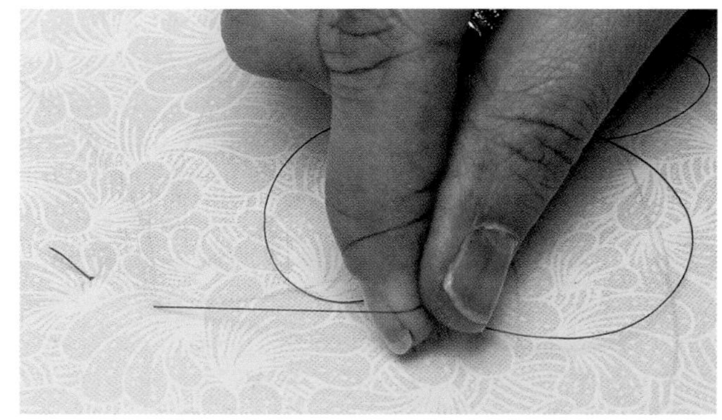

The Quilting Stitch

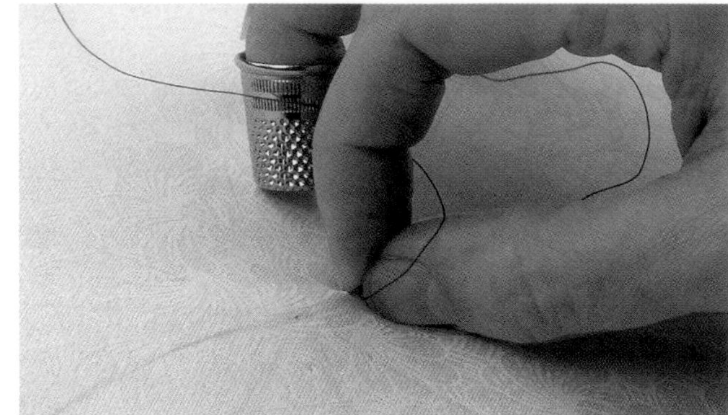

- Position yourself and the frame or hoop so that you will be quilting toward yourself or across your body. Place the non-quilting hand under the quilt with the pad of your index finger resting under the starting point. Pop the knot into the quilt layers and bring the needle up at the starting point.

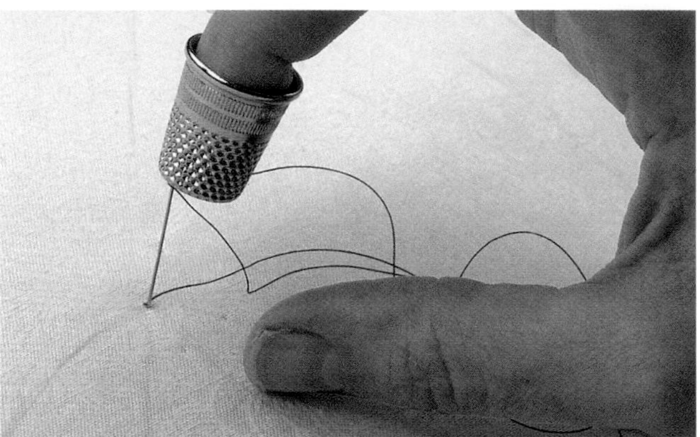

- To form the first stitch, insert the needle perpendicularly into the surface of the quilt, a stitch length away from where the needle came up.
- Place the quilting finger thimble on the eye of the needle and slightly push until you can feel the tip of the needle touch the underneath finger. Stop pushing.

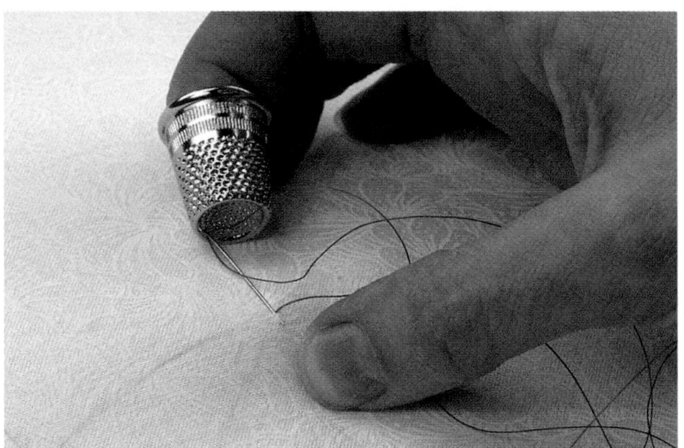

- Keep a constant pressure on the needle tip with the underneath finger. With only the thimble touching the needle, lay the needle back down, parallel to the quilt top. Place your upper hand's thumb on the quilt surface, in front of the tip of the needle, gently pushing the fabric down in front of where the needle will emerge up through the top.
- While pushing firmly and upward from underneath, slightly push the needle with the thimble until you can see its tip on top of the quilt. (Diana pushes and curls the end of her underneath finger forward, forcing the needle back up into the quilt.) There is your stitch. Stop pushing.

- Rock the eye of the needle upward at almost a perpendicular angle to the top and push until you feel the needle touch the underneath finger. Stop pushing and lay the needle back down on top of the quilt. Do not "let go" of the needle; it is being held by the thimble.

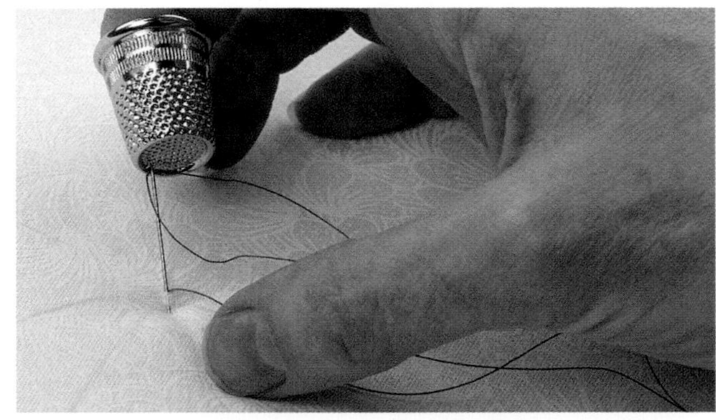

- Continue rocking the needle up and down until you have formed three to four stitches on the needle.

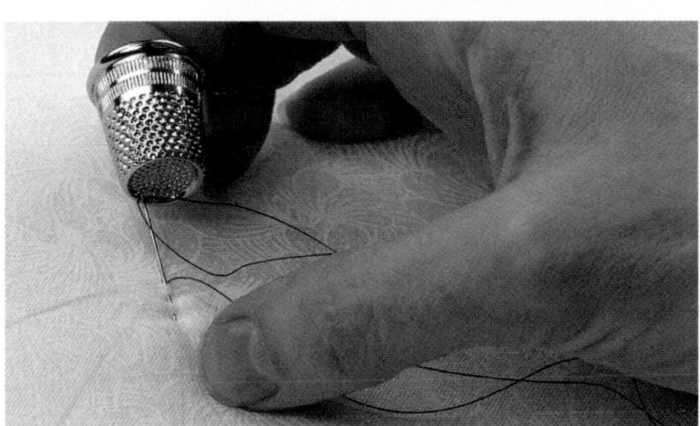

- With your thimble, push the needle all the way up and out through to the top.

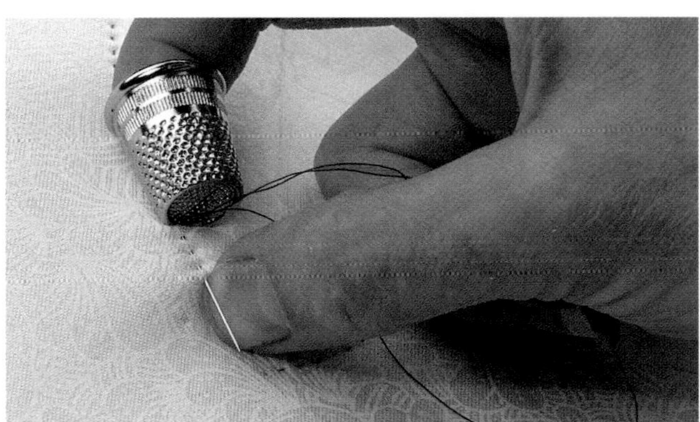

- Pull the thread all the way through with your fingers. Pull the thread just enough so the stitches sink into the surface, but not enough to gather or pucker the quilt.

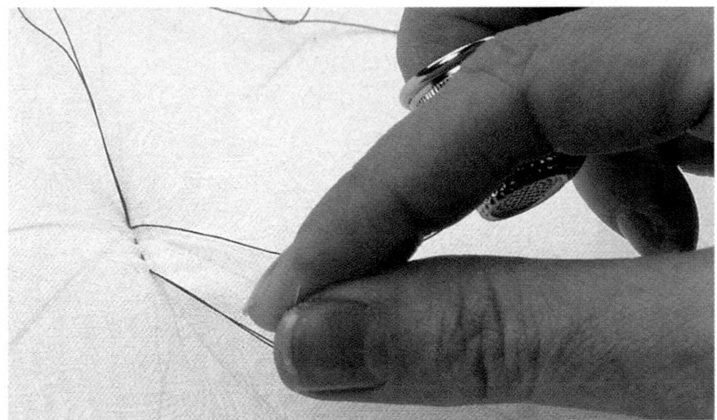

We have repeated the basic quilting stitch using clear bubble wrap, so you can see the underneath finger.

- To form the first stitch, insert the needle perpendicularly into the surface of the quilt, a stitch length away from where the needle came up.

- Place the quilting finger thimble on the eye of the needle and slightly push until you can feel the tip of the needle touch the underneath finger. Stop pushing.

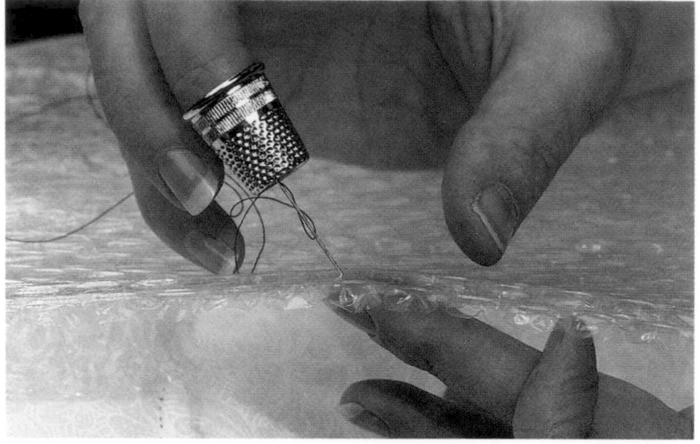

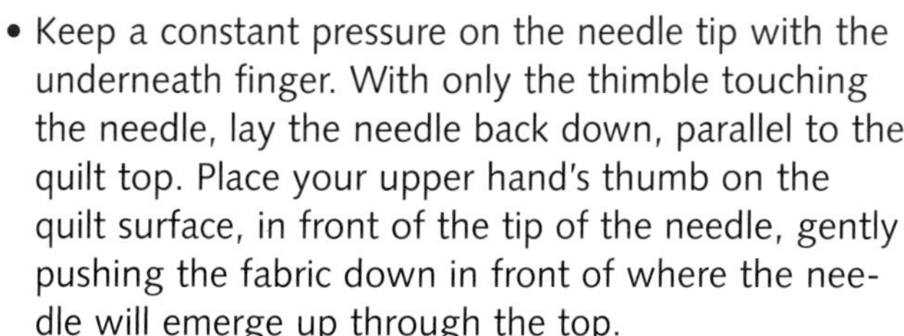

- Keep a constant pressure on the needle tip with the underneath finger. With only the thimble touching the needle, lay the needle back down, parallel to the quilt top. Place your upper hand's thumb on the quilt surface, in front of the tip of the needle, gently pushing the fabric down in front of where the needle will emerge up through the top.

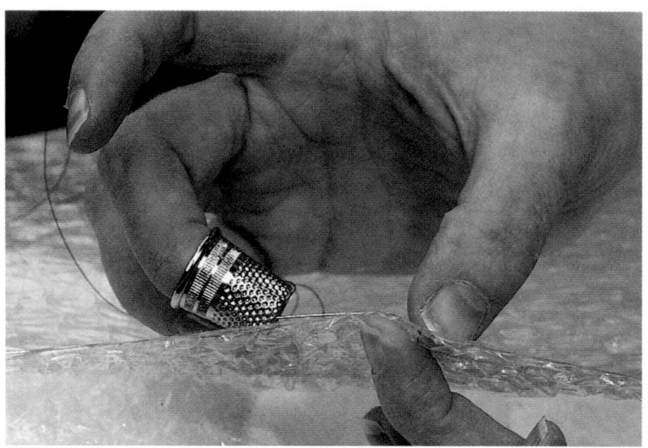

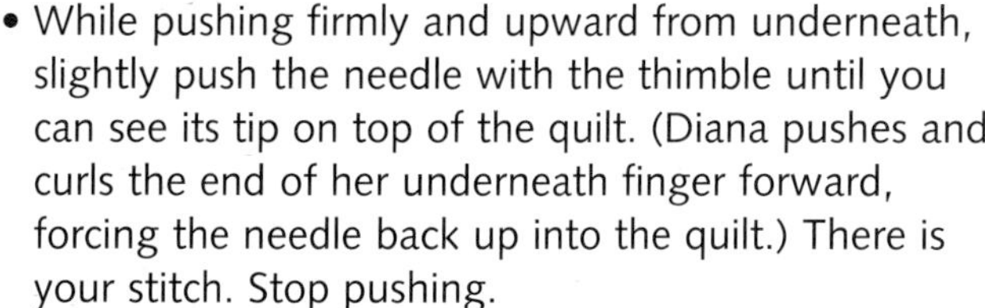

- While pushing firmly and upward from underneath, slightly push the needle with the thimble until you can see its tip on top of the quilt. (Diana pushes and curls the end of her underneath finger forward, forcing the needle back up into the quilt.) There is your stitch. Stop pushing.

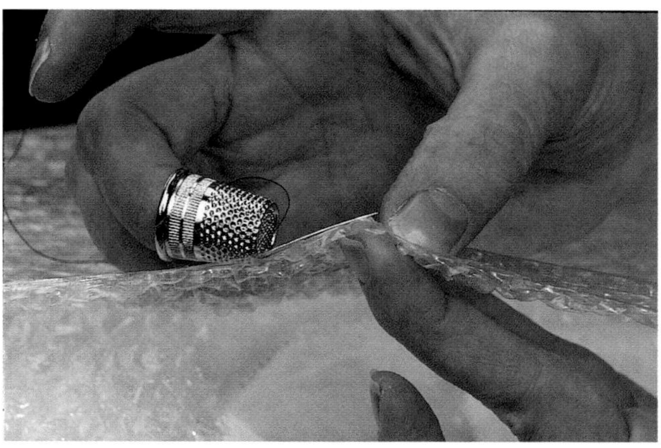

Tips from the Pros:

Glenda Hilluck, a quilter from Sanger, Texas, says, "I have been a quilter for about thirty years. My mother, grandmother, and two aunts let me help them sew pieces as a child. They also encouraged me to quilt on the tops. I use a metal thimble with a concave top and a 10 or 12 needle. The smaller the needle, the smaller the stitch you'll create. The more practice you get the better your stitches will become."

Tips from the Pros

Your index finger and thumb will eventually become sore and bruised from pulling the needle out of the quilt once it is loaded with multiple stitches. To prevent this from happening, learn to push the "loaded" needle out with your thimble. Diana's tip: Use a piece of a balloon or a "needle grabber" to pull the needle through the layers.

The Ending Knot

The knot is formed at the quilt's surface before ending the last stitch.

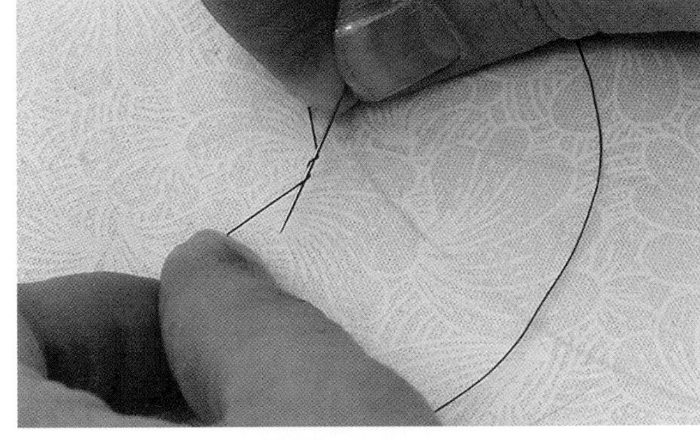

- To end the quilting, form a small knot in the thread at the quilt's surface.

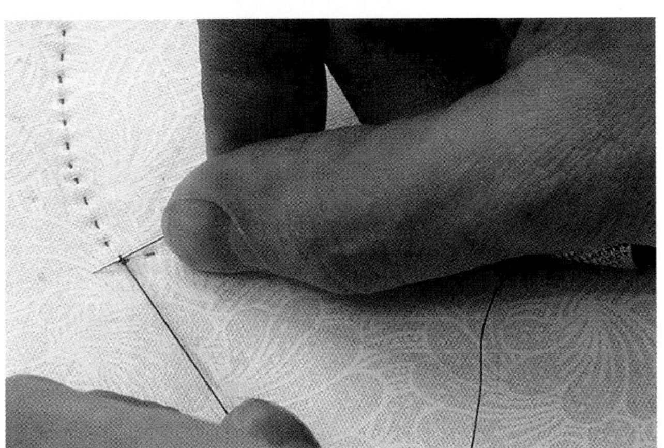

- Insert the needle back into the quilt. Bring the needle up through the top about 1 inch from the last stitch.

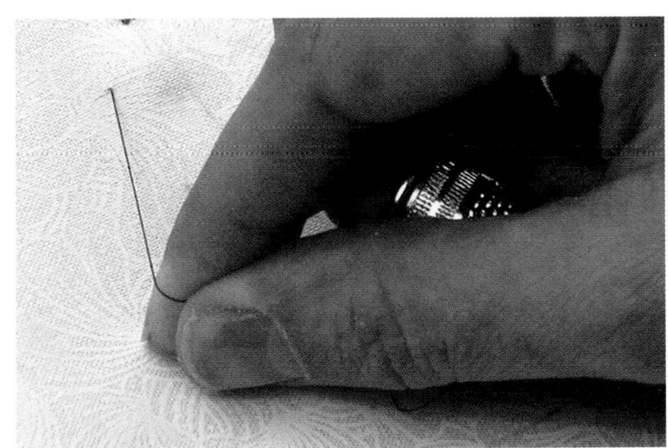

- Slightly tug on the thread, "popping" the knot between the layers. Trim the thread's tail.

Tips from the Pros:

Laverne Mathews, master quilter from Orange, Texas: "My daughter-in-law, a novice quilter at the time, opened my eyes to a wonderful way to start and stop the quilting thread. No knots! No jerking to bury the knots between the layers. Here's how: Insert the needle into the top and batting only, an inch in front of the starting point, and bring out at the starting point. Take a tiny backstitch and proceed with quilting in a regular manner. When the thread is used up, take another tiny backstitch, and send the needle between the layers to re-emerge a needle-length away. Clip thread close to the top. So simple."

Quilting Away from Yourself

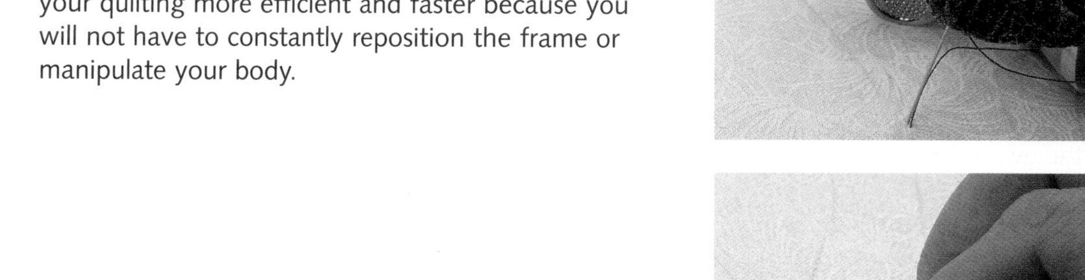

- Many quilters can only quilt toward themselves or across their body. It is certainly not mandatory to learn to quilt away from yourself, but it will make your quilting more efficient and faster because you will not have to constantly reposition the frame or manipulate your body.

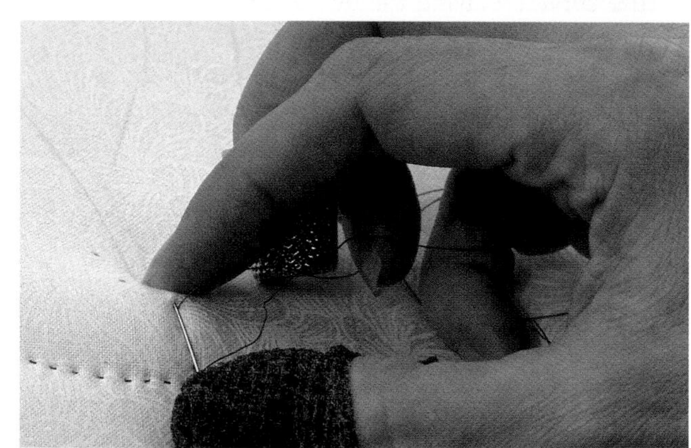

- Place a leather, or Wrap-it, thimble on your thumb. Use the thumb thimble to push the needle away from you, while your index finger pushes the fabric down in front of the needle's tip.

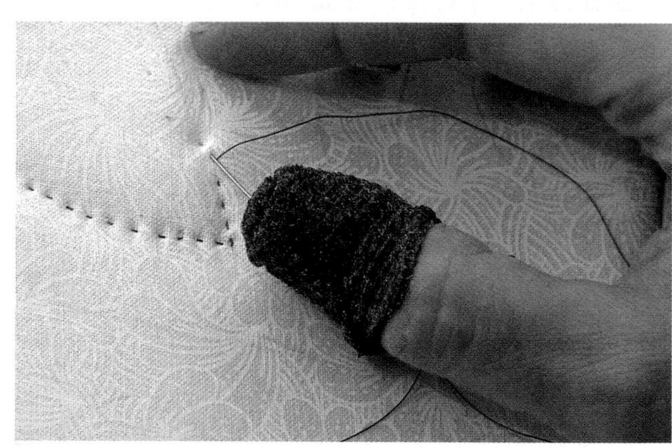

- It is the exact same movement as forward quilting; you are just using different fingers.

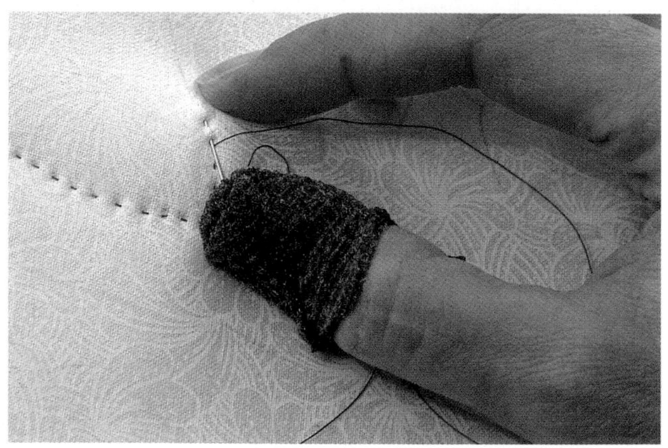

- Many quilters use their thumbnail instead of a thimble to push the needle. We do not recommend this because we have suffered damage to our nails with this method; it is best to use a thimble on your thumb.

Straight Stitches

Concentrate on straight stitches at first. The needle needs to enter the fabric in the direction you want to quilt. Most importantly, the eye end of the needle must be parallel to the quilting line. It is a common mistake for students to lay the eye end of the needle down, or pick it up, at an angle to the quilting line. This will result in crooked stitches or a crooked quilting line. Practice lifting the eye end of the needle straight up and down, on top of the quilting line. The technique is different for curved quilting lines. Follow the curve by laying the eye of the needle down at an angle so the tip can follow the angle of the line. When a quilting line curves, you may only be able to take one or two stitches at a time. This is a good place to practice forming one stitch at a time.

Short Stitches

A bonus of mastering even stitches, by concentrating on how many threads are on the needle, is your stitches will usually become shorter. You can directly control the length of your stitch by how hard you push, and angle, the needle. It will take time for you to gain control of all of the elements. It is important to gain control and build a smooth, methodical rhythm.

Even Stitches

After quilting for a few rows and concentrating on making straight stitches, try to make them even. "Even stitches" refers to the equal amount of thread appearing on the top of the quilt and the amount of fabric showing between each stitch. Try to form the stitches so the length of the stitch and the amount of fabric between each stitch are equal. To make the stitches even, concentrate on how much fabric appears on the needle and under the needle prior to inserting the tip again into the fabric for the next stitch. You will get to the point where you are actually aware of how many threads of fabric are on and under the needle of each stitch. The stitches on the back of the quilt may look different from those on the top. Diana's stitches on the back barely show and are smaller than the top stitches. Cindy's are the opposite. We both feel it is more important for you to concentrate on the look of the top stitches for the time being. A quilt in a judged show will seldom, if ever, lose points because of the stitches on the back.

Tips from the Pros:

Kathy Galos, master quilter, says even she can't make straight stitches without a hoop, so she recommends beginners use one. It also helps prevent puckers.

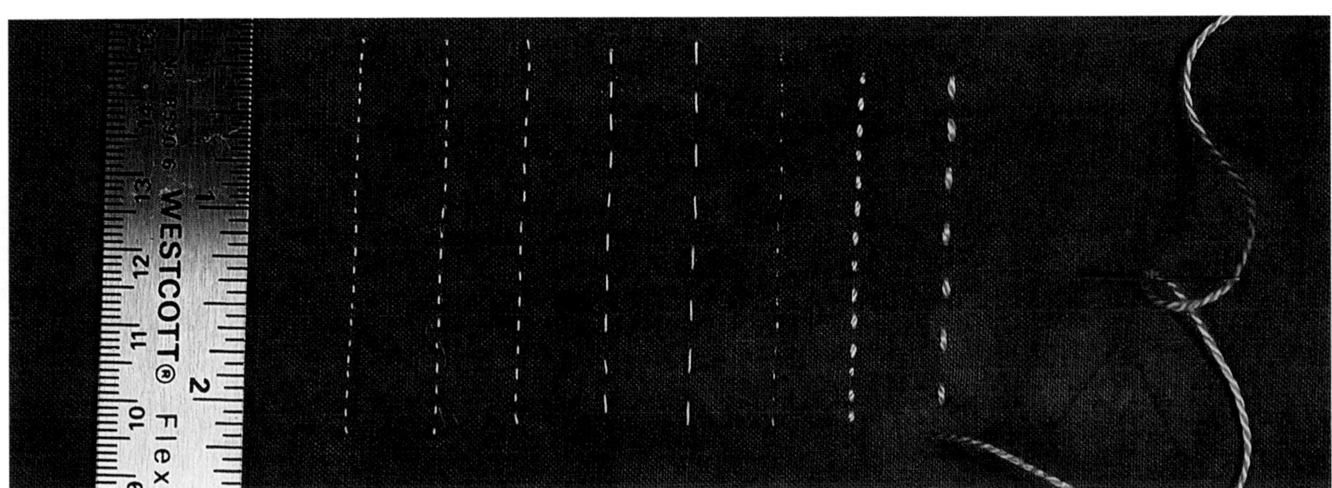

Various Thimble and Finger Positions

The combination of thimble uses and holding methods are endless. There is no right or wrong way to hold the needle or to make each stitch. Once you master the methods we recommend, make adjustments to suit your needs. Try all methods, including those shared with you by numerous quilters throughout the book. Our goals are for you to enjoy hand quilting and for you to be able to successfully complete your project.

Recently, a sore knuckle on Cindy's quilting finger (middle), forced her to try quilting with the thimble on her index finger. It worked! She could make small, even stitches with her index finger. It felt awkward but it was efficient, and she is happy to know she has a great alternative if her middle finger ever becomes permanently "out of commission."

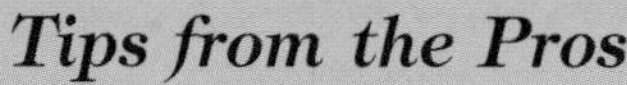

Tips from the Pros

Serene Miller, friend and author, has used two metal thimbles for over twenty years.

Penny Nii, a contemporary California quiltmaker, quilts with two thimbles but has taken this method a step further: she takes each stitch individually, but only pulls the thread through after taking four or five stitches. She is very fast.

Jenny Beyer, author and quiltmaker, can quilt equally well with both hands. Try it: you may be ambidextrous, too.

Diana can baste a quilt with either hand.

Doris Olds, a master quilter, uses a secretary's "rubber finger" on her quilting forefinger to pull the needle loaded with stitches through the quilt. She loads as many stitches on the needle as it will hold, maybe six to ten, then pushes the needle through the quilt layers with her thimble and pulls the needle through by gripping it with the rubber finger. Great idea!

You will find many quilters hold the needle between their thumb and index finger and use the thimble on their middle finger to push when they take only **one stitch at a time** on their needle. This may work for you, and you will stitch one stitch at a time when quilting through bulky seam areas.

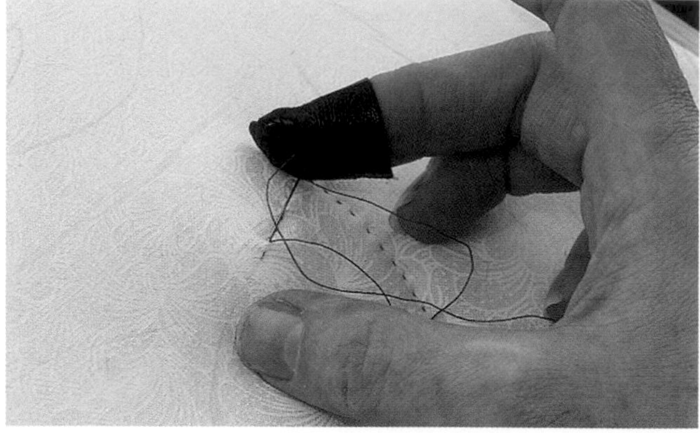

Leather thimble for a long fingernail.

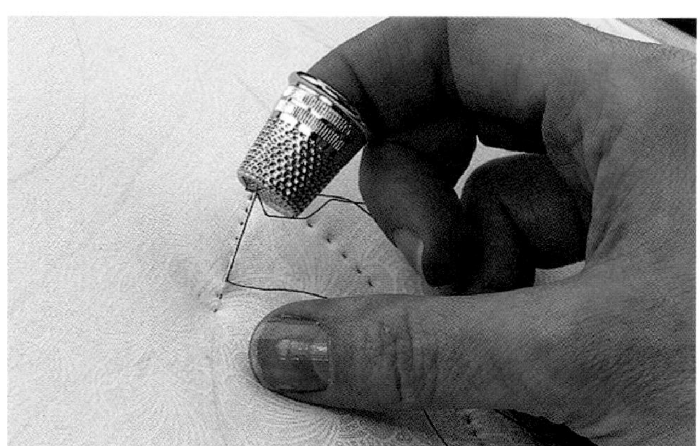

Using the thimble on the index finger.

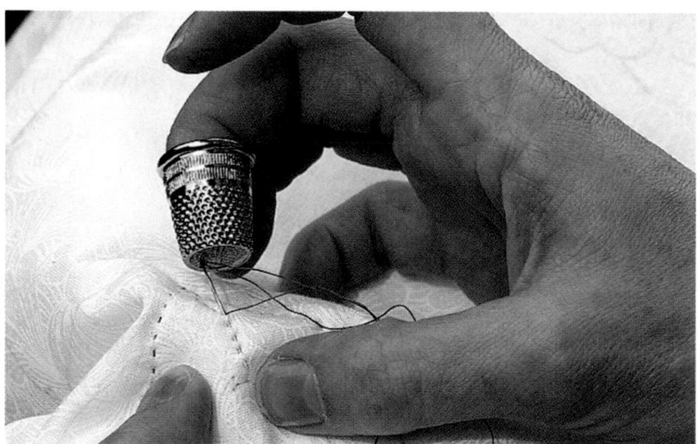

Quilting without a hoop or frame.

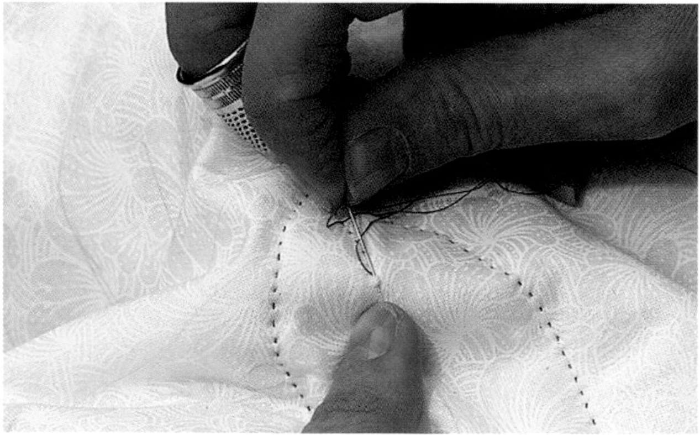

Making one stitch at a time with no hoop.

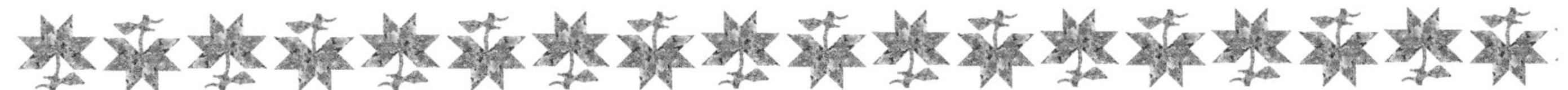

Chapter 5 Finishing

The binding is the edging sewn to the outer edges of the quilt to encase and finish the edge. The fabric should be of the same quality as was used on the quilt's front and back. You can use the same colored fabric as the quilt's outer border, chose a contrasting fabric, or the binding can also be pieced, using multiple colorful fabrics. If you do the latter, the eye will follow the active colors and bring the focus back to the center of the quilt. The binding serves as the final frame around your quilt.

When quilts have curved edges, cut the binding fabric from the fabric's bias (45-degree angle) and piece these strips together. Bias binding will ease and stretch around curved edges such as a Double Wedding Ring quilt. We have not included continuous bias cutting directions, because this method isn't used often today. (See *The New Sampler Quilt* for thorough bias binding instructions.)

When quilts have straight sides, the binding is cut on the straight of the grain (lengthwise preferred if you have enough fabric) to make the edges of the quilt as straight and squared as possible. A single-fold binding is used on wall quilts, thin quilts, and those receiving little wear, whereas double-fold binding is used on large bed quilts and those receiving more wear.

Make the binding strip by cutting parallel strips of fabric (1 1/2 inches for single, 2 3/4 inches for double) with scissors or rotary cutting equipment. Piece the strips together into one long, continuous strips. The length should match the project's perimeter, plus a little extra. For example, a double-sized quilt is 90 inches by 108 inches. You will need a binding that is 396 inches, plus about 12 inches extra, or about eleven strips of 40-inch wide fabric. For double binding, fold it in half, right sides out, and press.

We recommend that you use a walking foot (dual feed foot) to sew the binding to the quilt's edge.

Double-fold Straight Cut Binding

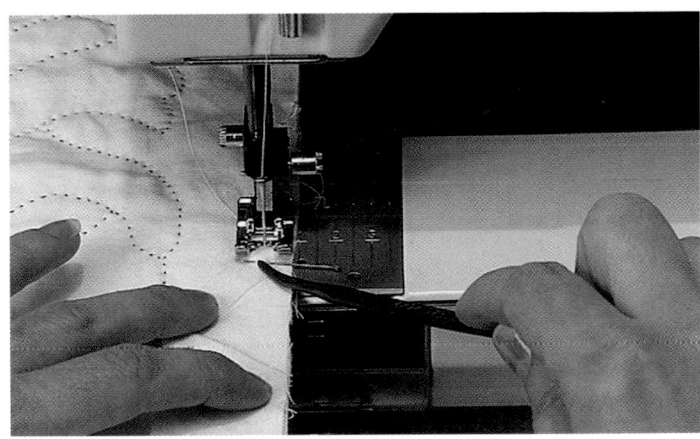

Align the raw edges of the binding with the front side edge of the quilt, beginning about 10 inches from a corner. Fold the end at a 45-degree angle. Insert a few pins at the beginning of the binding to hold it in place. Do not pin the binding to all of the quilt's edges. You may need to "ease" along the binding as you sew.

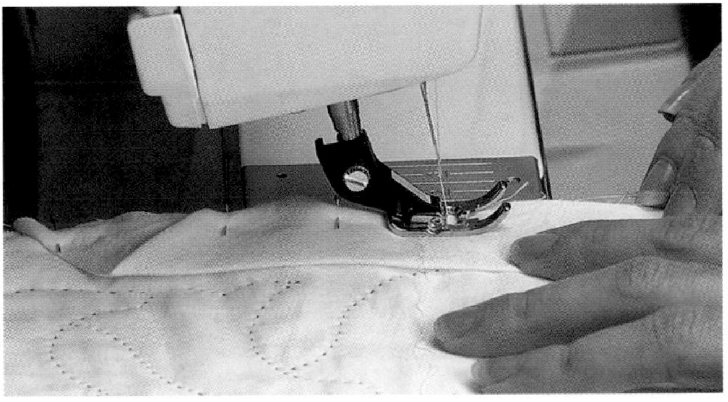

Begin sewing 3 inches down from the folded end. Sew 3/8 inch in from the raw edges.

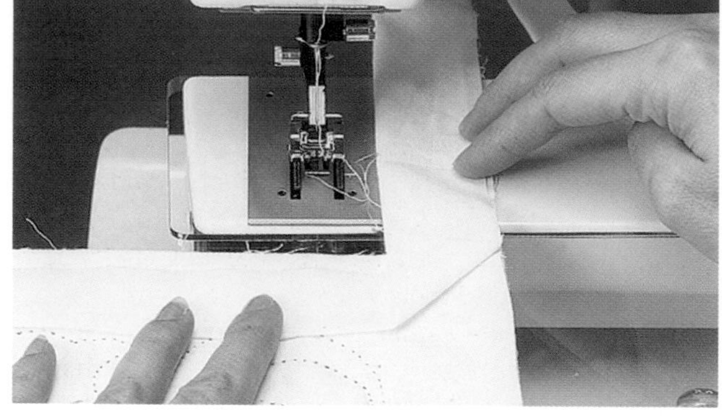

Stop stitching $^3/_8$ inch from the corner. Backstitch. Lift the needle out of the fabric (this is important). Pull the quilt a few inches away from the needle to loosen the threads. Turn the quilt one quarter counterclockwise. Fold the binding straight up (forming a 45-degree angle).

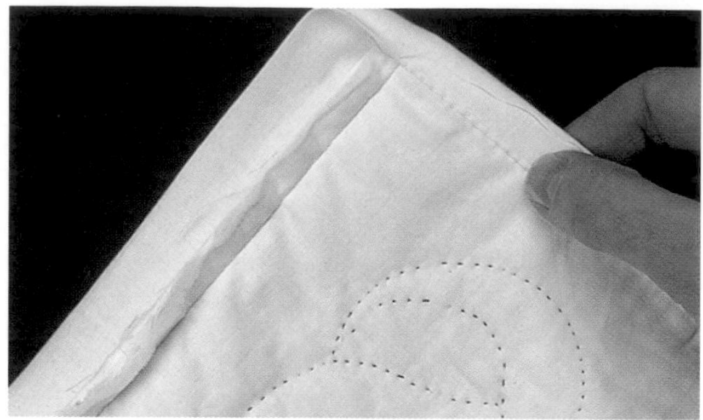

Bring the folded edge of the binding around to the back of the quilt.

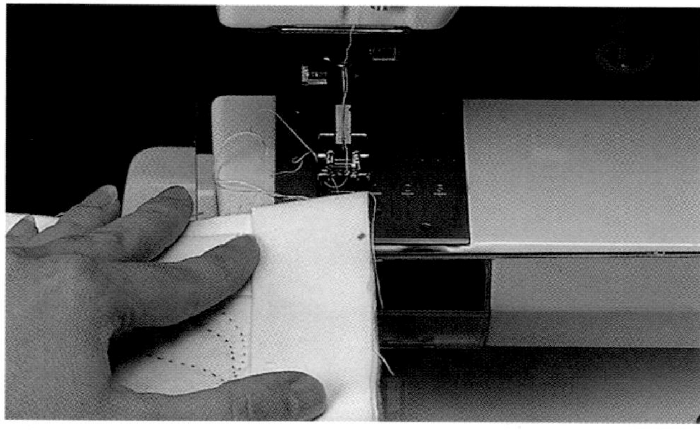

Fold the binding in front and down over the angle. The top folded edge must be even with the top edge of the quilt. Beginning at the top edge, sew all of the quilt's edges. Repeat the miter step at the corners.

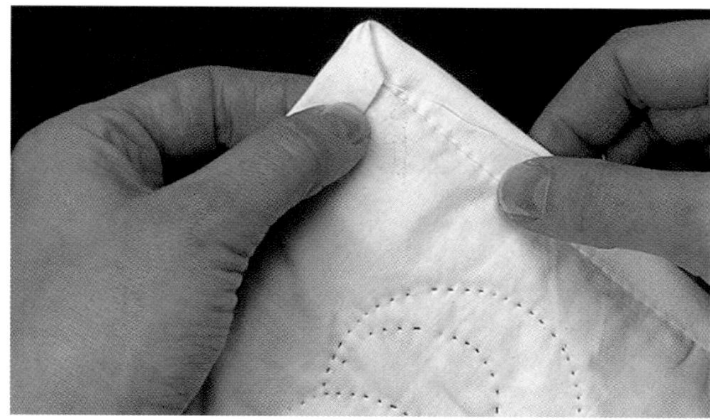

Tuck in the corner, forming a mitered corner of the front and back.

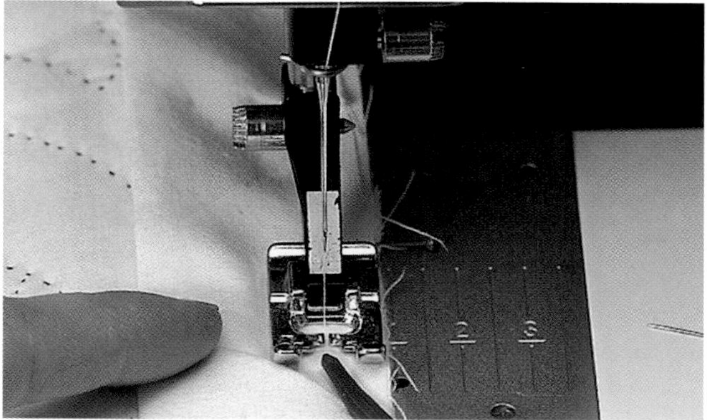

To finish the binding end, place the unsewn end over the beginning (folded end) of the binding. Cut the end $^1/_2$ inch longer than the beginning edge and insert the unsewn, cut end into the folded edge of the binding. For single-fold binding, simply place the end over the folded beginning edge. Pin and sew the seam across the overlapped ends to finish the seam.

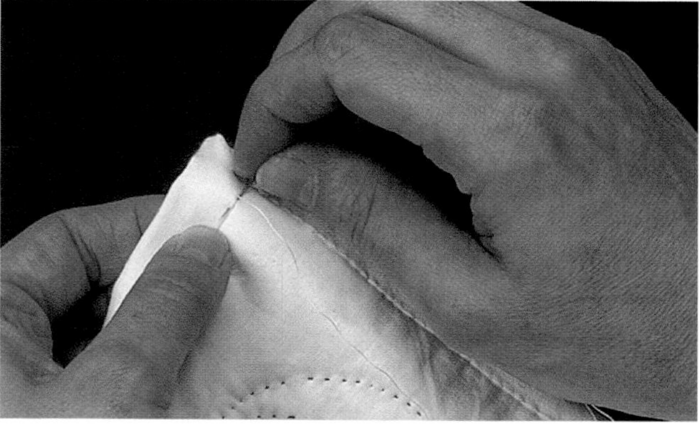

Hand-stitch the folded edge to the quilt back using a blind hemstitch.

Labeling the Quilt

It is important for you to document your work. One easy way to do this is to make a label. Write your name, address, and any important information on this piece of fabric with a waterproof pen and hand sew the label to the back of the quilt. There are also decorative pre-made labels available at your local quilt shop.

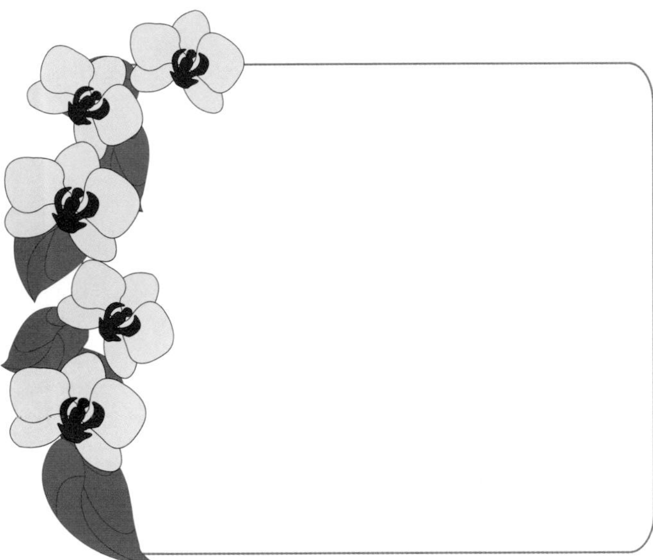

Custom labels, designed specifically for each quilt, add a great finishing touch to any quilt. Labels can be whimsical and fun, yet they can serve the purpose of documenting your and the quilt's personal history. A label may include what inspired you to make the quilt, special occasions, specially created designs, and, of course, an address or a way to contact the owner if the quilt is lost. Make your own or purchase a custom label.

Hanging the Quilt

Sew a sleeve, rod pocket, or casing to the quilt's top back edge. Cut the strip 9 inches wide from the same fabric as the backing fabric (if possible). Piece the strips if needed so the sleeve equals the exact width of the quilt's top edge. Hand sew it to the quilt about 1/2 inch from the top back edge. Slip a thin (1/4-inch x 1 1/2-inch) board through the sleeve, allowing 1/4 inch or more to show on each end. Nail the board to the wall on each end with a short, thin nail. If you are using a round dowel to hang the quilt, pinch a 1/2-inch fold of extra fabric along the outer side of the sleeve before sewing it to the quilt. The fold will absorb the dowel's roundness, and there will not be a bulge across the front of the quilt.

Cleaning the Quilt

A quilt, depending on its use, may need to be washed during its lifetime. If the quilt is stable and the fabric was prewashed, you will be able to hand or carefully machine-wash it; dry cleaning is not recommended. If the quilt is hanging on the wall, it can be lightly vacuumed to remove dust.

When washing a quilt, use a phosphorus-free soap, because detergents have harsh chemicals that may destroy the quilt. We recommend the purest soap available, called Orvus. Use one or two capfuls in a washing machine set on a gentle cycle. Lightly spin the quilt to remove excess water and place the quilt and a large towel in the dryer for 10 to 20 minutes. Remove the quilt before it is completely dry, straighten it on a large sheet on the floor, and allow it to finish drying.

Hand-wash a delicate or old quilt by using one or two capfuls of Orvus soap (or any other phosphorus-free soap) in a bathtub full of warm water. Gently place the quilt in the water and push it up and down until it is completely wet. Let it soak for 20 minutes (for a dirty quilt, you may have to repeat this process). Drain the bathtub and refill with clean water. Gently push the quilt up and down to rinse. Drain the bathtub and slightly squeeze the excess water from the quilt. Repeat this process until the water runs clear of soap. Dry the quilt outside on a warm day, away from direct sunlight. If drying on the ground, lay a clean sheet over a plastic sheet, and then position the quilt on top of the sheet. Check the quilt every hour or so, turning it until it is dry. If you have a clean clothesline out of the sun, use it, hanging the quilt over two lines.

Storing the Quilt

The best way to store a quilt is to lay it out flat on an unused bed. If the quilt is to be stored in a closet or cedar chest, place a large, clean sheet on the floor, fold the sheet and the quilt together, and place in the storage area. Unfold the quilt at least once a year and refold in a different area to prevent wear on the fold lines. If you have room, a tube about 6 inches in diameter and the width of the quilt is a perfect storage tool. Place the quilt on a sheet and roll the two around the tube. Never store a quilt in a sealed plastic bag. Take your quilts out of storage and enjoy them whenever possible.

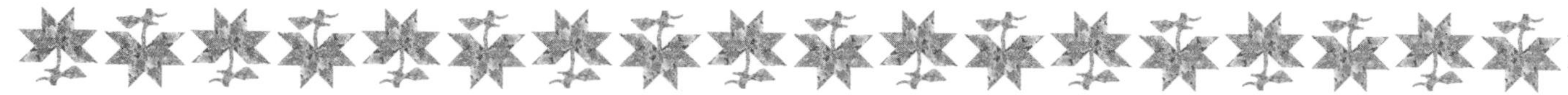

Chapter 6 How to Quilt This Quilt

Deciding on how to quilt your quilt will be an important decision; each type of quilt will require a different quilting line to complement the quilt's design. We are often asked for advice on what type of quilting line design someone should use to hand quilt his or her quilt. In this chapter, we have showcased several beautiful quilts and have reviewed what type of quilting line design the quilter used in each area of the quilt. Enjoy the quilts and use any of the following ideas when you are ready to quilt your quilt.

Traditional

As we discussed earlier, different quilting line styles traditionally lend themselves to certain types of quilts. For instance, a Sampler Quilt is usually quilted 1/4 inch in from the seam line around each piece of patchwork, the open areas of a Double Wedding Ring lend themselves to a more elaborate pattern, and A Trip Around the World is a perfect top for a beautiful diagonal grid. Observe the quilting lines used in the following traditional quilts and adapt the ideas to your needs.

Water Color Trip, 48" x 48", 1994, by Cindy Walter. Cindy was inspired to make this quilt when she read Colourwash *(TPP), by Deirdre Amsden. Marking the grid quilting lines was very quick with a yardstick. These lines enhance the diagonal design.*

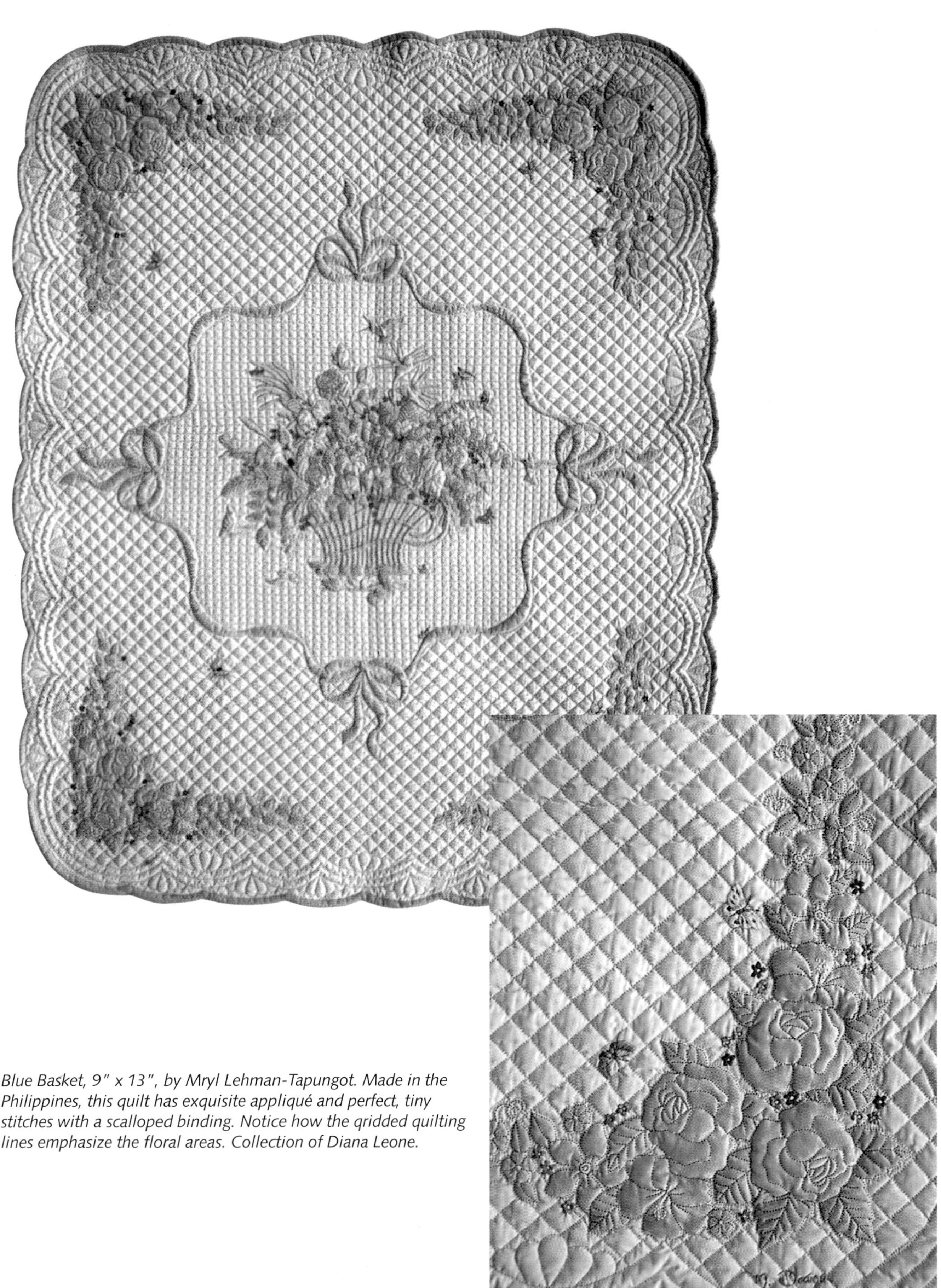

Blue Basket, 9" x 13", by Mryl Lehman-Tapungot. Made in the Philippines, this quilt has exquisite appliqué and perfect, tiny stitches with a scalloped binding. Notice how the qridded quilting lines emphasize the floral areas. Collection of Diana Leone.

Voices of the Past, 76" x 76", 1999, designed, pieced, and hand quilted by Judy Pleiss, machine quilting added by Cecelia Purciful. This quilt was inspired by a quilt from the 1820s, which hangs in the DAR Museum. Judy's workmanship is perfect. The patchwork blocks in the center and corners are from two books, Voices of the Past *and* Voices of the Past II, *both by Kaye England. All of the fabrics were designed by Kaye England for South Sea Imports. Left: Quilting detail.*

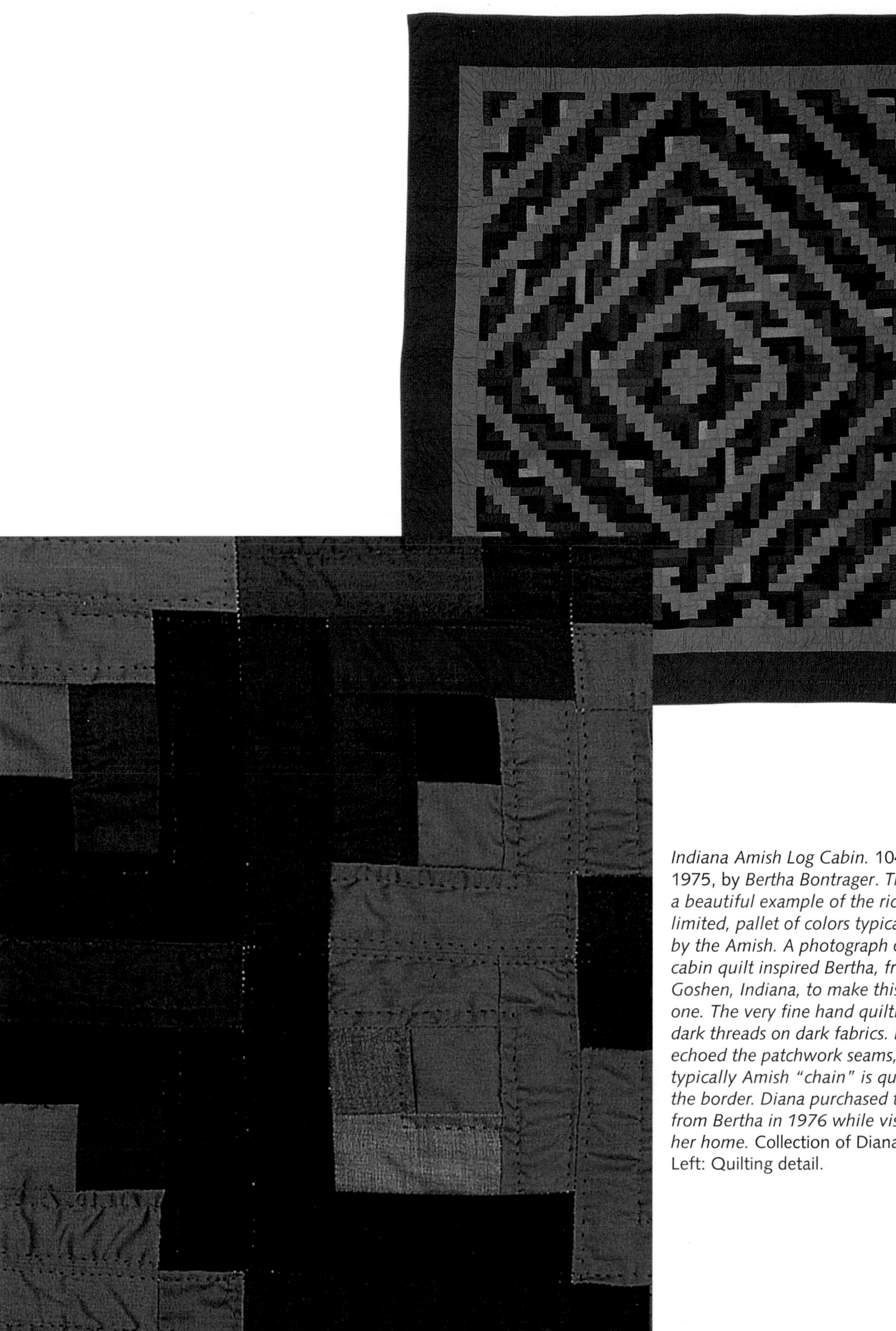

Indiana Amish Log Cabin. 104" x 104", 1975, by *Bertha Bontrager. This quilt is a beautiful example of the rich, yet limited, pallet of colors typically used by the Amish. A photograph of a log cabin quilt inspired Bertha, from Goshen, Indiana, to make this similar one. The very fine hand quilting used dark threads on dark fabrics. Bertha echoed the patchwork seams, and a typically Amish "chain" is quilted in the border. Diana purchased this quilt from Bertha in 1976 while visiting in her home.* Collection of Diana Leone. Left: Quilting detail.

Carolina Rose, 85" x 85". This Carolina Rose, or Carolina Lily, was appliquéd in 1870–1880. The top was quilted in 1993. Diana purchased the top and it became part of her private collection. When she discovered what magnificent hand quilting the quilters trained by Mryl Lehman-Tapungot in the Philippines did, she knew one of these lady's work would make this perfect top into an even more perfect quilt. The quilting took over a year; the design is original and by Mryl. The appliqué is outlined. A double grid appears behind the appliqué, and a rope is quilted into the border. The batting is thin cotton. Collection of Diana Leone. Right: Quilting detail.

Postage Stamps, 56" x 70", 1940–1996. This fine example of a postage stamp scrap quilt, made of 1/2-inch squares. If you quilt around the seams, it would be a tremendous amount of quilting and you would have to contend with all of the seam allowances. If you quilt on the diagonal, you will miss about half of the bulk of the seams, hence this quilt was quilted in that manner, on the diagonal. Collection of Diana Leone.

Flower Garden, 89" x 96", 1940. This is a typical example of the quilting style used in a Flower Garden. The quilting echoes each seam line. Try using 1/4-inch seam tape instead of marking the quilting lines. When a quilt is quilted next to each seam, you have to turn the hoop many times. Practice quilting with your thumb; up, away from your body and backwards. The quilting raises each piece of fabric and adds a secondary mosaic design. Collection of Diana Leone.

Quilts made by Native Americans are national treasures. These two quilts were generously loaned to us by Ann Pulford Wilson, daughter and curator of the collection of her late mother, Florence Pulford. Diana had the great pleasure of knowing Florence and documenting her collection of Native American quilts in the book of *Morning Star Quilts* (Leone Publications). Clouds are quilted into the border and/or background. Echo quilting follows the seam lines.

The quilts of the Northern Plains Indians were made primarily for The Giveaway. The quilts were made and freely given at a ceremony commemorating some great, significant event in another person's life, including the death of a relative, a birth, a wedding, graduating from college, and other such memorable events. The quilting is very significant and symbolic.

*Stars and Arrows, 90" x 90", by Artie Crazy Bull, Sioux. (*Morning Star Quilts *by Florence Pulford.) Artie Crazy Bull delights in color. This quilt amplifies her love of bold color. The hand quilted "clouds" fill the background, which makes it recede behind the double four-point/eight-point star with shooting arrows. The Native American Indian quiltmakers often use "cloud" style quilting. The quilting is done by marking radiating semi-circles using the hand and elbow as a compass. Collection of Mrs. Ann Wilson.*

*Point Star, 90" x 90", 1975, by Brigit Fast Horse, Sioux. (*Morning Star Quilts *by F. Pulford.) Cloud quilting, also called armchair or church quilting, fills the entire quilt. The quilter created the quilting design line by sweeping her forearm in an arch and marking the arcs with a pencil. This effective quilting design is a useful solution to a large quilt in a frame. It is fast and effective. Collection of Mrs. Ann Wilson.*

Currants & Coxcombs, 81" x 96", 1991, by Shirley Thompson. This original design was hand appliquéd and hand quilted by Shirley over a one-year period. Notice there is no border on the top; this is the "pillow tuck" area of the quilt. It has won numerous awards in local quilt shows. The pattern, including quilting designs, can be found in the book Quilts—Start to Finish *by Shirley Thompson and Jan Halgrimson (Powell Publications). Diana has used and recommended Shirley's quilting line design books for years (several of them are listed in the Bibliography). Left: Quilting detail.*

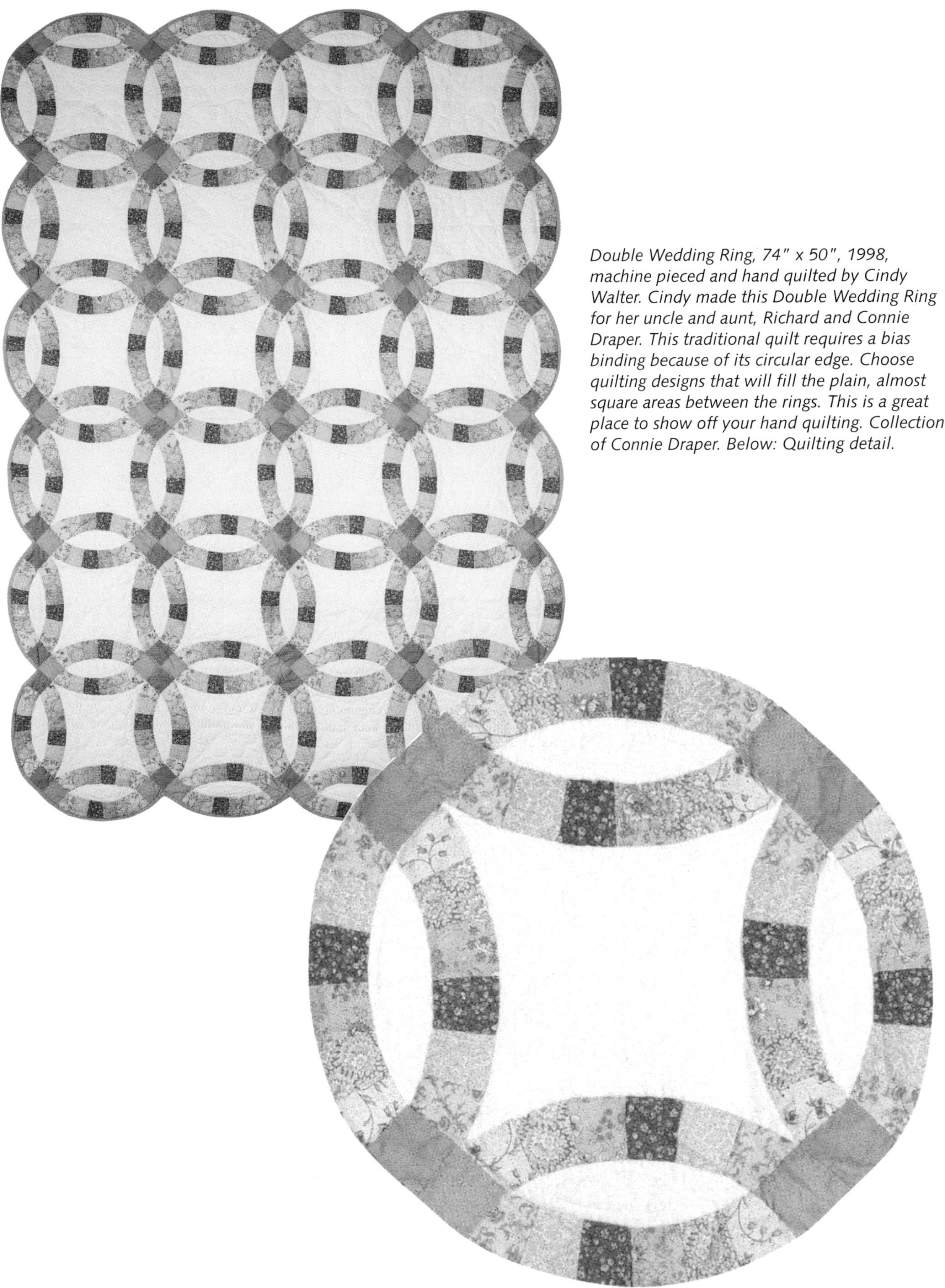

Double Wedding Ring, 74" x 50", 1998, machine pieced and hand quilted by Cindy Walter. Cindy made this Double Wedding Ring for her uncle and aunt, Richard and Connie Draper. This traditional quilt requires a bias binding because of its circular edge. Choose quilting designs that will fill the plain, almost square areas between the rings. This is a great place to show off your hand quilting. Collection of Connie Draper. Below: Quilting detail.

Hawaiian Appliqué, 62" x 45, 1989, appliqué cut by Deborah Kakalia, hand appliquéd by Diana Leone, hand quilted by Wendy Cameron. The Hawaiian quilting style showcases the hand quilting. Doris used teal-colored thread on the white areas and white thread on the teal areas, which emphasized the expertise of her fine hand quilting. The quilt was made for Diana's granddaughter, Gwendolyn, the year she was born. It was a gift from her grandmother as the first quilt for her collection. Below: Quilting detail.

Reminiscence, 80" x 80", 1997, by Laverne Mathews. This beautiful quilt, which was completely designed and made by Laverne, includes appliqué, embroidery, beadwork, and hand-dyed fabric. Laverne designed the fabrics, colors, and quilting lines to evoke flashbacks of quilts from the past and as a tribute to the famous quilter Betsey Totten, who packed her quilts with color, design, and hand quilting. Cindy Walter had the opportunity to visit Laverne's home in Texas in 1998. She was amazed not only by Laverne's large quilt collection, but she was duly impressed by the high quality of Laverne's fine hand quilting. Directly above: Quilting detail.

Baskets, 42" x 42," 1999, by Maxine Overman and Sara Hochhauser. This quilt combines machine and hand quilting. Maxine and Sara used a pattern from American Patchwork and Quilting *(December 1998) and Thimbleberry fabric (RJR Fashion Fabrics). It was quilted using Golden Threads' quilting line patterns from the Traditional Quilting Pack #1 and the Bold Beginning Border Pack, both designed by Keryn Emmerson of Australia (see Sources and Suppliers). Collection of Cheryl Barnes.*

Antique Square Sampler, 48" x 48", 1998, by Myra Mitchell. Myra was excited to find these nine old blocks in an antique store. For an authentic look, she set them together with reproduction 1950s fabric. She echo quilted around each patchwork seam in a traditional manner and used a simple diagonal quilting line in the border area. Myra learned to hand quilt in 1994 in a class taught by Cindy Walter. Her skills may have surpassed her teacher's!

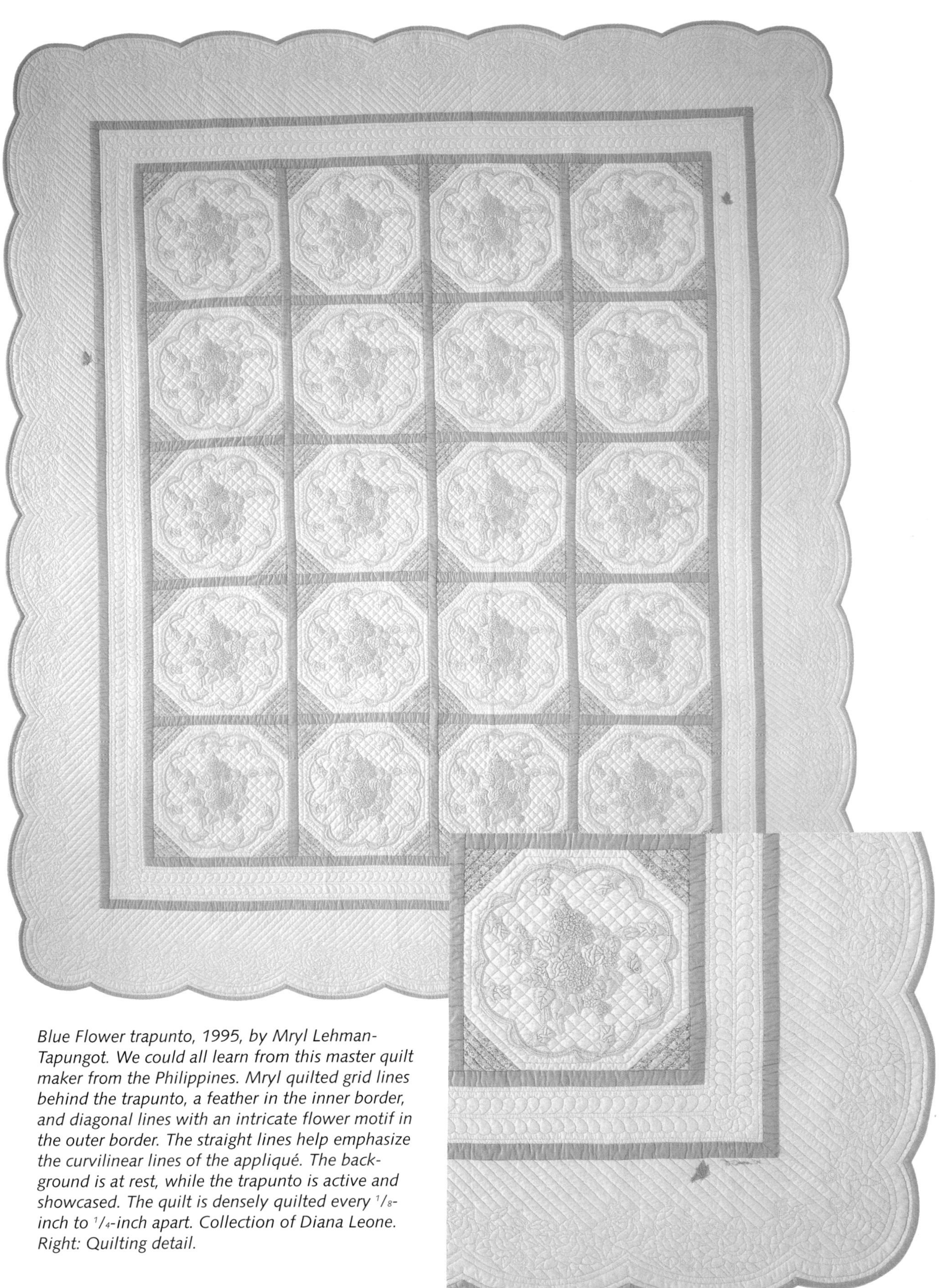

Blue Flower trapunto, 1995, by Mryl Lehman-Tapungot. We could all learn from this master quilt maker from the Philippines. Mryl quilted grid lines behind the trapunto, a feather in the inner border, and diagonal lines with an intricate flower motif in the outer border. The straight lines help emphasize the curvilinear lines of the appliqué. The background is at rest, while the trapunto is active and showcased. The quilt is densely quilted every 1/8-inch to 1/4-inch apart. Collection of Diana Leone. Right: Quilting detail.

Flowers from Friends, 72" x 72", 1998, designed by Anita Shackelford, hand appliquéd by Anita Shackelford, Sheila Kennedy, and friends (Glenda Clark, Janet Hamilton, Ruth Kennedy, Jo Lischynski, Connie St. Clair, and Rebecca Whetstone), and hand quilted by Barbara Yoder. This beautiful album quilt was made with a combination of two traditional appliqué techniques. Wreaths, leaves, and red centers were made using a variety of folded cutwork styles. The flowers were made with The Ruche Mark circular ruching guide (available from Thimble Works). The diagonal and grid quilting lines make the appliqué come alive. Instructions for this beautiful quilt are in Appliqué with Folded Cutwork, *by Anita Shackelford (AQS).*

Auntie's Garden, 50" x 62", 1998, machine pieced, hand appliquéd, and hand quilted by Cynthia Tomaszewski. Cynthia used Simple Pleasures pattern #111, which she designed. Originally inspired by the variety of flowers that grow in her mother's garden, she designed eighteen varieties of flowers and appliquéd them onto a white background with a climbing vine border, using 1930s reproduction printed fabrics.

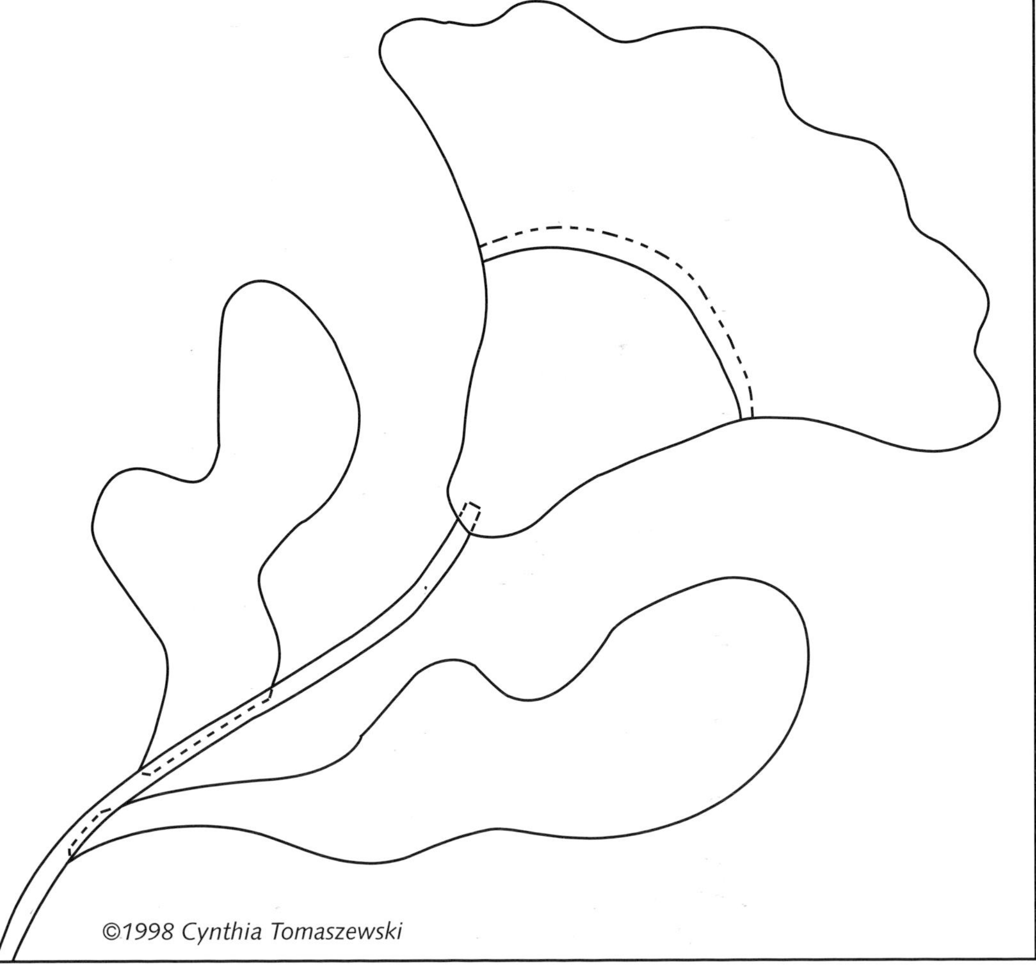

Cynthia Tomaszewski shares one of the appliqué flower patterns with us from her beautiful Auntie's Garden quilt. Add 1/8-inch seam allowances to all edges to allow for the "turn under" portion when you appliqué. Overlap the dotted-line areas.

Innovative and Contemporary

We are excited to include several innovative quilts from contemporary artists and pleased to be able to bring you quilts from around the world. You will find examples of finely hand quilted quilts, and you will also find more decorative styles of hand quilting and larger and longer stitches that form a surface embellishment. Thick and colorful threads create a secondary linear design element. Observe the variations contemporary quilters offer. Adapt any new ideas that may work for you. Study the quilting designs of these stunning quilts.

We both feel that hand quilting as an embellishment combined with machine quilting will be the quilting wave of the future. So, showcase your expertise and hand quilt some of your next project, finish it with machine quilting, and send us your pictures for our next book!

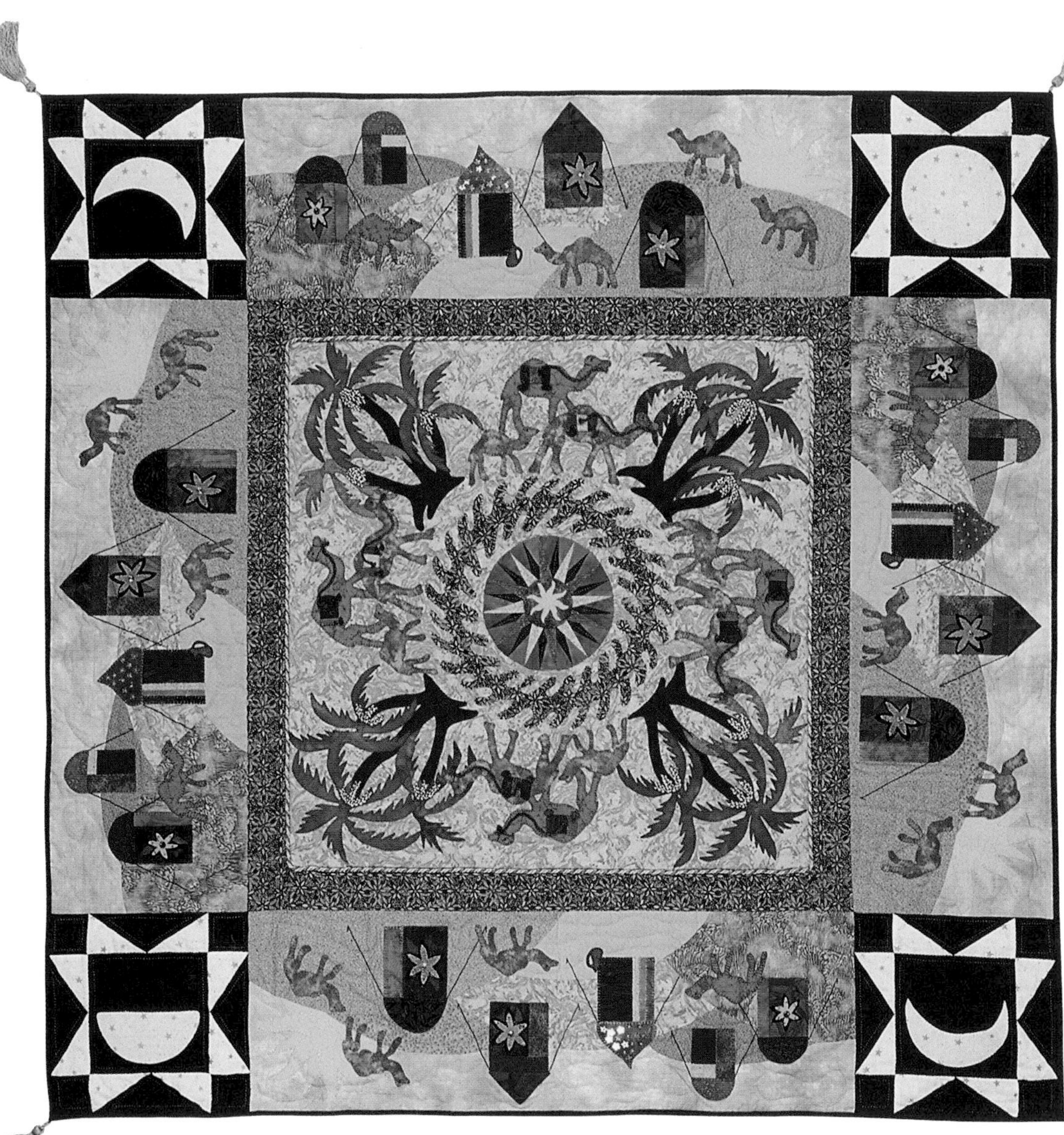

Shifting Sands, 50" x 50", 1998, hand pieced and hand quilted by Cynthia Tomaszewski. Cynthia used her original design Simple Pleasures pattern #203. The quilt was inspired by the customs and cultures of the Arabian Peninsula. An appliquéd desert oasis scene surrounds the center Mariners Compass with palm trees. The border depicts Arab camp life with stages of the moon. She quilted the entire quilt in a "free motion" style, echoing the appliqué area, and quilting motion lines around the clouds.

Garden Party, 50" x 50", 1999, hand pieced and hand quilted by Cynthia Tomaszewski. Cynthia used Simple Pleasures pattern #302, which she designed, for the quilting. Inspired by the show of spring flowers dancing in the breeze, this nine-patch block is surrounded by appliquéd flowers and borders of dancing leaves.

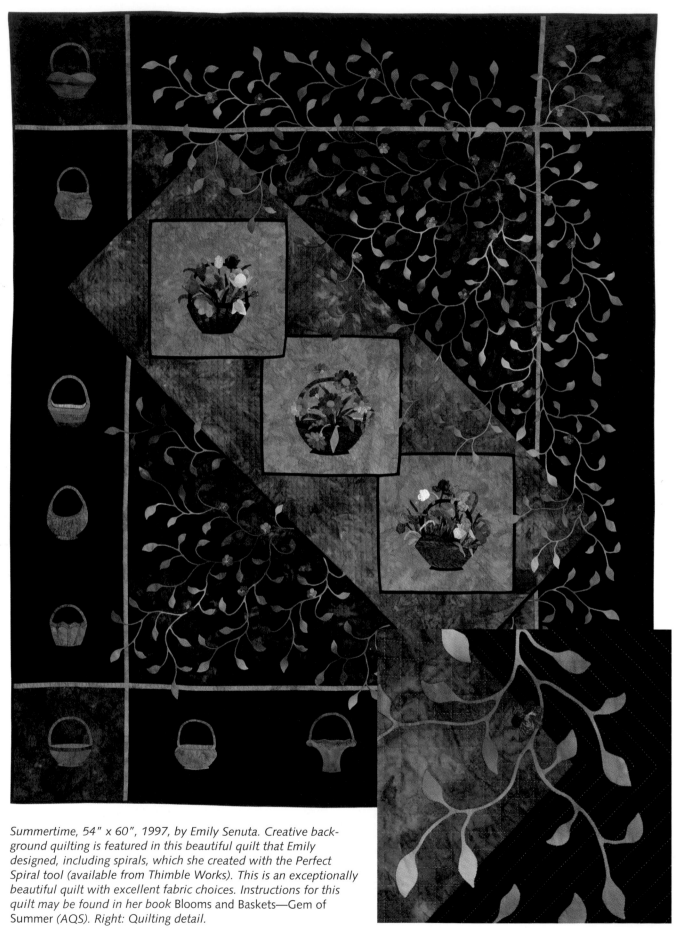

Summertime, 54" x 60", 1997, by Emily Senuta. Creative background quilting is featured in this beautiful quilt that Emily designed, including spirals, which she created with the Perfect Spiral tool (available from Thimble Works). This is an exceptionally beautiful quilt with excellent fabric choices. Instructions for this quilt may be found in her book Blooms and Baskets—Gem of Summer *(AQS). Right: Quilting detail.*

Afterglow, 82" x 68", 1997, by Barbara Oliver Hartman. The artist formed a central medallion by piecing together four blocks made using her favorite hand-dyed fabric. She enjoyed quilting this project and quilted in symbols and shapes throughout the entire quilt. In the Art Quilt category, this exceptional quilt has won 3rd place at AQS, 2nd place at IQA, and 1st place at the Dallas Quilt Festival. Photography by Barbara Oliver Hartman. Left: Quilting detail.

Papa Trostrud's Garden, 76" x 73", 1998, by Cheryl Trostrud-White. Cheryl's dad, Earl Trostrud, spent long hours working in his beautiful garden. "He was particularly fond of roses. One year, my family gave him one of the best Father's Day gifts he could receive. We all donated our labor for a day, helping him in the garden. Memories of the garden inspired me to make this quilt." It was machine pieced, machine quilted, hand quilted, and hand beaded in a random pattern. This quilt was exhibited at "Quilts in Bloom" on the island of Mainau, Konstanz, Germany. Photography by Heinz-Dieter Meier. Right: Quilting detail.

Uferidyll ("Idyllic Shoreline"), 47" x 63", 1999, machine pieced and hand quilted by the Baden Baden Patchwork Group in Germany. The group started the quilt with a single group of leaves and finally decided to make the entire shoreline of greens, integrating blossoms by appliqué. It was quilted "in the ditch" so as to not disturb the patchwork design. Notice the uneven bottom border. The quilt has been exhibited throughout Germany, including the prestigious "Quilts in Bloom" show at the Castle of Mainau, Konstanz, Germany. Photography by Heinz-Dieter Meier.

Fairy on Horse, 9" x 13", by Mryl Lehman-Tapungot. This magnificent quilt was hand painted (air brushed), appliquéd, and includes trapunto. The quilt is entirely hand quilted. Note the use of metallic threads.

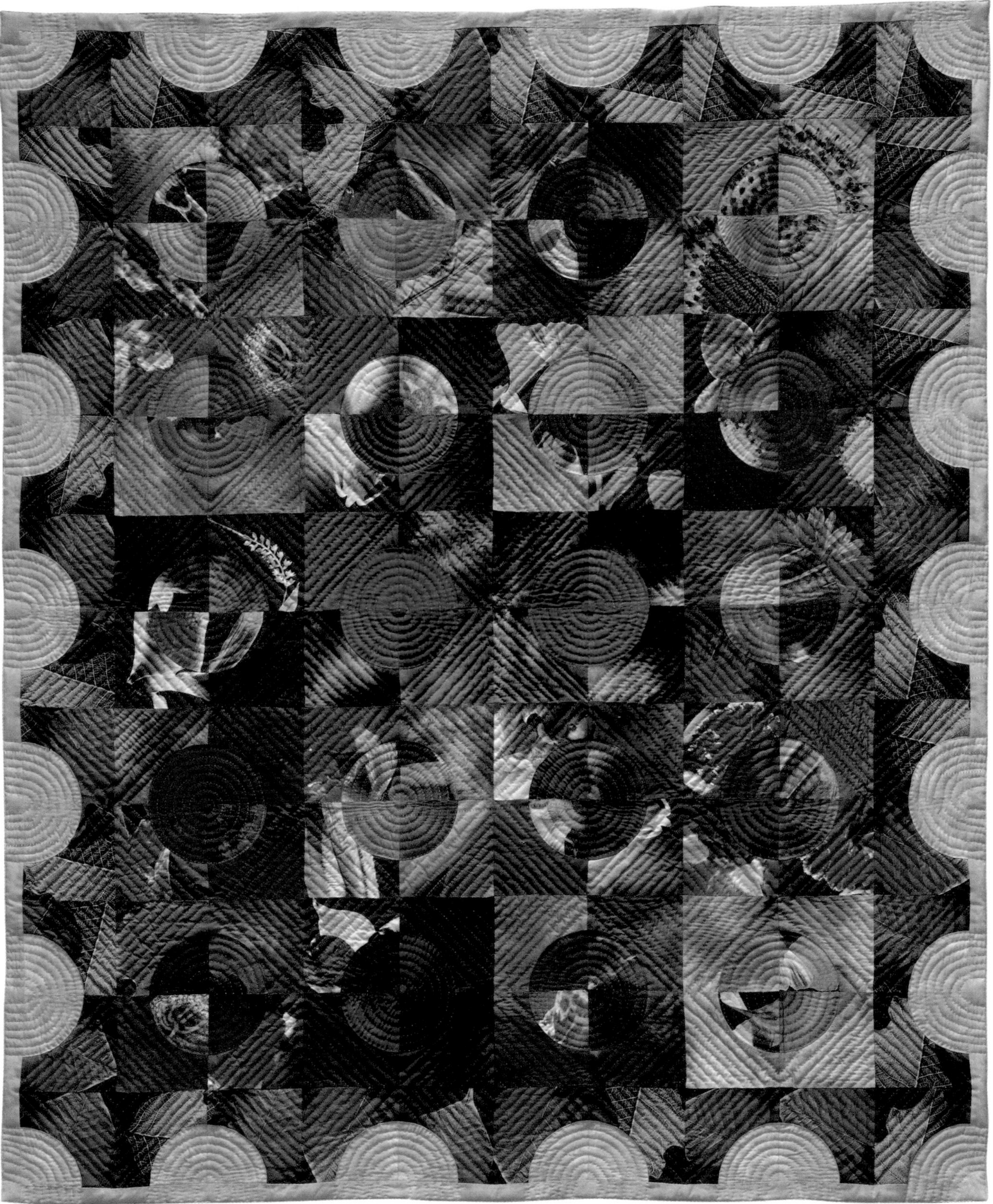

Mainaublumen, 65" x 43", 1998, by Genie Curtze. Genie is a quilting teacher from Konstanz, Germany, and the author of Ginie's Patchwork Fibel *and* Patchwork's Greatest Hits *(Curtze). Her patchwork templates were used to make this quilt. Mainaublumen was created for the Quilts in Bloom Exhibit at the Castle Gallery on the Island of the Mainau in April 1999. Photographs of flowers taken by the Count of the Castle, Count Bernadotte, inspired her to make this quilt. She photo-transferred his photographs onto fabric. The circular and straight-line hand quilting creates a visual path over the surface of the floral garden. Photography by Heinz-Dieter Meier.*

Stargate, 72" x 72", 1998, by Barbara Oliver Hartman. The four blocks that form the central medallion started with a computer-generated design. The quilting is a simple design of curved lines using black thread and larger stitches (using one strand of DMC floss). It won a blue ribbon at IQA and was also exhibited at AQS, Quilt America. Photography by Barbara Oliver Hartman. Below: Quilting detail.

Tips from the Pros

Barbara Oliver Hartman, master quilter from Flower Mound, Texas, says, "My favorite hand quilting thread is one strand of DMC embroidery floss. I love the sheen and the range of colors. For many years, I used a size 12 needle, but years of hand quilting caused problems with my hands. Now I use a size 8 John James quilting needle. I have shortened the hours that I hand quilt and stretch my hands and fingers frequently."

The Volcano Flows, 1995–1999, by Diana Leone. Diana designed her Hawaiian-style appliqué and she cut, appliquéd, and hand quilted this contemporary quilt. She wanted to try her hand at cutting a not-so-typical Hawaiian-style appliqué pattern. This is a two-fold, four-fold evolving pattern. The volcano erupts and the lava flows down the mountain slopes to the ocean's edge. The hand quilting used aubergine thread on aubergine fabric and red thread on the red fabric. It was quilted in a Hawaiian style, echoing the appliqué design to the edge. The rows are about 1/2 inch apart. This style of quilting is easy and fun, especially for beginners.

One of the most innovative quilters of our day, author of Colourwash (TPP), Deirdre Amsden, gives us this observation:

"I discovered the art of quilting one afternoon in the Victoria and Albert Museum in London while attending a short course on embroidery. I was utterly seduced by the texture and artistry wrought by simple running stitches: the first stitch learned as a child.

"I knew about patchwork from my Mother, but in the museum I could see the practical act of holding the quilt layers together and how it brought the patchwork to life. This is what inspired me to start making quilts.

"Some of my quilts could be described as being finely hand quilted. I know how to quilt a fine stitch but I do not always do so. Sometimes I machine quilt, sometimes I use thick threads, and sometimes I make big stitches. It all depends on the end effect I want to create. I make my quilting appropriate for the design as a whole.

"With this in mind at the design stage I treat patchwork and quilting as interdependent processes relating one to the other and paying equal attention to both. However, my designs are not rigid blueprints. I am ready to change my ideas at any stage. When I have finished piecing the quilt top, I test out my proposed quilting design by pinning a sheet of tracing paper over a section of the patchwork and marking out the design, full sized, in coloured pencils to match the colours of my quilting threads.

"I quilt most of my quilts these days in a hoop because it is portable and can easily be turned to avoid sewing in awkward directions. Also, every time I sit down to quilt I thank the person who invented the thimble with a ridge around the top edge, which prevents the needle from slipping off."

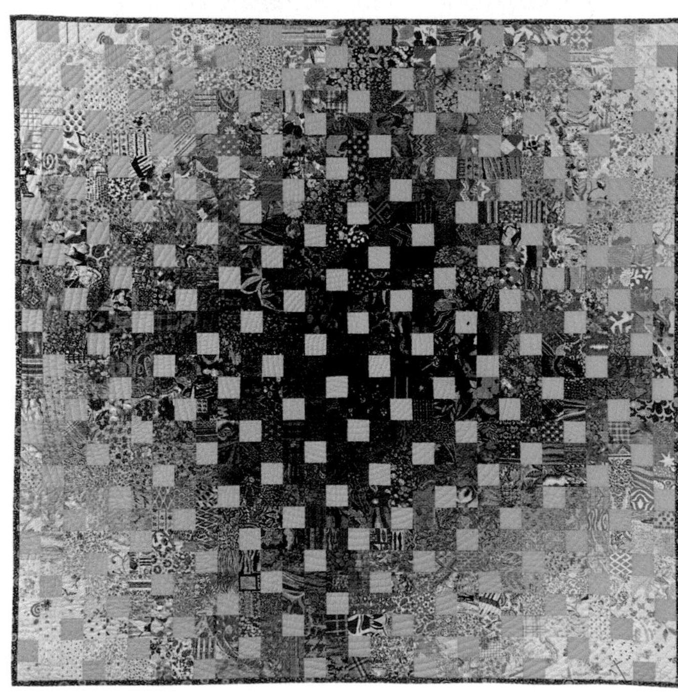

Summer Haze, 53" x 53", 1999, by Deirdre Amsden. This quilt depicts a summer day from early light to illuminated balmy night. Deirdre chose to quilt in a freehand spiral motion to give the impression of the sun and also the circle of illumination from a lantern. Photography by James Austin. Top: Quilting detail.

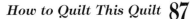

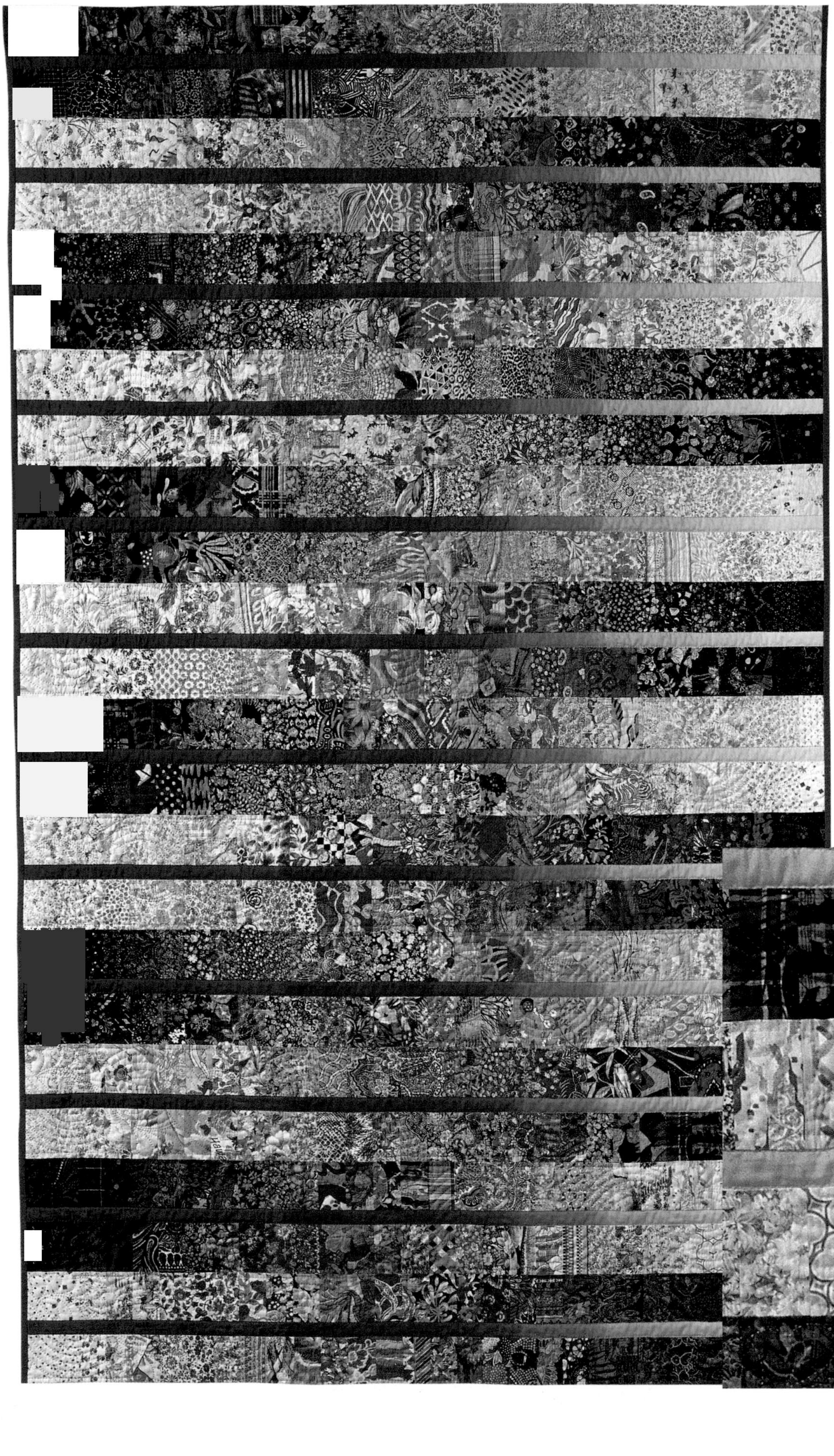

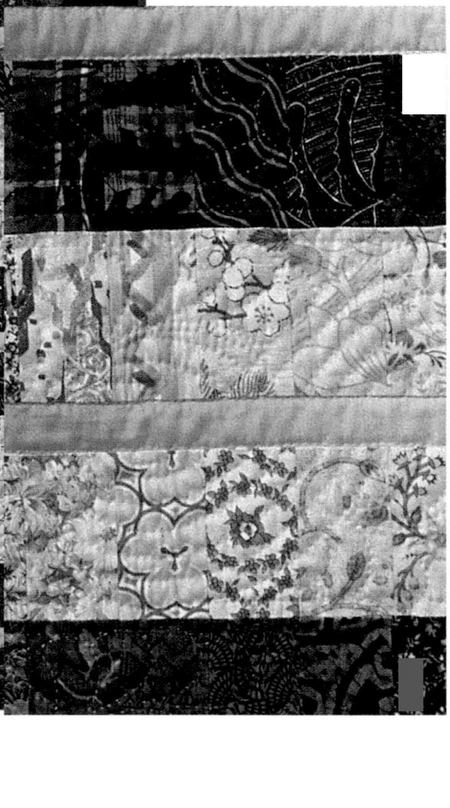

Colourwash and Electric Stripes, 46" x 77", 1999, by Deirdre Amsden. The shading of the "electric" stripes alternately contrast and repeat the shading of the broad "Colourwash" stripes, causing subtle visual alterations to the widths of both stripes. The electric stripes also create a visual difference between the left- and right-hand sides of the quilt—cool and warm. The colors of the quilting thread change from purple to red to orange, and to yellow across the quilt. The feather and cable quilting design is in memory of Mrs. Amy Emms MBE, a quilter from Durham, England, who used to border most of her beautiful quilts with this type of pattern. Mrs. Emms started quilting at the age of 14 and was still working at her frame a few weeks before her death at the age of 94. Photograph by James Austin.

Chapter 7 Three Easy Projects

We've included three projects for beginners or anyone wanting to brush up on his or her quilting skills. Project One has you quilting around the fabric's printed design, so there is very little preparation. In Project Two, you will trace a quilting line design onto a piece of fabric. Project Three incorporates machine piecing and tracing a quilting line design.

Project One: Printed Motif Whole Cloth

Habitat, 35" x 35", hand quilted by Diana Leone. Fabric design Habitat by Jane Kriss for Northcott/Monarch.

This is the perfect beginner's project. You will echo quilt around the design or motif printed on the fabric. Select from any of the hundreds of fabrics that are printed with a defined motif; choose one that you will enjoy quilting. Quilt around the motif's edges, echoing 3/4 inch away from the printed design's edge. This project is portable; you will finish it quickly because you can work on it wherever you are. Your project may vary in size depending on the size of the fabric you have chosen. Cut the borders and backing to fit the particular size of the motif fabric. Sew the borders to the central fabric. Layer the top, batting, and backing and baste as desired.

You will need

Rotary cutting tools: mat, rulers, and cutter

Sewing machine

General sewing machine supplies, including quality cotton thread and scissors

Iron and ironing board

Hand quilting supplies: 14" hoop, quilting thimble, between quilting needles (size 10 or 11), hand quilting thread, thread snips

Basting tools of your choice (see pages 42-44)

Follow these piecing instructions to create Habitat (finished size 35" x 35"):

Fabric A: print fabric with medium to large motifs

Need: 3/4 yard Cut: 1 square 22" x 22"

Fabric B: contrasting fabric for narrow inner border (optional)

Need: 1/3 yard Cut: 2 strips 1 1/2" x 22", 2 strips 1 1/2" x 24"

Fabric C: coordinating fabric for border and binding

Need: 1 yard Border cut: 2 strips 6" x 24", 2 strips 6" x 36"

Binding cut: 3 strips 1 1/2" wide

Fabric D: coordinating fabric for backing

Need: 1 yard

Batting: thin polyester

Need: 1 yard Cut: 36" x 36"

Using a 1/4" seam allowance, follow these directions to piece the top together:

1. Sew the 1 1/2" x 22" Fabric B (inner border) strips to each side of the Fabric A square. Iron the seam allowances away from the center.

2. Sew the 1 1/2" x 24" Fabric B strips to the top and bottom of the Fabric A square. Iron the seam allowances away from the center. Trim the excess fabric.

3. Sew the 6" x 24" Fabric C (border) strips to each side of the project. Iron the seam allowances away from the center. Trim any excess fabric.

4. Sew the 6" x 36" Fabric C strips to the top and bottom of the project. Iron the seam allowances away from the center. Trim all edges to be square.

5. Layer and baste the top, batting, and backing together.

6. Center the basted quilt in your hoop or lap frame and begin hand quilting. Move the hoop around as needed. When you have quilted as much as you wish, remove the basting and bind the quilt.

Congratulations! You have finished your first hand-quilted project!

Project Two: Whole Cloth With Marked Design

Feathers and Hearts in the Garden, 24" x 30", hand quilted, original quilting line design by Diana Leone.

Diana designed the Feathers and Heart quilting line design (found on the enclosed pattern sheet) for the beginner to practice straight line and curved hand quilting stitches. Try using different marking tools and different colored threads on this project—experiment.

We did not use a quilting line pattern in the border. Diana suggests that you quilt around the motifs in the border fabric, simply meandering in a free-motion fashion, or use a 4" wide border stencil to mark a pattern on the border once it is attached to the center piece.

You will need

Rotary cutting tools: mat, rulers, and cutter
Sewing machine
General sewing machine supplies, including quality cotton thread and scissors
Iron and ironing board
Light box or masking tape to hold project while tracing
Marking tools and 1/4" masking tape
Hand quilting supplies: 14" hoop, quilting thimble, between quilting needles (size 10), hand quilting thread, thread snips
Basting tools of your choice (see pages 42-44)
Quilting line design (found on pattern sheet)

Follow these instructions to create a quilt just like Feathers and Hearts (finished size 24" x 30"):

Fabric A: light color (solid-like print) fabric for center and binding

Need: 3/4 yard — Cut: 1 rectangle 15" x 21" for center piece; use the remaining fabric for the binding

Fabric B: print fabric for border and backing

Need: 1 1/4 yard — Cut 2 strips 5" x 21" for side borders, 2 strips 5" x 15" for top and bottom borders, 1 rectangle 26" x 32" for backing

Fabric C: contrasting fabric for border squares

Need: 1/4 yard — Cut: 4 squares 5" x 5" for corner blocks

Batting: 1/4" thick polyester

Need: 3/4 yard — Cut: 26" x 32"

Using a 1/4" seam allowance, follow these directions to piece the top together:

1. Fold the 15" x 21" center rectangle from Fabric A in half horizontally and in half vertically; finger press. Use these center line creases on the fabric to align the center edge of the quilting line design.
2. Trace the Feathers and Heart pattern from the pattern sheet; use a wax-based pencil.
3. Align the center line of the design to the center line of the fabric. Tape the paper design to a light box or window. Align the fabric to the design and tape securely to the light source. Trace the design onto the fabric. Note: Lightly transfer the design lines onto the fabric; the lines will appear darker when the light source is removed.
4. Pin and sew the 5" x 21" borders to the side of the center rectangle. Iron the seams away from the center.
5. For the top and bottom borders, sew one 5" square to each end of the 5" x 15" border strips. Iron the seams inward, toward the border strips.
6. Pin the border strips to the top and bottom of the center piece. Carefully match the seams at the 5" corner blocks. Sew the top and bottom borders to the center piece. Iron the seams away from the center.
7. Baste the top, batting, and backing together.
8. Center the basted quilt in your hoop or frame and begin hand quilting. Move the hoop around as needed. When you are finished quilting, remove the basting and bind the quilt.

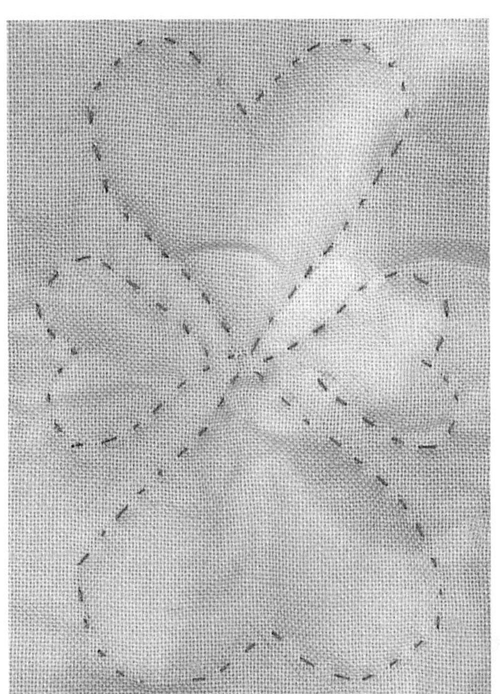

This full-size design can be found on the pattern sheet.

Project Three: Blue and Yellow Dolly Quilt

Blue and Yellow Dolly Quilt, 13½" x 13½", hand quilted by Cindy Walter.

Cindy designed this easy quilt to include the lesson of piecing triangles and squares together before hand quilting. The directions teach you a speedy method of sewing half-square triangles from strips of fabrics instead of making triangle templates. The soft curves of the quilting line designs and the ¼" echoing around the patchwork areas provide a perfect opportunity to practice hand quilting.

This full-size design can be found on the pattern sheet.

You will need

Rotary cutting tools: mat, rulers, and cutter
Sewing machine
General sewing machine supplies, including quality cotton thread and scissors
Iron and ironing board
Light box or masking tape to hold project while tracing
Pencil marking tools and ¼" masking tape
Hand quilting supplies: 8" hoop or lap frame, quilting thimble, between quilting needles (size 10), hand quilting thread, thread snips
Basting tools of your choice (see pages 42-44)
Quilting line design (found on pattern sheet)

Follow these instructions to create a quilt just like the Blue and Yellow Dolly Quilt.

Fabric A: white fabric

Need: 1/3 yard — Cut 1 square 8½" x 8½", 4 squares 2½" x 2½"

Fabric B: bold blue fabric

Need: 1/4 yard — Cut 1 strip 2½" x 42"; use remaining fabric for binding of choice

Fabric C: bright yellow fabric

Need: 1/4 yard — Cut 1 strip 2½" x 42"

Fabric D: floral fabric for border and backing

Need: 1/4 yard — Cut 2 strips 3½" x 12½", 2 strips 3½" x 18-½", 1 square 21" x 21"

Batting: light polyester

Need: 3/4 yard — Cut 1 square 21" x 21"

Using a 1/4" seam allowance, follow these directions to piece the top together.

1. Fold the 8 1/2" Fabric A white square in half horizontally and in half vertically to find the center line; finger press and open fabric. Tape the center quilting line design template to a light box or window. Align the white square fabric to the design and tape securely to the light source. Trace the design on the fabric. Note: Lightly transfer the design lines onto the fabric. The lines will appear darker when the light source is removed.
2. Place the 2 1/2" x 42" Fabric B and Fabric C strips on top of each other, with right sides together. From the strips, cut sixteen 2 1/2" segments, making sixteen 2 1/2" square sets.
3. Draw a diagonal line on each square set with a pencil. Sew on this line to create half-square triangles. Trim away the excess on one side of the seam line, leaving a 1/4" seam allowance.
4. Open up the square to find a blue and yellow triangle sewn together. Press the seams to the darker fabric.
5. Sew four of the blue and yellow squares together. Follow the photograph to make sure the triangles are going in the right direction. Repeat three more times to create the four inner border strips.

6. Sew an inner border strip to the right and left sides of the white 8 1/2" square. Press the seams away from the white center.
7. Sew a white 2 1/2" square to both ends of the two remaining border strips.

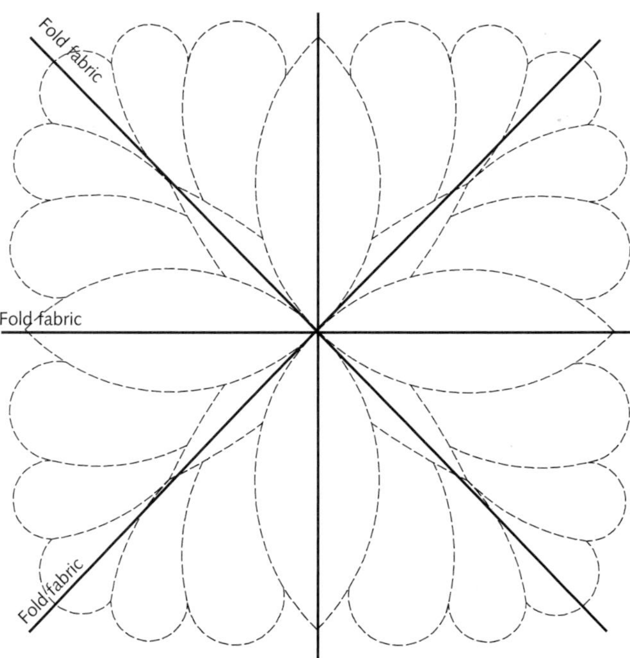

8. Pin and sew these longer borders to the top and bottom of the project. Press the seams away from the white center. Before sewing, check to make sure all of the triangles are going in the right direction according to the photograph.
9. For the outer border, sew a 3 1/2" x 12 1/2" Fabric D strip to the right and left sides of the project. Press the seams away from the center.
10. Sew the longer border strips to the top and bottom. Press the seams away from the center.
11. Tape the border quilting line design template to a light box or window. Align the borders to the design and tape securely to the light source. Trace the design on the fabric. Note: Lightly transfer the design lines onto the fabric; the lines will appear darker when the light source is removed.
12. Baste the top, batting, and backing together.
13. Center the basted quilt in your hoop or frame and you begin hand quilting. Move the hoop around if needed. When you are finished quilting, remove the basting and bind the quilt.

**A special thanks to the Golden Threads Company for sharing these wonderful quilting line patterns, designed by Keryn Emmerson of Australia, with us (see Sources and Suppliers). The center design on this quilt is from Traditional Design Pack #2 and the border design is from Traditional Design Pack #1.*

Bibliography and References

Amsden, Dierdre. *Colourwash Quilts*. Bothel, WA: That Patchwork Place.

Barber, Barbara. *Borderie Perse: The Elegant Quilt*. Paducah, KY: American Quilter's Society. 1997.

Better Homes and Garden's America's Heritage Quilts. Des Moines, IA: Meredith Corp.

Brandon, Reiko M. *The Hawaiian Quilt*. Honolulu, HI: Booklines Hawaii, Ltd. 1993.

Cory, Pepper. *Mastering the Art of Quilt Marking*. Lafayette, CA: C&T Publishing. 1999.

Curtze, Ginie. *Ginie's Patchwork Fibel*. Konstanz, Germany: Curtze. 1998.

Durcan, Philomena. *A Celtic Garden*. Celtic Design Company. 1995.

Fons, Marianne and Liz Porter. *Quilter's Complete Guide*. Birmingham, AL: Oxmoor House. 1993.

Hargrave, Harriet. *Heirloom Machine Quilting*. Lafayette, CA: C&T. 1995.

James, Michael. *The Quilter's Handbook*. Santa Clara, CA: Leone Publications, 1980. Mineola, NY: Dover Publications, 1992.

Leone, Diana and Cindy Walter. *Attic Windows*, 2nd Edition. Iola, WI: Krause Publications. 2000.

Leone, Diana. *Crazy with Cotton*. Lafayette, CA: C&T. 1996.

Leone, Diane. *The New Sampler Quilt*. Lafayette, CA: C&T. 1996.

McClun, Diana and Laura Nownes. *Quilts!, Quilts!!, Quilts!!!* Lincolnwood, IL: Quilt Digest. 1997.

Pulford, Florence. *Morning Star Quilts*. Santa Clara, CA: Leone Publications. Mineola, NY: Dover Publications, 1993.

QUILTER'S Newsletter Magazine. Leman Publications, Inc.

Sears, Roebuck and Co. *Century of Progress in Quilt Making*. 1937.

Senuta, Emily. *Blooms & Baskets—Gems of Summer*. Paducah, KY: American Quilter's Society.

Smith, Nancy and Lynda Milligan. *Time for a Chain*. Possibilities Publications.

Squire, Helen. *Create with Helen Squire: Hand and Machine Quilting*. Paducah, KY: American Quilter's Society 1999.

Walter, Cindy. *Snippet Sensations*. Iola, WI: Krause Publications. 1996.

Sources and Suppliers

For Seminars or Lectures Contact:

Diana Leone
21680 Leone Ct.
San Jose, CA 95120
dianaleone@hotmail.com
www.dianaleone.com
Seminars, lectures, and antique and new quilts.

Cindy Walter
c/o Krause Publications
700 E. State St.
Iola, WI 54990-0001
e-mail: snippetsensation@aol.com
Seminars and lectures.

All Materials and Supplies Available Through:

Eddie's Quilting Bee
264 Castor St.
Mountain View, CA 94041
1-888-QUILTER
www.Quiltingbee.com
e-mail: quiltbee@quiltingbee.com

Notions Supplied By:

Batting
Fairfield Processing Corp.
Hobbs Bonded Fibers
Kelsul, Inc./Quilter's Dream
Morning Glory Products
Mountain Mist/The Stearns
St. Peter Woolen Mill
The Warm Company

Frames and Hoops
Frank A. Edmunds & Co.
Grace Frame Company
Marie Products
Stearns and Foster

Fabric
Northcott/Monarch
Springs—For Quilter's Only

General Distributors
Aptex, Inc.
Checkers Dist., Inc.
E.E. Shenck Co.
Quilter's Rule Int'l Inc.
United Notions

Notions, Needles, and Thimbles
Clover Needlecraft, Inc.
Colonial Needle Co.
June Tailor
Prym-Dritz Corp.
Roxanne
W.H. Collins
Wrights

Scissors and Cutting Tools
Fiskars
Gingher
Olfa
Omnigrid

Thread
American & Efird, Inc.
Gutermann of America
Mettler
Sulky
YLI

Quilting Line Patterns:

Golden Threads
2 S 373 Seneca Dr.
Wheaton, IL 60187

Perfect Spiral Thimble Works
P.O. Box 462
Bucyrus, OH 44820

Powell Publications
8416 208th Ave. NE
Redmond, WA 98053

Quilting Patterns:

Kathy Galos Patterns
3454 Flora Vista Ave.
Santa Clara, CA 95051

Michell Marketing, Inc.
3525 Broad Street
Chamblee, GA 30341

Plum Creek Patchwork Patterns
14160 Country Hwy S
Walnut Creek, MN 56180

Possibilities Patterns
8970 E Hampton Ave.
Denver, CO 80231

Glossary

Backing: The fabric or underside of the quilt, which can be one piece of coordinating fabric lengths of similar fabrics seamed together to create the size needed or any pieced configuration. The backing fabric should be of the same quality as the quilt's top.

Basting: The process of temporarily holding three layers of a quilt together while it is being hand quilted. These basting stitches are removed after the quilting is completed. Basting may be done with a needle and thread, safety pins, a basting gun, or with spray adhesive.

Basting thread: A white cotton, fairly strong, inexpensive thread used to hand baste the layers of a quilt. A colored thread is not recommended because it may leave a dye mark on the quilt top.

Batting: In a quilt sandwich, this is the middle layer. There are many varieties available, including cotton, cotton polyester blend, 100-percent polyester, wool, and silk. Batting is used to add loft and warmth, and also to give the quilt the look of depth. The preferred batting for hand quilting should be "bonded." Use only a quality or premium batting.

Bearding: The occurrence of batting fibers working their way through the weave of the fabrics used to make the quilt's top and backing. Bearding occurs when the batting used is unbonded or not coated and when the fabric is thin and open weave.

Between needle: A short, size 8-12 needle recommended for hand quilting. Its eye size is between that of a larger crewel and a smaller sharp.

Binding: A narrow straight-on-grain or bias-cut narrow length of cotton fabric sewn to the front and back of the quilt's outer edges. Binding is used to encase or "bind" the quilt's open edges. Select a binding fabric that is similar in weight, weave, color, and print to the fabrics used throughout the quilt. Single-fold binding is used on small, thin projects (1/4 inch or less) and those that do not receive much wear, while double-fold binding is used on large, thicker (1/4 inch or more) projects that receive more wear.

Blocks: Any rectangle or similar shape made up of two or more pieced or appliquéd fabrics. Blocks may be pieced together with a separating strip of fabric (a sashing).

Border: A width and length comprised of a single or multiple pieced fabric selected to coordinate with the inner top and sewn to the outer edge of the quilt top. It acts as a frame, which can be as elaborate or as simple as the designer sees fit. The border also provides an area to feature any amount of quilting from simple to complex.

Cotton: A woven fabric made from the while fluff of the cotton plant; this is the quilter's fabric of choice. It is long lasting, washable, and easy to cut and needle. A 60-square weave is the most common.

Frame: A set of bars used to secure the quilt in a rectangular shape for quilting. Two long bars with fabric attached are secured to two shorter end bars; the quilt's layers are pinned or sewn to the frame's long bars. A frame supports the quilt and holds it up so the quilter can reach under and above to hand quilt.

Hand quilting: The process of forming one or more stitches that pass through the quilt's layers; it provides relief of the design on the quilt's surface. It is usually accomplished by using cotton thread and a short, sharp needle and forming a running stitch through the layers. The quilted line can be as simple or complex as the maker desires.

Hoop: A set of two circles, ovals, or rectangles, usually wooden or plastic, used to hold the quilt's layers together in a taut position while they are being quilted. Hoops may be held on the quilter's lap or braced on a floor stand.

Lap quilting: Also known as "quilt as you go." A portable process of making individually layered and semi-finished blocks. The blocks are sewn together into a large quilt only after all of the blocks have been made and quilted.

Lap quilts: The process of holding the quilt with the hoop on the lap and hand quilting.

Marking: The process of transferring a line or design onto the front surface of a quilt top. Markings are used to guide the quilter.

Marking tools: Items, including wax-based pencils and water-soluble felt pens, used to transfer quilting design lines onto the quilt top.

Milliner needle: A long (2-inch), thin needle used to hand baste a quilt. Sizes 4 to 8 are recommended.

Needles: A length of thin, hardened metal with one sharp end and a hole (eye) in the other that is used to carry the thread. A variety of lengths and thicknesses are available for hand quilting.

Pressing: The use of a hot iron to flatten fabric.

Prewashing: This is the process used to shrink fabric, to set its dye, and remove any finishes put into the fabric by the manufacturer before the top is quilted. Use a small amount of non-phosphorus soap and warm water (by hand or machine wash).

Quilt sandwich: A quilt's three layers: the top, batting, and backing.

Sampler quilt: A quilt top made up of dissimilar patterns. The Sampler provides a variety of techniques for the beginning quilter to learn the many possibilities of quiltmaking.

Sashing: A strip of fabric sewn between two or more blocks. Sashings provide an area to showcase hand quilting and gives unity and separation to the top.

Shears: Long (7 inches or more) scissors used to cut fabric. The blades are flat on one side and designed to be placed on a cutting surface when cutting fabric.

Snips: Small, short, bladed scissors used to clip thread.

Stencil: A thin sheet of cardboard or plastic with narrow slits cut through the surface, providing an area for a marking tool's tip to mark through onto the quilt top.

Template: A shape a quilter uses to trace around to transfer the shape's edge on the quilt top.

Thimble: A metal, leather, or stable device used to the upper hand's longest finger to protect its tip from injury while hand quilting. Always use a comfortable, well-fitting thimble when making a quilt.

Trapunto: The forming of a small shape or parallel lines on the quilt top, which are then stuffed or filled with batting or colored yarn to add a relief or raised design on the surface.

Pattern Sheet

The following section includes the quilting line patterns for Projects 2 and 3. As a bonus, we have also included several other quilting line patterns designed by Diana Leone. Use these quilting line designs for borders or center areas on your next quilt.

CONTENTS

Fodor's Features

MAPS

ABOUT THIS GUIDE

Fodor's Recommendations

Everything in this guide is worth doing—we don't cover what isn't—but exceptional sights, hotels, and restaurants are recognized with additional accolades. **Fodor'sChoice★** indicates our top recommendations; and **Best Bets** call attention to notable hotels and restaurants in various categories. Care to nominate a new place? Visit Fodors.com/contact-us.

Trip Costs

We list prices wherever possible to help you budget well. Hotel and restaurant price categories from **$** to **$$$$** are noted alongside each recommendation. For hotels, we include the lowest cost of a standard double room in high season. For restaurants, we cite the average price of a main course at dinner or, if dinner isn't served, at lunch. For attractions, we always list adult admission fees; discounts are usually available for children, students, and senior citizens.

Hotels

Our local writers vet every hotel to recommend the best overnights in each price category, from budget to expensive. Unless otherwise specified, you can expect private bath, phone, and TV in your room. For expanded hotel reviews, facilities, and deals visit Fodors.com.

Top Picks
★ Fodor'sChoice

Listings
✉ Address
Branch address
☎ Telephone
Fax
Website
E-mail
Admission fee
Open/closed times
Ⓜ Subway
Directions or Map coordinates

Hotels & Restaurants
Hotel
Number of rooms
Meal plans
✕ Restaurant
Reservations
Dress code
No credit cards
$ Price

Other
⇨ See also
☞ Take note
Golf facilities

Restaurants

Unless we state otherwise, restaurants are open for lunch and dinner daily. We mention dress code only when there's a specific requirement and reservations only when they're essential or not accepted. To make restaurant reservations, visit Fodors.com.

Credit Cards

The hotels and restaurants in this guide typically accept credit cards. If not, we'll say so.

EUGENE FODOR

Hungarian-born Eugene Fodor (1905–91) began his travel career as an interpreter on a French cruise ship. The experience inspired him to write *On the Continent* (1936), the first guidebook to receive annual updates and discuss a country's way of life as well as its sights. Fodor later joined the U.S. Army and worked for the OSS in World War II. After the war, he kept up his intelligence work while expanding his guidebook series. During the Cold War, many guides were written by fellow agents who understood the value of insider information. Today's guides continue Fodor's legacy by providing travelers with timely coverage, insider tips, and cultural context.

1

EXPERIENCE THE CARIBBEAN

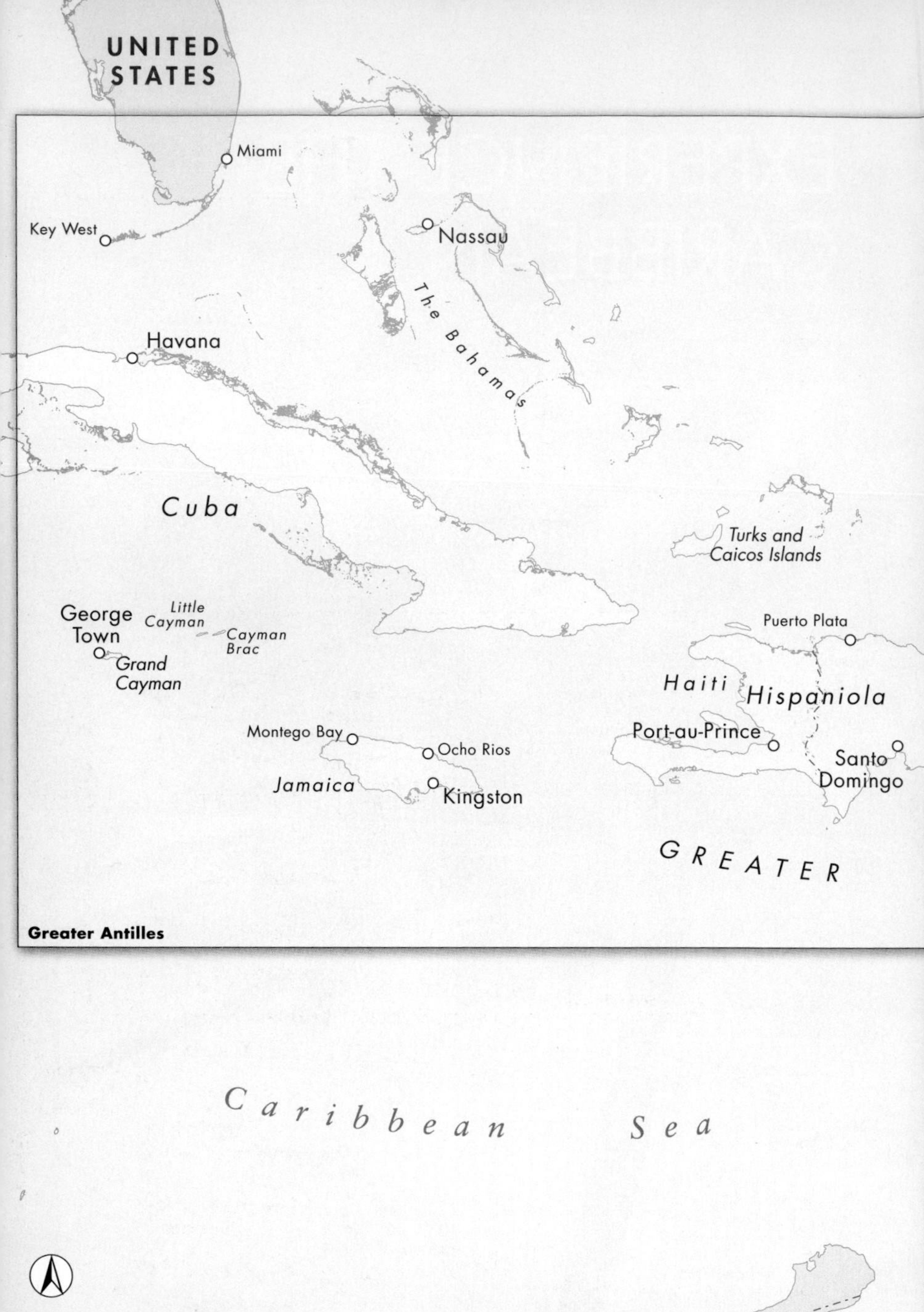
UNITED STATES
Miami
Key West
Nassau
The Bahamas
Havana
Cuba
Turks and Caicos Islands
George Town
Little Cayman
Cayman Brac
Grand Cayman
Puerto Plata
Haiti
Hispaniola
Montego Bay
Ocho Rios
Port-au-Prince
Santo Domingo
Jamaica
Kingston
GREATER
Greater Antilles
Caribbean Sea
0
200 mi
0
200 km
Cartagena
COLOMBIA
Maracaibo

The Caribbean

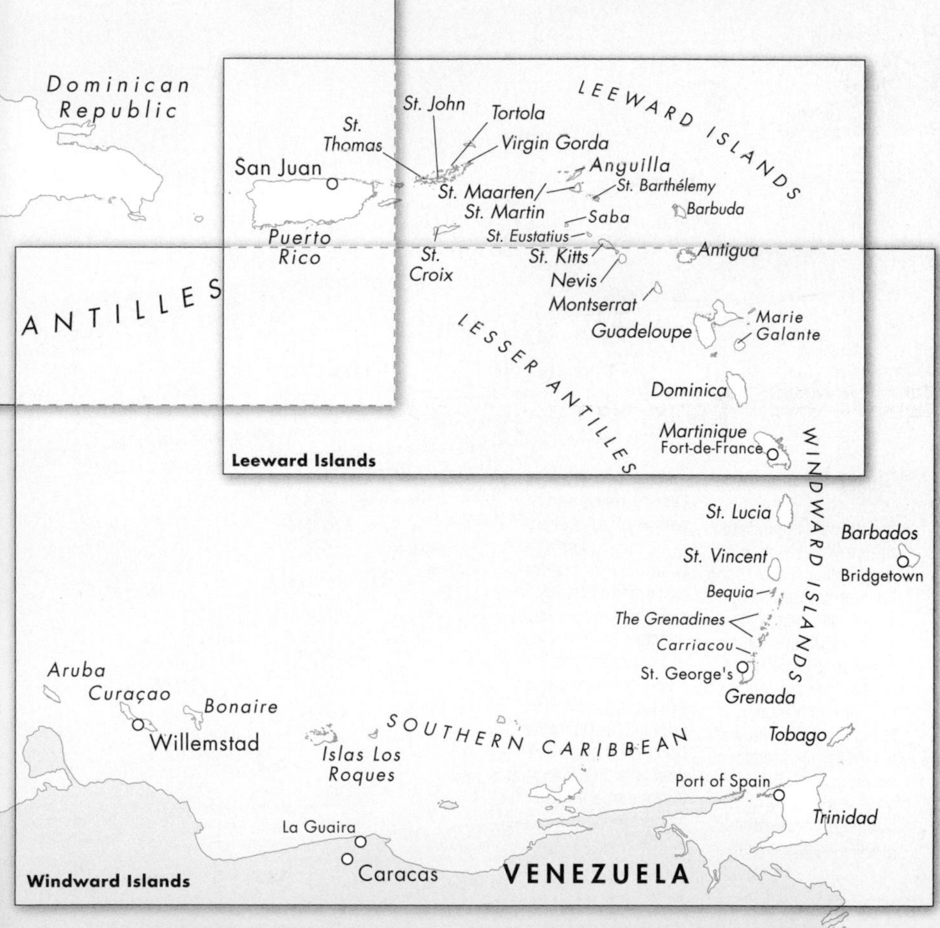

ATLANTIC OCEAN
Dominican Republic
LEEWARD ISLANDS
St. John
Tortola
St. Thomas
Virgin Gorda
San Juan
Anguilla
St. Maarten/ St. Martin
St. Barthélemy
Barbuda
Saba
St. Eustatius
Puerto Rico
St. Croix
St. Kitts
Antigua
Nevis
Montserrat
ANTILLES
LESSER ANTILLES
Marie Galante
Guadeloupe
Dominica
Martinique
Fort-de-France
Leeward Islands
WINDWARD ISLANDS
St. Lucia
Barbados
St. Vincent
Bridgetown
Bequia
The Grenadines
Carriacou
Aruba
St. George's
Curaçao
Grenada
Bonaire
SOUTHERN CARIBBEAN
Tobago
Willemstad
Islas Los Roques
Port of Spain
Trinidad
La Guaira
Caracas
VENEZUELA
Windward Islands

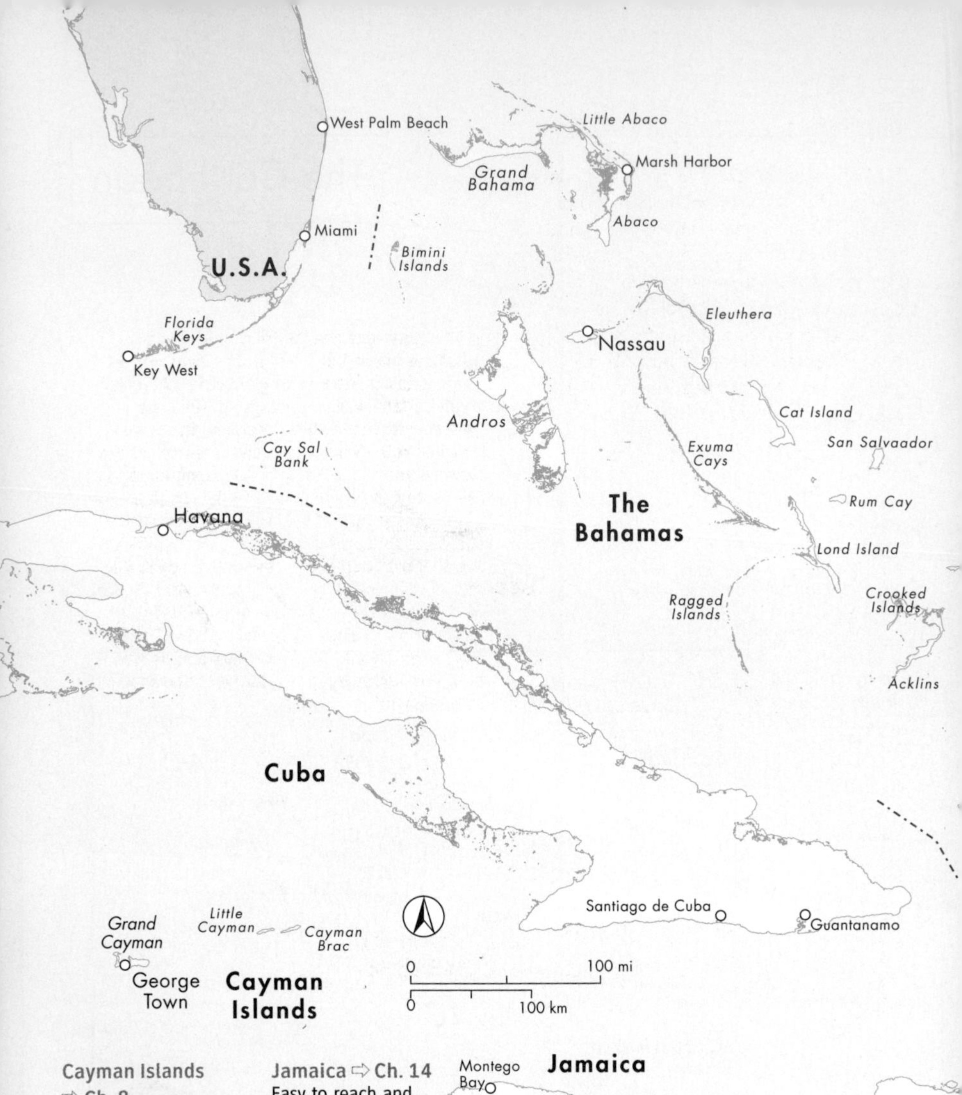

Cayman Islands ⇨ Ch. 8
Vacationers appreciate the mellow civility of these islands, and Grand Cayman's exceptional Seven Mile Beach has its share of fans. Divers come to explore the pristine reefs or perhaps to swim with friendly stingrays. Go if you want a safe, family-friendly vacation spot. Don't go if you're on a tight budget, because there are few bargains here.

Jamaica ⇨ Ch. 14
Easy to reach and with resorts in every price range, Jamaica is an easy choice for many travelers. Go to enjoy the music, food, beaches, and sense of hospitality that's made Jamaica one of the Caribbean's most popular destinations. Don't go if you can't deal with the idea that a Caribbean paradise still has problems of its own to solve.

WHAT'S WHERE

THE GREATER ANTILLES

The four islands closest to the United States mainland—Cuba, Jamaica, Hispaniola (Haiti and the Dominican Republic), and Puerto Rico—are the largest in the chain that stretches in an arc from the Florida Keys to Venezuela. The Cayman Islands, just south of Cuba, are usually included in the Greater Antilles group. We also include Turks and Caicos Islands. Haiti and Cuba aren't covered in this book

Dominican Republic ⇨ Ch. 11
Dominicans have beautiful smiles and warm hearts and are proud of their island, which is blessed with pearl-white beaches and a vibrant Latin culture. Go for the best-priced resorts in the Caribbean and a wide range of activities that will keep you moving day and night. Don't go if you can't go with the flow. Things don't always work here, and not everyone speaks English.

Turks and Caicos Islands ⇨ Ch. 26
Miles of white-sand beaches surround this tiny island chain, only eight of which are inhabited. The smaller islands are reminiscent of some long-forgotten era of Caribbean life. Go for deserted beaches and excellent diving on one of the world's largest coral reefs. Don't go for nightlife and a fast pace. And don't forget your wallet. This isn't a budget destination.

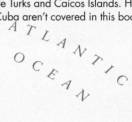

Puerto Rico ⇨ Ch. 17
San Juan is hopping day and night; beyond the city, you'll find a sunny escape and slower pace. Party in San Juan, relax on the beach, hike the rain forest, or play some of the Caribbean's best golf courses. You have the best of both worlds here, with natural and urban thrills alike. So go for both. Just don't expect to do it in utter seclusion.

WHAT'S WHERE

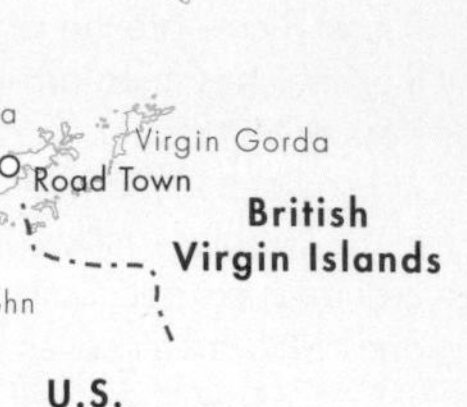

LESSER ANTILLES AND THE LEEWARD ISLANDS

Smaller in size but larger in number than the Greater Antilles, the Lesser Antilles make up the bulk of the Caribbean arc. From the Virgin Islands in the north to Grenada in the south, these islands form a barrier between the Atlantic Ocean and the Caribbean Sea. The Lesser Antilles are further divided into the Leeward Islands, the northernmost islands in the chain, and the Windward Islands, the southernmost islands in the chain. The Windwards are also referred to as the Eastern Caribbean. On any of these islands, the best beaches are usually located on the Caribbean side.

U.S. Virgin Islands ⇨ Ch. 27
A perfect combination of the familiar and the exotic, the U.S. Virgin Islands are a little bit of America surrounded by an azure sea. Go to St. Croix if you like history and interesting restaurants. Go to St. John if you crave a back-to-nature experience. Go to St. Thomas if you want a shop-'til-you-drop experience and a big selection of resorts, activities, and nightlife.

British Virgin Islands ⇨ Ch. 7
The lure of the British Virgins is exclusivity and personal attention, not lavish luxury. Even the most expensive resorts offer a state of mind rather than state-of-the-art. So go with an open mind, and your stress may very likely disappear. Don't go if you expect glitz or stateside efficiency. These islands are about getting away, not getting it all.

Anguilla ⇨ Ch. 2
With miles of brilliant beaches and a range of luxurious resorts (even a few that mere mortals can afford), Anguilla is where the rich, powerful, and famous go to chill out. Go for the fine cuisine in elegant surroundings, great snorkeling, and funky late-night music scene. Don't go for shopping and sightseeing. This island is all about relaxing and reviving.

St. Maarten/St. Martin ⇨ Ch. 23
Two nations (Dutch and French), many nationalities, one small island, and a lot of development—but there are also more white, sandy beaches than days in a month. Go for the awesome restaurants, excellent shopping, and wide range of activities. Don't go if you're not willing to get out and search for the really good stuff.

St. Barthélemy ⇨ Ch. 19
If you come to St. Barth for a taste of European village life, not for a conventional full-service resort experience, you will find yourself richly rewarded. Go for excellent dining and wine, great boutiques with the latest hip fashions, and an active, on-the-go vacation. Don't go for big resorts—and make sure your credit card is platinum.

St. Eustatius ⇨ Ch. 20
St. Eustatius (Statia) is the quintessential low-key island, where the most exciting thing is finding an elusive blue iguana while hiking the Quill. The real thrills are below the surface. Go to dive the wrecks, hike the island's extinct volcano, and mingle with the Caribbean's friendliest people. Don't go if you want to do much else.

0 100 mi

0 100 km

ATLANTIC OCEAN

Anguilla

West End Village

Marigot

St. Maarten
St. Martin

Philipsburg

Gustavia

St. Barthélemy

Barbuda

Saba

Oranjestad

St. Eustatius

St. Kitts

Basseterre

Nevis

Charlestown

St Johns

Antigua

English Harbour

LEEWARD ISLANDS

Montserrat

Guadeloupe

Grande-Terre

Le Désirade

Abymes

Pointe-à-Pitre

Petite Terre

Basse-Terre

Basse-Terre

Les Saintes

Marie Galante

Grande-Bourg

Portsmouth

Dominica

Roseau

Martinique

St Pierre

Fort-de-France

Antigua and Barbuda ⇨ Ch. 3

Beaches are bone-white and beckoning—there's one for every day of the year—and can be either secluded or hopping with activity. History buffs and nautical nuts will appreciate English Harbour, which sheltered Britain's Caribbean fleet in the 18th and 19th centuries. Go for those beaches but also for sailing. Don't go for local culture, because all-inclusives predominate. Lovely as they are, these islands are more for tourists than travelers.

Saba ⇨ Ch. 18

With few modern conveniences (no resorts, no fast food, no movie theaters), you can reacquaint yourself with Mother Nature or simply catch your breath. Go to dive in the clear water, hike to the top of Mt. Scenery, and enjoy the peace. Don't go if you want to lounge on the beach. There is no beach.

St. Kitts and Nevis ⇨ Ch. 21

Things are unhurried on lush, hilly St. Kitts and Nevis. And the locals seem more cordial and courteous—eager to share their paradise with you—than on more touristy Caribbean islands. Go to discover Caribbean history, stay in a small plantation inn, or just relax. Don't go for nightlife or shopping. These islands are about laid-back "liming" and maybe buying some local crafts.

Montserrat ⇨ Ch. 16

Montserrat has staged one of the best comebacks of the new century, returning to the tourism scene after a disastrous volcanic eruption in 1995. Go for exciting volcano ecotourism and great diving or just to have a taste of what the Caribbean used to be like. Don't go for splashy resorts or nightlife. You'll be happier here if you can appreciate simpler pleasures.

Guadeloupe ⇨ Ch. 13

An exotic, tropical paradise, Guadeloupe is covered by lush rain forest and blessed with a rich creole culture that influences everything from the dancing to the food. Go if you want to experience another culture—and still have your creature comforts and access to fine beaches. Don't go if you want five-star luxury, because it's rare here.

WHAT'S WHERE

THE WINDWARD AND SOUTHERN ISLANDS

The Windward Islands—Dominica, Martinique, St. Lucia, St. Vincent, and Grenada—complete the main Caribbean arc. These dramatically scenic southern islands face the trade winds head-on. The Grenadines—a string of small islands between Grenada and St. Vincent—are heaven for sailors. The Southern Caribbean islands—Trinidad, Tobago, Aruba, Bonaire, and Curaçao—are rarely bothered by hurricanes.

Aruba ⇨ Ch. 4
Some Caribbean travelers seek an undiscovered paradise, some seek the familiar and safe: Aruba is for the latter. On the smallest of the ABC islands, the waters are peacock blue and calm; the white beaches are broad, beautiful, and powdery soft. For Americans, Aruba offers all the comforts of home—including lots of casinos.

Bonaire ⇨ Ch. 6
With only 15,000 year-round citizens and huge numbers of visiting divers, Bonaire still seems largely untouched by tourism. Divers come for the clear water, profusion of marine life, and great dive shops. With a surreal, arid landscape, immense flamingo population, and gorgeous turquoise vistas Bonaire also offers a wonderful land-based holiday.

Curaçao ⇨ Ch. 9
Rich in heritage and history, Curaçao easily blends quaint island life and savvy city life, along with wonderful weather, spectacular diving, and charming beaches. Dutch and Caribbean influences are everywhere, but there's also an infusion of touches from around the world—particularly noteworthy in the great food. Willemstad is the picturesque capital and a treat for pedestrians, with shopping clustered in areas around the waterfront.

Dominica ⇨ Ch. 10
Dominica is the island to find your bliss exploring nature's bounty. Go to be active, either diving under the sea or hiking on land. Don't go for great beaches or a big-resort experience. This is one island that's delightfully behind the times.

Martinique ⇨ Ch. 15
Excellent cuisine, fine service, highly touted rum, and lilting Franco-Caribbean music are the main draws in Martinique. Go if you're a Francophile drawn to fine food, wine, and sophisticated style. Don't go if you are looking for a bargain and have little patience. Getting here is a chore, but there are definitely rewards for the persistent.

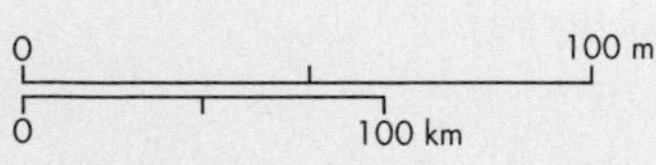

St. Kitts
Nevis
Antigua
Montserrat
LEEWARD ISLANDS
Grande-Terre
Guadeloupe
Le Désirade
Abymes
Pointe-à-Pitre
Basse-Terre
Basse-Terre
Marie Galante
Grande-Bourg
Les Saintes
Portsmouth
Dominica
Roseau
La Trinité
St Pierre
Fort-de-France
Martinique
Castries
St. Lucia
WINDWARD ISLANDS
Barbados
Bridgetown
Kingstown
St. Vincent
Bequia
The Grenadines
Carriacou
Grenada
St. George's
Tobago
Scarborough
Trinidad
Port of Spain
San Fernando

Barbados ⇨ **Ch. 5**
Broad vistas, sweeping seascapes, craggy cliffs, and acre upon acre of sugarcane make up the island's varied landscape. In this most British of all the Caribbean islands, a long, successful history of tourism has been forged from the warm, Bajan hospitality, welcoming hotels and resorts, sophisticated dining, lively nightspots, and, of course, magnificent sunny beaches.

St. Lucia ⇨ **Ch. 22**
One of the greenest and most beautiful islands in the Caribbean is, arguably, the most romantic. The scenic southwestern and central regions are mountainous and lush, with dense rain forest, endless banana plantations, and fascinating historic sites. In the north, some of the region's most appealing resorts are interspersed with dozens of delightful inns that welcome families as well as lovers and adventurers.

St. Vincent and the Grenadines ⇨ **Ch. 24**
Thirty-two perfectly endowed islands and cays have no mass tourism but amazing beaches, beautiful sailing waters, and authentic Caribbean charm; several of the Grenadines offer pure luxury. On mountainous St. Vincent itself, visitors can take a brisk walk through the rain forest or a more strenuous hike up a thankfully dormant volcano (last eruption in 1979) and spot rare species of island flora and fauna.

Grenada ⇨ **Ch. 12**
The spice business is going strong, but tourism is just as important. On this truly laid-back island, you'll spend your days exploring the lush rain forest, splashing in the surf on spectacular Grand Anse Beach, and enjoying nutmeg-flavored everything (drinks, ice cream, syrups, sauces . . .). Resorts are mostly small and charming. St. George's, the island's capital, boasts what is often called the most beautiful harbor in the Caribbean.

Trinidad and Tobago ⇨ **Ch. 25**
Trinidad and Tobago are two different islands but one nation. Trinidad is an effervescent mix of cultures—mostly descendants of African slaves and East Indian indentured workers—who like to party but also appreciate the island's incredibly diverse ecosystem. Little sister Tobago is laid-back and rustic; its broad vistas and beaches match any in the Caribbean.

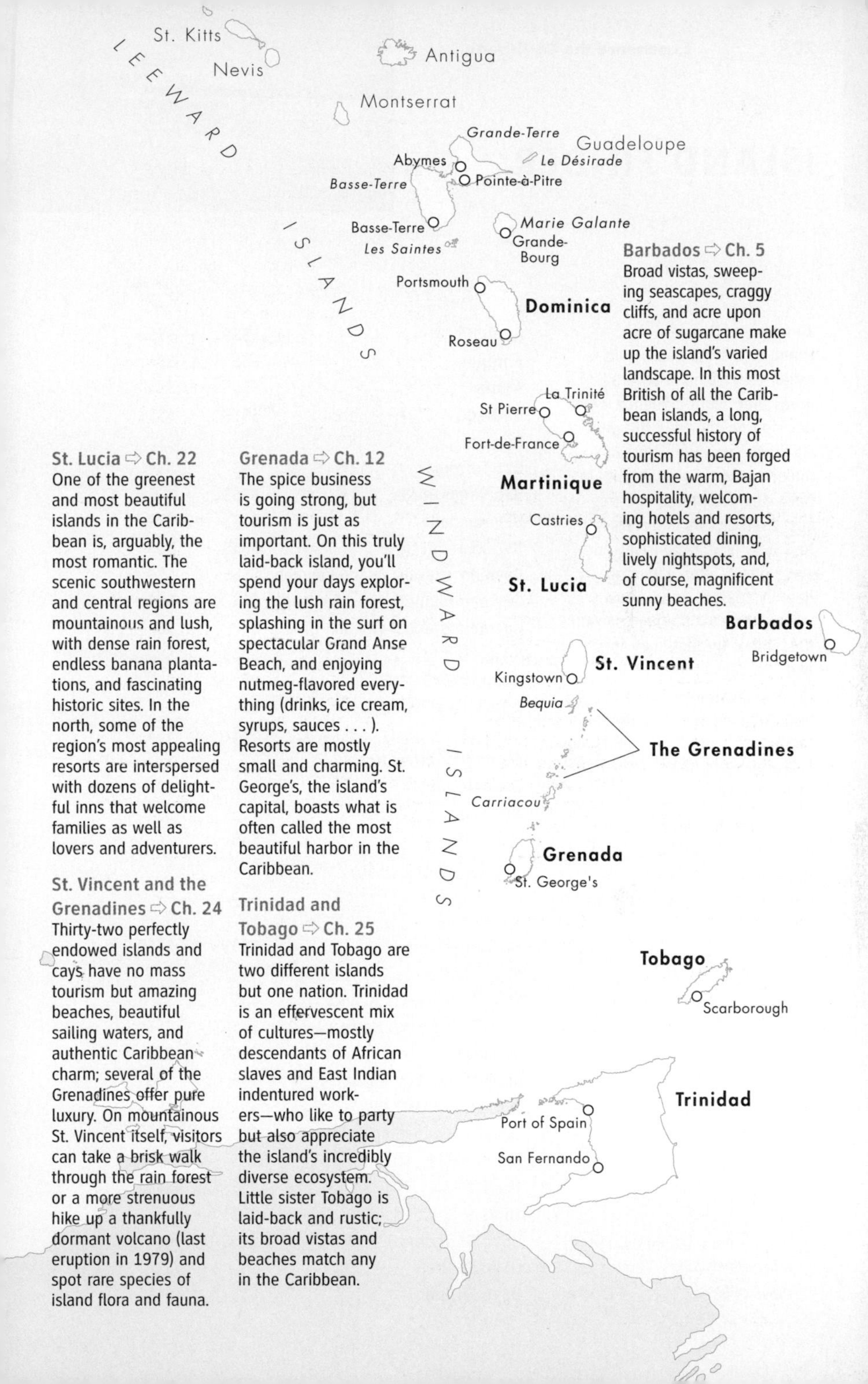

ISLAND FINDER

To help you decide which island is best for you, we've rated each island in several areas that might influence your decision on choosing the perfect Caribbean vacation spot. Each major island covered in this book has been rated in terms of cost from $ (very inexpensive) to $$$$$ (very expensive), and since prices often vary a great deal by season, we've given you a rating for the high season (December through mid-April) and low season (mid-April through November). We've also compared each island's relative strength in several other categories that might influence your decision.

If an island has no marks in a particular column (under "Golf" for example), it means that the activity is not available on the island.

	Cost High Season	Cost Low Season
Anguilla	$$$$	$$$
Antigua	$$$	$$
Aruba	$$$	$$
Barbados	$$$$	$$$$
Bonaire	$$	$$
BVI: Tortola	$$$	$$
BVI: Virgin Gorda	$$$$$	$$$$
BVI: Anegada	$$$$	$$$
BVI: Jost Van Dyke	$$$$	$$$
Cayman Islands: Grand Cayman	$$$$	$$$
Cayman Islands: Little Cayman	$$$	$$$
Cayman Islands: Cayman Brac	$$	$$
Curaçao	$$$$	$$$
Dominica	$$	$
Dominican Republic	$$	$
Grenada	$$$	$$$
Grenada: Carriacou	$$	$
Guadeloupe	$$	$$
Jamaica	$$$	$$
Martinique	$$$	$$
Montserrat	$	$
Puerto Rico	$$$	$$
Saba	$$	$
St. Barthélemy	$$$$$	$$$$
St. Eustatius	$$	$
St. Kitts & Nevis: St. Kitts	$$$	$$
St. Kitts & Nevis: Nevis	$$$$	$$$
St. Lucia	$$$$	$$$
St. Maarten/St. Martin	$$$	$$$
SVG: St. Vincent	$$	$$
SVG: The Grenadines	$$$$	$$$
T&T: Trinidad	$$$	$$
T&T: Tobago	$$$	$$
Turks & Caicos Islands	$$$$*	$$$*
USVI: St. Thomas	$$$$	$$$
USVI: St. Croix	$$	$
USVI: St. John	$$$	$$

* *Cost for Provo (Parrot Cay $$$$$, other islands $$)*

** *Provo Only*

Beautiful Beaches	Fine Dining	Shopping	Casinos	Nightlife	Diving	Golf	Eco-tourism	Good for Families
▲▲▲▲▲	▲▲▲▲	▲▲		▲▲	▲	▲▲▲	▲	▲▲
▲▲▲▲▲	▲▲▲▲▲	▲▲▲▲	▲▲▲	▲▲▲	▲▲	▲▲▲	▲▲▲	▲▲▲
▲▲▲▲	▲▲▲▲	▲▲▲▲	▲▲▲▲	▲▲▲▲▲	▲▲▲	▲▲	▲▲	▲▲▲▲
▲▲▲	▲▲▲▲▲	▲▲▲		▲▲▲	▲▲	▲▲▲▲▲	▲▲	▲▲▲▲
▲▲▲	▲▲▲	▲▲	▲	▲	▲▲▲▲▲		▲▲▲▲	▲▲▲▲
▲▲	▲▲▲	▲▲		▲▲	▲▲▲		▲▲▲	▲▲▲
▲▲▲▲▲	▲▲▲	▲		▲	▲▲▲▲		▲▲▲▲	▲▲▲
▲▲▲▲▲	▲▲▲			▲	▲▲▲▲		▲▲▲▲	▲▲▲
▲▲▲▲	▲▲▲	▲		▲▲▲▲	▲▲▲		▲▲▲	▲▲▲
▲▲▲▲▲	▲▲▲▲	▲▲▲▲▲		▲▲	▲▲▲▲	▲▲▲	▲▲	▲▲▲▲
					▲▲▲▲	▲▲▲▲▲	▲▲▲	▲▲▲
▲▲					▲▲▲▲		▲▲▲	▲▲▲
▲▲▲▲	▲▲▲▲	▲▲▲	▲▲▲	▲▲▲▲	▲▲▲▲	▲▲▲	▲▲▲▲	▲▲▲
▲	▲▲▲	▲▲▲		▲▲	▲▲▲▲▲		▲▲▲▲▲	▲▲▲
▲▲▲▲▲	▲▲▲	▲▲	▲▲▲	▲▲▲▲	▲▲▲	▲▲▲▲▲	▲▲▲	▲▲▲
▲▲▲▲	▲▲▲	▲▲		▲	▲▲▲	▲	▲▲▲▲	▲▲▲
▲▲▲	▲	▲			▲▲▲▲		▲▲▲	▲▲
▲▲▲▲	▲▲	▲▲▲	▲▲▲	▲▲▲	▲▲▲▲	▲▲▲	▲▲▲▲▲	▲▲▲
▲▲▲	▲▲▲	▲▲	▲	▲▲	▲▲▲	▲▲▲▲▲	▲▲▲▲▲	▲▲▲▲▲
▲▲▲▲	▲▲▲▲	▲▲▲	▲▲	▲▲▲	▲▲▲	▲▲▲	▲▲▲	▲▲
▲	▲	▲		▲	▲▲▲▲		▲▲▲▲	▲▲
▲▲▲	▲▲▲▲	▲▲▲▲	▲▲▲▲	▲▲▲▲▲	▲▲▲	▲▲▲▲	▲▲▲▲▲	▲▲▲▲▲
	▲▲▲▲	▲▲		▲	▲▲▲▲▲		▲▲▲▲▲	▲
▲▲▲▲	▲▲▲▲▲	▲▲▲▲▲		▲▲	▲▲▲			▲
▲	▲	▲▲		▲	▲▲▲▲▲		▲▲▲▲▲	▲▲▲
▲▲▲	▲▲▲	▲▲▲	▲▲▲▲	▲▲▲	▲▲▲▲	▲▲▲▲	▲▲▲▲▲	▲▲▲▲▲
▲▲▲	▲▲▲▲	▲▲		▲▲▲	▲▲▲▲	▲▲▲▲▲	▲▲▲▲▲	▲▲▲▲▲
▲▲▲	▲▲▲	▲▲▲		▲▲▲	▲▲▲	▲	▲▲▲▲▲	▲▲▲
▲▲▲▲	▲▲▲▲▲	▲▲▲▲	▲▲▲	▲▲▲▲	▲▲▲	▲	▲▲	▲▲▲
▲	▲▲	▲	▲	▲	▲▲▲▲		▲▲▲▲▲	▲▲▲
▲▲▲▲▲	▲▲▲▲	▲		▲	▲▲▲▲▲	▲▲▲▲▲	▲▲▲	▲▲▲▲
▲▲▲	▲▲▲	▲▲	▲▲▲	▲▲▲▲▲	▲▲▲▲	▲▲▲▲	▲▲▲▲	▲▲▲
▲▲▲▲	▲▲▲	▲▲	▲▲▲	▲▲▲	▲▲▲▲	▲▲▲▲	▲▲▲▲	▲▲▲
▲▲▲▲▲	▲▲**	▲	▲	▲	▲▲▲▲▲	▲▲▲▲**	▲▲▲▲	▲▲▲**
▲▲▲	▲▲▲▲	▲▲▲▲▲		▲▲	▲▲▲	▲▲▲▲	▲▲	▲▲▲▲
▲▲▲	▲▲▲	▲▲	▲▲	▲▲	▲▲▲	▲▲▲	▲▲▲	▲▲▲
▲▲▲▲▲	▲▲▲	▲▲		▲	▲▲▲	▲▲▲	▲▲▲▲	▲▲▲▲▲

CARIBBEAN LODGING

When to Reserve

At most hotels, the holiday season and school vacation periods generally require booking well in advance. The most popular properties book as much as a year in advance due to the high number of repeat guests, many of whom request the same room every year. Many high-end chain resorts, such as Ritz-Carlton and Four Seasons, also book well in advance during peak periods. The most difficult time to find a well-priced room is typically around the Christmas and New Year's holidays, when minimum-stay requirements of one to two weeks may be common and room rates, typically double.

But for the typical Caribbean resort, two months is usually sufficient notice. In popular mass-market destinations such as Punta Cana or Negril, a couple of weeks may be enough advance notice. Paradoxically, it's easiest to find an acceptable room in the busiest destinations by sheer virtue of the number of rooms available at any given time. Although waiting until the last minute doesn't always net bargains, flexibility and timing can sometimes pay off with either a deep discount (usually at a larger resort) or a room category upgrade.

Fees and Add-Ons

Every island charges an accommodations tax, whether you stay in a bed-and-breakfast inn, hotel, guesthouse, resort, or private villa. The tax ranges from 7% to 15%, depending on the destination (*you can find the exact surcharge listed in the individual chapters' hotel and restaurant price chart*). In addition, most Caribbean hotels and resorts tack on a service fee, usually 10%. The service fee isn't quite the same as a tip for service, so it is customary at most resorts (all-inclusives being an exception) to tip the staff. Generally, taxes and services charges will add at least 20% above the base rate for a room.

A growing trend is the "resort fee." You may encounter it anywhere, particularly at large resorts with lots of activities; resort fees are almost universal in San Juan, Puerto Rico. The fee, which can range from $5 to $50 per night, presumably covers the costs of services such as housekeeping (though you might sometimes see this on your bill, too, especially for villa rentals), utilities, and resort facilities. Resort fees are more common at larger hotels; and they depend more on the policy of the individual resort or hotel chain than on the island itself. These additional costs aren't always mentioned when you book, so be sure to inquire.

Picking the Best Room

On virtually every island, especially at beachfront lodgings, the better the beach access or ocean view, the higher the price. If you're the active type who really uses a room only to sleep, you could save $100 or more per night by choosing a garden-, mountain-, or town-view room. But regardless of view, be sure to ask about the property's layout. For example, if you want to be close to the "action" at many larger resorts, whether you have mobility concerns or just need to satisfy your gambling or gamboling itch, the trade-off might be noise—whether from screaming kids jumping in the pool or DJs pumping reggae in the bar. Likewise, saving that $100 may not be worth it if your room faces a busy thoroughfare. If you have any specific desires or dislikes, discuss them thoroughly and ahead of time with the reservations staff.

Types of Lodgings

Most islands offer the gamut of glitzy resorts, chic boutique hotels and inns, historic hostelries, family-run B&Bs, condo resorts, self-catering apartments, and private villas.

Condos and Time-Shares Condo resorts are increasingly popular and can offer both extra space and superior savings for families or small groups traveling together, with kitchens, sofa beds, and more. In fact, they dominate the sensuous sweeps of Grand Cayman's Seven-Mile Beach, Provo's amazing Grace Bay in the Turks and Caicos, Palm Beach in Aruba, and elsewhere. Some of these are time-share properties, but not all time-shares require you to sit through a sales pitch.

Inns and B&Bs Historic inns come in all shapes and sizes. The old Spanish colonial capitals of Santo Domingo and San Juan have converted monasteries. Puerto Rico also offers affordable lodgings in its paradors, patterned after the Spanish system, most of them historically and/or culturally significant buildings such as old-time thermal baths or working coffee plantations. Longtime sailing and whaling destinations such as Antigua or Bequia in the Grenadines offer their own bits of history adapted to modern comfort, and Guadeloupe and Martinique feature converted sugar plantations. St. Kitts and Nevis, in particular, are prized by Caribbean connoisseurs for their restored great house plantation inns, often with a resident expat owner who enhances your experience with amusing anecdotes and insider insights.

Private Villas Another increasingly popular option for families or those seeking a good bargain are private villas. Self-catering means saving on dining out on more expensive islands, such as St. Barth (where villas usually cost much less than hotels), though a car is often necessary. Many villas have private pools with stunning sea views and/or beachfront access.

Hotels and Resorts Most prevalent in the Caribbean are large resorts, including all-inclusives, that are usually positioned strategically on the beach or on a golf course or that may have a theme: couples, families, spa retreat, etc. You'll find familiar chain hotels in various price categories—from Ritz-Carlton to Comfort Suites.

All-Inclusive or Not?

The AI ("all-inclusive") concept is especially prominent in Jamaica, the Dominican Republic, Antigua, and St. Lucia. For those who have only a week for vacation, the allure is obvious: a hassle-free, prepaid vacation that includes accommodations, meals, unlimited drinks, entertainment, and most activities. And you tend to get what you pay for: AIs range from hedonistic, high-tech luxury to bare-bones, beachfront bang-for-the-buck, with prices to match. Some of these resorts are intimate romantic hideaways for couples, some emphasize sporting options, others cater to families, and still others cater to singles ready to mingle in a nonstop party atmosphere.

But there are caveats. Few AIs offer *everything* for free. That spa treatment, the scuba trip, the sunset cruise, or the tour of the nearby plantation may not be included. Moreover, there can be surcharges for dining in some restaurants (which also must be reserved).

AI resorts appeal mostly to travelers who just want to get away and bask in the sun, piña colada within easy reach. They're not for more adventuresome types who seek genuine interaction with the locals and immersion in their culture, nor are they good for people who want to eat local food, since most AI travelers rarely leave their resort boundaries.

CARIBBEAN LOGISTICS

Time

The Cayman Islands, Cuba, Haiti, Jamaica, and the Turks and Caicos Islands are all in the eastern standard time zone. All other Caribbean islands are in the Atlantic standard time zone, which is one hour later than eastern standard. Caribbean islands don't observe daylight saving time, so during that period (March through October) eastern standard time will be one hour behind; Atlantic standard Time and eastern daylight time will be the same.

Driving

Your own valid driver's license works in some countries. However, temporary local driving permits are required in several Caribbean destinations (Anguilla, Antigua, Barbados, the British Virgin Islands, Cayman Islands, Dominica, Grenada, Nevis, St. Kitts, St. Lucia, and St. Vincent and the Grenadines), which you can secure at rental agencies or local police offices on presentation of a valid license and a small fee. St. Lucia and St. Vincent and the Grenadines require a temporary permit only if you don't have an International Driving Permit (available from AAA).

Flights

Many carriers fly nonstop or direct routes to the Caribbean from major international airports in the United States, including Atlanta, Boston, Charlotte, Chicago, Dallas, Fort Lauderdale, Houston, Miami, New York (JFK), Newark, Philadelphia, Phoenix, and Washington (Dulles). If you live elsewhere in the United States, you'll have to make a connection to get to your Caribbean destination. It's also not uncommon to make a connection in the Caribbean, most often in San Juan, Montego Bay, Barbados, or St. Maarten.

Some interisland flights will be on small planes operated by local or regional carriers, some of which may have code-share arrangements with major airlines from the United States. Or you can confidently book directly with the local carrier, using a major credit card, either online or by phone.

Some regional airlines may make multiple stops, accepting and discharging passengers and/or cargo at each small airport or airstrip along the way. This is not unusual—nor is the sometimes-unreliable schedules that these smaller airlines can have. Flights can be late—or even depart early—without apology or explanation. Be sure to confirm your flights on interisland carriers, as you may be subject to their whims: for example, if no other passengers are booked on your flight, particularly if the carrier operates "scheduled charters," you'll be rescheduled on another flight or at a different departure time (earlier or later than your original reservation) that is more convenient for the airline. If you're connecting from an interisland flight to a major airline, be sure to include a substantial buffer of time for these kinds of delays.

TYPICAL NONSTOP TRAVEL TIMES BY AIR

	New York	Miami
Puerto Rico	3½ hours	2½ hours
Jamaica	4½ hours	1½ hours
St. Lucia	4½ hours	3½ hours
Trinidad	5 hours	3½ hours
Aruba	4¾ hours	2½ hours

Airlines

Major Airlines **American Airlines** (☎ *800/433–7300* 🌐 *www.aa.com*). **Caribbean Airlines** (☎ *800/920–4225* 🌐 *www.caribbean-airlines.com*). **Delta Airlines** (☎ *800/241–4141* 🌐 *www.delta.com*). **JetBlue** (☎ *800/538–2583* 🌐 *www.jetblue.com*). **Spirit Airlines** (☎ *801/401–2200 new reservations, fees apply, 801/400–2222 existing reservations* 🌐 *www.spirit.com*). **United Airlines** (☎ *800/864–8331* 🌐 *www.united.com*). **US Airways** (☎ *800/428–4322* 🌐 *www.usairways.com*).

Smaller/Regional Airlines **Air Antilles Express** (☎ *0890/648–648 in Guadeloupe* 🌐 *www.airantilles.com*). **Air Caraïbes** (☎ *0820/835–835 in Guyana* 🌐 *www.aircaraibes.com*). **Air Sunshine** (☎ *800/327–8900, 800/435–8900 in Florida* 🌐 *www.airsunshine.com*). **Bahamas Air** (☎ *242/702–4140 in Nassau, 800/222–4262 in U.S.* 🌐 *bahamasair.com*). **Caicos Express** (☎ *649/941–5730 in the Turks and Caicos, 305/677–3116 in U.S.* 🌐 *caicosexpressairways.com*). **Cape Air** (☎ *866/227–3247, 508/771–6944 outside U.S.* 🌐 *www.capeair.com*). **Cayman Airways** (☎ *345/949–2311 in the Cayman Islands, 800/422–9626 in U.S.* 🌐 *www.caymanairways.com*). **InselAir** (☎ *(599) 9/737–0444 in Curaçao, 855/493–6004 in U.S.* 🌐 *www.fly-inselair.com*). **InterCaribbean Airways** (☎ *888/957–3223 in U.S.,* 649/946–4999 in the Turks and Caicos 🌐 *intercaribbean.com*). **LIAT** (☎ *480–5582 in Antigua, 888/844–5428 within the Caribbean* 🌐 *www.liatairline.com*). **Mustique Airways** (☎ *718/618–4492 in U.S., 784/458–4380 in St. Vincent* 🌐 *www.mustique.com*). **Seaborne Airlines** (☎ *340/773–6442 in St. Thomas, 866/359–8784 in U.S.* 🌐 *www.seaborneairlines.com*). **St. Barth Commuter** (☎ *590/27–54–54 in St. Barth* 🌐 *www.stbarthcommuter.com*). **SVG Air** (☎ *784/457–5124 in St. Vincent, 315/507–8258 in U.S.* 🌐 *www.svgair.com*). **Winair** (*Windward Islands Airways* ☎ *866/466–0410* 🌐 *www.fly-winair.com*). **Windward Express Airways** (☎ *599/545–2001 in St. Maarten* 🌐 *www.windwardexpress.com*).

Ferries

Interisland ferries are an interesting and often less expensive way to travel around certain areas of the Caribbean, but they are not offered everywhere. A few destinations are reached only by ferry (St. John, for example). In most cases, where service is offered it is frequent (either daily or several times daily).

MAJOR FERRY ROUTES

Ferries connect Puerto Rico with the outlying islands of Vieques and Culebra; St. Thomas with Water Island, St. John, St. Croix, and the British Virgin Islands; the various islands of the British Virgin Islands with each other and with the U.S. Virgin Islands; St. Martin/St. Maarten with Anguilla, St. Barth, and Saba; St. Kitts with Nevis; Antigua with Barbuda and Montserrat; Guadeloupe with La Désirade, Marie-Galante, and Les Saintes, as well as Dominica, Martinique, and St. Lucia; St. Lucia with Guadeloupe, Martinique, and Dominica; St. Vincent with Bequia and the other islands of the Grenadines; Grenada with Carriacou and Petite Martinique; and Trinidad with Tobago; there's limited ferry service in the Turks and Caicos Islands (Provo and North Caicos, Grand Turk and Salt Cay). In most cases, service is frequent—either daily or several times daily.

RENTING A VILLA

In the Caribbean the term *villa* may describe anything from a traditional cottage to a luxurious architectural wonder, but it almost always means a stand-alone accommodation, often privately owned. Villa rentals provide some of the region's most desirable accommodations, from both a comfort and an economic point of view. We recommend considering this option, especially if you're traveling with your family or a group of friends. A villa accommodation provides a lot more space, much more privacy, and a better sense of the island than you would get at a hotel—and usually at a fraction of the per-person cost.

Factor in the ability to fix simple meals, snacks, and drinks, and the savings really add up. An additional advantage to Americans is that villa rates are generally negotiated in dollars, thus bypassing the unfavorable euro fluctuations in St. Martin, St. Barth, and Martinique.

What Does It Cost?

Rental rates vary widely by island and by season. In-season rates range from $1,200 for a simple one-bedroom cottage to more than $40,000 a week for a multiroom luxury home. Many full-service resorts also offer villas of varying sizes on their property and, although pricey, can be an excellent choice if you want the best of both worlds—full service and facilities but also space and privacy. In many cases, renting a villa at a resort will cost less than renting three or four individual rooms, and you can still have a waiter deliver your rum punch to a beach chair or enjoy access to a high-tech fitness room.

What's Included?

Villas are generally furnished nicely, have updated bathrooms and full kitchens, and are equipped with linens, kitchen utensils, CD and DVD players, a phone, TV, and, increasingly, Wi-Fi access. The sophistication of all of the above is factored into the price; the more luxurious the digs, the higher the price.

Upscale rental villas often have small, private plunge pools (rather few are beachfront); daily housekeeping service (except Sunday) is included in the quoted price. On some islands, including the Dominican Republic, Jamaica, Mustique, and Barbados, two or even three staff members are common. Inquire about the villa's staff and specify particular needs or expectations right from the start, including start times and specific or additional duties such as laundry, cooking, or child care.

How Do You Rent?

Some owners rent their properties directly (🌐 *www.vrbo.com*); but in general, we recommend renting a villa through a reputable local agency that both manages and maintains the properties and has an office with local staff to facilitate and troubleshoot on your behalf should something go wrong. Lavish catalogs or websites with detailed descriptions and photographs of each villa can help assuage any concerns about what to expect. The agent will meet you at the airport, bring you to the villa, explain and demonstrate the household systems, and (for a fee) stock the kitchen with starter groceries. Some agencies provide comprehensive concierge services, will arrange or recommend car rentals, and help you find additional staff such as chefs or babysitters or yoga instructors. Some of the larger companies even host a weekly cocktail party where renters can meet each other and form a community to share local information or socialize.

Specific villa-rental companies are listed and recommended throughout this guide.

Choosing a Villa

These days, your hunt will no doubt start on the Internet. A simple search for "villa rental [island name]" will get you started. The tourist board of each island can also provide a list of reputable local rental agents.

Villa-rental websites allow you to see pictures of available villas and often have a chat feature through which you can talk to a knowledgeable representative who can help you sort through the listings according to your requirements. But use caution: Sometimes the rental agent isn't personally familiar with the villas the agency is renting. Rather, they consolidate listings from other sources. It pays to seek out reputable companies, especially if you are a first-time renter.

Things to Consider When Searching for a Villa

How many people are in your family/group? How many bedrooms do you need? Do they have to be of equal size? Do they all have to be attached to the house? If you are two couples, you might want to specify that you'll need two master suites. If you are traveling with young children, you won't want them in a separate bedroom pavilion. Definitely confirm the types of beds in each room; couples may prefer queens or kings, whereas kids would be better in single beds. Those looking for a bit more privacy might prefer bedrooms in a guesthouse or small cottage that's separate from the main house.

What location do you prefer? Do you want to be right on a beach? Do you want to walk to town? Will proximity to a particular activity such as golf or scuba diving enhance your vacation? Are you willing to rent a car to get around?

What are your requirements for electronics and appliances? Do you require a TV? Wi-Fi? Or would you be okay with something less connected? Do you want a dishwasher? A microwave? How about an outdoor gas grill, or is charcoal sufficient?

Is the villa child-friendly? Ask whether the rooms have direct access to the pool area, as that might not be a safe choice for younger kids who could open a sliding door and enter the pool area unsupervised. Are you comfortable having a pool at all? Most Caribbean villas don't have childproof security gates around pools or pool alarms. If the villa has two floors, are the rooms best suited for kids on the same floor as the master suite?

What specific issues about your destination will affect your villa choice? Personal security may be an issue in some areas of the Caribbean. Evaluate the location of potential rentals in relation to known problem areas—and ask if the villa has an alarm system. A surprisingly low rental rate on an otherwise expensive island could be a red flag.

Will you really be comfortable on your own? The final thing to consider is your relative travel hardiness and that of your traveling companions. Is this your first time in the destination? Do you relish or dread the idea of navigating local markets? Will you miss having a concierge to help arrange things for you? Do you really want to be faced with a sink full of dishes a few times a day? Will your kids be happy without a hotel full of peers? What about you?

CARIBBEAN TOP EXPERIENCES

A

B

C

D

E

Diving in Bonaire

(A) Nautical buffs love Bonaire for its kaleidoscope of underwater activity, profusion of marine life, excellent environmental stewardship, and accessibility of its reefs, most of which are just 5 to 30 feet from shore in currents mild enough for snorkeling, too.

Hiking in Dominica

(B) Morne Trois Pitons National Park, a UNESCO World Heritage Site, epitomizes "The Nature Isle," which is Dominica's nickname. The island is so green that you can practically watch plants grow during the daily tropical spritz. Countless rivers and waterfalls flow from majestic mountains filigreed by waterfalls, crater lakes, and natural pools. All that beauty contrasts with the blast furnace Valley of Desolation, including the world's second-largest fumarole, Boiling Lake, which belches sulfurously.

Snorkeling the Cayman Islands

(C) Shore diving and snorkeling excels throughout all three islands. At Stingray City or wading at the adjacent sandbar, you can interact with gracefully balletic stingrays, so tame that you can feed them as they nuzzle you—practically begging pet-like for handouts. Numerous boats take you out for the ray-diant experience.

Shopping St. Thomas

(D) The Caribbean has colorful historic capitals known for duty-free shopping including Curaçao's Willemstad and St. Maarten's Philipsburg; but Charlotte Amalie on St. Thomas is like an elegant bazaar, with name-brand luxury boutiques tucked away in its charming arcaded historic alleys.

Birding in Trinidad

(E) Trinidad is noted for Carnival, calypso, oil, asphalt—and bountiful birdlife. More than 200 species flutter flirtatiously through the Asa Wright Nature Centre, a

glorious old plantation that is also home to bats and giant lizards. Come sunset, flocks of scarlet ibis turn the mangroves at Caroni Bird Sanctuary into a veritable Christmas decoration.

Whale-Watching in the Dominican Republic

(F) Samaná in the northeastern Dominican Republic is revered for its shimmering water, champagne-hue strands, and superior sportfishing. But its signature aquatic activity is world-class whale-watching in season (January through March), as pods of humpbacks mate and calve. The male whale's signature song echoes across the water.

Dining in St. Martin

(G) Few places rival the French West Indies for fine food and exotic ambience. One small St. Martin fishing village, Grand Case, has become the Caribbean's Restaurant Row. More than 40 eateries line the main beachfront drag, from humble *lolos* (shacks serving heaping helpings of creole fare at fair prices) to Michelin-worthy haute kitchens.

Sailing in the Grenadines

(H) Sailors forever compare sailing in the British Virgin Islands versus the Grenadines for their calm waters, exquisite anchorages, friendly islanders, even friendlier beach bars (such as Basil's on Mustique), and splendid diving and snorkeling (and beachcombing) at picturesque spots like the uninhabited Tobago Cays.

Viewing Colonial Architecture in Puerto Rico

(I) Old San Juan is a maze of cobblestone alleys that open onto broad tree-shaded plazas. Beautifully preserved 18th-century Spanish buildings range from stone mansions with wrought-iron balconies (now housing chic boutiques and restaurants) to the UNESCO World Heritage El Morro fortress that guards the bay.

CARIBBEAN TOP BEACHES

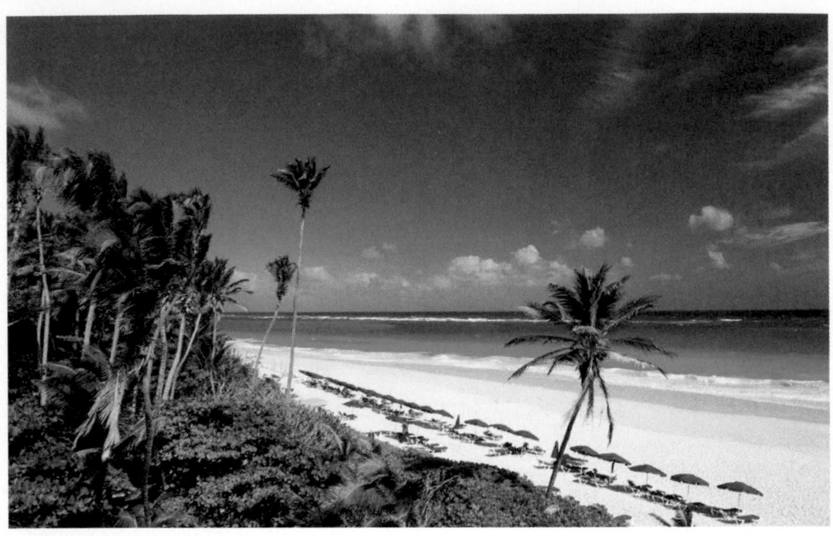

Maundays Bay, Anguilla
A dazzling, mile-long stretch of powdery soft sand on the island's southwest coast—great for swimming and long beach walks

Eagle Beach, Aruba
Bright sunshine, gleaming white sand, crystal clear water—sunglasses essential

Crane Beach, Barbados
A crescent of silky pink sand and ocean in varying shades of brilliant blue, accessible via 98 cliff-side steps—or a glass-walled elevator

Seven Mile Beach, Grand Cayman, Cayman Islands
Dominating the island's west coast, free of litter and peddlers, a sight to behold

Playa Grande, Dominican Republic
Dramatic, gorgeous, postcard-pretty, what more can we say?

Grand Anse Beach, Grenada
A 2-mile (3-km) semicircle of warm sand lapped by gentle surf, with mesmerizing views of the sea, cloud-capped mountains, and often a rainbow

Negril Beach, Jamaica
Miles of sand lined with beach bars, open-air restaurants, and resort hotels in westernmost Jamaica

Baie Orientale, St. Martin
Often crowded—often crowded with "naturalists"—but considered by many to be the island's most beautiful beach

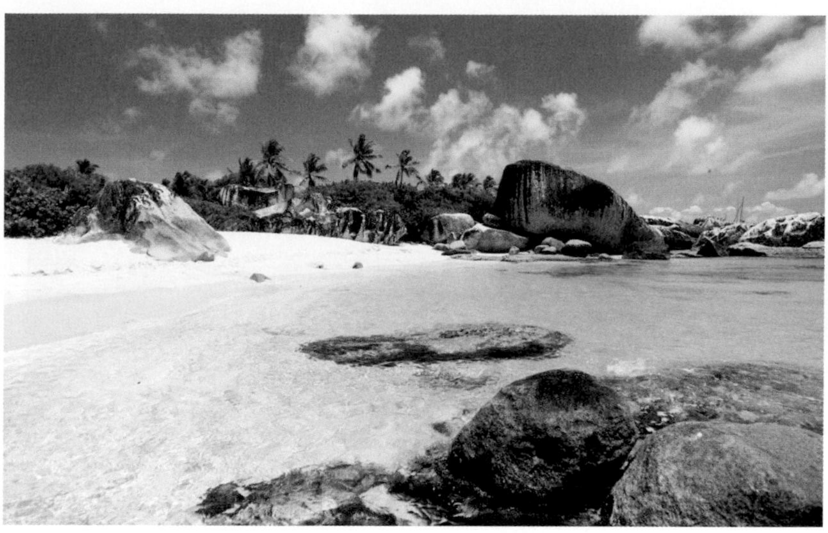

Saltwhistle Bay Beach, Mayreau, St. Vincent and the Grenadines
An exquisite and remote crescent of pure white sand—a popular anchorage for Grenadine sailors and paradise for snorkelers and swimmers

Half Moon Bay, Providenciales, Turks and Caicos Islands
A natural ribbon of ivory sand joins two tiny, uninhabited cays

Trunk Bay, U.S. Virgin Islands
A magnet for photographers, attracted to its stunning beauty, and swimmers, attracted to the underwater snorkeling trail

Other Top Spots
Bottom Bay Beach, Barbados; Pink Beach, Barbuda; Balneario La Monserrate and Playa Flamenco, Puerto Rico; Anse de Grande Saline, St. Barths; Magen's Bay, St. Thomas; Buck Island, St. Croix.

CARIBBEAN TOP GOLF COURSES

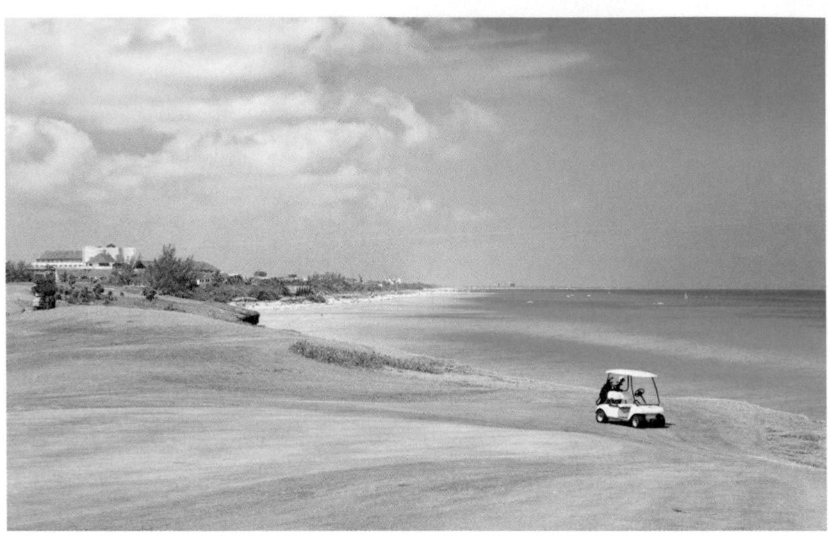

Tierra del Sol, Aruba

The island's native beauty—cacti, rock formations, and stunning views—embellish the abundant bunkers and water hazards on this Robert Trent Jones Jr.–designed course at the northwestern tip of one very windy island.

Country Club at Sandy Lane, Barbados

Perhaps the most prestigious club in the Caribbean, golfers can play The Old Nine, with its small greens and narrow fairways, or one of two Tom Fazio–designed courses—the modern-style Country Club Course or the spectacular Green Monkey (reserved for hotel guests and club members).

Casa de Campo Resort, Dominican Republic

The Teeth of the Dog course, one of the resort's three extraordinary courses, is touted as the number-one course in the Caribbean and one of the top courses in the world.

Punta Espada Golf Course, Dominican Republic

There's a Caribbean view from all the holes and eight play right along the sea at this Jack Nicklaus–designed championship course at the Cap Cana resort in Punta Cana.

Tryall Club Golf Course, Jamaica

Combine first-class golf and the island's storied history at this Ralph Plummer–designed course, beautifully laid out on the site of a 19th-century sugar plantation 15 miles west of Montego Bay.

Four Seasons Golf Course, Nevis

The majestic scenery, unbelievably lush landscaping, and Robert Trent Jones Jr.'s wicked layout incorporating ravines and sugar mills make this experience well above par even among classic golf resorts.

The Golf Links at Royal Isabela, Puerto Rico

One of the most dramatic courses built in recent years, this challenging course features an incomparable setting along the dramatic bluffs at the northwest edge of the island.

Grenadines Estate Golf Club, Canouan, St. Vincent and The Grenadines

Half the holes at this Jim Fazio-designed championship course, the only one in the Grenadines, has nine holes on a sloping green plain and nine carved into the mountainside.

Tobago Plantations Golf & Country Club, Trinidad and Tobago

An ocean-side course woven into the landscape of an old coconut plantation offers amazing views, not to mention challenging greens and fairways for golfers of all levels.

Provo Golf and Country Club, Turks and Caicos

Add stunning scenery—rugged limestone outcroppings and freshwater lakes—to the immaculate greens and lush fairways you'll find at this top-ranked championship course in Providenciales.

Buccaneer Golf Course, St. Croix, U.S. Virgin Islands

You'll have a spectacular Caribbean view from 13 of the 18 of the holes at this challenging yet very playable course on the east end of the island and not far from Christiansted.

IF YOU LIKE

Boating and Sailing

Whether you charter a crewed boat or are experienced enough to captain the vessel yourself, the waters of the Caribbean are excellent for boating and sailing. The many secluded bays and inlets provide ideal spots to drop anchor and picnic or explore. Once deemed an exclusive domain of the rich and famous, chartering a boat is now an affordable and attractive vacation alternative.

■ **Antigua.** Sailors put in regularly at Nelson's Dockyard, which hosts a colorful annual regatta in late April or early May.

■ **Grenada.** From Port Louis, on the lagoon in the capital city of St. George's, sail north to Carriacou and the nearby Grenadines.

■ **St. Lucia.** Rodney Bay Marina, the destination of the transatlantic Atlantic Rally for cruisers, is a premier yachting center that also provides easy access to open-water passages to nearby islands such as St. Vincent and the Grenadines.

■ **St. Martin.** Marigot's yacht harbor is a jumping-off spot for trips to the nearby islands of Anguilla and St. Barths.

■ **St. Thomas, U.S. Virgin Islands.** It's easy to charter a yacht in the Virgin Islands, which offer some of the best sailing opportunities in the world.

■ **St. Vincent and the Grenadines.** Thirty-two islands so close together give you more possibilities than you can possibly enjoy in one vacation.

■ **Tortola, British Virgin Islands.** The opportunity to sail the length and breadth of Drake's Channel, stopping at lovely islands en route, makes this, arguably, the best charter destination in the Caribbean.

Diving and Snorkeling

Many people would rather spend their days under the sea than on the beach. Here are some of the Caribbean's best dive destinations:

■ **Anegada, British Virgin Islands.** The reefs surrounding this flat coral-and-limestone atoll are a sailor's nightmare but a scuba diver's dream.

■ **Bonaire.** The reefs here begin about 30 feet offshore and quickly drop 100 feet, the current is mild, visibility is generally 60 feet to 100 feet, the marine life is magnificent, and most sites are accessible from shore.

■ **Dominica.** Serious divers know that the pristine, bubbly waters in Scotts Head Marine Reserve, a submerged volcanic crater, are among the best in the world.

■ **Little Cayman, Cayman Islands.** More than a dozen dive sites parallel the mile-long underwater ledge at Bloody Bay Wall, which drops from about 20 feet to several thousand feet.

■ **Saba.** Marine life is abundant, walls drop more than 1,000 feet just ½ mile from shore, and the visibility is extraordinary, making Saba one of the world's premier dive destinations.

■ **St. Eustatius.** Top sites for wreck diving and for exploring sunken 18th-century buildings, cannons, anchors, and seawalls.

■ **Tobago Cays, St. Vincent and the Grenadines.** A group of five uninhabited islands surrounds a beautiful lagoon studded with sponges, coral formations, and countless colorful fish.

■ **Turks and Caicos Islands.** The world's third-largest coral reef is visible from the air and packed with exotic marine life, dramatic wall drop-offs, colorful fans, and pristine coral formations.

Shopping

Whether it's jewelry in St. Maarten, fragrant spices in Grenada, high-end designer fashions in St. Barths, or island crafts almost anywhere, you're likely to come home with a bag full of treasures.

■ **Grenada.** Visit a historic spice plantation, tour a nutmeg-processing plant, and/or shop at Market Square in St. George's to replenish your spice rack with nutmeg, cinnamon sticks, cocoa, cloves, and more.

■ **Puerto Rico.** From the boutiques of Old San Juan and ateliers of young designers elsewhere in metro San Juan to galleries scattered all over the island, there's plenty to see and buy. You may also consider picking up some hand-rolled cigars in Old San Juan, handmade *mundilllo* lace from Moca, Carnival masks from Loíza and Ponce, or *santos* (small carved figures of saints or religious scenes) created in the southwestern village of San Germán.

■ **St. Barthélemy.** Without a doubt, the shopping here for luxury goods and fashion is the best in the Caribbean. The variety and quality are astounding. The prices here—all duty-free—are high but still less than what you'd pay in, say, Paris or St-Tropez.

■ **St. Maarten/St. Martin.** Hundreds of duty-free shops in Philipsburg make the Dutch side of the island the best in the Caribbean for bargain hunters, especially for high-quality jewelry and perfumes. Marigot, on the French side, has its fair share of boutiques with both locally made and French imported goods.

■ **St. Thomas, U.S. Virgin Islands.** The winding streets and alleys in Charlotte Amalie, the Caribbean's biggest cruise port, are lined with duty-free shops that sell everything from rum to designer fashions and gems.

Staying Active

■ **Bird-Watching, Trinidad and Tobago.** So the watching part isn't so active, but hiking through the rain forests and savannas on these sister islands will give you the opportunity to see more bird species than any other place in the Caribbean.

■ **Climbing La Soufriére Volcano, St. Vincent.** Called "The Queen of Climbs," St. Vincent's active volcano (last eruption, 1979) is approachable from either the windward or leeward side of the island. This is not a casual excursion; trekking to the peak (4,000 feet) and back will take all day.

■ **Horseback Riding at Chukka Cove, Jamaica.** Headquartered at the Ocho Rios polo fields, Chukka Caribbean Adventures is now Jamaica's top soft-adventure outfitter, having added canopy tours, river rafting, and more to its excellent horseback-riding program.

■ **Scaling Gros Piton, St. Lucia.** Reaching the top of the broader of the two Pitons, the iconic symbols of St. Lucia and a World Heritage Site, takes about two hours. It's a steep but safe trail, and the view from the summit (about 2,500 feet) is spectacular.

■ **Trekking to Boiling Lake, Dominica.** This bubbly, brackish cauldron is actually a flooded fumarole. A trek here is an unforgettable trip into an otherworldly place—but make sure you have a guide and allow plenty of time for the return trip. Night falls in the Caribbean by 6 pm.

■ **Windsurfing at Lac Bay, Bonaire.** With near-constant breezes and calm waters, Bonaire is one of the best places in the world for windsurfing. Lac Bay—a broad, protected cove on the east coast with relatively shallow water—is ideal.

IF YOU WANT

To Take It Easy on Your Wallet

The Caribbean isn't all about five-star resorts. You may want to save some of your vacation cash to eat in an elegant restaurant or shop for the perfect gift. Saving money in the Caribbean doesn't have to mean sacrificing comfort. Sometimes it just means choosing a less-expensive island, such as the Dominican Republic, Saba, or Dominica. Most islands, though, have some inns and resorts where you can pay much less and still have a great time.

■ **Bayaleau Point Cottages, Carriacou.** Owner Dave Goldhill built four colorful gingerbread guest cottages on this peaceful Windward hillside overlooking the Grenadines, as well as a 28-foot boat to take his guests on snorkeling trips.

■ **Bay Gardens Beach Resort, St. Lucia.** One of three Bay Gardens properties in Rodney Bay known for their friendly hospitality, this family-friendly hotel has a prime location on beautiful Reduit Beach.

■ **Beachcombers Hotel, St. Vincent.** Cheryl Hornsey's family home, once a tiny B&B, has morphed into a popular, 31-room beachfront hotel overlooking the sea at Villa Beach.

■ **Bellafonte Chateau de la Mer, Bonaire.** An oceanfront room at this chic, palazzo-style hotel will remind you why you came to the Caribbean.

■ **Carringtons Inn, St. Croix, U.S. Virgin Islands.** A stay at this spacious B&B harks back to a gentler time, when people spent the winter, rather than a week, in the Caribbean.

■ **Coco Palm, St. Lucia.** Rodney Bay is a beehive of activity, and this stylish boutique hotel is definitely the honey—beautiful rooms, amenities you'd expect at pricier resorts, a great restaurant, and nightly entertainment.

■ **Sugar Reef, Bequia.** Rustic splendor describes this adults-only, "eco-chic" boutique inn on Crescent Beach in Industry. Great restaurant, too.

■ **The Horny Toad, St. Maarten/St. Martin.** A marvelous little oceanfront guesthouse with a funky name offers the island's best value for those who want to keep costs down.

■ **La Sagesse, Grenada.** At this secluded country inn on La Sagesse Bay, 10 miles from town, guest rooms are 30 feet from the beach and a hop, skip, and jump from surrounding nature trails.

■ **Rockhouse Hotel, Jamaica.** Perched on the cliffs of Negril's West End, unique bungalows blend comfort and rustic style. Regular rooms keep costs down, but if you want to spend a bit more, the dramatic villas are worth every penny.

■ **Siboney Beach Club, Antigua.** This beachfront oasis is nestled in a tranquil corner of Dickenson Bay. Service is warm and friendly, and the surroundings are natural and secluded.

To Have the Perfect Honeymoon

Swaying palms, moonlight strolls on the beach, candlelit dinners: no wonder the Caribbean is a favorite honeymoon destination. You can certainly find whatever you are looking for in a honeymoon—seclusion, privacy, or more active fun—and it will usually be on a perfect beach. You can be pampered or just left alone, stay up late or get up with the sun, get out and stay active or simply rest and relax. Our favorites run the gamut; from easy access to remote, we have the perfect spot.

■ **Horned Dorset Primavera, Puerto Rico.** Whisk your beloved to this sunset-kissed

hotel and just disappear. You may never leave your elegant oceanfront room. When you do, the restaurant is one of the best in Puerto Rico.

■ **Palm Island, Grenadines.** Enjoy five dazzling beaches for water sports, nature trails for quiet walks, a pool with waterfall, sophisticated dining, impeccable service, exquisite accommodations—and privacy.

■ **Sandals Grande St. Lucian Spa & Beach Resort, St. Lucia.** Big, busy, and all-inclusive, this resort is a favorite of young honeymooners—particularly for its complimentary weddings.

■ **The Somerset, Turks and Caicos Islands.** Provo's most beautiful resort is more focused on your comfort than on attracting a celebrity clientele, so regular folks will still feel at home.

■ **Spice Island Beach Resort, Grenada.** Grenada's finest resort offers beautifully designed and decorated rooms, excellent dining, and impeccable service, placing it among the Caribbean's finest boutique resorts.

■ **Sugar Beach, A Viceroy Resort, St. Lucia.** You'll be hard put to find a more romantic spot. The resort's magnificent villas are tucked into dense tropical foliage that spills down a steep valley right between the Pitons. It's the most dramatic 192 acres in St. Lucia.

To Eat Well

Chefs in many of the Caribbean's finest restaurants—and there are many that are world-class—make local produce and spices the focal point of their dishes. Here are some of our favorite Caribbean restaurants:

Banana Tree Grille, St. Thomas, U.S. Virgin Islands. The eagle's-eye view of the Charlotte Amalie harbor from this breeze-cooled restaurant is as fantastic as the food.

■ **Blue by Eric Ripert, Cayman Islands.** Grand Cayman's best restaurant is brought to you by one of New York's finest chefs.

■ **Boston Jerk Centre, Port Antonio, Jamaica.** To enjoy the best Jamaican jerk in the place where it was invented, the place to go is this collection of open-air jerk pits on Boston Beach.

■ **The Cliff, Barbados.** Chef Paul Owens's mastery is the foundation of one of the finest dining experiences in the Caribbean, with prices to match.

■ **Coral Grill, Nevis, St. Kitts and Nevis.** The steak house at the Four Seasons Nevis is stunning and wildly successful—and a memorable place to eat.

■ **Coyaba Restaurant, Providenciales, Turks and Caicos Islands.** This posh eatery is one of the island's most romantic and inviting places to dine.

■ **Iguane Café, Guadeloupe.** Unquestionably original cuisine with influences from around the world is daring and dramatic, not to mention delicious.

■ **Le Tastevin, St. Martin.** In the heart of Grand Case, Le Tastevin is on everyone's list of favorites.

■ **Le Ti St. Barth Caribbean Tavern, St. Barthélemy.** Chef-owner Carole Gruson captures the funky, sexy spirit of the island in her wildly popular hilltop hot spot.

■ **Marmalade, Puerto Rico.** Old San Juan's hippest and finest restaurant, Marmalade's inventive menu is California-French.

■ **Rainforest Hideaway, St. Lucia.** A little ferry whisks you across pretty Marigot Bay to dine alfresco, on the waterfront, under a starry sky.

WHEN TO GO

The Caribbean high season is traditionally winter—from December 15 to April 14. During this season you're guaranteed the most entertainment at resorts and the most people with whom to enjoy it. It's also the most fashionable, the most expensive, and the most popular time to visit—and most hotels are heavily booked. You must make reservations at least two or three months in advance for the very best places (sometimes a year in advance for the most exclusive spots). Hotel prices can drop 20% to 50% after April 15; airfares and cruise prices also fall. Saving money isn't the only reason to visit the Caribbean during the off-season. Many islands now schedule their carnivals, music festivals, and other events during the off-season. Late August, September, October, and early November are the least crowded, while temperatures vary only a few degrees from season to season.

Climate

The Caribbean climate is fairly constant. The average year-round temperatures for the region are 78°F to 88°F. The temperature extremes are 65°F low, 95°F high; but, as everyone knows, it's the humidity, not the heat, that makes you suffer, especially when the two go hand in hand. The off-season months, particularly August through November, are the most humid. As part of the late-fall rainy season, hurricanes occasionally sweep through the Caribbean. Check the news daily and keep abreast of brewing tropical storms. The southernmost Caribbean islands are generally spared the threat of hurricanes, although they may experience storm-surge flooding. The rainy season consists mostly of brief showers interspersed with sunshine. You can watch the clouds thicken, feel the rain, then have brilliant sunshine dry you off, all while remaining on your lounge chair. A spell of overcast days or heavy rainfall is unusual.

HURRICANE SEASON

The Atlantic hurricane season lasts from June 1 through November 30, but it's fairly rare to see a large storm in either June or November. Most major hurricanes occur between August and October, with the peak season in September.

Avoiding Storms: Keep in mind that hurricanes are rarer the farther south you go. The ABC Islands (Aruba, Bonaire, and Curaçao), Trinidad and Tobago, and Grenada, are the least likely to get a direct hit from a hurricane, although it's never a certainty that you'll avoid storms by going south. Grenada, for example, was severely affected by Hurricane Ivan in 2004—the island's first direct hit in nearly 50 years. Similarly, Barbados is less likely to be affected by hurricanes, because it lies out in the Atlantic, all by itself, 100 miles east of its nearest neighbor, St. Lucia. Barbados can sometimes experience heavy rain and flooding in September and October; accordingly, many hotels close during that period.

Airlines: Airports are usually closed during hurricanes and flights are canceled, which results in a disruption of the steady flow of tourists in and out of affected islands. If you are scheduled to fly into an area where a hurricane is expected, check with your airline regularly and often. If flights are disrupted, airlines will usually allow you to rebook for a later date. You will not get a refund if you have booked a nonrefundable ticket nor, in most cases, will you be allowed to change your ticket to a different destination; rather, you will be expected to reschedule your trip for a later date.

Hotels and Resorts: If a hurricane warning is issued and flights to your destination are disrupted, virtually every Caribbean resort will waive cancellation and change penalties and allow you to rebook your trip for a later date. Some will allow you to cancel if a hurricane threatens to strike, even if flights aren't canceled. Some will give you a refund if you have prepaid for your stay, while others will expect you to rebook your trip for a later date. Some large resort companies—including Sandals and SuperClubs—have "hurricane guarantees," but they apply only when flights have been canceled or when a hurricane is sure to strike.

Travel Insurance: If you plan to travel to the Caribbean during the hurricane season, it is wise to buy travel insurance that allows you to cancel for any reason. This kind of coverage can be expensive (up to 10% of the value of the trip); but if you have to prepay far in advance for an expensive vacation package, the peace of mind may be worth it. Just be sure to read the fine print; some policies don't kick in unless flights are canceled and the hurricane strikes, something you may not be assured of until the day you plan to travel. To get a complete cancellation policy, you must usually buy your insurance within a week of booking your trip. If you wait until after the hurricane warning is issued to purchase insurance, it will be too late.

Track Those Hurricanes: To keep a close eye on the Caribbean during hurricane season, several websites track hurricanes as they progress: 🌐 *www.weather.com*, 🌐 *hurricanetrack.com*, 🌐 *www.nhc.noaa.gov*, and 🌐 *www.accuweather.com*.

WEDDINGS

The Caribbean has become one of the most popular venues for destination weddings. Many resorts offer attractive packages for couples to create their ultimate island-paradise wedding. As an added bonus, many islands and resorts either provide or will recommend an experienced wedding planner. Some will even lend you a dress! So whether you picture an intimate beachfront ceremony for two or a full-blown affair, you can confidently leave the details to a professional and simply concentrate on exchanging your vows.

Finding a Wedding Planner

Hiring a wedding planner to handle all the logistics—from the preliminary paperwork right down to the final toast—allows you to relax and truly enjoy your big day. The best planners will advise you about legalities (residency requirements, fees, etc.), help organize the marriage license, and hire the officiant, plus arrange for venues, flowers, music, refreshments, or anything else your heart desires. Planners typically have established relationships with local vendors and can bundle packages with them—which can save you money. Many resorts have on-site wedding coordinators. But there are also many independents available, including those who specialize in certain types of ceremonies—by locale, size, religious affiliation, and so on. Island tourism boards often maintain an online list of names, and a simple "Caribbean weddings" Google search will yield scores more. What's important is that you feel *comfortable* with your coordinator. Ask for references—and call them. Share your budget. Ask how long they've been in business, how much they charge, how often you'll meet with them, and how they select vendors. Above all, request a detailed, written list of what they'll provide. If your vision of the dream wedding doesn't match that vendor's services, try someone else. If you can afford it, you might even schedule a preliminary trip to meet the planner in person.

Making It Legal

Your goal is to tie the knot, not get tied up in red tape. So it is important to be mindful of the legalities involved. Specifics vary widely, depending on the type of ceremony you want (civil ones are invariably less complicated than religious services) and the island where you choose to wed. In the Dominican Republic, for example, key documents must be submitted in Spanish: unless you enlist a translator, your wedding will be conducted in Spanish, too. On the French-speaking islands (Guadeloupe, Martinique, St. Barths, and St. Martin) language issues are further compounded by stringent residency requirements, which can make marrying there untenable.

There are, however, **standard rules** that apply throughout the islands:

- Most places will expect you to produce valid passports and a certified copy of your birth certificates as proof of identification when applying for a marriage license (the exceptions being Puerto Rico and the U.S. Virgin Islands, where a government-issued picture ID will suffice for American citizens).
- If either partner is under 18 years old, parental consent is required unless otherwise stated *in the chart that follows*. If either partner is divorced, the original divorce or annulment decree is required.
- If either is a widow or widower, an original death certificate is required. (In certain locales, an *apostille* stamp confirming the authenticity of such documents must be attached.)

ISLAND	COSTS	WAITING PERIOD	GOOD TO KNOW
Anguilla ivisitanguilla.com/weddings	License and stamp fee, $284; ($40 if one partner resides in Anguilla for at least 15 days)	At least 2 business days to process license	Two witnesses are required in addition to the marriage officer.
Antigua www.antigua-barbuda.org/agmarr01.htm	License, $150; marriage officer's fee, $50; registration, $40	None	Couples landing in Antigua after 3 pm won't have enough time to get a license from the Ministry of Justice and wed the same day. Also, planning a church ceremony requires extra time.
Aruba www.aruba.com/aruba-vacations/weddings-honeymoons	License, $80 during office hours; $200 on Sat. or after hours	None, provided all documents are submitted at least one month in advance	Civil ceremonies may take place in Oranjestad's historic City Hall, on the beach, or at your venue of choice.
Barbados www.visitbarbados.org/weddings	License, $50 plus $7 stamp fee. Separate magistrate and court fees for civil ceremonies at the court, $63; at alternative venues, $175	None	All fees must be paid in cash. Couples may wait at the Ministry of Home Affairs in Wildey, St. Michael, for the license to be processed, but both parties must be present to take the oath.
Bonaire www.tourismbonaire.com/en/vacation-planner/specialized-vacations/wedding-honeymoons	License, $150	One partner must be resident on-island for at least 7 days before applying for a license, which takes 4 business days to process.	Two months in advance, couples must apply for a temporary residency permit for one partner. Official witnesses must do the same, but most wedding coordinators can arrange for local witnesses.
British Virgin Islands www.bvitourism.com/rules-requirements	Special license, $220; ordinary license, $120; marriage celebrated in the Registrar's Office, $120; marriage celebrated by a civil marriage officer, $220	One business day for a special license; 15 days or more for an ordinary license	You'll need 2 witnesses present when you sign your license application. They can be different from those in the ceremony. Don't be late for a wedding somewhere other than the Registrar's Office; there's a $75 late fee if you keep the Registrar General waiting!

ISLAND	COSTS	WAITING PERIOD	GOOD TO KNOW
Cayman Islands www.cayman-vows.ky	License, $250	None	When applying for a license, you must present a letter from the marriage officer who will officiate (obtain a list from the deputy chief secretary's office).
Curaçao www.curacao.com/en/directory/plan/getting-married/license-requirements	License, $308	Couple must be on the island 3 days before applying for license.	Curaçao is a stickler for paperwork, so hiring a wedding pro helps. Documents, which must be original, recent, and apostille-stamped, are to be with your planner at least 2 months in advance.
Dominica www.dominica.dm	License, $110; statutory declaration fee $185; stamp fee, $3; weekend/holiday supplement, $185	One partner must be on-island 2 days before the wedding.	Couples must complete and sign both the marriage application form and a statutory declaration of marital status in the presence of a local magistrate or notary public.
Dominican Republic www.godominicanrepublic.com	Combined fees, $450 for civil ceremonies in the registry office; $600 elsewhere	Notice of the intended marriage must be published before ceremony.	Both partners must present their sworn declarations of single status (translated into Spanish) at a Dominican Consulate. All paperwork should be submitted at least 6 months in advance.
Grenada www.grenadagrenadines.com/explore/wedding	License and stamps, $12	Couple must be on-island 3 days before applying for a license; 2 business days needed for processing.	Processing your license may take a bit longer if you've been married before. Parental consent required for either partner under age 21.
Jamaica www.visitjamaica.com/weddings-and-honeymoons	License, $50	24 hours	Accommodating laws and upscale couples-only resorts make Jamaica a top pick. Some all-inclusives offer complimentary weddings, complete with officiant and license.
Nevis www.nevisisland.com/weddings.htm	Application, $20; license, $80	None	You'll pay $20 to complete your application before a justice of the peace. If you've never been married, also be prepared to pop $20 for a notarized affidavit of single status.
Puerto Rico www.seepuertorico.com/en/experiences/lifestyle/weddings	License and stamp fees, $150	None	You must submit to the Demographic Registry Office a medical certification indicating that you met all the required tests for marriage back in your place of residence. The certification is valid for 10 days. Parental consent is required if either partner is under age 21.

ISLAND	COSTS	WAITING PERIOD	GOOD TO KNOW
St. Eustatius www.statiatourism.com/weddings.htm	License, marriage officer, and other fees, $300; after hours and on weekends, $328	14 days after document registration	Written request to marry required at least 3 weeks prior to the wedding ceremony. Marriages performed inside the courthouse require 2 witnesses; outside the courthouse, 6 witnesses.
St. Kitts stkittstourism.kn/love-st-kitts-weddings-honeymoons.php	License, $75	None	Civil weddings are performed only from 8 to 6. Church weddings may be held 6 to 6.
St. Lucia stlucianow.com/live/weddings	License, $125 for standard; $200 for special (same day); registrar and certificate fees, $60	None with a special license, 3 days with a standard license	St. Lucia, a leader in the destination wedding biz, has a streamlined process that makes marrying easy. Most lodgings have enticing packages and on-site planners.
St. Maarten www.st-maarten.com or www.stmartinisland.com	Combined cost of the license, civil ceremony, marriage book, certificate, and stamps ranges from $183 to $400.	Couples must submit a notice of intent to marry 14 days before the wedding.	It is slightly easier to marry in St. Maarten than in St. Martin. French St. Martin requires translated documents and requirements vary depending on the citizenships of the couple.
St. Vincent and the Grenadines www.discoversvg.com/index.php/en/whattodo/weddingshoneymoons	License, $185 plus approximately $8 for stamp fees	24 hours on-island	Blessed with postcard-pretty beaches, gorgeous gardens, private island resorts, and historic buildings, this archipelago of 32 islands boasts a range of likely venues.
Trinidad and Tobago www.gotrinidadandtobago.com/tobago/weddings.php	Special license, $55	3 days	To obtain a special license, both partners must be nonresidents. All fees must be paid in cash.
Turks and Caicos www.turksandcaicostourism.com/ license-requirements.html	License, $250; special license for cruise-ship passengers, $50 additional	Couples must be on the island 48 hours before submitting application. Cruise-ship passengers with a special license may be married the same day of arrival.	The marriage is registered here. To have it registered in your home country, you must make special arrangements. Parental consent needed if under 21.
U.S. Virgin Islands www.visitusvi.com/plan_events/weddings_honeymoons/stcroix	Marriage application and license fee $200; officiating fee, $200 if married by a judge.	8 days from receipt of application	Licenses must be picked up in person on weekdays, but you can shorten the wait by applying from home.

KIDS AND FAMILIES

Choosing a Place to Stay

Many resorts, except those that are exclusively for adults or couples, offer kids-free promotions, special restaurant menus, and programs for tots on up to teens.

Let them entertain you. If you prefer to relax while the kids are entertained, choose a major resort with all-inclusive meal plan and kids' program. For example, **Beaches Resorts** in Providenciales, Turks and Caicos, and in Ocho Rios and Negril, Jamaica, which offer kids' programs to match all ages from toddler to teen, outdoor playgrounds, gaming centers, field trips for ages 12 and up such as snorkeling and scuba diving, and *Sesame Street* character appearances. **Hyatt Regency Aruba Beach Resort & Casino** features Camp Hyatt, where kids ages 3 to 12 can participate in a variety of activities and adventures. **Club Med Punta Cana,** in the Dominican Republic, offers a baby gym, Crayola arts-and-crafts programs, hip-hop dance instruction, Petite Chef (ages 3 to 7) cooking classes, and The Ramp, an interactive club for 14- to 17-year-olds. The children's program at **Four Seasons Resort Nevis** offers cake baking, croquet, sea turtle watch, beach walks, and a supervised lizard hunt—along with story time, a playground with a pirate ship and tree house, a children's menu, even kid-size bathrobes in the bedroom.

DIY. Condos and villas provide an at-home atmosphere with full kitchens and separate bedrooms, and many include home entertainment systems.

At **Maho Bay Camps** on St. John in the U.S. Virgin Islands you stay in either a screen cottage or a canvas tent. There are cooking facilities in each unit and a cafeteria-style restaurant. Lifeguards are on duty, there are water-sports rentals, and there's plenty of white-sand beach for sand castles and swimming.

Top Attractions

Museums. Many kids have read about Christopher Columbus in history books; but at **El Faro a Colón** (Columbus Lighthouse), just outside Santa Domingo in the Dominican Republic, they can visit his tomb. The huge pyramid-shape complex has six museums that trace the history of the area from the ancient Indian days to the construction of the modern, multimillion-dollar structure. Kids will marvel over ancient maps, jewel-studded royal crowns, and replicas of dugout canoes. For a real treat, visit at night when the 688-foot-tall lighthouse projects a cross-shape beam of light some 44 miles into the sky. The **Barbados Museum** has a Children's Gallery with interactive exhibits on the island's Amerindian past, British colonialism, the development of the sugar industry, and island social life. The most fun: a "dress-up corner," where kids can don the garb of a Zouave soldier, an African prince, or a mulatto girl with full headgear.

Fortresses. A long grassy walk leads up to the 500-year-old **Castillo del Morro** (El Morro) Castle, an imposing structure in Puerto Rico's Old San Juan that looks like the Wicked Witch's scary fortress. Venture inside the thick walls and cruise the ramparts, tunnels, and dungeons. Wax mannequins model historic battle uniforms, and a video shows the history of building and defending this stronghold. Equally imposing is St. Kitts's **Brimstone Hill**, known as the Gibraltar of the West Indies. Ft. George, which sits atop the hill, is built of 7-foot-thick walls of black volcanic stone. Kids can woefully imagine being imprisoned here during a

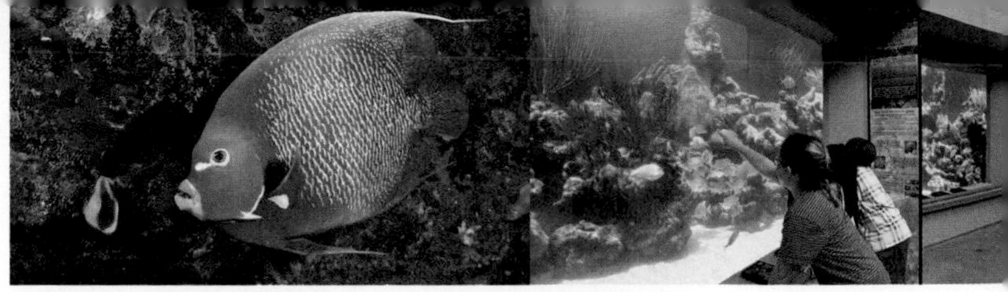

"time-out." From high atop the fort's cannon ways, kids can search the horizon for the islands of Nevis, Montserrat, Saba, St. Maarten/St. Martin, and St. Barths. It's also fun to try spotting the scampering green monkeys that play along the nature trails that wind around this 38-acre site.

Caves. An electric tram takes you into and through Barbados's **Harrison's Cave**, where specially lighted caverns illuminate the stalactites, stalagmites, and underground waterfalls so the caves don't seem too spooky. The **Hato Caves** in Curaçao date back to the Ice Age; but today, instead of cavemen, the inhabitants are long-nose fruit bats. Puerto Rico's **Rio Camuy Cave Park** tour begins with a short video and then a trolley ride right to the mouth of the cave. Though 200 feet high, the cave is only half a mile long. The walking tour is level and flat, allowing kids' eyes to roam all over without fear of stumbling.

Zoos. Roam freely with the animals at the **Barbados Wildlife Reserve.** This outdoor zoo keeps kids engaged as they walk along shady pathways and spot exotic animals, reptiles, and birds in their natural habitat. There are land turtles, fine-feathered peacocks, green monkeys, parrots, and even a caiman. After exploring outside, kids can check out the walk-in aviary and the many natural-history exhibits. On Grand Cayman, **Cayman Turtle Farm** is a marine theme park with tanks and ponds full of turtles; kids can touch and pick up the creatures, swim and snorkel among them, and learn about conservation, too. The **Emperor Valley Zoo**, named for Trinidad's native blue butterflies, is one of the best in the Caribbean. The island's president and prime minister have houses on this site, but most intriguing for kids is the 8-acre zoo that is filled with birds and other wildlife from the region, ranging from blue-and-gold macaws and small red brocket deer to giant anacondas. Not exactly zoos, but in Aruba, St. Martin, and St. Thomas, **Butterfly Farm**—a beautiful garden filled with fluttering butterflies from around the world—is a fascinating experience for the whole family. View, firsthand, the life cycle of these amazing insects from egg to caterpillar to butterfly.

Aquariums. **Curaçao Sea Aquarium** boasts more than 400 species of sea life. Some of the most fascinating creatures are the sharks—hand-fed daily, to the delight of kids of all ages. **Coral World Ocean Park,** on St. Thomas, is an interactive aquarium and water-sports center that has a 2-acre dolphin habitat, as well as several outdoor pools where you can pet baby sharks, feed stingrays, touch starfish, and view endangered sea turtles. You can also Snuba, swim with a sea lion, and view an 80,000-gallon coral reef exhibit. Get up close and personal with dolphins at either of two **Dolphin Discovery** locations, one on Tortola in the British Virgin Islands and another in Grand Cayman; kids can watch these amazing animals swim and do tricks—and even touch them. **Ocean World Adventure Park**, in Puerto Plata, Dominican Republic, has interactive marine and wildlife programs, including dolphin and sea lion shows, a double-dolphin swim, a tropical reef aquarium, stingrays, shark tanks, and more.

Fun parks. Kids will love **Kool Runnings Adventure Park** in Negril, Jamaica, which has 10 waterslides and a ¼-mile lazy-river float ride, as well as a go-kart track and kayaking. There are also outdoor laser combat games, bungee jumping, a "kool kanoe" adventure, a wave pool, and paintball.

FLAVORS OF THE CARIBBEAN

by Charyn Pfeuffer

As an entry point to the New World, the Caribbean has a rich culinary tradition reflecting the diversity of its immigrants. This melting pot of Spanish, African, French, English, and Dutch influences has created dishes packed with fresh ingredients and bold, spicy flavors and seasonings.

Local produce is varied and includes lima beans, black-eyed peas, corn, yams, sweet potatoes, cassava, and taro. Rice and beans are ever-present staples, commonly seasoned with ingredients like curry, cilantro, soy sauce, and ginger. The spice-forward "jerk" style of marinated and rubbed meat, fish, and fowl is prevalent. Jamaica, Haiti, Guadeloupe, and other French Caribbean islands savor goat meat in dishes like goat water, a tomato-based stew, which is the official national dish of Montserrat and a speciality on St. Kitts and Nevis. Fresh-caught seafood from local waters also figures prominently into the cuisine.

Modern menus don't stray too far from tradition, opting instead for clever twists rather than reinvention, like flavoring black beans with tequila and olive oil, or serving rice spiked with coconut and ginger. No matter where your culinary curiosities take you in the islands, plan on a well-seasoned eating adventure.

(opposite) Dasheene Restaurant at Ladera Resort, St. Lucia, (top) Jerk pork, a signature Jamaican dish, (bottom) scotch bonnet peppers.

THE ISLANDS' GLOBAL FLAVORS

Island cuisine developed through waves of wars, immigration, and natives' innovations from the 15th century through the mid-19th century. Early Amerindian native peoples, the Arawaks and the Caribs, are said to have introduced the concept of spicing food with chili peppers, a preparation that remains a hallmark of Caribbean cuisine. Pepper pot stew was a staple for the Caribs, who would make the dish with *cassareep*, a savory sauce made from cassava. The stew featured wild meats (possum, wild pig, or armadillo), squash, beans, and peanuts, which were added to the cassareep and simmered in a clay pot. The dish was traditionally served to guests as a gesture of hospitality. Today's recipes substitute meats like pig trotters, cow heel, or oxtail.

Caribbean-style curried goat

After Columbus' discovery of the New World, European traders and settlers brought new fruits, vegetables, and meats. Their arrival coincided with that of African slaves en route to the Americas. Every explorer, settler, trader, and slave brought something to expand the palette of flavors. Although Caribbean cooking varies from island to island, trademark techniques and spices unite the cuisine.

SPANISH INFLUENCES

The Caribbean islands were discovered by Christopher Columbus in 1492, while he was working for the Spanish crown. When he returned to colonize the islands a year later, he brought ships laden with coconut, chickpeas, cilantro, eggplant, onions, and garlic. The Bahamas, Hispaniola, and Cuba were among Columbus' first findings, and as a result, Cuba and nearby Puerto Rico have distinctly Spanish-accented cuisine, including *paella* (a seafood- or meat-studded rice dish), *arroz con pollo* or *pilau* (chicken cooked with yellow rice), and white-bean Spanish stews.

Arroz con Pollo

FRENCH TECHNIQUE

As tobacco and sugar crops flourished and the Caribbean became a center of European trade and colonization, the French settled Martinique and Guadeloupe in 1635 and later expanded to St. Barthélemy, St. Martin, Grenada, St. Lucia, and western Hispaniola. French culinary technique meets the natural resources of the islands to create dishes like whelk (sea snail) grilled in garlic butter, fish cooked *en papillote* (baked in parchment paper), and *crabs farcis*, land crab meat that is steamed, mixed with butter, breadcrumbs, ham, chilis, and garlic, then stuffed back into the crab shells and grilled.

DUTCH INGENUITY

Beginning in the 1620s, traders from the Dutch East India Company brought Southeast Asian ingredients like soy sauce to the islands of Curaçao and St. Maarten. Dutch influence is also evident throughout Aruba and Bonaire (all have been under Dutch rule since the early 19th century), where dishes like *keshi yeni*, or "stuffed cheese," evolved from stuffing discarded rinds of Edam cheese with minced meat, olives, and capers. Another Dutch-influenced dish is *boka dushi* (Indonesian-style chicken satay), which translates to "sweet mouth" in the islands' Papiamento dialect.

Paella

Boka dushi

Jerk meat

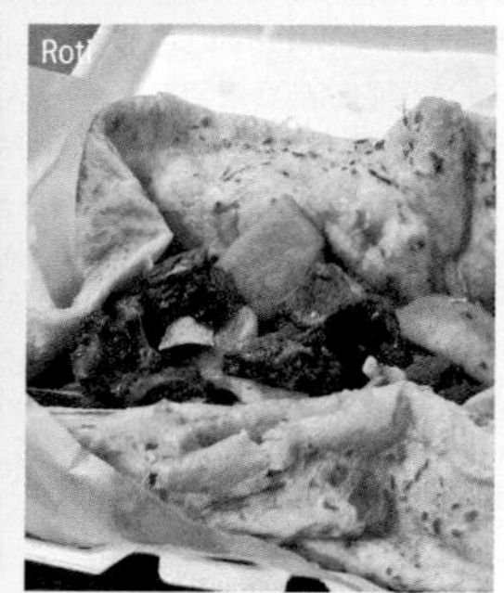
Roti

Whelk

ENGLISH IMPORTS
British settlers brought pickles, preserves, and chutneys to the Caribbean, and current-day chefs take advantage of the islands' indigenous fruits to produce these items. British influence also is evidenced by the Indian and Chinese contributions to Caribbean cuisine. British (and Dutch) colonists brought over indentured laborers from India and China to work on sugar plantations, resulting in the introduction of popular dishes like curry goat and *roti,* an Indian flatbread stuffed with vegetables or chicken curry.

AFRICAN INGREDIENTS
The African slave trade that began in the early 1600s brought foods from West Africa, including yams, okra, plantains, breadfruit, pigeon peas, and oxtail to the islands. Slave cooks often had to make do with plantation leftovers and scraps, yielding dishes like cow heel soup and pig-foot souse (a cool soup with pickled cucumber and meat), both of which are still popular today. One of the most significant African contributions to the Caribbean table is "jerking," the process of dry-rubbing meat with allspice, Scotch bonnet peppers, and other spices. Although the cooking technique originated with native Amerindians, it was the Jamaican Maroons, a population of runaway African slaves living in the island's mountains during the years of slavery, who developed and perfected it, resulting in the style of jerk meat familiar in restaurants today.

CARIBBEAN'S NATURAL BOUNTY

Soursop

Despite its spicy reputation, Caribbean food isn't always fiery; the focus is on enhancing and intensifying flavors with herbs and spices. Food plays a major role in island culture, family life, and traditions, and no holiday would be complete without traditional dishes prepared from the island's natural products.

TANTALIZING TROPICAL FRUIT

Breadfruit, a versatile starch with potato-like flavor, can be served solo—baked or grilled—or added to soups and stews.

With its rich, refreshing milk, **coconut** frequently appears in soups, stews, sauces, and drinks to help temper hot, spicy flavors with its rich, refreshing milk.

The bright orange tropical fruit **guava** tastes somewhat like a tomato when it's not fully ripe, but is pleasantly sweet when mature. It is used in compotes, pastes, and jellies.

The pungent smell of **jackfruit** may be off-putting for some, but its sweet fleshy meat is popular in milkshakes.

Papaya is sweet and floral when ripe; unripe, it can be shredded and mixed with spices and citrus for a refreshing salad. It is often used in fruit salsas that are served with seafood.

Tamarind

The brightly flavored **passion fruit** is commonly puréed and used in sauces, drinks, and desserts.

The dark-green skinned, creamy fleshed **soursop** is known for its sweet-tart juice used in drinks, sorbets, and ice creams.

The fibrous stalks of **sugarcane**, a giant grass native to India, are rich with sugar, which can be consumed in several forms, including freshly extracted juice and processed sugar.

Tamarind is the fruit of a large tree. The sticky pulp of its pod is used in chutneys and curries to impart a slightly sweet, refreshingly sour flavor.

FARM-FRESH VEGETABLES

Cassava (also called yucca) can be used much like a potato in purées, dumplings, soups, and stews. The flour of its roots is made into tapioca.

Chayote is a versatile member of the squash and melon family, often used raw in salads or stuffed with cheese and tomatoes and baked.

Dasheen (taro) is much like a potato, but creamier. It can be sliced thinly and fried like a potato chip.

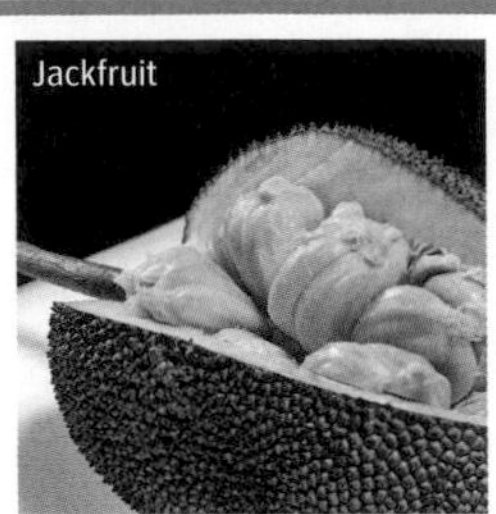
Jackfruit

Fitweed (or French thistle) is a tropical herb related to coriander (cilantro), and is popular in Caribbean seasonings.

Pod-like **okra** is commonly used in *callaloo*, the national dish of Trinidad and Tobago. The creamy, spicy stew is made of leafy greens, okra, and crabmeat.

Green plantain is a cooking staple across the Caribbean, often sliced, pounded, dipped in a seasoned batter, and deep-fried.

The leafy green **sorrel** is typically pureed in soups

Chayote

Curry powder

and stews, or used in salads.

SWEET AND SAVORY SPICES

Native **allspice**, also called Jamaican pepper, is commonly added to Caribbean curries. It is the dried unripe berry of the evergreen pimento tree. Native Jamaicans once used it to preserve meats. It is an essential ingredient in jerk preparations.

Curries are intensely seasoned gravy-based dishes originating from India—they are most prevalent on the islands of Jamaica, Trinidad, and Tobago.

Native Carib people pioneered the use of **chili peppers** in the islands for hot, spicy flavoring, using primarily habaneros and Scotch bonnet peppers.

Ginger can be used raw or dried and ground into a powder that adds flavor and heat to ginger beer, sweet potatoes, or coconut milk-based sauces.

The mix of spices in **jerk** seasoning vary, but typically include scallions, thyme, allspice, onions, and garlic.

The tiny island of Grenada is the second largest exporter of **nutmeg** in the world. It often accents sweet dishes, and is frequently added to vegetables in Dutch preparations.

Allspice

ISLAND FISH AND SEAFOOD

Bonito is a medium-sized fish in the mackerel family. Atlantic bonito is moderately fatty, with a firm texture and darker color. It is served blackened, grilled (sometimes with fruit-based salsas), or Jamaican jerk style.

On many islands, including the Bahamas, **conch**—a large shellfish—are made into conch fritters, a mix of conch meat, corn meal, and spices that are deep fried and make an excellent snack.

Cascadura fish is a small fish found in the freshwater swamps of Trinidad and Tobago. It is typically served in curry with a side of rice or dumplings.

Salt fish

Conch salad

Flying fish are named for the wing-like fins that enable them to glide or "fly" over water. Firm in texture, it is typically served steamed or fried. Flying fish is a staple in Bajan cuisine and is found in abundance off the coast of Barbados.

Kingfish is another word for wahoo, a delicate white fish commonly fished off the coasts of St. Croix and Barbados. It's served *escabeche* style, marinated in a vinegar mixture, then fried or poached.

Land crab is found throughout the islands. Delicate in flavor, its common preparations include curried crab stewed in coconut milk, stuffed crab, and crab soup.

Mahi mahi is fished off the coast of St. Croix. With a subtle, sweet flavor, its firm, dark flesh lends itself to soy sauce glazes and Asian preparations.

Salt fish is a dish made from dried cod, often seasoned with tomatoes, onions, and thyme. Stir-fried ackee (a tropical fruit with nutty-flavored flesh) and saltfish is Jamaica's national dish.

THE RISE OF RUM

The Caribbean is the world center for rum production, with many islands making their own brands and styles of rum. Dozens of rum companies operate throughout the islands. Although larger, mainstream brands like Bacardi, Captain Morgan, and Mount Gay are available on every island, you may have to look harder for the smaller brands. The best-quality rums are dark, aged rums meant for sipping, priced from $30 to $700 a bottle. For excellent sipping rum at the lower end of the spectrum, try Appleton or Rhum Barbancourt. For mixed drinks, use clear or golden-colored rums that are less expensive and pair well with fruit juices or cola. Spiced and flavored rums are also popular in cocktails. Here are some of the best rums you'll encounter at an island bar:

Appleton Estate (Jamaica) The Estate VX is an amber-colored rum with subtle brown sugar aromas and a smooth, toasted honey finish. Excellent mixer for classic cocktails.

Bacardi (Bermuda, PR) Superior is a clear, mild rum with subtle hints of vanilla and fresh fruits. It is smooth and light on the palate. Best in mixed drinks.

Captain Morgan (PR) Its Black Label Jamaica Rum is dark, rich, and smooth, with strong notes of vanilla. Sip it iced, or with a splash of water.

Clarke's Court (Grenada) The Original White is clear with a touch of sweetness and a hint of heat, best used as a mixer.

Mount Gay Rum

Ron Barceló

Cruzan (VI) Less strong and sweet than most rums, the White Rum is smooth, and best suited for mixing.

Havana Club (Cuba) The Añejo 3 Años is deceiving—light in color and body and delicate in flavor. It is a nice rum to sip neat.

Mount Gay Rum (Barbados) Eclipse, the brand's flagship rum, has a golden color with a butterscotch caramel nose and sweet taste on the palate with mouth-warming flavor.

Pusser's (BVI) Self-described as "the single malt of rum," the aged 15-year variety boasts notes of cinnamon, woody spice, and citrus. A good sipping rum.

Rhum Barbancourt (Haiti) Aged 15-years, this premium dark rum is distilled twice in copper pot stills and often called the "Cognac of Rum." Sip it neat.

Ron Barceló (DR) The Añejo is dark copper in color, with a rich flavor, while the aged Imperial boasts notes of toffee on the nose, and a buttery smooth finish.

Shillingford Estates (Dominica) Its most popular product, Macoucherie Spiced is a blend of rum, the bark of the Bois Bande tree, and spices.

(left) Pusser's Rum, (right) Havana Club

ISLANDS' BEST BREWS

Beer in the Caribbean was largely homemade for centuries, a tradition inherited from British colonial rulers. The first commercial brewery in the islands was founded in Trinidad and Tobago in 1947.

In the islands, do what the locals do: drink local beer. Whatever brand is brewed on-island is the one you'll find at every restaurant and bar. And no matter where you go in the Caribbean, there's a local island brew worth trying. Another plus: local brands are almost always cheaper than imports like Corona or Heineken. Most island beers are pale lagers, though you'll find a smattering of Dutch-style pilsners and English-style pale ales. The beers listed below are our top picks for beachside sipping:

Kalik

Banks Beer (Banks Breweries, Barbados) A straw-colored lager that is light tasting with a touch of maltiness on the nose and tongue.

Blackbeard Ale (Virgin Islands Brewing Co., Virgin Islands) This English pale ale-style beer is bright amber in color with a creamy white head. Well-crafted beer with a nice hoppy bite at the finish.

Balashi Beer (Brouwerij Nacional Balashi N.V., Aruba) Refreshingly light, this Dutch pilsner boasts mild flavor, slight sweetness, and subtle hop bitterness.

Legends Premium Lager (Banks Breweries, Barbados) One of the Caribbean's best brews, this golden yellow lager offers crisp hops and a clean finish. Distinctive toasty, malt character.

Carib Lager Beer (Carib Brewery, Trinidad and Tobago) This great beach refresher is pale yellow color with a foamy head. Fruity and sweet malty corn aromas, it is sometimes referred to as the "Corona of the Caribbean."

Kalik Gold (Commonwealth Brewery LTD., New Providence, Bahamas) Clear straw color with gentle hoppy, herbal notes, this is an easy drinking, warm weather lager.

Medalla Light (Puerto Rico) This bright gold lager is substantial for a light beer. It's a local favorite.

Red Stripe (Jamaica) The Jamaican lager pours golden yellow in color with lots of carbonation. Light bodied, crisp, and smooth.

Banks Beer

Carib Lager Beer

Piton (St. Lucia) Light and sparkly with subtle sweetness, this pale yellow lager is pleasant enough, but barely flavored.

Presidente (Domincan Republic) Slight citrus aroma, light body, and fizziness, plus a clean finish make for easy drinking. Perfect pairing for barbecued meats.

Wadadli (Antigua Brewery Ltd., Antigua and Barbuda) A crisp, light-bodied American-style lager. Toasty malt on the nose.

(left) Red Stripe, (right) Presidente

DID YOU KNOW?

In the varied habitats of Virgin Islands National Park, approximately 144 species of birds can be seen throughout the year.

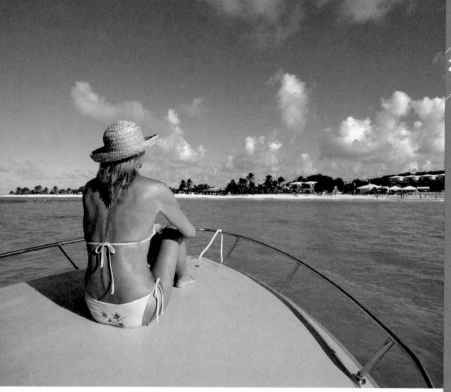

ANGUILLA

WELCOME TO ANGUILLA

TRANQUIL AND UPSCALE

This dry limestone isle is the most northerly of the Leeward Islands, lying between the Caribbean Sea and the Atlantic. The low-lying island is only 16 miles (26 km) long and 3 miles (5 km) wide, and its highest spot is 213 feet above sea level. Since there are neither streams nor rivers—only saline ponds used for salt production—water comes from desalinization plants and cisterns that collect rainwater.

In tiny Anguilla, where fishermen have been heading out to sea for centuries in handmade boats, the beaches are some of the Caribbean's best and least crowded. Heavy development has not spoiled the island's atmospheric corners, and independent restaurants still thrive, as do a few quaint inns, which share the island with some genuinely over-the-top palaces.

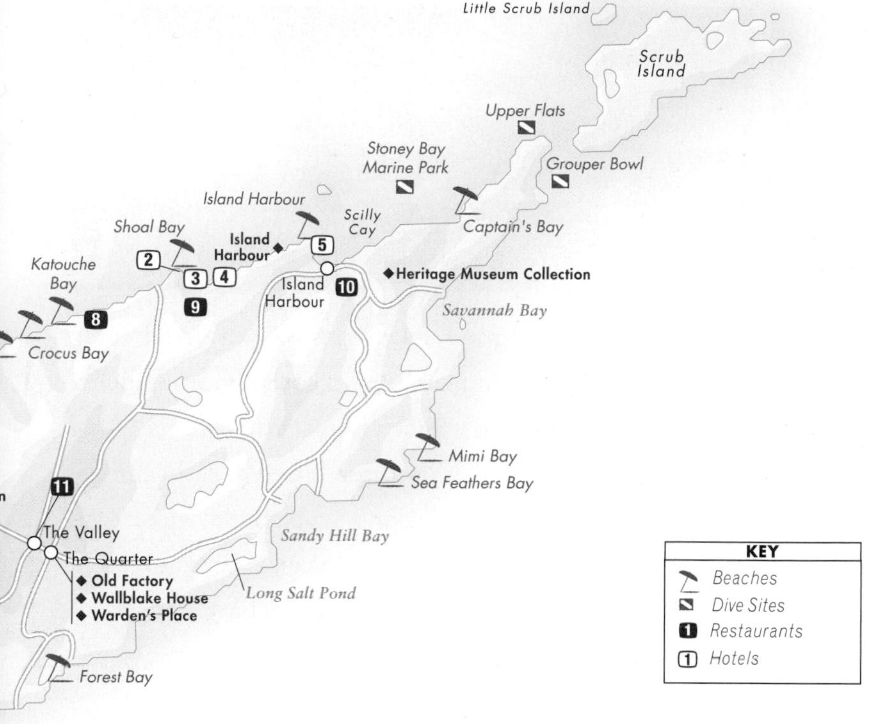

Restaurants ▼

- Blanchard's ... **18**
- Blanchard's Beach Shack ... **21**
- da'Vida ... **8**
- Dolce Vita ... **3**
- English Rose ... **11**
- Firefly ... **14**
- Geraud's Patisserie ... **6**
- Hibernia ... **10**
- Jacala Beach Restaurant ... **19**
- Mango's ... **15**
- Ocean Echo ... **20**
- Picante ... **17**
- Roy's Bayside Grille ... **4**
- Sand Bar ... **5**
- Smokey's ... **13**
- Straw Hat ... **1**
- Tasty's ... **7**
- Tokyo Bay ... **12**
- Trattoria Tramonto ... **16**
- Veya ... **2**
- Zara's ... **9**

Hotels & Rentals ▼

- Allamanda ... **3**
- Altamer ... **11**
- Anacaona ... **17**
- Anguilla Great House ... **6**
- Arawak Beach Inn ... **5**
- Cap Juluca ... **9**
- Caribella ... **13**
- Carimar Beach Club ... **14**
- CuisinArt Golf Resort & Spa ... **7**
- Frangipani Beach Club ... **1**
- Mead's Bay Beach Villas ... **16**
- Paradise Cove ... **8**
- Serenity Cottages ... **4**
- Sheriva Villa Hotel ... **10**
- Shoal Bay Villas ... **2**
- Turtle's Nest Beach Resort ... **15**
- Viceroy Anguilla ... **12**

TOP REASONS TO VISIT ANGUILLA

1 Beautiful Beaches: Miles of brilliant beach ensure you have a high-quality spot in which to lounge.

2 Great Restaurants: The dining scene offers both fine dining and delicious casual food.

3 Fun, Low-Key Nightlife: A funky late-night local music scene features reggae and string bands.

4 Upscale Accommodations: Excellent luxury resorts coddle you in comfort.

5 Hidden Bargains: You'll find a few relative bargains if you look hard enough.

Updated by Elise Meyer

Peace, pampering, great food, and a wonderful local music scene are among the star attractions on Anguilla (pronounced ang-*gwill*-a). Beach lovers may become giddy when they first spot the island from the air; its blindingly white sand and lustrous blue-and-aquamarine waters are intoxicating. And if you like sophisticated cuisine served in casually elegant open-air settings, this may be your culinary Shangri-la.

The island's name, a reflection of its shape, is most likely a derivative of *anguille,* which is French for "eel." (French explorer Pierre Laudonnaire is credited with having given the island this name when he sailed past it in 1556.) In 1631 the Dutch built a fort here, but so far no one has been able to locate its site. English settlers from St. Kitts colonized the island in 1650, with plans to cultivate tobacco and, later, cotton and then sugar. But the thin soil and scarce water doomed these enterprises. Except for a brief period of independence, when it broke from its association with St. Kitts and Nevis in the 1960s, Anguilla has remained a British colony ever since.

From the early 1800s various island federations were formed and disbanded, with Anguilla all the while simmering over its subordinate status and forced union with St. Kitts. Anguillians twice petitioned for direct rule from Britain and twice were ignored. In 1967, when St. Kitts, Nevis, and Anguilla became an associated state, the mouse roared; citizens kicked out St. Kitts's policemen, held a self-rule referendum, and for two years conducted their own affairs. To what *Time* magazine called "a cascade of laughter around the world," a British "peacekeeping force" of 100 paratroopers from the Elite Red Devil unit parachuted onto the island, squelching Anguilla's designs for autonomy but helping a team of royal engineers stationed there to improve the port and build roads and schools. Today Anguilla elects a House of Assembly and its own leader to handle internal affairs, and a British governor is responsible for public service, the police, the judiciary, and external affairs.

LOGISTICS

Getting to Anguilla: There are no nonstop flights to Anguilla (AXA) from the United States, so you will almost always have to fly through San Juan, St. Maarten, or some other Caribbean island. You'll ordinarily be making the hop on a smaller plane. You can also take a variety of boats and ferries from the airport in St. Maarten, or Marigot on the French side.

Hassle Factor: Medium.

On the Ground: Some hotels provide transfers from the airport or ferry pier, especially the more expensive ones. For everyone else, if you don't rent a car, the taxi ride from the airport to your hotel will be less than $25 even to the West End (and considerably less if you're going to Sandy Ground).

Getting Around the Island: It's possible to base yourself in Sandy Ground, Rendezvous Bay, Meads Bay, or Shoal Bay without a car, but restaurants and resorts are quite spread out, so for the sake of convenience you may wish to rent a car for a few days or for your entire stay. If you do, prepare to drive on the left. Taxis are fairly expensive on Anguilla, another reason to consider renting a car.

The territory of Anguilla includes a few islets (or cays, pronounced "keys"), such as Scrub Island, Dog Island, Prickly Pear Cay, Sandy Island, and Sombrero Island. The 16,000 or so residents are predominantly of African descent, but there are also many of Irish background, whose ancestors came over from St. Kitts in the 1600s. Historically, because the limestone land was unfit for agriculture, attempts at enslavement never lasted long; consequently, Anguilla doesn't bear the scars of slavery found on so many other Caribbean islands. Instead, Anguillians became experts at making a living from the sea and are known for their boatbuilding and fishing skills. Tourism is the stable economy's growth industry, but the government carefully regulates expansion to protect the island's natural resources and beauty. New hotels are small, select, casino-free, and generally expensive; Anguilla emphasizes its high-quality service, serene surroundings, and friendly people.

PLANNING

WHEN TO GO

As in much of the Caribbean, high season runs from mid-December through mid-April, and some resorts in Anguilla still close from September through mid-December, though many remain open year-round. A few resorts require long minimum stays until after New Year's Day.

GETTING HERE AND AROUND

AIR TRAVEL

There are no nonstop flights to Anguilla from the United States. Trans-Anguilla Airways offers daily flights from Antigua, St. Thomas, and St. Kitts. Air Sunshine flies several times a day from St. Maarten (SXM), and Anguilla Air Services also flies from St. Maarten. LIAT comes in

DID YOU KNOW?

Anguilla, about 150 miles east of Puerto Rico, has 33 beaches, each more beautiful than the last.

from Antigua. Cape Air has two daily flights from San Juan (three on peak travel days).

Local Airline Contacts Anguilla Air Services ☎ *264/498–5922* 🌐 *www.anguillaairservices.com.* **Cape Air** ☎ *264/498–2279, 508/771–6944* 🌐 *www.capeair.com.* **LIAT** ☎ *264/497–5000* 🌐 *www.liatairline.com.* **TransAnguilla Airways** ☎ *264/497–8690* 🌐 *www.transanguilla.com.*

Airport Clayton J. Lloyd International Airport ☎ *264/497–3510* 🌐 *www.anguillaairport.com.* **Air Sunshine** ☎ *800/327–8900* 🌐 *www.airsunshine.com.*

BOAT AND FERRY TRAVEL

Ferries run frequently between Anguilla and St. Martin. Boats leave from Blowing Point on Anguilla approximately every half hour from 7:30 am to 6:15 pm and from Marigot, St. Martin, every 45 minutes from 8 am to 7 pm. You pay a $20 departure tax before boarding ($5 for day-trippers coming through the Blowing Point terminal—but be sure to make this clear at the window where you pay), in addition to the $15 one-way fare. Children under 12 years of age are free. On very windy days the 20-minute trip can be bouncy. The drive between the Marigot ferry terminal and the airport is vastly improved thanks to a new bridge across Simpson Bay. Transfers by speedboat to Anguilla are available from a new terminal right at the airport, at a cost of about $75 per person (arranged directly with a company, or through your Anguilla hotel). Private ferry companies listed below run six or more round-trips a day, coinciding with major flights, between Blowing Point and the airport in St. Maarten. On the St. Maarten side they will bring you right to the terminal in a van, or you can just walk across the parking lot. These trips are $35 one-way or $60 round-trip (cash only), and usually include departure taxes. There are also private charters available.

A late-night sea shuttle service leaves St. Maarten for Anguilla at 10:30 pm. This sea shuttle meets the daily American flight from Miami, which arrives at 9:55 pm. It then takes you directly to Blowing Point in Anguilla. The trip costs $95 per person. Another sea shuttle, which departs at 7 pm, also goes from St. Maarten to Anguilla. This connects with JetBlue and InselAir flights originating in San Juan; the cost is $65 per person.

Contacts Funtime Ferry ☎ *866/334–0047* 🌐 *www.funtime-charters.com.* **GB Express** ☎ *264/584–6205* 🌐 *www.anguillaferryandcharter.com.* **Link Ferries** ☎ *264/497–2231* 🌐 *www.link.ai.* **Shauna Ferries** ☎ *264/476–6275.*

CAR TRAVEL

Although most of the rental cars on-island have the driver's side on the left as in North America, Anguillian roads are like those in the United Kingdom—driving is on the left side of the road. It's easy to get the hang of, but the roads can be rough, so be cautious, and observe the 30 mph (48 kph) speed limit. Roundabouts are probably the biggest driving obstacle for most. As you approach, give way to the vehicle on your right; once you're in the rotary, you have the right of way.

Car Rentals: A temporary Anguilla driver's license is required to rent a car—you can get into real trouble if you're caught driving without one. You get it for $20 (good for three months) at any of the car-rental agencies at the time you pick up your car; you'll also need your valid driver's license from home. Rental rates start at about $45 to $55 per day, plus insurance.

Car-Rental Contacts **Andy's Car Rental** ✉ *Blowing Point* ☎ *264/235–7010* 🌐 *www.andyrentals.com.* **Apex/Avis** ✉ *Airport Rd.* ☎ *264/497–2642* 🌐 *www.avisanguilla.com.* **Bryans Car Rental** ✉ *Blowing Point* ☎ *264/497–6407* 🌐 *www.bryanscarrentals.com.* **Triple K Car Rental/Hertz** ✉ *Airport Rd.* ☎ *264/497–2934* 🌐 *www.hertz.com/rentacar/location/axao60.*

TAXI TRAVEL

Taxis are fairly expensive, so if you plan to explore many beaches and restaurants, it may be more cost-effective to rent a car. Taxi rates are regulated by the government, and there are fixed fares from point to point, listed in brochures the drivers should have handy and published in local guides. It's $26 from the airport or $22 from Blowing Point Ferry to West End hotels. Posted rates are for one or two people; each additional passenger adds $5, and there is a $1 charge for each piece of luggage beyond the allotted two. You can also hire a taxi for $28 an hour. Surcharges of $4–$10 apply to trips after 6 pm. You'll always find taxis at the Blowing Point Ferry landing and the airport, but you'll need to call for hotel and restaurant pickups and arrange ahead with the driver who took you if you need a late-night return from a nightclub or bar.

Taxi Contacts **Blowing Point Ferry Taxi Stand** ☎ *264/497–6089* 🌐 *www.caribya.com/blowing.point/taxis.* **Maurice & Sons Exquisite Taxi Services** ☎ *264/235–2676* 🌐 *www.msexquisiteshuttle.com.*

ESSENTIALS

Banks and Exchange Services Legal tender is the Eastern Caribbean (EC) dollar, but U.S. dollars are widely accepted. ATMs dispense both U.S. and EC dollars. All prices quoted in this chapter are in U.S. dollars.

Electricity 110 volts, just as in the United States; no adapter required for American electronics.

Passport Requirements All visitors must carry a valid passport and have a return or ongoing ticket.

Phones Most hotels will arrange with a local provider for a cell phone to use during your stay (or you can rent one). A prepaid, local cell gives you the best rates. Some U.S. GSM phones will work in Anguilla; some will not. To call Anguilla from the United States, dial 1 plus the area code 264, then the local seven-digit number. To call the United States and Canada, dial 1, the area code, and the seven-digit number.

Safety Anguilla is a quiet, relatively safe island, but crime has been on the rise, and there's no sense in tempting fate by leaving your valuables unattended in your hotel room, on the beach, or in your car. Avoid remote beaches, and lock your car, hotel room, and villa. Most hotel rooms are equipped with a safe for stashing your valuables.

Taxes The departure tax is $20 for adults and kids 12 and older, payable in cash, at the airport and at the Blowing Point Ferry terminal. If you are staying in Anguilla but day-tripping to St. Martin, be sure to mention it, and the rate will be only $5. A 10% accommodations tax is added to hotel bills along with a $1-per-night marketing tax, plus whatever service charge the hotel adds (can be up to 10%).

Tipping Despite any service charge, it's usually expected that you will tip more—$5 per day for housekeeping, $20 for a helpful concierge, and $10 per day to beach attendants. Many restaurants include a service charge of 10% to 15% on the bill; if there's no surcharge, tip about 15%. Taxi drivers should receive 10% of the fare.

ACCOMMODATIONS

Anguilla is known for its luxurious resorts and villas, but there are also some places that mere mortals can afford (and a few that are downright bargains).

Hotel reviews have been shortened. For full information, visit Fodors.com.

WHAT IT COSTS IN U.S. DOLLARS

	$	$$	$$$	$$$$
Restaurants	under $12	$12–$20	$21–$30	over $30
Hotels	under $275	$275–$375	$376–$475	over $475

Restaurant prices are the average cost of a main course at dinner or, if dinner is not served, at lunch. Hotel prices are the lowest cost of a standard double room in high season.

VISITOR INFORMATION

Contacts Anguilla Tourist Board ✉ *Coronation Ave., The Valley* ☎ *264/497-2759, 800/553-4939 from U.S.* 🌐 *www.ivisitanguilla.com.*

WEDDINGS

Weddings are common, but there's a huge $241.80 (EC$650) fee for a license. Visit Anguilla's government website for more information:

Contacts Government of Anguilla Judicial Department ☎ *264/497-2377* 🌐 *www.gov.ai/marriage.php.*

EXPLORING

Exploring on Anguilla is mostly about checking out the spectacular beaches and resorts. The island has only a few roads. Locals are happy to provide directions, but using the readily available tourist map is the best idea. Visit the Anguilla Tourist Board, centrally located on Coronation Avenue in The Valley.

You can take a free, self-guided tour of the Anguilla Heritage Trail, comprising 10 important historical sights that can be explored independently in any order. Wallblake House, in The Valley, is the main information center for the trail, or you can just look for the large boulders with descriptive plaques.

TOP ATTRACTIONS

Heritage Museum Collection. A remarkable opportunity to learn about Anguilla, this tiny museum (complete with gift shop) is painstakingly curated by Colville Petty. Old photographs and local records and artifacts trace the island's history over four millennia, from the days of the Arawaks. High points include historical documents of the Anguilla Revolution and photo albums chronicling island life, from devastating hurricanes to a visit from Queen Elizabeth in 1964. You can see examples of ancient pottery shards and stone tools along with fascinating photographs of the island in the early 20th century—many depicting the heaping and exporting of salt and the christening of schooners—and a complete set of beautiful postage stamps issued by Anguilla since 1967. ✉ *East End at Pond Ground* ☎ *264/235–7440* 🎫 *$5* ⏲ *Mon.–Sat. 10–5.*

Sandy Ground. Almost everyone who comes to Anguilla stops by this central beach, home to several popular open-air bars and restaurants, as well as boat-rental operations. This is where you catch the ferry for tiny Sandy Island, 2 miles (3 km) offshore.

Bethel Methodist Church. Not far from Sandy Ground, this charming little church, which celebrated its 135th anniversary in 2013, is an excellent example of skillful island stonework. It also has some colorful stained-glass windows. ✉ *South Hill.*

WORTH NOTING

Island Harbour. Anguillians have been fishing for centuries in the brightly painted, simple, handcrafted fishing boats that line the shore of the harbor. It's hard to believe, but skillful pilots take these little boats out to sea as far as 50 or 60 miles (80 or 100 km). Late afternoon is the best time to see the day's catch. ■ **TIP→ Hail the free boat to Gorgeous Scilly Cay, a classic little restaurant offering sublime lobster and Eudoxie Wallace's knockout rum punches on Wednesday and Sunday.** ✉ *Island Harbor Rd.* 🌐 *www.scillycayanguilla.com.*

Old Factory. For many years the cotton grown on Anguilla and exported to England was processed in this beautiful historic building. Later it was a general store, and now it's the home of Sotheby's Real Estate. There is a small art gallery on the lower level in an old stone cellar. ✉ *Government Corner, The Valley* ☎ *264/497–2759* 🌐 *www.oldfactory-anguilla.ai* 🎫 *Free* ⏲ *Weekdays 10–noon and 1–4.*

Old Prison. The ruins of this historic jail on Anguilla's highest point (213 feet) have outstanding views. ✉ *Valley Rd. at Crocus Hill.*

Wallblake House. Anguilla's only surviving plantation house, Wallblake House was built in 1787 by Will Blake (Wallblake is probably a corruption of his name). The place is associated with many a tale involving murder, high living, and the French invasion in 1796. On the grounds are an ancient vaulted stone cistern and an outbuilding called the Bakery, which wasn't used for making bread at all but for baking turkeys and hams. You can only visit the thoroughly and thoughtfully restored house and grounds on a guided tour, usually offered three days a week. It's also the information center for the Anguilla Heritage Trail. ✉ *Wallblake Rd., The Valley* ☎ *264/497–6613* 🌐 *www.wallblake.ai* 🎫 *Free* ⏲ *Tours Mon., Wed., and Fri. at 10 and 2.*

Warden's Place. This former sugar-plantation great house, on the Anguilla Heritage Trail, was built in the 1790s and is a fine example of island architecture. For many years it served as the residence of the island's chief administrator, who also doubled as the only medical practitioner. Across the street is the oldest dwelling on the island, originally built as slave housing. ✉ *Coronation Ave., The Old Valley* ☎ *264/497–2930.*

BEACHES

Anguilla's beaches are among the best and most beautiful in the Caribbean. You can find long, deserted stretches suitable for sunset walks and beaches lined with lively bars and restaurants—all surrounded by crystal clear warm waters in several shades of turquoise. The sea is calmest at 2½-mile-long Rendezvous Bay, where gentle breezes tempt sailors. But Shoal Bay (East) is the quintessential Caribbean beach. The white sand is so soft and abundant that it pools around your ankles. Cove Bay and Maundays Bay must also rank among the island's best beaches. Maundays is the location of the island's famous resort, Cap Juluca. Meads Bay's arc is dominated by the tony Viceroy Resort, and smaller Cove Bay is just a walk away. In contrast to the French islands, Anguilla doesn't permit topless sunbathing.

NORTHEAST COAST

Captain's Bay. On the north coast just before the eastern tip of the island, this quarter-mile stretch of perfect white sand is bounded by a rocky shoreline where Atlantic waves crash. If you make the tough, four-wheel-drive-only trip along the dirt road that leads to the northeastern end of the island toward Junk's Hole, you'll be rewarded with peaceful isolation. The surf here slaps the sands with a vengeance, and the undertow is strong—so wading is the safest water sport. **Amenities:** none. **Best for:** solitude.

Island Harbour. For centuries Anguillians have ventured from these sands in colorful handmade fishing boats. Mostly calm waters are surrounded by a slender beach, not much for swimming or lounging, but there are several restaurants (Hibernia, Arawak Café, and Smitty's). This is also the departure point for a three-minute boat ride to Scilly Cay, where a thatched beach bar serves seafood. Just hail the restaurant's free boat and plan to spend most of the day (the all-inclusive lunch—Wednesday and Sunday only—starts at $40 and is worth the price). **Amenities:** food and drink. **Best for:** partiers.

NORTHWEST COAST

Little Bay. On the north coast, not far from The Valley, this small gray-sand beach is a favored spot for snorkeling and night dives. It's essentially accessible only by water, as it's backed by sheer cliffs lined with agave and creeping vines. The easiest way to get here is a five-minute boat ride from Crocus Bay (about $10 round-trip). The only way to access the beach from the road is to clamber down the cliffs by rope to explore the caves and surrounding reef—for young, agile, and experienced climbers only. Do not leave personal items in cars parked here, because theft can be a problem. **Amenities:** none. **Best for:** snorkeling.

Road Bay (*Sandy Ground*). The big pier here is where the cargo ships dock, but so do some pretty sweet yachts, sailboats, and fishing boats. The brown-sugar sand is home to terrific restaurants that hop from day through dawn, including Veya, Roy's Bayside Grille, Ripples, Barrel Stay, the Pumphouse, and Elvis', the quintessential beach bar. There are all kinds of boat charters available here. The snorkeling isn't very good, but the sunset vistas are glorious, especially with a rum punch in your hand. **Amenities:** food and drink. **Best for:** sunset.

Sandy Island. A popular day trip, tiny Sandy Island shelters a pretty lagoon nestled in coral reefs about 2 miles (3 km) from Road Bay, with a restaurant that serves lunch and great islandy cocktails. Fans of TV's *The Bachelor* may recall the Valentine's Day picnic date here in 2011. From November through August you can take the *Happiness* sea shuttle from Sandy Ground ($10 round-trip). There is mooring for yachts and larger sailboats. Small boats can come right in the channel. ■ **TIP→ The reef is great for snorkeling.** **Amenities:** food and drink. **Best for:** partiers; snorkeling; swimming. *www.mysandyisland.com* *Nov.–Aug., daily 10–4; Sept.–Oct. by reservation.*

FAMILY Fodor's Choice ★ **Shoal Bay.** Anchored by sea grape and coconut trees, the 2-mile (3-km) powdered-sugar strand at Shoal Bay (not to be confused with Shoal Bay West, at the other end of the island) is one of the world's prettiest beaches. You can park free at any of the restaurants, including Elodia's, Uncle Ernie's, or Gwen's Reggae Grill, most of which either rent or provide chairs and umbrellas for patrons for about $20 a day per person. There is plenty of room to stretch out in relative privacy, or you can barhop or take a ride on Junior's Glass Bottom Boat. The relatively broad beach has shallow water that is usually gentle, making this a great family beach; a coral reef not far from the shore is a wonderful snorkeling spot. Sunsets over the water are spectacular. **Amenities:** food and drink. **Best for:** sunset; swimming; walking.

SOUTHEAST COAST

Sandy Hill. You can park anywhere along the dirt road to Sea Feathers Bay to visit this popular fishing center. What's good for the fishermen is also good for snorkelers. But the beach here is not much of a lounging spot. The sand is too narrow and rocky for that. However, it's a great place to buy lobsters and fish fresh out of the water in the afternoon. **Amenities:** food and drink. **Best for:** walking.

SOUTHWEST COAST

Fodor's Choice ★ **Cove Bay.** Follow the signs to Smokey's at the end of Cove Road, and you will find water that is brilliantly blue and sand that's as soft as sifted flour. It's just as spectacular as its neighbors, Rendezvous Bay and Maundays Bay. You can walk here from Cap Juluca for a change of pace, or you can arrange a horseback ride along the beach. Weekend barbecues with terrific local bands at Smokey's are an Anguillian must. **Amenities:** food and drink. **Best for:** partiers; swimming; walking.

Fodor's Choice ★ **Maundays Bay.** The dazzling, mile-long platinum-white beach is especially great for swimming and long beach walks. It's no wonder that Cap Juluca, one of Anguilla's premier resorts, chose this as its location. Public parking is straight ahead at the end of the road near Cap Juluca's Pimms restaurant. You can have lunch or dinner here (be prepared for the cost) or, depending on the season, book a massage in one of the beachside tents. **Amenities:** food and drink; parking (no fee); toilets. **Best for:** partiers; swimming; walking.

FAMILY **Rendezvous Bay.** Follow the signs to Anguilla Great House for public parking at this broad swath of pearl-white sand that is some 1½ miles (2½ km) long. The beach is lapped by calm, bluer-than-blue water and a postcard-worthy view of St. Martin. The expansive crescent is home to three resorts; stop in for a drink or a meal at one, or rent a chair and umbrella at one of the kiosks. Don't miss the daylong party at the tree-house Dune Preserve, where Bankie Banx, Anguilla's most famous musician, presides. **Amenities:** food and drink; parking (no fee); toilets. **Best for:** partiers; swimming; walking.

Shoal Bay West. This glittering bay bordered by mangroves and sea grapes is a lovely place to spend the day. The mile-long beach is home to Covecastles villas. The tranquillity is sublime, with coral reefs for snorkeling not too far from shore. Punctuate your day with a meal at beachside Trattoria Tramonto and you can use their chairs and umbrellas. Reach the beach by taking the main road to the West End and bearing left at the fork, then continuing to the end. Note that similarly named Shoal Bay is a separate beach on a different part of the island. **Amenities:** food and drink; parking (no fee); toilets. **Best for:** solitude; swimming; walking.

WHERE TO EAT

Despite its small size, Anguilla has around 70 restaurants: stylish temples of haute cuisine; classic, barefoot beachfront grills; roadside barbecue stands; food carts; and casual cafés. Many have breeze-swept terraces for dining under the stars. Call ahead—in winter to make a reservation and in late summer and fall to confirm whether the place is open. Anguillian restaurant meals are leisurely events, and service often has a relaxed pace, so settle in and enjoy. Most restaurant owners are actively and conspicuously present, especially at dinner.

What to Wear: During the day, casual clothes are widely accepted: shorts will be fine, but don't wear bathing suits and cover-ups unless you're at a beach bar. In the evening, shorts are okay at the extremely casual eateries. Elsewhere, women wear sundresses or nice casual slacks; men will be fine in short-sleeve shirts and casual pants. Some hotel restaurants are slightly more formal, but that just means long pants for men.

$$$$ ECLECTIC Fodor's Choice ★ **Blanchards.** This delightful restaurant is one of the best in the Caribbean. Proprietors Bob and Melinda Blanchard moved to Anguilla from Vermont in 1994 to fulfill their culinary dreams. A festive atmosphere pervades the handsome, airy white room, accented with teal-blue,

floor-to-ceiling shutters to let in the breezes and colorful artwork by the Blanchards' son Jesse. Creative cuisine, an upscale atmosphere, attentive service, and an excellent wine cellar (including aged spirits) please the star-studded crowd. Ever changing but always good, the nuanced contemporary menu includes house classics like corn chowder, lobster and shrimp cakes, and a Caribbean sampler, and vegetarians have ample choices. You'll remember desserts like key lime "pie-in-a-glass" or the justly famous "cracked coconut" long after your suntan has faded. There is a also a three-course fixed-price menu ($48). *Average main: $49 Meads Bay 264/497–6100 www.blanchardsrestaurant.com Reservations essential Closed Sun. except late Dec., Mon. May–mid-Dec., and Sept.–Oct. No lunch.*

$$ AMERICAN FAMILY **Blanchards Beach Shack.** This spinoff on the sands of Meads Bay Beach is the perfect antidote to high restaurant prices. Right next to Blanchards, this chartreuse-and-turquoise cottage serves yummy lunches and dinners of lobster rolls, all-natural burgers, tacos, and terrific salads and sandwiches, and there are lots of choices for children and vegetarians. Frozen drinks like mango coladas and icy mojitos please grown-ups, while kids dig into fresh-made frozen yogurt concoctions. Organic produce and happy smiles are always on offer. You can dine at picnic tables or rent a beach chair. **TIP→ Diners are welcome to hang around on the beach.** *Average main: $12 Meads Bay 264/498–6100 www.blanchardsrestaurant.com Closed Sun. and Sept.–mid-Oct.*

$$$$ CARIBBEAN FAMILY **da'Vida.** You could spend the whole day dining, drinking, snorkeling, kayaking, shopping, and lounging on the comfortable chairs at this beautifully designed resort, restaurant, and club on exquisite Crocus Bay. Picnic at the Beach Grill (burgers, hot dogs, wraps, salads), or head inside the main building for dumplings, soups, pastas, and pizzas. Lunch starts at 11, tapas and sunset drinks at about 5. At dinner, the stylish wood interior (built by craftsmen from St. Vincent) is accented by candlelight. Tasty dishes include seared snapper with gingered kale, coconut-crusted scallops, and Angus steaks. The owners, siblings David and Vida Lloyd, who also operate Lloyd's Guest House, grew up right here, and they have taken pains to get it all just right. **TIP→ Call for information about live music and nightly shuttle service.** *Average main: $33 Crocus Bay 264/498–5433 www.davidaanguilla.com Closed Mon.*

$$$$ ITALIAN **Dolce Vita Italian Beach Restaurant & Bar.** Serious Italian cuisine and warm and attentive service are provided in a romantic beachside pavilion in Sandy Ground. Freshly made pasta stars in classic lasagna, fettuccini Bolognese, pappardelle with duck sauce, and a meatless eggplant parmigiana. A carnivorous quartet can pre-order suckling pig or sample first-quality chops and steaks. Pizza is offered only at lunch. Italian wine fans will discover new favorites. For dessert, how about Nutella cheesecake? *Average main: $31 Sandy Ground 264/497–8668 www.dolcevitasandyground.com Reservations essential Closed Sun. and Sept.–mid-Oct. No lunch Sat. and May–mid-Dec.*

$$ CARIBBEAN **English Rose Bar and Restaurant.** Lunchtime finds this neighborhood hangout packed with locals: cops flirting with sassy waitresses,

entrepreneurs brokering deals with politicos, schoolgirls in lime-green outfits doing their homework. The decor is nothing to speak of, but this is a great place to eavesdrop or people-watch while enjoying island-tinged specialties like beer-battered shrimp, fish-and-chips, jerk-chicken Caesar salad, snapper creole, and buffalo wings. [$] *Average main: $12* ✉ *Carter Rey Blvd., The Valley* ☎ *264/497–5353* ⏲ *Closed Sun.*

$$$ CARIBBEAN FAMILY ✕ **Firefly Restaurant.** Set on a breezy poolside patio, the restaurant at Anacaona Boutique Hotel turns out huge portions of tasty Caribbean fare by a longtime Anguillian chef. The pumpkin-coconut soup is a winner, as are the local snapper, mahimahi, and crayfish. Breakfast, lunch, and dinner are served, as are tasty drinks, bar snacks like buffalo wings and crispy calamari, and pizza to eat in or take away. Lunch and drinks can be delivered to the beach. For great value and fun, book a table at the Thursday night buffet, with a lively performance by the folkloric theater company Mayoumba. At Friday's Latin night, you can eat great food and practice salsa and merengue with a professional dancer. [$] *Average main: $30* ✉ *Anacaona Boutique Hotel, Meads Bay* ☎ *264/497–6827* 🌐 *www.anacaonahotel.com.*

$$ FRENCH FAMILY ✕ **Geraud's Patisserie.** A stunning array of delicious French pastries and breads—and universal favorites like cookies, brownies, and muffins—are produced by Le Cordon Bleu dynamo Geraud Lavest in this well-located shop. Come in the early morning for cappuccino and croissants or healthy fresh juices and smoothies, and pick up fixings for a wonderful and thrifty lunch, including the blackboard's daily specials. The little shop carries a small selection of condiments, teas, and gourmet goodies. December through May, a terrific Sunday brunch is available. Geraud also does off-site catering, from intimate villa and yacht dinners to weddings; his wedding cakes are an island wonder. [$] *Average main: $13* ✉ *South Hill Plaza, South Hill* ☎ *264/497–5559* 🌐 *www.anguillacakesandcatering.com* ⏲ *Closed Mon. No dinner.*

$$$$ ECLECTIC Fodor's Choice ★ ✕ **Hibernia Restaurant and Art Gallery.** Creative dishes are served in this wood-beam cottage restaurant overlooking the water at Anguilla's eastern end. The pretty garden has been redesigned with stone artifacts from Bali, and the intimate dining room (only nine tables) has been updated, also. Unorthodox yet delectable culinary pairings—inspired by chef-owners Raoul Rodriguez and Mary Pat's annual travels to Asia—bring new tastes and energy to the tables. Local organic products are used whenever possible. Long-line fish is served with a gratin of local pumpkin, shiitake mushrooms, and an essence of bitter oranges grown by the front gate. The owners' passion for life is expressed through the vibrant combination of setting, art, food, unique tableware, and thoughtful hospitality. A $12.50 per person shuttle service lets you enjoy the stellar wine collection at dinner. Hours vary seasonally. **■ TIP→ Mary Pat stocks the tiny art gallery here with amazing, and reasonable, finds from her travels.** [$] *Average main: $36* ✉ *Harbor Ridge Dr., Island Harbour* ☎ *264/497–4290* 🌐 *www.hiberniarestaurant.com* ✍ *Reservations essential* ⏲ *Closed mid-July–Nov.*

$$$ FRENCH Fodor's Choice ★ ✕ **Jacala Beach Restaurant.** On beautiful Meads Bay, this restaurant continues to receive raves, with Martha Stewart dubbing it her "new favorite Caribbean restaurant." Chef Alain (named one of the Caribbean's top 25 chefs in 2014) and maître d' Jacques (from the "old"

Mallioúhana) have created a lovely open-air restaurant that turns out carefully prepared and nicely presented French food accompanied by good wines and personal attention. A delicious starter terrine of feta and grilled vegetables is infused with pesto. Hand-chopped steak tartare and olive oil–poached mahimahi with curry-lemongrass sauce are entrée standouts. Lighter lunchtime options include a tart cucumber-yogurt soup garnished with piquant tomato sorbet. After lunch you can digest on the beach in a Fatboy lounger, but save room for the chocolate *pot de crème.* *Average main: $30 ✉ Meads Bay ☎ 264/498–5888 Reservations essential Closed Mon.–Tues. and Aug.–Sept.*

$$$$ SEAFOOD FAMILY **Mango's.** Sparkling-fresh fish specialties have starring roles here. Light and healthy choices include spicy grilled whole snapper and Cruzan rum–barbecued chicken, while the warm apple tart and coconut cheesecake are worth a splurge. Adding to the luxury are an extensive wine list and a Cuban cigar humidor. Lunch features sandwiches and burgers. *Average main: $36 ✉ Barnes Bay ☎ 264/497–6479 www.mangosseasidegrill.com Reservations essential Closed Tues. and Aug.–Sept.*

$$$ CARIBBEAN FAMILY **Ocean Echo.** It's nonstop every day from lunch until late at this relaxed and friendly restaurant, great for salads, burgers, grills, pasta, and fresh fish. Heartier appetites will enjoy the ribs and steaks. A couple of times a week there is live music as well as the possibility of dancing with an excellent islandy cocktail in hand. *Average main: $30 ✉ Meads Bay ☎ 264/498–5454 www.oceanechoanguilla.com.*

$$$ MEXICAN FAMILY **Picante.** This casual, wildly popular bright-red roadside Caribbean *taquería,* opened by a young California couple, serves huge, tasty burritos with a choice of fillings, fresh warm tortilla chips with first-rate guacamole, huge (and fresh) taco salads, seafood enchiladas, and tequila-lime chicken grilled under a brick. Passion-fruit margaritas are a must, and the creamy Mexican chocolate pudding makes a great choice for dessert. Seating is at picnic tables; the friendly proprietors cheerfully supply pillows on request. Reservations are recommended. *Average main: $21 ✉ West End Rd., West End ☎ 264/498–1616 www.picante-restaurant-anguilla.com Closed Tues. No lunch.*

$$$ CARIBBEAN FAMILY **Roy's Bayside Grill.** Come any time of day for good cooking and a friendly vibe. Try chocolate chip pancakes or an Anguillian breakfast of johnnycakes. At lunch enjoy the beachfront and grills, salads, and sandwiches. Some of the island's best grilled lobster is served here, along with tasty burgers, fish-and-chips, and home-style cooking. Every day but Sunday there's a happy hour with bar snacks, and Sunday brings roast beef and Yorkshire pudding. A prix-fixe menu ($35) has lots of choices, and kids and people with food allergies are accommodated. There's free Wi-Fi, too. *Average main: $27 ✉ Road Bay, Sandy Ground ☎ 264/497–2470 www.roysbaysidegrill.com.*

$$ TAPAS **SandBar.** Tasty and sharable small plates, a friendly beach vibe, and gorgeous sunsets are on offer here, as are cool music, gentle prices, a hammock on the beach, and potent tropical cocktails. The menu changes seasonally, but favorites include spicy fries, zucchini carpaccio, Carib beer–battered fish bites with lemon-caper aioli, pulled-pork

sliders, and a refreshing dish of watermelon, feta, and olives. *Average main: $13* *Sandy Ground* *264/498–0171* *Closed Sun. No lunch.*

$$$ CARIBBEAN FAMILY

Smokey's. This quintessential Anguillian beach barbecue, part of the Gumbs family mini-empire of authentic and delicious eateries, is on pretty Cove Bay. Lounges with umbrellas await on the beach. Hot wings, honey-coated smoked ribs, curried goat, smoked chicken salad, and grilled lobsters are paired with local-staple side dishes such as spiced-mayonnaise coleslaw, hand-cut sweet-potato strings, and crunchy onion rings. If your idea of the perfect summer lunch is a roadside lobster roll, try the one here, served on a home-baked roll with a kick of hot sauce. Dinner includes lobster fritters, grilled tuna with lemon-caper butter, and rum chicken. On Saturday afternoon, a popular local band enlivens the laid-back atmosphere and on Sunday this is party central, but there is entertainment every day but Thursday. *Average main: $25* *Cove Rd., Cove Bay* *264/497–6582* *www.smokeysatthecove.com.*

$$$$ ECLECTIC FAMILY Fodor's Choice ★

Straw Hat. Charming owners, a gorgeous oceanfront location, sophisticated and original food, and friendly service are why this stylish restaurant has been in business since the mid-1990s. Whether for breakfast, lunch, or dinner, you will find appealing, tasty, and fresh choices to mix up or share. Try Anguilla's only "real" bagel, tuna flatbread, jerk-braised pork belly, lobster spring rolls, or curried goat. Fish of the day is truly caught that day, and vegetarians and kids find many options, too. A small garden in back is the source of super-fresh greens. Big flat-screens with satellite TV make the bar a fine place to catch the game or make new friends. *Average main: $39* *Frangipani Beach Club, Meads Bay* *264/497–8300* *www.strawhat.com* *Reservations essential* *Closed Sept.–Oct.*

$$$ CARIBBEAN

Tasty's. Once your eyes adjust to the quirky kiwi, lilac, and coral color scheme, you'll find that breakfast, lunch, tapas, or dinner at Tasty's is, well, very tasty. It's open all day, so if you land midafternoon starving, head here—it's near the airport and ferry terminal. Chef-owner Dale Carty trained at Malliouhana, and his careful, confident preparation bears the mark of French culinary training, but the menu is classic Caribbean with a creole edge. It's worth leaving the beach at lunch for the lobster salad. A velvety pumpkin soup garnished with roasted coconut shards is superb, as are the seared jerk tuna and the garlic-infused marinated conch salad. Don't be stuffy—try the goat stew. Yummy desserts end meals on a high note. This is one of few nonsmoking restaurants, so take your Cubans elsewhere. The popular Sunday brunch buffet features island specialties like salt-fish cakes, and there is live music on Saturday night. *Average main: $23* *Main Rd., South Hill Village, South Hill* *264/497–2737* *www.tastysrestaurant.com* *Reservations essential* *Closed Thurs.*

$$$$ SUSHI FAMILY

Tokyo Bay. This chic sushi and teppanyaki restaurant, dramatically lit and perched at the top of CuisinArt's spa building, owes its raves to its Japanese chef. Chances are you will find local chefs and other restaurant people here on their night out. The sake bar features terrific cocktails with names like Eager Ninja and Saketini, and chefs slice up ocean-fresh fish for sushi both traditional and otherwise. Hot pots,

Straw Hat's outdoor patio on Forest Bay

rice dishes, Wagyu beef, and yakitori skewers round out the menu. "Chocolate sushi" is an amusing finale. *Average main: $42* *CuisinArt Golf Resort and Spa, Rendezvous Bay* *264/498–2000* *www.cuisinartresort.com* *Closed Tues. No lunch.*

$$$ ITALIAN FAMILY **Trattoria Tramonto and Oasis Beach Bar.** The island's beloved beachfront Italian restaurant features a dual (or dueling) serenade of Andrea Bocelli on the sound system and gently lapping waves a few feet away. Chef Valter Belli artfully adapts recipes from his home in Emilia-Romagna. Try the delicate lobster ravioli in truffle-cream sauce. For dessert, don't miss the tiramisu. If you wander in after a swim for lunch, when casual dress is OK, you'll still be treated to the same impressive menu. You can also choose from a luscious selection of champagne fruit drinks, a small and fairly priced Italian wine list, and homemade grappa at the beach bar. Come after 5 for sundowners and tasty bar snacks like truffle fries and prosciutto carrot zucchini bundles. Hang out on chairs on the spectacular beach before or after your meal. *Average main: $28* *Shoal Bay West* *264/497–8819* *www.trattoriatramonto.com* *Reservations essential* *Closed Mon. and Aug.–Oct.*

$$$$ ECLECTIC Fodor's Choice ★ **Veya.** On the suavely minimalist four-sided veranda, stylishly appointed tables glow with flickering candlelight from sea urchin–shape porcelain votive holders. Chic patrons mingle and sip mojitos to the purr of soft jazz in a lively lounge. Carrie Bogar's "cuisine of the sun" features ingenious preparations, first-rate provisions, and ample portions that are sharable works of art. Sample Moroccan-spiced shrimp "cigars" with roast tomato–apricot chutney or Vietnamese-spiced calamari. Jerk-spiced tuna is served with a rum-coffee glaze on a juicy slab of grilled pineapple, and crayfish in beurre blanc is divine, as is

warm chocolate cake with chili-roasted banana ice cream and caramelized bananas. Consider splurging on the $85 five-course tasting menu. Live music plays several nights a week. *Average main: $38 Sandy Ground 264/498–8392 www.veya-axa.com Reservations essential Closed Sun., Sat. June–Aug. and late Oct., and Sept.–mid-Oct. No lunch.*

$$$ ECLECTIC FAMILY **Zara's.** Chef Shamash Brooks presides at this under-the-radar but cozy restaurant with beamed ceilings, terra-cotta floors, and colorful artwork. His kitchen turns out tasty fare that combines Caribbean and Italian flavors with panache (Rasta Pasta is a specialty). Standouts include a velvety pumpkin soup with coconut milk, crunchy calamari, lemon pasta scented with garlic, herbed rack of lamb served with a roasted applesauce, and spicy fish fillet steamed in banana leaf. Follow the signs to Allamanda. *Average main: $25 Allamanda Beach Club, Shoal Bay 264/497–3229.*

WHERE TO STAY

Tourism on Anguilla is a fairly recent phenomenon—most development didn't begin until the early 1980s. The lack of native topography and, indeed, vegetation, and the blindingly white expanses of beach have inspired building designs of some interest; architecture buffs might have fun trying to name some of the most surprising examples. Inspiration largely comes from the Mediterranean: the Greek Islands, Morocco, and Spain, with some Miami-style art deco thrown into the mixture.

Anguilla accommodations basically fall into two categories: grand resorts and luxury resort-villas, or low-key, simple, locally owned inns and small beachfront complexes. The former can be surprisingly expensive, the latter surprisingly reasonable. In the middle are some condo-type options, with full kitchens and multiple bedrooms, which are great for families or for longer stays. Private villa rentals are becoming more common and are increasing in number and quality every season as development on the island accelerates.

A good phone chat or email exchange with the management of any property is a good idea, as units within the same complex can vary greatly in layout, accessibility, distance to the beach, and view. When calling to reserve a room, ask about special discount packages, especially in spring and summer. Most hotels include Continental breakfast in the price, and many have meal-plan options. But keep in mind that Anguilla is home to dozens of excellent restaurants before you lock yourself into an expensive meal plan that you may not be able to change. All hotels charge a 10% tax, a $1 per room/per day tourism marketing levy, and—in most cases—an additional 10% service charge. A few properties include these charges in the published rates, so check carefully when you are evaluating prices.

PRIVATE VILLAS AND CONDOS

The tourist office publishes an annual *Anguilla Travel Planner* with informative listings of available vacation apartment rentals.

CuisinArt Resort and Spa, Rendezvous Bay

RENTAL CONTACTS

Anguilla Luxury Collection. The Ricketts, longtime Anguilla residents, manage lovely luxury properties as well as the Anguilla Affordable Collection, a selection of less-expensive villas. ☎ *264/497–6049* 🌐 *www.anguillaluxurycollection.com.*

Ani Villas. Two stunning cliff-side villas for up to 24 guests offer breathtaking views and total luxury to families or groups looking for pampering. Included in the rental are private boat transfers from St. Martin, rental car, a full-service team (concierge, butler, chef, housekeepers), breakfast, and all beverages. A tennis court, bikes, fitness room, pool, cliff-side hot tubs, and playrooms mean you don't have to leave except for the beach. (Tennis pros, spa services, trainers, and guides are available on demand.) There is room for 100 guests for a party or wedding on the dramatic and romantic promontory. Promotions can include unlimited golf at the CuisinArt course. ✉ *Little Bay* ☎ *264/497–7888* 🌐 *www.anivillas.com.*

Kishti Villas. This group of stunning new four- and five-bedroom villas fuses Eastern and Western aesthetics. The name, from the Urdu for "canoe," expresses a mystic sense of being in tune with nature and the lords of creation. Appointed with lovely Asian artifacts, villas have huge windows and gorgeous views, giving the sense of actually being at sea. While rates are high, attention is paid to every detail, and everything from house managers, chefs, and sports equipment is included. This is a terrific choice for destination weddings and other large family gatherings. ✉ *Meads Bay* ☎ *264/497–6049* 🌐 *www.kishtivillacollection.com.*

RECOMMENDED HOTELS AND RESORTS

$ RENTAL FAMILY **Allamanda Beach Club.** Youthful, active couples from around the globe happily fill this casual, three-story, white-stucco building hidden in a palm grove just off the beach, opting for location and price over luxury. **Pros:** front row for Shoal Bay action; young crowd; good restaurant. **Cons:** location requires a car; rooms are pleasant but not fancy. *Rooms from: $189 The Valley 264/497–5217, 305/396–4472 www.allamanda.ai 20 units Closed Sept. No meals.*

$$$$ RENTAL **Altamer.** Architect Myron Goldfinger's geometric symphony of floor-to-ceiling windows, cantilevered walls, and curvaceous floating staircases is fit for any king (or CEO)—as is the price tag. **Pros:** plenty of space; lots of electronic diversions; great for big groups. **Cons:** a bit out of the way; you'll need a big group to make it worthwhile. *Rooms from: $3,200 Shoal Bay West 264/498–4000 www.altamer.com 3 5-bedroom villas Multiple meal plans.*

$$ RESORT FAMILY **Anacaona Boutique Hotel.** Imbued with island culture and traditions, this resort (its name is pronounced "an-nah-cah-*oh*-na") makes a low-key yet chic hideaway where guests feel like treasured friends. **Pros:** friendly clientele, sensitive to local culture; modern and good value; high-tech amenities. **Cons:** bit of a walk to beach; smallish rooms. *Rooms from: $280 Meads Bay 264/497–6827, 877/647–4736 www.anacaonahotel.com 27 rooms and suites Closed mid-Aug.–Oct. Multiple meal plans.*

$$ RESORT FAMILY **Anguilla Great House Beach Resort.** These traditional West Indian–style bungalows are strung along one of Anguilla's longest beaches. **Pros:** real, old-school Caribbean; right on the gorgeous beach; young crowd; good prices. **Cons:** very simple rooms; spotty Internet. *Rooms from: $310 Rendezvous Bay 264/497–6061, 800/583–9247 www.anguillagreathouse.com 31 rooms Multiple meal plans.*

$$ B&B/INN **Arawak Beach Inn.** These hexagonal two-story villas are a good choice for a funky, budget-friendly, low-key guesthouse experience. **Pros:** funky, casual crowd; friendly owners; very competitive rates. **Cons:** not on the beach; a/c only in premium rooms; isolated location makes a car a must. *Rooms from: $295 Island Harbour 264/497–4888, 877/427–2925 reservations www.arawakbeach.com 17 rooms Multiple meal plans.*

$$$$ RESORT **Cap Juluca.** Strung along 179 acres of breathtaking Maundays Bay, these romantic, domed, Moorish-style villas are an Anguilla favorite, thanks to caring staff, great sports facilities, and plenty of privacy and comfort. **Pros:** miles of talcum-soft sand; warm service; romantic. **Cons:** ongoing renovations, comparatively high rates, some units currently closed. *Rooms from: $995 Maundays Bay 264/497–6779, 888/858–5822 in U.S. www.capjuluca.com 69 rooms, 7 patio suites, 6 pool villas Some meals.*

$$$ RENTAL **Caribella.** These spacious Mediterranean-style villas on the broad sands of Barnes Bay are a good deal at the much-discounted weekly rate. **Pros:** huge amount of space for the cost; beautiful views from huge balconies. **Cons:** basic decor. *Rooms from: $450 Barnes Bay 264/497–6045 www.lambertventures.com 6 units No meals.*

$$$ RENTAL FAMILY **Carimar Beach Club.** This horseshoe of bougainvillea-draped Mediterranean-style buildings on beautiful Meads Bay has the look of a Sun Belt condo. **Pros:** tennis courts; easy walk to restaurants and spa; great beach location; laundry facilities. **Cons:** no pool or restaurant. *Rooms from: $425 Meads Bay 264/497–6881, 866/270-3764 www.carimar.com 24 apartments Closed Sept.–mid-Oct. Multiple meal plans.*

$$$$ RESORT FAMILY Fodor's Choice ★ **CuisinArt Golf Resort and Spa.** Anguilla's best family-friendly full-service resort has it all: miles of stunning beach, world-class golf, a gorgeous spa and health club, top dining, and sports galore. **Pros:** family-friendly; great spa and sports; gorgeous beach and gardens. **Cons:** food service can be slow; pool area is noisy. *Rooms from: $800 Rendezvous Bay 264/498–2000, 800/943–3210 www.cuisinartresort.com 100 rooms, 2 penthouses, 6 villas Closed Sept.–Oct. Multiple meal plans.*

$$$ RESORT FAMILY **Frangipani Beach Club.** This flamingo-pink Mediterranean-style property perches on the beautiful champagne sands of Meads Bay. **Pros:** great beach; good location for restaurants and resort hopping; first-rate on-site restaurant; helpful staff. **Cons:** some rooms lack a view, so be sure to ask if you care. *Rooms from: $400 Meads Bay 264/497–6442, 877/593–8988 www.frangipaniresort.com 19 rooms Closed Sept.–Oct. Breakfast.*

$$$$ RENTAL FAMILY **Meads Bay Beach Villas.** These gorgeous one-, two-, and three-bedroom villas right on Meads Bay have a cult following, so it can be hard to book them. **Pros:** big private apartments; beautiful beach; private plunge pools; free phone calls to United States. **Cons:** more condo than hotel in terms of service. *Rooms from: $550 Meads Bay Rd., Meads Bay 264/497–0271 www.meadsbaybeachvillas.com 4 villas No meals.*

$$ RENTAL FAMILY **Paradise Cove.** Located 500 yards away from Cove Beach, this simple complex of huge, reasonably priced studios and one- and two-bedroom apartments has two whirlpools, a large pool, and tranquil tropical gardens where you can pluck fresh guavas for breakfast. **Pros:** reasonable rates; great pool; lovely gardens. **Cons:** a bit far from the beach; bland decor. *Rooms from: $320 The Cove 264/497–6959, 264/497–6603 www.paradisecoveanguilla.com 12 studios, 17 1- and 2-bedroom apartments No meals.*

$$ RENTAL FAMILY **Serenity Cottages.** Despite the name, these aren't cottages but large, fully equipped, and relatively affordable one- and two-bedroom apartments (and studios created from them) in a small complex set in a lush garden at the far end of glorious Shoal Bay Beach. **Pros:** big apartments; quiet end of beach; snorkeling outside the door; weeklong packages. **Cons:** no pool; more condo than hotel in terms of staff; location requires a car and extra time to drive to the West End. *Rooms from: $325 Shoal Bay 264/497–3328 www.serenity.ai 2 1-bedroom suites, 8 2-bedroom apartments Closed Sept. No meals.*

$$$$ RENTAL FAMILY **Sheriva Villa Hotel.** This intimate, luxury-villa hotel is made up of three cavernous villas with a total of 20 guest rooms and seven private swimming pools, overlooking a broad swath of turquoise sea. **Pros:** incredible staff; all the comforts of home; good value for groups. **Cons:** not on the

beach; you risk being spoiled for life by the staff's attentions; expensive. *Rooms from: $1,500* ✉ *Maundays Bay Rd., West End* ☎ *264/498–9898* 🌐 *www.sheriva.com* *20 rooms* *Multiple meal plans.*

$$ RENTAL FAMILY **Shoal Bay Villas.** In this old-style property on Shoal Bay's incredible 2-mile (3-km) beach, studios and one- and two-bedroom apartments all have balconies over the water. **Pros:** friendly; casual; full kitchens; beachfront. **Cons:** not fancy; you'll want a car; there's construction in the area, so check before booking. *Rooms from: $365* ✉ *Shoal Bay* ☎ *264/497–2051* 🌐 *www.sbvillas.ai* *12 units* *No meals.*

$$ RENTAL FAMILY **Turtle's Nest Beach Resort.** This collection of studios and one- to three-bedroom oceanfront condos is right on Meads Bay Beach, with some of the island's best restaurants a sandy stroll away. **Pros:** beachfront; huge apartments; well-kept grounds and pool. **Cons:** no elevator, so fourth-floor units are a climb (but have great views). *Rooms from: $340* ✉ *Meads Bay* ☎ *264/462–6378* 🌐 *www.turtlesnestbeachresort.com* *29 units* *No meals.*

$$$$ RESORT FAMILY Fodor's Choice ★ **Viceroy Anguilla.** On a promontory over 3,200 feet of pearly sand on Meads Bay, Kelly Wearstler's haute-hip showpiece wows international sophisticates. **Pros:** state-of-the-art luxury; cutting-edge contemporary design; spacious rooms. **Cons:** international rather than Caribbean feel; very large resort; see-and-be-seen scene; really expensive. *Rooms from: $800* ✉ *Barnes Bay, West End* ☎ *264/497–7000, 866/270–7798 in U.S.* 🌐 *www.viceroyhotelsandresorts.com* *163 suites, 3 villas* *Closed Sept.* *Multiple meal plans.*

NIGHTLIFE

In late February or early March, on the first full moon before Easter, reggae star and impresario Bankie Banx stages Moonsplash, a three-day music festival that showcases local and imported talent. Anguilla Day's boat races, in May, are the most important sporting event of the year. At the end of July, the Anguilla Summer Festival has boat races by day and Carnival parades, calypso competitions, and parties at night. Some years bring a jazz festival.

Nightlife action doesn't really start until 11 and runs late into the night. Be aware that taxis are not readily available then. If you plan to take a cab back to your lodging at the end of the night, make arrangements in advance with the driver who brings you or with your hotel concierge.

Dune Preserve. There is music most nights at the funky driftwood-fabricated home of reggae star Bankie Banx, who often performs here weekends and during the full moon. There's a dance floor, beach bar, small menu, and potent rum cocktails, of course. In high season there's a $15 cover. ✉ *Rendezvous Bay* ☎ *264/497–6219* 🌐 *www.bankiebanx.net.*

Fodor's Choice ★ **Elvis' Beach Bar.** Actually a boat, this is a great place to hear music and sip the best rum punch on earth. You can also snack on Mexican food (try the goat tacos), play beach volleyball, or watch football on the big TV. The bar is closed Tuesday, and there's live music Wednesday through Sunday nights in high season—plus food until 1 am. The full-moon LunaSea party doesn't disappoint. ✉ *Sandy Ground* ☎ *264/772–0637.*

Viceroy Anguilla, Meads Bay

Johnno's Beach Stop. There's live music and alfresco dancing every night and on Sunday afternoon, when just about everybody drops by (on Sunday night, there's live jazz). This is *the* classic Caribbean beach bar, attracting a funky eclectic mix, from locals to movie stars. It's open Tuesday–Sunday from 11 to 9. ✉ *Sandy Ground* ☎ *264/497–2728.*

Fodor's Choice ★ **The Pumphouse.** In an old rock-salt factory, you can dance to live music most nights, drink craft beers, and dine on surprisingly good gastropub food (when they roast a whole steamship round of beef, make a reservation). A mini-museum has artifacts and equipment from 19th-century salt factories. Tuesday is ladies' night, and Monday is trivia. ✉ *Sandy Ground* ☎ *264/497–5154* 🌐 *www.pumphouse-anguilla.com.*

SHOPPING

Anguilla is by no means a shopping destination. In fact, if your suitcase is lost, you will be hard-pressed to secure even the basics. Hard-core shopping enthusiasts might like a day trip to nearby St. Martin. The island's tourist publication, *What We Do in Anguilla,* has shopping tips and is available free at the airport and in shops. For upscale designer sportswear, check out small boutiques in hotels (some are branches of larger stores in Marigot on St. Martin). Outstanding local artists sell their work in galleries, which often arrange studio tours (or check with the Anguilla Tourist Board).

ART AND CRAFTS

Cheddie's Carving Studio. Cheddie's showcases Cheddie Richardson's fanciful wood carvings and coral and stone sculptures, and bronzes cast from nature. It's closed Sunday. ✉ *Driftwood Haven, The Cove* ☎ *264/497–6027* 🌐 *www.news.ai/web/cheddie.*

2

Devonish Art Gallery. This gallery purveys the wood, stone, and clay creations of Courtney Devonish, an internationally known potter and sculptor, plus creations by his wife, Carolle, a bead artist. Works by other Caribbean artists and regional antique maps are also available. ✉ *West End Rd., George Hill* ☎ *264/497–2949* 🌐 *www.devonishart.com.*

The Galleria at World Art and Antiques. The peripatetic proprietor, Christy Douglas, displays a veritable United Nations of antiquities: exquisite Indonesian ikat hangings to Thai teak furnishings, Aboriginal didgeridoos to Dogon tribal masks, Yuan Dynasty jade pottery to Uzbeki rugs. There are also handcrafted jewelry and handbags, and Anguilla souvenirs. ✉ *West End Rd., West End* ☎ *264/497–5950, 264/497–2767.*

Hibernia Restaurant and Art Gallery. Striking pieces are culled from the owners' travels, from contemporary Eastern European art to traditional Indo-Chinese crafts. ✉ *Harbor Ridge Dr., Island Harbour* ☎ *264/497–4290* 🌐 *www.hiberniarestaurant.com.*

L. Bernbaum Art Gallery. Originally from Texas, Lynne Bernbaum has been working and living in Anguilla for more than a decade and exhibits around the world. Her paintings and prints are inspired by the island's natural beauty but have unusual perspectives and a hint of surrealism. The gallery is open Monday–Saturday 4–8 pm. ✉ *Sandy Ground* ☎ *264/497–5211* 🌐 *www.lynnebernbaum.com.*

Savannah Gallery. Adjacent historic houses contain high-quality works by Anguillian artists; other contemporary Caribbean and Central American art, including oil paintings by Marge Morani; works from the renowned Haitian St. Soleil school; Guatemalan textiles; Mexican pottery; and Haitian metal sculpture, some made from recycled oil drums. ✉ *Coronation St., Lower Valley* ☎ *264/497–2263* 🌐 *www.savannahgallery.com.*

CLOTHING

Irie Life. This popular boutique sells vividly hued beach and resort wear and flip-flops, as well as attractive handcrafts, jewelry, and collectibles from all over the Caribbean, many with a Rasta theme. ✉ *South Hill* ☎ *264/497–6526* 🌐 *www.irielife.com.*

ZaZaa. Sue Ricketts, the first lady of Anguilla marketing, owns boutiques on the Main Road in South Hill and near the entrance of Anacaona Boutique Hotel, on Meads Bay. They carry Anguillian crafts; wonderful ethnic jewelry and beachwear, such as sexy Brazilian bikinis and chic St. Barth goodies; and beach sundries and souvenirs. ✉ *Lower South Hill, South Hill* ☎ *264/235–8878* 🌐 *www.anguillaluxurycollection.com/zazaa-boutique.*

SPORTS AND THE OUTDOORS

Anguilla's expanding sports options include its beautiful first golf course (at the CuisinArt Golf Resort), designed by Greg Norman to accentuate the natural terrain and maximize the stunning ocean views over Rendezvous Bay. The Anguilla Tennis Academy, designed by noted architect Myron Goldfinger, operates in the Blowing Point area. The 1,000-seat stadium, equipped with pro shop and seven lighted courts, was created to attract major international matches and to provide a first-class playing option for tourists and locals.

DIVING

Sunken wrecks; a long barrier reef; walls, canyons, and hulking boulders; varied marine life, including greenback turtles and nurse sharks; and exceptionally clear water all make for excellent diving. **Prickly Pear Cay** is a favorite spot. **Stoney Bay Marine Park,** off the northeast end, showcases the *El Buen Consejo,* a 960-ton Spanish galleon that sank in 1772. Other good dive sites include **Grouper Bowl,** with exceptional hard-coral formations; **Ram's Head,** with caves, chutes, and tunnels; and **Upper Flats,** where you are sure to see stingrays.

Anguillian Divers. This full-service dive operator with a PADI five-star training center offers open-water certification, snorkel rentals, and diving equipment. Five-dive packages are a good deal. ✉ *Meads Bay* ☎ *264/497–4750* 🌐 *www.anguilliandiver.com.*

FAMILY **Shoal Bay Scuba and Watersports.** This highly rated PADI dive center runs up to six dives a day (closed Sundays) from two locations: at Roy's at Sandy Ground, and in West End. Single-tank dives start at $50, two-tank dives at $90. Snorkeling trips (1 pm) are $25. Kids' programs include a scuba intro in a pool and PADI Jr. certification. The shop sells masks, snorkels, fins, T-shirts, hats, shorts, and SPF-50 water shirts. Private dives, snorkel and sightseeing charters, private fishing charters, and sunset cruises are also offered. ✉ *Sandy Ground* ☎ *264/235–1482* 🌐 *www.shoalbayscuba.com.*

GOLF

Fodor'sChoice ★ **CuisinArt Golf Resort.** This Greg Norman course, a $50-million wonder, qualifies as one of the best golf courses in the Caribbean. Thirteen of its 18 holes are directly on the water, and it features sweeping sea vistas, elevation changes, and an ecologically responsible watering system of ponds and lagoons that snake through the grounds. Players including President Bill Clinton have thrilled to the spectacular vistas of St. Maarten and blue sea at the tee box of the 390-yard starting hole—the Caribbean's answer to Pebble Beach. An attractive Italian restaurant serves lunch. The course typically closes the second half of October for maintenance. Dress requirements include long shorts or slacks and a collared shirt. ✉ *Rendezvous Bay* ☎ *264/498–5602* 🌐 *www.cuisinartresort.com* 🎫 *$270 for 18 holes ($225 guests), $170 for 9 holes ($145 guests)* ⛳ *18 holes, 7200 yards, par 72.*

CLOSE UP

A Day at the Boat Races

If you want a different kind of trip to Anguilla, try for a visit during Carnival, which starts on the first Monday in August and continues for about 10 days. Colorful parades, beauty pageants, music, delicious food, arts-and-crafts shows, fireworks, and nonstop partying are just the beginning. The music starts with sunrise jam sessions—as early as 4 am—and continues well into the night. The high point? The boat races. They are the national passion and the official national sport of Anguilla.

Anguillians from around the world return home to race old-fashioned, made-on-the-island wooden boats that have been in use on the island since the early 1800s. Similar to some of today's fastest sailboats, these are 15 to 28 feet in length and sport only a mainsail and jib on a single 25-foot mast. The sailboats have no deck, so heavy bags of sand, boulders, and sometimes even people are used as ballast. As the boats reach the finish line, the ballast—including some of the sailors—gets thrown into the water in a furious effort to win the race. Spectators line the beaches and follow the boats on foot, by car, and from even more boats. You'll have almost as much fun watching the fans as you will the races.

2

GUIDED TOURS

A round-the-island tour by taxi takes about 2½ hours and costs about $55 for one or two people, $5 for each additional passenger.

Anguilla Access Tours. A three-hour tour gives an introduction to island heritage, food, nightlife, arts and crafts, or just beaches. You can get picked up from your lodging for the half-day tour ($45 per person). ✉ *Government Center, The Valley* ☎ *267/772–9827* 🌐 *www.anguillaaccess.com.*

Anguilla Tourist Board. Tuesdays at 10, Sir Emile Gumbs, the island's former chief minister, leads tours of the Sandy Ground area that highlight historic and ecological sites. Its $20 fee benefits the Anguilla Archeological and Historical Society. Gumbs also organizes bird-watching expeditions that spy everything from frigate birds to turtledoves. Tours tailored to almost any interest—sea turtle nesting sites, historic buildings, birding sites, gardens, and art galleries—can also be booked through the office. ✉ *Coronation Ave., The Valley* ☎ *264/497–2759, 800/553–4939* 🌐 *www.ivisitanguilla.com.*

Bennie's Travel & Tours. One of the island's more reliable tour operators also arranges private boat charters, event planning, real-estate tours, and personal security services. ✉ *Blowing Point* ☎ *264/497–2788.*

HORSEBACK RIDING

Seaside Stables. Ever dreamed of a sunset gallop (or slow clomp) on the beach? A bareback ocean romp or full-moon ride is $120, private rides any time of day are $90 per hour, and morning and afternoon group rides are $70. Prior riding experience is not required, as the horses are very gentle. Choose from English, Western, or Australian saddles. ✉ *Paradise Dr., Cove Bay* ☎ *264/235–3667* 🌐 *www.seaside-stables.com.*

SEA EXCURSIONS

A number of boating options are available for airport transfers, day trips to offshore cays or neighboring islands, night trips to St. Martin, or just whipping through the waves en route to a picnic spot.

Chocolat. This 35-foot EDEL catamaran, with four private cabins, is available for private charter or scheduled excursions to nearby cays. Captain Rollins is a knowledgeable, affable, safety-conscious guide. Rates for day sails with lunch (prepared by the captain's wife, Jacquie, of Ripples Restaurant) are about $80 per person. ✉ *Sandy Ground* ☎ *264/497–3394* 🌐 *www.sailinganguilla.com.*

Funtime Charters. With five powerboats from 32 to 38 feet, this charter and shuttle service arranges private and scheduled boat transport to the airport, including luggage services ($70 per person); day trips to St. Barth; and other powerboat excursions. The air-conditioned 42-seat *Sunshine Express* runs to SXM in the late night and early morning as well as interisland excursions. ✉ *The Cove* ☎ *264/497–6511, 866/334–0047* 🌐 *www.funtime-charters.com.*

FAMILY **Junior's Glass Bottom Boat.** For an underwater peek at sea turtles and stingrays without getting wet, catch a ride ($20 per person) on this boat. Guided snorkeling trips and instruction are available, too. Junior is great with kids and very knowledgable. Best to book in advance, especially during holidays. Hotel transport is available. ✉ *Sandy Ground* ☎ *264/497–4456* 🌐 *www.junior.ai.*

No Fear Sea Tours. In addition to private airport transportation, day snorkeling trips, sunset cruises, and fishing trips on three 32-foot speedboats and a 19-foot ski boat, this charter service offers water-sports rentals (tubing, skiing, knee-boarding). ✉ *The Cove* ☎ *264/235–6354.*

Sandy Island Enterprises. Picnic, swimming, and diving excursions to Prickly Pear Cay, Sandy Island, and Scilly Cay are available through this outfit, which also rents Sunfish and Windsurfers and arranges fishing charters. The Sandy Island sea shuttle *Happiness* leaves from the small pier in Sandy Ground daily November–August and by reservation September–October. ✉ *The Valley* ☎ *264/476–6534.*

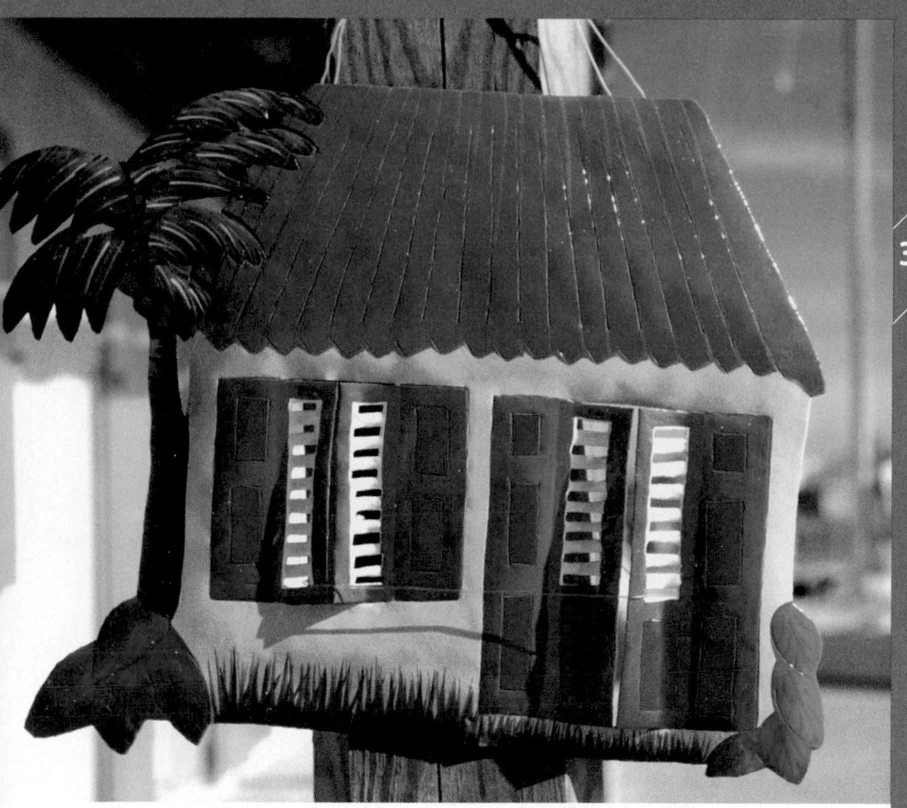

3

ANTIGUA AND BARBUDA

WELCOME TO ANTIGUA AND BARBUDA

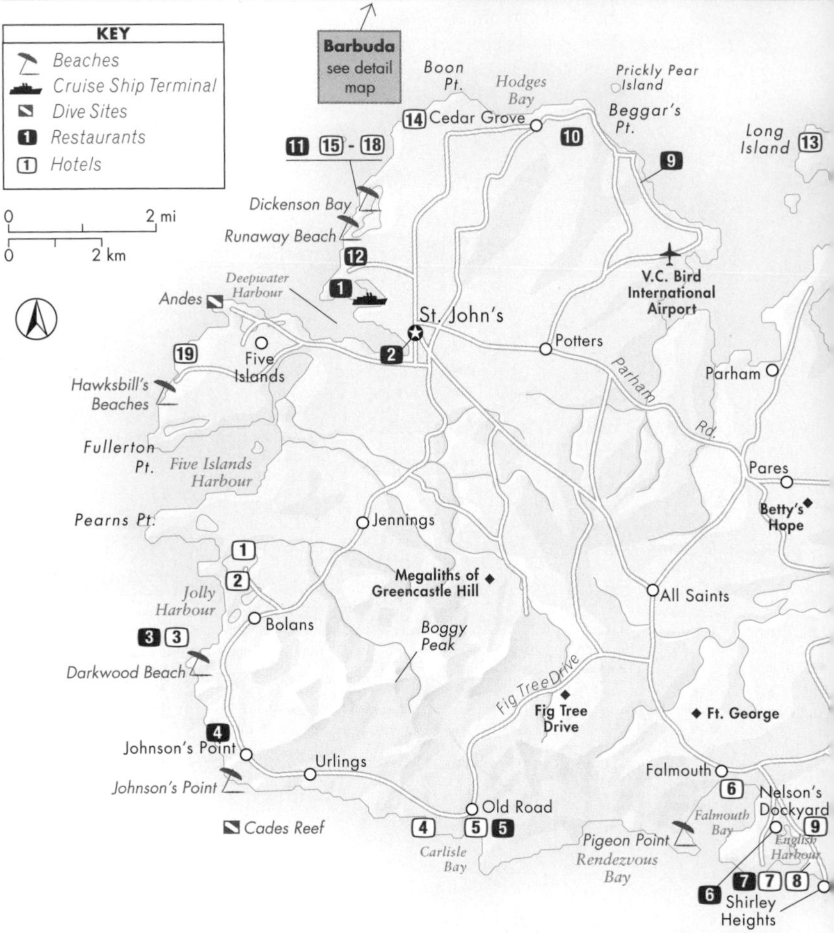

KEY
Beaches
Cruise Ship Terminal
Dive Sites
1 Restaurants
1 Hotels

0 2 mi
0 2 km

Barbuda see detail map
Boon Pt.
Hodges Bay
Prickly Pear Island
Beggar's Pt.
Long Island 13
14 Cedar Grove
10
9
11 15 - 18
Dickenson Bay
Runaway Beach
12
1
Deepwater Harbour
Andes
V.C. Bird International Airport
St. John's
Potters
19
Five Islands
2
Parham Rd.
Parham
Hawksbill's Beaches
Fullerton Pt.
Five Islands Harbour
Pares
Betty's Hope
Pearns Pt.
Jennings
1
2
Megaliths of Greencastle Hill
All Saints
Jolly Harbour
Bolans
3 3
Boggy Peak
Darkwood Beach
Fig Tree Drive
Fig Tree Drive
Ft. George
4
Johnson's Point
Urlings
Johnson's Point
Falmouth
6
Nelson's Dockyard
Falmouth Bay
9
English Harbour
Cades Reef
Old Road
4
5 5
Carlisle Bay
Pigeon Point
Rendezvous Bay
7 7 8
6
Shirley Heights

Excellent beaches—365 of them—might make you think that the island has never busied itself with anything more pressing than the pursuit of pleasure. But for much of the 18th and 19th centuries, English Harbour sheltered Britain's Caribbean fleet. These days, pleasure yachts bob where galleons once anchored.

A BEACH FOR EVERY DAY

At 108 square miles (280 square km), Antigua is the largest of the British Leeward Islands. Its much smaller sister island, Barbuda, is 26 miles (42 km) to the north. Together, they are an independent nation and part of the British Commonwealth. The island was under British control from 1667 until it achieved independence in 1981.

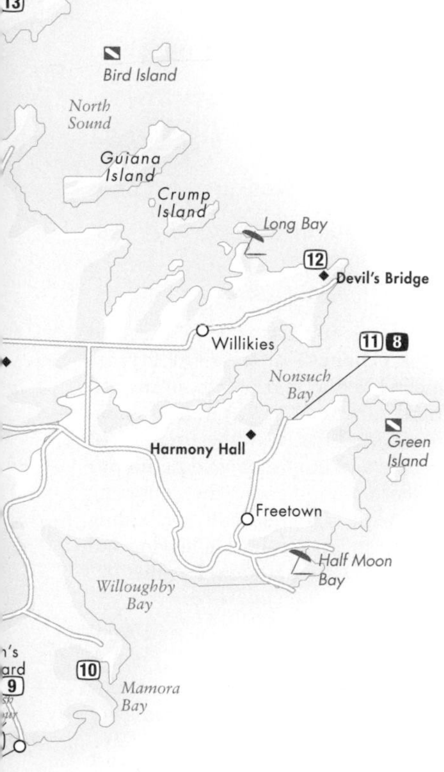

Restaurants	
The Bay @ Nonsuch	8
Big Banana	2
Cecilia's High Point	9
Coconut Grove	11
East	5
Jacqui O's	4
La Bussola	12
Le Bistro	10
Le Cap Horn	6
Pillar's Restaurant at the Admiral's Inn	7
Russell's	1
Sheer Rocks	3

Hotels	
Admiral's Inn	7
Blue Waters Hotel	14
Buccaneer Beach Club	17
Carlisle Bay	5
Catamaran Hotel	6
CocoBay	3
Curtain Bluff	4
Dickenson Bay Cottages	15
Galley Bay	19
Inn at English Harbor	9
Jolly Beach Resort	2
Jolly Harbour Villas	1
Jumby Bay	13
Nonsuch Bay Resort	11
Ocean Inn	8
St. James's Club	10
Sandals Grande	18
Siboney Beach Club	16
Verandah Resort & Spa	12

TOP REASONS TO VISIT ANTIGUA AND BARBUDA

1 **Beaches Galore:** So many paradisiacal beaches of every size provide a tremendous selection for an island its size.

2 **Nelson's Dockyard:** One of the Caribbean's best examples of historic preservation.

3 **Sailing Away:** With several natural anchorages and tiny islets to explore, Antigua is a major sailing center.

4 **Activities Galore:** Land and water sports, sights to see, and nightlife.

5 **Shopping Options:** A nice selection of shopping options, from duty-free goods to local artists and craftspeople (especially distinctive ceramics).

Updated by Jordan Simon

Travel brochures trumpet Antigua's 365 sensuous beaches, "one for every day of the year," as locals love saying, though when the island was first developed for tourism, the unofficial count was 52 ("one for every weekend"). Either way, even longtime residents haven't combed every stretch of sand.

The island's extensive archipelago of cays and islets is what attracted the original Amerindian settlers—the Ciboney—at least 4,000 years ago. The natural environment, which is rich in marine life, flora, and fauna, has been likened to a "natural supermarket." Antigua's superior anchorages and strategic location naturally caught the attention of the colonial powers. The Dutch, French, and English waged numerous bloody battles throughout the 17th century (eradicating the remaining Arawaks and Caribs in the process), with England finally prevailing in 1667. Antigua remained under English control until achieving full independence on November 1, 1981, along with Barbuda, 26 miles (42 km) to the north.

Boats and beaches go hand in hand with hotel development, and Antigua's tourist infrastructure has mushroomed since the 1950s. Though many of its grandes dames such as Curtain Bluff remain anchors, today all types of resorts line the sand, and the island offers something for everyone, from gamboling on the sand to gambling in casinos. Environmental activists have become increasingly vocal about preservation and limiting development, and not just because green travel rakes in the green. Antigua's allure is precisely that precarious balance and subliminal tension between its unspoiled, natural beauty and its sun-sand-surf megadevelopment. And the British heritage persists, from teatime (and tee times) to fiercely contested cricket matches.

PLANNING

WHEN TO GO

The high season runs from mid-December through April; after that time, you can find real bargains, as much as 40% off the regular rates, particularly if you book an air-hotel package. A fair number of the restaurants and properties close most of the time between August and October, especially around English Harbour.

GETTING HERE AND AROUND

AIR TRAVEL

Nonstop flights are available from Atlanta (Delta, twice weekly in season), Charlotte (US Airways), Miami (American, Caribbean Airlines, United), New York–JFK (American, Caribbean), and Newark (United).

Airport Contact V. C. Bird International Airport (*ANU*). ☎ *268/462–4672, 268/462–0358, 268/562–6798, 268/484–2300* 🌐 *www.vcbia.com.*

Airline Contacts American Airlines ☎ *268/462–0950, 268/481–4699* 🌐 *www.aa.com.* **Antigua Barbuda Montserrat Air** ☎ *268/562–8033, 268/562–7183* 🌐 *www.abm-air.com, www.antigua-flights.com, www.montserrat-flights.com.* **Caribbean Airlines** ☎ *268/480–2900, 800/744–2225* 🌐 *www.caribbean-airlines.com.* **United Airlines** ☎ *268/462–5355* 🌐 *www.united.com.* **Delta Airlines** ☎ *800/532–4777, 268/562–5951* 🌐 *www.delta.com.* **LIAT.** LIAT has daily flights to and from many other Caribbean islands. ☎ *268/480–5600* 🌐 *www.liatairline.com.*

BOAT AND FERRY TRAVEL

Barbuda Express. Barbuda Express runs five days a week (generally Tuesday–Saturday, but call for the changing schedule) from Antigua, departing St. John's Harbour at the bottom of High Street by the Heritage Quay Ferry Dock. ✉ *High St., St. John's* ☎ *268/560–7989* 🌐 *www.antiguaferries.com, www.barbudaexpress.com* 💳 *EC$130 one-way, EC$260 round-trip (day tour costs US$169).*

CAR TRAVEL

The main roads are mostly in good condition, with some bumpy dirt stretches at remote locations and a few hilly areas that flood easily and become impassable for a day. Driving is on the left. To rent a car, you need a valid license and a temporary permit ($20), available through the rental agent. Costs start at about $50 per day in season, with unlimited mileage, though multiday discounts are standard. Most agencies offer automatic or stick shift and right- and left-hand drive. Four-wheel-drive vehicles (from $55 per day) will get you more places and are useful because so many roads are full of potholes.

Contacts Avis ☎ *268/462–2840.* **Budget** ☎ *268/462–3009, 268/736–6400* 🌐 *budget-cars-antigua.com.* **Dollar** ☎ *268/462–0362* 🌐 *www.dollarantigua.com.* **Hertz** ☎ *268/481–4440 St. John's, 268/481–4455 airport branch.* **Thrifty** ☎ *268/462–9532 St. John's, 268/462–8803 airport.*

TAXI TRAVEL

Some cabbies may take you from St. John's to English Harbour and wait for about a half hour while you look around, for about $50.

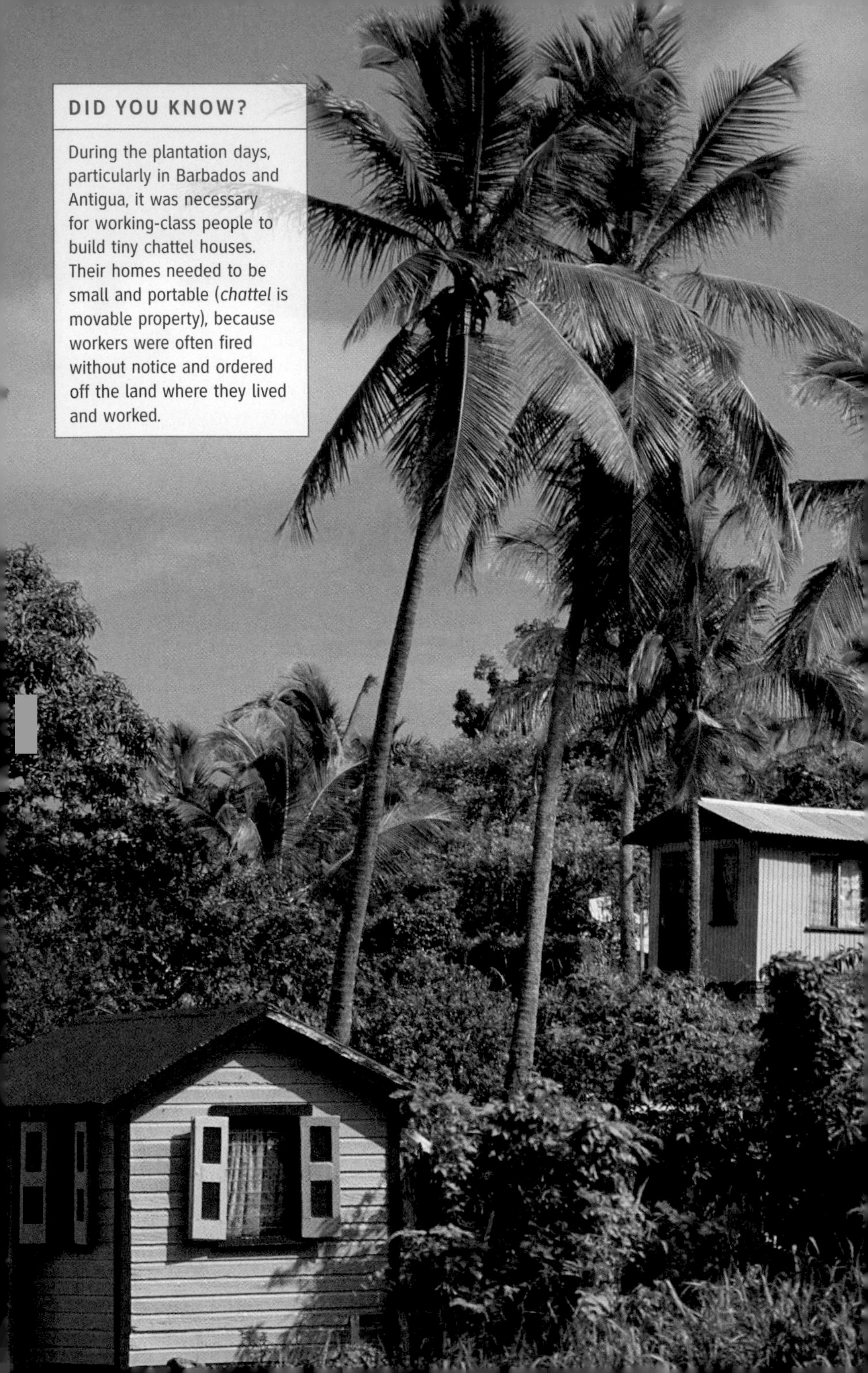

DID YOU KNOW?

During the plantation days, particularly in Barbados and Antigua, it was necessary for working-class people to build tiny chattel houses. Their homes needed to be small and portable (*chattel* is movable property), because workers were often fired without notice and ordered off the land where they lived and worked.

LOGISTICS

Getting to Antigua and Barbuda: Antigua is a Caribbean base, and several airlines fly there nonstop. There is ferry service to Barbuda several days a week, though it's geared for day-trippers. Antigua Barbuda Montserrat Air provides flights between the two islands. Good package deals are often available from resorts.

Hassle Factor: Low for Antigua, medium for Barbuda.

On the Ground: Taxis meet every flight, and drivers will offer to guide you around the island. Taxis are unmetered, but rates are posted at the airport. Drivers must carry a rate card with them. The fixed rate from the airport to St. John's is $12 (although drivers have been known to quote in Eastern Caribbean dollars), to Dickenson Bay $16, and to English Harbour $31.

If you are staying at an isolated resort or wish to sample the island's many fine restaurants, a car is a necessity, less so if you are staying at an all-inclusive with limited island excursions. It's possible to get by without a car if you are staying near St. John's or English Harbour, but taxi rates mount up quickly. A temporary driving permit is required on the island ($20), and you drive on the left.

Contact St. John's taxi stand. You can always call a cab from the St. John's taxi stand. ☎ *268/462–5190, 268/460–5353 for 24-hr service.*

ESSENTIALS

Banks and Exchange Services The local currency is the Eastern Caribbean dollar (EC$). American dollars are readily accepted, although change is often in EC dollars. Exchanging currency really isn't necessary, especially if you are staying in an all-inclusive resort. Most hotels, restaurants, and duty-free shops take major credit cards. ATMs (dispensing EC$) are available at the island's banks and at the airport.

Electricity 110 volts, 50 cycles.

Emergency Services **Ambulance** ☎ *268/462–0251, 999.* **Fire** ☎ *268/462–0044, 911.* **Police assistance** ☎ *268/462–0125.*

Passport Requirements All visitors must carry a valid passport and must have a return or ongoing ticket.

Phones GSM tri-band mobile phones from the United States and United Kingdom usually work on Antigua; you can also rent one from LIME (formerly Cable & Wireless) and APUA (Antigua Public Utilities Authority). Basic rental costs range between EC$25 and EC$50 per day. You can use the LIME Phone Card (available in $5, $10, and $20 denominations in most hotels and post offices) for local and long-distance calls.**APUA** ✉ *Long St., St. John's* ☎ *268/480–7000, 268/727–2782* 🌐 *www.apua.ag.* **LIME** ✉ *Clare Hall, St. John's* ☎ *268/480–4000* 🌐 *www.time4lime.com.*

Taxes and Service Charges The departure tax is $37.50, which should be included in your airfare; if not, your carrier's airport check-in agent will request payment in cash only—either U.S. or EC currency. Hotels collect an 8.5%–10.5% government room tax; some restaurants will add a 7% tax. Hotels and restaurants also usually add a 10% service charge to your bill.

Tipping Restaurants, 5% beyond the regular service charge added to your bill; taxi drivers 10%; porters and bellmen about $1 per bag; maids $2 to $3 per night. Staff at all-inclusives aren't supposed to be tipped unless they've truly gone out of their way.

ACCOMMODATIONS

In Antigua you're almost certain to have an excellent beach regardless of where you stay. Dickenson Bay and Five Islands Peninsula suit beachcombers who want proximity to St. John's, and Jolly Harbour offers affordable options and activities galore. English Harbour and the southwest coast have the best inns and several excellent restaurants—although many close from August well into October; it's also the yachting crowd's hangout. Resorts elsewhere on the island are ideal for those seeking seclusion; some are so remote that all-inclusive packages or rental cars are mandatory. Barbuda has one posh resort, one fairly upscale hotel, and several guesthouses. The new Labour government has aggressively pursued investment. There have been rumors of a $2-billion multi-property project on the east coast from Chinese developers. A memorandum of intent was signed with a UAE developer to invest $150 million in an upscale resort. And more is in the wings according to government sources. None of this is likely to impact travelers until 2017 at the earliest.

All-Inclusive Resorts: Most of the all-inclusives aim for a mainstream, package-tour kind of crowd—with varying degrees of success—though offerings such as Jumby Bay, Galley Bay, and Curtain Bluff are more upscale.

Luxury Resorts: A fair number of luxury resorts cater to the well-heeled in varying degrees of formality on both Antigua and Barbuda.

Small Inns: A few small inns, some historic, can be found around Antigua, mostly concentrated in or near English Harbour.

Hotel reviews have been shortened. For full information, visit Fodors.com.

WHAT IT COSTS IN U.S. DOLLARS

	$	$$	$$$	$$$$
Restaurants	under $12	$12–$20	$21–$30	over $30
Hotels	under $275	$275–$375	$376–$475	over $475

Restaurant prices are the average cost of a main course at dinner or, if dinner is not served, at lunch. Hotel prices are the lowest cost of a standard double room in high season.

VISITOR INFORMATION

Antigua & Barbuda Department of Tourism ✉ *Government Complex, Queen Elizabeth Hwy., St. John's* ☎ *268/462–0480, 268/462–0651* 🌐 *www.antigua-barbuda.org.*

Antigua and Barbuda Tourism Authority ✉ *ACB Financial Centre, High St., St. John's* ☎ *268/562–7600.*

Antigua & Barbuda Tourist Offices ☎ *212/541–4117 in New York City, 305/381–6762 in Miami, 888/268–4227* 🌐 *www.antigua-barbuda.org.*

Antigua Hotels & Tourist Association ✉ *Island House, Newgate St., St. John's* ☎ *268/462–0374, 268/462–3703* 🌐 *www.antiguahotels.org.*

Barbudaful.net 🌐 *www.barbudaful.net.*

WEDDINGS

No minimum residency or blood test is required. A license application fee is $150. You must have valid passports as proof of citizenship and, in the case of previous marriages, the original divorce or annulment decree. A marriage certificate registration fee is $40. The marriage officer receives $50.

EXPLORING

ANTIGUA

Hotels provide free island maps, but you should get your bearings before heading out on the road. Street names aren't listed (except in St. John's), though *some* easy-to-spot signs lead the way to major restaurants and resorts. Locals generally give directions in terms of landmarks (turn left at the yellow house, or right at the big tree). Wear a swimsuit under your clothes—one of the sights to strike your fancy might be a secluded beach.

ST. JOHN'S

Antigua's capital, with some 45,000 inhabitants (approximately half the island's population), lies at sea level at the inland end of a sheltered northwestern bay. Although it has seen better days, a couple of notable historic sights and some good waterfront shopping areas make it worth a visit.

At the far south end of town, where Market Street forks into Valley and All Saints roads, haggling goes on every Friday and Saturday, when locals jam the **Public Market** to buy and sell fruits, vegetables, fish, and spices. Ask before you aim a camera; your subject may expect a tip. This is old-time Caribbean shopping, a jambalaya of sights, sounds, and smells.

TOP ATTRACTIONS

Fodor's Choice ★ **Redcliffe Quay.** Redcliffe Quay, at the water's edge just south of Heritage Quay, is the most appealing part of St. John's. Attractively restored (and superbly re-created) 19th-century buildings in a riot of cotton-candy colors house shops, restaurants, galleries, and boutiques and are linked by courtyards and landscaped walkways. ✉ *Redcliff St., St. John's* 🌐 *www.historicredcliffequay.com.*

WORTH NOTING

Anglican Cathedral of St. John the Divine. At the south gate of the Anglican Cathedral of St. John the Divine are figures of St. John the Baptist and St. John the Divine, said to have been taken from one of Napoléon's ships and brought to Antigua. The original church was built in 1681, replaced by a stone building in 1745, and destroyed by an earthquake in 1843. The present neo-baroque building dates from 1845; the parishioners had the interior completely encased in pitch pine, hoping to forestall future earthquake damage. Tombstones bear eerily eloquent testament to the colonial days. ✉ *Between Long and Newgate Sts., St. John's* ☎ *268/461–0082.*

Heritage Quay. Shopaholics head directly for Heritage Quay, an ugly multimillion-dollar complex. The two-story buildings contain stores that sell duty-free goods, sportswear, down-island imports (paintings, T-shirts, straw baskets), and local crafts. There are also restaurants, a bandstand, and a casino. Cruise-ship passengers disembark here from the 500-foot-long pier. Expect heavy shilling. ✉ *High and Thames Sts., St. John's.*

Museum of Antigua and Barbuda. Signs at the Museum of Antigua and Barbuda say "Please touch," encouraging you to explore Antigua's past. Try your hand at the educational video games or squeeze a cassava through a *matapi* (grass sieve). Exhibits interpret the nation's history, from its geological birth to its political independence in 1981. There are fossil and coral remains from some 34 million years ago; models of a sugar plantation and a wattle-and-daub house; an Arawak canoe; and a wildly eclectic assortment of objects from cannonballs to 1920s telephone exchanges. The museum occupies the former courthouse, which dates from 1750. The superlative museum gift shop carries such unusual items as calabash purses, seed earrings, warri boards (warri being an African game brought to the Caribbean), and lignum vitae pipes, as well as historic maps and local books (including engrossing monographs on varied subjects by the late Desmond Nicholson, a longtime resident). ✉ *Long and Market Sts., St. John's* ☎ *268/462–1469, 268/462–4930* 🌐 *www.antiguamuseums.net* 🎟 *\$3; children under 12 free* 🕒 *Mon.–Fri. 8:30–4, Sat. 10–2. Closed Sun.*

ELSEWHERE ON ANTIGUA

TOP ATTRACTIONS

Fodor's Choice ★ **Nelson's Dockyard.** Antigua's most famous attraction is the world's only Georgian-era dockyard still in use, a treasure trove for history buffs and nautical nuts alike. In 1671 the governor of the Leeward Islands wrote to the Council for Foreign Plantations in London, pointing out the advantages of this landlocked harbor. By 1704 English Harbour was in regular use as a garrisoned station.

In 1784, 26-year-old Horatio Nelson sailed in on the HMS *Boreas* to serve as captain and second-in-command of the Leeward Island Station. Under him was the captain of the HMS *Pegasus*, Prince William Henry, duke of Clarence, who was later crowned King William IV. The prince acted as best man when Nelson married Fannie Nisbet on Nevis in 1787.

Nelson's Dockyard at English Harbour

When the Royal Navy abandoned the station at English Harbour in 1889, it fell into a state of decay, though adventuresome yachties still lived there in near-primitive conditions. The Society of the Friends of English Harbour began restoring it in 1951; it reopened with great fanfare as Nelson's Dockyard on November 14, 1961. Within the compound are crafts shops, restaurants, and two splendidly restored 18th-century hotels, the Admiral's Inn and the Copper & Lumber Store Hotel, worth peeking into. (The latter, occupying a supply store for Nelson's Caribbean fleet, is a particularly fine example of Georgian architecture, its interior courtyard evoking Old England.) The Dockyard is a hub for oceangoing yachts and serves as headquarters for the annual Boat Show in early December and the Sailing Week Regatta in late April and early May. Water taxis will ferry you between points for EC$5. The Dockyard National Park also includes serene nature trails accessing beaches, rock pools, and crumbling plantation ruins and hilltop forts.

The **Dockyard Museum,** in the original Naval Officer's House, presents ship models, mock-ups of English Harbour, displays on the people who worked there and typical ships that docked, silver regatta trophies, maps, prints, antique navigational instruments, and Nelson's very own telescope and tea caddy. ✉ *Dockyard Dr., English Harbour* ☎ *268/481–5027 for Dockyard Museum, 268/481–5021 for National Parks Authority, 268/460–1379 also for Dockyard Museum* 🌐 *www.nationalparksantigua.com* 🎫 *$2 suggested donation* ⏲ *Daily 9–5.*

Shirley Heights. This bluff affords a spectacular view of English Harbour and Falmouth Harbour. The heights are named for Sir Thomas

Shirley, the governor who fortified the harbor in 1781. At the top is Shirley Heights Lookout, a restaurant built into the remnants of the 18th-century fortifications. Most notable for its boisterous Sunday barbecues that continue into the night with live music and dancing, it serves dependable burgers, pumpkin soup, grilled meats, and rum punches. ✉ *Dockyard Dr., Shirley Heights* ☎ *268/481–5021* 🌐 *www.nationalparksantigua.com.*

Dows Hill Interpretation Centre. Not far from Shirley Heights is the Dows Hill Interpretation Centre, where observation platforms provide still more sensational vistas of the English Harbour area. A multimedia sound-and-light presentation on island history and culture, spotlighting lifelike figures and colorful tableaux accompanied by running commentary and music, results in a cheery, if bland, portrait of Antiguan life from Amerindian times to the present. ✉ *Shirley Heights* ☎ *268/481–5045, 268/481–5021* 🌐 *www.nationalparksantigua.com* 🎫 *EC$15* ⏲ *Daily 9–5.*

WORTH NOTING

Betty's Hope. Just outside the village of Pares, a marked dirt road leads to Antigua's first sugar plantation, founded in the 1670s. You can tour the twin windmills, various ruins, still-functional crushing machinery, and the visitor center's exhibits (often closed) on the island's sugar era. The private trust overseeing the restoration has yet to realize its ambitious, environmentally aware plans to replant indigenous crops destroyed by the extensive sugarcane plantings. Indeed, the site is somewhat neglected, with goats grazing the grounds. ✉ *Pares Village Main Rd., Pares* ☎ *268/462–1469* 🌐 *www.antiguamuseums.net* 🎫 *$2* ⏲ *Tues.–Sat. 10–4.*

Devil's Bridge. This limestone arch formation, sculpted by the crashing breakers of the Atlantic at Indian Town, is a national park. Blowholes have been carved by the hissing, spitting surf. The park also encompasses some archaeological excavations of Carib artifacts. ✉ *Dockyard Dr., Long Bay* 🌐 *www.nationalparksantigua.com.*

Falmouth. This town sits on a lovely bay backed by former sugar plantations and sugar mills. The most important historic site here is St. Paul's Church, which was rebuilt on the site of a church once used by troops during the Horatio Nelson period.

Fig Tree Drive. This often muddy, rutted, steep road takes you through the rain forest, which is rich in mangoes, pineapples, and banana trees (*fig* is the Antiguan word for "banana"). The rain forest is the island's hilliest area—1,319-foot Boggy Peak (renamed Mt. Obama), to the west, is the highest point. At its crest, Elaine Francis sells seasonal local fruit juices—ginger, guava, sorrel, passion fruit—and homemade jams at a stall she dubs the Culture Shop. A few houses down (look for the orange windows) is the atelier of noted island artist Sallie Harker (shimmering seascapes and vividly hued fish incorporating gold leaf). You'll also pass several tranquil villages with charming churches and Antigua Rainforest Canopy Tours here *(⇨ Zip-Lining under Sports and the Outdoors later in this chapter).* ✉ *Fig Tree Dr.*

Ft. George. East of Liberta—one of the first settlements founded by freed slaves—on Monk's Hill, this fort was built from 1689 to 1720. Among the ruins are the sites for 32 cannons, water cisterns, the base of the old flagstaff, and some of the original buildings. ✉ *Great Fort George Monk's Hill Trail, St. Paul.*

Harmony Hall. Northeast of Freetown (follow the signs), this art gallery/restaurant is built on the foundation of a 17th-century sugar-plantation greathouse. No longer affiliated with the original Jamaican outpost, the Antigua facility is run by enterprising Italians who operate a fine restaurant and six spare but chic cottage suites (with a villa development planned). Its remote location is a headache, but you can allot the whole afternoon to enjoy lunch (dinner Wednesday through Saturday), soak in the historic ambience and panoramic ocean views, browse through the exhibits, comb the beach, and perhaps even snorkel at nearby Green Island via the property's dragon boat, *Luna.* ✉ *Brown's Bay Mill, Dockyard Dr., Brown's Mill* ☎ *268/460–4120* 🌐 *www.harmonyhallantigua.com* ⏲ *Mid-Nov.–May, daily 10–6, later Wed., Fri., and Sat.*

Parham. This sleepy village is a splendid example of a traditional colonial settlement. St. Peter's Church, built in 1840 by English architect Thomas Weekes, is an octagonal Italianate building with unusual ribbed wooden ceiling, whose facade is richly decorated with stucco and keystone work, though it suffered considerable damage during an 1843 earthquake.

BARBUDA

This flat, 62-square-mile (161-square-km) coral atoll—with 17 miles (27 km) of gleaming white-sand beaches (sand is the island's main export)—is 26 miles (42 km) north of Antigua. Most of Barbuda's 1,200 people live in Codrington. Nesting terns, turtles, and frigate birds outnumber residents at least 10 to 1. Goats, guinea fowl, deer, and wild boar roam the roads, all fair game for local kitchens. There are a few very basic efficiencies and guesthouses, but most visitors stay overnight at the deluxe Coco Point Lodge or Lighthouse Bay (two other glam properties have closed). Pink Beach lures beachcombers, a bird sanctuary attracts ornithologists, caves and sinkholes filled with rain forest or underground pools (containing rare, even unique crustacean species) attract spelunkers, and reefs and roughly 200 offshore wrecks draw divers and snorkelers. Barbuda's sole historic ruin is the 18th-century, cylindrical, 56-foot-tall **Martello Tower,** which was probably a lighthouse built by the Spaniards before English occupation. The **Frigate Bird Sanctuary,** a wide mangrove-filled lagoon, is home to an estimated 400 species of birds, including frigate birds with 8-foot wingspans. Your hotel can make arrangements.

It's reachable by plane on ABM Air (🌐 *www.abm-air.com*)and by boat, the *Barbuda Express* (🌐 *www.antiguaferries.com*), although the 95-minute ride is extremely bumpy ("a chiropractor's nightmare—or fantasy," quipped one passenger).

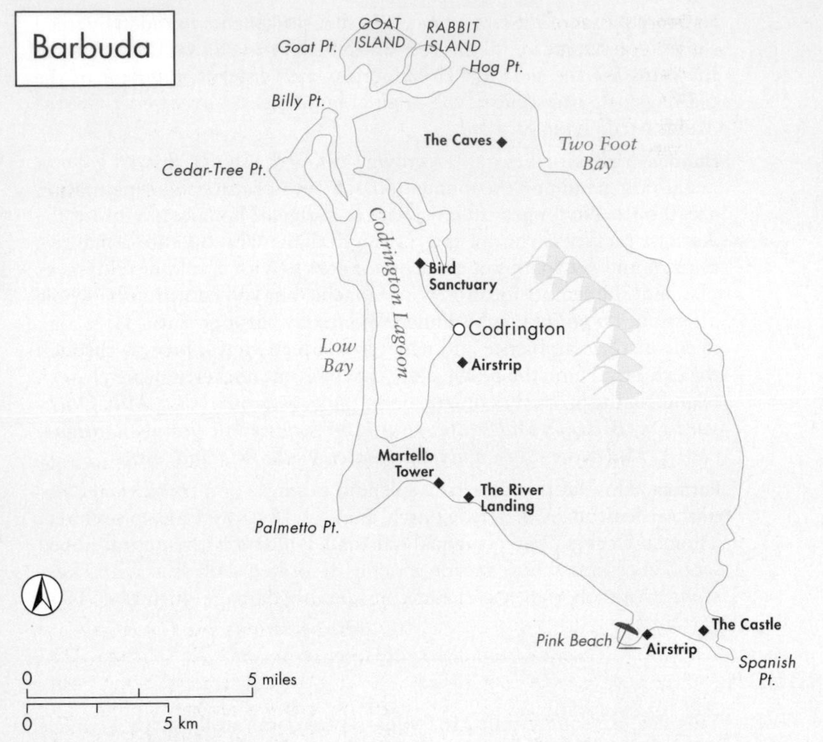

BEACHES

Antigua's beaches are public, and many are lined with resorts that have water-sports outfitters and beach bars. The government does a fairly good job of cleaning up seaweed and garbage. Most restaurants and bars on beaches won't charge for beach-chair rentals if you buy lunch or drinks; otherwise the going rate is $3 to $5. Access to some of the finest stretches, such as those at the Five Islands Peninsula resorts, is restricted to hotel guests (though, often, if you're polite, the guards will let you through). Sunbathing topless is strictly illegal except on one small beach at Hawksbill by Rex Resorts. When cruise ships dock in St. John's, buses drop off loads of passengers on most of the west-coast beaches. Choose such a time to visit one of the more remote east-end beaches or take a day trip to Barbuda.

ANTIGUA

Darkwood Beach. This ½-mile (1-km) beige ribbon on the southwest coast has stunning views of Montserrat. Although popular with locals and cruise-ship passengers on weekends, it's virtually deserted during the week. Waters are generally calm, but there's scant shade, little maintenance, no development other than Darkwood Beach Bar (and

Admiral's Bar across the coastal road), and little to do other than bask in solitude. **Amenities**: food and drink. **Best for**: solitude; swimming. ✉ *2 miles (3 km) south of Jolly Harbour and roughly ½ mile (1 km) southwest of Valley Church, off Valley Rd.*

Dickenson Bay. Along a lengthy stretch of well-kept powder-soft white sand and exceptionally calm water you can find small and large hotels (including Siboney Beach Club, Sandals, and Rex Halcyon Cove), water sports, concessions, and beachfront restaurants (Coconut Grove and Ana's on the Beach are recommended). There's decent snorkeling at either point. **Amenities**: food and drink; water sports. **Best for**: partiers; snorkeling; swimming; walking. ✉ *2 miles (3 km) northeast of St. John's, along main coast road.*

Half Moon Bay. This ½-mile (1-km) ivory crescent is a prime snorkeling and windsurfing area. On the Atlantic side, the water can be rough at times, attracting intrepid hard-core surfers and wakeboarders. The northeastern end, where a protective reef offers spectacular snorkeling, is much calmer. A tiny bar called Tibby's has restrooms, snacks, and beach chairs. Half Moon is a real trek, but one of Antigua's showcase beaches. **Amenities**: food and drink. **Best for**: snorkeling; sunrise; surfing; windsurfing. ✉ *On southeast coast, 1½ mile (2½ km) from Freetown, Dockyard Dr.*

Johnson's Point/Crabbe Hill. This series of connected, deserted beaches on the southwest coast looks out toward Montserrat, Guadeloupe, and St. Kitts. Notable beach bar–restaurants include OJ's, Jacqui O's Beach House, and Turner's. The water is generally placid, though not good for snorkeling. **Amenities**: food and drink. **Best for**: swimming; sunset; walking. ✉ *3 miles (5 km) south of Jolly Harbour complex, on main west-coast road.*

Pigeon Point. Near Falmouth Harbour lie two fine white-sand beaches reasonably free of seaweed and driftwood. The leeward side is calmer, the windward side is rockier, and there are sensational views and snorkeling around the point. Several restaurants and bars are nearby, though Bumpkin's (and its potent banana coladas) and the more upscale bustling Catherine's Cafe Plage satisfy most on-site needs. **Amenities**: food and drink. **Best for**: snorkeling; swimming; walking. ✉ *Off main south-coast road, southwest of Falmouth.*

Runaway Beach. An often unoccupied stretch of bone-white sand, this beach is still rebuilding after years of hurricane erosion, with just enough palms left for shelter. Both the water and the scene are relatively calm, the sand reasonably well-maintained, and beach restaurants such as Sandhaven and La Bussola offer cool shade and cold beer. Hug the lagoon past the entrance to Siboney Beach Club to get here; the Buccaneer Beach Club is the unofficial demarcation point between Dickenson and Runaway Bays. **Amenities**: food and drink. **Best for**: snorkeling; swimming; walking. ✉ *Approximately 2 miles (3 km) northwest of St. John's, down main north-coast road from Dickenson Bay, St. John's.*

BARBUDA

Fodor's Choice ★ **Pink Beach.** You can sometimes walk miles of this classic strand without encountering another footprint. It has a champagne hue, with sand soft as silk; crushed coral often imparts a rosy glint in the sun, hence its unofficial name (officially the part in front of the exclusive former K Club has been renamed Princess Diana Beach). The water can be rough with a strong-ish undertow in spots, though it's mainly protected by the reefs that make the island a diving mecca. Hire a taxi to take you here, since none of the roads are well marked. **Amenities**: none. **Best for**: solitude; snorkeling; walking. ✉ *1 mile (2 km) from ferry and airstrip along unmarked roads.*

WHERE TO EAT

Antigua's restaurants are almost a dying breed since the advent of all-inclusives. But several worthwhile hotel dining rooms and nightspots remain, especially in the English/Falmouth Harbour and Dickenson Bay areas. Virtually every chef incorporates local ingredients and elements of West Indian cuisine.

Most menus list prices in both EC and U.S. dollars; if not, ask which currency the menu is using. Always double-check whether credit cards are accepted and service is included. Dinner reservations are needed during high season.

What to Wear: Perhaps because of the island's British heritage, Antiguans tend to dress more formally for dinner than dwellers on many other Caribbean islands. Wraps and shorts (no beach attire) are de rigueur for lunch, except at local hangouts.

$$$ ECLECTIC ✕ **The Bay @ Nonsuch.** This restaurant's tiered wooden decks, swaddled in billowing white curtains, wrap around the bluff fronting Nonsuch Bay. Chef Mitchell Husbands deftly marries local ingredients to international techniques. His presentation alone is appetizing, the plates painted with swirls of red pepper coulis or basil reduction. The stellar starters are sometimes superior to the fine entrées. For lunch order several, tapas-style: perhaps the chunky yet silken crab cakes perfectly counterpointed by arugula aioli. Or try such creative wraps and panini as pulled pork and jerk mahimahi. For dinner, enjoy cocktails in the refined lounge with the lively mix of yachties and expats, then order soft-shell crab with pink peppercorn marmalade over sweet corn–flavored blini, segueing into blackened mahimahi with coconut- and saffron-infused risotto and *pico de gallo*. U.K.-based wine director Liam Stevenson's small, savvy list is admirably suited to the menu and climate, with selections like Eden Valley Rieslings and Albariños. Or look for the frequent four-course pairing menus and wine events. Finish with the dense, decadent banoffee (banana toffee) pie drowning in warm brandy sauce. [$] *Average main: $28* ✉ *Nonsuch Bay Resort, Hughes Point, Nonsuch Bay, St. Philips* ☎ *268/562–8000, 888/844–2480* 🌐 *www.nonsuchbayresort.com* *Reservations essential* ⊗ *Closed Sept.*

$$ PIZZA ✕ **Big Banana—Pizzas in Paradise.** This tiny, often crowded spot is tucked into one side of a restored 18th-century rum warehouse with broad

plank floors, wood-beam ceiling, and stone archways. Cool, Benetton-style photos of locals and musicians jamming adorn the brick walls. Big Banana serves some of the island's best pizza—try the lobster or the seafood variety—as well as fresh fruit crushes, classic pastas, wraps, burgers, and sub sandwiches bursting at the seams. There's live entertainment some nights, and a large-screen TV for sports fans. *Average main: $18 ✉ Redcliffe Quay, Redcliffe St., St. John's ☎ 268/480–6985 🌐 www.bigbanana-antigua.com ⏲ Closed Sun.*

$$$ ECLECTIC **Cecilia's High Point Café.** The eponymous owner, a vivacious, striking Swedish ex-model, floats (and once in a while flirts) about the tables in this cozy beachfront creole cottage plastered with vivid paintings of sailing and island scenes. An equally animated cross section of Antiguan life usually packs the coveted patio tables (it's a terrific spot to eavesdrop on island gossip), as well as the lounges on the point. The day's selections, including wine specials, are written on a blackboard. Stellar standbys run from goat cheese and caramelized apples in puff pastry to homemade gravlax on potato pancake to mushroom ravioli nestled in spinach with a gossamer creamy pesto, but the high points are the setting and Cecilia herself. As a bonus, Wi-Fi access is free. *Average main: $27 ✉ Dutchman's Bay, Texaco Dock Rd. ☎ 268/562–7070 🌐 www.highpointantigua.com Reservations essential ⏲ Closed Tues. and Wed. No dinner Fri.–Sun.*

$$$ ECLECTIC **Coconut Grove.** Coconut palms grow through the roof of this open-air thatched restaurant, flickering candlelight illuminates colorful local murals, waves lap the white sand, and the waitstaff provides just the right level of service. Jean-François Bellanger's dishes artfully fuse French culinary preparations with island ingredients. Top choices include pan-seared mahimahi served over cauliflower purée with fingerling potatoes and mango-pineapple chutney; and sautéed shrimp with roasted plantain and hickory bacon finished with champagne-Parmesan sauce. The signature coconut shrimp is the best lunch option. The kitchen can be uneven, the wine list is unimaginative and overpriced, and the buzzing happy-hour bar crowd lingering well into dinnertime can detract from the otherwise romantic atmosphere. Nonetheless, Coconut Grove straddles the line between casual beachfront boîte and elegant eatery with aplomb. *Average main: $30 ✉ Siboney Beach Club, Marina Bay Rd., Dickenson Bay ☎ 268/462–1538 🌐 www.coconutgroveantigua.com Reservations essential.*

$$$$ ASIAN FUSION **East.** Imposing Indonesian carved doors usher you into this bold and sexy Asian fusion spot. Flames flicker in the outdoor lily pond while candles illuminate lacquered dark-wood tables with blood-red napery and oversize fuchsia-color chairs. Exquisite pan-Pacific fare (with delicious detours to the Indian subcontinent) courts perfection through simplicity and precision: prawn spring rolls with hoisin–sweet chili sauce; superlative sashimi; entrées from Thai lobster curry to tandoori chicken; and green tea crème brûlée. The small main courses mandate tapas-style dining; the comprehensive wine list is pricey but offers values from intriguing lesser-known regions. Families appreciate the extensive, comparatively inexpensive children's menu. *Average main: $32*

✉ *Carlisle Bay, Old Road* ☎ *268/484–0000* ✍ *Reservations essential* ⏲ *No lunch.*

$$$$ ECLECTIC ✕ **Jacqui O's Love Beach.** A bevy of Bouviers would no doubt adore this stylish beachfront boite, which conjures a St-Tropez–gone-tropical vibe. The Aussie owner Lance Leonhardt visited six islands and 65 properties before settling on this spot. The turquoise throw pillows, fuschsia upholstery, and vivid abstract artworks are a sexy contrast with the giant white canopied beach chairs. The soundtrack, ranging from Pavarotti to Petty, duets harmoniously with the soothing surf; the almost ritualistic dancing between 6 and 8 is purely optional. Lance claims that his kitchen offers the Caribbean's only sous vide molecular cooking. The results are stunning, from tiger prawn ravioli in gossamer lobster sauce kissed with lemongrass and ginger to decadent foie gras burger with veal-truffle dipping sauce to velvety chocolate-crusted *panna cotta*. Pair your selections with the excellent if pricey wines, including superb rosés. Add stellar service and you might walk out feeling like a Kennedy. [$] *Average main: $35* ✉ *Off Valley Rd., Crab Hill* ☎ *268/562–2218* ⏲ *Closed 4 nights weekly; call ahead.*

$$$ ITALIAN Fodor's Choice ★ ✕ **La Bussola.** Blend a genuinely *simpatico* welcome with lapping waves, the murmur of jazz, and expert Italian fare and you have Omar Tagliaventi and family's recipe for the perfect beachfront bistro. Bleached-wood ceilings, old island photos of Antigua, boating paraphernalia, and brightly painted plates enhance the relaxed, romantic mood. The presentation is invariably pretty and Omar has a particularly facile touch with seafood; try the artichoke-shrimp pie in satiny garlic sauce, lobster-asparagus risotto, shark tartare with grapefruit nestling on a bed of arugula, mahimahi with olive "pâté" in filo, or the "fishermen's" spaghetti. Or savor the "true Italian-style" thin-crust pizzas. The carefully considered, affordable wine list showcases lesser-known Italian regions. Your evening ends with a complimentary grappa, Frangelico, or *limoncello* (lemon liqueur), representing northern, central, and southern Italy. La Bussola means "the compass" in Italian, and it certainly takes the right gastronomic direction. [$] *Average main: $25* ✉ *Rush Night Club Rd., Runaway Bay* ☎ *268/562–1545* 🌐 *www.labussolarestaurant.net* ✍ *Reservations essential* ⏲ *Closed Tues.*

$$$$ FRENCH ✕ **Le Bistro.** This Antiguan institution's peach, periwinkle, and pistachio accents subtly match the tile work, jade chairs, mint china, and painted lighting fixtures. Trellises divide the large space into intimate sections. Chef Patrick Gauducheau delights in blending classic regional fare with indigenous ingredients, displaying an especially deft hand with delicate sauces. The kitchen now runs smoothly after bouts of inconsistency. Opt for daily specials, such as smoked marlin carpaccio with pink peppercorns, prawns in a gossamer ginger white wine sauce laced with leeks, lobster medallions in roasted red bell pepper–lime sauce flamed with grappa, and almost anything swaddled in puff pastry. The fine wine list hits all the right spots, geographically and varietally, without outrageous markups. Co-owner Phillipa Esposito doubles as hostess and pastry chef; her passion-fruit mousse and chocolate confections are sublime. [$] *Average main: $34* ✉ *Hodges Bay Rd., Hodges Bay*

☎ 268/462–3881 🌐 *www.antigualebistro.com* ✍ *Reservations essential* ⊙ *Closed Mon. No lunch.*

$$$$ FRENCH ✕ **Le Cap Horn.** As Piaf and Aznavour compete with croaking tree frogs in a trellised, plant-filled room lighted by straw lamps, it's easy to imagine yourself in a tropical St-Tropez. Begin with escargots in tomato, onion, and pepper sauce (sop it up with the marvelous home-baked bread) or the ultimate in hedonism (and expense), lobster–foie gras millefeuille; then segue into tiger shrimp swimming in gossamer vanilla-lobster sauce or duck breast wrapped with mango in rice sheet floating in rum-tamarind sauce. Or cook your own seafood and/or beef on a hot volcanic stone at your table. Gustavo Belaunde (he's Peruvian of Catalan extraction) elicits delicate, almost ethereal flavors from his ingredients; his versatility is displayed in the restaurant's other half, a pizzeria replete with wood-burning oven (with much lower prices and rowdier ambience). Finish with wife Hélène's divine desserts or a cognac and cigar. $ *Average main: $39* ✉ *English Harbour* ☎ *268/460–1194* ⊙ *Closed Aug., Sept., and Thurs. Closed Wed. in low season (May–July, Oct. and Nov.). No lunch.*

$$$$ ECLECTIC ✕ **Pillars Restaurant & Bar.** This restaurant at the Admiral's Inn is a must for Anglophiles and mariners. Soak up the centuries at the inside bar, where 18th-century sailors reputedly carved their ships' names on the dark timbers. Most diners sit on the flagstone terrace under shady Australian gums to enjoy the views of the harbor complex (framed by the namesake pillars) and trendy exhibition kitchen; yachts seem close enough to eavesdrop. The menu is limited but expertly prepared; consider ordering two or three appetizers tapas-style. Specialties include ceviche, lobster toast and the pulled-pork open sandwich with chipotle mayo and red onion marmalade. $ *Average main: $35* ✉ *Dockyard Dr., Nelson's Dockyard, English Harbour* ☎ *268/460–1027* 🌐 *www.admiralsantigua.com* ✍ *Reservations essential.*

$$ CARIBBEAN ✕ **Russell's.** By restoring part of Ft. James, with its glorious views of the bay and headlands, and converting it into a semi-alfresco eatery, Russell's delivers a delightful dining experience. Jazz and reggae on the sound system (live music Friday and Sunday, with open mike Monday), beamed ceilings, cool canvases of musical instruments in fevered Fauvist hues, and red or black hurricane lamps lend a romantic aura to the stone-and-wood terrace. The limited menu—local specialties emphasizing seafood—includes fabulous chunky conch fritters and whelks in garlic butter. Danielle Russell maintains the tradition her father established at this restaurant. Russell's sister Faye co-owns Papa Zouk, and sister Valerie runs Shirley Heights Lookout; the Hodges might well be Antigua's first family of food. $ *Average main: $20* ✉ *Fort James* ☎ *268/462–5479* ⊙ *Closed Tues. No lunch Sun.*

$$$ ECLECTIC Fodor's Choice ★ ✕ **Sheer Rocks.** This sensuous eatery, a series of tiered wood decks carved into a sheer cliff side, showcases the setting sun from the staggered, thatched dining nooks, many separated by billowing white-gauze curtains. White four-poster beds surround infinity pools, making it equally sybaritic for daytime lounging. The menu encompasses a tapestry of creative tapas, many of which can be served in larger portions. Chef Alex Grimley's philosophy emphasizes simplicity, detail, and only the freshest

ingredients to create a symphonic counterpoint of flavors and textures—subtle to lusty, crispy to creamy. He's ably abetted by his new chef de cuisine, Simon Christey-French, who offers his own spin. Witness foie gras parfait with onion purée, lentil vinaigrette and seven-grain toast; decadent truffle mac-'n'-cheese infused with porcini stock; or slow-cooked mahimahi with bok choy, black olives, and saffron sauce. Add a dash of sultry music, season with smashing views, complement with an admirable wine list (not to mention inventive cocktails), and you have the recipe for a tropical St-Tropez experience. It closes more often in low season; call ahead. *Average main: $28 ✉ CocoBay Resort, Valley Rd. ☎ 268/562–4510, 268/464–5283 🌐 www.cocobayresort.com Reservations essential ⊙ Closed Tues. No dinner Sun.*

WHERE TO STAY

Scattered along Antigua's beaches and hillsides are exclusive, elegant hideaways; romantic restored inns; and all-inclusive hot spots for couples. Check individual lodgings for restrictions (many have minimum stays during certain high-season periods). Look also for specials on the Web or from tour packagers, since hotels' quoted rack rates are often negotiable (up to 45% off in season). There are several new condo and villa developments: At this writing, Keyonna Beach, Tamarind Hills, Hodges Bay Club, and South Point Resort are among several other major developments slated to open by late 2015.

$ B&B/INN Fodor's Choice ★ **Admiral's Inn.** This Georgian brick edifice, originally the shipwright's offices in what is now Nelson's Dockyard, has withstood acts of God and war since 1788. **Pros:** historic ambience yet contemporary boutique style; central English Harbour location; fine value; free Wi-Fi; charming restaurant setting. **Cons:** occasionally noisy when yachties take over the bar; recently remodeled bathrooms are still cramped; no beach; no air-conditioning in some units. *Rooms from: $195 ✉ Dockyard Dr., English Harbour ☎ 268/460–1027, 268/460–1153 🌐 www.admiralsantigua.com 18 rooms, 4 suites No meals.*

$$$$ RESORT **Blue Waters Hotel.** A well-heeled Brit crowd goes barefoot at this swank yet understated seaside retreat. **Pros:** pomp without pretension; exquisite setting; huge savings on week-long packages. **Cons:** small beachfront; little steps along the hillside make it less accessible for the physically challenged; difficult to obtain reservations at Bartley's at peak times. *Rooms from: $466 ✉ Boon Point, Atlantic Ave., Soldier's Bay ☎ 268/462–0290, 800/557–6536 reservations only 🌐 www.bluewaters.net 67 rooms, 32 suites, 3 villas, 4 penthouses ⊙ Closed Sept. Multiple meal plans.*

$ RENTAL **Buccaneer Beach Club.** This stylish compound opens onto the quieter part of Dickenson Bay, yet it's merely steps away from the rollicking restaurants and nightlife. **Pros:** free Wi-Fi; quieter part of beach; well-equipped units with flat-screen TVs in the living room and every bedroom; complimentary laundry facilities (individual washer/dryers in the cottages). **Cons:** few facilities on-site; hotel's section of beach sometimes eroded. *Rooms from: $229 ✉ Marina Bay Rd., Dickenson*

Bay ☎ *268/562–6785* 🌐 *www.buccaneerbeach.com* *15 1-bedroom suites, 2 2-bedroom cottages* 🍴 *No meals.*

$$$$ RESORT Fodor'sChoice ★ **Carlisle Bay.** This cosmopolitan, boutique sister property of London's trendy One Aldwych hotel daringly eschews everything faux colonial and creole. **Pros:** luxury resort; attentive service; family-friendly. **Cons:** aggressively hip; lovely beach but often murky water; pricey restaurants; no elevators. $ *Rooms from: $1,020* ✉ *Old Rd., Carlisle Bay* ☎ *268/484–0000, 866/502–2855 reservations only* 🌐 *www.carlisle-bay.com* *82 suites* ⏲ *Closed late Aug.–early Oct.* 🍴 *Breakfast.*

3

$ HOTEL **Catamaran Hotel.** The main building at the congenial cozy harborfront "Cat Club" evokes a plantation great house with verandas, white columns, and hand-carved doors. **Pros:** intimacy; central location; friendly staff; children under 12 stay free; free sailing lessons. **Cons:** small beach (swimming not advised); smallish rooms; surrounding area has limited dining and nightlife options during off-season (May–November). $ *Rooms from: $170* ✉ *Great Fort George Monks Hill Trail, Falmouth Harbour* ☎ *268/460–1036* 🌐 *www.catamaran-antigua.com* *12 rooms, 2 suites* 🍴 *No meals.*

$$$$ ALL-INCLUSIVE **CocoBay.** This healing, hillside hideaway aims to "eliminate all potential worries" by emphasizing simple natural beauty and West Indian warmth. **Pros:** emphasis on local nature and culture, including no room TVs; beautiful views; free Wi-Fi; nice main pool and bar; generally pleasant staff. **Cons:** mediocre food; stifling on breezeless days; difficult climb for those with mobility problems; smallish beaches; bar closes early; poor bedroom lighting. $ *Rooms from: $510* ✉ *Valley Rd., Valley Church* ☎ *268/562–2400, 877/385–6516, 508/506–1006 toll-free in U.S.* 🌐 *www.cocobayresort.com* *49 rooms, 4 2-bedroom houses* 🍴 *All-inclusive.*

$$$$ ALL-INCLUSIVE Fodor'sChoice ★ **Curtain Bluff.** An incomparable beachfront setting, impeccable service, superb extras (free scuba diving), effortless elegance: Curtain Bluff is that rare retreat that stays modern while exuding a magical timelessness. **Pros:** luxury lodging; sublime food, including the new Italian eatery on the beach; beautiful beaches; incredible extras. **Cons:** some find clientele standoffish; lodgings atop bluff not ideal for those with mobility problems; despite offering value, pricey by most standards. $ *Rooms from: $1,230* ✉ *Old Rd., Morris Bay* ☎ *268/462–8400, 888/289–9898 for reservations* 🌐 *www.curtainbluff.com* *18 rooms, 54 suites* ⏲ *Closed late Aug.–late Oct.* 🍴 *All-inclusive.*

$ RENTAL **Dickenson Bay Cottages.** Lush landscaping snakes around the two-story buildings and pool at this small hillside complex, which offers excellent value for families. **Pros:** relatively upscale comfort at down-home prices; walking distance to Dickenson Bay dining and activities. **Cons:** hike from beach; lacks cross-breeze in many units. $ *Rooms from: $170* ✉ *Anchorage Rd., Marble Hill* ☎ *268/462–4940* 🌐 *www.dickensonbaycottages.com* *11 units* 🍴 *No meals.*

$$$$ ALL-INCLUSIVE Fodor'sChoice ★ **Galley Bay.** This posh, adults-only all-inclusive channels the fictional Bali H'ai (with colonial architectural flourishes) on 40 lush acres. **Pros:** luxury lodging; gorgeous beach and grounds; impeccable maintenance; fine food by all-inclusive standards. **Cons:** some lodgings are small and lack a view; outdoor spa can get hot; surf is often too strong for weaker

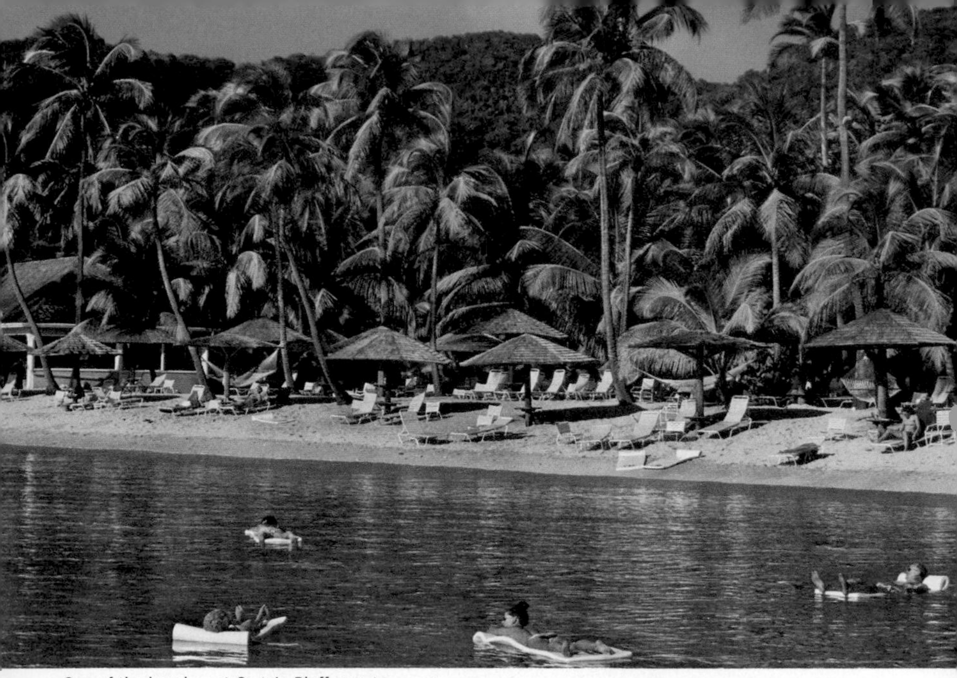
One of the beaches at Curtain Bluff resort

swimmers; only suites have tubs. 💲 *Rooms from: $1,020* ✉ *Grays Farm Rd., Five Islands* ☎ *268/462–0302, 866/237–1644, 800/858–4618 reservations only* 🌐 *www.galleybayresort.com* *98 rooms* ⏲ *Closed mid-Aug.–early Sept.* 🍽 *All-inclusive.*

$$$$ RESORT **Inn at English Harbour.** This genteel resort, long a favorite with Brits and the boating set, is ideal for those seeking beachfront accommodations near English Harbour's attractions, yet it suffers from a split personality. **Pros:** spectacular views; central English Harbour location; stylish rooms; complimentary water sports; appealing spa. **Cons:** tiny beach; uneven food and service; insufficient ventilation in most rooms; high prices. 💲 *Rooms from: $756* ✉ *Freeman's Bay, Dockyard Dr., English Harbour* ☎ *268/460–1014* 🌐 *www.theinn.ag* *28 units* ⏲ *Closed Sept. and Oct.* 🍽 *Some meals.*

$$$ RESORT **Jolly Beach Resort.** If you're looking for basic sun-sand-surf fun, this active resort—Antigua's largest—fits the bill luring a gregarious blend of honeymooners, families, and singles. **Pros:** inexpensive; great range of activities for the price; nice beach; good food for a cheaper all-inclusive; incredible online specials. **Cons:** many cramped, ugly rooms; overrun by tour groups; often impersonal service; lack of elevators and rambling layout make it difficult for the physically challenged. 💲 *Rooms from: $408* ✉ *Valley Rd., Jolly Harbour* ☎ *268/462–0061, 866/905–6559* 🌐 *www.jollybeachresort.com* *461 units, 2 2-bedroom cottages, 1 1-bedroom cottage* 🍽 *Multiple meal plans* ☞ *Supersaver rooms, which are not all-inclusive, cost substantially less.*

$ RENTAL **Jolly Harbour Villas.** These duplex, two-bedroom villas ring the marina of a sprawling, 500-acre compound offering every conceivable facility

CLOSE UP

Other Lodgings to Consider on Antigua

We can't include every property deserving mention without creating an encyclopedia. Consider the following accommodations, many of which are popular with tour operators.

Antigua Yacht Club Marina & Resort. Antigua Yacht Club Marina & Resort is a handsome collection of 19 hotel rooms and 30 studio and one-bedroom condos (for rent when owners are off-island), climbing a hill with stunning marina views. Accommodations are stylish if spare, with island crafts and the occasional high-tech amenity; the adjacent marina is a center of nautical hubbub with several restaurants, pubs, and shops. ✉ *Falmouth Harbour* ☎ *268/562-3030, 888/790-5264, 268/460-1544* 🌐 *www.aycmarina.com.*

Grand Pineapple Beach Resort. Grand Pineapple Beach Resort is a Sandals-owned, Sandals-branded all-inclusive (formerly Allegro/Occidental) on a tranquil beach and hillside amid lush landscaping. It's in the midst of ongoing renovations, restoring its sheen. Buildings containing 180 rooms feature almost edible pastel hues inside and out; the beachfront units and 500 block offer smashing east-coast views. ✉ *Long Bay* ☎ *268/463-2006, 800/327-1991* 🌐 *www.grandpineapple.com.*

Hermitage Bay. Hermitage Bay is a deluxe enclave of 30 beachfront and hillside cottages on a secluded, hard-to-reach but pretty stretch of sand. Affecting a look and ambience that borrow from both Carlisle Bay and Curtain Bluff, the enormous minimalist-chic lodgings include a garden shower and private plunge pool. The kitchen turns out admirable organic fare, much of it sourced from its gardens; the creative mixologists and the spa also utilize local ingredients where possible. ✉ *Hermitage Bay* ☎ *268/562-5500, 855/562-8080 toll-free* 🌐 *www.hermitagebay.com.*

from restaurants and shops to a golf course. **Pros:** nice beach; good value; plentiful recreational, dining, and nightlife choices nearby. **Cons:** mosquito problems; reports of hidden surcharges; inability to charge most restaurants and activities to your villa; some units have 220-volt outlets requiring adapters. 💲 *Rooms from: $170* ✉ *Jolly Harbour* ☎ *268/462-6166, 268/484-6100* 🌐 *www.hbkvillas.com* 🛏 *150 villas* 🍴 *No meals.*

$$$$ ALL-INCLUSIVE FAMILY Fodor's Choice ★

Jumby Bay. This refined resort proffers all the makings of a classic Caribbean private island hideaway, right from the stylish airport sedan pickup, private launch, dockside greeting, and registration at your leisure. **Pros:** isolated private island location; sterling cuisine; free bicycles; inventive, complimentary children's programs; thoughtful extras upon request such as cooking classes and wireless baby monitors; the lovely Sense by Rosewood spa. **Cons:** isolated private island location; jet noise occasionally disturbs the main beach. 💲 *Rooms from: $1,595* ✉ *Burma Rd., Long Island* ☎ *268/462-6000, 888/767-3966* 🌐 *www.jumbybayresort.com* 🛏 *40 suites, 14 villas* 🍴 *All-inclusive.*

$$ RESORT FAMILY Fodor's Choice ★ **Nonsuch Bay Resort.** This exclusive 40-acre compound's handsome, gabled Georgian-style buildings cascade down the lushly landscaped hillside to the eponymous bay, flecked with sails. **Pros:** contemporary luxury; fully equipped units; standout cuisine; lovely beach and setting; superlative sailing fleet and lessons; free Wi-Fi. **Cons:** remote settting mandates a car; pretty but poky beach; hilly layout presents mobility challenges. *Rooms from: $333* ✉ *Hughes Point, Nonsuch Bay, St. Philips* ☎ *268/562–8000, 888/844–2480* 🌐 *www.nonsuchbayresort.com* *13 1-bedroom apartments, 16 2-bedroom apartments, 8 3-bedroom apartments, 7 2-bedroom cottages, 7 3-bedroom residences, 4 villas* ⏲ *Closed Sept.* *Some meals.*

$ B&B/INN **Ocean Inn.** Views of English Harbour, affable management, and affordability distinguish this homey inn. **Pros:** fabulous views; affable staff; inexpensive. **Cons:** rickety paths down a steep hill linking cottages; worn rooms need updating; Wi-Fi dodgy; gym is very basic and public. *Rooms from: $110* ✉ *English Harbour* ☎ *268/463–7950* 🌐 *www.theoceaninn.com* *6 rooms, 4 with bath; 4 cottages* *Breakfast.*

$$$$ ALL-INCLUSIVE **St. James's Club.** Management has diligently smartened the public spaces and exquisite landscaping here, taking full advantage of the peerless location straddling 100 acres on Mamora Bay. **Pros:** splendid remote location; beautiful beaches and landscaping; complimentary Wi-Fi in public areas and Royal Suites; plentiful activities; additional adult pools offer more privacy. **Cons:** remote location makes a car a necessity for non-all-inclusive guests; tour groups can overrun the resort; uneven food and service; sprawling hilly layout not ideal for physically challenged. *Rooms from: $760* ✉ *Dockyard Dr., Mamora Bay* ☎ *268/460–5000, 800/858–4618 reservations only, 866/237–2071* 🌐 *www.stjamesclubantigua.com* *215 rooms, 72 villas (usually 40 in rental pool)* *All-inclusive.*

$$$$ ALL-INCLUSIVE **Sandals Grande Antigua Resort & Spa.** The sumptuous public spaces, lovely beach, glorious gardens, and plethora of facilities almost mask this resort's impersonal atmosphere. **Pros:** lively atmosphere; excellent spa; good dining options; huge online advance booking savings. **Cons:** sprawling layout; too bustling; uneven service. *Rooms from: $624* ✉ *Dickenson Bay* ☎ *888/726–3257 reservations only, 268/484–0100* 🌐 *www.sandals.com* *100 rooms, 257 suites, 16 rondavels* *All-inclusive* ☞ *3-night minimum.*

$$ HOTEL Fodor's Choice ★ **Siboney Beach Club.** This affordable beachfront oasis nestled in a tranquil corner of Dickenson Bay delights with intimacy and warmth, and knowledgeable Aussie owner Tony Johnson gladly acts as a de facto tourist board. **Pros:** friendly service; superb location; great value; well maintained with rooms smartly refurbished regularly. **Cons:** no TV in bedrooms; patios lack screens, thus forcing a choice between sweltering and swatting pests on rare still days; no elevator; inconsistent Wi-Fi signal. *Rooms from: $315* ✉ *Dickenson Bay* ☎ *268/462–0806, 800/533–0234, 620/420–0334 Vonage in U.S.* 🌐 *www.siboneybeachclub.com* *12 suites* *No meals.*

$$$$ ALL-INCLUSIVE FAMILY **Verandah Resort & Spa.** Verandah's splendid hillside setting overlooks calm, reef-protected Dian Bay, and hiking trails snake around the property to Devil's Bridge National Park. **Pros:** gorgeous remote location;

sprawling but cleverly centralized; good kids' club and facilities with own pool; frequent discounted packages. **Cons:** smallish beaches; noise carries between adjoining units; inconsistent service; though shuttles ply the resort, its hilly layout is problematic for the physically challenged. *Rooms from: $710* ✉ *Long Bay* ☎ *268/562–6848, 800/858–4618, 866/237–1785 reservations only* 🌐 *www.verandahresortandspa.com* *200 suites* *All-inclusive.*

NIGHTLIFE

Most of Antigua's evening entertainment takes place at the resorts, which occasionally present calypso singers, steel bands, limbo dancers, and folkloric groups. Check with the tourist office for up-to-date information. In addition, a cluster of clubs and bars pulsate into the night in season around English and Falmouth Harbours.

BARS

Abracadabra. It's always a party at busy, bright trattoria Abracadabra. Late nights often turn into a disco with live music from jazz to soca or DJs spinning reggae and 1980s dance music, while special events run from art exhibits to masquerades to fashion shows to fire-eating performances. There's even a fine late-night Italian snack menu and a fun, funky boutique. ✉ *Nelson's Dockyard, English Harbour* ☎ *268/460–2701* 🌐 *www.theabracadabra.com.*

Ana's on the Beach. This enormous, multi-tier, mostly alfresco beach bar–cum–art gallery styles itself a restaurant-lounge. Although the ramrod chrome-finished chairs make for rigid seating, the loud music begs for earplugs, and the globe-trotting menu is too ambitious, this is nonetheless a happening spot and prime meet market. The friendly staff is garbed in black pants and bubblegum pink shirts (stenciled "love is in the air"), the cocktails are fairly inventive, and the rotating art on the walls, including an epoxy-painted surfboard dangling from the white-beamed ceiling, displays a savvy selection of the hottest up-and-coming local artists in various media. ✉ *Dickenson Bay* ☎ *268/562–8562* 🌐 *www.anas.ag.*

Carmichael's. Carmichael's is the fine-dining hilltop aerie at the Sugar Ridge residential complex. Nestle into a banquette or lounge in the infinity pool while sipping luscious libations that match the setting sun's colorful display. It's also a splendid spot for a postprandial cigar and port or single malt. You can always head downhill to sister nightspot, the bustling, buzzing **Sugar Club** (by the resort entrance) for live music (jazz to funk) and DJ disco evenings. ✉ *Tottenham Park, across from Jolly Harbour* ☎ *268/562–7700* 🌐 *www.sugarridgeantigua.com.*

Indigo on the Beach. Indigo on the Beach is a soigné spot, yet it's relaxed and great any time of day for creative tapas, salads, grills, and burgers, but the beautiful people turn out in force come evening to pose at the fiber-optically lighted bar, or on white lounges scattered with throw pillows. ✉ *Carlisle Bay, Old Road* ☎ *268/480–0000.*

Inn at English Harbour Bar. The Inn at English Harbour Bar, with its green leather, wood beams, fieldstone walls, 19th-century maps, steering-wheel chandeliers, petit point upholstery, and maritime prints, is uncommonly refined. ✉ *English Harbour* ☎ *268/460–1014.*

Mad Mongoose. The Mad Mongoose is a wildly popular yachty (and singles') joint, splashed in vivid Rasta colors, with tapas and martini menus, live music Fridays (and some Tuesdays), joyous happy hours, a game room with foosball and pool tables, and satellite TV. ✉ *Falmouth Harbour* ☎ *268/463–7900* 🌐 *www.madmongooseantigua.com.*

Mainbrace Pub. The Mainbrace Pub has a historic ambience, right down to its warm brick walls and hardwood accents, and is known as a beer, darts, and fish-and-chips kind of hangout for the boating set. ✉ *Copper & Lumber Store Hotel, English Harbour* ☎ *268/460–1058.*

Fodor's Choice ★ **Shirley Heights Lookout.** Sunday-afternoon barbecues continue into the night with reggae, soca, and steel-band music and dancing that sizzles like the ribs on the grill. Residents and visitors gather for boisterous fun, the latest gossip, and great sunsets. Most tourist groups vanish by 7 pm, when the real partying begins. Admission is EC$20. There's occasionally another, less frenetic party Thursday evenings called Made in Pride in Antigua, which in addition to barbecue serves up traditional food, drink, crafts and music. ✉ *Shirley Heights* ☎ *268/460–1785, 268/728–0636, 268/764–0389* 🌐 *www.shirleyheightslookout.com* ⏲ *Closed Mon.*

Trappas. Trappas is a hipster hangout set in a bamboo-walled courtyard hung with huge hibiscus paintings. It serves delectable, sizable tapas (tuna sashimi, deep-fried Brie with blackcurrant jelly, Thai mango chicken curry, beer-batter shrimp with garlic dip) for reasonable prices (EC$26–EC$52) into the wee hours. Live music is often on the menu. ✉ *Main Rd., English Harbour* ☎ *268/562–3534.*

CASINOS

King's Casino. You can find abundant slots and gaming tables at the somewhat dilapidated, unintentionally retro (icicle chandeliers, Naugahyde seats, and 1970s soul crooners on the sound system) King's Casino. The best time to go is Friday and Saturday nights, which jump with energetic karaoke competitions, live bands, and dancing. ✉ *Heritage Quay, St. John's* ☎ *268/462–1727* 🌐 *www.kingscasino.com.*

SHOPPING

Antigua's duty-free shops are at Heritage Quay, one reason so many cruise ships call here. Bargains can be found on perfumes, liqueurs, and liquor (including English Harbour Antiguan rum), jewelry, china, and crystal. As for other local items, check out straw hats, baskets, batik, pottery, Susie's hot sauce, and hand-printed cotton clothing. Fine artists to look for include Gilly Gobinet (neo-postimpressionist island-scapes), Heather Doram (exquisite, intricately woven collage wall hangings), Jan Farara, Jennifer Meranto (incomparable hand-painted black-and-white photos of Caribbean scenes), and Heike Petersen (delightful dolls and quilts). Several artists and craftspeople have banded together to form 🌐 *www.antiguanartists.com*, which lists their information, including whether they accept atelier visits by appointment. **■ TIP→ Many businesses in the English/Falmouth Harbours area close from June to October. Call ahead to confirm hours of operation.**

3

SHOPPING AREAS

Fodor'sChoice ★ **Heritage Quay,** in St. John's, has 35 shops—including many that are duty-free—that cater to the cruise-ship crowd, which docks almost at its doorstep. Outlets here include Benetton, the Body Shop, Sunglass Hut, Dolce & Gabbana, and Oshkosh B'Gosh. There are also shops along **St. John's, St. Mary's, High,** and **Long Streets.** The tangerine-and-lilac-hue four-story **Vendor's Mall** at the intersection of Redcliffe and Thames streets gathers the pushy, pesky vendors who once clogged the narrow streets. It's jammed with stalls; air-conditioned indoor shops sell some higher-price, if not higher-quality, merchandise. On the west coast the Mediterranean-style, arcaded **Jolly Harbour Marina** holds some interesting galleries and shops, as do the marinas and the main road snaking around English and Falmouth Harbours.

Redcliffe Quay, on the waterfront at the south edge of St. John's, is by far the most appealing shopping area. Several restaurants and more than 30 boutiques, many with one-of-a-kind wares, are set around landscaped courtyards shaded by colorful trees.

ALCOHOL AND TOBACCO

Manuel Dias Liquor Store. Head to Manuel Dias Liquor Store for a wide selection of Caribbean rums and liqueurs. ✉ *Long and Market Sts., St. John's* ☎ *268/462–0490.*

Quin Farara. You'll find terrific deals on both liquor and wines as well as cigars at Quin Farara. ✉ *Long St. and Corn Alley, St. John's* ☎ *268/462–3869* ✉ *Jolly Harbour* ☎ *268/462–6245* ✉ *Heritage Quay, St. John's* ☎ *268/462–1737, 268/462–3197.*

ART

Fodor'sChoice ★ **Harmony Hall.** This is Antigua's top exhibition venue. A large space is used for one-person shows; other rooms display works in various media, from Aussie Aboriginal carvings to Antillean pottery. The sublime historic ambience, sweeping vistas, and fine Italian fare compensate for the remote location. ✉ *Brown's Mill Bay, Brown's Mill* ☎ *268/460–4120* 🌐 *www.harmonyhallantigua.com.*

BOOKS AND MAGAZINES

Best of Books. This bookstore is an excellent, extensive source for everything from local cookbooks and nature guides to international newspapers. Check out the works of Jamaica Kincaid, whose writing about her native Antigua has won international acclaim. You'll also find an intriguing selection of crafts and artworks. ✉ *Lower St. Mary's St., St. John's* ☎ *268/562–3198.*

CLOTHING

Exotic Antigua. This shop sells everything from antique Indonesian ikat throws to crepe de chine caftans to Tommy Bahama resort wear. ✉ *Redcliffe Quay, St. John's* ☎ *268/562–1288.*

Galley Boutique. At Galley Boutique, Janey Easton personally seeks out exclusive creations from both international (Calvin Klein, Adrienne Vittadini) and local Caribbean designers, ranging from swimwear to evening garb. She also sells handicrafts and lovely hammocks. There's also a small outpost at Pigeon Point beach. ✉ *Nelson's Dockyard, English Harbour* ☎ *268/460–1525.*

Jacaranda. This shop sells batik, sarongs, and swimwear as well as Caribbean food, perfumes, soaps, and artwork. ✉ *Redcliffe Quay, St. John's* ☎ *268/462–1888.*

New Gates. For duty-free threads, head to New Gates, an authorized dealer for such name brands as Ralph Lauren, Calvin Klein, and Tommy Hilfiger. ✉ *Redcliffe Quay, St. John's* ☎ *268/562–1627.*

Noreen Phillips. Glitzy appliquéd and beaded evening wear—inspired by the colors of the sea and sunset—in sensuous fabrics ranging from chiffon and silk to Italian lace and Indian brocade are created at Noreen Phillips. ✉ *Redcliffe Quay, St. John's* ☎ *268/462–3127.*

Sunseakers. At Sunseakers, you'll find every conceivable bathing suit and cover-up—from bikini thongs to sarongs—by top designers. ✉ *Heritage Quay, St. John's* ☎ *268/462–3618.*

DUTY-FREE GOODS

Abbott's. You'll find luxury items from Breitling watches to Belleek china to Kosta Boda art glass in a luxurious, air-conditioned showroom at Abbott's. ✉ *Heritage Quay, St. John's* ☎ *268/462–3107* 🌐 *www.abbottsjewellery.com.*

Lipstick. You'll find high-priced imported scents and cosmetics—from Clarins to Clinique and Gucci to Guerlain—at Lipstick. ✉ *Heritage Quay, St. John's* ☎ *268/562–1133.*

Passions. This shop gives Abbott's a run for its (and your) considerable money on luxury brands like Chanel, Hermès, and Lalique. ✉ *Heritage Quay, St. John's* ☎ *268/562–5295.*

HANDICRAFTS

Cedars Pottery. The airy studio of Michael and Imogen Hunt is Cedars Pottery. Michael produces a vivid line of domestic ware and Zen-simple teapots, vases, and water fountains featuring rich earth hues and sensuous lines. Imogen fashions ethereal paper-clay fish sculptures, and mask-shaped, intricately laced light fixtures and candelabras. Take time to savor their lush gardens where found objects and sculptural installations emerge like restless sprites from the ground. ✉ *St. Clare Estate, Buckleys Rd., Buckleys* ☎ *268/460–5293* 🌐 *www.cedarspottery.com.*

Eureka. The offerings at Eureka span the globe, from Azerbaijani hand-blown glass to Zambian weavings and carvings. ✉ *Thames St., St. John's* ☎ *268/560–3654.*

Isis. Island and international baubles and bric-a-brac, such as antique jewelry, hand-carved walking sticks, elaborate chess sets, and glazed pottery, are available at Isis. ✉ *Redcliffe Quay, St. John's* ☎ *268/462–4602.*

Pottery Shop. This shop sells the work of gifted potter Sarah Fuller, whose hand-painted tiles, wind chimes, and plates and cobalt-blue glazes are striking (as are her driftwood hangings mixed with clay and copper). You can also visit her studio–gallery on Dutchman's Bay. ✉ *Redcliffe Quay, St. John's* ☎ *268/562–1264 studio-gallery, 268/462–5503 shop* 🌐 *www.sarahfullerpottery.com.*

Rhythm of Blue Gallery. Nancy Nicholson co-owns Rhythm of Blue Gallery; she's renowned for her exquisite glazed and matte-finish ceramics, featuring Caribbean-pure shades, as well as her black-and-white yachting photos and flowing batik creations. You'll also find exhibitions showcasing leading regional artists working in media from batik to copper. ✉ *Dockyard Dr., English Harbour* ☎ *268/562–2230* 🌐 *www.rhythmofblue.com.*

JEWELRY

Colombian Emeralds. The Antiguan branch of the largest retailer of Colombian emeralds in the world also carries a wide variety of other gems. ✉ *Heritage Quay, St. John's* ☎ *268/462–3462* 🌐 *www.colombianemeralds.com/ourstores/antigua.*

Diamonds International. You'll find a huge selection of loose diamonds as well as a variety of watches, rings, brooches, bracelets, and pendants at Diamonds International. Several resorts have branches. ✉ *Heritage Quay, St. John's* ☎ *268/481–1880.*

Goldsmitty. Hans Smit is the Goldsmitty, an expert goldsmith who turns gold, black coral, petrified coral (which he dubs Antiguanite), and precious and semiprecious stones into one-of-a-kind works of art. ✉ *Redcliffe Quay, St. John's* ☎ *268/462–4601* 🌐 *www.goldsmitty.com.*

SPORTS AND THE OUTDOORS

Several all-inclusives offer day passes that permit use of all sporting facilities, from tennis courts to water-sports concessions, as well as free drinks and meals. The cost begins at $50 for singles (but can be as much as $200 for couples at Sandals), and hours generally run from 8 am to 6 pm, with extensions available until 2 am. Antigua has long been famed for its cricketers (such as Viv Richards and Richie Richardson); aficionados will find one of the Caribbean's finest cricket grounds right by the airport, with major test matches running January through June.

ADVENTURE TOURS

Antigua is developing its ecotourist opportunities, and several memorable offshore experiences involve more than just snorkeling. The archipelago of islets coupled with a full mangrove swamp off the northeast coast is unique in the Caribbean.

Adventure Antigua. The enthusiastic Eli Fuller, who is knowledgeable not only about the ecosystem and geography of Antigua but also about its history and politics (his grandfather was the American consul), runs Adventure Antigua. His thorough seven-hour excursion (Eli dubs it "re-creating my childhood explorations") includes stops at Guiana Island (for lunch and guided snorkeling; turtles, barracuda, and stingrays are common sightings), Pelican Island (more snorkeling), Bird Island (hiking to vantage points to admire the soaring ospreys and frigate and red-billed tropic birds), and Hell's Gate (a striking limestone rock formation where the more intrepid may hike and swim through sunken caves and tide pools painted with pink and maroon algae). The company also offers a fun "Xtreme Circumnavigation" variation on a racing boat catering to adrenaline junkies who "feel the need for speed" that also visits Stingray City and Nelson's Dockyard, as well as a more sedate Antigua Classic Yacht sail-and-snorkel experience that explains the rich West Indian history of boatbuilding. ☎ *268/727–3261, 268/726–6355* 🌐 *www.adventureantigua.com.*

"Paddles" Kayak Eco Adventure. "Paddles" Kayak Eco Adventure takes you on a 3½-hour tour of serene mangroves and inlets with informative narrative about the fragile ecosystem of the swamp and reefs and the rich diversity of flora and fauna. The tour ends with a hike to sunken caves and snorkeling in the North Sound Marine Park, capped by a rum punch at the fun creole-style clubhouse nestled amid botanic gardens. Experienced guides double as kayaking and snorkeling instructors, making this an excellent opportunity for novices. Conrad and Jennie's brainchild is one of Antigua's better bargains. ✉ *Seaton's Village* ☎ *268/463–1944* 🌐 *www.antiguapaddles.com.*

FAMILY **Stingray City Antigua.** Stingray City Antigua is a carefully reproduced "natural" environment nicknamed by staffers the "retirement home," though the 30-plus stingrays, ranging from infants to seniors, are frisky. You can stroke, feed, even hold the striking gliders ("they're like puppy dogs," one guide swears), as well as snorkel in deeper, protected waters. The tour guides do a marvelous job of explaining the animals' habits, from feeding to breeding, and their predators (including man). ✉ *Seaton's Village* ☎ *268/562–7297* 🌐 *www.stingraycityantigua.com.*

BOATING

Antigua's circular geographic configuration makes boating easy, and its many lovely harbors and coves provide splendid anchorages. Experienced boaters will particularly enjoy Antigua's east coast, which is far more rugged and has several islets; be sure to get a good nautical map, as there are numerous minireefs that can be treacherous. If you're just looking for a couple of hours of wave-hopping, stick to the Dickenson Bay or Jolly Harbour area.

Nicholson Yacht Charters. Nicholson Yacht Charters are real professionals, true pioneers in Caribbean sailing, with three generations spanning 60 years of experience. A long-established island family, they can offer you anything from a 20-foot ketch to a giant schooner. ✉ *English Harbour* ☎ *268/460–1530, 305/433–5533* 🌐 *www.nicholson-charters.com.*

Ondeck. Ondeck runs skippered charters on the likes of Farr and Beneteau out of the Antigua Yacht Club Marina in Falmouth Harbour, terrific one- and two-day sailing workshops, and eco-adventure trips to Montserrat on a racing yacht. You can even participate in official regattas. Instructors and crew are all seasoned racers. Bareboating options and sunset cruises are also available. ☎ *268/562–6696* 🌐 *www.ondeckoceanracing.com.*

Sunsail. Sunsail has an extensive modern fleet of dinghies and 32-foot day-sailers starting at $25 per half day, $50 for a full day (always call in advance, as the Nelson's Dockyard office is open sporadically). But its primary focus is bareboat yachting, often in conjunction with hotel stays; a week starts at $4,739. ☎ *268/460–2615, 888/350–3568, 877/651–4710* 🌐 *www.sunsail.com.*

DIVING

Antigua is an unsung diving destination, with plentiful undersea sights to explore, from coral canyons to sea caves. Barbuda alone features roughly 200 wrecks on its treacherous reefs. The most accessible wreck is the 1890s bark *Andes,* not far out in Deep Bay, off Five Islands Peninsula. Among the favorite sites are **Green Island, Cades Reef,** and **Bird Island** (a national park). Memorable sightings include turtles, stingrays, and barracuda darting amid basalt walls, hulking boulders, and stray 17th-century anchors and cannon. One advantage is accessibility in many spots for shore divers and snorkelers. Double-tank dives run about $90.

Dockyard Divers. Owned by British ex-merchant seaman Captain A.G. "Tony" Fincham, Dockyard Divers is one of the island's most established outfits and offers diving and snorkeling trips, PADI courses, and dive packages with accommodations. They're geared to seasoned divers (two-tank dives are a quite reasonable $89), but staff work patiently with novices. Tony is a wonderful source of information on the island; ask him about the "Fincham's Follies" musical extravaganza he produces for charity. ✉ *Nelson's Dockyard, English Harbour* ☎ *268/460–1178* 🌐 *www.dockyard-divers.com.*

FISHING

Antigua's waters teem with game fish such as marlin, wahoo, and tuna. Most boat trips include equipment, lunch, and drinks. Figure at least $495 for a half day, $790 for a full day, for up to six people.

Obsession. The 45-foot Hatteras Convertible Sportfisherman *Obsession* has top-of-the-line equipment, including an international-standard fighting chair, Rupp outriggers, and handcrafted rods. Also available is the new 55-foot Hatteras Sportfisherman, the *Double Header.* Beer and soft drinks are included in the rates. Captain Derek Biel is a seasoned sea salt, a certified I.G.F.A. Ambassador who has competed in many tournaments over the past quarter century. ☏ *268/462–3174* 🌐 *www.charternet.com/charters/obsession* 🎟 *$600 per half-day, $1,000 for 8 hrs.*

Overdraft. Frankie Hart, a professional fisherman who knows the waters intimately and regales clients with stories of his trade, operates *Overdraft,* a spacious, fiberglass 40-footer outfitted with the latest techno-gadgetry. He also rents the 26-foot *H2O,* a ProKat versatile enough to accommodate fly-fishing and deeper-water bay bait fishing. ✉ *English Harbour* ☏ *268/464–4954, 268/463–3112* 🌐 *www.antiguafishing.com* 🎟 *From $495.*

GOLF

Though Antigua hardly qualifies as a duffer's delight, its two 18-hole courses offer varied layouts.

Cedar Valley Golf Club. Finished as Antigua's first 18-hole golf course in 1977, Cedar Valley is not particularly well-maintained terrain, but nonethess offers some attractive vistas and challenges with narrow hilly fairways and numerous doglegs (Hole 7 is a perfect example). The 5th hole has exceptional ocean vistas from the top of the tee, and the par-5 9th offers the trickiest design with steep slopes and swales. Carts are $42 ($22 for 9 holes). And unlimited weekly golf pass costs $220. The Spinach! Cafe offers free Wi-Fi. ✉ *Friar's Hill* ☏ *268/462–0161* 🌐 *www.cedarvalleygolf.ag* 🎟 *$60 ($31 for 9 holes)* ⛳ *18 holes, 6157 yards, par 70.*

Jolly Harbour Golf Course. The flat Florida-style layout of Jolly Harbour was designed by Karl Litten. It's lushly tropical with the trade winds a challenge. Seven lakes add to the challenge, but the facility struggles with conditioning. The 15th is the signature hole, with a sharp dog-leg and long carry over two hazards. Unfortunately, despite improved maintenance, fairways are often dry and patchy, drainage is poor, and the pro shop and "19th hole" are barely adequate. Visitors can participate in regular tournaments and "meet-and-greet" events. ✉ *Jolly Harbour* ☏ *268/462–7771* 🌐 *www.jollyharbourantigua.com/golf* 🎟 *$57.50 ($97.75 including cart); $34.50 for 9 holes, $23 for cart* ⛳ *18 holes, 5587 yards, par 71.*

GUIDED TOURS

Almost all taxi drivers double as guides; an island tour with one costs about $25 an hour. Every major hotel has a cabbie on call and may be able to negotiate a discount, particularly off-season. Several operators specialize in off-road four-wheel-drive adventures that provide a taste of island history and topography.

Island Safaris. Four-wheel off-road adventures by Island Safaris, which also runs other land- and water-based excursions, enables you to fully appreciate the island's natural beauty, history, folklore, and cultural heritage as you zoom about the southwest part of Antigua. Hiking is involved, though it's not strenuous. Lunch and snorkeling are also included. Active adventurers will particularly enjoy the combo Land Rover–kayak outback ecotour. Prices start at $99 per adult, $60–$75 children 7–12. ☎ *268/480–1225* 🌐 *www.tropicaladventures-antigua.com.*

Scenic Tours. Scenic Tours gives affordable half- and full-day island tours, geared toward cruise passengers, that focus on such highlights as Devil's Bridge, Shirley Heights, and English Harbour, as well as soft adventure hikes. ✉ *Woods Mall, St. John's* ☎ *268/764–3060, 888/271–4004* 🌐 *www.scenictoursantigua.com.*

HORSEBACK RIDING

Comparatively dry Antigua is best for beach rides, though you won't find anything wildly romantic and deserted à la *Black Stallion.*

Antigua Equestrian Center. The former Spring Hill Riding Club specializes in equestrian lessons in show jumping and dressage but also offers $65 hour-long trail rides on the beach or through the bush past ruined forts, $125 for two hours (bareback riding in the ocean is an additional $45); half-hour private lessons from a British Horse Society instructor are $35. ✉ *Falmouth Harbour* ☎ *268/460–7787, 268/773–3139* 🌐 *www.antiguaequestrian.com.*

SAILING AND SNORKELING

Not a sailor yourself? Consider signing up for one of the following boat tours. Each tour provides a great opportunity to enjoy the seafaring life while someone else captains the ship.

Miguel's Holiday Adventures. Miguel's Holiday Adventures leaves every Tuesday, Thursday, and Saturday morning at 10 am from the Hodges Bay jetty for snorkeling, rum punches, and lunch at Prickly Pear Island, which offers both shallow and deepwater snorkeling, as well as hiking. In this comfortable family operation, Miguel's wife, Josephine, prepares an authentic, lavish West Indian buffet including lobster, and Miguel and his son Terrence are caring instructors. ☎ *268/460–9978, 268/772–3213, 268/723–7418 mobile* 🌐 *www.pricklypearisland.com.*

Tropical Adventures. Barbuda day trips on the catamaran *Excellence* overflow with rum and high spirits, as do circumnavigations of Antigua. Tropical Adventures also operates eco-kayaking tours and slightly more sedate, intimate catamaran cruises from sunset to snorkeling on the *Mystic.* ☎ *268/480–1225* 🌐 *www.tropicaladventures-antigua.com* 🎫 *From $105.*

Wadadli Cats. Wadadli Cats offers several cruises, including a circumnavigation of the island and snorkeling at Bird Island or Cades Reef, on its five sleek catamarans, including the handsome, fully outfitted *Spirit of Antigua.* Prices are fair ($95–$110), and advance direct bookers get a free T-shirt. ☎ *268/462–4792* 🌐 *www.wadadlicats.com.*

WINDSURFING AND KITEBOARDING

Most major hotels offer windsurfing equipment. The best areas are Nonsuch Bay and the east coast (notably Half Moon and Willoughby bays), which is slightly less protected and has a challenging juxtaposition of sudden calms and gusts.

KiteAntigua. KiteAntigua offers lessons in the Caribbean's hot new sport, kiteboarding, where a futuristic surfboard with harness is propelled only by an inflated kite; kiteboard rentals (for the certified) are also available at $30 per hour, $50 half day, $70 full day. The varied multiday lesson packages are expensive but thorough; a four-hour private beginners course is $280. KiteAntigua closes from September through November, when winds aren't optimal. The center is on a stretch near the airport, but road trips to secret spots are arranged for experienced kitesurfers seeking that sometimes harrowing "high." ✉ *Jabberwock Beach* ☎ *268/720–5483, 268/727–3983* 🌐 *www.kitesurfantigua.com.*

Windsurfing Antigua. Patrick Scales of Windsurfing Antigua has long been one of Antigua's, if not the Caribbean's, finest instructors; he now offers a mobile service in high season. He provides top-flight equipment for $30 per hour (first hour; $25 subsequent hours, $70 per half day, and $80 per day), two-hour beginner lessons for $90, and specialty tours to Half Moon Bay and other favorite spots for experienced surfers. ✉ *Jabberwock Beach* ☎ *268/461–9463, 268/773–9463* 🌐 *www.windsurfantigua.net.*

ZIP-LINING

Antigua Rainforest Canopy Tours. Release your inner Tarzan at Antigua Rainforest Canopy Tours. You should be in fairly good condition for the ropes challenges, which require upper-body strength and stamina; there are height and weight restrictions. But anyone (vertigo or acrophobia sufferers, beware) can navigate the intentionally rickety "Indiana Jones–inspired" suspension bridges, then fly (in secure harnesses) 200-300 feet above a rain-forest-filled valley from one towering turpentine tree to the next on lines with names like "Screamer" and "Leap of Faith." There are 23 stations, as well as a bar–café and interpretive signage. First-timers, fear not: the "rangers" are affable, amusing, and accomplished. Admission varies slightly, but is usually $85 and up. It's open Monday–Saturday from 8 to 6, with two scheduled tours at 9:15, 10:15, and 11:15 (other times by appointment). ✉ *Fig Tree Dr., Wallings* ☎ *268/562–6363* 🌐 *www.antiguarainforest.com.*

ARUBA

WELCOME TO ARUBA

California Pt.
Arashi Beach
Californian Wreck
Caribbean Sea
California Lighthouse
Tierra del Sol Golf Course
Malmok Beach
Malmok Reef
11
Antilla Shipwreck
Debbie II
1A/B
2A/B
Mt. Altovista
Alto Vista Chapel
Fisherman's Huts
Bushiribana
10
Butterfly Farm
Aruba Ostrich Farm
Pedernalis Wreck
9
Andicouri
Palm Beach
Noord
6-8
Tanki Leedert
Paradera
Eagle/Palm Beach Restaurants and Hotels see detail map
4A/B
Rock Formations
Eagle Beach
6A/B
J.E. Irausquin Blvd.
Mt. Hooiberg
7A/B
Santa Cruz
Manchebo Beach
Druif Bay
L.G. Smith Blvd.
Oranjestad
1-5
1
Reina Beatrix International Airport
Jane Sea Wreck

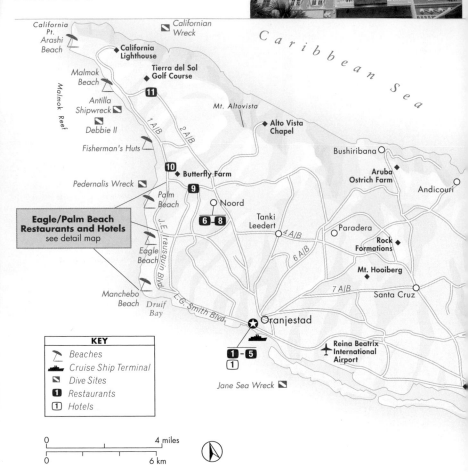

KEY
Beaches
Cruise Ship Terminal
Dive Sites
Restaurants
Hotels

0 4 miles
0 6 km

The pastel-color houses of Dutch settlers still grace the waterfront in the capital city of Oranjestad. Winds are fierce, even savage, on the north coast, where you'll find a landscape of cacti, rocky desert, and wind-bent divi-divi trees. On the west coast the steady breezes attract windsurfers to the shallow, richly colored waters.

THE A IN THE ABC ISLANDS

The A in the ABC Islands (followed by Bonaire and Curaçao), Aruba is small—only 19½ miles (31½ km) long and 6 miles (9½ km) across at its widest point. It became an independent entity (Status Aparte) within the Netherlands in 1986. The official language is Dutch, but the local language is Papiamento, though almost every native speaks English and Spanish as well. The island's population is 108,000.

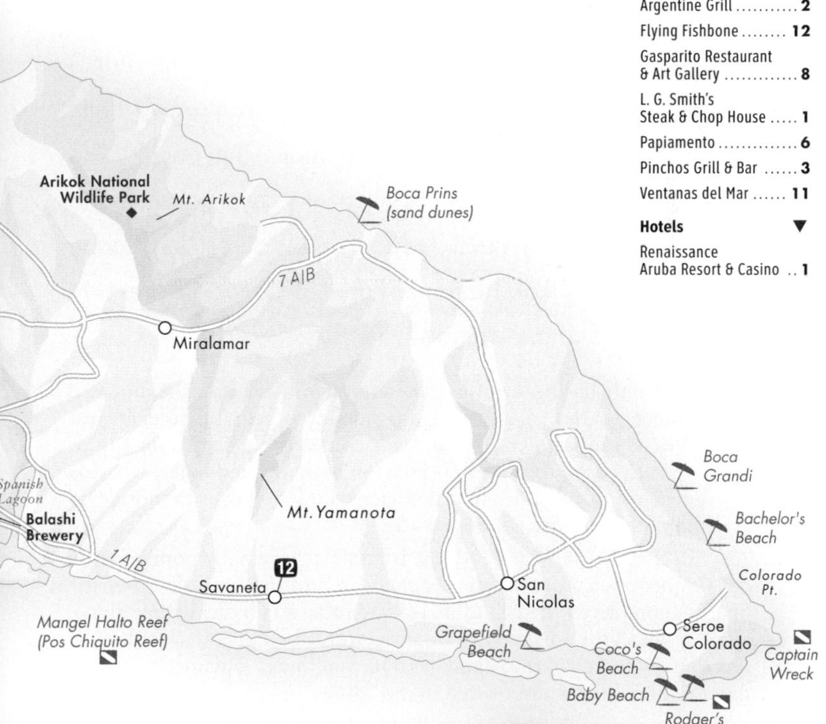

Restaurants ▼

2 Fools and a Bull 9
Amuse Bistro 10
Barefoot 5
Bucaneer 7
Cuba's Cookin' 4
El Gaucho Argentine Grill 2
Flying Fishbone 12
Gasparito Restaurant & Art Gallery 8
L. G. Smith's Steak & Chop House 1
Papiamento 6
Pinchos Grill & Bar 3
Ventanas del Mar 11

Hotels ▼

Renaissance Aruba Resort & Casino .. 1

TOP REASONS TO VISIT ARUBA

1 The Beaches: Powder-soft beaches and turquoise waters or wild waves crashing rocky cliffs.

2 The Nightlife: An after-dark vibe for everyone and dance-till-you-drop spots, plus party buses like the Kukoo Kunuku, which rolls the revelry right into the streets, make this island really move after sunset.

3 The Restaurants: Restaurants with fare from the around the world and local snack hideaways offer foodies much to discover.

4 The Casinos: Aruba's modern casinos will please both casual and serious gamblers.

5 The Welcome: A friendly multilingual population devoted to tourism guarantees smiles everywhere you go.

Updated by Susan Campbell

Cruise ships gleam in Oranjestad Harbour, and thousands of eager tourists spill out into downtown Oranjestad. The mile-long stretch of L.G. Smith Boulevard (aka "The Strip") is lined with cafés, designer stores, restaurants, and Palm Beach Plaza, a modern shopping mall. The countryside is dotted with colorful *cunucu* (country-style houses) and stretches out into a cacti-studded rocky desert landscape that becomes Arikok National Park—a protected preserve covering 20% of the island's landmass.

Aruba not only has beautiful beaches and world-class resorts, but also near-perfect weather: It's outside the hurricane belt and receives just 20 inches of rainfall per year and has constant cooling trade winds. On the south coast, the action is nonstop both day and night; whereas the rugged north coast boasts a desolate beauty that calls to those who seek solitude in nature.

As with Bonaire and Curaçao, the island was originally populated by the Caquetio, an Amerindian people related to the Arawak. After the Spanish conquered the island in 1499, Aruba was basically left alone, since it held little in the way of agricultural or mineral wealth. The Dutch took charge of the island in 1636, and things remained relatively quiet until gold was discovered in the 1800s.

Like the trademark *watapana* (divi-divi) trees that have been forced to bow to odd angles by the constant trade winds, Aruba has always adjusted to changes in the economic climate. Mining dominated the economy until the early part of the 20th century, when the mines became unprofitable. Shortly thereafter, Aruba became home to a major oil-refining operation, which was the economic mainstay until the early 1990s, when its contribution to the local economy was eclipsed by tourism. Today, after being so resolutely dedicated to attracting visitors for so many years, Aruba's national culture and tourism industry are inextricably intertwined.

LOGISTICS

Getting to Aruba: Many airlines fly nonstop to Aruba from several cities in North America and Canada; connections will usually be at a U.S. airport. Smaller airlines connect the Dutch islands in the Caribbean, often using Aruba as a hub. Travelers to the United States clear U.S. Customs and Immigration before leaving Aruba.

Hassle Factor: Low.

On the Ground: Aruba taxis are not metered; they operate on a flat rate by destination. Check the Aruba website (🌐 *www.aruba.com*) for more information on rates and grid. To explore the countryside at your leisure and see different beaches, rent a car. But for just getting to and around town, taxis are preferable, and you can use tour companies to arrange your activities. If you rent a car, try to make reservations before arriving, and rent a four-wheel-drive vehicle if you plan to explore the island's natural sights.

There is good reason why Aruba has more repeat visitors than any other island in the Caribbean. It offers something for everyone: a pleasant climate, excellent facilities, nightlife, nature, and warm and friendly locals. The hospitality industry here is of the highest order. The U.S. dollar is accepted everywhere, and English is spoken universally.

PLANNING

WHEN TO GO

Hotels are usually booked solid from mid-December through mid-April or early May, so advance booking during these months is essential. Other times of the year, rate reductions can be dramatic but Aruba also gets a big influx of visitors from Latin America for summer holidays, so it's advisable to book in advance any time of year.

FESTIVALS AND EVENTS

February through March witnesses a spectacular island-wide Carnival; enjoy a riot of color whirling to the tunes of steel bands, multiple pageants, musical competitions, lighting parades, and more, which all peaks during the Grand Parade in Oranjestad on the Sunday before Ash Wednesday.

Beyond the annual carnival, Aruba has a multitude of festivals and happenings year-round—most notably the Bon Bini festival (*see review in Exploring*)—including blues, jazz, and electronic music fests, an international film festival, marathons, golf events, and more. See the aruba.com calendar of events for full information (🌐 *www.aruba.com*).

GETTING HERE AND AROUND

AIR TRAVEL

Many airlines fly nonstop to Aruba's modern **Reina Beatrix International Airport** (AUA) from several cities in North America; connections will usually be at a U.S. airport.

Nonstop Flights: There are nonstop flights from Atlanta (Delta), Boston (American, JetBlue, US Airways), Charlotte (US Airways), Chicago (United), Fort Lauderdale (Spirit), Houston (United), Miami (American), Newark (United), New York–JFK (American, Delta, JetBlue), Philadelphia (US Airways), and Washington, D.C.–Dulles (United). Southwest Airlines has begun lift to Aruba from Baltimore and Houston as well.

Airline Contacts American Airlines ☎ *297/582–2700 on Aruba, 800/433–7300* 🌐 *www.aa.com.* **Delta Airlines** ☎ *297/800–1555 on Aruba, 800/221–1212 for U.S. reservations, 800/241–4141 for international reservations* 🌐 *www.delta.com.* **JetBlue** ☎ *800/538–2583* 🌐 *www.jetblue.com.* **KLM** ☎ *5999/868–0195 on Aruba, 31/20–4–747–747 in Amsterdam* 🌐 *www.klm.com.* **Spirit Airlines** ☎ *800/772–7117* 🌐 *www.spiritair.com.* **United Airlines** ☎ *297/562–9592 on Aruba, 800/538–2929 in North America* 🌐 *www.united.com.* **US Airways** ☎ *800/455–0123 for U.S. and Canada reservations, 001-800/622–1015 for international reservations* 🌐 *www.usairways.com.*

BUS TRAVEL

Public transportation with Arubus is excellent; it's a great way to explore the different resorts and beaches along the main tourist areas or get groceries to bring back to your hotel. A modern air-conditioned fleet of clean, well-scheduled buses travels from the downtown Oranjestad terminal and stops at every major resort all the way to the end of Palm Beach. Fare is less than $5. Schedules are online.

Contact Arubus 🌐 *www.arubus.com.*

CAR TRAVEL

To explore the countryside and try different beaches, you should rent a car. Try to make reservations before arriving, and rent a four-wheel drive if you plan to explore the island's natural sights. For just getting to and around town, taxis are preferable, and you can use tour companies to arrange your activities.

To rent a car a deposit of $500 (or a signed credit-card slip) is often required. Rates vary but can be between $47 and $75 a day (local agencies generally have lower rates).

International traffic signs and Dutch-style traffic signals (with an extra light for a turning lane) can be misleading if you're not used to them; use extreme caution, especially at intersections, until you grasp the rules of the road. Speed limits are rarely posted but are usually 50 mph (80 kph) in the countryside. Aside from the major highways, the island's winding roads are poorly marked. Gas prices average about $1 per liter (about $6 per gallon), which is reasonable by Caribbean standards. But this changes often.

Contacts Avis ✉ *330 J.E. Irausquin Blvd, Oranjestad* ☎ *297/586-2181, 800/522–9696* 🌐 *www.avis.com* 🖂 *Airport* ☎ *297/582-5496.* **Budget** ✉ *Camacuri 10, Oranjestad* ☎ *297/582–8600, 800/472–3325* 🌐 *www.budget.com.* **Dollar** ✉ *Queen Beatrix Airport, Oranjestad* ☎ *297/583–0101* 🌐 *www.dollar.com.* **Economy** ✉ *Bushiri 27, Oranjestad* ☎ *297/582–0009* 🌐 *www.economyaruba.com.* **Hertz** ✉ *Sabana Blanco 35, near airport, Oranjestad* ☎ *297/582-1845* 🌐 *www.arubarentcar.com.* **Thrifty** ✉ *Wayaca 33-F, Oranjestad* ☎ *297/583–4042* 🌐 *www.thriftycarrentalaruba.com* 🖂 *Airport* ☎ *297/583–4902.*

TAXI TRAVEL

There's a dispatch office at the airport; you can also flag down taxis on the street (look for license plates with a "TX" tag). Alternatively, ask at the front desk of any resort to call you a cab. Rates are fixed (i.e., there are no meters; the rates are set by the government and displayed on a chart), though you and the driver should agree on the fare before your ride begins. Add $2 to the fare after midnight and $3 on Sunday and holidays. An hour-long island tour costs about $45, with up to four people. Agree on a fare before heading out.

Contact Airport Taxi Dispatch ☎ *297/582–2116.*

ESSENTIALS

Banks and Exchange Services The local currency is the Aruban florin (AFl 1.79 to US$1). The florin is pegged to the U.S. dollar, and Arubans accept U.S. dollars readily, so you need acquire local currency only for pocket change. Note that the Netherlands Antilles florin used on Curaçao is not accepted on Aruba. ATMs are easy to find.

Electricity 110 volts, 50 cycles.

Emergency Services Dr. Horacio Oduber Hospital ✉ *L.G. Smith Blvd. 47, Manchebo Beach* ☎ *297/587–4300.*

Language Everyone on the island speaks English, but the official languages are Dutch and Papiamento. Most locals speak Papiamento—a rapid-fire mix of Spanish, Dutch, English, French, and Portuguese—in normal conversation. Here are a few helpful phrases: *bon dia* (good day), *bon nochi* (good night), *masha danki* (thank you very much).

Mail Main Post Office. The Main Post Office is in Oranjestad. There is also a branch office at Royal Plaza Mall, and others are scattered throughout the island. ✉ *9 J.E. Irausquinplein, Oranjestad* ☎ *297/582–1900.*

Taxes The airport departure tax is typically included in the price of your ticket. Hotels collect 9.5% in taxes (2% of which goes to marketing to tourists) on top of a typical 11% service charge, for a total of 20.5%. An additional $3 Environmental Levy per day was added in 2013. A 2.5% sales tax is included in the price charged in most shops.

Tipping Restaurants generally include a 10% to 15% service charge. If service isn't included, a 10% tip is standard; if it is included, it's customary to add something extra at your discretion. Taxi drivers, 10% to 15%; porters and bellhops, about $2 per bag; housekeeping, about $2 a day.

ACCOMMODATIONS

Almost all the resorts are along the island's southwest coast, along L.G. Smith and J.E. Irausquin Boulevards, with the larger high-rise properties being farther away from Oranjestad. A few budget places are in Oranjestad itself. Since most hotel beaches are equally fabulous, it's the resort, rather than its location, that's going to be a bigger factor in how you enjoy your vacation.

Boutique Resorts: You'll find a few small resorts that offer more personal service, though not always the same level of luxury as the larger places. But smaller resorts are better suited to the natural sense of Aruban hospitality you'll find all over the island.

Large Resorts: These all-encompassing vacation destinations offer myriad dining options, casinos, shops, water-sports centers, health clubs, and car-rental desks. The island has only a handful of all-inclusives, though these are gaining in popularity.

Time-shares: Large time-share properties are cropping up in greater numbers, luring visitors who prefer to prepare some of their own meals and have a bit more living space than in a typical resort hotel room.

Hotel reviews have been shortened. For full information, visit Fodors.com.

	WHAT IT COSTS IN U.S. DOLLARS			
	$	$$	$$$	$$$$
Restaurants	under $13	$13–$20	$21–$30	over $30
Hotels	under $275	$275–$375	$376–$475	over $475

Restaurant prices are the average cost of a main course at dinner or, if dinner is not served, at lunch. Hotel prices are the lowest cost of a standard double room in high season.

VISITOR INFORMATION

Aruba Tourism Authority ✉ *L.G. Smith Blvd. 172, Eagle Beach* ☎ *800/862–7822 in the U.S./international; 297/582–3777 in Aruba* 🌐 *www.aruba.com.*

WEDDINGS

You must be over 18 and submit the appropriate documents one month in advance. Couples are required to submit birth certificates with raised seals, through the mail or in person, to Aruba's Office of the Civil Registry. They also need an *apostille*—a document proving they are free to marry—from their country of residence. Most major hotels have wedding coordinators, and there are many independent wedding planners on the island.

Contacts Aruba Fairy Tales ☎ *297/583-8000* 🌐 *www.arubafairytales.com.* **Dream Weddings Aruba** ✉ *Catiri 29G, Oranjestad* ☎ *297/564-3289* 🌐 *www.dreamweddingsaruba.com.*

EXPLORING

Aruba's wildly sculpted landscape is replete with rocky deserts, cactus clusters, secluded coves, blue vistas, and the trademark divi-divi tree. To see the island's wild, untamed beauty, you can rent a car, take a sightseeing tour by bus, van, Jeep, and even motorcycle tours, or hire a cab for approximately $45 an hour (for up to four people). The main highways are well paved, but on the windward side (the north- and east-facing side) some roads are still a mixture of compacted dirt and stones. A four-wheel-drive vehicle is recommended to really explore the outback.

Traffic can get dense near Oranjestad and L.G. Smith Boulevard, especially at rush hour, but once out of the city it is sparse. Route 1A travels southbound along the western coast, and 1B is simply northbound along the same road. If you lose your way, just look to the divi-divi trees, which always lean southwest. Most rental cars have GPS now.

ORANJESTAD AND ENVIRONS

Aruba's capital is best explored by the free eco-trolley—hop on/hop off affair—and on foot. Major improvements downtown have opened up the back roads of Main Street and have created many resting spaces and pedestrian-only lanes. New small malls, restaurants, attractions, and museums can be explored there. Also worth exploring is the new linear park and boardwalk and the new outdoor art spaces along the waterfront.

TOP ATTRACTIONS

Aruba Aloe Museum & Factory. Aruba has the ideal conditions to grow the aloe vera plant. It's an important export, and there are aloe stores all over the island. The museum and factory tour reveals the process of extracting the serum to make many products used for beauty, health, and healing; and guided or self-guided tours are available in English, Dutch, Spanish, and Papiamento. There's also a store to purchase their products on-site. Products are also available online. ✉ *Pitastraat 115, Hato, Oranjestad* ☎ *800/952–7822* 🌐 *www.arubaaloe.com* 🎫 *Free* 🕑 *Mon.–Fri. 8–4:30, Sat. 9–4.*

Balashi Brewery & Beer Garden. Aruba is the only nation in the world to make beer out of desalinated seawater, and it's a really good beer! They also now make a version called "Chill" with added lemon flavor. See how it's done at their factory and sample some afterward. There is also a lovely outdoor beer garden for lunch, and sometimes they offer live music at their happy hour, too. Closed-toe shoes required for factory tour. ✉ *Balashi 75, Balashi* ☎ *297/592–2544* 🎫 *$6.*

Fodor's Choice ★ **Bon Bini Festival.** This year-round folklore event (the name means "welcome" in Papiamento), is held every Tuesday from 6:30 pm to 8:30 pm at Ft. Zoutman in Oranjestad. In the inner courtyard, you can check out the Antillean dancers in resplendent costumes, feel the rhythms of the steel drums, browse among the stands displaying local artwork, and sample local food and drink. ✉ *Ft. Zoutman, Oranjestad* 🌐 *www.aruba.com* 🎫 *$5.*

FAMILY Fodor's Choice ★ **DePalm Island.** A must-do for a full or half-day trip is a visit to this terrific little private island outpost full of incredible adventures for the entire family. Their all-inclusive offerings include snorkeling with giant neon blue parrotfish, a giant waterpark, banana boat rides, salsa lessons, beach volleyball, zip-lining, and a massive all-you-can-eat buffet plus open bar and snack shack. For additional cost, you can also try Snuba—deep snorkeling with an oxygen raft—and children 4–7 can join their parents with their unique SNUBA Doo® setup. Motorized Power Snorkel is another fun undersea option. They also have Seatrek®—underwater walking tours with air-supplied helmets—and have added zip lines over the water recently as well. There's also a small seaside spa on-site. Complimentary bus transportation from all major hotels includes access to the island by water taxi. ✉ *De Palm Island Way Z/N, Balashi* ☎ *297/522–4400* 🌐 *www.depalmtours.com.*

FAMILY Fodor's Choice ★ **National Archaeological Museum of Aruba.** Located in a multibuilding complex that once housed the Ecury Family Estate, this modern, air-conditioned museum showcases the island's beginnings right back to the indigenous Arawak people, including a vast collection of farm and domestic utensils dating back hundreds of years. Among the highlights are the re-created Arawak Village, multimedia and interactive presentations, and rotating exhibits of art, history, and cultural shows. ✉ *42 Schelpstraat, Oranjestad* ☎ *297/582–8979* 🌐 *namaruba.org* 🎟 *Free* 🕙 *Tues.–Fri. 10–5, Sat. and Sun. 10–2.*

WORTH NOTING

Ft. Zoutman. One of the island's oldest edifices, Aruba's historic fort was built in 1796 and played an important role in skirmishes between British and Curaçao troops in 1803. The Willem III Tower, named for the Dutch monarch of that time, was added in 1868 to serve as a lighthouse. Over time the fort has been a government office building, a police station, and a prison; now its historical museum displays Aruban artifacts in an 18th-century house. This is also the site of the weekly Tuesday night welcome party called the Bon Bini festival with local music, food, and dance. ✉ *Zoutmanstraat, Oranjestad* ☎ *297/582–5199* 🎟 *$5* 🕙 *Mon.–Fri. 8:30–4.*

MANCHEBO AND DRUIF BEACHES

One beach seamlessly merges with another resulting in a miles-long stretch of powdery sand peppered with a few low-rise resorts. This part of the island is much less crowded than Palm Beach and great for a morning or evening stroll.

EAGLE BEACH

Eagel Beach is often referred to as Aruba's low-rise hotel area. It's lined with smaller boutique resorts and time-share resorts. Eagle Beach is considered one of the best beaches in the Caribbean; the white-sand carpet here seems to stretch on forever. The water is great for swimming, and there are numerous refreshment spots along the beach. Although the beach can get busy during the day, there's never a problem finding a spot, but if you're looking for shade, it's best to stick near one of the hotel bar huts along the beach. Note: All beaches are open to public but the lounges and shade palapas are reserved for hotel guests.

PALM BEACH AND NOORD

The district of Noord is home to the strip of high-rise hotels and casinos that line Palm Beach. The hotels and restaurants, ranging from haute cuisine to fast food, are densely packed into a few miles running along the beachfront. When other areas of Aruba are shutting down for the night, this area is guaranteed to still be buzzing with activity. Here you can also find the beautiful **St. Ann's Church,** known for its ornate 19th-century altar. In this area Aruban-style homes are scattered amid clusters of cacti.

TOP ATTRACTIONS

FAMILY Fodor's Choice ★ **Butterfly Farm.** Hundreds of butterflies and moths from around the world flutter about this spectacular garden. Guided tours (included in the price of admission) provide an entertaining look into the life cycle of these insects, from egg to caterpillar to chrysalis to butterfly or moth. After your initial visit, you can return as often as you like for free during your vacation. **■ TIP→ Go early in the morning when the butterflies are most active; wear bright colors if you want them to land on you.** Early morning is also when you are most likely to see the caterpillars emerge from their cocoons and transform into butterflies or moths as well. ✉ *J.E. Irausquin Blvd., Palm Beach* ☎ *297/586–3656* 🌐 *www.thebutterflyfarm.com* 🎟 *$15* ⏲ *Mon.–Sun. 8:30–4:30 (last tour at 4).*

WESTERN TIP (CALIFORNIA DUNES)

No trip to Aruba is complete without a visit to the California Lighthouse and it's also worth exploring the rugged area of the island's western tip. This is the transition point between Aruba's calmer and rougher coasts. Malmok Beach and Arashi Beach are popular for windsurfing and are excellent for dramatic sunset photos. The California Lighthouse was designated a national monument in 2015 and at this writing is in the process of receiving a major restoration.

TOP ATTRACTIONS

California Lighthouse. Declared a national monument in 2014, the landmark lighthouse on the island's eastern tip is being restored to its original glory. It was named after a merchant ship that sunk nearby called the *Californian*, a tragedy that spawned its construction. Built in 1910, it has been a famous Aruba attraction for decades and a typical stop on most island tours. ✉ *Arashi, Noord, Oranjestad.*

WORTH NOTING

Alto Vista Chapel. Meaning "high view," Alto Vista was built in 1750 as the island's first Roman Catholic Church. The simple yellow and orange structure stands out in bright contrast to its stark desert-like surroundings, and its elevated location affords a wonderful panoramic view of the northwest coast. Restored in 1953, it's still in operation today with regular services and also serves as the culmination point of the annual walk of the cross at Easter. You will see small signposts guiding the faithful to the Stations of the Cross all along the winding road to its entrance. This landmark is a typical stop on most island tours. ✉ *Alto Vista Rd., Oranjestad* ⊕ *Follow the rough, winding dirt road that loops around the island's northern tip, or from the hotel strip, take Palm Beach Road through three intersections and watch for the asphalt road to the left just past the Alto Vista Rum Shop.*

SANTA CRUZ

Though not a tourist hot spot (by Aruba standards), this town in the center of the island offers a good taste of how the locals live. It's not architecturally interesting, but there are many restaurants and local shops offering something a bit different from the usual tourist fare (and at reasonable prices).

Mt. Hooiberg. Named for its shape (*hooiberg* means "haystack" in Dutch), this 541-foot peak lies inland just past the airport. If you have the energy, you can climb the 562 steps to the top for an impressive view of Oranjestad (and Venezuela on clear days). ✉ *Oranjestad.*

SAVANETA

The Dutch settled here after retaking the island in 1816, and it served as Aruba's first capital. Today it's a bustling fishing village with a 150-year-old *cas di torto* (mud hut), the oldest dwelling still standing on the island. Here you can watch local fisherman bring in the fresh catch of the day. They will fillet and cook it for you on the spot if you like at a small hut with cold beer and soft drinks. Many of the restaurants get their daily fish from these fishermen. Savaneta is also home to two gorgeous seaside-dining spots—The Old Man and the Sea and The Flying Fishbone, which are side by side.

SAN NICOLAS

During the oil refinery heyday, San Nicolas, Aruba's oldest village, was a bustling port; now its primary purpose is tourism. The major institution in town is Charlie's Restaurant & Bar. Stop in for a drink and advice on what to see and do in this little town. Aruba's main red-light district is here and will be fairly apparent to even casual observers.

The new Carnival Village in San Nicolas has a workshop where you can see costumes made and a new Carnival Museum were you can retrace its history. That's also where the sunrise jump-up at 4 am called "The Pajama Party" begins.

SEROE COLORADO

Originally established as a community for oil workers, San Nicholas is also known for its intriguing 1939 chapel. Here, organ-pipe cacti form the backdrop for sedate whitewashed cottages. The best reason to come here is the natural bridge. Keep bearing east past the community, continuing uphill until you run out of road. You can then hike down to the cathedral-like formation. It's not too strenuous, but watch your footing as you descend. Be sure to follow the white arrows painted on the rocks, as there are no other directional signs. Although this bridge isn't as spectacular as its more celebrated sibling (which collapsed in 2005), the raw elemental power of the sea that created it, replete with hissing blowholes, certainly is.

ARIKOK NATIONAL PARK AND ENVIRONS

The large, modern visitor center is the ideal place to begin exploring Arikok, a national park preserve that spans 18% of the island across the eastern interior and the northeast coast. Guided ranger hikes, exhibits, films, and maps will get you well started.

The park is the keystone of the government's long-term ecotourism plan to preserve Aruba's resources, and it showcases the island's flora and fauna as well as ancient Arawak petroglyphs, the ruins of a gold-mining operation at Miralmar, and the remnants of Dutch peasant settlements at Masiduri. Within the confines of the park are Mt. Arikok and the 620-foot Mt. Yamanota, Aruba's highest peak.

TOP ATTRACTIONS

Arikok National Park. There are more than 34 km (20 miles) of trails concentrated in the island's eastern interior and along its northeastern coast. Arikok Park is crowned by Aruba's second-highest mountain, the 577-foot Mt. Arikok, so you can also go climbing here.

Hiking in the park, whether alone or in a group led by guides, is generally not too strenuous. Look for different colors to determine the degree of difficulty of each trail. You'll need sturdy shoes to grip the granular surfaces and climb the occasionally steep terrain. You should also exercise caution with the strong sun—bring along plenty of water and wear sunscreen and a hat. On the rare occasion that it rains, the park should be avoided completely, as mud makes both driving and hiking treacherous. At the park's main entrance, the Arikok Center houses offices, restrooms, and food facilities. All visitors must stop here upon entering, so that officials can manage the traffic flow and distribute information on park rules and features. ☎ *297/582–8001* 🌐 *www.arubanationalpark.org.*

WORTH NOTING

Aruba Ostrich Farm. Everything you ever wanted to know about the world's largest living birds can be found at this farm. A large *palapa* (palm-thatched roof) houses a gift shop and restaurant that draws large bus tours, and tours of the farm are available every half hour. This operation is virtually identical to the facility in Curaçao; it's owned by the same company. ✉ *Makividiri Rd., Paradera* ☎ *297/585–9630* 🌐 *www.arubaostrichfarm.com* 🎫 *Adults $12, children under 12 $6* 🕒 *Daily 9–4.*

Rock Formations. The massive boulders at Ayo and Casibari are a mystery, as they don't match the island's geological makeup. You can climb to the top for fine views of the arid countryside. The main path to Casibari has steps and handrails, and you must move through tunnels and along narrow steps and ledges to reach the top. At Ayo you can find ancient pictographs in a small cave (the entrance has iron bars to protect the drawings from vandalism). At the base there is a new cafe/bar/restaurant open for lunch, and their dinner at night when lit up with colored lights around the rocks is surreal. Some party bus tours stop there for dinner at the end of their journey. ✉ *Paradera* ✣ *Access to the rock formations at Casibari is via Tanki Highway 4A; you can reach Ayo via Route 6A. Watch carefully for the turnoff signs near the center of the island on the way to the windward side.*

BEACHES

Virtually every popular Aruba beach has resorts attached, but because nearly all beaches are public, there is never a problem with access. However, lounges, showers, and shade palapas are reserved for hotel guests.

The major beaches, which back up to the hotels along the southwestern strip, are usually crowded but you can usually keep walking to find a secluded spot. Make sure you're well protected from the sun. Burning happens fast; you feel the intensity of the rays less because of the cool trade winds. Luckily, there are many covered bars and refreshment stands at every hotel and many piers with shade and bars as well. On the island's northeastern side, stronger winds make the waters too choppy for swimming, but the vistas are great, and the terrain is wonderful for exploring. You'll often find expert kitesurfers, bodyboarders, and windsurfers enjoying the wild surf there though.

Arashi Beach. This is the local favorite, a ½-mile (1-km) stretch of gleaming white sand with a rolling surf and good snorkeling. It can get busy on weekends, especially Sunday with local families bringing their own picnics, but during the week it is typically quiet, though Tierra del Sol Resort now provides transportation to it for their guests. **Amenities:** some shade palapas. **Best for:** swimming; walking. ✉ *West of Malmok Beach, on west end.*

FAMILY **Baby Beach.** On the island's eastern tip (near the now-closed refinery), this semicircular beach borders a placid bay of turquoise water that's just about as shallow as a wading pool—perfect for families with little ones. A small coral reef basin at the sea's edge offers superb snorkeling, but do not pass the barrier, as the current is extremely strong outside of the rocks. The new JADS dive shop offers snorkel and dive rentals, and their full-service bar and restaurant also offers a shower and washrooms and a small children's playground. **Amenities:** food and drink; clamshell shade rentals. **Best for:** snorkeling; swimming; walking. ✉ *Near Seroe Colorado, on east end, Seroe Colorado.*

Boca Grandi. This is *the* choice for the island's best kiteboarders and expert windsurfers, even more so than Fisherman's Huts. But the currents are strong so it's not safe for casual swimming. It's very picturesque though and a perfect spot for a picnic. It's a few minutes from San Nicolas; look for the big red anchor or the kites in the air. **Amenities:** none. **Best for:** walking; kiteboarding; windsurfing. ✉ *Near Seagrape Grove, on east end, San Nicolas.*

Druif Beach. Fine white sand and calm water make this beach a fine choice for sunbathing and swimming. It's the base beach for the Divi collections of all-inclusive resorts so amenities are reserved for guests. But the locals like it, too, and often camp out here as well with their own chairs and coolers. The beach is accessible by bus, rental car, or taxi, and it's walking distance to stores. **Amenities:** parking. **Best for:** swimming; sunbathing. ✉ *Parallel to J.E. Irausquin Blvd., near Divi resorts, south of Punta Brabo.*

Fodor's Choice ★ **Eagle Beach.** Aruba's most photographed beach and widest by far, especially in front of the Manchebo resort, Eagle Beach is not only a favorite with visitors and locals, but also of sea turtles. More sea turtles nest here than anywhere else on the island. This pristine stretch of blinding white sand and aqua surf frequently ranks among the best beaches in the world. Many of the hotels have facilities on or near the beach, and refreshments are never far away, but chairs and shade palapas are reserved for guests only. **Amenities:** food and drink; toilets. **Best for:** swimming; walking; sunset. ✉ *J.E. Irausquin Blvd., north of Manchebo Beach.*

Fisherman's Huts (*Hadicurari*). Beside the new Ritz-Carlton, Fisherman's Huts is a windsurfer's and kiteboarder's haven. Swimmers might have a hard time avoiding all the boards going by, as this is the nexus of where the lessons take place for both sports and it's always awash in students and experts and board hobbyists. It's a gorgeous spot to just sit and watch the sails on the sea. Only drinks and small snacks are available at the operator's shacks. No washrooms, but the Ritz lobby is nearby in a pinch. **Amenities:** food. **Best for:** windsurfing; kiteboarding. ✉ *North of Aruba Marriott Resort, Palm Beach.*

4

Malmok Beach (*Boca Catalina*). On the northwestern shore, this small, nondescript beach borders shallow waters that stretch 300 yards from shore. There are no snack or refreshment stands here, but shade is available under the thatched umbrellas. It's the perfect place to learn to windsurf. Right off the coast here is a favorite haunt for divers and snorkelers—the wreck of the German ship *Antilla,* scuttled in 1940. **Amenities:** none. **Best for:** solitude; snorkeling. ✉ *At end of J.E. Irausquin Blvd., Malmokweg.*

Manchebo Beach (*Punta Brabo*). Impressively wide, the white-sand shoreline in front of the Manchebo Beach Resort is where officials turn a blind eye to the occasional topless sunbather. This beach merges with Druif Beach, and most locals use the name Manchebo to refer to both. **Amenities:** food and drink; toilets. **Best for:** swimming. ✉ *J.E. Irausquin Blvd., at Manchebo Beach Resort.*

Palm Beach. This is the island's most populated and popular beach running along the high-rise resorts and it's crammed with every kind of water-sports activity and food and drink emporium imaginable. It's always crowded no matter the season, but it's a great place for people-watching, sunbathing, swimming, and partying, and there are always activities happening such as the increasingly popular beach tennis. The water is pond calm and the sand is powder fine. **Amenities:** food and drink; toilets; water sports; shade. **Best for:** swimming; partying; sunbathing; people-watching; water sports. ✉ *J.E. Irausquin Blvd., between Westin Aruba Resort and Marriott's Aruba Ocean Club.*

FAMILY **Rodger's Beach.** Near Baby Beach on the island's eastern tip, this beautiful curving stretch of sand is only slightly marred by its proximity to the tanks and towers of the now defunct oil refinery at the bay's far side. Swimming conditions are excellent here. The snack bar at the water's edge has beach-equipment rentals and a shop. Drive around the refinery perimeter to get here. **Amenities:** food and drink; water sports. **Best for:** swimming. ✉ *Next to Baby Beach, on east end, San Nicolas.*

CLOSE UP

Cunucu Houses

Pastel houses surrounded by cacti fences adorn Aruba's flat, rugged *cunucu* ("country" in Papiamento). The features of these traditional houses were developed in response to the environment. Early settlers discovered that slanting roofs allowed the heat to rise, and small windows helped to keep in the cool air. Among the earliest building materials was caliche, a durable calcium carbonate substance found in the island's southeastern hills. Many houses were also built using interlocking coral rocks that didn't require mortar (this technique is no longer used, thanks to concrete). Contemporary design combines some of the basic principles of the earlier homes with touches of modernization: windows, though still narrow, have been elongated; roofs are constructed of bright tiles; pretty patios have been added; and doorways and balconies present an ornamental face to the world beyond. Cacti fences are still used to keep meandering wild goats out of gardens.

WHERE TO EAT

Be sure to seek out spots where you can try Aruban specialties such as *pan bati* (a mildly sweet bread that resembles a pancake) and *keshi yena* (a baked concoction of Gouda or Edam cheese, spices, and meat or seafood in a rich brown sauce). Most restaurants are more international in style. Reservations are essential for dinner in high season. The larger restaurants don't typically close any day of the week, but if they do, Monday is usually the day of choice.

What to Wear. Cover-ups, shorts, and flip-flops should be reserved for casual beach bars. But formal dress is rarely required. The finest restaurants require at most a jacket for men and a sundress for women. If you plan to eat in the open air, bring along insect repellent—the mosquitoes can come out when the wind dies down.

Aruba Gastronomic Association: Dine-Around Program (*AGA*). To give visitors an affordable way to sample the island's eclectic cuisine, the Aruba Gastronomic Association has created a Dine-Around program involving more than 30 island restaurants. Savings abound with all kinds of different packages. Other programs, such as gift certificates and coupons for dinners at the association's VIP member restaurants are also available. You can buy Dine-Around tickets using the association's online order form, through travel agents, or at the De Palm Tours sales desk in many hotels. Participating restaurants and conditions change frequently; the AGA website has the latest information. ✉ *Rooi Santo 21, Noord* ☎ *297/586–1266, 914/595–4788 in U.S.* 🌐 *www.arubadining.com.*

$$$$ INTERNATIONAL

✕ **2 Fools and a Bull.** Friends Paul and Fred have teamed up to offer an evening of culinary entertainment that's more like a fun dinner party than a mere dining experience. Guests are assembled and introduced to one another. Then the evening's meal is explained before everyone sits down at the U-shaped communal dinner table for a five-course culinary adventure. The menu changes daily and there's a selection of suggested wine pairings available by the glass. This isn't a cheap eating-out experience, but it'll certainly be a cherished memory of Aruba. Reservations are advisable at least a few weeks in advance. **■ TIP→ Be sure to state any dietary restrictions in advance.** *$ Average main: $90 ✉ Palm Beach 17, Noord ☎ 297/586–7177 🌐 www.2foolsandabull.com ✍ Reservations essential ⏲ Closed Sat. and Sun.*

$$$ CONTEMPORARY Fodor's Choice ★ **✕ Amuse Bistro.** The chef-owner at Amuse Bistro provides creative French-inspired fusion cuisine, sometimes available in full and small portions, while his sommelier wife will help pair perfect choices of wine from their extensive selection. Pretention, however, is not on the menu here; it's a friendly spot where you can dine outside along Aruba's busiest tourist boulevard or inside in a warm and inviting enclave. The main menu offers mostly classic French dishes with surprising twists, but you're really better served to let the chef delight you with his daily three-course or five-course carte blanche surprise menu that can also be paired with the sommelier's choice of wines. The carte blanche menu can only be ordered for the whole table, not individually. *$ Average main: $28 ✉ J.E. Irausquin Blvd. 87, Palm Beach, ☎ 297/596–9949 ✍ Reservations essential.*

4

$$$$ SEAFOOD **✕ Aqua Grill.** Aficionados flock here to enjoy a wide selection of seafood and one of the largest raw bars on the island. The atmosphere is casual, with a distinctly New England feel. Maine lobster and Alaskan king crab legs are available, but why try the usual fare when you can order the Fisherman's Pot, which is filled with scallops, monkfish, and other seafood? The wood grill serves up great low-cal dishes, including mahimahi. There are cheaper restaurants that serve better-prepared seafood meals on the island, but the variety of offerings here sets it apart. *$ Average main: $32 ✉ J.E. Irausquin Blvd. 374, Palm Beach ☎ 297/586–5900 🌐 www.aqua-grill.com ⏲ No lunch.*

$$$ CONTEMPORARY Fodor's Choice ★ **✕ Barefoot.** In keeping with an "elegant dining in flip-flops" concept, Barefoot is a palapa restaurant with sand on the floor inside, and tables on the sand outside. Chef Gerco Aan het Rot and maitre d'/sommelier Luc Beerepoot excel at pairing food and wine or cocktails. Their menu of creative international fusion cuisine is complemented by superb signature cocktails and an impressive selection of wines, yet the atmosphere is never stuffy. This duo truly takes it up a notch above your basic toes-in-the-sand dining spot, and the sunset views are always spectacular. *$ Average main: $26 ✉ L.G. Smith Boulevard 1, across the street from the talk of the Town Hotel on Surfside Beach, Oranjestad ☎ 297/588–9824 🌐 www.barefootaruba.com ✍ Reservations essential ⏲ No lunch.*

$$$ ECLECTIC FAMILY **✕ Buccaneer.** Imagine you're in a sunken ship where sharks, barracudas, and grouper swim past the (rectangular) portholes. That's what you can find at Buccaneer, a restaurant dominated by a 10,000-gallon aquarium and where each table has its own individual aquarium. The best bet is the catch of the day or the rotating chef's special, but there is much more than fish and seafood. It's a great place for kids, and adults will also enjoy their new signature cocktail menu. The restaurant is a landmark family-run establishment that has been operating for more than 30

years. $ *Average main: $29* ✉ *Gasparito 11C, Noord* ☎ *297/586–6172* 🌐 *www.buccaneeraruba.com* ⏲ *Closed Sun. No lunch.*

$$$ CUBAN Fodor's Choice ★ ✕ **Cuba's Cookin'.** Old Havana meets the Caribbean here with authentic music and food from what locals call "The Big Island." The signature dish is the *ropa vieja,* a sautéed flank steak served with a rich sauce, and it's perfectly spiced and melts in your mouth. Vegetarian and gluten-free offerings are served as well. And their boast of the "the best mojitos in town" is a fair claim. There's live music some nights as well as interesting offerings like Poetry Night where locals get up and express themselves through spoken word. The atmosphere is fun and friendly and the location ideal for people-watching along the seaport marina. And it's the only place in town to get a famous Cuban sandwich for lunch. $ *Average main: $28* ✉ *Renaissance Marketplace, L.G. Smith Blvd. 82, Oranjestad* ☎ *297/588–0627* 🌐 *www.cubascookin.com.*

$$$$ STEAKHOUSE FAMILY ✕ **El Gaucho Argentine Grill.** Faux-leather-bound books, tulip-top lamps, wooden chairs, and tile floors decorate this Argentina-style steak house, which has been in business since 1977. The key here is meat served in mammoth portions (think 16-ounce steaks), and the "biggest shish kebab ever served" is also their specialty. But it's not all about meat; their seafood platters are something to consider as well. It's a boisterous and fun atmosphere with strolling musicians, and the kids will enjoy the separate children's playroom. Appropriate attire is appreciated. $ *Average main: $40* ✉ *Wilhelminastraat 80, Oranjestad* ☎ *297/582–3677* 🌐 *www.elgaucho-aruba.com.*

$$$$ SEAFOOD Fodor's Choice ★ ✕ **Flying Fishbone.** This friendly, relaxed beach restaurant is well off the beaten path in Savaneta, a small fishing town, so you know the fish is seriously fresh, often caught that day. You can dine with your toes in the sand (they have hooks for your shoes), or enjoy your meal on the wooden deck. The emphasis here is on fresh seafood—beautifully presented on colorful beds of vegetables—but there are good choices for landlubbers, too, like grilled maple leaf duck breast. The shrimp, shiitake, and blue-cheese casserole is a tried-and-true favorite kept on the menu to keep the regulars happy. For dessert, the chocolate ravioli with poached pear and ice cream is not to be missed. **■ TIP→ Arrive early for dinner to get a good table closer to the water.** $ *Average main: $34* ✉ *Savaneta 344, Savaneta* ☎ *297/584–2506* 🌐 *www.flyingfishbone.com* ✍ *Reservations essential.*

$$$ STEAKHOUSE ✕ **French Steakhouse & Omakase Sushi Bar.** A classic French restaurant with a modern sushi bar under the same roof in a landmark Aruba hotel might sound like a spot with something of an identity crisis, but it actually works. Well known as a place for high-end steak served with European flare, the recent addition of the Asian offerings brings the entire dining room into this century. The Omakase name of the sushi bar means "I will leave it to you," and you are expected to leave it to the sushi chef to delight you with the selection of dishes beginning with the lightest to the heaviest. Seating is limited so reservations at the sushi bar are essential. The French Steakhouse also offers an early-bird menu. Live piano music adds to the ambience. $ *Average main: $30* ✉ *Manchebo Beach Resort, J.E. Irausquin Blvd. 55, Manchebo Beach* ☎ *297/582–3444* ⏲ *No lunch. Sushi bar closed Mon.*

$$$ CARIBBEAN Fodor's Choice ★ **Gasparito Restaurant & Art Gallery.** You can find this enchanting hideaway in a beautifully restored 200-year-old *cunucu* (country) house in Noord. Dine indoors, where works by local artists are showcased on softly lit walls, or on the outdoor patio. Either way, the service is excellent. The Aruban specialties like *pan bati* and *keshi yena* come from centuries of tradition and the standout dish is the Gasparito chicken; the sauce recipe was passed down from the owner's ancestors and features seven special ingredients, including brandy, white wine, and pineapple juice. (The rest, they say, are secret.) Vegetarian entrées and American-style ribs round out the menu of local dishes that include fresh fish and seafood. Only 20 guests per evening—choice of seatings at 6, 7, or 8 pm. *Average main: $25 Gasparito 3, Noord 297/594–2550 www.gasparito.com Reservations essential Closed Sun. No lunch.*

$$$$ STEAKHOUSE Fodor's Choice ★ **L.G. Smith's Steak & Chop House.** A study in teak, cream, and black, this fine steak house offers some of the best beef on the island. Subdued lighting and cascading water create a pleasant atmosphere, and the view over L.G. Smith Boulevard to the harbor makes for an exceptional dining experience. Their comprehensive wine list has won a *Wine Spectator* Award of Excellence. The menu features high-quality cuts of meat, all superbly prepared. The casino is steps away if you fancy some slots after dinner. Nightcaps can be had at the trendy bar Blu just below. *Average main: $37 Renaissance Aruba Beach Resort & Casino, L.G. Smith Blvd. 82, Oranjestad 297/523–6195 www.lgsmiths.com No lunch.*

$$$$ EUROPEAN Fodor's Choice ★ **Madame Janette.** Named after the Scotch Bonnet pepper called Madame Janette in Aruba, the food here is surprisingly not Caribbean spicy but French-inspired from the classic haute cuisine–trained chef. Though they do fuse Caribbean flavors when they see fit, especially in the fish and seafood dishes, you'll find a lot of classic heavy butter and cream sauce offerings for the meats like Peppercorn Cognac, Béarnaise, and Hollandaise. They also have Aruba's largest selection of specialty beers due to one co-owner's avid interest in craft brewing. They also have a surprising number of specialty schnitzels. The commitment of the owners to serve only top quality in all of their offerings has won Madame Janette many prestigious culinary awards. You can be sure that a night at this spot will never disappoint when it comes to an over-the-top taste experience. *Average main: $33 Cunucu Abao 37, Cunucu Abao 297/587–0184 www.madamejanette.info Reservations essential No lunch. Closed Sun.*

$$$$ ECLECTIC **Papiamento.** The Ellis family converted its 126-year-old manor into a bistro with an atmosphere that is elegant, intimate, and always romantic. You can feast in the dining room, which is filled with antiques, or outdoors on the terrace by the pool (sitting on plastic patio chairs covered in fabric). The chef mixes Continental and Caribbean cuisines to produce sumptuous seafood and meat dishes and goes out of his way to source locally for fresh ingredients. Those seeking a bit of novelty can order one of the hot stone dishes, which come to the table sizzling. Service is unhurried and the atmosphere laid-back. Papiamento is one of the best spots on the island to try the famous local specialty *keshi yena*. *Average main: $32 Washington 61, Noord 297/586–4544*

Restaurants ▼
Aqua Grill 3
French Steakhouse 5
Madame Janette 4
Passions 2
Ruinas del Mar ..1
Windows on Aruba 6

Hotels ▼
Amsterdam Manor 9
Aruba Beach ... 12
Aruba Marriott ...1
Boardwalk Small 3
Bucuti & Tara Beach Resorts . 11
Divi Aruba Beach 13
Divi Aruba Phoenix 16
Divi Village 15
Holiday Inn 5
Hotel Riu Palace Aruba 8
Hyatt Regency Aruba 6
Marriott's Aruba Ocean Club 4
Occidental 7
Ritz-Carlton 2
Tamarijn Aruba 14
Tropicana Aruba 10

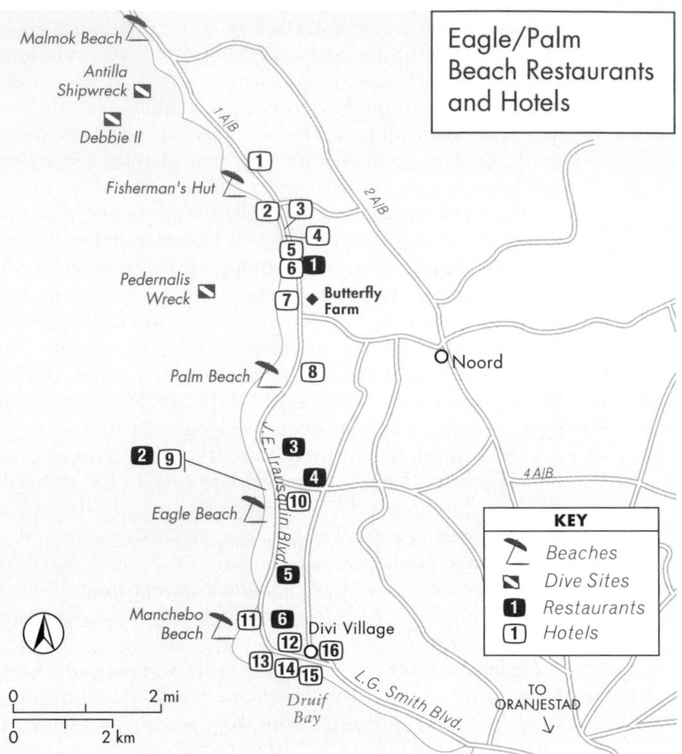

papiamentoaruba.com *Reservations essential* *Closed Mon. No lunch.*

$$$$ CARIBBEAN **Passions on the Beach.** Every night the Amsterdam Manor Beach Resort transforms the area of Eagle Beach in front of the hotel into a magical and romantic beach dining room. Tiki torches illuminate the white sand, and the linen-covered tables are within inches of the lapping water. Dine on imaginative dishes that are as beautiful as they are delicious. The huge tropical watermelon salad presented in a watermelon half is refreshing and whets the appetite with a slight chili heat. In this "reef cuisine," the main courses lean toward seafood, though meat lovers also are indulged. After dinner, relax with your toes in the sand and enjoy the best show that nature has to offer over signature cocktails. *Average main: $32* *Amsterdam Manor Beach Resort, J.E. Irausquin Blvd 252, Eagle Beach* *297/527–1100* *www.passions-restaurant-aruba.com* *Reservations essential.*

$$$ ECLECTIC Fodor's Choice ★ **Pinchos Grill & Bar.** Built on a pier, this casual spot with only 16 tables has one of the most romantic settings on the island. At night the restaurant glimmers from a distance as hundreds of lights reflect off the water. The restaurant's name comes from the Spanish word for a skewered snack so there are always a few of those on the menu. Guests can watch as the chef prepares delectable meals on the grill in his tiny kitchen while owners, Anabela and Robby, keep diners comfortable and happy. The

fish-cakes appetizer with a pineapple-mayonnaise dressing is a marriage made in heaven. The bar area is great for enjoying ocean breezes over one of their excellent signature cocktails or artisanal sangrias, and sometimes there's live entertainment. Magical at night is the lit-up water below the tables where you can see the colorful fish swimming by. Romance is always on tap here, especially with the lover's swing by the bar. *Average main: $24* *L.G. Smith Blvd. 7, Oranjestad* *297/583–2666* *No lunch.*

$$$$ CARIBBEAN **Ruinas del Mar.** Meaning "ruins by the sea," this scenic spot is the focal point of the grand dame Hyatt Regency hotel, famous for its gorgeous tropical grounds and water circuit of falls and pools leading to the sea. The trademark black swans swimming around the koi pond cresting the tiki-torch-lit terrace of the dining room make for a very romantic setting, and the interior is elegant and refined. Specialties include stone-hearth cooked items and basic international fare that changes at the chef's fancy and with the seasons. Not to be missed is the local pumpkin soup with coconut milk and cilantro. The Sunday champagne brunch buffet is also very popular, and the setting is unparalleled for breakfast weekdays as well. *Average main: $39* *Hyatt Regency Aruba Beach Resort & Casino, J.E. Irausquin Blvd. 85, Palm Beach* *297/586–1234* *www.aruba.hyatt.com* *Reservations essential* *No lunch. No dinner Sun.*

$$$$ ECLECTIC **Ventanas del Mar.** Floor-to-ceiling windows provide ample views across the lovely Tierra del Sol Golf Course and beyond to rolling sand dunes and the sea and the landmark California Lighthouse. Dining on the open-air terrace amid flickering candles inspires romance. Inside there's a distinctly country-club atmosphere. Sandwiches, salads, conch fritters, nachos, and quesadillas fill the midday menu; at night the emphasis is on seafood and meat. Crispy whole red snapper in a sweet-and-sour sauce and crab-and-corn chowder are specialties. Ask about their "All-you-can-taste" nights and early-bird menus that can change during the week. Before or after dinner, relax in style on their plush couches in their stylish lounge. *Average main: $32* *Tierra del Sol Resort, Malmokweg* *297/586–7800* *www.tierradelsol.com* *Closed Sun. Apr.–Nov.*

$$$$ INTERNATIONAL **Windows on Aruba.** Sunset views over the greens to the ocean beyond, live music, and impeccable service make this restaurant in the clubhouse of the Divi golf course one of the most romantic spots on the island. Menu items include the usual seafood and meat assortment but are exquisitely prepared and beautifully presented. The cauliflower and truffle soup—an excellent starter—reveals an understanding of turning simple ingredients into a complex taste experience. An excellent à la carte brunch experience with unlimited champagne draws locals and visitors alike every Sunday as well. *Average main: $36* *Divi Village Golf Resort, J.E. Irausquin Blvd. 41, Divi beach* *297/730–5017* *www.windowsonaruba.com* *Reservations essential* *No lunch Sat.*

4

WHERE TO STAY

Hotels on the island are categorized as low-rise or high-rise and are grouped in two distinct areas along L.G. Smith and J.E. Irausquin boulevards north of Oranjestad. The low-rise properties are closer to the capital, the high-rises in a swath a little farther north. Hotel rates, with the exception of those at a few all-inclusives, generally do not include meals or even breakfast. The larger resorts are destinations unto themselves, with shopping, entertainment, and casinos.

$ ALL-INCLUSIVE FAMILY **Amsterdam Manor Beach Resort.** Amsterdam Manor is an intimate, family-run hotel with a genuinely friendly staff, offering excellent value without too many frills. **Pros:** feels like a European village; friendly and helpful staff; mini-grocery on-site; public bus stop in front of hotel for easy access to downtown and the high-rise area. **Cons:** across the road from the beach; lacks the boutiques and attractions of a larger hotel; small pool; Jet Skis at beach can be noisy. *Rooms from: $225* ✉ *J.E. Irausquin Blvd. 252, Eagle Beach* ☎ *297/527–1100, 800/932–2310* 🌐 *www.amsterdammanor.com* *68 rooms, 4 suites* *All-inclusive.*

$ HOTEL FAMILY **Aruba Beach Club.** A favorite for families as well as those on a budget, Aruba Beach Club offers basic studios and one-bedroom units that attract repeat customers who enjoy a homey getaway on a great beach. **Pros:** family-friendly atmosphere; great beach; numerous activities; excellent value. **Cons:** pool area can be very busy; old-fashioned feel; service is uninspired except in the restaurant. *Rooms from: $200* ✉ *J.E. Irausquin Blvd. 51–53, Punta Brabo Beach* ☎ *297/582–3000* 🌐 *www.arubabeachclub.net* *131 suites* *No meals.*

$$$ RESORT Fodor's Choice ★ **Aruba Marriott Resort & Stellaris Casino.** One of the first landmark resorts on the high-rise beach strip, the Aruba Marriott combines family fun offerings with romance and business by offering an entirely separate luxury floor. **Pros:** every kind of amenity including full-service spa and beauty salon, large conference center/ballroom; shopping. **Cons:** charge for Wi-Fi beyond lobby; can be boisterous around the pool area; beach can become crowded in high season. *Rooms from: $411* ✉ *L.G. Smith Blvd. 101, Palm Beach* ☎ *297/586–9000, 800/223–6388* 🌐 *www.marriott.com* *388 rooms, 23 suites* *No meals.*

$ HOTEL Fodor's Choice ★ **Boardwalk Small Hotel Aruba.** A gorgeous luxury boutique oasis in an ex-coconut plantation, this family run gem is decorated in bright tropical hues with unique accents supplied by local artists. **Pros:** beautiful grounds and decor; intimate and romantic; highly personal service; eco-aware operation; free Wi-Fi. **Cons:** not right on the beach; limited views; fair walk from shopping. *Rooms from: $250* ✉ *Bakval 20, Palm Beach* ☎ *297/586–6654* 🌐 *www.boardwalkaruba.com* *11 1-bedroom suites, 2 2-bedroom suites* *No meals.*

$$$ HOTEL Fodor's Choice ★ **Bucuti & Tara Beach Resorts.** An extraordinary beach setting, impeccable personal service, and attention to detail help this elegant Green Globe resort easily outclass anything else on the island. **Pros:** sophisticated atmosphere; impeccable service; free self-service laundry; free Wi-Fi throughout; free use of netbooks during stay; outdoor bar is for exclusive use of hotel guests. **Cons:** beach can get busy because other hotels share it; no room service; no longer doing beach weddings. *Rooms*

Amsterdam Manor Beach Resort

from: $451 ✉ *L.G. Smith Blvd. 55B, Eagle Beach* ☎ *297/583–1100* 🌐 *www.bucuti.com* *63 rooms, 38 suites, 3 bungalows* *Breakfast.*

$$$$ ALL-INCLUSIVE FAMILY **Divi Aruba Beach Resort All Inclusive.** The free food and drinks here and the ability to use the facilities of the adjoining sister Tamarijn Resort mean you have very little reason to wander far from the idyllic beach location. **Pros:** on wonderful stretch of beach; common areas feel light and airy; great staff. **Cons:** buffet could use more variety; you must wear bracelets; charge for Wi-Fi. *Rooms from: $638* ✉ *L.G. Smith Blvd. 93, Manchebo Beach* ☎ *297/582–3300, 800/554–2008* 🌐 *www.diviaruba.com* *205 rooms, 4 suites* *All-inclusive* ☞ *5-night minimum.*

$$$ RESORT Fodor's Choice ★ **Divi Aruba Phoenix Beach Resort.** With incredible views from its high-rise tower, stunning rooms awash in tropical colors and state-of–the-art amenities, and comfortable, homey accommodations, Divi Aruba Phoenix offers something for everyone. **Pros:** beautifully appointed rooms; great beach; privacy from main Palm Beach frenzy; great vibe. **Cons:** children don't always stick to their appointed areas; Jet Skis from nearby operator can be noisy. *Rooms from: $414* ✉ *J.E. Irausquin Blvd. 75, Palm Beach* ☎ *297/586–1170* 🌐 *www.diviarubaphoenix.com* *140 luxury suites, 101 rooms* *No meals.*

$$ ALL-INCLUSIVE **Divi Village Golf & Beach Resort.** Although it's just across the road from its sister Divi properties, this all-suites version is quieter and more refined. **Pros:** excellent golf course; spacious rooms; lush grounds; free shuttles to sister Divi resorts on the beach; spa has the only hammam on the island. **Cons:** bit of a hike from some rooms to the lobby; it might be a bit too quiet for some; no ocean views. *Rooms from: $309* ✉ *J.E. Irausquin Blvd. 93, Oranjestad* ☎ *297/583–5000, 297/583–5000*

www.divivillage.com 250 suites All-inclusive 3-night minimum.

$$ RESORT FAMILY **Holiday Inn Resort Aruba.** Recipient of the 2014 "Renovation of the Year" award within the InterContinental Hotels Group Company, this is not your typical Holiday Inn. **Pros:** thematic zones provide distinct amenities; gorgeous pool area with sea views; lively vibe; free Wi-Fi. **Cons:** frequently fully booked; busy pool area; busy reception area. *Rooms from: $307 J.E. Irausquin Blvd. 230, Palm Beach 297/586–3600, 800/465–4329 www.holidayarubaresort.com 597 rooms, 7 suites Multiple meal plans.*

$$$$ ALL-INCLUSIVE **Hotel Riu Palace Aruba.** This white wedding cake of a resort towers over Palm Beach with one eight-story and two 10-story towers. **Pros:** beautiful vistas; drink dispensers in all rooms; large and lively pool area. **Cons:** pool area and beach is always crowded and loud; constant spring break party atmosphere; unimpressive à la carte restaurants; standard Riu interior decor is very out of place for Aruba; nothing locally inspired. *Rooms from: $674 J.E. Irausquin Blvd. 79, Palm Beach 297/586–3900, 800/345–2782 www.riuaruba.com 450 rooms All-inclusive.*

$$$$ RESORT FAMILY Fodor's Choice ★ **Hyatt Regency Aruba Beach Resort & Casino.** This 12-acre property is one the most lavishly landscaped resorts on the island, with a glorious array of bright tropical blooms and lush foliage surrounding a circuit of waterfalls culminating in a koi pond where black swans glide gracefully by. **Pros:** beautiful grounds; great for kids; excellent restaurants. **Cons:** small balconies for a luxury hotel; some rooms are quite a stretch from the beach. *Rooms from: $650 J.E. Irausquin Blvd. 85, Palm Beach 297/586–1234, 800/554–9288 aruba.hyatt.com 342 rooms, 24 suites, 29 regency club rooms No meals.*

$$$$ RENTAL FAMILY **Marriott's Aruba Ocean Club.** First-rate amenities and lavishly decorated villas have made this time-share the island favorite. **Pros:** relaxed atmosphere; feels more like a home than a hotel room; excellent beach. **Cons:** beach can get crowded; attracts large families, so kids are everywhere. *Rooms from: $700 L.G. Smith Blvd. 99, Palm Beach 297/586–2641 www.marriott.com 93 rooms, 213 suites No meals.*

$$$$ ALL-INCLUSIVE **Occidental Grand Aruba Resort & Casino.** From the spectacular beach to great nightly entertainment, and eclectic choice of dining and a dedicated Kids' Club, The Occidental Grand offers something for everyone. **Pros:** great beach location; lots of water sports in front; friendly; not spring-break style. **Cons:** non-stop action; few quiet escape spots; size can make it seem somewhat impersonal at times. *Rooms from: $640 J.E. Irausquin Blvd. 83, Palm Beach 297/586–4500, 800/448–8355 www.occidentalgrandaruba.com 368 rooms All-inclusive.*

$$$ RESORT Fodor's Choice ★ **Renaissance Aruba Resort & Casino.** This landmark property right on the port offers guests the best of both worlds—adults-only accommodations and family-friendly amenities with its own man-made beach. **Pros:** in the heart of the downtown shopping district; lobby and shopping areas are always lively; pool area offers an unmatched view of the port; free access to private island. **Cons:** rooms overlooking the atrium can be a bit claustrophobic; beach is off-site; no hotel grounds; no balconies in downtown section, nights can be noisy. *Rooms from: $397 L.G.*

Smith Blvd. 82, Oranjestad ☎ *297/583–6000, 800/421–8188* 🌐 *www.renaissancearuba.com* 🛏 *287 rooms, 269 suites* 🍴 *Multiple meal plans.*

$$$$ RESORT **Ritz-Carlton Aruba.** The high standards of Ritz-Carlton properties are well represented at the Aruba property with rooms that have private balconies, and ocean-view rooms that offer sweeping vistas of the Caribbean. **Pros:** absolute luxury; two pools so they never feel crowded; 24-hour room service; excellent restaurants on-site. **Cons:** far from downtown shopping at the end of Palm Beach; beach is off-site; lacks the intimate feel of smaller properties. 💲 *Rooms from: $650* ✉ *L.G. Smith Blvd. 107, Palm Beach* ☎ *297/527–2222* 🌐 *www.ritzcarlton.com/en/properties/aruba* 🛏 *265 rooms, 55 suites* 🍴 *No meals.*

$$$$ ALL-INCLUSIVE **Tamarijn Aruba All-Inclusive Beach Resort.** Sister property of the Divi Aruba All-Inclusive, this property is decidedly more laid-back and all rooms are oceanfront on a spectacular beach that is walking distance from town. **Pros:** stunning beach; access to the Divi Aruba All-Inclusive next door; nightly entertainment. **Cons:** Wi-Fi is an additional charge; daytime might be too quiet for some. 💲 *Rooms from: $614* ✉ *J.E. Irausquin Blvd. 41, Punta Brabo* ☎ *297/594–7888, 800/554–2008* 🌐 *www.tamarijnaruba.com* 🛏 *216 rooms, 20 suites* 🍴 *All-inclusive* ☞ *3-night minimum.*

$ RESORT FAMILY **Tropicana Aruba Resort & Casino.** An excellent waterslide, fast-food options, and a nearby supermarket make this complex of self-contained time-share units right across from Eagle Beach a popular choice for families. **Pros:** nice pools and waterfall; supermarket right across the street; price is hard to beat for a hotel so close to the beach. **Cons:** feels like an apartment complex; public areas are noisy and crowded; despite the attractions for children, there are no kids' programs available. 💲 *Rooms from: $191* ✉ *J.E. Irausquin Blvd. 250, Eagle Beach* ☎ *297/587–9000, 800/835–7193* 🌐 *www.troparuba.com* 🛏 *362 suites* 🍴 *No meals.*

4

NIGHTLIFE

Unlike many islands, Aruba's nightlife isn't confined to the touristy folkloric shows at hotels. Arubans like to party. They usually start celebrating late, and the action doesn't pick up until around midnight.

BARS

Iguana Joe's. The reptilian-themed decor is as colorful and creative as the specialty cocktails served here. A favorite hangout for those who want to enjoy the view of the port from the second-floor balcony. The crowd is primarily tourists during the early evening, and many locals enjoy the laid-back vibe on Friday and Saturday nights. Though famous for their potent drinks, especially their signature Pink Iguana, the food deserves a shout-out as well, especially the jerk chicken and coconut shrimp. ✉ *Royal Plaza Mall, L.G. Smith Blvd. 94, Oranjestad* ☎ *297/583–9373* 🌐 *www.iguanajoesaruba.com* ⊙ *Closed Sun.*

Fodor's Choice ★ **MooMba Beach Bar.** As the central party spot on the busiest part of Palm Beach, this open-air bar is famous for its Sunday night blowouts with big crowds of locals gathering to dance in the sand to live bands or DJs.

The barkeeps are flair and mixology masters, and happy hours are also very hot. Its sister dining establishment is also a wonderful surfside spot for breakfast, lunch, and dinner. ✉ *Between Holiday Inn and Marriott Surf Club, J.E. Irausquin Blvd. 230, Palm Beach* ☎ *297/586–5365* 🌐 *www.moombabeach.com.*

CASINOS

Aruban casinos offer something for both high and low rollers, as well as live, nightly entertainment in their lounges. Serious gamblers may want to look for the largest or the most active casinos, but many simply visit the casino closest to their hotel.

Alhambra Casino. Recently refurbished and refreshed as part of the new Alhambra Mall reconstruction, this is a lively popular casino with a big selection of modern slots, blackjack, craps, poker, roulette and more. Be sure to join their Player's Club—it's free and offers free slot credits, and you earn points with your card as well. Their new restaurant called The Cove serves light meals and drinks, and you'll also receive free drinks on the floor when you are playing the games. Special themes nights and promotions all week, and Saturday afternoons they have Super Bingo. It is owned by the Divi family of resorts. ✉ *L.G. Smith Blvd. 47, Oranjestad* ☎ *297/583–5000* 🌐 *www.casinoalhambra.com.*

Crystal Casino. Adorned with Austrian crystal chandeliers and gold-leaf columns, the Renaissance Aruba's glittering casino evokes Monaco's grand establishments. The Salon Privé offers serious gamblers a private room for baccarat, roulette, and high-stakes blackjack. This casino is popular among cruise-ship passengers, who stroll over from the port to watch and play in slot tournaments and bet on sporting events. Luxury car giveaways are also a big draw there. Open 11 am–6 am daily. ✉ *Renaissance Aruba Resort & Casino, L.G. Smith Blvd. 82, Oranjestad* ☎ *297/583–6000.*

Hyatt Regency Casino. Ablaze with neon, with a Carnival-in-Rio theme, the most popular games here are slots, blackjack, craps, and baccarat. In the heart of the main tourist strip in one of the nicest hotels along Palm Beach, this gambling emporium is also known for its live music Thursday through Sunday and lively party atmosphere. Don't forget to ask for your $10 free play card. Open until 4 am. ✉ *Hyatt Regency Aruba Beach Resort & Casino, J.E. Irausquin Blvd. 85, Palm Beach* ☎ *297/586–1234* 🌐 *www.aruba.hyatt.com.*

Fodor's Choice ★ **Stellaris Casino.** This is the largest casino on the island and boasts 500 modern interactive slots and 28 tables with games like craps, roulette, poker, and blackjack. They also have a state-of-the-art race and sports betting operation. Don't forget to join their VIP Club program where you can earn points, comps, and prizes. Free cocktails for gamers, and there are many special theme and entertainment nights. ✉ *Aruba Marriott Resort, L.G. Smith Blvd. 101, Palm Beach* ☎ *297/520–6428.*

DANCE AND MUSIC CLUBS

Fodor's Choice ★ **Gusto.** Definitely Aruba's most cosmopolitan, high-octane dance club, Gusto is where master bartenders show off excellent flair skills while serving up fabulous cocktails. Plenty of pretty people, the island's hottest DJ's, and dazzling light show keep the dancing going non-stop.

Late-night happy hour is from 9 pm to 11pm. All kinds of special events and theme nights add to Gusto's allure as a highly popular party spot. ✉ *J.E. Irausquin Boulevard 348-A, Palm Beach* ⊙ *Closed Mon.*

Nikky Beach. This upscale hot spot is party central on Friday night. Local bands perform on Sunday. The venue is often booked for special events so call ahead. ✉ *L.G. Smith Blvd. 2, Oranjestad* ☎ *297/582–0153* 🌐 *www.nikkybeacharuba.com.*

NIGHTLIFE TOURS AND FESTIVALS

Banana Bus. It's crazy touristy fun but if you are in the mood to bounce around the streets in a loud, colorful bus with a 20-foot banana on the roof, then this is your ride. Stop at three of Aruba's liveliest bars and enjoy revelry replete with supplied noisemakers along the way. Five drinks are included in the price. Reservations can be made at your hotel front desk. The bus makes pickups and drop-offs at all major resorts. It's run by Marlab Tours, which also does day-tripping adventures to major island attractions. 🌐 *www.bananabusaruba.com.*

4

Carubbian Festival. Every Thursday night in San Nicolas, the main streets of Aruba's old refinery town that locals called "Sunrise City" come to life in a spectacular fashion with a mini-carnival called the Carubbian Festival. It's a culture and heritage extravaganza featuring live music concerts, dancing shows, and even a big colorful parade finale where visitors are encouraged to fully participate. There are also arts and crafts stalls and food and drink kiosks that include local specialties set up for the occasion. There are activities planned for children as well. Festival runs from 6 pm to 10 pm. ■ **TIP→ You are best to take a hotel bus package as the roads at night are not lit, and navigation can be challenging.** ✉ *Main St., San Nicolas* 🎟 *Free.*

FAMILY Fodor's Choice ★ **Kukoo Kunuku Party Bus & Day Tours.** Aruba's premier wild and crazy party bus has been operating for almost two decades, and now they've added a new twist. Evenings it's all about shaking your maracas and bar-hopping through the town via their famous "Pub Krawl" tour or doing a new bar-hop and dinner night that culminates at the new Casibari Grill in the outback. But during the day, the bus now morphs into one big happy family-friendly vehicle that offers a trip to the surreal Casibari rock formations and Baby Beach in San Nicolas, or an "Animal Lover's" outing that goes to the Aruba Donkey Sanctuary, Phillips Animal Garden, and the Butterfly Farm. Either way, their guides are fabulous entertainers. Hotel pickup and drop-off included. No tours on Sunday. Private charters are also available. ■ **TIP→ Book direct by phone for a discount, or book a night tour at the same time as a day tour and receive $10 off.** ✉ *Noord 128 P, Noord* ☎ *297/586–2009* 🌐 *www.kukookunuku.com.*

SHOPS AND SPAS

The only real duty-free shopping is in the departure area of the airport. (Passengers bound for the United States should be sure to shop before proceeding through U.S. customs in Aruba.) Downtown stores do have very low sales tax though and some excellent bargains on high-end luxury items like gold, silver, and jewelry. Major credit cards are welcome everywhere, as are U.S. dollars. Aruba's souvenir and crafts stores are full of Dutch porcelains and figurines, as befits the island's heritage. Dutch cheese is a good buy, as are hand-embroidered linens and any products made from the native aloe vera plant. Local arts and crafts run toward wood carvings and earthenware emblazoned with "Aruba: One Happy Island" and the like, but there are many shops with unique Aruban items like designer wear and artwork. Don't try to bargain unless you are at a flea market. Arubans consider it rude to haggle.

AREAS AND MALLS

Alhambra Mall. There's an eclectic array of shops and dining in the Alhambra Mall with the casino as its focal point. Dotted with designer retail stores like The Lazy Lizard and the Aruba Aloe outlet, and a full service market and deli, the alfresco mall also has fast-food outlets like Juan Valdez Coffee Shop, Baskin Robbins, and Subway. Fusions Wine & Tapas Bar and popular new eateries Hollywood Smokehouse and Twist of Flavors restaurant round out the dining options. There's also a small full-service spa. ✉ *L.G. Smith Blvd. 47, Manchebo Beach.*

Caya G.F. Betico Croes. Oranjestad's original "Main Street" (behind the Renaissance Marina Resort) had been neglected since most cruise passengers preferred to stick to the front street near the marina where the high-end shops and open market souvenir stalls are. However, a recent massive renovation of the entire downtown region has breathed new life into the back streets with pedestrian-only stretches, compact malls, and open resting areas. A free eco-trolley now loops all through downtown, allowing you to hop on and off to shop at all kinds of stores. Fashions, souvenirs, specialty items, sporting goods, cosmetics . . . you name it, you'll find them all on this renewed street. ✉ *Oranjestad.*

Palm Beach Plaza. Aruba's newest and largest mall caters to shoppers with an eye for luxury. Stores include Mont Blanc, Ferragamo, Swarovski, and other high-end brands. Dining options range from burgers to sushi, and those seeking entertainment can enjoy a movie at the mall's megaplex. ✉ *Palm Beach* 🌐 *www.palmbeachplaza.com.*

FAMILY
Fodor's Choice ★
Paseo Herencia. A gorgeous old-fashioned colonial style courtyard and clock tower encases souvenir and specialty shops, cinemas, dining spots, cafés, and bars in this low-rise alfresco mall just off Palm Beach. Famous for its "liquid fireworks" shows when three times a night neon-lit water fountains waltz to music in a choreographed dance. Visitors can enjoy it for free from an outdoor amphitheater where many cultural events also take place. There's also a fancy carousel for children and a trendy bar with an outside dipping pool with neon-lit chairs that constantly change colors. A must visit—if not for the shopping—then for the water show. ✉ *J.E. Irausquin Blvd 382, Palm Beach* ☎ *297/586–6533* 🌐 *paseoherencia.com.*

Renaissance Mall. Upscale name-brand fashion and luxury brands of perfume, cosmetics, leather goods is what you'll find in the array of 60 stores spanning two floors in this mall located within and underneath the Renaissance Marina Resort. You'll also find specialty items like cigars and designer shoes plus high-end gold, silver, diamonds, and quality jewelry at low duty and no tax prices. Cafés and high-end dining, plus a casino and spa round out the offerings. Late-night shopping until 8 pm daily. ✉ *Renaissance Marina Resort, L.G. Smith Blvd. 82, Oranjestad* ☎ *297/582–4622* 🌐 *www.shoprenaissancearuba.com.*

Renaissance Marketplace. Five minutes from the cruise-ship terminal, the Renaissance Marketplace, also known as Seaport Mall, has more than 120 stores selling merchandise to meet every taste and budget; the Seaport Casino is also here. ✉ *L.G. Smith Blvd. 82, Oranjestad.*

Royal Plaza Mall. It's impossible to miss this gorgeous colonial-style, cotton-candy-colored building with the big gold dome gracing the front street along the marina. It's one of the most photographed in Oranjestad. Three levels of shops—indoor and outdoor—make up this artsy arcade full of small boutiques, cigar shops, designer clothing outlets, gift and jewelry stores, and souvenir kiosks. Great dining and bars are within as well. ✉ *L.G. Smith Blvd. 94, Oranjestad* ☎ *297/588–0351.*

4

ART GALLERIES

Gasparito Restaurant & Art Gallery. A permanent exhibition by a variety of Aruban artists is featured here, ranging from colorful landscapes to more abstract offerings. ✉ *Gasparito 3, Noord* ☎ *297/586–7044.*

Insight Art Studio. Owner Alida Martinez, a Venezuelan-born artist, likes more-avant-garde displays so don't expect to find the usual paintings of pastel-color skies here. Inventive works by local and international artists are featured. Martinez's own mixed-media creations juxtapose erotic and religious themes. The space, which includes a studio, is a magnet for the island's art community. Viewing is by appointment only. ✉ *Paradera Park 215, Paradera* ☎ *297/582–5882.*

CIGARS

Cigar Emporium. The Cubans come straight from the climate-controlled humidor at Cigar Emporium. Choose from Cohiba, Montecristo, Romeo y Julieta, Partagas, and more. ✉ *Renaissance Mall, L.G. Smith Blvd. 82, Oranjestad* ☎ *297/582–5479.*

CLOTHING

Fodor's Choice ★ **Wulfsen & Wulfsen.** In business for over 50 years, this sophisticated shop offers elegant European fashions for both women and men, and footwear for men as well. Plus sizes are also available for the ladies, and their on-site tailor makes this a rare made-to-measure emporium on the island. ✉ *Caya G.F. Betico Croes 52, Oranjestad* ☎ *297/582–3823.*

HANDICRAFTS

Artistic Boutique. The exclusive agents on the island for NAO by LLADRO collectible porcelain figurines and Aruba Lucky Stone, this little boutique also offers up a creative array of gold and silver jewelry, gems, pearls and fine watches, as well as unique giftware and decorative items like handcrafted local embroideries. ✉ *Caya G. F. Betico Croes 23, Oranjestad* ☎ *297/581–3842.*

Fodor'sChoice ★ **The Mask.** This shop specializes in original masks and crafty items called Mopa-Mopa Art. Originating with the Quillacingas Indians of Ecuador and Colombia, the art is made from the bud of the mopa-mopa tree, boiled down into a resin, colored with dyes, and applied to carved mahogany and other woods like cedar. Masks, jewelry boxes, coasters, whimsical animal figurines, and more make wonderfully unique gifts and souvenirs. The masks are also believed to ward off evil spirits. ✉ *Paseo Herencia, J.E. Irausquin Blvd. 382-A, Local C017, Palm Beach* ☎ *297/586–2900* 🌐 *www.mopamopa.com.*

JEWELRY

Colombian Emeralds. A trusted international jewelry dealer specializing in emeralds, this outlet also has a top-notch selection of diamonds, sapphires, tanzanite, rubies, ammolite, pearls, gold, semiprecious gems, luxury watches, and more at very competitive prices. A highly professional and knowledgeable staff adds to their credibility. ✉ *Renaissance Mall, L.G. Smith Blvd. 82, Oranjestad* ☎ *297/583–6238* 🌐 *www.colombianemeralds.com.*

Fodor'sChoice ★ **Diamonds International.** One of the pioneer diamond retailers in the Caribbean with over 130 stores throughout the chain, the Aruba outlet has been operating in the same spot since 1997. They are well known for their expertise, selection, quality, and competitive prices on diamonds, and they also sell high-end timepieces. The founders of Diamonds International are both graduates of the Gemological Institute of America. ✉ *Port of Call Marketplace, L.G. Smith Blvd. 17, Oranjestad* ☎ *800/515–3935* 🌐 *www.diamondsinternational.com.*

PERFUMES

Aruba Trading Company. Established in 1933, and located in the gorgeous Dutch colonial structure known as "La Casa Amarilla" (The Yellow House) in downtown Oranjestad, this shop specializes in fine perfumes, high-end cosmetics, and personal-care products. They also have beauty specialists and make-up artists on-site. ✉ *Caya G.F. Betico Croes 12, Oranjestad* ☎ *297/582–2602* 🌐 *www.arubatrading.com.*

J.L. Penha & Sons. Originating in Curacao in 1865, Penha has branched out throughout the Caribbean and has seven stores on Aruba. The largest is right next to the Renaissance Hotel. Known for good prices on high-end perfumes, cosmetics, skincare products, and more recently, eyewear and fashions. Brand and designer names include MAC, Lancôme, Estée Lauder, Clinique, Chanel, Dior, Montblanc, and Victoria's Secret to name just a few. Their newest store is in Plaza Daniel Leo in downtown Oranjestad. ✉ *Caya G.F. Betico Croes 11/13, Oranjestad* ☎ *297/582–4160, 297/582–4161* 🌐 *www.jlpenha.com.*

Fodor'sChoice ★ **Little Switzerland.** With five stores on the island—most in high-rise resorts and the original location in downtown Royal Plaza Mall—these outlets specialize in designer jewelry and upscale timepieces by big name designers like TAGHeuer, David Yurman, Breitling, Roberto Coin, Chopard, Pandora, Tiffany & Co., Cartier, Movado, Omega, and John Hardy. ✉ *Royal Plaza Mall, L.G. Smith Blvd. 94, Oranjestad* ☎ *284/809–5560* 🌐 *www.littleswitzerland.com.*

SPAS

Fodor's Choice ★ **Larimar Spa and Salon.** Larimar is a large and soul-soothing full-service spa with tropical Caribbean-inspired accents. Specializing in the use ESPA's natural products, they offer a comprehensive range of treatments from scrubs and wraps to facials for both women and men. All massages can also be enjoyed in the lovely seaside cabanas as well. Nail and hair salons are also on-site. ✉ *Radisson Aruba Resort & Casino, J.E. Irausquin Blvd. 81, Palm Beach* ☎ *297/586–6555* 🌐 *www.radisson.com.*

Nafanny Spa. Massage therapist Fanny Lampe's home and yard in Alto Vista provide a peaceful and picturesque backdrop for the pure relaxation to come. Thai, Swedish, bamboo, and hot-stone massages are all on offer as are various treatments including a 90-minute wine-therapy session and numerous facial treatments using soothing botanicals designed to ease away impurities and stress lines. The location is a bit remote but the tranquil setting makes that something of an advantage. Fanny will often pick up clients at their resort. Daily yoga classes are also offered. Though not offered as a package, customized half- and full-day spa bundles can be created. Nafanny Spa isn't the fanciest on the island, but the individual attention is unbeatable and so are the prices. ✉ *Alto Vista 39F, Noord* ☎ *297/586–3007* 🌐 *www.nafanny.com.*

Okeanos. The ocean provides the backdrop for this spa in the Renaissance, which has its own massage cove that seems a world apart from the rest of the resort. Outdoor massages and showers help to bring the calming effects of nature into the treatments. In addition to the usual assortment of massages and wraps, the spa also offers both anti-cellulite and anti-aging treatments. There are a huge number of packages available including one that combines Swedish massage with a meal served by your own butler. Pampering doesn't get much better than this. There are also optional packages to use the spa services at the Cove Spa located on the resort's private island. ✉ *Renaissance Aruba Resort & Casino, L.G. Smith Blvd. 82, Palm Beach* ☎ *297/583–6000* 🌐 *www.renaissancearubaspa.com.*

ZoiA Spa. It's all about indulgence at the Hyatt's upscale spa named after the Papiamento word for balance. Gentle music and the scent of botanicals make the world back home fade into the background. Newly arrived visitors to the island can opt for the jet lag massage that combines reflexology and aromatherapy, and those with the budget and time for a full day of relaxation can opt for the Serene package. There's even a mother-to-be package available. Island brides can avail themselves of a full menu of beauty services ranging from botanical facials (using local ingredients) to a full makeup job for the big day. The Pure High Tea package offers a delicious assortment of snacks and teas along with an hour of treatments. ✉ *Hyatt Regency Aruba Beach Resort &*

4

Casino, J.E. Irausquin Blvd. 85, Palm Beach ☎ *297/586–1234* 🌐 *www.aruba.hyatt.com.*

SPORTS AND THE OUTDOORS

Aruba has recently become the beach tennis capital of the world and now hosts many international tournaments on its beaches. As for water sports, there is little you cannot do on Aruba, including modern thrill activities such as Jetlev®, an overwater jet pack flight; the hoverboard, an air-propelled skateboard over the waves; and jet blades, ski boots on a board that lifts you over the water. Parasailing, banana boats, Jet Skis, kayaking, paddleboarding, yoga on paddleboard . . . Aruba has it all, even a real submarine.

DAY SAILS

There is a large variety of snorkeling, dinner, sunset, and party cruises to choose from. The larger operators offer the best experience, though the smaller ones might offer the best price.

Mi Dushi. This romantic, two-masted ship ("My Sweetheart") offers daytime snorkeling trips that include breakfast, lunch, and drinks for $59 per person. It also offers popular sunset happy-hour cruises. ✉ *Turibana Plaza, Noord 124, Noord* ☎ *297/586–2010* 🌐 *www.midushi.com.*

Octopus Sailing Charters. Captain Jethro Gesterkamp is at the helm for snorkel instruction and hosting aboard his small vessel—a 40-ft. trimaran that's limited to 22 passengers, so the experience is highly personal. Champagne brunch and sunset sails also available. It's an economical alternative to some of the bigger snorkel tour operators. Private charters are also available. ✉ *Pelican Pier, Palm Beach* ☎ *297/593–3739* 🌐 *www.octopusaruba.com.*

Tranquilo Charters Aruba. Captain Mike Hagedoorn, a legendary Aruban sailor, has recently handed the helm over to his son Captain Anthony after 20 years of running the family business. Today, *The Tranquilo*—a 43-foot sailing yacht—still takes small groups of passengers to a secluded spot at Spanish lagoon named "Mike's Reef" after his father where no other snorkel trips venture. The lunch cruise to the south side always includes "Mom's famous Dutch pea soup," and they also do private charters for dinner sails and sailing trips around Aruba's lesser-explored coasts. Look for the red boat docked at the Renaissance Marina beside the Atlantis Submarines launch. ✉ *Renaissance Marina, Oranjestad* ☎ *297/586–1418* 🌐 *www.tranquiloaruba.com.*

DIVING AND SNORKELING

With visibility of up to 90 feet, the waters around Aruba are excellent for snorkeling and diving. Advanced and novice divers alike will find plenty to occupy their time, as many of the most popular sites—including some interesting shipwrecks—are found in shallow waters ranging from 30 to 60 feet. Coral reefs covered with sensuously waving sea fans and eerie giant sponge tubes attract a colorful menagerie of sea

A bouquet of colorful reefs can be explored in the waters of Aruba.

life, including gliding manta rays, curious sea turtles, shy octopuses, and grunts, groupers, and other fish. Marine preservation is a priority on Aruba, and regulations by the Conference on International Trade in Endangered Species make it unlawful to remove coral, conch, and other marine life from the water, and the new Marine Park Foundation is ensuring the protection of the reefs. Many resorts lend or rent snorkel gear cheaply.

Scuba diving operator prices vary depending on the trip. If you want to go all the way, complete open-water certification takes at least four days worth of instruction.

Aruba Pro Dive. The fact that this is a small outfit that only caters to small groups (six maximum) helps make each dive more personal, flexible, and unique. They also do night dives and all levels of PADI certification. ⊠ *Ponton 90, Noord* ☎ *297/582–5520* 🌐 *www.arubaprodive.com.*

Dive Aruba. Resort courses, certification courses, and trips to interesting shipwrecks make Dive Aruba worth checking out. Small groups make it more personal. ⊠ *Wilhelminastraat 8, Oranjestad* ☎ *297/582–7337* 🌐 *www.divearuba.com.*

Native Divers Aruba. A small, personal operation, Native Divers Aruba specializes in PADI open-water courses. Ten different certification options include specialties like Multilevel Diver, Search & Recovery Diver, and Underwater Naturalist. Their boat schedule is also flexible and it's easy to tailor instruction to your specific needs. ⊠ *Marriott Surf Club, Palm Beach* ☎ *297/586–4763* 🌐 *www.nativedivers.com.*

FISHING

Deep-sea catches here include barracuda, kingfish, wahoo, bonito, and tuna. November to April is the catch-and-release season for sailfish and marlin. Many skippered charter boats are available for half- or full-day sails. Package prices vary but typically include tackle, bait, and refreshments. Some restaurants will cook your catch for you.

Teaser Charters. The expertise of the Teaser crew is matched by a commitment to sensible fishing practices, which include catch and release and avoiding ecologically sensitive areas. The company's two boats are fully equipped, and the crew seem to have an uncanny ability to locate the best fishing spots. Captain Kenny and Captain Milton run a thrilling expedition. ✉ *Renaissance Marina, Oranjestad* ☎ *297/582–5088* 🌐 *www.teasercharters.com.*

GOLF

The Links at Divi Aruba. This 9-hole course was designed by Karl Litten and Lorie Viola. The par-36 flat layout stretches to 2,952 yards and features paspalum grass (best for seaside courses) and takes you past beautiful lagoons. It's a testy little course with water abounding, making accuracy more important than distance. Amenities include a golf school with professional instruction, a swing-analysis station, a driving range, and a two-story golf clubhouse with a pro shop. Two restaurants are available: Windows on Aruba for fine dining and Mulligan's for a casual and quick lunch. ✉ *Divi Village Golf & Beach Resort, J.E. Irausquin Blvd. 93, Oranjestad* ☎ *297/581–4653* 🌐 *www.divilinks.com* 🏌 *9 holes, 2952 yards, par 36.*

Fodor's Choice ★ **Tierra del Sol.** Stretching out to 6,811 yards, this stunning course is situated on the northwest coast near the California Lighthouse and is Aruba's only 18-hole course. Designed by Robert Trent Jones Jr., Tierra del Sol combines Aruba's native beauty—cacti and rock formations, stunning views, and good conditioning. Wind can also be a factor here on the rolling terrain as are the abundant bunkers and water hazards. Greens fees include a golf cart equipped with GPS and a communications system that allows you to order drinks for your return to the clubhouse. The fully stocked golf shop is one of the Caribbean's most elegant, with an extremely attentive staff. ✉ *Caya di Solo 10, Malmokweg* ☎ *297/586–7800* 🌐 *www.tierradelsol.com* 🏌 *18 holes, 6811 yards, par 71.*

GUIDED TOURS AND MULTISPORT OUTFITTERS

FAMILY Fodor's Choice ★ **De Palm Tours.** Aruba's premier tour company covers every inch of the island on land and under sea, and they even have their own submarine (*Atlantis*) and semi-submarine (*Seaworld Explorer*) and their own all-inclusive private island destination (De Palm Island). Land exploration options include air-conditioned bus sightseeing tours and rough and rugged outback jaunts by Jeep safari to popular attractions like the natural pool. You can also do off-road tours in a UTV (two-seater utility task vehicle) via their guided caravan trips. On the waves, their luxury catamaran *DePalm Pleasure* offers romantic sunset sails and snorkel trips that include an option to try SNUBA®-deeper snorkeling with an air-supplied raft at Aruba's most famous shipwreck. DePalm also offers airport transfers. ✉ *L.G. Smith Blvd. 142, Oranjestad* ☎ *297/582–4400* 🌐 *www.depalmtours.com.*

Rancho Notorious. One of Aruba's oldest tour operators, Rancho Notorious offers horseback riding for all levels and many different guided tours, including ATV outback adventures and mountain biking. All adventures are a great way to experience the island's rugged arid outback and scenic rocky seasides where cars cannot venture. ✉ *Boroncana, Noord* ☎ *297/586–0508* 🌐 *www.ranchonotorious.com.*

Fodor's Choice ★ **Red Sail Sports Aruba.** A dynamic company established almost 15 years ago and experts in the field of water-sports recreation, Red Sail offers excellent diving excursions, snorkel sails, sunset sails, and full-dinner sails. They even have their own sports equipment shop. They are also the original operator to introduce the cool new sport of Jetlev®—a personal jet pack over the water—and jetblades—like roller blades on the waves. They also have the island's only certified instructors for these activities, and have recently opened their own beach tennis club with expert instruction as well. ✉ *Palm Beach, Noord, Oranjestad* ☎ *297/586–1603* 🌐 *www.aruba-redsail.com.*

HIKING

Aruba's arid and rugged countryside is full of flora and fauna. Arikok National Wildlife Park is an excellent place to glimpse the real Aruba; start at the visitor center to get guidance and maps, or see their website for online trails maps (🌐 *www.arubanationalpark.org*). The heat can be oppressive, so be sure to take it easy, wear a hat, wear plenty of sunscreen, and have lots of water handy. A guided hike will show you where to find the island's elusive but interesting wildlife in the arid outback.

FAMILY **Nature Sensitive Tours.** Eddy Croes, a former park ranger whose passion for nature is infectious runs this outfitter with care. Groups are never larger than eight people, so you'll see as much detail as you can handle. The hikes are done at an easy pace and are suitable for just about anyone. Moonlight tours also available. If you'd rather not hike, Eddy also has a 4x4 monster Jeep–guided tour of the arid outback for up to 20 people as well. ✉ *Pos Chiquito 13E, Savaneta* ☎ *297/585–1594* 🌐 *www.naturesensitivetours.com.*

HORSEBACK RIDING

Rancho Daimari. Rancho Daimari will lead your horse to water—either at Natural Bridge or Natural Pool—in the morning or afternoon for $80 per person. The "Junior Dudes" program is tailored to young riders. There are even ATV trips. ✉ *Palm Beach 33B, Noord* ☎ *297/586–6284.*

KAYAKING

Aruba Watersport Center. This family-run, full-service water activity center is right on Palm Beach. They offer a comprehensive variety of adventures including diving, snorkeling, parasailing, Jet Skis, WaveRunners, tubing, Hobie cat sailing, stand-up paddleboarding, kayaking, wakeboarding, and waterskiing, speedboat and bike rentals as well. ✉ *L.G. Smith Blvd. 81B, Noord* ☎ *297/586–6613* 🌐 *arubawatersportscenter.com.*

WINDSURFING

The southwestern coast's tranquil waters at Fishermen's Huts make windsurfing conditions ideal for both beginners and intermediates alike, and expert instruction and modern equipment rental will have you up on the waves in no time. Aruba has some of the best windsurfers in the world, and the annual Hi-Winds Competition also attracts the world's best each year and brings out big crowds to party on the beach.

Aruba Active Vacations. Aruba Active Vacations is a major windsurfing center on the island. ✉ *Near Fisherman's Huts, Malmok Beach* ☎ *297/586–0989* 🌐 *www.aruba-active-vacations.com.*

Sailboard Vacations. Complete windsurfing packages, including accommodations, can be arranged with Sailboard Vacations. Equipment rentals and full-week clinics are also available. ✉ *L.G. Smith Blvd. 462, Malmok Beach* ☎ *800/252–1070* 🌐 *www.sailboardvacations.com.*

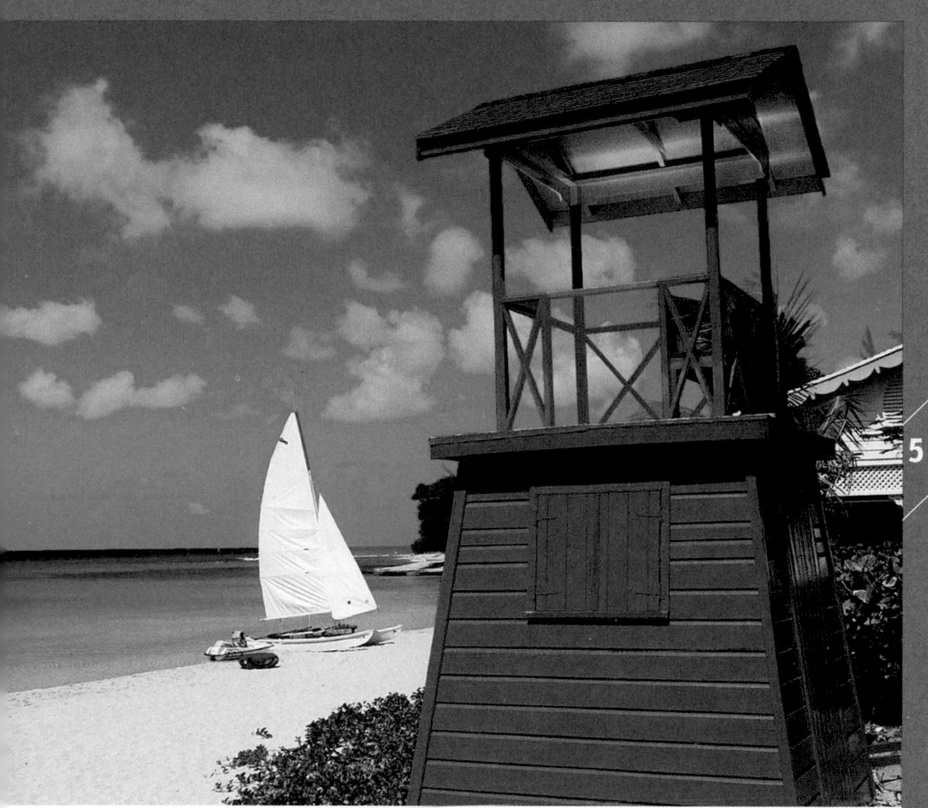

5

BARBADOS

WELCOME TO BARBADOS

Broad vistas, sweeping seascapes, craggy cliffs, and acre upon acre of sugarcane—that's Barbados. Beyond that, what draws visitors to the island is the Bajan hospitality, the welcoming hotels and resorts, the sophisticated dining, the never-ending things to see and do, the exciting nightspots, and, of course, the sunny beaches.

Restaurants ▼	
The Atlantis	9
Bellini's Trattoria	5
Brown Sugar	1
Café Luna	8
Café Sol	6
Champers	3
Fish Pot	12
L'Azure at the Crane	10
Naniki Restaurant	11
Shakers	2
Sweet Potatoes	4
Waterside Restaurant	7

Hotels ▼	
Accra Beach Hotel & Spa	2
The Atlantis Hotel	15
Bougainvillea Beach Resort	9
Cobblers Cove Hotel	17
Sandal's Barbados	7
Courtyard Bridgetown by Marriott	3
The Crane	14
Divi Southwinds Beach Resort	8
Hilton Barbados	1
Island Inn Hotel	4
Little Arches Hotel	12
Little Good Harbour	16
Ocean Two	10
Radisson Aquatica	5
Silver Point Hotel	13
SoCo Hotel	6
Turtle Beach Resort	11

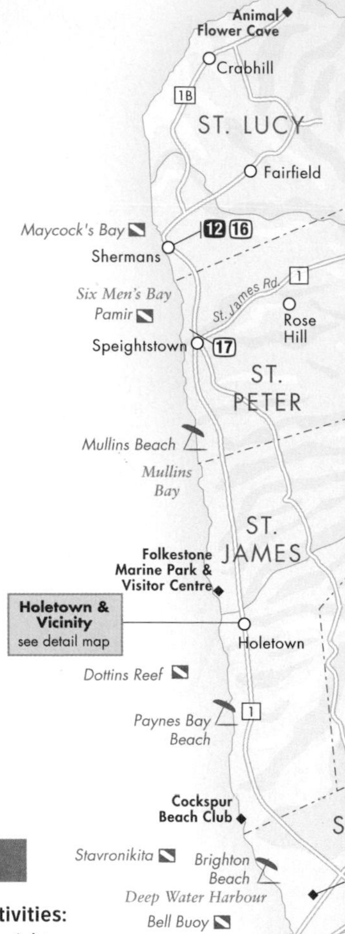

TOP REASONS TO VISIT BARBADOS

1 Great Resorts: They run the gamut—from unpretentious to knock-your-socks-off.

2 Great Golf: Tee off at some of the best championship courses in the Caribbean.

3 Restaurants Galore: Great food ranges from street-party barbecue to world-class dining.

4 Wide Range of Activities: Land and water sports, sightseeing options, and nightlife... there's always plenty to do.

5 Welcoming Locals: Bajans are friendly, welcoming, helpful, and hospitable. You'll like them; they'll like you.

BARBADOS BASICS

Barbados stands apart—both geographically and geologically—from its Caribbean neighbors; it's a full 100 miles (161 km) east of the Lesser Antilles chain. The top of a single submerged mountain of coral and limestone, Barbados is 21 miles (34 km) long, 14 miles (22½ km) wide, and relatively flat. The population is nearly 300,000, and the capital city is Bridgetown.

Updated by
Jane E. Zarem

Isolated in the Atlantic Ocean, 100 miles (161 km) due east of St. Lucia, Barbados stands apart from its neighbors in the Lesser Antilles archipelago, the chain of islands that stretches in a graceful arc from the Virgin Islands to Trinidad.

Geologically, most of the Lesser Antilles are the peaks of a volcanic mountain range, whereas Barbados is the top of a single, relatively flat protuberance of coral and limestone—the source of building blocks for many a plantation manor. Some of those historic "great houses," in fact, have been carefully restored. Two are open to visitors.

Bridgetown, both capital city and commercial center, is on the southwest coast of pear-shape Barbados. Most of the nearly 300,000 Bajans (*Bay*-juns, derived from the British pronunciation of *Barbadian*) live and work in and around Bridgetown, elsewhere in St. Michael Parish, or along the idyllic west coast or busy south coast. Others reside in tiny villages that dot the interior landscape. Broad sandy beaches, craggy cliffs, and numerous coves make up the coastline, and the interior is consumed by forested hills and gullies and acre upon acre of sugarcane.

Without question, Barbados is the "most British" island in the Caribbean. In contrast to the turbulent colonial past experienced by neighboring islands, including repeated conflicts between France and Britain for dominance and control, British rule in Barbados carried on uninterrupted for 340 years—from the first established British settlement in 1627 until independence was granted in 1966. That's not to say, of course, that there weren't significant struggles in Barbados, as elsewhere in the Caribbean, between 17th- and 18th-century British landowners and their African-born slaves and other indentured servants.

With that unfortunate period of slavery relegated to the history books, the British influence on Barbados remains strong today in local manners, attitudes, customs, and politics—tempered, of course, by the characteristically warm nature and Caribbean style of the Bajan people. In keeping with British-born traditions, many Bajans worship at the Anglican church, afternoon tea is a ritual, cricket is the national pastime (a passion, most admit), dressing for dinner is a firmly entrenched tradition, and patrons at some bars are as likely to order a Pimm's Cup or

LOGISTICS

Getting to Barbados: You can fly nonstop to Barbados from Atlanta, Miami, or New York. Grantley Adams International Airport (BGI) is in Christ Church Parish, on the south coast; the airport is about 15 minutes from hotels situated along the south coast, 45 minutes from the west coast, and 30 minutes from Bridgetown.

Hassle Factor: Low.

On the Ground: Ground transportation is available immediately outside the customs area. Airport taxis aren't metered, but fares are regulated ($38–$40 to Speightstown, $30–$35 to west-coast hotels, $16–$22 to south-coast hotels). Be sure, however, to establish the fare before getting into the taxi, and confirm whether the price quoted is in U.S. or Barbadian dollars.

Getting Around the Island: If you are staying in an isolated area, you may want to rent a car, but bus service is good, especially between Bridgetown and stops along the west and south coasts. Taxis, of course, are always an option.

5

a shandy as a rum and Coke. And yet, Barbados is hardly stuffy—this is still the Caribbean, after all.

Tourist facilities are concentrated on the west coast in St. James and St. Peter parishes (appropriately dubbed the "Platinum Coast") and on the south coast in Christ Church Parish. Traveling north along the west coast to historic Holetown, the site of the first British settlement, and continuing to the city of Speightstown, you can find posh beachfront resorts, luxurious private villas, and fine restaurants enveloped by tropical gardens and lush foliage. The trendier, more commercial south coast offers competitively priced hotels and beach resorts, and the St. Lawrence Gap area is known for its restaurants and nightlife. The relatively wide-open spaces along the southeast coast are proving ripe for development, and some wonderful inns and hotels already take advantage of those intoxicatingly beautiful ocean vistas. For their own vacations, though, Bajans escape to the rugged east coast, where the Atlantic surf pounds the dramatic shoreline with unrelenting force.

All in all, Barbados is a sophisticated tropical island with a rich history, lodgings to suit every taste and pocketbook, and plenty to pique your interest both day and night—whether you're British or not.

PLANNING

WHEN TO GO

Barbados is busiest in the high season, which extends from December 15 through April 15. Off-season hotel rates can be half of those charged during the busy period. During the high season, too, a few hotels may require you to buy a meal plan, which is usually not required in the low season. As noted in the listings, some hotels close in September and October, the slowest months of the off-season, for annual maintenance and renovations. Some restaurants may close for brief periods within that time frame, as well.

GETTING HERE AND AROUND

AIR TRAVEL

You can fly nonstop to Barbados from Atlanta (Delta), Miami (American), and New York–JFK (JetBlue). Caribbean Airlines offers connecting service from Miami and New York via Port of Spain, Trinidad, but this adds at least two hours to your flight time even in the best of circumstances and may not be the best option for most Americans. Barbados is also well connected to other Caribbean islands via LIAT. Mustique Airways and SVG Air connect Barbados to St. Vincent and the Grenadines. Many passengers use Barbados as a transit hub, sometimes spending the night each way.

Not all airlines flying into Barbados have local numbers. If your airline doesn't have a local contact number on the island, you will have to pay for the call.

Airline Contacts **American Airlines** ☎ *800/744–0006 in Barbados only, 246/428–4170* 🌐 *www.aa.com.* **Caribbean Airlines** ☎ *246/429–5929, 800/744–2225* 🌐 *www.caribbean-airlines.com.* **Delta Air Lines** ☎ *800/221–1212 in Caribbean, 800/241–4141 in U.S.* 🌐 *www.delta.com.* **JetBlue** ☎ *877/596–2413 in Barbados, landline only, 800/538–2583 in U.S.* 🌐 *www.jetblue.com.* **LIAT** ☎ *246/428–0986, 246/428–7101, 888/844–5428 in Caribbean* 🌐 *www.liat.com.* **Mustique Airways** ☎ *246/428–1638* 🌐 *www.mustique.com.* **SVG Air** ☎ *246/247–3712* 🌐 *www.svgair.com.*

Airport **Grantley Adams International Airport** (*BGI*). ✉ *Christ Church* ☎ *246/428–7101* 🌐 *www.gaia.bb.*

BUS TRAVEL

Bus service is efficient and inexpensive. Public buses are blue with a yellow stripe; yellow buses with a blue stripe are privately owned and operated; and "ZR" vans (so called for their ZR license plate designation) are white with a maroon stripe and also privately owned and operated. All buses travel frequently along Highway 1 (St. James Road) and Highway 7 (South Coast Main Road), as well as inland routes. The fare is Bds$2 for any one destination; exact change in either local or U.S. currency ($1) is appreciated. Buses run about every 20 minutes. Small signs on roadside poles that say "To City" or "Out of City," meaning the direction relative to Bridgetown, mark the bus stops. Flag down the bus with your hand, even if you're standing at the stop. Bridgetown terminals are at Fairchild Street for buses to the south and east and at Lower Green for buses to Speightstown via the west coast.

CAR TRAVEL

Barbados has good roads, but traffic can be heavy on main highways, particularly around Bridgetown. Be sure to keep a map handy, as the road system in the countryside can be very confusing—although the friendly Bajans are always happy to help you find your way. Drive on the left, British-style. When someone flashes headlights at you at an intersection, it means "after you." Be especially careful negotiating roundabouts (traffic circles). The speed limit is 45 mph (72 kph) on highways, 37 mph (60 kph) on minor roads in the countryside, and 20 mph (30 kph) in town. Bridgetown actually has rush hours: 7 to 9 am and 4 to 6 pm. Park only in approved parking lots or in parking spots marked with a P sign; downtown parking costs Bds$1 per hour.

Car Rentals: Most car-rental agencies require renters to be between 21 and either 70 or 75. Dozens of agencies rent cars, jeeps, or minimokes (small, open-sided vehicles). Rates range from about $50 per day for a minimoke to $65 per day for a four-wheel-drive vehicle and $85 or more for a luxury car (or $225 to $400 or more per week) in high season. Most firms also offer discounted three-day rates, and many require at least a two-day rental in high season. You'll need either an international driver's license or a temporary driving permit, available through the rental agency for Bds$10.

Car-Rental Contacts **Coconut Car Rentals** ✉ *Bayside, Bay St., Bridgetown, St. Michael* ☎ *246/437–0297* 🌐 *www.coconutcars.com.* **Courtesy Rent-A-Car** ✉ *Grantley Adams International Airport, Christ Church* ☎ *246/431–4160* 🌐 *www.courtesyrentacar.com.* **Drive-a-Matic Car Rental** ✉ *CWTS Complex, Lower Estate, St. George* ☎ *246/422–3000, 800/581–8773* 🌐 *www.carhire.tv.*

5

TAXI TRAVEL

Taxis operate 24 hours a day. They aren't metered but rates are fixed by the government. Taxis carry up to three passengers, and the fare may be shared. Sample one-way fares from Bridgetown are $20 to Holetown, $25 to Speightstown, $20 to St. Lawrence Gap, and $40 to Bathsheba. Drivers can also be hired for an hourly rate of about $35–$40 for up to three people.

ESSENTIALS

Banks and Exchange Services The Barbados dollar is pegged to the U.S. dollar at the rate of Bds$1.98 to $1. The U.S. dollar is widely accepted, although you will receive your change in local currency. Republic Bank Limited has a branch at Grantley Adams International Airport, open daily from 8 am until the last plane lands or departs. ATMs are available 24 hours a day throughout the island. *Unless otherwise indicated, all prices quoted in this chapter are in U.S. dollars.*

Electricity The electric current throughout Barbados is 110 volts, 50 cycles, U.S. standard.

Emergency Services **Ambulance** ☎ *511.* **Fire** ☎ *311.* **Hyperbaric Chamber in Barbados** ✉ *St. Ann's Fort, Garrison, St. Michael* ☎ *246/436–5483 to treat decompression illness in divers, 246/436–6185 for nonemergencies.* **Police** ☎ *211 emergencies, 246/430–7100 nonemergencies.*

Passport Requirements To enter Barbados, all visitors must have a valid passport and a return or ongoing ticket.

Phones The area code for Barbados is 246. Local calls from private phones are free; some hotels charge a small fee. For directory assistance, dial 411. Prepaid phone cards, which can be used throughout Barbados (and other Caribbean islands) to make local or international calls, are sold at shops, attractions, transportation centers, and other convenient outlets. Top-off services are available at several locations throughout the island. Most U.S. cell phones will work in Barbados, though roaming charges can be expensive. Your U.S. service provider may offer a reasonable short-term international talk, text, and data plan, but be sure to turn off the phone's "data roaming" feature when traveling internationally, as the application updates that continuously occur in the background whenever your phone is turned on are prohibitively expensive if you're not in a Wi-Fi environment.

Taxes and Service Charges A 7.5% government tax is added to all hotel bills. A 7.5% V.A.T. is also imposed on restaurant meals, admissions to attractions, and merchandise sales (other than those that are duty-free). Prices are often tax-inclusive; if not, the V.A.T. will be added to your bill. A 10% service charge is often added to hotel bills and restaurant checks.

Tipping If no service charge is added to your bill, tip waiters 10% to 15% and maids $2 per room per day. Tip bellhops and airport porters $1 per bag. Taxi drivers and tour guides appreciate a 10% tip.

ACCOMMODATIONS

Most people stay either in luxurious enclaves on the fashionable west coast—north of Bridgetown—or on the action-packed south coast with easy access to small, independent restaurants, bars, and nightclubs. A few inns on the remote southeast and east coasts offer ocean views and tranquillity, but those on the east coast don't have good swimming beaches nearby. Prices in Barbados are sometimes twice as high in season as during the quieter months. Most hotels include no meals in their rates; some include breakfast, many offer a meal plan, some require you to purchase the meal plan in the high season, and a few offer all-inclusive packages.

Resorts: Great resorts run the gamut—from unpretentious to knock-your-socks-off—in terms of size, intimacy, amenities, and price. Many are well suited to families.

Small Inns: A few small, cozy inns are located in the east and southeast regions of the island.

Villas and Condos: Families and long-term visitors may choose from a wide variety of condos (everything from busy time-share resorts to more sedate vacation complexes). Villas and villa complexes can be luxurious, simple, or something in between.

Hotel reviews have been shortened. For full information, visit Fodors.com.

WHAT IT COSTS IN U.S. DOLLARS

	$	$$	$$$	$$$$
Restaurants	under $12	$12–$20	$21–$30	over $30
Hotels	under $275	$275–$375	$376–$475	over $475

Restaurant prices are the average cost of a main course at dinner or, if dinner is not served, at lunch. Hotel prices are the lowest cost of a standard double room in high season.

VISITOR INFORMATION

Contacts Barbados Tourism Marketing, Inc. ✉ *Warrens Office Complex, Lodge Rd., 1st fl., West Wing, Warrens, St. Michael* ☎ *246/427–2623, 800/221–9831, 246/467–3600* 🌐 *www.visitbarbados.org* ✉ *Grantley Adams International Airport, Christ Church* ☎ *246/428–5570* ✉ *Cruise-ship terminal, Deep Water Harbour, Bridgetown, St. Michael* ☎ *246/426–1718.*

WEDDINGS

There are no minimum residency requirements to get married; however, you need to obtain a marriage license from the Ministry of Home Affairs (☎ *246/621–0227*). All wedding arrangements must be made with a magistrate or marriage officer (e.g., minister) prior to applying for the license, with a letter from the marriage officer who has consented to perform the ceremony presented with the application. The marriage license fee is Bds$100 plus Bds$13 for a stamp. For a civil marriage ceremony at the court, a separate fee of Bds$125 is payable to the court; for an alternative venue, Bds$350. A marriage certificate costs Bds$20. All fees must be paid in cash. If either person was divorced or widowed, a certified copy of the divorce decree or other appropriate paperwork is required.

5

EXPLORING

The terrain changes dramatically from each of the island's 11 parishes to the next, and so does the pace. Bridgetown, the capital, is a fairly sophisticated city. West-coast resorts and private estates ooze luxury, whereas the small villages and vast sugar plantations found throughout central Barbados reflect the island's history. The relentless Atlantic surf shaped the cliffs of the dramatic east coast, and the northeast is called Scotland because of its hilly landscape and broad vistas. Along the lively south coast, the daytime hustle and bustle produce a palpable energy that continues well into the night at restaurants, dance clubs, and nightspots.

BRIDGETOWN

This bustling capital city, inscribed along with its garrison on the UNESCO World Heritage List in 2011, is a duty-free port with a compact shopping area. The principal thoroughfare is Broad Street, which leads west from National Heroes Square. A shuttle service (☎ *246/227–2200*) operates between hotels and downtown during business hours.

TOP ATTRACTIONS

The Careenage. In the early days, Bridgetown's natural harbor was where schooners were turned on their sides (careened) to be scraped of barnacles and repainted. Today, the Careenage serves as a marina for pleasure yachts and excursion boats, as well as a gathering place for locals and tourists alike. A boardwalk skirts the north side of the Careenage; on the south side, a lovely esplanade has pathways and benches for pedestrians and a statue of Errol Barrow, the first prime minister of

Barbados. The Chamberlain Bridge and the Charles Duncan O'Neal Bridge span the Careenage.

Nidhe Israel Synagogue. Providing for the spiritual needs of one of the oldest Jewish congregations in the Western Hemisphere, this synagogue was formed by Jews who left Brazil in the 1620s and introduced sugarcane to Barbados. The adjoining cemetery has tombstones dating from the 1630s. The original house of worship, built in 1654, was destroyed in an 1831 hurricane, rebuilt in 1833, and restored in 1987 with the assistance of the Barbados National Trust. Friday-night services are held during the winter months, but the building is open to the public year-round. Shorts are not acceptable during services but may be worn at other times. ✉ *Synagogue La.* ☎ *246/436–6869* 🎫 *Donations requested* 🕓 *Weekdays 9–4.*

Queen's Park. Northeast of Bridgetown, Queen's Park has one of the island's two immense baobab trees. Brought to Barbados from Guinea, West Africa, around 1738, this tree has a girth of more than 60 feet. Queen's Park Art Gallery, managed by the National Culture Foundation, is the island's largest gallery; exhibits change monthly. Queen's Park House, built in 1783 and the historic home of the British troop commander, has been converted into a theater, with an exhibition room on the lower floor and a restaurant. Originally called King's House, the name was changed upon Queen Victoria's succession to the throne. ✉ *Constitution Rd.* ☎ *246/427–2345 gallery* 🎫 *Free* 🕓 *Daily 9–5.*

WORTH NOTING

Heroes Square. Across Broad Street from Parliament and bordered by High and Trafalgar Streets, this triangular plaza marks the center of town. Its monument to Lord Horatio Nelson, who visited Barbados only briefly in 1777 as a 19-year-old navy lieutenant, predates Nelson's Column in London's Trafalgar Square by 30 years (1813 versus 1843). There's also a war memorial and a fountain commemorating the advent of running water on Barbados in 1865. ✉ *Broad St., across from Parliament.*

FAMILY **Parliament Buildings.** Overlooking Heroes Square in the center of town, these Victorian buildings were constructed around 1870 to house the British Commonwealth's third-oldest parliament (after Britain and Bermuda). A series of stained-glass windows in the East Wing depicts British monarchs from James I to Victoria. The National Heroes Gallery & Museum is located in the West Wing. ✉ *Heroes Sq., Trafalgar St.* ☎ *246/427–2019* 🌐 *www.barbadosparliament.com* 🎫 *Donations welcome* 🕓 *Museum Mon. and Wed.–Sat. 9–4.*

St. Michael's Cathedral. Although no one has proven it, George Washington is said to have worshipped here in 1751 during his only trip outside the United States. By then, the original structure was already nearly a century old. Destroyed twice by hurricanes, the cathedral was rebuilt in 1784 and again in 1831. ✉ *Spry St., east of Heroes Sq.*

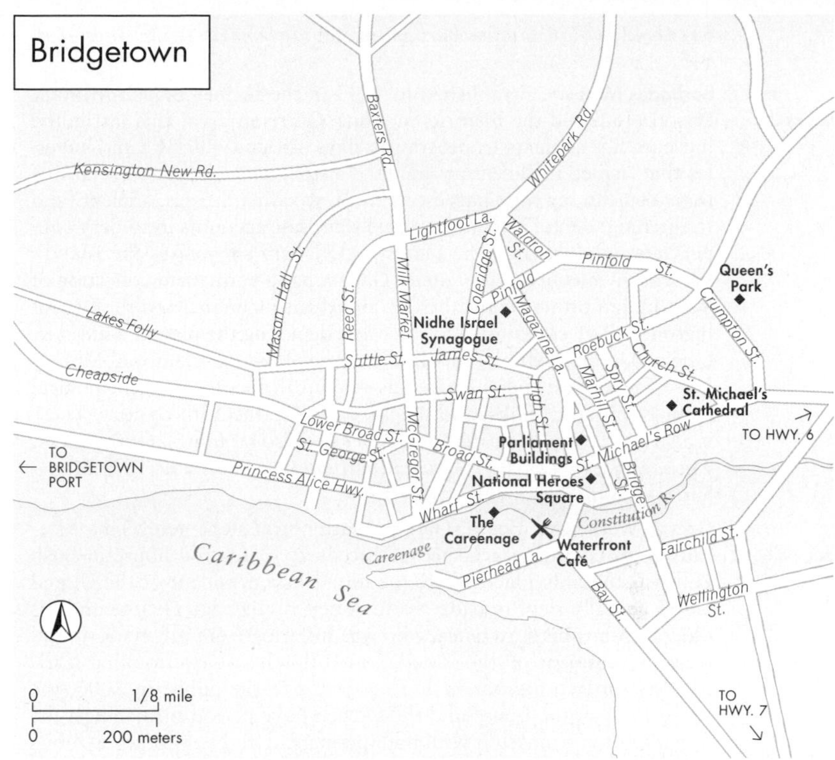

SOUTH COAST

Christ Church Parish, which is far busier and more developed than the west coast, is chockablock with condos, high- and low-rise hotels, and beach parks. It is also the location of St. Lawrence Gap, with its many places to eat, drink, shop, and party. As you move southeast, the broad, flat terrain comprises acre upon acre of cane fields, interrupted only by an occasional oil rig and a few tiny villages. Along the byways are colorful chattel houses, which were the traditional homes of tenant farmers. Historically, these typically Barbadian, ever-expandable small buildings were built so they could be dismantled and moved, as required.

TOP ATTRACTIONS

FAMILY **Barbados Concorde Experience.** Opened to the public in 2007, the Concorde Experience focuses on the British Airways Concorde G-BOAE (Alpha Echo, for short) that for many years flew between London and Barbados. The retired supersonic jet has made its permanent home here. Besides boarding the sleek aircraft itself, you'll learn about how the technology was developed and how this plane differed from other jets. You may or may not have been able to fly the Concorde when it was still plying the Atlantic, but this is your chance to experience some unique modern history—up close and personal. ✉ *Grantley Adams International Airport, adjacent to the terminal building, Christ Church*

☎ 246/420–7738 ⊕ *www.barbadosconcorde.com* 🎫 *$15* ⏲ *Tues.–Sat. 9–5.*

FAMILY Fodor'sChoice ★ **Barbados Museum.** Established in 1933 in the former British Military Prison (1815) in the historic St. Ann's Garrison area, this intriguing museum has artifacts from Arawak days (around 400 BC) and galleries that depict 19th-century military history and everyday social history. You can see cane-harvesting tools, wedding dresses, ancient (and frightening) dental instruments, and slave sale accounts in spidery copperplate handwriting. The Harewood Gallery showcases the island's natural environment, the Cunard Gallery has a permanent collection of West Indian prints bequeathed by Sir Edward Cunard, and the Warmington Gallery contains decorative arts depicting the planter's lifestyle. One gallery has exhibits for children. The Shilstone Memorial Library houses rare West Indian materials—archival documents, genealogical records, photos, books, and maps—dating to the 17th century. There is also a gift shop and café. ✉ *St. Ann's Garrison, Hwy. 7, Garrison, St. Michael* ☎ *246/427–0201* ⊕ *www.barbmuse.org.bb* 🎫 *$7.50* ⏲ *Mon.–Sat. 9–5, Sun. 2–6.*

FAMILY Fodor'sChoice ★ **George Washington House.** George Washington slept here! This carefully restored and refurbished 18th-century plantation house in Bush Hill was the only place where the future first president of the United States actually slept outside North America. Teenage George and his older half-brother Lawrence, who was suffering from tuberculosis and seeking treatment on the island, rented this house overlooking Carlisle Bay for two months in 1751. Opened to the public in 2007, the lower floor of the house and the kitchen have period furnishings; the upper floor is a museum with both permanent and temporary exhibits that display artifacts of 18th-century Barbadian life. The site includes an original 1719 windmill and bathhouse, along with a stable added to the property in the 1800s. Kids enjoy the network of secret tunnels. Guided tours begin with an informative 15-minute film appropriately called *George Washington in Barbados*. ✉ *Bush Hill, Garrison, St. Michael* ☎ *246/228–5461* ⊕ *www.georgewashingtonbarbados.org* 🎫 *$10* ⏲ *Weekdays 9–4:30.*

Fodor'sChoice ★ **Sunbury Plantation House and Museum.** Lovingly rebuilt after a 1995 fire destroyed everything but the thick flint-and-stone walls of this 300-year-old great house, Sunbury offers an elegant glimpse of the 18th and 19th centuries on a Barbadian sugar estate. Period furniture, old prints, and a collection of horse-drawn carriages lend an air of authenticity. A buffet luncheon ($22.50 per person, $34 on Sunday) and high tea ($14) are served daily in the Courtyard Restaurant. A five-course candlelight dinner ($100 per person, including drinks, minimum 12 people, reservations required) is served at the 200-year-old mahogany table in the dining room. ✉ *Off Hwy. 4B, Six Cross Roads, St. Philip* ☎ *246/423–6270* ⊕ *www.barbadosgreathouse.com* 🎫 *$7.50* ⏲ *Daily 9–5; last tour at 4:30.*

WORTH NOTING

Codrington Theological College. An impressive stand of cabbage palm trees lines the road leading to the coral-stone buildings and serene grounds of Codrington College, the oldest Anglican theological seminary in the Western Hemisphere, opened in 1745 on a cliff overlooking Conset Bay. The college's benefactor was Christopher Codrington III (1668–1710), a former governor-general of the Leeward Islands, whose antislavery views were unpopular in the plantocracy of the times. In an effort to "Christianize" the slaves and provide them with a general education, Codrington specified in his will that "300 negroes at least" would always be allowed to study at the institution; the planters who acted as trustees, however, were loath to teach slaves to read and write. You may tour the buildings, explore the grounds, and walk the nature trails, but remember that beachwear is not appropriate here. ✉ *Sargeant St., Conset Bay, St. John* ☎ *246/423–1140* 🌐 *www.codrington.org* 🎫 *Donations welcome* 🕓 *Daily 10–4.*

Emancipation Statue. This powerful statue of a slave—whose raised hands, broken chains hanging from each wrist, evoke both contempt and victory—is commonly referred to as the Bussa Statue. Bussa was the man who, in 1816, led the first slave rebellion on Barbados. The work of Barbadian sculptor Karl Brodhagen, the statue was erected in 1985 to commemorate the emancipation of the slaves in 1834. ✉ *St. Barnabas Roundabout, intersection of ABC Hwy. and Hwy. 5, Haggatt Hall, St. Michael.*

FAMILY **Harry Bayley Observatory.** Reopened in January 2014 with a fresh interior, high-tech fittings, a new dome, and new Meade 16-inch telescope equipped with the latest robotic controls and digital cameras, the observatory lets you view the moon, stars, planets, and other astronomical objects that may not be visible from mainland North America or Europe. The evening program, which starts with an informative presentation, is run by volunteers; call ahead to make sure it's open. The observatory has been the headquarters of the Barbados Astronomical Society since 1963. ✉ *Off Hwy. 6, Clapham, St. Michael* ☎ *246/426–1317, 246/422–2394* 🎫 *$10* 🕓 *Fri. 8–11:30 pm.*

Ragged Point. This is the location of East Coast Light, one of four strategically placed lighthouses on the island. Although civilization in the form of new homes is encroaching on this once-remote spot, the view of the entire Atlantic coastline is still spectacular, and the cool ocean breeze is refreshing on a hot day. ✉ *Marley Vale, St. Philip.*

Tyrol Cot Heritage Village. This coral-stone cottage just south of Bridgetown, constructed in 1854, is preserved as an example of period architecture. In 1929, it became the home of Sir Grantley Adams, the first premier of Barbados and the namesake of the island's international airport. Part of the Barbados National Trust, the cottage is filled with antiques and memorabilia that belonged to the late Sir Grantley and Lady Adams. It's also the centerpiece of an outdoor living museum, where artisans and craftspeople have workshops in a cluster of traditional chattel houses. Workshops are open, crafts are for sale, and refreshments are available at the "rum shop" primarily during the

Sunbury Plantation House

winter season and when cruise ships are in port. ✉ *Codrington Hill, St. Michael* ☎ *246/424–2074* 🎫 *$9* ⏲ *Weekdays 8–4:30; last tour at 4.*

CENTRAL BARBADOS

On the west coast, in St. James Parish, Holetown marks the center of the Platinum Coast—so called for the vast number of luxurious resorts and mansions that face the sea. Holetown is also where Captain John Powell and the crew of the British ship *Olive Blossom* landed on May 14, 1625, to claim the island for King James I (who had actually died of a stroke seven weeks earlier). On the east coast, the crashing Atlantic surf has eroded the shoreline, forming steep cliffs and exposing prehistoric rocks that look like giant mushrooms. Bathsheba and Cattlewash are favorite seacoast destinations for local folks on weekends and holidays. In the interior, narrow roads weave through tiny villages and along and between the ridges. The landscape is covered with tropical vegetation and is rife with fascinating caves and gullies.

TOP ATTRACTIONS

Fodor's Choice ★ **Andromeda Botanic Gardens.** More than 600 beautiful and unusual plant specimens from around the world are cultivated in 6 acres of gardens nestled among streams, ponds, and rocky outcroppings overlooking the sea above the Bathsheba coastline near Tent Bay. The gardens were created in 1954 with flowering plants collected by the late horticulturist Iris Bannochie (1914–1988). They're now administered by the Barbados National Trust. The Hibiscus Café serves snacks and drinks. ✉ *Foster Hall, Bathsheba, St. Joseph* ☎ *246/433–9384* 🌐 *andromeda.cavehill.uwi.edu* 🎫 *$12.50* ⏲ *Daily 9–5.*

Fodor's Choice ★ **Flower Forest.** It's a treat to meander among fragrant flowering bushes, canna and ginger lilies, puffball trees, and more than 100 other species of tropical flora in a cool, tranquil forest of flowers and other plants. A ½-mile (1-km) path winds through the 53.6-acre grounds, a former sugar plantation; it takes about 30 to 45 minutes to follow the path, or you can wander freely for as long as you wish. Benches throughout provide places to pause and reflect. There's also a snack bar, a gift shop, and a beautiful view of Mt. Hillaby, at 1,100 feet the island's highest point. ✉ *Hwy. 2, Richmond, St. Joseph* ☎ *246/433–8152* 🌐 *www.flowerforestbarbados.com* 🎫 *$12.50* ⏲ *Daily 8–4.*

FAMILY Fodor's Choice ★ **Gun Hill Signal Station.** The 360-degree view from Gun Hill, at 700 feet, was of strategic importance to the 18th-century British army. Using lanterns and semaphore, soldiers here could communicate with their counterparts at the south coast's Garrison and the north's Grenade Hill about approaching ships, civil disorders, or other emergencies. Time moved slowly in 1868, and Captain Henry Wilkinson whiled away his off-duty hours by carving a huge lion from a single rock—on the hillside below the tower. Come for a short history lesson but mainly for the view; it's so gorgeous that military invalids were sent here to convalesce. ✉ *Fusilier Rd., Gun Hill, St. George* ☎ *246/429–1358* 🎫 *$5* ⏲ *Weekdays 9–5.*

FAMILY Fodor's Choice ★ **Harrison's Cave.** This limestone cavern, complete with stalactites, stalagmites, subterranean streams, and a 40-foot waterfall, is a rare find in the Caribbean—and one of Barbados's most popular attractions. Tours include a nine-minute video and an hour-long underground journey via electric tram. The visitor center has interactive displays, life-size models and sculptures, a souvenir shop, restaurant, and elevator access to the tram for people with disabilities. Tram tours fill up fast, so book ahead. More intrepid visitors may like the 1½-hour walking tour or 4-hour eco-adventure tour, exploring nature trails and some of the cave's natural passages. ✉ *Hwy. 2, Welchman Hall, St. Thomas* ☎ *246/417–3700* 🌐 *www.harrisonscave.com* 🎫 *Tram tour $30, walking $20, eco-adventure $101* ⏲ *Tram tours daily 8:45–3:45, walking tour Sat. at 4, eco-adventure daily at 9 and noon.*

Fodor's Choice ★ **Hunte's Gardens.** Horticulturist Anthony Hunte spent two years converting an overgrown sinkhole (caused by the collapse of a limestone cave) into an extraordinary garden environment. Trails lead up, down, and around 10 acres of dense foliage—everything from pots of flowering plants and great swaths of thick ground cover to robust vines, exotic tropical flowers, and majestic 100-year-old cabbage palms reaching for the sun. Benches and chairs, strategically placed among the greenery, afford perfect (and fairly private) vantage points, while classical music plays overhead. Hunte lives on the property and welcomes visitors to his veranda for a glass of juice or rum punch. Just ask, and he'll be happy to tell you the fascinating story of how the gardens evolved. ✉ *Castle Grant, St. Joseph* ☎ *246/433–3333* 🌐 *www.huntesgardensbarbados.com* 🎫 *$15* ⏲ *Daily 9–4.*

Mount Gay Rum Visitors Centre. On this popular tour, you learn the colorful story behind the world's oldest rum, made in Barbados since 1703.

Although the modern distillery is in the far north, in St. Lucy Parish, tour guides here explain the rum-making process. Equipment, both historic and modern, is on display, and rows and rows of barrels are stored in this location. Tours conclude with a tasting and an opportunity to buy duty-free rum and gifts—and even have lunch or cocktails (no children on cocktail tour), depending on the time of day. ✉ *Spring Garden Hwy., Brandons, St. Michael* ☎ *246/425–8757* 🌐 *www.mountgayrum.com* 🎫 *$10, $50–$62 with cocktails or lunch and transportation* ⏲ *Weekdays 9:30–3:30, Sat. 10:30–2:30; tours every hr on half-hr.*

WORTH NOTING

Chalky Mount. This tiny east-coast village is perched high in the clay-yielding hills that have supplied local potters for about 300 years. A few working potteries are open daily to visitors, who can watch as artisans create bowls, vases, candleholders, and decorative objects—which are, of course, for sale. ✉ *Chalky Mount, St. Andrew.*

FAMILY **Cockspur Beach Club.** Just north of Bridgetown, the fun-loving folks at West Indies Rum Distillery, makers of Cockspur and Malibu rums, invite visitors to enjoy a day at the beach, a variety of water sports, and a complimentary rum punch. Changing rooms with lockers and showers are available, along with beach umbrellas and chairs. Snorkeling equipment may be rented for the day ($5). The beachside grill serves lunch and drinks. Since this is a popular outing for cruise-ship passengers, the beach gets crowded when ships are in port. ✉ *Brighton Beach, Black Rock, Brighton, St. Michael* ☎ *246/425–9393* 🎫 *$10* ⏲ *Daily 9–5.*

FAMILY **Folkestone Underwater Park & Marine Reserve.** The mission of this family-oriented marine park, located just north of Holetown, is to provide high-quality recreational activities in a sustainable way that will educate and entertain Barbadians and visitors alike. Facilities include a playground, basketball court, picnic area, beach with lifeguards, and museum (two rooms with artifacts and photos of how the sea is used for various purposes), which illuminates island marine life. For firsthand viewing, there's an underwater snorkeling trail (equipment rental, $10 for the day) around Dottins Reef, just off the beach in the 2.2-mile (3.5-km) protected marine reserve; nonswimmers can opt for a glass-bottom boat tour. A barge sunk in shallow water is home to myriad fish, making it a popular dive site. A canteen serves snacks and drinks. ✉ *Hwy. 1, Church Point, Holetown, St. James* ☎ *246/425–2871* 🎫 *Free, exhibits $1* ⏲ *Daily 9–5.*

Orchid World. Meandering pathways thread gardens filled with more than 30,000 colorful orchids and other tropical plants. You'll see Vandaceous orchids attached to fences or wire frames, Schomburgkia and Oncidiums stuck on mahogany trees, Aranda and Spathoglottis orchids growing in a grotto, and Ascocendas suspended from netting in shady enclosures as well as seasonal orchids, scented orchids, and multicolor Vanda orchids. Benches are well placed to rest, admire the flowers, or take in the expansive view of the surrounding cane fields and distant hills of Sweet Vale. Snacks, cold beverages, and other refreshments are served in the café. ✉ *Hwy. 3B, Groves, St. George* ☎ *246/433–0774* 🌐 *www.orchidworldbarbados.com* 🎫 *$12.50* ⏲ *Daily 9–5.*

Welchman Hall Gully. This 1½-mile-long (2-km-long) natural gully is really a collapsed limestone cavern, once part of the same underground network as Harrison's Cave. The Barbados National Trust protects the peace and quiet here, making it a beautiful place to hike past acres of labeled flowers and stands of trees. You can see and hear some interesting birds—and, with luck, a native green monkey. There are limited scheduled free guided tours, and a guide can be arranged with 24 hours' notice. Otherwise, the 30- to 45-minute walk is self-guided. ✉ *Welchman Hall, St. Thomas* ☎ *246/438–6671* 🌐 *www.welchmanhallgullybarbados.com* 🎫 *$12* ⏲ *Nov.–Aug., daily 9–4:30; Sept.–Oct., Mon.–Sat. 9–4:30; tours Nov., Fri. at 10:30, Dec.–Apr., weekdays at 10:30.*

NORTHERN BARBADOS

5

Speightstown, the north's commercial center and once a thriving port city, now boasts appealing local shops and informal restaurants. Many of Speightstown's 19th-century buildings, with traditional overhanging balconies, have been restored. The island's northernmost reaches, St. Peter and St. Lucy parishes, have a varied topography and are lovely to explore. Between the tiny fishing towns along the northwestern coast and the sweeping views out over the Atlantic to the east are forest and farm, moor and mountain. Most guides include a loop through this area on a daylong island tour—it's a beautiful drive.

TOP ATTRACTIONS

FAMILY **Animal Flower Cave.** Small sea anemones, or sea worms, resemble flowers when they open their tiny tentacles. They live in small pools in this sea cave at the island's very northern tip. The cave itself, discovered in 1780, has a coral floor that ranges from 126,000 to 500,000 years old, according to geological estimates. The view of breaking waves from inside the cave is magnificent. Steep stairs, uneven surfaces, and rocks make this an unwise choice for anyone with walking difficulties. ✉ *Flatfield, St. Lucy* ☎ *246/439–8797* 🎫 *$10* ⏲ *Daily 9–4.*

FAMILY **Barbados Wildlife Reserve.** This reserve at the top of Farley Hill is the habitat of herons, innumerable land turtles, screeching peacocks, shy deer, elusive green monkeys, brilliantly colored parrots (in a large walk-in aviary), snakes, and a caiman. Except for the snakes and the caiman, the animals run or fly freely—so step carefully and keep your hands to yourself. Late afternoon is your best chance to catch a glimpse of a green monkey. ✉ *Farley Hill, St. Peter* ☎ *246/422–8826* 🎫 *$12.50* ⏲ *Daily 10–5.*

Fodor's Choice ★ **St. Nicholas Abbey.** The island's oldest great house (circa 1650) was named after the original British owner's hometown, St. Nicholas Parish near Bristol, and Bath Abbey nearby. Its stone-and-wood architecture makes it one of only three original Jacobean-style houses still standing in the Western Hemisphere. It has Dutch gables, finials of coral stone, and beautiful grounds that include an "avenue" of mahogany trees, a "gully" filled with tropical trees and plantings, formal gardens, and an old sugar mill. The first floor, fully furnished with period furniture and portraits of family members, is open to the public. A fascinating home movie, shot by a previous owner's father, records Bajan life in the 1930s. Behind the great house is a rum distillery with a 19th-century steam press; cane grinding occurs Wednesdays and Thursdays February through mid-May. Visitors can purchase artisanal plantation rum, browse the gift shop's traditional Barbadian products, and enjoy light refreshments at the Terrace Café. ✉ *Cherry Tree Hill, St. Peter* ☎ *246/422–5357* 🌐 *www.stnicholasabbey.com* 🎟 *$17.50* ⏲ *Sun.–Fri. 10–3:30.*

WORTH NOTING

Cherry Tree Hill. Stop at the crest of this hill, just east of St. Nicholas Abbey, for a stunning panoramic view of the entire eastern coast and the Atlantic surf. ✉ *Cherry Tree Hill Rd., Cherry Tree Hill, St. Andrew.*

Farley Hill. At this national park in northern St. Peter, across from the Barbados Wildlife Reserve, gardens and lawns—along with an avenue of towering palms and gigantic mahogany, whitewood, and casuarina trees—surround the imposing ruins of a plantation great house built by Sir Graham Briggs in 1861 to entertain royal visitors from England. Partially rebuilt for the filming of *Island in the Sun,* the classic 1957 film starring Harry Belafonte and Dorothy Dandridge, the structure was destroyed by fire in 1965. Behind the estate is a sweeping view of the region called Scotland for its rugged landscape. The park is also the site of festivals and musical events. ✉ *Hwy. 2, Farley Hill, St. Peter* 🎟 *$2 per car, pedestrians free* ⏲ *Daily 8:30–6.*

FAMILY **Morgan Lewis Sugar Mill.** Built in 1727, the mill was operational until 1945. Today it's the only remaining windmill in Barbados with its wheelhouse and sails intact. No longer used to grind sugarcane, except for occasional demonstrations during crop season, the mill was donated to the Barbados National Trust in 1962 and eventually restored to original working specifications in 1998 by millwrights from the United Kingdom. Surrounding acres are used for dairy farming. ✉ *Southeast of Cherry Tree Hill, Morgan Lewis, St. Andrew* ☎ *246/426–2421* 🌐 *www.barbadosnationaltrust.org* 🎟 *$5* ⏲ *Dec.–Apr., daily 9–5.*

BEACHES

Geologically, Barbados is a coral-and-limestone island (not volcanic) with few rivers and, as a result, beautiful beaches, particularly along the island's southern and southeastern coastlines.

The west coast has some lovely beaches as well, but they're more susceptible to erosion after major autumn storms, if any, have taken their toll.

When the surf is too high and swimming becomes dangerous, a red flag will be hoisted on the beach. A yellow flag—or a red flag at half-staff—means swim with caution. Topless sunbathing—on the beach or at the pool—is not allowed anywhere in Barbados.

St. Nicholas Abbey

SOUTH COAST

A young, energetic crowd favors the south-coast beaches, which are broad and breezy, blessed with powdery white sand, and dotted with tall palms. The reef-protected areas with crystal clear water are safe for swimming and snorkeling. The surf becomes medium to high, and the waves get bigger and the winds stronger (windsurfers, take note) the farther southeast you go.

FAMILY **Accra Beach.** This popular beach, also known as Rockley Beach, is next to the Accra Beach Hotel. You'll find a broad swath of white sand with gentle surf and a lifeguard, plenty of nearby restaurants for refreshments, a playground, and beach stalls for renting chairs and equipment for snorkeling and other water sports. **Amenities**: food and drink; lifeguards; parking (no fee); water sports. **Best for:** snorkeling; swimming. ⊠ *Hwy. 7, Rockley, Christ Church.*

Fodor's Choice ★ **Bottom Bay Beach.** Popular for fashion and travel-industry photo shoots, Bottom Bay is the quintessential Caribbean beach. Secluded, surrounded by a coral cliff, studded with a stand of palms, and blessed with an endless ocean view, this dreamy enclave is near the southeasternmost point of the island. The Atlantic Ocean waves can be too strong for swimming, but it's the picture-perfect place for a day at the beach and a picnic lunch. Park at the top of the cliff and follow the steps down to the beach. **Amenities:** none. **Best for:** solitude; swimming; walking. ⊠ *Hwy. 5, Apple Hall, St. Philip.*

Fodor's Choice ★ **Crane Beach.** This exquisite crescent of pink sand on the southeast coast was named not for the elegant long-legged wading bird but for the crane used to haul and load cargo when this area served as a busy port. Crane Beach usually has a steady breeze and lightly rolling surf that varies in color from aqua to turquoise to lapis and is great for bodysurfing. Access to the beach is either down 98 steps or via a cliff-side, glass-walled elevator on The Crane resort property. **Amenities:** food and drink; lifeguards; parking (no fee); toilets. **Best for:** swimming; walking. ✉ *Crane Bay, St. Philip.*

Fodor's Choice ★ **Miami Beach.** Also called Enterprise Beach, this lovely spot on the coast road, just east of Oistins, is a slice of pure white sand with shallow and calm, crystal clear water on one side, deeper water with small waves on the other, and cliffs on either side. Located in a mainly upscale residential area, the beach is mostly deserted except for weekends, when folks who live nearby come for a swim. You can find a palm-shaded parking area, snack carts, and chair rentals. It's also a hop, skip, and jump from Little Arches Hotel. **Amenities:** food and drink; parking (no fee). **Best for:** solitude; swimming. ✉ *Enterprise Beach Rd., Enterprise, Christ Church.*

FAMILY Fodor's Choice ★ **Pebbles Beach.** On the southern side of Carlisle Bay, just south of Bridgetown, this broad half circle of white sand is one of the island's best beaches—and it can become crowded on weekends and holidays. The southern end of the beach wraps around the Hilton Barbados; the northern end is adjacent to the Radisson Aquatica Resort Barbados and a block away from Island Inn. Park at Harbour Lights or at the Boatyard Bar and Bayshore Complex, both on Bay Street, where you can also rent umbrellas and beach chairs and buy refreshments. **Amenities:** food and drink. **Best for:** snorkeling; swimming; walking. ✉ *Off Bay St., south of Bridgetown, Needham's Point, St. Michael.*

FAMILY **Sandy Beach** (*Dover Beach*). This beach has shallow, calm waters and a picturesque lagoon, making it an ideal location for families with small kids. Park right on the main road. You can rent beach chairs and umbrellas, and plenty of places nearby sell food and drinks. **Amenities:** food and drink. **Best for:** swimming; walking. ✉ *Hwy. 7, Worthing, Christ Church.*

FAMILY **Silver Sands–Silver Rock Beach.** Nestled between South Point, the southernmost tip of the island, and Inch Marlow Point, Silver Point Hotel overlooks this broad strand of beautiful white sand that always has a strong breeze. That makes this beach the best in Barbados for intermediate and advanced windsurfers and, more recently, kiteboarders. There's a small playground and shaded picnic tables. **Amenities:** parking (no fee); water sports. **Best for:** solitude; swimming; walking; windsurfing. ✉ *Off Hwy. 7, Christ Church.*

FAMILY **Turtle Beach.** Stretched from Turtle Beach Resort and Sandals Barbados at the eastern end of St. Lawrence Gap to Bougainvillea Beach Resort on Maxwell Coast Road, this broad strand of powdery white sand is great for sunbathing, strolling, and—with low to medium surf—swimming and boogie boarding. This beach is a favorite nesting place for turtles; if you're lucky, you may see hundreds of tiny hatchlings emerge from the sand and make their way to the sea . . . nature at its best! Find public access and parking on Maxwell Coast Road, near the Bougainvillea

Beach Resort. **Amenities:** food and drink; parking (no fee). **Best for:** swimming; walking. ✉ *Maxwell Coast Rd., Dover, Christ Church.*

EAST COAST

Be cautioned: Swimming at east-coast beaches is treacherous, even for strong swimmers, and is *not* recommended. Waves are high, the bottom tends to be rocky, the currents are unpredictable, and the undertow is dangerously strong.

Bathsheba Beach. Although not safe for swimming, the miles of untouched sand along the East Coast Road in St. Joseph Parish are great for beachcombing and wading. As you approach Bathsheba Soup Bowl, the southernmost stretch just north of Tent Bay, you'll see enormous mushroom-shape boulders and impressive rolling surf. Expert surfers from around the world converge on the Soup Bowl each November for the Barbados Independence Pro competition. **Amenities:** none. **Best for:** solitude; sunrise; surfing; walking. ✉ *East Coast Rd., Bathsheba, St. Joseph.*

5

Cattlewash Beach. Swimming is unwise at this windswept beach with pounding surf, which follows the Atlantic Ocean coastline in St. Andrew, but you can take a dip, wade, and play in the tide pools. Barclays Park, a 50-acre public park across the road, has a shaded picnic area. **Amenities:** none. **Best for:** solitude; sunrise; walking. ✉ *Ermy Bourne Hwy., Cattlewash, St. Andrew.*

WEST COAST

Gentle Caribbean waves lap the west coast, and leafy mahogany trees shade its stunning coves and sandy beaches. The water is perfect for swimming and water sports. An almost unbroken chain of beaches stretches between Bridgetown and Speightstown. Elegant homes and luxury hotels face much of the beachfront property in this area, dubbed Barbados's "Platinum Coast," although all beaches are open to the public.

West-coast beaches are considerably smaller and narrower than those on the south coast. Also, prolonged stormy weather in September and October may cause sand erosion, temporarily making the beaches even narrower. Even so, west-coast beaches are seldom crowded. Vendors stroll by with handmade baskets, hats, dolls, jewelry, even original watercolors; owners of private boats offer waterskiing, parasailing, and snorkeling excursions. Hotels and beachside restaurants welcome nonguests for terrace lunches (wear a cover-up), and you can buy picnic items at supermarkets in Holetown.

FAMILY **Brighton Beach.** Calm as a lake, this is where you can find locals taking a quick dip on hot days—particularly weekends. Just north of Bridgetown, Brighton Beach is also home to the Cockspur Beach Club. **Amenities:** food and drink; parking (no fee). **Best for:** swimming; walking. ✉ *Spring Garden Hwy., Brighton, St. Michael.*

FAMILY Fodor's Choice ★ **Mullins Beach.** At this lovely beach just south of Speightstown, the water is safe for swimming and snorkeling, there's easy parking on the main road, and Mullins Restaurant serves snacks, meals, and drinks—and rents chairs and umbrellas. **Amenities:** food and drink; toilets. **Best for:** sunset; swimming; walking. ✉ *Hwy. 1, Mullins Bay, St. Peter.*

Paynes Bay Beach. The stretch of beach just south of Sandy Lane is lined with luxury hotels—Tamarind, The House, and Treasure Beach among them. It's a very pretty area, with plenty of beach to go around, calm water, and good snorkeling. Public access is available at several locations along Highway 1, though parking is limited. **Amenities:** food and drink. **Best for:** snorkeling; sunset; swimming; walking. ✉ *Hwy. 1, Paynes Bay, St. James.*

WHERE TO EAT

First-class restaurants and hotel dining rooms serve quite sophisticated cuisine—often prepared by chefs with international experience and rivaling the dishes served in the world's best restaurants. Most menus include seafood: dolphin (mahimahi), kingfish, snapper, and flying fish prepared every way imaginable. Flying fish is so popular that it has become an official national symbol. Shellfish also abounds, as do steak, pork, and local black-belly lamb.

Specialty dishes include *buljol* (a cold salad of pickled codfish, tomatoes, onions, sweet peppers, and celery) and *conkies* (cornmeal, coconut, pumpkin, raisins, sweet potatoes, and spices, mixed together, wrapped in a banana leaf, and steamed). *Cou-cou,* often served with steamed flying fish, is a mixture of cornmeal and okra and usually topped with a spicy creole sauce made from tomatoes, onions, and sweet peppers. Bajan-style pepper pot is a hearty stew of oxtail, beef, and other meats in a rich, spicy gravy, simmered overnight.

For lunch, restaurants often offer a traditional Bajan buffet of fried fish, baked chicken, salads, macaroni pie (macaroni and cheese), and a selection of steamed or stewed provisions (local roots and vegetables). Be cautious with the West Indian condiments—like the sun, they're hotter than you think. Typical Bajan drinks—in addition to Banks Beer and Mount Gay, Cockspur, or Malibu rum—are *falernum* (a liqueur concocted of rum, sugar, lime juice, and almond essence) *mauby* (a nonalcoholic drink made by boiling bitter bark and spices, straining the mixture, and sweetening it), and Ponche Kuba, a creamy spiced rum liqueur (Caribbean eggnog) that's especially popular around the holidays. You're sure to enjoy the fresh fruit or rum punch, as well.

What to Wear: The dress code for dinner in Barbados is conservative, casually elegant, and, occasionally, formal—a jacket and tie for gentlemen and a cocktail dress for ladies in the fanciest restaurants and hotel dining rooms, particularly during the winter holiday season. Jeans, shorts, and T-shirts (either sleeveless or with slogans) are always frowned upon at dinner. Beach attire is appropriate only at the beach.

BRIDGETOWN

$$$ CARIBBEAN

✕ **Waterfront Café.** This busy bistro alongside the Careenage is the perfect place to enjoy a drink, snack, or meal—and to people-watch. Locals and tourists alike gather for alfresco all-day dining on sandwiches, salads, fish, pasta, pepperpot stew, and tasty Bajan snacks such as buljol, fish cakes, or plantation pork (plantains stuffed with spicy minced pork). The panfried flying-fish sandwich is an especially popular lunchtime treat. Dinner is served only Thursday, Friday, and Saturday nights; the menu is more extensive, and diners are treated to live jazz. *Average main: $30* ✉ *The Careenage, Bridgetown, St. Michael* ☎ *246/427–0093* *www.waterfrontcafe.com.bb* *No dinner Mon.–Wed. Closed Sun.*

BEST BETS FOR DINING

Fodor's Choice★
The Atlantis, Brown Sugar, Champers, The Cliff, Daphne's, Fish Pot, L'Azure at the Crane, The Tides, Waterside Restaurant

BEST VIEW
The Atlantis, Champers, L'Azure at the Crane, The Tides

BEST FOR FAMILIES
Bellini's Trattoria

MOST ROMANTIC
The Cliff, Daphne's, Lone Star, The Mews, Waterside Restaurant

5

SOUTH COAST

$$$ ITALIAN FAMILY

✕ **Bellini's Trattoria.** Classic Northern Italian cuisine is the specialty at Bellini's, located on the main floor of the Little Bay Hotel. Toast the evening with a Bellini cocktail (ice-cold sparkling wine with a splash of fruit nectar) and start your meal with bruschetta, an individual gourmet pizza, or perhaps a homemade pasta dish with fresh herbs and a rich sauce. Move on to the signature garlic shrimp entrée or the popular chicken parmigiana. Then top it off with a sweet extravagance such as chocolate mousse cake. Make reservations early, and request a table on the Mediterranean-style veranda for one of the most appealing dining settings on the south coast. *Average main: $27* ✉ *Little Bay Hotel, St. Lawrence Gap, Dover, Christ Church* ☎ *246/420–7587* *Reservations essential.*

$$$ CARIBBEAN FAMILY Fodor's Choice ★

✕ **Brown Sugar.** Set back from the road in a traditional Bajan home, the lattice-trimmed dining patios here are filled with ferns, flowers, and water features. Brown Sugar is a popular lunch spot for local businesspeople, who come for the nearly 30 delicious local and creole dishes spread out at the all-you-can-eat, four-course Planter's Buffet lunch ($27.50). Here's your chance to try local specialties such as flying fish, cou-cou, buljol, *souse* (pickled pork, stewed for hours in broth), fish cakes, and pepper pot. In the evening, the à la carte menu has dishes such as fried flying fish, coconut shrimp, plantain-crusted mahimahi, curried lamb, filet mignon, broiled pepper chicken, and seafood or pesto pasta. Bring the kids—there's a special children's menu with fried chicken, fried flying-fish fingers, and pasta dishes. Save room for the warm pawpaw (papaya) pie or Bajan rum pudding with rum sauce.

$ *Average main: $29* ✉ *Bay St., Aquatic Gap, Garrison, St. Michael* ☎ *246/426–7684* 🌐 *www.brownsugarbarbados.com* ⊗ *No lunch Sat.*

$$$$ ECLECTIC **Café Luna.** With a sweeping view of pretty Miami (Enterprise) Beach, the alfresco dining deck on top of the Mediterranean-style Little Arches Hotel is spectacular at lunchtime and magical in the moonlight. At lunch (for hotel guests only), sip on crisp white wine or a fruity cocktail while awaiting your freshly made salad, pasta, or sandwich. At dinner, the expertise of executive chef (and co-owner) Mark de Gruchy is displayed through contemporary dishes from around the world, including fresh Scottish salmon grilled to perfection, oven-roasted New Zealand rack of lamb, fresh seafood bouillabaisse, and local chicken breast with mango chutney. The special three-course menu ($40) is a good deal; sushi is a specialty on Thursday and Friday nights. $ *Average main: $33* ✉ *Little Arches Hotel, Enterprise Beach Rd., Oistins, Christ Church* ☎ *246/420–4689* 🌐 *www.littlearches.com* *Reservations essential.*

$$ MEXICAN FAMILY **Café Sol.** Have a hankerin' for good Tex-Mex food? Enjoy nachos, tacos, burritos, empanadas, fajitas, and tostadas in this Mexican bar and grill at the entrance to busy St. Lawrence Gap. Or choose a burger, honey-barbecue chicken, or flame-grilled steak from the gringo menu. Helpings of rice and beans, a Corona, and plenty of jalapeño peppers, guacamole, and salsa give everything a Mexican touch. Some people come just for the margaritas—15 fruity varieties rimmed with Bajan sugar instead of salt. With two happy hours every night, this place gets really busy; reservations are accepted only for parties of five or more. $ *Average main: $20* ✉ *St. Lawrence Gap, Dover, Christ Church* ☎ *246/420–7655* 🌐 *www.cafesolbarbados.com* *Reservations not accepted* ⊗ *No lunch Fri.–Mon.*

$$$$ ECLECTIC FAMILY Fodor's Choice ★ **Champers.** Chiryl Newman's snazzy seaside restaurant is in an old Bajan home just off the main road in Rockley. Luncheon guests—about 75% local businesspeople—enjoy repasts such as char-grilled beef salad, Champers fish pie, or fried flying fish with caper dressing. Dinner guests swoon over dishes such as the herb-crusted rack of lamb with spring vegetables and mint-infused jus, the grilled sea scallops with risotto primavera, and the Parmesan-crusted barracuda with whole-grain mustard sauce. The portions are hearty and the food is well seasoned with Caribbean flavors, "just the way the locals like it," says Newman. Dining out with the family? There's a kid's menu, too. The cliff-top setting overlooking the eastern end of Accra Beach offers diners a panoramic view of the sea and a relaxing atmosphere for daytime dining. Nearly all the artwork gracing the walls is by Barbadian artists and may be purchased through the on-site gallery. $ *Average main: $38* ✉ *Skeetes Hill, off Hwy. 7, Rockley, Christ Church* ☎ *246/434–3463* 🌐 *www.champersbarbados.com* *Reservations essential.*

$$$$ SEAFOOD Fodor's Choice ★ **L'Azure at the Crane.** Perched on an oceanfront cliff overlooking Crane Beach, L'Azure is an informal breakfast and luncheon spot by day that becomes elegant after dark. Enjoy seafood chowder or a light salad or sandwich while absorbing the breathtaking panoramic view of the beach and sea beyond. At dinner, candlelight and soft guitar music enhance tamarind-glazed snapper or a fabulous Caribbean lobster seasoned with herbs, lime juice, and garlic butter and served in its shell; if

you're not in the mood for seafood, try the crusted rack of lamb or herb-infused pork tenderloin. Sunday is really special, with a Gospel Brunch ($26) at 9 or 10 am and a Bajan Buffet ($40) at 12:30 pm. *Average main: $36 The Crane, Crane Bay, St. Philip 246/423–6220 www.thecrane.com Reservations essential No dinner Wed.*

$$ CARIBBEAN **Shaker's.** Locals and visitors gather at this no-frills hangout for drinks—perhaps a Banks beer or two, a margarita, a pitcher of sangria, or whatever wets their whistle—and the delicious local food. Simple dishes like beer-battered flying fish, grilled catch of the day, barbecued chicken, grilled steak, or a solid cheeseburger deliver the goods, but the ribs are the main event. All main dishes include crisp green salad, coleslaw, and either grilled or french-fried potatoes. It's a colorful, convivial place, full of laughter and chatter—partly because the tables are so close together and partly because of the rum-shop atmosphere. Arrive early or make a reservation if you want an outside table, as it fills up quickly; and be prepared to pay in cash. *Average main: $15 Browne's Gap, Rockley, Christ Church 246/228–8855 Reservations essential No credit cards Closed Sun. and Mon. No lunch.*

5

$$ CARIBBEAN **Sweet Potatoes.** "Good Old Bajan Cooking" is the slogan at this popular restaurant in the Gap, and that's what you can expect. Of course, you'll want to start everything off with a chilled rum punch. Then whet your appetite with some favorite local appetizers such as *buljol* (marinated codfish seasoned with herbs and onions), sweet plantains stuffed with minced beef, pumpkin-and-spinach fritters, or deep-fried fish cakes. A selection of Bajan appetizers will make a filling lunch as well. The dinner menu includes flying fish stuffed with local vegetables, grilled chicken breast in a Malibu Rum sauce, catch of the day bathed in a creole sauce, and jerk pork. Rum cake, flambéed bananas, and bread pudding with rum sauce are traditional desserts. *Average main: $20 St. Lawrence Gap, Dover, Christ Church 246/420–7668.*

$$$$ CONTEMPORARY Fodor's Choice ★ **Waterside Restaurant.** You won't get much closer to dining on the water without being on a boat. Tables here are set on a broad porch suspended over the beachfront and spaced generously to allow for pleasant and private conversation; all the bustle of St. Lawrence Gap is left at the door. Once inside, the setting becomes sophisticated, tranquil, and definitely picturesque; the mood, quiet and intimate. And then there's the food. Chef Keisha Hamblin's elegant cuisine ranges from homemade fettuccini, sweet potato gnocchi, and risotto with truffle oil and Parmesan to spiny lobster Thermidor, fire-roasted filet mignon, and char siu–marinated duck breast. For dessert, don't miss the warm sticky toffee pudding with honeycomb ice cream. *Average main: $55 St. Lawrence Gap, Dover, Christ Church 246/418–9750 www.watersiderest.com Reservations essential Closed Mon. No lunch.*

EAST COAST

$$ CARIBBEAN FAMILY Fodor's Choice ★ **The Atlantis.** For decades, an alfresco lunch on the Atlantis deck overlooking the ocean has been a favorite of both visitors and Bajans. Pleasant atmosphere and good food have always been the draw, with an elegant dining room and a top-notch menu that focuses on local produce, seafood, and meats. The Wednesday and Sunday Bajan buffet

lunch—with pepper pot, saltfish, chicken stew, peas and rice, cou-cou, yam pie, and breadfruit mash—is particularly popular. Lunch and dinner entrées include fresh fish, lobster (seasonal), curried goat or chicken, fricassee of rabbit, pepper-crusted flat-iron steak, and several main-course salads, pasta dishes, and panini sandwiches. There's a kids' menu, too. *Average main: $20 ✉ The Atlantis Hotel, Tent Bay, St. Joseph ☎ 246/433–9445 ⊕ www.atlantishotelbarbados.com Reservations essential ⊗ No dinner Sun.*

$$$ CARIBBEAN **Naniki Restaurant.** Rich wooden beams and stone tiles, clay pottery, straw mats, and colorful dinnerware set the style at Naniki (an Arawak word meaning "full of life"). Huge picture windows and outdoor porch seating allow you to enjoy the exhilarating view of surrounding hills and gardens along with your lunch of exquisitely prepared Caribbean standards. Seared flying fish, grilled dorado, stewed *lambi* (conch), and jerk chicken or pork are accompanied by cou-cou, peas and rice, or salad. For dinner (by special request only), start with conch fritters or Caribbean fish soup; then try roasted Bajan black-belly lamb or shrimp garnished with tarragon. Sunday brunch is a Caribbean buffet often featuring great jazz music by some of the Caribbean's best musicians. Vegetarian dishes are always available. *Average main: $28 ✉ Lush Life Nature Resort, off Hwy. 3, Suriname, St. Joseph ☎ 246/433–1300 ⊕ www.lushlife.bb/naniki Reservations essential.*

WEST COAST

$$$$ ECLECTIC Fodor's Choice ★ **The Cliff.** Chef Paul Owens's mastery creates one of the finest dining experiences in the Caribbean, with prices to match. Steep steps hug the cliff on which the restaurant sits to accommodate those arriving by yacht, and every candlelit table has a sea view. Starters may include spicy Thai-style beef salad, sashimi, or char-grilled white asparagus. For the main course, try swordfish with curry sauce and jasmine rice, seared tuna with saffron caper sauce and tomato coulis, or a prime strip steak with peppercorn sauce. Dessert falls into the sinful category, and service is impeccable. The prix-fixe menu will set you back $125 per person for a two-course meal or $145 per person for a three-course meal. Reserve days or even weeks in advance to snag a table at the front of the terrace for the best view. *Average main: $125 ✉ Hwy. 1, Derricks, St. James ☎ 246/432–1922 ⊕ www.thecliffbarbados.com Reservations essential ⊗ Closed Sun. Apr. 15–Dec. 15. No lunch.*

$$$$ ITALIAN Fodor's Choice ★ **Daphne's.** Executive chef Marco Festini Cromer whips up contemporary Italian cuisine at the House's beachfront restaurant, a chic outpost of the London eatery of the same name. Grilled mahimahi becomes "modern Italian" when combined with Marsala wine, *peperonata* (stewed peppers, tomatoes, onions, and garlic), and zucchini. Perfectly prepared *melanzane* (eggplant) and zucchini alla parmigiana is a delicious starter, a half portion of risotto with porcini mushrooms, green beans, and Parma ham is fabulously rich, and fettuccini with braised duck, red wine, and asparagus is a sublime pasta choice. There's even a gluten-free dinner menu and a "summer special" prix-fixe menu ($50, $60 with dessert). The extensive wine list features both regional Italian and fine French selections. *Average main: $36 ✉ The House, Hwy. 1,*

Paynes Bay, St. James ☎ *246/432–2731* 🌐 *www.daphnesbarbados.com* ✍ *Reservations essential* ⏲ *Closed Mon. June–Nov.*

$$ CARIBBEAN FAMILY ✕ **Fisherman's Pub.** As local as local gets, this open-air, waterfront beach bar (a former rum shop) is built on stilts a stone's throw from the Speightstown fish market. For years, fishermen and other locals have come here for the inexpensive, authentic Bajan lunch buffet. For $10 or so you can soak up the atmosphere and fill your plate with fried flying fish, stewed chicken or pork, curried goat or lamb, pepper pot, macaroni pie, fried plantain, peas and rice, sweet potatoes, cou-cou, and crisp green salad. Eat inside or on the deck. And on Wednesday nights, you can also dance—or simply listen—to catchy steel pan or calypso music. (Whether dinner is served varies from season to season, so call ahead.) [$] *Average main: $20* ✉ *Queen St., Speightstown, St. Peter* ☎ *246/422–2703* ✍ *Reservations not accepted.*

$$$$ MEDITERRANEAN Fodor's Choice ★ ✕ **Fish Pot.** Just north of the little fishing village of Six Men's Bay, on the northwestern coast of Barbados, this attractive seaside restaurant serves excellent Mediterranean cuisine and some of the island's freshest fish. Gaze seaward through windows framed with pale-green louvered shutters while lunching on a seafood crêpe, a grilled panini, snow-crab salad, or perhaps pasta with seafood or roasted-pepper-and-chili tomato sauce. In the evening, the menu may include seafood bouillabaisse; seared, herb-crusted tuna on garlic-and-spinach polenta; sun-dried-tomato risotto tossed with vegetables; or braised lamb shank with pan gravy. Bright and cheery by day and relaxed and cozy by night, the Fish Pot offers a tasty dining experience in a setting that's classier than its name might suggest. [$] *Average main: $35* ✉ *Little Good Harbour Hotel, Shermans, St. Lucy* ☎ *246/439–3000* 🌐 *www.littlegoodharbourbarbados.com* ✍ *Reservations essential.*

$$$$ EUROPEAN ✕ **Lone Star.** At the tiny but chic Lone Star Hotel, top chefs turn the finest local ingredients into gastronomic delights. At lunch, tasty salads, sandwiches, and homemade pizzas are served in the oceanfront bar. After sunset, the casual daytime atmosphere turns trendy. Start with open wild-mushroom and butternut-squash ravioli or jumbo crab cakes with grain mustard rémoulade, followed by seared yellowfin tuna Niçoise, panfried sea bass, roasted rack of lamb, simple tagliolini pasta *al limone,* or dozens of other land, sea, and vegetarian dishes. [$] *Average main: $36* ✉ *Lone Star Hotel, Hwy. 1, Mount Standfast, St. James* ☎ *246/419–0599* 🌐 *www.thelonestar.com.*

$$$$ EUROPEAN ✕ **The Mews.** Dining at the Mews is like being invited to a friend's very chic home for dinner. Once a private home, the front room is now an inviting bar, and an interior courtyard is an intimate, open-air dining area. The second floor is a maze of small dining rooms and balconies, but it's the food—classic, bistro, or tapas—that draws the visitors. A plump chicken breast, for example, may be stuffed with cream cheese, smoked salmon, and herb pâté and served on a garlic-and-chive sauce, while a braised lamb shank is presented on a bed of cabbage with a port-thyme jus and creamed potatoes. Some call the atmosphere avant-garde; others call it quaint. Everyone calls the food delicious. [$] *Average main: $39* ✉ *2nd St., Holetown, St. James* ☎ *246/432–1122* 🌐 *themewsbarbados.com* ✍ *Reservations essential* ⏲ *No lunch.*

$$$ CARIBBEAN

Ragamuffins. Tiny, funky, lively, and informal, this is the only Barbados restaurant in an authentic chattel house. Dine inside or out on seafood, perfectly broiled T-bone steaks, West Indian curries, and vegetarian dishes such as Bajan stir-fried vegetables with noodles. The kitchen is within sight of the bar, a popular meeting spot most evenings. Sunday night's Drag Show becomes a huge party that spills into the street. *Average main: $22* *1st St., Holetown, St. James* *246/432–1295* *www.ragamuffinsbarbados.com* *Reservations essential* *No lunch.*

$$$$ EUROPEAN Fodor's Choice ★

The Tides. After entering the courtyard of what was once a private mansion, have a cocktail at the cozy bar or visit the on-site art gallery before proceeding to your seaside table. Perhaps the most intriguing feature of this stunning setting—besides the sound of waves crashing onto the shore just feet away—is the row of huge tree trunks growing right through the dining room. The food is equally dramatic. Executive chef Guy Beasley and his team give a contemporary twist to fresh seafood, filet of beef, rack of lamb, and other top-of-the-line main courses by adding inspired sauces and delicate vegetables and garnishes. A full vegetarian menu is also available. Save room for the sticky toffee pudding—definitely worth the calories. *Average main: $50* *Balmore House, Hwy. 1, Holetown, St. James* *246/432–8356* *www.tidesbarbados.com* *Reservations essential* *No lunch Sat; no lunch Sun. May–Nov.*

WHERE TO STAY

Most visitors stay either on the fashionable west coast north of Bridgetown or on the action-packed south coast. On the west coast, the beachfront resorts in St. Peter and St. James Parishes are mostly luxurious, self-contained enclaves. Highway 1, a two-lane road with considerable traffic, runs past these resorts; strolling to a nearby bar or restaurant can be a bit difficult. Along the south coast in Christ Church Parish, several hotels are close to the busy strip known as St. Lawrence Gap, convenient to dozens of small restaurants, bars, and nightclubs. On the much more remote east coast, a few small inns offer oceanfront views and get-away-from-it-all tranquillity.

In keeping with the smoke-free policy enforced throughout Barbados, smoking is restricted to open outdoor areas such as the beach. It is not permitted in hotels (neither rooms nor public areas) or in restaurants.

Room rates in Barbados may be twice as high in season (December 15–April 15) compared with those in the quieter months; however, special promotions and vacation packages are available throughout the year. Most hotels include no meals in their rates, but some include breakfast and many offer a meal plan. Some require you to purchase a meal plan in the high season, and a few offer all-inclusive packages.

Resorts run the gamut—from unpretentious to exceedingly formal—in terms of size, intimacy, amenities, and price. Families and long-term visitors may choose from a wide variety of villas and condos. A few small, cozy inns are found along the east and southeast coasts, as well as the northwest, and these can be ultraluxurious, fairly simple, or something in between.

Villa and condo complexes, which continue to crop up along the south and west coasts, may be the most economical option for families, groups, or couples vacationing together. Nonowner vacationers rent units from property managers, the same as reserving hotel accommodations. Apartments are available for vacation rentals in buildings or complexes with from three or four units to 30, 40, or even more.

BEST BETS FOR LODGING

Fodor's Choice★
The Atlantis Hotel, Cobblers Cove Hotel, Colony Club Hotel, Coral Reef Club, Fairmont Royal Pavilion, Hilton Barbados, Ocean Two, Sandals Barbados, The Sandpiper, Sandy Lane Hotel and Golf Club, Sweetfield Manor

BEST FOR HONEYMOONERS
Cobblers Cove Hotel, Fairmont Royal Pavilion, The House, Sandals Barbados, Sweetfield Manor, Treasure Beach

BEST FOR FAMILIES
Bougainvillea Beach Resort, Divi Southwinds, Hilton Barbados, Tamarind, Turtle Beach

PRIVATE VILLAS AND CONDOS

Local real-estate agencies arrange vacation rentals of privately owned villas and condos along the west coast in St. James and St. Peter. All villas and condo units are fully furnished and equipped—including appropriate staff depending on the size of the villa or unit, which can range from one to eight bedrooms. The staff usually works six days a week. Most villas have TVs and other entertainment devices, all properties have telephones, and some have Internet access. International telephone calls are usually blocked; plan on using your cell phone, a phone card, or calling card. Vehicles generally are not included in the rates, but rental cars can be arranged for and delivered to the villa upon request. Linens and basic supplies (such as bath soap, toilet tissue, and dishwashing detergent) are normally included.

Villas or condos with one to eight bedrooms and as many baths run $250 to $1,500 per night in summer and at least double that in winter. Rates include utilities and government taxes. The only additional cost is for groceries and staff gratuities. A security deposit is required upon booking and refunded seven days after departure less any damages or unpaid miscellaneous charges.

Villa Rental Contacts **Altman Real Estate** ✉ *Hwy. 1, Derricks, St. James* ☎ *246/432–0840, 866/360–5292 in U.S.* 🌐 *www.altmanbarbados.com.* **Blue Sky Luxury** ✉ *Newton House, Hwy. 1B, Battaleys, St. Peter* ☎ *246/622–4466, 866/404–9600 in U.S.* 🌐 *www.blueskyluxury.com.* **Island Villas** ✉ *Trents Bldg., Holetown, St. James* ☎ *246/432–4627, 866/978–8499 in U.S.* 🌐 *www.island-villas.com.*

Apartment Rental Contacts **Barbados Tourism Marketing, Inc.** This office has a list of apartments in prime resort areas on the south and west coasts, complete with facilities offered and current rates. ✉ *Warrens Office Complex, 1st*

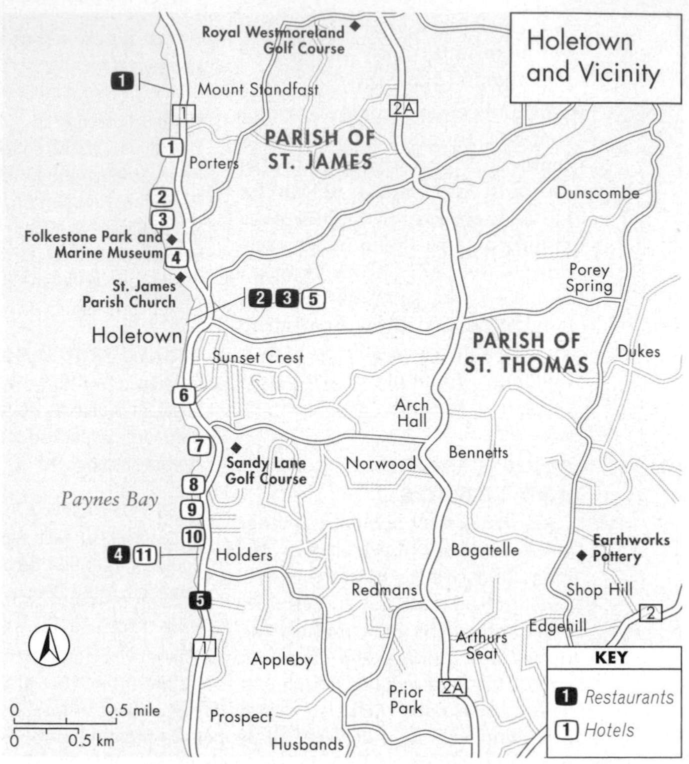

fl., West Wing, Warrens, St. Michael ☎ 246/427–2623 🌐 www.visitbarbados.org ▭ No credit cards.

RECOMMENDED HOTELS AND RESORTS

$ RESORT **Accra Beach Hotel and Spa.** A full-service resort in the middle of the busy south coast, Accra is large, it's modern, it faces a great beach, and it's competitively priced. **Pros:** on a great beach and, on the street side, near shopping, restaurants, and nightspots; good value; complimentary Wi-Fi. **Cons:** rooms facing the street have an unattractive view; rooms could use refreshing. *$ Rooms from: $235 ✉ Hwy. 7, Rockley, Christ Church ☎ 246/435–8920, 888/712–2272 in U.S. 🌐 www.accrabeachhotel.com ⇆ 190 rooms, 34 suites 🍽 No meals.*

$$ RESORT FAMILY **Bougainvillea Beach Resort.** Attractive seaside town houses, each with a separate entrance, wrap around the pool or face the beachfront; the suites are huge compared with hotel suites elsewhere in this price range, are decorated in appealing Caribbean pastels, and have full kitchens. **Pros:** great for families but also appeals to honeymooners; popular wedding venue; easy stroll to St. Lawrence Gap and Oistins; complimentary Wi-Fi. **Cons:** rooms are on four levels with no elevator; sea can be a little rough for swimming. *$ Rooms from: $290 ✉ Maxwell Coast Rd., Maxwell, Christ Church ☎ 246/628–0990, 800/495–1858 in U.S. 🌐 www.bougainvillearesort.com ⇆ 138 suites 🍽 Multiple meal plans.*

$ HOTEL **Courtyard Bridgetown by Marriott.** Comfortable, contemporary, convenient, and economical, this place is pleasant and the rooms are well appointed. **Pros:** good value; especially suited to business travelers; modern, attractive accommodations. **Cons:** walk to beach and restaurants; comparatively little "Caribbean resort" atmosphere; limited on-site dining options. *Rooms from: $225 Hwy. 7, Hastings Main Rd., set back a block from the road, Garrison Historic Area, Hastings, Christ Church 246/625–0000 www.marriott.com 118 rooms No meals.*

$$ RESORT **The Crane.** Hugging a seaside bluff on the southeast coast, The Crane incorporates the island's oldest hotel in continuous operation; the original coral-stone hotel building (1887) is the centerpiece of a luxurious, 40-acre villa complex. **Pros:** enchanting view; lovely beach; fabulous suites; great restaurants. **Cons:** remote location; rental car recommended; villas are considerably more expensive and more modern than historic hotel rooms. *Rooms from: $328 Crane Bay, St. Philip 246/423–6220 www.thecrane.com 4 rooms, 14 suites, 202 villas Multiple meal plans.*

$ RESORT FAMILY **Divi Southwinds Beach Resort.** This all-suites resort is situated on 20 acres of lawn and gardens bisected by action-packed St. Lawrence Gap. **Pros:** beautiful beach; three pools; beach villas are the best value; close to shopping, restaurants, and nightspots; kids' club; complimentary Wi-Fi. **Cons:** water sports cost extra; some rooms aching for renovations. *Rooms from: $244 St. Lawrence Main Rd., Dover, Christ Church 246/428–7181, 800/367–3484 www.divisouthwinds.com 121 1-bedroom suites, 12 2-bedroom suites Multiple meal plans.*

$$ HOTEL FAMILY Fodor's Choice ★ **Hilton Barbados.** Beautifully situated on the sandy Needham's Point peninsula, all 350 units in this high-rise resort hotel have private balconies overlooking either the ocean or Carlisle Bay; 77 rooms on executive floors offer a private lounge and concierge services. **Pros:** great location near town and on a beautiful beach; excellent accommodations; lots of services and amenities; accessible rooms available; frequent promotional deals. **Cons:** huge convention hotel; attracts groups; lacks island ambience. *Rooms from: $329 Needham's Point, St. Michael 246/426–0200 www.hiltonbarbadosresort.com 317 rooms, 33 suites Multiple meal plans.*

$$$ ALL-INCLUSIVE **Island Inn Hotel.** Constructed in 1804 as a rum storage facility for the British Regiment, this quaint, all-inclusive boutique hotel—less than a mile from Bridgetown and steps away from beautiful Pebbles Beach on Carlisle Bay—appeals to singles, couples, and families. **Pros:** friendly, accommodating atmosphere; smartly decorated rooms; excellent value. **Cons:** small pool; request a room near the pool, as rooms near the front may be noisier and don't have a patio. *Rooms from: $415 Aquatic Gap, Garrison, St. Michael 246/436–6393 www.islandinnbarbados.com 20 rooms, 4 suites All-inclusive.*

$$ HOTEL **Little Arches Hotel.** Just east of the fishing village of Oistins, this classy boutique hotel has a distinctly Mediterranean ambience and a perfect vantage point overlooking the sea. **Pros:** stylish accommodations; good restaurant; across from fabulous Miami Beach. **Cons:** fairly remote; rental car advised. *Rooms from: $310 Enterprise Beach Rd.,*

5

Oistins, Christ Church ☎ 246/420–4689 ⊕ www.littlearches.com ⇨ 8 rooms, 2 suites ¶◎| Multiple meal plans.

$$ RESORT FAMILY Fodor's Choice ★ **Ocean Two.** Couples and families are drawn to this sophisticated beachfront resort in the midst of lively St. Lawrence Gap. **Pros:** large, luxurious accommodations; beautiful beach; planned children's activities in summer and holiday season. **Cons:** showers only, no tubs; Taste could be tastier—and it's expensive—but plenty of dining options nearby. $ *Rooms from: $350 ✉ St. Lawrence Gap, Dover, Christ Church ☎ 246/418–1800 ⊕ www.oceantwobarbados.com ⇨ 18 rooms, 68 1- and 2-bedroom suites ¶◎| Some meals.*

$ HOTEL **Radisson Aquatica Resort Barbados.** Radisson invested $50 million to refurbish the former Grand Barbados Beach Resort and in 2013 reopened the renamed high-rise hotel overlooking pretty Carlisle Bay, just south of Bridgetown. **Pros:** lovely beach; comfortable rooms; complimentary Wi-Fi. **Cons:** noisy a/c; no room fridge; skip the Aquatic Club restaurant and opt for neighboring Brown Sugar or the Hilton. $ *Rooms from: $229 ✉ Aquatic Gap, Garrison, St. Michael ☎ 246/426–6000 ⊕ www.radisson.com/barbados ⇨ 124 rooms ¶◎| Breakfast.*

$$$$ ALL-INCLUSIVE Fodor's Choice ★ **Sandals Barbados.** Opened in January 2015 after $65 million was spent renovating, reconstructing, and redecorating what had been the venerable Casuarina Hotel, this newest Sandals resort, the first in Barbados, has three distinct "villages" surrounding an 8-acre garden and lagoon. **Pros:** great beach and beautiful garden; myriad activities, including scuba diving and golf; a magnet for weddings, honeymoons, and vow renewals; oceanfront and swim-up lagoon rooms are top choices; complimentary Wi-Fi. **Cons:** fabulously expensive so look for promotions. $ *Rooms from: $2,114 ✉ St. Lawrence Gap, at Maxwell Coast Rd., Dover, Christ Church ☎ 246/620–3600, 888/726–3257 ⊕ www.sandals.com ⇨ 280 rooms ¶◎| All-inclusive.*

$$ HOTEL **Silver Point Hotel.** This remote, gated community of modern condos at Silver Sands–Silver Rock Beach is operated as a trendy boutique hotel that appeals to singles, couples, and families—but especially to windsurfers and kitesurfers. **Pros:** stylish suites; perfect location for windsurfers and kitesurfers; gated community. **Cons:** not within walking distance of anything except the beach, so a rental car is recommended; sea can be rough for swimming. $ *Rooms from: $280 ✉ Silver Sands, Christ Church ☎ 246/420–4416 ⊕ www.silverpointhotel.com ⇨ 58 suites ¶◎| No meals.*

$$$$ ALL-INCLUSIVE **The SoCo Hotel.** Sophisticated couples love this ultramodern boutique hotel strategically poised on the beachfront in Hastings. **Pros:** stylish rooms; personalized service; excellent restaurant; lovely beach with long boardwalk; complimentary Wi-Fi. **Cons:** showers only, no tubs; very expensive. $ *Rooms from: $800 ✉ Hastings Main Rd., Hastings, Christ Church ☎ 246/228–6955 ⊕ www.thesocohotel.com ⇨ 24 rooms ¶◎| All-inclusive.*

$ B&B/INN Fodor's Choice ★ **Sweetfield Manor.** Perched on a ridge about a mile from Bridgetown, this lovely and romantic restored plantation house (circa 1900) was once the residence of the Dutch ambassador and is now the island's most delightful bed-and-breakfast. **Pros:** peaceful enclave primarily for adults; inviting pool and gardens; delicious gourmet breakfast;

Fairmont Royal Pavilion

perfect wedding venue; complimentary Wi-Fi. **Cons:** long walk (or short car ride) to beach; rental car advised; not a good choice for kids. *Rooms from: $177 Brittons New Rd., Brittons Hill, St. Michael 246/429–8356 www.sweetfieldmanor.net 6 rooms, 4 with bath; 1 suite Breakfast.*

$$$$
ALL-INCLUSIVE
FAMILY
Turtle Beach Resort. Families flock to this resort because it offers large, bright suites and enough all-included activities for everyone. **Pros:** perfect for family vacations; nice pools; roomy accommodations; lots of services and amenities. **Cons:** beach is relatively narrow; open vent between bedroom and hallway can be noisy at night. *Rooms from: $660 St. Lawrence Gap, Dover, Christ Church 246/428–7131 www.turtlebeachresortbarbados.com 161 suites All-inclusive.*

EASTERN BARBADOS

$$
B&B/INN
Fodor's Choice ★
The Atlantis Hotel. Renovated and reopened in 2009, this hotel, renowned for its spectacular oceanfront location, has been a fixture on the rugged east coast for more than a century. **Pros:** historical and modern blend beautifully; spectacular oceanfront location; excellent restaurant. **Cons:** from oceanfront rooms, smashing waves can be noisy at night; showers only, no tubs; remote location, so rental car advised; no beach for swimming. *Rooms from: $305 Tent Bay, St. Joseph 246/433–9445 www.atlantishotelbarbados.com 5 rooms, 3 suites, 2 apartments Closed Sept. Breakfast.*

$
B&B/INN
Sea-U Guest House. Uschi Wetzels, a German travel writer in an earlier life, became smitten with the wild and woolly east coast of Barbados while on assignment and returned in 1999 to build this tiny

guesthouse. **Pros:** peaceful and relaxing; couldn't be friendlier; complimentary Wi-Fi. **Cons:** remote location; few on-site activities; no TV or in-room telephone. *Rooms from: $239* *Tent Bay, St. Joseph* *246/433–9450* *www.seaubarbados.com* *8 rooms* *Breakfast.*

WEST COAST

$$$$ ALL-INCLUSIVE **The Club Barbados Resort & Spa.** This is one of the island's few adults-only (age 16 and up), all-inclusive resorts and the only one on the west coast; only spa and salon services and room service cost extra. **Pros:** intimate atmosphere; walk to Holetown and Sandy Lane Beach; waterskiing and boat trip included; complimentary Wi-Fi. **Cons:** beach erodes to almost nothing sometimes—usually after fall storms—but the sandy beach deck is a good substitute. *Rooms from: $790* *Hwy. 1, Vauxhall, St. James* *246/432–7840, 866/317–8009* *www.theclubbarbados.com* *96 rooms, 65 suites* *All-inclusive.*

$$$$ RESORT Fodor's Choice ★ **Cobblers Cove Hotel.** Flanked by tropical gardens on one side and the sea on the other, this English country-style resort has elegant suites, each with a comfy sitting room with sofa bed, a small library, and a wall of louvered shutters that open wide to a patio. **Pros:** very classy; lovely grounds; amazing penthouse suites; very quiet. **Cons:** small beach; too quiet for some; only bedrooms have a/c; adults-only Jan.–Mar. *Rooms from: $741* *Road View, Hwy. 1B, Speightstown, St. Peter* *246/422–2291* *www.cobblerscove.com* *40 suites* *Closed Sept.–mid-Oct.* *Multiple meal plans.*

$$$$ RESORT Fodor's Choice ★ **Colony Club Hotel.** The signature hotel of five Elegant Hotel properties on Barbados is certainly elegant, but with a quiet, friendly, understated style primarily targeted to adults. **Pros:** swim-up rooms; complimentary organic garden tour and cooking demo, historic Holetown walk, snorkel safari, and fishing with the chef; some ADA-compliant rooms; complimentary Wi-Fi. **Cons:** pricey; kid-friendly activities only summer and holidays; beach comes and goes, depending on storms. *Rooms from: $920* *Hwy. 1, Porters, St. James* *246/422–2335, 888/996–9948* *www.colonyclubhotel.com* *62 rooms, 34 junior suites* *Closed Sept.* *Multiple meal plans.*

$$$$ RESORT Fodor's Choice ★ **Coral Reef Club.** This upscale resort, with pristine coral-stone cottages scattered over 12 acres of flower-filled gardens, offers elegance in a welcoming, informal atmosphere. **Pros:** delightful appearance and atmosphere; beautiful suites with huge verandas; delicious dining. **Cons:** few room TVs; narrow beach sometimes disappears, depending on weather; no kids mid-January through February. *Rooms from: $847* *Hwy. 1, Porters, St. James* *246/422–2372* *www.coralreefbarbados.com* *29 rooms, 57 suites, 2 villas* *Closed mid-May–mid-July and Sept.* *Multiple meal plans.*

$$$$ RESORT Fodor's Choice ★ **Fairmont Royal Pavilion.** Every unit in this beautiful, luxurious adults-oriented resort (kids welcome mid-March through October) has immediate access to 11 acres of lovely tropical gardens and an uninterrupted sea view from a broad balcony or patio. **Pros:** excellent service—everyone remembers your name; excellent dining; complimentary Wi-Fi. **Cons:** dining—and everything else—is expensive. *Rooms from: $1,119* *Hwy. 1, Porters, St. James* *246/422–5555, 866/540–4485*

Coral Reef Club luxury cottage

www.fairmont.com/barbados *48 rooms, 24 suites, 1 3-bedroom villa* *Multiple meal plans.*

$$$$ HOTEL **The House.** Privacy, luxury, and service are hallmarks of this intimate adults-only sanctuary adjacent to sister resort Tamarind. **Pros:** trendy and stylish; privacy assured; pure relaxation; airport meet-and-greet, with one-way transfer included; complimentary Wi-Fi. **Cons:** atmosphere can be stuffy, but you can head next door to Tamarind for a reality check. *Rooms from: $979* *Hwy. 1, Paynes Bay, St. James* *246/432–5525, 888/996–9948 in U.S.* *www.thehousebarbados.com* *34 suites* *Breakfast.*

$$$ RENTAL FAMILY **Little Good Harbour.** A cluster of modern, spacious, self-catering cottages, built in updated chattel-house style with gingerbread balconies, overlooks a narrow strip of beach in far north Barbados—just beyond the fishing community of Six Men's Bay. **Pros:** spacious, beautifully decorated suites, laid-back atmosphere; good choice for families. **Cons:** busy road; tiny beach; remote location. *Rooms from: $425* *Hwy. 1B, Shermans, St. Peter* *246/439–3000* *www.littlegoodharbourbarbados.com* *21 suites* *Closed Sept.* *No meals.*

$$$$ ALL-INCLUSIVE **Mango Bay.** This boutique beachfront resort in the heart of Holetown is within walking distance of shops, restaurants, nightspots, historic sites, and the public bus to Bridgetown and Speightstown. **Pros:** pleasant accommodations; great food; friendly staff; excellent value. **Cons:** small pool; fairly narrow beach. *Rooms from: $495* *2nd St., Holetown, St. James* *246/432–1384* *www.mangobaybarbados.com* *64 rooms, 10 suites, 2 penthouse suites* *All-inclusive.*

$$$$ RESORT Fodor's Choice ★ **The Sandpiper.** An intimate vibe and (practically) private beach keep guests coming back to this west-coast hideaway with units spread over 7 acres of gardens. **Pros:** private and sophisticated; fabulous Tree Top Suites; jaw-dropping bathrooms; lots of included water activities. **Cons:** beach is small, typical of west-coast beaches; hotel is small and popular, so book far in advance. *Rooms from: $847 ✉ Hwy. 1, Holetown, St. James ☎ 246/422–2251 ⊕ www.sandpiperbarbados.com 22 rooms, 25 suites ⊗ Closed Sept. Multiple meal plans.*

$$$$ RESORT FAMILY Fodor's Choice ★ **Sandy Lane Hotel and Golf Club.** Few places in the Caribbean can compare to Sandy Lane's luxurious facilities and ultrapampering service—or to its astronomical prices. **Pros:** cream of the crop; excellent dining; lovely beach; amazing spa; great golf; complimentary Wi-Fi. **Cons:** over the top for most mortals; while you don't need to dress up to walk through the lobby, you'll feel that you should. *Rooms from: $2,450 ✉ Hwy. 1, Paynes Bay, St. James ☎ 246/444–2000 ⊕ www.sandylane.com 96 rooms, 16 suites, 1 5-bedroom villa Breakfast.*

$$$$ RESORT FAMILY **Tamarind.** This sleek Mediterranean-style resort, which sprawls along 750 feet of prime west-coast beachfront, is large enough to cater to active families and sophisticated couples, including honeymooners. **Pros:** very big resort, yet layout affords privacy; right on Paynes Bay Beach; lots of free water sports. **Cons:** some rooms could use a little TLC; uninspired buffet breakfast. *Rooms from: $592 ✉ Hwy. 1, Paynes Bay, St. James ☎ 246/432–1332, 888/917–9948 in U.S. ⊕ www.tamarindbarbados.com 57 rooms, 47 suites Multiple meal plans.*

$$$$ HOTEL **Treasure Beach.** Quiet, upscale, and intimate, this boutique hotel has a residential quality. **Pros:** cozy retreat; congenial crowd; swimming with the turtles just offshore. **Cons:** narrow beach; offshore turtles often attract boatloads of tourists. *Rooms from: $865 ✉ Hwy. 1, Paynes Bay, St. James ☎ 246/419–4200, 800/355–6161 in U.S. ⊕ www.treasurebeachhotel.com 35 suites ⊗ Closed Aug.–mid-Oct. Multiple meal plans.*

NIGHTLIFE

When the sun goes down, the locals "lime" (which can mean anything from getting together for a drink and casual chat to enjoying a full-blown "jump-up" or street party). Occasional performances by world-renowned stars and regional groups are major events, and tickets can be hard to come by—but give it a try. Most resorts have nightly entertainment in season, and nightclubs often have live bands for listening and dancing. The busiest bars and dance clubs rage until 3 am. On Saturday nights, some clubs—especially those with live music—charge a cover of $15 or more. Many bars and nightspots feature happy hours.

Barbados supports the rum industry with more than 1,600 "rum shops," simple bars where (mostly) men congregate to discuss the world or life in general, drink rum, and eat a cutter (sandwich). In more sophisticated establishments, you can find upscale rum cocktails made with the island's renowned Mount Gay and Cockspur brands—and no shortage of Barbados's own Banks Beer.

A local chef cooks up a fish fry at the Oistins fish market in Bridgetown.

BRIDGETOWN AREA

The Boatyard. There's never a dull moment at this popular beachside nightspot with both a DJ and live bands. From happy hour until the wee hours, the patrons at Sharkey's Bar are mostly local and visiting professionals. ✉ *Bay St., south of town, Carlisle Bay* ☎ *246/436–2622* 🌐 *www.theboatyard.com.*

Harbour Lights. This open-air, beachfront club claims to be the "home of the party animal." Wednesday and Friday nights are the hottest, with dancing under the stars to reggae and soca music. ✉ *Marine Villa, Bay St., south of town, Carlisle Bay* ☎ *246/436–7225* 🌐 *www.harbourlightsbarbados.com.*

Waterfront Café. From November through April, there's live jazz Thursday, Friday, and Saturday evenings. The location alongside the wharf and small dance floor are also draws. ✉ *The Careenage* ☎ *246/427–0093* 🌐 *www.waterfrontcafe.com.bb* ⏲ *Closed Sun.–Wed.*

SOUTH COAST

Bubba's Sports Bar. Merrymakers and sports lovers find live action on three 10-foot video screens and a dozen TVs, along with bar food and drinks. ✉ *Main Rd., Rockley, Christ Church* ☎ *246/435–8731* 🌐 *www.bubbassportsbar.net.*

FAMILY Fodor's Choice ★ **Oistins Fish Fry.** This is the place to be on Friday evenings, when the south-coast fishing village becomes a lively and convivial outdoor street party suitable for the whole family. Barbecued chicken and a variety of fish, along with all the traditional sides are served fresh from the grill and consumed at roadside picnic tables; servings are huge, and prices are inexpensive—about $10 per plate. Drinks, music, and dancing add to the fun. ✉ *Oistins, Christ Church.*

Reggae Lounge. This is a popular nightspot in the Gap, where live bands or DJs play the latest R&B hits and old and new reggae favorites every night until the wee hours. ✉ *St. Lawrence Gap, Dover, Christ Church* ☎ *246/435–6462.*

Sugar Ultra Lounge. This chic, upscale, techno nightspot—complete with light-show wall—attracts international talent in addition to the usual DJ and occasional local band on Tuesdays, Thursdays, and Saturdays from 10 pm to 3 or 4 am. The adjacent Rush Restaurant has casual dining. ✉ *St. Lawrence Gap, Dover, Christ Church* ☎ *246/420–7662.*

SHOPPING

WHAT TO BUY

One of the most long-lasting souvenirs to bring home from Barbados is a piece of authentic Caribbean art. The colorful flowers, quaint villages, mesmerizing seascapes, and fascinating cultural experiences and activities that are endemic to the region and familiar to visitors have been translated by local artists onto canvas and into photographs, sculpture, and other media. Gift shops and even some restaurants display local artwork for sale, but the broadest array of artwork will be found in a gallery. Typical Bajan crafts include pottery, shell and glass art, wood carvings, handmade dolls, watercolors, and other artwork (both originals and prints).

Although many of the private homes, great houses, and museums in Barbados are filled with priceless antiques, you'll find few for sale—mainly British antiques and some local pieces, particularly mahogany furniture. Look instead for old prints and paintings.

DUTY-FREE SHOPPING

Duty-free luxury goods—china, crystal, cameras, porcelain, leather items, electronics, jewelry, perfume, and clothing—are found at Bridgetown's Broad Street department stores and their branches, shops in the high-end Limegrove Lifestyle Centre in Holetown, the Bridgetown Cruise Terminal (for passengers only), and the departure lounge at Grantley Adams International Airport. Prices are often 30% to 40% less than full retail. To buy goods at duty-free prices, you must produce your passport, immigration form, or driver's license, along with departure information (such as flight number and date) at the time of purchase—or you can have your purchases delivered free to the airport or harbor for pickup; duty-free alcohol, tobacco products, and some electronic equipment *must* be delivered to you at the airport or harbor.

GROCERIES

If you've chosen self-catering lodgings, want some snacks, or just like to explore local grocery stores, you'll find large, modern supermarkets at Sunset Crest in Holetown on the west coast; in Oistins, at Sargeants Village (Sheraton Mall), and in Worthing on the south coast; and at Warrens (Highway 2, north of Bridgetown) in St. Michael.

CLOSE UP

Where de Rum Come From

For more than 300 years (from 1655 through "Black Tot Day," July 31, 1970), a daily "tot" of rum (2 ounces) was duly administered to each sailor in the British navy—as a health ration. At times, rum has also played a less appetizing—but equally important—role. When Admiral Horatio Nelson died in 1805 aboard ship during the Battle of Trafalgar, his body was preserved in a cask of his favorite rum until he could be properly buried.

Hardly a Caribbean island doesn't have its own locally made rum, but Barbados is truly "where de rum come from." Mount Gay, the world's oldest rum distillery, has continuously operated on Barbados since 1703, according to the original deed for the Mount Gay Estate, which itemized two stone windmills, a boiling house, seven copper pots, and a still house. The presence of rum-making equipment on the plantation at the time suggests that the previous owners were actually producing rum in Barbados long before 1703.

Today, much of the island's interior is still planted with sugarcane—where the rum really does come from—and several great houses on historic sugar plantations have been restored with period furniture and are open to the public.

To really fathom rum, however, you need to delve a little deeper than the bottom of a glass of rum punch. Mount Gay offers an interesting 45-minute tour of its main plant, followed by a tasting. You can learn about the rum-making process from cane to cocktail, hear more rum-inspired anecdotes, and have an opportunity to buy bottles of its famous Eclipse or Extra Old rum at duty-free prices. Bottoms up!

BRIDGETOWN

Bridgetown's **Broad Street** is the primary downtown shopping area. **DaCosta Manning Mall,** in the historic Colonnade Building on Broad Street, has more than 25 shops that sell everything from Piaget watches to postcards; across the street, **Mall 34** has 22 shops where you can buy duty-free goods, souvenirs, and snacks. At the **cruise-ship terminal** shopping arcade, passengers can buy both duty-free goods and Barbadian-made crafts at more than 30 boutiques and a dozen vendor carts and stalls. And the **airport departure lounge** is a veritable shopping mall.

DEPARTMENT STORES

Cave Shepherd. The main store sells an array of clothing and luxury goods. Branches are at Holetown's Sunset Crest and West Coast malls and Worthing's Vista shopping complex; the airport departure lounge and cruise-ship terminal have boutiques. ✉ *Broad St.* ☎ *246/431–2121.*

Harrison's. There are three large stores on Broad Street, one at the south coast's Sheraton Mall, and boutiques in the airport departure lounge and cruise-ship terminal. ✉ *Broad St.* ☎ *246/431–5500.*

HANDICRAFTS

Island Crafts. You'll find locally made pottery, wood carvings, straw items, glass art, batik, wire sculptures, and souvenirs. Additional shops are at Harrison's Cave and the airport courtyard and departure lounge. ✉ *Pelican Craft Centre, Shop No. 5* ☎ *246/435–0542.*

Pelican Village Craft Centre. Halfway between the cruise-ship terminal and downtown Bridgetown is this cluster of workshop studios where craftspeople create and sell locally made leather goods, batik, basketry, carvings, jewelry, glass art, paintings, pottery, and other items. It's open weekdays 9 to 5 and Saturday 9 to 2; things are most active when cruise ships are in port. ✉ *Princess Alice Hwy.* ☎ *246/427–5350.*

SOUTH COAST

At **Chattel House Village,** a cluster of boutiques in St. Lawrence Gap, you can buy locally made crafts and other souvenirs. In Rockley, Christ Church, **Quayside Centre** has a small number of boutiques.

Best of Barbados. Architect Jimmy Walker founded these shops to showcase the works of his artist wife. Products range from her frameable prints, housewares, and textiles to arts and crafts in both native style and modern designs. Everything is made or designed on Barbados. Branch shops are at Chattel Village in Holetown, at Southern Palms Resort in St. Lawrence Gap, at the cruise-ship terminal, and in the airport departure lounge. ✉ *Quayside Centre, Main Rd., Rockley, Christ Church* ☎ *246/435–6820* 🌐 *www.best-of-barbados.com.*

Tyrol Cot Heritage Village. In chattel houses, you can watch local artisans make hand-painted figurines, straw baskets, clothing, paintings, and pottery—and buy their wares. The workshops are open primarily during the winter season and when cruise ships are in port. ✉ *Codrington Hill, St. Michael* ☎ *246/424–2074.*

WEST COAST

Holetown has the upscale **Limegrove Lifestyle Centre,** a stylish shopping mall with high-end designer boutiques, as well as **Chattel House Village,** small shops in colorful cottages with local products, fashions, beachwear, and souvenirs. Also in Holetown, **Sunset Crest Mall** has two branches of the Cave Shepherd department store, a bank, a pharmacy, and several small shops; at **West Coast Mall** you can buy duty-free goods, island wear, and groceries.

Fodor'sChoice ★ **Earthworks Pottery.** At his family-owned and -operated pottery workshop, items range from dishes and knickknacks to complete dinner services and one-of-a-kind art pieces. The characteristically blue or green—and, more recently, peach and brown—pottery decorates hotel rooms and is sold in gift shops throughout the island, but the biggest selection (including "seconds") is here, where you also can watch the potters at work. ✉ *Edgehill Heights, St. Thomas* ☎ *246/425–0223* 🌐 *www.earthworks-pottery.com* ⊙ *Closed Sun.*

Gallery of Caribbean Art. This gallery is committed to promoting Caribbean art from Haiti and Cuba in the north to Curaçao and Guyana in the south—and, particularly, the works of Barbadian artists. ✉ *Northern Business Centre, Queen St., Speightstown, St. Peter* ☎ *246/419–0858* 🌐 *www.artgallerycaribbean.com* ⏲ *Closed Sun.*

On the Wall Art Gallery. Artist and gallery owner Vanita Comissiong offers an array of original paintings by Barbadian artists, along with handmade arts and crafts and jewelry products. An additional gallery is located in a dedicated space at Champers restaurant, on the south coast. ✉ *Earthworks Pottery, Edgehill Heights, St. Thomas* ☎ *246/234–9145* 🌐 *www.onthewallartgallery.com* ⏲ *Closed Sun.*

SPORTS AND THE OUTDOORS

5

Cricket, football (soccer), polo, and rugby are extremely popular sports in Barbados for participants and spectators alike, with local, regional, and international matches held throughout the year. Contact Barbados Tourism Marketing, Inc., or check newspapers for information.

DIVING AND SNORKELING

More than two-dozen dive sites lie along the west coast between Maycocks Bay and Bridgetown and off the south coast as far as the St. Lawrence Gap. Certified divers can explore flat coral reefs and see dramatic sea fans, huge barrel sponges, and more than 50 varieties of fish. Divers regularly explore nine sunken wrecks, and at least 10 more are accessible to experts. Underwater visibility is generally 80 to 90 feet. The calm waters along the west coast are also ideal for snorkeling. The marine reserve, a stretch of protected reef between Sandy Lane and the Colony Club, contains beautiful coral formations accessible from the beach.

On the west coast, **Bell Buoy** is a large, dome-shape reef where huge brown coral tree forests and schools of fish delight all categories of divers at depths of 20 to 60 feet. At **Dottins Reef**, off Holetown, you can see schooling fish, barracudas, and turtles at depths of 40 to 60 feet. **Maycocks Bay**, on the northwest coast, is particularly enticing; large coral reefs are separated by corridors of white sand, and visibility is often 100 feet or more. The 165-foot freighter *Pamir* lies in 60 feet of water off Six Men's Bay; it's still intact, and you can peer through its portholes at dozens of varieties of tropical fish. **Silver Bank** is a healthy coral reef with beautiful fish and sea fans; you may get a glimpse of the *Atlantis* submarine at 60 to 80 feet. Not to be missed, the *Stavronikita*, is a scuttled Greek freighter at about 135 feet; hundreds of butterfly fish hang out around its mast, and the thin rays of sunlight filtering down through the water make exploring the huge ship a wonderfully eerie experience.

Farther south, **Carlisle Bay** is a natural harbor and marine park just below Bridgetown. Here you can retrieve empty bottles thrown overboard by generations of sailors and see cannons and cannonballs, anchors, and six shipwrecks (*Berwyn, Fox, CTrek, Eilon,* the barge *Cornwallis,* and *Bajan Queen*) lying in 25 to 60 feet of water, all close enough to visit on the same dive. The *Bajan Queen*, a cruise vessel that sank in 2002, is the island's newest wreck.

Dive shops provide a two-hour beginner's "resort" course (about $100) followed by a shallow dive, or a weeklong certification course (about $450). Once you're certified, a one-tank dive costs about $70 to $80; a two-tank dive runs $120 to $125. All equipment is supplied, and you can purchase multidive packages. Gear for snorkeling is available (free or for a small rental fee) from most hotels. Snorkelers can usually accompany dive trips for $25 for a one- or two-hour trip. Most dive shops have relationships with hotels and offer dive packages to hotel guests, including round-trip transfers.

Dive Shop, Ltd. Near the Carlisle Bay marine park just south of Bridgetown, the island's oldest dive shop offers daily reef and wreck dives, plus beginner classes, certification courses, and underwater photography instruction. Underwater cameras are available for rent. Free transfers are provided between your hotel and the dive shop. ✉ *Amey's Alley, Upper Bay St., next to Nautilus Beach Apts., Bridgetown, St. Michael* ☎ *246/426–9947* 🌐 *www.thediveshopbarbados.com.*

Hightide Watersports. On the west coast, Hightide Watersports offers three dive trips daily—one- and two-tank dives and night reef–wreck–drift dives—for up to eight divers, along with PADI instruction, equipment rental, and free transportation. ✉ *Coral Reef Club, Hwy. 1, Holetown, St. James* ☎ *246/432–0931, 800/970–0016, 800/513–5763* 🌐 *www.divehightide.com.*

Reefers & Wreckers Dive Shop. The most northerly dive shop gives easy access to the north's unspoiled reefs and runs trips to dive sites and wrecks along the west coast and in Carlisle Bay. ✉ *Queen St., Speightstown, St. Peter* ☎ *246/422–5450* 🌐 *www.scubadiving.bb.*

FISHING

Fishing is a year-round activity in Barbados, but prime time is January through April, when game fish are in season. Whether you're a serious deep-sea fisher looking for marlin, sailfish, tuna, and other billfish or you prefer angling in calm coastal waters where wahoo, barracuda, and other small fish reside, you can choose from a variety of half- or full-day charters departing from the Careenage in Bridgetown. Expect to pay $175 per person for a shared half-day charter; for a private charter (up to six people), expect to pay $500 to $700 per boat for a four- to six-hour half-day charter or $900 to $1,000 for an eight-hour full-day charter. Spectators who don't fish are welcome for $50 per person.

***Billfisher* Deepsea Fishing.** *Billfisher III*, a 40-foot Viking Sport Fisherman, accommodates up to six passengers with three fishing chairs and five rods. Captain Winston ("The Colonel") White has been fishing these waters since 1975. His full-day charters include a full lunch; all trips include drinks and transportation to and from the boat. ✉ *Bridge House Wharf, the Careenage, Bridgetown, St. Michael* ☎ *246/431–0741.*

***Cannon* Charters.** *Cannon II*, a 42-foot Hatteras Sport Fisherman, has three chairs and five rods and accommodates six passengers; drinks and snacks are complimentary, and lunch is served on full-day charters.

Continued on page 200

SPORT FISHING

Marlise Kast

With its abundance of marlin, sailfish, tuna, and Mahi Mahi, the Caribbean has enough catch to beckon any angler. Crystal-blue waters, white-sand beaches, and tropical weather make this the perfect place to set sail. From Barbados and the Bahamas to Puerto Rico and the Virgin Islands, there is plenty of opportunity to cast your line.

Fishing on sailing boat, Grenadines Islands.

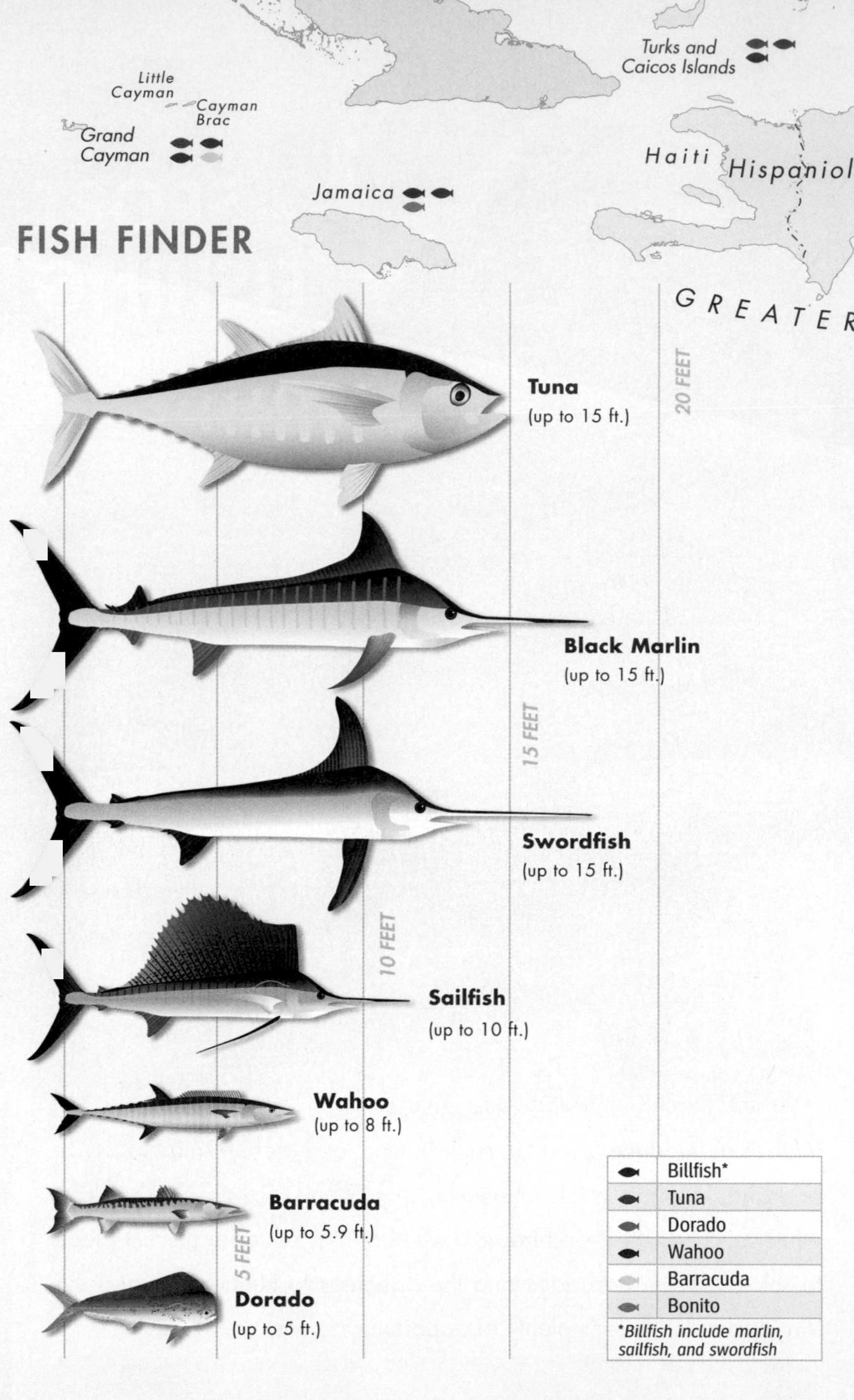

Little Cayman
Cayman Brac
Grand Cayman
Jamaica
Turks and Caicos Islands
Haiti
Hispaniola
GREATER
FISH FINDER
20 FEET
15 FEET
10 FEET
5 FEET
Tuna
(up to 15 ft.)
Black Marlin
(up to 15 ft.)
Swordfish
(up to 15 ft.)
Sailfish
(up to 10 ft.)
Wahoo
(up to 8 ft.)
Barracuda
(up to 5.9 ft.)
Dorado
(up to 5 ft.)
Billfish*
Tuna
Dorado
Wahoo
Barracuda
Bonito
*Billfish include marlin, sailfish, and swordfish

ATLANTIC OCEAN
LEEWARD ISLANDS
Dominican Republic
St. Thomas
St. John
Tortola
Virgin Gorda
Anguilla
St. Barthélemy
Barbuda
St. Maarten/ St. Martin
Saba
St. Eustatius
St. Kitts
Nevis
Antigua
Puerto Rico
St. Croix
Montserrat
Guadeloupe
Marie Galante
ANTILLES
Dominica
Martinique
St. Lucia
Barbados
St. Vincent
Bequia
The Grenadines
Carriacou
Grenada
Tobago
Trinidad
WINDWARD ISLANDS
LESSER ANTILLES
0 200 mi
0 200 km
Aruba
Curaçao
Bonaire
Islas Los Roques

So many islands, so little time. Among anglers' favorites are the **Virgin Islands**, known for bluefish, wahoo, swordfish, and shark. These deep-sea fishing waters host annual tournaments where eight world records for blue marlin have been set. Equally attractive to deep-sea fishermen are the **Cayman Islands**, home to tuna, wahoo, and marlin. Bottom dwellers, such as grouper and snapper are always an easy hook in this area.

For great bonefishing, head to nearby Little Cayman at Bloody Bay. Between January and June, the **Dominican Republic** is popular with sport fishermen in search of sailfish, bonito, marlin, and wahoo. Although the bonefish-laden **Bahamas** cater to fly-fishermen, **Barbados** is a paradise for both deep-sea anglers reeling in billfish, and for coastal catchers forging for wahoo, barracuda, and smaller fish. Luring fishermen from afar, **Puerto Rico's** coast has reeled in 30+ world records, making it the fishing capital of the Caribbean.

DEEP SEA VS. SHALLOW WATERS

Swordfish

Too deep or not too deep? That is the question!

From fly-fishing at the river mouth to sport fishing in the open waters, the Caribbean can satisfy any angler's longing to reel one in. It's a question of what type of experience you're looking for. How active vs. passive of an experience do you want?

If you're feeling strong head for the deep. Any quest for catch below 30 meters (98 ft) is considered deep-sea fishing. The massive sport fish that frequent the deeper waters are magnificent specimens, and it's a thrilling experience to wrestle one from the deep. Albacore, marlin, barracuda, and tuna are the common catch, and it requires a tremendous amount of patience, strength, and effort to properly hook and land these mighty creatures.

For a more tranquil way to enjoy the Caribbean waters, try shallow-water fishing over reefs and shipwrecks. Tarpon, permit, pompano, wahoo, and small barracuda are the primary catch. Casting your line inshore is both convenient and affordable because chartering a large boat is unnecessary.

TAKE THE BAIT

In the Caribbean, it is best to use natural bait such as ballyhoo, tuna strips, or flying fish. Because a variety of big game fish feed on ballyhoo, they are considered ideal enticers when trolling the open waters. Live bait will also help lure larger fish, which are attracted to the blood and movement on the line. Depending on the type of catch you are after, almost any baitfish can be used including squid, shrimp, conch, and sardines. Aiding in the hunt are digital fishfinders, commonly utilized by sport fishermen to detect schools of fish. Bait is the same for both inshore and deep-sea fishing, and rarely are artificial lures used in the Caribbean.

A golden catch from shallow waters.

PRACTICAL INFORMATION

TYPE OF FISHING	COSTS	CHARACTERISTICS
OFFSHORE TRIPS	From $325 for a half-day.	Many packages include roundtrip transportation to and from your hotel, a boat crew, food, beverages, bait, gear, taxes and licenses. Tips are not included.
REEF FISHING	From $300 per day. From $250 for a bonefishing guide.	An experienced captain to steady the boat directly over the reefs is recommended. Most reefs are home to large schools of fish, but some areas are barren. Use a braided line, which is more abrasion resistant than monofiliament lines, to keep your line from snapping between the crevices.
DEEP-SEA FISHING	From $500 for a half-day.	The open waters are where you'll find the big catch. Most operators offer half-day and full-day charters with an experienced crew that knows where to find that trophy fish. Packages generally include your captain, crew, fishing tackle, bait, license and fees.

Private boat owners who plan on fishing for tuna, shark, swordfish and billfish in the Atlantic Ocean, (including the Gulf of Mexico and Caribbean Sea), must obtain an **Atlantic Highly Migratory Species** (HMS) permit. Valid from the date of issue through December of that same year, permits can be ordered online through the **National Marine Fisheries Service** (🌐 www.hmspermits.noaa.gov).

MAN OVERBOARD: RULES/REGULATIONS

Although guidelines vary from island to island, it is safe to assume that a permit is required for fishing in the Caribbean. These licenses are usually included in sport fishing tours and packages, but it is best to inquire prior to booking. Because hundreds of fish can be hooked in a single day in the Caribbean waters, the catch-and-release method is vital for conservation. Throughout the entire region, spear fishing is illegal as is fishing within the boundaries of any marine park. It's advisable to utilize the services of licensed professionals.

Many of the Caribbean territories do not require a saltwater fishing license. One definite exception is the British Virgin Islands, where visitors must obtain permits, valid up to one month. Fishing permits are available from the Department of Conservation and Fisheries ☎284/494–5681 🌐 www.bvidef.org.

Deep-sea fishing boats.

STAYING AFLOAT: SAFETY

Before setting sail, be sure to inform someone of your intended whereabouts as well as the time of your scheduled return. If you're fishing solo, double check all safety equipment including your means of communication, life jackets, and emergency supplies. Above all, inquire about local weather conditions and policies before booking your charter.

✉ *The Careenage, Bridgetown, St. Michael* ☎ *246/424–6107* 🌐 *www.fishingbarbados.com.*

High Seas Charters. *Ocean Hunter*, a 42-foot custom-built sportfishing boat, has an extended cockpit that easily accommodates six people. Choose a four-, six-, or eight-hour charter. All tackle and bait are supplied, as well as drinks and snacks. Charter rates include hotel transfers. ✉ *The Careenage, St. Michael* ☎ *246/233–2598* 🌐 *www.sportfishingbarbados.com.*

GOLF

Barbadians love golf, and golfers love Barbados. Courses open to visitors are listed below.

Barbados Golf Club. The first public golf course on Barbados, an 18-hole championship course, was redesigned in 2000 by golf course architect Ron Kirby. The course has hosted numerous competitions, including the European Senior tour in 2003. Several hotels offer preferential tee-time reservations and reduced rates. Cart, trolley, club, and shoe rentals are all available. ✉ *Hwy. 7, Durants, Christ Church* ☎ *246/428–8463* 🌐 *www.barbadosgolfclub.com* 🎟 *$105 for 18 holes; $65 for 9 holes; 3-, 5-, and 7-day passes $255, $400, $525, respectively* 🏌 *18 holes, 6805 yards, par 72.*

Fodor's Choice ★ **Country Club at Sandy Lane.** At this prestigious club, golfers can play the Old Nine or either of two 18-hole championship courses: the Tom Fazio–designed Country Club Course and the spectacular Green Monkey Course, reserved for hotel guests and club members. The layouts offer a limestone quarry setting (Green Monkey), a modern style with lakes (Country Club), and traditional small greens and narrow fairways (Old Nine). Golfers can use the driving range for free. The Country Club Restaurant and Bar, overlooking the 18th hole, is open to the public. Caddies, trolleys, clubs, and shoes are available for rent, as are GPS-equipped carts, which alert you to upcoming hazards, give tips on how to play holes, and let you order refreshments! ✉ *Sandy Lane, Hwy. 1, Paynes Bay, St. James* ☎ *246/444–2500* 🌐 *www.sandylane.com/golf* 🎟 *$220 for 18 holes ($185 hotel guests); $145 for 9 holes ($125 guests); 7-day pass $1,250 ($1,150 guests)* 🏌 *Green Monkey: 18 holes, 7343 yards, par 72; Country Club: 18 holes, 7060 yards, par 72; Old Nine: 9 holes, 3345 yards, par 36.*

Royal Westmoreland Golf Club. This well-regarded Robert Trent Jones Jr.–designed, 18-hole championship course meanders through 500 acres. Highlights include challenging greens, a great set of par threes, and ocean views from every hole. The course is primarily for members and villa renters, with 10 to 11 am tee times for visitors subject to availability (no Saturdays). Greens fees include an electric cart (required); club and shoe rentals are available. ✉ *Royal Westmoreland Resort, Westmoreland, St. James* ☎ *246/419–7244* 🌐 *www.royal-westmoreland.com* 🎟 *$215 for 18 holes, $108 for 9 holes for villa renters or hotel guests with club privileges; $250 visitors* 🏌 *18 holes, 7045 yards, par 72.*

GUIDED TOURS

Taxi drivers give personalized tours for about $35 to $40 per hour for up to three people. Or you can choose an overland mountain-bike journey, a 4x4 safari expedition, or a full-day bus excursion. Prices vary by mode of travel and attractions included. Ask guest services at your hotel to help you make arrangements.

Highland Adventure Centre. Mountain-bike tours, for $60 per person including transportation, guides, and refreshments, are an exhilarating 7½-mile (12-km) ride (15% uphill) through the heart of northern Barbados, ending up at Barclays Park, on the east coast. ✉ *Cane Field, St. Thomas* ☎ *246/438–8069.*

Island Safari. This outfit takes you to all the popular spots via a 4x4 Land Rover—including some gullies, forests, and remote areas that are inaccessible by conventional cars and buses. The cost for half-day or full-day tours ranges from $50 to $92.50 per person, including snacks or lunch. ✉ *CWTS Complex, Salters Rd., Lower Estate, St. George* ☎ *246/429–5337* 🌐 *www.islandsafari.bb.*

5

HIKING

Hilly but not mountainous, the northern interior and the east coast are ideal for hiking.

Arbib Heritage and Nature Trail. Maintained by the Barbados National Trust, these are actually two trails. The Whim Adventure trail offers a rigorous hike (3½ hours) through gullies and plantations to old ruins and remote north-country areas; the shorter, easier Round-de-Town Stroll (2 hours) goes through Speightstown's side streets and past an ancient church and chattel houses. Guided hikes run from 9 am to 2 pm on Wednesdays, Thursdays, and Saturdays for $25 per person (minimum four people); group rates are available. Book ahead, preferably four days in advance. Not recommended for children under five. ✉ *Speightstown, St. Peter* ☎ *246/234–9010, 246/426–2421* 🌐 *www.barbadosnationaltrust.org.*

Hike Barbados. Free walks sponsored by the Barbados National Trust are led year-round on Sundays from 6 to 9 am and from 3:30 to 6 pm; once a month, a moonlight hike at 5:30 substitutes for the afternoon hike (bring a flashlight). Experienced guides group you with others of similar ability on Stop and Stare, 5 to 6 miles (8 to 10 km); Here and There, 8 to 10 miles (13 to 16 km); or Grin and Bear, 12 to 14 miles (19 to 23 km). Wear loose clothes, sensible shoes, sunscreen, and a hat, and bring a camera and water. Routes and locations change, but each hike is a loop, finishing where it began. Check newspapers, call the Trust, or check online for schedules and meeting places. ✉ *Wildey House, Wildey, St. Michael* ☎ *246/436–9033, 246/426–2421* 🌐 *www.barbadosnationaltrust.org.*

SEA EXCURSIONS

Mini-submarine voyages are enormously popular with families and those who enjoy watching fish but don't wish to get wet. Party boats depart from Bridgetown's Deep Water Harbour for sightseeing and snorkeling or romantic sunset cruises. Prices are $45 to $125 per person for four- or five-hour daytime cruises and $60 to $85 for three- or four-hour sunset cruises, depending on the type of refreshments and entertainment included; transportation to and from the dock is provided. For an excursion that may be less splashy in terms of a party atmosphere—but is definitely splashier in terms of the actual experience—turtle tours allow participants to feed and swim with a resident group of hawksbill and leatherback sea turtles.

FAMILY ***Atlantis* Submarine.** This 50-foot, 48-passenger submarine turns the Caribbean into a giant aquarium. The 45-minute voyage ($104 per person, including hotel transfer) takes in wrecks and reefs as deep as 150 feet. Children love the adventure, but they must be at least 3 feet tall. ✉ *Shallow Draught, Bridgetown, St. Michael* ☎ *246/436–8929* 🌐 *www.barbados.atlantissubmarines.com.*

FAMILY **Black Pearl Party Cruises.** The whole family will get a kick out of a "pirate" ship adventure on *Jolly Roger 1*. The four-hour day and sunset (Thursday only) cruises ($87.50) along the island's west coast include a barbecue lunch or dinner, free-flowing drinks, lively music, swimming with turtles, and pirate activities such as walking the plank and rope swinging. ✉ *Carlisle House, the Careenage, Bridgetown, St. Michael* ☎ *246/436–2885, 246/826–7245* 🌐 *www.barbadosblackpearl-jollyroger1.com.*

***Cool Runnings* Catamaran Cruises.** Owner Captain Robert Povey skippers a five-hour lunch cruise ($90) with stops to swim with the fishes, snorkel with sea turtles, and explore a shallow shipwreck. A four-hour sunset cruise ($80) includes swimming, snorkeling, and exploring underwater as the sun sinks. Delicious meals with wine, along with an open bar, are part of all cruises. ✉ *Carlisle House, Carlisle Wharf, Hincks St., Bridgetown, St. Michael* ☎ *246/436–0911* 🌐 *www.coolrunningsbarbados.com.*

Tiami Catamaran Cruises. Tiami operates five catamaran party boats for luncheon cruises to a secluded bay for swimming with turtles or for romantic sunset and moonlight cruises with catering and live music. ✉ *Shallow Draught, Bridgetown, St. Michael* ☎ *246/430–0900* 🌐 *www.tiamicatamarancruises.com.*

SURFING

The best surfing is at the east coast's Bathsheba Soup Bowl, where the Barbados Independence Pro competition is held each November, but note that the island's windward (Atlantic) side is safe only for the most experienced surfers. Surfers also congregate at Surfer's Point, at the southern tip of Barbados near Inch Marlow, where the Atlantic Ocean meets the Caribbean Sea.

Dread or Dead Surf Shop. This surf shop promises to get beginners from "zero to standing up and surfing" in one afternoon. The three-hour course—"or until you stand up or give up"—costs $75 per person and includes a board, wax, rash guard (if necessary), a ride to and from the surf break, and instruction; additional lessons cost $50 for 2½ hours of water time. More experienced surfers can rent boards for $25 a day. ✉ *Hastings Main Rd., Hastings, Christ Church* ☎ *246/228–4785* 🌐 *www.dreadordead.com.*

Zed's Surfing Adventures. This outfit rents surfboards, provides lessons, and offers surf tours including equipment, guide, and transportation to surf breaks appropriate for your experience. A two-hour group lesson costs $60. Surfboard rentals cost $30 for two hours, $40 per day. ✉ *Surfer's Point, Inch Marlow, Christ Church* ☎ *246/428–7873* 🌐 *www.zedssurftravel.com.*

5

WINDSURFING AND KITEBOARDING

Part of windsurfing's World Cup circuit, Barbados is a prime windsurfing spot. Winds are strongest November through April at Silver Sands–Silver Rock Beach, on the southern tip, where the Barbados Windsurfing Championships are held in mid-January. Windsurfing boards and equipment, as well as instruction, are often available at larger hotels and sometimes can be rented by nonguests. Kiteboarding is more difficult, requiring several hours of instruction to reach proficiency; Silver Sands is about the only location in Barbados with kiteboarding equipment and instruction.

deAction Surf Shop. Directly on Silver Sands–Silver Rock Beach, Brian "Irie Man" Talma's shop stocks a range of rental surfing equipment and offers beginner windsurfing, kiteboarding, surfing, and stand-up paddling lessons. Conditions are ideal, with waves off the outer reef and flat water in the inner lagoon. Kiteboarding, which isn't easy, generally involves six hours of instruction broken up into two or three sessions: from flying a small kite to getting the body dragged with a big kite to finally getting up on the board. All equipment is provided. ✉ *Silver Sands–Silver Rock Beach, Silver Sands, Christ Church* ☎ *246/428–2027* 🌐 *www.briantalma.com.*

6

BONAIRE

WELCOME TO BONAIRE

The landscape of Bonaire is littered with acres of cactus and aloe plants. This is an arid climate with a stark beauty. Divers come to explore some of the best sites this side of Australia's Great Barrier Reef. Above the water are more than 15,000 flamingos—the biggest flock in the Western Hemisphere.

Restaurants ▼		Hotels ▼	
Bistro de Paris	12	Bellafonte Luxury Oceanfront Hotel	3
Boudoir	9	Bruce Bowker's	2
Capriccio	5	Buddy Dive Resort	9
Hang Out Bar	7	Captain Don's Habitat	10
It Rains Fishes	6	Den Laman	1
La Guernica	4	Happy Holiday	5
Mi Banana	1	Harbour Village	8
Mona Lisa	2	Roomer	4
Patagonia Argentinian	10	Sorobon Beach Resort	7
Spice Beach	11	Windsock	6
Wil's Tropical Grill	3		
Wind & Surf	8		

TOP REASONS TO VISIT BONAIRE

1 **The Diving:** As locals say, you come here to dive, eat, dive, sleep, and dive.

2 **The Snorkeling:** You don't have to be a certified diver to appreciate Bonaire's reefs; snorkelers can see much of the beauty just below the surface of the water.

3 **The Quiet:** Visitors came to enjoy the tranquillity of the island long before they started exploring diving.

4 **The Dining:** Dining options are surprisingly good and varied for such a small island.

5 **The Smiles:** Bonaireans are genuinely friendly, offering salutations to friends and strangers alike.

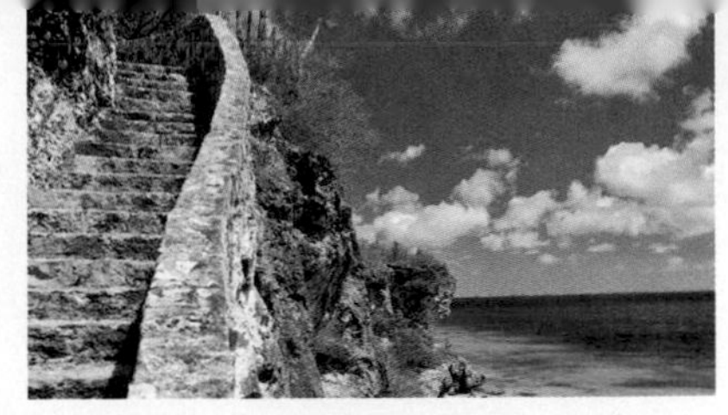

DIVER'S PARADISE

With just over 16,000 people, this unspoiled island (112 square miles [290 square km]) has a small-town atmosphere. Kralendijk, the capital, has just 3,000 inhabitants. The entire coastline—from the high-water tidemark to a depth of 200 feet—is protected as part of the Bonaire Marine Park, making it one of the best diving destinations in the Western Hemisphere.

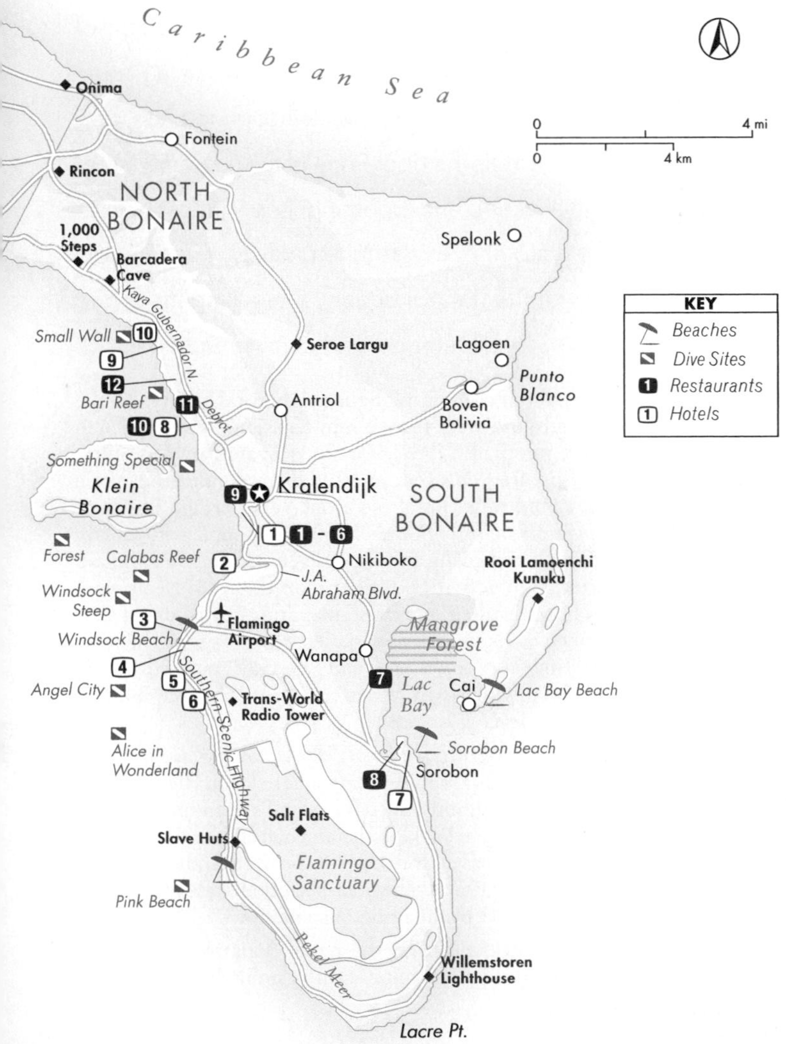

Caribbean Sea
Onima
Fontein
Rincon
NORTH BONAIRE
1,000 Steps
Barcadera Cave
Kaya Gubernador N. Debrot
Small Wall
10
9
12
Bari Reef
11
10 8
Something Special
Klein Bonaire
Seroe Largu
Antriol
Spelonk
Lagoen
Punto Blanco
Boven Bolivia
9
Kralendijk
SOUTH BONAIRE
1 1 - 6
Forest
Calabas Reef
2
J.A. Abraham Blvd.
Nikiboko
Rooi Lamoenchi Kunuku
Windsock Steep
3
Flamingo Airport
Windsock Beach
4
Mangrove Forest
Wanapa
5
6
Angel City
Southern Scenic Highway
Trans-World Radio Tower
7
Lac Bay
Cai
Lac Bay Beach
Alice in Wonderland
Sorobon Beach
Sorobon
8
7
Salt Flats
Slave Huts
Flamingo Sanctuary
Pink Beach
Pekel Meer
Willemstoren Lighthouse
Lacre Pt.
0
4 mi
0
4 km
KEY
Beaches
Dive Sites
Restaurants
Hotels

Updated by Ann L. Phelan

Bonaire is one of the best destinations in the Caribbean for shore diving. The dry climate and coral composition of the island mean that there's little soil runoff, allowing near-perfect visibility in the coastal waters. Although tourism, particularly diving tourism, is the backbone of the economy here, authorities strive to keep the booming hotel industry from damaging the precious ecosystem. Thankfully, most visitors come to Bonaire for the natural beauty, preventing the island from becoming overly developed and commercialized.

Islanders are serious about conserving Bonaire's natural beauty. All the coastal waters of the island were turned into a national park in 1979, and in 1999 Bonaire purchased the 1,500-acre privately owned outlying island of Klein Bonaire to prevent unwanted development. Anyone diving around the island must purchase a one-year permit, and park rangers patrol the waters, handing out hefty fines to people who violate park rules. Spearfishing, removing coral, and even walking on coral are just some of the restricted activities. Rather than restricting legitimate divers, these rules have resulted in a pristine marine environment that makes for a supremely satisfying dive experience. Damage to the reefs caused by rare passing hurricanes is usually quickly repaired by the healthy ecosystem. Small wonder that even the license plates in Bonaire declare it a diver's paradise.

Bonaire also offers a variety of experiences above the surface to those willing to explore its 112 square miles (290 square km). The southern salt flats give an interesting glimpse into the island's economic history. Washington–Slagbaai National Park, in the north, has the island's highest peak (784 feet) and is a haven for some of the thousands of flamingos that make Bonaire their home. The near-perfect climate also makes Bonaire the ideal destination for soaking in some sun.

Although many islanders claim that the name Bonaire comes from the French for "good air," this explanation is unlikely, particularly

LOGISTICS

Getting to Bonaire: Most flights from the United States connect in Houston, Newark, Miami and Atlanta. United Airlines and Delta Airlines both offer weekend service. Delta also offers a Friday flight seasonally. Insel Air has service from Charlotte and Miami with connections in Curacao. For those connecting in Curacao, local airline Divi Air offers the most reliable interisland service.

Hassle Factor: Low–medium

On the Ground: Rental cars and taxis are available, but try to arrange for pickup through your hotel. A taxi will run between $11 and $15 (for up to four people) to most hotels; $26 to the Sorobon Beach Resort. Fares are 25% extra from 7 pm to midnight and 50% extra from midnight to 6 am. Some physically motivated tourists ride bicycles but the majority rent cars.

because the island was never colonized by the French. The island was first inhabited by an Amerindian people (related to the Arawaks) called the Caquetios. Alonso de Ojeda and Amerigo Vespucci landed here in 1499 and claimed it for Spain. It seems likely that they adopted the Amerindian name for the island, which probably sounded very much like Bonaire and meant "low country." Because the Spanish found little use for the island except as a penal colony, the original inhabitants were shipped off to work on the plantations of Hispaniola, and Bonaire remained largely undeveloped. When the Dutch seized the islands of Aruba, Bonaire, and Curaçao in 1633, they started building the salt industry in Bonaire, which fueled the economy then and remains an important industry today.

The majority of the 16,000 inhabitants live in and around the capital, Kralendijk. Part of the BES Islands, Bonaire, St. Eustatius, and Saba were made special municipalities of the Netherlands in 2010. Before this change Bonaire was governed from neighboring Curaçao.

PLANNING

WHEN TO GO

Bonaire is a year-round destination largely due to dive and windsurf tourism. Bonaire is outside the hurricane belt with a brief rainy season, December through March.

GETTING HERE AND AROUND

AIR TRAVEL

Most North American tourists fly nonstop on United from Newark or Houston, on the weekend flights. Delta offers nonstop service from Atlanta weekends as well. KLM offers daily direct flights from Amsterdam.

Airline Contacts Delta ☎ *800/221–1212* 🌐 *www.delta.com.* **Insel Air** ☎ *800/386–4800* 🌐 *www.fly-inselair.com.* **KLM** ☎ *599/717–5600* 🌐 *www.klm.com.* **United Airlines** ☎ *800/864–8331* 🌐 *www.united.com.*

Airport Flamingo Airport. United Airlines offers once-weekly direct service to Flamingo Airport from Houston and Newark. Some flights only operate seasonally. Insel Air offers daily service to Bonaire via Curacao. Delta offers once-weekly service from Atlanta. Delta also offers seasonal Friday service to Bonaire. ✉ *BON* ☎ *599/717-3800.*

BIKE AND MOPED TRAVEL

Scooters are a fun way to get around the island by day. Rates are about $25 per day for a one-seater and up to $35 for a deluxe two-seater. A valid driver's license and cash deposit or credit card are required.

Contacts Bonaire Motorcycle Shop. Rent Harley-Davidson motorcycles at this shop. ✉ *Kaya Grandi 64, Kralendijk* ☎ *599/717-7790* 🌐 *www.motorcycleshopbonaire.com.* **Macho Scooter Rental.** Macho Scooters offers single-seaters and double-scooters. The owners upgrade their scooter line, maintaining a quality product. ✉ *Plaza Resort, J.A. Abrahamboulevard 80, Kralendijk* ☎ *599/701-1233* 🎫 *Single scooters $21.50 per day or 3 days for $55. Doubles $27.50 per day or $75 for 3 days.*

CAR TRAVEL

Minimum and maximum age to rent a car are 21 and 70. Some agencies rent to those 25 and older. There's a government tax of 5% per rental; no cash deposit is needed if you pay by credit card.

Gas prices are about double those of the United States. Traffic is to the right, and there's not a single traffic light.

Contacts Avis ✉ *Flamingo Airport, Kralendijk* ☎ *599/717-5795* 🌐 *www.avisbonaire.com.* **Bonaire Rent a Car** ✉ *Kaya International 1, Kralendijk* ☎ *599/786-6090* 🌐 *www.bonairerentacar.com.* **Budget** ✉ *Kaya Industria 10, Kralendijk* ☎ *599/717-4700* 🌐 *www.bonaire-budgetcar.com.* **Hertz** ✉ *Flamingo Airport, Kralendijk* ☎ *599/717-7221* 🌐 *www.interislandcarrental.com.* **Island Rentals** ✉ *Opposite Flamingo Airport, Kaya Internationaal 130, Kralendijk* ☎ *599/717-2100* 🌐 *www.islandrentalsbonaire.com.*

TAXI TRAVEL

Taxis are unmetered; fixed rates are controlled by the government. From most hotels into town it costs between $10 and $17. Fares increase from 7 pm to midnight by 25% and from midnight to 6 am by 50%. Drivers will conduct half-day tours; they charge about $28 per hour for up to four passengers. Airport taxi rates depend on distance and number in the party. Most fares are $10–$25 per route.

Contacts Airport Taxi Stand. ☎ *599/717-8100.* **Taxi Central Dispatch** ☎ *599/717-8100.*

ESSENTIALS

Banks and Exchange Services In 2010 the U.S. dollar became the official currency, replacing the NAf guilder. You can find ATMs at the airport, in Kralendijk, and at Hato branches of MCB, as well as at the Sand Dollar Condominium Resort and the Plaza Resort; at the Tourism Corporation Bonaire; and at Banco di Caribe on Kaya Grandi.

Electricity 120 AC/50 cycles. A transformer and occasionally a two-prong adapter are required. Some appliances may work slowly; hair dryers may overheat, and sensitive equipment may be damaged.

Emergency Services Ambulance ☎ *599/717–8900*. **Fire** ☎ *599/717–8000*. **Police emergencies** ☎ *599/717–8000*. **Scuba-diving emergencies** ☎ *114*.

Language The official language is Dutch, but the everyday language is Papiamento, a blend of Spanish, Portuguese, Dutch, and English. Locals will likely greet you with "*bon dia*," which translates to "good day." English is spoken by almost everyone on the island.

Passport Requirements U.S. citizens must carry valid passports. In addition, everyone must have a return or ongoing ticket, and you are advised to confirm reservations 48 hours before departure. The maximum stay is 90 days for nonresidents.

Phones The country code for Bonaire is 599; 717 is the exchange for every four-digit number on the island. Most U.S. cell phones work in Bonaire but roaming charges may apply. To call Bonaire from the United States, dial 011–599/717 plus the local four-digit number.

Taxes The departure tax is typically added into airline tickets. Hotels charge a room tax of $6.50 per person, per night. Many hotels add a 10% to 15% service charge to your bill.

ACCOMMODATIONS

Alongside the numerous lodges that offer only the basics (mostly catering to divers), you can now find a few larger resorts. Families can find self-catering accommodations which appeal to budget travelers. The best resorts are often on decent beaches, but these are mostly man-made. Almost all of the island's resorts are clustered around Kralendijk. There are also villa rentals for those seeking a more personal accommodation.

Hotel reviews have been shortened. For full information, visit Fodors.com.

WHAT IT COSTS IN U.S. DOLLARS

	$	$$	$$$	$$$$
Restaurants	under $12	$12–$20	$21–$30	over $30
Hotels	under $275	$275–$375	$376–$475	over $475

Restaurant prices are the average cost of a main course at dinner or, if dinner is not served, at lunch. Hotel prices are the lowest cost of a standard double room in high season.

WEDDINGS

One person must apply for temporary residency. Official witnesses must also apply for residency, but most wedding coordinators can arrange for local witnesses. After the marriage, an *apostille* (official seal) must be placed on the marriage license and certificate. Blood tests are not required.

EXPLORING

Two routes, north and south from Kralendijk, the island's small capital, are possible on the 24-mile-long (39-km-long) island; either route will take from a few hours to a full day, depending on whether you stop to snorkel, swim, dive, or lounge. Those pressed for time will find that it's easy to explore the entire island in a day if stops are kept to a minimum.

KRALENDIJK

Bonaire's small, tidy capital city (population 3,000) is five minutes from the airport. The main drag, J.A. Abraham Boulevard, turns into **Kaya Grandi** in the center of town. Along it are most of the island's major stores, boutiques, and restaurants. Across Kaya Grandi, opposite the Littman's jewelry store, is Kaya L.D. Gerharts, with several small supermarkets, a handful of snack shops, and some of the better restaurants. Walk down the narrow waterfront avenue called Kaya C.E.B. Hellmund, which leads straight to the **North and South piers.** In the center of town, the Harbourside Mall has chic boutiques. Along this route is **Ft. Oranje,** with its cannons. From December through April, cruise ships dock in the harbor once or twice a week. The diminutive ocher-and-white structure that looks like a tiny Greek temple is the produce market, where one can find plenty of fresh produce brought over from Venezuela. Pick up the brochure *Walking and Shopping in Kralendijk* from the tourist office to get a map and complete list of all the monuments and sights in the town.

SOUTH BONAIRE

The trail south from Kralendijk is chock-full of icons—both natural and man-made—that reveal part of Bonaire's history. Rent a vehicle and head out along the Southern Scenic Route. The roads wind through dramatic desert terrain, full of organ-pipe cacti and spiny-trunk mangroves—huge stumps of saltwater trees that rise from the marshes like witches. Watch for wild goats, wild donkeys, and lizards of all sizes.

TOP ATTRACTIONS

Salt Pans. You can't miss the salt flats—voluptuous white drifts that look like mountains of snow. Harvested once a year, the "ponds" are owned by Cargill, Inc., which has reactivated the 19th-century salt industry with great success (one reason for that success is that the ocean on this part of the island is higher than the land—which makes irrigation a snap). Keep a lookout for the three 30-foot obelisks—white, blue, and red—that were used to guide the trade boats coming to pick up the salt. Look also in the distance across the pans to the abandoned solar saltworks that's now a designated **flamingo sanctuary.** With the naked eye you might be able to make out a pink-orange haze just on the horizon; with binoculars you will see a sea of bobbing pink bodies. The sanctuary is completely protected, and no entrance is allowed (flamingos are extremely sensitive to disturbances of any kind). ⊠ *South Bonaire.*

WORTH NOTING

FAMILY **Rooi Lamoenchi Kunuku.** Owner Ellen Herrera restored her family's homestead north of Lac Bay, in the Bonairean *kadushi* (cactus) wilderness, to educate tourists and residents about the history and tradition of authentic Kunuku living and show unspoiled terrain in two daily tours. You must make an appointment in advance and expect to spend a couple of hours. ✉ *Kaya Suiza 23, Playa Baribe* ☎ *599/717–8489* 🎫 *$21* ⏲ *By appointment only.*

FAMILY **Slave Huts.** The salt industry's history is revealed in Rode Pan, the site of two groups of tiny slave huts. The white huts are on the right side of the road, opposite the salt flats; the second grouping, called the Red Slave, huts stretches across the road toward the island's southern tip. During the 19th century, slaves working the salt pans by day slept in the cramped huts. Each Friday afternoon they walked seven hours to Rincon to weekend with their families, returning each Sunday. The Red Slave area is a popular dive spot during low wind and calm seas. When the wind is strong and waves prevail, the local windsurf posse heads to Red Slave to catch the swell. ✉ *South Bonaire.*

Willemstoren Lighthouse. Bonaire's first lighthouse was built in 1837 and is now automated (but closed to visitors). Take some time to explore the beach and notice how the waves, driven by the trade winds, play a crashing symphony against the rocks. Locals stop here to collect pieces of driftwood in spectacular shapes and to build fanciful pyramids from objects that have washed ashore. ✉ *South Bonaire.*

6

NORTH BONAIRE

The Northern Scenic Route takes you into the heart of Bonaire's natural wonders—desert gardens of towering cacti (*kadushi*, used to prepare soup, and the thornier *yatu*, used to build cactus fencing), tiny coastal coves, and plenty of fantastic panoramas. The road also weaves between eroded pink-and-black limestone walls and eerie rock formations with fanciful names such as the Devil's Mouth and Iguana Head (you'll need a vivid imagination and sharp eye to recognize them). Brazil trees growing along the route were used by Indians to make dye (pressed from a red ring in the trunk). Inscriptions still visible in several island caves were made with this dye.

A snappy excursion with the requisite photo stops will take about 2½ hours, but if you pack your swimsuit and a hefty picnic basket (forget about finding fast food), you could spend the entire day exploring this northern sector. Head out from Kralendijk on Kaya Gobernador N. Debrot until it turns into the Northern Scenic Route. Once you pass the Radio Nederland towers, you cannot turn back to Kralendijk. The narrow road becomes one-way until you get to Landhuis Karpata, and you have to follow the cross-island road to Rincon and return via the main road through the center of the island.

TOP ATTRACTIONS

1,000 Steps. Directly across the road from the Radio Nederland towers on the main road north, you'll see a short yellow marker that points to the location of these limestone stairs carved right out of the cliff. If you trek down the stairs, you can discover a lovely coral beach and protected cove where you can snorkel and scuba dive. Actually, you'll count only 67 steps, but it feels like 1,000 when you walk back up carrying scuba gear. ✉ *Queen's Hwy., North Bonaire.*

Barcadera Cave. Once used to trap goats, this cave is one of the oldest in Bonaire; there's even a tunnel that looks intriguingly spooky. It's the first sight along the northern route; watch closely for a yellow marker on your left before you reach the towering Radio Nederland antennas. Pull off across from the entrance to the Bonaire Caribbean Club, and you can discover some stone steps that lead down into a cave full of stalactites and vegetation. **■TIP→ It's best to hire a local guide to traverse any cave in Bonaire. Hans from Outdoor Bonaire is an expert in caving in Bonaire.** 🌐 *www.outdoorbonaire.com.*

FAMILY **Gotomeer.** This saltwater lagoon near the island's northern end is a popular flamingo hangout. Bonaire is one of the few places in the world where pink flamingos nest. The shy, spindly-leg creatures—affectionately called "pink clouds"—are magnificent birds to observe, and there are about 15,000 of them in Bonaire (more than the number of human residents). The best viewing is January to June, when they tend to their gray-plumed young. For the best view take the paved access road alongside the lagoon through the jungle of cacti to the parking and observation area on the rise overlooking the lagoon and Washington–Slagbaai National Park beyond.

FAMILY **Washington–Slagbaai National Park.** Once a plantation producing divi-divi trees (the pods were used for tanning animal skins), aloe (used for medicinal lotions), charcoal, and goats, the park is now a model of conservation. It's easy to tour the 13,500-acre tropical desert terrain on the dirt roads. A truck or Jeep is recommended for clearance along the rutted roads. As befits a wilderness sanctuary, the well-marked, rugged routes force you to drive slowly enough to appreciate the animal life and the terrain. (Think twice about coming here if it has rained recently—the mud you may encounter will be more than inconvenient.) If you're planning to hike, bring a picnic lunch, camera, sunscreen, and plenty of water. There are two routes: the long one (22 miles [35½ km]) is marked by yellow arrows, the short one (15 miles [24 km]) by green arrows. Goats and donkeys may dart across the road, and if you keep your eyes peeled, you may catch sight of large iguanas camouflaged in the shrubbery.

Bird-watchers are really in their element here. Right inside the park's gate, flamingos roost on the salt pad known as **Salina Mathijs,** and exotic parakeets dot the foot of **Mt. Brandaris,** Bonaire's highest peak, at 784 feet. Some 130 species of birds fly in and out of the shrubbery in the park. Keep your eyes open and your binoculars at hand. Swimming, snorkeling, and scuba diving are permitted, but you're asked not to frighten the animals or remove anything from the grounds. Absolutely no hunting, fishing, or camping is allowed. A useful guide to the park is available at the entrance for about $6. To get here, take the secondary road north from the town of Rincon. The Nature Fee for swimming and snorkeling also grants you free admission to this park—simply present proof of payment and some form of photo ID. ✉ *North Bonaire* ☎ *599/717–8444* 🌐 *www.washingtonparkbonaire.org* 🎫 *Free with payment of scuba diving Nature Fee ($25) or $15 with non-scuba Nature Fee ($10). Otherwise $25 for one calendar year of entry* ⏲ *Daily 8–5; you must enter before 3.*

WORTH NOTING

Landhuis Karpata. This mustard-color building was the manor house of an aloe plantation in the 19th century. The site was named for the *karpata* (castor bean) plants that are abundant in the area—you can see them along the sides of the road as you approach. Notice the rounded outdoor oven where aloe was boiled down before the juice was exported. The handcrafted coral floor is quite a sight. There is a stand that sells beverages during high season. ✉ *North Bonaire.*

FAMILY **Mangazina di Rei.** Built around the second-oldest stone structure on Bonaire, this cultural park a few miles before Rincon provides a fascinating insight into the island's history. The museum commands an excellent view of the surrounding countryside and contains artifacts tracing the often-hard lives of the early settlers. There are numerous traditional structures built around the museum illustrating how living conditions have changed over the years. The park is usually filled with local schoolkids learning how to use traditional musical instruments and how to cook local foods. The last Saturday of each month features a cultural market. Enjoy local food and purchase crafts while listening to island music. Arrive early for the best selection of treats. ✉ *Kaya Rincon z/n, Rincon* ☎ *599/786–2101* 🌐 *www.mangazinadirei.org* 🎫 *$10 adults, $5 children under 12* ⏲ *Tues.–Sat. 10–5.*

6

Rincon. The island's original Spanish settlement, Rincon is where slaves brought from Africa to work the plantations and salt fields lived. Rincon is now a well-kept cluster of pastel cottages and 19th-century buildings that constitute Bonaire's oldest village.There are several local eateries and bars in town to enjoy libations. Dia de Rincon is an annual festival and legal holiday held April 30th each year. This massive street party features local food, music and revelry. Arrive early if traveling with children. By nighttime, it's a lively boisterous party vibe. ✉ *Rincon.*

Seroe Largu. Just off the main road, this spot, at 394 feet, is one of the highest on the island. A paved but narrow and twisting road leads to a magnificent daytime view of Kralendijk's rooftops and the island of Klein Bonaire. A large cross and figure of Christ stand guard at the peak, with an inscription reading *ayera* (yesterday), *awe* (today), and *semper* (always). ✉ *Rincon.*

BEACHES

Although most of Bonaire's charms are underwater, there are a few beautiful beaches. Don't expect long strands of white sand, but many dive and snorkel sites have suitable entries for swimmers. Bonaire's pristine water and protected reefs offer stunning settings for sunrise or sunset viewing. Several hotels have lovely beaches that are accessible for nonguests for a nominal entrance fee. Bonaire's National Parks

Foundation requires all nondivers to pay a $10 annual Nature Fee to enter the water anywhere around the island (divers pay $25). The fee can be paid at most dive shops, and the receipt will also allow access to Washington–Slagbaai National Park.

Boca Slagbaai. Inside Washington–Slagbaai Park is this beach of coral fossils and rocks with interesting offshore coral gardens that are good for snorkeling. Bring scuba boots or canvas sandals to walk into the water, because the beach is rough on bare feet. It is unlawful to touch or stand on coral. The gentle surf makes it an ideal place for swimming and picnicking. Sunday is a lively spot for locals who come to picnic. **Amenities:** parking; water sports. **Best for:** solitude; snorkeling; swimming; walking. ✉ *Off main park road, in Washington–Slagbaai National Park, North Bonaire.*

Klein Bonaire. Just a water-taxi hop across from Kralendijk, this little island offers picture-perfect white-sand beaches. Klein Bonaire is one of Bonaire's most popular snorkel spots. Local boat tours frequent the island in hopes of spotting turtles. The area is protected, so absolutely no development has been allowed. Make sure to pack everything before heading to the island, including water and an umbrella to hide under, because there are no refreshment stands or changing facilities, and there's almost no shade to be found. Boats leave from the pier, across from the Rains Fishes, and the round-trip water-taxi ride costs roughly $15 per person. **Amenities:** none. **Best for:** solitude; snorkeling; swimming

Lac Bay Beach. Once known for its Sunday music parties, Lac Bay Beach is mostly visited now for its peaceful setting. This open bay area with pink-tinted sand is dazzling by day. It's a bumpy drive (10 to 15 minutes on a dirt road) to get here, but you'll be glad you made the trip. It's a good spot for diving, snorkeling, and kayaking (local kayak companies lead tours from this spot). **Amenities:** parking. **Best for:** kayaking; snorkeling; and swimming. ✉ *Off Kaminda Sorobon, Lac Cai, Lac Bay.*

Playa Funchi. This Washington–Slagbaai National Park beach is notable for the lagoon on one side, where flamingos nest, and the superb snorkeling on the other, where iridescent green parrot fish swim right up to shore. All sea life including coral, is protected in Bonaire. Look but never touch. A vehicle with high clearance is recommended when driving into the park. **Amenities:** none. **Best for:** solitude; snorkeling; swimming. ✉ *Off main park road, in Washington–Slagbaai National Park, North Bonaire.*

Fodor's Choice ★ **Sorobon Beach.** This is *the* windsurfing beach on Bonaire and one of the most beautiful beaches on the island. The sand is powdery white and the water gin-clear. It's shallow, allowing swimmers to walk up to the reef on a calm-breeze day. Here, the snorkeling is quite amazing. Keep in mind all sea life is protected, so no touching or removing shells or creatures. There are two windsurf shops on-site offering rentals and lessons. Rent a stand-up paddleboard (SUP) and cruise the shallows looking for turtles. Two on-site restaurants offer diverse menus, including tropical drinks. The public beach area near the marina has restrooms and huts for shade. **Amenities:** food and drink; parking; showers; toilets; water sports. **Best for:** snorkeling; surfing; windsurfing. ✉ *Kaya I.R. Randolf Statuuis Van Eps, Sorobon Beach, Sorobon Beach* ✣ *Take E.E.G. Boulevard south from Kralendijk to Kaya I.R. Randolf Statuuis Van Eps, and then follow this route straight on to Sorobon Beach.*

Windsock Beach (*Mangrove Beach*). Near the airport (just off E.E.G. Boulevard), this pretty little spot looks out toward the north side of the island and has about 200 yards of white sand along a rocky shoreline. It's a popular dive site, and swimming conditions are good. **■ TIP→ There is often a food truck parked next door at Te Amo Beach, another great snorkeling beach. Amenities:** none. **Best for:** snorkeling; swimming. ✉ *Off E.E.G. Blvd., near Flamingo Airport.*

WHERE TO EAT

Dining on Bonaire is a food lover's dream as you can find everything from Caribbean to South American and Asian cuisines. Many restaurants serve only dinner—only a few establishments not affiliated with hotels are open for breakfast, so check ahead.

6

$$$ FRENCH ✕ **Bistro de Paris.** Owner Patrice Rannou has transformed a marina venue into a lovely bistro serving the best French food on the island. Their famous lamb shanks served with haricots verts and asparagus are outstanding. The dinner menu is reasonably priced, but lunch offerings are even more budget-friendly and great for an order of sandwiches to take along on a day of exploring. Wednesday night is Dive Master Night with $8 burger specials. Patrice posts his menu daily on the curbside chalkboard. If lionfish is on the menu, don't pass by. It's a local treat not to be missed. [$] *Average main: $23* ✉ *Kaya Gob. Debrot 71* ☎ *599/717–7070* ⊙ *Closed Sun. No lunch Sat.*

$ ECLECTIC ✕ **Boudoir.** Despite the nighttime-bedroom connotation, this excellent patio eatery at the Royal Palm Mall is only open for breakfast, lunch, and late-afternoon snacks. Besides having some of the best coffee on the island, Boudoir offers a range of soups, salads, sandwiches, and burgers that should please even the most discerning of diners. It's the perfect place to relax with an iced coffee and a smoked-salmon-and-capers sandwich after a day of exploring Kralendijk. [$] *Average main: $9* ✉ *Kaya Grandi 26 F/G, Royal Palm Mall* ☎ *599/717–4321.*

$$$ ITALIAN Fodor's Choice ★ ✕ **Capriccio.** This splendid, family-run Italian eatery has plenty to boast about. The pastas and breads are house-made. The wine cellar includes hundreds of labels and thousands of bottles. Ask for a a pairing with your meal to fit your taste and your budget. You can opt for casual à la carte dining on the terrace or a romantic meal in the tonier, air-conditioned dining room. If your appetite is hearty, go for the five-course prix-fixe menu. Otherwise, choose from 50 regular offerings. La Boutique has an abundance of lovely Italian specialty items including seasonal pannetone. [$] *Average main: $25* ✉ *Kaya Hellmund 5* ☎ *599/717–7230* 🌐 *www.capricciobonaire.com* ✍ *Reservations essential* ⊙ *Closed Tues. No lunch weekends.*

$ CARIBBEAN FAMILY Fodor'sChoice ★ ✕ **Hang Out Bar.** If your vision of a Caribbean vacation includes seaside dining with balmy trade winds and views of a gorgeous Caribbean bay, then Hang Out Bar is your spot. It overlooks Lac Bay, the training ground for the famous Bonaire Windsurf Team. Pros from around the globe come to train while tourists come to hone their skills and experience windsurf bliss. Hang Out Bar offers libations and tasty delights including fresh house-made smoothies and healthy and delicious salads and sandwiches, and there's always a daily special, usually fresh-caught fish. They also serve Dutch snack treats including *bitterballen* (meatballs) and *frikkendel* (hot dog). There's a lively bar scene, with a great happy hour. Free beach loungers and plenty of tables and chairs in the shade, as well as free Wi-Fi are available. Select evenings feature local and international music acts. Order a pitcher of their famous house-made sangria and you're all set. *Average main: $10 ✉ Kaminda Sorobon 12 ☎ 599/717–5064 Reservations not accepted No dinner.*

$$$ ECLECTIC Fodor'sChoice ★ ✕ **It Rains Fishes.** Those seeking upscale urban chic flock to this waterfront establishment where beautiful people serve beautiful food. Housed in a 100-year-old traditional home, the seafront setting is magical. Culinary delights feature grilled local fish. The menu is creative and diverse. Despite its popularity and large size, by Bonaire standards, service is impeccable and efficient. The restaurant now features a fish market selling local and Dutch delights. *Average main: $28 ✉ Kaya Jan N.E. Craane 24 ☎ 599/717–8780 www.itrainsfishesbonaire.com Reservations essential Closed Sun. No lunch Sat.*

$$$ TAPAS ✕ **La Guernica.** This trendy eatery overlooking the boardwalk and the harbor is great for people-watching; there's outdoor seating as well as a couch-and-pillow-filled lounge area. The interior is done in hacienda style, with terra-cotta tiles, clay decorations, and comfy lounge chairs. Though many come here for the excellent tapas, those with heartier appetites can choose from a variety of seafood and meat main courses, including an excellent beef tenderloin with a blue-cheese sauce. The lunch menu offers a range of sandwiches and salads. This is *the* place to sip a cocktail and be seen. *Average main: $27 ✉ Kaya Bonaire 4C ☎ 599/717–5022 www.laguernica.com.*

$$ CARIBBEAN Fodor'sChoice ★ ✕ **Mi Banana.** Hidden in an unassuming strip mall you'll find a wonderful Colombian eatery—Bonaire's best hole-in-the-wall. The owners specialize in Colombian fare and offer fresh locally caught fish along with other regional items. Try the house-made avocado sauce on your fish or chicken. The *lomito* (beef) is a house favorite, as is the whole red snapper in creole sauce. Choose the fried yucca as a side. House-made desserts include a sublime *tres leches* cake. *Average main: $15 ✉ Kaya Nikiboko, Noord 42C ☎ 599/717–4472.*

$$$$ EUROPEAN Fodor'sChoice ★ ✕ **Mona Lisa Bar & Restaurant.** This little dining spot features Continental, Caribbean, and Indonesian fare as well as throngs of regulars who would not dream of visiting Bonaire without a meal here. Located in the town center, diners can enjoy their meal on the sidewalk or inside. Popular bar dishes include Wiener schnitzel and fresh fish with saffron sauce. The lobster bisque is sublime. The intimate stucco-and-brick dining room, presided over by a copy of the famous painting of the lady with the mystic smile, is decorated with Dutch artwork, lace curtains,

and ceiling fans. The bar is popular with locals but visitors will feel at home under the care of Hank, the bartender. The bar menu, available outside or at the bar, features a fish item, saté, or a meat choice. Leave room for their house-made desserts, especially the passion-fruit cheesecake. *Average main: $38 Kaya Grandi 15 599/717–8718 Reservations essential Closed Sun. No lunch.*

$$$ SEAFOOD **Sebastian's Restaurant on the Sea.** Sebastian's is a romantic waterfront spot with a trendy chic decor. Chef Sebastian has created his own niche, offering an eclectic and international menu with a Mediterranean flair. DJ Miss Liv spins deep house music Saturday nights, adding to the ambience. The pier table is one of Bonaire's most sought-after tables. Reserve in advance for a sunset dining experience. *Average main: $29 J.A. Abraham Blvd. 60 599/717–1697 www.sebastiansrestaurantbonaire.com Closed Mon. No lunch.*

$$ CARIBBEAN FAMILY Fodor's Choice ★ **Spice Beach Club.** For a quintessential seaside dining setting head to Spice Beach Club. Tables, illuminated by torchlight, are set at water's edge. Service is friendly and mostly efficient. The menu features Caribbean–inspired tapas dishes. Flavors are bold and the plating is artistic. The wine list is simple and eclectic, featuring a number of international bottles. After dinner, walk next door to enjoy the lively vibe and DJ entertainment at the beach bar. Friday Happy Hour is a popular local spot. By day, the lunch menu is casual and best enjoyed on the beach in one of the cabanas. *Average main: $18 Bulevard. Gobernador Nicolaas Debrot 73 599/717–8060 www.spicebonaire.com.*

6

$$ CARIBBEAN **Wil's Tropical Grill.** This charming eatery is tucked away in a tranquil outdoor setting amid mature tropical trees and foliage. Chef Wil uses locally grown produce and fish from the sea, presenting a creative menu for his discerning clientele. The house-smoked marlin is delectable. Their wine list is impressive as well. Chef Wil also makes and bottles his own line of hot sauces and rubs called The Flaming Flamingo Hot Sauce Co. Be sure to take a few bottles home. *Average main: $20 L.D Gerharts 9 599/717–6616 Reservations essential Closed Sat. and Sun.*

$ CARIBBEAN **Wind & Surf Beach Hut Bar.** Part of Bonaire Windsurf Place—and located right on the beach—this fun eatery is one of the most casual dining experiences on the island. Tables and chairs are set directly in the sand under a straw-roof structure so that cooling winds sweep through the space. The food is simple but very good; the main offerings are sandwiches, salads, and burgers. The experience of dining with your toes in the sand is sure to leave lingering pleasant memories. *Average main: $10 Sorobon Beach 599/717–2288 No credit cards.*

WHERE TO STAY

Although meal plans are available at the larger hotels, the island has many excellent—and often inexpensive—restaurants. If you're planning a dive vacation, look into the many attractive dive packages. If you prefer a self-catering option, Bonaire has a large selection of condo- and apartment-style properties.

$ HOTEL Fodor's Choice ★ **Bellafonte Luxury Oceanfront Hotel.** Bellafonte is the quintessential Caribbean property complete with breathtaking ocean views, modern amenities and furnishings, and close proximity to all dining spots. **Pros:** well-designed rooms; diving straight from hotel pier; upper rooms have excellent views; free Wi-Fi; groceries can be ordered online before arrival. **Cons:** no restaurant or pool. *Rooms from: $145 ✉ E.E.G. Blvd. 10, Belnem ☎ 599/717–3333 ⊕ www.bellafontebonaire.com 4 studios, 8 1-bedroom suites, 8 2-bedroom suites, 2 penthouses No meals.*

$ B&B/INN **Bruce Bowker's Carib Inn.** The cozy rooms and owner–dive-instructor Bruce Bowker's personal touch have given his inn the highest return-visitor ratio on the island. **Pros:** intimate and friendly; excellent dive courses; Wi-Fi throughout. **Cons:** spare accommodations; nondivers will find little to entertain them. *Rooms from: $119 ✉ J.A. Abraham Blvd. 46 ☎ 599/717–8819 ⊕ www.caribinn.com 10 units No meals.*

$ RESORT FAMILY **Buddy Dive Resort.** Well-equipped rooms, a nicely landscaped compound, and excellent dive packages keep guests coming back to this large resort. **Pros:** excellent dive shop; rooms are spacious; open-air restaurant has one of the best ocean views on the island; excellent value for money. **Cons:** complex can feel like a maze; room amenities vary, depending on location. *Rooms from: $147 ✉ Kaya Gobernador N. Debrot 85 ☎ 599/717–5080, 866/462–8339 ⊕ www.buddydive.com 6 rooms, 72 apartments No meals.*

$ HOTEL **Captain Don's Habitat.** Bonaire's first hotel catering to divers remains a favorite, with a PADI five-star dive center offering more than 20 specialty courses. **Pros:** variety of accommodation types; pizzeria with wood-burning oven; excellent diving facilities. **Cons:** Wi-Fi coverage is spotty. *Rooms from: $126 ✉ Kaya Gobernador N. Debrot 113 ☎ 599/717–8290, 800/327–6709 ⊕ www.habitatbonaire.com 24 rooms, 12 junior suites, 5 villas, 19 cottages No meals.*

$ RENTAL **Den Laman Condominiums.** Though the exterior of this property will not win any design awards, the location and beautifully finished interiors are definitely first-class. **Pros:** rooms are chicly appointed; on-site dive shop. **Cons:** no elevator; common areas feel a little sterile; spotty Wi-Fi coverage. *Rooms from: $170 ✉ Kaya Gobernador N. Debrot 77 ☎ 599/717–1700 ⊕ www.denlaman.com 16 condos No meals.*

$ RENTAL **Happy Holiday Homes.** Catering to the seasoned traveler seeking budget accomodations, Happy Holiday Homes are charming bungalows just minutes away from Kite Beach, windsurfing, and a plethora of southern Bonaire dive sites. **Pros:** owner-managed; quiet residential neighborhood; good Wi-Fi. **Cons:** not on the water; 10 minutes to town; basic amenities. *Rooms from: $85 ✉ Punt Vierkant 9, Belnem ☎ 508/737–5245 ⊕ www.happyholidayhomes.com 13 units No meals.*

$$$ HOTEL FAMILY Fodor's Choice ★ **Harbour Village Beach Club.** This upscale enclave of ocher-color buildings is the benchmark for luxury accommodations on Bonaire. **Pros:** great for a secluded getaway; not awash with budget tourists; convenient to downtown. **Cons:** some rooms are small and cramped. *Rooms from: $390 ✉ Kaya Gobernador N. Debrot 71 ☎ 599/717–7500,*

Pool at the Harbour Village Beach Club

800/424–0004 ⊕ www.harbourvillage.com ⇆ 40 rooms, 14 1-bedroom suites, 6 2-bedroom suites 🍽 *No meals.*

$ HOTEL FAMILY **Roomer.** Nicole and Martin run a well-priced boutique hotel that features small but comfortable rooms, individually decorated with tasteful splashes of color. **Pros:** very family-oriented; excellent for budget travelers; kid-friendly pool area; free Wi-Fi; close to diving and kitesurfing; unique gift gallery with locally made and imported specialty items. **Cons:** not on the ocean. *$ Rooms from: $100 ✉ E.E.G. Blvd. 97, Belnem ☎ 599/717–7488 ⊕ www.roomerbonaire.com ⇆ 10 rooms* 🍽 *No meals.*

$ RESORT FAMILY **Sorobon Beach Resort.** Sorobon is the pefect oasis for relaxation with bungalows nestled in a rustic and natural landscape on picturesque Lac Bay. **Pros:** excellent beach bar and two restaurants, stunning beachfront; Wi-Fi; spa with yoga classes next to one of the island's most popular windsurfing centers. **Cons:** 15 minutes to town for shopping and restaurants; no radios or TVs in rooms. *$ Rooms from: $175 ✉ Sorobon Beach, Lac Bay ☎ 599/717–8080 ⊕ www.sorobonbeachresort.com ⇆ 28 1-bedroom chalets, 1 2-bedroom chalet, 1 3-bedroom house* 🍽 *Breakfast.*

$ RENTAL **Windsock.** Windsock is a casual, intimate Caribbean-inspired lowrise condo. **Pros:** private beach; dive shop; minutes to town. **Cons:** on busy street; close to airport; no restaurant on-site. *$ Rooms from: $150 ✉ E.E.G Boulevard 3, Belnem ☎ 508/737–5245 ⊕ www.gowindsockbonaire.com ⇆ 8 rooms.*

NIGHTLIFE

Most of Bonaire's nightlife consists of sitting on a quiet beach and sipping a Polar beer. Top island performers, including Moogie, migrate from one resort to another throughout the week. You can find information in the free magazines (published once a year) *Bonaire Affair* and *Bonaire Nights*. The twice-monthly *Bonaire Update Events and Activities* pamphlet is available at most restaurants.

BARS

Cuba Compagnie Bonaire. In a historic, traditional Dutch Antillean structure, this trendy club has a vibrant music scene. Latin Dance Night on Thursday is the place for sweaty, sexy dance music. Try to come when DJ Chrisbeat and DJ Mixup are in the house—it's a party when this duo hits the DJ booth. The beverages of choice are the House Mojito and Cuba Libre, and an extensive international menu features Pineapple Santiago de Cuba and Indonesian saté. The patio tables overlooking the waterfront district are perfect for sunsets and people-watching. ✉ *Kaya Grandi 1* ☎ *599/717–1822* 🌐 *www.cubacompagniebonaire.nl.*

Deco Stop Bar. Deco Stop is the place to be Monday night for Rum Punch Party with Moogie, live dance-band entertainment. Enjoy bar snacks and free rum punch as the sun sets. The Thursday-night happy hour is popular as well. Tourists and locals alike enjoy the seaside setting where dive gear and board shorts are appropriate attire! Next door you can enjoy one of Bonaire's best oceanfront dining spots, Rum Runners. ✉ *Captain Don's Habitat, Kaya Gobernador N. Debrot 113* ☎ *599/717–8286.*

Karel's. Karel's is one of Bonaire's best nighttime party spots—especially on Friday and Saturday, when there's live music until the wee hours. Deep House, Trance, and local music prevail at this beach bar right over the water. Often, international DJs visit Karel's, making it one of the island's hippest scenes. ✉ *Kaya J.N.E. Craane 12* ☎ *599/717–8434.*

Little Havana. Little Havana is the place to mix and mingle with locals and tourists while listening to DJs spin, jazz, or jam sessions. Prepare to get up close and personal with modelesque blondes, handsome Antilleans, and oldsters alike. The place gets so packed, crowds spill into the streets, drinking into the wee hours. Happy hour is a favorite but the witching hour is around 11 pm until 2 am. The bartenders mix up the best Caipirinha on island. Check out the cigar humidor, which is stocked with cigars from Cuba and the Dominican Republic. ✉ *Kaya Bonaire 4* ☎ *599/700–5927* 🌐 *www.littlehavanabonaire.com.*

SHOPPING

You can get to know all the shops in Kralendijk in an hour or so. Almost all the shops are on Kaya Grandi and adjacent streets and in tiny malls. Harbourside Mall is a pleasant, open-air mall with several fine air-conditioned shops. ■ **TIP→ Don't take home items made from tortoiseshell; they aren't allowed into the United States. Remember,**

too, that it's forbidden to take sea fans, coral, conch shells, and all other forms of marine life off the island.

CLOTHING

Benetton. This Benetton outpost claims that its prices for men's, women's, and children's clothes are 30% lower than in New York. The selection is small but the quality is typical Benetton. ✉ *Kaya Grandi 29* ☎ *599/717–5107.*

Bonaire Gift Shop. Bonaire Gift Shop is a mecca for those seeking a trinket or T-shirt to bring home. It's a one-stop shop for some of the island's best prices for liquor, tobacco, and tourist treasures. ✉ *Kaya Grandi 13* ☎ *599/717–2201.*

FAMILY **Island Fashions & Gifts.** Buy swimsuits, sunglasses, T-shirts, and costume jewelry at this stylish shop. There's a wonderful selection of whimsical ornaments and house decor. Shop for lovely Indonesian batik fashion. There's also a cute children's toy area in back. ✉ *Kaya Grandi 5* ☎ *599/717–7071.*

DUTY-FREE GOODS

Flamingo Airport Duty Free. Perfumes and cigarettes are available at Flamingo Airport Duty Free. This is the perfect spot to buy Dutch chocolates and local trinkets for last-minute shopping. ✉ *Flamingo Airport* ☎ *599/717–5563.*

HANDICRAFTS

JanArt Gallery. On the outskirts of town, JanArt Gallery sells unique paintings, prints, and art supplies; artist Janice Huckaby also hosts art classes. Jan also has a shop at Kaya Grandi 14 selling prints and crafts that are colorful and creative. ✉ *Kaya Gloria 7* ☎ *599/717–0955.*

Richter Art Gallery. This dedicated fine art gallery run by Linda Richter features a range of work from local artists including paintings by Linda and her late husband. In addition to paintings, the gallery also features prints and handmade jewelry. ✉ *Kaya Statius van Eps 17, Belnem* ☎ *599/717–4112* 🌐 *www.richterart.com* ☞ *Open by appointment only.*

Yenny's Art. Every visitor should make a point of visiting Yenny's Art. Roam around Jenny Rijna's house, which is a replica of a traditional Bonaire town complete with her handmade life-size dolls and the skeletons of all her dead pets. Fun (and sometimes kitschy) souvenirs made out of driftwood, clay, and shells are all handmade by Jenny. ✉ *Kaya Betico Croes 6, near post office* ☎ *599/717–5004.*

JEWELRY

Atlantis. This shop carries a large range of precious and semiprecious gems; the tanzanite collection is especially beautiful. You will also find Sector, Raymond Weil, and Citizen watches, among others, all at great savings. ✉ *Kaya Grandi 32B* ☎ *599/717–7730.*

Littman's. Owner Steven Littman handpicks many of the items available in this upscale jewelry and gift shop during his regular trips to Europe. Look for Rolex, Omega, Cartier, and Tag Heuer watches; fine gold jewelry; antique coins; nautical sculptures; resort clothing; and accessories. Typical savings are about 15% off U.S. prices. ✉ *Kaya Grandi 33* ☎ *599/717–8160* 🌐 *www.bonairelittmanstores.com* ✉ *Harbourside Mall, Kaya Grandi 31* ☎ *599/717–2130* 🌐 *www.bonairelittmanstores.com.*

SPORTS AND THE OUTDOORS

BICYCLING

Bonaire is generally flat, so bicycles are an easy way to get around if you are physically fit. Because of the heat it's essential to carry water if you're planning to cycle for any distance and especially if your plans involve exploring the deserted interior. There are more than 180 miles (290 km) of unpaved routes (as well as the many paved roads) on the island.

Bike Rental Delivery Bonaire. Opened in 2012, this service offers bike delivery to your door in their trademark yellow van. Rental prices start at $11 a day or $60 a week and tours can be arranged. Prices vary depending on duration of rental, size of group, and route. ☎ *599/786–2329* 🌐 *www.bikerentalbonaire.com.*

Tropical Travel. This tour operator offers bikes for $14 per day or $60 per week (a $300 deposit is required). ✉ *Plaza Resort Bonaire, J.A. Abraham Blvd. 80* ☎ *599/701–1232* 🌐 *www.tropicaltravelbonaire.com.*

DAY SAILS AND SNORKELING TRIPS

Regularly scheduled sunset sails and snorkeling trips are popular (prices range from $35 to $50 per person), as are private or group sails (expect to pay about $500 per day for a party of four).

Blue Bay Rental. Blue Bay Rentals offers half- and full-day charters aboard *Bowalie*, a luxurious 40-foot cabin sailor. Their three-hour sail includes refreshments and a snorkel stop. The full-day sail includes lunch. Those who want to go solo can rent one of their motorboats such as *Betty Boop*, an older six-person vessel, for half-day or full-day and cruise over to Klein Bonaire for a snorkel session and picnic. Wakeboarding is also available. ✉ *Plaza Resort, J.A. Abraham Blvd.* ☎ *599/701–5500* 🌐 *www.bluebayrentals.com* 🎫 *From $65 per person.*

Kantika de Amor Watertaxi. This company provides daily rides to Klein Bonaire and drift snorkel and evening cruises with complimentary cocktails. The taxi departs from the dock in front of It Rains Fishes Restaurant. There are three crossings daily. Bring a picnic and beach umbrella and make it a day. Avoid cruise-ship day, as the island and taxi are crowded. ✉ *Kaya J.N.E. Craane 24, opposite the restaurant It Rains Fishes* ☎ *599/796–7254* 🎫 *$15.*

Tropical Travel. Tropical Travel is a full-service tour company servicing the cruise-ship and tourism sector. They have large buses and small vans that whisk off guests for day excursions, touring the island's many attractions including Washington Park. They also offer scooter, moped, and bike rentals. ✉ *Plaza Resort Bonaire, J.A. Abraham Blvd. 80* ☎ *599/701–1232* 🌐 *www.tropicaltravelbonaire.com.*

Woodwind. The *Woodwind* is a 37-foot trimaran that offers sailing and snorkeling trips as well as charters. It departs from the dock at Divi Flamingo and offers a full-day cruise for $50 per person. Dee and Ulf will insure your trip is memorable. Many guests say they see turtles every time they sail with Woodwind. Group rates are available. Reservations recommended. ☎ *599/786–7055* 🌐 *www.woodwindbonaire.com.*

DIVING AND SNORKELING

Bonaire has some of the best reef diving this side of Australia's Great Barrier Reef. It takes only 5–25 minutes to reach many sites, the current is usually mild, and although some reefs have sudden, steep drops, most begin just offshore and slope gently downward at a 45-degree angle. General visibility runs 60 to 100 feet. You can see several varieties of coral: knobby-brain, giant-brain, elkhorn, staghorn, mountainous star, gorgonian, and black. You can also encounter schools of parrot fish, surgeonfish, angelfish, eel, snapper, and grouper. Shore diving is excellent just about everywhere on the leeward side. There are sites suitable for every skill level; they're clearly marked by yellow stones on the roadside.

The best snorkeling spots are on the island's leeward side, where you have shore access to the reefs, and along the west side of Klein Bonaire, where the reef is better developed. All snorkelers and swimmers must pay a $10 Nature Fee, which allows access to the waters around the island and Washington–Slagbaai National Park for one calendar year. The fee can be paid at most dive shops.

Fodor's Choice ★ **Bonaire Marine Park.** The waters surrounding Bonaire's Marine Park are pristine thanks to the efforts of the STINAPA which encompasses the entire coastline around Bonaire and Klein Bonaire. Several well-enforced rules include no: (1) spearfishing; (2) dropping anchor; or (3) touching, stepping on, or collecting coral. In order to dive (as opposed to simply swim and enter the water), you must pay a fee of $25 (used to maintain the park), for which you receive a colored plastic tag (to attach to an item of scuba gear) entitling you to one calendar year of unlimited diving. Checkout dives—dives you do first with a master before going out on your own—are required, and you can arrange them through any dive shop. All dive operations offer classes in free buoyancy control, advanced buoyancy control, and photographic buoyancy control. Tags are available at all scuba facilities and from the Marine Park Headquarters. Snorkelers, kiters, and windsurfers pay a $10 fee. ✉ *Barcadera 10* ☎ *599/717–8444* 🌐 *www.bmp.org.*

6

A Bonaire diver shows off her photographic buoyancy control.

DIVE SITES

The *Guide to the Bonaire Marine Park* lists 86 dive sites (including 16 shore-dive-only and 35 boat-dive-only sites). Another fine reference book is the *Diving and Snorkeling Guide to Bonaire,* by Jerry Schnabel and Suzi Swygert. Guides associated with the various dive centers can give you more complete directions. With more than 80 dive sites, there is something for every diver's needs. Here are a few of the better-known entries:

Angel City. Take the trail down to the shore adjacent to the Radio Nederland tower station; dive in and swim south to Angel City, one of the shallowest and most popular sites in a two-reef complex that includes Alice in Wonderland. The boulder-size green-and-tan coral heads are home to black margates, Spanish hogfish, gray snappers, stingrays, and large purple tube sponges.

Bari Reef. Catch a glimpse of the elkhorn and fire coral, queen angelfish, and other wonders of Bari Reef, just off the Sand Dollar Condominium Resort's pier. This is one of Bonaire's most diverse reefs.

Calabas Reef. Off the coast of the Divi Flamingo Resort, this is the island's busiest dive site. It's replete with Christmas-tree worms, sponges, and fire coral adhering to a ship's hull. Fish life is frenzied, with the occasional octopus putting in an appearance.

Forest. Forest is easily accessed via boat rental or a dive-shop boat trip. This diverse dive site is located off the southwest coast of Klein Bonaire. Named for the abundant black-coral forests found here, the site is best known for massive purple stovepipes, gorgonian fans, and plumes as well as some amazing turtles.

Rappel. This spectacular site is near the Karpata Ecological Center. The shore is a sheer cliff, and the lush coral growth is the habitat of some unusual varieties of marine life, including occasional orange sea horses, squid, spiny lobsters, and spotted trunkfish.

Small Wall. One of Bonaire's three complete vertical wall dives (and one of its most popular night-diving spots), Small Wall is in front of the Black Durgon Inn, near Barcadera Beach. Because the access to this site is on private property, this is usually a boat-diving site. The 60-foot wall is frequented by squid, turtles, tarpon, and barracuda and has dense hard and soft coral formations; it also allows for excellent snorkeling.

Windsock. This excellent shore-dive site (from 20 to 80 feet) is in front of the small beach opposite the airport runway. It's a popular place for snorkeling. The entrance is relatively easy to access. The current is moderate, the elkhorn coral profuse; you may also see angelfish and rays. An on-site food truck sells delicious lionfish burgers and cold beverages. There is plenty of shade to make this a day.

DIVE OPERATORS

Many of the dive shops listed *below* offer PADI and NAUI certification courses and SSI, as well as underwater photography and videography courses. Some shops are also qualified to certify dive instructors. Full certification courses cost approximately $385; open-water refresher courses run about $240; a one-tank boat dive with unlimited shore diving costs about $40; a two-tank boat dive with unlimited shore diving is about $65. As for equipment, renting a mask, fin, and snorkel costs about $12 altogether; for a BC (buoyancy compensator) and regulator, expect to pay about $20.

6

Most dive shops on Bonaire offer a complete range of snorkel gear for rent and will provide beginner training; some dive operations also offer guided snorkeling and night snorkeling. The cost for a guided snorkel session is about $50 and includes slide presentations, transportation to the site, and a tour. Gear rental is approximately $10 per 24-hour period.

FAMILY **Bonaire Dive & Adventure.** Bonaire Dive and Adventures is one of Bonaire's oldest dive operations. Jerry Ligon, Bonaire's best-known biologist, is reason alone to choose this dive shop. He knows everything about everything above and below the water. ✉ *Sand Dollar Condominium Resort, Kaya Gobernador N. Debrot 77A* ☎ *599/717–2229* 🌐 *www.bonairediveandadventure.com.*

Wannadive. Wannadive is a casual, efficient dive company with several locations around the island, offering daily boat dives to Klein Bonaire. They support the dive needs of beginners to professionals, from recreational to technical diving. Wannadive has an expansive rental inventory of dive and snorkel equipment and offers repair and retail at the various locations on island. ✉ *Kaya Gobernador N. Debrot 73* ☎ *599/717–8884* 🌐 *www.wannadive.com.*

Bruce Bowker's Carib Inn Dive Center. Carib Inn, run by The Bowkers, offers a homey casual and laid-back dive experience. The excellent retail shop is chock-full of all your dive needs, including regulators, skins, and snorkel gear. This full-service dive center is a one-stop shop for those in the know. It's rustic with no frills but has high repeat clientele. ✉ *J.A. Abraham Blvd. 46* ☎ *599/717–8819* 🌐 *www.caribinn.com.*

FAMILY **Buddy Dive Resort.** Buddy Dive is a large and lively resort, catering to groups. The property consists of 11 modern buildings featuring one-, two-, and three-bedroom apartments, a full-service dive center, activity desk, two swimming pools, restaurant, pool bar, vehicle rentals, and the famous drive-through air and Nitrox fill station. Friday nights, the property hosts a popular happy hour with house musician Moogie serenading the crowds. ✉ *Kaya Gobernador N. Debrot 85* ☎ *599/717–5080* 🌐 *www.buddydive.com.*

Captain Don's Habitat Dive Shop. Captain Don's Habitat, founded by the late, great underwater environmentalist Captain Don Stewart, is one of the island's most popular dive resort and dive centers for groups and dive enthusiasts. The dive center is a PADI 5-Star Gold Palm Resort and a SDI 5-Star Professional Development Center. With a full-service resort and conference facility, seaside bar and restaurant, and the renowned dive center, they have a high repeat rate for good reason. ✉ *Kaya Gobernador N. Debrot 113* ☎ *599/717–8290* 🌐 *www.habitatbonaire.com.*

Dive Friends Bonaire. Dive Friends is a full-service PADI 5-Star IDC Dive Center, catering to divers of every skill from beginners to technical divers. They have five locations and three retails shops around the island. Dive Friends is the proud organizer of quarterly cleanups attended by locals and tourists, devoting time to clean up various reefs around the island. ✉ *Playa Lechi 24* ☎ *599/727–2929* 🌐 *www.dive-friends-bonaire.com.*

Divi Dive Bonaire. Divi Dive Bonaire is a full-service PADI Gold Palm Resort dive center catering to the beginner and advanced dive enthusiast. Boat diving is offered daily. ✉ *Divi Flamingo Resort & Casino, J.A. Abraham Blvd. 40* ☎ *599/717–8285* 🌐 *www.diviflamingo.com.*

Touch the Sea with Dee Scarr. Dee Scarr offers education, dive tours, and professional expertise in all aspects of diving. She is an author of three books on the subject and is a local celebrity of sorts. She is based out of Captain Don's Habitat Resort. ✉ *Captain Don's Habitat, Kaya Gobernador N. Debrot 113* ☎ *599/717–8529* 🌐 *www.touchthesea.com.*

FISHING

Le Grand Bleu. You can rent the 44-foot *Striker* for $500 for a half day or $650 for a full day of deep-sea fishing. ☎ *599/795–1139* 🌐 *www.fishingbonaire.com.*

Piscatur Charters. Captain Chris is the man for all of your fishing needs. His company offers light-tackle angler reef fishing for jackfish, barracuda, and snapper. You can charter the 42-foot Sport Fisherman *Piscatur,* which carries up to six people. Captain Chris will also organize bonefishing tours. ✉ *Kaya H.J. Pop 3* ☎ *599/717–8774* 🌐 *www.piscatur.com.*

GUIDED TOURS

Achie Tours. Sue Felix runs one of Bonaire's best most reputable tour companies. On island since the '60s, Sue knows all of Bonaire's history, and passes her knowledge to all her well-trained tour guides. Achie Tours largely caters to the cruise ship clientele but is a popular tour company for island-based tourists as well. ✉ *Kaya Nikiboko Noord 33* ☎ *599/717–8630.*

Bonaire Tours & Vacations. Bonaire Tours and Vacations is one of the island's premiere tour companies offering a full array of tour services. They largely cater to the cruise ship clientele. They have brand new air-conditioned buses for the comfort of their guests. ✉ *Kaya Gobernador N. Debrot 79* ☎ *599/717–8778* 🌐 *www.bonairetours.com.*

Or simply ask any taxi driver for an island tour (be sure to negotiate the price up front).

HORSEBACK RIDING

FAMILY **Horse Ranch Club.** You can take hour-long trail rides at the 166-acre Horse Ranch Club (formerly the Riding Academy Club) for $120. A guide takes you through groves of cacti where iguanas, wild goats, donkeys, and flamingos reside; there is even an opportunity to swim with the horses. Reserve one of the gentle pintos or Paso Finos a day in advance, and try to go early in the morning, when it's cool. Tours are available by reservation only and are limited to two people. ✉ *Near airport, east of Kralendijk* ☎ *599/795–4851, 599/786–2094* 🌐 *www.horseranchbonaire.com.*

6

KAYAKING

Many tourists are discovering the natural wonders found in Bonare's extensive mangrove system. The mangroves are situated in Lac Bay. The mangrove harbors a myriad of sea life. This fragile ecosystem is the nursery for upside-down jelly fish, baby barracudas and other marine creatures. Almost all the kayaks used are of the sit-on-top variety, which are able to negotiate shallow waters.

Bonaire Dive and Adventure. This operator rents kayaks and also leads guided trips. ✉ *Kaya Gobernador N. Debrot 79* ☎ *599/717–2229* 🌐 *www.bonairediveandadventure.com.*

Jibe City. At Jibe City, which is primarily a windsurfing outfit, kayaks are free if you are renting surf equipment. Otherwise, they go for $10 (single) and $15 (double) for the first two hours; $25 and $30, respectively, per half day. ✉ *Sorobon Beach* ☎ *599/717–5233* 🌐 *www.jibecity.com.*

Mangrove Info and Kayak Center. Mangrove Kayak Center offers guided kayak tours of the spectacular mangroves of Bonaire. The mangroves are the nursery of Bonaire's diverse sea life, including baby rays, lobster, and baby seahorses. The tours are suited for all ages, offering single and double kayaks. There are several two-hour tours daily; all include snorkeling. Reservations recommended in advance during cruise ship season, April–November. ✉ *Kaminda Lac 141, on road to Lac Cai, Lac Bay* ☎ *599/780–5353* 🌐 *www.mangrovecenter.com.*

WINDSURFING

With gin-clear water and steady onshore trade winds, Bonaire is consistently ranked among the best places in the world for windsurfing. Lac Bay, a protected cove on the east coast, is ideal for windsurfing. Pros from around the world travel to Bonaire to train with Team Bonaire. This local group of sailors are some of the best windsurfers in the world. Beginners and novice sailors come to hone their skills. Lac Bay, a protected cove on the east coast, is ideal for windsurfing. The island's windsurfing companies are headquartered there on Sorobon Beach.

Bonaire Windsurf Place. Commonly referred to as "the Place," this shop rents the latest Hot Sails Maui, Starboard, and RRD equipment. The service is personalized and efficient. Local windsurfer Kenneth will insure you have the right rigged gear before you head into the tropical blue. The windsurf launch can be quite congested on cruise-ship days as the shop rents loungers, thus creating a large volume of non-windsurf beachgoers. ✉ *Sorobon Beach* ☎ *599/717–2288* 🌐 *www.bonairewindsurfplace.com.*

Jibe City. Jibe City is Bonaire's premiere windsurf center located on windy Lac Bay. They have assembled a crew of dedicated staff who cater to all levels of windsurfers. The shops feature state-of-the-art rigged and ready gear. They specialize in Severne Sails and Maui Sails and JP boards. Local pros from Team Bonaire are often on-site honing their skills, training for international events. The shop has rental gear by the day or by the week. They also have SUP rentals. ✉ *Sorobon Beach* ☎ *599/717–5233, 508/737–5245* 🌐 *www.jibecity.com.*

7

BRITISH VIRGIN ISLANDS

WELCOME TO BRITISH VIRGIN ISLANDS

NATURE'S LITTLE SECRETS

Most of the 60-some islands, islets, and cays that make up the British Virgin Islands (BVI) are remarkably hilly and volcanic in origin, having exploded from the depths of the sea some 25 million years ago. The exception is Anegada, which is a flat coral-limestone atoll. Tortola (about 10 square miles [26 square km]) is the largest member of the chain.

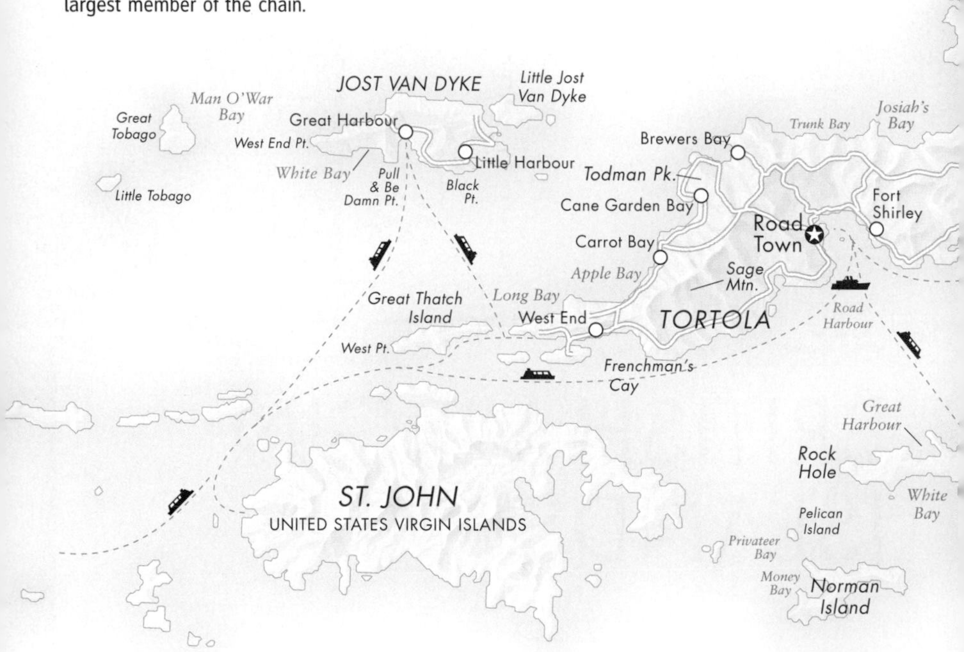

JOST VAN DYKE
Little Jost Van Dyke
Man O'War Bay
Great Tobago
Great Harbour
West End Pt.
Little Harbour
White Bay
Pull & Be Damn Pt.
Black Pt.
Little Tobago
Brewers Bay
Trunk Bay
Josiah's Bay
Todman Pk.
Cane Garden Bay
Fort Shirley
Road Town
Carrot Bay
Apple Bay
Sage Mtn.
Great Thatch Island
Long Bay
West End
TORTOLA
Road Harbour
West Pt.
Frenchman's Cay
Great Harbour
Rock Hole
ST. JOHN
UNITED STATES VIRGIN ISLANDS
White Bay
Pelican Island
Privateer Bay
Money Bay
Norman Island

The British Virgin Islands are mostly quiet and casual, so don't expect to party until dawn, and definitely leave the tux at home. Luxury here means getting away from it all rather than getting the trendiest state-of-the-art amenities. And the jackpot is the chance to explore the many islets and cays by sailboat.

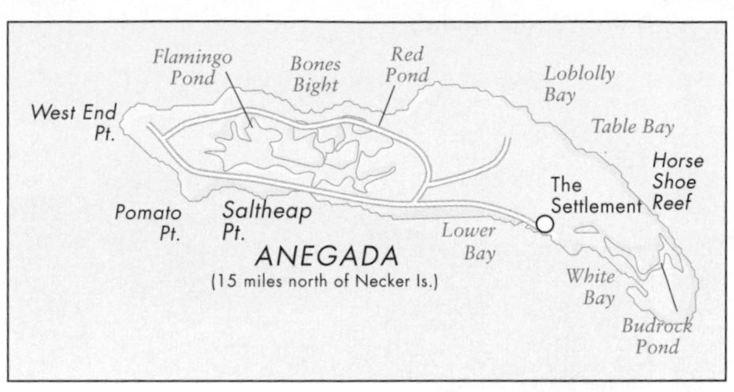

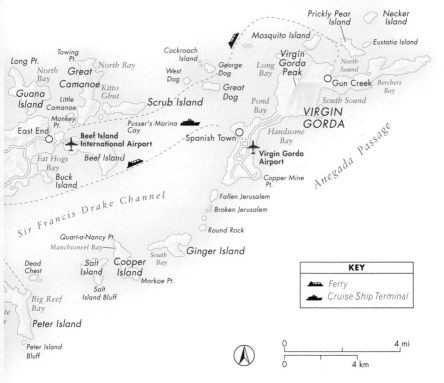

TOP REASONS TO VISIT BRITISH VIRGIN ISLANDS

1 The Perfect Place to Sail: With more than 60 islands in the chain, sailors can drop anchor at a different, perfect beach every day.

2 Low-Key Resorts: Laid-back (but luxurious) resorts offer a full-scale retreat from your everyday life.

3 Diving and Snorkeling: Both are great, and vibrant reefs are often just feet from the shore.

4 Jost Van Dyke: Your trip isn't complete until you've chilled at the casual beach bars here.

5 Few Crowds: There's no mass tourism; the farther you get from Tortola, the quieter things become.

Updated by Susan Zaluski

Once a collection of about 60 sleepy islands and cays, the British Virgin Islands now see huge cruise ships. Shoppers clog the downtown area, and traffic occasionally comes to a standstill. Even the second-largest island, Virgin Gorda, gets its share of smaller ships anchored off the main village of Spanish Town. Despite this explosive growth in the territory's tourism industry, it's still easy to escape the hubbub. Hotels outside Road Town usually provide a quiet oasis, and those on the other islands can be downright serene.

Each island has a different flavor. Want access to lots of restaurants and shopping? Make Tortola your choice. The largest of the BVIs, it covers 10 square miles (26 square km) and sits only a mile from St. John in the United States Virgin Islands (USVI). If you want to kick back at a small hotel or posh resort, try Virgin Gorda. Sitting nearly at the end of the chain, the 8-square-mile (21-square-km) island offers stellar beaches and a laid-back atmosphere. If you really want to get away from it all, the outermost islands, including Anegada and Jost Van Dyke, will fill the bill. Some of the smallest—Norman, Peter, Cooper, and Necker—are home to just one resort or restaurant. Others remain uninhabited specks on the horizon.

Visitors have long visited the BVI, starting with Christopher Columbus in 1493. He called the islands Las Once Mil Virgines—the 11,000 Virgins—in honor of the 11,000 virgin companions of St. Ursula, martyred in the 4th century AD. Pirates and buccaneers followed, and then came the British, who farmed the islands until slavery was abolished in 1834. The BVI are still politically tied to Britain, so the queen appoints a royal governor, but residents elect a local Legislative Council. Offshore banking and tourism share top billing in the territory's economy, but the majority of the islands' jobs are tourism-related. Despite the growth, you can usually find a welcoming smile.

LOGISTICS

Getting to the BVI: There are no nonstop flights to the BVI from the United States. Most travelers connect in San Juan or St. Thomas. You can fly to Tortola, Virgin Gorda, or Anegada, but only on a small plane. There are also ferries from St. Thomas, with regular service to Tortola, Jost Van Dyke, and Virgin Gorda.

Hassle Factor: Medium to high.

On the Ground: Although taxi service is good, you may wish to rent a car on Tortola or Virgin Gorda to explore farther afield or try many different beaches (you may need to if you are staying at an isolated resort). On Anegada it's possible to rent a car, but most people rely on taxis for transportation. Jost Van Dyke has a single road, and visitors travel on foot or by local taxi.

Getting Around the Islands: Most people take ferries to get from island to island, though flights are possible (some are regularly scheduled, or there are plenty of charter opportunities if you are traveling in a group).

PLANNING

7

WHEN TO GO

High season doesn't really get into full swing until Christmas and ends sooner (usually by April 1) than on most Caribbean islands. In the off-season, rates can be a third less. Locals and yachties gather at Foxy's bar on Jost Van Dyke for the annual Halloween party in October.

Glimpse the colorful spinnakers as sailing enthusiasts gather for the internationally known **BVI Spring Regatta and Sailing Festival,** which begins during the last week in March and continues until the first weekend in April. Tortola celebrates **Carnival** on and around August 1 to mark the anniversary of the end of slavery in 1834. A slew of activities culminating with a parade through the streets take place in Road Town. Hotels fill up fast, so make sure to reserve your room and rental car well in advance.

In August you can also try your hand at sportfishing, as anglers compete to land the largest catch at the **BVI Sportfishing Tournament.**

GETTING HERE AND AROUND

AIR TRAVEL

Several airlines have regularly scheduled service to either Tortola or Virgin Gorda. Although it may be cheaper to fly via Puerto Rico, the connections are better through St. Thomas. If you have seven or more people in your party, you can also charter a plane from St. Thomas or San Juan.

Airports Tortola (TOC), Virgin Gorda (VIJ), and Anegada (no code).

Airline Contacts **Air Sunshine** ☎ *800/327–8900, 800/435–8900 in Florida, 888/879–8900 in USVI, 284/495–8900 in BVI* 🌐 *www.airsunshine.com.* **American Airlines/American Eagle** ☎ *800/433–7300 in Tortola, 340/776–2560 in St. Thomas, 340/778–2000 in St. Croix* 🌐 *www.aa.com.* **Cape Air** ☎ *866/227–3247, 508/771–6944 Outside the US/USVI* 🌐 *www.capeair.com.* **Fly BVI**

☎ *284/495–1747 in BVI, 866/819–3146 in US* 🌐 *www.bviaircharters.com.* **LIAT** ☎ *888/844–5428, 866/549–5428 in USVI, 284/495–1693 in Tortola* 🌐 *www.liatairline.com.*

Airport Transfers **Mahogany Rentals and Taxi Service** ✉ *The Valley, Virgin Gorda* ☎ *284/495–5469* 🌐 *www.mahoganycarrentalsbvi.com.*

BOAT AND FERRY TRAVEL

Frequent daily ferries connect Tortola with St. Thomas (both Charlotte Amalie and Red Hook) and St. John. Ferries also link Tortola with Jost Van Dyke, Peter Island, and Virgin Gorda. Tortola has three ferry terminals—one at West End, one on Beef Island (at the airport), and one in Road Town. Schedules vary, and not all companies make daily trips. All Red Hook–bound ferries stop in Cruz Bay to clear customs and immigration.

Ferries also connect Virgin Gorda with St. Thomas (both Charlotte Amalie and Red Hook) and St. John, but not daily. All Red Hook–bound ferries stop in Cruz Bay to clear customs and immigration. Ferries to Virgin Gorda land in Spanish Town. Schedules vary by day, and not all companies make daily trips.

The BVI Tourist Board website 🌐 *www.bvitourism.com/inter-island-ferries* has links to all the ferry companies, and these sites are the best sources for ever-changing routes and schedules.

Boat and Ferry Contacts **Dohm's Water Taxi** ☎ *340/775–6501 in St. Thomas* 🌐 *www.watertaxi-vi.com.* **Inter-Island Boat Service** ☎ *340/776–6597 in St. John, 284/495–4166 in Tortola, 340/473–8567 St. John cell* 🌐 *www.interislandboatservices.com.* **Native Son** ☎ *340/774–8685 in St. Thomas (Charlotte Amalie), 284/495–4617 in Tortola (West End), 284/494–5674 in Tortola (Road Town), 340/775–3111 in St Thomas (Red Hook)* 🌐 *www.nativesonferry.com.* **New Horizon Ferry Service** ☎ *284/495–9278 in Tortola* 🌐 *www.newhorizonferry.com.* **North Sound Express** ☎ *284/495–2138 in Tortola.* **Peter Island Ferry** ☎ *284/495–2000 in Tortola, 800/346-4451* 🌐 *www.peterisland.com.* **Reefer** ☎ *340/776–8500 in St. Thomas* 🌐 *www.marriottfrenchmansreef.com.* **Smith's Ferry** ☎ *340/775–7292 in St. Thomas, 284/494–4454 in Tortola* 🌐 *www.bviferryservices.com.* **Speedy's Ferries** ☎ *284/495-5235 in Tortola* 🌐 *www.speedysbvi.com.* **Road Town Fast Ferry** ☎ *284/494–2323 in Tortola, 340/777-2800 in St. Thomas* 🌐 *www.tortolafastferry.com.* **Varlack Ventures** ☎ *340/776–6412 in St. John* 🌐 *www.varlack-ventures.com.*

CAR TRAVEL

Driving in the BVI is on the left, British-style, but your car will always have its steering wheel on the left, as in the United States. Your valid U.S. license will also do for driving in the BVI. The minimum age to rent a car is 25. Most agencies offer both four-wheel-drive vehicles and cars (often compacts). Both Tortola and Virgin Gorda have a number of car-rental agencies.

Tortola Car-Rental Contacts **Avis** ✉ *Opposite police station, Road Town* ☎ *284/494–2193* 🌐 *www.avis.com.* **D&D** ✉ *West End Rd., West End* ☎ *284/495–4765.* **Itgo Car Rental** ✉ *Wickham's Cay I, Road Town* ☎ *284/494–2639* 🌐 *www.itgobvi.com.* **National** ✉ *Airport, Beef Island* ☎ *284/495–2626* 🌐 *www.*

national.com ✉ *West End* ☎ *284/495–4877* ✉ *Waterfront Dr., Duff's Bottom, Road Town* ☎ *284/494–3197.*

Virgin Gorda Car-Rental Contacts L&S Jeep Rental ✉ *The Valley, Virgin Gorda* ☎ *284/495–5297* 🌐 *www.landsjeeprental.com.* **Mahogany Rentals & Taxi Service** ✉ *Spanish Town, Virgin Gorda* ☎ *284/495–5469* 🌐 *www.mahoganycarrentalsbvi.com.* **Speedy's Car Rentals** ✉ *The Valley, Virgin Gorda* ☎ *284/495–5240, 284/495–5235* 🌐 *www.speedyscarrentals.com.*

TAXI TRAVEL

Taxi rates aren't set in the BVI, so you should negotiate the fare with your driver before you start your trip. Fares are per destination, not per person here, so it's cheaper to travel in groups. The taxi number is always on the license plate.

Tortola Taxi Contacts BVI Taxi Association ☎ *284/494–3942.* **Waterfront Taxi Association** ☎ *284/494–6362.* **West End Taxi Association** ☎ *284/495–4934.*

Virgin Gorda Taxi Contacts Andy's Taxi and Jeep Rental ✉ *The Valley, Virgin Gorda* ☎ *284/495–5252* 🌐 *www.virgingordatours.com.*

ESSENTIALS

Banks and Exchange Services The currency in the BVI is the U.S. dollar. ATMs are common in Road Town, Tortola, and around Virgin Gorda Yacht Harbour.

Electricity 110 volts, the same as in North America, so American appliances work just fine.

Passport Requirements All travelers going to the British Virgin Islands need to have a valid passport, even if they are traveling by private yacht.

Phones The area code for the BVI is 284; when you make calls from North America, you need to dial only the area code and the number. To call anywhere in the BVI once you've arrived, dial all seven digits. A local call from a pay phone costs 25¢, but such phones are sometimes on the blink. An alternative is a Caribbean phone card, available in $5, $10, and $20 denominations. They're sold at most major hotels and many stores and can be used to call within the BVI, as well as all over the Caribbean, and to access **USADirect** (☎ *800/872–2881, 111 from a pay phone*) from special phone-card phones. For credit-card or collect long-distance calls to the United States, use a phone-card telephone or look for special USADirect phones, which are linked directly to an AT&T operator. USADirect and pay phones can be found at most hotels and in towns.

Taxes The departure tax is $15 per person by boat and $20 per person by plane. There are separate booths at the airport and ferry terminals to collect this tax, which must be paid in cash in U.S. currency. Most hotels add a service charge ranging from 5% to 18% to the bill. A few restaurants and some shops tack on an additional 10% charge if you use a credit card. There's no sales tax in the BVI. However, there's a 7% government tax on hotel rooms.

ACCOMMODATIONS

Pick your island carefully, because each is different, as are the logistics of getting there. **Tortola** gives you a wider choice of restaurants, shopping, and resorts. **Virgin Gorda** has fewer off-resort places to eat and shop, but the resorts themselves are often better, and the beaches are wonderful. **Anegada** is remote and better suited for divers. **Jost Van Dyke** has some classic Caribbean beach bars, along with fairly basic accommodations.

When you want to be pampered and pampered some more, consider a remote, **private-island resort** reached only by ferry, or even one of the appealing outer-island resorts that are still somewhat affordable for mere mortals.

If you want to enjoy everything the BVI have to offer, **charter a sailboat** so you can drop anchor where and when you want.

The largest resort in the British Virgin Islands has 120-some rooms, and most have considerably fewer. Luxury here is more about personal service than over-the-top amenities. The best places are certainly comfortable, but they aren't showy. You'll find **villas and condos** in abundance, and they are a good option for families.

Hotel reviews have been shortened. For full information, visit Fodors.com.

WHAT IT COSTS IN U.S. DOLLARS

	$	$$	$$$	$$$$
Restaurants	under $13	$13–$20	$21–$30	over $30
Hotels	under $275	$275–$375	$376–$475	over $475

Restaurant prices are the average cost of a main course at dinner or, if dinner is not served, at lunch. Hotel prices are the lowest cost of a standard double room in high season.

VISITOR INFORMATION

Contacts BVI Tourist Board ☎ *212/563–3117, 800/835–8530 in the U.S.* 🌐 *www.bvitourism.com.*

WEDDINGS

You must apply in person for your license ($110) weekdays at the attorney general's office in Road Town, Tortola. You must wait three days to pick it up at the registrar's office in Road Town. If you plan to be married in a church, announcements (called *banns* locally) must be published for three consecutive Sundays in the church bulletin. Only the registrar or clergy can perform ceremonies. The registrar charges $35 at the office and $100 at another location. No blood test is required.

Contacts BVI Wedding Planners and Consultants ☎ *284/494–5306* ✉ *enquiries@bviweddings.com* 🌐 *www.bviweddings.com.*

TORTOLA

Once a sleepy backwater, Tortola is definitely busy these days, particularly when several cruise ships tie up at the Road Town dock. Passengers crowd the streets and shops, and open-air jitneys filled with cruise-ship passengers create bottlenecks on the island's byways. That said, most folks visit Tortola to relax on its deserted sands or linger over lunch at one of its many delightful restaurants. Beaches are never more than a few miles away, and the steep green hills that form Tortola's spine are fanned by gentle trade winds. The neighboring islands glimmer like emeralds in a sea of sapphire. It can be a world far removed from the hustle of modern life, but it simply doesn't compare to Virgin Gorda in terms of beautiful beaches—or even luxury resorts, for that matter.

Initially settled by Taíno Indians, Tortola saw a string of visitors over the years. Christopher Columbus sailed by in 1493 on his second voyage to the New World, and ships from Spain, Holland, and France made periodic visits about a century later. Sir Francis Drake arrived in 1595, leaving his name on the passage between Tortola and St. John. Pirates and buccaneers followed, with the British finally laying claim to the island in the late 1600s. In 1741 John Pickering became the first lieutenant governor of Tortola, and the seat of the British government moved from Virgin Gorda to Tortola. As the agrarian economy continued to grow, slaves were imported from Africa. The slave trade was abolished in 1807, but slaves in Tortola and the rest of the BVI did not gain their freedom until August 1, 1834, when the Emancipation Proclamation was read at Sunday Morning Well in Road Town. That date is celebrated every year with the island's annual Carnival.

Visitors have a choice of accommodations, but most fall into the small and smaller-still categories. Only Long Bay Resort on Tortola's North Shore qualifies as a resort, but even some of the smaller properties add an amenity or two. A couple of new hotel projects are in the works, so look for more growth in the island's hotel industry over the next decade.

EXPLORING

Tortola doesn't have many historic sights, but it does have lots of beautiful natural scenery. Although you could explore the island's 10 square miles (26 square km) in a few hours, opting for such a whirlwind tour would be a mistake. There's no need to live in the fast lane when you're surrounded by some of the Caribbean's most breathtaking panoramas. Also, the roads are extraordinarily steep and twisting, making driving demanding. The best strategy is to explore a bit of the island at a time. For example, you might try Road Town (the island's tiny metropolis) one morning and a drive to Cane Garden Bay and the little town of West End the next afternoon. Or consider a visit to East End, a *very* tiny town exactly where its name suggests. The North Shore is where all the best beaches are found. Sights are best seen when you stumble on them on your round-the-island drive.

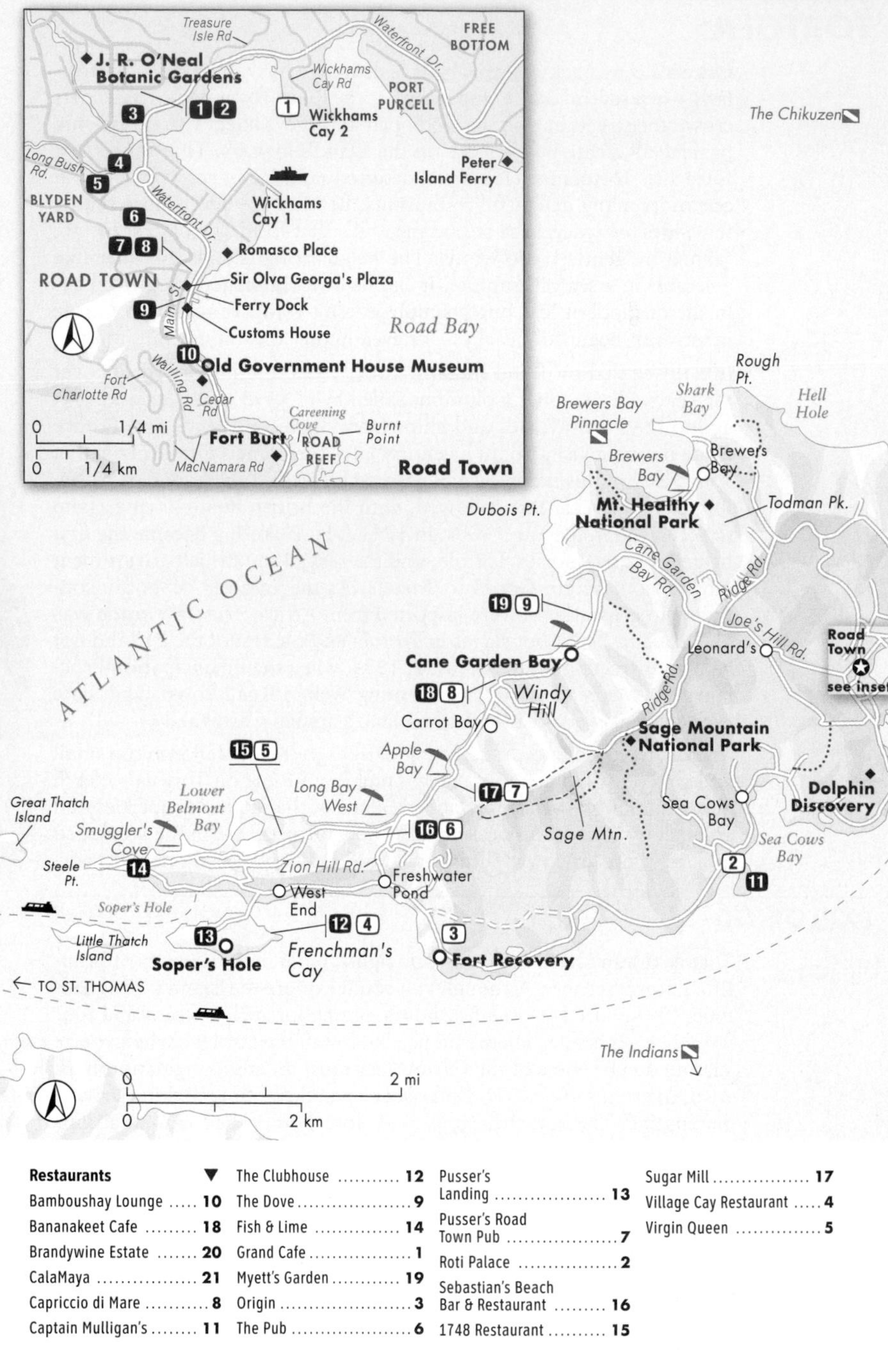

Restaurants ▼

- Bamboushay Lounge 10
- Bananakeet Cafe 18
- Brandywine Estate 20
- CalaMaya 21
- Capriccio di Mare 8
- Captain Mulligan's 11
- The Clubhouse 12
- The Dove 9
- Fish & Lime 14
- Grand Cafe 1
- Myett's Garden 19
- Origin 3
- The Pub 6
- Pusser's Landing 13
- Pusser's Road Town Pub 7
- Roti Palace 2
- Sebastian's Beach Bar & Restaurant 16
- 1748 Restaurant 15
- Sugar Mill 17
- Village Cay Restaurant 4
- Virgin Queen 5

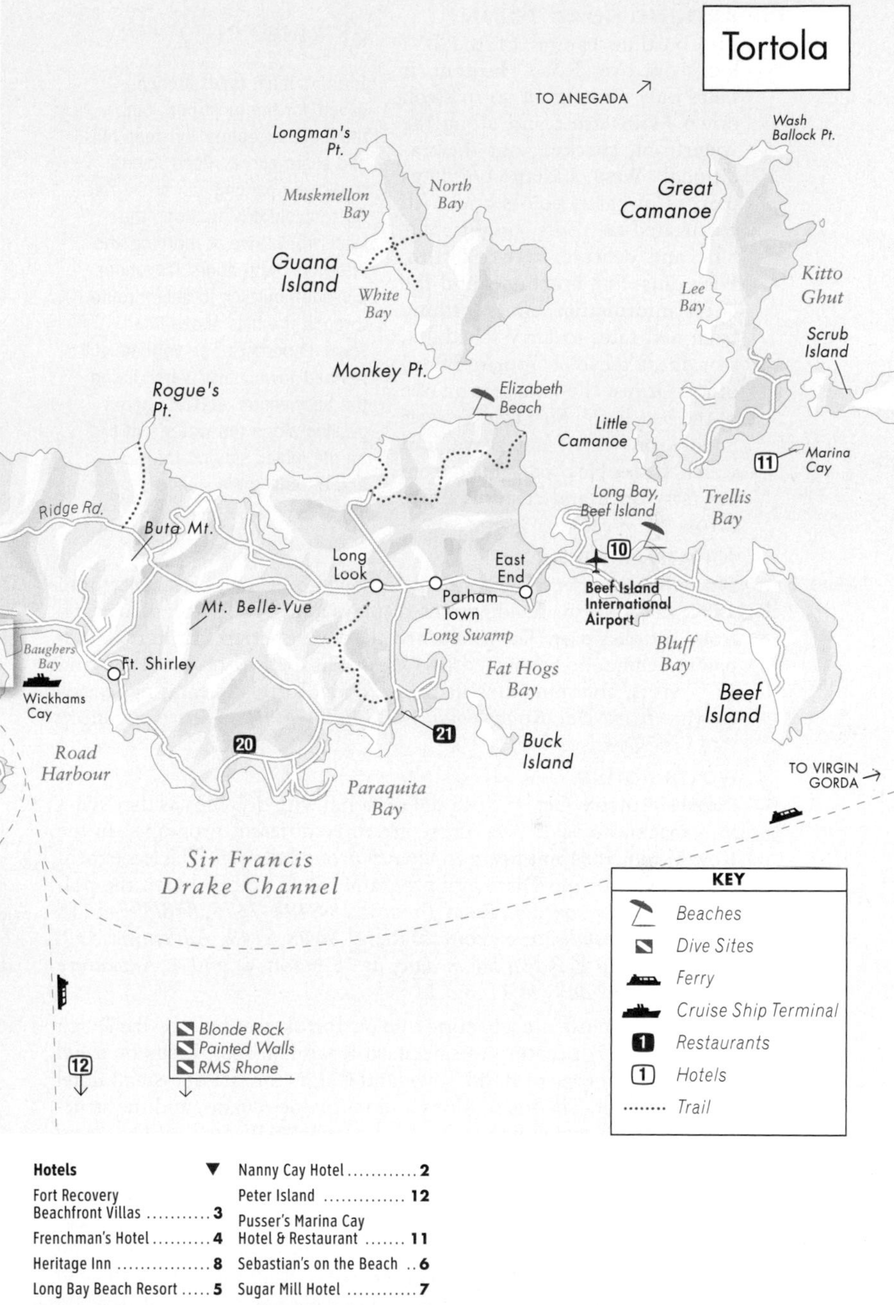

Hotels

Fort Recovery Beachfront Villas 3
Frenchman's Hotel 4
Heritage Inn 8
Long Bay Beach Resort 5
Moorings-Mariner Inn 1
Myett's 9
Nanny Cay Hotel 2
Peter Island 12
Pusser's Marina Cay Hotel & Restaurant 11
Sebastian's on the Beach .. 6
Sugar Mill Hotel 7
Surfsong Villa Resort 10

AROUND ROAD TOWN

The bustling capital of the BVI looks out over Road Harbour. It takes only an hour or so to stroll down Main Street and along the waterfront, checking out the traditional West Indian buildings painted in pastel colors and with corrugated-tin roofs, bright shutters, and delicate fretwork trim. For sightseeing brochures and the latest information on everything from taxi rates to ferry schedules, stop in at the BVI Tourist Board office. Or just choose a seat on one of the benches in Sir Olva Georges Square, on Waterfront Drive, and watch the people come and go from the ferry dock and customs office across the street.

DRIVING ON TORTOLA

Tortola's main roads are well paved, for the most part, but there are exceptionally steep hills and sharp curves. Road Town's traffic and parking can be horrific. Try to avoid driving along the Waterfront Drive at morning and afternoon rush hours. It's longer, but often quicker, to take a route through the hills above Road Town. Parking can be very difficult in Road Town, particularly during the busy winter season. There's parking along the waterfront and on the inland side on the eastern end of downtown.

TOP ATTRACTIONS

Fodor's Choice ★ **Old Government House Museum.** The official government residence until 1997, this gracious building now displays a nice collection of artifacts from Tortola's past. The rooms are filled with period furniture, hand-painted china, books signed by Queen Elizabeth II on her 1966 and 1977 visits, and numerous items reflecting Tortola's seafaring legacy. ✉ *Waterfront Dr., Road Town* ☎ *284/494–4091* 🌐 *www.oghm.org* 🎫 *$5* ⏲ *Weekdays 9–3.*

WORTH NOTING

Dolphin Discovery. Get up close and personal with dolphins as they swim in a spacious seaside pen. There are three different programs. In the Royal Swim, dolphins tow participants around the pen. The less expensive Adventure and Discovery programs allow you to touch the dolphins. ✉ *Waterfront Dr., Road Town* ☎ *284/494–7675, 888/393–5158* 🌐 *www.dolphindiscovery.com* 🎫 *Royal Swim $149, Adventure $99, Discovery $79* ⏲ *Royal Swim daily at 10, noon, 2, and 4. Adventure and Discovery daily at 11 and 1.*

Fort Burt. The most intact historic ruin on Tortola was built by the Dutch in the early 17th century to safeguard Road Harbour. It sits on a hill at the western edge of Road Town and is now the site of a small hotel and restaurant. The foundations and magazine remain, and the structure offers a commanding view of the harbor. ✉ *Waterfront Dr., Road Town* 🎫 *Free* ⏲ *Daily dawn–dusk.*

J.R. O'Neal Botanic Gardens. Take a walk through this 4-acre showcase of lush plant life. There are sections devoted to prickly cacti and succulents, hothouses for ferns and orchids, gardens of medicinal herbs, and plants and trees indigenous to the seashore. From the tourist office in Road Town, cross Waterfront Drive and walk one block over to Main Street and turn right. Keep walking until you see the high school. The

Old Government House Museum, Road Town

gardens are on your left. ✉ *Botanic Station, Road Town* ☎ *284/494–3650* 🌐 *www.bvinationalparkstrust.org* 🎟 *$3* ⏲ *Mon.–Sat. 8:30–4:30.*

WEST END

TOP ATTRACTIONS

Soper's Hole. On this little island connected by a causeway to Tortola's western end, you can find a marina and a captivating complex of pastel West Indian–style buildings with shady balconies, shuttered windows, and gingerbread trim that house art galleries, boutiques, and restaurants. Pusser's Landing is a lively place to stop for a cold drink (many are made with Pusser's famous rum) and a sandwich, and to watch the boats in the harbor. **Amenities:** food and drink; toilets. ✉ *Soper's Hole.*

WORTH NOTING

Fort Recovery. The unrestored ruins of a 17th-century Dutch fort sit amid a profusion of tropical greenery on the grounds of Fort Recovery Beachfront Villas and Suites. There's not much to see here, and there are no guided tours, but you're welcome to stop by and poke around. ✉ *Waterfront Dr., Pockwood Pond* ☎ *284/495–4467* 🎟 *Free.*

NORTH SHORE

TOP ATTRACTIONS

Fodor's Choice ★ **Cane Garden Bay.** Once a sleepy village, Cane Garden Bay has become one of Tortola's most important destinations. Stay at a small hotel or guesthouse here, or stop by for lunch, dinner, or drinks at a seaside restaurant. You can find a few small stores selling clothing and basics such as suntan lotion, and one of Tortola's most popular beaches is at your feet. Myett's offers hotel rooms almost directly on the beach. The roads in and out of this area are dauntingly steep, so use caution when driving. **Amenities:** food and drink. **Best for:** swimming; snorkeling; walking; partiers. ✉ *Cane Garden Bay.*

MID-ISLAND

WORTH NOTING

Mount Healthy National Park. The remains of an 18th-century sugar plantation can be seen here. The windmill structure has been restored, and you can see the ruins of a mill, a factory with boiling houses, storage areas, stables, a hospital, and many dwellings. It's a nice place to picnic. ✉ *Ridge Rd., Todman Peak* 🌐 *www.bvinpt.org* 🎫 *Free* ⏲ *Daily dawn–dusk.*

Sage Mountain National Park. At 1,716 feet, Sage Mountain is the highest peak in the BVI. From the parking area, a trail leads you in a loop not only to the peak itself (and extraordinary views) but also to a small rain forest that is sometimes shrouded in mist. Most of the forest was cut down over the centuries for timber, to create pastureland, or for growing sugarcane, cotton, and other crops. In 1964 this park was established to preserve what remained. Up here you can see mahogany trees, white cedars, mountain guavas, elephant-ear vines, mamey trees, and giant bullet woods, to say nothing of such birds as mountain doves and thrushes. Take a taxi from Road Town or drive up Joe's Hill Road and make a left onto Ridge Road toward Chalwell and Doty villages. The road dead-ends at the park. ✉ *Ridge Rd., Sage Mountain* ☎ *284/852-3650* 🌐 *www.bvinpt.org* 🎫 *$3* ⏲ *Daily dawn–dusk.*

BEACHES

WEST END

Long Bay Beach West. This beach is a stunning, mile-long stretch of white sand; have your camera ready to snap the breathtaking approach. Although Long Bay Resort sprawls along part of it, the entire beach is open to the public. The water isn't as calm here as at Cane Garden or Brewers Bay, but it's still swimmable. Rent water-sports equipment and enjoy the beachfront restaurant at the resort. Turn left at Zion Hill Road; then travel about half a mile. **Amenities:** food and drink; toilets; water sports. **Best for:** swimming. ✉ *Long Bay Rd., Long Bay.*

Smuggler's Cove Beach. A beautiful, palm-fringed beach, Smuggler's Cove is down a pothole-filled dirt road. After bouncing your way down, you'll feel as if you've found a hidden piece of the island. You probably won't be alone on weekends, though, when the beach fills with snorkelers and sunbathers. There's a fine view of Jost Van Dyke from the shore. The beach is popular with Long Bay Resort guests who want a change of scenery. Follow Long Bay Road past Long Bay Resort, keeping to the roads nearest the water until you reach the beach. It's about a mile past the resort. **Amenities:** parking. **Best for:** snorkeling; swimming. ✉ *Long Bay Rd., Long Bay.*

NORTH SHORE

Apple Bay Beach. Along with nearby Little Apple Bay and Capoon's Bay, this is your spot if you want to surf—although the white, sandy beach itself is narrow. Sebastian's, a casual hotel, caters to those in search of the perfect wave. The legendary Bomba's Surfside Shack—a landmark festooned with all manner of flotsam and jetsam—serves drinks and casual food. Otherwise, there's nothing else in the way of amenities. Good waves are never a sure thing, but you're more apt to find them in January and February. If you're swimming and the waves are up, take care not to get dashed on the rocks. **Amenities:** food and drink; toilets. **Best for:** surfing; swimming. ✉ *North Shore Rd. at Zion Hill Rd., Apple Bay.*

Brewers Bay Beach. This beach is easy to find, but the steep, twisting paved roads leading down the hill to it can be a bit daunting. An old sugar mill and ruins of a rum distillery are off the beach along the road. You can actually reach the beach from either Brewers Bay Road East or Brewers Bay Road West. **Amenities:** none. **Best for:** snorkeling; swimming. ✉ *Brewers Bay Rd. E, off Cane Garden Bay Rd., Brewers Bay.*

Cane Garden Bay Beach. A silky stretch of sand, Cane Garden Bay has exceptionally calm, crystalline waters—except when storms at sea turn the water murky. Snorkeling is good along the edges. Casual guesthouses, restaurants, bars, and shops are steps from the beach in the growing village of the same name. The beach is a laid-back, even somewhat funky place to put down your towel. It's the closest beach to Road Town—one steep uphill and downhill drive—and one of the BVI's best-known anchorages (unfortunately, it can be very crowded). Watersports shops rent equipment. **Amenities:** food and drink; toilets; water sports. **Best for:** snorkeling; swimming. ✉ *Cane Garden Bay Rd., off Ridge Rd., Cane Garden Bay.*

7

EAST END

Elizabeth Beach. Home to a small resort, Elizabeth Beach is a palm-lined, wide, and sandy beach with parking along its steep downhill access road. Other than at the hotel and its restaurant, which welcomes nonguests, there are no amenities aside from peace and quiet. Turn at the sign for Lambert Beach Resort. If you miss it, you wind up at Her Majesty's Prison. **Amenities:** food and drink; parking; toilets. **Best for:** solitude; swimming. ✉ *Lambert Rd., off Ridge Rd., on eastern end of island, Lambert Bay.*

Long Bay Beach, Beef Island. Long Bay on Beef Island has superlative scenery: the beach stretches seemingly forever, and you can catch a glimpse of Little Camanoe and Great Camanoe islands. If you walk around the bend to the right, you can see little Marina Cay and Scrub Island. Long Bay is also a good place to search for seashells. Swim out to wherever you see a dark patch for some nice snorkeling. There are no amenities, so come prepared with your own drinks and snacks. Turn left shortly after crossing the bridge to Beef Island. **Amenities:** none. **Best for:** snorkeling; swimming; bird-watching. ✉ *Beef Island Rd., Beef Island.*

WHERE TO EAT

Local seafood is plentiful on Tortola, and although other fresh ingredients are scarce, the island's chefs are a creative lot who apply their skills to whatever the boat delivers. Contemporary American dishes with Caribbean influences are very popular, but you can find French and

Italian fare as well. The more expensive restaurants have dress codes: long pants and collared shirts for men and elegant but casual resort wear for women. Prices are often a bit higher than they are back home, and the service can be a tad on the slow side, but enjoy the chance to linger over the view.

AROUND ROAD TOWN

$$ CAFÉ **Bamboushay Lounge.** Attached to the Bamboushay pottery boutique on Main Street, Bamboushay Lounge on adjacent Waterfront Drive serves weekday lunch options such as salads, pastas, rotis, and stuffed potatoes in an idyllic open-air garden-like setting. The free Wi-Fi seems to attract a lively mix of young local professionals, resident expats, visiting yachties, and tourists who have eagerly returned to lounge "after hours" on Thursdays and Fridays, helping Bamboushay Lounge gain itself a reputation as the new "it" spot. Call for dinner reservations; The Lounge offers dinner on Friday evenings and hopes to expand based on demand. *Average main: $16* *Waterfront Dr.* *284/342–0303* *Closed weekends.*

$$$$ MEDITERRANEAN Fodor's Choice ★ **Brandywine Estate.** At this Brandywine Bay restaurant, candlelit outdoor tables have sweeping views of nearby islands. With a Mediterranean flair, the menu changes often, but you might find a three-cheese tortellini with garlic-and-truffle sauce or scallops in a saffron sauce. Finish your meal with a delightful cheese platter. *Average main: $41* *Sir Francis Drake Hwy., east of Road Town, Brandywine Bay* *284/495–2301* *www.brandywinerestaurant.com* *Closed Tues.*

$$ ITALIAN Fodor's Choice ★ **Capriccio di Mare.** Stop by this casual, authentic Italian outdoor café for an espresso, a fresh pastry, a bowl of perfectly cooked penne, or a crispy tomato-and-mozzarella pizza. Drink specialties include a mango Bellini, an adaptation of the famous cocktail served at Harry's Bar in Venice. *Average main: $19* *Waterfront Dr.* *284/494–5369* *Reservations not accepted* *Closed Sun.*

$$ AMERICAN FAMILY **Captain Mulligan's.** Located at the entrance to Nanny Cay, this sports bar attracts expats, locals, and sailors with its promise to have "the second-best burger on the island," underlining the eatery's irreverent tone (we never found out who has the best!). Hot wings, pizza, ribs, and burgers are on the menu, and most people come to watch the game on the big screen. A mini-golf course has also been established and provides an activity for children of all ages, along with a children's recreation area. *Average main: $15* *Nanny Cay* *284/494–0602* *www.captainmulligans.com.*

$$$ ECLECTIC **The Dove.** The food matches the romantic feeling at this Road Town restaurant. Start with jumbo prawns sautéed with vanilla bean and almonds before moving on to the mushroom-and-parmesan-crusted rib-eye steak. Desserts are often new twists on old standards, as with the soursop (the fruit of a Caribbean evergreen tree) crème brûlée. Lunch offerings were added in 2014. *Average main: $29* *Waterfront Dr., Road Town* *284/494–0313* *www.thedovebvi.com* *Closed Sun. and Mon. No lunch on Sat.*

$$$ FRENCH **Grand Cafe.** Birds and bougainvillea brighten the patio of this breezy French restaurant and bar, a popular gathering spot for locals and visitors alike. French onion soup and smoked salmon salad are good

appetizer choices. From there, move on to the grilled tuna with wasabi sauce, sole in a brown butter sauce, or beef tenderloin with green peppercorn sauce. Save room for such tasty desserts as chocolate cake and crème brûlée, or opt for a platter of French cheeses. *Average main: $23 Waterfront Dr., Road Town 284/494–8660 Closed Sun.*

$ SUSHI **Origin.** Located in the heart of Road Town across from the Ferry Terminal, this lively sushi restaurant and cocktail bar offers high-quality, affordable sushi. The place jumps on Friday nights and can be a noisy dining experience; request a table on the rooftop for a more relaxed setting. *Average main: $12 Road Town 284/494–8295 www.originbvi.com Closed Sun. and Mon.*

$$$ ECLECTIC **The Pub.** At this lively waterfront spot, tables are arranged along a terrace facing a small marina and the harbor in Road Town. Hamburgers, salads, and sandwiches are typical lunch offerings, along with classic British fare such as shepherd's pie and liver and onions. In the evening you can also choose grilled fish, sautéed conch, sizzling steaks, or barbecued ribs. There's live entertainment Thursday and Friday, and locals gather here nightly for spirited games at the pool table. *Average main: $26 Waterfront Dr., Road Town 284/494–2608 Reservations not accepted No lunch Sun.*

$$ ECLECTIC FAMILY **Pusser's Road Town Pub.** Almost everyone who visits Tortola stops here at least once to have a bite to eat and to sample the famous Pusser's Rum Painkiller (fruit juice and rum). The nonthreatening menu includes cheesy pizza, shepherd's pie, fish-and-chips, and hamburgers. Dine inside in air-conditioned comfort or outside on the verandah, which looks out on the harbor. *Average main: $15 Waterfront Dr., Road Town 284/494–3897 www.pussers.com.*

$$ CARIBBEAN **Roti Palace.** You might be tempted to pass this tiny spot on Road Town's Main Street when you see the plastic tablecloths and fake flowers, but the restaurant's reputation for dishing up fantastic roti is known far and wide. Flatbread is filled with curried potatoes, onions, and either chicken, beef, conch, goat, or vegetables. Ask for the bones out if you order the chicken, to save yourself the trouble of fishing them out of your mouth. *Average main: $15 Main St., Road Town 284/494–4196 No credit cards Closed Sun. No dinner.*

$$$$ ECLECTIC **Village Cay Restaurant.** Docked sailboats stretch nearly as far as the eye can see at this busy Road Town restaurant. Its alfresco dining and convivial atmosphere make it popular with both locals and visitors. For lunch, try the grouper club sandwich with an ancho chili mayonnaise, or their extensive lunch buffet that is popular with local professionals and yachties alike. Dinner offerings run to fish served a variety of ways, including West Indian–style with okra, onions, and peppers, as well as a seafood jambalaya with lobster, crayfish, shrimp, mussels, crab, and fish in a mango–passion fruit sauce. *Average main: $32 Wickhams Cay I, Road Town 284/494–2771.*

$$ ECLECTIC **Virgin Queen.** The sailing and rugby crowds head here to play darts, drink beer, and eat Queen's Pizza—a crusty, cheesy pie topped with sausage, onions, green peppers, and mushrooms. Also on the menu is excellent West Indian and English fare: barbecued ribs with beans and rice, bangers and mash, shepherd's pie, and grilled sirloin steak.

7

Average main: $17 ✉ *Flemming St., Road Town* ☎ *284/494–2310* 🌐 *www.virginqueenbvi.com* ⏲ *Closed Sun. No lunch Sat.*

WEST END

$$$ FRENCH FUSION

✕ **The Clubhouse at Frenchman's Cay.** This idyllic, off-the-beaten-path restaurant nestled within the well-manicured grounds of Frenchman's Hotel offers exceptional food. Chef Paul Mason works diligently to incorporate fresh, local Caribbean ingredients and spices into traditional French meals. On Sundays, the restaurant offers a three-course fixed-price brunch that is one of the best values on-island and includes eggs Benedict, rum-and-coconut battered French toast, yellowfin tuna, and sirloin steaks. Brunch guests dine leisurely both indoors and by the small pool. Dinner items include piña colada–drunken duckling, conch pasta carbonara, Bajan seasoned filet mignon, and fresh seafood selections. *Average main: $29* ✉ *Frenchman's Cay* ☎ *284/494–8811* 🌐 *www.frenchmansbvi.com* ⏲ *Closed Mon.*

$$$ SEAFOOD

✕ **Fish and Lime Inn.** In walking distance of the West End Ferry terminal, this pleasantly breezy, waterside restaurant delights daytime visitors with burger, salad, and sandwich offerings that are accompanied by hand-cut french fries. After sunset, candles illuminate the picnic tables on the waterside deck and visiting yachties arrive by dinghy to enjoy menu items that include grilled lobster, Cornish game hen, Asian-marinated barbecue ribs, and a savory hot spinach-and-avocado cheesecake that will delight vegetarians. Occasional live music and happy hour specials also keep the bar lively, which fills with local expats on weekends. *Average main: $26* ✉ *West End* ☎ *284/495–4276* 🌐 *www.fishnlime.com.*

$$$ AMERICAN

✕ **Pusser's Landing.** Yachters navigate their way to this waterfront restaurant. Downstairs, from late morning to well into the evening, you can belly up to the outdoor mahogany bar or sit downstairs for sandwiches, fish-and-chips, and pizzas. At dinnertime, head upstairs for a harbor view and a quiet alfresco meal of grilled steak or fresh fish. *Average main: $26* ✉ *Soper's Hole* ☎ *284/495–4554* 🌐 *www.pussers.com.*

NORTH SHORE

$$$ INTERNATIONAL

✕ **1748 Restaurant.** Relax over dinner in this open-air eatery at Long Bay Beach Club. Tables are well spaced, offering enough privacy for intimate conversations. The menu changes daily, but several dishes show up regularly. Start your meal with a seafood cocktail, creamy carrot soup, or a mixed green salad. Entrées include grilled London broil served with a rosemary mushroom sauce, roasted potatoes and vegetables, grilled tuna steak in a spicy cilantro-coconut sauce, and a pesto-marinated grilled vegetable plate. There are always at least five desserts, and they might include Belgian chocolate mousse, strawberry cheesecake, or a fluffy lemon-and-coconut cake. *Average main: $28* ✉ *Long Bay Beach Club, Long Bay Rd., Long Bay* ☎ *284/495–4252* 🌐 *www.longbay.com.*

$$$ ECLECTIC Fodor's Choice ★

✕ **Bananakeet Cafe.** The sunset sea-and-mountain views are stunning, so arrive early for the predinner happy hour. "Caribbean fusion" best describes the fare, with an emphasis on seafood, including local Anegada conch swimming in an herb-butter broth. Those without a taste for seafood won't go hungry—the menu also includes lamb, beef, and chicken dishes. Locals and tourists alike come to enjoy the spectacular sunset, and enjoy a complimentary "sundowner" shot. *Average main: $24 ✉ North Coast Rd., Great Carrot Bay ☎ 284/494–5842 ⊗ No lunch.*

$$$$ ECLECTIC **Myett's Garden and Grille.** Partly because it's right on the beach, this bi-level restaurant and bar is hopping day and night for breakfast, lunch, and dinner. Chowder made with fresh conch is the specialty here, and the menu includes vegetarian dishes as well as grilled shrimp, steak, and tuna. There's live entertainment every night in winter. *Average main: $32 ✉ Cane Garden Bay ☎ 284/495–9649 ⊕ www.myetts.com.*

$$$ ECLECTIC **Sebastian's Seaside Grill.** The waves practically lap at your feet at this beachfront restaurant on Tortola's North Shore. The menu emphasizes seafood—especially lobster, conch, and local fish—but you can also find dishes such as ginger chicken and filet mignon. It's a perfect spot to stop for lunch on your around-the-island tour. Try the grilled dolphinfish (mahimahi) sandwich, served on a soft roll with an onion tartar sauce. Finish off with a cup of Sebastian's coffee, spiked with home-brewed rum. *Average main: $29 ✉ Sebastian's on the Beach, North Coast Rd., Apple Bay ☎ 284/495–4212 ⊕ www.sebastiansbvi.com.*

$$$$ ECLECTIC Fodor's Choice ★ **Sugar Mill Restaurant.** Candles gleam and the background music is peaceful in this romantic restaurant inside a 17th-century sugar mill. Well-prepared selections on the à la carte menu, which changes nightly, include some pasta and vegetarian entrées. Lobster bisque with basil croutons and a creamy conch chowder are good starters. Favorite entrées include fresh fish with soba noodles, shiitake mushrooms, and a scallion broth; filet mignon topped with an herb-cream sauce; grilled shrimp and scallops with mango salsa; and pumpkin-and–black bean lasagna. *Average main: $32 ✉ Sugar Mill Hotel, North Coast Rd., Apple Bay ☎ 284/495–4355 ⊕ www.sugarmillhotel.com ⊗ No lunch.*

EAST END

$$ ECLECTIC **CalaMaya.** Casual fare is what you can find at this waterfront restaurant. You can always order a burger or Caesar salad; the chicken wrap with sweet-and-sour sauce is a tasty alternative. For dinner, try the mahimahi with sautéed vegetables and rice. *Average main: $17 ✉ Hodge's Creek Marina, Blackburn Hwy., Hodge's Creek ☎ 284/495–2126.*

WHERE TO STAY

Luxury on Tortola is more about a certain state of mind—serenity, seclusion, gentility, and a bit of Britain in the Caribbean—than about state-of-the-art amenities and fabulous facilities. Some properties, especially the vacation villas, are catching up with current trends, but others seem stuck in the 1980s. But don't let a bit of rust on the screen door or a chip in the paint on the balcony railing mar your appreciation of the ambience. You will likely spend most of your time outside, so the location, size, or price of a hotel should be more of a factor to you than the decor.

7

Hotels in Road Town don't have beaches, but they do have pools and are within walking distance of restaurants, bars, and shops. Accommodations outside Road Town are relatively isolated, but most face the ocean. Tortola resorts are intimate—only a handful have more than 50 rooms. Guests are treated as more than just room numbers, and many return year after year. This can make booking a room at popular resorts difficult, even off-season, despite the fact that more than half of the island's visitors stay aboard their own or chartered boats.

A few hotels lack air-conditioning, relying instead on ceiling fans to capture the almost constant trade winds. Nights are cool and breezy, even in midsummer, and never reach the temperatures or humidity levels that are common in much of the United States. Note that all accommodations listed here have air-conditioning unless we mention otherwise. Remember that some places may be closed during the peak of hurricane season—August through October—to give their owners a much-needed break.

PRIVATE VILLAS

Renting a villa is growing in popularity. Vacationers like the privacy, the space to spread out, and the opportunity to cook meals. As is true everywhere, the most important thing is location. If you want to be close to the beach, opt for a villa on the North Shore. If you want to dine out in Road Town every night, a villa closer to town may be a better bet. Prices per week during the winter season run from around $2,000 for a one- or two-bedroom villa up to $10,000 for a five-room beachfront villa. Rates in summer are substantially less. Most, but not all, villas accept credit cards.

VILLA RENTAL CONTACTS

Areana Villas. Areana Villas represents top-of-the-line properties. Pastel-color villas with one to five bedrooms can accommodate up to 10 guests. Many have pools, whirlpool tubs, and tiled courtyards. ☎ *284/494–5864* 🌐 *www.areanavillas.com.*

McLaughlin-Anderson Luxury Villas. The St. Thomas–based McLaughlin-Anderson Luxury Villas manages nearly two-dozen properties around Tortola. Villas range from one to six bedrooms and come with full kitchens and stellar views. Most have pools. The company can hire a chef and stock your kitchen with groceries. ☎ *340/776–0635, 800/537–6246* 🌐 *www.mclaughlinanderson.com.*

Smiths Gore. Although Smiths Gore has properties all over the island, many are in the Smuggler's Cove area. They range from two to five bedrooms: all have stellar views, lovely furnishings, and lush landscaping. ☎ *284/494–2446* 🌐 *www.smithsgore.com.*

AROUND ROAD TOWN

$ HOTEL **Moorings-Mariner Inn.** If you enjoy the camaraderie of a busy marina, this inn on the edge of Road Town may appeal to you. **Pros:** good dining options; friendly guests; excellent spot to charter boats. **Cons:** busy location; long walk to Road Town; need car to get around. *Rooms from: $220* ✉ *Waterfront Dr.* ☎ *284/494–2333, 800/535–7289* 🌐 *www.bvimarinerinnhotel.com* *32 rooms, 7 suites* *No meals.*

CLOSE UP

American or British?

Yes, the Union Jack flutters overhead in the tropical breeze, schools operate on the British system, place-names have British spellings, Queen Elizabeth II appoints the governor—and the Queen's picture hangs on many walls. Indeed, residents celebrate the Queen's birthday every June with a public ceremony. You can overhear that charming English accent from a good handful of expats when you're lunching at Road Town restaurants, and you can buy "biscuits"—what Americans call cookies—in the supermarkets.

But you can pay for your lunch and the biscuits with American money, because the U.S. dollar is legal tender here. The unusual circumstance is a matter of geography. The practice started in the mid-20th century, when BVI residents went to work in the nearby USVI. On trips home, they brought their U.S. dollars with them. Soon they abandoned the barter system, and in 1959 the U.S. dollar became the official form of money. Interestingly, the government sells stamps (for use only in the BVI) that often carry pictures of Queen Elizabeth II and other royalty with the monetary value in U.S. dollars and cents.

The American influence continued to grow when Americans began to open businesses in the BVI because they preferred its quiet to the hustle and bustle of St. Thomas. Inevitably, cable and satellite TV's U.S.-based programming, along with Hollywood-made movies, further influenced life in the BVI. And most goods are shipped from St. Thomas in the USVI, meaning you can find more American products than British ones on the supermarket shelves.

$ HOTEL **Nanny Cay Hotel.** This quiet oasis is far enough from Road Town to give it a secluded feel but close enough to make shops and restaurants convenient. **Pros:** nearby shops and restaurant; pleasant rooms; marina atmosphere. **Cons:** busy location; need car to get around. *Rooms from: $150 Waterfront Dr., Nanny Cay 284/494–2512 www.nannycay.com 38 rooms No meals.*

WEST END

$$ RESORT FAMILY **Fort Recovery Beachfront Villas.** This is one of those small but special properties that stands out because of its friendly service and the chance to get to know your fellow guests rather than the poshness of the rooms and the upscale amenities. **Pros:** beautiful beach; spacious units; historic site. **Cons:** need car to get around; isolated location. *Rooms from: $345 Waterfront Dr., West End, Tortola 284/495–4354, 855/349–3355 www.fortrecoverytortola.com 30 suites No meals.*

NORTH SHORE

$$ RESORT **Frenchman's Hotel.** Small and tucked on a beautiful but often overlooked corner of Tortola (technically it's a separate island), Frenchman's Hotel is a quiet, intimate resort with stunning scenic vistas and beautifully landscaped, lush grounds. **Pros:** a tranquil spot. **Cons:** you need a car to get around. *Rooms from: $365 Frenchman's Cay, Tortola 284/494–8811 www.frenchmansbvi.com 8 villas Breakfast.*

$ B&B/INN **Heritage Inn.** The gorgeous sea and mountain views are the stars at this small hotel perched on the edge of a cliff. **Pros:** stunning views; fun vibe; room has kitchenette. **Cons:** need car to get around; close to road. *Rooms from: $225 North Coast Rd., Great Carrot Bay, Tortola 284/494–5842 heritageinnbvi.com 6 rooms No meals.*

$$$ RESORT **Long Bay Beach Club.** If you want all the resort amenities, including a beach, pool, spa, and tennis courts, in an intimate setting, then this is your only choice for Tortola. **Pros:** beach-club atmosphere; good restaurant on-site; many activities. **Cons:** need car to get around; sometimes-curt staff; uphill hike to some rooms. *Rooms from: $395 Long Bay Rd., Long Bay, Tortola 284/495–4252, 800/858–4618 www.longbay.com 20 villas, 10 suites, 10 cabanas Multiple meal plans.*

$ HOTEL **Myett's.** Tucked away in a beachfront garden, this tiny hotel puts you right in the middle of Cane Garden Bay's busy hustle and bustle. **Pros:** beautiful beach; good restaurant; shops nearby. **Cons:** busy location. *Rooms from: $200 Cane Garden Bay, Tortola 284/495–9649 www.myetts.com 6 rooms, 4 cottages, 1 villa No meals.*

$ RESORT **Sebastian's on the Beach.** Sitting on the island's north coast, Sebastian's definitely has a beachy feel, and that's its primary charm. **Pros:** nice beach; good restaurants; beachfront rooms. **Cons:** on busy road; some rooms nicer than others; need car to get around. *Rooms from: $135 North Coast Rd., Apple Bay, Tortola 284/495–4212, 800/336–4870 www.sebastiansbvi.com 26 rooms, 9 villas No meals.*

$$ RESORT Fodor's Choice ★ **Sugar Mill Hotel.** Though it's not a sprawling resort, the Sugar Mill Hotel has a Caribbean cachet that's hard to beat, and it's a favorite place to stay on Tortola. **Pros:** lovely rooms; excellent restaurants on-site; nice views. **Cons:** on busy road; small beach; need car to get around. *Rooms from: $350 North Coast Rd., Apple Bay, Tortola 284/495–4355, 800/462–8834 www.sugarmillhotel.com 19 rooms, 2 suites, 1 villa, 1 cottage No meals.*

EAST END

$$$ RESORT Fodor's Choice ★ **Surfsong Villa Resort.** Nested in lush foliage right at the water's edge, this small resort on Beef Island provides a pleasant respite for vacationers who want a villa atmosphere with some hotel amenities. **Pros:** lovely rooms; beautiful beach; chef on call. **Cons:** need car to get around; no restaurants nearby. *Rooms from: $465 Off Beef Island Rd., Beef Island, Tortola 284/495–1864 www.surfsong.net 1 suite, 7 villas Multiple meal plans.*

NIGHTLIFE AND PERFORMING ARTS

NIGHTLIFE

Like any other good sailing destination, Tortola has watering holes that are popular with salty and not-so-salty dogs. Many offer entertainment; check the weekly *Limin' Times* (*www.limin-times.com*) for schedules and up-to-date information. Bands change like the weather, and what's hot today can be old news tomorrow. The local beverage is the Painkiller, an innocent-tasting mixture of fruit juices and rums. It goes down smoothly but packs quite a punch, so give yourself time to recover before you order another.

Surfsong Villa Resort

Bomba's Surfside Shack. By day, you can see that Bomba's, which is covered with everything from crepe-paper leis to ancient license plates to spicy graffiti, looks like a pile of junk; by night it's one of Tortola's liveliest spots. There's a fish fry and a live band every Wednesday and Sunday. People flock here from all over on the full moon, when bands play all night long. ✉ *North Coast Rd., Apple Bay, Tortola* ☎ *284/495–4148.*

Fodor's Choice ★ **Myett's.** Local bands play at this popular spot, which has live music during happy hour. There's usually a lively dance crowd. ✉ *Cane Garden Bay, Tortola* ☎ *284/495–9649* 🌐 *www.myetts.com.*

The New Quito's Restaurant and Bar. BVI recording star Quito Rhymer sings island ballads and love songs at his rustic beachside bar–restaurant. Solo shows are on Tuesday and Thursday at 8:30; on Friday at 9:30 Quito performs with his band. ✉ *Cane Garden Bay, Tortola* ☎ *284/495–4837* 🌐 *www.quitorymer.com.*

The Pub. At this popular watering hole, there's a happy hour from 5 to 7 every day and live music on Thursday and Friday. ✉ *Waterfront St., Road Town, Tortola* ☎ *284/494–2608.*

Pusser's Road Town Pub. Courage is what people are seeking here—John Courage beer by the pint. Or try Pusser's famous mixed drink, called the Painkiller, and snack on the excellent pizza. ✉ *Waterfront St., Road Town, Tortola* ☎ *284/494–3897* 🌐 *www.pussers.com.*

Sebastian's. There's often live music at Sebastian's on Sunday evenings in season, and you can dance under the stars (but call ahead for the schedule). ✉ *North Coast Rd., Apple Bay, Tortola* ☎ *284/495–4212* 🌐 *www.sebastiansbvi.com.*

Most of Tortola's shops are in Road Town.

PERFORMING ARTS

Performing Arts Series. Musicians from around the world take to the stage during the island's Performing Arts Series, held annually October through May. Past artists have included Latin jazz artist Tito Puente Jr., gospel singer Kim Burrell, and pianist Richard Ormond. ✉ *H. Lavity Stoutt Community College, Blackburn Hwy., Paraquita Bay, Tortola* ☎ *284/494–4994* 🌐 *www.hlscc.edu.vg.*

SHOPPING

The BVI aren't really a shopper's delight, but there are many shops showcasing original wares, such as jams, spices, resort wear, and often-excellent artwork.

AREAS AND MARKETS

Many shops and boutiques are clustered along and just off Road Town's **Main Street.** You can shop in Road Town's **Wickham's Cay I** adjacent to the marina. The **Crafts Alive Market** on the Road Town waterfront is a collection of colorful West Indian–style buildings with shops that carry items made in the BVI. You might find pretty baskets or interesting pottery or perhaps a bottle of home-brewed hot sauce. A growing number of art and clothing stores are opening at **Soper's Hole** in West End.

ART

Allamanda Gallery. Photography by the gallery's owner, Amanda Baker, as well as books, gifts, and cards are on display and available to purchase. ✉ *124 Main St., Road Town, Tortola* ☎ *284/494–6680* 🌐 *www.virginportraits.com.*

Sunny Caribbee. This gallery has many paintings, prints, and watercolors by artists from around the Caribbean, and is also known for its collection of spices, hot sauces, and other food products. ✉ *119 Main St., Road Town, Tortola* ☎ *284/494–2178* 🌐 *www.sunnycaribbee.com.*

CLOTHES AND TEXTILES

Arawak. This boutique carries batik sundresses, sportswear, and resort wear for men and women. There's also a selection of children's clothing. ✉ *Nanny Cay Marina, Nanny Cay, Tortola* ☎ *284/494–3983.*

Latitude 18°. This store sells Maui Jim, Ray-Ban, and Oakley sunglasses; Freestyle watches; and a fine collection of beach towels, sandals, Crocs, sundresses, and sarongs. ✉ *Waterfront Drive, Road Town, Tortola* ☎ *284/494–6196* 🌐 *www.latitude18.com.*

Pusser's Company Store. The Road Town Pusser's sells nautical memorabilia, ship models, and marine paintings. There's also an entire line of clothing for both men and women, handsome decorator bottles of Pusser's rum, and gift items bearing the Pusser's logo. ✉ *Main St. at Waterfront Rd., Road Town, Tortola* ☎ *284/494–2467* 🌐 *www.pussers.com.*

Zenaida's of West End. Vivian Jenik Helm travels through South America, Africa, and India in search of batiks, hand-painted and hand-blocked fabrics, and interesting weaves that can be made into *pareus* (women's wraps) or wall hangings. The shop also sells unusual bags, belts, sarongs, scarves, and ethnic jewelry. ✉ *Soper's Hole Marina, West End, Tortola* ☎ *284/495–4867.*

7

FOOD

Ample Hamper. Head here to stock your yacht or rental villa—or have the staff do it for you. It carries an outstanding collection of cheeses, wines, fresh fruits, and canned goods from the United Kingdom and the United States. ✉ *Inner Harbour Marina, Road Town, Tortola* ☎ *284/494–2494.*

Best of British. This boutique has lots of nifty British food you won't find elsewhere. Shop here for Marmite, Vegemite, shortbread, frozen meat pies, and delightful Christmas "crackers" filled with surprises. ✉ *Wickham's Cay I, Road Town, Tortola* ☎ *284/494–3462.*

RiteWay. This market carries a good (but not massive) selection of the usual supplies. RiteWay will stock villas and yachts. ✉ *Waterfront Dr. at Pasea Estate, Road Town, Tortola* ☎ *284/494–2263* 🌐 *www.rtwbvi.com* ✉ *Flemming St., Road Town, Tortola* ☎ *284/347–1230* 🌐 *www.rtwbvi.com.*

GIFTS

Sunny Caribbee. In a brightly painted West Indian house, this store packages its own herbs, teas, coffees, vinegars, hot sauces, soaps, skin and suntan lotions, and exotic concoctions—Arawak Love Potion and Island Hangover Cure, for example. ✉ *119 Main St., Road Town, Tortola* ☎ *284/494–2178* 🌐 *www.sunnycaribbee.com.*

JEWELRY

Samarkand. The charming jewelry sold here includes gold-and-silver pendants, earrings, bracelets, and pins, many with island themes such as seashells, lizards, pelicans, and palm trees. There are also reproduction

Spanish pieces of eight (old Spanish coins) similar to those found on sunken galleons, and those including local Virgin Islands green jasper. ✉ *Main St., Road Town, Tortola* ☎ *284/494–6415* ⏲ *Closed Sun.*

SPORTS AND THE OUTDOORS

DIVING AND SNORKELING

Clear waters and numerous reefs afford some wonderful opportunities for underwater exploration. In some spots visibility reaches 100 feet, but colorful reefs teeming with fish are often just a few feet below the sea surface. The BVI's system of marine parks means the underwater life visible through your mask will stay protected.

There are several popular dive spots around the islands. **Alice in Wonderland** is a deep dive south of Ginger Island with a wall that slopes gently from 15 feet to 100 feet. It's an area overrun with huge mushroom-shape coral, hence its name. Crabs, lobsters, and shimmering fan corals make their homes in the tunnels, ledges, and overhangs of **Blonde Rock,** a pinnacle that goes from 15 feet below the surface to 60 feet deep. It's between Dead Chest and Salt Island. When the currents aren't too strong, **Brewers Bay Pinnacle** (20 to 90 feet down) teems with sea life. At the **Indians,** near Pelican Island, colorful coral decorates canyons and grottoes created by four large, jagged pinnacles that rise 50 feet from the ocean floor. The **Painted Walls** is a shallow dive site where coral and sponges create a kaleidoscope of colors on the walls of four long gullies. It's northeast of Dead Chest.

The *Chikuzen,* sunk northwest of Brewers Bay in 1981, is a 246-foot vessel in 75 feet of water; it's home to thousands of fish, colorful corals, and big rays. In 1867 the **RMS** *Rhone*, a 310-foot royal mail steamer, split in two when it sank in a devastating hurricane. It's so well preserved that it was used as an underwater prop in the 1977 movie *The Deep*. You can see the crow's nest and bowsprit, the cargo hold in the bow, and the engine and enormous propeller shaft in the stern. Its four parts are at various depths, from 30 to 80 feet. Get yourself some snorkeling gear and hop aboard a dive boat to this wreck near Salt Island (across the channel from Road Town). Every dive outfit in the BVI runs scuba and snorkel tours to this part of the BVI National Parks Trust; if you have time for only one trip, make it this one. Rates start at around $70 for a one-tank dive and $100 for a two-tank dive.

Your hotel probably has a dive company right on the premises. If not, the staff can recommend one nearby. Using your hotel's dive company makes a trip to the offshore dive and snorkel sites a breeze. Just stroll down to the dock and hop aboard. All dive companies are certified by PADI, the Professional Association of Diving Instructors, which ensures that your instructors are qualified to safely take vacationers diving. The boats are also inspected to make sure they're seaworthy. If you've never dived, try a short introductory dive, often called a resort course, which teaches you enough to get you underwater. In the unlikely event you get a case of the bends, a condition that can happen when you rise to the surface too fast, your dive team will take you to the decompression chamber at Roy L. Schneider Regional Medical Center in nearby St. Thomas.

Blue Waters Divers. If you're chartering a sailboat, Blue Waters Divers will meet yours at Peter, Salt, Norman, or Cooper Island for a rendezvous dive. The company teaches resort, open-water, rescue, and advanced diving courses, and also makes daily dive trips. Rates include all equipment as well as instruction. Reserve two days in advance. ✉ *Nanny Cay Marina, Nanny Cay, Tortola* ☎ *284/494–2847* 🌐 *www.bluewaterdiversbvi.com* ✉ *Soper's Hole Marina, Soper's Hole, Tortola* ☎ *284/495–1200* 🌐 *www.bluewaterdiversbvi.com.*

FISHING

Most of the boats that take you deep-sea fishing for bluefish, wahoo, swordfish, and shark leave from nearby St. Thomas, but local anglers like to fish the shallower water for bonefish. A half day for two people runs about $480, a full day around $850. Wading trips are $325.

Caribbean Fly Fishing ✉ *Nanny Cay Marina, Nanny Cay, Tortola* ☎ *284/494–4797, 284/499–1590* 🌐 *www.caribflyfishing.com.*

HIKING

FAMILY Sage Mountain National Park attracts hikers who enjoy the quiet trails that crisscross the island's loftiest peak. There are some lovely views and the chance to see rare species that grow only at higher elevations.

SAILING

FAMILY Fodor's Choice ★ The BVI are among the world's most popular sailing destinations. They're clustered together and surrounded by calm waters, so it's fairly easy to sail from one anchorage to the next. Most of the Caribbean's biggest sailboat charter companies have operations in Tortola. If you know how to sail, you can charter a bareboat (perhaps for your entire vacation); if you're unschooled, you can hire a boat with a captain. Prices vary depending on the type and size of the boat you wish to charter. In season, a weekly charter runs from $1,500 to $35,000. Book early to make sure you get the boat that fits you best. Most of Tortola's marinas have hotels, which give you a convenient place to spend the nights before and after your charter.

If a day sail to some secluded anchorage is more your cup of tea, the BVI have numerous boats of various sizes and styles that leave from many points around Tortola. Prices start at around $80 per person for a full-day sail, including lunch and snorkeling equipment.

Aristocat Charters. This company's 48-foot catamaran sets sail daily to Jost Van Dyke, Norman Island, and other small islands. ✉ *West End, Tortola* ☎ *284/499–1249* 🌐 *www.aristocatcharters.com.*

BVI Yacht Charters. The 31- to 52-foot sailboats for charter here come with or without a captain and crew. ✉ *Port Purcell, Road Town, Tortola* ☎ *284/494–4289, 888/615–4006* 🌐 *www.bviyachtcharters.com.*

The Catamaran Company. The catamarans here come with or without a captain. ✉ *Maya Cove Marina, Fat Hog's Bay, Tortola* ☎ *284/494–6661, 800/262–0308* 🌐 *www.catamarans.com.*

The Moorings. One of the world's best bareboat operations, The Moorings has a large fleet of both monohulls and catamarans. Hire a captain

7

or sail the boat yourself. ✉ *Wickham's Cay II, Road Town, Tortola* ☎ *800/535–7289* 🌐 *www.moorings.com.*

Regency Yacht Vacations. If you prefer a powerboat, call Regency Yacht Vacations. It handles captain and full-crew sail and powerboat charters. ✉ *Wickham's Cay I, Road Town, Tortola* ☎ *284/495–1970, 800/524–7676* 🌐 *www.regencyvacations.com.*

Sunsail. A full fleet of boats to charter with or without a captain is available here. ✉ *Wickham's Cay II, Road Town, Tortola* ☎ *888/350–3568, 800/327–2276* 🌐 *www.sunsail.com.*

Voyage Charters. Voyage has a variety of sailboats for charter, with or without a captain and crew. ✉ *Soper's Hole Marina, West End, Tortola* ☎ *284/494–0740, 888/869–2436* 🌐 *www.voyagecharters.com.*

White Squall II. This 80-foot schooner has regularly scheduled day sails to The Baths at Virgin Gorda, Cooper, the Indians, and the Caves at Norman Island. ✉ *Village Cay Marina, Road Town, Tortola* ☎ *284/541–2222* 🌐 *www.whitesquall2.com.*

SURFING

Surfing is big on Tortola's north shore, particularly when the winter swells come into Josiah's and Apple bays. Rent surfboards starting at $65 for a full day.

HIHO. Lots of good surfboards and stand-up paddleboards are available for rent as well as for sale. The staff will give you advice on the best spots to put in your board. ✉ *Trellis Bay, Trellis Bay, Tortola* ☎ *284/494–7694* 🌐 *www.go-hiho.com.*

WINDSURFING

Steady trade winds make windsurfing a breeze. Three of the best spots for sailboarding are Nanny Cay, Slaney Point, and Trellis Bay on Beef Island. Rates for sailboards start at about $25 an hour or $100 for a two-hour lesson.

Boardsailing BVI Watersports. This company rents equipment and offers private and group lessons. ✉ *Trellis Bay, Beef Island* ☎ *284/495–2447* 🌐 *www.adventures-bvi.com/.*

SIDE TRIPS FROM TORTOLA

There are several islands that make great side trips from Tortola, including lovely Marina Cay and tony Peter Island. Both have great accommodations, so you might want to spend the night.

MARINA CAY

FAMILY Beautiful little Marina Cay is in Trellis Bay, not far from Beef Island. Sometimes you can see it and its large J-shape coral reefs—a most dramatic sight—from the air soon after takeoff from the airport on Beef Island. Covering 8 acres, this islet is considered small even by BVI standards. On it there's a restaurant, Pusser's Store, and a six-unit hotel. Ferry service is free from the dock on Beef Island.

Continued on page 266

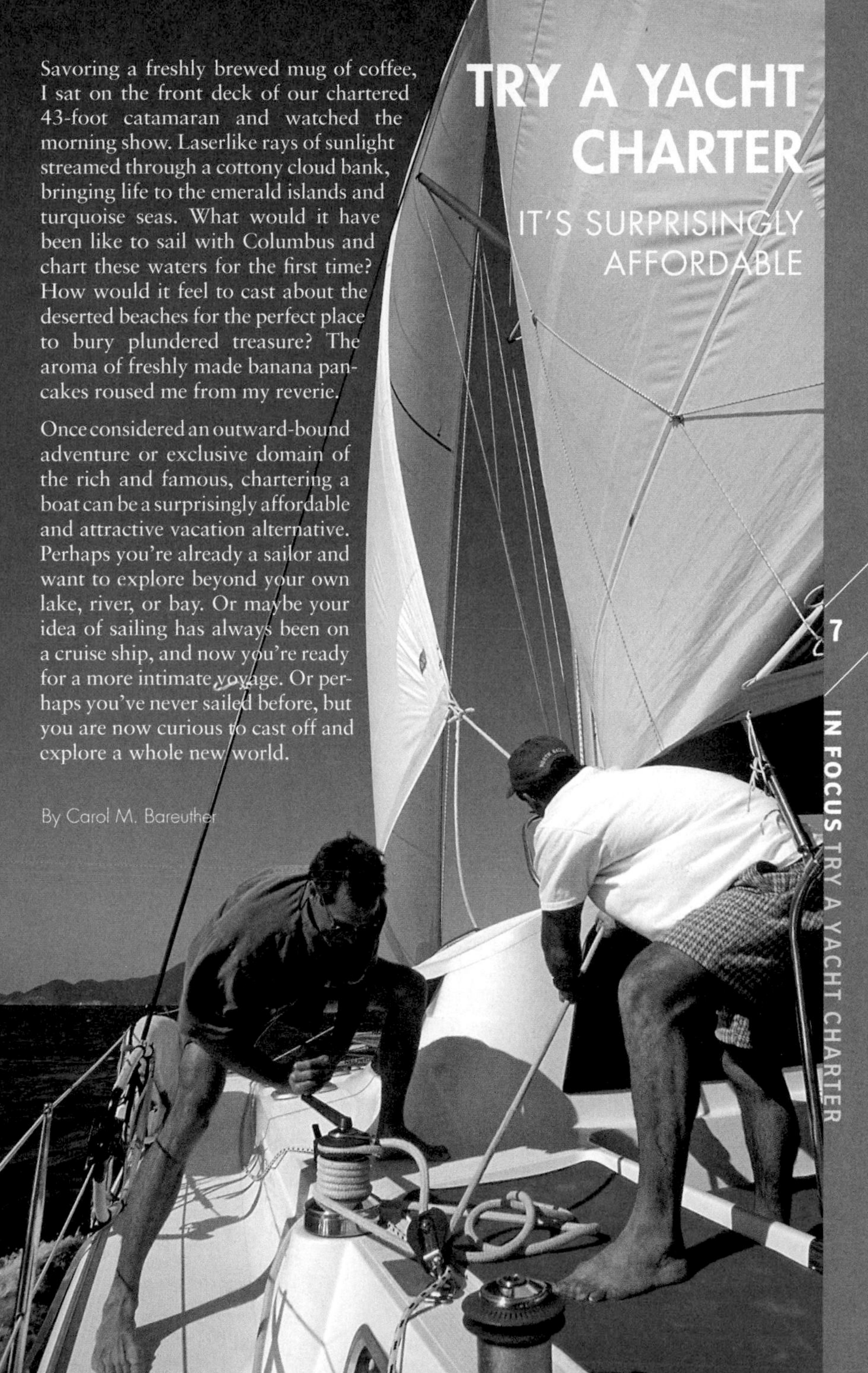

TRY A YACHT CHARTER

IT'S SURPRISINGLY AFFORDABLE

Savoring a freshly brewed mug of coffee, I sat on the front deck of our chartered 43-foot catamaran and watched the morning show. Laserlike rays of sunlight streamed through a cottony cloud bank, bringing life to the emerald islands and turquoise seas. What would it have been like to sail with Columbus and chart these waters for the first time? How would it feel to cast about the deserted beaches for the perfect place to bury plundered treasure? The aroma of freshly made banana pancakes roused me from my reverie.

Once considered an outward-bound adventure or exclusive domain of the rich and famous, chartering a boat can be a surprisingly affordable and attractive vacation alternative. Perhaps you're already a sailor and want to explore beyond your own lake, river, or bay. Or maybe your idea of sailing has always been on a cruise ship, and now you're ready for a more intimate voyage. Or perhaps you've never sailed before, but you are now curious to cast off and explore a whole new world.

By Carol M. Bareuther

CREWED CHARTER

On a crewed charter, you sit back and relax while the crew provides for your every want and need. Captains are licensed by the U.S. Coast Guard or the equivalent in the British maritime system. Cooks—preferring to be called chefs—have skills that go far beyond peanut butter and jelly sandwiches. There are four meals a day, and many chefs boast certificates from culinary schools ranging from the Culinary Institute of America in New York to the Cordon Bleu in Paris.

The advantage of a crewed yacht charter, with captain and cook, is that it takes every bit of stress out of the vacation. With a captain who knows the local waters, you get to see some of the coves and anchorages that are not necessarily in the guidebooks. Your meals are prepared, cabins cleaned, beds made up every day—and turned down at night, too. Plus, you can sail and take the helm as often as you like. But at the end of the day, the captain is the one who will take responsibility for anchoring safely for the night while the chef goes below and whips up a gourmet meal.

APPROXIMATE COSTS

From $4,300 for 2 people for 5 days

From $5,500 for 2 people for 7 days

From $8,600 for 6 people for 5 days

From $10,500 for 6 people for 7 days

Prices are all-inclusive for a 50- to 55-foot yacht in high season except for 15%–20% gratuity.

PROS

- Passengers just have to lay back and relax (unless they want to help sail)
- Most are catamarans, offering more space than monohulls
- You have an experienced, local hand on board if something goes wrong
- Water toys and other extras are often included
- Competively priced within an all-inclusive resort

CONS

- More expensive than a bareboat, especially if you get a catamaran
- Less privacy for your group than on a bareboat
- Captain makes ultimate decisions about the course
- Chance for personality conflicts: you have to get along with the captain and chef. This is where a charter yacht broker is helpful in determining what yachts and crews might be a good fit.

(top) Family sailing in the British Virgin Islands

BAREBOAT

If you'd like to bareboat, don't be intimidated. It's a myth that you must be a graduate of a sailing school in order to pilot your own charter boat. A bareboat company will ask you to fill out a resume. The company checks for prior boat-handling experience, the type of craft you've sailed (whether powerboat or sailboat), and in what type of waters. Real-life experience, meaning all those day and weekend trips close to home, count as valuable know-how. If you've done a bit of boating, you may be more qualified than you think to take out a bareboat.

Costs can be very similar for a bareboat and crewed charter, depending on the time of year and size of the boat. You'll pay the highest rates between Christmas and New Year's, when you may not be allowed to do a charter of less than a week. But there are more than 800 bareboats between the USVI and BVI, so regardless of your budget, you should be able to find something in your price range. Plus, you might save a bit by chartering an older boat from a smaller company instead of the most state-of-the-art yacht from a larger company.

APPROXIMATE COSTS

From $3,200 for a small monohull (2–3 cabins)

From $5,200 for a large monohull (4–5 cabins)

From $5,500 for a small catamaran (2 cabins)

From $7,500 for a large catamaran (4 cabins)

Prices exclude food, beverages, fuel, and other supplies. Most bareboat rates do not include water toys, taxes, insurance, and permits.

PROS

- The ultimate freedom to set the yacht's course
- A chance to test your sailing skills
- Usually a broader range of boats and prices to choose from
- More flexibility for meals (you can always go ashore if you don't feel like cooking)
- You can always hire a captain for a few days

CONS

- Must be able to pass a sailing test
- Those unfamiliar with the region may not find the best anchorages
- You have to cook for and clean up after yourself
- You have to do your own provisioning and planning for meals
- If something goes wrong, there isn't an experienced hand onboard

Three women rigging the sails.

WHAT TO CONSIDER

Whether bareboat or a crewed yacht, there are a few points to ponder when selecting your boat.

HOW BIG IS YOUR GROUP?

As a general rule, count on one cabin for every two people. Most people also prefer to have one head (bathroom) per cabin. A multihull, also called a catamaran, offers more space and more equal-size cabins than a monohull sailboat.

WHAT TYPE OF BOAT?

If you want to do some good old traditional sailing, where you're heeling over with the seas at your rails, monohulls are a good option. On the other hand, multihulls are more stable, easier to board, and have a big salon for families. They're also ideal if some people get seasick or aren't as gung-ho for the more traditional sailing experience. If you'd like to cover more ground, choose a motor yacht.

DO YOU HAVE A SPECIAL INTEREST?

Some crewed charter boats specialize in certain types of charters. Among these are learn-to-sail excursions, honeymoon cruises, scuba-diving adventures, and family-friendly trips. Your broker can steer you to the boats that fit your specific needs.

WHAT KIND OF EQUIPMENT DO YOU WANT ONBOARD?

Most charter boats have satellite navigation systems and autopilots, as well as regulation safety gear, dinghies with motors, and even stereos and entertainment systems. But do you want a generator or battery-drive refrigeration system? How about a/c? Do you want a satellite phone? Do you want water toys like kayaks, boogie boards, and Windsurfers?

Now that you've decided on bareboat versus crewed charter and selected your craft, all you need to do is confirm the availability of the date with the company or broker and pay a nonrefundable deposit equal to 50% of the charter price.

TO SAIL OR NOT TO SAIL?

If you're not sure whether a charter yacht vacation is right for you, consider this: would you enjoy a floating hotel room where the scenery outside your window changed according to your desires? A "yes" may entice wary companions to try chartering. A single one-week trip will have them hooked.

Two catamaran sailboats seen from behind.

CATAMARANS
Multihulls are more stable, easier to board and have a big salon for families. Seasickness is less of an issue.
MOTOR YACHT
Best if you want to cover more ground, but costs a lot more than a sailboat.
MONOHULLS
Good for more traditional and active sailing, but the movement may not appeal to non-sailors.

CHOOSING A CHARTER

Information on charters is much easier to find now than even a decade ago. Websites for bareboat companies show photos of different types of boats—both interiors and exteriors—as well as layout schematics, lists of equipment and amenities, and sample itineraries. Many sites will allow you to book a charter directly, while others give you the option of calling a toll-free number to speak with an agent first.

There are two types of websites for crewed charters. If you just want some information, the **Virgin Islands Charteryacht League** (🌐 *www.vicl.org*) and the **Charter Yacht Society of the British Virgin Islands** (🌐 *www.bvicrewedyachts.com*) both help you understand what to look for in a crewed charter, from the size of the boat to the amenities. You can't reserve on these sites, but they link to the sites of brokers, who are the sales force for the charter yacht industry. Most brokers, whether they're based in the Caribbean, the United States, or Europe, attend annual charter yacht shows in St. Thomas, Tortola, and Antigua. At these shows, brokers visit the boats and meet the crews. This is what gives brokers their depth of knowledge for "matchmaking," or linking you with a boat that will meet your personality and preferences.

The charter companies also maintain websites. About 30% of the crewed charter yachts based out of the U.S. and British Virgin Islands can be booked directly. This saves the commission an owner has to pay to the broker. But while "going direct" might seem advantageous, there is usually little difference in pricing, and if you use a broker, he or she can help troubleshoot if something goes wrong or find a replacement boat if the boat owner has to cancel.

Timing also matters. Companies may offer last-minute specials that are available only online. These special rates—usually for specific dates, destinations, and boats—are updated weekly or even daily.

PREPARING FOR YOUR CHARTER

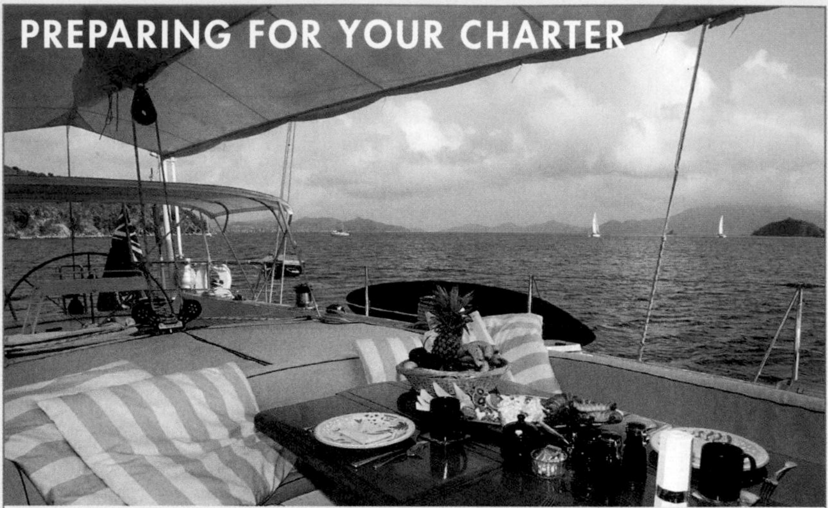

British Virgin Islands—anchorage in a tropical sea with breakfast on board.

PROVISIONING

Bareboaters must do their own provisioning. It's a good idea to arrange provisioning at least a week in advance.

Provisioning packages from the charter company are usually a bit more expensive, at $30 to $35 per person per day, but they save you the hassle of planning the details. You can also shop on arrival. Both St. Thomas and Tortola have markets, though larger grocery stores may require a taxi ride. If you shop carefully, this route can still save you money. Just be sure to allow yourself a few hours after arrival to get everything done.

PLANNING

For a crewed charter, your broker will send a preference sheet for both food and your wishes for the trip. Perhaps you'd like lazy days of sleeping late, sunning, and swimming. Or you might prefer active days of sailing with stops for snorkeling and exploring ashore. If there's a special spot you'd like to visit, list it so your captain can plan the itinerary accordingly.

PACKING TIPS

Pack light for any type of charter. Bring soft-sided luggage (preferably a duffle bag) since space is limited and storage spots are usually odd shapes. Shorts, T-shirts, and swimsuits are sufficient. Bring something a bit nicer if you plan to dine ashore. Shoes are seldom required except ashore, but you might want beach shoes to protect your feet in the water. Most boats provide snorkel equipment, but always ask. Bring sunscreen, but a type that will not stain cockpit cushions and decks.

WHAT YOU'LL SEE IN THE USBVI

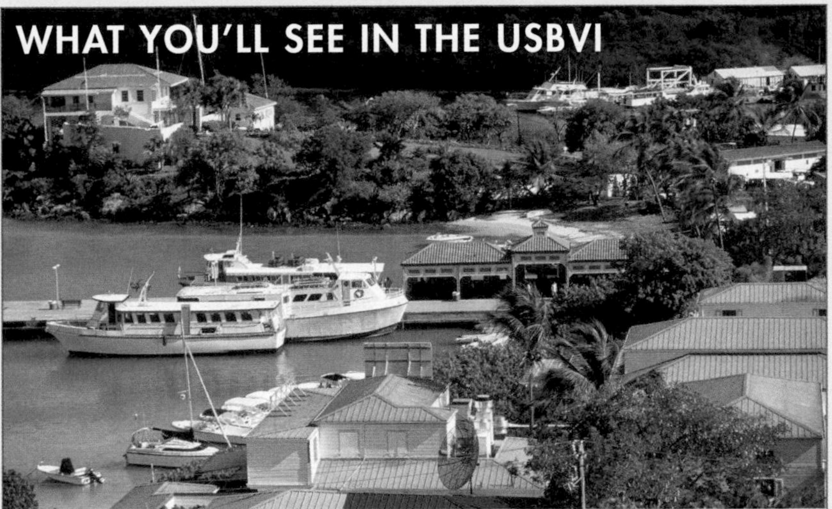

Cruz Bay in St. John

MAIN CHARTER BASES

The U.S. and British Virgin Islands boast more than 100 stepping-stone islands and cays within a 50-nautical-mile radius. This means easy line-of-sight navigation and island-hopping in protected waters, and it's rare that you'll spend more than a few hours moving between islands.

Tortola, in the British Virgin Islands, is the crewed charter and bareboat mecca of the Caribbean. This fact is plainly apparent from the forest of masts rising out from any marina.

The U.S. Virgin Islands fleet is based in **St. Thomas.** Direct flights from the mainland, luxurious accommodations, and duty-free shopping are drawing cards for departures from the U.S. Virgin Islands, whereas the British Virgins are closer to the prime cruising grounds.

POPULAR ANCHORAGES

On a typical weeklong charter you could set sail from Red Hook, St. Thomas, then cross Pillsbury Sound to St. John, which offers popular north-shore anchorages in Honeymoon, Trunk, or Francis bays. But the best sailing and snorkeling always includes the British Virgin Islands (which require a valid passport or passport card). After clearing customs in West End, Tortola, many yachts hop along a series of smaller islands that run along the south side of the Sir Francis Drake Channel. But some yachts will also visit Guana Island, Great Camanoe, or Marina Cay off Tortola's more isolated east end.

The islands south of Tortola include **Norman Island,** the rumored site of Robert Lewis Stevenson's *Treasure Island*. The next island over is **Peter Island,** famous for it's posh resort and a popular anchorage for yachters. Farther east, off Salt Island, is the wreck of the **RMS *Rhone***—the most magnificent dive site in the eastern Caribbean. Giant boulders form caves and grottos called The Baths at the southern end of **Virgin Gorda.**

A downwind run along Tortola's north shore ends at **Jost Van Dyke,** where that famous guitar-strumming calypsonian Foxy Callwood sings personalized ditties that make for a memorable finale.

WHERE TO STAY

$ HOTEL **Pusser's Marina Cay Hotel and Restaurant.** If getting away from it all is your priority, this may be the place for you, because there's nothing to do on this beach-rimmed island other than swim, snorkel, and soak up the sun—there's not even a TV to distract you. **Pros:** lots of character; beautiful beaches; interesting guests. **Cons:** older property; ferry needed to get here. *Rooms from: $175* *West side of Marina Cay* *284/494–2174* *www.pussers.com* *4 rooms, 2 2-bedroom villas* *Breakfast.*

$$$$ RESORT Fodor's Choice ★ **Scrub Island Resort, Spa and Marina.** Part of Marriott's Autograph Collection, this swanky resort is located on a 250-acre island near Tortola's Beef Island Airport. **Pros:** new property; lots of activities. **Cons:** need ferry to get there; expensive. *Rooms from: $480* *Scrub Island* *877/890–7444, 284/394–3440* *www.scrubisland.com* *52 rooms, 7 villas* *No meals.*

PETER ISLAND

Although Peter Island is home to the resort of the same name, it's also a popular anchorage for charter boaters and a destination for Tortola vacationers. The scheduled ferry trip from Peter Island's shore-side base outside Road Town runs $15 round-trip for nonguests. The island is lush, with forested hillsides sloping seaward to meet white sandy beaches. There are no roads other than those at the resort, and there's nothing to do but relax at the lovely beach set aside for day-trippers. You're welcome to dine at the resort's restaurants.

WHERE TO STAY

$$$$ RESORT Fodor's Choice ★ **Peter Island Resort & Spa.** Total pampering and prices to match are the ticket at this luxury resort. **Pros:** lovely rooms; nice beach. **Cons:** need ferry to get here; pricey rates. *Rooms from: $800* *284/495–2000, 800/346–4451* *www.peterisland.com* *52 rooms, 3 villas* *Multiple meal plans.*

VIRGIN GORDA

Virgin Gorda, or "Fat Virgin," received its name from Christopher Columbus. The explorer envisioned the island as a pregnant woman in a languid recline, with Gorda Peak being her big belly and the boulders of The Baths her toes. Different in topography from Tortola, with its arid landscape covered with scrub brush and cactus, Virgin Gorda has a slower pace of life, too. Goats and cattle own the right-of-way, and the unpretentious friendliness of the people is winning.

EXPLORING

One of the most efficient ways to see Virgin Gorda is by sailboat. There are few roads, and most byways don't follow the scalloped shoreline. The main route sticks resolutely to the center of the island, linking The Baths on the southern tip with Gun Creek and Leverick Bay at North Sound. The craggy coast, cut through with grottoes and fringed by palms and boulders, has a primitive beauty. If you drive, you can hit all the sights in one day. The best plan is to explore the area near your

The Baths

hotel (either Spanish Town or North Sound) first, then take a day to drive to the other end. Stop to climb Gorda Peak, which is in the island's center. There are few signs, so come prepared with a map.

THE VALLEY

TOP ATTRACTIONS

FAMILY Fodor's Choice ★ **The Baths National Park.** At Virgin Gorda's most celebrated sight, giant boulders are scattered about the beach and in the water. Some are almost as large as houses and form remarkable grottoes. Climb between these rocks to swim in the many placid pools. Early morning and late afternoon are the best times to visit if you want to avoid crowds. If it's privacy you crave, follow the shore northward to quieter bays—Spring Bay, the Crawl, Little Trunk, and Valley Trunk—or head south to Devil's Bay. ✉ *Off Tower Rd., The Valley* ☎ *284/852–3650* 🌐 *www.bvinationalparkstrust.org* 🎫 *$3* ⏲ *Daily dawn–dusk.*

WORTH NOTING

Copper Mine Point. A tall stone shaft silhouetted against the sky and a small stone structure that overlooks the sea are part of what was once a copper mine, now in ruins. Established 400 years ago, it was worked first by the Spanish, then by the English, until the early 20th century. The route is not well marked, so turn inland near LSL Restaurant and look for the hard-to-see sign pointing the way. ✉ *Copper Mine Rd., The Valley* 🌐 *www.bvinpt.org* 🎫 *Free.*

Spanish Town. Virgin Gorda's peaceful main settlement, on the island's southern wing, is so tiny that it barely qualifies as a town at all. Also known as The Valley, Spanish Town has a marina, some shops, and a couple of car-rental agencies. Just north of town is the ferry slip. At the

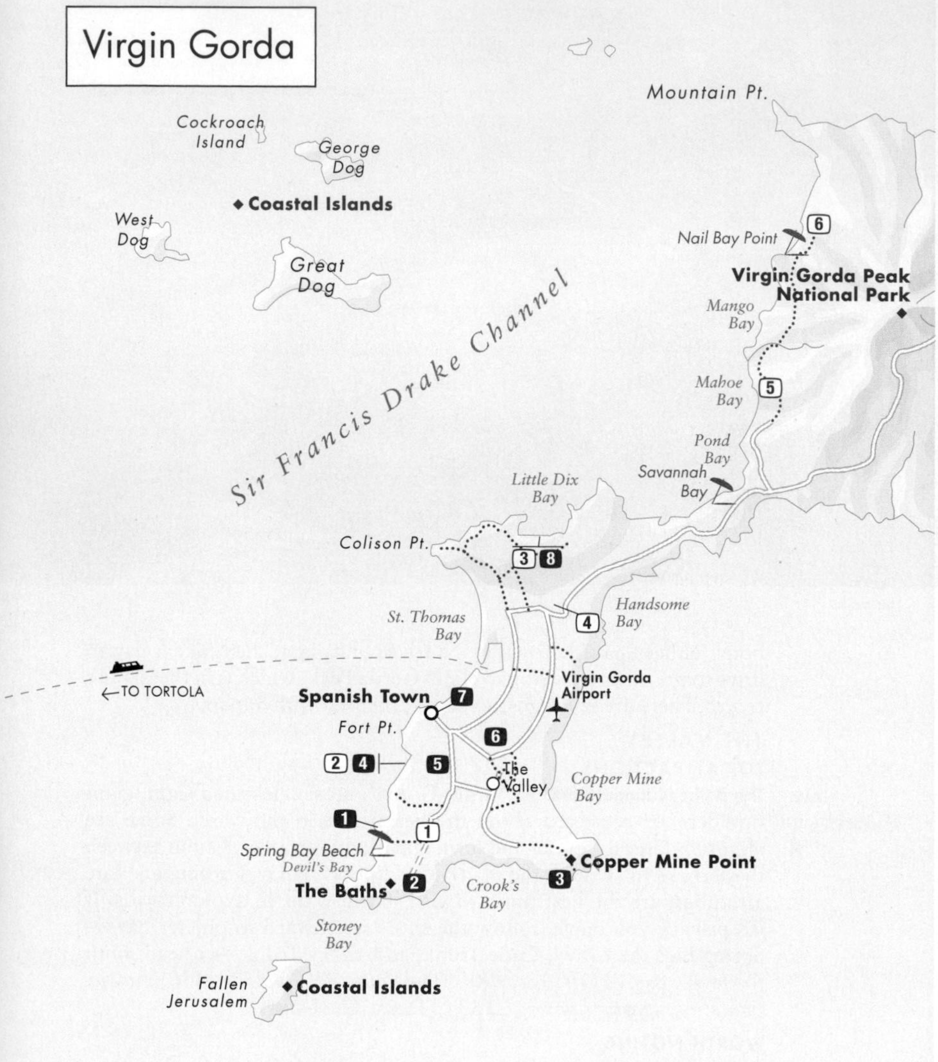

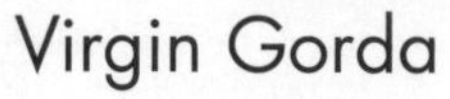

Restaurants ▼

- Bath and Turtle 7
- Biras Creek 11
- Chez Bamboo 6
- The Clubhouse 12
- Fat Virgin's Cafe 10
- Fischer's Cove Restaurant .. 4
- Little Dix Bay Pavilion 8
- LSL Bake Shop & Restaurant 5
- Mine Shaft Café 3
- Restaurant at Leverick Bay 9
- The Rock Café 1
- Top of the Baths 2

Hotels ▼

- Biras Creek Resort 10
- Bitter End Yacht Club 9
- Fischer's Cove Beach Hotel 2
- Guavaberry Spring Bay Vacation Homes 1
- Leverick Bay Resort & Marina 7
- Mango Bay Resort 5
- Nail Bay Resort 6
- Rosewood Little Dix Bay ... 3
- Saba Rock Resort 8
- Virgin Gorda Village 4

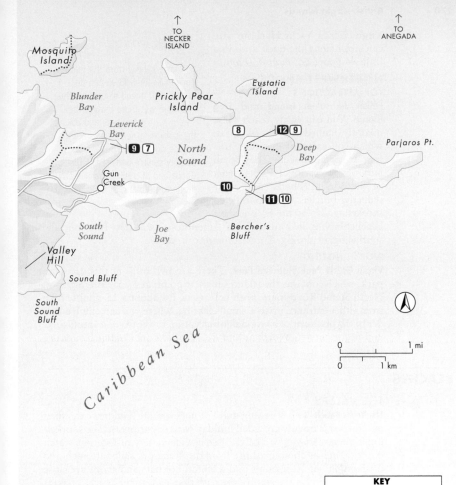

TO NECKER ISLAND

TO ANEGADA

Mosquito Island

Blunder Bay

Prickly Pear Island

Eustatia Island

Leverick Bay

9 7

North Sound

8

12 9

Deep Bay

Parjaros Pt.

Gun Creek

10

11 10

South Sound

Joe Bay

Bercher's Bluff

Valley Hill

Sound Bluff

South Sound Bluff

Caribbean Sea

0 1 mi

0 1 km

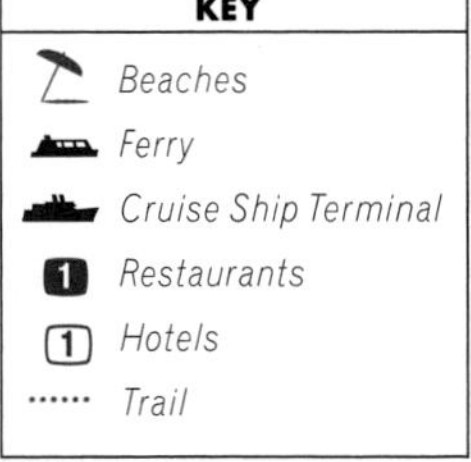

Virgin Gorda Yacht Harbour you can stroll along the dock and do a little shopping. ✉ *Spanish Town.*

VIRGIN GORDA FERRIES

The ferry service from the public dock in Spanish Town can be erratic. Call ahead to confirm the schedule, get there early to be sure it hasn't changed, and ask at the dock whether you're getting on the right boat. Thursday and Sunday service between Virgin Gorda and St. John is particularly prone to problems.

NORTHWEST SHORE

TOP ATTRACTIONS

Fallen Jerusalem Island and Dog Islands. You can easily reach these quaintly named islands by boat, which you can rent in either Tortola or Virgin Gorda. They're all part of the National Parks Trust of the Virgin Islands, and their seductive beaches and unparalleled snorkeling display the BVI at their beachcombing, hedonistic best. **Amenities:** none. **Best for:** solitude; snorkeling; exploring. 🌐 *www.bvinpt.org* 🎫 *Free.*

WORTH NOTING

Virgin Gorda Peak National Park. There are two trails at this 265-acre park, which contains the island's highest point, at 1,359 feet. Signs on North Sound Road mark both entrances. It's about a 15-minute hike from either entrance up to a small clearing, where you can climb a ladder to the platform of a wooden observation tower to see a spectacular 360-degree view. ✉ *North Sound Rd., Gorda Peak* 🌐 *www.bvinpt.org* 🎫 *Free.*

BEACHES

THE VALLEY

The Baths Beach. This stunning maze of huge granite boulders extending into the sea is usually crowded midday with day-trippers. The snorkeling is good, and you're likely to see a wide variety of fish, but watch out for dinghies coming ashore from the numerous sailboats anchored offshore. Public bathrooms and a handful of bars and shops are close to the water and at the start of the path that leads to the beach. Lockers are available to keep belongings safe. **Amenities:** food and drink; parking; toilets. **Best for:** snorkeling; swimming. ✉ *Tower Rd., about 1 mile (1½ km) west of Spanish Town ferry dock, The Valley* ☎ *284/852–3650* 🌐 *www.bvinpt.org* 🎫 *$3* 🕓 *Daily dawn–dusk.*

Spring Bay Beach. This national-park beach gets much less traffic than the nearby Baths, and has the similarly large, imposing boulders that create interesting grottoes for swimming. It also has no admission fee, unlike the more popular Baths. The snorkeling is excellent, and the grounds include swings and picnic tables. Guavaberry Spring Bay Vacation has villas and cottages right near the beach. **Amenities:** none. **Best for:** snorkeling; swimming. ✉ *The Valley* ☎ *284/852–3650* 🌐 *www.bvinpt.org* 🎫 *Free* 🕓 *Daily dawn–dusk.*

NORTHWEST SHORE

Nail Bay Beach. At the island's north tip, the three beaches at Nail Bay Resort are ideal for snorkeling. Mountain Trunk Bay is perfect for beginners, and Nail Bay and Long Bay beaches have coral caverns just offshore. The resort has a restaurant, which is an uphill walk but perfect for beach breaks. **Amenities:** food and drink; toilets. **Best for:** snorkeling; swimming. ✉ *Nail Bay Resort, off Plum Tree Bay Rd., Nail Bay* 🎫 *Free* ⏲ *Daily dawn–dusk.*

Savannah Bay Beach. This is a wonderfully private beach close to Spanish Town. It may not always be completely deserted, but you can find a spot to yourself on this long stretch of soft, white sand. Bring your own mask, fins, and snorkel, as there are no facilities. Villas are available through rental property agencies. The view from above is a photographer's delight. **Amenities:** none. **Best for:** solitude; snorkeling; swimming. ✉ *Off N. Sound Rd., ¾ mile (1¼ km) east of Spanish Town ferry dock, Savannah Bay* 🎫 *Free* ⏲ *Daily dawn–dusk.*

WHERE TO EAT

Most folks opt to have dinner somewhere at or near their hotel to avoid driving on Virgin Gorda's twisting roads at night. The Valley does have a handful of restaurants if you're sleeping close to town.

7

THE VALLEY

$$ ECLECTIC ✕ **Bath and Turtle.** You can sit back and relax at this informal tavern with a friendly staff (or enjoy the outdoor Rendezvous Bar on the waterfront), although the noise from the television can sometimes be a bit much. Well-stuffed sandwiches, homemade pizzas, pasta dishes, and daily specials such as conch soup round out the casual menu. Local musicians perform many Wednesday and Sunday nights. [$] *Average main: $19* ✉ *Virgin Gorda Yacht Harbour, Lee Rd., Spanish Town* ☎ *284/495–5239* 🌐 *www.bathandturtle.com.*

$$$ ECLECTIC ✕ **Chez Bamboo.** This pleasant little hideaway isn't difficult to find; look for the building with bamboo fencing. Candles in the dining room and on the patio help make this a mellow place where you can enjoy a bowl of lobster bisque, something from the tapas menu, or one of the specialties such as lobster curry. For dessert, try the chocolate cake or crème brûlée. Stop by Friday night for live music. [$] *Average main: $29* ✉ *Lee Rd., Spanish Town* ☎ *284/495–5752* 🌐 *www.chezbamboo.com.*

$$$$ ECLECTIC ✕ **Fischer's Cove Restaurant.** Dine seaside at this alfresco restaurant that's open to the breezes. If pumpkin soup is on the menu, give it a try for a true taste of the Caribbean. Although you can get burgers and salads at lunch, local fish (whatever is available) and *fungi* (a cornmeal-based side dish) are tasty alternatives. For dinner, try the Caribbean lobster or grilled mahimahi with lemon and garlic. [$] *Average main: $36* ✉ *Lee Rd., The Valley* ☎ *284/495–5252* 🌐 *www.fischerscove.com.*

$$$$ INTERNATIONAL ✕ **Little Dix Bay Pavilion.** For an elegant evening, you can't do better than this—the candlelight in the open-air pavilion is enchanting, the always-changing menu sophisticated, the service attentive. Superbly prepared seafood, meat, and vegetarian entrées draw locals and visitors alike. Favorites include a Cajun pork loin with mango salsa and

scallion potatoes, and mahimahi with warm chorizo and chickpea salad served with a zucchini-and-tomato chutney. The Monday evening buffet shines. *Average main: $33 Little Dix Bay Resort, Off Little Rd., Spanish Town 284/495–5555 www.littledixbay.com Reservations essential.*

$$ ECLECTIC **LSL Bake Shop & Restaurant.** Along the road to The Baths, this small restaurant with pedestrian decor is a local favorite. You can always find fresh fish on the menu, but folks with a taste for other dishes won't be disappointed. Try the pork tenderloin pesto with herb potatoes and a peppercorn sauce, or the banana curry shrimp with a coconut milk sauce. *Average main: $15 Tower Rd., The Valley 284/495–5151.*

$$ ECLECTIC **Mine Shaft Café.** Perched on a hilltop that offers a view of spectacular sunsets, this restaurant near Copper Mine Point serves simple, well-prepared food, including grilled fish, steaks, and baby back ribs. Tuesday night features an all-you-can-eat Caribbean-style barbecue. The monthly full-moon parties draw a big local crowd. *Average main: $20 Near Copper Mine Point, The Valley 284/495–5260.*

$$$$ ITALIAN **The Rock Café.** Good Italian cuisine and seafood is served among the waterfalls and giant boulders that form the famous Baths. For dinner at this open-air eatery, feast on saffron lobster pasta or fresh red snapper with a creamy risotto. For dessert, don't miss the chocolate mousse. *Average main: $39 Tower Rd., The Valley 284/495–5482 www.bvidining.com No lunch.*

$$$ ECLECTIC FAMILY **Top of the Baths.** At the entrance to The Baths, this popular restaurant has tables on an outdoor terrace or in an open-air pavilion; all have stunning views of the Sir Francis Drake Channel. The restaurant starts serving at 8 am; for lunch, hamburgers, coconut chicken sandwiches, and fish-and-chips are among the offerings. Sushi was recently added to the menu. For dessert, the key lime pie is excellent. The Sunday barbecue, served from noon until 3 pm, is an island event. *Average main: $23 The Valley 284/495–5497 www.topofthebaths.com.*

$$$ ECLECTIC **The Village Cafe and Restaurant.** Meals are served poolside under the shade of umbrellas at this casual eatery. The lunch menu includes salads, wraps, and burgers, but the lobster-and-crab salad (yes, it contains both!) is a must-have. A new dinner menu includes fish, chicken, and pork offerings with island spices. *Average main: $27 Virgin Gorda Village, North Sound Rd., The Valley 284/495–5350 Closed Mon.*

NORTH SOUND

$$$$ INTERNATIONAL **Biras Creek Restaurant.** This hilltop restaurant at the Biras Creek Hotel has eye-popping views of North Sound. For starters, there may be an artichoke, green bean, and wild mushroom salad topped with balsamic vinaigrette, or cream of sweet potato soup accompanied by potato straws. Entrées may include pan-seared snapper over horseradish pearl pasta. The desserts, including a lemon ricotta cheesecake with a spicy passion-fruit sauce, are stupendous. The restaurant also offers a fixed-price four-course meal that ends with Biras Creek's signature offering of cheese and port. Most days, lunch is a barbecue on the beach. *Average main: $37 Biras Creek Hotel, North Sound 284/494–3555 www.biras.com Reservations essential.*

$$$ ECLECTIC ✕ **The Clubhouse.** The Bitter End Yacht Club's open-air waterfront restaurant is a favorite rendezvous for sailors and their guests, so it's busy day and night. You can find lavish buffets for breakfast, lunch, and dinner, as well as an à la carte menu. Dinner selections include grilled mahimahi or tuna, local lobster, and porterhouse steak, as well as vegetarian dishes. *Average main: $29 ✉ Bitter End Yacht Club, North Sound ☎ 284/494–2745 🌐 www.beyc.com ✍ Reservations essential.*

$$$ ECLECTIC FAMILY ✕ **Fat Virgin's Café.** This casual beachfront eatery offers a straightforward menu of baby back ribs, chicken roti, vegetable pasta, grouper sandwiches, and fresh fish specials for lunch and dinner. You can also find a good selection of Caribbean beer. *Average main: $23 ✉ Biras Creek Resort, North Sound ☎ 284/495–7052 🌐 www.fatvirgin.com.*

$$$ ECLECTIC ✕ **Restaurant at Leverick Bay.** The laid-back menu at this beach restaurant draws cruise-ship passengers on tour as well as hotels guests and locals. The menu includes burgers, pizza, roti, chili, and fish-and-chips for lunch. Upstairs, there's an upscale restaurant that serves dinner with dishes that feature wild salmon and Anegada lobster. *Average main: $25 ✉ Leverick Bay Resort & Marina, Leverick Bay Rd., Leverick Bay ☎ 284/340–3005 🌐 www.leverickrestaurant.com.*

WORD OF MOUTH

"The Baths are incredible, especially since you'll be able to go when the cruise ships aren't there. First thing in the morning or later in the day is just perfect! We really enjoyed taking the ferries to both Saba Rock and the Bitter End for lunches. We wanted to rent a little dinghy to do a little exploring on our own from Leverick, but it was always too windy in February. Your daughter might enjoy the Friday night barbecue buffet and dancing with the [Moko Jumbie stilt dancers] at Leverick Bay, too!"

—Jayneann

WHERE TO STAY

Villas are scattered all over Virgin Gorda, but hotels are centered in and around The Valley, Nail Bay, and in the North Sound area. Except for Leverick Bay Resort, which is around the point from North Sound, all hotels in North Sound are reached only by ferry.

PRIVATE VILLAS

Those craving seclusion would do well at a villa. Most have full kitchens and maid service. Prices per week in winter run from around $2,000 for a one- or two-bedroom villa up to $10,000 for a five-room beachfront villa. Rates in summer are substantially less. On Virgin Gorda a villa in the North Sound area means you can pretty much stay put at night unless you want to make the drive on its narrow roads. If you opt for a spot near The Baths, it's an easier drive to town.

VILLA RENTAL AGENTS

McLaughlin-Anderson Luxury Villas. The St. Thomas–based McLaughlin-Anderson Luxury Villas represents about 15 properties all over Virgin Gorda. Villas range in size from one bedroom to five bedrooms, and come with full kitchens, pools, stellar views, and other amenities. The company can hire a chef and stock your kitchen with groceries. A seven-night minimum is required during the winter season. ☎ *340/776–0635, 800/537–6246* 🌐 *www.mclaughlinanderson.com.*

Villas Virgin Gorda. This management company's dozen properties stretch from The Baths to the Nail Bay area. Several budget properties are included among the pricier offerings. Most houses have private pools, and a few are right on the beach. A sister company at the same number, Tropical Nannies, provides babysitting services. ☎ *284/495–6493* 🌐 *www.villasvirgingorda.com.*

Virgin Gorda Villa Rentals. This company's 40 or so properties are all near Leverick Bay Resort and Mahoe Bay, so they are perfect for those who want to be close to activities. Many of the accommodations—from studios to six or more bedrooms—have private swimming pools and air-conditioning, at least in the bedrooms. All have full kitchens, are well maintained, and have spectacular views. ☎ *284/495–7421, 800/848–7081* 🌐 *www.virgingordabvi.com.*

THE VALLEY

$ RESORT **Fischer's Cove Beach Hotel.** The rooms are modest, the furniture is discount-store-style, and the walls are thin, but you can't beat the location right on the beach and within walking distance of Spanish Town's shops and restaurants. **Pros:** beachfront location; budget price; good restaurant. **Cons:** very basic units; thin walls; no air-conditioning in some rooms. *Rooms from: $145* ✉ *Lee Rd., The Valley* ☎ *284/495–5252* 🌐 *www.fischerscove.com* *12 rooms, 8 cottages* *No meals.*

$ RENTAL **Guavaberry Spring Bay Vacation Homes.** Rambling back from the beach, these hexagonal one- and two-bedroom villas give you all the comforts of home—and that striking boulder-fringed beach is just minutes away. **Pros:** short walk to The Baths (and excellent snorkeling); easy drive to town; great beaches nearby. **Cons:** few amenities; older property; basic decor. *Rooms from: $255* ✉ *Tower Rd., The Valley* ☎ *284/495–5227* 🌐 *www.guavaberryspringbay.com* *12 1-bedroom units, 6 2-bedroom units, 1 3-bedroom unit, 16 villas* *No credit cards* *No meals.*

$$$ RESORT FAMILY **Rosewood Little Dix Bay.** This laid-back luxury resort offers a gorgeous crescent of sand, plenty of activities, and good restaurants. **Pros:** convenient location; lovely grounds; near many restaurants. **Cons:** expensive; very spread out; insular though not isolated. *Rooms from: $405* ✉ *Off Little Rd., The Valley* ☎ *284/495–5555* 🌐 *www.littledixbay.com* *78 rooms, 20 suites, 7 villas* *No meals.*

$ RENTAL **Virgin Gorda Village.** All the condos in this upscale complex a few minutes' drive from Spanish Town have at least partial ocean views. **Pros:** close to Spanish Town; lovely pool; recently built units. **Cons:** no beach; on a busy street; some noisy roosters nearby. *Rooms from: $250* ✉ *North Sound Rd.* ☎ *284/495–5544* 🌐 *www.virgingordavillage.com* *30 condos* *No meals.*

NORTHWEST SHORE

$ RENTAL **Mango Bay Resort.** Sitting seaside on Virgin Gorda's north coast, this collection of contemporary condos and villas will make you feel right at home. **Pros:** nice beach; lively location; easy drive to restaurants. **Cons:** drab decor; some units have lackluster views; need car to get around.

Rooms from: $195 ✉ *Plum Tree Bay Rd., Pond Bay* ☎ *284/495–5672* 🌐 *www.mangobayresort.com* *17 condos, 5 villas* *No meals.*

$ RESORT **Nail Bay Resort.** On a hill above the coast, this beachfront resort offers a wide selection of rooms and suites. **Pros:** full kitchens; lovely beach; close to town. **Cons:** busy neighborhood; bit of a drive from main road; uphill walk from beach. *Rooms from: $240* ✉ *Off Nail Bay Rd., Nail Bay* ☎ *284/494–8000, 800/871–3551* 🌐 *www.nailbay.com* *4 rooms, 4 suites, 2 apartments, 7 villas* *No meals.*

NORTH SOUND

$$$$ RESORT **Biras Creek Resort.** Tucked out of the way on the island's North Sound, Biras Creek has a get-away-from-it-all feel that's a major draw for its well-heeled clientele. **Pros:** luxurious rooms; professional staff; good dining options; private, white-sand beach. **Cons:** very expensive; isolated; difficult for people with mobility problems. *Rooms from: $790* ✉ *North Sound* ☎ *284/394–1000, 877/883–0756* 🌐 *www.biras.com* *31 suites* *Multiple meal plans.*

$$$$ ALL-INCLUSIVE FAMILY Fodor's Choice ★ **Bitter End Yacht Club.** Sailing's the thing at this busy hotel and marina in the nautically inclined North Sound, and the use of everything from small sailboats to kayaks to windsurfers is included in the price. **Pros:** lots of water sports; good diving opportunities; friendly guests. **Cons:** expensive rates; isolated; lots of stairs. *Rooms from: $646* ✉ *North Sound* ☎ *284/494–2746, 800/872–2392* 🌐 *www.beyc.com* *85 rooms* *All-inclusive.*

$ RESORT **Leverick Bay Resort and Marina.** With its colorful buildings and bustling marina, Leverick Bay is a good choice for visitors who want easy access to water-sports activities. **Pros:** fun location; good restaurant; small grocery store. **Cons:** small beach; no laundry in units; 15-minute drive to town. *Rooms from: $149* ✉ *Off Leverick Bay Rd., Leverick Bay* ☎ *284/495–7421, 800/848–7081* 🌐 *www.leverickbay.com* *13 rooms, 4 apartments* *No meals.*

$ RESORT **Saba Rock Resort.** Reachable only by a free ferry or by private yacht, this resort on its own tiny cay is perfect for folks who want to mix and mingle with the sailors who drop anchor for the night. **Pros:** party atmosphere; convenient transportation; good diving nearby. **Cons:** tiny beach; isolated location; on a very small island. *Rooms from: $150* ✉ *North Sound* ☎ *284/495–7711, 284/495–9966* 🌐 *www.sabarock.com* *7 1-bedroom suites, 1 2-bedroom suites* *Breakfast.*

NIGHTLIFE

Pick up a free copy of the *Limin' Times* (🌐 *www.limin-times.com*)—available at most resorts and restaurants—for the most current local entertainment schedule.

Bath and Turtle. During high season, the Bath and Turtle is one of the liveliest spots on Virgin Gorda, hosting island bands Wednesday and Sunday from 8 pm until midnight. ✉ *Virgin Gorda Yacht Harbour, Lee Rd., Spanish Town* ☎ *284/495–5239* 🌐 *www.bathandturtle.com.*

Chez Bamboo. This is the place for calypso and reggae on Tuesday and Friday nights. ✉ *Lee Rd., Spanish Town* ☎ *284/495–5752* 🌐 *www.chezbamboo.com.*

7

Mine Shaft Café. The café has music on Tuesday and Friday. ✉ *Near Copper Mine Point, The Valley* ☎ *284/495–5260* 🌐 *www.mineshaftbvi.com.*

Restaurant at Leverick Bay. This resort's main restaurant hosts music on Tuesday and Friday in season. ✉ *Leverick Bay Resort & Marina, Leverick Bay Rd., Leverick Bay* ☎ *284/340–3005* 🌐 *www.therestaurantatleverickbay.com.*

Rock Café. There's live piano music nearly every night during the Rock Café's winter season. ✉ *Lee Rd., The Valley* ☎ *284/495–5482* 🌐 *www.bvidining.com.*

VIRGIN GORDA GROCERIES

Virgin Gorda's grocery stores barely equal convenience stores elsewhere. The selection is small, and the prices are high. Many Virgin Gorda residents head to Tortola or even to St. Thomas to do their shopping. If you're coming here from another island, you might want to bring along a few items you know you'll need.

SHOPPING

Most boutiques are within hotel complexes or at Virgin Gorda Yacht Harbour. Two of the best are at Biras Creek and Little Dix Bay. Other properties—the Bitter End and Leverick Bay—have small but equally good boutiques.

FOOD

Bitter End Emporium. This store at the Bitter End is the place for local fruits, cheeses, baked goods, and gourmet prepared food. ✉ *Bitter End Yacht Harbor, North Sound* ☎ *284/494–2746* 🌐 *www.beyc.com.*

Buck's Food Market. This market is the closest the island offers to a full-service supermarket, with an in-store bakery and deli as well as fresh fish and produce departments. ✉ *Virgin Gorda Yacht Harbour, Lee Rd., Spanish Town* ☎ *284/495–5423* 🌐 *bucksfoodmarket.homestead.com.*

Chef's Pantry. This store has the fixings for an impromptu party in your villa or on your boat—fresh seafood, specialty meats, imported cheeses, daily baked breads and pastries, and an impressive wine and spirit selection. ✉ *Leverick Bay Marina, Leverick Bay Rd., Leverick Bay* ☎ *284/495–7677.*

Rosy's Supermarket. This store carries the basics plus an interesting selection of ready-to-cook meals, such as a whole seasoned chicken. ✉ *Rhymer Rd., The Valley* ☎ *284/495–5245* 🌐 *www.rosysenterprisesvg.com* ⏲ *Closed Sun.*

Virgin Gorda Cash & Carry. The store isn't much to look at, inside or out, but it has the best wine prices on Virgin Gorda, along with the usual basic supermarket items. ✉ *Lee Rd., Spanish Town* ☎ *284/347–1200.*

GIFTS

Allamanda Gallery. This shop showcases owner Amanda Baker's tropical photography, but it's also a good place to browse for cards, magnets, and other take-home gifts. ✉ *The Baths, Tower Rd., The Valley* ☎ *284/495–5935* 🌐 *www.virginportraits.com.*

Caribbean Too. While this cozy store sells T-shirts and other vacation necessities, it's also a great place to shop for tropical wear in linen and other comfortable fabrics. ✉ *The Baths, Tower Rd., The Valley* ☎ *284/495–6288.*

Reeftique. This store carries island crafts and jewelry, clothing, and nautical odds and ends with the Bitter End logo. ✉ *Bitter End Yacht Harbor, North Sound* ☎ *284/494–2746* 🌐 *www.beyc.com.*

Thee Nautical Gallery. This boutique sells attractive handcrafted jewelry, paintings, and one-of-a-kind gift items, as well as books about the Caribbean. ✉ *Leverick Bay Marina, Leverick Bay Rd., Leverick Bay* ☎ *284/495–7479.*

SPORTS AND THE OUTDOORS

DIVING AND SNORKELING

Where you go snorkeling and what company you pick depends on where you're staying. Many hotels have on-site dive outfitters, but if they don't, one won't be far away. If your hotel does have a dive operation, just stroll down to the dock and hop aboard—no need to drive anywhere. The dive companies are all certified by PADI. Costs vary, but count on paying about $75 for a one-tank dive and $110 for a two-tank dive. All dive operators offer introductory courses as well as certification and advanced courses. Should you get an attack of the bends, which can happen when you ascend too rapidly, the nearest decompression chamber is at Roy L. Schneider Regional Medical Center in St. Thomas.

There are some terrific snorkel and dive sites off Virgin Gorda, including areas around The Baths, the North Sound, and the Dogs. The Chimney at Great Dog Island has a coral archway and canyon covered with a wide variety of sponges. At Joe's Cave, an underwater cavern on West Dog Island, huge groupers, eagle rays, and other colorful fish accompany divers as they swim. At some sites you can see 100 feet down, but divers who don't want to go that deep and snorkelers will find plenty to look at just below the surface.

FAMILY **Bitter End Yacht Club.** The BEYC schedules two snorkeling trips a day. ✉ *North Sound* ☎ *284/494–2746* 🌐 *www.beyc.com* 💵 *From $15.*

Dive BVI. In addition to day trips, Dive BVI also offers expert instruction and certification. ✉ *Virgin Gorda Yacht Harbour, Lee Rd., Spanish Town* ☎ *284/495–5513, 800/848–7078* 🌐 *www.divebvi.com* ✉ *Leverick Bay Marina, Leverick Bay Rd., Leverick Bay* ☎ *284/495–7328, 800/848–7078* 🌐 *www.divebvi.com.*

Sunchaser Scuba. Resort, advanced, and rescue courses are all available here. ✉ *Bitter End Yacht Club, North Sound* ☎ *284/495–9638, 800/932–4286* 🌐 *www.sunchaserscuba.com.*

SAILING AND BOATING

The BVI waters are calm, and terrific places to learn to sail. You can also rent sea kayaks, waterskiing equipment, dinghies, and powerboats, or take a parasailing trip.

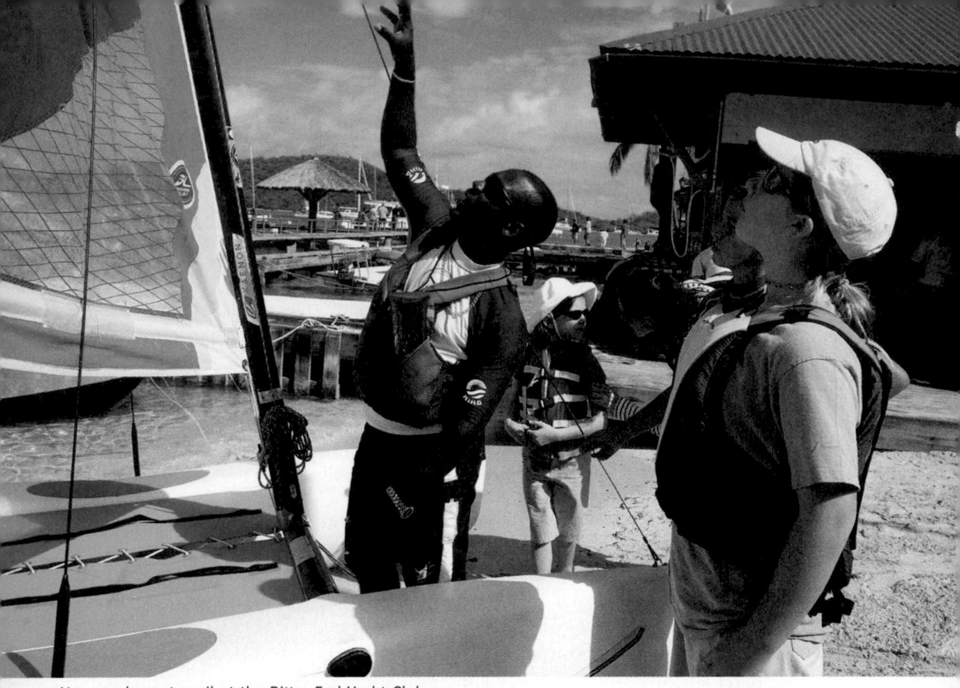

You can learn to sail at the Bitter End Yacht Club.

FAMILY **Bitter End Sailing School.** Classroom, dockside, and on-the-water lessons are available for sailors of all levels. Private lessons are $75 per hour. ✉ *Bitter End Yacht Club, North Sound* ☎ *284/494–2746* 🌐 *www.beyc.com.*

Double "D" Charters. If you just want to sit back, relax, and let the captain take the helm, choose a sailing or power yacht from Double "D" Charters. Rates run from $89 for a day trip. Private full-day cruises or sails for up to eight people run from $950. ✉ *Virgin Gorda Yacht Harbour, Lee Rd., Spanish Town* ☎ *284/499–2479* 🌐 *www.doubledbvi.com.*

JOST VAN DYKE

Named after an early Dutch settler, Jost Van Dyke is a small island northwest of Tortola. It's also a place to *truly* get away from it all. Mountainous and lush, the 4-mile-long (6½-km-long) island—with fewer than 200 full-time residents—has one tiny resort, some rental houses and villas, a campground, a few shops, a handful of cars, and a single road. There are no banks or ATMs on the island, and many restaurants and shops accept only cash. It's a good idea to buy groceries on St. Thomas or Tortola before arriving if you're staying for a few days. Life definitely rolls along on "island time," especially during the off-season from August to November, when finding a restaurant open for dinner can be a challenge. Water conservation is encouraged, as the source is rainwater collected in basement-like cisterns. Many lodgings will ask you to follow the Caribbean golden rule: "In the land of sun and fun, we never flush for number one." Jost is one of the Caribbean's most popular anchorages, and there are a disproportionately large number of informal bars and restaurants, which have helped earn Jost its reputation as the "party island" of the BVI.

BEACHES

FAMILY **Great Harbour Beach.** Great Harbour has an authentic Caribbean feel that's not just for tourists. Small bars and restaurants line the sandy strip of beach that serves as the community's main street. While the island's main settlement may not have the unspoiled natural beauty of some popular beaches, it holds a quaint charm. Activity picks up after dark, but many of the restaurants also serve excellent lunches without huge crowds. There are a few areas suited to swimming, with calm, shallow water perfect for children; however the attraction here is more about the facilities than the actual beach. Ali Baba and SeaCrest Inn have rooms on the bay. ⚠ **Bring your bug spray for sandflies in the early evenings. Amenities:** food and drink; toilets. **Best for:** walking; swimming. ✉ *Great Harbour*.

Sandy Cay Beach. Just offshore, the little islet known as Sandy Cay is a gleaming sliver of white sand with marvelous snorkeling and an inland nature trail. Previously part of the private estate of the late philanthropist and conservationist Laurance Rockefeller, the Cay recently became a protected area. You can hire any boatman on Jost Van Dyke to take you out; just be sure to agree on a price and a time to be picked up again. As this is a national park, visitors are asked to "take only photos and leave only footprints." Nevertheless, it's become an increasingly popular location for weddings, which require approval from the BVI National Parks Trust. ⚠ **Experienced boaters can rent a boat or dinghy to go here, but be aware that winter swells can make beach landings treacherous. Amenities:** none. **Best for:** walking; snorkeling; swimming.

FAMILY Fodor's Choice ★ **White Bay Beach.** On the south shore, this long stretch of picturesque white sand is especially popular with boaters who come ashore for a libation at one of the many beach bars that offer refuge from the sun. Despite the sometimes rowdy bar scene, the beach is large enough to find a quiet spot, particularly late in the day when most of the day-trippers disappear and the beach becomes serene. Accommodations directly on or just steps from the sand include the Sandcastle Hotel, White Bay Villas, Perfect Pineapple, and the Pink House Villas. ⚠ **Swimmers and snorkelers should be cautious of boat traffic in the anchorage. Amenities:** food and drink; toilets. **Best for:** partiers; swimming; walking. ✉ *White Bay*.

WHERE TO EAT

Restaurants on Jost Van Dyke are informal (some serve meals family-style at long tables) and often charming. The island is a favorite charter-boat stop, and you're bound to hear people exchanging stories about the previous night's anchoring adventures. Most restaurants don't take reservations (but for those that do, they are usually required). In all cases, dress is casual.

7

Boaters docking at Jost Van Dyke

$$$ ECLECTIC ✕ **Abe's by the Sea.** Many sailors who cruise into this quiet bay come so they can dock right at this open-air eatery to enjoy the seafood, conch, lobster, and other fresh catches. Chicken and ribs round out the menu, and affable owners Abe Coakley and his wife, Eunicy, add a pinch and dash of hospitality that makes a meal into a memorable evening. Casual lunches are also served, and an adjoining market sells ice, canned goods, and other necessities. Dinner reservations are required by 5 pm. *Average main: $29* ✉ *Little Harbour* ☎ *284/495–9329* *Reservations essential.*

$$$ SEAFOOD ✕ **Ali Baba's.** Lobster is the main attraction at this beach bar with a sandy floor, which is just some 20 feet from the sea. Grilled local fish, including swordfish, kingfish, and wahoo, are specialties and caught fresh daily. There's also a pig roast on Monday nights in season. Beware: Ali Baba's special rum punch is as potent as it is delicious. Reservations aren't mandatory for dinner, but you'll probably find yourself waiting a long time without them. *Average main: $29* ✉ *Great Harbour* ☎ *284/495–9280* *No credit cards.*

$$$ BARBECUE ✕ **Cool's Breeze Bar & Restaurant.** This brightly colored eatery is often frequented by island locals. The establishment offers full dinner options, serving fresh grilled lobster, barbecue, and baby back ribs. *Average main: $29* ✉ *Great Harbour* ☎ *284/496–0855* *No credit cards.*

$$$$ ECLECTIC ✕ **Corsairs Beach Bar and Restaurant.** On an island known for seafood, it's the pizza that draws raves at this friendly beach bar considered by some to be Jost's version of *Cheers*. If pizza doesn't appeal, the lunch and dinner menus have a wide variety of selections with an eclectic, Continental flare, and the owners brought a new chef on board in late 2013. Bring an appetite to breakfast, when the choices include hearty

omelets and breakfast burritos. The bar is easily recognized by its signature pirate paraphernalia and a restored U.S. military M37 Dodge truck parked next to the steps-from-the-sea dining room. [$] *Average main: $32 ✉ Great Harbour ☎ 284/495–9294 🌐 www.corsairsbvi.com.*

$$$$ ECLECTIC FAMILY ✕ **Foxy's Taboo.** It's well worth the winding hilly drive or sometimes-rough sail to get to Taboo, where there's a sophisticated menu and friendly staff with a welcoming attitude. Located on Jost's mostly undeveloped East End, Taboo is less of a party bar than Foxy's in Great Harbour but usually has a great breeze and scenic views. You'll find specialties with a Mediterranean twist like eggplant cheesecake, kebabs, and hot-from-the-oven pizza. The lunch menu differs from the standard island fare. Even the burgers are a step up from average, and the salads are the best on the island. Coupled with a walk to the nearby Bubbly Pool (ask for a map at the bar), a visit to Taboo is a good way to while away a few hours. Dinner reservations are required by 4 pm. [$] *Average main: $33 ✉ East End ☎ 284/340–9258.*

$$$ ECLECTIC FAMILY ✕ **Foxy's Tamarind Bar and Restaurant.** The big draw here is the owner, Foxy Callwood, a famed calypso singer who will serenade you with lewd and laugh-worthy songs as you fork into burgers, grilled chicken, barbecue ribs, and lobster. Check out the pennants, postcards, and weathered T-shirts that adorn every inch of the walls and ceiling of this large, two-story beach shack; they've been left by previous visitors. On Friday and Saturday nights in season, Foxy hosts a Caribbean-style barbecue with grilled fresh fish, chicken and ribs, peas and rice, salad, and more, followed by live music. Other nights choose from steak, fresh lobster, pork, or pasta; at lunch Foxy serves sandwiches and salads. Whether because of the sheer volume of diners or the experience of the management, Foxy's is one of the most reliable eating establishments on Jost. And it's also home to the only locally brewed beer in the BVI. You're unlikely to find Foxy performing at night, but he takes the mike many afternoons and makes time to mingle with guests—this a popular happy-hour pit stop. [$] *Average main: $29 ✉ Great Harbour ☎ 284/495–9258 🌐 www.foxysbar.com.*

$$$ BURGER ✕ **Gertrude's Beach Bar.** A casual bar right on White Bay Beach, Gertrude's will make you feel at home with burgers, conch fritters, and rotis. It's open for lunch and dinner, but it's a good idea to call ahead for dinner reservations. Sometimes Gertrude, and helpful staffer Olga, will let you pour your own drinks. [$] *Average main: $21 ✉ White Bay ☎ 284/495–9104.*

$$$$ ECLECTIC FAMILY ✕ **Harris' Place.** Owner Cynthia Harris is as famous for her friendliness as she is for her food. Lobster in a garlic butter sauce, and other freshly caught seafood, as well as pork, chicken, and ribs, are on the menu. Homemade key lime pie and expertly blended bushwackers are "to live for," as Cynthia would say, but diners also praise the fresh fish and lobster. Call for schedule of live music, which varies from season to season. Breakfast and lunch are served, too. Call ahead for reservations. [$] *Average main: $34 ✉ Little Harbour ☎ 284/495–9302.*

$$$ ECLECTIC ✕ **One Love Bar and Grill.** The Food Network's Alton Brown sought out this beachfront eatery and featured its stewed conch on a 2008 flavor-finding trip. Menu items include freshly caught seafood, quesadillas,

7

sandwiches, and salads. Try their specialty drink, a Bushwhacker. Seddy built the bar himself and decorated it with the flotsam and jetsam he collected during his years as a fisherman. *Average main: $28* *White Bay* *www.onelovebar.com.*

$$$$ ECLECTIC **Sydney's Peace and Love.** Here you can find great local lobster and fish, as well as barbecue chicken and ribs with all the fixings, including peas and rice, corn, coleslaw, and potato salad. Book early for all-you-can-eat lobster on Monday and Thursday nights. Meals are served on an open-air terrace or in an air-conditioned dining room at the water's edge. The find here is a sensational (by BVI standards) jukebox. The cognoscenti sail here for dinner, since there's no beach—and therefore no annoying sand fleas. Breakfast and lunch are served, too, and guests help themselves at the honor bar. *Average main: $33* *Little Harbour* *284/495–9271.*

WHERE TO STAY

$ B&B/INN **Ali Baba's Heavenly Rooms.** Just above Ali Baba's restaurant, owner Wayson "Baba" Hatchett has added three simple but attractive rooms, each equipped with air-conditioning and a private bath. **Pros:** convenient location. **Cons:** noisy area of Great Harbour. *Rooms from: $140* *Great Harbour* *284/495–9280* *3 rooms* *No meals.*

$ B&B/INN **Perfect Pineapple Guest Houses.** One-bedroom suites, as well as one- and two-bedroom guesthouses, all come equipped with private bath, air-conditioning, stove, satellite TV, and refrigerator. **Pros:** located just steps from the popular White Bay beach. **Cons:** rooms have only basic furnishings; in need of updating. *Rooms from: $160* *White Bay* *284/495–9401* *www.perfectpineapple.com* *6 rooms* *No meals.*

$$ HOTEL **Sandcastle.** Sleep steps from beautiful White Bay beach at this tiny beachfront hideaway, an island favorite for more than 40 years. **Pros:** beachfront rooms; near restaurants and bars; comfy hammocks. **Cons:** some rooms lack air-conditioning; beach sometimes clogged with day-trippers; no children allowed. *Rooms from: $310* *White Bay* *284/495–9888* *www.soggydollar.com* *2 rooms, 4 1-bedroom cottages* *Multiple meal plans.*

$ RENTAL FAMILY **White Bay Villas and Seaside Cottages.** Beautiful views and friendly staff keep guests coming back to these hilltop one- to three-bedroom villas and cottages. **Pros:** incredible views; full kitchens; friendly staff. **Cons:** 10- to 15-minute walk to White Bay and Great Harbour's restaurants and beaches; rental car recommended. *Rooms from: $220* *White Bay* *410/571–6692, 800/778–8066* *www.jostvandyke.com* *7 villas, 3 cottages* *No meals.*

NIGHTLIFE

Jost Van Dyke is the most happening place to go barhopping in the BVI, so much so that it is an all-day enterprise for some. In fact, yachties will sail over just to have a few drinks. All the spots are easy to find, clustered in three general locations: Great Harbour, White Bay, and Little Harbour *(⇨ see Where to Eat, above)*. On the Great Harbour side you can find Foxy's, Corsairs, and Ali Baba's; on the White Bay side are the One Love Bar and Grill and the Soggy Dollar Bar, where legend has it the famous Painkiller was first concocted; and in Little Harbour are Harris' Place, Sydney's Peace and Love, and Abe's by the Sea. If you can't make it to Jost Van Dyke, you can have a Painkiller at almost any bar in the BVI.

SPORTS AND THE OUTDOORS

Abe and Eunicy Rentals. This company's two-door Suzukis ($65 a day), four-door Suzukis ($75 a day), and four-door Monteros ($80 a day) will help you explore by land. There's pickup and drop-off service from anywhere on the island. ✉ *Little Harbour* ☎ *284/495–9329.*

Endeavour II Sailing. Built entirely from scratch on-island with local high school students, this 32-foot traditional sailing vessel was part of a maritime heritage project initiated by the Jost Van Dyke's Preservation Society. Day sails aboard help fund dive and sail training for young Jost Van Dyke islanders. ✉ *Great Harbour* ☎ *284/540–0861* 🌐 *www.jvdps.org.*

JVD Scuba and BVI Eco-Tours. Check out the undersea world around the island with dive master Colin Aldridge. One of the most impressive dives in the area is off the north coast of Little Jost Van Dyke. Here you can find the Twin Towers: a pair of rock formations rising an impressive 90 feet. A one-tank dive costs $95, a two-tank dive $115, and a four-hour beginner course is $120 plus the cost of equipment. Colin also offers day-trips to Sandy Cay and Sandy Spit, Norman Island, Virgin Gorda (The Baths), and custom outings. You can also rent snorkel equipment or dive gear. ✉ *Great Harbour* ☎ *284/495–0271* 🌐 *www.bvi-ecotours.com* ⏲ *Closed Sat.*

Paradise Jeep Rentals. Paradise Jeep Rentals offers the ideal vehicles to tackle Jost Van Dyke's steep, winding roads. Even though Jost is a relatively small island, you really need to be in shape to walk from one bay to the next. This outfit rents two-door Suzukis for $60 per day and four-door Grand Vitaras and Sportages for $70. Discounts are availble for rentals of six or more days. It's next to the Fire Station in Great Harbour. ■ **TIP→ Reservations are a must.** ✉ *Great Harbour* ☎ *284/495–9477.*

Paradise Powerboat Rental. Franky Chinnery, who was born and raised on Jost Van Dyke, owns Paradise Powerboat Rental. The company offers day-trip boat tours to Sandy Cay, Sandy Spit, Normal Island, The Baths, and custom trips, along with dinghy rentals, sportfishing, and other services on board the *Betram* and *Renegade* powerboats. It also provides water-taxi service between Jost Van Dyke and Tortola or USVI (call for prices). ✉ *Great Harbour* ☎ *284/442–4651.*

7

ANEGADA

Anegada lies low on the horizon about 14 miles (22½ km) north of Virgin Gorda. Unlike the hilly volcanic islands in the chain, this is a flat coral-and-limestone atoll. Nine miles (14 km) long and 2 miles (3 km) wide, the island rises no more than 28 feet above sea level. In fact, by the time you're able to see it, you may have run your boat onto a reef. (More than 300 captains unfamiliar with the waters have done so since exploration days; note that bareboat charters don't allow their vessels to head here without a trained skipper.) Although the reefs are a sailor's nightmare, they (and the shipwrecks they've caused) are a scuba diver's dream. Snorkeling, especially in the waters around Loblolly Bay on the North Shore, is a transcendent experience. You can float in shallow, calm water just a few feet from shore and see one coral formation after another, each shimmering with a rainbow of colorful fish. Many local captains are happy to take visitors out fishing for bonefish. Such watery pleasures are complemented by ever-so-fine, ever-so-white sand (the northern and western shores have long stretches of the stuff) and the occasional beach bar (stop in for burgers, local lobster, or a frosty beer). The island's population of about 180 lives primarily in a small south-side village called the Settlement, which has two grocery stores, a bakery, and a general store. In 2009 Anegada got its first bank, but it's open only one day a week, and there's still no ATM. Many restaurants and shops take only cash.

WHERE TO EAT

There are between 6 and 10 restaurants open at any one time, depending on the season and on whim. Check when you're on the island. Fresh fish and lobster are the island's specialties. The going rate for a lobster dinner is $50, and it's always the most expensive thing on any restaurant menu.

$$$$ SEAFOOD Fodor's Choice ★

Anegada Reef Hotel Restaurant. Seasoned yachters gather here nightly to share tales of the high seas; the open-air bar is the busiest on the island. Dinner is by candlelight under the stars and always includes famous Anegada lobster, steaks, and succulent baby back ribs—all prepared on the large grill by the little open-air bar. The ferry dock is right next door, so expect a crowd shortly after it arrives. Dinner reservations are required by 4 pm. Breakfast favorites include lobster omelets and rum-soaked French toast; at lunch the Reef serves salads and sandwiches. *Average main: $37 ✉ Setting Point ☎ 284/495–8002 Reservations essential.*

$$$ SEAFOOD FAMILY

Big Bamboo. This beachfront bar and restaurant tucked among sea grape trees at famous Loblolly Bay is the island's most popular destination for lunch. After you've polished off a plate of succulent Anegada lobster, barbeque chicken, or fresh fish, you can spend the afternoon on the beach, where the snorkeling is excellent and the view close to perfection. Fruity drinks from the cabana bar and ice cream from the freezer will round out your day. Dinner is by request only. If your heart is set on lobster, it's a good idea to call in the morning or day

Anegada has miles of beautiful white-sand beaches.

before to put in your request. *Average main: $29* *Loblolly Bay West* *284/495–2019* *www.bigbambooanegada.com.*

$$$$ SEAFOOD **Cow Wreck Bar and Grill.** Named for the cow bones that once washed up on shore, this wiggle-your-toes-in-the-sand beachside eatery on the northern shore is a fun place to watch the antics of surfers and kiteboarders skidding across the bay. Tuck into conch ceviche, lobster fritters, or the popular hot wings for lunch. The homemade coconut pie is a winner. Pack your snorkel gear and explore the pristine reef just a few strokes from the shore before you eat, or browse the on-site gift shop. Dinner is served by request; reservations required by 4 pm. *Average main: $36* *Cow Wreck Beach* *284/495–8047* *www.cowwreckbeach.com* *Reservations essential.*

$$$$ SEAFOOD FAMILY Fodor's Choice ★ **Neptune's Treasure.** The owners, the Soares family, have lived on the island for more than half a century, and the Soares men catch, cook, and serve the seafood at this homey bar and restaurant a short distance from Setting Point. The fresh lobster, swordfish, tuna, and mahimahi are all delicious. In 2013, Pam's Kitchen, a small bakery to the exterior of the property, was incorporated into the restaurant and rounds out offerings with freshly baked breads; sweet treats including made-from-scratch desserts (including key lime pie, chocolate brownies, and apple pie); and pizzas. Dinner is by candlelight at the water's edge, often with classic jazz playing softly in the background. If you've tired of seafood, Neptune's has a nice variety of alternatives, including vegetarian pasta, pork loin, and orange chicken. The view is spectacular at sunset. Breakfast and lunch are also served. Dinner reservations are essential by 4 pm. *Average main: $32* *Bender Bay* *284/495–9439* *www.neptunestreasure.com* *Reservations essential.*

$$$$ SEAFOOD ✕ **Pomato Point Restaurant.** This relaxed restaurant and bar sits on one of the best beaches on the island and enjoys Anegada's most dramatic sunset views. Entrées include lobster, stewed conch, and freshly caught seafood. It's open for lunch daily; call by 4 pm for dinner reservations. Be sure to take a look at owner Wilfred Creque's displays of island artifacts, including shards of Arawak pottery and 17th-century coins, cannonballs, and bottles. These are housed in a little one-room museum adjacent to the dining room. *Average main: $38 ⊠ Pomato Point ☎ 284/495–9466 Reservations essential Closed Sept.*

$$$$ SEAFOOD ✕ **Potter's By the Sea.** Owner Liston Potter, a great staff, and a lively atmosphere just a few steps from the dock complement freshly grilled lobster and other seafood selections such as snapper and grouper. Potter's also offers a beach shuttle, free Wi-Fi, pool tables, and live music (ask about the schedule when you call ahead for dinner reservations). *Average main: $37 ⊠ Setting Point ☎ 284/495–9182 Reservations essential.*

WHERE TO STAY

$$ RESORT **Anegada Beach Club.** This is a laid-back beach club setting where beach enthusiasts can enjoy beach volleyball and badminton. **Pros:** with the option of adjoining king and "junior" suites (with two twin beds) and plenty of outdoor activities, this is a great spot for families; there is a bar and restaurant on-site. **Cons:** some find Anegada too remote. *Rooms from: $276 ⊠ Keel Point ☎ 800/871–3551, 284/852–4500 www.anegadabeachclub.com 16 hotels, 7 luxury tents No meals.*

$ HOTEL **Anegada Reef Hotel.** Head here if you want to bunk in comfortable lodging near Anegada's most popular anchorage. **Pros:** everything you need is nearby; nice sunsets. **Cons:** basic rooms; no beach; often a party atmosphere at the bar. *Rooms from: $265 ⊠ Setting Point ☎ 284/495–8002 www.anegadareef.com 16 rooms Multiple meal plans.*

$$ RENTAL **Cow Wreck Beach Resort.** The resort's best attribute is its location at Cow Wreck Beach. **Pros:** secluded location; great snorkeling. **Cons:** the island's infamous, free-roaming livestock sometimes leave "presents" behind; location too remote for some. *Rooms from: $276 ⊠ Cow Wreck Beach ☎ 284/495–8047 www.cowwreckbeach.com 4 units No meals.*

$ B&B/INN FAMILY **Neptune's Treasure.** Basic waterfront rooms with simple furnishings and lovely views of the ocean are the hallmark of this family-owned guesthouse. **Pros:** waterfront property; run by a family full of tales of the island; nice sunset views. **Cons:** simple rooms; no kitchens; no beach. *Rooms from: $150 ⊠ Bender's Bay ☎ 284/495–9439 www.neptunestreasure.com 9 rooms, 2 cottages No meals.*

SPORTS AND THE OUTDOORS

Anegada Reef Hotel. Call the hotel to arrange bonefishing and sportfishing outings with seasoned local guides. *⊠ Setting Point ☎ 284/495–8002 www.anegadareef.com.*

Danny Vanterpool. Danny offers half-, three-quarter-, and full-day bonefishing excursions around Anegada. The cost ranges from $400 for a half day to $600 for a full day. ☎ *284/441–6334* 🌐 *www.dannysbonefishing.com.*

OTHER BRITISH VIRGIN ISLANDS

COOPER ISLAND

This small, hilly island on the south side of the Sir Francis Drake Channel, about 8 miles (13 km) from Road Town, Tortola, is popular with the charter-boat crowd. There are no paved roads (which doesn't really matter, as there aren't any cars), but you can find a beach restaurant, a casual hotel, a few houses (some are available for rent), and great snorkeling at the south end of Manchioneel Bay.

WHERE TO STAY

$ ALL-INCLUSIVE Fodor's Choice ★ **Cooper Island Beach Club.** Diving is the focus at this small resort, but folks who want to simply swim, snorkel, or relax can also feel right at home. **Pros:** lots of quiet; the Caribbean as it used to be. **Cons:** small rooms; island accessible only by ferry; there is no nightlife. *Rooms from: $225* ✉ *Manchioneel Bay* ☎ *284/495–9084, 800/542–4624* 🌐 *www.cooperislandbeachclub.com* *9 rooms* *All-inclusive.*

7

GUANA ISLAND

Guana Island sits off Tortola's northeast coast. Sailors often drop anchor at one of the island's bays for a day of snorkeling and sunning. The island is a designated wildlife sanctuary, and scientists often come here to study its flora and fauna. It's home to a back-to-nature resort that offers few activities other than relaxation. Unless you're a hotel guest or a sailor, there's no easy way to get here.

WHERE TO STAY

$$$$ RESORT Fodor's Choice ★ **Guana Island Resort.** Here's a good resort if you want to stroll the hillsides, snorkel around the reefs, swim at its seven beaches, and still enjoy some degree of comfort. **Pros:** secluded feel; lovely grounds. **Cons:** very expensive; need boat to get here. *Rooms from: $1,250* ✉ *Guana Island* ☎ *284/494–2354, 800/544–8262* 🌐 *www.guana.com* *15 rooms, 1 1-bedroom villa, 1 2-bedroom villa, 1 3-bedroom villa* *All meals.*

NORMAN ISLAND

This uninhabited island is the supposed setting for Robert Louis Stevenson's *Treasure Island.* The famed caves at Treasure Point are popular with day sailors and powerboaters. If you land ashore at the island's main anchorage in the Bight, you can find a small beach bar and behind it a trail that winds up the hillside and reaches a peak with a fantastic view of the Sir Francis Drake Channel to the north. The island boasts nearly 12 miles of hiking trails. Call Pirate's Bight for information on ferry service, which was being upgraded in late 2014 to accommodate day-trippers.

GETTING HERE AND AROUND

The only way to reach this island is by private boat or on a charter boat that puts you aboard the *Willy T.* for a meal and drinks.

WHERE TO EAT

$$$$ ECLECTIC ✕ **Pirate's Bight.** This breezy, open-air dining establishment boasts quirky beach-bar eccentricities (a cannon is fired at sunset and bargoers play games like "Giant Jenga"), while maintaining a slightly refined feeling that came with 2013 rennovations. Sail Caribbean operates a dive shop on the property and owners offer ferry service, giving the restaurant the feel of a casual day resort. Dinner offerings include a variety of seafood and poultry offerings, and appetizers and bar food include choices such as tuna tartar and coconut shrimp. The restaurant hosts live entertainment several nights a week. Call ahead for music schedule and for dinner reservations. [$] *Average main: $32* ✉ *The Bight* ☎ *284/443–1405* 🌐 *www.piratesbight.com.*

$$ ECLECTIC ✕ **Willy T.** *Willy T* is a floating bar and restaurant that's anchored to the north of the Bight. Lunch and dinner are served in a party-hearty atmosphere. Try the conch fritters for starters. For lunch and dinner, British-style fish-and-chips, West Indian roti sandwiches, and the baby back ribs are winners. Call ahead for dinner reservations. [$] *Average main: $17* ✉ *The Bight* ☎ *284/496–8603* 🌐 *www.williamthornton.com* ✍ *Reservations essential.*

CAYMAN ISLANDS

WELCOME TO CAYMAN ISLANDS

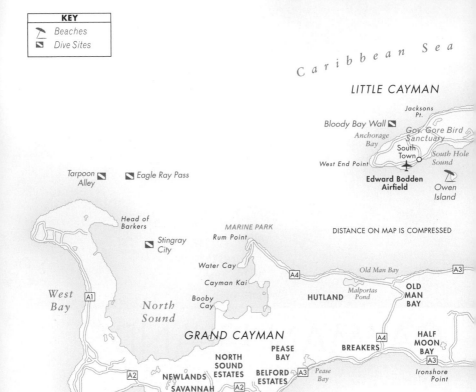

Grand Cayman may be the world's largest offshore finance hub, but other offshore activities have put the Cayman Islands on the map. Pristine waters, breathtaking coral formations, and plentiful and exotic marine creatures beckon divers from around the world. Other vacationers are drawn by the islands' mellow civility.

FUN ON AND OFF SHORE

Grand Cayman, which is 22 miles (36 km) long and 8 miles (13 km) wide, is the largest of the three low-lying islands that make up this British colony. Its sister islands (Little Cayman and Cayman Brac) are almost 90 miles (149 km) north and east. The Cayman Trough between the Cayman Islands and Jamaica is the deepest part of the Caribbean.

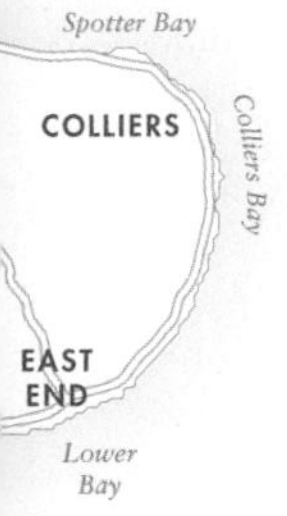

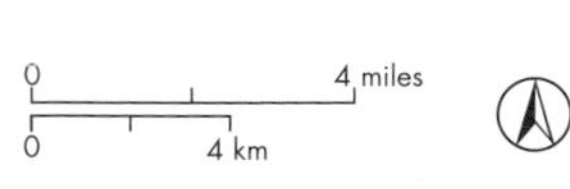

TOP REASONS TO VISIT CAYMAN ISLANDS

1 **Diving:** Underwater visibility is among the best in the Caribbean, and nearby reefs are healthy.

2 **Safety and Comfort:** With no panhandlers, little crime, and top-notch accommodations, it's an easy place to vacation.

3 **Dining Scene:** The cosmopolitan population extends to the varied dining scene, from Italian to Indian.

4 **Fabulous Snorkeling:** A snorkeling trip to Stingray City is an experience you'll always remember.

5 **Beaches:** Grand Cayman's Seven Mile Beach is one of the Caribbean's best sandy beaches.

Updated by Jordan Simon

This British Overseas Territory, which consists of Grand Cayman, smaller Cayman Brac, and Little Cayman, is one of the Caribbean's most popular destinations, particularly among Americans, who have become homeowners and constant visitors. The island's extensive array of banks also draws travelers.

Columbus is said to have sighted the islands in 1503 and dubbed them "*Las Tortugas*" after seeing so many turtles in the sea. The name was later changed to Cayman, referring to the caiman crocodiles that once roamed the islands. The Cayman Islands remained largely uninhabited until the late 1600s, when England seized them and Jamaica from Spain. Emigrants from England, Holland, Spain, and France arrived, as did refugees from the Spanish Inquisition and deserters from Oliver Cromwell's army in Jamaica; many brought slaves with them as well. The Cayman Islands' caves and coves were also perfect hideouts for the likes of Blackbeard, Sir Henry Morgan, and other pirates out to plunder Spanish galleons. Many ships fell afoul of the reefs surrounding the islands, often with the help of Caymanians, who lured vessels to shore with beacon fires.

Today's Cayman Islands are seasoned with suburban prosperity (particularly Grand Cayman, where residents joke that the national flower is the satellite dish) and stuffed with crowds (the hotels that line the famed Seven Mile Beach are often full, even in the slow summer season). Most of the 52,000 Cayman Islanders live on Grand Cayman, where the cost of living is at least 20% higher than in the United States, but you won't be hassled by panhandlers or fear walking around on a dark evening (the crime rate is very low). Add political and economic stability to the mix, and you have a fine island recipe indeed.

LOGISTICS

Getting to the Cayman Islands: There are plenty of nonstop flights to Grand Cayman (GCM) from the United States. Most people hop over to the Brac and Little Cayman (LYB) on a small plane from Grand Cayman; a weekly nonstop between the Brac and Miami was reinstated. Flights land at Owen Roberts Airport (Grand Cayman), Gerrard Smith Airport (Cayman Brac), or Edward Bodden Airstrip (Little Cayman).

Hassle Factor: Low for Grand Cayman; medium for Little Cayman and Cayman Brac.

On the Ground: In Grand Cayman you must take a taxi or rent a car at the airport, because most hotels are not permitted to offer airport shuttles. Hotel pickup is more readily available on Cayman Brac and Little Cayman.

Getting Around the Islands: It's possible to get by without a car on Grand Cayman if you are staying in the Seven Mile Beach area, where you could walk, take a local bus, or ride a bike. If you want to explore the rest of the island—or if you are staying elsewhere—you'll need a car. Though less necessary on Cayman Brac or Little Cayman, cars are available on both islands.

PLANNING

WHEN TO GO

High season begins in mid-December and continues through early to mid-April. During the low season you can often get a discount of as much as 40%.

GETTING HERE AND AROUND

AIR TRAVEL

You can fly nonstop to Grand Cayman from Atlanta (Delta), Boston (US Airways, once weekly; JetBlue), Charlotte (US Airways), Chicago (Cayman Airways, twice weekly), Detroit (Delta, once weekly), Fort Lauderdale (Cayman Airways), Houston (United, twice weekly), Miami (American, Cayman Airways), Minneapolis (Delta, once weekly), New York–JFK (Cayman Airways, Delta, JetBlue), New York–Newark (United, once weekly), Philadelphia (US Airways, once weekly), Tampa (Cayman Airways), and Washington, D.C. (United).

Almost all nonstop air service is to Grand Cayman, with connecting flights on Cayman Airways Express to Cayman Brac and Little Cayman on a small propeller plane; there's also interisland charter-only service on Island Air. A once-weekly nonstop on Cayman Airways links Miami and Cayman Brac.

Airline Contacts **American Airlines** ☎ *345/949–0666.* **Cayman Airways** ☎ *345/949–2311.* **Delta** ☎ *345/945–8430.* **JetBlue** ☎ *800/538–2583, 855/710–2951* 🌐 *www.jetblue.com.* **United** ☎ *345/916–5545.* **US Airways** ☎ *345/949–7488.*

Airports **Edward Bodden Airstrip** (*LYB*). ✉ *Little Cayman* ☎ *345/948–0021.* **Gerrard Smith International Airport** (*CYB*). ✉ *Cayman Brac* ☎ *345/948–1222.*

8

Owen Roberts International Airport (*GCM*). ✉ *Grand Cayman* ☎ *345/943–7070.*

BUS TRAVEL

On Grand Cayman, bus service—consisting of minivans marked "Omni Bus"—is efficient, inexpensive, and plentiful, running from 6 am to midnight (depending on route) roughly every 15 minutes in the Seven Mile Beach area and George Town, with fares from CI$1.50 to CI$3.

CAR TRAVEL

Driving is easy on Grand Cayman, but there can be considerable traffic, especially during rush hour. One major road circumnavigates most of the island. Driving is on the left, British-style, and there are roundabouts. Speed limits are 30 mph (50 kph) in the country, 20 mph (30 kph) in town. There's much less traffic on Cayman Brac and even less on Little Cayman. Gas is expensive.

Car Rentals: You'll need a valid driver's license and a credit card to rent a car. Most agencies require renters to be between 21 and 70, though some require you to be 25. If you are over 75, you must have a certified doctor's note attesting to your ability. A local driver's permit, which costs $20, is obtained through the rental agencies. Rates can be expensive (from $45 to $95 per day), but usually include insurance.

Car-Rental Contacts (Grand Cayman) Ace Hertz ☎ *345/949–2280, 800/654–3131, 855/212–1713 toll free, 345/943–4378.* **Andy's Rent a Car** ☎ *345/949–8111, 855/691–3991 toll free* 🌐 *www.andys.ky.* **Avis** ☎ *345/949–2468* 🌐 *www.aviscayman.com.* **Budget** ☎ *345/949–5605* 🌐 *www.budgetcayman.com.* **Dollar** ☎ *345/949–4790* 🌐 *www.dollarlac.com.* **Economy** ☎ *345/949–9550* 🌐 *www.economycarrental.com.ky.* **Thrifty** ☎ *345/949–6640, 800/367–2277* 🌐 *www.thrifty.com.*

Car-Rental Contacts (Cayman Brac) B&S Motor Ventures ☎ *345/948–1646* 🌐 *www.bandsmv.com.* **CB Rent-a-Car** ☎ *345/948–2424, 345/948–2847* 🌐 *www.cbrentacar.com.* **Four D's Car Rental** ☎ *345/948–1599, 345/948–0459.*

Car-Rental Contacts (Little Cayman) McLaughlin Rentals ☎ *345/948–1000* ✉ *littlcay@candw.ky.*

TAXI TRAVEL

On Grand Cayman, taxis operate 24 hours a day; if you anticipate a late night, however, make pickup arrangements in advance. You generally cannot hail a taxi on the street except occasionally in George Town. Fares are metered, and are not cheap, but basic fares include as many as three passengers. Taxis are scarcer on the Sister Islands; rates are fixed and fairly prohibitive. Your hotel can recommend drivers.

ESSENTIALS

Banks and Exchange Services You should not need to change money in Grand Cayman, since U.S. dollars are readily accepted. ATMs generally offer the option of U.S. or Cayman dollars. The Cayman dollar is pegged to the U.S. dollar at the rate of CI$1.25 to $1. Be sure you know which currency is being quoted when making a purchase.

Electricity Electricity is reliable and is the same as in the United States (110 volts/60 cycles).

Emergency Services Ambulance ☎ *911.* **Cayman Hyperbaric** ✉ *95 Hospital Rd., George Town, Grand Cayman* ☎ *345/949–2989.* **Fire** ☎ *911.* **Police** ☎ *911.*

Passport Requirements All visitors must have a valid passport and a return or ongoing ticket to enter the Cayman Islands. A birth certificate and photo ID are *not* sufficient proof of citizenship.

Phones The area code for the Cayman Islands is 345. To make local calls (on or between any of the three islands), dial the seven-digit number. Many international cell phones work in the Cayman Islands, though roaming charges can be significant. Mobile phone rental is available from LIME and Digicel, the two major providers; you can stay connected for as little as CI$5 per day plus the cost of a calling card (denominations range from CI$10 to CI$100). International per-minute rates usually range from CI35¢ to CI60¢.

Taxes At the airport, each adult passenger leaving Grand Cayman must pay a departure tax of $25 (CI$20), payable in cash. It's usually added to airfare—check with your carrier. A 10% government tax is added to all hotel bills.

Tipping At large hotels a service charge is generally included; smaller establishments and some villas and condos leave tipping up to you. Although tipping is customary at restaurants, note that some automatically include 10% to 15% on the bill—so check the tab carefully. Taxi drivers expect a 10% to 15% tip.

ACCOMMODATIONS

Grand Cayman draws the bulk of Cayman Island visitors. It's expensive during the high season but offers the widest range of resorts, restaurants, and activities both in and out of the water. Most resorts are on or near Seven Mile Beach, but a few are north in the West Bay Area, near Rum Point, or on the quiet East End. Both Little Cayman and Cayman Brac are more geared toward serving the needs of divers, who make up the majority of visitors. Beaches on the Sister Islands, as they are called, don't measure up (literally) to Grand Cayman's Seven Mile Beach. The smaller islands are cheaper than Grand Cayman, but with the extra cost of transportation, the overall savings are minimized.

Hotel reviews have been shortened. For full information, visit Fodors.com.

8

WHAT IT COSTS IN U.S. DOLLARS

	$	$$	$$$	$$$$
Restaurants	under $12	$12–$20	$21–$30	over $30
Hotels	under $275	$275–$375	$376–$475	over $475

Restaurant prices are the average cost of a main course at dinner or, if dinner is not served, at lunch. Hotel prices are the lowest cost of a standard double room in high season.

VISITOR INFORMATION

Contacts Cayman Islands Department of Tourism ☏ *305/599-9033 in Miami, 847/678-6446 in Chicago, 212/889-9009 in New York City, 713/461-1317 in Houston, 877/422-9626 in U.S., 345/949-0623 in Caymans* 🌐 *www.caymanislands.ky.*

WEDDINGS

Getting married in the Cayman Islands is a breeze. Documentation can be prepared ahead of time or in one day while on the island. There's no on-island waiting period. Larger resorts have on-site wedding coordinators.

GRAND CAYMAN

Grand Cayman has long been known for two offshore activities: banking (the new piracy, as locals joke) and scuba diving. With 296 banks, the capital, George Town, is relatively modern and usually bustles with activity, but never more so than when two to seven cruise ships are docked in the harbor, an increasingly common occurrence. Accountants in business clothes join thousands of vacationers in their tropical togs, jostling for tables at lunch. When they're not mingling in the myriad shops or getting pampered and pummeled in spas, vacationers delve into sparkling waters to snorkel and dive; increasingly, couples come to be married, or at least to enjoy their honeymoon.

The effects of recent devastating hurricanes such as Omar and Paloma, both in 2008, are visible only in the mangrove swamps and interior savanna. There is a lot of new construction and plenty of traffic, so check with a local to plan driving time. It can take 45 minutes during rush hours to go 8 miles (13 km).

EXPLORING

The historic capital of George Town, on the southwest corner of Grand Cayman, is easy to explore on foot. If you're a shopper, you can spend days here; otherwise, an hour will suffice for a tour of the downtown area. To see the rest of the island, rent a car or scooter or take a guided tour. The portion of the island called West Bay is noted for its jumble of neighborhoods and a few attractions. When traffic is heavy, it's about a half hour to West Bay from George Town, but the bypass road that runs parallel to West Bay Road has made the journey easier. The less-developed East End has natural attractions from blowholes to botanical gardens, as well as the remains of the island's original settlements. Plan at least 45 minutes for the drive out from George Town (more during rush hours). You need a day to explore the entire island—including a stop at a beach for a picnic or swim.

GEORGE TOWN

Begin exploring the capital by strolling along the waterfront Harbour Drive to **Elmslie Memorial United Church,** named after the first Presbyterian missionary to serve in Cayman. Its vaulted ceiling, wooden arches, and sedate nave reflect the religious nature of island residents.

Cayman Turtle Farm, Grand Cayman

In front of the court building, in the center of town, names of influential Caymanians are inscribed on the **Wall of History,** which commemorates the islands' quincentennial in 2003. Across the street is the **Cayman Islands Legislative Assembly Building,** next door to the **1919 Peace Memorial Building.** In the middle of the financial district is the **General Post Office,** built in 1939. Let the kids pet the big blue iguana statues.

TOP ATTRACTIONS

FAMILY Fodor's Choice ★ **Cayman Islands National Museum.** Built in 1833, the historically significant clapboard home of the national museum has had several different incarnations over the years, serving as courthouse, jail, post office, and dance hall. It features an ongoing archaeological excavation of the Old Gaol and excellent 3-D bathymetric displays, murals, dioramas, and videos that illustrate local geology, flora and fauna, and island history. The first floor focuses on natural history, including a microcosm of Cayman ecosystems, from beaches to dry woodlands and swamps, and offers such interactive elements as a simulated sub. Upstairs, the cultural exhibit features renovated murals, video history reenactments, and 3-D back panels in display cases holding thousands of artifacts ranging from a 14-foot catboat with animatronic captain to old coins and rare documents. These paint a portrait of daily life and past industries, such as shipbuilding and turtling, and stress Caymanians' resilience when they had little contact with the outside world. There are also temporary exhibits focusing on aspects of Caymanian culture, a local art collection, and interactive displays for kids. ✉ *Harbour Dr.* ☎ *345/949–8368* 🌐 *www.museum.ky* 🎟 *$8* 🕑 *Weekdays 9–5, Sat. 10–2.*

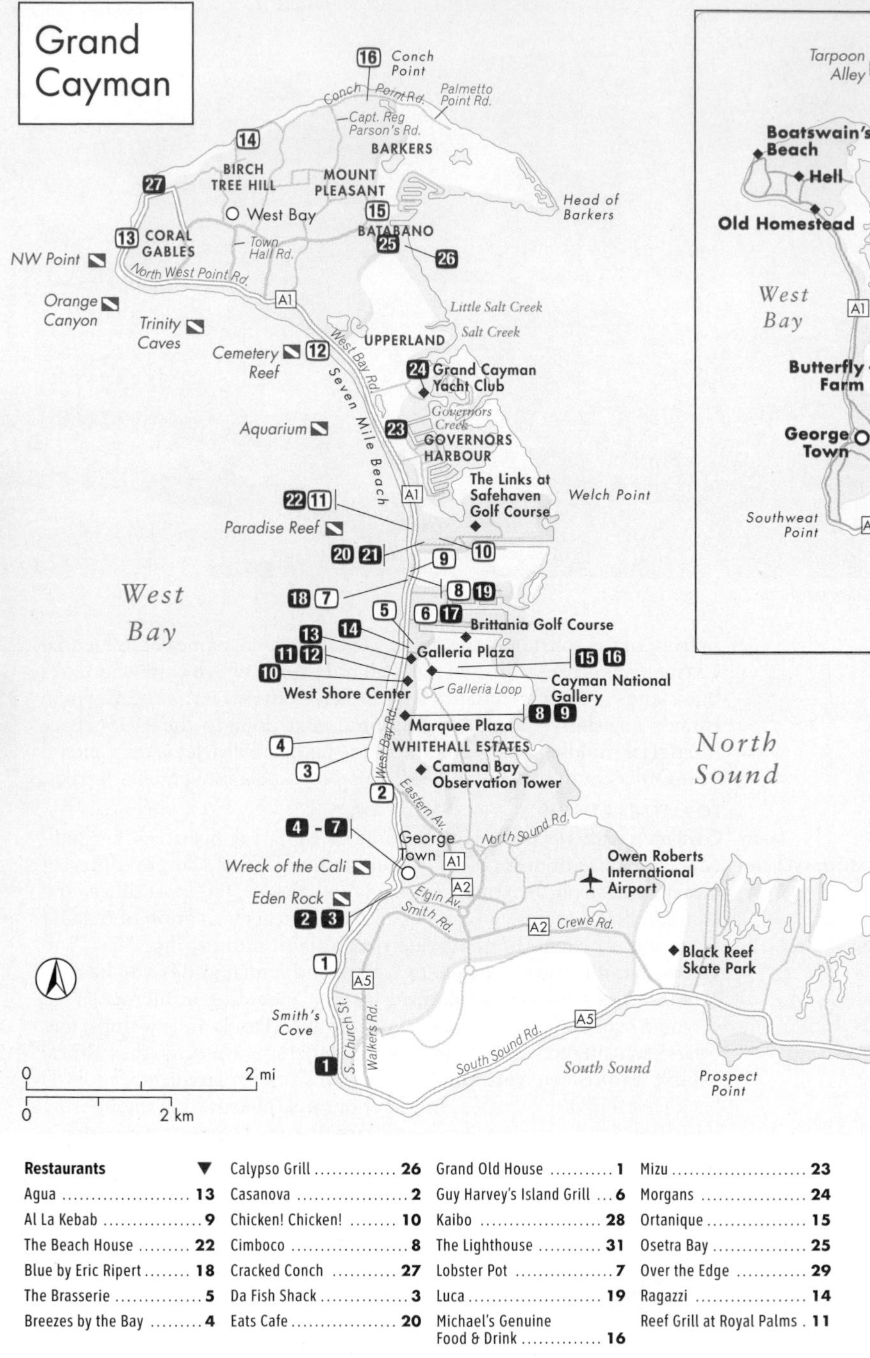

Grand Cayman
Conch Point
Conch Point Rd.
Palmetto Point Rd.
Capt. Reg Parson's Rd.
BARKERS
BIRCH TREE HILL
MOUNT PLEASANT
Head of Barkers
West Bay
CORAL GABLES
Town Hall Rd.
BATABANO
NW Point
North West Point Rd.
Orange Canyon
Trinity Caves
Cemetery Reef
Little Salt Creek
Salt Creek
UPPERLAND
West Bay Rd.
Seven Mile Beach
Grand Cayman Yacht Club
Governors Creek
Aquarium
GOVERNORS HARBOUR
The Links at Safehaven Golf Course
Welch Point
Paradise Reef
West Bay
Brittania Golf Course
Galleria Plaza
Cayman National Gallery
West Shore Center
Galleria Loop
Marquee Plaza
WHITEHALL ESTATES
Camana Bay Observation Tower
North Sound
Eastern Av.
George Town
North Sound Rd.
Wreck of the Cali
Owen Roberts International Airport
Eden Rock
Elgin Av.
Smith Rd.
Crewe Rd.
Black Reef Skate Park
Smith's Cove
S. Church St.
Walkers Rd.
South Sound Rd.
South Sound
Prospect Point
0 2 mi
0 2 km
Tarpoon Alley
Boatswain's Beach
Hell
Old Homestead
West Bay
Butterfly Farm
George Town
Southweat Point
Restaurants
Agua 13
Al La Kebab 9
The Beach House 22
Blue by Eric Ripert 18
The Brasserie 5
Breezes by the Bay 4
Calypso Grill 26
Casanova 2
Chicken! Chicken! 10
Cimboco 8
Cracked Conch 27
Da Fish Shack 3
Eats Cafe 20
Grand Old House 1
Guy Harvey's Island Grill 6
Kaibo 28
The Lighthouse 31
Lobster Pot 7
Luca 19
Michael's Genuine Food & Drink 16
Mizu 23
Morgans 24
Ortanique 15
Osetra Bay 25
Over the Edge 29
Ragazzi 14
Reef Grill at Royal Palms 11

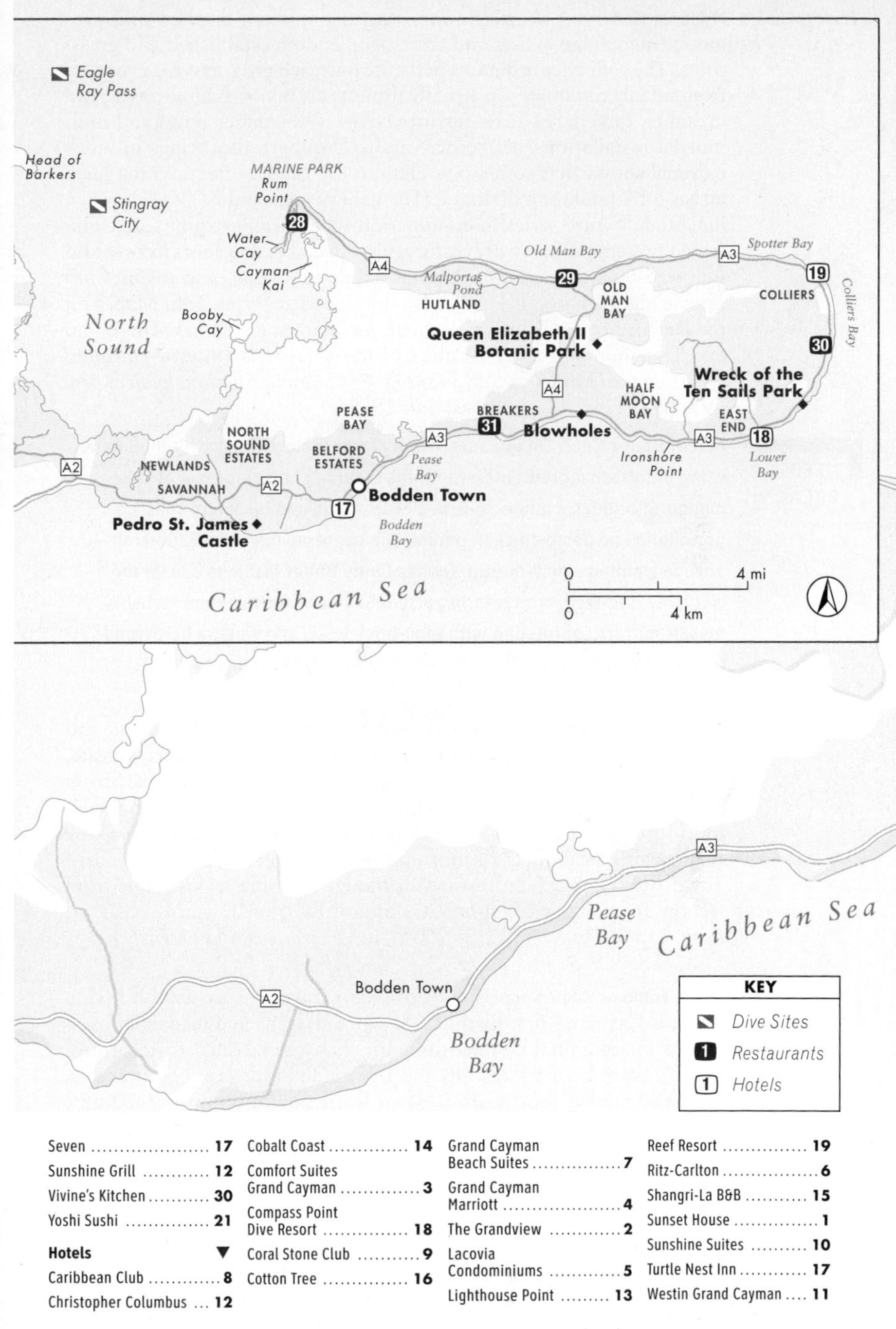

Seven **17**
Sunshine Grill **12**
Vivine's Kitchen **30**
Yoshi Sushi **21**

Hotels ▼

Caribbean Club **8**
Christopher Columbus ... **12**
Cobalt Coast **14**
Comfort Suites Grand Cayman **3**
Compass Point Dive Resort **18**
Coral Stone Club **9**
Cotton Tree **16**
Grand Cayman Beach Suites **7**
Grand Cayman Marriott **4**
The Grandview **2**
Lacovia Condominiums **5**
Lighthouse Point **13**
Reef Resort **19**
Ritz-Carlton **6**
Shangri-La B&B **15**
Sunset House **1**
Sunshine Suites **10**
Turtle Nest Inn **17**
Westin Grand Cayman **11**

Fodor'sChoice ★ **National Gallery.** A worthy nonprofit, this museum displays and promotes Caymanian artists and craftspeople, both established and grassroots. The gallery coordinates first-rate outreach programs for everyone from infants to inmates. It usually mounts six major exhibitions a year, including three large-scale retrospectives or thematic shows and multimedia installations. Director Natalie Urquhart also brings in international shows that somehow relate to the island, often inviting local artists for stimulating dialogue. The gallery hosts public slide shows, a lunchtime lecture series in conjunction with current exhibits, Art Flix (video presentations on art history, introduced with a short lecture and followed by a discussion led by curators or artists), and a CineClub (movie night). The gallery has also developed an Artist Trail Map with the Department of Tourism and can facilitate studio tours. There's an excellent shop and an Art Café. ✉ *Esterly Tibbetts Hwy. at Harquail Bypass, Seven Mile Beach* ☎ *345/945–8111* 🌐 *www.nationalgallery.org.ky* 🎫 *Free* 🕘 *Weekdays 10–5, Sat. 10–3.*

NEED A BREAK?

Full of Beans Cafe. On the surprisingly large, eclectic, Asian-tinged menu using ultrafresh ingredients, standouts include homemade carrot cake, mango smoothies, cranberry-Brie-pecan salad, and rosemary-roasted portobello and pesto chicken panini. The espresso martini will perk up anyone wanting a pick-me-up. Owner Cindy Butler fashions a feast for weary eyes as well, with rotating artworks (many for sale) and stylish mosaic mirrors contrasting with faux-brick walls and vintage hardwood tables. ✉ ***Pasadora Pl., Smith Rd.*** ☎ ***345/943–2326, 345/814–0157.***

WORTH NOTING

National Trust. This office provides a wonderful map of historic and natural attractions, books and guides to Cayman, and, on its website, more than 50 information sheets on cultural and natural topics from iguanas to schoolhouses. Regularly scheduled activities range from boat tours through the forests of the Central Mangrove Wetlands to cooking classes with local chefs to morning walking tours of historic George Town. Stop in, but be forewarned: though the office is walkable from George Town, it's an often-hot 20-minute hike from downtown. ✉ *Dart Park, 558 S. Church St.* ☎ *345/749–1121* 🌐 *www.nationaltrust.org.ky* 🕘 *Weekdays 9–5.*

Seven Fathoms Rum. Surprisingly, this growing company, established in 2008, is Cayman's first distillery. It's already garnered medals in prestigious international competitions for its artisanal small-batch rums. You can stop by for a tasting and self-guided tour (a more intensive, extensive guided tour costs $15) to learn how the rum is aged at 7 fathoms (42 feet) deep; supposedly the natural motion of the currents maximizes the rum's contact with the oak, extracting its rich flavors and enhancing complexity. Based on the results, it's not just yo-ho-hokum. ✉ *65 Bronze Rd.* ☎ *345/925–5379, 345/926–8186* 🌐 *www.sevenfathomsrum.com.*

SEVEN MILE BEACH

WORTH NOTING

FAMILY **Camana Bay Observation Tower.** This 75-foot structure provides striking 360-degree panoramas of otherwise flat Grand Cayman, sweeping from George Town and Seven Mile Beach to the North Sound. The double-helix staircase is impressive in its own right. Running alongside the steps (an elevator is also available), a floor-to-ceiling mosaic replicates the look and feel of a dive from seabed to surface. Constructed of tiles in 114 different colors, it's one of the world's largest marine-themed mosaics. Benches and lookout points let you take in the views as you ascend. Afterward you can enjoy 500-acre Camana Bay's gardens, waterfront boardwalk, and pedestrian paths lined with shops and restaurants, or frequent live entertainment. ✉ *Between Seven Mile Beach and North Sound, 2 miles (3 km) north of George Town, Camana Bay* ☎ *345/640–3500* 🌐 *www.camanabay.com* 🎟 *Free* ⏲ *Daily sunrise–10 pm.*

WEST BAY

WORTH NOTING

Cayman Motor Museum. This unexpected collection documents the magnificent obsession of one man, Norwegian magnate Andreas Ugland. More than 80 vehicles, preening like supermodels, gleam in ranks. "Holy hot-rod, Batman!" There's one of the three original Batmobiles from the 1960s TV series; the world's first produced auto, an 1886 Benz; and classic Ferraris, Jags, Corvettes, BMWs, and others dating back nearly a century, including Elton John's Bentley, the 1930 Phantom driven in the film *Yellow Rolls Royce*, and Queen Elizabeth II's first limo. You can go hog wild over Harleys and other bad-ass bikes. And well, just because, coffee grinders—more than kitchen kitsch: Peugeot started producing mills and grinders in the mid-19th century. An avid sailor, Ugland wants to start a boat museum as well, but it likely won't capture the unlikely charm of this Cayman oddity. ✉ *864 Northwest Point Rd., West Bay* ☎ *345/947–7741* 🌐 *www.caymanmotormuseum.com* 🎟 *$15* ⏲ *Oct.–Aug., Mon.–Sat. 8–3.*

FAMILY **Cayman Turtle Farm.** Cayman's premier attraction has been transformed into a marine theme park with souvenir shops and restaurants. Still, the turtles remain a central attraction, and you can tour ponds in the original research–breeding facility with thousands in various stages of growth, some up to 600 pounds and more than 70 years old. Four areas—three aquatic and one dry—cover 23 acres; different-color bracelets determine access (the steep full-pass admission includes snorkeling gear and water slides). The park helps promote conservation, encouraging interaction (a tidal pool houses invertebrates such as starfish and crabs) and observation. When turtles are picked up from the tanks, the little creatures flap their fins and splash the water. Animal Program events include Keeper Talks, where you might feed birds or iguanas, and biologists' conservation programs. The freshwater **Breaker's Lagoon,** replete with cascades plunging over moss-carpeted rocks, evokes Cayman Brac. The saltwater **Boatswain's Lagoon,** replicating all the Cayman Islands and the Trench, teems with 14,000 denizens of the deep milling about a cannily designed synthetic reef. You can snorkel here (lessons and guided tours are available). Both lagoons have underwater

4-inch-thick acrylic panels that look directly into **Predator Reef,** home to six brown sharks, four nurse sharks, and other predatory fish such as tarpons, eels, and jacks, which can also be viewed from terra (or terror, as one guide jokes) firma. Look for feeding times. The free-flight **Aviary**, designed by consultants from Disney's Animal Kingdom, is a riot of color and noise with feathered friends representing the entire Caribbean basin; it doubles as a rehabilitation center for Cayman Wildlife and Rescue. A winding interpretive **nature trail** culminates in the Blue Hole, a collapsed cave once filled with water. Audio tours are available with different focuses, from butterflies to bush medicine. The last stop is the living museum, **Cayman Street**, with facades duplicating vernacular architecture; an herb and fruit garden; porch-side artisans, musicians, and storytellers; model catboats; live cooking on an old-fashioned caboose (outside kitchen) oven; and interactive craft demonstrations from painting mahogany to thatch weaving. ✉ *786 Northwest Point Rd., Box 812, West Bay* ☎ *345/949–3894* 🌐 *www.turtle.ky, www.boatswainsbeach.ky* 🎫 *Comprehensive $45; Turtle Farm only, $18* ⏲ *Mon.–Sat. 8–5, Sun. 10–5; lagoons close ½ hr–2 hrs earlier.*

FAMILY **Dolphin Discovery.** If you ever dreamed of frolicking with Flipper, here's your (photo) opportunity, as the organizers of this global business promise a "touching experience." The well-maintained facility, certified by the Alliance of Marine Mammal Parks and Aquariums, offers three main options ($99–$169, less for kids, who must swim with an adult), depending on time spent splashing in the enormous pool with the dolphins and stingrays. The premium Royal Swim includes a dorsal tow and foot push, showcasing the amazing strength, speed, and agility of these majestic marine mammals. Other options offer a handshake, kiss, belly ride, and a new underwater dive experience dubbed Dolphin Trek. All participants receive free entrance to Stingray City or the Turtle Farm across the street, taking some of the sting out of the high prices. ✉ *Northwest Point Rd., West Bay* ☎ *345/769–7946, 866/393–5158 toll-free in U.S., 345/949–7946* 🌐 *www.dolphindiscovery.com/grand-cayman.*

Hell. Quite literally the tourist trap from Hell, especially when overrun by cruise-ship passengers, this attraction does offer free admission, fun photo ops, and sublime surrealism. Its name refers to the quarter-acre of menacing shards of charred brimstone thrusting up like vengeful spirits (actually blackened and "sculpted" by acid-secreting algae and fungi over millennia). The eerie lunarscape is now cordoned off, but you can prove you had a helluva time by taking a photo from the observation deck. The attractions are the small post office and a gift shop where you can get cards and letters postmarked from Hell, not to mention wonderfully silly postcards titled "When Hell Freezes Over" (depicting bathing beauties on the beach), "The Devil Made Me Do It" bumper stickers, Scotch bonnet–based Hell sauce, and "The coolest shop in Hell" T-shirts. Ivan Farrington, the owner of the Devil's Hang-Out store, cavorts in a devil's costume (horn, cape, and tails), regaling you with demonically bad jokes. ✉ *Hell Rd., West Bay* ☎ *345/949–3358* 🎫 *Free* ⏲ *Daily 9–6.*

NORTH SIDE

TOP ATTRACTIONS

Fodor's Choice ★ **Queen Elizabeth II Botanic Park.** This 65-acre wilderness preserve showcases a wide range of indigenous and nonindigenous tropical vegetation, approximately 2,000 species in total. Splendid sections include numerous water features from limpid lily ponds to cascades; a Heritage Garden with a traditional cottage and "caboose" (outside kitchen) that includes crops that might have been planted on Cayman a century ago; and a Floral Colour Garden arranged by color, the walkway wandering through sections of pink, red, orange, yellow, white, blue, mauve, lavender, and purple. A 2-acre lake and adjacent wetlands include three islets that provide a habitat and breeding ground for native birds just as showy as the floral displays: green herons, black-necked stilts, American coots, blue-winged teal, cattle egrets, and rare West Indian whistling ducks. The nearly mile-long Woodland Trail encompasses every Cayman ecosystem from wetland to cactus thicket, buttonwood swamp to lofty woodland with imposing mahogany trees. You'll encounter birds, lizards, turtles, and agoutis, but the park's star residents are the protected endemic blue iguanas, found only in Grand Cayman. The world's most endangered iguana, they're the focus of the National Trust's Blue Iguana Recovery Program, a captive breeding and reintroduction facility. This section of the park is usually closed to the public, though released "blue dragons" hang out in the vicinity. The Trust conducts 90-minute behind-the-scenes safaris Monday–Saturday at 11 am for $30. ✉ *367 Botanic Rd., North Side* ☎ *345/947–9462* 🌐 *www.botanic-park.ky* 🎫 *$10* 🕓 *Daily 9–5:30; last admission 1 hr before closing.*

BODDEN TOWN

In the island's original south-shore capital you can find an old **cemetery** on the shore side of the road. Graves with A-frame structures are said to contain the remains of pirates. There are also the ruins of a fort and a wall erected by slaves in the 19th century. The National Trust runs tours of the restored 1840s **Mission House.** A curio shop serves as the entrance to what's called the **Pirate's Caves** ($10), partially underground natural formations that are more hokey (decked out with fake treasure chests and mannequins in pirate garb, with an outdoor petting zoo) than spooky.

TOP ATTRACTIONS

Fodor's Choice ★ **Pedro St. James Castle.** Built in 1780, the great house is Cayman's oldest stone structure and the island's only remaining late-18th-century residence. In its capacity as courthouse and jail, it was the birthplace of Caymanian democracy, where in December 1831 the first elected parliament was organized and in 1835 the Slavery Abolition Act signed. The structure still has original or historically accurate replicas of sweeping verandas, mahogany floors, rough-hewn wide-beam ceilings, outside louvers, stone and oxblood- or mustard-color lime-wash-painted walls, brass fixtures, and Georgian furnishings (from tea caddies to canopy beds to commodes). Paying obsessive attention to detail, the curators even fill glasses with faux wine. The mini-museum also includes a hodgepodge of displays from slave emancipation to old stamps. The buildings are surrounded by 8 acres of natural parks and woodlands.

You can stroll through landscaping of native Caymanian flora and experience one of the most spectacular views on the island from atop the dramatic Great Pedro Bluff. First watch the impressive multimedia show, on the hour, complete with smoking pots, misting rains, and two screens. The poignant Hurricane Ivan Memorial outside uses text, images, and symbols to represent important aspects of the 2004 disaster. ✉ *Pedro Castle Rd., Savannah* ☎ *345/947–3329* 🌐 *www.pedrostjames.ky* 🎟 *$10* ⏲ *Daily 9–5.*

EAST END

WORTH NOTING

FAMILY **Blowholes.** When the easterly trade winds blow hard, crashing waves force water into caverns and send impressive geysers shooting up as much as 20 feet through the ironshore. The blowholes were partially filled during Hurricane Ivan in 2004, so the water must be rough to recapture their former elemental drama. ✉ *Frank Sound Rd., roughly 10 miles (16 km) east of Bodden Town, near East End.*

Cayman Islands Brewery. In this brewery occupying the former Stingray facility, tour guides explain the iconic imagery of bottle and label as well as the nearly three-week brewing process: seven days' fermentation, 10 days' lagering (storage), and one day in the bottling tank. The brewery's eco-friendly features are also championed: local farmers receive the spent grains to feed their cattle at no charge, while waste liquid is channeled into one of the Caribbean's most advanced water-treatment systems. Then enjoy your complimentary tasting knowing that you're helping the local environment and economy. ✉ *366 Shamrock Rd., Red Bay* ☎ *345/947–6699* 🌐 *caybrew.com* 🎟 *$6* ⏲ *Weekdays 9–5, tours 9–4 on the hr by appointment.*

Wreck of the Ten Sails Park. This lonely, lovely park on Grand Cayman's windswept eastern tip commemorates the island's most (in)famous shipwreck. On February 8, 1794, the *Cordelia,* heading a convoy of 58 square-rigged merchant vessels en route from Jamaica to England, foundered on one of the treacherous East End reefs. Its warning cannon fire was tragically misconstrued as a call to band more closely together due to imminent pirate attack, and nine more ships ran aground. Local sailors, who knew the rough seas, demonstrated great bravery in rescuing all 400-odd seamen. Popular legend claims (romantically but inaccurately) that King George III granted the islands an eternal tax exemption. Queen Elizabeth II dedicated the park's plaque in 1994. Interpretive signs document the historic details. The ironically peaceful headland provides magnificent views of the reef (including more recent shipwrecks); bird-watching is superb from here half a mile south along the coast to the Lighthouse Park, perched on a craggy bluff. ✉ *Gun Bay, East End* ☎ *345/949–0121 National Trust* 🎟 *Free* ⏲ *Daily.*

BEACHES

Limestone, coral, shells, water, and wind collaborated to fashion the Cayman Islands beaches. It's a classic example of the interaction between geology and marine biology. Most of the beaches in Cayman, especially on Grand and Little Cayman, resemble powdered ivory. A few, including those on Cayman Brac, are more dramatic, a mix of fine beige sand and rugged rocky "ironshore," which often signals the healthiest reefs and best snorkeling.

Barkers. Secluded, spectacular beaches are accessed via a dirt road just past Papagallo restaurant. There are no facilities (that's the point!), but some palms offer shade. Unfortunately, the shallow water and rocky bottom discourage swimming, and it can be cluttered at times with seaweed and debris. Kitesurfers occasionally come here for the gusts. **Amenities:** none. **Best for:** solitude; walking; windsurfing. ✉ *Conch Point Rd., Barkers, West Bay.*

Cemetery Beach. A narrow, sandy driveway takes you past the small cemetery to a perfect strand just past the northern end of Seven Mile Beach. The dock here is primarily used by dive boats during winter storms. You can walk in either direction. The sand is talcum-soft and clean, the water calm and clear (though local surfers take advantage of occasional small reef breaks), and the bottom somewhat rocky and dotted with sea urchins, so wear reef shoes if wading. You'll definitely find fewer crowds. **Amenities:** none. **Best for:** solitude; snorkeling; surfing. ✉ *West Bay Rd., Seven Mile Beach.*

East End Beaches. Just drive along and look for any sandy beach, park your car, and enjoy a stroll. The vanilla-hue stretch at Colliers Bay, by the Reef and Morritt's resorts (which offer water sports), is a good, clean one with superior snorkeling. **Amenities:** food and drink; water sports. **Best for:** solitude; snorkeling; sunrise; walking. ✉ *Queen's Hwy., East End.*

Old Man Bay. The North Side features plenty of hidden coves and pristine stretches of perfect sand, where you'll be disturbed only by seabirds dive-bombing for lunch and the occasional lone fishers casting nets for sprats, then dumping them into buckets. Over the Edge restaurant is less than 1 mile (1½ km) west. Otherwise, it's fairly undeveloped for miles, save for the occasional private home. Snorkeling is spectacular when waters are calm. **Amenities:** food and drink. **Best for:** solitude; snorkeling; walking. ✉ *Queen's Hwy., just off Frank Sound Rd., North Side.*

Rum Point. This North Sound beach has hammocks slung in towering casuarina trees, picnic tables, casual and "fancier" dining options, a well-stocked shop for seaworthy sundries, and Red Sail Sports, which offers various water sports and boats to explore Stingray City. The barrier reef ensures safe snorkeling and soft sand. The bottom remains shallow for a long way from shore, but it's littered with small coral heads, so be careful. The Wreck is an ultracasual hangout serving outstanding pub grub from fish-and-chips to wings, as well as lethal Mudslide cocktails. Just around the bend, another quintessential beach hangout, Kaibo, rocks during the day. **Amenities:** food and drink; parking (no fee); showers; toilets; water sports. **Best for:** partiers; snorkeling. ✉ *Rum Point, North Side.*

Fodor's Choice ★ **Seven Mile Beach.** Grand Cayman's west coast is dominated by this famous beach—actually a 6½-mile (10-km) expanse of powdery white sand overseeing lapis water stippled with a rainbow of parasails and kayaks. Free of litter and pesky peddlers, it's an unspoiled (though often crowded) environment. Most of the island's resorts, restaurants, and shopping centers sit along this strip. The public beach toward the north end offers chairs for rent ($10 for the day, including a beverage), a playground, water toys aplenty, beach bars, restrooms, and showers. The best snorkeling is at either end, by the Marriott and Treasure Island or off Cemetery Beach, to the north. **Amenities**: food and drink; showers; toilets; water sports. **Best for**: partiers; snorkeling. ✉ *West Bay Rd., Seven Mile Beach.*

Smith's Cove. South of the Grand Old House, this tiny but popular protected swimming and snorkeling spot makes a wonderful beach wedding location. The bottom drops off quickly enough to allow you to swim and play close to shore. Although slightly rocky (its pitted limestone boulders resemble Moore sculptures), there's little debris and few coral heads, plenty of shade, picnic tables, restrooms, and parking. Surfers will find decent swells just to the south. Note the curious obelisk cenotaph "In memory of James Samuel Webster and his wife Arabella Antoinette (née Eden)," with assorted quotes from Confucius to John Donne. **Amenities**: parking (no fee); toilets. **Best for**: snorkeling; sunset; swimming. ✉ *Off S. Church St.*

BEST BETS FOR DINING

Fodor's Choice ★
Agua, Blue by Eric Ripert, Grand Old House, Luca, Michael's Genuine Food & Drink, Mizu, Ortanique, Ragazzi

BEST VIEW
Cracked Conch, Reef Grill at Royal Palms

MOST ROMANTIC
Grand Old House

BEST FOR LOCAL CUISINE
Chicken! Chicken!, Cimboco, Over the Edge, Vivine's Kitchen

HOT SPOTS
Agua, Luca, Mizu, Ragazzi, Yoshi Sushi

WHERE TO EAT

Despite its small size, comparative geographic isolation, and British colonial trappings, Grand Cayman offers a smorgasbord of gastronomic goodies. With more than 100 eateries, something should suit and sate every palate and pocketbook (factoring in the fast-food franchises sweeping the islandscape like tumbleweed, and stands dispensing local specialties). The term *melting pot* describes both the majority of menus and the multicultural population. The sheer range of dining options from Middle Eastern to Mexican reflects the island's cosmopolitan clientele. Imported ingredients make up their own United Nations, with chefs sourcing salmon from Norway, foie gras from Périgord, and lamb from New Zealand. Wine lists can be equally global in scope. And don't be surprised to find both Czech and Chilean staffers at a remote East End restaurant. As one restaurateur quipped, "Cayman is the ultimate culture-shock absorber."

Prices are about 25% more than those in a major U.S. city. Many restaurants add a 10% to 15% service charge to the bill; be sure to check before leaving a tip. Alcohol with your meal can send the tab skyrocketing. Buy liquor duty-free before you leave the airport and enjoy a cocktail or nightcap from the comfort of your room or balcony. Cayman customs limits you to two bottles per person. You should make reservations at all but the most casual places, particularly during the high season. Note that many bars offer fine fare (and many eateries have hip, hopping bar scenes).

What to Wear: Grand Cayman dining is casual (shorts are okay, but *not* beachwear and tank tops). Mosquitoes can be pesky when you are dining outdoors, especially at sunset, so plan ahead or ask for repellent. Winter can be chilly enough to warrant a light sweater.

AROUND GEORGE TOWN

$$$$ ECLECTIC **The Brasserie.** Actuaries, bankers, and CEOs frequent this contemporary throwback to a colonial country club for lunch and "attitude adjustment" happy hours for creative cocktails and complimentary canapés. Inviting fusion sea-to-table cuisine, emphasizing local ingredients whenever possible (the restaurant has its own boat and garden), includes terrific bar tapas like chipotle-braised oxtail taco with pepper aioli and pickled vegetables, and melted Brie with white truffle–and-mango marmalade. Several evenings, you can get a five-course market-driven Random Acts of Cooking blind tasting. Dishes deftly balance flavors and textures without sensory overload: this is serious food with a sense of playfulness. Save room for dessert, from an artisanal cheese plate to an ice-cream-and-sorbet tasting menu to elaborate architectural confections. Lunch is more reasonably priced but equally creative; the adjacent Market excels at takeout, and the wine list is well considered. *Average main: $34 171 Elgin Ave., Cricket Sq. 345/945–1815 www.brasseriecayman.com Reservations essential Closed weekends.*

8

$$ CARIBBEAN **Breezes by the Bay.** There isn't a bad seat in the house at this nonstop fiesta festooned with tiny paper lanterns, Christmas lights, ship murals, model boats, and Mardi Gras beads (you're "lei'd" upon entering). Wraparound balconies take in a dazzling panorama from South Sound to Seven Mile Beach. It's happy hour all day every day, especially during Countdown to Sunset. Signs promise "the good kind of hurricanes," referring to the 23-ounce signature "category 15" cocktails with fresh garnishes. Chunky, velvety conch chowder served in a bread bowl or conch fritters are meals in themselves. Hefty sandwiches are slathered with jerk mayo or garlic aioli. Signature standouts include meltingly moist whole fish escoveitch, popcorn shrimp, sliders, and any pie from the pizza station. *Average main: $18 Harbour Dr. 345/943–8439 www.breezesbythebay.com No dinner May–Sept.*

$$$$ ITALIAN **Casanova Restaurant by the Sea.** Owner Tony Crescente and younger brother–maitre d' Carlo offer a simpatico dining experience, practically exhorting you to *mangia* and sending you off with a chorus of ciaos. There's some decorative *formaggio* (cheese): murals of grape clusters and cavorting cherubs, paintings of the Amalfi Coast, and *"una finestra sul mare"* ("window to the sea") stenciled redundantly over arches opening onto the harbor. The kitsch doesn't extend to the kitchen. Sterling Italian favorites include salmon marinated in citrus, olive oil, and basil; lemony veal piccata; gnocchetti in velvety four-cheese sauce

with a blush of tomato; and seafood grill in parsley-garlic-lemon sauce. Enjoy grappa at the marble bar of Il Bacio lounge amid its wooden wine racks (the impressive selection isn't overly Italian-centric). The patio juts over the harbor, and moonlight, abetted by a soundtrack of Bocelli to Bennett, can transform an amorous coward into a Casanova. *$ Average main: $35 ✉ 65 N. Church St. ☎ 345/949–7633 🌐 www.casanova.ky ✍ Reservations essential.*

$$$ SEAFOOD **✕ Da Fish Shack.** This classic clapboard seaside shanty couldn't be homier: constructed from an old fishing vessel, the structure is an authentic representation of original Caymanian architecture. The deck couldn't be better placed to savor the breezes and water views, and the chill Caribbean vibe makes it feel as if you're dining at a friend's home. The owners source fresh local ingredients wherever possible and developed relationships with Caymanian fishermen, who often cruise up to the dock with their catch. Savor jerk fish tacos, saltfish fritters, coconut shrimp with pineapple tomato salsa, and golden crunchy breadfruit fries. A wide array of non-seafood dishes is offered, from chicken schnitzel to a rib-eye with sauce chasseur. The place hops on Sundown Saturdays with a CI$20 waterfront barbecue. Free Wi-Fi and occasional DJs are bonuses. *$ Average main: $23 ✉ 127 N. Church St. ☎ 345/947–8126 🌐 www.dafishshack.com.*

$$$$ EUROPEAN Fodor's Choice ★ **✕ Grand Old House.** Built in 1908 as the Petra Plantation House and transformed into the island's first upscale establishment decades ago, this grande dame evokes bygone grandeur sans pretension. The interior rooms, awash in crystal, recall its plantation-house origins. Outside, hundreds of sparkling lights adorning the gazebos compete with the starry sky. Live nightly music and rumors of a charming blond ghost trailing white chiffon complete the picture. This is a place to propose or let someone down easily. Expertly executed classics include panfried foie gras with ice wine–raspberry compote, broiled lobster tail with smoked bell-pepper butter, and filet mignon with green peppercorn sauce. The subtle yet complex flavor interactions, stellar service, and encyclopedic if stratospherically priced wine list ensure legendary status. Nightly happy hours with discounted tapas are a sensational bargain. *$ Average main: $56 ✉ 648 S. Church St. ☎ 345/949–9333 🌐 www.grandoldhouse.com ✍ Reservations essential ⏲ Closed Sept. and Sun. in low season. No lunch weekends.*

$$$$ SEAFOOD **✕ Guy Harvey's Island Grill.** At this stylish, sporty, upstairs bistro, you half expect to find Hemingway regaling fellow barflies in the clubby interior with mahogany furnishings, ship's lanterns, porthole windows, fishing rods, and Harvey's action-packed marine art. The cool blues echo the sea and sky on display from the balcony. Seafood is carefully chosen to exclude overexploited and threatened species. Seasonally changing dishes are peppered with Caribbean influences but puréed through the original French chef's formal training. Hence, silken lobster bisque is served with puff pastry, scallops Rockefeller with spinach and béarnaise sauce, and the signature crab cakes with roasted-red-pepper aioli. You can select your fish baked, pan-sautéed, or grilled with any of eight sauces. Carnivores needn't despair, with rack of lamb provençale in balsamic glaze or intensely flavored filet mignon Roquefort

(frites optional). Many specialties are cheaper at lunch. Nightly specials for CI$9.99 and the four-course CI$30 dinner reel in savvy locals. *Average main: $38* *Aquaworld Duty-Free Mall, 55 S. Church St.* *345/946–9000* *www.guyharveysgrill.com.*

$$$$ SEAFOOD **Lobster Pot.** The nondescript building belies the lovely marine-motif decor and luscious seafood at this intimate, second-story restaurant overlooking the harbor. Enjoy lobster prepared several ways (market price, it can be as much as $60) along with reasonably priced wine, which you can sample by the glass in the cozy bar. The two musts are the Cayman Trio (lobster tail, grilled mahimahi, and garlic shrimp) and the Pot (lobster, giant prawns, and crab). The kitchen happily provides reduced-oil and -fat alternatives to most dishes; vegetarians love the flavorful chili-lime polenta with grilled artichoke in mango cream, and tofu, zucchini, and yellow-squash spaghetti. The balcony offers a breathtaking view of the sunset tarpon feeding. *Average main: $48* *245 N. Church St.* *345/949–2736* *www.lobsterpot.ky* *No lunch weekends.*

SEVEN MILE BEACH

$$$$ ITALIAN Fodor's Choice ★ **Agua.** This quietly hip spot plays up an aquatic theme with indigo glass fixtures, black-and-white photos of bridges and waterfalls, and cobalt-and-white walls subtly recalling foamy waves. Its young, international chefs emphasize seafood, preparing regional dishes from around the globe with a Caymanian slant, albeit emphasizing Italian specialties. Thai ceviche with kaffir lime and coconut milk and tuna tartare with avocado brunoise, white truffle oil, and sweet-and-sour sauce burst with flavor. Superlative pastas include lobster-shiitake-mascarpone ravioli with chive butter sauce. Presentation is painterly throughout, and authentic gelatos cap off the meal. Wine selections from lesser-known regions often represent good value, with 20 offered by the glass; the bartenders also creatively pair cocktails and food. Free tapas at happy hour and the CI$19.95 three-course lunch menu are steals. *Average main: $39* *Galleria Plaza, Seven Mile Beach* *345/949–2482* *www.agua.ky* *Reservations essential.*

$ MIDDLE EASTERN **Al La Kebab.** The Silvermans started by serving late-night kebabs and gyros. Today their eatery works miracles out of two makeshift lean-tos splashed in vibrant colors and is still open until 4 am weeknights, 2 am weekends. Alan calls it a building-block menu; you can modify the bread and sauce—a dozen varieties, including several curries, peanut satay, mango *raita* (yogurt, tomatoes, chutney), tahini, teriyaki, garlic cream, even gravy like Mom used to make. Food romps from Malaysia through the Mediterranean to Mexico: spicy chicken tikka, Thai chicken-lemongrass soup, and tzatziki as well as unusual salads (the Lebanese *fattoush*—toasted bread, mint, and parsley—is fabulous) and creative sides (addictive jalapeño-cheddar salsa for fries). *Average main: $9* *Marquee Plaza, West Bay Rd., Seven Mile Beach* *345/943–4343* *www.kebab.ky* *Reservations not accepted.*

$$$$ SEAFOOD **Beach House.** This refined eatery (aka Casa Havana) glamorously channels South Beach and Santa Monica, with a sexy black bar dispensing luscious libations, an earthy color scheme, and sparkly ecru curtains dividing dining spaces. Founding executive chef Michaell Farrell hails

8

from the Big Easy, and his coastal cuisine travels from Nantucket to New Orleans with aplomb. The menu offers mostly small plates and large plates to be shared family-style. Seafood is the star, unsurprisingly. Witness the sea bass with mojo, chipotle creamed corn, black beans, and roast pork croquettes, and wild tiger prawns with black pearl couscous, pickled cauliflower, tomato fondue, and saffron emulsion. Carnivores needn't despair: the sous-vide beef tenderloin practically dissolves in your mouth. Pairings are suggested for each dish, and the wine list features several fine $35 options and some surprising high-end bargains. Wine Master dinners pair several courses with wines (Marchese di Barolo to Gosset champagne), often introduced by guest winemakers or owners from as far afield as Tuscany, Australia, Napa, and Chile. *Average main: $40 ✉ Westin Grand Cayman Seven Mile Beach Resort & Spa, West Bay Rd., Seven Mile Beach ☎ 345/945–3800 www.westingrandcayman.com No lunch.*

$$$$ SEAFOOD Fodor's Choice ★ **Blue by Eric Ripert.** *Top Chef* judge Eric Ripert's trademark ethereal seafood (executed by his handpicked brigade), flawless but not fawning service, swish setting, and soothing, unpretentious sophistication make this one of the Caribbean's finest restaurants. Choose from hedonistic six- and seven-course tasting menus (with or without wine pairing); there are also trendy "almost raw" and "barely touched" options. Many dishes are clever riffs on the mother restaurant (New York's celebrated Le Bernardin), using the island's natural bounty; a tribute to the Bernardin tuna foie gras adds Cayman sea salt. Sensuous options might include melt-in-your-mouth lobster with purple cauliflower and macadamia nuts in truffle butter, seared turbot with braised endive in a clam–foie gras emulsion, and spicy pineapple–passion fruit–soy milk panna cotta with tequila sorbet. The vast wine list showcases heavy hitters, hot new regions, and lesser-known varietals. *Average main: $150 ✉ Ritz-Carlton Grand Cayman, West Bay Rd., Seven Mile Beach ☎ 345/943–9000 Reservations essential Closed Sun.–Mon. and Sept.–mid-Nov. No lunch.*

$$ CARIBBEAN FAMILY **Chicken! Chicken!** Devotees would probably award four exclamation points to the marvelously moist chicken, slow-roasted on a hardwood open-hearth rotisserie. Most customers grab takeout, but the decor is appealing for a fast-food joint; the clever interior replicates an old-time Cayman cottage. Bright smiles and home cooking from scratch enhance the authentic vibe. Hearty but (mostly) healthful heaping helpings of sides include scrumptious Cayman-style corn bread, honey-rum beans, jicama coleslaw, and spinach-pesto pasta. Prices are even cheaper at lunch. *Average main: $12 ✉ West Shore Centre, West Bay Rd., Seven Mile Beach ☎ 345/945–2290 www.chicken2.com.*

$$ ECLECTIC **Cimboco.** This animated space celebrates all things fun and Caribbean with walls saturated in orange, lemon, and lavender; cobalt glass fixtures; and flames dancing up the exhibition kitchen's huge wood-burning oven. The *Cimboco* was the first motorized sailing ship built in Cayman (in 1927) and for 20 years the lifeline to the outside world; National Archive photographs and old newspapers invest the space with still more character. Everything from breads (superlative bruschetta and jalapeño corn bread) to ice creams is made from scratch.

Artisanal pizzas come topped with balsamic-roasted eggplant, pesto, and feta or with jerk chicken with Bermuda onions. Signature items include banana-leaf-roasted snapper and fire-roasted bacon-wrapped shrimp. Amazingly good desserts include a sinfully rich brownie. The popular breakfast and brunch are equally creative. *Average main: $18 Marquee Plaza, West Bay Rd. at Harquail Bypass, Seven Mile Beach 345/947–2782 www.cimboco.com.*

$$
ECLECTIC
FAMILY

Eats Cafe. This happy, hopping hangout is more eclectic and stylish than any diner, with dramatic decor (crimson booths and walls, flat-screen TVs lining the counter, steel pendant lamps, an exhibition kitchen, gigantic flower paintings, and Andy Warhol reproductions) and vast menu (Cajun to Chinese), including smashing breakfasts. The 10-plus burgers alone (Sauteed 'Shroomer to Smokey Mountain BBQ, as well as fish and veggie versions) could satisfy almost any craving, but you could also get a Caesar salad or samosas, Philly cheese steak or chicken fajitas. It's noisy, busy, buzzing, and hip—but not aggressively so. *Average main: $16 Falls Plaza, West Bay Rd., Seven Mile Beach 345/943–3287 www.eatscafecayman.com.*

$$$$
ITALIAN
Fodor's Choice ★

Luca. Owners Paolo Polloni and Andi Marcher spared no expense in creating a smart beachfront trattoria that wouldn't be out of place in L.A. Everything was handpicked, from the wine wall of more than 3,000 international bottles to Murano glass fixtures, arty blown-up photographs, leather banquettes, and a curving onyx-top bar. Chef Frederico Destro delights in unorthodox pairings, all gorgeous. Tuna is served with pea pesto, wild rice, and Scotch bonnet aioli. Hudson Valley foie gras knits poached apple with sherry reduction and onion fondue. Homemade pastas like pumpkin ravioli in drawn thyme butter also shine, but the standout is a whole Mediterranean striped bass baked in salt crust. *Average main: $46 Caribbean Club, 871 West Bay Rd., Seven Mile Beach 345/623–4550 Reservations essential Closed Mon. Sept.–Oct. No lunch Sat.*

8

$$$$
ECLECTIC
Fodor's Choice ★

Michael's Genuine Food & Drink. James Beard Award–winning chef Michael Schwartz and original executive chef Thomas Tennant imported the slow-food philosophy of the groundbreaking Michael's Genuine in Miami. Seasonal menu items come from the on-site garden and from carefully chosen Cayman farmers, fishers, and ranchers. Living up to the Schwartz mantra of "fresh, simple, pure," the honest, uncluttered food sings with color and flavor down to the homemade sodas. Lunch offers a more traditional but lengthy selection, whereas dinner dishes come in small, medium, and large portions—perfect for sharing. The changing menu includes burrata (with seasonal heirloom tomato) and crispy yet unctuously fatty sweet-and-sour pork belly, and wood-oven-roasted dishes like pizza, snapper, or *poulet rouge* chicken. The well-considered wine list offers occasional bargains. Tennant devised an inspired solution to the invasive lionfish population: look for it as a menu special, and if you dive, ask about the Lionfish Safari. *Average main: $39 47 Forum La., Canella Court, Camana Bay 345/640–6433 www.michaelsgenuine.com.*

$$ ASIAN Fodor's Choice ★ ✕ **Mizu.** It's a toss-up as to which is sexier at this pan-Pacific bistro: the sleek decor, the model-worthy waitstaff, or the glistening, artfully presented food. The first, courtesy of Hong Kong designer Kitty Chan, is as sensuous as a 21st-century opium den, with a backlit dragon, contemporary Buddhas, glowing granite bar, and enormous mirrors. The bartenders have developed a loyal local following for their flair in more ways than one. The last trots effortlessly all over Asia for culinary inspiration: terrific tuna tartare, decadent duck gyoza, killer kung pao chicken, smashing Singapore fried noodles, heavenly honey-glazed ribs, beautifully crispy Okinawan-style pork belly, and two-dozen ultrafresh maki (try the signature roll). An extensive tea selection and a sake and wine list are also offered. *Average main: $20 ✉ Camana Bay ☎ 345/640–0001 🌐 www.mizucayman.com.*

$$$ ECLECTIC ✕ **Morgan's.** Energetic, effervescent Janie Schweiger patrols the front while husband Richard rules the kitchen at this simpatico marina spot with smashing Governor's Creek views. Locals and fishermen literally cruise into the adjacent dock for refueling of all sorts. You can sit in the cozy room decorated with Depression-era chandeliers and vivid aquatic artworks or admire the dexterous marine maneuverings from the deck. Richard's menu dances just as deftly from Asia to his Austrian home. Nimbly prepared nibbles include the wildly popular 10-ounce Brie-topped jerk burger and ceviche, but everything from chicken schnitzel to Thai seafood curry is expertly cooked to order. Lunch offers several of the restaurant's greatest hits at more palatable prices. *Average main: $26 ✉ Governor's Creek, Cayman Islands Yacht Club, Seven Mile Beach ☎ 345/946–7049 Reservations essential.*

$$$$ ECLECTIC Fodor's Choice ★ ✕ **Ortanique.** The vibrant food here lives up to its nickname: "cuisine of the sun." It's an outpost of chef Cindy Hutson and Delius Shirley's Miami Ortanique, which helped revolutionize Floribbean fusion fare. The interior gleams in rich yellows and oranges that subtly recall plantation living, though prize seating is on the patio, shaded by sea grape trees overlooking an islet. There is an emphasis on Caribbean and South American cuisine infused with Asian inspirations. The kitchen reinvents classics with an island twist: jerk-rubbed foie gras with burnt-orange marmalade, and the signature jerked double pork chop, fire-tamed by guava-spiced rum glaze. Save room for such decadent desserts as a deceptively airy Cloud of Coconut Joy or rum-soaked banana fritters. Best of all are almost nightly happy hour specials from Mojito Madness Mondays to Tapas Thursdays. *Average main: $36 ✉ 47 Forum La., The Crescent, Camana Bay ☎ 345/640–7710 🌐 www.ortaniquerestaurants.com ⏲ Closed Sun. June–Oct.*

$$$ ITALIAN Fodor's Choice ★ ✕ **Ragazzi.** The name means "good buddies," and this strip-mall jewel percolates with conversation and good strong espresso. The airy space is convivial: blond woods, periwinkle walls and columns, and handsome artworks of beach scenes, sailboats, and palm trees. Chef Adriano Usini meticulously prepares standards; the antipasto alone is worth a visit, as are homemade breadsticks and focaccia, carpaccio, and insalata Caprese. The shellfish linguine in a light, silken tomato sauce, with cherry-tomato skins pulled back and crisped, and gnocchi in four-cheese sauce with brandy and pistachios please pasta perfectionists. Two dozen

first-rate pizzas emerge from the wood-burning oven, and meat and seafood mains are beautifully done, never overcooked. The wine list is notable (400-odd choices) for a casual eatery, offering affordability even on heavy hitters such as Biondi Santi Brunello, Jermann Pinot Grigio, and Giacosa Barbaresco; the knowledgeable staff will gladly suggest pairings. *Average main: $24* ✉ *Buckingham Square, West Bay Rd., Seven Mile Beach* ☎ *345/945–3484* 🌐 *www.ragazzi.ky.*

$$$$ ECLECTIC **Reef Grill at Royal Palms.** This class act appeals to a casual, suave crowd, many of them regulars, who appreciate its consistent quality, efficient service, soothing seaside setting, top-notch entertainment, and surprisingly reasonable prices. The space is cannily divided into four areas, each with its own look and feel, including private beach cabanas (no extra charge). Co-owner–chef George Dahlstrom gives his perfectly prepared, familiar items just enough twist to satisfy jaded palates: calamari is fried in arborio rice batter with jalapeño aioli while Chilean sea bass swims amid Thai salad and homemade wontons. The Royal Palms menu offers more casual, inexpensive fare. Dance the calories off to the estimable reggae, calypso, and soca sounds of Coco Red or really sweat it out during Chill Wednesdays, and then adjourn to the cozy lounge for an aged rum or single malt. It's equally enticing at lunch, when it exudes a soigné beach-bar ambience. *Average main: $33* ✉ *537 West Bay Rd., Seven Mile Beach* ☎ *345/945–6358* 🌐 *www.reefgrill.com* ⏲ *No dinner Sun. May–Nov.*

$$$$ STEAKHOUSE **Seven.** The Ritz-Carlton's all-purpose dining room transforms from a bustling breakfast buffet to an elegant evening eatery. Tall potted palms, soaring ceilings, a black-and-beige color scheme, twin wine walls bracketing a trendy family-style table, and the tiered pool outside are lighted to stylish effect. Sinatra and Ella keep a sultry beat while the kitchen jazzes standard meat-and-potatoes dishes with inventive seasonings and eye-catching presentations. Splendid aged Niman Ranch steaks come with five sauces and rubs, from five-peppercorn to béarnaise. Even such sides as truffled mac-and-cheese redefine decadence. The calorie- and cholesterol-conscious can savor the likes of melt-in-your-mouth ahi tuna poke. Then surrender to the chocolate and sea-salt caramel candy bar. Nightly happy hour (5–7) offers superb bar snacks like tempura Brie with local pepper jelly and jerk maple-glazed pork belly. *Average main: $51* ✉ *Ritz-Carlton Grand Cayman, West Bay Rd., Seven Mile Beach* ☎ *345/943–9000* 🌐 *www.ritzcarlton.com.*

$$ CARIBBEAN FAMILY **Sunshine Grill.** This cheerful, cherished locals' secret serves haute comfort food at bargain prices. Even the chattel-style poolside building, painted a delectable lemon with lime shutters, whets the appetite. Sunshine ranks high in the island's greatest burger debate, while the chicken egg rolls with mango chutney and jerk mayo and fabulous fish tacos elevate pub grub to an art. Wash your food down with a signature libation like the Painkiller, and take advantage of affordable nightly dinner specials such as red snapper amandine in lemon butter caper sauce, and Cuban roast chicken marinated with sour orange, garlic, lime, and olive oil. *Average main: $18* ✉ *Sunshine Suites Resort, 1465 Esterley Tibbetts Hwy., Seven Mile Beach* ☎ *345/949–3000, 345/946–5848.*

8

$$ DINER FAMILY **The Waterfront.** Ultracontemporary design with industrial elements (exposed piping, raw timber, tugboat salvage) is a counterpoint to the down-home fare at this bustling glorified diner. Comfort food aficionados can launch into the splendid chicken and waffles, meat loaf, and poutine. The kitchen is also adept at sexier dishes, such as polenta-portobello burger with goat cheese and pork belly flatbread with cilantro and spicy kimchi sauce. Finish off your meal with the enormous cinnamon bun, though it might finish you off. *Average main: $19 ✉ The Crescent, Camana Bay ☎ 345/640–0002 🌐 www.waterfrontcayman.com.*

$$ JAPANESE **Yoshi Sushi.** This modish locals' lair serves superlative sushi. The main room's scarlet cushions, cherry blown-glass pendant lamps, leather-and-bamboo accents, orchids, and maroon walls create a sensuous, charged vibe. At the backlit bar, carefree customers try to work their chopsticks after a few kamikaze sake bomber missions (hot cups of sake plunged into frosty Kirin beer). Savvy diners literally leave themselves in Yoshi's hands (the rolls and nightly sushi "pizzas" are particularly creative), while the raw-phobic can choose from fine cooked items, from tuna tataki to tempura to teriyaki. The congenial staff recommends sake and beer pairings, but the wine and martini selections are also admirable for an Asian eatery. *Average main: $20 ✉ Falls Plaza, West Bay Rd., Seven Mile Beach ☎ 345/943–9674 🌐 www.yoshisushicayman.com Reservations essential.*

WEST BAY

$$$$ ECLECTIC **Calypso Grill.** Shack chic describes this inviting split-level space splashed in Dr. Seuss primary colors that contrast with brick walls, hardwood furnishings, terra-cotta floors, trompe l'oeil shutters, and (real) French doors opening onto sweeping North Sound vistas. If the interior is like a Caribbean painting, the outdoor deck, with a view of frigate birds circling fishing boats, is a Winslow Homer. George Fowler's menu emphasizes fish hauled in at the adjacent dock, fresh and rarely overcooked. You won't go wrong with the unvarnished catch of the day grilled, blackened, or sautéed. Though this is seafood turf, landlubbers can savor escargot bourguignon, beef carpaccio, or a proper rack of lamb. End with the sticky toffee pudding. *Average main: $43 ✉ Morgan's Harbour, West Bay ☎ 345/949–3948 🌐 www.calypsogrillcayman.com Reservations essential ⊙ Closed Mon.*

$$$$ ECLECTIC **Cracked Conch.** This island institution effortlessly blends upscale and down-home. The interior gleams from the elaborate light-and-water sculpture at the gorgeous mosaic-and-mahogany entrance bar to the plush booths with subtly embedded lighting. Take in the remarkable water views through large shutters, but for maximum impact, dine on the multitiered patio. Executive chef Gilbert Cavallaro reinvents familiar dishes to create such delectables as honey-jerk-glazed tuna tartare with tomato sorbet and crispy calamari with cardamom-marinated carrots and chipotle sauce. Stellar signature items include the conch chowder or ceviche, silken short rib ravioli with truffles and Parmesan foam, and sous-vide lobster over mango-orange demi-glace. Locals flock to Sunday brunch and hang out at the dockside Macabuca tiki bar (fab sunsets, sunset-hued libations), which lives up to its mellow name, indigenous

Taíno for "What does it matter?" *Average main: $45 Northwest Point Rd., West Bay 345/945–5217 www.crackedconch.com.ky Closed Sept.–mid-Oct. No lunch June–Aug.*

$$$$ ECLECTIC **Osetra Bay.** At sunset (when brightly colored fishing boats bob in the tourmaline North Sound) and at night (when Cayman Kai's lights twinkle and the moon dapples the water with gold doubloons), the view alone guarantees a memorable meal. The design is almost as appetizing—glowing columns strategically placed to flatter diners; intimate, billowingly draped dining cabanas; stark Starck-ish white-on-white ultralounges—infusing casual Caribbean underpinnings with a chic South Beach sensibility, literally bringing caviar to Cayman. The seasonal menu (sourced locally when possible) emphasizes seafood: blackened mahimahi with sweet potato in lemongrass curry and wahoo with pea and smoked-potato purées, pickled beets, and lemon butter sauce. Carnivores can stake out classic beef tartare, oxtail ravioli with red-wine veal jus and Parmesan foam, or dry-aged rib eye. *Average main: $45 Morgan's Harbour, West Bay 345/325–5000, 345/623–5100 www.osetrabay.com Reservations essential No lunch.*

EAST END

$$$ SEAFOOD **The Lighthouse.** This lighthouse surrounded by fluttering flags serves as a beacon for hungry East End explorers. The interior replicates a yacht: polished hardwood floors, ship's lanterns, mosaic hurricane lamps, steering wheels, portholes, and waiters in crew's garb with chevrons. Most tables afford sweeping sea vistas, but prized romantic seating is on a little deck. Starters include Miss Nell's red conch chowder and flash-fried calamari with sweet chili dip. Entrées include a platter of seafood floating on linguine Alfredo and a mustard/herb-crusted rack of lamb with Marsala-mint sauce. Vegetarian options include curries, tofu stir-fries, and pastas. Desserts include the Illy espresso crème brûlée. The comprehensive wine list extends to a superb postprandial selection of liqueurs, aged rums, ports, and grappas. Inexpensive prix-fixe lunch and dinner specials are CI$9.95 and CI$15, respectively. *Average main: $30 Bodden Town Rd., Oceanside, Breakers, East End 345/947–2047 www.lighthouse.ky.*

$$ CARIBBEAN **Vivine's Kitchen.** Cars practically block the road at this unprepossessing hot spot for classic Caymanian food—literally Vivine and Ray Watler's home. Prime seating is in the waterfront courtyard, serenaded by rustling sea grape leaves, crashing surf, and screeching gulls. The day's menu, sourced locally for freshness, is scrawled on a blackboard: perhaps stewed turtle, curried goat, barbecued chicken, and snapper, with cassava and sweet-potato cake sides. Burgers, dogs, and chicken-and-chips make a concession to more timid taste buds. Alcohol isn't served, but fresh tamarind, mango, and sorrel juices pack a flavorful punch. Vivine's generally closes early (and occasionally on Monday), but stays open if there's demand—and any food left. *Average main: $17 Austin Dr., Gun Bay, East End 345/947–7435 No credit cards.*

NORTH SIDE

$$$ CARIBBEAN **Kaibo Beach Bar and Grill.** Overlooking the North Sound, this beach hangout rocks days (fantastic lunches that cost half the price of dinner, festive atmosphere including impromptu volleyball tourneys, and free Wi-Fi) and serves murderous margaritas and mudslides well into the evening to boisterous yachties, locals, sports buffs, and expats. Enjoy New England–style conch chowder with a hint of heat, smoked mahimahi pâté, hefty burgers, and wondrous wraps, either on the multitiered deck garlanded with ships' rope and Christmas lights or in hammocks and thatched cabanas amid the palms. Swaddled in white muslin, the nautically themed Upstairs dining room (noted for its rare rum selection) is open Thursday through Sunday nights (reservations essential) and serves more creative fare at higher prices. Specialties include baked grouper with kaffir lime–leaf crust in sweet corn velouté. The ultimate in romance is the catered Luna del Mar on the Friday evening closest to the full moon. Tuesday beach barbecues are popular (including limbo dancing, live music, half-price drinks, and discounted water taxi service to the "mainland"). *Average main: $30 585 Water Cay Rd., Cayman Kai, North Side 345/947–9975 www.kaibo.ky.*

$$$ CARIBBEAN **Over the Edge.** This fun, funky seaside spot brims with character and characters. (A soused regular might welcome you by reciting "the daily lunch special: chilled barley soup . . . That's beer.") The nutty nautical decor—brass ships' lanterns dangle from the ceiling, and steering wheels, lacquered turtle shells, and fishing photos adorn the walls—contrasts with cool mirrored ads for Gitanes and Mumm Cordon Rouge and the trendily semi-open kitchen with fresh fish prominently displayed. The jukebox jumps (country music rules the roost), and the tiki-lighted terrace offers stunning views and fresh breezes. Expertly prepared local fare (Cajun chicken to conch steak to Cayman rock lobster escoveitch, served with rice and beans, plantains, and fried festival bread) is a bargain, especially at lunch, though the chef also surprises with such gussied-up fare as shrimp in Pernod sauce and turtle steak in port. *Average main: $21 312 North Side Rd., Old Man Bay, North Side 345/947–9568 www.overtheedgecayman.com.*

WHERE TO STAY

Brace yourself for resort prices—there are few accommodations in the lower price ranges. You'll find no big all-inclusive resorts on Grand Cayman (though the Reef Resort offers an optional AI plan to its guests), and very few offer a meal plan other than breakfast. Parking is always free at island hotels and resorts. Although the island has several resorts (mostly along Seven Mile Beach), the majority of accommodations are vacation rentals, and these are scattered throughout the island. Some of the condo complexes even offer resort-style amenities.

They may be some distance from the beach and short on style and facilities, but the island's guesthouses offer rock-bottom prices, a friendly atmosphere, and your best shot at getting to know the locals. Rooms are clean and simple, and most have private baths.

BEST BETS FOR LODGING

Fodor's Choice ★
Caribbean Club, Cotton Tree, Lighthouse Point, Reef Resort, Ritz-Carlton Grand Cayman, Westin Grand Cayman

BEST BEACHFRONT
Coral Stone Club, Lacovia Condominiums, Reef Resort, Southern Cross Club (Little Cayman), Westin Grand Cayman

BEST FOR AN ECO-FRIENDLY TRIP
Cobalt Coast, Compass Point, Lighthouse Point, Pirates Point (Little Cayman), Southern Cross Club (Little Cayman)

BEST FOR FAMILIES
Ritz-Carlton Grand Cayman

BEST SERVICE
Reef Resort, Ritz-Carlton Grand Cayman

BEST FOR ROMANCE
Caribbean Club, Cotton Tree, Shangri-La B&B, Turtle Nest Inn

PRIVATE VILLAS AND CONDOS

Most condo complexes are very similar, with telephones, satellite TV, air-conditioning, living and dining areas, patios, and parking. Differences are amenities, proximity to town and beach, and the views. As with resorts, rates are higher in winter, and there may be a three- or seven-night minimum. There are dozens of large private villas available on the beach, especially on the North Side near Cayman Kai. A growing trend: "green" condos. We no longer recommend individual private villas, especially since they frequently change agents. However, among the properties we've inspected, worth looking for are Coral Reef, Venezia, Villa Habana, Great Escapes, Fishbones, and Pease Bay House. Several of the condo and villa rental companies have websites where you can see pictures of the privately owned units and villas they represent.

RENTAL CONTACTS

Cayman Island Vacations. Longtime Cayman homeowners Don and Linda Martin represent more than 50 villas and condos (including their own). Extremely helpful with island suggestions, they can make arrangements for a rental car, diving discounts, and extras, and Linda is a leading wedding coordinator. ☎ *813/854–1201, 888/208–8935* 🌐 *www.caymanvacation.com.*

Cayman Villas. This locally owned agent represents top-notch villas and condos on Grand and Little Cayman. ✉ *177 Owen Roberts Dr.* ☎ *800/235–5888, 345/945–4144* 🌐 *www.caymanvillas.com.*

Grand Cayman Villas. Virginia resident Jim Leavitt carries listings for dozens of fine properties island-wide. He and his staff visit the island regularly to ensure quality and remain up-to-date. ☎ *866/358–8455* 🌐 *www.grandcaymanvillas.net.*

Wimco. The West Indies Management Company is synonymous with quality, especially in the Caribbean. ☎ *866/850–6140, 800/449–1553* 🌐 *www.wimco.com.*

8

AROUND GEORGE TOWN

$$ HOTEL **Sunset House.** This amiable seaside dive-oriented resort is on the ironshore south of George Town, close enough for a short trip to stores and restaurants yet far enough to feel secluded. **Pros:** great shore diving and dive shop; lively bar scene; fun international clientele; great package rates. **Cons:** often indifferent service; somewhat run-down; no real swimming beach; spotty Wi-Fi signal. *Rooms from: $300 ✉ 390 S. Church St. ☎ 345/949–7111, 800/854–4767 ⊕ www.sunsethouse.com 58 rooms, 2 suites Breakfast.*

SEVEN MILE BEACH

$$$$ RENTAL Fodor's Choice ★ **Caribbean Club.** This gleaming boutique facility has a striking lobby with aquariums, infinity pool, and contemporary trattoria, Luca. **Pros:** luxurious, high-tech facilities beyond the typical apartment complex; trendy Italian restaurant; service on the beach. **Cons:** stratospheric prices; poor bedroom reading lights; though families are welcome, they may find it imposing; smaller top-floor balconies (albeit amazing views). *Rooms from: $1,256 ✉ 871 West Bay Rd., Seven Mile Beach ☎ 345/623–4500, 800/941–1126 ⊕ www.caribclub.com 37 3-bedroom condos No meals.*

$$ RENTAL FAMILY **Christopher Columbus.** This enduring favorite on the peaceful northern end of Seven Mile Beach is a discovery for families. **Pros:** excellent snorkeling; fine beach; great value; complimentary Wi-Fi. **Cons:** car needed; often overrun by families during holidays and summer; top floors have difficult access for physically challenged. *Rooms from: $365 ✉ 2013 West Bay Rd., Seven Mile Beach ☎ 345/945–4354, 866/311–5231 ⊕ www.christophercolumbuscondos.com 30 2- and 3-bedroom condos No meals.*

$ HOTEL **Comfort Suites Grand Cayman.** This no-frills, all-suites hotel has an ideal location, next to the Marriott and near numerous shops, restaurants, and bars. **Pros:** affordable; complimentary buffet breakfast and Wi-Fi; fun young-ish crowd. **Cons:** rooms nearly a block from the beach; new condo blocks sea views; no balconies; bar closes early. *Rooms from: $212 ✉ West Bay Rd. ☎ 345/945–7300, 800/517–4000 ⊕ www.caymancomfort.com 108 suites Breakfast.*

$$$$ RENTAL **Coral Stone Club.** In the shadow of the Ritz-Carlton, this exclusive enclave still shines by offering understated barefoot luxury, stellar service, and huge condos. **Pros:** large ratio of beach and pool space to guests; walking distance to restaurants and shops; free airport transfers; excellent off-season deals. **Cons:** expensive in high season; Ritz-Carlton guests sometimes wander over to poach beach space. *Rooms from: $800 ✉ West Bay Rd., Seven Mile Beach ☎ 345/945–5820, 888/927–2322 ⊕ www.coralstoneclub.com 30 3-bedroom condos No meals.*

$$$$ RESORT **Grand Cayman Beach Suites.** The former Hyatt all-suites section, now locally run, offers a terrific beachfront location and trendy eateries. **Pros:** fine beach; superior dining and water-sports facilities; free use of gym (unusual on Grand Cayman); supermarkets and restaurants within walking distance; significant online discounts. **Cons:** most entrances face the street, making it noisy on weekends; small parking lot; several units need refurbishment; music often blaring around the pool.

Rooms from: $870 *West Bay Rd., Seven Mile Beach* *345/949–1234* *www.grand-cayman-beach-suites.com, www.gcbs.ky* *53 suites* *Multiple meal plans.*

$$$ RESORT **Grand Cayman Marriott Beach Resort.** The soaring, stylish, if impersonal marble lobby (with exquisite art glass, spectacular blown-up underwater photos, marine paraphernalia, and fun elements such as red British-style telephone boxes) sets the tone for this bustling beachfront property, which received a $16-million renovation in 2014. **Pros:** lively bars and restaurants; good snorkeling and water sports; free bike and kayak rentals; convenient to both George Town and Seven Mile Beach; airport connectivity lets you print your boarding pass. **Cons:** often overrun by tour groups and conventioneers; narrowest section of Seven Mile Beach; pool and bar often noisy late. *Rooms from: $393* *389 West Bay Rd., Seven Mile Beach* *345/949–0088, 800/223–6388* *www.marriott.com* *273 rooms, 22 suites* *No meals.*

$$$ RENTAL FAMILY **The Grandview.** Grand view, indeed: all 69 two- and three-bedroom units (sadly only 15 are generally in the rental pool) look smack onto the Caribbean and the beach past splendidly maintained gardens. **Pros:** restaurants and shops within walking distance; wine concierge dispenses advice; free Wi-Fi (when it's available); nice pool and hot tub. **Cons:** the long beach can be rocky; some units a tad worn though meticulously maintained; not all units have access to the free Wi-Fi signal. *Rooms from: $475* *95 Snooze La., Seven Mile Beach* *345/945–4511, 866/977–6766* *www.grandviewcondos.com* *69 2- and 3-bedroom condos* *No meals.*

$$$ RENTAL **Lacovia Condominiums.** The carefully manicured courtyard of this handsome arcaded Mediterranean Revival property could easily be mistaken for a peaceful park. **Pros:** central location; exquisite gardens; extensive beach. **Cons:** rear courtyard rooms can be noisy from traffic and partying from West Bay Road; pool fairly small (though most people prefer the beach). *Rooms from: $415* *697 West Bay Rd., Seven Mile Beach* *345/949–7599* *www.lacovia.com* *35 1-, 2-, and 3-bedroom condos* *No meals.*

$$$$ RESORT FAMILY Fodor's Choice ★ **Ritz-Carlton Grand Cayman.** This 144-acre resort, as exquisitely manicured as its clientele, offers unparalleled luxury and service infused with a sense of place, with works by local artists and craftspeople. **Pros:** exemplary service; exceptional facilities with complimentary extras. **Cons:** annoyingly high resort fee; sprawling with a confusing layout; long walk to beach (over an interior bridge) from most rooms. *Rooms from: $749* *West Bay Rd., Seven Mile Beach* *345/943–9000* *www.ritzcarlton.com* *353 rooms, 12 suites, 24 condos* *Breakfast.*

$ HOTEL **Sunshine Suites Resort.** This friendly, all-suites hotel is an impeccably clean money saver. **Pros:** good value and Internet deals; cheerful staff; rocking little restaurant; thoughtful free extras including business center and access to nearby World Gym. **Cons:** poor views; not on the beach. *Rooms from: $244* *1465 Esterley Tibbetts Hwy., off West Bay Rd., Seven Mile Beach* *345/949–3000, 877/786–1110* *www.sunshinesuites.com* *130 suites* *Breakfast.*

Shaded beach loungers at the Ritz-Carlton, Grand Cayman

$$$$ RESORT FAMILY Fodor's Choice ★ **Westin Grand Cayman Seven Mile Beach Resort & Spa.** The Westin offers something for everyone, from conventioneers to honeymooners to families, not to mention what the hospitality industry calls "location location location." **Pros:** terrific children's programs; superb beach (the largest resort stretch at 800 feet); better-than-advertised ocean views; heavy online discounts. **Cons:** occasionally bustling and impersonal when large groups book; daily $45 resort fee. *Rooms from: $499 West Bay Rd., Seven Mile Beach 345/945–3800, 800/937–8461 www.westingrandcayman.com 339 rooms, 8 suites No meals.*

WEST BAY

$$ RESORT **Cobalt Coast Resort and Suites.** This small eco-friendly hotel is perfect for divers who want a moderately priced spacious room or suite right on the ironshore far from the madding crowds. **Pros:** superb dive outfit; friendly service and clientele; free Wi-Fi; environmentally aware. **Cons:** poky golden-sand beach; unattractive concrete pool area; remote location, so a car (included in some packages) is necessary. *Rooms from: $290 18-A Sea Fan Dr., West Bay 345/946–5656, 888/946–5656 www.cobaltcoast.com 7 rooms, 15 suites Multiple meal plans.*

$$$$ RENTAL Fodor's Choice ★ **Cotton Tree.** Cayman-born owner Heather Lockington has created an authentic haven where guests can embrace Caymanian heritage and reconnect with nature without sacrificing comfort. **Pros:** peaceful and quiet setting; beautifully designed and outfitted accommodations; complimentary airport transfers; wonderful immersion in local culture. **Cons:** luxury comes with a price tag; remote location means a car is required; beach narrow and tangled with sea grape trees. *Rooms from: $980 375 Conch Point Rd., West Bay 345/943–0700,*

561/807–8566 in U.S. ⊕ *www.caymancottontree.com* ⇨ *4 2-bedroom cottages* ⏲ *Closed Sept.* 🍴 *No meals.*

$$$ RESORT Fodor's Choice ★ **Lighthouse Point.** Scuba operator DiveTech's stunning eco-development features sustainable wood interiors and recycled concrete, a gray-water system, energy-saving appliances and lights, and Cayman's first wind turbine generator. **Pros:** eco-friendly; fantastic shore diving (and state-of-the-art dive shop); creative and often recycled upscale look; superb eatery. **Cons:** no real beach; car necessary; bit difficult for physically challenged to navigate. [$] *Rooms from: $450* ✉ *571 Northwest Point Rd., West Bay* ☎ *345/949–1700* ⊕ *www.lighthouse-point-cayman.com* ⇨ *9 2-bedroom apartments* 🍴 *No meals.*

$ B&B/INN **Shangri-La B&B.** Accomplished pianist George Davidson and wife, Eileen, built this lavish lakeside retreat and truly make guests feel at home, along with dogs Roxie and Stella. **Pros:** use of kitchen; elegant decor; DVD players and Wi-Fi included. **Cons:** rental car necessary; not on the beach. [$] *Rooms from: $149* ✉ *1 Sticky Toffee La., West Bay* ☎ *345/526–1170* ⊕ *www.shangrilabandb.com* ⇨ *6 rooms, 1 apartment* 🍴 *Breakfast.*

EAST END

$$ RESORT **Compass Point Dive Resort.** This tranquil, congenial getaway run by the admirable Ocean Frontiers scuba operation would steer even nondivers in the right direction. **Pros:** top-notch dive operation; free bike/kayak use; good value, especially packages; affable international staff and clientele. **Cons:** isolated location requires a car; conservation is admirable but a/c can't go too low; poky beaches with poor swim access. [$] *Rooms from: $295* ✉ *Austin Conolly Dr., East End* ☎ *345/947–7500, 800/348–6096, 345/947–0000* ⊕ *www.compasspoint.ky* ⇨ *17 1-bedroom, 9 2-bedroom, and 3 3-bedroom condos* 🍴 *No meals.*

$ RESORT Fodor's Choice ★ **Reef Resort.** This exceedingly well-run time-share property seductively straddles a 600-foot beach on the less hectic East End. **Pros:** romantically remote; glorious beach; enthusiastic staff (including a crackerjack wedding coordinator); great packages and online discounts. **Cons:** remote; few dining options nearby; sprawling. [$] *Rooms from: $249* ✉ *Queen's Hwy., Colliers, East End* ☎ *345/947–3100, 888/232–0541* ⊕ *www.thereef.com* ⇨ *152 suites* 🍴 *Multiple meal plans.*

$ RENTAL **Turtle Nest Inn and Condos.** This affordable, intimate, Mediterranean-style seaside inn has roomy one-bedroom apartments and a pool overlooking a narrow beach with good snorkeling. **Pros:** wonderful snorkeling; thoughtful extras; caring staff; free Wi-Fi. **Cons:** car necessary; occasional rocks and debris on beach; ground-floor room views slightly obscured by palms; road noise in back rooms. [$] *Rooms from: $149* ✉ *166 Bodden Town Rd., Bodden Town* ☎ *345/947–8665* ⊕ *www.turtlenestinn.com, www.turtlenestcondos.com* ⇨ *8 apartments, 10 2-bedroom condos* 🍴 *No meals.*

8

NIGHTLIFE

Grand Cayman nightlife is surprisingly good for such a quiet-seeming island. Check the Friday edition of the *Caymanian Compass* for listings of music, movies, theater, and other entertainment. Bars are open during evening hours until 1 am, and clubs are generally open from 10 pm until 3 am, but none may serve liquor after midnight on Saturday and none can offer dancing on Sunday. Competition is fierce between Grand Cayman's many bars and restaurants. In addition to entertainment (fish feeding to fire-eating), even upscale joints host happy hours offering free hors d'oeuvres and/or drinks.

AROUND GEORGE TOWN

BARS AND MUSIC CLUBS

My Bar. Perched on the water's edge, this bar has great sunset views. The leviathan open-sided cabana is drenched in Rasta colors and crowned by an intricate South Seas–style thatched roof with about 36,000 palm fronds. Christmas lights and the occasional customer dangle from the rafters. Great grub and a mischievous mix of locals, expats, and tourists prove that ecocentric Cayman offers wild life alongside wildlife. ✉ *Sunset House, S. Church St.* ☎ *345/949–7111* 🌐 *www.sunsethouse.com.*

Rackam's Waterfront Pub and Restaurant. Fishermen to Who's-the-Hugo-Boss financiers savor sensational sunsets and joyous happy hours followed by exuberantly pirouetting tarpon feeding at this open-air, marine-theme happenin' bar on a jetty jutting into the harbor. Boaters—even snorkelers—cruise up the ladder for drinks, while anglers leave their catch on ice. There's complimentary snacks on Friday and pub fare at fair prices until midnight. ✉ *93 N. Church St.* ☎ *345/945–3860* 🌐 *www.rackams.com.*

SEVEN MILE BEACH

BARS AND MUSIC CLUBS

The Attic. This chic sports bar has three billiard tables, classic arcade games (Space Invaders, Donkey Kong), air hockey, and large-screen TVs (nab a private booth with its own flat-panel job). Events are daily happy hours, trivia nights, and the Caribbean's reputedly largest Bloody Mary bar on Sunday. Along with downstairs sister "O" Bar, it's ground zero for the Wednesday Night Drinking Club. For a $25 initiation (with T-shirt and personalized leather wristband, toga optional) and $10 weekly activity fee, you're shuttled by bus to three different bars, with free shots and drinks specials. ✉ *Queen's Court, 2nd fl., West Bay Rd., Seven Mile Beach* ☎ *345/949–7665* 🌐 *www.obar.attic.ky.*

Calico Jack's. This friendly outdoor beach bar at the public beach's north end has a DJ on Saturday, open mike on Tuesday, bands many Fridays, and riotous parties during the full moon, when even Ritz-Carlton guests let their hair down. ✉ *West Bay Rd., Seven Mile Beach* ☎ *345/945–7850.*

Deckers. Always bustling and bubbly, Deckers takes its name from the red English double-decker bus that forms the focal point of the main outdoor bar. You can luxuriate indoors on cushy sofas over a chess game and signature blood-orange mojito; hack your way through the 18-hole safari miniature-golf course; find a secluded nook in the garden terrace framed by towering palms, old-fashioned ornate street lamps, and colonial columns; or groove Thursday through Saturday nights to the easy-listening potpourri of pop, reggae, blues, and country courtesy of the Hi-Tide duo. Worthy Carib-Mediterranean fusion cuisine is a bonus (try the Caribbean lobster mac 'n' cheese or the coconut shrimp with citrus marmalade and green papaya salad). ✉ *West Bay Rd., Seven Mile Beach* ☎ *345/945–6600* 🌐 *www.deckers.ky.*

Duke's Seafood & Rib Shack. This is the ultimate in beach-shack chic (albeit a half block from the sand): awesome surfing photos, reclaimed driftwood patio bar, and a statue of the big kahuna with shades and board atop a manta ray. Locals and visitors belly up to the raw and real bars, especially at nightly happy hours, for "Cayman's endless summer." ✉ *West Bay Rd., across from public beach, Seven Mile Beach* ☎ *345/640–0000* 🌐 *www.dukescayman.com.*

Fidel Murphy's Irish Pub. Thanks to the unusual logo (a stogie-smoking Castro surrounded by shamrocks) and congenial Irish wit and whimsy, you half expect to find Fidel and Gerry Adams harping on U.S. and U.K. policy over a Harp. The Edwardian decor of etched glass, hardwood, and brass is prefabricated (constructed in Ireland, disassembled, and shipped), but everything else is genuine, from the warm welcome to the ales and cider on tap to the proper Irish stew (the kitchen also turns out conch fritters and chicken tikka curry). Sunday and Monday host all-you-can-eat extravaganzas (fish-and-chips, carvery) at rock-bottom prices. Trivia nights and live music lure regulars through the week. Weekends welcome live televised Gaelic soccer, rugby, and hurling, followed by karaoke and *craic* (if you go, you'll learn the definition). ✉ *Queen's Court, West Bay Rd., Seven Mile Beach* ☎ *345/949–5189* 🌐 *www.fidelscayman.com.*

Legendz. This sports bar with a clubby, retro feel (Marilyn Monroe and Frank Sinatra photos channel glamour days, while scarlet booths and bubble chandeliers add oomph) is a testosterone test drive with plentiful scoring of both types. Good luck wrestling a spot at the bar for pay-per-view and major sporting events, but 10 TVs, including two 6-by-8-foot screens, broadcast to every corner. Also an entertainment venue, Legendz books local bands, stand-up comics, and island DJs and serves grilled fare at fair prices. ✉ *Falls Centre, West Bay Rd., Seven Mile Beach* ☎ *345/943–3287* 🌐 *www.legendz.ky.*

Lone Star Bar and Grill. Calling itself Cayman's top dive (dive masters to dentists get down and occasionally dirty over kick-ass margaritas), the noisy bar glorifies sports, Texas, T&A, and the boob tube, from murals of Cowboys cheerleaders to an amazing sports memorabilia collection (with items signed by both Bushes) to 17 big-screen TVs tuned to different events. Trivia and Rock 'n' Roll Bingo nights lasso locals. ✉ *686 West Bay Rd., Seven Mile Beach* ☎ *345/945–5175* 🌐 *www.lonestarcayman.com.*

Stingers Resort and Pool Bar. Tasty, affordable food is served in an appealing setting (check out the stupendous "stinger" mosaic), with cover-free live music and dancing Thursday and Friday. Wednesday nights there's an all-you-can-eat Caribbean luau. The band Heat, a local institution, sizzles with energetic, emotional calypso, reggae, soca, salsa, and oldies; limbo dancers and fire-eaters keep the temperature rising. If you recoil from audience participation, stay far away. Exhibitionistic "spring break" sorts may find their photo on the Wall of Shame, but another blue-green Stingers punch is a worse fate. ✉ *Comfort Suites Grand Cayman, West Bay Rd., Seven Mile Beach* ☎ *345/945–3000.*

The Wharf. Dance near the water to mellow music on Saturday evenings; when there's a wedding reception in the pavilion, the crashing surf and twinkling candles bathe the proceedings in an almost Gatsby-esque glow. For something less sedate, Roger and Sarah conduct sizzling salsa dancing and lessons on Tuesday after dinner, while most Fridays morph into a wild 1970s disco night (after free hors d'oeuvres during happy hour). The stunning seaside setting on tiered decks compensates for often undistinguished food and service. The Ports of Call bar is a splendid place for sunset, and tarpon feeding off the deck is a nightly 9 pm spectacle. ✉ *West Bay Rd.* ☎ *345/949–2231* 🌐 *www.wharf.ky.*

CIGAR AND WINE LOUNGES

Nectar. Don't let the location in the back of a strip mall fool you. This is a chic New York–style martini lounge/sushi bar with a tapestry of tapas on tap and more than 30 drinks—including 'tinis with 'tude. Choose from bar, tall tables, or sofas in the sleek, slick, mostly monochrome space with chrome accents, blue seats, and red lighting. There's new art on the walls every month, special *shisha* (hookah) evenings, and DJs spinning Sexy Fridays and Tropical Saturdays, when it becomes a slim-hipper-than-thou club that delivers a dancing high for Jessica Alba wannabes poured into spandex and Gap poster-boy slackers (potential hell for those over 30 years old or 20% body fat). ✉ *Seven Mile Shops, Seven Mile Beach* ☎ *345/949–1802.*

Silver Palm Lounge. The Silver Palm drips with cash and cachet, with a model waitstaff and chic clientele. One section replicates a classic English country library (perfect for civilized, proper afternoon tea or a pre- or post-dinner champagne or single malt). The other forms Taikun, a sensuous sushi spot clad mostly in black, with a popular public table. Also on tap: fab cocktails, including specialty martinis (the Silver Palm cosmopolitan is a winner—Ketel One citron, triple sec, a squeeze of fresh lime juice, and a splash of cranberry topped off with Moët champagne); pages of wines by the glass; and an impressive list of cigars, cognacs, and aged drums. ✉ *Ritz-Carlton Grand Cayman, West Bay Rd., Seven Mile Beach* ☎ *345/943–9000.*

West Indies Wine Company. At this ultracontemporary wine store, you purchase tasting cards, allowing you to sample any of the 80-odd wines and even spirits available by the sip or half- or full glass via the argon-enhanced "intelligent dispensing system." Selections traverse a vast canny range of prices, regions, styles, and terroirs. "We slot in well-known labels so you don't feel lost, but also stay relatively obscure on beers, ales, and ciders for fun," notes manager Alex McClenaghan. Even better, the enterprising owners struck a deal with neighboring restaurants and gourmet shops to provide appetizers or cheese and charcuterie plates, best savored alfresco at the tables in front of the handsome space. Small wonder savvy locals congregate here after work or movies at the nearby cineplex. ✉ *Corner of Market St. and the Paseo, Camana Bay* ☎ *345/640–9492* 🌐 *www.wiwc.ky.*

DANCE CLUBS

"O" Bar. This trendy black-and-crimson, industrial-style dance club has mixed music (live on Saturdays), while juggling, flame-throwing bartenders—practically local celebs—flip cocktails every night. It's as close to a stand-and-pose milieu as you'll find on Cayman, with the occasional fashion fascist parading in Prada. An upper-level private loft is available by reservation. ✉ *Queen's Court, West Bay Rd., Seven Mile Beach* ☎ *345/943–6227* 🌐 *www.obar.attic.ky.*

WEST BAY

BARS AND LOUNGES

Macabuca Oceanside Tiki Bar. This classic hip-hopping happening beach bar has a huge deck over the water, thatched roof, amazing Asian-inspired mosaic murals of waves, spectacular sunsets (and sunset-colored libations), and tiki torches illuminating the reef fish come evening. Macabuca means "What does it matter?" in the indigenous Antillean Taíno language, perfectly encapsulating the mellow vibe. Big-screen TVs, live bands and DJs on weekends, excellent pub grub, and daily specials (CI$9 jerk dishes weekends; Monday all-night happy hour, DJ, and CI$17 all-you-can-eat barbecue) lure everyone from well-heeled loafers to barefoot bodysurfers animatedly discussing current events and dive currents in a Babel of tongues. ✉ *Northwest Point Rd., West Bay* ☎ *345/945–5217* 🌐 *www.crackedconch.com.ky.*

EAST END

BARS AND MUSIC CLUBS

Rusty Pelican. This spot draws an eclectic group of dive masters, expats, honeymooners, and mingling singles. The knockout, colorful cocktails pack quite a punch, making the sunset last for hours. The bar dialogue is entertainment enough, but don't miss local legend, country-calypsonian Barefoot Man, when he plays "upstairs" at Pelican's Reef—he's to Cayman what Jimmy Buffett is to Key West. ✉ *Reef Resort, Queen's Hwy., Colliers, East End* ☎ *345/947–3100* 🌐 *www.thereef.com.*

South Coast Bar and Grill. This delightful seaside slice of old Cayman (grizzled regulars slamming down dominoes, fabulous sea views, old model cars, Friday-night dances to local legend Lammie, karaoke Saturdays with Elvis impersonator Errol Dunbar, and reasonably priced red conch chowder and jerk chicken sausage) is also a big politico hangout. ("That big shark mural ain't just about nature," one bartender cackled.) Fascinating photos, some historical, show local scenes and personalities. The juke jives, from Creedence Clearwater Revival to Mighty Sparrow. ✉ *Breakers, East End* ☎ *345/947–2517* 🌐 *www.southcoastbar.com.*

8

SHOPPING

On Grand Cayman the good news is that there's no sales tax *and* there's plenty of duty-free merchandise. Locally made items to watch for include woven mats, baskets, jewelry made of a marble-like stone called Caymanite (from the cliffs of Cayman Brac), and authentic sunken treasure, though the latter is never cheap. In addition, there are several noteworthy local artists, some of whose atelier–homes double as galleries, such as Al Ebanks, Horacio Esteban, and Luelan Bodden. Unique items include Cayman sea salt and luxury bath salts (solar harvested in an ecologically sensitive manner) and Tortuga rum and rum cakes. Seven Fathoms is the first working distillery actually in Cayman itself, its award-winning rums aged underwater (hence the name). Cigar lovers, take note: some shops carry famed Cuban brands, but you must enjoy them on the island; bringing them back to the United States is illegal.

Although you can find black-coral products in Grand Cayman, they're controversial. Most of the coral sold here comes from Belize and Honduras; Cayman Islands marine law prohibits the removal of live coral from its own sea, so most of it has been taken illegally. Black coral grows at a very slow rate (3 inches every 10 years) and is an endangered species. Buy other products instead.

There are seven modern, U.S.-style supermarkets for groceries (three of them have full-service pharmacies) on Grand Cayman.

ART GALLERIES

Al Ebanks Studio Gallery. This gallery shows the eponymous artist's versatile, always provocative work in various media. Since you're walking into his home as well as atelier, everything is on display. Clever movable panels maximize space "like Art Murphy beds." His work, while inspired by his home, could never be labeled traditional Caribbean art, exhibiting vigorous movement through abstract swirls of color and textural contrasts. Though nonrepresentational (save for his equally intriguing sculpture and ceramics), the focal subject from carnivals to iguanas is always subtly apparent. Ask him about the Native Sons art movement he co-founded. ✉ *186B Shedden Rd.* ☎ *345/927–5365, 345/949–0693.*

Cathy Church's Underwater Photo Centre and Gallery. The store has a collection of the acclaimed underwater shutterbug's spectacular color and limited-edition, black-and-white underwater photos as well as the latest marine camera equipment. Cathy will autograph her latest coffee-table book, talk about her globetrotting adventures, and schedule private underwater photography instruction on her dive boat, with graphics-oriented computers to critique your work. She also does wedding photography, above and underwater. If you can't stop in, check out the world's largest underwater photo installation (9 by 145 feet) at the Owen Roberts Airport baggage claim, curated by Cathy and her team. ✉ *390 S. Church St.* ☎ *345/949–7415* 🌐 *www.cathychurch.com.*

Guy Harvey's Gallery and Shoppe. World-renowned marine biologist, conservationist, and artist Guy Harvey showcases his aquatic-inspired action-packed art in every conceivable medium, from tableware to sportswear (even logo soccer balls and Zippos). The soaring, two-story 4,000-square-foot space is almost more theme park than store, with monitors playing sportfishing videos, wood floors inlaid with tile duplicating rippling water, dangling catboats "attacked" by shark models, and life-size murals honoring such classics as Hemingway's *Old Man and the Sea.* Original paintings, sculpture, and drawings are expensive, but there's something (tile art, prints, lithographs, and photos) in most price ranges. ✉ *49 S. Church St.* ☎ *345/943–4891* 🌐 *www.guyharvey.com.*

Pure Art. About 1½ miles (2½ km) south of George Town, Pure Art purveys wit, warmth, and whimsy from the wildly colored front steps. Its warren of rooms resembles a garage sale run amok or a quirky grandmother's attic spilling over with unexpected finds, from foodstuffs to functional and wearable art. ✉ *S. Church St. and Denham-Thompson Way* ☎ *345/949–9133* 🌐 *www.pureart.ky.*

CLOTHING

Blue Wave. Your adrenaline starts pumping as soon as you enter this so-called lifestyle wear–surf shop. All the accoutrements you need to play the big kahuna are handsomely displayed, from sandals to sunglasses, Billabong plaid shirts to Quicksilver shorts, surfboards to ecosensitive Olukai footwear (talk to the clerks and you're ready to sign up for Greenpeace). ✉ *10 Shedden Rd.* ☎ *345/949–8166.*

FOODSTUFFS

Foster's Food Fair-IGA. The island's biggest chain has five supermarkets. The Airport Centre and Strand stores, with full-service pharmacies, are open Monday–Saturday 7 am–11 pm. ✉ *Airport Centre, 63 Dorcy Dr.* ☎ *345/949–5155, 345/945–3663* 🌐 *www.fosters-iga.com.*

Tortuga Rum Company. This company bakes, then vacuum-seals, more than 10,000 of its world-famous rum cakes daily, adhering to the original "secret" century-old recipe. There are eight flavors, from banana to Blue Mountain coffee. The 12-year-old rum, blended from private stock though actually distilled in Guyana, is a connoisseur's delight for after-dinner sipping. You can buy a fresh rum cake at the airport on the way home at the same prices as at the factory store. ✉ *Industrial Park, N. Sound Rd.* ☎ *345/943–7663* 🌐 *www.tortugarumcakes.com.*

8

MALLS AND SHOPPING CENTERS

Kirk Freeport Plaza. This downtown shopping center, home to the Kirk Freeport flagship department store, is ground zero for couture; it's also known for its boutiques selling fine watches and jewelry, china, crystal, leather, perfumes, and cosmetics, from Baccarat to Bulgari, Raymond Weil to Waterford and Wedgwood (the last two share their own autonomous boutique). Just keep walking—there's plenty of eye-catching, mind-boggling consumerism in all directions: Boucheron, Cartier (with its own mini-boutique), Chanel, Clinique, Christian Dior, Clarins, Estée Lauder, Fendi, Guerlain, Lancôme, Yves Saint Laurent, Issey Miyake, Jean Paul Gaultier, Nina Ricci, Rolex, Roberto Coin, Rosenthal and Royal Doulton china, and more. ✉ *Cardinal Ave.*

SEVEN MILE BEACH

MALLS AND SHOPPING CENTERS

The Strand Shopping Centre. This mall has branches of Tortuga Rum and Blackbeard's Liquor, and banks galore—the better to withdraw cash for shops with cachet like Polo Ralph Lauren and another Kirk Freeport (this branch particularly noteworthy for china and crystal, from Kosta Boda to Baccarat, as well as a second La Parfumerie). ✉ *West Bay Rd., Seven Mile Beach.*

CAYMAN DIVE DEVELOPMENTS

The Cayman Islands government acquired the 251-foot, decommissioned U.S. Navy ship **USS** *Kittiwake.* Sunk in 2011, it has already become an exciting new dive attraction (🌐 *www.kittiwakecayman.com*) while providing necessary relief for some of the most frequently visited dive sites. The top of the bridge is just 15 feet down, making it accessible to snorkelers. There's a single-use entry fee of $10 ($5 for snorkelers).

The **Cayman Dive 365** (🌐 *www.dive365cayman.com*) initiative is part of a commitment to protect reefs from environmental overuse. New dive sites will be introduced while certain existing sites are "retired" to be rested and refreshed. Visitors are encouraged to sponsor and name a new dive site from the list of selected coordinates.

SPORTS AND THE OUTDOORS

BIRD-WATCHING

Silver Thatch Tours. Geddes Hislop, who knows his birds and his island (though he's Trinidadian by birth), runs customizable five-hour natural and historic heritage tours ($60 an hour up to four people), including the Queen Elizabeth II Botanic Park's nature trail and lake and other prime birding spots. Serious birders leave at dawn, but you can leave whenever. Prearranged tours include the guide, pickup and return transport, and refreshments—a great excuse to discuss herbal medicinal folklore. ☎ *345/925–7401* 🌐 *www.earthfoot.org/places/ky001.htm.*

DIVING

One of the world's leading dive destinations, Grand Cayman's dramatic underwater topography features plunging walls, soaring skyscraper pinnacles, grottoes, arches, swim-throughs adorned with vibrant sponges, coral-encrusted caverns, and canyons patrolled by Lilliputian grunts to gargantuan groupers, hammerheads to hawksbill turtles.

There are more than 200 pristine dive sites, many less than half a mile from land and easily accessible, including wreck, wall, and shore options. Add exceptional visibility from 80 to 150 feet and calm, current-free water at a constant bathlike 80°F. Cayman is serious about conservation, with Marine Park, Replenishment, and Environmental Park zones and stringently enforced laws to protect the fragile, endangered marine environment (fines of up to $500,000 and a year in prison are the price for damaging living coral, which can take years to regrow). Most boats use biodegradable cleansers and environmentally friendly drinking cups; moorings at popular sites prevent coral and sponge damage caused by continual anchoring, and diving with gloves is prohibited to reduce the temptation to touch.

Pristine clear water, breathtaking coral formations, and plentiful marine life mark the **North Wall**—a world-renowned dive area along the North Side of Grand Cayman. **Trinity Caves,** in West Bay, is a deep dive with numerous canyons starting at about 60 feet and sloping to the wall at 130 feet. The South Side is the deepest, its wall starting 80 feet deep before plummeting, though its shallows offer a lovely labyrinth of caverns and tunnels in such sites as Japanese Gardens. The less-visited, virgin East End is less varied geographically beyond the magnificent Ironshore Caves and Babylon Hanging Gardens ("trees" of black coral plunging 100 feet) but teems with "Swiss cheese" swim-throughs and exotic life in such renowned gathering spots as the Maze.

Shore-entry snorkeling spots include **Cemetery Reef,** north of Seven Mile Beach, and the reef-protected shallows of the **north and south coasts.** Ask for directions to the shallow wreck of the *Cali* in the George Town harbor area; there are several places to enter the water, including a ladder at Rackam's Pub. Among the wreckage you'll find the winch and lots of friendly fish.

Fodor's Choice ★ **Devil's Grotto.** This site resembles an abstract painting of anemones, tangs, parrotfish, and bright purple Pederson cleaner shrimp (nicknamed the dentists of the reef, as they gorge on whatever they scrape off fish teeth and gills). Extensive coral heads and fingers teem with blue wrasse, horse-eyed jacks, butterfly fish, and Indigo hamlets. The cathedral-like caves are phenomenal, but tunnel entries aren't clearly marked, so you're best off with a dive master.

Fodor's Choice ★ **Eden Rock.** If someone tells you that the silverside minnows are in at Eden Rock, drop everything and dive here. The schools swarm around you as you glide through the grottoes, forming quivering curtains of liquid silver as shafts of sunlight pierce the sandy bottom. The grottoes themselves are safe—not complex caves—and the entries and exits are clearly visible at all times. Snorkelers can enjoy the outside of the grottoes as the reef rises and falls from 10 to 30 feet deep. Avoid carrying fish food unless you know how not to get bitten by eager yellowtail snappers. ✉ *S. Church St., across from Harbour Place Mall by Paradise Restaurant.*

Fodor's Choice ★ **Stingray City.** Most dive operators offer scuba trips to Stingray City in the North Sound. Widely considered the best 12-foot dive in the world, it's a must-see for adventurous souls. Here dozens of stingrays congregate—tame enough to suction squid from your outstretched palm. You can stand in 3 feet of water at **Stingray City Sandbar** as the gentle stingrays glide around your legs looking for a handout. Don't worry—these stingrays are so acclimated to tourist encounters that they pose no danger; the experience is often a highlight of a Grand Cayman trip. ✉ *Near West Bay, North Sound.*

Turtle Reef. The reef begins 20 feet out and gradually descends to a 60-foot mini-wall pulsing with sea life and corals of every variety. From there it's just another 15 feet to the dramatic main wall. Ladders provide easy entrance to a shallow cover perfect for pre-dive checks, and since the area isn't buoyed for boats, it's quite pristine. ✉ *West Bay.*

DIVE OPERATORS

As one of the Caribbean's top diving destinations, Grand Cayman is blessed with many top-notch dive operations offering diving, instruction, and equipment for sale and rent. A single-tank boat dive averages $80, a two-tank dive about $105 (discounts for multidive packages). Snorkel-equipment rental is about $15 a day. Divers are required to

Diving at one of the Cayman Islands' famous coral reefs

be certified and possess a C-card. If you're getting certified, save time by starting the book and pool work at home and finishing the open-water portion in warm, clear Cayman waters. Certifying agencies offer a referral service.

Strict marine-protection laws prohibit taking marine life from many areas.

Ambassador Divers. This on-call (around the clock), guided scuba-diving operation offers trips for two–eight persons. Co-owner Jason Washington's favorite spots include sites on the West Side and South and North Wall. Ambassador offers three boats: a 28-foot custom Parker (maximum six divers), a 46-foot completely custom overhauled boat, and a 26-footer primarily for snorkeling. Divers can be picked up from their lodgings. A two-tank boat dive is $105 ($90 for four or more days). ✉ *Comfort Suites, 22 Piper Way, West Bay Rd., Seven Mile Beach* ☎ *345/743–5513, 345/949–4530* 🌐 *www.ambassadordivers.com.*

Cayman Aggressor IV. This 110-foot live-aboard dive boat offers one-week cruises for divers who want to get serious bottom time, as many as five dives daily. Nine staterooms with en suite bathrooms sleep 18. The fresh food is basic but bountiful (three meals, two in-between snacks), and the crew offers a great mix of diving, especially when weather allows the crossing to Little Cayman. Digital photography and video courses are also offered (there's an E-6 film-processing lab aboard) as well as Nitrox certification. The price is $2,595 to $2,995 double occupancy for the week. ☎ *345/949–5551, 800/348–2628* 🌐 *www.aggressor.com.*

FAMILY Fodor's Choice ★ **DiveTech.** This outfit offers shore diving at its two north-coast locations, providing loads of interesting creatures, a mini-wall, and the North Wall, and comfortable boats with quick access to West Bay. Technical training (a specialty of owner Nancy Easterbrook) is unparalleled, and the company offers good, personable service as well as the latest gadgetry such as underwater DPV scooters and rebreathing equipment. They even mix their own gases. Options include extended cross-training Ranger packages, Dive and Art workshop weeks, photography-video seminars with Courtney Platt, deep diving, less disruptive free diving, search and recovery, stingray interaction, reef awareness, and underwater naturalist. Snorkel and diving programs are available for children eight and up, SASY (supplied-air snorkeling, with the unit on a personal flotation device) for five and up. Multiday discounts are a bonus. ✉ *Cobalt Coast Resort and Suites, 18-A Sea Fan Dr., West Bay* ☎ *345/946–5658, 888/946–5656* 🌐 *www.divetech.com* ✉ *Lighthouse Point, near Boatswain's Beach, 571 Northwest Point Rd., West Bay* ☎ *345/949–1700.*

Don Foster's Dive Cayman Islands. This operation offers a pool with shower, an underwater photo center, and snorkeling along the ironshore at Casuarina Point, easily accessed starting at 20 feet and extending to 55 feet. Night dives and Stingray City trips take divers and snorkelers in the same boat (good for families). Specialties include Nitrox, Wreck, and Peak Performance Buoyancy courses. Rates are competitive, and there's free shuttle pickup–drop-off along Seven Mile Beach. If you go out with Don, he might recount stories of his wild times as a drummer, but all crews are personable and efficient. The drawback is larger boats and groups. ✉ *218 S. Church St.* ☎ *345/949–5679, 345/945–5132* 🌐 *www.donfosters.com.*

Indigo Divers. This full-service, mobile PADI teaching facility specializes in exclusive guided dives from its 28-foot Sea Ray Bow Rider or 32-foot Donzi Express Cruiser, the *Cats Meow* and the *Cats Pyjamas*. Comfort and safety are paramount. Luxury transfers are included, and the boat is stocked with goodies like fresh fruit and homemade cookies. Captain Chris Alpers has impeccable credentials: a licensed U.S. Coast Guard captain, PADI master scuba diver trainer, and Cayman Islands Marine Park officer. Katie Alpers specializes in wreck, DPV, dry suit, boat, and deep diving, but her primary role is videographer. She edits superlative DVDs of the adventures with music and titles. They guarantee a maximum of six divers. The individual attention is pricier, but the larger the group, the more you save. ✉ *Seven Mile Beach* ☎ *345/946–7279, 345/525–3932* 🌐 *www.indigodivers.com.*

Fodor's Choice ★ **Ocean Frontiers.** This excellent ecocentric operation offers friendly small-group diving and a technical training facility, exploring the less trammeled, trafficked East End. The company provides valet service, personalized attention, a complimentary courtesy shuttle, and an emphasis on green initiatives and specialized diving, including unguided computer, Technical, Nitrox Instructor, underwater naturalist, and cave diving for advanced participants. You can even participate in lionfish culls. But even beginners and rusty divers (there's a wonderful Skills Review and Tune-Up course) won't feel over their heads. Special touches include hot chocolate and homemade muffins on night dives; the owner, Steve, will arrange for a minister to conduct weddings in full face masks. ✉ *Compass Point, 346 Austin Connelly Dr., East End* ☎ *345/640–7500, 800/348–6096, 345/947–0000, 954/727–5312 Vonage toll-free in U.S.* 🌐 *www.oceanfrontiers.com.*

FAMILY **Red Sail Sports.** Daily trips leave from most major hotels, and dives are often run as guided tours, good for beginners. If you're experienced and your air lasts long, ask the captain if you must come up with the group (when the first person runs low on air). Kids' options, ages five to 15, include SASY and Bubblemakers. The company also operates Stingray City tours, dinner and sunset sails, and water sports from Wave Runners to windsurfing. ☎ *345/949–8745, 345/623–5965, 877/506–6368* 🌐 *www.redsailcayman.com.*

Sunset Divers. At a hostelry that caters to the scuba set, this full-service PADI teaching facility has great shore diving and six dive boats that hit all sides of the island. Divers can be independent on boats as long as they abide by maximum time and depth standards. Instruction and packages are comparatively inexpensive. Though the company is not directly affiliated with acclaimed underwater shutterbug Cathy Church (whose shop is also at the hotel), she often works with the instructors on special courses. ✉ *Sunset House, 390 S. Church St.* ☎ *345/949–7111, 800/854–4767* 🌐 *www.sunsethouse.com.*

FISHING

If you enjoy action fishing, Cayman waters have plenty to offer. Experienced, knowledgeable local captains charter boats with top-of-the-line equipment, bait, ice, and often lunch included in the price (usually $700 to $950 per half day, $1,200 to $1,600 for a full day). Options include deep-sea, reef, bone, tarpon, light-tackle, and fly-fishing. June and July are good all-around months for blue marlin, yellow- and blackfin tuna, dolphinfish, and bonefish. Bonefish have a second season in the winter months, along with wahoo and skipjack tuna.

Black Princess Charters. Captain Chuckie Ebanks leads deep-sea and reef fishing as well as snorkel trips on his fully equipped and supplied eponymous 40-foot *Sea Ray*. Rates are reasonable, and he can arrange clean, inexpensive accommodations. ☎ *345/916–6319, 345/949–0400* 🌐 *www.fishgrandcayman.com.*

Oh Boy Charters. Charters include a 60-foot yacht with complete amenities (for day and overnight trips, sunset and dinner cruises) and a 34-foot Crusader. Alvin Ebanks—son of Caymanian marine royalty, the indomitable Captain Marvin Ebanks—jokingly claims he's been playing in and plying the waters for a century and tells tales (tall and otherwise) of his father reeling him in for fishing expeditions. No more than eight passengers on the deep-sea boats ensures the personal touch (snorkeling on the 60-footer accommodates more people). Guests always receive a good selection of their catch; if you prefer others to do the cooking, go night fishing (including catch-and-release shark safaris), which includes dinner. ☎ *345/949–6341, 345/926–0898* 🌐 *www.ohboycharters.com.*

R&M Fly Shop and Charters. Captain Ronald Ebanks is arguably the island's most knowledgeable fly-fishing guide, with more than 10 years' experience in Cayman and Scotland. He also runs light-tackle trips on a 24-foot Robalo. Everyone from beginners—even children—to experienced casters enjoy and learn, whether wading or poling from a 17-foot Stratos Flats boat. Free transfers are included. Captain Ronald even ties his own flies (he'll show you how). ☎ *345/947–3146, 345/946–0214* 🌐 *www.flyfishgrandcayman.com.*

Sea Star Charters. Friendly Caymanian Clinton Ebanks does what it takes to ensure a wonderful time on his 27- and 28-foot cabin cruisers and a 35-foot trimaran used primarily for snorkeling cruises. A good choice for beginners, he leads light-tackle, bone-, and bottom fishing and offers a nice cultural experience as well as sailing charters and snorkeling with complimentary transportation and equipment. Aka Captain Clinton's Watersports, the company only accepts cash and traveler's checks. ☎ *345/949–1016 evenings, 345/916–5234.*

GOLF

Britannia. Next to the Grand Cayman Beach Suites and designed by Jack Nicklaus, the course is really a 9-hole routing with two sets of tees so as to provide an 18-hole experience. The courses feature artificial abrupt mounding and lots of water, similar to what Nicklaus did early on in Florida. Tough holes include 3 and 10; beware tricky winds on 7 through 11. Amenities include a full pro shop and the Britannia Golf Grille (with particularly good breakfasts and local fare). ✉ *West Bay Rd., Seven Mile Beach* ☎ *345/745–4653* 🌐 *www.britannia-golf.com* 🎟 *$150 for 18 holes ($115 off-season), $100 for 9 holes ($75 off-season); twilight discounts* ⛳ *9-hole course w/2 tees, 5829 yards, par 70.*

North Sound Golf Club. Formerly the Links at Safehaven, this is Cayman's only 18-hole golf course and infamous among duffers for its strong wind gusts. Roy Case factored the wind into his design, which incorporates lots of looming water and sand bunkers. The handsome setting features many mature mahogany and silver thatch trees where iguana lurk. Wear shorts at least 14 inches long (15 inches for women) and collared shirts. Greens fees change seasonally, and there are twilight and walking discounts (though carts are recommended), a fine pro shop, and an open-air bar with large-screen TVs. ✉ *Off West Bay Rd., Seven Mile Beach* ☎ *345/947–4653* 🌐 *www.northsoundclub.com* 🎟 *$175 for 18 holes, $110 for 9 holes, including cart* ⛳ *18 holes, 6605 yards, par 71.*

GUIDED TOURS

Taxi drivers give personalized tours of Grand Cayman for about $25 per hour for up to three people. Hotels also arrange helicopter rides, horseback or mountain-bike journeys, 4x4 safari expeditions, and full-day bus excursions.

Costs and itineraries are about the same regardless of the tour operator. Half-day tours average $40 to $50 a person and generally include a visit to Hell and the Turtle Farm at Boatswain's Beach aquatic park in West Bay, as well as shopping downtown. Full-day tours ($70 to $90 per person) add lunch, a visit to Bodden Town (the first settlement), and the East End, with stops at the Queen Elizabeth II Botanic Park, blowholes (if the waves are high) on the ironshore, and the site of the wreck of the *Ten Sails* (not the wreck itself—just the site). The pirate graves in Bodden Town were destroyed during Hurricane Ivan in 2008, and the blowholes were partially filled. As you can tell, land tours here are low-key. Children under 12 often receive discounts.

A.A. Transportation Services. For taxis and tour buses, ask for Burton Ebanks. ☎ *345/949–6598, 345/926–8294, 345/949–7222.*

Cayman Safari. This hits the usual sights but emphasizes interaction with locals, so you learn about craft traditions, folklore, and herbal medicines; careening along in Land Rovers is incidental fun. Rates range from $79 to $99 ($69 to $79 for children under 12). ☎ *345/925–3001, 866/211–4677* 🌐 *www.caymansafari.com.*

Majestic Tours. The company caters mostly to cruise-ship and incentive groups but offers similar options to individuals and can customize tours, starting at $45 per person; it's particularly good for West Bay, including the Cayman Turtle Farm and Hell. ✉ *Industrial Park, 322 N. Sound Rd.* ☎ *345/949–7773* 🌐 *www.majestic-tours.com.*

McCurley Tours. This outfit is owned by B.A. McCurley, a free-spirited, freewheeling Midwesterner who's lived in Cayman since the mid-1980s and knows everything and everyone on the East End. Not only is she encyclopedic and flexible, but she also offers car rentals and transfers for travelers staying on the North Side or East End; don't be surprised if she tells you what to order at lunch, especially if it's off the menu. ☎ *345/947–9626, 345/916–0925.*

Tropicana Tours. With several excellent itineraries on large buses, tours include Stingray City stops as well as reef runner adventures across the North Sound through the mangrove swamps. ☎ *345/949–0944* 🌐 *www.tropicana-tours.com.*

HIKING

Mastic Trail. This significant trail, used in the 1800s as the only direct path to the North Side, is a rugged 2-mile (3-km) slash through 776 dense acres of woodlands, black mangrove swamps, savanna, agricultural remnants, and ancient rock formations. It embraces more than 700 species, including Cayman's largest remaining contiguous ancient forest (one of the heavily deforested Caribbean's last examples). A comfortable walk depends on weather—winter is better because it's drier, though flowering plants such as the banana orchid blaze in summer. Call the National Trust to determine suitability and to book a guide ($30); tours run daily 9 to 5 by appointment and Thursdays and Fridays at 9 (sometimes earlier in summer). Or walk on the wild side with a $5 guidebook covering the ecosystems, endemic wildlife, seasonal changes, poisonous plants, and folkloric uses of flora. The trip takes about three hours. ✉ *Frank Sound Rd., entrance by fire station at botanic park, Breakers, East End* ☎ *345/749–1121, 345/749–1124 for guide reservations* 🌐 *www.nationaltrust.org.ky.*

HORSEBACK RIDING

Coral Stone Stables. Leisurely 90-minute horseback rides take in the white-sand beaches at Barkers and inland trails at Savannah; photos are included. Your guide is Nolan Stewart, whose ranch contains 20 horses, chickens, and "randy" roosters. Nolan offers a nonstop narrative on flora, fauna, and history. He's an entertaining, endless font of local information, some of it unprintable. Rides are $80; swim rides cost $120. ✉ *Conch Point Rd., next to Restaurante Papagallo on the left, West Bay* ☎ *345/916–4799* 🌐 *www.csstables.com.*

FAMILY **Pampered Ponies.** Offering "the ultimate tanning machine"—horses walking, trotting, and cantering along the beach—the stable leads private tours and guided trips, including sunset, moonlight, and swim rides along the uninhabited beach from Conch Point to Morgan's Harbour on the north tip beyond West Bay. ✉ *355 Conch Point Rd., Barkers, West Bay* ☎ *345/945–2262, 345/916–2540* 🌐 *www.ponies.ky.*

KAYAKING

FAMILY **Cayman Kayaks.** This outfitter explores Grand Cayman's protected mangrove wetlands, providing an absorbing discussion of indigenous animals (including a mesmerizing stop at a gently pulsing, nonstinging Cassiopeia jellyfish pond) and plants, the effects of hurricanes, and conservation efforts. Even beginners find the tours easy (the guides dub it low-impact aerobics), and the sit-on-top tandem kayaks are stable and comfortable. The Bio Bay tour involves more strenuous paddling, but the underwater light show is magical as millions of bioluminescent microorganisms called dinoflagellates glow like fireflies when disturbed. It runs only on moonless nights and books well in advance. Tours ($39–$59 with some kids' and group discounts) depart from different locations, most from the public access jetty to the left of Rum Point. ✉ *Rum Point, Cayman Kai, North Side* ☎ *345/746–3249, 345/926–4467* 🌐 *www.caymankayaks.com.*

8

SEA EXCURSIONS

The most impressive sights in the Cayman Islands are on and underwater, and several submarines, semisubmersibles, glass-bottom boats, and Jules Verne–like contraptions allow you to see these wonders without getting your feet wet. Sunset sails, dinner cruises, and other theme (dance, booze, pirate) cruises are available from $30 to $90 per person.

FAMILY **Atlantis Submarines.** This submarine takes 48 passengers safely and comfortably along the Cayman Wall down to 100 feet. Peep through panoramic portholes as good-natured guides keep up a humorous but informative patter. A guide dons scuba gear to feed fish, who form a whirling frenzy of color rivaling anything by Picasso. At night, the 10,000-watt lights show the kaleidoscopic underwater colors and nocturnal stealth predators more brilliantly than during the day. Try to sit toward the front so you can watch the pilot's nimble maneuverings and the depth gauge. If that literally in-depth tour seems daunting, get up close and personal on the *Seaworld Observatory* semisubmersible (glorified glass-bottom boat), which just cruises the harbor (including glimpses of the *Cali* and *Balboa* shipwrecks). The cost is $89–$104 (children $49–$64) for the submarine, $39 (children $24) for the semisubmersible. There are frequent online booking discounts. ✉ *30 S. Church St.* ☎ *345/949–7700, 800/887–8571* 🌐 *www.caymanislandssubmarines.com.*

FAMILY ***Jolly Roger.*** This is a two-thirds-size replica of Christopher Columbus's 17th-century Spanish galleon *Niña*. (The company also owns the *Anne*

Bonny, a wooden Norwegian brig built in 1934 that holds more than 100 passengers.) On the afternoon snorkel cruise, play Captain Jack Sparrow while experiencing swashbuckling pirate antics, including a trial, sword fight, and walking the plank; kids can fire the cannon, help hoist the main sail, and scrub the decks (they will love it even if they loathe doing chores at home). Evening options (sunset and dinner sails) are more standard booze cruises, less appropriate for the kiddies. Food is more appropriate to the brig, and it's more yo-ho-hokum than remotely authentic, but it's fun. Prices are $45– $65 (children's discounts available). ✉ *South Terminal, next to Atlantis Submarines* ☎ *345/945–7245* 🌐 *www.jollyrogercayman.com, www.piratesofthecaymans.com.*

FAMILY **Sea Trek.** Helmet diving lets you walk and breathe 26 feet underwater for an hour—without getting your hair wet. No training or even swimming ability is required (ages eight and up), and you can wear glasses. Guides give a thorough safety briefing, and a sophisticated system of compressors and cylinders provides triple the amount of air necessary for normal breathing while a safety diver program ensures four levels of backup. The result at near-zero gravity resembles an exhilarating moonwalk ($89, $99 for Ultimate Stingray City excursion). ✉ *The Cabana, N. Church St.* ☎ *345/949–0008* 🌐 *www.seatrekcayman.com, www.snubacayman.com.*

SNORKELING

SNORKELING SITES

Fodor's Choice ★ **Stingray City Sandbar.** This site (as opposed to Stingray City, a popular 12-foot dive) is the island's stellar snorkeling attraction. Dozens of boats head here several times daily. It's less crowded on days with fewer cruise ships in port. ✉ *North Sound.*

Wreck of the *Cali.* You can still identify the engines and winches of this old sailing freighter, which settled about 20 feet down. The sponges are particularly vivid, and tropical fish, shrimp, and lobster abound. Many operators based in George Town and Seven Mile Beach come here. ✉ *About 50 yards out from Rackam's Waterfront Pub, 93 N. Church St.*

SNORKELING OPERATORS

Bayside Watersports. Offering half-day snorkel trips, North Sound beach lunch excursions, Stingray City and dinner cruises, and full-day deep-sea fishing, this company operates several popular boats out of West Bay's Morgan's Harbour. Full-day trips include lunch and conch diving November–April. ✉ *Morgan's Harbour, West Bay* ☎ *345/949–3200* 🌐 *www.baysidewatersports.com.*

FAMILY **Captain Crosby's Watersports.** Offering favorably priced snorkeling ($40–$73 including refreshments) and dive excursions on well-equipped 47- and 40-foot trimarans, Captain Crosby is one of the more colorful captains in a group of genuine characters. He's actively involved in preserving Cayman's maritime heritage as a founder of the Catboat Association. As a bonus, trips usually run a little long and often include a sing-along with the "singing captain." He also leads deep-sea fishing charters. ✉ *Cayman Islands Yacht Club, Dock C-29, Seven Mile Beach* ☎ *345/945–4049, 345/916–1725* 🌐 *www.captaincrosbywatersports.com.*

A group of stingrays patrols the grassy shallows of Grand Cayman.

FAMILY **Fantasea Tours.** Captain Dexter Ebanks runs tours on his 38-foot trimaran, *Don't Even Ask*, usually departing from the Cayman Islands Yacht Club ($40 including transfers). He doesn't pack you in like sardines (20 people max) and is particularly helpful with first-timers. Like many captains, he has pet names for the rays (ask him to find Lucy, whom he "adopted") and rattles off factoids during an entertaining, nonstop narration. It's a laid-back trip, with Bob Marley and Norah Jones playing, fresh fruit and rum punch on tap. ✉ *West Bay Rd., Seven Mile Beach* ☎ *345/916–0754* 🌐 *www.dexters-fantaseatours.com.*

8

FAMILY **Red Sail Sports.** Luxurious 62- and 65-foot catamarans (the *Spirits of Cayman, Poseidon, Calypso,* and *Ppalu)* often carry large groups on Stingray City, sunset, and evening sails ($40–$85, $20–$42.50 children under 12) including dinner in winter. Although the service may not be personal, it's efficient. A glass-bottom boat takes passengers to Stingray City/Sandbar and nearby coral reefs. Trips run from several hotels, including the Westin and Morritt's, in addition to the Rum Point headquarters. ☎ *345/949–8745, 345/623–5965, 877/506–6368* 🌐 *www.redsailcayman.com.*

CAYMAN BRAC

Cayman Brac is named for its most distinctive feature, a rugged limestone bluff (*brac* in Gaelic) that runs up the center of the 12-mile (19-km) island, pocked with caves and culminating in a sheer 140-foot cliff at its eastern end. The Brac, 89 miles (143 km) northeast of Grand Cayman, is a splendidly serene destination for eco-enthusiasts, offering world-class birding, scuba diving, bonefishing in the shallows or light-tackle and deep-sea angling, hiking, spelunking, and rock climbing. With only 1,800 residents—they call themselves Brackers—the island has the feel and easy pace of a small town. Brackers are known for their friendly attitude toward visitors, so it's easy to strike up a conversation. Locals wave on passing and might invite you home for a traditional rundown (a thick, sultry fish stew) and storytelling, usually about the sea, turtle schooners, and the great hurricane of 1932 (when the caves offered shelter).

Brackers are as calm and peaceful as their island is rugged, having been violently sculpted by sea and wind, most recently by Hurricane Paloma, which leveled the island in 2008 (locals quip that all 18 churches—but no bars—sustained significant damage).

EXPLORING

TOP ATTRACTIONS

Cayman Brac Museum. A diverse, well-displayed collection of historic Bracker implements ranges from dental pliers to pistols to pottery. A meticulously crafted scale model of the Caymanian catboat *Alsons* has pride of place. The front room reconstructs the Customs, Treasury, bank, and post office as they looked decades ago. Permanent exhibits include those on the 1932 hurricane, turtling, shipbuilding, and old-time home life. The back room hosts rotating exhibits such as one on herbal folk medicine. ✉ *Old Government Administration Bldg., Stake Bay* ☎ *345/948–2622, 345/244–4446* 🎟 *Free* ⏲ *Weekdays 9–4, Sat. 9–noon.*

Fodor's Choice ★ **Parrot Preserve.** The likeliest place to spot the endangered Cayman Brac parrot—and other indigenous and migratory birds—is along this National Trust hiking trail off Major Donald Drive, aka Lighthouse Road. Prime time is early morning or late afternoon; most of the day they're camouflaged by trees, earning them the moniker "stealth parrot." The loop trail incorporates part of a path the Brackers used in olden days to cross the bluff to reach their provision grounds on the south shore or to gather coconuts, once a major export crop. It passes through several types of terrain: old farmland under grass and native trees from mango to mahogany unusually mixed with orchids and cacti. Wear sturdy shoes, as the terrain is rocky, uneven, and occasionally rough. The 6-mile (10-km) gravel road continues to the lighthouse at the bluff's eastern end, where there's an astonishing view from atop the cliff to the open ocean—the best place to watch the sunrise. ✉ *Lighthouse Rd., ½ mile (1 km) south of town, Tibbetts Turn* ☎ *345/948–0319* 🎟 *Free* ⏲ *Daily sunrise–sunset.*

BEACHES

Much of the Brac's coastline is ironshore, though there are several pretty sand beaches, mostly along the southwest coast (where swimmers also find extensive beds of turtle grass, which creates less than ideal conditions for snorkeling). In addition to the hotel beaches, where everyone

Cayman Brac and Little Cayman

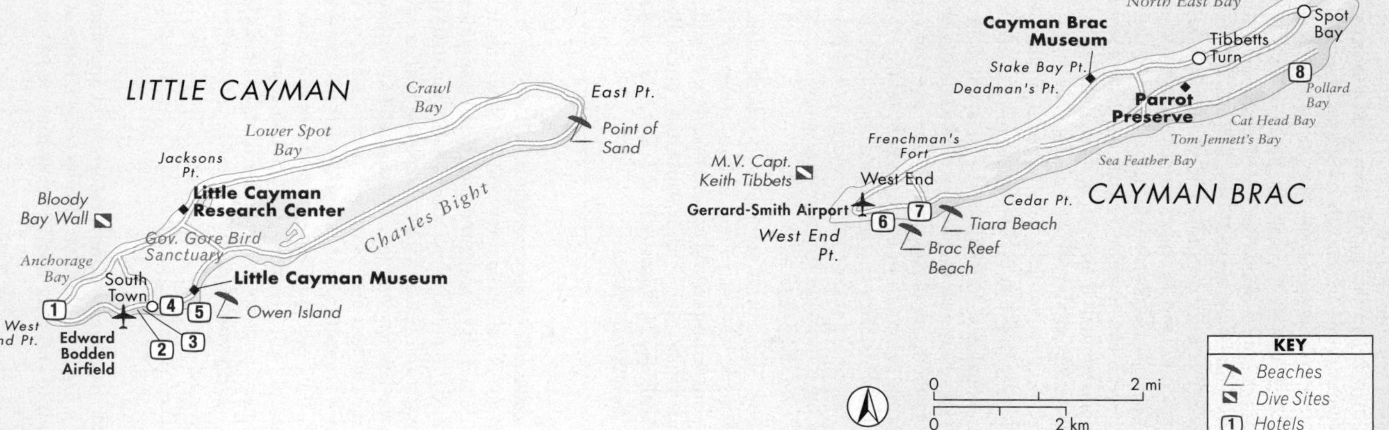

Brac Caribbean and Carib Sands 7
Brac Reef Beach Resort 6
Cayman Breakers 8
The Club 4
Little Cayman Beach Resort 3
Paradise Villas 2
Pirates Point Resort 1
Southern Cross Club 5

is welcome, there is a public beach with good access to the reef; it's well marked on tourist maps. The north-coast beaches, predominantly rocky ironshore, offer excellent snorkeling.

Pollard Bay. The beach by Cayman Breakers is fairly wide for this eastern stretch of the island. Start clambering east underneath the imposing bluff, past the end of the paved road, to strikingly beautiful deserted stretches accessible only on foot. The water here starts churning like a washing machine and becomes progressively rockier, littered with driftwood. Locals search for whelks here. Steps by the Breakers lead to shore dive sites. Flocks of seabirds darken the sun for seconds at a time, while blowholes spout as if answering migrant humpback whales. Don't go beyond the gargantuan rock called First Cay—the sudden swells can be hazardous—unless you're a serious rock climber. **Amenities:** none. **Best for:** solitude; walking. ✉ *South Side Rd. E, East End.*

Public Beach. Roughly 2 miles (3 km) east of the Brac Reef and Carib Sands/Brac Caribbean resorts, just past the wetlands (the unsightly gate is visible from the road; if you hit the Bat Cave you've passed it), lie a series of strands culminating in this beach, relatively deserted despite its name. The surf is calm and the crystalline water fairly protected for swimming. There are picnic tables and showers in uncertain condition. Snorkeling is quite good. **Amenities:** showers. **Best for:** snorkeling. ✉ *South Side Rd. W, South Side.*

Sea Feather Bay. The central section of the south coast features several lengthy ribbons of soft ecru sand, only occasionally maintained, with little shade aside from the odd coconut palm, no facilities, and blissful privacy (aside from some villas). **Amenities:** none. **Best for:** solitude; swimming, walking. ✉ *South Side Rd. just west of Ashton Reid Dr., Sea Feather Bay, South Side.*

WHERE TO EAT

$$$ EUROPEAN

✕ **Captain's Table.** This weathered, powder-blue, wooden building wouldn't be out of place on some remote New England shore, except perhaps for the garish pirate at the entrance. The nautical yo-ho-hokum continues inside (painted oars, model sailboats, faux portholes, mermaid painting, droll touches like a skeleton with a chef's toque), but fortunately the kitchen isn't lost at sea, despite voyaging from India to Italy. Teriyaki chicken and scampi Florentine are worthy house specialties. Lunch is cheaper, from standbys (wraps, burgers, nachos, Lolita's chicken-fried tacos) to more creative options like "honey-stung" chicken fried in chili powder and crushed corn chips. The outdoor poolside bar is a popular hangout for dive masters. *$ Average main: $21* ✉ *Brac Caribbean, South Side* ☎ *345/948–1418* *Reservations essential.*

WHERE TO STAY

Cayman Brac has several hotels, resorts, and apartments. Several private villas on Cayman Brac can also be rented, most of them basic but well maintained, ranging from one to four bedrooms. Most resorts offer optional meal plans, but there are several restaurants, some of which provide free transport from your hotel. Most restaurants serve island fare (local seafood, chicken, and curries). On Friday and Saturday nights the spicy scent of jerk chicken fills the air; several roadside stands sell take-out.

PRIVATE VILLAS AND CONDOS

Golden Sun/Le Soleil d'Or. Mirjana Mirjanic's company rents some of the Brac's newest, most luxurious homes but sets itself apart with the little extras (for a price): in-house spa treatments, personal training, gourmet chefs, even cooking classes. The rental office also doubles as a delightful shop, selling Mirjana's organic foodstuffs (sorrel flower jam, Meyer lemon marmalade), goat cheese soaps, and candles, all sourced from Golden Sun's own garden farm. (You can arrange a farm-to-table tour of the sustainable facility, too.) ✉ *403 Gerrard Smith Ave., Suite 4* ☎ *345/948–0555, 888/988–0521* 🌐 *www.goldensuncayman.com.*

HOTELS AND RESORTS

$ RESORT **Brac Caribbean and Carib Sands.** These neighboring, beachfront sister complexes offer condos with one to four bedrooms, all individually owned and decorated. **Pros:** lively restaurant-bar; excellent value for families with weekly discounts. **Cons:** pretty but narrow, often unmaintained beach; limited staff; Wi-Fi dodgy. $ *Rooms from: $165* ✉ *Bert Marson Dr.* ☎ *345/948–2265, 866/843–2722* 🌐 *www.caribsands.com, www.braccaribbean.com, www.866thebrac.com* *65 condos* *No meals.*

$$ RESORT **Brac Reef Beach Resort.** Popular with divers, this well-run eco-friendly resort features a beautiful sandy beach shaded by sea grape trees slung with hammocks. **Pros:** great dive outfit; friendly vibe; free Wi-Fi; good online packages; coin-operated laundry. **Cons:** noise from planes; view often obscured from ground-floor units; mandatory airport transfer of $20 per person. $ *Rooms from: $284* ✉ *West End* ☎ *345/948–1323, 727/323–8727 for reservations in Florida, 800/594–0843* 🌐 *www.bracreef.com* *40 rooms* *Multiple meal plans.*

$ RENTAL **Cayman Breakers.** This attractive, pink-brick, colonnaded condo development sitting between the bluff and the southeast coastal ironshore caters to climbers, who scale the bluff's sheer face, as well as divers, who appreciate the good shore diving right off the property. **Pros:** spectacular views; thoughtful extras like complimentary bikes, jigsaw puzzles, and climbing-route guides; very attentive managers who live on-site. **Cons:** nearest grocery is a 15-minute drive; gorgeous beach is rocky with rough surf; some units slightly musty and faded. $ *Rooms from: $150* ✉ *South Side Rd., near East End* ☎ *345/948–1463* 🌐 *www.caybreakers.com* *26 2-bedroom condos* *No meals.*

NIGHTLIFE

Divers are notoriously early risers, but a few bars keep things hopping if not quite happening, especially on weekends, when local bands (or "imports" from Grand Cayman) often perform. Quaintly reminiscent of *Footloose* (without the hellfire and brimstone), watering holes are required to obtain music and dancing permits. Various community

8

events including talent shows, recitals, concerts, and other stage presentations at the Aston Rutty Centre provide the rest of the island's nightlife.

Barracuda's Bar. New Yorker Terry Chesnard built his dream bar from scratch, endowing it with an almost 1960s Rat Pack ambience. Nearly everything is handcrafted, from the elegant bar itself to the blown-glass light fixtures to the shot specials (try the Barracuda "if you dare") and cocktails with *cojones* (though Terry takes greatest pride in his top-of-the-line espresso machine). The kitchen elevates pub grub to an art form, with Reubens and French melts. Locals flock here for free pasta Fridays, karaoke Wednesdays, and live music on Thursdays. You might walk in on a hotly contested darts or dominos tournament, but the vibe is otherwise mellow at this charming time-warp hangout. ✉ *West End* ☎ *345/948–8511* 🌐 *www.barracudas.ky.*

SPORTS AND THE OUTDOORS

DIVING AND SNORKELING

Cayman Brac's waters are celebrated for their rich diversity of sea life, from hammerhead and reef sharks to stingrays to sea horses. Divers and snorkelers alike will find towering coral heads, impressive walls, and fascinating wrecks. The snorkeling off the **north coast** is spectacular, particularly at West End, where coral formations close to shore attract all kinds of critters. The walls feature remarkable topography with natural gullies, caves, and fissures blanketed with Technicolor sponges, black coral, gorgonians, and sea fans. Some of the famed sites are the West Chute, Cemetery Wall, Airport Wall, and Garden Eel Wall. The South Wall is a wonderland of sheer drop-offs carved with a maze of vertical swim-throughs, tunnels, arches, and grottoes that divers nickname Cayman's Grand Canyon. Notable sites include Anchor Wall, Rock Monster Chimney, and the Wilderness. Many fish have colonized the 330-foot MV *Capt. Keith Tibbetts,* a Russian frigate—now broken in two—that was deliberately scuttled within swimming distance of the northwest shore. An artist named Foots has created an amazing underwater Atlantis off Radar Reef. The island's two dive operators offer scuba and snorkel training and PADI certification.

Brac Scuba Shack. Partners Martin van der Touw, wife Liesel, and Steve Reese form a tremedous troika at this PADI outfit, whose selling points include small groups (10 divers max on the custom Newton 36), flexible departures, valet service, and computer profiles. The 30-foot central console *Big Blue* takes no more than five divers and does double-duty for deep-sea fishing. Courses range from Discover Scuba through Divemaster Training, as well as such specialties as wreck, Nitrox, and night diving. Rates are competitive ($95 for two-tank dives), and multiday discounts are available. ✉ *West End* ☎ *345/948–8472* 🌐 *www.bracscubashack.com.*

Reef Divers. Pluses here include five Newton boats from 42 to 46 feet, valet service, and enthusiastic, experienced staff. Certified divers can purchase à la carte dive packages even if they aren't hotel guests. They also arrange snorkeling tours. ✉ *Brac Reef Beach Resort, West End*

☎ *345/948–1642, 345/948–1323* 🌐 *www.reefdiverscaymanbrac.com, www.bracreef.com.*

HIKING

Brac Tourism Office. Free printed guides to the Brac's many heritage and nature trails can be obtained here (and from the airport and hotels). Traditional routes across the bluff have been marked, as are trailheads along the road. It's safe to hike on your own, though some trails are fairly hard going (wear light hiking boots) and others could be better maintained. ✉ *West End Community Park, west of airport* ☎ *345/948–1649* 🌐 *www.itsyourstoexplore.com.*

Christopher Columbus Gardens. For those who prefer less-strenuous walking, these gardens have easy trails and boardwalks. The park showcases the unique natural flora and features of the bluff, including two cave mouths. This is a peaceful spot dotted with gazebos and wooden bridges comprising several ecosystems from cacti to mahogany trees. ✉ *Ashton Reid Dr. (Bluff Rd.), just north of Ashton Rutty Centre.*

Sister Islands District Administration. The administration arranges free, government-sponsored, guided nature and cultural tours with trained local guides. Options include the Parrot Reserve, nature trails, wetlands, Lighthouse/Bluff View, caving, birding, and heritage sites. You just supply the wheels and spirit of adventure. ☎ *345/948–2222.*

SPELUNKING

If you plan to explore Cayman Brac's caves, wear good sneakers or hiking shoes, as some paths are steep and rocky and some cave entrances are reachable only by ladders. **Peter's Cave** offers a stunning aerial view of the northeastern community of Spot Bay. **Great Cave,** at the island's southeast end, has numerous chambers and photogenic ocean views. In **Bat Cave** you may see bats hanging from the ceiling (try not to disturb them). **Rebecca's Cave** houses the grave site of a 17-month-old child who died during the horrific hurricane of 1932.

LITTLE CAYMAN

The smallest, most tranquil of the Cayman Islands, Little Cayman has a full-time population of only 170, most of whom work in tourism. This 12-square-mile (31-square-km) island is still unspoiled and has only a sand-sealed airstrip, no official terminal building, and few vehicles. The speed limit remains 25 mph (40 kph), as no one is in a hurry. In fact, the island's iguanas use roads more than residents; signs created by local artists read "Iguanas Have the Right of Way." With little commercial development, the island beckons ecotourists who seek wildlife encounters, not urban wildlife. It's probably best known for its spectacular diving on Bloody Bay Wall and adjacent Jackson Marine Park. The ravishing reefs and plummeting walls encircling the island teem with more than 500 species of fish and more than 150 kinds of coral. Fly-, lake-, and deep-sea fishing are also popular, as are snorkeling, kayaking, cycling, and hiking. And the island's certainly for the birds. The National Trust Booby Pond Nature Reserve is a designated wetland, protecting around 20,000 red-footed boobies, the Western

Hemisphere's largest colony. It's just one of many spots for avian aerial acrobatics. Pristine wetlands, secluded beaches, unspoiled tropical wilderness, mangrove swamps, lagoons, bejeweled coral reefs: Little Cayman practically redefines *escape*. Yet aficionados appreciate that the low-key lifestyle doesn't mean sacrificing high-tech amenities, and some resorts cater to a wealthy yet unpretentious crowd.

EXPLORING

TOP ATTRACTIONS

Fodor's Choice ★ **Little Cayman National Trust.** This traditional Caymanian cottage overlooks the Booby Pond Nature Reserve; telescopes on the breezy second-floor deck permit close-up views of their markings and nests, as well as other feathered friends. Inside are shell collections, panels and dioramas discussing endemic reptiles, models "in flight," and diagrams on the growth and life span of red-footed boobies, frigate birds, egrets, and other island "residents." The shop sells exquisite jewelry made from Caymanite and spider-crab shells, extraordinary duck decoys and driftwood carvings, and great books on history, ornithology, and geology. Mike Vallee holds an iguana information session and tour every Friday at 4. The cheeky movie *Calendar Girls* inspired a local equivalent: Little Cayman women, mostly in full, ripe maturity, going topless for an important cause—raising awareness of the red-footed booby and funds to purchase the sanctuary's land. Nicknamed, appropriately, "Support the Boobies," the calendar is tasteful, not titillating: the lasses strategically hold conch shells, brochures, flippers, tree branches, etc. ✉ *Blossom Village* 🌐 *www.nationaltrust.org.ky* ⏲ *Weekdays 3–5.*

WORTH NOTING

Little Cayman Museum. This newly renovated museum displays relics and artifacts, including a wing devoted to maritime memorabilia, that provide a good overview of this tiny island's history and heritage. ✉ *Across from Booby Pond Nature Reserve, Blossom Village* ☎ *345/948–1033 for Little Cayman Beach Resort* 🎟 *Free* ⏲ *Thurs. and Fri. 3–5, by appointment only.*

Little Cayman Research Center. Near the Jackson Point Bloody Bay Marine Park reserve, this vital research center supports visiting students and researchers, with a long list of projects studying the biodiversity, human impact, reef health, and ocean ecosystem of Little Cayman. Its situation is unique in that reefs this unspoiled are usually far less accessible; the National Oceanic and Atmospheric Administration awarded it one of 16 monitoring stations worldwide. The center also solicits funding through the parent U.S. nonprofit organization Central Caribbean Marine Institute; if you value the health of our reefs, show your support on the website. Chairman Peter Hillenbrand proudly calls it the "Ritz-Carlton of marine research facilities, which often are little more than pitched tents on a beach." Tours explain the center's mission and ecosensitive design (including Peter's Potty, an off-the-grid bathroom facility using compostable toilets that recycle fertilizer into gray water for the gardens); sometimes you'll get a peek at the upstairs functional wet labs and dormitories. To make it layperson-friendlier, scientists occasionally give talks and presentations. The Dive with a Researcher program (where you actually help survey and assess environmental impact and ecosystem health, depending on that week's focus) is hugely popular. ✉ *North Side* ☎ *345/948–1094* 🌐 *www.reefresearch.org* ⏲ *By appointment only.*

BEACHES

The southwest part of the island seems like one giant beach; this is where virtually all the resorts sit, serenely facing Preston Bay and South Hole Sound. But there are several other unspoiled, usually deserted strands that beckon beachcombers, all the sand having the same delicate hue of Cristal champagne and just as apt to make you feel giddy.

Fodor's Choice ★ **Owen Island.** This private, forested island can be reached by rowboat, kayak, or an ambitious 200-yard swim. Anyone is welcome to come across and enjoy the deserted beaches and excellent snorkeling. Nudity is forbidden as "idle and disorderly" in the Cayman Islands, though that doesn't always stop skinny-dippers (who may not realize they can be seen quite easily from shore). **Amenities**: none. **Best for**: solitude; snorkeling; swimming.

Fodor's Choice ★ **Point of Sand.** Stretching over a mile on the island's easternmost point, this secluded beach is great for wading, shell collecting, and snorkeling. On a clear day you can see 7 miles (11 km) to Cayman Brac. The beach serves as a green- and loggerhead turtle nesting site in spring, and a mosaic of coral gardens blooms just offshore. It's magical, especially at moonrise, when it earns its nickname, Lovers' Beach. There's a palapa for shade but no facilities. The current can be strong, so watch the kids carefully. **Amenities**: none. **Best for**: solitude; snorkeling; sunset; walking.

8

WHERE TO EAT

$$$ ECLECTIC ✕ **Hungry Iguana.** The closest thing to a genuine sports bar and nightclub on Little Cayman, the Iggy caters to the aquatically minded set with a marine mural, wood-plank floors, mounted trophy sailfish, lots of fishing caps, and yummy fresh seafood. Conch fritters are near definitive, while lionfish fingers with jerk mayo are mouth- and eye-watering. It's a great hangout for (relatively) cheap eats; prix-fixe theme nights between CI$20 and CI$40 offer fine value: pizza, fajitas, curry, and more. Drink in the smashing sunset views on the delightful patio overlooking the water, and also drink of the house specialty Iguana Punch (rum, rum, more rum, and coconut rum with orange and pineapple juices). [$] *Average main: $29* ✉ *Paradise Villas, Blossom Village* ☎ *345/948–0001* 🌐 *www.hungryiguana.com* ⏲ *No dinner Sun.*

WHERE TO STAY

Accommodations are mostly in small lodges, many of which offer meal and dive packages. The meal packages are a good idea; the chefs in most places create wonderful dishes with often limited resources.

$$ RENTAL **The Club.** These ultramodern, luxurious, three-bedroom condos are Little Cayman's nicest units, though only five are usually included in the rental pool. **Pros:** luxurious digs; lovely beach; hot tub. **Cons:** housekeeping not included; rear guest bedrooms dark and somewhat cramped; handsome but heavy old-fashioned decor. *Rooms from: $311 South Hole Sound 345/948–1033, 727/323–8727, 800/327–3835 www.theclubatlittlecayman.com 8 condos No meals.*

$$$ RESORT FAMILY **Little Cayman Beach Resort.** This two-story hotel, the island's largest, offers modern facilities in a boutique setting. **Pros:** extensive facilities; fun crowd; glorious LED-lit pool; great bone- and deep-sea fishing. **Cons:** less intimate than other resorts; tiny patios; bike rental fee. *Rooms from: $399 Blossom Village 345/948–1033, 800/327–3835 www.littlecayman.com 40 rooms Multiple meal plans.*

$ RENTAL **Paradise Villas.** Cozy, sunny, one-bedroom units with beachfront terraces and hammocks are simply but immaculately appointed with rattan furnishings, marine artwork, painted driftwood, and bright abstract fabrics. **Pros:** friendly staff; good value, especially online deals and dive packages. **Cons:** noisy some weekend nights in season; poky beach; small bike rental fee; off-site dive shop. *Rooms from: $200 South Hole Sound 345/948–0001, 877/322–9626 www.paradisevillas.com 12 1-bedroom villas Closed mid-Sept.–late Oct. No meals.*

$$$$ RESORT Fodor's Choice ★ **Pirates Point Resort.** Comfortable rooms and fine cuisine make this hideaway nestled between sea grape and casuarina pines on a sweep of sand one of Little Cayman's best properties. **Pros:** fabulous food; fantastic beach; dynamic dive program; fun-loving staff and owner. **Cons:** everyone respects honeymooners' privacy, but this isn't a resort for antisocial types; tasteful rooms are fairly spare; occasional Internet problems. *Rooms from: $484 Pirates Point 345/948–1010 www.piratespointresort.com 11 rooms Closed Sept.–mid-Oct. Multiple meal plans.*

$$$$ RESORT Fodor's Choice ★ **Southern Cross Club.** Little Cayman's first resort was founded in the 1950s as a private fishing club by the CEO of Sears-Roebuck and CFO of General Motors, and its focus is still on fishing and diving. **Pros:** barefoot luxury; free use of kayaks and snorkel gear; splendiferous beach; international staff tells of globetrotting exploits. **Cons:** not child-friendly (though families can rent a cottage); Wi-Fi not available in some rooms and spotty elsewhere. *Rooms from: $738 South Hole Sound 345/948–1099, 800/899–2582 www.southerncrossclub.com 12 suites, 1 2-bedroom cottage Closed mid-Sept.–mid-Oct. All meals.*

SPORTS AND THE OUTDOORS

BIRD-WATCHING

Little Cayman offers bountiful bird-watching, with more than 200 indigenous and migrant species on vibrant display, including red-footed boobies, frigate birds, and West Indian whistling ducks. Unspoiled wetland blankets more than 40% of the island, and elevated viewing platforms (carefully crafted from local wood to blend harmoniously with the environment) permit undisturbed observation—but then, it's hard to find an area that doesn't host flocks of warblers and waterfowl.

Brochures with maps are available at the hotels for self-guided bird-watching tours.

Fodor's Choice ★ **Booby Pond Nature Reserve.** The reserve is home to 20,000 red-footed boobies (the Western Hemisphere's largest colony) and Cayman's only breeding colony of magnificent frigate (man-of-war) birds. Other sightings include the near-threatened West Indian whistling duck and vitelline warbler. The RAMSAR Convention, an international treaty for wetland conservation, designated the reserve a wetland of global significance. Near the airport, the sanctuary also has a gift shop and reading library. ✉ *Next to National Trust, Blossom Village.*

Grape Tree Ponds. This splendid wetland spot on the North Side is great for observing West Indian whistling ducks and has some lovely shore walks.

Jackson's Pond. This is a vast mangrove-fringed body of water offering excellent viewing of herons, ducks, rails, stilt, plovers, and sandpipers. ✉ *Off North Coast Rd., near Jackson's Point, North Side.*

West End Lighthouse. The lighthouse offers magnificent sunset views and serves as arrivals check-in for migratory shorebirds. ✉ *West End Point, near Mahogany Bay, West End.*

DIVING AND SNORKELING

A gaudy, voluptuous tumble of marine life—lumbering grouper to fleet guppies, massive manta rays to miniature wrasse, sharks to stingrays, blue chromis to Bermuda chubs, puffers to parrot fish—parades its finery through the pyrotechnic coral reefs like a watery Main Street on Saturday night. Gaping gorges, vaulting pinnacles, plunging walls, chutes, arches, and vertical chimneys create a virtual underwater city, festooned with fiery sponges and sensuously waving gorgonians draped like come-hither courtesans over limestone settees.

8

Expect to pay around $105 for a two-tank boat dive and $25–$30 for a snorkeling trip. The island is small and susceptible to wind, so itineraries can change like a sudden gust.

Fodor's Choice ★ **Bloody Bay Wall.** This beach, named for being the site of a spectacular 17th-century sea battle, was declared one of the world's top three dive sites by the *maîtres* Jacques and Philippe Cousteau. Part of a protected marine reserve, it plunges dramatically from 18 to 6,000 feet, with a series of staggeringly beautiful drop-offs and remarkable visibility. Snorkelers who are strong swimmers can access the edge from shore, gliding among shimmering silver curtains of minnows, jacks, and bonefish. The creatures are amazingly friendly, including Jerry the Grouper, whom dive masters joke is a representative of the Cayman Islands Department of Tourism.

RECOMMENDED DIVE OPERATORS

Conch Club Divers. This is a personable, experienced outfit that often customizes trips on its 42-foot *Sea-esta.* ✉ *Conch Club, Blossom Village* ☎ *345/948–1026* 🌐 *www.conchclubdivers.com.*

Pirates Point Dive Resort. This popular resort has fully outfitted 42-foot Newtons with dive masters who excel at finding odd and rare creatures, and encourage computer diving so you can stay down longer. ✉ *Pirates Point Resort* ☎ *345/948–1010* 🌐 *www.piratespointresort.com.*

Reef Divers. Little Cayman Beach Resort's outfitter offers valet service and a full complement of courses, with Nitrox a specialty. The custom boats include AEDs (defibrillators). ✉ *Little Cayman Beach Resort, Blossom Village* ☎ *345/948–1033* 🌐 *www.littlecayman.com.*

Southern Cross Club. Each boat has its own dock and takes 12 divers max. The outfit has good specialty courses and mandates computer diving. ✉ *Southern Cross Club, 73 Guy Banks Rd., South Hole Sound* ☎ *345/948–1099, 800/899–2582* 🌐 *www.southerncrossclub.com.*

FISHING

Bloody Bay is celebrated equally for fishing and diving, and the flats and shallows including South Hole Sound Lagoon across from Owen Island, Tarpon Lake, and the Charles Bight Rosetta Flats offer phenomenal light-tackle and fly-fishing action: large tarpon, small bonefish, and permit (related to pompano) up to 35 pounds. Superior deep-sea fishing, right offshore, yields game fish such as blue marlin, dolphinfish, wahoo, tuna, and barracuda.

MAM's Tours. This reliable company is run by energetic local Maxine McCoy, who comes from fishing royalty of sorts (she, her mum, dad, and five brothers ran McCoy's Diving and Fishing Resort). Deep-sea fishing costs $125 per hour for up to four people; those angling for tarpon and bonefish pay $50 per hour ($75 per couple). Maxine also runs snorkeling trips to Owen Island and will take you conching in season. She's spending more time on the Brac, so call in advance to ensure she'll be on-island. ✉ *65 Mahogany Bay, Candle Rd., West End* ☎ *345/948–0104, 345/917–4582* 🌐 *www.mams.ky.*

Southern Cross Club. The resort offers light-tackle and deep-sea fishing trips. ✉ *Southern Cross Club, 73 Guy Banks Dr., South Hole Sound* ☎ *345/948–1099, 800/899–2582* 🌐 *www.southerncrossclub.com.*

HIKING

Flat Little Cayman is better suited to biking, but there are a few jaunts, notably the **Salt Rocks Nature Trail,** where you pass ancient mule pens, abandoned phosphate mines, and the rusting tracks of the original narrow-gauge railway, now alive with a profusion of flowering cacti and scrub brush.

CURAÇAO

WELCOME TO CURAÇAO

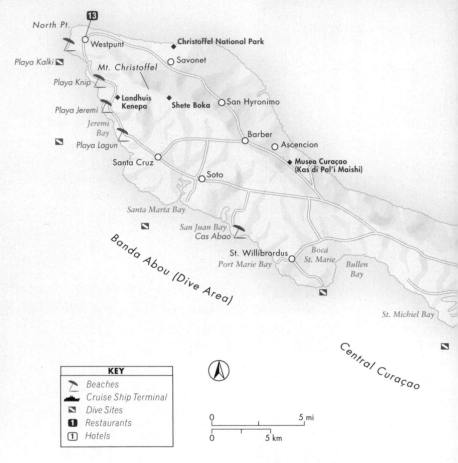

13
North Pt.
Westpunt
Christoffel National Park
Playa Kalki
Savonet
Mt. Christoffel
Playa Knip
Landhuis Kenepa
Shete Boka
San Hyronimo
Playa Jeremi
Jeremi Bay
Playa Lagun
Barber
Ascencion
Santa Cruz
Museo Curaçao (Kas di Pal'i Maishi)
Soto
Santa Marta Bay
San Juan Bay
Cas Abao
Banda Abou (Dive Area)
St. Willibrordus
Port Marie Bay
Boca St. Marie
Bullen Bay
St. Michiel Bay
Central Curaçao

KEY
Beaches
Cruise Ship Terminal
Dive Sites
Restaurants
Hotels

0 5 mi
0 5 km

Willemstad's fancifully hued, strikingly gabled town houses glimmer across Santa Anna Bay, and vendors at the Floating Market sell tropical fruit from their schooners. Curaçao's diverse population mixes Latin, European, and African ancestries. Religious tolerance is a hallmark here. All people are welcome in Curaçao, and even tourists feel the warmth.

AN ISLAND REBORN AND REDISCOVERED

The largest and most populous of the Netherlands Antilles is 38 miles (61 km) long and no more than 7½ miles (12 km) wide. Its capital, Willemstad, has been restored and revived over the past few years and is a recognized UNESCO World Heritage Site. The colorful waterfront town houses are unique to the island.

Restaurants ▼	
Bistro Le Clochard	**1**
Blues Bar	**9**
CRU Steak House	**7**
Fort Nassau Restaurant	**10**
Gouverneur de Rouville Restaurant & Café	**2**
Jaanchies	**13**
Kome	**8**
La Bahia	**3**
L'aldea Steakhouse	**12**
Primas	**4**
Royal Dutch Cheesery	**6**
Scampi's	**5**
Shore	**11**

Hotels ▼	
Avila Hotel	**8**
Baoase	**3**
Blue Bay Curaçao	**12**
Curaçao Marriott	**10**
Floris Suite Hotel	**11**
Hilton Curaçao	**13**
Hotel't Klooster	**1**
Lions Dive	**7**
PM78 Urban	**5**
Renaissance Curaçao Resort	**2**
Santa Barbara Beach & Golf Resort	**9**
Scuba Lodge	**4**
Sunscape Curaçao	**6**

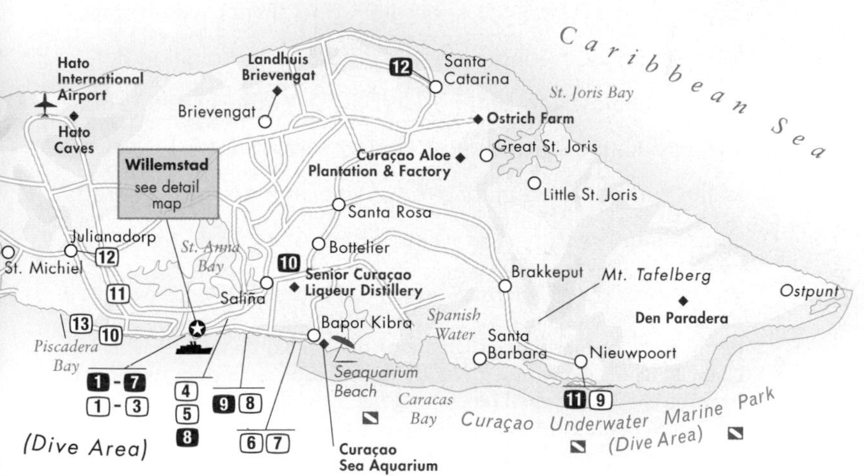

TOP REASONS TO VISIT CURAÇAO

1 Below the Belt: Because it sits below the hurricane belt, the weather in Curaçao is almost always alluring, even during the off-season.

2 Carnival: Curaçao's biggest party draws an increasingly large crowd.

3 Culture: The island's cultural diversity is reflected in the good food from many different cultures.

4 History You Can See: Striking architecture and fascinating historic sites give you something to see when you're not shopping or sunning on the charming beaches.

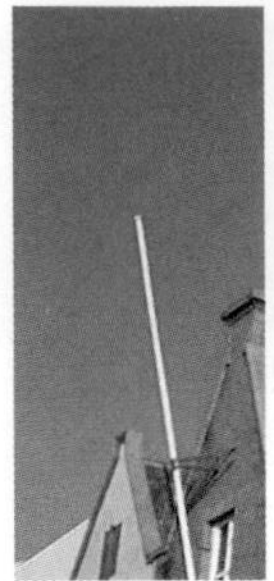

Updated by Susan Campbell

Curaçao is the most colorful and culture-rich of the Dutch Caribbean triumvirate of tropical islands called the ABCs (Aruba, Bonaire, and Curaçao). Fringed with 38 beaches and ringed with coral walls full of resplendent marine life, Curaçao is a haven for snorkelers and divers with first-rate facilities for both, and a wide range of cosmopolitan hotels that welcome all. From the UNESCO World Heritage harbor city to the arid interior dotted with plantation houses to the surf-pounded cliffs overlooking endless seas, there is something to satisfy every kind of traveler.

The UNESCO World Heritage city of Willemstad is divided by a deep natural harbor making it a perfect crossroads for trade, and a valuable destination for maritime powers that once ruled the high seas. It has changed hands many times over the centuries in a constant tug-of-war between the Dutch, the French, and the Spanish; and even the Americans once had a brief foothold there. Today, it still attracts voyagers from all over the globe, but their designs on the historic city are purely recreational, as tourism is slated to become an increasingly important driver of the economy.

Curaçao is continually awash in colorful celebrations; from the long-lasting Carnival to a multitude of live music events like the Curaçao North Sea Jazz Festival, there is always something additionally special to enjoy beyond the unique architecture and beautiful beaches.

The Handelskade—the long row of candy-colored buildings lining Santa Anna Bay—is the signature postcard shot one will see in reference to this island. Local lore has it that in the 1800s, the governor claimed he suffered from migraines and blamed the glare from the sun's reflection off the then-white structures. To alleviate the problem, he ordered the facades painted in colors. (It's also rumored he might have had an interest in the local paint company!) But there's so much more to Willemstad for history buffs and culture seekers than brightly colored buildings. The ancient neighborhoods are alive with history and interesting stories, with many of the colonial structures that house museums and heritage sites like the Maritime Museum. Restored forts now house entertainment complexes and resorts, and recently transformed neighborhoods like Pietermaai also invite visitors to take a walk through then-and-now contrasts sitting side by side in real time.

Though first inhabited by Arawak Indians, Curaçao was "discovered" by Alonzo de Ojeda (a lieutenant of Columbus) in 1499. The first Spanish settlers arrived in 1527. In 1634 the Dutch came via the Netherlands West Indies Company. Eight years later Peter Stuyvesant began his rule as governor (in 1647, Stuyvesant became governor of New Amsterdam, which later became New York). Twelve Jewish families arrived in Curaçao from Amsterdam in 1651, and by 1732 a synagogue had been built; the present structure is the oldest synagogue in continuous use in the Western Hemisphere. Over the years the city built fortresses to defend against French and British invasions—the standing ramparts now house restaurants and hotels. The Dutch claim to Curaçao was recognized in 1815 by the Treaty of Paris. From 1954 through 2006, Curaçao was the seat of government of the Netherlands Antilles, a group of islands under the umbrella of the Kingdom of the Netherlands. In 2010, after discussions with the Netherlands, Curaçao's island council granted the territory autonomy (the same status Aruba attained in 1986).

Today Curaçao's population derives from nearly 60 nationalities—an exuberant mix of Latin, European, and African roots speaking a Babel of tongues—resulting in superb restaurants and a flourishing cultural scene. Although Dutch is the official language, Papiamentu is the preferred choice for communication among the locals. English and Spanish are also widely spoken. The island, like its Dutch settlers, is known for its religious tolerance, and Curaçao is one of the most LGBT-friendly islands in the Caribbean.

PLANNING

WHEN TO GO

High season in Curaçao mirrors that in much of the Caribbean: basically from mid-December through mid-April. In the off-season, rates will be reduced at least 25% and often more. Hurricanes and severe tropical storms are very rare—though still possible—in Curaçao, which means the island has good weather almost year-round.

GETTING HERE AND AROUND

AIR TRAVEL

Curaçao is becoming easier to get to by air, as major North American and European carriers are adding more direct or one-stop connection flights like JetBlue and Air Canada.

JetBlue. ☎ *800/538–2583* 🌐 *www.jetblue.com.*

KLM ☎ *5999/861–0195.*

LOGISTICS

Getting to Curaçao:

From North America and Europe many major airlines now have direct flights from major hubs, and you can also connect through Aruba and San Juan on regional carriers.

The newly renovated Hato International Airport (CUR) offers a pleasant welcome and has car-rental facilities, duty-free shops, and restaurants.

Hassle Factor: Medium

On the Ground: It takes about 20 minutes to get to the hotels in Willemstad by taxi. Taxis have meters, but drivers still use set fares when picking passengers up at the airport. Verify which method your driver will use before setting off; fixed rates apply for up to four passengers in a single vehicle. Fares from the airport to Willemstad and the nearby beach hotels run about $18 to $22, and those to hotels at the island's western end about $40 to $47.

Airport Hato International Airport. The airport has car-rental facilities, duty-free shops, and restaurants. ✉ *CUR* ☎ *5999/839–1000.*

Nonstop Flights Atlanta (Delta, seasonal), Miami (American), and New York–Newark (United). American Airlines also offers service from San Juan.

CAR TRAVEL

Some of the larger hotels have free shuttles into Willemstad, or you can take a quick, cheap taxi ride; some hotels in Willemstad usually provide a free beach shuttle, so it's possible to get by without a car but if you want to really see the island contrasts a rental car is necessary. If you're planning to do country driving or rough it through Christoffel National Park, a four-wheel-drive vehicle is best. All you need is a valid driver's license. Driving in Curaçao is on the right-hand side of the road; right turns on red are prohibited. Seat belts are required, and motorcyclists must wear helmets. Children under age four must be in child safety seats.

Car Rental: You can rent a car from any of the major car agencies at the airport or have one delivered free to your hotel. Rates are about $40–$47 a day for a compact car to $55–$65 for a four-door sedan or four-wheel-drive vehicle; add 5% tax and optional daily insurance.

Contacts Avis ☎ *5999/461–1255, 800/331–1084* 🌐 *www.avis.com.* **Budget** ☎ *5999/868–3466, 800/472–3325* 🌐 *www.curacao-budgetcar.com.* **Hertz** ✉ *Rooseveltweg 503* ☎ *5999/888–0088* 🌐 *www.hertz.com.* **National Car Rental** ☎ *5999/869–4433* 🌐 *www.nationalcuracao.com.* **Thrifty** ☎ *5999/888–0188* 🌐 *www.thrifty.com.*

TAXI TRAVEL

Fares from the airport to Willemstad and the nearby beach hotels run about $18 to $22, and those to hotels at the island's western end about $40 to $47 (be sure to agree on the rate before setting off). The government-approved rates, which do not include waiting time, can be found in a brochure called "Taxi Tariff Guide," available at the airport, hotels, cruise-ship terminals, and the tourist board. Rates are for up to four passengers. There's a 25% surcharge after 11 pm. Note: If you call a taxi and then decide you do not want it, you will still have to pay a fee, typically $10.

Central Dispatch. Taxis are readily available at hotels and at taxi stands at the airport, in Punda, and in Otrobanda; in other cases, call Central Dispatch. ✉ *F.D. Rooseveltweg 32U* ☎ *5999/869–0747.*

ESSENTIALS

Addresses In street addresses that do not specify a house number, the *z/n* is a Dutch abbreviation for *zonder nummer* (no number).

Banks and Exchange Services U.S. dollars are accepted nearly everywhere. Currency in Curaçao is the florin (also called the guilder) and is indicated by *fl* or *NAf* on price tags. The official rate of exchange at this writing was NAf 1.75 to US$1. The government is considering changing the currency to the Caribbean guilder, but at press time, plans for this change were not definitive.

Electricity 110–130 volts/50 cycles.

Emergency Services **Ambulance** ☎ *912.* **Police and fire** ☎ *911.* **Tourist Emergencies** ☎ *917.*

Passport Requirements A valid passport is required. All visitors must be able to show an ongoing or return ticket as well as have proof of sufficient funds to support their stay on the island.

Phones To call Curaçao direct from the United States, dial 011–5999 plus the number in Curaçao. International roaming for most GSM mobile phones is available in Curaçao. Local companies are UTS (United Telecommunication Services) and Digicel. You can also rent a mobile phone or buy a prepaid SIM card for your own phone.

Taxes and Service Charges The departure tax for Aruba and St. Martin is US$20 (FL 36) and Bonaire is US$10 (FL 18). Children under the age of two are exempted of payment. Most major airlines now include the international departure tax (US$39) in their ticket price.

Hotels add a 12% service charge to the bill and collect a 7% government room tax; restaurants typically add 10% to 15%. Most goods and services purchased on the island will also have a 5% OB tax (a goods-and-services tax) added to the purchase price.

Tipping Service is usually included, but if you find the staff exemplary, you can add another 5% to 10% to the bill. Porters and bellhops, about $1 a bag; housekeeping, $2 to $3 per day; taxi, about 10%.

ACCOMMODATIONS

Resort development is concentrated around the capital, Willemstad, so most resorts are within easy reach of town, by shuttle or on foot. As the island becomes more developed, visitors have more options, and there are a few resorts farther removed as well, but it's the amenities that should drive your decision more than location. Choose the type of lodging that best appeals to your interests and style. Those spending a bit more time gravitate to villas and bungalows.

Resorts: Most of Curaçao's larger hotels are midsize resorts of 200 to 300 rooms, and many of them are within easy striking distance of town but some are secreted away in their own neighborhoods like Santa Barbara or Jan Thiel. The island offers a full range of resorts from the intimate and luxurious to historic properties—few other destinations offer a downtown hotel with a saltwater infinity pool complete with palm-lined beach.

Dive Resorts: Most of the resorts catering to divers are smaller operations of fewer than 100 rooms (often much smaller). Although some of these are in and around Willemstad, there are also a few on the secluded west end of the island, and that's where shore diving is best.

Villas and Bungalows: Though they are marketed primarily to European travelers who have more time to spend on the island, self-catering accommodations are an option for anyone who has at least a week to spend in Curaçao.

Hotel reviews have been shortened. For full information, visit Fodors.com.

WHAT IT COSTS IN U.S. DOLLARS				
	$	$$	$$$	$$$$
Restaurants	under $12	$12–$20	$21–$30	over $30
Hotels	under $275	$275–$375	$376–$475	over $475

Restaurant prices are the average cost of a main course at dinner or, if dinner is not served, at lunch. Hotel prices are the lowest cost of a standard double room in high season.

WEDDINGS

You and your partner must be living outside the Netherlands Antilles; you must report to the Office of the Registrar at least three days before your marriage. You'll need a birth certificate, passport, evidence that you are single, or evidence that you are divorced or a widow or widower.

EXPLORING

WILLEMSTAD

Dutch settlers came here in the 1630s, about the same time they sailed through the Verazzano Narrows to Manhattan, bringing with them original red-tile roofs, first used on the trade ships as ballast and later incorporated into the architecture of Willemstad. Much of the original colonial structures remain, but this historic city is constantly reinventing itself and the government monument foundation is always busy restoring buildings in one urban neighborhood or another. The salty air causes what is called "wall cancer" which causes the ancient abodes to continually crumble over time. The city is cut in two by Santa Anna Bay. On one side is Punda (the point)—crammed with shops, restaurants, monuments, and markets and a new museum retracing its colorful history. And on the other side is Otrobanda (literally meaning the "other side"), with lots of narrow, winding streets and alleyways

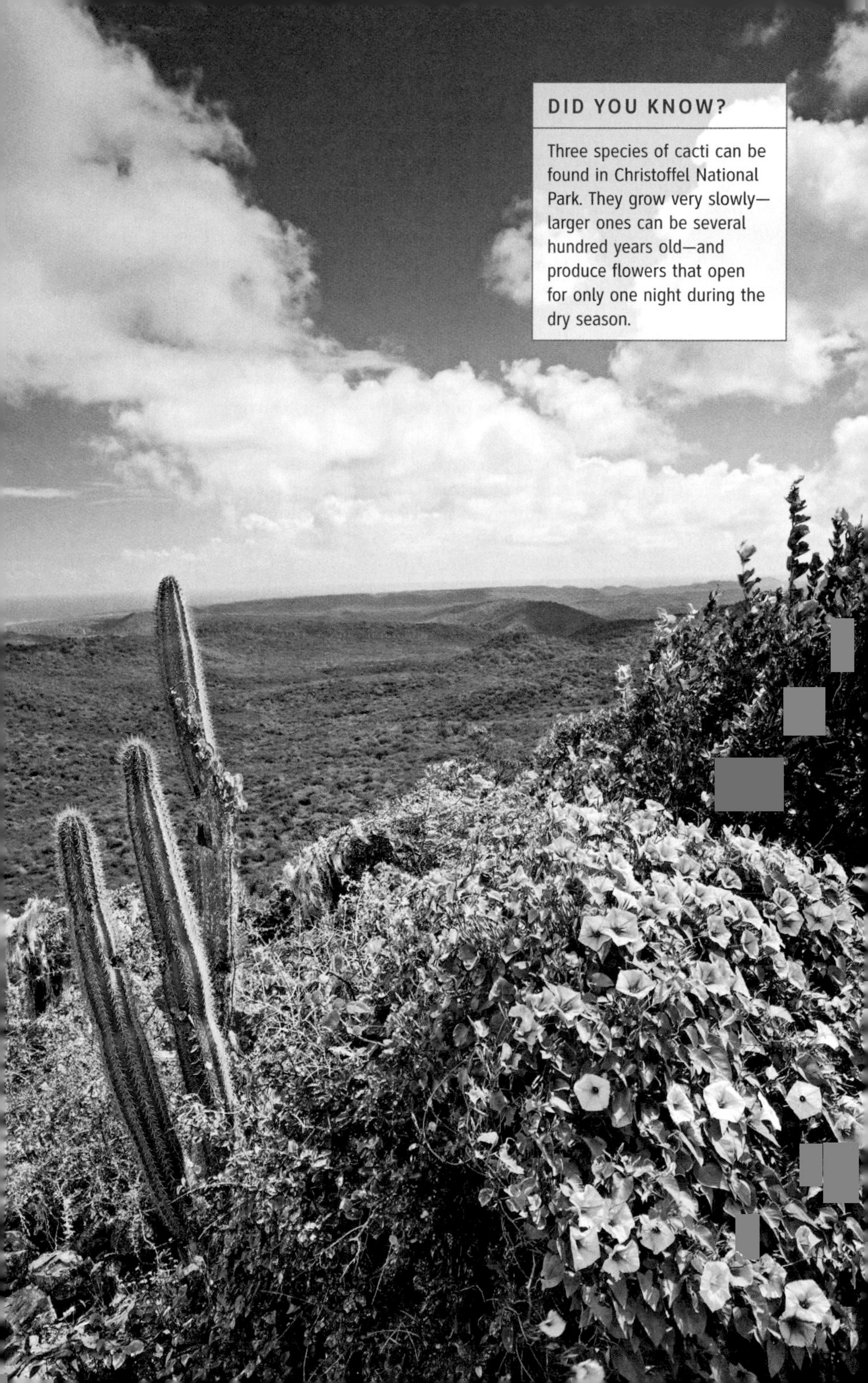

DID YOU KNOW?

Three species of cacti can be found in Christoffel National Park. They grow very slowly—larger ones can be several hundred years old—and produce flowers that open for only one night during the dry season.

(called "steekjes" in Dutch), full of private homes notable for their picturesque gables and Dutch-influenced designs. In recent years the ongoing regeneration of Otrobanda has been apparent, marked by a surge in development of new hotels, restaurants, and shops; the rebirth, concentrated near the waterfront, was spearheaded by the creation of the elaborate Kura Hulanda complex.

There are three ways to cross the bay: by car over the Juliana Bridge; by foot over the Queen Emma pontoon bridge (locally called "The Swinging Old Lady"); or by free ferry, which runs when the pontoon bridge is swung open for passing ships. All the major hotels outside town offer free shuttle service to town once or twice daily. Shuttles coming from the Otrobanda side leave you at Riffort. From here it's a short walk north to the foot of the pontoon bridge. Shuttles coming from the Punda side leave you near the main entrance to Ft. Amsterdam.

TOP ATTRACTIONS

Ft. Amsterdam. One of the island's first bastions of defense, built in 1635, this fort was crucial to protect the harbor, and there is still a cannonball stuck in its wall that was fired by the infamous Captain Bligh's men. Now Ft. Amerstdam houses the Governor's residence, the parliament, the United Protestant Church (Fortchurch) and museum, and some government offices. Many tours of Willemstad begin here. ✉ *Foot of Queen Emma Bridge, Punda* ☎ *5999/461–1139.*

Fodor's Choice ★ **Kura Hulanda Museum.** Pet project of Dutch billionaire philanthropist Jacob Gelt-Dekker who brought the Otrabanda neighborhood back to life in the '90s, this fascinating anthropological museum reveals the island's diverse roots. Housed in a restored 18th-century village, the museum is built around a former mercantile square (Kura Hulanda means "Holland courtyard"), where the Dutch once housed slaves mostly before they were sold and exported. Somber exhibits of the transatlantic slave trade are tempered by sections that highlight the origins of the diaspora, including relics from West African empires, examples of pre-Columbian gold, and Antillean art. Call ahead for guided tours or rent an audio guide. ✉ *Klipstraat 9, Otrobanda* ☎ *5999/434–7765* 🌐 *www.kurahulanda.com/en/museumx* 🎟 *$10* ⏲ *Mon.–Sat. 9:30–4:30.*

Mikvé Israel-Emanuel Synagogue. The temple—the oldest in continuous use in the Western Hemisphere—is one of Curaçao's most important sights and draws thousands of visitors per year. The synagogue was dedicated in 1732 by the Jewish community, which had already grown from the original 12 families who came from Amsterdam in 1651. They were later joined by Jews from Portugal and Spain fleeing persecution from the Inquisition. White sand covers the synagogue floor for two symbolic reasons: a remembrance of the 40 years Jews spent wandering the desert, and a re-creation of the sand used by secret Jews, or *conversos,* to muffle sounds from their houses of worship during the Inquisition. English and Hebrew services are held Friday at 6:30 pm and Saturday at 10 am. Men who attend should wear a jacket and tie. Yarmulkes are provided to men for services and tours. ✉ *Hanchi Snoa 29, Punda* ☎ *5999/461–1067* 🌐 *www.snoa.com* 🎟 *$10; donations also accepted* ⏲ *Weekdays 9–4:30*

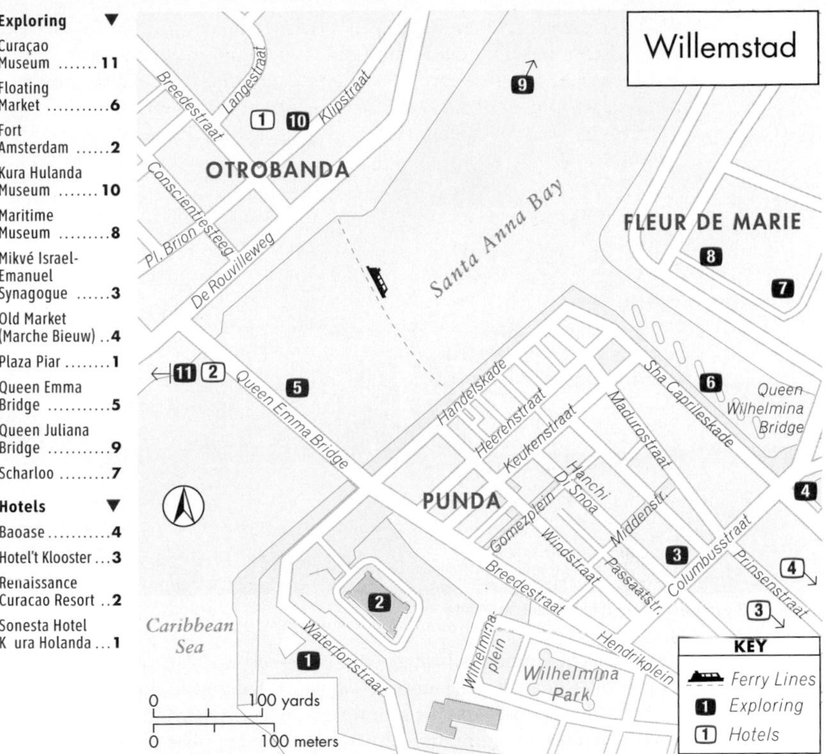

The Punda Museum. Opened in 2014, Curaçao's newest museum shows Punda through the ages, covering a century of change. View more than 400 photographs, slide shows, scale models of old neighborhoods, and interesting exhibits of life in the historic downtown center of Willemstad. Rotating exhibits of local artists are also displayed. English-language guided tours are offered daily at 10 am. Groups of six or more can reserve private tours. ✉ *Hanchi Snoa 1–5, Punda, Willemstad* ☎ *5999/465–2992* 🎟 *$8; guided tours $12.50* ⏲ *Mon.–Sat. 9:30–5:30.*

WORTH NOTING

The Curaçao Museum. Housed in an 1853 restored plantation house that later served as a military hospital, this small museum is filled with artifacts, paintings, and antiques that trace the island's history. The outdoor sculpture garden features local artists, and this is also a venue for local and international art exhibitions. ✉ *V. Leeuwenhoekstraat z/n, Otrobanda* ☎ *5999/462–3873* 🌐 *www.thecuracaomuseum.com* 🎟 *Free* ⏲ *Tues.–Fri. 8:30–4:30, Sat. 10–4.*

Floating Market. Curaçao is such an arid island that most of the fruit and vegetables need to be imported. The floating market consists of dozens of Venezuelan schooners laden with tropical fruits and vegetables that dock to sell their wares on the Punda side of the city. Mangoes, papayas, and exotic vegetables vie for space with freshly caught fish and herbs

A daring, mast-eye view of the Handelskade in Punda

and spices. The buying is best at 6:30 am—too early for many people on vacation—but there's plenty of action throughout the afternoon. Vendors will stay on-island for months away from their families—forming their own little community—awaiting fresh supplies each day, until they have enough to bring adequate money home to Venezeuala. ✉ *Sha Caprileskade, Punda.*

Maritime Museum. The museum—designed to resemble the interior of a ship—gives you a sense of Curaçao's maritime history that spans some 500 years using model ships, historic maps, nautical charts, navigational equipment, and audiovisual displays. Topics explored in the exhibits include the development of Willemstad as a trading city, Curaçao's role as a contraband hub, the remains of *De Alphen* (a Dutch marine freighter that exploded and sank in St. Anna Bay in 1778 and was excavated in 1984), the slave trade, the development of steam navigation, and the role of the Dutch navy on the island. The museum also offers a two-hour guided tour (Wednesday and Saturday, 1 pm) on its "water bus" through Curaçao's harbor—a route familiar to traders, smugglers, and pirates. The museum is wheelchair accessible. The bar/restaurant *Sails* on-site is open for lunch. ✉ *Van der Brandhofstraat 7, Scharloo* ☎ *5999/465–2327* 🌐 *www.curacaomaritime.com* 🎫 *Museum $6, museum and harbor tour $9* ⏲ *Tues.–Sat. 9–4 (also Sun. and Mon. during cruise season Nov.–Apr.).*

Old Market (*Marsche Bieuw*). Also known as the Marsche Bieuw, Old Market is a popular lunch stop for locals working downtown. Visitors appreciate the hearty, simple authentic Antillean lunches and good prices here. Enjoy such Curaçaoan specialties as *funchi* (polenta), goat stew, fried fish, stewed okra, fried plantains, and rice and peas prepared right in front of your eyes in open kitchens by local cooks. ✉ *De Ruyterkade, Punda.*

Plaza Piar. This plaza is dedicated to Manuel Piar, a native Curaçaoan who fought for the independence of Venezuela under the liberator Simón Bolívar. On one side of the plaza is the Waterfort, built in the late 1820s to help defend the old city. The original cannons are still positioned in the battlements. The foundation, however, now forms the walls of the Howard Johnson Plaza Hotel Curaçao & Casino.

Queen Emma Bridge. Affectionately called the Swinging Old Lady by locals, this bridge connects the two sides of Willemstad—Punda and Otrobanda—across the Santa Anna Bay. The bridge swings open at least 30 times a day to allow passage of ships to and from the sea. The original bridge, built in 1888, was the brainchild of the American consul Leonard Burlington Smith, who made a mint off the tolls he charged for using it: 2¢ per person for those wearing shoes, free to those crossing barefoot. But though that toll distinction was meant to help the poor, the rich often saved money by crossing barefoot, and the poor would often borrow shoes to cross because they were too proud to admit they could not afford the toll! Today it's free to everyone. The bridge was dismantled and completely repaired and restored in 2005.

Queen Juliana Bridge. This 1,625-foot-long bridge is the highest bridge in the Caribbean. It stands 200 feet above the water to accomodate the large ships crossing beneath it. It also allows for the motor traffic between Punda and Otrobanda. Panoramic views of the city below make it a popular spot to take photos from.

Scharloo. The Wilhelmina Drawbridge connects Punda with the once-flourishing district of Scharloo where the early Jewish merchants built stately homes. It was a tight-knit community and the architecture along Scharlooweg (much of it from the 17th century) is magnificent. Some of the neighborhood has been restored as part of the UNESCO heritage site and the Curaçao Monuments Foundation will be restoring more old mansions in the future. This neighborhood is also home to the island's most photographed building, a light-green mansion dubbed the "Wedding Cake House" since it looks like it's been frosted with white icing. Kleine Werf—the little wharf cresting Scharloo—has now become a venue for large-scale outdoor concerts. ✉ *Scharloo.*

ELSEWHERE ON CURAÇAO

As you drive out of town the arid, cacti-studded outback becomes rougher the farther you travel inland, and you might feel as if you have been transported into a stretch of Arizona desert. Wild donkeys and goats might step off onto the road, so use caution on curvy stretches, and be sure to bring plenty of water.

Many of Curaçao's secret attractions and tiny towns are pocketed within plain sight if you know where to go. One simple turnoff might lead to a spectacular beach like Cas Abao, or a beautiful plantation house like the Tula Museum at Kenepa or the art gallery at Jan Kok.

Or maybe it will lead to a natural wonder like the salt pool full of flamingoes at Salina St. Marie or the thunderous blowhole at Boca Pistol. Make sure to get a good map and clear directions to unearth all the unique adventures scattered throughout the *kunuku* (countryside) as few are easily sighted from the main roads, but often not very far from them. Christoffel Park and Shete Boka Park are protected preserves well worth exploring as well. And you'll find plenty of information and assistance at their new Savonet Museum there.

TOP ATTRACTIONS

Aquafari. You don't have to snorkel or dive to discover Curaçao's spectacular underwater world of coral reefs and tropical fish if you ride with Aquafari. Go 30 feet deep on Aquafari's unique eco-friendly, one-piece underwater scooter with an air-supplied helmet from which you breathe just as normally as you would on land. The instructors are also divers, and after a safty briefing, they accompany you down to one of the coolest underwater adventures on the island. Your underwater guide also takes photos of your journey for purchase. The journey including topside briefing takes approximately 1½ hours with 45 minutes underwater. There's full facilities—food, drink, and changing rooms right next door at Pirate's Bay Beach. ✉ *Piscaderaweg, Pirate Bay Beach, Willemstad* ☎ *5999/513–2625* 🌐 *aquafari.net* ☞ *Minimum age 10, minimun height 4 feet, maximum weight 275 pounds.*

Christoffel National Park. The 1,239-foot Mt. Christoffel, Curaçao's highest peak, is at the center of this 4,450-acre garden and wildlife preserve now under the protection of CARMABI (Caribbean Research and Management of Biodiversity). They offer many forms of touring the natural preserve, including guided hikes, Jeep safaris, mountain biking, deer-watching (the island's elusive white-tailed deer are very shy), animal presentations, cave explorations, and special activities like full-moon nature walks. Visitors can also hike the mountain on their own. The exhilarating climb takes about two hours for a reasonably fit person. On a clear day, the panoramic view from the peak stretches to the mountain ranges of Venezuela. CARMABI recommends an early start as it gets very hot later in the day. Throughout the park are eight hiking trails and a 20-mile (32-km) network of driving trails (use heavy-treaded tires if you wish to explore the unpaved stretches). The old Savonet plantation house there (one of the island's first plantations) has been restored and now serves as a modern museum with exhibits retracing the region's history as far back as the original Indian inhabitants. **■ TIP→ There's a separate entrance fee to the museum but you can also get a combo-entrance pass that includes park and museum for less.** ✉ *Savonet* ☎ *5999/864–0363 for information and tour reservations* 🌐 *www.christoffelpark.org* 💴 *$12* ⏲ *Mon.–Sat. 7:30–4, Sun. 6–3; last admission 90 min before closing.*

CurAloe Plantation & Factory. Visit the home of the island's thriving aloe product sold in shops and stores all over Curaçao where you'll see the 100,000 specimens of plants used in CurAloe's hundreds of cosmetic and medicinal applications. No reservations required and no admission fee. Information is provided by video, and staff are happy to answer questions. You can sample-purchase many products. ✉ *Kaminda*

Plantation house in Christoffel National Park with Mt. Christoffel in the distance

Mitologia, Groot St. Joris, Willemstad ☎ *5999/767–5577* 🌐 *www.ecocityprojects.com.*

FAMILY
Fodor's Choice ★
Curaçao Sea Aquarium. The Sea Aquarium is an original installation that became the island's largest marine life attraction. Though it's in the same physical location as the Dolphin Academy and Animal Encounters—all part of the SeaAquarium Park—it operates independently. Admission allows visitors to view dolphin shows and sea lion shows, and to view marine life in the Animal Encounter lagoon from an underwater observatory. A new Sea Lion Encounter program enables visitors to get up close under the supervision of a trainer as well (additional cost). The aquarium hall has over 40 saltwater tanks full of marine life and offers visitors the opportunity to feed sharks, interact with stingrays, sea turtles, flamingos . . . and lots more. Extremely educational for all ages. Snack bar and souvenir shop are also on-site. ✉ *Seaquarium Beach, Bapor Kibra z/n* ☎ *5999/461–6666* 🌐 *www.curacao-sea-aquarium.com/en* 🎫 *$20 adults* ⏲ *Daily 8–5.*

Dolphin Academy. The Dolphin Academy—run independently from the Sea Aquarium—specializes in up-close interactions with these friendly, ever-smiling mammals. There are many different kinds of encounters available, including swimming, free diving, snorkeling, scuba, and simple interactions in shallow water. There are also open-water dive opportunities. You can also become an assistant trainer for a day, or do an extremely in-depth dolphin course that takes two or three half-days. The trainers are extremely professional and knowledgable and the dolphins are very well cared for and thrive in a spacious, natural saltwater lagoon. (The scuba and dive encounters are offered in conjunction with Ocean Encounters dive operators.) ✉ *Seaquarium Beach, Bapor Kibra z/n* ☎ *5999/465–8900* 🌐 *www.dolphin-academy.com* 🎫 *From $99 depending on program* ⏲ *Daily 8–5.*

Hato Caves. Stalactites and stalagmites form striking shapes in these 200,000-year-old caves. Hidden lighting adds to the dramatic effect. Indians who used the caves for shelter left petroglyphs about 1,500 years ago. More recently, slaves who escaped from nearby plantations used the caves as a hideaway. Hour-long guided tours wind down to the pools in various chambers. Keep in mind that there are 49 steps to climb up to the entrance and the occasional bat might not be to everyone's taste. A new Indian Trail walking path and cactus garden enlighten visitors about local vegetation. The space is also available for special events. Located just two minutes from Hato International airport. ✉ *Rooseveltweg z/n, Hato* ☎ *5999/868–0379* 🌐 *www.hatocaves.com* 🎫 *$8* ⏲ *Daily 9–4.*

FAMILY **Ostrich Farm.** Though ostriches are not native to Curaçao, this is one of the largest Ostrich farms outside of Africa. Guided safari tours depart every hour. You'll learn about the bird's development from egg to maturity. Kids and adults alike will enjoy the chance to hold an egg, stroke a day-old chick, and sit atop an ostrich for a memorable photo. At the Restaurant Zambezi you can sample ostrich meat specialties and other African dishes. A combo safari and tour of the farm, which includes lunch or dinner, is also available. Quad tours that cover more of the countryisde are also offered. There's also a Special African Nights package, which include a visit to the aloe farm, ostrich facility tour, and three-course dinner with pickup and drop-off at your hotel. The souvenir shop sells crafts made by local artisans. ✉ *Groot St. Joris* ☎ *5999/747–2777* 🌐 *www.curacaoostrichfarm.com* 🎫 *Adults $16* ⏲ *Weekdays 9–5, Weekends 9 am–10 pm.*

FAMILY
Fodor's Choice ★ **Sea Aquarium Beach (Curaçao Beach Blvd.).** The liveliest, most full-service beach and entertainment spot on the island. There is something for all ages at the new Curaçao Beach Boulevard complex, which is part of the Sea Aquarium Beach and Park. Shoppers, sunbathers, swimmers, families, teens, couples, partiers, and even foodies will find their groove with upscale eateries like Fuoco Italian Chophouse sandwiched beside dozens of bars and cool boutiques like the Flip Flop Shop. And there are dive and activity operators, beauty salons, a spa, a children's playground, a small casino, and even an amusement park–style ride. There is a small fee to use the beach for just swimming and sunbathing and the water is calm due to a man-made breakwater. There is always some kind of special event going on here, and there's also a special tourism police force to keep it safe and secure. ✉ *Bapor Kibra z/n* 🌐 *www.blvdcuracao.com* 🎫 *$3.50 for beach use.*

Fodor's Choice ★ **Touracao Tourism Services.** Fabulous attractions on Curaçao are secreted all around the island, so tours are highly recommended. Touracao offers a wide range of choices from city tours and beach tours to off-road adventures to fun nights on the town. Their equipment is top-notch, and their guides are highly professional, multilingual, and well-informed. They can also customize private tours to your interests, and they specialize in VIP airport transfers, which means skipping the customs line so you have more time for fun in the sun! ✉ *Fokkerweg 5D, Willemstad* ☎ *5999/465–4611* 🌐 *www.touracao.com.*

WORTH NOTING

Den Paradera. Dazzle your senses at this organic herb garden, where traditional folk medicines used to treat everything from stomach ulcers to diabetes are grown. Owner Dinah Veeris is a renowned expert and author in the field of herbs and plants. The kitchen is a factory of sorts used to turn homegrown plants like cactus, aloe vera, and calabash into homemade body and skin care products like shampoos, ointments, and oils—all for sale at the gift shop. Reservations are essential for guided tours in English, Monday through Friday at 9:30 and 10:30 am, but you can take a self-guided tour with a brochure any time of day. (Santa Barbara Resort's spa uses ingredients made at Den Paradera.) ✉ *Seru Grandi 105A, Banda Riba* ☎ *5999/767–5608* 🌐 *www.dinahveeris.com* 🎫 *$8 self-guided tour; $9 guided* 🕒 *Mon.–Sat. 9–6.*

Kas di Pal'i Maishi (*Kas di Pal'i Maishi*). The thatch-roof cottage is filled with antique furniture, farm implements, and clothing typical of 19th-century colonial life. Out back is a small farm and vegetable garden. Look closely at the fence—it's made of living cacti. ✉ *Dokterstuin 27, on road to Westpunt from Willemstad, Westpunt* ☎ *5999/864–2742* 🌐 *www.fundashonmuseotula.com* 🎫 *$4* 🕒 *Tues.–Fri. 9–4, weekends 9–5.*

Landhuis Chobolobo. This is the distillery where the the famed Curaçao liqueur, which is made from the peels of the bitter Laraha oranges, is made. The family-run distillery is in a heritage mansion that dates to the 1800s. Self-guided factory tours include samples, and they also have a new terrace café that serves all kinds of delights including dishes and cocktails using the liqueurs. Though best known for its neon blue–colored spirit, the orginal liqueur was clear; it was colored later and also comes in green, red, and orange, and in different flavors including rum raisin, coffee, and chocolate. ✉ *Landhuis Chobolobo, Saliña* ☎ *5999/461–3526* 🌐 *www.curacaoliqueur.com* 🎫 *Free* 🕒 *Mon.–Fri. 8–12 and 1–5. Café Mon.–Fri. 8–5.*

National Park Shete Boka. Shete Boka means "seven inlets" in Papiamento and this national park by the sea is well worth exploring. The rugged coastline with scenic inlets is dramatic and wild—the incessantly crashing waves have sculptured the coral rock into fascinating natural works of art. The most impressive is Boka Tabla, where you can descend a natural rock stairway (take care, it's very slippery) to view an arched opening that looks out on the sea like a giant eye. Boka Pistol is also spectacular—jetting up into towering plumes of spray, often leaving rainbows lingering in the mist. And if you look closely as you walk upon the volcanic rock landscape, you will see coral fossil formations below your feet that are thousands of years old. This is also a popular nesting region for sea turtles. ✉ *Westpunt Hwy., just past village center, Soto* 🌐 *www.carmabi.org* 🎫 *$5.50* 🕒 *Daily 9–5.*

BEACHES

Curaçao's some 38 beautiful beaches run the gamut from isolated scenic small-cove escapes to party-hearty full-service entertainment venues, and include family-friendly gentle surf spots and wild and rugged cliff-ringed white-sand pockets. Klein Curaçao—the uninhabited satellite sister island only accessible by boat—also has some stellar stretches of sand. Beaches along the southeast coast tend to be rocky in the shallow water (wear reef shoes—some resorts lend them out for free), but they are typically the best spots to snorkel or dive—for where there are rocks, there are usually fish! The west side has more stretches of smooth sand at the shoreline. Exploring the beaches away from the hotels is a perfect way to soak up the island's character, and some have become attractions in their own right, famous for special events, like Kokomo Beach and its crazy full moon blow-out parties. There are snack bars and restrooms on most beaches, and some will have entrance fees or charge for loungers, while others are open to the public with few facilities but are popular with locals who bring their own picnics and outdoor grills on weekends. Some tour companies are now offering half- or full-day beach tours, so you can set foot on a lot of them to discover where you might like to return to spend more time.

WEST END

FAMILY **Cas Abao.** This white-sand gem has the brightest blue water in Curaçao, a treat for swimmers, snorkelers, and sunbathers alike. Full services include a Beach Bar and Restaurant, lockers, changing rooms on-site, and even full massages surfside are available. Can become crowded weekends, especially Sunday, when local families descend in droves. You can rent beach chairs, paddleboats, and snorkeling and diving gear. The entry fee is $5–$6 per car, more on weekends, and the beach is open from 8 am to 6 pm. Turn off Westpunt Highway at the junction onto Weg Naar Santa Cruz; follow until the turnoff for Cas Abao, and then drive along the winding country road for about 10 minutes to the beach. **Amenities:** food and drink; lifeguards; parking; showers; toilets; water sports. **Best for:** partiers; snorkeling; swimming. ✉ *West of St. Willibrordus, about 3 miles (5 km) off Weg Naar Santa Cruz* 🌐 *www.casabaobeach.com.*

FAMILY **Kokomo Beach.** The beach at Vaersenbaai, now better known as "Kokomo" after the restaurant/bar by the same name there, is famous for massive full-moon-party blow-outs with live music and thousands of partiers. Daytime it's a quiet, family-friendly public beach with lots of free lounges, shade, and full facilities. At night it kicks it up a notch with a young-adult party scene. Sunday happy hours are famous for DJ dance parties, and it's the only night Kokomo serves dinner. There is also a dive center on-site. **Amenities:** parking (free); food and drink; toilets. **Best for:** partiers; swimming; snorkeling. ✉ *Vaersenbaai* 🌐 *www.kokomo-beach.com.*

Playa Jeremi. No snack bar, no dive shop, no facilities, no fee—in fact, there's nothing but sheer natural beauty. Though the beach is sandy, there are rocky patches, so barefoot visitors should exercise care. The parking area is offset from the beach, and vehicle break-ins are common. Quite a bit of development is planned for this beach, so have a look before it's too late. **Amenities:** none. **Best for:** solitude; swimming; snorkeling; picnics. ✉ *Off Weg Naar Santa Cruz, west of Lagun.*

Playa Kalki. This beach is at the western tip of the island right under Kura Hulanda Lodge. Sunbathers may find the narrow and rocky beach less than ideal and there is a long steep staircase down to the sand, but go to GoWest Diving there for snorkel and dive trips to the Blue Room, a cool underwater cave. **Amenities:** food and drink; parking; toilets; water sports. **Best for:** solitude; snorkeling; swimming. ✉ *Near Jaanchi's, Westpunt.*

FAMILY **Playa Knip.** Two protected coves offer crystal clear turquoise waters. Big (Groot) Knip, also known as Playa Kenepa, is an expanse of alluring white sand, perfect for swimming and snorkeling. You can rent beach chairs and hang out under the *palapas* (thatch-roof shelters) or cool off with ice cream at the snack bar. There are restrooms here but no showers. It's particularly crowded on Sunday and school holidays. Just up the road, also in a protected cove, sister beach Little (Klein) Knip is a charmer, too, with picnic tables and palapas. There's no fee for these beaches. **Amenities:** food and drink; lifeguards; parking; toilets; water sports. **Best for:** snorkeling; sunrise; sunset; swimming. ✉ *Just east of Westpunt, Banda Abou.*

FAMILY **Playa PortoMari.** Set beneath a historic plantation site, you'll find calm, clear water and a long stretch of white sand and full facilities on this beach. A decent bar and restaurant, well-kept showers, changing facilities, and restrooms are all on-site; a nature trail is nearby. The double coral reef—explore one, swim past it, explore another—is a special feature that makes this spot popular with snorkelers and divers. The entrance fee is $3, children under 12 are free. From Willemstad, drive west on Westpunt Highway for 4 miles (7 km); turn left onto Willibrordus Road at the PortoMari billboard, and then drive 3 miles (5 km) until you see a large church; follow signs on the winding dirt road to the beach. **Amenities:** food and drink; lifeguards; parking; showers; toilets. **Best for:** partiers; snorkeling; swimming; walking. ✉ *Off Willibrordus Rd.*

WHERE TO EAT

Curaçao's culinary scene has become seriously cosmopolitan in the past few years. Though you can still find places to get traditional, local dishes like iguana soup, *keshi yena*, and goat stew, the emerging generation of chefs has really raised the bar. Caribbean meets international with a side of nouvelle cuisine or farm-to-fork organic offerings. All combine for a cornucopia of tastes and flavors that meet world-class standards. And the range of locations where you can enjoy these creations is as eclectic as the fare. You'll find romantic toes-in-the-sand surfside spots, family-friendly air-conditioned emporiums, lush countryside gardens, and unique historic sites like forts and plantation houses all hosting diners. For authentic local-style lunches drop by the Old Market in Punda, or after the nightclubs seek out one of the late-night snack trucks (*truki pan*) for cheap, yet satisfying, eats. Many beach bars also have fabulous fare for less than you'd expect to pay. But on the most part, fine dining will cost you what it's typically worth, especially since almost every kind of food on this island needs to be imported from elsewhere.

What to Wear. Dress in restaurants is almost always casual (though beachwear isn't acceptable). Some of the resort dining rooms and more elegant restaurants require that men wear jackets, especially in high season; ask when you make reservations.

$$$$ EUROPEAN

Bistro Le Clochard. Built into a 19th-century fort, this romantic gem anchors the entrance to the 21st-century Rif Fort complex and the waterside terrace offers an enchanting view of the harbor. They present French cuisine with a Caribbean twist, but there are many international specialities as well like Swiss fondue, raclette, and Wiener schnitzel. The menu differs depending on where you sit—for example, you can only order their bouillabiasse on the terrace. But both inside and out, you can order their most famous decadent dessert, Swiss Toblerone chocolate mousse with strawberry foam. *Average main: $40 Rif Fort Unit 1, Otrobanda, Willemstad 5999/462–5666 www.bistroleclochard.com Reservations essential.*

$$ CONTEMPORARY Fodor's Choice ★

Blues Bar & Restaurant. Jutting out onto a pier over the ocean at the Avil Hotel, this legendary perch is famous for their live jazz and blues nights on Thursdays, and the fact that the band is also perched over the bar. Recently refreshed with a new look and a new menu featuring *pinchos* (skewers), the cuisine is also beginning to steal the show with a tasty selection of fish, seafood, and meat specialties, and the ribs are first-rate as well. The vibe is always convivial, and it's a popular place for locals to gather, especially on Thursday at happy hour. *Average main: $20 Avila Hotel, Penstraat 130, Punda, Willemstad 5999/461–4377 www.avilahotel.com Closed Mon. No lunch.*

$$$ STEAKHOUSE

CRU Steak House & Wine Bar. It's all about steak and wine at this legendary dining spot in the Renaissance Mall. In fact they boast they are the island's only genuine U.S. steak house. From small 6-ounce to whopping 24-ounce cuts of meat, beef is perfectly prepared to order and paired with the perfect foil from a vast selection of quality wines from their comprehensive cellar. They also sell wines by the bottle for take-away. Fish and seafood are also on the menu, and they also offer a decent vegetarian ravioli. *Average main: $25 Renaissance Mall, Otrobanda, Willemstad 5999/435–5090 www.crusteakhousecuracao.com.*

$$$$ EUROPEAN Fodor's Choice ★

Fort Nassau Restaurant. On a hill above Willemstad, this elegant restaurant is built into an 18th-century fort with a 360-degree view. Among the highlights of the diverse menu is the medley of Caribbean seafood, but the best bets come from their special menu—three courses with a fixed price—your choice of appetizer, main course, and dessert. Entrées include a chicken and a beef dish, but most interesting is the carmelized salmon with sugared bacon. The watermelon soup with honey, rum, basil, and mint is certainly a unique creation for dessert. Vegetarian main also available. Superb views of the sunset over the port can be enjoyed from the terrace. *Average main: $31 Schottegatweg*

82, near Juliana Bridge, Otrobanda, Willemstad ☎ *5999/461–3450, 5999/461–3086* 🌐 *www.fortnassau.com* ⚠ *Reservations essential* ⏲ *No lunch weekends.*

$$$ ECLECTIC Fodor's Choice ★

✕ **Gouverneur de Rouville Restaurant & Café.** Dine on the veranda of a restored 19th-century Dutch mansion overlooking the Santa Anna Bay and the resplendent Punda skyline. Though often busy and popular with tourists, the ambience makes it worth a visit. Intriguing soup options include Cuban banana soup and Curaçao-style fish soup. *Keshi yena* (seasoned meat wrapped in cheese and then baked) and spareribs are among the savory entrées. After dinner, you can stick around for live music at the bar, which stays open until 1 am. The restaurant is also popular for lunch and attracts crowds when cruise ships dock. Reserve ahead if you would like a balcony table. Wine-tasting room available for special events. $ *Average main: $22* ✉ *De Rouvilleweg 9, Otrobanda, Willemstad* ☎ *5999/462–5999* 🌐 *www.de-gouverneur.com.*

$$$ CARIBBEAN

✕ **Jaanchies Restaurant.** Over the years this has become something of a road marker on Curaçao's beaten tourist path, with prices to match. You'll be greeted by the owner, Jaanchi himself, a self-described "walking, talking menu," who will recite your choices of authentic local dishes for lunch. Jaanchi's iguana soup, touted in folklore as an aphrodisiac, is one of their specialities. Although predominantly a lunch spot, the restaurant will accommodate groups of four or more for dinner by prior arrangement. $ *Average main: $23* ✉ *Westpunt 15, Westpunt* ☎ *5999/864–0126.*

$$$$ CONTEMPORARY Fodor's Choice ★

✕ **Kome.** Ask any local foodie where to get creative fusion fare with a Curaçao twist, and Kome will be the first spot they mention. It's not super fancy, in fact it's no-nonsense rustic with basic wooden tables and chairs, but it's the food that attracts. They are always changing specialties due to constant efforts to source locally, and the results are often surprising. The menu is divided into small plates and big plates and the dishes can range from pork belly confit and tamarind-glazed pork tenderloin to smoked beef brisket to seafood paella. And don't forget to leave room for dessert because one of the owners is a talented pastry chef! They are also known for their tapas nights on Wednesday with creative small bites to go with superb signature cocktails and excellent sangrias. $ *Average main: $40* ✉ *Johan van Walbeeckplein 6, Pietermaai* ☎ *5999/465–0413* ⏲ *Closed Sun.*

$$$ SEAFOOD FAMILY

✕ **La Bahia Seafood & Steakhouse.** The sheltered terrace at La Bahia features a remarkable view of the harborfront and is so close to the passing ships you'll feel you can almost touch them. The menu runs the gamut from burgers and pastas to *keshi yena* (seasoned meat wrapped in cheese and then baked) and other local specialties. This is also a great spot to relax with a cup of coffee or a cocktail after a day of exploring. Part of the renewed Otrabanda Hotel, it is a short walk from the Queen Emma Bridge. $ *Average main: $22* ✉ *Otrobanda Hotel & Casino, Breedestraat, Otrobanda, Willemstad* ☎ *5999/462–7400* 🌐 *www.otrobandahotel.com.*

$$$$ STEAKHOUSE

✕ **L'aldea Steakhouse/Rainforest Mystery.** A very unique installation on such an arid island, L'aldea is in a small rain-forest reserve, replete with lizards, animals, fish, and birds that you would find typically in lusher

9

climes. But what is most impressive here is the handcrafted design of absolutely everything including faux Mayan and other ancient culture recreations, caves and tropical atmospheres by local craftsmen (some of whom are the owners) using wood and cement to recreate a "lost world" in the middle of nowhere. They have also recently added a few small rooms as eco-accommodation stays there. The easiest way to visit is to take a tour that includes a facility visit and then staying for their Latin American-themed dinner. The fare is incredible—largest salad bar on the island—plus a carnivore's heaven with grilled meats served Argentinian grill-style until you burst. Live music also adds to the full-on experience. For day-trippers though, it would be great if they served some kind of lunch. *Average main: $58* *Sta. Catharina 66, Willemstad* *5999/767–6777* *laldeacur.com* *Reservations essential* *Closed Mon. No lunch.*

$$ ECLECTIC Fodor's Choice ★ **Primas.** In a restored plantation mansion called Landhuis Vredenberg on a lush estate, Primas is a family-run restaurant that offers authentic homemade lunch fare in a superb setting. The menu is up to the chef, but typically, hearty savory meat stews, fresh fish dishes, and Curaçaon specialties like *keshi yena* will pop up. You can view their daily menu on their Facebook page. They're typically not open for dinner (private parties abound), but on Thursday nights Primas is one of the only places left on the island where you can sample real *rijsttafel* (rice table), a Surinamese-influenced extravaganza of dozens of small dishes served community-style. It's also worth the trip just to see the magnificent restored mansion full of exquisite antiques. Groups of 15 or more can make special dinner arrangements. *Average main: $14* *Bramendiweg 200, Willemstad* *5999/461–2901* *Reservations essential* *Closed Sun. No dinner except Thurs.*

$$ DUTCH **Royal Dutch Cheesery.** Tucked away in the corner of the historic Rif Fort Village courtyard, Royal Dutch Cheesery is much more than a cheese shop. Of course they do sell cheese and are the only suppliers of Reypenaer cheese on the island, but it's more of a dining spot and tasting emporium replete with a large wine list and even artisanal spirits. A wine pairing along with various types of cheese (on a wooden plank shaped like Curaçao) is a must, as are their gourmet grilled-cheese sandwiches, fondues, and raclette. Weekend nights, this is a perfect spot to enjoy outdoor live music on the courtyard while sipping some of their unique small-batch limoncello. *Average main: $15* *Rif Fort Village, Otrobanda, Willemstad* *5999/788–5599.*

$$$ SEAFOOD **Scampi's Restaurant.** Part of the Waterfort Terrace complex, this open-air dining spot serves an interesting selection of international fare, steak, seafood, and some dishes with Asian twists or Latin American heat. Daily specialties like freshly caught lobster are a best bet. Their evening setting can be very romantic with a stellar view of the sunset and the port at night and their signature cocktails like Coastal Kiss and Fancy Scampis will get you in the mood. Families aren't left out as there is also a children's menu. *Average main: $22* *Waterfortstraat 41-42, Punda* *5999/465–0769.*

$$$ CONTEMPORARY **Shore.** The main dining room of Santa Barbara Beach & Golf Resort is set upon a hill beside the golf course with stunning sea views. A

gourmet burger and sandwich emporium by day, it morphs into a causal yet romantic dining enclave by night with cool tropical breezes wafting in from the open design, and incredible aromas coming from the open-air kitchen. Chef Hortencia suprises daily with fabulous fusions of local and international flavors. His specials are top-notch and often involve fresh fish and seafood. Try the short ribs, seasoned to perfection. Falling off the bone, they melt in your mouth. Top it off with a decadent chocolate trio of delights for dessert. Finish with a special digestif under the stars at their cocktail lounge. *Average main: $30* ✉ *Santa Barbara Beach & Golf Resort, Santa Barbara Plantation, Nieuwpoort* ☎ *5999/840–1234.*

WHERE TO STAY

Simple beachside relaxation, culture and history, snorkel and dive-centered, adult-only romantic solitude, or fun family-friendly activity spots: On Curaçao you'll find it all, including small boutique-style stays and all-inclusive full-service complexes. You'll generally find that hotels at all price levels provide friendly, prompt, detail-oriented service and clean, well-maintained accommodations, and English is spoken by staff just about everywhere. Many of the large-scale resorts east and west of Willemstad proper have lovely beaches and provide a free shuttle to the city, five to 10 minutes away, but there are also fine hotels right in the city center should you want to be in the heart of the action. There are also resorts in their own self-maintained neighborhoods just out of town in Santa Barbara and Jan Thiel.

Villas and Rentals. Villa and bungalow rentals are especially popular with divers and European visitors and are generally good options for large groups or longer stays. The Curaçao Tourist Board (*www.curacao.com*) has a complete list of rental apartments, villas, and bungalows on its website.

9

RECOMMENDED HOTELS AND RESORTS

$$ HOTEL Fodor's Choice ★

Avila Hotel. Even though it's been around for over six decades, beautifully restored Dutch colonial architecture and a lively contemporary vibe keep this legendary complex from ever feeling dated. **Pros:** superb on-site dining and entertainment; calm protected waters; gorgeous location; free Wi-Fi. **Cons:** main beach overcrowds easily due to insuffficent lounges on second beach; not all rooms are ocean view. *Rooms from: $310* ✉ *130 Penstraat, Punda, Willemstad* ☎ *5999/461–4377* *www.avilahotel.com* *154 rooms, 11 suites* *Multiple meal plans.*

$$$ RESORT Fodor's Choice ★

Baoase. No other resort on Curaçao can match this Balinese-inspired gem for understated elegance and attention to detail. **Pros:** beautiful landscaping; complete privacy; unsurpassed luxury. **Cons:** lacks some of the distractions of a larger resort; exclusivity can sometimes become isolating. *Rooms from: $425* ✉ *Winterswijkstraat 2, Willemstad* ☎ *8884/409–3506* *www.baoase.com* *9 villas, 3 1-bedroom suites, 10 beachfront suites* *Breakfast.*

$ RENTAL FAMILY **Blue Bay Curaçao.** Set in a storied plantation estate and on a beautiful beach, Blue Bay's accommodations range from luxury apartment–style rooms to stand-alone villas and bungalows—hillside or beachfront. **Pros:** spacious units; ideal location for golfers, divers, and families. **Cons:** a bit isolated, so a car is absolutely necessary; little nightlife. *Rooms from: $180 ✉ Landhuis Blauw z/n, Willemstad ☎ 5999/888–8800 🌐 www.bluebay-curacao.com 48 apartments, 36 3-bedroom villas No meals.*

$ RESORT FAMILY Fodor's Choice ★ **Curaçao Marriott Beach Resort & Emerald Casino.** The cream of the crop of Curaçao's resorts beckons you to live it up from the moment you arrive. **Pros:** no need to leave the compound for anything but sightseeing; excellent beach location; first-class fitness center; five-star PADI dive shop. **Cons:** feels big and impersonal; pool area can get very busy. *Rooms from: $219 ☎ 5999/736–8800 🌐 www.curacaomarriott.com 237 rooms, 10 suites Breakfast.*

$ HOTEL **Floris Suite Hotel.** Dutch interior designer Jan des Bouvrie has used warm mahogany shades offset by cool, sleek stainless-steel adornments in the suites of this modernist hotel, all of which have a balcony or porch and a full kitchen. **Pros:** great for a quiet escape; beautifully designed rooms and public spaces. **Cons:** decor lacks romantic feel; bit of a hike to decent shopping and restaurants. *Rooms from: $195 ✉ Piscaderaweg, Piscadera Bay, Willemstad ☎ 5999/462–6111 🌐 www.florissuitehotel.com 72 suites No meals.*

$ RESORT FAMILY **Hilton Curaçao.** Two beautiful beaches of pillowy white sand beyond the open-air lobby make this resort a jewel in its price range. **Pros:** gorgeous beachfront; lots of on-site facilities; friendly staff. **Cons:** lacks the intimacy of smaller resorts; not all rooms are ocean view. *Rooms from: $200 ✉ Piscaderaweg, Willemstad ☎ 5999/462–5000 🌐 www.hiltoncuracaoresort.com 196 rooms, 12 suites Multiple meal plans.*

$ HOTEL **Hotel 't Klooster.** Located in a former monastery (*klooster* means cloister), this bright yellow structure looks impressive from the outside, but it's a more spartan hotel within. **Pros:** historical charm; reasonable price. **Cons:** small rooms; can be noisy. *Rooms from: $110 ✉ Veerstraat 12, Punda, Willemstad ☎ 5999/461–2650 🌐 www.hotelklooster.com 24 rooms Multiple meal plans.*

$ RESORT FAMILY **Lions Dive & Beach Resort.** Divers are lured by the first-rate program here, but this low-key resort has a lot to offer nondivers as well. **Pros:** ideal for diving; beautiful private beach and access to Seaquarium Beach; family-friendly, Olympic-length pool. **Cons:** beach can get busy; kids everywhere; noisy weekends. *Rooms from: $199 ✉ Seaquarium Beach, Bapor Kibra z/n ☎ 5999/434–8888 🌐 www.lionsdive.com 102 rooms, 10 suites, 1 penthouse No meals.*

$ RESORT Fodor's Choice ★ **Lodge Kura Hulanda & Beach Club-GHL Hotel.** On the island's remote western tip, this sprawling resort with tranquil gardens will make you feel far removed from the daily grind. **Pros:** perfect for a complete escape; unparalleled ocean views; great value; beautifully appointed rooms; free Wi-Fi. **Cons:** a bit quiet for some tastes; miles away from everything; although there's a shuttle, a rental car is necessary if you want to explore the island. *Rooms from: $179 ✉ Playa Kalki 1,*

Westpunt ☎ *5999/839–3600* 🌐 *www.kurahulanda.com* *30 rooms, 69 suites* 🍽 *Multiple meal plans.*

$$ RESORT

Papagayo Beach Hotel. Set upon its own private beach with a massive infinity pool overlooking the sea, the sleek white and steel structure is no-nonsense modern with a South Beach feel and popular with European visitors seeking a classy escape in an upscale neighborhood. **Pros:** great spa on-site; spacious pool; modern amenities; fine dining. **Cons:** though adults-only, lots of children/families go to the public beach right next door on weekends; far from Willemstad; traffic can be an issue. *Rooms from: $220* ✉ *Jan Thiel* ☎ *5999/747–4333* 🌐 *www.papagayo-designhotel.com/nl/home.html* *75 bungalows* 🍽 *No meals.*

$ B&B/INN Fodor's Choice ★

PM78 Urban Oasis Curacao. Set within a stunning three-story cobalt-blue mansion right in the heart of trendy Pietermaai, this small family-run luxury boutique property offers some special stay options. **Pros:** sleek modern design; homey and inviting with friendly family owners on-site. **Cons:** occasional noise from restaurant next door at night; sea is too rough for swimming. *Rooms from: $125* ✉ *Punda, Pietermaai* ☎ *5999/528–6118* 🌐 *www.pietermaai78.com* *4 rooms* 🍽 *No meals.*

$$ RESORT Fodor's Choice ★

Renaissance Curaçao Resort & Casino. The four gabled buildings of this downtown resort are painted in colors that seem to mirror those of Punda across the harbor and fit in perfectly with the historic surroundings. **Pros:** coolest (and only) pool-beach in town; every amenity imaginable; walking distance to all the attractions of both Otrobanda and Punda; exceptionally helpful staff. **Cons:** Rif Fort area is a major tourist draw and can get busy; common-area color scheme is not exactly calming. *Rooms from: $280* ✉ *Pater Euwensweg, Otrobanda, Willemstad* ☎ *5999/435–5000* 🌐 *www.renaissancecuracao.com* *223 rooms, 14 suites* 🍽 *Breakfast.*

$$ RESORT FAMILY Fodor's Choice ★

Santa Barbara Beach & Golf Resort. The sprawling hacienda-style complex is set along a beautiful stretch of ocean and their first-class Pete Dye–designed golf course has spectacular views of the sea and countryside. **Pros:** gorgeous location; elegant public areas; top-flight dining; first-rate spa. **Cons:** long distance from town; rental car required to explore island. *Rooms from: $300* ✉ *Santa Barbara Plantation, Nieuwpoort* ☎ *5999/840–1234* 🌐 *www.santabarbararesortcuracao.com* *335 rooms, 15 suites* 🍽 *Multiple meal plans.*

$ HOTEL

Scuba Lodge and Suites. An interesting surprise in the residential neighborhood of Pietermaai, spanning three brightly painted renovated heritage homes, this small seaside resort and full PADI diving center combines casual chic with bohemian boutique. **Pros:** homey vibe; great staff; house reef and expert dive instruction. **Cons:** far from shopping; not swimmable beach; few amenities. *Rooms from: $155* ✉ *Punda, Pietermaai* ☎ *5999/465–2575* 🌐 *www.scubalodge.com* *44 rooms* 🍽 *No meals.*

$ HOTEL Fodor's Choice ★

Sonesta Hotel Kura Hulanda Spa & Casino. Sonesta's luxury boutique accommodations include modern amenities surrounded by unique antiques and bespoke decor—different in every room and suite—gleaned from owner Jacob Gelt-Dekker's personal collection. **Pros:** UNESCO heritage site property; walking distance to all downtown attractions; unique museum also on-site. **Cons:** not near a beach;

narrow alleyways and small rooms can become somewhat confining. *Rooms from: $159* ✉ *Langestraat 8, Otrobanda, Willemstad* ☎ *5999/434–7700* 🌐 *www.kurahulanda.com* *68 rooms, 14 suites* *Multiple meal plans.*

$$$ ALL-INCLUSIVE FAMILY **Sunscape Curaçao Resort, Spa & Casino.** This family-friendly all-inclusive resort has its own house reef and great snorkeling steps from your room. **Pros:** ample distractions for the whole family; renovated rooms are beautifully appointed and airy; nice laid-back atmosphere. **Cons:** beach gets very busy; no-reservations dining can also mean long waits for tables at prime times. *Rooms from: $404* ✉ *Martin Luther King Blvd. 78, Willemstad* ☎ *5999/736–7888, 866/SUNSCAPE* 🌐 *www.sunscaperesorts.com/curacao* *285 rooms, 56 suites* *All-inclusive* ☞ *3-night minimum.*

NIGHTLIFE

There are hundreds of bars and nightlife hot spots scattered about the island in different neighborhoods, and something different going on every night of the week. But there is no one "nightlife" district per say. Your best bet it to seek out the Curaçao Party Guide (🌐 *www.curacaopartyguide.com*) for complete up-to-date events and music and theme nights to find your style and where it's happening. There are a few pockets however that are always nightlife-lively like Curaçao Beach Boulevard, Jan Thiel, and more recently, the newly transformed neighborhood of Pietermaai where you can barhop in one spot without having to drive anywhere. And most resorts have some kind of nightly entertainment on-site weekends.

BARS AND CLUBS

Grand Café de Heeren. This is a great spot to grab a locally brewed Amstel Bright and meet a happy blend of tourists and transplanted Dutch locals. Live music DJs keep it hopping. ✉ *Zuikertuintjeweg, Bloempot* ☎ *5999/736–0491.*

Miles Jazz Cafe. Curaçao is addicted to jazz, and there are many live jazz festivals throughout the year, but if you really want to get into the swing of it any night of the week, head to Miles Jazz Vinyl and Cigars Cafe. Named after the legendary musician Miles Davis, it's a cool little getaway in the heart of Pietermaai where you can hear jazz played on vinyl, play board games, and have a cigar and a drink. Local musicians occasionally stop by to jam as well. ✉ *Nieuwestraat 42, Pietermaai* ☎ *5999/520–5200* 🌐 *www.milescuracao.com.*

Fodor's Choice ★ **Mundo Bizarro.** As the name suggests, the decor here is definitely bizarre—a hodgepodge of paraphernalia with no rhyme or reason but a lot of creativity. Locals and visitors alike flock here weekends for super signature cocktails, live music, great snacks, and an unparalleled offbeat atmosphere. ✉ *Nieuwestraat 12, Pietermaai* ☎ *5999/461–6767* 🌐 *www.mundobizarrocuracao.com.*

Rif Fort Bar & Terrace. Located within the stone walls of Rif Fort, there's usually a lively crowd on weekends. A good place to sit outside and enjoy the evening breezes with one of their signature cocktails like the Rifortini or killer shooters like the Devil's Breath. Live entertainment in the courtyard weekends give the historic scene a vibrant party atmosphere. ✉ *Rif Fort, Otrobanda, Willemstad* ☎ *5999/462–5666.*

Fodor's Choice ★ **Rock Beach.** One of Curaçao's coolest concept bars is Rock Beach—an old shipping container turned into a seaside bar on the rocks in Pietermaai. Live bands turn this spot into a party on Fridays, and DJs move the crowds on Saturday and Sunday nights. In addition there are many special musical events. The food is pub fare, mainly ribs and burgers, and Sunday there is a fun brunch. ✉ *Pietermaaiweg 44-50, Pietermaai* ☎ *5999/512–8131* ⏲ *Fri.–Sun.*

Saint Tropez Ocean Club. Part of the Saint Tropez Suites resort in Pietermaai, this unique day club is where French Riviera–style meets Dutch Caribbean cool. A gorgeous infinity pool crests a rocky coast with crashing waves and is surrounded by plush daybeds, private cabanas, and loungers. A trendy bar and open-air dining spot serve small bites and full lunch, and there's also surfside bottle service and tapas by the pool. Access is free to resort guests, and some neighboring hotels also have complimentary access; others must buy a pass. At night, it morphs into a cool open-air lounge and dinner spot often featuring hot DJs and special events, and every Monday night sushi and signature cocktails are on special. ✉ *Pietermaai 152, Pietermaai* ☎ *5999/461–7727* 🌐 *www.sainttropezcuracao.com.*

Waterfort Terrace (*Waterfort Arches*). This collection of bars and dining spots gathered in the historic stone bastion affords glorious views of the harbor and sea by day and morphs into a magical strip by night with twinkling lights and live music emanating from the many different venues. ✉ *Waterfortstraat Boog 1, Punda, Willemstad* ☎ *5999/465–0769.*

CASINOS

The following hotels have casinos that are open daily: Sunscape Curaçao, the Curaçao Marriott Beach Resort & Emerald Casino, the Hilton Curaçao, Holiday Beach Hotel & Casino, Plaza Hotel & Casino, Otrobanda Hotel & Casino, Trupial Inn Hotel & Casino, and there is a new casino at Papagayo Beach Plaza. And Veneto Casino at the Holiday Beach Resort is newly renovated and also the largest on the island. Slot machines open earlier than table games, between 10 am and 1 pm, and most of the rooms have penny and nickel slots in addition to the higher-priced machines. Tables generally open at 3 pm or 4 pm. Casinos close about 1 am or 2 am weekdays; some stay open until 4 am on weekend nights. Some have sports betting.

DANCE AND MUSIC CLUBS

Mambo Beach. With an expansive surfside emporium and a huge stage on the beach, Mambo Beach has always been one of this island's main party spots. A new menu and cushy seaside lounges make it a hot spot by day as well. ✉ *Seaquarium Beach, Bapor Kibra z/n* ☎ *5999/516–6946.*

SHOPPING

From Dutch classics like embroidered linens, Delft earthenware, and cheeses to local artwork and handicrafts, shopping in Willemstad can turn up some fun finds. But don't expect major bargains on watches, jewelry, or electronics; Willemstad is not a duty-free port (the few establishments that claim to be "duty-free" are simply absorbing the cost of some or all of the tax rather than passing it on to consumers); however, if you come prepared with some comparison prices, you might still dig up some good deals. But there are new complexes out of downtown now for ultimate retail therapy—Curaçao Beach Boulevard has an eclectic collection of trendy shops at the Sea Aquarium Park and the brand-new Sambil megamall is a massive multilevel shopping and entertainment complex in Veeris Commerical Park with hundreds of modern stores and trendy boutiques.

AREAS AND MALLS

Willemstad's **Punda** is a treat for pedestrians, with most shops concentrated within a bustling area of about six blocks. Closed to traffic, Heerenstraat and Gomezplein are pedestrian malls covered with pink inlaid bricks. Other major shopping streets are Breedestraat and Madurostraat. Here you can find jewelry, cosmetics, perfumes, luggage, and linens—and no shortage of trinkets and souvenirs. Savvy shoppers don't skip town without a stop across the bay to Otrobanda, where the Riffort Village Shopping Mall houses a variety of retailers. It's worth noting that many of the bargain-price designer labels found in smaller clothing shops are just knockoffs from Latin America. The Renaissance Mall right next to Rif Fort has retailers such as Guess and Tiffany & Co. next to local shops offering a range of jewelry and fashion. Curaçao Beach Boulevard is a new shopping spot as is Sambil megamall in Veeris.

ART GALLERIES

Gallery Alma Blou. The oldest established gallery on the island located in Landhouse Habaai showcases works by top local artists in rotating exhibits. You can find shimmering landscapes, dazzling photographs, ceramics, even African-inspired Carnival masks here, and there is also a separate gift shop with artsy souvenirs. ✉ *Frater Radulphusweg 4, Otrobanda* ☎ *5999/462–8896* 🌐 *www.galleryalmablou.com* ⏲ *Closed Sun.*

Fodor's Choice ★ **Nena Sanchez Gallery.** At the Nena Sanchez Gallery, you can find this local artist's cheerful paintings in characteristically bright yellows, reds, greens, pinks, and blues. Her work depicting marine life and island scenes is available in various forms, including posters, mouse pads, and picture frames. She often gives art classes at her workshop and gallery at restored historic plantation Landhuis Jan Kok. ✉ *Bloempot Shopping Mall, Windstraat 15, Punda* ☎ *5999/461–2882* 🌐 *www.nenasanchez.com.*

Serena's Art Factory. You might have noticed brightly painted sculptures of colorful Caribbean women with highly exaggerated physical features in many public places around the island and minature versions of them for sale as souvenirs in many shops. These are Chichis®—creations by artist Serena Janet Israel that are unique to Curaçao. "Chi Chi" means big sister in the local lingo, and the figures are meant to exude the warmth of matronly Caribbean women. Many different local female artists have been trained by Serena to custom-paint them, but visitors are welcome to create their own for a one-of-a-kind souvenir at Serena's Art Factory near the Ostrich Farm. Group workshops and walk-in workshops for non-tour visitors are available on a regular basis. Workshop is about two hours. ✉ *Jan Louis 87a* ☎ *5999/738–0648* 🌐 *www.chichi-curacao.com* 🎫 *Free tour of factory.*

CIGARS

Cigar Emporium. A sweet aroma permeates Cigar Emporium, where you can find the largest selection of Cuban cigars on the island, including H. Upmann, Romeo y Julieta, and Montecristo. Visit the climate-controlled cedar cigar room. ✉ *Gomezplein 4, Punda, Willemstad* ☎ *5999/465–3955.*

CLOTHING

Bamali. This shop sells fabulous women's apparel in natural fabrics and international styles including Indonesian batik. Lots of stunning jewelry and unique accessories as well—beads, shells, gemstones, silver, and handbags. Custom-made clothing is available as they have their own workshop on-site. ✉ *Breedestraat 2, Punda, Willemstad* ☎ *5999/461–2258* 🌐 *www.bamali-fashion.com.*

Tommy Hilfiger. This label's Curaçao outposts carry the full designer line for men, women, and children. Stores located in Punda and Zuikertuin Mall. Hilfiger Denim is a specialty store in the Rif Fort. ✉ *Willemstad* ☎ *5999/461–2266.*

GIFTS

Boolchand's. The best-known brand for electronics in the Caribbean, Boolchand's is a legendary family-run chain and their main store is in Punda, though they have many other outlets around Curaçao. Beyond electronics and tech, they also sell fine jewelry, Swarovski crystal, Swiss watches, cameras, and more with a good repuation for fair price and good quaility. ✉ *Breedstraat 50, Punda, Willemstad* ☎ *5999/461–6233* 🌐 *www.boolchand.com/locations.*

Penha Curaçao. Founded in 1865, and still run by the Penha family, this landmark store is housed in one of Punda's most iconic structures and specializes in offering a wide range of duty-free items, including French perfumes, cosmetics, clothing, eyewear, watches, and high-end lingerie and accessories. It's also a UNESCO property and one of the most photographed on the island, another reason why it draws tourists in droves. ✉ *Heerenstraat 1, Punda, Willemstad* ☎ *5999/461–2266* 🌐 *www.jlpenha.com.*

Little Switzerland. A well-established high-end chain offering designer jewelry, watches, crystal, china, and leather goods with outlets throughout the Caribbean, Little Swizerland's three Curaçao outlets are located in the Renaissance complex and at Rif Fort. Top-quality brands include Tiffany, Cartier, Movado, Tag Heuer, and more, at prices much lower than on the mainland. ✉ *Renaissance and Rif Fort, Punda, Willemstad* ☎ *877/800–9988* 🌐 *www.littleswitzerland.com.*

HANDICRAFTS

Landhuis Groot Santa Martha. Run by the Tayor Soshal Foundation this ex-plantation houses a project designed to help people with disabilities train and receive education and paid employment in a beneficial environment. The program takes place in a 17th-century land house that has been converted into an artisan's factory and museum where visitors can purchase creative handmade crafts, and souvenirs made by the residents. ✉ *Soto, Santa Martha Bay* ☎ *5999/864–1323, 5999/864–2969* 🌐 *www.tayersoshal.com* 🎫 *$10.*

JEWELRY

Freeport Jewelers. The Freeport Jeweler's Group consists of six stores around the island featuring high-end brands of fine jewelry, watches, and collectibles. They have four stores in Willemstad (two on the Handelsakde), one in Punda, and one in Otrabanda at the Renaissance Mall. The other two are located in the Zuikertuin Mall. Their newest outlet there, Fashion Zone by Freeport, offers good prices on trendy watches by names like Calvin Klein, Swatch, Armani, Diesel, and more. ✉ *Punda, Willemstad* ☎ *800/617–0766* 🌐 *www.freeportjewelers.com.*

PERFUMES AND COSMETICS

The Yellow House and Zylo. Also known as La Casa Amarilla, The Yellow House specializes in high-end duty-free perfumes and cosmetics with exclusive rights to big names like Guerlain. They have recently teamed up with Zylo (another retail chain) under the same roof to expand their range of wares. Now with their new partner, shoppers can also purchase high-end fashion watches, jewelry, handbags, and sunglasses there. ✉ *Breedestraat 46, Punda, Willemstad* ☎ *5999/461–3222* 🌐 *www.theyellowhouse-zylo.com.*

SPORTS AND THE OUTDOORS

FAMILY **Curaçao Buggy Adventures.** Strap on a helmet for an adventurous, guided excursion called a "Scooby Tour" around the island's most popular sites. Visit caves and forts, stop for a swim or snorkel; you can even design your own tour if you're a group of four or more. Daily tours average two and a half hours. No experience required, but drivers must be 18 or older with a valid driver's license. Children over five can ride as passengers. Hotel pickup also available. ✉ *SeaAquarium Beach & Zanzibar Beach–Jan Thiel, Willemstad* ☎ *5999/696–2182* 🌐 *www.curacaobuggyadventures.com.*

Eric's ATV Adventures. Hit the road in rugged style behind the wheel of an all-terrain vehicle with Eric's ATV Adventures. All you need for a guided tour of the countryside is a regular driver's license. If you're 10 or older, you can ride as a passenger in the back seat. Helmets and goggles are provided. ✉ *Babor Kibra z/n, Seaquarium Beach, Willemstad* ☎ *5999/524–7418* 🌐 *www.curacao-atv.com.*

DIVING AND SNORKELING

The **Curaçao Underwater Marine Park** includes almost a third of the island's southern diving waters. Scuba divers and snorkelers can enjoy more than 12½ miles (20 km) of protected reefs and shores, with normal visibility from 60 to 150 feet. With water temperatures ranging from 75°F to 82°F (24°C to 28°C), wet suits are generally unnecessary. No coral collecting, spearfishing, or littering is allowed. Some of the most popular dive sites are the Mushroom Forest, the wreck of the *Superior Producer*, and the Blue Room secret cave at Westpunt. Snorkelers and divers also enjoy the little sunken tugboat at Spanish Water. Wall diving is good around the Sea Aquarium Park and they also offer open-water dives with dolphins. The north coast—where conditions are dangerously rough—is not recommended for diving.

Introductory scuba resort courses run about $75 for one dive and $140 for two dives. Open-water certification courses run about $425 for the five-dive version. Virtually every operator charges $40 to $55 for a single-tank dive and $70 to $85 for a two-tank dive. One day of unlimited shore diving runs about $22 to $25. Snorkeling gear commonly rents for $10 to $16 per day.

DiveVersity Piscadera. This outfitter specializes in intimate one-on-one instruction with an additonal focus on marine life and coral awareness education due to their affiliation with CARMABI their eco-centered research neighbor. They offer a full range of dive services and equipment rental and are a fully certified PADI diving school. ✉ *Piscadera Bay z/n, Piscadera* ☎ *5999/684–0434* 🌐 *www.diveversity-piscadera.com.*

Fodor's Choice ★ **Ocean Encounters.** This is the largest dive operator on Curaçao, and they offer a vast menu of scheduled shore and boat dives and packages as well as certified PADI instruction. They cover the island's most popular dive sites including the *Superior Producer* wreck—where barracudas hang out—an adorable little tugboat wreck, the renowned Mushroom Forest, and much more. In July, the dive center sponsors a children's

9

sea camp in conjunction with the Sea Aquarium and they also now run the unique Animal Encounters experience in the Sea Aquarium lagoon. ✉ *Seaquarium Park, Bapor Kibra z/n* ☎ *5999/461–8131* 🌐 *www.oceanencounters.com.*

FISHING

Miss Ann Boat Trips. A wide range of seaborne adventures including day trips with barbecue lunch and diving and/or snorkeling ops at sister satellite island uninhabited Klein Curaçao. Fishing trips, private charters, and more available as well with their modern fleet of motor yachts. ✉ *Jan Sofat 232, Van Engelen* ☎ *5999/767–1579* 🌐 *www.missannboattrips.com.*

GOLF

Blue Bay Golf. Part of the Blue Bay Hotel, an ex-plantation house turned resort, the golf course is famous for its incredible sea views. Designed by Rocky Roquemore, it measures 6,735 yards from the tips and beckons experts and novices alike. You will be sure to enjoy the par-3 5th, which plays across and is guarded by the sea the entire left-hand side. Facilities include a golf shop, locker rooms, and a snack bar. You can rent carts, clubs, and shoes, though don't expect too much with any of them or the facilities. If you'd like to drive your game to a new level, take a lesson from the house pro ($50 for a half hour). With Pay & Play no membership is required. Rates vary depending on time of day and high or low season. ✉ *Blue Bay Hotel, Blue Bay z/n* ☎ *5999/868–1755* 🌐 *www.bluebay-curacao.com* 🏌 *18 holes, 6735 yards, par 72.*

Old Quarry Golf Course. This lush course designed by Pete Dye has incredible vistas on the sheltered bay known as Spanish Water. The course features a breathtaking mixture of ocean views and various forms of desert cactus along with Dye's dramatic bunkering. The 6,920-yard layout is the best and toughest on the island and includes an 8,000-square-foot clubhouse. There is a full range of facilities, and with the Santa Barbara Resort nearby, drinks and fine dining are mere steps away. Greens fees feature multiple play packages as well as resort discounts. You can rent carts, clubs, and shoes. They also offer offbeat glow-in-the-dark fun golf on the Friday night before the full moon each month. ✉ *Santa Barbara Plantation, Porta Blancu, Nieuwpoort z/n* ☎ *5999/840–6886* 🌐 *www.oldquarrygolfcuracao.com* 🏌 *18 holes, 6920 yards, par 72.*

GUIDED TOURS

Most tour operators have pickups at the major hotels and offer tours in several languages including English. Tour offerings have expanded beyond simple island tours in air-conditioned motor coaches to include themes such as beach-hopping, nightlife, culture, culinary, or history—some in combinations covering more than one theme.

Atlantis Adventures. A novel way to explore the historic city of Willemstad is via the Trolley Train, which is as brightly colored in pastel hues as the Handelskade buildings. It begins and ends at Fort Amsterdam and winds through the neighborhoods of Punda, Scharloo, and Pietermaai with many points of local color and interest throughout. ✉ *Punda* ☎ *5999/461–0011* 🌐 *www.curacao-atlantisadventures.com.*

PeterTrips Curaçao. Small and large air-conditioned buses transport visitors for full-day or half-day outings to beaches, natural wonders, historical sights, and points of interest like the Ostrich Farm or Landhuis Chobolobo for Curaçao liqueur tastings. Special group adventures are also possible. They offer pickup at most major hotels. ☎ *5999/561–5368, 5999/465–2703* 🌐 *www.petertrips.com.*

WALKING TOURS

When making reservations for any tour, mention that you speak English.

Anko van der Woude. Walking tours of historic Otrobanda, focusing on the unique architecture of this old section of town, are led by architect Anko van der Woude upon request. ☎ *5999/461–3554.*

Gigi Scheper Tours. Gigi Scheper leads expert walking tours of Willemstad focusing on Jewish heritage and architecture, including an insider's look at the synagogue. ✉ *Punda, Willemstad* ☎ *5999/697–0290.*

SEA EXCURSIONS

Many sailboats, motorboats, and catamarans offer sunset cruises and daylong snorkeling and picnic trips to Klein Curaçao, the uninhabited island between Curaçao and Bonaire, and other destinations. Prices are around $50 to $90 for a half-day trip (including food and drinks).

Insulinde. The 120-foot Dutch sailing ketch is very popular for weddings and special event charters but also offers up many snorkeling/swimming/scenic-tour combos, and sunset sails. ✉ *Handelskade z/n* ☎ *5999/560–1340* 🌐 *www.insulinde.com.*

Bounty Adventures. Two custom-built, high-speed catamarans and a luxury motor yacht take guests for snorkel sails, sunset trips, day trips to Klein Curaçao, and deep-sea fishing adventures that include an open bar and barbecue lunch. Charters also available. ✉ *Jan Thiel beach* ☎ *5999/767–9998* 🌐 *www.bountyadventures.com.*

Mermaid. The *Mermaid* is a 66-foot motor yacht that carries up to 60 people to deserted island Klein Curaçao four times a week. A buffet lunch, beer, and soft drinks are provided at the boat's exclusive beach house; they are the only tour operator that goes there with their own picnic tables, shade huts, and facilities. ☎ *5999/560–1530* 🌐 *www.mermaidboattrips.com.*

FAMILY ***Seaworld Explorer.*** For a unique vantage point, soak up the local marine life on a 1½-hour-long tour of the coral reefs aboard the glass-bottom, semisubmersible *Seaworld Explorer.* ☎ *5999/461–0011* 🌐 *www.curacao-atlantisadventures.com/Seaworld_Explorer.html.*

WATER SPORTS

FAMILY **Caribbean Sea Sports.** This company runs a tight ship when it comes to all sorts of water sports, including kayaking, windsurfing, banana boats, tube rides, diving, and snorkeling. ✉ *Curaçao Marriott Beach Resort, Piscadera Bay* ☎ *5999/462–2620* 🌐 *www.caribseasports.com.*

Let's Go Watersports. Captain "Goodlife" at Let's Go Watersports will help you plan kayaking and other boat outings so you can live it up on the water and snorkel in some special spots. He also grills up a tasty lunch at the dock. ✉ *Santa Cruz Beach 1, Santa Cruz* ☎ *5999/520–1147, 5999/864–0438* 🌐 *www.facebook.com/capt.goodlife.*

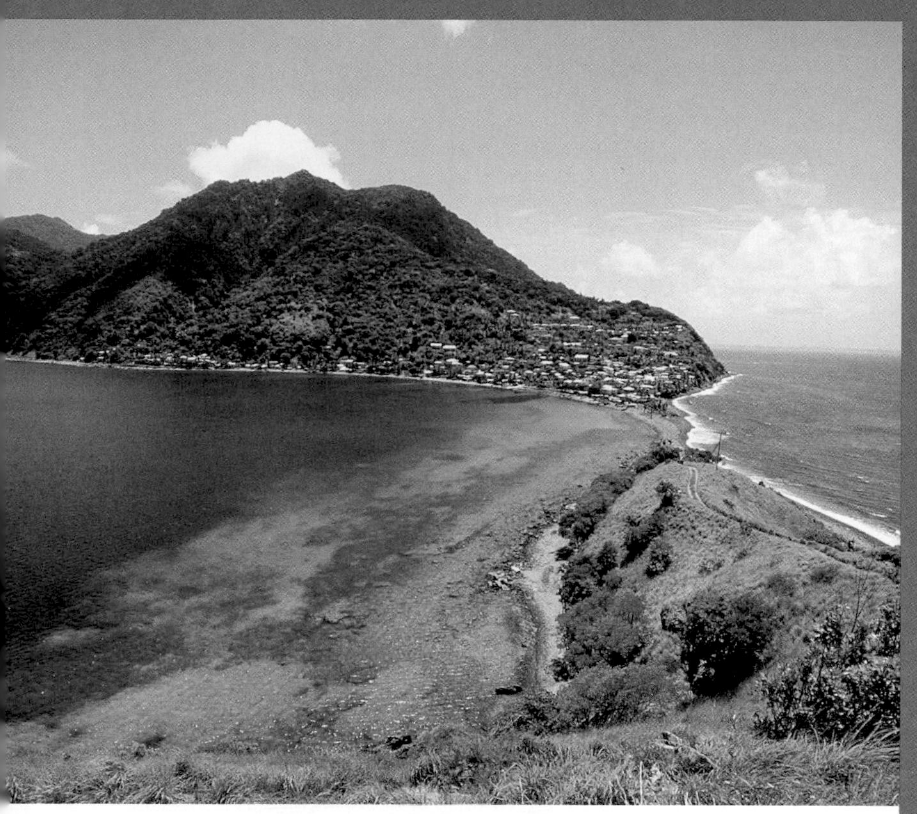

DOMINICA

10

WELCOME TO DOMINICA

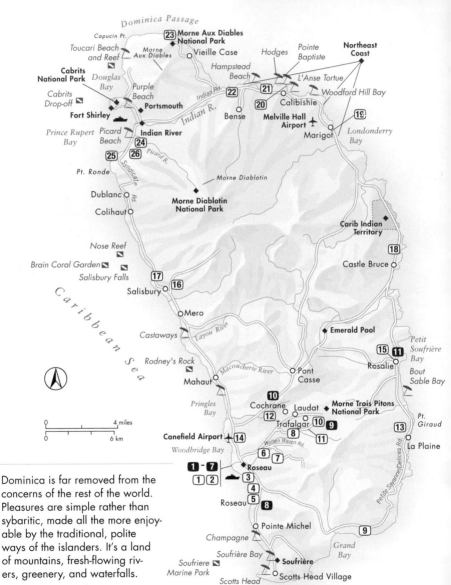

Dominica Passage
Capucin Pt.
23 Morne Aux Diables National Park
Toucari Beach and Reef
Morne Aux Diables
Vieille Case
Hodges
Pointe Baptiste
Northeast Coast
Cabrits National Park
Douglas Bay
Hampstead Beach
L'Anse Tortue
Cabrits Drop-off
Purple Beach
Indian Rd.
22
21
Woodford Hill Bay
Portsmouth
20
Calibishie
Fort Shirley
Indian R.
Bense
Melville Hall Airport
19
Prince Rupert Bay
Picard Beach
Indian River
Marigot
Londonderry Bay
24
26
25
Picard R.
Pt. Ronde
Syndicate Rd.
Morne Diablotin
Dublanc
Morne Diablotin National Park
Colihaut
Carib Indian Territory
Nose Reef
18
Brain Coral Garden
Castle Bruce
Salisbury Falls
17
16
Caribbean Sea
Salisbury
Mero
Emerald Pool
Castaways
Layou River
Petit Soufrière Bay
15
11
Rodney's Rock
Rosalie
Mahaut
Macoucherie River
Pont Casse
Bout Sable Bay
10
Pringles Bay
Cochrane
Laudat
Morne Trois Pitons National Park
0 4 miles
0 6 km
12
Trafalgar
10
9
Pt. Giraud
8
13
Canefield Airport
14
11
Petite Savanne/Delices Rd.
Wotten Waven Rd.
La Plaine
Woodbridge Bay
6
7
1 - 7
Roseau
1 2
3
4
Roseau
5
8
Pointe Michel
9
Champagne
Grand Bay
Soufrière Bay
Soufrière
Soufriere Marine Park
Scotts Head Village
Scotts Head
Martinique Passage

Dominica is far removed from the concerns of the rest of the world. Pleasures are simple rather than sybaritic, made all the more enjoyable by the traditional, polite ways of the islanders. It's a land of mountains, fresh-flowing rivers, greenery, and waterfalls.

THE NATURE ISLAND

The island is 29 miles (47 km) long and 16 miles (26 km) wide, with approximately 73,000 citizens. Because it was a British colony (achieving independence in 1978), you may wonder about the prevalence of French names. Although the English first claimed Dominica in 1627, the French controlled it from 1632 until 1759, when it passed back into English hands.

Restaurants ▼

The Banana Tree **2**
Cocorico **4**
Guiyave **5**
Miranda's Corner **10**
Old Stone **6**
Palisades Restaurant **3**
Pearl's Cuisine **1**
Rainforest Restaurant ... **9**
Sea Surge **8**
TAO **7**
Zamaan Restaurant **11**

Hotels ▼

Anchorage Hotel **3**
Atlantique View **23**
Beau Rive **18**
Calibishie Lodges **21**
Castle Comfort Lodge ... **4**
Cocoa Cottage **11**
Comfort Cottages **22**
Crescent Moon **12**
Evergreen Hotel **5**
Fort Young Hotel **1**
Garraway Hotel **2**
Hummingbird Inn **14**
Itassi Cottages **7**
Jungle Bay **13**
Pagua Bay House **19**
Papillote Wilderness Retreat **10**
Picard Beach Cottages **26**
Red Rock Haven **20**
Rejens Hotel **24**
Rosalie Bay **15**
Roseau Valley Hotel **6**
Secret Bay **25**
Sunset Bay Club **17**
Tamarind Tree **16**
Tia's Bamboo Cottages .. **8**
Zandoli Inn **9**

KEY

Beaches
Cruise Ship Terminal
Dive Sites
Restaurants
Hotels

TOP REASONS TO VISIT DOMINICA

1 **Fewer Crowds:** Dominica is a delightful respite from the more crowded, commercial islands.

2 **Unspoiled Nature:** The island's natural environment is the major draw.

3 **Great Dives:** Diving pristine reefs full of colorful sea life or in bubbly, volcanic water is amazing.

4 **Natural Spas:** Dominica has an abundance of natural sulfur pools, some of which have become makeshift spas.

THE ORIGINAL CARIBBEANS

Blame Christopher Columbus: his logs give accounts of the "gentle, laughing" Arawak and the "ferocious, cannibalistic" Carib, both stereotypes that pigeonholed the Caribbean's two indigenous peoples and persist to this day. Historians have had to wade through a lot of colonial romanticism to get at the truth.

Archaeologists have determined that the first Amerindian migration to the islands took place around 1000 BC from northern South America. "War and Peace" could describe the divergence between the agrarian Arawak and the more militant Carib. The Arawak—the umbrella term encompassed many smaller groups, most notably the Taíno people on the larger islands—were easily subjugated by Spanish explorers; the Carib, less so, but eventually they succumbed, too. Warfare and disease—the indigenous peoples had never encountered smallpox until the Europeans' arrival—caused populations of both groups to dwindle to a few thousand by the end of the 18th century.

Language. Carib warfare resulted in the capture of many Arawak women. As a result, early Spanish arrivals were puzzled by what appeared to be gender-specific languages, with men speaking the Carib Kalinago language, and women, one of several Arawakan tongues. Historians debate the notion of a persistent gender-communication divide between what the British would later call Island Carib and Island Arawak. The languages gave several of the islands their names: Bequia ("cloud"), Canouan ("turtle"), Carriacou ("reef"), Saba ("rock"), and

Tobago ("tobacco"). The English words *barbecue*, *hurricane*, and *potato* have their roots in indigenous Caribbean languages, too.

Religion. The Carib adopted many of the tenets of Arawak religion, essentially a system of animism and ancestor worship. Shamans held the keys to unlocking contact with the spirit world, thus occupying esteemed roles in their communities. Tobacco played a prominent role in worship ceremonies. Petroglyphs, rock carvings dedicated to objects of indigenous veneration, can be seen today in Puerto Rico, St. Kitts, St. John, and Grenada.

Innovations. With the construction of their *canoas*—source of the word *canoe*—indigenous Caribbean peoples were able to establish interisland transport. (The Arawak used their vessels for trade; the Carib, for warfare.) And the next time you laze in a hammock, acknowledge the Arawak. *Hamacas* were a regular fixture in their homes.

Women. Carib and Arawak women participated in surprisingly egalitarian societies. Women were eligible to be a community's *cacique* (chief) and frequently served on its ruling council. Society did, however, ascribe gender roles: men went off to war while women tended agriculture and took care of domestic chores.

Food. Fishing was a major source of nourishment for the Carib and Arawak. Perhaps no food is more identified with Caribbean indigenous peoples than the cassava or yucca, a starchy tuber and a major source of carbohydrates, with one major god even being the patron of this important crop.

Cannibalism? What of the charges of cannibalism among the Carib people? Columbus wrote that he saw the practice, but most historians side with today's Carib descendants who insist it never went on. They suggest that Spanish explorers had religious and economic motives for perpetuating the myth of cannibalism. Conversion to Christianity and even slavery would have to be better than such "barbarism" in their eyes.

—Jeffrey Van Fleet

Updated by Roberta Sotonoff

Wedged between the two French islands of Guadeloupe and Martinique, Dominica (pronounced dom-in-ee-ka) is as close to the Garden of Eden as you're likely to get. Wild orchids, anthurium lilies, ferns, heliconia, and myriad fruit trees sprout profusely. Much of the interior is still covered by luxuriant rain forest and remains inaccessible by road.

With this bountiful natural abundance, there's also a lot of active watching—flying birds and butterflies, turtles hatching, plus jumping dolphins and breaching whales. Even when you're not looking, something is sure to capture your gaze. The sensory overload isn't just visual. Your soul may be soothed by the refreshing smell of clean river water and cleaner air, your taste buds will be tantalized by the freshest fruits and vegetables, and your skin will be caressed by the purest natural soaps.

A natural fortress, the island protected the Caribs (the region's original inhabitants) against European colonization. The rugged northeast is still reserved as home to the last survivors of the Caribs, along with their traditions and mythology.

Dominica—with a population of approximately 72,000—did eventually become a British colony. It attained independence in November 1978 and has a seat in the United Nations as the central Caribbean's only natural World Heritage Site. Its official language is English, although most locals communicate with each other in Creole; roads are driven on the left; family and place-names are a mélange of English, Carib, and French; and the economy is still heavily dependent on agriculture.

Dominica is an ideal place to be active—hike, bike, trek, kayak, dive, snorkel, or sail in marine reserves. Explore the rain forests, waterfalls, and geothermal springs, or search for whales and dolphins. Discover Dominica's vibrant Carib culture. To experience Dominica is really to know Earth as it was created.

LOGISTICS

Getting to Dominica: There are no nonstops from the United States, so you'll have to transfer in the British Virgin Islands, Antigua, Barbados, Martinique, San Juan, St. Maarten. There is also a ferry (90 minutes) from Guadeloupe or Martinique.

Hassle Factor: High.

On the Ground: Taxis and minibuses are available at the airports and in Roseau as well as at most hotels and guesthouses. Rates are fixed by the government (if you share a taxi with other passengers going in the same direction, you can negotiate a special price; a trip from Douglas-Charles Airport to Roseau can cost as little as $30 per person). Taxi drivers also offer tours anywhere on the island beginning at $30 an hour for up to four people; a four- to five-hour island tour costs approximately $150. It's best to get a recommendation from your hotel. You can recognize a taxi or minibus by the H, HA, and HB plates; simply flag them down or make your way to the nearest bus stop.

PLANNING

WHEN TO GO

Dominicans boast that they have the most spontaneous carnival in the region, Mas Domnik. It's fun to join a band, get all costumed and painted, and revel in the streets during Carnival Monday and Tuesday. Celebrations usually heat up the last 10 days or so before Ash Wednesday. Independence Day on November 3 celebrates not only Dominica's independence from Great Britain, but also the creole culture. On the last weekend in October or first weekend of November, the awesome, three-day Annual World Creole Music Festival draws performers and creole music enthusiasts from around the globe.

The high season is December to April, when many Americans and Europeans come. May 1 to November 1 is hurricane season.

GETTING HERE AND AROUND

AIR TRAVEL

There are no nonstops from the United States. Note that LIAT is not the most reliable airline; if you're flying them, it pays to double-check your reservation and to get to the airport with lots of time to spare.

Airport Contacts Canefield Airport (*DCF*). Canefield Airport (DCF) is served by only a few small Caribbean-based airlines. ⚠ **There is no longer a tourist information office at this airport.** ✉ *Canefield.* **Douglas-Charles Airport** (*DOM*). Douglas-Charles Airport (DOM)—formerly known as Melville Hall Airport—where most flights arrive, is 75 minutes from Roseau. ✉ *Marigot* ☎ *767/445–7101.*

Airline and Travel Agent Contacts Air Sunshine. Air Sunshine flies daily from San Juan via St. Thomas, USVI. Depending on the departure, flights take from two to four hours. ☎ *800/327–8900 in U.S. and Canada, 954/434–8900 in Dominica* 🌐 *www.airsunshine.com.* **BVI Airlines.** BVI Airlines flies from Tortola, in the British Virgin Islands, and from St. Maarten to Dominica (Douglas-Charles

Airport) on Mondays, Wednesdays, and Saturdays. Flights can be booked online or through the Witchurch Travel Agency. ☎ *919/523–7094 in Tortola* 🌐 *www.bvi-airlines.com.* **LIAT.** LIAT flies from Douglas-Charles Airport. ☎ *767/445–7242* 🌐 *www.liatairline.com.* **Seaborne Airlines.** Seaborne Airlines flies daily from San Juan, Puerto Rico. SuperSaver fares are sometimes offered online. ☎ *866/359–8784, 767/445–8936* 🌐 *www.seaborneairlines.com.* **Winair.** Depending on the season, Winair flies from St. Maarten to Dominica two to four times per week. ☎ *866/466–0410 in U.S.* 🌐 *www.fly-winair.sx.*

BOAT AND FERRY TRAVEL

There is a ferry (90 minutes) from Guadeloupe or Martinique.

Express des Isles. Express des Isles has regularly scheduled interisland jet catamaran ferry service connecting Dominica to Martinique, Guadeloupe, and St. Lucia. The ferry departs from Roseau and travels to Martinique on Monday, Wednesday, Friday, Saturday, and Sunday. (Schedules are subject to change.) From Guadeloupe, it continues south to St. Lucia. The Martinique round-trip crossing costs €129 and takes approximately 90 minutes. The voyage offers superb views of the other islands. Tickets can be booked through Whitchurch Travel Agency. ✉ *H.V. Whitchurch & Co. Ltd., Old St., Roseau* 🌐 *www.express-des-iles.com.*

CAR TRAVEL

Unless you are staying in Roseau or doing extensive guided tours, a car may be a necessity. Cabs can be very expensive. Daily car-rental rates begin at about $35 to $70 (weekly and long-term rates can be negotiated). A refundable US$1,200 deposit or credit card confirmation is required at the time of pickup. You'll need to buy a visitor's driving permit for $12 at one of the airports or at the Traffic Division office on High Street in Roseau or at vehicle-rental offices. Gasoline stations are all over the island; gas costs considerably more than in the United States. Driving in Dominica is on the left side, though you can rent vehicles with a steering wheel on either the left or the right.

Contacts Best Deal Rent-A-Car ✉ *15 Hanover St., Roseau* ☎ *767/449–9204, 767/616–3325* 🌐 *bestdealrentacar.dm.* **Courtesy Car Rental.** There are two locations: one at that Douglas-Charles Airport and one in the town of Roseau. ✉ *10 Winston La., Goodwill* ☎ *767/448–7763 Roseau, 767/445–7677 Melville Hall Airport* 🌐 *www.dominicacarrentals.com.* **Island Car Rentals** ✉ *Canefield Airport, Canefield Hwy., Canfield* ☎ *767/255–6844* 🌐 *www.islandcar.dm.* **Road Runner Car Rental.** At all its non-Portsmouth locations, the reasonably priced Road Runner Car Rental will deliver and pick up cars at no charge. ✉ *Canefield Airport, Canefield Hwy., Canfield* ☎ *767/275–5337* 🌐 *www.roadrunnercarrental.com.*

TAXI TRAVEL

Contacts CombineTaxi. There are fixed rates from Douglas-Charles Airport to different parts of the island. To Picard/Portsmouth, it's $26; a shared taxi from the airport to Roseau runs $30–$35. Other prices are calculated by distance. ☎ *767/275-6005.* **Dominica Taxi Association.** Dominica Taxi Association has fixed rates from the airport to different parts of the island. From Douglas-Charles Airport to Portsmouth/Picard, rates are $26. A shared taxi from Douglas-Charles to Roseau is $30–$35. Other destinations run from $15–$40. ☎ *767/275–8533, 767/449–8533.*

ESSENTIALS

Banks and Exchange Services The official currency is the Eastern Caribbean dollar (EC$). The exchange rate hovers around EC$2.70 to the US$1. U.S. dollars and major credit cards are widely accepted. You can find ATMs in all the banks in Roseau and airports as well as some in larger villages such as Portsmouth. They dispense EC dollars only and accept international bank cards.

Passport Requirements Valid passport plus a return or onward ticket.

Phones To call Dominica from the United States, dial the area code (767) and the local access code (44), followed by the five-digit local number. On the island, dial only the seven-digit number that follows the area code.

Safety Petty crime can be a problem on Dominica, as with nearly all destinations in the world. It's always wise to secure valuables in the hotel safe and not carry too much money or many valuables around. Remember that if you rent a car to tour the island, you may have to park it in a remote area; don't leave valuables in your vehicle while you're off on a hike or a tour.

Taxes and Service Charges The departure-embarkation tax is EC$59, or about US$23, payable in cash only at the airport at the time of departure from the island. Hotels collect 10%, plus a 10% service charge. Restaurants collect a 15% government V.A.T. (value-added tax).

Tipping Most hotels and restaurants add a 10% service charge to your bill. A 5% tip for exceptionally good service on top of the service charge is always welcome; otherwise just tip accordingly.

Travel Agents **Whitchurch Travel Agency.** This local travel agency can help you book flights on local airlines and passage on ferries. It's open weekdays from 8 am to 4:30 pm, Saturday from 8 am to 1 pm. ✉ *Old St.* ☎ *767/448–2181* ✉ *customerservice@whitchurch.com.*

ACCOMMODATIONS

There are a few upscale options in Dominica and no large resorts. Most accommodations are in small lodges and guesthouses, but you can also arrange a homestay in the Carib Territory.

Hotel reviews have been shortened. For full information, visit Fodors.com.

WHAT IT COSTS IN U.S. DOLLARS

	$	$$	$$$	$$$$
Restaurants	under $12	$12–$20	$21–$30	over $30
Hotels	under $275	$275–$375	$376–$475	over $475

Restaurant prices are the average cost of a main course at dinner or, if dinner is not served, at lunch. Hotel prices are the lowest cost of a standard double room in high season.

VISITOR INFORMATION

Discover Dominica Authority. The main tourism office is in the Financial Centre (open year-round Monday through Wednesday until 4 pm and later during the high season), but there's also a small branch at the airport and another at the ferry terminal in Roseau. The Discover Dominica Authority's information offices at the bay front (Dame Charles Boulevard) can recommend hiking guides. ✉ *Financial Centre, Kennedy Ave.* ☎ *767/448–2045, 866/522–4057 in U.S.* 🌐 *www.discoverdominica.com.*

WEDDINGS

Two days' minimum residency, a valid passport, original birth certificate, and divorce decree or death certificate for the former spouse (if applicable) is required. The parties must sign a statutory declaration on marital status, which must be obtained and sworn in Dominica in the presence of a local lawyer. At least two witnesses must be present at the ceremony.

EXPLORING

Despite the small size of this island, it can take a couple of hours to travel between the popular destinations. Many sights are isolated and difficult to find; you may be better off taking an organized excursion. If you do go it alone, drive carefully; roads can be narrow and winding. Plan at least eight hours to see the highlights. To fully experience the island, set aside about five days so you can enjoy the water and take some hikes.

ROSEAU

Although it's one of the smallest capitals in the Caribbean, Roseau has the highest concentration of inhabitants of any town in the eastern Caribbean. Caribbean vernacular architecture and a bustling marketplace transport visitors back in time. Although you can walk the entire town in about an hour, you'll get a much better feel for the place on a leisurely stroll.

For some years now, the Society for Historical Architectural Preservation and Enhancement (SHAPE) has organized programs and projects to preserve the city's architectural heritage. Several interesting buildings have already been restored. **Lilac House,** on Kennedy Avenue, has three types of gingerbread fretwork, latticed veranda railings, and heavy hurricane shutters. The **J.W. Edwards Building,** at the corner of Old and King George V streets, has a stone base and a wooden second-floor gallery. The **Old Market Plaza** is the center of Roseau's historic district, which was laid out by the French on a radial plan rather than a grid, so streets such as Hanover, King George V, and Old radiate from this area. South of the marketplace is the Fort Young Hotel, built as a British fort in the 18th century; the nearby statehouse, public library, and Anglican cathedral are also worth a visit. New developments at the bay front on Dame M.E. Charles Boulevard have brightened up the waterfront.

TOP ATTRACTIONS

FAMILY **Botanical Gardens.** The 40-acre Botanical Gardens, founded in 1891 as an annex of London's Kew Gardens, is a great place to relax, stroll, or watch a cricket match. In addition to the extensive collection of tropical plants and trees, there's also a parrot aviary. At the Forestry Division office, which is also on the garden grounds, you can find numerous publications on the island's flora, fauna, and national parks. The forestry officers are particularly knowledgeable on these subjects and can also recommend good hiking guides. ✉ *Valley Rd., Roseau* ☎ *767/266–3807, 767/266–3812* 🌐 *www.da-academy.org/dagardens.html* 🎫 *Free* 🕐 *Daily 8–4.*

WORTH NOTING

Dominica Museum. The old post office now houses the Dominica Museum. This labor of love by local writer and historian Dr. Lennox Honychurch contains furnishings, documents, prints, and maps that date back hundreds of years; you can also find an entire Carib hut as well as Carib canoes, baskets, and other artifacts. Normally closed on Sunday, the museum will open up when a cruise ship is in town. ✉ *Dame M.E. Charles Blvd., opposite cruise-ship berth, Roseau* ☎ *767/448–2401* 🎫 *$3* 🕐 *Weekdays 9–4, Sat. 9–noon.*

Old Mill Cultural Centre Museum. At this landmark, the island's first sugarcane processing mill and rum distillery, you can see exhibits of the island's heritage including costumes worn during Carnival and posters of sugar and coffee processing. ✉ *Canefield* ☎ *767/449–1804, 767/266–3421* 🎫 *Free (donations accepted)* 🕐 *Mon. 8–5; Tues.–Fri. 8–4.*

SOUFRIÈRE

Tourism is quietly mingling with the laid-back lifestyle of the residents of this gently sunbaked village in the southwest, near one of the island's two marine reserves. Although it was first settled by French lumbermen in the 17th century, it's mainly fishermen you'll find here today. In the village sits one of the island's prettiest churches, a historic 18th-century Catholic church built of volcanic stone. The ruins of the L. Rose Lime Oil factory; Sulphur Springs, with its hot mineral baths to the east; and some of the best diving and snorkeling on the island is within the **Soufrière/Scotts Head Marine Reserve.** To the west is Bois Cotlette (a historic plantation house) and to the south the Scotts Head Peninsula—at the island's southern tip—which separates the Caribbean from the Atlantic.

WORTH NOTING

The Waitukubuli National Trail. On an island that already brims with fabulous hiking tracks, this 114-mile trail is like the icing on the cake. In its 14 segments, paths wind from the southern part of the island at Scotts Head to Capuchin up north. As they make their way down rivers and up mountains, trekkers pass through woodlands, gorges, waterfalls, and lush rain forests. The trails weave through Ft. Shirley and Carib villages, in some places following old runaway-slave trails. Paths and signage are sometimes hard to find, as the project is still a work in progress. Yellow and blue markings are on rocks, sticks, poles, and sometimes embedded into the ground. Pick and choose the segments that most interest you. Those ambitious enough to do the whole trail—which can take about a week—will come away with an intimate knowledge of the island's terrain and unique history. Via the Kalinago Home Stay, you can even stay overnight in a house or hut in Carib Territory. It is US$12 for a day pass or US$40 for a 15-day pass on any of the 14 segments. Passes are mandatory and available at the Forestry and Wildlife Division, the Waitukubuli Trail Headquarters in Pont Casse, and at vendors near the trail segments (see ⇨ *Where to Stay*). ☏ *767/266–3593, 767/440–6125* 🌐 *www.waitukubulitrail.com.*

NORTHEAST COAST

Steep cliffs, dramatic reefs, and rivers that swirl down through forests of mangroves and fields of coconut define this section of Dominica. The road along the Atlantic, with its red cliffs, whipped-cream waves, and windswept trees, crosses the Hatton Garden River before entering the village of Marigot. In the northeastern region there are numerous estates—old family holdings planted with fruit trees. Beyond Marigot and the Douglas-Charles Airport is the beautiful Londonderry Estate. The beach here is inspiring, with driftwood strewn about its velvety black sands, which part halfway where the Londonderry River spills into the Atlantic (swimming isn't advised because of strong currents, but a river bath here is a memorable treat). Farther along the coast, beyond the village of Wesley (which has a gas station and a shop that sells wonderful bread) and past Eden Estate, there are still more beautiful beaches and coves. The swimming is excellent at Woodford Hill Bay, Hodges Beach, Hampstead Estate, Batibou Bay, and L'Anse Tortue (Turtle Bay), where you might glimpse a turtle plodding on the beach to lay her eggs. At the charming community of Calibishie you'll find beach bars and restaurants, as well as laid-back villas and guesthouses. At Bense, a village in the interior just past Calibishie, you can take a connector road to Chaudiere, a beautiful swimming spot in a valley; the only crowd you're likely to encounter is a group of young villagers frolicking in the 15-foot-deep pool and diving off the 25-foot-high rocks.

PORTSMOUTH

In 1782, Portsmouth was the site of the Battle of Les Saintes, a naval engagement between the French and the English. The English won the battle but lost the much tougher fight against malaria-carrying mosquitoes that bred in the nearby swamps. Once intended to be the capital, thanks to its superb harbor on Prince Rupert Bay, Portsmouth saw as many as 400 ships in port at one time in its heyday. But because of those swamps, Roseau, not Portsmouth, is the capital today. Maritime traditions are continued here by the yachting set, and a 2-mile (3-km) stretch of sandy beach fringed with coconut trees runs to the Picard Estate area.

ELSEWHERE ON DOMINICA

TOP ATTRACTIONS

FAMILY **Cabrits National Park.** Along with Brimstone Hill in St. Kitts, Shirley Heights in Antigua, and Ft. Charlotte in St. Vincent, the Cabrits National Park's Ft. Shirley ruins are among the most significant historic sites in the Caribbean. Just north of the town of Portsmouth, this 1,300-acre park includes a marine park and herbaceous swamps, which are home to several species of rare birds and plants. At the heart of the park is the Ft. Shirley military complex. Built by the British between 1770 and 1815, it once comprised 50 major structures, including storehouses that were also quarters for 700 men. With the help of the Royal Navy (which sends sailors ashore to work on the site each time a ship is in port) and local volunteers, historian Dr. Lennox Honychurch restored the fort and its surroundings, incorporating a small museum that highlights the natural and historic aspects of the park and an open canteen-style restaurant. ✉ *Portsmouth* 🎫 *$5* ⏲ *Museum daily 9–5.*

FAMILY **Emerald Pool.** Quite possibly the most visited nature attraction on the island, this emerald-green pool fed by a 50-foot waterfall is an easy trip to make. To reach this spot in the vast Morne Trois Pitons National Park, you follow a trail that starts at the side of the road near the reception center (it's an easy 20-minute walk). Along the way, there are lookout points with views of the windward (Atlantic) coast and the forested interior. If you don't want a crowd, check whether there are cruise ships in port before going out, as this spot is popular with cruise-ship tour groups. ✉ *Morne Trois Pitons National Park* 🎫 *US$3 for pre-organized tours; US$5 for private and stay-over visitors; US$12 weekly-site pass for all national parks.*

Morne Trois Pitons National Park. A UNESCO World Heritage Site, this 17,000-acre swath of lush, mountainous land in the south-central interior (covering 9% of Dominica) is the island's crown jewel. Named after one of the highest (4,600 feet) mountains on the island, it contains the island's famous "boiling lake," majestic waterfalls, and cool mountain lakes. There are four types of vegetation zones here. Ferns grow 30 feet tall, wild orchids sprout from trees, sunlight leaks through green canopies, and a gentle mist rises over the jungle floor. A system of trails has been developed in the park, and the Division of Forestry and Wildlife works hard to maintain them—with no help from the excessive rainfall and the profusion of vegetation that seems to grow right before your eyes. Access to the park is possible from most points, though the easiest approaches are via the small mountaintop villages of Laudat (pronounced lau-*dah*) and Cochrane.

About 5 miles (8 km) out of Roseau, the Wotten Waven Road branches off toward Sulphur Springs, where you can see the belching, sputtering, and gurgling releases of volcanic hot springs. At the base of Morne Micotrin you can find two crater lakes: the first, at 2,500 feet above sea level, is **Freshwater Lake.** According to a local legend, it's haunted by a vindictive mermaid and a monstrous serpent. Farther on is **Boeri Lake,** fringed with greenery and purple hyacinths floating on its surface.

On your way to Boiling Lake you pass through the **Valley of Desolation,** a sight that definitely lives up to its name. Harsh sulfuric fumes have destroyed virtually all the vegetation in what must once have been a lush forested area. Small hot and cold streams with water of various colors—black, purple, red, orange—web the valley. Stay on the trail to avoid breaking through the crust that covers the hot lava. During this hike you'll pass rivers where you can refresh yourself with a dip (a particular treat is a soak in a hot-water stream on the way back). At the beginning of the Valley of Desolation trail is the **TiTou Gorge,** where you can swim in the pool or relax in the hot-water springs along one side. If you're a strong swimmer, you can head up the gorge to a cave (it's about a five-minute swim) that has a magnificent waterfall; a crack in the cave about 50 feet above permits a stream of sunlight to penetrate the cavern.

Also in the national park are some of the island's most spectacular waterfalls. The 45-minute hike to **Sari Sari Falls,** accessible through the east-coast village of La Plaine, can be hair-raising. But the sight of water cascading some 150 feet into a large pool is awesome. So large are these falls that you feel the spray from hundreds of yards away. Just beyond the village of Trafalgar and up a short hill is the reception facility, where you can purchase passes to the national park and find guides to take you on a rain-forest trek to the twin **Trafalgar Falls**; the 125-foot-high waterfall is called the Father, and the wider, 95-foot-high one, the Mother. If you like a little challenge, let your guide take you to the riverbed and the cool pools at the base of the falls (check whether there's a cruise ship in port before setting out; this sight is popular with the tour operators). You need a guide for the arduous 75-minute hike to **Middleham Falls.** It's best if you start at Laudat (the turnoff for the trailhead is just before the village); the trip is much longer from Cochrane Village. The trail takes you to another spectacular waterfall, where water cascades 100 feet over boulders and vegetation and then into an ice-cold pool (a swim here is absolutely exhilarating). Guides for these hikes are available at the trailheads; still, it's best to arrange a tour before setting out. *US$3 for pre-organized tours; US$5 per site for private and stay-over visitors; US$12 weekly pass for all national parks.*

WORTH NOTING

FAMILY **Carib Indian Territory.** In 1903, after centuries of conflict, the Caribbean's first settlers, the Kalinago (more popularly known as the Caribs), were granted approximately 3,700 acres of land on the island's northeast coast. Here a hardened lava formation, **L'Escalier Tête Chien** (Snake's Staircase), runs down into the Atlantic. The name is derived from a snake whose head resembles that of a dog. The ocean alongside Carib Territory is particularly fierce, and the shore is full of countless coves and inlets. According to Carib legend, every night the nearby Londonderry Islets transform into grand canoes to take the spirits of the dead out to sea.

A chief administers the Carib Territory, where about 3,000 natives reside. The reservation's Catholic church in Salybia has a canoe as its altar, which was designed by Dr. Lennox Honychurch, a local historian, author, and artist.

The Kalinago people resemble native South Americans and are mostly farmers and fishermen. Others are entrepreneurs who have opened restaurants, guesthouses, and little shops that offer exquisite baskets and handcrafted items. Craftspeople have retained their knowledge of basket weaving, wood carving, and canoe building through generations. They fashion long, elegant canoes from the trunk of a single *gommier* tree. 🌐 *www.caribterritory.com.*

FAMILY **Indian River.** The mouth of the Indian River, which flows into the ocean at Portsmouth, was once a Carib Indian settlement. A rowboat ride down this river, which was featured in *Pirates of the Caribbean: Dead Man's Chest,* is both relaxing and educational. The river is lined with trees whose buttress roots spread up to 20 feet. Clear, brackish water is a playground for young barracudas and crayfish. Except for singing yellow warblers, flitting hummingbirds, or wing-flapping egrets, there is an eerie silence. To arrange such a trip, stop by the visitor center in Portsmouth and ask for one of the "Indian River boys," of the Portsmouth Indian River Tour Guides Association. Most boat trips take you up as far as Rahjah's Jungle Bar. You can usually do an optional guided walking tour of the swamplands and the remnants of one of Dominica's oldest plantations. Tours last one to three hours, for roughly $20–40 per person, but the actual price depends on your guide.

Kalinago Barana Autê. You might catch canoe builders at work at Kalinago Barana Autê, the Carib Territory's place to learn about Kalinago customs, history, and culture. A guided, 45-minute tour explores the village, stopping along the way to see some traditional dances and to learn about plants, dugout canoes, basket weaving, and cassava bread making. The path offers wonderful views of the Atlantic and a chance to glimpse Isukulati Falls. There's also a good souvenir shop. ✉ *Crayfish River, Salybia* ☎ *767/445–7979* 🌐 *www.kalinagobaranaaute.com* 🎟 *$10* ⏲ *Daily 9–5.*

FAMILY **Morne Diablotin National Park.** Here Dominica's highest mountain, Morne Diablotin, soars 4,747 feet. The peak takes its name from a bird known in English as the black-capped petrel. Now extinct on the island, it was prized by hunters in the 18th century. Dominica is still a major birding destination with many exotic—and endangered—species such as the green-and-purple Sisserou parrot (*Amazona imperialis*) and the Jaco, or red-neck, parrot (*Amazona arausiaca*). Before this national park was established, its Syndicate Nature Trail was aided by some 6,000 schoolchildren—each donated 25¢ to protect the area's habitat. The west-coast road (at the bend near Dublanc) runs through three types of forest and leads to the park. The trail offers a casual walk; just bring a sweater and binoculars. But the five- to eight-hour hike up Morne Diablotin is no walk in the park. You will need a guide, sturdy hiking shoes, warm clothing, and a backpack with refreshments and a change of clothes (including socks). All should be wrapped in plastic to keep them dry.

Emerald Pool is one of Dominica's most popular natural attractions.

BEACHES

Most of Dominica's beaches are in the north and east; they are windswept, dramatic, and uncrowded, lending themselves more to relaxing than swimming. That is because many have undercurrents. Slightly farther north there are beautiful secluded beaches and coves. Although northeast-coast beaches offer excellent shallow swimming, their wind-tossed beauty can be dangerous; there are sometimes strong currents with the frothy waves. From these beaches you can see the islands of Marie-Galante and Les Saintes and parts of Guadeloupe. On the southwest coast, beaches are fewer and made mostly of black sand and rounded volcanic rocks. In general, the west coast is more for scuba diving and snorkeling than for lounging on the beach.

FAMILY **Champagne.** On the west coast, just south of the village of Pointe Michel, this stony beach is hailed as one of the best spots for swimming, diving, and (especially) snorkeling. Forget the sunning, though, because the beach is strewn with rocks. Champagne gets its name from volcanic vents that constantly puff steam into the sea, which makes you feel as if you are swimming in warm champagne. A boardwalk leads to the beach from Soufrière/Scotts Head Marine Reserve. **Amenities:** none. **Best for:** snorkeling; swimming. ⊠ *1 mile (1½ km) south of Pointe Michel, Soufrière.*

FAMILY **Hampstead Beach.** This isolated gold-with-speckled-black-sand shoreline on the northeast coast actually encompasses three bays. It is divided into two beaches. The Red River meets the sea at Hampstead Beach I. This is where Johnny Depp was chased by natives in *Pirates of the Caribbean:*

Dead Man's Chest. The palm tree–lined Hampstead Beach II is on the sheltered and calm Batibou Bay. A 4x4 is the preferred mode of transportation to get here—or be prepared to hike in from the road. Both beaches ooze with charm and are worth the effort. **Amenities:** none. **Best for:** solitude; swimming. ✉ *Off Indian Rd., west of Calibishie.*

L'Anse Tortue. On the northeast coast, this isolated, golden-sand beach with dabs of black is also known as Turtle Bay. It is a favorite for egg-laying turtles and for those who want seclusion without having to drive all the way out to Hampstead Beach. Sitting on a cove just past Woodford Hill, it's an easy, although sometimes steep, walk down from the road. There is no sign marking the trail or the beach, but it starts just across the road from a brown-building snack shop with Fanta signs. This is another BYOBC (bring your own beach chair) beach with no amenities. It's charm is its solitude and beauty. **Amenities:** none. **Best for:** solitude. ✉ *East of Calibishie.*

Mero Beach. The closest beach to Roseau, this silver-gray stretch of beach on the west coast, is just outside the village of Mero. Waters are warm and calm. The entire community comes here on Sunday. This is one of the few beaches with amenities. **Amenities:** food and drink; showers; toilets. **Best for:** partiers; swimming. ✉ *Near Roseau, Mero.*

FAMILY **Pointe Baptiste.** Extravagantly shaped red-sandstone boulders surround this beautiful golden-sand beach. Access is a 15-minute walk, entering through private property (Pointe Baptiste Guest House or Red Rock Haven), so the beach is quiet and unpopulated. It is the place to relax, take a dip, or climb the incredible rock formations. The Red Rock Haven luxury hotel is just behind it, so you can grab a snack at its Escape Beach Bar & Grill. **Amenities:** food and drink. **Best for:** solitude; swimming. ✉ *Calibishie.*

Scotts Head. At the southernmost tip of the island, a small landmass is connected to the mainland by a narrow stretch of stony beach. It's a fantastic spot for snorkeling and diving. You can lunch at one of the village restaurants, where you'll always find fresh-caught red snapper and mahimahi. On the beach, there's also a small snack shop and a couple of vendors. **Amenities:** food and drink. **Best for:** snorkeling; swimming. ✉ *Near Soufriére, Scotts Head Village.*

WHERE TO EAT

You can expect an abundance of vegetables, fruits, and root crops to appear on menus around the island. Dominica's economy, after all, is based on agriculture. Sweet ripe plantains, *kushkush* (cornmeal), yams, breadfruit, dasheen (also called taro), fresh fish, and chicken prepared at least a dozen different ways are all staples. The local drink is a spiced rum steeped with herbs such as anisette (called nanny) and *pweve* (lemongrass). Dominican cuisine is also famous for its use of local game, such as the *manicou* (a small opossum) and the *agouti* (a large indigenous rodent), but you'll have to be an intrepid diner to go that route. The government has banned "mountain chicken" (a euphemism for a large frog called *crapaud*) because a fungal disease, overhunting, and other problems have greatly reduced its numbers.

What to Wear: Most Dominicans dress nicely but practically when eating out—for dinner it's shirts and trousers for men and modest dresses for women. During the day, nice shorts are acceptable at most places; beach attire is frowned on unless you're eating on the beach.

$$ ECLECTIC **The Banana Tree.** This former garage has become the only true grill on the island. It boasts "cool drinks, great food." The menu includes prime steaks, pasta, and seafood as well as creole food and jerk chicken. The bar stools here are anchored by old tires, and a selection of vittles like the 4x4 (ribs) and 6 Cylinders (spicy chicken wings) also recall the space's former incarnation. In early evening, it is a very happening place with the locals. Breakfast, lunch, and dinner are served. *Average main: US$14 ✉ 15 Hanover St., at Kennedy Ave., Roseau ☎ 767/448–5433.*

$ ECLECTIC FAMILY **Cocorico.** It's hard to miss this bright yellow-and-blue Parisian-style café on a prominent bay-front corner in Roseau. Breakfast crepes, croissants, baguette sandwiches, and piping-hot café au lait are available beginning at 8:30 am. Dinner is now served on Friday and Saturday (about US$17). Throughout the day you can relax indoors or out and enjoy any of the extensive menu selections with the perfect glass of wine. You can also surf the Internet on its computers. In the cellar downstairs, the Cocorico wine store has a reasonably priced selection from more than eight countries, plus a wide assortment of pâtés and cheeses, crepes, sausages, cigars, French bread, and chocolates. *Average main: US$10 ✉ Bay front at Kennedy Ave., Roseau ☎ 767/449–8686 cocoricocafe.com Closed Sun. unless a ship is in port. No dinner Mon.–Thurs. and Sun.*

$$ CARIBBEAN **Guiyave.** This popular restaurant in a quaint Caribbean town house also has a shop downstairs serving a scrumptious selection of sweet and savory pastries, tarts, and cakes, which can also be ordered upstairs, along with breakfast and a Caribbean buffet for lunch. Choose to dine either in the airy dining room or on the sunny, narrow balcony perched above Roseau's colorful streets—the perfect spot to have a freshly squeezed tropical juice. *Average main: US$16 ✉ 15 Cork St., Roseau ☎ 767/448–2930 Closed Sun. No dinner.*

$ CARIBBEAN **Miranda's Corner.** Just past Springfield on the way to Pont Casse, you'll begin to see hills full of flowers. At a big bend, a sign on a tree reads "Miranda's Corner," referring to a bar, rum shop, and diner all in one. Here Miranda Alfred is at home, serving everyone from Italian tourists to banana farmers. Many of her ingredients are grown in her adjacent garden. The specialties are numerous, including tropical juices and *titiree,* fish balls made from a type of fish called titiree, which are served only in season. All the dishes are prepared with a potion of passion and a fistful of flavor. Miranda's is open for breakfast, lunch, and dinner and is a great pit stop if you are in the area; call ahead to make sure it's open. *Average main: US$11 ✉ Mount Joy, Springfield ☎ 767/449–2509.*

$$$$ ECLECTIC **Old Stone Bar and Grill.** Stone walls, lots of plants, and red accents make this restaurant near the waterfront a very cozy place. The menu offers tasty chicken, pork, seafood, and local dishes like coconut battered fish

is very good. The Old Stone's owner, Leonard Lewis, says they serve the biggest selection of specialty drinks on the island; many are made with fresh fruit. The very friendly waitstaff only enhances the experience. *Average main: US$32 ✉ 15 Castle St., Roseau ☎ 767/440–7549, 767/277–3652 ⊙ Closed Sun. No lunch.*

$$$ ECLECTIC FAMILY Fodor's Choice ★

Palisades Restaurant. At the southern end of Roseau's bay front, this elegant and romantic restaurant overlooks the Caribbean coastline. You can dine outdoors on the wraparound veranda while listening to the sounds of the sea or indoors in the air-conditioned formal dining room. The restaurant's menu incorporates spa-vegetarian choices alongside the traditional international and local dishes. The dishes range widely, including creole specialties like callaloo soup; beef, lamb, and duck dishes; and even skewered shrimp with a Thai sauce. Tropical desserts include cheesecake and guava tart. No matter what your choice, it will be served by a friendly and efficient waitstaff. Monday-night manager's cocktail is served in the Bala's Bar, followed by a Caribbean fusion buffet in the Marquis Restaurant. The steel pan band adds a nice touch to the night's events. Palisades Restaurant is closed in September and early October, but meals are served in the Marquis Restaurant, which has a regular Monday-night buffet. Snacks are available all day. *Average main: US$25 ✉ Fort Young Hotel, Victoria St., Roseau ☎ 767/448–5000 🌐 www.fortyounghotel.com ✍ Reservations essential ⊙ No lunch weekends. No dinner Mon.*

$$ CARIBBEAN

Pearl's Cuisine. Located in downtown Roseau, chef Pearl, with her robust and infectious character, prepares some of the island's best local cuisine, such as callaloo soup, fresh fish, and rabbit. Her menu changes daily, but she offers such local delicacies as souse (pickled pigs' feet), blood pudding, and rotis. When sitting down, ask for a table on the open-air gallery that overlooks Roseau. Servings are large here, but make sure you leave space for dessert. If you're on the go, enjoy a quick meal from the daily, varied menu in the ground-floor snack bar. You're spoiled for choice when it comes to the fresh fruit juices. *Average main: US$12 ✉ Sutton Place Hotel, 25 Old St., Roseau ☎ 767/448–8707 ⊙ Closed Sun. No dinner.*

$$ CARIBBEAN

Rainforest Restaurant at Papillote. Dine at an altitude cool enough to demand a throw blanket and warm enough to inspire after-dinner conversation. First, try a strong rum punch while lounging in a hot mineral bath in the Papillote Wilderness Retreat gardens. The menu has expanded but still offers the bracing callaloo soup, dasheen puffs, fish "rain forest" (marinated with papaya and wrapped in banana leaves), or other creole-style delicacies. This handsome Caribbean restaurant has quite possibly one of the best views in the region. *Average main: US$20 ✉ Papillote Wilderness Retreat, Trafalgar Falls Rd., Trafalgar ☎ 767/448–2287 🌐 www.papillote.dm ✍ Reservations essential ⊙ Closed Sept. and Oct.*

$$$ CARIBBEAN

Sea Surge Terrace Restaurant & Bar. You can find classic local food with a very elegant twist at this restaurant in the Evergreen Hotel. Selections include starters like fresh soup or salad made with local produce, authentic creole and international main courses, and, when in season, tasty crab backs. Breakfast, lunch, and dinner are served

10

daily. On Friday evenings there is entertainment as well as a special menu. The Lazy Sunday buffet, from 1 to 4 pm, features live music by one of Dominica's finest. *Average main: US$30 Evergreen Hotel, Castle Comfort 767/448–3288 www.evergreenhoteldominica.com Daily 7:15 am–9 pm.*

$$$$ ECLECTIC **TAO Lounge Bar & Grill.** Just across from the water sits a cottage that has been converted into a small bistro that's as lovely inside as it is on the patio. Dark woods decorate the interior; above the small bar is a portrait of Johnny Depp as Jack Sparrow in *Pirates of the Caribbean*. The menu features a mix of Peruvian, Japanese, Italian and international dishes as well as the more usual steaks, fish, and pork entrées. All are tastefully presented. Tao is the only place in Roseau that serves sushi—it's not quite traditional, but it is delicious. *Average main: US$34 7 Victoria St., south of Fort Young Hotel, Roseau 767/316–6666 No lunch Sat. Closed Sun.*

$$$ ECLECTIC **Zamaan Restaurant.** The setting, whether you sit out on the covered, open-air patio or inside the comfortable, beamed-ceiling dining room, is sublime, and the food is delicious and healthful. The chef is happy to accommodate any special dietary requests, including vegan, vegetarian, and gluten-free dishes. Expect a variety of entrées from roasted duck and lobster tail to curried goat (local-style) and coconut-curried seasonal vegetables. Many ingredients are grown in Rosalie Bay's own garden. *Average main: US$26 Rosalie Bay Resort, Rosalie 767/446–1010, 767/275–2680 www.rosaliebay.com Reservations essential.*

WHERE TO STAY

Many properties offer packages with dives, hikes, tours, and meal plans included, along with all the usual amenities. Some advertise winter rates with a discount for either summer or longer stays. You may also want to look into a stay among the Caribs, via Kalinago Territory Home Stay.

Kalinago Home Stays. Now you can experience life as the Kalinago (Carib) Indians live it by spending the night with a family and learning firsthand about their culture. Three different kinds of accommodations are offered: rooms in conventional residential homes (US$30 per night per person), with shared kitchens and bathrooms; in conventional/traditional homes (US$40), with their own facilities; and the most traditional option, thatched roof/wooden huts (US$50). Reservations must be made in advance, and meals are extra (breakfast and dinner US$10, lunch US$15, and snacks US$6). For more information, contact the program's organizer Kevin Dangleben by email. *Carib Territory kbamanger@cwdom.dm.*

$ HOTEL FAMILY **Anchorage Hotel.** Pioneers in Dominica's diving and whale-watching industry, the Anchorage Hotel attracts adventure seekers of every age, who come for these and other activities led by the in-house tour company. **Pros:** a fine range of water activities; wheelchair accessible; upstairs rooms have balconies; small meeting room. **Cons:** no-frills accommodations. *Rooms from: US$95 Castle Comfort*

☎ 767/448–2638, 888/790–5264 in U.S. 🌐 www.anchoragehotel.dm 🛏 32 rooms 🍴 No meals.

$ HOTEL **Atlantique View Resort & Spa.** Perched high on a hill overlooking the water, one of Dominica's newest properties has a lot to offer. **Pros:** free airport pickup; room service, breakfast included; entertainment, including live music and movies; a nonsmoking hotel. **Cons:** though there is a small private beach, it's a five-minute walk down the hill. *$ Rooms from: US$150 ✉ Anse De Mai ☎ 767/445–6719 🌐 atlantiqueview.com 🛏 35 rooms 🍴 Breakfast ☞ 2-night minimum.*

$ B&B/INN **Beau Rive.** Owner Mark Steele puts Zen-like elegance and creative soul into every detail of this secluded boutique hotel. **Pros:** lovely rooms; very good food; all rooms have fans and awesome ocean views; swimming pool. **Cons:** ocean is too rough for swimming; no TVs or room phones; no guests under 16 or a/c (though the latter is not needed). *$ Rooms from: US$190 ✉ Between Castle Bruce and Sineku ☎ 767/445–8992 🌐 www.beaurive.com 🛏 10 rooms ⏲ Closed Aug. and Sept. unless special arrangements made 🍴 Multiple meal plans ☞ 2-night minimum.*

BEST BETS FOR LODGING

BEST FOR ROMANCE
Beau Rive, Red Rock Haven, Secret Bay

BEST BEACHFRONT
Red Rock Haven

BEST POOL
Fort Young Hotel

BEST SERVICE
Calibishie Lodges, Fort Young Hotel

BEST FOR KIDS
Calibishie Lodges, Fort Young Hotel

$ HOTEL FAMILY Fodor's Choice ★ **Calibishie Lodges.** Within walking distance from one of Dominica's most picturesque seaside villages, these six self-contained one-bedroom suites emerge from behind terraced lemongrass. **Pros:** plenty of charm; people-pleasing owners; meal plans available; 20 minutes from Douglas-Charles airport. **Cons:** at least an hour's drive from Roseau; no a/c. *$ Rooms from: US$129 ✉ Calibishie Main Rd., Calibishie ☎ 767/445–8537 🌐 www.calibishie-lodges.com 🛏 6 suites 🍴 Multiple meal plans.*

$ HOTEL **Castle Comfort Lodge.** The boats anchored just off the pier, the telltale dive log, and the guests with mask imprints on their foreheads give it all away—this is the best dive lodge in Dominica. **Pros:** a favorite retreat for divers; good location; free Wi-Fi. **Cons:** rooms are very basic. *$ Rooms from: US$100 ✉ Castle Comfort ☎ 767/448–2188, 646/502–6800 in U.S., 888/414–7626 in U.S. 🌐 www.castlecomfortdivelodge.com 🛏 13 rooms ⏲ Closed Sept. 🍴 Some meals.*

$ B&B/INN **Cocoa Cottage.** This eco-sensitive, hand-built wood-and-stone lodge has a cozy tree-house feel, and, though very basic, it's still comfortable. **Pros:** immersive tropical mountain experience; artistic vibe; only 10 minutes from Roseau and 10 minutes from Morne Piton National Park. **Cons:** no-frills accommodations. *$ Rooms from: US$125 ✉ Trafalgar ☎ 767/448–0412, 767/276–2920 🌐 www.cocoacottages.com 🛏 6 rooms 🍴 Multiple meal plans.*

$ HOTEL **Comfort Cottages.** Like to do your own thing? **Pros:** a great deal; immersive tropical mountain experience; artistic vibe. **Cons:** a bit far removed and somewhat difficult to find. *Rooms from: US$149 Terre Platte, Blenhiem 767/445–3245 comfortcottages.com 4 rooms Breakfast.*

$ HOTEL FAMILY **Crescent Moon Cabins.** In a hidden valley full of waterfalls and a river, this small, family-run, forest resort is so deep in the bush that you might almost believe you're camping—except you have the benefit of basic, eco-friendly facilities with balconies and hammocks. **Pros:** one-of-a-kind property; excellent food. **Cons:** facilities are about two steps above camping; road here is difficult to navigate but recently improvements have been made. *Rooms from: US$140 Sylvania 767/449–3449 www.crescentmooncabins.com 4 cabins Closed Aug. and Sept. Multiple meal plans 2-night minimum.*

$ HOTEL FAMILY **Evergreen Hotel.** This family-run, modern, oceanfront inn is a non-diver's oasis in diver-friendly Castle Comfort. **Pros:** friendly staff; pleasant surroundings; breakfast included. **Cons:** though it's close to Roseau, it's a good idea to take a cab at night. *Rooms from: US$120 Castle Comfort 767/448–3288 www.evergreenhoteldominica.com 16 rooms, 1 cottage Breakfast.*

$ RESORT FAMILY Fodor's Choice ★ **Fort Young Hotel.** This hotel's street-level entrance and lobby are in an old stone fort, cannons and all. **Pros:** lovely property that is well located; cosmopolitan, friendly staff. **Cons:** issues for guests with disabilities. *Rooms from: US$131 Victoria St., Dutchman's Bay, Roseau 767/448–5000 www.fortyounghotel.com 73 rooms No meals.*

$ HOTEL FAMILY **Garraway Hotel.** Fronted by the bay, this city-style hotel on the western edge of Roseau offers lovely views from its higher floors—the rooms take in the town's quaint buildings, the ocean, and the imposing mountains. **Pros:** spacious rooms; well located in the heart of Roseau; free Wi-Fi. **Cons:** rooms are a bit sparse; lower-level rooms do not have good views. *Rooms from: US$95 Place Heritage, 1 Dame Eugenia Charles Blvd., Roseau 767/449–8800 garrawayhotel.com 20 rooms, 10 suites No meals.*

$ B&B/INN **Hummingbird Inn.** The ocean vistas, lushly fragrant garden, and naturally sensuous atmosphere at this hillside retreat provide the perfect setting for honeymooners and, needless to say, hummingbirds. **Pros:** gorgeous view; if you are into lizards, this is a sanctuary for the rare local iguana. **Cons:** very basic rooms; a charge for in-room TV; road to the property has a very steep turn and is challenging after it rains; no a/c. *Rooms from: US$75 Rock-A-Way, Canefield 767/449–1042 767/285–4285 www.thehummingbirdinn.com 9 rooms, 1 suite Breakfast.*

$ RENTAL FAMILY **Itassi Cottages.** You forget how close these three cottages are to Roseau as you swing on your hammock overlooking the ocean. **Pros:** very friendly atmosphere; great bang for your buck; weekly and monthly rates available. **Cons:** 20-minute drive to Mero, the closest beach. *Rooms from: US$60 Morne Bruce 767/449–8700 www.avirtualdominica.com/itassi 3 cottages No meals.*

Fort Young Hotel

$ RESORT **Jungle Bay Resort & Spa.** Sweeping views of the untamed Atlantic surround this luxury eco-resort, which sits on 55 acres of the only developed section of the island's southeast.

Pros: perfect for active vacationers; lovely rooms; outdoor showers; tours of the island offered. **Cons:** facility is remote; water is too rough for swimming; no a/c; long trek to many of the rooms; not wheelchair accessible. *Rooms from: US$244* *Point Mulatre* *767/446–1789, 917/338–3749* *www.junglebaydominica.com* *35 cottages* *Closed Sept.* *Multiple meal plans.*

$ B&B/INN **Pagua Bay House.** If you're after privacy and beautiful views, this is your place. **Pros:** nonmotorized sports equipment is complimentary, as is airport drop-off. **Cons:** because of the strong currents, you can't swim in the ocean; breakfast not included. *Rooms from: US$200* *Pagua Bay, Marigot* *767/445–8888* *www.paguabayhouse.com* *7 rooms* *No meals.*

10

$ B&B/INN FAMILY **Papillote Wilderness Retreat.** Luxuriant vegetation abounds in this retreat's 4 acres of gardens. **Pros:** lovely grounds; adjacent to Morne Trois Pitons National Park and close to Trafalgar Falls; only 10 minutes by car from Roseau. **Cons:** though bus service to and from Roseau is available, you'll probably want to rent a car. *Rooms from: US$139* *Trafalgar Falls Rd., Trafalgar* *767/448–2287* *www.papillote.dm* *3 rooms, 4 suites, 1 villa* *Closed Sept. and Oct.* *Some meals.*

$ B&B/INN FAMILY **Picard Beach Cottages.** Eighteen cottages, on the grounds of an old 6-acre coconut plantation and its lovely landscaped gardens, are just steps away from Dominica's longest grayish-sand beach. **Pros:** has some spa facilities; nice beach; free Wi-Fi. **Cons:** property is not well lit so it can be difficult to navigate at night without a flashlight; mosquitoes love this section of the island. *Rooms from: US$120 Prince Rupert Bay 767/445–5131 picardbeachcottages.dm 18 1-bedroom cottages No meals.*

$ HOTEL FAMILY **Red Rock Haven.** Perched above the secluded Pointe Baptise Beach and surrounded by lush landscape, these posh accommodations are accented with wood, stone, and bamboo, and also have laddered lofts for the kids. **Pros:** modern and lovely. **Cons:** steep paths, so difficult for people with mobility problems; you'll need a car. *Rooms from: US$125 Calibishie 767/445–7997 3 1-bedroom suites, 1 2-bedroom villa Breakfast.*

$ HOTEL **Rejens Hotel.** Located between the airport and Roseau, this group of Dominican-style suites is in quiet surroundings. **Pros:** very reasonably priced; nice set of amenities and handicap-accessible rooms. **Cons:** not on the beach. *Rooms from: US$91 Portsmouth 767/445–5577 www.rejens.com 6 standard suites, 3 deluxe suites, 4 social suites No meals.*

$ HOTEL Fodor'sChoice ★ **Rosalie Bay Resort.** It's hard not to be charmed by this boutique hotel, which is on 22 acres along the Atlantic Ocean and overlooks the Rosalie River. **Pros:** tranquil; beautiful surroundings; kid-friendly; discounts for stays of four nights or more. **Cons:** beach is small, and the currents make swimming dangerous. *Rooms from: US$225 Rosalie 767/446–1010, 877/732–2864 www.rosaliebay.com 28 rooms Breakfast.*

$ HOTEL FAMILY **Roseau Valley Hotel.** With tile floors and cheerful decor, this little hotel is quite inviting. **Pros:** reasonable and pleasant; kid-friendly; free parking, local calls, and Wi-Fi. **Cons:** a long walk to Roseau (but there is local bus service). *Rooms from: US$60 2 miles (3 km) east of Roseau, Roseau 767/449–8176, 767/225–7038 www.roseauvalleyhotel.com 11 rooms Breakfast.*

$$$ B&B/INN Fodor'sChoice ★ **Secret Bay.** Private and luxurious, the four villas and two bungalows here come with stunning panoramas and outdoor showers, plus lots of amenities—even a chef to cook two daily meals, which can be delivered to your accommodation ($55 per day fee plus cost of food). **Pros:** perfect honeymoon hideaway; open veranda; free Wi-Fi; nonmotorized sports complimentary. **Cons:** tiny beach; no children under 12; pricey for Dominica; no restaurant. *Rooms from: US$402 Tibay Beach, northwest part of island, Portsmouth 767/445–4444 www.secretbay.dm 6 rooms Some meals.*

$ HOTEL FAMILY **Sunset Bay Club & Seaside Dive Resort.** The simple but comfortable Sunset Bay Club & Seaside Dive Resort sits alongside the Batalie River on a stretch of Dominica's spectacular west coast. **Pros:** beautiful gardens and views; great food; kid-friendly; promotion rates for weeklong stays; kids under 12 stay free. **Cons:** very basic rooms; in-room TVs are extra. *Rooms from: US$132 Batalie Beach, Coulibistrie 767/446–6522 www.sunsetbayclub.com 12 rooms, 1 suite Breakfast.*

$ B&B/INN FAMILY **Tamarind Tree Hotel & Restaurant.** The warmth and friendliness of owners Annette and Stefan Loerner-Peyer are this small inn's most valuable asset. **Pros:** extremely friendly owners; good food; one of the owners is a certified tour guide. **Cons:** no-frills rooms. *Rooms* *from: US$94* ✉ *Salisbury* ☎ *767/449–7395, 767/449–7007* 🌐 *www.tamarindtreedominica.com* *15 rooms* ⏲ *Closed Sept.* 🍴 *Breakfast.*

$ HOTEL **Tia's Bamboo Cottages.** Tia himself built these charming but rustic cabins, which sit on the side of a hill, amid a picturesque, natural setting. **Pros:** proximity to river and natural springs; extremely helpful staff. **Cons:** cottages are sparsely furnished; strictly cash only. $ *Rooms from: US$65* ✉ *Wotton Waven, in Roseau Valley* ☎ *767/225–4823, 767/448–1998* *3 cottages* ▭ *No credit cards* ⏲ *Closed June* 🍴 *No meals.*

$ HOTEL **Zandoli Inn.** Overlooking a 111-foot cliff on the southeast Atlantic coast, this small inn has a stunning view—water and mountains. **Pros:** drop-dead vistas; full-service bar and restaurant. Snorkeling in the area is great. **Cons:** though there is a staircase, it's a steep walk to the beach, which is not the best place to take a plunge. $ *Rooms from: US$145* ✉ *Roche Cassée, Stowe* ☎ *767/446–3161* 🌐 *www.zandoli.com* *5 rooms* 🍴 *No meals.*

NIGHTLIFE AND PERFORMING ARTS

The friendly, intimate atmosphere and colorful patrons at the numerous bars and hangouts will keep you entertained for hours. Jazz, calypso, reggae, steel band, soca (a variation of calypso), and cadence-zouk, or jing ping—a type of folk music featuring the accordion, the *quage* (a kind of washboard instrument), drums, and a "boom boom" (a percussion instrument)—are all heard on the island. Wednesday through Saturday nights are really lively, and during Carnival, Independence, and summer celebrations, things can be intense. Indeed, Dominica's Carnival, the pre-Lenten festival, is the most spontaneous in the Caribbean. Other big cultural events include Emancipation celebrations hosted by the National Cultural Council each August.

NIGHTLIFE

Banana Leaf. Very popular with locals, this bar doesn't close until the last person leaves. ✉ *15 Hanover St., Roseau* ☎ *767/448–5433.*

Melvina's Champagne Bar & Restaurant. Melvina's Champagne Bar & Restaurant is a popular hangout for locals and tourists, especially on Friday and Saturday nights. ✉ *Pointe Michel Rd., Pointe Michel* ☎ *767/440–5480.*

Symes Zee's. At this crowd-pleasing bar, there's no cover, and the food, drinks, and cigars are reasonably priced. ✉ *34 King George V St., Roseau* ☎ *767/448–2494.*

PERFORMING ARTS

Arawak House of Culture. Arawak House of Culture, managed by Harry Sealy at the Cultural Division, is Dominica's main performing-arts theater. A number of productions are staged here throughout the year, including plays, recitals, and dance performances. ✉ *Kennedy Ave., near Government Headquarters, Roseau.*

Fodor's Choice ★ **World Creole Music Festival.** During the World Creole Music Festival, held for three days in late October or early November, fans come from all over the world to listen to the likes of Kassav, Aswad, and Tabou Combo. 🌐 *www.wcmfdominica.com.*

SHOPS AND SPAS

Dominicans produce distinctive handicrafts, with various communities specializing in their specific products. The crafts of the Carib Indians include traditional baskets made of dyed *larouma* reeds and waterproofed with tightly woven *balizier* leaves. These are sold in the Carib Indian Territory and Kalinago Barana Autê as well as in Roseau's shops. Vertivert straw rugs, screw-pine tableware, *fwije* (the trunk of the forest tree fern), and wood carvings are just some examples. Also notable are local herbs, spices, condiments, and herb teas. Café Dominique, the local equivalent of Jamaican Blue Mountain coffee, is an excellent buy, as are the Dominican rums Macoucherie and Soca. Proof that the old ways live on in Dominica can be found in the number of herbal remedies available. One stimulating memento of your visit is rum steeped with *bois bandé* (scientific name *Richeria grandis*), a tree whose bark is reputed to have aphrodisiacal properties. It's sold at shops, vendors' stalls, and supermarkets.

One of the easiest places to pick up a souvenir is the Old Market Plaza, just behind the Dominica Museum, in Roseau. Slaves were once sold here, but today handcrafted jewelry, T-shirts, spices, souvenirs, batik, and trays, plus lacquered and woven bamboo boxes, are available from a group of vendors in open-air booths set up on the cobblestones.

ART

Indigo. The tree-house studio and café at Indigo sells works by in-house artists Clem and Marie Frederick and also serves fresh sugarcane juice or bush teas. ✉ *Grandby Dr., Bournes* ☎ *767/445–3486* 🌐 *www.mariefrederickgallery.com.*

CLOTHING

For classic Caribbean and international designer clothing, there are several reliable boutiques to try. Kai-K, on the Dame Eugenia Charles Boulevard (bay front), is good for clothes made of linen. Desiderata, on King George V Street, has a good selection of clothing.

GIFTS AND SOUVENIRS

Achipelago Trading Ltd. For high-quality leather goods, alcohol, tobacco, Victrinox/Swiss Army products, and clothing, this is your place. Located next to the Royal Bank. ✉ *Leopold House, Bay Front, Roseau* ☎ *767/448–3394.*

Jewellers International. Jewellers International carries crystalware, liquor, and other gift items, such as gold and silver jewelry and baubles with emeralds, diamonds, and other gems. ✉ *Fort Young Hotel Complex, Dame Eugenia Charles Blvd., Bay Front, Roseau* ☎ *767/440–3319, 767/448–3394.*

Pirates. Pirates is the place for booze, Cuban cigars, cheese, watches, and souvenirs. It's open weekdays from 8 to 5. ✉ *6 Long La., Dupigmy Bldg., Roseau* ☎ *767/449–9774.*

Whitchurch Duty-Free. Whitchurch Duty-Free sells perfumes, leather goods, designer sunglasses, and many other items. ✉ *Fort Young Hotel, Victoria St., Roseau* ☎ *767/448–7177* 🌐 *www.whitchurch.com.*

HANDICRAFTS

Kalinago Barana Autê. Kalinago Barana Autê sells carvings, pottery, and lovely hand-woven baskets, which you can watch the women weave. ✉ *Salybia, Carib Territory* ☎ *767/445–7979* 🌐 *www.kalinagobaranaaute.com.*

Papillote Wilderness Retreat Gift Shop. Papillote Wilderness Retreat has a small gift shop with local handcrafted goods and particularly outstanding wood carvings by Louis Desire. ✉ *Trafalgar* ☎ *767/448–2287.*

SPAS

Screw's Sulfur Spas. Hidden in the bush here are sulfur-enriched, burping waters, fumaroles, and cascades—and Screw's. Experience mudpacks and wraps plus six pools, each a different temperature and depth. Screw—and that's his real name—doesn't let you leave without giving you fresh juice or fruit. Dominica's spas are a far reach from California's Golden Door or other lavish places, but then again that is their charm. ✉ *Wooten Waven* ☎ *767/440–4478* 🌐 *screwsspa.com* ⏲ *Tues.–Sun. 10–10.*

SPORTS AND THE OUTDOORS

10

ADVENTURE SPORTS

Extreme Dominica. Rappel alongside waterfalls, jump into clear pools, explore canyons in Dominica's lush rain forests or hike to Boiling Lake. Extreme Dominica will pick you up from Roseau, supply the necessary equipment, and offer a short training session before setting out on your wet adventure. All levels of experience can be accommodated. Prices begin at $75 per person for Boiling Lake to $160 per person for canyoning tours. ✉ *Cocoa Cottages, Trafalgar* ☎ *767/295–7272, 767/295–6828* 🌐 *www.extremedominica.com.*

FAMILY **Wacky Rollers.** Wacky Rollers will make you feel as if you are training for the marines as you swing on a Tarzan-style rope and grab onto a vertical rope ladder, rappel across zip lines, and traverse suspended log bridges, a net bridge, and four monkey bridges (rope loops). Including transportation, it costs $75 per person for the adult course and should take from 1½ to 3½ hours to conquer the 28 "games." There is also an abbreviated kids' course for $25 (kids 10 and under). Wacky Rollers also organizes adventure tours around the island plus kayak and tubing trips. Although the office is in Roseau, the park itself is in Hillsborough Estate, about 20 to 25 minutes north of Roseau. ✉ *Front St., Roseau* ☎ *767/440–4386, 767/616–8276* 🌐 *www.wackyrollers.com.*

DIVING AND SNORKELING

Fodor's Choice ★ Not only is Dominica considered one of the top 10 dive destinations in the world by *Skin Diver* and *Rodale's Scuba Diving* magazines, but it has won many other awards for its underwater sites. They are truly memorable. The west coast of the island has awesome sites, but the best are those in the southwest—within and around **Soufrière/Scotts Head Marine Reserve.** This bay is a submerged volcanic crater. The Dominica Watersports Association has worked along with the Fisheries Division for years to establish this reserve and has set stringent regulations to prevent the degradation of the ecosystem. Within ½ mile (¾ km) of the shore there are vertical drops from 800 feet to more than 1,500 feet, with visibility frequently extending to 100 feet. Shoals of boga fish, creole wrasse, and blue cromis are common, and you might even see a spotted moray eel or a honeycomb cowfish. Crinoids (rare elsewhere) are also abundant here, as are giant barrel sponges. There is a $2 fee per person to dive, snorkel, or kayak in the reserve. Other noteworthy dive sites include **Salisbury Falls, Nose Reef, Brain Coral Garden,** and—even farther north—**Cabrits Drop-Off** and **Toucari Reef.** The conditions for underwater photography, particularly macrophotography, are unparalleled. Rates start at about $55 for a single-tank dive and about $90 for a two-tank dive or from about $75 for a resort course with one open-water dive. All scuba-diving operators also offer snorkeling. Equipment rents for $10 to $25 a day; trips with gear range from $15 to $35. A 10% tax is not included.

Anchorage Dive & Whale Watch Center. The Anchorage Dive & Whale Watch Center has two dive boats that can take you out day or night. It also offers PADI instruction (all skill levels), snorkeling and whale-watching trips, and shore diving. It has many of the same trips as Dive Dominica. ✉ *Anchorage Hotel, Castle Comfort* ☎ *767/448–2638, 888/790–5264 in U.S.* 🌐 *www.anchoragehotel.dm.*

Cabrits Dive Center. Cabrits Dive Center is the only PADI five-star dive center in Dominica. Nitrox courses are also available for $250. Since Cabrits is the sole operator on the northwest coast, its dive boats have the pristine reefs almost to themselves, unlike other operations, whose underwater territories may overlap. ✉ *Picard Estate, Portsmouth* ☎ *767/445–3010* 🌐 *www.cabritsdive.com.*

Dive Dominica. Dive Dominica, one of the island's dive pioneers, conducts PADI courses as well as Nitrox certification courses. With four boats, it offers diving, snorkeling, and whale-watching trips and packages, including accommodations at the Castle Comfort Lodge. Its trips are similar to Anchorage's. ✉ *Castle Comfort Lodge, Castle Comfort* ☎ *767/448–2188, 646/502–6800 in U.S.* 🌐 *www.divedominica.com.*

Fort Young Dive Centre. Fort Young Dive Centre conducts snorkeling, diving, and whale-watching trips that depart from the hotel's private dock.

A diver pauses to admire a lavender stovepipe sponge (*aplysina archeri*).

✉ *Fort Young Hotel, Victoria St., Roseau* ☎ *767/448–5000* 🌐 *www.fortyounghotel.com/dive.*

Irie Safari. Irie Safari takes snorkelers to Champagne and the nearby tall grasses, where turtles like to hang out. ✉ *Soufrière/Scotts Head Marine Reserve, Soufrière* ☎ *767/440–5085.*

FISHING

Anchorage Hotel. Contact the Anchorage Hotel for information about fishing excursions. Fees are $550 for a half-day trip and $1,050 for a full day. ✉ *Castle Comfort* ☎ *767/448–2638, 888/790–5264 in U.S.* 🌐 *www.anchoragehotel.dm.*

GUIDED TOURS

Generally tours start off in the Roseau area, but most operators will arrange convenient pickups. Prices range between $35 and $75 per person, depending on the duration and the destination, amenities provided, and the number of people on the excursion.

Dominica Tours. Dominica Tours is one of the island's largest tour companies, offering a range of hikes and bird-watching trips. ☎ *767/448–2638* 🌐 *www.experience-dominica.com.*

Ken's Hinterland Adventure Tours & Taxi Service. Ken's Hinterland Adventure Tours & Taxi Service offers a range of island tours and guided hikes, including some specifically for families with children. ✉ *Fort*

Young Hotel, Victoria St., Roseau ☎ *767/448–4850, 767/448–1660, 866/880–0508 in U.S.* 🌐 *www.khattstours.com.*

HIKING

Dominica's majestic mountains, clear rivers, and lush vegetation conspire to create adventurous hiking trails. The island is crisscrossed by ancient footpaths of the Arawak and Carib Indians and of the Nègres Maroons, escaped slaves who established camps in the mountains. Existing trails range from easygoing to arduous. To make the most of your excursion, you'll need sturdy hiking boots, insect repellent, a change of clothes (kept dry), and a guide. Hikes and tours run $25 to $80 per person, depending on destinations and duration. A poncho or light raincoat is recommended. Some of the natural attractions within the island's national parks require visitors to purchase a site pass. These are sold for varying numbers of visits. A single-entry site pass costs $5, and a week pass $12. The Discover Dominica Authority's information offices at the Bayfront (Dame Charles Boulevard) can recommend guides.

Bertrand Jno Baptiste. Local bird and forestry expert Bertrand Jno Baptiste leads hikes up Morne Diablotin and along the Syndicate Nature Trail; if he's not available, ask him to recommend another guide. ☎ *767/245–4768.*

Forestry Division. The Forestry Division, which is responsible for the management of forests and wildlife, has numerous publications on Dominica as well as a wealth of information on reputable guides. ✉ *Dominica Botanical Gardens, between Bath Rd. and Valley Rd., Roseau* ☎ *767/266–5852, 767/266–5853.*

WHALE-WATCHING

FAMILY
Fodor's Choice ★

Dominica records the highest species counts of resident cetaceans in the southern Caribbean region, so it's not surprising that tour companies claim 90% sighting success for their excursions. Humpback whales, false killer whales, minke, and orcas are all occasionally seen, as are several species of dolphin. But the resident sperm whales (they calve in Dominica's 3,000-foot-deep waters) are truly the stars of the show. During your 3½-hour expedition, which costs about $55 plus tax, you may be asked to assist in recording sightings, data that can be shared with local and international organizations. Although there are resident whale and dolphin populations, more species can be observed from November through February. Turtle-watching trips are also popular.

Anchorage Dive & Whale Watch Center. The Anchorage Dive & Whale Watch Center can arrange whale-watching trips. ✉ *Anchorage Hotel, Castle Comfort* ☎ *767/448–2638, 767/440–2639* 🌐 *www.anchoragehotel.dm.*

Dive Dominica. Dive Dominica is a major whale-watching operator as well as a dive operator on the island. ✉ *Castle Comfort Lodge, Castle Comfort* ☎ *767/448–2188* 🌐 *www.divedominica.com.*

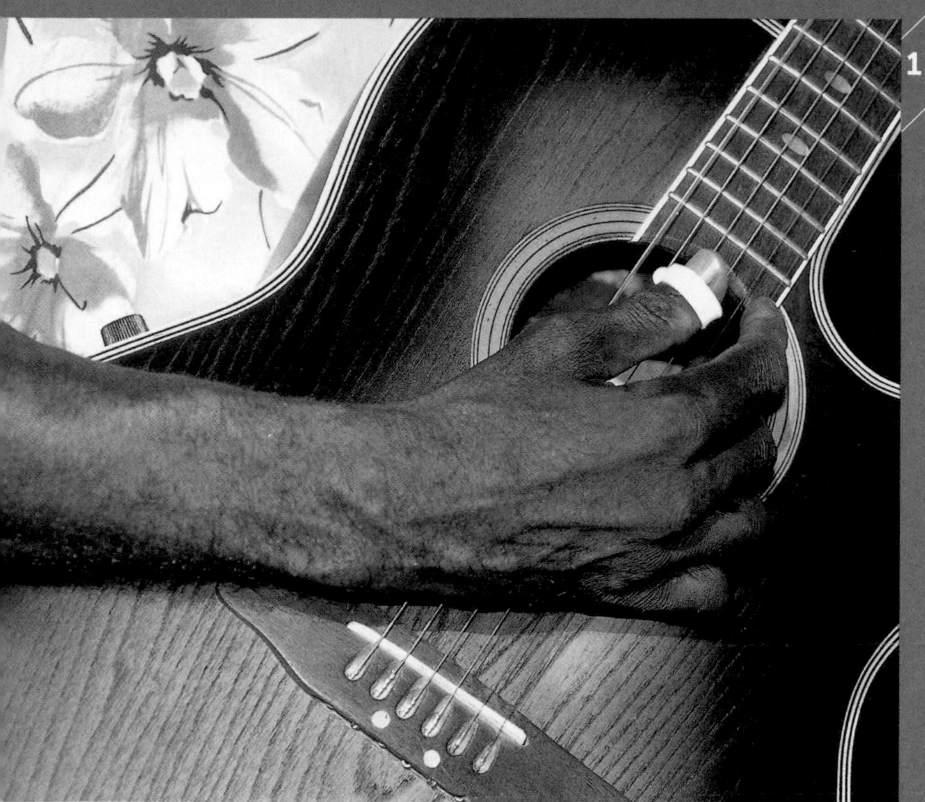

DOMINICAN REPUBLIC

WELCOME TO DOMINICAN REPUBLIC

Ocean World Adventure Park
Cofresí Beach
Luperón Beach
Playa Dorada
Playa Cabarete
Montecristi
Puerto Plata
Museo de Ambar Dominicano
Sosúa
Cabarete
Cabo Francés Viejo
Laguna Grí-Grí
Guayubin
Mt. Isabel de Torres
Gregorie Luperón International Airport
Cabrera
Playa Grande
Bahía Escocesa
Las Terrenas
HAITI
Santiago
Moca
Pico Duarte
La Vega Vieja
San Francisco de Macorís
Playa Cosón
Nagua
Los Haitises National Park
Taino Park
Bahía de Samaná
Jarabacoa
Sabana de la Mar
← TO HAITI
HISPANIOLA
San Juan
Monte Plata
Las Américas International Airport
Lago Enriquillo
Neiba
Azua
San Cristóbal
Duvergé
Bahia de Ocoa
Bani
Boca Chica
Juan Dolio
Santo Domingo see detail map
Barahona
Playa Bahoruco
Pto. Palenque
Caribbean Sea
Oviedo
Cabo Beata

Like the merengue seen on all the dance floors in Santo Domingo, the Dominican Republic is charismatic yet sensuous, energetic yet elegant. The charm of the people adds special warmth: a gracious wave of greeting here, a hand-rolled cigar tapped with a flourish there. Dazzling smiles just about everywhere will quickly beguile you.

LA ISLA ESPAÑOLA

The Dominican Republic covers the eastern two-thirds of the island of Hispaniola (Haiti covers the other third). At 18,765 square miles (48,730 square km), it's the second-largest Caribbean country (only Cuba is larger), and with more than 8.8 million people, the second-most-populous country, too. It was explored by Columbus on his 1492 voyage to the New World.

Restaurants ▼		Hotels ▼	
The Beach	9	Balcones del Atlantico	6
The Beach Club	5	The Bannister Hotel	5
bliss	1	Casa Colonial	13
B.Y.O.W. Restaurant	6	Casa de Campo	1
Il Pasticcio	4	Dreams La Romana	2
Lucía	7	Gran Ventana Beach Resort	12
Mares Restaurant	8	Grand Palladium Baváro	4
Miró's	2	Hotel El Magnifico	10
Natura Restaurant at Natura Cabana	3	Natura Cabana	9
Peperoni	11	Peninsula House	7
Porto	10	Sea Horse Ranch	11
		Sublime Samaná	8
		Westin	3

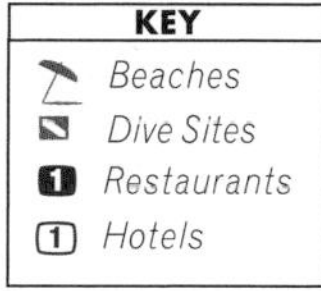

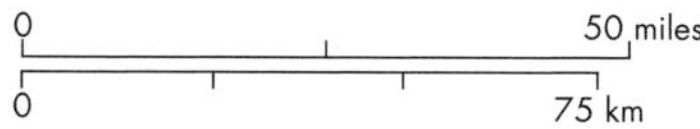

TOP REASONS TO VISIT DOMINICAN REPUBLIC

1 Great Beaches. There are some 1,000 miles of excellent beaches, many of which are white.

2 Great Value. You'll find the best-value all-inclusive resorts in the Caribbean here.

3 Myriad Water Sports. Every imaginable activity—world-class golf, horseback riding, white-water rafting, surfing, diving, windsurfing—is available here.

4 Friendly People. The genuine hospitality of the people and their love of *norteamericanos.*

5 Happening Nightlife. The Dominicans love to party, dance, drink, and have a good time at happening bars and clubs.

Updated by Eileen Robinson Smith

Dominicans will extend a gracious welcome, saying, "This is your home!" and indeed are happy to share their beautiful island bathed by the Atlantic Ocean to the north and the Caribbean Sea to the south. Among its most precious assets are 1,000 miles (1,600 km) of gorgeous beaches studded with coconut palms and sands ranging from pearl-white to golden brown to volcanic black. The Caribbean sun kisses this exotic land, which averages 82°F year-round. It's a fertile country blessed with resources, particularly cocoa, coffee, rum, tobacco, and sugarcane.

A land of contrasts, the Dominican Republic has mountain landscapes, brown rivers with white-water rapids, rain forests full of wild orchids, and fences of multicolor bougainvillea. Indigenous species from crocodiles to the green cockatoo, symbol of the island, live in these habitats. Bird-watchers, take note: there are 29 endemic species flying around here.

The contrasts don't stop with nature. You can see signs of wealth, for the upper strata of society lives well indeed. In the capital, the movers and shakers ride in chauffeur-driven silver Mercedes. On the country roads you'll be amazed that four people with sacks of groceries and a stalk of bananas can fit on a smoky old *motoconcho* (motorbike–taxi). This is a land of mestizos who are a centuries-old mix of native Indians, Spanish colonists, and African slaves, plus every other nationality that has settled here, from Italian to Arabic.

Accommodations offer a remarkable range—surfers' camps, exclusive boutique hotels, and amazing megaresorts that have brought the all-inclusive hotel to the next level of luxury. Trendy restaurants, art galleries, boutique hotels, and late-night clubs help make Santo Domingo a superb urban vacation destination. Regrettably, most Dominican towns and cities are neither quaint nor pretty, and poverty still prevails. However, the standard of living has come up along with the growth of North

LOGISTICS

Getting to the Dominican Republic: The D.R. has seven international airports. Plan your air travel carefully so you don't end up flying into Santo Domingo when you are staying in Punta Cana, a 90-minute, $150 taxi ride away. Travel between the island's many developed tourism zones can be arduous and expensive, with few domestic flights available.

Hassle Factor: Low for popular destinations. High for off-the-beaten-path places.

Getting Around the Island: Most travelers to the Dominican Republic take guided tours or participate in organized excursions. Independent travel is easier if you rent a car, but car rentals are expensive and signage is bad (and some working knowledge of Spanish is strongly advisable). For longer distances, buses are the best alternative, but locally, taxis are widely available in all major resort areas.

On the Ground: Most travelers book packages that include airport transfers. Otherwise, you'll have to take a local taxi, which can be quite expensive.

American tourism. Food prices are higher, which means prices at all-inclusive resorts are up; however, a vacation in the D.R. can still be a relative bargain. Even the new boutique hotels are still well priced for the Caribbean. Nevertheless, government taxes on hotels and restaurants increased to 18% in 2013 and must be considered when budgeting.

The vibrant lifestyle of this sun-drenched Latin-Caribbean country, where Spanish is the national language and where people are hospitable, makes the Dominican Republic a different cultural experience. If you pick up the rhythm of life here, as freewheeling as the trademark merengue, this can be a beguiling destination.

PLANNING

WHEN TO GO

The D.R. is busy year-round. During the somewhat quieter summer season, Europeans keep rates high from mid-June through August. However, in late spring (after Easter until early June) and early fall (September to October—peak rainy season, with hurricanes a threat) you can get good deals.

Unlike on many islands, where rain showers are usually passing things, the rains in the D.R. can linger, especially from June through November.

GETTING HERE AND AROUND

AIR TRAVEL

You can fly nonstop to the Dominican Republic from Atlanta (Delta, Southwest), Baltimore (Southwest), Boston (JetBlue, US Airways), Charlotte (American), Chicago–Midway (Southwest), Chicago–O'Hare (United), Detroit (Delta), Fort Lauderdale (Spirit), Miami (American), Minneapolis (Delta), New York–JFK (Delta, JetBlue), New York–Newark (United), Orlando (JetBlue), Philadelphia (American), and

Washington Dulles (United). However, not all airlines fly to all the destinations in the D.R., and some flights connect in San Juan or airports throughout the United States.

Many visitors fly nonstop on charter flights direct from the U.S. East Coast and Midwest, particularly into Punta Cana; these charters are part of a package and can be booked only through a travel agent.

Airport Transfers: If you book a package through a travel agent or vacation provider, your airport transfer will almost certainly be included. If you book independently, you will have to take a taxi, rent a car, or hire a private driver-guide. DominicanShuttles.com offers drivers and private transfers in addition to scheduling domestic airline flights and excursions.

Airports **Cibao International Airport** (STI) in Santiago; **El Catey International Airport** (AZS) in Samaná; **Gregorio Luperón International Airport** (POP) in Puerto Plata; **La Isabella International Airport** (JBQ) in Higüero; **La Romana/Casa de Campo International Airport** (LRM) in La Romana; **Las Américas International Airport** (SDQ) in Santo Domingo; and **Punta Cana International Airport** (PUJ) in Punta Cana.

Domestic and Charter Airlines **Aerodomca** ✉ *La Isabella International Dr. Joaquin Balaguer, Higuero* ☎ *809/931-4073 DomShuttle, 829/410-3326 DomShuttle, 809/826-4141 airport* 🌐 *www.aerodomca.com.* **Air Century** ✉ *La Isabella International Dr. Joaquin Balaguer, Av. Presidente Antonio Guzmán Fernández, Higuero* ☎ *809/826-4333 charters, 305/677-9641 in U.S., 809/931-4073 DominicanShuttles reservations* 🌐 *www.aircentury.com.* **Dominican Shuttles.com** ✉ *Torre Empresarial Forum, Av. 27 de Febrero at Av. Privada, Cuarto Inclinado, Santo Domingo* ☎ *809/931-4073, 829/410-3326* 🌐 *www.dominicanshuttles.com.* **Helidosa Helicopters** ✉ *Punta Cana International Airport, Punta Cana* ☎ *809/552-6069* 🌐 *www.helidosa.com.*

International Airline Contacts **Air Antilles Express** ☎ *809/688-6661 air ticket agency, 809/560-0168 call center/agency* 🌐 *www.flyairantilles.com.* **Air Caraïbes** ☎ *809/621-8888 general services, 0590/82-47-00 in Guadeloupe* 🌐 *www.aircaraibes.com, www.aircaraibes-usa.com.* **American Airlines** ☎ *809/959-2420 in Punta Cana, 800/433-7300 in U.S., 800/222-2377 Web help, 809/200-5151 toll-free, 809/542-5151 in Santo Domingo* 🌐 *www.aa.com.* **Delta** ☎ *809/549-8151 in D.R., 800/221-1212 in U.S.* 🌐 *www.delta.com.* **JetBlue** ☎ *809/200-9898 in D.R. (SDQ), 800/538-2583 in U.S.* 🌐 *www.jetblue.com.* **Southwest** ☎ *800/435-9792* 🌐 *www.southwest.com.* **Spirit Airlines** ☎ *801/401-2200 in U.S.* 🌐 *www.spirit.com.* **United** ☎ *809/262-1060 in D.R., 800/538-2929 in U.S., 800/864-8331 in U.S.* 🌐 *www.united.com.*

CAR TRAVEL

Driving in the D.R. can be a harrowing and expensive experience; we don't recommend that the typical vacationer rent a car. It's best if you don't drive outside the major cities at night. If you must, use extreme caution, especially on narrow, unlighted mountain roads.

Local agencies exist, but it is highly advisable to rent only from internationally known companies. U.S. citizens should really consider only U.S.–based chains, so that if you have a problem you have easier recourse. Major agencies are in most of the island's airports. At Las Americas International Airport, most agencies are open 7 am–11 pm.

Car-Rental Contacts **Budget** ☎ *800/472–3325* 🌐 *www.budget.com* ✉ *Gregorio Luperón International Airport, Puerto Plata* ☎ *809/586–0413* 🌐 *www.budget.com* ✉ *Las Américas International Airport, Santo Domingo* ☎ *809/549–0351, 800/527–0700 in U.S.* 🌐 *www.budget.com.* **Europcar** ✉ *Las Américas Airport, Santo Domingo* ☎ *809/549–0942 in the D.R.* 🌐 *www.europcar.com.* ✉ *Punta Cana International Airport, Bavaro, Punta Cana* ☎ *809/959–0177, 809/480–8188* **National** ✉ *Casa de Campo, La Romana* ☎ *809/523–3333, 809/523–8191* 🌐 *www.nationalcar.com.*

TAXI TRAVEL

Wherever you are, hotel taxis are generally the best option. Carry small bills; drivers rarely have change. Recommendable radio-taxi companies in Santo Domingo are Tecni-Taxi (which also operates in Puerto Plata) and Apolo. You can use taxis to travel to out-of-town destinations at quoted rates. Check with your hotel or the dispatcher at the airport. From the Zona Colonial in Santo Domingo to Playa Dorada with Tecni-Taxi is $160. If you book through your hotel concierge, it can be more. Dominican Shuttles (🌐 *www.dominicanshuttles.com*) provides safe and reliable service.

Contacts **Apolo Taxi** ☎ *809/537–0000, 809/537–1245 for high-end cars or SUVs* 🌐 *www.apolotaxi.com.* **Taxi-Cabarete** ☎ *809/571–0767 in Cabarete.* **Taxi-Queen Santiago** ☎ *809/570–0000 in Santiago.* **Taxi-Sosúa** ☎ *809/571–3097 in Sosúa.* **Tecni-Taxi** ☎ *809/567–2010 in Santo Domingo, 809/320–7621 in Puerto Plata.*

ESSENTIALS

Banks and Exchange Services Currency is the Dominican peso (written RD$). You will not need to change money unless you plan to travel independently around the D.R. Banco Popular has many locations throughout the country, with ATMs that accept international cards.

Electricity 110–120 volts/60 cycles, the same as in the United States.

Health Never drink tap water in the D.R. (look for a hotel or restaurant that has earned an *H* for food-service hygiene or that has a Crystal America certification). Don't buy food or even juice from the street vendors. Use mosquito repellent to protect yourself from mosquito-borne illnesses like Dengue fever; long sleeves and long pants also help.

Language Spanish is spoken in the D.R. Most staff at major tourist attractions and front-desk personnel in most major hotels speak English. Outside the popular tourist establishments, English is spoken less frequently.

Passport Requirements All U.S. citizens must carry a valid passport. Additionally, all visitors must have a valid tourist card, which costs US$10 (purchased on arrival in cash with U.S. currency only).

Phones To call the D.R. from the United States, dial 1–809, and the local number. From the D.R. you also need dial only 1–809, then the number. To make a local call, you must dial 809 plus the seven-digit number (dial 1–809 if you are calling a cell phone). Directory assistance is 1411.

Safety Violent crime is rare. Nevertheless, poverty is everywhere in the D.R., and petty theft, pickpocketing, and purse snatching are an increasing concern, particularly in Santo Domingo. Pay attention, especially when leaving a bank or casino. Take hotel-recommended taxis at night.

Taxes The departure tax of $20 is almost always included in the price of your airline ticket. The government tax (IBIS) is a whopping 18% and is added to almost everything—bills at restaurants, hotels, sports activities, rental cars, and even many items at the supermarkets, definitely on anything imported.

Tipping A 10% service charge is included in all hotel and restaurant bills. In restaurants, the bill will say *propino incluido* or simply *servis*. Even then it's still expected that you will tip an extra 5% to 10% if the service was good. Hotel maids typically get $2 per day; taxi drivers, 10%; skycaps and hotel porters, $1 per bag.

ACCOMMODATIONS

All-inclusive resorts predominate in Punta Cana; some of these are quite luxurious. All-inclusives also make up the lion's share of resorts in Playa Dorada on the north coast, but Sosúa and Cabarete still have a few charming independent inns and small resorts. The Southeast Coast has nice beaches but some of the most mediocre resorts on the island, though the area around La Romana (Casa de Campo in particular) and nearby Bayahibe, has both wonderful beaches and some good resorts. Santo Domingo offers both large and small hotels with access to the capital's great restaurants, nightlife, and historical sights. Samaná is a bit more isolated, though becoming less so, and it offers a range of all-inclusive resorts as well as smaller properties both luxurious and simple.

Hotel reviews have been shortened. For full information, visit Fodors.com.

WHAT IT COSTS IN U.S. DOLLARS

	$	$$	$$$	$$$$
Restaurants	under $12	$12–$20	$21–$30	over $30
Hotels	under $275	$275–$375	$376–$475	over $475

Restaurant prices are the average cost of a main course at dinner or, if dinner is not served, at lunch. Hotel prices are the lowest cost of a standard double room in high season.

VISITOR INFORMATION

Contacts Dominican Republic One. Dominican Republic One is a "trusted site" of the Secretariat de Turismo. It's written by bilingual staffers at the ministry and delivers the official word on the latest news, travel, and airline information. *www.dr1.com*. **Dominican Republic Tourist Office** *212/588–1012 in New York City, 888/358–9594 in Miami* *www.godominicanrepublic.com*.

WEDDINGS

There are no residency requirements. Blood tests are not mandatory. Original birth certificates and passports are required. Divorce certificates and proof that the bride and groom are single must be stamped by the Dominican Consulate. Documents must be submitted two weeks

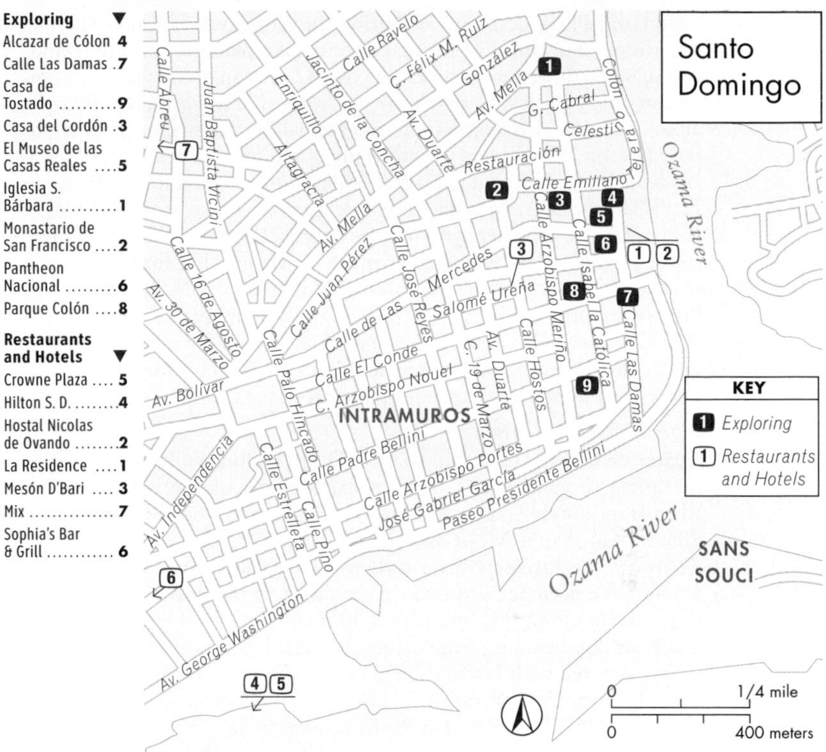

before the wedding and translated into Spanish. Many couples are opting to marry in the United States, then hold a ceremony at the resort of their choice followed by a reception.

EXPLORING

SANTO DOMINGO

Parque Independencia separates the old city from modern Santo Domingo, a sprawling, noisy city with a population of close to 2 million. The 12 cobblestone blocks of Santo Domingo's **Zona Colonial** contain most of the major sights in town. It's one of the most appealing historic districts in the Caribbean and is best explored on foot. The Zona ends at the seafront, called the Malecón.

Spanish civilization in the New World began in Santo Domingo's 12-block Zona Colonial. As you stroll its narrow streets, it's easy to imagine this old city as it was when the likes of Columbus, Cortés, and Ponce de León walked the cobblestones, pirates sailed in and out, and colonists started settling. Tourist brochures claim that "history comes alive here"—a surprisingly truthful statement. Almost every Thursday to Sunday night at 8:30 a typical "folkloric show" is staged at Parque

Colón and Plaza de España. During the Christmas holidays there is an artisans' fair and live-music concerts take place. A fun horse-and-carriage ride throughout the Zona costs $25 for an hour, with any commentary in Spanish. The steeds are no thoroughbreds, but they clip right along. You can also negotiate to use them as a taxi, say, to go down to the Malecón. The drivers usually hang out in front of the Hostal Nicolas de Ovando. You can get a free walking-tour map and brochures in English at the Secretaria de Estado de Turismo office at Parque Colón (Columbus Park), where you may be approached by freelance, English-speaking guides who will want to make it all come alive for you. They'll work enthusiastically for $25 an hour for four people. At the time of this writing, the major reconstruction of so many of the streets in the Zona is expected to come to an end soon. Yet simply put, the Zona is not as safe as it once was—particularly at night and during festivals. Don't carry a lot of cash or your passport (leave them in the hotel safe).

TOP ATTRACTIONS

Alcázar de Colón. The castle of Don Diego Colón, built in 1517, was the home to generations of the Christopher Columbus family. The Renaissance-style structure, with its balustrade and double row of arches, has strong Moorish, Gothic, and Isabelline influences. The 22 rooms are furnished in a style to which the viceroy of the island would have been accustomed—right down to the dishes and the vice regal shaving mug. The mansion's 40-inch-thick coral-limestone walls make air-conditioning impossible. Bilingual guides are on hand for tours peppered with fascinating anecdotes, like weddings once-upon-a time. ✉ *Plaza de España, off Calle Emiliano Tejera, Zona Colonial* ☎ *809/682–4750* 🎫 *RD$100* ⏲ *Tues.–Sun. 9–5.*

Calle Las Damas. "Ladies Street" was named after the elegant ladies of the court: in the Spanish tradition, they promenaded in the evening. Here you can see a sundial dating from 1753 and the Casa de los Jesuitas, which houses a fine research library for colonial history as well as the **Institute for Hispanic Culture**; admission is free, and it's open weekdays from 8 to 4:30. The boutique Hostal Nicolas de Ovando is on this street, across from the French Embassy. If you follow the street going toward the Malecón, you will pass a picturesque alley, fronted by a wrought-iron gate, where there are perfectly maintained colonial structures owned by the Catholic Church. ✉ *Calle las Damas, Zona Colonial.*

WORTH NOTING

Iglesia Santa Bárbara. This combination church and fortress, the only one of its kind in Santo Domingo, was completed in 1562. **■ TIP→ For Mass times, be sure to check the day before you want to attend.** ✉ *Av. Mella, between Calle Isabel la Católica and Calle Arzobispo Meriño, Zona Colonial* ☎ *809/682–3307* 🎫 *Free* ⏲ *Mon.–Sat. 6 am–6:45 pm; Sun. Masses begin at 8 am, last Mass at 6 pm.*

Monasterio de San Francisco. Constructed between 1512 and 1544, the St. Francis Monastery contained the church, convent, and hospital of the Franciscan order. Sir Francis Drake's demolition squad significantly damaged the building in 1586, and in 1673 an earthquake nearly

The architecture in the town of Altos de Chavón re-creates a 16th-century Mediterranean village.

finished the job, but when it's floodlit at night, the eerie ruins are dramatic indeed. The Spanish government has donated money to turn this into a beautiful cultural center, but we are still waiting. In the meantime, there's music many nights at 7 pm (often live), and it becomes an old-fashioned block party. Zona residents mingle with expats and tourists, who snap pictures of the octogenarians dancing the merengue and the bachata. Others who come are content to just sit in white plastic chairs, swaying and clapping. It's nice. ✉ *Calle Hostos at Calle Emiliano, Zona Colonial.*

Pantheon Nacional. The National Pantheon (circa 1714) was once a Jesuit monastery and later a theater. The real curiosity here is the military guard, who stays as still as the statues, despite the schoolchildren who try to make him flinch. ✉ *Calle Las Damas, near Calle de Las Mercedes, Zona Colonial* ☎ *809/689–6010* 🎫 *Free* ⏲ *Mon.–Sat. 8 am–9 pm.*

Parque Colón. The huge statue of Christopher Columbus in the park named after him dates from 1897, and is the work of sculptor Ernesto Gilbert. At the far end, the Catedral Primada de America is a landmark and most worthy of a visit. Like all the parks in the Zona Colonial, this one is quite a social gathering place. ✉ *El Conde at Calle Arzobispo Meriño, Zona Colonial.*

Plaza de España. This wide esplanade, which goes past the Casas de Reales in front of Don Diego Columbus's former palace, El Alcazar de Colón, is the area in the Zona Colonial where national holidays are celebrated. The annual Coca-Cola–sponsored Christmas tree is here. It's bordered by what once were the ramparts of the original walled city. People enjoy the views of the Ozama River from here, and watch the cruise-ship activity below at the terminal. Lovers stroll by night, sharing a kiss under the gas lamps. When many people talk about the Plaza de España, they are often referring to the half-dozen restaurants in a row, which are on the upper level of these 16th- and 17th-century warehouses. The popular tables are on their outdoor decks. Cultural performances are held on a stage across from the plaza on certain weekends. **■TIP→ Make dinner reservations on those nights and you'll have a special Santo Domingo experience.** ✉ *Calle La Atarazana, Zona Colonial.*

SOUTHEAST COAST

Las Américas Highway (built by the dictator Rafael Trujillo so his son could race his sports cars) runs east along the coast from Santo Domingo to La Romana—previously a two-hour drive. Midway are the well-established beach resorts such as Juan Dolio, and Sammy Sosa's hometown, San Pedro de Macorís. Much farther east are Punta Cana and Bávaro, glorious beaches on the sunrise side of the island. Along the way, between La Romana and Punta Cana, is Higüey, the capital city of the province called La Altagracia. It is a short detour (15 minutes) off the new highway. An undistinguished city with heavy traffic, Higuey is notable for its giant concrete cathedral and shrine to the country's virgin saint. It is one of the country's most visited monuments.

LA ROMANA

48 miles (78 km) east of Juan Dolio.

Neither pretty nor quaint, La Romana has a central park, an interesting market, a couple of good restaurants, banks and small businesses, a public beach, and Jumbo, a major supermarket. **■TIP→ If you are staying for a week or more you may want to buy a Dominican cell phone at Jumbo. It's a mere $20 for a basic one, plus minutes. It can save you untold money if you'll be making local calls from your hotel/resort.** It is, at least, a real slice of Dominican life. Casa de Campo is just outside La Romana, and other resorts are found in the vicinity of nearby Bayahibe. Although there are now more resorts in the area, this 7,000-acre luxury enclave put the town on the map. Casa de Campo Marina, with its Mediterranean design and impressive yacht club and villa complex, is as fine a marina facility as can be found anywhere; the shops and restaurants at the marina are a big draw for all tourists to the area.

Fodor's Choice ★ **Altos de Chavón.** This re-creation of a 16th-century Mediterranean village sits on a bluff overlooking the Río Chavón, on the grounds of Casa de Campo but about 3 miles (5 km) east of the main facilities. There are cobblestone streets lined with lanterns, wrought-iron balconies, wooden shutters, courtyards swathed with bougainvillea, and **Iglesia St. Stanislaus,** the romantic setting for many a Casa de Campo wedding. More than a museum piece, this village is a place where artists live, work, and play. Emilio Robba, a famous European designer, is now directing the art studios. Visitors can visit the ateliers and see the talented artisans making pottery, tapestry and serigraphy art. The artists sell their finished wares at the Art Studios Boutique. The village also has an amber museum, an archaeological museum, a handful of restaurants, and a number of unique shops. Strolling musicians enliven the rustic ambience of ceramic tiles and cobblestone terrace. Big names, like Elton John, perform at the amphitheater. Christmastime is sheer magic, what with the lights, music concerts, giant Christmas tree, and Santa making a cameo appearance. ✉ *Casa de Campo* 🌐 *www.casadecampo.com.do.*

FLAT TIRE

Blowout? A *gomero* can make a flat tire round! There are many such fellows, because the rough roads are rubber-eaters. You will see their signs on the highways and if stranded in a town, just ask: *¿Donde esta un gomero?*

Amphitheater at Altos de Chavon. A 5,000-seat, Grecian-style amphitheater features *Kandela,* a spectacular musical extravaganza showcasing the island's sensuous Afro-Caribbean dance moves, music, and culture (December–April only). The production has been enhanced by both new music and choreography yet the price remains the same! Concerts and celebrity performances by such singers as Elton John, Julio Iglesias, his son Enrique, Sting, and the Pet Shop Boys share the amphitheater's schedule of events. Show dates vary to coincide with cruise-ship arrivals, presently Sunday and Monday nights. Many people make dinner reservations at **La Piazzetta** (*Altos de Chavón,* ☎ *809/523–3333)*, the high-end Italian restaurant that is closest to the amphitheater. It's known for its antipasto selections, homemade pasta, and authentic regional dishes; outside guests are welcome. ✉ *Casa de Campo* ☎ *809/523–2424 for Kandela tickets* 🌐 *www.kandela.com.do* 🎫 *$35 for Kandela; other concert prices vary.*

Isla Saona. Off the east coast of Hispaniola and part of Parque Nacional del Este lies this island, inhabited by sea turtles, pigeons, and other wildlife. Indigenous people once used the caves here. The beaches are beautiful, and legend has it that Columbus once stopped over. However, the island is not nearly as pristine as one might expect for a national park. Getting here, on catamarans and other excursion boats, is half the fun, but it can be a crowd scene once you arrive. Vendors are allowed to sell to visitors, and there are a number of beach shacks serving lunch and drinks. Most boats traveling here leave out of the beach at Bayahibe Village. Most tourists book through their hotel. ⚠ **Please note that there is little to no refrigeration on the island and the sun is strong, so take caution when dining.** ✉ *20 mins from Bayahibe harbor by boat.*

PUNTA CANA

The larger area known as Punta Cana encompasses Cabeza de Torres, Playa Bávaro, and continues all the way around the peninsula to Playa de Uvero Alto. Development continues in Galerias Punta-Cana Village, a shopping center that is a draw for visitors from around the area. A Four Points by Sheraton just opened across from the area and is the only "airport" hotel in the region. Five minutes from the village on a gorgeous stretch of beach within the Punta Cana Group's domain, is the new (2014) Westin Punta Cana Resort & Club. Characteristic of this American chain, it is an upscale, non–all inclusive property.

This stretch between Club Med, the Westin, and the Puntacana Resort & Club is one of the most beautiful. Farther up the coast, Playa El Cortecito is more how life used to be, with fishermen bringing in their catch, and it is where the wild and crazy restaurant Capitán Cook's is located. Farther north along the coast is a stretch of beach known as Arena Gorda, literally "fat sand," and Bavaro. About 20 miles (32 km) from Punta Cana International Airport, it's an area brimming with coconut groves and the location of many resorts. Each has its own strip of sand with rows of chaises longues, and most of these hotels will grant outsiders day passes for a fee. Macao is a pastoral village, but its public beach is no longer a good option, having first been taken over by four-wheeler excursions and now dominated by the huge Hard Rock Hotel & Casino Punta Cana.

NORTH COAST

The farther east you go from Puerto Plata and Sosúa, the prettier and less spoiled the scenery becomes. The autopista runs past Cabarete, a town that's a popular windsurfing haunt, and Playa Grande, which has a miraculously unspoiled white-sand beach with amenities now being gentrified, a famous golf course (now under major renovation until fall 2015), and a development project underway. Surrounded by high cliffs, this incredibly beautiful stretch of sand had food shacks and cheapie souvenir stands that marred its beauty. Vendors now have brightly painted, cutesy, Victorian-style huts that have been relocated to the end of the beach. There is now a proper parking area and vehicles can no longer drive on the beach. The Playa Grande Beach Club has a new collection of high-end bungalows available for rent.

PUERTO PLATA

Although it has been sleeping for decades, this was a dynamic city in its heyday, and it is coming back. You can get a feeling for this past in the magnificent Victorian gazebo in the central **Parque Independencia.** Painted a crisp white, the park looks postcard pretty, with gleaming new statuary. On Puerto Plata's own Malecón, which has had a multimillion-dollar refurbishment, the **Fortaleza de San Felipe** protected the city from many a pirate attack and was later used as a political prison. Nearby, a new amphitheater is in the planning stages. The nearby **lighthouse** has been restored.

Mt. Isabel de Torres. Southwest of Puerto Plata, this mountain soars 2,600 feet above sea level and is notable for its huge statue of Christ. Up there also are botanical gardens that, despite efforts, still are not memorable. You can choose to hire a knowledgeable English-speaking guide for $5 per person. A cable car takes you to the top for a spectacular view. The cars usually wait until filled to capacity before going up—which can make them crowded; and should the electricity happen to go off, there is no backup generator. You should visit in the morning, preferably by 9 am; by afternoon, the cloud cover rolls in, and you can see practically nothing. ■ **TIP→ The vendors are particularly tenacious here. Wear comfortable walking shoes.** ✉ *Manolo Tavarez Justo, off*

Autopista Duarte, follow signs, Puerto Plata ☎ 809/970–0501 🌐 telefericopuertoplata.com 🎫 Cable car RD$350 ⏲ Mon.–Sun. 9–6.

Museo de Ambar Dominicano (*Dominican Amber Museum*). In an opulent, galleried mansion, restored to its former Victorian glamour, the museum displays and sells the Dominican Republic's national stone: semiprecious, translucent amber. Amber is essentially prehistoric hardened tree sap, and Dominican amber is considered the best in the world. Many pieces are fascinating for what they have trapped inside, and the second-floor museum contains a piece with a lizard reported to be 50 million years old, give or take a few millennia. The museum's English text is informative. Shops on the museum's first floor sell amber, souvenirs, and ceramics. ✉ *Calle Duarte 61, Puerto Plata ☎ 809/586–2848 museum, 809/320-2215 gift shop 🌐 www.ambermuseum.com 🎫 RD$50 ⏲ Mon.–Sat. 9–6 multilingual guided tours.*

Ocean World Adventure Park. This multimillion-dollar aquatic park in Cofresí has marine and wildlife interactive programs, including dolphin and sea lion shows and encounters, a double-dolphin swim, a tropical reef aquarium, stingrays, shark tanks, an aviary, a rain forest, and the Tiger Grotto inhabited by Bengal tigers. You must make advance reservations if you want to participate in one of the swims or encounters; children must be at least six and accompanied by an adult. The exhilarating (albeit expensive) double-dolphin swim will produce lifelong memories. If you are brave enough for the (nurse) shark encounter, you will feed them and touch them in the shark cove; the stingray encounter is also included. A photo lab and video service can capture the moment, but there is a charge. If you're staying at nearby Lifestyle resorts, or hotels in Puerto Plata, transfers are free. If in Sosua or Cabarete, transfers are $5 per person; hotels should have the tour schedules. ■ **TIP→ There's a private beach, showers, and a locker room on-site.** ✉ *Calle Principal 3, 3 miles (5 km) west of Puerto Plata, Cofresi, Puerto Plata ☎ 809/291–1000 🌐 www.oceanworld.net 🎫 $69 entrance includes lunch; extra charge for some activities/encounters; $54 for children 6–12 and seniors ⏲ Tues.–Sun. 9–6.*

SOSÚA

15 miles (24 km) east of Puerto Plata.

Sosúa is called Puerto Plata's little sister, and consists of two communities—El Batey, the more modern hotel development, and Los Charamicos, the old quarter—separated by a cove and one of the island's prettiest beaches. The sand is soft and nearly white, the water crystal clear and calm. The walkway above the beach is packed with tents filled with souvenirs, pizzas, and even clothing for sale. The town had developed a reputation for prostitution, but much is being done to eliminate that and to clean up the more garish elements. Conversely, there are many fine, cultured types here, both Dominican and expats, and the recent opening of a cultural center, Casa del Arte de Sosua, was a major coup for them.

Casa del Arte de Sosua. The new cultural center of Sosúa, inaugurated with much celebration by Mayor Llana in 2013, continues to "grow up." Classical concerts and choral performances by area residents characterized the long-awaited event. Open to the public and free of charge, the ground-floor gallery has rotating exhibitions that primarily feature work by Sousa and Dominican artists, such as Teddy Tejada. Music and dance lessons, from violin to ballet, are offered to local children on the second floor, as are other culturally minded activities. During the 2014 Dominican Republic Jazz Festival—which continues to grow—musicians offered free music workshops to local kids. ✉ *Pedro Clisante, across from the casino, Sosúa* ⏲ *Mon.–Fri. 9–5.*

Museo Judio Sosúa. Sosúa is not a destination known for its sights; however, this museum stands as one of the exceptions, chronicling the immigration and settlement of the Jewish refugees in the 1940s. This is a fascinating place, and depending on the docent, you may hear that the Jewish settlers fleeing from Hitler experienced a certain amount of prejudice here when they arrived. The fascinating website says no. The adjacent small wooden synagogue is the wedding spot for many Jewish couples from abroad. At this writing there wasn't a working telephone and hours were irregular, but chances are good that someone will be at the museum to let you in if you get there early in the day. **■ TIP→ You can try phoning Sosua Villas or the accommodating Hotel Casa Valeria nearby to confirm if the museum is open.** ✉ *Near Banco Popular, Calle Dr. Rosen at David Stern, Sosúa* ☎ *809/377–2038 Sosua Villas, 809/477–2038 Sosua Villas, 809/571–3565 Hotel Casa Valeria* 🌐 *www.sosua-villas.com/jewish-museum* 🎫 *RD$75* ⏲ *Sun.–Fri. 10–1 (but hrs are irregular).*

CIBAO VALLEY

The heavily trafficked four-lane highway north from Santo Domingo, known as the Autopista Duarte, cuts through the banana plantations, rice and tobacco fields, and royal poinciana trees of the Cibao Valley. Along the road are stands where a few pesos buy pineapples, mangoes, avocados, *chicharrones* (fried pork rinds), and fresh-fruit drinks.

SANTIAGO

Although an industrial center, Santiago has a surprisingly charming, provincial feel; the women of Santiago are considered among the country's most beautiful. High on a plateau is an impressive monument honoring the restoration of the republic. Traditional yet progressive, Santiago is still relatively new to the tourist scene but already has several thriving restaurants and hotels. It's definitely worth setting aside some time to explore the city. Colonial-style buildings—with wrought-iron details and tiled porticoes—date from as far back as the 1500s. Others are from the Victorian era, with the requisite gingerbread latticework and fanciful colors, and recent construction is nouveau Victorian. Santiago is the DR's cigar-making center; the Fuente factory is here, though its cigars can be bought on the island only in special designated cigar stores and clubs. (If you see them for sale on the streets, they are counterfeit.)

Fodor's Choice ★ **Centro León.** Without question, this is a world-class cultural center for Dominican arts and culture. A postmodern building full of light from a crystal dome, the center includes several attractions, galleries for

Hand-rolling cigars in the Cibao Valley

special exhibits, a sculpture garden, and an aviary. It has a replica of La Aurora's first cigar factory, too. Presently, an exhibition celebrates the biennial Eduardo Jimenes Art Contest; 2014 was the contest's 50th anniversary. There's even a first-rate cafeteria and a museum shop where you can buy high-quality, artsy souvenirs and jewelry. Check the website for activities and night events. Friday night there is a free soirée, with live music or a music video (from Spanish pop to R&B). The café stays open and serves beer, wine, and light fare. It can be a fine way to meet sophisticated Santiagueros who have a high level of fluency in English. ■ **TIP→ It's best to give advance notice if you want a guided tour in English.** ✉ *Av. 27 de Febrero 146, Villa Progreso, Santiago* ☎ *809/582–2315* 🌐 *www.centroleon.org.do* 🎫 *RD$150, guides in English RD$300 per person* 🕐 *Exhibitions Tues.–Sun. 10–7.*

SAMANÁ PENINSULA

Samaná (pronounced sah-mah-NAH) is a dramatically beautiful peninsula, like an island unto itself, of coconut trees stretching into the sea. It's something of a microcosm of the Dominican Republic: here you'll see poverty and fancy resorts, brand-new highways as well as bad roads, verdant mountainsides, tropical forests, tiny villages lined with street-side fruit vendors, secluded beaches, and the radiant warmth of the Dominican people. A visit here is really about two things: exploring the preserved natural wonders and relaxing at a small beachfront hotel. The latter is most readily accomplished in **Las Terrenas,** the only true tourist center, where you can find picturesque restaurants, accommodations of all types (including the new oceanfront Sublime Samaná and the luxury condo-hotel, Balcones del Atlantico), and great beaches. At Las Terrenas you can enjoy peaceful *playas,* take advantage of the vibrant nightlife, and make all your plans for expeditions on the peninsula. The other pleasures are solitary—quiet beaches, the massive national park Los Haitises, and water sports and hiking. A relatively new toll road connects Santo Domingo to the peninsula; it's now less than a two-hour drive. Small El Catey International Airport is near Las Terrenas and is now being served by twice-weekly JetBlue flights (Wednesday and Saturday).

Salto el Limón Waterfall. Provided that you're fit and willing to deal with a long and slippery path, an adventurous guided trip (three hours) to the spectacular Salto el Limón Waterfall is a delight. It's mostly on horseback but includes walking down rocky, sometimes muddy trails. Horse paths are slippery, and the trek is strenuous. The well-mannered horses take you across two rivers and up mountains to El Limón, the 165-foot waterfall amid luxuriant vegetation. Some snacks and drinks are usually included, but a grilled chicken lunch is only a few more pesos. The outpost for the trek, a local guide service called Santi Rancho, is difficult to find; it's best to arrange a tour from a professional operator like Flora Tours in Las Terrenas. Their price remains a reasonable $50. ✉ *Santi Rancho, Limon* ☎ *829/923–2792, 809/240–5482* 🌐 *flora-tours.net.*

SANTA BÁRBARA DE SAMANÁ

22 miles (35 km) southeast of Las Terrenas.

The official name of the city is Santa Bárbara de Samaná; but these days it's just called "Samaná." An authentic port town, it's getting its bearings as a tourist zone, and still is not a tourist magnet like Las Galeras and Las Terrenas. It has a typical *malecón* (seaside promenade) that's ideal for strolling and watching the boats in the harbor. Lookout "towers" have been built; ascend the stairs and see the whales in season or just look out to the horizon. Strong night lighting has been added, too, so you will see Dominicans and tourists alike taking walks after dinner. A small but bustling town, Samaná is filled with friendly residents, skilled local craftsmen selling their wares, and a handful of outdoor, sea-view, and courtyard restaurants.

A big all-inclusive resort, the Bahía Príncipe Cayacoa, is on one end of the bay road up on a hill. Day passes are available (and the resort has the only beach in town). The hotel also operates a block of colorful gift shops and a small casino.

Fodor's Choice ★ **Los Haitises National Park.** A highlight of a visit to the Samaná Peninsula is Los Haitises National Park (pronounced High-tee-sis), which is across Samaná Bay. The park is famous for its karst limestone formations, caves, and grottoes filled with pictographs and petroglyphs left by the indigenous Taínos.

The park is accessible only by boat, and a professionally guided kayaking tour is highly recommended, plus a licensed guide from a tour company or the government is mandatory. You'll paddle around dozens of dramatic rock islands and spectacular cliff faces, while beautiful coastal birds—magnificent frigate birds, brown pelicans, brown booby, egrets, and herons—swirl around overhead. A good tour will also include the caverns, where your flashlight will illuminate Taíno petroglyphs. It's a continual sensory experience, and you'll feel tiny, like a human speck surrounded by geological grandeur. DominicanShuttles.com can arrange a park tour and a stay at the adjacent, and rustic, Paraiso Caño Hondo Ecolodge, which has authentic creole cuisine and multiple waterfalls. ✉ *Samaná Bay* ☎ *809/472–4204* 🎫 *$4, not including manadatory use of licensed guide* ⏲ *Daily dawn–dusk.*

Taíno Park. This unique park tells the story of a lost civilization. The Taíno Indians, the indigenous people of this island, were the inhabitants here some 1,500 years ago . . . that is, until Christopher Columbus discovered it. And then came the inevitable clash between the Spanish colonials and these peaceful natives. The major exhibits comprise 25 animated scenes with life-size figures depicting the life of the Taínos and their conflict with the Spanish conquistadors. Their costumes came from the best movie-company makers in Europe. The museum has an archaeological exhibition of more than 200 pieces—bone, clay, stone, and wood. If it's raining, the tour is fully roofed. Plan on at least one hour with a personal audio guide (available in five languages). ✉ *Before the Arrollo Airport, 15 minutes west of Santa Barbara de Samaná, Los Róbalos* ☎ *809/729–1514, 809/267–9531* 🌐 *www.tainopark.com* 🎫 *$15* ⏲ *9–6, last entrance at 4:30.*

BEACHES

SOUTHEAST COAST

Playa Boca Chica. You can walk far out into warm, calm, clear waters protected by coral reefs here. On weekends, the strip with the midrise resorts is busy, drawing mainly Dominican families and some Europeans. But midweek is better, when the beaches are less crowded. Sadly, on the public beach you will be pestered and hounded by a parade of roving vendors of cheap jewelry, sunglasses, hair braiders, seafood cookers, ice-cream men, and masseuses (who are usually peddling more than a simple beach massage). Young male prostitutes also roam the beach and often hook up with older European and Cuban men. The best section of the public beach is in front of Don Emilio's (the blue hotel), which has a restaurant, bar, decent bathrooms, and parking. Better, go to one of the nicer waterfront restaurants—Boca Marina Restaurant & Lounge, El Pelicano, Neptuno's Club—and skip the public beach altogether. **Amenities:** Food and drink; toilets; parking. **Best For:** partiers; sunset; swimming; walking. ✉ *Autopista Las Américas, 21 miles (34 km) east of Santo Domingo, Boca Chica.*

BAYAHIBE

Playa Bayahibe. Playa Bayahibe, where several seafood restaurants are situated, is somewhat thin, with hard-packed taupe sand and no lounge chairs. However, as you move away from the village, a 10-minute walk along the shoreline, you'll reach the glorious, half-moon cove where you'll find the Dreams resort. Although you'll be able to get to the cove and the soft sand, bring a towel (the resort's security won't let you use the facilities). At night, when no one is on the playa and the silver moon illuminates the phosphorescence, it's the stuff that Caribbean dreams are made of. **Amenities:** food and drink; toilets. **Best for:** partiers; sunset; swimming; walking; windsurfing. ✉ *Starts in the center of town, near the Dreams resort, Bayahibe.*

PUNTA CANA

Playa Bávaro. Bávaro is the most developed stretch of the 35 miles (56 km) of white-sand beach in the Punta Cana area, which is lined with massive all-inclusive resorts. Although it encompasses many smaller towns, the main area, which is past Cabeza de Toro, is thought to begin with the massive Barcelo Bávaro Beach Resort and extend to the funky, fun fishermen's beach, Playa El Cortecito, known for the landmark restaurant Capitán Cook's. The water is characteristically warm and fairly shallow, with seaweed kept in check by hotels. Each resort has its own designated area with its chaises longues lined up in neat rows. Although there are stretches that are idyllically quiet, for the most part it is nonstop action. Boats and water sports provide the entertainment, wandering beach vendors the aggravation. In several areas there are designated, makeshift markets. **Amenities:** food and drink; toilets; water sports. **Best for:** walking; swimming; windsurfing. ✉ *Playa Bávaro, Bávaro.*

Playa Punta Cana. This long stretch of sandy coastline on the Caribbean side of the peninsula is where tourism first began in Punta Cana. This undulating beach with powdery white sand is shaded by lilting coconut palms. Much of it still looks like virgin beach since there is not the proliferation of all-inclusive hotels you find farther north in Bávaro. The beach extends south to Playa Juanillo, which is similarly incredible and now the site of the Cap Cana development. The waters are generally calm, with more wave action in the winter and during hurricane season. Seaweed has become more of a problem in recent years, and resorts have crews that rake their stretch of sand. Coral rock can make areas difficult to walk in the water, which is often shallow close to shore; however, the reefs are super for snorkeling and one can walk or swim from shore. The new Westin Punta Cana has fresh contemporary food offerings at their beachside restaurant and Playa Blanca, is a delightful seafood restaurant adjacent to the Kite-Club. **Amenities:** food and drink; toilets; water sports. **Best for:** snorkeling; swimming; walking; windsurfing; kitesurfing. ✉ *Playa Punta Cana, Punta Cana.*

NORTH SHORE

Playa Cabarete. This is the main business district of Cabarete. If you follow the coastal road east from Playa Dorada, you can't miss it. The beach, which has strong waves after a calm entrance, and ideal, steady wind (from 15 to 20 knots), is an integral part of the international windsurfing circuit. Segments of this long beach are strips of sand punctuated only by palm trees. The regeneration of Cabarete Beach was a massive engineering project that made the beach some 115 feet wider, adding an infusion of white sand. In the most commercial area, restaurants and bars are back-to-back, spilling onto the sand. The informal scene is young and fun, with expats and tourists from everywhere. **Amenities:** food and drink; lifeguards; toilets; water sports. **Best for:** partiers; surfing; swimming; windsurfing; kitesurfing. ✉ *Sosúa–Cabarete Rd., Cabarete.*

Playa Dorada. Playa Dorada is one of the island's most established resort areas. Each hotel has its own slice of the beach, which is covered with soft sand, nearly white now thanks to its participation in a $6-million beach rejuvenation. Reefs for snorkeling are right offshore. Gran Ventana Beach Resort, which is on a point, marks the easternmost end of the beach, followed by Casa Colonial and Blue Bay Villa Doradas. If you're not staying at one of the resorts in the Playa Dorada complex, then it's best to enter the beach before this point. Zealous hotel security guards try to keep you off "their" stretch of beach, but by law they cannot if you walk along the water's edge. They can keep you off the chaises longues and the resort's property. This is a good swimming beach with mild wave action. **Amenities:** none (though resorts on the beach offer full service). **Best for:** fishing; swimming; walking; waterskiing; windsurfing. ✉ *Off Autopista Luperón, at the entrance to the Playa Dorada Complex, approximately 10-min drive east of town, Playa Dorada* 🌐 *www.playadorada.com.do.*

Fodor's Choice ★ **Playa Grande.** This dramatic, mile-long stretch is widely considered to be one of the top beaches in the world. Many a photo shoot was made at this picture-perfect beach with off-white sands and turquoise water. Just east of the famous golf course of the same name, Playa Grande's drama comes from craggy cliffs dropping into the crystalline sea. Shade can be found in the palm trees that thicken into Parque Nacional Cabo Frances Viejo, a jungle preserve south of the beach.

This simply gorgeous stretch of sand had food shacks and cheapie souvenir stands that marred its beauty, but the vendors now have brightly-painted, cutesy, Victorian-style huts that have been relocated to the end of the beach where a large parking area was constructed. Some are selling fried fish, tostones, lobster, avocado salad, and cold Presidente beer. Security is present, and there are clean restrooms. Surfboards, paddleboards, and bodyboards are for rent; although the surf can swell, it can also be smooth. The days of driving your car onto the beach are definitely over (a good thing since islanders with huge speaker systems in their cars would park right next to your table.) Just behind the beach, screened by a palm-frond fence, the Playa Grande Beach Club is a new collection of buildings and bungalows available for rent. **Amenitites:** food and drink; restrooms. **Best for:** surfing; swimming; walking. ✉ *Carretera Río San Juan–Cabrera, Km 12, Río San Juan* 🌐 *www.playagrande.com* 🎫 *Free* ⛳ *Playa Grande Golf & Reserve.*

Playa Sosúa. This gorgeous beach on Sosúa Bay, renowned for its coral reefs and dive sites, is a 20-minute drive east of Puerto Plata. Here, calm waters gently lap at a shore of soft, golden sand. Swimming is delightful—except after a heavy rain, when litter floats in. But beware of sea urchins in the shallow water—beach shoes are definitely recommended—and bring your own mask and snorkel if possible. You can see mountains in the background, the cliffs that surround the bay, and seemingly miles of coastline. Snorkeling from the beach can be good, but the best spots are offshore, closer to the reefs. The beach is backed by a string of tents where hawkers push souvenirs, snacks, drinks, and water-sports equipment rentals. The weekend scene here is incredible—local families pack the beach, and the roar of Dominican fun fills the air. Alas, with the closing of the Sosua Bay Resort, the tourist presence has diminished. Don't bring valuables or leave your belongings unattended. There is a small parking area on the beach's north end near the Big Blue Dive Center, at the south end of La Puntilla Street. **Amenities:** food and drink; parking (free). **Best for:** snorkeling; swimming; walking. ✉ *Carretera Puerto Plata–Sosúa, El Batey, Sosúa.*

SAMANÁ PENINSULA

On the north coast of the Samaná Peninsula, tall palms list toward the sea, and the beaches are extensive and postcard perfect, with crystalline waters and soft, golden sand. There's plenty of color—vivid blues, greens, and yellows—as well as colorful characters. To the west is Playa El Cosón, opposite Cayo Ballena, a great whale-watching spot (from January to April). Samaná has some of the country's best beaches and drop-dead scenery, the rough roads notwithstanding.

LAS TERRENAS

Fodor's Choice ★ **Playa Cosón.** This is a long, wonderful stretch of nearly white sand and the best beach close to the town of Las Terrenas. Previously undeveloped, it's now reachable by a new highway, Carretera Cosón, and there are a number of condo developments under construction (so the current sense of solitude probably won't last). One excellent restaurant, The Beach, serves the entire 15-mile (24-km) shore, and there's the European-owned boutique hotel Casa Cosón and its restaurant and bar. If beachgoers buy lunch and/or drinks at either, then they can use the restrooms. **Amenities:** food and drink; parking; toilets. **Best for:** swimming; sunset; walking; windsurfing. ✉ *Las Terrenas.*

WHERE TO EAT

The island's culinary repertoire includes Spanish, Italian, Middle Eastern, Indian, Japanese, and *nueva cocina Dominicana* (contemporary Dominican cuisine). If seafood is on the menu, it's bound to be fresh. The dining scene in Santo Domingo is the best in the country and probably offers as fine a selection of restaurants as you will find in most Caribbean destinations. Keep in mind that the touristy restaurants, such as those in the Zona Colonial, with mediocre fare and just-okay service, are becoming more and more costly, while the few fine-dining options here have lowered some of their prices. For example, La Residence now offers a daily prix-fixe chef's menu with three courses. Or you can order two generous appetizers for even less. You will have caring service and be sequestered in luxe surroundings away from the tourist hustle. Know that *capitaleños* (residents of Santo Domingo) dress for dinner and dine late. The crowds pick up after 9:30 pm.

What to Wear: In resort areas, shorts and bathing suits under beach wraps are usually (but not always) acceptable at breakfast and lunch. For dinner, long pants, skirts, and collared shirts are the norm. Restaurants tend to be more formal in Santo Domingo, both at lunch and at dinner, with trousers required for men and dresses suggested for women. Ties aren't required anywhere, but jackets are (even at the midday meal) in some of the finer establishments.

SANTO DOMINGO

ZONA COLONIAL

$$$ FRENCH Fodor's Choice ★ **La Residence.** This fine-dining enclave has the setting—Spanish-colonial architecture, with pillars and archways overlooking a courtyard—but with the classically grounded French chef, Dominique David, serving remarkably innovative cuisine, it has really grown into a destination restaurant. An amuse-bouche arrives before your meal, and there is an excellent bread service. Available for lunch and dinner, the three-course daily Menu de Chef is about $26, including tax. It could feature brochettes of spit-roasted duck, chicken au poivre, or vegetable risotto. Veer from this menu, and prices go higher, but they remain fair. A luscious foie gras parfait with a port wine velouté and house-made brioche will start you on your way; segue to grilled scallop skewers with a strong passion-fruit jus and spinach tagliatelle. For a finale, we suggest the strawberry soup with basil and mint infusion. A guitarist romantically serenades diners Friday through Sunday nights and during Saturday and Sunday brunch. *Average main: $23* *Hostal Nicolas de Ovando, Calle Las Damas, Zona Colonial* *809/685–9955* *www.hostal-nicolas-de-ovando-santo-domingo.com* *Reservations essential.*

ON THE MENU

Among the best Dominican specialties are *queso frito* (fried cheese), *sancocho* (a thick stew of meats and chicken, served with rice and avocado slices), *arroz con pollo* (rice with beans and chicken), *pescado al coco* (fish in coconut sauce), *platanos* (plantains), and *tostones* (fried green plantains). Presidente is the best local beer. Brugal rum is popular with the Dominicans, but Barceló *añejo* (aged) rum is as smooth as cognac, and Barceló Imperial is so special that it was sold only around Christmastime. But now, due to demand, it is on the shelves all year-round.

$$ CARIBBEAN **Mesón D' Bari.** Dominicans call this one a "long hitter"—as in baseball, which will inevitably be on the TV at the bar. For some 30 years, owner Señor Marisol has been feeding the local Zoners his grandmother's recipes. This simple, two-story Dominican restaurant is still a hangout for artists, baseball players, politicians, businessmen, tourists, and even unaccompanied gringas, who feel comfortable here. Really flavorful dishes include creole-style eggplant, empanadas of crab and conch, grilled crabs, and stewed, sweet orange peels. Prices are up even though the culinary ambition is not. You'll hear bachata and American music from decades past (think "Moonglow"). *Average main: $15* *Calle Hostos 302, corner of Salomé Ureña, Zona Colonial* *809/687–4091.*

$$ INTERNATIONAL FAMILY

✕ **Mix.** Mix, match, and *compartir* (share) is the thought behind this trendy restaurant that is in presently, with well-heeled capitaleños. Best enjoyed with a group, the round tables with banquette seating can easily accommodate six or more. Two-tops prevail out on the terrace, which is not as loud as the dining room. Neighboring tables talk back and forth. It's: "Pass the *Cocoloco* (ceviche with lime and green plantains)" and "Where is the Popeye (a spinach dip au gratin with hot tortillas)?" "Did you finish the great balls of rice (risotto balls stuffed with pork and covered with a creamy Italian sauce)?" It's a fun atmosphere, though you might want your very own tamarind-grilled chicken salad. Italian-Dominican influences often prevail in the main courses. The cultivated wine list offers many fine Italian and Spanish bottles and to finish, there are grappas. Family-friendly, with a convivial bar and late-night scene, this is a crowd-pleaser (translation: always packed). **■TIP→ Check out the new casual, sister restaurant Market. Coming soon is their trendy new steak house to be named Meatpacking.** $ *Average main: $17* ✉ *Gustavo Mejia Ricart 69, Torre Washington Local 102, Serralles* ☎ *809/472–0100* ⏲ *Sun.–Thurs. noon–midnight, Fri.–Sat. noon–2 am.*

PIANTINI

$$$ ECLECTIC

✕ **Sophia's Bar & Grill.** Don't look for a sign that read's "Sophia's"; it reads simply "SBG." And don't ask for Sophia; she doesn't exist. "Her" high-profile restaurant is actually owned by a prime Dominican family that appreciates fine food, wine, and art. Prices are surprisingly reasonable at this elegant, fairly formal venue (dress accordingly). Gourmet burgers and creative sandwiches go for around $12, but main courses can get quite expensive; sides are extra. To keep expenses down, order an innovative appetizer such as Japanese-style miso eggplant or a ceviche of shrimp, octopus, and calamari, accompanied by a memorable bottle from the extensive wine list. End your meal with a slice of warm guava cheesecake and an aged port. One can relax in this classy environment, in an armchair, even a Bali bed or take a seat on the outdoor terrace. If so inclined, you can join the young lovelies and the *guapos* (handsomes) at the granite bar until late (3 am on Friday and Saturday and about 1 am the rest of the week.) **■TIP→ Kitchen closes about two hours before the bar.** $ *Average main: $25* ✉ *Paseo de los Locutores 9, Piantini* ☎ *809/620–1001* 🌐 *www.sbg.com.do.*

LA ROMANA

$$$ ECLECTIC Fodor's Choice ★

✕ **Peperoni.** Although the name may sound as Italian as *amore*, this restaurant's menu is much more eclectic than Italian. It has a classy, contemporary, white-dominated decor in a dreamy, waterfront setting. Strolling musicians perpetuate the mood. Astounding appetizers are found under the Asian section, like the sweet plantain roll or the Peperoni roll. Pasta dishes and risottos with rock shrimp or porcinis taste authentic, and the more inventive items such as house-made pear-and-goat-cheese ravioli with pine nuts and a key-lime emulsion are delectable. *Pulpo* (octopus) with fava beans stewed in limoncello vinaigrette is highly recommended. You can also opt for stylishly simple charcoal-grilled steaks (sauce or no), burgers, gourmet wood-oven pizzas, sandwiches, or even sushi and sashimi. Desserts are worthy here. Long-term ownership has sold but in a recent visit all was still the same. $ *Average* *main: $21 ✉ Casa de Campo, Plaza Portafino 16, Casa de Campo Marina, La Romana ☎ 809/523–2227, 809/523–3333.*

PUNTA CANA

$$$ SEAFOOD **Blue Marlin.** You dine here beneath a palapa-shaded table on a pier that sits over the Caribbean's gentle waters—truly a paradisical island experience. The restaurant's own small fleet of fishing boats harvests the waters daily for fresh catch, which are among the most popular menu items, though other specialties come from around the world. The menu offers everything from ceviche to Asian calamari rolls with sweet-and-spicy chili sauce and cilantro to Caribbean lobster cakes. Healthful, vegetarian, or vegan offerings are flagged. Lunch offerings have such innovations as wasabi or spicy chipotle mayonnaise. Some may think the portions are small but on the all-inclusive plan you can order as much as you like. Service is caring and attentive. The blue Euro-tiles around the fireplace at the bar add an unexpected, decorative element. Non-hotel guests must have a reservation to pass through security. **TIP→ Lobster and other high-ticket seafood items do come with a supplement if you have the Sanctuary Cap Cana AI plan.** *$ Average main: $24 ✉ Sanctuary Cap Cana, Cap Cana, Playa Juanillo ☎ 809/562–9191 ⊕ www.sanctuarycapcana.com Reservations essential.*

$$$ SEAFOOD **La Palapa by Eden Roc.** If you crave waterfront dining, this is a great option. Especially close to the blue-green is the deck with its sushi menu. The main restaurant with its palapa (thatched) roof exudes Caribbean charisma, yet has an Italian accent. The aromas promise exceptional seafood specialties, even hard finds like baby octopus, which is enhanced by the deft preparations of the Italian chef. The quality of product is immediately apparent from the Parmigiano-Reggiano to wines by the glass from the international wine list. Experience burrata cheese, best with grilled portobello mushrooms, arugula salad, and tomatoes. Details such as the contemporary Campari cocktails bespeak the high style of Eden Roc at Cap Cana, the boutique hotel that has proud ownership. The manager and waiters are professionals, yet here it is as casual as the pareos on the beachgoers who come and the golf guys when they finish the nearby 18th hole of Punta Espada. *$ Average main: $22 ✉ Caleton Beach Club, Cap Cana, Juanillo ☎ 809/469–7593, 809/695–5555 ⊕ www.edenroccapcana.com.*

$$ SEAFOOD Fodor's Choice ★ **Playa Blanca.** On a white-sand beach shaded by coconut palms, this understatedly cool seafood restaurant is efficient, friendly, and fun. Start with a perfectly executed cocktail—like a lime or mango daiquiri. Food is savvy and simple—fresh fish is a staple; opt for baked or grilled with a sauce on the side; shrimp is done three ways. Each winter season the offerings have become more creative. The prices are an excellent value for the amount of creativity and skill involved in dish creations. And there are paellas, pasta, risotto, ravioli, and grilled lobster and meats, to fill out the rest of the menu. You usually have to pay for the sides, but a bit more for some yucca mashed with blue cheese—why not? The best dessert is the chocolate fondant filled with molten *dulce de leche,* with vanilla ice cream. Live music weekly is just one aspect of the beachfront

entertainment; another is watching the kitesurfers—poetry in motion. You could try it yourself . . . it is available "next door." *Average main: $20* ✉ *Puntacana Resort & Club, Playa Blanca* ☎ *809/959–2262* 🌐 *www.puntacana.com.*

$$$ SEAFOOD

✕ **Restaurante Club Acquamare.** As the name depicts, the dominant color is aqua and the view of the marina and its moored yachts is a major draw. Seafood is the obvious choice and you may never find a better lobster bisque, with chunks of lobster meat and whipped cream. Yes, it costs $17, but couple it with a salad or another appetizer such as Thai tuna ceviche, and you will be double happy. Save a few pesos and calories by not having dessert, which is not memorable. However, sea bass with a citrus salsa is. Wraps and burgers are also good options. The DJ goes mellow with the music during dinner service and the waiters are professionals. Another bonus of this upscale dining venue? It has affordable pricing, and a shiny, white van that will transfer you to and from your accommodations within Cap Cana, complimentary. *Average main: $21* ✉ *Marina Cap Cana, Cap Cana, Playa Juanillo* ☎ *809/469–7342, 829/762–9988* ⏲ *No lunch.*

$$$ CONTEMPORARY Fodor'sChoice ★

✕ **Simon Mansion.** This unique dining experience is found within the Hard Rock Hotel, nearly adjacent to its casino; it is the only full-service restaurant that is open to outside guests. Celebrity chef Simon Kerry has contracted with Hard Rock to design the menu and train the chefs at this signature restaurant featuring his brand of contemporary American cuisine. The setting is cleverly designed as a mythical rock star's mansion and the various dining rooms are decadent, lavishly furnished like a living room, a library, even a bedroom, and a patio. Your dining experience will be a sensory rush from an innovative rum cocktail to a Pacific Rim appetizer, followed by a rack of lamb (seasonal) that is perfection. All meats are natural, the produce organic, so feel no guilt when you order a luscious dessert. Follow the wine and other suggestions of the savvy manager and prepare to be pampered. *Average main: $25* ✉ *Hard Rock Hotel & Casino Punta Cana, Blvd. Turistico del Este 74, Km 28, Playa Macao* ☎ *809/731–0094 restaurant, 809/687–0000 hotel* ⏲ *6 pm–midnight* ⏲ *No lunch.*

NORTH COAST

The Cabarete area in particular—where all-inclusive resorts don't yet totally dominate the scene—has some fun, original restaurants, but these are often small places, so it's important that you make reservations in advance. Expat residents complain that the prices in this town have moved past the good-value-for-money mark. Also, more and more restaurants are insisting on cash only, be it pesos, dollars, or euros. The area has lovely fine-dining options, *listed below.*

PUERTO PLATA

$$$ CARIBBEAN Fodor'sChoice ★

✕ **Lucía.** Lucia's menu is comprehensive and contemporary; billed as Caribbean Fusion cuisine, the Italian chef has put his own accent on it. The setting is as artistic as a gallery—befitting its location within Casa Colonial, a refined boutique hotel. Picture orchids galore, crisp white linens, and waiters in white guayabera shirts giving impeccable service. Guests love the one-of-a-kind appetizers, like the Seis-Viche, six varieties of ceviche presented in individual spoons. A main course might be a grilled duck breast, crispy leg confit, and foie gras served with rum-mango sauce and mashed pumpkin. Carnivores with more basic tastes can order an Angus fillet. The molten chocolate volcano with vanilla ice cream is the dessert you want. When the digestif cart is rolled over, be daring with a Brunello grappa or the local Brugal Unico rum, and look through the glass wall to the orchids clinging to the trees and the tropical mangrove garden. It's the good life at Lucía. $ *Average main: $25* ✉ *Casa Colonial, Playa Dorada* ☎ *809/320–3232* 🌐 *www.casacolonialhotel.com* ⏲ *No lunch.*

$$ CONTEMPORARY Fodor's Choice ★

✕ Mares Restaurant & Pool Lounge. This residence-cum-restaurant is the home of the D.R.'s most acclaimed chef, Rafael Vasquez. Guests "knock the door," decorated with an oversized fork and spoon; it's indicative of this charismatic chef's mantra—he is a rule breaker. The indoor dining room is sophisticated with classy china, glassware and cutlery and lots of white, with contemporary art by Rafael's father, a recognized painter. The outdoor seating is arranged between the bar and the swimming pool and the twinkle lights of the former play on the latter. The candles make it as romantic as Valentine's Day. Vasquez's Dominican heritage always is represented in his global repertoire; his island version of sushi is a sweet plantain roll with tempura shrimp, and mofonguitos have goat marinated with local Brugal rum. The mains are more international, such as salmon or baby lobsters in a creamy pastis sauce that is so French. The staff is mature, discreet, and professional. Ask if a dessert sampler is available . . . mmm. Mares can be like a house party or it can be your venue for a landmark celebration. $ *Average main: $18* ✉ *Francisco J. Peynado 6A, Puerto Plata* ☎ *809/261–3330, 809/224–1998* 🌐 *www.maresrestaurant.com* *Reservations essential* ⏲ *No lunch. Closed Mon.*

SOSÚA

$$ EUROPEAN

✕ B.Y.O.W. Restaurant. This be the place if it's your birthday, for your meal and those of your close, personal friends (up to six) will be discounted by your age, i.e., 50 years, half off. This cozy restaurant's name stands for "Bring Your Own Wine," a concept that has evolved into a popular dining establishment offering a moderately-priced, international-inspired menu. A palm tree snakes its way through the thatched roof that rises above the salmon-colored adobe walls. From the kitchen come such classics as Wiener schnitzel (even fish schnitzel), as well as other innovations like avocado salad with feta, tomato, and cucumbers. Chill with the soothing CDs as you move on to Italian tiramisu (about US$3.50). Breakfast is also very popular here, notably the yogurt parfaits and frittatas, and served every day. $ *Average main: $12* ✉ *Casa Valeria, Calle Dr. Rosen 28, El Batey, Sosúa* ☎ *809/571–3565, 809/949–3845* 🌐 *hotelcasavaleria.com* ⏲ *No lunch or dinner Wed.*

CABARETE

$$ INTERNATIONAL

✕ The Beach Club. Overlooking a craggy shoreline, this restaurant has seen a number of evolutions but this reincarnation is the best ever. The couple in charge, the Avakians, are a well-known entity in the

Cabarete expat community, with roots in Armenia, Ethiopia, and Italy. Consequently, the menu is international and runs the global gamut from Thai beef salad to Middle-Eastern baklava, lobster ravioli, and fragrant chicken Tikka Tandoori. Grilled tuna is served atop caramelized onions with a fresh herb sauce, and do ask what *zil zil* is. A lunch favorite is the salad of grilled mango, avocado, shrimp, and cilantro, which you should pair with the signature yucca fries. Product quality is high, from the pancetta to the house-made gelato and gourmet pizzas. The monthly music nights are sceney, and you may even see musicians from the annual jazz festival perform. As the music grooves, savor the panna cotta drizzled with caramel. **■TIP→ Reservations are essential when there's live music; otherwise just tell the security gate that you are going to the Beach Club.** *Average main: $18 ✉ Sea Horse Ranch, Carretera Principal Sosua-Cabarete, Cabarete ☎ 809/571–4995 ⊕ www.sea-horse-ranch.com ⊙ Daily noon–10 pm ⊙ Closed Wed. in low season.*

$$ MEDITERRANEAN **bliss Restaurant–Lounge Bar Pool.** A white, stucco home where tables flank the night-lighted pool and soft, chill music plays—this is the kind of intimate place where wedding proposals are staged. Like its name, the mood is *tranquillo* and the restaurant is ideally suited to the concept of slow food. Charming and passionate, the young owners are Italian so anything from Italy is a wise choice. Start with antipastos, carpaccios, and tartares or a salad, like one with tomino cheese, prosciutto, almonds, and a strawberry vingairette. For mains, try the gnocchi or ravioli four cheeses with avocado sauce; pair it with a Tuscan red. Panna cotta with a berry sauce is just like you hope to find and marries well with a mild grappa or sambuca. The chic set come to dinner and leave with an art piece under their arm—an adjacent room is an unexpected gallery. *Average main: $19 ✉ Callejón de la Loma 1, Cabarete ✣ This home is at the entrance of a residential neighborhood off the Sosua-Cabareta Highway 5. The side street is directly across from the Ocean Dreams complex on the other side of the highway ☎ 809/571–9721 ⊕ www.activecabarete.com/bliss ⊙ Daily 6 pm–10:30 pm. Closed Wed. ⊙ No lunch.*

$$ ECLECTIC **Eze Bar & Restaurant.** This little beach oasis doesn't look like much, but it has an intensely loyal following, from wallet-watching windsurfers to wealthy *capitaleño* families. Menu names, which reflect the jargon of its surfers, include the Rocker (grilled marinated beef with onions, peppers, tomato, and tzatziki on a soft pita). Get an energy kick from yogurt-and-mango smoothies and organic vegetable drinks. Fresh-squeezed juices have morphed into the most interesting, tropical cocktails. An extremely family- and dog-friendly place, there's an extensive children's menu and beach toys to entertain. The new owner, Antonello Cannistra, a restaurant pro, has kept all of the Eze *positivos* by day but by night Eze transforms into "Antonello," with a chic and romantic ambience. The Mediterranean menu is full of fresh carpaccios, seafood, pasta, and meat dishes. There are a wide variety of events now, including jazz nights and on the first Saturday of every month a theme party with DJs and often an art installation. *Average main: $15 ✉ Cabarete Beach, Plaza Carib Wind, Cabarete ✣ Adjacent to*

Carib Wind ☎ *829/601–8892* 🌐 *www.facebook.com/ezebarcabarete* ▭ *No credit cards.*

$$ ECLECTIC **Miró's on the Beach.** Miró's is going back to its origins, honoring both its Spanish namesake, with classic tapas and paellas, and owner Lydia Wazana's Moroccan roots, offering kebabs and tagines. You can almost hear the castenets when the Andalusian gazpacho, *patatas bravas*, and octopus à la Gallega arrive at your table. Authentic paellas (for two) can follow, even a combination of seafood and chicken and vegetarian. As Middle Eastern food is now in vogue, it shares the menu with the aromatic tagines, with vegetarian and vegan dishes. Lydia has also kept house faves (and mine) like Thai shrimp curry and beef tenderloin with three-pepper cream sauce. This landmark restaurant is smack on the beach with its share of contemporary lounge furniture. Take a table on the sand and listen to the gentle jazz. [$] *Average main: $18* ✉ *Cabarete Beach, Cabarete* ☎ *809/853–6848, 809/571–9709* ⏲ *Sometimes no lunch in low season.*

$$ SEAFOOD **Natura Restaurant at Natura Cabana.** If you're staying at this beachfront eco-lodge, you'll likely take most of your meals here. If not, definitely go, not only for the freshest of seafood, but for the soothing ambience. Seafood is at the heart of the menu here, and appropriately so, because diners listen to the sounds of the waves crashing on coral rock as they fork the catch of the day. The menu changes with the seasons while holding tight to some perennial favorites. The vegetables and herbs are farmed at Natura's organic garden. An innovative ceviche has octopus and conch marinated with pineapple juice, honey, and tiger milk. That appetizer could be coupled with a filet mignon in a coconut-blue cheese sauce. For dessert, enjoy a classic such as tiramisu with a tropical twist—passion fruit. Know that rich, flavorful soups, many pastas, vegetarian (and vegan) dishes round out the menu. The handmade pasta is delicious and everything possible is made from scratch—bread, burger buns, pastries, etc. The wines are French, Spanish, and Chilean (go for the *reservas*). Service is warm, caring, and efficient, the international music atmospheric. Just renovated, with an emphasis on the bar, a "chill out" deck on the beach side has been added. [$] *Average main: $16* ✉ *Natura Cabana, Perla Marina, Cabarete* ☎ *809/571–1507, 809/858–5822* 🌐 *www.naturacabana.com* ✍ *Reservations essential.*

SANTIAGO

$$ ITALIAN Fodor's Choice ★ **Il Pasticcio.** Everyone from college students to cigar kings, presidents to politicos, photographers, and movie stars pack this eccentrically decorated culinary landmark. Tourists take photos of the bathrooms, with their ornate mirrors and Romanesque plaster sinks. Chef-owner Paolo's mouthwatering creations are authentic and fresh. Ask about the tasting menu, or try the great antipasto selections; commence with the Pasticcio salad. Even the bread service comes with three sauces; the best is a creamy anchovy sauce. Finish with a shot of limoncello and cheesecake. And if it's too dim to read the menu, just look up—it's also written on the ceiling. Who said Paolo is off the wall? He just celebrated his 20th anniversary with his amigos (check out his site). The outdoor terrace seating is new, along with a wall of black-and-white

photos of former film stars. ■ **TIP→ The value here is remarkable and it has won the hospitality award for Latin America and the Caribbean by the Italian Chamber of Commerce.** *Average main: $15* ✉ *Av. El Lano, corner Calle 3, Gurabo* ☎ *809/582–6061* 🌐 *www.ilpasticciord.com* ⏲ *Closed Mon.*

SAMANÁ PENINSULA

LAS TERRENAS

$$$ SEAFOOD Fodor's Choice ★

✕ **The Beach.** Some of the best food in Samaná is served up for lunch (and lunch only) in a wooden, Victorian-style bungalow on Playa Cosón—decidedly not the usual beach shack. Hidden past a long stretch of lawn and behind a grove of coconut trees, it's on a 12-mile (19-km) stretch of virgin beach. The Beach is an alfresco terrace restaurant decorated with the same exquisite taste as its big sister, The Peninsula House. The new Columbian executive chef has cooked in Michelin three-star restaurants in Europe. The daily menu changes based on what fresh ingredients, fish, and lobster are available. Cooking is refined: a terrine of roasted beets and fresh goat cheese, or langostinos in passion-fruit butter. Lunch here on fine china makes for a cherished travel memory. After you finish, you can dream about it while taking a siesta on the golden beach. *Average main: $22* ✉ *Playa Cosón, Antiqua carretera de Playa Coson (Old Beach Rd.), Las Terrenas* ☎ *809/962–7447* ▭ *No credit cards* ⏲ *Closed Mon. No dinner.*

$$ SEAFOOD Fodor's Choice ★

✕ **Porto.** This jaw-dropping, beachfront beauty is one of the best players in the ever-evolving, European-accented restaurant scene in Las Terrenas. Sectioned off by ceiling-to-floor shell mobiles that divide the space, the nautically themed dining room is by the well-known Dominican designer Patricia Reid. Smart servers take pride in providing the kind of service that normally is found only in Santo Domingo's finest restaurants. Though beautiful, the setting is decidedly casual; in between courses, guests who come in their cover-ups can dive into the crystalline waters just past the sea grape trees. The Peruvian-influenced cuisine has roots in Italian cooking, with Asian undertones and focuses primarily on fresh seafood, including delightful Peruvian-style ceviche. The wine cave is impressive as well. There are new fire pits and oftenimes live entertainment, usually a jazz trio. ■ **TIP→ In low season the hours are cut back some.** *Average main: $18* ✉ *Across from its hotel, Balcones del Atlántico, Playa Las Terrenas, Las Terrenas* ☎ *809/682–0954* 🌐 *www.balcones.com.do.*

WHERE TO STAY

The Dominican Republic has the largest hotel inventory (at this writing some 70,000 rooms, with even more under construction) in the Caribbean and draws large numbers of stateside visitors. Surfers can still find digs for $25 a night in Cabarete, and the new generation of luxurious all-inclusives in Punta Cana and Uvero Alto is simply incredible.

Santo Domingo properties generally base their tariffs on the European Plan (no meals)—though many include breakfast—and maintain the same room rates year-round. Beach resorts have high winter rates, with prices reduced for the shoulder seasons of late spring and early fall (summer has become another strong season). All-inclusives dominate in Punta Cana. Cabarete was a stronghold of the small inn, but it does have all-inclusives. Villa rentals are gaining in popularity all over the island, particularly in Cabarete and the Cabrera area.

During your stay your patience may be tested at times, particularly at all-inclusives. Even in the touristic zones, the D.R. still has vestiges of a third-world country. The nodding in and out of the electricity is one annoyance, and sometimes the *plantas* (generators) either don't kick in or wheeze and hiss from age. Service lapses and the language barrier can also be frustrating. But when an employee sincerely says, "How can I serve you, missus?" followed by, "It's a pleasure to help you. Have a happy day!" you're pleasantly reminded of the genuine hospitality of the locals. You gotta love it!

BEST BETS FOR LODGING

BEST FOR ROMANCE
Eden Roc Cap Cana, The Peninsula House

BEST POOL
Casa Colonial Beach & Spa, The Westin Punta Cana Resort & Club.

BEST SERVICE
Tortuga Bay

BEST FOR KIDS
Casa de Campo, Club Med Punta Cana

SANTO DOMINGO

The seaside capital of the country is in the middle of the island's south coast. In Santo Domingo, most of the better hotels are on or near the Malecón, with several small, desirable properties in the trendy Zona Colonial, allowing you to feel part of that magical environment. The capital is where you'll find some of the most sophisticated hotels and restaurants, not to mention nightlife. However, such an urban vacation is best coupled with a beach stay elsewhere on the island.

ZONA COLONIAL

$ HOTEL Fodor's Choice ★ **Hostal Nicolas de Ovando–M Gallery Collection.** This historic, boutique hotel was sculpted from the residence of the first governor of the Americas, and it just might be the best thing to happen in the Zona since Diego Columbus's palace was finished in 1517. **Pros:** lavish breakfast buffet; beautifully restored historic section; its La Residence is one of the capital's best restaurants. **Cons:** breakfast, no longer included in rates, is $25; some rooms could be larger. *Rooms from: $185* ✉ *Calle Las Damas, Zona Colonial* ☎ *809/685–9955, 800/763–4835* 🌐 *www.hostal-nicolas-de-ovando-santo-domingo.com* *97 rooms* *No meals.*

$ B&B/INN **Hotel Villa Colonial.** Owner Lionel Biseau turned this circa-1920s town house into a lovely boutique hotel, keeping as much of the original structure as possible, including a second-floor veranda and old-timey, patterned tile floors. **Pros:** stylish breakfast room and bar overlooking the petite pool; low rates make this an exceptional value; plush towels.

Cons: the small street sign is easy to miss and only reads "Villa Colonial"; not haute luxury; Wi-Fi can be intermittent—best in 1st-floor rooms—which are the better ones. $ *Rooms from: $85* ✉ *Calle Sanchez 157, between Calles Padre Bellini and Arzobispo Noel, Zona Colonial* ☎ *809/221–1049, 809/849–3104 mobile* 🌐 *www.villacolonial.net* *11 rooms* *Breakfast.*

$ HOTEL **Hotel Frances Santo Domingo—M Gallery Collection.** Discerning business travelers, American vacationers, celebs, and other luminaries opt for the intimate, refined luxury of this small, well-run hotel. **Pros:** long-term stays available; many hospitable, veteran staffers; historic Zona ambience. **Cons:** some heavy furnishings remain dated; a romantic hideaway that's not the best place for children; many rooms are dark; maintenance problems associated with age. $ *Rooms from: $119* ✉ *Calles Las Mercedes, at the corner of Arzobispo Meriño, Zona Colonial* ☎ *809/685–9331, 800/763–4835* 🌐 *www.hotel-frances-santo-domingo.com* *19 rooms* *Breakfast.*

GAZCUE

$ HOTEL **Crowne Plaza Santo Domingo.** Leisure-minded guests may now find little reason to leave this stylish 15-story hotel, especially with the second-story outdoor pool and Jacuzzi that overlook the Caribbean. **Pros:** class-A professional service throughout; on-site convenience store and beauty salon, day-care and children's activities available. **Cons:** this busy hotel can get noisy late into the evening; geared for convention groups (13 salons), which may bother some independent guests. $ *Rooms from: $149* ✉ *Av. George Washington 218, Gazcue* ☎ *809/221–0000, 877/859–5095 toll-free* 🌐 *www.ihg.com/crowneplaza* *196 rooms* *No meals.*

$ HOTEL **Hilton Santo Domingo.** On the Malecón, it manages to please business people, convention attendees, and leisure travelers (the pool has sea views). **Pros:** The lobby renovation is both colorful, and tasteful; luxe bedding; totally soundproof rooms; the executive-level lounge. **Cons:** little about the property is authentically Dominican; Malecón neighborhood is sketchy by night; some rooms are looking tired and at this writing they are due to be renovated. $ *Rooms from: $129* ✉ *Av. George Washington 500, Gazcue* ☎ *809/685–0000* 🌐 *hiltoncaribbean.com/santodomingo* *260 rooms* *No meals.*

SOUTHEAST COAST

LA ROMANA

$$$$ ALL-INCLUSIVE FAMILY Fodor's Choice ★ **Casa de Campo.** The country's most illustrious resort, which set the benchmark for luxury travel in the Caribbean, has had a dramatic renovation of its public spaces, rooms, and suites. **Pros:** excellent golf and tennis; La Cana by Il Circo, and La Casita in the marina are on the meal plan are fine choices; food continues to upgrade to please the clientele. **Cons:** not the largest beach; food's expensive if not on an inclusive plan; a bit too sprawling although *gratis* golf carts minimize this; the standard accommodations have not enjoyed the same renovations as the higher categories. $ *Rooms from: $820* ✉ *Casa de Campo Resort*

809/523–3333, 305/856–5405, 800/877–3643 *www.casadecampo.com.do* *173 rooms, 12 suites, 50 villas* *All-inclusive.*

BAYAHIBE

$$ ALL-INCLUSIVE FAMILY Fodor's Choice ★ **Dreams La Romana.** This outstanding resort sits on an exceptional palm-fringed ribbon of white sand protected by a coral reef that offers great snorkeling from the beach, and a professional PADI dive school. **Pros:** with the new highway, the hotel is now a 50-minute drive from Las Americas Airport and 40 minutes from Punta Cana Airport; top-shelf liquors available at the lobby bar; free Wi-Fi in lobby and in-room at the club level; Cristal program for the food outlets. **Cons:** large and busy property can feel overly full; constant entertainment—if room is next to the main pool and stage, it will be noisy until about 11 pm; lots of local groups book in August–October and can be noisy; caring and efficient staff is sometimes overwhelmed. *Rooms from: $310* *Playa Bayahibe, Box 80, Bayahibe* *809/221–8880* *www.dreamsresorts.com/la-romana* *788 rooms* *All-inclusive.*

PUNTA CANA

The easternmost coast of the island has 35 miles (56 km) of incredible beach punctuated by coconut palms; add to that a host of all-inclusive resorts, an atmospheric thatch-roof airport, and many more direct flights than any other D.R. resort area, and it's easy to see why this region—despite having almost 50,000 hotel rooms (more than on most other Caribbean islands)—can regularly sell out. It has become the Cancún of the D.R. Most hotels in the region are clustered around Punta Cana and Bávaro beaches, where more than 90% of the existing properties are all-inclusive. But development continues to press outward—northward to the more remote locations of Macao and Uvero Alto, and southward to the nearby Juanillo—and several of the newer offerings are more luxurious and not all-inclusive, like the Eden Roc Cap Cana.

The region commonly referred to as Punta Cana actually encompasses the beaches and villages of Juanillo, Punta Cana, Bávaro, Cabeza de Toro, El Cortecito, Arena Gorda, Macao, and Uvero Alto, which hug an unbroken stretch of the eastern coastline; however, Uvero Alto, the farthest developed resort area to the north, lies some 45 minutes from the Punta Cana International Airport, less than before that road was significantly improved

Big news in November 2014 was the inauguration of the second terminal at Punta Cana International Airport (PUJ). With this expansion, PUJ is slated to be the Caribbean's largest airport hub. Designated Terminal B, it will be able to accommodate 6,500 passengers daily, with a capacity of handling more than 2 million passengers annually.

A main goal of the new project was to elevate passenger ease to the region, as wait lines for incoming passengers to clear customs and immigration were too long. The Passenger Departure Area will have 50 check-in counters, an air-conditioned concourse equipped with seven jet bridges, associated parking, and nine departure gates. Passengers

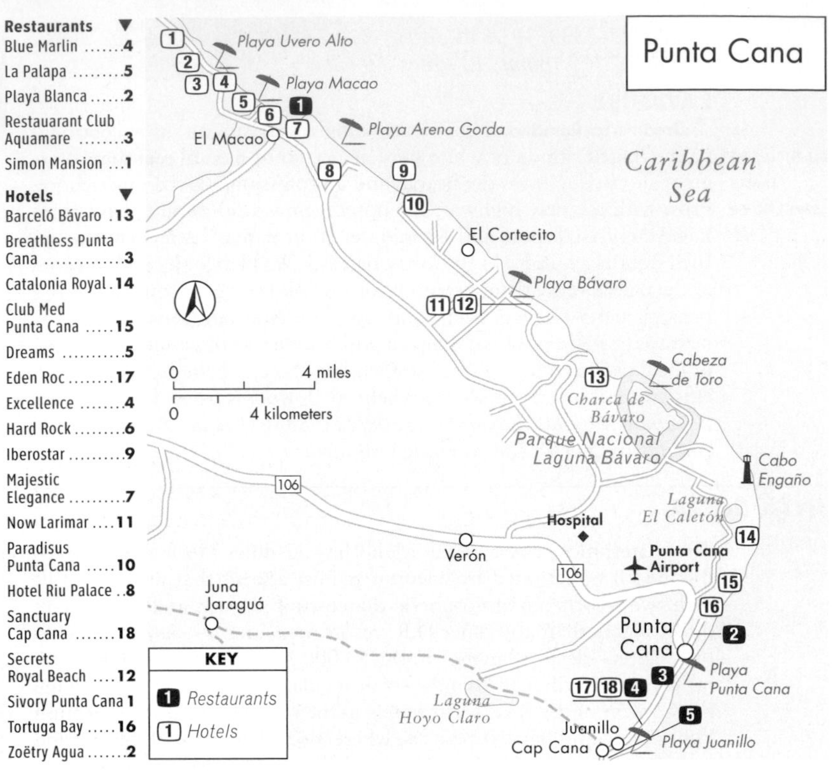

will find a food court, a VIP lounge, duty-free stores, champagne bar, kid's playground, a designated smoking area, access to Wi-Fi, and a recharging area for electronic equipment.

PLAYA PUNTA CANA

$$ ALL-INCLUSIVE FAMILY Fodor'sChoice ★ **Club Med Punta Cana.** Whimsy and camaraderie are characteristic of this family-friendly resort—Punta Cana's original all-inclusive—redesigned and situated on 75 tropical acres, with a coastline of incredible white-sandy shores. **Pros:** upscale, two-bedroom Trident Tiara suites ($790) are the best choice; animated, fun, interesting, global staff; themed weeks for music, dance, and sports. **Cons:** although buffets are praiseworthy, dining options are limited; Wi-Fi is expensive both in-room and in public spaces (free in Tiara suites); most guest complaints seem to occur during peak holiday times; complaints cited are that standard rooms are aging (although being renovated in stages) and maintenance issues. *Rooms from: $360 ✉ Playa Punta Cana ☎ 809/686–5500, 800/258–2633 🌐 www.clubmed.com 553 rooms All-inclusive.*

$$$$ RENTAL Fodor'sChoice ★ **Tortuga Bay.** Shuttered French windows that open to grand vistas of the sea and a cotton-white private beach are hallmarks of this yellow, luxury-villa enclave within the grounds of Puntacana Resort & Club. **Pros:** sprawling grounds with virgin beaches; VIP check-in at airport;

breakfast poolside with fresh squeezed OJ. **Cons:** little nightlife; Bamboo restaurant is pricey; too isolating for singles unless you roll on over to Playa Blanca. *Rooms from: $905 ✉ Punta Cana Resort & Club, Playa Punta Cana ☎ 809/959–8229, 888/442–2262 www.puntacana.com 30 suites Breakfast.*

$$$ RESORT **The Westin Punta Cana Resort & Club.** The Punta Cana Group has eschewed the all-inclusive in favor of a beautiful Westin property on a glorious stretch of beach with ocean views from floor-to-ceiling windows and private balconies in every guestroom. **Pros:** well-trained staff; incredible breakfast buffet; gorgeous dual-pool complex that faces the ocean; bartenders put the happy in the happy hour. **Cons:** in-room Wi-Fi inconsistent; hotel shuttle has few runs to Punta Cana Village during dinner hours; not for party-hearty types or budget travelers. *Rooms from: $389 ✉ Playa Blanca, Punta Cana www.westinpuntacana.com 206 rooms, 7 suites No meals.*

PLAYA BÁVARO

$$$ ALL-INCLUSIVE FAMILY **Barceló Bávaro Beach Resort.** Barceló deserves loud applause for the incredible face-lift that has totally transformed this property from an aging, middle-of-the-road has-been to a glamorous complex worthy of gushing praise. **Pros:** the whole place has been reinvented; enormous range of entertainment and activity options; no other kids' club is this contemporary; exceptionally comfortable beds; guests appreciate cleanliness, gorgeous beach. **Cons:** pool gets crowded and noisy, music loud, heavy animation; high-volume resort draws large conventions; tacky go-go girls have been moved from the disco to the casino; Dominican residents flock here on holidays; complaints include slow restaurant service, some bathrooms; cost and regularity of Wi-Fi. *Rooms from: $413 ✉ Carretera Bávaro, Km 1, Bávaro ☎ 809/686–5797 www.barcelo.com 2,887 rooms All-inclusive.*

$$$ ALL-INCLUSIVE Fodor's Choice ★ **Catalonia Royal Bavaro.** This adults-only haven is a perfect example of how an all-inclusive resort can offer top-tier hospitality without the herd mentality. **Pros:** all rooms have hammocks on terraces; three restaurants at Royal, eight at the Bávaro, make 11 dining options; less expensive than other deluxe/luxurious AIs. **Cons:** even the bi-level suites need some maintenance and better lighting; busier than a comparable boutique hotel would be; the other Royal restaurants are not as wonderful as Cata Tapa. *Rooms from: $403 ✉ Playa Bávaro, Bávaro ☎ 809/412–0011 www.hoteles-catalonia.com 255 rooms All-inclusive.*

$$ ALL-INCLUSIVE FAMILY **Dreams Palm Beach Punta Cana.** This fine Dreams has a fabulous new look after its 2013 renovation—most notably in its new room category, 75 Premium Deluxe rooms with luxurious decor and the new Dreams Pevonia Spa. **Pros:** unlimited top-shelf alcohol; handsome redecoration of bars and restaurants plus a music lounge; close to the airport; free Wi-Fi for all; management is especially conscientious. **Cons:** complaints that not enough chaises or floats at pool; often party-hardy atmosphere; time-share sales can be agressive. *Rooms from: $338 ✉ Cabeza de Toro, Bávaro ☎ 809/552–6000 www.dreamsresorts.com/palmbeach 500 rooms All-inclusive.*

$$ ALL-INCLUSIVE FAMILY **Grand Palladium Bávaro Suites Resort & Spa.** Four sprawling, contiguous resorts (with a shuttle service until 2 am) share these well-kept grounds and feel like a beachside village, and three of these—Grand Palladium Bávaro, Grand Palladium Punta Cana, and Grand Palladium Palace—share one another's facilities. **Pros:** excellent offshore snorkeling (extra charge); guest rooms are exceptionally spacious, and quiet, because of solid, quality construction and location far from activity centers; complete spa and health club. **Cons:** few rooms have sea views; the attractive lobby at Turquesa serves as the club lounge with the bar/café offering drinks but no contemporary hors d'oeuvres; the Royal section doesn't have a strong fun quotient but rather focuses on calm relaxation; staff has minimal English and must guests are not Anglos. *Rooms from: $336 ✉ Carretera El Cortecito, El Cortecito, Bávaro ☎ 809/221–8149 Grand Palladiuim Bávaro, 809/221–0719 Grand Palladium Palace, 800/961–7661 in U.S. www.fiestahotelgroup.com, www.palladiumhotelgroup.com 1,823 rooms All-inclusive.*

$$$$ ALL-INCLUSIVE FAMILY **Iberostar Bávaro Resort.** Like its two sister resorts, this Spanish entry has panache—evidenced in its lobby, an artistic showpiece, and newly refurbished guest accommodations with contemporary style and bedding—making it competitive with Punta Cana's newer properties. **Pros:** fun entertainment—not too aggressive; a kids' water playground; good specialty restaurants; extra-special management keeps the staff in fine spirits. **Cons:** buffet not quite as good as it once was; the property is showing its age. *Rooms from: $480 ✉ Playa Bávaro, Bávaro ☎ 809/221–6500, 888/923–2722 809/688–6186 www.iberostar.com 596 rooms All-inclusive.*

$$$$ ALL-INCLUSIVE Fodor's Choice ★ **Iberostar Grand Bavaro Hotel.** Iberostar's adults-only resort—an architectural gem—is a knockout from the moment you walk into the glamorous lobby and is one resort where the term "no expense was spared" is actually true. **Pros:** impressive selection of designer restaurants with contemporary cuisine; excellent lunch buffet at beach; idyllic beach weddings and honeymoons. **Cons:** although improving, there are still service lapses from lack of English-language skills; chefs don't always let servers know when items are unavailable; cuisine is not gastronomic; the hotel is pricey for an all-inclusive in this area. *Rooms from: $784 ✉ Playa Bávaro, Bávaro ☎ 809/221–6500, 888/923–2722 iberostar.com 260 suites, 13 grand suites, 1 presidential All-inclusive.*

$$$$ ALL-INCLUSIVE **Majestic Elegance.** The younger of Punta Cana's two Majestic resorts, which is an all-suites property, is the more sophisticated sister—and a busy one. **Pros:** fun and welcoming staff; premium liquors at all bars and à la carte restaurants; at holidays decoration is full throttle as is the fun quotient; free Wi-Fi and in-room, too. **Cons:** guests not in the VIP Club may feel second-class; high occupancy makes it feel crowded; rooms are not soundproof and there have been some bathroom plumbing issues. *Rooms from: $495 ✉ Majestic St., Arena Gorda, Bávaro ☎ 809/221–9898 www.majestic-resorts.com 596 rooms All-inclusive.*

$$ ALL-INCLUSIVE FAMILY **Now Larimar Punta Cana.** This relatively new, moderately priced branch of the AMResorts family—which welcomes children—has style as well as a gorgeous 700-yard beachfront. **Pros:** within walking

distance of shops and off-site cafés; close to the airport; large housekeeping and entertainment team. **Cons:** some complaints about maintenance and repairs, uncomfortable beds; in-room Wi-Fi is expensive (free at the Club level); many adults without children prefer its sister, Secrets, adjacent. *Rooms from: $310 ✉ El Cortecito, Ave. Alemania s/n, Bávaro ☎ 809/221–4646 ⊕ www.nowresorts.com 720 rooms All-inclusive.*

$$$$ ALL-INCLUSIVE FAMILY Fodor's Choice ★ **Paradisus Palma Real Resort.** This luxury all-inclusive is a visual showstopper especially its central plaza by night, which sparkles under dramatic lighting. **Pros:** wonderful spa; adjacent to the Palma Real Shopping Center; fantastic on-site restaurant. **Cons:** restaurants and nightlife are far from some rooms; rooms at The Reserve do not have sea views and guests must take a shuttle to the private beach. *Rooms from: $478 ✉ Bavaro Beach, Bávaro ☎ 809/688–5000 ⊕ www.paradisuspalmareal.com 554 rooms All-inclusive.*

$$$ ALL-INCLUSIVE FAMILY Fodor's Choice ★ **Paradisus Punta Cana.** Paradisus has so many new, innovative amenities, while also exuding a charismatic quality—like vintage wine—that produces the warm feeling that makes for loyal, repeat guests. **Pros:** some impressive architecture and decor; professional and caring management strives for good service; the newly renovated YHI spa which allows one to de-stress and revitalize. **Cons:** at The Reserve, kids can make the dining room noisy and the only water views are of the pool; no elevators; some rooms have yet to be renovated but all are spacious; guest complaints vary, sporadic Wi-Fi, etc; during the fall rainy season avoid ground floor rooms even at Royal level. *Rooms from: $460 ✉ Bavaro Beach, Bávaro ☎ 809/687–9923 ⊕ www.paradisuspuntacana.solmelia.com 686 rooms All-inclusive.*

$$$ ALL-INCLUSIVE Fodor's Choice ★ **Secrets Royal Beach.** The lobby at this sceney, adults-only all-suites resort is like a modern art gallery, with suspended fish sculptures immediately attracting the eye; however, the Caribbean-accented guest rooms do not quite match. **Pros:** idyllic for weddings and honeymoons; nightly entertainment at the main plaza; good fun quotient with activities like cooking competitions on the beach; exceptional 17,000-square-foot Spa by Pevonia. **Cons:** beach vendors, excursion salespeople and overzealous entertainment crew can be annoying; some clients think food is not as stellar as the environment; tropical view rooms don't compare to more expensive accommodations; Wi-Fi is slow and costly. *Rooms from: $453 ✉ El Cortecito, Avenida Alemania s/n, Bávaro ☎ 809/221–4646 ⊕ www.secretsresorts.com 372 rooms All-inclusive.*

PLAYA MACAO

$$$$ ALL-INCLUSIVE Fodor's Choice ★ **Hard Rock Hotel & Casino Punta Cana.** Hard Rock's first all-inclusive property has its own unique identity, different from any other Domincan resort, and themed like its cafés. **Pros:** there is a large fun quotient here; mostly good service, particularly wait staff; baby boomers love to rock, roll, and remember. **Cons:** complaints balloon when the resort is overly full particularly on long Dominican weekends and traditional holidays (although customer service has definitely bumped up); some maintenance needed due to high occupancy; doesn't have a Caribbean feel except at the beach, which can have a bad undertow; not for those who prefer a small, boutique property. *Rooms from: $508 ✉ Blvd.*

Excellence Punta Cana

Turístico del Este 74, Km 28, Playa Macao ☎ 809/687–0000 ⊕ www.hardrockhotels.com ⇨ 1,787 rooms ¶◎| All-inclusive.

$$$ ALL-INCLUSIVE Fodor's Choice ★ **Hotel Riu Palace Macao.** After a major, much-needed renovation, this adults-only resort has gone from dowdy to stellar, having been brought up to a completely new level. **Pros:** the exterior which replicates a grand, white, Victorian edifice; good for a girls' getaway for the mannerly staff will ask you to dance to the live music in the lounge; fun and friendly staffers like the one dressed in a chauffer's uniform who opens the nightly buffet by reciting welcome in 25 languages. **Cons:** limited room views of the gorgeous beach (worth upgrading to one); it is such a good value for the price, but don't expect luxury; its new popularity equals high occupancy. ($) *Rooms from: $408 ✉ Playa Arena Gorda, Bávaro ☎ 809/221–7171 ⊕ www.riu.com ⇨ 328 rooms, 36 suites ¶◎| All-inclusive.*

PLAYA UVERO ALTO

$$$$ ALL-INCLUSIVE **Breathless Punta Cana Resort & Spa.** Enter the lobby and the contemporary decor with its explosion of vibrant colors—orchid, orange, flamingo pink—strong lighting, dangling sculptures, and retro-styled furniture may leave you breathless. **Pros:** everything new, clean and unique; premium liquors are served in the lobby bar, Wink; Xhale level makes everything better; well suited for the wedding market and for conferences; many enjoy the E-Team that keeps the party going. **Cons:** some find the interior design overwhelming; standard rooms are basic and smallish; no reservations needed for à la cartes can mean wait time; some staffers lack sufficient English. ■ **TIP→ Room suggestions are Master Ocean Suites and swim-up rooms.** ($) *Rooms from: $550 ✉ Playa*

Uvero Alto, Km 275, Uvero Alto ☎ 809/551–0000 ⊕ breathlessresorts.com ⇆ 750 rooms 🍴 *All-inclusive.*

$$ ALL-INCLUSIVE FAMILY **Dreams Punta Cana Resort & Spa.** This fun resort in a remote, pastoral setting is super for families, young couples, wedding entourages, honeymooners, ladies getaways—yes, even singles. **Pros:** all-around camaraderie; nightly entertainment is a cut above; lovely guest rooms, most have been redecorated. **Cons:** some rooms still need updating as do some of older public spaces; complaints are few, like insufficient outdoor furniture and beach towels; expensive Wi-Fi (Club level, it's free); resort runs at high occupancy. ■ **TIP→ For quiet's sake, no children are booked into second-floor rooms.** $ *Rooms from: $329* ✉ *Playa Uvero Alto, Km 269.5, Uvero Alto* ☎ *809/682–0404* ⊕ *www.dreamsresorts.com/punta-cana* ⇆ *620 rooms* 🍴 *All-inclusive.*

$$$$ ALL-INCLUSIVE Fodor's Choice ★ **Excellence Punta Cana.** Originally known to be a sumptuous lovers' lair, this adults-only all-inclusive is particularly appealing to couples (honeymooners, for sure) and wedding parties, and it now attracts a younger, fun clientele. **Pros:** no reservations are required at any of the individualistic restaurants; super-sized, renovated Excellence Club suites (about $185 more a night); the bi-level Excellence Club lounge has had its total redecoration and serves laudible food and liquors. **Cons:** far from shopping, other restaurants, and nightlife; isolating for singles. $ *Rooms from: $530* ✉ *Playa Uvero Alto, Uvero Alto* ☎ *809/685–9880* ⊕ *www.excellence-resorts.com* ⇆ *456 rooms* 🍴 *All-inclusive.*

$$$$ RESORT **Sivory Punta Cana Boutique Hotel.** The best things really do come in small packages for this boutique hotel, which delivers on its promise of expressly personal service and utter tranquillity. **Pros:** caring and accommodating staff (mostly); free, strong Wi-Fi throughout; near virgin beach albeit not calm. **Cons:** guests from high-stress areas like New York City appreciate the slowness here (others not always); food is frequently cited as disappointing; if accustomed to all-inclusive resorts, paying for each drink and meal can be painful; too many maintenance issues. $ *Rooms from: $500* ✉ *Uvero Alto Rd., Playa Sivory, Uvero Alto* ☎ *809/333–0500* ⊕ *www.sivorypuntacana.com* ⇆ *55 rooms* 🍴 *No meals.*

$$$$ ALL-INCLUSIVE **Zoëtry Agua Punta Cana.** At this serene, oceanfront resort, rustic natural beauty and high architectural style blend seamlessly. **Pros:** the wellness spa has hydrotherapy, yoga, and Reiki classes and complimentary 20-minute massage; the petite gourmet room with its fusion menu, top shelf liquors, and "wine cellar"; barista-style coffee shop/bakery. **Cons:** bathrooms can have too much nature and bugs can get into suites with thatched roofs, especially when it rains; some low-key entertainment but limited nightlife here or in the Uvero Alto area; guest reviews range from outstanding to lacking, with complaints ranging from service to food, lack of English, and original rooms needing renovations. $ *Rooms from: $705* ✉ *Playa Uvero Alto, Uvero Alto* ☎ *809/468–0000* ⊕ *www.zoetryresorts.com/agua* ⇆ *89 rooms, 5 villas* 🍴 *All-inclusive.*

PLAYA JUANILLO

$$$$ HOTEL Fodor's Choice ★ **Eden Roc Cap Cana.** This new star in the Cap Cana luxury resort category is an all-suites boutique hotel with interior decor straight from the French Riviera. **Pros:** pampering, discreet service; a golf cart is included for zipping around to reception and the beach; full-board

plans available (drinks extra); the new glamour spa and gym. **Cons:** suites don't have sea views; only eight one-bedrooms, which are in demand; expensive, but keep an eye out for promotions on its website. *Rooms from: $1104 ✉ Cap Cana, Juanillo ☎ 809/469–7469 🌐 www.edenroccapcana.com 34 suites Breakfast.*

$$$ ALL-INCLUSIVE **Sanctuary Cap Cana By AlSol.** This stellar resort, the keystone of Cap Cana, welcomes families with the Fortress wing reserved for adults only; both all-inclusive and EP plans are offered. **Pros:** famous white-sand beach; professional management with many exceptional staffers; a wonderful spirit and fun quotient, especially in the Love Bar. **Cons:** the standard junior suites are long but narrow; beach by main pool has coral, shallow and milky water but to the left of the Fortress is a phenomonal beach but B.Y.O. towel, etc. *Rooms from: $450 ✉ Cap Cana, Blvd. Zona Hotelera, Playa Juanillo, Juanillo ☎ 809/562–9191 🌐 www.sanctuarycapcana.com 142 rooms, 33 villas All-inclusive.*

NORTH COAST

The northern coast of the island, with mountains on one side, is also called the Amber Coast because of the large quantities of amber found in the area. The sands on its 75 miles (121 km) of beach are also golden. Major resort areas are Playa Dorada, Cabarete, and Sosúa. Plan to fly into Puerto Plata's Gregorio Luperon International Airport.

PUERTO PLATA

$$ HOTEL Fodor's Choice ★ **Casa Colonial Beach & Spa.** Designed by architect Sara Garcia, sophisticated Casa Colonial, a boutique property exuding refinement and relaxation on the quiet end of the long beach, is a surprise among the all-inclusives of Playa Dorada. **Pros:** architectural gem offering the full luxury, boutique experience; glorious spa; exceptional gourmet room (Lucia). **Cons:** can feel empty during the low season; large suites could use a splash of color; service is attentive but sometimes a bit off. *Rooms from: $295 ✉ Playa Dorada, Puerto Plata ☎ 809/320–3232, 866/376–7831 🌐 www.casacolonialhotel.com 50 rooms No meals.*

$ ALL-INCLUSIVE FAMILY **Gran Ventana Beach Resort.** This all-inclusive is filled primarily with English-speaking clientele who like its sophisticated lobby, the colorfully painted facades, and easy beach access. **Pros:** consistently good food and service for this price point; particulary efficient and caring front-desk staff; renovation has given the resort a rebirth. **Cons:** some aspects are still dated; charge for safes; can only dine once a week in each of three á la carte restaurants. *Rooms from: $189 ✉ Playa Dorada ☎ 809/320–2111, 809/320–3232 🌐 www.granventanahotel.com 506 rooms All-inclusive.*

$$$$ ALL-INCLUSIVE **Presidential Suites—Puerto Plata Lifestyle.** This hilltop enclave consists mainly of apartment-style, two-bedroom suites decorated in a modern, masculine style with black leather chairs, cherry wood, and bedroom Jacuzzis. **Pros:** the sexy, *moderne* suites; pool with cascading waterfall and the fabric-draped lounging beds; variety of lounges and restaurants; VIP beach club; caring employees and management try hard to please. **Cons:** a fast shuttle from the beach; heavily occupied, so can

Peninsula House, Las Terrenas

feel overly crowded; restaurants can jam up; relentless time-share sellers. *Rooms from: $660* ✉ *1 Paradise Dr., Cofresí* ☎ *809/970–7777* 🌐 *www.lhvcresorts.com* *60 suites* *All-inclusive.*

SOSÚA

$$$$ RENTAL **Sea Horse Ranch.** This enclave of private homes, each with large front- and backyards and private pool, is an elite bastion set within a vast country club–like setting. **Pros:** one of the country's most organized, well-managed groups of villas; potent security makes your vacation worry-free; location close to Cabarete and the airport; all villas have free, unlimited Wi-Fi. **Cons:** guests usually feel the need to rent a car or hire a driver; it's a walk or short drive to reach two petite, communal beaches; if your laptop has to be configured for the Wi-Fi, you will need to pay for a tech. *Rooms from: $700* ✉ *Coastal Hwy., Cabarete* ☎ *809/571–3880, 800/635–0991* 🌐 *www.sea-horse-ranch.com* *20 villas* *No meals.*

CABARETE

$ HOTEL **Hotel El Magnifico.** You will find a healthy dose of unexpected pleasure at this stellar, boutique condo-hotel. **Pros:** never feels crowded; the interior decor is très chic in many units; the spaces are large and contemporary; children under 15 stay free. **Cons:** steep spiral staircases and no elevators; no restaurant (next door is a breakfast/lunch restaurant) or bar; no in-room phones and no way to communicate with reception unless you have a cell phone or rent one here. *Rooms from: $94* ✉ *Calle del Cementario, Cabarete* ☎ *809/571–0868* 🌐 *www.hotelmagnifico.com* *30 units* *No meals.*

$ RENTAL FAMILY Fodor's Choice ★ **Le Reef Beach Condos.** Le Reef is a small condominium complex with Euro-style and furnishings that reflect Cabarete's surfing craze (kite, wind, and otherwise). **Pros:** rooms are spacious and stylin'; beautiful beach; super food and service at the Front Loop Café. **Cons:** smaller property than some people may want; no elevator and three floors; some water views are hindered by the café's structure. *Rooms from: $160 Cabarete Beach, next to The Palms condos, Cabarete 809/571–0848, 809/858–2589 cell www.le-reef.com 6 condos Breakfast.*

$ B&B/INN **Natura Cabana.** If your idea of perfection is thatched-roof cabanas and a quiet, private beach, then this is your oceanfront eco-lodge. **Pros:** natural, peaceful, beachfront stay; fresh seafood and innovative cuisine for dinner; caring owner, manager and long-term staff; spa with "Magic Mushroom" steam bath; free Wi-Fi. **Cons:** no TVs, phones, or air-conditioning, but sea breezes; car is an asset but taxis to town are safer; boutique touches, yet not for those who crave luxurious creature comforts. *Rooms from: $180 Playa Perla Marina, Cabarete 809/571–1507 www.naturacabana.com 10 rooms Breakfast.*

$ HOTEL **Velero Beach Resort.** You'll appreciate the location of this well-managed hotel and residential enclave with its own beachfront and gardens, just a few minutes' walk east of the noise of town yet also just minutes from the happening bars and restaurants. **Pros:** blenders, microwaves, and DVDs in the junior suites and above; draped Balinese sun beds at the pool are dreamy. **Cons:** no elevators—it's a climb up the spiral staircases; standard rooms are not spacious; showing some signs of age. *Rooms from: $140 Calle la Punta 1, Cabarete 809/571–9727, 888/770–9886 www.velerobeach.com 29 units No meals.*

CABRERA

$ B&B/INN Fodor's Choice ★ **Villa Castellamonte.** When not rented in its entirety, this elegant villa in Orchid Bay Estates operates as a high-end B&B. **Pros:** for all its grandeur, it's as laid-back as the garden hammock; sumptuous master suites have gas fireplaces; 24-hour security guards; three rooms have been updated with Italian-themed murals. **Cons:** beach is rocky and best visited with reef shoes; the staff of eight can be too much service. *Rooms from: $195 Orchid Bay Estates, Casa 10, Cabrera 829/629–1012 cell, 888/589–8455 toll-free in U.S. and Canada, 702/900–3121 U.S. direct www.villa-castellamonte.com 8 rooms Breakfast.*

SAMANÁ

Samaná is the name of both the peninsula that curves around the eponymous bay and of the largest town. Conveniently, El Catey Airport (AZS) is served regularly by JetBlue from New York–JFK; otherwise, *www.dominicanshuttles.com* offers regular flights from several D.R. airports.

LAS TERRENAS

$$$ RENTAL FAMILY **Balcones del Atlantico.** A condo hotel on a large tract of virgin land; its spacious accommodations are beyond stellar, with exceptional interior design, dreamy bedding, and private Jacuzzis on terraces that are basically outdoor rooms. **Pros:** intelligent and caring concierge staff; everything is nearly new, clean, and fresh; ideal for longer stays. **Cons:** not smack on the beach, with marginal views; some planned

amenities are still not in place; a second restaurant and minimart closer to accommodations is needed; best with a rental car for trips to town and shopping; maintenance problems continue. *Rooms from: $434 ✉ Carretera El Limon, across from Porto on Playa Las Terrenas, Las Terrenas ☎ 809/240–5011 ⊕ www.balconesdelatlantico.com.do 26 units No meals.*

$$$$ B&B/INN Fodor'sChoice ★ **The Peninsula House.** The gorgeous Victorian-style plantation house with wraparound verandas overlooks acres of coconut palms down to the ocean and is one of the best B&Bs in the Caribbean. **Pros:** quiet and remote; ideal for honeymoons and babymoons; many English TV channels and DVDs. **Cons:** pricey; you may worry that you'll break something; unmarked entrance, just off a dirt road. *Rooms from: $650 ✉ Camino Cosón, Las Terrenas ☎ 809/962–7447, 809/847–7540 ⊕ www.thepeninsulahouse.com 6 rooms Breakfast.*

SANTA BÁBARA DE SAMANÁ

$ HOTEL Fodor'sChoice ★ **The Bannister Hotel at Puerto Bahia Marina & Residences.** This stylish marina complex smack on the Bay of Samaná has changed the face of tourism in this area and become the social center for the upscale residents, a safe harbor for visiting yachtsmen, and a reasonable option for international visitors. **Pros:** wonderful ambience; natural beauty everywhere. **Cons:** the bedrooms in the one-bedroom accommodations could be more spacious; too far from town to walk. *Rooms from: $170 ✉ Puerto Bahia, Carretera Sanchez, Km 5, Santa Bárbara de Samaná ☎ 809/503–6363 ⊕ www.thebannisterhotel.com 30 rooms No meals.*

LAS GALERAS

$$$$ HOTEL Fodor'sChoice ★ **Sublime Samaná.** With dramatic, contemporary architecture that allows each suite water views, this resort offers large two- and three-bedroom condo accommodations with designer kitchens and living rooms, two LCD TVs and a balcony that looks down upon the labyrinth of swimming pools. **Pros:** the beach bar offers a great lunch, tropical cocktails, and fresh juices; chic interior furnishings are designed with taste and Caribbean spirit; the pool complex is so inviting especially with new gazebo bar. **Cons:** relatively isolated (a taxi into town, 4.3 miles [7 km] is $45 round-trip); restaurant options are limited and main dining rom has no water views; not a lot of on-site activities. *Rooms from: $580 ✉ Bahia de Coson, Ramal Viva, Las Terrenas ☎ 809/240–5050 ⊕ www.sublimesamana.com 15 suites (number in rental pool fluctuates) Breakfast.*

$ HOTEL **Villa Serena.** Decidedly one of the better hotels in the eastern corner of the peninsula, Villa Serena makes for a wonderful, stress-free Samaná vacation. **Pros:** private beachfront without vendors or loud music; reliable Wi-Fi in lobby; Croatian manager speaks English, as do front-desk staff. **Cons:** main section feels dated; most rooms have a/c but no TVs; no blackout drapes. *Rooms from: $140 ✉ Las Galeras Beach, Las Galeras ☎ 809/538–0000 ⊕ www.villaserena.com 21 rooms Breakfast.*

NIGHTLIFE

Santo Domingo's nightlife is vast and ever changing. Check with the concierges and hip capitaleños. At this writing, there is still a curfew for clubs and bars; they must close at midnight during the week, and 2 am on Friday and Saturday nights. There are some exceptions to the latter, primarily those clubs and casinos in hotels. Sadly, the curfew has put some clubs out of business, but it has cut down on the crime and late-night noise, particularly in the Zona Colonial. Some clubs are now pushing the envelope and staying open until 3, but they do get in trouble with the authorities when caught, and you probably don't want to be there then.

Dancing is as much a part of the culture here as eating and drinking. As in other Latin countries, after dinner it's not a question of *whether* people will go dancing but *where* they'll go. Move with the rhythm of the merengue and the pulsing beat of salsa (adopted from neighboring Puerto Rico). Among the young, the word is that there's no better place to party in the Caribbean than Santo Domingo. Almost every resort in Puerto Plata and Punta Cana has live entertainment, dancing, or both.

The action can heat up—and the island does have casinos—but gambling in the Dominican Republic is more a sideline than a raison d'être. Most casinos are in the larger hotels of Santo Domingo, with a couple on the North Coast, plus many more in Punta Cana. All offer slot machines, blackjack, craps, and roulette and are generally open daily from 3 pm to 4 am, the exception being those in Santo Domingo, which, for now, must close at midnight (2 am on Friday and Saturday). You must be 18 to enter.

PUNTA CANA

BARS AND CLUBS

Fodor's Choice ★ **Imagine.** Imagine you were dancing the night away in a natural cave, with earth-rocking acoustics. You can bounce back and forth between the various "cave" rooms with their stalactites and stalagmites, with equally hot dance floors, featuring house/club jams, merengue/salsa/world beats, current Top 40, and more. Theme nights change, like Crazy Thursday might switch to Brazil's Carnaval. Come late and stay early: things start getting steamy well after midnight, when many club crawlers descend via shuttle (round-trip) from the local resorts. (The free bus is great, but know that it stops at every resort in the area, beginning around 11 pm. Service from Uvero Alto resorts is $10 extra. Taxis wait outside for those who can't hang.) Special rates (from $60) are offered for a weekly, multiple-entrance pass, with one night including an open bar. Although most disco-goers are in awe, others say that it's a lot of hype. ✉ *Carretera Cocoloco–Riu, Coco Loco/Friusa, Bávaro* ☎ *809/466–1049, 809/466–1079* 🌐 *www.imaginepuntacana.com* 🎫 *$40 (includes cover, transportation, 2 drinks, and even Wi-Fi)* ⏲ *11 pm–after 4 am.*

Pacha. A favorite among locals and still one of the best resort-based dance spots, Pacha plays more merengue and bachata than most of the

Continued on page 462

PIRATES IN THE CARIBBEAN

Susan MacCallum Whitcomb & Julie Collazo Schwietert

Peg legs, parrots, and an easy-to-imitate "ahoy matey" lexicon: these are requisite elements in any pirate tale, but so are avarice and episodes of unspeakable violence. The combination is clearly compelling. Our fascination with pirates knows no bounds.

The true history of piracy has largely been obscured by competing pop-culture images. On one hand, there is the archetypal opportunist—fearsome, filthy, and foul-mouthed. On the other is the lovable scallywag epitomized by Captain Jack Sparrow in Disney's *Pirates of the Caribbean* franchise. Actual pirates, however, usually fell somewhere between these two extremes.

They could be uneducated men with limited life choices or crewmen from legitimate commercial and exploratory vessels left unemployed in the wake of changing political agendas. In either case, the piratical career path offered tempting benefits. Making a fast doubloon was only the beginning. Piracy also promised adventure plus egalitarian camaraderie—a kind of social equality unlikely to be found elsewhere during that class-conscious period.

Life aboard ship was governed by majority, as opposed to autocratic, rule. Pirates moreover, adhered to the Pirate's Code (a sort of "honor among thieves" arrangement). On the ships, at least, the common good took precedence.

X MARKS THE SPOT

Movie *Pirates of the Caribbean.*

Anegada
St. Thomas
Tortola
Virgin Gorda
Isla de Culebra
British Virgin Islands
Puerto Rico
St. John
U.S. Virgin Islands
Isla de Vieques
St. Croix
Tortola
St. Thomas
St. John

The Caribbean offered easy pickings for pirates because Spanish imperialists had already done the heavy lifting, extracting gems and precious metals from their South American colonies. Pirates from competing powers (namely England and France) could simply grab the spoils as Spanish ships island-hopped homeward.

Jamaica

Calico Jack Rackham, his lover Anne Bonny, and Mary Read were ultimately captured in **Bloody Bay** near Negril. Reportedly the male crew members were too busy drinking rum to mount a proper defense.

Dominican Republic

The centuries-old Spanish architecture in Santo Domingo's **Zona Colonial** is so well-preserved you can almost picture the area populated with tankard-toting buccaneers and corset-clad wenches.

Santo Domingo, Dominican Republic

Puerto Rico

Massive fortifications, like **Castillo San Felipe del Morro** in Old San Juan, show just how far the Spanish were prepared to go to protect their assets from seagoing attackers, whether authorized or otherwise.

British Virgin Islands

Sir Francis Drake Channel, Jost Van Dyke, and Great Thatch Island were named for pirates or privateers. Ditto for **Norman Island**, which reputedly inspired the setting for R.L. Stevenson's *Treasure Island.*

St. Thomas

A strategic location, protected anchorages, plus easy-to-hide-in inlets made the U.S. Virgin Islands an ideal habitat for plunderers. High points like **Drake's Seat** and Blackbeard's Castle were used to survey the terrain.

Anguilla

Underwater heritage preserves let divers explore vessels that sailed during piracy's Golden Age. **Stoney Ground Marine Park** contains a Spanish galleon wrecked in 1772, plus cannons, anchors, and other artifacts.

Stoney Ground Marine Park

Pirate ship arrives for Pirates Week, the Cayman Islands.

Peppered Pickled Pirate Party, Nevis.

Castillo de San Felipe del Morro, Puerto Rico.

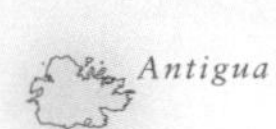

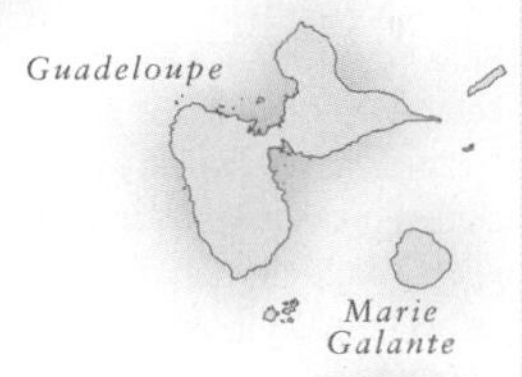

PIRATES OF THE CARIBBEAN

Dominica

Convoys of booty-filled Spanish ships often stopped at this lush island. Pirates followed—and so did Hollywood. Key scenes for the second and third *Pirates of the Caribbean* movies were shot here.

St. Vincent

Sequences for the first three *Pirates of the Caribbean* installments were filmed on location here. The meticulously detailed cluster of buildings built to represent Port Royal can be seen at **Wallilabou Bay**.

PIRATE PARTIES

Cayman Islands

In mid-November, islanders celebrate their piratical past with an 11-day festival featuring treasure hunts, mock trials, and other themed events. The highlight is an invasion of **George Town** staged by *faux* pirates.

Nevis

Taking a page from the Cayman Islands book, Nevis introduced the weeklong **Peppered Pickled Pirate Party**. Held twice during the last week of October and November, It celebrates William Kidd and Black Bart with an "invasion," regattas, cooking and cocktail competitions, treasure hunts, and more

St. Barthélemy

Logically enough, Frenchman Daniel Montbars used this French island as his home base. Legend has it some of his treasure remains hidden in the beachfront caves around **Anse du Gouverneur**.

St. Lucia

Now a peaceful national park, **Pigeon Island** (on St. Lucia's northern tip) was once the hideout of François Le Clerc. This peg-legged pirate orchestrated attacks from his hilly vantage point in the late 16th century.

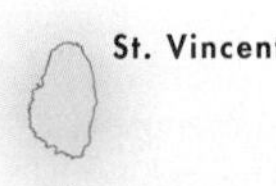

TIMELINE

1523 First Spanish treasure ships seized

1577 Francis Drake begins circumnavigating the globe

1604 James I revokes Letters of Marque

1500

1550

1600

1492 onward exploitation of New World resources

1585–1604 Anglo-Spanish War

FAMOUS PIRATES

Years after they wreaked havoc on the high seas, history still remembers some of the most notorious pirates of the Caribbean.

SIR FRANCIS DRAKE

Drake was a busy fellow. The first Englishman to circumnavigate the globe, he popularized tobacco, led slave-trading expeditions, helped destroy the Spanish Armada, and still had time to terrorize treasure-laden ships with Queen Elizabeth's blessing. Drake led his country's fleet in epic encounters throughout the Caribbean.

HENRY MORGAN

Captain Morgan led a colorful life before lending his name to a ubiquitous brand of rum. Leaving Wales for the West Indies as a young man, he successfully segued from debauched buccaneer to semi-respectable privateer and, after dodging piracy charges in England, ended up as the Lieutenant Governor of Jamaica.

Captin Morgan

Edward "Blackbeard" Teach

BLACKBEARD

Born Edward Teach, Blackbeard was notable for his business savvy (which included making profit-sharing deals with politicos) as well as his fiendish looks. His signature beard was braided and often laced with lit fuses to terrify enemies. Alas, in 1718 Blackbeard's head was severed in a dramatic showdown with Lt. Robert Maynard of the Royal Navy. It was mounted on Maynard's ship as a warning to others.

WILLIAM KIDD

Life was a roller-coaster ride for the legendary Captain Kidd. Kidd was a retired privateer living in New York when he accepted a commission to hunt pirates and then became one himself with the encouragement of a mutinous crew. He was executed in London in 1701, but hopefuls still hunt for the treasure he supposedly left buried.

PIRATES, PRIVATEERS, AND BUCCANEERS

The "pirate" label is generally applied to sailors engaging in any type of maritime marauding. Yet there are variations on the theme.

Privateers such as Sir Francis Drake were licensed looters, their escapades were authorized by a royal Letter of Marque, which issued private commissions for strategic naval operations. Privateers were sanctioned to attack only specific enemy ships, with the goodies gained benefitting their government. Since this rogue diplomacy was intended to challenge Spain's dominance in the Americas, many privateers felt they were protecting national interests. Hence, they were pirates… but patriotic.

Buccaneers, conversely, were a motley crew. The word, originally reserved for pirates from Hispaniola (the island shared by Haiti and the Dominican Republic), eventually included anyone from

Sir Francis Drake

1655 Jamaica established as privateer base

1674 Henry Morgan knighted

1650 1700 1750

1618–1648 Thirty Years War

1689–1697 King William's War

1701–1714 War of Spanish Succession

William Kidd

Calico Jack Rackman

Anne Bonny

BLACK BART ROBERTS

Though not the most famous pirate, he is often considered the most successful. He racked up impressive credits, plundering some 400 ships between 1719 and 1722. A snappy dresser who was fashionably attired even in battle, he was also a strict disciplinarian. Roberts quashed onboard gambling and banned music on Sunday.

DANIEL MONTBARS

Montbars proved Brits didn't hold a monopoly on bad behavior. French lineage aside, he differed from his 17th-century peers in that he was affluent and educated. His manners needed polishing, though. Violent outbursts (disemboweling Spaniards was a favorite sport) earned Montbars the nickname "The Exterminator."

CALICO JACK RACKHAM

An Englishman who ascended from mate to captain, Rackham, secured his legend by adding women to his crew. Workwise, his favorite tactic was attacking small vessels close to shore. Such boldness led to an inglorious end. Rackham was hung then tarred, feathered, and displayed in a cage in Port Royal, Jamaica.

ANNE BONNY AND MARY READ

Thought to be unlucky, female pirates were rare. Yet the comely Bonny and cross-dressing Read were respected by their shipmates... and feared by their victims. Captured together in 1720, they were sentenced to death. Both, however, escaped the noose by claiming to be pregnant.

the "Boys Gone Wild" school. Coming from diverse ethnic backgrounds, many buccaneers were fugitive slaves, escaped criminals, or other social outcasts who became plunderers by choice or force. Operating solely in their own interests and typically lacking a strategy or social order, they were the bottom feeders.

Political shifts could turn privateers into pirates (James I's decision to revoke Letters of Marque was a case in point). Desperation or moral degeneration could just as easily turn pirates into buccaneers.

PIRATE FLAGS

Flashy flags were to pirates what coats of arms were to royal families: visible signs of group identity. Each crew flew its own, depending on what attributes the captain wanted to emphasize or the degree of menace he wanted to convey.

The most recognizable is the "Jolly Roger": an iconic white-on-black skull cradled by crossbones.

other clubs, but still is geared to "young" contemporary music. The later it gets, typically the louder it gets. The place is not that large and is handsome in its decor, especially the bar. Drinks here are cheaper, too. For a beer, expect to pay about 80 pesos (about $2.50); the price can be double in some of the other clubs. Cover charges apply when live bands perform; otherwise it's free to enter, and non-resort guests are welcome. ■ **TIP→ If you're staying at the Riu Macao complex, it's an easy, safe enough walk.** ✉ *Riu Naiboa Resort, Av. Estados Unidos, on Caribbean St., Bávaro* ☎ *809/221–7575.*

NORTH COAST

BARS AND CLUBS

LAX Ojo Cabarete. LAX, that perennially popular bar that really comes alive by night, has made a move down the beach into new digs. You can sit in the sand in lounge chairs or jump into the action on the outdoor deck or on the second level where a DJ will be spinning madly or a live band might be playing. A dance club without a cover charge, you will see American free style and Latin salsa. Guests say "it rocks, so fun." There's good grazing chow, too, and special theme nights. Carefully made mojitos and other drinks (two-for-one specials from 5 to 7) mean you must be patient: getting one can take time when the bar backs up. Food is inexpensive then, too, and if you have kids they will be happy with the pizza, pasta, or wings. ✉ *Cabarete Beach, Cabarete* ☎ *829/745–8811.*

Onno's Bar Cabarete. Onno's remains a serious party place. It is usually wall-to-wall and back-to-back as the young and fit pack the dance floor and groove to techno sounds while other multinational youth sit at the tables in the sand. It's easier to get served at the beach bar than the main one, and as you chill, people will pass by, introduce themselves, chat, and then move on. It's fun and friendly, with theme nights, like Mexican night (fish tacos, mmm) and ladies night. Happy Hour is daily from 6–9 pm and Killer Hour is from 9–10 pm . . . don't ask, just go. A DJ cranks it up on Friday and Saturday nights, however, in high season, when it stays open until 3 am, the scene can get rowdy. (In fact, some local expats say that the crowd that it is now attracting is less than wonderful.) Cabarete's Onno's now has sister establishments in Bavaro, Altos de Chavon, and Santo Domingo's Zona Colonial. ✉ *Cabarete Beach, Calle Principal, Cabarete* ☎ *809/571–0461* 🌐 *www.onnosbar.com.*

SHOPS AND SPAS

Cigars continue to be the hottest commodity coming out of the D.R. Many exquisite, hand-wrapped smokes come from the island's rich Cibao Valley, and Fuente Cigars—handmade in Santiago—are highly prized. Only reputable cigar shops sell the real thing, and many you will see sold on the street are fakes. You can also buy and enjoy Cuban cigars here, but they can't be brought back to the United States legally. Dominican rum and coffee are also good buys. *Mamajuana*, an herbal liqueur, is said to be the Dominican answer to Viagra. The D.R. is the homeland of designer Oscar de la Renta, and you may want to stop at the chic shops that carry his creations. La Vega is famous for its *diablos cajuelos* (devil masks), which are worn during Carnival. Look also for the delicate, faceless ceramic figurines that symbolize Dominican culture.

Though locally crafted products are often of a high caliber (and very affordable), expect to pay hundreds of dollars for designer jewelry made of amber and larimar. Larimar—a semiprecious stone the color of the Caribbean Sea—is found on the D.R.'s south coast in the hills above the city of Barahona. Prices vary according to the stone's hue and category, AAA being the highest. Amber has been mined extensively between Puerto Plata and Santiago. A fossilization of resin from a prehistoric pine tree, it often encases ancient animal and plant life, from leaves to spiders to tiny lizards. Beware of fakes, which are especially prevalent in street stalls. A reputable dealer can show you how to tell the difference between real larimar and amber and imitations.

Bargaining is both a game and a social activity in the D.R., especially with street vendors and at the stalls in El Mercado Modelo. Vendors are disappointed and perplexed if you don't haggle. They're also tenacious so unless you really plan to buy, don't even stop to look.

SANTO DOMINGO

AREAS AND MALLS

Acropolis Mall, between Avenida Winston Churchill and Calle Rafael Augusto Sanchez, has become a favorite shopping arena for the young and/or hip capitaleños. Stores like Zara and Mango (both from Spain) have today's look without breaking your budget.

One of the main shopping streets in the Zona is **Calle El Conde,** a pedestrian thoroughfare. With the advent of so many restorations, the dull and dusty stores with dated merchandise are giving way to some hip new shops. However, many of the offerings, including local designer shops, are still of a caliber and cost that the Dominicans can afford. Some of the best shops are on **Calle Duarte,** north of the Zona Colonial, between Calle Mella and Avenida de Las Américas. **El Mercado Modelo,** a covered market, borders Calle Mella in the Zona Colonial; vendors here sell a dizzying selection of Dominican crafts.

Piantini is a swanky residential neighborhood that has an increasing number of fashionable shops and clothing boutiques, often housed in contemporary shopping malls. Its borders run from Avenida Winston Churchill to Avenida Lope de Vega and from Calle Jose Amado Soler to Avenida 27 de Febrero.

RECOMMENDED STORES

Casa Virginia. One of the Dominican Republic's leading department stores, Casa Virginia was founded in 1945 by the mother of the present Virginia, who took it to the next level, adding a great day spa. The store is stocked mostly with high-end designer clothing (including a Jenny Polanco department) and fashion finds, but also has Italian jewelry and some moderately priced gift items. ✉ *C/Av. Roberto Pastoriza*

255, Naco ☎ 809/566–4000, 809/566–1535 spa 🌐 casavirginia.com ⊙ Closed Sun.

Galería de Arte Nader. Top Dominican artists in various mediums are on display here. The gallery staff are well known in Miami and New York, and work with Sotheby's. ✉ *Rafael Augusto Sanchez 22, Ensanche Piantini, Piantini ☎ 809/544–0878.*

La Leyenda del Cigarro, S.R.L. This shop along El Conde in the Zona Colonial makes and sells its own branded premium cigars to clients worldwide and anyone who happens to walk into the cozy store. Enjoy the leather couch in the seating area, and let owner Julio Vilchez Rosso or a member of his personable staff regale you with the history of cigar making in the Dominican Republic and learn what makes a good cigar a good cigar. This store is perfect for experienced connoisseurs or those who'd like to become one. There's another branch in the Malecón Center. ✉ *Calle El Conde 4, Zona Colonial ☎ 809/686–5489, 809/445–3728.*

L'Ile Au Tresor. L'Ile Au Tresor has a *Pirates of the Caribbean* theme, but that aside, it's fun. The owner, a talented trilingual Frenchman named Patrick, has some of the most attractive and creative designer pieces in native larimar and amber. If you have never bought any of these lovely stones because of cheesy settings or too high a price tag, then this is your chance. His innovative custom work, with sterling or gold, can be done in 48 hours. The shop crew does not speak English, but will call Patrick if he is not there. ✉ *Arzobispo Meriño 258, Zona Colonial ⊕ In front of the Colonial Tour Agency ☎ 829/688–8751, 809/688–8751.*

Lyle O. Reitzel Art Contemporaneo. Lyle O. Reitzel Art Contemporaneo has, since 1995, specialized in contemporary art. The gallery showcases mainly Latin artists from Mexico, South America, and Spain, and some of the most controversial Dominican visionaries. Their rotating collection can include the new, the strange, and the daring. ✉ *Torre Piantini, Gustavo Mejia Ricart, Suites 1 and 2 A, Piantini ☎ 809/227–8361, 809/519–9214 cell for L.O.R 🌐 www.lyleoreitzelgallery.com.*

Plaza Toledo Bettye's Galeria. A fascinating array of artwork, including Haitian voodoo banners and metal sculpture, and souvenirs, chandeliers, and estate jewelry, are sold at Plaza Toledo Bettye's Galeria. The gallery's second room is dedicated to Dominican fine art. The American expat owner, Bettye Marshall, has a great eye, and can also rent you a room in one of her bed-and-breakfasts; which are basic, but historic with some kind of art hanging on the walls and just $50 for two including breakfast. ✉ *Isabel la Católica 163, Zona Colonial ☎ 809/688–7649.*

SOUTHEAST COAST

AREAS AND MALLS

Altos de Chavón. Altos de Chavón is a re-creation of a 16th-century Mediterranean village on the grounds of the Casa de Campo resort, where you can find a church, art galleries, boutiques, restaurants, and souvenir shops, and a 5,000-seat amphitheater for concerts grouped around a cobbled square. At the Altos de Chavón Art Studios you can find ceramics, weaving, and screen prints made by local and resident artists. Extra special is the Jenny Polanco Project. She, a top Dominican fashion designer, has made an outlet for Dominican, Haitian, and Caribbean craftsmen to sell their wares, from Carnival masks to baskets and carved plates. Tienda Batey sells fine linens handcrafted by woman from the sugar plantation *bateys* (poor villages). ✉ *Casa de Campo.*

Casa de Campo Marina. Casa de Campo's top-ranked marina is home to shops and international boutiques, galleries, and jewelers scattered amid restaurants, an ice-cream parlor, bars, banks, a beauty salon, the Caribbean Mall & Theaters, a sailing school, and a yacht club. It's a great place to spend some time shopping, sightseeing, and staring at the extravagant yachts. The chic shopping scene at the marina includes Carmen Sol NY and Kiwi St. Tropez for French bathing suits. Everett Designs showcases high-end larimar and amber jewelry, gold and silver Spanish treasure coins. Polanco-Leon with Dominican designer Jenny Polanco's has resortwear, purses, and jewelry and Bibi Leon's tropical-themed home accessories. There's also a marvelous Italian antiques shop, Nuovo Rinascimento, and for cigars, the Tienda (Fumo). The *supermercado* Nacional has not only groceries but sundries, postcards, and snacks. ✉ *Casa de Campo Marina, Calle Barlovento* 🌐 *www.marinacasadecampo.com.do.*

PUNTA CANA

AREAS AND MALLS

Fodor's Choice ★ **Galerias at Puntacana Village.** The Galerias at Puntacana Village lie within a still-blossoming shopping, dining, and residential complex built on the road to the Punta Cana International Airport. Originally the village was built to house employees of the Puntacana Group, but now the shops and restaurants are also a tourist draw. The village is comprised of churches, an international school, and this commercial area with its restaurants, shops, a supermarket, banks (with ATMs), a beauty salon, and doctors' offices. Family-oriented, there is an ice-cream parlor, a playground, and a children's clothing boutique as well as those for ladies. The restaurants, often ethnic, and even a Wendy's, are less expensive than those at most resorts, and usually convivial. The Sheraton Four Points Puntacana Village is across the street, just a two-minute drive to the airport. ✉ *Blvd. Primero de Noviembre* 🌐 *www.puntacanavillage.com.*

Fodor's Choice ★ **Palma Real Shopping Village.** A standout among the region's shopping centers, Palma Real Shopping Village is a swanky, partially enclosed mall (similar to something you would see in Southern California) that is also overall the most expensive. Fountains and tropical plants infuse life into the bright and airy interiors beneath the blue-tile roof. Music pipes through the stone-floor plaza in the center, where seating is available and security is tight. Upscale retail shops, which sell beachwear, clothing, skin-care products, and jewelry, line the walls. Several restaurants give visitors welcome dining alternatives beyond the gates of their resorts. There are two banks, ATMs, and a money exchange outlet.

Stores are open 10–10, but the restaurants stay open later. It has the best pharmacy in the area. Shuttle buses run to and from many of the hotels, with pickups every two hours. ✉ *Bávaro* ☎ *809/552–8725* 🌐 *www.palmarealshoppingvillage.com.*

Plaza Uvero Alto. You won't find brand-name shops at Plaza Uvero Alto, which is a convenient shopping center for the hotels in the remote Uvero Alto area of Punta Cana. Especially useful are a bank, outdoor ATM, and a money exchange, followed by Internet access, a small pharmacy, gift shops, and two minimarkets (one in the front, the other in the back row of booths). Here you can get sundries like sunscreen and deodorant at prices much cheaper than in the hotels. Behind the first row of enclosed stores, visit the colorful kiosks full of handicrafts, paintings, ceramics, and other gift items. Most shopkeepers here, although very friendly, don't speak much English, so be prepared to practice your Spanish. For beautifully designed jewelry with larimar and amber as well as other locally made novelties, visit **Tesoro Caribeño** (Suite 5, front row of stores), where the owner speaks fluent English. There's also a branch of the Politur (tourist police) in the plaza. ✉ *Carretera Uvero Alto, Uvero Alto.*

JEWELRY

Harrison's Fine Jewelry. It's hard to walk by the windows of Harrison's Fine Jewelry without stepping in to admire the collection of jewelry, including a large selection of larimar and amber pieces in striking settings, as well as diamonds and other classic gems. Outlets of this renowned chain are also in several resorts of Punta Cana. Like the Palma Real Shopping Village itself, Harrison's is open 10 am–10 pm daily. ✉ *Palma Real Shopping Village, Bávaro* ☎ *809/552–8721* 🌐 *www.harrisons.com.*

SPAS

Fodor's Choice ★ **Six Senses Spa.** This spa offers the best treatments in the Dominican Republic. Period. Here you will find master Thai therapists; you will melt in the hands of these gifted women and be transported to another zone. Whether you have a special manicure or facial with fresh product, a hot stone massage, or go on a magical Spa Sensory Journey, it will be exceptional. This exotic wellness center also has couples' accommodations, which include luxurious baths. The spa belongs to the Puntacana Resort and is housed in its gorgeous golf club; gentlemen as well as ladies are made welcome, as are outside guests. **■ TIP→ An added bonus for resort guests: you can book therapies in your guest rooms or villas.** ✉ *Puntacana Resort and Club, La Cana Golf & Beach Club* 🌐 *www.puntacana.com, sixsensesspa.com* ⏲ *Daily 9–8.*

SPORTS AND THE OUTDOORS

Although there's hardly a shortage of activities here, the resorts have virtually cornered the market on sports, including every conceivable water sport. In some cases, facilities may be available only to guests of the resorts.

BASEBALL

Baseball is a national passion, the cultural icon of the D.R., and yes, Sammy Sosa is still a legend in his own time. But he is just one of many celebrated Dominican baseball heroes, including pitcher Odalis Revela. Triple-A Dominican and Puerto Rican players and some American major leaguers hone their skills in the D.R.'s professional Winter League, which plays from October through January. Some games are held in the Tetelo Vargas Stadium, in the town of San Pedro de Macorís, east of Boca Chica.

Estadio Francisco A. Michelli. Estadio Francisco A. Michelli is La Romana's baseball stadium. Know that *la temporada* (the season) is short; your window of opportunity is just October through December, with an occasional game in January. ✉ *Av. Padre Abreu, near monument, La Romana* ☎ *809/556–6188.*

Liga de Béisbol Stadiums. Liga de Béisbol Stadiums can be a helpful information source if you're planning an independent trip to a baseball game. ✉ *Santo Domingo* ☎ *809/567–6371* 🌐 *lidom.com.*

BIKING AND HIKING

Pedaling is easy on pancake-flat beaches, but there are also some steep hills in the D.R. Several resorts rent bikes to guests and nonguests alike.

NORTH COAST

Fodor's Choice ★ **Iguana Mama.** Iguana Mama's offerings include mountain-bike tours that will take you along the coastal flats or test your mettle on steeper climbs in the National Parks. Downhill bike rides—which include a taxi up to 3,000 feet, breakfast, and lunch—cost $99 for a full-day trip, $70 for a half-day trip without lunch. Advanced rides, on- and off-road, are $55 to $95.

Other half- and full-day trips—which range in price from $89 to $195—include hiking, swimming, climbing up and jumping off various waterfalls, rappelling, and natural waterslides. Guided day hikes cost $35 to $75; a three-day hike to the Caribbean's tallest peak, Pico Duarte in Jarabacoa, is $450. This well-established, safety-oriented company also offers horseback riding on the beach of Cabarete and in the countryside (from $45 for two hours), white-water rafting, ecotours, and lots of other adventure sports. ✉ *Calle Principal 74, across from Scotia Bank, Cabarete, Dominican Republic* ☎ *809/571–0908, 809/571–0734, 809/654–2325* 🌐 *www.iguanamama.com.*

BOATING

Sailing conditions are ideal, with constant trade winds. Favorite excursions include day trips to Catalina and Saona Islands—both in La Romana area—and sunset cruises on the Caribbean. Prices for crewed sailboats of 26 feet and longer, with a capacity of four to 12 people, are fixed according to size and duration, from a low of $200 a day to the norm of $700 a day. Examples of other prices, taken from the fleet at the upscale Cap Cana Marina, are as follows: sportfishermen from 47 to 51 feet accommodating up to eight people (crewed with all equipment, snacks, and beverages with sandwiches on all-day trips), $1,800 for four hours, $2,500 for eight hours; a 62-foot custom, luxury power-sail catamaran, $1,650 for two hours (everything included for Cap Cana guests); a 56-foot Sea Ray Sedan Bridge motor yacht, $2,000 for two hours, $2,500 for four hours, $3,500 for eight hours (everything included); and a luxury 90-foot custom motor yacht, ideal for an incentive group, $3,500 for two hours, $5,000 for four hours, $8,500 for eight hours.

SOUTHEAST COAST

Casa de Campo Marina. Casa de Campo Marina has much going on, from sailing to motor yachting and socializing at the Casa de Campo Yacht Club. And now there is a sailing school for kids from 12 years to adults. A first for the marina was hosting the Rolex FARR 40 World's Championship in 2010. One of the world's most important annual sailing events, this was the first time it had come to the Caribbean. With everything from a laundry to ship chandlery and shipyard, as well as video surveillance that guarantees security, this is a safe haven for yachtsmen. ✉ *Casa de Campo, Calle Barlovento 3, La Romana* ☎ *809/523–3333, 809/523–3333* 🌐 *www.marinacasadecampo.com.do.*

NORTH COAST

Carib Wind Cabarete. A renowned windsurfing center (known for decades as BIC Center) Carib Wind Cabarete has been operating since 1988. In the last decade it has transformed into a high-performance Olympic training center for Laser sailors from around the world. Here you can rent Lasers, 17-foot catamarans, bodyboards, ocean kayaks, and paddleboards. ✉ *Cabarete* ☎ *809/571–0640* 🌐 *www.caribwind.com.*

SAMANÁ PENINSULA

Puerto Bahia Marina. This stunning marina on the north end of pristine Samaná Bay is a relatively new entity and is a first-class, full-service facility with slips from 40 to 150 feet. This marina not only has the necessary amenities, including fuel, restrooms with showers, 24-hour security, garbage pickup, Internet access, water taxis, and car rentals, but all the services and facilities of the Bannister Hotel. ✉ *Carretera Sanchez-Samaná, Km.5, Santa Bárbara de Samaná* ☎ *809/503–6363, 855/503–6363 toll-free* 🌐 *www.puertobahiasamana.com.*

DIVING

Ancient sunken galleons, undersea gardens, and offshore reefs are among the lures here. Most divers head to the north shore. In the waters off Sosúa alone you can find a dozen dive sites (for all levels of ability) with such catchy names as Three Rocks (a deep, 163-foot dive), Airport Wall (98 feet), and Pyramids (50 feet). Some dive schools are represented on or near Sosúa Beach, in the town of Bayahibe and in Las Terrenas and Las Galeras on the Samaná Peninsula resorts have dive shops on-site or can arrange trips for you.

NORTH COAST

Northern Coast Aquasports. Located on the main street of Sosúa, it is a PADI 5-Star IDC Resort, a full-service dive center offering valet service—not a shack on the beach. It offers all levels of PADI courses from Discover Scuba Diving to Instructor, with diving and snorkeling seven days a week. Professionalism is apparent in the initial classroom and pool training; classroom has air-conditioning and DVDs. Successful completion of a three-day course earns one a lifetime PADI Open Water Diver certification!

The selection of outstanding sites in the calm, protected waters of Sosúa Bay features reefs, walls, wrecks, coral heads, and swim-throughs, from 25 to 130 feet. The mecca of diving on the north coast, Sosúa is close to Cabarete and not too far from Puerto Plata, Costambar, and Cofresi. All activities are guided by (multilingual) PADI professionals. For experienced divers, there are day excursions to DuDu Caverns (near Cabrera). For groups of four or more, private diving excursions to Monte Cristi can be arranged; VIP snorkeling excursions can be arranged (minimum four) to Paradise Island, and more. ✉ *Calle Pedro Clisante 8, Sosúa* ☎ *809/571–1028* 🌐 *www.northerncoastdiving.com.*

SAMANÁ

In 1979 three atolls disappeared after a seaquake off Las Terrenas, providing an opportunity for truly memorable dives. Also just offshore from Las Terrenas are the Islas Las Ballenas (the Whale Islands), a cluster of four little islands with good snorkeling. A coral reef is off Playa Jackson, a beach accessible only by boat.

Las Galeras Divers. This is a professional, safety-conscious operation. Owner Serge is a PADI, OWSI, and Nitrox instructor, and every level of PADI course is offered. Diving lessons and trips are offered in English, French, and Spanish, and diving equipment rentals are also available. Single-tank dives are $45, two-tank dives $75, but equipment charge for either is an extra $10. Exciting night dives cost $70. Discounts are given to groups, families, and divers who want a package deal. ✉ *Calle Principal, Las Galeras* ☎ *809/538–0220* 🌐 *www.las-galeras-divers.com.*

FISHING

Big-game fishing is big in Punta Cana, with blue and white marlin, wahoo, sailfish, and dorado among the most common catches in these waters. Several fishing tournaments are held every summer. The Punta Cana Resort & Club hosted the ESPN Xtreme Billfishing Tournament for many years. Blue-marlin tournaments are held at La Mona Channel in Cabeza de Toro. Several tour operators offer organized deep-sea fishing excursions.

LA ROMANA

Casa de Campo Marina. Casa de Campo Marina is the best charter option in the La Romana area. Yachts (22- to 60-footers) are available for deep-sea fishing charters for half or full days. Prices go from $824 for a half day on Scorpio, to $3,555 for a full day on Gabriella. They can come equipped with rods, bait, dinghies, drinks, and experienced guides.

Going out for the big billfish that swim the depths of the Caribbean is a major adrenaline rush. In 2014 (March 21–24) the marina hosted the annual Casa de Campo International Blue Marlin Classic Tournament, which was celebrated with a round of parties. ✉ *Casa de Campo, Calle Barlovento 3, La Romana* ☎ *809/523–3333, 809/523–3333.*

PUNTA CANA

Puntacana Marina. At the Puntacana Marina, on the southern end of the resort, there are many, many nautical options available for rent, from banana boats and waterskiing craft to sportfishing and diving charters. ✉ *Puntacana Resort & Club, Punta Cana* ☎ *809/959–2262* 🌐 *www.puntacana.com.*

GOLF

Fodor's Choice ★ The D.R. has some of the best courses in the Caribbean, designed by top golf architects; among these leading designers are Pete Dye, P.B. Dye, Jack Nicklaus, Robert Trent Jones, Gary Player, Tom Fazio, and Nick Faldo. The country's courses have won awards for customer satisfaction, quality of courses and accommodations, value for money, support from suppliers and tourist boards, and professional conduct. Most courses charge higher rates during the winter high season; some, but not all, reduce their rates between April and October, so be sure to ask. Also, some have cheaper rates in the afternoon (mornings are cooler). And guests of certain hotels get better prices.

SOUTHEAST COAST

Fodor's Choice ★ **Casa de Campo Resort.** The resort is considered by most to be the premier multiple-course golf resort in the Caribbean. The famed 18-hole Teeth of the Dog course at Casa de Campo, with seven holes on the sea, is usually ranked as the number-one course in the Caribbean and is among the top courses in the world. Pete Dye regards Teeth of the Dog as one of his best designs and has long enjoyed living there part-time. The Teeth of the Dog requires a caddy for each round and an additional $25 (plus tip). Pete Dye has designed this and two other globally acclaimed courses here. Dye Fore, now with a total of 27 holes, is close to Altos de Chavón, hugging a cliff that features commanding vistas of the sea, a river, Dominican mountains, and the marina. The Links is a gamey 18-hole inland course. Resort guests must reserve tee times for all courses at least one day in advance; nonguests should make reservations earlier. Jim McLean operates a golf school at Casa de Campo; an instructor is on-site year-round. Half- and full-day lessons are available to individuals and groups; one-hour private lessons for adults cost $150. ✉ *Casa de Campo, La Romana* ☎ *809/523–3333 resort, 809/523–8115 golf director* 🌐 *www.casadecampo.com.do* 🎫 *Teeth of the Dog: for non-hotel guests, $325 per round per golfer; for guests, $185 per round per player. Dye Fore: $295 for nonguests, $218 for guests. The Links: $206.50 for nonguests; $182.90 for hotel guests* 🏌 *Teeth of the Dog: 18 holes, 6989 yards, par 72; Dye Fore: 18 holes, 7740 yards, par 72; The Links: 18 holes, 6664 yards, par 71.*

PUNTA CANA

Barceló Bávaro Golf. Integrated within the Barceló Bávaro Beach Golf & Casino Resort complex in the Punta Cana region, this course is open to both resort and non-resort guests. The course traverses a lush inland mangrove forest and features 22 inland lakes and 122 bunkers, and totals 6,655 yards. It was actually the first course in the area and was designed by Juan Manuel Gordillo. Complete renovations, executed by designer P. B. Dye in 2010, breathed new life to the layout. The best rates are available for guests of the more upscale Barceló hotels, such as the Barceló Palace Deluxe. Walking is not permitted. ✉ *Barceló Bávaro Beach Golf & Casino Resort, Bávaro* ☎ *809/686–5797* 🌐 *www.barcelobavarogolf.net* 🎫 *Barceló guests, $65 for 18 holes; nonguests, $145* ⛳ *18 holes, 6655 yards, par 72.*

Catalonia Caribe Golf Club. Challenging and reasonably priced, Catalonia Caribe Golf Club is spread out on greens surrounded by five lakes and an abundance of shady palms. It's a relatively short course and features an island green. The architect, Alberto Sola, designed it to be challenging for both experienced and novice golfers. Rates include a cart. ✉ *Catalonia Bávaro Resort, Cabeza de Toro, Bávaro* ☎ *809/321–7059* 🌐 *www.cataloniabavaro.com* 🎫 *Catalonia Resort guests: $80 for 18 holes; non-resort guests: $130* ⛳ *18 holes, 6950 yards, par 72.*

Cocotal Golf Course. Named for the coconut plantation on which it was built, Cocotal Golf Course, designed by Spaniard José "Pepe" Gancedo, has an 18-hole championship layout. It's a challenging par-72 course dotted with palm trees and serene lakes within the residential community Palma Real. There's also a driving range, clubhouse, pro shop, and golf academy. Fees include a golf cart. Advance booking is mandatory. Lessons and club rentals are available. ✉ *Palma Real Villas, Bávaro* ☎ *809/687–4653, 809/221–1290* 🌐 *www.cocotalgolf.com* 🎫 *$112 for 18 holes, $65 for 9 holes* ⛳ *18 holes, 7285 yards, par 72.*

Corales Golf Club. Corales Golf Club is "the Augusta National of the Caribbean" with expansive finely landscaped grounds. Designed by Tom Fazio it's a dramatic 18-hole course with six Caribbean seaside holes with a finishing hole that encourages players to cut off as much of the Caribbean as they dare off the tee. Laid out along the natural cliffs and coves of the sea and inland lakes and Coralina quarries, the 700 acres here are part of the extensive Puntacana Resort & Club. The club is open to its members and their guests, guests of Tortuga Bay, and Puntacana Resort guests who purchase the resort's Golf Experience packages. Caddies are mandatory at Corales. Inquiries and tee-time requests can be made by emailing *golfcorales@puntacana.com.* ✉ *Puntacana Resort & Club, Punta Cana* ☎ *809/959–4653* 🌐 *www.puntacana.com* 🎫 *Resort guests: from $275 in season and $195 during off-season. Subject to availability, the Corales Golf Club accepts a limited number of external guests with a rate of $380 in season and $280 off-season.* ⛳ *18 holes, 7555 yards, par 72.*

Fodor's Choice ★ **La Cana Golf Club.** You will enjoy the ocean views on 14 of the La Cana Golf Club's 27 holes of championship golf designed by P. B. Dye. The three 9s: Tortuga, Hacienda, and Arrecife make for a very popular offering, particularly the ocean-side finish on the La Cana Nine. The latest nine, Hacienda, opened in 2012 not as a full course but rather a set of nine individual holes; it is punctuated with many lakes amidst an unspoiled tropical landscape, a challenging addition to the existing, spectacular courses. All fees include a golf cart, taxes, and use of the expansive practice facility. Multiple round/twilight packages are available as well. Caddies are optional. Lessons and golf schools are offered by PGA professional staff. Rental clubs are available and reserve two weeks in advance from November through April. Golf packages may also include the nearby Corales Golf Course. ✉ *Puntacana Resort & Club, Punta Cana* ☎ *809/959–4653* 🌐 *www.puntacana.com* 🎫 *Resort guests: $135 for 18 holes in season, $105 off-season; nonguests: $175 in season, $140 off-season.* ⛳ *27 holes; Tortuga Nine: 9 holes, 3483 yards, par 36; Arrecife Nine: 9 holes, 3676 yards, par 36; Hacienda Nine: 9 holes, 3768 yards, par 36.*

Fodor's Choice ★ **Punta Espada Golf Course.** Jack Nicklaus casts his mark in the Caribbean with the magnificent Punta Espada Golf Course. You will discover a par-72 challenge with striking bluffs, lush foliage, and many gently tumbling fairways with spectacular water vistas. Incidentally, the water often does come into play. Having hosted the Champions Tour, the course is even better in person than it looks on TV, and you won't find smoother putting surfaces! Yes, there's a Caribbean view from all the holes, and eight of them play right along the sea. The course's length can be extended to nearly 7,400 yards, but it's advisable to play a more forward tee. This exceptional golf club has concierge services, a restaurant, the Hole 19 bar, a pro shop, a members' trophy gallery, a library, lockers, an equipment repair shop, and a meeting room. Rates are discounted for guests in any of Cap Cana's accommodations and include golf cart, caddy, tees, water, and practice on the driving range. In high season, reservations are required and it's best to make them two weeks in advance for tee times. ✉ *Cap Cana, Carretera Juanillo, Playa Juanillo* ☎ *809/221–1290* 🌐 *www.capcana.com* 🎫 *Resort guests: $225 ($160 after 2 pm); nonguests: $375 ($250 after 2 pm)* ⛳ *18 holes, 7396 yards, par 72.*

NORTH COAST

Playa Dorada Golf Club. *Golf Digest* has named Playa Dorada Golf Club one of the top 100 courses outside the United States. It's open to guests of all the hotels in the area. Greens fees for 9 holes are $50, 18 holes $75; caddies are mandatory for foursomes and will cost about $15 for 18 holes, $8 for 9 (plus tip); carts are optional, at $25 and $15, for 18 or 9 holes, respectively. The attractive clubhouse has lockers, a pro shop, a bar, and a restaurant. Reservations during high season should be made as far in advance as possible. Guests at certain hotels in the Playa Dorada complex get discounts. ✉ *Playa Dorada* ☎ *809/320–4262* 🌐 *www.playadoradagolf.com.*

Playa Grande Golf Course. Imagine 10 holes that interface with the Atlantic at the Playa Grande Golf Course, the most of any course in the Western Hemisphere. Some describe the layout, located between Río San Juan and Cabrera on the North Coast, as "the Pebble Beach of the Caribbean" because it also features ocean-side cliffs reaching 60 feet.

The challenge has lots of muscle extending to over 7,000 yards and carries the signature of Robert Trent Jones Sr. At this writing, the course is being renovated. It is experiencing a glorious revival under the care of Jones's son, Rees. He is directing the renovation of the course, with respect for the legacy created by his father, and with a goal of enhancing the experience and challenging golfers at every skill level. It is expected to be completed in fall 2015 together with the opening of the Aman Resort in Playa Grande, currently under way. It will be the first golf-integrated Amanresort in the world, and it will be setting a new standard for luxury in the Caribbean. (Note: The Playa Grande Golf Course and the Playa Grande Beach Club, now operating, are owned and managed by different companies. Playa Grande Golf Course is part of the development in Dominican Republic of Dolphin Capital Investors.) ✉ *Carretera Río San Juan–Cabrera, Km 9, Cabrera* ☎ *809/582–0860* 🌐 *www.playagrande.com* 🏌 *18 holes, 7090 yards, par 72.*

GUIDED TOURS

Visitors to the Dominican Republic will have a plethora of excursions to choose from, but many options are not wonderful and are overpriced. Wait until you arrive before booking anything. As for group excursions, "interview" fellow guests to find out if their tour was worth the money and effort. Often the full-day excursions are too long and leave too early. Best are half-day trips—particularly boat excursions. Horseback riding can sound appealing, as the trails usually include some stretches of beach, but do not envision superior horseflesh, tack, instruction, or even guides who can speak English. And whatever, just enjoy! Clients traveling on a tour-company package tend to book excursions with the same company, or through the company affiliated with their resort.

SANTO DOMINGO

Private tours are a good option in Santo Domingo, but you will have to pay more than $125 a day for a guide—more if the tour guide works with a driver. Your hotel concierge can best arrange these for you, and he or she will know the best English-speaking guides. Be sure you hire a guide who is licensed by the government.

SOUTHEAST COAST

FAMILY **Tropical Tours.** The primary tour operator on the Southeast Coast is Tropical Tours (at Casa de Campo), whose prices are even less than some non-pros and cruise-ship excursions. Their vans are new or nearly new and well maintained. Also, most of their staff speaks English as well as other languages. They can take you on a tour of Santo Domingo, and to fascinating caves (⇨ *see Cuevas Las Marvillas*). Guys particularly enjoy taking in a game at La Romana's baseball stadium, as it is unlike nany they have ever witnessed. Price for a group (four minimum, 15 maximum) is $35 for the ticket and transportation, $40 for VIP seating, which is what you want!

Although most water-based excursions (outback safaris and zip-lining, too) now go through the concierges at Casa; they do have a trip to the Marinarium and Reef Explorer where bravehearts can swim with the sharks. The company also provides transfers to Las Americas and Punta

Cana International Airports; $140 for 1–4 persons or a mere $28 per person for 5 or more. ✉ *Casa de Campo, La Romana* ☎ *809/523–2029, 809/523–2028* 🌐 *tropicaltoursromana.com.do.*

PUNTA CANA

Fodor's Choice ★ **Amstar DMC–Apple Vacations.** Amstar is well managed and reliable, and it is associated with Apple Vacations, a major player that packages all-inclusive vacations in the D.R., particularly in Punta Cana. They also offer transfers. ✉ *Carretera Bávaro, Bávaro* ☎ *809/221–6626* 🌐 *www.amstardmc.com.*

Fodor's Choice ★ **Go Golf Tours (GGT).** Go Golf has services tailored to clients seeking to make golf part of their getaway—whether it's the primary focus or just a one-time outing; the company will help arrange tee times, golf instruction, and transport to courses in Punta Cana or Casa de Campo by private driver at costs that are usually considerably less than those in a private taxi. They can also provide airport transfers. ✉ *Cocotal Golf & Country Club, Bávaro* ☎ *809/687–4653, 855/374–4653 toll-free in U.S., 809/200–9556 toll-free in D.R.* 🌐 *www.golfreservationcenter.com.*

NORTH COAST

Alf's Tours. In Sosúa, Alf's Tours has been a mainstay for years. Why? It only has multilingual, licensed tour guides, and it's open daily (9–7). Plus, it has excursions all over the island for moderate prices, and they offer complimentary pickup service at any hotel in Sosua, Puerto Plata, and Cabarete. Vehicles are closer to new than old, and guests are insured whether they are going to the famous waterfall, El Limon in Las Terrenas, or hopping aboard a Funny Buggy. They are now booking hotels, too. ✉ *Eugenio Kunhardt 68, El Batey, Sosúa* ☎ *809/571–1461.*

Flora Tours. Considered one of the better tour operators in Las Terrenas, Flora Tours can arrange boating and guided hiking trips to cacao plantations, mountain biking to beaches and mountains, and zip-line adventures. A trip to the El Limón waterfall includes taxi pickup at your hotel, round-trip transportation, a horse, a meal, and guides' tips. The company also arranges snorkeling trips to various beaches nearby. Their specialty is excursions to Los Haitises National Park, which leave on Wednesday and Saturday, but they also take clients whale-watching (January 15–March 15), on a safe catamaran with dual engines. In addition, this well-established, safety-oriented company offers daily ATV excursions into the mountains, where you rarely encounter any other tourists. They also go to Playa Moron by ATV. Flora will begin a new adventure, kayaking on a river coupled with a safari to a rice plantation and beyond. ✉ *Suite 278, Calle Principal Duarte, Las Terrenas* ☎ *809/240–5482* 🌐 *www.flora-tours.net.*

HORSEBACK RIDING

SOUTHEAST COAST

Equestrian Center at Casa de Campo. The 250-acre Equestrian Center at Casa de Campo has something for both Western and English riders—a dude ranch, a rodeo arena (where Casa's trademark "Donkey Polo" is played), three polo fields, guided trail rides, riding, jumping, and polo lessons. Guided rides run about $57 an hour, $90 for two hours; polo lessons cost $155 an hour by a pro, $77 with an assistant, and both riding and jumping lessons are $90 an hour or $56 a half hour.

There are early morning and sunset trail rides, too. Handsome, old-fashioned carriages are available for hire as well. Unlimited horseback riding is included if you are a hotel guest staying on the all-inclusive plan. Great for families, trail rides are offered through the property's private cattle ranch, and upon request, can include a classy, catered lunch. ✉ *Casa de Campo, La Romana* ☎ *809/523–3333* 🌐 *www.casadecampo.com.do.*

PUNTA CANA

Adventures Land. Long established, the former Southfork Ranch (Rancho Pat), which has been the stable of choice, is now a part of the Barceló resort complex (French owners are still the same). Trail rides are along Barceló's "private" beach and on open country roads. Prices begin at $55 per hour. Morning rides start out at 9 am (and include a mojito break at a typical bar). Another includes an exploratory mission to Taíno caves and culminates in a lobster beach cookout ($130). Then there is the memorable sunset beach ride, which can end with a beach bonfire barbecue ($100). If you like speed and don't mind getting dusty, go for the outback adventures on the powerful quads or tamer buggies— and discover the Dominican countryside. These multi-option activities are ideal for families. There is a new white marriage (horse) carriage and classic car (1932 Pontiac) for weddings or romantic surprises. ✉ *Barceló Resort Complex, Bávaro* ☎ *809/223–8896* ✐ *contacto@adventures-puntacana.com* 🌐 *adventures-puntacana.com.*

El Rancho in Punta Cana. El Rancho in Punta Cana is across from the main entrance of the resort. A one-hour trail ride winds along the beach, the golf course, and through tropical forests. The two-hour jungle trail ride has a stopover at a lagoon fed by a natural spring, so wear your swimsuit under your long pants. You can also do a one-hour sunset excursion (weekly) or take riding lessons. There are new adult riding classes for beginners that include basic horse care. ✉ *Puntacana Resort & Club, Punta Cana* ☎ *809/959–9221* 🌐 *www.puntacana.com.*

NORTH COAST

Sea Horse Ranch Equestrian Center. This equestrian center is a professional, well-staffed operation. The competition ring is built to international regulations, and there is a large schooling ring. Private lessons for experienced riders, including dressage or jumping instruction, are $40 per half hour; "laissez faire" rides are $35 for 90 minutes, $60 for three hours, including drinks and snacks—but make reservations. The most popular ride includes stretches of beach and a bridle path across a neighboring farm's pasture that's full of wildflowers and butterflies. Feel free to tie your horse to a palm tree and jump into the waves. ✉ *Sea Horse Ranch, Coastal Hwy., Cabarete* ☎ *809/571–3880, 809/571–4462* 🌐 *www.sea-horse-ranch.com.*

WHALE-WATCHING

SAMANÁ PENINSULA

Humpback whales come to Samaná Bay to mate and give birth each year for a relatively limited period, from approximately January 15 through March 30. Samaná Bay is considered one of the top 10 destinations in the world to watch humpbacks. If you're here during the brief season, this can be the experience of a lifetime. You can listen to the male humpback's solitary courting song and witness incredible displays as the whales flip their tails and breach (humpbacks are the most active species of whales in the Atlantic).

Fodor's Choice ★ **Whale Samaná.** Whale Samaná is owned by Kim Beddall, a Canadian who is incredibly knowledgeable about whales and Samaná in general, having lived here for decades. Her operation is far and away the region's best, most professional, and environmentally sensitive. On board *Pura Mia*, a 55-foot motor vessel, a marine mammal specialist narrates and answers questions in several languages. Kim herself conducts almost all the English-speaking trips. The $59 price does not include the $3 Marine Mammal Sanctuary entrance fee (price is subject to change). Normal departure times are 9 am for the morning trip and 1:30 pm for the afternoon trip, but she is flexible whenever possible for cruise-ship passengers yet does require advance reservations. Online bookings are now taken at *whalesamana.com*. ✉ *Across street from town dock, beside park, Calle Sra. Morellia Kelly, Santa Bárbara de Samaná* ☎ *809/538–2494* ✉ *kim.beddall@whalesamana.com* 🌐 *www.whalesamana.com.*

WIND- AND KITESURFING

Laurel Eastman Kiteboarding. One of the best-known and most respected schools in the Caribbean, Laurel Eastman Kiteboarding School (LEK) offers a free lesson with certified instructors, usually from 10:30 to 11 am daily. In four days, beginners can learn the theory of the wind and start using the smaller kite trainers. It may be exhilarating, but it isn't cheap. In four days, beginners can usually get all the way up to having their first rides on the board, a thrill that just must be experienced. Four days of private lessons with the certified instructor and all the gear costs about $508.

Eastman was a pioneer in this sport and among the characteristics students love about "flying high in the sky" with her team is that it's fun and safe. She donates time to local charities, such as Mariposa, and teaches those girls involved how to kite. Staff dispenses fresh fruit and their knowledge about local marine life. ✉ *Millennium Resort & Spa, Cabarete* ☎ *809/571–0564* 🌐 *www.laureleastman.com.*

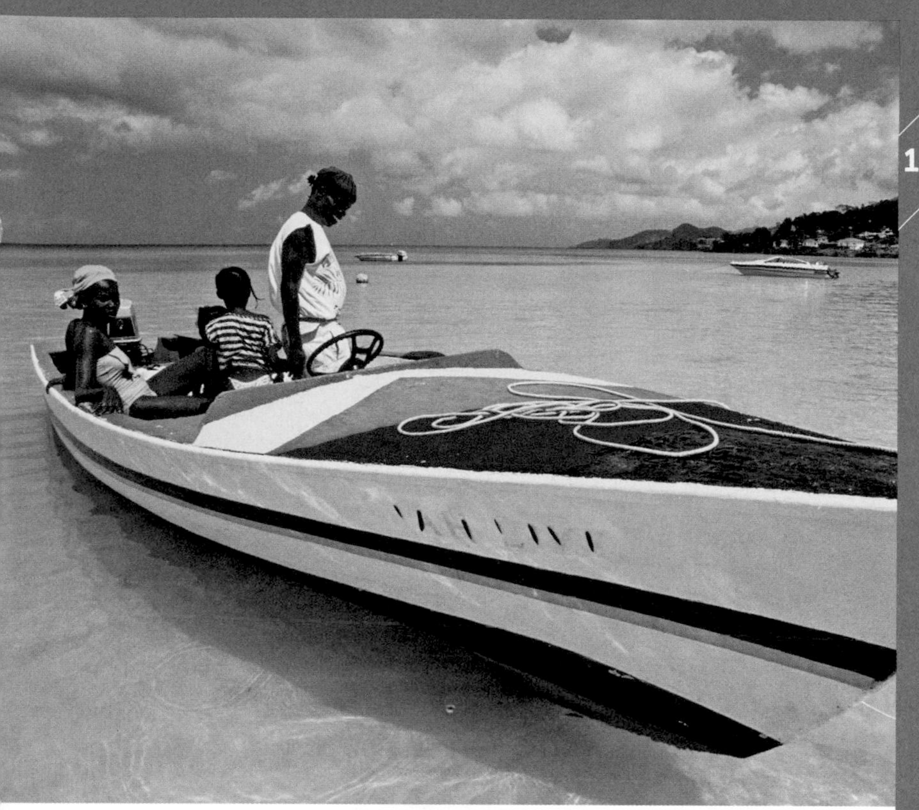

GRENADA

with Carriacou

WELCOME TO GRENADA

THE SPICE ISLAND

A small, mountainous island, Grenada is 21 miles (34 km) long and 12 miles (19 km) wide; much of the interior is covered by verdant rain forest. Grenada is a major producer of nutmeg, cinnamon, mace, cocoa, and other spices and flavorings. Carriacou—23 miles (37 km) north of Grenada—comprises just 13 square miles (34 square km). Tiny Petite Martinique is 2 miles (3 km) farther north.

0 5 mi
0 5 km

20
Sauteurs Bay
David Bay
Carib's Leap
Sauteurs
Morne Fendue
St. Mark Bay
Victoria
15
Gouyave Nutmeg Processing Station
Gouyave
Mt. St. Catherine
Dougaldston Spice Estate
Gouyave Bay
Mt. Granby
Concord Falls
Mt. Qua Qua
Black Bay Pt.
Flamingo Bay
Grand Étang National Park and Forest Reserve
Halifax Harbour
Marquis
Annandale Falls
Mt. Lebanon
Molinère Reef
Molinère Pt.
Constantine
Mt. Sinai
Grand Mal Bay
Pomme Rose
St. George's
St. George's Harbour
De La Grenade Industries
St. David's
Bianca C
3 4
1 2
Laura Herb and Spice Garden
Boss Reef
Belmont
La Sagesse Beach
7 - 9
1 - 7
Grand Anse Beach
5
Westerhall Estate
Grand Anse
6
Morne Rouge Bay
Morne Rouge Beach
8
14 18
Magazine Beach
La Sagesse Bay
St. George's U.
Pink Gin Beach
13
L'Anse aux Epines
Westerhall Bay
Pt. Salines
11 12
Maurice Bishop International Airport
12 13
10 9 - 11
Prickly Bay
14 - 17

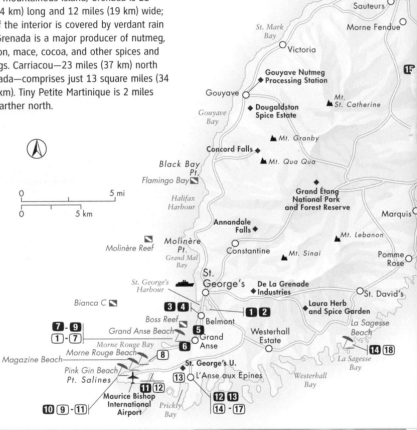

These days, local people on the Isle of Spice busy themselves cultivating nutmeg, cloves, and other spices. Renowned for its natural beauty, its fragrant air, and its friendly people, Grenada has lovely beaches and plenty of outdoor and cultural activities. Vestiges of its briefly turbulent past have all but disappeared.

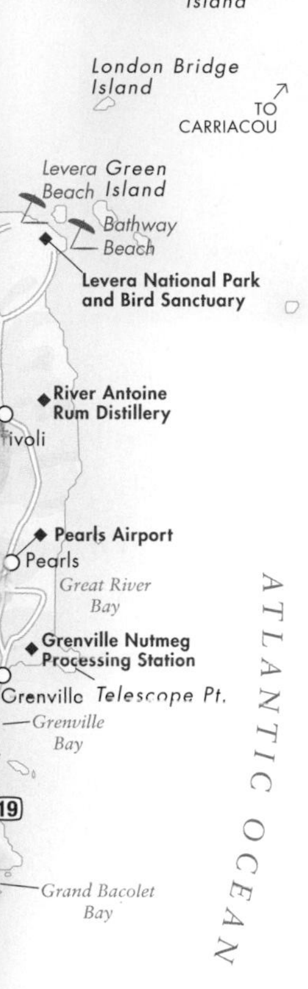

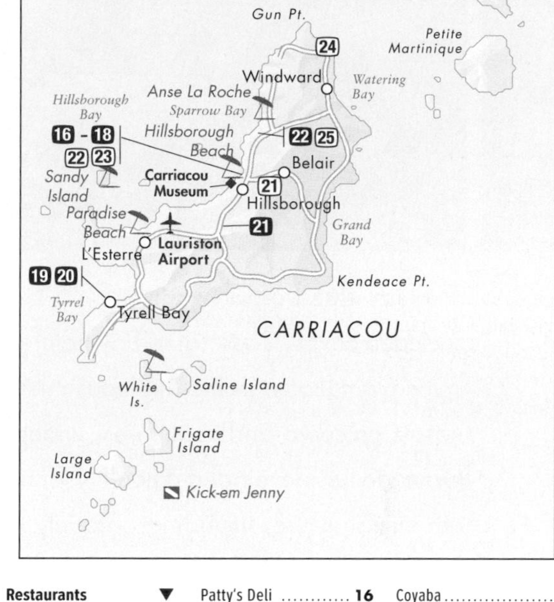

KEY

- Beaches
- Cruise Ship Terminal
- Dive Sites
- Restaurants
- Hotels

Restaurants

- Aquarium 10
- BB's Crabback 2
- Beach House 11
- Belmont Estate 15
- Bogles Round House .. 22
- Coconut Beach 9
- Kayak Kafé 17
- La Belle Creole 7
- La Boulangerie 8
- La Sagesse 14
- Laurena II 21
- Lazy Turtle 20
- Moringa 18
- The New Nutmeg 1
- Oliver's 5
- Patrick's 3
- Patty's Deli 16
- The Red Crab 12
- Rhodes' Restaurant 13
- Slipway 19
- Umbrellas Beach Bar 6
- Victory Bar & Grill 4

Hotels

- Allamanda 2
- Bayaleau Point Cottages 24
- Blue Horizons 5
- Bogles Round House .. 25
- Cabier 19
- Calabash Hotel 15
- Carriacou Grand View 21
- Coral Cove 17
- Coyaba 3
- Flamboyant 6
- Green Roof Inn 22
- Grenadian by Rex 11
- Hotel Laurena 23
- Kalinago Beach Resort .. 8
- Laluna 12
- La Sagesse 18
- Maca Bana 9
- Mount Cinnamon 7
- Mount Hartman 14
- Petite Anse Hotel 20
- Radisson Grand 1
- Sandals 10
- Spice Island 4
- True Blue Bay 13
- Twelve Degrees North . 16

TOP REASONS TO VISIT GRENADA

1 Old and New: Grenada successfully blends a "pure" Caribbean atmosphere with all of the comforts and amenities that you expect.

2 The Aroma: The scent of spices fills the air, perfumes the soap, enriches the drinks, and even flavors the ice cream.

3 Nature Abounds: Spot monkeys in the mountains, watch birds in the rain forest, join fish in the sea, and build sand castles on the beach.

4 Local Hospitality: Grenadians go out of their way to make you feel welcome.

5 A Great Getaway: With no megaresorts, you really can get away from it all.

Updated by Jane E. Zarem

The lush island of Grenada has 45 beaches and countless secluded coves. Crisscrossed by nature trails and laced with spice plantations, its mountainous interior consists mostly of nature preserve and rain forest. Independent since 1974, Grenada has developed a healthy tourism sector and a modern infrastructure, including a variety of hotels and resorts, good roads, up-to-date technology, and reliable utilities.

The nation of Grenada actually consists of three islands: Grenada, the largest, has a population of about 103,000; Carriacou (*car*-ree-a-coo), north of Grenada, has a population of just over 6,000; and Petite Martinique has a population of about 500. Carriacou and Petite Martinique are popular for day trips, fishing adventures, sailing destinations, or diving and snorkeling excursions, but most of the tourist activity is on the island of Grenada itself. People interested in a really quiet, get-away-from-it-all vacation will, however, appreciate the simple pleasures of Carriacou during an extended stay.

St. George's, the capital, is a busy city with buildings and landmarks that date back centuries; its harbor is one of the most picturesque in the Caribbean. Grand Anse, south of the capital, boasts one of the region's finest beaches.

Although Christopher Columbus never set foot on Grenada, he did cruise by in 1498, naming the island Concepción. Spanish sailors following in his wake renamed it Granada, after the city in the hills of their homeland. Adapted to Grenade by French colonists, the transformation of the name to Grenada was completed by the British in the 18th century.

Throughout the 17th century, Grenada was the scene of many bloody battles between the indigenous Carib Indians and the French. Rather than surrender to the Europeans after losing their last battle in 1651, the Caribs committed mass suicide by leaping off a cliff that's now called Carib's Leap or Leapers Hill. The French were later overwhelmed by the British in 1762, the beginning of a seesaw of power between the two nations. The Treaty of Versailles in 1783 ultimately granted Grenada to the British. Almost immediately, thousands of African slaves were brought in to work the sugar plantations (although slavery in Grenada actually began with the French colonization in 1650). Slavery on the island was finally abolished in 1834.

Forts on which the French began construction, in order to protect St. George's Harbour during their colonization of Grenada, were later completed and used by the British during theirs. Today Ft. George and Ft. Frederick are two of the most visited sites in St. George's. Besides their historical interest, the two locations have magnificent views of the harbor, the capital city itself, and the distant mountains and countryside. Not a single shot was fired from either fort for more than two centuries. In 1983, however, Prime Minister Maurice Bishop and seven others were murdered at Ft. George during a coup d'état. That event triggered the request from Grenada's governor-general and the heads of state of neighboring islands for U.S. troops to intervene, which they did on October 25, 1983. The insurrection came to an immediate halt, perpetrators were imprisoned, and peace was restored.

From that time forward, Grenada's popularity as a vacation destination has increased with each decade, as travelers continue to seek welcoming, exotic islands to visit. Most hotels, resorts, and restaurants in Grenada are family-owned and -run (mostly by Grenadians); their guests often become good friends. All Grenadians, in fact, have a well-deserved reputation for their friendliness, hospitality, and entrepreneurial spirit.

PLANNING

WHEN TO GO

The high season stretches from December 15 to April 15. In the off-season, prices at Grenada resorts may be discounted by up to 40%. In September and early October, some hotels close for annual maintenance and renovations. There are fewer seasonal rate changes on Carriacou, where the small hotels and guesthouses are all relatively inexpensive anyway.

GETTING HERE AND AROUND

AIR TRAVEL

Nonstop flights to Grenada are available from New York on Caribbean Airlines and Delta and from Miami on American Airlines. Regional flights between Grenada and Carriacou and between Grenada and neighboring islands operate several times each day.

Airline Contacts American Airlines. American flies nonstop to Grenada from Miami several times a week, with connecting service through Miami from other major cities. ☎ *473/444–2121, 800/744–0006* 🌐 *www.aa.com.* **Caribbean Airlines.** Caribbean Airlines provides nonstop service from New York and connecting service from Miami via Port-of-Spain, Trinidad. ☎ *800/523–5585* 🌐 *www.caribbean-airlines.com.* **Delta Air Lines.** Delta provides nonstop service from New York every Saturday. ☎ *800/221–1212* 🌐 *www.delta.com.* **LIAT.** LIAT offers frequent scheduled service linking Grenada with more than a dozen neighboring islands. ☎ *473/444–4121, 888/844–5428* 🌐 *www.liat.com.* **SVG Air.** SVG Air flies between Grenada and Carriacou and between Grenada and Union Island, with connecting

LOGISTICS

Getting to Grenada and Carriacou: Nonstop flights to Grenada are available from New York on Caribbean Airlines and Delta and from Miami on American Airlines. Otherwise, connect through Barbados or another nearby island via LIAT. Fairly frequent air service (20 minutes each way) and a daily ferry (1½–2½ hours each way, depending on the boat) connect Grenada and Carriacou.

Hassle Factor: Medium for Grenada, medium-high for Carriacou.

On the Ground: Maurice Bishop International Airport (GND), at Point Salines on the southwestern tip of Grenada, is a modern facility suitable for the largest jets. Best of all, it's no more than a 10-minute drive from most hotels and resorts. On Carriacou, Lauriston Airport (CRU) is located just west of Hillsborough, the main town, and has a lighted landing strip that accommodates small planes and a small building for ticket sales and shelter. A $4 departure tax is payable in cash when leaving Carriacou by air.

On Grenada, taxis are always available for transportation between the airport and hotels.

At Carriacou's airport, taxis meet every plane.

flights between Union Island and Canouan, Mustique, Bequia, St. Vincent, and Barbados. ☎ *473/444–3549, 473/443–8519 in Carriacou* 🌐 *www.svgair.com.*

Airport Contacts Lauriston Airport (*CRU*). ✉ *Carriacou* ☎ *473/443–6306.* **Maurice Bishop International Airport** (*GND*). ✉ *Point Salines, St. George* ☎ *473/444–4101* 🌐 *www.mbiagrenada.com.*

Transfers On Grenada, taxis are always available for transportation between the airport and hotels. Fares to St. George's are $25; to the hotels of Grand Anse and L'Anse aux Épines, $15. Rides taken between 6 pm and 6 am incur a $4 surcharge. On Carriacou, taxis meet every plane; the fare to Hillsborough is $8; to Bogles, $10; to Tyrell Bay, $12; to Windward, $15.

CAR TRAVEL

On Grenada, having a car or jeep is a real convenience if you're staying at a resort in a location other than Grand Anse, which has frequent minibus service. If you don't have a car of your own, the round-trip taxi rides can get expensive if you plan to leave the resort frequently for shopping, meals, or visiting other beaches. Driving is also a reasonable option if you want to explore the island on your own. Most of Grenada's 650 miles (1,050 km) of paved roads are kept in fairly good condition—although they are steep, curving, and narrow beyond the Grand Anse area. Driving is on the left, British-style. You'll find gas stations in St. George's, Grand Anse, Grenville, Gouyave, and Sauteurs.

Renting a Car: To rent a car on Grenada, you need a valid driver's license and a temporary local permit (available at the Central Police Station on the Carenage in the capital city of St. George's and at most car-rental firms), which costs $12 (EC$30). You can rent a car on Carriacou, even for just a few hours, but it's easier to take taxis.

Some rental agencies impose a minimum age (18 or 21). Rental cars, including four-wheel-drive vehicles, cost $75 to $85 a day or $475 to $500 a week with unlimited mileage—rates are slightly lower in the low season. In high season there may be a three-day minimum rental. Rental agencies offer free pickup and drop-off at either the airport or your hotel.

Contacts on Grenada David's Sun Car Rental ☎ *473/444-3399* 🌐 *www.davidscars.com.* **Indigo Car Rentals** ☎ *473/439-3300* 🌐 *www.indigocarsgrenada.com.* **McIntyre Bros. Ltd.** ☎ *473/444-3944* 🌐 *www.caribbeanhorizons.com.* **Y & R Car Rentals** ☎ *473/444-4448* 🌐 *www.carrentalgrenada.com.* **Vista Rentals** ✉ *Spice Island Beach Resort, Grand Anse, St. George* ☎ *473/439-8105* 🌐 *www.grenadavistarentals.com.*

Contacts on Carriacou Barba's Auto Rentals ✉ *Harvey Vale, Carriacou* ☎ *473/443-7454.* **Wayne's Auto Rentals** ✉ *The Esplanade, Main St., Hillsborough, Carriacou* ☎ *473/443-6120.*

FERRY TRAVEL

Osprey Express. The high-speed ferry Osprey Express makes one round-trip voyage daily from Grenada to Carriacou and on to Petite Martinique. The trip takes 1½ to 2½ hours, depending on the boat. On either vessel, the fare from Grenada to Carriacou is $31 each way. For the 15-minute trip from Carriacou to Petite Martinique, the fare is $12 each way. The ferry departs Grenada from The Carenage in St. George's Monday–Saturday at 9 am and Sunday at 8 am; the return trip leaves from the jetty in Hillsborough, Carriacou, at 3:30 pm. ✉ *The Carenage, St. George's, St. George* ☎ *473/440-8126* 🌐 *www.ospreylines.com.*

TAXIS

On Grenada, taxis are plentiful, and rates are set. The trip between Grand Anse and St. George's is $20. A $4 surcharge is added for rides taken between 6 pm and 6 am. Taxis can be hired at an hourly rate of $30, as well.

In Carriacou the taxi fare from the jetty in Hillsborough to Belair is $10; to Prospect, Tyrell Bay, or Windward, $13. Carriacou minibus drivers will take up to four people on a 2½-hour full-island tour for $75 or a 1½-hour half-island tour for $40.

ALTERNATIVE TRANSPORTATION

The best way to travel between Grenada and Carriacou is by air; the high-speed ferry is the next-best choice as long as you aren't prone to motion sickness. The outbound voyage gets a little rough once you've cleared the island of Grenada. Reservations for the ferry aren't necessary, but get to the wharf well before the departure time of 9 am in Grenada and 3:30 pm in Carriacou to be sure you don't miss the boat.

Water taxis are available along the Esplanade, near the port area. For about $8 (EC$20) a motorboat will transport you on a quick and picturesque cruise between St. George's and the jetty at Grand Anse Beach. Water taxis are privately owned, unregulated, and don't follow any particular schedule—so make arrangements for a pickup time if you need a return trip.

ESSENTIALS

Banks and Exchange Services Grenada uses the Eastern Caribbean dollar (EC$). The official exchange rate is fixed at EC$2.67 to US$1; for convenience, taxis, shops, and hotels sometimes use a lower rate (EC$2.50). You can exchange money at banks and hotels, but major credit cards and U.S. paper currency (no coins) are widely accepted—although you'll get your change in local currency.

Electricity Current on Grenada is 220 volts/50 cycles. U.S. standard appliances (110 volts) require a transformer and adapter plug. For dual-voltage computers and other devices, you'll still need an adapter plug; most hotels will lend adapters and some have installed 110 outlets.

Language English is the official language in Grenada.

Passport Requirements To enter Grenada, visitors must produce a valid passport and a return or onward ticket.

Phones The area code for Grenada and Carriacou is 473. Prepaid phone cards can be used for local or international calls from special card phones located throughout the Caribbean; the phone cards are sold in denominations of EC$20 ($7.50), EC$30 ($12), EC$50 ($20), and EC$75 ($28) at shops, attractions, transportation centers, and other convenient outlets. For international calls using a major credit card, dial 111; to place a collect call or use a calling card, dial 800/225–5872 from any telephone.

Taxes and Service Charges Grenada has a 10% V.A.T. (value-added tax) on hotel bills and a 15% V.A.T. on restaurant bills and retail sales. In addition, a 10% service charge is often added to hotel and restaurant bills.

Tipping If there is no service charge, then tip 10%; if a service charge has been included, additional tipping is optional: bellhops, $1 per bag; housekeeping, $2 per night; taxi drivers and tour guides, 10% of the fare or fee.

ACCOMMODATIONS

Grenada's tourist accommodations are located, for the most part, in the southwestern part of the island—primarily on or near Grand Anse Beach or overlooking small bays along the island's southern coast. Carriacou is a small island, and its hotels and guesthouses are primarily in or around Hillsborough.

Guesthouses: Small guesthouses predominate on Carriacou, where no property has more than 25 rooms.

Luxury Resorts: Grenada has a handful of luxurious inns and resorts. Spice Island Beach Resort on Grand Anse Beach is one of the finest boutique resorts in the Caribbean.

Modest Resorts and Apartment Complexes: Most resorts and hotels on Grenada are small, and many are modest; that is part of their charm.

Hotel reviews have been shortened. For full information, visit Fodors.com.

WHAT IT COSTS IN U.S. DOLLARS				
	$	$$	$$$	$$$$
Restaurants	under $12	$12–$20	$21–$30	over $30
Hotels	under $275	$275–$375	$376–$475	over $475

Restaurant prices are the average cost of a main course at dinner or, if dinner is not served, at lunch. Hotel prices are the lowest cost of a standard double room in high season.

VISITOR INFORMATION

Contacts Grenada Hotel & Tourism Association ☎ *473/444–1353* 🌐 *www.gogrenada.gd.* **Grenada Tourism Authority** ☎ *561/948–6925* 🌐 *www.puregrenada.com.* **Grenada Tourism Authority** ✉ *Burns Point, south end of The Carenage, St. George's* ☎ *473/440–2001, 473/440–2279* 🌐 *www.puregrenada.com* ✉ *Main St., Hillsborough, Carriacou* ☎ *473/443–7948* 🌐 *www.puregrenada.com* ✉ *Maurice Bishop International Airport, Point Salines, St. George* ☎ *473/444–4140* 🌐 *www.puregrenada.com.*

WEDDINGS

Three days' residency is required to apply for a marriage license, and securing the license can take two additional days; no blood test is necessary. You'll need to present valid passports, birth certificates, proof of single status (e.g., an affidavit or letter from a clergyman or lawyer) and original or certified copies of divorce decrees or death certificates, if applicable. The license fee is $4 (EC$10) plus a $6 (EC$15) stamp fee and a $3 (EC$7) registration search and stamp fee. Contact the registrar's office (☎ *473/330–2649*) for specific information regarding marriage licenses and marriage certificates.

EXPLORING

GRENADA

Grenada is divided into six parishes, including one named St. George that includes the communities of Grand Anse, Morne Rouge, True Blue, L'Anse aux Épines, and the capital city of St. George's. When exploring this beautiful island, please note that removing bark from trees, taking wildlife from the forest, and taking coral from the sea are all against the law.

ST. GEORGE'S

Grenada's capital is a bustling West Indian city, much of which remains unchanged from colonial days. Narrow streets lined with shops wind up, down, and across steep hills. Brick warehouses cling to the waterfront, and pastel-painted homes rise from the waterfront and disappear into steep green hills.

Horseshoe-shape **St. George's Harbour,** a submerged volcanic crater, is arguably the prettiest harbor in the Caribbean. Schooners, ferries, and tour boats tie up along the seawall or at the small dinghy dock. **The Carenage** (pronounced car-a-*nahzh*), which surrounds the harbor, is the capital's center. Warehouses, shops, and restaurants line the waterfront. The *Christ of the Deep* statue sits on the pedestrian plaza at the center of the Carenage; it was presented to Grenada by Costa Cruise Line in remembrance of its ship, *Bianca C,* that burned and sank in the harbor in 1961; *Bianca C* is now a popular dive site.

An engineering feat for its time, the 340-foot-long **Sendall Tunnel** was built in 1895 and named for Walter Sendall, an early governor. The narrow tunnel, used by both pedestrians and vehicles, separates the harbor side of St. George's from the Esplanade on the bay side of town, where you will find the markets (produce, meat, and fish), the Cruise Ship Terminal, the Esplanade Mall, and the public bus station.

TOP ATTRACTIONS

Ft. Frederick. Overlooking the city of St. George's and the picturesque harbor, historic Ft. Frederick provides a panoramic view of about one-fourth of Grenada. The French began construction of the fort; the British completed it in 1791. Ft. Frederick was the headquarters of the People's Revolutionary Government before and during the 1983 coup. Today, it's simply a peaceful spot with a bird's-eye view of much of Grenada. ✉ *Richmond Hill, St. George.*

FAMILY Fodor's Choice ★ **Ft. George.** Ft. George is perched high on the hill at the entrance to St. George's Harbour. Grenada's oldest fort was built by the French in 1705 to protect the harbor, yet no shots were ever fired here until October 1983, when Prime Minister Maurice Bishop and several of his followers were assassinated in the courtyard. The fort now houses police headquarters but is open to the public daily. The 360-degree view of the capital city, St. George's Harbour, and the open sea is spectacular. ✉ *Church St., St. George's* 🎫 *$2.*

FAMILY **Grenada National Museum.** A block from the Carenage, the Grenada National Museum is built on the foundation of a French army barracks and prison that was originally built in 1704. The small museum has exhibitions of news items, photos, and proclamations relating to the 1983 intervention, along with fragments of Amerindian pottery, the childhood bathtub of Empress Joséphine (who was born on Martinique), and other memorabilia. ✉ *Young and Monckton Sts., St. George's, St. George* ☎ *473/440–3725* 🌐 *www.grenadamuseum.gd* 🎫 *$5* 🕒 *Weekdays 9–5, Sat. 10–1.*

Fodor's Choice ★ **Market Square.** Definitely plan to visit St. George's Market Square, a block from the Cruise Ship Terminal and Esplanade Mall in downtown St. George's. This is the place to buy fresh spices, bottled sauces, and handcrafted gifts and souvenirs to take home. In addition to local spices and heaps of fresh produce, vendors sell baskets, brooms, clothing, knickknacks, coconut water, and more. The market is open every weekday morning but really comes alive on Saturday from 8 to noon. Market Square is also where parades begin and political rallies take place. ✉ *Granby St., St. George's, St. George.*

WORTH NOTING

Cathedral of the Immaculate Conception. The Roman Catholic cathedral, high on a hill overlooking the harbor, is the city's most visible landmark. The Gothic tower dates from 1818. ✉ *Church St., St. George's, St. George* ☎ *473/435–9808.*

ELSEWHERE ON GRENADA

TOP ATTRACTIONS

Fodor'sChoice ★ **Concord Falls.** About 8 miles (13 km) north of St. George's, a turnoff from the West Coast Road leads to Concord Falls—actually three separate waterfalls. The first is at the end of the road; when the currents aren't too strong, you can take a dip under the 35-foot cascade. Reaching the two other waterfalls requires a hike into the forest reserve. The hike to the second falls (Au Coin) takes about 30 minutes. The third and most spectacular waterfall (Fountainbleu) thunders 65 feet over huge boulders and creates a small pool. It's smart to hire a guide for that trek, which can take an hour or more. The path is clear, but slippery boulders toward the end can be treacherous without assistance. ⊠ *Off West Coast Rd., Concord, St. John* *Changing room $2* *Daily 9–5.*

FAMILY Fodor'sChoice ★ **Gouyave Nutmeg Processing Station.** Touring the nutmeg-processing co-op, right in the center of the west-coast fishing village of Gouyave (pronounced *gwahv*), is a fragrant, fascinating way to spend a half-hour. You can learn all about nutmeg and its uses, see the nutmegs laid out in bins, and watch the workers sort them by hand and pack them into burlap bags for shipping worldwide. The three-story plant turned out 3 million pounds of Grenada's most famous export each year before Hurricane Ivan's devastating effect on the crop in 2004, when most of the nutmeg trees were destroyed. Production has finally begun to reach pre-hurricane levels. ⊠ *Central Depradine St., Gouyave, St. John* ☎ *473/444–8337* *$1* *Weekdays 10–1 and 2–4.*

FAMILY Fodor'sChoice ★ **Grand Étang National Park & Forest Reserve.** A rain forest and wildlife sanctuary deep in the mountainous interior of Grenada, Grand Étang has miles of hiking trails for all levels of ability. There are also lookouts to observe the lush flora and many species of birds and other fauna (including the Mona monkey) and a number of streams for fishing. **Grand Étang Lake** is a 36-acre expanse of cobalt-blue water—1,740 feet above sea level—that fills the crater of an extinct volcano. Although legend has it that the lake is bottomless, maximum soundings have been recorded at just 18 feet. The informative **Grand Étang Forest Center** has displays on the local wildlife and vegetation. A forest ranger is on hand to answer questions; a small snack bar and souvenir stands are nearby. ⊠ *Main interior road, between Grenville and St. George's, St. Andrew* ☎ *473/440–6160* *$1* *Daily 8:30–4.*

FAMILY **Laura Herb & Spice Garden.** The 6½ acres of gardens here are part of an old plantation at Laura, near the village of Perdmontemps in St. David Parish and about 6 miles (10 km) east of Grand Anse. On the 20-minute tour, you will learn all about spices and herbs grown in Grenada—including cocoa, clove, nutmeg, pimiento, cinnamon, turmeric, and tonka beans (sometimes used in vanilla substitutes)—and how they're used for flavoring and for medicinal purposes. ⊠ *Laura Rd., Perdmontemps, St. David* ☎ *473/443–2604* *$2* *Weekdays 8–4.*

FAMILY **Spice Basket.** Half of the small but fascinating museum at this cultural center and performance venue covers Grenada's heritage—its Amerindian beginnings, its geology (including samples of sand representing all the different hues represented on local beaches), local birds and animals, early tools and implements, sugar and slavery, and the 1979–1983 Grenada Revolution. The other half of the museum is dedicated to cricket, making it "the world's first and only display offering an insight into Caribbean social history through cricket." The memorabilia, some dating to the 1800s, includes uniforms, bats, equipment, and more. It's all very fascinating and definitely worth a visit. A gift shop features locally made items. Spice Basket is in the countryside, not far from Annandale Falls. ✉ *Beaulieu, St. George* ☎ *473/437–9000, 473/232–9000* 🌐 *www.spicebasketgrenada.com* 🎫 *$10.*

WORTH NOTING

Annandale Falls. This is a lovely, cool spot for swimming and picnicking. A mountain stream cascades 40 feet into a natural pool surrounded by exotic vines. A paved path leads to the bottom of the falls, and a trail leads to the top. You'll often find local boys diving from the top of the falls—and hoping for a small tip. ✉ *Main interior road, 15 mins northeast of St. George's, Annandale, St. George* ☎ *473/440–2452* 🎫 *$1* ⏲ *Daily 9–5.*

Carib's Leap. At Sauteurs (the French word for "leapers") on the island's northernmost tip, Carib's Leap (or Leaper's Hill) is the 100-foot vertical cliff from which the last of the indigenous Carib Indians flung themselves into the sea in 1651. After losing several bloody battles with European colonists, they chose suicide over surrender to the French. ✉ *Sauteurs, St. Patrick.*

De La Grenade Industries. In the suburb of St. Paul's, five minutes east of St. George's, De La Grenade produces syrups, jams, jellies, and a liqueur from nutmeg and other homegrown fruits and spices. You're welcome to watch the manufacturing process and stroll around the adjacent herb and spice gardens. ✉ *Morne Délice, St. Paul's, St. George* ☎ *473/440–3241* 🌐 *www.delagrenade.com* 🎫 *$5* ⏲ *Weekdays 8–5, Sat. 9–12:30.*

FAMILY **Dougaldston Spice Estate.** Just south of Gouyave, this historic plantation still grows and processes spices the old-fashioned way. You can see cocoa, nutmeg, mace, cloves, and other spices laid out on giant racks to dry in the sun. A worker will be glad to explain the process (and will appreciate a small donation). You can buy spices for about $5 a bag. ✉ *Gouyave, St. John* 🎫 *Free* ⏲ *Weekdays 9–4.*

FAMILY **Grand Anse.** A residential and commercial area about 5 miles (8 km) south of downtown St. George's, Grand Anse is named for the world-renowned beach it surrounds. Grenada's tourist facilities—resorts, restaurants, some shopping, and most nightlife—are concentrated in this general area. **Grand Anse Beach** is a 2-mile (3-km) crescent of sand, shaded by coconut palms and sea grape trees, with gentle turquoise surf. A public entrance is at Camerhogne Park, just a few steps from the main road. Water taxis carry passengers between the Esplanade in St. George's and a jetty on the beach. **St. George's University,** which for years held classes at its enviable beachfront location in Grand Anse, now has its sprawling main campus in True Blue, a nearby residential community. The original beachside building in Grand Anse is currently used for student housing. ✉ *Grand Anse, St. George.*

12

FAMILY **Grenville Nutmeg Processing Station.** Like its counterpart in Gouyave, this nutmeg-processing plant is open to the public for guided tours. You can see and learn about the entire process of receiving, drying, sorting, and packing nutmeg. ✉ *Grenville, St. Andrew* ☎ *473/442–7241* 🎫 *$1* ⏲ *Weekdays 10–1 and 2–4.*

Levera National Park & Bird Sanctuary. This portion of Grenada's protected parkland encompasses 450 acres at the northeastern tip of the island, where the Caribbean Sea meets the Atlantic Ocean. A natural reef protects swimmers from the rough Atlantic surf at Bathway Beach. Thick mangroves provide food and protection for nesting seabirds and seldom-seen parrots. The southernmost islets of the Grenadines are visible from the beach. ✉ *Levera, St. Patrick* 🎫 *Free* ⏲ *Daily dawn–dusk.*

WORD OF MOUTH

"Grenada really does have it all. I love the island and the incredibly friendly people. Having visited the Caribbean extensively, I always tell people that Grenada is the best of St. Lucia and Barbados put together on one island. It has the dramatic scenery and wildlife that St. Lucia has and the beautiful white sandy beaches of Barbados—a true gem!"

—sunflower12

River Antoine Rum Distillery. At this rustic operation, kept open primarily as a museum, a limited quantity of Rivers rum is produced by the same methods used since the distillery opened in 1785. River Antoine (pronounced An-*twyne*) is the oldest functioning water-propelled distillery in the Caribbean. The process begins with the crushing of sugarcane from adjacent fields; the discarded canes are then used as fuel to fire the boilers. The end result is a potent overproof rum, sold only in Grenada, that will knock your socks off. (A less strong version is also available.) ✉ *River Antoine Estate, St. Patrick* ☎ *473/442–7109* 🎫 *Guided tour $2* ⏲ *Mon.–Sat. 9–5.*

Westerhall Estate. Back in the late 1800s, cocoa, sugarcane, coconuts (the oil was used for soap), and limes (used in perfume) were produced on the 951-acre Westerhall Estate, which was then called Bacaye. More recently, Westerhall has focused on rum. The Westerhall Estate tour includes an explanation of the ruins and sugar-processing machinery on the grounds, along with a small museum comprising the eclectic collection of the Grenadian journalist Dr. Alistair Hughes (1919–2005). Particularly interesting items on display in the museum include old rum bottles and labels, Carib artifacts, a number of vintage sewing machines, a World War I Maxim machine gun, and a 1915 Willys Overland automobile. ✉ *Westerhall* ☎ *473/443–5477* 🌐 *www.westerhallrums.co.uk* 🎫 *$4* ⏲ *Mon.–Fri. 9–3.*

CARRIACOU

Carriacou, the land of many reefs, is a hilly island with neither lakes nor rivers, so its drinking water comes from rainwater caught in cisterns. It gets quite arid during the dry season (January through May). Nevertheless, pigeon peas, corn, and fruit are grown here, and the climate seems to suit the mahogany trees used for furniture making and the white cedar that's critical to the island's famed boatbuilding industry.

Hillsborough is Carriacou's main town. Just offshore, Sandy Island is a tiny spit of land and one of the nicest beaches around. Almost anyone with a boat will give you a ride from Paradise Beach or Hillsborough to Sandy Island for a small fee (about $25 round-trip). Rolling hills cut a wide swath through the middle of Carriacou, from Gun Point in the north to Tyrell Bay in the south.

Despite its tiny size, Carriacou has several distinct cultures. Hillsborough is decidedly English; the southern region, around L'Esterre, reflects French roots; and the northern town of Windward has Scottish ties. African culture, though, is the overarching influence.

TOP ATTRACTIONS

Belair. For a great bird's-eye view of Hillsborough and Carriacou's entire west coast, drive to Belair in the north-central part of the island. The vantage point for the magnificent view, 700 feet above sea level, is adjacent to Princess Royal Hospital. On the way to Belair, you'll pass by the photogenic ruins of an old sugar mill. ✉ *Belair.*

High North Nature Reserve. At 955 feet, the highest peak on Carriacou is in the High North Nature Reserve, a designated national park site that allows breathtaking views as far as Grenada to the south and St. Vincent and all its Grenadines to the north. Visitors can hike the trails, either alone or with a guide, and are likely to encounter iguanas, land tortoises, soldier crabs, and various birds—perhaps even a few macaws—along the way. ✉ *Windward.*

Tyrell Bay. Tyrell Bay, a waterfront village in Harvey Vale, is a large protected harbor in southwest Carriacou and the official port of entry for yachts. The bay is almost always full of sailboats, powerboats, and working boats—coming, going, or bobbing at their moorings. Restaurants, cafés, and grocery stores face the waterfront. If you take a short boat ride, you will find yourself in the middle of one of the few pristine ecosystems in the region, with oysters growing on the roots of the mangrove trees. ✉ *Tyrell Bay, Harvey Vale.*

WORTH NOTING

Carriacou Museum. Housed in a building that once held a cotton gin (the second-oldest cotton ginnery in the world) and just one block from the waterfront, Carriacou's little museum has exhibitions of Amerindian, European, and African artifacts, a collection of watercolors by native folk artist Canute Caliste, and a small gift shop with local items. Founded in 1976, the museum is supported by the Carriacou Historical Society. Museum manager Clemencia Alexander, one of Caliste's daughters, has worked for the museum for more than 30 years and is happy to give a guided tour. ✉ *Paterson St., Hillsborough* ☎ *473/443–8288* 🌐 *www.carriacoumuseum.org* 🎫 *$2* ⏲ *Weekdays 10–4.*

Windward. The small town of Windward is a boatbuilding community on the northeast coast of Carriacou. At certain times of year, primarily during school vacations, you may encounter a work in progress along the roadside. ✉ *Windward.*

The lookout from Belair, with Hillsborough and Carriacou's western coast below

PETITE MARTINIQUE

Ten minutes north of Carriacou by boat or ferry lies the tiny residential island of Petite Martinique. There's a guesthouse or two but no tourist facilities or attractions—just peace and quiet. Meander along the beachfront and watch boatbuilders at work. If by chance there's a boat launching, sailboat race, traditional wedding, holiday, or festival taking place while you're there, you're in for a treat. The music is infectious, the food bountiful, and the spirit lively.

BEACHES

GRENADA

Grenada has some 80 miles (130 km) of coastline, 65 bays, and 45 beaches—many in little coves. The best beaches are just south of St. George's, facing the Caribbean, where many resorts are clustered. Nude or topless bathing that's done in view of others is against the law.

Bathway Beach. This broad strip of white sand on the northeastern tip of Grenada is part of Levera National Park. A natural coral reef protects swimmers and snorkelers from the rough Atlantic surf; swimming beyond the reef is dangerous. A magnet for local folks on national holidays, the beach is almost deserted at other times. Changing rooms are located at the park headquarters. A vendor or two sometimes sets up shop near the beach, but you're smart to bring your own refreshments.

Amenities: parking (no fee); toilets. **Best for:** solitude; snorkeling; swimming; walking. ✉ *Levera National Park, Levera, St. Patrick.*

FAMILY Fodor's Choice ★ **Grand Anse Beach.** Grenada's loveliest and most popular beach is Grand Anse: a gleaming 2-mile (3-km) semicircle of white sand, lapped by gentle surf and punctuated by sea grape trees and coconut palms that provide shady escapes from the sun. Brilliant rainbows frequently spill into the sea from the high green mountains that frame St. George's Harbour to the north. Several resorts face the beach, from Flamboyant and Mount Cinnamon at the southern end of the beach to Spice Island Beach Resort, Coyaba Beach Resort, Allamanda Beach Resort, and Radisson Grenada Beach Resort as you head north. Several of these hotels have dive shops for arranging dive trips or renting snorkeling equipment. A water-taxi dock is at the midpoint of the beach, along with the Grand Anse Craft & Spice Market, where vendors also rent beach chairs and umbrellas. Restrooms and changing facilities are available at Camerhogne Park, which is the public entrance and parking lot. Hotel guests, cruise-ship passengers, and other island visitors love this beach, as do local people who come to swim and play on weekends. There's plenty of room for everyone. **Amenities:** food and drink; parking (no fee); toilets; water sports. **Best for:** sunset; swimming; walking. ✉ *3 miles (5 km) south of St. George's, Grand Anse, St. George.*

La Sagesse Beach. Surrounding a sheltered bay along the southeastern coast at La Sagesse Nature Centre, this secluded crescent of the finest (gray) sand on the island is a 30-minute drive from Grand Anse. Surrounded by tropical vegetation, it provides a lovely, quiet refuge. The water is fairly shallow and always calm along the shoreline. Plan a full day of swimming, sunning, and nature walks, with lunch at La Sagesse Inn's restaurant, which is adjacent to the beach. **Amenities:** food and drink; parking (no fee); toilets. **Best for:** solitude; swimming; walking. ✉ *La Sagesse Nature Center, La Sagesse, St. David.*

Magazine Beach. Not far from the international airport in Point Salines, Magazine Beach is a magnificent strip of pure white sand that stretches from Aquarium Restaurant and Maca Bana Villas at its southern end to the Grenadian by Rex Resort, farther north. Never crowded, it's excellent for swimming and sunbathing; the surf ranges from gentle to spectacular. Cool drinks, snacks, or a full lunch are available at the Aquarium's La Sirena Beach Bar—or stick around for happy hour. You can also rent snorkeling equipment and kayaks there. Access to the beach is next to the restaurant or next to the Rex. **Amenities:** food and drink; toilets; water sports. **Best for:** snorkeling; sunset; swimming; walking. ✉ *Point Salines, St. George.*

FAMILY **Morne Rouge Beach.** One mile (1½ km) south of Grand Anse, a ½-mile-long (¾-km-long) crescent of pure white sand is tucked away on Morne Rouge Bay. The clear turquoise water is excellent for swimming, and the gentle surf makes this beach perfect for families with small children. Light meals and snacks are available at Gem Holiday Resort's beachfront bar and grill. **Amenities:** food and drink; parking (no fee); toilets. **Best for:** sunset; swimming. ✉ *Morne Rouge, St. George.*

CARRIACOU

On Carriacou, you'll find some beaches within walking distance of the ferry jetty in Hillsborough—miles of soft, white sand that slopes gently down to the warm (average 83°F), calm sea. Carriacou's best beach experience, though, is a day spent swimming, snorkeling, and picnicking on one of the otherwise uninhabited islands just offshore.

Anse La Roche. About a 15-minute hike north from the village of Prospect, on the northwestern tip of Carriacou, this often-deserted beach has white sand, sparkling clear water, and abundant marine life for snorkelers. The beach was named for a huge rock where pelicans gather, so bird-watchers will also be thrilled. And because of its relative inaccessibility, Anse La Roche is never crowded. **Amenities:** none. **Best for:** solitude; snorkeling; swimming; walking. ✉ *Prospect, Carriacou.*

Hillsborough Beach. Day-trippers (and others) can take a dip at this strip of sand adjacent to the jetty where the ferry docks, right in the center of town. The beach extends for quite a distance in each direction, so there's plenty of room to swim without interference from the boat traffic. The best part of the beach is at the northern end, along what's called the Esplanade. Ade's Dream House is across the street from the beach, and snack bars and restaurants are nearby. **Amenities:** food and drink. **Best for:** swimming. ✉ *Hillsborough, Carriacou.*

Paradise Beach. This long, narrow stretch of beautiful sandy beach in L'Esterre, between Hillsborough and Tyrell Bay, has calm, clear, inviting water. Popular with local folks on weekends, it's very quiet—often deserted—at other times. The Hardwood Bar, at the southern end of the parking lot, serves local specialties for lunch. **Amenities:** food and drink; parking (no fee); showers; toilets. **Best for:** snorkeling; swimming; walking. ✉ *L'Esterre, Carriacou.*

Fodor's Choice ★ **Sandy Island.** This is a truly deserted sandbar off Paradise Beach—just a few young palm trees on a spit of pure white, powdery soft sand—except for those who come by boat to snorkel and swim in the sparkling clear water. A 5-square-mile (3-square-km) Marine Protected Area surrounds the island. Arrange transportation to the island (about $25 round-trip) with a local boat owner at Paradise Beach; be sure to arrange the pickup time! Wear your bathing suit and bring along snorkeling gear and everything else you'll need (sunscreen, towel, hat, shirt, food and water, etc.), making sure to leave only your footprints when you leave. **Amenities:** none. **Best for:** solitude; snorkeling; swimming. ✉ *L'Esterre Bay, off Paradise Beach, Carriacou.*

White Island. On this deserted island off Carriacou's southeastern coast, your choice of beautiful white sandy beaches and calm Caribbean waters awaits you. The island is surrounded by reefs and has beaches on all sides except for the eastern (Atlantic Ocean) side, which has a high cliff. Arrange transportation from Tyrell Bay for about $25 to $30 (EC$70) round-trip, and be sure to bring everything you may need. **Amenities:** none. **Best for:** solitude; snorkeling; swimming; walking. ✉ *Cassada Bay, off the southeastern coast, Carriacou.*

WHERE TO EAT

Grenada's crops include all kinds of citrus, mangoes, papaya (pawpaw), callaloo (similar to spinach), dasheen (taro, a root vegetable), christophene (a squash, also known as chayote), yams (white, green, yellow, and orange), and breadfruit. All restaurants prepare dishes with local produce and season them with the many spices grown throughout the island. Be sure to try the local flavors of ice cream: soursop, guava, rum raisin, coconut, or nutmeg.

Soups—especially pumpkin and callaloo—are divine and often start a meal. Pepper pot is a savory stew of pork, oxtail, vegetables, and spices. *Oildown,* the national dish, combines salted meat, breadfruit, onions, carrots, celery, dasheen, and dumplings all boiled in coconut milk until the liquid is absorbed and the savory mixture becomes "oily." A roti—curried chicken, beef, or vegetables wrapped in pastry and baked—is similar to a turnover and more popular in Grenada than a sandwich.

Fresh seafood of all kinds is plentiful, including lobster in season (September–April). Conch, known here as *lambi,* often appears curried or in a stew. Crab back, though, is not seafood—it's land crab. Most Grenadian restaurants serve seafood and at least some local dishes.

Rum punches are ubiquitous and always topped with grated nutmeg. Clarke's Court, Rivers, and Westerhall are local rums. Carib, the local beer, is refreshing, light, and quite good. If you prefer a nonalcoholic drink, opt for fruit punch—a delicious mixture of freshly blended tropical fruit.

What to Wear: Dining in Grenada is casual. At dinner, collared shirts and long pants are appropriate for men (even the fanciest restaurants don't require jacket and tie), and sundresses or dress pants are fine for women. Reserve beachwear and other revealing attire for the beach.

GRENADA

$$$ SEAFOOD FAMILY Fodor's Choice ★

Aquarium Restaurant. As the name suggests, fresh seafood is the specialty here. Spend the day at the adjacent Magazine Beach (you can rent kayaks or snorkeling gear) and then break for a cool drink or satisfying lunch—a salad, sandwich or burger, fresh fish, or pasta—served on the waterfront deck at the restaurant's La Sirena Beach Bar. Tropical plants and palms surround the dining room, and a waterfall adds a touch of romance in the evening. The dinner menu always includes fresh fish, grilled lobster, and specialties such as callaloo cannelloni. On Sunday, there's a beach barbecue with live reggae music. *Average main: $25* *Maurice Bishop Memorial Hwy., overlooking Magazine Beach, Point Salines, St. George* *473/444–1410* *www.aquarium-grenada.com* *Closed Mon.*

$$$ CARIBBEAN FAMILY

BB's Crabback Caribbean Restaurant. Overlooking St. George's Harbour, on the north side of The Carenage, BB's Crabback features Grenadian and West Indian dishes prepared with special flair. Born in Grenada and trained in England, Chef BB (Brian Benjamin) turns out some of the best meals in town. Crab back (local land crab) is a house specialty, of course, but you'll want to try some of his seafood dishes, as well. Prawns in lobster sauce come to mind. Or try the signature curried goat, the breast of chicken marinated in 12 herbs and spices, or the pan-fried barracuda in a crab and lobster sauce. Dining is alfresco here, and the views of the harbor and out to sea are nothing short of spectacular. It's definitely a premier place to go for lunch or dinner in downtown St. George's. *Average main: $23 Progress House, The Carenage, St. George's 473/435–7058.*

$$$ ECLECTIC **The Beach House.** At this family-owned restaurant in an iconic Caribbean beach house, the gleaming white sand and sea views are the perfect backdrop for a casual salad or pasta lunch on the deck or a burger or ribs at the bar. At dinner, the casually elegant surroundings, the delectable entrées—rack of lamb, blackened fish, or prime rib—and superb wines give new meaning to the term beach party. There's a kid's menu available, and a quick snack menu is available anytime in high season. On Friday and Saturday nights, there's a happy hour from 10 pm to midnight. Get to the restaurant via a short walk down the beach from Laluna resort, a longer walk up the beach from the Grenadian by Rex resort, a water taxi ride from the Carenage in St. George's, or a drive from the airport road. *Average main: $30 Off Maurice Bishop Memorial Hwy., on Dr. Groom's Beach, Portici Bay, Point Salines, St. George 473/444–4455 www.beachhousegrenada.com Reservations essential Closed Sun. No lunch Apr.–Nov.*

$$ CARIBBEAN FAMILY **Belmont Estate.** If you're visiting the northern reaches of Grenada, plan to stop at Belmont Estate, a 400-year-old working nutmeg and cocoa plantation. Settle into the breezy open-air dining room, which overlooks enormous trays of nutmeg, cocoa, and mace drying in the sunshine. A waiter will offer some refreshing local juice and a choice of callaloo or pumpkin soup. Then head to the buffet and help yourself to salad, rice, stewed chicken, beef curry, stewed fish, local vegetables, and more. Dessert may be homemade ice cream, ginger cake, or another delicious confection. Afterward, feel free to take a tour of the museum, cocoa fermentary, sugarcane garden, and old cemetery. Farm animals (and a couple of monkeys) roam the property, and there's often folk music and dancing on the lawn. *Average main: $18 Belmont, St. Patrick 473/442–9524 www.belmontestate.net Closed Sat. No dinner.*

$$$ CARIBBEAN **Coconut Beach Restaurant.** Take local seafood, add butter, wine, and Grenadian spices, and you have excellent French-creole cuisine. Throw in a beautiful location at the northern end of Grand Anse Beach, and this West Indian cottage becomes a perfect spot for either an alfresco lunch or a dinner by moonlight. Lobster is a specialty, whether it's lobster Thermidor or perhaps wrapped in a crepe, dipped in garlic butter, or added to pasta. Homemade coconut pie is a winner for dessert. Dine "wet or fine" at a table on the beach or inside. At lunch, you can walk down Grand Anse Beach to the restaurant; at night, either drive or opt for a taxi. And on Saturdays, stick around for late-night drinks and DJ music. *Average main: $25 Grand Anse Main Rd., on the beach, Grand Anse, St. George 473/444–4644 www.thecoconutbeachgrenada.com Closed Tues.*

$$$$ CARIBBEAN Fodor's Choice ★ **La Belle Creole.** The marriage of contemporary and West Indian cuisines and a splendid view of the twinkling lights in distant St. George's are the delights of this romantic hillside restaurant. The always-changing five-course menu is based on original recipes from the owner's mother,

a pioneer in incorporating local fruits, vegetables, and spices into "foreign" dishes. Try, for instance, Grenadian caviar (roe of the white sea urchin), green-banana soup, callaloo quiche, creole fish, baked chicken roulade, or shrimp in coconut/ginger sauce—with homemade mango cheesecake for dessert. The inspired cuisine, romantic setting, and gracious service are impressive. Lunch is served poolside. *Average main: $35 ✉ Blue Horizons Garden Resort, Morne Rouge Rd., Grand Anse, St. George ☎ 473/444–4316 ⊕ www.grenadabluehorizons.com ✍ Reservations essential.*

$$ CAFÉ FAMILY ✕ **La Boulangerie.** This combination French bakery and Italian pizzeria, convenient to the hotels at Grand Anse, is perfect for an inexpensive breakfast or light meal—to eat in, take out, or have delivered. You'll find freshly baked croissants and Danish pastry, focaccia and baguette sandwiches, homemade pizza and pasta, fresh-squeezed juice or house wine, coffee and espresso, and homemade gelato. *Average main: $18 ✉ Le Marquis Complex, across from Spiceland Mall, Grand Anse, St. George ☎ 473/444–1131.*

$$$ SEAFOOD ✕ **La Sagesse Restaurant.** The perfect spot to soothe a frazzled soul, this open-air seafood restaurant is on a secluded cove in a nature preserve. Combine your lunch or dinner with a nature walk or a day at the beach. Linger over sandwiches, salads, or grilled lobster for lunch. *Lambi* (conch), smoked marlin, tuna steak, chicken piccata, filet mignon, and a daily vegetarian platter may be joined on the dinner menu by Chef Cecilia's specials, such as flying fish or an upscale version of Grenada's national dish, oildown. All fish is locally caught; all vegetables, fruit, and spices are grown on La Sagesse's own organic farm in the rain forest. La Sagesse is a 25-minute drive from St. George's or Grand Anse; public transportation is available. *Average main: $24 ✉ La Sagesse Nature Centre, La Sagesse, St. David ☎ 473/444–6458 ⊕ www.lasagesse.com ✍ Reservations essential.*

$$ CARIBBEAN FAMILY ✕ **The New Nutmeg.** West Indian specialties, fresh seafood, hamburgers, and a waterfront view make the New Nutmeg a favorite with locals and visitors alike. It's on the Carenage, with large, open, second-floor windows from which you can view the harbor activity and catch a cool breeze as you eat. Try the callaloo soup, curried lambi, fresh seafood, or a steak—or just stop by for a roti and a cold beer or rum punch, with grated nutmeg on top, of course. *Average main: $18 ✉ The Carenage, St. George's ☎ 473/435–9525.*

$$$$ CONTEMPORARY Fodor's Choice ★ ✕ **Oliver's.** Enjoy a memorable dining experience at Oliver's, the seaside restaurant at Spice Island Beach Resort. Head Chef Jesson Church, a Grenadian, turns out some of the most delicious, savory, and elegant culinary creations that you'll find on this island. The prix-fixe menu, which changes each evening, lets you choose from a pair of appetizers, a hot or cold soup, a salad or sorbet, and a half-dozen entrées—such as roasted rib of beef with rosemary roast potatoes and Shiraz reduction, nutmeg-glazed stuffed chicken breast with cassoulet of vegetables and Cajun gnocchi, or panfried snapper with bell pepper mash and pineapple and spring onion salsa—along with one "light" and a couple of vegetarian options. Desserts are made in-house, as are the ice creams and sorbets, and reflect local fruits, flavors, and spices. Service is impeccable,

as it is throughout the hotel. Most nights, dinner is accompanied by soft music from a local calypso, reggae, or steel pan band. (No children under five.) *Average main: $75 ✉ Spice Island Beach Resort, Grand Anse, St. George ☎ 473/444–4258 🌐 www.spiceislandbeachresort.com ✍ Reservations essential.*

$$$ CARIBBEAN ✕ **Patrick's Local Homestyle Cooking.** The fixed tasting menu of 20 or so local dishes, served family-style, will astound you—it's Grenadian homestyle cooking at its casual best. The restaurant, in a tiny cottage on the outskirts of St. George's, is named for the late and very charismatic chef Patrick Levine. You'll sample successive helpings of superb callaloo or pumpkin soup, lobster salad, codfish fritters, breadfruit salad, ginger pork, fried jacks (fish), *cou-cou* (cornmeal cakes), lambi creole, curried goat, stir-fried rabbit, oildown, rice *pelau* (layered with meat and vegetables), starchy tannia (yautia) cakes with shrimp, green papaya in cheese sauce, carrot or banana cake, and more—all for $23 per person. Everything is cooked fresh, so you must call ahead for reservations. *Average main: $23 ✉ Lagoon Rd., opposite Port Louis Marina, St. George's ☎ 473/449–7243 🌐 www.patrickslocalgrenada.wix.com/eat ✍ Reservations essential.*

$$$ SEAFOOD ✕ **The Red Crab.** West Indian basics such as curried lambi and garlic shrimp—and classics such as lobster Newburg, Coquilles St. Jacques, and veal Cordon Bleu—keep the regulars coming back to this family-run restaurant that's been serving locals and expats for decades. Seafood, particularly lobster, and steak (imported from the United States) are staples of the menu; hot garlic bread comes with every order. Dine inside or outside on the front patio. *Average main: $24 ✉ L'Anse aux Épines Rd., L'Anse aux Épines, St. George ☎ 473/444–4424 ⏲ Closed Sun.*

$$$$ INTERNATIONAL ✕ **Rhodes Restaurant.** Named for the acclaimed British chef Gary Rhodes, this open-air restaurant is surrounded by palms, flowering plants, and twinkling lights—a wonderful setting for a romantic dinner or special occasion. Local produce and spices have never appeared (or tasted) more elegant. Past menus have featured citrus-cured salmon with a lime, fennel, and pawpaw (papaya) salad as a starter, followed by grilled swordfish steak with Caribbean paella risotto or fillet of beef on a roasted potato cake with whole-grain-mustard cream. The passion-fruit panna cotta, light as a soufflé, is nothing short of divine. *Average main: $40 ✉ Calabash Hotel, L'Anse aux Épines, St. George ☎ 473/444–4334 🌐 www.calabashhotel.com ✍ Reservations essential ⏲ No lunch.*

$$ ECLECTIC FAMILY ✕ **Umbrellas Beach Bar.** Whether you're spending the day on Grand Anse Beach or just looking for a quick bite, Umbrellas is the place to go. Right on the beach, next to Coyaba Beach Resort, this classic beach bar is open from breakfast until well into the evening. The burgers and sandwiches are great, the salads are freshly made, and there's barbecued fish or steak with wedge potatoes or sweet potato fries. Everything's reasonably priced—yet another reason it's so busy. Of course, you can also just sit on the top deck with a beer or rum punch and a plate of appetizers and stare at the waves—or watch the sunset. *Average main: $20 ✉ Grand Anse Beach, next to Coyaba Beach Resort, Grand Anse, St. George ☎ 473/439–9149 ⏲ Closed Mon.*

$$$ INTERNATIONAL

The Victory Bar & Grill. Boaters, businesspeople, vacationers, and anyone else looking for good food in a waterfront atmosphere close to town keep the Victory busy. Overlooking the docks at Port Louis Marina, with views of the lagoon and masts swaying in the breeze, the restaurant is open every day for all-day dining, starting with breakfast and ending with a lively bar. The extensive lunch and dinner menus include pizza, pasta, salads, burgers, sandwiches, steaks, chops, and, of course, fresh seafood. Friday nights feature Texas-style barbecue. *Average main: $22 Port Louis Marina, Lagoon Rd., St. George's, St. George 473/435–7431.*

CARRIACOU

$$$ CARIBBEAN Fodor's Choice ★

Bogles Round House. Surrounded by gardens and a handful of cottages for rent, this small round structure was built with a concrete-filled tree trunk as its central support and a long bench that was once the jawbone of a whale. The food is less peculiar: Chef Roxanne Russell is celebrated for her elegant style of Caribbean cuisine. Her three-course menu, which changes according to market availability, may include starters such as local goat cheese tart and cream of coconut and callaloo soup and entrées such as slowly braised lamb shank and butter-poached lobster with a garlic-lime glaze. The take-away menu offers beer-battered fish and chips, spicy chicken or shrimp curry, and grilled lobster tail. Desserts, including the ice cream, are all homemade. *Average main: $30 Sparrow Bay, Bogles 473/443–7841 www.boglesroundhouse.com Reservations essential Closed Wed. No dinner Sun.*

$ CARIBBEAN

Kayak Kafé & Juice Bar. A tiny spot just steps from the jetty, the "dining room" is simply the back porch of a Main Street building with a handful of tables overlooking the scene on Hillsborough Bay. Enjoy freshly prepared local food—callaloo soup, lambi (conch) fritters, cracked lambi, fish cakes, fresh fish, fish chowder—or staples such as a good burger, fish-and-chips, delicious sandwiches, tasty wraps, and freshly prepared salads. Wash it down with local juice or a fresh fruit smoothie. All baked goods—wonderful bread and even better pies, cakes, and pastries—are homemade each day. Breakfast—try a sausage roll—is served from 7:30 to 11 am, lunch until about 3 or 4 pm, and dinner (just three evenings per week) from 7:30 to 9 pm. *Average main: $12 Main St., Hillsborough 473/406–2151 Closed Tues. No dinner Sun.–Wed.*

$$ CARIBBEAN FAMILY

Laurena II. As you approach this popular restaurant and bar, just a few giant steps from the ferry wharf and adjacent to Ade's Dream House, you're greeted by the unmistakable scent of authentic Jamaican jerk chicken and pork. That's the specialty (and personal favorite) of Chef Purgeon Reece, who hails from Negril, although his menu also includes other local and regional dishes such as curried goat, baked chicken, or grilled fish with rice and peas. Daily specials are posted on a street-side blackboard. This "jerk center" is definitely a casual spot, the best bet for a delicious lunch, and a good place to catch the local vibe. *Average main: $14 Main St., Hillsborough 473/443–8333 Closed Sun.*

$$ PIZZA FAMILY Fodor's Choice ★

Lazy Turtle. On the waterfront at the edge of Tyrell Bay, Lazy Turtle has been a favorite eatery and watering hole for divers, yachting families, and vacationers for years. New owners from Jersey (in the UK) took over the open-air restaurant in 2013 and boast "the best thin-crusted pizza in the Caribbean." Perhaps so, as Chef Alison has a brand-new, Italian-made pizza oven in which to bake her delicious creations. The 12-inch pizzas range from the usual—and simply delicious—toppings of tomato/cheese/oregano to the Lazy Turtle Special (artichoke/fresh tomato/onion/mushroom) or seafood (lobster sautéed in garlic and butter/anchovies/lambi) and more. In addition to pizzas, the menu offers a full range of pastas, salads, seafood (lobster in season, deep-fried or curried shrimp, fresh-caught fish), and chicken dishes. Desserts are all homemade. *Average main: $16 ✉ Tyrell Bay ☎ 473/443–8322 🌐 www.lazyturtlewi.com ⏲ Closed Tues. and Sept.*

$$$ BISTRO

Moringa Restaurant & Creperie. Caribbean cuisine with a French twist is how Chef JB (Jean-Baptiste Bocquel), a long-term expat from Brittany, characterizes his cooking style at Moringa. Locally sourced ingredients—fresh fish, meat, and produce—are the stars of the menu. Lunch choices may include beef burger "en baguette," croque monsieur, salad Nicoise, and catch of the day. At dinner, you might start with Vietnamese spring rolls or goat cheese and carmelized red onion tartlet and then move on to fresh seafood (try the lionfish), breadnut stuffed chicken, lobster risotto, or perhaps fish curry. And given JB's heritage, there's a separate crepe menu, both savory (callaloo and cheese, ratatouille) and sweet (banana flambée, chestnut and whipped cream, crepe suzette. Despite the rich and accomplished menu, though, this is a casual, friendly bistro. *Average main: $21 ✉ The Esplanade, Main St., Hillsborough ☎ 473/443–8300 🌐 www.moringacarriacou.com ⏲ No lunch Tues. and Sun.*

$ DELI

Patty's Deli. At this delicatessen, a short walk from the ferry jetty, you can get takeout sandwiches made to order with freshly sliced meats (ham, smoked turkey, herbed chicken, etc.) and cheeses. Baguettes, croissants, and pastries are fresh daily—and on Friday, there's usually cheesecake. Anyone provisioning a boat or a house will find a wide selection of coffee, tea, preserves, condiments, locally smoked fish, and a freezer full of USDA meats. *Average main: $12 ✉ Main St., Hillsborough ☎ 473/443–6258 🌐 www.pattysdeli.com.*

$$ ECLECTIC

Slipway Restaurant. Slip right in for lunch or dinner—or Sunday brunch—overlooking the waterfront activity on Tyrell Bay. The menu depends on what's fresh that day, but you can depend upon a juicy American-style hamburger, fresh salad, or creative pasta dish at lunch and fresh-caught seafood at night—lobster in season, pan-seared tuna, mahimahi . . . you name it. You can choose to dine inside or beachside. It's hard to decide what's most appealing—the outstanding food, the nautical ambience, the friendly service, or the very reasonable prices. Plus, the bar is open all day. *Average main: $20 ✉ Tyrell Bay ☎ 473/443–6500 🌐 www.slipwayrestaurant.com ⏲ Closed Mon. No dinner Sun. Closed Thurs. (May–Nov.).*

WHERE TO STAY

Hotels and resorts in Grenada tend to be small, with friendly and attentive management and staff. All guest rooms are equipped with air-conditioning, an in-room TV, and telephone unless indicated otherwise. Most also offer complimentary Wi-Fi. During the off-season (April 15 to December 15), rates may be discounted up to 40%.

PRIVATE VILLAS AND CONDOS

Grenada was one of the last islands to have private villa communities, in which privately owned units are rented to nonowner vacationers through management companies. Only a few such properties are here now or in progress. Laluna Estate in Morne Rouge has opened seven waterfront villas, and an extensive villa development is under way at Bacolet Bay in St. David (265 villas expected on completion) and is part of the long-term plan for Port Louis on the lagoon in St. George's. Otherwise, villas, apartments, and houses are available for rent for a week or longer on both Grenada and Carriacou. The minimum staff includes a maid and laundress, but a cook, housekeeper, gardener, and others can be arranged.

In Grenada, many rental properties are located in and around L'Anse aux Épines, a beautiful residential peninsula that juts into the sea. In-season rates range from $1,000 a week for a small, two-bedroom house with no pool or air-conditioning to $8,000 a week for a five-bedroom house full of amenities, including a pool and beach access. In Carriacou, in-season rates range from $80 a day for a small cottage or in-town apartment suitable for two people to $350 a day for a two-bedroom villa with panoramic views and a swimming pool.

RENTAL CONTACTS

Altman Real Estate (Grenada) ✉ *Le Marquis Shopping Complex, Grand Anse, St. George* ☎ *473/435–2081* 🌐 *www.altmangrenada.com.*

Down Island Villa Rentals ✉ *Craigston, Carriacou* ☎ *473/443–8182* 🌐 *www.islandvillas.com.*

Spice Isle Villas ✉ *Grand Anse, St. George* ☎ *473/439–2486* 🌐 *www.spiceislevillas.com.*

GRENADA

$ HOTEL FAMILY **Allamanda Beach Resort.** Well-situated facing Grand Anse Beach, many rooms in this small hotel have connecting doors, making Allamanda a good choice for families. **Pros:** location, location, location; great value; room rates include breakfast and complimentary Wi-Fi. **Cons:** don't expect luxury at this price; rooms are attractive but somewhat dated; you have to walk down the beach for water sports. [$] *Rooms from: $165* ✉ *Grand Anse, St. George* ☎ *473/444–0095* 🌐 *www.allamandaresort.com* *50 rooms* *Breakfast.*

$ RESORT FAMILY **Blue Horizons Garden Resort.** Just 300 yards from Grand Anse Beach, "Blue" is especially popular among divers, nature lovers, and family vacationers looking for roomy self-catering accommodations. **Pros:** peaceful and quiet; walk to shopping and restaurants; lovely garden environment; complimentary two-hour babysitting once during stay; complimentary

Wi-Fi. **Cons:** not directly on the beach; lots of steps up to the hilltop units—which also offer the best view. *Rooms from: $220 ✉ Morne Rouge Rd., Grand Anse, St. George ☎ 473/444–4316, 473/444–4592 🌐 www.grenadabluehorizons.com 26 suites, 6 studios Multiple meal plans.*

BEST BETS FOR LODGING

BEST FOR ROMANCE
Calabash Hotel & Spa, Laluna, Petite Anse Hotel, Spice Island Beach Resort

BEST BEACHFRONT
Coyaba Beach Resort, Grenadian by Rex Resorts, Laluna, La Sagesse, Radisson Grenada Beach Resort, Spice Island Beach Resort

$ B&B/INN FAMILY **Cabier Ocean Lodge.** Definitely off the beaten path and in a truly natural environment, Cabier Ocean Lodge is a combination guesthouse, restaurant/bar, petting zoo, and donkey ranch—all on a remote point of land high above the sea on Grenada's windward (eastern) coast. **Pros:** perfect place to unwind; all rooms have a sea view; kids love the little zoo and the donkey rides; snorkeling and fishing equipment provided; complimentary Wi-Fi. **Cons:** a long drive (45 minutes) from the airport or St. George's; rooms are simply furnished, as guests seem more attracted to the outdoors; limited restaurant facilities in September; TV only in the lounge. *Rooms from: $120 ✉ Crochu, St. Andrew ☎ 473/444–6013 🌐 www.cabier.com 11 rooms, 2-unit villa No meals.*

$$$$ HOTEL Fodor'sChoice ★ **Calabash Hotel & Spa.** The posh suites here are in 10 two-story cottages distributed in a horseshoe around 8 acres of lawn and gardens that hug the beach on Prickly Bay (L'Anse aux Épines). **Pros:** excellent service; love those treats; breakfast served on your veranda. **Cons:** small beach, small pool, large lawn and gardens; rental car suggested to get around the island; no kids under 12 January 15–March 15. *Rooms from: $620 ✉ L'Anse aux Épines Rd., L'Anse aux Épines, St. George ☎ 473/444–4334, 800/738–4752 in U.S. 🌐 www.calabashhotel.com 30 suites Closed Aug.–Sept. Multiple meal plans.*

$ RENTAL **Coral Cove.** Peace and quiet are all yours at Coral Cove, a group of 11 one- and two-bedroom self-catering cottages and apartments perched high on a grassy hillside on the windward side of the Lance aux Épines peninsula. **Pros:** all units have fully equipped kitchens; tennis courts; weekly rates available; complimentary Wi-Fi. **Cons:** room furnishings are rather basic; bathrooms have showers only; rental car advised. *Rooms from: $150 ✉ Coral Cove Rd., L'Anse aux Épines, St. George ☎ 473/444–4422 🌐 www.coralcovecottages.com 5 cottages, 6 apartments No meals.*

$$ RESORT **Coyaba Beach Resort.** Rooms at Coyaba, one of a handful of hotels with direct access to beautiful Grand Anse Beach, are in pavilion-style buildings that surround a 5½-acre beachfront garden of palm trees, hibiscus, frangipani, and bougainvillea. **Pros:** excellent beachfront location; spacious grounds; pool with swim-up bar; on-site dive center. **Cons:** rooms are attractive but not extraordinary; "free" water sports have time limits, usually 1 hour per day; restaurant meals mediocre, better to eat elsewhere. *Rooms from: $360 ✉ Grand Anse, St. George*

☎ *473/444–4129, 855/626–9222 in U.S.* 🌐 *www.coyaba.com* ⇨ *80 rooms* 🍴 *Multiple meal plans.*

$ RESORT FAMILY **Flamboyant Hotel & Villas.** Draped over the hillside at the southern end of Grand Anse Beach, Flamboyant offers roomy, reasonably priced accommodations—all with private verandas that have stunning, panoramic views of the sea. **Pros:** reasonable prices; friendly staff; nightlife at the Owl bar; on-site dive center. **Cons:** rooms are pleasant but decidedly unflamboyant; hilly terrain. $ *Rooms from: $250* ✉ *Morne Rouge Rd., Grand Anse, St. George* ☎ *473/444–4247* 🌐 *www.flamboyant.com* ⇨ *38 rooms, 27 suites, 2 cottages* 🍴 *Multiple meal plans.*

$$ ALL-INCLUSIVE FAMILY **Grenadian by Rex Resorts.** This massive, beachfront resort on a huge piece of property on Tamarind Bay is particularly popular with Europeans. **Pros:** large play area for kids; two excellent beaches—one quiet, the other for water sports; minutes from the airport. **Cons:** rooms are unremarkable; quite a hike from room to beach to lobby; rooms could use some TLC. $ *Rooms from: $345* ✉ *Tamarind Bay, Point Salines, St. George* ☎ *473/444–3333* 🌐 *www.rexresorts.com* ⇨ *152 rooms, 20 suites* 🍴 *All-inclusive.*

$ HOTEL FAMILY **Kalinago Beach Resort.** This contemporary beachfront hotel on Morne Rouge Bay, next to Gem Holiday Resort and with the same ownership, has stylish suites—all with a patio or deck and a view of the ocean. **Pros:** modern rooms; great beach; dive packages; complimentary Wi-Fi. **Cons:** walking to Grand Anse—or anywhere—requires negotiating a steep hill; a rental car is a good idea. $ *Rooms from: $210* ✉ *Morne Rouge Rd., Morne Rouge, St. George* ☎ *473/444–5255* 🌐 *www.kalinagobeachresort.com* ⇨ *29 rooms* 🍴 *Multiple meal plans.*

$$$$ RESORT Fodor's Choice ★ **Laluna.** You may think you've landed on an island in the South Pacific when you reach this upscale getaway, hidden away on a pristine beach near Grenada's Quarantine Point. **Pros:** nifty 650 square-foot cottages; great restaurant; fabulous beach; free Wi-Fi. **Cons:** the long, bumpy, dirt access road; total seclusion could seem confining (if it weren't such a divine spot!). $ *Rooms from: $495* ✉ *Morne Rouge, St. George* ☎ *473/439–0001* 🌐 *www.laluna.com* ⇨ *16 cottages, 7 villas* 🍴 *Multiple meal plans.*

$ B&B/INN **La Sagesse.** Secluded on La Sagesse Bay, this country inn boasts its own restaurant and beach bar, along with a salt-pond bird sanctuary, thick mangroves, nature trails, and ½ mile (¾ km) of palm-lined beach—one of the prettiest beaches in the entire Caribbean. **Pros:** perfect out-of-the-way escape; great place to commune with nature; excellent restaurant, complimentary Wi-Fi. **Cons:** far from everything; no TV, no phones, no Internet access, no noise; not the best choice for families with kids. $ *Rooms from: $185* ✉ *La Sagesse Nature Center, La Sagesse, St. David* ☎ *473/444–6458* 🌐 *www.lasagesse.com* ⇨ *9 rooms, 3 suites* 🍴 *No meals.*

$$$$ RENTAL Fodor's Choice ★ **Maca Bana.** Clustered on a 2-acre hillside overlooking mile-long Magazine Beach, each of Maca Bana's seven private villas ("banas") has a great view—of the white sand below, out to sea, up the coastline to pretty St. George's Harbour, and beyond toward cloud-capped mountains. **Pros:** roomy villas with huge kitchens; enormous decks with amazing views; fabulous beach. **Cons:** steep hill down to the restaurant and beach;

expensive; tiny pool. *Rooms from: $515 Maurice Bishop Memorial Hwy., Point Salines, St. George 473/439–5355 www.macabana.com 2 1-bedroom villas, 5 2-bedroom villas No meals.*

$$$$ RESORT FAMILY **Mount Cinnamon.** On a hillside overlooking Grand Anse Beach, Mount Cinnamon's spacious one-, two-, or three-bedroom villas have full kitchens with a breakfast bar, Bose entertainment systems, cable TV, and convenient extras that include washers and dryers. **Pros:** amazing views; great choice for families; pool, private beach club on Grand Anse Beach, on-site dive shop; grocery stocking service. **Cons:** villas are on a steep hill, but golf-cart transport to restaurant or beach is available. *Rooms from: $495 Morne Rouge Rd., Grand Anse, St. George 473/439–4400, 866/720–2616 www.mountcinnamongrenadahotel.com 21 units Multiple meal plans.*

$$$ B&B/INN Fodor's Choice ★ **Mount Hartman Bay Estate.** This architecturally intriguing boutique inn (formerly a private home), perched on a cliff overlooking peaceful Mount Hartman Bay, is a perfect spot for a honeymoon, anniversary, or romantic getaway. **Pros:** lovely locale off the beaten track; personalized service; kayak or snorkel from the private beach or jetty. **Cons:** not recommended for kids; lots of stairs; rental car advised. *Rooms from: $399 Reef View Dr., L'Anse aux Épines, St. George 473/407–4504 www.mounthartmanbayestate.com 10 suites Multiple meal plans.*

$$ HOTEL **Petite Anse Hotel.** Experienced travelers love this delightful oceanfront hotel at the northern tip of Grenada; it's surrounded by beautiful gardens on one side and an unobstructed view of the southern Grenadines on the other. **Pros:** romantic setting; secluded palm-studded beach; inviting and woodsy trails; complimentary Wi-Fi. **Cons:** remote; rental car advised; it's a trek down to the beach. *Rooms from: $283 Sauteurs, St. Patrick 473/442–5252 www.petiteanse.com 2 rooms, 9 cottages Multiple meal plans.*

$ RESORT FAMILY **Radisson Grenada Beach Resort.** On 20 landscaped acres that stretch along 1,200 feet of Grand Anse Beach, the Radisson Grand offers comfortable rooms and extensive amenities at a reasonable price. **Pros:** huge hotel full of amenities, including water sports and a dive shop; beautiful beachfront location; walking distance to Grand Anse shops and restaurants; excellent value; elevators; complimentary Wi-Fi. **Cons:** rooms are comfortable but not extraordinary; gets crowded when meetings are scheduled. *Rooms from: $205 Grand Anse, St. George 473/444–4371 www.radisson.com 229 rooms Multiple meal plans.*

$$$$ ALL-INCLUSIVE **Sandals LaSource Grenada Resort & Spa.** Young couples, honeymooners, and second honeymooners love Sandals, and this particular Sandals—a sophisticated, attractive, well-designed enclave on pretty Pink Gin Beach—is one of the company's newest resorts. **Pros:** excellent beachfront location with lots to do; congenial atmosphere; brand-new; Wi-Fi access. **Cons:** expensive for Grenada, though it's all-inclusive and a reliable brand; somewhat isolated; a rental car or island tour suggested (extra cost). *Rooms from: $717 Pink Gin Beach, near the airport, Point Salines, St. George 473/444–2556, 888/726–3257 www.sandals.com 150 rooms, 75 suites All-inclusive.*

$$$$ RESORT FAMILY Fodor's Choice ★ **Spice Island Beach Resort.** Presenting the most luxurious resort experience in Grenada: exquisite rooms fill gleaming white buildings that extend along 1,600 feet of Grand Anse Beach, and the personalized service is impeccable. **Pros:** casually elegant and luxurious, yet family-friendly; perfect beachfront location; personalized service; fabulous dining. **Cons:** luxury doesn't come cheap; all the pampering makes it very hard to go home. *Rooms from: $914 Grand Anse, St. George 473/444–4258 www.spiceislandbeachresort.com 64 suites Multiple meal plans.*

$$ RESORT FAMILY **True Blue Bay Resort & Villas.** Families with kids appreciate the lawns and gardens at this family-run resort, a former indigo plantation that overlooks True Blue Bay. **Pros:** pleasant environment at reasonable prices; convenient to St. George's University; complimentary shuttle to Grand Anse Beach; complimentary Wi-Fi. **Cons:** on the water but no beach for swimming; rental car recommended. *Rooms from: $275 Old Mill Ave., True Blue Bay, True Blue, St. George 473/443–8783, 888/883–2482 www.truebluebay.com 33 rooms, 5 villa suites Multiple meal plans.*

$ B&B/INN **Twelve Degrees North.** Named for the latitude here, this small, secluded, adults-only inn on 3 acres of hillside has one- and two-bedroom self-contained suites, all of which face the sea—and also face west, providing beautiful sunset views from the balcony or patio. **Pros:** private getaway; personalized service; excellent snorkeling off the dock; complimentary Wi-Fi. **Cons:** reef makes the beach unsuitable for swimming; suites are comfortable but not stylish. *Rooms from: $225 L'Anse aux Épines, St. George 473/444–4580 www.twelvedegreesnorth.com 8 suites No meals.*

CARRIACOU

$ RENTAL FAMILY **Bayaleau Point Cottages.** In a laid-back environment on a quiet hillside estate on the easternmost point of Windward Bay, four colorful gingerbread cottages are within earshot of one another but partially hidden by trees and other foliage. **Pros:** ideal for small groups or families (up to 16 people); swinging in your hammock is an "active" sport; beautiful Grenadines view; Wi-Fi access. **Cons:** very rustic; way off the beaten path; rental car advised. *Rooms from: $110 Bayaleau, Windward 473/443–7984 www.carriacoucottages.com 4 cottages No meals.*

$ B&B/INN **Bogles Round House.** Three quaint cottages—called Lime, Mango, and Plum—are in a garden setting about 60 feet from Sparrow Bay, where guests enjoy swimming, snorkeling, and walks on the beach. **Pros:** the price; the restaurant; the ambience; complimentary Wi-Fi. **Cons:** one step up from camping out; not much of a beach; no phone, no TV (although that may appeal to some). *Rooms from: $95 Sparrow Bay, Bogles 473/443–7841 www.boglesroundhouse.com 3 cottages Closed May Breakfast.*

$ HOTEL **Carriacou Grand View Hotel.** Island visitors and local businesspeople alike relish the lovely view, particularly at sunset, from this perch high above Hillsborough Harbour. **Pros:** truly a grand view, even from the swimming pool; popular restaurant with late-night piano bar; complimentary Wi-Fi. **Cons:** accommodations are basic; it's a hot walk uphill from town and the beach. Ⓢ *Rooms from: $65* ✉ *Beausejour* ☎ *473/443–6348* 🌐 *www.carriacougrandview.com* 🛏 *7 rooms, 7 suites* 🍴 *No meals.*

$ B&B/INN **Green Roof Inn.** You're guaranteed beautiful views of Hillsborough Bay and the offshore cays at this small inn, which is the perfect location for a scuba-diving, snorkeling, or beachcombing vacation. **Pros:** pick a room with a sea view; homey atmosphere; close to town; Wi-Fi access. **Cons:** rooms are small and very basic; no a/c; showers only. Ⓢ *Rooms from: $95* ✉ *Hillsborough Bay, Hillsborough* ☎ *473/443–6399* 🌐 *www.greenroofinn.com* 🛏 *5 rooms, 2 cottages* 🍴 *Breakfast.*

$ HOTEL FAMILY **Hotel Laurena.** The family-owned, family-operated Hotel Laurena is within walking distance of downtown Hillsborough, the ferry jetty, shops, and some beaches. **Pros:** convenient to town; good dining at the on-site restaurant and the nearby Laurena II Jerk Center; some rooms are wheelchair accessible; complimentary Wi-Fi. **Cons:** not particularly attractive town views; no pool; walk to beach. Ⓢ *Rooms from: $95* ✉ *Hillsborough* ☎ *473/443–8759, 877/755–4386 in U.S.* 🌐 *www.hotellaurena.com* 🛏 *20 rooms, 6 apartments* 🍴 *Breakfast.*

12

NIGHTLIFE

Grenada's nightlife consists mainly of live music at resort hotels, a dinner theater in the countryside, a very popular street party, and a handful of nightspots. During the winter season, some resorts present a steel band or other local entertainment several nights a week.

BARS

Bananas. The students at nearby St. George's University like to "lime" (hang out) at this casual restaurant and nightspot, especially on Friday night when there's a DJ and Tuesday night when drinks are half-price. Other nights, sports events on big-screen TVs in the sports bar get much of the attention, as does the menu of wood-fired pizza, burgers, wings, and cold beer. ✉ *True Blue Rd., True Blue, St. George* ☎ *473/444–4662* 🌐 *www.bananas.gd.*

West Indies Beer Company. Enjoy craft ales, bitter, porter, or cider brewed on site at the tiny West Indies Beer Company. Awarded Grenada's first new brewery license in 50 years, the brewery is in the beer garden's back room. Drinks are served from the tap in ice-cold Mason jars. A favorite hangout of university students and vacationers alike, the beer garden is open from 1 pm to about 10 pm on weekdays and until 1 am on weekends. On Friday evenings, from midday to midnight, you can watch the brewing in progress. ✉ *L'Anse aux Épines Main Rd., L'Anse aux Épines, St. George* ☎ *473/443–8783* 🌐 *www.westindiesbeercompany.com* ⏲ *Closed Sun. and Mon.*

DANCE CLUBS

Fantazia 2001. On weekends, you can hear disco, soca, reggae, and international pop music from 9:30 pm until the wee hours at this spot. Wednesday night is "Oldie Goldies" night. There may be a cover charge of EC$10 to EC$30, depending on the entertainment, although admission is often free. Friday night is always ladies night—no charge.

✉ *Morne Rouge Beach, adjacent to Gem Holiday Beach Resort, Morne Rouge, St. George* ☎ *473/444–2288* 🌐 *fantazia2001niteclub.com.*

The Owl. This club, at the Flamboyant Hotel, features crab racing on Monday night, karaoke on Thursday night, calypso on Friday night, and two happy hours (4–7 and 11–midnight) every night. It's open until 3 am nightly. ✉ *Flamboyant Hotel, Morne Rouge Rd., Grand Anse, St. George* ☎ *473/444–4247* 🌐 *www.owlgrenada.com.*

SUNSET CRUISES

Rhum Runner. *Rhum Runner*, a 60-foot twin-deck catamaran and *Rhum Runner II,* a 72-foot sister ship, are floating party boats. The boats depart the Carenage and the cruise dock on most weekends for day, sunset, and moonlight cruises—with plenty of rum and snacks—in and around St. George's and Grand Anse. Reservations are required. ✉ *The Carenage, St. George's* ☎ *473/440–4386* 🌐 *www.rhumrunner.gd.*

THEME NIGHTS

FAMILY Fodor's Choice ★ **Gouyave Fish Friday.** Every Friday from 4 pm until 1 am, the town of Gouyave—the very proud hometown of 2012 Olympic gold medalist Kirani James—celebrates its deep-sea fishing heritage. Street vendors sell freshly caught fish, lobster, and other seafood cooked on open fires, as well as your favorite beverages. Local music and cultural performances make it an entertaining family event—and the place to be on a Friday night. It's about 45 minutes north of St. George's. ✉ *St. Francis and St. Dominic Sts., Gouyave, St. John* ☎ *473/444–8430, 473/444–9490* 🌐 *www.gogouyave.com.*

FAMILY **Spice Basket.** In the Spice Basket theater every Tuesday night, beginning at 7:15 pm, a colorful and family-friendly musical journey through history explores the sweep of Grenadian culture. The admission price for the buffet dinner, drinks, and the show is $50 per person, with an additional $10–$15 for transportation from your hotel, depending on its location. Reservations are recommended. Spicy Fridays, every Friday evening beginning at 5 pm, enjoy a live band, drink specials, and a buffet with local foods; admission is free except for special events or when the live entertainment is a major headliner. ✉ *Beaulieu, St. George* ☎ *473/437–9000* 🌐 *www.spicebasketgrenada.com.*

Spicy Fridays and Oldie Goldies at Spice Basket. At the Spice Basket cultural center, Spicy Fridays begin at 5 pm with a live band, drink specials, and a buffet with local foods; on Saturday, Oldie Goldies night begins at 8 pm. Admission is free except for special events or when the live entertainment is a major headliner. ✉ *Beaulieu, St. George* ☎ *473/437–9000, 473/232–9000* 🌐 *www.spicebasketgrenada.com.*

SHOPPING

Some unique, locally made goods to look for in gift shops and supermarkets are locally made chocolate bars, nutmeg jam and syrup, spice-scented soaps and body oils, and (no kidding) Nut-Med Pain-Relieving Spray. Grenada's best souvenirs or gifts for friends back home, though, are spice baskets in a variety of shapes and sizes that are filled with cinnamon, nutmeg, mace, bay leaves, cloves, turmeric, and ginger. You can buy them for as little as $5 to $10 in practically every shop, at the open-air produce market at **Market Square** in St. George's, at vendor stalls along the Esplanade near the port, and at the Vendor's Craft & Spice Market on Grand Anse Beach. Vendors also sell handmade fabric dolls, coral jewelry, seashells, spice necklaces, and hats and baskets handwoven from green palm fronds.

Here's some local terminology you should know. If someone asks if you'd like a "sweetie," you're being offered a candy. When you buy spices, you may be offered "saffron" and "vanilla." The "saffron" is really turmeric, a ground yellow root rather than the (much more expensive) fragile pistils of crocus flowers; the "vanilla" is extracted from locally grown tonka beans rather than from actual (also much more expensive) vanilla beans. No one is trying to pull the wool over your eyes; these are common local terms. That said, the U.S. Food and Drug Administration warns that "vanilla" extracts made from tonka beans can have toxic effects and may pose a significant health risk for individuals taking certain medications.

AREAS AND MALLS

In St. George's, on the northern side of the harbor, **Young Street** is a main shopping thoroughfare; it rises steeply uphill from the Carenage and then descends just as steeply to **Market Square.** On Melville Street adjacent to the Cruise Ship Terminal, **Esplanade Mall** has shops that offer duty-free jewelry, electronics, liquor, and gift items, as well as local crafts. In Grand Anse, a short walk from the resorts, **Excel Plaza** has shops and services to interest locals and tourists alike, including a three-screen movie theater. **Grand Anse Shopping Centre** has a supermarket and liquor store, a clothing store, a fast-food restaurant, a pharmacy, an art gallery, several small gift shops, and a doctor's office. **Le Marquis Complex** has restaurants, shops, and tourist services. **Spiceland Mall** has a modern supermarket with a liquor section, clothing and shoe boutiques for men and women, housewares stores, a wineshop, gift shops, an art gallery, a food court, a bank, and a video-game arcade.

ART

Art and Soul Gallery. Owned by noted Grenadian artist Susan Mains, Art and Soul is a full-service gallery with original works by local, regional, and international artists—including Mains herself. You can commission a portrait of yourself, your child, or even your pet. ✉ *Spiceland Mall, Grand Anse, St. George* ☎ *473/439–3450* 🌐 *www.artandsoulgrenada.com.*

FOODS

FAMILY **Grenada Chocolate Company.** The small Grenada Chocolate Company, founded in 1999, initially produced its now-famous chocolate bars in a small house-turned-factory in the village of Hermitage. Now the chocolate bars are produced in alliance with the nearby Belmont Estate cocoa farm and fermentary. Employees use antique machinery powered by solar energy to roast cocoa beans supplied by a local cooperative of growers representing more than 150 acres of organic cocoa farms—the largest of which is Belmont Estate. They mix and temper small batches of rich, dark chocolate that are then molded and wrapped by hand into high-quality, organic chocolate bars (cocoa powder and cocoa butter are also available). The 82% chocolate bar was awarded the silver medal in 2011 by the London Academy of Chocolate. Buy the candy bars at Belmont Estate or in supermarkets or gift shops for about $6 each. ✉ *Belmont Estate, Belmont, St. Patrick* ☎ *473/442–0050* 🌐 *www.grenadachocolate.com, www.belmontestate.net.*

De La Grenade Industries. Nutmeg and guava jams and jellies, nutmeg syrup, nutmeg liqueur (from a 200-year-old family recipe), and a dozen other kinds of delicious jellies, marmalades, and condiments are all available from this famous local manufacturer. You can buy De La Grenade products at the processing plant, in food stores and gift shops throughout Grenada, and at duty-free shops in the airport departure lounge. ✉ *Morne Délice, St. Paul's, St. George* ☎ *473/440–3241* 🌐 *www.delagrenade.com.*

Food Fair. The local supermarket chain is a great spot to buy spices, hot sauce, candy, snacks, and other edible gifts. Prices of locally produced goods are very reasonable, while familiar brands imported from the United States may cost twice as much as back home. ✉ *The Carenage, St. George's* ☎ *473/440–2488.* ✉ *Grand Anse Shopping Center, Grand Anse Main Rd., Grand Anse, St. George* ☎ *473/444–4573*

Fodor's Choice ★ **Market Square.** This bustling produce market is open mornings and the best place to stock up on fresh fruit to enjoy during your stay and to buy packets of baskets of island-grown spices to take home. Saturday morning is busiest. Vendors also sell crafts, leather goods, and decorative objects. ✉ *Foot of Young St., on the north side of town, St. George's.*

GIFTS

Arawak Islands. This workshop's spice-scented soaps, body oils, perfumes, insect repellents, balms, beeswax candles, and incense are all made by hand from 100% natural products, most of which are grown in Grenada. Visitors are welcome to watch the small group of workers sorting, blending, cutting, shaping, bottling, and labeling the products—and even cutting, sewing, hand-painting, and ironing the little cotton bags used for packaging. Arawak Islands products, including gift baskets, are sold in most gift shops. ✉ *Frequente Industrial Park, Airport Rd., Point Salines, St. George* ☎ *473/444–3577.*

Imagine. The main draws at this gift shop are straw work, ceramics, island fashions, and batik fabrics. ✉ *Grand Anse Shopping Centre, Grand Anse Main Rd., Grand Anse, St. George* ☎ *473/444–4028.*

HANDICRAFTS

Art Fabrik. At Art Fabrik, you'll find batik fabric created by hand by as many as 45 home workers. It's sold by the yard or fashioned into pareus, dresses, shirts, shorts, hats, scarves, and bags. Part of the boutique is dedicated to demonstrating the batik process. ✉ *Young St., St. George's* ☎ *473/440–0568* 🌐 *www.artfabrikgrenada.com.*

Fidel Productions. At this little gift shop at Port Louis Marina, you'll find locally made gifts and souvenirs—hand-printed T-shirts, hand-painted calabashes, Arawak Islands soaps and lotions, handmade jewelry, caps, and more. There's also a location on Carriacou inside a bright green shipping container in the Paradise Beach parking lot. ✉ *Port Louis Marina, Lagoon Rd., St. George's, St. George* ☎ *473/435–8866.*

Tikal. Regional artwork, carvings, jewelry, home goods, batik items, and a few fashions are the specialties at Tikal, established in 1959 as one of the first arts and crafts shops in Grenada. ✉ *Young St., St. George's* ☎ *473/440–2310.*

Vendor's Craft & Spice Market at Grand Anse. Managed by the Grenada Tourism Authority, this market has 82 booths for vendors who sell arts, crafts, spices, music tapes, clothing, produce, and refreshments. It's open daily from 7 to 7. ✉ *Grand Anse Beach, toward the north end, Grand Anse, St. George* ☎ *473/444–3780.*

Veronica's Vision. Find colorful silk-screened lengths of fabric, along with handmade totes, bags, women's dresses, men's shirts and ties, T-shirts, scarves, belts, and cushions at this shop. The fabrics and other products are all designed and created by artist/designer Jessie-Ann Jessamy and hand-printed in her on-site workshop. The colors and themes celebrate the isle of spice—particularly the ubiquitous nutmeg. ✉ *Corner Limes Gap and Main Rd., opposite Excel Plaza, Grand Anse, St. George* ☎ *473/437–8154* 🌐 *www.grenadaspicecloth.com.*

SPORTS AND THE OUTDOORS

BOATING AND SAILING

As the "Gateway to the Grenadines," Grenada attracts boatloads of seasoned sailors to its waters. Large marinas are located at Port Louis along the lagoon in St. George's, at Prickly Bay and True Blue on Grenada's southern coast, at Petite Calivigny Bay and St. David's in southeastern Grenada, and at Tyrell Bay in Carriacou. You can charter a yacht, with or without crew, for weeklong sailing vacations through the Grenadines. Scenic day sails along Grenada's coast cost about $145 per person (with a minimum of four passengers), including lunch or snacks and an open bar; a bareboat charter will cost $575 to $1,400 per day, while a crewed charter will cost $1,500 to $2,000 per day (both with a five-day minimum), depending on the boat, for up to six people.

Carib Cats. Departing from Grand Anse Beach, Carib Cats' 60-foot sailing catamaran takes passengers on a full-day sail along the southwest coast, a half-day snorkel cruise to the Underwater Sculpture Park at Molinère Bay, or a two-hour sunset cruise along the west coast. ✉ *Grand Anse Beach, St. George's* ☎ *473/444–3222.*

Footloose Yacht Charters. Operating from the lagoon in St. George's, Footloose Yacht Charters has a catamaran spacious enough for three couples, as well as a 71-foot ocean ketch. Both are available for day trips around Grenada or longer charters to the Grenadines. ✉ *Lagoon Rd., St. George's* ☎ *473/440–7949.*

Horizon Yacht Charters. Arrange either bareboat or crewed charters (there's a four-day minimum) on monohulls or catamarans through Horizon. ✉ *True Blue Bay Marina, True Blue, St. George* ☎ *473/439–1000, 866/463–7245 in U.S.* 🌐 *www.horizonyachtcharters.com.*

Moorings. Based at Port Louis Marina in St. George's, Moorings offers bareboat or crewed charters on its custom-built 35-foot to 51-foot catamarans and monohulls. The diverse itinerary options include one-way charters through the Grenadines to the company's base in St. Lucia. ✉ *Port Louis Marina, Lagoon Rd., St. George's* ☎ *800/535–7289* 🌐 *www.moorings.com.*

DIVING AND SNORKELING

You can see hundreds of varieties of fish and some 40 species of coral at more than a dozen sites off Grenada's southwestern coast—only 15 to 20 minutes away by boat—and another couple of dozen sites around Carriacou's reefs and neighboring islets. Depths vary from 20 to 120 feet, and visibility varies from 30 to 100 feet.

OFF GRENADA

For a spectacular dive, visit the ruins of *Bianca C,* a 600-foot cruise ship that caught fire in 1961, sank to 100 feet, and is now a coral-encrusted habitat for giant turtles, spotted eagle rays, barracuda, and jacks. **Boss Reef** extends 5 miles (8 km) from St. George's Harbour to Point Salines, with a depth ranging from 20 to 90 feet. **Flamingo Bay** has a wall that drops to 90 feet. It teems with fish, sponges, sea horses, sea fans, and coral. **Molinère Reef** slopes from about 20 feet below the surface to a wall that drops to 65 feet. Molinère is also the location of the **Underwater Sculpture Park**, a rather odd artificial reef consisting of more than 55 life-size figures that were sculpted by artist and scuba instructor Jason Taylor and placed on the sea bottom. An underwater bench gives divers a good view of the art gallery. Its most recent addition is a replica of *Christ of the Deep*, the statue that's on the promenade along the Carenage in St. George's. Molinère is a good dive for beginners; advanced divers can continue farther out to view the wreck of the *Buccaneer,* a 42-foot sloop.

OFF CARRIACOU

There's an active underwater volcano known as **Kick-em Jenny**, with plentiful coral and marine life in the vicinity and, usually, visibility up to 100 feet, though you can't dive down the 500 feet required to reach the actual volcano. **Sandy Island,** in Hillsborough Bay, is especially good for night diving and has fish that feed off its extensive reefs 70 feet below. For experienced divers, **Twin Sisters of Isle de Rhonde** is one of the most spectacular dives in the Grenadines, with walls and drop-offs of up to 185 feet and an underwater cave.

PADI-certified dive operators offer scuba and snorkeling trips to reefs and wrecks, including night dives and special excursions to the *Bianca C.* They also offer resort courses for beginning divers and certification instruction for more experienced divers. It costs about $60 for a one-tank dive, $110 for a two-tank dive, $65 for trips to the *Bianca C,* $145 to dive Isle de Rhonde, and $65 to $70 for night dives. Discounted 5- and 10-dive packages are usually offered. Resort courses cost about $100, and open-water certification runs from $265 to $460.

Most dive operators will take snorkelers along on dive trips or offer special snorkeling adventures. The best snorkeling in Grenada is at Molinère Point, north of St. George's; in Carriacou, magnificent Sandy Island is just a few hundred yards offshore. Snorkeling trips cost $25 to $35 per person.

GRENADA DIVE OPERATORS

Aquanauts Grenada. Every morning Aquanauts Grenada heads out on two-tank dive trips, each accommodating no more than eight divers, to both the Caribbean and Atlantic sides of Grenada. Also available: guided snorkel trips; beach snorkeling; and special activities, courses, and equipment for children. ✉ *Spice Island Beach Resort, True Blue, St. George* ☎ *473/444–1126, 850/303–0330 in U.S.* 🌐 *www.aquanautsgrenada.com* 📨 *True Blue, St. George* 🌐 *www.aquanautsgrenada.com.*

Dive Grenada. Specializing in wreck diving, particularly the *Bianca C,* and in family snorkeling trips, Dive Grenada heads out twice daily (at 10 am and 2 pm) to local dive sites. ✉ *Flamboyant Hotel, Morne Rouge Rd., Morne Rouge, St. George* ☎ *473/444–1092* 🌐 *www.divegrenada.com.*

EcoDive. This full-service PADI dive shop offers two trips daily for both drift and wreck dives, as well as weekly trips to dive Isle de Rhonde and a full range of diving courses. EcoDive employs two full-time marine biologists who run Grenada's marine-conservation and education center and conduct coral-reef monitoring and restoration efforts. ✉ *Coyaba Beach Resort, Grand Anse Beach, Grand Anse, St. George* ☎ *473/444–7777* 🌐 *www.ecodiveandtrek.com.*

ScubaTech Grenada. With three full-time diving instructors, ScubaTech Grenada offers the complete range of PADI and TDI programs—from "discover scuba," which allows novices to learn the basics and dive for the length of their vacation, to "dive master," the highest level a diver can achieve. Dive trips to local sites leave each morning. ✉ *Calabash Hotel, Prickly Bay Beach, L'Anse aux Épines, St. George* ☎ *473/439–4346* 🌐 *www.scubatech-grenada.com.*

CARRIACOU DIVE OPERATORS

Arawak Divers. This company has its own jetty at Tyrell Bay. Arawak takes small groups on daily dive trips and night dives, offers a full range of courses in both German and English, and provides pickup service from yachts. ✉ *Tyrell Bay, Harvey Vale, Carriacou* ☎ *473/443–6906* 🌐 *www.arawakdivers.com.*

Deefer Diving. Deefer Diving has two PADI dive masters and two PADI instructors that provide a full range of diving instruction on their 30-foot catamaran, which accommodates up to 11 divers. The itinerary is flexible, so you can dive when, where, and for as long as you like. There are two guided single-tank dives daily, as well as individually scheduled excursions. ✉ *Main St., Hillsborough, Carriacou* ☎ *473/443–7882* 🌐 *www.deeferdiving.com.*

Lumbadive. The folks who operate Lumbadive share their enthusiasm for safe, exciting scuba-diving adventures with both new and experienced divers. Lumbadive, located adjacent to Lazy Turtle Restaurant at the southern end of Tyrell Bay, offers open-water diving courses that range from "discover" to "dive master." ✉ *On the beachfront, Tyrell Bay, Harvey Vale, Carriacou* ☎ *473/443–8566* 🌐 *www.lumbadive.com.*

FISHING

Deep-sea fishing around Grenada is excellent. The list of likely catches includes marlin, sailfish, yellowfin tuna, and dorado (also known as mahimahi or dolphin). You can arrange sportfishing trips that accommodate up to six people starting at $500 for a half day and $750 for a full day.

True Blue Sportfishing. British-born Captain Gary Clifford, who has been fishing since the age of six, has run True Blue Sportfishing since 1998. He offers big-game charters for up to six passengers on the 31-foot *Yes Aye.* The boat has an enclosed cabin, a fighting chair, and professional tackle. Refreshments and transportation to the marina are included. ✉ *Port Louis Marina, Lagoon Rd., St. George's, St. George* ☎ *473/407–4688* 🌐 *www.yesaye.com.*

GOLF

Grenada Golf & Country Club. Determined golfers might want to try the 9-hole course at the Grenada Golf & Country Club. Separate tees allow for an 18-hole configuration. Located halfway between St. George's and Grand Anse, the layout features lateral hazards and challenging rough and small, elevated, sloping putting surfaces. Spread over the top of a hill, with strong winds fairly common, the course is more challenging than you might expect. Your hotel can make arrangements for you. Popular with local businessmen, this course is convenient to most hotels and is the only public course on the island. The club has changing rooms as well as club rental, a bar, and a restaurant. ✉ *Golf Course Hill, Belmont, St. George* ☎ *473/444–4128* 🎫 *$16; $24 to play the course twice (from separate tees)* 🏌 *9 holes (18 when played twice from different tees), 5165 yards, par 67.*

GUIDED TOURS

Guided tours offer the historical sights of St. George's, Grand Étang National Park & Forest Reserve, spice plantations and nutmeg-processing stations, rain-forest hikes and treks to waterfalls, snorkeling trips to local islands, and day trips to Carriacou. A full-day sightseeing tour costs $70 to $90 per person, usually including lunch and admissions; a half-day tour, $45 to $60; a guided hike to Concord or Mt. Qua Qua, $55 to $60 per person. Grenada taxi drivers will conduct island sightseeing tours for $150 per day or $25 to $35 per hour for up to four people. Carriacou

Take an exciting safari-style tour of Grenada on an Adventure Jeep Tour.

minibus drivers will take up to four people on a full-island tour for $75 (2½ hours) or a half-island tour for $40 (1½ hours).

Adventure Jeep Tour. On a full-day Adventure Jeep Tour you ride in the back of a Land Rover, safari fashion, along scenic coastal roads, trek in the rain forest, have lunch at a plantation, take a swim or two, and skirt the capital. The company also combines the full-day Jeep tour ($95 per person, hotel pickup included) with river tubing (add $45 per person) and offers guided bike tours ($15 an hour). ✉ *St. George's, St. George* ☎ *473/444–5337* 🌐 *www.adventuregrenada.com.*

Caribbean Horizons. Personalized half- or full-day tours of historic and natural island sites, market and garden tours, rain-forest hikes, and sailing excursions to Carriacou are all available from this company. ✉ *True Blue, St. George* ☎ *473/444–1555* 🌐 *www.caribbeanhorizons.com.*

Edwin Frank's Tours. After 22 years as public relations officer for the Grenada Board of Tourism—and as a radio and TV personality in his own right—Edwin Frank brings to his daily island tours a wealth of information about Grenada's history, geography, politics, culture, flora, fauna, and cuisine, along with a range of contemporary perspectives about life in and on this lovely island. ✉ *Calvigny, St. George* ☎ *473/407–5393.*

Henry's Safari Tours. Denis Henry knows Grenada like the back of his hand. He leads adventurous hikes and nature safaris in four-wheel-drive vehicles, or you can design your own half- or full-day "as you like it" tour for $30–35 per hour, depending on the number of people. ✉ *Woburn, St. George* ☎ *473/444–5313* 🌐 *www.henrysafari.com.*

Isle of Reefs Tours. A soft adventure tour operator, Isle of Reefs specializes in guided hiking treks, turtle-watching, boat trips to Sandy Island, White Island, or the Tobago Cays Marine Park, mountain-bike rentals, offshore camping expeditions, dingy sailing lessons, and cookery classes. ✉ *L'Esterre, Carriacou* ☎ *473/404–0415* 🌐 *www.isleofreefstours.com.*

Mandoo Tours. Whether for one or two people or for a busload, Mandoo (Simon Seales) offers half- or full-day standardized island tours that follow northern, southern, or eastern routes. An environmentalist at heart and determined advocate for the preservation of the island's heritage, he will gladly arrange customized tours, as well as hikes to waterfalls, the rain forest, and the mountains. ✉ *Mt. Moritz, St. George* ☎ *473/440–1428* 🌐 *www.grenadatours.com.*

Sunsation Tours. You can visit all the usual sites in Grenada or go as far off the beaten track as you want to go on Sunsation Tours' customized island tours, market tours, home and garden tours, challenging hikes, and day sails. ✉ *Le Marquis Complex, Grand Anse, St. George* ☎ *473/444–1594* 🌐 *www.grenadasunsation.com.*

HIKING

EcoTrek. This company takes small groups on day trips to the heart of the rain forest, where you'll find hidden waterfalls and hot-spring pools. A half-day hike to Seven Sisters Waterfall ($55 per person) is suitable for the reasonably fit; full-day adventures to other destinations are more strenuous. **■ TIP→ Make arrangements at the main location at Coyaba Beach Resort in Grand Anse or at Port Louis Marina on Lagoon Rd. in St. George's.** ✉ *Coyaba Beach Resort, Grand Anse, St. George* ☎ *473/444–7777 at Coyaba, 473/232–7777 at Port Louis* 🌐 *www.ecodiveandtrek.com.*

Fodor's Choice ★ **Grand Étang National Park & Forest Reserve.** Mountain trails wind through Grand Étang National Park & Forest Reserve; if you're lucky, you may spot a Mona monkey or some exotic birds on your hike. There are trails for all levels—from a self-guided nature trail around Grand Étang Lake to a demanding hike through the bush to the peak of Mt. Qua Qua (2,373 feet) or a major trek up Mt. St. Catherine (2,757 feet). Long pants and hiking shoes are recommended. Expect to pay $25 per person for a four-hour guided hike up Mt. Qua Qua, $20 each for two or more, or $15 each for three or more; the Mt. St. Catherine hike starts at $35 per person. ✉ *Grand Étang, St. Andrew* ☎ *473/440–6160.*

Henry's Safari Tours. The personalized hiking excursions here include trips through rich agricultural land and rain forest to remote waterfalls, the summit of Mt. Qua Qua, and other fascinating spots. ✉ *Woburn, St. George* ☎ *473/444–5313, 347/721–9271 in U.S.* 🌐 *www.henrysafari.com.*

Telfor Bedeau Hiking Tours. Telfor Bedeau has walked up, down, or across nearly every mountain, trail, and pathway on the island. His experience and knowledge of the trails and his inexhaustible energy and patience make him an excellent guide, whether it's an easy walk with novices or a strenuous hike with experts. ✉ *Soubise, St. Andrew* ☎ *473/442–6200.*

GUADELOUPE

WELCOME TO GUADELOUPE

Guadeloupe Passage
Plage de la Chapelle á Anse Bertrand
La Pointe de la Grande Vigie
Anse Bertrand
D122
N8
N6
Campêche
Port Louis
Les Mangles
N8
Beauport
N6
N6
Gros-Cap
Anse du Vieux Fort
Pte. Allègre
Petit-Canal
D120
La Grande-Anse
12
11
13
10 10
Ilet à Fajou
Anse du Canal
GRANDE
Ste-Rose
Vieux-Bourg
Morne-à-l'Eau
N5
Grand Cul-de-Sac Marin
14
Deshaies
N2
N2
Jabrun du Sud
Jabrun du Nord
Abymes
9
9
Airport
Lamentin
Rivière Salée
Pointe-Noire
N1
Destrelan
BASSE
Pointe-à-Pitre
Anse Caraïbe
Cascade aux Ecrevisses
N1
Fort Fleur d'Epée
1 2
1 2
Bas-du-Fort
Mahaut
La Traversée
D23
Plage Caravelle
Les Mamelles
Ilet de Pigeon
Pigeon Island
Vernou
Petit-Bourg
Aquarium de la Guadeloupe
Malendure
Pigeon
Parc National de la Guadeloupe
Bouillante
11
Goyave
TERRE
La Soufrière
Marigot
Ste-Marie
N2
N1
15
Vieux-Habitants
Le Musée Volcanologique
Capesterre-Belle-Eau
Carbet
Matouba
Plage de Rocroy
St-Claude
Chutes du Carbet
Anse Chapelle
Caribbean Sea
D11
St-Sauveur
Gourbeyre
N1
Bananier
Basse-Terre
D6
Trois-Rivières
D6
16
Anse Turlet
Vieux Fort
12 - 14
17 - 20
Iles des Saintes (Les Saintes)
Pompierres
21
22
Terre-de-Haut
23
Anse Crawen
Terre-de-Bas
La Coche
Grand Ilet

KEY

- Beaches
- Cruise Ship Terminal
- Dive Sites
- Restaurants
- Hotels
- Ferry

A heady blend of Afro-Caribbean customs, French style, and tropical delights, butterfly-shape Guadeloupe is actually two islands divided by a narrow channel: smaller, flatter, and drier Grande-Terre (Large Land) and wetter and more mountainous Basse-Terre (Low Land). Sheltered by palms, the beaches are beguiling, and the waterfront sidewalk cafés are a bit like the Riviera.

THE BUTTERFLY ISLAND

Guadeloupe, annexed by France in 1674, is not a single island but rather an archipelago. The largest parts of the chain are Basse-Terre and Grande-Terre, which together are shaped somewhat like a large butterfly. The "out" islands are the Iles des Saintes, La Désirade, and Marie-Galante.

Restaurants

- Café Wango 4
- Chez Clara 10
- Chez Henri 15
- Couleurs du Monde 12
- Iguane Café 6
- La Toubana 3
- La Porte 7
- Le Mabouya 5
- Le Rocher de Malendure 11
- Le Touloulou 16
- Manman'dlo 9
- Oualiri Breeze 8
- Restauarant La Savane 17
- Restaurant Les Petits Saints 13
- Restaurant de la Vielle Tour 2
- Ti Kaz La 14
- Zawag 1

Hotels

- Au Village de Menard .. 25
- Auberge de la Vieille Tour 1
- Bwa Chik Hotel 7
- Caraib Bay Hotel 13
- Club Med La Caravelle .. 3
- Habitation du Comté ... 10
- Habitation Getz 15
- Hotel Amundo 5
- Hotel Bois Joli 22
- Hotel Cap Reva 28
- Hotel Les Petits Saints 18
- Langley Hotel 12
- La Cocoteraie 6
- La Créole Beach 2
- La Rose de Bresil 26
- La Toubana Hôtel 4
- Le Jardin de Malanga . 16
- Le Neem 8
- Le Soleil Levant 27
- Le Village de Canada .. 24
- Les Hauts de Grand Anse 21
- L'Habitation Tabanon 9
- Lô Bleu Hôtel 17
- Paradis Saintois 19
- Residence Anse Caraibe 20
- Residence Grand Baie . 23
- Tainos Cottages 11
- Tendacayou Ecolodge . 14

TOP REASONS TO VISIT GUADELOUPE

1 Creole Flavors: Guadeloupe's restaurants and hotel dining rooms highlight the island's fine creole cuisine.

2 Small Inns: Also called *relais* and *gites* (apartments) these intimate accommodations give you a genuine island experience.

3 Adventure Sports: Parc National has plenty of activities to keep the adrenaline pumping.

4 La Désirade: Remote and affordable, this friendly island provides an escape-from-it-all experience.

EATING AND DRINKING WELL IN THE FRENCH WEST INDIES

Creole cuisine, a sultry mélange of African, European, Arawak, even Asian traditions, reflects the islands' turbulent territorial tugs-of-war.

Deceptively simple yet robustly flavored, authentic "kweyol" cuisine demands patience to make: continual macerating and marinating, then seasoning as the food simmers. Many dishes developed in response to economic necessities, recycling leftovers and incorporating ingredients such as starches (both hardy and impervious to spoilage). The indigenous Arawaks provided tubers such as tannia and yucca; lemongrass and capsicum for seasoning; arrowroot for thickening; and *roucou* (annatto, a yellowish-reddish seed) for coloring. The Africans imported plantains, pigeon peas, potatoes, and peppers. The French and British introduced tomatoes, onions, and less perishable salt cod. East Indian indentured servants brought cumin, cardamom, and coriander, notably used in *colombo*, a meat (try *cabri*, goat), poultry, or seafood dish that detonates the palate. Wash it down with fresh local juices from pulpy papaya to puckering passion fruit or the fine rums. Bon appétit!

Blaff. This typical method of preparation is usually used for firm, flaky, white fish such as mahimahi or grouper. The fish is poached in a seasoned broth, often a classic court-bouillon (a quick stock perfumed with fresh herbs). The incendiary "condiment" *sauce chien* is served with accras, grilled fish, chicken, and "whatever." The components are: vegetable oil, chopped chives, crushed garlic, hot pepper, lemon juice, salt, and pepper. Consensus has it that the derivation of the name came from the brand name of the knife, "Chien," which is used to cut the ingredients. However, as its etymology is obscure, it may indeed have been named "dog's sauce" because it would render even canines edible.

Cod. France contributed many basic ingredients over time to economize, notably dried salt cod, which required no refrigeration and became a staple in creole cooking. *Accras de morue*, fluffy cod fritters, grace every menu. Other popular traditional dishes include *chiquetaille*, shredded cod usually served with a spicy vinaigrette, and *ferocé* (saltfish mixed with avocado and peppers, deep-fried in manioc flour). *Tinnain morue*, grilled cod and bananas believed to energize, still jump-starts many locals' days.

Crayfish. This spiky freshwater crustacean, both wild and, increasingly, farmed, is usually served whole with a variety of sauces. It goes by many names in the French West Indies, including the more Gallic *écrevisse*, patois *z'habitant* or *crebiche*, and *ouassou* (generally larger). A favorite preparation is stewed with *dombrés* (manioc dumplings served pancake-style); you may also see it *étouffée* (stewed with vegetables, served over rice), underscoring the similarity to Cajun cuisine (alongside such dishes as *boudin*, blood sausage).

Poulet Boucané. "Buccaneer's chicken" is smoked slowly over burnt sugarcane (a centuries-old warning signal that pirates were coming) in a closed, chimney-topped barbecue. *Boucanage* is also a French preservation technique, "drying" seasoned meats and poultry on a wood fire (in this case using sugarcane husks). Roughly similar to Jamaica's jerk, it mingles smokiness, sweetness, and spiciness; the marinade typically is a variant of the combustible sauce chien, though milder versions might combine vinegar, lime, garlic, and clove.

'Ti Punch. The primary ingredient in this aperitif is 100-proof rum, occasionally fruit-infused, muddled with lime and simple cane syrup. Novices can request the lighter (weight) *ti-bete*. Another concoction worth sampling is the classic *planteur* (rum with fruit juices and spices); finish dinner with a *rhum vieux* (aged, cognac-quality rum) like Reimonenq's Ste. Rose, or *shrubb*, an orange-and-spice-tinged rum-based liqueur.

Tripe. Another old-fashioned method of economizing was the use of internal organs, offal, which eventually became appropriated by haute cuisine. Tripe (small intestines) is particularly popular. The classic dish is *bébélé*, a stew of tripe, green bananas, tubers (usually breaded as croquettes or *domblés*), and gourds such as *giraumon* (similar to pumpkin).

—Jordan Simon

Updated by Eileen Robinson Smith

Sail the waters around the Isles of Guadeloupe and you'll observe nuances in the ocean's color palette as you glide through the gin-clear sea. Things look better from the bow of a sailboat, from the storybook islands of Les Saintes to towns not as postcard pretty. This Caribbean coastline is dramatic with white and golden beaches, rocky promontories, and rugged cliffs that span the horizon.

Although Guadeloupe is thought of as one island, it is several, each with its own personality. "The mainland" consists of the two largest islands in the Guadeloupe archipelago: Basse-Terre and Grande-Terre, which look something like a butterfly. The outer islands—Les Saintes, Marie-Galante, and La Désirade—are acknowledged as wonderfully unique, unspoiled travel destinations. Tourism officials are now wisely marketing their country as a plural, Les Iles de Guadeloupe. See which one is your place in the sun. *Vive les vacances!*

It's no wonder that in 1493 Christopher Columbus welcomed the sight of this emerald paradise, where fresh, sweet water flows in cascades. And it's understandable why France annexed it in 1674 and why the British schemed to wrench it from them. In 1749 Guadeloupe mirrored what was happening in the motherland. It, too, was an island divided between royalists and revolutionaries.

The resident British sided with the royalists, so Victor Hugues was sent to banish the Brits. While here, he sent to the guillotine more than 300 planters loyal-to-the-royals and freed the slaves, thus all but destroying the plantocracy. An old saying of the French Caribbean refers to *les grands seigneurs de la Martinique et les bonnes gens de la Guadeloupe* (the lords of Martinique and the bourgeoisie of Guadeloupe), and that still rings true. You'll find more aristocratic descendants of the original French planters on Martinique (known as *békés*) and also more "expensive" people both living and vacationing there. That mass beheading is one of the prime reasons. Napoléon—who ultimately ousted the

LOGISTICS

Getting to Guadeloupe: You can connect in Miami with American Airlines direct flight on Saturday or go through San Juan or another Caribbean island. Some travelers prefer the regularly scheduled ferry service from Dominica, St. Lucia, and Martinique, but the extra travel time certainly increases the hassle factor. The smaller islands—though charming and rewarding—are harder to reach; even with regular ferries and air service, you will almost always need to spend some time on Guadeloupe both coming and going. Aéroport International Pôle Caraïbes, 3 miles (5 km) from Pointe-à-Pitre (PTP), is a fairly modern airport by Caribbean standards.

Hassle Factor: Medium for Guadeloupe to high for the smaller islands.

On the Ground: Cabs meet flights at the airport if you decide not to rent a car. The metered fare is about €30 to Pointe-à-Pitre, €35 to Gosier, and as much as €70 to St-François. Fares go up 40% on Sunday and holidays and from 7 pm to 7 am. You can take a public bus from the airport to downtown Pointe-à-Pitre, but that's not a good option if you have a lot of luggage. And there are no recommendable hotels in the city.

royals—also ousted Hugues and reestablished slavery. It wasn't until 1848 that an Alsatian, Victor Schoelcher, abolished it for good.

Guadeloupe became one of France's *départements d'outremer* in 1946, meaning that it's a dependent of France. It was designated a region in 1983, making it a part of France, albeit a distant part. This brought many benefits to the islanders, from their fine highway systems to the French social services and educational system, as well as a high standard of living. Certain tensions still exist, though the anticolonial resentment harbored by the older generations is dying out. Guadeloupe's young people realize the importance of tourism to the island's future, and you'll find them welcoming, smiling, and practicing the English and tourism skills they learn in school. Some *français* is indispensable, though you may receive a bewildering response in Creole.

Guadeloupe has more than a bit of France, but the culture of this tropical paradise is more Afro-influenced. Savor the earthier pleasures here, exemplified by the wonderful potpourri of whole spices whose heady aromas flood the outdoor markets.

PLANNING

WHEN TO GO

The tourism industry thrives during the high season, which goes from mid-November through May; the island is quiet the rest of the year. Prices decline 25% to 40% in the off-season.

GETTING HERE AND AROUND

AIR TRAVEL

The nonstop service now available is from Miami on American Airlines and on Seaborne Airlines, flying out of San Juan direct, three times weekly. It has similar inter-line agreements (codeshares) with both American Airlines, Delta, United and JetBlue. Air Canada flies weekly nonstops between Montreal and Pointe-à-Pitre. Air Antilles Express has service to Martinique; St. Martin; Cayenne, French Guiana; St. Lucia; and Santo Domingo, Dominican Republic.

Air Caraïbes connects the island to St. Maarten; Martinique; Haiti; St. Barth; French Guiana, St. Lucia; Santo Domingo, Dominican Republic; Havana, Cuba; and Paris.

Air France's weekly flights between Miami and Guadeloupe stop in Haiti before landing in Pointe-a-Pitre. Air France is a Parisian connection, of course, and from the islands you can sometimes get good prices to France.

LIAT mainly services the English-speaking Caribbean islands, including Antigua, Barbados, and St. Lucia. St. Lucia has direct service from New York, Miami, Atlanta, and Toronto. These flights are one way for U.S. and Canadian travelers to get to Guadeloupe with fewer stopovers. LIAT codeshares with Air Caraïbes.

A carrier relatively new to the French Islands, Seaborne Airlines now flies to Guadeloupe three times a week out of San Juan on Monday, Tuesday, Thursday, and Saturday. Flights are timed for connections to and from the United States and Canada. A new codeshare program between American Airlines and Seaborne Airlines allows you to book your American Airlines and Seaborne Airlines combined itinerary on 🌐 *www.aa.com* while earning AAdvantage program miles. They have a similar online agreement with JetBlue, United, and Delta.

Airline Contacts Air Antilles Express. Air Antilles Express has service to Martinique; St. Martin; Cayenne, French Guiana; St. Lucia; and Santo Domingo, Dominican Republic. ☎ *0890/64-86-48* 🌐 *www.airantilles.com.* **Air Canada.** Air Canada services Guadeloupe flies weekly nonstop flights, between Montreal (YUL) and Pointe-a-Pitre (PAP). Residents of states that border Canada might find it convenient to go north in order to go south. ☎ *888/247-2262, 0590/21-12-77* 🌐 *www.aircanada.com.* **Air Caraïbes.** Air Caraïbes connects the island to St. Maarten; Martinique; Haiti; St. Barth; French Guiana, St. Lucia; Santo Domingo, Dominican Republic; Havana, Cuba; and Paris. ■ **TIP→ This airline offers substantial discounts for seniors on some routes.** ☎ *0820/83-58-35* 🌐 *www.aircaraibes.com.* **Air France.** Air France's weekly flights between Miami and Guadeloupe stop in Haiti before landing in Pointe-à-Pitre, and then go on to Martinique. Air France is a Parisian connection, of course, and from the islands you can sometimes get good prices to France. ☎ *0590/21-13-03, 0820/82-08-20, 800/237-27-47* 🌐 *www.airfrance.com.* **American Airlines.** American flies direct from Miami to Guadeloupe on Saturday. 🌐 *www.aa.com.*

LIAT. LIAT mainly services the English-speaking Caribbean islands, including Antigua, Barbados, and St. Lucia. St. Lucia has direct service from New York, Miami, Atlanta, and Toronto. These flights are another option for U.S. and Canadian travelers to get to Guadeloupe with fewer stopovers. LIAT codeshares with Air Caraïbes. ☎ *0590/21–13–93, 888/844–5428 in Guadaloupe* 🌐 *www.liatairline.com.* **Seaborne Airlines.** Seaborne Airlines flies to Guadeloupe three times a week out of San Juan. Flights are timed for connections to and from the United States and Canada. A codeshare program between American Airlines and Seaborne Airlines allows you to book your American Airlines and Seaborne Airlines combined itinerary on *www.aa.com* while earning AAdvantage program miles. They have entered into a similar online agreement with JetBlue, Delta, and United. ☎ *866/359–8784* 🌐 *www.seaborneairlines.com.*

AIRPORTS AND TRANSFERS

Aéroport International Pôle Caraïbes (PTP). Aéroport International Pôle Caraïbes (PTP), usually called the Pointe-à-Pitre Airport, is one of the largest and most modern in the Caribbean. Excellent signage makes it very manageable. It has shops, restaurants, and car-rental agencies. There is a tourism information booth in the terminal with bilingual staffers, an ATM, and a currency exchange. The staff can help with last-minute lodging and a wealth of brochures. Ask your resort if airport transfers can be arranged, as they are almost always cheaper than taking a taxi. ✉ *Morne Mamiel, Abymes* ☎ *0590/21–71–71, 0590/21–14–00* 🌐 *www.guadeloupe.aeroport.fr.*

Taxi fare to Pointe-à-Pitre is about €30, to Gosier resorts about €35, to Ste-Anne as much as €60, and to St-François nearly €70. Cabs meet flights at the airport if you decide not to rent a car.

CAR TRAVEL

Renting a Car: If you're based in Gosier or at a large resort, you'll probably need a car only for a day or two of sightseeing. That may be enough, since roundabouts, mountain roads, and fast, aggressive drivers are stressful. Your valid driver's license will suffice for up to 20 days. You can get a rental car from the airport or your hotel. Count on spending between €48 and €80 a day for a small car with standard shift; automatics are considerably more expensive and must be reserved in advance. Note that some companies, including Europcar, charge a €25 drop-off fee for the airport, even if you pick the car up there. Allow at least 30 to 60 minutes to drop off your car at the end of your stay. The chances of your getting lost on the way to the airport and to where you need to leave the car (at a car rental box near the airport, where you then wait for a shuttle to bring you and your luggage back to the airport) are such that you should probably allow a full hour. Conscientiously follow every sign that has a picture of a plane. An alternative is to return it in Gosier and put that €25 drop-off fee saved toward a €35 stress-free, taxi ride. Return your vehicle with the same amount of gas or you'll be charged an exorbitant rate.

Captheo. New to Guadeloupe, electric cars can solve the transportation issues. Scooters can also be rented at this reputable agency. Expect to pay about €70 for a car that seats four, €25 for a scooter. A credit card deposit of €382 for a scooter is required, €650 for a car. ✉ *Terre-de-Haut, Iles des Saintes* ✢ *From the ferry dock, turn left, walk a couple of blocks. This is on the right, sea side of the street, near the pharmacy* ☎ *0590/81–49–82, 0690/63–58–13.*

Car Rental Contacts Avis ☎ *0590/21–13–54, 800/331–1212* 🌐 *www.avis.fr.* **Budget** ☎ *0590/21–46–57* 🌐 *www.budget-antilles.com.* **Europcar.** Europcar, like most companies, charges a €25 drop-off fee for the airport, even if you pick the car up there. Employees speak English and are very professional; convertibles go for €113 per day. ☎ *0590/21–13–52, 0690/35–29–52* 🌐 *www.europcar-guadeloupe.com.* **Hertz.** Hertz has some automatics, convertibles, and various high-end models. They charge a €30 drop-off fee at the airport, even if you picked up there. ☎ *0590/21–13–46, 0590/89–28–05* 🌐 *www.hertzantilles.com.* **Jumbo Car** ☎ *0820/22–02–30, 0590/91–91–66* 🌐 *www.jumbocar.com.*

Sixt. Sixt has a number of convertibles and high-end cars, including some from high-end German automobiles. ☎ *0590/21–13–44* 🌐 *www.sixt.com.*

DRIVING TIPS

Guadeloupeans are fast and often impatient drivers and they tailgate. Driving around Grande-Terre is relatively easy for there is a well-maintained system of highways. Basse-Terre requires more skill to navigate the hairpin bends in the mountains and around the eastern shore; at night the roads are unlighted and treacherous. Roundabouts (*rond-pointes*) are everywhere. Use your turn signal and proceed cautiously. If you're lost, don't ask people standing on the side of the road; they are waiting for a lift and may jump in. Try to find a gas station. *"Je suis perdue!"* (I am lost!) is a good phrase to know.

FERRY TRAVEL

Ferry schedules and fares often change, so phone ahead to confirm. You normally travel to the outlying islands in the archipelago in the morning, returning in the afternoon. Both Comatrile and Express des Isles operate ferries between Terre-de-Haut and Marie-Galante.

One of the newer ferries, *Jeans for Freedom*, is owned by L'Express des Isles. Its ferries go between Pointe-à-Pitre, Guadeloupe, and St-Pierre, Martinique; they also make a brief stop in Dominica. The price is approximately €79. Jeans also connects Fort-de-France to St. Lucia (€70). In Guadeloupe, service is also available between Pointe-à-Pitre and Marie-Galante or Les Saintes for €19. Round-trip tickets are discounted, as are children's. **C.T.M. DEHER.** C.T.M. DEHER goes between Trois-Rivieres and Terre-de-Haut, Les Saintes, which is a shorter distance, for about €11.

BABOU One. This ferry runs between St-François and La Désirade and on certain days, Marie-Galante and/or Les Saintes and now even Petite-Terre. As an example of prices, it is just €25 round-trip to Desirade, on a boat that leaves St-François at 8 am and returns at 4:45 pm. ☎ *0690/26–60–69, 0590/47–50–31, 0690/63–46–39* 🌐 *www.babouone.fr.*

Comatrile. Comatrile travels from St-François on Grande Terre to Désirade, to St-Louis on Marie-Galante and Terre de Haut on Les Saintes. January through March the boat leaves St-François at 7:05 am and returns from Marie-Galante at 3:45 pm. From April onwards the schedule will be 7:15 am from St-François and 3 pm from Marie-Galante.The cost is €56 round-trip if you are staying more than one night. If you are doing a day trip (coming back the same day) then the promotion is

€38. Bwa Chik, the eco-hotel in St-François, is offering a special package with the newly refreshed Cap Reva property in Marie-Galante.

Year-round the schedule to Les Saintes is Monday–Sunday 7:15 am, St-François departure; at 3 pm it returns from Terre de Haut. Fare: €58 round-trip. If doing a same-day round-trip, there is a promotion for €39.

To and from Desirade, the schedule is Monday–Sunday the ferry leaves St-François at 4:45 pm and departs from Desirade at 5:06 am. Cost is €28 RT. ✉ *Marina de St-François, St-François, Grande-Terre* ☎ *0690/50–05–09 port, 0590/22–26–31.*

C.T.M. DEHER. C.T.M. DEHER goes between Trois-Rivieres and Terre-de-Haut, Les Saintes, departing at 9 am and returning to Guadeloupe at 4 pm daily. ☎ *0590/99–50–68, 0590/92–06–39* 🌐 *www.ctmdeher.com.*

Jeans for Freedom. This company is owned by L'Express des Isles and operates two ferries to Martinique and Les Saintes, also. ✉ *St-Pierre, Martinique* ☎ *0825/01–01–25* 🌐 *www.jeansforfreedom.com.*

L'Express des Isles. L'Express des Isles runs ferries to Marie-Galante and to Les Saintes (about €19), from Pointe-à-Pitre. Longer trips to other islands like Dominica, Martinique, and St. Lucia cost about €79 one-way (€109 round-trip) and take between three and four hours. **■ TIP→ Be prepared for bad weather and choppy seas, which are especially likely on longer runs, when the boats are in open water.** That said, the company uses larger ferries when heading to and from Dominica and Martinique, and that makes for a smoother ride. French films (sometimes R-rated) on flat-screen TVs help pass the time. There are extra departures on weekends and holidays and for special events, when the ferries can be crowded. Note that the company enforces its overweight baggage rules and uses the same limits as the airlines. A snack bar on board sells beverages, including snacks and oftentimes simple sandwiches which they sometimes run out of. Be prepared and B.Y.O. food. ☎ *0825/35–90–00* 🌐 *www.express-des-iles.com.*

TAXI TRAVEL

Taxis are metered and fairly pricey. Fares jump by 40% between 7 pm and 7 am and on Sunday and holidays.

CDL Taxi. If your French is in order, you can call this company which has "radio cabs" (or ask your hotel receptionist to call them for you). ☎ *0590/20–74–74.*

Jean Luc Renault Taxi of St-François. Accommodating and punctual, this pleasant driver has multiple vehicles and speaks English well. ☎ *0690/57–59–40.*

ESSENTIALS

Banks and Exchange Services Few places accept U.S. dollars, so plan on exchanging them for euros. You must exchange cash at a bank, your hotel, or a *bureau de change*, which has a better exchange rate. One favorite company is Change Caraïbe, with branches near the tourist office and market in Pointe-à-Pitre. It's easier to use your ATM card to get euros. There are a number of banks that have outdoor ATMs in downtown Pointe-à-Pitre. To use them, make sure you have a four-digit

PIN, and be aware that they will charge a fee of about €2 for withdrawals and your own bank as much as $5. ATMs, particularly those in smaller towns, don't always accept foreign bank cards. Visa and MasterCard are most often accepted, followed by American Express. There are just two ATMs on the main island of Iles des Saintes, one at the ferry dock and the other at the post office, which has erratic hours. Come with extra cash reserve, because it's not unusual for ATMs to run out of euros or to malfunction during electrical blackouts.

Electricity 220 volts/50 cycles. North American electronics and laptops (sometimes) require an adapter and a plug converter.

Emergency Services **Ambulance** ☎ *15, 0590/90–13–13*. **Fire** ☎ *18*. **Police emergencies** ☎ *17*. **SAMU.** SAMU is a medical service for when you need to see a doctor fast. ☎ *0590/89–11–00*.

Etiquette Guadeloupeans are often religious and traditional, particularly the older generations. Revealing shorts or swimwear away from the beach may be considered indecorous by some, and you should ask before taking a picture of any islander. The children, however, will probably flash you one of their happy smiles. Observe the courtesy of saying *bonjour* or *bonsoir* when you enter or leave a place or before asking someone a question or directions.

Language The official language is French, though most of the islanders also speak Creole, a lyrical patois that you won't be able to understand. Often, their French has a heavy Creole accent. Most of the staff in hotels knows some English as do some taxi drivers, but communicating is decidedly more difficult in the countryside. Arm yourself with a phrase book, a dictionary, patience, and a sense of humor.

Passport Requirements You must have a valid passport as well as a return or ongoing ticket to enter Guadeloupe.

Phones To make on-island calls, dial 0590 (0690 if it is a cellular phone) and then the six-digit phone number. To call Guadeloupe from the United States, dial 00–590–590, then the local number. For cell phone numbers, dial 00–590–690, then the local number. If you're on one of the other islands in the French West Indies, dial 0590 and then the local number.

Taxes and Service Charges The *taxe de séjour* (room tax), which varies by hotel, is usually €1 but never exceeds €1.80 per person per day. Most hotel prices include a 10% to 15% service charge in their rates; if not, it'll be added to your bill. A 15% service charge is included in all restaurant prices, as are taxes.

Tipping Restaurants are required to include that 15% service charge in the menu price. No additional gratuity is necessary (although it's appreciated if service is particularly good). Tip skycaps and porters about €2 a bag, cabdrivers 10% of the fare (if they work for a cab company rather than having their own taxi), and housekeeping €2 per night.

ACCOMMODATIONS

Guadeloupe is actually an archipelago of large and small islands. Grande-Terre has the big package hotels that are concentrated primarily in four or five communities on the south coast, whereas wilder

Basse-Terre has more locally owned hotels. More distant and much quieter are the Iles des Saintes, Marie-Galante, and La Désirade, in that order. On each of these smaller islands tourism is only a part of the economy and development is light, and any of them will give you a sense of what the Caribbean used to be.

Relais and Gites: These small inns offer a more personal—and authentic—kind of Caribbean experience.

Resorts: You can certainly opt for a big, splashy resort with all the amenities. Many of the island's large chain hotels cater to French package groups and are relatively bare-bones, though an increasing number of them are being renovated to the degree that they will appeal more to Americans as well.

Villas: Private villas are another option—particularly for families—but the language barrier is often a deterrent for Americans. Best to go through one of the rental agencies recommended here.

Hotel reviews have been shortened. For full information, visit Fodors.com.

13

WHAT IT COSTS IN EUROS

	$	$$	$$$	$$$$
Restaurants	under €12	€12–€20	€21–€30	over €30
Hotels	under €275	€275–€375	€376–€475	over €475

Restaurant prices are the average cost of a main course at dinner or, if dinner is not served, at lunch. Hotel prices are the lowest cost of a standard double room in high season.

VISITOR INFORMATION

Contacts Comité du Tourisme des Iles de Guadeloupe ✉ *5 sq. de la Banque, Pointe-à-Pitre, Grande-Terre* ☎ *0590/82-09-30* 🌐 *www.lesilesdeguadeloupe.com.*

Office de Tourisme de Désirade ✉ *La Capitainerie-Beausejour, waterfront at ferry dock, La Désirade* ☎ *0590/85-00-86.* **Office du Tourisme de Marie-Galante.** Located right in town, this office has staff who speak English and who are quite helpful. ✉ *Rue du Fort, BP 15, Grand-Bourg, Marie-Galante* ☎ *0590/97-56-51* 🌐 *www.ot-mariegalante.com.* **Office du Tourisme de St-François** ✉ *Av. de l'Europe, St-François, Grande-Terre* ☎ *0590/68-66-81* 🌐 *www.destination-stfrancois.com* ⏲ *Mon.–Fri. 8–12 and 2–5, Sat. and Sun. 9–12 and 3–5.* **Office du Tourisme de Terre de Haut** ✉ *Ferry Dock, Jean Calot St., PB 10, Terre-de-Haut, Iles des Saintes* ☎ *0590/94-30-61* 🌐 *www.lessaintes.fr.*

WEDDINGS

A long residency requirement makes weddings prohibitive.

EXPLORING

To see each "wing" of the butterfly, you'll need to budget at least one day. They are connected by a bridge, and Grande-Terre has pretty villages along its south coast and the spectacular Pointe des Châteaux.

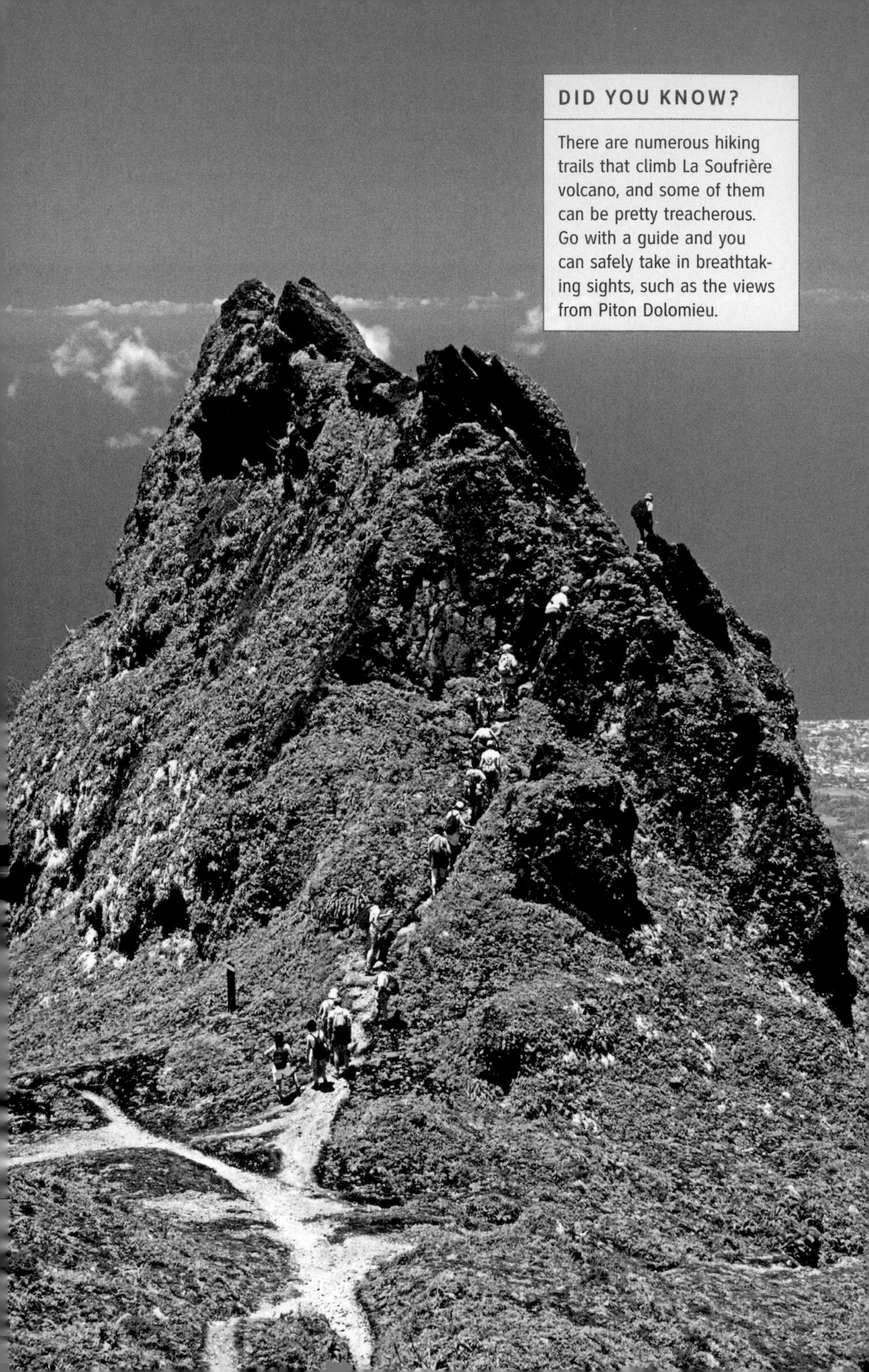

DID YOU KNOW?

There are numerous hiking trails that climb La Soufrière volcano, and some of them can be pretty treacherous. Go with a guide and you can safely take in breathtaking sights, such as the views from Piton Dolomieu.

You can see the main sights in Pointe-à-Pitre in a half day. Touring the rugged, mountainous Basse-Terre is a challenge. If time is a problem, head straight to the west coast; you could easily spend a day traveling its length, stopping for sightseeing, lunch, and a swim. You can make day trips to the islands, but an overnight or more works best. Leave your heavy luggage in the baggage room of your "mainland" hotel and take a small bag on the ferry.

GRANDE-TERRE

POINTE-À-PITRE

Although not the capital, this is the island's largest city, a commercial and industrial hub in the southwest of Grande-Terre. The Isles of Guadeloupe have 450,000 inhabitants, 99.6% of whom live in the cities. Pointe-à-Pitre is bustling, noisy, and hot—a place of honking horns and traffic jams and cars on sidewalks for want of a parking place. By day its pulse is fast, but at night, when its streets are almost deserted, you may not want to be there.

The heart of the old city is Place de la Victoire; surrounded by wooden buildings with balconies and shutters (including the tourism office) and by sidewalk cafés, it was named in honor of Victor Hugues' 1794 victory over the British. During the French Revolution Hugues ordered the guillotine set up here so that the public could witness the bloody end of 300 recalcitrant royalists, mainly the prosperous plantation owners.

Even more colorful is the bustling marketplace, between rues St-John Perse, Frébault, Schoelcher, and Peynier. It's a cacophonous place, where housewives bargain for spices, herbs (and herbal remedies), and a bright assortment of papayas, breadfruits, christophenes, and tomatoes.

WORTH NOTING

Cathédrale de St-Pierre et St-Paul. If you like churches, then make a pilgrimage to the imposing Cathédrale de St-Pierre et St-Paul, built in 1807. Although battered by hurricanes, it has fine stained-glass windows and creole-style balconies. ✉ *Rue Alexandre Isaac at rue de l'Eglise.*

Musée Schoelcher. Established in a colonial-style building, Musée Schoelcher celebrates Victor Schoelcher, an abolitionist from Alsace who fought against slavery in the French West Indies in the 19th century. The first museum in Guadeloupe, it was inaugurated in 1887, following a substantial donation in 1883 by "himself." New are 17 ethnographic objects that are part of a collection assembled by the abolitionist during his travels in the Caribbean, Egypt, and Africa, between 1830 and 1847. Eventually a total of 52 objects will be in trust and for the completion of the museum extension project. Presently, the museum contains many of his personal effects, and exhibits trace his life and work. ✉ *24 rue Peynier, Pointe-à-Pitre* ☎ *0590/82–08–04* 🎫 €2 ⏲ *Weekdays 9–5.*

ELSEWHERE ON GRANDE-TERRE

TOP ATTRACTIONS

Ft. Fleur d'Épée. The main attraction in Bas-du-Fort is this fortress, built between 1759 and 1763. It hunkers down on a hillside behind a deep moat. The fort was the scene of hard-fought battles between the French and the English in 1794. You can explore its well-preserved dungeons and battlements and take in a sweeping view of Iles des Saintes and Marie-Galante. The free guided tour here explores the fort's history and architecture and helps explain the living conditions of the soldiers who lived here. Included on the tour is an exploration of its underground galleries, now decorated with graffiti. If a bilingual person is on duty, she will explain it all in English. Call ahead, and to make certain of that day's hours. Registered as a historic monument since 1979, the fort also provides superb views for walkers. ✉ *Bas-du-Fort* ☎ *0590/90–94–61* 🎫 *Free* ⏲ *Daily 9–5.*

Gosier. Gosier was still a tiny village in the 1950s, a simple stopping place between Pointe-à-Pitre and Ste-Anne. However, it grew rapidly in the 1960s, when the beauty of the southern coastline began to bring tourists in ever-increasing numbers. Today Gosier is one of Guadeloupe's premier tourist areas while at the same time serving as a chic suburb of Pointe-à-Pitre. People sit at sidewalk cafés reading *Le Monde* as others flip-flop their way to the beach. This resort town has several hotels, nightclubs, shops, a casino, rental-car agencies, and a long stretch of sand.

Pointe des Châteaux. A National Grand Site, the island's easternmost point offers a breathtaking view of the Atlantic crashing against huge rocks, carving them into shapes resembling pyramids. A rocky arm reaching out to the ocean, it is a spectacular display of sea versus land. A 9-ton crucifix can be seen for miles out at sea and was erected for the centennial of the Catholic diocese in 1946. There are spectacular views of Guadeloupe's southern and eastern coasts and the island of La Désirade. The beach has few facilities now that vendors have been relocated to Petit Anse Kahouanne, about a mile up the road, so bring your own food and drink. The Village Artisanal is open 9–7. In high season taxis run every hour. ✉ *St-François.*

WORTH NOTING

FAMILY **Aquarium de la Guadeloupe.** Unique in the Antilles, this aquarium in the marina near Pointe-à-Pitre is a good place to spend an hour. Its motto is: "Visit the sea." The well-planned facility has an assortment of tropical fish, crabs, lobsters, moray eels, coffer fish, and some live coral. It's also a turtle rescue center, and the shark tank is spectacular. A restaurant serves kid-friendly fare, snacks, salads, pastas, etc. A small shop stocks marine toys and souvenirs.

The aquarium also offers a half-day ecotour, in which small boats travel through the mangroves, reefs, and a lagoon, with a biologist guide and a diving instructor on board. Leaving daily at 8:30 am and 1 pm, the tours are €59. Snorkeling gear is included, and kids are more than welcome. A full-day ecotour includes lunch and a visit to the aquarium (€95). ✉ *Place Créole, off Rte. N4, Marina, Gosier* ☎ *0590/90–92–38,*

0690/90–92–38, 0690/57–60–69 🌐 *www.aquariumdelaguadeloupe.com* 🎫 *€11.50* 🕑 *Daily 9–6:30.*

Le Moule. On the Atlantic coast, and once the capital city of Guadeloupe, this port city of 24,000 has had more than its share of troubles: it was bombarded by the British in 1794 and 1809 and by a hurricane in 1928. An important tourist center in past decades, it's experiencing a comeback. A large East Indian population, which originally came to cut cane, lives here. Canopies of flamboyant trees hang over the narrow streets, where colorful vegetable and fish markets do a brisk business. The town hall, with graceful balustrades, and a small 19th-century neoclassical church are on the main square. Le Moule's beach, protected by a reef, is perfect for windsurfing.

13

Musée Camélia Costumes et Traditions. This museum is a labor of love by its creators, and seeing the dress of black, white, and *métisseé* (mixed-race, or "maroon") societies is a fascinating way to visualize the island's tumultuous history and fascinating heritage. Items that you will remember: madras headdresses; baptism outfits; embroidered maternity dresses; colonial pith helmets and other various chapeaux as well as the doll collection. Make sure to go out back and visit the replica of a Guadeloupean case circa 1920. A film now depicts life of yesteryear. The small museum is privately owned; the founder, Camelia Bausivoir, is a retired English teacher, and she can act as your guide. This represents a collection accrued over decades, and Bausivoir sewed many of the costumes. Call before you go for directions and to make sure that a school group is not there. ✉ *1 Perinette, Gosier* ☎ *0590/83–21–70, 0690/41–51–90* 🎫 *€9* 🕑 *Tues.–Sun. 9–1 and 3–5.*

NEED A BREAK?

If you don't want to take time for a two-hour French lunch, watch for gas stations such as Shell Boutique, Total Boutique, and Esso Tigermart, which sell food. The VITO station on the left going into St-François has good pizza for about €8, as well as tables and chairs. A Total "fillin' station" might have barbecue ribs, chicken, and turkey.

Port Louis. This fishing village of about 7,000 people is best known for Le Soufleur Plage. It was once one of the island's prettiest, but it has become a little shabby. Yet the road construction is finally coming to an end, and it is looking better. Although the beach is crowded on weekends, it's blissfully quiet during the week. The sand is fringed by flamboyant trees, and there are also spectacular views of Basse-Terre. Near the dock, Chez Henri is a good, restaurant, friendly and hip.

Ste-Anne. In the 18th century this town, 8 miles (13 km) east of Gosier, was a sugar-exporting center. Sand has replaced sugar as the town's most valuable asset. La Caravelle and the other beaches are among the best in Guadeloupe. On its main drag, which parallels the waterfront, is a lively group of inexpensive eateries, shops, and artisan stalls. On a more spiritual note, Ste-Anne has a lovely cemetery with stark-white tombs.

St-François. This was once a simple little village, primarily involved with fishing and harvesting tomatoes. The fish and tomatoes are still here, as are the old creole houses and the lively market with recommendable food stalls in the *centre ville*, but increasingly, the St-François marina district is overtaking Gosier as Guadeloupe's most fashionable tourist resort area. Its avenue de l'Europe runs between the marina and the fairways and water obstacles of the municipal golf course, which was designed by Robert Trent Jones Sr. On the marina side is a string of shops (including a huge supermarket), hotels, bars, and restaurants. The Bwa Chik Hotel & Golf, an eco-chic study in recyclable materials, is here; it's a favorite with golfers. Other attractions include an array of beaches, a lagoon, and the St. François casino. St-François was designated as a Station Balnéaire (nautical resort) by the French government. With its 220-slip marina, it's a sailing mecca and a departure point for catamaran day sails to the out islands, which are in close proximity.

Vanibel. Guadeloupean coffee is considered some of the best in the world. Joel Nelson will tell you all about it if you take one of his tours around the grounds of his Domaine de Vanibel. Dress comfortably as you will be going into the bush, picking vanilla and coffee beans from the trees. His enthusiasm and passion for what he grows and produces makes what could be a ho-hum walk through the woods, a pleasurable learning experience. After some 30 minutes or more you will be brought back to the stone cottage that is the Habitation Sucrerie for a coffee tasting and fresh tropical fruits. You might want to buy a bag or two of Mr. Nelson's coffee. And the precious vanilla beans are four pods for €7.50 or a vanilla powder for €9. Also, there are simple *gîtes* (holiday cottages) for two to four persons on the estate. ✉ *Cousinière Caféière, Vieux-Habitants, Basse-Terre* ☎ *0590/98–40–79, 0690/30–21–37, 0690/48–92–06* 🌐 *www.vanibel.fr* 🎫 *€7* ⏲ *Mon.–Sat. 8–noon, and 2–5. Guided tours Mon.–Sat. 2:30 and 3:30 (Jan.–Apr.), 3 pm (May–Dec.).*

NEED A BREAK?

There's no wagering at Hyper Casino, a *supermarché* on l'avenue de l'Europe at the St-François Marina, but there are esoteric cheeses and baked goods such as pie-size, tropical-fruit tarts. Other supermarkets with good deli or bakery departments are those in the Leader Price and Carrefour chains.

BASSE-TERRE

Basse-Terre (which translates as "low land") is by far the highest and wildest of the two wings of the Guadeloupe butterfly, with the peak of the Soufrière volcano topping off at nearly 4,811 feet. Basse-Terre, where you can find the island's national park, is also an ecotourist's treasure, with lush, equatorial plant life and adventurous opportunities for hikers and mountain bikers on the old *traces*, routes that porters once took across the mountains. You can still find numerous fishing villages and banana plantations stretching as far as the eye can see. The northwest coast, between Bouillante and Grande-Anse, is magnificent; the road twists and turns up steep hills smothered in vegetation and then drops down and skirts deep-blue bays and colorful seaside towns. Constantly changing light, towering clouds, and frequent rainbows only add to the beauty. In fact, Basse-Terre is gaining in popularity each year, and is especially appreciated by young, sporty couples.

BASSE-TERRE

Because Pointe-à-Pitre is so much bigger, few people suspect that this little town of 15,000 is the capital and administrative center of Guadeloupe. But if you have any doubts, walk up the hill to the state-of-the-art Théâtre Nationale, where some of France's finest theater and opera companies perform.

FAMILY **Jardin Botanique.** This exquisite 10-acre park is filled with parrots and flamingos. A circuitous walking trail takes you by ponds with floating lily pads, cactus gardens, and every kind of tropical flower and plant, including orchids galore. Amid the exotic ferns and and gnarled, ancient trees are little wooden bridges and a gazebo. A panoramic restaurant with a surprisingly sophisticated lunch menu plus a snack bar are housed in terraced gingerbread buildings, one overlooking the park's waterfall, the other the mountains. The restaurant has authentic yet innovative creole cuisine for a moderate price, served on madras tablecloths. The garden has a children's park and nature-oriented playthings in the shop. A local juice and a snack is included with admission. This excursion is delightful and serene, ideal on an overcast day. ✉ *Deshaies* ☎ *0590/28–43–02* 🌐 *www.jardin-botanique.com* 🎫 *€15.50* 🕒 *Daily 9–5:30 Last tickets sold at 4:30.*

VIEUX-HABITANTS

This was the island's first colony, established in 1635. Beaches, a restored coffee plantation, and the oldest church on the island (1666) make this village worth a stop.

Musée du Café/Café Chaulet. From the riverfront Musée du Café/Café Chaulet, dedicated to the art of coffee making, the tantalizing aroma of freshly ground beans reaches the highway. Plaques and photos tell of the island's coffee history. The shop sells excellent Arabic coffee, rum punches, Schrubb, (an orange liqueur), hot sauces, sachets of spices, bay-rum lotion, marmalades, and jewelry made from natural materials. Cocoa beans are also grown here. The "resident" chocolate-maker, a young French woman, also crafts bonbons and festive holiday candies with lots of dark chocolate and tropical fruit from the island. You will even see the coffee cars—emblazoned Volkswagen Beetles. The Chaulet family respects traditional procedures while bowing to modernity. Their latest product is coffee capsules. ✉ *The Bouchu, Vieux-Habitants* ☎ *0590/98–54–96* 🌐 *www.cafe-chaulet.com* 🎫 *Museum €6; shop free* 🕒 *Daily 9–5.*

POINTE-NOIRE

Pointe-Noire is a good jumping-off point from which to explore Basse-Terre's little-visited northwest coast. A road skirts magnificent cliffs and tiny coves, dances in and out of thick stands of mahogany and gommier trees, and weaves through unspoiled fishing villages with boats and ramshackle houses as brightly colored as a child's finger painting. This town has two small museums devoted to local products.

STE-ROSE

In addition to a sulfur bath, there are two good beaches (Amandiers and Clugny) and several interesting small museums in Ste-Rose.

Domaine de Séverin Distillery. At this historic rum distillery, a new, "Petit Train" crosses the plantation at 9:30, 10:30, and 11:30 am and again at 2 and 3 pm. (Hours are abbreviated in the low season, as is the train schedule.) The train passes by crayfish ponds (they farm the jumbo *ouassous*), golden fields of sugarcane, the distillery's working waterwheel, and the Big House, the former mansion of the Marsolle family, which has owned the habitation since 1928. The impressive great house, white-pillared with verandas on two stories, is now a museum open for touring. The estate is so picturesque and atmospheric—even a white gazebo with a red roof—that it was recently a film site for the Franco-British series, *Murder in Paradise*. A combination tasting room and gift shop sells rum, rum punches (liqueurs) spices, and hot sauces. The simple, open-air dining room here has a good menu and sometimes offers the jumbo crayfish. ✉ *Ste-Rose* ☎ *0590/28–91–86* 🌐 *www.severinrhum.com* 🎫 *€7 visit and rum tasting, €11 complete tour on the Petit Train and tasting* ⏲ *Daily 8:30–5:30 for the distillery and La Cave* ⏲ *La Cave and restaurant closed Sun. Restaurant closed Sept.*

ELSEWHERE ON BASSE-TERRE

TOP ATTRACTIONS

Cascade aux Ecrevisses. Within the Parc National de la Guadeloupe, Crayfish Falls is one of the island's loveliest (and most popular) spots. There's a marked trail (walk carefully—the rocks can be slippery) leading to this splendid waterfall, which dashes down into the Corossol River—a good place for a dip. Come early, though; otherwise you definitely won't have it to yourself. ✉ *St-Claude* 🌐 *www.guadeloupe-parcnational.com.*

Chutes du Carbet. You can reach three of the Carbet Falls (one drops from 65 feet, the second from 360 feet, the third from 410 feet) via a long, steep path from the village of Habituée. On the way up you pass the Grand Étang (Great Pond), a volcanic lake surrounded by interesting plant life. For horror fans there's also the curiously named Étang Zombi, a pond believed to house evil spirits. If there have been heavy rains, though, don't even think about going here. ✉ *St-Claude.*

Ilet de Pigeon. This tiny, rocky island a few hundred yards off the coast is the site of the Jacques Cousteau Underwater Park, the island's best scuba and snorkeling site. Although the reefs here are good, they don't rank among the top Caribbean dive spots. Several companies conduct diving trips to the reserve, and it's on the itinerary of some sailing and snorkeling trips *(⇨ Diving section in Sports and the Outdoors).* ✉ *Bouillante.*

Parc National de la Guadeloupe. This 74,100-acre park has been recognized by UNESCO as a Biosphere Reserve. Before going, pick up a *Guide to the National Park* from the tourist office; it rates the hiking trails according to difficulty, and most are quite difficult indeed. Most mountain trails are in the southern half. The park is bisected by the route de la Traversée, a 16-mile (26-km) paved road lined with masses of tree ferns, shrubs, flowers, tall trees, and green plantains. It's the ideal point of entry. Wear rubber-soled shoes and take along a swimsuit, a sweater, water, and perhaps food for a picnic. Try to get an early start to stay ahead of the hordes of cruise-ship passengers making a day of it. Check on the weather; if Basse-Terre has had a lot of rain, give it up. In the past, after intense rainfall, rockslides have closed the road for months. ✉ *Habitation Beausoleil-Montéran, BP-93, St-Claude* ☎ *0590/80–86–00* 🌐 *www.guadeloupe-parcnational.com* 🎫 *Free* 🕓 *Weekdays 8–5:30.*

DRAINAGE DITCHES

Whether you're driving a car or walking on an unlighted street at night, be aware that there are drainage ditches on the side of the road meant to catch the runoff after a rain. Because parking is at a premium, you will see cars straddling the ditches. Don't do it.

WORTH NOTING

Bouillante. The name means "boiling," and so it's no surprise that hot springs were discovered here. However, the biggest attraction is scuba diving on nearby Pigeon Island, which is accessed by boat from Plage de Malendure. There's a small information kiosk on the beach at Plage de Malendure that can help you with diving and snorkeling arrangements. ✉ *Bouillante.*

Les Mamelles. Two mountains—Mamelle de Petit-Bourg, at 2,350 feet, and Mamelle de Pigeon, at 2,500 feet—rise in the Parc National de la Guadeloupe. *Mamelle* means "breast," and when you see the mountains, you'll understand why they got their name. Trails ranging from easy to arduous lace up into the surrounding mountains. There's a glorious view from the lookout point 1,969 feet up Mamelle de Pigeon. If you're a climber, plan to spend several hours exploring this area. If there have been heavy rainfalls, cancel your plans. ✉ *St-Claude* 🌐 *www.guadeloupe-parcnational.com.*

ILES DES SAINTES

The eight-island archipelago of Iles des Saintes, often referred to as Les Saintes, dots the waters off the southern coast of Guadeloupe. The islands are Terre-de-Haut, Terre-de-Bas, Ilet à Cabrit, Grand Ilet, La Redonde, La Coche, Le Pâté, and Les Augustins. Columbus discovered them on November 4, 1493, and christened them Los Santos (Les Saintes in French) for All Saints' Day.

Only Terre-de-Haut and Terre-de-Bas are inhabited, with a combined population of little more than 3,000. Many of the Saintois are fair-haired, blue-eyed descendants of Breton and Norman sailors. Unless they are in the tourism industry, they tend to be taciturn and standoffish. Fishing still is their main source of income, and they take pride in their work. The shores are lined with their boats and *filets bleus* (blue nets dotted with orange buoys).

TERRE-DE-HAUT

With 5 square miles (13 square km) and a population of about 1,500, Terre-de-Haut is the largest and most developed of Les Saintes. Its "big city" is Bourg, with one main street lined with bistros, cafés, and shops. Clutching the hillside are trim white houses with bright red or blue doors, balconies, and gingerbread frills.

Terre-de-Haut's ragged coastline is scalloped with lovely coves and beaches, including the semi-nude beach at Anse Crawen. The beautiful bay, complete with a "sugarloaf" mountain, has been called a mini Rio. There are precious few vehicles or taxis on-island, so you'll often find yourself walking, despite the hilly terrain. Or you can add to the din and rent a motorbike. Take your time on these rutted roads, as around any bend there might be a herd of goats chomping on a fallen palm frond. Two traffic lights have brought a small amount of order to the motorbike hordes. When aggressively soliciting you, the scooter agencies will not tell you that it is prohibited to scoot in town from 9 to noon and from 2 to 4.

This island makes a great day trip, but you can really get a feel for Les Saintes if you stay overnight. It's not unlike St. Barths, but for a fraction of the price. Note: most shops and restaurants close for two hours in the afternoon. **■TIP→ A wonderful introduction to the island as well as a travel keepsake, is the coffee-table book *Carnet de Route-Les Saintes* on sale in shops for €20.**

Fort Napoléon. Also known as Louis Castle, this fort was built in 1777 by order of King Louis XVI, and was first known as a military tower. Renamed Napoléon Castle in 1805, it was strengthened by Vauban, a famous architect. However, it was never used for military purposes, although it did serve as a penitentiary in wartime. The museum here is notable for its exhaustive exhibit of the greatest sea battles ever fought. You can also visit the well-preserved barracks and prison cells, or admire the botanical gardens, which specialize in cacti. **■TIP→ This is a hill climb, and if you decide to walk, allow 30 minutes from the village, wear comfortable footwear, and bring water. You will be rewarded with outstanding views of the bay and neighboring islands.** ✉ *Grand Bourg* ☎ *0690/50–73–43* 🎫 *€5* ⏲ *Daily 9–12:30.*

MARIE-GALANTE

Columbus sighted this 60-square-mile (155-square-km) island on November 3, 1493, named it after his flagship, the *Maria Galanda,* and sailed on. It's dotted with ruined 19th-century sugar mills, and sugar is still its major product. Honey and 59% rum are its other favored harvests. You should make it a point to see one of the distilleries. With its rolling hills of green cane still worked by oxen and men with broad-brim straw hats, it's like traveling back in time to when all of Guadeloupe was still a giant farm.

Although it's only an hour by high-speed ferry from Pointe-à-Pitre, for the most part, the country folk here are still sweet and shy, and crime is a rarity. That said, driving, can be stressful thanks to young men in dark cars, rudely intimidating tourist-drivers.You can see swarms of yellow butterflies, and maybe a marriage carriage festooned with flowers, pulled by two white oxen. A daughter of the sea, Marie-Galante has some of the archipelago's most gorgeous, uncrowded beaches. Take time to explore the dramatic coast. You can find soaring cliffs—such as the Gueule Grand Gouffre (Mouth of the Giant Chasm) and Les Galeries (where the sea has sculpted a natural arcade)—and enormous sun-dappled grottos, such as Le Trou à Diable, whose underground river can be explored with a guide. Port Louis, the island's "second city," is the new hip spot. The ferry dock is in Port Louis, and it's also on the charts for yachts and regattas. After sunset, the no-see-ums and mosquitoes can be a real irritation, so always be armed with repellent. At different times of year, you might experience a lot of nature trying to enter your hotel.

TOP ATTRACTIONS

Fodor's Choice ★ **Domaine de Bellevue.** If time allows just one distillery, choose the modern Domaine de Bellevue. It's rum has taken home the gold during official French competitions. Free tastings are just one inviting element here. There are award-winning, pure rums (50%–59%); excellent tropical liqueurs (punches); coffee-table books; and local organic products. Bellevue is the top rum exporter of Guadeloupe/Marie-Galante with the only eco-positive distillery in the world.

Down from one of only two restored windmills (c. 1821) on-island, is a boutique with everything made from natural materials, such as calabash gourds. ✉ *Section Bellevue, Capesterre* ☎ *0590/97–26–50* 🎫 *Free* 🕒 *Daily 9:30–1.*

Kreol West Indies. This fascinating museum, in a renovated bungalow, houses information and graphics on Guadeloupe's early Indians, as well as some pirate artifacts. Rooms are furnished with antiques and collectibles that depict island life during various eras, up through the 1950s. Devoted to creole culture, the museum also doubles as an art gallery, with attractive contemporary paintings by island artists. This labor of love, displays furnishings and descriptives owned by a professional French hotelier, Vincent Nicaudie. The gift shop carries quality, Marie-Galante logoized T-shirts and caps, beach wear, and island food products. Also, this is a Wi-Fi hotspot. ✉ *Plage de Grand Bourg, rue Beaurenon prolongee, Grand-Bourg* ✣ *100 meters after exiting the town, continue in the direction of Capesterre and it is right on the road, on the right* ☎ *0590/97–21–56* 🌐 *www.kreolwestindies.com* 🎫 *Free* 🕒 *Daily 9:30–noon and 2–6:30.*

WORTH NOTING

Château Murat. A mile from town, the Château Murat is a 19th-century sugar plantation and rum distillery housing exhibits on the history of rum making and sugarcane production that goes back three centuries. This former habitation was once the grandest sugar plantation in Guadeloupe. Various hurricanes left the chateau in ruins, with just remnants of the kitchen, etc., still standing. From the rubble rose the eco-museum which celebrates island crafts and there is a garden for medicinal local plants. ✉ *Rte. de Capesterre, Grand-Bourg* ☎ *0590/97–48–68* 🎫 *Free* 🕒 *Weekdays 9–1 and 2:30–5:30, weekends 9–1.*

Distillerie Poisson "Rhum du Père Labat." The Poisson Distillery produces rum (nearly 200,000 liters a year) that is considered some of the finest in the Caribbean, and its atelier turns out lovely pottery. Tastings are available, but watch out—those samples are quite strong, especially considering that it is only open in the morning! ✉ *Section Poisson, Grand-Bourg* 🎫 *Free* 🕒 *Mon.–Sat. 7–noon.*

LA DÉSIRADE

Desirable is the operative word here. This small, safe, somewhat remote island is an absolute find for those who prefer a road less traveled, who want their beaches long and white, and who don't mind that accommodations are simple if the price is right. The Désirade populace (all 1,700 of them) welcome tourism and these dear hearts have a warm, old-fashioned sense of community.

> **COMPETITIONS DES BOEUFS TIRANTS**
>
> The annual ox-pulling competitions on Marie-Galante go on for two weeks in November. Oxen were used for the sugar mills and still power the agriculture. Where else will you see this in your lifetime?

According to legend, the "desired land" was so named by the crew of Christopher Columbus, whose tongues were dry for want of fresh water when they spied the island; alas, it was the season for drought. The 8-square-mile (21-square-km) island, 5 miles (8 km) east of St-François, is a chalky plateau, with an arid climate, perennial sunshine, cacti, and iguanas. You may even see two male iguanas locked in a prehistoric-looking battle. Rent a four-wheel drive to climb the zigzag road that leads to the Grande Montagne. Make a photo stop at the diminutive white chapel, which offers a panorama of the sea below. Afraid that you might zig instead of zag down the precipice? Then take a fun, informative van tour that you join near the tourist office at the harbor near the ferry dock. The ruins of the original settlement—a leper colony—are on the tour.

Only one road runs around the perimeter of the island, and if you're interested in visiting one of the many gorgeous beaches shaded by coconut palms and sea grape trees, you can do that on a scooter. Driving is safer here than most anywhere.

BEACHES

Guadeloupe is an archipelago of five paradises surrounded by both the Caribbean and the Atlantic. Its beaches run the spectrum from white to black. There are idyllic beaches, long stretches of unspoiled beach shaded by coconut palms, with soft, warm sand. Hotel beaches are generally narrow, although well maintained. Some hotels allow nonguests who patronize their restaurants to use their beach facilities. The popular public beaches tend to be cluttered with campers-turned-cafés and cars parked in impromptu lots on the sand. Sunday is the big day, but these same (free) beaches are often quiet during the week.

On the southern coast of Grande-Terre, from Ste-Anne to Pointe des Châteaux, you can find stretches of soft white sand and some sparsely visited areas. The Atlantic waters on the northeast coast are too rough for swimming. Along the western shore of Basse-Terre signposts indicate small beaches. The sand starts turning gray in Malendure; it becomes volcanic black farther south. There's only one official nude beach, Pointe Tarare, but topless bathing is common.

Looking out over Marie-Galante

GRANDE-TERRE

L'Autre Bord. The waves on this Atlantic beach give the long expanse of sand a wild look. The beach is protected by an extensive coral reef, which makes it safe for children. Further out, the waves draw surfers and windsurfers. From its location right in the town of Moule, you can stroll along a seaside promenade fringed by flamboyant trees (also known as flame trees). Many shade trees offer protection; the swaying coconut palms are more for photo composition. Sidewalk cafes provide sustenance. **Amenities:** food and drink; parking (no fee); toilets. **Best for:** surfing; swimming; walking; windsurfing. ✉ *Moule, Grande-Terre.*

Plage Caravelle. Just southwest of Ste-Anne is one of Grande-Terre's longest and prettiest stretches of sand, the occasional dilapidated shack notwithstanding. Protected by reefs, it's also a fine snorkeling spot. Club Med occupies one end of this beach, and nonguests can enjoy its beach and water sports, as well as lunch and drinks, by buying a day pass. You can also have lunch on the terrace of La Toubana Hotel & Spa, then descend the stairs to the beach or enjoy lunch at its beach restaurant, wildly popular on Sunday. **Amenities:** food and drink; parking (no fee); toilets; water sports. **Best for:** partiers; snorkeling; sunset; swimming; walking; windsurfing. ✉ *Rte. N4, southwest of Ste-Anne, Ste-Anne, Basse-Terre.*

Plage de la Chapelle à Anse-Bertrand. If you want a delightful day trip to the northern tip of Grande-Terre, aim for this spot, one of the loveliest white-sand beaches, whose gentle midafternoon waves are popular with families. It's shaded by coconut palms, there are the ruins of a chapel to explore, and the sea kayaking's excellent. When the tide rolls in, it's equally popular with surfers. Several little terrace restaurants are at the far end of the beach, but you might want to bring your own mat or beach towel, because no one rents chaises longues. The town has remained relatively undeveloped. **Amenities:** food and drink; showers; toilets. **Best for:** solitude; sunrise; sunset; surfing; swimming; walking; windsurfing. ✉ *4 miles (6½ km) south of La Pointe de la Grand Vigie, Grande-Terre.*

Plage du Helleux. Except on Sunday, this long stretch of wild beach—framed by dramatic cliffs—is often completely deserted in the morning or early afternoon. By 4 pm, though, you might find 70 or so young surfers. Many locals take their young children here, but use caution with your own, because the current can be strong. The beach has no facilities of its own, but you can get lunch and drinks at the Hotel Eden Palm. To get here, follow the signs to Hotel Eden Palm and pass the hotel; the beach is down the dirt road to the right. **Amenities:** none. **Best for:** solitude; partiers; surfing; swimming; walking. ✉ *Rte. N4, Lieu-dit le Helleux, St. Anne, Grande-Terre.*

Pointe Tarare. This secluded strip just before the tip of Pointe des Châteaux is the island's only nude beach. (Technically, this is not allowed by French law.) Small bar-cafés are in the parking area, but it's still best to bring some water, snacks, and beach chairs, because there's no place to rent them. What you do have is one of the coast's most dramatic landscapes; looming above are rugged cliffs topped by a huge crucifix. When approaching St-François Marina, go in the direction of Pointe des Châteaux at the roundabout and drive for about 10 minutes. **Amenities:** food and drink; parking (no fee); toilets. **Best for:** solitude; partiers; sunset; swimming; walking. ✉ *Rte. N4, southeast of St-François, Grande-Terre.*

BASSE-TERRE

Plage de la Grande-Anse. One of Guadeloupe's widest beaches has soft beige sand sheltered by palms. To the west it's a round verdant mountain. It has a large parking area and some food stands, but no other facilities. The beach can be overrun on Sunday, not to mention littered, due to the food carts. Right after the parking lot, you can see signage for the creole restaurant Le Karacoli; if you have lunch there (it's not cheap), you can *sieste* on the chaises longues. At the far end of the beach, which is more virgin territory, is Tainos Cottages, which has a restaurant. **Amenities:** food and drink; parking (no fee). **Best for:** partiers; solitude; swimming; walking. ✉ *Rte. N6, north of Deshaies, Deshaies, Basse-Terre.*

Plage de Malendure. Across from Pigeon Island and the Jacques Cousteau Underwater Park, this long, gray, volcanic beach on the Caribbean's calm waters has restrooms, a few beach shacks offering cold drinks and snacks, and a huge parking lot. There might be some litter, but the beach is cleaned regularly. Don't come here for solitude, as the beach is a launch point for many dive boats. The snorkeling's good. Le Rocher de Malendure, a fine seafood restaurant, is perched on a cliff over the bay. Food carts work the parking lot. **Amenities:** food and drink; parking (no fee); toilets. **Best for:** partiers; snorkeling; swimming. ✉ *Rte. N6, Bouillante, Basse-Terre.*

ILES DES SAINTES

FAMILY **Pompierre Bay.** This beach is particularly popular with families with small children, as there's a gradual slope, no drop-off, and a long stretch of shallow water. The calm water also makes for good snorkeling. The isles of Les Saintes offer outstanding snorkeling and scuba diving. On the other end of the island, the conditions are not as good as at Pain de Sucre, but the shouldered sandy bay is larger and there are a lot of fish. Saintois women may be at the entrance selling snacks and drinks. The curve of the beach is called the Bridge of Stone and you can walk it—carefully—taking a dip in the crater that fills with water from the Atlantic. Morning sun is best; then, return to Salako for some grilled fresh fish and a cold one. **Amenities:** food and drink. **Best for:** snorkeling; sunrise; swimming; walking. ✉ *Terre-de-Haut, Iles des Saintes* ✣ *Go to the seamen's church near the main plaza, and then head in the direction of Marigot. Continue until you see Le Salako Snack Bar and voilà! you'll spy a palm-fringed, half-moon bay with some 2,600 feet of tawny sand.*

LA DÉSIRADE

Le Soufleur Plage. To reach one of La Désirade's longest and best beaches from the ferry dock, face town and follow the main road to the right. It's about 15 minutes by car or motor scooter (about €20 a day). White sand, calm waters, and snacks and cold drinks from the beach restaurant await, but there are no chaises, so BYO beach towel or mat. **Amenities:** food and drink; toilets. **Best for:** solitude; snorkeling; sunset; swimming; walking. ✉ *Rd. 207, La Désirade.*

MARIE-GALANTE

Anse de Vieux Fort. This gorgeous Marie-Galante beach stretches alongside crystal clear waters that border a large body of freshwater that is ideal for canoeing. It's a surprising contrast from the nearby mangrove swamp you can discover on the hiking trails. The beaches in this area are wide because of the erosion of the sand dunes. It's known as a beach for lovers because of the solitude. Bring your own everything. You can pair a visit to Château Murat with your beach day. **Amenities:** none. **Best for:** solitude; snorkeling; sunset; swimming; walking. ✉ *Rte. D205, Marie-Galante.*

Plage de Petite-Anse. This long, golden beach on Marie-Galante is punctuated with sea grape trees. It's idyllic during the week, but on weekends the crowds of locals and urban refugees from the main island arrive. Le Touloulou's great creole seafood restaurant provides the only facilities. The golden sands are ideal for shelling. **Amenities:** food and drink; parking (no fee); toilets. **Best for:** partiers; snorkeling; sunset; swimming; walking. ✉ *6½ miles (10 km) north of Grand-Bourg via rte. D203, Marie-Galante.*

WHERE TO EAT

Creole cooking is the result of a fusion of influences: African, European, Indian, and Caribbean. It's colorful, spicy, and made up primarily of local seafood and vegetables (including squash-like christophines), root vegetables, and plantains, always with a healthy dose of pepper sauce. Favorite appetizers include *accras* (salted codfish fritters), *boudin* (highly seasoned blood sausage), and *crabes farcis* (stuffed land crabs). *Langouste* (lobster), *lambi* (conch), *chatrou* (octopus), and *ouassous* (crayfish) are considered delicacies. *Souchy* (Tahitian-style ceviche), raw fish that is "cooked" when marinated in lime juice or similar marinades, is best at seafront restaurants. *Moules et frites* (mussels in broth served with fries) can be found at cafés, both in the Marina in St-François and Bas du Fort Marina. Also in the marina is Rótisseur des Isles, with aromatic roasted meats, a salad bar, and classic French desserts. The chef/owner, Gerard Lopinto has received awards for his cooking skills. Many of the most contemporary, gastronomic restaurants are in Jarry, a commercial area near Pointe-à-Pitre. All restaurants and bars are smoke-free, as decreed by French law.

Diverse culinary options range from pizza and crepes to Indian cuisine. For a quick and inexpensive meal, visit a *boulangerie,* where you can buy luscious French pastries and simple baguette sandwiches. Look for the recommendable chain Baguet. Good news: menu prices seem high but include tax and service (which is split among the entire staff). If service is to your liking, be generous and leave some extra euros, and they will think of Americans as "the good guys." In most restaurants in Guadeloupe (as throughout the Caribbean), lobster is the most expensive item on the menu. It can easily top €40 and often comes as part of a prix-fixe menu*; price ranges for the restaurants listed in this chapter do not include lobster for this reason.*

What to Wear: Dining is casual at lunch, but beach attire is a "not" except at the more laid-back marina and beach eateries. Dinner is slightly more formal. Long pants, collared shirts, and skirts or dresses are appreciated, although not required. Guadeloupean ladies like to "dress," particularly on weekends, so don't arrive in flip-flops—they'll be in heels.

GRANDE-TERRE

$$$ ECLECTIC

Café Wango. At this alfresco hot spot, Asian wok dishes, sushi, skewers, fish carpaccios, and tartares dominate the menu, and there are no fewer than nine better-than-average salads. There are also pricey pastas and daily specials like a classic sirloin in a Roquefort-poivre sauce. Kids are crazy for the ice cream and beg parents for *un coupe* (a sundae). So many flavors, so little time. Facing the marina's boat slips, the modern furnishings are charcoal gray and burnt orange juxtaposed with flamingo pink walls and napkins. The seats are often filled with a fun, discerning crowd of mainly French expats; parked nearby there may be a couple of Harleys, flying tiny American flags. $ *Average main:*

€21 ✉ St-François Marina, Marines 1, St-François ☎ 0590/83–50–41 🌐 www.cafewango.com ⊙ Closed June 17–July 6.

$$$ ECLECTIC Fodor's Choice ★ ✕ **Iguane Café.** Iguanas are indeed the theme here, and you can still spy them in unexpected places—but their numbers have diminished and the room now has a clean, contemporary appeal, just like the china and glassware. The salon seating for cocktails has a homey feel, with basket-weave rattan furniture and hot-pink accent pillows. Unquestionably original cuisine with Asian, Indian, Creole, and African influences is chef Sylvain Serouart's trademark. Two amuse-bouches will arrive, and there is usually a wonderful foie-gras appetizer—with a vintage-rum crème brûlée and a papaya compote. Follow with a lobster ravioli dashed with lime, tinted with saffron. The menu is always evolving. Desserts are contemporary marvels like a cacao ice-orange-cake. This is a pricey place, but recently it's become a bit more egalitarian, now allowing guests to compose their own three-course prix fixe. $ *Average main: €30 ✉ Rte. de La Pointe des Châteaux, ½ mile (¾ km) from airport, St-François ☎ 0590/88–61–37 🌐 www.iguane-cafe.com ⊙ Closed Tues. No lunch Mon.–Sat. ☞ Prix fixe €45.*

13

$$$ INDIAN ✕ **La Porte des Indes.** Dining here is truly a departure: the open-air pergola, the blue gates, the pungent aromas, and the bust of Ganesha. Within the paisley-covered menu you can find authentic Indian dishes alongside such adaptations as boneless curried chicken with crème fraîche, cashews, and raisins. Vegetarian are catered to here, and an eggplant purée is one of the better options. Children may fill up on the addictive Indian cheese naan bread and be too stuffed for *kulfi,* Indian ice cream that's topped here with ginger confit. The welcome here is always warm, and the service dignified. The Indian chef-owner, Karious Arthur, has a culinary degree from Paris and worked for years in France. Consistently good, the restaurant's perennial popularity means that on weekends you really should make reservations. $ *Average main: €30 ✉ Desvarieux, St-François ☎ 0590/21–30–87 ⊙ Closed mid-Sept.–mid-Oct. and Mon. No lunch Tues.–Sat. No dinner Sun.*

$$$$ FRENCH ✕ **La Toubana Restaurant** (*Le Gran Bleu*). Fresh lobsters, which swim in the canals that beautify the deck, draw many diners. There is always foie gras, both hot and cold. The French food here often gets a delicious Caribbean infusion, as in the fillet of *daurade* with a vanilla sauce, or the passion-fruit tart with a meringue. The inside dining room, although open-air, has deep leather chairs, and, on occasion, a piano player and live music by pop-rock vocalists; local music is the norm on Thursday night. You can listen whether you just "take a pop" (drink) or have dinner. Lunch patrons dine on the terrace near the infinity pool. With your feet dangling in the water and an exotic cocktail in hand, you can watch the sea churn below. The hotel's other lunch option is the beach restaurant, not going full tilt every day, but surely on the weekends. It's more casual, with grilled brochettes as one example. $ *Average main: €35 ✉ La Toubana Hotel & Spa, BP-63-Fonds Thezan, Ste-Anne, Basse-Terre ☎ 0590/88–25–57.*

$$$ FRENCH FUSION ✕ **Le Mabouya dans la Bouteille.** This fine dining restaurant in St-François has consistently good Franco-fusion cuisine. The French couple who owned a Parisian restaurant for eight years before setting up shop here

don't always extend the same hospitality to English-speaking tourists as French patrons, but that and the impractical, silky, maroon napkins aside, this open-air venue is cozy and inviting with displays of vintage corkscrews, etc. (The wine cave doubles as a bottle shop.) More good news, an amuse-bouche may be offered and a mint punch as a digestive. *$ Average main: €27 ✉ 17 Saline Est, St-François ⊕ 5-min walk from marina ☎ 0590/21–31–14 ✍ Reservations essential ⊗ Closed Tues. night. No lunch.*

$$$ FRENCH

✕ **Restaurant la Vieille Tour.** A historic sugar mill is the backdrop for the artistic creations here, which take refined French cuisine and incorporate culinary trends and local produce. As the hotel's only restaurant, it tries to be all things to all guests. The lunch menu is a mix of classic restaurant food and lighter dishes. A *formule* (prix fixe) of a main course, a starter or dessert, a glass of wine, and coffee is available for €42. A creole menu is available on Thursday and Sunday nights; other evenings feature a more classically French menu. Roasted veal rib with chanterelles and seared sea scallops topped with passion-fruit butter are elegantly delicious. Desserts are dazzling, with the pastry chef turning out towers, sauces, and glacés. On Friday and Saturday nights, a piano man plays in the lounge. *$ Average main: €26 ✉ Auberge de la Vieille Tour, Rte. 1, Montauban 97, Gosier ☎ 0590/84–23–23 ✍ Reservations essential.*

$$$ SEAFOOD Fodor's Choice ★

✕ **Zawag.** At this secret hideaway you'll see the churning sea below and hear the waves crashing against the coral rock upon which it sits. The interior architecture is all hardwood with matching furniture and white linen napkins at dinnertime. Primarily a grill, the simplicity is reflected in the food offerings. Kids are particularly fascinated when the lobster net is dipped into the tank and the thrashing begins. The fish of the night is fresh from the waters below, often accompanied by creole or tropical-fruit sauces. Creole dishes and sides that were gently contemporized by a French chef, are offered as nightly specials. Chef Nicolas Bonnot has impressive credentials, and he honed his seafood cooking while in Tahiti. His presentations are beautifully exotic. And what's a Zawag? Why, that's a tropical fish that swims in the water that guests see through the open shutters. *$ Average main: €22 ✉ La Créole Beach Hotel & Spa, Pointe de la Verdure, Gosier ☎ 0590/90–46–46 ✍ Reservations essential ⊗ Closed Sun. and Sept.*

BASSE-TERRE

$$$ CARIBBEAN

✕ **Chez Clara.** As a jazz dancer, Clara worked her way through Europe's capitals. She was always a colorful character, and her restaurant is equally vivid; even the napkins offer a splash of color. Her brother has taken over, keeping the landmark restaurant in the family, and Clara still makes cameo appearances. The food here is is haute creole. The curries are intoxicating, and the chef has a remarkable way of preparing *lambi* (conch), octopus, and local fish, as well as preparing delicious paella and couscous. The apricot tarte tatin is *tres bonne*. A dessert surprise is sweet potato pie, a recipe from a Carolina girl who was Clara's roomie in Paris. *$ Average main: €21 ✉ Bord de Mer, Ste-Rose ☎ 0590/28–72–99 ⊗ No dinner Wed. and Sun.*

$$$ SEAFOOD ✕ **Le Rocher de Malendure.** Guests first climb the worn yellow stairs, and the decks of various levels because of the panoramic sea views, but they return again and again for the food. The view is gorgeous in daylight, and you watch the dive boats going to Pigeon islands and a veritable parade of marine action. Begin with a perfectly executed mojito. Fish is fresh off the boat, so don't hesitate to try the sushi *antillaise* or grilled crayfish; or better yet have these jumbos in a rich cream and rum-laced sauce—a two-napkin affair as the shells are left on. Select your lobster from a pool. The fresh fish is the way to go here, served with a passion-fruit sauce, a vanilla sauce, or sauce chien (spicy creole sauce.) *[$] Average main: €25 ✉ Bord de Mer, Malendure de Pigeon, Bouillante ☎ 0590/98–70–84 ⏲ Closed Tues. and Sept.–early Oct. ☞ Reserve ahead of time for tables with views.*

$$$ FRENCH ✕ **Restaurant La Savane.** Even if there's a downpour, a terrace table right on the crystalline Deshaies Bay is a dream fulfilled. Besides, La Savane's roof overhang (with gingerbread fretwork) will keep you dry, and the music and food does a lot to keep spirits high here. Part of the fascination with this gastronomique outpost is that the owning family has a most unusual, vastly international background that influences the operation. Emilia, the mother, is Portuguese, yet she lived in Angola (Africa) for 15 years, thus the African decor and name. The father, Vincent, is French and was a candy maker in Switzerland. Daughter Tatiana is the welcoming English-speaking server. Her dad's desserts are not to be missed, like the tarte tatin with Calvados-infused butter. Among the mains, the giant crayfish in red curry/coconut milk has proved successful. Chef Vincent prides himself on the freshest fish and product; lobster must be ordered in advance as he gets them in live. Some diners feel that Savane is expensive, but quality ingredients coupled with creativity make for happy forks. *[$] Average main: €22 ✉ Blvd. des Poissonniers, Deshaie ☎ 0690/75–70–57 🌐 www.restaurant-la-savane-deshaies.com ✍ Reservations essential ⏲ Closed Wed. No lunch in low season. No lunch Mon.–Thurs. in high season.*

ILES DES SAINTES

$$$ CAFÉ ✕ **Couleurs du Monde.** Vivid Caribbean colors of pink, yellow, and green all pop at this fun waterfront café, where the free Wi-Fi, books and newspapers, teas and coffees, wine, and icy rum cocktails all encourage lounging. Sushi, smoked-fish plates, and smoked duck salad often appear on the appetizer menu. The catch of the day with an exotic sauce is usually a good choice. After sunset there are aperitifs, and although reservations are requested for dinner, the friendly, accommodating staff also takes walk-ins. Finish off with the house-made punch *du monde*. This is one of the few island restaurants that does not close between lunch and dinner. To get here from the main dock, take a left to the main street and walk two blocks. It's across from the kayak-rental company. *[$] Average main: €25 ✉ Le Mouillage, Terre-de-Haut ☎ 0590/92–70–98 ⏲ Closed Sept. and Oct.*

$$$ ECLECTIC ✕ **Restaurant Les Petits Saints.** Chef Xavier Simon is remarkably inventive with the fresh local produce and seafood, as in his Asian-style *lambi* (conch) with noodles, conch lasagna, crab canneloni. Grilled lobster

is a signature dish of the restaurant, and he does a lobster salad with citrus. The meat selection changes as does the vegan, no-gluten special. Contemporary dinnerware brought from France complements the menu and presentation. A lot of effort has gone into the wine menu, and the selection of a full range of aged rums from Guadeloupe. For the finale, there are some dazzling desserts, like panna cotta with hibiscus sauce. Service is on the veranda, where the night sounds of the tropics vie with jazz and French music. Guests could benefit from more selections on the menu and some feel it's too pricey. *Average main: €24* *Hotel Restaurant les Petits Saints, La Savane, Terre-de-Haut* *0590/99–50–99* *www.petitssaints.com* *Reservations essential* *Closed Mon. and Sept. No lunch. Check ahead for summer hrs, which vary.*

$$$ FRENCH

Ti Kaz La. This small, convivial waterfront restaurant has a lot to recommend. It's artsy, with contemporary, original works, hanging plants, hip music, and a talented chef-owner, Philippe Dade. Fresh fish grilled, accompanied by chien and passion-fruit sauces—plus authentic *pomme frites,* makes an ideal lunch out on the beach terrace. *Le choucroute de la mer* has fish, scallops, and mussels in a white wine sauce. There are two well-priced, three-course, prix-fix menus; the €20 one has a choice of mains—either chicken in coconut sauce or a fricassee of octopus. For €40 you can have baked lobster plus a starter and a dessert. For dessert, one pouffed marvel—a mango soufflé with raspberry coulis—must be ordered in advance. (If having a prix fixe, there is a supplement.) *Average main: €22* *10 rue Benoit Cassin, Terre-de-Haut* *0590/99–57–63, 0690/65–52–28* *www.tikazla.com* *Closed 2–7. Closed Wed.*

MARIE-GALANTE

$$ CARIBBEAN

Chez Henri. This hip place on the water, flanked by the town pier, is named for its passionate chef-owner, Henri Vergerolle. An island character, he spent much of his life in France and returned to create this combination restaurant and cultural center. Begin with a rum and fresh-squeezed juice. Smoked fish can be a component of a salad or an appetizer; the creole omelet is quite an original, with breadfruit and sweet potatoes. Another innovation is the fish of the day with a Caribe sauce. Everything is fresh here, but alas, the menu might only have three main courses available. But just kick back and listen to African blues and view the latest art or sculpture exhibits. You might have the good luck to be here when there's a live music concert. They rock. *Average main: €17* *8 rue des Caraibes, St-Louis, Marie-Galante* *0590/97–04–57* *www.chezhenri.net* *Closed Mon. No lunch Tues.–Thurs. from Sept.–early Oct.*

$$ SEAFOOD Fodor's Choice ★

Le Touloulou. On the curve of Plage de Petite-Anse, this casual eatery has tables in the sand. Stylish Euro furnishings are here, as are marine-blue hammocks—perfect for chilling between courses. Chef José Viator serves the freshest, most delicious seafood. like fish carpaccio; his standout dish just might be fricassee of conch or octopus with breadfruit. And you may never see Bebele, a flavorful creole dish with dumplings, anywhere else. Set menus start at €20-something, and a simple, fresh lobster prix fixe is €35. For lunch, the best value is the *formule rapid.* Both the chicken and the *ouassous* (jumbo crayfish) in coconut sauce are exceptional, as is the smoked chicken in pineapple sauce. You can be assured that the fish carpaccios are fresh. On Saturday and Sunday, the Creole Brunch (from 11 to 4) is particularly celebratory. Pergola's, the circular bar, with its new blue sail installation overhead, has the best rum cocktails. On weekend nights the anteroom is a dance club, with salsa lessons on Friday and a disco beat on Saturday. *Average main: €18 Plage de Petite-Anse, Capesterre 0590/97-32-63 www.letouloulou.com Closed mid-Sept.–mid-Oct. No dinner Sun.*

$$$ FRENCH FUSION Fodor's Choice ★ **Manman'dlo Restaurant.** If on Marie-Galante you may hear that one of the best tables is found at the small *hotel de charme* La Rose du Brésil, the rumor is true. Chef Bertrand, who came by way of Corsica, is an international talent. First, order a fresh-squeezed lime daiquiri. You will likely want two. A surprising appetizer is a delicate samosa filled with lightly curried chicken and side greens dressed with a sweet vinaigrette–salty 'n' sweet! The pièce de la résistance is a fresh, grilled lobster tail accompanied by a perfect risotto and bisque. The flaky pineapple tart with pineapple ice cream is a delightful palate cleanser. *Average main: €28 La Rose du Brésil, Rte. du litoral, Capesterre 0590/97–47–39 www.larosedubresil.com Reservations essential.*

LA DÉSIRADE

$$ CARIBBEAN FAMILY **Oualiri Breeze Restaurant.** On tables in the sand, on the covered terrace, and under a conical tent, this beachfront eatery lays out a bountiful creole buffet on Friday nights and for Sunday brunch. Both are accompanied by live entertainment. You can always grab a Continental breakfast, lunch, or dinner, and customize your own €15.50 prix fixe. Seafood is the obvious specialty, particularly creole fricassees of lambi (conch) and chatrou. Sidle up to the fieldstone bar for a perfect planter's punch, and between courses, jump into the sea. Children have their own menus and love that this is also a *glacier* (ice-cream shop) with a litany of flavors; drizzle your scoops with cajou (cashew) syrup. P.S. You can check your email here. Also, the affable, English-speaking owner, Theodore Compper, will pick you up at the dock or airport. *Average main: €15 Plage Beausejour, Beau Sejour, Le Désirade 0590/20–20–08, 0690/71–24–76 www.im-caraibes.com/oualiri.*

WHERE TO STAY

Most of the island's resort hotels are on Grande-Terre: Gosier, St-François, and Bas-du-Fort are generally considered major resort areas, as is Ste-Anne. With each passing year, the hotels here improve. The Swedish-owned Langley Resort Fort Royal has breathed new life into the north of Basse-Terre, the closest area of that island to Pointe-à-Pitre and Grande-Terre. In general, more tourists are discovering this area, loving the small hotels and unspoiled nature.

Often, hotel rates include a generous buffet breakfast; ask whether this is included in your rate quote. (It usually is.) Many smaller properties do not accept American Express. As dictated by French law, all public spaces in hotels are no-smoking, but hotel rooms are considered private, and properties can choose to offer smoking rooms.

PRIVATE VILLAS AND RENTALS

French Caribbean International. French Caribbean International handles hotel arrangements and private villa rentals, from charming cottages in Basse-Terre ($130 to $350 a night) to deluxe sea-view villas in Grande-Terre ($2,600 to $7,000 per week), all with pools. With three decades of experience in the French Caribbean, including Les Saintes and Marie-Galante, the company has a global reputation for honesty, exceptional service, and professionalism. They can also dispense information on just about everything you need to know about the French islands. ☎ *805/967–9850 in U.S.* 🌐 *www.frenchcaribbean.com.*

prestigevillarental.com. An online agency that provides luxury villa rental services to the French Caribbean, their site is contemporary and comprehensive with an excellent English version, photos of every room and detailed descriptions. Rental properties range from deluxe to over-the-top, such as the most high-end rental in Terre de Haut, Villa Les Saintes. It's a real blend of luxury and the island's unique charm. Prestige has villas that are handpicked for celebratory occasions, everything from honeymoon hideaways to contemporary mansions for family reunions. They have handled corporate retreats and anniversaries. Their concierge service can provision villas or arrange private chefs and housekeepers, orchestrate tours and shopping excursions and in-house spa services. Villas can have everything from Wi-Fi to pool guys. The agency's young bilingual owner, who grew up on Guadeloupe, writes an impressive blog giving tips on "doing" the French islands. He honed his rental skills in St. Barts, where he became a villa specialist. ✉ *Grande-Terre* ☎ *917/720–3120 in U.S.* 🌐 *www.prestigevillarental.com.*

GRANDE-TERRE

$ HOTEL **Auberge de la Vieille Tour.** At this island classic built around an historic sugar mill, everyone loves the initial welcome: a cool drink and citrus-scented towels dispensed by ladies in white-eyelet uniforms. **Pros:** most rooms have great views; breakfast is a highlight; restaurant is one of the better ones on-island. **Cons:** exteriors of some sections are unattractive 1960s-style; it's a hill climb back from the beach and pool, which is slated to be redone, but not soon enough. *Rooms from: €250* ✉ *Rte. de Montauban, Gosier, Grande-Terre* ☎ *0590/84–23–23* 🌐 *www.auberge-vieille-tour.fr* *70 rooms, 32 deluxe rooms, 1 suite* *Breakfast.*

$ HOTEL **Bwa Chik Hotel & Golf.** This eco-chic, boutique hotel at the marina is the buzz in St-François for its unique decor; recycled wood and driftwood are juxtaposed with ultracontemporary Euro furnishings and gauzy, salmon-hued drapes. **Pros:** ideal location; car unnecessary; welcoming staff; live jazz nights in season. **Cons:** small pool; no elevators or bellmen; standard rooms could be larger. *Rooms from: €146* ✉ *Ave. d'l Europe, St-François, Grande-Terre* ☎ *0590/88–60–60* 🌐 *www.bwachik.com* *43 rooms, 11 duplexes* *Breakfast.*

$$ ALL-INCLUSIVE FAMILY Fodor's Choice ★ **Club Med La Caravelle.** Facing the island's best white-sand beaches, La Caravelle is one of the original clubs in the Caribbean, yet all the facilities—including the seafront restaurant and its deck—have a smashing, contemporary look. **Pros:** a large fun quotient; exceptional boutique; good service. **Cons:** Club Med experience and kid-friendly atmosphere is not for everyone; older standard rooms are small; Wi-Fi is extra. *Rooms from: €345 Quartier Caravelle, Ste-Anne, Basse-Terre 0590/85–49–50, 800/258–2633 www.clubmed.us 260 rooms, 37 suites All-inclusive.*

$ B&B/INN **Hotel Amaudo.** This *hôtel de charme* (boutique hotel) is a small *madam-et-monsieur* operation, the mom 'n' pop being the sophisticated French managers. **Pros:** a moderate price tag for unobstructed sea views; safe (mechanized security gate); well-maintained and renovated when needed. **Cons:** you need a car, as it is not in the tourist zone of St-François; no bar, restaurant, or activities; could be too quiet and peaceful. *Rooms from: €154 Anse à la Barque, St-François, Grande-Terre 0590/88–87–00 www.amaudo.fr 9 rooms, 1 suite Breakfast.*

$$ HOTEL **La Cocoteraie.** This boutique hotel's lobby, overlooking a glorious pool and with basket-weave rattan furnishings and decorative masks, is a study in refinement. **Pros:** by a calm lagoon; sophisticated clientele; international crowd and light fare at the Indigo Bar; excellent location in St-François. **Cons:** generic, white-plastic furniture on terraces; some ongoing maintenance issues; not as fun as it used to be; simply, this property has to be revitalized—as in major refurbishment. *Rooms from: €300 Av. de l'Europe, St-François, Grande-Terre 0590/88–79–81 www.lacocoteraie.com 52 suites Breakfast.*

$ RESORT Fodor's Choice ★ **La Créole Beach Hotel & Spa.** This 10-acre complex has a contemporary, colorful lobby, cosmopolitan bar, and dual pools that are surrounded by gray market umbrellas and silver patio furniture. **Pros:** excellent management and long-term staff; lovely tropical gardens; exceptionally good buffets and the entire restaurant has been refreshed. **Cons:** some rooms quite a hike from lobby; beach is nice but small; Wi-Fi costs extra and needs code. *Rooms from: €230 Pointe de la Verdure, Gosier, Grande-Terre 0590/90–46–46 www.deshotelsetdesiles.com 276 rooms, 16 junior suites, 6 suites, 13 apartments No meals.*

$$ RESORT Fodor's Choice ★ **La Toubana Hôtel & Spa.** Few hotels on Guadeloupe command such a panoramic view of the sea—spanning four islands, no less. **Pros:** a special boutique experience with sophisticated style; glass-enclosed cocktail lounge–library has remarkable views; praise-worthy restaurant continues to evolve. **Cons:** the little beach is down the hill, via a very steep paved path; bedrooms and TVs are small by American standards; some bungalows need renovation. *Rooms from: €304 Grande-Terre 0590/88–25–57 www.toubana.com 32 bungalows, 1 studio suite, 5 1-bedroom suites, 9 2-bedroom suites, 3 4-bedroom villas Breakfast.*

BASSE-TERRE

$ B&B/INN FAMILY **Caraïb'Bay Hotel.** This complex of colorful duplex bungalows may not impress you at first, but its service and customer satisfaction have earned it many kudos. **Pros:** homey feel with multilingual library;

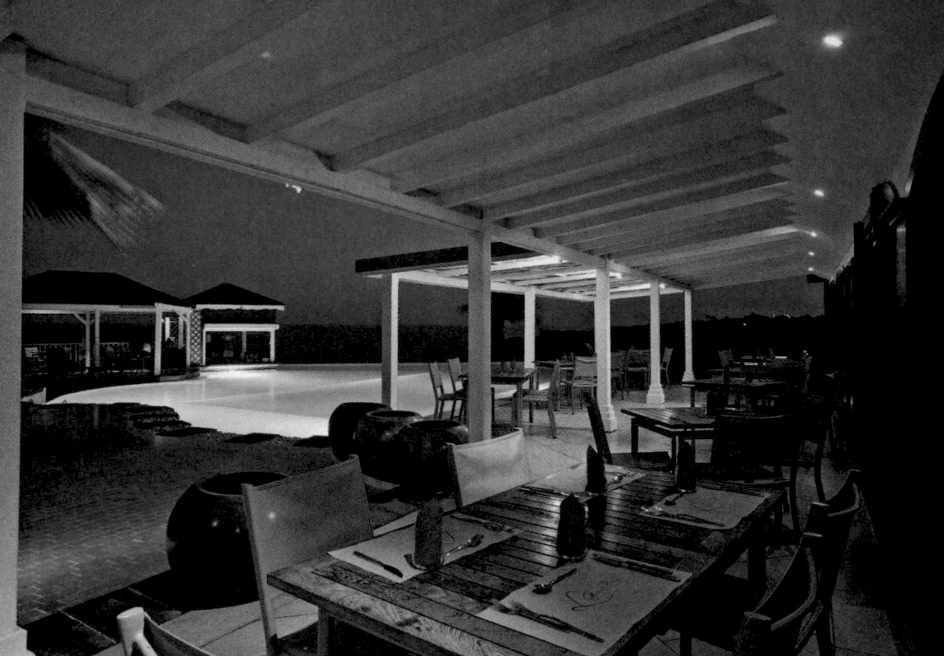
La Toubana Hotel & Spa

moderate prices, especially with weekly offers; innovative bar and flavorful, creole specialties by night. **Cons:** good, long beach, but it's down and across the road; not luxe; statesiders sometimes consider furnishings in duplexes dated. *Rooms from: €148 ✉ Allée du Coeur, Ziotte, Deshaies ☎ 0590/28–41–71 12 duplex bungalows (for 2–5 persons), 4 villas (3–8 persons) Multiple meal plans.*

$ B&B/INN **Habitation Du Comté.** A decidedly special place, this was the great house for the owner of a sugarcane plantation, but the stalwart, hurricane-proof manson wasn't built eons ago, but rather in 1948. **Pros:** shutters for sleeping that block out any light; blissfully quiet; in-room Wi-Fi is strong and free. **Cons:** not much goes on; need a car; no resort-style amenities. *Rooms from: €140 ✉ Comté de Lohéac, Ste-Rose ☎ 0590/21–78–81 www.hotelducomte.com 7 rooms, 1 2-bedroom suite, 1 2-bedroom, 2-bath bungalow Restaurant closed Sun. night, Tues. night, and all day Wed. Breakfast.*

$ RENTAL **Habitation Getz.** Marketed as a Chambres d' Hotes, this former coffee plantation is unique for its atmospheric guest rooms in the great house and deluxe tree houses—ideal for a family that wants to play Swiss Family Robinson. **Pros:** one marvels at the sweat-equity and exceptional taste apparent in this labor of love; the one-of-a-kind tree-house experience for children. **Cons:** to ascend to a tree house, one has to climb a swaying ladder—children should be older; the great house is not so close to the beaches and guests need a car. *Rooms from: €90 ✉ Route de Gery, Vieux-Habitants ☎ 0590/24–46–86, 0690/58–70–20 www.chambrescabanesguadeloupe.com 2 rooms, 3 tree houses Restaurant open for dinner only on Wed. and Sun. afternoon Breakfast.*

$ RENTAL **L'habitation Tabanon.** This new complex is located in a small market town in the heart of Basse-Terre, the mountainous, wild side of Guadeloupe, where eco-sports and scuba diving are practiced. **Pros:** a hip, place to call home for a week; manager is accommodating and acts as a concierge to guests; for self-catering, these well-equipped units are exceptional for Basse-Terre. **Cons:** you will need a car; Petite Borg is not a touristic destination; no resort services and amenities. *Rooms from: €94 Moulin de Tabanon, Petit Borg 0690/29–94–99 www.habitation-tabanon.com 5 apartments No meals.*

$ ALL-INCLUSIVE FAMILY **Langley Hotel Fort Royal.** This well-priced, friendly, and fun hotel was formed by a major renovation of a 1970s seafront mid-rise with the addition of conical bungalows (14 beachfront). **Pros:** nonguests can sample the fun by paying €49 for a day pass; free Internet; food and service surprisingly good. **Cons:** not all hotel rooms have a sea view; bungalows are small and some close to the beach, are subject to noise from the restaurant and bar; the single restaurant, which mainly serves buffets, gets crowded; bedding and beds in main building need to be refreshed. *Rooms from: €250 Petit Bas Vent, Deshaies 0590/68–76–70 www.fortroyal.eu 126 rooms, 7 suites, 82 bungalows Closed Sept. and Oct. All-inclusive.*

$ B&B/INN **Le Jardin de Malanga.** At this former coffee plantation, trees laden with fruit are like the temptations of the Garden of Eden. **Pros:** a romantic hideaway with history and character; lovely food (half-board is a good option). **Cons:** no TV or Internet in the bungalows; beds and pillows in bungalows more comfortable than those in the colonial house. *Rooms from: €233 60 Rte. de l'Hermitage, Hermitage, Trois-Rivières 0590/92–67–57 www.deshotelsetdesiles.com 9 rooms, 1 suite Restaurant Le Panga closed Sun. night Breakfast.*

$ RENTAL **Le Neem Bungalows.** Le Neem has really "grown up" from three bungalows to five suites, a seven-person spa, and a swimming pool, and in addition to the petite restaurant, the chef/owner Joel Kitchen, also gives creole cooking lessons. **Pros:** fine beach just across the street; young owning couple is caring, and Joel's wife, Ancette, speaks English; Nutmeg and Clove have a seaview terrace, well-equipped full kitchen, and are disability accessible. **Cons:** no space between the original suites, nor sea views; some noise from the adjacent suites; no full-service, hotel amenities. *Rooms from: €125 Rte. de la Pointe des Chateaux, St-François, Grande-Terre www.leneem.com 5 suites No meals.*

$$ B&B/INN **Tainos Cottages.** Now *this* is a story: a globe-trotting Frenchman designed seven teakwood cottages resembling Guadeloupean *cases* from the 1920s, had them constructed in Indonesia, and imported the cottages to a site overlooking a long unspoiled beach, Plage de Grande-Anse. **Pros:** from the smallest to the largest, the cottages are spacious; a discount is available by booking online. **Cons:** the mosquito netting's there for a reason; no glass on the windows and most interiors are not sunny; the dark wood and some other features need maintenance; the rustic experience is not for everyone. *Rooms from: €300 Plage de Grande-Anse, Deshaies 0590/28–44–42 www.tainos-cottages.com 7 bungalows Closed end of Aug.–Oct. 25 Breakfast.*

Le Jardin de Malanga

$ B&B/INN **Tendacayou Ecolodge & Spa.** This complex is the result of a remarkable 10-year saga, as an expat French family learned to live off a parcel of rain forest, building tree houses for their large brood, then constructing additional ones for paying guests, as well as a seafood restaurant, Le Poisson Rouge. **Pros:** boardwalks rather than scary ladders to the tree houses; fun, funky, quirky and inventive; ample homemade breakfast; a boutique jammed with wonderfully exotic clothes and treasures from Thailand and elsewhere. **Cons:** open-air sleeping not for everyone; no beach (but sea views and a pool); no phones, TVs, or in-room Wi-Fi; need a car *Rooms from: €260* *Matouba La Hauf, Deshaies* *0590/28–42–72* *www.tendacayou.com* *7 1-bedroom bungalows, 2 3-bedroom bungalows* *Breakfast.*

ILES DES SAINTES

$ HOTEL **Hotel Bois Joli.** The new residence at Bois Joli houses the best guest rooms on-island, aside from those in private villas. **Pros:** fairly close to some of the better beaches; the pool complex traversed by a diminutive bridge; the hotel is organized, clean, and well-serviced. **Cons:** the distance to town (beyond a long walk) is a transportation dilemma and an electric car or motor scooter should be considered; no bellmen, no elevators at the residence and it's a walk to the main campus; English is lacking throughout (a manager or two is bilingual). *Rooms from: €152* *Terre-de-Haut* *0590/99–50–38, 0590/99–55–05* *www.hotelboisjoli.fr* *5 rooms, 8 bungalows, 17 new rooms in La Residence* *Breakfast.*

$ **Hotel Restaurant Les Petits Saints.** This charismatic landmark inn, which draws mainly couples and families, was bought by a French couple who discovered the property while on vacation from their home in California. **Pros:** reminiscent of the island guesthouses of the 1970s; village just down the hill; free Wi-Fi, in some rooms, but mainly in lobby. **Cons:** do not expect luxury, though improvements continue; not the house party it once was; breakfast ends early, 9:30, and checkout is also early, 11 am. *Rooms from: €134* *La Savane, Terre-de-Haut* *0590/99–50–99* *www.petitssaints.com* *3 bungalows, 3 suites, 2 studios, 2 rooms* *Closed Sept. Restaurant may close in summer until Oct.* *Breakfast.*
B&B/INN

$ **Les Hauts de Grand Anse.** No neighbors and no noise other than the sound of the sea is what guests can expect at this property on pristine Grand Anse and Anse Rodrigue Beaches. **Pros:** gorgeous beaches; nearly new and well maintained; incredible sea views. **Cons:** if renting the main three-bedroom know that the other units may be occupied; no landlines; distance to town may necessitate an electric car/scooters. *Rooms from: €68* *Route de l'Anse Rodrigue, Terre-de-Haut* *0683/05–63–67, 0690/46–29–19* *www.grandbaie.com* *3 apts, 1 studio* *No meals.*
RENTAL

$ **Lô Bleu Hôtel.** This cheerful hotel is painted sunset orange with marine-blue trim; dramatic nightlights illuminate the beach area, which is furnished with chaises. **Pros:** right on the bay; large front rooms with sea view and balconies; family-friendly, with baby monitors and some bunk beds. **Cons:** no grounds or resort amenities; no restaurant; the front desk does not always speak English. *Rooms from: €122* *Fond de Curé, Terre-de-Haut* *0590/92–40–00, 0690/63–80–36* *www.lobleuhotel.com* *9 rooms, 1 suite* *No meals.*
HOTEL

$ **Paradis Saintois.** You'll feel like the king of the hill as you rock yourself to sleep in your hammock while gazing down on the Caribbean below. **Pros:** lots of fun; super managers; TVs in apartments and some studios. **Cons:** no phones or TVs in some rooms; a hike up the hill from town. *Rooms from: €70* *211 Rte. des Pres Cassin, Terre-de-Haut* *0590/99–56–16* *www.paradissaintois.com* *5 apartments, 3 studios, 1 room* *No meals* *3-night minimum.*
RENTAL

$ **Residence Anse Caraibe.** This residence, which in French means a rental complex, is perched on a hill right in the village, a five-minute walk from the ferry dock. **Pros:** English-speaking, acommodating French manager, who can even arrange transportation on the mainland; four apartments (F2 is the best) open onto spacious, private terraces that look to the bay; Wi-Fi is now in all units. **Cons:** no phones nor cable channels for little TVs; steep hill; no cushy creature comforts; three-night minimum in high season, two in low season. *Rooms from: €57* *Emmanuel Laurent St., Terre-de-Haut* *0690/46–29–19, 0683/05–63–67* *www.grandbaie.com* *4 studio apartments, 1 2-bedroom apartment, 1 3-bedroom apartment* *No meals.*
RENTAL

$ **Résidence Grand Baie.** A luxe hilltop complex that houses several different accommodations, it offers privacy and a seafront existence, 15 minutes from the village. **Pros:** everything is new; outstanding water views: quiet and private. **Cons:** distance from town and its restaurants
RENTAL

and markets necessitates an electric car and/or scooters. *Rooms from: €68 Route du Figuier, Terre-de-Haut 0690/46–29–19, 0690/57–68–13 www.grandbaie.com 5 units No meals.*

MARIE-GALANTE

Accommodations here run the gamut from inexpensive, locally owned beachfront bungalows to complexes with international owners. For an overnight or longer, a special promotion put together by Bwa Chik Hotel in St-François involves the ferry BABOU that runs from that town. There is one to Marie-Galante and one to a new hotel option, Cap Reva.

$ HOTEL **Hotel Cap Reva.** Hotel Cap Reva is most likely the largest property on Marie-Galante and it faces one of the island's best beaches. **Pros:** friendly staff and manager; snack bar offers salads, crepes, etc., so you can hang by the pool. **Cons:** no Wi-Fi in rooms; too much nature keeps coming in as the lobby is open; not all receptionists speak English and the desk is deserted by night; restaurant not getting raves; bedding and much throughout needs updating. *Rooms from: €185 Plage de la Feuillere, Capesterre 0590/97–20–01 www.deshotelsetdesiles.com 22 studios, 12 duplexes Breakfast.*

$ B&B/INN **La Rose du Bresil.** At this pretty, diminutive hotel d'charme, you will want one of the newly renovated, large rooms with an impressive kitchen. **Pros:** flat-screen, satellite TV; free Wi-Fi even in-room; quality mattresses are replaced every three years. **Cons:** no sea views; no resort amenities; older rooms not as lovely. *Rooms from: €85 Route du litoral, Capesterre 0590/97–47–39 www.larosedubresil.com 7 rooms, two 2-bedroom suites; 1 3-bedroom suite No meals.*

$ HOTEL **Le Soleil Levant Hotel and Resort.** Several features keep this simple, family-owned complex filled, the first being its low price, followed by its hilltop views and dual pools. **Pros:** family-friendly; good air-conditioning; free, reliable Wi-Fi in rooms. **Cons:** need a car; hotel rooms are not large and get some noise; staff not accustomed to American guests. *Rooms from: €55 Section Marie-Louise, 42 Rue de la Marine, Les Hauteurs de Capesterre, Capesterre 0590/97–31–55 www.hotel-soleil-levant.fr 8 rooms, 5 apartments, 10 bungalows No meals.*

$ RENTAL **Le Touloulou.** Le Touloulou has four simple stucco one-bedroom bungalows, two of which have kitchenettes, as well as a two-bedroom bungalow, also with a kitchenette. **Pros:** beachfront location at a budget price; adjacent restaurant and fun bar; genial, bilingual chef-owner. **Cons:** simple, no-frills place; lacks the usual resort amenities. *Rooms from: €60 Plage de Petite-Anse 0590/97–32–63 www.letouloulou.com 5 bungalows No meals.*

$ RENTAL **Le Village de Canada.** Le Village de Canada has studios, bungalows, and apartments, some with sea views; there's a pool but no beach, though one is close by. **Pros:** friendly; private terraces; moderate prices, especially on a weekly basis; good central location, being equidistant between Grand Bourg and St-Louis. **Cons:** not on the beach; furnishings, TVs, and bedding dated; self-catering only; no restaurant. *Rooms* *from: €70* ✉ *Section Canada, Grand-Bourg* ☎ *0590/97–86–11* 🌐 *www.villagedecanada.com* 5 *studios, 3 villas, 7 apartments* 🍽 *No meals.*

$ B&B/INN **Oualiri Beach Hotel.** This pioneer from the 1930s, a feet-in-the-sand bed-and-breakfast, has sling-back chairs on the beach. $ *Rooms from: €104* ✉ *Beausejour* ☎ *0590/20–20–08* 📠 *0590/91–25–10* 🌐 *www.im-caraibes.com/oualiri* 6 *rooms* 🍽 *Breakfast.*

NIGHTLIFE

Guadeloupeans maintain that the beguine began here, and for sure, the beguine and mazurkas were heavily influenced by the European quadrille and orchestrated melodies. Their merging is the origin of West Indian music, and it gave birth to zouk (music with an African-influenced Caribbean rhythm) at the beginning of the 1980s. Still the rage here, it has spread not only to France but to other European countries. Many resorts have dinner dancing or offer regularly scheduled entertainment by steel bands and folkloric groups.

BARS AND NIGHTCLUBS

Club Med By Night. Club Med sells night passes that include all cocktails, dinner with wine, and a show in the theater, followed by admission to the disco. Go on Friday for the gala dinner and the most creative show, or on a Tuesday, another special night. A night pass is a good option for single ladies, who will feel comfortable and safe at the disco, where there are plenty of fun staffers (G.O.s) willing to be dance partners. ✉ *Quartier Caravelle, Ste-Anne, Basse-Terre* ☎ *0590/85–49–50* ⏲ *Closed Sept.– early Nov.*

Eden Palm Theater Spectacles. The jazzed-up Eden Palm Theater usually presents Cuban-influenced Caribbean musical reviews on Saturday nights (though phone ahead to make sure, as it is tending to happen more on major holidays). The fast-moving, grand *spectacle*—like nothing else on the island—has plumage, imaginative costumes, a super sound system, special effects, a bevy of dancers, and sometimes even trapeze artists. The cost varies along with what one receives for it. The program (and the price) escalates during the Christmas holidays and on New Year's Eve; both are celebratory happenings here. Always there is the dinner—multicourse and Franco-Caribbean, and some alcoholic beverage. The wine carte encompasses many countries with some fine bottles. ✉ *Hotel Eden Palm, Ste-Anne, Basse-Terre* ☎ *0590/88–48–48* 🌐 *www.edenpalm.com.*

La Rhumerie Bar & Lounge. Something is always happening at this hotel. The entertainment is often bands playing beguine and zouk, or piano with bass, all of which are very danceable and add to the hotel's conviviality. The tom-tom drummers accompanied by a bevy of native dancers are exciting. A steel band also plays, usually on Monday and Wednesday. The busy bar specializes in quality rums from various Caribbean islands, and serves creole tapas including traditional *accras* (dried codfish fritters). ✉ *La Créole Beach Hotel & Spa, Pointe de la Verdure, Gosier, Grande-Terre* ☎ *0590/90–46–46.*

Bar de la Vieille Tour. The atmospheric piano bar with its planters' chairs and whirring fan blades is as memorable as Rick's Café in *Casablanca*. The terrace tables give you the best views of the Caribbean through the multicolored bougainvillea. *Accras* (salt-fish fritters), peanuts, and olives usually arrive with your cocktail, which will be as tasty as it is pretty. A bar menu offers a selection of tapas and the rum carte is extensive, some are available by the flight. On Friday and Saturday evenings there's live piano, and in high season, there's often more live music, like a jazz trio. ✉ *Rte. de Montauban, Gosier, Grande-Terre* ☎ *0590/84–23–23*.

Zoo Rock Café. Open nightly, this bar, *rhumerie* (rum distillery), restaurant, and café usually has live music on Thursday, from 10 pm to 1 am—often a pop-rock duo. Theme nights are a house party, be it Havana night, Halloween, or their takeoff on Mardi Gras. The crowd is young and mostly French European. Food is secondary to the fun and good humor—on a busy night, the crowd spills out of this alfresco café as they rock to the DJ's sounds.The disco action is always Friday and Saturday nights (11 pm –5 am!). Go early and have one of their signature beef brochettes off the grill. Doors open at 6 pm. ✉ *La Marina Gosier, Gosier, Grande-Terre* ☎ *0590/90–77–77* 🌐 *www.zoo-rock-cafe.com*.

CASINOS

Both of the island's casinos are on Grande-Terre and have American-style roulette, blackjack, and stud poker. The legal age for gambling is 21, and French law dictates that everyone show a passport, or for locals, a driver's license. Jacket and tie aren't required, but "proper attire" means no shorts, T-shirts, jeans, flip-flops, or sneakers.

DISCOS

Night owls should note that carousing here isn't cheap. On the weekend and when there's live music, most discos charge a cover of at least €10, which might go up to as much as €20. Your cover usually includes a drink, and other drinks cost about €12 each.

SHOPPING

The island has a lot of desirable French products, from designer fashions for women and men and sensual lingerie to French china and liqueurs. As for local handicrafts, you can find attractive wood carvings, madras table linens, island dolls dressed in madras, woven straw baskets and hats, and *salakos*—fishermen's hats made of split bamboo, some covered in madras—which make great wall decorations. Of course, the favorite Guadeloupean souvenir is rum. Look for *rhum vieux*, the top of the line. Be aware that the only liquor bottles allowed on planes have to be bought in the duty-free shops at the airport. Usually the shops have to deliver purchases to the aircraft. For foodies, the market ladies sell aromatic fresh spices, crisscrossed with cinnamon sticks, in little baskets lined with madras.

AREAS AND MALLS

Bas-du-Fort. Bas-du-Fort's two shopping areas are the Cora Shopping Center and the marina, where there are 20 or so shops and some restaurants, many right on the water. This marina has an active social scene. ✉ *Pointe-à-Pitre, Grande-Terre.*

Destreland. Grande-Terre's largest, most modern shopping mall, Destreland, has more than 180 boutiques, restaurants and stores. This commercial center is a few minutes from the airport, which is a shopping destination in its own right. ✉ *Abymes, Grande-Terre* 🌐 *www.destreland.com.*

Pointe-à-Pitre. This bustling metropolis obtained the prestigious French label of *Ville d'Art et d'Histoire* (town of art and history). It's home to museums, monuments, ruins, libraries, center for the arts and culture, entertainment venues, churches, squares, and fountains. In Pointe-à-Pitre you can browse in the street stalls around the harbor quay and at the two markets (the best is the Marché de Frébault). The town's main shopping streets with lots of French merchandise, from pâte to sexy lingerie, are rue Schoelcher, rue de Nozières, and the busy rue Frébault. At the St-John Perse Cruise Terminal, there's an attractive mall with about two-dozen shops. ✉ *Pointe-à-Pitre, Grande-Terre.*

St-François. In St-François there are more than a dozen shops surrounding the marina, some selling French lingerie, swimsuits, and fashions. The supermarket has particularly good prices on French wines and cheeses, and if you pick up a fresh baguette, you'll have a picnic. (Then you can go get lost at a secluded beach.) Don't forget some island chocolates or individual fruit and custard tarts. ✉ *St-François, Grande-Terre.*

ART

Kreol West Indies Guadeloupe. Housed in a white, stucco bungalow with lavender and aqua trim, Kreol West Indies Guadeloupe is Grand-Terre's first museum/art gallery/shop. This genuinely unique concept melds an historic exhibition with colonial furnishings, such as planters' chairs, with hundreds of high-level sculptures and contemporary paintings. A colorful shop, it also specializes in beach bags from recycled materials and island artifacts. ✉ *Pointe-des-Châteaux Road, St-François, Grande-Terre* ☎ *0590/24–41–92* 🌐 *www.kreolwestindies.com* 🎫 €2 ⏲ *Daily 9–6.*

Pascal Foy. Artist Pascal Foy produces stunning homages to traditional creole architecture: paintings of houses that incorporate collage make marvelous wall hangings. As his fame has grown, his media attention has expanded, so prices have risen. You are more likely to find a family member manning the shop nowadays. ✉ *Rte. à Pompierres, Terre-de-Haut, Iles des Saintes* ☎ *0690/43–13–09.*

CLOTHING

Boutique Le Gall. Boutique Le Gall handles a line of fashionable resort wear for women and children, designed by French painter Jean Claude Le Gall, that has hand-painted figures like turtles and dolphins on high-quality cotton knits. There are several other branches of this French favorite across the island, at the Bas-du-Fort Marina and even on Les Saintes. A gift from this store is considered prestigious back in mainland France. ✉ *La Marina–La Coursive, St-François, Grande-Terre* ☎ *0590/55–46–95* ⏲ *Daily 9:30–12:30 and 3:30–7:30.*

Dody. Across from the market, Dody is the place to go if you want white eyelet lace (blouses, skirts, dresses, even bustiers). A single item can cost from €100 to €300. Madras clothing is both traditional and contemporary. There's lots of madras, too, which is especially cute in children's clothing. Hark! Now those who love designer ensembles based in Guadeloupean tradition, can shop online. Online models include Miss Guadeloupe. A new line of colorful, Carnival-inspired, tropical dresses is knockout. And for men there are creole suits and cool, madras shirts and a line of Bebe Creole. Many styles have reduced prices and there are special-occasion "costumes"—wedding, communion, and confirmation dresses all in white eyelet. ✉ *Spice Market Sq., 31 rue Frébault, Pointe-à-Pitre, Grande-Terre* ☎ *0590/82–18–73* 🌐 *www.dodyshop.com.*

Maogany Boutique. At this shop, which resembles a yacht, the best of the offerings are batiks and clothing in luminescent seashell- and blue shades. Ladies love *pareus* (wraparound fabric for skirts) in the colors of the sea, from pale green to deep turquoise, as well as the jewelry. For men and ladies, there are authentic Panama hats—tropical fedoras in classic white *and* tropical colors. There are also several lines of women's clothing by French designers (like Nathalie Joubert), tunics, crocheted tops, and tiered long skirts. Many items are quite expensive but cool—and lightweight. And here the silkscreen is the real deal. ✉ *26 rue Jean Calot, Terre-de-Haut, Iles des Saintes* ☎ *0590/99–50–12, 0690/74–19–00* 🌐 *www.maogany.com* ⏲ *Daily 9–7, except Mon. during low season.*

Tata Somba. This boutique has an African name but is owned by a classy French woman with characteristic good taste. Ladies will find French and Italian fashions here, cool, lightweight skirts and dresses, stylish shade hats for the island's strong sun, jewelry, sandals, accessories, and hip clothes for little girls. ✉ *Terre-de-Haut, Iles des Saintes* ☎ *0590/99–51–65, 0690/64–48–13, 0670/87–14–55.*

COSMETICS AND PERFUME

L'Atelier du Savon. L'Atelier du Savon makes all of its soaps from vegetable products, with scents including marine spice and mandarin orange. Beautifully packaged gift baskets include bath salts and aromatic oils. You never know when the sign "Closed today, we are making soap" will go up. ✉ *Impasse du Mouillage, near the pharmacy on rue Jean Calot, Terre-de-Haut, Iles des Saintes* ☎ *0590/99–56–24.*

FOOD

Cap Creole. "Invite the sea to your table" is Cap Creole's motto. This shop just across from the sea, sells smoked fish par excellence. Since 1996 it has been taking the catch of the local fishermen—tuna, marlin, mahimahi, thazard—smoking it, and vaccum packing it. More recently, they have added other products, notably *boudin* (sausage) of fish, conch, and crab in 1-kilo packets. And there are a lot more local gourmet products. This is great stuff if you're in a self-catering villa and want to have appetizers before going out to dinner, or if you want to pack a picnic for a secluded beach. ✉ *La Lise, Bouillante, Basse-Terre* ☎ *0590/95–45–66* 🌐 *www.capcreole.com.*

HANDICRAFTS

Centre Artisanat. The Centre Artisanat offers a wide selection of local crafts, including art composed of shells, wood, and stone. One of the outlets sells authentic Panama hats. It is located under a tent across from the waterfront as you first drive into the village. ✉ *Ste-Anne, Basse-Terre.*

Madras Bijoux. Bijoux is the French word for jewelry and Madras Bijoux specializes in replicas of authentic creole jewelry, like the multistrand gold bead necklaces. The shop also creates custom designs and does repairs. ✉ *115 rue Nozières, Pointe-à-Pitre, Grande-Terre* ☎ *0590/82–88–03.*

SPORTS AND THE OUTDOORS

BOATING AND SAILING

Generally speaking, most of the towns and cities of Guadeloupe are not beautiful; however, the craggy coastline and the waters of variegated blues and greens are gorgeous. If you plan to sail these waters, you should be aware that the winds and currents tend to be strong. There are excellent, well-equipped marinas in Pointe-à-Pitre, Bas-du-Fort, Deshaies, St-François, and Gourbeyre. You can rent a yacht (bareboat or crewed) from several companies. To make a bareboat charter, companies will evaluate your navigational and seamanship skills. If you do not pass, you must hire a skipper or be left on dry land.

Antilles Sail. Antilles Sail is a charter operation specializing in catamarans from 40 to 62 feet, which can accommodate eight guests. A new, exciting addition to their fleet is a 45-foot Neel trimaran. For those who don't qualify to captain their own ship, or for those who want to just relax and be pampered, a skipper and crew can be hired. Provisioning and meal service can be arranged and VIP, dive, and other packages are available. The fleet also contains monohulls from 35 to 55 feet, which are used mainly for bareboating. Antilles Sail can also arrange flights, land stays, and other arrangements. ✉ *Bas-du-Fort Marina, Quai No. 9, Boutique des Moulins, Bas-du-Fort, Grande-Terre* ☎ *0590/90–16–81* 🌐 *www.antilles-sail.com.*

DIVING

The main diving area at the **Cousteau Underwater Park,** just off Basse-Terre near Pigeon Island, offers routine dives to 60 feet. The numerous glass-bottom boats and other craft make the site feel like a marine parking lot; however, the underwater sights are spectacular. Guides and instructors are certified under the French CMAS (some also have PADI, but none have NAUI). Most operators offer two-hour dives three times per day for about €50 to €55 per dive; three-dive packages are €120 to €145. Hotels and dive operators usually rent snorkeling gear.

FAMILY **Les Heures Saines.** Les Heures Saines is the premier operator for dives in the Cousteau Underwater Park. Trips to Les Saintes offer one or two dives for average and advanced divers, with plenty of time for lunch and sightseeing. Wreck, night, and Nitrox diving are also available. Despite its popularity, it has kept its prices moderate—€45 for a standard, supervised dive, with many packages available. The instructors, young and fun types from The Metropole, many of them English speakers, are excellent with children. The company also offers winter whale- and dolphin-watching trips with marine biologists as guides. These tours, aboard a 60-foot catamaran, cost about €55 (less for children). Inquire also about going canyoning and/or hiking with Les Heures Saines. ✉ *Le Rocher de Malendure, Plage de Malendure, Bouillante, Basse-Terre* ☎ *0590/98–86–63* 🌐 *www.heures-saines.gp.*

FAMILY **Pisquettes Club de Plongée Des Saintes.** With more than 15 years of experience, dive master Cedric Phalipon of Pisquettes Club de Plongée Des Saintes knows all the best sites. He gives excellent lessons, and in English, too. Equipment is replaced frequently and is of a high caliber. Small tanks are available for kids, who are taken buddy-diving. PADI divers are welcomed. Sec Pate is a famous underwater mountain, off the island's coast, in open seas. Les Saintes is known for its underwater hills, caves, canyons, and wall dives. Divers can see sponges of varied colors and gorgeous underwater trees that sway. ✉ *Le Mouillage, Terre-de-Haut, Iles des Saintes* ✣ *From the main ferry dock, leaving it behind you, turn left and walk up Main St. Pisquettes is just past the kayak rental shop on the right* ☎ *0590/99–88–80* 🌐 *www.pisquettes.com.*

Plaisir Plongee Karokera (PPK). Plaisir Plongee Karokera (PPK) has a good reputation and is well established among those who dive off Pigeon Island. One dive boat departs three times daily and charges €35 a dive, which is less than its competition. A second dive boat goes to Les Saintes, with two dives, one at a wreck, the other at a reef. The cost of snorkel gear is a low €15. The €85 price includes lunch. English-speaking dive masters are PADI-certified. Show your Fodor's guide and ask for a discount. ✉ *Plage de Malendure, Bouillante, Basse-Terre* ☎ *0590/98–82–43* 🌐 *www.ppk-plongee-guadeloupe.com.*

FISHING

Not far offshore from Pigeon-Bouillante, in Basse-Terre, is a bounty of big-game fish such as bonito, dolphinfish, captain fish, barracuda, kingfish, and tuna. You can also thrill to the challenge of the big billfish such as marlin and swordfish. Anglers have been known to come back with as many as three blue marlins in a single day. For Ernest Hemingway wannabes, this is it. To reap this harvest, you'll need to charter one of the high-tech sportfishing machines with flying bridges, competent skippers, and mates. The price is $430 to $600 a day, with lunch and drinks included. The boats can accommodate up to six passengers.

Captain Tony. Like father, like son: Tony Burel has officially taken over the sportfishing boat that he and his dad, Michel, worked for years. It's outfitted to go into combat with the big game fish and he has hauled many a billfish aboard. It has the latest generation of electronics and is considered the most commodious sportfisherman on the island. This Burel has 10 fishing years to his credit, five as a guide. Not only does he know where to find blue marlin but yellow-fin tuna, wahoo—"what you like." Rates are €160 for each fisherman, and €90 if someone is just coming along for the ride. This reliable big-fishing charter outfit can usually pick anglers up at their hotel for an extra €30. The skipper will be happy to take your picture with your catch of the day. And if you are not into jigging or chumming, check the website for snorkeling adventures and other excursions. ✉ *Les Galbas, Ste-Anne, Basse-Terre* ☎ *0690/55–21–35* 🌐 *captaintonyb.com.*

EN ROUTE

If you're driving from Ste-Anne to the St-François Marina area, follow signs first to St-François, then look for signs to the marina and Pointe des Châteaux, not St-François centre ville. That is the old town, and although it's a nice detour to see the market, it's also a circuitous route to the marina.

GOLF

Golf Municipal St-François. Golf Municipal St-François is a par-72 course that was designed by Robert Trent Jones in 1978, with later alterations that made it more challenging, though many feel that the putting surfaces could use improvement. The course has an English-speaking pro and electric carts for rent. It's best to reserve tee times a day or two in advance. There are no caddies. Clubs can be rented for about €2. Guests at Bwa Chik Hotel & Golf get a 10% discount. Le Birdy restaurant serves lunch daily and dinner Wednesday and Friday through Sunday and tapas are offered at the bar. Sunday buffets in season or during competitions are €35. ✉ *Ave. d'l Europe, St-François, Grande-Terre* ☎ *0590/88–41–87* *€45 for 9 holes, €65 for 18 holes* *18 holes, 6755 yards, par 71* ⏲ *Daily 7 am–6:30 pm.*

HIKING

Fodor's Choice ★

With hundreds of trails and countless rivers and waterfalls, the **Parc National de la Guadeloupe** on Basse-Terre is the main draw for hikers. Some of the trails should be attempted only with an experienced guide. All tend to be muddy, so wear a good pair of boots. Know that even the young and fit can find these outings arduous; the unfit may find them painful. Start off slowly, with a shorter hike, and then go for the gusto. All water sports—even canoeing and kayaking—are forbidden in the center of the park. Scientists are studying the impact of these activities on the park's ecosystem.

Vert Intense. Vert Intense organizes hikes in the national park and to the volcano. You move from steaming hot springs to an icy waterfall in the same hike. Guides are patient and safety-conscious, and can bring you to heights that you never thought you could reach, including the top of Le Soufrière. The volcano hike costs €30 and must be booked four days in advance. Note that when you are under the fumaroles you can smell the sulfur (like rotten eggs) and you, your hair and clothes will smell like sulfur until you take a shower. A mixed-adventure package spanning three days costs €225. The two-day bivouac and other adventures can be extreme, so before you decide to play Indiana Jones, know what is expected. The French-speaking guides, who also know some English and Spanish, can take you to other tropical forests and rivers for canyoning (climbing and scrambling on outcrops, usually along and above the water). If you are just one or two people, the company can team you up with a group. Vert Intense now has a guesthouse, les Bananes Vertes, (The Green Bananas) where you can combine a stay with trekking and other activities. ⊠ *Rte. de la Soufrière, Mourne Houel, Basse-Terre* ☎ *0590/99–34–73, 0690/55–40–47* 🌐 *www.vert-intense.com.*

HORSEBACK RIDING

Le Haras de Saint-François. A 50-horse stable, Le Haras de Saint-François has English lessons and Western trail rides for two hours (€50) or three hours (€60). The latter will take you to the beach, where you can go bareback into the sea. ⊠ *Chemin de la Princesse, St-François, Grande-Terre* ☎ *0690/39–90–00.*

KAYAKING AND OTHER WATER SPORTS

Centre Nautique. On the beach, Centre Nautique rents sea kayaks for €10 an hour and Hobie Cats for €40 an hour, even flyboards and stand-up paddleboards. Staff can arrange fishing, catamaran, kayaking, diving, and motorboat excursions. It also runs water taxis to the Islet du Gosier (€10). A motorized catamaran excursion to the gorgeous Grand Cul de Sac is €90 and includes lunch and drinks. There are PADI instructors for the dive segment of the operation, and certifications are possible. Jet Ski rentals include a guide, and range from 20 minutes for €70 to €270 for one Jet Ski for five hours including lunch. Nonguests are welcome but must call in advance. ⊠ *La Créole Beach Hotel & Spa, Pointe de la Verdure, Gosier, Grande-Terre* ☎ *0590/90–46–59.*

Centre Éconautique. Centre Éconautique aka Clear Blue Caraibes has mastered the art of underwater exploration without ever getting your hair wet. Rent a transparent kayak, which allows you to see the myriad colors of one of the world's most beautiful bays here. Paddleboards and clear-bottom, dinghy-like inflatables also enable you to play in the water. The tours, which last either two hours or a half day, will let you be privy to the marine beauty of the coral reefs and sea life. The cost is €20 per person, with special family and group rates available. Also, trips to the nearby Isle de Cabrito for a picnic and snorkeling are offered. To find Centre Éconautique, take a left from the main dock, go two blocks and look for its colorful signage on the right. It is across from Couleurs du Monde. ✉ *Ruelle Lasserre, Mouillage, Terre-de-Haut, Iles des Saintes* ☎ *0690/65–79–81* 🌐 *www.clearbluecaraibes.fr.*

SEA EXCURSIONS

Cool Caraibes. Relatively new to the catamaran excursion scene, Cool Caraibes has acquired a 27- passenger cat (three crew). It plies the turquoise waters to both Les Saintes, and Marie-Galante, yet not on the same day. For full-day trips, you must be at the dock by 7 am, returning between 5:30 and 6 pm. Coffee and a simple lunch prepared by the crew are served. It is generally crudités, mahimahi with a creole sauce, rice and tropical fruit for dessert. And yes, there is rum aboard—Planter's Punch. Once on Les Saintes, you are on your own to explore, or you can opt for a mini-bus tour, which is a good choice, especially if you are not one to hike hills or if you have children in tow. There is snorkeling gear and most guests utilize it and swim off the boat. On Marie-Galante, passengers disembark for a 90-minute mini-van tour, which includes a tasting at a rum distillery and a swim and snorkel at a gorgeous white-sand beach. ✉ *Marina de Bas-du-Fort, Bas-du-Fort, Grande-Terre* ✣ *If you are facing the marina where all the restaurants are, continue left on that street until you see the boat's dock on the right hand side, near the l'Aquarium au Gosier* ☎ *0690/70–47–18* 🌐 *www.coolcaraibes.com.*

FAMILY **Evasion Tropicale.** Evasion Tropicale operates daylong, ecotouristic, whale-watching cruises. With the help of the onboard hydrophone and the skipper's and researchers' 20 years of experience, sperm whales are easy to find all year long and humpback whales from December through March. Food and drinks are served and when you arrive back in port, you follow the leader to the small whale museum "Balen ka Souflé." Trips on the 51-foot motor sailor cost €65 per person (10 passengers maximum), but every passenger must also buy an annual membership in the Association for Study and Census of Turtles, Marine and Mammals of the Caribbean for €25. Contributing to the conservation of marine life is a good way to discover and learn about the underwater world, especially for children. Evasion Tropicale received the biodiversity Conservation Award Special Mention in 2013. ✉ *Rue des paletuviers, Pigeon-Bouillante, Basse-Terre* ☎ *0590/92–74–24, 0690/57–19–44* 🌐 *www.evasiontropicale.org.*

Paradoxe Croisieres. A top-of-the-line catamaran, *Paradoxe* sails to Marie-Galante (anchoring at the idyllic beach, Anse Canot) for €90 in high season, usually on Thursday, but most days it departs from St-François for Petite-Terre (€80), an uninhabited island that's a nature preserve. This isn't your typical booze cruise. Bottles of rum aboard? Sure, but passengers are more likely to be in it for the sailing experience and to see an out island. In the morning when it anchors off Petite-Terre, the passengers take guided walking tours, always on the lookout for iguanas. Then it's back to the beach to eat lunch. Normally lunch is grilled fish with side dishes, which is served on the beach and prepared by the boat's crew. In the afternoon guests can snorkel in the lagoon. The lunch is tasty, and the music on board's soothing. The trip to Marie-Galante usually includes a bus tour around the island and a visit to a distillery. Marina ticket booth is open from 8 am–noon and 4 pm–7 pm. ✉ *St-François Marina, St-François, Grande-Terre* ☎ *0590/88–41–73* 🌐 *paradoxe-croisieres.com.*

WIND- AND KITESURFING

Most beachfront hotels can help you arrange lessons and rentals.

LookaSurf. This retail surf shop also rents surf and stand-up paddleboards (SUP). The action takes place on the remarkable Caravelle Beach. ✉ *Ste-Anne Lagoon, 17 Lot Marguerite-Valette, Ste-Anne, Basse-Terre* ☎ *0590/88–15–17* 🌐 *www.lookasurf.com.*

UCPA Hotel Club. Windsurfing buffs congregate at the UCPA Hotel Club, where for moderate weekly rates (beginning at €845 or €125 a day) they sleep in hostel-style quarters, eat three meals a day, and do a lot of windsurfing. Lessons and boards (also available to nonguests) are included in the package, as are bikes to pedal to the lagoon. UCPA has a water-sports center in the middle of town, though the hotel itself is out on isolated Baie de Marigot. There is a lot of action at *le centre* UCPA, where island visitors can rent windsurfing equipment for €25, take a lesson for €30, or take a kitesurfing lesson for €70 (€20 if part of a group). Kayaks, Hobie Cats, and dive tanks are available, too, and you can explore the beautiful seabeds and remote beaches of the archipelago. ■ **TIP→ The hotel club markets to 18–39-year-olds, sporty types who don't mind roughing it.** ✉ *Terre-de-Haut, Iles des Saintes* ☎ *0590/99–56–34 in-town sport center; hotel reservations, 0590/99–54–94* 🌐 *www.ucpa.com.*

JAMAICA

WELCOME TO JAMAICA

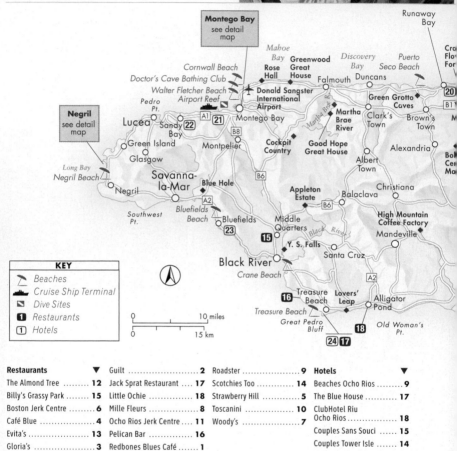

Montego Bay see detail map
Negril see detail map
Runaway Bay
Maboe Bay
Rose Hall
Greenwood Great House
Discovery Bay
Puerto Seco Beach
Cornwall Beach
Doctor's Cave Bathing Club
Walter Fletcher Beach
Airport Reef
Pedro Pt.
Donald Sangster International Airport
Falmouth
Duncans
Green Grotto Caves
Lucea
Sandy Bay
Montego Bay
Martha Brae River
Clark's Town
Brown's Town
Green Island
Glasgow
Montpelier
Cockpit Country
Good Hope Great House
Alexandria
Albert Town
Long Bay
Negril Beach
Negril
Savanna-la-Mar
Blue Hole
Appleton Estate
Balaclava
Christiana
Bluefields Beach
Bluefields
Southwest Pt.
Middle Quarters
Black River
High Mountain Coffee Factory
Mandeville
Y. S. Falls
Santa Cruz
Black River
Crane Beach
Treasure Beach
Lovers' Leap
Alligator Pond
Great Pedro Bluff
Old Woman's Pt.

KEY
- Beaches
- Cruise Ship Terminal
- Dive Sites
- Restaurants
- Hotels

0 10 miles
0 15 km

Restaurants ▼
- The Almond Tree **12**
- Billy's Grassy Park **15**
- Boston Jerk Centre **6**
- Café Blue **4**
- Evita's **13**
- Gloria's **3**
- Guilt **2**
- Jack Sprat Restaurant **17**
- Little Ochie **18**
- Mille Fleurs **8**
- Ocho Rios Jerk Centre **11**
- Pelican Bar **16**
- Redbones Blues Café **1**
- Roadster **9**
- Scotchies Too **14**
- Strawberry Hill **5**
- Toscanini **10**
- Woody's **7**

Hotels ▼
- Beaches Ocho Rios **9**
- The Blue House **17**
- ClubHotel Riu Ocho Rios **18**
- Couples Sans Souci **15**
- Couples Tower Isle **14**

Chances are you will never fully understand Jamaica in all its delightful complexity, but you will probably have a good time trying. You can party in Montego Bay, enjoy the sunset in Negril, or simply relax at one of the island's many all-inclusive resorts. One thing's for sure: along the way you'll discover a rich culture and delicious island cuisine that you'll not soon forget.

OUT OF MANY, ONE PEOPLE

The third-largest island in the Caribbean (after Cuba and Hispaniola), Jamaica is 146 miles (242 km) long and is slightly smaller than the state of Connecticut. It has a population of 2.7 million. With about 800,000 people, the capital, Kingston, is the largest English-speaking city south of Miami (in the Western Hemisphere, at least). The highest point is Blue Mountain Peak at 7,402 feet.

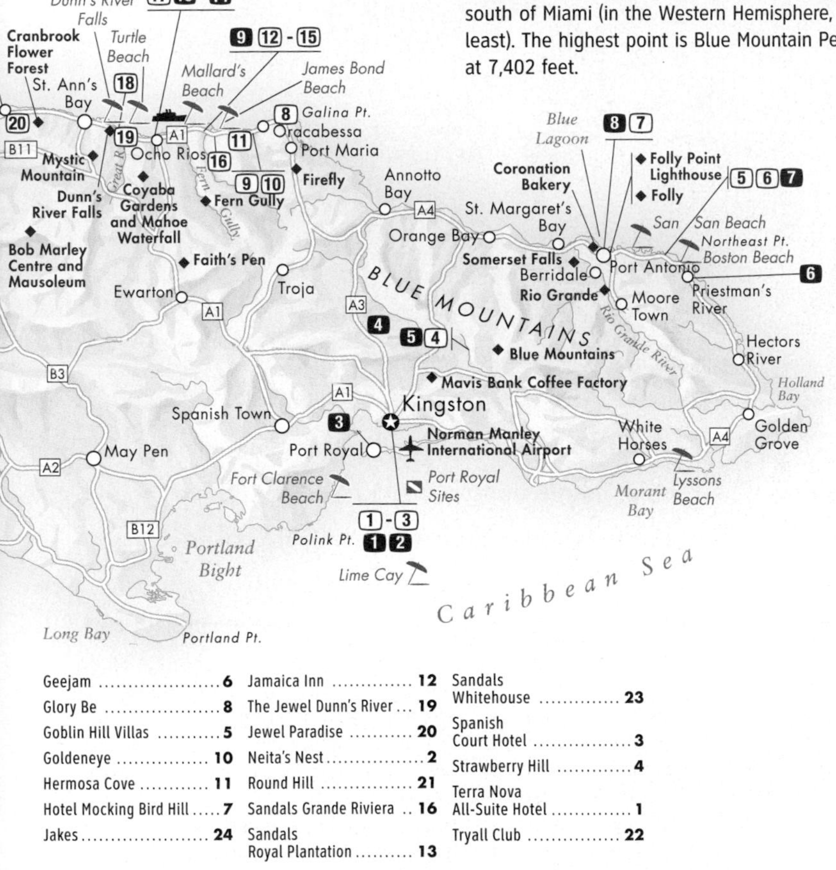

Geejam 6
Glory Be 8
Goblin Hill Villas 5
Goldeneye 10
Hermosa Cove 11
Hotel Mocking Bird Hill 7
Jakes 24
Jamaica Inn 12
The Jewel Dunn's River ... 19
Jewel Paradise 20
Neita's Nest 2
Round Hill 21
Sandals Grande Riviera .. 16
Sandals Royal Plantation 13
Sandals Whitehouse 23
Spanish Court Hotel 3
Strawberry Hill 4
Terra Nova All-Suite Hotel 1
Tryall Club 22

TOP REASONS TO VISIT JAMAICA

1 All-Inclusive Resorts: Come to where they were invented.

2 Great Golf: Golfers will be delighted by the many wonderful courses.

3 Fun for the Kids: Every conceivable activity, great beaches, and many child-friendly resorts appeal to families.

4 Negril Beach: It's simply one of the Caribbean's best.

5 Unique Culture: Jamaica has rich cultural traditions—particularly local music, art, and cuisine.

EATING WELL IN JAMAICA

The multicultural values embodied in Jamaica's national motto, "Out of Many, One People," serve equally well to describe its melting-pot cuisine: a savvy, savory fusion of African, Asian, Arawak-Taíno, and European influences, ingredients, techniques, and traditions.

Even the humble patty blends African peppers, Chinese soy sauce, and Cornish pasties. Sizzling Scotch bonnet peppers are indigenous, as are pimento—from which allspice is produced (Jamaica produces 80% of the world's supply), and the liberally used native ginger is stronger in Jamaica than elsewhere. Aspiring Anthony Bourdains should try beachfront or roadside vans, kiosks, and shacks dishing out darkly bubbling grub from cow foot to curried goat. They offer authentic fare such as succulent slow-cooked jerk with heaping helpings of rice 'n' peas (beans) and provisions (tubers such as yam and cassava).

JERK

Arguably Jamaica's most famous export after reggae and Olympic-caliber runners, jerk (usually chicken or pork but now including goat, fish, and even conch) is marinated for hours in a fiery blend of peppers, pimento, scallion, and thyme, then cooked over an outdoor pit lined with pimento wood. Low, slow heating retains the natural juices while infusing the meat with the flavor of the wood and spices and ensures that the meat lasts in the tropical heat.

The Culinary Jerk Trail spans the island from Negril through Mo'Bay and Ocho Rios to Kingston and Port Antonio. The attraction features 10 of the hottest jerk spots, where diners can interact with chefs and learn the origins behind jerk cooking. For more information, go to ⊕ *www.visitjamaica.com/jerk*.

ACKEE AND SALTFISH

The British brought salt cod with them as a cheap, long-lasting foodstuff for sailors and slaves alike. Ackee, a red tree fruit introduced to Jamaica from western Africa via Britain, is actually poisonous in its natural state. Once the pear-shape fruit's tough, toxic, ruddy membrane is removed, however, the boiled, yellowish, pulpy arils surprisingly resemble scrambled eggs in taste and texture.

EXOTICA (TO SOME)

Goat figures in incendiary curries, as well as in "mannish water," a lusty soup, believed to be an aphrodisiac, that's traditionally served on wedding nights, wakes, and other festive occasions. The soup includes the head, brains, and other organs slow-cooked with various seasonings and tubers. Oxtail is a culinary constant from Italy to Indonesia. Jamaicans serve it stewed, braised, or in soup; inventive chefs might toss it with pasta in rum-cream sauce or use it to stuff quesadillas.

SEAFOOD ESCOVEITCH

Freshly caught fish—including snapper, tuna, wahoo, grouper, and marlin—is often served as *escoveitch* aka *escoveech*

(fried to a golden crisp then topped with pickled hot peppers, onions, chayote, carrots, and pimento). Despite the linguistic and gastronomic similarity to ceviche and *escabeche*, escoveitch is rarely served cold, though it is usually marinated in vinegar and lime juice before it is cooked.

PROVISIONS

Farmers traditionally cultivated carb-rich crops that could furnish energy for islanders' hardscrabble heavy labor without requiring refrigeration. Pumpkins, coconuts, plantains, breadfruit, sweet potatoes, cassava, yams, and other "provisions" (root and gourd vegetables as well as some fruits) became staples, sometimes replacing expensive imported ingredients (chayote was used in mock-apple crumble). Most homeowners still have kitchen gardens; the Olympic sprinter Usain Bolt credits yams from his native Trelawny Parish for his speed. Today lots of sophisticated chefs here are returning to the "grow what you eat" locavore ethos.

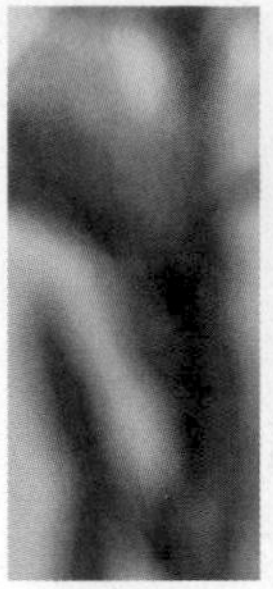

Updated by Jonique Gaynor

Jamaicans define enthusiasm. Whether the topic is track and field or politics, the spirit of this island comes out in every interaction. Although the country is well known for its tropical beauty, reggae music, and cuisine, you may find that your interactions with local residents are what you truly remember.

The island is rich in beauty, but a quick look around reveals widespread poverty and a disparity between the lives of resort guests and resort employees that is often staggering. Where vacationers opt to stay in Jamaica depends on factors ranging from vacation length to personal interests. With its direct air connections to many U.S. cities, Montego Bay (or Mo'Bay) is favored by Americans taking short trips; many properties are just minutes from the airport. Other parts of Jamaica can be reached from Montego Bay in 60 to 90 minutes, while eastern areas may be more accessible from the other major airport—in the capital, Kingston.

Some of the island's earliest residents were the Arawak Indians, who arrived from South America around AD 650 and named the island Xaymaca, or "land of wood and water." Centuries later, the Arawaks welcomed Christopher Columbus on his second voyage to the New World. Later, when the Spanish arrived, the peaceful inhabitants were executed or taken as slaves.

The Spanish maintained control of the island until 1655, when the English arrived. Soon, slavery increased as sugar became a booming industry. In 1834 slavery was abolished, but the sugar as well as banana industries continued. Jamaica's plantation owners looked for another source of labor. From 1838 to 1917, more than 30,000 Indians immigrated here, followed by about 5,000 Asians as well as Middle Easterners, primarily from what is now Lebanon. (Today although 95% of the population traces its bloodlines to Africa, Jamaica is a stockpot of cultures, including those of other Caribbean islands, Great Britain, the Middle East, India, China, Germany, Portugal, and South America.)

LOGISTICS

Getting to Jamaica: Donald Sangster International Airport (MBJ), in Montego Bay, is the most efficient point of entry for travelers destined for Mo'Bay, Ocho Rios, Runaway Bay, the South Coast, and Negril. Norman Manley International Airport (KIN), in Kingston, is the best arrival point for travelers headed to the capital or to Port Antonio.

Hassle Factor: Low–high, depending on your distance from the resort areas of Montego Bay, Ocho Rios, and Negril.

On the Ground: Most all-inclusive resorts include transfers. If transfers are not included for your trip, you can get shared-van service or charter a taxi from the airport in Montego Bay to your final destination. You can rent a car at either airport.

Getting Around the Island: Most travelers to Jamaica take guided tours on trips outside their resorts. The average traveler will not want to rent a car, which can be expensive. In most places, a taxi may suffice for occasional trips around town, but your resort may have a free shuttle, so ask.

In the early 1900s the boats that took the banana crop off the island began returning with travelers. By 1960 the tourism industry was the most important form of income, and in 1962, Jamaica gained independence. Along with tourism, agriculture and mining contribute to the island's considerable self-sufficiency.

PLANNING

WHEN TO GO

High season in Jamaica runs roughly from mid-December through mid-April. From May through mid-December, you can save from 20% to as much as 40% on rates, more if you use value-oriented travel packagers. There are several annual events in Jamaica that draw huge numbers of visitors.

GETTING HERE AND AROUND

AIR TRAVEL

You can fly to Jamaica from Atlanta (Delta, Southwest), Boston (JetBlue, US Airways), Charlotte (US Airways), Chicago (American), Dallas (American), Detroit (US Airways), Fort Lauderdale (Caribbean Airlines, Spirit), Houston (United), Baltimore–Washington (Southwest), Las Vegas (American), Los Angeles (American), Miami (American, Cayman Airways), New York–JFK (American, Caribbean Airlines, JetBlue), New York–Newark (United), Orlando (JetBlue), Philadelphia (US Airways), Phoenix (US Airways), San Diego (American), or Tampa (American, Cayman Airways). Most international flights come into Montego Bay, but some go to Kingston.

Domestic Airline Contacts Captain John's Island Hoppers. With more than 200 landing sites and offices in Kingston, Ocho Rios, and Montego Bay, Captain John offers transportation from Montego Bay and Kingston airports to hotels and villas across the island. ☎ *876/974–1285* 🌐 *www.jamaicahelicopterservices.com.* **Tim Air.** Charter service connects Montego Bay's Sangster International Airport to airports in Port Antonio, Ocho Rios, Kingston, Negril, and Treasure Beach. ☎ *876/952–2516, 876/979–1114* 🌐 *www.timair.com.*

Domestic Airports **Ian Fleming International Airport** (*OCJ*). ✉ *8 miles (14 km) east of Ocho Rios, Oracabessa* ☎ *876/975–3101* 🌐 *www.ifia.aero.* **Negril Aerodrome** ✉ *Norman Manley Blvd., Negril* ☎ *876/957–5016.* **Port Antonio Ken Jones Aerodrome** ✉ *North Coast Hwy., Port Antonio* ☎ *876/913–3926, 876/913–3173.*

International Airline Contacts **American Airlines** ☎ *800/744–0006* 🌐 *www.aa.com.* **Caribbean Airlines** 🌐 *www.caribbean-airlines.com.* **Cayman Airways** 🌐 *www.caymanairways.com.* **Delta Airlines** ☎ *800/221–1212* 🌐 *www.delta.com.* **JetBlue** ☎ *800/963–3014* 🌐 *www.jetblue.com.* **Spirit Airlines** ☎ *877/211–1546* 🌐 *www.spirit.com.* **Southwest Airlines** ☎ *800/435–5792* 🌐 *www.southwest.com.* **United Airlines** ☎ *800/538–2929* 🌐 *www.united.com.* **US Airways** ☎ *800/455–0123* 🌐 *www.usairways.com.*

International Airports **Donald Sangster International Airport** (*MBJ*). ✉ *Montego Bay* ☎ *876/952–3124* 🌐 *www.mbjairport.com.* **Norman Manley International Airport** (*KIN*). ✉ *Kingston* ☎ *876/924–8452* 🌐 *www.nmia.aero.*

CAR TRAVEL

Driving in Jamaica can be an extremely frustrating endeavor. You must constantly be on guard—for enormous potholes, people and animals darting out into the street, and aggressive drivers. Local drivers are quick to pass other cars—and sometimes two cars will pass simultaneously. Gas stations are open daily, and some now accept credit cards, though you shouldn't count on it. Driving in Jamaica is on the left, British-style.

Car Rentals To rent a car, you must be at least 23 years old, have a valid driver's license (from any country), and have a valid credit or debit card. You may be required to post a security deposit of several hundred dollars before taking possession of your car; ask about it when you make the reservation. Rates average $70 to $120 a day after the addition of the compulsory insurance, which you must usually purchase even if your credit card offers it.

Car-Rental Contacts **Avis** ✉ *Donald Sangster International Airport* ☎ *876/952–0762, 876/979–1060* 🌐 *www.avis.com.jm.* **Budget** ✉ *Donald Sangster International Airport* ☎ *877/825–2953* 🌐 *www.budgetjamaica.com.* **Fiesta Car Rentals** ☎ *876/926–0133 in Kingston, 876/684–9444 in Montego Bay* 🌐 *www.fiestacarrentals.com.* **Hertz** ☎ *876/979–0438.* **Island Car Rentals** ☎ *876/924–8075 in Kingston, 876/952–7225 in Montego Bay* 🌐 *www.islandcarrentals.com.*

TAXI TRAVEL

Some but not all of Jamaica's taxis are metered. If you accept a driver's offer of his services as a tour guide, be sure to agree on a price before the vehicle is put into gear. (Note that a one-day tour should run about $150 to $200, in U.S. dollars, depending on distance traveled.) All licensed taxis display red Public Passenger Vehicle (PPV) plates. Your hotel concierge can call a taxi for you, or you can flag one down on the street. Rates are per car, not per passenger, and 25% is added to the rate between midnight and 5 am. Licensed minivans are also available and bear the red PPV plates. JUTA is the largest taxi franchise, with offices in most resort areas.

Taxi Contacts JCAL Tours ☎ *876/952–7574, 876/952–8277* 🌐 *www.jcaltours.com.* **JUTA Montego Bay** ☎ *876/952–0813* 🌐 *www.jutatoursltd.com.* **Pat's Car Rental and Taxi** ✉ *5 Lewis St., Savanna-la-Mar* ☎ *876/918–0431, 876/955–3335* 🌐 *www.patscarrentaljamaica.com.*

ESSENTIALS

Banks and Exchange Services The official currency is the Jamaican dollar, but few Americans bother to exchange money, since U.S. dollars are widely accepted. At this writing, an American dollar is worth roughly 114 Jamaican dollars. Most ATMs in Jamaica accept American ATM cards and will dispense either U.S. or Jamaican dollars. Major credit cards are widely accepted, although cash is often required at gas stations, in markets, and in many small stores.

Electricity As in North America, the current in Jamaica is 110 volts but only 50 cycles, with outlets that take two flat prongs. Some hotels provide 220-volt plugs as well as special shaver outlets.

Emergency Services Police, Ambulance, and Fire ☎ *110, 911.* **Police Emergencies & Air Rescue** ☎ *119.* **Scuba-Diving Emergencies** ✉ *St. Ann's Bay Hospital, Edge Hill Rd., St. Ann's Bay* ☎ *876/972–2272.*

Passport Requirements All visitors must have a valid passport.

Phones Cellular service is available throughout Jamaica. GSM cell phones equipped with tri-band or world-roaming service will find coverage throughout much of the coastal region. Cellular service averages about J$1.50 to J$2 per minute on the island. Rates for local calls start at about 10¢ per minute, and incoming calls are free. Outgoing international calls to the United States start at about 19¢ per minute. Prepaid SIM cards cost about J$500. Providers Digicel and Lime also offer prepaid international calling to the United States and Canada. Cellular-phone rentals are also available starting at about $20 per week.

Safety Crime in Jamaica is a persistent problem, so don't let the island's beauty cause you to abandon caution. Most headlines are grabbed by murders in Kingston, often gang-related; violent crimes are largely a problem for residents in certain areas of the city. Visitors should be extremely cautious about visiting Kingston neighborhoods outside the business district of New Kingston.

Property crime is an island-wide problem. Use your in-room safe and lock all doors—including balconies—when you leave your room or villa. Never leave your car unlocked, and never leave valuables inside it, even when it is locked. Ignore efforts, however persistent, to sell you drugs, including ganja (marijuana), which is illegal.

Taxes Almost all airline ticket prices include a departure tax, which varies by country; otherwise, it must be paid in cash. A General Consumption Tax (G.C.T.) of 17.5% is included in the cost of most goods and services; there is also a $1 per room hotel tax.

Tipping Most hotels and restaurants add a 10% service charge to your bill. When a service charge isn't included, a 10% to 20% tip is expected, as it is for tour guides and drivers. However, many all-inclusives have a strict no-tipping policy.

ACCOMMODATIONS

Montego Bay has the largest concentration of resorts on the island; Negril, known as the Capital of Casual, is a more relaxed haven on the west coast. Both offer a mix of large and small resorts, plus good nightlife. Runaway Bay and Ocho Rios are more than an hour east of Mo'Bay. Port Antonio, a sleepy, laid-back haven, has a few resorts and a quiet atmosphere and is usually accessed by a short flight or long drive from Kingston. The South Coast has a few small resorts, uncrowded beaches, and only one large resort. Few vacationers choose to stay in **Kingston,** the capital, but it can be a good weekend-break destination, and the surrounding area includes the Blue Mountains, home of the luxe Strawberry Hill resort. Jamaica was the birthplace of the Caribbean all-inclusive resort, which is still the most popular vacation option here. Several of these are open only to couples. The island also has some high-end villas for rent, many near Runaway Bay.

Hotel reviews have been shortened. For full information, visit Fodors.com.

WHAT IT COSTS IN U.S. DOLLARS				
	$	$$	$$$	$$$$
Restaurants	under $12	$12–$20	$21–$30	over $30
Hotels	under $275	$275–$375	$376–$475	over $475

Restaurant prices are the average cost of a main course at dinner or, if dinner is not served, at lunch. Hotel prices are the lowest cost of a standard double room in high season.

VISITOR INFORMATION

Contacts Jamaica Tourist Board ☎ *305/665–0557 in Miami, 876/929–9200 in Kingston, 876/952–4425 in Montego Bay* ⊕ *www.visitjamaica.com.*

WEDDINGS

A 24-hour waiting period is required; many resorts offer free weddings.

EXPLORING

Touring Jamaica can be both thrilling and frustrating. Rugged (albeit beautiful) terrain and winding (often potholed) roads make for slow going. *Always* check conditions before you set off by car, but especially in the rainy season, June through October, when roads can be washed out. Two-lane primary roads that loop around and across the island are not particularly well marked. Numbered addresses are seldom used outside major townships, locals drive aggressively, and people and animals have a knack for appearing out of nowhere. That said, Jamaica's scenery shouldn't be missed. To be safe and avoid frustration, stick to guided tours and licensed taxis.

If you're staying in Kingston or Port Antonio, set aside at least one day for the capital and another for a guided excursion to the Blue Mountains. There's at least three days of activity along Mo'Bay's boundaries, but also consider a day trip to Negril or Ocho Rios. If you're based in Ocho Rios, be sure to visit Dunn's River Falls; you may also want to stop by Bob Marley's birthplace, Nine Mile, or Firefly, the restored home of Noël Coward. If Negril is your hub, take in the South Coast, including Y.S. Falls and the Black River.

MONTEGO BAY

As home of the north-shore airport and a busy cruise pier west of town, Jamaica's second-largest city is the first taste most visitors have of the island. Travelers from around the world come and go year-round, drawn to the bustling community's all-inclusive resorts and great beaches. Montego Bay's relative proximity to resort towns like Ocho Rios and Negril also make the town a popular choice. Adventures and one-of-a-kind experiences, not to mention interesting colonial sights, await in surrounding areas.

TOP ATTRACTIONS

Greenwood Great House. Unlike Rose Hall, Greenwood has no spooky legend to titillate, but it's much better than Rose Hall at evoking life on a sugar plantation. The Barrett family, from whom the English poet Elizabeth Barrett Browning descended, once owned all the land from Rose Hall to Falmouth; on their vast holdings they built this and several other great houses. (The poet's father, Edward Moulton Barrett, "the Tyrant of Wimpole Street," was born at nearby Cinnamon Hill, later the estate of country singer Johnny Cash.) Highlights of Greenwood include oil paintings of the Barretts, china made for the family by Wedgwood, a library filled with rare books from as early as 1697, fine antique furniture, and a collection of exotic musical instruments. There's a pub on-site as well. It's 15 miles (24 km) east of Montego Bay. ✉ *Greenwood* ☎ *876/631–4701* 🌐 *www.greenwoodgreathouse.com* 🎟 *$20* 🕘 *Daily 9–6; last tour at 5.*

Fodor's Choice ★ **Rose Hall.** In the 1700s it may well have been one of the greatest great houses in the West Indies. Today it's popular less for its architecture than for the legend surrounding its second mistress, Annie Palmer. As the story goes, she was born in 1802 in England, but when she was 10, her family moved to Haiti. Soon after, her parents died of yellow fever. Adopted by a Haitian voodoo priestess, Annie became skilled in the practice of witchcraft. She moved to Jamaica, married, and became mistress of Rose Hall, an enormous plantation spanning 6,600 acres with more than 2,000 slaves. You can take a spooky nighttime tour of the property—recommended if you're up for a scare—and then have a drink at the White Witch pub, in the great house's cellar. The house is 15 miles (24 km) east of Montego Bay. ✉ *North Coast Hwy., St. James* ☎ *876/953–2323* 🌐 *www.rosehall.com* 🎟 *$20* 🕘 *Daily 9:15–5:15; night tours, daily 6:30–9:15 pm.*

WORTH NOTING

Martha Brae River. This gentle waterway about 25 miles (40 km) southeast of Montego Bay takes its name from an Arawak woman who killed herself because she refused to reveal the whereabouts of a local gold mine. According to legend, she agreed to take her Spanish inquisitors there and, on reaching the river, used magic to change its course, drowning herself and the greedy Spaniards with her. Her *duppy* (ghost) is said to guard the mine's entrance. Rafting on this river is a very popular activity—many operators are on hand to take you for a glide downstream. ✉ *Trelawny.*

Rocklands Bird Sanctuary. A great place to spot birds, this sanctuary is south of Montego Bay. The station was the home of the late Lisa Salmon, one of Jamaica's first amateur ornithologists. Here you can sit quietly and feed a variety of birds—including the doctor bird (also known as the streamer-tail hummingbird), recognizable by its long tail—from your hand. ✉ *Rock Pleasant District, Anchovy, Montego Bay* ☎ *876/952–2009* 🎫 *$15* ⏲ *Daily 10–5.*

FALMOUTH

Fodor's Choice ★ **Good Hope Estate.** About a 20-minute drive inland from Falmouth, this estate on more than 2,000 acres provides a sense of Jamaica's rich history as a sugar-estate island, incredible views of the Martha Brae River, and loads of fun. An adventure park offers zip-lining, river tubing, a great house tour, access to a colonial village, an aviary, swimming pool, challenge course for adults, and kids' play area with its own challenge course. Guests may get a taste of Jamaica at the Appleton Estate Jamaica Rum Tavern and Jablum Cafe or enjoy spicy goodness from the Walkerswood Jerk Hut. Adventure park passes entitle visitors to all estate activities. ✉ *Falmouth* ☎ *876/356–8502, 876/276–2082* 🌐 *chukka.com* 🎫 *$55.*

RUNAWAY BAY

WORTH NOTING

Green Grotto Caves. A good choice for rainy days, these caves offer 45-minute guided tours that include a look at a subterranean lake. The cave has a long history as a hiding place for everyone from fearsome pirates to runaway slaves to the Spanish governor (he was on the run from the British at the time). It's a good destination if you want to see one of Jamaica's caves without going too far off the beaten path. You'll feel like a spelunker, since you must wear a hard hat throughout the tour. ✉ *North Coast Hwy., 2 miles (3 km) east of Discovery Bay, Runaway Bay* ☎ *876/973–2841* 🌐 *www.greengrottocavesja.com* 🎫 *$20* ⏲ *Daily 9–4.*

OCHO RIOS

Although Ocho Rios isn't near eight rivers, as its name would seem to indicate, it does have a seemingly endless series of cascades that sparkle from limestone rocks along the coast. (The name Ocho Rios came about because the English misunderstood the Spanish *las chorreras*—"the waterfalls.") The town itself isn't very attractive and can be traffic-clogged, but the area has several worthwhile attractions, including the very popular Dunn's River Falls. A few steps from the main road in Ocho Rios are some of the Caribbean's most charming inns and ocean-front restaurants. Lying on the sand of what seems to be your own cove or swinging gently in a hammock while sipping a tropical drink, you'll soon forget the traffic that's just a stroll away. The original "defenders" stationed at the Old Fort, built in 1777, spent much of their time sacking and plundering as far afield as St. Augustine, Florida, and sharing their booty with the local plantation owners who financed their missions. In Discovery Bay, 15 miles (24 km) west, where Columbus landed, there's a small museum with such artifacts as ships' bells and cannons and iron pots used for boiling sugarcane. Don't miss a drive through Fern Gully, south of Ocho Rios via the A3 highway.

TOP ATTRACTIONS

Bob Marley Centre and Mausoleum. The reggae legend was born and is buried at Nine Mile, in the parish of St. Ann, and today his former home is a shrine to his music and values. Tucked behind a tall fence, the site is marked with green and gold flags. Tours are led by Rastafarians, who take visitors through the house and point out the single bed that Marley wrote about in "Is This Love." Visitors also step inside the mausoleum where the singer is interred with his guitar, and there is a restaurant and gift shop. It is best to take a guided excursion from one of the resorts. If you're driving here yourself, be ready for some bad roads, and the hustlers outside the center are some of Jamaica's most aggressive. ✉ *Nine Mile, St. Ann* ☎ *876/843–0498* 🎫 *$19* ⏲ *Daily 9–5.*

Coyaba Gardens and Mahoe Waterfalls. Jamaica's national motto is "Out of Many, One People," and exhibits here show the many cultural influences that have contributed to that "one." The museum covers island history from the time of the Arawak Indians to the present. A guided 45-minute tour through the lush 3-acre garden, 1½ miles (2⅓ km) south of Ocho Rios, introduces the island's flora and fauna. The complex includes a crafts and gift shop and a snack bar, and Mahoe Falls is a good spot for a quiet picnic or swim. ✉ *Shaw Park Estate, Shaw Park Ridge Rd., Ocho Rios* ☎ *876/974–6235* 🌐 *www.coyabagardens.com* 🎫 *$10* ⏲ *Daily 8–5.*

Fodor's Choice ★ **Dunn's River Falls.** One of Jamaica's most popular attractions is an eye-catching sight: 600 feet of cold, clear mountain water splashing over a series of stone steps to the warm Caribbean Sea. The best way to enjoy the falls is to climb the slippery steps: don a swimsuit, take the hand of the person ahead of you, and trust that the chain of hands and bodies leads to an experienced guide. The leaders of the climbs are personable fellows who reel off bits of local lore while telling you where to step; you can hire a guide's service for a tip of a few dollars. After the climb, you exit through a crowded market, another reminder that this is one of Jamaica's top tourist attractions. If you can, try to visit on a day when no cruise ships are in port. ■ **TIP→ Always climb with a licensed guide at Dunn's River Falls. Freelance guides might be a little cheaper, but the experienced guides can tell you just where to**

Climbing Dunn's River Falls, Ocho Rios

plant each footstep—helping you prevent a fall. ✉ *Off Rte. A1, between St. Ann's Bay and Ocho Rios, Ocho Rios* ☎ *876/974–4767* 🌐 *www.dunnsriverfallsja.com* 🎫 *$20* 🕒 *Daily 8:30–5; last entry at 4.*

Fern Gully. Don't miss this natural canopy of vegetation, which sunlight barely penetrates. (Jamaica has the world's largest number of fern species—more than 570.) The winding road through the gully has been resurfaced, making for a smoother drive, and most tours of the area include a drive through this natural wonder. But to really experience it, stop and take a walk. The 3-mile (5-km) stretch of damp, fern-shaded forest includes many walking paths as well as numerous crafts vendors. ✉ *Rte. A3, south of Ocho Rios.*

Mystic Mountain. This attraction covers 100 acres of mountainside rain forest near Dunn's River Falls. Visitors board the Rainforest Sky Explorer, a chairlift that soars through and over the pristine rain forest to the apex of Mystic Mountain. On top, there is a restaurant with spectacular views of Ocho Rios, arts-and-crafts shops, and the attraction's signature tours, the Rainforest Bobsled Jamaica ride and the Rainforest Zipline Canopy ride. Custom-designed bobsleds, inspired by Jamaica's Olympic bobsled team, run downhill on steel rails with speed controlled by the driver, using simple push-pull levers. Couples can run their bobsleds in tandem. The zip-line tours streak through lush rain forest under the care of an expert guide who points out items of interest. The entire facility was built using environmentally friendly techniques and materials in order to leave the native rain forest undisturbed. ✉ *North Coast Hwy., Ocho Rios* ☎ *876/974–3990* 🌐 *www.rainforestbobsledjamaica.com* 🎫 *$47–$137* 🕒 *Daily 9–5; activities 9–3:30.*

WORTH NOTING

Faith's Pen. To combine a cultural experience with lunch, stop by these stalls with names like Johnny Cool No. 1 and Shut's Night and Day, which offer local specialties. For just a few dollars, buy jerk chicken, curried goat, roasted fish, or mannish water (a goat's-head soup and reported aphrodisiac). Faith's Pen is 12 miles (19½ km) south of Ocho Rios. ✉ *Rte. A1, about 4 miles (6½ km) south of Rte. A3.*

Firefly. About 20 miles (32 km) east of Ocho Rios, Noël Coward's vacation home is now a national monument managed by Chris Blackwell's Island Outpost company. Although the setting is Eden-like, the house is surprisingly spartan. Coward decamped uphill from his original home at Blue Harbour to escape the jet-setters who came to visit. He wrote *High Spirits, Quadrille,* and other plays here, and his simple grave is next to a small stage where his works are occasionally performed. Recordings of Coward singing about "mad dogs and Englishmen" echo over the lawns. Tours include a walk through the house and grounds. The view from the house's hilltop perch, which was a lookout for Captain Morgan, is one of the best on the North Coast. ✉ *Port Maria* ☎ *876/420–5544* 🌐 *www.firefly-jamaica.com* 🎫 *$10* ⏲ *Daily 9–4.*

Prospect Plantation. This working plantation east of town teaches about Jamaica's agricultural heritage, but it's not just for history lovers. Everyone enjoys the views over the White River Gorge; a tour in a tractor-pulled cart; grounds full of exotic flowers and tropical trees, some planted by such celebrities as Winston Churchill and Charlie Chaplin; and a small aviary with free-flying butterflies. You can saddle up for horseback rides and camel safaris on the plantation's 900 acres, but times are usually geared toward cruise-ship schedules. There's also a Segway tour, and you can take a lesson in cooking Jamaican style. Tour prices vary. ✉ *Rte. A1, 4 miles (3 km) east of Ocho Rios, Ocho Rios* ☎ *876/994–1058.*

Shaw Park Gardens and Waterfalls. Originally used for growing sugarcane and later oranges, this estate became the original site of the exclusive Shaw Park Hotel (today relocated to the beach). The owner's daughter, appropriately named Flora, worked to create the lush gardens, which now fill the 25-acre site with flame flowers, birds of paradise, and orchids. ✉ *Shaw Park Rd., Ocho Rios* ☎ *876/974–2723, 876/893–5899* 🎫 *$10* ⏲ *Daily 8–5.*

PORT ANTONIO

Port Antonio is one of Jamaica's quietest getaways, primarily preferred by long-staying Europeans. Even with improvement of the North Coast Highway from Ocho Rios, tourism remains slow here. However, in 2013, Trident Castle reopened as part of the Geejam chain, which is expected to boost area tourism.

Port Antonio has also long been a center for some of the Caribbean's finest deep-sea fishing. Dolphin (the delectable fish, not the lovable mammal) is the likely catch here, along with tuna, kingfish, and wahoo. In October the weeklong International Marlin Tournament attracts anglers from around the world. By the time they've all had their fill of beer, it's the fish stories—rather than the fish—that carry the day.

TOP ATTRACTIONS

Blue Lagoon. One of Port Antonio's best-known attractions, the azure waters of this spring-fed lagoon are a contrast to the warmer waters of the ocean. Catch some rays on the floating docks, or relax on the small beach. Just how deep is the lagoon? You might hear it's bottomless, but it's been measured at 180 feet. Guests of nearby hotels may have access to the lagoon, while those staying farther away can hire an operator for rafting trips. ✉ *9 miles (13 km) east of Port Antonio, 1 mile (1½ km) east of San San Beach, Port Antonio.*

Boston Beach. A short drive east of Port Antonio is this destination for lovers of jerk pork. The recipe's origins go back to the Arawak, the island's original inhabitants, but modern jerk was perfected by the Maroons. Eating almost nothing but wild hog preserved over smoking coals enabled these former slaves to survive years of fierce guerrilla warfare with the English. Jerk resurfaced in the 1930s, and the spicy barbecue drew diners from around the island. Today a handful of jerk stands, known as the Boston Jerk Centre, offers fiery flavors cooled by *festival* (like a Southern hush puppy) and Red Stripe beer. ✉ *Rte. A4, east of Port Antonio, Port Antonio.*

QUICK BITES

Coronation Bakery. Grab some hard-dough bread (originally brought to Jamaica by the Chinese), an unleavened bun called *bulla*, or spicy patties. The bakery's been open for more than seven decades. ✉ *18 West St., Port Antonio* ☎ *876/993–2710.*

WORTH NOTING

Folly. A favorite photo stop, this structure, little more than ruins, was home to a Tiffany heiress. Built in 1905 and spanning 60 rooms, the house didn't last long because seawater, rather than freshwater, was used in the cement. The ruins have been featured in music videos. In July, the Portland Jerk Festival is held here. ✉ *Folly Point, Port Antonio.*

Folly Lighthouse. Since 1888, this red-and-white-stripe masonry lighthouse has stood watch at the tip of Folly Point. Administered by the Jamaica National Heritage Trust, the lighthouse is an often-photographed site near Port Antonio's East Harbour. ✉ *Folly Point, Port Antonio* 🌐 *www.jnht.com/site_folly_point_lighthouse.*

Rio Grande. Jamaica's river-rafting operations began here, on an 8-mile-long (13-km-long), swift, green waterway from Berrydale to Rafter's Rest. (Beyond that, the Rio Grande flows into the Caribbean Sea at St. Margaret's Bay.) The trip of about three hours is made on bamboo rafts pushed along by a guide who is likely to be quite a character. You can pack a picnic lunch to enjoy on the raft or on the riverbank; wherever you lunch, a Red Stripe vendor is likely to appear. A restaurant, a bar, and several souvenir shops can be found at Rafter's Rest. ✉ *Rte. A4, 5 miles (8 km) west of Port Antonio, Port Antonio.*

Somerset Falls. On the Daniels River, these falls are in a veritable botanical garden. A concrete walk to the falls takes you past the ruins of a

Spanish aqueduct and Genesis Falls before reaching Hidden Falls. At Hidden Falls, you board a boat and travel beneath the tumbling water; more daring travelers can swim in a whirlpool or jump off the falls into a pool of water. The bar and restaurant specializing in local seafood here is a great place to catch your breath. ✉ *Rte. A4, 13 miles (21 km) west of Port Antonio, Port Antonio* ☎ *876/913–0046* 🎟 *$12* ⏲ *Daily 9–5.*

KINGSTON

Few travelers—particularly Americans—take the time to visit Kingston, although organized day trips make the city accessible from Ocho Rios and Montego Bay. That's understandable, as Kingston can be a tough city to love. It's big and has a bad reputation, with gang-controlled neighborhoods that erupt into violence. However, New Kingston is a vibrant and exciting business district with many places to enjoy. If you yearn to know more about the heart and soul of Jamaica, Kingston is worth a visit. This government and business center is also a cultural capital, home to numerous dance troupes, theaters, and museums. It's also home to the University of the West Indies, one of the Caribbean's largest universities. In many ways, Kingston reflects the true Jamaica—a wonderful cultural mix—more than the sunny havens of the North Coast. As one Jamaican put it, "You don't really know Jamaica until you know Kingston."

The Blue Mountains are a magnificent backdrop for the city, with fabulous homes in the foothills. Views get grander as roads wind up into one of the island's least developed yet most beautiful regions.

TOP ATTRACTIONS

Bob Marley Museum. At the height of his career, Bob Marley purchased a house on Kingston's Hope Road and added a recording studio—painted Rastafarian red, yellow, and green. It now houses this museum, the capital's best-known tourist site. The guided tour takes you through rooms wallpapered with magazine and newspaper articles that chronicle his rise to stardom. There's a 20-minute biographical film on Marley's career. You can also see the bullet holes in the walls from a politically motivated assassination attempt in 1976. ✉ *56 Hope Rd., Kingston* ☎ *876/927–9152* 🌐 *www.bobmarley-foundation.com* 🎟 *$20* ⏲ *Mon.–Sat. 9:30–5; last tour at 4.*

Devon House. Built in 1881 as the mansion of the island's first black millionaire, who made his fortune from gold mining in South America, Devon House was bought and restored by the Jamaican government in the 1960s. You can only visit the two-story mansion, furnished with Venetian-crystal chandeliers and period reproductions, on a guided tour. On the grounds there are two restaurants, crafts shops, a bakery, a wine bar, and one of the few mahogany trees to survive Kingston's ambitious but not always careful development. ✉ *26 Hope Rd., Kingston* ☎ *876/929–6602* 🌐 *www.devonhousejamaica.com* 🎟 *$10.*

Hope Royal Botanic Gardens. The largest botanical garden in the Caribbean, originally called the Hope Estate, was founded in the 1600s by an English army officer. Today it's often referred to as Hope Gardens and features areas devoted to orchids, cacti, and palm trees. The gardens are also home to the Hope Zoo Kingston. ✉ *Old Hope Rd., Kingston* ☎ *876/927–1257, 876/970–3505* 🎫 *Gardens free* ⏲ *Daily 6–6.*

FAMILY **Hope Zoo Kingston.** Lucas, a regal male lion, is the zoo's most popular sight, but there are many interesting animals, including a colorful array of parrots and other tropical birds. Current exhibits also include zebras, crocodiles, monkeys, and deer. There are plans afoot to add more programs and attractions. ✉ *Hope Gardens, Kingston 6, Kingston* ☎ *876/927–1085* 🎫 *J$1,500.*

Jamaica Defence Force Museum. This museum is dedicated to Jamaica's military history. Exhibits include plans of the forts built around Kingston in the 18th century, as well as information, weapons, medals, and uniforms of the West Indies Regiment and the Jamaica Infantry Militia. ✉ *S. Camp Rd., north of Kingston's National Heroes Park at Arnold Rd., Kingston* ☎ *876/818-4725, 876/920–0186* 🌐 *www.jdfmil.org* 🎫 *J$100* ⏲ *Wed.–Sun. 10–4.*

WORTH NOTING

Bank of Jamaica Money Museum. You don't have to be a numismatist to enjoy the exhibits at this museum, which offer a fascinating look at Jamaica's history through its monetary system. It includes everything from glass beads used as currency by the Taíno Indians to Spanish gold pieces to currency of the present day. Ultraviolet lights enable the viewing of detailed features of historic bank notes. There's also a parallel exhibit on the general history of currency through world history. ✉ *Duke St., at Nethersole Pl., Kingston* ☎ *876/922–0750* 🌐 *www.boj.org.jm* 🎫 *Free* ⏲ *Weekdays 10–4.*

Emancipation Park. Seven acres of lush greenery make a popular respite from New Kingston's concrete jungle. Locals come to jog, play table tennis, see concerts, and relax. Clowns entertain children, and photographers take romantic pictures of couples by the fountain. At the south entrance, Redemption Song is a pair of monumental statues of slaves, a reminder of the island's colonial past. ✉ *Knutsford Blvd., at Oxford Rd., Kingston* ☎ *876/926–6312* 🌐 *www.emancipationpark.org.jm* 🎫 *Free* ⏲ *Closes at 6 pm on public holidays.*

Institute of Jamaica. Dating to 1879, this museum covers early Arawak residents to modern times. Collections span art, literature, and natural history, with exhibits from Jamaican furniture to Marcus Garvey. ✉ *10–16 East St., Kingston* ☎ *876/922–0620* 🌐 *www.instituteofjamaica.org.jm* 🎫 *J$400* ⏲ *Mon.–Thurs. 9–4:30, Fri. 9–3:30.*

National Gallery of Jamaica. The artists represented may not be household names, but their paintings are sensitive and moving. You can find works by such Jamaican masters as painter John Dunkley and sculptor Edna Manley, and visitors are introduced to the work of contemporary Jamaican artists through events such as the National Biennial and the National Visual Arts Competition and Exhibition, staged each July and August, respectively. Guided tours (J$3,000 for groups of up to 25) must be booked in advance. ✉ *12 Ocean Blvd., near waterfront, Kingston* ☎ *876/922–1561* 🌐 *www.natgalja.org.jm/ioj_wp* 🎫 *J$400; free last Sun. of month* ⏲ *Tues.–Thurs. 10–4:30, Fri. 10–4, Sat. 10–3, last Sun. of month 10–3.*

BLUE MOUNTAINS

Fodor'sChoice ★ Best known as the source of Blue Mountain coffee, these mountains rising out of the lush jungle north of Kingston are a favorite destination with adventure travelers, as well as hikers, birders, and anyone looking to see what lies beyond the beach. You can find guided tours to the mountains from the Ocho Rios and Port Antonio areas, as well as from Kingston. **■TIP→ Unless you're traveling with a local, don't try to go on your own; the roads wind and dip without warning, and hand-lettered signs blow away, leaving you without a clue as to which way to go. It's best to hire a taxi (look for red PPV license plates to identify a licensed cab) or book a guided tour.**

WORTH NOTING

Holywell. In this recreation area, part of the Blue and John Crow Mountains National Park, nature trails wind through rugged terrain and offer the chance to spot reclusive creatures, including the streamertail hummingbird (known as the doctor bird) and the rare swallowtail butterfly. Rustic camping facilities are available, including showers and shelters. It's about 15 miles (25 km) north of Kingston on a very slow and winding road. ✉ *Rte. B1, northwest of Newcastle, Kingston* ☎ *876/960–2849, 876/960–2848* 🌐 *www.blueandjohncrowmountains.org, www.jcdt.org.jm* 🎫 *$5* ⏲ *Tues.–Sun. 9–5.*

Mavis Bank Coffee Factory. An hour-long guided tour (ask at the main office) takes you through coffee processing from planting to distribution and includes a sample. Mavis Bank is high up in the Blue Mountains. ✉ *Gordon Town Rd., Mavis Bank* ☎ *876/977–8005, 876/977–8527* 🌐 *www.jablumcoffee.com* 🎫 *$8* ⏲ *Weekdays 9–3 (with a break 12–1).*

SOUTH COAST

TOP ATTRACTIONS

Appleton Estate. Before the rise of tourism, the island was prized for sugarcane. Vast fortunes were made during colonial times, and many of the island's historic great houses remain as reminders. Much of the sugarcane was processed into molasses, the main ingredient in rum. Appleton Estate, still one of the Caribbean's premier rum distillers, offers guided tours illustrating the history of rum making in the region. After a lively discussion of the days when sugarcane was crushed by donkey power, the tours move on to a behind-the-scenes look at the modern facility. After the tour, samples flow freely, and every visitor receives a complimentary bottle. ✉ *Hwy. B6, Siloah* ☎ *876/963–9215* 🌐 *appletonrumtour.com* 🎫 *$25, lunch (reservations required) $15 more* ⏲ *Mon.–Sat. 9–3:30.*

WORTH NOTING

High Mountain Coffee Factory. Coffee beans grown on nearby plantations are brought here for processing. Call ahead for tours, or just stop by the gift shop for a sample taste. The factory is around 5 miles (8 km) east of Mandeville. ✉ *Winston Jones Hwy., Mandeville* ☎ *876/963–4211* 🌐 *www.jamaicastandardproducts.com* 🎫 *J$200* ⏲ *Mon.–Thurs. 8–5, Fri. 8–4:30.*

Peter Tosh Mausoleum. In the small community of Belmont, this simple white-concrete building contains the grave of reggae great Peter Tosh (born Winston Hubert McIntosh), who was murdered in Jamaica in 1987. Together with Bob Marley and Bunny Wailer, Tosh formed the seminal reggae group the Wailers in 1967. In contrast to the Marley memorials in Kingston and Nine Mile, Tosh's burial place is quiet and uncrowded. ✉ *Rte. A2, Belmont* 🎫 *Donation suggested* ⏲ *Daily 9–5.*

FAMILY **Y.S. Falls.** A quiet alternative to Dunn's River Falls in Ocho Rios, these falls are part of a cattle and horse farm and are reached via a tractor and trailer. An exhilarating zip line zooms over the cascading falls. Companies in Negril offer excursions for those not staying on the South Coast. ✉ *North of A2, just past town of Middle Quarters* ☎ *876/997–6360* 🌐 *www.ysfalls.com* 🎫 *$17, zip line $42* ⏲ *Tues.–Sun. 9:30–4:30; last admission 3:30.*

NEGRIL

Negril stretches along the coast south from horseshoe-shape Bloody Bay (named when it was a whale-processing center) along the calm waters of Long Bay to the lighthouse. Nearby, divers spiral downward off 50-foot-high cliffs into the deep green depths as the sun turns into a ball of fire and sets the clouds ablaze with color. Sunset is also the time when Norman Manley Boulevard and West End Road, which intersect, come to life with busy waterside restaurants and reggae stage shows.

TOP ATTRACTIONS

Blue Hole Mineral Spring. At this mineral spring about 20 minutes from Negril, near the community of Little Bay, you can jump 22 feet off a cliff or climb down a ladder to swim in the hole's icy water. Mud around the water's edge is said to be good for your skin, and the water itself is reputed to have therapeutic properties. For those who cannot jump or climb, water is pumped into a swimming pool at the surface. A bar, grill, cabanas, and a volleyball court add to the attractions. Take a chartered taxi from Negril, or call to organize a pickup. ✉ *Brighton, Negril* ☎ *876/860–8805* 🎫 *$10.*

FAMILY **Kool Runnings Adventure Park.** Billing itself as the place where "Jamaica comes to play," this park has 10 waterslides and a ¼-mile lazy-river float ride, as well as a go-kart track and kayaking. An adventure zone features outdoor laser combat games and Jamboo rafting (on floating bamboo). There is also bungee jumping, a "kool kanoe" adventure, a wave pool, and paintball. Admission varies by age and area, and the All For One Plan covers both the water park and fun zone. ✉ *Norman Manley Blvd., Negril* ☎ *876/957–5400* 🌐 *www.koolrunnings.com* 🎫 *$33; All For One Plan $75* ⏲ *Labor Day (May)–early Sept., daily 11–5:30.*

BEACHES

Although hotel beaches are generally private and restricted to guests above the high-water mark, other beaches are public and open to all kinds of vendors, who can sometimes get aggressive. At resort areas, even if the beach area is considered private, the area below the high-water mark is always public, so vendors will roam longer beaches looking for business. In most cases, a simple "no thanks" will do.

MONTEGO BAY

FAMILY **Doctor's Cave Bathing Club.** Montego Bay's tourist scene has its roots on the Hip Strip, the bustling entertainment district along Gloucester Avenue. Here, a sea cave whose waters were said to have healing powers drew travelers from around the world. Although the cave was destroyed by a hurricane long ago, the busy beach has a perpetual spring-break feel. The clubhouse has changing rooms, showers, a gift shop, and restaurant. You can rent beach chairs, pool floats, and umbrellas. Its location within the Montego Bay Marine Park—with protected coral reefs and plenty of marine life—makes it good for snorkeling and glass-bottom boat rides. **Amenities:** food and drink; lifeguards; parking (fee); showers; toilets; water sports. **Best for:** partiers; snorkeling; sunset; swimming. ✉ *Gloucester Ave., Montego Bay* ☎ *876/952–2566* 🌐 *www.doctorscavebathingclub.com* 🎟 *$6* ⏲ *Daily 8:30–5.*

14

FAMILY **Walter Fletcher Beach.** Although not as pretty as Doctor's Cave Beach, this strand is home to Aquasol Theme Park, which offers a large beach (with lifeguards and security personnel) and for an additional cost, glass-bottom boats, snorkeling, go-kart racing, a skating rink at night, and a bar and restaurant. Near the center of town, the beach has unusually fine swimming; the calm waters make it good for children. **Amenities:** food and drink; lifeguards; parking (no fee); showers; toilets; water sports. **Best for:** partiers; snorkeling; sunset; swimming. ✉ *Gloucester Ave., Montego Bay* ☎ *876/979–9447* 🎟 *J$400* ⏲ *Daily 9–6.*

RUNAWAY BAY

FAMILY **Puerto Seco Beach.** This public beach looks out on Discovery Bay, the location where, according to tradition, Christopher Columbus first came ashore on this island. The explorer sailed in search of freshwater but found none, naming the stretch of sand Puerto Seco, or "dry port." Today the beach is anything but dry; concession stands sell Red Stripe beer and local food, including jerk and patties, to a primarily local beach crowd. **Amenities:** food and drink; lifeguards; parking (no fee); showers; toilets. **Best for:** snorkeling; swimming. ✉ *Discovery Bay, 5 mile (8 km) west of Runaway Bay, Runaway Bay.*

OCHO RIOS

Dunn's River Falls Beach. You'll find a crowd (especially if there's a cruise ship in town) at the small beach at the foot of the falls, one of Jamaica's most-visited landmarks. Although tiny—especially considering the crowds—the beach has a great view. Look up for a spectacular vista of the cascading water, the roar from which drowns out the sea as you approach. All-day access to the beach is included in the falls' entrance fee. **Amenities:** lifeguards; parking (no fee); toilets. **Best for:** swimming. ✉ *Rte. A1, between St. Ann's Bay and Ocho Rios, Ocho*

Rios ☎ *876/974–4767* 🌐 *www.dunnsriverfallsja.com* 🎫 *$20* ⏲ *Daily 8:30–5; last entry at 4.*

PORT ANTONIO

Boston Bay Beach. Considered the birthplace of jerk-style cooking, Boston Bay is the beach that some locals visit just to buy dinner. You can get peppery jerk pork at any of the shacks spewing scented smoke along the small beach, perfect for an after-lunch dip, though these waters are occasionally rough and much more popular for surfing. **Amenities:** food and drink; parking (no fee); toilets; showers. **Best for:** snorkeling; sunrise; surfing; windsurfing. ✉ *11 miles (18 km) east of Port Antonio, Port Antonio.*

FAMILY **Frenchman's Cove.** This beautiful, petite, somewhat secluded beach is protected by two outcroppings, creating calm waters good for families. A small stream trickles into the cove. You'll find a bar and restaurant serving fried chicken right on the beach. If this stretch of sand looks familiar, it might be because you've seen it in the movies: *Club Paradise, Treasure Island* (the 1990 TV-movie version), and *The Mighty Quinn.* **Amenities:** food and drink; lifeguards; parking (no fee); showers; toilets. **Best for:** partiers; sunrise; swimming. ✉ *Rte. A4, 5 miles (8 km) east of Port Antonio* ☎ *876/993–7270* 🎫 *$8 for those not staying at Frenchman's Cove Resort.*

SOUTH COAST

If you're looking for something off the main tourist routes, head for Jamaica's largely undeveloped South Coast. Because the population in this region is sparse, these isolated beaches are some of the island's safest, with hustlers practically nonexistent. You should, however, use common sense; never leave valuables unattended on the beach.

Bluefields Beach Park. On the South Coast road to Negril, this relatively narrow stretch of sand and rock near the small community of Bluefields is typically crowded only on weekends and local holidays. The swimming here is good, although the sea is sometimes rough. **Amenities:** food and drink; lifeguards; parking (fee); showers; toilets. **Best for:** sunset; swimming. ✉ *Bluefields.*

FAMILY **Treasure Beach.** The most atmospheric beach in the southwest is in the community of Treasure Beach. Here there are several long stretches of sand and many small coves. With more rocks and darker sand, the beach isn't as pretty as those to the west or north, but it's a bit of the "real" Jamaica. Both locals and visitors use the beach, though you're as likely to find it deserted, beyond a friendly beach dog. Treasure Beach attracts a bohemian crowd, and you won't find as many hustlers as in North Coast resort towns. **Amenities:** food and drink; parking (no fee). **Best for:** solitude; sunset; walking. ✉ *Treasure Beach.*

NEGRIL

Fodor's Choice ★ **Negril Beach.** Stretching for 7 miles (11 km)—from Bloody Bay in the north along Long Bay to the cliffs on the southern edge of town—this long, white-sand beach is probably Jamaica's finest. Some stretches remain undeveloped, but these are increasingly few. Along the main stretch, the sand is public to the high-water mark, and visitors and vendors parade from end to end. The walk is sprinkled with good beach bars and open-air restaurants, some of which charge a small fee to use their beach facilities. Bloody Bay is lined with large all-inclusive resorts; these sections are mostly private. Jamaica's best-known nude beach, at Hedonism II, is always among the busiest; only resort guests or day-pass holders may sun here. **Amenities:** food and drink; lifeguards; parking (no fee); toilets; showers; water sports. **Best for:** partiers; sunset; swimming; walking. ✉ *Norman Manley Blvd., Negril.*

WHERE TO EAT

Probably the most famous Jamaican dish is jerk pork—the ultimate island barbecue. The pork (purists cook a whole pig) is covered with a paste of Scotch bonnet peppers, pimento berries (also known as allspice), and other herbs, and cooked slowly over a coal fire. Many aficionados believe the best jerk comes from Boston Beach, near Port Antonio. Jerk chicken and fish are also seen on many menus. The ever-so-traditional rice and peas is similar to the *moros y cristianos* of Spanish-speaking islands: white rice cooked with red kidney beans, coconut milk, scallions, and seasonings.

There are fine restaurants in all the resort areas, many in Kingston and in the resorts themselves. Many restaurants outside the hotels in Mo'Bay and Ocho Rios will provide complimentary transportation.

What to Wear: Dinner dress is usually casual chic (or just plain casual at many local hangouts, especially in Negril). There are a few exceptions in Kingston and at the top resorts; some require semiformal wear (no shorts; collared shirts for men) in the evening during high season. People tend to dress up for dinner; men might be more comfortable in nice slacks, women in a sundress.

MONTEGO BAY

$$ BARBECUE **Biggs BBQ Restaurant & Bar.** On the Hip Strip, this authentic barbecue joint features pulled pork, corn bread, mac-and-cheese, baked beans, and, of course, good ol' Memphis-style ribs—a taste of Americana in paradise. Diners have the option of sitting outside for amazing views of the Montego Bay coastline or inside around wooden tables draped in checkered fabric. Drinks like the must-try Bluegrass Lemonade, a heady mix of house-made lemonade and "bluebeery" vodka, are served in traditional jars, and meals are served in half-pound and one-pound portions. $ *Average main: $15* ✉ *Gloucester Ave., Montego Bay* ☎ *876/952–9488.*

$$$$ SEAFOOD ✕ **Marguerites Seafood By the Sea.** At this romantic seaside restaurant, lobster, shrimp, and fish are the specialties, as is the Caesar salad. Dine on the patio-style terrace or at the water's edge. Walk-in guests can often be accommodated, but it's best to make a reservation. *Average main: $40 ✉ Gloucester Ave., Montego Bay ☎ 876/952–4777 🌐 www.margaritavillecaribbean.com Reservations essential No lunch.*

$$$ CARIBBEAN ✕ **Pier 1.** After tropical drinks at the deck bar, you'll be ready to dig into the international variations on fresh seafood; the best are the grilled lobster and any preparation of island snapper. Occasional party cruises leave from the marina here, and on Friday night the restaurant is mobbed by locals who come to dance at the weekly Pier Pressure party. *Average main: $22 ✉ Off Howard Cooke Blvd., Montego Bay ☎ 876/952–2452 🌐 www.pieronejamaica.com.*

BEST BETS FOR DINING

Fodor's Choice★

Boston Jerk Centre, Evita's Italian Restaurant, Ivan's Restaurant, Jack Sprat Restaurant, Kuyaba on the Beach, Pelican Bar, Pork Pit, Redbones Blues Cafe, Rockhouse Restaurant, Strawberry Hill, Toscanini

BEST LOCAL FOOD

Boston Jerk Centre, Just Natural, Pork Pit, Scotchies, Scotchies Too,

BEST FOR A SPECIAL OCCASION

Rockhouse Restaurant, Strawberry Hill

$$ JAMAICAN Fodor's Choice ★ ✕ **Pork Pit.** A favorite with many Mo'Bay locals, this no-frills eatery serves Jamaican specialties including some fiery jerk—note that it's spiced to local tastes, not watered down for tourists. Many people get their food to go, but you can also eat at picnic tables. *Average main: $12 ✉ 27 Gloucester Ave., Montego Bay ☎ 876/940–3008 Reservations not accepted.*

$ JAMAICAN ✕ **Scotchies.** Many call this open-air jerk eatery the best in Jamaica, but the Scotchies Too branch in Ocho Rios makes it a tough call. Both serve genuine jerk—chicken, pork, fish, sausage, and more—with fiery sauce and delectable side dishes including festival (bread similar to a hush puppy) and rice and peas. This restaurant is a favorite with Montego Bay residents and tourists; you're likely to see a slap-the-table game of dominoes. *Average main: $10 ✉ North Coast Hwy., across from Holiday Inn SunSpree, 10 miles (16 km) east of Montego Bay, Montego Bay ☎ 876/953–3301.*

$$$$ INTERNATIONAL ✕ **Seagrape Terrace.** Named for the trees that line the beach at the Half Moon resorts, this beachside restaurant is open to the public. At lunchtime, a superb buffet and à la carte menu are available. Standout buffet options include roast meats and freshly baked breads. At dinner there's a good selection of seafood, steaks, and ribs including the herb-roasted Angus beef tenderloin, red wine–braised short ribs and grilled yellowfin tuna. *Average main: $38 ✉ Half Moon, North Coast Hwy., 7 miles (11 km) east of Montego Bay, Montego Bay ☎ 876/953–2211 🌐 www.halfmoon.com.*

$$$$ ECLECTIC ✕ **Sugar Mill.** Caribbean dishes with an Asian twist are served with flair at this terrace restaurant on the Half Moon golf course. The menu

includes the likes of coconut- and saffron-poached snapper fillet, pork tenderloin infused with island spices, and a tea-smoked duck breast. A well-stocked wine cellar rounds out the experience. The dress code is "casual elegant." *Average main: $38 Half Moon, North Coast Rd., 7 miles (11 km) east of Montego Bay, Montego Bay 876/953–2211 www.halfmoon.com Reservations essential No lunch.*

OCHO RIOS

$$$ ECLECTIC **Almond Tree.** This restaurant is named for the massive tree growing through the roof. For many diners, the evening starts with a drink at the terrace bar overlooking the sea. Dinner, which can be enjoyed on the terrace or in the dining room, begins with pumpkin or pepperpot soup before moving on to seafood, pasta, and dishes with a Jamaican flavor, such as jerk lamb. *Average main: $21 Hibiscus Lodge Hotel, 83–85 Main St., Ocho Rios 876/974–2813 www.hibiscusjamaica.com.*

14

$$$ ECLECTIC Fodor's Choice ★ **Evita's Italian Restaurant.** Set in an 1860s' gingerbread house, Evita's has a commanding view of Ocho Rios. The chic and charming restaurant—an island institution—is the self-proclaimed "Best Little Pasta House in Jamaica." The pasta has a spicy zing, a mash-up of the best of Italian and Jamaican cuisine. The friendly staff, and sometimes the proprietor herself (the effervescent Eva Myers), will guide you through the many inventive choices, which include lasagna Rastafari, jerk spaghetti, and One-Love Penne. Make time for dessert and enjoy the view from the veranda. *Average main: $25 Eden Bower Rd., Ocho Rios 876/974–2333 www.evitasjamaica.com.*

$ JAMAICAN **Ocho Rios Jerk Centre.** This canopied, open-air eatery is a great place for fiery jerk pork, chicken, or seafood such as fish and conch. Frosty Red Stripe beer and cocktails such as the special Jerk Center Cooler—a colorful mix featuring rum and vodka—are perfect complements to the island fare. Milder barbecued meats, also sold by weight (typically, a quarter or half pound makes a good serving), turn up on the daily chalkboard menu posted on the wall. It's busy at lunch, especially when passengers from cruise ships swamp the place. *Average main: $8 Da Costa Dr., Ocho Rios 876/974–2549.*

$ JAMAICAN **Roadster.** This simple, rustic eatery across from Jamaica Inn serves good Jamaican food at unbeatable prices. You can eat under a tree or inside the restaurant, which is run by German-turned-Jamaican-resident Marion Rose and her Jamaican husband. The menu has local favorites such as fried chicken and oxtail. Go early or call ahead with your order, because there's a limited amount of food prepared each day. *Average main: $8 Hibiscus Dr., Ocho Rios 876/974–2910, 876/402–1602 No credit cards.*

$ JAMAICAN **Scotchies Too.** The Ocho Rios branch of the longtime Montego Bay favorite has been lauded by international chefs for its excellent jerk. The plates of jerk chicken, sausage, fish, pork, and ribs at this open-air restaurant are all accompanied by festival, *bammy* (flatbread), and some fire-breathing hot sauce. Be sure to step over to the kitchen to watch the preparation of the jerk over the pits. *Average main: $10 Drax Hall, North Coast Hwy., Ocho Rios 876/794–9457.*

Fresh shrimp offered at a colorful roadside stand

$$$ INTERNATIONAL Fodor's Choice ★

✕ **Toscanini.** At Harmony Hall, this longtime favorite offers seating in the dining room and on the garden veranda. The menu features classic Italian dishes and Jamaican fusion cuisine, all made with fresh, local produce. Look out for marinated marlin, caught in local waters, and tuna, which customers come from Kingston to enjoy. Huge juicy South Coast prawns also draw customers. Desserts such as tiramisu, chocolate profiteroles, and a wicked affogato round off the meal beautifully. Call for a complimentary shuttle in Ocho Rios. *Average main: $25 ✉ Harmony Hall, North Coast Hwy., Ocho Rios ☎ 876/975–4785 ⊕ www.harmonyhall.com.*

PORT ANTONIO

$ JAMAICAN Fodor's Choice ★

✕ **Boston Jerk Centre.** Actually a collection of about half a dozen open-air stands, this is a culinary landmark thanks to its popular jerk pits. Stroll up to the open pits, fired by pimento logs and topped with a piece of corrugated roofing metal, locally known as zinc, and order meat by the quarter, half, or full pound; chicken, pork, goat, and fish are top options. Side dishes are few but generally include festival and rice and peas. *Average main: $10 ✉ Boston Beach, Rte. A4, east of Port Antonio, Port Antonio ▭ No credit cards.*

$$$ JAMAICAN

✕ **Mille Fleurs.** Enjoy European, Jamaican, and Carribean cuisine while watching the sunset on a terrace surrounded by tropical vegetation. Dishes made with local ingredients change daily, perhaps ackee-fruit soufflé or plantain fritters with black-bean dip. Lobster medallions in a creamy passion-fruit sauce is a favorite. Innovative vegetarian options, such as ratatouille with feta and herb crumble, are always on the menu, and Meatless Mondays are a weekly feature. *Average main: $29 ✉ Hotel Mockingbird Hill, Port Antonio ☎ 876/993–7267 🌐 www.hotelmockingbirdhill.com.*

$ JAMAICAN

Woody's Low Bridge Place Fast Food Restaurant & Bar. Positive vibes and burgers are featured at this roadside eatery. Charles "Woody" Cousins and wife Cherry serve up simple fare from a whitewashed shack whose walls bear Cherry's handwritten affirmations. Besides quintessential American fare from fries to hot dogs, you can order veggie or plantain burgers or a traditional Jamaican dinner made to order. A full range of beverages includes homemade ginger beer and blended drinks. *Average main: $8 ✉ Drapers Main Rd., Port Antonio ☎ 876/993–7888 No credit cards.*

14

KINGSTON

$$ JAMAICAN

Gloria's. The unassuming setting belies the excellent food served at this restaurant, frequented by Kingston residents who happily drive to Port Royal for its seafood. Fresh fish is served up steamed, fried, escoveitched, or in brown stew. Garlic or curry lobster and shrimp are other delicious offerings. Sit on the upper deck to catch the cooling sea breeze. *Average main: $12 ✉ 15 Foreshore Rd., Port Royal ☎ 876/967–8220.*

$$ JAMAICAN

Guilt Restaurant. Bold creations that transform traditional Jamaican cuisine into novel, sumptuous meals please the most discerning palate. Eat on the terrace of the venerable Devon House or in exclusive private dining in the vault. Do not pass up dessert, as imaginative chef/owner Colin Hylton made his name and reputation as a pastry chef. *Average main: $12 ✉ Devon House, 26 Hope Rd., Kingston ☎ 876/968–5488 Closed Mon.*

$$ JAMAICAN Fodor's Choice ★

Redbones Blues Cafe. At this hip restaurant and bar, there's a lively music and arts scene, and the family owners take their social and environmental responsibilities seriously. Not only is the food some of the best in Kingston, but much of the produce is grown on the owners' farm in the hills above the city. The pork is raised at a children's home in Mandeville that has its own farm, and the waiters attended a children's home in Kingston. Choose from delicious dishes such as lamb chops or jerked chicken kebabs, served with a Caribbean fruit salsa. Redbones comes alive at night, with movies nights, literary evenings, music, and other events. There is also a gallery with revolving exhibitions. *Average main: $20 ✉ 1 Argyle Rd., Kingston ☎ 876/978–8262, 876/978–6091 🌐 www.redbonesbluescafe.com Closed Sun. No lunch Sat.*

BLUE MOUNTAINS

$ CAFÉ

Cafe Blue. Perched on a hillside more than 3,000 feet up in Irish Town, Cafe Blue could be one of the most stunning places to enjoy a cup of coffee in the region where it's produced. It's a hip hideaway for Kingstonians and is popular with Strawberry Hill guests. On offer are many different styles of Blue Mountain, from espresso to latte, as well as a selection of freshly baked cakes. Other café branches are in the Shoppes at Rosehall and Fairview in Montego Bay and the Sovereign

Centre in Kingston. $ *Average main: $8* ✉ *Irish Town* ☎ *876/944–8918* 🌐 *www.jamaicacafeblue.com.*

$$$$ JAMAICAN Fodor's Choice ★ ✕ **Strawberry Hill.** A favorite with Kingstonians for its elegant Sunday brunch, Strawberry Hill has a stunning location; the open-air terrace has spectacular views of the city and countryside. The restaurant serves a prix-fixe menu with constantly changing dishes for lunch and dinner. Entrées include curried shrimp, coconut-crusted snapper, and Jamaican favorites such as curried goat and jerk chicken. The greens, the milk, and much of the other ingredients come from the Island Outpost farm in the parish of Trelawny and from local farmers. The bar area, a good place for cocktails or after-dinner drinks, features a piano and a fireplace that's usually ablaze in the cool evenings of the Blue Mountains. $ *Average main: $38* ✉ *Strawberry Hill, New Castle Rd., Irish Town* ☎ *876/944–8400* 🌐 *www.islandoutpost.com* ✍ *Reservations essential.*

SOUTH COAST

$ JAMAICAN ✕ **Billy's Grassy Park.** In the Middle Quarters strip along the South Coast Highway, this side-of-the-road stop serves fiery Jamaican food, including scorching peppered shrimp caught just behind the kitchen. Billy cooks favorites such as fried fish, curried goat, and chicken over a wood fire. Also on the menu is peanut porridge, a popular, hearty Jamaican breakfast. $ *Average main: $8* ✉ *A2, about 30 mins east of Whitehouse, Middle Quarters* ☎ *876/366–4182* ▭ *No credit cards.*

$$ ECLECTIC Fodor's Choice ★ ✕ **Jack Sprat Restaurant.** It's no surprise that this restaurant shares its home resort's bohemian style (it's the beachside dining spot at Jakes). From the casual outdoor tables to the late-night dance-hall rhythm, it's a place to come and chill out. Jerk crab, conch, fish, and lobster join favorites like pizzas and jerk chicken on the menu, all followed by Devon House ice cream. Tables are either shaded by trees or in the open-sided dining porch. $ *Average main: $15* ✉ *Jakes, Calabash Bay, Treasure Beach* ☎ *876/965–3000* 🌐 *www.jakeshotel.com.*

$$ JAMAICAN ✕ **Little Ochie.** This casual beachside eatery, a favorite with locals and travelers, is known for its genuine Jamaican dishes like "fish tea" (a spicy bouillon), escoveitch fish, peppered shrimp, jerk chicken, seapuss (octopus), and lobster. Most of the seafood is brought in by fishermen just yards away. For those staying in Treasure Beach, a popular way to reach Little Ochie is by boat. Each year in the second week of July, the place comes alive with the Little Ochie Seafood Fest, a veritable paradise for seafood lovers featuring several stalls serving fresh seafood with all the trimmings, music, and all-day entertainment. $ *Average main: $17* ✉ *About 7 miles (11 km) south of A2, Alligator Pond* ☎ *876/852–6430, 876/508–3578* 🌐 *www.littleochie.com.*

$ SEAFOOD Fodor's Choice ★ ✕ **Pelican Bar.** One of the funkiest places to down a cold Red Stripe, this whimsical structure sits on stilts ½ mile (1 km) offshore between Treasure Beach and Black River, atop a small sandbar, and reachable only by boat. It has become a local legend and a mandatory stop for many visitors to the South Coast. The place serves platters of lobster and other fresh seafood for lunch and dinner. Floyde Forbes (who runs the bar) and local hotels can arrange boat transportation, but the short rides can be pricey. $ *Average main: $10* ✉ *St. Elizabeth* ☎ *876/354–4218* ▭ *No credit cards.*

NEGRIL

$$ INTERNATIONAL ✕ **Annie's Restaurant.** For a special occasion or a night of romantic indulgence, book the private dining cave overlooking the sea at this casual but upscale small restaurant at Moon Dance Cliffs. You'll be set up with an intimate table in the small cavern underneath the main dining area, where wait staff will pamper you with flowers, candles, champagne, and your own music system. The restaurant's main menu is also first-class, with appetizers such as creamy pumpkin soup, cracked conch, and grilled tomatoes topped with goat cheese. The filet mignon is melt-in-your-mouth tender, and the shrimp is also a great option. There's a good mix of seafood, international, local, and vegetarian dishes. $ *Average main: $20* ✉ *Moon Dance Cliffs, West End Rd., Negril* ☎ *876/957–0872* 🌐 *www.moondanceresorts.com/cliffs.*

$$$ INTERNATIONAL ✕ **Bongos Restaurant.** A grand piano and a well-stocked premium bar add to the upscale feeling at this restaurant, with stylish indoor seating and patio tables. The cuisine is a fusion of the foods from the many cultures that have settled in the Caribbean—from Africa, Spain, the Netherlands, France, Portugal, Denmark, Great Britain, and, later, India and China. The resulting melting pot of flavors makes for mouthwatering contemporary cuisine. The seafood paella for two is a good bet, as is the Lime 'n' Thyme–grilled chicken breast with ackee, callaloo, and a mango broad-bean sauce. Alternatively, opt for the vegetarian choice such as the ackee, vegetable, and mixed-bean stew with a cilantro-tomato sauce. $ *Average main: $25* ✉ *Sandy Haven Resort, Norman Manley Blvd., Negril* ☎ *876/957–3200* 🌐 *www.sandyhavenresort.com* ⏱ *No lunch.*

$$$$ JAMAICAN ✕ **The Caves Restaurant.** With a reservation, nonguests can savor authentic Jamaican cuisine with a twist at this gorgeous boutique resort on Negril's West End. The price ($100 per person) covers a three-course dinner, welcome drink, and bottle of wine, or you can book a private, romantic candlelit five-course dinner in a sea-front cave ($300 per couple). When the hotel bar, the Sands, is open (Wednesday and Saturday 4–7), you can join in cliff-jumping, a popular West End pastime, and enjoy exotic cocktails and fare from the smoky jerk grill, and on Thursdays it offers dining under the stars ($100 per person) to a mento band. The Blackwell Rum Bar, in a private cave, is open Wednesday–Saturday 5–10. Much of the produce comes from the hotel's organic farm in the parish of Trelawny. $ *Average main: $100* ✉ *The Caves, West End, Negril* ☎ *876/957–0270, 876/618–1081* 🌐 *www.islandoutpost.com* ✍ *Reservations essential* ⏱ *No lunch.*

$$ SEAFOOD ✕ **Cosmo's Seafood Restaurant and Bar.** Owner Cosmo Brown has made this seaside, open-air bistro a pleasant place to spend the afternoon—and maybe stay on for dinner. Fish is the main attraction, and the conch soup—a house specialty—is a meal in itself. You can also find lobster (grilled, Thermidor, or curried), fish-and-chips, and the catch of the morning. After lunch, customers often drop cover-ups to take a dip before coffee and dessert and return to lounge in chairs scattered under

almond and sea grape trees (there's an entrance fee of J$400 for the beach if you want to use the facilities and J$150 to rent a lounge chair). This is where many Jamaicans chill out when they come to Negril. *Average main: $14* ✉ *Norman Manley Blvd., Negril* ☎ *876/957–4330, 876/957–4784.*

$$ ECLECTIC **The Hungry Lion.** This small but intimate restaurant with stylish decor has long been a West End favorite. An eclectic crowd comes to enjoy excellent vegetarian fare and seafood, though Jamaican jerk-chicken kebabs are also available. With the Thai tofu—in a coconut-curry-and lemongrass sauce—you may be tempted to lick the plate. Other favorites include "shepherd's pie" (a spicy lentil stew topped with mashed potatoes) and Killer Shrimp, marinated and grilled in herbs and coconut milk. There is also a good selection of fresh juices. The good-health accent is set to the tune of world music, jazz and blues, and roots reggae. *Average main: $17* ✉ *West End Rd., Negril* ☎ *876/957–4486* *No lunch.*

$$$ CARIBBEAN Fodor's Choice ★ **Ivan's Restaurant.** Upscale Caribbean cuisine, stunning cliff-side dining, and romance make this one of the best places to eat on Negril's West End. Watch the spectacular sunset while enjoying a cocktail by the simple thatched bar and eatery, decorated with funky art. Dinner opens with a delicious complimentary conch soup. Beautifully presented appetizers include the Calypso Trio—three of the most requested dishes: chicken, sweet pepper, tomato, and pineapple skewer; jerk shrimp; and a Caribbean crab cake with Ivan dip. Don't miss entrées like grilled lobster with garlic butter and mashed potatoes and the seafood linguine: shrimp, lobster, and snapper in a creamy white-wine sauce. For the flambéed banana or pineapple dessert, over-proof rum is set on fire for you to blow out and pour over ice cream. Frozen cheesecakes like chocolate mocha, key-lime pie, and peanut butter swirl are also available. You can dress up or dine in casual wear. *Average main: $25* ✉ *Catcha Falling Star, West End Rd., Negril* ☎ *876/957–0390, 876/967–0045* *www.catchajamaica.com* *No lunch.*

$ VEGETARIAN **Just Natural.** This low-key eatery with the motto "come and relax" serves vegetarian and seafood dishes as well as fresh fruit and vegetable juices, but it's the surroundings—an enchanting garden on Negril's West End—that make it stand out. Tables and chairs are mismatched, some of them made from recycled materials. They're scattered in the garden, surrounded by orange trees, pretty flowers, and lush vegetation, so that each dining area is private. All food is made to order and well priced. A small soup and dessert are included with dinner. *Average main: $8* ✉ *Hylton Ave., ½ mile (1 km) after the lighthouse, Negril* ☎ *876/957–0235, 876/354–4287* *No credit cards.*

$$ JAMAICAN Fodor's Choice ★ **Kuyaba on the Beach.** Open all day and right on the beach, this charming thatch-roofed restaurant is one of the top spots for dinner on Negril's 7-mile (11-km) strip of sand. The menu specializes in Jamaican cuisine with an international twist, with meals covering sea, breeze, and land. There are a few good vegetarian options like the veggie stewed peas and the Rasta pasta. All food is cooked to order, so come prepared for a long languorous meal. During the day you can lounge on beach chairs. The restaurant will bring you here for free if you're staying in Negril.

$ *Average main: $20* ✉ *Norman Manley Blvd., Negril* ☎ *876/957–4318* 🌐 *www.kuyaba.com.*

$$ INTERNATIONAL ✕ **LTU Pub.** This thatched bar and eatery is one of the prettiest on the West End. Right on the cliffs and practically next door to Rick's Cafe, it has dazzling views during the day and at sunset and steps down to the water. At night, you can dine under the stars. Expats and long-term visitors hang out here to enjoy the laid-back vibe that put Negril on the map. Appetizer highlights include chicken-and-cheese quesadillas and coconut shrimp. Entrées feature beef tenderloin in red-wine sauce, chicken Lola, and snapper stuffed with callaloo. There are lots of pasta choices, too. Dinners come with a delicious pumpkin soup. $ *Average main: $15* ✉ *West End Rd., Negril* ☎ *876/957–0382.*

BEST BETS FOR LODGING

Fodor's Choice★
The Blue House, Catcha Falling Star, The Caves, Geejam, Goldeneye, Hermosa Cove, Hotel Mockingbird Hill, Jakes, Jamaica Inn, Rockhouse, Round Hill, Sandals Royal Plantation Ocho Rios, Spanish Court Hotel, Strawberry Hill, Tensing Pen

BEST FAMILY RESORTS
Beaches Ocho Rios, Hilton Rose Hall, Holiday Inn SunSpree, Sunset Beach Resort

BEST FOR ROMANCE
Catcha Falling Star, The Caves, Strawberry Hill, Tensing Pen

$$ CARIBBEAN Fodor's Choice ★ ✕ **Rockhouse Restaurant.** This restaurant is a must for dinner at least once. The open-air dining area has huge comfy bamboo sofas where you can relax for an aperitif or after-dinner drink; tables are arranged near the cliff for sensational seaside dining. For special occasions, private tables for groups can be set up in a cabana, on an intimate terrace, or on a lower deck. The menu features both traditional Jamaican cooking and Rockhouse's interpretation of "new Jamaican cuisine," inspired by the many cultures that have come to the island. Staff are friendly and attentive. $ *Average main: $17* ✉ *Rockhouse, West End Rd., Negril* ☎ *876/957–4373* 🌐 *www.rockhousehotel.com.*

$ JAMAICAN ✕ **Shark's Restaurant.** This nicely decorated thatched roadside restaurant with just three tables is opposite Tensing Pen. It's one of the best places to sample local cooking in a friendly and laid-back atmosphere. Juliet, who owns and runs the tiny place, also cooks. All the food is delicious including chicken fricassee, curried goat, panfried snapper, and grilled lobster with lashings of garlic butter. $ *Average main: $8* ✉ *West End Rd., Negril* ☎ *876/428–8411* ▭ *No credit cards.*

WHERE TO STAY

Jamaica is the birthplace of the Caribbean all-inclusive resort, a concept that started in Ocho Rios and later spread throughout the island, so that now most hotel rates are all-inclusive. Package prices usually include airport transfers, accommodations, three meals a day, snacks, all bar drinks (often including premium liquors) and soft drinks, a full menu of sports options (including scuba diving and golf at high-end resorts), nightly entertainment, and all gratuities and taxes. At most all-inclusives, the only surcharges are for such luxuries as spa and beauty treatments, telephone calls, tours, vow-renewal ceremonies, and weddings (often included at high-end establishments).

The all-inclusive market is especially strong with couples. To maintain a romantic atmosphere (no Marco Polo games in the pool), some resorts have minimum age requirements from 12 to 18. Other properties court families with supervised kids' programs, family-friendly entertainment, and in-room amenities for young travelers.

PRIVATE VILLAS

Ocho Rios is filled with private villas, especially in the Discovery Bay area. In Jamaica, most luxury villas come with a full staff, including a housekeeper, cook, butler, gardener, and often a security guard. Many can arrange for a driver for airport transfers, daily touring, or a prearranged number of days of sightseeing.

Demand for larger, more luxurious properties has increased. Numerous villas have five or more bedrooms in different parts of a building—or in different buildings altogether for extra privacy.

Most villas come with linens, and you can often arrange for the kitchen to be stocked with groceries upon your arrival. Air-conditioning, even in the most luxurious villas, is typically limited to bedrooms.

A four-night minimum is average for many villas though this can vary by season and property. Gratuities, usually split among the staff, are typically 10%–15%. Several private companies specialize in finding vacationers rentals at the right size and price.

RENTAL CONTACTS

Jamaica Association of Villas and Apartments. Since 1967, this company, based in Ocho Rios, has handled villas, cottages, apartments, and condos across the island. ☎ *876/452–1268* 🌐 *www.javavillas.org.*

Jamaica Villas by Linda Smith. More than 90 fully staffed villas are available. ✉ *8029 Riverside Dr., Cabin John, Maryland, United States* ☎ *301/229–4300* 🌐 *www.jamaicavillas.com.*

Luxury Retreats International. This outfit offers numerous luxury villa rentals in Negril, Montego Bay, Ocho Rios (including Discovery Bay), and Port Antonio. ✉ *5530 St. Patrick St., Suite 2210, Montréal, Québec, Canada* ☎ *877/993–0100* 🌐 *www.luxuryretreats.com/search/caribbean/jamaica.*

MONTEGO BAY

Mo'Bay has miles of hotels, villas, apartments, and duty-free shops. Although without much in the way of must-see culture, at least for the average visitor, it presents a comfortable island backdrop for the many conventions it hosts. And it has the added advantage of being the closest resort area to the Donald Sangster International Airport.

$$ RESORT **Coyaba Beach Resort and Club.** Privately owned, this intimate property is relaxing, welcoming, and just 10 minutes east of Montego Bay airport. **Pros:** quiet atmosphere of an inn; excellent restaurants; good-size private beach. **Cons:** directly on North Coast Highway; fairly small

Restaurants ▼

Biggs BBQ **1**

Marguerites Seafood By The Sea **2**

Pier 1 ....**4**

Pork Pit **3**

Scotchies **5**

Seagrape Terrace **7**

Sugar Mill **6**

Hotels ▼

Coyaba Beach Resort and Club **5**

Half Moon, a Rockresort **7**

Hilton Rose Hall .**1**

Holiday Inn SunSpree Resort **6**

Iberostar Rose Hall Beach **2**

Riu Palace **3**

Sandals Royal Caribbean **4**

Sunset Beach Resort **8**

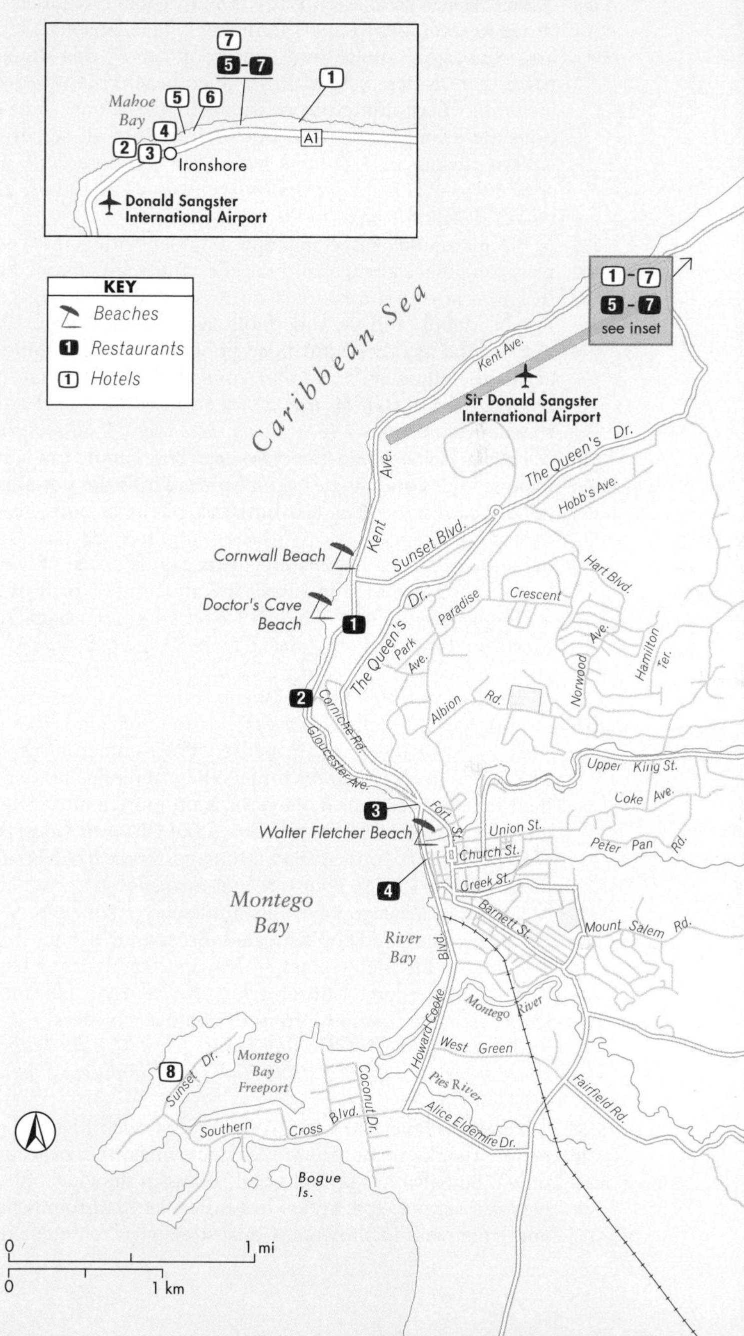

pool: climb to third-floor rooms can be difficult without elevator. *Rooms from: $369 Little River, Montego Bay 876/953–9150 www.coyabaresortjamaica.com 50 rooms Multiple meal plans.*

$$$$ HOTEL FAMILY **Half Moon, a RockResort.** With its many room categories, massive villas (three to seven bedrooms), shopping village, hospital, school, dolphin attraction, golf course, and equestrian center, this seems more like a town than a mere resort. **Pros:** huge beach; many room categories, including villas; numerous on-site activities. **Cons:** some accommodations are a long walk from public areas, not all activities are within walking distance. *Rooms from: $499 Rose Hall, Montego Bay 876/953–2211 www.halfmoon.com 45 rooms, 152 suites, 33 villas Multiple meal plans.*

$$$ ALL-INCLUSIVE FAMILY **Hilton Rose Hall Resort and Spa.** Popular with romance-minded couples, conference groups, and families, this self-contained resort 4 miles (6 km) east of the airport is on Rose Hall's 400-acre grounds. **Pros:** family-friendly dining and pool; easy access to golf. **Cons:** beach is not as good as others; kid-filled pool can be noisy; some activities are across the highway. *Rooms from: $448 Rose Hall Main Rd., 15 miles (24 km) east of Montego Bay, St. James 876/953–2650 www.rosehallresort.com 488 rooms, 14 suites All-inclusive.*

$$$ ALL-INCLUSIVE FAMILY **Holiday Inn SunSpree Resort Montego Bay.** Family fun is tops here, but many couples and singles are also drawn to the not-crazy prices and good location, 6 miles (10 km) east of the airport. **Pros:** good family atmosphere; easy access to shopping; free self-serve laundry. **Cons:** numerous children mean some areas can be noisy; only nonmotorized water sports included in rates; directly beside North Coast Highway. *Rooms from: $408 North Coast Hwy., 10 miles (16 km) east of Montego Bay, Montego Bay 876/953–2485 www.caribbeanhi.com/jamaica 524 rooms, 27 suites All-inclusive.*

$$ ALL-INCLUSIVE FAMILY **Iberostar Rose Hall Beach.** Twenty minutes east of the Montego Bay airport, this all-inclusive resort was the first (and least expensive) of three adjacent Ibersotar properties. **Pros:** numerous on-site activities; easy access to airport and Montego Bay; complimentary minibar. **Cons:** high-rise setup can mean elevator wait; more limited all-inclusive program than some. *Rooms from: $324 North Coast Hwy., 8 miles (13 km) east of Montego Bay, Montego Bay 876/680–0000 www.iberostar.com 366 rooms All-inclusive.*

$$$$ ALL-INCLUSIVE **Riu Palace Montego Bay.** This adult-only resort with well-appointed rooms is trendy and sophisticated. **Pros:** on the beach and near activities; free Wi-Fi; double-glass, noise-canceling doors and hydro-massage tubs in every room. **Cons:** parking lot at resort entrance takes away from aesthetics; contemporary design overpowers the expected island flavor; small gym. *Rooms from: $518 Blue Mahoe Bay, Ironshore, Montego Bay 800/810–9822 www.riu.com 238 rooms All-inclusive.*

$$$$ HOTEL Fodor's Choice ★ **Round Hill Hotel and Villas.** A favorite of celebrities and other wealthy people thanks to its private, elegant villas, this peaceful resort west of Mo'Bay also has stylish hotel rooms in the Pineapple House. **Pros:** personal service; spa; stylish rooms; quiet; bathrooms have deep tubs and large walk-in showers. **Cons:** somewhat remote; expensive; some

villas do not have pools. $ *Rooms from: $819* ✉ *North Coast Hwy., 8 miles (13 km) west of Montego Bay, Montego Bay* ☎ *876/956–7050* 🌐 *www.roundhill.com* 36 *rooms, 27 villas* *Multiple meal plans.*

$$ ALL-INCLUSIVE **Sandals Carlyle.** If you can forgo a private beach at your doorstep (there's a public one across the street, and an hourly shuttle that takes you to other Sandals properties), you can stay here for much less than at the other Sandals resorts. **Pros:** moderate price; complimentary shuttle to sister properties; convenient location. **Cons:** no private beach; small pool; limited on-site dining. $ *Rooms from: $275* ✉ *Kent Ave., Montego Bay* ☎ *876/952–4140* 🌐 *www.sandals.com* *52 rooms and suites* *All-inclusive.*

$$$$ ALL-INCLUSIVE **Sandals Royal Caribbean Resort & Private Island.** Four miles (6 km) east of the airport, this elegant resort has Jamaican-style buildings around attractive gardens. **Pros:** lots of room categories; offshore dining; complimentary shuttles to airport and other Sandals resorts. **Cons:** too quiet for some; smaller beach than Sandals Montego Bay. $ *Rooms from: $505* ✉ *North Coast Hwy., 6 miles (9 km) east of Montego Bay, Montego Bay* ☎ *876/953–2231* 🌐 *www.sandals.com* *197 rooms and suites* *All-inclusive.*

$$$ ALL-INCLUSIVE FAMILY **Sunset Beach Resort.** Often packed with charter groups, this expansive resort can be a good value if you don't mind mass tourism. **Pros:** excellent beaches; good restaurants; numerous on-site activities. **Cons:** can be crowded; high-rise setup means lines for the elevator; too far to walk to other Montego Bay attractions. $ *Rooms from: $440* ✉ *Freeport, Montego Bay* ☎ *876/979–8800* 🌐 *www.sunsetresortsjamaica.com/sunset-beach-resort-montego-bay* *430 rooms, 16 suites* *All-inclusive.*

$$$$ RESORT **Tryall Club.** The sumptuous villas—each with a private pool—and pampering staff lend a home-away-from-home feel to this golfers' haven west of Mo'Bay. **Pros:** excellent golf; villa experience with convenience of a resort; complimentary kids' club plus a nanny service. **Cons:** nonmembers pay $20 a day for temporary membership to Tryall Club; shared public facilities; somewhat formal atmosphere. $ *Rooms from: $550* ✉ *North Coast Hwy., 15 miles (24 km) west of Montego Bay, Sandy Bay* ☎ *876/956–5660, 800/238–5290 in U.S.* 🌐 *www.tryallclub.com* *86 villas* *No meals.*

RUNAWAY BAY

The smallest of the resort areas, Runaway Bay, 50 miles (80 km) east of Montego Bay and about 12 miles (19 km) west of Ocho Rios, has a handful of modern hotels, a few all-inclusive resorts, and an 18-hole golf course.

$$$ ALL-INCLUSIVE **Jewel Paradise Cove Beach Resort & Spa.** A full-service spa is the centerpiece of this resort, which focuses on fitness, health, and well-being. **Pros:** free Wi-Fi; complimentary greens fees at Runaway Bay Golf Club; excellent fitness facilities. **Cons:** spa treatments cost extra; beach not the best. $ *Rooms from: $469* ✉ *Paradise Cove Dr., Runaway Bay* ☎ *876/972–7400* 🌐 *www.jewelresorts.com* *225 rooms* *All-inclusive.*

$$$ RESORT **Jewel Runaway Bay Beach & Golf Resort.** Geared to active adults and families, this luxury all-inclusive has a championship golf course. **Pros:** extensive sports and water sports; complimentary airport shuttle and greens fees. **Cons:** small property; low-rise layout blocks easy beach access. *Rooms from: $399 North Coast Hwy., Runaway Bay 876/973–6099 www.jewelresortsrunawaybay.com 266 rooms, 20 suites Multiple meal plans.*

OCHO RIOS

Rivers, waterfalls, fern-shaded roads, and tropical lushness fill this fertile North Coast region, halfway between Port Antonio and Mo'Bay. It's a favorite with honeymooners as well as Jamaicans who like to escape crowded Kingston for the weekend. Resorts, hotels, and villas are all a short drive from the frenetic, traffic-clogged downtown, which has a crafts market, boutiques, duty-free shops, restaurants, and several scenic attractions. Ocho Rios is 67 miles (111 km) east of Montego Bay, just under two hours by car.

$$$$ ALL-INCLUSIVE FAMILY **Beaches Ocho Rios Resort and Golf Club.** The company that specializes in the all-inclusive resort brings its brand of luxury, attention to detail, and attentive staff to this family-oriented property. **Pros:** excellent children's program; numerous dining options; great spa; compact, enclosed property. **Cons:** no room service without butler service; restaurants not always open; charge for Wi-Fi. *Rooms from: $608 North Coast Hwy., St. Ann's Bay 876/975–7777 www.beaches.com 223 rooms, 90 suites All-inclusive 2-night minimum.*

$ B&B/INN Fodor's Choice ★ **The Blue House.** This stylish boutique B&B is a nice alternative to North Coast all-inclusives. **Pros:** homey; great for single travelers; pool. **Cons:** not many rooms, so you need to book early during busy season; not on the beach; far from amenities. *Rooms from: $240 Marcliff, White River Estate, Ocho Rios 876/994–1367 www.thebluehousejamaica.com 5 rooms Multiple meal plans.*

$ ALL-INCLUSIVE **ClubHotel Riu Ocho Rios.** This sprawling resort, built in two U-shape wings each overlooking a pool, is one of the largest in Jamaica. **Pros:** lots of places to eat; large rooms; expansive beach. **Cons:** long walk to beach; some public areas feel cramped; all-inclusive package is limited. *Rooms from: $178 North Coast Hwy., Mammee Bay 876/972–2200 www.riu.com 478 rooms, 386 junior suites All-inclusive.*

$$$$ ALL-INCLUSIVE **Couples Sans Souci Resort and Spa.** This classy all-inclusive encourages you to check your cares at the entrance and indulge in soul-nurturing pampering. **Pros:** excellent spa; expansive all-inclusive package: free weddings, Montego Bay airport shuttle, trips to Dunn's River Falls and Ocho Rios shopping. **Cons:** some rooms are very isolated and a long walk from public areas; beaches are not as good as others. *Rooms from: $950 North Coast Hwy., 2 miles (3 km) east of Ocho Rios, Ocho Rios 876/994–1206 www.couples.com 150 suites All-inclusive.*

$$$$ ALL-INCLUSIVE **Couples Tower Isle.** This all-inclusive has beautiful contemporary decor. **Pros:** some free weddings; excellent beach facilities; reciprocal deal with Couples Sans Souci on Monday, Wednesday, and Friday. **Cons:** far from

Montego Bay airport. *Rooms from: $950* ✉ *Tower Isle, Rte. A3, 5 miles (8 km) east of Ocho Rios, St. Mary* ☎ *876/975–4271* 🌐 *www.couples.com* *280 rooms, 14 suites* *All-inclusive.*

$ RENTAL **Glory Be.** When owner Karen Schleifer's aunt Marion Simmons first set eyes on this property, she exclaimed, "Glory be," and that's what the house, frequented by a fashionable 1950s and '60s art and literary crowd, became known as. **Pros:** private; pool; great location on the cliffs; close to Reggae Beach. **Cons:** no natural-sand beach on property; 4 miles (6½ km) from Ocho Rios town center. *Rooms from: $150* ✉ *Tower Isle, Ocho Rios* ☎ *876/975–4213* *3 cottages* *No meals.*

$$$$ RENTAL Fodor's Choice ★ **Goldeneye.** Whether you're a fan of James Bond or luxury getaways, this exclusive address 20 minutes east of Ocho Rios holds special appeal. **Pros:** spacious; plenty of privacy. **Cons:** remote location; limited dining options; may be too quiet for some. *Rooms from: $840* ✉ *North Coast Hwy., Oracabessa* ☎ *876/622–9007* 🌐 *www.goldeneye.com* *1 5-bedroom villa, 20 villas/cottages* *No meals.*

$$ RESORT Fodor's Choice ★ **Hermosa Cove Villa Resort & Suites.** Secluded in a walled-in complex, contemporary one- and two-story villas are artfully decorated and set in verdant, lush grounds. **Pros:** quiet, stylish, and comfortable suites and villas; safe and secure. **Cons:** small beach; limited menu at restaurant; isolated; walled-in. *Rooms from: $295* ✉ *Hermosa Cove, Hermosa St., Ocho Rios* ☎ *876/974–3699* 🌐 *www.hermosacove.com* *9 cottages* *Breakfast.*

14

$$$$ HOTEL Fodor's Choice ★ **Jamaica Inn.** Attracting such luminaries as Marilyn Monroe, who honeymooned here with playwright Arthur Miller, this inn exemplifies the elegance, luxury, and exquisite service of Jamaica's tourism heyday. **Pros:** elegant accommodations; exceptional service; good spa; all-inclusive plans available. **Cons:** no in-room TV. *Rooms from: $529* ✉ *North Coast Hwy., 2 miles (3 km) east of Ocho Rios, Ocho Rios* ☎ *876/974–2514* 🌐 *www.jamaicainn.com* *48 suites, 4 two-bedroom cottages* *Multiple meal plans.*

$$$ ALL-INCLUSIVE **Jewel Dunn's River Beach Resort & Spa.** From the waterfall in the main pool, inspired by the famous nearby attraction, to the bag of jewels placed on your pillow by the attentive staff, this upscale resort for adults lives up to its name. **Pros:** more intimate than most all-inclusives; 9-hole golf course; high-quality service and amenities. **Cons:** crowded beach. *Rooms from: $429* ✉ *Mammee Bay, Ocho Rios* ☎ *876/972–7400* 🌐 *www.jewelresorts.com* *234 rooms, 16 suites* *All-inclusive.*

$$$ ALL-INCLUSIVE **Sandals Grande Riviera Beach & Villa Golf Resort.** This sprawling resort began years ago as two separate properties, and today it continues to have a split personality. **Pros:** airport shuttle; lots of privacy; numerous swimming options; romantic dining options. **Cons:** villas a long way from the beach; some rooms removed from public areas; long wait for the shuttle. *Rooms from: $471* ✉ *Main St., Ocho Rios* ☎ *876/974–5691* 🌐 *www.sandals.com* *260 rooms, 268 villas* *All-inclusive.*

$$$$ ALL-INCLUSIVE Fodor's Choice ★ **Sandals Royal Plantation Ocho Rios.** During its heyday, guests at what was then called Plantation Inn included British royals, Winston Churchill, and authors Noël Coward and Ian Fleming. **Pros:** expansive, stylish accommodations; good dining; room service available. **Cons:** guest rooms and beach are on different levels; small pool and beach.

Rooms from: $655 ✉ *Main St., Ocho Rios* ☎ *876/974–5601* 🌐 *www.sandals.com* *74 suites, 1 villa* *All-inclusive.*

PORT ANTONIO

For an alternative to the hectic tourist scene in the bustling resort towns of Montego Bay and Ocho Rios, head to this quiet community on Jamaica's east end, 133 miles (220 km) east of Montego Bay. Don't look for mixology classes or limbo dances here. The fun is usually found outdoors, followed by a fine evening meal. The area's must-do activities include rafting Jamaica's own Rio Grande, taking an eco-hike, and having lunch or a drink at the Jamaica Palace.

$ HOTEL **Demontevin Lodge Hotel.** On Titchfield Hill, this fine example of elegant 19th-century Victorian architecture has period decor and furnishings. **Pros:** a taste of old Jamaica; central location. **Cons:** limited amenities beyond a modest restaurant; some rooms share bathroom. *Rooms from: $40* ✉ *21 Fort George St., Port Antonio* *876/993–2604* ☎ *876/715–5987* *13 rooms* *Some meals.*

$ RESORT **Frenchman's Cove Resort.** This resort has a pristine location and decor that feels like a time capsule, but a far cry from when Queen Elizabeth II stayed in Villa 18. **Pros:** excellent beach; privacy; large accommodations; kitchens in villas; Continental breakfast included. **Cons:** dated decor; long walk to public areas and beach; some rooms don't have TV. *Rooms from: $140* ✉ *Rte. A4, 5 miles (8 km) east of Port Antonio, Port Antonio* ☎ *876/993–7270* 🌐 *www.frenchmanscove.com* *10 rooms, 2 suites, 16 villas* *Breakfast.*

$$$$ HOTEL Fodor's Choice ★ **Geejam.** Located 10 minutes east of Port Antonio, this stylish rockers' getaway (Gwen Stefani recorded an album here, and it's a favorite of Grace Jones) was once a music producer's hideaway. **Pros:** five-night stay includes ground transfer from Kingston airport; complimentary transportation to nearby beaches; personalized service; Apple TV in all rooms. **Cons:** remote location; limited on-site amenities; may be too quiet for some. *Rooms from: $595* ✉ *North Coast Hwy., San San, Port Antonio* ☎ *876/993–7000* 🌐 *www.geejam.com* *1 3-bed villa, 1 suite, 3 cabins* *Breakfast.*

$ RESORT FAMILY **Goblin Hill Villas at San San.** Hummingbirds flit about this property, consisting of one- and two-story villas with the conveniences of a hotel. **Pros:** full maid service; roomy; family-friendly. **Cons:** no restaurant; not right on the beach. *Rooms from: $225* ✉ *Rte. A4, 3 miles (5 km) east of Port Antonio, San San* ☎ *876/925–8108* 🌐 *www.goblinhill.com* *28 villas* *No meals.*

$$ HOTEL Fodor's Choice ★ **Hotel Mockingbird Hill.** This eco-friendly boutique hotel is a delight for those who are environmentally conscious and socially aware, with luxury bound to please anyone. **Pros:** numerous ecotourism options; environmentally conscious; carbon offsetting; excellent (but limited) dining. **Cons:** somewhat remote; not directly on the beach. *Rooms from: $345* ✉ *North Coast Hwy., Point Ann, Port Antonio* ☎ *876/993–7267* 🌐 *www.hotelmockingbirdhill.com* *10 rooms* *Some meals.*

$$$$ HOTEL **Trident Hotel.** What was once a stiff, formal, and traditional hotel has been remade into a stylish contemporary resort, part of the

Geejam collection. **Pros:** stylish; movie-screening room; full-service spa; nanny service; private beach. **Cons:** few rooms can make it hard to book at busy times. *Rooms from: $600 North Coast Hwy., Point Ann, Port Antonio 876/993–2602 www.geejam.com, www.tridentportantonio.com 14 suites Breakfast 5-night minimum Dec. 20–26 and Easter, 7-night minimum Dec. 26–Jan. 3.*

KINGSTON

14

Visited by few vacationers but a frequent destination for business travelers and visitors with a deep interest in Jamaican heritage and culture, the sprawling city of Kingston is home to some of the island's finest business hotels. Skirting the city are the Blue Mountains, a completely different world from the urban frenzy of the capital city.

$ HOTEL **The Courtleigh Hotel & Suites.** Aimed at business people, this hotel is in the city's financial district, in the heart of New Kingston and less than a half-hour from Norman Manley International Airport. **Pros:** large rooms; lively nightlife; good business facilities. **Cons:** limited dining options; noisy location; most rooms lack balconies. *Rooms from: $195 85 Knutsford Blvd., Kingston 876/929–9000 www.courtleigh.com 127 rooms, 38 suites Breakfast.*

$ HOTEL **Knutsford Court Hotel.** This modest business-district hotel combines business services with a garden-style atmosphere. **Pros:** good value; business amenities; friendly staff. **Cons:** limited leisure amenities; small pool area, no free Wi-Fi. *Rooms from: $120 16 Chelsea Ave., Kingston 876/929–1000 www.knutsfordcourt.com 143 rooms, 18 suites, 5 townhouses Breakfast.*

$ B&B/INN **Neita's Nest.** This B&B is for those who want to avoid a corporate hotel and the bustle of the city. **Pros:** inexpensive; intimate experience in a Jamaican family's house; quiet location; free Wi-Fi. **Cons:** far from restaurants and attractions; no amenities within walking distance. *Rooms from: $160 Bridgemount, Stony Hill, Kingston 876/469–3005 www.neitasnest.com 3 rooms No credit cards Breakfast.*

$ HOTEL Fodor's Choice ★ **Spanish Court Hotel.** Quickly becoming the go-to hotel in Kingston, providing service to business travelers, wedding parties, and tourists, Spanish Court is a calm oasis in New Kingston. **Pros:** great city-center location; 24-hour business center; reasonable prices; energy-conserving features. **Cons:** limited dining options. *Rooms from: $189 1 St. Lucia Ave., Kingston 876/926–0000 www.spanishcourthotel.com 122 rooms Breakfast.*

$ HOTEL **Terra Nova All Suite Hotel.** This graceful former colonial mansion has refurbished rooms and elegant touches to please the discerning traveler. **Pros:** elegant; great open-air dining; near shops and restaurants. **Cons:** fills up quickly on weekends. *Rooms from: $220 17 Waterloo Rd., Kingston 876/926–2211 www.terranovajamaica.com 49 suites Breakfast.*

BLUE MOUNTAINS

$$ HOTEL Fodor's Choice ★ **Strawberry Hill.** A 45-minute drive from Kingston—but worlds apart in terms of atmosphere—this exclusive resort was developed by Chris Blackwell, former head of Island Records (the label of Bob Marley, among many others). **Pros:** stylish accommodations with breathtaking mountain views; cool retreat from the heat; great for hiking or exploring nearby coffee plantations. **Cons:** remote location a distance from beaches; limited on-site dining options. *Rooms from: $355 New Castle Rd., Irish Town 876/944–8400 www.islandoutpost.com 12 cottages Multiple meal plans.*

SOUTH COAST

In the 1970s Negril was Jamaica's most relaxed place to hang out. Today that distinction is held by the South Coast, a long stretch of coastline ranging from Whitehouse to Treasure Beach. Here local residents wave to cars, and travelers spend their days exploring local communities and their nights in local restaurants. The best way to reach the South Coast is from Montego Bay, driving overland, or via Savanna-la-Mar from Negril. Both methods take around 90 minutes to two hours, depending on your final destination.

$ HOTEL Fodor's Choice ★ **Jakes.** Seaside charm combines with art to create a chic place that oozes personality. **Pros:** unique accommodations; South Coast friendliness; personalized service. **Cons:** can feel cramped when occasional rainy periods keep you inside; long drive from Montego Bay and Kingston airports. *Rooms from: $115 Calabash Bay, Treasure Beach 876/965–3000 www.jakeshotel.com 50 rooms, including villas No meals.*

$$$$ ALL-INCLUSIVE **Sandals Whitehouse European Village and Spa.** The first major resort on the South Coast, this property is one of the most upscale properties in the Sandals chain. **Pros:** great private beach; lots of restaurants; extensive all-inclusive package includes airport shuttle; stylish rooms at all levels. **Cons:** some travelers won't like Disney-ish re-creation of Euro styles; far from independent restaurants and attractions. *Rooms from: $585 Whitehouse, Westmoreland 876/640–3000 www.sandals.com 360 rooms and suites All-inclusive.*

NEGRIL

Some 50 miles (80 km) west of Mo'Bay, the so-called Capital of Casual was once a hippie hangout, favored for its inexpensive mom-and-pop hotels and laid-back atmosphere. Today there's still a little bohemian flair, but the town is one of the biggest tourist draws on the island, with several large all-inclusives along Bloody Bay, northeast of town. The main strip of Negril Beach and the cliffs are still favored by vacationers who like to get out and explore.

$$ ALL-INCLUSIVE **Breezes Grand Resort and Spa Negril.** Fancy touches and an expansive clothing-optional beach (with its own hot tub, bar, and grill) make it equally tempting to dress for dinner or strip down for some fun in the sun. **Pros:** excellent beaches; super-inclusive package, including 24-hour

Restaurants ▼

Annie's **10**
Bongos **3**
Cosmo's **1**
The Hungry Lion **5**
Ivan's Restaurant & Bar **7**
Just Natural **9**
Kuyaba on the Beach **2**
LTU Pub **8**
The Rockhouse Restaurant **4**
Shark's Restaurant **6**

Hotels ▼

Breezes Grand Resort and Spa Negril **4**
Catcha Falling Star **14**
The Caves **12**
Charela Inn **9**
ClubHotel Riu Negril **1**
Country Country **8**
Couples Negril **2**
Couples Swept Away **6**
Grand Pineapple Beach Negril .. **10**
Hedonism II **5**
Rockhouse **11**
Sandy Haven **7**
Sunset at the Palms **3**
Tensing Pen **13**

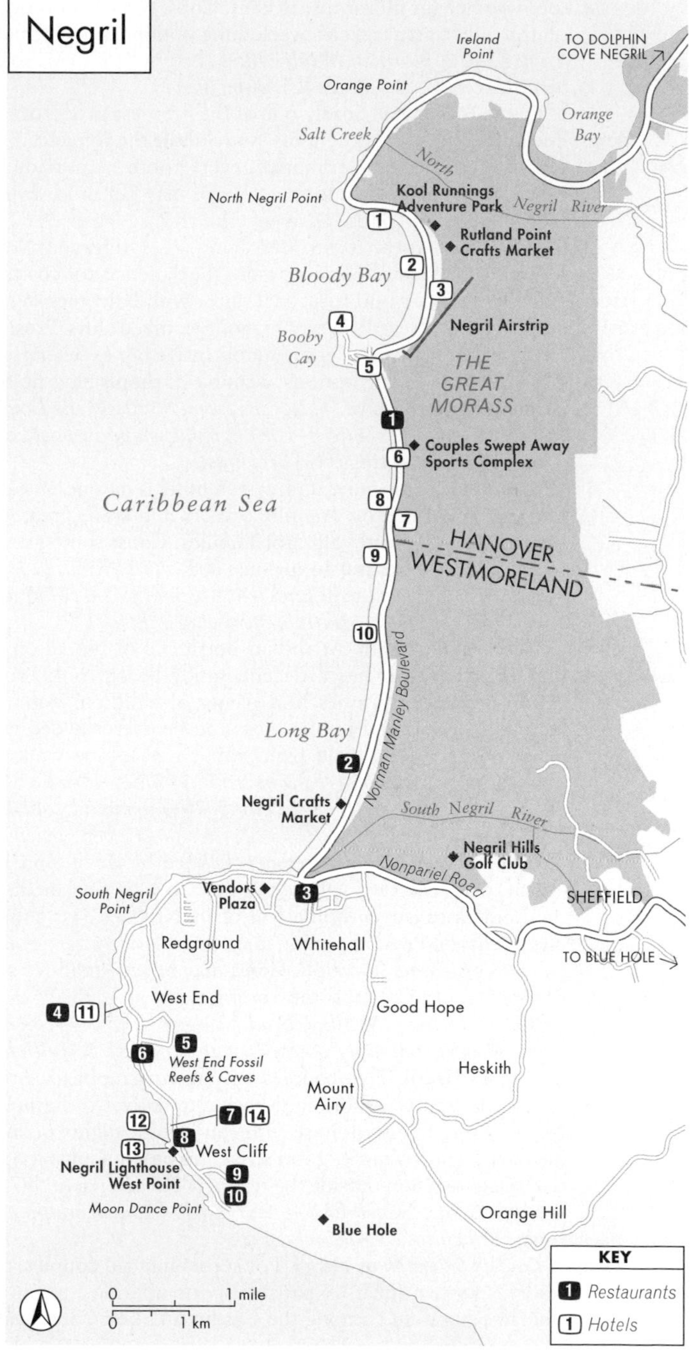

14

room service for all rooms; elegant. **Cons:** some rooms need updating; central public area lacks view; clothing-optional pool is small. *Rooms from: $340 ⊠ Norman Manley Blvd., Negril ☎ 876/957–5010 www.breezes.com 210 suites All-inclusive.*

$ HOTEL Fodor's Choice ★ **Catcha Falling Star.** Surely one of the prettiest properties on the West End cliffs, this place proclaims "to rekindle the romance." **Pros:** rooms for different budgets; romantic; every room is individual. **Cons:** no beach; the cheapest gatehouse cottage may get noise from the street. *Rooms from: $135 ⊠ West End Rd., Negril ☎ 876/957–0390 www.catchajamaica.com 6 suites, 11 cottages No meals.*

$$$$ RESORT Fodor's Choice ★ **The Caves.** At this boutique resort, the thatched-roof cottages are individually designed and furnished, most with balconies overlooking the deep water off Negril's West End honeycombed cliffs. **Pros:** intimate spa on clifftop; quiet and friendly; unobtrusive but excellent service. **Cons:** limited on-site dining options; a couple of rooms have no sea views; no beach; really expensive. *Rooms from: $690 ⊠ One Love Dr., Negril ☎ 876/957–0270, 876/618–1081 www.islandoutpost.com/the_caves 13 villas and cottages Breakfast.*

$ HOTEL **Charela Inn.** This quiet, family-run hotel is on one of the nicest parts of Negril Beach. **Pros:** friendly owners and staff; great dining; good beach location; good value for families. **Cons:** some guest rooms are small; facilities are not luxurious. *Rooms from: $210 ⊠ Norman Manley Blvd., Negril ☎ 876/957–4648, 876/957–4277 www.charela.com 50 rooms Multiple meal plans.*

$ ALL-INCLUSIVE FAMILY **ClubHotel Riu Negril.** At the far north end of Negril on Bloody Bay, this massive resort has a decent, sandy beachfront. **Pros:** economical all-inclusive; families find plenty of children; good on-site dining. **Cons:** pools and public areas can be overcrowded with families; many rooms a long walk from public areas; long walk from attractions of Negril Beach. *Rooms from: $171 ⊠ Norman Manley Blvd., Negril ☎ 876/957–5700, 876/940–8020 www.riu.com 400 rooms All-inclusive.*

$ B&B/INN **Country Country Beach Cottages.** Owned by Kevin and Joanne Robertson, who also own Montego Bay's Coyaba, this small hotel carries the home-away-from-home feel of its North Coast cousin but with Negril charm. **Pros:** charming guest rooms; oversize accommodations; good Negril Beach location. **Cons:** may be too small for some; nearby Margaritaville makes some rooms noisy at night. *Rooms from: $200 ⊠ Norman Manley Blvd., Negril ☎ 876/957–4273 www.countrynegril.com 17 cottages, 2 apartments Multiple meal plans.*

$$$$ ALL-INCLUSIVE **Couples Negril.** This couples-only resort emphasizes romance and relaxation and is a more laid-back alternative to the nearby Sandals Negril. **Pros:** free weddings with stays of six nights or more; complimentary airport shuttle; good stretch of beach. **Cons:** long walk along the beach to action outside the resort. *Rooms from: $975 ⊠ Norman Manley Blvd., Negril ☎ 876/957–5960 www.couples.com 234 rooms, 18 suites All-inclusive.*

$$$$ ALL-INCLUSIVE **Couples Swept Away Negril.** For sports-minded couples, this all-suites resort is known for its expansive sports offerings, top-notch facilities (Jamaica's best and among the Caribbean's best), and healthy cuisine.

The Rockhouse Hotel in Negril has thatched villas on cliffs overlooking the sea.

Pros: excellent fitness and sports facilities; complimentary airport shuttle; great spa. **Cons:** the healthy angle's not for everyone; some facilities are across the road; expensive. *Rooms from: $1000 ✉ Norman Manley Blvd., Negril ☎ 876/957–4061 🌐 www.couples.com 312 suites 🍴 All-inclusive ☞ 3-night minimum.*

$ ALL-INCLUSIVE **Grand Pineapple Beach Resort Negril.** This low-rise resort, dubbed "the cutest little resort in Negril" epitomizes the relaxed and funky style that Negril is still known for. **Pros:** nice pool on the garden side with snacks available; good value; lovely beach; helpful staff; nice spa. **Cons:** some rooms don't have balconies; nearby bars can be noisy; limit of three to a room. *Rooms from: $205 ✉ Norman Manley Blvd., Negril ☎ 876/957–4408 🌐 www.grandpineapple.com 65 rooms 🍴 All-inclusive.*

$$$ ALL-INCLUSIVE **Hedonism II.** Promising a perpetual spring break for adults drawn to the legendary party atmosphere, this resort gets a lot of repeat business. **Pros:** good beaches; more economical than some adult all-inclusives; numerous activities. **Cons:** bacchanalian atmosphere not for everyone; nude beach and pool frequently overcrowded; basic rooms. *Rooms from: $466 ✉ Norman Manley Blvd., Rutland Point, Negril ☎ 876/957–5200 🌐 www.hedonism.com 268 rooms, 12 suites 🍴 All-inclusive.*

$ HOTEL Fodor's Choice ★ **Rockhouse Hotel.** Attracting discerning travelers, honeymooners, and celebrities, this boutique hotel has its cottages and villas placed along a cliff. **Pros:** unique accommodations; beautiful setting; natural, tropical style throughout; great dining options. **Cons:** no beach; may be too quiet for some. *Rooms from: $180 ✉ West End Rd., Negril ☎ 876/957–4373 🌐 www.rockhousehotel.com 9 rooms, 20 villas, 5 studios 🍴 No meals.*

$$ HOTEL **Sandy Haven Resort.** This small boutique hotel, opened in 2012, is a good value, particularly since it's on a lovely stretch of Negril's famed beach. **Pros:** good value; lovely beach location; good restaurant. **Cons:** beach is not private; limited on-site lunch options. *Rooms from: $315* *Norman Manley Blvd., Negril* *876/957–3200, 800/583–8365 toll free in U.S.* *www.sandyhavenresort.com* *17 rooms, 18 suites* *Multiple meal plans.*

$$ HOTEL **The Spa Retreat.** This boutique resort on the cliffs features seven seaside cottages and five rooftop cottages with sea views as well as five similar garden cottages. **Pros:** large groups and wedding parties can rent the whole property; shuttle to beach; on-site restaurant; lovely yoga deck. **Cons:** no natural beach; sea's sometimes too rough for swimming; no relaxation area in spa section. *Rooms from: $325* *West End Rd., Negril* *876/957–4329, 855/843–7725* *www.thespajamaica.com* *17 cottages, one suite* *Multiple meal plans.*

$$$ ALL-INCLUSIVE **Sunset at the Palms Resort.** A sister of the Sunset Resorts in Montego Bay and Ocho Rios—but far different in scale and atmosphere—this relaxed all-inclusive is a favorite with ecotourists thanks to its emphasis on environmental sustainability. **Pros:** environmentally conscious; beautiful grounds. **Cons:** beach is across street; eco-theme not for everyone; expensive; not within walking distance of many Negril Beach attractions and restaurants. *Rooms from: $422* *Norman Manley Blvd., Negril* *876/957–5350* *www.sunsetatthepalms.com* *85 rooms* *All-inclusive.*

$ B&B/INN Fodor's Choice ★ **Tensing Pen.** At this rustic but elegant resort, the cottages are made of stone and wood with thatch roofs; some are on stilts, and they all have big beds. **Pros:** unique accommodations; great snorkeling; spa; spacious rooms. **Cons:** not on beach; barking dogs and other noise sometimes interrupts the quiet. *Rooms from: $160* *West End Rd., Negril* *876/957–0387* *www.tensingpen.com* *21 rooms* *Breakfast.*

NIGHTLIFE

For the most part, the liveliest late-night happenings that tourists take part in are in the major resort hotels and on the beach in Negril. Some all-inclusives offer a dinner-and-entertainment pass for $50–$100; call ahead and bring a photo ID. *Daily Gleaner,* the *Jamaica Observer,* and the *Star* (online and at newsstands) list who's playing when and where. In Negril, cars with loudspeakers sometimes drive the streets in the afternoon announcing that evening's hot spot.

MONTEGO BAY

ANNUAL EVENTS

Fodor's Choice ★ **Jamaica Jazz & Blues.** Held in a stadium 25 minutes east of Montego Bay on the last Thursday–Saturday of January, the music festival attracts followers from around the world. Previous headliners include Mary J. Blige, Michael Bolton, Celine Dion, Kenny Rogers, and Alicia Keys. Tickets usually go on sale online in late November or early December. *Greenfield Stadium, Trelawny* *www.jamaicajazzandblues.com.*

Fodor's Choice ★ **Reggae Sumfest.** Those who know and love reggae should visit Montego Bay between mid-July and August for this weeklong concert, which attracts big names. Tickets are sold for each night's performances or by multi-event passes. ✉ *Catherine Hall, Montego Bay* ☎ *876/953–8360* 🌐 *www.reggaesumfest.com.*

BARS AND CLUBS

Blue Beat. This lounge moves to a jazz groove on Friday nights and features techno and house music on others. It closes around 10:30 most nights but goes until the wee hours on Friday and Saturday. ✉ *Gloucester Ave., Montego Bay* ☎ *876/952–4777.*

Club Ville. After 10, the Margaritaville restaurant turns into a hip and happening nightspot. DJs play reggae, house, and R&B along with occasional live performances. Thursday night is Ladies Night and is especially popular among locals. ✉ *Margaritaville, Gloucester Ave., Montego Bay* ☎ *876/952–4777* 🌐 *www.margaritavillecaribbean.com.*

14

CASINOS

Mosino Gaming Lounge. The newest gaming lounge to open in Montego Bay, this has become a favorite for gamers and non-gamers alike. It houses a full restaurant and sports bar serving tasty apps and entrées. Visitors may try their luck at any of the 214 machines available here, including an assortment of virtual tables and slot machines. ✉ *Catherine Hall, Montego Bay* ☎ *876/620–9202.*

Treasure Hunt Gaming Lounge. One of the newer additions to Montego Bay's gaming scene, this lounge is in Ironshore's Whitter Village shopping complex. Guests can try their luck at slot machines or roulette tables or have a drink from the well-stocked bar. ✉ *Whitter Village, Ironshore, Montego Bay.*

OCHO RIOS

ANNUAL EVENTS

Jamaican Epicurean Escape. This two day festival showcases Jamaica's best culinary offerings. Restaurants from around the island set up food stations with dishes that are hard to resist. There are also chefs' demonstrations, cultural craft booths, and other events and entertainment, such as traditional drumming. ✉ *Grizzly's Plantation Cove, St. Ann* ☎ *876/815–8500* 🌐 *www.jamaicaepicureanescape.com.*

Jamaica Ocho Rios International Jazz Festival. The biggest event in Ocho Rios, June's jazz festival has been running since 1991, when it was one day. Now nine days, it draws top names. ✉ *Ocho Rios* ☎ *876/927–3544* 🌐 *www.ochoriosjazz.com.*

Fodor's Choice ★ **Rebel Salute.** Over the years, this has grown to be one of Jamaica's biggest reggae festivals. As a family-oriented, roots-reggae event, no meat or alcohol is served at the two-day celebration, held in January. ✉ *Richmond Estate, St. Ann.*

BARS AND CLUBS

Club Ville. After 10, Margaritaville transforms into this club, with a mix of the hottest tunes of the moment, along with occasional live performances from local entertainers. ✉ *Margaritaville, Island Village, Ocho Rios* ☎ *876/675–8800* 🌐 *www.margaritavillecaribbean.com.*

KINGSTON

As the cultural hub, Kingston has Jamaica's largest selection of nightlife. Unlike the more tourist-oriented resort communities, nightlife here is aimed at locals, and varies from live music to DJs. Because of Kingston's high crime rate, check with your concierge or a local who knows the scene before heading out.

BARS AND CLUBS

Friday nights in Kingston bring on the Friday Night Jam, an impromptu street party that begins when office doors close and entrepreneurial chefs roll out oil drums transformed into jerk pits. Street corners sizzle with spicy fare, music blares, and the city launches into weekend mode.

The *Daily Gleaner*, the *Jamaica Observer*, and the *Star* have listings of who's playing when and where. Also look out for roadside posters.

Redbones Blues Cafe. You can't beat the sophisticated jazz, world music, and other low-key performances on Thursdays at this café and performance space. On Friday, it's rock, reggae, or alternative fusion, and once a month sees house music—this is one of the few venues for electronic music in Kingston. The Redbones Gallery rotates art shows once or twice a month, showcasing paintings, photography, sculptures, and sometimes even furniture. Films are screened once a week in the movie garden, usually Tuesday or Saturday. And the last Wednesday of the month brings an evening of poetry or fiction. Some events have a cover. ✉ *1 Argyle Rd., Kingston* ☎ *876/978–8262, 876/978–6091* 🌐 *www.redbonesbluescafe.com.*

Usain Bolt's Tracks and Records. For fans of sprint superstar Usain Bolt, no trip to Kingston would be complete without a visit to his club, a combination casual restaurant and sports bar that's designed to look like a stadium. There are (of course) large-screen TVs. Upstairs, on the mezzanine, you can see the running shoes Bolt wore on many of his record-breaking runs as well as signed outfits from medal-winning events. A gift shop sells Bolt gear. When not breaking records or outrunning competitors, the big man himself regularly shows up at the bar. ✉ *The Marketplace, Constant Spring Rd., Kingston* ☎ *876/906–3903* 🌐 *www.tracksandrecords.com.*

NEGRIL

BARS AND CLUBS

Alfred's Ocean Palace. You can find some of Negril's best live music at this bar, which stages reggae band performances right on the beach on Sunday, Tuesday, and Friday nights. ✉ *Norman Manley Blvd., Negril* ☎ *876/957–4669* 🌐 *www.alfreds.com.*

Continued on page 616

REGGAE

Julie Schwietert Collazo
& Eric Wechter

There's an undeniable, universal appeal to reggae music. Its feel-good beat and impassioned lyrics resonate with listeners across the globe, but experiencing reggae in the country of its birth is the best way to enjoy the music.

Widely considered to be Jamaica's seminal music form, reggae was born out of other genres, including ska and rocksteady, and is relatively young compared to other Jamaican musical styles. In fact, the history of Jamaican music is as long as the history of the island itself. Reggae's origins are firmly rooted in traditions of African music, and its lyrics are inspired by Jamaicans' fervid resistance to colonialism and imperialism. Reggae can be distinguished from earlier music forms by its comparatively faster beat, its experimental tendencies, and a more prominent role for the guitar. Reggae is also more "ragged"—both in sound and in concept. That is it's both more earthy and down to earth, or folkloric. Lyrically, reggae is rife with social themes, primarily those that explore the plight of the working classes.

BUILDING A BEAT

Sly Dunbar, touring with Peter Tosh, 1979

Robbie Shakespeare, on tour with Peter Tosh, 1978

Pioneering reggae musicians, such as drummer **Sly Dunbar** and bassist **Robbie Shakespeare**, shaped the genre by distilling what they viewed as the best elements of ska and rocksteady. Reggae is not complex in terms of chord structure or rhythmic variation. There may be only one to three chords in a typical reggae song, and the danceable feel is propelled most commonly by a rhythm—or "riddim"—called the "drop beat" or "one drop." The bass drum emphasizes the third beat in a four-beat cycle, creating an anchor, or a pull, that the guitar and bass play on top of. For a more propulsive feel, the drummer may equally emphasize all four beats in each measure. Layered on top of this repetitive, solid foundation are socially conscious lyrics, which often preach resistance to the establishment or beseech listeners to love one another.

REGGAE AND RASTA

Reggae is a musical genre of, by, and for the people, and the influence of Rastafarianism has expanded its folk appeal. Rasta became pervasive in Jamaica in the 1950s, when resistance to colonialism peaked. Rasta, combining spiritual, political, and social concerns, had its origins in the crowning of **Haile Selassie I** as the emperor of Ethiopia in 1930. Selassie, the only black man to head an independent African nation at the time, became a vital figure and symbol of freedom for Africans in the diaspora. Greatly inspired by Selassie, Jamaicans integrated his empowering messages into many aspects of their culture. Musically, the Rasta influence is felt in reggae in two ways. The lyrics often advocate the idea of returning to Africa, and minor chords and a simple "riddim" structure characterize the songs. In the words of music historian Lloyd Bradley, Rastas were the "underclass of the underclass," and by 1959 more than one in every 25 Jamaicans identified with Rastafarianism. One of them was Bob Marley.

Haile Selassie I of Ethiopia

BOB MARLEY

Bob Marley is reggae's oracle, a visionary who introduced the world to the music of Jamaica and the struggles of its people. A stirring performer with a preternatural talent for connecting with audiences, Marley revealed the oppression of his countrymen and their indomitable spirit through his songs of hope, freedom, and redemption. His legacy extends far beyond reggae, influencing generations of artists across multiple genres.

Born in February 1945, Robert Nesta Marley left his home in rural St. Ann's Parish, Jamaica, at 14 to pursue a music career in Kingston. In 1963 Marley joined with singers Peter Tosh and Bunny Livingston to form the group the Wailers, and they began recording singles with a renowned local producer. After a series of stops and starts and a strengthened devotion to the teachings of the Rastafari faith, Bob Marley and the Wailers released *Catch a Fire* in 1973. It was their first release outside of Jamaica, and nearly instantly it became an international success. Marley's global popularity and acclaim grew with albums like *Burnin'* and *Natty Dread.* As Marley's stardom increased abroad, his influence at home became transcendent. Regarded by many of his countrymen as a prophet, Marley, whose songs of freedom and revolution reverberated throughout Jamaica, was perceived as threat in some corridors. In December 1976, he was wounded in an assassination attempt. Marley left Jamaica for more than a year and in 1977 released his biggest record thus far, *Exodus,* which included the hits "Jammin" and "One Love/People Get Ready." By 1980, Marley was poised to reach even greater heights with an extensive U.S. tour, but while jogging in New York he suddenly collapsed. Cancer had silently invaded his brain and lungs. He died in May, 1981, at age 36. Marley's spirit and music endure in the hearts and minds of fans worldwide. His greatest hits collection, *Legend,* is the top-selling reggae album of all time.

Bob Marley at Reggae Sunsplash

COMMUNING WITH THE SPIRIT

Bob Marley Museum, Kingston

Whether you're a serious enthusiast or have just a passing curiosity, Jamaica offers visitors plenty of opportunities to experience the music and culture of reggae.

Zion Bus Line Tour to Nine Mile. Marley fans won't want to miss this bus pilgrimage to the reggae icon's birthplace and final resting place. With the sounds of familiar reggae tunes thumping through the bus speakers, the guided tour takes you through the mountains to the small town of Nine Mile. The half-day tour includes a visit to Marley's house, a stop at Mount Zion (a rock where Marley meditated) and the opportunity to view Marley's mausoleum. The tour leaves from Ocho Rios. On the return trip from Nine Mile, the group stops at the Jerk Center for an authentic Jamaican lunch.

Reggae Sumfest in Montego Bay. This week-long reggae festival is held each July. In addition to featuring musical line-ups of the most popular reggae, dance hall, R&B, and hip hop acts, the Sumfest offers traditional Jamaican food and local crafts. Recent festivals have featured local favorite Tarrus Riley, as well as international performers, like LL Cool J and Mary J. Blige.

DID YOU KNOW?

The first appearance of the word *reggae* is widely attributed to the 1968 single by the Maytals called "Do the Reggay."

Burning Spear

Jimmy Cliff

The Congos

Bob Marley Museum in Kingston (☎ *876/630–1588*). If the Zion Bus Tour only whets your appetite for Marley, visit the Bob Marley Museum for a glimpse at another chapter of his life. Housed inside the former headquarters of Marley's label, Tuff Gong Records, it is also the site of the failed attempt on Marley's life that inspired his song, "Ambush."

And, of course, your Jamaican reggae experience would not be complete without catching some live bands. Local acts play at **Bourbon Beach** (☎ *876/957–4432*) in Negril on Monday, Thursday, and Saturday nights. Also in Negril is **Rick's Cafe** (☎ *876/957–0380*), which features an in-house reggae band nightly, and **Alfred's Ocean Palace** (☎ *876/957–4669*) where you can dance on the beach to live reggae.

REGGAE LINGO

Dancehall. A modern style that introduces elements of electronic dance music and improvised singing or rapping by DJs to raw reggae tracks.

Dub. A form of reggae characterized by the use of remixes of previously recorded material.

One-drop rhythm. The definitive beat of reggae characterized by a steady "drop" of the bass drum on the strong beat in each measure.

Ragamuffin (ragga). Similar to dancehall, ragga combines electronic dance music, hip-hop, and R&B with reggae for a more contemporary, club feel.

Riddim. The rhythmic foundation for nearly all reggae styles, characterized by a repetitive, driving drum and bass feel.

Rocksteady. A style of reggae that followed ska, rocksteady is marked by a slower tempo.

Ska. Precursor to reggae that combines traditional Caribbean rhythms, jazz, and calypso

RECOMMENDED LISTENING

Bob Marley
Uprising, Legend, Exodus, Burnin', Catch a Fire

Peter Tosh
Legalize It

Toots and the Maytals
Funky Kingston

Jimmy Cliff
The Harder They Come

Burning Spear
Marcus Garvey

Alton Ellis
Alton Ellis Sings Rock and Soul

The Congos
The Heart of the Congos

Bourbon Beach. This beach bar is popular for its live reggae music on Monday, Thursday, and Saturday nights. ✉ *Norman Manley Blvd., Negril* ☎ *876/957–4432, 876/374–4982* 🌐 *www.bbnegril.com.*

Hedonism II. The sexy, always-packed disco here is a wild night out. Non-guest passes ($100 for couples and single men, $50 for single women) include meals, drinks, and use of the facilities from 6 pm to 2 am. (Bring a photo ID, and call for a reservation.) ✉ *Norman Manley Blvd., Negril* ☎ *876/957–5200* 🌐 *www.hedonism.com.*

The Jungle. This hot nightspot has two raised bars and a circular dance floor. ✉ *Norman Manley Blvd., Negril* ☎ *876/957–4005.*

Margaritaville Negril. This popular party spot is right on the beach, so there is plenty of barefoot fun. ✉ *Norman Manley Blvd., Negril* ☎ *876/957–4467.*

Rick's Cafe. Sunset brings the crowds for live reggae. ✉ *West End Rd., Negril* ☎ *876/957–0380.*

SHOPPING

Shopping is not really one of Jamaica's high points, though you will certainly find things to buy. Good choices include Jamaican crafts, which range from artwork to batik fabrics to baskets. Wood carvings are a top purchase; the finest are made from the Jamaican national tree, lignum vitae, or tree of life, a dense, blond wood that requires a talented carver to transform it into dolphins, heads, or fish. Bargaining is expected with crafts vendors. Naturally, Jamaican rum is another top souvenir, as is Tia Maria, the Jamaican-made coffee liqueur. Coffee (both Blue Mountain and the less expensive High Mountain) is sold at nearly every gift shop, but the cheapest prices are often found at local grocery stores, where you can buy coffee beans or ground coffee.

Unless you have an extremely early flight, you'll find plenty of shopping at the Sangster International Airport, which has a large shopping mall. Fine handmade cigars are available there and at the island's many cigar stores. You can buy Cuban cigars almost anywhere, though they can't be taken back legally into the United States. As a rule, only rum distilleries, such as Appleton's and Sangster's, have better deals than the airport stores. Best of all, if you buy your rum at the airport, you don't have to tote all those heavy, breakable bottles. (Note that if you purchase rum—or other liquids, such as duty-free perfumes—outside the airport, you'll need to place them in your checked luggage when returning home. If you purchase liquids inside the secured area of the airport, you may board with them, but, after clearing U.S. Customs on landing, you will need to place them in your checked bag if continuing on another flight.)

MONTEGO BAY

HANDICRAFTS

In Montego Bay, the largest crafts market can be found on Fort Street and **Market Street.** Both have a bunch of stalls selling pretty much the same thing. Be prepared to haggle and to be given the hard sell; if you're in the right mood, though, it can be a fun peek into Jamaican commerce away from the resorts.

SHOPPING CENTERS

Half Moon Shopping Village. The bright yellow buildings at Half Moon hotel contain some of the finest and most expensive wares money can buy, as well as more affordable boutiques, a post office, bank, and restaurants. ✉ *Half Moon, North Coast Hwy., 7 miles (11 km) east of Montego Bay, Montego Bay* ☏ *876/953–2211* 🌐 *www.halfmoon.com.*

Holiday Shopping Centre. Directly across the street from the Holiday Inn Sunspree Resort, this casual shopping area has jewelry, clothing, and crafts stores. ✉ *Holiday Inn SunSpree Resort, North Coast Hwy., 10 miles (16 km) east of Montego Bay, Montego Bay.*

The Shoppes at Rose Hall. This upscale, open-air shopping center was designed to resemble an old-fashioned main street. Five minutes from the Hilton Rose Hall, it sells jewelry, cosmetics, and designer clothing. Some hotels offer shuttles. ✉ *Rose Hall, North Coast Hwy., 7 miles (11 km) east of Montego Bay, St. James.*

14

OCHO RIOS

Ocho Rios has several malls that draw day-trippers from the cruise ships. The best are **Soni's Plaza** and the **Taj Mahal,** two malls on the main street with stores selling jewelry, cigars, and clothing. Another popular mall on the main street is **Ocean Village.** On the North Coast Highway slightly east of Ochos Rios are **Pineapple Place** and **Coconut Grove.**

HANDICRAFTS

Harmony Hall. Eight minutes east of town, a restored 19th-century minister's house now carries original works of art. On sale are owner Annabella Proudlock's wooden boxes, their covers decorated with reproductions of Jamaican paintings; magnificently displayed larger reproductions of paintings, lithographs, and signed prints of Jamaican scenes; and hand-carved wooden combs. Harmony Hall is also well known for its shows of local artists. It's closed Mondays. ✉ *Rte. A3, Ocho Rios* ☏ *876/974–2870* 🌐 *www.harmonyhall.com.*

Wassi Art Handcrafted Caribbean Home Accessories. You'll find ceramics and other arts and crafts, all of which are made in Jamaica. ✉ *Bonham Spring, Ocho Rios* ☏ *876/974–5044* 🌐 *www.wassiart.com.*

MARKETS

Musgrave Market. This traditional market, unlike those in Ocho Rios and Montego Bay, is primarily aimed at locals. Although you can find some crafts here, look for luscious fruits and vegetables, household goods, and clothing in these stalls. ✉ *West St., Port Antonio.*

Ocho Rios Crafts Market. This largest market has stalls selling everything from straw hats to wooden figurines to T-shirts. Vendors can be aggressive, and haggling is expected. Your best chance of getting a good price is to come on a day when there's no cruise ship in port. ✉ *Main St., Ocho Rios.*

Pineapple Craft Market. This small, casual market on the outskirts of Ocho Rios has everything from carved figurines to coffeebean necklaces. ✉ *Main St., Ocho Rios.*

KINGSTON

Unlike the island's North Coast towns, Kingston isn't known for its duty-free stores. Shopping here is mostly limited to shops for residents. The city's Constant Spring Road and King Street are home to a growing roster of shopping malls offering fashions, housewares, and more.

MARKETS

Kingston Crafts Market. A large assortment of Jamaican handicrafts, including paintings, sculptures, and inexpensive jewelry, can be found in the market's stalls. Although pickpockets have been a problem in the past, it's much safer now. Some bargaining is tolerated, but don't expect many concessions. ✉ *Harbour St. and Ocean Blvd., Kingston.*

SHOPPING CENTERS

Shops at Devon House. This cluster of mostly upscale shops sells clothing, crafts, and other items. The location, at the historic Devon House, makes it a pleasant spot to spend a morning or afternoon. Don't miss the famous Devon House ice cream. ✉ *26 Hope Rd., Kingston* ☎ *876/929–6602.*

SPECIALTY ITEMS

Starfish Oils. Find aromatherapy products, such as fragrant oils, scented candles, and soaps here. Lemongrass, which grows locally, goes in one of the most popular oils, and Blue Mountain coffee is a favorite ingredient in both soap and candles. Another Starfish Oils shop is in Manor Park Plaza, and its products are sold in shops throughout the island. ✉ *Devon House, Kingston* ☎ *876/901–7113* 🌐 *www.starfishoils.com* ✉ *Manor Park Plaza, Kingston.*

Tuff Gong Record Shop. Housed in a studio that's part of the Bob Marley group of companies, this shop carries an impressive collection featuring the legend himself and other reggae greats. Marley and Tuff Gong merchandise is also on sale. The building itself is a tourist attraction, since the studio's international clients include Maxi Priest, Steele Pulse, and Sinéad O'Connor. ✉ *220 Marcus Garvey Dr., Kingston* ☎ *876/923–9380* 🌐 *www.tuffgong.com.*

NEGRIL

MARKETS

Craft Market by Beach Park. This market on the beach side of the bridge at Negril's town center roundabout sells arts and crafts aplenty. ✉ *Norman Manley Blvd., Negril.*

Rutland Point. With Negril's laid-back atmosphere, it's no surprise that most shopping involves straw hats, woven baskets, and T-shirts, all plentiful at this crafts market on the northern edge of town. The atmosphere is less aggressive here than at similar establishments in Montego Bay and Ocho Rios. ✉ *Norman Manley Blvd., Negril.*

SHOPPING CENTERS

The Boardwalk Village. Set right on the beach in Negril, this is a nice place to spend half a day perusing souvenir stores and clothing boutiques, and perhaps also having lunch at the restaurant. ✉ *Norman Manley Blvd., Negril* 🌐 *www.theboardwalkvillagenegril.com.*

Time Square. The mall is known for its luxury goods and souvenirs, including cigars and jewelry. ✉ *Norman Manley Blvd., Negril* ☎ *876/957–9263* 🌐 *www.timesquareplaza.com.*

14

SPORTS AND THE OUTDOORS

The tourist board licenses all recreational activity operators and outfitters, which should assure you of fair business practices as long as you deal with companies that display its decals.

BIRD-WATCHING

Jamaica is a major bird-watching destination, thanks to its various natural habitats. The island is home to more than 200 species, some seen only seasonally or in particular parts of the island. Many bird-watchers flock here for the chance to see the vervain hummingbird (the world's second-smallest bird, larger only than Cuba's bee hummingbird) and the Jamaican tody (which nests underground).

PORT ANTONIO

Jamaica Explorations. Hotel Mockingbird Hill is the starting point for guided bird tours in the Reach Falls area ($130) and the Blue Mountains ($330). Transportation is included. In addition to the conventional Reach Falls tour, a more adventurous option includes hiking up the river and swimming across pools and mini-falls. ✉ *Hotel Mockingbird Hill, Port Antonio* ☎ *876/993–7267* 🌐 *www.jamaicaexplorations.com.*

KINGSTON AND THE BLUE MOUNTAINS

Arrowhead Birding Tours. This company runs birding tours across the island, including one-day outings ($130), customized trips, and eight-day trips in November, February, and March. ✉ *Kingston* ☎ *876/260–9006* 🌐 *www.arrowheadbirding.com.*

Birdlife Jamaica. This nonprofit organizes bird-watching trips into the Blue Mountains and nearby John Crow Mountains, as well as other parts of the island. ✉ *University of the West Indies Mona, Dept. of Life Sciences, Mona Rd., Kingston* ☎ *876/260–9006.*

Sun Venture Tours. This outfit offers 25 different special-interest tours for nature lovers, including bird-watching, across the island. ✉ *30 Balmoral Ave., Kingston* ☎ *876/960–6685, 876/408–6973 after office hrs and weekends* 🌐 *www.sunventuretours.com.*

DIVING AND SNORKELING

Jamaica isn't a major dive destination, but you can find a few rich underwater regions with a wide array of marine life, especially off the North Coast, which is on the edge of the Cayman Trench. Mo'Bay, known for its wall dives, has **Airport Reef** at its southwestern edge. The site has coral caves, tunnels, and canyons. The first marine park in Jamaica, the **Montego Bay Marine Park,** was established to protect the natural resources of the bay; it's easy to see the treasures that lie beneath the surface.

Thanks to a marine area protected since 1966, the Ocho Rios region is also a popular diving destination. Through the years, the protected area grew into the **Ocho Rios Marine Park,** stretching from Mammee Bay and Drax Hall in the west to Frankfort Point in the east. Top dive sites in the area include **Jack's Hall,** a 40-foot dive dotted with all types of coral; **Top of the Mountain,** a 60-foot dive near Dunn's River Falls with many coral heads and gorgonians; and the **Wreck of the *Katryn*,** a 50-foot dive to a deliberately sunk 140-foot former minesweeper.

With its murkier waters, the southern side of the island isn't as popular for diving. However, **Port Royal,** near Kingston's airport, is filled with sunken ships that are home to many varieties of tropical fish; a special permit is required to dive some sites here.

A one-tank dive costs \$45–\$80. Most large resorts have dive shops, and the all-inclusives sometimes include scuba diving. To dive, you need a certification card, though it's possible to get a taste of scuba and do a shallow dive—usually from shore—after a one-day resort course, which almost every resort with a dive shop offers.

MONTEGO BAY

Jamaica Scuba Divers. With serious scuba facilities for dedicated divers and beginners, this PADI and NAUI outfit offers Nitrox diving and instruction as well as instruction in underwater photography, night diving, and open-water diving. Operations are based at Travellers Beach Resort in Negril and Franklyn D. Resort in Runaway Bay. Pickup can be arranged from most hotels and other locations along the North Coast. ☎ *876/381–1113* 🌐 *www.scuba-jamaica.com.*

PORT ANTONIO

Lady G'Diver. The only dive operator in Port Antonio runs trips to interesting sites almost every day. Two-tank dive trips depart at around 11 am. Call two or three days in advance. ✉ *Errol Flynn Marina, Ken Wright Dr., Port Antonio* ☎ *876/995–0246* 🌐 *www.ladygdiver.com.*

FISHING

Port Antonio makes deep-sea-fishing headlines with its annual International Marlin Tournament in fall, and Mo'Bay and Ocho Rios have devotees who exchange tales (tall and otherwise) about sailfish, yellowfin tuna, wahoo, dolphinfish, and bonito. Licenses aren't required, and you can arrange to charter a boat at your hotel. A chartered boat (with captain, crew, and equipment) costs \$500–\$900 for a half day or \$900–\$1,500 for a full-day excursion, depending on the size of the boat.

MONTEGO BAY

No Problem Sport Fishing. Charter fishing excursions are available aboard the *E-Zee*. Half- and full-day excursions take anglers in search of big catch. Plan on $600 for a half-day charter and $1,200 for a full day on the seas. A discount is available if paying by cash. Fees include drinks and equipment. ✉ *The Yacht Club, Montego Bay* ☎ *876/381–3229* 🌐 *www.montego-bay-jamaica.com/ajal/noproblem.*

FALMOUTH

Glistening Waters Marina. Offering deep-sea fishing and other charter trips from Glistening Waters (20 minutes east of Montego Bay), this marina also runs night tours of the lagoon, which is iridescent due to microscopic dinoflagellates that glow when they move. ✉ *North Coast Hwy., Falmouth* ☎ *876/954–3229* 🌐 *www.glisteningwaters.com.*

GOLF

Some of Jamaica's best courses are near Mo'Bay. Many resorts have their own courses (including several of the Sandals resorts) and allow both guests and nonguests to play. Caddies ($15–$45) are almost always mandatory, and cart rentals ($20–$40) are available at most courses.

MONTEGO BAY

Cinnamon Hill Gold Course. On 400 lush acres on the Rose Hall estate, this course, designed by Robert von Hagge and Rick Baril, takes you to the water's edge and up into the hilly jungles. Rates include greens fees, cart, caddy, and tax, and Nike clubs are available for rent. ✉ *Rose Hall, North Coast Hwy., St. James* ☎ *876/953–2984* 🌐 *www.cinnamonhilljamaica.com* 🎫 *$169 in winter, $49 replay* ⛳ *18 holes, 6828 yards, par 72.*

Half Moon Golf Course. Swaying palms, abundant bunkering, and large greens greet you on this flat Robert Trent Jones, Sr.–designed course, home of the Jamaica Open. The course was renovated in 2005 by Jones protégé Roger Rulewich to better position the hazards for today's longer hitters. The Half Moon Golf Academy offers one-day sessions, multiday retreats, and hour-long private sessions. ✉ *Half Moon, North Coast Hwy., 7 miles (11 km) east of Montego Bay, Montego Bay* ☎ *876/953–2211* 🌐 *www.halfmoongolf.com* 🎫 *Nonguests $181 for 18 holes, $118 for 9 holes* ⛳ *18 holes, 7141 yards, par 72.*

Fodor's Choice ★ **Tryall Club Golf Course.** At an exclusive country club 15 miles (24 km) west of Montego Bay, this championship course on the site of a 19th-century sugar plantation blends first-class golf with traces of history. The ambience is peaceful; no one is hurried and playing with a caddy is the norm. The layout takes in the Caribbean coast—the 4th-hole green hugs the sea—before heading up into the hills for expansive vistas. Designed by Ralph Plummer, the course has hosted events such as the Johnnie Walker World Championship. ✉ *Tryall Club, North Coast Hwy., Sandy Bay* ☎ *876/956–5601* 🌐 *www.tryallclub.com* 🎫 *$150 for 18 holes ($105 guests), $115 for 9 holes ($75 guests)* ⛳ *18 holes, 6836 yards, par 71.*

Constant Spring Golf Club. Designed by Stanley Thompson, a mentor of Robert Trent Jones Sr., in 1920, this short course is in one of Kingston's nicest neighborhoods. There's a clubhouse, restaurant, bar, and pro shop. ✉ *152 Constant Spring Rd., Kingston* ☎ *876/924–1610* *J$4,500 weekdays, J$5,000 weekends and public holidays* *18 holes, 6094 yards, par 70.*

NEGRIL

Negril Hills Golf Club. Inland from Jamaica's longest stretch of private beach, this course is 1½ hours west of Montego Bay. High points are the lush tropical foliage, picturesque water hazards, elevated tees, gently rolling fairways, tropical mountain vistas, and hard-sloping greens. The 6,333-yard course is walkable but plays longer due to elevated putting surfaces. ✉ *Sheffield, Negril* ☎ *876/957–4638* 🌐 *www.negrilhillsgolfclub.com* *$60* *18 holes, 6333 yards, par 72.*

GUIDED TOURS

Because most vacationers avoid renting cars for safety and cost reasons, guided tours with hotel pickup are popular options for exploring. Jamaica's size and slow interior roads mean that you can't expect to see the entire island on one trip; even full-day tours concentrate on one part of the island. Most tours are similar in both content and price. From Montego Bay, tours often include one of the area's plantation houses. Several Negril-based companies offer tours to Y.S. Falls on the South Coast. Tours from Ocho Rios might include top attractions such as Dunn's River Falls or Kingston. In almost all cases, you arrange the tour through your resort.

MONTEGO BAY

Most of the large resorts have tour desks where you can book a number of excursions and activities. Guided plantation and countryside visits are popular. Almost all tour operators will pick you up if you are staying at a large resort.

Croydon Plantation Tour. Tour the birthplace of the Jamaican hero Sam Sharpe, who led the rebellion that helped put an end to slavery on the island. The tour ($70), run on Tuesday, Thursday, and Friday, visits the plantation, an hour and a half from Montego Bay, where pineapples, sugarcane, and citrus fruits are grown in the foothills of the Catadupa Mountains. Pickup is available from hotels around Montego Bay and the Grand Palladium Resort in Hanover. ☎ *876/979–8267* 🌐 *www.croydonplantation.com.*

Glamour Destination Management. One of the island's large tour operators, this company offers a wide selection of guided visits to Rose Hall and Greenwood Great House. ✉ *1225 Providence Dr., Montego Bay* ☎ *876/953–3810* 🌐 *www.glamourtoursdmc.com.*

Island Routes Caribbean Adventures. Run by Sandals, this company provides a host of luxury group and private guided tours (with certified partners) to guests and nonguests. Guests can book via the website or at an Island Routes tour desk at participating resorts. ✉ *Queens Dr.,*

Montego Bay ☎ *888/768–8370 in U.S. and Canada, 888/429–5478 in Jamaica* 🌐 *www.islandroutes.com.*

JUTA. The island's largest tour operator offers a great house tour and a rafting tour, as well as tours to other parts of the island like Black River, Negril, and Ocho Rios. ☎ *876/952–0813* 🌐 *www.jutatoursltd.com.*

OCHO RIOS

Chukka Caribbean Zion Bus Tour. A country-style bus painted in bright colors travels inland to the village of Nine Mile and the simple house where Bob Marley was born and is now buried. The five-hour tour ($100, including lunch at a jerk stand) is for those 18 and older. ✉ *Ocho Rios* ☎ *876/619–1441 Digicel in Jamaica, 876/656–8026 Lime in Jamaica, 877/424–8552 in U.S.* 🌐 *chukka.com.*

Jamaica Tours Limited. This operator offers several tours with stops that include gardens and Dunn's River Falls. ☎ *876/974–6447* 🌐 *www.jamaicatoursltd.com.*

PORT ANTONIO

Tours in Port Antonio. Joanna Hart leads an in-depth cultural and historical tour of the Port Antonio area, incorporating the history of the Maroons. ✉ *Port Antonio* ☎ *876/859–3758* 🌐 *www.toursinportantonio.com.*

KINGSTON

Numerous operators offer tours of the Kingston area, as well as excursions into the Blue Mountains. Professional tour operators provide a valuable service, as neither destination is particularly suited to exploration without a guide. In Kingston, certain areas can be dangerous; an organized tour provides a measure of security. Think twice before roaming in the Blue Mountains, as roads are narrow or in poor condition and signs are few and far between.

Typical city tours include a city overview with stops at Devon House, the Bob Marley Museum, and Port Royal. Niche operators such as Olde Jamaica Tours provide theme tours, including a tour of churches and museums and one that visits the athletic grounds where Usain Bolt and other sprinters have trained.

Jessa Tours, Ltd. Tours visit the Bob Marley Museum, National Gallery, craft market, and other heritage sites. ✉ *19 Herb McKenley Dr., Kingston* ☎ *876/978–2259* 🌐 *www.jessatours.com.*

Olde Jamaica Tours. This company runs heritage and cultural tours—churches, great houses, and the like—as well as visits to a cricket field and the training ground where Usain Bolt and others have developed their sporting prowess. Though island-wide trips are offered, the focus is on Kingston. ✉ *5 Cowper Dr., Kingston* ☎ *876/371–3613, 876/328–1385* 🌐 *www.oldejamaicatours.com.*

Sun Island Executive Tours & Services Ltd. This company offers tours to places of interest around Jamaica and can work with you to design an itinerary. ✉ *8 Bower Bank Ave., Kingston* ☎ *876/931–8826.*

SOUTH COAST

Countrystyle Community Experiences Tours. Combining your choice of accommodation—whether homestay or hotel—with your interests, these tour packages match you with residents to showcase rural community lifestyles, helping you enjoy Jamaican culture, heritage, cuisine, and music. Additional experiences such as the Jamaica Roots Experience, Jamaica Taste Experience, and Jamaica Nature Experience are offered in Kingston and Montego Bay. ✉ *62 Ward Ave., Mandeville* ☎ *876/507–6326, 876/488–7207* 🌐 *www.jamaica-no-problem.com/community-tours.html, www.villagesasbusinesses.com.*

Jakes Biking Tour. Jakes offers various area bike tours. In one three-hour tour ($60), a guide leads the way to the gorgeous stretch of sand at Fort Charles or Great Bay, and since Treasure Beach is flat, almost all fitness levels can participate. Jakes also runs hiking tours. ✉ *Treasure Beach* ☎ *876/965–3000* 🌐 *www.jakeshotel.com.*

NEGRIL

Rhodes Hall Eco Tours. Just 15 minutes from Negril, this former sugar plantation offers ecotours in a nature reserve with a crocodile lake and bird sanctuary. Other adventures include horseback riding, snorkeling and scuba diving, glass-bottom boating, and bathing in Rhodes Hall's Magic Blue Mud Mineral Spring Bath. Help arranging transportation from Negril area hotels is provided. ✉ *Green Island, Hanover* ☎ *876/957–6422* 🌐 *www.rhodesresort.com.*

Tropical Tours. One tour takes in the lighthouse and shopping, another Rick's Cafe. Tours leave from Club Riu at 2 for the former, at 4 for the latter. ✉ *Norman Manley Blvd., Negril* ☎ *876/957–4110 in Negril* 🌐 *www.tropicaltours-ja.com.*

HORSEBACK RIDING

MONTEGO BAY

Braco Stables. These stables are in the Braco area near Duncans in Trelawny, between Montego Bay and Ocho Rios. Two daily estate rides ($70) include complimentary refreshments served poolside at the Braco great house. Experienced riders can also opt for a mountain ride ($100) for a more-rugged two-hour tour. ✉ *Braco, Duncans* ☎ *876/954–0185* 🌐 *www.bracostables.com, www.bracotours.com.*

OCHO RIOS

Fodor's Choice ★

Chukka Caribbean Adventures. The two-hour ride-and-swim tour ($74) travels along Papillion Cove (where the 1973 movie *Papillion* was filmed) as well as to locations used in *Return to Treasure Island* (1985) and *Passion and Paradise* (1988). The trail continues along the coastline to Chukka Beach and a bareback ride in the sea. Chukka has a location west of Montego Bay and handles other activities and tours, too. ✉ *Ocho Rios* ☎ *876/619–1441 Digicel in Jamaica, 876/656–8026 Lime in Jamaica, 877/424–8552 in U.S.* 🌐 *chukka.com.*

Hooves. This stable offers several guided tours, including a popular 2½-hour beach ride ($95 from Boscobel, $85 from Ocho Rios, $90 from Runaway Bay—including transportation) suitable for adults

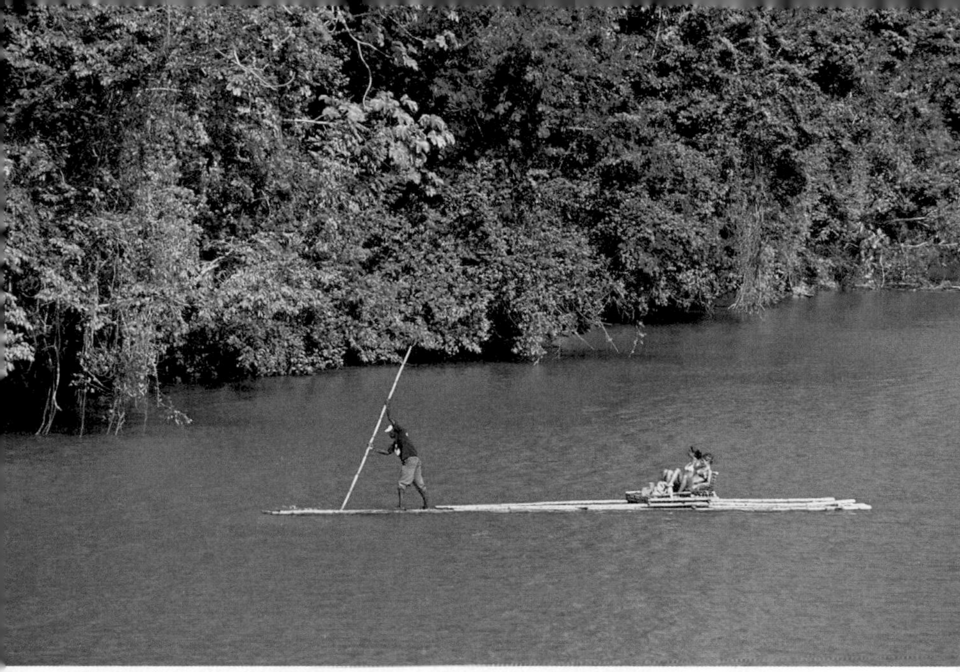

Rafting on the Rio Grande, near Port Antonio

and children taller than three feet. The trip begins with a visit to the Seville Great House estate before making its way to the beach for a ride. Hooves is home to many rescue horses that have been rehabilitated. ✉ *Windsor Rd., St. Ann's Bay* ☎ *876/972–0905* 🌐 *www.hooves-jamaica.com.*

Prospect Plantation. The plantation offers horseback rides ($64) for ages eight and older, including use of helmets; reservations are required. For the adventurous, there are also guided camel rides. ✉ *Rte. A1, about 3 miles (5 km) east of Ocho Rios* ☎ *876/974–5335.*

SOUTH COAST

Paradise Park. This working farm has been owned and operated by the same family for more than 100 years. Visitors can take horseback rides ($50) to explore the farm's fields and pastures and the beaches on the property. Afterward you can take a dip in Sweet River and have a picnic if you bring your own food. Reservations must be made at least 24 hours in advance. ✉ *Rte. A2, 1 mile (2 km) west of Ferris Cross, Savanna-la-Mar* ☎ *876/955–2675.*

RIVER BOATING AND RAFTING

Fodor's Choice ★

Jamaica's many rivers mean a multitude of freshwater experiences, from mild to wild. The island's first tourist activity off the beaches was relaxing rafting trips aboard bamboo rafts poled by local boatmen, which originated on the **Río Grande.** Jamaicans had long used rafts to transport bananas downriver. Decades ago actor and local resident Errol Flynn saw the rafts and thought they'd make a good tourist attraction. Today the slow rides are a favorite with romantic travelers and anyone looking to get off the beach for a few hours. The popularity of the Río Grande's trips spawned similar trips down the **Martha Brae River,** about 25 miles (38 km) from Mo'Bay. Near Ocho Rios, the **Great River** has lazy river rafting as well as energetic kayaking.

MONTEGO BAY

Jamaica Tours Limited. This big tour company conducts raft trips down the Martha Brae, approximately 25 miles (38 km) east of Mo'Bay; the excursion can include lunch if requested. Price depends on number of people and pickup location. Hotel tour desks can book it. ✉ *Providence Dr., Montego Bay* ☎ *876/953–3700* 🌐 *www.jamaicatoursltd.com.*

Rio Grande Tours. Guided raft trips down the Rio Grande ($72 plus $5–$10 tip) depart around 9 am and take about two hours, unless you stop to swim and have lunch. ✉ *St. Margaret's Bay* ☎ *876/993–5778.*

River Raft Ltd. This company leads 1½-hour trips ($60) down the Martha Brae River, about 25 miles (38 km) from most Mo'Bay hotels. ✉ *Martha Brae* ☎ *876/940–6398* 🌐 *www.jamaicarafting.com.*

SOUTH COAST

FAMILY **South Coast Safaris Ltd.** On slow boat cruises ($20) up the river, keep an eye peeled for crocodiles basking on the banks and swimming in the water—the captain has pet names for some of them. The cruise also passes through a thick mangrove area with egrets and other birds. Back at the landing stage there is a crocodile nursery where you can see young crocs being raised for release. ✉ *1 Crane St., Black River* ☎ *876/965–2513* 🌐 *www.jamaica-southcoast.com.*

SAILING

MONTEGO BAY

Dreamer Catamaran Cruises. Four catamarans, from 53 to 65 feet, take cruises ($83) that include a snorkel stop and visit to Margaritaville. Foot massages for women are followed by dance instruction for all. Children are allowed on only the morning and sunset cruises. ✉ *Cornwall Beach, Gloucester Ave., Montego Bay* ☎ *876/979–0102* 🌐 *www.dreamercatamarans.com.*

OCHO RIOS

Five Star Watersports. Several sailing and partying options are available through this company's Cool Runnings catamaran cruises: romantic dinner sails, the Wet and Wild Cruise, and a popular trip to Dunn's River Falls. Boats only run on Sundays with a minimum number of bookings; check when making reservations. ✉ *121 Main St., Ocho Rios* ☎ *876/974–2446, 876/974–4593* 🌐 *www.fivestarwatersports.com.*

PORT ANTONIO

Errol Flynn Marina. This official port of entry has 24-hour customs and immigration services, 24-hour security, an Internet center, pool, laundry, and 100-ton boat lift—the only area facility that can handle vessels of 600 feet. Scuba diving and other water-sports attractions are also here. ✉ *Ken Wright Dr., Port Antonio* ☎ *876/715–6044* 🌐 *www.errolflynnmarina.com.*

MARTINIQUE

WELCOME TO MARTINIQUE

PARIS IN THE TROPICS

The largest of the Windward Islands, Martinique is 425 square miles (1,101 square km). The southern part of the island is all rolling hills and sugarcane fields; it's also where you'll find the best beaches and most development. In the north are craggy cliffs, lush vegetation, and one of the Caribbean's largest volcanoes, Mont Pelée.

Restaurants ▼	
Atomic Food	9
Chez Les Pecheurs	4
Coup d'Coeur	12
La Baraqu'Obama	8
La Cave à Vins	1
La Table Restaurant	5
Le Bélem	7
Le Foyaal	2
Le Petibonum	3
Le Pitaya	13
Le Plein Soleil	6
Le Zandoli	10
Restaurant Le Golf	11

Hotels ▼	
Cap Est Lagoon	9
Club Med Buccaneer's Creek	10
Domaine de la Palmeraie	11
Engoulevent	4
Fort Savane	2
Hotel Bakoua	12
Hotel L'Impératrice	1
Hotel La Caravelle	7
Hôtel Le Pagerie	14
Hotel Plein Soleil	8
Hotel Villa St. Pierre	5
La Suite Villa	15
Le Domaine St. Aubin	6
L'Hôtel la Batelière	3
Résidence Le Village	13

Joie de vivre is the credo in this French enclave, which is often characterized as a Caribbean suburb of Paris. Exotic fruit grows on the volcanoes' forested flanks amid a profusion of wild orchids and hibiscus. The sheer lushness of it all inspired the tropical paintings of onetime resident Paul Gauguin.

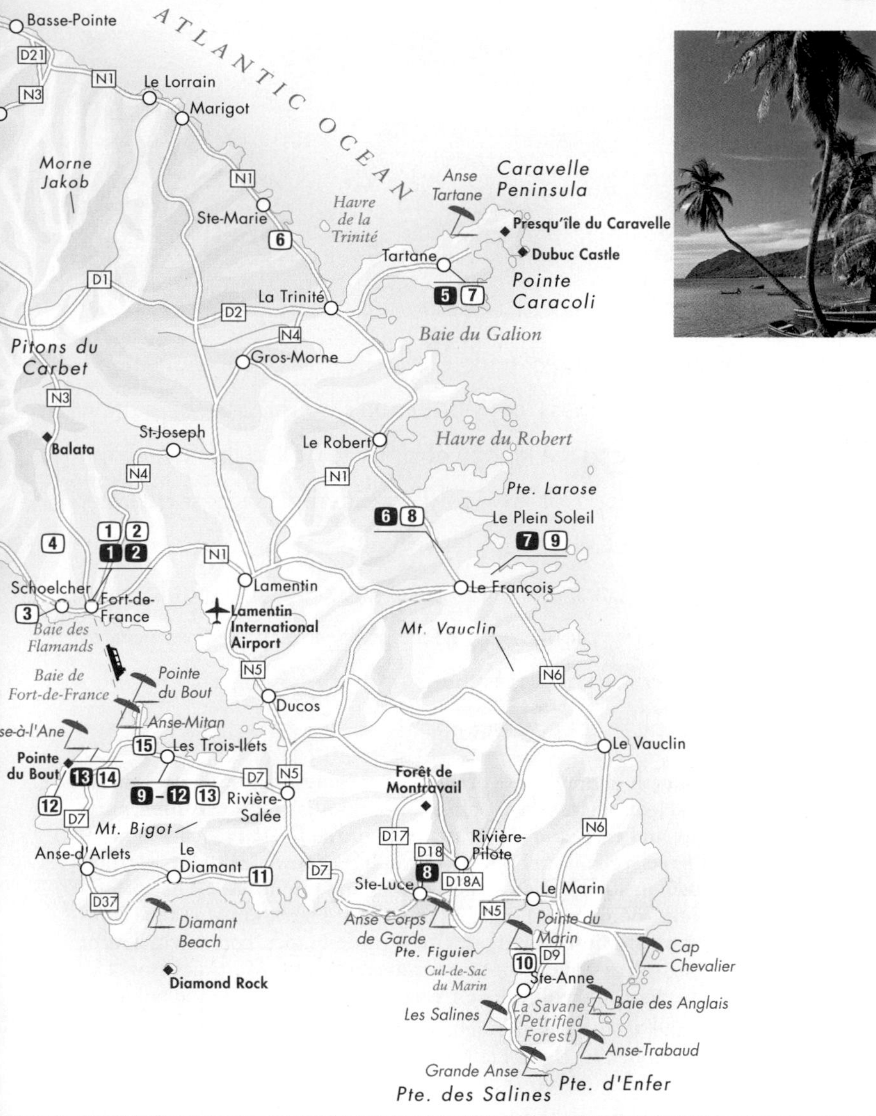

TOP REASONS TO VISIT MARTINIQUE

1 The Romance: A magical sensuality infuses everything; it will awaken dormant desires and fuel existing fires.

2 Beautiful Beaches: A full roster of beautiful beaches will let you enjoy sun and sand.

3 The French Connection: Excellent French food, not to mention French music and fashion, make the island a paradise for those in search of the finer things.

4 Range of Accommodations: Hospitable, stylish small hotels abound; big resorts, too. Or play expat in a private, luxe villa.

5 Inviting Waters: The sea, Caribbean; the ocean, Atlantic—experience the water in a kayak or on a sailboat. Even a ferry works.

Updated by Eileen Robinson Smith

Numerous scattered ruins and other historical monuments reflect the richness of Martinique's sugarcane plantation past, *rhum,* and the legacy of slavery. Called the Rum Capital of the World, it is widely considered the best gourmet island in the Caribbean. It stirs the passions with its distinctive brand of culinary offerings. If you believe in magic, Martinique has it, along with a sensuality that fosters romance. It has become known as the island of *revenants,* those who always return. *Et pourquoi non?*

Martinique is simply one of the most enchanting destinations in the Western Hemisphere. Francophiles adore this island for its food, rum, *musique*, and élan, and the availability of the finest French products, from Chanel fashions to Limoges china. It is endowed with lots of tropical beauty, including white-sand beaches and rain forests. The volcano Mont Pelée looms over the harbor town of St-Pierre, known as the Pompeii of the Caribbean. Its largest city, Fort-de-France, comes with lots of charm as well as some great restaurants and clubs. Martinicans will be glad you came, and you will be greeted with warm smiles and politesse.

Christopher Columbus first sighted this gorgeous island in 1502, when it was inhabited by the fierce Caraïbes, who had terrorized the peace-loving Arawaks. The Arawaks called their home Madinina (the Isle of Flowers), and for good reason. Exotic wild orchids, frangipani, anthurium, jade vines, flamingo flowers, and hundreds of vivid varieties of hibiscus still thrive here.

The island reflects its rich cultural history. In colonial days Martinique was the administrative, social, and cultural center of the French Antilles; this rich, aristocratic island was famous for its beautiful women. The island even gave birth to an empress, Napoléon's Joséphine. It saw the full flowering of a society ruled by planters, with servants and soirées, wine cellars, and lots of snobbery.

Martinique's economy still depends on *les bananes* (bananas), *l'ananas* (pineapples), cane sugar, rum, and fishing. It's also the largest remaining stronghold of the *békés*—the descendants of the original French planters—and they are still the privileged class on any of the French-Caribbean islands. Numbering around 4,000, many control Martinique's most profitable businesses, from banana plantations and rum distilleries to car dealerships. The elite dress in designer outfits straight off the Paris runways. In general, the islanders have style. In the airport waiting room you can almost always tell the Martiniquaises by their fashionable clothes.

Of the island's 400,000 inhabitants, 100,000 live in Fort-de-France and its environs. It has 34 separate municipalities. Though the actual number of French residents from the Metropole (France) does not exceed 15% of the total population, Martinique is a part of France, an overseas *département* to be exact; and French is the official language, though the vast majority of the residents also speak Creole.

Thousands are employed in government jobs offering more paid holidays than most Americans can imagine. Martinicans work hard and enjoy their time off, celebrating everything from *le fin de la semaine* (the weekend) to Indian feast days, sailboat races, and Carnival. Their joie de vivre is infectious. Once you experience it, you'll be back.

PLANNING

WHEN TO GO

High season runs from mid-December through mid-April, and the island can be quiet the rest of the year, with some hotels closing down for months, particularly in September and October. Those places that remain open offer discounts. Check 🌐 *www.martinique.org* for the latest deals.

GETTING HERE AND AROUND

AIR TRAVEL

There are now nonstop flights from the United States on American Airlines, flying out of Miami twice a week. New service by Seaborne Airlines has flights leaving four times a week from San Juan. Most travelers are able to connect in San Juan or in Miami and to Air France, as well, which departs Miami three times a week with a stop in a neighboring island.

Contacts Air Antilles Express. ☎ *0890/64–86–48, 0596/42–18–07* 🌐 *www.airantilles.com.* **Air Canada.** ☎ *888/247–2262* 🌐 *www.aircanada.com.* **Air Caraïbes.** ☎ *0820/83–58–35, 0590/82–47–47 in Guadeloupe, reservations* 🌐 *www.aircaraibes.com; www.aircaraibes-usa.com.* **Air France.** ☎ *0892/68–29–72, 0596/55–34–72, 800/237–27–47 in U.S., 0596/82–61–61* 🌐 *www.airfrance.com.* **American Airlines.** ☎ *800/433–7300* 🌐 *www.aa.com.* **LIAT.** ☎ *0596/42–16–11* 🌐 *www.liatairline.com.* **Seaborne Airlines.** ☎ *866/359–8784* 🌐 *www.seaborneairlines.com.*

LOGISTICS

Getting to Martinique: There are now nonstop flights from the United States aboard American Airlines, departing from Miami twice weekly. There are also year-round, nonstop, direct flights from Montreal, with connections from most major cities. A new carrier, Seaborne Airlines, now flies to Martinique four times a week out of San Juan; it code-shares with American Airlines which allows you to book your American Airlines and Seaborne Airlines combined itinerary on the AA website while earning AAdvantage program miles.

Many travelers can connect in San Juan or Miami. Air Canada flies to Martinique every Sunday. A second flight on Tuesday is available January 8–April 9. Air Antilles Express flies from Guadeloupe (also connected to Martinique by ferries), St. Maarten, and St. Barth. Air Caraïbes flies from Guadeloupe, St. Maarten, St. Barth, and Santo Domingo. (This airline offers substantial discounts for seniors on its shorter flights.) Air France is another connection option; during the peak tourist season (winter), it has service from Miami three times a week, with stops in neighboring islands. LIAT connects Martinique with the English-speaking "down islands" such as St. Lucia.

Hassle Factor: Medium–high.

On the Ground: Taxis in Martinique are expensive, so factor airport-transfer costs into your vacation budget. From the airport to Fort-de-France, you'll pay at least €30 (€40 at night or on Sunday); from the airport to Pointe du Bout, it's about €50 (€60 at night or on Sunday); fares to François or Tartane are approximately €60 (€70 at night or on Sunday). If you arrive at night or on Sunday, depending on where your hotel is, it may be cheaper (although not safer) to rent a car from the airport and keep it for 24 hours than to take a taxi to your hotel. ■ **TIP→ Better yet, stay closer to the airport or in Fort de France, pick up your rent-a-car after a good night's sleep, and then navigate to your resort.**

AIRPORT

Martinique Aimé Césaire Airport (FDF). Martinique Aimé Césaire Airport, in the commercial area of Lamentin, is relatively small and easy to maneuver; some staff members speak English. The tourist office has a desk staffed with an English-speaking person(s). There are food outlets, shops, and numerous rent-a-car desks. The airport is 15 minutes from Fort-de-France via taxi; it's 40 minutes from Les Trois-Ilets Peninsula. ✉ *Lamentin* ☎ *0596/42–16–00* 🌐 *www.martinique.aeroport.fr.*

CAR TRAVEL

The main highways, about 175 miles (280 km) of well-paved and well-marked roads, are excellent, but only in a few areas are they lighted at night. Many hotels are on roads that are barely passable, so get wherever you're going by nightfall or you could lose your way. Then tell a stranger, "*Je suis perdu!*" ("I am lost!"). It elicits sympathy. If they say, "*Suivez-moi!*"—that's "Follow me!"—stay glued to their bumper. Finally, drive defensively; although Martinicans are polite and lovely people, they drive with aggressive abandon.

Martinique, especially Fort-de-France and environs, is plagued with heavy traffic; if you must drive into Fort-de-France, do it on a weekend. Absolutely avoid the Lamentin Airport area and Fort-de-France during weekday rush hours, roughly 7 to 10 am and 4 to 7:30 pm, and on Sunday night going in the direction of Fort-de-France. That's when everyone comes off the beaches and heads back to the city. Even smaller towns such as La Trinité have rush hours. Watch, too, for *dos d'ânes* (literally, donkey backs), speed bumps that are hard to spot—particularly at night. Gas is costly, some $US7 per gallon. Diesel is somewhat cheaper, around $5.20, but if you rent an economy car for a full week, you should budget at least $100 for fuel.

Be aware that the French gendarmes set up roadblocks, often on Sunday, to stop speeders and drunk drivers, and just to check papers. Now they even have video cameras on the highways. Visitors are not absolved from speeding tickets, because you can be tracked down through the rental car's license plate.

Renting a Car: It's worth the hassle to rent a car—if only for a day or two—so that you can explore more of this beautiful island. Just be prepared for a manual shift, steep mountainous roads, and heavy traffic. Prices are expensive, "in season" about €80 per day or €450 per week (unlimited mileage) for a manual shift, perhaps more for an automatic, which must be ordered in advance (and not all agencies have them). You may save money by waiting to book your car rental on the island for a reduced weekly rate from a local agency. Some of the latter, though, make up their own rules, and they will not be in your favor. There's an extra charge (about $20) if you drop the car off at the airport after having rented it somewhere else on the island. A valid U.S. driver's license or International Driver's Permit is needed to rent a car for up to 20 days. ■**TIP➜ Often, the airline you fly in with will have a discount coupon for a rental car, right on the ticket, or in their in-flight magazine. Also, local publications have ads with discounts that can be as much as 40% off (in low season). You can find these at the Tourism Information counter in the airport.**

Contacts Avis. This is one of the agencies that will have an automatic; reserve it as far in advance as possible. ☎ *0596/42–11–00* 🌐 *www.avis-antilles.fr.* **Budget.** A presence on island for 20 years, Budget has three locations; the airport location is the one that is open the latest. ✉ *Martinique Aimé Césaire Airport, Lamentin* ☎ *0596/42–04–04* 🌐 *www.budget-martinique.com.* **Europcar.** Europcar will sometimes deliver the car to you and pick it up when finished, and its rates are usually among the lowest. The downside is that employees don't usually speak English. That said, at its location near the airport, which is behind a gas station on the national road, there are several English-speaking employees who are particularly helpful. If you go first to the Europcar counter at the airport, a shuttle will transport you to the site. With advance notice, you can get an automatic. ☎ *0596/42–42–42* 🌐 *www.europcar-martinique.com.* **Hertz.** Hertz has the advantage of three locations, more multilingual staffers, and the assurance that you are dealing with a U.S. franchise. As in the states, it's more expensive than most, but they have some automatics including BMWs, as well as French cars, both economy and higher-end models. ✉ *Martinique Aime Cesare Airport, Lamentin* ☎ *0596/51–01–01, 0810/32–31–13* 🌐 *www.hertzantilles.com,* *www.hertzantilles.com/location_voiture_martinique.* **JumboCar.** Of the many agencies, JumboCar is the most likely to cut a deal (but few of its staffers speak English). The airport location is open until 10 pm. They have a large selection of cars, more standard and economy models, but they do have some convertibles; automatics may be possible with advance reservations. ✉ *Martinique Aimé Césaire Aéroport, Lamentin* ☎ *0596/42–17–01, 0820/22–02–30* 🌐 *www.jumbocar.com.* **Sixt.** This well-oiled operation is the agency most likely to have automatics and higher-end cars, notably BMWs, as well as more affordable options. ✉ *Martinique Aimé Césaire Airport, Lamentin* 🌐 *www.sixt.fr.*

FERRY TRAVEL

Weather permitting, *vedettes* (ferries) operate daily between Quai d'Esnambuc in Fort-de-France and the marinas in Pointe du Bout, Anse-Mitan, and Anse-à-l'Ane and are the best way to go into the capital. Any of these trips takes about 20 minutes. Ferries depart every 30 minutes on weekdays; less often in the low season and weekends. Round-trip tickets cost €6.50.

Compagnie Maritime West Indies. Compagnie Maritime West Indies provides rapid sea shuttle service from neighboring St. Lucia. Boats (capacity 15 persons) usually depart daily at 11 am and 4 pm from Castries, St. Lucia, to Le Marin, Fort-le-France. Fares are approximately €89 round-trip for adults and €69 round-trip for children under 12. It departs from Le Marin at 8 am and from St. Lucia at 11 am. **■ TIP→ A number of airlines fly into St. Lucia, so making arrangements to land there and take Compagnie can be a good way to get to Martinique (especially if you are staying at Club Med or another resort in the south or chartering a sailboat from the marina in Le Marin).** ☎ *0696/21–77–76, 0596/74–93–38, 0758/452–8757 in St. Lucia.*

Jeans for Freedom. This branch of the L'Express des Îles company goes between Pointe-à-Pitre, Guadeloupe, and St-Pierre, Martinique; it also makes a brief stop in Dominica; the price is now up to €79. In Guadeloupe, service is also available between Pointe-à-Pitre and Marie-Galante or Les Saintes for €19. Jeans also runs specials like a day-trip out of Fort-de-France to St. Lucia and Antigua. ✉ *Pl. du Marche, rue Victor Hugo, St-Pierre* ☎ *0825/01–01–25, 0596/78–11–50* 🌐 *www.jeansforfreedom.com.*

L'Express des Îles. *L'Express des Îles* connects Martinique with Dominica, St. Lucia, Guadeloupe—it also services Guadeloupe's out islands, Marie-Galante and Les Saintes—from Pointe-à-Pitre, Guadeloupe (one-way €26, round-trip €43). Each one-way trip is €79, but round-trip tickets are just €119. The crossings generally take between three and four hours. Most of these services are daily, with extra departures on weekends and holidays or for special events—the ferries can often get crowded then. Boats depart from the Terminal Inter Îles–Quai Ouest in Fort-de-France. If traveling from Martinique to Dominica, Guadeloupe, or St. Lucia, a passenger is allowed three pieces of luggage that weigh no more than 25 kg (55 pounds) each; if traveling from Guadeloupe to its out islands, Les Saintes and Marie-Galante you're allowed one less bag. In either direction, you're also allowed to carry on one piece of baggage that weighs 10 kg (22 pounds) or less. Be aware that this ferry company also follows airline rules for what you're allowed to pack inside checked and carry-on baggage; check the website for more information. ✉ *Terminal Inter Isles Quai Ouest, Fort-de-France* ☎ *0825/35–90–00, 0590/91–98–53 in Guadeloupe* 🌐 *www.express-des-iles.com.*

TAXI TRAVEL

Taxis, which are metered, are expensive, though you can try bargaining by offering to pay a flat rate to your destination or offering them an hourly rate—try for €40, but you may have to compromise at €50.

Contacts J. Peloponese Taxis. J. Peloponese Taxis provides luxury service in new Mercedes-Benz cars. The taxis have meters but you can also arrange an hourly rate for touring. English speaking, politeness, and patience are characteristics. ☎ *0696/25–61–02.* **M. Martial Mercedes Taxis.** Drivers of M. Martial Mercedes Taxis speak English, Spanish, and German as well as French. ☎ *0596/64–20–24, 0696/45–69–07 mobile.* **Taxi de Place.** At this government-designated stand, you will find some English-speaking drivers, lots of courtesy, and new SUVs. ✉ *Rue Victoire sévre, Fort-de-France* ☎ *0696/31–91–05.*

15

ESSENTIALS

Banks and Exchange Services The euro is the official currency in Martinique. U.S. dollars are accepted in some hotels, but generally at an unfavorable rate. You can usually get the best rate by withdrawing euros from ATMs, which you'll find at the airport and at branches of the Crédit Agricole and other major banks. Be aware that your bank will probably charge $5 for each foreign withdrawal; the ATM will advise you of its fee before they release the cash. Consequently, it may make sense to take the maximum amount allowed out at one time, but be diligent about stashing the cash in your hotel safe. Most hotels and restaurants accept major credit cards, but this is somewhat less common once you get away from Fort-de-France and Pointe du Bout. Many establishments don't accept American Express in any case. There is a change office at the beginning of Ernest Deproge Street next to the Banque Francaise. Change Caraïbes is at 14 rue Victor Hugo and Le Bord de Mer.

Electricity 220-volt outlets. North American appliances require a converter and an adapter.

Passport Requirements All visitors must have a valid passport and a return or ongoing ticket.

Phones To call Martinique from the United States, dial 011–596–596 plus the local six-digit number (yes, you must dial 596 *twice*). To call the United States from Martinique, dial 001, then the area code, then the local number.

Taxes and Service Charges A resort tax varies from city to city. Each has its own tax, with most between €0.76 and €1.25 per person per day; the maximum is €2.25. Rates quoted by hotels usually include a 10% service charge.

Tipping All restaurants include a 15% service charge in their menu prices. You can always add to this if you feel that service was particularly good. Although you may have some initial sticker shock at the prices, remember that they include the tax and tip.

ACCOMMODATIONS

At Martinique, you can stay in tiny inns called *relais créoles,* boutique hotels, and private villas as well as splashy tourist resorts and restored plantation houses. Several hotels are clustered in Pointe du Bout on Les Trois-Ilets Peninsula, which is connected to Fort-de-France by ferry. Other clusters are in Ste-Luce, and Le François has become known for its boutique properties. Hotels and relais can be found all over the island. Because Martinique is the largest of the Windward Islands, this can mean a substantial drive to your hotel after a long flight or ferry trip. You may want to stay closer to the airport on your first night—for instance, at the Hotel Galleria, a no-nonsense hotel within a shopping mall just 10 minutes from the airport, or at a hotel in Fort-de-France. If you need to make a last-minute hotel reservation, head for the Tourism Information counter in the airport arrival hall (☎ *0596/42–18–05*); it is open between 8 am and 9 pm every day except Sunday, when it's open from 2 pm to 9 pm.

Large Resorts: There are only a few deluxe properties on the island. Those that lack megastar ratings offer an equally appealing mixture of charisma, hospitality, and French style. Larger hotels often have the busy, slightly frenetic feel that the French seem to like.

Relais Créoles: Small, individually owned inns are still available on Martinique, though they may be far removed from the resorts.

Villas: Groups and large families can save money by renting a villa, but the language barrier can be problematic, and often you will need a car.

Hotel reviews have been shortened. For full information, visit Fodors.com.

WHAT IT COSTS IN EUROS

	$	$$	$$$	$$$$
Restaurants	under €12	€12–€20	€21–€30	over €30
Hotels	under €275	€275–€375	€376–€475	over €475

Restaurant prices are the average cost of a main course at dinner or, if dinner is not served, at lunch. Hotel prices are the lowest cost of a standard double room in high season.

VISITOR INFORMATION

Contacts Comité Martiniquais du Tourisme ✉ *Immeuble Beaupre, Pointe de Jaham, Schoelcher, Fort-de-France* ☎ *0596/61–61–77* 🌐 *www.martiniquetourisme.com.* **Martinique Promotion Bureau** ✉ *825 3rd Ave., 29th fl., New York, New York, United States* ☎ *212/838–6887 in New York* 🌐 *www.martinique.org.* **Office du Tourisme de Fort-de-France** ✉ *76 rue Lazare Carnot, Fort-de-France* ☎ *0596/60–27–73* 🌐 *www.tourismefdf.com.*

MARTINIQUE TRANSPORTATION TIPS

Taxi: Taxis in Martinique are expensive, and you will pay more after dark. From the airport to Fort-de-France you'll pay at least €30 during the day, €40 at night; from the airport to Pointe du Bout, it's about €50 (€60 at night); to François or Tartane, the fare is approximately €60 (€70 at night). A 40% surcharge is levied between 7 pm and 6 am and on Sunday. If you arrive at night, depending on where your hotel is, it may be cheaper (although not safer) to rent a car from the airport and keep it for 24 hours than to take a taxi to your hotel.

Car Rental: Be prepared for a manual shift, steep mountainous roads, and heavy traffic. Prices are about €80 per day or €450 per week (unlimited mileage) in high season, substantially more for an automatic, which is rare. Usually, you won't find them unless you book in advance.

Alternative Transportation: Locals take *collectifs* (white vans holding up to 10 passengers) that cost just a few euros and depart from Pointe Simon, on the waterfront in Fort-de-France, to all parts of the island. Don't be shy; the difference can be €3 versus, say, €60 for a taxi to reach the same destination. Drivers don't usually speak English, and there's no air-conditioning.

Bus Mozaik. The air-conditioned buses of this private company stop within the city; they service Lamentin, Fort-de-France suburbs such as Schoelcher, and as far into the interior of the island as St. Joseph. Buses leave from Pointe Simon, on the waterfront, where the public buses and shared-taxis (white vans) congregate. Fares start at €1.25 one-way; €2.30 for round-trip, if tickets are purchased at a Moziak Kiosk. If bought on the bus, those same rates would be €1.80 and €2.50. For schedules, visit 🌐 *www.aquelleheure.fr/bus.htm.*

The tourist offices can help with maps and information.

15

WEDDINGS

Martinique has a long residency requirement, so it's not really feasible to plan a wedding on the island. It is, however, a very romantic place for honeymoons.

EXPLORING

The northern part of the island will appeal to nature lovers, hikers, and mountain climbers. The drive from Fort-de-France to St-Pierre is particularly impressive, as is the one across the island, via Morne Rouge, from the Caribbean to the Atlantic. This is Martinique's wild side—a place of waterfalls, rain forest, and mountains. The highlight is Mont Pelée. The south is the more developed half of the island, where the resorts and restaurants are located, as well as the beaches.

FORT-DE-FRANCE

With its historic fort and superb location beneath the towering Pitons du Carbet on the Baie des Flamands, Martinique's capital—home to about one-quarter of the island's 400,000 inhabitants—should be a grand place. It wasn't for decades, but it's now coming up fast. The bay has received the designation One of the Most Beautiful Bays in the World. An ambitious redevelopment project, still under way, hopes to make it one of the most attractive cities in the Caribbean.

There is a small Office of Tourism de Fort-de-France at 76 rue Lazare Carnot. It has some brochures in English and helpful, English-speaking staffers. They can organize English-language tours with advance notice. Walking tours are scheduled for Wednesday and Friday at 9 am. They take in a number of historic sites in about an hour and 45 minutes and cost €12. Another Point d'Information Touristique is near the cathedral, at the junction of rues Antoine Siger and Victor Schoelcher. Also, Kiosk number 1 in La Savane is another location for the helpful tourism people; one can now arrange a tour to Fort Louis at that kiosk.

The Stewards Urbains, easily recognized by their red caps and uniforms, are able to answer most visitor questions about the city and give directions. These young gals and *garçons* are multilingual and knowledgeable. When a large cruise ship is in port, they are out in force, positioned in heavily trafficked tourist zones and at the front entrance of Lafayette's department store.

The most pleasant districts of Fort-de-France—Didier, Bellevue, and Schoelcher—are up on the hillside, and you need a car (or a taxi) to reach them. But if you try to drive here, you may find yourself trapped in gridlock in the narrow streets downtown. Parking is difficult, and it's best to try for one of the garages or—as a second choice—outdoor public parking areas. Come armed with some euro coins for this purpose. A taxi or ferry from Pointe du Bout may be a better alternative. Even if your hotel isn't there, you can drive to the marina and park nearby.

There are some fine shops with Parisian wares (at Parisian prices), including French lingerie, St. Laurent clothes, Cacharel perfume, and sexy stiletto heels. Near the harbor is a lively indoor marketplace (*grand marché*), where produce and spices are sold.

A playground on the Malecón, which now has a half-mile wooden boardwalk, has swings, trampolines, benches, and grounds for playing *pétanque*. The urban beach between the Malecón and the fort, La Française, is covered with white sand that was brought in.

TOP ATTRACTIONS

La Savane. The heart of Fort-de-France, La Savane is a 12½-acre park filled with trees, fountains, and benches. A massive revitalization made it the focal point of the city again, with entertainment, shopping, and a pedestrian mall. Attractive wooden stands have been constructed along the edge of the park that house a tourism information office, public restrooms, arts-and-crafts vendors, a crepe stand, an ice-cream stand, and numerous other eateries. There are some homeless types around, but everyone considers them harmless.

The Hotel L'Imperatrice, directly across from the park, has become a real gathering place—particularly for its café, which opens to the sidewalk. The hotel also has one of the best kiosks in the Savanne for lunch and snacks.

Diagonally across from La Savane, you can catch the ferries for the 20-minute run across the bay to Pointe du Bout and the beaches at Anse-Mitan and Anse-à-l'Ane. It's relatively cheap as well as stress-free—much safer, more pleasant, and faster than by car.

The most imposing historic site in Fort-de-France is **Ft. St-Louis**, which runs along the east side of La Savane. Now a military installation, it's again open to the public. However you have to arrange a guided tour in advance at the Tourism kiosk.

WORTH NOTING

Fort St. Louis. Fort Saint Louis (Lou-ee), an imposing stone fortress that has guarded the island's principal port city for some 375 years, was closed to the public after 9/11 when it was reinstated as an active naval base by the French Navy. The fort officially reopened on July 20, 2014.

15

On a hilltop, originally carved out from a rocky promontory jutting out into the Bay of Fort-de-France, at its highest point, it towers nearly 200 feet over the city, affording visitors panoramic views of the surrounding seaside urban landscape. A view-experience and photo op, with a spyglass one could see any threatening warships coming for miles in advance . . . location, location.

Guided tours are available in English, French, Spanish, and Italian. Walking shoes are recommended. Visitors must first check in at the Fort-de-France Office de Tourisme information kiosk 1, at the northwest corner of La Savane, at the intersection of rue de la Liberté and boulevard Alfassa. ✉ *Boulevard Chevalier, Sainte-Marthe* ☎ *0596/75–41–44* 🌐 *www.tourismefdf.com* 🎫 *Adults €8, €4 for children, who must be at least 6 years old* ⏲ *Tues.–Sat. 9–4* ⏲ *Fort closed for tours Sun. and Mon.*

Musée d'Histoire et d'Ethnographie. This museum is best undertaken at the beginning of your vacation, so you can better understand the history, background, and people of the island. Housed in an elaborate, former military residence (circa 1888) with balconies and fretwork, the museum displays some of the garish gold jewelry that prostitutes wore after emancipation as well as the sorts of rooms that a proper, middle-class Martinican would have lived in. Oil paintings, engravings, and old historical documents also help sketch out the island's culture. ✉ *10 bd. Général de Gaulle* ☎ *0596/72–81–87* 🎫 *€3* ⏲ *Mon. and Wed.–Fri. 8:30–5, Tues. 2–5, Sat. 8–noon.*

Musée d'Archéologie Précolombienne et de Préhistoire. A hidden treasure with an unassuming entrance, it is just down the street from the hotel l'Imperatrice. A multistory archaeological museum, it houses some 2,000 artifacts that go way back to the era when Indians were the indigenous inhabitants. If luck is with you, an English-speaking guide will make it all come alive. Young boys take to this museum, "digging" the early pea shooters, poison darts, hammocks that took a year to make, and the shaman's headdress. Women are fascinated by the jewelry fashioned from natural materials, boar tusks, and exotic bird feathers. A good time to sample this dose of prehistory is on a typically hot city day, for the air-conditioning is frigid. ✉ *9 rue de Liberté* ☎ *0596/71–57–05* 🎫 *€4.*

Rue Victor Schoelcher. Stores sell Paris fashions and French perfume, china, crystal, and liqueurs, as well as local handicrafts along this street running through the center of the capital's primary shopping district, a six-block area bounded by rue de la République, rue de la Liberté, rue Victor Severe, and rue Victor Hugo.

St-Louis Cathedral. This Romanesque cathedral with lovely stained-glass windows was built in 1878, the sixth church on this site (the others were destroyed by fires, hurricanes, and earthquakes). Classified as a historical monument, it has a marble altar, an impressive organ, and carved wooden pulpits. ✉ *Rue Victor Schoelcher* ☎ *0596/60–59–00* 🕓 *Daily 6:30 am–11:30 am. Church services Sun. 7:30–10:30 am; Tues., Wed., and Fri. 6:45 am; Sat. 6:30 pm.*

SOUTH OF FORT-DE-FRANCE

LE FRANÇOIS

With some 16,000 inhabitants, this is the main city on the Atlantic coast. Many of the old wooden buildings remain and are juxtaposed with concrete structures. The classic West Indian cemetery, with its black-and-white tiles, is still here, and a marina is at the end of town. Two of Martinique's best hotels are in this area (Cap Est and Hotel Plein Soleil), as well as some of the island's most upscale residences and most visited distillery/museum, Habitation Clément. Le François is also noted for its snorkeling. Offshore are the privately owned Ilets de l'Impératrice. The islands received that name because, according to legend, this is where Empress Joséphine came to bathe in the shallow basins known as *les fonds blanc* because of their white-sand bottoms. Group boat tours leave from the harbor and include lunch and drinks and one can even buy a package that includes an overnight stay on the remote and romantic, Isle de Oscar. Prices vary *(⇨ Sports and the Outdoors)*. The town itself is rather lackluster but authentic, and you'll find a number of different shops and supermarkets, owned by truly lovely, helpful residents.

TOP ATTRACTIONS

Fodor's Choice ★ **Habitation Clément.** Get a glimpse into Martinique's colonial past. Visitors are given a multilingual audio headset, which explains tour highlights. Signage further describes the rum-making process and other aspects of plantation life. The Palm Grove, with an avenue of palms and park benches, is delightful. It was all built with the wealth generated by its rum distillery, and its 18th-century splendor has been lovingly preserved. The plantation's creole house illustrates the adaptation to life in the tropics up through the 20th century. An early French typewriter, a crank-up telephone, and decades-old photos of the Clements and Hayots (béké families) are juxtaposed with modern Afro-Caribbean art. Enjoy the free tastings at the bar of the retail shop. Consider the Canne Bleu, Grappe Blanche, or one of the aged rums, some bottled as early as 1952. ■ **TIP→ Children get a discount, but so do parents with children!**

Also, allow 1½–2 hours to see everything. The ticket office closes at 5. ⊠ *Domaine de l'Acajou* ☎ *0596/54–62–07* 🌐 *www.habitation-clement.fr* 🎫 *€12* ⏲ *Daily 9–5.*

LES TROIS-ILETS

Named after the three rocky islands nearby, this lovely little village (population 3,000) has unusual brick-and-wood buildings roofed with antique tiles. It's known for its pottery, straw, and woodwork, but above all as the birthplace of Napoléon's empress, Joséphine. In the square, where there's also a market and a fine *mairie* (town hall), you can visit the simple church where she was baptized Marie-Joseph Tascher de la Pagerie. The Martinicans have always been enormously proud of Joséphine, even though her husband reintroduced slavery on the island and most historians consider her to have been rather shallow.

ELSEWHERE SOUTH OF FORT-DE-FRANCE

TOP ATTRACTIONS

15

Le Marin. The yachting capital of Martinique, Le Marin is also known for its colorful August carnival and its Jesuit church, circa 1766. From Le Marin a narrow road leads to picturesque Cap Chevalier, about 1 mile (1½ km) from town. Most of the buildings are white and very European. The marina, a hub for charter boats, is often busy. There are waterfront restaurants and clubs that are a magnet for the younger crowd as well as for sailors and tourists at large. 🌐 *www.marin-martinique.fr/fr/agenda.*

Pointe du Bout. This tourist area has a marina and several resort hotels, among them the deluxe Hotel Bakoua and the newly renovated Hotel Le Pagerie. The ferry to Fort-de-France leaves from here. The Village Creole complex with its "residences" for tourists, its cluster of boutiques, ice-cream parlors, and rental-car agencies, forms the hub from which various restaurants and hotels radiate. It's a pretty quiet place in the low season. The beach at Anse-Mitan, which is a little west of Pointe du Bout proper, is one of the best on the island. There are also several small restaurants, and inexpensive guesthouses there. ⊠ *Les Trois-Ilets.*

WORTH NOTING

Forêt de Montravail. A few miles north of Ste-Luce, this tropical rain forest is ideal for a short hike. Look for the interesting group of Carib rock drawings. ⊠ *Le Diamant.*

NEED A BREAK?

Le Grand Trianon Boulangerie. If you need a fast French lunch break in Le François, try this bakery, which is in town, near the Carrefour Supermarket. Crisp baguettes and luscious pastries and ice cream are sold, as are prix-fixe lunches with sandwiches or salads. French ladies love to "do lunch" here. ⊠ ***Centre Cial Ancienne Usine, Le François*** ☎ ***0596/77–46–01.***

Ste-Luce. This quaint fishing village has a sleepy main street with tourist shops and markets, and you can see some cool types taking a Pernod. Many young, single people live in this town. From the sidewalk cafés there are panoramic sea views of St. Lucia. Nearby are excellent beaches, nearly white, and several resorts, including three from the Karibea Hotel chain. To the east is Pointe Figuier, an excellent spot for

Diamond Rock

scuba diving. On the way, the Trois-Rivieres Distillery is just off the highway, and Club Med is nearby, on its own peninsula.

NORTH OF FORT-DE-FRANCE

Jardin de Balata (*Balata Gardens*). The Jardin de Balata has thousands of varieties of tropical flowers and plants; its owner is a dedicated horticulturist. There are shaded benches from which to take in the mountain views and a plantation-style house furnished with period furniture. An aerial path gives visitors an astounding, bird's-eye view of the gardens and surrounding hills, from wooden walkways suspended 50 feet in the air. There is no restaurant, though beverages are for sale. This worthy site shows why Martinique is called the Island of Flowers. It's 15 minutes from Fort-de-France, in the direction of St-Pierre. You can order anthuriums and other tropical flowers to be delivered to the airport from the mesmerizing flower boutique here. ■ **TIP→ The gardens close at 6, but the ticket office will not admit anyone after 4:30. Children get a discount.** ✉ *Km. 10, Rte. de Balata, Balata* ☎ *0596/64–48–73* 🌐 *www.jardindebalata.fr* 🎟 *€12.80* ⏲ *Daily 9–6.*

ST-PIERRE

The rise and fall of St-Pierre is one of the most remarkable stories in the Caribbean and one of its worst disasters. Martinique's modern history began here in 1635. By the turn of the 20th century St-Pierre was a flourishing city of 30,000, known as the Paris of the West Indies. As many as 30 ships at a time stood at anchor. By 1902 it was the most modern town in the Caribbean, with electricity, phones, and a tram. On May 8, 1902, two thunderous explosions rent the air. As the nearby volcano erupted, Mont Pelée split in half, belching forth a cloud of burning ash, poisonous gas, and lava that raced down the mountain at 250 mph. At 3,600°F, it instantly vaporized everything in its path; 30,000 people were killed in two minutes.

The **Cyparis Express**, a small tourist train, will take you around to the main sights with running narrative (in French) for an hour Monday through Saturday, starting at 11 am, with reservations (☎ *0596/55–50–92, 0696/81–88–70*) for €12 (€6 for children).

An Office du Tourisme is on the *moderne* seafront promenade. Stroll the main streets and check the blackboards at the sidewalk cafés before deciding where to lunch. At night some places have live music. Like stage sets for a dramatic opera, there are the ruins of the island's first church (built in 1640), the imposing theater, and the toppled statues. This city, situated on its naturally beautiful harbor and with its narrow, winding streets, has the feel of a European seaside hill town. With every footstep you touch a page of history. Although many of the historic buildings need work, stark modernism has not invaded this burg.

15

TOP ATTRACTIONS

Fodor's Choice ★ **Depaz Distillery.** An excursion to Depaz Distillery is one of the best things to do on the island. Established in 1651, it sits at the foot of the volcano. After a devastating eruption in 1902, the fields of blue cane were replanted, and in time, the rum making began all over again. A self-guided tour includes the workers' gingerbread cottages. The tasting room sells its rums, including golden and aged rum, and liqueurs made from orange, ginger, and basil, among other flavors, that can enhance your cooking. Unfortunately, the plantation's great house, or château, is still closed to the public. Allow time and make a reservation for Depaz's restaurant, **Le Moulin a Canne** (*0596/69–80–44*). Open only for lunch—even on Sunday when the distillery is closed, it has the views, the service, and flavorful creole specialties as well as some French classics on the menu, plus—you guessed it—Depaz rum to wash it down. It's "on the house." ■ **TIP→ Shutters are drawn at the tasting room and the staff leaves at exactly 5 pm (or 4 on Saturday), so plan to be there at least an hour before.** ✉ *Mont Pelée Plantation* ☎ *0596/78–13–14* 🌐 *www.depazrhum.com* 🎟 *Distillery free* ⏲ *Weekdays 10–5, Sat. 9–4.*

FAMILY **Musée Vulcanologique Frank Perret.** For those interested in Mont Pelée's eruption of 1902, the Musée Vulcanologique Frank Perret is a must. It was established in 1933 by Frank Perret, a noted American volcanologist. Small but fascinating, the museum houses photographs of the old town before and after the eruption, documents, and a number of relics—some gruesome—excavated from the ashy ruins, including molten glass, melted iron, the church bell, and contorted clocks stopped at 8 am. The 30-minute film is a good way to begin. An English-speaking guide is often available and may tell you that the next lava flow is expected within 50 years. (No wonder the price of real estate in St-Pierre is among the lowest in the island.) ✉ *Rue Victor Hugo (D10) at rue du Theatre* ☎ *0596/78–15–16* 🎟 *€3* ⏲ *Daily 9–5 with a lunch hr closure.*

STE-MARIE

The winding, hilly route to this town of some 20,000 offers breathtaking views of the rugged Atlantic coastline. Ste-Marie is the commercial capital of the island's north. Look for a picturesque mid-19th-century church here. Most come to the area to visit the St. James Distillery and its Musée du Rhum, but the north is also filled with immense natural beauty.

Nearby in Marigot, Habitation La Grange, originally the Great House on a grand banana plantation that was converted into a deluxe, historical hotel in the '90s, changed hands. The present owner, an architect, is currently involved in a major restoration and it is slated to reopen as a boutique property in spring 2015.

Fodor's Choice ★ **La distillerie J.M.** This distillery wins the prize for the most innovative and contemporary exhibits as well as its tastings. Firstly, for those in the know, J.M rum has long been considered on the top echelon of Martinique rums. It does not have the same name recognition as some of the other popular labels, like Clement, for example. That is partly because the best that they offer are their *rhum vieux* (aged), which is considerably more expensive than your average bottle of white rum. Their 10-year-old vintages (44.8 proof) truly rival France's fine cognacs. It is among the complimentary tastings offered.

The displays that they have created allow one to inhale the various aromas of the products, from vanilla and orange to almonds and exotic fruits flambé. It is a sensory learning experience. And then there are high-tech visuals, a film, and an unexpected water installation. It is said that the pure mountain water of Macouba is what makes J.M rums so special.

In the far north, there is little in this immediate area as far as sightseeing, other than some outstanding rain forests, with monster trees and hanging lanai vines—sometimes right overhead the mountain road. **■ TIP→ Plan to couple a visit to this destination distillery with one to Carbet and St-Pierre, then the Depaz Distillery, in time to take lunch at their fine restaurant. Then proceed to J.M. It is best to either have a designated driver or hire an English-speaking driver for a half or full day.** ✉ *Macouba* ☎ *0596/78–92–55* 🌐 *www.rhum-jm.com.*

St. James Distillery & Rum Museum. The Musée du Rhum, operated by the St. James Rum Distillery, is housed in a graceful, galleried creole house. Interestingly, the distillery was founded in 1765 in St-Pierre by a priest who was also an alchemist. It was relocated to Ste-Marie after the 1902 eruption of Mont Pelée. Guided tours can take in the plantation and the displays of the tools of the trade, the art gallery, and include a visit and tasting at the distillery. You can opt to take a little red train tour for €5 that traverses the cane fields and runs between here and the nearby banana museum, while a guide narrates. This runs on Tuesday and Thursday mornings and Saturday afternoons—maybe.

The museum is known for its "happenings," including beauty contests as well as the huge Fête du Rhum, in December. The party can get somewhat wild when a dozen or more tour buses pull in. **■ TIP→ The museum and distillery are closed during the cane harvest, and weekend**

hours sometimes change; tours may not happen during December. It's a good idea to call ahead. ✉ *Plan d l'union, St. James Distillery* ☎ *0596/69–30–02* 🎟 *Free* ⏲ *Daily 9–5.*

OTHER ATTRACTIONS NORTH OF FORT-DE-FRANCE

TOP ATTRACTIONS

Le Morne Rouge. This town sits on the southern slopes of the volcano that destroyed it in 1902. Today it's a popular resort spot and offers hikers some fantastic mountain scenery. From Le Morne Rouge you can start the climb up the 4,600-foot **Mont Pelée.** But don't try scaling this volcano without a guide unless you want to get buried alive under pumice stones. Instead, drive up to L'Auberge de la Montagne Pelée. (Ask for a room with a view.) From the parking lot it's 1 mile (1½ km) up a well-marked trail to the summit. Bring a hooded sweatshirt because there's often a mist that makes the air damp and chilly. From the summit follow the route de la Trace (Route N3), which winds south of Le Morne Rouge to St-Pierre. It's steep and winding, but that didn't stop the *porteuses* (female porters) of old: balancing a tray, these women would carry up to 100 pounds of provisions on their heads for the 15-hour trek to the Atlantic coast.

15

WORTH NOTING

Ajoupa-Bouillon. Near pineapple fields and filled with flowers, this 17th-century village is the jumping-off point for several sights. The Saut Babin, a 40-foot waterfall, is a half-hour walk from Ajoupa-Bouillon. The Gorges de la Falaise is a river gorge where you can swim. ✉ *Ajoupa-Bouillon.*

Basse-Pointe. On the route to this village, on the Atlantic coast at the island's northern end, you pass many banana and pineapple plantations. Just south of Basse-Pointe is a **Hindu temple**, which was built by descendants of the East Indians who settled in this area in the 19th century. The view of Mont Pelée from the temple is memorable.

Bellefontaine. This colorful fishing village has pastel houses on the hillsides and beautifully painted *gommiers* (fishing boats) bobbing in the water. Look for the restaurant built in the shape of a boat.

Le Prêcheur. This quaint village, the last on the northern Caribbean coast, is surrounded by volcanic hot springs. It was the childhood home of Françoise d'Aubigné, who later became the Marquise de Maintenon and the second wife of Louis XIV. At her request, the Sun King donated the handsome bronze bell that still hangs outside the church. The Tomb of the Carib Indians commemorates a sadder event. It's a formation of limestone cliffs, from which the last of the Caraïbes are said to have flung themselves to avoid capture by the marquise's forebears.

Neisson Distillery. The producers of one of the best rums on the island, Neisson is a small, family-run operation. Its rum is distilled from pure sugarcane juice rather than molasses. It's open for tours and tastings, and the shop sells *rhum extra-vieux* (vintage rum) that truly rivals cognac. Neisson is one of the distilleries that consistently bring home the gold (and the silver) from rum competitions in France. A passion for history and tradition characterizes the distillery, as does the design of its bottles. Proud of its independence, at a time when most distilleries

Le Morne Rouge

are absorbed by large groups, the distillery is now run by the daughter and grandson of Hildevert Pamphille Neisson, who founded the distillery in 1931. ✉ *Domaine Thieubeurt-Bourg, Carbet* ☎ *0596/78–03–70* 🌐 *www.neisson.com* 🎫 *Free* 🕒 *Weekdays 8:30–5, Sat. 8–noon.*

Presqu'île du Caravelle. Much of the Caravelle Peninsula, which juts 8 miles (13 km) into the Atlantic Ocean, is under the protection of the Regional Nature Reserve and offers places for trekking, swimming, and sailing. This is also the site of Anse-Spoutourne, an open-air sports and leisure center operated by the reserve. The town of Tartane has a popular surfing beach with brisk Atlantic breezes. Hotel La Caravelle is one of the beter places to stay in this area. ✉ *Tartane.*

DID YOU KNOW?

One man survived the eruption of Mont Pelée. His name was Cyparis, and he was a prisoner in an underground cell in the town's jail, locked up for public drunkenness. Later, he went on the road with the Barnum & Bailey Circus as a sideshow attraction. Le Petit Train, that gives tours of the town, is named after him, "Cyparis Express."

BEACHES

Take to the beach in Martinique and experience the white sandbars known as Josephine's Baths, where Napoléon's Joséphine would bathe. All of Martinique's beaches are open to the public, but hotels charge a fee for nonguests to use chaises longues, changing rooms and other facilities. There are no official nudist beaches, but topless bathing is prevalent, as is the case on most French islands. Unless you're an expert swimmer, steer clear of the Atlantic waters, except in the area of Cap Chevalier (Cape Knight) and the Presqu'île du Caravelle (Caravelle Peninsula). The white-sand beaches are south of Fort-de-France; to the north, the sand turns darker, and there are even beaches with silvery-black volcanic sand. Some of the most pleasant strips of sand are around Ste-Anne, Ste-Luce, and Havre du Robert. Some 15 minutes from Le François harbor, the white sandbars that form Josephine's Baths stand in the middle of the sea.

SOUTH OF FORTE DE-FRANCE

Anse Corps de Garde. On the southern Caribbean coast, this is one of the island's best long stretches of white sand. The public beach has picnic tables, restrooms, sea grape trees (which offer some shade), and crowds on weekends, when you'll also usually find plenty of wandering food vendors and the litter that follows them. During the week, the beach is much less busy, usually just with a few tourists and some local kids after school. The water is calm, with just enough wave action to remind you that it's the sea. There are no beach-chair rentals. From Fort-de-France, exit to the right before you get to the town of Ste-Luce. You first see signs for the Karibea Hotels and then one for Corps de Garde, which is on the right. At the stop sign take a left. **Amenities:** food and drink; toilets. **Best for:** swimming; walking; partiers. ✉ *Ste-Luce.*

Anse-Mitan. There are often yachts moored offshore in these calm waters. This long stretch of beach can be particularly fun on Sunday. Small, family-owned seaside restaurants are half-hidden among palm trees and are footsteps from the lapping waves. Nearly all offer grilled lobster and some form of music on weekends, perhaps a zouk band. Inexpensive waterfront hotels line the clean, golden beach, which has excellent snorkeling just offshore. Chaises longues are available for rent from hotels for about €7, and there are also usually vendors on weekends. When you get to Pointe du Bout, take a left at the yellow office of Budget Rent-A-Car, then the next left up a hill, and park near the little white church. **Amenities:** food and drink. **Best for:** partiers; snorkeling; swimming; walking. ✉ *Pointe du Bout, Les Trois-Ilets.*

Diamant Beach. The island's longest beach has a splendid view of Diamond Rock, but the Atlantic waters are rough, with lots of wave action—it's not known as a surfers' beach, though. Diamant is often deserted, especially midweek, which is more reason to be careful if you do go swimming. The sand is black here, and it is an experience to snorkel above it. Happily, it's a great place for picnicking and beachcombing; there are shade trees aplenty, and parking is abundant and free. The hospitable, family-run Diamant les Bains hotel is a good lunch spot; if you eat lunch there, the management may let you wash off in the pool overlooking the beach. From Les Trois-Ilets, go in the direction of Rivière Salée, taking the secondary road to the east, toward Le Diamant. A coastal route, it leads to the beach. **Amenities:** food and drink; parking. **Best for:** solitude; snorkeling; walking. ✉ *Le Diamant.*

FAMILY **Les Salines.** A short drive south of Ste-Anne brings you to a mile-long (1½-km-long) cove lined with soft white sand and coconut palms. The

The town of St-Pierre is beneath the 4,600-foot Mont Pelée.

beach is awash with families and children during holidays and on weekends, but quiet during the week. The far end—away from the makeshift souvenir shops—is most appealing. The calm waters are safe for swimming, even for the kids. You can snorkel, but it's not that memorable. Food vendors roam the sand, and there are also pizza stands and simple seafood restaurants. From Le Marin, take the coastal road toward Ste-Anne. You will see signs for Les Salines. If you see the sign for Pointe du Marin, you have gone too far. **Amenities:** food and drink; parking; showers; toilets. **Best for:** partiers; swimming; walking. ✉ *Ste-Anne.*

FAMILY **Pointe du Bout.** The beaches here are small, man-made, and lined with resorts. Each little strip is associated with its resident hotel, and security guards and closed gates make access difficult. However, if you take a left across from the main pedestrian entrance to the marina—after the taxi stand—then go left again, you will reach the beach for Hotel Bakoua, which has especially nice facilities and several options for lunch and drinks. If things are quiet—particularly during the week—one of the beach boys may rent you a chaise; otherwise, just plop your beach towel down, face forward, and enjoy the delightful view of the Fort-de-France skyline. The water is dead calm and quite shallow, but it eventually drops off if you swim out a bit. **Amenities:** food and drink; showers. **Best for:** snorkeling; sunset; swimming. ✉ *Pointe du Bout, Les Trois-Ilets.*

Pointe du Marin. Stretching north from Ste-Anne, this is a good windsurfing and waterskiing spot. It's also a popular family beach, with restaurants, campsites, and clean facilities available for a small fee. Club Med is on the northern edge, and you can purchase a day pass.

From Le Marin, take the coastal road to Ste-Anne. Make a right before town, toward Domaine de Belfond. You can see signs for Pointe du Marin. **Amenities:** food and drink; toilets. **Best for:** swimming; walking; windsurfing. ✉ *St. Anne.*

NORTH OF FORT DEFRANCE

Anse Tartane. This patch of sand is on the wild side of the Presqu'île du Caravelle. Ungroomed and in a fairly natural state, it's what the French call a *sauvage* beach. The only people you are likely to see are brave surfers who ride the high waves or some local families. Bliss, the surf school here, has taught many kids. Résidence Oceane looks down on all of this action; it doesn't have a restaurant, but you can get a drink. **Amenities:** parking; toilets (at surf school); water sports. **Best for:** partiers; surfing; walking. ✉ *Tartane, La Trinité* ✣ *Turn right before you get to La Trinité, and follow the route de Château past the Caravelle hotel. Instead of following the signs to Résidence Oceane, veer left and go downhill when you see the ocean. The road runs right beside the beach. There are several bays and points here, but if you keep heading to the right, you can reach the surf school.*

15

WHERE TO EAT

Martinique cuisine, a fusion of African and French, is certainly more international and sophisticated than that of its immediate island neighbors. The influx of young chefs, who favor a contemporary and lighter approach, has brought exciting innovations to the table. This haute-nouvelle creole cuisine emphasizes local products, predominantly starchy tubers such as plantains, white yams, yucca, and island sweet potatoes, as well as vegetables such as breadfruit, christophene (also known as chayote), and taro leaves. Many creole dishes have been Frenchified, transformed into mousselines, terrines, and gratins topped with creamy sauces. And then there's the bountiful harvest of the sea—*lambi* (conch), *langouste* (clawless local lobsters), and dozens of species of fish predominate, but you can also find *écrevisses* (freshwater crayfish, which are as luscious as jumbo prawns).

Some local creole specialties are *accras* (cod or vegetable fritters), which are the signature appetizer of Martinique, *crabes farcis* (stuffed land crab), and *feroce* (avocado stuffed with saltfish and farina). You can perk up fish and any other dish with a hit of hot *chien* (dog) sauce. Not to worry—it's made from onions, shallots, hot peppers, oil, and vinegar. To cool your jets, have a 'ti punch—four parts white rum and one part sugarcane syrup.

In Fort-de-France's city market, ladies serve up well-priced creole prix-fixe meals that can include accras, fricassee of octopus and conch, chicken in coconut milk, or grilled whole fish.

As for euro sticker shock, the consolation is that although menu prices may seem steep, they include tax and service. Prix-fixe menus, sometimes with wine, can help keep costs in line.

What to Wear. For dinner, casual resort wear is appropriate. Generally, men wear collared shirts. Women typically wear light cotton sundresses, short or long. At dinnertime, beach attire is too casual for most restaurants. Both the French (expats) ladies and the Martiniquais often "dress." They have an admirable French style, and almost always wear high heels.

SOUTH OF FORT-DE-FRANCE

$$$ FRENCH FUSION ✕ **Atomic Food.** Those who loved Fleur de Sel are sampling the difference between it and Atomic Food, a recent evolution by the same talented chef-owner, Damien Pelé, at his original venue, a 19th-century maison bourgeoise just past the village of Trois Ilets. For the uninitiated, the term "atomic food" means the opposite of nuclear fallout and altered, processed food. It is pure food, both organic and vegan, as iterated in David Guetta's popular song, "Atomic Food." (Google it and listen.) Previously, the cuisine, music, and the service all came together. It was coupled with innovative French dishes, the hallmark of this young Frenchman who has worked in five-star hotels and prestigious restaurants in Europe. A new dining terrace has been added in the garden, and manning a bar constructed with recycled wood and local bamboo, is a flamboyant barman, Antoine, a true mixologist. Tapas are served from 5 pm on (€8–€18). As there is a Latin ambience, start the party with a cucumber mojito! *[$] Average main: €24 ✉ 27 ave. de l'Impératrice Josephine, Les Trois-Ilets ☎ 0596/68–42–11 ⊗ No lunch (except for brunch during Jan./Feb.). Closed Sun. in low season.*

$ BAKERY ✕ **Coup d'Coeur.** If perusing the Poterie Village, look no farther for a lunch spot or a tea break. This *patisserie–salon de thé* is on the right, as you first enter the village. In fact, you might make this your daytime go-to restaurant if you are staying in Trois Ilets. When you open the front door, the aromas of fresh-baked goods will have you pressing your finger against the glass display case, euros clutched in your left hand, just like a little kid. Lunch can be a quiche (many varieties), pizza, or creative sandwiches, and if you clean your plate then you can be rewarded with a Viennoiserie. Only French butter is used and all products are made in an artisanal manner. There's table seating but not waiter service as such. *[$] Average main: €10 ✉ Village de la Poterie, Trois-Ilets ☎ 0596/69–70–32 ⊗ Mon.–Sat. 9:30–6; Sun. 9:30–1 pm ⊗ No dinner.*

$$$ SEAFOOD ✕ **La Baraqu' Obama.** If you're looking for a seafront restaurant that specialized in conch and lobster, Obama's is recommended. During lunchtime the alfresco terrace fills up mainly with French tourists supping on grilled lobster (€35). Aromas are drool-worthy with hints of lemon and melted butter. Mains come with frites or rice, and some vegetables and greenery dressed with vinaigrette. Red Desperados (local beer) and French rosé wash it all down. The kitchen is across the street as is the ice cream (tropical fruit flavors), and The Special Bar. Owner Patrick Henry put it together for his son who rocks it on weekends, with salsa on Friday nights. A four-foot poster of Obama is the major work of art. *[$] Average main: €21 ✉ Bord de mer, blvd.*

Kennedy, St-Luce ☎ 0696/80–78–75 ⊙ Tues.–Sat. lunch and dinner; Sun. lunch only ⊙ Closed Mon.

$$$$ FRENCH **Le Bélem.** To really experience Le Bélem, start with a cocktail in the super-chic bar lined with old black-and-white photographs of the island; a simple 'ti punch gets an elaborate presentation. At this special-occasion restaurant for the well-heeled, the innovative cuisine is served in a contemporary setting, with a bevy of servers who try hard to please, although some diners feel that the menu is too limited. It's all definitely expensive, but the complimentary amuse-bouche may save you an appetizer. However, most clients just love being there, especially if they are having a romantic interlude. A cylindrical wine "cave" is the dramatic focal point. The menu changes seasonally: the latest favorite is red snapper with lime crust, socca pancake, and eggplant caviar. Grand cru chocolate soufflé with tonka beans, tangerine and *cumbava* (kaffir lime) sorbet, is an unexpected dessert. **TIP→ Although less glamorous, lunch at Campeche, the beach restaurant, is still a treat, and provides a more affordable alternative.** It opens for dinner in high season. Hotel guests take their "wonderful breakfast" at Le Bélem, and during the season, it's open seven nights a week. *$ Average main: €32 ✉ Cap Est Lagoon Resort & Spa, Quartier Cap Est, Le François ☎ 0596/54–80–80 Reservations essential ⊙ No lunch. Closed some nights in low season.*

$$ FRENCH FUSION **Le Pitaya.** This is onc hotel restaurant that is not only surprisingly good but affordable. Hotel Le Pagerie markets it as "semi gastronomic," but that may be selling it short. The menu changes nightly but many items find their way back. They offer a menu du jour, a prix-fixe of three courses, for a modest €29. A favorite appetizer is the salmon gravlax with cream of wasabi; a €17 main could be duck en croute of herbs with a bigarde sauce. Desserts range from a panna-cotta to a classic tiramisu. Lobster is always available—as a grilled half lobster with an assortment of sauces. Relatively small, but open-air and overlooking the dramatically lit pool, it is best for outside guests to reserve. *$ Average main: €17 ✉ Hotel Le Pagerie, rue Chacha, Pointe du Bout, Les Trois-Ilets ☎ 0596/66–05–30 ⊕ www.hotel-lapagerie.com.*

$$$$ FRENCH FUSION Fodor's Choice ★ **Le Plein Soleil Restaurant.** Perennially popular with the chic set, Le Plein Soleil has a smashing contemporary, creole look. But it's the inventive, beautifully executed menu that cements its well-deserved reputation. It continues to draw applause for the use of the latest techniques from France coupled with remarkable twists on local products. Take a long and leisurely lunch (€45) on the terrace, which has a hilltop sea view; by night the mood is romantic, the service fine, the music heady. Soups are like a mixed-media collage. A velouté can be the canvas for ravioli made of foie gras or pineapple. For the evening's three-course prix fixe dinner (€45), a thick tuna steak roasted with lemon confit and stacked on mushroom risotto might be the main. At dinner, guests can choose from five main courses, two of which are fresh lobster and a steak. A memorable finale is a basil custard topped with a red berry coulis. *$ Average main: €45 ✉ Hôtel Le Plein Soleil, Pointe Thalèmont, Le François ☎ 0596/38–07–77 Reservations essential ⊙ No lunch Mon., Tues., Wed. and Thurs. No dinner Sun.*

15

$$$$ FRENCH FUSION Fodor's Choice ★ **Le Zandoli.** Although "le zandoli" is the creole term for the lowly gecko, there's nothing humble about the culinary presentation or the wildly colorful dining room here, which are as slick as anything you might encounter in Paris. The executive chef has worked in Michelin three-star restaurants in France, and the owning couple has artistic taste that is off the charts. At the start of the meal, an amuse-bouche—even two—will arrive, one in a tall shooter glass, another on a white, contemporary spoon. The three-course, prix-fixe menu is continually evolving, affected by seasonal market finds and influenced by five continents—one favorite main is the fillet of beef with girolles (chanterelle mushrooms). **■TIP→ One can opt for just two courses for €33.** You may want to arrive for your dinner reservation early, so that you can sit at the bar, which looks like an avant-garde movie set, and have a fanciful, fresh juice cocktail with tiny accoutrement. And in any given month there may be a reception and art exhibition, fashion show, or a gala party, like their Fifth Anniversary fete, when all comers, male and female alike had to wear a chapeau. *Average main: €42* *La Suite Villa, Rte du Fort d'Alet, Anse Mitan, Les Trois-Ilets* *0596/59–88–00* *www.la-suite-villa.com* *Reservations essential* *No lunch.*

$$ MODERN FRENCH **Restaurant Le Golf.** A golf course isn't the usual place for a great restaurant, but once you're at this terraced, alfresco location, you might find yourself wowed. It opens to acres of rolling greens, followed by the turquoise blue of the Caribbean. The interior is bright with colorful place settings, but the real eye candy is on the plates the French chef sends out—he can elevate a red snapper fillet to art with a purée of sweet potato here and a colorful (and spicy) rouille sauce there. Golfers sit down to torchon de foie gras with spiced fruit condiments, or cold avocado soup with apples and citronelle. And the food's usually light enough to allow for a rich and satisfying dessert like caramel "Lutti." *Average main: €18* *Golf de Trois-Ilets, Quartier la Pagerie, Trois-Ilets* *0596/48–20–84* *No dinner Sun. and Mon.*

FORT-DE-FRANCE AND POINTS NORTH

$$ SEAFOOD **Chez Les Pecheurs.** At the sign of the billfish, you'll find the kind of beach restaurant you search for but seldom find. It's your basic "feet-in-the-sand" spot, but it's authentic and it opened when owner M. Palmont still made his living by fishing. Now Palmont's pink-and-blue boat is the best one bobbin'. People come for the fisherman's platter, *literally* the catch of the day (which could be *loup de mer* [branzino], flying fish, marlin, even sea bass or tuna) with a flavorful red sauce, ripe tomatoes, perfect red beans and rice, and lentil salad. Grilled crayfish can usually be had Thursday through Saturday. In fact, the best offerings are on the weekend; these might include the fricassee of octopus or conch, which are among the more expensive dishes. Bottles of Neisson rum are plunked in front of a table of the convivial groups of diners here. Service, mostly pleasant, slows when 30 people sit down. Also, it is often plastic cutlery. Friday nights are the big nights as local bands usually play; they get everyone up and dancing in the sand. *Average main: €17* *Le Bord de Mer, Carbet* *0596/76–98–39, 0696/23–95–59* *No dinner Sun.*

CLOSE UP

Dining in Martinique

Dining in Martinique is a delightful culinary experience, but as with driving here, it is best to get some directions before you head out. First of all, as in France, *entrées* are appetizers; the main courses will usually be labeled as follows: *poissons* (fish); *viandes* (meat); or *principal plats* (main dishes). The appetizers are almost as expensive as the mains—and if the appetizer is foie gras, you'll pay just as much as for a main course, but it is oh so worth it.

Entrecôte is a sirloin steak, usually cut too thin. A filet mignon is a rarity, but you will see *filet mignon du porc*, which is pork tenderloin. *Ecrivesses* (known also as *ouassous* or *z'habitants*) are incredible freshwater crayfish, usually served with their heads on. Similarly, if a fish dish does not specify fillet, it will be served whole—bones, stones, and eyeballs.

Every respectable restaurant has an admirable wine *carte*, and the offerings will be almost completely French, with few half bottles. Wines by the glass are often swill and best avoided.

Finally, don't ever embarrass yourself by asking for a doggie bag, unless you're willing to risk being considered gauche.

15

$$$ FRENCH **La Cave à Vins.** You must ring the bell, someone will peek out (like a speakeasy), and the front door of this landmark restaurant will open on a small shop selling French food items, chocolates, and fine wine. What follows are two dining rooms, the first modern and whimsical, the second with murals of the French countryside and an impressive, domed skylight that compensates somewhat for the lack of windows. Meals begin with an amuse-bouche, such as coriander sorbet. One signature dish is duck breast Rossini (with foie gras) finished with a sauce of morels. Contemporary desserts complement such richness; mango pie topped with vanilla ice cream is Martinique's answer to our apple pie. The menu is the same for lunch and dinner, with not much in the way of light fare. It is likely the proprietress, Madame Clementine, will serve you well; it all makes for a most gracious experience. *Average main: €30 124 rue Victor-Hugo, Fort-de-France 0596/70–33–02 No dinner Sun. and Mon. Closed Aug.*

$$$ FRENCH **Restaurant La Table de Mamy Nounou.** Although the name may sound like a local eatery, it's actually quite a civilized setting with cuisine *raffinée*. Sip an aperitif while listening to the mesmerizing music and admiring the view from the lounge decorated with African art. (Free Wi-Fi, too.) Chef Jean-Paul Mahler has been the recipient of a number of culinary awards and is a member of Euro-Toques. His à la carte menu becomes increasingly inventive, like foie gras served with house-made mango chutney and prunes in an orange sauce. An amuse-bouche arrives before the outstanding appetizers. New additions include roast monkfish with smoked duck breast, creamy Ceps sauce, mashed potatoes,and foie gras. Finish with a mirabelle and vanilla parfait with caramelized hazel nuts. Lunch is served outdoors on the terrace and has a simpler, less pricey menu, and includes some salads, even one with smoked chicken. [$] *Average main: €22* ✉ *L'Anse L'Etang, Tartane, La Trinité* ☎ *0596/58–07–32* 🌐 *hotel-la-caravelle-martinique.com* ✍ *Reservations essential* ⌚ *Closed Tues. and June and Sept.*

$$ BISTRO ✕ **Le Foyaal Bar & Brasserie.** At this versatile place on the main drag, you can choose your experience. Downstairs is a brasserie or a gastropub, while upstairs, at Le Cesaire, things are more refined, elegant, and expensive. The first floor has a large open dining space and seating on a covered terrace with a view of the sea. However, the traffic, noise, and dust make it a bad choice. For a light lunch there are many possibilities, including a crepe with shrimp in coconut sauce and a small salad, smoked marlin, fried Camembert with jam and nuts, and a perfect burger. If you want to go with something more substantial, and creative, there's local octopus with green papaya and passion-fruit sauce or duck in a citrusy sauce. Some waiters speak English, and most are fun and helpful. **■ TIP→ Foyaal serves from 7 am into the late night, 1:30 am, even on Sundays when most of the town is closed up.** Try sitting at the bar; it's fun and for a lot of French expats, this is their "Cheers." [$] *Average main: €20* ✉ *Bord de Mer, 38 rue de Ernest Proges, Fort-de-France* ☎ *0596/63–00–38.*

$$ SEAFOOD ✕ **Le Petibonum.** Billed as an artisan restaurant, Le Petibonum is a marriage of French island funkiness and Miami's South Beach. It's a one-of-a-kind in Martinique. So is charismatic owner Guy Ferdinand, a tall Martinican with curly, blond-streaked hair who has made this a destination restaurant in the north coast's tiny town of Carbet. Smack on the beach, it's an ideal stopover if you're visiting nearby St-Pierre. Remember to wear your swimsuit. Kick off your shoes and order a perfect mojito. You can lounge on coral rubber chaises, shaded by umbrellas, and be sprayed intermittently with a gentle, cool mist. The appetizers—blue marlin tartare or fried flying fish right from the Carbet shore—are appropriate for a feet-in-the-sand restaurant. For mains, the signature dish is jumbo crayfish in a vanilla cream sauce flambéed with rhum vieux and it is decadently rich. There's lobster on Friday nights, when local bands play. It's a scene.

The first Saturday night of the month is the big party; a music event that could be live salsa in the sand, or Cuban music, Puerto Rican, merengue, cha-cha, or reggaeton. And there is no entrance fee. [$] *Average main: €18* ✉ *Le Coin, Le Bord de Mer, Carbet* ☎ *0596/78–04–34* 🌐 *www.babaorum.net.*

WHERE TO STAY

Larger hotels usually include a big buffet breakfast of eggs, fresh fruit, cheese, yogurt, croissants, baguettes, jam, and café au lait. Smaller relais (inns) often have open-air, terrace kitchenettes. There are only a few hotels that still have rooms in which smoking is allowed. Most hotels do not have elevators and many are built on hillsides, so if you have issues with stairs or with climbing paths, be sure to ask about that.

PRIVATE VILLAS AND CONDOS

If you're staying a week or longer, you can often save money by renting a villa or apartment with a kitchen for preparing your own meals. The more upscale rentals come with French-speaking maids and cooks. Don't forget to add the cost of a car rental to your vacation budget.

RENTAL CONTACTS

French Caribbean International. French Caribbean International, a highly professional English-speaking reservation service operated for decades by Gerard Hill, can help you with both villa rentals and hotel rooms in Martinique; it covers all of the French West Indies. ✉ *Santa Barbara, California, United States* ☎ *800/322–2223, 805/967–9850 U.S. office* 🌐 *www.frenchcaribbean.com.*

prestigevillas.com. An online agency that provides luxury villa rental services to the French Caribbean, their site is contemporary and comprehensive with an excellent English version, photos of every room, and detailed descriptions. Rental properties range from deluxe to over-the-top. Prestige has villas that are handpicked for celebratory occasions, everything from honeymoon hideaways to contemporary mansions for family reunions. They have handled corporate retreats and anniversaries. Two new (2014) luxury villas are Alice Bay in Le François (five bedrooms) with a salon and patio overlooking its pool and the ocean, and Le Domaine des Fonds Blancs in Pointe Cerisier. The complex can accommodate 18 persons with a huge swimming pool and unobstructed views of the Atlantic.

Their concierge service can provision villas or arrange for private chefs and housekeepers, and orchestrate tours, shopping excursions, and in-house spa services. Villas can have everything from Wi-Fi to pool guys. The agency's young bilingual owner, who grew up on Guadeloupe, writes an impressive blog giving tips on "doing" the French islands. He honed his rental skills in St. Bart's, where he became a villa specialist. ✉ *Santa Barbara, California, United States* ☎ *917/720-3120, 336/851–853–01* 🌐 *www.prestigevillarental.com.*

15

SOUTH OF FORT-DE-FRANCE

$$$$ RESORT Fodor's Choice ★ **Cap Est Lagoon Resort & Spa.** At Martinique's most exclusive resort, the caring staff strives to make sure that guests leave satisfied. **Pros:** large central infinity pool; really special lounge/bar, with a Martinican feel and an array of rums. **Cons:** somewhat isolated and both taxis and rent-a-cars are expensive; beach is not that big; some suite renovations are needed and only cosmetic ones being done; pricey and some clients question the value factor. ■ **TIP→ Suites 26 through 30 have incredible views of water and mountains.** 💲 *Rooms from: €795* ✉ *Quartier Cap Est, Le François* ☎ *0596/54–80–80, 800/735–2478* 🌐 *www.capest.com* *50 suites spread throughout 18 villas* 🍴 *Breakfast.*

$$$ ALL-INCLUSIVE Fodor's Choice ★ **Club Med Buccaneer's Creek.** This is one of the French chain's most upscale, sophisticated resorts, and the huge, seaside pool has sensual Indonesian beds. **Pros:** on one of the island's best beaches; Club Med energy is contagious; even waterskiing is included; enjoyable, professional entertainment in lounge before dinner; always a safe haven.

Cons: no small catamarans or windsurfing; no in-room Wi-Fi; in-room elements are dated, like the bedding; some first-timers just don't like the Club Med style. **■TIP→ As one guest puts it "not all rooms are created equal." Choose carefully; standard rooms should not be your first choice. Ocean-view with a balcony or beachfront should be. Tower rooms are popular for their view and individuality but are petite.** *Rooms from: US$400 ✉ Pointe Marin, Ste-Anne ☎ 0596/76–72–72 ⊕ www.clubmed.us ⇨ 250 rooms, 44 suites 🍴 All-inclusive.*

$ RENTAL **Domaine de la Palmeraie.** Unique in Martinique, this new complex of six villas is contemporary yet Caribbean, secluded amid acres of Zen-like gardens yet a short drive to Diamant's beach and town, which is not touristic, but rather a real slice of island life. **Pros:** private enclave; owner speaks English; whimsical children's rooms; desks and strong Wi-Fi. **Cons:** some might prefer to be closer to Trois Ilets or other touristic zones; a rental car is almost a necessity; no a/c in second-floor bedrooms except in the spacious Villa Papaye. *Rooms from: €165 ✉ Quartier Thoraille, Diamant ☎ 0696/98–97–17 ⊕ www.domainedelapalmeraie.com ⇨ 6 villas 🍴 No meals.*

$ RESORT **Hotel Bakoua.** Wrought-iron gates open to what's one of Martinique's best resorts, what French guests call a "human hotel," where you can cocoon. **Pros:** the Bakoua exudes vintage Caribbean charisma; it's a classy classic; you don't necessarily need a car; the breakfast buffet with omelet and crepe stations is memorable. **Cons:** constructed in stages, so some rooms show age; facades are not all pretty; the hotel awaits its long-promised renovation, 2016 hopefully. *Rooms from: €220 ✉ Pointe du Bout, Les Trois-Ilets ☎ 0596/66–02–02 ⊕ www.hotel-bakoua.fr/en ⇨ 132 rooms, 6 suites 🍴 Breakfast.*

$ HOTEL **Hôtel Le Pagerie.** For many years the keystone hotel for Pointe du Bout, it had deteriorated to the point where loyal guests went elsewhere, only to return when they heard of its massive—really a metamorphosis. **Pros:** spacious, renovated guest rooms with everything nearly new, like the bed and bedding; the helpful management and staff that warmly welcomes you; free Wi-Fi, it is well-priced and conveniently located. **Cons:** some question its four-star rating; among guest complaints are no sea vistas (but pool views); in-room furnishings are not high-end; the marauding birds at breakfast. *Rooms from: €195 ✉ Rue Chacha, Pointe de Bout, Trois-Ilets ☎ 0596/66–05–30 ⊕ hotel-lapagerie.com ⇨ 96 rooms 🍴 No meals.*

$ B&B/INN Fodor's Choice ★ **Hotel Plein Soleil.** Long one of our favorites, this heavenly hideaway is now a modern Martinique landmark. **Pros:** stimulating client mix; owner Jean Christophe is on-site and accessible; sophisticated and artistic ambience is unique in Martinique; deluxe breakfast. **Cons:** rough road (particularly in rainy season) to somewhat remote, hilltop location; smallest rooms have small bathrooms; Wi-Fi is free but seldom works within accommodations. *Rooms from: €200 ✉ Pointe Thalèmont, Le François ☎ 0596/38–07–77 ⊕ www.hotelpleinsoleil.fr ⇨ 12 rooms, 4 suites ⊗ Closed Sept.–mid-Oct. 🍴 No meals.*

$$ HOTEL Fodor's Choice ★ **La Suite Villa.** This hilltop *hôtel de charme* (boutique hotel) gives Les Trois-Ilets some art-infused glamour. **Pros:** inimitable, whimsical style with a profusion of Caribbean colors; entertaining and artistic owners; the upbeat social scene. **Cons:** great house has three floors and no

FRENCH PLUMBING

If you aren't familiar with handheld showers and intricate levers, you can easily flood the bathroom and scald yourself. The French are not big on shower curtains either. So when the bellman gives you the walk-through, ask him to explain the plumbing. For example, toilets have two depressors; one is for a quick flush, the other a strong and serious flush, and you'd better step aside. You can try for too long to figure out how to get the stopper in a bathtub to hold the water. Step into the tub and stomp down on that silver stopper. That should do it. It's as difficult to drain it. Leave it for the maid and tip heavily? Bidets are common. In self-catering villas, if there is a washing machine or a dishwasher, make sure you have a lesson before touching those dials or you'll be sorry. In some *toilettes* (public restrooms) there are new sanitary sinks where you depress a lever on the left, or a foot pedal. If you are looking to get some water and don't see any handles near the faucet, look down.

elevator; no beach (nearest one is 2,000 feet away); great views are seen best from the smaller rooms in the great house than from the more expensive and spacious villas; pool is petite with few chaises. *Rooms from: €275 Rte. du Fort d'Alet, Anse Mitan, Les Trois-Ilets 0596/59–88–00 www.la-suite-villa.com 6 suites, 9 villas (6 2-bedrooms, 3 3-bedrooms) Breakfast.*

$ RENTAL **Résidence Le Village Créole.** A residence brushed with tropical colors and enhanced with Victorian accents, it surrounds a courtyard that is the central hub for some 20 shops and 10 restaurants/bars. **Pros:** a lot of square footage for the euro; budget prices yet caring, English-speaking management; plump pillows from the United States replace flat ones and new double-paned glass. **Cons:** not a lot of furniture; inexpensive couches with brown faux suede and bedding not stylish. *Rooms from: €126 Village Créole, Pointe du Bout, Trois-Ilets 0596/66–03–19 www.villagecreole.com 23 apartments No meals.*

FORT-DE-FRANCE AND POINTS NORTH

$ B&B/INN **Engoulevent.** This small B&B in a suburban house (about 10 minutes from Fort-de-France) has deluxe suites with contemporary decor, as well as Wi-Fi and other attractive amenities and high-end touches. **Pros:** rooms are attractive, particularly Nos. 2 and 5; unique on the island. **Cons:** not all the benefits of a hotel; best with a car; no restaurant here, but many are nearby; charming manager does not speak English—owners do. *Rooms from: €135 22 rte. de l'Union Didier, Fort-de-France 0596/64–96–00 5 suites Closed Aug. Breakfast.*

$ RENTAL **Fort Savane.** Not to be confused with the military installation (Fort Louis) up on the hill, this new entity bills itself as a residence for business (clients) and tourism since it does not have the usual amenities of a hotel, like a restaurant, bar, etc. **Pros:** personalized concierge service can even obtain a bottle of champagne after midnight; cordial, English-speaking receptionists; excellent location across from the Savane. **Cons:** "simple" rooms are small; some interior accommodations have no windows and might be claustrophobic; beds and bedding new but not luxe; reception desk is not manned after 8 pm or on weekends and guests must enter with a code. *Rooms from: €110 ✉ 5 rue de la Liberté, Le François ☎ 0596/80–75–75 🌐 www.fortsavane.fr ⇨ 4 rooms, 9 studios, 2 suites 🍽 No meals.*

$ HOTEL **Hotel La Caravelle.** The energetic Mahler family transformed this simple hotel with a renovation and their artwork from Africa, where patriarch Jean-Paul worked for several decades as a manager of five-star hotels. **Pros:** caring service; interesting international family; very good food; free Wi-Fi in lounge. **Cons:** no pool; still a simple French hotel; you'll need a car. *Rooms from: €84 ✉ Anse L'Etang, Tartane, La Trinité ☎ 0596/58–07–32 🌐 www.hotel-la-caravelle-martinique.com ⇨ 14 studios, 1 apartment 🍽 No meals.*

$ HOTEL **Hôtel L'Impératrice.** Right across from La Savane stands this hotel; like the park, it's another landmark that's been revived in recent years. **Pros:** personalized service; shades of a small Parisian hotel with diminutive elevator and narrow hallways; some English is spoken. **Cons:** the small standard rooms in back are not desirable albeit quiet; narrow hallways; some maintenance worries, mainly window a/c units breaking down. *Rooms from: €117 ✉ 15 rue de la Libert, Fort-de-France ☎ 0596/63–06–82 🌐 www.limperatricehotel.fr ⇨ 22 rooms 🍽 Breakfast.*

$ HOTEL **Hotel Villa Saint Pierre.** A simple, modern decor typifies this modest bay-front property that is somewhere between a hôtel de charme (boutique hotel) and a French business hotel. **Pros:** caring managers Maryse and Andre; downtown location. **Cons:** little English spoken; not luxurious; price is somewhat high for the relatively small accommodations. *Rooms from: €135 ✉ 108 rue Bouillé, St-Pierre ☎ 0596/78–68–45 🌐 www.hotel-villastpierre.fr ⇨ 9 rooms ⊙ Closed Sept. 🍽 Breakfast.*

$ HOTEL **Le Domaine Saint Aubin.** This former estate perched on a verdant hilltop has breathtaking views overlooking the Atlantic.
Pros: daydream yourself into a more gracious era; hip owners make scintillating company; wheelchair-accessible rooms (and the pool has a chair-lift). **Cons:** somewhat remote location requires a car; original rooms have character but are not stylin'; breakfast is an additional €14; no lunch, bar or snacks, so BYO. *Rooms from: €124 ✉ Petite Rivière Salée, off Rte. 1, La Trinité ☎ 0596/69–34–77, 0696/41–88–23 🌐 www.ledomainesaintaubin.com ⇨ 30 rooms, 6 2-bedroom apartments 🍽 No meals.*

$ HOTEL **L'Hôtel la Batelière.** Mixed emotions are how most hotel guests describe their experiences, in what is considered the best of the full-service hotels in the Fort de France arena. **Pros:** lovely pool deck that looks down to the sea and small, man-made beach; good and ample breakfast buffet with sea views (wire-net covers have almost solved the bird invasion); safe suburban location with free parking and a public bus close by that goes downtown (€1.20). **Cons:** the hotel cries for a total reno' or for an American chain to take it over; not all of the front desk or other staffers speak fluent English; this somewhat generic property with a large convention center, caters predominantly to the business trade. *Rooms from: €109 ✉ 20 rue des Alizés, Schoelcher ☎ 0596/61–49–49 🌐 www.hotel-bateliere-martinique.com ⇨ 190 rooms, 3 suites 🍽 Breakfast.*

NIGHTLIFE AND PERFORMING ARTS

To enter a casino, French law requires everyone to show a passport; the legal gambling age is now 21.

There are lively discos and nightclubs in Martinique, but a good deal of the fun is to be had by befriending Martinicans and French residents and other expats and hoping they will invite you clubbing or to their private parties. For art openings and other cultural events, check with the Fondation Clément (🌐 *www.fondation-clement.org*), which runs the Habitation Clément, to see what's coming up. In addition to its art exhibits, the foundation throws some of the best parties on the island, which are a chance to toast and clink rum glasses with some of Martinique's leading citizens and culture mavens.

CASINOS

Casino Trois-Ilets. The interior of this casino was designed in a French Quarter style. It houses 70 slot machines, blackjack, U.S. roulette, stud poker, and craps (Friday and Saturday). The casino is open daily 10 am to 3 am, but the gaming tables don't start cranking until 9 pm. On weekends in high season a DJ spins Caribbean, creole, and international beats, and there's a dance floor. Happenings that occur range from chocolate tastings to fashion shows and live local entertainment. The casino restaurant serves up a marriage of refined creole and international fare, with fresh local product. The menu is much improved and one can eat well for about €20. The caveat is that the tables are right in the middle of the floor, which is not conducive to fine dining. ■ **TIP→ The gaming age is now 21. Everyone must remember to bring their passport, and be prepared for a possible entrance fee of about US$7, if there is an event.** ✉ *Rte. de Pointe du Bout, near rte. de Trois-Ilets, Trois-Ilets* ☎ *596/66–00–30.*

DANCE CLUBS

Your hotel or the tourist office can put you in touch with the current popular places. It's also wise to check on opening and closing times and cover charges. Several free tourist publications that can be found at hotels tell of the latest happenings at the clubs. For the most part, the discos draw a mixed crowd of Martinicans and tourists, and although a younger crowd is the norm, people of all ages go dancing here

Infinity. Infinity is the latest tenant on the first and second-story of the building previously occupied by a Mexican restaurant. On the ground floor is a gourmet food boutique, and on the second a sophisticated bar with tables, some on a small terrace. Called a concept bar and an art gallery, there is to be live entertainment during peak season and weekends. The concept is that one chooses from the menu of chichi cocktails (not inexpensive) and then orders some foodstuffs from the shop below. ✉ *Village Creole, Pointe du Bout, Trois-Ilets* ☎ *0596/38–71–68.*

Jet Set. One of the newest clubs in Fort-de-France, this hot ticket has salsa going on and live bands that play mainly Caribbean music. It has an inviting ambience and decor and is known for having a courteous crowd. Tourists can feel welcome and will not be hassled. Drinks are less expensive than at many of the clubs. The best is its convenient, easy-to-find location right across from the Savane. Guests at l'Imperatrice or the new Fort Savane can walk to it for it is on the same street. If you are having trouble finding it, look up . . . it is not on the ground floor. ✉ *Rue de la Liberté at rue Perrinon, Fort-de-France* 🌐 *www.aux-antilles.fr/martinique/sortir/info-jet-set-1019.htm.*

GOOD TO KNOW

You may see billboards that say "Casino" or even "Geante Casino," with directionals. Do not follow them if you are looking for a gambling casino. *Casino* is the name of a supermarket chain. *Geante* means a mega-supermarket.

L' Bar 'Oc. This sophisticated lounge is the ground floor of a lovely, white home that has some history. The tile floors put it in another era, and thus the name of its former restaurant, Le Belle Epoque, which for decades was a gastronomic favorite on island. The same owner, Martine, a charming, charismatic French woman came back out of retirement to open instead what is primarily a cocktail lounge with world music and some food served. The house is her home (upstairs) and the neighborhood, Didier, is an upscale suburb of Fort de France, but close, not far from the Hotel Bateliere. It attracts the after-work crowd who live in the neighborhood, those staying at The Bat' and the small B&B Engoulevent close by, and those savvy, older tourists who hear tell of it. ✉ *97 rte. de Didier, Didier, Fort-de-France* ☎ *0596/48–52–52* ⏲ *Mon.–Sat. 5 pm–midnight.*

Le Milk / Le Club. A well-thought-out concept, it is one address with two spaces. Le Milk, with its trendy decor, appeals to a younger clientele, from 18 to 45 years old, but predominantly twentysomethings. They are into the electro and dance music, and a little soul in the form of R'n'B.

Le Club welcomes patrons from 25 to 60s, with retro music and an atmosphere that promotes nostalgia. And no one objects if you wander back 'n' forth between the two, from old-school to techno. Interestingly, a soda costs as much as hard liquor—€8. ✉ *20 blvd. Alegre, Fort-de-France* ☎ *0696/27–93–19.*

Le Negresco. This is a prime example of a French Antilles urban disco. You will hear zouk, salsa, and kompas. It's hot, it rocks, there are lots of glam outfits, and on busy nights when people are feeling their dances and waving their arms in the air, well, you just have to be there. The weekend is when it really cranks up. On most nights you can expect a cover charge, especially when there's live entertainment. This club, which plays a fair share of Caribbean music, appeals to a crowd in their 30s and 40s. Security is tight, and there's a free parking lot just across the street. ✉ *10 rue Commerce, Fort-de-France* ☎ *0596/70–07–03.*

Le Paparazzi Club. You may see Paparazzi advertised as a private club, but anyone looking cool is seldom refused entrée. You may hear that this disco is frequented by kids—the 18–25-year-olds—while others categorize it as for those 30-plus. Marc Martial, an English-speaking taxi

Traditional madras costumes in Martinique

driver with a late-model Mercedes, says that it is one of the clubs that he takes his American clients to when doing a noctural bar crawl. ✉ *8 rue Joseph Compete, Fort-de-France* ☎ *0696/54–05–30, 0696/00–47–81.*

FOLKLORIC PERFORMANCES

Most leading hotels offer nightly entertainment in season, including the marvelous **Grands Ballets de Martinique,** one of the finest folkloric dance troupes in the Caribbean. Consisting of a bevy of musicians and dancers dressed in traditional costume, the ballet revives the Martinique of yesteryear through dance rhythms such as the beguine and the mazurka. They usually appear on Tuesday at the Hotel Carayou & Spa in Les Trois-Ilets in a dinner performance coupled with an authentic creole buffet. Call first to be sure of the time, and to make reservations (or have your hotel make them). You can sometimes catch a performance elsewhere.

ISLAND CULTURE

Aimé Césaire Theatre. This ornate, historical building—built around 1901—is the main theater downtown. Now named after Martinique's literary great, Aimé Césaire, it has an Italian proscenium stage with excellent acoustics. This impressive building (circa 1912), with classic design and Italian architectural theater inspirations, was the old city hall (interesting translation: Hotel de Ville).

Césaire's former office has been arranged as an exhibition space, open for visits. The schedule of events includes national and international music and/or dance companies, and more. ✉ *Rue Victor Sévère, Fort-de-France* ☎ *0596/59–43–29* 🌐 *www.fortdefrance.fr.*

MUSIC CLUBS AND LOUNGES

Hotel Cap Macabou, in Vauclin, has "dancing dinners" and theme nights, most often on Friday and Saturday. On Sunday, there's usually a midday buffet with dancing to a band—you can even bring your bathing suit. Check the site for holiday parties.

Calebasse Café. A diverse, mostly older, crowd gravitates to Calebasse Café. Jazz is the norm, but there may be soul or R&B, and there's often a talented local singer. Concerts may be combined with art exhibitions, like "percussion and painting." Funky and hip, the interior is a bit rough but convivial, albeit artsy. If you don't make a reservation on Saturday night, you won't have a seat. The food here isn't wonderful, but if you have the conch tart and the grilled lobster, you'll leave satisfied and avoid the cover charge. Friday and Saturday nights are banging, but call before you go on other nights. Doors open at 6 pm, but the music doesn't start till later in the evening. **■TIP→ If an event is destined to be a big draw, a white tent is erected outside.** ✉ *19 bd. Allègre, Le Marin* ☎ *596/74–91–93* ⊗ *Closed Mon. Low season: closed Tues., Thurs., and Sun.*

Club Med Buccaneer's Creek. At Club Med Buccaneer's Creek, you can buy a night pass that, at €93, extends from 7 pm until the bar closes at midnight or 1 am. It includes an extensive buffet dinner with wine, a show in the theater, and drinks and dancing afterwards. Friday is the best night to come. Called the gala, it boasts elaborate food and the most impressive show. Single women feel comfortable here. ✉ *Pointe du Marin, Ste-Anne* ☎ *0596/76–83–36.*

Hotel Bakoua. The entertainment here ranges from concerts of just a pianist and vocalist or a jazz combo on up to bathing-suit fashion shows or *spectacles* (splashy variety shows, often with special effects). The quality of the entertainment is known island-wide. You can go to Le Gommier and order a tropical cocktail there. There's a litany of island rums, from white to amber and rhum vieux. Call the hotel first to learn what's on the schedule, since events taper off during the low season. ✉ *Pointe du Bout, Les Trois-Ilets* ☎ *0596/66–02–02.*

Hotel Cap Macabou. Hotel Cap Macabou in Vauclin has "dancing dinners" and theme nights, most often on Friday and Saturday. On Sunday, there's usually a midday buffet with dancing to a band—you can even bring your bathing suit. There are often salsa soirées with Latin music, as well as holiday parties in season, which are quite celebratory. ✉ *Petit Macabou, Le Vauclin* ☎ *0596/74–24–24* 🌐 *www.capmacabou.com.*

La Marine. La Marine is a busy bar and restaurant with live entertainment, mainly a local band on Saturday nights. Open daily, expats and boaters hang here for the reasonably priced, good pizza and old-world Italian and French classics. There's nothing contemporary about this place—on quiet nights you can hear the wind in the riggings and check out the boat action on the docks. ✉ *Marina Pointe du Bout, Les Trois-Ilets* ☎ *0596/66–02–32.*

La Villa Créole. This restaurant's Martinican owner, Guy Bruere-Dawson, has been singing and strumming the guitar since the 1980s—in five languages, everything from François Cabrel to Elton John, some Italian and creole ballads, even original ditties. Other singers perform, too, on Friday and Saturday nights, when there might also be a limbo show, a Brazilian group, Caribbean musicians, and perhaps an art expo. To see the show, you must order dinner; grilled lobster from the tank is often the best option. That said, the present chef has a fine repertoire of contempory French-creole cuisine. ✉ *Anse Mitan* ☎ *0596/66–05–53* 🌐 *la-villa-creole.restaurantmartinique.info* ⏲ *Closed Sun. and Mon.*

Le Kano Bar–Lounge Restaurant. At this trendy, beachfront bar, lounge/restaurant, creole-influenced tapas and brochettes as well as creative Caribbean cocktails with lyrical creole names, are happily consumed while listening to weekend music events—a full menu is available, too. Spacious with several open rooms leading to the beach, the contemporary Euro furniture is inviting. In season, a DJ cranks until 2:30 on Saturday night and on Sundays the music is live. Kano is handy to the Casino des Trois-Ilets across the street and the ample parking there makes it easy to visit both. ✉ *On the beach at Anse Mitan, 31 rue des Bougainvilliers, facing the casino, Les Trois-Ilets* ☎ *0596/78–40–33.*

Lili's Beach Bar. At this thatched-roof beach bar, DJs spin local and international sounds, making this a good alternative to clubbing downtown, and there are special theme nights and happenings. Lili's attracts a mainly young crowd, and now, predominantly, a local one as well as guests from L'Hotel La Bateliere. Food is less expensive than the hotel's restaurant and is a cut above the usual beach fare. With free parking and tight security because of the casino, it is a safe haven for tourists and one sexy party place. ✉ *The Beach at l'Hôtel La Batelière, Schoelcher* ☎ *0596/42–89–02.*

SHOPPING

French fragrances; designer clothes, scarves, and sunglasses; fine china and crystal; leather goods; wine (inexpensive at supermarkets); and liquor are all good buys in duty-free Fort-de-France. Purchases are further sweetened by the 20% discount on luxury items when paid for with certain credit cards. Among the items produced on the island, look for *bijoux creole* (local jewelry, such as hoop earrings and heavy bead necklaces); white, dark, and aged rum; and handcrafted straw goods, pottery, and tapestries.

AREAS AND MALLS

The striking 215,000-square-foot Cour Perrinon Mall in Fort-de-France, bordered by rue Perrinon, houses a Carrefour supermarket, a bookstore, perfume shops, designer boutiques, a French bakery, and a café–brasserie. The area around the cathedral in Fort-de-France has a number of small shops that carry luxury goods. Of particular note are the shops on rue Victor Hugo, rue Moreau de Jones, rue Antoine Siger, and rue Lamartine. The **Galleries Lafayette** department store on rue Schoelcher in downtown Fort-de-France sells everything from perfume to pâté. On the outskirts of Fort-de-France, the **Centre Commercial de Cluny, Centre Commercial de Dillon, Centre Commercial de Bellevue,** and **Centre Commercial la Rond Point** are among the major shopping malls.

You can find more than 100 thriving businesses—from shops and department stores to restaurants, pizzerias, fast-food outlets, a superb supermarket, and the simple Galleria Hotel (the closest hotel to the airport)—at **La Galleria** in Lamentin. In Pointe du Bout there are a number of appealing tourist shops and boutiques, both in and around **Village Créole**, which alone has more than 20, plus some 10 restaurants–bars, an ice-cream shop, free Wi-Fi, and the Residence Village Creole, with small and family-size furnished apartments, available by the night, the week, or longer, for moderate prices. Village Creole often has live entertainment at night in the courtyard.

CLOTHING

Coté Plage Sarl. Stop in here for French sailor jerseys in creative colors, youthful straw purses in bold hues, fun teenage jewelry, and ladies' bathing suits. ✉ *Village Créole, Pointe du Bout, Les Trois-Ilets* ☎ *0596/66–13–00.*

fashion bay. The newly painted walls of this marina boutique are as fresh as the fashions on the racks. They carry name brands from France and Italy and "hot" teeny, weeny bikinis and big-girl shoes from Rio, like: Bogdanoff; Valerie; Best Montain (Parisian); Pako Litto and Replay (Italian); Anti Flirt and Brigitte Bardot (France); Au Soleil de St-Tropez; Galibelle Shoes, and Brazilian designer high heels; and exclusive in Martinique, bikinis and bracelets from *www.hipanema.com*. French, English, and Italian are spoken and the sales staff is fun. ✉ *Marina Pointe du Bout, Pointe du Bout, Les Trois-Ilets* ☎ *0596/66–13–81.*

La Chamade. So you wanna look French? *Femmes,* this urban boutique is a good start, although the chic doesn't come cheap here. You will recognize some well-known brands like Saint-Hillaire, Escada, and Blue Label, and the sexy French shoes are nearly irresistible. The shop does have some good *soldes* (sales), though—and make sure you check the second level. ✉ *25 rue Schoelcher, Fort-de-France* ☎ *0596/73–28–78.*

La Petite Boutique. La Petite Boutique offers a unique children's collection, including jewelry, madras dollies, and teeny underwear. There are also contemporary mini-styles from Hip Up and Funky Family. ✉ *Village Créole, Pointe du Bout, Les Trois-Ilets* ☎ *0596/38–00–65.*

Lynx Optique. Lynx Optique has the latest designer sunglasses from Chanel, Gucci, Dior, Cartier, and Versace. (French designer brands are less expensive here.) And if you need a pair of prescription lenses, or a repair, they can take care of that, too. Staff is professional, polite, and English is spoken. ✉ *20 rue Lamartine, Fort-de-France* ☎ *0596/71–38–48.*

Mounia. Owned by a former Yves St. Laurent model, Mounia carries the top French designers for women and men, including Yves St. Laurent as well as her very own Mounia collection. It will have you opening your wallet wide. Hope for a *solde* (sale). ✉ *26 rue Perrinon, near old House of Justice, Fort-de-France* ☎ *0596/73–77–27* ⊙ *Closed Sun.*

HANDICRAFTS

Antan Lontan. The work of Antan Lontan has to be seen. Sculptures, busts, statuettes, and artistic lamps portray Creole women and the story of the Martiniquaise culture. ✉ *Centre Commercial, La Veranda, Rue du Professeur Raymond Garcin, Fort-de-France* ☎ *0596/65–52–72.*

Art et Nature. Art et Nature carries unique wood paintings, daubed with 20 to 30 shades of earth and sand. They depict simple Martinican scenes. This dedicated French artist has moved his location from Distillerie Trois Rivieres to Le Potterie. ■ **TIP→ The small-size artwork makes good take-home gifts. If you want more, his website is set up to take PayPal.** ✉ *Village de la Poterie, Trois-Ilets* ☎ *0596/62–59–19* 🌐 *www.artetnaturemartinique.com.*

Artisanat & Poterie des Trois-Ilets. This complex lets you watch the creation of Arawak- and Carib-style pots, vases, and jars. On the site of an old Jesuit compound, this group of shops is now a major tourist attraction in thc area. There are shops with interesting gifts, jewelry, and clothing, especially pareus (wraparound skirts). Several appealing restaurants (particularly the bakery) also make it a good stopover for lunch, ✉ *Rte. des Trois-Ilets, Les Trois-Ilets* ☎ *0596/68–03–44.*

Bois Nature. This place is all about mood and mystique and eco-sensitivity. Gift items at Bois Nature begin with scented soap, massage oil, aromatherapy sprays, and perfumes. Then there are wind chimes, mosquito netting, shell mobiles, and sun hats made of coconut fiber. The interior decor accessories are unique and worth carrying home on the plane, but they can also ship things home for you. The big stuff includes natural wood-frame mirrors and furniture à la Louis XV. ✉ *Parking Centre, commercial place d'armes, Lamentin* ☎ *0596/65–77–65* 🌐 *www.boisnature.fr.*

Caz' Art. This is one of those artsy souvenir shops that is so chockablock full that you are fascinated, amazed at every turn. Now there are many small items that would fit in luggage, like colorful, metallic sculptures. Some of the most fanciful items are home accessories. ✉ *Village de la Poterie, Trois-Ilets* ✣ *When you first drive in the village you pass the bakery (patissiere) and then this shop is next, also on the right* ☎ *0596/68–53–56.*

Galerie de Sophen. Across from the Village Créole, this gallery combines Sophie and Henry, both in name and content. On sale are the originals and limited prints of a French couple who live aboard their sailboat and paint the beauty of the sea and the island, from exotic birds to banana trucks. ✉ *Pointe du Bout, Les Trois-Ilets* ☎ *0596/66–13–64.*

JEWELRY

Thomas de Rogatis. Authentic creole jewelry, popularized after the abolition of slavery and seen in many museums, is for sale here at the number-one jewelry store in Martinique. ✉ *22 rue Antoine Siger, Fort-de-France* ☎ *0596/71–36–78.*

PERFUME

Créez Votre Parfum. "Create Your Own Perfume" is an attention-getting name in any language, as is this fascinating new shop in Village Creole. Now not only Hollywood celebrities are able to have their own scent customized for them. The trained staff here can formulate your very own eau du parfume from more than 50 available fragrances. The ingredients are natural and from the island. Among the various soaps and body oils is a natural bronzer with oil of roucou and a coconut oil base. One purse-size spray that everyone should carry is an anti-mosquito oil with eucalyptus, citronelle, etc. Many of the spray atomizers (non-aerosol) are less than 3 ounces and can be carried aboard your homebound plane. ✉ *Au Village Creole, Pointe du Bout, Trois-Ilets* ☎ *0696/80–80–04* 🌐 *www.parfums-des-iles-martinique.com.*

SALON

Hair du Temps. If you want to look French, you can put on the right designer resort wear, but the secret is a cool, sexy French haircut. Both ladies and men vie for appointments at Hair du Temps. Note that haircut prices are reasonable but do not include a blow-dry—that's extra, as are hairspray and mousse—€6 extra for whichever you choose. ✉ *Arcade La Pagerie, Point du Bout, Les Trois-Ilets* ☎ *0596/66–02–51.*

SPORTS AND THE OUTDOORS

BOATING AND SAILING

You can rent Hobie Cats, Sunfish, and Sailfish by the hour from most hotel beach shacks. As for larger craft, bareboat charters (that is, ones with no crew) can be had for $1,900 to $7,000 a week, depending on the season and the size of the craft. The Windward Islands are a joy for experienced sailors, but the channels between islands are often windy and have high waves. You must have a sailing license or be able to prove your nautical prowess, though you can always hire a skipper and crew. Before setting out, you can get itinerary suggestions; the safe ports in Martinique are many. If you charter for a week, you can go south to St. Lucia or Grenada or north to Dominica, Guadeloupe, and Les Saintes. One-way sailing to St. Martin or Antigua is a popular choice.

⚠ **Don't even consider striking out on the rough Atlantic side of the island unless you're an experienced sailor. The Caribbean side is much calmer—more like a vast lagoon.**

Punch Croisières. A local, French-owned charter company, Punch Croisières has a fleet of 17 sailboats, 14 of which are catamarans from 40 to 47 feet; they go out bareboat or crewed, and you can take a boat to a neighboring island. They are comfortably equipped to go down to the Grenadines or just over to Guadeloupe. This company has been here since 1995 while other charter operations, from the Moorings to Windward Islands Cruising, have pulled out. The staff is really accommodating and English is spoken. Rentals from one week to 11 months are available. ✉ *Marina, Bd. Allègre, Le Marin* ☎ *0596/74–89–18* 🌐 *www.punch-croisieres.com.*

CANOPY TOURS

Mangofil. This professionally run zip-line park is overseen by Frenchmen who came from a similar park in France. All the platforms, ladders, and stations were installed by members of a special union in France that specializes in such work. Safety is key here, but there's also a lot of fun; there are upgraded food offerings and a picnic area. The cost is €25 per person for adults, €15–€20 for children, depending on height. It's open Wednesday–Sunday 9–5 and every day during French school holidays. For kids, age 18 months and up, there's also a huge safety net for them to frolic and "dance" among the trees, with toys galore to bounce around with. Here Happy Hour on the weekends refers to discounted prices for their mini-golf. And mini-golf is open until 11 pm on Fridays, Saturdays, and Sundays. **■ TIP→ If a Big Mango (adult) comes with a little Parcabout (kid), it is €25 + €5. They also rent quads (4x4s) Wednesdays, Saturdays, and Sundays.** ✉ *Forêt Rateau, Rte. de Trois-Ilets, near Le Potterie, Les Trois-Ilets* ☎ *0596/68–08–08* 🌐 *www.mangofil.eu.*

15

CANYONING

Bureau de la Randonnée et du Canyoning. Since 1995, the professionals at this company have been leading hikes that take in the island's gorge, canyons, and volcanic landscape. The tours also include some canyoning, which involves climbing up, down, in, and around rocky areas, which are usually near falls or along a stream. For this adrenaline rush, you must be fit and able to hike in the forest for hours. If you are not sure about that, book just the half-day trip, not the full day. These tropical adventures can take you to the Presqu'île du Caravelle, through canals, to Mont Pelée, even to the borders of the craters. Price depends on the destination and the duration. For example, a hike to the volcano Mont Pelée takes six hours and is €45—should you want to test fate, that is. ✉ *Jolimont, Morne Vert* ☎ *0596/55–04–79, 0696/24–32–25, 0696/35–91–28* 🌐 *www.bureau-rando-martinique.com.*

DAY SAILS

Kata Mambo. The catamaran *Kata Mambo* offers two full-day excursions now. For €80, you can sail north to historic St-Pierre and snorkel in clear, Atlantic waters. For €85, you can have a sail coupled with a 4x4 adventure through sugarcane and banana plantations in the south

Kayaking is a popular activity on Martinique.

of the island. The full-day trips include rum drinks and a good, multi-course creole lunch. The boat pulls into its slip at the marina at 5 pm. This is a fun day; and although there's no guarantee, chances are you'll meet some dolphins. And someone in the crew will speak English. The fact that it's been in the biz since the early 1990s attests to its professionalism. ✉ *Pointe du Bout Marina, Les Trois-Ilets* ☎ *0696/25–23–16, 0596/66–11–83* 🌐 *www.kata-mambo.com.*

La Belle Kréole. La Belle Kréole runs one of the most popular excursion boats to *les fonds blanc*, also known as Empress Joséphine's baths. (These are natural, shallow pools with white-sand bottoms.) You can experience the unique Martinican custom of "baptism by rum" (tilt your head back while standing in waist-deep water, and one of the crew pours rum into your mouth). The cost of the day trip depends in part on what you choose to have for lunch, which is taken on the remote Isle de Thierry. There's Planter's Punch and dancing to Martinican CDs. Yes, it is touristy—you're basically on a booze cruise that lasts from 9 am to 5 pm, with lots of loud music. The price, which starts at around €50–60, varies depending on what you choose for lunch. A two-hour excursion directly to the baths is also available in a smaller boat with capacity for nine guests. ✉ *Baie du Simon, slip 36, Le François* ☎ *0596/54–95–57, 0696/29–93–13* 🌐 *www.baignoiredejosephine.com.*

Fodor's Choice ★ **Les Ballades du Delphis.** This civilized full-day tour (€80) uses one of three commodious catamarans, with two departure points: François Bay and Anse Spoutourne (Tartane). The sail from François takes in the famous *fonds blancs* and then the Baie du Robert and I'let Chancel to see sea iguanas and ruins. The Tartane route heads to Treasure Bay, one of the most appealing nature preserves on the island. You'll be served Planter's Punch, accras (fritters), and a creole-style lunch with fish or chicken. A new offering is a day cruise with an overnight at the guesthouse on islet Oscar, a magical setting, with meals included. All of these cruises can be idyllic, travel memories, especially when you are sailing from islet to islet, between coral reefs and swimming in shallow pools with white-sand bottoms. The boats are available for private party charters, or a romantic couple sail. These comfortable catamarans have a capacity for 23 guests and are even wheelchair accessible. ✉ *La Marina du François, Baie du Simon, Le François* ☎ *0696/90–90–36* 🌐 *www.catadelphis.com.*

DIVING AND SNORKELING

Martinique's underwater world is decorated with multicolor coral, crustaceans, turtles, and sea horses. Expect to pay €50 to €55 for a single dive; a package of three dives is around €120.

Okeanos Club. This landmark dive operation has a morning trip close to shore; in the afternoon the boats go farther into open water. Lessons (including those for kids eight to 12) with a PADI-certified instructor can be conducted in English. It's always a fun experience. The dive shop looks out to Diamant Rock, which has wonderful underwater caves and is one of the preferred dives on the island. Okeanos Club goes to 12 different sites, many with catchy names like Little Turtle, and the Gardens of St. Luce, an underwater spot chock-full of colorful sponges. Trips are geared to the level of the clients, from rank beginners to certified divers. A single, one-tank dive costs €55, and there are a variety of discounted packages. Guests from all hotels are welcome, and Okeanos provides pickup from some of them. ✉ *Pierre & Vacances, Pavilion-Pointe Philippeau Rte. de Gros Raisin, Ste-Luce* ☎ *0696/71–94–41* 🌐 *www.okeanos-martinique.com.*

Planète Bleue. Planète Bleue has a big up-to-date dive boat, hand-painted with tropical fish and waves, so it's impossible to miss. The English-speaking international crew is proud to have been in business since the early 1990s. The company hits 20 sites, including the Citadel and Salomon's Pool, and you'll also see the quaint town of Anses d'Arlet. A boat goes out mornings and afternoons. Thursday is a full day on the north coast, with breakfast, lunch, and all drinks included. A one-tank dive is €50; a half-day dive includes gear and a 'ti punch. Sunday is a day of rest, except for the first one in the month, when it's off to Diamant Rock. ✉ *Pointe du Bout Marina, Pointe du Bout, Les Trois-Ilets* ☎ *0596/58–61–43.*

GOLF

Golf de l'Impératrice Josephine (*Martinique Golf and Country Club*). Although it's named in honor of Empress Joséphine Napoléon, this Robert Trent Jones Sr. course is completely American in design, with an English-speaking pro, a pro shop, a bar, and an especially good restaurant. The best hole on the course may just be the par-five 15th. Sandwiched between two good par-threes, the 15th plays to an island fairway and then to a green situated by the shore. Try not to be mesmerized by the turquoise waters (You can finish your visit here with foie gras torchon or a full meal at Le Golf Restaurant.) The club offers special greens fees to cruise-ship passengers. Club trolleys (called "chariots") are €6 for 18 holes, €4 for 9. There are no caddies. ✉ *Quartier la Pagerie, Les Trois-Ilets* ☎ *0596/61–05–24* *€15 for 9 holes, €22.50 for 18; €25 for a cart, 9 holes; €40 for cart, 18 holes* *18 holes, 6640 yards, par 71.*

HIKING

Parc Naturel Régional de la Martinique. Two-thirds of Martinique is designated as protected land. Trails, all 31 of them, are well marked and maintained. At the beginning of each, a notice is posted advising on the level of difficulty, the duration of a hike, and any interesting facts. The Parc Naturel Régional de la Martinique organizes inexpensive guided excursions year-round. If there have been heavy rains, though, give it up. The tangle of ferns, bamboo trees, and vines is dramatic, but during rainy season, the wet, muddy trails will temper your enthusiasm. ✉ *9 bd. Général de Gaulle, Fort-de-France* ☎ *0596/64–45–64 communications department.*

HORSEBACK RIDING

Ranch Jack. Ranch Jack has a large stable of some 30 horses. Its trail rides (English-style) cross some beautiful country for €38 for an hour and a half (to two); half-day excursions for €55 (inquire about transfers from nearby hotels) go through the fields and forests to the beach. Short rides can range from €16 to €25. They also have a wonderful program to introduce kids ages 3–7 to horses. Online comments reflect riders' satisfaction with the professionalism of the stable and the beautiful acreage that they traverse. ✉ *Morne habitué, Trois-Ilets* ☎ *0596/68–37–69, 0696/92–26–58* *ranch.jack@wanadoo.fr.*

KAYAKING

Les Kayaks du Robert. You'll receive one of the island's warmest welcomes at Les Kayaks du Robert. After a memorable paddle through shallow lagoons and mangrove swamps chasing colorful fish, you can enjoy a complimentary glass of juice or Planter's Punch, all for €15 per person for a half day; a full day is €23 per person. An English-speaking guide is available with advance reservation. If you're going without a guide, ask how to get to various small islets, especially Iguana Island. A waterproof box for your belongings is complimentary; masks and fins are available and it's a joy to snorkel in the *fonds blancs.* ✉ *Pointe Savane, Le Robert* ☎ *0596/65–33–89.*

16

MONTSERRAT

WELCOME TO MONTSERRAT

Although the Soufrière Hills volcano continues to rumble, the island is otherwise a paragon of Caribbean peacefulness—almost a throwback to another time, with the occasional modern convenience (and convenience store) thrown in. Montserrat draws ecotourists, divers, adventure seekers, and those who simply want to experience the Caribbean as it once was.

Restaurants ▼		Hotels ▼	
Olveston House	2	Erindell Villa	4
Tina's	1	Gingerbread Hill	2
Ziggy's	3	Grand View Bed & Breakfast	5
		Olveston House	3
		Tropical Mansion	1

TOP REASONS TO VISIT MONTSERRAT

1 Geology: Volcano lovers will experience a landscape that's been unsullied for more than a decade.

2 Diving: The diving is one of the Caribbean's unsung secrets: Montserrat's underwater terrain has also remained largely undisturbed.

3 Peace and Quiet: You'll find tranquillity in abundance; if you want to kick back and relax, this is the place for you.

4 Peace of Mind: There's virtually no crime, and you won't find a friendlier place in the Caribbean.

THE EMERALD ISLE OF THE CARIBBEAN

Montserrat is a small island about 25 miles (40 km) southwest of Antigua. Named by Columbus after a Catholic abbey near Barcelona—Santa Maria de Montserrate—the island was settled predominantly by Irish Catholics who had once been indentured servants in the West Indies. The numbers of Irish waned, but their influence remained. The island rumbled into the media in 1995, when the Soufriére Hills volcano suddenly erupted and covered the capital, Plymouth, in ash.

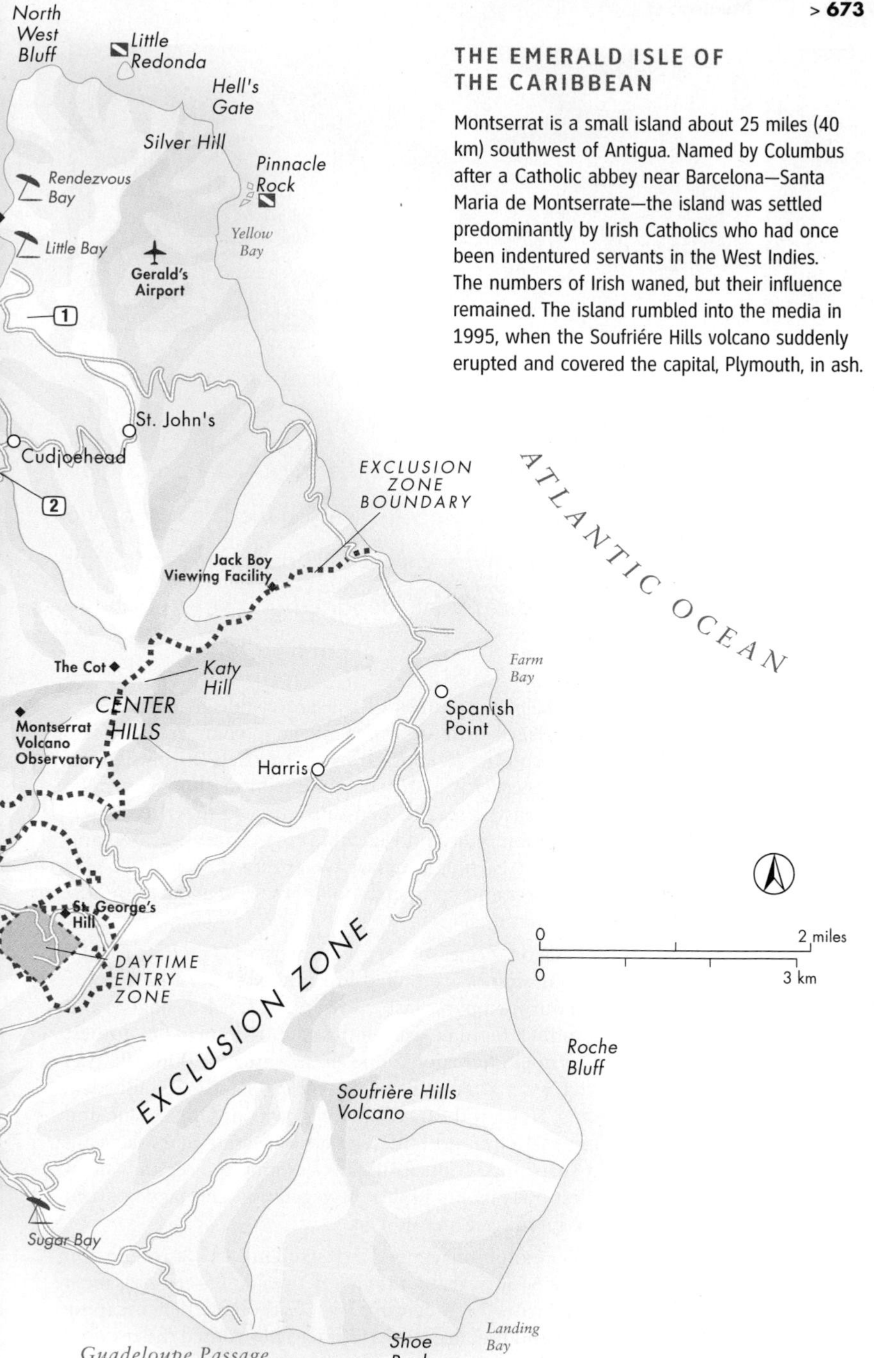

Updated by Jordan Simon

Aficionados have always regarded Montserrat as an idyllic, fairy-tale island. But in 1995, Grimm turned grim when the Soufrière Hills volcano erupted. The frilly Victorian gingerbreads of the capital, Plymouth, were buried, much of the tourism infrastructure was wiped out, and more than half the original 11,000 residents departed and have not been able to return.

When the volcano belches, plumes of ash are visible from as far as Antigua; plucky locals joke that new beachfront is being created. The volcano itself is an ecotourism spot, drawing travelers curious to see nature's incredible capacity for destruction and rejuvenation. Ironically, other fringe benefits exist. Volcanic deposits enriched the already fertile soil; locals claim their fruit and vegetable crops have increased and improved. The slightly warmer waters have attracted even more varied marine life for divers and snorkelers to appreciate, along with new underwater rock formations.

Although an "Exclusion Zone" covers half the island, the rest is safe; in fact, the zone was slightly retracted after the volcano's lava dome partially collapsed during a pyroclastic flow in 2003. Seismologists and volcanologists conduct regular risk analyses and simulation studies; as a result, the Daytime Exclusion Zone shrank after a 2006 collapse, and then expanded again after activity in early 2008 and 2009. Borders retracted slightly in 2010 and 2011, opening parts of Old Towne and Isles Bay to as far as Richmond Hill. Visitors expecting mass devastation are in for a surprise; Montserrat ranks among the region's most pristine, serene destinations, its luxuriant vegetation and jagged green hills justifying the moniker Emerald Isle.

Though Christopher Columbus named the island in 1493 (after the hillside Santa Maria de Montserrate monastery outside Barcelona), most locals are descended from 17th-century Irish Catholic settlers escaping English persecution and indentured servitude. They routed the resident Caribs (who themselves had "evicted" the indigenous Saladoids and

LOGISTICS

Getting to Montserrat: There are no nonstop flights to Montserrat from North America. You can transfer on Antigua for a FlyMontserrat flight or the ABM/SVG Air service. You can also take a ferry from Antigua.

Hassle Factor: Medium–high.

Getting Around the Island: The fixed taxi fare from the airport ranges from $10 (for Tropical Mansion) to $26 (to the Olveston/Salem area villas). Though you can take taxis, you'll best appreciate Montserrat's quiet beauty if you rent a car and do some exploring on your own. Rates start at around $35 a day, but gas is expensive, so be sure to budget for that.

One main road runs from the north, down each side of the island, with little unnamed side roads streaming inland. Most addresses don't have street names or house numbers. Driving is on the left; the well-paved main road zigs, zags, climbs, and plummets precipitously, and many equally winding side roads are pocked with potholes. There are no traffic lights, but there are a few zebra pedestrian crossings; beware wandering pigs and goats.

Arawaks) and eventually imported slaves to work the plantations. The Gaelic influence lingers in the names of families and places, as well as in folklore, jigs, and even a wispy brogue.

The island's captivating beauty, low profile, and difficult access made it a hip destination in the 1970s and '80s. Sir George Martin (The Beatles' producer) fell in love with Montserrat and founded AIR Studios on the island in 1979, luring icons such as Eric Clapton, Sir Paul McCartney, and Stevie Wonder to record. Destroyed by Hurricane Hugo in 1989, it was never rebuilt. But locals and expats alike still like a good band. The combined Carnival and Christmas festivities go on for nearly a month, when the island is awash with color, with calypso competitions, parades, and pageants.

Other than the volcano, the steamiest activities are the fiercely contested domino games outside rum shops. That may soon change. The government speaks optimistically of building a new golf course, developing spa facilities to offer volcanic mud baths, even running tours—pending safety assessments—of Plymouth as a haunting Caribbean answer to Pompeii. An airport was constructed, partly in the hope of recapturing the villa crowd that once frequented the island. But these developments—as well as debates over the new capital and threatened lawsuits against the British government for restricting access and utility service to homesites—will simmer for quite some time. One thing won't change: the people, whether native-born or expat, are among the kindest anywhere. Hit it off with them, and don't be surprised if you're invited to a family dinner or beach picnic.

PLANNING

WHEN TO GO

The year's big event is **St. Patrick's Day,** which ushers in more than a week of festivities, highlighted by musical concerts and masquerades à la Carnival. July's annual weeklong Calabash Festival is becoming quite popular. Late October's **Police, Fire, Search, and Rescue Services Community Week** also explodes with sound and color, as jump-ups, concerts, and barbecues lure hundreds of revelers. Early December welcomes the literary celebration, Alliouagana Festival of the Word. Mid-December into the New Year sees **Christmas festival celebrations,** from calypso competitions to pageants and parades.

GETTING HERE AND AROUND

AIR TRAVEL

There are nonstop flights to Antigua, where you can transfer to a Fly-Montserrat flight (most departures are scheduled to coincide with the international flight schedule) into the John A. Osborne Airport (MNI) in Geralds. ABM Air, a sister carrier of well-known SVG Air, also offers flights from Antigua.

Airline Contacts ABM/SVG Air. A service and subsidiary of SVG Air, ABM flies twice daily between Antigua and Montserrat. ☎ *268/562–8033* 🌐 *www.abm-air.com.* **FlyMontserrat.** FlyMontserrat offers daily flights from Antigua on nine-seat Britten Norman Islanders, and charter service to and from other destinations. ☎ *664/491–3434* 🌐 *www.flymontserrat.com.*

CAR TRAVEL

A temporary driver's license is required if you wish to drive on the island; you can get one for $20 at the police headquarters in Brades, which is open 24 hours on weekdays. You can rent Jeeps and cars for roughly $35–$50 per day. Even if you rent a car, you're best off hiring a local guide, who will know where the best views are—and which parts of the island are off-limits because of volcanic activity. Respect the signs and closed gates that indicate the Exclusion Zone boundaries; though the Daytime Entry Zone is usually open 24/7, you should avoid it at night.

Car-Rental Contacts Montserrat Enterprises ✉ *Old Towne* ☎ *664/491–2431.* **Yvette Lee's Agency** ✉ *Olveston* ☎ *664/491–5270, 664/493–1947.*

FERRY TRAVEL

There's year-round ferry service between Little Bay and Antigua's **Bryson's Pier at Heritage Quay** in St. John's, though the schedule changes periodically and has halted abruptly in the past. The one-hour-long trip takes place Wednesday–Sunday on the 195-passenger *Caribe Sun.* The fare is EC$150 each way. Call Ferry Agent Roosevelt Jemmotte (☎ *664/496–9912*) on Montserrat or Jennifer Burke (☎ *268/788–9786*) on Antigua for more info. Also check the Montserrat Development Corporation Tourism Division's website for updates and schedule.

Ferry Contact Carib World Travel ✉ *Antigua* ☎ *268/480–2999* 🌐 *www.caribworldtravel.com.*

TAXI TRAVEL

Taxis don't have meters. Rates are fixed, and drivers can often serve as useful guides. Many have set rates for this service.

ESSENTIALS

Banks and Exchange Services Local currency is the Eastern Caribbean dollar (EC$). US$1 is worth approximately EC$2.70. American dollars are readily accepted, although you usually receive change in EC$. If you decide to change money, you will get a slightly better exchange rate if you change your money in a bank than at your hotel (the exchange is sometimes rounded down to EC$2.50 in simpler transactions). Major credit cards are widely accepted. ATMs (dispensing EC$) are available at the Royal Bank of Canada and the Bank of Montserrat.

Electricity 220 volts, 50 to 60 cycles, but most lodgings also use 110 volts, permitting use of small North American appliances such as electric shavers. Outlets may be either two- or three-pronged, so bring an adapter.

Emergency Services **Ambulance** ☎ *411, 664/491–2802*. **Fire** ☎ *911*. **Glendon Hospital** ✉ *St. John's* ☎ *664/491–2552, 664/491–7404*. **Police** ☎ *999*.

16

Passport Requirements All visitors need a valid passport. All visitors must present a return or ongoing ticket.

Phones To place a local call, simply dial the local seven-digit number. To call Montserrat from the United States, dial 1 + 664 + the local seven-digit number. To call the United States and Canada from Montserrat, dial 1 + the area code + the seven-digit number. Digicel provides the island's cell-phone service.

Taxes and Service Charges The departure–airport-security tax is US$21—cash only. Most flights come through Antigua, as it is the main hub; be sure to bring copies of your onward travel documents for check-in on both flight legs (you may also be asked to fill out a form upon check-in) to avoid the US$37.50 Antiguan airport tax, normally assessed each way. Day-trippers from Antigua spending less than 24 hours on Montserrat or people with onward connections to and from Montserrat within 24 hours pay only an EC$10 "security charge" and no departure tax on Antigua. Hotels collect a 10% government room tax, guesthouses and villas 7%. Hotels and restaurants also usually add a 10% service charge to your bill.

Tipping In restaurants, it's customary to leave 5% beyond the regular service charge added to your bill if you're pleased with the service. Taxi drivers expect a 10% tip; porters and bellmen, about $1 per bag; maids are not often tipped, but if you do, leave $2 to $3 per night.

ACCOMMODATIONS

With a few small guesthouses, villas, and one small hotel, Montserrat has no large-scale development.

Hotel reviews have been shortened. For full information, visit Fodors.com.

WHAT IT COSTS IN U.S. DOLLARS				
	$	$$	$$$	$$$$
Restaurants	under $12	$12–$20	$21–$30	over $30
Hotels	under $150	$150–$250	$251–$350	over $350

Restaurant prices are the average cost of a main course at dinner or, if dinner is not served, at lunch. Hotel prices are the lowest cost of a standard double room in high season.

VISITOR INFORMATION

Contact Tourism Division of Montserrat Development Corporation. The MDC's Tourism Division keeps track of accommodations, restaurants, activities, car-rental agencies, and tours available on the island and will prove to be an invaluable resource for those traveling to Montserrat. ✉ *E. Karney Osborne Bldg., Little Bay* ☎ *664/491–2230, 664/491–4700* 🌐 *www.visitmontserrat.com* ✉ *Montserrat Government Office, 180-186 King's Cross Rd., London, England* ☎ *0207/031–0317, 0207/520–2622.*

WEDDINGS

Getting married on Montserrat is relatively easy. No blood test is required. For adults 18 years and over, the minimum residency is three days. Apply for a special or Governor's marriage license through the Department of Administration Human Resource Unit via email or by calling between 8 am and 4 pm weekdays. They will ask you to bring valid passports as proof of citizenship and, in the case of previous marriages, the original divorce or annulment decree; widows or widowers will need the original marriage and death certificates. Given the lack of on-island wedding planners and difficulty in transportation, most visitors choose to get married on Antigua and then take a honeymoon trip to Montserrat, which would certainly allow you to spend some quiet time together.

Contact Department of Administration. You can reach the Department of Administration Human Resource Unit via email or or by calling between 8 am and 4 pm weekdays. ☎ *664/491–2365* ✉ *hrmu@gov.ms.*

EXPLORING

Though the more fertile—and historic—southern half of Montserrat was destroyed by the volcano, emerald hills still reward explorers. Hiking and biking are the best ways to experience this island's unspoiled rain forest, glistening black-sand beaches, and lookouts over the devastation.

TOP ATTRACTIONS

Jack Boy Viewing Facility. This vantage point—replete with telescope, barbecue grill and tables for picnickers, landscaped grounds, and washrooms—provides bird's-eye views of the old W.H. Bramble airport and eastern villages damaged by pyroclastic flows. ✉ *Jack Boy Hill.*

Montserrat National Trust Botanical Gardens. The MNT's main headquarters and collections relocated to Little Bay's new Montserrat National

Museum in 2012. But the lovingly tended botanical gardens and nature trails at the original site make for a pleasant, self-guided stroll. Among the plants are herbs used in folkloric medicine, former economic staples like Sea Island cotton and limes, and uniquely indigenous flora. You'll also find charming local keepsakes in the gift shop on the premises. ✉ *Main Rd., Olveston* ☎ *664/491–3086* 🌐 *www.montserratnationaltrust.ms* 🎫 *$2* ⏲ *Weekdays 10–4.*

Montserrat Volcano Observatory. The island's must-see sight occupies capacious, strikingly postmodern quarters with stunning vistas of the Soufrière Hills volcano—a lunarscape encircled by brilliant green—and Plymouth in the distance. Unfortunately, the MVO staff no longer offers tours that explain monitoring techniques on sophisticated computerized equipment in riveting detail. But you can see graphic photos, artifacts like rock and ash, and diagrams that describe the various pyroclastic surge deposits. The Interpretation Center screens a high-impact film with IMAX footage. ✉ *Flemings* ☎ *664/491–5647* 🌐 *www.mvo.ms* 🎫 *Observatory free, screening EC$10* ⏲ *Mon.–Thurs. 10:15–3.*

St. George's Hill/Garibaldi Hill. The only access to this incredible vantage point over the devastation is across the Belham Valley, through a once-beautiful golf course now totally covered by volcanic mudflow, resembling a lunarscape. The area is sometimes reinstated in the Daytime Entry Zone when decreased volcanic activity permits. If it's accessible on your visit, be aware that routes aren't signposted on the rough road, which is often impassable after heavy rains, so it's best to hire an experienced guide. You'll drive through Cork Hill and Weekes, villages for the most part spookily intact (there's no way to provide utilities, though geothermal drilling as an alternate energy source is under way). Close to the summit, the equally eerie, abandoned, stark-white wind-generator project and the giant satellite dishes of the Gem and Antilles radio stations resemble abstract-art installations awaiting completion by Christo. At the top, Ft. St. George contains sparse ruins, including a few cannons, but the overwhelming sight is the panorama of destruction, an unrelenting swath of gray offset by vivid emerald fields and the turquoise Caribbean. If access is restricted to St. George's, you may be able to drive partway to Garibaldi Hill, which also affords sweeping vistas of the devastation. ✉ *St. George's Hill* ⏲ *Daylight hrs when open.*

WORTH NOTING

The Cot. A fairly strenuous Centre Hills trail leads to one of Montserrat's few remaining historic sites—the ruins of the once-influential Sturges family's summer cottage—as well as a banana plantation. Its Duck Pond Hill perch, farther up the trail, dramatically overlooks the coastline, Garibaldi Hill, Old Towne, abandoned villages, and Plymouth.

National Museum of Montserrat. The National Trust, which aims to conserve and enhance the island's natural beauty and cultural heritage, moved its headquarters and collection to this handsome new building in March 2012. The museum features permanent and rotating exhibits on Arawak canoe building, colonial sugar and lime production (the term limey was first applied here to English sailors trying to avoid scurvy), indigenous marine life, West Indian cricket, the annual

Calabash Festival, island folklore like mocko jumbies (spirits), and the history of Sir George Martin's Air Studios, which once lured top musicians from Dire Straits to Stevie Wonder and Paul McCartney. The back room houses a charming small-scale re-creation of pre-eruption Plymouth via blown-up photos, cutouts, and dioramas. Eventually one archival exhibit will screen videos of Montserrat's oral history related by its oldest inhabitants. ✉ *Little Bay* ☎ *664/491–3086* 🌐 *www.montserratnationaltrust.ms* 🎫 *$2, children 12 and under free* 🕒 *Weekdays 10–2.*

Plymouth. Montserrat's former capital has been off-limits to general tourists because of volcanic activity since the 2006 dome collapse. Before that, the adventuresome could stroll its streets, albeit at their own risk; check with the police department to see if the situation has changed again. Once one of the Caribbean's loveliest towns, facing the vividly hued sea, it now resembles a dust-covered lunarscape, with elegant Georgian buildings buried beneath several feet of ash, mud, and rubble (though rain is slowly washing layers away). Entry is officially possible only with a police escort (lest you fall through a rickety roof), and can be arranged with the police headquarters in Salem if you are able to obtain clearance from the Volcano Observatory (generally, permission is restricted to scientists and historians). A hazard allowance of EC$150 is charged per individual or group. ✉ *Plymouth* ☎ *664/491–2230 Montserrat Tourist Board.*

Richmond Hill. This once-affluent suburb of Plymouth, which is back in the Daytime Entry Zone, is just north of the former capital and also offers a riveting panorama. You can see the 18th-century sugar mill that once housed the Montserrat Museum and poke around the abandoned Montserrat Springs Hotel, where a few items remain just as they were left on the front desk during the mass exodus in 1997. You might encounter a goat or cow nibbling mushrooms growing through the cracks in the pool and tennis court. The hotel's hot springs are down the hill by the beach, which has grown substantially and was long a favorite liming spot of locals and expats. ✉ *Richmond Hill* 🕒 *Daylight hrs when open.*

Runaway Ghaut. Montserrat's *ghauts* (pronounced guts) are deep ravines that carry rainwater down from the mountains to the sea. This natural spring, a short, well-marked walk into the hilly bush outside Woodlands, was the site of bloody colonial skirmishes between the British and French. The legend is more interesting than the trail: "Those that drink its water clear they spellbound are, and the Montserrat call they must obey." If you don't want to hike or picnic, a drink from the roadside faucet should ensure that you return to Montserrat in your lifetime. ✉ *Main Rd., just south of Woodlands.*

BEACHES

Montserrat's beaches are public and, with one exception, composed of soft, light- to dark-gray volcanic sand.

Little Bay. Boats chug in and out of the port at the northern end of this otherwise comely crescent with calm waters. Several beach bars—Pont's (fine cheap local lunch Tuesday–Sunday), Soca Cabana, Seaside and Sylvia's—provide cool shade and cooler drinks. Carlton's Fish Net Bar specializes in barbecued stuffed trunkfish (a shellfish delicacy). A number of bars and restaurants were recently built in the adjacent section dubbed "Marine Village," including Monty's Bar and Dive Centre, which opened January 2014. You may see locals casting lines for their own dinner. **Amenities:** food and drink. **Best for:** partiers; snorkeling; swimming. ✉ *Approximately 1½ miles (2½ km) north of Brades off main road; look for turnoffs to Little Bay.*

Rendezvous Bay. The island's sole white-sand beach is a perfect cove tucked under a forested cliff whose calm, unspoiled waters are ideal for swimming and offer remarkable snorkeling. It's accessible only via the sea or a steep trail that runs over the bluff to adjacent Little Bay (you can also negotiate boat rides from the fishermen who congregate there). There are no regular facilities or shade, but its very remoteness and pristine reef teeming with marine life lend it exceptional charm. Quan Jo Boat Tours and Camping offers Sunday beach activities including boat rides and snorkeling, as well as food, music and tents for shade. **Amenities:** none. **Best for:** snorkeling; solitude; swimming. ✉ *Rendezvous Bay.*

16

Woodlands. The only drawback to this secluded strand is the occasionally rough surf (children should be closely monitored). The breezy but covered picnic area on the cliff is one of the best vantage points to watch migratory humpback whales in spring and nesting green and hawksbill turtles in early fall. From here, you can hike north, then down across a wooden bridge to even less trammeled Bunkum Bay, which has a friendly guesthouse and beach bar. **Amenities:** none. **Best for:** solitude; surfing. ✉ *At turnoff just outside Woodlands Village.*

WHERE TO EAT

Restaurants are casual affairs indeed, ranging from glorified rum shops to hotel dining rooms. Most serve classic Caribbean fare, including such specialties as goat water (a thick stew of goat meat, tubers, and vegetables that seems to have been bubbling for days), salt fish cake (codfish fritters), home-brewed ginger beer, and freshly made juices from soursop, mango, blackberry (different from the North American species), guava, tamarind, papaya, and gooseberry.

What to Wear: Dress is informal even at dinner, though skimpy attire is frowned upon by the comparatively conservative islanders. Long pants are preferred, albeit not required, for men in the evening.

$$ ECLECTIC

Olveston House. Five different rums power the knockout Olveston Rum Punch, but the animated chatter of locals, expats, and international guests also generates its own potent buzz. Picture windows overlook the handsome veranda and gardens at this popular eatery. Chef Margaret Wilson creatively uses whatever ingredients are available. You might luck into fresh wahoo in orange-ginger sauce, scrumptious garlic shrimp, pork tenderloin glazed with homemade preserves, or flaky savory pies that elevate traditional English pub grub to an art form. The sublime sticky toffee pudding, mango-ginger crumble, and pear tart justify Margaret's declaration, "I'd rather make desserts than clean the house," though daughter Sarah's luscious cheesecakes (mango, chocolate hazelnut) are also winners. Sailing etchings, period cabinets with mismatched china, and serenading tree frogs create the ambience of dining at someone's country estate, Caribbean-style. Wednesday barbeque, Friday Pub Night, and Sunday classic English brunch are casual and cheap, with no reservations required. *Average main: US$18 Olveston 664/491–5210, 664/495–5210 www.olvestonhouse.com Reservations essential Closed Jan., Mon., and dinner Sun.*

$$ CARIBBEAN **Tina's.** This pretty, coral-and-white wooden building is garlanded year-round with Christmas lights, a harbinger of the good vibes within. It's the best place to eavesdrop on island gossip, as government functionaries file in for lunch (at least when day-trippers don't take over). Dine either in a trim room or on a breezy veranda (admittedly sans view). Occasionally you'll find old-time dishes like souse, but the menu is generally more upscale: specialties include velvety pumpkin soup, proper escargots, and tender lobster in sultry creole sauce or (even better) tangy garlic sauce. Entrées are served with heaping helpings of salads and sides. Fine desserts (moist carrot cake, cheesecake, and wonderfully textured coconut pie) end the meal and, surprisingly, good take-out pizza is available. *Average main: US$18 Brades 664/491–3538 No credit cards Closed Sun.*

$$$ ECLECTIC **Ziggy's.** Vivacious owners John and Marcia Punter literally hacked Montserrat's most elegant eatery from the rain forest. They poured a concrete floor and dressed it with a billowing, white, rectangular tent, pergolas, palm fronds, potted plants, hardwood chairs, jade hurricane shutters, bronze sculpted candlesticks, and colorful Moroccan-inspired table settings: the ultimate in shack chic. The menu (posted on a blackboard) changes daily, but always offers one red meat, one white meat, and one seafood entrée. Generally well-executed dishes lean more toward bistro fare (emphasizing beef entrecôte or goat cheese soufflé over such island staples as fish, though specials like oxtail ravioli happily marry both culinary traditions); the signature butterfly shrimp usually precedes entrées. A decent wine list enhances the meal; save room for the Chocolate Sludge. Despite an erratic schedule (reconfirm reservations), hard-to-find location, and overly relaxed service, the ambience is appealingly serene and upscale. *Average main: US$28 Mahogany La., Woodlands 664/491–8282 www.ziggysrestaurant.com Reservations essential No lunch.*

WHERE TO STAY

Currently, the island primarily offers villas (housekeepers and cooks can be arranged) or guesthouses, the latter often incorporating meals in the rate by request (ask if the 7% tax and 10% service charge are included), and there is one small hotel. Note that inns rarely have air-conditioning, relying instead on hillside breezes.

PRIVATE VILLA RENTALS

Fodor'sChoice ★ In the pre-volcano (and pre–Hurricane Hugo) days, when an international roster of celebrity musicians (Elton to Eric, the Rolling Stones to Sting) recorded at Sir George Martin's AIR Studios, Montserrat was a favored spot for many rich and famous Britons (and the occasional American) to vacation. Today you can luxuriate in one of the handsome villas they called home when visiting and do so for comparatively affordable rates.

Montserrat Enterprises. In business since 1962, Montserrat Enterprises has a generally smaller inventory but most of its properties offer splendid views and amenities. ✉ *Bishop's View Rd., Old Towne* ☎ *664/491–2431* 🌐 *www.montserratenterprises.com.*

Tradewinds Real Estate. The leading villa rental company in Montserrat is Tradewinds Real Estate. Many of its 20-plus deluxe properties, ranging from one to four bedrooms, have plunge pools, amazing water vistas, and ultramodern conveniences from DVD players and Internet access to gourmet kitchens. Recommended properties with beach access and/or strategic hillside locations include Mango Falls, Vest View, Cythera, and Mango Pointe (owned by the former drummer of The Turtles). Caring owner Susan Edgecombe really tries to match guest to villa, remaining available throughout your stay to make any additional arrangements and offer touring and activity suggestions; she'll keep you updated back home with her informative newsletter. Rates run from $700 to $3,000 per week in high season. ✉ *Main Rd., Olveston* ☎ *664/491–2004* 🌐 *www.tradewindsmontserrat.com.*

16

RECOMMENDED HOTELS AND INNS

$ B&B/INN **Erindell Villa Guesthouse.** This tranquil rain-forest retreat is a photo album in the making, overflowing with character and characters. **Pros:** engaging owners; beautiful landscaping; fun, makeshift entertainment; abundant freebies. **Cons:** hike to beach; occasionally raucous, fun, makeshift entertainment; occasional ash dustings. [$] *Rooms from: US$75* ✉ *Gros Michel Dr., Woodlands* ☎ *664/491–3655* 🌐 *www.erindellvilla.com* *2 rooms* *No credit cards* *Breakfast.*

$ HOTEL **Gingerbread Hill.** This secluded mountainside retreat offers remarkable value, splendid views, utter tranquillity, and exquisite grounds. **Pros:** environmentally conscious; fascinating owners; delightful menagerie, including birds; free Wi-Fi and airport transfers; access to washer/dryer. **Cons:** car necessary; no beachfront; perhaps too "granola" for some. [$] *Rooms from: US$125* ✉ *Virgin Island Road, St. Peter's* ☎ *664/491–5812, 813/774–5270* 🌐 *www.volcano-island.com* *2 rooms, 2 villas, 1 cottage* *No meals.*

$ B&B/INN **Grand View Bed & Breakfast.** This aptly named inn is run by energetic dynamo Theresa Silcott, who prides herself on being Montserrat's top hostess. **Pros:** splendid views; delightful gardens; congenial hostess; excellent local food (ask about medicinal folklore); free Wi-Fi. **Cons:** no beachfront; very basic if clean rooms. [$] *Rooms from: US$55* ✉ *Baker Hill* ☎ *664/491–2284* 🌐 *www.mnigrandview.com* *2 suites, 8 rooms* *No credit cards* *Breakfast.*

$ HOTEL Fodor'sChoice ★ **Olveston House.** This 1950s villa, rented to island hotelier Carol Osborne by Beatles producer Sir George Martin, brims with history (including the owner's fabled AIR Studios where Sting, Elton John, Eric Clapton, and Paul McCartney recorded). **Pros:** incredible value; gorgeous pool; glorious views of the glowing Soufrière; invigorating blend of locals, expats, and guests at the bar and dining room. **Cons:** no beach; occasional dusting of ash; Wi-Fi spotty. *Rooms from: US$119 ✉ Olveston ☎ 664/491–5210, 664/495–5210 www.olvestonhouse.com 6 rooms Closed Jan. Breakfast.*

$ HOTEL **Tropical Mansion Suites.** Despite the grandiose name, this is little more than a motel with neocolonial architectural pretensions and clean, spacious rooms. **Pros:** currently the island's only full-service lodging; centrally located. **Cons:** far from beaches; extra charge for air-conditioning; mediocre and comparatively pricey food. *Rooms from: US$139 ✉ 404 Sweeney's Rd., Sweeney's ☎ 664/491–8767 www.tropicalmansion.com 17 rooms, 1 suite Breakfast.*

NIGHTLIFE AND PERFORMING ARTS

Although Montserrat is better known for another kind of wildlife, Friday-night revelers lime in roadside rum shops scattered around the island, often spilling out on the street as part of the informal evening culture. There's no closing time, and many bars serve yummy, authentic local food. Salem is party central (the roadside sign says, "Welcome to fun and revelry"). Little Bay is being developed as the island capital (the government will remain in Brades); in season the Hot Spot is a collection of a dozen watering holes between the "town" and Cultural Center; Festival Village is a gathering of pop-up bars during festivals.

NIGHTLIFE

Garry Moore's Wide Awake Bar. This perennial favorite doesn't close as long as customers are thirsty. The name was a teasing reference to Garry's penchant for napping at the bar (when he wasn't complaining—mostly humorously—about a plumber's hard life and long hours). Sadly, Garry passed in 2012, but his son carries on the tradition. *✉ Salem ☎ 664/491–7156.*

Howe's Rum Shop. This is the best spot on the island for shooting pool and the breeze; get here early for luscious fried and barbecued chicken, liberally daubed with mouth- and eye-watering homemade sauces and seasonings, accompanied by frosty beers and local firewater liqueurs. *✉ St. John's ☎ 664/491–3008.*

Let's Go Limin'. In season, artist Harriet Peakes runs a rollicking "Rumshop Tour" of three to four truly local watering holes where you can lime, drink, sample local fare, and play spirited dominoes. *☎ 664/491–7156.*

Soca Cabana. This hot spot offers live Caribbean beats, as the name implies. But expat owner Tom Walker is passionate about the island's musical heritage, including the halcyon days of Air Studios. He salvaged the "Bar of the Stars" from Sir George Martin's celebrated recording space, where weekly Montserrat Idol competitions take place. It's a delightful liming spot, with the bamboo bar and whitewashed patio accented in mint and turquoise overlooking the beach. Seemingly half the island descends on the hot spot Sunday for meals, music, and merriment. Karaoke Saturdays also reel partiers in. ✉ *Little Bay* ☎ *664/492–1677* 🌐 *www.socacabana.com* 🎫 *Admission varies* ⏲ *Open for lunch daily; dinner by request and live music Wed., Fri., and Sat. nights; dinner Sun.*

Treasure Spot Cafe. Lydia, the owner of the Treasure Spot, often books the island's up-and-coming musicians (usually One Man Band but also Pops Morris, Hero, and Basil—reggae and soca artists beginning to develop a reputation outside Montserrat) to play weekends. Locals also savor breakfast, lunch, and weekend barbecues. ✉ *Cudjoe Head* ☎ *664/493–2003.*

PERFORMING ARTS

Montserrat Cultural Centre. Eight years in development, the impressive, colonnaded Montserrat Cultural Centre and its 500-seat, state-of-the-art Sir George Martin Auditorium present craft demonstrations, folkloric and fashion shows, pageants, movies (with popcorn and hot dogs), and the occasional dance and theatrical performance. During intermission, check out the Wall of Fame (bronzed handprints of musicians who recorded or performed on Montserrat, such as Sir Paul McCartney, Sir Elton John, and Mark Knopfler). Check with the tourist board or local newspaper listings for the current schedule. ✉ *Little Bay* ☎ *664/491–4242, 664/491–4700.*

16

SHOPPING

Montserrat offers a variety of local crafts and does a brisk trade in vulcanology mementos (many shops sell not only postcards and striking photographs but also small bottles of gray ash capped by colorful, homemade cloth).

David Lea. David Lea has chronicled Montserrat's volcanic movements in a fascinating eight-part video–DVD series, *The Price of Paradise,* each entry a compelling glimpse into the geological and social devastation—and regeneration. These, as well as rollicking local-music CDs by his son (named Sun) and other musicians, are available at his studio. ✉ *Gingerbread Hill, St. Peter's* ☎ *664/491–5812* 🌐 *www.volcano-island.com.*

Luv's Cotton Store. This is the island's best source for sportswear made from Sea Island cotton, celebrated for its softness and high quality. ✉ *Salem* ☎ *664/491–3906.*

Montserrat Philatelic Bureau. Occupying the Government Headquarters Building, the Montserrat Philatelic Bureau sells a wealth of highly prized unusual stamps, including handsome first-day covers, that highlight local treasures from the Montserrat Oriole to the late great musician, the Mighty Arrow. ✉ *Government Headquarters Bldg., 7 Farara Plaza, Brades* ☎ *664/491–2042, 664/491–2996.*

Oriole Gift Shop. Oriole Gift Shop in the National Museum, run by the Montserrat National Trust, is an excellent source for books on Montserrat (look for the *Montserrat Cookbook* and works by the island's former acting governor, Sir Howard Fergus), as well as trail maps, handicrafts (wonderful dolls, hand-painted boxes, and calabash purses) and locally made food products. ✉ *Little Bay* ☏ *664/491–3086.*

Woolcock's Craft & Photo Gallery. This gallery promotes the work of local artists such as Donaldson Romeo and sells spectacular photos of the volcano as well as of indigenous birds and other wildlife. ✉ *BBC Bldg., Little Bay Public Market, Little Bay* ☏ *664/491–2025.*

SPORTS AND THE OUTDOORS

BIKING

Mountain biking is making a comeback, with a wide network of trails through the lush Centre Hills. Bikes are also a wonderful way to explore the island and enjoy the lovely coastal vistas along the main road.

DIVING

More than 30 practically pristine dive sites surround Montserrat. The even more bountiful marine life has had time to recover from the predations of human activities, and the pyroclastic flows have formed boulders, pinnacles, ledges, and walls that anchor new coral reefs. **Carr's Bay** is a favorite for shore dives, with arrow crabs, basket stars, turtles, and shimmering blue tang darting about hulking boulders and a small, colorful cave; night dives are particularly memorable, as millions of bioluminescent microorganisms glow when disturbed. The shallow reefs surrounding **Woodlands Bay** feature varied underwater topography, including a small, colorful cave that houses thousands of banded coral shrimp, copper sweepers, sergeant majors, four-eyed butterfly fish, jackknife, attenuated trumpetfish, and turtles. **Rendezvous Bay** may be the finest spot for both snorkeling and diving, thanks to a sheltered reef and lack of ash or silt. In its depths, you may come face-to-face with spotted morays, porcupine fish, snake eels, octopuses, and more. You can even hang out with thousands of (harmless) fruit bats in partially submerged caves. Other top dive sites include **Lime Kiln Bay** and **Bunkum Bay,** as well as the spectacular submarine rock formations around **Little Redonda** and the **Pinnacles** off the rougher, more challenging northeastern shores.

FAMILY **Scuba Montserrat.** Andrew Myers and Emmy Aston of Scuba Montserrat provide experienced PADI certification; lengthy shore, boat, and kayak dives; snorkeling excursions (including a stop at a very cool bat cave); specialty courses from drift diving to digital underwater photography; and down the road the possibility of helping regenerate volcano-damaged sites. They're particularly family focused, stocking underwater Frisbees, torpedoes, and specialized children's gear. They also rent inflatable two-person Hanauma kayaks. ✉ *Little Bay* ☏ *664/496–7807* 🌐 *www.scubamontserrat.com.*

FISHING

Danny Sweeney. Deep-sea fishing (wahoo, bonito, shark, marlin, and yellowfin tuna) is superb, since the waters aren't disturbed by leviathan cruise ships. Affable Danny Sweeney (ask him why Dire Straits' "Walk of Life" allegedly memorializes him) has won several regional tournaments, including Montserrat's Open Fishing Competition. Half-day charters (up to four people) are $300. Though schools of game fish amazingly cavort just 2 to 3 miles (3 to 5 km) offshore, Danny's depth sounder picks up action in deeper waters. An extra bonus on the open sea is the gripping views of the volcanic devastation. He also runs Plymouth/island circumnavigation boat tours for $50 per person. ✉ *Olveston* ☎ *664/491–5645.*

GUIDED TOURS

Avalon Tours. Joe "Fergus" Phillip, who operates Avalon Tours, often emails updates on Montserrat to visitors. ✉ *Manjack* ☎ *664/491–3432, 664/492–1565* ✉ *joephillip@live.com.*

Furlonge Taxi & Tours. Reuben Furlonge of Furlonge Taxi & Tours is another hardy helpful local (and a "goat water specialist"; you may be stopped along the way by locals inquiring if he's made a batch). All the staff here are friendly, knowledgeable, and reliable taxi and tour drivers. ✉ *Gerald's* ☎ *664/491–4376, 664/492–2790.*

16

HIKING

Montserrat's lush, untrammeled rain forest teeming with exotic flora, fauna, and birdlife is best experienced on foot. The tourist office provides lists of hiking trails, from easy to arduous. The most dramatic routes are gradually being upgraded as part of the Montserrat Tourism Development Project; in addition to improving their definition, the government will also be building viewing platforms and providing interpretative information at strategic points. Still, if you're not experienced or fit, go with a guide; always wear sturdy shoes and bring water. Most marked trails run through the biologically diverse, scenic Centre Hills region, offering stirring lookouts over the volcano's barren flanks, surrounding greenery, and ash-covered villages in the Exclusion Zone. The rain forest is home to many regionally endemic wildlife species (tree frogs, dwarf geckos, anoles, mountain chicken—actually a type of frog—and the half-snake, half-lizard galliwasp), as well as most of the 34 resident birds, from red-billed tropic birds to the rare national bird, the Montserrat oriole, with its distinctive orange-and-black plumage. The Silver Hills in the north are vastly different, with dry and deciduous forests and open plains blanketing a defunct, heavily faulted and eroded volcano; views here might provide a glimpse of how southern Montserrat will look millions of years from now.

Scriber's Adventure Tours. These excellent tours are run by James "Scriber" Daley ("a describer since I was little"), an employee of the Agricultural Department legendary for his uncanny birdcalls. He leads nature hikes through the rain forest for $20 to $50; he'll hire additional guides if there are more than 10 people per group, ensuring personal attention. Scriber also explains indigenous flora, from 42 fern species (kids love when he "tattoos" them with silver fern leaves) to others prized for medicinal properties (you might collect the makings of bush tea for back pain or menstrual cramps). He also conducts a memorable, if brief, evening mountain-chicken tour, distributing flashlights to find the foot-long frogs. ☎ *664/491–2546, 664/491–3412, 664/492–2943.*

17

PUERTO RICO

WELCOME TO PUERTO RICO

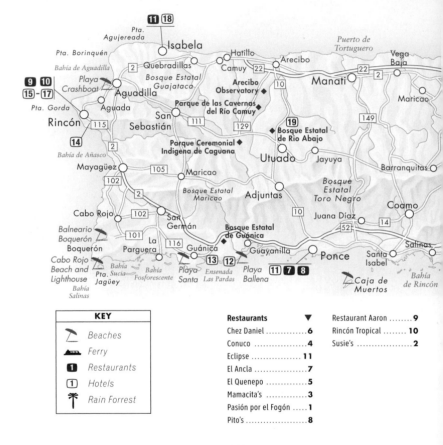

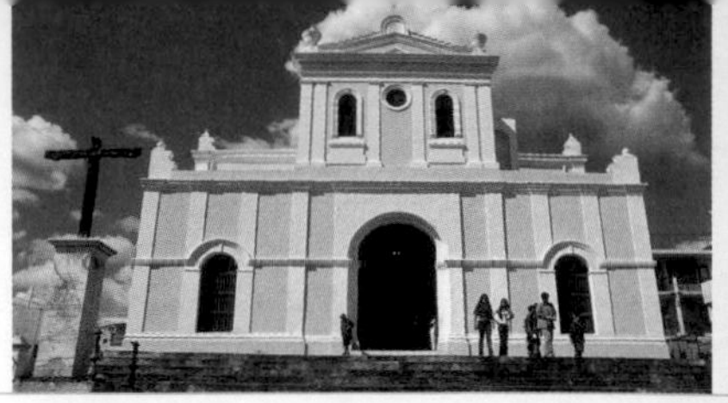

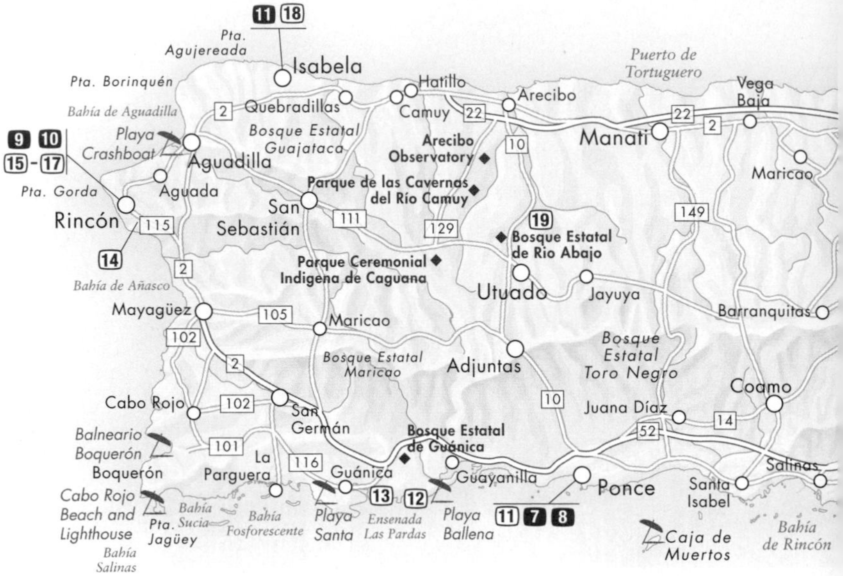

11 18
Pta. Agujereada
Isabela
Pta. Borinquén
Bahía de Aguadilla
2
Quebradillas
Hatillo
Camuy
22
Arecibo
Puerto de Tortuguero
Vega Baja
22
2
Manatí
9 10 15-17
Playa Crashboat
Aguadilla
Bosque Estatal Guajataca
Arecibo Observatory
10
Maricao
Pta. Gorda
Aguada
Parque de las Cavernas del Río Camuy
Rincón
115
San Sebastián
111
129
19
Bosque Estatal de Rio Abajo
149
14
2
Bahía de Añasco
Parque Ceremonial Indígena de Caguana
Utuado
Jayuya
Barranquitas
Mayagüez
105
Maricao
102
Bosque Estatal Maricao
Adjuntas
Bosque Estatal Toro Negro
2
Coamo
Cabo Rojo
102
San Germán
10
Juana Díaz
14
Balneario Boquerón
52
Bosque Estatal de Guánica
101
Boquerón
La Parguera
116
Guánica
Guayanilla
Salinas
Ponce
Santa Isabel
Cabo Rojo Beach and Lighthouse
Bahía Sucia
Pta. Jagüey
Bahía Fosforescente
Playa Santa
13 12
Ensenada Las Pardas
Playa Ballena
11 7 8
Caja de Muertos
Bahía de Rincón
Bahía Salinas

KEY

- Beaches
- Ferry
- Restaurants
- Hotels
- Rain Forrest

Restaurants ▼

Chez Daniel 6
Conuco 4
Eclipse 11
El Ancla 7
El Quenepo 5
Mamacita's 3
Pasión por el Fogón 1
Pito's 8
Restaurant Aaron 9
Rincón Tropical 10
Susie's 2

Mother Spain is always a presence here—on a sun-dappled cobblestone street, in the shade of a colonial cathedral or fort. Yet multifaceted Puerto Rico pulses with New World energy. The rhythms of the streets are of Afro-Latin salsa and bomba. And the U.S. flag flaps in the salty breezes wherever you go.

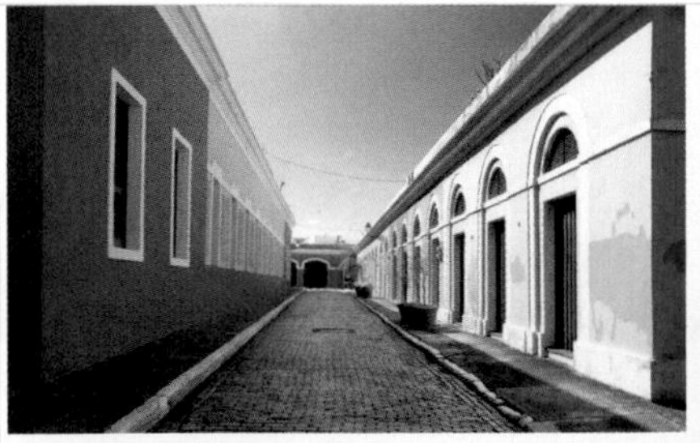

SPANISH AMERICAN

Puerto Rico is 110 miles (177 km) long and 35 miles (56 km) wide. With a population of almost 4 million, it's among the biggest of the Caribbean islands. The first Spanish governor was Juan Ponce de León in 1508; he founded Old San Juan in 1521. The United States won the island in the Spanish-American War in 1898 and made it a commonwealth in 1952.

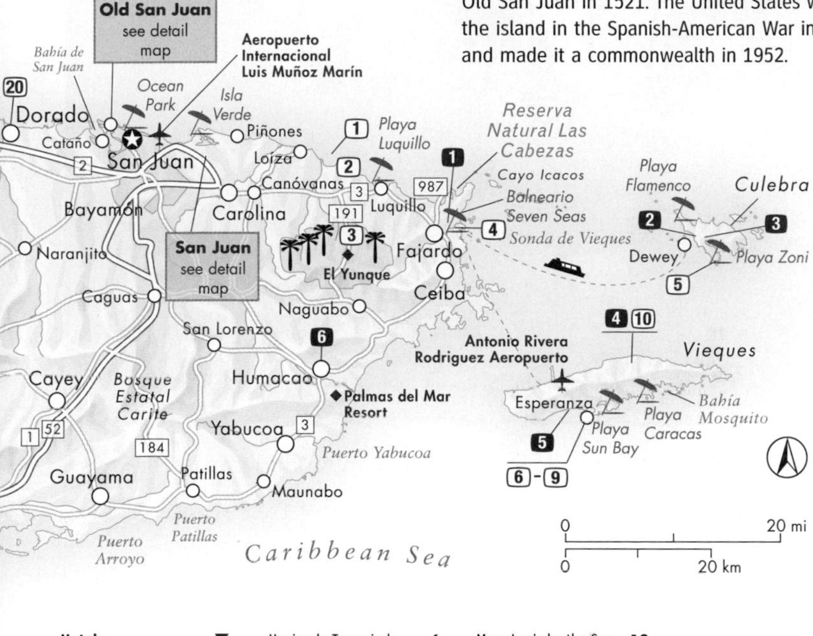

Hotels ▼	
Casa Grande	19
Club Seaborne	5
Copamarina Beach Resort	13
Dorado Beach, A Ritz Carloton Resort	20
El Conquistador	4
Gran Meliá Puerto Rico	2
Hacienda Tamarindo	6
Hix Island House	9
Horned Dorset Primavera	15
Hotel Meliá	11
Inn on the Blue Horizon	7
Lazy Parrot	17
Lemontree	14
Malecón House	8
Mary Lee's by the Sea	12
Río Mar Beach Resort & Spa	1
St. Regis Bahia	3
Tres Sirenas	16
Villa Montaña	18
W Retreat & Spa	10

TOP REASONS TO VISIT PUERTO RICO

1 The Nightlife: Happening clubs, discos, and bars make San Juan one of the Caribbean's nightlife capitals, rivaling even Miami.

2 The Food: Great restaurants run the gamut from elegant places in San Juan to simple spots serving delicious *comida criolla.*

3 The Beaches: Both developed and wild, beaches here suit the needs of surfers, sunbathers, and families.

4 The Nature: Nature abounds, from the underground Río Camuy to El Yunque, the only Caribbean national forest.

5 The Unexpected: Puerto Mosquito—kayak after dark on the astounding bioluminescent bay on Vieques.

EATING AND DRINKING WELL IN PUERTO RICO

More chefs and restaurateurs are fusing international ingredients with traditional dishes. However, even the most avant-garde chefs use local produce as an homage to classic *comida criolla*.

Standard meats like chicken, pork, and lamb are given an added zest by sauces made from such tropical fruits as tamarind, mango, or guava. Puerto Rican cooking uses a lot of local vegetables: plantains are cooked a hundred different ways, and yams and other root vegetables are served baked, fried, stuffed, boiled, and mashed. Rice and beans are accompaniments to almost every dish. *Sofrito*—a garlic, onion, sweet pepper, cilantro, oregano, and tomato purée—is used as a base for practically everything. *Arroz con pollo* (chicken with rice), *pernil* (roasted pork shoulder), *sancocho* (beef, chicken, or pork feet and tuber soup), and *bistec encebollado* (steak and onions) are all typical plates. Also look for fritters served along highways and beaches. You may find *empanadillas* (stuffed fried turnovers), *sorullitos* (cheese-stuffed corn sticks), and *bacalaítos* (codfish fritters).

Cocina Criolla: *Cocina or comida criolla* (creole cooking), the local Puerto Rican food, is an aggregate of Caribbean cuisines, sharing basic ingredients common to Cuban, Dominican, and even Brazilian culinary traditions. Conventional wisdom says that the secret of the cocina criolla depends on the use of sofrito, achiote (the inedible fruit of a small Caribbean shrub whose seeds are sometimes ground as a spice or simmered in oil to release their color), lard, and the *caldero* (cooking pot).

Coffee: Cultivated at high altitudes in cool, moist air and mineral-rich soil, the island's coffee beans (called cherries) are black and aromatic. Look for local brands: Yaucono Selecto, Rioja, Yaucono, Hacienda San Pedro, Café Rico, Crema, Adjuntas, Coqui, and Alto Grande Super Premium.

Fruits and Vegetables: Tropical fruits often wind up at the table in the form of delicious juices. A local favorite is pineapple juice from crops grown in the north of the island. Coconut, mango, acerola (Caribbean cherry), papaya, lime, and tamarind are other local favorites. Puerto Rico is home to terrific lesser-known fruits; these include the *caimito* (also called a star apple), *quenepa* (a Spanish lime with a yellow sweet-tart pulp surrounded by a tight, thin skin), and *zapote* (a plum-size fruit that tastes like peach, avocado, and vanilla). The Plaza del Mercado in Río Piedras is a good place to look for the unusual.

Local Seafood: The freshest seafood is to be found on the northern and western coasts, where seaside shacks and kiosks serve up red snapper, grouper, conch, crab, and spiny lobster in traditional recipes. Fried fish is also popular, served with *mojo isleño*, a sauce made with olives, onions, pimientos, capers, tomatoes, and vinegar.

Plantains and Mofongo: *Plátanos,* or plantains, are related to bananas but are larger and starchier. They are

served mostly as side dishes and may be eaten green or ripe. They can be fried, baked, boiled, or roasted and served either whole or in slices. Of all the delicious plantain preparations, one of the tastiest is also the simplest—*mofongo.* Fried green plantains are mashed with a wooden *pilón*, mixed with garlic, pork fat, and other flavorings. Served plain, it's often a side dish. But when it's stuffed with chicken, beef, or some other meat, *mofongo* becomes one of Puerto Rico's signature entrées.

Rice: Rice is omnipresent, and most often it's served with *habichuelas* (beans). Rice stuck to the pot, known as *pegao,* is the most highly prized, full of all the ingredients that have sunk to the bottom.

Rum: Although rum was first exported in 1897, it took a bit longer for it to become the massive industry it is today. The Bacardí family set up shop near San Juan in 1959, after fleeing Cuba. The company's product, lighter-bodied than those produced by most other distilleries, gained favor around the world. Today Puerto Rico produces more than 35 million gallons of rum a year. You might say it's the national drink.

Updated by Paulina Salach

Sunrise and sunset are both worth waiting for when you're in Puerto Rico. The pinks and yellows that hang in the early-morning sky are just as compelling as the sinewy reds and purples that blend into the twilight. It's easy to compare them, as Puerto Rico is small enough to have breakfast in Fajardo, looking eastward over the boats headed to Vieques and Culebra, and lobster dinner in Rincón as the sun is sinking into the inky-blue water.

Known as the Island of Enchantment, Puerto Rico conjures a powerful spell. Here traffic actually leads you to a "Road to Paradise," whether you're looking for a pleasurable, sunny escape from the confines of urbanity or a rich supply of stimulation to quench your cultural and entertainment thirst. On the island you have the best of both worlds, natural and urban thrills alike, and although city life is frenetic enough to make you forget you're surrounded by azure waters and warm sand, traveling a few miles inland or down the coast can easily make you forget you're surrounded by development.

Puerto Rico was populated primarily by Taíno Indians when Columbus landed in 1493. In 1508 Ponce de León established a settlement and became the first governor; in 1521 he founded what is known as Old San Juan. For centuries, while Africans worked on the coastal sugarcane fields, the French, Dutch, and English tried unsuccessfully to wrest the island from Spain. In 1898, as a result of the Spanish-American War, Spain ceded the island to the United States. In 1917 Puerto Ricans became U.S. citizens, and in 1952 Puerto Rico became a semiautonomous commonwealth.

Since the 1950s, Puerto Rico has developed exponentially, as witnessed in the urban sprawl, burgeoning traffic, and growing population (estimated at nearly 4 million); yet *en la isla* (on the island) a strong Latin sense of community and family prevails. Puertorriqueños are fiercely proud of their unique blend of heritages.

Music is another source of Puerto Rican pride. Like wildflowers, *vellon-eras* (jukeboxes) pop up almost everywhere, and when one is playing, somebody will be either singing or dancing along—or both. Cars often vibrate with *reggaetón,* an aggressive beat with lyrics that express social malaise. Salsa, a fusion of West African percussion, jazz, and other Latin beats, is the trademark dance. Although it may look difficult to master, it's all achieved by just loosening your hips. You may choose to let your inhibitions go by doing some clubbing *a la vida loca* made famous by pop star Ricky Martin. Nightlife options are on par with any cosmopolitan city—and then some.

By day you can drink in the culture of the old world; one of the richest visual experiences in Puerto Rico is Old San Juan. Originally built as a fortress by the Spaniards in the early 1500s, the Old City has myriad attractions that include restored 16th-century buildings and 200-year-old houses with balustraded balconies of filigreed wrought iron that overlook narrow cobblestone streets. Spanish traditions are also apparent in the countryside festivals celebrated in honor of small-town patron saints. For quiet relaxation or experiences off the beaten track, visit coffee plantations, colonial towns, or outlying islets where nightlife is virtually nonexistent.

And you don't come to a Caribbean island without taking in some of the glorious sunshine and natural wonders. In the coastal areas the sun mildly toasts your body, and you're immediately healed by soft waves and cool breezes. In the misty mountains, you can wonder at the flickering night flies and the star-studded sky while the *coquís* (tiny local frogs) chirp their legendary sweet lullaby. On a moonless night, watch the warm ocean turn into luminescent aqua-blue speckles on your skin. Then there are the island's many acres of golf courses, numerous tennis courts, rain forests, and dozens of beaches that offer every imaginable water sport.

PLANNING

WHEN TO GO

San Juan in particular is very expensive—many would say overpriced—during the busy tourist season from mid-December through mid-April; during the off-season, you can get good deals all over the island, with discounts of up to 40% off high-season rates.

GETTING HERE AND AROUND

AIR TRAVEL

San Juan's busy Aeropuerto Internacional Luis Muñoz Marín (SJU) receives flights from all major American carriers, and there are dozens of daily flights to Puerto Rico from the United States. Nonstop options include American Airlines from Chicago, Dallas, Miami, and New York–JFK; Delta from Atlanta and New York–JFK; JetBlue from Boston, Chicago, Fort Lauderdale, Hartford, Newark, New York–JFK, Orlando, and Tampa; Southwest from Atlanta, Baltimore, Fort Lauderdale, Houston, Orlando, and Tampa; Spirit Airlines from Fort Lauderdale; United from Chicago, Houston, Newark, Philadelphia, and

LOGISTICS

Getting to Puerto Rico: There are dozens of daily flights to Puerto Rico from the United States. San Juan's international airport is a major regional hub, so many travelers headed elsewhere in the Caribbean make connections here. Fares to San Juan are among the most reasonably priced in the region. The island also has airports in Aguadilla (BQN), Fajardo (FAJ), Ponce (PSE), and Mayagüez (MAZ), and on the islands of Vieques (VQS) and Culebra (CPX). Culebra and Vieques can also be reached by ferry.

Hassle Factor: Low.

On the Ground: Before arriving, check with your hotel about transfers: some hotels and resorts provide transport from the airport—free or for a fee—to their guests; some larger resorts run regular shuttles. Otherwise, your best bets are *taxis turísticos* (tourist taxis). Uniformed officials at the airport can help you make arrangements. They will give you a slip with your exact fare to hand to the driver. Rates are based on your destination. There's a $1 charge for each bag handled by the driver.

Washington, D.C.–Dulles; and US Airways from Charlotte, Chicago, Philadelphia, and Washington, D.C.–Dulles.

SJU is a major regional hub; many travelers make connections here to other islands in the Caribbean. Sometimes known as Isla Grande, San Juan's other airport, the Aeropuerto Fernando L. Ribas Dominicci (SIG), is in Miramar near the Convention Center. It handles mainly short hops to Vieques and other nearby islands, though both airports offer flights to Culebra, Vieques, and other destinations on Puerto Rico and throughout the Caribbean. Air Flamenco and Vieques Air Link offer daily flights from SJU and SIG to Vieques and Culebra. Cape Air flies from SJU to Vieques and Culebra.

International Airline Contacts **American Airlines** ☎ *800/433–7300* 🌐 *www.aa.com.* **Delta Airlines** ☎ *800/221–1212 U.S. reservations, 800/241–4141 international reservations* 🌐 *www.delta.com.* **JetBlue** ☎ *800/538–2583* 🌐 *www.jetblue.com.* **Spirit Airlines** ☎ *801/401–2200* 🌐 *www.spirit.com.* **Southwest Airlines** ☎ *800/435–9792* 🌐 *www.southwest.com.* **United Airlines** ☎ *800/864–8331* 🌐 *www.united.com.* **US Airways** ☎ *800/428–4322* 🌐 *www.usairways.com.*

Regional Airline Contacts **Air Flamenco** ☎ *787/724–1818, 877/535–2636* 🌐 *www.airflamenco.net.* **Cape Air** ☎ *800/227–3247* 🌐 *www.capeair.com.* **Vieques Air Link** ☎ *787/741–8331, 888/901–9247* 🌐 *www.viequesairlink.com.*

Airports **Aeropuerto Internacional Luis Muñoz Marín** (*SJU*). ✉ *Carolina, San Juan* ☎ *787/253–2329* 🌐 *www.aeropuertosju.com.* **Aeropuerto Fernando L. Ribas Dominicci** (*SIG*). ✉ *Calle Lindbergh, San Juan* ☎ *787/729–8715.*

BOAT AND FERRY TRAVEL

Part of the Department of Transportation, the Autoridad de Transporte Marítimo (Maritime Transport Authority) runs passenger and cargo ferries from Fajardo, about a 90-minute drive from San Juan, to Culebra and Vieques. There are a limited number of seats on the ferries, so get to the terminal in plenty of time.

Contact Autoridad de Transporte Marítimo ✉ *Carr De Maternillo, Fajardo* ☎ *787/494–0934* 🌐 *www.dtop.gov.pr.*

CAR TRAVEL

In San Juan it's often more trouble than it's worth to rent a car. Elsewhere a car is probably a necessity. A valid driver's license from your country of origin can be used in Puerto Rico for three months. Rates start as low as $25 a day. Several well-marked multilane highways link population centers. Driving distances are posted in kilometers, but speed limits are posted in miles per hour. Road signs are in Spanish.

International Agencies Avis ✉ *San Juan International Airport, Terminal Bldg., Carolina* ☎ *787/253–5926* 🌐 *www.avis.com.* **Hertz** ☎ *800/654–3030* 🌐 *www.hertz.com.* **National** ☎ *787/791–1805* 🌐 *www.nationalcar.com.* **Thrifty** ☎ *800/847–4389* 🌐 *www.thrifty.com.*

Local Agencies Charlie Car Rental ☎ *787/728–2418* 🌐 *www.charliecars.com.* **Vias** ☎ *787/791–4120* 🌐 *www.viascarrental.com.*

TAXI TRAVEL

The Puerto Rico Tourism Company has instituted a well-organized taxi program. White taxis with the "taxi turistico" logo run from the airport or the cruise-ship piers to Isla Verde, Condado/Ocean Park, and Old San Juan, with fixed "zone" rates ranging from $10 to $24. If you take a cab going somewhere outside the fixed zones, insist on setting the meter. City tours start at $36 per hour. In other towns you can flag down cabs on the street, but it's easier to have your hotel call one for you. ■ **TIP→ Make sure the driver is clear on whether he or she will charge a flat rate or use a meter to determine the fare.**

Contacts Major Cab Company ☎ *787/723–2460.* **Metro Taxi** ☎ *787/725–2870* 🌐 *www.metrotaxipr.com.*

ESSENTIALS

Banks and Money The U.S. dollar is the official currency. Major credit cards are widely accepted, and ATMs are readily available and reliable in the cities, less frequently in rural areas. Look to local banks such as Banco Popular and First Bank.

Electricity 110 volts/60 cycles.

Emergencies Dial 911. For nonemergencies, the Tourist Zone Police are particularly helpful to visitors. **Tourist Zone Police** ☎ *787/726–7020 for Condado, 787/726–2981 for Isla Verde.*

Language Puerto Rico is officially bilingual, but Spanish dominates, particularly outside the tourist areas of San Juan. Although English is widely spoken, you'll probably want to take a Spanish phrase book along for your travels throughout the island.

Passport Requirements U.S. citizens don't need passports. You will not pass through immigration, but there is an agriculture inspection before you check in for your flight home.

Phones Most U.S. mobile phone users will not pay roaming charges in Puerto Rico; confirm with your company. Area codes are 787 and 939. Toll-free numbers (prefix 800, 888, or 877) are widely used, and many can be accessed from North America (and vice versa). To make a local call in Puerto Rico, you must dial 1, the area code, and the seven-digit number. For international calls, dial 011, the country code, the city code, and the number. Dial 00 for an international long-distance operator. Phone cards are widely available (most drugstores carry them).

Taxes Accommodations incur a tax: for hotels with casinos it's 11%, for other hotels it's 9%, and for government-approved paradores it's 7%. The tax, in addition to the standard 5%–12% service charge or resort fee applied by most hotels, can add a hefty 20% or more to your bill. Puerto Rico's sales tax is 7%.

Tipping Tips are expected, and appreciated, by restaurant waitstaff (15% to 20% if a service charge isn't included), hotel porters ($1 per bag), maids ($1 to $2 a day), and taxi drivers (15% to 18%).

ACCOMMODATIONS

If you want easy access to shopping, dining, and nightlife, then you should stay in San Juan, which also has decent—though by no means the island's best—beaches. Most other large, deluxe resorts are along the northeast coast, but there are a few along the southern coast. Rincón, in the west, has a concentration of resorts and great surfing. Other small inns and hotels are in the interior, including a few around El Yunque. Look to Vieques and Culebra if you want to find excellent beaches and little development. Many larger resorts in Puerto Rico charge resort fees, which are uncommon elsewhere in the Caribbean.

Big Hotels: San Juan's beaches are lined with large-scale hotels that include happening restaurants and splashy casinos. Most are spread out along Condado and Isla Verde beaches.

Paradores: Small inns (many offering home-style comida criolla cooking) are spread around the island, though they are rarely on the beach.

Upscale Beach Resorts: All over the island—but particularly along the north coast—large tourist resorts offer all the amenities along with a hefty dose of isolation. Just be prepared for expensive food and few off-resort restaurants nearby.

Hotel reviews have been shortened. For full information, visit Fodors.com.

WHAT IT COSTS IN U.S. DOLLARS

	$	$$	$$$	$$$$
Restaurants	under $12	$12–$20	$21–$30	over $30
Hotels	under $275	$275–$375	$376–$475	over $475

Restaurant prices are the average cost of a main course at dinner or, if dinner is not served, at lunch. Hotel prices are the lowest cost of a standard double room in high season.

VISITOR INFORMATION

Contact Puerto Rico Tourism Company ✉ *Ochoa Bldg., Calle Tanca and Calle Comercio, across from Pier 1, Old San Juan, San Juan* ☎ *787/721–2400* 🌐 *www.seepuertorico.com* ✉ *Luis Muñoz Marín International Airport, Carolina, San Juan* ☎ *787/791–1014.*

WEDDINGS

There are no residency requirements, but U.S. citizens must produce a birth certificate, as well as a driver's license or other state-issued photo ID. Both parties must appear together at the office to purchase a marriage license. A judge or any member of the clergy may then perform the ceremony. The fee is usually $150–$350. Most large hotels have marriage coordinators who can explain the necessary paperwork and help you complete it on time.

EXPLORING

OLD SAN JUAN

17

Old San Juan, the original city founded in 1521, contains carefully preserved examples of 16th- and 17th century Spanish colonial architecture. More than 400 buildings have been beautifully restored. Graceful wrought-iron and wooden balconies with lush hanging plants extend over narrow streets paved with *adoquines* (blue-gray stones originally used as ballast on Spanish ships). The Old City is partially enclosed by walls that date from 1633 and once completely surrounded it. Designated a U.S. National Historic Zone in 1950, Old San Juan is chockablock with shops, open-air cafés, homes, tree-shaded squares, monuments, and people. You can get an overview on a morning's stroll, which includes some steep climbs. However, if you plan to immerse yourself in history or to shop, you'll need a couple of days.

TOP ATTRACTIONS

FAMILY Fodor'sChoice ★ **Castillo San Cristóbal.** This huge stone fortress, built between 1634 and 1790, guarded the city from land attacks from the east. The largest Spanish fortification in the New World, San Cristóbal was known in the 17th and 18th centuries as the Gibraltar of the West Indies. Five freestanding structures divided by dry moats are connected by tunnels. You're free to explore the gun turrets (with cannon in situ), officers' quarters, re-created 18th-century barracks, and gloomy passageways. Along with El Morro, San Cristóbal is a National Historic Site administered by the U.S. Park Service; it's a World Heritage Site as well. Rangers conduct tours in Spanish and English. ✉ *Calle Norzagaray at Av. Muñoz Rivera, Old San Juan* ☎ *787/729–6777* 🌐 *www.nps.gov/saju* 🎫 *$5 includes admission to El Morro* ⏲ *Daily 9–6.*

FAMILY Fodor'sChoice ★ **Castillo San Felipe del Morro** (*El Morro*). At the northwestern tip of the Old City, El Morro ("the promontory") was built by the Spaniards between 1539 and 1786. Rising 140 feet above the sea, the massive six-level fortress was built to protect the port and has a commanding

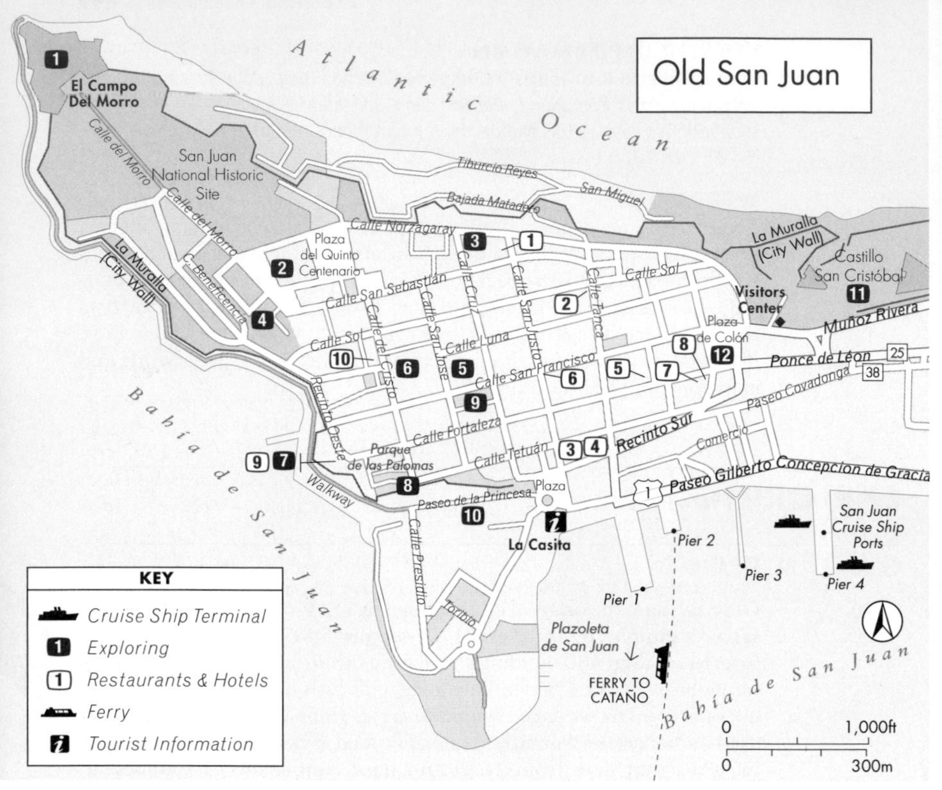

Exploring ▼

Alcaldía **5**
Capilla del Cristo **8**
Casa Blanca **4**
Castillo San Cristóbal **11**
Castillo San Felipe del Morro **1**
Catedral de San Juan Bautista **6**
Galería Nacional **3**
La Fortaleza **7**
Museo de las Américas **2**
Paseo de la Princesa **10**
Plaza de Armas **9**
Plaza de Colón **12**

Restaurants ▼

Aguaviva **8**
Café Cuatro Sombras **4**
Casa Cortés Chocobar **6**
Dragonfly **7**
La Fonda del Jibarito **2**
Marmalade **5**
Verde Mesa **3**
Waffle-era Tea Room **9**

Hotels ▼

El Convento **10**
Gallery Inn **1**

view of the harbor. It is a labyrinth of cannon batteries, ramps, barracks, turrets, towers, and tunnels, which you're free to wander. The cannon emplacement walls and the dank secret passageways are a wonder of engineering. A small but enlightening museum displays ancient Spanish guns and other armaments, military uniforms, and blueprints for Spanish forts in the Americas, although Castillo San Cristóbal has more extensive and impressive exhibits. There's also a gift shop. The fort is a National Historic Site administered by the U.S. Park Service and is a World Heritage Site as well. Various tours and a video are available in English. ✉ *Calle del Morro, Old San Juan* ☎ *787/729–6960* 🌐 *www.nps.gov/saju* 🎫 *$5 includes admission to Castillo San Cristóbal* ⏲ *Daily 9–6.*

La Fortaleza. Sitting atop the fortified city walls overlooking the harbor, La Fortaleza was built between 1533 and 1540 as a fortress, but it proved insufficient, mainly because it was built inside the bay. It was attacked numerous times and occupied twice, by the British in 1598 and the Dutch in 1625. When the city's other fortifications were finished, this became the governor's palace. Changes made over the past four centuries have resulted in the current eclectic yet eye-pleasing collection of marble and mahogany, medieval towers, and stained-glass galleries. Still the official residence of the island's governor, it is the Western Hemisphere's oldest executive mansion in continual use. Guided tours of the gardens and exterior are conducted several times a day in English and Spanish. Call ahead, as the schedule changes daily. Proper attire is required: no sleeveless shirts or very short shorts. Tours begin near the main gate in a yellow building called the Real Audiencia, housing the Oficina Estatal de Preservación Histórica. ✉ *Western end of Calle Fortaleza, Old San Juan* ☎ *787/721–7000* 🌐 *www.fortaleza.gobierno.pr* 🎫 *Free* ⏲ *Weekdays 9–4:30.*

17

Paseo de la Princesa. Built in the mid-19th century to honor the Spanish princess of Asturias, this street has a broad pedestrian walkway and is spruced up with flowers, trees, benches, and street lamps. Unfurling westward from Plaza del Inmigrante along the base of the fortified city walls, it leads to the Fuente Raíces, a striking fountain depicting the various ethnic groups of Puerto Rico. Take a seat and watch the boats zip across the water. Beyond the fountain is the beginning of Paseo del Morro, a well-paved shoreline path that hugs Old San Juan's walls and leads past the city gate at Calle San Juan and continues to the tip of the headland, beneath El Morro. ✉ *Paseo de la Princesa, Old San Juan.*

WORTH NOTING

Alcaldía. San Juan's city hall was built between 1602 and 1789. In 1841, extensive alterations made it resemble Madrid's city hall, with arcades, towers, balconies, and an inner courtyard. Renovations have refreshed the facade and some interior rooms, but the architecture remains true to its colonial style. Only the patios are open to public viewings. A municipal tourist information center and an art gallery with rotating exhibits are in the lobby. Call ahead to schedule a free tour. ✉ *153 Calle San Francisco, Plaza de Armas, Old San Juan* ☎ *787/480–2910* 🎫 *Free* ⏲ *Weekdays 8–4.*

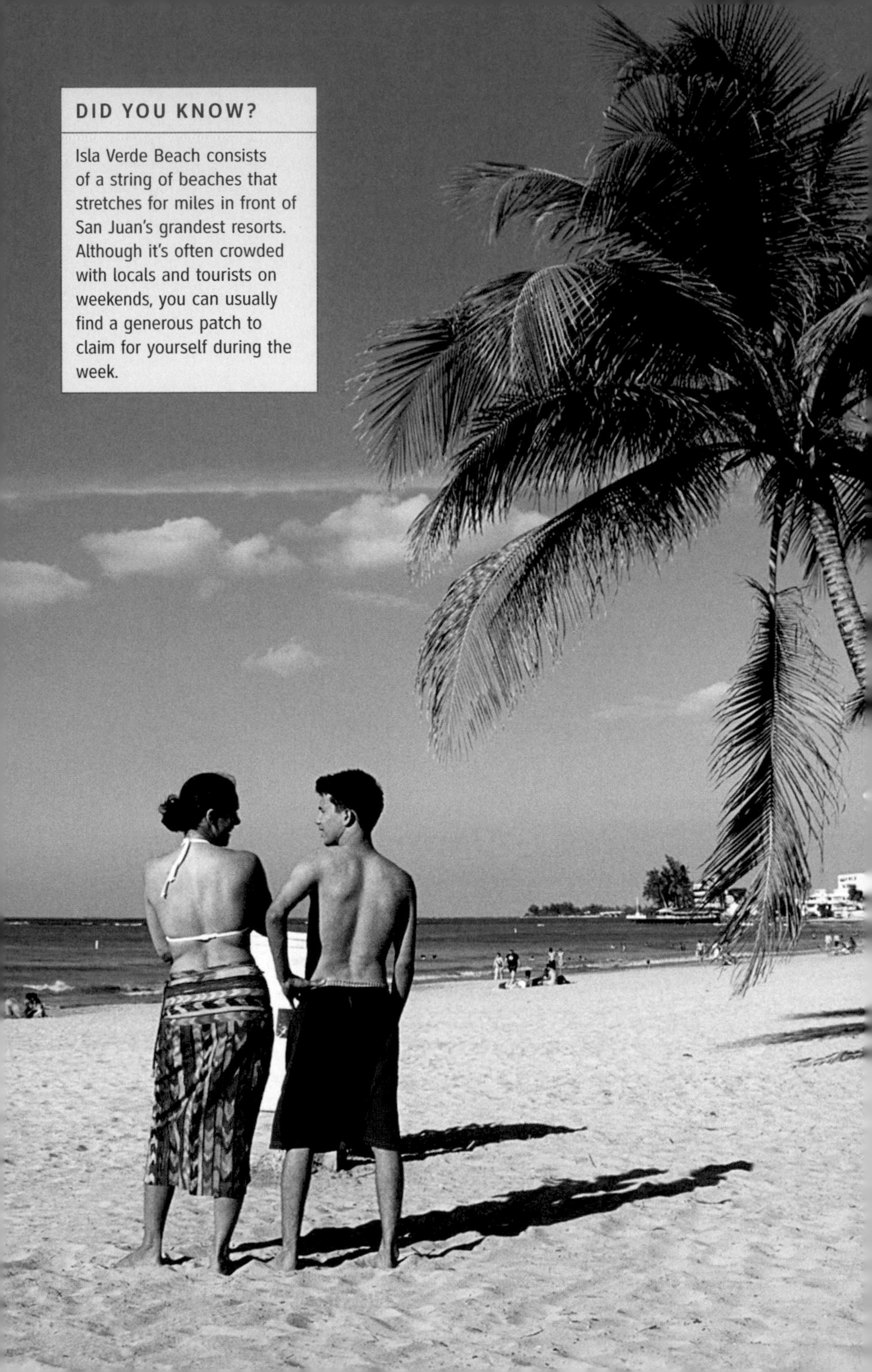
DID YOU KNOW?
Isla Verde Beach consists of a string of beaches that stretches for miles in front of San Juan's grandest resorts. Although it's often crowded with locals and tourists on weekends, you can usually find a generous patch to claim for yourself during the week.

Casa Blanca. The original structure here was a wooden house built in 1521 as a home for Ponce de León; he died in Cuba without ever living here. His descendants occupied the house's sturdier replacement, a lovely colonial mansion with tile floors and beamed ceilings, for more than 250 years. It was the home of the U.S. Army commander in Puerto Rico from the end of the Spanish-American War in 1898 to 1966. Several rooms decorated with colonial-era furnishings are open to the public. A guide will show you around, and then you can explore on your own. Don't miss the stairway descending from one of the bedrooms. (Despite local lore, this leads to a small room and not to a tunnel to nearby El Morro.) The lush garden, complete with watchtower, is a quiet place to unwind. ✉ *1 Calle San Sebastián, Old San Juan* ☎ *787/725–1454* 🌐 *www.icp.gobierno.pr* 🎫 *Free* 🕐 *Wed.–Sun. 8:30–4:15.*

Catedral de San Juan Bautista. The Catholic shrine of Puerto Rico had humble beginnings in the early 1520s as a thatch-roofed, wooden structure. After a hurricane destroyed the church, it was rebuilt in 1540, when it was given a graceful circular staircase and vaulted Gothic ceilings. Most of the work on the present cathedral, however, was done in the 19th century. The remains of Ponce de León are behind a marble tomb in the wall near the transept, on the north side. The trompe l'oeil work on the inside of the dome is breathtaking. Unfortunately, many of the other frescoes suffer from water damage. ✉ *151 Calle Cristo, Old San Juan* ☎ *787/722–0861* 🎫 *$1 donation suggested* 🕐 *Mon.–Sat. 9–5, Sun. 9–1.*

17

Museo de las Américas. On the second floor of the imposing former military barracks, Cuartel de Ballajá, this museum houses four permanent exhibits: Folk Arts, African Heritage, the Indian in America, and Conquest and Colonization. You'll also find a number of temporary exhibitions of works by regional and international artists. A wide range of handicrafts is available in the gift shop. ✉ *Calle Norzagaray and Calle del Morro, Old San Juan* ☎ *787/724–5052* 🌐 *www.museolasamericas.org* 🎫 *$3* 🕐 *Tues.–Sat. 9–noon and 1–4; Sun. noon–5.*

Plaza de Armas. The Old City's original main square was once used as military drilling grounds. Bordered by Calles San Francisco, Rafael Cordero, San José, and Cruz, it has a fountain with 19th-century statues representing the four seasons as well as a bandstand, a small café, and kiosk selling snacks and fruit frappés. The Alcaldía commands the north side. This is a popular, bustling meeting place, often filled with artists sketching caricatures, pedestrians in line at the food stands, and hundreds of pigeons waiting for handouts. ✉ *Calle San José, Old San Juan.*

Plaza de Colón. The Americas' tallest statue of Christopher Columbus stands atop a soaring column and fountain in this bustling Old San Juan square, kitty-corner to Castillo San Cristóbal. Once called St. James Square, it was renamed in 1893 to honor the 400th anniversary of Columbus's arrival in Puerto Rico. Bronze plaques on the statue's base relate episodes in his life. Local artisans often line the plaza, so it's a good place for souvenirs. Cool off with a fresh fruit frappé or smoothie at the kiosk. ✉ *Old San Juan.*

Hear your footsteps echo throughout Castillo San Felipe's vast network of tunnels, designed to amplify the sounds of approaching enemies.

GREATER SAN JUAN

Taxis, buses, *públicos* (shared vans), or a rental car are needed to reach the "new" San Juan. Avenidas Muñoz Rivera, Ponce de León, and Fernández Juncos are the main thoroughfares that cross Puerta de Tierra, east of Old San Juan, to the business and tourist districts of Santurce, Condado, Ocean Park, and Isla Verde. Dos Hermanos Bridge connects Puerta de Tierra with Miramar, Condado, and Isla Grande. Isla Grande Airport, from which you can take short hops, is on the bay side of the bridge. On the other side, the Condado Lagoon is bordered by Avenida Ashford, which goes past the high-rise Condado hotels, and Avenida Baldorioty de Castro Expreso, which barrels east to the airport and beyond. Due south of the lagoon is Miramar, a residential area with fashionable turn-of-the-20th-century homes and a few hotels and great restaurants. Isla Verde, with its glittering beachfront hotels, casinos, discos, and public beach, is to the east, near the airport.

TOP ATTRACTIONS

Museo de Arte Contemporáneo de Puerto Rico. This Georgian-style structure, once a public school, displays a dynamic range of works by established and up-and-coming Latin American artists. Many works have strong political messages, including pointed commentaries on Puerto Rico's status as a commonwealth. Only part of the permanent collection's more than 900 works is on display at a time, but it might be anything from ceramics to videos. ✉ *1220 Av. Ponce de León, at Av. R.H. Todd, Santurce* ☎ *787/977–4030* 🎟 *$5* 🕓 *Tue.–Fri. 10–4, Sat. 11–4, Sun. 1–5.*

Continued on page 708

WALKING OLD SAN JUAN

Old San Juan is Puerto Rico's quintessential colonial neighborhood. Narrow streets and plazas are still enclosed by thick fortress walls, and bougainvillea bowers spill over exquisite facades. A walk along streets paved with slate-blue cobblestones leads past colonial mansions, ancient churches, and intriguing museums and galleries. Vivacious restaurants and bars that teem with life young and old are always nearby, making it easy to refuel and reinvigorate anytime during your stroll.

by Christopher P. Baker

left, strolling down Calle del Cristo; top right, a view from El Morro; bottom right, dancers in front of Castillo San Cristóbal

A STROLL THROUGH OLD SAN JUAN

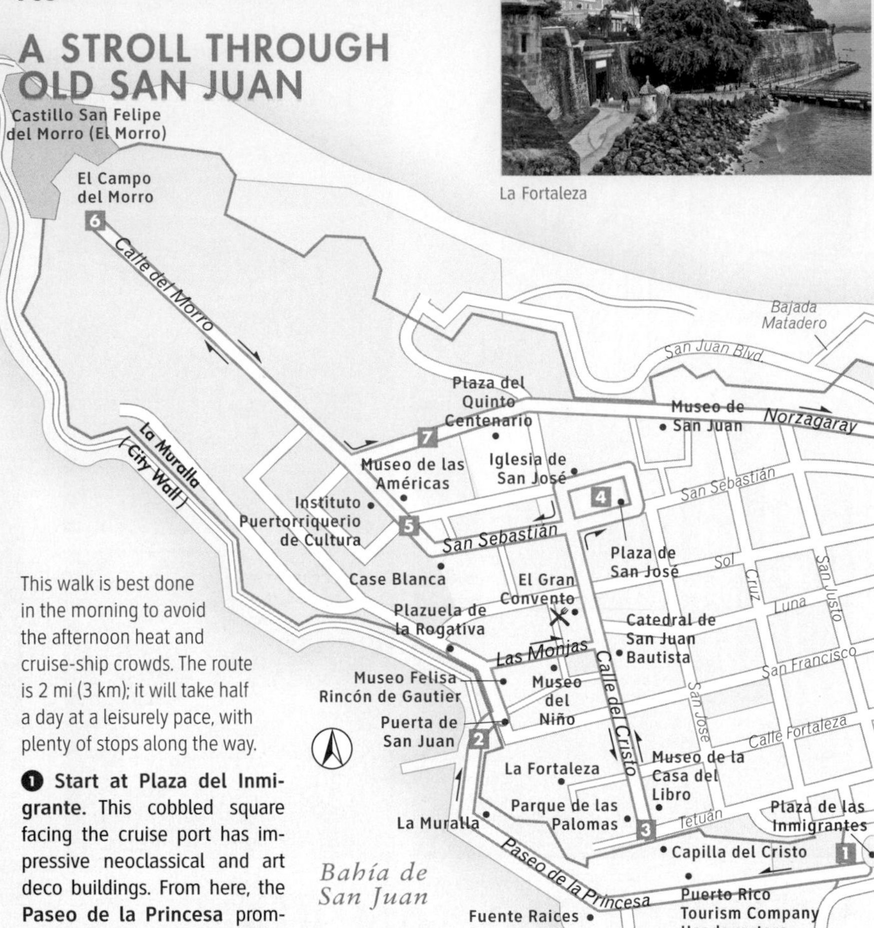

La Fortaleza

This walk is best done in the morning to avoid the afternoon heat and cruise-ship crowds. The route is 2 mi (3 km); it will take half a day at a leisurely pace, with plenty of stops along the way.

❶ **Start at Plaza del Inmigrante.** This cobbled square facing the cruise port has impressive neoclassical and art deco buildings. From here, the **Paseo de la Princesa** promenade unfurls west beneath the ancient city wall, **La Muralla.** Artisans set up stalls under the palms on weekends. Midway along the brick-paved walkway, stop to admire the **Fuente Raices** monument and fountain: dolphins cavort at the feet of figures representing Puerto Rico's indigenous, Spanish, and African peoples.

Puerta de San Juan

❷ **Pass through the Puerta de San Juan.** This fortified entrance in La Muralla was built in 1520 and still retains its massive wooden gates, creaky on their ancient hinges. Immediately beyond, turn left and ascend to **Plazuela de la Rogativa**, a tiny plaza where a contemporary statue recalls the torch-lit procession that thwarted an English invasion in 1797. The harbor views are fantastic. Then, walk east one block to reach the **Catedral de San Juan Bautista**, the neoclassical 19th-century cathedral containing the mausoleum of Ponce de León.

❸ **Head south on Calle del Cristo.** Sloping gradually, this lovely cobbled street is lined with beautifully restored colonial mansions housing cafés, galleries, and boutiques. Pass-

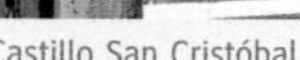

Castillo San Cristóbal

Calle del Cristo

Catedral de San Juan Bautista

Castillo San Felipe del Morro

ing Calle Fortaleza, note **La Fortaleza,** the official residence of the Puerto Rican Governor at the end of the street. Calle del Cristo ends at **Capilla del Cristo**, a chapel adorned within by silver *milagros* (token requests).

❹ **Return via Calle del Cristo and continue to Plaza de San José.** Catercorner to the cathedral you'll find **El Gran Convento**, a former convent turned hotel, with an excellent restaurant, tapas bar, and café. At **Plaza de San José** visit the **Iglesia de San José**, a simple church dating from 1532.

❺ **Walk west on Calle San Sebastián.** This narrow street with colonial mansions painted in vibrant pastels ends at the gleaming white **Casa Blanca**. The oldest continually occupied residence in the Americas was originally the home of Ponce de León. Today it's a delightful museum furnished with period pieces. The garden is a tranquil spot for contemplation.

❻ **Follow Calle del Morro north.** One block from Casa Blanca you'll emerge upon a broad grassy headland—the Campo del Morro—popular with kite-flying families. It's skewered by an arrow-straight gravel path that aims at the imposing **Castillo San Felipe del Morro (El Morro)**, guarding the harbor entrance. Allow one-hour to roam the small museum, turrets, labyrinthine tunnels, and six levels of ramparts soaring 140 feet above the ocean.

❼ **Retrace your steps and turn left on Calle Norzagaray.** This street runs atop the Atlantic shoreline, offering sweeping ocean vistas. On your right you'll pass the **Plaza del Quinto Centenario**, pinned by an impressive statue: the *Tótem Telúrico.* Beyond, stroll past the Convento de los Dominicos to reach the **Museo de San Juan**. Housed in a former market, it traces the city's history and displays works by Puerto Rico's master painters.

❽ **Continue east to Castillo San Cristóbal.** Spanning 27 acres, this multitiered fortress was completed in 1771 with mighty bulwarks that protected the city from eastern attack by land. It features superb historical exhibits and reenactments by soldiers in period costumes.

❾ **Exit the castle, turn south and walk one block to Plaza de Colón**, This leafy square is lined with excellent cafés and restaurants where you can rest your feet and enjoy a great meal.

Fodor's Choice ★ **Museo de Arte de Puerto Rico.** One of the Caribbean's biggest museums, this beautiful neoclassical building was once the San Juan Municipal Hospital. The collection of Puerto Rican art starts with the colonial era, when most art was commissioned for churches. Works by José Campeche, the island's first great painter, include his masterpiece, *Immaculate Conception,* finished in 1794. Also well represented is Francisco Oller y Cestero, who was the first to move beyond religious subjects to paint local scenes. Another room has works by artists inspired by Oller. The original building, built in the 1920s, proved too small to house the collection; a newer east wing is dominated by a five-story stained-glass window by local artist Eric Tabales. The museum also has a beautiful garden with native flora and a 400-seat theater with a remarkable hand-crocheted lace curtain. ✉ *299 Av. José de Diego, Santurce* ☎ *787/977–6277* 🌐 *www.mapr.org* 🎫 *$6; free Wed. 2–8* 🕘 *Tues. and Thurs.–Sat. 10–5, Wed. 10–8, Sun. 11–6.*

WORTH NOTING

El Capitolio. The white-marble Capitol, a fine example of Italian Renaissance style, dates from 1929. The grand rotunda, which can be seen from all over San Juan, was completed in the late 1990s. Fronted by eight Corinthian columns, it's a dignified home for the commonwealth's constitution. Although the Senate and House of Representatives have offices in the more modern buildings on either side, the Capitol is where the legislators meet. Guided tours, which last about an hour and include the rotunda, are by appointment only. ✉ *Av. Constitución, Puerta de Tierra* ☎ *787/724–2030, 787/721–5200 guided tours* 🎫 *Free* 🕘 *Weekdays 8:30–4:30.*

Museo de Historia, Antropología y Arte. The Universidad de Puerto Rico's small Museum of History, Anthropology and Art offers rotating exhibitions in three areas. Its archaeological and historical collection covers the Native American influence on the island and the Caribbean, the colonial era, and the history of slavery. There's also a small collection of Egyptian antiquities. Art holdings include a range of Puerto Rican popular, graphic, folk, and fine art; the museum's prize exhibit is the painting *El Velorio* (*The Wake*), by the 19th-century artist Francisco Oller. If you're looking to see something in particular, call before you go, as only a small portion of the collection is on display at a time. Guided tours in English are available; call for reservations. ✉ *Universidad de Puerto Rico, Av. Ponce de León, Río Piedras* ☎ *787/763–3939* 🎫 *Free* 🕘 *Mon.–Tues. and Thurs.–Fri. 9–4:30, Wed. 9–9, Sun. 11:30–5.*

SAN JUAN ENVIRONS

WORTH NOTING

Casa Bacardí Visitor Center. Exiled from Cuba, the Bacardí family built a small rum distillery here in the 1950s. Today it's the world's largest, able to produce 100,000 gallons of spirits a day and 21 million cases a year. A basic tour of the visitor center includes one free drink, or you can opt for a mixology class or rum tasting. If you don't want to drive, you can take a ferry from Pier 2 for 50¢ and then a *público* (public van service) from the ferry pier to the factory for about $3 per person.

✉ Bay View Industrial Park, Rte. 165, Km 2.6, at Rte. 888, Cataño ☎ 787/788–1500 🌐 www.casabacardi.org 🎟 Tour $12; class or tasting $35 ⏲ Mon.–Sat. 9–6, last tour at 4:15; Sun. 10–5, last tour at 3:45.

EASTERN PUERTO RICO

EL YUNQUE

FAMILY Fodor's Choice ★ El Yunque is the only tropical rain forest in the U.S. National Forest System, spanning 28,000 acres, reaching an elevation of more than 3,500 feet, and receiving an estimated 200–240 inches of rain each year. The forest's 13 hiking trails are extremely well maintained; many are easy to navigate and less than 1 mile (1½ km) long. It's about 73°F year-round, but expect rain nearly every day. Post-shower times bring the best bird-watching. For easy parking and fewer crowds, arrive early in the day, although the park rarely gets crowded by U.S. National Park standards.

Carve out some time to stop at the cathedral-like **El Portal Visitor Center** (*✉ Rte. 191, Km 4.3, off Rte. 3 ☎ 787/888–1880 🌐 www.fs.usda.gov/elyunque 🎟 $4 ⏲ Daily 9–4:30*). Enter via an elevated walkway that transports visitors across the forest canopy, 60 feet above the ground. Signs identify and explain the birds, animals, and other treasures seen among the treetops. Below the walkway, there's a ground-level nature trail with stunning views of the lower forest and coastal plain. Inside the center, interactive exhibits explain the El Yunque National Forest's history, topography, flora, and fauna. The facility also has a well-stocked bookstore and gift shop.

17

The trails on the north side of El Yunque, the park's main tourist hub, tend toward folks with minimal or no hiking experience. There are several short trails (about ½ mile [.8 km]) that are completely paved. On the south side, expect fewer people and moderate to challenging hikes. These trails are not maintained as well as the marked trails found lower in the forest. Regardless of where you go, you'll be immersed in the sounds, smells, and scenic landscape of the park. For avid outdoor adventurers, it's possible to hike between the north and south sides of El Yunque. If you prefer to see the sights from a car, as many people do, simply follow Route 191 as it winds into the mountains, and stop at several observation points along the way.

FAJARDO

Founded in 1772, Fajardo was once known as a port where pirates stocked up on supplies. It later developed into a fishing community and an area where sugarcane flourished. (There are still cane fields on the city's fringes.) Today it's a hub for the yachts that use its marinas; the divers who head to its good offshore sites; and the day-trippers who travel by catamaran, ferry, or plane to the offshore islands of Culebra and Vieques. With the most significant docking facilities on the island's eastern side, Fajardo is often congested and difficult to navigate.

Reserva Natural Las Cabezas de San Juan. The 316-acre reserve on a headland north of Fajardo is owned by the nonprofit Conservation Trust of Puerto Rico. You ride in open-air trolleys and wander down boardwalks through seven ecosystems, including lagoons, mangrove swamps, and dry-forest areas. Green iguanas skitter across paths, and guides identify other endangered species. A half-hour hike down a wooden walkway brings you to the mangrove-lined **Laguna Grande**, where bioluminescent microorganisms glow at night. The restored **Fajardo Lighthouse** is the final stop on the tour; its Spanish-colonial tower has been in operation since 1882, making it Puerto Rico's second-oldest lighthouse. The first floor houses ecological displays, and a winding staircase leads to an observation deck. The only way to see the reserve is on a guided tour; reservations are required through the trust website. ✉ *Rte. 987, Km 6* ☎ *787/722–5882* 🌐 *www.paralanaturaleza.org* 🎫 *$10.*

VIEQUES AND CULEBRA

VIEQUES

This island off Puerto Rico's east coast is famed for its Playa Sun Bay, a gorgeous stretch of sand with picnic facilities and shade trees. In 2003 the U.S. Navy withdrew its military operations and turned over two-thirds of Vieques to the local government. It's being transformed into the Vieques National Wildlife Refuge. Vieques has two communities—Isabel Segunda, where the ferries dock, and the smaller Esperanza. Both have restaurants and hotels with surprising sophistication.

Fodor's Choice ★ **Puerto Mosquito Bioluminescent Bay.** East of Esperanza, this is one of the world's best spots for a glow-in-the-dark experience with undersea dinoflagellates. Local operators offer kayak trips or excursions on nonpolluting boats to see the bay's microorganisms, which light up when the water around them is agitated. Look behind your boat at the twinkling wake. Even the fish that swim through and jump from the water bear an eerie glow. The high concentration of dinoflagellates sets the bay apart from other spots (including in Puerto Rico) that are home to these microorganisms. The bay is at its best when there's little or no moonlight; rainy nights are beautiful, too, because raindrops hitting the water produce ricochets that shimmer like diamonds. ✉ *Unpaved roads off Rte. 997, Vieques.*

CULEBRA

Culebra is known around the world for its curvaceous coastline. Playa Flamenco, the tiny island's most famous stretch of sand, is considered one of the best beaches in the world. If Playa Flamenco gets too crowded, as it often does around Easter and Christmas, you can find many other nearly deserted beaches. There's archaeological evidence that Taíno and Carib peoples lived on Culebra long before the late-15th-century arrival of the Spanish, who didn't bother laying claim to it until 1886. Its dearth of freshwater made it an unattractive location for a settlement. Although the island now has modern conveniences, its pace seems little changed from a century ago. There's only one town, Dewey, named after U.S. Admiral George Dewey. When the sun goes down, Culebra winds down as well. But during the day it's a delightful place to stake out a spot on Playa Flamenco or Playa Zoni and read, swim, or search for shells. So what causes stress on the island? Nada.

SOUTHERN PUERTO RICO

Bosque Estatal de Guánica (*Guánica State Forest*). This 9,900-acre United Nations Biosphere Reserve is a great place for hiking. An outstanding example of a tropical dry coastal forest, it has some 700 species of plants, from the prickly-pear cactus to the gumbo-limbo tree, and offers superb bird-watching; its more than 100 species include the pearly-eyed thrasher, lizard cuckoo, and nightjar.

The popular **Ballena Trail,** which begins at the ranger station on Route 334, is an easy 1¼-mile (2-km) walk that follows a partially paved road past a mahogany plantation to a dry plain covered with stunted cactus. A sign reading "Guayacán centenario" leads you to an extraordinary guayacán tree with a six-foot-wide trunk. The moderately difficult, 3½-mile (5½-km) **Fuerte Trail** leads to an old fort built by the Spanish Armada. It was destroyed in the Spanish-American War in 1898, but you can see ruins of the old observatory tower.

In addition to using the main entrance on Route 334, you can enter on Route 333, which skirts the forest's southwestern quadrant, or try the less explored western section, off Route 325. ✉ *Rte. 334, Guánica* ☎ *787/821–5706* 🎫 *Free* ⏲ *Daily 8:30–4:30.*

PONCE

The island's second-largest urban area, Ponce shines in 19th-century style with pink-marble-bordered sidewalks, painted trolleys, and horse-drawn carriages. Stroll around the main square, the Plaza de las Delicias, with its perfectly pruned India-laurel fig trees, graceful fountains, gardens, and park benches. View the Catedral de Nuestra Señora de la Guadalupe (Our Lady of Guadalupe Cathedral), perhaps even attend the 6 am Mass, and walk down Calles Isabel and Cristina to see turn-of-the-20th-century wooden houses with wrought-iron balconies.

TOP ATTRACTIONS

Castillo Serrallés. This lovely Spanish-style villa—so massive that townspeople dubbed it a castle—was built in the 1930s for Ponce's wealthiest family, the makers of Don Q rum. Guided tours provide a glimpse into the lifestyle of a sugar baron, and a permanent exhibit explains the area's sugarcane and rum industries. The dining room, with original hand-carved furnishings, and the extensive garden, with sculptured bushes and a shimmering reflection pool, are highlights. A large cross looming over the house is an observatory; from the top, you can see the Caribbean. ✉ *17 El Vigía, El Vigía* ☎ *787/259–1774* 🌐 *www.castilloserralles.org* 🎫 *$8.50, $12.80 with Japanese garden and cross* ⏲ *Wed.–Sun. 9:30–5:30.*

FAMILY Fodor's Choice ★ **Hacienda Buena Vista.** Built by Salvador de Vives in 1838, this was one of the area's largest coffee plantations. It's a technological marvel—water from the nearby Río Canas was funneled into narrow brick channels that could be diverted to perform any number of tasks, including turning the waterwheel. (Seeing the two-story wheel slowly begin to turn is fascinating, especially for kids.) Nearby is the two-story manor house, with a kitchen dominated by a massive hearth and furniture that hints at life on a coffee plantation nearly 150 years ago. In 1987 the plantation

17

was restored by the Puerto Rican Conservation Trust, which leads four tours a day (at least one in English) by reservation only (call several days ahead). A gift shop sells coffee beans and other souvenirs. Allow an hour to drive the winding road from Ponce. ✉ *Rte. 123, Km 16.8, Sector Corral Viejo* ☎ *787/722–5882 weekdays* 🌐 *www.paralanaturaleza.org* 🎫 *$10* ⏲ *Wed.–Sun., tours at 10, 1:30, and 3:30.*

Fodor's Choice ★ **Museo de Arte de Ponce.** Designed by Edward Durrell Stone, who also designed the original Museum of Modern Art in New York City and the Kennedy Center in Washington, D.C., Ponce's art museum is easily identified by the hexagonal galleries on the second story. The museum has one of the best art collections in Latin America, which is why residents of San Juan frequently make the trip. The 4,500-piece collection includes works by famous Puerto Rican artists such as Francisco Oller, represented by a lovely landscape called *Hacienda Aurora*. European works include paintings by Peter Paul Rubens and Thomas Gainsborough as well as pre-Raphaelite paintings, particularly the mesmerizing *Flaming June*, by Frederick Leighton, which has become the museum's unofficial symbol. The museum also offers special exhibits, three sculpture gardens, and Restaurant Al Sur. ✉ *2325 Blvd. Luis A. Ferre Aguayo, Sector Santa María* ☎ *787/840–1510* 🌐 *www.museoarteponce.org* 🎫 *$6* ⏲ *Mon. and Wed.–Sat. 10–5, Sun. noon–5.*

FAMILY Fodor's Choice ★ **Parque de Bombas.** After El Morro in Old San Juan, this distinctive red-and-black-stripe building may be the second-most-photographed structure in Puerto Rico. Built in 1882 as a pavilion for an agricultural and industrial fair, it was converted the following year into a firehouse. Today it's a museum tracing the history—and glorious feats—of Ponce's fire brigade. Kids love the antique fire truck on the lower level. Short tours in English and Spanish are given on the hour starting at 10; you can sign up for free trolley tours of the historic downtown here. Helpful tourism officials staff a small information desk inside. ✉ *Plaza de las Delicias, Ponce Centro* ☎ *787/284–3338* 🌐 *www.visitponce.com* 🎫 *Free* ⏲ *Daily 9–5:30.*

WORTH NOTING

Centro Ceremonial Indígena de Tibes (*Tibes Indian Ceremonial Center*). This archeological site, discovered after flooding from a tropical storm in 1975, is the island's most important. Dating from AD 300–700, it includes nine playing fields used for a ritual ball game that some think was similar to soccer. The fields are bordered by smooth stones, some of which are engraved with petroglyphs that might have ceremonial or astronomical significance. In the eye-catching *Plaza de Estrella* (Plaza of the Star), stones are arranged in a pattern resembling a rising sun, perhaps used to chart the seasons. A village with thatched huts has been reconstructed. Visit the small museum before taking a walking tour of the site. ✉ *Rte. 503, Km 2.5, Barrio Tibes* ☎ *787/840–2255, 787/840–5685* 🌐 *www.ponce.inter.edu/tibes/tibes.html* 🎫 *$3* ⏲ *Tues.–Sun. 9–3.*

Museo de la Historia de Ponce. Housed in two adjoining neoclassical mansions, this museum includes 10 rooms with exhibits covering the city's residents, from Taíno Indians to Spanish settlers to the mix of the present. Guided tours in English and Spanish give an overview of the city's

Today it's a museum, but for more than 100 years Parque de Bombas served as Ponce's main firehouse.

history. Though descriptions are mostly in Spanish, displays of clothing from different eras are interesting. ✉ *53 Calle Isabel, at Calle Mayor* ☎ *787/844–7071* 🎟 *Free* ⏲ *Tues.–Sun. 9–4.*

SAN GERMÁN

Around San Germán's (population 39,000) two main squares—Plazuela Santo Domingo and Plaza Francisco Mariano Quiñones (named for an abolitionist)—are buildings done in every conceivable style of architecture found on the island, including mission, Victorian, creole, and Spanish colonial. The city's tourist office offers a free, guided trolley tour. Students and professors from the Inter-American University often fill the center's bars and cafés.

Capilla de Porta Coeli (*Heaven's Gate Chapel*). One of the oldest religious buildings in the Americas, this mission-style chapel overlooks the long, rectangular Plazuela de Santo Domingo. It's not a grand building, but its position at the top of a stone stairway gives it a noble air. Queen Isabel Segunda decreed that the Dominicans should build a church and monastery in San Germán, so a rudimentary building was erected in 1609, replaced in 1692 by the structure seen today. (Sadly, most of the monastery was demolished in 1866, leaving only a vestige of its facade.) The chapel functions as a museum of religious art, displaying painted wooden statuary by Latin American and Spanish artists. ✉ *East end of Plazuela Santo Domingo* ☎ *787/892–5845* 🎟 *$3* ⏲ *Weekdays 9–noon and 1–4:30.*

CENTRAL PUERTO RICO

Fodor's Choice ★ **Arecibo Observatory.** Hidden among pine-covered hills, this observatory is home to the world's largest radar-radio telescope. Operated by the National Astronomy and Ionosphere Center of Cornell University, the 20-acre dish lies in a 563-foot-deep sinkhole in the karst landscape. If the 600-ton platform hovering eerily over the dish looks familiar, it may from the movie *Contact*. You can walk around the viewing platform and explore two levels of interactive exhibits on planetary systems, meteors, and weather phenomena in the visitor center. There's also a gift shop. Note that the trail leading to the observatory is extremely steep. Those with difficulty walking or a medical condition can ask at the gate about a courtesy shuttle. ✉ *Rte. 625, Km 3, Arecibo* ☎ *787/878–2612* 🌐 *www.naic.edu* 🎫 *$10* ⏲ *Mid-Jan.–May and Aug.–mid-Dec., Wed.–Sun. 9–4; June–July and mid-Dec.–mid-Jan., daily 9–4.*

FAMILY Fodor's Choice ★ **Parque de las Cavernas del Río Camuy.** This 268-acre park contains one of the world's largest cave networks. After watching an introductory film, you take a tram down a trail shaded by bamboo and banana trees to Cueva Clara, where stalactites and stalagmites turn the entrance into a toothy grin. Hour-long guided tours in English and Spanish take you on foot through the 180-foot-high cave teeming with wildlife. You're likely to see blue-eyed river crabs and long-legged tarantulas. Elusive bats don't come out until dark, but you can feel their heat at the cave entrance. The visit ends with a tram ride to the Tres Pueblos sinkhole, where the world's third-longest underground river passes from one cave to another. Tours are first-come, first-served; arrive early on weekends, when locals join the crowds. There's a picnic area, cafeteria, and gift shop. ✉ *Rte. 129, Km 18.9, Camuy* ☎ *787/898–3100* 🌐 *www.parquesnacionalespr.com* 🎫 *$15* ⏲ *Wed.–Sun. 8:30–5; last tour at 3:30.*

WESTERN PUERTO RICO

MAYAGÜEZ

With a population of slightly more than 100,000, this is the largest city on Puerto Rico's west coast. Although bypassed by the mania for restoration that has spruced up Ponce and Old San Juan, Mayagüez is graced by some lovely turn-of-the-20th-century architecture, such as the landmark art deco Teatro Yagüez and the Plaza de Colón.

FAMILY **Zoológico de Puerto Rico.** Puerto Rico's only zoo is just north of downtown. Its 45-foot-tall aviary lets you walk through a rain-forest environment as tropical birds fly overhead. There's also a butterfly park where you can let brilliant blue morphos land on you, and an arthropodarium where you can get up close and personal with spiders and their kin. Video monitors in the floor show the bugs that normally get trampled underfoot. The older section of the 45-acre park has undergone an extensive renovation, with most cages replaced by fairly natural-looking environments. A popular resident is Mundi, a female elephant who arrived as a baby more than two decades ago. There are also plenty of lions, tigers, and even bears. ✉ *Rte. 108, north of Rte. 65, Miradero*

☎ *787/834–8110* 🌐 *www.parquesnacionalespr.com* 🎫 *$13; parking $3* ⏲ *Wed.–Sun. 8:30–4.*

RINCÓN

Jutting into the ocean along the rugged western coast, Rincón, meaning "corner" in Spanish, may have gotten its name because it's tucked into a bend of the coastline. Some, however, trace the name to Gonzalo Rincón, a 16th-century landowner who let poor families live on his land. Whatever the truth, the name suits the town, which is like a little world unto itself.

Though now home to resorts, including the luxurious Horned Dorset Primavera—Puerto Rico's only Relais & Chateaux property—Rincón remains laid-back. The town is still a mecca for wave-seekers, particularly surfers from the East Coast of the United States, who often prefer the relatively quick flight to Aguadilla's airport instead of the long haul to the Pacific. One of Rincón's greatest attractions is the diving and snorkeling at nearby Desecheo Island, but the town caters to all sorts of travelers, from budget-conscious surfers to families to honeymooners seeking romance.

BEACHES

In Puerto Rico the Foundation for Environmental Education, a nonprofit agency, designates Blue Flag beaches. They have to meet 27 criteria, focusing on water quality, the presence of a trained staff, and the availability of facilities such as water fountains and restrooms. Surprisingly, two such beaches are in San Juan: Balneario El Escambrón, in Puerta de Tierra, and Balneario de Carolina, in Isla Verde. The government maintains 13 *balnearios* (public beaches), which are gated and equipped with dressing rooms, lifeguards, parking, and, in some cases, picnic tables, playgrounds, and camping facilities.

SAN JUAN

The city's beaches can get crowded, especially on weekends. There's free access to all of them, but parking can be an issue in the peak sun hours—arriving early or in the late afternoon is a safer bet.

FAMILY **Balneario de Carolina.** When people talk about a "beautiful Isla Verde beach," this is it. East of Isla Verde, this Blue Flag beach is so close to the airport that leaves rustle when planes take off. Thanks to an offshore reef, the surf is not as strong as other nearby beaches, so it's good for families. There's plenty of room to spread out underneath the palm and almond trees, and there are picnic tables and barbecue grills. Though there's a charge for parking, there's not always someone to take the money. On weekends, the beach is crowded; get here early to nab parking. **Amenities:** lifeguards; parking (fee); showers; toilets. **Best for:** swimming; walking. ✉ *Ave. Los Gobernadores, Carolina* ☎ *787/791–2410* 🎫 *$3 parking* ⏲ *Tues.–Sun. 8–5.*

FAMILY **Balneario El Escambrón.** In Puerta de Tierra, this government-run beach has a patch of honey-colored sand shaded by coconut palms. An offshore reef generally makes surf gentle, so it's favored by families. Nearby restaurants make picnicking easy. **Amenities:** food and drink;

lifeguards, parking (fee); showers; toilets. **Best for:** swimming; walking. ✉ *Ave. Muñoz Rivera, Puerta de Tierra* *$5 parking* ⏲ *Daily 8–5:30.*

EASTERN PUERTO RICO

FAMILY **Balneario Seven Seas.** One of Puerto Rico's prized Blue Flag beaches, this long stretch of powdery sand near the Reserva Natural Las Cabezas de San Juan has calm, clear waters that are perfect for swimming. There are plenty of picnic tables, as well as restaurants just outside the gates. **Amenities:** food and drink; parking (fee); showers; toilets. **Best for:** swimming. ✉ *Rte. 195, Km. 4.8, Las Croabas* ☎ *787/863–8180* 🌐 *www.parquesnacionalespr.com* *$5 parking* ⏲ *Apr.–Aug., daily 8:30–6; Sept.–Mar., Wed.–Sun. 8:30–5.*

FAMILY **Luquillo Beach** (*Balneario La Monserrate*). Signs refer to this gentle beach off Route 3 as Balneario La Monserrate, but everyone simply calls it Luquillo Beach. Lined with colorful lifeguard stations and shaded by soaring palm trees, it's a magnet for families and has picnic areas and 60+ kiosks serving fritters and drinks—a local hangout. Lounge chairs and umbrellas are available to rent, as are kayaks and Jet Skis. Its most distinctive facility is the Mar Sin Barreras (Sea Without Barriers), a low-sloped ramp into the water that allows wheelchair users to take a dip. Unfortunately, the beach has become a crowded, and littered, party beach. **Amenities:** food and drink; lifeguards, parking (fee); showers; toilets; water sports. **Best for:** partiers; swimming; walking. ✉ *Off Rte. 3, Luquillo* ☎ *787/889–5871* 🌐 *www.parquesnacionalespr.com* *$4 per car* ⏲ *Wed.–Sun. 8:30–5.*

VIEQUES AND CULEBRA

Balneario Sun Bay. Just east of Esperanza, this mile-long stretch of sand skirts a perfect crescent-shape bay. Dotted with picnic tables, this beach gets packed on holidays and weekends. On weekdays, when crowds are thin, you might see wild horses grazing among the palm trees. Parking is $2, but often there is no one at the gate to take your money. **Amenities:** food and drink; parking (fee); showers; toilets. **Best for:** snorkeling; swimming; walking. ✉ *Rte. 997, Esperanza, Vieques* ☎ *787/741–8198* 🌐 *www.parquesnacionalespr.com* *$2 parking* ⏲ *Wed.–Sun. 8:30–5.*

Playa Caracas (*Red Beach*). One of the first stretches of sand east of Esperanza, this well-maintained beach boasts covered cabanas for lounging. Less rustic than other nearby beaches, it is sheltered from waves. **Amenities:** parking (free), toilets. **Best for:** snorkeling; swimming; walking. ✉ *Off Rte. 997, Vieques.*

FAMILY Fodor's Choice ★ **Playa Flamenco.** Consistently ranked one of the most beautiful beaches in the world, this beach has snow-white sands, turquoise waters, and lush hills rising on all sides. During the week, it's pleasantly uncrowded; on weekends it fills up with day-trippers from the mainland. With kiosks selling simple dishes and vendors for lounge-chair and umbrella rentals, it's easy to make a day of it. There's great snorkeling past the old dock. Tanks on the northern end of the beach are a reminder that the area was once a military base. **Amenities:** food and drink; parking (free); showers; toilets. **Best For:** snorkeling; swimming; walking. ✉ *Rte. 251, west of the airport, Culebra* ☎ *787/742–0700.*

SOUTHERN PUERTO RICO

Isla Caja de Muertos (*Coffin Island*). Named for its shape, this island, which stretches for 2 miles 5 miles off the coast, has the best beaches near Ponce and some of the best snorkeling in southern Puerto Rico, second only to La Parguera. Due to hawksbill turtle nesting (May–December), the island is protected by the Reserva Natural Caja de Muertos, but you can still swim, snorkel, and dive here. A 30-minute hike across the island leads to a small lighthouse dating to 1887. Scheduled boats leave La Guancha Friday–Sunday at 8:30 am, daily in high season. Pack in what you need (drinks and food) and pack out your garbage. **Amenities:** toilets. **Best for:** snorkeling; swimming; walking. ✉ *Boats leave from La Guancha, at the end of Rte. 14, Ponce.*

WESTERN PUERTO RICO

Balneario de Rincón. Families enjoy the tranquil waters, playground, and shelters for seaside picnics. The beach is within walking distance of the center of town. **Amenities:** parking (free); showers; toilets. **Best for:** sunset; swimming. ✉ *Calle Caubija, Rincón.*

Playa Crashboat. Here you'll find the colorful fishing boats pictured on postcards. Named for rescue boats used when nearby Ramey Air Force Base was in operation, the beach has soft, sugary sand and water as smooth as glass. A food stand serves the catch of the day with cold beer. Right before you cross the bridge leading to the beach, a lookout point on your left makes a great photo op. **Amenities:** food and drink; parking (free); showers; toilets. **Best for:** partiers; snorkeling; swimming. ✉ *End of Rte. 458, off Rte. 107, Aguadilla.*

WHERE TO EAT

In cosmopolitan San Juan, European, Asian, Middle Eastern, and chic fusion eateries vie for attention with family-owned restaurants specializing in seafood or *comida criolla* (creole cooking). Many of the most innovative chefs here have restaurants in the city's large hotels, but don't be shy about venturing into stand-alone establishments—traditionally concentrated in Condado and Old San Juan. The historic center is also home to new restaurants and cafés offering artisanal cuisine—crop-to-cup coffee, rustic homemade pizzas, and creative vegetarian food—at affordable prices. But as the San Juan metro area develops, great restaurants are popping up in other parts of the city, including Santurce, Miramar, and Ocean Park. Throughout the island, there's a radiant pride in what the local land can provide, and enthusiastic restaurateurs are redefining what Puerto Rican food is, bite by tasty bite.

What to Wear: Dress codes vary greatly, though a restaurant's prices are a fairly good indicator of its formality. For less expensive places, anything but beachwear is fine. Ritzier eateries will expect collared shirts for men (jacket and tie requirements are rare) and chic attire for women. When in doubt, do as the Puerto Ricans often do and dress up.

OLD SAN JUAN

$$$$ SEAFOOD

Aguaviva. The name means "jellyfish," which explains why this ultra-modern place has dim blue lighting and jellyfish-shape lamps floating overhead. Eating here is like being submerged in the sea. The extensive, ever-changing menu by chef Hector Crespo features inventive ceviches, including truffle tuna tartare with cucumber and green apple. For something more filling, try the lobster yucca gnocchi or orzo paella, with generous seafood, chicken, chorizo, and a saffron beurre blanc—oh so tasty and enough for two. Another splurge, the gravity-defying *torres del mar* (towers of the sea) comes hot or cold and includes oysters, mussels, shrimp—you name it. The oysters Rockefeller alone are worth the trip. *Average main: $31* *364 Calle Fortaleza, Old San Juan* *787/722–0665* *www.oofrestaurants.com* *No lunch.*

$ CAFÉ Fodor's Choice ★

Café Cuatro Sombras. If you want to try locally grown, single-origin, shade-grown coffee, this micro-roastery and café is the place to do it. Owners Pablo Muñoz and Mariana Suárez grow their beans in the mountains of Yauco on a hacienda that has been in the Muñoz family since 1846. The wood planks lining the banquette are from coffee storage pallets, and red accents recall perfectly ripe coffee beans. *Cuatro sombras* (four shades) refers to the four types of trees traditionally used in Puerto Rico to provide shade for coffee plants. And although it's the delicious, medium-bodied brew that steals the show, there's also a small but tasty menu of pastries and sandwiches. *Average main: $7* *259 Calle Recinto Sur, Old San Juan* *787/724–9955* *www.cuatrosombras.com* *No dinner.*

$ CONTEMPORARY

Casa Cortés ChocoBar. The Cortés family has been making bean-to-bar chocolate for more than 85 years. In 2013, they opened Puerto Rico's first "choco bar" to share their passion. The walls in this vivid, modern space are decorated with ads from the '50s, original chocolate bar molds, a timeline of chocolate, and two flat screens showing the chocolate-making process. From pastries to tapas, breakfast dishes to panini sandwiches, the chef integrates chocolate into every bite without overpowering. Ripe plantain *mofonguitos* are filled with chocolate and bacon bits. The panfried jumbo shrimp with a chocolate lemon sauce are delicious. Bonbons, chocolate bars, and even chocolate soaps are also for sale. Locals from all over the metro area flock here for weekend brunch; arrive early to avoid a long wait. On Thursday, Saturday, and Sunday an upstairs gallery offers a glimpse of the family's private contemporary Caribbean art collection. *Average main: $10* *210 Calle San Francisco, Old San Juan* *787/722–0499* *www.casacortespr.com* *Closed Mon. No dinner.*

$$$ ASIAN

Dragonfly. Dark and sexy, this popular Latin-Asian restaurant, all done up in Chinese red, feels more like a fashionable after-hours lounge than a restaurant. The romantic ambience, created partly through tightly packed tables and low lighting, is a big draw. Small plates, meant to be shared, come in generous portions. Don't miss the Peking duck nachos, pork and sweet plantain dumplings, and inventive cocktails that complement the food. Reservations aren't accepted, but you can call ahead to get put on the waiting list. *Average main: $21* *364 Calle*

Fortaleza, Old San Juan ☎ 787/977–3886 ⊕ www.oofrestaurants.com ✍ Reservations not accepted ⊙ No lunch.

$$ PUERTO RICAN ✕ **La Fonda del Jibarito.** The menus are handwritten and the tables wobble, but sanjuaneros have favored this casual, no-frills, family-run restaurant—tucked away on a quiet cobbled street—for years. The *bistec encebollado,* goat fricassee, and shredded beef stew are among the specialties on the menu of typical Puerto Rican comida criolla dishes. The tiny back porch is filled with plants, and the dining room is filled with fanciful depictions of life on the street outside. Troubadours serenade patrons, which include plenty of cruise-ship passengers when ships are in dock. *$ Average main: $14 ✉ 280 Calle Sol, Old San Juan ☎ 787/725–8375.*

$$$$ ECLECTIC Fodor's Choice ★ ✕ **Marmalade.** Peter Schintler, the U.S.-born owner-chef of Old San Juan's hippest—and finest—restaurant, apprenticed with Raymond Blanc and Gordon Ramsay. Here he's created a class act famous for its ultra-chic lounge bar. The restaurant's sensual and minimalist orange-and-white decor features high-back chairs and cushioned banquettes. The menu uses many sustainable and non-modified ingredients prepared California-French fashion, resulting in complex flavors and strong aromas. The yellowtail is served with lemongrass and compressed watermelon while the pork cheeks are served with a peach-poblano marmalade. For dessert, indulge in the Millionaire's ice cream, topped with honeycomb and shaved truffles. You can build your own four- to six-course tasting menu, with or without pairings from the *Wine Spectator* Award of Excellence wine list, or order à la carte. The restaurant is accommodating to vegetarians, vegans, and those with dietary restrictions. *$ Average main: $32 ✉ 317 Calle Fortaleza, Old San Juan ☎ 787/724–3969 ⊕ www.marmaladepr.com ✍ Reservations essential ⊙ No lunch.*

$$$ VEGETARIAN Fodor's Choice ★ ✕ **Verde Mesa.** With punched-tin ceilings, mason-jar light fixtures, and eclectic decor inspired by Versailles' Petit Trianon, this vegetarian restaurant focuses on pleasing the senses. Much of the organic produce used in the changing menu comes from the owners' farm and other local sources. Flavor combinations are anything but accidental. Start with a garlicky "hummus" of local pigeon peas. The signature Verde Mesa rice is a mixture of in-season vegetables and chickpeas that the owners say has gotten many a skeptic to explore the culinary potential of vegetables. There are also quite a few expertly prepared tuna, salmon, and scallop dishes. Salmon might be cured with lavender and ginger, and scallops might be served on a bed of parsnip mash, dressed with fig foam. Reservations are not accepted, so arrive early for dinner. *$ Average main: $22 ✉ 107 Calle Tetuán, at Calle San José, Old San Juan ☎ 787/390–4662 ⊕ www.verdemesa.com ✍ Reservations not accepted ⊙ Closed Sun.–Mon. No lunch Sat.*

$ CAFÉ ✕ **Waffle-era Tea Room.** The only tearoom in Puerto Rico is hugely popular, and its relocation to a larger space (with reservations) made locals very happy. You can choose from nearly 30 loose teas, including white and fruity blends as well as black, or a carefully crafted cocktail menu, but you may be more curious about the coffee setup, which looks like a mad scientist's experiment. It's a siphon fire-brewing system, a painstaking process popular in Japan. Food consists of house-made sweet or savory waffles or smaller "wafflitos" (the crème brûlée wafflito is decadent) and a tapas menu with signature ham-hugged dates (stuffed with Gorgonzola and cherry tomatoes, wrapped in fire-torched, brandy-infused prosciutto). A "waffle-izza" has fresh tomato sauce and blowtorch-melted mozzarella. At writing, there are plans to open another restaurant at the original location, 103 Calle Tetuán. *Average main: $9 ✉ 252 Calle San José, Old San Juan ☎ 787/721–1512 🌐 www.waffle-era.com ⏲ No dinner.*

GREATER SAN JUAN

$$$$ ECLECTIC Fodor's Choice ★

1919. Michelin-starred, Puerto Rico–born chef José Cuevas successfully operates this fine-dining restaurant in San Juan's most striking hotel, once home to the Vanderbilt family. The main dining room is set on the Atlantic Ocean; elegant and sophisticated, it is large yet intimate, with tables spread out to allow for privacy and comfort. Brazilian-tigerwood tables, dark wood floors, and three striking chandeliers with drooping pearl shells are reminiscent of the Gatsby era. The international cuisine—prix fixe or à la carte—changes seasonally and focuses on local ingredients, perhaps eggplant confit in tomato water with local cucumber, clams escabeche, calabaza ravioli with sage brown butter, or chicharrones gremolata. For pairings, choose from 200+ wines or take advantage of the champagne table service. *Average main: $36 ✉ Vanderbilt Hotel, 1055 Av. Ashford, Condado ☎ 787/724–1919 🌐 www.1919restaurant.com ⏲ Closed Sun.–Mon. No lunch Sat.*

$$$ PUERTO RICAN Fodor's Choice ★

Jose Enrique. Since 2007, chef Jose Enrique's eponymous restaurant has been the preferred choice of locals. In 2013, the world started catching on when José was nominated for *Food & Wine* magazine's Best New Chefs. He is also the first Puerto Rican chef to receive the prestigious James Beard award nomination, for two consecutive years. The elevated Puerto Rican cuisine fits the very casual setting. The menu, on an eraser board, changes all the time, but crab fitters are a staple, as is whole fried yellowtail snapper served over a root mash with avocado and papaya salsa. The no-reservation policy means you'll wait for a table. Put your name on the list and wander around La Placita, where you can sip cheap drinks and mingle with locals. *Average main: $30 ✉ 176 Calle Duffaut, La Placita de Santurce, Santurce ☎ 787/725–3518 🌐 www.joseenriquepr.com Reservations not accepted ⏲ Closed Sun.–Mon. No lunch Sat.*

$$ CAFÉ

Kasalta. Those who think coffee can never be too strong should make a beeline to Kasalta and its amazing pitch-black brew. Display cases are full of luscious pastries, including the *quesito* (cream cheese–filled puff pastry), and sandwiches include the Medianoche, made famous when President Obama ordered one while campaigning. For dinner, dive into a fish dish or paella, or do like the locals and make a meal out of savory Spanish tapas. Quality is occasionally uneven, and some staff members are curt with tourists. *Average main: $16 ✉ 1966 Calle McLeary, Ocean Park ☎ 787/727–7340 🌐 www.kasalta.com.*

$$$ CARIBBEAN

Pamela's. If you dream of dining right on the beach, head to this Ocean Park favorite. If you prefer air-conditioning, opt for the elegant glassed-in solarium, with black cobblestone floors and slow-turning ceiling fans. The menu—a contemporary, creative mix of Caribbean spices and other tropical ingredients with an accent on fresh seafood—has red snapper, blackened salmon with a Caribbean vegetable medley, and a bouillabaisse-like seafood sofrito with shrimp, mussels, clams, and calamari. *Average main: $30* ✉ *Numero Uno Guest House, 1 Calle Santa Ana, Ocean Park* ☎ *787/726–5010* 🌐 *www.numero1guesthouse.com.*

$$$$ ECLECTIC Fodor's Choice ★

Pikayo. Celebrity chef and Puerto Rico native Wilo Benet's flagship restaurant makes the most of its elegant surroundings at the Condado Plaza Hilton. Works from local artists line the walls, and the atmosphere is formal but never hushed. The menu offers a twist on traditional Puerto Rican classics as well as more international flavors. Choose from the thoughtfully crafted tasting menu or order à la carte. Of the large selection of starters, the pork-belly sliders, spicy tuna on crispy rice (known as *pegao*), and foie gras with ripe plantains and black-truffle honey are particularly good. Main course options include succulent petit duck magret with cremini mushrooms and a raspberry vinegar gastrique and North Atlantic swordfish in a pigeon pea escabeche with a ripe plantain emulsion. Don't be surprised if Benet stops by to make sure everything is to your liking. *Average main: $37* ✉ *Condado Plaza Hilton, 999 Ashford Ave., Condado* ☎ *787/721–6194* 🌐 *www.wilobenet.com/pikayo* ⊙ *No lunch.*

EASTERN PUERTO RICO

$$$$ FRENCH

Chez Daniel. When the stars are out, it would be hard to find a more romantic setting than this eatery in a marina. Dozens of gleaming white boats are anchored so close that you could practically hit them with a baguette. The dining room has a chummy atmosphere, probably because many patrons seem to know each other. For alone time, ask for a table on one of the private terraces. Chef Daniel Vasse's French-country-style dishes are some of the island's best. The Marseille-style bouillabaisse is full of fresh fish and bursts with the flavor of a white garlic sauce. Something less French? Choose steak or fish simply prepared on the grill, and pair it with a bottle from the extensive wine cellar. Sunday brunch ($45 including one brunch cocktail), with its seemingly endless seafood bar, draws people from all over the island. *Average main: $33* ✉ *Palmas del Mar, Anchor's Village Marina, Rte. 906, Km 86.4, Humacao* ☎ *787/850–3838* *Reservations essential* ⊙ *Closed Mon.–Tues. No lunch.*

$$$ CARIBBEAN

Pasión por el Fogón. At this beloved Fajardo restaurant, chef Myrta Pérez Toledo transforms traditional dishes into something special. Succulent cuts of meat and fish are presented in unexpected ways. A perfectly cooked flank steak, rolled into a cylinder standing on one end, has a slightly sweet tamarind sauce that brings out the meat's earthy flavors. If you're a seafood lover, start with the lime-infused red-snapper ceviche and move on to lobster medallions broiled in butter. For dessert, order the Caribbean Sun, an ice cream sundae that blends caramel, cinnamon, and chocolate toppings. *Average main: $28* ✉ *Rte. 987, Km 2.3, Barrio Sardinera, Fajardo* ☎ *787/863–3502* 🌐 *www.pasionporelfogon.net* *Reservations essential* ⊙ *No lunch weekdays.*

17

VIEQUES AND CULEBRA

$$ PUERTO RICAN Fodor's Choice ★ **Conuco.** A mix of locals and gringos frequent Conuco, soft-spoken Puerto Rico native Rebecca Betancourt's homage to local food with an upscale twist. Barnlike open windows look out onto one of Isabel Segunda's main streets, and within, the airy room is simple but cozy, enhanced by bright yellow walls, seafoam chairs, white table tops, and ceiling fans. A back patio offers alfresco dining. Start with sangria rum punch, then move onto *any* of the menu's many selections; they're all that wonderful. Piping-hot arepas are piled high with pepper and octopus salad, while small *tostones rellenos* (fried plantains) are shaped into cups filled with a citrusy ceviche. *Sorullitos* (cheesy corn fritters) and *bacalaítos* (cod fritters) are re-imagined with modern flair. The only thing trumping the flavors of a juicy *churrasco* (skirt steak) and overflowing seafood mofongo is the wow factor of Betancourt's presentations. *Average main: $15* *110 Luis Muñoz Rivera, Isabel Segunda, Vieques* *787/741–2500* *www.restauranteconuco.com* *Closed Sun.–Mon. No lunch.*

$$$ ECLECTIC Fodor's Choice ★ **El Quenepo.** This elegant yet unpretentious spot brings fine dining and a touch of class to the Esperanza waterfront. Six stable doors on a powder-blue building open to ocean views. The menu, which changes yearly, features local herbs and fruits such as quenepas and breadfruit in artfully prepared dishes that owners Scott and Kate Cole call "fun, funky island food." Scott is the chef, known for seafood specials highlighting the daily catch; Kate is the consummate hostess. Start with the popular grilled Caesar salad followed by sensational mofongo stuffed with shrimp and lobster in sweet-and-spicy criollo sauce. There's a large wine list, and the sangria is delicious. Lucky walk-ins can grab a seat at the more casual high bar tables, but for a true experience, make a reservation. *Average main: $25* *148 Calle Flamboyan, Esperanza, Vieques* *787/741–1215* *Reservations essential* *Closed Sun. No lunch.*

$$ CARIBBEAN **Mamacita's.** Pull your dinghy up to the dock and watch the resident iguanas plod past at this simple open-air, tin-roofed restaurant on a rough-plank deck beside the Dewey canal. Painted pink, purple, and green, the space is littered with palm tree trunks. Tarpon cruise past in the jade waters, and the to and fro of boaters add to the show at Culebra's favorite watering hole and gringo hangout. Mamacita's down-home menu changes nightly. It's heavy on burgers and sandwiches but includes an excellent mahimahi. Open times vary by season. *Average main: $12* *66 Calle Castelar, Dewey, Culebra* *787/742–0090* *www.mamacitasguesthouse.com.*

$$$ ECLECTIC **Susie's.** Sanjuanera owner-chef Susie Hebert learned her culinary skills at San Juan's swank Caribe Hilton and Ritz-Carlton before settling on Culebra and opening her casual and unpretentious fine-dining restaurant, a soothing Zen space filled with banquettes, pillows, and couches. A huge courtyard is perfect for dining under the stars. The Caesar salad excels. Follow with sautéed jumbo shrimp in a lemongrass, ginger, and coconut cream sauce; grilled lobster with a Spanish-style butter; sesame-crusted blackfin tuna; or whole fried red snapper in a lemon-lime vinaigrette. Feeling carnivorous? The filet mignon with a

simple truffle jus is divine. Susie's is seasonal, so call ahead. $ *Average main: $21* ✉ *Rte. 250, Las Delicias, Dewey, Culebra* ☎ *787/742–1141* 🌐 *www.susiesculebra.com* *Reservations essential* *Closed Wed.–Thurs. No lunch.*

SOUTHERN PUERTO RICO

$$ SEAFOOD **El Ancla.** Families favor this laid-back restaurant at water's edge. Generous and affordable plates of fish, crab, and other fresh seafood come with *tostones* (fried plantains), french fries, and garlic bread. Try the shrimp in garlic sauce, salmon fillet with capers, or delectable mofongo stuffed with seafood, and finish with a fantastic flan. The piña coladas—with or without rum—are exceptional. The area needs improvement, but the views are worth it. $ *Average main: $20* ✉ *805 Av. Hostos Final, Ponce Playa, Ponce* ☎ *787/840–2450* 🌐 *www.restauranteelancla.com.*

DID YOU KNOW?

The seafood shacks of Joyuda are so well known for fresh fish that locals flock there from as far away as Ponce and San Juan. In Boquerón people line up at pushcarts where vendors sell oysters on the half shell.

WESTERN PUERTO RICO

17

$$$ ECLECTIC Fodor's Choice ★ **The Eclipse.** Beautiful beachfront dining, farm-to-table ingredients, and fantastic service are worth a drive from San Juan. The setting is rustic yet elegant, and the view is ideal. Executive chef Jeremie Cruz flawlessly executes dishes full of local flavors. Wonderful sweet and savory brunch selections range from coconut brioche French toast with caramelized bananas and nuts to pizza frittatas. Lunch brings delicious classic Neapolitan pizzas baked in a handmade brick oven. The catch of the day (from Isabela) ceviche is perfectly marinated. On top of the varied dinner menu, chef Jeremie creates a three-course menu daily that highlights the freshest products he can find. Wine pairings are optional and suggested, given the spectacular wine list. Enjoy live Caribbean jazz on Sunday and Wednesday nights. $ *Average main: $28* ✉ *Villa Montaña, Carretera 4466, Km 1.9, Isabela* ☎ *787/872–9554* 🌐 *www.villamontana.com.*

$$$$ CARIBBEAN **Restaurant Aaron at the Horned Dorset Primavera.** A pair of stone stairways leads up to the elegant dining room, with black-and-white marble floors, chandeliers with ruby-red shades, and a 1901 Steinway piano. The extravagant seven-course tasting menu ($125) might include foie gras with maple berry glaze, pan-seared scallops with asparagus risotto, or poached *chillo* (red snapper) with apricot gnocchi. Adding Caribbean accents to classical French cuisine, the à la carte menu changes weekly but might include roasted rack of lamb and wahoo (a kind of mackerel) in a pistachio crust. Dress is formal by island standards, except in the downstairs Blue Room, with a similar menu. Lunch (dessert and after-dinner drinks often, too) is served on the terrace to the crash of the waves. $ *Average main: $36* ✉ *Horned Dorset Primavera, Rte. 429,*

Km 3, Rincón ☎ *787/823–4030* 🌐 *www.horneddorset.com* ✍ *Reservations essential* ⊗ *Closed Mon.–Wed. Apr.–Nov.*

$$ PUERTO RICAN ✕ **Rincón Tropical.** Don't be scared off by the cheap plastic tables and chairs. They are almost always full of locals enjoying the fresh seafood. The kitchen keeps it simple, preparing dishes with a light touch. Highlights include mahimahi with onions and peppers as well as fried red snapper with rice and bean and octopus salad. Fried plantains make a nice accompaniment to almost anything. Weekdays bring an affordable lunch special. [$] *Average main: $15* ✉ *Rte. 115, Km 12, Rincón* ☎ *787/823–2017* 🌐 *www.rinconpr.com/rincontropical.*

WHERE TO STAY

In San Juan, the best beaches are in Isla Verde, though Condado is more centrally located. Old San Juan offers easy access to dining and nightlife. Outside San Juan, particularly on the east coast, you can find self-contained luxury resorts that cover hundreds of acres. Around the island, government-sponsored *paradores* are rural inns, others offer no-frills apartments, and some are large hotels close to either an attraction or beach.

PRIVATE VILLAS AND CONDOS

In the west, southwest, and south—as well as on the islands of Vieques and Culebra—smaller inns and condominiums for short-term rentals are the norm. Villa and apartment rentals are increasingly popular.

RENTAL CONTACTS

Island West Properties. Around for years, this office has cornered the market for renting villas in Rincón by the day, week, or month. ✉ *Rte. 413, Km 0.7, Rincón* ☎ *787/823–2323* 🌐 *www.islandwestrentals.com.*

Rainbow Realty. A list of rental properties is available from this gay-friendly company. ✉ *278 Calle Flamboyán, Esperanza, Vieques* ☎ *787/741–4312* 🌐 *www.viequesrainbowrealty.com.*

San Juan Vacations. Many properties in Condado and Isla Verde can be rented from this real estate company. ✉ *Marbella del Caribe Oeste, Av. Isla Verde, S-5, Isla Verde, San Juan* ☎ *787/727–1591* ✉ *sanjuvac@gmail.com.*

OLD SAN JUAN

$ B&B/INN **The Gallery Inn.** No two rooms in this 200-year-old mansion are alike, but all have four-poster beds, hand-woven tapestries, and quirky antiques in every nook and cranny. **Pros:** one-of-a-kind lodging; ocean views; wonderful classical music concerts. **Cons:** several narrow, winding staircases; an uphill walk from rest of Old San Juan; sometimes-raucous pet macaws and cockatoos. [$] *Rooms from: $160* ✉ *204–206 Calle Norzagaray, Old San Juan* ☎ *787/722–1808* 🌐 *www.thegalleryinn.com* *20 rooms, 5 suites* 🍽 *Breakfast.*

$$ HOTEL Fodor's Choice ★ **Hotel El Convento.** There's no longer anything austere about this 350-year-old former convent. **Pros:** lovely building; atmosphere to spare; plenty of nearby dining options. **Cons:** near some noisy bars; small pool; small bathrooms. [$] *Rooms from: $285* ✉ *100 Calle Cristo,*

Hotel El Convento

Old San Juan ☎ *787/723–9020* 🌐 *www.elconvento.com* ⇨ *52 rooms, 6 suites* 🍴 *No meals.*

GREATER SAN JUAN

$ B&B/INN **Andalucía.** In a Spanish-style house, this friendly little inn evokes its namesake region with such details as hand-painted tiles and ceramic pots filled with greenery. **Pros:** terrific value; helpful hosts; gorgeous courtyard. **Cons:** not right on the beach; some rooms are smaller than others. $ *Rooms from: $99* ✉ *2011 Calle McLeary, Ocean Park, San Juan* ☎ *787/309–3373* 🌐 *www.andalucia-puertorico.com* ⇨ *11 rooms* 🍴 *No meals.*

$ B&B/INN **At Wind Chimes Inn.** Hidden behind a whitewashed wall covered with bougainvillea, this Spanish-style villa feels like an exclusive retreat. **Pros:** charming architecture; on the edge of Condado; on-site bar (opens at 5); use of Acacia Seaside Inn facilities. **Cons:** busy street; old-fashioned rooms; only a few rooms have closets. $ *Rooms from: $109* ✉ *1750 Av. McLeary, Condado, San Juan* ☎ *787/727–4153, 800/946–3244* 🌐 *www.atwindchimesinn.com* ⇨ *17 rooms, 5 suites, 1 apartment* 🍴 *No meals.*

$$$ RESORT FAMILY Fodor's Choice ★ **El San Juan Resort & Casino.** Much of the classical appeal remains; the lobby's intricately carved mahogany walls and ceiling date to 1955. **Pros:** beautiful pool; great dining options in and near hotel; fantastic beach. **Cons:** noise in lobby from bars and casino; parking lot a long walk from hotel entrance; small bathrooms. $ *Rooms from: $450* ✉ *6063 Av. Isla Verde, Isla Verde, San Juan* ☎ *787/791–1000* 🌐 *www.elsanjuanhotel.com* ⇨ *386 rooms, 22 suites* 🍴 *No meals.*

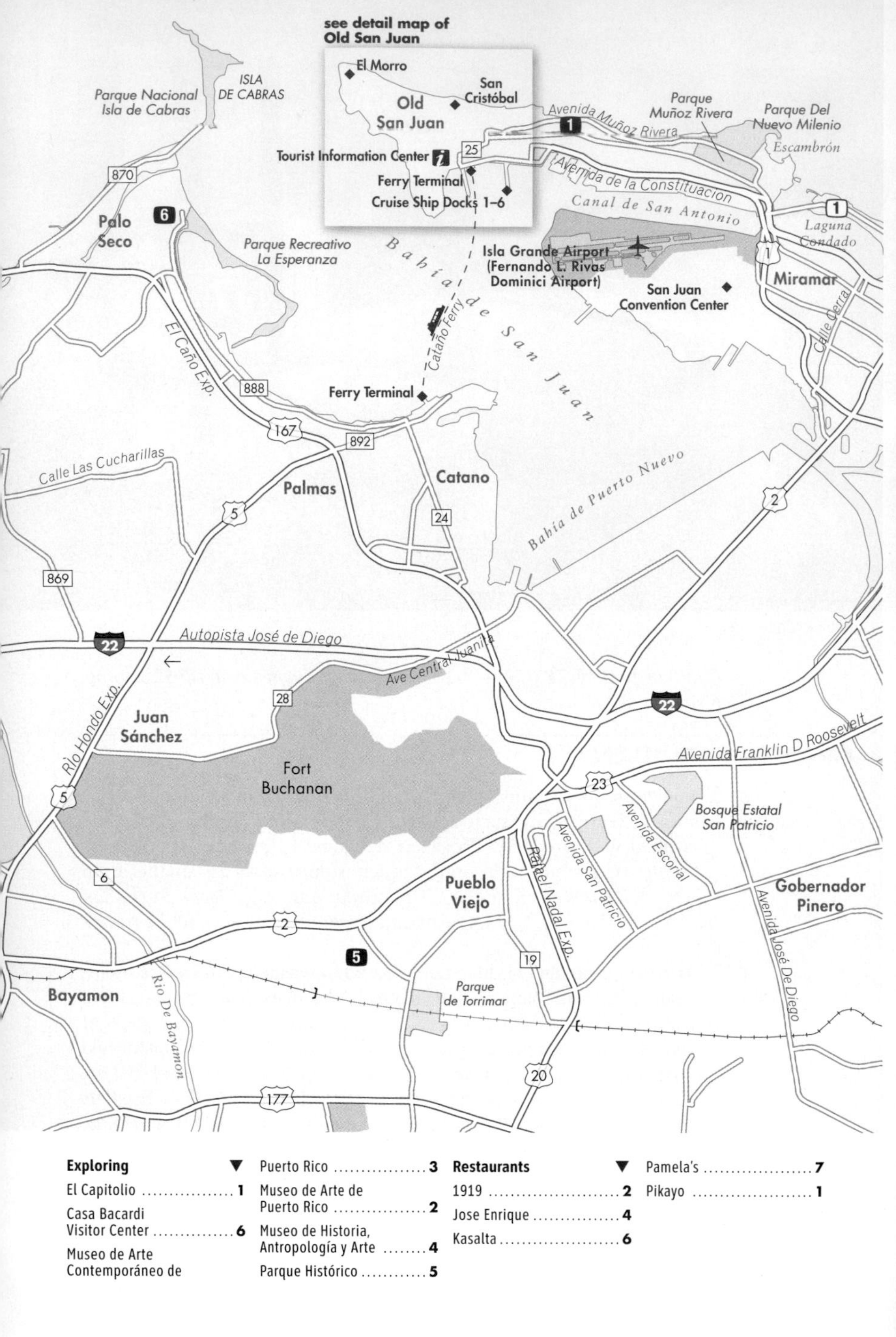

Exploring

El Capitolio ... **1**

Casa Bacardi Visitor Center ... **6**

Museo de Arte Contemporáneo de Puerto Rico ... **3**

Museo de Arte de Puerto Rico ... **2**

Museo de Historia, Antropología y Arte ... **4**

Parque Histórico ... **5**

Restaurants

1919 ... **2**

Jose Enrique ... **4**

Kasalta ... **6**

Pamela's ... **7**

Pikayo ... **1**

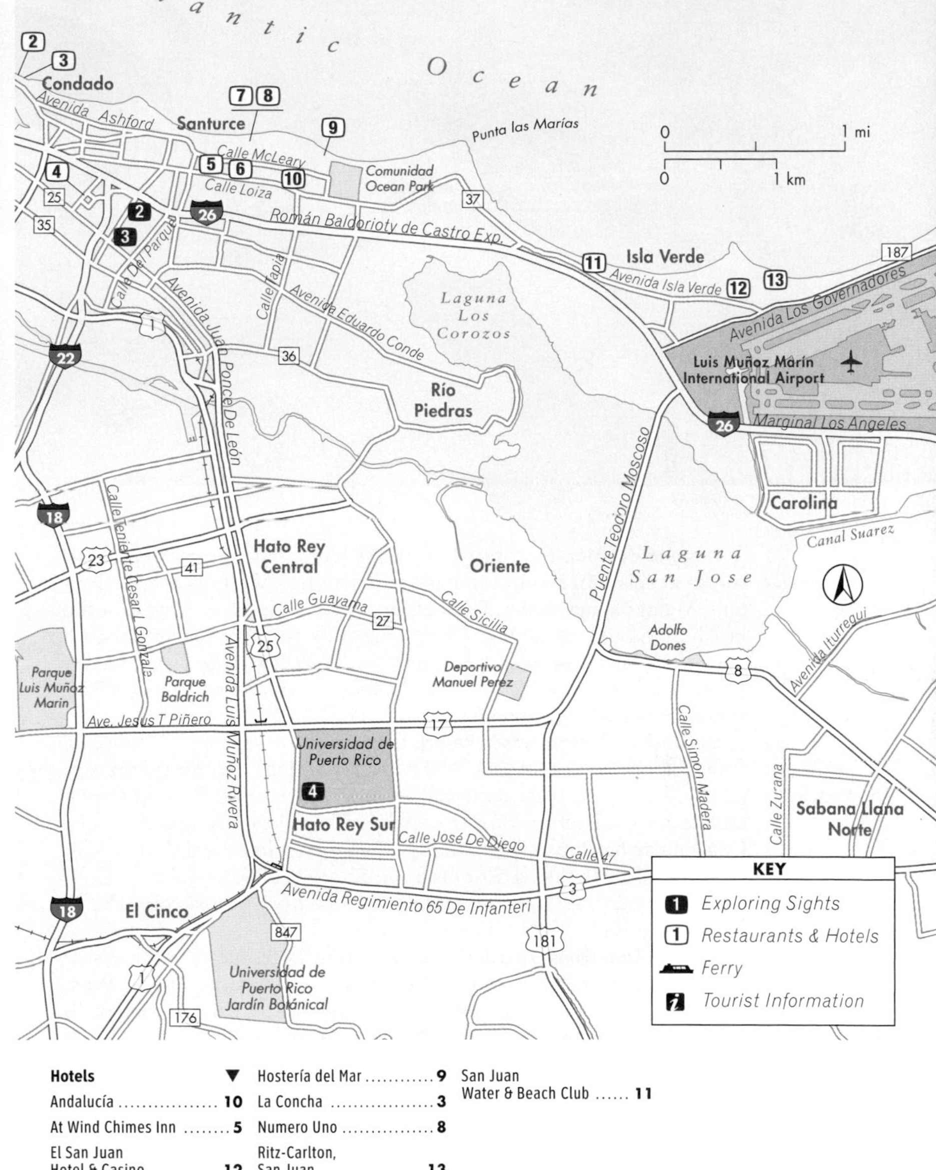

Hotels ▼

Andalucía **10**

At Wind Chimes Inn **5**

El San Juan Hotel & Casino **12**

Hostería del Mar **9**

La Concha **3**

Numero Uno **8**

Ritz-Carlton, San Juan **13**

San Juan Water & Beach Club **11**

El San Juan Resort & Casino

$ B&B/INN **Hostería del Mar.** Decorated in bright blues and whites, the stylish rooms at this beachfront inn have an Asian feel, with influences from Bali, Malaysia, and India. **Pros:** plasma-screen televisions; right on the beach; good on-site dining. **Cons:** long walk to other restaurants; no pool; Wi-Fi in lobby only. *Rooms from: $139* ✉ *1 Calle Tapia, Ocean Park, San Juan* ☎ *787/727–3302* 🌐 *www.hosteriadelmarpr.com* *23 rooms, 2 suites* *No meals.*

$$ RESORT Fodor's Choice ★ **La Concha—A Renaissance Resort.** Every detail feels tropical and sexy, from the undulating ceiling in the sprawling lobby to Perla, the signature shell-shape restaurant and architectural marvel. **Pros:** stunning architecture; numerous on-site social activities; beautiful guest rooms. **Cons:** noisy bar/lobby, particularly when there's live music; beach can be narrow at high tide. *Rooms from: $299* ✉ *1077 Av. Ashford, Condado, San Juan* ☎ *787/721–7500* 🌐 *www.laconcharesort.com* *257 rooms, 226 suites* *No meals.*

$ HOTEL Fodor's Choice ★ **Numero Uno Guest House.** It's common to hear guests trading stories about how often they've returned to this relaxing retreat. **Pros:** friendly atmosphere; great restaurant; on the beach. **Cons:** a long walk to other restaurants; small pool. *Rooms from: $150* ✉ *1 Calle Santa Ana, Ocean Park, San Juan* ☎ *787/726–5010, 866/726–5010* 🌐 *www.numero1guesthouse.com* *11 rooms* *Breakfast.*

$$$$ RESORT FAMILY Fodor's Choice ★ **The Ritz-Carlton, San Juan.** Elegant marble floors and fountains don't undermine the beach getaway feel. **Pros:** top-notch service; excellent restaurant options; spruce guest rooms; modern spa and fitness center. **Cons:** not much within walking distance; expensive. *Rooms from: $629* ✉ *6961 Av. de los Gobernadores, Isla Verde, San Juan*

787/253–1700, 800/241–3333 www.ritzcarlton.com/sanjuan 416 rooms, 11 suites No meals.

$ HOTEL **San Juan Water Beach Club Hotel.** Water is everywhere at this boutique hotel, from droplets in the reception area to a deluge running down the elevators' glass walls. **Pros:** fun atmosphere; interesting design; great nightlife; on the beach. **Cons:** dark hallways; small pool. *Rooms from: $219 2 Calle Tartak, Islá Verde, San Juan 787/728–3666, 888/265–6699 www.waterbeachhotel.com 80 rooms, 4 suites No meals.*

BEYOND SAN JUAN

$$$$ RESORT Fodor'sChoice ★ **Dorado Beach, A Ritz-Carlton Reserve.** Following a $342-million renovation, this resort's big draws include a restaurant from Fodor's Travel Tastemaker chef José Andres and an incredible setting along 3 miles of Puerto Rican coastline. **Pros:** all rooms are beachfront; top-notch facilities; golf, tennis, and water activities; award-winning spa; gourmet dining. **Cons:** daily $95 resort fee; 45-minute drive from San Juan. *Rooms from: $1,399 100 Dorado Beach Dr., Dorado 787/626–1100 www.ritzcarlton.com/en/properties/doradobeach 100 rooms, 14 suites, 1 villa No meals.*

EASTERN PUERTO RICO

$$$ RESORT **El Conquistador Resort.** Perched on a bluff overlooking the ocean, this sprawling complex on the northern tip of the island is one of its most popular destination resorts. **Pros:** bright, spacious rooms; unbeatable views of nearby islands; good dining options. **Cons:** must take boat to reach beach; long waits at funicular running between levels; self-parking far from hotel entrance; hidden fees like parking ($16/day) and kids club ($70/day). *Rooms from: $400 1000 Av. El Conquistador, Fajardo 787/863–1000, 888/543–1282 www.elconresort.com 750 rooms, 15 suites, 234 villas Breakfast.*

$$ RESORT **Gran Meliá Puerto Rico.** This massive resort, on a stretch of pristine coastline, has an open-air lobby with elegant floral displays that resemble a Japanese garden, while the swimming pool's columns recall ancient Greece. **Pros:** beautiful setting; lovely pool area; short walk to beach. **Cons:** scarce parking; blank and uninviting facade. *Rooms from: $319 200 Coco Beach Blvd., Coco Beach 787/809–1770, 877/476–3542 www.gran-melia-puerto-rico.com 544 suites, 6 villas Multiple meal plans.*

$$ RESORT FAMILY **Rio Mar Beach Resort & Spa, a Wyndham Grand Resort.** This sprawling 500-acre resort offers a host of outdoor activities, including championship golf and tennis and hiking excursions in the nearby rain forest. **Pros:** expansive beachfront; good restaurants; casino; plenty of outdoor activities. **Cons:** dark and depressing parking garage; occasionally long lines at check-in; far from off-site restaurants. *Rooms from: $305 6000 Río Mar Blvd., Río Grande 787/888-6000 www.wyndhamriomar.com 600 rooms, 72 suites No meals.*

17

$$$$ RESORT Fodor's Choice ★ **St. Regis Bahia Beach Resort.** Between El Yunque National Forest and the Río Espíritu Santo, this luxurious, environmentally aware property has raised the bar for lodgings in Puerto Rico. **Pros:** privacy; impeccable service; luxurious amenities. **Cons:** isolated location; slim off-property restaurant selection; very, very expensive. *Rooms from: $800 Rte. 187, Km 4.2, Río Grande 787/809–8000 www.stregisbahiabeach.com 139 rooms, 35 suites No meals.*

VIEQUES AND CULEBRA

$ HOTEL Fodor's Choice ★ **Club Seaborne.** The most sophisticated place in Culebra, this cluster of slate-blue plantation-style cottages paints a pretty picture on a hilltop overlooking Fulladoza Bay. **Pros:** lovely cottages; lush gardens; airport or ferry transfers included. **Cons:** some steps to negotiate; no elevator; spotty Internet and cell phone reception. *Rooms from: $249 Rte. 252, northwest of town, Culebra 787/742–3169 www.clubseabourne.com 3 rooms, 8 villas, 1 cottage Breakfast.*

$ HOTEL **Hacienda Tamarindo.** The 250-year-old tamarind tree rising more than three stories through the center of the main building gives this plantation-style house and former dance hall its name. **Pros:** beautiful views; nicely designed rooms; excellent breakfasts. **Cons:** drive to beaches; small parking lot; no full-service restaurant; no elevator. *Rooms from: $199 Rte. 997, Km 4.5, Esperanza, Vieques 787/741–8525 www.haciendatamarindo.com 16 rooms, 1 penthouse suite Breakfast.*

$ HOTEL **Hix Island House.** Constructed entirely of concrete and set in tropical forest, the four buildings of this hotel echo the gray granite boulders strewn around Vieques and blend seamlessly with the environment. **Pros:** acclaimed architecture; secluded setting; friendly staff. **Cons:** the lack of windows means bugs (especially pesky mosquitos) get in; damp linens and clothing after tropical showers; no elevator. *Rooms from: $175 Rte. 995, Km 1.5, Vieques 787/741–2302 www.hixislandhouse.com 19 rooms Breakfast.*

$ B&B/INN **Malecón House.** Posh boutique spots like this seaside escape in Esperanza are raising the bar on Vieques lodging. **Pros:** affordable waterfront property; tasty breakfasts; welcoming hosts. **Cons:** in-town location not for those seeking seclusion. *Rooms from: $175 105 Calle Flamboyan, Esperanza, Vieques 787/741–0663 www.maleconhouse.com 13 rooms Breakfast.*

$$$$ RESORT Fodor's Choice ★ **W Retreat & Spa.** Hovering over two gorgeous beaches, this überhip resort is the island's hot spot for urbane fashionistas, yet manages to still be family-friendly. **Pros:** sensational decor; full-service spa; free transfers to/from airport. **Cons:** high prices even in low season; $60 daily resort fee. *Rooms from: $885 Rte. 200, Km 3.2, Isabel Segunda, Vieques 787/741–4100 www.wvieques.com 156 rooms, 20 suites No meals.*

SOUTHERN PUERTO RICO

$ RESORT Fodor's Choice ★ **Copamarina Beach Resort & Spa.** The most beautiful resort on the southern coast is set on 16 palm-shaded acres facing the Caribbean. **Pros:** tropical decor; plenty of activities; great dining options; 10-minute boat ride to Gilligan's Island. **Cons:** somewhat distant from other attractions; 20% resort fee. *Rooms from: $190 Rte. 333, Km 6.5, Guánica 787/821–0505, 800/468–4553 www.copamarina.com 104 rooms, 2 villas Multiple meal plans.*

$ HOTEL **Hotel Meliá.** In the heart of the city, this family-owned hotel has been a local landmark for over a century. **Pros:** great location on the main square; walking distance to downtown sites; good dining options nearby. **Cons:** somewhat dated decor; front rooms can be noisy. *Rooms from: $145 75 Calle Cristina, Ponce Centro, Ponce 787/842–0260 www.meliacenturyhotel.com 68 rooms, 10 suites Multiple meal plans.*

$ RENTAL **Mary Lee's by the Sea.** This meandering cluster of apartments sits on quiet grounds full of brightly colored flowers. **Pros:** home away from home; warm and friendly owner; near pristine beaches and forests. **Cons:** weekly maid service unless requested daily; no nightlife; no pool; rooms a bit dated. *Rooms from: $110 Rte. 333, Km 6.7, Guánica 787/821–3600 www.maryleesbythesea.com 10 apartments No meals.*

17

CENTRAL PUERTO RICO

$ HOTEL **Casa Grande Mountain Retreat.** This is as close as you can get to sleeping in a tree house. **Pros:** unspoiled setting with spectacular views; accessible for people with disabilities; outdoor activities. **Cons:** no a/c; long drive to other sights/restaurants; pool closes at 6. *Rooms from: $126 Rte. 612, Km 0.3, Utuado 787/894–3939 www.hotelcasagrande.com 20 rooms No meals.*

WESTERN PUERTO RICO

$$$$ RESORT Fodor's Choice ★ **Horned Dorset Primavera.** Whitewashed villas scattered throughout the tropical gardens are designed to provide privacy whether you are relaxing in your private plunge pool or admiring the sunset from one of your balconies. **Pros:** unabashed luxury; lovely setting; pet-friendly; beautiful decor; yoga "tree house." **Cons:** very narrow beach; long staircase to some villas; some repairs needed. *Rooms from: $770 Rte. 429, Km 3, Rincón 787/823–4030, 800/633–1857 www.horneddorset.com 17 villas Multiple meal plans.*

$ HOTEL **The Lazy Parrot.** Painted in eye-popping tropical hues, this mountainside hotel doesn't take itself too seriously. **Pros:** economy rooms available; tropical setting; microwaves in rooms. **Cons:** not on the beach; stairs to climb; some may consider the whimsical style tacky. *Rooms from: $135 Rte. 413, Km 4.1, Rincón 787/823–5654, 800/294–1752 www.lazyparrot.com 21 rooms No meals.*

$ HOTEL **Lemontree Oceanfront Cottages.** Right on the beach, this pair of lemon-yellow buildings holds six apartments with names like Mango, Cocoa,

Tres Sirenas

Banana, and Piña. **Pros:** far from the crowds; on-call massage therapist; spacious balconies. **Cons:** very narrow beach; it's a drive to shops and restaurants; no elevator. *Rooms from: $155* ✉ *Rte. 429, Km 4.1, Rincón* ☎ *787/823–6452* 🌐 *www.lemontreepr.com* *6 apartments* *No meals.*

$ B&B/INN Fodor's Choice ★ **Tres Sirenas.** Waves gently lap against the shore at this boutique inn named Three Mermaids for the owners' daughters. **Pros:** in-room massage; spotless; tastefully decorated; discounted rates May–October. **Cons:** usually booked; Wi-Fi occasionally drops. *Rooms from: $230* ✉ *26 Seabeach Dr., Rincón* ☎ *787/823–0558* 🌐 *www.tressirenas.com* *2 rooms, 1 studio, 2 apartments* *Breakfast.*

$ RESORT Fodor's Choice ★ **Villa Montaña.** This cluster of villas, on a deserted stretch of beach between Isabela and Aguadilla, feels like a little town. **Pros:** bikes and playground; secluded beach; great food. **Cons:** a bit pricey; far from off-site restaurants; airplane noise; some dated rooms. *Rooms from: $255* ✉ *Rte. 4466, Km 1.9, Isabela* ☎ *787/872–9554* 🌐 *www.villamontana.com* *74 rooms, 52 villas* *No meals.*

NIGHTLIFE AND PERFORMING ARTS

Qué Pasa, the official visitor's guide, has listings of events in San Juan and out on the island. The local blog 🌐 *puertoricodaytrips.com* is another great source for event listings.

NIGHTLIFE

Wherever you go, dress to impress. Puerto Ricans have flair, and both men and women love getting dressed up to go out. Bars are usually casual, but if you have on jeans, sneakers, and a T-shirt, you may be refused entry at swankier nightclubs and discos.

In Old San Juan, Calle San Sebastián is lined with bars and restaurants. Evenings begin with dinner and stretch into the wee hours (often until 3 or 4) at bars at the more upscale, SoFo (south of Fortaleza) end. An eclectic crowd heads to the Plaza del Mercado in Santurce after work to hang out in the plaza or enjoy drinks and food in one of the small establishments skirting the farmers' market. Condado and Ocean Park have their share of nightlife, too. Most are restaurant-and-bar environments.

Just east of San Juan along Route 187, funky Piñones has a collection of open-air seaside eateries that are popular with locals. On weekend evenings many places have merengue combos, Brazilian jazz trios, or reggae bands. In Ponce, people embrace the Spanish tradition of the *paseo,* an evening stroll around the Plaza de las Delicias, and the boardwalk at La Guancha is also a lively scene. Live bands often play on weekends. Elsewhere *en la isla,* nighttime activities center on the hotels and resorts.

OLD SAN JUAN AND GREATER SAN JUAN

BARS AND MUSIC CLUBS

Mist. On the roof of the San Juan Water Beach Club Hotel, this sexy spot offers some of Isla Verde's best ocean views. On the weekends there's a DJ, and locals pack in to relax at the bar or on the white leather beds reserved for bottle service. The eclectic Socializers menu includes Serrano ham flatbread with fig marmalade and goat cheese, and pork belly *banh mi.* ✉ *San Juan Water Beach Club Hotel, 2 Calle Tartak, Isla Verde* ☎ *787/725–4664* 🌐 *www.waterbeachhotel.com.*

Nuyorican Café. Something interesting happens nearly every night (it's closed Monday and Tuesday) at this hipper-than-hip, no-frills, wood-paneled performance space, be it an early evening play, poetry reading, or talent show or, later on, a band playing Latin jazz, Cuban *son,* Puerto Rican salsa, or rock. On Wednesday nights, the owner plays the conga drums with the house salsa band, Comborican. During breaks the youthful, creative crowd chats in an alley outside. There is usually a $5 cover. ✉ *312 Calle San Fransico, entrance on Callejón de la Capilla, Old San Juan* ☎ *787/977–1276* 🌐 *www.nuyoricancafepr.com.*

CASINOS

By law, all casinos must be in hotels, and most of them are in San Juan. The government keeps a close eye on them. Dress for the larger casinos is on the formal side, and the atmosphere is refined, particularly in the Isla Verde resorts. Casinos set their own hours but are generally open from noon to 4 am. In addition to slot machines, typical games include blackjack, roulette, craps, Caribbean stud (a five-card poker game), and *pai gow* poker (a combination of American poker and the Chinese game pai gow). Hotels with casinos have live entertainment most weekends, as well as restaurants and bars. The minimum age to gamble (and to drink) is 18.

DANCE CLUBS

Atlantic Beach. This oceanfront hotel deck bar is famed in the gay community for its weekday happy hours (5–10), but the pulsating tropical music, exotic drinks, and pleasant ocean breeze would make it a hit in any case. ✉ *Atlantic Beach Hotel, 1 Calle Vendig, Condado, San Juan* ☎ *787/721–6900* 🌐 *www.atlanticbeachhotel.com.*

Brava. Dress to impress at this chic hotel dance club, where a long line of young people (21+) waits to get in Thursday–Saturday. Two levels each have their own DJ and dance floor. ✉ *El San Juan Resort & Casino, 6063 Av. Isla Verde, Isla Verde, San Juan* ☎ *787/791–2781* 🌐 *www.bravapr.com.*

PERFORMING ARTS

Orquesta Sinfónica de Puerto Rico (*Puerto Rico Symphony Orchestra*). Under the direction of conductor Maximiano Valdés, this 80-member orchestra performs a 52-week season that includes classical music, operas, ballets, and popular music. The orchestra plays mostly at Centro de Bellas Artes Luis A. Ferré but also gives outdoor concerts at museums and universities around the island as well as doing educational outreach in island schools. Pablo Casals helped create the group in 1956. ✉ *San Juan* ☎ *787/918–1107* 🌐 *www.sinfonicapr.gobierno.pr.*

Teatro Tapia. Named for Puerto Rican playwright Alejandro Tapia y Rivera, this is the oldest theater in Puerto Rico. It hosts traveling and locally produced theatrical and musical productions. Matinee performances for families are also held, especially around the holidays. ✉ *Plaza Colón, Calle Fortaleza, Old San Juan, San Juan* ☎ *787/480–5004* 🌐 *www.teatropr.com.*

SHOPPING

San Juan has the island's best range of stores (many closed on Sunday), but it isn't a free port, so you won't find bargains on electronics and perfumes. You can, however, find excellent prices on china, crystal, clothing, and jewelry. When shopping for local crafts, you'll find tacky along with treasures; in many cases you can watch the artisans at work. Popular items include *santos* (small carved figures of saints or religious scenes), hand-rolled cigars, handmade *mundillo* lace from Moca, *vejigantes* (colorful masks used during Carnival and local festivals) from Loíza and Ponce, and fancy men's shirts called guayaberas.

Old San Juan—especially Calles Fortaleza and Cristo—has T-shirt emporiums, crafts stores, bookshops, art galleries, jewelry boutiques, and even shops that specialize in made-to-order Panama hats. Calle Cristo has factory outlets, including Coach and Dooney & Bourke.

With many stores selling luxury items and designer fashions, the shopping spirit in the San Juan neighborhood of Condado is reminiscent of Miami. Avenida Ashford, the heart of San Juan's fashion district, has plenty of high-end clothing stores.

OLD SAN JUAN AND GREATER SAN JUAN

ART

Galería Botello. This influential gallery displays art by the late Angel Botello, who was hailed as the Caribbean Gauguin as far back as 1943. (His works also hang in the Museo de Arte de Puerto Rico.) His paintings often feature the bright colors of the tropics and usually depict island scenes. Also on display here are works by other prominent local artists, Puerto Rican santos, and sculptures by Botello. ✉ *208 Calle Cristo, Old San Juan* ☎ *787/723–9987* 🌐 *www.botello.com.*

CLOTHING

Cappalli. Noted local designer Lisa Cappalli sells her feminine, sensuous designs in this elegant boutique, which specializes in ready-to-wear and custom fashions including a small collection of whimsical, lacy wedding gowns. ✉ *206 Calle O'Donnell, Old San Juan* ☎ *787/289–6565.*

Nativa. The window displays are almost as daring as the clothes at this shop catering to trendy young ladies looking for party dresses, jumpers, accessories, and shoes. ✉ *55 Calle Cervantes, Condado* ☎ *787/724–1396* 🌐 *www.nativaboutique.net.*

Nono Maldonado. Known for high-end, elegant men's and women's clothes, particularly in linen, Nono Maldonado worked for many years as the fashion editor of *Esquire* and presents a periodic couture collection. This second-floor store also serves as the designer's studio. ✉ *1112 Av. Ashford, 2nd fl., Condado* ☎ *787/721–0456* 🌐 *www.nonomaldonado.com.*

17

Otto. Otto Bauzá stocks international lines of casual and formal wear for younger men. His shop is closed Sunday and Monday. ✉ *69 Av. Condado, Condado* ☎ *787/722–4609.*

GIFTS

Eclectika. This boutique carries a variety of items, mostly from Indonesia, from bedspreads to beaded and wooden jewelry, furnishings to hand fans. Everything is reasonably priced. ✉ *204 Calle O'Donnell, Plaza Colón, Old San Juan* ☎ *787/721–7236.*

Spicy Caribbee. Kitchen items, cookbooks, jams, spices, and sauces from around the Caribbean are on offer. ✉ *154 Calle Cristo, Old San Juan* ☎ *888/725–7259* 🌐 *www.spicycaribbee.com.*

JEWELRY

Bared & Sons. The store carries Rolex, Cartier, Bulgari, and Brietling watches and a large selection of fine jewelry. Look for the massive clock face on the corner. ✉ *206 San Justo, Old San Juan* ☎ *787/724–4811.*

Catalá Joyeros. Family-run since the 1930s, the store is known for its large selection of pearls and precious stones, and for its jewelry design. ✉ *Plaza de Armas, 152 Calle Rafael Cordero, Old San Juan* ☎ *787/722–3231* 🌐 *www.catalajoyeros.com.*

SOUVENIRS

Mi Pequeño San Juan. You might find a reproduction of your hotel at this shop, which specializes in tiny ceramic versions of San Juan doorways. The works are created by hand in the shop, which also carries fine art prints. ✉ *152 Calle Fortaleza, Old San Juan* ☎ *787/721–5040* 🌐 *www.mipequenosanjuan.com.*

SPORTS AND THE OUTDOORS

BOATING AND SAILING

East Island Excursions. This outfit operates 45- to 65-foot catamarans, two of the which are powered to cut down on travel time to outlying islands. Trips may include offshore snorkeling, stops at isolated beaches, and a lunch buffet. An evening excursion to Vieques to see the bioluminescent bay includes dinner at a local restaurant. All of the plush craft are outfitted with swimming decks, freshwater showers, and full-service bars. ✉ *Marina Puerto del Rey, Rte. 3, Km 51.4, Fajardo* ☎ *787/860–3434, 877/937–4386* 🌐 *www.eastislandpr.com.*

DIVING AND SNORKELING

The diving is excellent off Puerto Rico's south, east, and west coasts, as well as its nearby islands. Particularly striking are dramatic walls created by a continental shelf off the south coast near La Parguera and Guánica. There's also some fantastic diving near Fajardo and around Vieques and Culebra, two small islands off the east coast. It's best to choose specific locations with the help of a guide or outfitter. Escorted half-day dives range from $65 to $120 for one or two tanks, including all equipment; in general, double those prices for night dives. Packages that include lunch and other extras are more. Snorkeling excursions, which include transportation, equipment rental, and sometimes lunch, start at $50. Equipment rents for about $5 to $10.

Aquatic Adventures. Captain Taz Hamrick takes guests out on snorkeling and PADI-certified scuba trips, as well as charters to the surrounding keys. ✉ *372 Sector Fulladoza, Dewey, Culebra* ☎ *515/290–2310, 787/209–3494* 🌐 *www.diveculebra.com.*

Culebra Divers. Run by Monika and Walter Rieder, the island's premier dive shop caters to those new to scuba as well as those adept at underwater navigation. The company's 25-foot cabin cruisers travel to more than 50 local sites to see spotted eagle rays, octopus, moray eels, and turtles. Spring for an underwater scooter, which propels you through the sea like James Bond. You can also rent a mask and snorkel to explore on your own. ✉ *4 Calle Pedro Marquez, Dewey, Culebra* ☎ *787/742–0803* 🌐 *www.culebradivers.com.*

Sea Ventures Dive Center. Here you can get diving certification, arrange dive trips to 20 offshore sites, and organize boating and sailing excursions. ✉ *Marina Puerto del Rey, Rte. 3, Km 51.4, Fajardo* ☎ *787/863–3483, 800/739–3483* 🌐 *www.divepuertorico.com.*

GOLF

Aficionados may know that Puerto Rico is the birthplace of golf legend Chi Chi Rodríguez—and that he had to hone his craft somewhere. There are nearly 20 courses, including many championship links. Call ahead for tee times, as hours vary and several hotel courses give preference to guests. Greens fees are $20–$165.

The **Puerto Rican Golf Association** (✉ *264 Av. Matadero, Suite 11, San Juan* ☎ *787/793–3444* 🌐 *www.prga.org*) is a good source for information on courses and tournaments.

Arthur Hills Golf Course at El Conquistador Resort & Waldorf Astoria Spa. Named for its designer, the 18-hole course is famous for its mountainous terrain with elevation changes of more than 200 feet—rare in the Caribbean. From the highest spot, on the 15th hole, you have great views of the surrounding mountains and rain forest. The trade winds make every shot challenging—if the gorgeous views, strategic bunkering, and many water hazards haven't already distracted you. You are also likely to spot the harmless and generally timid iguanas that populate the area. ✉ *El Conquistador Resort, 1000 Av. El Conquistador, Fajardo* ☎ *787/863–6784* 🌐 *www.elconresort.com* *Up to $185* *18 holes, 6746 yards, par 72.*

Dorado Beach Resort Golf. Four 18-hole regulation courses blend Caribbean luxury and great golf at this icon with a storied tradition. Designed by Robert Trent Jones Sr., the famous East and West courses (West is closed for renovation at this writing) are in a secluded seaside sanctuary along 2 miles of northeasterly shore within the former Rockefeller estate. Two Plantation Courses—the Sugarcane (more challenging) and Pineapple (easier)—complete the offerings. ✉ *5000 Plantation Dr., Dorado* ☎ *787/262–1010* 🌐 *www.doradobeachclubs.com* *East/West $255, Plantation Courses $154* *East Course: 18 holes, 7000 yards, par 72; West Course: 18 holes, 6975 yards, par 72; Sugarcane: 18 holes, 7119 yards, par 72; Pineapple: 18 holes, 7030 yards, par 72.*

Fodor's Choice ★ **Golf Links at Royal Isabela.** Mixing luxurious service, ecological sensitivity, and an incomparable setting along dramatic bluffs at Puerto Rico's northwest edge, this 18-hole course, which opened in 2011, is already considered among the Caribbean's best. Designed and developed by Stanley and Charlie Pasarell with assistance from course architect David Pfaff, it can play to as much as 7,667 yards and a par of 72 or 73 depending upon how you play the Fork in the Road sixth. The course doesn't have one signature moment; it has many, from the sixth to the island green at nine to the carry over the sea at 12, to name a few. Carts are available, though walking is encouraged, and caddies are mandatory. ✉ *396 Ave. Noel Estrada, Isabela* ☎ *787/609–5888* 🌐 *www.royalisabela.com* *$250 ($125 guests); caddie $90 for two players* *18 holes, 7667 yards, par 73.*

HORSEBACK RIDING

Horseback riding is a well-established family pastime in Puerto Rico, with *cabalgatas* (group day rides) frequently organized on weekends through mountain towns.

Carabalí Rainforest Park. A family-run operation, this hacienda is a good place to jump in the saddle and ride one of Puerto Rico's Paso Fino horses. Hourlong rides take you around the 600-acre ranch, while two-hour treks take you to a river where you and your horse can take a dip. If you prefer something more high-tech, rent a four-wheeler for an excursion through the foothills of El Yunque. ✉ *Rd. 3, Km. 31.6, Luquillo* ☎ *787/889–4954* 🌐 *www.carabalirainforestpark.com.*

SURFING

The best surfing beaches are along the northwestern coast from Isabela south to Rincón, which gained notoriety by hosting the World Surfing Championship in 1968. Today the town draws surfers from around the globe, especially in winter, when the waves are at their best.

Desecheo Surf & Dive Shop. This shop rents bodyboards and a variety of short and long surfboards as well as snorkeling equipment; sets up surfing lessons; and sells swimwear, sandals, sunglasses, and surf gear. ✉ *Rte. 413, Km 2.5, Maria's Beach, Rincón* ☎ *787/823–0390* 🌐 *www.desecheosurfshop.com.*

Mar Azul. One of the best surf shops on the entire island has Rincon's best selection of performance surfboards and stand-up paddleboards to buy or rent. Paddleboard lessons are also available. ✉ *Rte. 413, Km 4.4, Rincón* ☎ *787/823–5692* 🌐 *www.puertoricosurfinginfo.com.*

18

SABA

WELCOME TO SABA

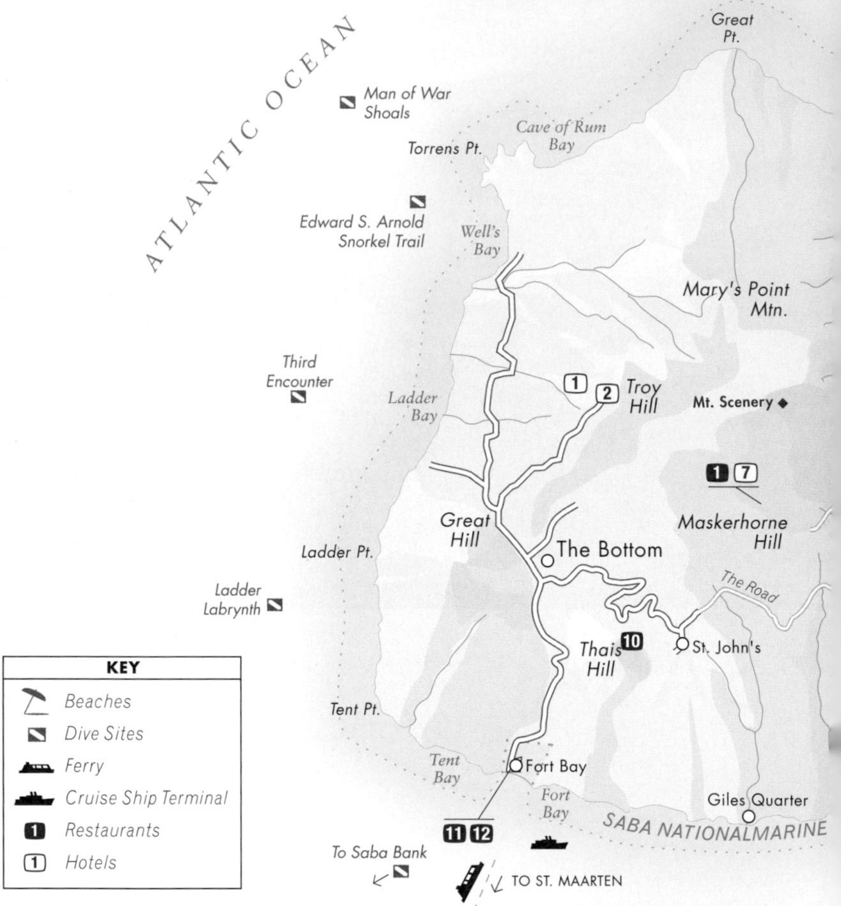

ATLANTIC OCEAN

Great Pt.

Man of War Shoals

Cave of Rum Bay

Torrens Pt.

Edward S. Arnold Snorkel Trail

Well's Bay

Mary's Point Mtn.

Third Encounter

Ladder Bay

Troy Hill

Mt. Scenery

Maskerhorne Hill

Great Hill

The Bottom

Ladder Pt.

The Road

Ladder Labrynth

Thais Hill

St. John's

Tent Pt.

Tent Bay

Fort Bay

Fort Bay

Giles Quarter

SABA NATIONALMARINE

To Saba Bank

TO ST. MAARTEN

KEY
Beaches
Dive Sites
Ferry
Cruise Ship Terminal
1 Restaurants
1 Hotels

Mountainous Saba's precipitous terrain allows visitors to choose between the heights and the depths. The Bottom, the island's capital, was once thought to be the crater of a dormant volcano. From here a trail of 400 rough-hewn steps drops to the sea. Divers can take a different plunge to view the pristine reef.

THE UNSPOILED QUEEN

Tiny Saba—an extinct volcano that juts out of the ocean to a height of 2,855 feet—is just 5 square miles (13 square km) in size and has a population of about 1,500. Part of the Dutch Caribbean, it's 28 miles (45 km) south of St. Maarten and surrounded by some of the richest dive sites in the Caribbean.

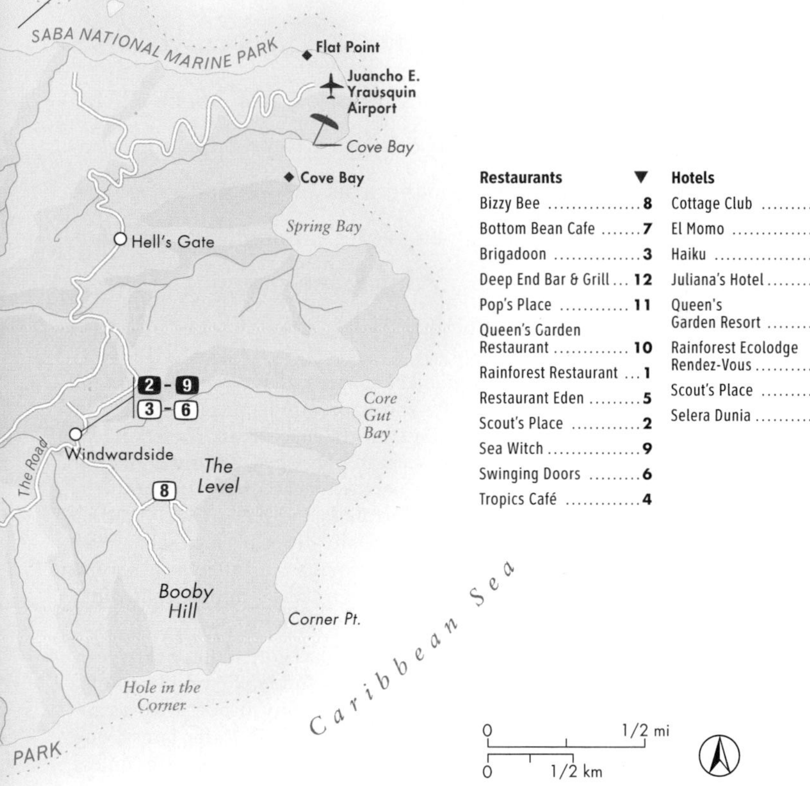

TOP REASONS TO VISIT SABA

1 Diving: Divers flock to Saba because of the clear water and spectacular ocean life.

2 Hiking: Hikers can climb the island's pinnacle, Mt. Scenery, but the less intense trails offer many sweeping vistas as well.

3 Authenticity: The locals in Saba are genuine, and tourist traps are just about nonexistent.

4 Ecotourism: Several hotels cater to ecotourists, with resident nature pros who can tell you everything about local flora and fauna.

5 Quirkiness: On this unusual island, the airport landing and "the Road" are thrill rides, Wells Bay beach disappears at the end of every summer, and the Bottom is not on the bottom.

Updated by Roberta Sotonoff

Though Saba (pronounced *say*-ba) is just south of St. Maarten (if you've seen the original *King Kong,* you may recognize its majestic silhouette from the beginning of the film), the islands couldn't be more different. St. Maarten is all beaches, gambling, and duty-free shopping; Saba is ecotourism, diving, and hiking.

Nearly half of Saba's 5 square miles (13 square km) is covered in verdant tropical rain forest; the other half is sprinkled with hamlets composed of white, green-shuttered houses trimmed with gingerbread, roofed in red, and built on grades so steep, they seem to defy physics. Flower-draped walls and neat picket fences border narrow paths among the bromeliads, palms, hibiscus, orchids, and Norfolk Island pines. The land dips and climbs à la San Francisco and eventually drops off into sheer cliffs that fall right into the ocean, the fodder for some of the world's most striking dive sites and the primary reason for Saba's cultlike following. Divers seem to relish the fact that they're in on Saba's secret.

But word about this Dutch Caribbean island has gotten out. Every year, more tourists are turned on to Saba's charms and make the 11-minute, white-knuckle flight from St. Maarten into the tiny airport with a runway not much larger than an aircraft carrier's. Indeed, traffic jams along the winding, narrow road (yes, there's really just one) are rare, unless the driver in front of you stops to chat. The past few years have seen the opening of more restaurants and, most recently, a minimall (big advances, considering around-the-clock electricity was established only in 1970). But don't come expecting a booming metropolis; even as it changes, Saba retains an old-world charm.

A major point of local pride is that many Saban families can be traced all the way back to the island's settlement in 1640 (the surnames Hassell, Johnson, and Peterson fill the tiny phone book). And Sabans hold their traditions dear. Saba lace—a genteel art that dates back to the 1870s—is still hand-stitched by local ladies who, on the side, also distill potent, 151-proof Saba Spice. It is for sale in most of the island's mom-and-pop shops. And islanders like to keep their ancestors close in a very literal sense: in keeping with a generations-old tradition, the dead are buried in local families' neatly tended gardens.

Like the residents of most small towns, Sabans are a tight-knit group; nothing happens without everyone hearing about it, making crime pretty much a nonissue. That said, they welcome newcomers and tend to make travelers feel less like tourists and more like old friends. After all, they're proud to show off their home, which they lovingly call "the unspoiled queen."

LOGISTICS

Getting to Saba: There are no nonstops from the United States. Connections for the short flight to the island are made in St. Maarten.

Hassle Factor: Medium to high.

On the Ground: Taxis can take you around, or you can rent a car. There's just one road, so it's not as if you could get lost. Some people even hitchhike.

PLANNING

WHEN TO GO

High season runs from mid-December through April. The Saba Day long weekend is usually at the end of the first week of December, and Carnival is in the summer (July or August).

GETTING HERE AND AROUND

AIR TRAVEL

All flights from the United States arrive in St. Maarten, where you transfer for a short flight on Winair, the only airline to fly to Saba. The approach to the tiny airstrip is as thrilling as a roller-coaster ride; luckily, the de Havilland Twin Otter aircraft are built for it. In fact, the pilot needs only half the length of the runway to land properly. (If you're nervous, don't sit on the right side of the plane. The wing seems almost to scrape the cliff side on the approach.) Once you've touched down, the pilot taxis an inch or two, turns, and deposits you just outside the airport.

Airline Contact Winair. Round-trip fees start at $132. ☎ *599/416–2255* 🌐 *www.fly-winair.com.*

Airport Juancho E. Yrausquin Airport (*SAB*). ☎ *599/416–2222 control tower, 599/416–2860 airport manager.*

BOAT AND FERRY TRAVEL

Dawn II. This 50-person, 65-foot aluminum vessel runs on Tuesday, Thursday, and Saturday between Philipsburg and Fort Bay. It leaves Saba at 7 am, arriving at St. Maarten at 8:30, and departs St. Maarten at 4:30 pm, arriving at Fort Bay at 6. The one-way fare from St. Maarten to Saba is $58 plus a $7 harbor fee; the opposite direction is $55 plus a $10 harbor fee. A same-day round-trip is $100 plus a $17 harbor fee. Call to check current schedules. ✉ *Fort Bay Ferry Terminal* ☎ *599/416–2299, 607/846–7222 in U.S.* 🌐 *www.sabactransport.com.*

The Edge. This high-speed ferry leaves St. Maarten's Pelican Marina in Simpson Bay for Fort Bay on Saba every Wednesday, Friday, and Sunday at 9 am (check in an hour before) and leaves Saba at 3:30 pm (check-in at 3). The journey, which can be rough, takes an hour and 20 minutes. A day trip costs $80 per person plus a $15 port fee, and a round-trip (overnight stay) costs $110 plus $17 port feet. Reservations are recommended. ✉ *Fort Bay Ferry Terminal* ☎ *721/544–2631, 321/422–7037 in U.S.* 🌐 *www.stmaarten-activities.com.*

CAR TRAVEL

You won't need long to tour the island by car—you can cover the entire circuitous length of the Road in the space of a morning. If you want to shop, have lunch, and do some sightseeing, plan on a full day. The island has only one gas station, in Fort Bay. If you are renting a car—one from Morgan's Car Rental averages $55–$65 a day—don't let the tank run too low, as the station has abbreviated hours (weekdays 8–3:30, Saturdays 8–noon). At this writing, gas costs $5.75 per gallon.

Car-Rental Contact Morgan's Car Rental ✉ *Breadline Plaza, Windwardside* ☎ *599/416–2881 ICS (Island Communication Services), 599/416–5893.*

TAXI TRAVEL

Taxis charge a set rate for up to four people per taxi, with an additional cost for each extra person. The fare from the airport to Hell's Gate is $10, to Windwardside it's $12.50, and to the Bottom it's $20. The fare from the Fort Bay ferry docks to Windwardside is $15. A taxi from Windwardside to the Bottom is $10.

ESSENTIALS

Banks and Exchange Services Saba's official currency is the U.S. dollar, but the Netherlands Antillian guilder (ANG) is sometimes used. The exchange rate is fixed at ANG 1.79 to $1. The RBC Bank, in Windwardside, and Windward Island Bank (WIB), in the Bottom, offer full banking services, weekdays 8:30–3:30.

Electricity 110 volts/60 cycles; visitors from North America should have no trouble using their electronics or travel appliances.

Emergency Services Ambulance ☎ *911, 599/416–2210, 599/416–3710.* **Fire** ☎ *599/416–3710, 599/416–2210.* **Police** ✉ *The Bottom* ☎ *599/416–3737.*

Passport Requirements Visitors must carry a valid passport and have an ongoing or return ticket.

Phones Phones take prepaid phone cards, which can be bought at stores throughout the island, or local coins. To call Saba from the United States, dial 011 + 599 + 416, followed by the four-digit number.

Taxes and Service Charges You must pay a $10 departure tax when leaving Saba by plane. There is also a $5 departure tax by boat, which is sometimes covered in the cost of the ticket. Several of the larger hotels will tack on a 10%–15% service charge; others include it in rates. Hotels add a 5% government tax plus a 3% turnover tax to the cost of a room. A $1 per person, per night nature fee is automatically added to your hotel bill.

ACCOMMODATIONS

There are no big resorts on Saba, just some small hotels and guesthouses, as well as a few rental apartments and villas.

Hotel reviews have been shortened. For full information, visit Fodors.com.

	WHAT IT COSTS IN U.S. DOLLARS			
	$	$$	$$$	$$$$
Restaurants	under $12	$12–$20	$21–$30	over $30
Hotels	under $275	$275–$375	$376–$475	over $475

Restaurant prices are the average cost of a main course at dinner or, if dinner is not served, at lunch. Hotel prices are the lowest cost of a standard double room in high season.

VISITOR INFORMATION

Saba Tourist Office ✉ *Windwardside* ☎ *599/416–2231, 599/416–2322* 🌐 *www.sabatourism.com.*

WEDDINGS

If you want to be married somewhere other than the Government Building's courtroom, you must submit a written request to the lieutenant governor of Saba. Same-sex marriages are now the norm.

Lt. Governor of Saba ☎ *599/416–3313, 599/416–3311, 599/416–3312.*

EXPLORING

18

Getting around the island means negotiating the narrow, twisting roadway that clings to the mountainside and rises from sea level to almost 2,000 feet. Although driving isn't difficult, be sure to go slowly and cautiously. If in doubt, leave the driving to a cabbie so you can enjoy the scenery.

TOP ATTRACTIONS

FAMILY **Harry L. Johnson Museum.** Small signs mark this 160-year-old former sea captain's home, surrounded by lemongrass, clover, and a playground for small children. It has been renovated, but period pieces like the handsome mahogany four-poster bed, an antique organ, and the kitchen's rock oven still remain. You can also look at old documents, such as a letter a Saban wrote after the hurricane of 1772, in which he sadly says, "We have lost our little all." The delightful stroll to the museum down the stone-walled Park Lane is one of the prettiest walks in the Caribbean. ✉ *Windwardside* 🎟 *$2* ⏲ *Weekdays 11–4.*

Fodor's Choice ★ **Mt. Scenery.** Stone and concrete steps—1,064 of them—rise to a mahogany grove at the summit. En route, the steps pass giant elephant ears, ferns, begonias, mangoes, palms, and orchids—six identifiable ecosystems in all. Staff at the Trail Shop in Windwardside can provide a field guide. Have your hotel pack a lunch, wear sturdy shoes, and take a jacket and water. The three-hour round-trip is best begun in the early morning.

WORTH NOTING

The Bottom. Sitting in a bowl-shape valley 820 feet above the sea, this town is the seat of government and the home of the lieutenant governor. The governor's mansion, next to Wilhelmina Park, has fancy fretwork, a steeply pitched roof, and wraparound double galleries.

On the other side of town is the Wesleyan Holiness Church, a small stone building with white fretwork. Though it's been renovated and virtually reconstructed over the years, its original four walls date from 1919; go inside and look around. Stroll by the church, beyond a place called the Gap, to a lookout point where you can see the 400 rough-hewn steps leading down to Ladder Bay. This and Fort Bay were the two landing sites from which Saba's first settlers had to haul themselves and their possessions up to the heights. Sabans sometimes walk down to Ladder Bay to picnic. Think long and hard before you do: climbing back requires navigating the same 400 steps.

Cove Bay. Near the airport on the island's northeastern side, this 20-foot-long strip of rocks and pebbles laced with gray sand is really the only place for sunning. There's also a small tide pool here for swimming. Sand has been added to make it look more beachy. ⊠ *Cove Bay.*

Flat Point. This is the only place on the island where planes can land. The runway here is one of the world's shortest, with a length of approximately 1,300 feet. Only STOL (short takeoff and landing) prop planes dare land here, as each end of the runway drops off more than 100 feet into the crashing surf below. ⊠ *Flat Point.*

Fort Bay. The end of the Road is also the jumping-off point for Saba's dive operations and the site of the St. Maarten ferry dock. The island's only gas station is here, as is a 277-foot pier that accommodates tenders from ships. On the quay is a decompression chamber, which at this writing is not in use, and three dive shops. At Deep End Bar and Grill and Pop's Place, you can catch your breath while enjoying refreshments and a view of the water. ⊠ *Fort Bay.*

Hell's Gate. The Road makes 14 hairpin turns up nearly 2,000 vertical feet to Hell's Gate. Holy Rosary Church, on Zion's Hill, is a stone structure that looks medieval but was built in 1962. In the community center behind the church, village ladies sell their intricate lace. The same ladies make the potent rum-based Saba Spice, each according to her old family recipe. The intrepid can venture to Lower Hell's Gate, where the Old Sulphur Mine Walk leads to bat caves (with a sulfuric stench) that can—with caution—be explored. ⊠ *Holy Rosary Church.*

Saba National Marine Park. Established in 1987 to preserve and manage the island's marine resources, this marine park encircles the island, dipping down to 200 feet. It's zoned for diving, swimming, fishing, boating, and anchorage. A unique aspect of Saba's diving is the submerged pinnacles at about 70 feet deep. Here all forms of sea creatures rendezvous. The information center offers talks and slide shows for divers and snorkelers and provides literature on marine life. (Divers are charged $3 per dive to help maintain the park facilities.) Before you visit, call to see if anyone is around. ⊠ *Saba Conservation Foundation/Marine Park*

Looking down from Mt. Scenery

Visitors Center, Fort Bay ☎ *599/416–3295, 599/416–2709* 🌐 *www.sabapark.org* ⏲ *Weekdays 8–5.*

Windwardside. The island's second-largest village, perched at 1,968 feet, commands magnificent views of the Caribbean. Here amid the oleander bushes are rambling lanes and narrow alleyways that wind through the hills; clusters of tiny, neat houses and shops; and the Saba Tourist Office. At the village's northern end, the Church of St. Paul's Conversion is a colonial building with a red-and-white steeple. ■ **TIP→ With the exception of Sunday, expect traffic jams.** ✉ *Windwardside.*

WHERE TO EAT

The island might be tiny, but there's no shortage of mouthwatering fare, including French dishes, fresh seafood, and Caribbean specialties. Reservations are necessary, as most of the restaurants are quite small. In addition, some places provide transportation.

What to Wear: Restaurants are informal. Shorts are fine during the day, but for dinner you may want to wear pants or a sundress. Just remember that Windwardside's elevation can make nights cool.

$ BAKERY FAMILY ✕ **Bizzy Bee Bakery.** Chat with the locals while you buy sandwiches or something sweet to have with your tea or coffee. The turkey panini and breads such as cornbread, multigrain, sunflower seed, pumpkin seed, and milk bread are also tasty. 💲 *Average main: $7* ✉ *Breadline Plaza, Windwardside* ☎ *599/416–2900* ▭ *No credit cards* ⏲ *No dinner. Closed Sun.*

$ CAFÉ **✕ Bottom Bean Café.** Saba's answer to Starbucks, this local hangout roasts its own coffee. And there are lots to choose from—15 to be exact—as well as mochas, cappuccinos, lattes, and frozen drinks like chais and smoothies. Salads, soup, sandwiches, ice cream, beer, and wine are also served, and there's free Wi-Fi. *Average main: $3 ✉ The Bottom ☎ 599/416–3636 No credit cards No dinner.*

$$$ ECLECTIC **✕ Brigadoon.** The exceptional fare here draws as many people as the entertaining atmosphere. Eccentric co-owner Tricia Chammaa livens things up with jokes and brassy banter while her husband, Michael, toils in the kitchen. The result is a great experience. Brigadoon's glass-top tables are accented with Caribbean-style runners and string lights. Specialties include Chowder Michael, Shrimp Michael (a pasta dish that includes mushrooms and olives), and an encrusted, lightly seared yellowfin tuna served on a salad. Thursday is prime rib night, but you must preorder before 3 pm. As for desserts, the cheesecake—in a variety of flavors—and the peanut-butter pie are standouts. Also worth a try: Madagascar vanilla bean–ginger rum, made in-house (as are all the ice creams). *Average main: $23 ✉ Windwardside ☎ 599/416–2380 Reservations essential Closed Tues. and Aug. or Sept. No lunch.*

$$ AMERICAN **✕ Deep End Restaurant and Bar.** Owned by Queen's Garden Resort, the restaurant has a $10 breakfast special that lets you choose your egg style, bread, and enhancer (Gouda cheese, bacon, sausage, ham, or cream cheese). Lunch features a variety of customized pastas, sandwiches, salads, and wok dishes. *Average main: $15 ✉ Fort Bay ☎ 599/416–3438 Closed Mon. No dinner.*

$ AMERICAN **✕ Pop's Place.** This itty-bitty come-as-you-are, Caribbean-flavor shack is directly on the water, overlooking the pier in Fort Bay. It's cozy, it's fun, and its bar resembles a ship. Fast food and sandwiches are on offer. Note that Pop's sometimes closes on slow days. *Average main: $8 ✉ Fort Bay ☎ 599/416–3640 No credit cards Closed Mon.*

$$$ ECLECTIC Fodor's Choice ★ **✕ Queen's Garden Restaurant.** Set in a lovely garden and showcasing sweeping views of the Bottom, this dimly lit venue is perfect for a romantic meal, especially in the Bird's Nest, a tree house for private dining. Regardless of where you sit, you can expect excellent service to go with superb Saban lobster or some other tasty offering. Nothing that excites your taste buds? Let the chef create something for you. The smoked-duck-breast salad starter is mouthwatering. Come early for cocktails at the outdoor bar, overlooking the pool—and, below that, the ocean—then stay and be awed by the star-studded sky. Poolside parties, musical events, and theme nights with international flavors spice things up. A jacket is required for dinner. *Average main: $30 ✉ Queen's Garden Resort, 1 Troy Hill Dr., Troy Hill ☎ 599/416–3494 www.queensaba.com/theresort Reservations essential No dinner Mon.*

$$ CARIBBEAN **✕ Rainforest Restaurant.** You might need a flashlight for the five-minute hike down the Crispeen Track, by way of the Mt. Scenery Trail, to find this restaurant in the middle of the rain forest. It's truly away from it all. There's a different menu every week. At night, you are surrounded by music—the lilting sound of tree frogs. *Average main: $15 ✉ Rainforest Ecolodge Rendez-Vous, Crispeen Track, Windwardside ☎ 599/416–7012, 599/416–7032 www.ecolodge-saba.com Closed Mon.*

$$$$ EUROPEAN Fodor's Choice ★ **Restaurant Eden.** On a rooftop amid a lovely garden, chef Norbert Schippers concocts an eclectic, European-French menu that might include anything: risotto, seafood, steaks. Sample the Frutti del Mare, pasta with seafood and garden vegetables topped with a lobster cream sauce. The restaurant prides itself on the freshness of its ingredients. *Average main: $31 Lambee's Place, above Sea Saba Dive Center, Windwardside 599/416–2539 Reservations essential Closed Tues. No lunch.*

$$ CARIBBEAN **Scout's Place.** At this spacious, fun-loving restaurant and bar, you'll find dishes like goat stew and spit-roasted chicken. Theme nights include Friday fish-and-chips or gyros ($18) and Saturday barbecue ($19). In addition to the good food, there's great atmosphere. Locals flock here on Friday for karaoke, but there's bound to be a group looking for fun other nights, too. The veranda has stunning views of the water, the tiny houses, and the lush forest. *Average main: $19 Windwardside 599/416–2740, 599/416–2205 www.scoutsplace.com No dinner Sun.*

$$ ECLECTIC **Sea Witch Bar & Grill.** Eat indoors or out at this eatery (formerly Saba's Treasure). Start with a cocktail or imported beer. Then enjoy pizza, pasta, steak, or seafood. Desserts are homemade. *Average main: $19 Windwardside 599/416–2013.*

$$ BARBECUE **Swinging Doors.** A cross between an English pub and an Old West saloon (yes, there are swinging doors), this busy watering hole serves not-to-be-missed barbecue on Tuesday and Friday nights. Pick from ribs, chicken, or ribs and chicken ($12), and ask for peanut sauce—you'll be glad you did. Steak night is Sunday ($16–$18); if you'd like to cook your own, you're welcome to. The rest of the week, it's just drinks. Expect plenty of conversation, including local gossip. *Average main: $15 Windwardside 599/416–2506 No credit cards No lunch. No dinner Mon., Wed., Thurs., and Sat.*

$$ ECLECTIC **Tropics Café.** Breakfast and lunch are served in the cabana-style, open-air dining room by the pool or in a small room dominated by a bar. Lunch comprises sandwiches, salads, and specials, while dinner brings fresh fish, steaks, and a changing three-course menu. Every Friday at 4, a TGIF party mixes snack platters and music by local DJs. Free wine is available Tuesday–Sunday 4–5, and a daily happy hour (4–6) features half-price beers. *Average main: $20 Juliana's Hotel, Windwardside 599/416–2469, 888/289–5708 www.sabatropics.com No lunch and dinner Mon.*

18

WHERE TO STAY

Saba's few hotel rooms are primarily in a handful of friendly, tidy inns or guesthouses perched on ledges or tucked into tropical gardens. Because the island is so small, it doesn't much matter where you stay. Among the choices are a couple of delightful small inns and eco-resorts. There are also more than a dozen apartments, cottages, and villas for rent. Cable TV is common, but air-conditioning is rare.

$ HOTEL FAMILY **Cottage Club.** Form follows function at these gingerbread bungalows, where the price is right and the proximity to downtown is ideal. **Pros:** walking distance to Windwardside; lushly landscaped pool with a gorgeous view; majestic lobby–reception room. **Cons:** stark suites; no on-site dining; some of the walks to the rooms are steep; no a/c. *Rooms from: $130 Windwardside 599/416–2386 www.cottage-club.com 6 cottages No meals 4 additional cottages are long-term rentals.*

$ HOTEL **El Momo.** If you want to do your ecological part without giving up modern convenience, consider these tiny cottages, hidden among tropical flora 1,500 feet up Booby Hill. **Pros:** buried in the woods; smoke-free property; free Wi-Fi; gift shop. **Cons:** tiny accommodations; 60+ steep steps to the property, so not handicap accessible. *Rooms from: $75 Booby Hill 599/416–2265 www.elmomocottages.com 7 cottages No meals.*

$$$$ RENTAL **Haiku House.** Hidden on a hilltop and constructed of redwood—no gingerbread here—this three-bedroom, three-bath rental was built to resemble a 16th-century Japanese villa. **Pros:** remote location ensures privacy; one of the island's nicest properties. **Cons:** taxi or car needed to get around; minimum three-night stay. *Rooms from: $545 Troy Hill www.sabavillas.com 1 cottage No meals.*

$ HOTEL FAMILY **Juliana's Hotel.** Reasonable prices, in town, great views, and accommodations from good to luxurious—it's all here. **Pros:** across from Tropics Café; outdoor, in-rock shower in Orchid Cottage; on-site computer with free Internet; full breakfast. **Cons:** close quarters; a hike to get off property; not all rooms have a/c. *Rooms from: $130 Windwardside 599/416–2269, 888/783–3319 in U.S. www.julianas-hotel.com 9 rooms, 1 apartment, 4 cottages Breakfast.*

$ HOTEL Fodor's Choice ★ **Queen's Gardens Resort.** Everything about this romantic mini-resort reflects Saba, from the quaint stone stairway that winds past the island's largest pool to the patio in front of the main building, which houses the Queen's Garden Restaurant, serving fresh island fare. **Pros:** local flavor; large pool with bar; private Jacuzzis with sweeping views. **Cons:** not wheelchair accessible or kid-friendly. *Rooms from: $230 1 Troy Hill Dr., Troy Hill 599/416–3494 www.queenssaba.com 12 1- or 2-bedroom suites No meals.*

$ HOTEL **Rainforest Ecolodge Rendez-Vous Saba.** If you like hiking and getting back to nature, then this lodge, a five-minute walk deep in the rain forest, is for you. **Pros:** quiet; candlelit restaurant; nature-theme cottages. **Cons:** it's a hike to get here and a steep climb to rooms; only three cottages have ocean views; no electricity or Internet. *Rooms from: $60 Crispeen Track, Windwardside 599/416–7428 www.ecolodge-saba.com 12 cottages No meals.*

$ HOTEL **Scout's Place.** Owned by dive instructors Wolfgang and Barbara Tooten, this all-in-one dive resort is especially good for the diver on a tight budget. **Pros:** on-site dive shop; free Nitrox diving with packages; multilingual owners; Friday Sabaoke. **Cons:** smallish rooms, some with little sunlight. *Rooms from: $114 Windwardside 599/416–2740, 599/416–2205, 866/656–7222 for reservations www.scoutsplace.com 10 rooms, 1 2-bedroom cottage Breakfast.*

$ B&B/INN Fodor's Choice ★ **Selera Dunia.** The managing director, Hemmie van Xanten, has traveled the world amassing a vast collection of objects from Africa, Asia, and Colombia, and the hotel's spacious themed rooms reflect those travels. **Pros:** very well appointed accommodations; tranquillity and privacy. **Cons:** car or taxi needed to explore the island. *Rooms from: $135* ✉ *The Level, Windwardside* ☎ *599/416–5443* 🌐 *www.seleradunia-saba.com* *2 rooms* *No meals.*

NIGHTLIFE

Guido's. There's often dancing and local DJs on weekends here. ✉ *Windwardside* ☎ *599/416–2230.*

Scout's Place. When night rolls around, the convivial bar here can get crowded, and sometimes there's dancing. Go on Friday for "Sabaoke" (the Saban version of karaoke), when people swarm the spacious dining area. ✉ *Windwardside* ☎ *599/416–2740.*

SHOPPING

The history of Saba lace, one of the island's most popular goods, goes back to the late 19th century. Gertrude Johnson learned lace making at a Caracas convent school. She returned to Saba in the 1870s and taught the art that has endured ever since. Saban ladies display and sell their creations at the community center in Hell's Gate and from their houses; just follow the signs. Collars, tea towels, napkins, and other small articles are relatively inexpensive; larger ones, such as tablecloths, can be pricey. The fabric requires some care—it's not drip-dry. Saba Spice is another island buy. Although it *sounds* as delicate as lace, and the aroma is as sweet as can be, the base for this liqueur is 151-proof rum.

Breadline Plaza. Saba's one and only minimall contains Bluemint Boutique, Bizzy Bee Bakery, Eye Care Optical, and Island Communication Service (a business and Internet café). ✉ *Windwardside.*

El Momo Folk Art. The shelves here overflow with regional crafts, local postcards, handmade jewelry, knickknacks, and anything else El Momo can find a spot for. It's next door to the Peanut Gallery and has the same owners. ✉ *Lambee's Place, Windwardside* ☎ *599/416–2518* 🌐 *www.emfa-saba.com.*

JoBean Glass. Artist-owner Jo Bean makes delicate glass-bead jewelry and sterling silver and gold pieces. Workshops in beadwork are available, and there's a branch in the main part of Windwardside. ✉ *Booby Hill* ☎ *599/416–2490.*

Peanut Gallery. From watercolors of local houses to ocean-inspired sculpture, this gallery has Saba's best selection of local and Caribbean art. Browse its offerings, and you might end up with something better than a refrigerator magnet to remember your trip. ✉ *Lambee's Place, Windwardside* ☎ *599/416–2509, 599/416–6088* 🌐 *www.thepeanutgallery.vpweb.co.uk.*

Divers will find spectacular marine life and coral in Saba's 28 dive sites.

Saba Artisan Foundation. Here you can buy hand-screened fabrics by the yard or already made into resort clothing. The foundation also serves as a central location for buying the famous Saba lace as well as T-shirts and spices. It's open weekdays only. ✉ *The Bottom* ☎ *599/416–3260.*

SPORTS AND THE OUTDOORS

DIVING AND SNORKELING

Fodor's Choice ★ Saba is one of the world's premier scuba-diving destinations. Visibility is extraordinary, and dive sites are alive with corals and other sea creatures. Within ½ mile (¾ km) of shore, seawalls drop to depths of more than 1,000 feet. The Saba National Marine Park, which includes shoals, reefs, and seawalls rich with corals and fish, is dedicated to preserving its marine life.

Divers have a pick of 28 sites, including **Third Encounter,** a top-rated pinnacle dive (usually to about 110 feet) for advanced divers, with plentiful fish and spectacular coral; **Man of War Shoals,** another popular pinnacle dive (70 feet), with myriad fish and coral; and **Ladder Labyrinth,** a formation of ridges and alleys (down to 80 feet), where likely sightings include grouper, sea turtles, and sharks.

Snorkelers shouldn't feel left out: the marine park has several marked spots where reefs or rocks sit in shallow water. Among these sites is **Torrens Point,** on the northwest side of the island. Waterproof maps are available from the marine park, the Saba Conservation Foundation, and dive shops.

Expect to pay about $60 for a one-tank dive, around $110 for a two-tank dive. There is also a mandatory $3 dive fee imposed by the marine park and a $1 charge per dive for the hyperbaric chamber.

FAMILY **Sea and Learn.** Every October, local dive operator Lynn Costenaro, of Sea Saba, orchestrates an event that has become an international attraction. Pharmacologists, biologists, and other nature experts from all over the world descend on Saba to give presentations, lead field trips, and show off research projects, all of which are designed to increase environmental awareness, mostly about the sea. Past events have included monitoring undersea octopus checkpoints and studying the medicinal value of indigenous plants. There are even special events for kids. And best of all, it's free. You can sign up online. ☎ *599/416–2246* 🌐 *www.seaandlearn.org.*

DIVE OPERATORS

Saba Deep. For a personal one-on-one dive experience, try this outfit, which tends to take out smaller groups. The company provides PADI certifications from beginner to dive master and offers Nitrox diving and equipment if needed. A one-tank dive is $60; two tanks, $110. ✉ *Fort Bay* ☎ *599/416–3347, 866/416–3347 in U.S.* 🌐 *www.sabadeep.com.*

Saba Divers. Offering multilingual instruction, this company is a great option for those interested in meeting international divers or in practicing their language skills. It's the only outfit on the island that lets customers dive with Nitrox for free. ✉ *Windwardside* ☎ *599/416–2740* 🌐 *www.sabadivers.com.*

Sea Saba. All excursions are accompanied by at least two dive instructors and can include up to 10 divers on one of two 40-foot boats. The staff is both knowledgeable and jovial, making a day on the boat illuminating and enjoyable for any diver. ✉ *Windwardside* ☎ *599/416–2246, 800/883–7222 in U.S.* 🌐 *www.seasaba.com.*

GUIDED TOURS

The taxi drivers who meet the planes at the airport or the boats at Fort Bay conduct tours of the island. Tours can also be arranged by dive shops and hotels. A full-day trek costs $50 for one to four passengers and $12.50 per person for groups larger than four. If you're in from St. Maarten for a day trip, you can do a full morning of sightseeing, stop off for lunch (have your driver make reservations before starting), complete the tour afterward, and return to the airport in time to make the last flight back to St. Maarten. Guides are available for hiking; arrangements may be made through the tourist office or the Trail Shop in Windwardside. Or check out the island in a guided boat tour available for groups of up to 10 on Tuesday, Thursday, and Saturday. In an hour and a half you can circle the island while learning about its history, its local seabirds, and its coral reefs.

HIKING

On Saba you can't avoid hiking, even if you just go to mail a postcard. The big deal, of course, is Mt. Scenery, with 1,064 steps leading to its top.

Saba Conservation Foundation. The foundation maintains Saba's trails and provides information about 18 recommended botanical hikes at its office in Fort Bay or its shop in Windwardside. The charges for trail use are $1 per day or $3 per stay, automatically added to your hotel bill. Botanical tours are available on request, and Crocodile James (James Johnson) will explain the local flora and fauna. A guided, strenuous, full-day hike through the undeveloped side of Mt. Scenery costs about $50. ✉ *Fort Bay* ☎ *599/416–2630 trail shop, 599/416–3295* 🌐 *www.sabapark.org* 🎫 *$3 donation requested.*

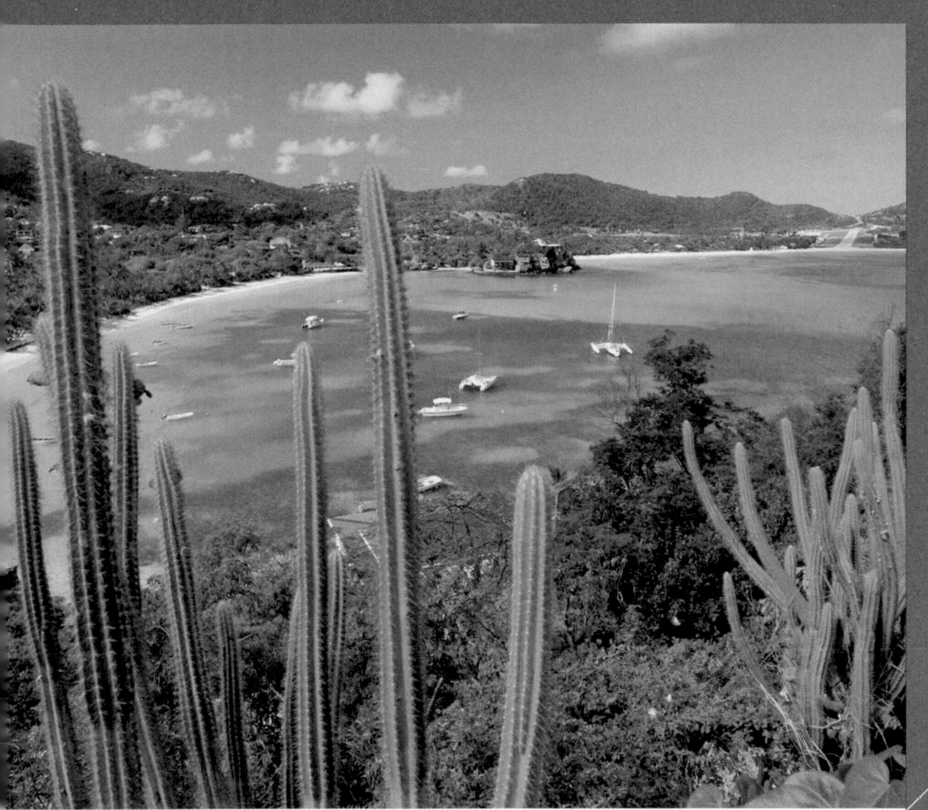

ST. BARTHÉLEMY

19

WELCOME TO ST. BARTHÉLEMY

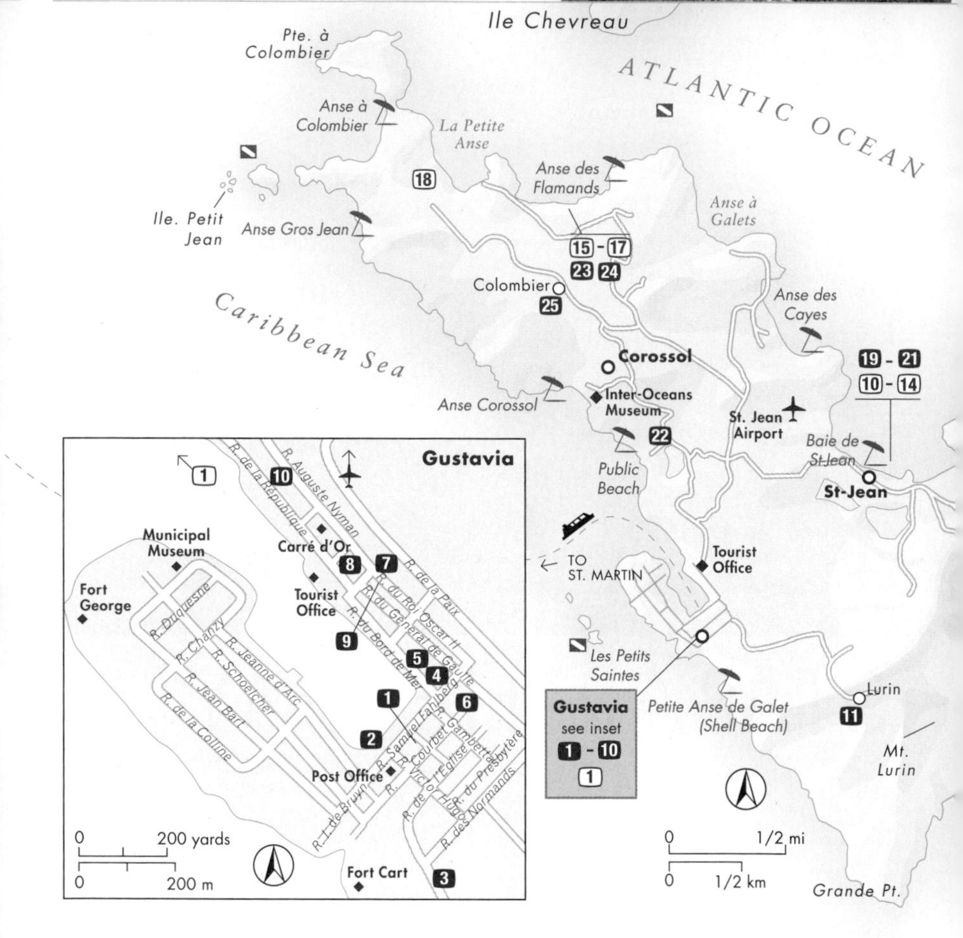

Chic travelers put aside their cell phones long enough to enjoy the lovely beaches—long, surf-pounded strands; idyllic crescents crowned by cliffs or forests; glass-smooth lagoons perfect for windsurfing. Nothing on St. Barth comes cheap. But on a hotel's awning-shaded terrace St. Barth's civilized ways seem worth every penny.

Restaurants

Bagatelle St. Barth 2
Bartolomeo 16
Les Bistroy/ Absolutely Wine 21
Bonito 6
Dō Brazil 3
Eddy's 4
La Case de L'Isle 24
La Gloriette 17
La Langouste 23
La Plage 19
La Table de Jules 14
Le Carré Lounge 8
Le Gaïac 15
Le Palace 5
Le Repaire 10
Le Ti St. Barth 18
Les Bananiers 25
L'Esprit 12
L'Isola 7
L'Isoletta 9
Maya's 22
Meat and Potatoes 13
Ocean 1
Restaurant La Santa Fé ... 11
The Sand Bar 20

Hotels

Cheval Blanc St-Barth Isle de France 15
Christopher 7
Eden Rock 12
Emeraude Plage 10
Hôtel Baie des Anges 16
Hotel Guanahani 6
Hôtel Le Toiny 3
Hôtel le Village St-Jean .. 14
Hotel Les Ondines Sur La Plage 4
Hotel Taïwana 17
Le P'tit Morne 18
Le Sereno 5
Le Tom Beach Hôtel 11
Les Îlets de la Plage 13
Les Mouettes 8
Normandie 9
Salines Garden Cottages ... 2
Sunset Hotel 1

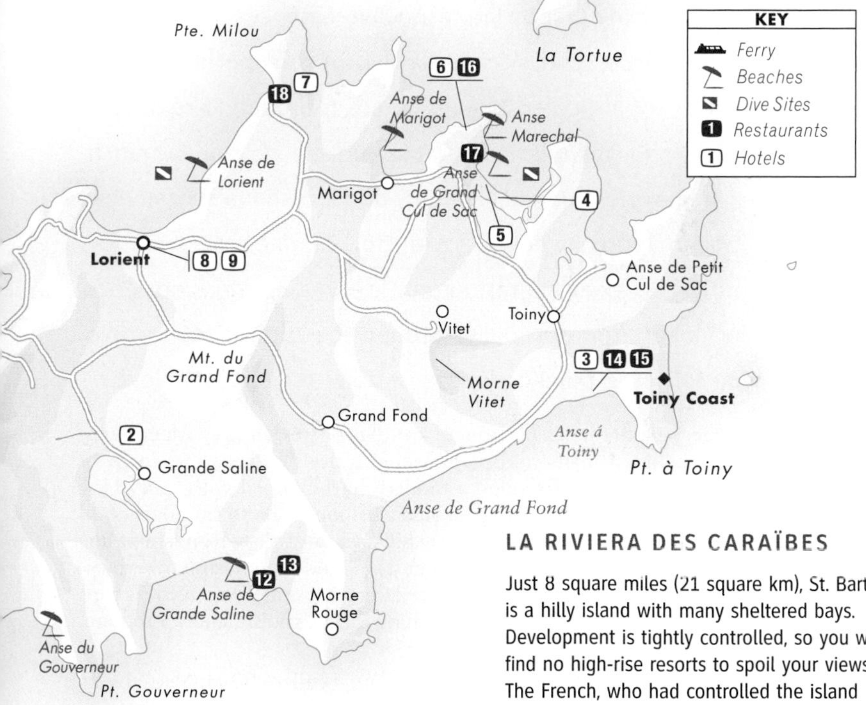

KEY
Ferry
Beaches
Dive Sites
Restaurants
Hotels

LA RIVIERA DES CARAÏBES

Just 8 square miles (21 square km), St. Barth is a hilly island with many sheltered bays. Development is tightly controlled, so you will find no high-rise resorts to spoil your views. The French, who had controlled the island since the late 17th century, gave it to Sweden in 1784 but reclaimed it in 1877.

TOP REASONS TO VISIT ST. BARTHÉLEMY

1 The Scene: The island is active, sexy, hedonistic, and hip, and the human scenery is as beautiful as the sparkling-blue sea vistas.

2 Super Style: St. Barth continues to change and evolve, becoming ever more chic.

3 Great Dining: New restaurants continue to tempt gourmets and gourmands.

4 Shopping Galore: If you're a shopper, you'll find bliss stalking the latest in clothes and accessories in dozens of the Caribbean's best boutiques.

5 Getting Out on the Water: Windsurfing, kitesurfing, and other water sports make going to the beach more than just a lounging experience.

Updated by Elise Meyer

St. Barthélemy blends the respective essences of the Caribbean, France, and *Architectural Digest* in perfect proportions. A sophisticated but unstudied approach to relaxation and respite prevails: you can spend the day on a beach, try on the latest French fashions, and watch the sunset while nibbling tapas over Gustavia Harbor, then choose from nearly 100 excellent restaurants for an elegant or easy evening meal. You can putter around the island, scuba dive, windsurf on a quiet cove, or just admire the lovely views.

A mere 8 square miles (21 square km), St. Barth is a hilly island, with many sheltered inlets and picturesque, quiet beaches. The town of Gustavia wraps itself around a modern harbor lined with everything from size-matters megayachts to rustic fishing boats to sailboats of all descriptions. Red-roof villas dot the hillsides, and glass-front shops line the streets. Beach surf runs the gamut from kiddie-pool calm to serious-surfer dangerous, beaches from deserted to packed. The cuisine is tops in the Caribbean, and almost everything is tidy, stylish, and up-to-date. French *savoir vivre* prevails.

Christopher Columbus came to the island—called "Ouanalao" by its native Caribs—in 1493; he named it for his brother Bartolomé. The first French colonists arrived in 1648, drawn by its location on the West Indian Trade Route, but they were wiped out by the Caribs, who dominated the area. Another small group from Normandy and Brittany arrived in 1694. This time the settlers prospered—with the help of French buccaneers, who took advantage of the island's strategic location and protected harbor. In 1784 the French traded the island to King Gustav III of Sweden in exchange for port rights in Göteborg. The king dubbed the capital Gustavia, laid out and paved streets, built three forts, and turned the community into a prosperous free port. The island thrived as a shipping and commercial center until the 19th century, when earthquakes, fires, and hurricanes brought financial ruin.

Many residents fled for newer lands of opportunity, and Oscar II of Sweden returned the island to France. After briefly considering selling it to America, the French took possession of St. Barthélemy again on August 10, 1877.

Today the island is a free port, and in 2007 it became a Collectivity, a French-administered overseas territory. Arid, hilly, and rocky, St. Barth was unsuited to sugar production and thus never developed an extensive slave base. Some of today's 3,000 current residents are descendants of the tough Norman and Breton settlers of three centuries ago, but you are more likely to encounter attractive French twenty- and thirtysomethings from Normandy and Provence, who are friendly, English speaking, and here for the sunny lifestyle.

PLANNING

WHEN TO GO

High season in St. Barth is typical for the Caribbean, from mid-December through mid-April (or until after Easter). During busy holiday periods prices can shoot up to the highest levels, but in the summer (particularly June and July), there are some remarkable bargains on the island, though some restaurants still close over the summer months, and hotels tend to do their annual maintenance during this time as well.

GETTING HERE AND AROUND

AIR TRAVEL

There are no direct flights to St. Barth. Most North Americans fly first into St. Maarten's Queen Juliana International Airport *(⇨ Chapter 23, St. Maarten/St. Martin for more information)*, from which the island is 10 minutes by air. Winair, which celebrated its 50th anniversary of service to St. Barth in 2013, has regularly scheduled flights from St. Maarten. Tradewind Aviation has regularly scheduled service from San Juan and also does V.I.P charters. Anguilla Air Services and St. Barth Commuter have scheduled flights and also do charters. You must reconfirm your return interisland flight, even in an off-peak season, or you may very well lose your reservation. Leave ample time between your scheduled flight and your connection in St. Maarten—three hours is the minimum recommended (and be aware that luggage frequently doesn't make the trip; your hotel or villa-rental company may be able to send someone to retrieve it). It's a good idea to pack a change of clothes, required medicines, and a bathing suit in your carry-on—or better yet, pack very light and don't check baggage at all.

Airports Gustaf III Airport (SBH) ✉ *St-Jean Rd., St-Jean* ☎ *0590/27-75-81.*

Local Airline Contacts Anguilla Air Services ☎ *264/498-5922* 🌐 *www.anguillaairservices.com.* **St. Barth Commuter** ☎ *0590/27-54-54* 🌐 *www.stbarthcommuter.com.* **Tradewind Aviation** ☎ *800/376-7922, 203/267-3305 in Connecticut* 🌐 *www.tradewindaviation.com.* **Winair** ☎ *0590/27-61-01, 866/466-0410* 🌐 *www.fly-winair.com.*

DID YOU KNOW?

The largest hotel on St. Barth has only about 70 rooms, which means you get a great deal of personal service and attention wherever you stay.

LOGISTICS

Getting to St. Barth: There are no direct flights to St. Barth (SBH). You must fly to another island and then catch a smaller plane for the hop over, or you can take a ferry. Most Americans fly first to St. Maarten and take the 10-minute flight to St. Barth, but you can connect through St. Thomas or San Juan as well.

Hassle Factor: Medium–high.

On the Ground: Many hotels offer free airport transfers; they will need your arrival information in advance. Otherwise, there's a taxi stand at the airport; unmetered taxis cost about €10 to €25 to reach most hotels. If you are renting a car, you may pick it up from the airport, or rental agents will meet you at the ferry if you have a reservation (strongly recommended in high season).

Getting Around the Island: Most people coming to St. Barth rent a car. Taxis are expensive, but some visitors prefer to let an experienced driver negotiate the roads at night (restaurants are happy to call a cab for you after dinner). It's also possible to rent a motorbike, but steep roads can make driving stressful if you aren't experienced. There is no other transportation on the island.

BOAT AND FERRY TRAVEL

St. Barth can be reached via ferry service from St. Maarten/St. Martin to Quai de la République in Gustavia. Voyager offers several daily round-trips for about $110 per person from either Marigot or Oyster Pond. Great Bay Express has two or three round-trips a day from Bobby's Marina in Philipsburg for €90 if reserved in advance, €95 for same-day tickets, and €56 for a same-day round-trip. Private boat charters are also available, but they are very expensive; Master Ski Pilou offers transfers from St. Maarten.

Boat and Ferry Contacts Great Bay Express ✉ *Quai Gustavia, Gustavia* ☎ *599/542–0032, 347/568–0574* 🌐 *www.greatbayferry.com.* **Master Ski Pilou** ☎ *0590/27–91–79* 🌐 *www.masterski-pilou.com.* **Voyager** ☎ *0590/87–10–68* 🌐 *www.voy12.com.*

19

CAR TRAVEL

Roads are sometimes unmarked, so get a map and look for signs, nailed to posts at all crossroads, pointing to a destination. Roads are narrow and sometimes very steep, but have been improved; even so, check the brakes and gears of your rental car before you drive away. Maximum speed is 30 mph (50 kph). Driving is on the right, as in the United States and Europe. Parking is an additional challenge. There are two gas stations on the island, one near the airport and one in Lorient. They aren't open after 5 pm or on Sunday, and pumps at the station near the airport accept chip-and-pin credit cards (at this writing many U.S. credit cards don't have the chip required). Considering the short distances, a full tank should last most of a week.

Car Rentals: You must have a valid driver's license and be 25 or older to rent, and in high season there may be a three-day minimum. During peak periods, such as Christmas week and February, arrange for your car rental ahead of time. Rental agencies operate out of Gustaf III

Airport, and some will bring cars to your hotel. Alternately, when you make your hotel reservation, ask if the hotel has its own cars available to rent; some hotels provide 24-hour emergency road service—something most rental companies don't. A tiny but powerful Smart car is a blast to buzz around in, and also a lot easier to park than larger cars. Expect to pay at least $55 per day.

Car-Rental Contacts Avis ☎ *0590/27–71–43, 0590/27–71–52* 🌐 *www.st-barths.com/avis-car-rental-st-barts.* **Budget** ☎ *0590/29–62–40* 🌐 *www.st-barths.com/budget.* **Cool Rental** ✉ *Maison I, Flamands* ☎ *0590/27–52–58* 🌐 *www.cool-rental.com.* **Europcar** ☎ *0590/27–74–34* 🌐 *www.st-barths.com/europcar.* **Gumbs** ☎ *0590/27–75–32* 🌐 *www.gumbs-car-rental.com.* **Hertz** ☎ *0590/27–71–14* 🌐 *www.hertzstbarth.com.* **Turbé** ☎ *0590/27–71–42* 🌐 *www.turbe-car-rental.com.*

BACKUP FERRY

Even if you are flying to St. Barth, it's a good idea to keep the numbers and schedules for the three ferry companies handy in case your flight is delayed. If you are planning to spend time in St. Maarten before traveling on to St. Barth, the ferry is half the cost and somewhat more reliable than the puddle-jumper, and you can leave from Marigot, Oyster Pond, or Philipsburg. Check at the St. Barth Tourist Information counter at Princess Juliana Airport for specifics.

MOPED, SCOOTER, AND BIKE TRAVEL

Several companies rent motorbikes, scooters, mopeds, and mountain bikes. Motorbikes go for about $30 per day and require a $100 deposit. Helmets are required. Scooter and motorbike rental places are mostly along rue de France in Gustavia and around the airport in St-Jean.

Rental Contacts Barthloc Rental ✉ *Rue de France, Gustavia* ☎ *0590/27–52–81* 🌐 *www.barthloc.com.* **Chez Béranger** ✉ *21 rue du Général de Gaulle, Gustavia* ☎ *0590/27–89–00* 🌐 *www.beranger-rental.com.*

TAXI TRAVEL

Taxis are expensive and not particularly easy to arrange, especially in the evening. There's a taxi station at the airport and another at the ferry dock in Gustavia; from elsewhere you must contact a dispatcher in Gustavia or St-Jean. Fares are regulated by the Collectivity, and drivers accept both dollars and euros. If you go out to dinner by taxi, let the restaurant know if you will need a taxi at the end of the meal, and they will call one for you. Limo-style private car-and-driver service is available 24/7 through Taxi Prestige.

Taxi Contacts Gustavia taxi dispatcher ☎ *0590/27–66–31.* **St-Jean taxi dispatcher** ✉ *Gustaf III Airport, St-Jean* ☎ *0590/27–66–31.* **Taxi Prestige** ☎ *0590/27–70–57* 🌐 *www.stbarts-limousine.com.*

ESSENTIALS

Banks and Exchange Services Legal tender is the euro, but U.S. dollars are widely accepted. ATMs are common and dispense only euros.

Electricity Voltage is 220 AC/60 cycles, as in Europe. You'll need a converter and perhaps a transformer for electronic devices. Most hotels have converters available for guests' use.

Emergency Services **Ambulance and Fire** ☎ *18, 590/27–66–13.* **Hospital Emergency** ☎ *590/27–60–35.* **Police** ☎ *0590/27–11–70.*

Language French, but English is widely spoken.

Passport Requirements All visitors must carry a valid passport and have a return or ongoing ticket. A visa is not necessary for stays of up to a month. Passports must be valid for at least three months from the date of entry to the territory of St. Barthélemy.

Phones Many hotels provide or rent cell phones for use during stays. Some U.S. cell phones work in St. Barth, but ask your provider before you leave; you may need to have your phone authorized for international use. The country code for St. Barth is 590, as are most "area codes" (some cell phones use 690). Thus, to call St. Barth from the United States, dial 011 + 590 + 590 and the local six-digit number. When on St. Barth, you dial 0590 plus the local six-digit number.

Taxes and Service Charges The island charges a $5 departure tax when your next stop is another French island, $10 to anywhere else, payable in cash only (dollars or euros). Some hotels add a 10% service charge. Sometimes it is included in the room rate, so check. There is a 5% room tax on hotels and villa rentals.

Tipping Restaurants include a 15% service charge in their published prices, but it's common French practice to leave 5% to 10% more in cash, even if you have paid by credit card. Most taxi drivers expect about 15%.

ACCOMMODATIONS

Most hotels on St. Barth are small (the largest has about 70 rooms) and stratospherically expensive, but there are some reasonable options. About half the accommodations on St. Barth are in private villas. Prices drop dramatically after March, and summer is a great time for a visit. Check hotel websites for discounts and special offers.

Hotel reviews have been shortened. For full information, visit Fodors.com.

WHAT IT COSTS IN EUROS

	$	$$	$$$	$$$$
Restaurants	under €12	€12–€20	€21–€30	over €30
Hotels	under €275	€275–€375	€376–€475	over €475

Restaurant prices are the average cost of a main course at dinner or, if dinner is not served, at lunch. Hotel prices are the lowest cost of a standard double room in high season.

VISITOR INFORMATION

Contact **Office du Tourisme** ✉ *Quai Général de Gaulle, Gustavia* ☎ *0590/27–87–27* 🌐 *www.saintbarth-tourisme.com.*

WEDDINGS

Because of the long legal residency requirement, it's not really feasible to get married on St. Barth unless you're a French citizen.

19

EXPLORING

With practice, negotiating St. Barth's narrow, steep roads soon becomes fun. Infrastructure upgrades and small, responsive rental cars have improved driving. Free maps are everywhere, and roads are smooth and well marked. The tourist office has annotated maps with walking tours that highlight sights of interest.

WORD OF MOUTH

"If you've been to France and like the culture then I'm sure you will enjoy St. Barth. It's France in the tropics."

—Sharona

GUSTAVIA

You can easily explore all of Gustavia during a two-hour stroll. Some shops close from noon to 3 or 4, so plan lunch accordingly, but stores stay open past 7 in the evening. Parking in Gustavia is a challenge, especially during vacation times. A good spot to park is rue de la République, alongside the catamarans, yachts, and sailboats.

FAMILY **Le Musée Territorial de Saint Barthélemy.** On the far side of the harbor known as La Pointe, the charming Municipal Museum has watercolors, portraits, photographs, traditional costumes, and historic documents detailing the island's history as well as displays of the island's flowers, plants, and marine life. Summer hours often change. ✉ *La Pointe, Gustavia* ☎ *0590/29–71–55* 🎫 *€2* ⏲ *Mon., Tues., Thurs., and Fri. 8:30–12:30 and 2:30–6; Wed. 8:30–12:30; Sat. 9–12:30.*

Le P'tit Collectionneur. Encouraged by family and friends, André Berry opened this private museum to showcase his lifelong passion for collecting fascinating objects such as 18th-century English pipes and the first phonograph to come to the island. He will happily show you his treasures. ✉ *La Pointe, Gustavia* 🎫 *€2* ⏲ *Mon.–Sat. 10–noon and 4–6.*

COROSSOL

Traces of the island's French provincial origins are evident in this two-street fishing village with a little rocky beach.

LORIENT

Site of the first French settlement, Lorient is one of the island's two parishes; a restored church, a school, and a post office mark the spot. Note the gaily decorated graves in the cemetery.

ELSEWHERE ON THE ISLAND

St-Jean. There is a monument at the crest of the hill that divides St-Jean from Gustavia. Called *The Arawak,* it symbolizes the soul of St. Barth. A warrior, one of the earliest inhabitants of the area (AD 800–1800), holds a lance in his right hand and stands on a rock shaped like the island; in his left hand he holds a conch shell, which sounds the cry of nature; perched beside him are a pelican (which symbolizes the air and survival by fishing) and an iguana (which represents the earth). The half-mile-long crescent of sand at St-Jean is the island's favorite beach. A popular activity is watching and photographing the hair-raising airplane landings (but it is extremely dangerous to stand at the beach end of the runway). Some of the best shopping on the island is here as are several restaurants. ⊠ *St-Jean.*

Toiny Coast. Over the hills beyond Grand Cul de Sac is this much-photographed coastline. Stone fences crisscross the steep slopes of Morne Vitet, one of many small mountains on St. Barth, along a rocky shore that resembles the rugged coast of Normandy. Nicknamed the "washing machine" because of its turbulent surf, it is not recommended even to expert swimmers because of the strong undertow. ■ **TIP→ There is a tough but scenic hike around the point. Take the road past Le Toiny hotel to the top to the start of the trail.**

BEACHES

There is a beach in St. Barth to suit every taste. Wild surf, a dreamy white-sand strand, and a spot at a chic beach club close to shopping and restaurants—they're all within a 20-minute drive.

There are many *anses* (coves) and nearly 20 *plages* (beaches) scattered around the island, each with a distinct personality; all are open to the public, even if they front a tony resort. Because of the number of beaches, even in high season you can find a nearly empty one, despite St. Barth's tiny size. That's not to say that all beaches are equally good or even equally suitable for swimming, but each has something to offer. Unless you are having lunch at a beachfront restaurant with lounging areas set aside for patrons, you should bring an umbrella, beach mat, and water (all of which are easily obtainable all over the island). Topless sunbathing is common, but nudism is supposedly forbidden—although both Grande Saline and Gouverneur are de facto nude beaches, albeit less than in the past. Shade is scarce.

Anse à Colombier. The beach here is the island's least accessible, thus the most private; to reach it you must take either a rocky footpath from Petite Anse or brave the 30-minute climb down (and back up) a steep, cactus-bordered trail from the top of the mountain behind the beach. Appropriate footgear is a must, and on the beach, the only shade is a rock cave. But this is a good place to snorkel. Boaters favor this cove for its calm anchorage. **Amenities:** none. **Best for:** snorkeling; swimming. ⊠ *Colombier.*

Anse de Grand Cul de Sac. The shallow, reef-protected beach is nice for small children, fly-fishermen, kayakers, and windsurfers—and for the amusing pelican-like frigate birds that dive-bomb the water fishing for their lunch. There is a good dive shop. You needn't do your own fishing; you can have a wonderful lunch at one of the excellent restaurants, and use their lounge chairs for the afternoon. **Amenities:** food and drink; parking (no fee); toilets; water sports. **Best for:** swimming; walking. ⊠ *Grand Cul de Sac.*

FAMILY Fodor's Choice ★ **Anse de Grande Saline.** With its peaceful seclusion and sandy ocean bottom, this is just about everyone's favorite beach and is great for swimming, too. Without any major development (although there is some talk of developing a resort here), it's an ideal Caribbean strand, though there can be a bit of wind at times. In spite of the prohibition, young and old alike go nude. The beach is a 10-minute walk up a rocky dune trail, so wear sneakers or water shoes, and bring a blanket, umbrella, and beach towels. There are several good lunch restaurants near the parking area, but the beach itself is just sand, sea, and sky. The big salt ponds here are no longer in use, and the place looks a little desolate on approach, but don't despair. **Amenities:** parking (no fee). **Best for:** nudists; swimming; walking. ✉ *Grande Saline.*

PICKING THE RIGHT BEACH

For long stretches of talcum-soft pale sand choose La Saline, Gouverneur, or Flamands. For seclusion in nature, pick the tawny grains of Corossol. But the most remarkable beach on the island, Shell Beach, is right in Gustavia and hardly has sand at all! Millions of tiny pink shells wash ashore in drifts, thanks to an unusual confluence of ocean currents, sea-life beds, and hurricane action.

FAMILY **Anse de Lorient.** This beach is popular with families and surfers, who like its waves and central location. Be aware of the level of the tide, which can come in very quickly. Hikers and avid surfers like the walk over the hill to Pointe Milou in the late afternoon, when the waves roll in. **Amenities:** parking (no fee). **Best for:** snorkeling; surfing; swimming. ✉ *Lorient.*

Anse des Flamands. This is the most beautiful of the hotel beaches—a roomy strip of silken sand. Come here for lunch and then spend the afternoon sunning, enjoying long beach walks, and swimming in the turquoise water. From the beach, you can take a brisk hike along a paved sidewalk to the top of the now-extinct volcano believed to have given birth to St. Barth. **Amenities:** food and drink; toilets. **Best for:** snorkeling; swimming; walking. ✉ *Flamands.*

FAMILY **Anse du Gouverneur.** Because it's so secluded, this beach is a popular place for nude sunbathing. Truly beautiful, it has blissful swimming and views of St. Kitts, Saba, and St. Eustatius. Venture here at the end of the day and watch the sun set behind the hills. The road here from Gustavia also offers spectacular vistas. Legend has it that pirates' treasure is buried in the vicinity. There are no restaurants, toilets, or other services here, so plan accordingly. **Amenities:** parking (no fee). **Best for:** nudists; sunset; swimming; walking. ✉ *Gouverneur.*

FAMILY **Baie de St-Jean.** Like a mini–Côte d'Azur—beachside bistros, terrific shopping, bungalow hotels, bronzed bodies, windsurfing, and day-trippers who tend to arrive on BIG yachts—the reef-protected strip is divided by Eden Rock promontory. Except when the hotels are filled, you can rent chaises and umbrellas at La Plage restaurant or Eden Rock, where you can lounge for hours over lunch. **Amenities:** food and drink; toilets. **Best for:** partiers; walking. ✉ *St-Jean.*

WHERE TO EAT

Dining on St. Barth compares favorably to almost anywhere in the world. Varied and exquisite cuisine, a French flair in the decor, sensational wine, and attentive service make for a wonderful epicurean experience in almost any of the more than 80 restaurants. On most menus, freshly caught local seafood mingles on the plate with top-quality provisions that arrive regularly from Paris. Interesting selections on the Cartes de Vins are no surprise, but don't miss the sophisticated cocktails whipped up by island bartenders. They are worlds away from cliché Caribbean rum punches with paper umbrellas. The signature drink of St. Barth is called "'ti punch," a rum concoction similar to a Brazilian Caipirinha. It's also fun to sit at a bar and ask the attractive bartender for his or her own signature cocktail.

Most restaurants offer a chalkboard of daily specials, usually a good bet. But even the pickiest eaters will find something on every menu. Some level of compliance will be paid to dietary restrictions, especially if explained in French; just be aware that French people generally let the chef work his or her magic. Expect meals to be costly, but you can dine superbly and somewhat economically if you limit pricey cocktails, watch wine selections, share appetizers or desserts, and pick up snacks and picnics from one of the well-stocked markets. Or you can follow the locals to small *crêperies,* cafés, sandwich shops, and pizzerias in the main shopping areas. Lunch is usually less costly than dinner. *Ti creux* means "snack" or "small bite."

Lavish publications feature restaurant menus and contacts. Ask at your hotel or look on the racks at the airport. Reservations are strongly recommended and, in high season, essential. Lots of restaurants now accept reservations on their website or by email. Check social media. Except during the Christmas–New Year's season it's not usually necessary to book far in advance. A day's—or even a few hours'—notice is usually sufficient. At the end of the meal, as in France, you must request the bill. Until you do, you can feel free to linger at the table and enjoy the complimentary vanilla rum that's likely to appear.

Check restaurant bills carefully. A *service compris* (service charge) is always added by law, but you should leave the server 5% to 10% extra in cash. You'll usually come out ahead if you charge restaurant meals on a credit card in euros instead of paying with American currency, as your credit card might offer a better exchange rate than the restaurant (unless your credit card charges a conversion surcharge). Many restaurants serve locally caught *langouste* (lobster); priced by weight, it's usually the most expensive item on a menu and, depending on its size and the restaurant, will range in price from $40 to $60. *In menu prices below, it has been left out of the range.*

What to Wear: A bathing suit and *gauzy top or shift* is acceptable at beachside lunch spots, but not really in Gustavia. Jackets are never required and are rarely worn by men, but most people do dress fashionably for dinner. Casual chic is the idea; women wear whatever is hip, current, and sexy. You can't go wrong in a tank dress or a sexy top with white jeans and high sandals. The sky is the limit for high fashion at nightclubs and lounges in high season, when you might (correctly) think everyone in sight is a model. Leave some space in your suitcase; you can buy the perfect outfit here on the island. Nice shorts (not beachy ones) at the dinner table may label a man *américain,* but many locals have adopted the habit, and nobody cares much. Wear them with a pastel shirt to really fit in (never tucked in). Pack a light sweater or shawl for the occasional breezy night.

ANSE DE TOINY

$$$$ MODERN FRENCH Fodor's Choice ★

Le Gaïac. Hôtel Le Toiny's dramatic, tasteful, cliff-side dining porch showcases gastronomic art. Less stuffy than in the past, the food is notable for its innovation and extraordinary presentation, and the warm but consummately professional service sets a high standard. The menu changes frequently, but rare ingredients and unique preparations always delight: spaghetti with black truffles, tamarind-glazed duck breast, lamb fillet with eggplant caviar, and chocolate soufflé for dessert. Tuesday is Fish Market Night, when you choose your own fish to be grilled, and Sunday (11–2) there's a €43 buffet brunch. *Average main: €36 Hôtel Le Toiny, Anse de Toiny 590/29–77–47 www.letoiny.com Reservations essential Closed Sept.–mid-Oct.*

FLAMANDS

$$$$ MODERN FRENCH Fodor's Choice ★

La Case de L'Isle. You can't top the view or the service at this waterfront restaurant at the renowned Cheval Blanc St-Barth Isle de France, and at night there is no more romantic spot on the island. Lightened traditional French fare is served. At lunch you can have your toes in the sand while enjoying a composed salad or club sandwich. For dinner, choose from tender suckling lamb with sweet-pepper creamy polenta or flambéed local lobster fricassee. Amazing desserts include pistachio-raspberry panna cotta with fresh red fruits and a crispy grilled pistachio crêpe. Occasional fashion shows featuring the lovely beachwear from the on-site boutique are a fun diversion. *Average main: €45 Cheval Blanc St-Barth Isle de France, Flamands Beach, Flamands 0590/27–61–81 www.isle-de-france.com Reservations essential.*

$$$ FRENCH FUSION

La Langouste. This tiny but friendly beachside restaurant in the pool courtyard of Hôtel Baie des Anges lives up to its name by serving fresh-grilled local lobster, and lobster Thermidor, at prices that are somewhat gentler than at most other island venues. Try starters like creole stuffed crab, scallop carpaccio, a warm goat cheese salad, or one of the five soups including classic Caribbean fish soup and lobster bisque. The well-prepared fish and pasta dishes are great main options, and there are choices for meat fans as well. Classic French desserts like Floating Island with vanilla sauce, crêpes suzette, and mango tart are worth the calories. *Average main: €27 Hôtel Baie des Anges, Anse des Flamands 0590/27–63–61 www.hotel-baie-des-anges.com Reservations essential Closed late Aug.–mid-Oct.*

Le Gaïac, Anse de Toiny

GRAND CUL DE SAC

$$$$ ITALIAN FAMILY ✕ **Bartolomeo.** Locavores will like the pretty restaurant in the gardens of the Guanahani hotel, which showcases the refined cuisine of executive chef Philippe Masseglia. Influenced by Provence and Italy, beautifully presented dishes use some organic and local products. Try the lemon-and-cheese ravioli or scallop risotto followed by cheesecake with apricot sauce or pistachio crisp. If the whole table is adventurous and likes to eat on the early side, you can opt for a €75, €90, or €120 tasting menu. (There is a €20 children's menu, too.) Veggie and gluten-free items are marked on the menu. ■ **TIP→ Long pants are required.** *Average main: €38 ✉ Hotel Guanahani, Grand Cul de Sac ☎ 0590/27–66–60 Reservations essential ⊙ Closed Mon.–Tues. No lunch.*

$$$ CARIBBEAN ✕ **La Gloriette.** Everyone has a great time eating a beachside lunch at shady picnic tables under coccoloba trees. Those who remember the original creole restaurant here will be happy to know that the *accras* (salt-cod fritters with spicy sauce) are as good as ever. There are huge, fresh salads and many daily specials on the blackboard. Grilled fish is super-fresh, and the sushi-style tatakis are light and delicious. At dinner there are good pizzas for dining in or taking back to your villa. Artisanal, island-flavored rums are offered after the meal and available at the tiny shop. *Average main: €23 ✉ Plage de Grand Cul de Sac, Grand Cul de Sac ☎ 0590/29–85–71 ⊙ Closed Wed.*

GRANDE SALINE

$$$$ MODERN FRENCH FAMILY Fodor's Choice ★

✕ L' Esprit. Renowned chef Jean-Claude Dufour (formerly of Eden Rock) brings innovative dishes to a romantic terrace close to Saline Beach. The menu has lots of variety, from light French dishes with a Provençal twist to interesting salads (like soba noodles with shrimp and lime), roasted pigeon with foie gras, veal burgers, steak, and tasty vegetarian options. The chocolate tart is a pleasing dessert, but the memory of the sweet service will last longer. *Average main: €38 ✉ Anse de Grande Saline, Grande Saline ☎ 0590/52–46–10 ⏲ No lunch Wed. and Sun.*

$$$$ STEAKHOUSE

✕ Meat and Potatoes. If you think that St. Barth is sometimes too "girly," you will love this restaurant at the end of the road to Saline Beach. The white interior is lined with banquettes heaped with red, black, and gray pillows. A half-dozen cuts of steak, from tenderloins to T-bones, can be paired with 15 sauces, at least a dozen starchy sides (including the Provençal *pommes ratte,* potato wedges cooked in duck fat, fresh rosemary, and sea salt), and some vegetables for good measure—all à la carte. People love the Burger Party on Thursdays. For the red meat averse, there is fresh fish and a vegetarian menu. The wine list is full of complementary bottles, heavy on Bordeaux's best. *Average main: €35 ✉ Grande Saline ☎ 0590/51–15–98 ⏲ No lunch.*

$$$$ FRENCH FAMILY

✕ Restaurant La Santa Fé. Perched at the top of the Lurin hills on the way to Gouverneur Beach, this relaxed and scenic restaurant serves panoramic views with both lunch and dinner. The chef comes from Provence and trained at some its best restaurants before moving to the Caribbean. Salads and light lunch offerings are great before the beach, but come for dinner—especially if you are a fan of authentic French cuisine—for delicious osso buco, coq au vin, and crisp tomato tarts with pesto. *Average main: €34 ✉ Rte. de Lurin, Lurin ☎ 0590/27–61–04 ⏲ Closed Wed. and Sept.–mid-Oct.*

GUSTAVIA

$$$$ MODERN FRENCH

✕ Bagatelle St Barth. The sophisticated St. Tropez–inspired eatery, right on the harbor, is a scene-y place to watch big boats and enjoy pizzas (try the truffle one) and simple favorites like duck breast, steak, and local fish. You can book a table on the terrace, and cocktails are special and strong. Fans of sister establishments in New York's Meatpacking District and Los Angeles will recognize the friendly service, lively atmosphere, and great music provided by resident DJs. Come late—the party and champagne get going after 11. *Average main: €34 ✉ Rue Samuel Fahlberg, Gustavia ☎ 0590/27–51–51 🌐 www.bistrotbagatelle.com ✍ Reservations essential ⏲ Closed Sun. No lunch.*

$$$$ LATIN AMERICAN Fodor's Choice ★

✕ Bonito. Decorated like a chic beach house, Bonito features big white canvas couches for lounging, in the center; tables around the sides; an open kitchen; and three bar areas—all on a hill above Gustavia Harbor. The young Venezuelan owners go to great lengths to see that guests are having as much fun as they are. The specialty is ceviche (eight varieties), in combos that are prettily arrayed on poured-glass platters. Try octopus and shrimp, or wahoo garnished with sweet potatoes and popcorn. Traditionalists might like the fricassee of escargots or foie gras served with pear chutney. Carnivores love the olive-crusted rack of lamb. French pastry classics are on the dessert menu. **■ TIP→ A sister location, with the same terrific food but a quieter ambience, is in the chic beachside Le Sereno resort.** *Average main: €41 ✉ Rue Lubin Brin, Gustavia ☎ 0590/27–96–96 🌐 www.ilovebonito.com Reservations essential ⊙ Closed Wed. and late Aug.–early Nov. No lunch.*

$$$ ECLECTIC **✕ Dõ Brazil.** In addition to lunch and dinner, this restaurant on Shell Beach has live music for sundown cocktail hour Thursday–Saturday as well as top DJs spinning the latest club mixes for evening events. Tasty fare includes chilled soups, Caesar salad, burgers, wok noodles and vegetables, and grilled fresh fish for lunch. The Dõ Brazil hot pot is mahimahi, shrimp, and sea scallops in a sauce of lemongrass and coconut milk. The extensive cocktail menu tempts, but at €12 each, the bar bill can quickly exceed the price of dinner. There is a €10 children's menu. *Average main: €26 ✉ Shell Beach, Gustavia ☎ 0590/29–06–66 🌐 www.dobrazil.com ⊙ Closed Sept.–Oct.*

$$$ ASIAN **✕ Eddy's.** By local standards, dinner in the pretty, open-air, tropical garden here is reasonably priced. The cooking is French-creole-Asian. Fish specialties, especially the sushi tuna sampler, are fresh and delicious, and there are always plenty of daily specials. Just remember some mosquito repellent for your ankles. *Average main: €24 ✉ 12 rue Samuel Fahlberg, Gustavia ☎ 0590/27–54–17 Reservations not accepted ⊙ Closed Sun. and Sept.–Oct. No lunch.*

$$$ ECLECTIC **✕ Le Carré.** Franck Mathevet, the esteemed Burgundy-born chef formerly of Wall House, situated this attractive and lively outdoor restaurant in the center of Le Carré d'Or, Gustavia's glam shopping enclave. Team terrific cocktails with tasty and modern small plates, fresh seafood from the raw bar, or sandwiches like Caribbean lobster rolls, grilled chicken, and smoked salmon on bagels. Fun sharable appetizers and simple grills are great at night. The restaurant is open for breakfast, lunch, snacks, dinner, and Sunday brunch—and for special events, too. *Average main: €21 ✉ Le Carré d'Or, rue Auguste Nyman, Gustavia ☎ 0590/52–46–11.*

19

$$$ CARIBBEAN **✕ Le Palace.** Tucked into a tropical garden, this popular restaurant, also known as Pipiri Palace, is famous for its barbecued ribs, beef fillet, and rack of lamb. Lunch brings omelets, kabobs, and croque monsieur. For dinner, fish-market specialties like curried red snapper cooked in a banana leaf and grilled tuna are good, as are grilled duck with mushroom sauce and a skewered surf-and-turf with green curry sauce. The blackboard's daily specials, like St-Marcellin cheese roasted in a crock of honey, are usually a great choice, and the island's best tarte Tatin is made with salted caramel. *Average main: €30 ✉ Rue du Général de Gaulle, Gustavia ☎ 0590/27–53–20 Reservations essential ⊙ Closed Sun. and mid-June–July.*

$$ BRASSERIE FAMILY **✕ Le Repaire.** Overlooking the harbor, this friendly classic French brasserie is busy from its early morning opening to its late-night closing. The flexible hours are great if you arrive on the island midafternoon and need a substantial snack. Grab a cappuccino, pull a captain's chair up to the street-side rail, and watch the pretty people go by. The menu ranges from cheeseburgers, served only at lunch along with the island's

best fries, to simply grilled fish and meat, pastas, risottos, mixed salads, and wonderful ice cream sundaes. Le Repaire carries on the island tradition of *moules frites* (mussels and fries) on Thursday night. *Average main: €19 ✉ Rue de la République, Gustavia ☎ 0590/27–72–48 ⊙ Closed Sun.*

$$$ FRENCH **Les Bananiers.** Ask the locals where to eat, and they will surely recommend this casual spot in Colombier, adjacent to a wonderful bakery. The food is classic French, the service is warm, the prices are gentle, and you can eat in or take out. Choose from dishes like classic fish soup, grilled duck breast, escargots in garlic butter, thin-crust pizza, and fresh fish. Order early in the day for takeout pizza. *Average main: €23 ✉ Rte. de Colombier, Colombier ☎ 0590/27–93–48.*

$$$$ ITALIAN Fodor's Choice ★ **L'Isola.** The chic sister of Santa Monica, California's Via Veneto packs in happy guests for classic Italian dishes, dozens of house-made pasta dishes, prime meats, and a huge, well-chosen wine list. Restaurateur Fabrizio Bianconi wants it to feel like a big Italian party, and with all the celebrating in this pretty and romantic room, it sounds like he succeeded. Favorite dishes include a hearty veal chop in a sage-butter sauce and heavenly risotto with either wild mushrooms or wild boar. *Average main: €38 ✉ 33 rue du Roi Oscar II, Gustavia ☎ 0590/51–00–05 ⊕ www.lisolastbarth.com Reservations essential ⊙ Closed Sept.–Oct. No lunch.*

$ PIZZA **L'Isoletta.** This casual Roman-style pizzeria run by the popular L'Isola restaurant is a chic lounge-style gastropub serving delicious thin-crust pizzas by the slice or the meter. There are even dessert pizzas. Lasagnas and focaccia sandwiches are also available to eat in or take out. It's open from lunch until 11 pm. *Average main: €10 ✉ Rue du Roi Oscar II, Gustavia ☎ 0590/52–02–02 ⊕ www.lisolettastbarth.com Reservations not accepted.*

$$$$ FRENCH **Maya's.** New Englander Randy Gurley and his wife, Maya (the French-born chef), provide returning guests with a warm welcome and a very pleasant, albeit expensive, dinner on their cheerful dock decorated with big round tables and crayon-color canvas chairs, all overlooking Gustavia Harbor. A market-inspired menu of good, simply prepared and garnished dishes—like roast quail and Indian-spiced fish—changes daily, assuring the restaurant's ongoing popularity. *Average main: €39 ✉ Public, Gustavia ☎ 0590/27–75–73 ⊕ www.mayas-stbarth.com Reservations essential ⊙ Closed Sun. No lunch.*

$$$ SEAFOOD **Ocean.** This romantic and delicious family-run seafood restaurant features fresh-caught local fish and attentive, friendly service. Plates are distinctive, creative, refined, and beautifully presented—think a whole sea bass baked in a salt-pastry shell. There are also beautiful steaks for non–fish lovers and spectacular, classic French desserts. A daily prix-fixe lunch, including main course and dessert, costs €11–€19. *Average main: €26 ✉ 13 rue Samuel Fahlberg, Gustavia ☎ 0590/52–45–31 Reservations essential.*

POINTE MILOU

$$$$ ECLECTIC Fodor's Choice ★ ✕ **Le Ti St. Barth Caribbean Tavern.** Chef-owner Carole Gruson captures the island's funky, sexy spirit in her wildly popular hilltop spot. Come to dance to great music with the attractive bar crowd, lounge at a pillow-strewn banquette, or chat on the torch-lighted terrace. By the time your appetizers arrive, you'll be best friends with the next table. Top-quality fish and meats are cooked on the traditional charcoal barbecue. Big spenders love the Angus beef fillet Rossini with truffles, but there are lighter options like wok shrimp with Chinese noodles, and seared tuna with caviar. Provocatively named desserts, such as Nymph Thighs (airy lemon cake with vanilla custard), Daddy's Balls (passion-fruit sorbet and ice cream), and Sweet Thai Massage (kiwi, pineapple, mango, and lychee salad) end the meal on a fun note. By then someone is sure to be dancing on the tables. There's an extensive wine list. The famously raucous full-moon parties, cabarets, and Monday Plastic Boots ladies' nights are all legendary. *$ Average main: €53 ✉ Pointe Milou ☎ 0590/27–97–71 🌐 www.letistbarth.com ✍ Reservations essential ⏲ Closed Sun.–Mon. No lunch.*

ST-JEAN

$$$$ FRENCH ✕ **La Plage.** Dining in St. Barth–style is spot-on at this eatery in Le Tom Beach Hôtel, a prime place to watch people and the action on St-Jean Beach. Passion-fruit martinis are a must, as is the fresh-caught grilled spiny lobsters and roasted beet "carpaccio." There are beach lounges for daytime and music all day long. Special events include Full Moon White Parties and Saturday Bikini Brunch. *$ Average main: €36 ✉ Le Tom Beach Hôtel, Plage de St-Jean, St-Jean ☎ 0590/27–53–13 🌐 www.tombeach.com.*

$$$$ ECLECTIC Fodor's Choice ★ ✕ **The Sand Bar.** At this Eden Rock hotel eatery, lunch on the terrace with the beautiful blue water sparkling beyond is incomparable. Star chef Jean Georges Vongerichten's cuisine is tailored to the setting—all the things you'd be tempted to eat at the beach. Delicious light salads, soups, and carpaccio are highlights, but there are also heartier salads with fish and chicken, simple grilled fish and meat entrées, and delicious wood-oven pizzas, such as fontina and truffle. Beautiful desserts include chocolate and lemon tart, and there's brunch on Sundays. With the Eden Rock's world-class people-watching, you never know who'll be checking out a menu next to you. *$ Average main: €41 ✉ Eden Rock, Baie de St-Jean, St-Jean ☎ 0590/29–79–99 🌐 www.edenrockhotel.com ✍ Reservations essential.*

WHERE TO STAY

There's no denying that hotel rooms and villas on St. Barth carry high prices. You're paying primarily for the privilege of staying on the island, and even at $800 a night the bedrooms tend to be small. Still, if you're flexible—in terms of timing and in your choice of lodgings—you can enjoy a holiday in St. Barth and still afford to send the kids to college.

CLOSE UP

St. Barth's Spas

Visitors to St. Barth can enjoy more than the comforts of home by taking advantage of the myriad spa and beauty treatments available on the island. Major hotels—the Cheval Blanc St-Barth Isle de France, Guanahani, and Christopher—have beautiful, comprehensive, on-site spas. Others, including the Hôtel le Village St. Barth, Le Sereno, and Hôtel Le Toiny, have added spa cottages, where treatments and services can be arranged on-site. Depending on availability, all island visitors can book services at these. In addition, scores of independent therapists will come to your hotel room or villa and provide any therapeutic discipline you can think of, including yoga, Thai massage, shiatsu, reflexology, and even manicures, pedicures, and hairdressing. You can get recommendations at the tourist office in Gustavia.

The most expensive season falls during the holidays (mid-December to early January), when hotels are booked far in advance, may require a 10- or 14-day stay, and can be double the high-season rates. A 5% government tourism tax on room prices (excluding breakfast) is in effect; be sure to ask if it is included in your room rate or added on.

When it comes to booking a hotel on St. Barth, the reservation manager can be your best ally. Rooms within a property can vary greatly. It's well worth the price of a phone call or the time invested in emails to make a personal connection, which can lead to a room that meets your needs or preferences. Details of accessibility, views, recent redecorating, meal options, and special package rates are topics open for discussion. Quoted hotel rates are per room, not per person, and include service charges and often airport transfers. Bargain rates found on Internet booking sites can sometimes yield unpleasant surprises in terms of the actual room you get. Consider contacting the hotel and mentioning the rate you found. Often they will match it, and you'll end up with a better room.

PRIVATE VILLAS AND CONDOS

On St. Barth the term *villa* describes anything from a small cottage to a luxurious, modern estate. Today almost half of St. Barth's accommodations are in villas, a great option, especially if traveling with friends or family. Even more advantageous to Americans, villa rates are usually quoted in dollars, thus bypassing unfavorable euro fluctuations. Most villas have a small private swimming pool and maid service daily except Sunday. They are well furnished with linens, kitchen utensils, and such electronic playthings as smart-phone docks, CD and DVD players, satellite TV, and broadband Internet. Weekly in-season rates range from $1,400 to "oh-my-gosh." Most villa-rental companies are based in the United States and have extensive websites that allow you to see pictures or panoramic videos of the place you're renting; their local offices oversee maintenance and housekeeping and provide concierge services. Just be aware that there are few beachfront villas, so if you have your heart set on "toes in the sand" and a cute waiter delivering your Kir Royale, stick with the hotels or villas operated by hotel properties.

RENTAL CONTACTS

Marla. This local St. Barth villa-rental company represents more than 100 villas, many of which are not listed with other companies. ✉ *Rue du Roi Oscar II, Gustavia* ☎ *0590/27–62–02* 🌐 *www.marlavillas.com.*

St. Barth Properties, Inc. Owned by American Peg Walsh, a regular on St. Barth since 1986, this company represents more than 120 properties. The excellent website offers virtual tours of most of the villas and even details on availability. ✉ *Gustavia* ☎ *508/528–7727, 800/421–3396* 🌐 *www.stbarth.com.*

Wimco. Based in Rhode Island, Wimco oversees bookings for more than 230 properties, at $2,000–$10,000 a week for two- and three-bedroom villas and from $7,000 for larger villas. The website, which occasionally lists last-minute specials, has interactive floor plans, and a catalog is available by mail. The company can arrange for babysitters, massages, chefs, and other in-villa services as well as private air charters. ☎ *800/932–3222* 🌐 *www.wimco.com.*

ANSE DE TOINY

$$$$ HOTEL Fodor's Choice ★

Hôtel Le Toiny. Privacy, serenity, and personalized service please the international mogul set; it's remote, but you never have to leave if you don't want to. **Pros:** extremely private; luxurious rooms; flawless service; environmental awareness. **Cons:** not on the beach; isolated (at least half an hour's drive from town). $ *Rooms from: €1,390* ✉ *Anse de Toiny* ☎ *0590/27–88–88* 🌐 *www.letoiny.com* *14 1-bedroom villas, 1 3-bedroom villa* ⏲ *Closed Sept.–late Oct.* 🍴 *Breakfast.*

COLOMBIER

$ B&B/INN

Le P'tit Morne. Each of the modestly furnished but clean and freshly decorated, painted mountainside studios has a private balcony with panoramic views of the coastline. **Pros:** reasonable rates; great area for hiking. **Cons:** rooms are basic; remote location. $ *Rooms from: €204* ✉ *Colombier* ☎ *0590/52–95–50* 🌐 *www.timorne.com/fr* *14 rooms* 🍴 *Breakfast.*

FLAMANDS

$$$$ RESORT Fodor's Choice ★

Cheval Blanc St-Barth Isle de France. Nestled along a pristine white-sand beach, in tropical gardens, or on a hillside, the spacious rooms, suites, and villas of this intimate, casual, and refined resort are private and luxurious. **Pros:** prime beach location; terrific management; great spa; excellent restaurant. **Cons:** car needed to get around; one day you'll have to leave this paradise. $ *Rooms from: €890* ✉ *B.P. 612 Baie des Flamands, Flamands* ☎ *0590/27–61–81* 🌐 *www.isle-de-france.com* *40 rooms, suites, villas, and bungalows* ⏲ *Closed Sept.–mid-Oct.* 🍴 *Breakfast.*

19

Hotel Guanahani and Spa, Grand Cul de Sac

$$ HOTEL FAMILY **Hôtel Baie des Anges.** Everyone is treated like family at this casual retreat with 10 clean, spacious units, two of which are two-bedroom oceanfront suites. **Pros:** on St. Barth's longest beach; family-friendly; excellent value. **Cons:** a bit remote from town, necessitating a car. *Rooms from: €300 Anse des Flamands 0590/27–63–61 www.hotel-baie-des-anges.com 10 rooms Closed Sept. No meals.*

$$$$ RESORT FAMILY Fodor's Choice ★ **Hotel Taïwana.** This classic island retreat delights young international guests who appreciate spiffy updates in spacious rooms and suites around a charming atrium garden. **Pros:** busy social scene; great beach access. **Cons:** maybe too scene-y for some; every room is different, so choose carefully. *Rooms from: €740 Baie De Flamands, Anse des Flamands 0590/29–80–08 www.hoteltaiwana.com 7 rooms, 15 suites Breakfast.*

GRAND CUL DE SAC

$$$$ RESORT FAMILY Fodor's Choice ★ **Hotel Guanahani and Spa.** St. Barth's largest full-service resort has lovely rooms and suites (14 have private pools) and impeccable service, not to mention one of the island's only children's programs (actually more of a nursery). **Pros:** fantastic spa; beachside sports; family-friendly; great service. **Cons:** lots of walking around property; steep walk to beach. *Rooms from: €895 Grand Cul de Sac 0590/52–90–00 www.leguanahani.com 36 suites, 31 rooms Closed Sept. Breakfast.*

$$$$ RENTAL FAMILY **Hotel Les Ondines Sur La Plage.** Right on the beach, this reasonably priced, intimate gem comprises modern, comfortable apartments with room to spread out. **Pros:** spacious beachfront apartments; close to

restaurants and water sports; pool; airport transfers. **Cons:** not a resort; narrow beach; you'll need a car. *Rooms from: €550 Grand Cul de Sac 590/27–69–64 www.st-barths.com/les-ondines 7 rooms, suites, and villas Closed Sept.–mid-Oct. Breakfast.*

$$$$ RESORT Fodor's Choice ★ **Le Sereno.** Those seeking a restorative, sensuous escape discover nirvana at the quietly elegant, aptly named Le Sereno, set on a beachy cove of turquoise sea, between the island's highest mountain and the foamy waves. **Pros:** romantic rooms; beach location; super-chic comfort; friendly atmosphere. **Cons:** no a/c in bathrooms; construction planned nearby. *Rooms from: €790 B.P. 19 Grand-Cul-de-Sac, Grand Cul de Sac 590/29–83–00 www.lesereno.com 37 suites and villas Closed late Aug.–mid-Oct. Multiple meal plans.*

GRANDE SALINE

$ RENTAL FAMILY **Salines Garden Cottages.** Budget-conscious beach lovers who don't require a lot of coddling need look no further than these petite garden cottages, a short stroll from St. Barth's best beach. **Pros:** only property walkable to Salines Beach; quiet; reasonable rates; good restaurants nearby. **Cons:** far from town; not very private; strict cancellation policy. *Rooms from: €180 Grand Saline 0590/51–04–44 www.salinesgarden.com 5 cottages Closed mid-Aug.–mid-Oct. Breakfast.*

GUSTAVIA

$ HOTEL **Sunset Hotel.** Ten simple, utilitarian rooms (one can accommodate three people) sit across from Gustavia's harbor and offer an economical and handy, if not luxurious, option for those who want to stay in town. **Pros:** reasonable rates; in town. **Cons:** no elevator; not resort-like in any way. *Rooms from: €110 Rue de la République, Gustavia 0590/27–77–21 www.saint-barths.com/sunset-hotel 10 rooms No meals.*

LORIENT

$ RENTAL FAMILY **Les Mouettes.** This guesthouse offers clean, simply furnished, and economical bungalows that open directly onto the beach. **Pros:** on the beach; family-friendly. **Cons:** basic rooms; near road; strict prepayment and cancellation policies; no pool; no TV. *Rooms from: €158 Lorient Beach 0590/27–77–91 www.lesmouetteshotel.com 7 bungalows No credit cards No meals.*

$ B&B/INN **Normandie Hotel.** There's nothing in this price range that compares to these small but stylish and immaculate rooms. **Pros:** friendly management; pleasant atmosphere; good value. **Cons:** tiny rooms; small bathrooms. *Rooms from: €210 Lorient 0590/27–61–66 www.normandiehotelstbarts.com 8 rooms (7 double, 1 single) Breakfast.*

Eden Rock, St-Jean

POINTE MILOU

$$$$ RESORT FAMILY **Christopher.** This longtime favorite of European families delivers a high standard of professionalism and courteous service. **Pros:** comfortable elegance; family-friendly; reasonable price. **Cons:** on the water but not on a beach; three-night minimum. *Rooms from: €510 Pointe Milou 590/27–63–63 www.hotelchristopher.com 42 rooms Closed Sept.–mid-Oct. Breakfast.*

ST-JEAN

$$$$ RESORT FAMILY Fodor's Choice ★ **Eden Rock.** Even on an island known for gourmet cuisine and luxury hotels, this icon stands out—thanks to two Jean-Georges Vongerichten eateries, spacious rooms, stunning bay views, and cosseting service. **Pros:** two Vongerichten restaurants; great service; chic clientele; beach setting; stylish facilities; walk to shopping and restaurants. **Cons:** some suites near street are noisy. *Rooms from: €850 Baie de St-Jean, St-Jean 0590/29–79–99, 877/563–7015 in U.S. www.edenrockhotel.com 32 rooms, 2 villas Closed late Aug.–mid-Oct. Breakfast.*

$$$ HOTEL FAMILY Fodor's Choice ★ **Emeraude Plage.** Right on the beach of Baie de St-Jean, this petite resort consists of small but immaculate bungalows and villas with modern, fully equipped outdoor kitchens on small private patios. **Pros:** beachfront and in-town location; good value; cool kitchens on each porch. **Cons:** smallish rooms. *Rooms from: €425 Baie de St-Jean, St-Jean 0590/27–64–78 www.emeraudeplage.com 28 bungalows Closed Sept.–mid-Oct. No meals.*

$ HOTEL FAMILY Fodor'sChoice ★ **Hôtel le Village St. Barth.** For two generations the Charneau family has offered friendly hotel service, villa advantages, and reasonable rates, making guests feel like a part of the family. **Pros:** great value; convenient location; wonderful management; friendly clientele. **Cons:** steep walk to hotel; rooms close to street can be noisy. *Rooms from: €265 ✉ Colline de St-Jean, St-Jean ☎ 0590/27–61–39, 800/651–8366 🌐 www.villagestjeanhotel.com 5 rooms, 20 cottages, 1 3-bedroom villa, 2 2-bedroom villas Breakfast.*

$$$ RENTAL FAMILY **Les Îlets de la Plage.** On the far side of the airport and the far corner of Baie de St-Jean, these well-priced, island-style one-, two-, and three-bedroom bungalows (four on the beach, seven up a small hill) have small kitchens, open-air sitting areas, and comfortable bathrooms. **Pros:** beach location; apartment conveniences; front porches. **Cons:** TVs by request and with limited French programming; a/c only in bedrooms; next to airport. *Rooms from: €465 ✉ Plage de St-Jean, St-Jean ☎ 0590/27–88–57 🌐 www.lesilets.com 11 bungalows Closed Sept.–Oct. Multiple meal plans.*

$$ HOTEL **Le Tom Beach Hôtel.** This chic but casual boutique hotel on busy St-Jean beach is fun for social types; the nonstop house party often spills onto the terraces and lasts into the wee hours. **Pros:** party central at beach, restaurant, and pool; in town. **Cons:** trendy social scene is not for everybody, especially light sleepers. *Rooms from: €320 ✉ Plage de St-Jean, St-Jean ☎ 0590/52–81–20 🌐 www.tombeach.com 12 rooms Breakfast.*

NIGHTLIFE

Most of the nightlife in St. Barth is centered on Gustavia, though there are a few places to go outside of town. "In" clubs change from season to season, so you might ask around for the hot spot of the moment, but none really get going until about midnight. Theme parties are the current trend. Check the daily *St. Barth News* or *Le Journal de Saint-Barth* for details. A late (10 pm or later) reservation at one of the club–restaurants will eventually become a front-row seat at a party. *Saint-Barth Collector Guest Book* contains current information about sports, spas, nightlife, and the arts.

19

GUSTAVIA

Bar de l'Oubli. Where young locals gather for drinks is a great breakfast option, too (cash only). *✉ Rue du Roi Oscar II, Gustavia ☎ 0590/27–70–06 🌐 www.bardeloubli.com.*

Le Repaire. This restaurant lures a crowd for cocktail hour and its pool table. *✉ Rue de la République, Gustavia ☎ 0590/27–72–48.*

Le Sélect. Commemorated in Jimmy Buffett's "Cheeseburger in Paradise," St. Barth's original hangout recently turned 65. The Facebook page has vintage photos. In the boisterous garden, the barefoot boating set gathers for a cold Carib beer at lower-than-usual prices. *✉ Rue du Centenaire, Gustavia ☎ 0590/27–86–87.*

St. Barth Yacht Club. Although ads call this a private club, dress right and you can probably get in. Nothing much happens till midnight, when the terrific DJs get things going. Above the Yacht Club, the First is a newer hot spot with tapas, drinks, and music. The club's Facebook page and local papers have details on current events. ✉ *Rue Jeanne d'Arc, Gustavia* ☎ *0590/51–15–88* 🌐 *www.caroleplaces.com.*

ST-JEAN

Le Nikki Beach. This place rocks on weekends at lunch—especially Sundays—when the scantily clad young and beautiful lounge on the white canvas banquettes. Check out crazy theme nights on Facebook, including one inspired by *Happy Days.* ✉ *St-Jean* ☎ *0590/27–64–64* 🌐 *www.nikkibeach.com.*

SHOPPING

Fodor's Choice ★ St. Barth is a duty-free port, and its sophisticated visitors find shopping in its 200-plus boutiques a delight, especially for beachwear, accessories, jewelry, and casual wear. It's no overstatement to say that shopping for fashionable clothing, jewels, and designer accessories is better in St. Barth than anywhere else in the Caribbean. New shops open all the time, so there's always something to discover. Some stores close from noon to 3, but they are open until 7 pm. Many are closed on Sunday. A popular afternoon pastime is strolling the two major shopping areas in Gustavia and St-Jean.

In Gustavia, boutiques line the three major shopping streets. Quai de la République, which is right on the harbor, rivals New York's Madison Avenue or Paris's avenue Montaigne for high-end designer retail, including shops for **Louis Vuitton, Bulgari, Cartier, Chopard,** Eres, and **Hermès.** These shops often carry items that are not available in the United States. The elegant Carré d'Or plaza is great fun to explore. Shops are also clustered in **La Savane Commercial Center** (across from the airport), **La Villa Créole** (in St-Jean), and **Espace Neptune** (on the road to Lorient). It's worth working your way from one end to the other at these shopping complexes—just to see or, perhaps, be seen. Boutiques in all three areas carry the latest in French and Italian sportswear and some haute couture. Bargains may be tough to come by, but you might be able to snag that *Birkin* that has a long waiting list stateside, and in any case, you'll have a lot of fun hunting around.

For locally made art and handicrafts, the tourist office can provide information and arrange visits to studios of island artists, including Christian Bretoneiche, Robert Danet, Nathalie Daniel, Patricia Guyot, Rose Lemen, Aline de Lurin, and Marion Vinot. Gustavia, La Villa Créole, and the larger hotels have a few good gallery/craft boutiques.

GUSTAVIA

BOOKS

La Case Aux Livres. This full-service bookstore and newsstand has hundreds of English titles for adults and kids. Its blog lists author appearances. ✉ *9 rue de la République, Gustavia* ☎ *0590/27–15–88* 🌐 *www.lacaseauxlivres.com.*

CLOTHING

Black Swan. This shop has an unparalleled selection (in size and style) of bathing suits for men, women, and children plus souvenir-appropriate island logo-wear and whatever beach equipment you might require. ✉ *Le Carré d'Or, Gustavia* ☎ *0590/52–48–30* 🌐 *www.blackswanstbarth.com.*

Boutique Lacoste. This store has a huge selection of the once-again-chic alligator-logo wear, while a shop next door has a complete selection of the Petit Bateau line of T-shirts popular with teens. ✉ *Rue du Bord de Mer, Gustavia* ☎ *0590/27–66–90.*

Calypso. This well-known retailer carries sophisticated, sexy resort wear and accessories by Balenciaga, Chloe, and D Squared, among others. ✉ *Le Carré d'Or, Gustavia* ☎ *0590/27–69–74* 🌐 *www.calypsostbarth.com/boutiques/st-barth.*

Hermès. This independently owned franchise (closed September–October) has prices slightly below those in the States. ✉ *Rue de la République, Gustavia* ☎ *0590/27–66–15.*

Kokon. This boutique offers a nicely edited mix of designs for on-island or off, including the bo'em, Lotty B. Mustique, and Day Birger lines, and cute shoes to go with them by Heidi Klum for Birkenstock. ✉ *Rue Samuel Fahlberg, Gustavia* ☎ *0590/29–74–48.*

La Chemise Tropezienne. Beautiful tailored cotton shirts in fun prints and stripes for men and women, and colorful Bermuda shorts to coordinate, are popular in St-Tropez and St. Barth. ✉ *Le Carré d'Or, Gustavia* ☎ *0590/27–54–33.*

19

Linde Gallery. In addition to vintage sunglasses, accessories, and ready-to-wear from the 1970s and '80s, Linde carries a well-edited collection of women's and men's fashion from international designers such as Emilio Pucci, Rick Owens, Commune, John de Maya, Maison Martin Margiela, and Comme des Garçons as well as books, CDs, and DVDs. A sister boutique is at the Christopher. ✉ *Les Hauts de Carré d'Or, Gustavia* ☎ *0590/29–73–86* 🌐 *www.lindegallery.com.*

Linen. This shop offers tailored linen shirts for men in a rainbow of soft colors and soft slip-on driving mocs in classic styles. ✉ *Rue Lafayette, Gustavia* ☎ *0590/27–54–26* 🌐 *www.linensbh.com.*

Lolita Jaca. This store has trendy, tailored sportswear and floaty silk charmeuse and cotton gauze tunics perfect for the beach. ✉ *Le Carré d'Or, Gustavia* ☎ *0590/27–59–98* 🌐 *www.lolitajaca.com.*

Mademoiselle Hortense. Charming tops and dresses for the young and young at heart in pretty Liberty prints are made on the island. Great

Shops on rue de France, Gustavia

crafty bracelets and necklaces to accent your new styles are also here. ⊠ *Rue de la République, Gustavia* ☎ *590/27–13–29.*

Marina St. Barth. The trendy, sexy resort wear here, worn by the young and the beautiful, ranges from floaty beachwear to Havaianas. Lines include Ondade, Façonnable, and Caffé, and there are unusual ponchos by Lotus London, high-fashion T-shirts by Eleven Paris, and elegant silk tunics by Jodé. ⊠ *Rue du Roi Oscar II, Gustavia* ☎ *0590/29–37–30* 🌐 *www.marina-stbarth.com.*

Pati de Saint Barth. This is the largest of the three shops that stock the chic, locally made T-shirts, totes, and beach wraps that have practically become the logo of St. Barth. The newest styles have hand-done graffiti-style lettering. The shop also has some handicrafts and other giftable items, like Sobral resin jewelry and great sandals. ⊠ *Rue du Bord de Mer, Gustavia* ☎ *0590/29–78–04* 🌐 *www.madeinstbarth.com.*

Poupette St. Barth. All the brilliant color-crinkle silk, chiffon batik, and embroidered peasant skirts and tops are designed by the owner. There also are great belts and beaded bracelets. An outpost is at Hotel Taïwana. ⊠ *Rue de la République, Gustavia* ☎ *0590/27–55–78* 🌐 *www.poupettestbarth.com.*

Saint-Barth Stock Exchange. On the far side of Gustavia Harbor, the island's consignment and discount shop is a blast to explore. ⊠ *La Pointe, Gustavia* ☎ *0590/27–68–12.*

Stéphane & Bernard. A large, well-edited selection of fashion designers includes Rykiel, Missoni, Valentino, Versaci, Ungaro, Christian Lacroix, and Eres beachwear. ✉ *Rue de la République, Gustavia* ☎ *0590/27–65–69* 🌐 *www.stephaneandbernard.com.*

Vanita Rosa. This store showcases beautiful lace and linen sundresses, peasant tops, accessories galore, and very cool designer vintage. ✉ *Rue du Roi Oscar II, Gustavia* ☎ *0590/52–43–25* 🌐 *www.vanitarosa.com.*

Victoire. Classic, well-made sportswear in luxurious fabrics and great colors has a French twist on preppy that plays as well in Nantucket and Greenwich as it does on St. Barth. A small sidewalk café has Wi-Fi. ✉ *Rue du Général de Gaulle, Gustavia* ☎ *590/29–84–60* 🌐 *www.victoire-paris.com.*

FOODSTUFFS

A.M.C. This supermarket is a bit older than Marché U in St-Jean but can supply nearly anything you might need. It's closed Sunday. ✉ *Quai de la République, Gustavia.*

HOME FURNISHINGS

French Indies Design. This beautiful shop on the far side of Gustavia Harbor is the brainchild of Karine Bruneel, a St. Barth–based architect and interior designer. There are lovely items to accent your home (or yacht) including furniture, textiles, glassware, and unusual decorative baskets, candles, and pottery. ✉ *Maison Suédoise, Gustavia* ☎ *0590/29–66–38* 🌐 *www.frenchindiesdesign.fr.*

JEWELRY

Bijoux de la Mer. South Sea pearls in wonderful hues are strung in clusters on leather to wrap around the neck or arms. ✉ *Rue de la République, Gustavia* ☎ *0590/52–37–68* 🌐 *bijouxdelamersbh.com.*

Donna del Sol. This designer carries beautiful handmade gold chains, Tahitian pearl pieces, and baubles in multicolor diamonds. Have something special in mind? She'll design and produce custom items. ✉ *Rue Auguste Nyman, Gustavia* ☎ *0590/27–90–53* 🌐 *www.donnadelsol.com.*

Fabienne Miot. Unusual and artistic jewelry features rare stones and natural pearls. ✉ *Rue de la République, Gustavia* ☎ *0590/27–73–13* 🌐 *www.fabiennemiot.com.*

Kalinas Perles. Beautiful freshwater pearls are knotted onto the classic St. Barth–style leather thongs by artist Jeremy Albaledejo, who also showcases other artisans' works. ✉ *23 rue du Général de Gaulle, Gustavia* ☎ *0690/65–93–00* 🌐 *www.kalinasperles.com.*

Sindbad. This tiny shop, an island favorite since 1977, curates funky couture jewelry by Gaz Bijou of St-Tropez, crystal collars for pampered pooches, and other reasonably priced, up-to-the-minute styles, including South Sea pearls strung on leather thongs or colorful silky cords. ✉ *Le Carré d'Or, Gustavia* ☎ *0590/27–52–29* 🌐 *www.sindbad-st-barth.com.*

LEATHER GOODS AND ACCESSORIES

Human Steps. Two boutiques, one for women and one for men, have a well-edited selection of chic shoes and leather accessories from names like YSL, Prada, Balenciaga, Miu Miu, and Jimmy Choo. ✉ *39 rue de la République, Gustavia* ☎ *0590/27–85–57* 🌐 *www.human-steps.fr.*

Longchamp. Fans of the popular travel bags, handbags, and leather goods will find a good selection at about 20% off stateside prices. ✉ *Rue de France, Gustavia* ☎ *0590/51–96–50.*

LIQUOR AND TOBACCO

La Cave du Port Franc. This store has a huge selection of wine, especially from France. ✉ *Rue de la République, Gustavia* ☎ *0590/27–65–27* 🌐 *www.lacaveduportfranc.com.*

M'Bolo. Sample infused rums, including lemongrass, ginger, and the island favorite, vanilla, and bring some home in beautiful handblown bottles. Laguiole knives and local spices are sold, too. ✉ *Rue du Général de Gaulle, Gustavia* ☎ *0590/27–90–54.*

LORIENT

COSMETICS

Ligne St. Barth. Superb skin-care products are made on-site from local tropical plants. Call to request a visit from a beautician or therapist to your villa or yacht. ✉ *Rte. de Saline, Lorient* ☎ *0590/27–82–63* 🌐 *www.lignestbarth.com.*

FOODSTUFFS

JoJo Supermarché. This well-stocked counterpart to Gustavia's supermarket gets daily deliveries of bread and produce. JoJoBurger, next door, is the local surfers' spot for a (very good) quick burger. ✉ *Lorient* ☎ *0590/27–63–53.*

ST-JEAN

CLOTHING

Bamboo St. Barth. Beach fashions like cotton tunics, cocktails-on-the-yacht dresses, and sexy Australian swimsuits by Nicole Olivier and Seafolly can be paired with sassy sandals and costume jewelry. ✉ *Pelican Beach, St-Jean* ☎ *0590/52–08–82.*

Black Swan. This shop has an unparalleled selection of bathing suits. ✉ *La Villa Créole, St-Jean* 🌐 *www.blackswanstbarth.com.*

Filles des Iles. In addition to high-quality, flattering attire and sophisticated swimwear that even women of a certain age can wear, the shop stocks delicious artisanal fragrances and chic accessories, like bejewelled sandals. ✉ *8 Villa Créole, St-Jean* ☎ *0590/29–04–08.*

Iléna. Incredible beachwear and lingerie by Chantal Thomas, Sarda, and others includes Swarovski crystal–encrusted bikinis for the young and gorgeous. ✉ *La Villa Créole, St-Jean* ☎ *0590/29–84–05.*

KIWI St. Tropez. This popular resort-wear boutique has a branch in Gustavia, too. ✉ *3 Villa Créole, St-Jean* ☎ *0590/27–57–08* 🌐 *www.kiwi.fr.*

Lili Belle. The nice selection comprises wearable and current styles. ✉ *Pelican Beach, St-Jean* ☎ *0590/87–46–14.*

Morgan. This shop has a line of popular casual wear in the trendy vein. ✉ *La Villa Créole, St-Jean* ☎ *0590/27–71–00.*

SUD SUD.ETC. This store stocks everything for the beach: inflatables, mats, bags, and beachy shell jewelry, as well as bikinis and gauzy cover-ups. ✉ *Les Galeries du Commerce, St-Jean* ☎ *0590/27–98–75.*

FOODSTUFFS

Maya's to Go. This is the place to go for prepared picnics, meals, salads, and rotisserie chickens from the kitchen of the popular restaurant in Gustavia. It's closed Monday. ✉ *Les Galeries du Commerce, St-Jean* ☎ *0590/29–83–70* 🌐 *www.mayastogo.com* ⏲ *Closed Mon.*

SPORTS AND THE OUTDOORS

BOATING AND SAILING

Gustavia's harbor, 13 to 16 feet deep, has mooring and docking facilities for 40 yachts. There are also good anchorages at Public, Corossol, and Colombier. You can charter sailing and motorboats in Gustavia Harbor for as little as a half day, staffed or bareboat. Ask at the Gustavia tourist office or your hotel for a list of recommended charter companies.

Carib Waterplay. On St-Jean beach for over 30 years, this outfit lets you try windsurfing, kayaking, and stand-up paddling; rents waterbikes; and gives kids' windsurf lessons. ✉ *St-Jean* ☎ *0590/61–80–81* 🌐 *www.caribwaterplay.com.*

Jicky Marine Service. This company offers full-day outings (starting at $160) on motorboats, Zodiacs, and 42- or 46-foot catamarans to the uninhabited Île Fourchue for swimming, snorkeling, cocktails, and lunch. Fishing trips are also offered, as is private transport from St. Martin. An unskippered motor rental runs about $260 a day. ✉ *26 rue Jeanne D'Arc, Gustavia* ☎ *0590/27–70–34* 🌐 *www.jickymarine.com.*

19

DIVING AND SNORKELING

Several dive shops arrange scuba excursions. Depending on weather conditions, you may dive at **Pain de Sucre, Coco Island,** or toward nearby **Saba.** There's also an underwater shipwreck, plus sharks, rays, sea tortoises, coral, and the usual varieties of colorful fish. The waters on the island's leeward side are the calmest. For the uncertified, there's a shallow reef right off the beach at Anse de Cayes, which you can explore with mask and fins, and a hike down to the beach at Corossol brings you to a very popular snorkeling spot.

La Bulle Diving Center. PADI certification, day and night dives, and snorkeling trips with friendly and watchful supervision make this a popular outfit. A beginners' package (€210) includes instruction and two dives. ✉ *La Pointe, Gustavia* ☎ *0690/77–76–55* 🌐 *www.labullesbh.com.*

FAMILY **Plongée Caraïbe.** This company is recommended for its up-to-the-minute equipment, dive boat, and scuba discovery program. It also runs two-hour group snorkeling trips on the *Blue Cat Catamaran* (€60). ✉ *Rue Victor Schoelcher, Gustavia* ☎ *0590/27–55–94* 🌐 *www.plongee-caraibes.com.*

Réserve Naturelle de Saint-Barthélemy. Most of the waters surrounding St. Barth are protected in the island's nature reserve, which provides information from its Gustavia office. The diving here isn't nearly as rich as in more dive-centered destinations like Saba and St. Eustatius, but the options aren't bad either. ✉ *Gustavia* ☎ *0590/27–88–18* 🌐 *www.reservenaturellestbarth.com.*

Splash. This company offers PADI and CMAS (Confédération Mondiale des Activités Subaquatiques—World Underwater Federation) diver training at all levels. All instructors speak French, Russian, and English. Although the boat normally leaves daily at 9, 11:30, 2, and in the evening for a night dive, times are adjusted to suit preferences. Seabob scuba scooters run €150 per hour. ✉ *Gustavia* ☎ *0590/56–90–24.*

FISHING

Most fishing is done in the waters north of Lorient, Flamands, and Corossol. Popular catches are tuna, marlin, wahoo, and barracuda. The annual St. Barth Open Fishing Tournament, organized by Océan Must, is in mid-July.

Océan Must Marina. This outfitter arranges deep-sea fishing expeditions as well as bareboat and staffed boat charters. ✉ *La Pointe, Gustavia* ☎ *0590/27–62–25* 🌐 *www.oceanmust.com.*

GUIDED TOURS

You can arrange island tours by minibus or car at hotel desks or through taxi operators in Gustavia or at the airport. The tourist office runs a variety of tours for about €46 for a half day for up to eight people. You can also download up-to-the-minute walking and driving tour itineraries from the office's website.

JC Taxi. Since 1986, native-born Jean-Claude has been providing safe and comfortable transportation in a 10-passenger minivan. Island tours and night driving are available. ✉ *Gustavia* ☎ *0690/49–02–97.*

St. Barth Jetski. This company leads tours of the island by water on a Jet Ski or Flyboard, St. Barth's newest water-play craze. Kids love the banana-boat rides. ✉ *Quai du Yacht Club, Rue Jeanne d'Arc, Gustavia* ☎ *0690/49–54–72* 🌐 *www.stbarthjetski.com.*

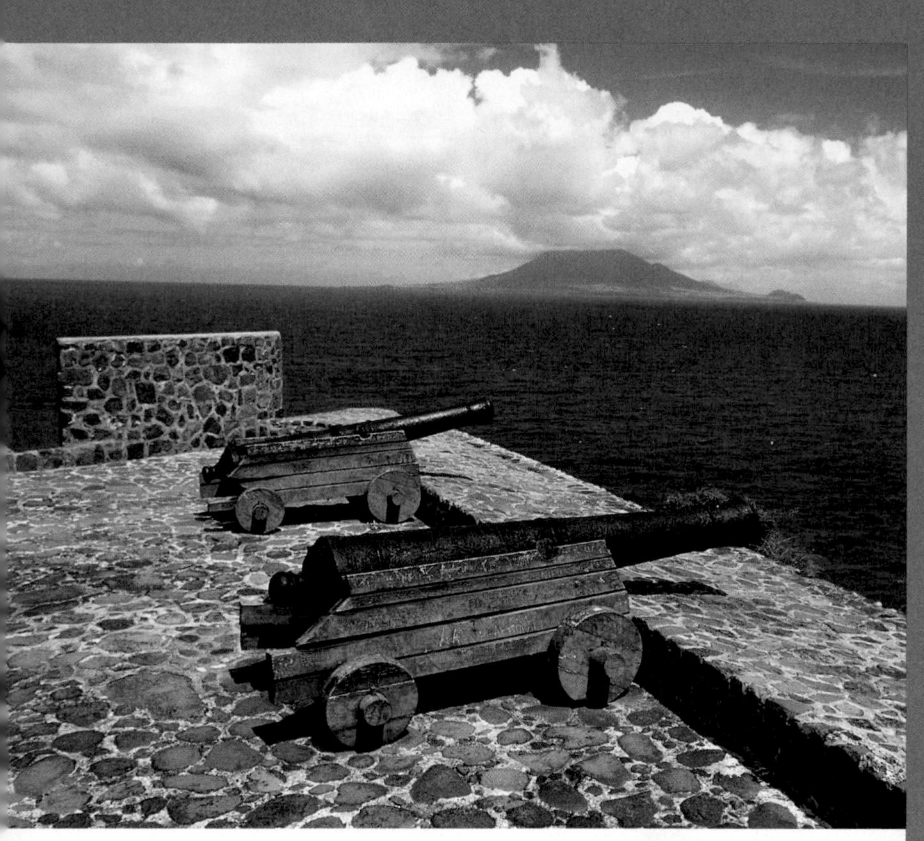

ST. EUSTATIUS

20

WELCOME TO ST. EUSTATIUS

FRIENDLY TRANQUILLITY

A tiny part of the Dutch Caribbean, St. Eustatius (often just called "Statia") is just under 12 square miles (30 square km), which is still twice as large as Saba. The island, which is 38 miles (63 km) south of St. Maarten, has a population of a bit more than 4,000. And although there are some beaches, they are better for strolling than swimming.

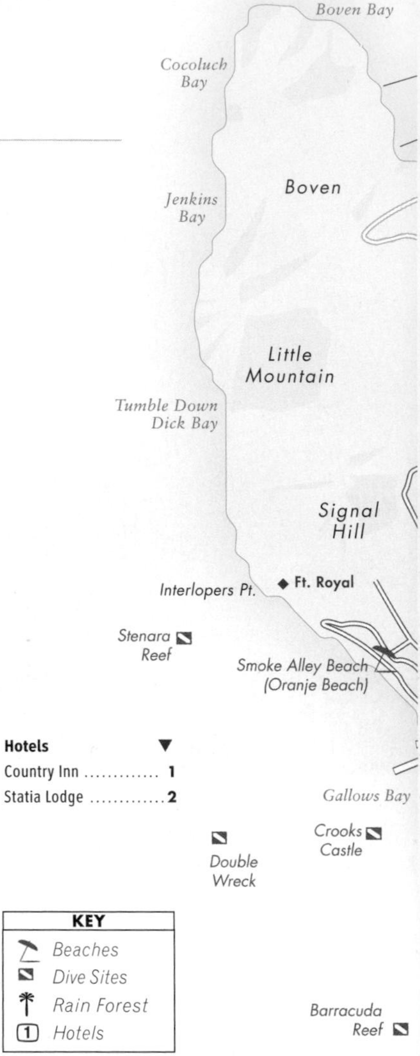

Boven Bay
Cocoluch Bay
Boven
Jenkins Bay
Little Mountain
Tumble Down Dick Bay
Signal Hill
Interlopers Pt.
Ft. Royal
Stenara Reef
Smoke Alley Beach (Oranje Beach)
Gallows Bay
Crooks Castle
Double Wreck
Barracuda Reef

Hotels	▼
Country Inn	1
Statia Lodge	2

KEY
- Beaches
- Dive Sites
- Rain Forest
- Hotels

Like Saba, tiny Statia is a quiet Caribbean haven for scuba divers and hikers. When the island was called the Emporium of the Western World, warehouses stretched for miles along the quays, and 200 merchant ships could anchor at its docks. These days it's the day-trippers from St. Maarten who walk the quays.

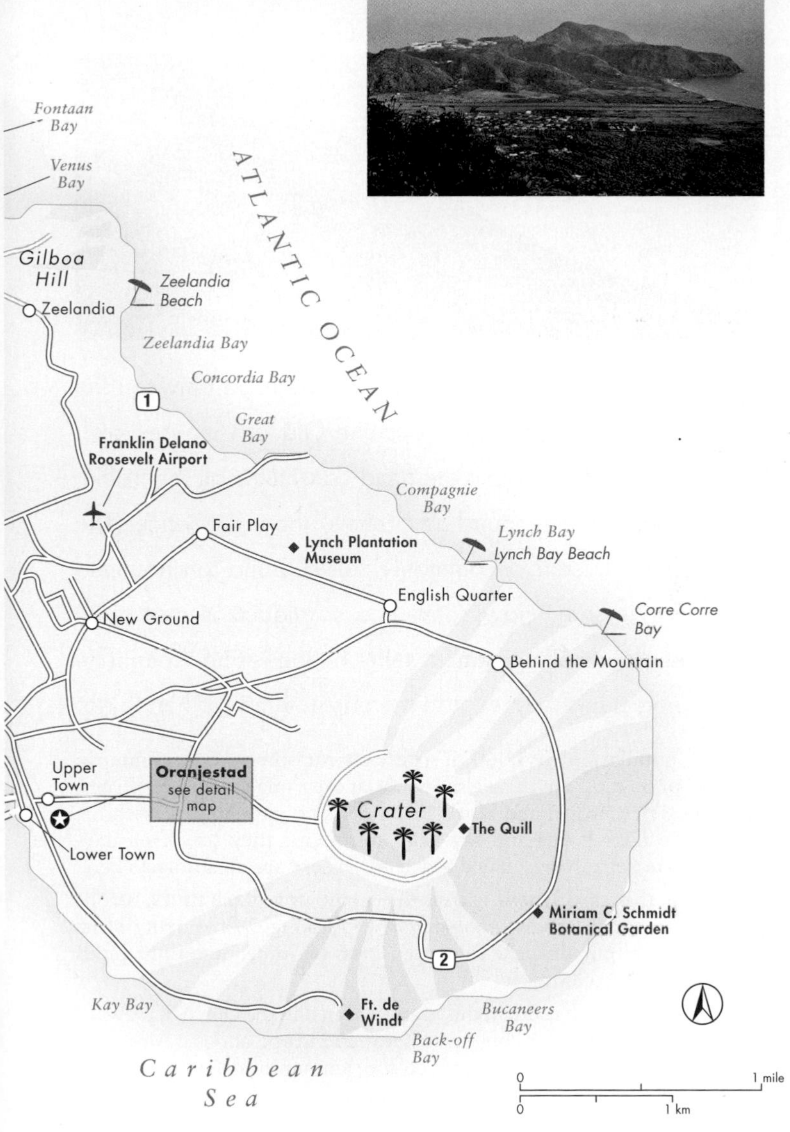

TOP REASONS TO VISIT ST. EUSTATIUS

1 Diving: Visiting the many varied wrecks in Statia's protected waters is a highlight.

2 Hiking: Hiking the Quill, an extinct volcano that holds a primeval rain forest, is the top activity for landlubbers.

3 Welcoming: The genuine friendliness of the people here is overwhelming.

4 History: For anyone interested in 18th-century history, even a day trip from St. Maarten is a satisfying experience.

Updated by Roberta Sotonoff

The stars are ablaze, but it's dark on the road between the Blue Bead Bar & Restaurant and the Old Gin House hotel. A chicken running across the road constitutes all the traffic, and except for the sound of crickets, there is silence. The island of St. Eustatius, commonly called Statia (pronounced *stay*-sha), is safe. How safe? The scuttlebutt is that a St. Maarten police officer sent to serve on the island thought he was being punished because there is nothing for him to do.

With a population of 4,060, it's difficult for someone to commit a crime—or do most anything else—without everyone finding out. Everyone knows everyone, and that's also a blessing. Statians are friendly; they beep their horns and say hello to anyone they see. Even day-trippers are warmly welcomed as friends. There are no strangers here.

Think of this tiny Dutch Caribbean island for quiet times, strolls through history, and awesome diving and hiking. While many of its neighbors are pursuing the tourist business big-time, Statia just plods along. That's its charm.

During the late 18th century, this island, located in the Dutch Windward Triangle, was a hub for commerce between Europe and the Americas. When ships carrying slaves, sugar, cotton, ammunition, and other commodities crowded its harbor, it was known as the Emporium of the Western World and the Golden Rock.

With an 11-gun salute to the American Stars and Stripes on the brig-of-war *Andrew Doria* on November 16, 1776, Statia's golden age ended. Statia's noteworthy role as the first country to recognize U.S. independence from Great Britain was not a gesture appreciated by the British. In 1781, British Admiral George Rodney looted and economically destroyed the island. It has never really recovered.

Indeed, chaos ensued between 1781 and 1816 as the Dutch, English, and French vied for control of the island. It changed hands 22 times. The Netherlands finally won out, and Statia has been a Dutch possession since 1816. Today, it's part of the Dutch Caribbean and a special municipality of the Netherlands.

Remnants of those bygone days are evident around the island. Hanging off the cliff at the only village, Oranjestad, is the nearly 370-year-old Fort Oranje, the site from where the famous shots were fired. The original Dutch Reformed Church, built in 1755, sits in its courtyard. Oranjestad itself, on a ridge above the sea, is lush with greenery and bursting with bougainvillea, oleander, and hibiscus. The rest of the island is rather pristine. The eastern side, bordered by the rough waters of the Atlantic, has an untamed quality to it. Extinct volcanoes and dry plains anchor the north end. Statia's crown is the Quill, a 1,968-foot extinct volcano, its verdant crater covered with a primeval rain forest. Hiking to the peak is a popular pastime.

LOGISTICS

Getting to St. Eustatius: There are no nonstop flights here from the United States, and the only way to get here is a Winair flight from St. Maarten.

Hassle Factor: Medium–high.

On the Ground: This is a small place. You can rent a car or scooter for trips out of town, or you can take a taxi.

Beaches on the island come and go as the waters see fit, but first-class dive sites lure most visitors to the island. Wrecks and old cannons are plentiful at archaeological dive sites, and modern ships, such as the cable-laying *Charles L. Brown*, have been sunk into underwater craters. Stingrays, eels, turtles, and barracudas live in the undersea Caribbean neighborhood where giant pillar coral, huge yellow sea fans, and reef fingers abound. The sea has reclaimed the walls of Dutch warehouses that have sunk into the Caribbean over the past several hundred years, but these underwater ruins serve as a day-care center for abundant schools of juvenile fish.

On land, beachcombers hunt for blue beads. The 17th-century baubles, found only on Statia, were used to barter for rum, slaves, tobacco, and cotton. The chance of finding one is slim, though you can see them at the island's museum. Pre-Columbian artifacts, dating back to 500 BC, are also on display there.

Statia is mostly a short-flight, day-trip destination from nearby St. Maarten. That might be just enough for some visitors. But those who linger can appreciate the unspoiled island, its history, and its peacefulness. Most of all, it's the locals who make a visit to the island special.

PLANNING

GETTING HERE AND AROUND

AIR TRAVEL

The only way to get to Statia is on one of the five daily Winair flights from St. Maarten, timed to coincide with the arrival of international flights. The flight takes 16 minutes. You'll have to book directly with Winair, by phone or online. Prices are $150–$200. Reconfirm your flight, because schedules can change abruptly. The departure fee from the island is $10. If flying out of St. Maarten, check to see if the international departure fee has already been added into your airline ticket. There is no regularly scheduled ferry service.

Airline Contact **Winair** ☎ *599/318–2381, 866/466–0410* 🌐 *www.fly-winair.com.*

Airport **Franklin Delano Roosevelt Airport** (*EUX*). ✉ *Oranjestad* ☎ *599/318–2620.*

CAR TRAVEL

Driving in Statia is not difficult, mostly because there are not that many places to go. Street signs are not plentiful, but anyone you ask for directions will be more than happy to help you. The roads are generally in good condition. Daily rates for a car rental begin at $35.

Car-Rental Contacts **ARC Car Rental** ✉ *Airport Rd., Oranjestad* ☎ *599/318–2595.* **Brown's** ✉ *White Wall Rd. 8, Oranjestad* ☎ *599/318–2266, 599/318–5564.* **Rainbow Car Rental** ✉ *Statia Mall, Oranjestad* ☎ *599/318–1480, 599/318–2444.*

SCOOTER TRAVEL

Zipping around by scooter is another option. Scooter rentals start at $25 per day, including insurance.

Contacts **Elly's Scooter** ✉ *Golden Rock* ☎ *599/318–1476.* **LNP Scooter and Bike Rental** ☎ *599/318–1476.*

TAXI TRAVEL

You could literally walk from the airport runway into town; one or two taxis are usually waiting for arriving passengers at the airport, and you'll be whisked into Oranjestad for about $8.

ESSENTIALS

Banks and Exchange Services The U.S. dollar has been the legal tender here since 2011. **Windward Islands Bank.** The bank has an ATM at the airport and at Mazinga Square, as well as exchange services in town. ☎ *599/318–2847* 🌐 *www.wib-bank.net* 🕓 *Weekdays 8–3:30.*

Emergency Services **Ambulance** ☎ *912, 599/318–2211.* **Fire** ☎ *912, 599/318–2360.* **Police** ☎ *911, 599/318–2333.*

Mail The post office is on Ruby Hassell Road, Upper Town. Airmail letters to North America and Europe are $1.59, postcards 92¢. When sending letters to the island, be sure to include "Dutch Caribbean" in the address.

Passport Requirements All visitors must present a valid passport and a return or ongoing ticket for entry to Statia.

Phones To call Statia from North America, dial 011 + 599 + 318, followed by the four-digit number. To call the United States using an AT&T card, the access number is 001–800–872–2881. To call within the island, dial only the five-digit number that starts with an 8.

Taxes and Service Charges The departure tax—$10 for flights to Dutch Caribbean islands and foreign destinations—is payable in cash only. Note: When flying home through St. Maarten, list yourself as "in transit" to avoid paying the tax levied in St. Maarten if you will be there for less than 24 hours. Hotels collect a 7% government tax and 3% turnover tax. Restaurants charge a 3% government tax and a 10% service charge.

Tipping: Taxi drivers, 10%; housekeeping, a dollar or two per day; waitstaff, an extra 5%–10%.

ACCOMMODATIONS

Statia has only five hotels, with 20 rooms or fewer—and except for Statia Lodge, all are within Oranjestad. There are also a handful of bed-and-breakfasts. Nothing on the island could be described as luxurious.

Hotel reviews have been shortened. For full information, visit Fodors.com.

WHAT IT COSTS IN U.S. DOLLARS

	$	$$	$$$	$$$$
Restaurants	under $12	$12–$20	$21–$30	over $30
Hotels	under $275	$275–$375	$376–$475	over $475

Restaurant prices are the average cost of a main course at dinner or, if dinner is not served, at lunch. Hotel prices are the lowest cost of a standard double room in high season.

Visitor Information In addition to the main tourist office, a tourist information booth at the airport is open daily.

Contacts St. Eustatius Tourism Development Foundation ✉ *Fort Oranje, Oranjestad* ☎ *599/318–2433, 599/318–2620 airport tourism booth* 🌐 *www.statiatourism.com* ⏲ *Mon.–Thurs. 8–noon and 1–5, Fri. 8–noon and 1–4:30.*

WEDDINGS

Foreign couples must be at least 21 and Dutch nationals at least 18. Documents should be received 14 days before the wedding date. The application requires notarized original documents, including birth certificates, passports (for non-Dutch people), divorce decrees, and death certificates of deceased spouses. The ceremony can be performed in English, Dutch, Spanish, or Papiamento. For more information, visit 🌐 *www.statiatourism.com*.

20

EXPLORING

Statia is an arid island with a valley between two mountain peaks. Most sights lie in the valley, making touring the island easy. From the airport you can rent a car or take a taxi and be in Oranjestad in minutes; to hike the Quill, Statia's highest peak, you can drive to the trailhead in less than 15 minutes from just about anywhere. Other trails with breathtaking views include Boven, 450 feet elevation, Gilboa, 400 feet, and Venus Bay.

TOP ATTRACTIONS

Fodor's Choice ★ **Oranjestad.** Statia's only town, Oranjestad sits on the west coast facing the Caribbean. Both Upper Town—with cobblestone streets that designate its historic section—and Lower Town are easy to explore on foot.

Ft. Oranje. Three bastions have clung to these cliffs since 1636. In 1976, Statia participated in the U.S. bicentennial celebration by restoring the fort, and now the black cannons extend beyond the ramparts. In the parade grounds a plaque, presented in 1939 by Franklin D. Roosevelt, reads "Here the sovereignty of the United States of America was first formally acknowledged to a national vessel by a foreign official."

Built in 1775, the partially restored **Dutch Reformed Church,** on Kerkweg (Church Way), has lovely stone arches that face the sea. Ancient tales can be read on the gravestones in the adjacent 18th-century cemetery, where people were often buried atop one another. On Synagogepad (Synagogue Path) off Kerkweg is **Honen Dalim** ("She Who is Charitable to the Poor"), one of the Caribbean's oldest synagogues. Dating from 1738, it has a partially restored exterior.

Lower Town sits below Fort Oranjestraat (Fort Orange Street) and some steep cliffs. It is accessible from Upper Town on foot via the zigzagging, cobblestone Fort Road or by car via Van Tonningenweg. Warehouses and shops that were piled high with European imports in the 18th century are either abandoned or simply used to store local fishermen's equipment. One of them has been restored and now holds the **Mazinga-on-the-Bay Gift Shop.**

Along the waterfront is a lovely park with palms, flowering shrubs, and benches—the work of the historical foundation. Peeking out from the shallow waters are the crumbling ruins of 18th-century buildings, reminders of Statia's days as the merchant hub of the Caribbean. The sea has slowly advanced since then, and it now surrounds many of the stone-and-brick ruins, making for fascinating snorkeling. ✉ *Oranjestad.*

Fodor's Choice ★ **The Quill.** This extinct, perfectly formed, 1,968-foot volcano has a primeval rain forest in its crater. Hike and be surrounded with giant elephant ears, ferns, flowers, wild orchids, and fruit trees, and if you're lucky, glimpse the elusive, endangered *iguana delicatissima* (a large—sometimes several feet long—greenish-gray lizard with spines down its back). The volcanic cone rises 3 miles (5 km) south of Oranjestad on the main road. Local boys go up to the Quill at night to catch delectable land crabs. The tourist board or St. Eustatius National Parks will help you make hiking arrangements, and you must purchase a $6 permit before beginning the hike. Figure on two to four hours to hike the volcano.

St. Eustatius National Parks (*STENAPA*). There are three national parks in Statia: St. Eustatius National Marine Park, Quill/Boven National Park, and Miriam C. Schmidt Botanical Garden. To hike the Quill or Boven or dive in the marine park, you must purchase a permit ($6 per day or $30 annually) at the STENAPA office, the information booth at the airport, or your hotel. ✉ *STENAPA office, Gallows Bay* ☎ *599/318–2884* 🌐 *www.statiapark.org.*

WORTH NOTING

Lynch Plantation Museum. Also known as the Berkel Family Plantation and the Berkel's Domestic Museum, these two one-room buildings give a detailed perspective of life on Statia almost 100 years ago. A remarkable collection preserves this family's history: pictures, eyeglasses, original furnishings, and farming and fishing implements. Call Ismael Berkel to

St. Eustatius Historical Foundation Museum

arrange a private tour. Since it's on the northeast side of the island, you need a taxi or car to get here. ✉ *Lynch Bay* ☎ *599/318–2338* 🎫 *Free* ⏲ *By appointment only.*

FAMILY **Miriam C. Schmidt Botanical Garden.** Relaxation and quiet abound on these 52 acres, with a greenhouse, a palm garden, a kitchen garden, and an observation bird trail. Its location, on the Atlantic side of the Quill on a plot called Upper Company, reveals a superb view of St. Kitts. For a picnic, there's no better place, but the only way to get here is by car or taxi, and some of the road is not well paved. ☎ *599/318–2884 STENAPA* 🌐 *www.statiapark.org* 🎫 *Suggested donation $5* ⏲ *Daily sunrise–sunset.*

St. Eustatius Historical Foundation Museum. In the center of Upper Town is the former headquarters of Lord George Rodney, a British admiral during the American Revolution. While here, Rodney confiscated everything from gunpowder to wine in retaliation for Statia's gallant support of the fledgling country. The completely restored house is Statia's most important intact 18th-century dwelling. Exhibits trace the island's history from the pre-Columbian 6th century to the present. You can also buy a booklet with a self-guided walking tour, beginning in Lower Town at the marina and ending at the museum. ✉ *Doncker House, 3 Wilhelminaweg, Upper Town, Oranjestad* ☎ *599/318–2288* 🌐 *www.steustatiushistory.org* 🎫 *$3* ⏲ *Mon.–Sat. 9–5.*

DID YOU KNOW?

The Quill's highest point is known as Mazinga. The last eruption of the now-dormant volcano was in AD 400.

BEACHES

If you desire a white sandy beach, calm waters, and a place to cool yourself off with a quick dip, you're looking at the wrong island. Statia's beaches are mostly deserted, rocky stretches of pristine shoreline. Many of the beaches on the Caribbean side are here today and reclaimed by the sea tomorrow. The Atlantic side is an untamed mass of wild swells and vicious undertow. Walking, shelling, and searching for the elusive blue beads are popular pastimes for beachgoers. It's more likely, however, that the only place you will find real blue beads is at the St. Eustatius Historical Foundation Museum.

Lynch Bay Beach. Just two bends north of Corre Corre Bay on the island's Atlantic side, light-brown sand and rock cover this small beach, which is really an extension of Zeelandia Beach. Opt for walking instead of swimming here. There are turbulent swells, and there's a strong undertow. **Amenities:** none. **Best for:** walking. ✉ *Lynch Bay.*

Smoke Alley Beach (*Oranje Beach*). The color of the sand varies from light beige to black at this beach on the Caribbean side near Gallows Bay. Much of the beach is claimed by ebb and flow. The waters are sometimes calm, so snorkeling is possible, but it's usually a better place for a swim or sunning. **Amenities:** none. **Best for:** swimming. ✉ *North end of Bay Rd., Oranjestad.*

Zeelandia Beach. Walking, shelling, and sunbathing are popular pastimes on this 2-mile (3-km) stretch of black-and-tan sand. Its Atlantic-side location makes it dangerous for swimming. **Amenities:** none. **Best for:** walking. ✉ *Oranjestad.*

WHERE TO EAT

As with most everything on the island, low-key and casual is the name of the game when it comes to Statia's restaurants.

$$ ECLECTIC Fodor's Choice ★

✕ **Blue Bead Bar & Restaurant.** This delightful little blue-and-yellow restaurant, a favorite with locals, is the perfect place to watch the sunset. It is one of those places where everyone talks to everyone. There are always daily specials; the menu includes pizza, seafood, and Italian and French food. [$] *Average main: $18* ✉ *Bay Rd., Gallows Bay, Lower Town, Oranjestad* ☎ *599/318–2873* ⏲ *Closed Mon.*

$$ ECLECTIC

✕ **Franky's Bar & Restaurant.** There isn't much more to this nondescript place than a bar, some tables, and a patio. But its goat dishes have made it well known. Every Saturday there is a barbecue and a DJ. The barbecue is a great deal—ribs, chicken, potatoes, satay rice, vegetables, and salad—all for $13. [$] *Average main: $12* ✉ *Black Harry La., Oranjestad* ☎ *599/318–0166* ▭ *No credit cards* ⏲ *Closed Mon.*

$$ CARIBBEAN

✕ **Golden Era Hotel Restaurant.** The surroundings may be bland, but the tasty seafood and fine creole dishes are anything but. It has another thing going for it: it's alongside the water, so the sound of the Caribbean is always playing in the background. Wednesday is chicken night; Friday is pasta. [$] *Average main: $15* ✉ *Golden Era Hotel, Bay Rd., Lower*

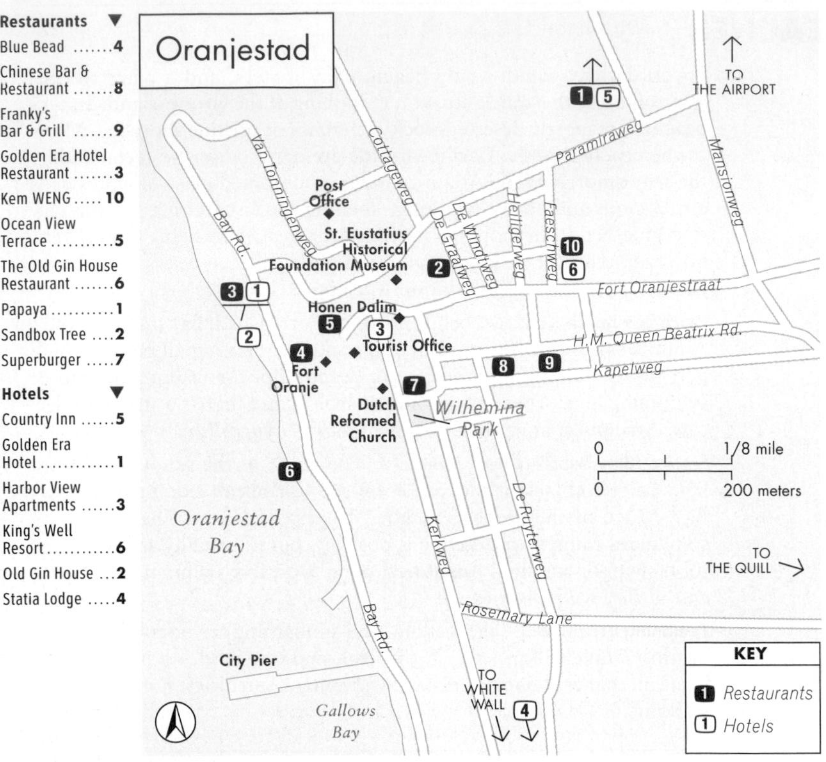

Town, Oranjestad ☎ 599/318–2445, 599/318–2345, 599/318–2355 ⊕ www.goldenerahotel.com.

$$ CHINESE ✕ **Kem WENG Chinese Bar & Restaurant.** Unless you're into Formica, don't expect to be wowed by the atmosphere at this simple spot. What you will find are large portions of dishes such as *bami goreng* (Indonesian-style noodles with bits of beef, pork, or shrimp as well as tomatoes, carrots, bean sprouts, cabbage, soy sauce, and spices) and pork chops with a spicy sauce. It's do-it-yourself table hauling if you want to eat outside. *$ Average main: $12 ✉ Queen Beatrix Rd., Upper Town, Oranjestad ☎ 599/318–2389 ▭ No credit cards ⏲ Closed Sun.*

$ CARIBBEAN ✕ **Ocean View Terrace.** In the courtyard overlooking Fort Oranje, this is a favorite of those who like to watch the sunset. It hasn't changed over the years. Owner Lauris Redan serves sandwiches and burgers for lunch and local dishes—baked snapper with shrimp sauce, spicy chicken, tenderloin steak—at dinner. Every now and then there's a succulent barbecue. *$ Average main: $11 ✉ Fort Oranjestraat, Upper Town, Oranjestad ☎ 599/318–2934 ▭ No credit cards ⏲ No lunch Sun.*

$$ ECLECTIC ✕ **The Old Gin House Ocean View Restaurant.** This extension of the Old Gin House faces the water. The simple menu includes great scrambled eggs for breakfast and sandwiches and tasty salads for lunch. Caribbean Cuisine BBQ Night is every Wednesday. **■ TIP→ Service is slow, but on this island there is no reason to rush.** *$ Average main: $13*

Across from the Old Gin House, Bay Rd., Lower Town, Oranjestad 599/318–2319 No lunch Wed.; no dinner Mon.–Tues.

$ BAKERY **Sandbox Tree Bakery.** This is the spot to get a quick sandwich, satisfy your sweet tooth, or order a wedding, birthday, or other special-occasion cake. It's open to 7:30 weekdays but closes at noon on Saturday. *Average main: $4 Kerkweg, across from Dutch Reformed Church, Upper Town, Oranjestad 599/318–2404 No credit cards Closed Sun.*

$ BURGER FAMILY **Superburger.** Statia's version of fast food, this little hangout serves burgers, shakes, and ice cream as well as local West Indian dishes. It's a local favorite for lunch. *Average main: $6 De Graaffweg, Upper Town, Oranjestad 599/318–2412 No credit cards Closed Sun.*

WHERE TO STAY

Statia has several basic rental apartments available as alternatives to hotel rooms, and a few are available for $60 or less per night. Don't expect much beyond cable TV, a bathroom, and a kitchenette. Check with the tourist office for options.

$ B&B/INN Fodor's Choice ★ **Country Inn.** Facing Zeelandia Bay and close to the airport, this folksy little inn is surrounded by a lush tropical garden. **Pros:** very homey; lovely tropical garden. **Cons:** not on water; 15-minute walk to town, so a vehicle is recommended. *Rooms from: $70 3 Passionfruit Rd., Concordia 599/318–2484 www.countryinn-statia.com 6 rooms No credit cards Multiple meal plans.*

$ HOTEL **Golden Era Hotel.** On the waterfront across from the Old Gin House, this property has a funky, retro-1960s feel. **Pros:** friendly staff; right on the waterfront; breakfast included. **Cons:** rooms are basic and dark. *Rooms from: $115 Bay Rd., Lower Town, Oranjestad 599/318–2555, 599/318–2345, 599/318–2545 www.goldenerahotel.com 20 rooms, 1 suite Breakfast.*

$ RENTAL **Harbor View Apartments.** Each of these newly constructed accommodations has lots of modern conveniences, but the best part is the beautiful ocean view. **Pros:** modern facilities; walking distance to most downtown restaurants and attractions. **Cons:** maid service only twice a week. *Rooms from: $250 Kerkweg 8, Lower Town, Oranjestad 599/586–0923 www.statiaharborviewapartments.com 4 apartments No meals.*

20

$ B&B/INN **King's Well Resort.** Win and Laura Piechutzki, along with their macaws, iguanas, fishponds, cats, and Great Danes, warmly welcome visitors to their little inn, on the wooded cliffs between Upper and Lower Town. **Pros:** cliff-side patio overlooks Fort Oranje, the bay, and the sunsets; breakfast included; observatory with telescope. **Cons:** not for those who don't love animals, particularly iguanas; not on the water or in town. *Rooms from: $150 On curve of Van Tonningenweg, Smoke Alley, Oranjestad 599/318–2538 www.kingswellstatia.com 5 rooms, 2 apartments Breakfast.*

$ HOTEL **The Old Gin House.** Built from 17th- and 18th-century cobblestones, this old cotton warehouse is now a hotel and restaurant with a renovated lobby. **Pros:** conveniently located; American breakfast included.

Cons: dark rooms could use some sprucing up; pricey for what you get. *Rooms from: $195* ✉ *Bay Rd., Lower Town, Oranjestad* ☎ *599/318–2319* 🌐 *www.oldginhouse.com* *20 rooms and suites* *Breakfast.*

$ RENTAL FAMILY Fodor's Choice ★ **Statia Lodge.** From your cottage patio at the island's best digs, the views of St. Kitts and Nevis are drop-dead-gorgeous; do an about-face and the Quill volcano looms. **Pros:** the best views and most modern accommodations on the island; lovely landscaping; French, English, and German spoken. **Cons:** no a/c; not near the water or town, so car or scooter needed; not accessible for people with disabilities. *Rooms from: $145* ✉ *White Wall* ☎ *599/318–1900* 🌐 *www.statialodge.com* *8 1-bedroom bungalows, 2 2-bedroom bungalows* *Closed Aug. and Sept.* *No meals.*

NIGHTLIFE

Cool Corner Bar & Restaurant. The island's oldest bar, this tiny but lively after-work and weekend hangout is across from the St. Eustatius Historical Foundation Museum. ✉ *Wilhelminaweg, Oranjestad* ☎ *599/318–3386.*

SHOPPING

The limited shopping here is all duty-free. But other than the predictable souvenirs, there's not much to buy. Several shops carry Dutch cheeses and chocolates.

Mazinga-on-the-Bay Gift Shop. Beads and other souvenirs are for sale at this store in a refurbished warehouse, open Wednesday–Saturday afternoons. It's on the seaside across from the Old Gin House. ✉ *Gallows Bay, Oranjestad* ☎ *599/318–2245.*

Paper Corner. Magazines, a few books, computer accessories, and stationery supplies are for sale here weekdays. ✉ *Van Tonningenweg, Upper Town, Oranjestad* ☎ *599/318–2208.*

SPORTS AND THE OUTDOORS

DIVING AND SNORKELING

Fodor's Choice ★ Forget about glitz and nightlife. Statia is the quintessential low-key island. Finding an elusive *iguana delicatissima* on the Quill is probably the most exciting thing you can do on land. Statia's real thrills are underwater.

Long ago the ocean reclaimed the original seawall built by the Dutch in the 1700s. The sunken walls, remnants of old buildings, cannons, and anchors are now part of an extensive reef system populated by reef fingers, juvenile fish, and other sea creatures.

STATIA HAS MORE THAN 30 dive sites protected by the St. Eustatius National Marine Park, part of the St. Eustatius National Parks. Barracuda swim around colorful coral walls at **Barracuda Reef**, off the island's southwest coast. At **Double Wreck**, just offshore from Lower Town, you can find two tall-masted ships that date from the 1700s. The coral has taken on the shape of these two disintegrated vessels, and the site attracts spiny lobsters, stingrays, moray eels, and large schools of fish. About 100 yards west of Double Wreck is the Japanese ship ***Cheng Tong***, which was sunk in 2004. Off the south end of the island, the sinking of the ***Charles L. Brown***, a 1957 cable-laying vessel that was once owned by AT&T, created another artificial reef when it was sunk in a 135-foot underwater crater. Off the island's western shore, **Stenapa Reef** is an artificial reef created from the wrecks of barges, a harbor boat, and other ship parts. Large grouper and turtles are among the marine life you can spot here. For snorkelers, **Crooks Castle** has several stands of pillar coral, giant yellow sea fans, and sea whips just southwest of Lower Town.

Dive shops along Bay Road rent gear (including snorkeling gear for about $14 a day), offer certification courses, and organize dive trips. One-tank dives start at $49; two-tank dives are about $98.

Dive Statia/Scubaqua. This fully equipped dive shop in a remodeled warehouse features PADI and CMAS certification plus Nitrox diving and underwater photography courses. DVPs (diver propulsion vehicles) are available for diving or snorkeling. Dive courses are offered in several different languages. ✉ *Bay Rd., Lower Town, Oranjestad* ☎ *599/318–5450* 🌐 *www.scubaqua.com.*

Golden Rock Dive Center. Operated by Glenn and Michele Faires, this dive center offers PADI certification and personal service. A one-tank dive is $50, two tanks $95, plus a $1 harbor fee and $6 per dive marine park fee. ✉ *Gallows Bay, Lower Town, Oranjestad* ☎ *599/318–2964* 🌐 *www.goldenrockdive.com.*

GUIDED TOURS

Statia's four taxis and two large buses are available for island tours. A 2½-hour outing costs $20 per person per vehicle for five people (extra people are $5 each), usually including airport transfer. (If you'd rather head out on your own, there's a self-guided walking tour booklet available from the St. Eustatius Historical Foundation Museum.)

HIKING

Trails range from the easy to the "Watch out!" The big thrill here is the Quill, the 1,968-foot extinct volcano whose crater cradles a rain forest. Give yourself two to four hours to complete the hike. The tourist office has a list of 12 marked trails and can put you in touch with a guide. Quill/Boven National Park includes a trail into the crater, which is a long, winding but safe walk. Maps and the necessary $6 permit ($30 for a year) are available at the St. Eustatius National Parks office at Gallows Bay. Wear layers: it can be cool on the summit and steamy in the interior.

ST. KITTS AND NEVIS

TOP REASONS TO VISIT ST. KITTS AND NEVIS

1 History: Both St. Kitts and Nevis are steeped in history; Brimstone Hill Fortress is a man-made UNESCO World Heritage Site.

2 Luxury: Luxurious, restored plantation inns can be found on both islands.

3 Landscape: Both islands have extinct volcanoes and luxuriant rain forests ideal for hikes, as well as fine diving and snorkeling sites.

4 Unspoiled: You'll find less development—particularly on Nevis—and more cordial and courteous islanders than on more touristy islands.

5 Water Activities: Both islands feature aquatic activities aplenty, with fine sailing, deep-sea fishing, diving (especially off St. Kitts), and windsurfing (especially around Nevis).

WELCOME TO ST. KITTS AND NEVIS

THE MOTHER COLONY AND HER SISTER

St. Kitts, a 65-square-mile (168-square-km) island, is 2 miles (3 km) from smaller Nevis, about 40 square miles (121 square km). The two former British colonies are joined in a sometimes strained independence. St. Kitts is often called "The Mother Colony," because it was the first permanent English settlement in the Caribbean.

Muddy Pt.
Frigate Bay
6
4
Frigate Bay
7
8
9 10 5
Friar's Bay
River Taw
Sand Bank Bay
Mosquito Bluff
St. Anthonys Peak
13
ATLANTIC OCEAN
Great Salt Pond
Turtle Bay
White House Bay
11
12
Cockleshell Bay
Banana Bay
Major's Bay
Major's Bay
Tamarind Bay
Newcastle Beach
Long Haul Bay
Mosquito Bay
The Narrows
Oualie Beach
Newcastle
Vance W. Amory International Airport
Jones Bay
Nags Head
Brick Kiln
Nevis see detail map
Cades Bay
Huggins Bay
Pinney's Beach
ST. THOMAS LOWLAND
ST. JAMES WINDWARD
Cotton Ground
Nevis Peak
Jamestown
NEVIS
Zion
ST. PAUL CHARLESTOWN
Charlestown
ST. GEORGE GINGERLAND
White Bay
Nelson Museum
Fig Tree
Long Pt.
Saddle Hill
Red Cliff
ST. JOHN FIG TREE
Dogwood Pt.
The Devil's Caves

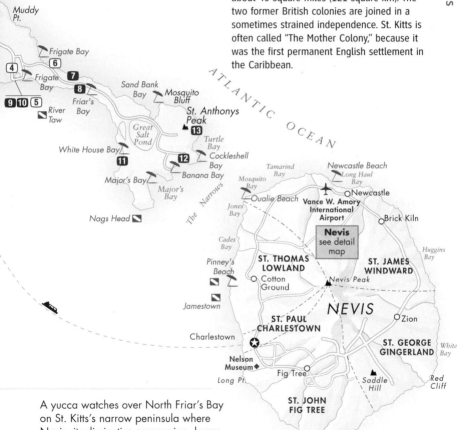

A yucca watches over North Friar's Bay on St. Kitts's narrow peninsula where Nevis, its diminutive companion, looms on the horizon. On both islands, green fields of sugarcane run to the sea, once-magnificent plantation houses are now luxurious inns, and lovely stretches of uncrowded beach stretch before you.

Updated by Jordan Simon

These idyllic sister islands, 2 miles (3 km) apart at their closest point, offer visitors a relatively authentic island experience. Both have luxuriant mountain rain forests; uncrowded beaches; historic ruins; towering, long-dormant volcanoes; charming if slightly dilapidated Georgian capitals in Basseterre (St. Kitts) and Charlestown (Nevis); intact cultural heritage; friendly if shy people; and restored 18th-century sugar plantation inns run by elegant, if sometimes eccentric, expatriate owners.

The islands' history follows the usual Caribbean route: Amerindian settlements, Columbus's voyages, fierce colonial battles between the British and French, a boom in sugar production second only to that of Barbados. St. Kitts became known as the mother colony of the West Indies: English settlers sailed from there to Antigua, Barbuda, Tortola, and Montserrat, and the French dispatched colonists to Martinique, Guadeloupe, St. Martin, and St. Barth.

St. Kitts and Nevis, in addition to Anguilla, achieved self-government as an associated state of Great Britain in 1967. Anguillians soon made their displeasure known, separating immediately, whereas St. Kitts and Nevis waited until 1983 to become an independent nation. The two islands, despite their superficial similarities, have taken increasingly different routes regarding tourism. Nevis received an economic boost from the Four Seasons, which helped establish it as an upscale destination. St. Kitts, however, had yet to define its identity at a time when most islands have found their tourism niche but is now making up for lost time and notoriety with several high-profile high-end projects, including Kittitian Hill and Christophe Harbour. A fierce sibling rivalry has ensued.

Though its comparative lack of development is a lure, the Kittitian government is casting its economic net in several directions. Golf, ecotourism, and scuba diving are being aggressively promoted. And the government hopes the number of available rooms will increase roughly

30% by 2016 to more than 2,000, according to the "build it and they will come" philosophy. But is St. Kitts ready to absorb all this? The island offers a surprisingly diverse vacation experience while retaining its essential Caribbean flavor. Divers have yet to discover all its underwater attractions, and nature lovers will be pleasantly surprised by the hiking. There's now every kind of accommodation, as well as gourmet dining, golf, and gaming.

Meanwhile, Nevis seems determined to stay even more unspoiled (there are still no traffic lights). Its natural attractions and activities certainly rival those of St. Kitts, from mountain biking and ecohiking to windsurfing and deep-sea fishing, though lying in a hammock and dining on romantic candlelit patios remain cherished pursuits. Pinney's Beach, despite occasional hurricane erosion, remains a classic Caribbean strand. Its historic heritage, from the Caribbean's first hotel to Alexander Hamilton's childhood home, is just as pronounced, including equally sybaritic plantation inns that seem torn from the pages of a romance novel.

Perhaps it's a warning sign that many guests call the catamaran trip to Nevis the high point of their stay on St. Kitts—and many Kittitians build retirement and second homes on Nevis. The sister islands' relationship remains outwardly cordial if slightly contentious. Nevis papers sometimes run blistering editorials advocating independence, though one plebiscite has already failed. St. Kitts and Nevis may separate someday, but for now their battles are confined to ad campaigns and political debates. Fortunately, well-heeled and barefoot travelers alike can still happily enjoy the many energetic and easygoing enticements of both blissful retreats.

PLANNING

WHEN TO GO

The high season is relatively short, starting in mid-December and stretching into early or mid-April. The shoulder season (roughly April to mid-June and November to mid-December) offers lower rates. Rates are lower still from mid-June through November, but some establishments close for a month or longer.

GETTING HERE AND AROUND

AIR TRAVEL

Many travelers connect in Antigua, San Juan, St. Maarten, or St. Thomas. To Nevis, it's almost always cheaper to fly into St. Kitts and then take a regularly scheduled ferry, but check the schedules or book a transfer from your resort (if available) in advance. St. Kitts unveiled the YU Lounge, available not just to private jet passengers but any commercial travelers willing to pay for a restful, hassle-free executive retreat that eliminates the need to go through Customs and Immigration (and offering its own approved security screening).

There are nonstop flights to St. Kitts from Atlanta (Delta), Charlotte (US Airways), Miami (American), and New York–JFK (American). There are no nonstops from the United States to Nevis.

LOGISTICS

Getting to St. Kitts and Nevis: Many travelers connect in Antigua, San Juan, St. Maarten, or St. Thomas. When going to Nevis, it's almost always cheaper to fly into St. Kitts and then take a regularly scheduled ferry to Nevis, but check the schedules. Robert L. Bradshaw International Airport on St. Kitts (SKB) and the smaller, simpler Vance W. Armory International Airport on Nevis (NEV) are still fairly sleepy.

Hassle Factor: Low–medium for St. Kitts, medium for Nevis.

On the Ground: Taxis meet every ferry and flight to St. Kitts or Nevis. The taxis are unmetered, but fixed rates, in EC dollars, are posted at the airport and at the jetty. Note that rates are the same for one to four passengers. On St. Kitts the fares from the airport range from EC$32 to Frigate Bay to EC$72 for the farthest point. From the airport on Nevis it's EC$27 to Nisbet Plantation, EC$54 to the Four Seasons, and EC$67 to Montpelier. There is a 50% surcharge between 10 pm and 6 am. Before setting off in a cab, be sure to clarify whether the rate quoted is in EC or U.S. dollars.

Airline Contacts American. American has daily flights from Miami into St. Kitts (twice daily Thursday–Sunday) and weekly flights from New York's JFK. ☎ *869/465–2273, 869/469–8995.* **LIAT.** Other major domestic airlines (US Airways once-weekly nonstop from Charlotte and Delta once-weekly from Atlanta) fly from their eastern hubs either into Antigua, St. Maarten, San Juan, or St. Thomas, where connections to St. Kitts (and, less frequently, to Nevis) can be made on LIAT. ☎ *869/465–1330, 869/469–5238 on Nevis* 🌐 *www.liatairline.com.* **Robert L. Bradshaw International Airport** (*SKB*). St. Kitts's airport is Robert L. Bradshaw International Airport. ✉ *Golden Rock* ☎ *465–8013.* **Vance W. Amory International Airport** (*NEV*). The Nevis airport is Vance W. Amory International Airport. ✉ *Newcastle, Nevis* ☎ *869/469–9343.* **Winair.** Nevis connections can also be made from St. Maarten on Winair. ☎ *869/469–5302* 🌐 *www.fly-winair.com.*

BOAT AND FERRY TRAVEL

There are several ferry services between St. Kitts and Nevis, all with schedules that are subject to abrupt change. Most companies make two or three daily trips. All the ferries take about 30 to 45 minutes and cost $8–$10.

Contacts Ferry Schedule 🌐 *www.thestkittsnevisobserver.com/ferry-schedules.html.*

There's an additional EC$1 tax for port security, paid separately on departure.

CAR TRAVEL

Driving Tips: One well-kept main road circumnavigates St. Kitts and is usually clearly marked, making it difficult to get lost, though the northeast can get a bit bumpy and the access roads to the plantation inns are notoriously rough.

The roads on Nevis are generally smooth, at least on the most traveled north, west, and south sides of the island. The east coast has some potholes, and pigs, goats, and sheep still insist on the right-of-way all around the island. Drivers on both islands tend to travel at a fast clip and pass on curves, so drive defensively. Driving is on the left, British-style, though you will probably be given an American-style car.

Renting a Car: You can get by without a car if you are staying in the Frigate Bay–Basseterre area, but elsewhere you'll need to rent a car. On Nevis it's often easier to just take taxis and guided tours. On St. Kitts, present your valid driver's license and $24 at the police station traffic department on Cayon Street in Basseterre or Fire Station in Frigate Bay to get a temporary driving permit (on Nevis the car-rental agency will help you obtain the $24 local license at the police station). The license is valid for three months on both islands. On either island, car rentals start at about $45 per day for a compact; expect to pay a few extra bucks for air-conditioning. Most agencies offer substantial multiday discounts.

Avis. Avis has the best selection of Hyundai and Daihatsu four-wheel-drive vehicles on St. Kitts, as well as rental exchange on Nevis and complimentary pickup. ✉ *South Independence Sq., Basseterre* ☎ *869/465–6507* 🌐 *www.avisstkitts.com.*

Delisle Walwyn. Delisle Walwyn provides an excellent selection and the option of a replacement car for one day on Nevis if you rent for three days or more on St. Kitts. ✉ *Liverpool Row, Basseterre* ☎ *869/465–8449.*

Funky Monkey Tours and Rentals. Funky Monkey Tours and Rentals lets you ride on the wild side in Polaris Ranger and Razor 4x4s; prices start at $115 per half day. You can also rent Vespas for $75 per day, as well as Sea-Doo wave runners. Or follow in their tire tracks, off-roading through the island on a three-hour Funky Monkey tour ($105). ✉ *Nelson Springs, Nevis* ☎ *869/665–6045, 869/665–6245* 🌐 *www.funkymonkeytours.com.*

Nevis Car Rentals. Nevis Car Rentals has quality vehicles and service. ✉ *Newcastle, Nevis* ☎ *869/469–9837.*

Striker's Car Rental. Striker's Car Rental has a good selection of vehicles. ✉ *Hermitage Rd., Gingerland, Nevis* ☎ *869/469–2654* 🌐 *www.strikerscarrentals.com.*

TDC/Thrifty Rentals. TDC/Thrifty Rentals has a wide selection of vehicles and outstanding service; it offers a three-day rental that includes a car on both islands. ✉ *West Independence Sq., Central St., Basseterre* ☎ *869/465–2991* 🌐 *www.tdclimited.com* ✉ *Bay Rd., Charlestown, Nevis* ☎ *869/469–5430* 🌐 *www.tdclimited.com.*

TAXI TRAVEL

Taxi rates are government regulated and posted at the airport, the dock, and in the free tourist guide. Be sure to clarify whether the fare is in EC or U.S. dollars. There are fixed rates to and from all the hotels and to and from major points of interest.

Airport Transfers: On St. Kitts the fares from the airport range from EC$32 to Frigate Bay to EC$72 for the farthest point. From the airport on Nevis it's EC$27 to Nisbet Plantation, EC$54 to the Four Seasons, and EC$67 to Montpelier. There is a 50% surcharge between 10 pm and 6 am.

Contacts St. Kitts Taxi Association ☎ *869/465–8487, 869/465–4253, 869/465–7818 after hrs.* **Nevis Taxi Service.** Nevis Taxi Service provides taxi information for Nevis, but does not operate a fleet of taxis. ☎ *869/469–5631, 869/469–9790 for the airport, 869/469–5515 after dark.*

ESSENTIALS

Banks and Exchange Services Legal tender is the Eastern Caribbean (EC) dollar. The rate of exchange at this writing is EC$2.70 to US$1. U.S. dollars are accepted everywhere, but change is usually EC currency. Most large hotels, restaurants, and shops accept major credit cards, but small inns and shops often do not. All banks, including the Royal Bank of St. Kitts and Scotia Bank, have ATMs. There are ATMs on Nevis at the airport, Bank of Nova Scotia, First Caribbean International Bank, Royal Bank of Trinidad & Tobago, and St. Kitts–Nevis National Bank.

Electricity 110 volts, 60 cycles.

Emergency Services Ambulance and Emergencies ☎ *911.* **Fire emergencies on St. Kitts** ☎ *869/465–2515, 333.* **Fire emergencies on Nevis** ☎ *869/469–3444.* **Police** ☎ *869/465–2241 on St. Kitts, 869/469–5391 on Nevis, 911 on St. Kitts.*

Passport Requirements All travelers must have a valid passport and a return or ongoing ticket. Canadian citizens (not connecting through U.S. territory) need either a valid passport or a birth certificate (with a raised seal) accompanied by a government-issue photo ID.

Phones Phone cards, which you can buy in denominations of EC$5, $10, and $20, are handy for making local phone calls, calling other islands, and accessing U.S. direct lines. To call St. Kitts and Nevis from the United States, dial area code 869, then access code 465, 466, 468, or 469 and the local four-digit number.

Taxes The departure tax of US$22 is included in your plane ticket; if it isn't, the gate agent will request payment, in cash only. There's no sales tax on either St. Kitts or Nevis. Hotels collect a 9% government tax.

Tipping Hotels add a 10%–12% service charge to your bill. Restaurants occasionally do the same; ask if it isn't printed on the menu; a 15% tip is appropriate when it isn't included. Taxi drivers typically receive a 10% tip, porters and bellhops $1 per bag; housekeeping staff, $2 to $3 per night.

ACCOMMODATIONS

St. Kitts has a wide variety of places to stay—beautifully restored plantation inns, full-service affordable hotels, simple beachfront cottages, comfortable condos, and all-inclusive resorts. One large resort—the Marriott—is more midrange than upscale and attracts large groups and package tourists. Choose St. Kitts if you want a wider choice of activities and accommodations (you can always do Nevis as a day trip). Nevis is a small island with no large resorts, and most accommodations are upscale—primarily plantation inns and the luxurious Four Seasons. It's much quieter than St. Kitts, so choose it if you want to get away from the hectic island scene and simply relax in low-key comfort and surprisingly high style.

Four Seasons Resort Nevis: Really in a class by itself, the Four Seasons is the only sizable, lavish, high-end property on either island until the Park Hyatt opens on Banana Bay (the first phase is tentatively scheduled to debut by 2016) as part of the massive upscale Christophe Harbour development. If you can afford it, the resort is certainly one of the Caribbean's finest; recent post-hurricane renovations improved on near-perfection.

Plantation Inns: St. Kitts and Nevis feature renovated, historic plantation houses that have been turned into upscale inns. On Nevis, the inns are the most distinctive form of lodging. They are usually managed by hands-on owner-operators and offer fine cuisine and convivial hospitality; though not usually on a beach, most of these inns have beach clubs with free private shuttle service.

Hotel reviews have been shortened. For full information, visit Fodors.com.

WHAT IT COSTS IN U.S. DOLLARS

	$	$$	$$$	$$$$
Restaurants	under $12	$12–$20	$21–$30	over $30
Hotels	under $275	$275–$375	$376–$475	over $475

Restaurant prices are the average cost of a main course at dinner or, if dinner is not served, at lunch. Hotel prices are the lowest cost of a standard double room in high season.

VISITOR INFORMATION

Contacts Nevis Tourism Authority ✉ *Elm House, Park La., Lower Froyle, Alton, Hampshire, England* ☎ *01420/520810* 🌐 *www.nevisisland.com.* **St. Kitts Tourism Authority** ☎ *212/535–1234 in New York City, 800/582–6208, 866/556–3847 for Nevis alone* 🌐 *www.stkittstourism.kn.* **St. Kitts–Nevis Hotel and Tourism Association** ✉ *Sands Complex, Box 438, Unit C9, Basseterre* ☎ *869/465–5304* 🌐 *www.stkittsnevishta.org.*

WEDDINGS

Two-business-day residency requirement. License and application are EC$200. Valid passport or birth certificate required; if divorced, a divorce decree; if widowed, a death certificate of the deceased spouse.

ST. KITTS

EXPLORING

You can explore Basseterre, the capital city, in a half hour or so, and should allow four hours for an island tour. Main Road traces the northwestern perimeter of the island through seas of sugarcane and past breadfruit trees and stone walls. Villages with tiny pastel-color houses of stone and weathered wood are scattered across the island, and the drive back to Basseterre around the island's other side passes through several of them. The most spectacular stretch of scenery is on Dr. Kennedy Simmonds Highway, which goes to the tip of the Southeast Peninsula. This modern road twists and turns through the undeveloped grassy hills that rise between the calm Caribbean and the windswept Atlantic, passing the shimmering pink Great Salt Pond, a volcanic crater, and seductive beaches. Major developments are under way, including the Kittitian Hill and Christophe Harbour megadevelopments. The 6-furlong Belmont Park racetrack and state-of-the-art stables opened in 2009 but, despite the exciting equine environment that lured as many as 9,000 spectators, has closed indefinitely, its planned entertainment complex, with an upscale restaurant as well as polo grounds, go-karts, a retail complex, and bird and butterfly parks, on hold.

BASSETERRE

On the south coast, St. Kitts's walkable capital is graced with tall palms and flagstone sidewalks; although many of the buildings appear rundown, there are interesting shops, excellent art galleries, and some beautifully maintained houses. Duty-free shops and boutiques line the streets and courtyards radiating from the octagonal **Circus,** built in the style of London's famous Piccadilly Circus.

WORTH NOTING

Independence Square. There are lovely gardens and a fountain on the site of a former slave market at Independence Square. The square is surrounded on three sides by 18th-century Georgian buildings. ✉ *Off Bank St.*

National Museum. In the restored former Treasury Building, the National Museum presents an eclectic collection of artifacts reflecting the history and culture of the island. ✉ *Bay Rd.* ☎ *869/465–5584* 🎫 *US$3* 🕒 *Mon.–Fri. 9:15–5, Sat. 9:15–1.*

Port Zante. Port Zante is an ambitious, ever-growing 27-acre cruise-ship pier and marina in an area that has been reclaimed from the sea. The domed welcome center is an imposing neoclassical hodgepodge, with columns and stone arches, shops, walkways, fountains, and West Indian–style buildings housing luxury shops, galleries, restaurants, and a small casino. A second pier, 1,434 feet long, has a draft that accommodates even leviathan cruise ships. The selection of shops and restaurants (Twist serves global fusion cuisine and rocks with DJs several nights of the week) is expanding as well. ✉ *Waterfront, behind Circus.*

St. George's Anglican Church. This handsome stone building has a crenellated tower originally built by the French in 1670 that is called Nôtre-Dame. The British burned it down in 1706 and rebuilt it four years later, naming it after the patron saint of England. Since then it has suffered a fire, an earthquake, and hurricanes and was once again rebuilt in 1869. ✉ *Cayon St.*

ELSEWHERE ON ST. KITTS

TOP ATTRACTIONS

Brimstone Hill. This 38-acre fortress, a UNESCO World Heritage Site, is part of a national park dedicated by Queen Elizabeth in 1985. After routing the French in 1690, the English erected a battery here; by 1736 the fortress held 49 guns, earning it the moniker Gibraltar of the West Indies. In 1782, 8,000 French troops laid siege to the stronghold, which was defended by 350 militia and 600 regular troops of the Royal Scots and East Yorkshires. When the English finally surrendered, they were allowed to march from the fort in full formation out of respect for their bravery (the English afforded the French the same honor when they surrendered the fort a mere year later). A hurricane severely damaged the fortress in 1834, and in 1852 it was evacuated and dismantled. The beautiful stones were carted away to build houses.

The citadel has been partially reconstructed and its guns remounted. It's a steep walk up the hill from the parking lot. A seven-minute orientation film recounts the fort's history and restoration. You can see remains of the officers' quarters, redoubts, barracks, ordnance store, and cemetery. Its museum collections were depleted by hurricanes, but some pre-Columbian artifacts, objects pertaining to the African heritage of the island's slaves (such as masks and ceremonial tools), weaponry, uniforms, photographs, and old newspapers remain. The spectacular view includes Montserrat and Nevis to the southeast; Saba and St. Eustatius to the northwest; and St. Barth and St. Maarten to the north. Nature trails snake through the tangle of surrounding hardwood forest and savanna (a fine spot to catch the green vervet monkeys—inexplicably brought by the French and now outnumbering the residents—skittering about). ✉ *Main Rd., Brimstone Hill* ☎ *869/465–2609* 🌐 *www.brimstonehillfortress.org* 🎫 *$10* ⏲ *Daily 9:30–5:30.*

FAMILY **St. Kitts Eco Park.** Created in collaboration with the Taiwanese government, St. Kitts Eco Park essentially functions as an agro-tourism demonstration farm, with soaring, light-filled glass and fiber-reinforced concrete structures that are powered by state-of-the-art solar trackers. Antique cannons and old-fashioned gas lamps lead to the handsome Victorian plantation-style visitors center, divided into Kittitian and Taiwanese sections, each selling local foodstuffs and specialty items (ceramics for St. Kitts, tea and technology for Taiwan). You can stroll through the greenhouse, viewing orchids in the working nursery, then scale the watchtower for scintillating views of the farm and Caribbean, with Saba and Statia in the distance. Kids will love challenging the map mazes (plantings shaped like the partner nations), while parents can wander the orchards and desert garden or savor bush tea in the herb gazebo. The property provides environmental edutainment while delivering on its so-called "4G" promise: greenhouse, green beauty, green energy, green landscape. ✉ *Sir Gillies Estate, Sandy Point* ☎ *869/465–8755* 🎫 *$8* ⏲ *Daily 9:30–5:30.*

St. Kitts Scenic Railway. The old narrow-gauge train that had transported sugarcane to the central sugar factory since 1912 is all that remains of the island's once-thriving sugar industry. Two-story cars bedecked in bright Kittitian colors circle the island in just under four hours (a Rail and Sail option takes guests going or on the return via catamaran). Each passenger gets a comfortable, downstairs air-conditioned seat fronting vaulted picture windows and an upstairs open-air observation spot. The conductor's running discourse embraces not only the history of sugar cultivation but also the railway's construction, local folklore,

Cannons at Brimstone Hill, a UNESCO World Heritage Site on St. Kitts

island geography, even other agricultural mainstays from papayas to pigs. You can drink in complimentary tropical beverages (including luscious guava daiquiris) along with the sweeping rain-forest and ocean vistas, accompanied by an a cappella choir's renditions of hymns, spirituals, and predictable standards like "I've Been Workin' on the Railroad." ✉ *Needsmust* ☎ *869/465–7263* 🌐 *www.stkittsscenicrailway.com* *$89, children 4–12 $44.50* ⏲ *Departures vary according to cruise-ship schedules (call ahead, but at least once daily Dec.–Apr., usually 8:30 am).*

WORTH NOTING

Black Rocks. This series of lava deposits was spat into the sea ages ago when the island's volcano erupted. It has since been molded into fanciful shapes by centuries of pounding surf. ✉ *Atlantic coast, outside town of Sadlers, Sandy Bay, Sand Bank Bay.*

Fairview Great House & Botanical Gardens. Parts of this French colonial greathouse set on more than 2 lush tropical acres date back to 1701, with an impeccably restored interior in period fashion. Each room is painted in different colors from pomegranate to lemon. Furnishings include a 16-seat mahogany dinner table set with china and silver; docents relate fascinating factoids (chaises were broadened to accommodate petticoats—or "can-can skirts," in local parlance). Cross the cobblestone courtyard to the original kitchen, replete with volcanic stone and brick oven, and bathing room (heated rocks warmed spring water in the tub). The fieldstone cellar now contains the gift shop, offering local pottery, art, and honey harvested on-site at the apiary. You can wander meticulously maintained gardens with interpretive signage, filled with chattering birds and monkeys. The Nirvana restaurant offers pan-Asian food; dips in the pool are a bonus. ✉ *Artist's Level Hill, Boyd's* ☎ *869/465–3141* 🌐 *www.nirvanafairview.com* 🎫 *$10* 🕑 *Daily 9–5 (last entrance 4:30).*

Old Road. This site marks the first permanent English settlement in the West Indies, founded in 1624 by Thomas Warner. Take the side road toward the interior to find some Carib petroglyphs, testimony of even earlier habitation. The largest depicts a female figure on black volcanic rock, presumably a fertility goddess. Less than a mile east of Old Road along Main Road is **Bloody Point,** where French and British soldiers joined forces in 1629 to repel a mass Carib attack; reputedly so many Caribs were massacred that the stream ran red for three days. ✣ *Main Rd. west of Challengers.*

Romney Manor. The ruins of this somewhat restored house (reputedly once the property of Thomas Jefferson) and surrounding replicas of chattel-house cottages are set in 6 acres of glorious gardens, with exotic flowers, an old bell tower, and an enormous, gnarled 350-year-old saman tree (sometimes called a rain tree). Inside, at **Caribelle Batik,** you can watch artisans hand-printing fabrics by the 2,500-year-old Indonesian wax-and-dye process known as batik. You can also stroll to the 17th-century ruins of Wingfield Manor, site of the first land grant in the British West Indies, and home to a zip-lining outfit. A new bar offers splendid panoramic vistas of the rain forest. Look for signs indicating a turnoff for Romney Manor near Old Road. ✉ *Old Road* ☎ *869/465–6253* 🌐 *www.caribellebatikstkitts.com* 🎫 *Free* 🕑 *Daily 9–5.*

BEACHES

Beaches on St. Kitts are free and open to the public (even those occupied by hotels). The best beaches, with powdery white sand, are in the Frigate Bay area or on the lower peninsula. The Atlantic waters are rougher, and many black-sand beaches northwest of Frigate Bay double as garbage dumps.

Banana/Cockleshell Bays. These twin connected eyebrows of glittering champagne-color sand—stretching nearly 2 miles (3 km) total at the southeastern tip of the island—feature majestic views of Nevis and are backed by lush vegetation and coconut palms. The first-rate restaurant–bar Spice Mill (next to Rasta-hue Lion Rock Beach Bar—order the knockout Lion Punch) and Reggae Beach Bar & Grill bracket either end of Cockleshell. At this writing, plans for a 125-room mixed-use Park Hyatt (with additional residential condos and villas) are back on schedule for development by late 2015. The water is generally placid, ideal for swimming. The downside is irregular maintenance, with seaweed (particularly after rough weather) and occasional litter, especially on Banana Bay. Follow Simmonds Highway to the end and bear right, ignoring the turnoff for Turtle Beach. **Amenities**: food and drink; parking. **Best for**: partiers; snorkeling; swimming; walking. ✉ *Banana Bay.*

Friar's Bay. Locals consider Friar's Bay, on the Caribbean (southern) side, the island's finest beach. It's a long, tawny scimitar where the water always seems warmer and clearer. The upscale Carambola Beach Club has co-opted roughly one third of the strand. Still, several happening bars, including Jam Rock (great grouper and jerk), ShipWreck and Sunset, serve terrific, inexpensive local food and cheap, frosty drinks. Chair rentals cost around $3, though if you order lunch, you can negotiate a freebie. Friar's is the first major beach along Southeast Peninsula Drive (aka Simmonds Highway), approximately a mile (1½ km) southeast of Frigate Bay. **Amenities**: food and drink. **Best for**: snorkeling; swimming; walking. ✉ *Friar's Bay.*

Frigate Bay. The Caribbean side offers talcum-powder-fine beige sand framed by coconut palms and sea grapes, and the Atlantic side (a 15-minute stroll)—sometimes called North Frigate Bay—is a favorite with horseback riders. South Frigate Bay is bookended by the Timothy Beach Club's Sunset Café and the popular, pulsating Buddies Beach Hut. In between are several other lively beach spots, including Cathy's (fabulous jerk ribs), Chinchilla's, Vibes, and Mr. X Shiggidy Shack. Most charge $3 to $5 to rent a chair, though they'll often waive the fee if you ask politely and buy lunch. Locals barhop late into Friday and Saturday nights. Waters are generally calm for swimming; the rockier eastern end offers fine snorkeling. The incomparably scenic Atlantic side is—regrettably—dominated by the Marriott (plentiful dining options), attracting occasional pesky vendors. The surf is choppier and the undertow stronger here. On cruise-ship days, groups stampede both sides. **Amenities**: food and drink; water sports. **Best for**: partying; snorkeling; swimming; walking. ✉ *Frigate Bay* ✣ *Less than 3 miles (5 km) from downtown Basseterre.*

Sand Bank Bay. A dirt road, nearly impassable after heavy rains, leads to a long mocha crescent on the Atlantic. The shallow coves are protected here, making it ideal for families, and it's usually deserted. Brisk breezes lure the occasional windsurfer, but avoid the rocky far left area because of fierce sudden swells and currents. This exceptionally pretty beach lacks shade; Christophe Harbour has constructed several villas and a beach club (whose upscale Pavilion restaurant is open to the public only for dinner). As you drive southeast along Simmonds Highway, approximately 10 miles (16 km) from Basseterre, look for an unmarked dirt turnoff to the left of the Great Salt Pond. **Amenities**: none. **Best for**: solitude; swimming; windsurfing. ✉ *Sand Bank Bay.*

White House Bay. The beach is rocky, but the snorkeling, taking in several reefs surrounding a sunken tugboat, as well as a recently discovered 18th-century British troop ship, is superb. It's usually deserted, though the calm water (and stunning scenery) makes it a favorite anchorage of yachties. There is little shade, but also little seaweed. Christophe Harbour's sexy new beach bar (open from late afternoon), Salt Plage anchors one end. A dirt road skirts a hill to the right off Simmonds Highway approximately 2 miles (3 km) after Friar's. **Amenities**: food and drink. **Best for**: snorkeling; solitude. ✉ *White House Bay.*

Royal Palm

WHERE TO EAT

St. Kitts restaurants range from funky beachfront bistros to elegant plantation dining rooms (most with prix-fixe menus); most fare is tinged with the flavors of the Caribbean. Many restaurants offer West Indian specialties such as curried mutton, pepperpot (a stew of vegetables, tubers, and meats), and Arawak chicken (seasoned and served with rice and almonds on breadfruit leaf).

What to Wear. Throughout the island, dress is casual at lunch (but no bathing suits). Dinner, although not necessarily formal, definitely calls for long pants and sundresses.

$$$$ ECLECTIC ✕ **Carambola Beach Club.** This ultrastylish restaurant unfurls sensuously down South Friar's Bay, like something out of St-Tropez. More casual lunches take full advantage of the beachfront setting, with white tents and hedonistic beach beds. But nighttime is truly spectacular, as outdoor fiber-optic fountains enhance the visual flair of the vast, sleek-but-not-slick interior replete with eat-in wine cellar and tile-and-layered-wood sushi bar. You might start with intensely flavored butternut squash ravioli or one of the original maki, such as the fiery Calypso Bay roll (lobster, eel, avocado, chili paste, and honey-mustard sauce). Seafood such as breaded grouper in orange beurre blanc is masterfully executed; nothing at Carambola is overcooked. The sole letdown is the wine list. Although it's the island's largest, it lacks imagination; however, the by-the-glass selections are at least reasonably priced (the stylish Provence rosé, M de Minuty, is just $6), as are such prizes as the 2007 Antinori Cervaro della Sala. *Average main: US$31* ✉ *Friar's Bay* ☎ *869/465–9090* 🌐 *www.carambolabeachclub.com* *Reservations essential* ⏲ *No*

dinner Mon. and Tues. ☞ Lunch is only offered on cruise-ship days; call ahead to confirm hrs of operation.

$ CARIBBEAN

✕ **El Fredo's.** This humble wood shack across from the waterfront dishes out some of the finest local fare on St. Kitts. No surprise you'll find politicians and expats grabbing a quick lunch (it's a terrific place to eavesdrop on local gossip) alongside local workers shyly flirting with the waitresses. With just a few genre paintings for atmosphere, the decor is basic. The draw is the traditional stewed oxtail, curry goat, or swordfish creole served with heaping helpings of fungi (cornmeal), rice and peas, and dumplings. Join the locals for bounteous dishes that they swear will cure—or at least absorb—any hangover. *Average main: US$10 ✉ Newtown Bay Rd. at Sanddown Rd., Basseterre ☎ 869/764–9228 No credit cards ⊙ No dinner. Closed Sun.*

$$$ SEAFOOD

✕ **Fisherman's Wharf.** Part of the Ocean Terrace Inn, this extremely casual waterfront eatery, completely reinvented in late 2013, is decorated in contemporary nautical style, with sail rigging, walls splashed with aqua waves, illuminated water features, a mauve Plexiglas marine display case, and a stylish open kitchen whose mosaic-work gleams like fish scales. Try the excellent conch chowder, followed by fresh grilled lobster or other shipshape seafood, and finish off your meal with a slice of the memorable banana cheesecake. The place is generally hopping, especially on weekend nights between karaoke and live bands jamming atop the split-level, breeze-swept bar. *Average main: US$24 ✉ Ocean Terrace Inn, Wigley Ave., Fortlands, Basseterre ☎ 869/465–2754 ⊕ www.oceanterraceinn.com ⊙ No lunch.*

$$$$ CARIBBEAN Fodor's Choice ★

✕ **The Kitchen.** Fans of the great terroir-driven European three-star Michelin restaurants Noma, Steirereck, and De Librije will devour this stunner set in the so-called Great House—the soaring stone-steel-and-wood space of Belle Mont Farm at Kittitian Hill. The ultimate in farm-to-table cuisine, The Kitchen offers a series of sustainable seasonal treats, sourced from Kittitian Hill's 400 acres of organic farmland and local suppliers who share their vision for responsible and ethical farming, fishing, and animal husbandry. Begin your evening with handcrafted ultrafresh cocktails in the Mill Bar, set in a handsome faux sugar mill. Then repair to the main dining room or terrace overlooking the Caribbean to savor the multicourse repast. Executive chef Christophe Letard's parade of dishes teases and titillates the taste buds, with daring counterpoints of color, flavor, and texture. You might begin with a silken carrot soup goosed with coconut, avocado, cilantro, lime, and ginger whipped to a hint of molecular foam. Then segue to callaloo wrap (marlin, avocado, pineapple, and plantain swirled with passion fruit–peanut emulsion) or yam ravioli with local goat cheese and bok choy stir fry. Lobster is dazzlingly tinged with lime and coconut over dasheen risotto (the tuber cut and cooked until you'd swear it was Arborio rice), while pork is braised in Cabernet Sauvignon and finished with pumpkin, coconut, and chocolate. Finish with a sublime pumpkin tarte Tatin beautifully textured with crisp arugula and crunchy cashew. Champagne Sunday brunch is already an island mover-and-shaker tradition. The all-organic wine list was curated by Isabelle Legeron MW, France's only female master of wine, who co-founded London's RAW

Natural Wine Fair. *Average main: US$85* ✉ *Frigate Bay* ☎ *869/465–7388* 🌐 *www.bellemontfarm.com* *Reservations essential.*

$$$$ FRENCH **La Belle Vie.** This *très sympa* nod to St. Kitts's French heritage is aptly titled "the good life." The cozy antiques-strewn lobby–bar leads to the semi-enclosed garden dining patio. Everything brims with brio from the brioches baked on-site to Brel and Aznavour on the soundtrack (accompanied by tree frogs). Nantes-born Fabien Richard deftly executes bistro fare at fair prices. You could feast on appetizers alone: salad *chabichoux* (warm goat cheese, *lardons*, mesclun) or velvety tomato *bavarois* with prosciutto. But opt for the bargain $41 three-course prix fixe; main courses might include salmon with aniseed emulsion, duck "steaklet" with green- and black-peppercorn sauce, or rack of lamb in thyme jus. Even the old-fashioned veggies delight, including smashing potatoes *dauphinoise*. Save room for an unimpeachable peach sable (tart) with crème anglaise. A few minor complaints include: mosquitoes on still nights, limited wine selection, and the occasional overcooked if tasty entrée. *Average main: US$34* ✉ *19 Golf View, Frigate Bay* ☎ *869/465–5216, 869/764–6035* 🌐 *www.labelleviestkitts.com* *Reservations essential* *No lunch. Closed Sun.*

$$$ ECLECTIC **Marshall's.** The pool area of Horizons Villa Resort is transformed into a stylish eatery thanks to smashing ocean views, potted plants, serenading tree frogs, and elegant candlelit tables. Jamaican chef Verral Marshall fuses ultrafresh local ingredients with global influences. Recommended offerings include grilled swordfish with passion-fruit beurre blanc, pan-roasted duck breast with raspberry-balsamic sauce, or homemade sorbets. Most dishes are regrettably orthodox (rack of lamb in port reduction) if artfully plated, and the execution is uneven. *Average main: US$30* ✉ *Horizons Villa Resort, Frigate Bay* ☎ *869/466–8245* 🌐 *www.marshalls-stkitts.com* *Reservations essential* *No lunch.*

$$$$ ECLECTIC Fodor's Choice ★ **The Pavilion.** Imagine a semi-alfresco cathedral constructed of raw limestone coral overlooking a palm-fringed sandy crescent: that's The Pavilion, the ritzy Christophe Harbour beach club open to nonmembers for dinner only. The soaring interior blends colonial and contemporary with aplomb: a curved exhibition kitchen, streamlined bar stools, and abstract pendant lamps contrast with "found" sculptural sea fans and driftwood, antique settees, and 19th-century black-and-white photos of Kittitian scenes. Executive chef Damien Heaney similarly blends tradition and innovation, taking the confusion out of fusion cuisine. Even such "traditional" fare as conch fritters is goosed with pickled ginger and passion-fruit coulis and artfully presented with swirls of jerk mayo. Stunners such as beef tenderloin rubbed with five peppercorns, accompanied by fresh figs, local greens, and sorrel glaze or creole-spiced swordfish with clams, pale-ale sofrito, and sweet pea risotto provide textbook examples of how to juxtapose textures, flavors, even colors. Wednesday night's $39 Chef's Appreciation prix fixe is an amazing buy. The wine list features some surprising bargains, especially among whites, and you can finish your meal in style with one of a dozen aged rums. *Average main: US$33* ✉ *Christophe Harbour, Sandy Bank Bay* ☎ *869/465–8304* 🌐 *www.christopheharbour.com* *No lunch unless member. Closed Sun.–Mon. dinner.*

$$ ITALIAN ✕ **PJ's Bar and Restaurant.** "Garbage pizza"—topped with everything but the kitchen sink—is a favorite, or you can create your own pie at this longtime hangout owned by three expats (two Canadians and a Texan: Pat, Jude, and Janet). Sandwiches, calzones, simple but lustily flavored pastas (try the goat cheese ravioli in sun-dried tomato sauce or spaghetti with humongous garlicky meatballs), and mamma-mia classics (eggplant Parmesan to chicken piccata) are also served. Finish your meal with delicious, moist rum cake. This casual spot, bordering the golf course and open to cooling breezes, is always boisterous (especially during the 9–10 pm happy hour, overseen with good spirits by bartending fixture Ashton). *$ Average main: US$18 ✉ Frigate Bay ☎ 869/465–8373 🌐 www.pjsrestaurantstkitts.com ⏲ Closed Mon. and Sept. No lunch.*

$$$ ECLECTIC ✕ **Reggae Beach Bar & Grill.** Treats at this popular daytime watering hole include honey-mustard ribs, coconut shrimp, grilled lobster, decadent banana bread pudding with rum sauce, and an array of tempting tropical libations. Business cards and pennants from around the world plaster the bar, and the open-air space is decorated with nautical accoutrements, from fishnets and turtle shells to painted wooden crustaceans. You can snorkel here, spot hawksbill turtles and the occasional monkey, visit the enormous house pig Wilbur (who once "ate" beer cans whole, then moved to "lite" beers—but feeding is no longer encouraged), laze in a palm-shaded hammock, or rent a kayak, Hobie Cat, or snorkeling gear. Beach chairs and Wi-Fi are free. Locals come Friday nights for bonfire dinners and Sunday afternoons for dancing to live bands. *$ Average main: US$21 ✉ S.E. Peninsula Rd., Cockleshell Beach ☎ 869/762–5050 🌐 www.reggaebeachbar.com ⏲ No dinner.*

$$$$ ECLECTIC Fodor's Choice ★ ✕ **Royal Palm.** A 65-foot, spring-fed pool bisects this elegant restaurant at Ottley's Plantation Inn into a semi-enclosed lounge with sea views and a breezy alfresco stone patio. Delectable dishes (prix fixe menus are also available) blend indigenous ingredients with Asian, Mediterranean, and Latin touches: sweet potato, chili, and lime soup; portobello-caramelized onion ravioli with creamy spinach pesto; crab salpicon on Caribbean crab cake with mango vinaigrette and ginger remoulade. Finish with simple yet sinful indulgences such as coconut-cream cheesecake or mango mousse with raspberry coulis. The combination of superb food, artful presentation, romantic setting, and warm bonhomie is unbeatable. *$ Average main: US$39 ✉ Ottley's Plantation Inn, Ottley's Village, Basseterre ☎ 869/465–7234 🌐 www.ottleys.com ✍ Reservations essential ☞ Prix-fixe $66.*

$$$ ECLECTIC ✕ **Serendipity.** This stylish restaurant occupies an old creole home whose charming enclosed patio offers lovely views of Basseterre and the bay. The interior lounge is even more conducive to romantic dining, with cushy sofas, patterned hardwood floors, porcelain lamps, and African carvings. The menu reflects co-owner–chef Alexander James's peripatetic postings: you might start with wonderfully crispy fried Brie with sweet-and-sour blackberry chutney or beautifully presented spring rolls with plum-soy dipping sauce. Mahimahi crusted with cheddar, Parmesan, basil, and garlic floating on pools of creole and saffron cream sauces; or tiger shrimp glazed with teriyaki-ginger sauce sitting in

creamy garlic butter typify the ambitious main courses. The wine list is well considered; vegetarians will be delighted by the many creative options; and very affordable lunches feature gargantuan tapas-style selections. *Average main: US$29* *3 Wigley Ave., Fortlands, Basseterre* *869/465–9999* *www.serendipitystkitts.net* *Reservations essential* *Closed Mon. No lunch weekends.*

$$$$ ECLECTIC Fodor's Choice ★ **Spice Mill.** This beachfront beauty references the Caribbean's multiethnic cuisine, a melting pot of African, French, English, Iberian, Asian, and Dutch influences. But the kitchen also stays home in proper locavore fashion, as does the bar, sourcing as much local produce as possible from Kittitian farmers and fishermen (who might troop through the restaurant with 30 just-caught snapper for "De Bossman"). Spice Mill merrily marries those gastronomic traditions, juxtaposing colors, tastes, and textures right from the dips served with scrumptious homemade breads. Panko-crusted crab cake might be served with mango-lemon aioli. Seafood risotto contrasts sweet pumpkin with savory truffle oil. The culinary globetrotting approach also dictates the decor—a mix of regional (coconut-wood-top bar, Carib canoe, and crayfish baskets from Dominica) and cosmopolitan (white beach beds, cushioned couches) elements, making even the bar (open daily and serving light snacks) a barefoot-chic hangout. Lunch is considerably cheaper and more island-flavored. *Average main: US$35* *Cockleshell Beach* *869/465–6455* *www.spicemillrestaurant.com* *Reservations essential* *Closed Sun. No dinner Mon.*

$$ SEAFOOD **Sprat Net.** This simple cluster of picnic tables—sheltered by a brilliant-turquoise corrugated-tin roof and decorated with driftwood, life preservers, photos of coastal scenes, and fishnets—sits on a sliver of sand. Nonetheless, it's an island hot spot. There's nothing fancy on the menu: just grilled fish, lobster, ribs, and chicken served with mountains of coleslaw and peas and rice. But the fish is amazingly fresh: the fishermen–owners heap their catches on a center table from which you choose your own dinner, then watch it grilled to your specification before dining family-style on paper plates. An adjacent hut serves up the final food group: pizza, Wednesday–Sunday. Sprat Net offers old-style Caribbean flavor, with the cheapest drinks and best bands on weekends. No wonder cars line up along the road, creating an impromptu jump-up. *Average main: US$15* *Main Rd., Old Road Town* *869/466–7535* *No credit cards* *Closed Sept. No lunch.*

WHERE TO STAY

St. Kitts has an appealing variety of places to stay—beautifully restored plantation inns (where a meal plan including afternoon tea in addition to breakfast and dinner is the norm), full-service, affordable hotels, simple beachfront cottages, and all-inclusive resorts. There are also several guesthouses and self-serve condos. Increasing development has been touted (or threatened) for years. At this writing, the ritzy Park Hyatt plans to debut its first Caribbean property on Banana Bay, in partnership with the grand Christophe Harbour development that will sprawl across the Southeast Peninsula replete with spectacular villas, beach clubs, celebrity restaurants, megayacht marina, Tom Fazio–designed golf course, and other boutique hotels. Several upscale villa compounds are being developed, such as the culture-oriented, eco-centric Kittitian Hills (architect Bill Bensley designed some of Thailand's most remarkable resorts), which will include an "edible" golf course (greens will intersect with farmland), spa, cosmopolitan retail village, farm-to-table restaurants, and a variety of sustainable lodgings in vernacular style, most with fabulous views. The first phase of spectacular hillside cottages opened in 2014; the resort is scheduled for completion in 2016. Another deluxe condo complex, the sparkling 185-unit Ocean's Edge on the Atlantic side of Frigate Bay, opened its first two beachfront blocks in late 2012; plans for hillside villas, a stunning tiered pool, additional water features, and a high-end restaurant have been temporarily shelved.

$$$$ RESORT Fodor's Choice ★ **Belle Mont Farm on Kittitian Hill.** Spectacularly perched atop a hill with sweeping views, Belle Mont Farm is the opening salvo in the eco-centric Kittitian Hill development. **Pros:** eco-friendly; remote; luxurious; technologically state-of-the-art. **Cons:** pricey; still-water design features attract mosquitoes; too "techy" for some; remote; beach club a bumpy ride away. *Rooms from: US$2,250 ☎ 855/846–3951 reservations, 869/465–7388 🌐 www.bellemontfarm.com 85 rooms, 75 cottages Multiple meal plans.*

$ RESORT **Bird Rock Beach Resort.** This basic scuba-set resort crowns a bluff above Basseterre, delivering amazing views of the town, sea, and mountains from every vantage point. **Pros:** exuberant clientele; great diving; excellent value; superb views; bike and kayak rental; complimentary Frigate Bay shuttle. **Cons:** small man-made beach; insufficient parking; difficult for physically challenged to maneuver; several rooms leased long-term to students; poor lighting; dilapidated decor. *Rooms from: US$90 ✉ 2 miles (3 km) east of Basseterre, Basseterre Bay ☎ 869/465–8914, 877/244–6285 🌐 www.birdrockbeach.com 30 rooms, 18 studios Multiple meal plans.*

$$ HOTEL Fodor's Choice ★ **Ottley's Plantation Inn.** You're treated like a beloved relative rather than a commercial guest at this quintessential Caribbean hotel, formerly a sugar plantation, at the foot of Mt. Liamuiga. **Pros:** posh yet unpretentious luxury; wonderfully helpful staff and owners; gorgeous gardens; excellent dining. **Cons:** no beach; bumpy access road; long walk from farthest cottages to office. *Rooms from: US$276 ✉ Southwest of Nicola Town, Ottley's Village, Basseterre ☎ 869/465–7234, 800/772–3039 🌐 www.ottleys.com 24 rooms Some meals.*

$ B&B/INN **Rock Haven Bed & Breakfast.** This restful, cozy bed-and-breakfast, a two-minute drive from Frigate Bay beaches (airport transfers are included), provides true local warmth, courtesy of Judith and Keith Blake. **Pros:** genuine island hospitality; immaculately maintained; delicious breakfasts. **Cons:** long walk to beach; car recommended to get around. *Rooms from: US$199 ✉ Frigate Bay ☎ 869/465–5503 🌐 www.rock-haven.com 2 rooms Breakfast.*

$$ RESORT **St. Kitts Marriott Resort.** This big, bustling beachfront resort offers something for everyone from families to conventioneers, golfers to gamblers. **Pros:** great range of activities; good bars; recently refurbished rooms; plentiful on-site duty-free shopping; enormous main

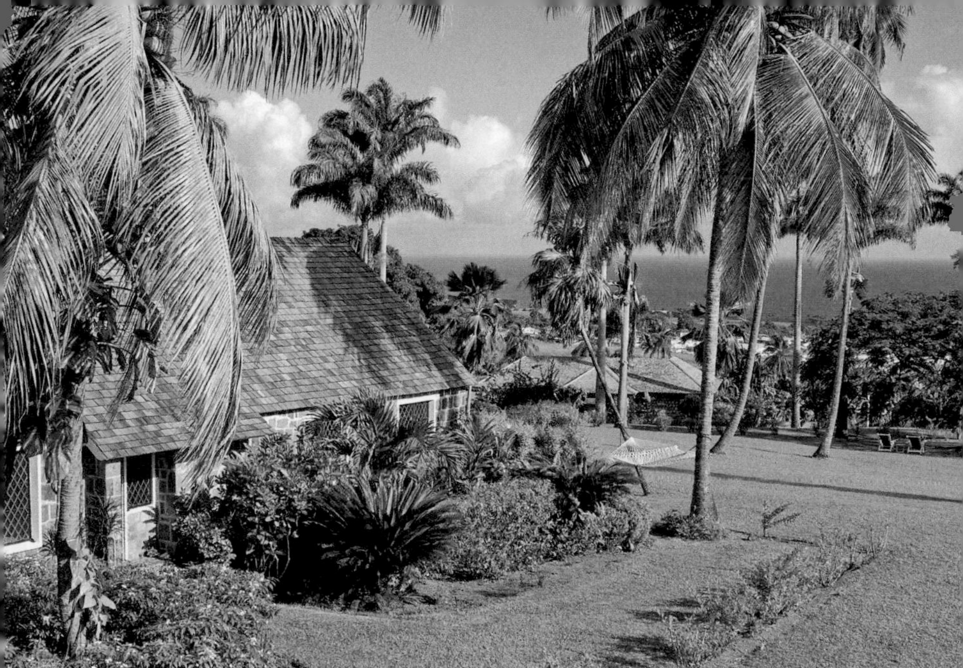

Ottley's Plantation Inn

pool. **Cons:** impersonal service; occasional time-share pitches; surprise extra charges; mostly mediocre food; not enough units feature ocean views. *Rooms from: US$289* *858 Frigate Bay Rd., Frigate Bay* *869/466–1200, 800/223–6388* *www.stkittsmarriott.com* *320 rooms, 73 suites* *No meals.*

$ RENTAL **Timothy Beach Resort.** The only St. Kitts resort sitting directly on a Caribbean beach is incomparably located and restful, a great budget find thanks to smiling service and simple but sizable apartments. **Pros:** complimentary Wi-Fi; close to the beach action; pleasant on-site restaurant and bar; plentiful deals. **Cons:** occasionally worn decor; can hear boisterous beach bar music weekend nights; no view from most bedrooms. *Rooms from: US$160* *1 South Frigate Bay Beach, Frigate Bay* *869/465–8597, 845/201–0047, 888/229–2747* *www.timothybeach.com* *60 apartments* *No meals.*

NIGHTLIFE

Most nightlife revolves around the hotels, which host folkloric shows and calypso and steel bands of the usual limbo-rum-and-reggae variety. The growing Frigate Bay "strip" of beach bars, including Mr. X Shiggidy Shack, Patsy's, Monkey Bar, Inon's, Buddies Beach Hut, Chinchilla, and Vibes, is the place to party hearty on weekend nights.

Look for such hard-driving local exponents of soca music as Nu-Vybes, Grand Masters, Small Axe, and Royalton 5; and "heavy dance-hall" reggae group House of Judah. The Marriott's large, glitzy casino has table games and slots.

BARS AND CLUBS

Circus Grill. A favorite happy-hour watering hole is the Circus Grill, a second-floor eatery whose veranda offers views of the harbor and the activity on the Circus. ✉ *Bay Rd., Basseterre* ☎ *869/465–0143.*

Keys Lounge. This low-key, classy hangout has jazz-salsa duos, cushy sofas, high-back straw chairs, chess-set tables, and a superlative selection of aged rums. If it's packed, try the hotel's Lobby Bar for tapas on tap or 'tinis with 'tude. ✉ *St. Kitts Marriott Resort, Frigate Bay* ☎ *869/466–1200.*

Mr. X Shiggidy Shack. Mr. X Shiggidy Shack is known for its sizzling Thursday-night bonfire parties replete with fire-eaters, and raucous karaoke Saturdays. For locals it's a must-stop on the Friday-night liming circuit of Frigate Bay bars. ✉ *Frigate Bay* ☎ *869/762–3983, 869/465–0673* 🌐 *www.mrxshiggidyshack.com.*

Salt Plage. This happening beachfront nightspot merges with the handsomely recycled, rusting ruins of a former salt storage chattel house (the lavatories are particularly creative, incorporating old depth meters and a reclaimed engine room). Turquoise tables and white chairs dot the multitiered bleached wood deck, all optimally placed for sunset viewing. DJs and live bands are on tap most nights; boaters often anchor at the dock, joining in the fun. The menu and drinks list conjure a Cannes in the Caribbean feel. Savory light bites (priced between $10 and $20) include fish tacos, ceviches, and lobster kebabs. There's bottle service (but of course!), and a small but savvy wine selection to help further loosen inhibitions. ✉ *White House Bay* ☎ *869/466–7221* 🌐 *www.christopheharbour.com* ⏲ *Wed.–Sun. 4–12.*

SHOPPING

St. Kitts has limited shopping, but several duty-free shops offer good deals on jewelry, perfume, china, and crystal. Numerous galleries sell excellent paintings and sculptures. The batik fabrics, scarves, caftans, and wall hangings of Caribelle Batik are well known. British expat Kate Spencer is an artist who has lived on the island for years, reproducing its vibrant colors on everything from silk pareus (beach wraps) and scarves to note cards. Other good island buys include crafts, jams, and herbal teas. Don't forget to pick up some CSR (Cane Spirit Rothschild), which is distilled from fresh wild sugarcane right on St. Kitts. The Brinley Gold Company has made a splash among spirits connoisseurs with its coffee, mango, coconut, lime, and vanilla rums (there is a tasting room at Port Zante).

AREAS AND MALLS

Most shopping plazas are in downtown Basseterre, on the streets radiating from the Circus.

All Kind of Tings. All Kind of Tings, a peppermint-pink edifice on Liverpool Row at College Street Ghaut, functions as a de facto vendors' market, where several booths sell local crafts and cheap T-shirts. Its courtyard frequently hosts folkloric dances, fashion shows, poetry readings, and steel-pan concerts. ✉ *Liverpool Row, Basseterre.*

Pelican Mall. This shopping arcade, designed to look like a traditional Caribbean street, has more than 20 stores (purveying mostly resort wear, souvenirs, and liquor), a restaurant, tourism offices, and a bandstand near the cruise-ship pier. ✉ *Bay Rd., Basseterre.*

Port Zante. Directly behind Pelican Mall, on the waterfront, is Port Zante, the deepwater cruise-ship pier where a much delayed upscale shopping–dining complex is becoming a 30-shop area (including the usual ubiquitous large jewelry concerns like Abbott's, Diamonds International, and Kay Jewelers); the Amina Market here is a fine source for cheap local crafts. If you're looking for inexpensive, island-y T-shirts and souvenirs, check out the series of vendors' huts behind Pelican Mall to the right of Port Zante as you face the sea. ✉ *Cruise Ship Pier, Basseterre.*

Shoreline Plaza. Shoreline Plaza is next to the Treasury Building, right on Basseterre's waterfront. The shops mainly sell locally made souvenirs and handicrafts, as well as T-shirts. ✉ *Basseterre.*

TDC Mall. TDC Mall is just off the Circus in downtown, with a few boutiques, selling mostly island wear. ✉ *Bank St., Basseterre.*

ART

Spencer Cameron Art Gallery. Spencer Cameron Art Gallery has historical reproductions of Caribbean island charts and prints, in addition to owner Rosey Cameron's popular Carnevale clown prints and a wide selection of exceptional artwork by Caribbean artists. It also showcases the work of Glass Island (exquisite Italianate art glass from frames to plates in sinuous shapes and seductive colors) and various local craftspeople, including the marvelous pottery of Carla Astaphan. The gallery will mail anywhere. ✉ *10 N. Independence Sq., Basseterre* ☎ *869/465–1617, 869/664–4157.*

HANDICRAFTS

Caribelle Batik. Caribelle Batik sells gloriously colored batik wraps, kimonos, caftans, T-shirts, dresses, wall hangings, and the like; you can watch the process in back. ✉ *Romney Manor, Old Road Town* ☎ *869/465–6253* 🌐 *www.caribellebatikstkitts.com.*

Crafthouse. The Crafthouse is one of the best sources for local dolls, wood carvings, and straw work. ✉ *Southwell Industrial Site, Bay Rd., Basseterre* ☎ *869/465–7754.*

Palms Court Gardens. Talk about multitasking: this little oasis offers a restaurant, an infinity pool and hot tub with bay views, miniature botanical gardens, and the Shell Works atelier and gift shop, where artisans fashion graceful napkin holders, candlesticks, stemware, wall hangings, and jewelry from coral, sea fans, mother-of-pearl, and other marine materials. ✉ *Corner of Wilkin and Wigley Sts., Basseterre* ☎ *869/465–6060* 🌐 *www.palmscourtgardens.com.*

SPORTS AND THE OUTDOORS

BOATING AND FISHING

Most operators are on the Caribbean side of Frigate Bay, known for its gentle currents. Turtle Bay offers stronger winds and stunning views of Nevis. Though not noted for big-game fishing, several steep offshore drop-offs do lure wahoo, barracuda, shark, tuna, yellowtail snapper, and mackerel. Rates are occasionally negotiable; figure approximately $400 for a four-hour excursion with refreshments.

Leeward Island Charters. The knowledgeable Todd Leypoldt of Leeward Island Charters takes you out on his charter boats, *Spirit of St. Kitts, Caona,* and *Eagle.* He's also available for snorkeling charters, beach picnics, and sunset-moonlight cruises. ✉ *Basseterre* ☎ *869/465–7474* 🌐 *www.leewardislandscharters.com.*

Mr. X Watersports. Found within Mr. X Shiggidy Shack *(⇨ see Nightlife above),* this shop rents small craft, including motorboats (waterskiing and jet skiing are available). Paddleboats are $15 per hour, sailboats $25 per hour. Deep-sea fishing charters, snorkeling tours, water taxis, sunset cruises, and private charters with captain and crew are available. Mr. X and his cohorts are usually hanging out at the adjacent open-air Monkey Bar. ✉ *Frigate Bay* ☎ *869/465–0673* 🌐 *www.mrxshiggidyshack.com.*

Reggae Beach Bar & Grill. This establishment rents kayaks and snorkeling equipment from the restaurant, offers sailing lessons, and can also arrange fishing trips, as well as water taxis to Nevis. ✉ *S.E. Peninsula Rd., Cockleshell Beach* ☎ *869/762–5050* 🌐 *www.reggaebeachbar.com.*

DIVING AND SNORKELING

Though unheralded as a dive destination, St. Kitts has more than a dozen excellent sites, protected by several new marine parks. The surrounding waters feature shoals, hot vents, shallows, canyons, steep walls, and caverns at depths from 40 to nearly 200 feet. The St. Kitts Maritime Archaeological Project, which surveys, records, researches, and preserves the island's underwater treasures, has charted several hundred wrecks of galleons, frigates, and freighters dating back to the 17th century. **Bloody Bay Reef** is noted for its network of underwater grottoes daubed with purple anemones, sienna bristle worms, and canary-yellow sea fans that seem to wave you in. **Coconut Tree Reef,** one of the largest in the area, includes sea fans, sponges, and anemones, as well as the Rocks, three enormous boulders with impressive multilevel diving. The only drift-dive site, **Nags Head,** has strong currents, but experienced divers might spot gliding rays, lobsters, turtles, and reef sharks. Since it sank in 50 feet of water in the early 1980s, the *River Taw* makes a splendid site for less experienced divers. **Sandy Point Reef** has been designated a National Marine Park and includes Paradise Reef, with swim-through 90-foot sloping canyons, and Anchors Away, where anchors have been encrusted with coral formations. The 1985 wreck of the *Talata* lies in 70 feet of water; barracudas, rays, groupers, and grunts dart through its hull.

Dive St. Kitts. This PADI–NAUI facility, offers competitive prices, computers to maximize time below, a wide range of courses from refresher to technical, and friendly, laid-back dive masters. The Bird Rock location features superb shore diving (unlimited when you book packages): common sightings 20 to 30 feet out include octopuses, nurse sharks, manta and spotted eagle rays, sea horses, even barracudas George and Georgianna. It also offers kayak and snorkeling tours. ✉ *2 miles (3 km) east of Basseterre, Frigate Bay* ☎ *869/465–1189, 869/465–8914* 🌐 *www.divestkitts.com.*

Kenneth's Dive Center. Kenneth Samuel, the owner of this PADI company, takes small groups of divers with C cards to nearby reefs on his two custom-built catamarans. Rates average $70 for single-tank dives, $105 for double-tank dives; add $10 for equipment. Night dives, including lights, are $80–$100, and snorkeling trips (four-person minimum) are $40, drinks included. After nearly 30 years' experience, former fisherman Samuel is considered an old pro (Jean-Michel Cousteau requested his guidance upon his first visit in the 1990s) and strives to keep groups small and prices reasonable. ✉ *Bay Rd., Newtown* ☎ *869/465–2670* 🌐 *www.kennethdivecenter.com.*

Pro-Divers. Owned by Auston Macleod, a PADI-certified dive master–instructor, this outfitter offers resort and certification courses running $125–$600, including specialty options from deep diving to digital underwater photography. Dive computers are included gratis. He offers introductory scuba courses Sunday through Thursday at 10 am and Friday and Saturday at 2:30 pm at the Marriott for guests only (the $20 fee is refunded if you purchase dives). He also takes groups to snorkeling sites accessible only by boat via his custom-built 38-foot catamaran, *Kuriala.* ✉ *Fisherman's Wharf, Ocean Terrace Inn, Basseterre* ☎ *869/660–3483* 🌐 *www.prodiversstkitts.com.*

GOLF

St. Kitts hopes to market itself as a golf destination with the remodeling of the Royal St. Kitts Golf Course and two upcoming resort and villa developments that include 18-hole courses, one called Irie Fields, an edible layout with sweeping water views at Kittitian Hill, and the other designed by Tom Fazio (which promises to be one of the Caribbean's most spectacular, with huge elevation drops, ruins, extraordinary sweeping vistas, and carries over ravines: "Scottsdale meets Pebble Beach").

Royal St. Kitts Golf Club. This 18-hole links-style championship course underwent a complete redesign by Thomas McBroom to maximize Caribbean and Atlantic views and increase the challenge (there are 12 lakes and 83 bunkers). Holes 15 through 17 (the latter patterned after Pebble Beach No. 18) skirt the Atlantic in their entirety, lending new meaning to the term sand trap. The sudden gusts, wide but twisting fairways, and extremely hilly terrain demand pinpoint accuracy and finesse, yet holes such as 18 require pure power. The development includes practice bunkers, a putting green, a short-game chipping area, and the fairly high-tech Royal Golf Academy. Twilight and super-twilight discounts are offered. ✉ *St. Kitts Marriott Resort, 858 Zenway Blvd., Frigate*

Bay ☎ 869/466–2700, 866/785–4653 ⊕ www.royalstkittsgolfclub.com *$150 for Marriott guests in high season, $165 for nonguests* *18 holes, 6900 yards, par 71.*

GUIDED TOURS

The taxi driver who picks you up will probably offer to act as your guide to the island. Each driver is knowledgeable and does a three-hour tour of Nevis for $75 or a four-hour tour of St. Kitts for $80. He can also make a lunch reservation at one of the plantation restaurants, and you can incorporate this into your tour.

Kantours. On St. Kitts, Kantours offers comprehensive general island tours, as well as a variety of specialty excursions, including ATV expeditions. ✉ *Liverpool Row, Basseterre* ☎ *869/465–2098, 869/465–3141 in St. Kitts, 869/469–0136 in Nevis* ⊕ *www.kantours.com.*

Tropical Tours. The friendly guides at Tropical Tours can run you around St. Kitts (from $27 per person), arrange kayaking and snorkeling, deep-sea fishing (from $145 per person), and take you to the volcano or rain forest for $52 per person and up. ☎ *869/465–4167, 869/465–4039* ⊕ *www.tropicaltoursstkitts-nevis.com.*

HIKING

Trails in the central mountains vary from easy to don't-try-it-by-yourself. Monkey Hill and Verchild's Peak aren't difficult, although the Verchild's climb will take the better part of a day. Don't attempt Mt. Liamuiga without a guide. You'll start at Belmont Estate—at the west end of the island—on horseback, and then proceed on foot to the lip of the crater, at 2,600 feet. You can go down into the crater—1,000 feet deep and 1 mile (1½ km) wide, with a small freshwater lake—clinging to vines and roots and scaling rocks, even trees. Expect to get muddy. There are several fine operators (each hotel recommends its favorite); tour rates generally range from $50 for a rain-forest walk to $95 for a volcano expedition and usually include round-trip transportation from your hotel and picnic lunch.

Duke of Earl's Adventures. Owner Earl "The Duke of Earl" Vanlow is as entertaining as his nickname suggests—and his prices are slightly cheaper ($50 for a rain-forest tour includes refreshments, $75 volcano expeditions add lunch; hotel pickup and drop-off is complimentary). He genuinely loves his island and conveys that enthusiasm, encouraging hikers to swing on vines or sample unusual-looking fruits during his rain-forest trip. He also conducts a thorough volcano tour to the crater's rim and a drive-through eco-safari tour ($55 with lunch). ☎ *869/465–1899, 869/663–0994.*

Greg's Safaris. Greg Pereira of Greg's Safaris, whose family has lived on St. Kitts since the early 19th century, takes groups on half-day trips into the rain forest and on full-day hikes up the volcano and through the grounds of a private 18th-century greathouse. The rain-forest trips include visits to sacred Carib sites, abandoned sugar mills, and an excursion down a 100-foot coastal canyon containing a wealth of Amerindian petroglyphs. The Off the Beaten Track 4x4 Plantation Tour provides a thorough explanation of the role sugar and rum played in the Caribbean economy and colonial wars. He and his staff relate fascinating historical, folkloric, and botanical information. ☎ *869/465–4121* 🌐 *www.gregsafaris.com.*

HORSEBACK RIDING

Wild North Frigate Bay and desolate Conaree Beach are great for riding, as is the rain forest.

Trinity Stables. Guides from Trinity Stables offer beach rides ($50) and trips into the rain forest ($60), both including hotel pickup. The latter is intriguing, as guides discuss plants' medicinal properties along the way (such as sugarcane to stanch bleeding) and pick oranges right off a tree to squeeze fresh juice. Otherwise, the staffers are cordial but shy; this isn't a place for beginners' instruction. ✉ *Palmetto Point* ☎ *869/465–3226* 🌐 *www.trinityinnapartments.com/stables.asp.*

SEA EXCURSIONS

In addition to the usual snorkeling, sunset, and party cruises (ranging in price from $40 to $100), most companies offer whale-watching excursions during the winter migrating season, January through April. And on land, turtle-watches during nesting season are becoming popular.

Blue Water Safaris. Blue Water Safaris offers half-day snorkeling trips or beach barbecues on deserted cays, as well as sunset and moonlight cruises on its 65-foot catamarans *Irie Lime* and *Swaliga,* and the smaller *Falcon.* Prices include refreshments and/or meals. It also runs kayaking tours. Boats depart from Port Zante. ✉ *Princess St., Basseterre* ☎ *869/466–4933* 🌐 *www.bluewatersafaris.com* 🎫 *From $50.*

Leeward Island Charters. This reliable outfit offers day and overnight charters on two catamarans—the 67-foot *Eagle* and 78-foot *Spirit of St. Kitts*, as well as the 47-foot *Caona*. Day sails are from 9:30 to 4:30 and include a barbecue, an open bar, and use of snorkeling equipment. The Nevis trip stops at Pinney's Beach for a barbecue and at Shooting Bay, a tiny cove in the bullying shadow of a sheer cliff, where petrels and frigate birds inspect your snorkeling skills. The crews are mellow, affable, and knowledgeable about island life. ✉ *586 Fort St., Basseterre* ☎ *869/465–7474* 🌐 *www.leewardislandscharters.com.*

ZIP-LINING

FAMILY **Sky Safari Tours.** On these popular tours, would-be Tarzans and Janes whisk through the "Valley of the Giants" (so dubbed for the towering trees) at speeds up to 50 mph (80 kph) along five cable lines; the longest (nicknamed "The Boss") stretches 1,350 feet through towering turpentine and mahogany trees draped thickly with bromeliads, suspended 250 feet above the ground. Following the Canadian-based company's mantra of "faster, higher, safer," it uses a specially designed trolley with secure harnesses attached. Many of the routes afford unobstructed views of Brimstone Hill and the sea beyond. The outfit emphasizes environmental and historic aspects. Guides provide nature interpretation and commentary, and the office incorporates Wingfield Estate's old sugar plantation, distillery, and church ruins, which visitors can explore. Admission is usually $65–$85, depending on the tour chosen. It's open daily 9–6, with the first and last tours departing at 10 and 3. ✉ *Wingfield Estate, Wingfield Estate* ☎ *869/466–4259, 869/465–4347* 🌐 *www.skysafaristkitts.com.*

NEVIS

Nevis's charm is its rusticity: there are no traffic lights, goats still amble through the streets of Charlestown, and local grocers announce whatever's in stock on a blackboard (anything from pig snouts to beer).

EXPLORING

Nevis's Main Road makes a 21-mile (32-km) circuit through the five parishes; various offshoots of the road wind into the mountains. You can tour Charlestown, the capital, in a half hour or so, but you'll need three to four hours to explore the entire island.

CHARLESTOWN

About 1,200 of Nevis's 10,000 inhabitants live in the capital. If you arrive by ferry, as most people do, you'll walk smack onto Main Street from the pier. It's easy to imagine how tiny Charlestown, founded in 1660, must have looked in its heyday. The weathered buildings still have fanciful galleries, elaborate gingerbread fretwork, wooden shutters, and hanging plants. The stone building with the clock tower (1825, but mostly rebuilt after a devastating 1873 fire) houses the courthouse and second-floor library (a cool respite on sultry days). The little park next to the library is Memorial Square, dedicated to the fallen of World Wars I and II. Down the street from the square, archaeologists have discovered the remains of a Jewish cemetery and synagogue (Nevis reputedly had the Caribbean's second-oldest congregation), but there's little to see.

Alexander Hamilton Birthplace. The Alexander Hamilton Birthplace, which contains the Hamilton Museum, sits on the waterfront. This bougainvillea-draped Georgian-style house is a reconstruction of what is believed to have been the American patriot's original home, built in 1680 and likely destroyed during a mid-19th earthquake. Born here in 1755, Hamilton moved to St. Croix when he was about 12. He moved to the American colonies to continue his education at 17; he became George Washington's Secretary of the Treasury and died in a duel with political rival Aaron Burr in 1804. The Nevis House of Assembly occupies the second floor; the museum downstairs contains Hamilton memorabilia, documents pertaining to the island's history, and displays on island geology, politics, architecture, culture, and cuisine. The gift shop is a wonderful source for historic maps, crafts, and books on Nevis. ✉ *Low St., Charlestown* ☎ *869/469–5786* 🌐 *www.nevisheritage.org, www.nevis-nhcs.org* 🎫 *$5, with admission to Museum of Nevisian History $7* 🕓 *Weekdays 9–4, Sat. 9–noon.*

ELSEWHERE ON NEVIS

TOP ATTRACTIONS

Botanical Gardens of Nevis. In addition to terraced gardens and arbors, this remarkable 7.8-acre site in the glowering shadow of Mt. Nevis has natural lagoons, streams, and waterfalls, superlative bronze mermaids, Buddhas, egrets and herons, and extravagant fountains. You can find a proper rose garden, sections devoted to orchids and bromeliads, cacti, and flowering trees and shrubs—even a bamboo garden. The entrance to the Rain Forest Conservatory—which attempts to include every conceivable Caribbean ecosystem and then some—duplicates an imposing Mayan temple. A splendid re-creation of a plantation-style greathouse contains the appealing Oasis in the Gardens Thai restaurant with sweeping sea views (and wonderfully inventive variations on classic cocktails utlizing local ingredients), and the upscale World Art & Antiques Gallery selling artworks, textiles, jewelry, and Indonesian teak furnishings sourced during the owners' world travels. ✉ *Montpelier Estate* ☎ *869/469–3509* 🌐 *www.botanicalgardennevis.com* 🎟 *$13; $8 children 6–12* ⏲ *Mon.–Sat. 9–4.*

Museum of Nevis History. Purportedly this is the Western Hemisphere's largest collection of Lord Horatio Nelson memorabilia, including letters, documents, paintings, and even furniture from his flagship. Nelson was based in Antigua but came on military patrol to Nevis, where he met and eventually married Frances Nisbet, who lived on a 64-acre plantation here. Half the space is devoted to often-provocative displays on island life, from leading families to vernacular architecture to the adaptation of traditional African customs, from cuisine to Carnival. The shop is an excellent source for gifts, from homemade soaps to historical guides. ✉ *Bath Rd., Charlestown* ☎ *869/469–0408* 🌐 *www.nevis-nhcs.org, www.nevisheritage.org* 🎟 *$5, with Hamilton Museum $7* ⏲ *Weekdays 8:30–4, Sat. 10–1.*

WORTH NOTING

Bath Springs. The Caribbean's first hotel, the Bath Hotel, built by businessman John Huggins in 1778, was so popular in the 19th century that visitors, including such dignitaries as Samuel Taylor Coleridge and Prince William Henry, traveled two months by ship to "take the waters" in the property's hot thermal springs. It suffered extensive hurricane and earthquake damage over the years and long languished in disrepair. Local volunteers have cleaned up the spring and built a stone pool and steps to enter the waters; now residents and visitors enjoy the springs, which range from 104°F to 108°F, though signs still caution that you bathe at your own risk, especially if you have heart problems. The development houses the Nevis Island Administration offices; there's still talk of adding massage huts, changing rooms, a restaurant, and a cultural/history center on the original hotel property. ✉ *Charlestown* ✥ *Follow Main St. south from Charlestown.*

Eden Brown Estate. This government-owned mansion, built around 1740, is known as Nevis's haunted house, or haunted ruins. In 1822 a Miss Julia Huggins was to marry a fellow named Maynard. However, come wedding day, the groom and his best man killed each other in a duel. The bride-to-be became a recluse, and the mansion was closed down. Local residents claim they can feel the presence of "someone" whenever they go near the eerie old house with its shroud of weeds and wildflowers. Though memorable more for the story than the hike or ruins, it's always open, and it's free. ✉ *East Coast Rd., between Lime Kiln and Mannings, Eden Brown Bay.*

Ft. Ashby. Overgrown with tropical vegetation, this site overlooks the place where the settlement of Jamestown fell into the sea after a tidal wave hit the coast in 1680. Needless to say, this is a favorite

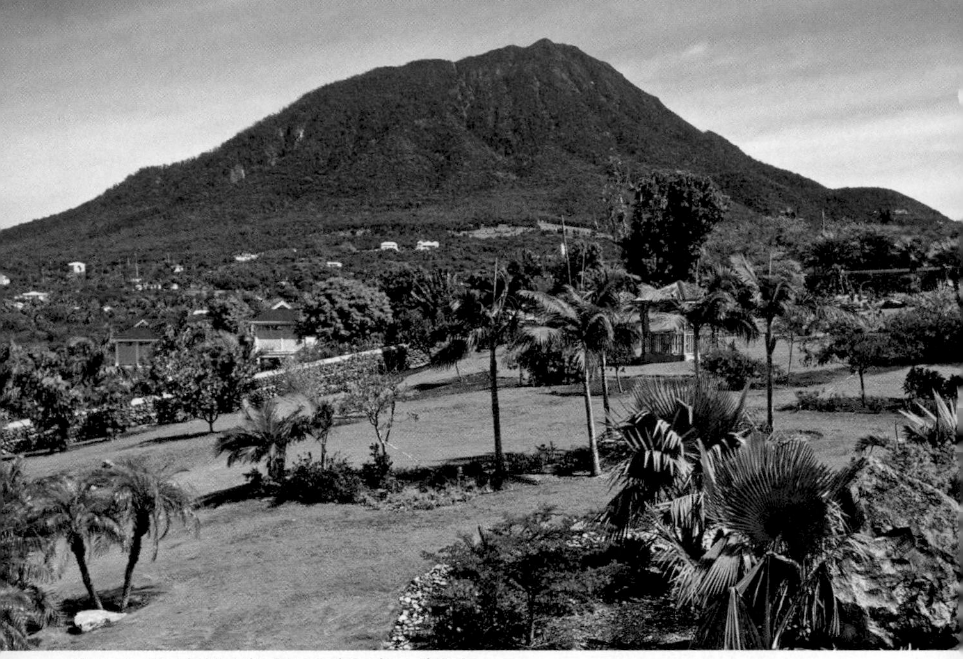

Mt. Nevis rising behind the Botanical Gardens of Nevis

scuba-diving site. ✉ *Main Rd., 1½ miles (2½ km) southwest of Hurricane Hill, Fort Ashby Beach.*

Fothergills Nevisian Heritage Village. On the grounds of a former sugar plantation–cotton ginnery, this ambitious, ever-expanding project traces the evolution of Nevisian social history, from the Caribs to the present, through vernacular dwellings that re-create living conditions over the centuries. The Carib chief's thatched hut includes actual relics such as weapons, calabash bowls, clay pots, and cassava squeezers. Wattle-and-daub structures reproduce slave quarters; implements on display include coal pots and sea fans (used as sieves). A post-emancipation gingerbread chattel house holds patchwork quilts and flour-bag dresses. There's a typical sharecropper's garden explaining herbal medicinal folklore and blacksmith's shop. Docents are quite earnest and go on at great (mostly fascinating) length. ✉ *Gingerland* ☎ *869/469–5521, 869/469–2033* 🎫 *$3* ⏲ *Mon.–Sat. 9–4; sometimes closes early, call ahead.*

Mansa's Farm. Anyone who wants a real sense of island daily life and subsistence should call Mervin "Mansa" Tyson. He'll take you past his fruit trees and herb gardens through rows of tomatoes, cucumbers, string beans, eggplant, zucchini, sweet pepper, melons, and more. Discussing the needs for at least partial organic growing practices, he passionately explains how he adapted traditional folk pesticides and describes the medicinal properties of various plants, cultivated and wild. He'll prepare a lunch using his produce, including delectable refreshing fruit drinks at his Mansa's Last Stand grocery across from the beach. Weekend barbecues are a highlight. All in all, this agritourism foray redefines food for thought. ✉ *Cades Bay* ☎ *869/469–8520* 🎫 *Varies* ⏲ *Call for appointment.*

St. John's Figtree Church. Among the records of this church built in 1680 is a tattered, prominently displayed marriage certificate that reads "Horatio Nelson, Esquire, to Frances Nisbet, Widow, on March 11, 1787." ✉ *Church Ground* ✣ *Located about 10 mins south of Charlestown on the main road.*

St. Thomas Anglican Church. The island's oldest church was built in 1643 and has been altered many times over the years. The gravestones in the old churchyard have stories to tell, and the church itself contains memorials to Nevis's early settlers. ✉ *Main Rd. just south of Cotton Ground, Jessups.*

BEACHES

All beaches on Nevis are free to the public (the plantation inns cordon off "private" areas on Pinney's Beach for guests), but there are no changing facilities, so wear a swimsuit under your clothes.

Newcastle Beach. This broad swath of soft ecru sand shaded by coconut palms is near Nisbet Plantation, on the channel between St. Kitts and Nevis. It's popular with snorkelers, but beware stony sections and occasional strong currents that kick up seaweed and roil the sandy bottom. **Amenities:** food and drink. **Best for:** snorkeling. ✉ *Newcastle, St. Kitts.*

Oualie Beach. South of Mosquito Bay and north of Cades and Jones Bays, this beige-sand beach lined with palms and sea grapes is where the folks at Oualie Beach Hotel can mix you a drink and fix you up with water-sports equipment. There's excellent snorkeling amid calm water and fantastic sunset views with St. Kitts silhouetted in the background. Several beach chairs and hammocks (free with lunch, $3 rental without) line the sand and the grassy "lawn" behind it. Oualie is at the island's northwest tip, approximately 3 miles (5 km) west of the airport. **Amenities:** food and drink; water sports. **Best for:** snorkeling; sunset. ✉ *Oualie Beach, St. Kitts.*

Pinney's Beach. The island's showpiece has soft, golden sand on the calm Caribbean, lined with a magnificent grove of palm trees. The Four Seasons Resort is here, as are the plantation inns' beach clubs and casual beach bars such as Sunshine's, Chevy's, and the Lime (which morphs into the island's disco Friday nights). Beach chairs are gratis when you purchase a drink or lunch. Regrettably, the waters can be murky and filled with kelp if the weather has been inclement anywhere within a hundred miles, depending on the currents. **Amenities:** food and drink; water sports. **Best for:** swimming; walking. ✉ *Pinney's Beach, St. Kitts.*

WHERE TO EAT

Dinner options range from intimate meals at plantation guesthouses (where the menu is often prix fixe) to casual eateries. Seafood is ubiquitous, and many places specialize in West Indian fare. The island is trying to raise its profile as a fine-dining destination by holding NICHE (Nevis International Culinary Heritage Exposition), a gastronomic festival with guest chefs and winemakers offering cooking seminars and tastings during the second half of October.

What to Wear. Dress is casual at lunch, although beach attire is unacceptable. Dress pants and sundresses are appropriate for dinner.

$$$ ECLECTIC

Bananas. Peripatetic English owner Gillian Smith has held jobs with Disney and Relais & Châteaux, and everything about Bananas (read lovably nuts) borrows from her wildly diverse experiences. Even the setting is delightfully deceptive: the classic stone, brick, and wood plantation greathouse nestled amid extravagant gardens was painstakingly built by Gillian herself in 2006. Her fun, shabby-chic sensibility informs every aspect of the restaurant and adjacent art gallery in a faux chattel house. The colonial look (pith helmets, steamer trunks, beamed ceiling, chandeliers dangling from a corrugated tin roof) contrasts with Turkish kilims and Moroccan lamps. The food is equally eclectic and globe-trotting, running from bourbon-glazed guava ribs to baked gnocchi in roast pumpkin-Gorgonzola or portobello sauce. Despite the improvisational ambience, there's no monkeying around with quality at Bananas. *Average main: US$27 Upper Hamilton Estate 869/469–1891 www.bananasrestaurantnevis.com Reservations essential No lunch. Closed Sun.*

$$$$ ECLECTIC Fodor's Choice ★

Coconut Grove. This thatched-palm roof, rough-timber structure sports a sensuous South Seas look, best appreciated on the deck as the sun fireballs across the Caribbean. Inside, handsome teak furnishings are animated by Buddhas, parrot-hue throw pillows, batik hangings, and gauzy curtains. The service is warm, the champagne is properly chilled, and the splendid Pacific Rim–Mediterranean fusion fare seems designed to complement the admirable, 8,000-bottle wine cellar rather than the other way around. Stephen "Chef Steve" Smith, a CIA grad and registered dietitian, introduced heart-healthier options such as curry-scented pumpkin soup with fat-free soy cream and a miraculously fiber-licious 100-calorie whole-wheat-flour–and–black-bean brownie. Nonetheless, the menu also includes such indulgences as homemade foie gras steeped in aged rum and candied cherries served with a balsamic reduction or baby Camembert baked in Calvados with cranberry confiture. Happy hour, 11 pm–midnight, often ushers in impromptu dancing, continuing the "Bali high" theme. The downstairs "Coco Beach" has an infinity pool for use, sensational St. Kitts views, affordable, creative, lighter daytime fare when open for lunch (call ahead), and live music many evenings. *Average main: US$36 Nelson's Spring, Pinney's Beach 869/469–1020 www.coconutgroverestaurantnevis.com Reservations essential Closed Aug.–Oct.*

$$$$ STEAKHOUSE Fodor's Choice ★

Coral Grill. Coral Grill is Four Seasons' successful "de-formalized" conversion of its former haute Dining Room into a stunning steak house. It eschews the venue's typical men's-club decor, lightening and brightening the original's imposing space. The graceful patio, beamed cathedral ceilings, flagstone hearth, and parquet floors remain; yet an open contemporary lounge that wouldn't be out of place in Santa Monica bisects the vast interior. The grilled items shine here, from Wagyu steak that dissolves in your mouth to gossamer lobster tails. Or opt for the decadent foie gras burger perfectly set off by mushroom-onion fricassee and tomato jam. Meats are served with a choice of Shiraz reduction, béarnaise, or chimichurri; seafood with rum-citrus glaze, lemongrass emulsion, or hollandaise. The streamlined but comprehensive wine list features some surprisingly fair prices. The hotel can arrange a unique interactive dive-and-dine experience, plunging you into the deep to pluck lobster and other marine creatures that the chefs will cook for you later. *Average main: US$43 Four Seasons Nevis, Pinney's Beach 869/469–1111, 869/469–6238 www.fourseasons.com/nevis Reservations essential No lunch.*

$$ SEAFOOD **Double Deuce.** Mark Roberts, the former chef at Montpelier, decided to chuck the "five-star lifestyle" and now co-owns this jammed, jamming bar just off Pinney's, which lures locals with fine, fairly priced fare and creative cocktails. The overgrown shack is plastered with sailing and fishing pictures, as well as Balinese masks, fishnets, license plates, and wind chimes. Behind the cool mauve bar is a gleaming modern kitchen where Mark (and fun-loving firebrand partner Lyndeta) prepare sublime seafood he often catches himself, as well as organic beef burgers, velvety pumpkin soup, inventive pastas, and lip-smacking ribs. The "DD" is as cool and mellow as it gets. Stop by for free Wi-Fi and proper espresso, a game of pool, riotous karaoke Thursdays, Sunday bingo, or just to hang out with a Double Deuce Stinger (Lyndy's answer to Sunshine's Killer Bee punch). Kids have their own trampoline. Dinner can be arranged for parties of six to 10. *Average main: US$18 Pinney's Beach 869/469–2222 www.doubledeucenevis.com Reservations essential No credit cards Closed Mon.*

$$$ ECLECTIC Fodor's Choice ★ **Hermitage Plantation Inn.** After cocktails in the inn's antiques-filled parlor (the knockout rum punches are legendary), dinner is served on the veranda. Many ingredients are harvested from the inn's herb garden, fruit trees, piggery, and livestock collection; the scrumptious cured meats, baked goods, preserves, and ice creams are homemade. Sumptuous dishes prepared by long-time expat maestro Janice Ryan might include breadfruit-cheddar soufflé, ginger-and-lime conch cakes, scallops in gossamer lemon beurre blanc, herb-crusted lamb with rosemary and guava, and passion fruit–ginger cheesecake. A traditional wood-burning oven yields savory items as well, including what may be the best thin-crust pizzas within hundreds of miles. Wednesday night pig roasts are an island must. The ever-growing wine list is exceptionally priced. Bon mots and bonhomie serve as prelude, intermezzo, and coda for a lively evening. *Average main: US$30 Gingerland 869/469–3477 www.hermitagenevis.com Reservations essential.*

$$$$ CARIBBEAN **Mango.** This sophisticated beach bar at the Four Seasons is a perennial hot spot, thanks to a gorgeous outdoor deck overlooking the illuminated water, sizzling music, fab drinks (as well as an extensive rum bar with more than 100 selections), hip decor, and a farm-and-sea-to-table menu showcasing local ingredients, many grown by the staff. You can savor artfully presented, robustly flavored Caribbean classics with inventive accents such as barbecue pork-and-plantain empanada with avocado aïoli, lobster fritters with chipotle-mango dip, and mouth- and eye-watering mango–Myers's rum barbecued baby back ribs with cooling coconut coleslaw and yummy sweet potato jerk fries. The kitchen

also delights with updated twists, such as swirls of jalapeño-cilantro salsa floating in silken, chilled corn-and-coconut soup. Half the menu is gluten-free. $ *Average main: US$36* ✉ *Four Seasons Resort, Pinney's Beach* ☎ *869/469–1111, 869/469–6238* ⊗ *No lunch.*

$$$$ ECLECTIC Fodor's Choice ★ **✕ Montpelier Plantation & Beach.** The Hoffman family presides over a scintillating evening, starting with canapés and cocktails in the civilized plantation great room. Dinner is served on the breezy west veranda, dubbed Restaurant 750, overlooking the lights of Charlestown and St. Kitts. Executive chef Stéphane Caumont uses the inn's organic herb gardens and fruit trees to full advantage. The changing three-course menu might present vanilla-scented parsnip soup with morel powder; signature pan-seared sea scallops with green asparagus cream, Serrano ham crisp, and apple chutney; and dark chocolate tart with caramelized banana, vanilla milk shake, and almond crumble. The exemplary wine list is perfectly matched to the cuisine. The Mill Privée opens with sufficient reservations, offering a different set multicourse menu accompanied by champagne and sorbets. Torches illuminate cobblestone steps up to this theatrical sugar mill with crystal sconces, floating candles, and an antique mahogany gear wheel suspended from the ceiling. Tapas, salads, and grilled items are available at the poolside Indigo. Finish with one of the infused rums. Stéphane offers cooking classes as well as tasty souvenirs under the M logo. $ *Average main: US$60* ✉ *Montpelier Estate* ☎ *869/469–3462* 🌐 *www.montpeliernevis.com* ✍ *Reservations essential* ⊗ *Closed late Aug.–early Oct.*

$$$$ ECLECTIC **✕ Mount Nevis Hotel & Beach Club.** Mount Nevis's sublime open-air dining room by the pool offers a splendid view of St. Kitts. Before dinner, savor cocktails in the distinctive lounge, accented by sisal rugs, mosaic tiles, towering bamboo stalks, and a cool mostly blue color scheme. Maine-born chef Nick Gratton apprenticed with such top toques as Clark Frazier and Justin Walker; he deftly blends local ingredients, many grown in the organic garden, with a cornucopia of Caribbean-Continental cuisines. Sterling starters on the ever-changing menu might include wahoo poke accented by white soy sauce, tobiko, sesame, and cilantro, from which you might segue to duck breast with potato, green banana, and curried pumpkin. Finish with tropical variations on classics such as coconut flan. $ *Average main: US$32* ✉ *Shaws Rd., Mt. Nevis Estates* ☎ *869/469–9373* 🌐 *www.mountnevishotel.com* ✍ *Reservations essential.*

$$$$ ECLECTIC **✕ Nisbet Plantation Beach Club.** The blissfully air-conditioned great house is an oasis of polished hardwood floors, mahogany and cherrywood furnishings, equestrian bronzes, antique hurricane lamps, wicker furnishings, and works by famed Nevisian artist Eva Wilkin. Tables on the veranda look down the palm-tree-lined fairway to the sea. The four-course menu combines Continental, Pacific Rim, and Caribbean cuisines with local ingredients. The more mature clientele dictates less complex options from house-cured gravlax to filet mignon with chipotle butter in zinfandel reduction. But executive chef Antonio Piani might sneak in conch-breadfruit-and-dumpling soup, lobster stuffed with king crab leg ragout in coconut creole glaze, and lemon-and-vanilla mascarpone mousse with hazelnut praline. Enjoy an impressively

cosmopolitan selection of cocktails or coffee with soft live music in the front bar. Witty, dapper maître d' Patterson Fleming (his cravat collection, more than 1,000 augmented by guests over the years, is enviable!) ensures a smooth, swank experience. *Average main: US$65 Newcastle 869/469–9325 www.nisbetplantation.com Reservations essential.*

$$$ ECLECTIC **The Rocks at Golden Rock.** This glam eatery's tiered setting may be a genuine artistic and engineering masterpiece. Glass panels and ceilings display the night sky while reflecting patio lights. A series of cascading waterfalls, chutes, limpid pools, lily ponds, and fountains filigree the surrounding landscaped jungle with liquid silver. Strategically placed boulders resemble hulking Henry Moore sculpture; even the cut stone was painstakingly joined without mortar. Decor playfully contrasts classic and modern. A stone gazebo recalls an upside-down plantation-era copper boiler (the patio's barrel-vaulting also slyly mimics sugar equipment). Contemporary and colonial artworks from Mali and Afghanistan grace the interior. Sadly the kitchen doesn't quite match the setting's splendor or creativity. But the atmosphere more than compensates, and solid choices include jerk pork with pineapple relish or pan-roasted snapper with crispy risotto cake and red-pepper coulis. *Average main: US$28 Gingerland 869/469–3346 www.goldenrocknevis.com Reservations essential No lunch.*

$$ CARIBBEAN **Sunshine's.** Everything about this shack overlooking (and spilling onto) the beach is larger than life, including the Rasta man Llewelyn "Sunshine" Caines himself. Flags and license plates from around the world complement the international patrons (including an occasional movie or sports star wandering down from the Four Seasons). Picnic tables are splashed with bright sunrise-to-sunset colors; even the palm trees are painted, though "it gone upscaled," as locals say, with VIP cabanas. Fishermen cruise up with their catch—you might savor lobster rolls or snapper creole. Don't miss the lethal house specialty, Killer Bee rum punch. As Sunshine boasts, "One and you're stung, two, you're stunned, three, it's a knockout." *Average main: US$18 Pinney's Beach 869/469–5817 www.sunshinesnevis.com.*

WHERE TO STAY

Many lodgings are in restored manor or plantation houses scattered throughout the island's five parishes (counties). The owners often live at these inns, and it's easy to feel as if you've been personally invited down for a visit. Before dinner you may find yourself in the drawing room having a cocktail and conversing with the family, other guests, or visitors who have come for a meal. Meal plans for most inns include breakfast and dinner (plus afternoon tea) and offer a free shuttle service to their "private" stretch of beach. If you require TVs and air-conditioning, you're better off staying at hotels and simply dining with the engaging inn owners. Two major (by Nevisian standards) condo developments, with at least Phase 1 completed by late 2015, will nearly double the island's room inventory. Hamilton Beach Villas & Spa opened its first fully equipped condos on Cotton Ground Beach in 2013; the 10-building project will comprise a total of 79 self-catering units, as

Restaurants ▼
Bananas 3
Coconut Grove ... 9
Coral Grill 11
Double Deuce ... 2
Hermitage Plantation Inn ... 4
Mango 10
Montpelier Plantation 6
Mount Nevis Hotel & Beach Club 8
Nisbet 7
The Rocks 5
Sunshine's 1

Hotels ▼
Four Seasons 7
Golden Rock 3
Hermitage 1
Lindbergh Landing 9
Montpelier Plantation 2
Mount Nevis Hotel & Beach Club 5
Nisbet 4
Oualie Beach 6
Paradise Beach Nevis 8

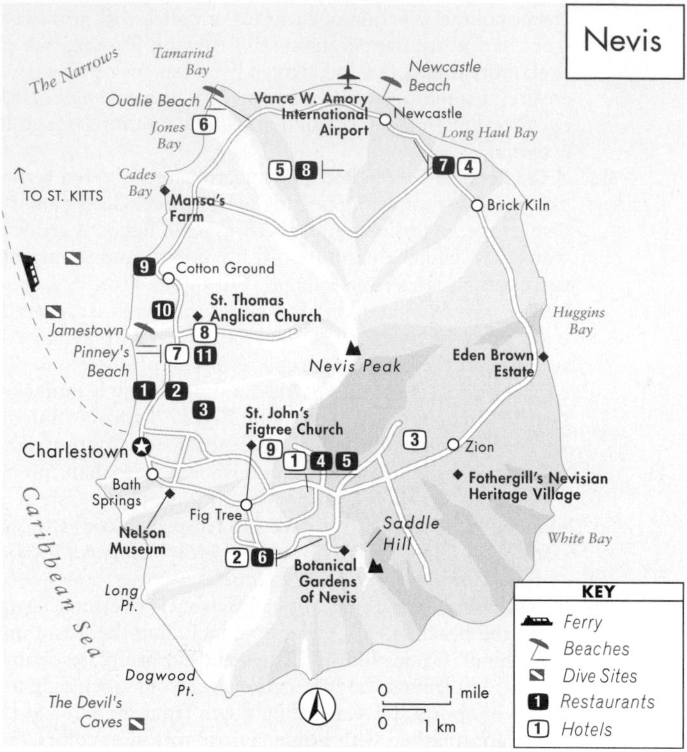

Nevis
The Narrows
Tamarind Bay
Newcastle Beach
Oualie Beach
Vance W. Amory International Airport
Newcastle
Jones Bay
Long Haul Bay
Cades Bay
TO ST. KITTS
Mansa's Farm
Brick Kiln
Cotton Ground
St. Thomas Anglican Church
Huggins Bay
Jamestown
Pinney's Beach
Nevis Peak
Eden Brown Estate
St. John's Figtree Church
Charlestown
Zion
Bath Springs
Fothergill's Nevisian Heritage Village
Fig Tree
Saddle Hill
Nelson Museum
White Bay
Caribbean Sea
Botanical Gardens of Nevis
Long Pt.
Dogwood Pt.
The Devil's Caves
0 1 mile
0 1 km
KEY
Ferry
Beaches
Dive Sites
Restaurants
Hotels

well as a spa, gym, pool, and tennis courts upon expected completion in 2015. The even more ambitious Tamarind Cove broke ground in 2012; plans call for six buildings housing 91 units, plus a pool, clubhouse with restaurant and shopping arcade, seafront boardwalk with more retail and dining, and a 120-berth marina. Other small upscale compounds are in various stages of development, including the Paradise Villa development (not to be confused with Paradise Beach), the overhauled Cliffdwellers at Tamarind Bay and the Zenith Beach houses, connected with the delightful Chrishi Beach Club on Cades Bay.

$$$$ RESORT FAMILY Fodor's Choice ★ **Four Seasons Resort Nevis.** This beachfront beauty impeccably combines world-class elegance with West Indian hospitality while scrupulously maintaining and upgrading facilities. **Pros:** luxury without attitude; superlative service; marvelous food; dazzling golf and spa; **Cons:** pricey; sometimes overrun by conventions and incentive groups (off-season mainly); berms added as secondary defense against storm surges impede some beachfront room views. *Rooms from: US$795 ✉ Pinney's Beach ☎ 869/469–1111, 869/469–6238, 800/332–3442 in U.S., 800/268–6282 in Canada 🌐 www.fourseasons.com/nevis 179 rooms, 17 suites, 61 villas No meals.*

$$ HOTEL **Golden Rock Plantation Inn.** Acclaimed artists Brice Marden and wife Helen Harrington have imparted a chic, modernist sensibility to this

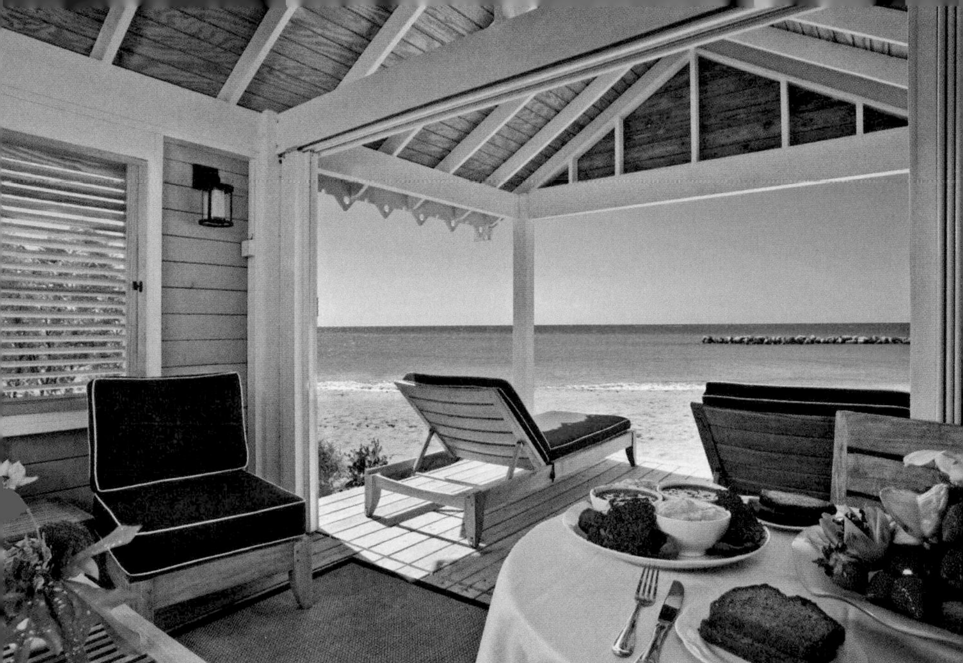
Four Seasons Resort Nevis

18th-century estate property while respecting its storied past. **Pros:** eco-friendly; arty crowd; glorious grounds; free Wi-Fi. **Cons:** no actual beach, though there are two beach clubs; lack of air-conditioning can be a problem on still days. *Rooms from: US$290* ✉ *Gingerland* ☎ *869/469–3346* 🌐 *www.goldenrocknevis.com, www.golden-rock.com* *16 rooms, 1 suite* *Closed mid-Aug.–mid-Oct.* *Breakfast.*

$ HOTEL Fodor's Choice ★ **Hermitage Plantation Inn.** A snug 1670 great house—reputedly the Caribbean's oldest surviving wooden building—forms the heart of this breeze-swept hillside hideaway. **Pros:** wonderful sense of history; delightful owners and clientele; delicious food. **Cons:** long drive to beach; hillside setting difficult for physically challenged to negotiate. *Rooms from: US$255* ✉ *Hermitage Rd., Gingerland* ☎ *869/469–3477, 800/682–4025* 🌐 *www.hermitagenevis.com* *8 rooms, 8 cottages, 1 house* *Multiple meal plans.*

$ B&B/INN **Lindbergh Landing.** Spencer and Jacqueline "Jackie" Harvey's charming and chill hillside inn abounds in color and personality. **Pros:** affordable; warm hospitality; sensational views. **Cons:** no air-conditioning can be problematic on rare still days; dicey Wi-Fi signal; three-day minimum stay required. *Rooms from: US$150* ✉ *Dr. Penn Heights, Church Ground, Gingerland* ☎ *869/469–3398* 🌐 *www.lindberghlandingnevis.com* *2 rooms* *Multiple meal plans.*

$$$ RESORT Fodor's Choice ★ **Montpelier Plantation & Beach.** This Nevisian beauty, a Rélais & Châteaux property, epitomizes understated elegance and graciously updated plantation living. **Pros:** impeccable service and attention to detail; lovely cuisine; exquisite gardens; trendily minimalist decor; complimentary Wi-Fi. **Cons:** some may find it a little stuffy; no beach on-site. *Rooms from: US$445* ✉ *Montpelier Estate* ☎ *869/469–3462, 800/735–2478*

www.montpeliernevis.com *17 rooms, 2 one-bedroom villas, 1 two-bedroom villa* *Closed mid-Aug.–mid-Oct.* *Multiple meal plans.*

$$ HOTEL **Mount Nevis Hotel & Beach Club.** The personable, attentive Meguid family blends the intimacy of the plantation inns, contemporary amenities of the Four Seasons, and typical Nevisian warmth in this hilltop aerie. **Pros:** friendly staff; fantastic views; free Wi-Fi; complimentary cell phone (pay for card). **Cons:** lacks beach; long drive to many island activities; occasional plane noise. *Rooms from: US$350* *Shaws Rd., Mount Nevis* *869/469–9373, 800/756–3847* *www.mountnevishotel.com* *32 rooms, 32 suites, 10 villas* *Breakfast.*

$$$$ RESORT Fodor's Choice ★ **Nisbet Plantation Beach Club.** At this beachfront plantation inn, pale yellow cottages face a regal, palm-lined grass avenue that sweeps to a lovely champagne-hue beach. **Pros:** beautiful setting; environmentally conscious practices; plentiful recreational options; free Wi-Fi; complimentary afternoon tea. **Cons:** long drive to most activities on island; airplanes occasionally whoosh by; food is variable. *Rooms from: US$712* *Newcastle* *869/469–9325, 800/742–6008* *www.nisbetplantation.com* *36 rooms* *Some meals.*

$ RESORT **Oualie Beach Hotel.** These creole-style gingerbread cottages daubed in cotton-candy colors sit just steps from a beach overlooking St. Kitts and are carefully staggered to ensure sea views from every room. **Pros:** fantastic water-sports operations; affordable (especially with recreational packages); appealing beach; Green Globe-certified. **Cons:** showing some wear; not ideal for less active types. *Rooms from: US$180* *Oualie Beach* *869/469–9735* *www.oualiebeach.com* *32 rooms* *Multiple meal plans.*

$$$$ RENTAL **Paradise Beach Nevis.** This exclusive villa enclave cascades down a lushly landscaped hill to Pinney's Beach. **Pros:** luxurious; well-equipped; private and quiet. **Cons:** pricey; few on-site facilities; not the nicest stretch of Pinney's Beach. *Rooms from: US$3,100* *Pinney's Beach* *869/469–7900* *www.paradisebeachnevis.com* *2 3-bedroom villas, 5 4-bedroom villas* *No meals* *3-night minimum stay.*

NIGHTLIFE

In season it's usually easy to find a local calypso singer or a steel or string band performing at one of the hotels, notably the Four Seasons and Oualie Beach (which also features string musicians on homemade instruments Tuesday evening), as well as at the Pinney's bars. Scan the posters plastered on doorways announcing informal jump-ups. Though Nevis lacks high-tech discos, many restaurants and bars have live bands or DJs on weekends.

FAMILY Fodor's Choice ★ **Chrishi Beach Club.** Though more a daytime hangout (especially Sunday when Nevisians descend on the lovely beach with their families), Chrishi Beach Club remains happening through sunset thanks to vivacious Norwegian expats Hedda and Christian "Chrishi" Wienpahl. You can sprawl on beach waterbeds in the shady "Love Shack + Bar," or on comfy chaises in the "stripper" lounge, replete with pole for shimmying. Enjoy the righteous lounge mix (and mixology), the movie nights, the glorious St. Kitts views, and what Hedda calls "European

CLOSE UP

Nevis's Day at the Races

One of the Caribbean's most festive, endearingly idiosyncratic events is the Nevis Turf and Jockey Club's Day at the Races, held nine to 12 times a year on the wild and windswept Indian Castle course. I first experienced the event in the mid-1990s, when I met club president Richard "Lupi" Lupinacci, owner of the Hermitage Plantation Inn. Before even introducing himself, Richard sized me up in the driveway: "You look about the right size for a jockey. How's your seat?" His equally effervescent wife, Maureen, then interceded, "Darling, if you loathe horses, don't worry. In fact, Lupi and I have an agreement about the Jerk and Turkey Club. I get major jewels for every animal he buys."

Since my riding skills were rusty, it was decided that I should be a judge (despite questionable vision, even with glasses). "If it's really by a nose, someone will disagree with you either way," I was reassured. The next day presented a quintessential Caribbean scene. Although a serious cadre of aficionados (including the German consul) talked turf, the rest of the island seemed more interested in liming and enjoying lively music. Local ladies dished out heavenly barbecued chicken and devilish gossip. Sheep and cattle unconcernedly ambled across the course. But when real horses thundered around the oval, the wooden stands groaned under the weight of cheering crowds, and bookies hand-calculated the payouts.

The irregularly scheduled races continue, albeit now on a properly sodded track, as does the equine hospitality.

Hermitage Stables. Here you can opt for everything from horseback riding to jaunts in hand-carved mahogany carriages. ✉ *Hermitage Plantation Inn, Hermitage Rd., Gingerland* ☎ *869/469–3477* 🌐 *www.hermitagenevis.com.*

Nevis Equestrian Centre. The Nevis Equestrian Centre offers leisurely beach rides as well as more demanding canters through the lush hills, starting at $75. Lessons are sometimes available ($30 group, $40 private). ✉ *Clifton Estate, Cotton Ground, Pinney's Beach* ☎ *869/662–9118* 🌐 *www.nevishorseback.com.*

—Jordan Simon

café-style" food (salads, pizzas, sandwiches like Brie with sun-dried tomatoes and cranberries, and more substantial dishes like butterflied prawns in garlic-parsley sauce). Kids have their own club with fresh-fruit smoothies, DJs spin on Sexy Saturday Nights, and Hedda's fun funky HWD jewelry line (incorporating leather, coins, found objects) is on sale. Their new Zenith Resort, an adjacent villa development, has some spectacular units. No surprise that the menu boasts it's "The Place to See and Be Seen." ✉ *Next to Sea Bridge and Mansa's, Cades Bay* ☎ *869/662–3958, 869/662–3959* 🌐 *www.chrishibeachclub.com.*

Water Department Barbecue. The Water Department Barbecue is the informal name for a lively Friday-night jump-up that's run by two fellows (nicknamed The Pump Boys) from the local water department. Friday afternoons the tents go up and the grills are fired. Cars line the streets and the guys dish up fabulous barbecue ribs and chicken—as certain customers lobby to get their water pressure adjusted. It's a classic Caribbean scene. ✉ *Pump Rd., Charlestown.*

Yachtsman Grill. This beachfront eatery features nautical decor (sailboat models, keels, fishing rods, outboard motors) and seafood to match (pick your own lobster from the tank). It overflows with good cheer, especially during the joyous happy hours. Oenophiles will appreciate the Cruvinet dispensing several wines by the glass; the convivial owners, Greg and Evelyn, adore Austrian bottlings ("Not Australian, Austrian . . . as in *The Sound of Music*, brthplace of coffeehouses, lederhosen, dirndl dresses, schnitzel, and so on. . . ."). ✉ *At Hamilton Beach Villas, Nelson Spring* ☎ *869/469–1382* 🌐 *www.yachtsmangrill.com.*

SHOPPING

CLOTHING

Most hotels have their own boutiques.

Island Fever. The island's classiest shop carries an excellent selection of everything from bathing suits and dresses to straw bags and jewelry. ✉ *Main St., Charlestown* ☎ *869/469–0867.*

HANDICRAFTS

CraftHouse. This marvelous source for local specialties, from vetiver mats to leather moccasins, also has a smaller branch in the Cotton Ginnery. ✉ *Pinney's Rd., Charlestown* ☎ *869/469–5505.*

Nevis Handicraft Co-op Society. This shop across from the tourist office offers works by local artisans (clothing, ceramic ware, woven goods) and locally produced honey, hot sauces, and jellies (try the guava and soursop). ✉ *Main St., Charlestown* ☎ *869/469–1746.*

Newcastle Pottery. This cooperative has continued the age-old tradition of hand-built red-clay pottery fired over burning coconut husks. It's possible to watch the potters and purchase wares at their small Newcastle factory. ✉ *Main Rd., Newcastle* ☎ *869/469–9746.*

Philatelic Bureau. St. Kitts and Nevis are famous for their decorative, and sometimes valuable, stamps. Collectors will find real beauties here including the butterfly, hummingbird, and marine-life series. ✉ *Cotton Ginnery, opposite the tourist office, Charlestown* ☎ *869/469–0617.*

SPORTS AND THE OUTDOORS

BIKING

Windsurfing Nevis/Wheel World. This shop offers mountain-bike rentals, apparel, and specially tailored tours on Gary Fisher, Trek, Hybrid, and MTB bikes. The tours ($60–$80), led by Winston Crooke, a master windsurfer and competitive bike racer, encompass lush rain forest, majestic ruins, and spectacular views. Costs vary according to itinerary and ability level but are aimed generally at experienced riders. Winston and his team delight in sharing local knowledge, from history to culture. For those just renting (rates from $25 daily, $150 weekly), Winston determines your performance level and suggests appropriate routes. ✉ *Oualie Beach* ☎ *869/469–9682* 🌐 *www.bikenevis.com.*

DIVING AND SNORKELING

The **Devil's Caves** make up a series of grottoes where divers can navigate tunnels, canyons, and underwater hot springs while viewing lobsters, sea fans, sponges, squirrelfish, and more. The village of **Jamestown,** which washed into the sea around Ft. Ashby, just south of Cades Bay, makes for superior snorkeling and diving. Reef-protected Pinney's Beach offers especially good snorkeling. Single-tank dives are usually $80, two-tank dives $100; packages provide deep discounts.

FAMILY **Scuba Safaris.** This PADI Five Star facility and NASDS Examining Station is staffed by experienced dive masters who offer everything from a resort course to full certification to Nitrox. Their equipment is always state-of-the-art, including underwater scooters. It also provides a snorkeling learning experience that enables you not only to see but to listen to sea life, including whales and dolphins, as well as an exhilarating underwater scooter safari, night dives, and kids' bubblemakers. ✉ *Oualie Beach* ☎ *869/469–9518* 🌐 *www.scubanevis.com.*

FISHING

Fishing here focuses on kingfish, wahoo, grouper, tuna, and yellowtail snapper, with marlin occasionally spotted. The best areas are Monkey Shoals and around Redonda. Charters cost approximately $450–$500 per half day, $850–$1,000 per full day, and usually include an open bar.

Deep Venture. Run by fisherman–chef Matt Lloyd, Deep Venture does day-fishing charters (he keeps the catch), providing a real insight into both commercial fishing and the Caribbean kitchen. ✉ *Oualie Beach* ☎ *869/469–5110.*

GOLF

Fodor's Choice ★ **Four Seasons Golf Course.** The Robert Trent Jones Jr.–designed Four Seasons Golf Course is beautiful and impeccably maintained. The front 9 holes are fairly flat until Hole 8, which climbs uphill after your tee shot. Most of the truly stunning views are along the back 9. The signature hole is the 15th, a 660-yard monster that encompasses a deep ravine; other holes include bridges, steep drops, rolling pitches, extremely tight and unforgiving fairways, sugar-mill ruins, and fierce doglegs. Attentive attendants canvas the course with beverage buggies, handing out chilled, peppermint-scented towels and preordered Cubanos that help test the wind. There are huge kids', twilight, and off-season discounts. ✉ *Four Seasons Resort Nevis, Pinney's Beach* ☎ *869/469–1111* 🌐 *www.fourseasons.com/nevis* *$235 for hotel guests, $240 for nonguests high season* *18 holes, 6766 yards, par 72.*

GUIDED TOURS

TC's Island Tours. TC, a Yorkshire lass who used to drive a double-decker bus in England and has been married to a Nevisian for more than a decade, offers entertaining explorations via TC's Island Tours. ☎ *869/469–2911.*

HIKING

The center of the island is Nevis Peak—also known as Mt. Nevis—which soars 3,232 feet and is flanked by Hurricane Hill on the north and Saddle Hill on the south. If you plan to scale Nevis Peak, a daylong affair, it's highly recommended that you go with a guide. Your hotel can arrange it (and a picnic lunch) for you. The 9-mile (15-km) **Upper Round Road Trail** was constructed in the late 1600s and cleared and restored by the Nevis Historical and Conservation Society. It connects the Golden Rock Plantation Inn, on the east side of the island, with Nisbet Plantation Beach Club, on the northern tip. The trail encompasses numerous vegetation zones, including pristine rain forest, and impressive plantation ruins. The original cobblestones, walls, and ruins are still evident in many places.

Sunrise Tours. Run by Lynell and Earla Liburd (and their son Kervin), Sunrise Tours offers a range of hiking trips, but their most popular is Devil's Copper, a rock configuration full of ghostly legends. Local people gave it its name because at one time the water was hot—a volcanic thermal stream. The area features pristine waterfalls and splendid bird-watching. They also do a Nevis village walk, a Hamilton Estate Walk, a Charlestown tour, an Amerindian walk along the wild southeast Atlantic coast, and trips to the rain forest and Nevis Peak. They love highlighting Nevisian heritage, explaining time-honored cooking techniques, the many uses of dried grasses, and medicinal plants. Hikes range from $25 to $40 per person, and you receive a certificate of achievement. ☎ *869/469–2758* 🌐 *www.nevisnaturetours.com.*

WINDSURFING

Windsurfing Nevis. Waters are generally calm and northeasterly winds steady yet gentle, making Nevis an excellent spot for beginners and intermediates. Windsurfing Nevis offers top-notch instructors (Winston Crooke is one of the best in the islands) and equipment for $30 per hour. Beginners get equipment and two-hour instruction for $60. Groups are kept small (eight maximum), and the equipment is state-of-the-art from Mistral, North, and Tushingham. It also offers kayak rentals and tours along the coast, stopping at otherwise inaccessible beaches. ✉ *Oualie Beach* ☎ *869/469–9682.*

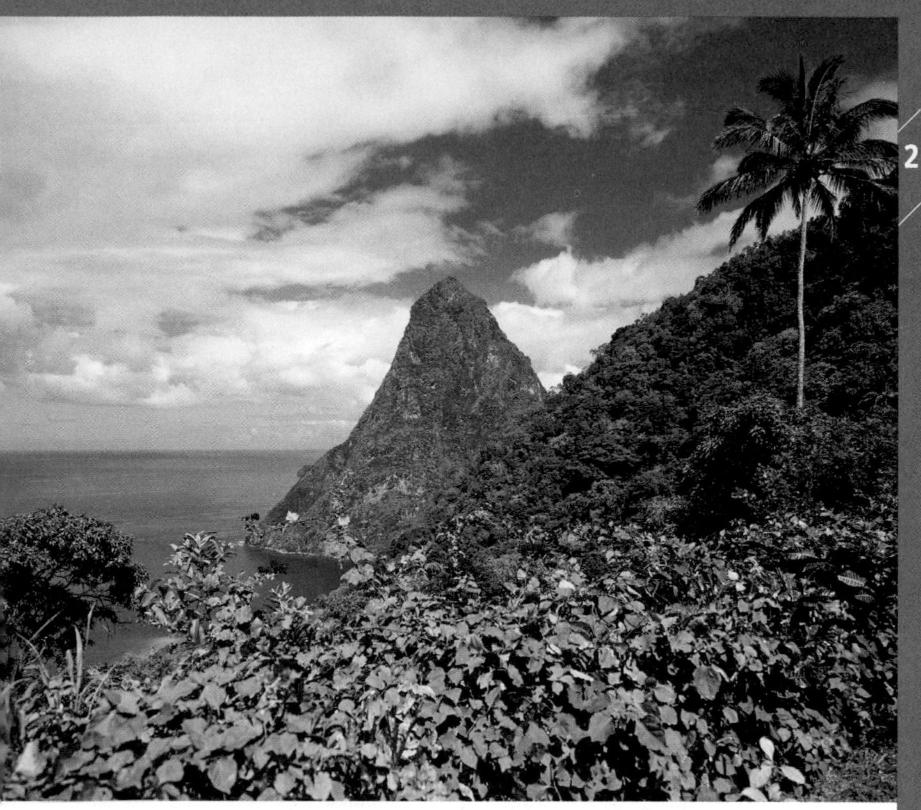

ST. LUCIA

WELCOME TO ST. LUCIA

THE CARIBBEAN'S TWIN PEAKS

St. Lucia, 27 miles (43.5 km) by 14 miles (22.5 km), is a volcanic island covered to a large extent by lush rain forest, much of which is protected as a national park. The most notable geological features are the Pitons, some 2,600-foot-high twin peaks designated a UNESCO World Heritage Site in 2004.

Restaurants ▼

Apsara **18**
Boucan **15**
Buzz **5**
Chateau Mygo **9**
The Cliff at Cap **6**
Coal Pot **1**
Dasheene **16**
Doolittle's **11**
The Edge **3**
The Hummingbird **12**
Jacques Waterfront Dining **2**
Jardin Cacao **17**
KoKo Cabana **4**
Orlando's **13**
Rainforest Hideaway **8**
Rowley's Café **10**
The Still **14**
Tao **7**

Hotels ▼

Anse Chastanet **20**
Bay Gardens Beach Resort **11**
Bay Gardens Hotel **10**
blu St. Lucia **12**
The Body Holiday **18**
Boucan by Hotel Chocolat **25**
Calabash Cove **7**
Cap Maison **15**
Coco Palm **9**
Coconut Bay **28**
Cotton Bay Village **17**
East Winds Inn **5**
Fond Doux Holiday Plantation **27**
Hummingbird **22**
Jade Mountain **21**
Ladera **24**
The Landings **14**
Rendezvous **2**
Royal St. Lucia by Rex **8**
St. James Club Morgan Bay **4**
Sandals Grande **13**
Sandals Halcyon **3**
Sandals Regency La Toc **1**
Smugglers Cove Resort & Spa **16**
Stonefield Estate **23**
Sugar Beach, A Viceroy Resort **26**
Ti Kaye Resort **19**
Windjammer Landing **6**

KEY

- *Beaches*
- *Dive Sites*
- *Ferry*
- *Cruise Ship Terminal*
- *Restaurants*
- *Hotels*
- *Rain Forest*

Explorers, pirates, soldiers, sugar planters, and coal miners have made their mark on this lovely landfall, and the lush tropical peaks known as the Pitons (Gros and Petit) have witnessed them all. Today's visitors come to snorkel and scuba dive in St. Lucia's calm cobalt-blue waters, sun themselves on its multihued beaches, and experience nature at its finest.

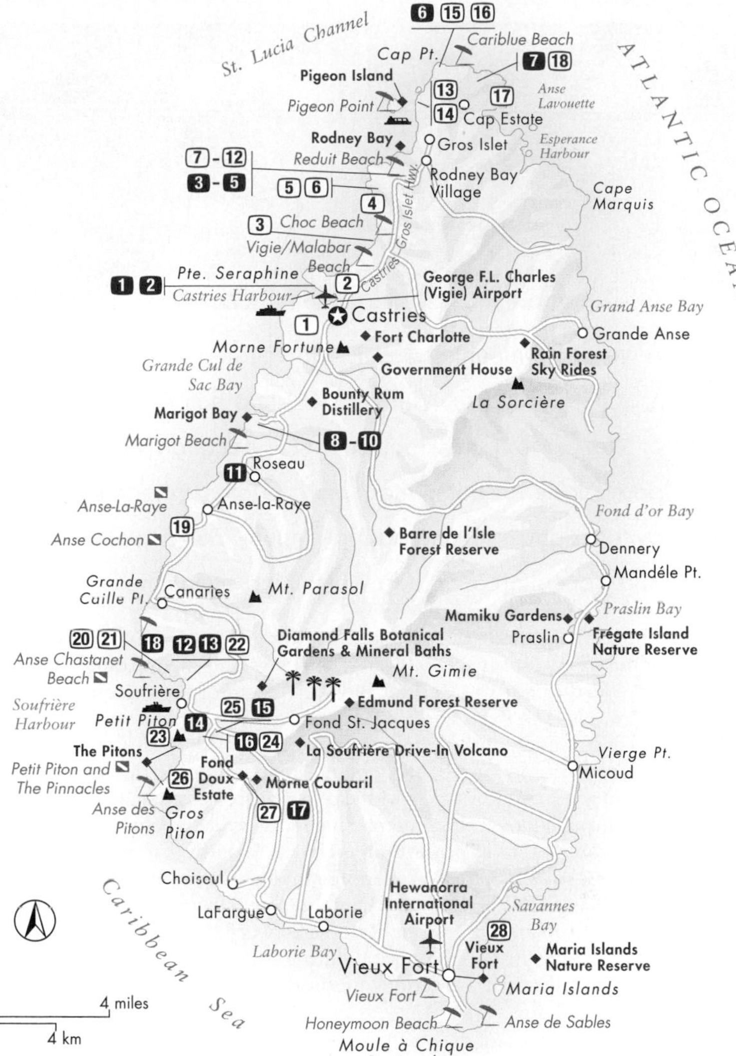

TOP REASONS TO VISIT ST. LUCIA

1 The Beauty: Magnificent, lush scenery makes St. Lucia one of the most beautiful Caribbean islands.

2 The Romance: A popular honeymoon spot, St. Lucia has abundant romantic retreats.

3 Indulgent Accommodations: Sybaritic lodging options include an all-inclusive spa resort, a posh sanctuary sandwiched between a mountain and the beach, and two resorts with prime locations between the Pitons.

4 St. Lucia Jazz: Performers and fans come from all over the world for this annual music festival.

5 The Welcome: The friendly St. Lucians love sharing their island and their cultural heritage with visitors.

Updated by Jane E. Zarem

A verdant, mountainous island located halfway between Martinique and St. Vincent, St. Lucia has evolved into one of the Caribbean's most popular vacation destinations—particularly for honeymooners and other romantics enticed by the island's striking natural beauty, many splendid resorts and appealing inns, and welcoming atmosphere.

The capital city of Castries and nearby villages in the northwest are home to 40% of the 180,000 St. Lucians. This area, Rodney Bay Village (farther north), Marigot Bay (just south of the capital), and Soufrière (southwestern coast) are the destinations of most vacationers. In central and southwestern areas, dense rain forest, jungle-covered mountains, and vast banana plantations dominate the landscape. A tortuous road follows most of the coastline, bisecting small villages, cutting through mountains, and passing fertile valleys. Petit Piton and Gros Piton, unusual twin peaks that anchor the southwestern coast and rise to more than 2,600 feet, are familiar landmarks for sailors and aviators as well as a UNESCO World Heritage Site. Divers are attracted to the reefs in the National Marine Reserve between the Pitons and extending north past Soufrière, the capital during French colonial times. Most of the natural tourist attractions are in this area, along with several fine resorts and inns.

The pirate François Le Clerc, nicknamed Jambe de Bois (Wooden Leg) for obvious reasons, was the first European "settler." In the late 16th century Le Clerc holed up on Pigeon Island, just off St. Lucia's northernmost point, using it as a staging ground for attacking passing ships. Now, Pigeon Island National Landmark is a public park connected by a causeway to the mainland; Sandals Grande St. Lucian Spa & Beach Resort, one of the largest resorts in St. Lucia, and the Landings, a luxury villa community, sprawl along that causeway.

Like most of its Caribbean neighbors, St. Lucia was first inhabited by Arawaks and then the Carib people. British settlers attempted to colonize the island twice in the early 1600s, but it wasn't until 1651, after the French West India Company suppressed the local Caribs,

LOGISTICS

Getting to St. Lucia: St. Lucia's primary gateway is Hewanorra International Airport (UVF) in Vieux Fort, on the island's southern tip. Regional airlines fly into George F.L. Charles Airport (SLU) in Castries, commonly called Vigie Airport, which is more convenient to resorts in the north. The 40-mile (64 km) drive between Hewanorra and resorts in the north takes about 90 minutes; the trip between Hewanorra and Soufrière takes about 45 minutes.

Hassle Factor: Medium–high due to the long and winding drive from Hewanorra International Airport.

On the Ground: Taxis are available at both airports, although transfers may be included in your travel package. It's an expensive ride to the north from Hewanorra—$80–$90 for up to four passengers—and $75–$80 to Soufrière. A helicopter shuttle cuts the transfer time to about 10 minutes, but the cost doubles.

Getting Around the Island: A car is more important if you are staying at a small inn or hotel away from the beach. If you're staying at an all-inclusive beach resort and you don't plan to leave for meals, taxis may be the better bet.

that Europeans gained a foothold. For 150 years, battles between the French and the British over the island were frequent, with a dizzying 14 changes in power before the British finally took possession in 1814. The Europeans established sugar plantations, using slaves from West Africa to work the fields. By 1838, when the slaves were emancipated, more than 90% of the population was of African descent—roughly the same proportion as today.

On February 22, 1979, St. Lucia became an independent state within the British Commonwealth of Nations, with a resident governor-general appointed by the queen. Still, the island appears to have retained more relics of French influence—notably the island's patois, cuisine, village names, and surnames—than of the British. Most likely, that's because the British contribution primarily involved the English language, the educational and legal systems, and the political structure, whereas the French culture historically had more influence on the arts—culinary, dance, and music.

PLANNING

WHEN TO GO

The high season runs from mid-December through mid-April and during the annual St. Lucia Jazz and Carnival events; at other times of the year, hotel rates may be significantly lower. December and January are the coolest months, and June through August are the hottest. Substantial rain (more than just a tropical spritz) is more likely from June through November; September and October are the most humid.

GETTING HERE AND AROUND

AIR TRAVEL

American Airlines flies nonstop from Miami, with connecting service from major cities. Delta flies nonstop from Atlanta and New York–JFK. JetBlue flies nonstop from New York–JFK and Philadelphia. United flies weekly nonstops from New York–Newark. US Airways flies nonstop from Charlotte and Philadelphia, with connecting service from major cities. Air Caraïbes flies from Guadeloupe and Martinique; LIAT flies from several neighboring islands.

Airline Contacts Air Caraïbes ☎ *758/453–0357* 🌐 *www.aircaraibes-usa.com.* **American Airlines** ☎ *800/744–0006, 758/459–6500* 🌐 *www.aa.com.* **Delta** ☎ *758/454–5594, 800/221–1212* 🌐 *www.delta.com.* **JetBlue** ☎ *877/766–9614* 🌐 *www.jetblue.com.* **LIAT** ☎ *888/844–5428, 758/452–2348* 🌐 *www.liat.com.* **United** ☎ *800/534–0089 in Caribbean, 800/864–8331 in U.S.* 🌐 *www.united.com.* **US Airways** ☎ *800/622–1015* 🌐 *www.usairways.com.*

Airports George F.L. Charles Airport (*SLU*). ✉ *Vigie, Castries* ☎ *758/457–6149.* **Hewanorra International Airport** (*UVF*). ✉ *Vieux Fort* ☎ *758/457–6160.*

Air Transfers St. Lucia Helicopters ☎ *758/453–6950* 🌐 *www.stluciahelicopters.com.*

BOAT AND FERRY TRAVEL

When cruise ships are in port in Castries, a water taxi shuttles back and forth between Pointe Seraphine (on the north side of the harbor) and La Place Carenage (on the south side) for $2 per person each way. L'Express des Iles travels between St. Lucia and Martinique, Dominica, and Guadeloupe.

Contacts L'Express des Iles ☎ *758/456–5000* 🌐 *www.express-des-iles.com.*

BUS TRAVEL

Privately owned and operated minivans constitute St. Lucia's bus system, an inexpensive and efficient means of transportation used primarily by local people. Buses have green number plates beginning with the letter "M." They are a good way to travel between Castries and the Rodney Bay area; the fare is EC$2 (ideally payable in local currency). You can also travel from Castries to Soufrière (two-plus hours, EC$10), but that is definitely an arduous ride. Wait at a marked stop and hail the passing minivan. Let the conductor or driver know where you need to go, and he'll stop at the appropriate place.

CAR TRAVEL

Roads throughout St. Lucia, except north of Castries, are winding and mountainous, making driving a challenge for timid or apprehensive drivers and exhausting for everyone else. You drive on the left, British-style. Seat belts are required, and speed limits are enforced, especially in Castries.

Car Rentals To rent a car you must be at least 25 years old and provide a valid driver's license and a credit card. If you don't have an international driver's license, you must buy a temporary St. Lucia driving permit for $21 (EC$54), which is valid for three months, at the car-rental office or the immigration office at either airport. Car-rental rates are usually quoted in U.S. dollars and range from $80 to $90 per day or $400 to $540 per week.

Car-Rental Contacts Avis ✉ *Vide Bouteille, Castries* ☎ *758/452–2700* 🌐 *www.avisstlucia.com* ✉ *Hewanorra International Airport, Vieux Fort* ☎ *758/454–6325* ✉ *George F. L. Charles Airport, Vigie* ☎ *758/452–2046.* **Cool Breeze Jeep/Car Rental** ✉ *Soufrière* ☎ *758/459–7729* 🌐 *www.coolbreezecarrental.com.* **Cost-Less Rent-a-Car & Internet Café** ✉ *Harmony Suites, Rodney Bay Village, Gros Islet* ☎ *758/450–3416* 🌐 *www.costless-rentacar.com.* **Courtesy Car Rental** ✉ *Rodney Bay Village, Gros Islet* ☎ *758/452–8140* 🌐 *www.courtesycarrentals.com.*

TAXI TRAVEL

Fully licensed taxis have number plates beginning with "TX." They are unmetered, although fares are fairly standard. Sample fares for up to four passengers are: Castries to Rodney Bay, $25; Rodney Bay to Cap Estate, $12; Castries to Cap Estate, $25; Castries to Marigot Bay, $30; Castries to Anse la Raye, $40; Castries to Soufrière, $80–$100; Castries to Vieux Fort, $80; and Soufrière to Vieux Fort, $75–$80. Always ask the driver to quote the price *before* you get in, and be sure that you both understand whether it's quoted in EC or U.S. dollars. Drivers are generally careful, knowledgeable, and courteous.

ESSENTIALS

Banks and Exchange Services The official currency is the Eastern Caribbean dollar (EC$), but U.S. dollars (not coins) are accepted nearly everywhere—although you will likely receive your change in local currency. Major credit cards and traveler's checks are also widely accepted. ATMs dispense only local currency. Major banks on the island include Bank of St. Lucia, Bank of Nova Scotia (Scotiabank), FirstCaribbean International Bank, and Royal Bank of Canada.

Electricity The electric current on St. Lucia is 220 volts, 50 cycles, with a square, three-pin plug (U.K. standard). You'll need a transformer to convert voltage and a plug adapter to use most North American appliances; dual-voltage computer and phone chargers or other appliances will still need a plug adapter, which you can often borrow from the hotel. More and more hotels and resorts have added 110-volt outlets for general use but sometimes only for electric razors. Many hotels and resorts also provide iPod docking stations.

Emergency Services Ambulance and Fire ☎ *911, 758/452–2373 nonemergencies.* **Police** ☎ *999, 758/452–2854 nonemergencies.*

Passport Requirements U.S. and Canadian citizens must have a valid passport to enter St. Lucia and a return or ongoing ticket.

Phones The area code for St. Lucia is 758. You can make direct-dial overseas and interisland calls from St. Lucia, and the connections are excellent. You can charge an overseas call to a major credit card with no surcharge; from public phones and many hotels, dial 811 to charge the call to your credit card. Some hotels charge a small fee (usually about EC$1) for local calls. Many retail outlets sell phone cards to use for either local or international calls from any touch-tone telephone (including pay phones) in St. Lucia. Your cell phone will likely work in St. Lucia, but the international roaming charges are expensive. Your U.S. service provider may offer reasonable short-term international talk, text, and data plans. Also, be sure to turn off the "data roaming" feature on your phone when traveling internationally, as the application updates that continuously occur in the background whenever your phone is turned on are prohibitively expensive if you're not in a Wi-Fi environment.

Safety Although crime isn't a significant problem, take the same precautions that you would at home—lock your door, secure your valuables, and don't carry too much money or flaunt expensive jewelry on the street or at the beach.

Taxes and Service Charges A government V.A.T. (value-added tax) of 10% is added to all hotel and restaurant bills, as well as services such as tours, excursions, tram rides, zip lines, hair braiding, and massages. Most restaurants and some hotels also add a service charge of 10% in lieu of tipping.

ACCOMMODATIONS

Nearly all St. Lucia's resorts and small inns face unspoiled beaches or are hidden away on secluded coves or tucked into forested hillsides in three locations along the calm Caribbean (western) coast. They're in the greater Castries area between Marigot Bay, a few miles south of the city, and Labrelotte Bay in the north; in and around Rodney Bay Village and north to Cap Estate; and in and around Soufrière on the southwest coast near the Pitons. There's only one resort in Vieux Fort, near Hewanorra. The advantage of being in the north is that you have access to a wider range of restaurants and nightlife; in the south, you may be limited to your hotel's offerings and a few other restaurants—albeit some of the best—in and around Soufrière.

Hotel reviews have been shortened. For full information, visit Fodors.com.

WHAT IT COSTS IN U.S. DOLLARS

	$	$$	$$$	$$$$
Restaurants	under $12	$12–$20	$21–$30	over $30
Hotels	under $275	$275–$375	$376–$475	over $475

Restaurant prices are the average cost of a main course at dinner or, if dinner is not served, at lunch. Hotel prices are the lowest cost of a standard double room in high season.

VISITOR INFORMATION

Contacts St. Lucia Tourist Board ☎ *212/867–2950, 800/456–3984 in U.S.* ⊕ *www.stlucianow.com.* **Soufrière Tourist Information Centre** ✉ *Maurice Mason St., Soufrière* ☎ *758/459–7419* ⊙ *Weekdays 8–4:30.*

WEDDINGS

Wedding licenses cost $125 with a required three-day waiting period or $200 with no waiting period, plus $60 for the associated registrar and certificate fees. You'll need to produce valid passports and original or certified copies of divorce decrees or death certificates, if applicable.

Some resorts offer free weddings when combined with a honeymoon stay.

EXPLORING

Except for a small area in the extreme northeast, one main highway circles all of St. Lucia. The road snakes along the coast, cuts across mountains, makes hairpin turns and sheer drops, and reaches dizzying heights. It takes at least four hours to drive the whole loop. Even at a leisurely pace with frequent sightseeing stops, and whether you're driving or being driven, the curvy roads make it a tiring drive in a single outing.

The West Coast Road between Castries and Soufrière (a 1½-hour journey) has steep hills and sharp turns, but it's well marked and incredibly scenic. South of Castries, the road tunnels through Morne Fortune, skirts the island's largest banana plantation (more than 127 varieties of bananas, called "figs" in this part of the Caribbean, grow on the island), and passes through tiny fishing villages. Just north of Soufrière the road negotiates the island's fruit basket, where most of the mangoes, breadfruit, tomatoes, limes, and oranges are grown. In the mountainous region that forms a backdrop for Soufrière, you will notice 3,118-foot Mt. Gimie (pronounced Jimmy), St. Lucia's highest peak. Approaching Soufrière, you'll have spectacular views of the Pitons; the spume of smoke wafting out of the thickly forested mountainside just east of Soufrière emanates from the so-called "drive-in" volcano.

The landscape changes dramatically between the Pitons and Vieux Fort on the island's southeastern tip. Along the South Coast Road traveling southeasterly from Soufrière, the terrain starts as steep mountainside with dense vegetation, progresses to undulating hills, and finally becomes rather flat and comparatively arid. Anyone arriving at Hewanorra International Airport, which is in Vieux Fort, and staying at a resort near Soufrière will travel along this route, a journey of about 45 minutes each way.

From Vieux Fort north to Castries, a 1½-hour drive, the East Coast Road twists through Micoud, Dennery, and other coastal villages. It then winds up, down, and around mountains, crosses Barre de l'Isle Ridge, and slices through the rain forest. Much of the scenery is breathtaking. The Atlantic Ocean pounds against rocky cliffs, and acres and acres of bananas and coconut palms blanket the hillsides. If you arrive at Hewanorra and stay at a resort in Marigot Bay, Castries, Rodney Bay, or Cap Estate, you'll travel along the East Coast Road.

CASTRIES AND THE NORTH

Castries, the capital city, and the area north and just south of it are the island's most developed areas. The roads are mostly flat, straight, and easy to navigate. The beaches are some of the island's best. Rodney Bay Marina and most of the resorts, restaurants, and nightspots are north of Castries. Pigeon Island, one of the important historical sites, is at the island's northwestern tip. Picturesque Marigot Bay, about 15

DID YOU KNOW?

Dunstan St. Omer, whose frescoes can be seen in Castries's Cathedral of the Immaculate Conception, also designed the nation's flag.

CLOSE UP

Embracing Kwéyòl

English is St. Lucia's official language, but most St. Lucians speak Kwéyòl—a French-based Creole language—and often use it for informal conversations among themselves. Primarily a spoken language, Kwéyòl in its written version doesn't look at all like French; pronounce the words phonetically, though—*entenasyonnal* (international), for example, or the word *Kwéyòl* (Creole) itself—and you indeed sound as if you're speaking French.

Pretty much the same version of the Creole language, or patois, is spoken in the nearby island of Dominica. Otherwise, the St. Lucian Kwéyòl is quite different from that spoken in other Caribbean islands that have a French and African heritage, such as Haiti, Guadeloupe, and Martinique—or elsewhere, such as Mauritius, Madagascar, and the state of Louisiana. The Kwéyòl spoken in St. Lucia and Dominica is mostly unintelligible to people from those other locations—and vice versa.

St. Lucia embraces its Creole heritage by devoting the month of October each year to celebrations that preserve and promote Creole culture, language, and traditions. Events and performances highlight Creole music, food, dance, theater, native costumes, church services, traditional games, folklore, native medicine—a little bit of everything, or *tout bagay,* as you say in Kwéyòl.

Creole Heritage Month culminates at the end of October with all-day events and activities on Jounen Kwéyòl Entenasyonnal, or International Creole Day, which is recognized by all countries that speak a version of Creole.

minutes south of Castries, is both a yacht haven and a lovely destination for landlubbers.

TOP ATTRACTIONS

Castries. The capital, a busy commercial city of about 65,000 people (one-third of the island's population), wraps around sheltered Castries Bay. Morne Fortune rises sharply to the south, creating a dramatic green backdrop. The charm of Castries lies in its liveliness rather than its architecture, since four fires between 1796 and 1948 destroyed most of the colonial buildings. Freighters (exporting bananas, coconut, cocoa, mace, nutmeg, and citrus fruits) and cruise ships come and go frequently, making Castries Harbour one of the Caribbean's busiest ports. **Pointe Seraphine** is a duty-free shopping complex on the north side of the bay, about a 20-minute walk or two-minute cab ride from the city center; a launch ferries passengers across the harbor when cruise ships are in port. Pointe Seraphine's attractive Spanish-style architecture houses more than 20 duty-free shops, a tourist information kiosk, and a taxi stand. **La Place Carenage,** on the south side of the harbor near the pier and markets, is another duty-free shopping complex with a dozen or more shops and a café. **Derek Walcott Square,** a green oasis bordered by Brazil, Laborie, Micoud, and Bourbon streets, honors the hometown poet who won the 1992 Nobel Prize in Literature—one of two Nobel laureates from St. Lucia (the late Sir W. Arthur Lewis won the 1979 Nobel in economics). Some of the few 19th-century buildings that survived fire, wind, and rain can be seen on Brazil Street, the square's southern border. On the Laborie Street side, there's a huge, 400-year-old samaan (monkeypod) tree with leafy branches that shade a good portion of the square. Directly across Laborie Street from Derek Walcott Square is the Roman Catholic **Cathedral of the Immaculate Conception,** which was built in 1897. Though it's rather somber on the outside, colorful murals by St. Lucian artist Dunstan St. Omer decorate the interior walls. The murals were reworked prior to the visit of Pope John Paul II in 1985. The church has an active parish and is open daily for both public viewing and religious services. ✉ *Castries.*

Castries Market. Under a brilliant orange roof, this bustling market is at its liveliest on Saturday morning, when farmers bring their produce and spices to town—as they have for more than a century. (It's closed Sunday.) Next door to the produce market is the **Craft Market,** where you can buy pottery, wood carvings, and handwoven straw articles, and innumerable souvenirs, trinkets, and gewgaws. At the **Vendors' Arcade**, across Peynier Street from the Craft Market, you'll find still more handicrafts and souvenirs. ✉ *Jeremie and Peynier Sts., Castries.*

Fodor's Choice ★ **Marigot Bay.** This is one of the prettiest natural harbors in the Caribbean. In 1778, British admiral Samuel Barrington sailed into this secluded bay-within-a-bay and, the story goes, covered his ships with palm fronds to hide them from the French. Today this small community is a favorite anchorage for boaters and a peaceful destination for landlubbers, with a luxury resort, several small inns and restaurants, and a marina village with a snack shop, grocery store, bakery, and boutiques. A 24-hour ferry ($2 round-trip) connects the bay's two shores—a voyage that takes a minute or two each way. ✉ *Marigot Bay.*

FAMILY **Rainforest Adventures.** Ever wish you could get a bird's-eye view of the rain forest? Or at least experience it without hiking up and down miles of mountain trails? Here's your chance. Depending on your athleticism and spirit of adventure, choose a two-hour aerial tram ride, a zip-line experience, or both. Either activity guarantees a magnificent view as you peacefully ride above or actively zip through the canopy of the 3,442-acre Castries Waterworks Rain Forest in Babonneau, 30 minutes east of Rodney Bay. On the tram ride, eight-passenger gondolas glide slowly among the giant trees, twisting vines, and dense thickets of vegetation accented by colorful flowers as a tour guide explains and shares anecdotes about the various trees, plants, birds, and other wonders of nature found in the area. The zip line, on the other hand, is a thrilling experience in which you're rigged with a harness, helmet, and clamps that attach to cables strategically strung through the forest. Short trails connect 18 platforms, so riders come down to earth briefly and hike to the next station before speeding through the forest canopy to the next stop. There's even a nighttime zip-line tour. **■ TIP→ Bring binoculars and a camera.** ✉ *Chassin, Babonneau* ☎ *758/458–5151, 866/759–8726 in U.S.* 🌐 *www.rainforestadventure.com* 🎫 *Tram $95, zip line $85, combo $100, night zip $87* ⏲ *Tues.–Thurs. and Sun. 9–4, night zip at 6.*

Rodney Bay. Hotels, popular restaurants, a huge mall, and the island's only casino surround a natural bay and an 80-acre man-made lagoon named for Admiral George Rodney, who sailed the British navy out of Gros Islet Bay in 1780 to attack and ultimately destroy the French fleet. With 253 slips, Rodney Bay Marina is one of the Caribbean's premier yachting centers; each December, it's the destination of the Atlantic Rally for Cruisers (a transatlantic yacht crossing). Yacht charters and sightseeing day trips can be arranged at the marina. Rodney Bay is about 15 minutes north of Castries. ✉ *Rodney Bay Village, Gros Islet.*

WORTH NOTING

Bounty Rum Distillery. St. Lucia Distillers, which produces the island's own Bounty and Chairman's Reserve rums, offers 90-minute Rhythm of Rum tours that cover the history of sugar, the background of rum, a detailed description of the distillation process, colorful displays of local architecture, a glimpse at a typical rum shop, Caribbean music, and a chance to sample the company's rums and liqueurs. The distillery is at the Roseau Sugar Factory in the Roseau Valley, on the island's largest banana plantation, a few miles south of Castries and not far from Marigot. Reservations for the tour are essential. ✉ *Roseau Sugar Factory, West Coast Rd., near Marigot, Roseau* ☎ *758/456–3148* 🌐 *www.saintluciarums.com* 🎫 *$10* 🕘 *Weekdays 9–3.*

Ft. Charlotte. Begun in 1764 by the French as the Citadelle du Morne Fortune, Ft. Charlotte was completed after 20 years of battling and changing hands. Its old barracks and batteries are now government buildings and local educational facilities, but you can drive around and look at the remains of redoubts, a guardroom, stables, and cells. You can also walk up to the Inniskilling Monument, a tribute to the 1796 battle in which the 27th Foot Royal Inniskilling Fusiliers wrested the Morne from the French. At the military cemetery, first used in 1782, faint inscriptions on the tombstones tell the tales of French and English soldiers who died in St. Lucia. Six former governors of the island are also buried here. From this point atop Morne Fortune, you have a beautiful view of Castries Harbour, Martinique farther north, and the Pitons to the south. ✉ *Morne Fortune, Castries.*

Government House. The official residence of the governor-general—and one of the island's few remaining examples of Victorian architecture—is perched high above Castries, halfway up Morne Fortune (Hill of Good Fortune), which forms a backdrop for the capital city. Morne Fortune has also seen more than its share of *bad* luck, including devastating hurricanes and four fires that leveled Castries. Within Government House is **Le Pavillon Royal Museum,** which houses important historical photographs and documents, artifacts, crockery, silverware, medals, and awards; original architectural drawings of the house are displayed on the walls. Note that you must make an appointment to visit. ✉ *Morne Fortune, Castries* ☎ *758/452–2481* 🎫 *Free* 🕘 *Tues. and Thurs. 10–noon and 2–4, by appointment only.*

FAMILY **Pigeon Island National Landmark.** Jutting out from the northwest coast, Pigeon Island connects to the mainland via a causeway. Tales are told of the pirate Jambe de Bois (Wooden Leg), who once hid out on this

44-acre hilltop islet—a strategic point during the French and British struggles for control of St. Lucia. Now Pigeon Island is a national park and a venue for concerts, festivals, and family gatherings. There are two small beaches with calm waters for swimming and snorkeling, a restaurant, and picnic areas. Scattered around the grounds are ruins of barracks, batteries, and garrisons that date from 18th-century French and English battles. In the Museum and Interpretative Centre, housed in the restored British officers' mess, a multimedia display explains the island's ecological and historical significance. The site is administered by the St. Lucia National Trust. ✉ *Pigeon Island, Gros Islet* ☎ *758/452–5005* 🌐 *www.slunatrust.org* 💲 *$7* 🕐 *Daily 9–5.*

SOUFRIÈRE AND THE WEST COAST

The oldest town in St. Lucia and the island's former colonial capital, Soufrière was founded by the French in 1746 and named for its proximity to the volcano of the same name. The wharf is the center of activity in this sleepy town (population, 9,000), particularly when a cruise ship anchors in pretty Soufrière Bay. French colonial influences are evident in the second-story verandas, gingerbread trim, and other appointments of the wooden buildings that surround the market square. The market building itself is decorated with colorful murals.

The site of much of St. Lucia's renowned natural beauty, Soufrière is the destination of most sightseeing trips. Here you can get up close to the iconic Pitons and visit St. Lucia's "drive-in" volcano, botanical gardens, working plantations, waterfalls, and countless other examples of the natural beauty for which the island is deservedly famous. Note that souvenir vendors station themselves outside some of the popular attractions in and around Soufrière, and they can be persistent. Be polite but firm if you're not interested.

TOP ATTRACTIONS

Fodor's Choice ★ **Diamond Falls Botanical Gardens and Mineral Baths.** These splendid gardens are part of Soufrière Estate, a 2,000-acre land grant presented by King Louis XIV in 1713 to three Devaux brothers from Normandy in recognition of their services to France. The estate is still owned by their descendants; Joan DuBouley Devaux maintains the gardens. Bushes and shrubs bursting with brilliant flowers grow beneath towering trees and line pathways that lead to a natural gorge. Water bubbling to the surface from underground sulfur springs streams downhill in rivulets to become Diamond Waterfall, deep within the botanical gardens. Through the centuries, the rocks over which the cascade spills have become encrusted with minerals tinted yellow, green, and purple. Near the falls, mineral baths are fed by the underground springs. King Louis XVI of France provided funds in 1784 for the construction of a building with a dozen large stone baths to fortify his troops against the St. Lucian climate. It's claimed that the future Joséphine Bonaparte bathed here as a young girl while visiting her father's plantation nearby. During the Brigand's War, just after the French Revolution, the bathhouse was destroyed. In 1930 André DuBoulay had the site excavated, and two of the original stone baths were restored for his use. Outside baths were added later. For a small fee, you can slip into your swimsuit and soak for 30 minutes in one of the outside pools; a private bath costs slightly more. ✉ *Soufrière Estate, Diamond Rd.* ☎ *758/459–7155* 🌐 *www.diamondstlucia.com* 🎫 *$7, public bath $6, private bath $7* ⏲ *Mon.–Sat. 10–5, Sun. 10–3.*

22

Fodor's Choice ★ **The Pitons.** Rising precipitously from the cobalt-blue Caribbean just south of Soufrière Bay, these two unusual mountains—named a UNESCO World Heritage Site in 2004—have become the symbol of St. Lucia. Covered with thick tropical vegetation, the massive outcroppings were formed by a volcanic eruption 30 to 40 million years ago. They are not identical twins, since 2,619-foot Petit Piton is taller than 2,461-foot Gros Piton (Gros Piton is broader). It's possible to climb the Pitons, but it's a strenuous trek. Gros Piton is the easier climb and takes about four hours round-trip. Either climb requires permission and a guide ($30); register at the base of Gros Piton.

WORTH NOTING

Edmund Forest Reserve. Dense tropical rain forest that stretches from one side of St. Lucia to the other, sprawling over 19,000 acres of mountains and valleys, is home to a multitude of exotic flowers, other plants, and rare birds—including the brightly feathered Jacquot parrot. The Edmund Forest Reserve, on the island's western side, is most easily accessible from the road to Fond St. Jacques, which is just east of Soufrière. A trek through the verdant landscape, with spectacular views of mountains, valleys, and the sea beyond, can take three or more hours. The ranger station at the reserve entrance is a 30-minute drive from Soufrière and 90 minutes or more from the northern end of St. Lucia. You'll need a 4-wheel drive vehicle to drive inland to the trailhead, which can take another hour. The trek itself is a strenuous hike, requiring stamina and sturdy hiking shoes. Your hotel can help you obtain permission from the St. Lucia Forestry Department to access reserve trails and to arrange for a naturalist or forest officer guide—necessary because the vegetation is so dense. ☎ *758/468–5648 Forestry Dept.* 🎫 *Guide for nature trails $10, hiking trails $25, bird-watching $30* ⏲ *Daily by appointment only.*

FAMILY **Fond Doux Estate.** One of the earliest French estates established by land grants (1745 and 1763), this plantation still produces cocoa, citrus, bananas, coconut, and vegetables on 135 hilly acres. The restored 1864 plantation house is still in use as well. A 30-minute walking tour begins at the cocoa fermentary, where you can see the drying process. You then follow a trail through the cultivated area, where a guide points out various fruit- or spice-bearing trees and tropical flowers. Additional trails lead to old military ruins, a religious shrine, and a vantage point for viewing the spectacular Pitons. Cool drinks and a creole buffet lunch are served at the Cocoa Pod restaurant. Souvenirs, including just-made chocolate sticks, are sold at the boutique. ✉ *Vieux Fort Rd., Chateaubelair* ☎ *758/459–7545* 🌐 *www.fonddouxestate.com* 🎫 *$30, including lunch* ⏲ *Daily 11–2.*

FAMILY **La Soufrière Drive-In Volcano.** As you approach the volcano, your nose will pick up the strong scent of sulfur from more than 20 belching pools of murky water, crusty sulfur deposits, and other multicolor minerals

DID YOU KNOW?

The Devaux family has owned Diamond Falls Botanical Gardens since 1713; the sulfurous water has stained the surrounding rocks different colors.

baking and steaming on the surface. Despite its name, you don't actually drive all the way in. Rather, you drive within a few hundred feet of the gurgling, steaming mass and then walk behind your guide—whose service is included in the admission price—around a fault in the substratum rock. It's a fascinating, educational half-hour, though it can also be pretty stinky on a hot day. ☎ *758/459–7686* ⊕ *www.soufrierefoundation.org* 🎫 *$5* ⏲ *Daily 9–5.*

FAMILY **Morne Coubaril.** On the site of an 18th-century estate, a 250-acre land grant by Louis XIV of France in 1713, the original plantation house has been rebuilt and a farm workers' village has been re-created. It does a good job of showing what life was like for both the owners (a single family owned the land until 1960) and those who did all the hard labor over the centuries producing cotton, coffee, sugarcane, and cocoa. Cocoa, coconuts, and manioc are still grown on the estate using traditional agricultural methods. On the 30-minute estate tour, guides show how coconuts are opened and roasted for use as oil and animal feed and how cocoa is fermented, dried, crushed by dancing on the beans, and finally formed into chocolate sticks. Manioc roots (also called cassava) are grated, squeezed of excess water, dried, and turned into flour used for baking. The grounds are lovely for walking or hiking, and the views of mountains and Soufrière Harbour are spellbinding. More adventurous visitors will enjoy Soufrière Hotwire Rides, an hourlong zip-line excursion with eight stations, taking you by Petit Piton and through the adjacent rain forest. A large, open-air restaurant serves a creole buffet luncheon by reservation only. ✉ *West Coast Rd., 2 miles (3 km) south of town* ☎ *758/459–7340, 758/712–5808 reservations* ⊕ *www.mornecoubarilestate.com, www.stluciaziplining.com* 🎫 *$7, with lunch $21; zip line $69; all 3 and transportation $99* ⏲ *Daily 8–5.*

VIEUX FORT AND THE EAST COAST

Although less developed for tourism than the island's north and west, the area around Vieux Fort and points north along the eastern coast are home to some of St. Lucia's unique ecosystems and interesting natural attractions.

WORTH NOTING

Barre de l'Isle Forest Reserve. St. Lucia is divided into eastern and western halves by Barre de l'Isle ridge. A mile-long (1½-km-long) trail cuts through the reserve, and four lookout points provide panoramic views. Visible in the distance are Mt. Gimie, immense green valleys, both the Caribbean Sea and the Atlantic Ocean, and coastal communities. The trailhead is about a half-hour drive from Castries. It takes about an hour to walk the trail—an easy hike—and another hour to climb Mt. LaCombe Ridge. Permission from the St. Lucia Forestry Department is required to access the trail in Barre de l'Isle; a naturalist or forest officer guide ($10) will accompany you. ✉ *Micoud Hwy., midway between Castries and Dennery, Ravine Poisson* ☎ *758/468–5648 Forestry Dept.* ⊕ *www.malff.com* ⏲ *Daily by appointment only.*

Mamiku Gardens. One of St. Lucia's largest and loveliest botanical gardens surrounds the hilltop ruins of the Micoud Estate. Baron Micoud, an 18th-century colonel in the French Army and governor-general of St. Lucia, deeded the land to his wife, Madame de Micoud, to avoid confiscation by the British during one of the many times when St. Lucia changed hands. Locals abbreviated her name to "Ma Micoud," which, over time, became Mamiku. (The estate did become a British military outpost in 1796, but shortly thereafter was burned to the ground by slaves during the Brigand's War.) The estate is now primarily a banana plantation, but the gardens themselves—including several secluded or "secret" gardens—are filled with tropical flowers and plants, delicate orchids, and fragrant herbs. ✉ *Micoud Hwy., just north of Micoud, Praslin* ☎ *758/455–3729* 🎟 *$8, guided tour $10* ⏲ *Daily 9–5.*

Maria Islands Nature Reserve. Two tiny islands in the Atlantic Ocean off St. Lucia's southeastern coast make up the reserve, which has its own interpretive center. The 25-acre Maria Major and the 4-acre Maria Minor are inhabited by two rare species of reptiles: the colorful Zandoli Terre ground lizard and the harmless Kouwes grass snake. They share their home with frigate birds, terns, doves, and other wildlife. There's a small beach for swimming and snorkeling, as well as an undisturbed forest, a vertical cliff covered with cacti, and a coral reef for snorkeling or diving. The St. Lucia National Trust offers tours, including a boat trip to the islands, by appointment only; bring your own picnic lunch, as there are no facilities. ✉ *Vieux Fort* ☎ *758/454–5014 for tour reservations* 🌐 *www.slunatrust.org* 🎟 *$35* ⏲ *Aug.–mid-May, Wed.–Sun. 9:30–5 by appointment only.*

Vieux Fort. St. Lucia's second-largest town is also the location of Hewanorra International Airport. From the Moule à Chique Peninsula, the island's southernmost tip, you can see much of St. Lucia to the north and the island of St. Vincent 21 miles (34 km) to the south. This is where the waters of the clear Caribbean Sea blend with those of the deeper blue Atlantic Ocean. ✉ *Vieux Fort.*

BEACHES

The sand on St. Lucia's beaches ranges from warm gold to volcanic black, and the island has some of the best off-the-beach snorkeling in the Caribbean—especially along the western coast north of Soufrière.

St. Lucia's longest, broadest, and most popular beaches are in the north, which is also the flattest part of this mountainous island and the location of most resorts, restaurants, and nightlife. Many of the island's biggest resorts front the beaches from Choc Bay to Rodney Bay and north to Cap Estate. Elsewhere, tiny coves with inviting crescents of sand offer great swimming and snorkeling opportunities. Beaches are all public, but hotels flank many along the northwestern coast. A few secluded stretches of beach on the southwestern coast, south of Marigot Bay and accessible primarily by boat, are popular swimming and snorkeling stops on catamaran day sails or powerboat sightseeing trips. Don't swim along the windward (eastern) coast, as the Atlantic Ocean is too rough—but the views are spectacular. At Coconut Bay Beach Resort, which has a beautiful beach facing the Atlantic at the southernmost tip of the island, the water is rough—but an artificial reef makes it safe for swimming and water sports, especially kitesurfing.

Anse Chastanet. In front of the resort of the same name and Jade Mountain, this palm-studded, dark-sand beach just north of Soufrière has a backdrop of green mountains, brightly painted fishing skiffs bobbing at anchor, calm waters for swimming, and some of the island's best reefs for snorkeling and diving right from shore. Anse Chastanet Resort's gazebos are among the palms; its dive shop, restaurant, and bar are on the beach and open to the public. The mile-long dirt road from Soufrière, though, is a challenge even for taxi drivers, given its usual (and colossal) state of disrepair. **Amenities:** food and drink; parking (no fee); toilets; water sports. **Best for:** snorkeling; sunset; swimming. ✉ *Anse Chastanet Rd., 1 mile (1½ km) north of town, Soufrière.*

Anse Cochon. This dark-sand beach in front of Ti Kaye Resort & Spa is accessible by boat or via Ti Kaye's mile-long, tire-crunching access road. The calm water and adjacent reefs, part of the National Marine Reserve, are superb for swimming, diving, and snorkeling. In fact, most catamaran cruises to Soufrière stop here for day-trippers to take a quick swim on the northbound leg. Moorings are free, and boaters and swimmers can enjoy refreshments at Ti Kaye's beach bar. Snorkeling equipment is available at the dive shop on the beach. **Amenities:** food and drink; toilets; water sports. **Best for:** snorkeling; swimming. ✉ *Off West Coast Rd., 3 miles (5 km) south of Anse la Raye, Anse la Raye.*

Anse des Pitons (*Sugar Beach*). The white sand on this crescent beach, snuggled between the Pitons, was imported years ago and spread over the natural black sand. Accessible through the Sugar Beach, a Viceroy Resort, property or by boat, Anse des Pitons offers crystal clear water for swimming, excellent snorkeling and diving, and breathtaking scenery—you're swimming right between the Pitons, after all. The underwater area here is protected as part of the National Marine Reserve. Neighboring resorts Ladera and Boucan provide shuttle service to the beach. **Amenities:** food and drink; toilets; water sports. **Best for:** snorkeling; sunset; swimming. ✉ *Val des Pitons, 3 miles (5 km) south of Soufrière, Soufrière.*

Marigot Beach (*Labas Beach*). Calm waters rippled only by passing yachts lap a sliver of sand on the north side of Marigot Bay adjacent to the Marigot Beach Club & Dive Resort, across the bay from Capella Marigot Bay, and a short walk from Mango Beach Resort. Studded with palm trees, the tiny but extremely picturesque beach is accessible by a ferry ($2 round-trip) that operates continually from one side of the bay to the other, with pickup at the Marina Village; you can find refreshments at adjacent restaurants. **Amenities:** food and drink; toilets; water sports. **Best for:** swimming. ✉ *Marigot Bay.*

FAMILY **Pigeon Point.** This small beach within the national landmark, on the northwestern tip of St. Lucia, has golden sand, a calm sea, and a view that extends from Rodney Bay to Martinique. It's a perfect spot for picnicking, and you can take a break from the sun by visiting the nearby Museum and Interpretive Centre. **Amenities:** food and drink; toilets.

Best for: solitude; snorkeling; swimming. ✉ *Pigeon Island National Landmark, Pigeon Island, Gros Islet* 🎫 *$7 park admission.*

FAMILY Fodor's Choice ★ **Reduit Beach.** Many feel that Reduit (pronounced red-wee) is the island's finest beach. The long stretch of golden sand that frames Rodney Bay is within walking distance of many hotels and restaurants in Rodney Bay Village. Bay Gardens Beach Resort, Royal St. Lucia by Rex Resorts, and St. Lucian by Rex Resorts all face the beachfront; blu St. Lucia, Harmony Suites, and Ginger Lily hotels are across the road. At the Royal's water-sports center, you can rent sports equipment and beach chairs and take windsurfing or waterskiing lessons. **Amenities:** food and drink; toilets; water sports. **Best for:** snorkeling; sunset; swimming; walking; windsurfing. ✉ *Rodney Bay Village, Gros Islet.*

Vigie/Malabar Beach. This 2-mile (3-km) stretch of lovely white sand runs parallel to the George F. L. Charles Airport runway in Castries and continues on past the Rendezvous resort, where it becomes Malabar Beach. In the area opposite the airport departure lounge, a few vendors sell refreshments. **Amenities:** food and drink. **Best for:** swimming. ✉ *Adjacent to George F.L. Charles Airport runway, Castries.*

WHERE TO EAT

Bananas, mangoes, passion fruit, plantains, breadfruit, okra, avocados, limes, pumpkins, cucumbers, papaya, yams, christophenes (also called chayote), and coconuts are among the fresh fruits and vegetables that grace St. Lucian menus. The French influence is strong, and most chefs cook with a creole flair. Resort buffets and restaurant fare include standards like steaks, chops, pasta, and pizza—and every menu lists fresh fish along with the ever-popular lobster, which is available in season—August through March.

Soups and stews are traditionally prepared in a coal pot—unique to St. Lucia—a rustic clay casserole on a matching clay stand that holds the hot coals. Chicken and pork dishes and barbecues are also popular here. As they do throughout the Caribbean, local vendors set up barbecues along the roadside, at street fairs, and at Friday-night "jump-ups" and do a bang-up business selling grilled fish or chicken legs, bakes (fried biscuits), and beer. You can get a full meal for less than $10.

Guests at St. Lucia's many popular all-inclusive resorts take most meals at hotel restaurants—which are generally quite good and in some cases exceptional—but it's fun when vacationing to try some of the local restaurants as well—for lunch when sightseeing or for a special night out.

What to Wear: Dress on St. Lucia is casual but conservative. Shorts are usually fine during the day, but bathing suits and immodest clothing are frowned upon anywhere but at the beach. Nude or topless sunbathing is prohibited. In the evening, the mood is casually elegant, but even the fanciest places generally expect only a collared shirt and long pants for men and a sundress or slacks for women.

CASTRIES AND THE NORTH

$$$ SEAFOOD **✕ Buzz.** Opposite the Royal St. Lucia by Rex Resorts hotel and Reduit Beach, this is part of Rodney Bay's "restaurant central." Starting with cool drinks (maybe a Buzz cooler) and warm appetizers (perhaps lobster and crab cakes, crispy calamari, or tempura shrimp) at the bar, diners make their way to the dining room or garden for some serious seafood or a good steak, baby back ribs, West Indian pepperpot stew, spicy lamb shanks, or simple chicken-and-chips. The seared yellowfin tuna, potato-crusted red snapper, and seafood creole are big hits, too. There's also a vegetarian menu. Fresh lobster is available in season (September–April). *Average main: US$30 ✉ Reduit Beach Ave., Rodney Bay Village, Gros Islet ☎ 758/458–0450 ⊕ www.buzzstlucia.com ✍ Reservations essential ⊗ Closed Mon. No lunch.*

$$$$ ECLECTIC Fodor's Choice ★ **✕ The Cliff at Cap.** High on top of a cliff at the northern tip of St. Lucia, the open-air dining room at Cap Maison welcomes diners to what executive chef Craig Jones calls "nouveau" French West Indian cuisine. True, he incorporates local vegetables, fruits, herbs, and spices with the best meats and fresh-caught seafood you'll find on the island, but the technique and presentation—and the service—lean more toward the French. In addition to the mouthwatering à la carte menu, there's a five-course, prix-fixe Tasting Menu ($89, $134 with course-matching wines). Lucky Cap Maison guests who choose a meal plan get to dine here daily, but nonguests make up about 40% of the dinner clientele. Day or night, this is one of the loveliest dining venues on St. Lucia. At lunch, the view on a clear day stretches to Martinique; in the evening, twinkling stars and waves crashing far below lend an air of romance. *Average main: US$36 ✉ Cap Maison, Smuggler's Cove Dr., Cap Estate ☎ 758/457–8681 ⊕ www.thecliffatcap.com ✍ Reservations essential.*

$$$$ FRENCH Fodor's Choice ★ **✕ Coal Pot.** Popular since the early 1960s, this tiny waterfront restaurant overlooks pretty Vigie Cove. For a light lunch, opt for a bowl of creamy pumpkin soup, Greek or shrimp salad, or broiled fresh fish. Dinner might start with a divine lobster bisque, followed by fresh seafood accompanied by one (or more) of the chef's fabulous sauces—ginger, coconut-curry, lemon-garlic butter, or wild mushroom. Heartier eaters may prefer duck, lamb, beef, or chicken laced with peppercorns, red wine, onion, or Roquefort sauce. *Average main: US$32 ✉ Vigie Cove, Castries ☎ 758/452–5566 ⊕ www.coalpotrestaurant.com ✍ Reservations essential ⊗ Closed Sun. No lunch Sat.*

$$$$ ECLECTIC Fodor's Choice ★ **✕ The Edge.** Innovative Swedish chef Bobo Bergstrom has brought "Eurobbean" cuisine to his own restaurant, which overlooks the harbor at Harmony Suites hotel. The contemporary fusion style combines the chef's European heritage, Caribbean traditions and ingredients, and a touch of Asian influence. Raves are doled out to chef Bobo's culinary feats, the excellent wine list, and the sushi bar. Follow one of a dozen starters with pan-seared red snapper and lobster medallions au gratin, jerk-marinated-and-grilled beef tenderloin, or pecan- and cardamom-rubbed rack of lamb. Or you might want to consider the five-course tasting menu. There's sure to be a dish on the extensive menu (or at the sushi bar) to suit all, including vegetarians. **■ TIP→ Leave room for**

a fabulous "dessert creation." $ *Average main: US$37 ✉ Harmony Suites, Reduit Beach Ave., Rodney Bay Village, Gros Islet ☎ 758/450–3343 🌐 www.edge-restaurant.com ✍ Reservations essential.*

$$$$ FRENCH ✕ **Jacques Waterfront Dining.** Chef-owner Jacky Rioux creates magical dishes in his waterfront restaurant overlooking Rodney Bay. The cooking is decidedly French, as is Rioux, but fresh produce and local spices create a memorable fusion cuisine. You might start with a bowl of Mediterranean fish soup, a grilled portobello mushroom, or tomato-and-basil tart. Main dishes include fresh seafood, perhaps oven-baked kingfish with a white wine–and–sweet pepper sauce, and breast of chicken stuffed with smoked salmon in a citrus-butter sauce. The wine list is impressive. Coming by boat? You can tie up at the dinghy dock. $ *Average main: US$32 ✉ Reduit Beach Ave., end of road, Rodney Bay Village, Gros Islet ☎ 758/458–1900 🌐 www.jacquesrestaurant.com ✍ Reservations essential.*

$$$ CARIBBEAN ✕ **KoKo Cabana.** Poolside at the Coco Palm hotel, this open-air bistro and bar attracts mostly hotel guests for breakfast but a wider clientele for lunch or dinner. Lunch is a good bet if you're poking around Rodney Bay, need a break from Reduit Beach, or are just looking for a good meal in an attractive spot. In the evening, the magic happens in the breezy dining room. The dinner menu focuses on Caribbean favorites such as jerk baby back ribs with guava barbecue sauce, perfectly grilled fish or steak with local vegetables, tamarind-glazed chicken breast, and always a pasta dish or two. Dessert could be a dark chocolate truffle cake or vanilla profiteroles with chocolate sauce. A live band entertains most evenings and always at the Friday night barbecue buffet. $ *Average main: US$27 ✉ Coco Palm, Rodney Bay Village, Gros Islet ☎ 758/456–2866 🌐 www.coco-resorts.com ✍ Reservations essential.*

$$$$ ASIAN Fodor's Choice ★ ✕ **Tao.** For exquisite dining, head for this Cap Estate restaurant on the premises of the Body Holiday resort. As you dine on a second-floor balcony at the edge of Cariblue Beach, you're guaranteed a pleasant breeze and a starry sky while you enjoy fusion cuisine—mouthwatering Asian tastes with a Caribbean touch. Appetizers such as seafood dumplings, sashimi salad, or miso-eggplant timbale can be followed by tender slices of pork loin teriyaki, twice-cooked duck, wok-seared calves' liver, or tandoori chicken. Fine wines accompany the meal, desserts are extravagant, and service is superb. Seating is limited and hotel guests have priority, so reserve early. $ *Average main: US$35 ✉ The Body Holiday, Cap Estate ☎ 758/457–7800 🌐 www.thebodyholiday.com ✍ Reservations essential ⊗ No lunch.*

SOUFRIÈRE AND THE WEST COAST

$$$ INDIAN ✕ **Apsara.** India has had an important influence on the islands, from the heritage of their people to colorful madras plaids to the curry flavors that are a staple of Caribbean cuisine. At night, Anse Chastanet's Trou au Diable restaurant transforms into Apsara, an extraordinarily romantic, candlelit, beachfront dining experience with modern Indian cuisine. The innovative menu, mixing East Indian and Caribbean cooking, produces food that's full of flavor but not too spicy, although you can opt for some hotter dishes. Mulligatawny soup with cumin yogurt

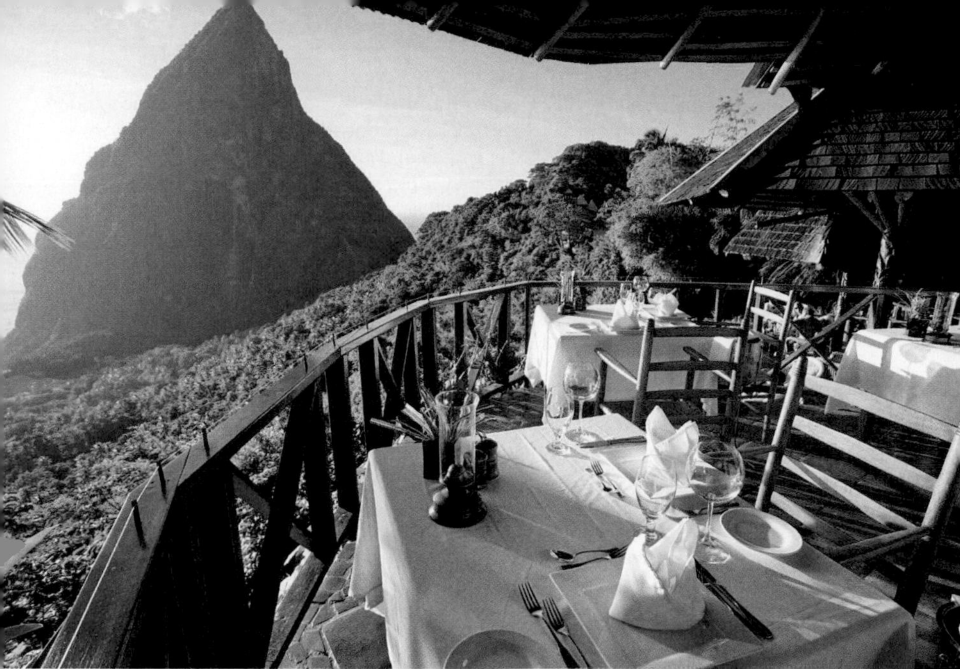

Amazing views at Dasheene at Ladera

or vegetable samosas might be followed by coconut-chili king prawns, pork vindaloo, or tandoori-roasted salmon, lamb chops, chicken, or lobster. Definitely order the naan, either plain or flavored with almond, coconut, or raisin. For dessert, choose the mango, saffron, or sea moss *kulfi* (Indian-style ice cream) or go all the way with Apsara's Temptation (tandoori-baked pineapple with honey, saffron, and passion-fruit syrup, kulfi, and sun-blushed chili). $ *Average main: US$28* ✉ *Anse Chastanet* ☎ *758/459–7354* 🌐 *www.ansechastanet.com* ✍ *Reservations essential* ⏲ *Closed Tues. No lunch.*

$$$ CARIBBEAN ✕ **Boucan.** Ahh . . . chocolate! Here on the Rabot Estate, a working cocoa plantation, that heavenly flavor is infused into just about every dish—cacao gazpacho or citrus salad with white chocolate dressing for starters. The main course might be red snapper roasted in cacao butter, rib-eye steak "matured and infused" with cacao nibs, cacao- and herb-encrusted pork medallions, or handmade cocoa ravioli with a tomato and fresh herb sauce. You get the picture. Dessert, of course, is the grand chocolate finale: cacao crème brûlée, meringue floating in a sea of chocolate crème anglaise, dark chocolate mouse . . . even cacao sorbet. Yum. $ *Average main: US$29* ✉ *Boucan by Hotel Chocolat, Rabot Estate, West Coast Rd., 3 miles (5 km) south of Soufrière* ☎ *758/572–9600* 🌐 *www.hotelchocolat.com* ✍ *Reservations essential.*

$$ SEAFOOD FAMILY ✕ **Chateau Mygo.** Walk down a garden path to Chateau Mygo (a colloquial corruption of "Marigot"), pick out a table on the deck, and soak up the waterfront atmosphere of what may be the Caribbean's prettiest bay. The tableau is mesmerizing—and that's at lunch, when you can order a sandwich, burger, roti, fish- or chicken-and-chips, salads, or grilled fish or savory coconut chicken with peas and rice and vegetables.

At dinner, chef-owner Doreen Rambally—whose family has owned and operated this popular dockside restaurant since the mid-1970s—draws on three generations of East Indian and creole family recipes. Beautifully grilled fresh tuna, red snapper, kingfish, mahimahi, and local lobster are embellished with flavors such as ginger, mango, papaya, or passion fruit, and then dished up with regional vegetables—perhaps callaloo, okra, dasheen, breadfruit, christophene, or yams. You can also have roast pork, beef, a chicken dish, pizza, or sushi. This is a very casual restaurant with delicious, reasonably priced meals. And oh, that view! *Average main: US$20 ✉ Marigot Bay ☎ 758/451–4772.*

$$$ CARIBBEAN Fodor's Choice ★ **Dasheene at Ladera.** The terrace restaurant at Ladera resort has breathtakingly close-up views of the Pitons and the sea between them, especially beautiful at sunset. The ambience is casual by day and magical at night. Appetizers may include silky sweet potato–and–coconut soup or Caribbean lamb salad. Typical entrées are "fisherman's catch" with a choice of flavored butters or sauces, shrimp Dasheene (panfried with local herbs), grilled rack of lamb with coconut risotto and curry sauce, or pan-seared fillet of beef marinated in a lime-and-pepper seasoning. Light dishes, pasta dishes, and fresh salads are also served at lunch—along with that million-dollar view. *Average main: US$30 ✉ Ladera, 2 miles (3 km) south of Soufrière ☎ 758/459–6623 🌐 www.ladera.com.*

$$$ SEAFOOD FAMILY **Doolittle's.** Named for the protagonist in the original (1967) *Dr. Dolittle* movie, part of which was filmed in Marigot Bay, this indoor-outdoor restaurant at Marigot Beach Club & Dive Resort is on the north side of the bay. You'll have a beautiful waterside view—watch yachts quietly slip by—as you enjoy your meal. The menu includes light meals such as sandwiches, burgers, grilled chicken, and salads at lunchtime and, in the evening, seafood, steak, chicken, and Caribbean specials such as curries and stews. Take the little ferry across the bay to get here. During the day, bring your bathing suit; the beach is just outside. **TIP→ In the evening, it's a great spot for drinks and entertainment.** *Average main: US$26 ✉ Marigot Beach Club & Dive Resort, Marigot Bay ☎ 758/451–4974 🌐 www.marigotbeachclub.com.*

$$ CARIBBEAN **The Hummingbird.** The cheerful restaurant-bar in the Hummingbird Beach Resort specializes in French creole cuisine, starting with fresh seafood or chicken seasoned with local herbs and accompanied by fresh-picked vegetables from the Hummingbird's garden. Sandwiches (on homemade bread) and salads are also available. At lunch, sit outside by the pool for a magnificent view of the Pitons (you're welcome to take a dip). Wednesday night is Creole Night, with live entertainment, dancing, and special dishes. **TIP→ Stop in at the batik studio and art gallery of proprietor Joan Alexander Stowe, next to the dining room.** *Average main: US$20 ✉ Hummingbird Beach Resort, Anse Chastanet Rd. ☎ 758/459–7985 🌐 www.hummingbirdbeachresort.com.*

$$$ CARIBBEAN FAMILY **Jardin Cacao at Fond Doux Estate.** The small, rustic restaurant at Fond Doux Estate—a working plantation—is one of the most popular spots to enjoy a creole lunch when touring the natural sights in and around Soufrière. Help yourself to the buffet containing stewed chicken, grilled fish, rice and beans, macaroni and cheese, caramelized plaintains, figs (green bananas), breadfruit balls, purple yams, salad, and more. Nearly

all ingredients are locally sourced. Wash it all down with a rum punch or local fruit juice, and finish with something sweet such as coconut or banana cake. Dinner, by candlelight, is à la carte: a choice of seafood, chicken, beef, and pasta dishes with a local twist—pepperpot, for example. Most people who come for lunch also take a short tour and learn about how the cacao growing on the plantation is turned into delicious chocolate. **■TIP→ You can buy chocolate in the gift shop to take home.** *Average main: US$25* ✉ *Fond Doux Holiday Plantation, Chateaubelair* ☎ *758/459–7545* 🌐 *www.fonddouxestate.com* *Reservations essential.*

$$$ CARIBBEAN **Orlando's.** British-born of Jamaican/Barbadian heritage, chef Orlando Satchell is a man on a mission. He opened his restaurant in downtown Soufrière to present his "Share the Love" (or STL) style of cooking, which focuses on Caribbean cuisine. Orlando supports local farmers and fishers by using only locally grown meats and organic produce and freshly caught fish in his delicious—and world-class—dishes. Dinner offers a choice of two set five-course menus—starting with soup (pumpkin is *the* best!) and salad, then a fish dish followed by beef or chicken, and ultimately dessert. It's clear that Orlando loves St. Lucia, especially Soufrière. *Average main: US$30* ✉ *Bridge St.* ☎ *758/572–6613* *Reservations essential* *Closed Mon.–Tues.*

$$$$ INTERNATIONAL Fodor's Choice ★ **Rainforest Hideaway.** Exotic Caribbean tastes and flavors are paired with classical French techniques and recipes at this romantic and upscale hideaway on the north shore of pretty Marigot Bay. It's definitely worth the 20-minute-or-so drive from Castries. A little ferry whisks you to the alfresco restaurant, perched on a dock, where you're greeted with complimentary champagne. Fresh local fish—including the ubiquitous (and foreign) lionfish that is the scourge of local waters but tastes delicious—and prime meats are enhanced by fresh herbs grown in the backyard garden, which is also the source of exotic local vegetables and fruits featured in various dishes. Entrées such as panfried mahimahi with creole buerre blanc; marinated loin of lamb with cucumber relish; and grilled beef tenderloin with papaya confit are impressive. The menu is prix-fixe: $48 for two courses; $59 includes dessert. Dinner is accompanied by a blanket of stars overhead and live jazz on Wednesday, Thursday, and Saturday nights. *Average main: US$35* ✉ *Marigot Bay* ☎ *758/286–0511* 🌐 *www.rainforesthideawaystlucia.com* *Reservations essential* *Closed Sun.–Tues. in June–Sept. No lunch.*

$ CAFÉ FAMILY **Rowley's Café/Baguet Shop.** Join the yachties and nearby hotel guests for breakfast, lunch, afternoon tea, an evening snack, or just dessert at this French bakery and café in the Marina Village on Marigot Bay. Open every day from 7 to 7, it offers freshly baked French bread, crusty croissants, juicy steakburgers with fries, pizza, deli wraps, and delicious French pastries. Sandwiches are prepared on a baguette, croissant, or focaccia—your choice. A cup of cappuccino, mocha, or latte goes well with a fruit tart, *pain au chocolat*, or coconut flan. Eat in (well, outside on the dock) or take it out. Even if you eat in, you'll probably also want a baguette—or a bagful—to take out. *Average main: US$10* ✉ *Marina Village, Marigot Bay* ☎ *758/451–4275* *Reservations not accepted.*

$$ CARIBBEAN ✕ **The Still.** When you're visiting Diamond Falls and other Soufrière attractions, this makes a convenient (buffet) lunch spot. Located on a 400-acre working plantation just outside town, the two dining rooms here seat up to 400 people, so it's also a popular stop for tour groups and cruise passengers. The emphasis is on local cuisine, using vegetables such as christophene, breadfruit, yam, and callaloo along with grilled fish or chicken; there are also pork and beef dishes. All fruits and vegetables used are organically grown on the estate. 💲 *Average main: US$20* ✉ *The Still Plantation, La Perle Estate* ☎ *758/459–7224* 🌐 *www.thestillplantation.com* ⊗ *No dinner.*

WHERE TO STAY

Most people—particularly honeymooners—stay in grand beach resorts, most of which are upscale and pricey. Several are all-inclusive, including the three Sandals resorts, two resorts owned or managed by Sunswept (the Body Holiday and Rendezvous), St. James's Club Morgan Bay, East Winds Inn, and Smuggler's Cove Resort & Spa. Smaller and less expensive, St. Lucia's dozens of small inns and hotels are primarily locally owned and frequently quite charming. They may or may not be directly on the beach. Luxury villa communities and independent private villas are other alternatives.

PRIVATE VILLAS AND CONDOS

Luxury villa and condo communities can be an economical option for families, couples vacationing together, and other groups. Villa units are privately owned, but nonowners can rent from property managers for short-term stays, much like reserving hotel accommodations.

Rental villas are staffed with a housekeeper and cook who specializes in local cooking; in some cases, a caretaker lives on the property and a gardener and night watchman are on staff. All properties have telephones, and some have Internet access. Telephones may be barred against outgoing overseas calls; plan to use a phone card, calling card, or your own cell phone. Most villas have TVs, DVDs, and CD players. All private villas have a swimming pool; condos share a community pool. Vehicles are generally not included in the rates, but rental cars can be arranged and delivered to the villa upon request. Linens and basic supplies (such as bath soap, toilet tissue, and dishwashing detergent) are included. Pre-arrival grocery stocking can be arranged.

Units with one to nine bedrooms and the same number of baths run $200 to $2,000 per night, depending on the size of the villa, the amenities, the number of guests, and the season. Rates include utilities and government taxes. Your only additional cost will be for groceries and staff gratuities. A security deposit is required upon booking and refunded after departure less any damages or unpaid miscellaneous charges.

Rental Contacts Discover Villas of St. Lucia ✉ *Cap Estate* ☎ *758/484–3066* 🌐 *www.a1stluciavillas.com.* **Tropical Villas** ✉ *Cap Estate* ☎ *758/450–8240* 🌐 *www.tropicalvillas.net.*

Sandals Grande St. Lucian Spa & Beach Resort

CASTRIES AND THE NORTH

$ RESORT FAMILY Fodor's Choice ★ **Bay Gardens Beach Resort & Spa.** One of three Bay Gardens properties in Rodney Bay Village, this family-friendly resort has a prime location on beautiful Reduit Beach. **Pros:** on St. Lucia's best beach; self-catering suites; excellent value; complimentary Wi-Fi in public areas. **Cons:** very popular, so book ahead in season. *Rooms from: US$240 ✉ Reduit Beach Ave., Rodney Bay Village, Gros Islet ☎ 758/457–8006, 877/620–3200 in U.S. www.baygardensbeachresort.com 36 rooms, 36 suites Multiple meal plans.*

$ HOTEL **Bay Gardens Hotel.** Independent travelers and regional businesspeople swear by this cheerful, well-run boutique hotel at Rodney Bay Village. **Pros:** terrific value; Croton suites are best bet; complimentary Wi-Fi. **Cons:** not beachfront, although there's a beach shuttle; heavy focus on business travelers. *Rooms from: US$128 ✉ Castries–Gros Islet Hwy., Rodney Bay Village, Gros Islet ☎ 758/457–8010, 877/620–3200 www.baygardenshotel.com 59 rooms, 28 suites Multiple meal plans.*

$ RESORT **blu St. Lucia.** Singles, couples, families, and business travelers all find this a good base in Rodney Bay Village across from Reduit Beach—and a reasonably priced one, too. **Pros:** excellent location; a peaceful refuge close to the Rodney Bay restaurants and action; complimentary Wi-Fi. **Cons:** not beachfront, although pretty close; rooms have showers only. *Rooms from: US$175 ✉ Reduit Beach Ave., Rodney Bay Village, Gros Islet ☎ 758/456–9800, 855/212–1972 in U.S. www.harlequinblu.com 72 rooms Multiple meal plans.*

$$$$ ALL-INCLUSIVE Fodor's Choice ★ **The Body Holiday.** At this adults-only spa resort on picturesque Cariblue Beach—where daily treatments are included in the rates—you can customize your own "body holiday" online even before you leave home. **Pros:** daily spa treatments included; excellent dining; interesting activities, such as archery, include free instruction. **Cons:** expensive; unremarkable rooms; small bathrooms; lots of steps to the spa, though you can get a ride. *Rooms from: US$1,300 Cariblue Beach, Cap Estate 758/457–7800, 800/544–2883 www.thebodyholiday.com 152 rooms, 3 suites All-inclusive.*

$$$$ RESORT Fodor's Choice ★ **Calabash Cove Resort & Spa.** The luxurious suites and Balinese-inspired cottages at this inviting boutique resort spill gently down a tropical hillside to a secluded beach on Bonaire Bay, just south of Rodney Bay. **Pros:** stylish, sophisticated, and friendly; great food; wedding parties can reserve the entire resort. **Cons:** the long, bone-crunching dirt road at the entrance; the many steps to the cottages and beach may be difficult for those with physical challenges. *Rooms from: US$826 Bonaire Estate, off Castries–Gros Islet Hwy., south of Rodney Bay, Marisule, Gros Islet 758/456–3500, 800/917–2683 in U.S. www.calabashcove.com 17 suites, 9 cottages Multiple meal plans.*

$$$ RESORT Fodor's Choice ★ **Cap Maison.** Prepare to be spoiled by the doting staffers at this intimate villa resort—the luxurious service includes unpacking (if you wish) and a personal butler for any little needs that arise. **Pros:** private and elegant; outstanding service; rooftop plunge pools; cocktails with a view at Cliff Bar or surfside at Rock Maison. **Cons:** a/c in bedrooms only; many steps to the beach. *Rooms from: US$417 Smuggler's Cove Dr., Cap Estate 758/457–8670, 888/765–4985 in U.S. www.capmaison.com 10 rooms, 39 suites in 22 villas Multiple meal plans.*

$ HOTEL FAMILY **Coco Palm.** This boutique hotel in Rodney Bay Village overlooks an inviting pool and a separate cozy guesthouse, Kreole Village, at the edge of the property. **Pros:** excellent value; fabulous swim-up rooms; family suites; complimentary Wi-Fi. **Cons:** not directly on the beach; nightly entertainment can get noisy. *Rooms from: US$200 Rodney Bay Village, Gros Islet 758/456–2800, 877/655–2626 in U.S. www.coco-resorts.com 91 rooms, 12 suites Multiple meal plans.*

$ RESORT FAMILY **Cotton Bay Village.** Wedged between a quiet ocean beach and the St. Lucia Golf Resort & Country Club, luxurious, individually designed and decorated colonial-style town houses and château-style villas surround a village center and a free-form lagoon pool. **Pros:** beautiful remote beach; very private surroundings; family-friendly. **Cons:** a/c in bedrooms only; bathrooms have showers only; you'll probably need a car to leave the grounds. *Rooms from: US$230 Cotton Bay, Cap Estate 758/456–5700, 866/460–5755 www.cottonbayvillage.com 206 suites in 74 villas No meals.*

$$$$ ALL-INCLUSIVE **East Winds Inn.** Guests keep returning to this small all-inclusive resort on a secluded beach halfway between Castries and Rodney Bay, where 7 acres of botanical gardens surround 13 duplex gingerbread-style cottages, three ocean-view rooms, and a suite. **Pros:** lovely beach; excellent dining; peaceful and quiet. **Cons:** not best choice for families, though children welcome; very expensive; six-night minimum. *Rooms from:*

US$935 ✉ *Gros Islet* ☎ *758/452–8212* 🌐 *www.eastwinds.com* 🛏 *30 rooms* 🍽 *All-inclusive.*

$$$$ RESORT FAMILY **The Landings.** On 19 acres along the Pigeon Point Causeway at the northern edge of Rodney Bay, this villa resort surrounds a private, 80-slip harbor where residents can dock their own yachts, literally, at their doorstep. **Pros:** spacious, beautifully appointed units; perfect for yachties; personal chef service; kids' club. **Cons:** condo atmosphere; little hike to beach from some rooms. $ *Rooms from: US$510* ✉ *Pigeon Island Causeway, Gros Islet* ☎ *758/458–7300, 866/252–0689 in U.S.* 🌐 *www.landingsstlucia.com* 🛏 *122 units* 🍽 *Multiple meal plans.*

22

$$$$ ALL-INCLUSIVE **Rendezvous.** Romance is alive and well at this easygoing, all-inclusive, couples resort that stretches along the dreamy white sand of Malabar Beach at the end of the George F.L. Charles Airport runway. **Pros:** convenient to Castries and Vigie Airport; romance in the air; popular wedding venue. **Cons:** no room TVs; occasional flyover noise. $ *Rooms from: US$835* ✉ *Malabar Beach, Castries* ☎ *758/457–7900, 800/544–2883 in U.S.* 🌐 *www.theromanticholiday.com* 🛏 *57 rooms, 35 suites, 8 cottages* 🍽 *All-inclusive.*

$$$ RESORT FAMILY **Royal St. Lucia by Rex Resorts.** This luxurious all-suites resort on St. Lucia's best beach caters to every whim—for the whole family. **Pros:** great beachfront; roomy rooms; family-friendly; convenient to restaurants, clubs, and shops; two suites equipped for disabled guests. **Cons:** don't expect all-day dining—get snacks at the nearby supermarket. $ *Rooms from: US$440* ✉ *Reduit Beach Ave., Rodney Bay Village, Gros Islet* ☎ *758/452–8351, 305/471–6170* 🌐 *www.rexcaribbean.com* 🛏 *96 suites* 🍽 *Multiple meal plans.*

$$$$ ALL-INCLUSIVE FAMILY **St. James's Club Morgan Bay.** Singles, couples, and families enjoy tons of sports and activities at this all-inclusive resort on 22 secluded acres surrounding a stretch of white-sand beach. **Pros:** lots to do; children's club with organized activities; free waterskiing, sailing, and tennis lessons; great dining atmosphere evenings at Morgan's Pier. **Cons:** huge resort can be very busy, especially when full; relatively small beach given resort's size; Wi-Fi only in some rooms and for a fee. $ *Rooms from: US$720* ✉ *Choc Bay, Castries* ☎ *758/450–2511, 866/830–1617* 🌐 *www.morganbayresort.com* 🛏 *245 rooms, 100 suites* 🍽 *All-inclusive.*

$$$$ ALL-INCLUSIVE **Sandals Grande St. Lucian Spa & Beach Resort.** Couples—particularly young honeymooners and those getting married here—love this busy, busy, busy resort, the biggest and splashiest of the St. Lucia Sandals. **Pros:** excellent beach; lots of activities; free scuba for certified divers; service with a smile. **Cons:** really long ride (at least 90 minutes) to Hewanorra; beach can be crowded; uninspired buffet meals. $ *Rooms from: US$720* ✉ *Pigeon Island Causeway, Gros Islet* ☎ *758/455–2000* 🌐 *www.sandals.com* 🛏 *272 rooms, 29 suites* 🍽 *All-inclusive.*

$$$$ ALL-INCLUSIVE **Sandals Halcyon Beach Resort & Spa.** This is the most intimate and low-key of the three Sandals resorts on St. Lucia; like the others, it's beachfront, all-inclusive, for couples only, and loaded with amenities and activities. **Pros:** all the Sandals amenities in a more intimate setting; lots of dining and activity choices; exchange privileges (including golf) at other Sandals properties. **Cons:** it's Sandals, so it's a theme property that's not for everyone; it's small, so book well in advance. $ *Rooms*

Sandals Halcyon Beach, Kelly's Dockside Seaside Bar & Grill

from: US$545 ✉ Choc Bay, Castries ☎ 758/453–0222, 888/726–3257 ⊕ www.sandals.com ⇨ 169 rooms 🍴 All-inclusive.

$$$$ ALL-INCLUSIVE **Sandals Regency La Toc Golf Resort & Spa.** The second largest of the three Sandals, this resort distinguishes itself with a 9-hole golf course (for guests only). **Pros:** lots to do; picturesque; on-site golf; airport shuttle. **Cons:** somewhat isolated; expert golfers will prefer the St. Lucia Golf Resort & Country Club. $ *Rooms from: US$535 ✉ La Toc Rd., La Toc, Castries ☎ 758/452–3081 ⊕ www.sandals.com ⇨ 212 rooms, 116 suites 🍴 All-inclusive.*

$$$$ ALL-INCLUSIVE FAMILY **Smuggler's Cove Resort & Spa.** This huge all-inclusive resort on 60 acres overlooking pretty Smuggler's Cove has more food, fun, and features than your family will have time to enjoy in a week. **Pros:** family rooms sleep five; excellent children's program; family-friendly nightly entertainment. **Cons:** busy, busy, busy; not the place for a quiet getaway; guest rooms spread far and wide on the hillside. $ *Rooms from: US$735 ✉ Smuggler's Cove Dr., Cap Estate ☎ 758/457–4140, 866/297–1685 in U.S. ⊕ www.smugglersbeachresorts.com ⇨ 251 rooms, 100 suites 🍴 All-inclusive.*

$$ RESORT FAMILY **Windjammer Landing Villa Beach Resort.** As appropriate for a family vacation as for a romantic getaway, this resort offers lots to do while still providing privacy. **Pros:** lovely, spacious units; beautiful sunset views; family-friendly; in-unit dining. **Cons:** some units have living rooms with no a/c; far from main road, so you'll need a car if you plan to leave the property often. $ *Rooms from: US$308 ✉ Trouya Point Rd., Labrelotte Bay, Castries ☎ 758/456–9000, 877/522–0722 in U.S. ⊕ www.windjammer-landing.com ⇨ 41 suites, 72 villas 🍴 Multiple meal plans.*

SOUFRIÈRE AND THE WEST COAST

$$$$ RESORT **Anse Chastanet Resort.** This resort is magical; spectacular rooms—some with fourth walls open to the stunning Pitons view—peek out of the thick rain forest that cascades down a steep hillside to the beach. **Pros:** great for divers; Room 14B has a huge tree growing through the bathroom; the open-wall Piton views. **Cons:** no pool; entrance road is annoying even in a 4WD vehicle; steep hillside not conducive to strolling; no in-room TVs, phones, or a/c. *Rooms from: US$560 ✉ Anse Chastanet Rd. ☎ 758/459–7000, 800/223–1108 in U.S. www.ansechastanet.com 49 rooms Multiple meal plans.*

$$$$ HOTEL Fodor's Choice ★ **Boucan by Hotel Chocolat.** Anyone who loves chocolate will love this themed boutique hotel just south of Soufrière and within shouting distance of the Pitons. **Pros:** small and sophisticated; chocolate lover's dream; complimentary Wi-Fi. **Cons:** no a/c; no TV; no children under 12; car advised; not for anyone allergic to or less than thrilled by chocolate. *Rooms from: US$550 ✉ Rabot Estate, Soufrière–Vieux Fort Rd., 2 miles (3 km) south of town ☎ 758/572–9600 www.thehotelchocolat.com 14 rooms Multiple meal plans.*

$$$$ RESORT Fodor's Choice ★ **Capella Marigot Bay.** Five miles (8 km) south of Castries, this ultra-chic—yet laid-back—villa resort climbs the hillside overlooking what author James Michener called "the most beautiful bay in the Caribbean." **Pros:** peaceful; stunning bay view; oversize villa accommodations; ground-level units good for those with difficulty negotiating stairs; complimentary Wi-Fi. **Cons:** a/c in bedrooms only; car recommended to explore beyond Marigot Bay; nearby beach is lovely but tiny. *Rooms from: US$550 ✉ Marigot Bay ☎ 758/458–5300, 877/384–8037 in U.S. www.capellahotelgroup.com 67 rooms, 57 suites Multiple meal plans.*

$$ RESORT **Fond Doux Holiday Plantation.** Here at one of Soufrière's most active agricultural plantations, a dozen historic homes salvaged from all around the island have been rebuilt on the 135-acre estate and refurbished as guest accommodations. **Pros:** an exotic, eco-friendly experience; striking location on an 18th-century plantation. **Cons:** no a/c; no TV; a car is advised, as beach and local sights are a few miles away; not all cottages have a kitchen. *Rooms from: US$300 ✉ Fond Doux Estate, 4 miles south of Soufrière ☎ 758/459–7545 www.fonddouxestate.com 12 cottages Multiple meal plans.*

$ B&B/INN **Hummingbird Beach Resort.** Unpretentious and welcoming, this delightful little inn on Soufrière Harbour has simply furnished rooms—a traditional motif emphasized by four-poster beds and African wood sculptures—in small seaside cabins. **Pros:** local island hospitality; small and quiet; small beach; good food. **Cons:** few resort amenities—but that's part of the charm. *Rooms from: US$250 ✉ Anse Chastanet Rd. ☎ 758/459–7985 www.hummingbirdbeachresort.com 9 rooms, 2 with shared bath; 1 suite; 1 cottage Some meals.*

$$$$ RESORT Fodor's Choice ★ **Jade Mountain.** This premium-class, premium-priced, adults-only hotel is an architectural wonder perched on a picturesque mountainside overlooking the Pitons and the Caribbean. **Pros:** amazing accommodations; huge in-room pools; incredible Pitons view from every "sanctuary." **Cons:** sky-high rates; no a/c; not a good choice for anyone with

Jade Mountain

disabilities. $ *Rooms from: US$1,375* ✉ *Anse Chastanet, Anse Chastanet Rd.* ☎ *758/459–4000* 🌐 *www.jademountainstlucia.com* ⇆ *28 rooms* 🍽 *Multiple meal plans.*

$$$$ B&B/INN Fodor's Choice ★ **Ladera.** The elegantly rustic Ladera, perched 1,100 feet above the sea directly between the two Pitons, is one of the most sophisticated small inns in the Caribbean but, at the same time, takes a local, eco-friendly approach to furnishings, food, and service. **Pros:** local flavor and style; breathtaking Pitons vista; in-room pools; excellent cuisine; complimentary Wi-Fi. **Cons:** expensive; small communal infinity pool; open fourth walls and steep drops make this the wrong place for kids or those with disabilities; no a/c (but no real need); car suggested. $ *Rooms from: US$1,045* ✉ *Rabot Estate, Soufrière–Vieux Fort Hwy., 3 miles (5 km) south of town* ☎ *758/459–6600* 🌐 *www.ladera.com* ⇆ *32 suites* ⏲ *Closed Sept.* 🍽 *Multiple meal plans.*

$ B&B/INN FAMILY **La Haut Plantation.** It's all about the view—the Pitons, of course—and the appeal of staying in an intimate and affordable family-run inn. **Pros:** lovely for weddings and honeymoons but also for families; stunning Piton views; complimentary fresh fruit daily. **Cons:** very quiet, especially at night, unless that's the point; spotty Wi-Fi access; vehicle recommended. $ *Rooms from: US$260* ✉ *West Coast Rd., just north of town* ☎ *758/459–7008* 🌐 *www.lahaut.com* ⇆ *17 rooms* 🍽 *Breakfast.*

$$$ RESORT **Stonefield Estate Resort.** The 18th-century plantation house and several gingerbread-style cottages that dot this 26-acre family-owned estate, a former lime and cocoa plantation that spills down a tropical hillside, have eye-popping views of Petit Piton. **Pros:** very private; beautiful pool; great sunset views from villa decks; lovely wedding venue; complimentary Wi-Fi. **Cons:** car is recommended. $ *Rooms from: US$400*

✉ *West Coast Rd., 1 mile (1½ km) south of Soufrière* ☎ *758/459–7037, 800/420–5731 in U.S.* 🌐 *www.stonefieldvillas.com* ⇨ *17 villas* 🍴 *Multiple meal plans.*

$$$$ ALL-INCLUSIVE FAMILY Fodor's Choice ★ **Sugar Beach, A Viceroy Resort.** Located in Val des Pitons, the steep valley (once a sugar plantation) between the Pitons and the most dramatic 192 acres in St. Lucia, magnificent private villas are tucked into the dense tropical foliage that covers the hillside and reaches down to the sea. **Pros:** incomparable accommodations, scenery, service, and amenities; huge infinity pool; complimentary Wi-Fi and use of iPad during stay. **Cons:** very expensive; fairly isolated, so meal plan makes sense; car advised. $ *Rooms from: US$1,200* ✉ *Val des Pitons, 2 miles (3 km) south of town* ☎ *800/235–4300 in U.S., 758/456–8000* 🌐 *www.viceroyhotelsandresorts.com/sugarbeach* ⇨ *11 rooms, 59 villas, 8 bungalows* 🍴 *All-inclusive.*

$$$ RESORT Fodor's Choice ★ **Ti Kaye Resort & Spa.** Rustic elegance is not an oxymoron at this upscale cottage community that spills down a hillside above Anse Cochon Beach. **Pros:** great for a wedding, honeymoon, or getaway; garden showers; good restaurant; excellent snorkeling; on-site dive shop. **Cons:** far from anywhere; long, bumpy dirt access road; all those steps to the beach; not for those with physical challenges; no kids under 12. $ *Rooms from: US$390* ✉ *Off the West Coast Rd., halfway between Anse la Raye and Canaries, Anse Cochon* ☎ *758/456–8101* 🌐 *www.tikaye.com* ⇨ *33 rooms* 🍴 *Multiple meal plans.*

VIEUX FORT

$$$$ ALL-INCLUSIVE FAMILY **Coconut Bay Beach Resort & Spa.** The only resort in Vieux Fort, Coconut Bay is a sprawling (85 acres), family-friendly, seaside retreat minutes from Hewanorra International Airport. **Pros:** great for families; excellent kitesurfing; friendly and sociable atmosphere. **Cons:** bathrooms have showers only; rough surf. $ *Rooms from: US$689* ✉ *Micoud Hwy.* ☎ *758/459–6000, 877/352–8898 in U.S.* 🌐 *www.cbayresort.com* ⇨ *223 rooms, 27 suites* 🍴 *All-inclusive.*

NIGHTLIFE AND PERFORMING ARTS

PERFORMING ARTS

Fodor's Choice ★ **St. Lucia Jazz and Arts Festival.** This weeklong festival held in early May is one of the premier events in the Caribbean. International jazz greats perform at outdoor venues on Pigeon Island and at hotels, restaurants, and nightspots throughout St. Lucia; free concerts are also held at Derek Walcott Square in downtown Castries. ✉ *Pigeon Island* 🌐 *www.stluciajazz.org.*

NIGHTLIFE

Most resort hotels have entertainment—island music, calypso singers, or steel bands, as well as disco, karaoke, or staff/guest talent shows—every night in high season and a couple of nights per week in the off-season. Otherwise, Rodney Bay Village is the best bet for nightlife. The many restaurants and bars there attract a crowd nearly every night.

BARS

Jambe de Bois. Enjoy live jazz on Sunday evenings at this cozy Old English–style pub within the Pigeon Island National Landmark. ✉ *Pigeon Island, Gros Islet* ☎ *758/450–8166.*

CASINOS

Treasure Bay Casino. St. Lucia's first (and only, so far) casino has more than 250 slot machines, 22 gaming tables (poker, blackjack, roulette, and craps), and a sports bar with 31 screens. ✉ *Baywalk Mall, Reduit Beach Ave., off Castries–Gros Islet Hwy., Rodney Bay Village, Gros Islet* ☎ *758/459–2901* 🌐 *www.treasurebaystlucia.com* ⏲ *Sun.–Thurs. 10 am–3 am, Fri.–Sat. 10 am–4 am.*

DANCE CLUBS

Most dance clubs with live bands have a cover charge of $10–$20 (EC$25–EC$50), and the music usually starts at 11 pm.

Delirius. Visitors and St. Lucians alike "lime" over cocktails at the horseshoe-shape bar and at tables in the garden. The atmosphere is casual, the decor is contemporary, and the music (live bands or DJs on Wednesday, Friday, and Saturday nights) is often from the 1960s, '70s, and '80s. It's closed Sunday. ✉ *Reduit Beach Ave., Rodney Bay Village, Gros Islet* ☎ *758/451–3354* 🌐 *www.deliriusstlucia.com.*

Doolittle's. The music changes nightly. Expect live bands and a mix of calypso, soul, salsa, steel band, reggae, limbo, and other dance music. ✉ *Marigot Beach Club & Dive Resort, Marigot Bay* ☎ *758/451–4974* 🌐 *www.marigotbeachclub.com.*

STREET PARTIES

Anse la Raye Seafood Friday. For a taste of St. Lucian village life, head for this street festival, held every Friday night beginning at 6:30. The main street in this tiny fishing village—about halfway between Castries and Soufrière—is closed to vehicles, and residents prepare what they know best: fish cakes, grilled or stewed fish, hot bakes (biscuits), roasted corn, boiled crayfish, and lobster (grilled before your eyes). Prices range from a few cents for a fish cake or bake to $10 or $15 for a whole lobster. Walk around, eat, chat with locals, and listen to live music until the wee hours. ✉ *Main St., off West Coast Rd., Anse la Raye.*

Fodor's Choice ★ **Gros Islet Jump-Up.** The island's largest street party is a Friday-night ritual. Huge speakers set up on the street blast Caribbean music all night long. Sometimes there are live bands. When you take a break from dancing, you can buy barbecue fish or chicken, rotis, beer, and soda from villagers who set up grills along the roadside. It's the ultimate "lime" experience. ✉ *Dauphin St., off Castries–Gros Islet Hwy., Gros Islet.*

SHOPPING

The island's best-known products are artwork and wood carvings, straw mats, clay pottery, and clothing and household articles made from batik and silk-screened fabrics that are designed and produced in island workshops. You can also take home straw hats and baskets and locally grown cocoa, coffee, spices, sauces, and flavorings.

AREAS AND MALLS

Baywalk Mall, at Rodney Bay Village, is a 60-store complex of boutiques, restaurants, banks, a beauty salon, jewelry and souvenir stores, and the island's first (and only, so far) casino.

Along the harbor in Castries, rambling structures with bright-orange roofs house several markets that are open from 6 am to 5 pm Monday through Saturday. Saturday morning is the busiest and most colorful time to shop. For more than a century, farmers' wives have gathered at the **Castries Market** to sell produce—which you can enjoy on the island but, alas, can't bring to the United States. You can take spices (such as cocoa sticks or balls, turmeric, cloves, bay leaves, ginger, peppercorns, cinnamon sticks, nutmeg, and mace), though, as well as locally bottled hot-pepper sauces—all of which cost a fraction of what you'd pay back home. The adjacent **Craft Market** has aisles and aisles of baskets and other handmade straw work, rustic brooms made from palm fronds, wood carvings, leather work, clay pottery, and souvenirs—all at affordable prices. The **Vendors' Arcade,** across the street from the Craft Market, is a maze of stalls and booths where you can find handicrafts among the T-shirts and costume jewelry.

Gablewoods Mall, on the Gros Islet Highway in Choc Bay, a couple of miles north of downtown Castries, has about 35 shops that sell groceries, wines and spirits, jewelry, clothing, crafts, books and overseas newspapers, music, souvenirs, household goods, and snacks.

Along with 54 boutiques, restaurants, and other businesses that sell services and supplies, a large supermarket is the focal point of each **J.Q.'s Shopping Mall**; one is at Rodney Bay Village, and another is at Vieux Fort.

Marigot Marina Village, in Marigot Bay, has shops and services for boaters and landlubbers alike, including a bank, grocery store, business center, art gallery, assortment of boutiques, and French bakery and café.

Duty-free shopping areas are at **Pointe Seraphine,** an attractive Spanish-motif complex on Castries Harbour with a dozen shops, and **La Place Carenage,** an inviting three-story complex on the opposite side of the harbor. You can also find duty-free items at Baywalk Mall, in a few small shops at the arcade at the Royal St. Lucia by Rex Resorts hotel in Rodney Bay Village, and, of course, in the departure lounge at Hewanorra International Airport. You must present your passport and airline ticket to purchase items at the duty-free price.

Vieux Fort Plaza, near Hewanorra International Airport in Vieux Fort, is the main shopping center in the southern part of St. Lucia. It has a bank, supermarket, bookstore, toy shop, and clothing stores.

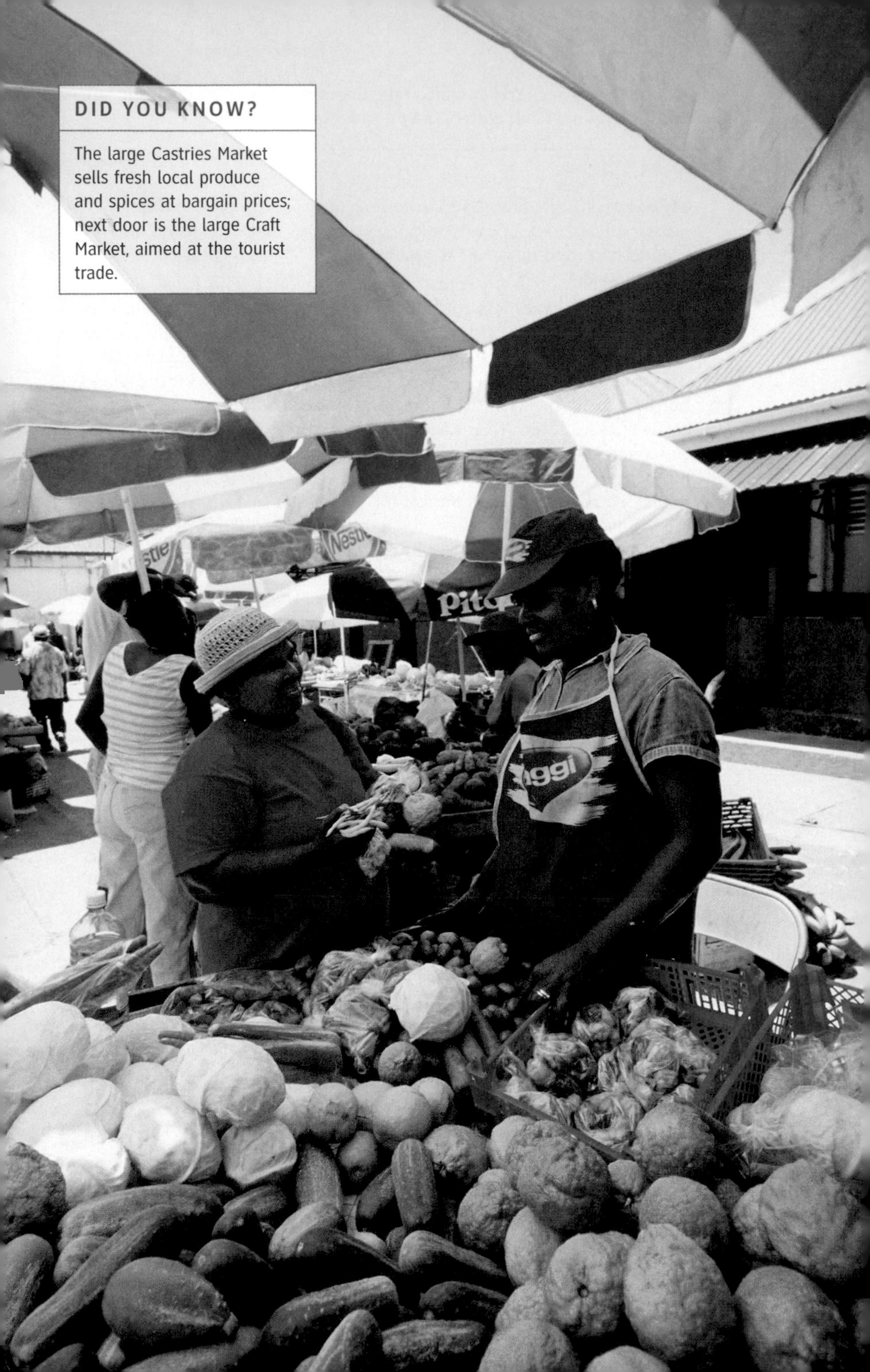

DID YOU KNOW?

The large Castries Market sells fresh local produce and spices at bargain prices; next door is the large Craft Market, aimed at the tourist trade.

ART

Caribbean Art & Antiques. On offer here are original artwork by local artists, including Llewellyn Xavier and Mervyn Charles, antique maps and prints, and hand-painted silk. ✉ *Rodney Bay Marina, Gros Islet* ☎ *758/450–9740.*

Llewellyn Xavier. World-renowned St. Lucian artist Llewellyn Xavier creates modern art, ranging from vigorous oil abstracts that take up half a wall to small objects made from beaten silver and gold. Much of his work has an environmental theme and is created from recycled materials. Xavier's work is owned by major museums in New York and Washington, D.C. Other pieces are sold in gift shops throughout the island. ■ **TIP→ Call to arrange a studio visit.** ✉ *Mount du Cap, Cap Estate* ☎ *758/450–9155* 🌐 *www.llewellynxavier.com.*

BOOKS AND MAGAZINES

Sunshine Bookshop. In addition to newspapers and magazines, this shop carries novels and titles of regional interest, including books by the St. Lucian Nobel laureate Derek Walcott and other Caribbean authors. ✉ *Gablewoods Mall, Sunny Acres, Castries* ☎ *758/452–3222.*

Valmont. This shop carries West Indian literature and picture books, as well as stationery. ✉ *Jeremie St. at Laborie St., Castries* ☎ *758/452–3817.*

CLOTHING AND TEXTILES

The Bagshaws of St. Lucia. Using Sydney Bagshaw's original designs, this shop sells clothing and table linens in colorful tropical patterns. The fabrics are silk-screened by hand in an adjacent workroom. You can also find Bagshaw boutiques at Pointe Seraphine and La Place Carenage, as well as a selection of items in gift shops at Hewanorra Airport. Visit the workshop to see how the designs are turned into colorful silk-screened fabrics, which are then fashioned into clothing and household articles. It's open weekdays from 8:30 to 5, Saturday 8:30 to 4, and Sunday 10 to 1. Weekend hours may be extended if a cruise ship is in port. ✉ *La Toc Rd., La Toc, Castries* ☎ *758/451–9249.*

The Batik Studio. The superb batik sarongs, scarves, and wall panels sold here are designed and created on-site by the shop's proprietor, Joan Alexander Stowe. ✉ *Hummingbird Beach Resort, Anse Chastanet Rd., Soufrière* ☎ *758/459–7985.*

Caribelle Batik. Craftspeople demonstrate the art of batik and silk-screen printing, while seamstresses use the batik fabric to make clothing and wall hangings, which you can buy in the shop. The studio is in an old Victorian mansion, high atop Morne Fortune and a 10-minute drive south of Castries. There's a terrace where you can have a cool drink and a garden full of tropical orchids and lilies. Caribelle Batik creations are also available in many gift shops throughout St. Lucia. ✉ *Howelton House, Old Victoria Rd., Morne Fortune, Castries* ☎ *758/452–3785* 🌐 *www.caribellebatikstlucia.com.*

Sea Island Cotton Shop. High-quality T-shirts, Caribelle Batik clothing and other resort wear, and colorful souvenirs are sold at attractive prices. ✉ *Baywalk Mall, Reduit Beach Ave., off Castries–Gros Islet Hwy., Rodney Bay Village, Gros Islet* ☎ *758/458–4220* 🌐 *www.seaislandstlucia.com.*

HANDICRAFTS

Choiseul Arts & Crafts Centre. A project of the Ministry of Education to encourage skill development and local crafts, this center carries handmade furniture, clay pots, wood carvings, and straw items. Many of St. Lucia's artisans come from the area—on the southwest coast, halfway between Soufrière and Vieux Fort. It's closed Sunday. ✉ *South Coast Hwy., 5 miles (8 km) south of Choiseul Village, La Fargue* ☎ *758/454–3226.*

Eudovic's Art Studio. This workshop, studio, and art gallery has wall plaques, masks, and abstract figures hand-carved by sculptor Vincent Joseph Eudovic from local mahogany, red cedar, and eucalyptus wood. ✉ *West Coast Rd., south of Morne Fortune, Goodlands, Castries* ☎ *758/452–2747* 🌐 *www.eudovicart.com.*

Fodor's Choice ★ **Zaka.** You may get a chance to talk with artist and craftsman Simon Gajhadhar, who fashions totems and masks from driftwood, branches, and other environmentally friendly wood sources—taking advantage of the natural nibs and knots that distinguish each piece. Once the "face" is carved, it is painted in vivid colors to highlight the exaggerated features and provide expression. ✉ *Jalousie Rd., off Soufrière–Vieux Fort Rd., Malgretoute, Soufrière* ☎ *758/457–1504* 🌐 *www.zaka-art.com.*

PERFUME

Caribbean Perfumes. Using exotic flowers, fruits, tropical woods, and spices, Caribbean Perfumes blends eight lovely scents for women and two aftershaves for men. The reasonably priced fragrances, all made in St. Lucia, are available at the perfume and duty-free shops at Baywalk Mall in Rodney Bay and at most gift shops. ✉ *Castries* ☎ *758/453–7249* 🌐 *www.caribbeanperfumes.com.*

SPORTS AND THE OUTDOORS

BIKING

Bike St. Lucia. Small groups of bikers are accompanied on jungle biking tours along 8 miles (13 km) of trails that meander through the remnants of the 18th-century Anse Mamin Plantation, part of the 600-acre Anse Chastanet Estate in Soufrière. Stops are made to explore the French colonial ruins, study the beautiful tropical plants and fruit trees, have a picnic lunch, and take a dip in a river swimming hole or at the beach. There's a training area for learning or brushing up on off-road riding skills. If you're staying in the north, you can arrange a tour that includes transportation to the Soufrière area. ✉ *Anse Mamin*

Plantation, adjacent to Anse Chastanet, Soufrière ☎ *758/457–1400* 🌐 *www.bikestlucia.com.*

Palm Services Bike Tours. Tour participants first take a jeep or bus across the central mountains to Dennery, on the east coast. After cycling 3 miles (5 km) through the countryside, bikes are exchanged for shoe leather. A short hike into the rain forest ends with a cool drink and refreshing swim by a sparkling waterfall—then the return to Dennery. All gear is included, and the four-hour tours are suitable for all fitness levels. ✉ *Rodney Bay Marina, Rodney Bay, Gros Islet* ☎ *758/458–0908* 🌐 *www.adventuretoursstlucia.com.*

BOATING AND SAILING

Rodney Bay and Marigot Bay are both centers for bareboat and crewed yacht charters. Charter prices range from $1,700 to $8,000 per week, depending on the season and the type and size of vessel, plus $130 extra per day if you want a skipper and $100 per day for a cook. Some boat charter companies do not operate in August and September due to possible weather issues.

Bateau Mygo. Choose a monohull or catamaran for your half- or full-day cruise along the west coast, or charter by the week and explore neighboring islands. ✉ *Chateau Mygo Villas, Marigot Bay* ☎ *758/721–7007* 🌐 *www.sailsaintlucia.com.*

Destination St. Lucia Ltd. (*DSL*). For its bareboat yacht charters, DSL's vessels include two 42-foot catamarans and several monohulls ranging in length from 32 to 50 feet. ✉ *Rodney Bay Marina, Rodney Bay, Gros Islet* ☎ *758/452–8531* 🌐 *www.dsl-yachting.com.*

Moorings Yacht Charters. Bareboat and crewed catamarans and monohulls ranging from Beneteau 39s to Morgan 60s are available for charter. You can also plan a one-way sail through the Grenadines, either picking up or dropping off at the company's facility in Grenada. ✉ *Rodney Bay Marina, Rodney Bay, Gros Islet* ☎ *758/451–4357, 888/952–8420 in U.S.* 🌐 *www.moorings.com.*

DIVING AND SNORKELING

Fodor's Choice ★

On-site dive shops at resorts include the Body Holiday, Sandals Grande, Royal St. Lucia by Rex, and Rendezvous in the north; Ti Kaye farther south; and Anse Chastanet and Sugar Beach, a Viceroy Resort, in Soufrière. Nearly all dive operators, regardless of their location, provide transportation from Rodney Bay, Castries, Marigot Bay, or Soufrière. Depending on the season and the particular trip, prices range from about $35 for a one-tank shore dive or $65 for a one-tank boat dive to $175–$250 for a six-dive package over three days and $350–$400 for a 10-dive package over five days—plus a National Marine Reserve permit fee of $6 per day. Dive shops provide instruction for all levels. For beginners, a resort course (pool training followed by an open-water dive) runs about $100–$130, depending on the number of days and dives included. Snorkelers can rent equipment for $5–$10 and are generally welcome on dive trips for $50–$70. All prices generally include taxi/boat transfers, lunch, and equipment.

Anse Chastanet, near the Pitons on the southwestern coast, is the best beach-entry dive site. The underwater reef drops from 20 feet to nearly 140 feet in a stunning coral wall.

A 165-foot freighter, *Lesleen M,* was deliberately sunk in 60 feet of water near **Anse Cochon** to create an artificial reef; divers can explore the ship in its entirety and view huge gorgonians, black coral trees, gigantic barrel sponges, lace corals, schooling fish, angelfish, sea horses, spotted eels, stingrays, nurse sharks, and sea turtles.

Anse la Raye, midway up the west coast, is one of St. Lucia's finest wall and drift dives and a great place for snorkeling.

At the **Pinnacles,** four coral-encrusted stone piers rise to within 10 feet of the surface.

Superman's Flight is a dramatic drift dive along the steep walls beneath the Pitons. At the base of **Petit Piton,** a spectacular wall drops to 200 feet, where you can view an impressive collection of huge barrel sponges and black coral trees; strong currents ensure good visibility.

DIVE OPERATORS

Dive Fair Helen. In operation since 1992 and owned by a St. Lucian environmentalist, this PADI center offers half- and full-day excursions on two custom-built dive boats to wreck, wall, and marine reserve areas, as well as night dives and instruction. ✉ *Marina Village, Marigot Bay* ☎ *758/451–7716* 🌐 *www.divefairhelen.com.*

Island Divers. At the edge of the National Marine Park at Soufrière, with two reefs and an offshore wreck accessible from shore, this dive shop at Ti Kaye Resort & Spa offers shore dives, boat dives, PADI certification, equipment rental, and an extensive list of specialty courses. ✉ *Ti Kaye Resort & Spa, off West Coast Rd., between Anse la Raye and Canaries, Anse Cochon* ☎ *758/456–8110* 🌐 *www.tikaye.com.*

Scuba St. Lucia. Daily beach and boat dives and resort and certification courses are available from this PADI Five Star facility on Anse Chastanet Beach, and so is underwater photography and snorkeling equipment. Day trips from the north of the island include round-trip speedboat transportation. ✉ *Anse Chastanet Resort, Anse Chastanet Rd., Soufrière* ☎ *758/459–7755, 800/223–1108 in U.S.* 🌐 *www.scubastlucia.com.*

FISHING

Among the deep-sea creatures you can find in St. Lucia's waters are dolphin (the fish, also called dorado or mahimahi), barracuda, mackerel, wahoo, kingfish, sailfish, and white and blue marlin. Sportfishing is generally done on a catch-and-release basis, but the captain may permit you to take a fish back to your hotel to be prepared for your dinner. Neither spearfishing nor collecting live fish in coastal waters is permitted. Half- and full-day deep-sea fishing excursions can be arranged at Vigie Marina. A half day of fishing on a scheduled trip runs about $85–$90 per person; a private charter costs $500–$1,200 for up to six or eight people, depending on the size of the boat and the length of time. Beginners are welcome.

Captain Mike's. Named for Captain Mike Hackshaw and run by his family, Bruce and Andrew, this operation has a fleet of Bertram powerboats (31 to 46 feet) that accommodate up to eight passengers for half-day or full-day sportfishing charters; tackle and cold drinks are supplied. Customized sightseeing or whale/dolphin-watching trips ($50 per person) can also be arranged for four to six people. ✉ *Vigie Marina, Vigie, Castries* ☎ *758/452–7044* 🌐 *www.captmikes.com.*

Hackshaw's Boat Charters. In business since 1953, this company runs charters on *Blue Boy,* a 31-foot Bertram; *Lady Hack,* a 50-foot custom-built Newton; and *Party Hack,* a 64-foot double-deck power catamaran also used for snorkeling, whale-watching, and party cruises. ✉ *Vigie Marina, Seraphine Rd., Vigie, Castries* ☎ *758/453–0553* 🌐 *www.hackshaws.com.*

GOLF

St. Lucia has only one 18-hole championship course: **St. Lucia Golf Resort & Country Club**, which is in Cap Estate. **Sandals Regency La Toc Golf Resort & Spa** has a 9-hole course for its guests.

St. Lucia Golf Resort & Country Club. St. Lucia's only public course is at the island's northern tip and features broad views of both the Atlantic and the Caribbean as well as many spots adorned with orchids and bromeliads. Wind and the demanding layout present challenges. The Cap Grill serves breakfast and lunch until 7 pm; the Sports Bar is a convivial meeting place all day long. You can arrange lessons at the pro shop and perfect your swing at the 350-yard driving range. Fees include carts, which are required; club and shoe rentals are available. Reservations are essential. Complimentary transportation from your hotel (north of Castries) is available for parties of three or more. ✉ *Cap Estate* ☎ *758/450–8523* 🌐 *www.stluciagolf.com* *$100 for 18 holes, $75 for 9 holes* *18 holes, 6685 yards, par 71.*

GUIDED TOURS

Taxi drivers are well informed and can give you a full tour and often an excellent one, thanks to government-sponsored training programs. Full-day island tours cost about $140 for up to four people, depending on the route and whether entrance fees and lunch are included; half-day tours, $100. If you plan your own day, expect to pay the driver $40 per hour plus tip.

Island Routes. This Sandals partner offers a variety of adventure tours, including guided, drive-it-yourself dune buggy safaris of Soufrière's natural sites and attractions (six hours, $199; 10 hours, $230). The longer adventure includes a cruise down the west coast from Rodney Bay. Drivers must be at least 23, have a valid driver's license, and be able to drive a manual transmission. Other tours include ATV adventures (two hours, $140) and a guided historical tour beginning in Marigot Bay (eight hours, $125). ✉ *Gros Islet* ☎ *877/768–8370 in U.S., 758/452–3081* 🌐 *www.islandroutes.com.*

Jungle Tours. This company specializes in rain-forest hiking tours for all ability levels. You're required only to bring hiking shoes or sneakers and have a willingness to get wet and have fun. The cost is $95 per person and includes lunch, fees, and transportation via an open Land Rover truck. ✉ *Cas en Bas, Gros Islet* ☎ *758/715–3438* 🌐 *www.jungletoursstlucia.com.*

St. Lucia Helicopters. How about a bird's-eye view of the island? A 10-minute North Island tour ($98 per person) leaves from the hangar in Castries, continues up the west coast to Pigeon Island, then flies along the rugged Atlantic coastline before returning inland over Castries. The 20-minute South Island tour ($160 per person) starts at Pointe Seraphine and follows the western coastline, circling beautiful Marigot Bay, Soufrière, and the majestic Pitons before returning inland over the volcanic hot springs and tropical rain forest. A complete island tour combines the two and lasts 30 minutes ($200 per person). All tours require a minimum of four passengers. ✉ *George F. L. Charles Airport, Island Flyers Hangar, Vigie, Castries* ☎ *758/453–6950* 🌐 *www.stluciahelicopters.com.*

St. Lucia Heritage Tours. The Heritage Tourism Association of St. Lucia (HERITAS), a volunteer group that represents local sites and institutions, puts together "authentic St. Lucia experiences" that focus on local culture and traditions. Groups are kept small, and the tours can be tailored to your interests. Some of the sites visited include a 19th-century plantation house surrounded by nature trails, a 20-foot waterfall hidden away on private property, and a living museum presenting Creole practices and traditions. Other options include bird-watching, turtle-watching, horseback riding, garden walks, culinary experiences, and rain-forest treks. ✉ *John Compton Hwy., Castries* ☎ *758/458–1454* 🌐 *www.heritagetoursstlucia.org.*

St. Lucia National Trust. Among the trust's fascinating educational programs and tours are a hike through a mangrove forest, a boat trip and trek to Maria Islands Nature Reserve, a native fishing tour on a traditional pirogue, handicraft production, horseback riding, and sea moss harvesting. ✉ *Castries* ☎ *758/452–5005* 🌐 *www.slunatrust.org.*

Sunlink Tours. This huge tour operator offers dozens of land, sea, and combination sightseeing tours, as well as shopping tours, plantation and rain-forest adventures via Jeep safari, deep-sea fishing excursions, and day trips to other islands. Prices range from $30 for a half-day shopping tour in Castries to $135 for a full-day land-and-sea Jeep safari to Soufrière. ✉ *Reduit Beach Ave., Rodney Bay Village, Gros Islet* ☎ *758/456–9100* 🌐 *www.sunlinktours.com.*

HIKING

St. Lucia Forestry Department. Trails under this department's jurisdiction include the Barre de L'Isle Trail (just off the highway, halfway between Castries and Dennery), the Forestiere Trail (20 minutes east of Castries), the Des Cartiers Rain Forest Trail (west of Micoud), the Edmund Rain Forest Trail and Enbas Saut Waterfalls (east of Soufrière), the Millet Bird Sanctuary Trail (east of Marigot Bay), and the Union Nature Trail (north of Castries). Most are two-hour hikes on 2-mile (3-km) loop trails; the bird-watching tour lasts four hours. The Forestry Department provides guides ($2–$30, depending on the hike), who explain the plants and trees that you'll encounter and keep you on the right track. Seasoned hikers climb the Pitons, the two volcanic cones rising 2,461 feet and 2,619 feet from the ocean floor just south of Soufrière. Hiking is recommended only on Gros Piton, which offers a steep but safe trail to the top. The first half of the hike is moderately difficult; reaching the summit is challenging and should be attempted only by those who are physically fit. The view from the top is spectacular. Tourists are also permitted to hike Petit Piton, but the second half of the hike requires a good deal of rock climbing, and you'll need to provide your own safety equipment. Hiking either Piton requires permission and a knowledgeable guide ($45), both arranged through the St. Lucia Forestry Department. ✉ *Stanislaus James Bldg., Waterfront, Castries* ☎ *758/468–4104, 758/450–2231 for Piton permission* 🌐 *www.malff.com.*

HORSEBACK RIDING

Creole horses, a breed native to South America and popular on St. Lucia, are fairly small, fast, sturdy, and even-tempered animals suitable for beginners. Established stables can accommodate all skill levels. They offer countryside trail rides, beach rides with picnic lunches, plantation tours, carriage rides, and lengthy treks. Prices run about $40 for a one-hour guided ride, $60 for two hours, and $70–$90 for a three- or four-hour beach ride with swimming (with the horses) and lunch. Transportation is usually provided between the stables and nearby hotels. Local people sometimes appear on beaches with their steeds and offer 30-minute rides for $10 to $15; ride at your own risk.

Atlantic Shores Riding Stables. Two-hour trail rides roam along the beach and through the countryside. Beginners are welcome. ✉ *Savannes Bay, Vieux Fort* ☎ *758/285–1090.*

Trim's National Riding Stable. At the island's oldest riding stable there are four sessions per day, plus beach tours, trail rides, and carriage tours to Pigeon Island. ✉ *Cas en Bas, Gros Islet* ☎ *758/450–8273* 🌐 *www.horserideslu.50megs.com.*

SEA EXCURSIONS

Fodor's Choice ★ A day sail or sea cruise from Rodney Bay or Vigie Cove to Soufrière and the Pitons is a wonderful way to see St. Lucia and get to its distinctive natural sites. Prices for a full-day sailing excursion to Soufrière run about $100 per person and include a land tour to the Diamond Falls Botanical Gardens, lunch, a stop for swimming and snorkeling, and a visit to pretty Marigot Bay. You can even add zip-lining! Half-day cruises to the Pitons, three-hour whale-watching tours, and two-hour sunset cruises along the northwest coast cost $45–$60 per person.

Captain Mike's Whale/Dolphin Watching Tours. With 20 species of whales and dolphins living in Caribbean waters, your chances of sighting some are very good on these three-hour trips ($50 per person) aboard *Free Willie*, a 60-foot Defender. ✉ *Vigie Marina, Ganthers Bay, Castries* ☎ *758/452–7044* 🌐 *www.captmikes.com.*

FAMILY ***Endless Summer* Cruises.** *Endless Summer*, a 56-foot party catamaran, runs day trips along the coast to Soufrière—hotel transfers, tour, entrance fees, lunch, and drinks included—for $110 per person. A half-day swimming and snorkeling trip is also available. For romantics, there's a sunset cruise for $60, including dinner and entertainment. ✉ *Reduit Beach Ave., Rodney Bay Village, Gros Islet* ☎ *758/450–8651* 🌐 *www.stluciaboattours.com.*

Mystic Man Tours. Glass-bottom boat, sailing, catamaran, deep-sea fishing, snorkeling, and/or whale- and dolphin-watching tours are all great family excursions; there's also a sunset cruise. Most trips depart from Soufrière. ✉ *Maurice Mason St., Soufrière* ☎ *758/459–7783, 800/401–9804* 🌐 *www.mysticmantours.com.*

Sea Spray Cruises. Sail down the west coast from Rodney Bay to Soufrière on *Mango Tango* (a 52-foot catamaran), *Tango Too* (an 80-foot cat'), or *Jus Tango* (a 65-foot cat'). The all-day Tout Bagay (a little bit of everything) tour includes a visit to the sulfur springs, drive-in volcano, and Morne Coubaril Estate. The view of the Pitons from the water is majestic. You'll have lunch and drinks on board, plenty of music, and an opportunity to swim at a remote beach. Tout Bagay operates Monday, Wednesday, and Saturday. Sea Spray operates several other boat tours, including a sunset cruise, on other days. ✉ *Rodney Bay Marina, Rodney Bay, Gros Islet* ☎ *758/458–0123, 321/220–9423 in U.S.*

WINDSURFING AND KITEBOARDING

Reef Kite and Surf Centre. This water-sports center offers equipment rental and lessons from certified instructors. Windsurfing equipment rental is $50 for a half day, $70 full day. Kitesurfing equipment rents for $60 half day, $80 full day. A three-hour beginning windsurfing course costs $100, including equipment; a two-hour "taster" session is $75. For kitesurfing, the three-hour starter costs $200, including equipment and safety gear, the two-hour taster, $90. Kitesurfing is particularly strenuous, so participants must be excellent swimmers and in good health. ✉ *The Reef Beach Café, Anse de Sables, Vieux Fort* ☎ *758/454–3418.*

ST. MAARTEN/ ST. MARTIN

WELCOME TO ST. MAARTEN/ ST. MARTIN

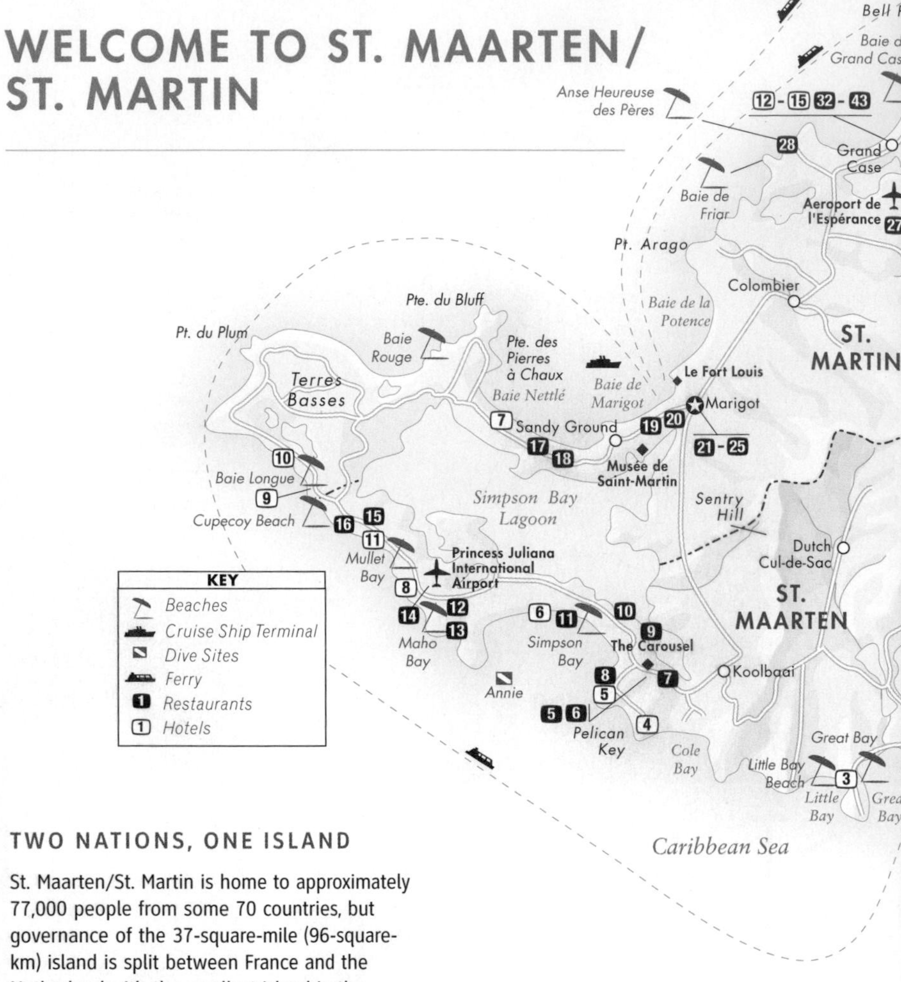

TWO NATIONS, ONE ISLAND

St. Maarten/St. Martin is home to approximately 77,000 people from some 70 countries, but governance of the 37-square-mile (96-square-km) island is split between France and the Netherlands. It's the smallest island in the world divided between two ruling powers. The Dutch capital is Philipsburg; the French capital is Marigot.

TOP REASONS TO VISIT ST. MAARTEN/ST. MARTIN

1 Great Food: The island has so many good places to dine that you could eat out for a month and never repeat a restaurant visit.

2 Lots of Shops: Philipsburg is one of the top shopping spots in the Caribbean, and Marigot brings a touch of France.

3 Beaches Large and Small: Thirty-seven picture-perfect beaches are spread out all over the island.

4 Water Sports Galore: The wide range of water sports will satisfy almost any need and give you the perfect excuse to finally try stand-up paddleboarding or kitesurfing.

5 Nightlife Every Night: There is a wide variety of nightlife: shows, discos, beach bars, and casinos.

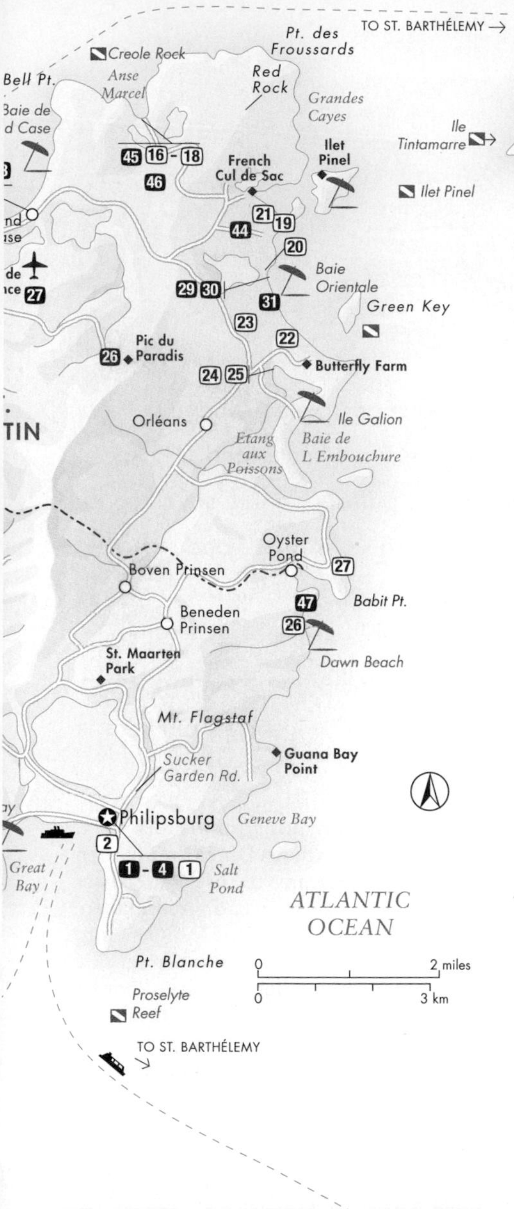

Restaurants ▼

Restaurant	Map no.
Anse Marcel Beach	45
Bacchus	35
Bamboo	13
Big Fish	47
Chesterfield's	4
Enoch's Place	23
Friar's Bay Beach Cafe	28
The Greenhouse	3
Hidden Forest Café	26
Izi Ristorante	5
Karakter Beach Lounge	11
La Belle Epoque	21
La Cigale	17
La Source	25
La Table d'Antoine	31
L'Astrolabe	29
L'Auberge Gourmande	38
Le Dateau Ivre	16
Le Cottage	40
Le Marrakech	24
Le Mini-Club	22
Le Moulin Fou	12
Le Pressoir	33
Le Sand	18
Le Shamabala	41
Le Ti Bouchon	46
Le Tastevin	37
L'Effet Mer	39
L'Estaminet	32
Ma Ti' Beach	27
Mario's Bistro	19
Ocean Lounge	2
Palm Beach	30
Panlaan Thai	6
Pineapple Pete	7
Sky's the Limit	43
Sol é Luna	44
Spiga	34
Tai Chi	42
Talk of the Town	36
Taloula Mango's	1
Temptation	15
Top Carrot	8
Tropicana	20
Trattoria Italiana	14
Vesna Taverna	9
Zee Best	10

Hotels ▼

Hotel	Map no.
Alamanda Resort	23
Belmond La Samanna	10
Bleu Emeraude	14
Blue Pelican	5
Captain Oliver's Resort	27
Caribbean Princess	19
The Cliffs at Cupecoy	9
Divi Little Bay Beach Resort	3
Esmeralda	20
Grand Case Beach Club	15
Green Cay Village	24
Holland House Beach Hotel	1
The Horny Toad	6
Hotel La Plantation	22
Hotel L'Esplanade	12
Hotel Mercure	7
Hotel Riu Palace St. Martin	18
Karibuni Lodge	21
La Vista	4
Le Domaine de Lonvilliers by Christophe Leroy	16
Le Petit Hotel	13
Marquis Boutique Hotel	17
Palm Court	25
Sonesta Great Bay	2
Sonesta Maho Beach Resort	8
Towers at Mullet Bay	11
Westin St. Maarten, Dawn Beach Resort & Spa	26

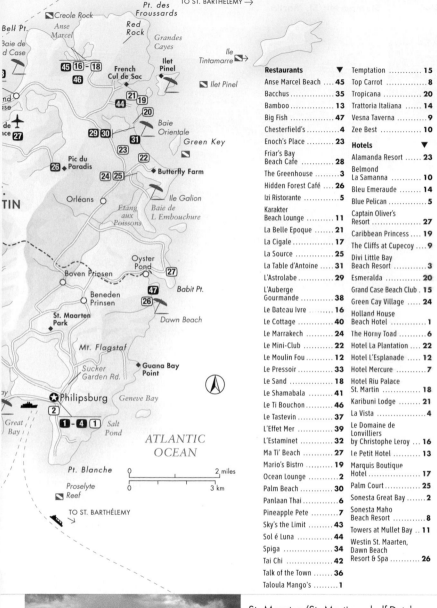

St. Maarten/St. Martin, a half-Dutch, half-French island, is a place where gastronomy flourishes, where most resorts are large rather than small, where casinos draw gamblers, where sporting opportunities are plentiful, and where the sunning, as on the south end of Orient Beach, is sometimes au naturel.

Updated by Elise Meyer

St. Maarten/St. Martin is unique among Caribbean destinations. The 37-square-mile (96-square-km) island is a seamless place (there are no border gates), but it is governed by two nations—the Netherlands and France—and has residents from 70-some countries. A call from the Dutch side to the French is an international call, currencies are different, and even the vibe is different. Only the island of Hispaniola, which encompasses Haiti and the Dominican Republic, is in a similar position in the Caribbean.

Happily for Americans, who make up the majority of visitors to St. Maarten/St. Martin, English works in both nations. Dutch St. Maarten might feel particularly comfortable for Americans: the prices are lower (not to mention in U.S. dollars), the big hotels have casinos, and there is more nightlife. Huge cruise ships disgorge masses of shoppers into the Philipsburg shopping area at midmorning, when roads can quickly become congested. But once you pass the meandering, unmarked border to the French side, you find a hint of the south of France: quiet countryside, fine cuisine, and in Marigot, a walkable harbor area with outdoor cafés, an outdoor market, and plenty of shopping and cultural activities.

Almost 4,000 years ago, it was salt and not tourism that drove the little island's economy. Arawak Indians, the island's first known inhabitants, prospered until the warring Caribs invaded, adding the peaceful Arawaks to their list of conquests. Columbus spotted the isle on November 11, 1493, and named it after St. Martin (whose feast day is November 11), but it wasn't populated by Europeans until the 17th century, when it was claimed by the Dutch, French, and Spanish. The Dutch and French finally joined forces to claim the island in 1644, and the Treaty of Concordia partitioned the territory in 1648. According to legend the border was drawn along the line where a French man and a Dutch man, running from opposite coasts, met.

Both sides of the island offer a touch of European culture along with a lot of laid-back Caribbean ambience. Water sports abound—diving, snorkeling, sailing, windsurfing, and in early March, the Heineken Regatta. With soft trade winds cooling the subtropical climate, it's easy to while away the day relaxing on one of the 37 beaches, strolling Philipsburg's boardwalk, and perusing the shops on Philipsburg's Front Street or the *rues* (streets) of the very French town of Marigot. Although luck is an important commodity at St. Maarten's 13 casinos, chance plays no part in finding a good meal at the excellent eateries or after-dark fun in the subtle to sizzling nightlife. Heavy development—especially on the Dutch side—has stressed the island's infrastructure, but slowly some of the more dilapidated roads are showing signs of improvement. A series of large roundabouts, with the beginnings of some decent signage, and attractive monumental sculptures has improved traffic flow (remember, the cars already in the roundabout have right-of-way). At long last, the eyesore of hurricane-wrecked buildings that lined the golf course at Mullet Bay have been demolished, and most welcome is the new swing bridge that crosses Simpson Bay Lagoon, connecting the airport and Cole Bay.

When cruise ships are in port (and there can be as many as seven at once), shopping areas are crowded and traffic moves at a snail's pace. Instead spend days on the beach or the water, and plan shopping excursions for the early morning or at cocktail hour, after "rush hour" traffic calms down. Still, these are minor inconveniences compared with the feel of the sand between your toes or the breeze through your hair, gourmet food sating your appetite, and being able to crisscross between two nations on one island.

PLANNING

WHEN TO GO

The high season begins in December and runs through the middle of April. During the off-season, hotel rooms can be had for as little as half the high-season rates.

GETTING HERE AND AROUND

AIR TRAVEL

There are nonstop flights from Atlanta (Delta, seasonal), Charlotte (US Airways), Miami (American), New York–JFK (American, Delta, JetBlue), New York–Newark (United), and Philadelphia (US Airways). There are also some nonstop charter flights (including GWV/Apple Vacations from Boston). You can also connect in San Juan on Air Sunshine, JetBlue, or LIAT. Many smaller Caribbean-based airlines, including Air Caraïbes, Anguilla Air Services, Caribbean Airlines, Copa, Insel, LIAT, St. Barth Commuter, and Winair (Windward Islands Airways), offer service from other islands in the Caribbean.

Airline Contacts Air Caraïbes ✉ *St. Martin* ☎ *0590/52–05–10* 🌐 *www.aircaraibes-usa.com.* **Air Sunshine** ✉ *Airport Rd., Simpson Bay, St. Martin* ☎ *800/434–8900* 🌐 *www.airsunshine.com.* **American Airlines** ✉ *St. Martin* ☎ *721/545–2040, 800/433–7300* 🌐 *www.aa.com.* **Anguilla Air**

LOGISTICS

Getting to St. Maarten/St. Martin: There are nonstop flights to St. Maarten from the mainland United States, as well as connecting service through San Juan. Further, St. Maarten is a hub for smaller, regional airlines. The island's main airport is Princess Juliana International Airport (SXM), on the Dutch side. Aeroport de L'Espérance (SFG), on the French side, is small and handles only small planes.

Hassle Factor: Low–medium.

On the Ground: Most visitors rent a car upon arrival, but taxi service is available at the airport with fixed fares to all hotels on the island, and you'll be able to pay in U.S. dollars. Although the island is small, it's still a long drive to many hotels on the French side, and fares add up.

Getting Around the Island: Most visitors rent a car because rates are fairly cheap and the island is easy to navigate. It's possible to get by with taxis if you are staying in a major hub such as Philipsburg or Baie Orientale, but you may spend more money than if you rented a car.

Services ✉ *Airport Rd., Simpson Bay, St. Martin* ☎ *264/498–5922* 🌐 *www.anguillaairservices.com.* **Caribbean Airlines** ✉ *St. Martin* ☎ *721/546–7660* 🌐 *www.caribbean-airlines.com.* **Copa Airlines** ✉ *Airport Rd., Simpson Bay, St. Martin* ☎ *877/389–3606* 🌐 *www.copaair.com.* **Delta Airlines** ✉ *St. Martin* ☎ *721/546–7615* 🌐 *www.delta.com.* **Insel Air** ✉ *St. Martin* ☎ *599/546–7621* 🌐 *www.fly-inselair.com.* **JetBlue** ✉ *St. Martin* ☎ *721/546–7797, 877/306–4939* 🌐 *www.jetblue.com.* **LIAT** ✉ *St. Martin* ☎ *721/546–7621* 🌐 *www.liatairline.com.* **St. Barth Commuter** ✉ *St. Martin* ☎ *0590/87–80–73* 🌐 *www.stbarthcommuter.com.* **United Airlines** ✉ *St. Martin* ☎ *800/864–8331* 🌐 *www.united.com.* **US Airways** ✉ *St. Martin* ☎ *721/546–7680* 🌐 *www.usairways.com.* **Winair** ✉ *St. Martin* ☎ *721/545–4237* 🌐 *www.fly-winair.com.*

Airports **Aéroport de L'Espérance** (*SFG*). This airport, on the French side, is small and handles only island-hoppers. ✉ *Rte. de l'Espérance, Grand Case, St. Martin* ☎ *0590/27–11–00* 🌐 *www.aeroport-saintmartin.com.* **Princess Juliana International Airport** (*SXM*). This airport on the Dutch side handles all the large jets. ✉ *St. Maarten* ☎ *721/546–7542* 🌐 *www.sxmairport.com.*

BOAT AND FERRY TRAVEL

You can take ferries to St. Barth (45–80 minutes, €67–€93 from the Dutch or French side, though you can pay in dollars); to Anguilla (20 minutes, $25 from the French side); and to Saba (one to two hours, $90–$100 from the Dutch side).

Contacts **Aqua Mania Adventures.** Boats run day trips to Saba, St. Barth, and Anguilla. ✉ *Pelican Marina, Simpson Bay, St. Maarten* ☎ *721/544–2640, 721/544–2631* 🌐 *www.stmaarten-activities.com.* **Great Bay Express.** A high-speed ferry goes to St. Barth several times a day. ✉ *Bobby's Marina Village, Phillipsburg, St. Maarten* ☎ *721/542–0032* 🌐 *www.greatbayferry.com.* **Link Ferries.** Ferry service to Anguilla runs from both Marigot and Princess Juliana Airport. ✉ *Marigot, St. Martin* ☎ *264/497–2231 in Anguilla, 264/497–3290 in Anguilla* 🌐 *www.link.ai.* ***Shauna.*** Service to Anguilla is offered. ✉ *Simpson Bay,*

St. Maarten ☎ *599/553–1820 in Anguilla.* ***Voyager II.*** Service from both Marigot and Oyster Pond connects to St. Barth. ✉ *Marigot, St. Martin* ☎ *0590/87–10–68* 🌐 *www.voy12.com.*

CAR TRAVEL

It's easy to get around the island by car. Most roads are paved and in generally good condition. However, they can be crowded, especially when the cruise ships are in port; you might experience traffic jams, particularly around Marigot and Philipsburg. Be alert for potholes and speed bumps, as well as the island tradition of stopping in the middle of the road to chat with a friend or yield to someone entering traffic. Few roads are identified by name or number, but most have signs indicating the destination. Driving is on the right. There are gas stations in Simpson Bay near the airport as well as in Cole Bay, and on the French side, in Sandy Ground and Marigot.

Car Rentals: You can book a car at Juliana International Airport, where all major rental companies have booths, but it is often much cheaper to reserve a car in advance from home. A shuttle to the rental-car lot is provided. Rates are among the best in the Caribbean, as little as $20–$35 per day. You can rent a car on the French side, but this rarely makes sense for Americans because of the unfavorable exchange rates.

Car-Rental Contacts Avis ✉ *Simpson Bay, St. Maarten* ☎ *721/545–2847, 800/331–1084* 🌐 *www.avis-sxm.com.* **Dollar/Thrifty Car Rental** ✉ *102 Airport Rd., St. Maarten* ☎ *721/545–2393* 🌐 *www.thriftycarrentalsxm.com.* **Empress Rent-a-Car** ✉ *St. Maarten* ☎ *721/520–2391* 🌐 *www.empressrentacar.com.* **Golfe Car Rental** ✉ *Rte. de l'Espérance, Grand Case, St. Martin* ☎ *0690/35–04–75* 🌐 *www.golfecarrental.com.* **Hertz** ✉ *82 Airport Rd., Simpson Bay, St. Maarten* ☎ *721/545–4541* 🌐 *www.hertz.sxmrentacar.com.***Unity** ✉ *6 Sister Modesta Rd., Simpson Bay, St. Maarten* ☎ *721/520–5767* 🌐 *www.unitycarrental.com.*

SCOOTER TRAVEL

Though traffic can be heavy, speeds are generally slow, so a moped can be a good way to get around. Scooters rent for as low as €30 per day and motorbikes for €37 a day at Eugene Moto, on the French side. The Harley-Davidson dealer, on the Dutch side, rents hogs for $150 a day or $900 per week.

Contacts Eugene Moto ✉ *Sandy Ground Rd., Sandy Ground, St. Martin* ☎ *0590/87–13–97.* **Harley-Davidson** ✉ *71 Union Rd., Cole Bay, St. Maarten* ☎ *721/544–2704* 🌐 *www.h-dstmartin.com.*

TAXI TRAVEL

There is a government-sponsored taxi dispatcher at the airport and the harbor. Posted fares are for one or two people. Add $5 for each additional person, half price for kids. The first bag is free; after that it's $1 per bag. It costs about $18 from the airport to Philipsburg or Marigot, and about $30 to Dawn Beach. After 10 pm fares go up 25%, and after midnight 50%. Licensed drivers can be identified by the "taxi" license plate on the Dutch side and the window sticker on the French. You can hail cabs on the street or call the taxi dispatch to have one sent. Fixed fares apply from Juliana International Airport and the Marigot ferry to hotels around the island.

ESSENTIALS

Banks and Exchange Services Legal tender on the Dutch side is the Netherlands Antilles guilder (also called the florin), but almost everyone accepts dollars. On the French side, the currency is the euro, but most establishments accept dollars. At this writing, quite a few restaurants continue to offer one euro-for-one dollar exchanges in cash. ATMs dispense dollars or euros, depending on where you are.

Electricity Generally, 110 volts AC (60-cycle) on the Dutch side, just as in the United States. The French side operates on 220 volts AC (60-cycle), with round-prong plugs (many hotels can supply adapters).

Language Dutch is the official language of St. Maarten and French is the official language of St. Martin, but almost everyone speaks English.

Passport Requirements A valid passport and a return ticket are required for all visitors.

Phones Calling from one side of the island to another is an international call. To phone from the Dutch side to the French, you first must dial 00–590–590 for local numbers, or 00–590–690 for cell phones, then the six digit number. To call from the French side to the Dutch, dial 00–721, then the local number. To call a local number on the French side, dial 0590 plus the six-digit number. On the Dutch side, just dial the seven-digit number with no prefix. Any of the local carriers—and most hotel concierges—can arrange for a prepaid rental phone for your use while you are on the island for about $5 a weekday plus a per-minute charge.

Taxes and Service Charges Departure tax from Juliana Airport is $10 to destinations within the Netherlands Antilles and $30 to all other destinations. It is usually included in your air ticket. It will cost you €3 (usually included in the ticket price) to depart by plane from Aéroport de L'Espérance and $5 (the rate can change) by ferry to Anguilla from Marigot's pier. Hotels on the Dutch side add a 15% service charge to the bill as well as a 5% government tax. Hotels on the French side add 10%–15% and generally 5% tax.

Tipping Service charges may be added to hotel and restaurant bills on the Dutch side (otherwise tip 15%–18%). Check bills carefully so you don't inadvertently tip twice. On the French side, a service charge is customary; on top of the included service it is customary to leave 5%–10% *in cash* for the server. Taxi drivers, porters, and maids depend on tips. Give 10%–15% to cabbies, $1 per bag for porters, and $2–$5 per night per guest for chambermaids.

ACCOMMODATIONS

The island, though small, is well developed—some say overdeveloped—and offers a wide range of lodging. The larger resorts and time-shares are mostly on the Dutch side; the French side has more intimate properties. Just keep in mind that the popular restaurants around Grand Case, on the French side, are a long drive from most Dutch-side hotels. French-side hotels often charge in euros. Be wary of very low–price alternatives, as some of these can be run-down time-shares, short-term housing for temporary workers, or properties used by very low-end tour companies. Additionally, note locations very close to the airport to avoid unpleasant, noisy surprises. In general, the newer a property, the better.

Hotel reviews have been shortened. For full information, visit Fodors.com.

WHAT IT COSTS				
	$	**$$**	**$$$**	**$$$$**
Restaurants	under $12	$12–$20	$21–$30	over $30
	under €12	€12– €20	€21–€30	over €30
Hotels	under $275	$275–$375	$376–$475	over $475

Restaurant prices are the average cost of a main course at dinner or, if dinner is not served, at lunch. Hotel prices are the lowest cost of a standard double room in high season.

VISITOR INFORMATION

Contacts Dutch-side Tourist Information Bureau ✉ *Vineyard Park Bldg., 33 W. G. Buncamper Rd., Philipsburg, St. Maarten* ☎ *721/542-2337* 🌐 *www.vacationstmaarten.com.* **French-side Office de Tourisme** ✉ *Rte. de Sandy Ground, facing Marina de la Port-Royale, Marigot, St. Martin* ☎ *0590/87-57-21* 🌐 *www.iledesaintmartin.org.*

WEDDINGS

There's a three-day waiting period on the Dutch side. Getting married on the French side is not a viable option because of long wait times.

EXPLORING

The best way to explore St. Maarten/St. Martin is by car. Though often congested, especially around Philipsburg and Marigot, the roads are fairly good, though narrow and winding, with some speed bumps, potholes, roundabouts, and an occasional wandering goat herd. Few roads are marked with their names, but destination signs are common. Besides, the island is so small that it's hard to get really lost—at least that is what locals tell you.

If you're spending a few days, get to know the area with a scenic loop around the island. Be sure to pack a towel and some water shoes, a hat, sunglasses, and sunblock. Head up the east shoreline from Philipsburg, and follow the signs to Dawn Beach and Oyster Pond. The road winds past soaring hills, turquoise waters, quaint West Indian houses, and wonderful views of St. Barth. As you cross over to the French side, turn into Le Galion for a stop at the calm sheltered beach, the stables, the butterflies, or the windsurfing school; then keep following the road toward Orient Bay, the St-Tropez of the Caribbean. Continue to Anse Marcel, Grand Case, Marigot, and Sandy Ground. From Marigot, the flat island of Anguilla is visible. Completing the loop brings you past Cupecoy Beach, through Maho and Simpson Bay, where Saba looms in the horizon, and back over the mountain road into Philipsburg.

DUTCH SIDE

PHILIPSBURG

The capital of Dutch St. Maarten stretches about a mile (1½ km) along an isthmus between Great Bay and the Salt Pond and has five parallel streets. Most of the village's dozens of shops and restaurants are on Front Street, narrow and cobblestone, closest to Great Bay. It's generally congested when cruise ships are in port, because of its many duty-free shops and several casinos. Little lanes called *steegjes* connect Front Street with Back Street, which has fewer shops and considerably less congestion. Along the beach is a ½-mile-long (1-km-long) boardwalk with restaurants and several Wi-Fi hot spots.

St. Maarten Museum. Hosting rotating cultural exhibits addressing the history, industry, geology, and archaeology of the island, the museum contains artifacts ranging from Arawak pottery shards to objects salvaged from the wreck of the HMS *Proselyte.* An interesting exhibit about hurricanes focuses on Hurricane Luis, which devastated the island in 1995. There is a good reference and video library as well. ✉ *7 Front St., Philipsburg* ☎ *721/542–4917* 🌐 *www.museumsintmaarten.org* 🎫 *Free* ⏲ *Weekdays 10–4.*

Yoda Guy Movie Exhibit. This odd-sounding exhibit is actually a nonprofit museum run by Nick Maley, a movie-industry artist who was involved in the creation of Yoda and other icons. You can learn how the artist worked while enjoying the models and memorabilia on display—a must-see for *Star Wars* fans but of interest to most movie buffs. Maley is happy to autograph souvenirs for sale. ✉ *19a Front St., Philipsburg* ☎ *721/542–4009* 🌐 *www.netdwellers.com/mz/planetp/home.*

ELSEWHERE IN ST. MAARTEN

FAMILY **The Carousel.** After riding this beautiful restored Italian carousel, you can enjoy homemade Italian gelato or French pastries. There's even an espresso bar with great coffee drinks and a small cocktail bar. ✉ *60 Welfare Rd., Cole Bay* ☎ *721/544–3112* 🌐 *www.carouselstmaarten.com* 🎫 *$2* ⏲ *Daily 2–10.*

FAMILY **St. Maarten Park.** A good break from sand and sea, this little enclave houses animals and plants indigenous to the Caribbean and South America, including many birds that were inherited from a former aviary. There are also a few strays from other parts of the world and a snake house with boa constrictors and other slithery creatures. A pair of collared peccaries and a family of cotton-topped tamarins have taken up residence. All the animals live among more than 100 different plant species. The Monkey Bar is the charming souvenir shop, selling Caribbean and zoo mementos. ✉ *Madame Estate, Arch Rd., Philipsburg* ☎ *721/543–2030* 🌐 *www.stmaartenzoo.com* 🎫 *$10* ⏲ *Weekdays 9–5.*

FRENCH SIDE

MARIGOT

It is great fun to spend a few hours exploring the bustling harbor, shopping stalls, open-air cafés, and boutiques of St. Martin's biggest town, especially on Wednesday and Saturday, when the daily open-air

CLOSE UP

Concordia

The smallest island in the world to be shared between two different countries, St. Maarten/St. Martin has existed peacefully in its subdivided state for more than 360 years. The Treaty of Concordia, which subdivided the island, was signed in 1648 and was really inspired by the two resident colonies of French and Dutch settlers (not to mention their respective governments) joining forces to repel a common enemy, the Spanish, in 1644. Although the French were promised the side of the island facing Anguilla and the Dutch the south side of the island, the boundary itself wasn't firmly established until 1817 and only then after several disputes (16 of them, to be exact).

Visitors to the island will likely not be able to tell that they have passed from the Dutch to the French side unless they notice that the roads on the French side feel a little smoother. In 2003 the population of St. Martin (and St. Barthélemy) voted to secede from Guadeloupe, the administrative capital of the French West Indies. That detachment became official in 2007, and St. Martin is now officially known as the Collectivité de Saint-Martin.

crafts markets expand to include fresh fruits and vegetables, spices, and all manner of seafood. The market might remind you of Provence, especially when aromas of delicious cooking waft by. Be sure to climb up to the fort for the panoramic view, stopping at the museum for an overview of the island. **Marina Port La Royale** is the shopping–lunch-spot central to the port, but rue de la République and rue de la Liberté, which border the bay, have duty-free shops, boutiques, and bistros. The West Indies Mall offers a deluxe (and air-conditioned) shopping experience. There's less bustle here than in Philipsburg, but the open-air cafés are still tempting places to sit and people-watch. From the harbor front you can catch ferries for Anguilla and St. Barth. Parking can be a real challenge during the business day, and even at night during the high season.

Fort Louis. Though not much remains of the structure itself, Fort Louis, which was completed by the French in 1789, is great fun if you want to climb the 92 steps to the top for the wonderful views of the island and neighboring Anguilla. On Wednesday and Saturday there is a market in the square at the bottom. ✉ *Marigot.*

FAMILY **Saint Martin Museum.** At the southern end of Marigot, next to the Marina Port La Royale, is a museum dedicated to preserving St. Martin's history and culture. A new building houses a variety of pre-Columbian treasures unearthed by the Hope Estate Archaeological Society. ✉ *Rue Fichot, Marigot* ☎ *0690/29–48–36* 🌐 *museesaintmartin.e-monsite.com* 🎫 *$5* 🕒 *Weekdays 9–5.*

FRENCH CUL DE SAC

North of Orient Bay Beach, the French colonial mansion of St. Martin's mayor is nestled in the hills. Little red-roof houses look like open umbrellas tumbling down the green hillside. The area is peaceful and good for hiking. From the beach here, shuttle boats make the five-minute trip to **Ilet Pinel,** an uninhabited island that's fine for picnicking, sunning, and swimming. There are full-service beach clubs there, so just pack the sunscreen and head over.

GRAND CASE

The Caribbean's own Restaurant Row is the heart of this French-side town, a 10-minute drive from either Orient Bay or Marigot, stretching along a narrow beach overlooking Anguilla. You'll find a first-rate restaurant for every palate, mood, and wallet. At lunchtime, or with kids, head to the casual *lolos* (open-air barbecue stands) and feet-in-the-sand beach bars. Twilight drinks and tapas are fun. At night, stroll the strip and preview the sophisticated offerings on the menus posted outside before you settle in for a long and sumptuous meal. If you still have the energy, there are lounges with music (usually a DJ) that get going after 11 pm.

ORLÉANS

North of Oyster Pond and the Étang aux Poissons (Fish Lake) is the island's oldest settlement, also known as the French Quarter. You can still see a few vibrantly painted West Indian–style homes with the original gingerbread fretwork. There are also large areas of the nature and marine preserve trying to save the island's fragile ecosystem.

PIC DU PARADIS

Fodor's Choice ★ Between Marigot and Grand Case, Paradise Peak, at 1,492 feet, is the island's highest point. There are two observation areas. From them, the tropical forest unfolds below, and the vistas are breathtaking. The road is quite isolated and steep, best suited to a four-wheel-drive vehicle. There have also been some problems with crime in this area, so it might be best to go with an experienced local guide.

FAMILY Fodor's Choice ★ **Loterie Farm.** Halfway up the road to Pic du Paradis is a peaceful 150-acre private nature preserve, opened to the public in 1999 by American expat B.J. Welch. There are trail maps, so you can hike on your own or hire a guide. Marked trails traverse native forest with tamarind, gum, mango, and mahogany trees. With luck you can see a greenback monkey. L'Eau Lounge is a lovely spring-fed pool and Jacuzzi area with lounge chairs, great music, and chic tented cabanas with a St. Barth–meets–Wet 'n' Wild atmosphere; groups should consider the VIP package. A delicious, healthy treetop lunch or dinner can be had at **Hidden Forest Café** (⇨ *Where to Eat, below*), and if you are brave—and over 4 feet 5 inches tall—you can try soaring over trees on one of the longest zip lines in the Western Hemisphere. There is a mild version, but people love the extreme one. ✉ *103 rte. de Pic du Paradis, Rambaud* ☎ *0590/87–86–16, 0590/57–28–55* 🌐 *www.loteriefarm.com* 🎫 *Hiking €5, guide €25, zip line €35–€55* ⏲ *Tues.–Sun. 9–3:30.*

ELSEWHERE IN ST. MARTIN

FAMILY Fodor's Choice ★ **Butterfly Farm.** If you arrive early in the morning when the butterflies first break out of their chrysalis, you can marvel at butterflies and moths from around the world and the host plants with which each evolved. At any given time, some 40 species of butterflies—and as many as 600 individual insects—flutter inside the lush screened garden and hatch on the plants housed there. Butterfly art and knickknacks are for sale in the gift shop. In case you want to come back, your ticket, which includes a guided tour, is good for your entire stay. ✉ *Le Galion Beach Rd., Quartier d'Orléans* ☎ *0590/87–31–21* 🌐 *www.thebutterflyfarm.com* 🎫 *$12* ⏲ *Daily 9–3:30, last tour at 3.*

BEACHES

For such a small island, St. Maarten/St. Martin has a wide array of beaches, from the long expanse of Baie Orientale on the French side to powdery-soft Mullet Bay on the Dutch side.

Warm surf and a gentle breeze can be found at the island's 37 beaches, and every one of them is open to the public. Try several. Each is unique: some bustling and some bare, some refined and some rocky, some good for snorkeling and some for sunning. Whatever your fancy, it's here, including a clothing-optional beach at the south end of beautiful Baie Orientale. And several of the island's gems don't have big hotels lining their shores. ⚠ **Petty theft from cars in beach parking lots is an unfortunate fact of life in St. Maarten and St. Martin. Leave nothing in your parked car, not even in the glove compartment or trunk.**

DUTCH SIDE

Several of the best Dutch-side beaches are developed and have large-scale resorts. But others, including Simpson Bay and Cupecoy, have little development. You'll sometimes find vendors or beach bars to rent chairs and umbrellas (but not always).

Cupecoy Beach. Near the Dutch-French border, this picturesque area of sandstone cliffs, white sand, and shoreline caves is a necklace of small beaches that come and go according to the whims of the sea. Even though the western part is more developed, the surf can be rough. It's popular with gay locals and visitors. Break-ins have been reported in cars, so don't leave anything at all in your vehicle. **Amenities:** food and drink. **Best for:** solitude; sunset. ✉ *Between Baie Longue and Mullet Bay, Cupecoy, St. Maarten.*

Dawn Beach. True to its name, this is the place to be at sunrise. On the Atlantic side of Oyster Pond, just south of the French border, it's a first-class beach for sunning and snorkeling, but the winds and rough water mean only strong swimmers should attempt to take a dip. It's not usually crowded, and there are several good restaurants nearby. To find it, follow the signs to the Westin or Mr. Busby's restaurant. **Amenities:** food and drink. **Best for:** snorkeling; sunrise. ✉ *South of Oyster Pond, Dawn Beach, St. Maarten.*

Great Bay. This bustling, white-sand beach curves around Phillipsburg just behind Front Street, making it easy to find. Here you'll find boutiques, eateries, a pleasant boardwalk, and even Segway tours. Busy with cruise-ship passengers, the beach is best west of Captain Hodge Pier or around Antoine Restaurant. **Amenities:** food and drink. **Best for:** swimming; walking. ✉ *Philipsburg, St. Maarten.*

Guana Bay. If you're looking for seclusion, you'll find it five minutes northeast of Philipsburg. There are no umbrellas and no lounge chairs; even the beach shack has no regular service. What this bay does have is a long expanse of soft sand. The surf is strong, making the beach a

The view from Fort Louis, high above Marigot

popular surfer hangout and not recommended for kids. Turn on Guana Bay Road, behind Great Bay Salt Pond. **Amenities:** none. **Best for:** solitude; surfing; walking. ✉ *Upper Prince's Quarter, St. Maarten.*

Little Bay. Despite its popularity with snorkelers, divers, kayakers, and boating enthusiasts, Little Bay isn't usually crowded, perhaps due to its gravelly sand. It does boast panoramic views of St. Eustatius, Philipsburg, the cruise-ship terminal, Saba, and St. Kitts. The beach is west of Fort Amsterdam and accessible via the Divi Little Bay Beach Resort. **Amenities:** food and drink; parking; toilets. **Best for:** snorkeling; swimming; walking. ✉ *Little Bay Rd., Little Bay, St. Maarten.*

Mullet Beach. Many believe that this mile-long, powdery white-sand beach behind the Mullet Bay Golf Course is the island's best. Swimmers like it because the water is usually calm, but when the swell is up, surfers take over. Listen for the "whispering pebbles" as the waves wash up. **Amenities:** food and drink. **Best for:** snorkeling; surfing; swimming. ✉ *South of Cupecoy, Mullet Bay, St. Maarten.*

Simpson Bay Beach. This secluded, half-moon stretch of white sand on the island's Caribbean side is a hidden gem. It's mostly surrounded by private residences, with no big resorts, no jet-skiers, and no crowds. It's just you, the sand, and the water (along with one funky beach bar to provide some nourishment). Southeast of the airport, follow the signs to Mary's Boon and the Horny Toad guesthouses. **Amenities:** food and drink; showers; toilets. **Best for:** solitude; swimming; walking. ✉ *Simpson Bay, St. Maarten.*

FRENCH SIDE

Almost all of the French-side beaches, whether busy Baie Orientale or less busy Baie des Pères (Friar's Bay), have beach clubs and restaurants. For about $25 a couple you get two chaises (*transats*) and an umbrella (*parasol*) for the day, not to mention chair-side service for drinks and food. Only some beaches have bathrooms and showers, so if that is your preference, inquire.

Anse Heureuse (*Happy Bay*). Not many people know about this romantic, hidden gem. Happy Bay has powdery sand, gorgeous luxury villas, and stunning views of Anguilla. The snorkeling is also good. To get here, turn left on the rather rutted dead-end road to Baie des Péres (Friar's Bay). The beach itself is a 10- to 15-minute walk from the last beach bar. **Amenities:** food and drink; toilets. **Best for:** solitude; snorkeling; swimming; walking. ✉ *Happy Bay, St. Martin.*

Baie de Grand Case. Along this skinny stripe of a beach bordering the culinary capital of Grand Case, the old-style gingerbread architecture sometimes peeps out between the bustling restaurants. The sea is calm, and there are tons of fun lunch options from bistros to beachside barbecue stands (called *lolos*). Several of the restaurants rent chairs and umbrellas; some include their use for lunch patrons. In between there is a bit of shopping—for beach necessities but also for the same kinds of handicrafts found in the Marigot market. **Amenities:** food and drink; toilets. **Best for:** swimming; walking. ✉ *Grand Case, St. Martin.*

FAMILY **Baie des Pères** (*Friar's Bay*). This quiet cove close to Marigot has beach grills and bars, with chaises and umbrellas, calm waters, and a lovely view of Anguilla. Kali's Beach Bar, open daily for lunch and (weather permitting) dinner, has a Rasta vibe and color scheme—it's the best place to be on the full moon, with music, dancing, and a huge bonfire, but you can get lunch, beach chairs, and umbrellas anytime. Friar's Bay Beach Café is a French bistro on the sand, open from breakfast to sunset. To get to the beach, take National Road 7 from Marigot, go toward Grand Case to the Morne Valois hill, and turn left on the dead-end road at the sign. **Amenities:** food and drink; toilets. **Best for:** partiers; swimming; walking. ✉ *Baie des Pères, St. Martin.*

Baie Longue (*Long Bay*). Though it extends over the French Lowlands, from the cliff at La Samanna to La Pointe des Canniers, the island's longest beach has no facilities or vendors. It's a great place for a romantic walk, but be warned that car break-ins are a particular problem here. To get here, take National Road 7 south of Marigot. Baie Longue Road is the first entrance to the beach. It's worth a splurge for lunch or a sunset cocktail at the elegant La Samanna. **Amenities:** none. **Best for:** solitude; walking. ✉ *Baie Longue, St. Martin.*

Fodor's Choice ★ **Baie Orientale** (*Orient Bay*). Many consider this the island's most beautiful beach, but its 2 miles (3 km) of satiny white sand, underwater marine reserve, variety of water sports, beach clubs, and hotels also make it one of the most crowded. Lots of "naturists" take advantage of the clothing-optional policy, so don't be shocked. Early-morning nude beach walking is de rigueur for the guests at Club Orient, at the southeastern end of the beach. Plan to spend the day at one of the clubs; each bar has different color umbrellas, and all boast terrific restaurants and lively bars. You can have an open-air massage, try any sea toy you fancy, and stay until dark. To get here from Marigot, take National Road 7 past Grand Case, past the Aéroport de L'Espérance, and watch for the left turn. **Amenities:** food and drink; parking; toilets; water sports. **Best for:** partiers; nudists; swimming; walking; windsurfing. ✉ *Baie Orientale, St. Martin.*

Baie Rouge (*Red Bay*). Here you can bask with the millionaires renting the big-ticket villas in the "neighborhood." The gorgeous beach and its salt ponds make up a nature preserve, site of the oldest habitation in the Caribbean. This area is widely thought to have the best snorkeling on the island. You can swim the crystal waters along the point and explore a swim-through cave. The beach is fairly popular with gay men in the mornings and early afternoons. There are two restaurants; only Chez Raymond is open every day, and cocktail hour starts when the conch shell blows, so keep your ears open. There is a sign and a right turn after you leave Baie Nettlé. **Amenities:** food and drink; toilets. **Best for:** snorkeling; swimming; walking. ✉ *Baie Rouge, St. Martin.*

FAMILY Fodor's Choice ★ **Ilet Pinel.** A protected nature reserve, this kid-friendly island is a five-minute ferry ride from French Cul de Sac ($7 per person round-trip). The ferry runs every half hour from midmorning until dusk. The water is clear and shallow, and the shore is sheltered. If you like snorkeling, don your gear and paddle along both coasts of this pencil-shaped speck in the ocean. You can rent equipment on the island or in the parking lot before you board the ferry for about $10. Plan for lunch any day of the week at a palm-shaded beach hut, Karibuni (except in September, when it's closed) for the freshest fish, great salads, tapas, and drinks—try the frozen mojito. **Amenities:** food and drink; parking. **Best for:** snorkeling; swimming. ✉ *Ilet Pinel, St. Martin.*

FAMILY **Le Galion.** A coral reef borders this quiet beach, part of the island's nature preserve. The water is calm, clear, and quite shallow, so it's paradise with young kids. It's a full-service place, with chair rentals, restaurants, and water-sports operators. Kiteboarders and windsurfers like the trade winds at the far end of the beach. On Sunday there are always groups picnicking and partying. To get here, follow signs to the Butterfly Farm and continue toward the water. **Amenities:** food and drink; parking; toilets; water sports. **Best for:** partiers; swimming; windsurfing. ✉ *Quartier d'Orléans, St. Martin.*

WHERE TO EAT

Although most people come to St. Maarten/St. Martin for sun and fun, they leave praising the cuisine. On an island that covers only 37 square miles (96 square km), there are more than 400 restaurants. You can sample the best dishes from France, Thailand, Italy, Vietnam, India, Japan, and, of course, the Caribbean.

Many of the best restaurants are in Grand Case (on the French side), but you should not limit your culinary adventures to that village. Great dining thrives throughout the island, from the bistros of Marigot and the hopping restaurants of Cupecoy to the low-key eateries of Simpson

BEST BETS FOR DINING

Fodor's Choice★
Bacchus, Bamboo, Hidden Forest Café, Karakter Beach Lounge, La Cigale, L'Effet Mer, Le Pressoir, L'Estaminet, Mario's Bistro, Sky's The Limit, Top Carrot

MOST ROMANTIC
Le Marrakech, Le Pressoir, Sol é Luna, Temptation

BEST VIEW
La Cigale, Sol é Luna, Taloula Mango's

BEST LOCAL FOOD
Chesterfield's

BEST FOR FAMILIES
Taloula Mango's, Top Carrot

BEST FOR A SPECIAL OCCASION
Le Pressoir

HIP AND YOUNG
Bamboo, Hidden Forest Café, Karakter Beach Lounge, Palm Beach, Temptation

Bay and the many *lolos* (roadside barbecue stands) throughout. Loyalists on both "sides" will cheerfully try to steer you to their favorites, and though it's common to cite high euro prices to deter exploration, quite a few restaurants still offer a one-to-one exchange rate if you use cash. Besides, main-course portions are often large enough to be shared.

During high season, it's essential to make reservations; a month in advance is advisable for some of the best places. Dutch-side restaurants sometimes include a 15% service charge, so check your bill before tipping. On the French side, service is usually included (worth checking, here, too), but it is customary to leave 5%–10% extra. Don't leave tips on your credit card—it's customary to tip in cash. A taxi is probably the easiest solution to the parking problems in Grand Case, Marigot, and Philipsburg. Grand Case has two lots—each costs $4—at each end of the main boulevard, but they're often packed by 8 pm.

What to Wear: Although appropriate dining attire ranges from swimsuits to sport jackets, casual dress is usually appropriate. For men, a nice shirt and khakis or jeans will take you anywhere; for women, dressy pants, a skirt, or even fancy shorts are usually acceptable. Jeans are fine in the less formal eateries.

DUTCH SIDE

CUPECOY

$$$$ ECLECTIC **✕ Temptation.** Supercreative chef Dino Jagtiani, who trained at the Culinary Institute of America, is the mastermind behind dishes like seared foie gras PB and J (melted foie gras accented with peanut butter and homemade port-wine fig jam), spicy tuna, and lobster paella. The chef, who compares dessert to lovemaking ("both intimate, and not to be indulged in lightly") created tempura apple pie with cinnamon ice cream and caramel sauce. The extensive wine list features a number of reasonably priced selections. The dining room is pretty and intimate, in spite of its location behind the casino. There's outdoor seating as well. *$ Average main: $36 ✉ Atlantis Casino Courtyard, 106 Rhine*

Rd., Cupecoy ☎ *721/545–2254* 🌐 *www.chefdino.com* ✍ *Reservations essential* ⊙ *No lunch.*

MAHO

$$$ ASIAN Fodor's Choice ★ ✕ **Bamboo.** This dramatic, hip addition to the top level of the Maho central shopping area features red lacquer walls, lounging tables, Indonesian art, a first-rate bar, and electro-house tunes. You can get terrific sushi and sashimi, both classic Japanese varieties and Americanized ones like California roll. Asian hot appetizers and exotic cocktails like the Tranquillity (citrus vodka and smoky oolong tea) are good, too. If you're not into Asian fare, try the salmon, ribs, or beef. The young crowd keeps this place hopping way past midnight. Solo visitors have a great time hanging and even dining at the bar. There is a sake and sushi happy hour 5–7 nightly. $ *Average main: $25* ✉ *Sonesta Maho Beach Resort & Casino, 1 Rhine Rd., Maho* ☎ *721/545–3622* 🌐 *www.bamboo-sxm.com* ⊙ *No lunch Sat.–Sun.*

$$$ MEDITERRANEAN FAMILY ✕ **Le Bateau Ivre.** In the middle of an anonymous-looking plaza in the new-ish Porto Cupecoy Marina complex, this place is a good choice for an easy lunch thanks to big salads, American-style sandwiches, and varied crêpes. Night brings all the French bistro classics plus seafood specials, all frequently accompanied by a singer performing Edith Piaf. You can sit outdoors and admire the yachts, or indoors for a more lounge-y feel. $ *Average main: $26* ✉ *Marina Porto Cupecoy, Maho* ☎ *721/526–2157* ⊙ *Closed Tues.*

$$$$ ECLECTIC ✕ **Le Moulin Fou.** This busy restaurant towards the back of the Maho complex serves French food like onion soup and escargot as well as fish, pasta, steaks, and good sushi. It's open every day and serves late. You can choose your lobster from the tank and explore a vast wine selection. Eating on the outdoor terrace provides a good view of the nightly party at Cheri's. $ *Average main: $38* ✉ *Maho Village, Maho* ☎ *721/545–5777* 🌐 *www.moulinfou.com* ⊙ *No lunch.*

$$$ ITALIAN FAMILY ✕ **Trattoria Italiana.** Tucked behind Casino Royale, this plain Italian eatery is extremely popular with locals. The menu includes favorites like penne Bolognese and eggplant Parmesan, but the real winners are the thin-crust pizzas. The freshly brewed iced tea is great on a hot day. With its laid-back atmosphere and friendly staff, this is a cozy spot for families with small children or a place where you just run in and grab a quick bite. $ *Average main: $22* ✉ *Maho Village, Maho* ☎ *721/545–4034* ⊙ *No lunch Sun.*

OYSTER POND

$$$ SEAFOOD FAMILY ✕ **Big Fish.** A chic, white interior; fresh-caught fish; and friendly, if sometimes relaxed, service are the draw at this Oyster Pond restaurant, also convenient to Dawn Beach. Stick with whatever was most recently in the sea, and you will be happy. If offered, grouper in curry-coconut is a yummy option, and the hurricane shrimp is a local favorite. Light eaters love the huge fresh salads. The owners also run a fishing-charter outfit and will happily cook up your catch here. $ *Average main: $28* ✉ *14 Emerald Merrit Rd., Oyster Pond* ☎ *721/543–6288* ⊙ *No lunch.*

23

PHILIPSBURG

$$ CARIBBEAN FAMILY **Chesterfield's.** Both locals and tourists seem to love this restaurant at Great Bay Marina. Seafood is the main focus, but steaks, burgers, pasta, and poultry are all on the dinner menu. You can also come for breakfast, lunch, or happy hour (5–7). If you love sophisticated cuisine, look elsewhere; but the portions are big and the prices are reasonable. Delivery to area condos and time-shares is available. *Average main: $19 Great Bay Marina, Philipsburg 721/542–3484.*

$$$ ECLECTIC FAMILY **The Greenhouse.** Two-for-one happy hour drinks are just one reason people flock to this waterfront restaurant, which balances a relaxed atmosphere, reasonable prices, and favorites like burgers, prime rib, and steaks. If you're seeking something spicy, try the creole shrimp. Daily specials, like the Friday-night Lobster Mania, are popular. *Average main: $21 Bobby's Marina, Philipsburg 721/542–2941 www.thegreenhouserestaurant.com.*

$$$$ ECLECTIC FAMILY **Ocean Lounge.** An airy modern veranda perched on the Philipsburg boardwalk gives a distinct South Beach vibe. You'll want to linger over fresh fish and steaks as you watch tourists pass by on romantic strolls by night or determined cruise-ship passengers surveying the surrounding shops by day. Daily three-, four-, and five-course tasting menus are a pretty good deal. There is also a fun menu of bar snacks and martinis. It's a bit hard to park here so consider taking a taxi at night. *Average main: $34 Holland House Beach Hotel, 43 Front St., Philipsburg 721/542–2572 www.hhbh.com.*

$$ ECLECTIC FAMILY **Taloula Mango's.** Ribs and burgers are the specialty at this casual beachfront restaurant, but the jerk chicken and thin-crust pizza, not to mention a few vegetarian options like tasty falafel, are not to be ignored. On weekdays lunch is accompanied by (warning: loud) live music; every Friday during happy hour a DJ spins tunes. In case you're wondering, the restaurant got its name from the owner's golden retriever. *Average main: $17 Sint Rose Shopping Mall, off Front St. on boardwalk, Philipsburg 721/542–1645 www.taloulamango.com.*

SIMPSON BAY

$$$ ITALIAN FAMILY **Izi Ristorante Italiano.** The former chef of La Gondola serves up huge, shareable portions of more than 400 dishes in this cheerful, centrally located space. For something fun, diners are invited to create their own menu: pick a pasta and sauce; then add your choice of meat, fish, and veggies. *Average main: $23 Paradise Mall, 67 Welfare Rd., Simpson Bay 721/544–3079 www.iziristoranteitaliano.com Reservations essential Closed Tues. May–Nov. No lunch.*

$$ ECLECTIC FAMILY Fodor's Choice ★ **Karakter Beach Lounge.** This funky and charming modern beach bar, right behind the airport, serves up fun, great music, relaxation, and a lot of style. The vibe is more like St-Tropez than St. Maarten. Open from 9 am till 10 pm, the restaurant serves up fresh fruit smoothies, tropical cocktails, fresh fruit salads, healthy sandwiches, and tapas. There is live music in the evening. A sign near the shower/bathhouse invites you to "come hang out here and shower before you go to the airport"—in case you want to spend every second possible on the sand. *Average main: $14 121 Simpson Bay Rd., Simpson Bay 721/523–9983 www.karakterbeach.com.*

$$$ THAI FAMILY

✕ **Panlaan Thai on the Bay.** On a pretty, centrally located waterfront deck on Simpson Bay, this restaurant serves up big portions of fresh-tasting and nicely presented classic Thai dishes like curries and satays. There's delivery and take-out if you don't have time for a sit-down meal. Happy hour in high season (November–June) features $4 martinis served with $5 appetizers, and there is live music on Sunday nights. ■ **TIP→ It can be breezy at night, so bring a light sweater.** *Average main: $22 ✉ Welfare Rd., Simpson Bay ☎ 721/559–2811 ⊕ www.panlaansxm.com.*

$$ SEAFOOD FAMILY

✕ **Pineapple Pete.** This popular, casual, and fun (if slightly touristy) place is well located and has a game room with seven pool tables, four dart boards, an arcade, and flat-screen TVs tuned to sports. A friendly, efficient staff serves up burgers, seafood, and ribs; for a real treat, try one of the specialties, like the tasty crab-stuffed shrimp appetizer. Follow it up with succulent, herb-crusted rack of lamb. There's free Wi-Fi and live entertainment Tuesday–Sunday. It's good for a bite near the airport. Note the 15% service charge included in the check. There's also a little shop with T-shirts and local crafts. *Average main: $20 ✉ 56 Welfare Rd., Simpson Bay ☎ 721/544–6030 ⊕ www.pineapplepete.com Reservations essential.*

$ VEGETARIAN FAMILY Fodor's Choice ★

✕ **Top Carrot.** Open from 7:30 am to 6 pm, this friendly café and juice bar is a popular breakfast and lunch stop. It features fresh and tasty vegetarian entrées, sandwiches, salads, homemade pastries, and fresh fish. Favorites include a pastry stuffed with pesto, avocado, red pepper, and feta cheese, and a cauliflower, spinach, and tomato quiche. The house-made granola and yogurt are popular, but folks also drop in just for espresso and the large selection of teas. Many also come for the free Wi-Fi. Adjacent to the restaurant is a gift shop with Asian-inspired items, spiritual books, and half-price cotton beach cover-ups. *Average main: $8 ✉ Airport Rd., near Simpson Bay Yacht Club, Simpson Bay ☎ 721/544–3381 Closed Sun. No dinner.*

$ DELI FAMILY

✕ **Vesna Taverna and Bagel House.** Centrally located near the Simpson Bay Bridge, this casual eatery is open all day long, with tasty but healthy options like smoothies, bagel sandwiches, omelets, crêpes, pancakes, and salads (burgers available for dinner). Saturday is Greek Night. The patio makes for great outdoor eating, plus there's free Wi-Fi. *Average main: $10 ✉ 9 La Palapa Marina, Simpson Bay ☎ 721/524–5283 ⊕ www.vesnataverna.com No dinner Sun.–Tues.*

$ CAFÉ

✕ **Zee Best.** This friendly bistro serves one of the best breakfasts on the island. There's a huge selection of fresh-baked pastries—try the almond croissants—plus sweet and savory crêpes, omelets, quiches, and other treats from the oven. When you sit down, a basket of assorted pastries arrives, and you are charged for the ones you select. Specialties include the St. Martin omelet, filled with ham, cheese, mushrooms, onions, green peppers, and tomatoes. Best of all, breakfast is served until 2. Lunch includes sandwiches, salads, and the chef's famous spaghetti Bolognese. ■ **TIP→ There are also locations near the airport and at Port de Plaisance.** *Average main: $8 ✉ Plaza del Lago, Simpson Bay ☎ 721/544–2477 ⊕ www.zeebestrestaurant.com No credit cards No dinner.*

FRENCH SIDE

BAIE DES PÈRES

$$ BISTRO

Friar's Bay Beach Café. There is a sophisticated vibe at this quiet, rather elegant beach club that may make you feel as if you're on a private beach. You can rent lounge chairs and umbrellas and spend the whole day relaxing, drinking, and dining. With decor less funky than some other beach-club restaurants, it is open from breakfast through the spectacular sunset, offering a menu reminiscent of a French bistro. A blackboard lists specials, carpaccios of meat and fish are sparklingly fresh, and the salads are terrific. French standbys include tomato and goat cheese tartlets, and "international" ones add burgers and sandwiches. Sunday evenings have live music until 9. Watch for the red and black signs on the road between Grand Case and Marigot, and drive slowly because the road is rough. *Average main: $18 Friar's Bay Rd., Baie des Pères 0590/49–16–87 No credit cards No dinner.*

23

BAIE NETTLÉ

$$$$ FRENCH Fodor's Choice ★

La Cigale. On the edge of Baie Nettlé, this restaurant has wonderful views of the lagoon from its dining room and open-air patio, but the charm comes from the devoted attention of adorable owner Olivier, helped by his mother and brother, and various cousins, too. The delicious food is edible sculpture: ravioli of lobster with wild mushrooms and foie gras is poached in an intense lobster bisque, and house-smoked gravlax and salmon is garnished with a garlic cream sauce. For dessert, the house-made ginger ice cream with flambéed pineapple is a favorite. *Average main: €43 101 Laguna Beach, Baie Nettlé 0590/87–90–23 www.restaurant-lacigale.com Reservations essential Closed Sun. and Sept.–Oct. No lunch.*

$$$$ FRENCH FAMILY Fodor's Choice ★

Le Sand. A stylish St. Barth vibe and beachfront location make this a great choice. Relax on the terrace for cocktails and snacks, or park yourself on a lounge chair on the beach with an umbrella (no charge if you're dining), and enjoy the music and ambience. The refined food is fresh and nicely presented; the snapper and fish tartares are standouts, but real credit is due to the management and staff who are friendly and attentive. *Average main: $35 Sandy Bay, Baie Nettlé 0690/73–14–38.*

$$$ FRENCH FAMILY

Ma Ti' Beach. On the road to Marigot, this casual beach bar has better-than-average food and great views across the turquoise water to Anguilla. You can always get fresh lobster from the tank, and the traditional French onion soup with a cheesy crust is excellent. If the *moules frites* (fresh mussels) are a special, snap them up. *Average main: €23 Anse Marigot, across from Mercure resort, Baie Nettlé 0590/87–01–30.*

BAIE ORIENTALE

$$$ FRENCH

L'Astrolabe. Chef Maxime Orea gets raves for his modern interpretations of classic French cuisine served around the pool at this cozy, relaxed restaurant in the Esmeralda Resort. Corn soup, foie gras terrine with apricot and quince jam, an amazing roast duck with pineapple-ginger sauce, and deliciously fresh fish dishes are just some of the offerings. There are also lots vegetarian choices, a €45 three-course prix fixe, a children's menu, Monday night jazz, and a lobster party with live music every Friday night. *Average main: $26 ✉ Esmeralda Resort, Baie Orientale ☎ 0590/87–11–20 ⊕ www.astrolabe-sxm.com Reservations essential ⊙ No lunch. No dinner Wed.*

$$$$ FRENCH FAMILY ✕ **La Table d'Antoine.** Settle in here for an evening of attentive, friendly service and hearty French-country food with a side dish of lively people-watching. The varied menu features slightly unfamiliar dishes that are worth a try, like the *Tartiflette* (a kind of cheese and potato gratin), beef baked in a salt crust, and duck magret with foie gras. Desserts are delicious, as is the selection of house-made infused rums. *Average main: €35 ✉ Pl. de la Baie Orientale, Baie Orientale ☎ 0590/52–97–57 ⊙ Closed Tues. in Aug.–Oct.*

$$$ FRENCH FUSION FAMILY ✕ **Palm Beach.** As stylish as its Florida namesake, this beach club sets the stage with Balinese art and furniture, big comfy chaises on the beach, and an active bar. There are three big tree-house-like lounges for lunch or to spend the afternoon, plus a spa for beachside massages. Salads, tartares, and Thai-influenced salads and noodle specialties are served in a pavilion shaded by sail-like awnings. The Sunday night beach party is the place to be, and there are monthly daytime beach parties, too. *Average main: €21 ✉ Baie Orientale ☎ 0690/35–99–06 ⊕ www.palmbeachsxm.net ⊙ No dinner.*

$$$ ASIAN ✕ **Tai Chi.** Thai-fusion dishes are served with flashy cocktails at the end of the Orient Bay Plaza on the way from the beach. There are lots of choices for vegetarians and vegans and congenial happy hours. *Average main: $23 ✉ Place du Parc de la Baie Orientale, Baie Orientale ☎ 0590/87–73–98.*

FRENCH CUL DE SAC

$$$ MODERN FRENCH ✕ **Anse Marcel Beach.** Beachside calm with a side order of chic is on the menu at this lovely and private cove restaurant/beach club, good for a beach day, a sunset cocktail, and great swimming. You can dine and lounge all day, either in the tented pavilion or on the beach. The food changes according to market availabilities, but there are always salads, tasty mussels, fresh grilled fish and lobster, steaks, and sandwiches; try the smoked salmon and bagel combo if it's offered. The desserts are amazing, especially the crêpes. There is safe, private parking for cars and moorings available for boats. *Average main: €24 ✉ Anse Marcel Beach, Anse Marcel ☎ 0690/26–38–50 ⊕ www.ansemarcelbeach.com.*

$$$ FRENCH ✕ **Le Ti Bouchon.** This tiny restaurant, close to Anse Marsel hotels, captures the spirit of Lyon, the capital of French gastronomy, where casual small restaurants serve hearty traditional cuisine, wine comes by the pitcher, and the patron is very much part of the party. The eight tables are set on the porch of a traditional cottage, and the menu (written on a chalkboard) changes frequently. Chances are you will become fast friends with the owner, Momo; join in conversations with the next table; and linger over your chocolate mousse. Dietary restrictions are handled with grace and accuracy. There are two seatings for dinner. *Average main: €30 ✉ 110 rte. de Cul de Sac, French Cul de Sac ☎ 0690/64–84–64 ⊕ www.tibouchonrestaurant.com Reservations essential ⊙ Closed late July–mid Oct. No lunch.*

$$$ CARIBBEAN

Sol é Luna. Charming and romantic, with modern decor, this restaurant puts its best tables on the balcony, from which you can best appreciate the great views. Begin with an appetizer like curry tuna carpaccio, monkfish spring rolls, or roasted vegetables with goat cheese; then move on to an entrée such as fresh pasta with mixed seafood or beef tenderloin flamed with Cognac. Try the chocolate soufflé for dessert. Don't be surprised if you see a proposal or two during your meal, as this is one of the most romantic restaurants on the island. The €20 three-course lunch is a bargain. **TIP→ Before ordering one of the "specials," ask about the prices; sometimes they can be surprisingly high compared to regular menu items.** *Average main: €28 61 Rte. de Mont Vernon, French Cul de Sac 0590/29–08–56 www.solelunarestaurant.com Reservations essential Closed mid-June–early July and Sept.–early Oct.*

GRAND CASE

$$ FRENCH Fodor's Choice ★

Bacchus. If you want to lunch with the savviest locals, you have to scrape yourself off the beach and head into an industrial park outside Grand Case, where Benjamin Laurent, the best wine importer in the Caribbean, has built this lively, deliciously air-conditioned reconstruction of a wine cellar. First-rate starters, salads, and main courses made from top ingredients brought in from France are lovingly prepared. You can also buy gourmet groceries or order from the extensive takeout menu. Smokers hang in the cigar–rum lounge. Naturally, the wines are sublime, and you can get an amazing education along with a great lunch. Enter at the "Hope Estate" sign in the roundabout across from the road that leads to the Grand Case airport. *Average main: $20 18–19 Hope Estate, Grand Case Rd., Grand Case 0590/87–15–70 www.bacchussxm.com Closed Sun. No dinner.*

$$$ FRENCH

L'Auberge Gourmande. With a formal dining room framed by elegant arches, this fixture is in one of the island's oldest creole houses. The light Provençal cuisine includes roasted rack of lamb with an herb crust over olive mashed potatoes, Dover sole in almond butter, and pork filet mignon stuffed with apricots and walnuts. There are vegetarian options, a kids' menu, and a good selection of wines. Ask for an outside table. *Average main: $21 89 bd. de Grand Case, Grand Case 0590/87–73–37 www.laubergegourmande.com Closed Sept. No lunch.*

$$$ FRENCH

Le Cottage. Inventive French cuisine is prepared with a light touch and presented with flair, and perhaps a bit of humor, here. There are lots of themed "tasting" plates with interesting variations on an ingredient. Alternatively, try a prix-fixe meal. Huge portions of hearty French food are served by a genial staff to a lively community gathered on the street-front porch. The caramel dessert tasting features a perfect soufflé or the house-made salted caramel meringues. *Average main: $29 97 bd. de Grand Case, Grand Case 0590/29–03–30 www.lecottagesxm.com Reservations essential No lunch.*

$$$$ MODERN FRENCH Fodor's Choice ★

L'Effet Mer. Longtime visitors to St. Martin remember the award-winning cuisine of chef Stephane Decluseau at L'Astrolabe. Now, along with partner Damien Pointeau, he's opened this Grand Case waterfront restaurant. You can hang out on beach chairs outside, but the real action is inside, where creative and first-rate cooking is served with charm, precision, and panache. A tasting plate of foie gras or the incomparable foamy lobster cappuccino soup are fine starters, mains are lively, and desserts are gorgeous edible art. The crème brûlée tasting has three variations on the theme. The €29 prix fixe is a good deal. $ *Average main: €34* ✉ *48 bd. de Grand Case, Grand Case* ☎ *0590/87–05–65* 🌐 *www.effetmer.net* ✍ *Reservations essential* ⏲ *Closed Sun.*

> **WORD OF MOUTH**
>
> "You should not visit St. Martin without enjoying at least one dinner at Le Pressoir (we chose to eat there twice on our last visit). Each course was outstanding, and the wine list is superb. Though the menu is a bit pricey, the food, service, and charm of the place make it worth every penny."
>
> —AddieLangdon

$$$$ FRENCH Fodor's Choice ★ ✕ **Le Pressoir.** This restaurant in a carefully restored West Indian house painted in brilliant reds and blues has charm to spare. The name comes from the historic salt press that sits opposite the restaurant, but the thrill comes from the culinary creations of chef Franc Mear and the hospitality of his beautiful wife, Melanie. If you are indecisive, or just plain smart, try any (or all) of the degustations (tastings) of four soups, four foie gras preparations, or four fruit desserts—all sophisticated preparations with adorable presentations. Foie gras is served in a dollhouse-size terrine with a teensy glass of Sauternes. There is a €15 kids' dinner. $ *Average main: $35* ✉ *30 bd. de Grand Case, Grand Case* ☎ *0590/87–76–62* 🌐 *www.lepressoirsxm.com* ✍ *Reservations essential* ⏲ *Closed mid-Sept.–mid-Oct. and Sun. in May–Dec. No lunch.*

$$$$ FRENCH FUSION ✕ **Le Shambala.** Romantic and beachy-chic, this waterfront restaurant has a lavish south-of-France vibe, with prices to match. Come for the sunset and start with an interesting cocktail before moving on to bruschetta, quiche, steak tartare, roast chicken, or simply prepared fish with fresh veggies. Sophisticated desserts—all made in-house—can be paired with a glass of champagne (more than a dozen types to choose from). $ *Average main: €31* ✉ *28 bd. de Grand Case, Grand Case* ☎ *0590/29–17–09* 🌐 *www.leshambala.com* ✍ *Reservations essential.*

$$$ FRENCH Fodor's Choice ★ ✕ **L'Estaminet.** The name of this restaurant is an old-fashioned word for "tavern" in French, but the food is anything but archaic. The creative, upscale cuisine served in this modern, clean space is fun and surprising, utilizing plenty of molecular gastronomy. Intense liquid garnishes might be inserted into your goat cheese appetizer or served in a tiny toothpaste tube or plastic syringe. The Melting Apple is one of the best desserts on the island. The bright flavors, artistic plating, and novelty make for a lively meal to be remembered fondly. $ *Average main: €25* ✉ *139 bd. de Grand Case, Grand Case* ☎ *0590/29–00–25* 🌐 *www.lestaminetsxm.com* ⏲ *Closed Mon. in June–Nov. No lunch.*

$$$$ FRENCH ✕ **Le Tastevin.** In the heart of Grand Case and on everyone's list of favorites, this attractive wood-beam room has "real" St. Martin style. Tasty food served on a breezy porch over a glittering blue sea is enhanced by Joseph, the amiable owner. Salads and simple grills rule for lunch; at dinner, try one of the seasonal specials featuring what's best in the local markets. $ *Average main: $32* ✉ *86 bd. de Grand Case, Grand Case*

☎ *0590/87–55–45* 🌐 *www.letastevin-restaurant.com* *Reservations essential* *Closed mid-Aug.–Sept.*

$$ CARIBBEAN Fodor's Choice ★ ✕ **Sky's the Limit.** Although St. Martin is known for upscale dining, each town has its barbecue stands, called lolos—even Grand Case. Locals flock to the half-dozen stands in the middle of town, on the waterside, for a fun, relatively cheap, and iconic St. Martin meal. With plastic utensils and paper plates, Sky's the Limit couldn't be more informal. The menu includes everything from succulent grilled ribs to stewed conch, fresh snapper, and grilled lobster at the most reasonable prices on the island. All come with several tasty sides, like plantains, curried rice, beans, and coleslaw. Don't miss the johnnycakes. The service is friendly, if a bit slow; sit back with a $1.50 beer and enjoy the experience. On weekends there is often live music. At this writing, a 1:1 euro-dollar exchange rate is offered. ■ **TIP→ Come earlier in the day for fresher fare.** *Average main: €14* ✉ *Bd. de Grand Case, Grand Case* ☎ *0590/35–67–84* *Reservations not accepted* *No credit cards.*

$$$$ ITALIAN ✕ **Spiga.** In a beautifully restored creole house, tasty cuisine fuses Italian and Caribbean ingredients and cooking techniques. Follow one of the ample appetizers with an excellent pasta, fresh fish, or meat dish, such as the pesto-crusted rack of lamb. Vegetarian and gluten-free options are noted on the menu. Try the tiramisu or one of the grappas. *Average main: $36* ✉ *4 rte. de L'Espérance, Grand Case* ☎ *0590/52–47–83* 🌐 *www.spiga-sxm.com* *Reservations essential* *Closed mid-Sept.–late Oct. and Tues. in June–mid-Sept. No lunch.*

MARIGOT

$$ CARIBBEAN ✕ **Enoch's Place.** The blue-and-white-stripe awning on a corner of the Marigot Market makes this place hard to miss. But Enoch's lolo-style creole cooking is what draws crowds. Specialties include garlic shrimp, fresh lobster, and rice and beans like your St. Martin mother used to make. Try the saltfish and fried johnnycake—a great breakfast option. The food more than makes up for the lack of decor. *Average main: €13* ✉ *Marigot Market, Front de Mer, Marigot* ☎ *0590/29–29–88* *Reservations not accepted* *No credit cards* *Closed Sun. No dinner.*

$$ ECLECTIC FAMILY ✕ **La Belle Epoque.** This brasserie at the Marigot marina is a favorite among locals. Whether for a drink or a meal, it's a great spot for boat- and people-watching. The menu has a bit of everything: big salads, traditional fish soup, thin-crust pizza, seafood, and rave-worthy desserts. There's also a good wine list, and it's open nonstop from breakfast through late dinner. *Average main: €20* ✉ *Marina Port La Royale, Marigot* ☎ *0590/87–87–70* 🌐 *www.sxm-marinaroyale.com/belle_epoque* *Closed Sun.*

$$ CONTEMPORARY ✕ **La Source.** Somewhat hidden behind the boutiques in Marina Port La Royale (look near Vilbrequin), this tiny "healthy" restaurant features a French seasonal menu as well as sandwiches, salads, soups, fair-trade coffee and teas, and organic pastries. A bargain lunch special includes the special of the day and a drink, and the organic pasta dishes are delicious and inventive. The light choices, which include crab tartare with seaweed and organic-chicken salad, are terrific. *Average main: $14* ✉ *Marina Port La Royale, Marigot* ☎ *0590/27–17–27.*

$$$ MOROCCAN **Le Marrakech.** Some 20 years ago, the charming owners renovated this historic St. Martin *case*. After several other restaurant ventures, they returned to the cottage to serve up delicious, authentic Moroccan cuisine in a beautiful and romantic space with an open garden that feels like Morocco. The food is fragrant and delicious, with portions so huge you'll have enough for lunch the next day. The couscous and tagines are authentically spiced and delivered in Moroccan serving pieces by the affable and professional staff. The mixed appetizers (*meze*) are delectable, and the royal couscous is justly popular. Lounge in the tented courtyard after dinner—you may be entertained by a talented belly dancer. The restaurant is on Marigot's main road across from the stadium. *Average main: $24* *169 rue de Hollande, Marigot* *0590/27–54–48* *www.marrakechsxm.wordpress.com* *Reservations essential* *Closed Sun. No lunch.*

$$$ CARIBBEAN **Le Mini-Club.** This institution has served up a blend of creole and French food since 1969 but now has new owners and a fresh paint job. The whole place is built tree-house style around the trunks of coconut palms, and the lofty perch results in great views of Marigot Harbor. The dinner buffet on Wednesday and Saturday nights is an island tradition. It comprises more than 30 dishes, often including conch soup, grilled lobster, roast leg of lamb, black Angus roast beef, and roast pig. Prix-fixe menus are something of a bargain, and there's live dance music on Fridays. *Average main: €24* *49 bd. de France, Marigot* *0590/87–50–69* *Closed Sun. No lunch.*

$$$ FRENCH **Tropicana.** This bustling bistro at the Marina Port La Royale is busy all day long, thanks to a varied menu, (relatively) reasonable prices, and friendly staff. Salads are superb lunch options, especially the salad Niçoise with medallions of crusted goat cheese. Dinner brings some exceptional steak and seafood dishes, and the wine list is quite extensive. Desserts are tasty, including old standbys like crème brûlée. You can dine outside or in. *Average main: $21* *Marina Port La Royale, Marigot* *0590/87–79–07.*

PIC DU PARADIS

$$ CARIBBEAN FAMILY Fodor's Choice ★ **Hidden Forest Café.** Schedule your trip to Loterie Farm to take in lunch or dinner in lovely tree-house pavilions with a safari vibe the hip clientele can appreciate. The yummy, locally sourced food is inventive and fresh. Curried-spinach chicken with banana fritters is a popular pick, but there are great choices for vegetarians, too, including cumin lentil balls. Those with stouter appetites dig into the massive Black Angus tenderloin. Loterie Farm's other eatery, Treelounge, features great cocktails and tapas, is open Monday through Saturday, and stays open late with frequent live music. *Average main: $20* *Loterie Farm, 103 rte. de Pic du Paradis, Rambaud* *0590/87–86–16* *www.loteriefarm.com* *Closed Mon.*

SANDY GROUND

$$$$ FRENCH FUSION Fodor's Choice ★ **Mario's Bistro.** Dinner here is favored for the ravishing cuisine, romantic ambience, and, most of all, the marvelously friendly owners. Didier Gonnon and Martyne Tardif are out front, while chef Mario Tardif is in the kitchen creating bouillabaisse with green Thai curry, a duet of

CLOSE UP

St. Maarten vs. St. Martin

If this is your first trip to St. Maarten/St. Martin, you're probably wondering which side will better suit your needs. That's hard to say, because in some ways the difference between the two can seem as subtle as the hazy boundary dividing them. But there are some major distinctions.

St. Maarten, the Dutch side, has the casinos, more nightlife, smaller price tags, and bigger hotels. St. Martin, the French side, has no casinos, less nightlife, and hotels that are smaller and more intimate. Many have kitchenettes, and most include breakfast. There are many good restaurants on the Dutch side, but if fine dining makes your vacation, the French side rules.

The biggest difference might be currency—the Netherlands Antilles guilder (also called the florin) on the Dutch side, the euro on the French side. And the relative strength of the euro can translate to some expensive surprises. Many establishments on both sides (even the French) accept U.S. dollars.

grilled lamb chops and braised lamb shank shepherd's pie, and sautéed jumbo scallops with crab mashed potatoes and leek tempura. The upside-down banana coconut tart with caramel sauce and coconut ice cream is heavenly. The restaurant is rather strict about reservations for large groups, and there are set seatings for the waterside tables. *Average main: $31 At the Sandy Ground Bridge, Sandy Ground 0590/87–06–36 www.mariosbistro.com Reservations essential Closed Sun., Aug., and Sept. No lunch.*

WHERE TO STAY

St. Maarten/St. Martin accommodations range from modern mega-resorts such as the Hotel Riu Palace and the Westin St. Maarten to condos and small inns. On the Dutch side many hotels cater to groups, and although that's also true to some extent on the French side, you can find a larger collection of intimate accommodations there. **TIP→ Off-season rates (April through the beginning of December) can be as little as half the high-season rates.**

TIME-SHARE RENTALS

Time-share properties are scattered around the island, mostly on the Dutch side. There's no reason to buy a share, as these condos are rented out whenever the owners are not in residence. If you stay in one, be prepared for a sales pitch. Most rent by the night, but there's often substantial savings if you secure a weekly rate. Not all offer daily maid service. As some properties are undergoing renovations at this writing, ask about construction conditions, and in any case, ask for a recently renovated unit.

PRIVATE VILLAS

Villas are a great lodging option, especially for families who don't need to keep the kids occupied, or groups of friends who like hanging out together. Since these are for the most part freestanding houses, their greatest advantage is privacy. Properties are scattered throughout the island, often in gated communities or on secluded roads. Some have bare-bones furnishings, whereas others are over-the-top luxurious, with gyms, theaters, game rooms, and several different pools. There are private chefs, gardeners, maids, and other staffers to care for both the villa and its occupants.

Villas are secured through rental companies. They offer weekly prices that range from reasonable to more than many people make in a year. Check around, as prices for the same property vary from agent to agent. Because of the economy, many villas are now offered by the night rather than the week. Rental companies usually provide airport transfers and concierge service, and for an extra fee will even stock your refrigerator.

RENTAL CONTACTS

French Caribbean International. This company offers rental properties on the French side. ☎ *800/322–2223 in U.S.* 🌐 *www.frenchcaribbean.com.*

HomeAway. This listing service is the world's leading vacation rentals marketplace. To rent a condo, you contact the owner directly. ☎ *512/684–1098* 🌐 *www.homeaway.com.*

Island Hideaways. The island's oldest rental company rents villas on both sides. ☎ *800/832–2302 in U.S.* 🌐 *www.islandhideaways.com.*

Island Properties. This company's properties are scattered around the island. ✉ *62 Welfare Rd., Simpson Bay, St. Maarten* ☎ *599/544–4580, 866/978–5852 in U.S.* 🌐 *www.remaxislandproperties.com.*

Jennifer's Vacation Villas. You can rents villas on both sides of the island from this company. ✉ *Plaza Del Lago, Simpson Bay Yacht Club, Simpson Bay, St. Maarten* ☎ *631/546–7345 in New York, 721/544–3107 in St. Maarten* 🌐 *www.jennifersvacationvillas.com.*

Pierres Caraïbes. Owned by American Leslie Reed and associated with Christies Great Estates, this company rents upscale St. Martin villas. First-rate properties are available in all sizes and prices. ✉ *Plaza Caraibes, rue Kennedy, Bldg. A, Marigot, St. Martin* ☎ *0590/51–02–85* 🌐 *www.pierrescaraibes.com.*

Villas of Distinction. This is one of the oldest villa-rental companies on both the French and Dutch sides. The website can have special deals. ☎ *800/289–0900 in U.S.* 🌐 *www.villasofdistinction.com.*

WIMCO. This outfit has more hotel, villa, apartment, and condo listings in the Caribbean than most other companies. ☎ *800/449–1553 in U.S.* 🌐 *www.wimco.com.*

BEST BETS FOR LODGING

Fodor's Choice★
Belmond La Samanna, Blue Pelican, Caribbean Princess, The Horny Toad, Hotel L'Esplanade, Hotel Riu Palace St. Martin, Karibuni Lodge, Le Petit Hotel, Palm Court.

BEST FOR ROMANCE
Belmond La Samanna, Le Domaine Beach Resort and Spa, Marquis Boutique Hotel, Palm Court.

BEST BEACHFRONT
Belmond La Samanna, Esmeralda Resort, The Horny Toad, Hotel Riu Palace St. Martin, Le Petit Hotel.

BEST POOL
Hotel Riu Palace St. Martin, Westin St. Maarten Dawn Beach Resort & Spa

BEST SERVICE
Belmond La Samanna, Hotel Riu Palace St. Martin

BEST FOR KIDS
Alamanda Resort, Hotel Mercure St. Martin and Marina, Hotel Riu Palace St. Martin

DUTCH SIDE

CUPECOY

$$$ RENTAL **The Cliff at Cupecoy Beach.** These luxurious, high-rise condos are rented out when the owners are not in residence; depending on the owner's personal style, they can be downright fabulous. **Pros:** great views; good for families; close to Maho casinos and restaurants; tight security. **Cons:** it's apartment living, so if you're looking for resorty, this is not for you; no hotel services other than concierge. *Rooms from: $425 ✉ Rhine Rd., Cupecoy ☎ 866/978–5839, 721/546–6633 🌐 www.cliffsxm.com 72 apartments No meals.*

LITTLE BAY

$ RESORT FAMILY **Divi Little Bay Beach Resort.** Bordering the lovely but sparsely populated Little Bay, this semi-renovated property is well located and awash with water sports. **Pros:** good location; lovely beach; kids stay and eat free. **Cons:** ongoing renovations; pool areas not great. *Rooms from: $269 ✉ Little Bay Rd., Little Bay ☎ 721/542–2333, 800/367–3484 in U.S. 🌐 www.divilittlebay.com 218 rooms No meals.*

$$ RESORT FAMILY **Sonesta Maho Beach Resort & Casino.** The island's largest hotel, which is on Maho Beach and typically caters to big groups, isn't luxurious or fancy, but this full-service resort offers everything right on the premises at reasonable rates, and it is located very close to the airport. **Pros:** huge resort complex; lots of shopping; nonstop nightlife. **Cons:** resort is aging and requires renovations; not for a quiet getaway; limited dining choices on all-inclusive plan. *Rooms from: $366 ✉ 1 Rhine Rd., Box 834, Maho ☎ 721/545–2115, 800/223–0757, 800/766–3782 🌐 www.sonesta.com/mahobeach 537 rooms Multiple meal plans.*

$ RENTAL FAMILY **Towers at Mullet Bay.** Near powdery Mullet Bay Beach, this time-share resort has the island's only (poorly maintained) golf course. **Pros:** close to restaurants and shops; on a gorgeous beach; units have Nintendo

The Westin St. Maarten Dawn Beach Resort & Spa

Wii and on-demand movies. **Cons:** disappointing golf course; no on-site restaurant; ongoing renovations. *Rooms from: $240 ✉ 28 Rhine Rd., Mullet Bay ☎ 599/545–3069, 800/235–5889 ⇨ 81 units ¶◎| No meals.*

OYSTER POND

$ RESORT FAMILY **Westin St. Maarten Dawn Beach Resort & Spa.** Straddling the border between the Dutch and French sides, the modern Westin sits on one of the island's best beaches. **Pros:** on Dawn Beach; plenty of activities; no smoking. **Cons:** very big; a bit off the beaten track; time-share salespeople can be bothersome; rooms need some updating. *Rooms from: $199 ✉ 144 Oyster Pond Rd., Oyster Pond ☎ 599/543–6700, 800/228–3000 in U.S. ⊕ www.westinstmaarten.com ⇨ 317 rooms, 15 suites, 99 1-, 2-, and 3-bedroom condos ¶◎| No meals.*

PELICAN KEY

$$ RENTAL Fodor's Choice ★ **Blue Pelican.** The 13 modern and chic apartment units hidden in this private enclave in Pelican Key were built by the owners of Hotel L'Esplanade and Le Petit Hotel, on the French side, and share the French management's vision, graciousness, obsessive attention to detail, and concern for guest comfort and safety. **Pros:** nicest place in the area; great pool; excellent management and security. **Cons:** residence, not a resort; not on the beach; no restaurant; need a car to get around; seven-night minimum. *Rooms from: $290 ✉ Billy Folly Rd., Pelican Key ☎ 0690/50–60–20 ⊕ www.bluepelicansxm.com ⇨ 13 apartments ¶◎| No meals.*

PHILIPSBURG

$ HOTEL **Holland House Beach Hotel.** This historic hotel is in an ideal location for shoppers and sun worshippers; it faces the Front Street pedestrian mall, and to the rear are the boardwalk and a long stretch of Great Bay Beach. **Pros:** easy access to beach and shops; free Wi-Fi; young, engaging management. **Cons:** in a busy, downtown location; no pool; not very resorty. *Rooms from: $170 ✉ 43 Front St., Philipsburg ☎ 721/542–2572 ⊕ www.hhbh.com 48 rooms, 6 suites Multiple meal plans.*

$$$ ALL-INCLUSIVE FAMILY **Sonesta Great Bay Beach Resort and Casino.** St. Maarten's adults-only all-inclusive is well positioned even if it doesn't offer the height of luxury: away from the docks that are usually crawling with cruise ships, but only a 10-minute walk from downtown Philipsburg. **Pros:** unlimited food and bar; nice beach and pool; enough activities to keep you busy. **Cons:** white, bare hallways have hospital-like feel; expensive Wi-Fi; although beach is beautiful, pollution can be a problem; staff can be indifferent. *Rooms from: $384 ✉ 19 Little Bay Rd., Philipsburg ☎ 721/542–2446, 800/223–0757 in U.S. ⊕ www.sonesta.com/greatbay 257 rooms All-inclusive.*

SIMPSON BAY

$ B&B/INN Fodor's Choice ★ **The Horny Toad.** Because of its stupendous view of Simpson Bay and the simple but comfortable rooms with creative decor, this lovely guest-house is widely considered the best on this side of the island. **Pros:** tidy rooms; friendly vibe and fantastic owner; beautiful beach is usually deserted. **Cons:** rooms are very basic; need a car to get around; no kids under seven; no pool. *Rooms from: $218 ✉ 2 Vlaun Dr., Simpson Bay ☎ 721/545–4323, 800/417–9361 in U.S. ⊕ www.thtgh.com 8 rooms No meals.*

$ RENTAL **La Vista.** Hibiscus and bougainvillea line brick walkways that connect the wood-frame bungalows and beachfront suites of this intimate and friendly, family-owned time-share resort perched at the foot of Pelican Key. **Pros:** close to restaurants and bars. **Cons:** no-frills furnishings; need a car to get to more swimmable beaches. *Rooms from: $180 ✉ 53 Billy Folly Rd., Simpson Bay ☎ 721/544–3005, 888/790–5264 in U.S. ⊕ www.lavistaresort.com 50 suites, penthouses, and cottages No meals.*

FRENCH SIDE

ANSE MARCEL

$$$$ ALL-INCLUSIVE FAMILY Fodor's Choice ★ **Hotel Riu Palace St. Martin.** Now under the RIU brand, this family-friendly all-inclusive (including alcoholic beverages) is well located: on a great beachy cove on 18 acres in a quiet part of St. Martin. **Pros:** all-inclusive; activities galore; great beach; huge pool. **Cons:** rooms face garden or marina, not ocean; need a car to get around; lots of families at school-vacation times; beach can be busy; ongoing renovations. *Rooms from: $564 ✉ BP 581, Anse Marcel ☎ 0590/87–67–09, 800/333–3333 in U.S. ⊕ www.riu.com/en/Paises/saint-martin/saint-martin-island/hotel-riu-palace-st-martin 189 rooms, 63 suites All-inclusive.*

Le Domaine Beach Resort and Spa

$ RESORT FAMILY **Le Domaine Beach Resort and Spa.** This classic property on 148 acres of lush gardens borders the exceptionally beautiful and secluded beach in Anse Marcel. **Pros:** all-inclusive option; lovely gardens; beachfront setting. **Cons:** some rooms have round bathtubs in middle of room; need a car to get around; beach is shared with busy Hotel Riu Palace. *Rooms from: $147 Anse Marcel 0590/52–35–35 www.hotel-le-domaine.com 124 rooms, 5 suites Closed Sept.–Oct. Multiple meal plans.*

$$ HOTEL **Marquis Boutique Hotel.** This fun property with a funky St. Barth vibe has spectacular vistas and intimate surroundings, but be warned of the heights and steep walks. **Pros:** romantic; doting staff; amazing views. **Cons:** not on beach; on a steep hill. *Rooms from: $280 Pigeon Pea Hill, Anse Marcel 0590/29–42–30 www.hotel-marquis.com 17 rooms Breakfast.*

BAIE LONGUE

$$$$ RESORT FAMILY Fodor's Choice ★ **Belmond La Samanna.** A long stretch of pretty, white-sand beach borders this classic resort, where service is warm and professional. **Pros:** chic decor; great beach; beach cabanas, convenient location; romantic; excellent spa. **Cons:** rather pricey for standard rooms; small pools. *Rooms from: $845 Baie Longue 0590/87–64–00, 800/854–2252 in U.S. www.belmond.com/la-samanna-st-martin 27 rooms, 54 suites Closed Sept.–Oct. Breakfast.*

BAIE NETTLÉ

$ RESORT FAMILY **Hotel Mercure St. Martin and Marina.** This modern option by a quiet beach bay is centrally located. **Pros:** good location; pet- and family-friendly; great spa; lots of activities, including for kids. **Cons:** beach

Belmond La Samanna

isn't great for swimming; ground-floor rooms are noisy and have no view; no elevators. *Rooms from: $174* *Baie Nettlé* *0590/87–54–54* *www.mercure.com/gb/hotel-1100-hotel-mercure-saint-martin-marina/* *170 rooms* *Breakfast.*

BAIE ORIENTALE

$$ RESORT FAMILY **Alamanda Resort.** One of the few resorts directly on the white-sand beach of Orient Bay, this hotel has a funky feel and spacious, colonial-style suites with terraces that overlook the pool, beach, or ocean. **Pros:** pleasant property; friendly staff; right on Orient Beach. **Cons:** some rooms are noisy; could still use some updating despite renovations. *Rooms from: $316* *Baie Orientale* *0590/52–87–40, 800/622–7836* *www.alamanda-resort.com* *42 rooms* *Breakfast.*

$$$ RENTAL FAMILY Fodor's Choice ★ **Caribbean Princess.** These 12 large, well-equipped, and updated two- and three-bedroom condos have big kitchens and living rooms and lovely balconies over Orient Beach (a few steps away), and they share a pretty pool. **Pros:** comforts of home; nice interior design; direct beach access. **Cons:** not a full-service resort; maid service every three days. *Rooms from: $400* *C5 Parc de la Baie Orientale, Baie Orientale* *0590/52–94–94* *www.caribbeanprincesscondos.com* *12 condos* *Closed Sept.* *No meals.*

$$$ RESORT FAMILY **Esmeralda Resort.** Almost all these traditional Caribbean-style, kitchen-equipped villas, which can be configured to meet guest needs, have their own pool, and the fun of Orient Beach and the hotel's beach club is a two-minute walk away. **Pros:** beachfront location; private pools; plenty of activities; frequent online promotions. **Cons:** need a car to get around; iffy Wi-Fi service. *Rooms from: $415* *Baie Orientale*

Palm Court

☎ *0590/87–36–36, 800/622–7836* 🌐 *www.esmeralda-resort.com* ⇨ *65 rooms* ⏲ *Closed Sept.–Oct.* 🍴 *Breakfast.*

$$$$ RENTAL FAMILY **Green Cay Village.** Surrounded by 5 acres of lush greenery high above Baie Orientale, these villas are a great deal for families or other groups looking for privacy and the comforts of home. **Pros:** beautiful setting near Baie Orientale; good for families with teens or older kids. **Cons:** need a car to get around; beach is a five-minute walk; need to be vigilant about locking doors, as there have been reports of crime in the area. 💲 *Rooms from: $660* ✉ *Parc de la Baie Orientale, Baie Orientale* ☎ *0590/87–38–63* 🌐 *www.greencay.com* ⇨ *9 villas* 🍴 *Breakfast.*

$ HOTEL FAMILY **Hotel La Plantation.** Perched high above Baie Orientale, this colonial-style hotel is a charmer. **Pros:** relaxing atmosphere; eye-popping views; lots of area restaurants. **Cons:** small pool; beach is a 10-minute walk away. 💲 *Rooms from: $167* ✉ *C5 Parc de La Baie Orientale, Baie Orientale* ☎ *0590/29–58–00* 🌐 *www.la-plantation.com* ⇨ *51 rooms* ⏲ *Closed Sept.–mid-Oct.* 🍴 *Breakfast.*

$$ HOTEL Fodor's Choice ★ **Palm Court.** The romantic beachfront units of this *hotel de charme* are steps from the fun of Orient Beach yet private, quiet, and stylish. **Pros:** big rooms; fresh and new; nice garden. **Cons:** across from, but not on the beach. 💲 *Rooms from: $330* ✉ *Parc de la Baie Orientale, Baie Orientale* ☎ *0590/87–41–94* 🌐 *www.sxm-palm-court.com* ⇨ *24 rooms* ⏲ *Closed Sept.* 🍴 *Breakfast.*

FRENCH CUL DE SAC

$$ B&B/INN Fodor's Choice ★ **Karibuni Lodge.** Lovely in every way, this super-chic yet reasonably priced enclave of spacious suites surrounded by gorgeous tropical gardens offers stunning views of tiny Ilet Pinel. **Pros:** stylish; eco-friendly; lushly comfortable; amazing views. **Cons:** removed from the action;

need a car; not a resort; not on the beach. *Rooms from: $352 ✉ 29 Terrasses de Cul de Sac, French Cul de Sac ☎ 0690/64–38–58 ⊕ www.lekaribuni.com ⇒ 6 suites ¦ Breakfast.*

GRAND CASE

$$ RENTAL FAMILY **Bleu Emeraude.** The 11 spacious apartments in this tidy complex sit right on a sliver of Grand Case Beach. **Pros:** modern and updated; walk to restaurants; attractive decor. **Cons:** not resorty. *Rooms from: $360 ✉ 240 bd. de Grand Case, Grand Case ☎ 0590/87–27–71 ⊕ www.bleuemeraude.com ⇒ 4 studios, 6 1-bedroom apartments, 1 2-bedroom apartment ¦ Breakfast.*

$$ RESORT FAMILY **Grand Case Beach Club.** This beachfront property on a cove at the east end of Grand Case has a friendly staff and spectacular sunset views. **Pros:** reasonably priced; comfortable rooms; walking distance to restaurants. **Cons:** small beach; dated decor and buildings; need a car to explore. *Rooms from: $345 ✉ 21 rue de la Petite Plage, at north end of bd. de Grand Case, Grand Case ☎ 0590/87–51–87, 800/344–3016 in U.S. ⊕ www.grandcasebeachclub.com ⇒ 72 apartments ¦ Breakfast.*

$$$ HOTEL FAMILY Fodor's Choice ★ **Hôtel L'Esplanade.** Fans return again and again to the classy, loft-style suites in this immaculate boutique hotel. **Pros:** attentive management; very clean; updated room decor; family-friendly feel. **Cons:** lots of stairs to climb; not on the beach. *Rooms from: $415 ✉ Grand Case ☎ 0590/87–06–55, 866/596–8365 in U.S. ⊕ www.lesplanade.com ⇒ 24 units ¦ No meals.*

$$$ HOTEL FAMILY Fodor's Choice ★ **Le Petit Hotel.** Surrounded by some of the best restaurants in the Caribbean, this beachfront boutique hotel oozes charm and has the same caring, attentive management as Hotel L'Esplanade. **Pros:** walking distance to everything in Grand Case; friendly staff; clean, updated rooms. **Cons:** many stairs to climb; no pool. *Rooms from: $435 ✉ 248 bd. de Grand Case, Grand Case ☎ 0590/29–09–65 ⊕ www.lepetithotel.com ⇒ 9 rooms, 1 suite ¦ Breakfast.*

OYSTER POND

$ HOTEL **Captain Oliver's Resort.** This cluster of older pink bungalows is perched high on a hill above a lagoon with lots of lush landscaping and a fine view of the Caribbean and St. Barth. **Pros:** reasonably priced restaurant; ferry trips leave from the hotel. **Cons:** not on beach; not fancy or modern; could use some updating; must have a car. *Rooms from: $241 ✉ Oyster Pond ☎ 0590/87–40–26 ⊕ www.captainolivers.com ⇒ 50 suites ⊗ Closed Sept.–Oct. ¦ Breakfast.*

NIGHTLIFE

St. Maarten has lots of evening and late-night action. To find out what's doing, pick up *St. Maarten Nights* or *St. Maarten Events,* both distributed free in the tourist office and hotels. The glossy *Discover St. Martin/ St. Maarten* magazine, also free, has articles on island history and on the newest shops, discos, and restaurants. Or buy a copy of Thursday's *Daily Herald* newspaper, which lists the week's entertainment.

The island's 13 casinos are only on the Dutch side. All have craps, blackjack, roulette, and slot machines. You must be 18 or older to gamble.

Dress is casual (but not bathing suits or skimpy beachwear). Most casinos are in hotels, but there are also some independents.

DUTCH SIDE

CUPECOY

CASINOS

Atlantis World Casino. With some of the best restaurants on the Dutch side, this casino is popular even with people who don't gamble. It has more than 400 slot machines and gaming tables offering roulette, baccarat, three-card poker, Texas Hold'em poker, and Omaha high poker. ✉ *106 Rhine Rd., Cupecoy* ☎ *721/545–4601* 🌐 *www.atlantisworld.com.*

MAHO

BARS AND CLUBS

Cheri's Café. Across from Maho Beach Resort and Casino, this open-air club (you can't miss it—look for pink) features Sweet Chocolate, a lively band that will get your toes tapping and your tush twisting. Snacks and hearty meals are available all day long on a cheerful veranda decorated with hundreds of inflatable beach toys. ✉ *45 Rhine Rd., Maho* ☎ *721/545–3361* 🌐 *www.cheriscafe.com* ⊗ *Closed Tues.*

Fodor's Choice ★ **Sky Beach.** For those who don't want to leave the beach vibe after the sun goes down, this elegant rooftop pulses with techno and house music while guests lounge on beds in cabanas. (In case of rain, there's a tent.) Sand volleyball is fun, and the happening bar serves delicious cocktails. Great views and stargazing come with the territory. In-the-know clubbers come here before Tantra starts to wake up after midnight. It's open every day from 4 pm until 1 am. The website lists special events and parties. ✉ *Sonesta Maho Beach Resort & Casino, 1 Rhine Rd., Maho* ☎ *721/520–1757* 🌐 *www.theskybeach.com.*

Soprano's. Starting each night at 8, the pianist takes requests for oldies, romantic favorites, or smooth jazz. Come for happy hour (8–9), with a full menu that includes pizza. The bar is open until 3. Special events are posted on the website. ✉ *Sonesta Maho Beach Resort & Casino, 1 Rhine Rd., Maho* ☎ *721/545–2485* 🌐 *www.sopranospianobar.com.*

Sunset Bar and Grill. This popular spot offers a relaxed, anything-goes atmosphere. Enjoy live music Wednesday through Sunday as you watch planes from the airport next door fly directly over your head. Bring your camera for stunning photos, but expect a high noise level. ✉ *Maho Beach, Beacon Hill No. 2, Maho* ☎ *721/545–2084* 🌐 *www.sunsetsxm.com.*

Tantra Nightclub & Sanctuary. This is definitely the hottest nightclub at the Sonesta Maho. Come late—things don't really get going until after 1 am. On Wednesday nights, ladies drink champagne for free, and drinks are $2 for everyone on Fridays. Celebrity DJs spin on Saturdays. Feel free to dress up. There is bottle and table service by reservation. It's closed Monday, Tuesday, and Thursday. ✉ *Sonesta Maho Beach Resort & Casino, 1 Rhine Rd., Maho Bay* ☎ *721/545–2861* 🌐 *www.tantrasxm.com.*

Gambling is the most popular indoor activity in St. Maarten.

CASINOS

Casino Royale. This is the largest casino on the island, with some 1,300 square meters of gaming and a full theater with 750 seats for events and shows. There are 21 tables for gaming, including roulette (American and French), craps, blackjack, and poker (three-card and Caribbean). The 410 slot machines include a variety of classics and modern video slots. ✉ *Sonesta Maho Beach Resort & Casino, 1 Rhine Rd., Maho* ☎ *721/545–2590* 🌐 *www.playmaho.com.*

OYSTER POND

CASINOS

Westin Casino. This is somewhat more sedate than other island casinos. If you get tired of the slot machines and gaming tables, beautiful Dawn Beach is just outside. ✉ *Westin St. Maarten Dawn Beach Resort & Spa, 144 Oyster Pond Rd., Oyster Pond* ☎ *721/543–6700* 🌐 *www.westinstmaarten.com.*

PHILIPSBURG

BARS AND CLUBS

Ocean Lounge. Sip a guavaberry colada and point your chair toward the boardwalk at this quintessential people-watching venue. There's free parking for patrons until midnight; enter on Back Street, and look for the Holland House banner. ✉ *Holland House Beach Hotel, 43 Front St., Philipsburg* ☎ *721/542–2572* 🌐 *www.hhbh.com.*

CASINOS

Beach Plaza Casino. In the heart of the shopping area, this casino has more than 180 slots, a sports book, and multigame machines with touch screens. Because of its location, it is popular with cruise-ship passengers. ✉ *Front St., Philipsburg* ☎ *721/543–2031* 🌐 *www.atlantisworld.com.*

SIMPSON BAY

BARS AND CLUBS

FAMILY **Buccaneer Beach Bar.** Conveniently located on Kim Sha Beach, this family-friendly bar can provide you a BBC (Bailey's banana colada), a slice of pizza, a sunset, and a nightly fireball show. ✉ *10 Billy Folly Rd., behind Festiva Atrium Beach Resort, Simpson Bay* ☎ *721/522–9700* 🌐 *www.buccaneerbeachbar.com.*

Le Shore. With special events and parties almost every night, this nighttime hot spot in the middle of Simpson Bay is reminiscent of Miami or Vegas. It's billed as a private club, but if you call for a reservation or just dress nicely, you shouldn't have a problem getting in. ✉ *111 Welfare Rd, Simpson Bay* ☎ *721/586–4499* 🌐 *www.shoreclubsxm.com.*

Pineapple Pete. You can groove to live music or hit the game room for a couple of rounds of pool. ✉ *Airport Rd., Simpson Bay* ☎ *721/544–6030* 🌐 *www.pineapplepete.com.*

Red Piano. This bar has a great pool room, terrific live music, and tasty cocktails every night from 8 until 3. ✉ *Hollywood Casino, 35 Billy Folly Rd., Simpson Bay* ☎ *721/544–6008* 🌐 *www.theredpianosxm.com.*

CASINOS

Paradise Plaza Casino. Betting on sporting events is the big thing here, which explains the 20 televisions tuned to whatever game happens to be on. There are also 250 slots and multigame machines. ✉ *69 Welfare Rd., Simpson Bay* ☎ *721/543–4721* 🌐 *www.atlantisworld.com/paradise-plaza-casino-sports-book-simpson-bay.*

FRENCH SIDE

GRAND CASE

Calmos Café. Join the young local crowd by walking through the boutique and around the back to the sea. Then pull up a beach chair or park yourself at a picnic table. It's open all day, but the fun really begins at the cocktail hour, when everyone enjoys tapas. The little covered deck at the end is romantic. On Thursday and Sunday there is often live reggae on the beach. ✉ *40 bd. de Grand Case, Grand Case* ☎ *0590/29–01–85* 🌐 *www.lecalmoscafe.com.*

SHOPPING

Shopaholics are drawn to the huge array of stores, and jewelry in particular is big business on both sides of the island. (Many stores have outlets in both places.) Duty-free shops can offer substantial savings—about 15% to 30% below U.S. and Canadian prices—on cameras, expensive jewelry, watches, liquor, cigars, and designer clothing, but not always, so make sure you know U.S. prices to know if you're getting a deal, and be prepared to bargain hard. Stick with the big vendors that advertise in the tourist press, and you will be more likely to avoid today's ubiquitous fakes and replicas. On both sides of the island, be alert for idlers. They can snatch unwatched purses.

Prices are in dollars on the Dutch side, in euros on the French side. As for bargains, there are more to be had on the Dutch side; prices on the French side may be higher than those back home, and being in euros doesn't help. Merchandise may not be from the newest collections, especially with regard to clothing; there are items available on the French side that are not available on the Dutch side.

DUTCH SIDE

MAHO

You'll find a moderately good selection of stores in Maho Village, near the Sonesta resort. The glitzy Blue Mall opened in 2013.

PHILIPSBURG

Philipsburg's **Front Street** has reinvented itself. Now it's mall-like, with a redbrick walk and streets, palm trees lining the sleek boutiques, jewelry stores, souvenir shops, outdoor restaurants, and the old reliables, such as McDonald's and Burger King. Here and there a school or a church appears to remind visitors there's more to the island than shopping. On Back Street, the **Philipsburg Market Place** is a daily open-air market where you can haggle on handicrafts, souvenirs, and beachwear. **Old Street,** near the end of Front Street, has stores, boutiques, and open-air cafés offering French crêpes, rich chocolates, and island mementos.

Façonnable. The refined men's line of cheery, well-fitting shirts is well represented, with a smattering of women's items in back. ✉ *16 Sint Rose Arcade, Front St., Philipsburg* ☎ *721/542–2444* 🌐 *www.faconnable.com.*

Polo Ralph Lauren. Polo Ralph Lauren has men's, women's, and children's sportswear in preppy styles, as well as a small selection of home goods. ✉ *48 Front St., Philipsburg* ☎ *721/543–0197.*

HANDICRAFTS

Shipwreck Shop. With outlets all over the island, this chain stocks a little of everything: colorful hammocks, handmade jewelry, and lots of the local Guavaberry liqueur. But the main store has the largest selection. ✉ *42 Front St., Philipsburg* ☎ *721/542–2962, 721/542–6710* 🌐 *www.shipwreckshops.com.*

JEWELRY AND GIFTS

Little Europe. Come here to buy fine jewelry, crystal, and china. There is also a branch in Marigot. ✉ *80 Front St., Philipsburg* ☎ *721/542–4371* 🌐 *www.littleeurope.com* ✉ *2 Front St., Philipsburg* ☎ *721/542–4371* 🌐 *www.littleeurope.com.*

Little Switzerland. The large Caribbean duty-free chain sells watches, fine crystal, china, perfume, and jewelry. There are five locations on the island, one a Tiffany boutique. ✉ *52 Front St., Philipsburg* ☎ *721/542–3530* 🌐 *www.littleswitzerland.com.*

Oro Diamante. This store carries loose diamonds, jewelry, watches, perfume, and cosmetics. It specializes in natural colored diamonds and also sells the popular stackable rings by Gabriel & Co. ✉ *62-B Front St., Philipsburg* ☎ *599/543–0342, 800/635–7950 in U.S.* 🌐 *www.oro-diamante.com.*

LIQUOR

Guavaberry Emporium. Visitors come for free samples at the small factory where the Sint Maarten Guavaberry Company makes its famous liqueur. The many versions include one made with jalapeño peppers. Check out the hand-painted bottles. The store also sells a gourmet barbecue and hot-sauce collection and souvenir hats. ✉ *8–10 Front St., Philipsburg* ☎ *721/542–2965* 🌐 *www.guavaberry.com.*

FRENCH SIDE

GRAND CASE

ART

Tropismes Gallery. Contemporary Caribbean artists showcased here include Paul Elliot Thuleau, who is a master of capturing the sunshine of the islands, and Nathalie Lepine, whose portraits show a Modigliani influence. This is a serious gallery with some very good artists. It's open 10–1 and 5–9 daily. ✉ *107 bd. de Grand Case, Grand Case* ☎ *0690/54–62–69* 🌐 *www.tropismesgallery.com.*

MARIGOT

Wrought-iron balconies, colorful awnings, and gingerbread trim decorate smart shops, tiny boutiques, and bistros in the **Marina Port La Royale** complex and on the main streets, **rue de la Liberté** and **rue de la République.** Also in Marigot are the pricey **West Indies Mall** and the **Plaza Caraïbes,** which house designer shops.

ART

Galerie Camaïeu. This gallery sells both originals and copies of works by Caribbean artists. It's closed Sunday, plus Saturday May–November. ✉ *8 rue de Kennedy, Marigot* ☎ *0590/87–25–78* 🌐 *www.camaieu-artgallery.com.*

CLOTHING

Some of the best luxury-brand shops are in the modern, air-conditioned West Indies Mall and the Plaza Caraïbes center across from Marina Port La Royale.

Vilebrequin. This shop on the marina has a vast selection of brighly patterned status swimsuits for men and boys. ✉ *Marina Port La Royale, Marigot* ☎ *0590/29–13–09.*

JEWELRY AND GIFTS

Art of Time. This reputable shop carries Mikimoto, Pandora, and David Yurman, among many others, as well as high-end designer watches, including Chanel, Baum & Mercier, Technomarine, Bidat, and Chopard. ✉ *3 rue du Général de Gaulle, Marigot* ☎ *0590/52–24–80* 🌐 *www.artoftimejewelers.com.*

Manek's. Two floors house electronics, luggage, perfume, jewelry, Cuban cigars, duty-free liquors, and tobacco products. ✉ *Rue de la République, Marigot* ☎ *0590/87–54–91.*

SPORTS AND THE OUTDOORS

BOATING AND SAILING

The island is surrounded by water, so why not get out and enjoy it? The water and winds are perfect for skimming the surf. It'll cost you around $1,200 to $1,500 per day to rent a 28- to 40-foot powerboat, considerably less for smaller boats or small sailboats. Drinks and sometimes lunch are usually included on crewed day charters, and some tours are eco-oriented.

DUTCH SIDE

Random Wind. This company offers full-day sailing and snorkeling trips on a traditional 54-foot clipper. Charter prices depend on the size of the group and whether lunch is served. The regularly scheduled Paradise Daysail ($109 adults, $75 kids) includes food and drink, snorkeling equipment, and stand-up paddleboard. Departures, weekdays at 9:45, are from SkipJack's at Simpson Bay. Everyone loves "flying" from the Tarzan Swing. ■ **TIP→ You can get the best rates from the website rather than hotels or cruises.** ✉ *Ric's Place, Simpson Bay* ☎ *721/587–5742* 🌐 *www.randomwind.com.*

St. Maarten 12-Metre Challenge. Sailing experience is not necessary as participants compete on 68-foot racing yachts, including Dennis Connor's *Stars and Stripes* (the actual boat that won the America's Cup in Freemantle, Australia, in 1987), *Canada II,* and *True North I.* Everyone is allocated a crew position, either grinding winches, trimming sails, punching the stopwatch, or bartending. The thrill is priceless, but book well in advance; this is the most popular shore excursion in the Caribbean. It is offered up to five times daily and lasts 2½–3 hours. Children over 12 (7 with sailing experience) may participate. ✉ *Bobby's Marina, Philipsburg* ☎ *721/542–0045* 🌐 *www.12metre.com.*

FRENCH SIDE

MP Yachting. You can rent boats of all sizes, with or without a crew, for short trips and long. ✉ *Marina Port La Royale, Marigot* ☎ *0690/53–37–40* 🌐 *www.mpyachting.com.*

Sun Evasion. This charter company has locations all over the world. You can take a half- or full-day charter to Tintamarre, St. Barth, or Ilet Pinel on a mono- or multihull powerboat, available with or without a skipper. ■ **TIP→ Book online for a 10% discount.** ✉ *Marina Port La Royale, Marigot* ☎ *0690/35–03–18* 🌐 *www.sun-evasion.com.*

DIVING

Diving in St. Maarten/St. Martin is mediocre at best, but those who want to dive will find a few positives. The water temperature here is rarely below 70°F (21°C) and visibility is often 60 to 100 feet. The island has more than 30 dive sites, from wrecks to rocky labyrinths. Right outside Philipsburg, 55 feet under the water, is the HMS *Proselyte,* once explored by Jacques Cousteau. Although it sank in 1801, the boat's cannons and coral-encrusted anchors are still visible.

Off the north coast, in the protected and mostly current-free Grand Case Bay, is **Creole Rock.** The water here ranges in depth from 10 feet to 25 feet. Other sites off the north coast include **Ilet Pinel,** with its good shallow diving; **Green Key,** with its vibrant barrier reef; and **Tintamarre,** with its sheltered coves and geologic faults. On average, one-tank dives start at $55; two-tank dives are about $100. Certification courses start at about $400.

The Dutch side offers several full-service outfitters and SSI (Scuba Schools International) and/or PADI certification. There are no hyperbaric chambers on the island.

DUTCH SIDE

Dive Safaris. Certified divers who have dived within the last two years can watch professional feeders give reef sharks a little nosh in a half-hour shark-awareness dive. The company also offers a full PADI training program and can tailor dive excursions and sophisticated, sensitive instruction to any level. ✉ *16 Airport Blvd., Simpson Bay* ☎ *721/545–2401* 🌐 *www.divestmaarten.com.*

Ocean Explorers Dive Shop. St. Maarten's oldest dive shop offers different types of certification courses. Serious divers like the six-person maximum policy on trips, but this means you should reserve in advance. ✉ *113 Welfare Rd., Simpson Bay* ☎ *721/544–5252* 🌐 *www.stmaartendiving.com.*

FRENCH SIDE

Octopus. The well-stocked dive shop offers PADI diving certification courses and all-inclusive dive packages, as well as highly recommended private and group snorkel trips starting at $55, including all necessary equipment. The shop also services regulators. ✉ *3 rue de la Petite Plage, Grand Case* ☎ *914/487–1315* 🌐 *www.octopusdiving.com.*

FISHING

You can angle for yellowtail snapper, grouper, marlin, tuna, and wahoo on deep-sea excursions. Costs range from $150 per person for a half day to $250 for a full day. Prices usually include bait and tackle, instruction for novices, and refreshments. Ask about licensing and insurance.

DUTCH SIDE

Lee's Deepsea Fishing. When you return from an excursion with this outfit, Lee's Roadside Grill will cook the tuna, wahoo, or mahi you catch. Rates start at $800 for a half-day trip for six people. ✉ *84 Welfare Rd., Cole Bay* ☎ *721/544–4233* 🌐 *www.leesfish.com.*

Private Yacht Charter. This company leads deep-sea fishing, snorkeling, and catamaran trips, including snacks and drinks. ✉ *Oyster Pond Great House Marina, 14 Emerald Merit Rd., Oyster Pond* ☎ *721/581–5305* 🌐 *www.privateyachtcharter-sxm.com.*

Rudy's Deep Sea Fishing. One of the more experienced sport-angling outfits runs private charter trips. Half-day excursions for up to four people start at $575, $50 each additional for up to six. Three-quarter- and full-day trips are also available. ■TIP→ **Check the website for great tips on fishing around St. Maarten.** ✉ *14 Airport Rd., Simpson Bay* ☎ *721/545–2177* 🌐 *www.rudysdeepseafishing.com.*

GOLF

DUTCH SIDE

Mullet Bay Golf Course. St. Maarten is not a golf destination. Nevertheless, there have been improvements to this golf course, which is again 18 holes (and the island's only choice), though hardly a must-play. ✉ *Airport Rd., north of airport, Mullet Bay* ☎ *721/545–2850* 🎫 *$93* *18 holes, 6200 yards, par 70.*

HORSEBACK RIDING

Island stables offer riding packages for everyone from novices to experts. A 90-minute ride along the beach typically costs $100 or more for group rides. Private treks are available, too. Reservations are necessary and can be arranged directly or through most hotels.

DUTCH SIDE

Lucky Stables. These stables in Cay Bay offer hourlong rides every hour on the hour. For a romantic treat, book a sunset ride with champagne and a bonfire (complete with marshmallows) for $100 per person. All experience levels are welcome, as the horses only walk, but advanced riders can book private rides if they want to trot and canter. ✉ *64 Traybay Dr., Cay Bay* ☎ *721/544–5255* 🌐 *www.seasidenaturepark.com.*

Bayside Riding Club. This established outfit can accommodate all levels on group beach rides around a nature preserve; one to 1½ hours costs €80 (cash only). You actually take the horses into the water, so bring a towel and a plastic bag for your clothes, and leave your valuables behind. It's closed Sunday and Monday. ✉ *Galion Beach Rd., Baie Orientale* ☎ *721/581–0206 on Dutch side, 0690/62–36–18 on French side* 🌐 *www.baysideranch.com.*

KAYAKING

Kayaking is becoming very popular and is almost always offered at the many water-sports operations on both the Dutch and the French sides. Rental starts at about $15 per hour for a single and $19 for a double.

DUTCH SIDE

TriSports. This company organizes kayaking and snorkeling excursions in addition to its biking operation. ✉ *Airport Rd. 14B, Simpson Bay* ☎ *721/545–4384* 🌐 *www.trisportsxm.com.*

FRENCH SIDE

FAMILY **Wind Adventures.** Near Le Galion Beach, this outfitter offers rentals and instruction in kayaking, kitesurfing, windsurfing, Hobie Cats, and stand-up paddleboarding as well as ecotours. ✉ *Baie Orientale* ☎ *0590/29–41–57* 🌐 *www.wind-adventures.com.*

SEA EXCURSIONS

DUTCH SIDE

Bluebeard II. The 60-foot custom-built day-sail catamaran is specially designed for maximum safety and comfort. *Bluebeard II* sails around Anguilla's south and northwest coasts to Prickly Pear Cay, where there's a coral reef for snorkeling and powdery white sands for sunning. Thrill-seekers might prefer the three-hour racing trip aboard a 52-footer built for speed. Private charters are also available. ✉ *Simpson Bay* ☎ *721/587–5935* 🌐 *www.bluebeardcharters.com.*

Celine. For low-impact sunset and dinner cruises, try the catamaran *Celine.* ✉ *SkipJack's Restaurant, Simpson Bay* ☎ *721/526–1170, 721/552–1335* 🌐 *www.sailstmaarten.com.*

FAMILY ***Golden Eagle.*** The sleek 76-foot catamaran *Golden Eagle* takes day-sailors on eco-friendly excursions to outlying islets and reefs for snorkeling and partying. They can pick you up from your hotel or condo. ✉ *Bobby's Marina, Philipsburg* ☎ *721/542–3323* 🌐 *www.sailingsxm.com.*

SNORKELING

Some of the best snorkeling on the Dutch side can be found around the rocks below Fort Amsterdam off Little Bay Beach, in the west end of Maho Bay, off Pelican Key, and around the reefs off Oyster Pond Beach. On the French side, the area around Baie Orientale—including Caye Verte, Ilet Pinel, and Tintamarre—is especially lovely and is officially classified and protected as a regional underwater nature reserve. Sea creatures also congregate around Creole Rock at the point of Baie de Grand Case. The average cost of an afternoon snorkeling trip is $45–$55 per person.

DUTCH SIDE

FAMILY **Blue Bubbles.** This company offers both boat and shore snorkel excursions as well as jet-skiing, parasailing, and Snuba for beginner divers. ✉ *153 Front St., Philipsburg* ☎ *721/556–8484* 🌐 *www.bluebubblessxm.com.*

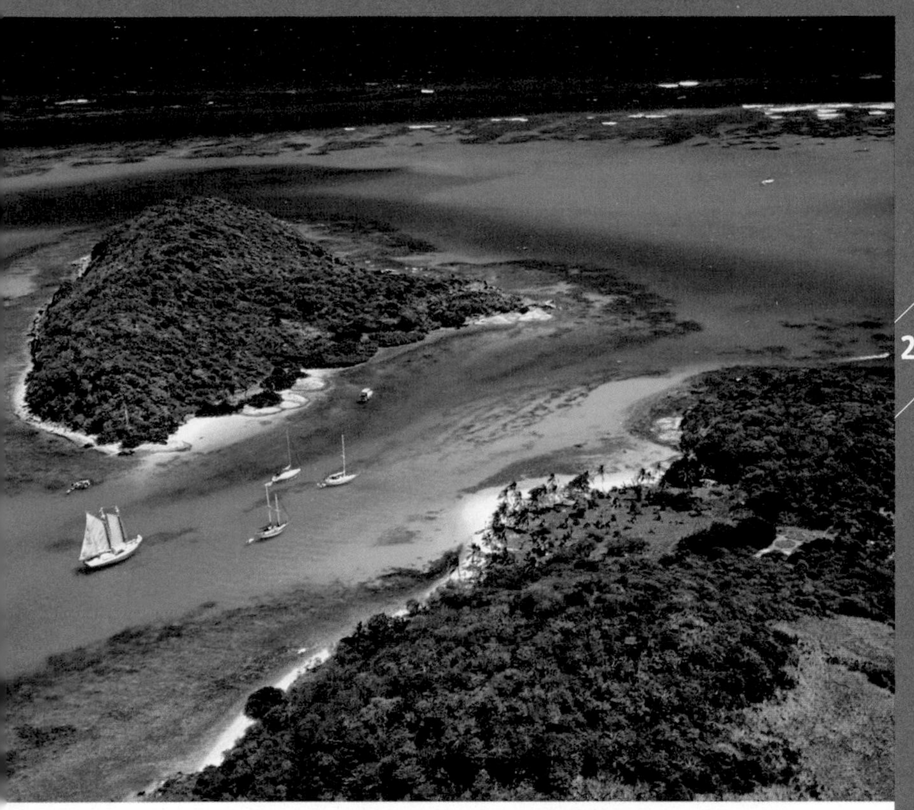

ST. VINCENT AND THE GRENADINES

WELCOME TO ST. VINCENT AND THE GRENADINES

A STRING OF PEARLS

St. Vincent, which is 18 miles (29 km) long and 11 miles (18 km) wide, is the northernmost and largest of the chain of 32 islands that make up St. Vincent and the Grenadines and extend 45 miles (72 km) southwest toward Grenada. What these islands all have in common is a get-away-from-it-all atmosphere.

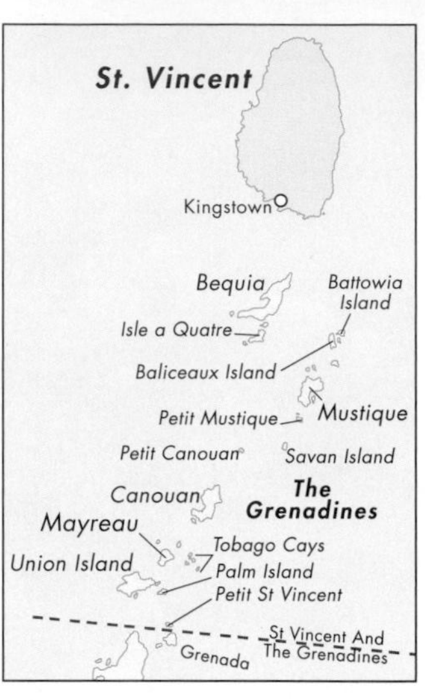

Restaurants	▼
Basil's Bar & Restaurant	2
Cobblestone Roof-Top	3
The French Verandah	6
High Tide	7
Paradise Beach Hotel Restaurant	8
The Sapodilla Room	5
Vee Jay's Restaurant & Bar	4
Wallilabou Anchorage	1
Young Island Resort	9

Hotels	▼
Beachcombers Hotel	5
Blue Lagoon	12
Buccament Bay Resort	1
Cobblestone Inn	2
Grand View Beach Hotel	4
Grenadine House	3
Hotel Alexandrina	11
Mariners Hotel	9
Paradise Beach Resort	10
Rosewood Apartment Hotel	8
Sunset Shores Beach Hotel	6
Young Island Resort	7

The 32 Grenadine islands and cays have some of the Caribbean's best anchorages and prettiest beaches.

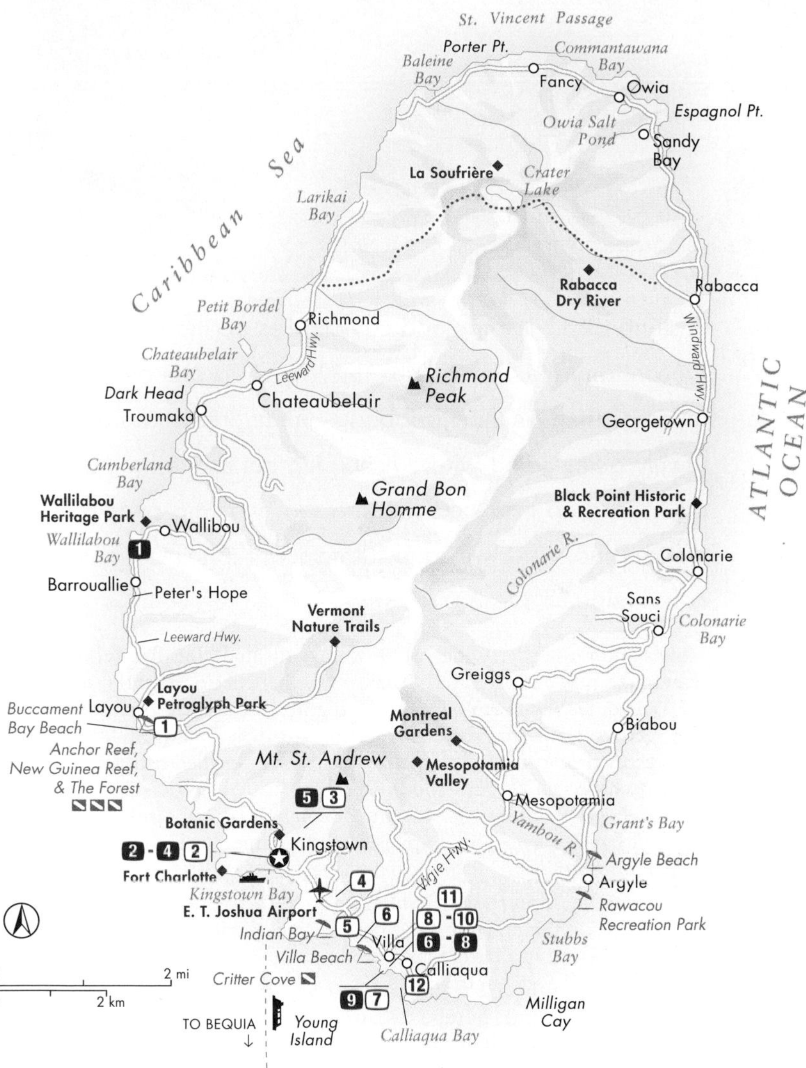

TOP REASONS TO VISIT ST. VINCENT AND THE GRENADINES

1 Diverse Landscape: St. Vincent offers a lush landscape, extraordinary hiking trails, remarkable botanical gardens, majestic waterfalls, and intriguing dive sites.

2 Tranquillity: With few large resorts and no crowds, you're guaranteed peace and quiet.

3 Sail Away: Island-hopping sailing charters are the premier way to travel through the beautiful Grenadines.

4 Beach Paradise: Grenadine beaches have brilliant-white, powdery-soft sand washed by gentle waves in several shades of blue.

Updated by Jane E. Zarem

A string of 32 islands and cays makes up the nation of St. Vincent and the Grenadines. St. Vincent is one of the least touristy islands in the Caribbean—an unpretentious and relatively quiet island where fishermen get up at the crack of dawn to drop their nets into the sea, working people conduct business in town, and farmers work their crops in the countryside.

Hotels and inns on St. Vincent are almost all small, locally owned and operated, and definitely not glitzy. So far, there are only two resorts—one on a quiet bay north of Kingstown and another on a private island 600 feet from the mainland. Restaurants (other than at St. Vincent's two resort properties) serve mainly local food—grilled fish, stewed or curried chicken, rice, and root vegetables (called "provisions"). And the beaches are either tiny crescents of black or brown sand on remote leeward bays or sweeping expanses of the same black sand pounded by Atlantic surf.

The Grenadines, on the other hand, dazzle vacationers with amazing inns and resorts, fine white-sand beaches, excellent sailing waters, and a get-away-from-it-all atmosphere.

Bequia, just south of St. Vincent and an efficient hour's voyage by ferry, has many inns, hotels, restaurants, shops, and activities; it's a popular vacation destination in its own right. Bequia's Admiralty Bay is one of the prettiest anchorages in the Caribbean. With superb views, snorkeling, hiking, and swimming, the island has much to offer the international mix of backpackers, landlubbers, and boaters who frequent its shores.

South of Bequia, on the exclusive and very private island of Mustique, elaborate villas are tucked into lush hillsides. Mustique does not encourage wholesale tourism, least of all to those hoping for a glimpse of the rich and famous who own or rent villas here. The appeal of Mustique is its seclusion.

Boot-shape Canouan, mostly quiet and unspoiled and with only 1,200 or so residents, is nevertheless a busy venue for chartered yachts. It also accommodates well-heeled guests of the villa community that takes up the entire northern third of the island along with one of the Caribbean's most challenging and scenic golf courses.

Tiny Mayreau (fewer than 200 residents) has one of the area's most beautiful (and unusual) beaches. At Saltwhistle Bay, the Caribbean Sea is usually as calm as a mirror; just yards away, the rolling Atlantic surf washes the opposite shore. Otherwise, Mayreau has a single unnamed village, one road, rain-caught drinking water, and an inn—but no airport, no bank, and no problems!

Union Island, with its dramatic landscape punctuated by Mt. Taboi, is the transportation center of the southern Grenadines. Its small but busy airport serves landlubbers, and its yacht harbor and dive operators serve sailors and scuba divers. Clifton, the quaint main town, has shops, restaurants, and a few guesthouses. Ashton, the second significant town, is mainly residential.

Meanwhile, it took decades to turn the 100-acre, mosquito-infested mangrove swamp called Prune Island, a virtual stone's throw from Union Island, into the upscale private resort now known as Palm Island. Today, well-healed vacationers lounge on the island's five palm-fringed white-sand beaches.

Petit St. Vincent, another private resort island, was reclaimed from the overgrowth by the late Hazen K. Richardson II. The luxury resort's cobblestone cottages are so private that, if you wish, you could spend your entire vacation completely undisturbed.

And finally, there are the Tobago Cays, five uninhabited islands south of Canouan and east of Mayreau that draw snorkelers, divers, and boaters. Surrounded by a shallow reef, the tiny islands have rustling palm trees, pristine beaches with powdery sand, the clearest water imaginable in varying shades of brilliant blue—and plenty of resident fish and sea turtles.

PLANNING

WHEN TO GO

High season runs from mid-December through mid-April; in the off-season, rates at larger resorts may be reduced by up to 40%. Seasonal discounts vary dramatically by resort and by island, with some of the luxury resorts offering specials periodically throughout the year; the most extravagant resorts, however, are always expensive. The small, less-expensive hotels and guesthouses have little or no seasonal variation in their rates.

GETTING HERE AND AROUND

AIR TRAVEL

Until Argyle International Airport begins operations (scheduled for mid-2015), there are no nonstop flights between the United States and St. Vincent and the Grenadines. Instead, travelers from North America

LOGISTICS

Getting to St. Vincent and the Grenadines: Until Argyle International Airport begins operations (expected in mid-2015), there are no nonstop flights between the United States and St. Vincent and the Grenadines. Travelers from North America arrive at airports in St. Vincent, Bequia, Canouan, Mustique, or Union Island via regional airlines that connect to major airlines serving Barbados, Grenada, Puerto Rico, or St. Lucia. Some of the smaller Grenadines require both a flight and a boat transfer. Unless you're on a private jet, it's an exhausting, time-consuming trip (and fairly expensive); yet people still make the effort to reach some of the most wonderful, unspoiled islands in the Caribbean. Once you've landed on St. Vincent, it's also possible to hop to several different islands for a day or longer by air or by an interisland ferry.

Hassle Factor: High, but worth it.

On the Ground: St. Vincent's Argyle International Airport, expected to begin operations in midsummer 2015, is on the southeastern coast of the island and a 20- to 30-minute drive from Kingstown. The new airport will accommodate large commercial jets arriving from overseas, as well as general aviation planes. In the meantime, E.T. Joshua Airport in Arnos Vale, about halfway between Kingstown and Villa Beach, is a small but busy airport that accommodates only turboprop passenger aircraft and small private jets. In the Grenadines, Canouan's modern airport has an extended runway that can accommodate jets as large as 737s. Bequia, Mustique, and Union islands each have an airstrip with frequent regional service. Taxis and buses are readily available at the airport on St. Vincent. The taxi fare to Kingstown or the Villa Beach area is $12 (or EC$30); from Argyle, twice that amount. Taxi service is available from the airports on Bequia, Mustique, Canouan, and Union islands.

arrive at **E.T. Joshua International Airport** (SVD) in St. Vincent or the airports in Bequia (BQU), Canouan (CIW), Mustique (MQS), or Union Island (UNI) via regional airlines that connect with major carriers serving Barbados, Grenada, Puerto Rico, or St. Lucia.

Airline Contacts **Grenadine Air Alliance.** Operating a shared-charter service via SVG Air and Mustique Airways, Grenadine Air Alliance links Barbados with St. Vincent and the four airports in the Grenadines. ☎ *246/418–1650 in Barbados, 784/458–4380 in Mustique, 784/457–4124 in St. Vincent* ⊕ *www.grenadine-air.com.* **LIAT.** LIAT flights connect St. Vincent and Canouan with Antigua, Barbados, Grenada, St. Lucia, St. Maarten, Tortola, and Trinidad. ☎ *268/480–5601 in U.S., 888/844–5428 throughout the Caribbean* ⊕ *www.liat.com.* **Mustique Airways.** This regional airline operates scheduled shared-charter service between Barbados and Mustique (with meet-and-greet service at the Barbados airport for in-transit passengers), as well as inter-Grenadine scheduled service and private charter flights to points around the Caribbean. ☎ *784/458–4380, 718/618–4492 in U.S.* ⊕ *www.mustique.com.* **SVG Air.** SVG Air operates twice-daily flights between St. Vincent and Barbados (through Grenadine Air Alliance), as well as frequent service between St. Vincent and the four airports in the Grenadines. ☎ *784/457–5124, 246/247–3712 in Barbados* 🌐 *www.svgair.com.* **SVG Air (Grenada).** SVG Air (Grenada) operates scheduled flights between Grenada and Union Island, sometimes including Carriacou. ☎ *473/444–3549 in Grenada, 784/457–5124* 🌐 *www.svgair.com/grenada.*

Airport Contacts Grantley Adams International Airport (*BGI*). An official tourist information desk for St. Vincent and the Grenadines is in the connecting-travelers area of the Barbados airport. ✉ *Christ Church, Barbados* ☎ *246/428–0961.*

CAR TRAVEL

Car rental is available on St. Vincent, Bequia, or Mustique. Rental cars in St. Vincent and Bequia cost about $55 to $85 per day or $300 to $400 a week. Unless you already have an international driver's license, you'll need to buy a temporary driving permit for $24 (EC$65), valid for six months. To get one, present your valid driver's license at the police station on Bay Street or the Licensing Authority on Halifax Street, both in Kingstown, on St. Vincent, or at the Revenue Office in Port Elizabeth, Bequia. If you're planning an extended stay on St. Vincent and expect to travel frequently between Kingstown and, say, the Villa Beach area, a rental car might be useful—although both taxis and buses are inexpensive and readily available. On Bequia, a rental car will be handy if you're staying for several days in a remote location—that is, anywhere beyond Port Elizabeth. On Mustique, you'll get a kick out of driving around in a rented "mule" (beach buggy).

About 360 miles (580 km) of paved roads wind around St. Vincent's perimeter—except for a section in the far north with no road at all, which precludes a circle tour of the island. A few roads jut into the interior a few miles, and a single east–west road (through the Mesopotamia Valley) bisects the island.

Driving Tips: Roads in the country are often not wide enough for two cars to pass, and people (including schoolchildren), dogs, goats, and chickens often share the roadway with cars, minibuses, and trucks. Outside populated areas, roads can be bumpy and potholed; be sure your rental car has tire-changing equipment and a spare. Drive on the left, and honk your horn before you enter blind curves out in the countryside, where you'll encounter plenty of steep hills and hairpin turns.

Bequia Contacts Bequia Jeep Rentals ✉ *Friendship, Bequia* ☎ *784/458–3760* 🌐 *www.bequiajeeprentals.com.* **Challenger** ✉ *Belmont, Bequia* ☎ *784/458–3811.*

Mustique Contacts Mustique Mechanical Services ✉ *Mustique Company, Britannia Bay, Mustique* ☎ *784/488–8555.*

St. Vincent Contacts Avis ✉ *E.T. Joshua International Airport, Arnos Vale, St. Vincent* ☎ *784/456–6861* 🌐 *www.avis.com.* **Ben's Auto Rental** ✉ *Arnos Vale, St. Vincent* ☎ *784/456–2907* 🌐 *www.bensautorentals.com.* **David's Auto Clinic** ✉ *Upper Sion Hill, St. Vincent* ☎ *784/456–4026.* **Star Garage** ✉ *Grenville St., Kingstown, St. Vincent* ☎ *784/456–1743.*

FERRY TRAVEL

Traveling by ferry between St. Vincent and the Grenadine islands—particularly Bequia—is easy and relatively inexpensive. A fast ferry makes the trip between St. Vincent and Union in less than 90 minutes, though not every day, stopping in Bequia and Canouan (and Mayreau, as needed) along the way. A one-way trip between St. Vincent and Bequia on the more conventional ferries takes 60 minutes and costs $9.50 (EC$25) each way or $17 (EC$45) round-trip with the same ferry company.

Contacts Admiralty Transport. This ferry makes several round-trips daily between Kingstown and Bequia. ✉ *Grenadines Wharf, Kingstown, St. Vincent* ☎ *784/458–3348* 🌐 *www.admiraltytransport.com.* ***Jaden Sun.*** This ferry's reliable, comfortable service goes between mainland St. Vincent and Bequia (25 minutes), Canouan (1½ hours), and Union islands (2 hours), with an "as needed" stop in Mayreau. There is no service on Tuesday, Thursday, or Saturday or on Wednesday afternoon. The one-way fare between Kingstown and Bequia is $15; between Kingstown and Canouan, $34; between Kingstown and Union, $38. ✉ *Grenadines Wharf, Kingstown, St. Vincent* ☎ *784/451–2192* 🌐 *www.jadeninc.com.* **M/V *Bequia Express.*** This ferry runs several round-trips daily between Kingstown and Bequia. ✉ *Grenadines Wharf, Kingstown, St. Vincent* ☎ *784/457–3539* 🌐 *www.bequiaexpress.net.*

TAXI TRAVEL

Taxis are not metered. Settle on the price—and the currency—before entering the taxi. Taxis are always available at the airport in St. Vincent; the fare from the airport to Kingstown or Villa is $12 (EC$30). In Bequia, the taxis—usually pickup trucks with their beds fitted with benches accommodating four to six people under an awning—will take you to Port Elizabeth, to the various hotels, or on a day of sightseeing. On Canouan, resorts generally provide airport transfers, although taxis are available. On Mustique, transfers are usually provided, but taxis are available. On Union Island, it's a short walk or jitney ride from the airport to the Anchorage Yacht Club dock (a two-minute trip) or a taxi ride to the dock in Clifton, the main town, to meet the launch from Palm Island or Petit St. Vincent.

ESSENTIALS

Banks and Exchange Services ATMs are located at banks in Kingstown and their branches. U.S. dollars are accepted nearly everywhere, although you'll receive change in Eastern Caribbean currency (EC$). U.S. coins are not accepted anywhere. The exchange rate is fixed at EC$2.67 to US$1. Hotels, car-rental agencies, and most shops and restaurants also accept major credit cards and traveler's checks.

Dress Don't pack camouflage clothing. It is illegal to wear any form of camouflage clothing in St. Vincent and the Grenadines (as it is on most Caribbean islands), as that pattern is reserved for the local police. The law is strictly enforced, and the clothing may be confiscated.

Electricity Electric current is generally 220–240 volts, 50 cycles. Some large resorts, such as Petit St. Vincent, have 110 volts, 60 cycles (U.S. standard); many have 110-volt shaver outlets. A few small hotels or inns are equipped with 110-volt outlets, as well.

Passports Requirements You need a valid passport and an ongoing or return ticket to enter St. Vincent and the Grenadines.

Phones The area code is 784. If making a collect call to the United States, dial 800/CALLUSA (☎ *800/225–5872*). For international credit-card calling, dial 800/744–2000.

Taxes and Service Charges The departure tax from St. Vincent and the Grenadines is now incorporated into the price paid for airfare, as it is on most other Caribbean islands. A government tax of 10% is added to the room cost on hotel bills, a 15% V.A.T. (value-added tax) is added to restaurant checks and other purchases, and a 10% service charge is often added to hotel bills and restaurant checks.

DOLLAR BUSES

"Dollar buses" on St. Vincent are privately owned, brightly painted minivans; fares range from EC$1 to EC$6 (40¢ to $2.50). Routes are indicated on the windshield, and the bus will stop on demand. Just wave from the road or point your finger to the ground as a bus approaches. To get off, signal by tapping your knuckles twice above the window by your seat or ask the conductor, usually a young boy who rides along to open the door and collect fares; it's helpful to have the correct change in EC coins. In Kingstown, the central departure point is the bus terminal at the New Kingstown Fish Market.

Tipping If a 10% service charge has not been added to your restaurant tab, a gratuity at that rate is appropriate. Otherwise, tipping is expected only for special service. For bellmen and porters, tip $1 per bag; housekeeping, $2 per day; taxi drivers and tour guides, 10% of the fare.

ACCOMMODATIONS

Mass tourism hasn't come to St. Vincent and the Grenadines, but that could change after the Argyle International Airport begins operations in mid-2015. With two exceptions, hotels and inns on St. Vincent are modest. Luxury and privacy can be found in great abundance, however, at the exclusive resorts found throughout the Grenadines. If you have the time to island-hop by air or ferry, staying in simple guesthouses will maximize both your budget and your experiences.

Luxury Resorts: On Young Island just a stone's throw from St. Vincent's shore, at Buccament Bay on St. Vincent, and scattered throughout the Grenadines, luxury resorts offer a laid-back vacation experience without sacrificing service, comfort, and privacy.

Simple Resorts and Guesthouses: Most lodgings in St. Vincent are simple, small, and relatively inexpensive. You'll also find small hotels and guesthouses with similarly attractive rates throughout the Grenadines—on Bequia and Union, in particular.

Villas: Luxurious villas, which make up the majority of accommodations on Mustique, offer every amenity you can imagine. Private villas are also available for rent on St. Vincent, Bequia, Palm Island, and Canouan.

Hotel reviews have been shortened. For full information, visit Fodors.com.

WHAT IT COSTS IN U.S. DOLLARS				
	$	$$	$$$	$$$$
Restaurants	under $12	$12–$20	$21–$30	over $30
Hotels	under $275	$275–$375	$376–$475	over $475

Restaurant prices are the average cost of a main course at dinner or, if dinner is not served, at lunch. Hotel prices are the lowest cost of a standard double room in high season.

VISITOR INFORMATION

Contacts St. Vincent and the Grenadines Tourism Authority ☎ *212/687–4981, 800/729–1726 in U.S.* 🌐 *www.discoversvg.com.* **St. Vincent & the Grenadines Hotel & Tourism Association** 🌐 *www.svghotels.com.*

WEDDINGS

At least a 24-hour residency is required. A special governor-general's marriage license ($185 plus an $8 stamp fee) must be obtained in person from the attorney general's office at the Ministry of Justice in Kingstown, St. Vincent. Bring valid passports, return or ongoing plane tickets, certified and notarized divorce decrees if applicable, and an appropriate death certificate if either party is widowed. An official marriage officer, priest, or minister registered in St. Vincent and the Grenadines must officiate at the ceremony, and two witnesses must be present.

ST. VINCENT

EXPLORING

You can explore Kingstown's shopping and business district, historic churches and cathedrals, and other points of interest in a half day, with another couple of hours spent in the Botanic Gardens. The coastal roads of St. Vincent offer spectacular panoramas and scenes of island life. The Leeward Highway follows the scenic Caribbean coastline; the Windward Highway follows the more dramatic Atlantic coast. A drive along the windward coast requires a full day. Exploring La Soufrière or the Vermont Nature Trails is also a major undertaking, requiring a very early start and a full day of strenuous hiking.

TOP ATTRACTIONS

FAMILY Fodor's Choice ★ **Botanic Gardens.** One of the oldest botanical gardens in the Western Hemisphere is just north of downtown Kingstown—a few minutes by taxi. The garden was created in 1765 by General Robert Melville, governor of the British Caribbean islands, after Captain Bligh—of *Bounty* fame—brought the first breadfruit tree to this island for landowners to propagate. The prolific bounty of the breadfruit trees was used to feed the slaves. You can see a direct descendant of the original tree among the specimen mahogany, rubber, teak, and other tropical trees and shrubs in the 20 acres of gardens. Two-dozen rare St. Vincent parrots (*Amazona* *guildingii*), confiscated from illegal collections, live in the small aviary. Guides explain all the medicinal and ornamental trees and shrubs; they also appreciate a tip (about $5 per person) at the end of the tour. A gift shop, open Monday through Friday, has local crafts, artwork, books, confections, and a traditional creole lunch menu. ✉ *Off Leeward Hwy., northeast of town, Montrose, Kingstown* ☎ *784/453–1623* 🎫 *Free* 🕑 *Daily 6–6.*

FAMILY Fodor's Choice ★ **Ft. Charlotte.** Started by the French in 1786 and completed by the British in 1806, the fort was ultimately named for Britain's Queen Charlotte, wife of King George III. It sits on Berkshire Hill, a dramatic promontory 2 miles (3 km) north of Kingstown and 636 feet above sea level, affording a stunning view of the capital city and the Grenadines. Interestingly, its cannons face inland, as the fear of attack—by the French and their Carib allies—from the ridges above Kingstown was far greater than any threat approaching from the sea. In any case, the fort saw no action. Nowadays, it serves as a signal station for ships; the ancient cells house historical paintings of the island by Lindsay Prescott. ✉ *Berkshire Hill, 2 miles (3 km) north of town, Kingstown* 🕑 *Daily 6–6.*

24

WORTH NOTING

Barrouallie. Once an important whaling village, Barrouallie (*bar*-relly) today is home to fishermen earning their livelihoods trawling for blackfish, which are actually small pilot whales. The one-hour drive north from Kingstown on the Leeward Highway takes you along ridges that drop to the sea, through small villages and lush valleys, and beside quiet bays with black-sand beaches and safe bathing. ✉ *Barrouallie.*

FAMILY **Black Point Historic and Recreation Park.** In 1815, under the supervision of British Colonel Thomas Browne, Carib and African slaves drilled a 360-foot tunnel through solid volcanic rock—an engineering marvel at the time—to facilitate the transportation of sugar from estates in the north to the port in Kingstown. Today, Jasper Rock Tunnel is the centerpiece of Black Point Historic and Recreation Park, which also has an interpretation center, children's playground, and washrooms. The tunnel, just off beautiful Black Point Beach between Georgetown and Colonarie (pronounced con-a-*ree*), links Grand Sable with Byrea Bay. The park is open daily, 8 am to 6 pm. ✉ *Windward Hwy., north of Colonarie, Black Point.*

Georgetown. St. Vincent's second-largest city (and former capital), halfway up the island's windward (Atlantic) coast and surrounded by acres and acres of coconut groves, is a convenient place to stop for a cool drink or snack or other essential shopping while traveling along the windward coast. It is also the site of the now-defunct Mount Bentinck sugar factory. A tiny, quiet town with a few small shops, a restaurant or two, and modest homes, Georgetown is completely unaffected by tourism. ✉ *Georgetown.*

Kingstown. The capital of St. Vincent and the Grenadines, a city of 13,500 residents, wraps around Kingstown Bay on the island's southwestern coast; a ring of green hills and ridges studded with homes forms a backdrop for the city. This is very much a working city, with a busy harbor and few concessions to tourists. Kingstown Harbour is the only deepwater port on the island.

A few gift shops can be found on and around **Bay Street,** near the harbor. Upper Bay Street, which stretches along the bay front, bustles with daytime activity—workers going about their business and housewives doing their shopping. Many of Kingstown's downtown buildings are built of stone or brick brought to the island as ballast in the holds of 18th-century ships (and replaced with sugar and spices for the return trip to Europe). The Georgian-style stone arches and second-floor overhangs on former warehouses—which provide shelter from midday sun and the brief, cooling showers common to the tropics—have earned Kingstown the nickname "City of Arches."

Grenadines Wharf, at the south end of Bay Street, is busy with ships loading supplies and ferries loading people bound for the Grenadines. The **Cruise-Ship Complex,** just south of the commercial wharf, has a mall with a dozen or more shops, plus restaurants, a post office, communications facilities, and a taxi-minibus stand.

A huge selection of produce fills the **Kingstown Market,** a three-story building that takes up a whole city block on Upper Bay, Hillsboro, and Bedford Streets in the center of town. It's noisy, colorful, and open Monday through Saturday—but the busiest times (and the best times to go) are Friday and Saturday mornings. In the courtyard, vendors sell local arts and crafts. On the upper floors, merchants sell clothing, household items, gifts, and other products.

St. George's Cathedral, on Grenville Street, is a pristine, creamy-yellow Anglican church built in 1820. The dignified Georgian architecture includes simple wooden pews, an ornate chandelier, and beautiful stained-glass windows; one was a gift from Queen Victoria, who actually commissioned it for London's St. Paul's Cathedral in honor of her first grandson. When the artist created an angel with a red robe, she was horrified by the color and sent the window abroad. The markers in the cathedral's graveyard recount the history of the island. Across the street is **St. Mary's Roman Catholic Cathedral of the Assumption,** built in stages beginning in 1823. The strangely appealing design is a blend of Moorish, Georgian, and Romanesque styles applied to black brick. Nearby, freed slaves built the **Kingstown Methodist Church** in 1841. The exterior is brick, simply decorated with quoins (solid blocks that form the corners), and the roof is held together by metal straps, bolts, and wooden pins. **Scots Kirk** was built from 1839 to 1880 by and for Scottish settlers but became a Seventh-Day Adventist church in 1952. ⊠ *Kingstown.*

La Soufrière. This towering volcano, which last erupted in 1979, is 4,048 feet high and so huge in area that its surrounding mountainside covers virtually the entire northern third of the island. The eastern trail to the rim of the crater, a two-hour ascent, begins at Rabacca Dry River. ⊠ *Rabacca Dry River, Rabacca.*

Layou Petroglyph Park. Just off the main road beyond the small fishing village of Layou, about 30 minutes north of Kingstown and just north of Buccament Bay, petroglyphs (rock carvings) were carved into a giant

A waterfall near Wallilabou Bay, St. Vincent

boulder by pre-Columbian inhabitants sometime between AD 300 and 600. ✉ *Leeward Hwy., Rutland Vale* ☎ *784/454–8686* 💰 *$2; $8 with guided tour* ⏲ *Daily 9–5.*

Mesopotamia Valley. The rugged, ocean-lashed scenery along St. Vincent's windward coast is the perfect counterpoint to the calm leeward coast. In between, the fertile Mesopotamia Valley (nicknamed "Mespo") affords a view of dense rain forests, streams, and endless banana and coconut plantations. Breadfruit, sweet corn, peanuts, and arrowroot also grow in the rich soil here. Mountain ridges, including 3,181-foot Grand Bonhomme Mountain, surround the valley. ✉ *Mesopotamia.*

Owia Salt Pond. In the village of Owia on the island's far northeastern coast and at least a two-hour drive from Kingstown, Owia Salt Pond is a natural saltwater pool created by the pounding surf of the Atlantic Ocean overflowing a barrier reef of lava rocks and ridges. The village itself is the home of many descendants of the indigenous Carib people, as well as the home of the **Owia Arrowroot Processing Factory.** Long used to thicken sauces and flavor cookies, arrowroot is now also used in pharmaceutical products. St. Vincent produces 90% of the world's supply of arrowroot, but that is only a tiny fraction of the maximum levels exported in the 1960s. Take a pleasant swim in Owia Salt Pond and enjoy a picnic lunch on the adjacent grounds before the long return trip to Kingstown. ✉ *Owia* ⏲ *Daily 9–6.*

Rabacca Dry River. This rocky gulch just north of Georgetown was carved from the earth by lava flow from the 1902 volcanic eruption of nearby **La Soufrière.** When it rains in the mountains, the riverbed changes from dry moonscape to a trickle of water to a gushing river—all within minutes—and then simply dries up again. Before the Rabacca Dry River Bridge opened in 2007, drivers would often get stranded on one side or the other whenever it rained. ✉ *Rabacca.*

FAMILY **Wallilabou Heritage Park.** The Wallilabou Estate, halfway up the island's leeward coast, once produced cocoa, cotton, and arrowroot. Today, it is Wallilabou Heritage Park, a recreational site with a river and small waterfall, which creates a small pool where you can take a freshwater plunge. You can also sunbathe, swim, picnic, or buy your lunch at Wallilabou Anchorage—a favorite stop for boaters staying overnight. The *Pirates of the Caribbean* movies left their mark on Wallilabou (pronounced wally-la-*boo*), a location used for filming the opening scenes of *The Curse of the Black Pearl* in 2003. Many of the buildings and docks built as stage sets remain, giving Wallilabou Bay (a port of entry for visiting yachts) an intriguingly historic (yet ersatz) appearance. ✉ *Wallilabou.*

BEACHES

Aside from the beach on private Young Island, just offshore, all beaches on St. Vincent are public. Indian Bay is a popular swimming and snorkeling spot. Villa Beach, on the mainland opposite Young Island, is more of a waterfront area than a beach—except at the northern end, where the sand broadens considerably. The southern end of Villa Beach is sometimes so narrow that it becomes nonexistent; nevertheless, boats bob at anchor in the channel and dive shops, inns, and restaurants line the shore, making this an interesting place to be. At Buccament Bay, north of Kingstown, the owners of the huge villa community of the same name have covered the natural black beach with imported white sand. On the windward coast, dramatic swaths of broad black sand are strewn with huge black boulders, but the water is rough and unpredictable. Even on the leeward coast, swimming is recommended only in the lagoons, rivers, and bays.

Buccament Bay Beach. A long strand of (imported) white sand stretches in front of Buccament Bay Resort, about a half hour northwest of Kingstown. The water is calm, and snorkeling is very good. **Amenities:** food and drink; parking. **Best for:** snorkeling; sunset; swimming; walking. ✉ *Buccament Bay.*

Indian Bay Beach. South of Kingstown and separated from Villa Beach by a rocky hill, Indian Bay has golden sand but is slightly rocky; it's very good for snorkeling. Grand View Hotel, high on a cliff overlooking Indian Bay Beach, operates a beach bar and grill. **Amenities:** food and drink. **Best for:** snorkeling; swimming. ✉ *Villa.*

Rawacou Recreation Park. At Rawacou Bay, close to the new Argyle International Airport, two stunning black-sand, high-surf beaches are separated by a rocky headland with a trail down to a man-made lagoon—a swimming pool created by placing huge boulders in the sea to prevent the high surf from smashing against the shore. The water by the beaches isn't safe for swimming, but the lagoon pool is; however, be cautious when the surrounding water is particularly rough. The beautiful grounds of Rawacou Recreation Park, shaded by coconut and sea grape trees, include a performance venue and vendor huts. The park is a popular site for picnics, weekend parties, and special events. **Amenities:** food and drink; parking; showers; toilets. **Best for:** partiers; swimming; walking. ✉ *8½ miles (13½ km) southeast of Kingstown, Argyle* ⏲ *Daily 8–5.*

Villa Beach. The long stretch of sand in front of the row of hotels facing the Young Island Channel (Mariners, Paradise Beach, Sunset Shores, and Beachcombers hotels on the "mainland" and Young Island Resort across the channel) varies from 20 to 25 feet wide to practically nonexistent. The broadest, sandiest part is in front of Beachcombers Hotel, which is also the perfect spot for sunbathers to get lunch and liquid refreshments. It's a popular beach destination for cruise-ship passengers when a ship is in port. **Amenities:** food and drink; water sports. **Best for:** swimming. ✉ *Villa.*

WHERE TO EAT

Nearly all restaurants in St. Vincent specialize in local West Indian cuisine, although you can find chefs with broad culinary experience at a few hotel restaurants. Local dishes to try include callaloo (similar to spinach) soup, curried goat or chicken, rotis (turnovers filled with curried meat or vegetables), fresh-caught seafood (lobster, kingfish, snapper, and mahimahi), local vegetables such as the squash-like christophene (also known as chayote) and pumpkin, "provisions" (roots such as yams and dasheen), and tropical fruit (including avocados, breadfruit, mangoes, soursop, pineapples, and papaya). Fried or baked chicken is available everywhere, often accompanied by "rice 'n' peas" or *pelau* (a stew made with rice, coconut milk, and either chicken or beef seared in caramelized sugar). At Campden Park, just north of Kingstown, the local beer, Hairoun, is brewed in accordance with a German recipe. Sunset is the local rum.

What to Wear. Restaurants are casual. You may want to dress up a little—long pants and collared shirts for gents, summer dresses or dress pants for the ladies—for an evening out at a pricey restaurant, *but none of the establishments listed below require men to wear a jacket or tie.* Beachwear, however, is never appropriate in restaurants.

$$$ CARIBBEAN ✕ **Basil's Bar and Restaurant.** It's not just the air-conditioning that makes this restaurant cool. Basil's, at street level at the Cobblestone Inn, is owned by Basil Charles, whose Basil's Beach Bar on Mustique is a hangout for the vacationing rich and famous. This is the Kingstown power-lunch venue. Local businesspeople gather for the daily buffet (weekdays) or full menu of salads, sandwiches, barbecued chicken, or fresh seafood platters. Dinner entrées of pasta, local seafood, and chicken are served at candlelit tables. [$] *Average main: $24* ✉ *Upper Bay St., below Cobblestone Inn, Kingstown* ☎ *784/457–2713* 🌐 *www.basilsbar.com* ⏲ *Closed Sun.*

$$ CARIBBEAN ✕ **Cobblestone Roof-Top Bar & Restaurant.** To reach what is perhaps the most pleasant, the breeziest, and the most satisfying breakfast and lunch spot in downtown Kingstown, diners must climb the equivalent of three flights of interior stone steps within the historic Cobblestone Inn. But

getting to the open-air rooftop restaurant is half the fun, as en route diners get an up-close view of a 19th-century sugar (and later arrowroot) Georgian warehouse that's now a very appealing boutique inn. A full breakfast menu is available to hotel guests and the public alike. The luncheon menu ranges from homemade soups, salads (tuna, chicken, fruit, or tossed), sandwiches, or burgers and fries to full meals of roast beef, stewed chicken, or grilled fish served with rice, plantains, macaroni pie, and fresh local vegetables. *Average main: $15* ✉ *Cobblestone Inn, Upper Bay St., Kingstown* ☎ *784/456–1937* 🌐 *www.thecobblestoneinn.com* ⏲ *No dinner.*

$$$ FRENCH Fodor's Choice ★ **The French Verandah.** Dining by candlelight on the waterfront terrace of Mariners Hotel means excellent French cuisine with Caribbean flair—and one of the best dining experiences on St. Vincent. Start with a rich soup (piping hot French onion, fish with aioli, creamy pumpkin, or callaloo and conch) or escargots, stuffed crab back, or conch salad. Main courses include fresh fish and shellfish grilled with fresh herbs, garlic butter and lime, or creole sauce. Landlubbers may prefer sautéed chicken paillard with mushroom or Thai peanut sauce, grilled lamb chops, or beef tenderloin with béarnaise, Roquefort, or pepper sauce. For dessert, there's the wonderful *mi-cuit,* a warm chocolate delicacy with vanilla ice cream. Lighter, equally delicious fare is served at lunch—and you can enjoy a full seaside breakfast. *Average main: $28* ✉ *Mariners Hotel, Young Island Cut, Villa Beach, Villa* ☎ *784/453–1111* 🌐 *www.marinershotel.com* *Reservations essential.*

$$ ECLECTIC FAMILY **High Tide Bar & Grill.** Enjoy simple, well-prepared fare dockside alongside the Young Island Cut, where you'll see boats maneuvering during the day and the twinkling lights of Young Island Resort in the evening. There's something on the menu that will appeal to everyone, kids included—burgers and fries, pizza, sandwiches, salads, or main courses of steak, chicken, or fresh fish. Dine inside or on the terrace. *Average main: $18* ✉ *Young Island Cut, Villa Beach, Villa* ☎ *784/456–6700.*

$$$ CARIBBEAN **Paradise Beach Hotel Restaurant.** Settle in for lunch on the patio, with a view of Young Island and the sea beyond, or dinner inside or alfresco. Enjoy local specialties—crab back, creole chicken, grilled just-caught fish, or the absolutely freshest lobster that you select from the live lobster pool. Latin dance classes on Tuesday night, Grillin' With the Captain (Earl Halbich of Fantasea Tours) on Friday night, Havana Night with live entertainment on Saturday night, and happy hour at the bar every night all add to the joie de vivre. The ambience and view definitely make up for the service, which can be a little slow. Plan to linger! *Average main: $22* ✉ *Paradise Beach Hotel, Villa* ☎ *784/457–4795* 🌐 *www.paradisesvg.com.*

$$$ EUROPEAN **The Sapodilla Room.** The Sapodilla Room at the historic Grenadine House (1765) is a hidden gem. Whet your appetite with a fruity cocktail at the West Indies Bar—the actual bar is from an old English pub, and a gallery of classic black-and-white stills of movie stars graces the walls. Move inside to the stonewalled dining room and enjoy grilled fresh fish, creamy seafood risotto, or tasty beef, lamb, and chicken entrées that reflect Caribbean flavors. Local people come here for special occasions and business dinners, as this is one of the few elegant dining spots on

St. Vincent. They also enjoy the live jazz in the bar on Friday night. *Average main: $26* ✉ *Grenadine House, Kingstown Park, Kingstown* ☎ *784/458–1800* 🌐 *www.grenadinehouse.com* *Reservations essential* ⏲ *No lunch.*

$$ CARIBBEAN **Vee Jay's Restaurant & Bar.** Come here for "authentic Vincy cuisine." Specials are chalked onto the blackboard: mutton or fish stew, chicken or vegetable rotis, curried goat, souse, and *buljol* (sautéed codfish, breadfruit, and vegetables). Not-so-Vincy sandwiches, fish-and-chips, and burgers can be authentically washed down with *mauby,* a bittersweet drink made from tree bark; linseed, peanut, passion-fruit, or sorrel punch; local Hairoun beer; or your choice of tropical cocktails. Lunch is buffet-style. *Average main: $12* ✉ *Lower Bay St., Kingstown* ☎ *784/457–2845* ⏲ *Closed Sun.*

24

$$$ CARIBBEAN **Wallilabou Anchorage.** Halfway up St. Vincent's Caribbean coast, this is a favorite lunch stop for boaters sailing the Grenadines and for landlubbers touring the leeward coast. The picturesque view of the bay is enhanced by the period stage sets left behind by the *Pirates of the Caribbean* filmmakers. Open all day from 8 am, the bar-and-restaurant serves snacks, sandwiches, tempting West Indian dishes, locally caught fish, and lobster in season. Ice, telephones, business services, and shower facilities are available to boaters. *Average main: $21* ✉ *Leeward Hwy., Wallilabou* ☎ *784/458–7270* 🌐 *www.wallilabou.com.*

$$$$ CONTEMPORARY Fodor's Choice ★ **Young Island Resort Restaurant.** Take the little ferry (a two-minute ride from the dock at Villa Beach) to Young Island for a delightful lunch or a very special romantic evening. Stone paths lead to candlelit tables—some in breezy, thatch-roof kiosks—and gentle waves lap the shore. Five-course, prix-fixe dinners of grilled seafood, roast pork, succulent beef tenderloin, duck breast, and sautéed chicken are accompanied by local vegetables. Two or three choices are offered for each course, and freshly made breads (coconut, raisin, banana, country white, cinnamon, or whole-grain wheat) are sliced at your table. Wednesday is local buffet night; Saturday is a barbecue buffet. Lunch is à la carte—soups, salads, grilled meats, or fish—and served on the beachfront terrace. Tuesday and Sunday lunch is buffet-style. *Average main: $62* ✉ *Young Island Cut, Young Island* ☎ *784/458–4826* 🌐 *www.youngisland.com* *Reservations essential.*

WHERE TO STAY

With a few exceptions—most notably, Buccament Bay Resort northwest of the capital city—tourist accommodations and facilities on St. Vincent are in either Kingstown or the Villa Beach area. All guest rooms have air-conditioning, TV, and phone unless stated otherwise.

PRIVATE VILLAS AND CONDOS

Because the island's air service has been limited to small planes operated by regional carriers, huge villa communities and condo complexes have been late to arrive in St. Vincent—though the international airport set to begin operations in mid-2015 will likely change that. The island's first villa community at Buccament Bay opened in 2010; many of the one- and two-bedroom town houses are available for vacation rentals.

$ HOTEL **Beachcombers Hotel & Spa.** Guests choose Beachcombers for its comfortable beachfront rooms, friendly service, and lively atmosphere both day and night. **Pros:** great value and location; best beachfront in the area, the place to be on weekends; complimentary Wi-Fi. **Cons:** popular with small groups, so book well ahead; standard rooms are very standard—deluxe or penthouse rooms cost only slightly more; the beach gets busy when a cruise ship is in port. *Rooms from: $99 ✉ Villa Beach, Villa ☎ 784/458–4283 🌐 www.beachcombershotel.com 27 rooms, 4 suites No meals.*

$ HOTEL **Blue Lagoon Hotel & Marina.** Whether you arrive by yacht, plan to charter a yacht for a sail through the Grenadines, or just like to be in a marina environment, Blue Lagoon is the place for you. **Pros:** everything brand-new and attractive; port of entry for boaters; good dining; complimentary Wi-Fi. **Cons:** dockside location requires close supervision of young children; small beach with boat traffic nearby. *Rooms from: $199 ✉ Windward Hwy., Calliagua ☎ 784/458–4308 🌐 www.bluelagoonsvg.com 19 rooms No meals.*

$$$$ ALL-INCLUSIVE FAMILY Fodor's Choice ★ **Buccament Bay Resort.** This luxury villa community, by far the largest resort in St. Vincent, is on a pretty bay about a half-hour drive northwest of Kingstown. **Pros:** huge accommodations; lots of amenities and activities; great spot for soccer-playing kids. **Cons:** very expensive; some units have a/c only in bedrooms; quite remote—a rental car is advised. *Rooms from: $900 ✉ Buccament Bay, off the Leeward Hwy., 5 miles (8 km) north of Kingstown, Buccament ☎ 784/457–4100 🌐 www.buccamentbay.com 102 villas All-inclusive.*

$ B&B/INN **Cobblestone Inn.** This boutique hotel is cozy, convenient, inexpensive, and loaded with historic charm—but it's nowhere near a beach. **Pros:** convenient for an overnight stay if you're taking an early ferry to the Grenadines; historical atmosphere; fascinating architecture, complimentary Wi-Fi. **Cons:** mostly tiny rooms; wandering around downtown streets at night is not recommended; not near a beach. *Rooms from: $80 ✉ Upper Bay St., Kingstown ☎ 784/456–1937, 800/413–3120 in U.S. 🌐 www.thecobblestoneinn.com 20 rooms, 6 suites No meals.*

$ HOTEL **Grand View Beach Hotel.** The unobstructed view of the Grenadines from this stylish, family-run hotel perched on a very private promontory is very grand indeed. **Pros:** friendly, boutique vibe; beautiful (grand) sunset views; on-site amenities include a pool, squash court, gym, and yoga classes. **Cons:** hike down to the beach; a rental car would be handy. *Rooms from: $154 ✉ Villa Point, Villa ☎ 784/458–4811 🌐 www.grandviewhotel.com 19 rooms, 2 suites Multiple meal plans.*

$ B&B/INN **Grenadine House.** Especially favored by business travelers, rooms in this Victorian-style mansion are also perfect for vacationers who want modern comforts in an elegant setting but don't require planned activities or beachfront resort features. **Pros:** attractive rooms; excellent dining; on-site spa and gym. **Cons:** quiet, residential area far from any beach and a $5 taxi ride to town. *Rooms from: $170 ✉ Kingstown Park, Kingstown ☎ 784/458–1800 🌐 www.grenadinehouse.com 20 rooms Breakfast.*

$ HOTEL **Hotel Alexandrina.** Guests are made to feel right at home at Hotel Alexandrina, because it actually is—and was—home to the owners; in fact, you may find that you're sharing the hotel with a whole team of cricketers, who prefer its private, relaxing atmosphere when visiting St. Vincent. **Pros:** warm and welcoming owners; no request is too much trouble; excellent local chef in the on-site restaurant; year-round rates; 110-volt electricity in guest rooms; complimentary Wi-Fi. **Cons:** about 20 minutes to Kingstown, but a short hop to the new international airport (when it opens); far from a beach; rental car advised. *Rooms from: $90 Ribishi, Prospect 784/456–9788, 917/829–8354 in U.S. www.hotelalexandrina.com 25 rooms Multiple meal plans.*

$ HOTEL **Mariners Hotel.** This small, pleasant hotel on the Villa Beach waterfront, opposite Young Island, has large rooms with either a balcony or terrace facing the water or overlooking the small pool. **Pros:** the on-site French restaurant; access to Young Island beach; many water sports and tours available nearby; complimentary Wi-Fi. **Cons:** rooms are simply decorated; bathrooms have showers, no tubs; small pool (but certainly refreshing). *Rooms from: $95 Villa Beach, Villa 784/457–4000 www.marinershotel.com 20 rooms No meals.*

24

$ B&B/INN **Paradise Beach Hotel.** Painted bright yellow with white gingerbread trim, the waterfront porches and balconies at Paradise Beach Hotel offer a million-dollar view of Young Island, the activity at Villa Beach, and an amazing sunset every evening. **Pros:** friendly, welcoming atmosphere; the view, particularly at sunset; the waterfront restaurant and bar; complimentary Wi-Fi. **Cons:** beach is narrow to nonexistent but gets broader nearby; no pool. *Rooms from: $85 Villa Beach, Villa 784/457–4795, 784/570–0000 www.paradisesvg.com 14 rooms, 4 apartments Multiple meal plans.*

$ RENTAL **Rosewood Apartment Hotel.** Perched high on a hillside overlooking Villa Beach and Young Island, every one of these self-contained apartments has a mesmerizing view of the Grenadines from its patio or terrace—particularly at sunset. **Pros:** year-round rates; accommodating management; what a view! **Cons:** not on the beach; very steep driveway and hillside location may complicate casual strolls. *Rooms from: $74 Rose Cottage, Villa 784/457–5051 www.rosewoodsvg.com 9 rooms, 1 suite No meals.*

$ HOTEL FAMILY **Sunset Shores Beach Hotel.** Down a long, steep driveway off the main road, this lemon-yellow, low-rise, family-owned hotel faces a narrow curve of Villa beachfront. **Pros:** picturesque location opposite Young Island; pool–bar area lovely at sundown; the price is right. **Cons:** room decor is attractive but a bit bland; beach is slim. *Rooms from: $120 Villa Beach, Villa 784/458–4411 www.sunsetshores.com 32 rooms Multiple meal plans.*

$$$$ RESORT FAMILY Fodor's Choice ★ **Young Island Resort.** One of St. Vincent's two true resorts is actually 200 yards offshore on its own private 35-acre island ringed by powder-soft beaches, offering 29 airy, hillside cottages and a pool, spa, tennis court, and superb alfresco restaurant. **Pros:** St. Vincent's best white-sand beach; casually elegant; romantic but also appropriate for families; excellent dining. **Cons:** pricey, even though rates include breakfast and dinner; no a/c in some cottages; no phones or TVs in rooms (though this might be a plus for some). *Rooms from: $532 Young Island*

Young Island Resort

Cut, Young Island ☎ 784/458–4826, 800/223–1108 in U.S. 🌐 www.youngisland.com ⇨ 23 cottage rooms, 6 cottage suites 🍴 Some meals.

NIGHTLIFE

Nightlife in St. Vincent consists mostly of once-a-week (in season) hotel barbecue buffets with a steel band or a local string band (usually older gents who play an assortment of string instruments). Jump-ups, so called because the lively calypso music makes listeners jump up and dance, happen around holidays, festivals, and Vincy Mas—St. Vincent's Carnival—which begins in June and is the biggest cultural event of the year.

SHOPPING

The 12 small blocks that hug the waterfront in **downtown Kingstown** make up St. Vincent's main shopping district. Among the shops that sell goods to fulfill household needs are a few that sell local crafts, gifts, and souvenirs. Bargaining is neither expected nor appreciated. The **cruise-ship complex,** on the waterfront in Kingstown, has a collection of a dozen or so boutiques, shops, and restaurants that cater primarily to cruise-ship passengers but welcome all shoppers. The best souvenirs of St. Vincent are intricately woven straw items, such as handbags, hats, slippers, baskets, and grass mats that range in size from place mats to room-size floor mats. If you're inclined to bring home a floor mat, they aren't heavy and roll or fold rather neatly; wrapped tightly and packed in an extra (soft-sided) suitcase or tote, it can be checked as luggage for the flight home. Local artwork and carvings are available in galleries, from street vendors, and in shops at the cruise-ship complex. Hot sauce and other condiments, often produced in St. Vincent and sold in markets and gift shops, make tasty souvenirs to bring back home.

DUTY-FREE GOODS

Voyager. Among the few duty-free shops in St. Vincent, Voyager I has a small selection of cameras, electronics, watches, china, and jewelry. A second shop, Voyager II, is nearby on Bay St. ✉ *R. C. Enterprises Ltd., Halifax St., Kingstown* ☎ *784/456–1686.*

FOOD

C. K. Greaves Supermarket. Whether you're putting together a picnic, stocking your kitchenette, provisioning a yacht, looking for recognized brands or locally made seasonings and sauces, or just want some snacks, C. K. Greaves Supermarket is the main supermarket and your best bet. **Sunrise Supermarket**, in Arnos Vale and across the road from the E.T. Joshua Airport, is owned by the same company. Both can be reached by the same phone number, and either store will deliver your order to the dock. ✉ *Upper Bay St., Kingstown* ☎ *784/457–1074* 🌐 *www.ckgreaves.com.*

Market Square. Don't miss visiting the Kingstown market, a three-story enclosed building that really bustles on Friday and Saturday mornings when vendors bring their produce, meats, and fish to market. ✉ *Bay and Bedford Sts., Kingstown* ⏲ *Closed Sun.*

LOCAL ART AND HANDICRAFTS

Nzimbu Browne. This self-taught craftsman, artist, musician, and drum maker is best known for his original banana art, which he creates from dried banana leaves, carefully selecting and snipping varicolored bits and arranging them on pieces of wood to depict intricate local scenes. Prices range from $35 for smaller items to several thousands of dollars for larger works sold in galleries. Browne has a kiosk in front of his house, but sometimes sets up shop on Bay Street, near the Cobblestone Inn. ✉ *McKie's Hill, Kingstown* ☎ *784/457–1677* 🌐 *www.nzimbu-browne.com.*

St. Vincent Craftsmen's Centre. Locally made grass floor mats, place mats, and other straw articles, as well as batik cloth, handmade West Indian dolls, hand-painted calabashes, and framed artwork are all available at this store that's three blocks from the wharf. Cash only; no credit cards. ✉ *Frenches St., Kingstown* ☎ *784/457–2516.*

Wallilabou Craft Centre. Established in 1986, this local cooperative teaches villagers various techniques for weaving straw and other natural fibers. Workers create baskets, handbags, hats, toys, and other items that are sold in the Kingstown market; they make good souvenirs of a visit to St. Vincent. The workshop is on the leeward coast, about a 45-minute drive north of Kingstown. ✉ *Leeward Hwy., Wallilabou* ☎ *784/456–0078.*

SPORTS AND THE OUTDOORS

BICYCLING

Bicycles can be rented for about $25 per day, but roads aren't conducive to leisurely cycling. Serious cyclists, however, will enjoy mountain biking in wilderness areas.

Sailor's Wilderness Tours. Individuals or groups can head out for half-day guided mountain-bike tours through the Mesopotamia Valley and around Argyle and the Atlantic coast or a full-day trip from Kingstown north along the west coast to Chateaubelair and Richmond Vale. The price, which starts at about $50 per person, includes 21-speed mountain-bike rental and refreshments. ✉ *Middle St., Kingstown* ☎ *784/457–1712, 784/457–9207 after hrs* 🌐 *www.sailorswildernesstours.com.*

BOATING

Fodor's Choice ★ From St. Vincent you can charter a monohull or catamaran (bareboat or complete with captain, crew, and cook) to weave you through the Grenadines for a day or a week of sailing or for a full- or half-day fishing trip. One of the most spectacular cruising areas in the world, particularly for sailing, the islands of the Grenadines are close enough to allow landfall at a different island nearly every day, yet some are far enough apart to allow for true blue-water sailing. Bequia and Union Island have excellent yacht services and waterfront activity. Mustique is a dream destination, as is Mayreau. Visitors on yachts can dine at the private Palm Island and Petit St. Vincent resorts. Canouan is a prime yacht-chartering locale, and many of its beaches are accessible only by boat. The nearby Tobago Cays are a don't-miss destination for snorkeling and diving.

Boats of all sizes and degrees of luxury are available for charter. Bareboat charter rates in high season start at about $350 and go up to $1,000 or more per day for monohull sailing yachts and $600-plus per day for catamarans; add $130 per day for a captain and $120 per day for a chef. Rates for a crewed luxury sailing yacht begin at about $7,500 per week for two guests and $18,500 or more per week for boats that accommodate eight guests.

Barefoot Yacht Charters. Barefoot's owners, the Barnard family, have been sailing the Grenadines for seven generations. The company's bareboat fleet of 25 catamarans and monohulls are in the 32- to 50-foot range. ✉ *Blue Lagoon, Ratho Mill* ☎ *784/456–9526* 🌐 *www.barefootyachts.com.*

Horizon Yacht Charters. Luxury bareboat or crewed charters, either monohull or catamaran that range from 37 to 51 feet, are available for sailing the Grenadines or for one-way charters through the Grenadines to Horizon's base in Grenada. ✉ *Blue Lagoon Hotel & Marina, Ratho Mill* ☎ *473/439–1000, 866/463–7245 in U.S.* 🌐 *www.horizonyachtcharters.com.*

TMM Yacht Charters. The fully equipped yachts and catamarans here range from 38 to 51 feet and come either bareboat or crewed. ✉ *Blue Lagoon, Ratho Mill* ☎ *784/456–9608, 800/633–0155 in U.S.* 🌐 *www.sailtmm.com.*

DIVING AND SNORKELING

Fodor's Choice ★ Novices and advanced divers alike will be impressed by the marine life in the waters around St. Vincent—brilliant sponges, huge deepwater coral trees, and shallow reefs teeming with colorful fish. Many sites in the Grenadines are still virtually unexplored. It can't be emphasized enough, however, that the coral reef is extremely fragile; you must only look and never touch.

Most dive shops offer three-hour beginner "resort" courses, full certification courses, and day and night excursions to reefs, walls, and wrecks throughout the Grenadines. A single-tank dive costs $60 to $75; a two-tank, $100 to $135; a 10-dive package, $650. A half-day snorkel trip on a dive boat will cost $16 to $20. All prices include equipment.

St. Vincent, "the critter capital of the Caribbean," is ringed by one long, almost continuous reef. The best dive spots are in the small bays along the western coast between Kingstown and Layou; many are within 20 yards of shore and only 20 to 30 feet down. **Anchor Reef** has excellent visibility for viewing a deep-black coral garden, schools of squid, sea horses, and maybe a small octopus. **Critter Corner,** just 600 feet off Indian Bay Beach, is St. Vincent's hallmark "muck" dive site—a wealth of marine life lurks in and among the sand, silt, sea grass, and boulders. The **Forest,** although a shallow dive, is still dramatic with soft corals in pastel colors and schools of small fish. **New Guinea Reef** slopes to 90 feet and can't be matched for its quantity of corals and sponges. The pristine waters surrounding the **Tobago Cays,** in the southern Grenadines, provide a spectacular diving or snorkeling experience.

Dive Fantasea. Earl Halbich takes guests on dive and snorkeling trips along the St. Vincent coast and to the Tobago Cays on his custom-built 42-foot snorkel/dive boat, *Get Wet.* ✉ *Villa Beach, Villa* ☎ *784/457–4477* 🌐 *www.fantaseatours.com.*

Dive St. Vincent. Two PADI-certified dive masters offer beginner and certification courses for ages eight and up, advanced water excursions along the St. Vincent coast and to the southern Grenadines for diving connoisseurs, and an introductory scuba course for novices. ✉ *Young Island Dock, Villa Beach, Villa* ☎ *784/457–4714, 784/457–4948* 🌐 *www.divestvincent.com.*

Indigo Dive. Indigo specializes in tailor-made dive experiences that match your experience level. PADI dive instructors offer a broad range of courses, from introductory through dive master. Dive shops are located at Buccament Bay Resort and at Blue Lagoon Hotel & Marina. ✉ *Buccament Bay Resort, Buccament* ☎ *784/493–9494* 🌐 *www.indigodive.com.*

GUIDED TOURS

Several operators on St. Vincent offer sightseeing tours on land or by sea. Per-person prices range from $30 for a two-hour tour to the Botanic Gardens to $150 for a day sail to the Grenadines. A full-day tour around Kingstown and either the leeward or windward coast, including lunch, will cost about $65 per person. You can arrange for informal land tours through taxi drivers, who double as knowledgeable guides. Expect to pay $30 per hour for up to four people.

Fantasea Tours. A fleet of four powerboats—ranging from a 28-foot Bowen to a 60-foot party catamaran—are ready to take you on a cruise to Bequia and Mustique, along the St. Vincent coast, whale- or dolphin-watching, or snorkeling in the Tobago Cays and Mayreau. Alternatively Fantasea offers land tours along the windward coast to Owia Salt Pond, along the leeward coast to Dark View Falls, or hikes either along the Vermont Nature Trail or up La Soufrière volcano. ✉ *Villa Beach, Villa* ☎ *784/457–4477* 🌐 *www.fantaseatours.com.*

Sailor's Wilderness Tours. Options from this company include a comfortable sightseeing drive (by day or by moonlight), mountain biking on remote trails, or a strenuous hike up La Soufrière volcano—and the tours are usually under the expert guidance of Trevor "Sailor" Bailey himself. ✉ *Middle St., Kingstown* ☎ *784/457–1712* 🌐 *www.sailorswildernesstours.com.*

Sam's Taxi Tours. In addition to half- and full-day tours of St. Vincent, Sam's also offers hiking tours to La Soufrière and scenic walks along the Vermont Nature Trails. Also available: a day trip to Mustique and a tour on Bequia that includes snorkeling at Friendship Bay. ✉ *Sion Hill, Cane Garden, Kingstown* ☎ *784/456–4338, 703/738–6461 in U.S.* 🌐 *www.samtaxiandtours.com.*

HIKING

St. Vincent offers hikers and trekkers a choice of experiences: easy, scenic walks near Kingstown; moderately difficult nature trails in the central valleys; and exhilarating climbs through a rain forest to the rim of an active volcano. Bring a hat, long pants, and insect repellent if you plan to hike in the bush.

Fodor's Choice ★ **La Soufrière.** La Soufrière, the queen of climbs, is St. Vincent's active volcano (last eruption, 1979). Approachable from either the windward or leeward coast, this is *not* a casual excursion for the inexperienced—the massive mountain covers nearly the entire northern third of the island. Climbs take all day. You'll need stamina and sturdy shoes to reach the top (at just over 4,000 feet) and peek into the mile-wide (1½-km-wide) crater. Be sure to check the weather before you leave; hikers have been disappointed to find a cloud-obscured view at the summit. You can arrange for a guide ($25 to $30) through your hotel, the SVG Tourism Authority, or tour operators. The eastern approach is most popular. In a four-wheel-drive vehicle, you pass through Rabacca Dry River, north of Georgetown, and the Bamboo Forest; then it's a two-hour, 3½-mile (5½-km) hike to the summit. If you're approaching from the west, near Châteaubelair, the climb is longer—6 miles (10 km)—and rougher, but even more scenic. If you hike up one side and down the other, you must arrange in advance to be picked up at the end. ✉ *Rabacca.*

Vermont Nature Trail. The hiking trail begins near the top of the Buccament Valley, 9 miles (14½ km) north of Kingstown. A 2-mile (3¼-km) loop passes through bamboo, evergreen, and rain forest. In the late afternoon you may be lucky enough to see the rare St. Vincent parrot, *Amazona guildingii.* The trail, which is suitable for all ages and abilities, is open daily from 7 am to 5 pm; a visitor center, washrooms, and gift shop are open between 9 am and 5 pm. ✉ *Buccament* ☎ *784/453–1623* 🌐 *www.nationalparks.gov.vc* 🎫 *$2.*

THE GRENADINES

The Grenadine islands are known for great sailing, excellent scuba diving and snorkeling, magnificent beaches, and unlimited chances to relax with a picnic, watch the sailboats, and watch the sun set. Each island has a different appeal. Whether you like quiet relaxation, nonstop activity, or socializing (as long as you're not looking for wild nightlife), the Grenadines will hit the spot.

BEQUIA

Bequia (pronounced *beck*-way) is a Carib word meaning "island of the cloud." Hilly and green with several golden-sand beaches, Bequia is 9 miles (14½ km) south of St. Vincent's southwestern shore; with a population of 5,000, it's the largest of the Grenadines. Although boatbuilding, whaling, and fishing have been the predominant industries here for generations, sailing has now become almost synonymous with Bequia. Admiralty Bay is a favored anchorage for both privately owned and chartered yachts. Lodgings range from comfortable resorts and small hotels to luxurious villas and cozy West Indian–style inns. Bequia's airport and the frequent ferry service from St. Vincent make this a favorite destination for day-trippers, as well. The ferry docks in Port Elizabeth, a tiny town with waterfront bars, restaurants, and shops where you can buy handmade souvenirs—including the exquisitely detailed model sailboats that are a famous Bequia export. The Easter Regatta is held during the four-day Easter weekend, when revelers gather to watch boat races and celebrate the island's seafaring traditions with food, music, dancing, and competitive games.

EXPLORING BEQUIA

To see the views, villages, beaches, and boatbuilding sites around Bequia, hire a taxi at the jetty in Port Elizabeth. Several usually line up under the almond trees to meet each ferry from St. Vincent. The driver will show you the sights in a couple of hours, point out a place for lunch, and (if you wish) drop you at a beach for swimming and snorkeling and pick you up later on. Negotiate the fare in advance, but expect to pay about $30 per hour for the tour. Water taxis are available for transportation between the jetty in Port Elizabeth and the beaches. The cost is $6 (EC$15) per person each way, but keep in mind that most of these operators are not regulated; ride at your own risk.

WORTH NOTING

Admiralty Bay. This huge sheltered bay on the leeward side of Bequia is a favorite yacht anchorage. Year-round it's filled with boats; in season, they're moored transom to bowsprit. It's the perfect spot for watching the sun dip over the horizon each evening—either from your boat or from the terrace bar at one of Port Elizabeth's waterfront hotels or restaurants. ✉ *Port Elizabeth.*

The Grenadines

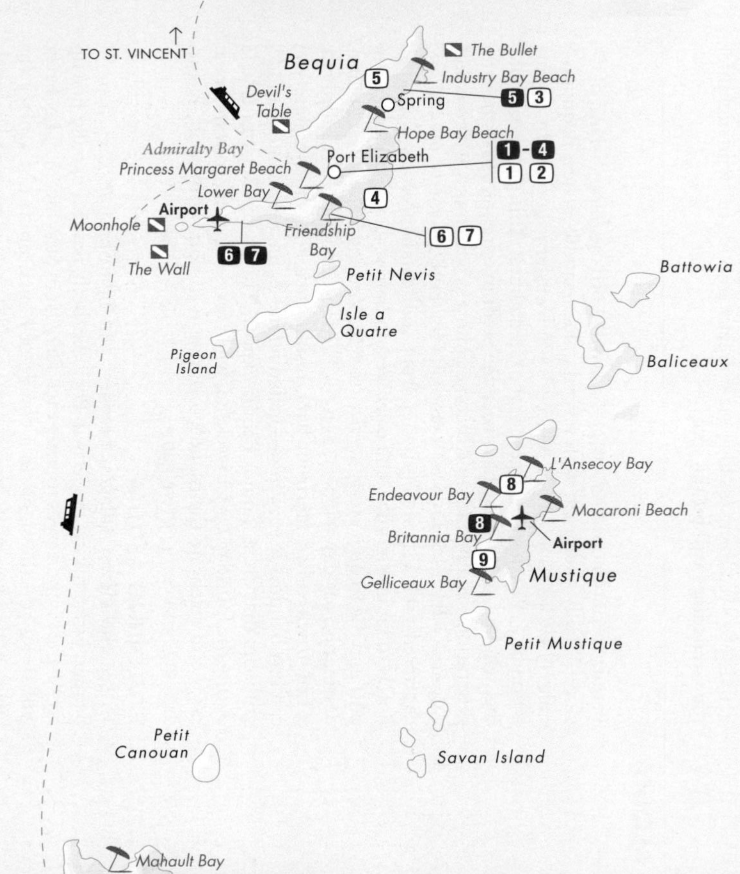

TO ST. VINCENT
Bequia
The Bullet
Industry Bay Beach
Spring
Hope Bay Beach
Devil's Table
Admiralty Bay
Princess Margaret Beach
Port Elizabeth
Lower Bay
Airport
Moonhole
The Wall
Friendship Bay
Petit Nevis
Isle a Quatre
Pigeon Island
Caribbean Sea
Battowia
Baliceaux
L'Ansecoy Bay
Endeavour Bay
Macaroni Beach
Britannia Bay
Airport
Gelliceaux Bay
Mustique
Petit Mustique
Petit Canouan
Savan Island
Mahault Bay
Grenadines Estate Golf Club

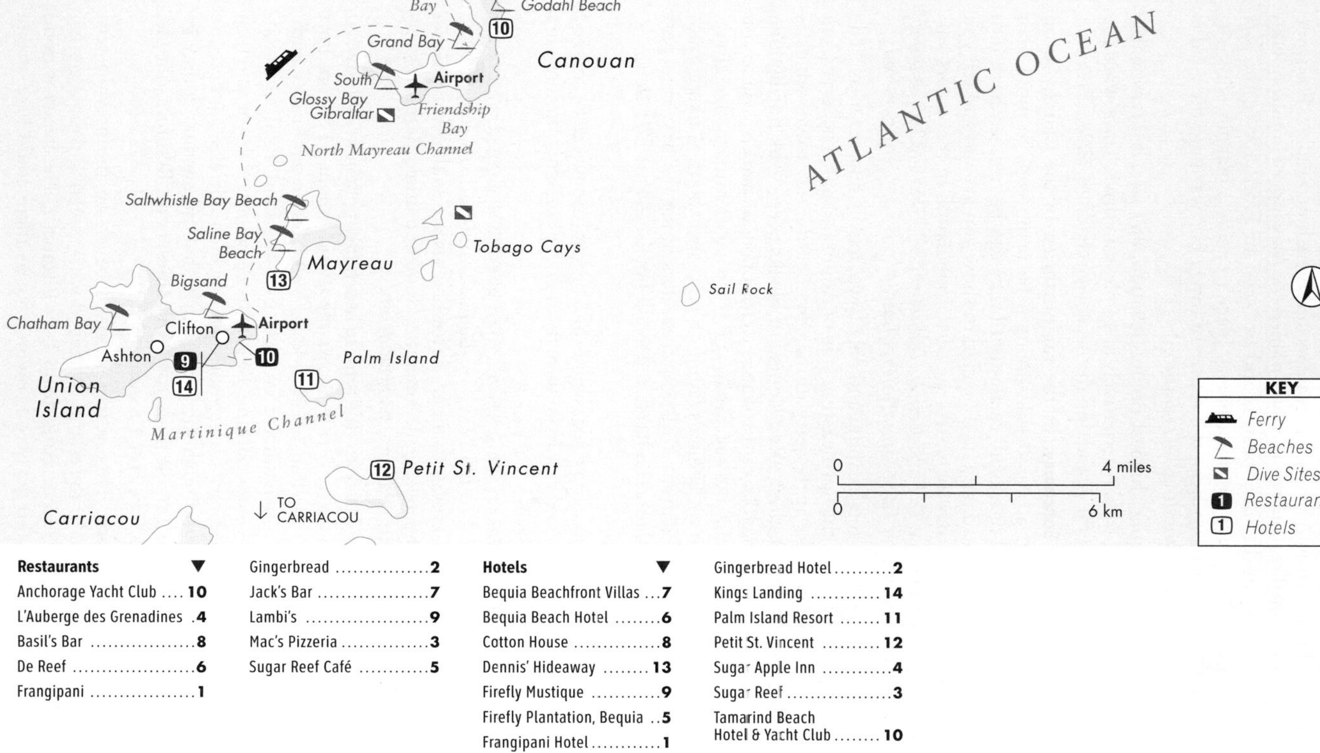

Restaurants ▼		Hotels ▼	
Anchorage Yacht Club 10	Gingerbread 2	Bequia Beachfront Villas ... 7	Gingerbread Hotel 2
L'Auberge des Grenadines . 4	Jack's Bar 7	Bequia Beach Hotel 6	Kings Landing 14
Basil's Bar 8	Lambi's 9	Cotton House 8	Palm Island Resort 11
De Reef 6	Mac's Pizzeria 3	Dennis' Hideaway 13	Petit St. Vincent 12
Frangipani 1	Sugar Reef Café 5	Firefly Mustique 9	Sugar Apple Inn 4
		Firefly Plantation, Bequia .. 5	Sugar Reef 3
		Frangipani Hotel 1	Tamarind Beach Hotel & Yacht Club 10

Hamilton Battery/Ft. Hamilton. Just north of Port Elizabeth, 300 feet above Admiralty Bay, a British fort constructed in the late 1700s protected the harbor from American privateers and French marauders. For some unexplained reason, the fort was named for Alexander Hamilton, who was born on the Caribbean island of Nevis in 1755. Today, the fort is gone; the spot is simply a breezy place to enjoy a magnificent view. Hike or take a taxi from the center of town; fair warning, the road is very steep and winding. ✉ *Hamilton.*

Mt. Pleasant. Bequia's highest point (elevation, 881 feet) is a reasonable goal for a hiking trek. Alternatively, it's a pleasant drive. The reward is a stunning view of the island and the nearby Grenadines. ✉ *Mt. Pleasant.*

FAMILY **Old Hegg Turtle Sanctuary.** In the far northeast of the island, Orton "Brother" King, a retired skin-diving fisherman, tends to more than 200 endangered hawksbill turtles until they can be released back into the sea. Call ahead, and he'll be glad to show you around and tell you how his project has increased the turtle population in the waters surrounding Bequia. ✉ *Park Beach, Industry* ☎ *784/458–3245* 🌐 *www.turtles.bequia.net* 🎫 *$5 donation requested* 🕑 *By appointment only.*

Port Elizabeth. Bequia's capital and only town, locally referred to as "The Harbour," is on the northeastern side of Admiralty Bay. The ferry from St. Vincent docks at the jetty in the center of the tiny town, which is only a few blocks long and a couple of blocks deep. Walk north along Front Street (which faces the water) to the open-air market, where you can buy local fruits and vegetables and some handicrafts; farther along, you will find some of Bequia's famous model-boat shops. Walking south from the jetty, Belmont Walkway meanders along the bay front past shops, cafés, restaurants, bars, and small hotels. ✉ *Port Elizabeth.*

BEACHES

Bequia has clean, uncrowded, white-sand beaches. Some can be reached via a short water-taxi ride from the jetty at Port Elizabeth; others require land transportation.

FAMILY Fodor's Choice ★ **Friendship Bay Beach.** This spectacular horseshoe-shaped, mile-long (1½-km-long), protected beach on Bequia's midsouthern coast can be reached by land taxi or by boat. Refreshments are available at Bequia Beach Hotel's Bagatelle grill. **Amenities:** food and drink. **Best for:** snorkeling; swimming; walking. ✉ *Friendship.*

Hope Bay Beach. Getting to this remote beach facing Bequia's windward side involves a long taxi ride across the island (about $12 from Port Elizabeth) and a mile-long (1½-km-long) walk down a semi-paved path. Your reward is a magnificent crescent of white sand, total seclusion, and—if you like—nude bathing. Be sure to ask your taxi driver to return at a prearranged time. Bring your own lunch and drinks, as there are no facilities. Even though the surf is fairly shallow, swimming may be dangerous because of the undertow. **Amenities:** none. **Best for:** solitude; nudists. ✉ *Hope Bay, Hope Estate.*

Industry Bay Beach. This nearly secluded beach on the northeastern (windward) side of the island is fringed with towering palms; getting here requires transportation from Port Elizabeth. The beach is good for snorkelers who are strong swimmers, as there could be a strong

Port Elizabeth, Bequia

undertow. Bring a picnic; the nearest facilities are at Firefly Bequia or Sugar Reef resorts, about a 10- to 15-minute walk. **Amenities:** none. **Best for:** solitude; snorkeling. ✉ *Industry.*

FAMILY Fodor's Choice ★ **Lower Bay Beach.** This broad, palm-fringed beach on the southern shore of Admiralty Bay, south of Port Elizabeth and Princess Margaret Beach, is reachable by land or water taxi or a healthy hike from town. It's an excellent beach for swimming and snorkeling. Refreshments are available at beachfront restaurants, including La Plage and De Reef. **Amenities:** food and drink; toilets; water sports. **Best for:** snorkeling; swimming. ✉ *Lower Bay.*

FAMILY Fodor's Choice ★ **Princess Margaret Beach.** Quiet and wide with a natural stone arch at one end, the beach is not far from Port Elizabeth's Belmont Walkway—but you still need to take a water or land taxi to get here. When you tire of the water, snoozing under the palm and sea grape trees is always an option. Plan to have lunch at Jack's Bar. **Amenities:** food and drink; toilets. **Best for:** snorkeling; swimming; walking. ✉ *Between Port Elizabeth and Lower Bay, Port Elizabeth.*

WHERE TO EAT

Dining on Bequia ranges from casual local-style meals to more elaborate cuisine, and both the food and the service are consistently good. Barbecues at Bequia's hotels mean spicy West Indian seafood, chicken, and beef, plus a buffet of side salads, vegetable dishes, and desserts.

$$ CARIBBEAN **✕ De Reef.** This casual beach bar and restaurant on Lower Bay is the primary feeding station for long, lazy beach days. When the beach bar closes at dusk, the restaurant starts to fill up with those who have made reservations. For breakfast (from 7) or a light lunch, De Reef bakes

its own breads, croissants, coconut cake, and cookies—and blends fresh juices to accompany them. For a full lunch or dinner, conch, lobster, whelk, and shrimp are treated the West Indian way; the curried conch and the lobster salad are favorites. Every other Saturday in season, there's a seafood buffet dinner accompanied by live music; on Sunday afternoon, a jam session. *Average main: $16 ✉ Lower Bay ☎ 784/458–3958 Reservations essential No credit cards.*

$$$ CARIBBEAN **Frangipani.** By day, this is the perfect spot for a harborside breakfast or lunch; just before sunset, boaters comes ashore to what is arguably the most popular gathering place in Bequia—the Frangipani Hotel's open-air waterfront bar. After a drink and a chat, the mood turns romantic with candlelight and Caribbean cuisine in the open-air dining room. The à la carte menu emphasizes seafood and local dishes—and be sure to have a slice of Frangi's lime pie for dessert. On Monday night in high season, a local string band plays catchy tunes; on Friday night, folksingers entertain. At the Thursday Jump-Up, the Frangi barbecue buffet (about $35) is accompanied by steel-band music. *Average main: $25 ✉ Frangipani Hotel, Belmont Walkway, Port Elizabeth ☎ 784/458–3255 www.frangipanibequia.com Reservations essential.*

$$$ CARIBBEAN FAMILY **Gingerbread.** The airy dining veranda at the Gingerbread Hotel offers all-day dining and a panoramic view of the waterfront activity on Admiralty Bay. The lunch crowd enjoys barbecued beef kebabs or chicken with fried potatoes or onions, grilled fish, homemade soups, salads, and sandwiches. In the evening, steaks, seafood, and curries are specialties of the house. Save room for warm, fresh gingerbread—served here with lemon sauce. In season, dinner is often accompanied by live music. *Average main: $22 ✉ Gingerbread Hotel, Belmont Walkway, Port Elizabeth ☎ 784/458–3800 www.gingerbreadhotel.com Reservations essential.*

$$ AMERICAN FAMILY **Jack's Bar.** Jack's is a perfect spot for lunch when you're enjoying a day at Princess Margaret Beach . . . or any day when you're on Bequia. The sandwiches, salads, burgers and fries, or the grilled catch of the day along with a refreshing cold drink will certainly satisfy. Dinner by the water is always a delight, but you'll have to maneuver some rough terrain (in your car or on foot) down from the main road and then navigate a lot of stairs farther down to the beachside restaurant—and back up, of course, after your meal. The Tuesday night barbecue is particularly popular. *Average main: $18 ✉ Princess Margaret Beach, between Port Elizabeth and Lower Bay, Port Elizabeth ☎ 784/457–3160.*

$$$ FRENCH **L'Auberge des Grenadines.** Owned by French-born Jacques Thevenot and his Vincentian wife, Eileen, this fine French restaurant is convenient for the yachting crowd, day-trippers, and anyone staying awhile. The extensive menu marries French and West Indian cuisines: seafood and local vegetables are prepared with a French twist. Lobster is the specialty; select yours from the live lobster pool. Light salads and sandwiches are available at lunch. Choose dinner from either the à la carte or prix-fixe menu. Delicious baguettes and delicate pastries round out any meal. *Average main: $25 ✉ On the north shore of Admiralty Bay, Hamilton ☎ 784/458–3555 www.caribrestaurant.com Reservations essential.*

$$ PIZZA FAMILY

Mac's Pizzeria. Mac's has been serving brick-oven pizza in Bequia since 1980. Choose from 17 mouthwatering toppings (including lobster) or opt for homemade lasagna, quiche, conch fritters, pita sandwiches, or soup and salad. Mac's home-baked cookies, muffins, and banana bread (by the slice or the loaf) are great for dessert or a snack. Or top off your meal with a scoop or two of Maranne's homemade ice cream in tropical flavors. The outdoor terrace has water views. Take-out is also available. *Average main: $20 Belmont Walkway, Port Elizabeth 784/458–3474 Reservations essential Closed Mon.*

$$ SEAFOOD

Sugar Reef Café. Put Sugar Reef Café on your "must do" list when visiting Bequia. The hotel's bar and restaurant is strategically placed in the Beach House lounge and sitting room, where French doors open to the sound of crashing waves. While perfect for a romantic dinner, it's also an excellent choice for a delightful lunch of savory seafood (try the lobster or fish roti or an open-faced fish steak on foccacia bread), a vegetarian dish (tangy callaloo soup, callaloo lasagna, cassava flat bread with grilled vegetables, or the light but filling fire-roasted corn salad with goat cheese and spinach), or settle for a perfectly cooked hamburger with cheese, bacon, and grilled onion. The chef's lime pie is the perfect dessert, with passion-fruit mousse a close runner-up. All produce, fish, and meat are locally sourced. Although the hotel is for adult guests only, children are welcome in the restaurant—particularly at lunch. *Average main: $18 Sugar Reef Beach House, Crescent Beach, Industry 784/458–3400 www.sugarreefbequia.com Reservations essential.*

24

WHERE TO STAY

In addition to several small hotels and inns in Port Elizabeth, Friendship Bay, and elsewhere on the island, a number of villas are available for vacation rental in Spring, Friendship Bay, Lower Bay, and other scenic areas of Bequia. The villas are suitable for two people or as many as a dozen, and the weekly rentals in high season run from as low as $560 a week for a "sweet and simple" villa to $9,000 or more for an elaborate villa with an Italian-style courtyard, gardens, and pool.

RENTAL CONTACT

Grenadine Island Villas *Belmont Walkway, Port Elizabeth 784/457–3739, 784/529–8046 after hrs www.grenadinevillas.com.*

RECOMMENDED HOTELS AND RESORTS

$$ HOTEL FAMILY Fodor's Choice ★

Bequia Beach Hotel. With an ideal location on pretty Friendship Bay, this sparkling boutique property is a great choice for a relaxing beach getaway or family vacation. **Pros:** classy, luxurious accommodations in an overall casual atmosphere; a beach lover's dream; good food; complimentary Wi-Fi. **Cons:** no TVs except in three cottages—is that a problem? *Rooms from: $350 On Friendship Bay, Friendship 784/458–1600 www.bequiabeach.com 11 rooms, 30 suites, 7 villas Multiple meal plans.*

$$ B&B/INN Fodor's Choice ★

Firefly Plantation Bequia. This small inn, under the same ownership as the Firefly in Mustique, is about 2 miles (3 km) north of Port Elizabeth on a 28-acre sugar plantation that dates back to the late 18th century. **Pros:** exquisitely designed rooms with fabulous views; pool, books, and games available to amuse you; good restaurant and friendly bar; complimentary Wi-Fi. **Cons:** you'll want to rent a vehicle; five-minute walk to the beach and tennis court; negotiating the steep hillside and many steps to the upper-floor rooms can be daunting for the elderly or those with disabilities. *Rooms from: $375 Spring 784/488–8414 www.fireflybequia.com 5 rooms Breakfast.*

$ HOTEL **Frangipani Hotel.** The venerable Frangipani, once a sea captain's home and also the birthplace of James Mitchell, former prime minister of St. Vincent and the Grenadines, is known for its welcoming waterfront bar and restaurant. **Pros:** great waterfront location; beautiful harbor view from hillside rooms; lively bar and restaurant at night; complimentary Wi-Fi. **Cons:** steep hillside not easy for anyone with disabilities; no air-conditioning in most rooms; "original" rooms—and the cold-water bath—are really basic. *Rooms from: $85 Belmont Walkway, Port Elizabeth 784/458–3255 www.frangipanibequia.com 15 rooms, 10 with bath No meals.*

$ HOTEL FAMILY **Gingerbread Hotel.** Breezy waterfront suites—each suitable for up to three guests—are large and modern, with bedroom alcoves, adjoining salons, and full kitchens (but no air-conditioning). **Pros:** in the middle of all the action; lovely waterfront suites; good casual restaurant; discounted weekly rates available. **Cons:** you might miss air-conditioning if the breeze isn't brisk; no TV, if that matters. *Rooms from: $230 Belmont Walkway, Port Elizabeth 784/458–3800 www.gingerbreadhotel.com 7 suites No meals.*

$ B&B/INN **Sugar Apple Inn.** On a hillside overlooking Friendship Bay (and Bequia Beach Hotel), each room in this small inn offers a different view and a different color scheme—but all have a kitchen and airy sitting room. **Pros:** right on the main road—and on the dollar (EC$1) bus route for easy access to town; one complimentary night with a week's stay; 110-volt electricity available in rooms; lovely staff; complimentary Wi-Fi. **Cons:** a/c in bedrooms only, but all rooms catch a good breeze. *Rooms from: $132 Friendship 784/457–3148 www.sugarappleinn.com 8 rooms, 2 cottage apartments No meals.*

$ HOTEL Fodor's Choice ★ **Sugar Reef.** "Rustic splendor" is one way to describe Sugar Reef, an adults-only, "eco-chic" boutique inn near the northeastern tip of Bequia. **Pros:** a perfect spot to relax, unwind, chill out; kayaks, bikes, boccie, badminton, and snorkeling equipment are available for guest use; area is good for long walks, runs, or forest "rambles"; excellent restaurant. **Cons:** no a/c, but a constant breeze diminishes that as an issue; pool available only to French House guests. *Rooms from: $150 Crescent Beach, Industry 784/458–3400 www.sugarreefbequia.com 8 rooms No meals.*

SHOPPING

Long renowned for their boatbuilding skills, Bequians have translated that craftsmanship to building model boats. In their workshops in Port Elizabeth, you can watch as hair-thin lines are attached to delicate sails or individual strips of wood are glued together for decking. Other Bequian artisans create scrimshaw, carve wood, throw pottery, crochet, or work with fabric—designing or hand-painting it first, then creating clothing and gift items for sale. Bequia's shops are mostly on

Front Street and Belmont Walkway, its waterfront extension, just steps from the jetty where the ferry arrives in Port Elizabeth. North of the jetty there's an open-air market; farther along that road, you'll find the model-boat workshops. Opposite the jetty, at Bayshore Mall, shops sell ice cream, baked goods, stationery, gifts, and clothing; there's also a grocery, liquor store, pharmacy, travel agent, and bank. On Belmont Walkway, south of the jetty, shops and studios showcase gifts and handmade articles. Shops are open weekdays from 8 to 5, Saturday 8 to noon.

Bequia Bookshop. Head here for Caribbean literature, cruising guides and charts, Caribbean flags, beach novels, souvenir maps, and exquisite scrimshaw and whalebone penknives carved by Bequian scrimshander Sam McDowell. ✉ *Belmont Walkway, Port Elizabeth* ☎ *784/458–3905.*

Claude Victorine's Art Studio. A small roadside sign marks the studio of French artist Claude Victorine. Stop by and admire her delicate, hand-painted, silk wall hangings and scarves. ✉ *Lower Bay* ☎ *784/458–3150* ⏲ *By appointment only.*

Local Color. This shop stocks an excellent and unusual selection of handmade jewelry, wood carvings, scrimshaw, and resort clothing. It's above the Porthole restaurant, near the jetty. Note that it's closed in October. ✉ *Belmont Walkway, Port Elizabeth* ☎ *784/458–3202.*

Fodor's Choice ★ **Mauvin Model Boat Shop.** At this workshop, you can purchase a Bequia trademark—a handmade model "Bequia boat"—or special-order a replica of your own yacht. The models are incredibly detailed and quite expensive—priced from a few hundred to several thousand dollars. The simplest models take about a week to make. ✉ *Front St., Port Elizabeth* ☎ *784/458–3669.*

Noah's Arkade. Gifts, souvenirs, and contemporary arts and crafts from around the Caribbean are available at this small shop. ✉ *Frangipani Hotel, Belmont Walkway, Port Elizabeth* ☎ *784/458–3424.*

Oasis Art Gallery. "Made in SVG" is the mandate of curator L.D. Lucy, whose paintings are among those on display. In addition to paintings of other local artists, Nzimbu Brown's banana leaf art, "Prop" King's model boats, and Mike Goddard's pottery, you can buy greeting cards, jewelry, ceramics, sculpture, photos, and more. ✉ *Belmont Walkway, behind Porthole Restaurant, Port Elizabeth* ☎ *784/497–7670.*

Fodor's Choice ★ **Sargeant Brothers Model Boat Shop.** In addition to handcrafted, expertly rigged, and authentically detailed model boats, the artisans at Sargeant Brothers also build custom models on commission. ✉ *Front St., Port Elizabeth* ☎ *758/458–3344.*

SPORTS AND THE OUTDOORS

BOATING AND SAILING

Fodor's Choice ★ With regular trade winds, visibility for 30 miles (48 km), and generally calm seas, Bequia is a big draw for those sailing the Grenadines—which easily rates among the best blue-water sailing anywhere in the world. At Port Elizabeth, you'll find all kinds of options: day sails or weekly charters, bareboat or fully crewed, monohulls or catamarans. Prices for day trips start at about $140 per person.

FAMILY Fodor's Choice ★ ***Friendship Rose.*** This 80-foot schooner spent its first 25 years ferrying both passengers and mail between Bequia and neighboring islands. In the late 1960s it was refitted, and the *Friendship Rose* now takes passengers on day trips from Bequia to Mustique, Mayreau, and the Tobago Cays. Breakfast, lunch, snacks, drinks, and snorkeling gear are included in the price. One child per adult sails free. ✉ *Waterfront, Port Elizabeth* ☎ *784/457–3888, 784/457–3739, 784/529–8046* 🌐 *www.friendshiprose.com.*

DIVING AND SNORKELING

About 35 dive sites around Bequia and nearby islands are accessible within 15 minutes by boat. The leeward side of the 7-mile (11-km) reef that fringes Bequia has been designated a marine park. The **Bullet,** off Bequia's northeast point, has limited access because of rough seas, but it's a good spot for spotting rays, barracuda, and the occasional nurse shark. **Devil's Table** is a shallow dive at the northern end of Admiralty Bay that's rich in fish and coral and has a sailboat wreck nearby at 90 feet. The **Wall** is a 90-foot drop off West Cay. Expect to pay dive operators $60 to $70 for a one-tank and $100 or so for a two-tank dive, including equipment. Dive boats welcome snorkelers for about $20 per person, but for the best snorkeling in Bequia, take a water taxi to the bay at Moonhole and arrange a pickup time.

Bequia Dive Adventures. This company offers PADI instruction courses and takes small groups on three dives daily. Rates include all equipment; harbor pickup and return is included for customers staying on yachts. ✉ *Belmont Walkway, Port Elizabeth* ☎ *784/458–3826* 🌐 *www.bequiadiveadventures.com.*

Dive Bequia. Dive and snorkel tours, night dives, and full equipment rental is available from Dive Bequia. PADI instructors provide resort and certification courses—including several interactive e-learning courses. ✉ *Gingerbread Hotel, Belmont Walkway, Port Elizabeth* ☎ *784/458–3504* 🌐 *www.divebequia.com.*

CANOUAN

Halfway down the Grenadines chain, this tiny boot-shape island—3½ miles (5½ km) long and 1¼ miles (2 km) wide—has only about 1,200 residents. But don't let its historically slow pace and quiet ways fool you. Canouan (pronounced *can*-o-wan), which is the Carib word for "turtle," has a modern airport with an extended runway suitable for small to midsize jets. The island has one of the region's largest and nicest villa communities, a championship golf course, a delightful small resort, and four of the most pristine beaches in the Caribbean. Canouan is also a busy port for yacht charters and diving expeditions to the Tobago Cays. Mt. Royal, the highest point on the island at 900 feet, offers panoramic 360-degree views of St. Vincent, all the Grenadines, and even St. Lucia on a clear day.

BEACHES

Canouan has four exquisite white-sand beaches, although land access to two of them is difficult because entry to the entire northern two-thirds of the island (where those two beaches are located) is controlled

Tamarind Beach Hotel

by a private villa community. Canouan faces a mile-long (1½-km-long) coral reef—one of the longer barrier reefs in the Caribbean—that offers excellent diving and snorkeling opportunities. The island's proximity to several of the other Grenadines (Mayreau and the Tobago Cays, in particular) makes excursions to other beautiful beaches relatively easy.

Godahl Beach. This lovely stretch of white-sand beach (pronounced *Gud*-ul) at the southern end of Carenage Bay is surrounded by private property owned by Canouan Resort (Pink Sands Club is scheduled to open in mid-2015) and Grenadines Estate Villas. Those who are not resort guests or villa residents may access the beach only by boat. **Amenities:** none for nonguests/nonresidents. **Best for:** swimming; walking. ✉ *Carenage Bay.*

Grand Bay Beach. In central Canouan on the leeward coast, Grand Bay is the island's longest beach and the site of Charlestown, the largest town, where ferries dock; it's alternatively called Charlestown Bay beach. Tamarind Beach Hotel & Yacht Club faces Grand Bay Beach. **Amenities:** food and drink; toilets. **Best for:** swimming. ✉ *Charlestown Bay.*

Mahault Bay Beach. This lovely but remote expanse of beach (pronounced *mah*-ho) is at the northern tip of the island, surrounded by Mt. Royal; the beach is accessible through the private property of Canouan Resort (Pink Sands Club is scheduled to open in mid-2015) and Grenadines Estate Villas—or by sea. **Amenities:** none. **Best for:** solitude; swimming. ✉ *Mahault Bay.*

South Glossy Bay Beach. This and other beaches along Glossy Bay, on the southwest (windward) coast of Canouan, are absolutely spectacular.

South Glossy Bay is within walking distance of the airport. **Amenities:** none. **Best for:** swimming; walking. ✉ *Glossy Bay.*

WHERE TO STAY

$$ RESORT FAMILY **Tamarind Beach Hotel & Yacht Club.** Thatched roofs are a trademark of this Italian-owned beachfront hotel. **Pros:** good value; excellent location for diving and boating enthusiasts; complimentary airport transfers; complimentary Wi-Fi. **Cons:** no pool; standard rooms are small. $ *Rooms from: $295* ✉ *Charlestown* ☎ *784/458–8044* 🌐 *www.tamarindbeachhotel.com* *32 rooms, 8 suites* ⊙ *Closed Sept.* 🍽 *Multiple meal plans.*

SPORTS AND THE OUTDOORS

BOATING

Fodor's Choice ★ The Grenadines have some of the most superb cruising waters in the world. Canouan is at the midpoint of the Grenadines, so it's an easy sail north to St. Vincent, Bequia, and Mustique or south to Mayreau, the Tobago Cays, and beyond.

DIVING AND SNORKELING

The mile-long (1½-km-long) reef protecting Canouan offers excellent snorkeling, as well as spectacular sites for both novice and experienced divers. **Gibraltar,** a giant stone almost 30 feet down, is a popular site; plenty of colorful fish and corals are visible. **Windward Bay,** on Canouan's southeastern coast, is a large lagoon protected by a barrier reef, making it perfect for snorkeling. The crystalline waters surrounding the nearby **Tobago Cays** are filled with fish and sea turtles and offer marvelous diving and snorkeling.

One-tank dives cost $110 per dive; two-tank dives, $175 per dive; night dives, $130 per dive. A full range of PADI courses are offered; novices can take a Discover Scuba Diving course for $175. Three-hour snorkeling trips to the Tobago Cays cost $110 per person, including equipment.

Canouan Scuba Center. Specializing in taking small groups of divers, whether beginners or experts, to the Tobago Cays and other nearby sites, Canouan Scuba Center is a full-service PADI facility that also offers resort and certification courses. The dive center is located on the grounds of Tamarind Beach Hotel. ✉ *Tamarind Beach Hotel & Yacht Club, Charlestown* ☎ *784/532–8073, 917/796–1100 in U.S.* 🌐 *www.canouandivecenter.com.*

GOLF

Fodor's Choice ★ **Grenadines Estate Golf Club.** This 18-hole, par-72 championship course is spread over 60 acres within the private Canouan Resort property and Grenadines Estate Villas, a private villa community. It is open to residents staying at the resort and patrons purchasing a daily ticket. The first 9 holes of the Jim Fazio–designed course, along with holes 10 and 18, are in a pretty, green plain that slopes down to the sea. The rest have been carved into the mountainside, affording spectacular views of Canouan Island and the surrounding Grenadines. The 13th hole offers a wraparound view of the Grenadines; it's also the most challenging, because its unforgiving green is at the edge of a cliff. Greens fees for 18 holes are $195 for resort guests and $450 for nonresident patrons; rates include a golf cart. Golf instruction and rental clubs are available, and a pro shop and lounge are on-site. ✉ *Canouan Resort, at the northern tip of the island, Carenage Bay* ☎ *784/458–8000* 🌐 *www.canouan.com/golf.asp.*

MAYREAU

Mayreau (pronounced *my*-row) is minuscule—1½ square miles (4 square km). With the exception of 22 acres at its northern tip that is privately owned and 21 acres that comprise the island's single (unnamed) village and were acquired by St. Vincent and the Grenadines, Mayreau remains in the hands of heirs of the original French plantation owners. Only about 250 residents live in the little village on Station Hill, and there are no proper roads. Visitors enjoy these natural surroundings in one of the prettiest locations in the Grenadines—and a rather unique spot where the calm Caribbean is separated from the Atlantic surf by only a narrow strip of beach. It's a favorite stop for boaters, as well, who anchor in Saltwhistle Bay. Except for water sports and hiking, there's not much to do—but everyone prefers it that way. For a day's excursion, you can hike up Mayreau's only hill (wear sturdy shoes) for a stunning view of the Tobago Cays. Then stop for a drink at Dennis' Hideaway and enjoy a swim at Saline Bay beach, where you may be joined by a boatload of cruise-ship passengers. The only access to Mayreau is by boat (ferry, private, or hired), which you can arrange at Union Island.

BEACHES

Mayreau's primary beach, Saltwhistle Bay, is unique because the calm water of the Caribbean is on one side, and the more powerful Atlantic surf is on the other; a few yards of white-sand beach is all that separates them. Saline Bay Beach, also magnificent, is popular with small cruise ships that ply the waters of the Grenadines and anchor offshore for the day.

Saline Bay Beach. This beautiful 1-mile (1½-km) crescent of pure white sand on the southwestern coast of Mayreau has no facilities, but you can walk up the hill to Dennis' Hideaway for lunch or drinks. The adjacent dock is where the ferry that travels between St. Vincent and Union Island ties up, and small cruise ships occasionally anchor offshore to give passengers a beach break. **Amenities:** none. **Best for:** swimming. ✉ *Saline Bay.*

Fodor's Choice ★ **Saltwhistle Bay Beach.** This beach at the northwestern tip of Mayreau takes top honors—it's an exquisite, 2½-mile-long (4-km-long) crescent of powdery white sand shaded by perfectly spaced palms, sea grape trees, and flowering bushes. It's a popular anchorage for the yachting crowd, as well as for day trips en route to or from the Tobago Cays. **Amenities:** none. **Best for:** snorkeling; swimming. ✉ *Saltwhistle Bay.*

WHERE TO STAY

$ B&B/INN **Dennis' Hideaway.** Each room in this hilltop guesthouse has a private balcony with a perfect view of the sun as it sets over Saline Bay. **Pros:** great value; stunning views; excellent local food; good base for boaters and divers; complimentary Wi-Fi. **Cons:** no frills; little in the way of amenities; village life can get noisy at night (unless you're participating!). $ *Rooms from: $85* ✉ *Above Saline Bay* ☎ *784/458–8594* 🌐 *www.dennis-hideaway.com* 5 *rooms* 🍽 *No meals.*

SPORTS AND THE OUTDOORS

BOATING AND FISHING

Dennis' Hideaway Charters. Yacht charters, drift-fishing trips, dive trips, and day sails can be arranged at Dennis' Hideaway. Expect to pay $40 per person for drift fishing for 1½ hours and $75–$100 per person (depending on the number of passengers) for a full day of sailing, swimming, and snorkeling—lunch included. ✉ *Near Saline Bay* ☎ *784/458–8594* 🌐 *www.dennis-hideaway.com.*

MUSTIQUE

This upscale haven, 18 miles (29 km) southeast of St. Vincent, is 3 miles (5 km) by 1¼ miles (2 km) at its widest point. The island is hilly and has several green valleys, each with a sparkling white-sand beach facing an aquamarine sea. The permanent population is about 300. Back in the 1960s, Britain's Princess Margaret put this small, private island on the map after the owner, the late Colin Tennant (Lord Glenconner), presented her with a 10-acre plot of land as a wedding gift. Tennant had bought the entire 1,400-acre island in 1958 for $67,500 (the equivalent of about $450,000 today). The Mustique Company—which Tennant formed in 1968 to develop the copra, sea-island cotton, and sugarcane estate into the glamorous hideaway it has become—now manages the privately owned villas, provides housing for all island employees, and operates Mustique Villa Rentals. Arrangements must be made about a year in advance to rent one of the luxury villas that now pepper the northern half of the island.

Sooner or later, stargazers see the resident glitterati at Basil's Bar, the island's social center. Proprietor Basil Charles also runs a boutique crammed with clothes and accessories from Bali. A pair of cotton-candy-color, gingerbread-style buildings, the centerpiece of the tiny village, house a gift shop and clothing boutique. There's also an antiques shop with fabulous objets d'art and a deli–grocery stocked with Brie and champagne.

The Mustique Blues Festival, held during the first two weeks of February, features artists from North America, Europe, and the Caribbean; shows occur nightly at Basil's Bar. The festival is quite a draw.

BEACHES

Mustique has a number of beautiful white-sand beaches at the foot of each of its lovely green valleys, one reason for its appeal to the rich and famous. Villas are strung out along the northern half of the island, but the best beach, the picture-perfect Macaroni Beach, is on the south side.

Britannia Bay Beach. This beach on Mustique's western coast is right next to the Brittania Bay jetty, and Basil's Bar is convenient for lunch. Firefly Mustique, on a steep hillside overlooking Britannia Bay, has steps leading down to the beach. **Amenities:** food and drink; toilets. **Best for:** swimming.

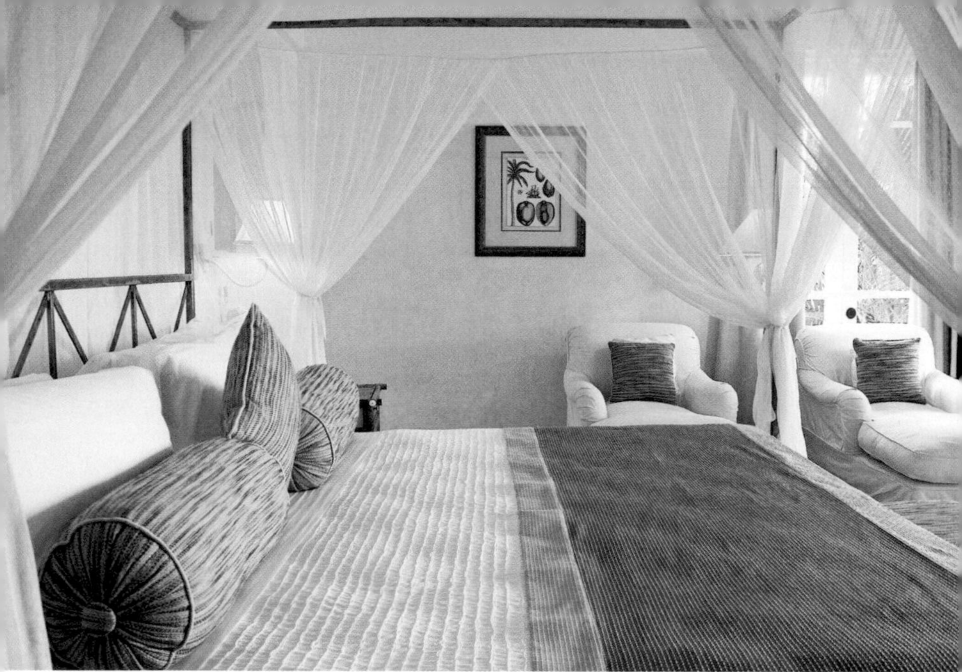

Cotton House

Endeavour Bay Beach. On the northwestern tip of Mustique, this is the main beach used by Cotton House guests. Swimming and snorkeling are ideal, and a dive shop with water-sports equipment rental is available on-site. The resort's Beach Café restaurant and bar are convenient for lunch or snacks. **Amenities:** food and drink; toilets; water sports. **Best for:** snorkeling; swimming.

Gelliceaux Bay Beach. This rather remote beach on the southwestern coast, one of 10 marine conservation areas designated by St. Vincent and the Grenadines, provides the best snorkeling on Mustique. **Amenities:** none. **Best for:** snorkeling; swimming.

L'Ansecoy Bay Beach. At the island's very northern tip, adjacent to the Cotton House, this broad crescent of white sand fringes brilliant turquoise water. Just offshore, the French liner *Antilles* went aground in 1971. **Amenities:** none. **Best for:** snorkeling; swimming.

FAMILY Fodor's Choice ★ **Macaroni Beach.** Macaroni is Mustique's most famous stretch of fine white sand—offering swimming (no lifeguards) in moderate surf that's several shades of blue, along with a few palm huts and picnic tables in a shady grove of trees. **Amenities:** parking. **Best for:** swimming.

WHERE TO EAT

$$$$ SEAFOOD FAMILY ✕ **Basil's Bar.** Basil's is *the* place to be—only partly because it's just about the *only* place to be in Mustique. It's mainly a wooden deck perched on bamboo stilts over the waves; there's a thatched roof, a congenial bar, and a dance floor that's open to the stars—in every sense. You never know what celebrity may show up at the next table. The food is simple and good—mostly seafood, homemade ice cream, burgers, and salads, great French toast and banana pancakes, the usual cocktails,

and unusual wines. Wednesday is Jump Up & Barbecue Night, with live music; Sunday, enjoy cocktails and jazz as the sun goes down. *Average main: $34 ✉ Britannia Bay ☎ 784/488–8350 🌐 www.basilsbar.com ✍ Reservations essential.*

WHERE TO STAY

$$$$ RESORT Fodor's Choice ★ **Cotton House.** Mustique's only full-service resort allows travelers to enjoy the sun-kissed glam and idyllic beaches of this famous island in an intimate, island-chic setting that also shelters those-in-the-know and the rich and famous (at least those without their own Mustique homes). **Pros:** direct beach access; beautiful rooms; personalized service with great attention to detail; excellent dining; a familial vibe. **Cons:** quite expensive; more sedate than, say, Firefly. *Rooms from: $750 ✉ Endeavor Bay ☎ 784/456–4777 🌐 www.cottonhouse.net 5 rooms, 8 suites, 3 cottages, 1 villa Closed Sept. and Oct. Multiple meal plans.*

$$$$ ALL-INCLUSIVE **Firefly Mustique.** Tiny and charming, this three-story hotel is wedged into dense tropical foliage on a steep hillside above Britannia Bay. **Pros:** relaxed and friendly spot; open-air ocean views from each amazing room; the bar—a hangout for guests and visiting celebrities—features martini and champagne menus; complimentary Wi-Fi. **Cons:** very expensive; house-party atmosphere at the bar can get noisy at night. *Rooms from: $1,250 ☎ 784/488–8414 🌐 www.fireflymustique.com 5 rooms All-inclusive.*

$$$$ RENTAL **Mustique Villa Rentals.** Except for Cotton House and Firefly, Mustique is an island of privately owned villas—more than 85 of them; rentals can be arranged through Mustique Villa Rentals. *Rooms from: $5,000 ☎ 784/488–8500, 855/261–1316 in U.S. 🌐 www.mustique-island.com 85+ villas No meals.*

SPORTS AND THE OUTDOORS

Water-sports facilities are available at Cotton House, and most villas include sports equipment. Four floodlighted tennis courts are near the airport for those whose villa lacks its own; there's a cricket field (matches on Sunday afternoon) and an equestrian center. Motorbikes or "mules" (beach buggies) to ride around the bumpy roads rent for $75 per day.

DIVING AND SNORKELING

FAMILY **Mustique Watersports.** Mustique is surrounded by coral reefs, and nearly 20 dive sites are nearby. Mustique Watersports, on Endeavour Bay Beach, offers PADI instruction and certification and has a 28-foot, fully equipped dive boat. Rates are $80 for an introductory course, $95 for a one-tank dive, and $400 for a five-dive package. A special "bubble maker" introduction-to-diving course ($65) is available for children ages 8–11. Snorkelers can rent a mask and fins for the day for $10 or join a snorkeling trip where equipment is provided. *✉ Cotton House, Endeavour Bay Beach ☎ 784/456–3486 🌐 www.mustique-island.com.*

HORSEBACK RIDING

FAMILY **Mustique Equestrian Centre.** Mustique is the only island in the Grenadines where you can find a fine thoroughbred horse or pony to ride. Daily excursions leave from the Mustique Equestrian Centre, which is one block from the airport. All rides are accompanied, and children five years or older are allowed to ride—or kids can attend Pony Camp and learn horsemanship, tack maintenance, and care of the pony itself. ☎ *784/488–8316* 🌐 *www.mustique-island.com.*

PALM ISLAND

A private speck of land (only 135 acres), exquisite Palm Island used to be an uninhabited, mosquito-infested swamp called Prune Island. One intrepid family put heart and soul—as well as muscle and brawn and lots of money—into taking the wrinkles out of the prune and rechristened it Palm Island. The Caldwell family cleaned up the five surrounding beaches, built bungalows, planted palm trees, and irrigated the swamp with seawater to kill the mosquitoes. The rustic getaway existed for 25 years before Palm Island's current owners, Elite Island Resorts, dolled up the property. Now it's one of the finest resorts in the Caribbean. Other than the resort, the island is populated by a handful of privately owned villas. Access is via Union Island, 1 mile (1½ km) to the west and a 10-minute ride in the resort's launch.

24

WHERE TO STAY

$$$$ ALL-INCLUSIVE Fodor's Choice ★

Palm Island Resort. Perfect for a honeymoon, rendezvous, or chic escape, this palm-studded resort island offers peace and tranquillity, along with five dazzling white-sand beaches, a calm aquamarine sea for swimming and water sports, nature trails for quiet walks, a pool with waterfall, a "pitch-and-putt" golf course, sophisticated dining, impeccable service, and exquisite accommodations. **Pros:** private and romantic; fabulous beach; great snorkeling right outside beachfront cottages 15 and 16; free scuba resort course. **Cons:** quiet nights (early to bed and early to rise); fairly isolated; very expensive. 💲 *Rooms from: $960* ☎ *784/458–8824, 866/237–2157 in U.S.* 🌐 *www.palmislandcaribbean.com* *33 rooms, 8 suites, 2 villas* *All-inclusive.*

PETIT ST. VINCENT

The southernmost of St. Vincent's Grenadines, tiny (115 acres), private Petit St. Vincent—pronounced "Petty" St. Vincent and affectionately called PSV—is ringed with white-sand beaches and covered with tropical foliage. The late Hazen Richardson created the resort in 1968. The current owners made extensive renovations (cottage upgrades, a casual beachside restaurant, an air-conditioned fitness and yoga center, an open-air spa, an air-conditioned library with a TV and Internet access, a new children's center, and landscaping upgrades) but have not changed the design or, more importantly, the nature of the property. To get to PSV, you fly from Barbados to Union Island, where the resort's motor launch meets you for the 20-minute voyage.

WHERE TO STAY

$$$$ RESORT Fodor's Choice ★

Petit St. Vincent. The lack of phones, room TVs, outside interference, and even planned activities is particularly appealing when indulging in your most luxurious, private-island fantasies. **Pros:** private island experience with secluded white-sand beaches; very accommodating service; spacious cottages; excellent cuisine (including the large jar of homemade cookies placed in your room upon arrival). **Cons:** you're pretty much a captive here, so bring a good, long book; some of the beaches adjacent to the cottages are rocky or have high surf; Wi-Fi and Internet available only in the front office; all this luxury and solitude is pricey. $ *Rooms from: $1,400* ☎ *784/458–8801, 800/654–9326 in U.S.* 🌐 *www.petitstvincent.com* *22 cottages* *Closed Aug.–Oct.* *All meals.*

SPORTS AND THE OUTDOORS

DIVING AND SNORKELING

Jean-Michel Cousteau, son of the legendary Jacques-Yves Cousteau, opened this state-of-the-art PADI 5-Star dive center on PSV at the end of 2014—a perfect place to share the wonders of coral reefs with both guests and locals, he would say, and a first step in an ongoing program to protect the waters and aquatic life in the region.

Jean-Michel Cousteau Caribbean Diving Center. Guided dives, diving instruction, and PADI certifications are offered for all levels of divers. For qualified divers, a one-tank dive costs $85; two-tank dive, $150; night dive, $100; a full week, $525. The half-day resort course with two guided dives costs $170. ✉ *Petit St. Vincent Resort* ☎ *784/458–8984* 🌐 *www.jeanmichelcousteaudiving-caribbean.com.*

TOBAGO CAYS

Fodor's Choice ★ Tobago Cays, a small group of five uninhabited islands (Petit Rameau, Petit Bateau, Baradal, Petit Tabac, and Jamesby) just east of Mayreau in the southern Grenadines, was declared a wildlife reserve—Tobago Cays Marine Park—in 2006 by the St. Vincent and the Grenadines government to preserve the natural beauty and biodiversity of the cays and to allow visitors to experience some of the best snorkeling in the world. The sparkling-clear water within Horseshoe Reef, which surrounds four of the islands, is studded with sponges and coral formations and populated by countless colorful fish and sea turtles. All the major dive operators and sailing and snorkeling day trips stop here, sometimes making it a little overcrowded, but the Tobago Cays remain everyone's version of a tropical paradise and one unforgettable place. All visitors to the Tobago Cays Marine Park, including those on private or chartered yachts and dive boats, are required to pay a user fee of $4 ($EC10) per person; a yacht mooring costs $17 (EC$45) for 24 hours.

UNION ISLAND

Union Island is the commercial center of the southern Grenadines—a popular anchorage for those sailing the Grenadines and a crossroads for those heading to surrounding islands. Clifton, the main town and a port of entry for yachts, is small, with a bustling harbor, a quaint town square with a busy market, a few simple beachfront inns and restaurants, businesses that cater to yachts, and the regional airstrip—the busiest in the Grenadines. Hugh Malzac Square, in the center of town, honors a local islander and the first black man to captain a merchant-marine ship. The ship was the *Booker T. Washington*, the time, 1942.

Taxis and minibuses are available to get around the island, and water taxis go between islands—including Happy Island, a man-made islet in the harbor where you can get a good stiff rum punch and even some grilled lobster or fish. The Easterval Regatta occurs during the Easter weekend with festivities that include boat races, sports and games, a calypso competition, a beauty pageant, and a cultural show featuring the Big Drum Dance (derived from French and African traditions). Union Island has several small inns and hotels, some directly on the waterfront and others inland.

BEACHES

Although it's an important hub for travelers heading to some of the smaller islands in the Grenadines (especially the private retreats of Petit St. Vincent and Palm Island and also Mayreau, which does not have an airstrip), the hilly, volcanic island has few beaches that compare with those on its closest neighbors. The best beach, Big Sands Beach, has powdery white sand and is easily accessible from Clifton.

FAMILY **Big Sands Beach.** Union has relatively few good beaches, but this one on Belmont Bay—on the island's northern shore and a five-minute drive from Clifton—is a pretty crescent of powdery white sand, protected by reefs, with lovely views of Mayreau and the Tobago Cays. **Amenities:** none. **Best for:** solitude; snorkeling; swimming. ✉ *Richmond Bay.*

Chatham Bay Beach. The desolate but lovely golden-sand beach at Chatham Bay, on the leeward side of Union Island, offers good swimming. **Amenities:** none. **Best for:** solitude; swimming. ✉ *Chatham Bay.*

WHERE TO EAT

$$$ SEAFOOD FAMILY ✕ **Anchorage Yacht Club.** You can't get much closer to waterfront dining than here at the AYC. This is the yachting crowd's favorite stop for land-side meals—breakfast, lunch, or dinner. Freshly baked croissants and other pastries, along with pitchers of fresh-squeezed juice and piping-hot coffee, present the perfect wake-up. At lunch, the sandwiches, salads, burgers, pasta grilled fish, and more are served within striking distance (figuratively speaking) of the shark pool. And at dinner, you can enjoy fresh seafood cooked to order or, perhaps, a lobster prepared to your liking. 💲 *Average main: $22* ✉ *Clifton* ☎ *784/458–8821* 🌐 *www.anchorage-union.com* ✍ *Reservations essential.*

$$ CARIBBEAN ✕ **Lambi's.** Lambi's, which overlooks the waterfront in Clifton, offers a daily buffet for all meals from November through May. The dinner buffet includes some 50 dishes, including the specialty: delicious conch creole. From June through October, dining is à la carte—with the same menu for both lunch and dinner. Choose from fish, chicken, conch, pork, lobster, shrimp, and beef dishes. *Lambi* is Creole patois for "conch," and the restaurant's walls are constructed from conch shells. Yachts and dinghies can tie up at the wharf, and there's steel-band music and limbo dancing every night in season. 💲 *Average main: $18* ✉ *Clifton* ☎ *784/458–8549* 🌐 *www.lambisunion.weebly.com.*

WHERE TO STAY

$ HOTEL **Anchorage Yacht Club.** The popular AYC offers convenient, inexpensive land-side accommodations to boaters looking for a night or two on dry land, as well as to those beginning or ending a sailing vacation through the Grenadines. **Pros:** two minutes from airport via jitney; convenient for all boating activities; good restaurant; convivial atmosphere; Kite Beach apartment (4–6 guests) offers monthly rates. **Cons:** standard rooms are comfortable but not luxurious; entrance into some beach cottages is through the bathroom! *Rooms from: $98* ⊠ *Clifton* ☎ *784/458–8221* *www.anchorage-union.com* *10 rooms, 3 cottages* *No meals.*

$ HOTEL **Kings Landing Hotel.** Divers flock to Kings Landing, because Grenadines Dive—the busiest dive operator in the region—is based here. **Pros:** great for divers; excellent waterfront location; year-round rates; good value. **Cons:** tiny beach; bathrooms have showers only. *Rooms from: $105* ⊠ *Clifton* ☎ *784/485–8823* *www.kingslandinghotel.com* *15 rooms, 2 cottages* *Breakfast.*

SHOPPING

L'Atelier Turquoise. On the waterfront in Clifton, in the center of town next to Erika's Marine and adjacent to the main dock, this tiny shop sells a variety of Caribbean arts and crafts, colorful gifts and souvenirs, hats, T-shirts, and more. ⊠ *Hugh Mulzac Sq., Clifton* ☎ *784/458–8734.*

SPORTS AND THE OUTDOORS

BOATING AND SAILING

Yannis Day Tours. Yannis catamaran trips depart from Clifton Harbour for day sails to Saltwhistle Bay on Mayreau and the Tobago Cays. Snorkeling gear, drinks, and a buffet lunch are included. ⊠ *Clifton* ☎ *784/458–8513.*

DIVING AND SNORKELING

Grenadines Dive. Glenroy Adams, a Bequia native who claims to know "every dive site in the Grenadines," is the dive master here. The company offers Tobago Cays snorkeling trips and wreck dives at the *Purina*, a sunken World War I English gunboat. Single-tank dives cost $65; multidive packages are discounted. Beginners can take a four-hour resort course, which includes a shallow dive. Certified divers can rent equipment by the day or week. ⊠ *Next to Kings Landing Hotel, Clifton* ☎ *784/458–8138* *www.grenadinesdive.com.*

Wind and Sea. Based at the Bougainvilla Hotel complex, Wind and Sea has a fleet of catamarans that are available for private charters and can accommodate up to 90 people, depending on the size of the boat. Snorkeling equipment, buffet lunch, and a fully stocked bar are all included. ⊠ *Bougainvilla Hotel, Clifton* ☎ *784/458–8344.*

25

TRINIDAD AND TOBAGO

WELCOME TO TRINIDAD AND TOBAGO

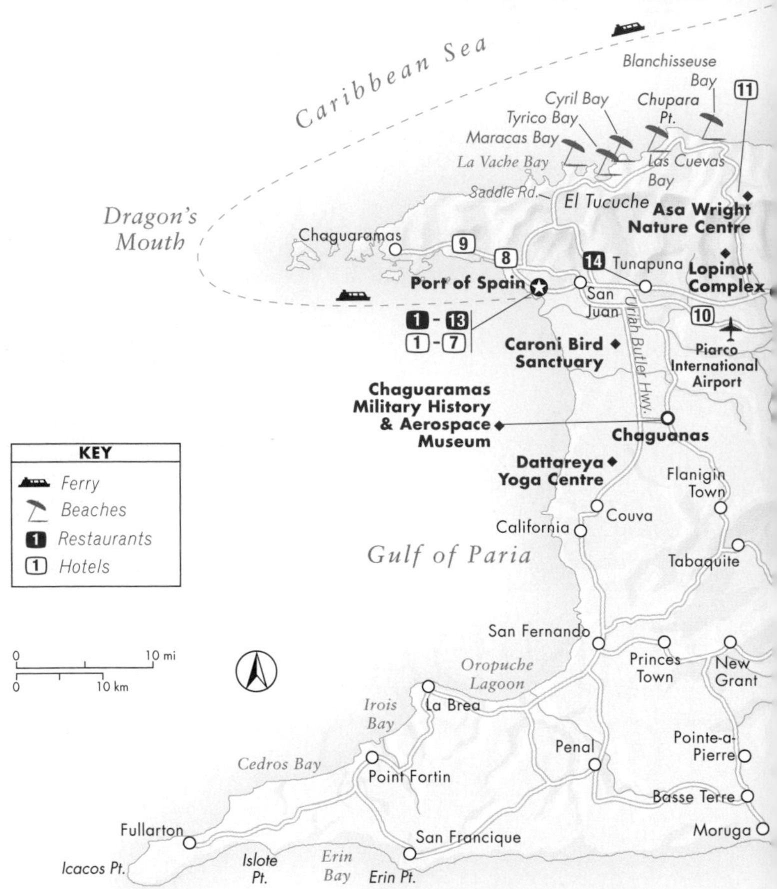

Caribbean Sea
Blanchisseuse Bay
Cyril Bay
Chupara Pt.
Tyrico Bay
Maracas Bay
La Vache Bay
Las Cuevas Bay
Saddle Rd.
El Tucuche
Asa Wright Nature Centre
Dragon's Mouth
Chaguaramas
Tunapuna
Lopinot Complex
Port of Spain
San Juan
Uriah Butler Hwy.
Caroni Bird Sanctuary
Piarco International Airport
Chaguaramas Military History & Aerospace Museum
Chaguanas
Dattareya Yoga Centre
Flanigin Town
Couva
California
Gulf of Paria
Tabaquite
San Fernando
Oropuche Lagoon
Princes Town
New Grant
Irois Bay
La Brea
Penal
Pointe-a-Pierre
Cedros Bay
Point Fortin
Basse Terre
Fullarton
San Francique
Moruga
Icacos Pt.
Islote Pt.
Erin Bay
Erin Pt.

KEY
Ferry
Beaches
Restaurants
Hotels

0 10 mi
0 10 km

The most southerly of the Caribbean islands, Trinidad is also the most colorful. Islanders trace their roots to Africa, India, China, Lebanon, and Europe, and they speak English, Spanish, Hindi, and French patois. On much quieter Tobago, the most exciting event is often the palm trees swaying high above a gentle arc of a beach.

BUSINESS AND PLEASURE

The two-island republic is the southernmost link in the Antillean island chain, some 7 miles (11 km) off the coast of Venezuela, but Tobago's Main Ridge and Trinidad's Northern Range are believed to represent the farthest reaches of the Andes Mountains. Trinidad is a large petroleum and natural-gas producer. Tiny Tobago is known more for its quiet atmosphere and gorgeous, wild beaches.

Restaurants	▼
Aioli	13
Angelo's	5
Apsara	6
Buzo Osteria	12
Chaud	9
Joseph's	4
Mélange	8
More Vino More Sushi	11
Prime Restaurant	1
Tiki Village	2
Town Restaurant & Bar	7
Trotters	10
Veni Mangé	3
Wings Restaurant	14

Hotels	▼
Asa Wright Nature Centre Lodge	11
The Carlton Savannah	7
Coblentz Inn	3
Courtyard by Marriott	8
Crews Inn	9
Radisson Trinidad	4
Hilton Trinidad	1
Holiday Inn Express	10
Hyatt Regency Trinidad	6
Kapok Hotel	2
Le Grande Almandier	12
Monique's	5

TOP REASONS TO VISIT TRINIDAD AND TOBAGO

1 Carnival: Trinidad's Carnival is the Caribbean's biggest and best party, but nightlife is hopping the rest of the year, too.

2 Bird-Watching: Both Trinidad and Tobago are major bird-watching destinations; Trinidad itself has more resident species than any other Caribbean island.

3 Culture Sharing: A melding of many cultures means lively festivals year-round and a fabulous mix of cuisines.

4 Music: The steel pan was invented in Trinidad, and excellent bands play all over the island.

EATING WELL IN TRINIDAD AND TOBAGO

Food here blends indigenous, British, French, Spanish, African, South American, East Indian, Chinese, and Middle Eastern influences.

Referencing the national dish, acclaimed second-generation chef Debra Sardinha-Metivier notes, "We are a callaloo in people form. Maybe you had a Chinese grandmother or Indian grandfather who helped broaden, sophisticate your palate."

Today there's a growing awareness, pun intended, of returning to roots: "Everything comes full circle; organic-farm-to-table sustainability was always a necessity. More people then had a backyard garden . . . and shared. If I had a mango tree, and my neighbor had a coconut, we would barter. . . . Adapting to modern life while creatively meeting the needs of three square meals (including a rushed lunch for workers) began fusion cuisine." It's the fusion (particularly of Indian and Caribbean) that sets Trinidad apart.

STREET FOOD

Although much of what you'll find in restaurants and stalls here resembles variations on Caribbean standards, street food, which rules rushed Trini life, stands out. You'll find fresh rotis (akin to wraps) stuffed with curried meat, seafood, or chicken; chicken *geera* (an Indian dish heavily seasoned with cumin); pies—beef, cheese, fish, *aloo* (Hindi for potato); and *pows* (from the Cantonese *pao-tzu*, steamed wrapped buns with savory or sweet filling, typically pork).

CALLALOO

Reflecting the island's pronounced African influence, this hearty stew is the national dish (variants are found throughout the islands). Into the pot go the leaves of the dasheen, which resembles slightly bitter spinach and is also called taro or "callaloo bush," along with okra, chili peppers, coconut milk, *chadon bene* (an herb also known as culantro), garlic, onion, and sometimes crab. It's often served with macaroni pie (essentially pasta baked with cheese and eggs).

CRAB AND DUMPLING

Tobagonian cuisine mimics Trinidad's, for the most part, but its signature dish is messy, marvelous curried crab with dumpling. The sweet blue crabs and dumplings are simmered in a rich coconut sauce. Tobago is also celebrated for its sumptuously prepared "provisions" (often-starchy vegetables), soups, and stews.

PELAU

Pelau is another mainstay, its roots dating back to 5th-century-BC Mesopotamia and brought to Europe by Alexander the Great's army. International variations run from rice pilaf to Spain's paella; Trinidad's version borrows from several cultures. Chicken, beef, pork, or goat is cooked down with rice, pigeon peas, pumpkin, brown sugar, onions, garlic, and often the ubiquitous curry powder (which Trinis consider a metaphor for the spiciness of their lives).

ROTI

One of the great Indian contributions to Trinidad, this is unleavened flatbread cooked on an iron griddle called a *tawa*/*tava* and stuffed with a variety of filling fillings. *Sada* roti is the simplest kind, filled with curried lentils, fire-roasted tomato, eggplant, potato, and other vegetables. It's a popular breakfast option, along with *paratha* roti (aka "Buss-Up-Shut"), rubbed with clarified butter to enhance flavor and grilled until crisp, brown, and crumbly, and usually served with fried eggs. The classic roti, *dhalpuri,* is stuffed with ground yellow split peas, garlic, cumin, and pepper; meats are often added.

SWEETS

Guava paste, sticky-sweet but delectable candied tamarind or papaya balls, and Indian snacks like *gulab jamon* (creamy fried dough in sugar syrup scented with cardamom and rosewater) are common. Pone, which is similar to bread pudding, derives its consistency from ground provisions such as cassava (manioc), sweet potato, or pumpkin. Grated cinnamon, nutmeg, raisins, coconut, and sugar are added and baked in a casserole. Tobago chefs often add a pinch of black pepper to provide an edgy counterpoint.

—Jordan Simon

(top left) Curried crab; (bottom right) Ingredients for a roti; (top right) Creole-style pelau

CARNIVAL IN TRINIDAD

On Carnival Monday and Tuesday the traffic lights of Port of Spain are turned off and the streets are turned over to a human traffic jam of costumed revelers. They jump and dance to the pounding sound of music trucks and turn Port of Spain into a pulsing celebration of island life that they call the *mas.*

Trinidad's celebration has evolved through the years. What was once a two-day affair has turned into a lengthy party season starting in early January and lasting until Ash Wednesday. The biggest and best parties are held in and around Port of Spain, where locals max out their credit cards and even take out bank loans to finance their costumes and attend as many parties as possible.

THE FETE

Huge outdoor parties—called fetes—are held in the months before Carnival; during the final week, there are usually several fetes every day. You can get tickets for many of them through the major hotels, but some exclusive fetes may require an invitation from a well-connected Trinidadian.

THE PANORAMA

While fetes are important to Carnival, the Panorama Steelband Preliminaries and finals are essential. Two weeks before Carnival, the "Prelims" are held, when dozens of steel drum orchestras compete for a place in the finals held on Carnival Saturday. Music lovers go to hear the throbbing sound of hundreds of steel pans beating out a syncopated rhythm, and the rum-fueled party often rivals even the best fetes.

THE COSTUMES

To be a true part of Carnival, you need a costume. Every mas band has its own costumes, which must be reserved months in advance (these days online). You pick up yours at the band's mas "camp" and find out where and when to meet your band. Then all you have to do is jump, walk, or wave in the Carnival procession as the spirit moves you. Drinks and food may be included.

THE MUSIC

Carnival is powered by music, and though the steel pan still plays a big part, it's the soca performers who draw the biggest crowds. You can hear the most popular performers at the bigger fetes and at the Soca Monarch competition held on Carnival Friday before the more prestigious Calypso Monarch contest.

THE MAS BANDS

Trinis are passionate about their favorite mas band. The most popular have costumes largely comprised of beaded bikinis and feathered headdresses and are called "pretty mas." Very large bands such as Tribe, Island People, and Hart's fall into this category. If you're not willing to show that much skin or want more theater, then choose a band like K2K & Associates, which offers more elaborate costumes with a thematic story. As has always been the case, women greatly outnumber men in the bands.

TOP FETES

Safety is an increasing concern in Trinidad, especially at Carnival time. Fetes that attract a better-heeled crowd offer more security and sufficient bars to cater to the thousands of revelers who attend. They usually command higher prices but are worth the cost.

Beach House. This fete attracts an upscale crowd at a different spot each year. The party runs till about 10 pm with catered food and premium drinks.

Eyes Wide Shut is held at The Oval (home of Trinidad cricket) and tends to attract a younger crowd.

Insomnia is an overnight fete held in Chaguaramas, just West of Port of Spain, on Carnival Saturday, and the partying doesn't stop till sunrise.

The **Brian Lara** and **Moka** all-inclusive fetes are both held on the afternoon of Carnival Sunday. Tickets for both are highly sought. Brian Lara is considered the most exclusive of all fetes and is the most expensive.

(top left) Young stilt walkers stride the streets of Port of Spain during Carnival; (bottom right) Carnival celebrations during the Junior Parade of the Bands; (top right) Fancy, playful, and revealing are the characteristics of many Carnival costumes.

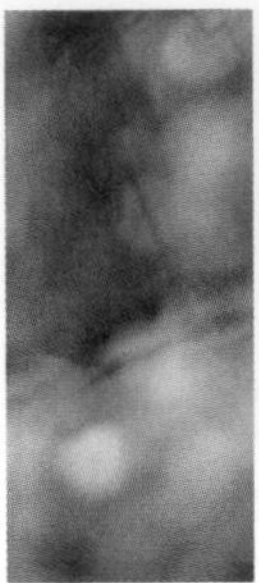

Updated by Vernon O'Reilly-Ramesar

These lush islands lay claim to being the economic powerhouse of the Caribbean. Vast oil and gas reserves have led to a high standard of living, and tourism is not the mainstay of the economy. Indeed, the word *tourist* is seldom used here; the preference is for the much friendlier (and perhaps vaguer) *visitor*.

Trinidad's Northern Range is thought to be part of the Andes in South America (it was connected to the mainland as recently as the last Ice Age). This geological history helps explain why the range of flora and fauna is much greater than on other Caribbean islands.

The two islands have very different histories, although both islands' Amerindian populations were virtually wiped out by the arrival of Europeans. After Columbus landed in Trinidad in 1498, the island came under Spanish rule. In an attempt to build the population and provide greater numbers to fend off a potential British conquest, the government at the time encouraged French Catholics from nearby islands to settle in Trinidad. This migration can be seen in the large number of French place-names scattered around the island. Despite this effort, the British conquered the island in 1797.

Tobago had a much more turbulent history. Named after the tobacco that was used by the native Amerindian population, the island changed hands more than a dozen times before eventually coming under British rule in 1814.

The two islands were merged into one crown colony in 1888, with Tobago being made a ward of Trinidad. Independence was achieved in 1962 under the leadership of Dr. Eric Williams, who became the first prime minister. The islands became an independent republic in 1976, with a bicameral parliament and an appointed president.

Trinidad's capital city, Port of Spain, is home to some 300,000 of the island's 1.3 million inhabitants. Downtown Port of Spain is a bustling commercial center complete with high-rise office buildings and seemingly perpetual traffic. Happily, the northern mountain range rises just behind the city and helps to take much of the edge off the urban clamor.

The majority of Trinidad's population is of either African or East Indian background—the descendants of African slaves and indentured East Indian laborers, who came to work the plantations in the 19th century. The island is always buzzing with a variety of celebrations and arts performances that might include African drumming and classical Indian dance. Although these two groups compose more than 80% of the population, other groups such as the French, Spanish, Chinese, and even Lebanese have left their mark.

Many of the art forms that are considered synonymous with the Caribbean were created on this relatively small island. Calypso was born here, as were soca, limbo, and the steel pan (steel drum). The island can also claim two winners of the Nobel Prize in Literature—V.S. Naipaul (2001), who was born in Trinidad and wrote several of his earlier books about the island, and Derek Walcott (1992), a St. Lucian who moved to Trinidad in 1953. Many tourists make a pilgrimage simply to trace the places mentioned in Naipaul's most famous novel, *A House for Mr. Biswas* (1961), which was partially based on his father's life.

Physically, the island offers an exact parallel to the rain forests of South America, which allows for interesting—and sometimes challenging—adventures. Beach lovers accustomed to the electric blue water and dazzling white sand of coral islands may be disappointed by the beaches on Trinidad. The best beaches are on the north coast, with peach sand, clean blue-green water, and the forest-covered Northern Range as a backdrop. Beaches are almost completely free of hotel development.

Tobago is 23 miles (37 km) northeast of Trinidad. The population here is much less ethnically diverse than that of Trinidad, with the majority being of African descent. Tobagonians have their own dialect and distinct culture. Tourism is much more a part of the island's economy, and you can find excellent resorts and facilities—along with pretty white-sand beaches.

PLANNING

WHEN TO GO

Trinidad is more of a business destination than a magnet for tourists, so hotel rates (particularly in Port of Spain) are fairly stable year-round; nevertheless, you can usually get a price break during the traditional Caribbean low season (from May to December). Carnival (in January, February, or March) brings the highest rates.

Tobago is much more of a tourist destination, but since the island is more popular with Europeans than Americans, its busy periods are sometimes different from those of islands with more of an American presence.

GETTING HERE AND AROUND

AIR TRAVEL

There are nonstops to Trinidad from Houston (United), Miami (American, Caribbean Airlines), Ft. Lauderdale (Caribbean Airlines, JetBlue), New York–JFK (American, Caribbean Airlines), and New York–Newark (United). There are no nonstop flights to Tobago from the United

LOGISTICS

Getting to Trinidad and Tobago: You can fly nonstop to Trinidad from several U.S. cities, but there are no nonstop flights to Tobago from the United States; to get to Tobago, you will have to take a short flight from Trinidad on Caribbean Airlines. Trinidad's Piarco International Airport (POS), about 30 minutes east of Port of Spain (take Golden Grove Road north to the intersection with the Churchill-Roosevelt Highway and then follow it west for about 10 miles [16 km] to Port of Spain), is a modern facility with 14 air bridges. Tobago's small Crown Point Airport (TAB) is the gateway to the island.

Hassle Factor: Medium-high.

On the Ground: Few hotels provide airport transfers, but you can always ask when you make your reservations. If you've booked a package, sometimes transfers are included. In Trinidad, taxis are readily available at Piarco Airport; the fare to Port of Spain is set at $50 ($100 after 10 pm). In Tobago the fare from Crown Point Airport to Scarborough or Grafton Beach is about $65.

States; to get to Tobago, you will have to fly from Trinidad to the A.N.R. Robinson International Airport on Caribbean Airlines or LIAT.

Airports A.N.R. Robinson International Airport (*Crown Point International Airport*). ✉ *TAB, Tobago* ☎ *868/639–0509* 🌐 *www.tntairports.com.* **Piarco International Airport.** Trinidad's airport is modern, with 14 air bridges. It's about 30 minutes east of Port of Spain. ✉ *POS, Trinidad* ☎ *868/669–4101* 🌐 *www.tntairports.com.*

Local Airline Contacts American Airlines ☎ *868/821–6000* 🌐 *www.aa.com.* **British Airways** ☎ *800/247–9297* 🌐 *www.ba.com.* **Caribbean Airlines** ☎ *868/625–7200, 868/669–3000* 🌐 *caribbean-airlines.com.* **JetBlue** ☎ *800/538–2583 in U.S., 801/449–2525 international.* **LIAT** ☎ *868/627–2982, 888/844–5428* 🌐 *www.liatairline.com.* **United Airlines** ☎ *800/461–2744* 🌐 *www.united.com.* **WestJet** ☎ *888/937–8538.*

FERRY TRAVEL

The seas between Trinidad and Tobago can be very rough, and flights are frequent and only 20 minutes long, so it's better to fly than take a ferry.

Contact Port Authority of Trinidad and Tobago. Trips between Trinidad and Tobago are made on one of the two high-speed CAT ferries and take 2½ hours. The ferries leave twice a day from the jetty at the foot of Independence Square in Port of Spain and three times a day from the cruise-ship complex in Scarborough. The round-trip fare is TT$100. There is also a water-taxi service that travels between Port of Spain and San Fernando in southern Trinidad for TT$15 each way. ☎ *868/625–2901* in Port of Spain, *868/639–2181* in Scarborough 🌐 *www.patnt.com.*

CAR TRAVEL

Don't rent a car if you're staying in Port of Spain, but if you're planning to tour Trinidad, you'll need some wheels, as you will if you end up staying out on the island. In Tobago you're better off renting a four-wheel-drive vehicle than relying on expensive taxi service. On either island, driving is on the left, British-style. Be aware that Tobago has very few gas stations—the main ones are in Crown Point and Scarborough. Be cautious driving on either island, because despite the introduction of the Breathalyzer, many people still take their chances driving after drinking, and erratic driving is the norm rather than the exception.

Tobago Car Rentals Baird's Rentals ✉ *A.N.R. Robinson International Airport, Crown Point, Tobago* ☎ *868/639–7054.* **Rattan's Car Rentals** ✉ *A.N.R. Robinson International Airport, Crown Point, Tobago* ☎ *868/639–8271.* **Rollock's Car Rentals** ✉ *A.N.R. Robinson International Airport, Crown Point, Tobago* ☎ *868/639–0328.* **Thrifty** ✉ *A.N.R. Robinson International Airport, Crown Point, Tobago* ☎ *868/639–8507.*

Trinidad Car Rentals Auto Rentals ✉ *Piarco International Airport, Piarco, Trinidad* ☎ *868/669–2277.* **Southern Sales Car Rentals** ✉ *Piarco International Airport, Piarco, Trinidad* ☎ *868/669–2424, 269 from courtesy phone in airport baggage area.* **Thrifty** ✉ *Piarco International Airport, Piarco, Trinidad* ☎ *868/669–0602.*

TAXI TRAVEL

In Trinidad, taxis are readily available at Piarco Airport; the fare to Port of Spain is set at $50 ($100 after 10 pm). In Tobago the fare from Crown Point Airport to Scarborough or Grafton Beach is about $65. Taxis in Trinidad and Tobago are easily identified by their license plates, which begin with the letter *H*. Passenger vans, called Maxi Taxis, pick up and drop off passengers as they travel (like a bus) and are color-coded according to which of the six areas they cover. Rates are generally less than $1 per trip. (Yellow is for Port of Spain, red for eastern Trinidad, green for south Trinidad, and black for Princes Town. Brown operates from San Fernando to the southeast—Erin, Penal, Point Fortin. The only color for Tobago is blue.) They're easy to hail day or night along most of the main roads near Port of Spain. For longer trips you need to hire a private taxi. Cabs aren't metered, and hotel taxis can be expensive.

ESSENTIALS

Banks and Exchange Services At this writing, the exchange rate for the Trinidadian dollar (TT$) is about TT$6.40 to US$1. Most businesses on the islands will accept U.S. currency and credit cards are almost universally accepted. Though foreign ATM cards can be used to withdraw cash from ATM machines they will not work for retail purchases. There are far fewer bank branches in Tobago than in Trinidad. Trinidad has ATMs in all but the most remote areas. In Tobago there are only a few in Scarborough and at the airport in Crown Point.

Electricity 110 volts/60 cycles (U.S. standard).

Emergency Services Ambulance and Fire ☎ *990.* **Police** ☎ *999.*

Phones The area code for both islands is 868 ("TNT" if you forget). This is also the country code if you're calling to Trinidad and Tobago from another country. From the United States, just dial 1 plus the area code and number. To make a local call to any point in the country, simply dial the seven-digit local number. Most hotels and guesthouses will allow you to dial a direct international call. To dial a number in North

America or the Caribbean, dial 1 and the U.S. or Canadian area code before the number you're calling, but watch out for the hefty surcharge for overseas calls that most hotels add.

Taxes The departure tax is TT$100, but is required by law to be included in the ticket price. All hotels add a 10% government tax. Prices for almost all goods and services include a 15% V.A.T. (value-added tax).

Tipping Almost all hotels will add a 10% to 15% service charge. Most restaurants include a 10% service charge, which is considered standard on these islands. If it isn't on the bill, tip according to service: 10% to 15% is fine. Tip taxi drivers 10%; housekeeping staff $1 to $2 per night.

ACCOMMODATIONS

Resorts in Trinidad are few and far between, and many are a long drive from Port of Spain and the airport. However, a few eco-conscious options are worth the hassle, particularly if you are a bird-watcher. Tobago has many lodging options, and it's a much smaller island with better beaches, so your choice of resort there is driven more by the amenities you want and your budget than by the resort's location.

Beach Resorts: Tobago has a nice mix of midsize resorts, including several offering a fair degree of luxury, but there are also many choices for budget-oriented tourists, as is the case in Trinidad, where fewer tourists mean better value at the small beach resorts that cater primarily to locals. Few hotels on either island offer anything but room-only rates, though there are two all-inclusive resorts on Tobago.

Eco-resorts: An especially good option for nature lovers, particularly bird-watchers, is Trinidad's Asa Wright Nature Centre Lodge. Several of Tobago's small resorts are particularly green.

Hotels: Though they have nice pools and other resort-type amenities, Trinidad's hotels are geared more for business travelers. Options for beachgoers are more limited and farther removed from Port of Spain.

Hotel reviews have been shortened. For full information visit Fodors.com.

WHAT IT COSTS IN U.S. DOLLARS

	$	$$	$$$	$$$$
Restaurants	Under $12	$12–$20	$21–$30	over $30
Hotels	Under $275	$275–$375	$376–$475	over $475

Restaurant prices are the average cost of a main course at dinner or, if dinner is not served, at lunch. Hotel prices are the lowest cost of a standard double room in high season.

SAFETY

Travelers should exercise caution in Trinidad, especially in the highly populated east–west corridor and downtown Port of Spain, where walking on the streets at night is not recommended unless you're with a group. Trinidad has recorded more than 400 homicides annually for the past few years, but these do not generally involve tourists. As a general rule, Tobago is safer than its larger sister island but there have been isolated attacks on tourists over the last few years. There is little visible police presence in most areas of Trinidad. Petty theft occurs on both islands, so don't leave cash or other easy-to-steal valuables in bags that you check at the airport, and use your hotel's safe.

VISITOR INFORMATION

Contacts TDC ✉ *Maritime Centre, Level 1, 9 10th Ave., Barataria* ☎ *868/638-7962* 🌐 *www.tdc.co.tt* ✉ *Piarco International Airport, Piarco, Trinidad* ☎ *868/669-5196.* **Tobago Division of Tourism** ✉ *N.I.B. Mall, Level 3, Wilson St., Scarborough, Tobago* ☎ *868/639-2125* 🌐 *www.visittobago.gov.tt* ✉ *A.N.R. Robinson Airport, Crown Point, Tobago* ☎ *868/639-0509.*

WEDDINGS

There is a three-day residency requirement. A passport, airline ticket, and proof of divorce (if you've been married before) are all required, as is a $55 license fee.

Registrar General ✉ *Jerningham St., Scarborough, Tobago* ☎ *868/639-3210* ✉ *72–74 South Quay, Port of Spain, Trinidad* ☎ *868/624-1660.*

TRINIDAD

EXPLORING

The intensely urban atmosphere of Port of Spain belies the tropical beauty of the countryside surrounding it. You'll need a car and three to eight hours to see all there is to see. Begin by circling the Queen's Park Savannah to Saddle Road, in the residential district of Maraval. After a few miles the road begins to narrow and curve sharply as it climbs into the Northern Range and its undulating hills of dense foliage. Stop at the lookout on North Coast Road; a camera is a must-have here, and be sure to try some of the sweet or savory snacks sold under the tents. You pass a series of lovely beaches, starting with Maracas. From the town of Blanchisseuse there's a winding route to the Asa Wright Nature Centre that takes you through canyons of towering palms, mossy grottoes, and imposing bamboo. In this rain forest keep an eye out for vultures, parakeets, hummingbirds, toucans, and, if you're lucky, maybe red-bellied, yellow-and-blue macaws. Trinidad also has more than 600 native species of butterflies and far more than 1,000 varieties of orchids.

PORT OF SPAIN

Most organized tours begin at the port. If you're planning to explore on foot, which will take two to four hours, start early in the day; by midday the port area can get very hot and crowded. It's best to end your tour on a bench in the Queen's Park Savannah, sipping a cool coconut water bought from one of the vendors operating out of flatbed trucks. For about $2 he'll lop the top off a green coconut with a deft swing of the machete and, when you've finished drinking, lop again, making a bowl and spoon of coconut shell for you to eat the young pulp. Take extra care at night; women should not walk alone. Local police advise tourists and locals to avoid the neighborhoods just east of Port of Spain.

The town's main dock, **King's Wharf,** entertains a steady parade of cruise and cargo ships, a reminder that the city started from this strategic harbor. When hurricanes threaten other islands, it's not unusual to see as many as five large cruise ships taking advantage of the safety of the harbor. It's on Wrightson Road, the main street along the water on the southwest side of town. The government embarked on a massive development plan to turn the area into a vibrant and attractive commercial and tourism zone. Many spanking-new high-rises have already been built, and others are in various stages of completion.

Across Wrightson Road and a few minutes' walk from the south side of King's Wharf, the busy **Independence Square** has been the focus of the downtown area's major gentrification. Flanked by government buildings and the familiar twin towers of the Financial Complex (they adorn all T&T dollar bills), the square (really a long rectangle) is a lovely park with trees, flagstone walkways, chess tables, and the Brian Lara Promenade (named after Trinidad's world-famous cricketer). On its south side is the International Waterfront Centre, with its gleaming skyscrapers and fast-ferry dock. On the eastern end of the square is the Cathedral of the Immaculate Conception; it was by the sea when it was built in 1832, but subsequent landfill around the port gave it an inland location. The imposing Roman Catholic structure is made of blue limestone from nearby Laventille.

Frederick Street, Port of Spain's main shopping drag, starting north from the midpoint of Independence Square, is a market street of scents and sounds—perfumed oils sold by sidewalk vendors and CDs (mostly pirated) being played from vending carts.

At Prince and Frederick Streets, **Woodford Square** has served as the site of political meetings, speeches, public protests, and occasional violence. It's dominated by the magnificent Red House, a Renaissance-style building that takes up an entire city block. Trinidad's House of Parliament takes its name from a paint job done in anticipation of Queen Victoria's Diamond Jubilee in 1897. The original Red House was burned to the ground in a 1903 riot, and the present structure was built four years later. The building is undergoing a multiyear refurbishment, so the parliament is currently using one of the buildings at the International Waterfront Centre for sittings.

The view of the south side of the square is framed by the Gothic spires of Trinity, the city's Anglican cathedral, consecrated in 1823; its mahogany-beam roof is modeled after that of Westminster Hall in London. On the north are the impressive former Public Library, the Hall of Justice, and City Hall.

QUEEN'S PARK SAVANNAH

If the downtown port area is the pulse of Port of Spain, the great green expanse of Queen's Park Savannah, roughly bounded by Maraval Road, Queen's Park West, Charlotte Street, and Saddle Road, is the city's soul. You can walk straight north on Frederick Street and get there within 20 minutes. Its 2-mile (3-km) circumference is a popular jogger's track. The northern end of the Savannah is devoted to plants. A rock garden, known as the Hollows, and a fishpond add to the rusticity. In the middle of the Savannah, you will find a small graveyard where members of the Peschier family—who originally owned the land—are buried. The southern end near the National Academy for the Performing Arts turns into a massive food court every evening. Although the perimeter of the Savannah is busy and safe, you should take care when walking across the park, as there have been occasional reports of muggings. The sheer size of the Savannah makes it difficult for local authorities to patrol, so it is best avoided altogether at night.

A series of astonishing buildings constructed in several 19th-century styles—known collectively as the **Magnificent Seven**—flanks the western side of the Savannah. Notable are Killarney, patterned (loosely) after Balmoral Castle in Scotland, with an Italian-marble gallery surrounding the ground floor; Whitehall, constructed in the style of a Venetian palace by a cacao-plantation magnate and, until recently, the office of the prime minister; Roomor (named for the Roodal and Morgan families—it's still occupied by the Morgans), a flamboyantly baroque colonial house with a preponderance of towers, pinnacles, and wrought-iron trim that suggests an elaborate French pastry; and the Queen's Royal College, in German Renaissance style, with a prominent tower clock that chimes on the hour. Sadly, several of these fine buildings have fallen into advanced decay.

Emperor Valley Zoo & Botanical Gardens. The cultivated expanse of parkland north of the Savannah is the site of the president's and prime minister's official residences and also the Emperor Valley Zoo & Botanical Gardens. A meticulous lattice of walkways and local flora, the parkland was first laid out in 1820 for Governor Ralph Woodford. In the midst of the serene wonderland is the 8-acre zoo, which exhibits mostly birds and animals of the region—including the brilliantly plumed scarlet ibis as well as slithering anacondas and pythons; you can also see (and hear) the wild parrots that breed in the surrounding foliage. Two African giraffes and several big cats were added to the collection in 2013 and have proven to be hugely attractive with locals. The zoo is undergoing a major renovation to make it more of a naturalistic setting. The zoo draws a quarter of a million visitors a year. Tours are free. ✉ *Northern side of Queen's Park Savannah, Port of Spain* ☎ *868/622–3530, 868/622–5343* 🎫 *Zoo TT$30 adults; TT$15 kids under 12, gardens free* ⏲ *Daily 9–6.*

National Academy for the Performing Arts. Head over to the southeast corner of the Savannah, which is dominated by the shiny National Academy for the Performing Arts. It opened in 2009 in time to host the opening ceremony for the Commonwealth Heads of Government Meeting. The Chinese-built structure looks something like a rounded glass-and-metal version of Sydney's famous opera house. ✉ *Queen's Park, Port of Spain.*

National Museum & Art Gallery. Be sure to see the National Museum & Art Gallery, especially its Carnival exhibitions, the Amerindian collection and historical re-creations, and the fine 19th-century paintings of Trinidadian artist Cazabon. Tours are free. ✉ *117 Upper Frederick St., Port of Spain* ☎ *868/623–5941* 🎫 *Free* ⏲ *Tues.–Sat. 10–6, Sun. 2–6.*

CLOSE UP

East Indians in Trinidad

With the abolition of slavery in the British colonies in 1838, many plantation economies such as Trinidad were left looking for alternative sources of cheap labor. Trinidad tried to draw Europeans, but the heat made them ineffective. Attention finally turned to the Indian subcontinent, and in 1845 the first ship of Indian laborers arrived in Trinidad. These indentured workers came mainly from the poorer parts of Uttar Pradesh. They undertook the three-month journey to the New World with the understanding that after their five-year work stint was over, they could re-indenture themselves or return to India. The system stayed in place until 1917.

The Indians proved effective on the sugarcane and cocoa plantations, helping them return to prosperity. In an effort to discourage the Indians from returning home, the colony eventually offered a land grant as an incentive to stay. Many took up the offer and stayed to make new lives in their adopted homeland. Their descendants still maintain many traditions and, to some extent, language. East Indian culture is a vibrant component of T&T's national culture, and you can find Indian festivals and music sharing center stage at all national events. East Indians compose about half the islands' population.

NEARBY PORT OF SPAIN

TOP ATTRACTIONS

Fodor's Choice ★ **Asa Wright Nature Centre.** Nearly 200 acres are covered with plants, trees, and multihued flowers, and the surrounding acreage is atwitter with more than 200 species of birds, including the gorgeous blue-crowned motmot and the rare (and protected) nocturnal oilbird. If you stay at the center's inn for two nights or more, take one of the guided hikes (included in your room price if you are staying here) to the oilbirds' breeding grounds in Dunston Cave (reservations for hikes are essential). Those who don't want to hike can relax on the inn's veranda and watch birds swoop about the porch feeders. You are also more than likely to see a variety of other animal species, including agoutis (similar to large guinea pigs) and alarmingly large golden tegu lizards. This stunning plantation house looks out onto the lush, untouched Arima Valley. Even if you're not staying over, book ahead for lunch (TT$160), offered Monday through Saturday, or for the noontime Sunday buffet (TT$240). The center is an hour outside Blanchisseuse. ✉ *Blanchisseuse Rd., Arima Valley* ☎ *868/667–4655* 🌐 *www.asawright.org* 🎫 *$10* ⏲ *Daily 9–5. Guided tours at 10:30 and 1:30.*

FAMILY **Caroni Bird Sanctuary.** This large swamp with mazelike waterways is bordered by mangrove trees, some plumed with huge termite nests. If you're lucky, you may see lazy caimans idling in the water and large snakes hanging from branches on the banks, taking in the sun. In the middle of the sanctuary are several islets that are home to Trinidad's national bird, the scarlet ibis. Just before sunset the ibis arrive by the thousands, their richly colored feathers brilliant in the gathering dusk, and as more flocks alight, they turn the mangrove foliage a brilliant

More than 200 species of birds can be spotted at the Asa Wright Nature Centre.

scarlet. Bring a sweater and insect repellent. The sanctuary's only official tour operator is Winston Nanan (⇨ *Bird-watching in Sports and the Outdoors*). ✉ *Port of Spain* ✣ *½ hr from Port of Spain; take Churchill Roosevelt Hwy. east to Uriah Butler south; turn right and in about 2 mins, after passing Caroni River Bridge, follow sign for sanctuary* ☎ *868/645–1305* 🎫 *$10* ⏲ *Daily dawn–dusk.*

WORTH NOTING

Chaguaramas Military History & Aerospace Museum. Although this museum covers everything from Amerindian history to the Cold War, the emphasis is on the two World Wars, and it's a must-see for history buffs. The exhibits, on a former U.S. military base, are in a large hangar-like shed without air-conditioning, so dress appropriately. There's a decidedly charming and homemade feel to the place; in fact, most exhibits were made by the curator and founder, Commander Gaylord Kelshall of the T&T Coast Guard. The museum is set a bit off the main road but is easily spotted by the turquoise BWIA L1011 jet parked out front (Trinidad and Tobago's former national airline). ✉ *Western Main Rd., Chaguaramas* ☎ *868/634–4391* 🌐 *www.militarymuseumtt.com* 🎫 *TT$30* ⏲ *Mon.–Sat. 9–5.*

FAMILY **Dattatreya Yoga Centre.** This impressive temple site was constructed by artisans brought in from India. It is well worth a visit to admire the intricate architectural details of the main temple, learn about Trinidad Hinduism, and marvel at the towering 85-foot statue of the monkey deity, Hanuman. Krishna Ramsaran, the compound manager, is extremely helpful and proud to explain the history of the center and the significance of the various *murtis* (sacred statues). Kids are welcome, so this makes for a pleasant and educational family outing (kids seem especially interested in the giant elephant statues that guard the temple doors). This is a religious site, so appropriate clothing is required (no shorts), and shoes must be left outside the temple door. It's fine to take pictures of the statue and the temple exterior and grounds, but permission is required to take pictures inside, as it's an active place of worship. The temple is half an hour from Port of Spain; take Churchill Roosevelt Highway east to Uriah Butler south; turn right until the Chase Village flyover (overpass); follow the signs south to Waterloo; then follow signs to the temple. ✉ *Datta Dr. at Orangefield Rd., Carapichaima* ☎ *868/673–5328* 🎫 *Free* 🕒 *Daily dawn–dusk, services daily.*

FAMILY **Galera Point Lighthouse.** This essential stop when touring the northeast was constructed in 1897 on a stunning cliff. It's still used to warn ships about the rough waters below, the point where the Atlantic Ocean and Caribbean Sea meet. You can walk out onto a nearby rocky outcropping that marks Trinidad's easternmost point. On most days Tobago is clearly visible from here. A local legend (unprovable) tells that a group of Arawaks jumped off this point to their deaths rather than be captured by the Spanish. You'll pass several beautiful beaches on the drive from Toco to the lighthouse. The journey from Port of Spain takes about two hours; take Churchill Roosevelt Highway east to Valencia Road; follow the road east to Toco Main Road sign; take this road all the way to Toco; from the Toco intersection, follow the sign to Galera Point. ✉ *Galera Rd., 3 miles (5 km) from triangular Toco intersection* 🎫 *Free* 🕒 *Daily dawn–dusk.*

Lopinot Complex. It's said that the ghost of the French count Charles Joseph de Lopinot prowls his former home on stormy nights. Lopinot came to Trinidad in 1800 and chose this magnificent site to plant cocoa. His restored estate house has been turned into a museum—a guide is available from 10 to 6—and a center for *parang*, the Venezuelan-derived folk music. Although worthwhile for those interested in the finer points of Trinidad history, this may not be worth the long and winding drive for most visitors. ✉ *Lopinot Rd.* ✣ *Take Eastern Main Rd. from Port of Spain to Arouca; look for sign that points north* 🎫 *Free* 🕒 *Daily 6–6.*

BEACHES

Trinidad has some good beaches for swimming and sunning, particularly on the north coast, though none as picture perfect as those in Tobago. Although popular with some locals, the beaches of the western peninsula (such as Maqueripe) are not particularly attractive. All beaches on Trinidad are free and open to the public. Many locals are fond of playing loud music wherever they go, and even the most serene beach may suddenly turn into a seaside party.

Balandra Bay. On the northeast coast, this beige-sand beach—popular with locals on weekends—is sheltered by a rocky outcropping and is a favorite of bodysurfers. Much of the beach is suitable for swimming. It can be rather noisy on the weekends. Take the Toco Main Road from the Valencia Road, and turn off at the signs indicating Balandra (just

CLOSE UP

The Steel Pan

The sound of a steel pan playing poolside has become emblematic of the Caribbean. What you may not know is that the fascinating instrument has an interesting and humble history that began in Trinidad.

In 1883 the British government banned the playing of drums on the island, fearful that they were being used to carry secret messages. Enterprising Afro-Trinidadians immediately found other means of creating music. Some turned to cut bamboo poles beaten rhythmically on the ground; these were called Tambu Bamboo bands, and they soon became a major musical force on the island. With the coming of industry, new materials such as hubcaps and biscuit tins were added as "instruments" in the bands. These metal additions were collectively known as "pan." Later, after the Americans established military bases on the islands during World War II, empty oil drums became available and were quickly put to musical use.

At some point it was discovered that these drums could be cut down, heated in a fire, and beaten into a finely tuned instrument. The steel pan as we know it was thus born. Soon there were entire musical bands playing nothing but steel pans. For years the music gestated in the poorer districts of Port of Spain and was seen as being suitable only for the lower classes of society, a reputation not helped by the fact that the loyal followers of early steel bands sometimes clashed violently with their rivals. Eventually, the magical sound of the pan and its amazing ability to adapt to any type of music won it widespread acceptance.

Today the government recognizes the steel pan as the official musical instrument of Trinidad and Tobago. It's played year-round at official functions and social gatherings, but the true time for the steel pan is Carnival. In the annual Panorama festival, scores of steel bands from around the country compete for the "Band of the Year" title. Some have fewer than a dozen steel pans, whereas others number in the hundreds. The performance of the larger bands creates a thunderous wall of sound.

after Salybia). **Amenities:** lifeguards. **Best for:** surfing; swimming. ✉ *Off Valencia Rd. near Salybia.*

Blanchisseuse Bay. The facilities are nonexistent at this narrow, palm-fringed beach, but it's an ideal spot for a romantic picnic. A lagoon and river at the east end of the beach allow you to swim in fresh water, but beware of floating logs in the river, as they sometimes contain mites that can cause a body rash (called *bete rouge* locally). You can haggle with local fishermen to take you out in their boats to explore the coast. This beach is about 14 miles (23 km) after Maracas; just keep driving along the road until you pass the Arima turnoff. The coastal and rain-forest views here are spectacular. **Amenities:** none. **Best for:** swimming; walking. ✉ *North Coast Rd. just beyond Arima turnoff.*

NEED A BREAK?

Kay's Pot. On the long drive to Point Galera, be sure to stop at Kay's Pot for a great meal en route. Many consider it worth the drive all by itself. In

The steel pan is the official musical instrument of Trinidad and Tobago.

a corner of the front parking lot of Arthur's Grocery and Bar, Kay serves an incredible array of local food such as *souse* (pickled pigs' feet in a lime-and-cucumber sauce), curried crab, and many kinds of grilled and jerk meats. The informal atmosphere, low prices, and music pouring out of the bar make for a fun and unusual dining experience. ✉ ***Toco Main Rd., Rampanalgas.***

Grande Riviere. On Trinidad's rugged northeast coast, Grande Riviere is well worth the drive. Swimming is good, and there are several guesthouses nearby for refreshments, but the main attractions here are turtles. Every year up to 500 giant leatherback turtles a night come onto the beach to lay their eggs. If you're here at night, run your hand through the black sand to make it glow—a phenomenon caused by plankton. **Amenities:** food and drink. **Best for:** swimming; walking. ✉ *End of Toco Main Rd., Grande Riviere.*

Las Cuevas Bay. This narrow, picturesque strip on North Coast Road is named for the series of partially submerged and explorable caves that ring the beach. A food stand offers tasty snacks, and vendors hawk fresh fruit across the road. You can also buy fresh fish and lobster from the fishing depot near the beach. You have to park your car in the small parking lot and walk down a few steps to get to the beach, so be sure to take everything from the car (it will be out of sight once you are on the beach). There are basic changing and toilet facilities. It's less crowded here than at nearby Maracas Bay and seemingly serene, although, as at Maracas, the current can be treacherous. **Amenities:** food and drink;

parking; toilets. **Best for:** swimming; walking. ✉ *North Coast Rd., 7 miles (11 km) east of Maracas Bay.*

Manzanilla Beach. You can find picnic facilities and a pretty view of the Atlantic here, though the water is occasionally muddied by Venezuela's Orinoco River. The Cocal Road running the length of this beautiful beach is lined with stately palms. This is where many well-heeled Trinis have vacation houses. The Nariva River, which enters the sea just south of this beach and the surrounding Nariva Swamp, is home to the manatee and other rare species, including the much-maligned anaconda. To get here take the Mayaro turnoff at the town of Sangre Grande. Manzanilla is where this road first meets the coast. The road was badly damaged following heavy rains at the end of 2014 but is expected to be completely restored by early 2015. **Amenities:** food and drink; lifeguards. **Best for:** sunrise; walking. ✉ *Southeast of Sangre Grande.*

BAKE AND SHARK

Maracas Bay in Trinidad is famous for its bake and shark (about $5), a deep-fried piece of shark stuffed into fried homemade bread. To this, you can add any of dozens of toppings, such as tamarind sauce and coleslaw. Local conservationists have expressed concern about the depletion of the shark population in recent years, so ordering a bake and kingfish might be a "greener" option. There are dozens of beach huts serving the specialty, as well as stands in the nearby parking lot. Richard's is by far the most popular.

25

Fodor's Choice ★ **Maracas Bay.** This stretch of peach-colored sand has a cove and a fishing village at one end. It's the local favorite, so it can get crowded on weekends. Lifeguards will guide you away from strong currents. Parking sites are ample, and there are snack bars selling the famous bake and shark, a must-try. Take the winding North Coast Road from Maraval (it intersects with Long Circular Road right next to KFC Maraval) over the Northern Range; the beach is about 7 miles (11 km) from Maraval. **Amenities:** food and drink; lifeguards; parking; toilets. **Best for:** partiers; swimming; walking. ✉ *North Coast Rd.*

Salibea Bay (Salybia Bay). This gentle beach has shallows and plenty of shade—perfect for swimming. Snack vendors abound in the vicinity. Like many of the beaches on the northeast coast, this one is packed with people and music trucks blaring soca and reggae on weekends. It's off the Toco Main Road, just after the town of Matura. **Amenities:** food and drink; parking; toilets. **Best for:** partiers; swimming; walking. ✉ *Off Toco Main Rd. south of Toco.*

WHERE TO EAT

The food on T&T is a delight to the senses and has a distinctively creole touch, though everyone has a different idea about what creole seasoning is (just ask around, and you'll see). Bountiful herbs and spices include bay leaf, chadon bene (aka culantro, and similar in taste to cilantro), nutmeg, turmeric, and different varieties of peppers. The cooking also involves a lot of brown sugar, rum, plantain, and local fish and meat.

If there's fresh juice on the menu, be sure to try it. You can taste Asian, Indian, African, French, and Spanish influences, among others, often in a single meal. Indian-inspired food is a favorite: rotis (ample sandwiches of soft dough with a filling, similar to a wrap) are served as a fast food; a mélange of curried meat or fish and vegetables frequently makes an appearance, as do vindaloos (spicy meat, vegetable, and seafood dishes). Pelau (rice, peas, and meat stewed in coconut milk) is another local favorite. Crab lovers will find large bluebacks curried, peppered, or in callaloo (Trinidad's national dish), a stew made with green dasheen leaves, okra, and coconut milk. Shark and bake (lightly seasoned, fried shark meat) is the sandwich of choice at the beach.

What to Wear. Restaurants are informal: you won't find any jacket-and-tie requirements. Beachwear, however, is too casual for most places. A nice pair of shorts is appropriate for lunch, and pants or sundresses are probably a better choice for dinner.

$$$$ MEDITERRANEAN Fodor's Choice ★

Aioli. Executive Chef and owner Johnny Aboud set a new benchmark for fine dining and attentive service in Trinidad when he opened Aioli. Deep earth tones and subtle lighting make the interior of the restaurant seem miles away from its location in an upscale suburban mall. The Mediterranean-inspired menu features beautifully presented dishes ranging from reasonable risottos to extravagant favorites like Magret de Canard (a crispy duck breast). While Caribbean spiny lobster is the norm in most restaurants in T&T, fans of Maine lobster will find their beloved crustacean on offer here. Budget-minded diners can opt for the tapas menus offered on Thursdays and Fridays. The three-course lunch is prix fixe ($35) from Monday to Wednesday. *Average main: $35* ✉ *Ellerslie Plaza, Maraval* ☎ *868/222–4564* *Closed Sun. No lunch weekends.*

$$$$ ITALIAN

Angelo's. Calabrian chef Angelo Cofone married a Trinidadian and soon found himself in the restaurant business. Popular with locals and visiting businesspeople alike, Angelo's has an innovative Italian menu that changes regularly, and there's always a daily special. The restaurant is on Ariapita Avenue, which locals now refer to as the strip or simply "The Avenue." *Average main: $32* ✉ *38 Ariapita Ave., Woodbrook, Port of Spain* ☎ *868/628–5551* *Closed Sun. No lunch Sat.*

$$$$ INDIAN

Apsara. This upscale Indian eatery is one of the few in Trinidad that features genuine Indian cuisine and not the local (though equally tasty) version. The name means "celestial dancer," and the food here is indeed heavenly. At the time of writing, the restaurant is undergoing renovations and has been temporarily relocated upstairs in the Tamnak Thai section of the building. The inviting terra-cotta interior is decorated with hand-painted interpretations of Moghul art. Choosing dishes from the comprehensive menu is a bit daunting, so don't be afraid to ask for help. The *Husseini boti kebab* (lamb marinated in poppy seeds and masala) is an excellent choice. Service can be a bit slow at times, and the prices are fairly high. *Average main: $43* ✉ *13 Queen's Park E, Belmont, Port of Spain* ☎ *868/627–7364, 868/623–7659* *Closed Sun.*

$$ ITALIAN Fodor's Choice ★ **Buzo Osteria Italiana.** This chic eatery and bar is tucked away on a side street in the Newtown area of uptown Port of Spain, but every taxi driver in town will know where it is. Italian chef-patron Cristian Grini always has a selection of classic Italian favorites on offer—the authentic pizza is probably the best on the island and is surprisingly affordable. The bar attracts young professionals and local hipsters who come for the excellent cocktails and late-night desserts. This restaurant is associated with the even more upscale Prime Restaurant, so the service is impeccable. *Average main: $17 6A Warner St., Port of Spain 868/223–2896 Reservations essential.*

$$$$ ECLECTIC Fodor's Choice ★ **Chaud.** Style meets substance at veteran chef Khalid Mohammed's restaurant. The restaurant moved from its Queen's Park Savannah location to a quiet nearby suburb in January 2015. Famous for his extravagance, Mohammed presents food that rises off the plate like a Manhattan skyscraper. There is an obsession with freshness here, and satisfaction is virtually guaranteed. Although the prices are high, it's well worth it for a special romantic evening. Those on a budget might want to try a meal at its sister property Chaud Café located at 1 Woodbrook Place. *Average main: $43 6 Nook Ave., St. Ann's, Port of Spain 868/623–0375 www.chaudkm.com Reservations essential Closed Sun. No lunch Sat.*

$$$ ECLECTIC Fodor's Choice ★ **Joseph's.** Lebanese-born chef Joseph Habr has been serving fine cuisine at his Maraval location for over a decade and has more than 25 years of experience under his belt. The restaurant is a lovely open affair with a dining room that looks out on a lush garden—complete with the sound of flowing water. Joseph visits every table and is always happy to offer helpful advice. The menu is comprehensive, and somehow there seems to be an Arabic element in even seemingly conventional dishes. If in doubt, it's impossible to go wrong with any of the lamb offerings. The truly adventurous may special order Joseph's renowned *kibbeh nayeh*—a generous portion of Lebanese lamb tartare. *Average main: $29 3A Rookery Nook, Maraval, Port of Spain Take Saddle Rd. into Maraval and follow it to RBTT Bank. Rookery Nook is on left 868/622–5557 Closed Sun. No lunch Sat.*

$$$ ECLECTIC **Mélange.** Some of the most imaginative food on the island is to be found at this elegant establishment on restaurant row. Chef and owner Moses Ruben uses his years of experience as head chef at the Hilton to create delightfully balanced meals. The tuna or steak *river rock* appetizer is prepared on a seasoned hot stone at the table and makes for a dramatic photo op. There's also a good selection of sushi on offer. *Average main: $29 40 Ariapita Ave., Woodbrook, Port of Spain 868/628–8687 Closed Sun. No lunch Sat. No dinner Mon.*

$$$ JAPANESE **More Vino More Sushi.** This popular after-work drinking and dining spot serves consistently excellent sushi. This was the first sushi establishment on the popular dining strip known to locals as "The Avenue." Choose to dine on the wooden outdoor deck and take in the sights (and traffic sounds) of Ariapita Avenue or sit indoors for a cooler and more intimate experience with a view of the sushi masters at work. *Average main: $28 23 O'Connor St., at Ariapita Ave., Port of Spain 868/622–8466 www.morevino.com Closed Sun.*

$$$$ ECLECTIC **Prime Restaurant.** Occupying the ground floor of the BHP Billiton tower, this upscale establishment caters to businesspeople armed with large expense accounts and demanding tastes. The subtle lighting, understated decor, and attentive staff also make this the ideal spot for a romantic dinner or a special-occasion splurge. Though a variety of options are available, most diners come for the excellent Angus steaks, and not without reason. The wine cellar is one of the best on the island, and a well-chosen vintage may help take some of the edge off the inevitably large bill. The restaurant is behind the Marriott and next door to the Movietowne complex. *Average main: $60 Ground fl., BHP Billiton Bldg., Invaders Bay 868/624–6238 www.trentrestaurants.com/prime Reservations essential Closed Sun.*

$$$ ASIAN **Tiki Village.** Port of Spainers in the know flock to the eighth floor of the Kapok Hotel, where the views of the city from this teak-lined dining room are simply spectacular, day and night. The solid menu includes the best of Polynesian and Asian fare. The Sunday dim sum—with tasting-size portions of dishes such as pepper squid and tofu-stuffed fish—is very popular. *Average main: $30 Kapok Hotel, 16–18 Cotton Hill, St. Clair, Port of Spain 868/622–5765 www.kapokhotel.com/dining No dinner Sun.–Tues. No lunch Mon. and Tues.*

$$ ECLECTIC **Town Retaurant & Bar.** Though the menu is skewed towards Chinese cuisine, this extremely popular eatery on Cipriani Boulevard offers everything from ravioli to lobster Thermidor. Young professionals flock here on evenings to enjoy the lively atmosphere, attentive but laid-back service, and consistently good (and reasonably priced) food. Parking is always an issue in the area, but don't be fooled by the men on the roadside offering to find you a parking spot and "look after your car" for a price. It's also a great place to enjoy a cocktail or two. *Average main: $19 51 Cipriani Blvd., Tunapuna 868/627-8696 www.towntrinidad.com Closed Sun.*

$$$ AMERICAN **Trotters.** Although Trinidad has many American sports-bar chain restaurants, this local version easily beats them at their own game. There is often a lively crowd watching the more than 20 giant screens featuring all the latest in soccer and international sports. The huge square bar in the middle of the restaurant is where folks gather. Dining areas branch off from the bar area, and though some are more isolated than others, it is virtually impossible to escape the cheers of the throng of sports enthusiasts. The food includes excellent burgers, hearty salads, and Italian favorites and steaks. The standard is consistently excellent, and the servers, bedecked in pins and wearing safari hats, are efficient and attentive. *Average main: $22 Maraval Rd. at Sweetbriar Rd., St. Clair 868/627–8768 www.trotters.net.*

$$$ CARIBBEAN FAMILY Fodor's Choice ★ **Veni Mangé.** The best lunches in town are served in this traditional West Indian house. The restaurant is the creation of Rosemary (Roses) Hezekiah and her late sister, Allyson Hennessy—a Cordon Bleu–trained chef who was a local television celebrity. The creative creole menu changes regularly, but there's always an unusual and delicious vegetarian entrée (Roses is vegetarian). Veni's version of Trinidad's national dish, callaloo, is considered one of the best on the island. The *chip chip* (a small local clam) cocktail is deliciously piquant and is a restaurant

rarity. The restaurant's signature dish, stewed oxtail with dumplings, is not served every day but is worth ordering if it's available. The bar area is a popular hangout for local artists and sports celebrities. If you can only visit one restaurant and want to get a truly Trinidadian experience this is the place. *Average main: $25 ✉ 67A Ariapita Ave., Woodbrook, Port of Spain ☎ 868/624–4597 🌐 www.venimange.com ⊗ Closed weekends. No dinner Mon., Tues., and Thurs.*

$ CARIBBEAN **Wings Restaurant & Bar.** Rum shops and good food are an intrinsic part of Trinidad life, and both are combined in this colorful eatery, which is open from 10 to 6. Regulars from the nearby university and industrial park flock here at lunchtime to enjoy a wide selection of local Indian food. It can get a bit loud, but at least there are fans to keep the heat under control—just barely. If the atmosphere is a bit too much there's always the option of takeout. To get here, turn off the Churchill Roosevelt Highway at the FedEx building (north side of the highway) in Tunapuna, and take the first left. *Average main: $8 ✉ 16 Mohammed Terr., Tunapuna ☎ 868/645–6607 ▭ No credit cards ⊗ Closed Sun. No dinner.*

25

WHERE TO STAY

Because Trinidad is primarily a business destination, most accommodations are in or near Port of Spain. Standards are generally good, though not lavish. Port of Spain has a small downtown core—with a main shopping area along Frederick Street—and is surrounded by inner and outer suburbs. The inner areas include Belmont, Woodbrook, Newtown, St. Clair, St. Ann's, St. James, and Cascade. The nearest beach to most hotels is Maracas Bay, which is a half-hour drive over the mountains. Carnival visitors should book many months in advance and be prepared to pay top dollar for even the most modest hotel.

$$$ HOTEL **Asa Wright Nature Centre Lodge.** This hotel, an hour's drive from the nearest beach or town, is designed for serious bird-watchers and is surrounded by 200 acres of wilderness, streams, waterfalls, and natural pools. **Pros:** best bird-watching on the island; main house has a wonderful colonial feel; peaceful setting. **Cons:** miles from anything else on the island; no dining choices; the lack of entertainment options at night can be unnerving; no shopping for miles. *Rooms from: $430 ✉ Blanchisseuse Rd., Arima Valley ☎ 868/667–4655, 800/426–7781 🌐 www.asawright.org 24 rooms All meals.*

$ HOTEL **The Carlton Savannah.** Those looking for a boutique hotel at a reasonable price away from the noise of downtown may find this property the perfect fit. **Pros:** convenient and quiet location; free Wi-Fi; stylish, modern feeling. **Cons:** not within walking distance of shopping; while staff are eager, the service can sometimes be erratic and even infuriating. *Rooms from: $120 ✉ 2–4 Coblentz Ave., Cascade ☎ 868/621–5000 🌐 www.thecarltonsavannah.com 155 rooms, 10 suites No meals.*

$ HOTEL **Coblentz Inn.** Just a short drive from downtown in the quiet suburb of Cascade, this small boutique hotel offers peace, quiet, and style at a relatively affordable price. **Pros:** rooms have genuine charm; small but attentive staff; common areas are relaxing and great for catching up on reading. **Cons:** restaurant's food can be unreliable; small compound can feel cramped; no pool on compound. *Rooms from: $145 ✉ 44 Coblentz Ave., Cascade, Port of Spain ☎ 868/621–0541 www.coblentzinn.com 17 rooms Breakfast.*

$ HOTEL **Courtyard by Marriott.** This large hotel in the capital offers excellent facilities and a great location. **Pros:** excellent location for shopping and dining; large and airy rooms; high service standards. **Cons:** just off busy highway; the many business travelers can make it feel a bit uncomfortable for leisure guests. *Rooms from: $194 ✉ Invaders Bay, Audrey Jeffers Hwy., Port of Spain ☎ 868/627–5555 www.marriott.com 116 rooms, 3 suites No meals.*

$ HOTEL **Crews Inn Hotel & Yachting Centre.** On Trinidad's western peninsula, this hotel is in the middle of the island's main yachting marina, about 20 minutes from downtown. **Pros:** great view of marina; airy rooms are tastefully decorated and very large; great for yachting enthusiasts. **Cons:** far from Port of Spain; limited shopping and dining nearby. *Rooms from: $224 ✉ Point Gourde, Chaguaramas ☎ 868/634–4384 www.crewsinn.com 42 rooms, 4 suites Breakfast.*

$ HOTEL **Hilton Trinidad & Conference Centre.** The Hilton was the most upscale hotel on the island before the arrival of the Hyatt Regency, and it still commands a loyal following. **Pros:** great view; contemporary rooms; full range of hotel services; reliable and consistent service; the thrill of saying you stayed at the hotel where the U.S. president stayed. **Cons:** pool area can get very lively—especially at Carnival time; taxi ride needed to get to shopping; Wi–Fi isn't free. *Rooms from: $179 ✉ Lady Young Rd., Port of Spain ☎ 868/624–3211, 800/445–8667 in U.S. www.hiltoncaribbean.com 385 rooms, 27 suites No meals.*

$ HOTEL **Holiday Inn Express & Suites Trincity.** Just five minutes from the airport and with a complimentary shuttle service before midnight, this handy hotel is popular with short-stay travelers. **Pros:** convenient to the airport; close to Trincity Mall (free shuttle available). **Cons:** not close to the major urban centers; nearby traffic can be horrendous; no restaurant on property; has that bland chain-hotel feeling. *Rooms from: $139 ✉ 1 Exposition Dr., Trincity ☎ 868/669–6209 www.ichotelsgroup.com 62 rooms, 20 suites Breakfast.*

$ HOTEL Fodor'sChoice ★ **Hyatt Regency Trinidad.** Trinidad's only full-service hotel on the waterfront is a striking high-rise structure and part of the government's dramatic makeover of the Port of Spain waterfront. **Pros:** easily the most upscale full-service hotel on the island; view from the rooftop pool is unbeatable; convenient to downtown and shopping; excellent restaurants. **Cons:** right on the city's busiest commuter road; waterfront area is usually teeming with people; Wi-Fi not free. *Rooms from: $219 ✉ 1 Wrightson Rd., Port of Spain ☎ 868/623–2222 trinidad.hyatt.com 418 rooms, 10 suites No meals.*

$ HOTEL **Kapok Hotel.** In a good neighborhood just off Queen's Park Savannah, the Kapok is a good all-around value if you want to stay in the city; it offers a high level of comfort and service. **Pros:** great location away from downtown noise; walking distance to shopping; smaller alternative to Hilton and Hyatt; one of the best restaurants on the island. **Cons:** lacks some of the services of larger hotels; some rooms are much smaller than others; pool is a bit small. *Rooms from: $149* ✉ *16–18 Cotton Hill, St. Clair, Port of Spain* ☎ *868/622–5765, 800/344–1212* *www.kapokhotel.com* *73 rooms, 12 suites, 9 studios* *No meals.*

$ B&B/INN **Le Grande Almandier.** This low-priced hotel is on Trinidad's remote and beautiful northeast coast in an area that is a popular weekend escape for locals seeking a lush rain-forest backdrop and expansive beach. **Pros:** right on the beach; great for turtle-watching in season; small, with a friendly-family vibe; Wi-Fi. **Cons:** far from the capital; no bar, and restaurant serves only wine; limited shopping and dining options; car is definitely required for any exploring. *Rooms from: $151* ✉ *2 Hosang St., Grande Riviere* ☎ *868/670–1013* *www.legrandealmandier.com* *10 rooms* *Breakfast.*

$ B&B/INN **Monique's.** Spacious but simple rooms and proximity to Port of Spain ensure the popularity of this guesthouse, which consists of two separate buildings. **Pros:** huge rooms; in a generally quiet area; family ownership shows in the concern for the comfort of guests; on the main road to Maracas Beach. **Cons:** rooms feel dated; no bar; not within walking distance of shopping or dining; neighborhood dogs can get noisy at night. *Rooms from: $90* ✉ *114–116 Saddle Rd., Maraval, Port of Spain* ☎ *868/628–3334, 868/628–2351* *www.moniquestrinidad.com* *20 rooms* *Breakfast.*

$ HOTEL **Radisson Trinidad.** Trinidad's newest downtown hotel features the largest rooms on the island in a completely renovated property that has housed other hotels in the past. **Pros:** close to downtown and the business core; much cheaper than the Hyatt even though it is quite literally across the road; 24-hour room service; free Wi-Fi. **Cons:** there's traffic noise by the pool area; located on Port of Spain's most traffic congested roadway. *Rooms from: $152* ✉ *Wrightson Rd., Port of Spain* ☎ *868/625–3366* *www.radisson.com* *243 rooms, 12 suites* *Breakfast.*

NIGHTLIFE AND PERFORMING ARTS

NIGHTLIFE

There's no lack of nightlife in Port of Spain, and spontaneity plays a big role—around Carnival time look for the handwritten signs announcing the "Panyard," where the next informal gathering of steel-drum bands is going to be. Gay and lesbian travelers can take advantage of an increasingly lively gay scene in Trinidad, with parties drawing upward of 200 people on most weekends.

51° Lounge. At this stylish club, there's entertainment on most nights, and Thursday is always packed to the rafters (go after 11 if you want to avoid the karaoke crowd). Don't even think about showing up in shorts, as there's a strict "elegant casual" dress code. Admission varies and sometimes requires an invitation be picked up ahead of time, so call ahead—and be prepared to stand in line for a bit. ✉ *51 Cipriani Blvd., Woodbrook, Port of Spain* ☎ *868/627–0051.*

Aria Lounge. This is Ariapita's most popular hot spot for the well-heeled crowd on a weekend. Music goes on well into the night and the drink of choice is vintage champagne. There is a strict dress code in effect so no shorts, and tank tops are a definite no-no. ✉ *Cor. Fitt St. & Ariapita Ave., Woodbrook, Port of Spain* ☎ *868/225–2742.*

Coco Lounge. This busy hangout on the popular Ariapita Avenue strip caters to upscale nightlifers who come to sip cocktails in the elegant, modern-plantation-style interior or watch the world go by from the huge veranda. ✉ *35 Carlos St., Woodbrook, Port of Spain* ☎ *868/622–6137.*

De Nu Pub (Mas Camp Pub). Port of Spain's most dependable nightspot for local entertainment and color features a large stage where a DJ or live band reigns, along with an ample bar and a kitchen that serves reasonably priced creole lunches. ✉ *Ariapita Ave. at French St., Woodbrook, Port of Spain* ☎ *868/627–4042.*

Drink! Wine Bar. A large and varied selection of wines and reasonably priced nibbles makes this cozy lounge popular with locals and visitors alike. There are snacks on offer and frequent performances from visiting DJs and musicians. It's a great place to meet members of the local arts community. ✉ *63 Rosalino St., Woodbrook, Port of Spain* ☎ *868/622–2895* ⊙ *Closed Mon.*

More Vino. Young professionals head here to network while sipping one of the more than 100 varieties of wine. Although most people choose to sit outside during the evening, seating is also available in the air-conditioned interior. Inside, you will also find an astonishing number of bottles on display for consumption on the premises or to take away. Cheeses and other items for nibbling are also available. Smoking is allowed on the deck and cigars are sold here. ✉ *23 O'Connor St., Woodbrook, Port of Spain* ☎ *868/622–8466.*

Trotters. An abundance of TV screens, as well as more than 30 varieties of beer from around the globe, await at this sports bar in a two-story atrium. It's incredibly popular on weekends—despite the pricey drinks. It's also one of the few establishments on the island that offers a free ride home for any patron who feels too intoxicated to drive. ✉ *Maraval Rd. at Sweetbriar Rd., St. Clair, Port of Spain* ☎ *868/627–8768.*

Zen. What was once a movie theater now holds a very popular club with a stylish interior and a varied crowd. On the balcony is a VIP area (open to anyone who pays the extra admission charge) where the well-heeled keep track of the action on the dance floor below. The beat goes on until the sun comes up. The club underwent a major renovation in 2014. ✉ *9–11 Keate St., Port of Spain* ☎ *868/625–9936.*

Tzar Nightlife. This new club on The Avenue draws a lively and well-heeled crowd on Friday and Saturday nights. Hit the dance floor or just relax on one of the many couches and enjoy the specialty cocktails. ✉ *33 Carlos Street, Woodbrook, Port of Spain* ☎ *868/684–8927.*

CARNIVAL

Fodor's Choice ★ Trinidad always seems to be anticipating, celebrating, or recovering from a festival. Visitors are welcome at these events, which are a great way to explore the island's rich cultural traditions.

Trinidad's version of the pre-Lenten bacchanal may be the oldest in the Western Hemisphere; there are festivities all over the country, but the most lavish are in Port of Spain. Trinidad's Carnival has the warmth and character of a massive family reunion and is billed by locals (not unreasonably) as "The Greatest Show on Earth." The season begins right after Christmas, and the parties, called *fêtes,* don't stop until Ash Wednesday. Listen to a radio station or go online for five minutes, and you can find out where the action is. The Carnival event itself officially lasts only two days, from *J'ouvert* (2 am) on Monday to midnight the following day, Carnival Tuesday. But if you really want to *experience* Carnival, then you need to arrive in Trinidad a week or two early to enjoy the preliminary events. (Hotels fill up quickly, so be sure to make reservations months in advance, and be prepared to pay premium prices for a minimum five-night stay. Even bedrooms in private houses have been known to go for as much as $300 per night.) If you visit during Carnival, try to get tickets to one of the all-inclusive parties where thousands of people eat and drink to the sound of music all night long. And although the festivities are mostly of the adult variety, children can parade in a kiddie carnival that takes place on the Saturday morning the week before the official events.

Carnival is a showcase for performers of calypso, which mixes dance rhythms with social commentary—sung by characters with such evocative names as Shadow, the Mighty Sparrow, and Black Stalin—and soca, which fuses calypso with a driving dance beat. As Carnival approaches, many of these singers perform nightly in calypso tents around the city. Many hotels also have special concerts by popular local musicians. You can also visit the city's "panyards," where steel orchestras such as the Renegades, Desperadoes, Neal and Massy All-Stars, Invaders, and Phase II rehearse their musical arrangements (most can also be heard during the winter season).

From the Sunday before Lent until midnight on Carnival Tuesday, when Port of Spain's exhausted merrymakers finally go to bed, it's basically one big nonstop party. The next day, feet are sore, but spirits have been refreshed. Lent (and theoretical sobriety) takes over for a while.

SHOPPING

Good buys in Trinidad include Angostura bitters, Old Oak or Vat 19 rum, and leather goods, all widely available throughout the country. Thanks in large part to the costumes needed for Carnival, there's no shortage of fabric shops. The best bargains for Asian and East Indian silks and cottons can be found in downtown Port of Spain, on Frederick Street and around Independence Square. Recordings of local calypsonians and steel-pan performances as well as *chutney* (local East Indian music) are available throughout the islands and make great gifts. Note that duty-free goods are available only at the airport upon departure or arrival.

AREAS AND MALLS

Downtown Port of Spain, specifically **Frederick, Queen,** and **Henry Streets,** is full of fabrics and shoes. **Ellerslie Plaza** is an attractive outdoor mall well worth a browse. **Excellent City Centre** is set in an old-style oasis under the lantern roofs of three of downtown's oldest commercial buildings. Look for cleverly designed keepsakes, trendy cotton clothes, and original artwork. The upstairs food court overlooks bustling Frederick Street. The **Falls at West Mall,** just west of Port of Spain, is a dazzling temple to upscale shopping that could hold its own anywhere in the world. **Long Circular Mall** has upscale boutiques that are great for window-shopping. **Trincity Mall,** near the airport, is the largest mall on the island and has everything from souvenirs to high-end fashion. The **Market at the Normandie Hotel** is a small collection of shops that specialize in indigenous fashions, crafts, jewelry, basketwork, and ceramics. You can also have afternoon tea in the elegant little café.

CLOTHING

Meiling. Acclaimed local designer Meiling Esau showcases her classically detailed Caribbean resort clothing here. ✉ *6 Carlos St., Woodbrook, Port of Spain* ☎ *868/627–6975.*

Radical. Radical is a good spot for T-shirts and original men's and women's casual clothing. ✉ *The Falls at West Mall, Western Main Rd., Westmoorings* ☎ *868/632–5800.* ✉ *Excellent City Centre, Independence Sq., Port of Spain* ☎ *868/627–6110*

DUTY-FREE GOODS

De Lima's. All the traditional duty-free luxury goods are available from De Lima's. ✉ *Piarco International Airport, Piarco* ☎ *868/669–4738.*

Stecher's. The branch at Ellerslie Plaza in Maraval carries only perfumes and cosmetics, but the Stecher's at the airport also carries china, crystal, handcrafted pieces, cigars, and jewelry. ✉ *Piarco International Airport, Piarco* ☎ *868/669–4793.*

T-Wee Liquor Store. The deals on alcohol here would be hard to find in many other parts of the world. ✉ *Piarco International Airport, Piarco* ☎ *868/669–4748.*

HANDICRAFTS

The tourism office can provide a list of local artisans who sell straw and cane work, miniature steel pans, and other crafts.

101 Art Gallery at Holder's Studio. Trinidad's foremost gallery showcases Jackie Hinkson (figurative watercolors), Peter Sheppard (stylized realist local landscapes in acrylic), Sundiata (semi-abstract watercolors), and other local artists. Openings are usually held Tuesday evenings; the gallery is closed Sunday and Monday. ✉ *84 Woodford St., Newtown, Port of Spain* ☎ *868/628–4081.*

Cockey. For painted plates, ceramics, aromatic candles, wind chimes, and carved-wood pieces and instruments, check out Cockey. ✉ *Level 3, Long Circular Mall, Long Circular Rd., St. James, Port of Spain* ☎ *868/628–6546.*

Rainy Days Gift Shop. Stylish handmade batik items, *Ajoupa* (an attractive, local terra-cotta pottery), CDs, local art, T-shirts and many other gift items are available here. ✉ *Ellerslie Plaza, Long Circular Rd., Maraval, Port of Spain* ☎ *868/628–4387.*

MUSIC

Just CDs and Accessories. This shop carries a good selection of popular local musicians as well as other music genres. ✉ *Long Circular Mall, Long Circular Rd., St. James, Port of Spain* ☎ *868/622–7516.*

Rhyner's. The soca and steel-pan recordings and other local music from this airport store (it's in duty-free) make great last-minute souvenirs. ✉ *Piarco International Airport, Piarco* ☎ *868/669–3064.*

SPORTS AND THE OUTDOORS

BIRD-WATCHING

Fodor's Choice ★ Trinidad and Tobago are among the top 10 spots in the world in terms of the number of species of birds per square mile—more than 430, many living within pristine rain forests, lowlands and savannas, and fresh- and saltwater swamps. If you're lucky, you might spot the collared trogon, Trinidad piping guan (known locally as the common pawi), or rare white-tailed Sabrewing hummingbird. Restaurants often hang feeders outside on their porches, as much to keep the birds away from your food as to provide a chance to see them. Both the Asa Wright Nature Centre and Caroni Bird Sanctuary (⇨ *Exploring Trinidad*) are major bird-watching destinations.

Point-a-Pierre Wildfowl Trust. This 26-acre haven for rare bird species is within the unlikely confines of a petrochemical complex; you must call in advance for a reservation. ✉ *Petrotrin Complex, Point-a-Pierre* ☎ *868/658–4200.*

Winston Nanan. Nanan, a self-taught ornithologist, knows the local fauna as well as his own children. He will arrange personal tours in his own car anywhere on the island. His business is based at the Caroni Bird Sanctuary, but his expertise makes a trip with him to the Northern Range or the northeast a must for just about any true bird-watcher. It won't be cheap (figure on $400–$500 a day), but the personal attention and his willingness to try to find rare species are well worth the expense. ☎ *868/645–1305.*

FISHING

The islands off the northwest coast of Trinidad have excellent waters for deep-sea fishing; you may find wahoo, kingfish, and marlin, to name a few. The ocean here was a favorite angling spot of Franklin D. Roosevelt.

Bayshore Charters. Through Bayshore Charters you can fish for an afternoon or hire a boat for a weekend; the *Melissa Ann* is fully equipped for comfortable cruising, sleeps six, and has an air-conditioned cabin, a refrigerator, cooking facilities, and fishing equipment. Captain Sa Gomes is one of the most experienced charter captains on the islands. ✉ *29 Sunset Dr., Bayshore, Westmoorings* ☎ *868/637–8711.*

GOLF

St. Andrew's Golf Club. The best course in Trinidad is just outside Port of Spain. Picture a valley setting adorned with beautiful mature tropical trees and you get an idea of St. Andrews. Established in 1892, it qualifies as one of the region's oldest layouts. As one might expect, this vintage course is not particularly long at 6,555 yards, but narrow tree-lined fairways and contoured putting surfaces place a premium upon accuracy and make it a sporting challenge. The most convenient tee times are available on weekdays. Golf shoes with soft spikes are required. ✉ *Moka, Saddle Rd., Maraval, Port of Spain* ☎ *868/629–0066* 🌐 *golftrinidad.com* *$40 for 9 holes, $75 for 18 holes* *18 holes, 6555 yards, par 72.*

GUIDED TOURS

Although any taxi driver in Trinidad or Tobago can take visitors to the major attractions, using a tour company often makes for a more leisurely and educational adventure. Tour operators are also more mindful of the sensitivities of tourists and are much less likely to subject passengers to breakneck speeds and "creative" driving.

Banwari Experience. Andrew Welch and his knowledgeable staff have numerous, customizable tour packages to serve your needs in T&T. They specialize in cultural experiences that immerse you in island customs, history, nature, and most of all food. A number of their tours reveal the best-kept secrets in Trinidad's dining scene. Mr. Welch has friends all over the island, and these friends are some of Trinidad's best chefs, artists, and adventurers. Individual and group tours as well as family packages are available, all at reasonable rates. ✉ *Bourg Mulatresse, Santa Cruz* ☎ *868/675–1619, 868/624–8687.*

Caribbean Discovery Tours Ltd. Stephen Broadbridge's tours are completely personalized and can include both on- and offshore activities. Tours can range from the strenuous to the leisurely, with prices based on the duration of the expedition and the number of participants. ✉ *9B Fondes Amandes, St. Ann's, Port of Spain* ☎ *868/624–7281, 868/620–1989* 🌐 *www.caribbeandiscoverytours.com.*

Kalloo's. Tours from Kalloo's include a fascinating three-hour tour of Port of Spain as well as an overnight one devoted to turtle-watching. ✉ *Piarco International Airport, Piarco* ☎ *868/669–5673, 868/622–9073* 🌐 *www.kalloos.com.*

Sensational Tours & Transport. This is one of the best choices for island tours. The affable owner Gerard Nicholas worked for the tourist board for many years and knows the island intimately. Tour prices are reasonable, too. ✉ *47 Reservoir Rd., La Pastora, Santa Cruz* ☎ *868/702–4129, 868/315–3652.*

TOBAGO

EXPLORING

A driving tour of Tobago, from Scarborough to Charlotteville and back, can be done in about four hours, but you'd never want to undertake this spectacular, and very hilly, ride in that time. The switchbacks can induce nausea as well as awe, so it's a good idea to take some motion-sickness pills along with you. Plan to spend at least one night at the Speyside end of the island, and give yourself a chance to enjoy this largely untouched country and seaside at leisure.

TOP ATTRACTIONS

Charlotteville. This delightful fishing village in the northeast is within a series of steep hills. Fishermen here announce the day's catch by sounding their conch shells. A view of Man O' War Bay with Pigeon Peak (Tobago's highest mountain) behind it at sunset is an amazing sight.

Flagstaff Hill. One of the highest points on the island sits at the northern tip of Tobago. Surrounded by ocean on three sides and with a view of other hills, Charlotteville, and St. Giles Island, this was the site of an American military lookout and radio tower during World War II. It's an ideal spot for a sunset picnic. The turnoff to the hill is at the major bend on the road from Speyside to Charlotteville. It's largely unpaved, so the going may be a bit rough.

Ft. King George. On Mt. St. George, a short drive up the hill from Scarborough, Tobago's best-preserved historic monument clings to a cliff high above the ocean. Ft. King George was built in the 1770s and operated until 1854. It's hard to imagine that this lovely, tranquil spot commanding sweeping views of the bay and landscaped with lush tropical foliage was ever the site of any military action, but the prison, officers' mess, and several stabilized cannons attest otherwise. Just to the left of the tall wooden figures dancing a traditional Tobagonian jig is the former barrack guardhouse, now housing the small **Tobago Museum.** Exhibits include weapons and other pre-Columbian artifacts found in the area; the fertility figures are especially interesting. Upstairs are maps and photographs of Tobago's past. Be sure to check out the gift display cases for the perversely fascinating jewelry made from embalmed and painted lizards and sea creatures; you might find it hard to resist a pair of bright-yellow shrimp earrings. The **Fine Arts Centre** at the foot of the Ft. King George complex shows the work of local artists. ✉ *84 Fort St., Scarborough* ☎ *868/639–3970* 🎟 *Fort free, museum $2* ⏲ *Weekdays 9–5.*

25

WORTH NOTING

Kimme Sculpture Museum. The diminutive and eccentric German-born sculptress Luise Kimme fell in love with the form of Tobagonians and devoted her life to capturing them in her sculptures. Her pieces can exceed 12 feet in height and are often wonderfully whimsical. Much of her work is done in wood (none of it local), but there are many bronze pieces as well. Ms. Kimme passed away in 2013 but her work remains on permanent display at her former home. The museum itself is a turreted structure with a commanding view of the countryside. Most locals refer to it as "The Castle." There are numerous signs in Mt. Irvine directing visitors to the museum. ✉ *Mt. Irvine* ☎ *868/639–0257* 🌐 *www.luisekimme.com* 🎟 *TT$20* ⏲ *Sun. 10–2 or by appointment.*

Scarborough. Around Rockley Bay on the island's leeward hilly side, this town is both the capital of Tobago and a popular cruise-ship port, but it feels as if not much has changed since the area was settled two centuries ago. It may not be one of the delightful pastel-color cities of the Caribbean, but Scarborough does have its charms, including several interesting little shops. Whatever you do, be sure to check out the busy Scarborough Market, an indoor and outdoor affair with fresh

A cannon at Ft. King George, Tobago

vegetables, live chickens, and clothing. Note the red-and-yellow Methodist church on the hill, one of Tobago's oldest churches.

NEED A BREAK?

Ciao Pizza. With more than 20 flavors of gelato, Ciao Pizza is an essential stop on any visit to the capital. You can also get pizza slices and sandwiches if you're looking for a quick snack. There's seating in the air-conditioned interior and a lovely outdoor perch from which to absorb the downtown action sheltered from the blazing sun. In addition to the usual complement of coffees, cocktails are also available. ✉ ***20 Burnett St., Scarborough*** ☎ ***868/639–3001.***

Speyside. At the far reach of Tobago's windward coast, this small fishing village has a few lodgings and restaurants. Divers are drawn to the unspoiled reefs in the area and to the strong possibility of spotting giant manta rays. The approach to Speyside from the south affords one of the most spectacular vistas of the island. Glass-bottom boats operate between Speyside and **Little Tobago Island,** an important seabird sanctuary.

St. Giles Island. The underwater cliffs and canyons here off the northeastern tip of Tobago draw divers to this spot, where the Atlantic meets the Caribbean. ✉ *Take Windward Rd. inland across mountains from Speyside.*

BEACHES

Tobago has many beautiful beaches ranging from the popular to the completely isolated. Store Bay near the airport is also a popular area for local food and entertainment. The beach most associated with Tobago—and certainly the most photographed—is Pigeon Point Beach, which is a beautiful stretch of white sand lined with palm trees and perfect for swimming. Because of the crime levels on both islands, exercise caution if planning to explore some of the more remote beaches.

Bacolet Beach. This dark-sand beach was the setting for the films *Swiss Family Robinson* and *Heaven Knows, Mr. Allison.* If you are not a guest at the Blue Haven Hotel, access is down a track next door to the hotel. The bathroom and changing facilities are for hotel guests only. **Amenities:** food and drink. **Best for:** swimming; walking. ⊠ *Windward Rd., east of Scarborough.*

Englishman's Bay. This mile-long crescent of sand looks like a frame ripped from a classic pirate movie. The somewhat steep sandy beach almost always has calm waters and backs onto unspoiled tropical rain forest. The beach is usually deserted but there are a few shacks offering food, drink, and souvenirs. **Amenities:** food and drink; toilets. **Best for:** snorkeling; solitude; walking. ⊠ *North Side Rd., east of Castara Bay.*

Great Courland Bay. This bay near Ft. Bennett has clear, tranquil waters. Along the sandy beach—one of Tobago's longest—you can find several hotels. A marina attracts the yachting crowd. **Amenities:** none. **Best for:** swimming; walking. ⊠ *Leeward Rd., northeast of Black Rock, Courland.*

King's Bay. Surrounded by steep green hills, this is the prettiest swimming site off the road from Scarborough to Speyside. The crescent beach is marked by a sign about halfway between the two towns. Just before you reach the bay, there's a bridge with an unmarked turnoff that leads to a parking lot; beyond that, a landscaped path leads to a waterfall with a rocky pool. Locals will likely offer to guide you to the top of the falls; however, you may find the climb not worth the effort. **Amenities:** food and drink; lifeguards; parking; showers. **Best for:** swimming; walking. ⊠ *Winward Rd., Delaford.*

Lovers Beach. You have to hire a local to bring you to this isolated retreat of pink sand. Ask one of the fishermen in Charlotteville to arrange a ride for you, but be sure to haggle. It should cost no more than TT$30 per person, round-trip. **Amenities:** none. **Best for:** solitude; snorkeling. ⊠ *North coast, reachable only by boat from Charlotteville.*

Mt. Irvine Beach. The beach across the street from the Mt. Irvine Bay Hotel has great surfing in July and August, and the snorkeling is excellent, too. It's also ideal for windsurfing in January and April. There are picnic tables surrounded by painted concrete pagodas and a snack bar. **Amenities:** food and drink; showers; toilets. **Best for:** snorkeling; surfing; swimming; windsurfing. ⊠ *Shirvan Rd., Mt. Irvine.*

Parlatuvier. On the north side of the island, the beach is best approached via the road from Roxborough. It's a classic Caribbean crescent, a scene peopled by villagers and fishermen. Local food and souvenir shops are literally steps from the sand, as the village fronts the beach. The local fishermen bringing in their catch is a photo opportunity not to be missed. **Amenities:** none. **Best for:** swimming. ✉ *Parlatuvier.*

Pigeon Point Beach. This stunning locale is often displayed on Tobago travel brochures. The white-sand beach is lined with swaying coconut trees, and there are changing facilities and food stalls nearby. The beach is public but there is an admission fee (about TT$20). **Amenities:** food and drink; showers; toilets. **Best for:** partiers; swimming, tanning. ✉ *Pigeon Point.*

Stone Haven Bay. This gorgeous stretch of sand is literally across the street (a small secondary road) from the Grafton Beach Resort and is great for tanning. There are strong currents and no lifeguards on duty so bear in mind that swimming poses risks. A better bet is to relax with a cocktail from the hotel beach bar and wait for one of the locals to come by offering handmade souvenirs. **Amenities:** food and drink. **Best for:** walking. ✉ *Shirvan Rd., Black Rock.*

Store Bay. The beach, where boats depart for Buccoo Reef, is little more than a small sandy cove between two rocky breakwaters, but the food stands here are amazing: several huts licensed by the tourist board to local ladies who sell roti, pelau, and curried crab and dumplings. There are also souvenirs ranging from carvings to soap as well as local sweets. It's near the airport; just walk around the Crown Point Hotel to the beach entrance. There's also free parking just off Milford Rd. **Amenities:** food and drink; showers; toilets. **Best for:** partiers; swimming. ✉ *Crown Point.*

Turtle Beach. This beach is named for the leatherback turtles that lay their eggs here at night between February and June. (If you're very quiet, you can watch; the turtles don't seem to mind.) It's 8 miles (13 km) from the airport between Black Rock and Plymouth. **Amenities:** solitude. **Best for:** walking. ✉ *Southern end of Great Courland Bay between Black Rock and Plymouth, Courland.*

WHERE TO EAT

Curried crab and dumplings is a Sunday-dinner favorite in Tobago. *Oildown*—a local dish—tastes better than it sounds: it's a gently seasoned mixture of boiled breadfruit and salt beef or pork flavored with coconut milk. Mango ice cream or a sweet-and-sour tamarind ball makes a tasty finish. You may want to take home some hot-pepper sauce or chutney to a spice-loving friend or relative.

$$$ CARIBBEAN Fodor'sChoice ★

✕ **Blue Crab Restaurant.** The Sardinha family has been serving the best local lunches at their home since the 1980s. The ebullient Alison entertains and hugs diners while her husband, Ken, does the cooking. The food is hearty and usually well seasoned in the creole style. The only bad news is that the restaurant is primarily a lunch spot—it's only open for dinner three days a week; the good news is that you may not have room for dinner after lunch here. [$] *Average main: $23* ✉ *Robinson and Main Sts., Scarborough* ☎ *868/639–2737* 🌐 *www.tobagobluecrab.com* ⊙ *Closed weekends. No dinner Tues. and Thurs.*

$$ ECLECTIC FAMILY ✕ **Bonkers.** This restaurant at the Toucan Inn is atmospheric and excellent. Designed by expat British co-owner Chris James, the architecture is a blend of Kenyan and Caribbean styles, executed entirely in local teak and open on all sides. The menu is comprehensive and kid-friendly. The nightly entertainment attracts a lively crowd on weekends. Open for breakfast, lunch, and dinner seven days a week, this is the busiest eatery on the island. *Average main: $20 ✉ Toucan Inn, Store Bay Local Rd., Crown Point ☎ 868/639–7173 ⊕ www.toucan-inn.com.*

$$$$ ECLECTIC ✕ **Café Coco.** This stylish eatery seats 200, but it's divided into multiple levels, so there's still a sense of intimacy. Statuary is strewn about with carefree abandon, and the sound of flowing water permeates the room. The main courses vary widely and may include Cuban stewed beef as well as shrimp tempura. The restaurant is seldom full, so getting a table is usually not a problem. *Average main: $32 ✉ TTEC Substation Rd. off Crown Point Rd., Crown Point ☎ 868/639–0996.*

25

$$$ CARIBBEAN ✕ **The Fish Pot.** Beautifully presented dishes made with the freshest of fish is the big draw at this cozy eatery. The surf and turf, featuring Caribbean spiny lobster, is excellent. The bar is usually lively and populated with regulars who consider this an essential Tobago dining experience. *Average main: $24 ✉ Pleasant Prospect, Grafton ☎ 868/635–1728 ⊗ Closed Sun.*

$$$ CARIBBEAN ✕ **Kariwak Village Restaurant.** Recorded steel-band music plays gently in the background at this romantic, candlelit spot in the Kariwak Village complex. In a bamboo pavilion that resembles an Amerindian round hut, Cynthia Clovis orchestrates a very original menu. Whatever the dish, it will be full of herbs and vegetables picked from her organic garden. Be sure to try the delicious homemade ice cream and the reasonably priced but potent cocktails. Friday and Saturday buffets, with live jazz or calypso, are a Tobagonian highlight. *Average main: $30 ✉ Crown Point ☎ 868/639–8442 ⊕ www.kariwak.com.*

$$ ITALIAN Fodor's Choice ★ ✕ **La Tartaruga.** Milanese owner Gabriele de Gaetano has created the island's most prominent Italian eatery. Sitting on the large patio surrounded by lush foliage with Gabriele rushing from table to table chatting in Italian-laced English is all the entertainment you'll need. Cuisine ranges from basic but tasty pizzas to elaborate Northern Italian pasta dishes. The carpaccio with Gabriele's trademark Tuscan sauce is excellent. The impressive cellar stocks only Italian wines. *Average main: $18 ✉ Buccoo Rd., Buccoo ☎ 868/639–0940 ⊕ www.latartarugatobago.com ⚠ Reservations essential ⊗ Closed Sun. No lunch.*

$$ ITALIAN ✕ **The Pasta Gallery.** This tiny gem specializes in hearty servings of beautifully prepared homemade pasta at a budget-friendly price. It's on the main road to Pigeon Point Beach, with three outside tables and about an equal number inside. The funky decor, small size and attentive casual service makes it feel like you're at a small dinner party with friends. The *Spaghetti alla Carbonara* is comfort food done right. It's within walking distance of most Crown Point hotels. *Average main: $12 ✉ Pigeon Point Rd., Crown Point ☎ 868/727–8200.*

$$ SOUTH AMERICAN

Salsa Kitchen. This charming little establishment offers tasty tapas in a magical little space in the heart of Scarborough. Distressed ochre walls and seemingly random strings of lights create the perfect dining experience for those lucky enough to bag one of the five tables. The seafood and pork dishes are stars, and daily specials are displayed on a chalkboard. The owners close the restaurant when they are on vacation so be sure to call ahead. *Average main: $19 ✉ 8 Pump Mill Rd., Scarborough ☎ 868/639–1522 ⊙ Closed Monday. No lunch.*

$ CAFÉ Fodor's Choice ★

Shore Things Café & Craft. With a dramatic setting over the ocean on the Milford Road between Crown Point and Scarborough, this is a good spot to stop for lunch or a coffee break. Survey the view from the deck tables while enjoying a variety of freshly prepared juices (the tamarind is particularly refreshing) and nibbling on excellent sandwiches. The whole-wheat pizza is great and owner Giselle Beaubrun takes special pride in her indulgent desserts. While waiting for your meal, you can shop for local crafts in the lovely and comprehensive gift shop. *Average main: $10 ✉ 25 Old Milford Rd., Lambeau ☎ 868/635–1072 ⊙ Closed Sun. No dinner.*

$$$$ CARIBBEAN

Shutters on the Bay. The warm-yellow dining area of this hotel restaurant is on the second floor of a colonial-style building and surrounded by white push-out shutters that frame a magical view of Bacolet Bay. The menu features a variety of dishes, all with a contemporary Caribbean twist. Don't be afraid to try some of the more exotic local offerings, such as callaloo soup, or some of the local starches (called "ground provisions"), such as dasheen (taro) or breadfruit. *Average main: $31 ✉ Blue Haven Hotel, Bacolet Bay, Scarborough ☎ 868/660–7500 Reservations essential.*

$$$$ ECLECTIC

Tamara's. At the elegant Coco Reef Resort you can dine on contemporary cuisine with an island twist. The peach walls and whitewashed wooden ceiling make the resort's restaurant feel airy and light, and island breezes waft through the palm-lined terrace. The menu changes seasonally, and the fish dishes are worth special attention. A full tropical buffet breakfast is served daily; dinner is served nightly. There's a lavish buffet spread on Wednesday and Sunday evenings. A dress code is enforced but casual chic is fine and men are not required to wear jackets for dinner. *Average main: $35 ✉ Coco Reef Resort, Crown Point, Scarborough ☎ 868/639–8571 Reservations essential ⊙ No lunch.*

$$$ CARIBBEAN

Watermill. Lush surroundings, great food, and impeccable service make this alfresco eatery a popular choice. Despite the romantic atmosphere, beautifully presented fare here will likely not break the bank. The fresh seafood offerings are always a good choice and those seeking a luxurious and special treat may want to try the butter-poached lobster. Be sure to leave room for one of their homemade desserts such as guava or coconut cheesecake. This restaurant has no connection to the one that previously occupied the same site. *Average main: $25 ✉ Shirvan Rd., Mt. Pleasant ☎ 868/639–0000 ⊙ Closed Sun.*

WHERE TO STAY

Tobago is much more of a tourist destination than Trinidad, and this is reflected in the range of accommodations. Those seeking luxury can find a number of upscale resorts and villas, and the budget-minded can take advantage of several more intimate establishments.

$ HOTEL Fodor's Choice ★ **Blue Haven Hotel.** Justifiably celebrated, this 1940s-era luxury hotel overlooks a spectacular secluded beach on Bacolet Bay just outside Scarborough. **Pros:** historic charm; beautiful beach; more European flair than any other hotel on the island. **Cons:** lacks the range of services of the larger hotels; far from the attractions of Crown Point; some maintenance issues; beach is a short walk down a hillside. *Rooms from: $200 Bacolet Bay, Scarborough 868/660–7400 www.bluehavenhotel.com 51 rooms, 8 suites Multiple meal plans.*

$ HOTEL **Blue Waters Inn.** A tropical rain forest creeps up behind this eco-friendly hotel, which sits on sheltered, turquoise Batteaux Bay; it's just east of Speyside and a 90-minute drive from Scarborough. **Pros:** rooms open onto the beach; rooms and common areas renovated in 2014; enthusiastic and friendly staff; simple but delicious food. **Cons:** it's a long drive from Scarborough; may be too quiet for some. *Rooms from: $240 Batteaux Bay, Speyside 868/660–4341 www.bluewatersinn.com 31 rooms, 3 suites, 4 bungalows Multiple meal plans.*

$$$ RESORT FAMILY Fodor's Choice ★ **Coco Reef Resort.** Although it's just a short distance from the airport, this expansive enclave feels remote, with pink buildings that are sprawled along a perfect stretch of coast. **Pros:** beautifully appointed rooms; the only private beach on the island; impeccable and understated service. **Cons:** pool area can get a bit too busy; limited Wi-Fi; some rooms are far from the beach and reception; expensive. *Rooms from: $445 Milford Rd., Coconut Bay, Crown Point 868/639–8571, 800/221–1294 www.cocoreef.com 100 rooms, 27 suites, 8 villas Breakfast.*

$ RESORT FAMILY **Grafton Beach Resort.** The first all-inclusive in Tobago—Grafton Beach is very popular with young couples who are attracted by the all-inclusive option. **Pros:** large rooms; lively pool area. **Cons:** so-so food; the free drinks plan can sometimes make for a rowdy crowd. *Rooms from: $150 Shirvan Rd., Black Rock 868/639–0191 102 rooms, 4 suites Breakfast.*

$ HOTEL Fodor's Choice ★ **Kariwak Village.** Owner Cynthia Clovis personally oversees this intimate, tranquil oasis that draws guests who return year after year. **Pros:** cozy and intimate throughout; excellent restaurant; beautiful grounds. **Cons:** the New Age concept not for everyone (although it isn't imposed on guests); no beach. *Rooms from: $205 Store Bay Rd. 868/639–8442 www.kariwak.com 24 rooms Breakfast.*

$$ HOTEL **Magdalena Grand Beach & Golf Resort.** This impressive seafront resort (formerly the Hilton Tobago) is located in a lovely gated residential area complete with golf course; the beach, however, is minuscule, requiring a complimentary shuttle to the much better Pigeon Point Beach. **Pros:** gorgeous ocean views; pool area is stunning; excellent restaurants and entertainment options. **Cons:** on-site beach is tiny; long walk from some

Tobago

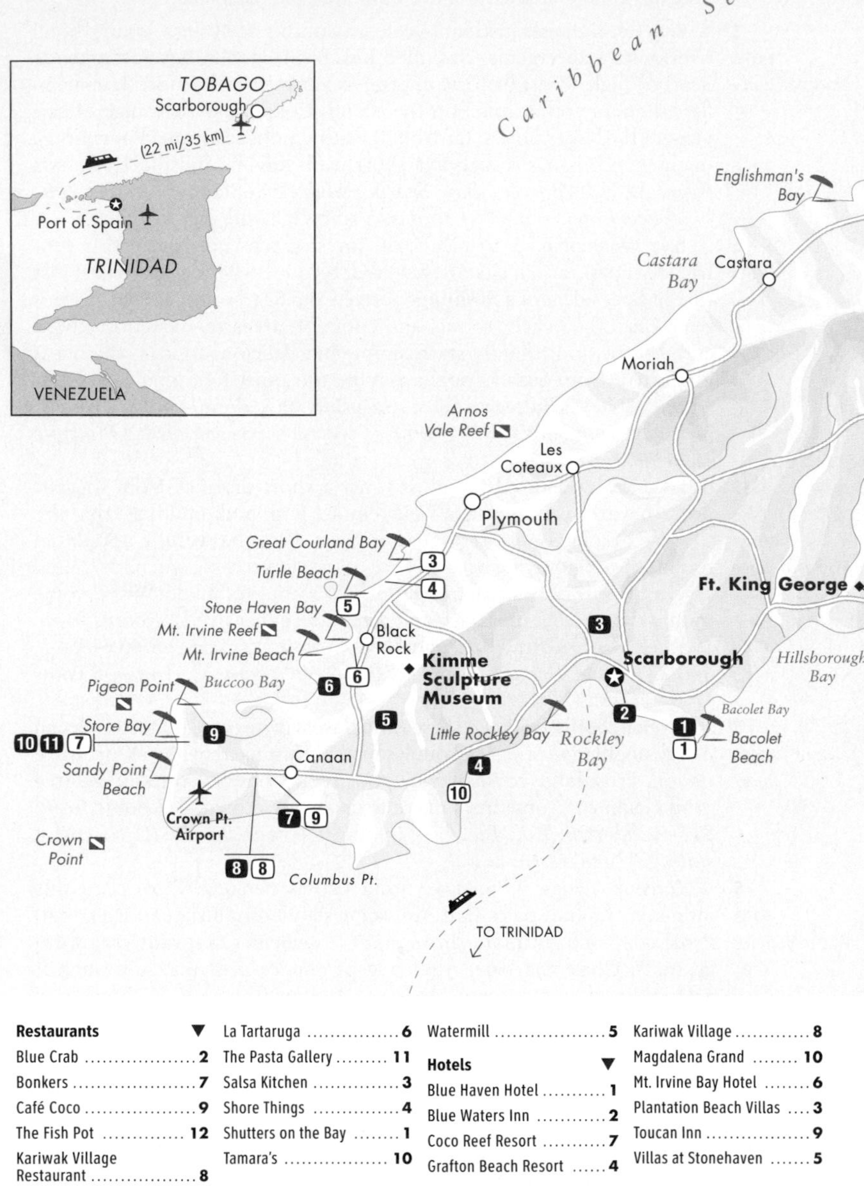

Restaurants ▼

- Blue Crab ... 2
- Bonkers ... 7
- Café Coco ... 9
- The Fish Pot ... 12
- Kariwak Village Restaurant ... 8
- La Tartaruga ... 6
- The Pasta Gallery ... 11
- Salsa Kitchen ... 3
- Shore Things ... 4
- Shutters on the Bay ... 1
- Tamara's ... 10
- Watermill ... 5

Hotels ▼

- Blue Haven Hotel ... 1
- Blue Waters Inn ... 2
- Coco Reef Resort ... 7
- Grafton Beach Resort ... 4
- Kariwak Village ... 8
- Magdalena Grand ... 10
- Mt. Irvine Bay Hotel ... 6
- Plantation Beach Villas ... 3
- Toucan Inn ... 9
- Villas at Stonehaven ... 5

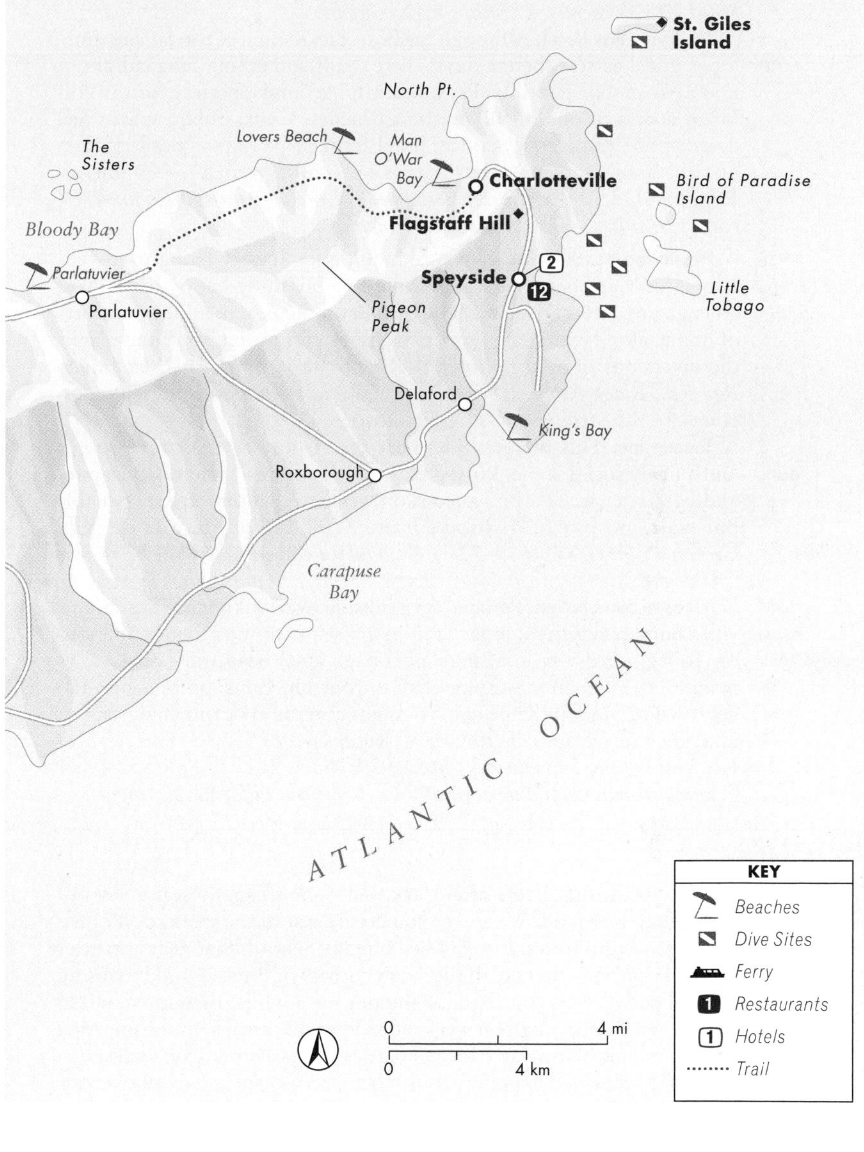
St. Giles
Island
North Pt.
The
Sisters
Lovers Beach
Man
O'War
Bay
Charlotteville
Bird of Paradise
Island
Bloody Bay
Flagstaff Hill
Parlatuvier
Parlatuvier
Speyside
2
12
Little
Tobago
Pigeon
Peak
Delaford
King's Bay
Roxborough
Carapuse
Bay
ATLANTIC OCEAN
KEY
Beaches
Dive Sites
Ferry
Restaurants
Hotels
Trail
0
4 mi
0
4 km

rooms to reception. *Rooms from: $300* ✉ *Milford Rd.* ☎ *868/660–8800* *178 rooms, 22 suites* *No meals.*

$ HOTEL **Mt. Irvine Bay Hotel.** Although the hotel lacks some of the fancier amenities and has seen better days, there's still something magical about its 1970s shabby gentility. **Pros:** beautiful grounds; perfect for the golf lover; access to one of the prettiest beaches. **Cons:** public spaces feel dated; poor restaurant service; hotel frequently empty; pool is often out of commission and needs repairs. *Rooms from: $150* ✉ *Shirvan Rd., Box 222, Mt. Irvine* ☎ *868/639–8871* 🌐 *www.mtirvine.com* *53 rooms, 6 suites, 46 cottages* *No meals.*

$$ RENTAL FAMILY **Plantation Beach Villas.** If you're looking for luxury living in a well-appointed Caribbean villa, you should be blissfully happy here. **Pros:** an engaging alternative to a hotel room; on the beach; all the comforts of home, along with maid service. **Cons:** no restaurant for dinner; lacks the diversions of a large hotel. *Rooms from: $300* ✉ *Stone Haven Bay Rd., Black Rock* ☎ *868/639–9377* 🌐 *www.plantationbeachvillas.com* *6 3-bedroom villas* *No meals.*

$ HOTEL **Toucan Inn.** This budget hotel near the airport offers simple rooms and a lively social scene. **Pros:** great value; good restaurant. **Cons:** pool and bar area can be a bit raucous on weekends; rooms are serviceable but plain; no beach. *Rooms from: $100* ✉ *Store Bay Local Rd., Crown Point* ☎ *868/639–7173* 🌐 *www.toucan-inn.com* *20 rooms* *Breakfast.*

$$$$ RENTAL Fodor's Choice ★ **Villas at Stonehaven.** Perched on a hillside overlooking the ocean, this villa complex sets the standard for luxury self-catering accommodations on Tobago. **Pros:** as luxurious as Tobago gets; beautiful ocean views from every villa; an infinity pool all to yourself. **Cons:** bit of a climb to get to villas; not on the beach; five-night minimum during high season; amenities vary from villa to villa. *Rooms from: $520* ✉ *Bon Accord, Grafton Estate, Shirvan Rd., Box 1079, Black Rock* ☎ *868/639–0361* 🌐 *www.stonehavenvillas.com* *14 3-bedroom villas* *No meals.*

NIGHTLIFE

Tobago is not that lively after dark, but there's usually some form of nightlife to be found. Whatever you do the rest of the week, don't miss the huge impromptu party, dubbed Sunday School, that gears up after midnight on Saturday on all the street corners of Buccoo and breaks up around dawn. Pick your band, hang out for a while, then move on. In downtown Scarborough on weekend nights you can also find competing sound systems blaring at informal parties that welcome extra guests. In addition, "blockos" (spontaneous block parties) spring up all over the island; look for the hand-painted signs. Tobago also has harvest parties on Sunday throughout the year, when a particular village extends its hospitality and opens its doors to visitors.

Bonkers. There's live entertainment every night except Sunday at this usually busy club. ✉ *Toucan Inn, Store Bay Local Rd., Crown Point* ☎ *868/639–7173.*

Grafton Beach Resort. Grafton Beach Resort has some kind of organized cabaret-style event every night. Even if you hate that touristy stuff, check out Les Couteaux Cultural Group, which does a high-octane dance version of Tobagonian history. ✉ *Shirvan Rd., Black Rock* ☎ *868/639–0191.*

Kariwak Village. As many locals as visitors frequent Kariwak Village on Friday and Saturday nights, when one of the better local jazz-calypso bands almost always plays. Expect more of an older crowd. ✉ *Crown Point* ☎ *868/639–8442.*

Shade. This sure bet for raucous late-night fun is open from 7 pm to 4 am Thursday through Saturday. It's across the road from Crown Point's only gas station. ✉ *Milford Rd. at Robert St., Bon Accord Village, Crown Point* ☎ *868/639–9651.*

SHOPPING

Souvenir seekers will do better in Trinidad than in Tobago, but determined shoppers ought to be able to find a few things to take home. Scarborough has the largest collection of shops, and Burnett Street, which climbs sharply from the port to St. James Park, is a good place to browse.

FOOD

Forro's Homemade Delicacies. Eileen Forrester, wife of the Anglican archdeacon of Trinidad and Tobago, supervises a kitchen full of good cooks who boil and bottle the condiments sold here and pack them in little straw baskets—or even in bamboo. Most of the jars of tamarind chutney, lemon and lime marmalade, hot sauce, and guava and golden-apple jelly are small, easy to carry, and inexpensive. ✉ *The Andrew's Rectory, Bacolet St., opposite the fire station, Scarborough* ☎ *868/639–2485.*

HANDICRAFTS

Anthea's Treasure Trove. The sights and scents of homemade soaps and lotions in this delightful little store are sure to please. Soaps come in a variety of shapes and sizes and the soap cupcake display makes for a great photo opportunity. ✉ *Store Bay Beach Facility, Store Bay, Crown Point* ☎ *868/304–1256.*

Batiki Point. Tina Louis offers batik, imaginative local crafts, footwear, and clothing at this charming little store in Buccoo, which is conveniently also open on Sunday during the area's raucous "Sunday School" evening party. ✉ *Opposite Beach, Main Rd., Buccoo* ☎ *868/631–0111.*

Shore Things Café & Crafts. Masks and music are just two of the many kinds of souvenirs you can pick up at Shore Things Café & Crafts. ✉ *25 Old Milford Rd., Lambeau* ☎ *868/635–1072.*

Store Bay. The stalls at Store Bay sell T-shirts, local handicrafts, homemade candy, and lots of other souvenirs. It's also convenient to the airport for any last-minute purchases. ✉ *Store Bay, Crown Point.*

SPORTS AND THE OUTDOORS

BIRD-WATCHING

Some 200 varieties of birds have been documented on Tobago: look for the yellow oriole, scarlet ibis, and the comical motmot—the male of the species clears sticks and stones from an area and then does a dance complete with snapping sounds to attract a mate. The flora is as vivid as the birds. Purple-and-yellow *poui* trees and spectacular orange immortelles splash color over the countryside, and something is blooming virtually every season.

NG & Company Nature Tours. Newton George spent 23 years with the Forestry Division and knows the island intimately. He offers a variety of tours and will even provide bird-watching tours of Trinidad. He also has a delightful hummingbird gallery at his home. ✉ *3 Top Hill St., Speyside* ☎ *868/660–5463* 🌐 *www.newtongeorge.com.*

Pioneer Journeys. Pat Turpin and Renson Jack at Pioneer Journeys can give you information about their bird-watching tours of Bloody Bay rain forest and Louis d'Or River valley wetlands. ☎ *868/660–4327* ✉ *pturpin@tstt.net.tt.*

BOAT TOURS

Tobago offers many wonderful spots for snorkeling. Although the reefs around Speyside in the northeast are becoming better known, **Buccoo Reef,** off the island's southwest coast, is still the most popular—perhaps too popular. Over the years the reef has been badly damaged by the ceaseless boat traffic and by thoughtless visiting divers who take pieces of coral as souvenirs. Still, it's worth experiencing, particularly if you have children. Daily 2½-hour tours by glass-bottom boats let you snorkel at the reef, swim in a lagoon, and gaze at Coral Gardens—where fish and coral are as yet untouched. Most dive companies in the Black Rock area also arrange snorkeling tours. There's also good snorkeling near the former **Arnos Vale Hotel** and the **Mt. Irvine Bay Hotel.**

Hew's Glass Bottom Boat Tours. These tours are perfect for those who want to see sea life but who neither snorkel nor dive. Boats leave daily at 11:30 am. ✉ *Pigeon Point* ☎ *868/639–9058.*

DIVING

An abundance of fish and coral thrives on the nutrients of Venezuela's Orinoco River, which are brought to Tobago by the Guyana current. Off the west coast is **Arnos Vale Reef,** with a depth of 40 feet and several reefs that run parallel to the shore. Here you can spot French and queen angelfish, moray eels, southern stingrays, and even the Atlantic torpedo ray. Much of the diving is drift diving in the mostly gentle current. **Crown Point,** on the island's southwest tip, is a good place for exploring the Shallows—a plateau at 50 to 100 feet that's favored by turtles, dolphins, angelfish, and nurse sharks. Just north of Crown Point on the southwest coast, **Pigeon Point** is a good spot to submerge. North of Pigeon Point, long, sandy beaches line the calm western coast; it has a gradual offshore slope and the popular **Mt. Irvine Wall,** which goes down to about 60 feet.

A short trip from Charlotteville, off the northeast tip of the island, is **St. Giles Island.** Here are natural rock bridges—London Bridge, Marble Island, and Fishbowl—and underwater cliffs. The **waters off Speyside** on the east coast draw scuba divers who come for the many manta rays in the area. Exciting sites in this area include Batteaux Reef, Angel Reef, Bookends, Blackjack Hole, and Japanese Gardens—one of the loveliest reefs, with depths of 20 to 85 feet and lots of sponges.

Tobago is considered a prime diving destination, as the clear waters provide maximum visibility. Every species of hard coral and most soft corals can be found in the waters around the island. Tobago is also home to the largest-known brain coral. Generally, the best diving is around the Speyside area. Many hotels and guesthouses in this area cater to the diving crowd with basic accommodations and easy access to the water. You can usually get the best deals with these "dive-and-stay" packages.

Blue Waters Dive'n. On the northeast coast, Dive'n is friendly, laid-back, and caters to divers of all levels. ✉ *Blue Waters Inn, Batteaux Bay, Speyside* ☎ *868/660–5445* 🌐 *www.bluewatersinn.com.*

Tobago Dive Experience. Class sizes at Tobago Dive Experience are kept small to ensure that all divers get the attention they need. It has the most comprehensive range of courses, including PADI, NAUI, and BSAC, and prices are very competitive. ✉ *Manta Lodge, Speyside* ☎ *868/660-5268* 🌐 *www.mantalodge.com.*

FISHING

Dillon's Deep Sea Charters. This company is excellent for full- and half-day trips for kingfish, barracuda, wahoo, mahimahi, blue marlin, and others. A full day on the sea with either a beach stop for lunch or a cruise around the island runs about $750, including equipment. ✉ *Crown Point* ☎ *868/639–8765.*

Hard Play Fishing Charters. The colorful skipper at Hard Play, Gerard "Frothy" De Silva, helps you bag your own marlin. ✉ *13 The Evergreen, Old Grange, Mt. Irvine Bay* ☎ *868/639–7108.*

GOLF

Tobago Plantations Golf & Country Club. The 18-hole, par-72 course is set on rolling greens. It offers some amazing views of the ocean as a bonus. Greens fees are $100 for 18-holes, $50 for 9-holes. This is the newer of the two main courses on the island and is by far the most popular. The course is well maintained and contains areas of mangrove and forest that are home to many bird species. The course and clubhouse were placed under the management of the Magdalena Grand Beach & Golf Resort in 2013 and, at this writing, are scheduled to undergo a $2-million upgrade in 2015. ✉ *Tobago Plantations Golf & Country Club, Lowlands* ☎ *868/387-0287.*

GUIDED TOURS

Frank's Glass Bottom Boat & Birdwatching Tours. In addition to glass-bottom-boat and snorkeling tours of the shores of Speyside, Frank and his son also conduct guided tours of the rain forest and Little Tobago. As natives of Speyside, they are extremely knowledgeable about the island's flora, fauna, and folklore. ✉ *Speyside* ☎ *868/660–5438.*

Tobago Travel. The island's most experienced operator is almost certain to have the perfect tour for you. ✉ *TTEC Substation Rd off Crown Point Rd., Crown Point* ☎ *868/639–8105.*

HIKING

Eco-consciousness is strong on Tobago, where the rain forests of the Main Ridge were set aside for protection in 1764, creating the first such preserve in the Western Hemisphere. Natural areas include Little Tobago and St. Giles islands, both major seabird sanctuaries. In addition, the endangered leatherback turtles maintain breeding grounds on some of Tobago's leeward beaches.

Harris Jungle Tours. The knowledgeable Harris McDonald offers tours that range from strenuous to laid-back. The more adventurous might want to try the rain-forest-at-night tour, which promises the possibility of encounters with some of Tobago's folklore characters, including La Diablesse (a beautifully dressed she-devil with one cow's foot). ✉ *Golden Grove Rd., Canaan* ☎ *868/639–0513* 🌐 *www.harris-jungle-tours.com.*

Yes Tourism. Among the many tours from this company is an excellent guided hike through the rain forest—the off-road Jeep safari is hair-raising but memorable. Sightseeing tours around Tobago as well as to Trinidad are also possible. ✉ *7 De Freitas Dr., Lowlands* ☎ *868/631–0286* 🌐 *www.yes-tourism.com.*

TURKS AND CAICOS ISLANDS

WELCOME TO TURKS AND CAICOS ISLANDS

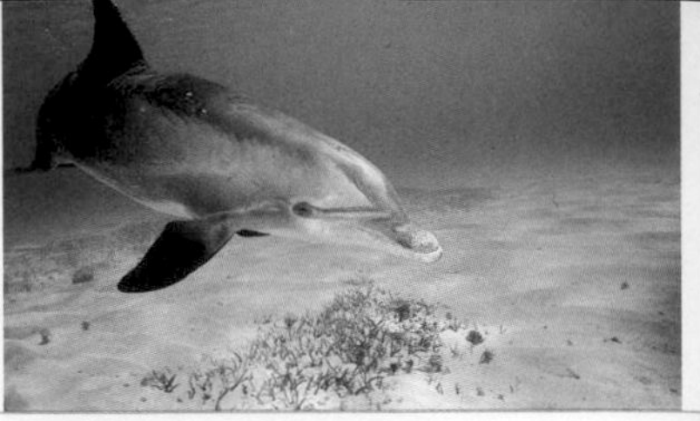

TO BAHAMAS
Caicos Passage
Three Mary's Cays
Parrot Cay
Fort George Cay
Football Fields
Pine Cay
Little Water Cay
Northwest Point
Providenciales
Grace Bay
Cheshire Hall
Sapodilla Hill
Caicos Conch Farm
Juba Point
Southwest Bluff
Providenciales see detail map
West Caicos
Southwest Reef
North Caicos
North Caicos
Spanish Point
Highas Cay
Juniper Hole
Platico Point
Middle Caicos
Middle Caicos
Ocean Hole
Vine Point
Toll Crawl Point
CAICOS ISLANDS
Molasses Reef
0
14 miles
0
21 km
CAICOS BANK
Little Ambergris Cay
SEAL CAYS
White Cay
KEY
Dive Sites
Restaurants
Hotels

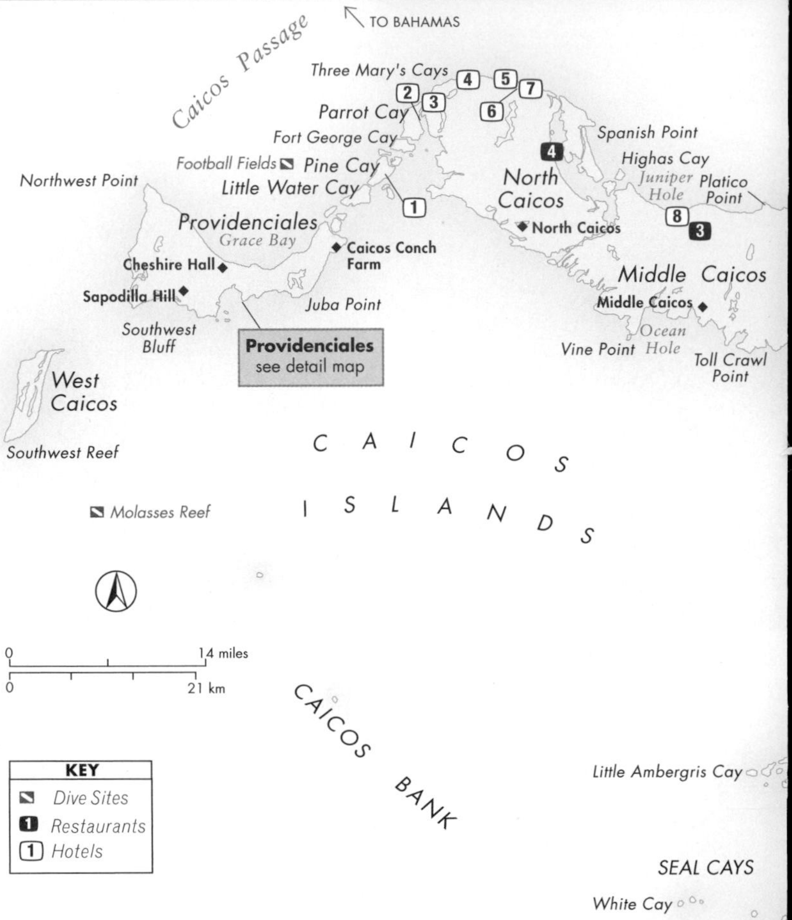

The Turks and Caicos Islands make up the southern extension of the Lucayan archipelago, just north of Hispaniola; only eight of the 40 islands are inhabited. Divers and snorkelers can explore one of the world's largest coral reefs. Land-based pursuits don't get much more taxing than teeing off at the Provo Golf and Country Club or sunset-watching from the seaside terrace of a laid-back resort.

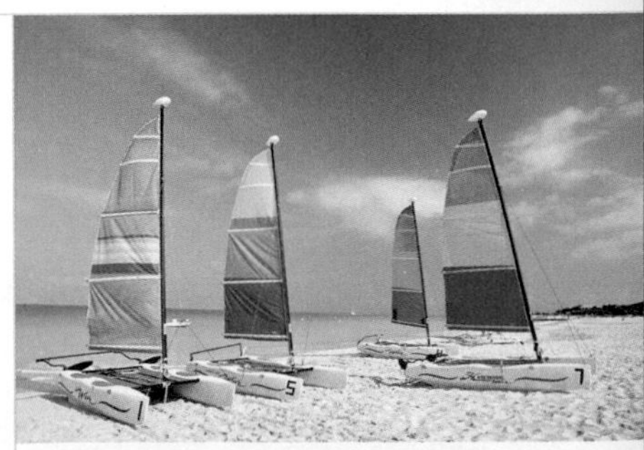

GEOGRAPHICAL INFO

Though Providenciales is an offshore banking center, sea creatures far outnumber humans in this archipelago of 40 islands, where the total population is a mere 32,000. From developed Provo to sleepy Grand Turk to sleepier South Caicos, the islands offer miles of undeveloped beaches, crystal clear water, and laid-back luxury resorts.

Restaurants ▼	
Last Chance	4
Mudjin Bari	3
Pat's Place	2
Porter's Island Thyme Bistro	1

Hotels ▼	
Blue Horizon Resort	8
Castaway	12
Couch Cottage	6
Datai Villa	4
Hollywood Beach Suites	5
Jodo Resort	3
Meridian Club	1
Parrot Cay Resort	2
Pelican Beach Hotel	7
Pirate's Hideaway	13
South Caicos Ocean & Beach Resort	9
Tradewinds Guest Suites	10
Villas of Salt Cay	11

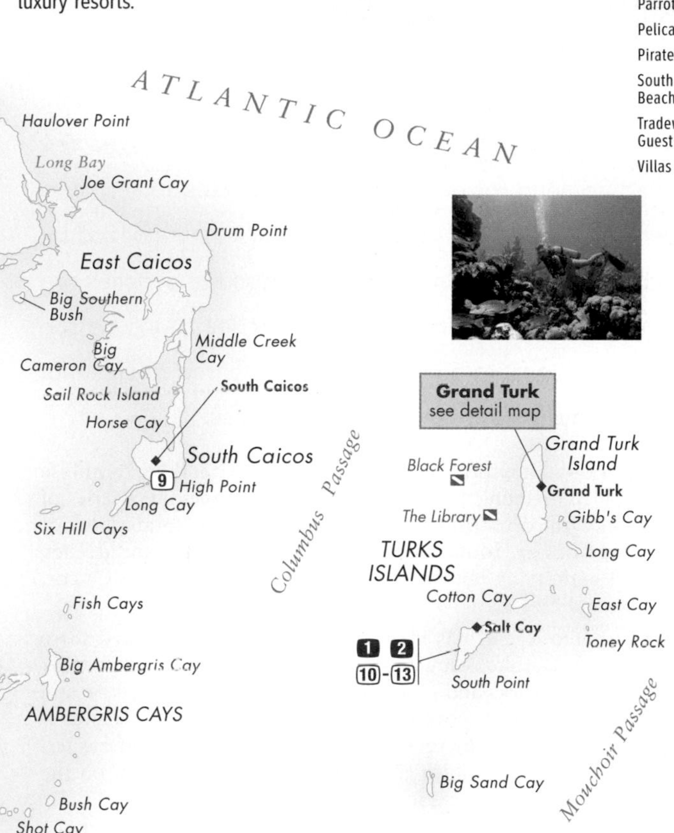

TOP REASONS TO VISIT TURKS AND CAICOS ISLANDS

1 Beautiful Beaches: Even on Provo, there are miles of deserted beaches without any beach umbrellas in sight.

2 Excellent Diving: The third-largest coral-reef system in the world is among the world's top dive sites.

3 Easy Island-Hopping: Island-hopping beyond the beaten path will give you a feel for the islands.

4 The Jet Set: Destination spas, penthouse suites, and exclusive villas and resorts make celebrity-spotting a popular sport.

5 Exploring on the Sea: You'll find excellent fishing and boating among the uninhabited coves and cays.

Updated by David Fenimore and Laura Brander

With water so turquoise that it glows, you may find it difficult to stray far from the beach in the Turks and Caicos. You may find no need for museums, and no desire to see ruins or even to read books. You may find yourself hypnotized by the water's many neon hues. And because the beaches are among the most incredible you will ever see, don't be surprised if you wake up on your last morning and realize that you didn't find a lot of time for anything else.

Although ivory-white, soft, sandy beaches and breathtaking turquoise waters are shared among all the islands, the landscapes are a series of contrasts, from the dry, arid bush and scrub on the flat, coral islands of Grand Turk, Salt Cay, South Caicos, and Providenciales to the greener, foliage-rich undulating landscapes of Middle Caicos, North Caicos, Parrot Cay, and Pine Cay.

A much-disputed legend has it that Columbus first discovered these islands in 1492. Despite being on the map for longer than most other island groups, the Turks and Caicos Islands (pronounced *kay*-kos) still remain part of the less-discovered Caribbean. More than 40 islands—only eight inhabited—make up this self-governing British overseas territory that lies just 575 miles (925 km) southeast of Miami on the third-largest coral-reef system in the world.

The political and historical capital island of the country is Grand Turk, but most of the tourism development, which consists primarily of boutique hotels and condo resorts, has occurred in Providenciales, thanks to the beauty of its North Shore, and in particular Grace Bay, one of the world's most talked about beaches. Once home to a population of around 500 people plus a few donkey carts, Provo has now become the hub of activity, where one may enjoy resorts, spas, restaurants, and water sports. It's the temporary home for the majority of visitors who come to the Turks and Caicos.

LOGISTICS

Getting to the Turks and Caicos: Several major airlines fly nonstop to Providenciales from the United States. If you're going to one of the smaller islands, you'll usually need to make a connection in Provo. All international flights arrive at Providenciales International Airport (PLS), but you can hop over to the other islands from there.

Hassle Factor: Low–high, depending on the island and your home airport.

On the Ground: You can find taxis at the airports, and most resorts provide pickup service as well. Taxi fares are fairly reasonable on Provo and Grand Turk; on the smaller islands transfers can cost more since gas is much more expensive.

Getting Around the Islands: If you are staying on Provo, you'll probably want a car, at least for a couple of days. On Grand Turk, you can rent a car, but you probably won't need to.

Marks of the country's colonial past can be found in the wooden-and-stone, Bermudian-style clapboard houses—often wrapped in deep-red bougainvillea—that line the streets on the quiet islands of Grand Turk, Salt Cay, and South Caicos. Donkeys roam free in and around the salt ponds, which are a legacy from a time when residents of these island communities worked hard as both slaves and then laborers to rake salt (then known as "white gold") bound for the United States and Canada. In Salt Cay, the remains of wooden windmills are now home to large osprey nests. In Grand Turk and South Caicos, the crystal-edge tidal ponds are regularly visited by flocks of rose-pink flamingos hungry for the shrimp to be found in the shallow, briny waters.

In all, only 32,000 people live in the Turks and Caicos Islands; less than half are "Belongers," the term for the native population, mainly descended from Loyalist and Bermudian slaves who settled here beginning in the 1600s. The majority of residents work in tourism, fishing, and offshore finance, as the country is a tax haven. Indeed, for residents and visitors, life in "TCI" is anything but taxing. But even though most visitors come to do nothing—a specialty in the islands—it does not mean there's nothing to do.

PLANNING

WHEN TO GO

High season in Turks and Caicos runs roughly from November through April, with the usual extra-high rates during the Christmas and New Year's holiday period. Several hotels on Provo offer shoulder-season rates at the end of April and May. During the off-season, rates are reduced substantially, as much as 40%.

GETTING HERE AND AROUND

AIR TRAVEL

You can fly nonstop from Atlanta (Delta), Dallas (American), Charlotte (US Airways), Miami (American), New York–JFK (Delta and JetBlue), Newark–EWR (United), and Philadelphia (US Airways).

Although carriers and schedules can vary seasonally, there are many nonstop and connecting flights to Providenciales from several U.S. cities on American, Delta, JetBlue, and US Airways. There are also flights from other parts of the Caribbean on Air Turks & Caicos; this airline also flies to some of the smaller islands in the chain from Provo. There are also flights from Nassau on Bahamas Air, to Canadian cities on WestJet and Air Canada, and to London on British Airways.

Airports: The main gateways into the Turks and Caicos Islands are Providenciales International Airport (PLS) and Grand Turk International Airport (GDT). For private planes, Provo Air Center is a full-service FBO (Fixed Base Operator) offering refueling, maintenance, and short-term storage, as well as on-site customs and immigration clearance, a lounge, and concierge services. There are smaller airports on Grand Turk (GDT), North Caicos (NCS), South Caicos (XSC), and Salt Cay (SLX). Even if you are going on to other islands in the chain, you will probably stop in Provo first for customs, then take a domestic flight from there.

Airline Contacts Air Turks & Caicos ☎ *649/946–4999* 🌐 *www.intercaribbean.com.* **American Airlines** ☎ *800/433–7300* 🌐 *www.aa.com.* **Bahamas Air** ☎ *800/222–4262* 🌐 *up.bahamasair.com.* **Caicos Express** ☎ *649/941-5730* 🌐 *caicosexpressairways.com.* **Delta** ☎ *800/241–4141* 🌐 *www.delta.com.* **JetBlue** ☎ *800/538–2583* 🌐 *www.jetblue.com.* **United Airlines** ☎ *800/864–8331* 🌐 *www.united.com.* **US Airways** ☎ *800/428–4322* 🌐 *usairways.com.*

Airport Contacts Turks & Caicos Islands Airport Authority. The TCIAA website has a schedule of all flights coming into and out of the islands, along with real-time delay information. 🌐 *www.tciairports.com.*

BOAT AND FERRY TRAVEL

Despite the islands' relative proximity, ferry service is limited in the Turks and Caicos. You can take a ferry from Provo to North Caicos and South Caicos. There's also a ferry from Grand Turk to Salt Cay, but seemingly only when the planets align; the service is often inconsistent due to weather. Air service is your best bet.

Contacts Caribbean Cruisin' ✉ *Walkin Marina, Leeward, Providenciales* ☎ *649/946–5406, 649/231–4191* 🌐 *www.tciferry.com.* **Salt Cay Ferry** ✉ *Salt Cay* ☎ *649/244–1407* 🌐 *www.turksandcaicoswhalewatching.com.*

CAR TRAVEL

Driving here is on the left side of the road, British-style; when pulling out into traffic, remember to look to your right. Give way to anyone entering a roundabout, as roundabouts are still a relatively new concept in the Turks and Caicos; stop even if you are on what appears to be the primary road. The maximum speed is 40 mph (64 kph), 20 mph (30 kph) through settlements; speed limits, as well as the use of seat belts, are enforced.

If you are staying on Provo, you may find it useful to have a car; it's nice to enjoy a few days of exploring or also to get away from your hotel for dinner. On Grand Turk, you can rent a car, but you probably won't need to. Car- and jeep-rental rates average $39 to $100+ per day on Provo, plus a $15 surcharge per rental as a government tax. Be sure to check if the company you are renting from includes insurance with your rental. Many do not include liability. Reserve well ahead of time during the peak winter season. Most agencies offer free mileage and airport pickup service. Avis and Budget have offices on the islands. You might also try local Provo agencies such as Grace Bay Car Rentals, Rent a Buggy, Tropical Auto Rentals, and Caicos Wheels—the latter rents scooters, colorful ATVs, cars, and even cell phones. Pelican Car Rentals is on North Caicos, as well as a number of other operators who meet the ferries when they arrive at Sandy Point.

Contacts Avis ✉ *Airport, Providenciales* ☎ *649/946-4705, 649/941-7557, 649/946-8570* 🌐 *www.avis.tc.* **Budget** ✉ *Airport, Providenciales* ☎ *649/946-4079* 🌐 *www.global.budget.com/tc.* **Caicos Wheels** ✉ *Ports of Call, Grace Bay Rd., Grace Bay, Providenciales* ☎ *649/242-6592, 649/946-8302* 🌐 *www.CaicosWheels.com.* **Grace Bay Car Rentals** ✉ *Grace Bay Plaza, Grace Bay Rd., Grace Bay, Providenciales* ☎ *649/941-8500* 🌐 *www.gracebaycarrentals.com.* **Island Auto Rentals** ✉ *Carnival Cruise Center, Grand Turk* ☎ *649/232-0933, 649/231-4214, 649/946-2042.* **Pelican Car Rentals** ✉ *Whitby, North Caicos* ☎ *649/241-8275, 649/946-7112.* **Rent a Buggy** ✉ *1081 Leeward Hwy., Leeward, Providenciales* ☎ *649/946-4158, 649/231-6161* 🌐 *www.rentabuggy.tc* ☞ *Jeep rentals.* **Scooter Bob's** ✉ *Turtle Cove, Providenciales* ☎ *649/946-4684* 🌐 *www.scooterbobstci.com.* **Tropical Auto Rentals** ✉ *Tropicana Plaza, Leeward Hwy., Leeward, Providenciales* ☎ *649/946-5300* 🌐 *www.tropicalautorentaltci.com.*

26

TAXI TRAVEL

You can find taxis at the airports on both Provo and Grand Turk. You will also be able to organize a ride at the ferry dock on North Caicos. Most resorts have their own pickup service; those that don't are happy to prearrange a taxi for your arrival. When booking your accommodations, be sure to ask upfront about airport transfers to and from your hotel. A trip via taxi between Provo's airport and most major hotels runs between $15–$20 per person. On Grand Turk a trip from the airport to Cockburn Town is about $8; it's $8–$15 to hotels outside town on Grand Turk. Transfers usually cost more on the smaller islands, where gas is much more expensive. Taxis (actually large vans) in Providenciales are metered, and rates are regulated by the government at $2 per person per mile traveled. In the family islands, taxis may not be metered, so it's best discuss the cost for your trip in advance.

ESSENTIALS

Banks and Exchange Services The official currency on the islands is U.S. dollars. On Provo, there are ATMs at all bank branches (Scotiabank and First Caribbean), at the Graceway IGA Supermarket, as well as at Graceway's Gourmet in the Grace Bay area, and at Ports of Call shopping center. There are also Scotiabank and First Caribbean branches on Grand Turk. It's useful to have cash on hand when you visit the other islands because not everyone accepts credit cards.

Electricity Current is suitable for all U.S. appliances (120/240 volts, 60 Hz).

Guided Tours Big Blue Unlimited's educational ecotours include three-hour kayak trips and other guided journeys around the family islands. Its Coastal Ecology and Wildlife tour is a kayak adventure through red mangroves to bird habitats, rock iguana hideaways, and natural fish nurseries. The North Caicos Mountain Bike Eco Tour gets you on a bike to explore the island, the plantation ruins, the inland lakes, and at flamingo pond with a stop for lunch along the way. Package costs range from $85 to $225 per person. For an exciting overview of Provo, try an air tour with TCI Helicopters.

WHERE WHEN HOW

Check out *www.wherewhenhow.com*, a terrific source with links to restaurants, places to stay, excursions, and transportation. You can pick up the printed version of the magazine all around the island.

Contacts **Big Blue Unlimited** *Leeward Marina, Leeward, Providenciales* *649/946–5034, 649/231-6455* *www.bigblue.tc.* **TCI Helicopters.** Aerial tours of Providenciales are available for $195–$385 per person, depending on time in the air. *Provo Air Centre, Providenciales* *649/941–5079, 649/432–4354* *www.tcihelicopters.tc.*

Passport Requirements A valid passport is required to fly to the Turks and Caicos. Everyone must have an ongoing or return ticket.

Phones The country code for the Turks and Caicos is 649. To call the Turks and Caicos from the United States, dial 1, the area code (649), plus the seven-digit local number. Be aware that this is an international call. Calls from the islands are expensive, and many hotels add steep surcharges for long distance.

Taxes The departure tax is $60, but it is usually included in the cost of your airline ticket; you don't need to pay at the airport. Restaurants, hotels, and all tourism related activities, add a 12% government tax, and they typically add 10% to 15% for service. Be sure to check your bill to see if it has already been tacked on before leaving additional monies.

ACCOMMODATIONS

The Turks and Caicos can be a fairly expensive destination. Most hotels on Providenciales are pricey, but there are some moderately priced options; most accommodations are condo-style, but not all resorts are family-friendly. You'll find several upscale properties on the outer islands—including the famous Parrot Cay—but the majority of places are smaller inns. What you give up in luxury, however, you gain back tenfold in island charm. Though the smaller islands are relatively isolated, that's partly what makes them so attractive in the first place.

Resorts: Most of the resorts on Provo are upscale; many are condo-style, so at least you will have a well-furnished kitchen for breakfast and a few quick lunches. There are two all-inclusive resorts on Provo. A handful of other luxury resorts are on the smaller islands. Many resorts are closed from one to six weeks a year, depending on economics, the hurricane season, and employee vacations. Some resorts may also use slow periods (usually October) to refurbish, so ask questions when booking, particularly if you're booking in the fall.

Small Inns: Aside from the exclusive, luxury resorts, most of the places on the outlying islands are smaller, modest inns with relatively few amenities. Some are devoted to diving.

Villas and Condos: Villas and condos are plentiful, particularly on Provo, and usually represent good value for families. However, you need to plan a few months in advance to get what suits you best.

Hotel reviews have been shortened. For full information, visit Fodors.com.

WHAT IT COSTS IN U.S. DOLLARS				
	$	$$	$$$	$$$$
Restaurants	under $12	$12–$20	$21–$30	over $30
Hotels	under $275	$275–$375	$376–$475	over $475

Restaurant prices are the average cost of a main course at dinner or, if dinner is not served, at lunch. Hotel prices are the lowest cost of a standard double room in high season.

VISITOR INFORMATION

The tourist offices on Grand Turk and Providenciales are open daily from 9 to 5.

Contacts Turks & Caicos Reservations. On-island service handles reservations for hotels, resorts, villas, restaurants, and more. Locals know. ✉ *Providenciales* ☎ *877/774–5486, 649/941–8988* 🌐 *www.turksandcaicosreservations.tc.*

WEDDINGS

The residency requirement for both parties is 24 hours, after which you can apply for a marriage license to the registrar in Grand Turk. You must present a passport, original birth certificate, and proof of current marital status, as well as a letter stating both parties' occupations, ages, addresses, and fathers' full names. No blood tests are required. The license fee is $50.

Nila Destinations Wedding Planning ☎ *649/231–3986* 🌐 *www.niladestinations.com.*

PROVIDENCIALES

Passengers typically become silent when their plane starts its descent, mesmerized by the shallow, crystal clear turquoise waters of Chalk Sound National Park. This island, nicknamed Provo, was once called Blue Hills after the name of its first settlement. Just south of the airport and downtown area, Blue Hills is the closest thing you can get to a more typical Caicos island settlement on what's now the most developed of the islands in the chain. Most of the modern resorts, exquisite spas, water-sports operators, shops, business plazas, restaurants, bars, cafés, and the championship golf course are on or close by the stretch of Grace Bay beach. In spite of the ever-increasing number of taller and grander condominium resorts, it's still possible to find deserted stretches on the ivory-white shoreline. For guaranteed seclusion, rent a car and go explore the southern shores and western tip of the island, but be wary in your isolation; never carry valuables on your person or in your vehicle. And never go alone. Another wonderful option is to set sail for a private island getaway on one of the many deserted cays nearby.

26

Progress and beauty come at a price: with plenty of new visitors arriving each year, the country's charms are no longer a secret, but don't worry—you'll still enjoy the gorgeous beaches and wonderful dinners. Although you may start to believe that every road leads to a big resort development, there are, happily, plenty of sections of beach where you can escape the din.

Although you may be kept quite content enjoying the beachscape and top-notch amenities of Provo itself, it's also a great starting point for island-hopping tours by sea or by air as well as fishing and diving trips. Resurfaced roads should help you get around and make the most of the main tourism and sightseeing spots.

EXPLORING

WORTH NOTING

FAMILY **Caicos Conch Farm.** More than 3 million conchs are farmed at this commercial operation on the northeast tip of Provo. It's a popular tourist attraction, too, with guided tours and a small gift shop selling conch-related souvenirs, jewelry, and freshwater pearls. You can even meet Jerry and Sally, the resident conchs that are brought out on demand. Fish farming is also part of the operation. ✉ *Leeward-Going-Through, Leeward, Providenciales* ☎ *649/946–5330* 🌐 *www.caicosconchfarm.net/* 🎫 *$12* ⏲ *Weekdays 9–4, Sat. 9–2:30.*

Chalk Sound National Park. As you drive toward Sapodilla Bay on South Dock Road, on your right you will get glimpses of Chalk Sound. The water here is the brightest turquoise you'll ever see, and the mushroom-like tiny islands make the colors even bolder. There are a couple of places to stop for pictures, or you can enjoy lunch overlooking it at Las Brisas Restaurant. No matter how many times you see it, it still manages to take your breath away. ✉ *Chalk Sound Rd., Chalk Sound, Providenciales.*

Cheshire Hall. Standing eerily just west of downtown Provo are the remains of a circa-1700 cotton plantation owned by the Loyalist Thomas Stubbs. A trail weaves through the ruins, where a few interpretive signs tell the story of the island's doomed cotton industry, with little information about the plantation itself. A variety of local plants are also identified. The lack of context can be disappointing for history buffs; a visit to North Caicos Wades Green plantation or the Turks & Caicos National Museum could well prove a better fit. ✉ *Leeward Hwy., across from Royal Jewels, Downtown, Providenciales* ☎ *649/941–5710 for National Trust* 🌐 *www.tcinationaltrust.com* 🎫 *$5* ⏲ *Mon.–Fri. 8:30–4:30, 9-1 Sat. (guided tour required).*

FAMILY **Sapodilla Hill.** On this cliff overlooking the secluded Sapodilla Bay, you can discover rocks carved with the names of shipwrecked sailors and dignitaries from TCI's maritime and colonial past. There are carvings on the rocks that some claim are secret codes and maps to hidden treasures; many have tried in vain to find these treasures. The hill is known by two other names, Osprey Rock and Splitting Rock. The less adventurous can see molds of the carvings at Provo's International Airport. It's best to go by boat with Captain Bill's Adventures, as cars in the parking area are occasionally broken into. ✉ *Off South Dock Rd., west of South Dock, Chalk Sound, Providenciales.*

BEACHES

All the beaches of Turks and Caicos have bright white sand that's soft like baby powder. An added bonus is that no matter how hot the sun gets, your feet never burn. The sand is soft and clean, even in the water, so there is little fear of stepping on rocks or corals. Even the beach areas with corals for snorkeling have clear, clean sand for entry until you reach them.

Fodor's Choice ★ **Grace Bay.** The 12-mile (18-km) sweeping stretch of ivory-white, powder-soft sand on Provo's north coast is simply breathtaking. It's home to migrating starfish as well as shallow snorkeling trails. The majority of Provo's beachfront resorts are along this shore, and it's the primary reason the Turks and Caicos is a world-class destination. **Amenities:** food and drink; parking (free); water sports. **Best for:** sunset; swimming; walking. ✉ *Grace Bay Rd., along the north shore, Grace Bay, Providenciales.*

Fodor's Choice ★ **Half Moon Bay.** This natural ribbon of sand links two uninhabited cays; it's only inches above the sparkling turquoise waters and one of the most gorgeous beaches on the island. There are limestone cliffs to explore as well as small, sandy coves; there's even a small wreck offshore for snorkeling. It's only a short boat ride away from Provo, and most of the island's tour companies run excursions here or simply offer a beach drop-off. These companies include Silverdeep and Caicos Dream Tours *(⇨ Boating and Sailing, in Sports and the Outdoors)*. **Amenities:** none. **Best for:** solitude; snorkeling; swimming; walking. ✉ *Between Pine Cay and Little Water Cay, Providenciales* 🌐 *Accessible only by boat, 15 minutes from Leeward Marina.*

Lower Bight Beach. Lower Bight Beach is often confused with Grace Bay Beach because it seems to blend right into it. Although the beach is gorgeous, it gets rocky here. It also has the best off-the-beach snorkeling—not just in Provo, but possibly the Caribbean. Thursday evening "fish fries" offer local food and music. **Amenities:** food and drink; parking (free). **Best for:** snorkeling; walking. ✉ *Lower Bight Rd., The Bight, Providenciales.*

Malcolm's Beach. It's one of the most stunning beaches you'll ever see, but you'll need a high-clearance vehicle to reach it. Bring your own food and drinks, because it doesn't have any facilities or food service unless you have made a reservation to eat at the very expensive Amanyara resort. There have been reports of break-ins at the parking lot in years past, so it's best to not keep any valuables in your car. From Malcolm's parking lot, for the best beach area, walk towards Amanyara, where there are no boulders in the water. **Amenities:** parking (free). **Best for:** solitude; swimming; walking. ✉ *Malcolm's Beach Rd., beyond the Amanyara turnoff, Northwest Point, Providenciales* ✣ *On Leeward Highway, take Fuller Walken Round-About towards Blue Hills. Keep following the road after it turns into rolled packed sand. Take the second unpaved*

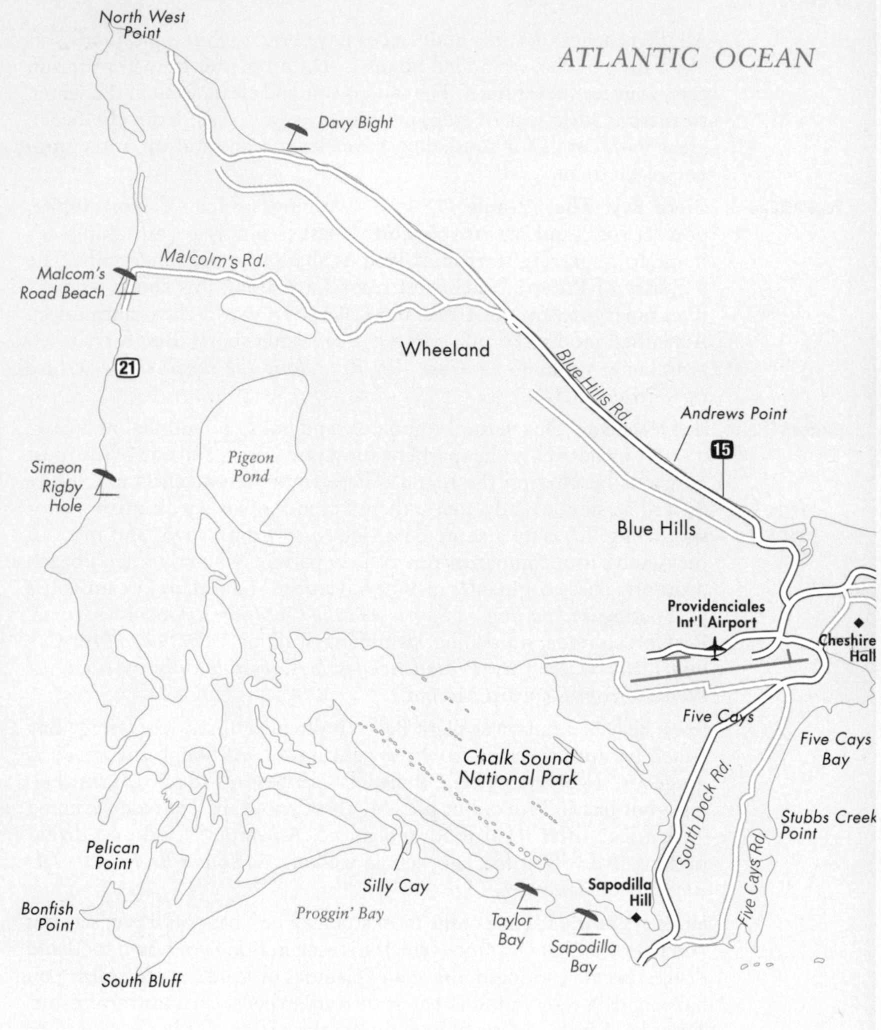

Restaurants ▼

- Anacaona **13**
- Angela's Top o' the Cove ... **3**
- Bay Bistro **6**
- Caicos Café **12**
- Coco Bistro **7**
- Coyaba Restaurant **9**
- Da Conch Shack **15**
- Fairways **14**
- Grace's Cottage **11**
- Hemingway's **10**
- Magnolia Wine Bar & Restaurant **2**
- Somewhere Café and Lounge **5**
- Stelle **4**
- Tiki Hut **1**
- The Vix **8**

Hotels ▼

- The Alexandra Resort **7**
- Amanyara **21**
- Beach House Turks and Caicos **20**
- Beaches Turks & Caicos **6**
- Club Med Turkoise **16**
- Gansevoort Turks and Caicos **2**
- Grace Bay Club **14**
- Harbour Club Villas **19**
- Island Club Townhouses ... **4**
- Ocean Club **17**
- Point Grace **12**

Water Cay

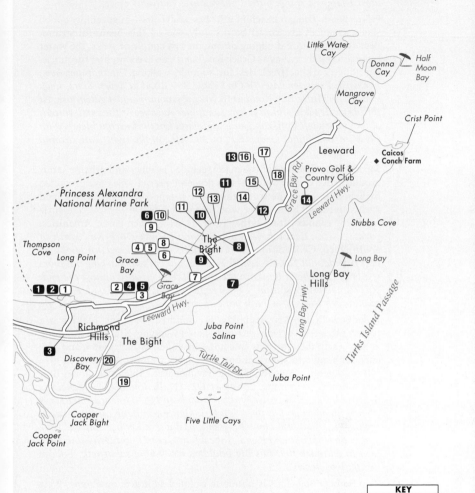

Little Water Cay

Donna Cay

Half Moon Bay

Mangrove Cay

Crist Point

Leeward

Caicos Conch Farm

Provo Golf & Country Club

Grace Bay Rd.

Leeward Hwy.

Princess Alexandra National Marine Park

Stubbs Cove

The Bight

Thompson Cove

Long Point

Grace Bay

Long Bay

Long Bay Hills

Long Bay Hwy.

Turks Island Passage

Richmond Hills

The Bight

Juba Point Salina

Turtle Tail Dr.

Discovery Bay

Juba Point

Cooper Jack Bight

Five Little Cays

Cooper Jack Point

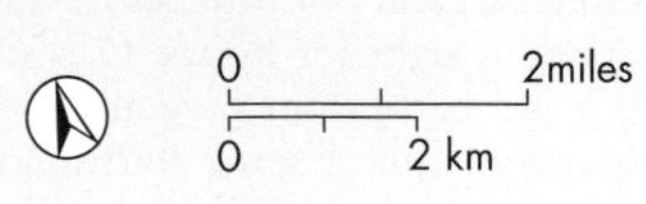

KEY

Beaches

Restaurants

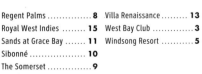

Hotels

road on the left. Follow road until the end, which takes about 20 minutes. There is a rough patch that requires caution.

Pelican Beach. Pelican Beach has the best souvenirs—huge, empty conch shells. Chances are you'll be the only one on this beautiful strand. Because of offshore dredging during the last couple of years, the water is not as crystal clear as at Grace Bay, but it's an even brighter turquoise. **Amenities:** parking (free). **Best for:** solitude; walking. ✉ *Sandpiper Ave., Leeward, Providenciales* ⊕ *On Grace Bay Road at Seven Stars, keep straight on Grace Bay Road until you pass an unmanned gatehouse. At the big circle take your first left, Sandpiper Avenue. At the small roundabout, take a left until road ends and park. On the beach it blends with Leeward Beach and Grace Bay on the left, on the right walk around to Pelican Beach.*

Sapodilla Bay. The best of the many secluded beaches and pristine sands around Provo can be found at this peaceful quarter-mile cove protected by Sapodilla Hill. The soft strand here is lapped by calm waves, and yachts and small boats move with the gentle tide. During low tide, little sandbar "islands" form—they're great for a beach chair. **Amenities:** parking (free). **Best for:** walking. ✉ *End of South Dock Rd., north of South Dock, Chalk Sound, Providenciales* ⊕ *From Leeward Highway take roundabout No. 6 towards Five Cays (there's no marking but there is a First Caribbean Bank on the corner). Follow until almost the end, past a small police station. Take a right at Chalk Sound Road. First dirt road on left leads to a small parking area.*

Taylor Bay. Taylor Bay is shallow for hundreds of yards, making it a perfect place for a private picnic or sunset wedding. Kids become giddy at this beach; they can play in a huge area of chest-high water, and parents don't have to worry about dangerous drop-offs. The beach also offers gorgeous views for the many villas here. **Amenities:** none. **Best for:** solitude; swimming. ✉ *Sunset Dr., Chalk Sound, Providenciales* ⊕ *From Leeward Highway, take roundabout No. 6 towards Five Cays (there's no marking but there is a First Caribbean Bank on the corner). Follow the road until almost the end, past a small police station. Take a right on Chalk Sound Road. Take left at Ocean Point Drive and park next to entrance that has big boulders blocking a sand path. Follow this path to beach.*

West Harbour Bay. This is about as isolated as it gets on Provo. West Bay has long stretches of beaches to walk and explore, and there's no other person in sight for hours. Occasionally Captain Bill's Outback Adventure excursion stops here and explores the nearby pirate caves. Not only can you find big red starfish in the water here but you might find a buried pirate's treasure if you correctly interpret the "maps" in the rock carvings. ⚠ **We can only recommend going by boat excursion, as there have been persistent break-ins at the parking lot.** **Amenities:** none. **Best for:** solitude; walking. ✉ *West Harbour, Providenciales.*

WHERE TO EAT

Whichever Provo restaurant you eat at (and there are more than 50), you'll be able to spot the islands' own influence in fresh seafood specials, colorful presentations, and a tangy dose of spice. Some restaurants close during the slow season (September through late October), with the exact dates fluctuating yearly.

Pick up a free copy of *Where When How's Dining Guide*, which you will find all over the island; it has menus, websites, and pictures of all the restaurants.

GRACE BAY

$$$$ MEDITERRANEAN

Anacaona. At Grace Bay Club, this thatch-roofed restaurant has the best setting in the Turks and Caicos, and perhaps in the entire Caribbean. Despite its elite clientele and high prices, the restaurant continues to offer a memorable dining experience minus any formality and attitude (and minus the air-conditioning). That said, children under 12 are not allowed, and long pants and collared shirts are required for men. Oil lamps on the tables, gently revolving ceiling fans, and the murmur of the trade winds add to the Edenic environment. The entrancing ocean views and the careful service make this an ideal choice when you want to be pampered. The kitchen uses the island's bountiful seafood and fresh produce to craft healthy, Mediterranean-influenced cuisine. It's a good thing the setting is amazing, though; the portions are tiny for what you pay. *Average main: $40 Grace Bay Club, Grace Bay Circle Rd., Grace Bay, Providenciales 649/946–5050 www.gracebayresorts.com/gracebayclub Reservations essential Closed Sept. No lunch.*

$$$$ INTERNATIONAL FAMILY Fodor's Choice ★

Bay Bistro. You simply can't eat any closer to the beach than here, the only restaurant in all of Provo to be built directly on the sand. You dine on a covered porch (or on one of three individual platforms) surrounded by palm trees and the sound of lapping waves. The spring-roll appetizer is delicious, and the oven-roasted chicken is the best on the island. At the very popular weekend brunch, which includes such favorites as eggs Benedict with mimosas (included), lines can be long if you don't have a reservation. Around the time of the full moon, ask about the memorable beach barbecue: all-you-can-eat ribs, pig roast, and bonfire on the sand. *Average main: $31 Sibonné Beach Hotel, Princess Dr., Grace Bay, Providenciales 649/946–5396 sibonne.com/grace-bay-bistro Reservations essential.*

$$$ ITALIAN

Caicos Café. At what's probably the most popular restaurant with locals, the island dishes come with an Italian twist. The bruschetta that everyone gets at the start of the meal is delicious enough that you may ask for seconds, and the bread is baked fresh every day at the bakery next door. Blackened fish and jerk chicken on top of pasta are popular, but we think that ravioli with cream sauce is the tastiest dish. On windy nights, the inland setting offers protection from the breezes. Be sure to wear bug spray at night. *Average main: $30 Caicos Café Plaza, Grace Bay Rd., Grace Bay, Providenciales 649/946–5278 caicoscafe@tciway.tc Closed Sun.*

26

$$$$ INTERNATIONAL Fodor's Choice ★ ✕ **Coco Bistro.** With tables under palm trees, Coco Bistro has a divine setting, and the food is just as good. Though not directly on the beach, the location under the tropical tree grove still reminds you that you are on vacation. Main courses are complemented by both French flourishes (served *au poivre*, for example) and West Indian (such as with mango chutney) and are accompanied by fried plantains and mango slaw to maintain a Caribbean flair. Consider conch soup, soft-shell-crab tempura, and sun-dried tomato pasta from the internationally influenced menu. Do not miss this restaurant; it is the best of the best on the island. ■ **TIP→ Make reservations at least 1 week ahead during non-peak season, 2 to 3 weeks ahead in peak season, as this is the most popular restaurant on island.** *Average main: $40 ✉ Grace Bay Rd., Grace Bay, Providenciales ☎ 649/946–5369 🌐 www.CocoBistro.tc Reservations essential ⏲ Closed Mon. No lunch.*

$$$$ INTERNATIONAL Fodor's Choice ★ ✕ **Coyaba Restaurant.** Directly behind Grace Bay Club at Caribbean Paradise Inn, this posh restaurant is in a palm-fringed setting. The nostalgic favorites here are served with tempting twists in conversation-piece crockery. Chef Paul Newman uses his culinary expertise for the daily-changing main courses, which include exquisitely presented dishes such as crispy, whole, yellow snapper fried in Thai spices. One standout is lobster Thermidor in a Dijon-mushroom cream sauce. You may want to try several different appetizers instead of an entrée for dinner; guava-and-tamarind barbecue ribs and coconut-shrimp tempura are two good choices if you go that route. If you enjoy creative menus, this is the place for you. Coyoba keeps the resident expat crowd happy with traditional favorites such as lemon meringue pie, albeit with his own tropical twist. Don't skip dessert; Paul makes incredible chocolate fondant. *Average main: $34 ✉ Caribbean Paradise Inn, Bonaventure Crescent, off Grace Bay Rd., Grace Bay, Providenciales ☎ 649/946–5186 🌐 www.coyabarestaurant.com Reservations essential ⏲ Closed Tues. and Sept.–Oct.*

$$$$ STEAKHOUSE Fodor's Choice ★ ✕ **Fairways Bar & Grill.** If you're a steak lover, there is no better steak to be found on the island. Located at the golf course, during the day they serve casual fare, at night it converts to fine dining. Rib eyes are aged different dates; you pick the aging. Pick a special chef's butter and accompanied sauce such as Bearnaise, port wine or peppercorn. Start with the amazing avocado bruschetta, add the delectable onion soup (do not miss!), and you will not have room for dessert. The weekend brunch is one of the best on the island. Lauren, the executive chef, can also host private-event parties. *Average main: $35 ✉ Grace Bay Rd., Grace Bay, Providenciales ☎ 649/946-5833 fairways@provogolfclub.com 🌐 www.provogolfclub.com.*

$$$$ INTERNATIONAL ✕ **Grace's Cottage.** At one of the prettiest dining settings on Provo, the tables are artfully set under wrought-iron cottage-style gazebos and around the wraparound veranda, which skirts the gingerbread-covered main building. The tangy and exciting entrées may include lobster lasagna with diced veggies or melt-in-your-mouth grilled beef tenderloin with truffle fries. The portions are small, but the quality is high. You might want to end with the mango-infused cheesecake, because after all, you're at the beach. Service is impeccable (ladies are given a small stool

so that their purses do not touch the ground). On Tuesday nights, live music adds to the good vibes. [$] *Average main: $40* ✉ *Point Grace, Off Grace Bay Rd., Grace Bay, Providenciales* ☎ *649/946–5096* 🌐 *www.pointgrace.com* *Reservations essential* ⏲ *No lunch.*

$$$ ECLECTIC ✕ **Hemingway's.** The casual and gorgeous setting, with a patio and deck offering views of Grace Bay, makes this one of the most popular tourist restaurants. At lunch don't miss the best fish tacos with mango chutney. For dinner there is an excellent kids' menu and something for everyone, including vegetarians. Order the popular "Old Man of the Sea," which features the freshest fish of the day. It's known for great sauces such as the wine reduction for the filet mignon, the creole for fish dishes, and a delicious curry for chicken. If you're on a budget, go right before 6 pm, when you can still order the less expensive lunch menu items. On Mondays NaDa sings while you dine; Thursday and Friday nights there's additional live music that adds to the ambience. [$] *Average main: $25* ✉ *The Sands at Grace Bay, Grace Bay Rd., Grace Bay, Providenciales* ☎ *649/946–8408* 🌐 *www.thesandstci.com.*

$$ MEXICAN ✕ **Somewhere Café and Lounge.** The Tex-Mex breakfasts here are enhanced by great views. Try the breakfast burrito, a light tortilla filled with scrambled eggs, peppers, and homemade salsa, best enjoyed while overlooking thatched umbrellas and snorkelers on the reef. For lunch, the black bean salsa and homemade guacamole score high marks. A three-tier outdoor terrace makes for terrific sunset dining, drawing a fun adult-only crowd into the evening for steak and fish with Mexican spice. The portions are always huge. There's live music many nights—Thursdays are the best. [$] *Average main: $18* ✉ *Coral Gardens Resort, Lower Bight Rd., The Bight, Providenciales* ☎ *649/941–8260* 🌐 *www.somewherecafeandlounge.com.*

$$$$ MODERN ITALIAN ✕ **Stelle.** At Stelle, chef Matthew Doerner serves modern Mediterranean cuisine with island touches, including local conch, grouper, and spiny lobster. You can choose either indoor dining or outdoor seating overlooking the pool at Gansevoort resort. Side dishes cost extra for the meat, poultry, and seafood entrées, but you can also get pasta dishes. There are interesting items among the small plates, such as charcuterie, peppered beef carpaccio, and conch ceviche. [$] *Average main: $37* ✉ *Gansevoort Resort, Grace Bay Beach, Providenciales* ☎ *649/941–7555* 🌐 *www.gansevoorttc.com.*

TURTLE COVE

$ DELI ✕ **Angela's Top o' the Cove New York Style Delicatessen.** Order deli sandwiches, salads, enticingly rich desserts, and freshly baked pastries at this island institution on Leeward Highway, just south of Turtle Cove. The location's not close to where most tourists stay, but it's worth the drive. From the deli case you can buy the fixings for a picnic; the shelves are stocked with a broad selection of fancy foodstuffs, as well as beer and wine. It's open at 6:30 am for a busy trade in coffees and cappuccinos. There's even a cheesesteak comparable to what you get in Philly. [$] *Average main: $9* ✉ *Leeward Hwy., Turtle Cove, Providenciales* ☎ *649/946–4694* 🌐 *www.provo.net/topothecove* ⏲ *No dinner.*

$$$$ ECLECTIC ✕ **Magnolia Wine Bar and Restaurant.** The hands-on owners here, Gianni and Tracey Caporuscio, make success seem simple. Expect

well-prepared, uncomplicated dishes from all over. You can construct an excellent meal from the outstanding appetizers, which might include spring rolls and a grilled-vegetable-and-fresh-mozzarella stack. Finish your meal with the mouthwatering molten chocolate cake. The atmosphere is romantic, the presentations are attractive, and the service is careful. It's easy to see why the Caporuscios have a loyal following. The adjoining wine bar includes a handpicked list of specialty wines, which can be ordered by the glass. The marine setting is a great place to watch the sunset. *Average main: $35 ✉ Miramar Resort, Lower Bight Rd., Turtle Cove, Providenciales ☎ 649/941–5108 🌐 www.magnoliaprovo.com ⏲ Closed Mon. No lunch.*

$$ AMERICAN FAMILY **✕ Tiki Hut.** From a location overlooking the marina, the ever-popular Tiki Hut serves consistently tasty, value-priced meals in a fun atmosphere. Locals take advantage of the Wednesday night chicken-and-rib special, and the lively bar is a good place to sample local Turks Head brew. There's a special family-style menu (the best kids' menu in Provo) and kids' seating. Don't miss pizzas made with the signature white sauce, or the jerk wings, coated in a secret barbecue sauce and then grilled—they're out of this world. The restaurant can be busy, with long waits for a table, and you can reserve only with five people or more. *Average main: $20 ✉ Turtle Cove Marina, Suzy Turn, Turtle Cove, Providenciales ☎ 649/941–5341 🌐 tikihut.tc.*

ELSEWHERE ON PROVIDENCIALES

$$ CARIBBEAN **✕ Da Conch Shack.** An institution in Provo for many years, this brightly colored beach shack is justifiably famous for its conch and seafood. The conch is fished fresh out of the shallows and broiled, spiced, cracked, or fried to absolute perfection. This is the freshest conch anywhere on the island, as the staff dive for it only after you've placed your order, but if you don't like seafood, there's also chicken. Go on a Tuesday night, when jerk chicken, peas and rice, and slaw are only $10.99, or a Wednesday night when there's live music on the sand. *Average main: $15 ✉ Blue Hills Rd., Blue Hills, Providenciales ☎ 649/946–8877 🌐 www.conchshack.tc.*

WHERE TO STAY

Most of the resorts on Providenciales are on Grace Bay, but a few are off the beaten track. You will find choices dotted along smaller bays around the island or even off the beach.

PRIVATE VILLA RENTALS

On Provo you can rent a self-catering apartment or a private house. For the best villa selection, make your reservations six months to a year in advance, or you may not get your first choice. Most villas can be rented on multiple villa-rental sites, which act as booking agents, and most have property managers or owners on-island to assist you. Vacation Rentals By Owners (VRBO) is an excellent overview of what is available.

Rental Contacts Coldwell Banker TCI. The agents at Coldwell Banker list some of the most beautiful vacation homes in Provo. ☎ *649/946–4969* 🌐 *www.coldwellbankertci.com.* **Prestigious Properties.** Modest to magnificent condos and houses in the Leeward, Grace Bay, and Turtle Cove areas of Providenciales are available from this company. ☎ *649/946–4379* 🌐 *www.prestigiousproperties.com*. **T.C. Safari.** This company manages numerous properties around Provo. ☎ *649/941–5043, 904/491-1415* 🌐 *www.tcsafari.tc.*

GRACE BAY

$$ RESORT FAMILY **The Alexandra Resort.** Situated on the most popular stretch of Grace Bay Beach, the Alexandra is within walking distance of shops, Coral Garden's snorkeling, and excellent restaurants. **Pros:** luxury for (somewhat) less, with lots of good amenities. **Cons:** some rooms have only queen beds, not kings. *Rooms from: $325* ✉ *Princess Dr., Grace Bay, Providenciales* ☎ *649/946–5807, 877/703–3303, 800/704–9424* 🌐 *www.alexandraresort.com* *88 rooms* *No meals.*

$$$$ ALL-INCLUSIVE FAMILY Fodor's Choice ★ **Beaches Turks & Caicos Resort Villages & Spa.** The largest resort in the Turks and Caicos Islands can satisfy families who might be just as eager to spend some time apart as together, and a recent major expansion and renovation has made it even better. **Pros:** great place for families; gorgeous pools. **Cons:** with an all-inclusive plan you miss out on the island's other great restaurants; excursions such as catamaran trip can get crowded; very expensive. *Rooms from: $884* ✉ *Lower Bight Rd., Grace Bay, Providenciales* ☎ *649/946–8000, 800/BEACHES* 🌐 *www.beaches.com* *758 rooms and suites* *All-inclusive.*

$$$$ ALL-INCLUSIVE **Club Med Turkoise.** In contrast to the other, more tranquil Grace Bay resorts, this energetic property has a vibrant party atmosphere, nightly entertainment, and even a flying trapeze—it caters mainly to fun-loving singles and couples. **Pros:** all-inclusive; active; good value; adults only (of all ages, not just young); numerous languages spoken. **Cons:** even with some renovations, the rooms are dorm-like and need updates and TLC; food just so-so. *Rooms from: $554* ✉ *Grace Bay Rd., Grace Bay, Providenciales* ☎ *649/946–5500, 888/932–2582* 🌐 *www.clubmed.com* *293 rooms* *All-inclusive.*

$$$$ RESORT **Gansevoort Turks + Caicos.** South Beach Miami–chic meets island time at this gorgeous resort with modern, comfortable furnishings. **Pros:** service is pleasant and eager to please; gorgeous heated pool and beautiful rooms; great ambience. **Cons:** since this is one of Provo's few nightlife venues, Friday and Saturday nights can get a little lively; need transportation for shops and exploring. *Rooms from: $750* ✉ *Lower Bight Rd., The Bight, Providenciales* ☎ *649/941–7555, 888/844–5986* 🌐 *www.gansevoorttc.com* *55 rooms, 32 suites, 4 penthouses* *Breakfast.*

$$$$ RESORT FAMILY **Grace Bay Club.** This stylish resort retains a loyal following because of its helpful, attentive staff and unpretentious elegance. **Pros:** gorgeous pool and restaurant lounge areas with outdoor couches, daybeds, and fire pits; all guests receive a cell phone to use on the island. **Cons:** no children allowed at Anacaona restaurant; have to stay in Estates section to get to its pool; expensive. *Rooms from: $995* ✉ *Grace Bay Rd., behind Grace Bay Court, Grace Bay, Providenciales* ☎ *649/946–5050, 800/946–5757* 🌐 *www.gracebayclub.com* *59 suites* *Breakfast.*

$ RENTAL **Harbour Club Villas.** Although not on the beach, this small complex of villas is by the marina, making it a good base for scuba diving and bonefishing. **Pros:** nice value; great base for divers; personable and

26

CLOSE UP

What Is a Potcake?

Feral dogs in the Bahamas and Turks and Caicos Islands are called potcakes. Traditionally, they would be fed from the leftover scraps of food that formed at the bottom of the pot in yesteryears; this is how they got their name. Much is being done these days to control the stray dog population. The TCSPCA and Potcake Place are two agencies working to adopt out the puppies. You can "travel with a cause" by adopting one of these gorgeous pups; they come with all their shots and all the papers required to bring them back home to the United States. Even if you don't adopt, you can help by volunteering as a carrier—bringing one back to its adoptive family. Customs in the States is actually easier when you are bringing back a potcake! You can also choose to borrow a pup for a couple of hours to take it for a walk, an activity that has become increasingly popular with those who are sad to have had to leave their canines back at home. For more information on how you can help, check out the website for Potcake Place (*www.potcakeplace.com*).

friendly hosts. **Cons:** need a car to get around island; not close to the better beaches; accommodations are a bit rustic. *Rooms from: $255 ✉ 36 Turtle Tail Dr., Turtle Tail, Providenciales ☎ 649/941–5748, 866/456–0210 www.harbourclubvillas.com 6 villas No meals.*

$ RENTAL **Island Club Townhouses.** If you're on a budget you won't find a place that gives you more for your money than this small condo complex. **Pros:** you can't get a better deal in Provo; centrally located so you can walk everywhere. **Cons:** the few condos for short-term rental go fast; no phones in the room; a block from the beach. *Rooms from: $240 ✉ Grace Bay Rd., Grace Bay, Providenciales ☎ 649/946–5866, 877/211–3133 www.islandclubgracebay.com 12 2-bedroom apartments No meals.*

$$ RESORT FAMILY **Ocean Club.** Enormous, locally painted pictures of hibiscus make a striking first impression as you enter the reception area at one of the island's most well-established condominium resorts. **Pros:** family-friendly resort with shuttles between the two shared properties; screened balconies and porches allow a respite from incessant air-conditioning. **Cons:** although clean, furniture is dated; if no car rental, you have to take the shuttle to get closer to the "hub." *Rooms from: $309 ✉ Grace Bay Rd., Grace Bay, Providenciales ☎ 649/946–5880, 800/457–8787 www.oceanclubresorts.com 86 suites No meals.*

$$$$ RESORT **Point Grace.** Asian-influenced rooftop domes blend with Romanesque stone pillars and wide stairways in this plush resort, which offers spacious beachfront suites and romantic cottages surrounding the centerpiece: a turquoise infinity pool with perfect views of the beach. **Pros:** relaxing environment; beautiful pool. **Cons:** can be extremely quiet (there are signs reminding you around the pool). *Rooms from: $656 ✉ Grace Bay Rd., Grace Bay, Providenciales ☎ 649/946–5096, 888/209-5582 www.pointgrace.com 23 suites, 9 cottage suites, 2 villas Closed Sept. Breakfast.*

$$$$ RESORT FAMILY **Regent Palms.** High on luxury and glitz, this is a place where glamour meets the beach. **Pros:** great people-watching; lively; one of the best spas in the Caribbean, and lots of other amenities. **Cons:** in the summer, the pool bar can get hot in the sunken area; kind of formal around the pool; sky-high rates. *Rooms from: $1,250* *Princess Dr., Grace Bay, Providenciales* *649/946–8666* *www.regentpalmstci.com* *72 suites* *Breakfast.*

$$ RESORT **Royal West Indies Resort.** With a contemporary take on colonial architecture and the outdoor feel of a botanical garden, this unpretentious resort on Grace Bay Beach has plenty of garden-view and beachfront studios and suites for moderate self-catering budgets. **Pros:** the best bang for the buck on Provo; on one of the widest stretches of Grace Bay Beach. **Cons:** Club Med next door can be noisy. *Rooms from: $310* *Bonaventure Crescent, Grace Bay, Providenciales* *649/946–5004, 800/332–4203* *www.royalwestindies.com* *99 suites* *No meals.*

$$ RESORT FAMILY **Sands at Grace Bay.** Spacious gardens and winding pools set the tone for one of Provo's most popular family resorts. **Pros:** one of the best places for families; central to shops and numerous restaurants; screened balconies and porches give an escape from incessant air-conditioning. **Cons:** the pool deck is dark wood, so keep your sandals or flip-flops handy; avoid courtyard rooms, which are not worth the price. *Rooms from: $360* *Grace Bay Rd., Grace Bay, Providenciales* *649/941–5199, 877/777–2637* *www.thesandstc.com* *118 suites* *No meals.*

26

$$$$ RESORT FAMILY Fodor's Choice ★ **Seven Stars.** Fronting gorgeous Grace Bay Beach, the tallest property on the island also sets a high mark for luxury with several buildings, an enormous heated pool, and huge in-room bathrooms—just about everything at Seven Stars is bigger and better than its competitors. **Pros:** beachside location; gorgeous inside and out; walking distance to everything in Grace Bay; terrific deck bar by the beach. **Cons:** some find the giant scale of the resort too big for the rest of the island. *Rooms from: $618* *Grace Bay Rd., Grace Bay, Providenciales* *649/941–7777, 866/570–7777* *www.sevenstarsgracebay.com* *107 suites* *Breakfast.*

$ HOTEL **Sibonné Beach Hotel.** Dwarfed by most of the nearby resorts, the smallest hotel on Grace Bay Beach has snug (by Provo's spacious standards) but pleasant rooms with Bermuda-style balconies and a tiny circular pool that's hardly used because the property is right on the beach. **Pros:** closest property to the beach; the island's best bargain directly on the beach. **Cons:** pool is small and dated. *Rooms from: $175* *Princess Dr., Grace Bay, Providenciales* *649/946–5547, 800/528–1905* *www.sibonne.com* *29 rooms, 1 apartment* *No meals.*

$$$$ RESORT **The Somerset.** This luxury resort has the wow factor, starting with the architecture and ending in your luxuriously appointed suite. **Pros:** the most beautiful architecture on Provo; located in middle, so you can still walk to snorkel, still walk to shops. **Cons:** the cheapest lockout rooms are not worth the cost—they can get noisy; service has suffered during management changes. *Rooms from: $950* *Princess Dr., Grace Bay, Providenciales* *649/946–5900, 877/887–5722* *www.thesomerset.com* *53 suites* *Breakfast.*

West Bay Club

$$$$ HOTEL **Beach House Turks and Caicos.** New owners as well as tastefully redesigned rooms and facilities at the former Turks and Caicos Club have created a tranquil, upscale hideaway on Grace Bay. **Pros:** gorgeous hues throughout offer tranquillity; true intimate boutique hotel. **Cons:** room service not offered all day; need transportation to the best restaurants and shops. *Rooms from: $545 Lower Bight Rd. 218, Providenciales 649/946–5800, 855/946–5800 www.beachhousetci.com 21 suites Breakfast.*

$$$$ RESORT **The Tuscany.** This self-catering, quiet, upscale resort is the place for independent travelers to unwind around one of the prettiest pools on Provo. **Pros:** luxurious; all condos have ocean views; beautiful pool. **Cons:** no restaurant, and it's at the far end of the hub; very expensive for a self-catering resort. *Rooms from: $950 Grace Bay Rd., Grace Bay, Providenciales 649/941–4667, 866/359–6466 www.thetuscanyresort.com 30 condos No meals.*

$$$$ RENTAL **Villa Renaissance.** Modeled after a Tuscan villa, this luxury property is self-catering and not really a full-service resort; nevertheless, you do get daily maid service, afternoon tea or coffee at the Pavilion Bar, and a weekly manager's cocktail reception. **Pros:** luxury for less; one of the prettiest courtyards in Provo. **Cons:** the pool bar is not consistently manned; not a full-service resort. *Rooms from: $760 Ventura Dr., Grace Bay, Providenciales 649/941–5300, 877/285–8764 www.villarenaissance.com 20 suites No meals.*

$$ RESORT Fodor's Choice ★ **West Bay Club.** One of Provo's newest resorts has a prime location on a pristine stretch of Grace Bay Beach just steps away from the best off-the-beach snorkeling. **Pros:** all rooms have a beach view; contemporary architecture makes it stand out from other resorts; amazing

luxury for the price. **Cons:** you'll need transportation to go shopping and to get to the main hub. *Rooms from: $365 ⊠ Lower Bight Rd., The Bight, Providenciales ☎ 649/946–8550, 866/607–4156 🌐 www.thewestbayclub.com 46 suites Breakfast.*

$$$ RESORT Fodor's Choice ★ **Windsong Resort.** On a gorgeous beach lined with several appealing resorts, Windsong stands out for two reasons: the Sail Provo program and a magnificent pool. **Pros:** the pool is the coolest; Sail Provo; gorgeous huge bathrooms. **Cons:** studios only have a refrigerator and microwave; thinner stretch of beachfront here. *Rooms from: $390 ⊠ Stubbs Rd., Lower Bight, Providenciales ☎ 649/941–7700 🌐 www.windsongresort.com 16 studios, 30 suites No meals.*

TURTLE COVE

$ B&B/INN **Turtle Cove Inn.** This pleasant two-story inn is affordable and comfortable. **Pros:** very reasonable prices for Provo; nice marina views. **Cons:** not on the beach; requires a car to get around. *Rooms from: $125 ⊠ Turtle Cove Marina, Turtle Cove, Providenciales ☎ 649/946–4203, 888/495–6077 🌐 www.turtlecoveinn.com 28 rooms, 2 suites No meals.*

ELSEWHERE ON PROVIDENCIALES

$$$$ RESORT Fodor's Choice ★ **Amanyara.** If you seek seclusion, peace, and tranquillity in a Zen-like atmosphere—and you're ready to pay a lot for it—this is your place. **Pros:** on one of the best beaches on Provo; resort is quiet and secluded. **Cons:** isolated; far from restaurants, excursions, and other beaches; probably the most expensive place to stay in Provo. *Rooms from: $1,650 ⊠ Northwest Point, Providenciales ☎ 649/941–8133 🌐 www.amanresorts.com 40 pavilions No meals.*

26

NIGHTLIFE

Although Provo is not known for its nightlife, there are some live bands and bars worth checking out. Popular singers such as Brentford Handfield, Justice, Corey Forbes, and Quinton Dean perform at numerous restaurants and barbecue bonfires. Danny Buoy's, where you can always watch the latest game on big video screens, gets going late at night. Be sure to see if any ripsaw bands—aka rake-and-scrape—are playing while you're on island; this is one of the quintessential local music genres: it's popular at local restaurants in Blue Hills. You can also find karaoke around the island if you enjoy holding the mike. Give the Turks & Caicos Miniature Golf Club a try; weekend evenings usually bring out the local songbirds and many more.

Late-night action can be found at Gansevoort Turks + Caicos (*see hotel review*), where DJs play until the wee hours on weekends, and Casablanca Casino, where everyone ends the night. The best time to come is wherever Daniel and Nadine are singing; this crowd-pleasing couple has developed a real following. And on Sunday, a barbecue bonfire at Seven Stars offers music while you dine on the sand.

Keep abreast of events and specials by checking **TCI eNews** (🌐 *www.tcienews.com*).

BARS AND CLUBS

Danny Buoy's. A popular Irish pub, Danny Buoy's has pool tables, darts, and big-screen TVs. It's a great place to watch sports broadcasts from all over. Different nights feature different nightlife; Tuesdays is karaoke, other nights have live music. It's open late every night. ✉ *Grace Bay Rd., across from Carpe Diem Residences, Grace Bay, Providenciales* ☎ *649/946–5921* 🌐 *www.dannybuoys.com.*

Somewhere on the Beach. A Tex-Mex alternative that gives the wallet a break from fine dining becomes the hot spot on Thursday nights with live music. Three levels of outdoor decks turn into adults-only bars at 4 pm, after 4 children allowed on bottom floor only. ✉ *Coral Gardens on Grace Bay, The Bight, Providenciales* ☎ *649/941–8260.*

Casablanca Casino. Slots, blackjack, American roulette, poker, craps, and baccarat are all here. Open until very late, this is often the last stop for the night. During slow season they may close on Sundays. ✉ *Grace Bay Rd., Grace Bay, Providenciales* ☎ *649/941–3737* ⏲ *Closed Sun. in summer.*

SHOPS AND SPAS

Handwoven straw baskets and hats, polished conch-shell crafts, paintings, wood carvings, model sailboats, handmade dolls, and metalwork are crafts native to the islands and nearby Haiti. The natural surroundings have inspired local and international artists to paint, sculpt, print, craft, and photograph; most of their creations are on sale in Providenciales.

AREAS AND MALLS

There are several main shopping areas in Provo: Grace Bay has the newer **Saltmills** complex and **La Petite Place** retail plaza, the new **Regent Village**, and the original **Ports of Call** shopping village.

ART AND CRAFTS GALLERIES

Anna's Art Gallery and Studio. Anna's sells original artworks, silk-screen paintings, sculptures, and handmade sea-glass jewelry. ✉ *The Saltmills, Grace Bay, Providenciales* ☎ *649/941–8841.*

ArtProvo. This is the island's largest gallery of designer wall art, but native crafts, jewelry, handblown glass, candles, and other gift items are also available. Featured artists include Trevor Morgan, from Salt Cay, and Dwight Outten. ✉ *Regent Village, Regent St., Grace Bay, Providenciales* ☎ *649/941–4545* 🌐 *www.artprovo.tc.*

Making Waves Art Studio. At this gallery, Sara the proprietor paints turquoise scenes, often on wood that doesn't require framing—they're surprisingly affordable. She also gives group art lessons at the studio. ✉ *Regent Village, Regent St., Grace Bay, Providenciales* ☎ *649/242–9588* 🌐 *www.makingwavesart.com.*

FOOD

After 5 Island Concierge. Sometimes you just need help before or during your trip. After 5 Island Concierge can do everything from find you a villa rental to provide grocery delivery or arrange a talented personal chef to cook during your condo or villa stay. Virtually any service you can think of is available from this company. ☎ *649/232–3483, 649/231–0731, 877/404–9535* 🌐 *www.islandconciergetc.com.*

Graceway IGA. With a large fresh-produce section, a bakery, gourmet deli, and extensive meat counter, the Provo's largest supermarket is likely to have what you're looking for. The most consistently well-stocked store on the island carries lots of known brands from the United Kingdom and North America, as well as a good selection of prepared foods, including rotisserie chicken, pizza, and potato salad. Expect prices to be much higher than at home. ✉ *Leeward Hwy., Providenciales* ☎ *649/941–5000* 🌐 *www.gracewayiga.com.*

LIQUOR

Wine Cellar. Visit this store for its large selection of duty-free liquor, at very good prices. ✉ *1025 Leeward Hwy., east of Suzie Turn Rd., Providenciales* ☎ *649/946–4536* 🌐 *www.winecellar.tc* ⏲ *Mon.–Sat. 8–6.*

SPAS

Except for Parrot Cay, Provo is the best destination in the Turks and Caicos if you are looking for a spa vacation. The spas here offer treatments with all the bells and whistles, and most get very good word of mouth. Most of Provo's high-end resorts have spas, but if you're staying at a villa, Spa Tropique or Teona Spa will bring their services to you.

Anani Spa at Grace Bay Club. Anani Spa at Grace Bay Club is on the Villas side of the complex; the six treatment rooms have alfresco showers, but treatments can also be performed on your balcony at Grace Bay Club facing the ocean. One of the most popular treatments is the Exotic Lime and Ginger Salt Glow; not only will it polish your skin, but the aroma it leaves on your skin is worth the treatment. ✉ *Villas at Grace Bay Club, Bonaventure Crescent, Grace Bay, Providenciales* ☎ *649/946–5050* 🌐 *www.gracebayresorts.com.*

Beaches Red Lane Spa. Open to nonresort guests, this spa has one hot plunge pool and one cold plunge pool to get the circulation going. During special hours, it offers kids' treatments, too. Although Beaches is an all-inclusive resort, spa treatments are an additional charge to guests. ✉ *Beaches Turks & Caicos Resort Villages & Spa, Lower Bight Rd., Grace Bay, Providenciales* ☎ *649/946–8000* 🌐 *www.beaches.com.*

Como Shambhala at Parrot Cay. Asian holistic treatments, yoga with the world's leading teachers in a stunning pavilion, and a signature health-conscious cuisine are all part of the program here. The infinity pool, Pilates studio, steam room, sauna, and outdoor Jacuzzi make you feel complete. If you're staying in Provo, you can call for reservations, but you have to pay for the boat ride to Parrot Cay. Some consider this one of the finest spas in the world, and you'd be hard-pressed to find a better one in the Turks and Caicos. ✉ *Parrot Cay Resort, Parrot Cay, Parrot Cay* ☎ *649/946–7788* 🌐 *www.comoshambhala.com.*

Regent Spa. Regent Spa is so gorgeous that it has been featured on several travel magazine covers. A reflecting pool with majestic date palms sets the scene. The signature treatment, a "Mother of Pearl Body Exfoliation," uses hand-crushed local conch shells to revitalize and soften skin. On an island with several terrific spas, the combination of a beautiful setting and treatments incorporating local ingredients makes this a standout. ✉ *Regent Palms, Princess Dr., Grace Bay, Providenciales* ☎ *649/946–8666, 866/877–7256* 🌐 *www.regentpalmstci.com.*

Spa Sanay. Spa Sanay recently moved into Alexandra Resort, where it offers facials, massages, body treatments and nail services. There is also a line of men-only treatments. ✉ *Alexandra Resort, Grace Bay Beach, Grace Bay, Providenciales* ☎ *649/432–1092, 649/946–5807* 🌐 *www.spasanay.com.*

Spa Tropique. You pick the place, and this spa comes to you—an ideal option for those in more isolated villas who can't bear to leave their island paradise; the spa can also come to your hotel room (provided your hotel has no spa of its own). Have your treatment on your balcony, or on the beach or by the pool, which will make the treatments seem extra special. Spa Tropique's one-of-a-kind Turks Island Salt Glow incorporates local salts from Grand Turk and Salt Cay. The spa also has locations at Ocean Club West and the Sands Resort. ✉ *Ports of Call Shopping Center, Grace Bay Rd., Grace Bay, Providenciales* ☎ *649/331–2400* 🌐 *www.spatropique.com.*

Teona Spa. Treatments here include the "Two Hot to Handle" couples massage, which includes a warming Boreh mask and Mediterranean hot-oil massage. Afterwards you can wind down with spice tea or a glass of wine. ✉ *The Regent Grand Resort, Regent St., Grace Bay, Providenciales* ☎ *649/941–5051* 🌐 *www.theregentgrandresort.com.*

Thalasso Spa at Point Grace. Thalasso Spa at Point Grace has three white-washed open-air cabanas on the dunes looking out to the beach. French skin oils and the latest European techniques are incorporated in all skin treatments, along with elements of the ocean, including sea mud, seaweed, and sea salt. The setting alone, with the breezes and views of Grace Bay, is worth the stop. ✉ *Point Grace Resort, Grace Bay Rd., Grace Bay, Providenciales* ☎ *649/946–5096* 🌐 *www.pointgrace.com.*

SPORTS AND THE OUTDOORS

BICYCLING

Most hotels have bicycles available for guests, or you can rent one from an independent company. Stick to the sidewalks on Grace Bay Road; drivers don't pay much attention to bikes, and you'll create less dust on this dry island.

BOATING AND SAILING

Provo's calm, reef-protected seas combine with constant easterly trade winds for excellent sailing conditions. Several multihulled vessels offer charters with snorkeling stops, food and beverage service, and sunset vistas. Prices range from $89 per person for group trips (subject to passenger minimums) to upwards of $600 or more for private charters.

FAMILY
Fodor's Choice ★
Island Vibes. Shaun Dean makes these excursions stand out, since he grew up on these waters. If conditions are right, he'll have you snorkel the "abyss," where the reef drops 6,000 feet. The sight is amazing. His boat is also the best on Provo, with a diving board on the roof as

well as a bathroom. ✉ *Turtle Cove Marina, Turtle Cove, Providenciales* ☎ *649/231–8423* 🌐 *www.islandvibestours.com.*

Sail Provo. Very popular for private charters, Sail Provo also runs 52-foot and 48-foot catamarans on scheduled half-day, full-day, sunset, and kid-friendly glowworm cruises (these are held in the first few days after full moons, when underwater creatures light up the sea's surface for several days). ✉ *Heaving Down Rock, Leeward, Providenciales* ☎ *649/946–4783* 🌐 *www.sailprovo.com.*

Silver Deep. Silver Deep sailing trips include time for snorkeling and beachcombing at a secluded beach. If you're thinking of fishing, keep in mind that Captain Arthur Dean here is said to be among the Caribbean's finest bonefishing guides. ✉ *Ocean Club West Plaza, Grace Bay Rd., Grace Bay, Providenciales* ☎ *649/946–5612* 🌐 *www.silverdeep.com.*

Sun Charters. The *Atabeyra,* operated by Sun Charters, is a retired rumrunner and the choice of residents for special events. Sunset rum punch parties and glowworm excursions are its specialty. There are also regularly scheduled sunset and half-day snorkeling cruises if you don't want to do a charter. ✉ *Leeward Marina, Leeward, Providenciales* ☎ *649/231-0624* 🌐 *www.suncharters.tc.*

26

Undersea Explorer. For sightseeing below the waves, try a semi-submarine, the *Undersea Explorer,* operated by Caicos Tours out of the Turtle Cove Marina. You can stay dry within the small, lower observatory as it glides along on a one-hour tour of the reef, with large viewing windows on either side. ✉ *Turtle Cove Marina, Turtle Cove, Providenciales* ☎ *649/231–0006* 🌐 *www.caicostours.com* 🎫 *$70.*

Water Play Provo. Right on the beach, they have windsurfing, stand-up paddleboards, and kayaks for multiple day or weekly rentals. ✉ *Ocean Club, Grace Bay Rd., Grace Bay, Providenciales* ☎ *649/331–3122* 🌐 *www.waterplayprovo.com.*

DIVING AND SNORKELING

Fodor's Choice ★ The island's many shallow reefs offer excellent and exciting snorkeling relatively close to shore. Try **Smith's Reef** over Bridge Road east of Turtle Cove, or the Bight Reef in front of Coral Gardens, to explore the reef as it comes in to touch the shoreline. A third option is the patch coral just off Babalua Beach, located between the north shore's Turtle Cove and Thompson Cove; you will need a car to get there.

Scuba diving in the crystalline waters surrounding the islands ranks among the best in the Caribbean. The reef and wall drop-offs thrive with bright, unbroken coral formations and lavish numbers of fish and marine life. Mimicking the idyllic climate, waters are warm all year, averaging 76°F to 78°F in winter and 82°F to 84°F in summer. With minimal rainfall and soil runoff, visibility is usually very good and frequently superb, ranging from 60 feet to more than 150 feet. An extensive system of marine national parks and boat moorings, combined with an eco-conscious mind-set among dive operators, contributes to an uncommonly pristine underwater environment.

Diving with stingrays

Dive operators in Provo regularly visit sites at **Grace Bay** and **Pine Cay** for spur-and-groove coral formations and bustling reef diving. They make the longer journey to the dramatic walls at **North West Point** and **West Caicos** depending on weather conditions. Instruction from the major diving agencies is available for all levels and certifications, including technical diving. An average one-tank dive costs $45; a two-tank dive, $90; they go upwards from there depending on the number of divers aboard, where the dive sites are, and what services are included. There are also two live-aboard dive boats available for charter working out of Provo.

Big Blue Unlimited. The educational ecotours from Big Blue include three-hour kayak trips and land-focused guided journeys around the family islands. Its Coastal Ecology and Wildlife tour is a kayak adventure through red mangroves to bird habitats, rock iguana hideaways, and natural fish nurseries. The Middle Caicos Bicycle Adventure gets you on a bike to explore the island, touring limestone caves in Conch Bar with a break for lunch with the Forbes family in the village of Bambarra. A new package explores South Caicos. Packages start at $255 for adults. No children under 12 are allowed. ✉ *Leeward Marina, Marina Rd., Leeward, Providenciales* ☎ *649/946–5034, 649/231-6455* 🌐 *www.bigblueunlimited.com.*

Caicos Adventures. Run by the friendly Frenchman Fifi Kuntz, Caicos Adventures offers daily trips to West Caicos, French Cay, and Molasses Reef. The company owns several boats, including the *Lady K*, a luxury motorboat available for private charters. ✉ *Regent Village, Grace Bay Rd., Grace Bay, Providenciales* ☎ *649/941–3346* 🌐 *www.caicosadventures.com.*

CLOSE UP

Diving the Turks and Caicos Islands

Scuba diving was the original water sport to draw visitors to the Turks and Caicos Islands in the 1970s. Aficionados are still drawn by the abundant marine life, including humpback whales in winter, sparkling clean waters, warm and calm seas, wall diving, and the coral reefs around the islands. Diving in the Turks and Caicos—especially off Grand Turk, South Caicos, and Salt Cay—remains among the best in the world.

Off Providenciales, dive sites are along the north shore's barrier reef. Most sites can be reached in anywhere from 10 minutes to 1½ hours. Dive sites feature spur-and-groove coral formations atop a coral-covered slope. Popular stops such as **Aquarium, Pinnacles,** and **Grouper Hole** have large schools of fish, turtles, nurse sharks, and gray reef sharks. From the south side, dive boats go to **French Cay, West Caicos, South West Reef,** and **Northwest Point.** Known for typically calm conditions and clear water, the West Caicos Marine National Park is a favorite stop. The area has dramatic walls and marine life, including sharks, eagle rays, and octopus, with large stands of pillar coral and huge barrel sponges.

Off Grand Turk, the 7,000-foot coral wall is actually within swimming distance of the beach. Buoyed sites along the wall have swim-through tunnels, cascading sand chutes, imposing coral pinnacles, dizzying vertical drops, and undercuts where the wall goes beyond the vertical and fades beneath the reef.

26

Fodor's Choice ★ **Caicos Dream Tours.** Caicos Dream Tours offers several snorkeling trips, including one that has you diving for conch before lunch on a gorgeous beach. The company also offers private charters. ✉ *Alexandra Resort, Princess Dr., Grace Bay, Providenciales* ☎ *649/231–7274* 🌐 *www.caicosdreamtours.com.*

Dive Provo. Dive Provo is a PADI Five Star operation that runs daily one- and two-tank dives to popular Grace Bay sites as well as West Caicos. ✉ *Ports of Call, Grace Bay Rd., Grace Bay, Providenciales* ☎ *649/946–5040, 800/234–7768* 🌐 *www.diveprovo.com.*

Provo Turtle Divers. Provo Turtle Divers, which also operates out of the Ocean Club and Ocean Club West, has been on Provo since the 1970s. The staff is friendly, knowledgeable, and unpretentious. ✉ *Turtle Cove Marina, Turtle Cove, Providenciales* ☎ *649/946–4232, 800/833–1341* 🌐 *www.provoturtledivers.com.*

FISHING

The islands' fertile waters are great for angling—anything from bottom- and reef-fishing (most likely to produce plenty of bites and a large catch) to bonefishing and deep-sea fishing (among the finest in the Caribbean). Each July the Caicos Classic Catch & Release Tournament attracts anglers from across the islands and the United States, who compete to catch the biggest Atlantic blue marlin, tuna, or wahoo. For any fishing activity, you are required to purchase a $15 visitor's fishing license; operators generally furnish all equipment, drinks, and snacks.

Prices range from $100 upwards, depending on the length of trip and size of boat.

Grand Slam Fishing Charters. For deep-sea fishing trips in search of marlin, sailfish, wahoo, tuna, barracuda, and shark, look up this company. ✉ *Turtle Cove Marina, Turtle Cove, Providenciales* ☎ *649/231–4420* 🌐 *www.gsfishing.com.*

Gwendolyn Fishing Charters. Gwendolyn sets up deep-sea fishing trips for marlin, sailfish, wahoo, tuna, barracuda, and shark. ✉ *Turtle Cove Marina, Turtle Cove, Providenciales* ☎ *649/946–5321* 🌐 *www.fishtci.com.*

Silverdeep ✉ *Leeward Marina, Leeward, Providenciales* ☎ *649/946–5612* 🌐 *www.silverdeep.com.*

GOLF

Fodor's Choice ★ **Provo Golf and Country Club.** The par-72, 18-hole championship course at Provo Golf and Country Club is a combination of lush greens and fairways, rugged limestone outcroppings, and freshwater lakes. Designed by Karl Litten, it is ranked among the Caribbean's top courses. Premium golf clubs are available ✉ *Governor's Rd., Grace Bay, Providenciales* ☎ *649/946–5991, 877/218–9124* 🌐 *www.provogolfclub.com* *$185 for 18 holes, $95 for 9 holes with shared cart.* *18 holes, 6705 yards, par 72.*

HORSEBACK RIDING

Provo Ponies. Provo Ponies offers morning and afternoon rides for all levels. A 60-minute ride costs $75; a 90-minute ride is $90. Reservations are required, and there is a 200-pound weight limit. You can get a pickup at your Grace Bay hotel or villa (Grace Bay area only) for an additional $10 per person, which is a good deal if you don't have a rental car. It's closed on weekends. ⚠ **If you are staying at Beaches, make your own reservations; bookings through the excursion desk are not accepted.** ✉ *Long Bay, Providenciales* ☎ *649/946–5252, 649/241–6350* 🌐 *www.provoponies.com.*

PARROT CAY

Once said to be a hideout for Calico Jack Rackham and his fellow pirates Mary Read and Anne Bonny, the 1,000-acre cay, between Fort George Cay and North Caicos, is now the site of a luxury resort.

The only way to reach Parrot Cay is by private boat or the resort's private ferry from its own dock

WHERE TO STAY

$$$$ RESORT Fodor's Choice ★ **Parrot Cay Resort.** This private paradise, on its own island, pairs tranquillity with the best service in Turks and Caicos. **Pros:** impeccable service; gorgeous, secluded beach; the spa is considered one of the best in the world. **Cons:** only two restaurants on the entire island; it's expensive to get back and forth to Provo for excursions, as there is only private ferry service. $ *Rooms from: $750* ✉ *Parrot Cay, Parrot*

Parrot Cay Resort

Cay ☎ *649/946–7788, 877/754–0726* 🌐 *www.parrotcay.como.bz* ⇨ *42 rooms, 4 suites, 14 villas* 🍽 *Breakfast.*

PINE CAY

15 to 20 minutes by boat from Provo.

Pine Cay's 2½-mile-long (4-km-long) beach is among the most beautiful in the archipelago. The 800-acre private island, which is in the string of small cays between Provo and North Caicos, is home to a secluded resort and almost 40 private residences. The beach alone is reason to stay here: the sand seems a little whiter, the water a little brighter than beaches on the other cays. Nonguests of the Meridian Club can make reservations for lunch. Expect to pay $85 plus taxes for the day, plus a fee for the boat transfer; there are themed buffets on Sunday.

WHERE TO STAY

$$$$ RESORT Fodor's Choice ★

Meridian Club. Feeling like a private club, this resort on the prettiest beach in Turks and Caicos is *the* place to de-stress, with no phones, no TVs, no air-conditioning, no worries. **Pros:** the finest beach in Turks and Caicos; rates include some of the best food in the Turks and Caicos as well as snorkeling trips. **Cons:** no TVs or phones, so you are really unplugged here; expensive to get back to Provo for shopping or other Provo-based excursions or activities; all this simplicity costs a great deal. $ *Rooms from: $1,060* ✉ *Pine Cay* ☎ *649/946–7758, 866/746–3229,*

CLOSE UP

Local Souvenirs

What should you bring home after a fabulous vacation in the Turks and Caicos Islands? Here are a few suggestions, some of which are free.

You can bring home up to three conch shells (shells only). The Middle Caicos Co-op shop, in addition to its Conch Bar location, sells its local crafts at a market in front of Gourmet IGA on Grace Bay Road the second Saturday of each month. You'll find locally made ceramics at Art Provo and at Turks & Caicos National Trust (at Town Center Mall or next to Island Scoop Ice Cream).

The Conch Farm sells beautiful, affordable jewelry made from conch shells and freshwater pearls.

One of the best souvenirs is the hardcover coffee-table cookbook from the Red Cross. Not only is it gorgeous, featuring recipes from all the great chefs of the Turks and Caicos, but the proceeds help the Red Cross.

If you're a dog lover, then maybe the best free souvenir would be to adopt a potcake puppy. Dogs come with a carrier, papers, and all their shots—and one will remind you year after year of your terrific vacation.

888/286–7993 🌐 www.meridianclub.com 12 rooms, 1 cottage, 7 villas ⏲ Closed Aug.–Oct. 🍴 All meals.

NORTH CAICOS

Thanks to abundant rainfall, this 41-square-mile (106-square-km) island is the lushest in the Turks and Caicos chain. With an estimated population of only 1,500, the expansive island allows you to get away from it all. Bird-lovers can see a large flock of flamingos here, anglers can find shallow creeks full of bonefish, and history buffs can visit the ruins of a Loyalist plantation. Although there's little traffic, almost all the roads are paved, so bicycling is an excellent way to sightsee. Even though it's a quiet place, you can find some small eateries around the settlements and in Whitby, giving you a chance to try local and seafood specialties, sometimes served with homegrown okra or corn. The beaches are in a natural state here, as they are often sprinkled with seaweed and pine needles, as there are no major resorts to rake them daily. Nevertheless, some of these secluded, less manicured strands are breathtaking.

North Caicos is definitely rustic, especially in comparison with shiny new Provo. Accommodations are clean but fairly basic. Locals are consistently friendly, and life always seems to move slowly.

EXPLORING NORTH CAICOS

WORTH NOTING

Flamingo Pond. This is a regular nesting place for the beautiful pink birds. They tend to wander out into the middle of the pond, so bring binoculars to get a better look. ✉ *North Caicos.*

Kew. This settlement has a school, a church, and ruins of old plantations—all set among lush tropical trees bearing limes, papayas, and custard apples. Visiting Kew will give you a better understanding of the daily life of many islanders. ✉ *North Caicos.*

Three Mary Cays. Three small rocks within swimming distance from Whitby Beach give you some of the best secluded snorkeling in all of the Turks and Caicos. You will often find ospreys nesting here, too. This is a protection area for wildlife, so do not fish or touch any of the corals. ✉ *Off Whitby Beach, North Caicos.*

FAMILY **Wades Green.** Visitors can view well-preserved ruins of the great house, overseer's house, and surrounding walls of one of the most successful plantations of the Loyalist era. A lookout tower provides views for miles. Contact the National Trust for tour details. ✉ *Kew, North Caicos* ☎ *649/941–5710* 🎫 *$8* ⏲ *Daily, by appointment only.*

WHERE TO EAT

$ AMERICAN ✕ **Last Chance Bar and Grill.** Overlooking the calm waters of Bottle Creek, this little place makes a great stop for day-trippers going to or from Middle Caicos. In addition to making smaller items such as conch fritters and burgers, owner Howard Gibbs provides four-course meals of grouper and local lobster at reasonable prices, with the desserts made by his wife, Cheryl. $ *Average main: $30* ✉ *Bottle Creek, North Caicos* ☎ *649/232-4141* 🌐 *www.greatbonefishing.com* 💳 *No credit cards* ⏲ *Closed Sun.*

WHERE TO STAY

$$ RENTAL 🏨 **Hollywood Beach Suites.** With seven miles of secluded beaches and few others to share them with, this property with four self-contained units is completely relaxing. **Pros:** secluded; tranquil; upscale furnishings. **Cons:** might feel a little quiet if you're after a busy vacation or active social scene. $ *Rooms from: $341* ✉ *Hollywood Beach Dr., Whitby, North Caicos* ☎ *649/231–1020, 800/551–2256* 🌐 *www.hollywoodbeachsuites.com* 🛏 *4 suites* 🍽 *No meals.*

$$ RENTAL 🏨 **Jodo Resort.** This new villa sits on 7 acres of the leeward side of the island, giving calm waters to its 400 feet of beachfront. $ *Rooms from: $275* ✉ *Sandy Point, North Caicos* ☎ *609/513–6363* 🌐 *www.jodoresort.com* 🛏 *1 villa* 💳 *No credit cards* 🍽 *No meals.*

$ HOTEL 🏨 **Pelican Beach Hotel.** North Caicos islanders Susan and Clifford Gardiner built this small, palmetto-fringed hotel in the 1980s on the quiet, mostly deserted Whitby Beach. **Pros:** the beach is just outside your room; linens are crisp and clean. **Cons:** location may be too remote and sleepy for some people; beach is in a natural state, meaning seaweed and pine needles. $ *Rooms from: $165* ✉ *Whitby, North Caicos* ☎ *649/946–7112, 877/774–5486* 🌐 *www.pelicanbeach.tc* 🛏 *14 rooms, 2 suites* ⏲ *Closed Aug. 15–Sept. 15* 🍽 *Some meals.*

26

MIDDLE CAICOS

At 48 square miles (124 square km) and with fewer than 300 residents, this is the largest and least developed of the inhabited islands in the Turks and Caicos chain. A limestone ridge runs to about 125 feet above sea level, creating dramatic cliffs on the north shore and a cave system farther inland. Middle Caicos has rambling trails along the coast; the **Crossing Place Trail,** maintained by the National Trust, follows the path used by the early settlers to go between the islands. Inland are quiet settlements with friendly residents. This is the real thing.

EXPLORING MIDDLE CAICOS

FAMILY **Conch Bar Caves.** These limestone caves have eerie underground lakes and milky-white stalactites and stalagmites. Archaeologists have discovered Lucayan artifacts in the caves and the surrounding area. The caves are now inhabited only by some harmless bats. If you visit, don't worry—they don't bother visitors. It's best to get a guide. If you tour the caves, be sure to wear sturdy shoes, not sandals. ✉ *Middle Caicos.*

WHERE TO EAT

$$$$ SEAFOOD ✕ **Mudjin Bar and Grill.** After a long wait, this restaurant at Blue Horizon Resort is finally open. The view is wonderful, as it sits overlooking the spectacular Mudjin Harbour. Daily lunches concentrate on seafood items such as lobster bites, cracked conch, and fish-and-chips, although there are also burgers, chicken and ribs, and some vegetarian options (rare in these parts). Dinner is by reservation only and features a choice of several daily specials. [$] *Average main: $35* ✉ *Blue Horizon Resort, Mudjin Harbour, Middle Caicos* ☎ *649/946–6141* 🌐 *www.bhresort.com* *Reservations essential* ⏲ *Closed Sun. evening.*

WHERE TO STAY

$$ HOTEL Fodor's Choice ★ **Blue Horizon Resort.** At this property, undulating cliffs skirt one of the most dramatic beaches in the Turks and Caicos. **Pros:** breathtaking views of Mudjin Harbour from the rooms; lack of development makes you feel like you're away from it all. **Cons:** need a car to explore; probably too isolated for some; three-night minimum. [$] *Rooms from: $290* ✉ *Mudjin Harbour, Middle Caicos* ☎ *649/946–6141* 🌐 *www.bhresort.com* *5 cottages, 2 villas* *No meals.*

SPORTS AND THE OUTDOORS

CAVE TOURS

Cardinal Arthur. Although exploring Middle Caicos on your own can be fun, a guided tour with Cardinal can illuminate the island's secret spots, from caves to the spots where flamingos flock. He can also show you the sandbars that make vacationers giddy and that can't be found by car. By skiff he can show off all the hidden beaches reached only by water, too. ☎ *649/946–6107, 649/241-0730.*

Ernest Forbes. Local cave specialist and taxi driver Ernest Forbes can give you a cave tour and may even arrange for you to have a prix-fixe lunch at his house afterward if you ask nicely. ✉ *Middle Caicos* ☎ *649/946–6140.*

George Gibbs. George Gibbs knows all the crevices in the reefs and will take you lobster hunting: fun during the day followed by a delicious night. ✉ *Middle Caicos* ☎ *649/243–8371.*

SOUTH CAICOS

This 8½-square-mile (21-square-km) island was once an important salt producer; today it's the heart of the fishing industry. Nature prevails, with long, white beaches, jagged bluffs, quiet backwater bays, and salt flats. Diving and snorkeling on the pristine wall and reefs are a treat enjoyed by only a few.

In 2008 hurricanes Hanna and Ike gave South Caicos a one-two punch. Although the island has recovered, the few dive operators that were here disappeared. The best way to dive (other than independently) is through a charter with Big Blue Unlimited out of Providenciales.

The major draw for South Caicos is its excellent diving and snorkeling on the wall and reefs (with an average visibility of 100 feet). It's practically the only thing to do on South Caicos other than to lie on the lovely beaches, enjoy a mountain bike ride, or go for a kayak. Several local fishermen harvest spiny lobsters for the Turks and Caicos and for export. Making up the third-largest reef in the world, the coral walls surrounding South Caicos are dramatic, dropping dramatically from 50 feet to 6,000 feet in the blink of an eye.

EXPLORING SOUTH CAICOS

At the northern end of the island are fine white-sand beaches; the south coast is great for scuba diving along the drop-off, and there's excellent snorkeling off the windward (east) coast, where large stands of elkhorn and staghorn coral shelter several varieties of small tropical fish. An eroded, sunken plane makes an excellent site. Spiny lobster and queen conch are found on the shallow Caicos Bank to the west and are harvested for export by local processing plants. The bonefishing here is some of the best in the West Indies.

Boiling Hole. Abandoned salinas (natural salt pans) make up the center of this island—the largest, across from the downtown ballpark, receives its water directly from an underground source connected to the ocean through this "boiling" hole. ✉ *South Caicos.*

Cockburn Harbour. The best natural harbor in the Caicos chain hosts the South Caicos Regatta, held each year in May. ✉ *South Caicos.*

WHERE TO EAT

Restaurant choices on South Caicos are limited and no one takes credit cards, so you most definitely should bring cash. The Dolphin Pub at South Caicos Ocean & Beach Resort is truly the only restaurant that operates with regular hours. There you can find a wide range on the menu including fresh catch and a fully stocked bar. **Darryl's** (on Stubbs Road) is a more casual restaurant, along with the Chicken Shack; expect to pay $10 to $20 for what they have available. Ask around to find out when (or if) these local favorites will be open; if you are staying over on the island, your accommodations will assist you in making "reservations." There are a couple of other dining spots operated directly out of an owner's home; advance notice must be given so that the proprietor can prepare in advance.

$$ ECLECTIC ✕ **Dolphin Grill.** The only real restaurant on the island serves casual, crowd-pleasing food: you'll find burgers, chicken, and fish. There is some Asian influence in the sauces and rice, and there are certainly Caribbean influences in the jerk sauce on the fish. At night this turns into a gathering place for guests to tell their tales about the sea, the fish that they caught, or the sea eagle ray that they spotted while diving. If you are around for lunch (most visitors to South Caicos will be scuba diving), this is your only choice. [$] *Average main: $15* ✉ *South Caicos Ocean & Beach Resort, Tucker Hill, South Caicos* ☎ *649/946–3219.*

$ CARIBBEAN ✕ **Muriel's.** Muriel serves dinner most nights in her home but has no fixed menu. This is the most reliable of the three home-based businesses on the island, though you must call ahead. Dinner will likely be the catch of the day. [$] *Average main: $8* ✉ *Graham St., Cockburn Harbour, South Caicos* ☎ *649/946–3535* *Reservations essential* *No credit cards* *No lunch.*

WHERE TO STAY

$ HOTEL **South Caicos Ocean & Beach Resort.** Rustic and basic—though perfectly acceptable—this is your only lodging option in South Caicos at this writing. **Pros:** each room has stunning views of the Caicos Banks; the best scuba diving off South Caicos is in front of the hotel; it has the only real restaurant on the island. **Cons:** you need cash for everything but your room; not on the beach; no dive shop at the resort. [$] *Rooms from: $125* ✉ *Tucker Hill, South Caicos* ☎ *649/946–3219* *oceanandbeachresort.com* *24 rooms, 6 apartments* *No meals.*

GRAND TURK

Just 7 miles (11 km) long and a little more than 1 mile (1½ km) wide, this island, the capital and seat of the Turks and Caicos government, has been a longtime favorite destination for divers eager to explore the 7,000-foot-deep pristine coral walls that drop down only 300 yards out to sea. On shore, the tiny, quiet island is home to white-sand beaches, the National Museum, and a small population of wild horses and donkeys, which leisurely meander past the white-walled courtyards, pretty churches, and bougainvillea-covered colonial inns on their daily

CLOSE UP

All in the Family

Belongers, as local islanders are sometimes known, from the taxi driver meeting you to the chef feeding you, are often connected. "Oh, him?" you will hear. "He my cousin!" Development has been slow here, and as a result such family connections, as well as crafts, bush medicine, ripsaw music, storytelling, and even recipes, have remained constant. But where do such traditions come from? Recently, researchers came closer to finding out. Many Belongers had claimed that their great-great-grandparents told them their forebears came directly from Africa. For decades their stories were ignored. Indeed, most experts believe that Belongers were descendants of mostly second-generation Bermudian and Caribbean slaves.

In 2005, museum researchers continued their search for a lost slave ship called *Trouvadore*. The ship, which wrecked off East Caicos in 1841, carried a cargo of 193 Africans, captured to be sold into slavery, almost all of whom miraculously survived the wreck. As slavery had been abolished in this British territory at the time, all the Africans were found and freed in the Turks and Caicos Islands. Since there were only a few thousand inhabitants in the islands at the time, these first-generation African survivors were a significant minority (about 7% of the population then).

During one expedition, divers found a wrecked ship of the right time period. If these remains are the *Trouvadore*, many Belongers may finally have a physical link to their past to go with their more intangible cultural traditions. So while you're in the islands, look closely at the intricately woven baskets, and listen carefully to the African rhythms in the ripsaw music and the stories you hear. For more information, check out the website 🌐 *www.trouvadore.org*.

commute into town. But things aren't entirely sleepy: a cruise-ship complex at the southern end of the island brings about 600,000 visitors per year. That said, the dock is self-contained and is about 3 miles (5 km) from the tranquil, small hotels of Cockburn Town, Pillory Beach, and the Ridge and far from most of the western-shore dive sites.

EXPLORING GRAND TURK

Pristine beaches with vistas of turquoise waters, small local settlements, historic ruins, and native flora and fauna are among the sights on Grand Turk. Fewer than 4,000 people live on this 7½-square-mile (19-square-km) island, and it's hard to get lost, as there aren't many roads.

COCKBURN TOWN

WORTH NOTING

The buildings in the colony's capital and seat of government reflect a 19th-century Bermudian style. Narrow streets are lined with low stone walls and old street lamps. The once-vital *salinas* (natural salt pans, where the sea leaves a film of salt) have been restored, and covered benches along the sluices offer shady spots for observing wading birds, including flamingos that frequent the shallows. Be sure to pick up a

Restaurants ▼

Birdcage Restaurant 4

Guanahani Restaurant & Bar 1

Mookie Pookie Pizza Palace 2

Sand Bar 3

Secret Garden ...5

Hotels ▼

Bohio Drive Resort 2

Island House 1

Osprey Beach Hotel 4

Salt Raker Inn ...3

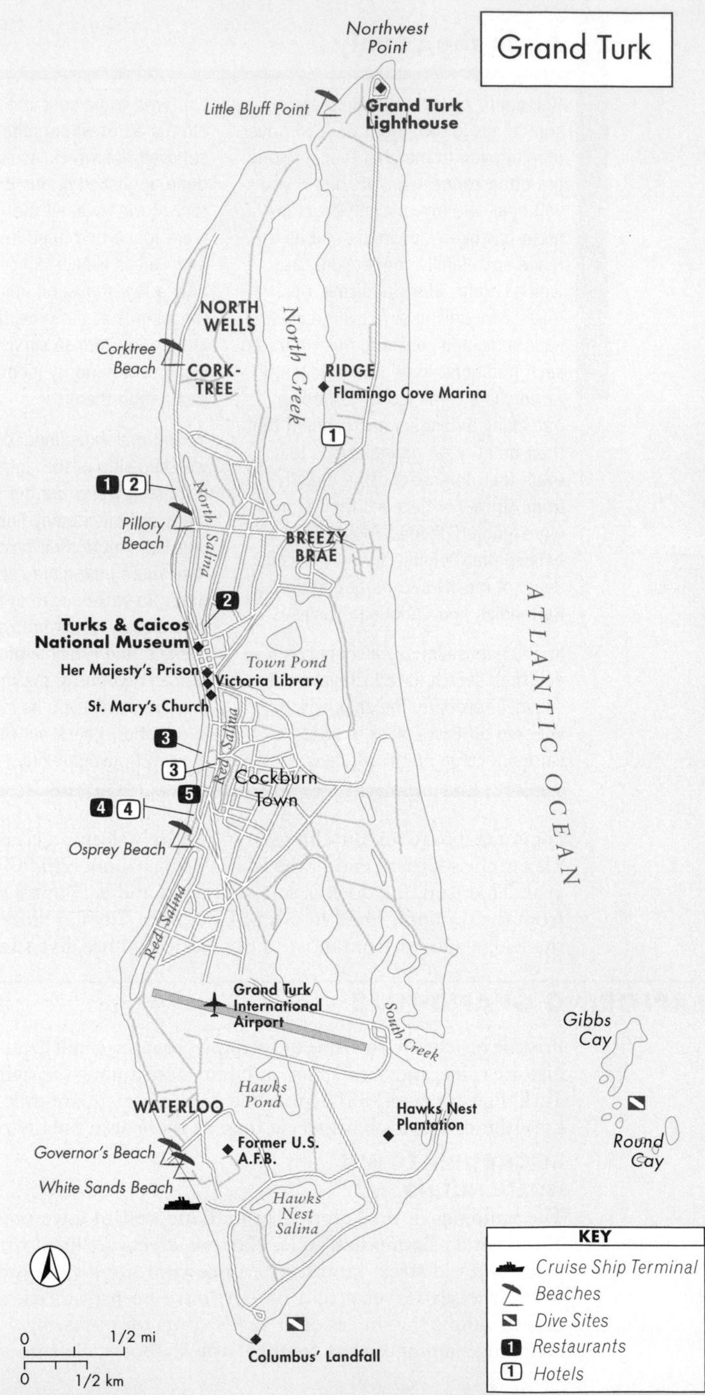

copy of the TCI Tourist Board's *Heritage Walk* guide to discover Grand Turk's rich architecture.

Her Majesty's Prison. This prison was built in the 19th century to house runaway slaves and slaves who survived the wreck of the *Trouvadore* in 1841. After the slaves were granted freedom, the prison housed criminals and even modern-day drug runners until it closed in the 1990s. The last hanging here was in 1960. Now you can see the cells, solitary-confinement area, and exercise patio. The prison is open only when there is a cruise ship at the port. ✉ *Pond St., Cockburn Town, Grand Turk.*

FAMILY **Turks and Caicos National Museum.** In one of the oldest stone buildings on the islands, the national museum houses the Molasses Reef wreck, the earliest shipwreck—dating to the early 1500s—discovered in the Americas. The natural-history exhibits include artifacts left by Taíno, African, North American, Bermudian, French, and Latin American settlers. The museum has a 3-D coral-reef exhibit, a walk-in Lucayan cave with wooden artifacts, and a gallery dedicated to Grand Turk's little-known involvement in the Space Race (John Glenn made landfall here after being the first American to orbit the Earth). An interactive children's gallery keeps knee-high visitors "edutained." The museum also claims that Grand Turk was where Columbus first landed in the New World. The most original display is a collection of messages in bottles that have washed ashore from all over the world. ✉ *Duke St., Cockburn Town, Grand Turk* ☎ *649/946–2160* 🌐 *www.tcmuseum.org* 🎫 *$7* 🕐 *Mon.–Wed. 9–1; Thurs. 1–5, plus all cruise-ship days.*

26

BEYOND COCKBURN TOWN

Grand Turk Lighthouse. More than 150 years ago, the lighthouse, built in the United Kingdom and transported piece by piece to the island, protected ships from wrecking on the northern reefs. Use this panoramic landmark as a starting point for a breezy cliff-top walk by following the donkey trails to the deserted eastern beach. ✉ *Lighthouse Rd., North Ridge, Grand Turk.*

BEACHES

Governor's Beach. A beautiful crescent of powder-soft sand and shallow, calm turquoise waters front the official British governor's residence, called Waterloo, framed by tall casuarina trees that provide plenty of natural shade. To have it all to yourself, go on a day when cruise ships are not in port (but bring your own water). On days when ships are in port, the beach is lined with lounge chairs, and bars and restaurants are open. **Amenties:** parking (free), toilets. **Best for:** swimming, walking. ✉ *South Caicos.*

Little Bluff Point Beach. Just west of the Grand Turk Lighthouse is a low, limestone-cliff-edged, shell-covered beach that offers more of a beachcombing experience and looks out onto shallow waters, mangroves, and often flamingos, especially in spring and summer. ✉ *North Ridge, Grand Turk.*

WHERE TO EAT

Conch in every shape and form, fresh grouper, and lobster (in season) are the favorite dishes at the laid-back restaurants that line Duke Street. Away from these more touristy areas, smaller and less expensive eateries serve chicken and ribs, curried goat, peas and rice, and other native island specialties. Prices are more expensive than in the United States, as almost all the produce has to be imported.

COCKBURN TOWN

$$$ CARIBBEAN **Birdcage Restaurant.** This has become the place to be on Sunday and Wednesday nights, when a sizzling barbecue of ribs, chicken, and lobster combines with live "rake-and-scrape" music from a local group called High Tide to draw an appreciative crowd. Arrive before 8 pm to secure beachside tables and an unrestricted view of the band; the location around the Osprey pool is lovely. The rest of the week, enjoy more elegant and eclectic fare accompanied by a well-chosen wine list. *Average main: $24 Osprey Beach Hotel, Duke St., Cockburn Town, Grand Turk 649/946–2666 www.ospreybeachhotel.com/dining.*

$$ PIZZA **Mookie Pookie Pizza Palace.** Local husband-and-wife team "Mookie" and "Pookie" have created a wonderful backstreet restaurant that has gained well-deserved popularity over the years as much more than a pizza place. At lunchtime, the tiny eatery is packed with locals ordering specials such as steamed beef, curried chicken, and curried goat. You can also get burgers and omelets, but stick to the specials if you want fast service, and dine in if you want to get a true taste of island living. By night, the place becomes Grand Turk's only take-out pizza place. *Average main: $12 Hospital Rd., Cockburn Town, Grand Turk No credit cards Closed Sun.*

$$ AMERICAN **Sand Bar.** Run by two Canadian sisters, this popular beachside bar is a good value; the menu is limited to fish-and-chips, quesadillas, and similarly basic bar fare. The tented wooden terrace jutting out onto the beach provides shade during the day, making it an ideal lunch spot, but it's also a great place to watch the sunset. The service is friendly, and the local crowd often spills into the street. *Average main: $14 Duke St., Cockburn Town, Grand Turk.*

$$ SEAFOOD **Secret Garden.** Simply prepared garlic shrimp or grilled grouper are among the more popular dishes at this local favorite. Located behind Salt Raker Inn in a pretty courtyard garden, it more than lives up to its name. Friday nights feature live music by rake-and-scrape bands. *Average main: $17 Cockburn Town, Grand Turk 649/946–2260.*

ELSEWHERE ON GRAND TURK

$$$ INTERNATIONAL **Guanahani Restaurant and Bar.** Off the town's main drag, this restaurant sits on a stunning but quiet stretch of beach. The food goes beyond the usual Grand Turk fare and is some of the best in town, thanks to the talents of executive chef Jorika Mhende, who takes care of the evening meals. The menu changes daily, based partly on the fresh fish catch. Thursday nights feature a different country's cuisine every time, so sauces and spices are based on that pick. *Average main: $26 Bohio Dive Resort & Spa, Pillory Beach, Grand Turk 649/946–2135 www.bohioresort.com.*

Cockburn Town, Grand Turk

WHERE TO STAY

COCKBURN TOWN

$ HOTEL Fodor's Choice ★ **Osprey Beach Hotel.** The veteran hotelier Jenny Smith has transformed this two-story oceanfront hotel with artistic touches: palms, frangipani, and deep-green azaleas frame it like a painting. **Pros:** best hotel on Grand Turk; walking distance to Front Street, restaurants, and excursions. **Cons:** rocky beachfront. *Rooms from: $225 ✉ Duke St., Cockburn Town, Grand Turk ☎ 649/946–2666 🌐 www.ospreybeachhotel.com 11 rooms, 16 suites No meals.*

$ B&B/INN **Salt Raker Inn.** A large anchor on the sun-dappled pathway marks the entrance to this 19th-century house, which is now an unpretentious inn. **Pros:** excellent location that is an easy walk to Front Street, restaurants, and excursions. **Cons:** the lack of no-smoking rooms. *Rooms from: $115 ✉ Duke St., Cockburn Town, Grand Turk ☎ 649/946–2260 🌐 www.saltrakerinn.com 10 rooms, 3 suites No meals.*

ELSEWHERE ON GRAND TURK

$ RESORT **Bohio Dive Resort and Spa.** Divers are all drawn to this basic yet comfortable hotel. **Pros:** Guanahani is probably the best restaurant in Grand Turk; on a gorgeous beach; steps away from awesome snorkeling. **Cons:** three-night minimum doesn't allow for quick getaways from Provo. *Rooms from: $195 ✉ Pillory Beach, Grand Turk ☎ 649/946–2135 🌐 www.bohioresort.com 12 rooms, 4 suites No meals ☞ 3-night minimum.*

$ RENTAL FAMILY **Island House.** Years of business-travel experience helped Colin Brooker create the comfortable, peaceful suites that overlook North Creek. **Pros:** full condo units feel like a home away from home. **Cons:**

not on the beach; you need a car to get around. *$ Rooms from: $150 ✉ Lighthouse Rd., North Ridge, Grand Turk ☎ 649/232–1439 🌐 www.islandhouse.tc ⇨ 5 suites 🍴 No meals ☞ 3-night minimum.*

NIGHTLIFE

Grand Turk is a quiet place where you come to relax and unwind, and most of the nightlife consists of little more than happy hour at sunset, giving you the chance to glimpse the elusive green flash. Most restaurants turn into gathering places where you can talk with the new friends you have made that day—for instance, every Wednesday and Sunday, there's lively rake-and-scrape music at the Osprey Beach Hotel, and similar bands visit the Salt Raker Inn on Friday. On some evenings, you'll be able to catch Mitch Rollings of Blue Water Divers; he often headlines the entertainment at the island's different restaurants.

SHOPPING

Shopping in Grand Turk is hard to come by—choices are slim. Let's just say that no true shopaholic would want to come here for vacation. You can get the usual T-shirts and dive trinkets at all the dive shops, but there are only a few options for more interesting shopping opportunities. When a ship is in port, the shops at the pier will be open, and these increase your options dramatically.

SPORTS AND THE OUTDOORS

BICYCLING

Out of all the islands in Turks and Caicos, Grand Turk is the perfect island for biking: it's small enough that it is possible to tour it all that way. The island's mostly flat terrain isn't very taxing, and most roads have hard surfaces. Take water with you: there are few places to stop for refreshments. Most hotels have bicycles available, but you can also rent them for $20 a day from Grand Turk Diving across from the Osprey; there is also a $200 deposit.

DIVING AND SNORKELING

In these waters you can find undersea cathedrals, coral gardens, and countless tunnels, but note that you must carry and present a valid certificate card before you'll be allowed to dive. As its name suggests, the **Black Forest** offers staggering black-coral formations as well as the occasional black-tip shark. In the **Library** you can study fish galore, including large numbers of yellowtail snapper. At the Columbus Passage separating South Caicos from Grand Turk, each side of a 22-mile-wide (35-km-wide) channel drops more than 7,000 feet. From January through March, thousands of Atlantic humpback whales swim through en route to their winter breeding grounds. **Gibb's Cay,** a small cay a couple of miles off Grand Turk, where you can swim with stingrays, makes for a great excursion.

Blue Water Divers. In operation on Grand Turk since 1983, Blue Water Divers is the only PADI Gold Palm Five Star dive center on the island.

The owner, Mitch, may put some of your underwater adventures to music in the evenings when he plays at the Osprey Beach Hotel or Salt Raker Inn. ✉ *Duke St., Cockburn Town, Grand Turk* ☎ *649/946–2432* 🌐 *www.grandturkscuba.com.*

Grand Turk Diving. The outfitter offers full-service dives and trips to Gibbs Cay and Salt Cay. ✉ *Cockburn Town, Grand Turk* ☎ *649/946–1559* 🌐 *www.gtdiving.com.*

Oasis Divers. Oasis Divers provides complete gear handling and pampering treatment. It also supplies Nitrox and rebreathers. The company also offers a wide variety of other tours, as well as renting bicycles and operating Segway tours. ✉ *Duke St., Cockburn Town, Grand Turk* ☎ *649/946–1128* 🌐 *www.oasisdivers.com.*

KAYAKING

Oasis Divers offers glass-bottom kayak and eco-safari tours. Check out their website for the options available, as something the whole family can enjoy.

SALT CAY

Fewer than 100 people live on this 2½-square-mile (6-square-km) dot of land, maintaining an unassuming lifestyle against a backdrop of stucco cottages, stone ruins, and weathered wooden windmills standing sentry in the abandoned salinas. The beautifully preserved island is bordered by beaches where weathered green and blue sea glass and pretty shells often wash ashore. Beneath the waves, 10 dive sites are minutes from shore.

EXPLORING SALT CAY

Salt sheds and salinas are silent reminders of the days when the island was a leading producer of salt, actually once considered to be the largest harvester of salt in the world. Now the salt ponds attract abundant birdlife. Island tours are often conducted by motorized golf cart. From January through April, humpback whales pass by on the way to their winter breeding grounds.

What little development there is on Salt Cay is found in its main community, Balfour Town. It's home to several small hotels and a few stores, as well as the main dock and the Coral Reef Bar & Grill, where locals hang out with tourists to watch the sun set and drink a beer. As a visitor, you can cover the entire island on foot if you are so inclined. Renting a sea kayak to explore the coastline is an appealing alternative.

White House. This grand stone house, which once belonged to a wealthy salt merchant, is testimony to the heyday of Salt Cay's eponymous industry. Still owned by the descendants of the original family, it's sometimes opened up for tours. Ask Tim Dunn, a descendant of the original owners, as he may give you a personal tour to see the still-intact, original furnishings, books, and medicine cabinet that date back to the early 1800s. ✉ *Victoria St., Balfour Town, Salt Cay* ☎ *649/243-9843* 🎟 *Free* 🕒 *By appointment only.*

WHERE TO EAT

$$$ CARIBBEAN **Pat's Place.** Island native Pat Simmons can give you a lesson in the medicinal qualities of her garden plants and periwinkle flowers, as well as provide excellent native cuisine for a very reasonable price in her comforting Salt Cay home. Home cooking doesn't get any closer to home than this. Try conch fritters for lunch and steamed grouper with okra rice for dinner. Pat also has a small grocery shop selling staples. As with all places to eat in Salt Cay, put in your food order and tell them what time you want to eat in the morning. Pat only cooks when there's someone to cook for. *Average main: $25 South District, Salt Cay 649/946–6919 Reservations essential No credit cards.*

$$$ ECLECTIC Fodor's Choice ★ **Porter's Island Thyme Bistro.** Owner Porter Williams serves potent alcoholic creations as well as fairly sophisticated local and international cuisine. Try steamed, freshly caught snapper in a pepper-wine sauce with peas and rice, or spicy-hot chicken curry served with tangy chutneys. Or you can order the "Porter" house steak. You can take cooking lessons from the chef, enjoy the nightly Filipino fusion tapas during happy hour, and join the gang for Friday-night pizza. This is a great place to make friends and the best place to catch up on island gossip. The airy, trellis-covered spot overlooks the salinas. There's a small shop with gifts and tourist information; you can also get a manicure or pedicure here. Reservations are essential here; put in your order for food in the morning and tell Porter what time you want to eat. Then explore, food will be waiting for you. *Average main: $26 Balfour Town, Salt Cay 649/946–6977 www.islandthyme.tc Reservations essential Closed Wed. mid-May–June and Sept.–late Oct.*

WHERE TO STAY

$$ RENTAL Fodor's Choice ★ **Castaway, Salt Cay.** This only lodging that sits directly on the stunning 3-mile (5-km) North Beach might just be what the doctor ordered if you're in need of total relaxation—it can be hard to fathom having one of the world's most beautiful beaches all to yourself. **Pros:** on a spectacular beach; truly a get-away-from-it-all, perfect for relaxing. **Cons:** it's a dark, secluded road into town at night. *Rooms from: $299 North Beach, Salt Cay 649/946–6977 www.castawayonsaltcay.com 4 suites Multiple meal plans.*

$ RENTAL **Pirates Hideaway and Blackbeard's Quarters.** Owner Candy Herwin—true to her self-proclaimed pirate status—has smuggled artistic treasures across the ocean and created her own masterpieces to deck out this lair. **Pros:** island personality throughout; great snorkling off the beachfront. **Cons:** the closest swimming beach is a five-minute walk. *Rooms from: $175 Victoria St., Balfour Town, Salt Cay 649/244–1407 www.saltcay.tc 3 suites, 1 cottage No meals.*

$ RENTAL **Tradewinds Guest Suites.** A grove of whispering casuarina trees surrounds these five single-story basic apartments, which offer a moderate-budget option on Salt Cay with the option of dive packages. **Pros:** walking distance to diving, fishing, dining. **Cons:** a/c costs extra; too isolated for some people. *Rooms from: $161 Victoria St., Salt Cay,*

Balfour Town, Salt Cay ☎ *649/241-1009* 🌐 *www.tradewinds.tc* *5 apartments* *No meals.*

$ RENTAL **Villas of Salt Cay.** One of the most convinient places to stay in Salt Cay is centrally located on Victoria Street, in the middle of everything. **Pros:** bedrooms are set up for extra privacy; on Victoria Street within walking distance of everything; on a private stretch of beach. **Cons:** not all rooms have a/c; cabanas don't have kitchens; shared pool. *Rooms from: $225* ✉ *Victoria St., Balfour Town, Salt Cay* ☎ *649/343–2157* 🌐 *www.villasofsaltcay.tc* *1 2-bedroom villa, 1 1-bedroom cottage, 3 cabanas* *No meals.*

SPORTS AND THE OUTDOORS

DIVING AND SNORKELING

Scuba divers can explore the wreck of the *Endymion,* a 140-foot wooden-hull British warship that sank in 1790; you can swim through the hull and spot cannons and anchors. It's off the southern point of Salt Cay.

Salt Cay Divers. Salt Cay Divers conducts daily dive trips and rents out all the necessary equipment. In season, they run whale-watching trips. They can also help get you to Salt Cay from Provo or Grand Turk, and stock your villa with groceries. ☎ *649/241–1009* 🌐 *www.saltcaydivers.tc.*

26

KAYAKING

If you fancy exploring the coastline of Salt Cay, renting sea kayaks from Salt Cay Divers (🌐 *www.saltcaydivers.tc*) is another option for visitors to this tiny island.

WHALE-WATCHING

FAMILY During the winter months (January through April), Salt Cay is a center for whale-watching, when some 2,500 humpback whales migrate past close to shore. Whale-watching trips can most easily be organized through your inn or guesthouse.

Fodor's Choice ★ **Crystal Seas Adventures.** Proprietor Tim Dunn, whose family descends from the original owners of Salt Cay's historic White House, knows these waters as well as anybody. His company offers a variety of excursions: diving with stingrays at Gibbs Cay, and trips to Grand Turk and secluded beaches, such as Great Sand Cay. Whale-watching is also very popular, and Dunn is the only outfitter with diving trips to South Caicos, reputed to be one of the best places in the world for this. ☎ *649/431–9585* 🌐 *www.crystalseasadventures.com.*

UNITED STATES VIRGIN ISLANDS

WELCOME TO UNITED STATES VIRGIN ISLANDS

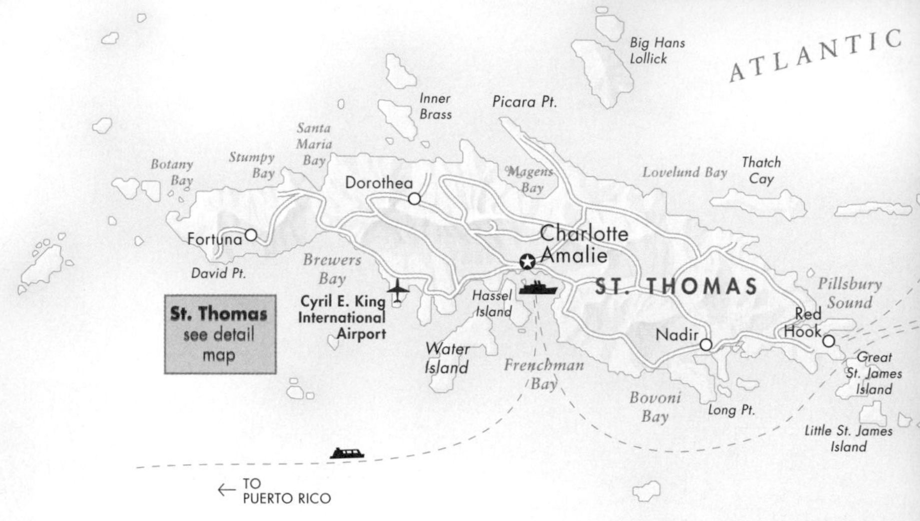

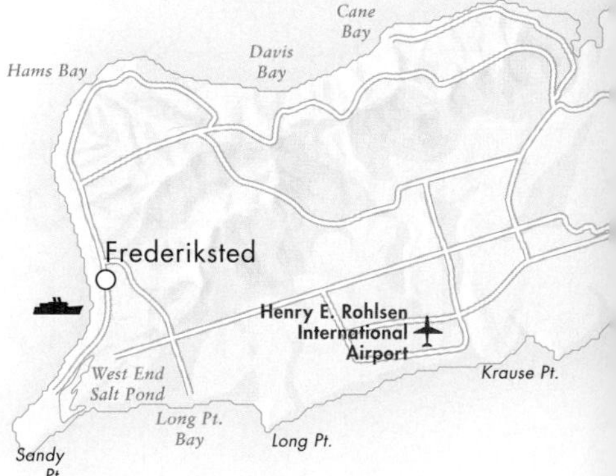

AMERICA'S CARIBBEAN

About 1,000 miles (1,600 km) from the southern tip of Florida, the U.S. Virgin Islands were acquired from Denmark in 1917. St. Croix, at 84 square miles (218 square km), is the largest of the islands; St. John, at 20 square miles (52 square km), is the smallest. Together, they have a population of around 110,000, half of whom live on St. Thomas.

A perfect combination of the familiar and the exotic, the U.S. Virgin Islands are a little bit of home set in an azure sea. With hundreds of idyllic coves and splendid beaches, chances are that on one of the three islands you'll find your ideal Caribbean vacation spot.

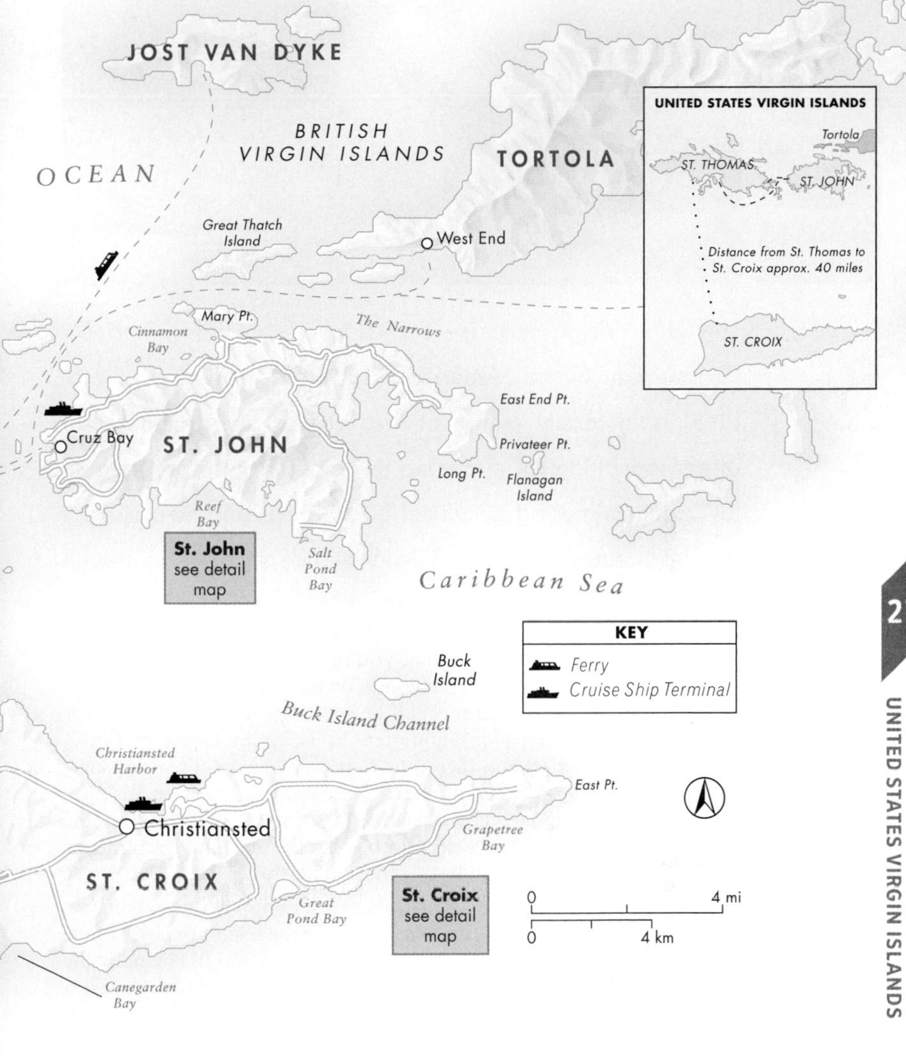

TOP REASONS TO VISIT UNITED STATES VIRGIN ISLANDS

1 **Incomparable Sailing:** St. Thomas is one of the Caribbean's major sailing centers.

2 **Great Hiking:** Two-thirds of St. John is a national park that's crisscrossed by excellent hiking trails.

3 **Beaches:** Though Magens Bay on St. Thomas and Trunk Bay on St. John are two of the most perfect beaches you'll ever find, St. Croix's West End beaches are fetching in their own way.

4 **Shopping:** Shopping on both St. Thomas and St. Croix is stellar.

5 **Deep-Sea Fishing:** St. Thomas is one of the best places to catch Atlantic blue marlin between the months of June and October.

Updated by Carol M. Bareuther, Carol Buchanan, Lynda Lohr, and Susan Zaluski

The U.S. Virgin Islands—St. Thomas, St. John, and St. Croix—may fly the American flag, but "America's Paradise" is in reality a mix of the foreign and familiar that offers something for everyone to enjoy. The history, beautiful beaches, myriad activities, good food, and no-passport-required status make the Virgin Islands an inviting beach destination for many Americans.

With three islands to choose from, you're likely to find your piece of paradise. Check into a beachfront condo on the East End of St. Thomas; then eat burgers and watch football at a beachfront bar and grill. Or stay at an 18th-century plantation great house on St. Croix, go horseback riding at sunrise, and then dine that night on local seafood classics. Rent a tent or a cottage in the pristine national park on St. John; then take a hike, kayak off the coast, read a book, or just listen to the sounds of the forest. Or dive deep into "island time" and learn the art of limin' (hanging out, Caribbean-style) on all three islands.

History books give credit to Christopher Columbus for discovering the New World. In reality, the Virgin Islands, like the rest of the isles in the Caribbean chain, were populated as long ago as 2000 BC by nomadic waves of seagoing settlers as they migrated north from South America and eastward from Central America and the Yucatàn Peninsula.

Columbus met the descendants of these original inhabitants during his second voyage to the New World, in 1493. He anchored in Salt River, a natural bay west of what is now Christiansted, St. Croix, and sent his men ashore in search of fresh water. Hostile arrows rather than welcoming embraces made for a quick retreat, but Columbus did have time to name the island Santa Cruz (Holy Cross) before sailing north. He eventually claimed St. John, St. Thomas, and what are now the British Virgin Islands for Spain and at the same time named this shapely silhouette of 60-some islands Las Once Mil Virgenes, for the 11,000 legendary virgin followers of St. Ursula. Columbus believed the islands barren of the costly spices he sought, so he sailed off, leaving more than a century's gap in time before the next Europeans arrived.

Pioneers, planters, and pirates from throughout Europe ushered in the era of colonization. Great Britain and the Netherlands both claimed St. Croix in 1625. This peaceful coexistence ended abruptly when the Dutch governor killed his English counterpart, thus launching years of battles for possession that would see seven flags fly over this southernmost Virgin isle. Meanwhile, St. Thomas's sheltered harbor proved a magnet for pirates such as Blackbeard and Bluebeard. The Danes first colonized the island in 1666, naming their main settlement Taphus for its many beer halls. In 1691 the town received the more respectable name of Charlotte Amalie in honor of Danish king Christian V's wife. It wasn't until 1718 that a small group of Dutch planters raised their country's flag on St. John. As on the other Virgin Islands, a plantation economy soon developed.

Plantations depended on slave labor, and the Virgin Islands played a key role in the triangular route that connected the Caribbean, Africa, and Europe in the trade of sugar, rum, and human cargo. By the early 1800s a sharp decline in cane prices because of competing beet sugar and an increasing number of slave revolts motivated Governor-General Peter von Scholten to abolish slavery in the Danish colonies on July 3, 1848. This holiday is now celebrated as Emancipation Day.

After emancipation, the island's economy slumped. Islanders owed their existence to subsistence farming and fishing. Meanwhile, during the American Civil War the Union began negotiations with Denmark for the purchase of the Virgin Islands in order to establish a naval base. However, the sale didn't happen until World War I, when President Theodore Roosevelt paid the Danes $25 million for the three largest islands; an elaborate Transfer Day ceremony was held on the grounds of St. Thomas's Legislature Building on March 31, 1917. A decade later, Virgin Islanders were granted U.S. citizenship. Today the U.S. Virgin Islands is an unincorporated territory, meaning that citizens govern themselves and vote for their own governors, but cannot vote for president or congressional representation.

Nowadays, Virgin Islanders hail from more than 60 nations. The Danish influence is still strong in architecture and street names. Americana is everywhere, too, most notably in recognizable fast-food chains, familiar TV shows, and name-brand hotels. Between this diversity and the wealth that tourism brings, Virgin Islanders struggle to preserve their culture. Their rich, spicy West Indian–African heritage comes to full bloom at Carnival time, when celebrating and playing *mas* (with abandon) take precedence over everything else.

There's evidence, too, of growing pains. Traffic jams are common, a clandestine drug trade fuels crime, and there are few beaches left that aren't fronted by a high-rise hotel. Despite fairly heavy development, wildlife has found refuge here. The brown pelican is on the endangered list worldwide but is a common sight here. The endangered native boa tree is protected, as is the hawksbill turtle, whose females lumber onto the beaches to lay eggs.

LOGISTICS

Getting to the USVI: There are many nonstop flights to St. Thomas from the United States, and there are a few nonstops to St. Croix; often, you'll have to change planes in Miami, San Juan, or St. Thomas to reach St. Croix. There are no flights at all to St. John; you have to take a ferry from St. Thomas.

Hassle Factor: Low to high, depending on your flight schedule.

On the Ground: Many travelers do just fine without a car in St. Thomas, but it's much harder if you are renting a villa; also be aware that taxis can be expensive when used every day. In St. John you must rent a car if you are staying in a villa or in Coral Bay, but you might be able to get by without one if you are staying elsewhere. A car is more of a necessity in St. Croix, regardless of where you stay.

Getting Around the Islands: Frequent, convenient ferries connect St. Thomas and St. John. St. Croix is farther removed, so a flight from St. Thomas is the most common mode of transport.

PLANNING

WHEN TO GO

High season coincides with that on most other Caribbean islands, from December through April or May; before and after that time, rates can drop by as much as 25% to 50%, depending on the resort.

GETTING HERE AND AROUND

AIR TRAVEL

Fly nonstop to St. Thomas from Atlanta (Delta), Boston (American, seasonal; JetBlue via San Juan, seasonal), Charlotte (US Airways), Chicago (United), Fort Lauderdale (Spirit), Miami (American), New York–JFK (American), New York–Newark (Continental; United), Philadelphia (US Airways), or Washington, D.C.–Dulles (United). Fly nonstop to St. Croix from Miami (American). In the winter, US Airways flies nonstop from Charlotte, N.C.

If you can't fly nonstop, then you can connect in San Juan on Seaborne Airlines or Cape Air. You can also take a seaplane between St. Thomas and St. Croix. The only option for St. John is a ferry from either Red Hook or Charlotte Amalie in St. Thomas. Both Caneel Bay and the Westin have private ferries.

Airline Contacts American Airlines/Enjoy. On American, you can fly direct to St. Thomas from Miami and New York–JFK year-round and from Boston during the winter season. Envoy offers several daily nonstops between St. Thomas and San Juan, Puerto Rico, and other Caribbean islands. ☎ *800/474–4884* 🌐 *www.aa.com.* **Delta Airlines.** Delta flies direct from Atlanta. ☎ *800/221–1212* 🌐 *www.delta.com.* **JetBlue.** JetBlue flies direct from Boston five times a week, with a connection in San Juan. ☎ *800/538–2583* 🌐 *www.jetblue.com.* **Seaborne Airlines** ☎ *787/949–7800* 🌐 *www.seaborneairlines.com.* **Spirit Airlines.** Spirit flies direct from Ft. Lauderdale. ☎ *800/772–7117* 🌐 *www.spiritair.com.* **United Airlines.** United flies direct from Chicago, Dulles, and Newark. ☎ *800/241–6522,*

340/774–9190 in St. Thomas 🌐 *www.united.com.* **US Airways.** US Airways offers direct flights from Charlotte and Philadelphia. ☎ *800/622–1015* 🌐 *www.usairways.com.*

Airports Cyril E. King Airport (*STT*). ✉ *Rte. 30, Lindbergh Bay, St. Thomas* ☎ *340/774–5100.* **Henry Rohlsen Airport** (*STX*). ✉ *Airport Rd., off Rte. 66, Anguilla, St. Croix* ☎ *340/778–1012.*

BOAT AND FERRY TRAVEL

There's frequent service between St. Thomas and St. John and their neighbors, the BVI. Check with the ferry companies for the current schedules. These schedules are also printed in the free *St. Thomas + St. John This Week* magazine and on the website of the **Virgin Islands Vacation Guide & Community** (🌐 *www.vinow.com*).

There's frequent daily service from both Red Hook and Charlotte Amalie to Cruz Bay, St. John. About every hour there's a car ferry, which locals call the barge. You should arrive at least 15 minutes before departure.

Ferry Contacts Inter-Island Boat Service. Inter-Island has daily and weekly service between St. John and the British Virgin Islands of Jost Van Dyke, Tortola, Virgin Gorda, and Anegada. ☎ *340/776–6597 in St. John.* **Native Son.** Ferries operate daily between Charlotte Amalie and Red Hook, in St. Thomas, and West End and Road Town, in Tortola. ☎ *340/774–8685 in St. Thomas* 🌐 *www.nativesonferry.com.* **Smith's Ferry.** Smith's operates multiple trips daily between Charlotte Amalie and Red Hook in St. Thomas, and West End and Road Town, in Tortola. ☎ *340/775–7292 in St. Thomas* 🌐 *www.smithsferry.com.* **Speedy's.** Speedy's offers weekly ferry service to Virgin Gorda. The company also runs seasonal three-day weekend trips to Fajardo, Puerto Rico. ☎ *284/495–5235 in Tortola* 🌐 *www.speedysbvi.com.*

27

CAR TRAVEL

Driving is on the left, British-style. The law requires that *everyone* wear a seat belt. Traffic can be bad during rush hour on all three islands.

Car Rentals in St. Thomas: Avis, Budget, and Hertz all have counters at Cyril E. King Airport, but there are some other offices as well; in addition, there are local companies.

Car Rentals in St. John: All the car-rental companies in St. John are locally owned. Most companies are just a short walk from the ferry dock. Those a bit farther away will pick you up.

Car Rentals in St. Croix: There are both local and national companies on St. Croix; if your company doesn't have an airport location, you'll be picked up or a car will be delivered to you.

St. Thomas Car Rental Contacts Avis ✉ *Cyril E. King Airport, 70 Lindbergh Bay, 4 miles west of Charlotte Amalie, Lindbergh Bay, St. Thomas* ☎ *340/774–1468* 🌐 *www.avis.com* ✉ *Al Cohens Mall, Rte. 30, Havensight Cruise Ship Dock, Havensight, St. Thomas* ☎ *340/777–8888* ✉ *Across from Windward Passage Hotel, 3400 Veterans Dr., at Seabourne Airlines terminal, Charlotte Amalie, St. Thomas* ☎ *340/776–7329* 🌐 *www.avis.com.* **Budget** ✉ *Cyril E. King Airport, 70 Lindbergh Bay, 4 miles west of Charlotte Amalie, Lindbergh Bay, St. Thomas* ☎ *340/776–5774* 🌐 *www.budgetstt.com* ✉ *Havensight Cruise Ship Dock, Rte.*

30, Havensight, St. Thomas ☎ *340/776–5774* 🌐 *www.budgetstt.com.* **Dependable Car Rental** ✉ *Estate Contant, 12 Lindbergh Bay, 1.5 miles east of Cyril E. King Airport off Rte. 308, turning north at the Medical Arts Building, Lindbergh Bay, St. Thomas* ☎ *340/774–2253, 800/522–3076* 🌐 *www.dependablecar.com.* **Discount Car Rental.** The main office of this local family-owned business is in Lindbergh Bay, but they pick up at the Cyril E. King Airport as well as from most resorts and hotels. ✉ *Cyril E. King Airport, 70 Lindbergh Bay, 4 miles west of Charlotte Amalie, car rental is located adjacent to the entrance road of the airport, 1 min from the terminal* ☎ *340/776–4858, 877/478–2833* 🌐 *www.discountcar.vi.* **Hertz** ✉ *Cyril E King Airport, Airport Rd., 8100 Lindbergh Bay, 4 miles west of Charlotte Amalie, Lindbergh Bay, St. Thomas* ☎ *340/774–1879* 🌐 *www.hertz.com.*

St. John Car Rental Contacts Best ✉ *Near library, Cruz Bay, St. John* ☎ *340/693–8177* 🌐 *www.bestcarrentalvi.com.* **Cool Breeze** ✉ *1 block east of the passenger ferry dock, Cruz Bay, St. John* ☎ *340/776–6588* 🌐 *www.coolbreezecarrental.com.* **Courtesy** ✉ *Near St. Ursula's Church, Cruz Bay, St. John* ☎ *340/776–6650* 🌐 *www.courtesycarrental.com.* **Delbert Hill Taxi & Jeep Rental Service** ✉ *King St., Cruz Bay, St. John* ☎ *340/776–6637* 🌐 *www.delberthillcarrental.com.* **Denzil Clyne** ✉ *North Shore Rd., across from creek, Cruz Bay, St. John* ☎ *340/776–6715.* **O'Connor Car Rental** ✉ *Rte. 104, near the roundabout, Cruz Bay, St. John* ☎ *340/776–6343* 🌐 *www.oconnorcarrental.com.* **St. John Car Rental** ✉ *Bay St., near Wharfside Village, Cruz Bay, St. John* ☎ *340/776–6103* 🌐 *www.stjohncarrental.com.* **Spencer's Jeep** ✉ *Boulon Center Rd., near creek, Cruz Bay, St. John* ☎ *340/693–8784, 888/776–6628.*

St. Croix Car Rental Contacts Avis ✉ *Henry E. Rohlsen Airport, St. Croix* ☎ *340/778–9355, 800/354–2847* 🌐 *www.avis.com* ✉ *Seaplane, Christiansted, St. Croix* ☎ *340/713–9355* 🌐 *www.avis.com.* **Budget** ✉ *Henry E. Rohlsen Airport, St. Croix* ☎ *340/778–9636, 888/264–8894* ✉ *Prince St., across from Seaplane, Christiansted, St. Croix* ☎ *340/713–9289* 🌐 *www.budgetstcroix.com.* **Hertz** ✉ *Henry E. Rohlsen Airport, St. Croix* ☎ *340/778–1402, 888/248–4261* 🌐 *www.rentacarstcroix.com.* **Judi of Croix** ☎ *340/773–2123, 877/903–2123* 🌐 *www.judiofcroix.com.* **Midwest** ✉ *Centerline Rd., Estate Carlton, Frederiksted, St. Croix* ☎ *340/772–0438, 877/772–0438* 🌐 *www.midwestautorental.com.* **Olympic** ✉ *Rte. 70, Christiansted, St. Croix* ☎ *340/718–3000, 888/878–4227* 🌐 *www.olympicstcroix.com.*

TAXI TRAVEL

USVI taxis don't have meters; fares are per person, set by a schedule, and drivers usually take multiple fares, especially from the airport, ferry docks, and cruise-ship terminals. Many taxis are open safari vans, but some are air-conditioned vans.

St. Thomas East End Taxi ✉ *Urman Victor Fredericks Marine Terminal, 6117 Red Hook Quarters, off Rte. 38 in Red Hook, St. Thomas* ☎ *340/775–6974* 🌐 *eastendtaxi.cbt.cc.* **Islander Taxi Services** ✉ *Fortress Storage, Building K Ste. 2025, at the intersection of Rtes. 313 and 38, Sugar Estate, St. Thomas* ☎ *340/774–4077* 🌐 *www.islandertaxiservice.com.* **Virgin Islands Taxi Association** ✉ *68A Estate Contant, Charlotte Amalie, St. Thomas* ☎ *340/774–4550, 340/774–7457* 🌐 *vitaxiassociation.com.*

St. John Paradise Taxi ✉ *Waterfront, Cruz Bay, St. John* ☎ *340/714–7913.*

St. Croix Antilles Taxi Service ✉ *Christiansted, St. Croix* ☎ *340/773-5020.* **St. Croix Taxi Association** ✉ *Henry E. Rohlsen Airport, St. Croix* ☎ *340/778-1088* 🌐 *www.stcroixtaxi.com.*

ESSENTIALS

Banks and Exchange Services The U.S. dollar is used throughout the U.S. Virgin Islands. All major credit cards are accepted by most hotels, restaurants, and shops. ATMs are common on St. Thomas. Banks on St. Thomas include Banco Popular, Scotia Bank, and First Bank. St. John has First Bank and Banco Popular in Cruz Bay and Scotia Bank at the Marketplace shopping center. St. Croix has branches of Banco Popular in the Orange Grove and Sunny Isle. V.I. Community Bank is in Sunny Isle, Frederiksted, Estate Diamond, Orange Grove, and Christiansted. Scotia Bank has branches in Sunny Isle, Frederiksted, Christiansted, and Sunshine Mall.

Electricity Electricity is the U.S. standard.

Safety Keep your hotel or vacation villa door locked at all times, and stick to well-lighted streets at night. Keep your rental car locked wherever you park, and lock possessions in the trunk. Don't leave valuables lying on the beach while you snorkel. Don't wander the streets of the main towns alone at night, whether you are in Charlotte Amalie, Cruz Bay, Christiansted, or Frederiksted.

Although crime is not as prevalent in St. John as it is on St. Thomas and St. Croix, it does exist. There are occasional burglaries at villas, even during daylight hours. Lock doors even when you're lounging by the pool. It's not a good idea to walk around Cruz Bay late at night. If you don't have a car, plan on taking a taxi. Because it can be hard to find a taxi in the wee hours of the morning, arrange in advance for a driver to pick you up.

ACCOMMODATIONS

St. Thomas is the most developed of the Virgin Islands; choose it if you want extensive shopping opportunities and a multitude of activities and restaurants. St. John, the least developed of the three, has a distinct following; it's the best choice if you want a small-island feel and easy access to great hiking. However, most villas there aren't directly on the beach. St. Croix is a sleeper. The diversity of the accommodations means that you can stay in everything from a simple inn to a luxury resort, but none of the beaches is as breathtaking as those on St. Thomas and St. John.

Resorts: Whether you are looking for a luxury retreat or a moderately priced vacation spot, there's going to be something for you in the USVI. St. Thomas has the most options. St. John has only two large resorts, both upscale; others are small, but it has two unique eco-oriented camping options. St. Croix's resorts are more midsize.

Small Inns: Particularly on St. Croix, you'll find a wide range of attractive and accommodating small inns; if you can live without being directly on the beach, these friendly, homey places are a good option. St. Thomas also has a few small inns in the historic district of Charlotte Amalie.

Villas: Villas are plentiful on all three islands, but they are especially popular on St. John, where they represent the majority of the available lodging. They're always a good bet for families who can do without a busy resort environment.

Hotel reviews have been shortened. For full information, visit Fodors.com.

WHAT IT COSTS IN U.S. DOLLARS				
	$	$$	$$$	$$$$
Restaurants	under $12	$12–$20	$21–$30	over $30
Hotels	under $275	$275–$375	$376–$475	over $475

Restaurant prices are the average cost of a main course at dinner or, if dinner is not served, at lunch. Hotel prices are the lowest cost of a standard double room in high season.

VISITOR INFORMATION

Contacts USVI Department of Tourism ☎ *340/774–8784, 800/372–8784* 🌐 *www.visitusvi.com.*

WEDDINGS

Apply for a marriage license at the Superior Court. There's a $100 application fee and $100 license fee. You have to wait eight days after the clerk receives the application to get married, and licenses must be picked up in person weekdays or on weekends for an additional $150, though you can apply by mail. A marriage ceremony at the Superior Court costs $400 in St. John and $200 in St. Thomas.

St. Croix Superior Court ☎ *340/778–9750.*

St. Thomas Superior Court ☎ *340/774–6680.*

ST. THOMAS

Updated by Carol M. Bareuther

If you fly to the 32-square-mile (83-square-km) island of St. Thomas, you land at its western end; if you arrive by cruise ship, you come into one of the world's most beautiful harbors. Either way, one of your first sights is the town of Charlotte Amalie. From the harbor you see an idyllic-looking village that spreads into the lower hills. If you were expecting a quiet hamlet with its inhabitants hanging out under palm trees, you've missed that era by about 300 years. Although other islands in the USVI developed plantation economies, St. Thomas cultivated its harbor, and it became a thriving seaport soon after it was settled by the Danish in the 1600s.

The success of the naturally perfect harbor was enhanced by the fact that the Danes—who ruled St. Thomas with only a couple of short interruptions from 1666 to 1917—avoided involvement in some 100 years' worth of European wars. Denmark was the only European country with colonies in the Caribbean to stay neutral during the War of the Spanish Succession in the early 1700s. Thus, products of the Dutch, English, and French islands—sugar, cotton, and indigo—were traded through Charlotte Amalie, along with the regular shipments of slaves. When the Spanish wars ended, trade fell off, but by the end of the 1700s Europe was at war again, Denmark again remained neutral, and St. Thomas continued to prosper. Even into the 1800s, while the economies of St. Croix and St. John foundered with the market for sugarcane, St. Thomas's economy remained vigorous. This prosperity led to the development of shipyards, a well-organized banking system, and a large merchant class. In 1845 Charlotte Amalie had 101 large importing houses owned by the English, French, Germans, Haitians, Spaniards, Americans, Sephardim, and Danes.

Charlotte Amalie is still one of the world's most active cruise-ship ports. On almost any day at least one and sometimes as many as eight cruise ships are tied to the docks or anchored outside the harbor. Gently rocking in the shadows of these giant floating hotels are just about every other kind of vessel imaginable: sleek sailing catamarans that will take you on a sunset cruise complete with rum punch and a Jimmy Buffett soundtrack, private megayachts for billionaires, and barnacle-bottom sloops—with laundry draped over the lifelines—that are home to world-cruising gypsies. Huge container ships pull up in Sub Base, west of the harbor, bringing in everything from breakfast cereals to tires. Anchored right along the waterfront are down-island barges that ply the waters between the Greater Antilles and the Leeward Islands, transporting goods such as refrigerators, VCRs, and disposable diapers.

HOP ON THE BUS

On St. Thomas the island's large buses make public transportation a very comfortable—though slow—way to get from east and west to Charlotte Amalie and back (service to the north is limited). Buses run about every 30 minutes from stops that are clearly marked with "Vitran" signs. Fares are $1 between outlying areas and town and 75¢ in town. There are also safari taxis (open-air seats with a roof built on the back of a pickup truck) or "dollar buses" that run the same routes for $1 a ride.

The waterfront road through Charlotte Amalie was once part of the harbor. Before it was filled in to build the highway, the beach came right up to the back door of the warehouses that now line the thoroughfare. Two hundred years ago those warehouses were filled with indigo, tobacco, and cotton. Today the stone buildings house silk, crystal, and diamonds. Exotic fragrances are still traded, but by island beauty queens in air-conditioned perfume palaces instead of through open market stalls. The pirates of old used St. Thomas as a base from which to raid merchant ships of every nation, though they were particularly fond of the gold- and silver-laden treasure ships heading to Spain. Pirates are still around, but today's versions use St. Thomas as a drop-off for their contraband: illegal immigrants and drugs.

EXPLORING

To explore outside Charlotte Amalie, rent a car or hire a taxi. Your rental car should come with a good map; if not, pick up the pocket-size "St. Thomas–St. John Road Map" at a tourist information center. Roads are marked with route numbers, but they're confusing and seem

Fort Christian (1672–80) is the oldest surviving structure in St. Thomas.

to switch numbers suddenly. Roads are also identified by signs bearing the St. Thomas–St. John Hotel and Tourism Association's mascot, Tommy the Starfish. More than 100 of these color-coded signs line the island's main routes. Orange signs trace the route from the airport to Red Hook, green signs identify the road from town to Magens Bay, Tommy's face on a yellow background points from Mafolie to Crown Bay through the north side, red signs lead from Smith Bay to Four Corners via Skyline Drive, and blue signs mark the route from the cruise-ship dock at Havensight to Red Hook. These color-coded routes are not marked on most visitor maps, however. Allow yourself a day to explore, especially if you want to stop to take pictures or to enjoy a light bite or refreshing swim. Most gas stations are on the island's more populated eastern end, so fill up before heading to the north side. And remember to drive on the left!

CHARLOTTE AMALIE

Look beyond the pricey shops, T-shirt vendors, and bustling crowds for a glimpse of the island's history. The city served as the capital of Denmark's outpost in the Caribbean until 1917, an aspect of the island often lost in the glitz of the shopping district.

Emancipation Gardens, right next to the fort, is a good place to start a walking tour. Tackle the hilly part of town first: head north up Government Hill to the historic buildings that house government offices and have incredible views. Several regal churches line the route that runs west back to the town proper and the old-time market. Virtually all the alleyways that intersect Main Street lead to eateries serving frosty drinks, sandwiches, and West Indian fare. There are public restrooms in this area, too. Allow an hour for a quick view of the sights.

A note about the street names: In deference to the island's heritage, the streets downtown are labeled by their Danish names. Locals will use both the Danish name and the English name (such as Dronningens Gade and Norre Gade for Main Street), but most people refer to things by their location ("a block toward the waterfront off Main Street" or "next to the Little Switzerland Shop"). You may find it more useful if you ask for directions by shop names or landmarks.

TOP ATTRACTIONS

99 Steps. This staircase "street," built by the Danes in the 1700s, leads to the residential area above Charlotte Amalie and to Blackbeard's Castle, a U.S. National Historic Landmark. If you count the stairs as you go up, you'll discover, as thousands have before you, that there are more than the name implies. ✉ *Look for steps heading north from Government Hill.*

FAMILY **Fort Christian.** St. Thomas's oldest standing structure, this remarkable building was built between 1672 and 1680 and now has U.S. National Landmark status. Over the years, it was used as a jail, governor's residence, town hall, courthouse, and church. In 2005, a multimillion-dollar renovation project started to stabilize the structure and halt centuries of deterioration. The fort re-opened for public tours in 2014. Inside you can visit the inner courtyard and rooms, and from the outside, you can see the four renovated faces of the famous 19th-century clock tower. ✉ *Waterfront Hwy., east of shopping district* ☎ *340/774–5541* 🌐 *stthomashistoricaltrust.org.*

Hassel Island. East of Water Island in Charlotte Amalie harbor, Hassel Island is part of the Virgin Islands National Park. On it are the ruins of a British military garrison (built during a brief British occupation of the USVI during the 1800s) and the remains of a marine railway (where ships were hoisted into dry dock for repairs). Daily guided kayak tours to the island are available from VI Ecotours. The St. Thomas Historical Trust also leads walking tours throughout the year. ✉ *Charlotte Amalie harbor* ☎ *340/776–6201 Virgin Islands National Park main office* 🌐 *www.nps.gov/viis.*

Pissarro Building. Housing several shops and an art gallery, this was the birthplace and childhood home of the acclaimed 19th-century impressionist painter Camille Pissarro, who lived for most of his adult life in France. The art gallery on the second floor contains three original pages from Pissarro's sketchbook and two pastels by Pissarro's grandson, Claude. ✉ *14 Dronningens Gade (Main St.), between Raadets Gade and Trompeter Gade.*

FAMILY **Roosevelt Park.** The former Coconut Park was renamed in honor of Franklin D. Roosevelt in 1945. It's a great place to put your feet up and people-watch. Five granite pedestals represent the five branches of the military, bronze urns commemorate special events and can be lighted, and inscribed bronze plaques pay tribute to the territory's veterans who died defending the United States. There's also a children's playground. ✉ *Intersection of Norre Gade and Rte. 35, adjacent to the Memorial*

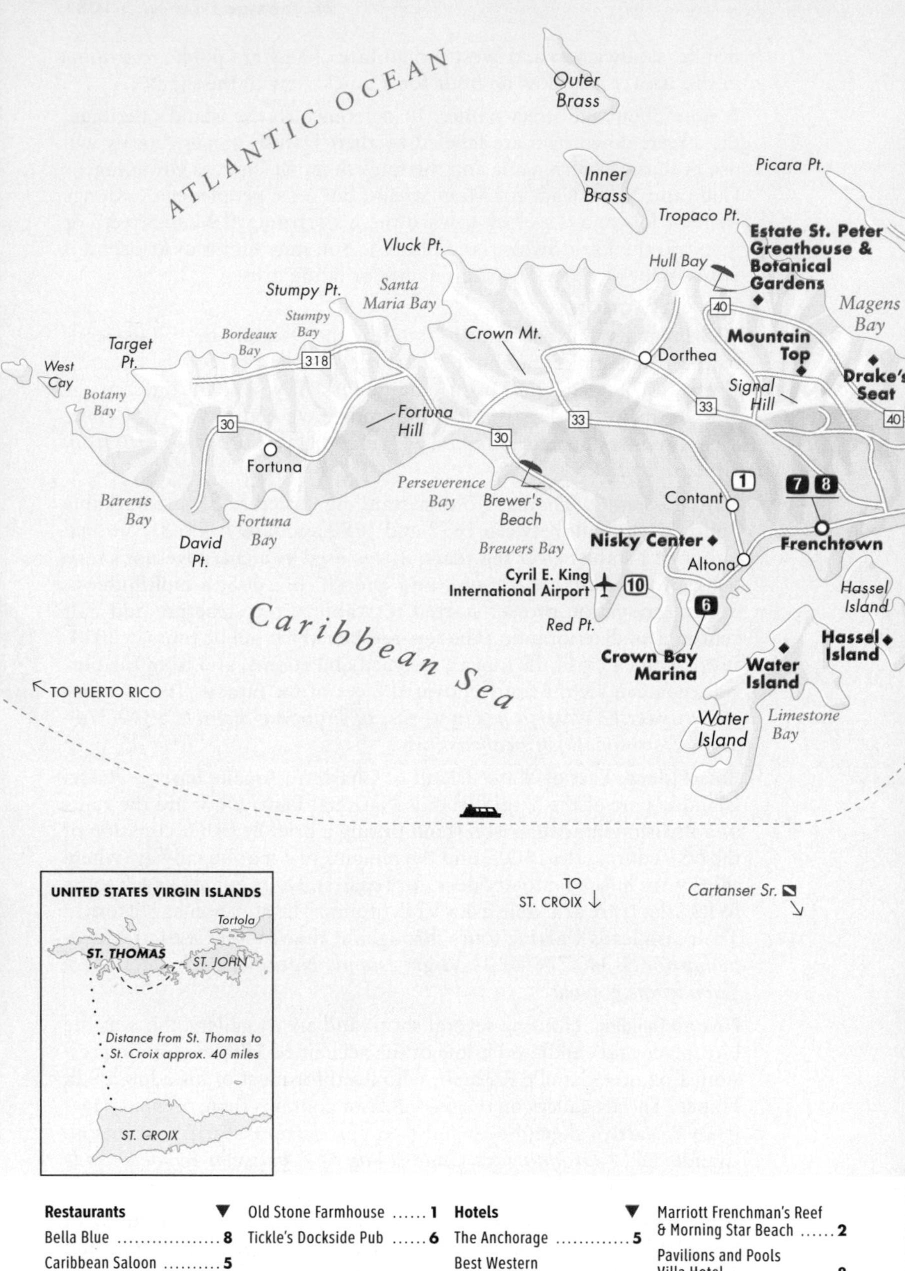

Restaurants ▼

- Bella Blue 8
- Caribbean Saloon 5
- Duffy's Love Shack 3
- Havana Blue 2
- Hook, Line & Sinker 7
- Molly Molone's 4
- Old Stone Farmhouse 1
- Tickle's Dockside Pub 6

Hotels ▼

- The Anchorage 5
- Best Western Emerald Beach 10
- Bolongo Bay 3
- Island View Guesthouse 1
- Marriott Frenchman's Reef & Morning Star Beach 2
- Pavilions and Pools Villa Hotel 8
- Point Pleasant Resort 9
- Ritz-Carlton 6
- Secret Harbour 4
- Sugar Bay Resort & Spa 7

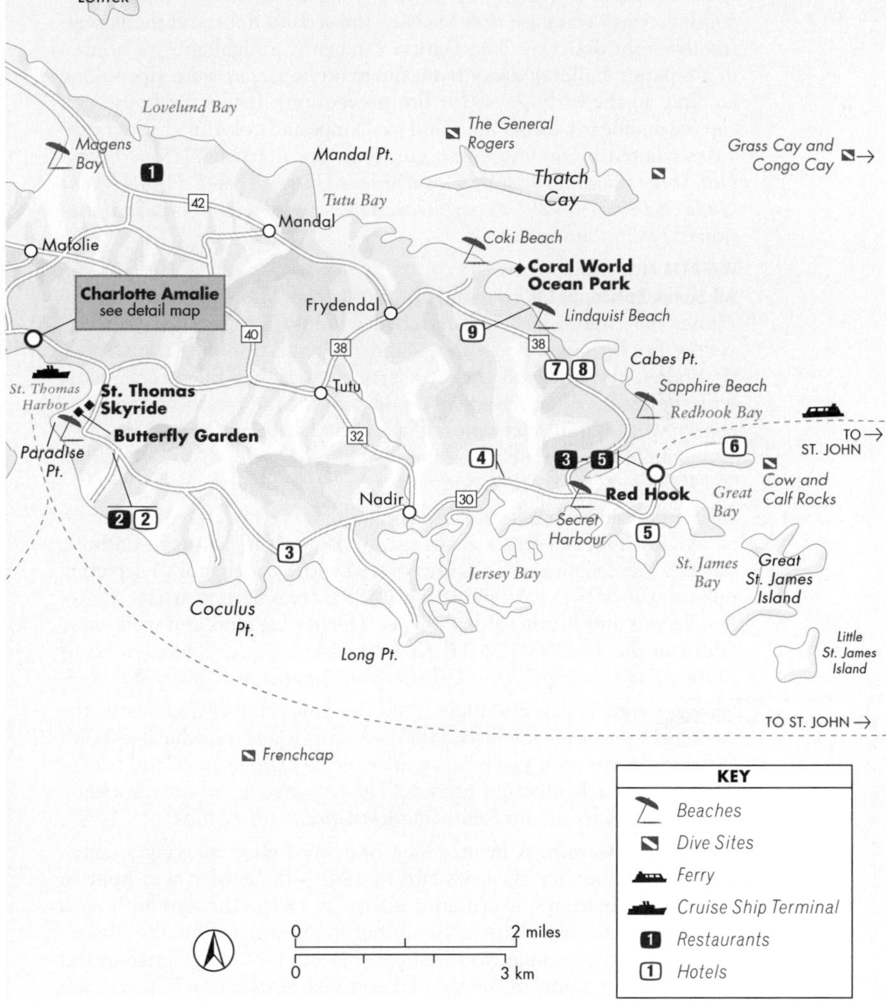
St. Thomas
Hans Lollick
Lovelund Bay
Magens Bay
The General Rogers
Mandal Pt.
Grass Cay and Congo Cay
Thatch Cay
Tutu Bay
Mandal
Mafolie
Coki Beach
Coral World Ocean Park
Charlotte Amalie
see detail map
Frydendal
Lindquist Beach
Cabes Pt.
St. Thomas Harbor
St. Thomas Skyride
Tutu
Sapphire Beach
Redhook Bay
Butterfly Garden
TO ST. JOHN
Paradise Pt.
Cow and Calf Rocks
Red Hook
Great Bay
Nadir
Secret Harbour
St. James Bay
Great St. James Island
Jersey Bay
Coculus Pt.
Long Pt.
Little St. James Island
TO ST. JOHN
Frenchcap
KEY
Beaches
Dive Sites
Ferry
Cruise Ship Terminal
Restaurants
Hotels
0
2 miles
0
3 km

Moravian Church ☎ *340/774–5541* 🌐 *www.stthomashistoricaltrust.org.*

Seven Arches Museum and Gallery. This restored 18th-century home is a striking example of classic Danish–West Indian architecture. There seem to be arches everywhere—seven to be exact—all supporting a "welcoming arms" staircase that leads to the second floor and the flower-framed front doorway. The Danish kitchen is a highlight: it's housed in a separate building away from the main house, as were all cooking facilities in the early days (for fire prevention). Inside the house you can see mahogany furnishings and gas lamps and colorful abstract canvases painted by the museum's curator, a local artist. ✉ *Government Hill, three buildings east of Government House, 18A–B Dronningens Gade* ☎ *340/774–9295* 🌐 *www.sevenarchesmuseum.com* 🎫 *$5 donation* ⏲ *By appointment only.*

WORTH NOTING

All Saints Episcopal Church. Built in 1848 from stone quarried on the island, the church has thick, arched window frames lined with the yellow brick that came to the islands as ballast aboard ships. Merchants left the brick on the waterfront when they filled their boats with molasses, sugar, mahogany, and rum for the return voyage. The church was built in celebration of the end of slavery in the USVI. ✉ *13 Commandant Gade, near the Emancipation Garden U.S. Post Office* ☎ *340/774–0217* ⏲ *Mon.–Sat. 9–3.*

Saints Peter and Paul Cathedral. This building was consecrated as a parish church in 1848, and serves as the seat of the territory's Roman Catholic diocese. The ceiling and walls are covered with a dozen murals depicting biblical scenes; they were painted in 1899 by two Belgian artists, Father Leo Servais and Brother Ildephonsus. The marble altar and walls were added in the 1960s. ✉ *22-AB Kronprindsens Gade, 1 block west of Market Square* ☎ *340/774–0201* 🌐 *cathedralvi.com* ⏲ *Mon.–Sat. 8–5.*

Educators Park. A peaceful place amid the town's hustle and bustle, the park has memorials for three famous Virgin Islanders: educator Edith Williams, J. Antonio Jarvis (a founder of the *Daily News*), and educator and author Rothschild Francis. The last gave many speeches here. ✉ *Main St., across from Emancipation Garden post office.*

Emancipation Garden. A bronze bust of a freed slave blowing a conch shell commemorates slavery's end in 1848—the garden was built to mark emancipation's 150th anniversary in 1998. The gazebo here is used for official ceremonies. Two other monuments show the island's Danish-American connection—a bust of Denmark's King Christian and a scaled-down model of the U.S. Liberty Bell. ✉ *between Tolbod Gade and Fort Christian, next to Vendor's Plaza.*

Frederick Evangelical Lutheran Church. This historic church has a massive mahogany altar, and its pews—each with its own door—were once rented to families of the congregation. Lutheranism is the state religion of Denmark, and when the territory was without a minister, the governor—who had his own elevated pew—filled in. ✉ *7 Norre Gade, across from Emancipation Garden and the Grand Hotel* ☎ *340/776–1315* 🌐 *www.felc1666.org* ⏲ *Mon.–Sat. 9–4.*

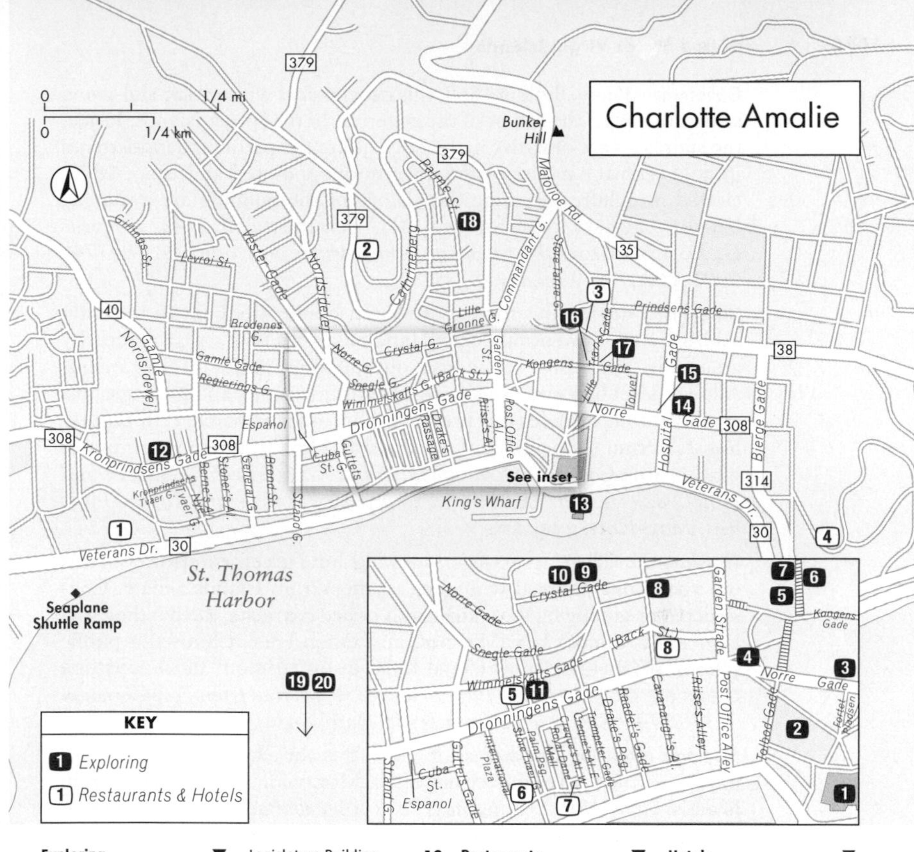

Exploring	▼
99 Steps	6
All Saints Episcopal Church	18
Cathedral of St. Peter and St. Paul	12
Educators Park	4
Emancipation Garden	2
Fort Christian	1
Frederick Evangelical Lutheran Church	3
Government House	16
Haagensen House	7
Hassel Island	20
Hotel 1829	5
Legislature Building	13
Memorial Moravian Church	15
Pissarro Building	11
Roosevelt Park	14
St. Thomas Reformed Church	8
Seven Arches Museum	17
Synagogue of Beracha Veshalom Vegmiluth Hasidim	9
Water Island	19
Weibel Museum	10

Restaurants	▼
Banana Tree Grille	4
Cuzzin's Caribbean Restaurant & Bar	8
Gladys' Cafe	7
Greenhouse	6
Virgilio's	5

Hotels	▼
The Green Iguana	3
Villa Santana	2
Windward Passage	1

Government House. Built in 1867, this neoclassical white brick-and-wood structure houses the offices of the governor of the Virgin Islands. Inside, the staircases are of native mahogany, as are the plaques, hand-lettered in gold with the names of the governors appointed and, since 1970, elected. Brochures detailing the history of the building are available, but you may have to ask for them. ✉ *Government Hill, 21–22 Kongens Gade, across from the Emancipation Garden post office* ☎ *340/774–0001* 🎫 *Free* ⏲ *Weekdays 8–5.*

Haagensen House. This lovingly restored house was built in the early 1800s by Danish entrepreneur Hans Haagensen. It's surrounded by an equally impressive cookhouse, outbuildings, and terraced gardens. A lower-level banquet hall showcases antique prints and photographs. A guided tour includes this property, plus other restored 19th-century houses, a rum factory, amber museum, and finally, the lookout tour at Blackbeard's Castle. ✉ *Government Hill, 29–30 Kongens Gade, behind Hotel 1829* ☎ *340/776–1234* 🎫 *Tours $10* ⏲ *Dec.–Apr., Tues.–Thurs. 9–3; May–Nov., weekdays 9–2.*

Legislature Building. Its pastoral-looking lime-green exterior conceals the vociferous political wrangling of the Virgin Islands Senate. Constructed originally by the Danish as a police barracks, the building was later used to billet U.S. Marines, and much later it housed a public school. ■ **TIP→ You're welcome to sit in on sessions in the upstairs chambers.** ✉ *Waterfront Hwy. (aka Rte. 30), across from Fort Christian* ☎ *340/774–0880* 🌐 *www.legvi.org* ⏲ *Daily 8–5.*

Memorial Moravian Church. Built in 1884, this church was named to commemorate the 150th anniversary of the Moravian Church in the Virgin Islands. ✉ *17 Norre Gade, next to Roosevelt Park* ☎ *340/776–0066* 🌐 *www.memorialmoravianvi.org* ⏲ *Weekdays 8–5.*

St. Thomas Historical Trust Museum. Tours of the museum take 30 minutes and include a wealth of pirate artifacts, as well as West Indian antique furniture, old-time postcards, and historic books. The Trust office, also located at the museum, is where you can book reservations for the one-hour historic Charlotte Amalie walking tour and three-hour Hassel Island tour, both of which have to be scheduled by appointment. ✉ *West end of Roosevelt Park* ☎ *340/774–5541* 🌐 *www.stthomashistoricaltrust.org* ⏲ *Tues., Thurs. 10–2.*

St. Thomas Reformed Church. This church has an austere loveliness that's amazing considering all it's been through. Founded in 1744, it's been rebuilt twice after fires and hurricanes. The unembellished cream-color hall is quite peaceful. The only other color is the forest green of the shutters and the carpet. Call ahead if you wish to visit at a particular time, as the doors are sometimes locked. Services are held at 9 am each Sunday. ✉ *5 Crystal Gade at Nye Gade, 1½ blocks north of Main St.* ☎ *340/776–8255* 🌐 *www.stthomasreformedchurch.org* ⏲ *Weekdays 9–5.*

Synagogue of Beracha Veshalom Vegmiluth Hasidim. The synagogue's Hebrew name translates as the Congregation of Blessing, Peace, and Loving Deeds. The small building's white pillars contrast with rough stone walls, as does the rich mahogany of the pews and altar. The sand on the floor symbolizes the exodus from Egypt. Since the synagogue first opened its doors in 1833, it has held a weekly service, making it the oldest synagogue building in continuous use under the American flag and the second-oldest (after the one on Curaçao) in the Western Hemisphere. Guided tours can be arranged. Brochures detailing the key structures and history are also available. Next door the Weibel Museum showcases Jewish history on St. Thomas. ✉ *Synagogue Hill, 15 Crystal Gade ✣ From Main St., walk up Raadet's Gade (H. Stern is on the corner) to the top of the hill, turn left and synagogue is the 2nd bldg. on right* ☎ *340/774–4312* 🌐 *www.onepaper.com/synagogue* ⏲ *Weekdays 9–4.*

Weibel Museum. In this museum next to the synagogue, 300 years of Jewish history on St. Thomas are showcased. The small gift shop sells a commemorative silver coin celebrating the anniversary of the Hebrew congregation's establishment on the island in 1796. There are also tropically inspired items, such as menorahs painted to resemble palm trees. ✉ *Synagogue Hill, 15 Crystal Gade ✣ From Main St., walk up Raadet's Gade (H. Stern is on the corner) to the top of the hill, turn left and it's the 2nd building on right* ☎ *340/774–4312* 🌐 *www.onepaper.com/synagogue* 🎫 *Free* ⏲ *Weekdays 9–4.*

EAST END

Although the eastern end has many major resorts and spectacular beaches, don't be surprised if a cow or a herd of goats crosses your path as you drive through the relatively flat, dry terrain.

TOP ATTRACTIONS

FAMILY
Fodor's Choice ★

Coral World Ocean Park. This interactive aquarium and water-sports center lets you experience a variety of sea life and other animals. There's a new two-acre dolphin habitat under construction, as well as several outdoor pools where you can pet baby sharks, feed stingrays, touch starfish, and view endangered sea turtles. During the Sea Trek Helmet Dive, you walk along an underwater trail wearing a helmet that provides a continuous supply of air. You can also try Snuba, a cross between snorkeling and scuba diving. Swim with a sea lion and have a chance at playing ball or getting a big, wet, whiskered kiss. You can also buy a cup of nectar and let the cheerful lorikeets perch on your hand and drink. The park also has an offshore underwater observatory, an 80,000-gallon coral reef exhibit (one of the largest in the world), and a nature trail with native ducks and tortoises. Daily feedings take place at most exhibits. ✉ *Coki Point north of Rte. 38, 6450 Estate Smith Bay, Estate Frydendal* ☎ *340/775–1555* 🌐 *www.coralworldvi.com* 🎫 *$19, Sea Lion Splash $126, Sea Lion Encounter $86, Sea Trek $79, Snuba $73, Shark and Turtle Encounters $53, Semi-Submarine $41* ⏲ *Daily 9–4. Off-season (May–Oct.) hrs may vary, so call to confirm.*

WORTH NOTING

Red Hook. The IGY American Yacht Harbor marina here has fishing and sailing charter boats, a dive shop, and powerboat-rental agencies. There are also several bars and restaurants, including Molly Molone's, Fish Tails, Duffy's Love Shack, and the Caribbean Saloon. Ferries depart

Coral World Ocean Park offers interactive sea-life encounters.

from Red Hook en route to St. John and the British Virgin Islands. ✉ *Red Hook, intersection of Rtes. 38 and 32.*

SOUTH SHORE

TOP ATTRACTIONS

FAMILY **Skyride to Paradise Point.** Fly skyward in a 7-minute gondola ride to Paradise Point, an overlook with breathtaking views of Charlotte Amalie and the harbor. You'll find several shops, a bar, a restaurant, and a wedding gazebo. A ¼-mile (½-km) hiking trail leads to spectacular views of St. Croix. Wear sturdy shoes, as the trail is steep and rocky. You can also skip the $21 gondola ride and taxi to the top for $6 per person from the Havensight Dock. ✉ *Rte. 30, across from Havensight Mall, Havensight* ☎ *340/774–9809* 🌐 *www.ridetheview.com* 🎫 *$21* ⏲ *Thurs.–Tues. 9–5, Wed. 9–9.*

WORTH NOTING

FAMILY **Butterfly Garden.** Step into this 10,000-square-foot mesh enclosure and watch hundreds of colorful, exotic butterflies flutter all around you. A 25-minute tour takes you through their life cycle. Outside the enclosure, you can wander a garden of native plants designed to attract local butterflies and hummingbirds. The butterflies are most active in the morning. If you're a photographer, you'll probably prefer the afternoon, when the butterflies move more slowly and are more easily captured in pictures. ✉ *Havensight Mall, 9016 Havensight Mall, adjacent to West Indian Company cruise-ship dock, Havensight* ☎ *340/715–3366* 🌐 *www.butterflygardenvi.com* 🎫 *$12* ⏲ *Nov.–Apr. 8:30–4 on days a cruise ship is at the Havensight Dock. Off-season (May–Oct.) hrs may vary, so call to confirm.*

Frenchtown. Popular for its bars and restaurants, Frenchtown is also the home of descendants of immigrants from St. Barthélemy (St. Barths). You can watch them pull up their brightly painted boats and display their equally colorful catch of the day along the waterfront. If you chat with them, you can hear speech patterns slightly different from those of other St. Thomians. Get a feel for the residential district of Frenchtown by walking west to some of the town's winding streets, where tiny wooden houses have been passed down from generation to generation. ✉ *Turn south off Waterfront Hwy. (Rte. 30) at post office, Frenchtown.*

French Heritage Museum. Next to Joseph Aubain Ballpark, the museum houses fishing nets, accordions, tambourines, mahogany furniture, photographs, and other artifacts illustrating the lives of the French descendants during the 18th through 20th centuries. Admission is free, but donations are accepted. ✉ *Rue de St. Anne and Rue de St. Barthélemy, next to Joseph Aubain Ballpark, Frenchtown* ☎ *340/714–2583* 🌐 *www.frenchheritagemuseum.com* 🎫 *Free* ⏲ *Mon.–Sat. 9–6.*

FAMILY **Water Island.** This island, the fourth-largest of the U.S. Virgin Islands, floats about a ¼ mile (½ km) out in Charlotte Amalie harbor. A ferry between Crown Bay Marina and the island operates several times daily Monday through Saturday 6:30–6 and Sunday and holidays 8–5 at a cost of $10 round-trip. (On cruise-ship days, a ferry goes directly from the West India Company dock, but only for those passengers on the bike trip.) From the ferry dock, it's a hike of less than a half mile to Honeymoon Beach (though you have to go up a big hill), where Brad Pitt and Cate Blanchett filmed a scene of the movie *The Curious Case of Benjamin Button.* Get lunch from a food truck that pulls up on weekends. ✉ *Charlotte Amalie harbor, Charlotte Amalie* ☎ *340/690–4159 for ferry information.*

27

WEST END

WORTH NOTING

Drake's Seat. Sir Francis Drake was supposed to have kept watch over his fleet, looking for enemy ships from this vantage point. The panorama is especially breathtaking (and romantic) at dusk, and if you arrive late in the day, you can miss the hordes of day-trippers on taxi tours who stop here to take pictures. ✉ *Rte. 40, located ¼ mile west of the intersection of Rtes. 40 and 35, Estate Zufriedenheit.*

Estate St. Peter Greathouse and Botanical Gardens. This unusual spot is perched on a mountainside 1,000 feet above sea level, with views of more than 20 islands and islets. You can wander through a gallery displaying local art, sip a complimentary rum punch while looking out at the view, or follow a nature trail that leads you past nearly 70 varieties of tropical plants, including 17 varieties of orchids. ✉ *Rte. 40, directly across from Tree Limin' Extreme Zipline, Estate St. Peter* ☎ *340/774–4999* 🌐 *www.greathousevi.com* 🎫 *$8.*

FAMILY **Magic Ice Gallery.** This is one cool gallery! Life-size ice carvings feature sea life, a pirate ship, a chapel, a bar (a complimentary drink is included in the tour), a slide you can ride down, and much more. Insulated ponchos with hoods and mittens are provided, but you don't get to keep them. ✉ *Charlotte Amalie Waterfront, 21 Dronningens Gade, located* *next to the Pizza Hut on the Waterfront* ☎ *340/422–6000* ⊕ *www.magicice.vi* 🎫 *$22* ⊙ *Weekends 10–5, weekdays 11–5.*

FAMILY **Mountain Top.** Head out to the observation deck—more than 1,500 feet above sea level—to get a bird's-eye view that stretches from Puerto Rico's out island of Culebra in the west all the way to the British Virgin Islands in the east. There's also a restaurant, restrooms, and duty-free shops that sell everything from Caribbean art to nautical antiques, ship models, and touristy T-shirts. Kids will like talking to the parrots—and hearing them answer back. ✉ *Head north off Rte. 33, look for signs, Mountain Top* ☎ *340/774–2400* ⊕ *www.mountaintopvi.com* 🎫 *Free* ⊙ *Daily 8–5.*

BEACHES

All 44 St. Thomas beaches are open to the public, although you can reach some of them only by walking through a resort. Hotel guests frequently have access to lounge chairs and floats that are off-limits to nonguests; for this reason you may feel more comfortable at one of the beaches not associated with a resort, such as Magens Bay (which charges an entrance fee to cover beach maintenance) or Coki Beach, the latter abutting Coral World Ocean Park and offering the island's best off-the-beach snorkeling. Remember to remove all your valuables from the car and keep them out of sight when you go swimming. Break-ins are possible on all three of the U.S. Virgin Islands; most locals recommend leaving your windows down and leaving absolutely nothing in your car.

EAST END

FAMILY
Fodor's Choice ★
Coki Beach. Funky beach huts selling local foods such as pâtés (fried turnovers with a spicy ground-beef filling), quaint vendor kiosks, and a brigade of hair braiders and taxi men make this beach overlooking picturesque Thatch Cay feel like an amusement park. But this is the best place on the island to snorkel and scuba dive. Fish, including grunts, snappers, and wrasses, are like an effervescent cloud you can wave your hand through. **Amenities:** food and drink; lifeguards; parking; showers; restrooms; water sports. **Best for:** partiers; snorkeling. ✉ *Rte. 388, next to Coral World Ocean Park, Estate Smith Bay.*

Lindquist Beach. The newest of the Virgin Islands' public beaches has a serene sense of wilderness that isn't found on the more crowded beaches. A lifeguard is on duty between 8 am and 5 pm. Picnic tables are available. Try snorkeling over the offshore reef. **Amenities:** lifeguards; parking; toilets. **Best for:** solitude; snorkeling. ✉ *Rte. 38, at end of a bumpy dirt road* 🎫 *$2 per person.*

FAMILY **Sapphire Beach.** A steady breeze makes this beach a board sailor's paradise. The swimming is great, as is the snorkeling, especially at the reef near Pettyklip Point. Beach volleyball is big on the weekends. Sapphire Beach Resort and Marina has a snack shop, a bar, and water-sports rentals. **Amenities:** parking; restrooms. **Best for:** snorkeling; swimming; windsurfing. ✉ *Rte. 38, ½ mile north of Red Hook, Sapphire Bay.*

Secret Harbour. Placid waters make it easy to stroke your way out to a swim platform offshore from the Secret Harbour Beach Resort & Villas. Nearby reefs give snorkelers a natural show. There's a bar and restaurant, as well as a dive shop. **Amenities:** food and drink; parking; restrooms; water sports. **Best for:** snorkeling; sunset; swimming. ✉ *Rte. 322, take first right off Rte. 322, Red Hook.*

Vessup Beach. This wild, undeveloped beach is lined with sea grape trees and century plants. It's close to Red Hook harbor, so you can watch the ferries depart. The calm waters are excellent for swimming. It's popular with locals on weekends. **Amenities:** parking; water sports. **Best for:** swimming. ✉ *Off Rte. 322, Vessup Bay.*

SOUTH SHORE

Brewer's Beach. Watch jets land at the Cyril E. King Airport as you dip into the usually calm seas. Rocks at either end of the shoreline, patches of grass poking randomly through the sand, and shady tamarind trees 30 feet from the water give this beach a wild, natural feel. Civilization has arrived, in the form of one or two mobile food vans parked on the nearby road. Buy a fried-chicken leg and johnnycake or burgers and chips to munch on at the picnic tables. **Amenities:** food and drink; lifeguards; parking; restrooms. **Best for:** sunset; swimming. ✉ *Rte. 30, west of University of the Virgin Islands.*

27

Morningstar Beach. Nature and nurture combine at this ¼-mile-long (½-km-long) beach between Marriott Frenchman's Reef and Morning Star Beach Resorts, where the amenities include beachside bar service. A concession rents floating mats, snorkeling equipment, sailboards, and Jet Skis. Swimming is excellent; there are good-size rolling waves year-round, but do watch the undertow. If you're feeling lazy, rent a lounge chair with umbrella and order a libation from one of two full-service beach bars. At 7 am and again at 5 pm, you can catch the cruise ships gliding majestically out to sea from the Charlotte Amalie harbor. **Amenities:** food and drink; parking; restrooms; water sports. **Best for:** partiers; surfing; swimming. ✉ *Rte. 315* ✣ *2 miles (3 km) southeast of Charlotte Amalie, past Havensight Mall and cruise-ship dock.*

WEST END

FAMILY
Fodor's Choice ★

Magens Bay. Deeded to the island as a public park, this heart-shape stretch of white sand is considered one of the most beautiful in the world. The bottom of the bay is flat and sandy, so this is a place for sunning and swimming rather than snorkeling. On weekends and holidays the sounds of music from groups partying under the sheds fill the air. There's a bar, snack shack, and beachwear boutique; and bathhouses with restrooms, changing rooms, and saltwater showers are close by. Sunfish, kayaks, and paddleboards are the most popular rentals at the water-sports kiosk. East of the beach is Udder Delight, a one-room shop that serves a Virgin Islands tradition—a milk shake with a splash of Cruzan rum. (Kids can enjoy virgin versions, which have a touch of soursop, mango, or banana flavoring). If you arrive between 8 am and 5 pm, you pay an entrance fee of $4 per person, $2 per vehicle; it's free for children under 12. **Amenities:** food and drink; lifeguards; parking (fee); showers; restrooms; water sports. **Best for:** partiers; swimming;

walking. ✉ *Magens Bay, Rte. 35, at end of road on north side of island* ☎ *340/777–6300* 🌐 *www.magensbayauthority.com.*

WHERE TO EAT

The beauty of St. Thomas and its sister islands has attracted a cadre of professionally trained chefs who know their way around fresh fish and local fruits. You can dine on terrific cheap local dishes such as goat water (a spicy stew) and fungi (a cornmeal side dish that's similar to polenta) as well as imports that include hot pastrami sandwiches and raspberries in crème fraîche.

Restaurants are spread all over the island, although fewer are found on the west and northwest parts of the island. Most restaurants out of town are easily accessible by taxi and have ample parking. If you dine in Charlotte Amalie, take a taxi. Parking close to restaurants can be difficult to find, and walking around after dark isn't always safe.

If your accommodations have a kitchen and you plan to cook, there's good variety in St. Thomas's mainland-style supermarkets. Just be prepared for grocery prices that are about 20% to 30% higher than those in the United States. As for drinking, a beer in a bar that's not part of a hotel will cost between $5 and $6 and a piña colada $8 or more.

What to Wear: Dining on St. Thomas is informal. Few restaurants require a jacket and tie. Still, at dinner in the snazzier places shorts and T-shirts are inappropriate; men would do well to wear slacks and a shirt with buttons. Dress codes on St. Thomas rarely require women to wear skirts, but you can never go wrong with something flowing.

CHARLOTTE AMALIE

$$$$ ECLECTIC Fodor's Choice ★

✕ **Banana Tree Grille.** The eagle's-eye view of the Charlotte Amalie harbor from this breeze-cooled restaurant is as fantastic as the food. Linen tablecloths, china, and silver place settings combine with subdued lighting to make an elegant space. To start, try the flamed-grilled oysters or crispy calamari dipped in tangy lemon aioli. The signature dish here—and worthy of its fame—is a grass-fed pasture-raised filet mignon topped with plump shrimp and served with velvety Bearnaise sauce and fresh asparagus. Arrive before 6 pm to watch the cruise ships depart from the harbor while you enjoy a drink at the bar. [$] *Average main: $40* ✉ *Bluebeard's Castle, Bluebeard's Hill, 1331 Estate Taamburg* ☎ *340/776–4050* 🌐 *www.bananatreegrille.com* ✍ *Reservations essential* ⏲ *Closed Mon. No lunch.*

$$ CARIBBEAN

✕ **Cuzzin's Caribbean Restaurant and Bar.** In a 19th-century livery stable on Back Street, this restaurant is hard to find but well worth it if you want to sample bona fide Virgin Islands cuisine. For lunch, order tender slivers of conch stewed in a rich onion-and-butter sauce, savory braised oxtail, or curried chicken. At dinner the island-style mutton, served in thick gravy and seasoned with locally grown herbs, offers a tasty treat that's deliciously different. Side dishes include peas and rice, boiled green bananas, fried plantains, and potato stuffing. [$] *Average main: $15* ✉ *7 Wimmelskafts Gade, also called Back St.* ☎ *340/777–4711* 🌐 *cuzzinsvi.com* ⏲ *Closed Sun.*

$$ CARIBBEAN Fodor's Choice ★ **Gladys' Cafe.** Even if the local specialties—conch in butter sauce, jerk pork, panfried yellowtail snapper—didn't make this a recommended café, it would be worth coming for Gladys's smile. Her cozy alleyway restaurant is rich in atmosphere with its mahogany bar and native stone walls, making dining a double delight. While you're here, pick up a $5 or $10 bottle of her special hot sauce. There are mustard-, oil and vinegar–, and tomato-based versions; the tomato-based sauce is the hottest. *Average main: $14 Waterfront, 28A Dronningens Gade, west side of Royal Dane Mall 340/774–6604 No dinner Only Amex credit cards accepted.*

$$ AMERICAN FAMILY **Greenhouse Bar and Restaurant.** Fun-lovers come to this waterfront restaurant to eat, listen to music, and play games, both video and pool. Even the most finicky eater should find something to please on the eight-page menu that offers burgers, salads, and pizza served all day long, along with peel-and-eat shrimp, Maine lobster, Alaskan king crab, and Black Angus prime rib for dinner. This is generally a family-friendly place, though the Two-for-Tuesdays happy hour and Friday-night live reggae music that starts thumping at 10 pm draw an occasionally rambunctious young-adult crowd. *Average main: $18 Waterfront Hwy. at Storetvaer Gade 340/774–7998 www.thegreenhouserestaurant.com.*

$$$$ ITALIAN **Virgilio's.** For the island's best Northern Italian cuisine, don't miss this intimate, elegant hideaway that's on a quiet side street. Eclectic art covers the two-story brick walls, and the sound of opera sets the stage for a memorable meal. Come here for more than 40 homemade pastas topped with superb sauces—capellini with fresh tomatoes and garlic or peasant-style spaghetti in a rich tomato sauce with mushrooms and prosciutto. House specialties include osso buco and tiramisu, which are expertly crafted by chef Ernesto Garrigos, who has prepared these two dishes on the Discovery Channel's *Great Chefs of the World* series. *Average main: $34 5150 Dronnigens Gade 340/776–4920 www.virgiliosvi.com Reservations essential Closed Sun.*

27

EAST END

$$$ AMERICAN **Caribbean Saloon.** Sports on wide-screen TVs and and live music on weekends are two added attractions at this hip sports bar that's in the center of the action in Red Hook. The menu ranges from finger-licking barbecue ribs to more sophisticated fare, such as the signature filet mignon wrapped in bacon and smothered in melted Gorgonzola cheese. There's always a catch of the day; the fishing fleet is only steps away. A late-night menu is available from 10 pm until 4 am. *Average main: $28 American Yacht Harbor, Rte. 32, Bldg B., Red Hook 340/775–7060 www.caribbeansaloon.com.*

$$ ECLECTIC **Duffy's Love Shack.** If the floating bubbles don't attract you to this zany eatery, the lime-green shutters, loud rock music, and fun-loving waitstaff just might. It's billed as the "ultimate tropical drink shack," and the bartenders shake up such exotic concoctions as the Love Shack Volcano—a 50-ounce flaming extravaganza. The menu has a selection of burgers, tacos, burritos, and salads. Try the grilled fish tacos or Caribbean Pu-Pu platter that includes conch fritters, coconut shrimp, and Puerto Rican–style *pinonos* (sweet plantains stuffed with savory

CLOSE UP

Where to Shop for Groceries

High food prices in Virgin Islands supermarkets are enough to dull anyone's appetite. According to a report by the U.S. Virgin Islands Department of Labor, food is significantly more expensive than on the mainland.

Although you'll never match the prices back home, you can shop around for the best deals. If you're traveling with a group, it pays to stock up on the basics at warehouse-style stores like Pricesmart (membership required) and Cost-U-Less. Even the nonbulk food items here are sold at lower prices than in the supermarkets or convenience stores. Good buys include beverages, meats, produce, and spirits.

After this, head to supermarkets such as Plaza Extra, Pueblo, and Food Center. Although the prices aren't as good as at the big-box stores, the selection is better.

Finally, if you want to splurge on top-quality meats, exotic produce and spices, and imported cheeses and spirits, finish off your shopping at high-end shops such as Moe's Fresh Market or Gourmet Gallery.

The Fruit Bowl is the place for fresh produce. The prices and selection are unbeatable.

For really fresh tropical fruits, vegetables, and seasoning herbs, visit the farmers' markets in Smith Bay (daily), at Market Square (daily), at Yacht Haven Grande (first and third Sunday of the month), and in Estate Bordeaux (second and fourth Sunday of every month).

meat or cheese and deep fried). $ *Average main: $15* ✉ *Red Hook Shopping Center, Rte. 32 and 6500 Red Hook Plaza, located in the parking lot, Red Hook* ☎ *340/779–2080* 🌐 *www.duffysloveshack.com.*

$$$ IRISH FAMILY ✕ **Molly Molone's.** This dockside eatery has a devoted following among local boaters, who swear by the traditional American and Irish fare. Opt for eggs Benedict or rashers of Irish sausages and eggs for breakfast, or fork into fish-and-chips, Irish stew, or bangers and mash (sausage and mashed potatoes) for lunch or dinner. ⚠ **Beware: the resident iguanas will beg for table scraps—bring your camera.** $ *Average main: $24* ✉ *American Yacht Harbor, Bldg. D, Rte. 32, Red Hook* ☎ *340/775–1270* 🌐 *mollymalonesstthomas.com.*

$$$$ ECLECTIC Fodor's Choice ★ ✕ **Old Stone Farmhouse.** Dine in the splendor of a beautifully restored plantation house. Come early and sidle up to the beautiful mahogany bar, where you can choose from an extensive wine list. Then, start with a first course of heirloom tomato gazpacho, move on to Wagyu beef and local lobster surf and turf or perfectly seared scallops; and finish with a thick rich pineapple crème brûlée. Exotic meats such as camel and kangaroo are available on the special Butcher's Block entrée selections. Personalized attention makes dining here a delight. $ *Average main: $36* ✉ *Rte. 42, 1 mile (1½ km) west of entrance to Mahogany Run Golf Course, Estate Lovenlund* ☎ *340/777–6277* 🌐 *oldstonefarmhouse.com* ✍ *Reservations essential* ⏲ *Closed Mon.*

SOUTH SHORE

$$$$ ECLECTIC Fodor's Choice ★ **Havana Blue.** The cuisine here is described as Latin America meets Pacific Rim, but however you describe it, the dining experience is outstanding. A glowing wall of water meets you as you enter this beachfront eatery, and then you're seated at a table laid with linen and silver that's illuminated in a soft blue light radiating from above. Be sure to sample the mango mojito, made with fresh mango, crushed mint, and limes. Tapas-style entrées include slow-roasted pulled-pork Cuban sliders, seared tuna with Szechuan peppercorn, and shiitake spring rolls. Hand-rolled cigars and aged rums finish the night off in true Latin style. For something really special, request an exclusive table for two set on Morning Star Beach—you get a seven-course tasting menu, champagne, and your own personal waiter, all for $350 for two. *$ Average main: $36 ✉ Marriott Morningstar Beach Resort, Rte. 315, 2nd Fl., above front desk, Estate Bakkeroe ☎ 340/715–2583 ⊕ www.havanabluerestaurant.com ⚠ Reservations essential ⊙ No lunch.*

WEST END

$$$ AUSTRIAN **Bella Blu.** In a quaint building in Frenchtown, this place has an ever-changing display of local art on the walls and delicious specials to match. The Austrian-inspired menu includes six varieties of schnitzel and boasts a Caribbean flair with fresh-fish dishes such as house specialty snapper Provençal. Lunchtime attracts a business crowd that breaks bread and brokers deals at the same time. Fork into omelets, pancakes, or waffles during Saturday's Jazz Brunch from 10 am to 3 pm. *$ Average main: $26 ✉ Frenchtown Mall, 24-A Honduras St., across from the ballpark, Frenchtown ☎ 340/774–4349 ⊕ www.bellabludining.com ⚠ Reservations essential ⊙ Closed Sun.*

$$$ SEAFOOD FAMILY **Hook, Line and Sinker.** Anchored on the breezy Frenchtown waterfront and close to the pastel-painted boats of the local fishing fleet, this harbor-view eatery serves high-quality fish dishes. The almond-crusted yellowtail snapper is a house specialty. Spicy jerk-seasoned swordfish and grilled tuna topped with a yummy mango-rum sauce are also good bets. This is one of the few independent restaurants serving Sunday brunch. *$ Average main: $24 ✉ Frenchtown Mall, 2 Honduras St., at the head of the Frenchtown Marina docks, Frenchtown ☎ 340/776–9708 ⊕ www.hooklineandsinkervi.com.*

$$ AMERICAN FAMILY **Tickles Dockside Pub.** Nautical types as well as the local working crowd come here for casual fare with homey appeal: chicken-fried steak, meat loaf with mashed potatoes, and baby back ribs. Hearty breakfasts feature eggs and pancakes, and lunch is a full array of burgers, salads, sandwiches, and soups. From November through April, the adjacent marina is full of enormous yachts, which make for some great eye candy while you dine. *$ Average main: $17 ✉ Crown Bay Marina, 8168 Crown Bay Marina, Ste. 308, off Rte. 304, Estate Contant ☎ 340/777–8792 ⊕ ticklesdocksidepub.com.*

WHERE TO STAY

Of the USVI, St. Thomas has the most rooms and the greatest number and variety of resorts. You can let yourself be pampered at a luxurious resort—albeit at a price of $400 to more than $600 per night, not including meals. For much less, there are fine hotels (often with rooms that have a kitchen and a living area) in lovely settings throughout the island. There are also guesthouses and inns with great views and great service at about half the cost of what you'll pay at the beachfront pleasure palaces. Many of these are east and north of Charlotte Amalie or overlooking hills—ideal if you plan to get out and mingle with the locals. There are also inexpensive lodgings (most right in town) that are perfect if you just want a clean room to return to after a day of exploring or beach bumming.

East End condominium complexes are popular with families. Although condos are pricey (winter rates average $350 per night for a two-bedroom unit, which usually sleeps six), they have full kitchens, and you can definitely save money by cooking for yourself—especially if you bring some of your own nonperishable foodstuffs. (Virtually everything on St. Thomas is imported, and restaurants and shops pass shipping costs on to you.) Though you may spend some time laboring in the kitchen, many condos ease your burden with daily maid service and on-site restaurants; a few also have resort amenities, including pools and tennis courts. The East End is convenient to St. John, and it's a hub for the boating crowd, with some good restaurants. The prices *below* reflect rates in high season, which runs from December 15 to April 15. Rates are 25% to 50% lower the rest of the year.

PRIVATE VILLAS AND CONDOMINIUMS

St. Thomas has a wide range of private villas. Most will require that you book for seven nights during high season, five in low season. A minimum stay of up to two weeks is often required during the Christmas season. The agents who represent villa owners usually have websites and brochures that show photos of the properties they represent. Some villas are suitable for travelers with disabilities, but be sure to ask specific questions about your own needs.

RENTAL CONTACTS

Calypso Realty ☎ *340/774–1620, 800/747–4858* 🌐 *www.calypsorealty.com.*

McLaughlin-Anderson Luxury Caribbean Villas. Handling rental villas throughout the U.S. Virgin Islands, British Virgin Islands, and Grenada, McLaughlin-Anderson has a good selection of complexes in St. Thomas's East End. ☎ *340/776–0635, 800/537–6246* 🌐 *www.mclaughlinanderson.com.*

CHARLOTTE AMALIE

Accommodations in and near town mean that you're close to the airport, shopping, and a number of restaurants. The downside is that this is the most crowded and noisy area of the island. Crime can also be a problem. Don't go for a stroll at night in the heart of town. Use common sense and take the same precautions you would in any major city.

Properties along the hillsides are less likely to have crime problems, and they also get a steady breeze from the cool trade winds. This is especially important if you're visiting in summer and early fall.

$ HOTEL **The Green Iguana.** Atop Blackbeard's Hill, this value-priced small hotel offers the perfect mix of gorgeous harbor views, proximity to shopping (five-minute walk), and secluded privacy provided by the surrounding showy trees and bushy hibiscus. **Pros:** personalized service; near the center of town; laundry on premises. **Cons:** need a car to get around; town may be noisy at night depending on seasonal events. *Rooms from: $150* *1002 Blackbeard's Hill* *340/776–7654, 855/473–4733* *www.thegreeniguana.com* *9 rooms* *No meals.*

$ HOTEL Fodor's Choice ★ **Villa Santana.** Built by exiled General Antonio López Santa Anna of Mexico, this 1857 landmark provides a panoramic view of the harbor and plenty of West Indian charm, which will make you feel as if you're living in a charming slice of Virgin Islands history. **Pros:** historic charm; plenty of privacy. **Cons:** not on a beach; no restaurant; need a car to get around. *Rooms from: $170* *2602 Bjerge Gade, 2D Denmark Hill* *340/776–1311* *www.villasantana.com* *6 rooms* *No meals.*

$ HOTEL **Windward Passage Hotel.** Business travelers, tourists on their way to the British Virgin Islands, and laid-back vacationers who want the convenience of being able to walk to duty-free shopping, sights, and restaurants, stay at this harborfront hotel. **Pros:** walking distance to Charlotte Amalie; nice harbor views; across from BVI ferry terminal. **Cons:** basic rooms; on a busy street; no water sports, but dive shop is on property. *Rooms from: $220* *Waterfront Hwy.* *340/774–5200, 800/524–7389* *www.windwardpassage.com* *140 rooms, 11 suites* *No meals.*

27

EAST END

You can find most of the large, luxurious beachfront resorts on St. Thomas's East End. The downside is that these properties are about a 30-minute drive from town and a 45-minute drive from the airport (substantially longer during peak hours). On the upside, they tend to be self-contained, plus there are a number of good restaurants, shops, and water-sports operators in the area. Once you've settled in, you don't need a car to get around.

$$$ RENTAL FAMILY **The Anchorage Beach Resort.** A beachfront setting and homey conveniences that include full kitchens and washer–dryer units are what attract families to these two- and three-bedroom suites on Cowpet Bay next to the St. Thomas Yacht Club. **Pros:** on the beach; good amenities. **Cons:** small pool; noisy neighbors; need a car to get around; petty theft is a problem in the neighborhood. *Rooms from: $395* *Rte. 317, Estate Nazareth* *800/874–7897* *www.antillesresorts.com* *11 suites* *No meals.*

$ RENTAL **Pavilions and Pools Villa Hotel.** Perfect for couples craving privacy, the villas here have full kitchens, lots of space, and sunken garden showers. **Pros:** intimate atmosphere; friendly host; private pools. **Cons:** on a busy road; long walk to beach; rooms could use a bit of refurbishment. *Rooms from: $260* *6400 Estate Smith Bay, off Rte. 38, Estate*

The Ritz-Carlton St. Thomas

Smith Bay ☎ *340/775–6110, 800/524–2001* ⊕ *www.pavilionsandpools.com* ⇆ *25 1-bedroom villas* 🍴 *Breakfast.*

$$ RESORT **Point Pleasant Resort.** Hilltop suites give you an eagle's-eye view of the East End and beyond, and those in a building adjacent to the reception area offer incredible sea views. **Pros:** lush setting; convenient kitchens; pleasant pools. **Cons:** steep climb from beach; need a car to get around; some rooms need refurbishing. $ *Rooms from: $320* ✉ *6600 Estate Smith Bay, off Rte. 38, Estate Smith Bay* ☎ *340/775–7200, 800/524–2300* ⊕ *www.pointpleasantresort.com* ⇆ *128 suites* 🍴 *No meals.*

$$$$ RESORT FAMILY Fodor's Choice ★ **Ritz-Carlton, St. Thomas.** Everything sparkles at the island's most luxurious resort, from the in-room furnishings and amenities to the infinity pool, white-sand beach, and turquoise sea beyond. **Pros:** gorgeous views; great water-sports facilities; beautiful beach; airport shuttle. **Cons:** service can sometimes be spotty for such an upscale (and pricey) hotel; food and drink can lack flair and are expensive ($19 hamburger, $12 piña colada); half-hour or more drive to town and airport. $ *Rooms from: $610* ✉ *6900 Estate Great Bay, off Rte. 317, Estate Great Bay* ☎ *340/775–3333, 800/241–3333* ⊕ *www.ritzcarlton.com* ⇆ *255 rooms, 20 suites, 2 villas, 81 condos* 🍴 *No meals.*

$$ RENTAL **Secret Harbour Beach Resort.** There's not a bad view from these low-rise studios and one- and two-bedroom condos, which are either beachfront or perched on a hill overlooking an inviting cove. **Pros:** beautiful beach and great snorkeling; good restaurant; secluded location. **Cons:** car needed to get around; condo owners are territorial about beach chairs. $ *Rooms from: $355* ✉ *Rte. 317, Estate Nazareth* ☎ *340/775–6550, 800/524–2250* ⊕ *www.secretharbourvi.com* ⇆ *73 suites* 🍴 *No meals.*

$$$$ ALL-INCLUSIVE FAMILY **Sugar Bay Resort & Spa.** The only completely all-inclusive resort on St. Thomas, this terra-cotta high-rise is surrounded by palm trees and lush greenery, but the rooms and the walkways between them feel a little generic. **Pros:** gorgeous pool area; full-service spa; on-site casino. **Cons:** some steps to climb; lawn by pool teems with iguanas; limited dining options. *Rooms from: $525 6500 Estate Smith Bay, Estate Smith Bay 340/777–7100, 800/927–7100 www.sugarbayresortandspa.com 294 rooms, 7 suites All-inclusive.*

SOUTH SHORE

The South Shore of St. Thomas connects town to the East End of the island via a beautiful road that rambles along the hillside with frequent peeks between the hills for a view of the ocean and, on a clear day, of St. Croix some 40 miles (64 km) to the south. The resorts here are on their own beaches. They offer several opportunities for water sports, as well as land-based activities, fine dining, and evening entertainment.

$$$ RESORT **Bolongo Bay Beach Resort.** All the rooms at this family-run resort tucked along a 1,000-foot-long palm-lined beach have balconies with ocean views; down the beach are nine condos with full kitchens. **Pros:** family-run property; on the beach; water sports abound. **Cons:** a bit run-down; on a busy road; need a car to get around. *Rooms from: $385 Rte. 30, Estate Bolongo 340/775–1800, 800/524–4746 www.bolongobay.com 71 rooms, 9 condos Multiple meal plans.*

$$$ RESORT FAMILY **Frenchman's Reef & Morning Star Marriott Beach Resort.** Set majestically on a promontory overlooking the east side of Charlotte Amalie's harbor, Frenchman's Reef is a high-rise full-service superhotel; Morning Star is the even more upscale boutique property that's closer to the fine white-sand beach. **Pros:** beachfront location; good dining options; plenty of activities. **Cons:** musty smell on lower levels; long walk between resorts; a crowded-cruise-ship feel. *Rooms from: $430 Rte. 315, Estate Bakkeroe 340/776–8500, 800/233–6388 www.marriott.com 479 rooms, 27 suites; 220 2- and 3-bedroom time-share units No meals.*

27

WEST END

A few properties are in the hills overlooking Charlotte Amalie to the west or near French Town, which is otherwise primarily residential.

$ HOTEL **Best Western Emerald Beach Resort.** You get beachfront ambience at this reasonably priced mini resort tucked beneath the palm trees, but the tradeoff is that it's directly across from a noisy airport runway. **Pros:** beachfront location; good value; great Sunday brunch. **Cons:** airport noise until 10 pm; on a busy road; limited water sports. *Rooms from: $220 8070 Lindberg Bay, Lindbergh Bay 340/777–8800, 800/780–7234 www.emeraldbeach.com 90 rooms Breakfast.*

$ B&B/INN **Island View Guesthouse.** Perched 545 feet up the face of Crown Mountain, this small, homey inn has hands-on owners who can book tours or offer tips about the best sightseeing spots. **Pros:** spectacular views; friendly atmosphere; good value. **Cons:** small pool; need a car to get around. *Rooms from: $115 Rte. 332, Estate Contant 340/774–4270, 800/524–2023 www.islandviewstthomas.com 12 rooms, 10 with bath Breakfast.*

NIGHTLIFE AND PERFORMING ARTS

On any given night, especially in season, you can find steel-pan bands, rock and roll, piano music, jazz, broken-bottle dancing (actual dancing atop broken glass), disco, and karaoke. Pick up a free copy of the bright yellow *St. Thomas–St. John This Week* magazine (🌐 *www.virginislandsthisweek.com*) when you arrive (it can be found at the airport, in stores, and in hotel lobbies). The back pages list who's playing where. The Friday edition of the *Daily News* carries complete listings for the upcoming weekend.

NIGHTLIFE

CHARLOTTE AMALIE

Greenhouse Bar and Restaurant. Once this popular eatery puts away the salt-and-pepper shakers after 10 pm, it becomes a rock-and-roll club with a DJ or live reggae bands bringing the weary to their feet six nights a week. ✉ *Waterfront Hwy. at Storetvaer Gade, Charlotte Amalie* ☎ *340/774–7998* 🌐 *www.thegreenhouserestaurant.com.*

EAST END

Duffy's Love Shack. At this island favorite, a live band and dancing under the stars are the big draws for locals and visitors alike. ✉ *Red Hook Plaza, Rte. 32, Red Hook* ☎ *340/779–2080* 🌐 *www.duffysloveshack.com.*

SOUTH SHORE

Epernay Bistro & Wine Bar. Sometimes you need nothing more than small tables for easy chatting and wine and champagne by the glass. You can also mix and mingle with island celebrities here. The action at this intimate nightspot runs from 4 pm until the wee hours Monday through Saturday. ✉ *Frenchtown Mall, 24-A Honduras St., Frenchtown* ☎ *340/774–5348.*

Iggies Beach Bar. Bolongo Bay's beachside bar offers karaoke on Saturday nights, so you can sing along to the sounds of the surf or the latest hits here. There are live bands on weekends, and you can dance inside or kick up your heels under the stars. On Wednesday it's Carnival Night, complete with steel-pan music, a limbo show, and a West Indian buffet. ✉ *Bolongo Bay Beach Club & Villas, Rte. 30, Estate Bolongo* ☎ *340/775–1800* 🌐 *www.iggiesbeachbar.com.*

PERFORMING ARTS

SOUTH SHORE

FAMILY **Pistarkle Theater.** This theater in the Tillett Gardens complex is air-conditioned and has more than 100 seats; it hosts a half-dozen productions annually, plus a children's summer drama camp. ✉ *Tillett Gardens, Rte. 38, across from Tutu Park Shopping Mall, Estate Tutu* ☎ *340/775–7877* 🌐 *pistarckletheater.com.*

Reichhold Center for the Arts. St. Thomas's major performing arts center has an amphitheater, and its more expensive seats are covered by a roof. Throughout the year there's an entertaining mix of local plays, dance exhibitions, and music of all types. ✉ *Rte. 30, across from Brewers Beach, Estate Lindberg Bay* ☎ *340/693–1559* 🌐 *www.reichholdcenter.com.*

SHOPPING

Fodor's Choice ★ St. Thomas lives up to its billing as a duty-free shopping destination. Even if shopping isn't your idea of how to spend a vacation, you still may want to slip in on a quiet day (check the cruise-ship listings—Monday and Sunday are usually the least crowded) to browse. Among the best buys are liquor, linens, china, crystal (most stores will ship), and jewelry. The amount of jewelry available makes this one of the few items for which comparison shopping is worth the effort. Local crafts include shell jewelry, carved calabash bowls, straw brooms, woven baskets, and dolls. The local doll maker Gwendolyn Harley makes costumed West Indian market women and other creations who have become little goodwill ambassadors, bought by visitors from as far away as Asia. Spice mixes, hot sauces, and tropical jams and jellies are other native products.

On St. Thomas stores on Main Street in Charlotte Amalie are open weekdays and Saturday 9 to 5. The hours of the shops in the Havensight Mall (next to the cruise-ship dock) and the Crown Bay Commercial Center (next to the Crown Bay cruise-ship dock) are the same, though occasionally some stay open until 9 on Friday, depending on how many cruise ships are anchored nearby. You may also find some shops open on Sunday if cruise ships are in port. Hotel shops are usually open evenings as well.

There's no sales tax in the USVI, and you can take advantage of the $1,200 duty-free allowance per family member (remember to save your receipts). Although you can find the occasional salesclerk who will make a deal, bartering isn't the norm.

CHARLOTTE AMALIE

The prime shopping area in **Charlotte Amalie** is between Post Office and Market Squares; it consists of two parallel streets that run east–west (Waterfront Highway and Main Street) and the alleyways that connect them. Particularly attractive are the historic **A.H. Riise Alley, Royal Dane Mall, Palm Passage,** and pastel-painted **International Plaza.**

Vendors Plaza, on the waterfront side of Emancipation Gardens in Charlotte Amalie, is a central location for vendors selling handmade earrings, necklaces, and bracelets; straw baskets and handbags; T-shirts; fabrics; African artifacts; and local fruits. Look for the many brightly colored umbrellas.

ART

Camille Pissarro Art Gallery. This second-floor gallery, at the birthplace of St. Thomas's famous artist, offers a fine collection of original paintings and prints by local and regional artists. ✉ *14 Main St., Charlotte Amalie* ☎ *340/774–4621.*

Gallery St. Thomas. The gallery in this charming space has a nice collection of fine art and collectibles, including paintings, wood sculptures, glass, and jewelry that are from or inspired by the Virgin Islands. ✉ *Palm Passage, 5143 Palm Passage, Suite A-13, Charlotte Amalie* ☎ *340/777–6363* 🌐 *gallerystthomas.com.*

27

CLOSE UP

Made in St. Thomas

Date-palm brooms, frangipani-scented perfume, historically clad dolls, sun-scorched hot sauces, aromatic mango candles: these are just a few of the handicrafts made in St. Thomas.

Justin Todman, aka the Broom Man, keeps the art of broom making alive. It's a skill he learned at the age of six from his father. From the fronds of the date palm, Todman cuts, strips, and dries the leaves. Then he weaves them into distinctively shaped brooms with birch-berry wood for handles. There are feather brooms, cane brooms, multicolor-yarn brooms, tiny brooms to fit into a child's hand, and tall, long-handled brooms to reach cobwebs on the ceiling. Some customers buy Todman's brooms—sold at the **Native Arts and Crafts Cooperative**—not for cleaning but rather for celebrating their nuptials. It's an old African custom for the bride and groom to jump over a horizontally laid broom to start their new life.

Gail Garrison puts the essence of local flowers, fruits, and leaves into perfumes, powders, and body splashes. Her Island Fragrances line includes frangipani-, white ginger–, and jasmine-scented perfumes; aromatic mango, lime, and coconut body splashes; and bay rum after-shave for men. Garrison compounds, mixes, and bottles the products herself in second-floor offices on Charlotte Amalie's Main Street.

Gwendolyn Harley preserves Virgin Islands culture in the personalities of her hand-sewn, softly sculptured historic dolls for sale at the Native Arts & Crafts Cooperative. There are quadrille dancers clad in long, colorful skirts; French women with their neat peaked bonnets; and farmers sporting handwoven straw hats. Each one-of-kind design is named using the last three letters of Harley's first name; the dolls have names like Joycelyn, Vitalyn, and Iselyn.

Cheryl Miller cooks up ingredients such as sun-sweetened papayas, fiery Scotch bonnet peppers, and aromatic basil leaves into the jams, jellies, and hot sauces she sells under her Cheryl's Taste of Paradise line. Five of Miller's products—Caribbean Mustango Sauce, Caribbean Sunburn, Mango Momma Jam, Mango Chutney, and Hot Green Pepper Jelly—have won awards at the National Fiery Foods Show in Albuquerque, New Mexico. You can buy her products at Cost-U-Less, the Native Arts and Crafts Cooperative, and the farmers' market at Yacht Haven Grande on the first and third Sunday of each month.

Jason Budsan traps the aromas of the islands, such as ripe mango and night jasmine, into sumptuous candles he sells at his **Tillett Gardens** workshop.

CAMERAS AND ELECTRONICS

Boolchand's. This store sells brand-name cameras, audio and video equipment, and binoculars. ✉ *31 Main St., 5124 Dronningens Gade, Charlotte Amalie* ☎ *340/776–0794* 🌐 *www.boolchand.com* ⏲ *Closed Sun. (if no cruise ship is in port).*

Royal Caribbean. Find a wide selection of cameras, camcorders, stereos, watches, and clocks at this store. ✉ *33 Main St., Charlotte Amalie* ☎ *340/776–4110* 🌐 *www.royalcaribbeanvi.com* ✉ *Havensight Mall,* *off Rte. 30, Bldg. A, Havensight* ☎ *340/776–8890* 🌐 *royalcaribbeanvi.com.*

CHINA AND CRYSTAL

Little Switzerland. This popular Caribbean chain carries crystal from Baccarat, Waterford, and Orrefors; and china from Kosta Boda, Rosenthal, and Wedgwood. There's also an assortment of Swarovski cut-crystal animals, gemstone globes, and many other affordable collectibles. It also does a booming mail-order business. ✉ *5 Dronningens Gade, across from Emancipation Garden, Charlotte Amalie* ☎ *340/776–2010* 🌐 *www.littleswitzerland.com* ✉ *Havensight Mall, 9002 Havensight Shop Ctr., Rte. 30, Ste. D, Havensight* ☎ *340/776–2198* 🌐 *littleswitzerland.com.*

CLOTHING

FAMILY **Fresh Produce Sportswear.** This clothing store doesn't sell lime-green mangoes, peachy-pink guavas, or sunny-yellow bananas, but you will find these fun, casual colors on its clothing for children and adults. This is one of 30 stores nationwide to stock all of the California-created, tropical-feel line of women's separates. The dresses, shirts, slacks, and skirts are in small to plus sizes, and bags and hats and other accessories are also available. ✉ *Riise's Alley, 5189 Dronnigens Gade, across from the Rolex store, Charlotte Amalie* ☎ *340/774–0807* 🌐 *www.freshproduceclothes.com.*

FAMILY **Local Color.** This St. Thomas chain has clothes for men, women, and children among its brand names, which include Jams World, Fresh Produce, and Urban Safari. You can also find St. John artist Sloop Jones's colorful, hand-painted island designs on cool dresses, T-shirts, and sweaters. The tropically oriented accessories include big-brimmed straw hats, bold-color bags, and casual jewelry. ✉ *Waterfront Hwy., at Raadets Gade, Charlotte Amalie* ☎ *340/776–5860* 🌐 *www.localcolorvi.com* ✉ *Route 315, at Coco Joe's restaurant at the Morning Star Marriott Beach Resort, Charlotte Amalie* ☎ *340/776–5860* 🌐 *www.localcolorvi.com* ✉ *Havensight Mall, Rte. 30, Bldg 7, 2 stores north of post office, Charlotte Amalie* ☎ *340/776–5860* 🌐 *localcolorvi.com.*

HANDICRAFTS

Native Arts and Crafts Cooperative. This crafts market is made up of a group of more than 40 local artists—including schoolchildren, senior citizens, and people with disabilities—who create the handcrafted items for sale here: African-style jewelry, quilts, calabash bowls, dolls, soaps, carved-wood figures, woven baskets, straw brooms, note cards, and cookbooks. ✉ *48B Tolbod Gade, across from Emancipation Garden, Charlotte Amalie* ☎ *340/777–1153.*

JEWELRY

Cardow Jewelers. You can get gold in several lengths, widths, sizes, and styles, along with jewelry made of diamonds, emeralds, and other precious gems from this small chain's main store. You're guaranteed 40% to 60% savings off U.S. retail prices, or your money will be refunded within 30 days of purchase. ✉ *5195 Dronningens Gate, across from Emancipation Garden, Charlotte Amalie* ☎ *340/776–1140* 🌐 *www.*

cardow.com ✉ *Marriott Frenchman's Reef Resort, Rte. 315, Estate Bakkeroe* ☎ *340/774–0434.*

Diamonds International. At this large chain with several outlets on St. Thomas, just choose a diamond, emerald, or tanzanite gem and a mounting, and you can have your dream ring set in an hour. Famous for having the largest inventory of diamonds on the island, this shop welcomes trade-ins, has a U.S. service center, and includes diamond earrings with every purchase. ✉ *31 Main St., Charlotte Amalie* ☎ *340/774–3707* 🌐 *www.diamondsinternational.com* ✉ *3A Main St., Charlotte Amalie* ☎ *340/774–1516* 🌐 *www.diamondsinternational.com* ✉ *1 Dronningens Gade, Charlotte Amalie* ☎ *340/775–1202* 🌐 *www.diamondsinternational.com.*

H. Stern Jewelers. The World Collection of jewels set in modern, fashionable designs and an exclusive sapphire watch have earned this Brazilian jeweler a stellar reputation. There is another location in Havensight. ✉ *5332 Dronningens Gade, Charlotte Amalie* ☎ *340/776–1146* 🌐 *www.hstern.net* ✉ *Marriott Frenchman's Reef Resort, Rte. 315, Estate Bakkeroe* ☎ *340/776–3550.*

Jewels. This jewelry store sells name-brand jewelry and watches in abundance. Designer jewelry lines include David Yurman, Bulgari, Chopard, and Penny Preville. The selection of watches includes Jaeger le Coultre, Tag Heuer, Breitling, Movado, and Gucci. ✉ *Main St., at Riise's Alley, Charlotte Amalie* ☎ *248/809–5560* 🌐 *www.jewelsonline.com* ✉ *Havensight Mall, Rte. 30, Bldg. 2, Havensight* ☎ *248/809–5560* 🌐 *www.jewelsonline.com.*

Rolex Watches at A. H. Riise. A.H. Riise is the official Rolex retailer of the Virgin Islands, and this shop offers one of the largest selections of these fine timepieces in the Caribbean. An After Sales Service Center helps you keep your Rolex ticking for a lifetime. ✉ *37 Main St., at Riise's Alley, Charlotte Amalie* ☎ *340/777–6789* 🌐 *www.ahriise.com.*

LEATHER GOODS

Coach. This designer leather store has a full line of fine leather handbags, belts, gloves, and more for women, plus briefcases and wallets for men. Accessories for both sexes include organizers, travel bags, and cell-phone cases. ✉ *Yacht Haven Grande, 5328 Yacht Haven Grande, Ste. 104, Charlotte Amalie* ☎ *340/776–1930* 🌐 *www.coach.com.*

LINENS

Fabric in Motion. Fine Italian linens share space with Liberty London's silky cottons, colorful batiks, cotton prints, ribbons, and accessories in this small shop. ✉ *7 Store Tvaer Gade, Charlotte Amalie* ☎ *340/774–2006.*

Mr. Tablecloth. This store has prices to please, and the friendly staff here will help you choose from the floor-to-ceiling selection of linens, which include Tuscan lace tablecloths and Irish linen pillowcases. ✉ *6–7 Main St., Charlotte Amalie* ☎ *340/774–4343* 🌐 *mrtablecloth-vi.com.*

LIQUOR AND TOBACCO

A.H. Riise Liquors and Tobacco. This giant duty-free liquor outlet carries a large selection of tobacco (including imported cigars), as well as cordials, wines, and rare vintage Armagnacs, cognacs, ports, and Madeiras. It also stocks fruits in brandy and barware from England. Enjoy rum samples at the tasting bar. The prices are among the best in St. Thomas. ✉ *37 Main St., at Riise's Alley, Charlotte Amalie* ☎ *340/777–2222* 🌐 *www.ahriise.com.*

EAST END

Red Hook has **American Yacht Harbor,** a waterfront shopping area with a dive shop, a tackle store, clothing and jewelry boutiques, a bar, and a few restaurants.

ART

The Color of Joy Art & Framing. This gallery offers locally made arts and crafts, including pottery, batik, hand-painted linen-and-cotton clothing, glass plates and ornaments, and watercolors by owner Corinne Van Rensselaer. There are also original prints by many local artists. Framing is available. ✉ *Rte. 322, about 100 yards west of Ritz-Carlton, Red Hook* ☎ *340/775–4020* 🌐 *www.thecolorofjoyvi.com.*

FOODSTUFFS

Food Center. This supermarket sells fresh produce, meats, and seafood. There's also an on-site bakery and deli with hot and cold prepared foods, which are the big draw here, especially for those renting villas, condos, or charter boats in the East End area. ✉ *Rte. 32, 1 mile west of Red Hook, Estate Frydenhoj* ☎ *340/777–8806* 🌐 *www.foodcentervi.com.*

Moe's Fresh Market. This gourmet market near the ferry to St. John has the best deli cheeses, prepared-to-order subs, and selection of organic foods, coffees, and wines on the island. ✉ *Rte. 32, 6502 Smith Bay Road, Red Hook* ☎ *340/693–0254* 🌐 *moesvi.com.*

JEWELRY

Jewels. Designer jewelry available in this major chain include David Yurman, Bulgari, Chopard, and Penny Preville. The selection of watches is also extensive. ✉ *Ritz-Carlton St. Thomas, Rte. 322, Estate Nazareth* ☎ *248/809–5560* 🌐 *www.jewelsonline.com.*

SOUTH SIDE

West of Charlotte Amalie, the pink-stucco **Nisky Center,** on Harwood Highway about ½ mile (1 km) east of the airport, is more of a hometown shopping center than a tourist area, but there's a bank, clothing store, and Radio Shack.

At the Crown Bay cruise-ship pier, the **Crown Bay Center,** off the Harwood Highway in Sub Base about ½ mile (1 km), has quite a few shops.

Havensight Mall, next to the cruise-ship dock, may not be as charming as downtown Charlotte Amalie, but it does have more than 60 shops. It also has a bank, a pharmacy, a gourmet grocery, and smaller branches of many downtown stores. The shops at **Port of $ale,** adjoining Havensight Mall (its buildings are pink instead of brown), sell discount goods. Next door to Port of $ale is the **Yacht Haven Grande** complex, a

27

stunning megayacht marina with beautiful, safe walkways and many upscale shops.

East of Charlotte Amalie on Route 38, **Tillett Gardens** (🌐 *www.tillettgardens.com*) is an oasis of artistic endeavor. The late Jim and Rhoda Tillett converted this Danish farm into an artists' retreat in 1959. Today you can watch artisans produce silk-screen fabrics, candles, pottery, and other handicrafts. Something special is often happening in the gardens as well, including concerts and an arts-and-crafts fair, held in November and May.

Tutu Park Shopping Mall, across from Tillett Gardens, is the island's only enclosed mall. More than 50 stores and a food court are anchored by Kmart and the Plaza Extra grocery store. Archaeologists have discovered evidence that Arawak Indians once lived near the grounds.

ART

Mango Tango. This gallery sells and displays works by popular local artists—originals, prints, and note cards. There's a one-person show at least one weekend a month. ✉ *Al Cohen's Plaza, ½ mile (¾ km) east of Charlotte Amalie, Raphune Hill* ☎ *340/777–3060* ✉ *Yacht Haven Grande, Rte. 38, Crown Bay* ☎ *340/777–3060.*

CAMERAS AND ELECTRONICS

Boolchand's. This store sells brand-name cameras, audio and video equipment, and binoculars. There's also a location on Main Street, Charlotte Amalie. ✉ *Havensight Mall, Rte. 30, Bldg. II, Suite C, Havensight* ☎ *340/776–0302* 🌐 *www.boolchand.com.*

CHINA AND CRYSTAL

Scandinavian Center. Find the best of Scandinavia here, including Royal Copenhagen, Georg Jensen, Kosta Boda, and Orrefors. Owners Søren and Grace Blak make regular buying trips to northern Europe and are a great source of information on crystal. Online ordering is available if you want to add to your collection once home. ✉ *Havensight Mall, Rte. 30, Bldg. III, last store closest to cruise-ship dock, Havensight* ☎ *340/777–8620, 877/454–8377* 🌐 *www.scandinaviancenter.com* ✉ *Crown Bay Center, Route 305, Crown Bay* ☎ *340/777–8620* 🌐 *www.scandinaviancenter.com* ✉ *Crown Bay Commercial Center, Rte. 30, Crown Bay* ☎ *340/777–8620.*

FOODSTUFFS

Fruit Bowl. This grocery store is the best place on the island to go for fresh fruits and vegetables. There are many ethnic, vegetarian, and health-food items as well as a fresh meat area, seafood department, and salad bar. ✉ *Wheatley Center, intersection of Rtes. 38 and 313, Charlotte Amalie* ☎ *340/774–8565* 🌐 *www.thefruitbowlvi.com.*

Gourmet Gallery. This is where visiting megayacht owners (or their staff) go to buy their caviar. There's also an excellent and reasonably priced wine selection, as well as specialty ingredients for everything from tacos to curries to chow mein. A full-service deli offers imported meats, cheeses, and in-store prepared foods that are perfect for a picnic. ✉ *Crown Bay Marina, Rte. 304, Estate Contant* ☎ *340/776–8555* 🌐 *gourmetgallery.net* ✉ *Havensight Mall, Bldg. VI, Rte. 30, Havensight* ☎ *340/774–4948* 🌐 *www.gourmetgallery.net.*

HANDICRAFTS

JEWELRY

H. Stern Jewelers. This Brazilian jeweler is known for the modern settings and designs of its offerings. The jewelry vault design center is located on Main Street, Charlotte Amalie. ✉ *Havensight Mall, Bldg. II, Rte. 30, Havensight* ☎ *340/776–1223* 🌐 *www.hstern.net.*

Jewels. Head here for name-brand jewelry and designer watches in abundance. Locations also at Havensight Mall, Crown Bay Center, and the Ritz-Carlton, St. Thomas. ✉ *38 Dronnigans Gade (Main St.), Charlotte Amalie* ☎ *248/809–5560* 🌐 *www.jewelsonline.com.*

LIQUOR AND TOBACCO

Al Cohen's Discount Liquor. This warehouse of a store holds an extremely large wine and liquor selection. ✉ *Rte. 30, across from the main entrance to Havensight Mall, Havensight* ☎ *340/774–3690.*

Tobacco Discounters. This duty-free outlet carries a full line of discounted brand-name cigarettes, cigars, and tobacco accessories. ✉ *9100 Port of $ale Mall, Rte. 30, next to Havensight Mall, Havensight* ☎ *340/774–2256.*

MUSIC

Music Shoppe II. This is a good place to buy CDs of the latest Caribbean releases—steel pan, reggae, and calypso, plus contemporary tunes in a broad range of genres. ✉ *Havensight Mall, Bldg. III, Rte. 30, Suite D, Havensight* ☎ *340/774–1900* 🌐 *musicshoppe2.com.*

27

TOYS

FAMILY **Kmart.** This giant discount chain store has five aisles of toys for boys and girls: Barbie dolls, hula hoops, computer games, dollhouses, talking teddies, and more. ✉ *Tutu Park Shopping Mall, Rte. 38, Estate Tutu* ☎ *340/714–5839* 🌐 *www.kmart.com* ✉ *Lockhart Gardens, Rte. 38, Estate Long Bay* ☎ *340/774–4046* 🌐 *www.kmart.com.*

SPORTS AND THE OUTDOORS

AIR TOURS

Caribbean Buzz Helicopters. Near to the UVI field, Caribbean Buzz Helicopters offers a minimum 30-minute tour that includes St. Thomas, St. John, and Jost Van Dyke. It's a nice ride if you can afford the splurge (tours are from $600 for up to three people), but in truth, you can see most of the aerial sights from Paradise Point, and there's no place you can't reach easily by car or boat. ✉ *Jet Port, 8202 Lindbergh Bay, Charlotte Amalie* ☎ *340/775–7335* 🌐 *www.caribbean-buzz.com.*

BOATING AND SAILING

Calm seas, crystal waters, and nearby islands (perfect for picnicking, snorkeling, and exploring) make St. Thomas a favorite jumping-off spot for day- or weeklong sails or powerboat adventures. With more than 100 vessels from which to choose, St. Thomas is the charter-boat center of the U.S. Virgin Islands. You can go through a broker to book a sailing vessel with a crew or contact a charter company directly. Crewed charters start at approximately $3,100 per person per week, and bareboat charters can start at $2,000 per person for a 50- to 55-foot sailboat (not including provisioning), which can comfortably accommodate up to six people. If you want to rent your own boat, hire a captain. Most local captains are excellent tour guides.

Single-day charters are also a possibility. You can hire smaller boats for the day, including the services of a captain if you wish to have someone take you on a guided snorkeling trip around the islands.

Island Yachts. The sailboats and powerboats from Island Yachts are available for charter with or without crews. ✉ *6100 Red Hook Quarter, 18B, Red Hook* ☎ *340/775–6666, 800/524–2019* 🌐 *www.iyc.vi.*

Magic Moments. *Luxury* is the word at Magic Moments, where crews aboard the 45-foot Sea Ray and 52-foot Sunseeker offer pampered island-hopping snorkeling cruises for $475 per person (children ages 2–10 are half price). Nice touches include a wine-and-lobster lunch and icy-cold eucalyptus-infused washcloths for freshening up. ✉ *American Yacht Harbor, 6501 Red Hook Plaza, Ste. 201, Docks B and C, Red Hook* ☎ *340/775–5066* 🌐 *www.yachtmagicmoments.com.*

Nauti Nymph. A large selection of 28- to 35-foot powerboats and power catamarans are available from this company. Rates, which vary from $700 to $945 a day, include snorkeling gear, water skis, and outriggers, but not fuel. You can hire a captain for $140 more per day. ✉ *American Yacht Harbor Marina, 6501 Red Hook Plaza, Ste. 201, Dock C, Red Hook* ☎ *540/775–5066, 800/734–7345* 🌐 *www.nautinymph.com.*

Stewart Yacht Charters. Run by longtime sailor Ellen Stewart, this company is skilled at matching clients with yachts and crews for weeklong charter holidays. ✉ *6501 Red Hook Plaza, Ste. 20, Red Hook* ☎ *340/775–1358, 800/432–6118* 🌐 *www.stewartyachtcharters.com.*

VIP Yacht Charters. Forty-eight- to 59-foot powerboats, including a selection of stable trawlers, are available for bareboat charter. Professional captains are available at request, for an extra charge. ✉ *Compass Point Marina, 6300 Estate Frydenhoj, south off Rte. 32, Ste. 27, Estate Frydenhoj* ☎ *340/774–9224, 866/847–9224* 🌐 *www.vipyachts.com.*

BICYCLING

Water Island Adventures. In this company's fun biking trip, you first take a ferry ride from Crown Bay to Water Island and then jump on a Cannondale for 90 minutes of biking over rolling hills on dirt and paved roads. (On cruise-ship days, a direct ferry goes from the West India Company Docks, but this is only for cruise passengers who have booked the bike tour.) Explore the remains of the Sea Cliff Hotel, reputedly the inspiration for Herman Wouk's book *Don't Stop the Carnival,* and then take a cooling swim at beautiful Honeymoon Beach. Helmets, water, guides, and ferry fare are included in the $85 cost. Bike rentals are available on days when no tours are scheduled: call for details. ✉ *Water Island* ☎ *340/626–9815, 340/690–4019* 🌐 *www.waterislandadventures.com.*

DIVING AND SNORKELING

Popular dive sites include such wrecks as the *Cartanser Sr.,* a beautifully encrusted World War II cargo ship sitting in 35 feet of water, and the *General Rogers,* a Coast Guard cutter resting at 65 feet. Here you can find a gigantic resident barracuda. Reef dives offer hidden caves

Continued on page 1118

BELOW THE WAVES

By Lynda Lohr

Colorful reefs and wrecks rife with corals and tropical fish make the islands as interesting underwater as above. Brilliantly colored reef fish vie for your attention with corals in wondrous shapes. Scuba diving gets you up close and personal with the world below the waves.

Bright blue tangs and darting blue-headed wrasses. Corals in wondrous shapes—some look like brains, others like elk antlers. Colorful, bulbous sponges. All these and more can be spotted along the myriad reefs of the U.S. and British Virgin Islands. You might see a pink conch making its way along the ocean bottom in areas with seagrass beds. If you're really lucky, a turtle may swim into view, or a lobster may poke its antennae out of a hole in the reef or rocks. If you do a night dive, you might run into an octopus. But you may be surprised at how much you can see by simply hovering just below the surface, with nothing more than a mask and snorkel. It's a bird's-eye view, but an excellent one. Whether scuba diving or snorkeling, take along an underwater camera to capture memories of your exciting adventure. You can buy disposable ones at most dive shops or bring one from home.

DIVE AND SNORKELING SITES IN BRITISH VIRGIN ISLANDS

TORTOLA

Although a major base for dive operations in the BVI (due to its proximity to so many exceptional dive sites), Tortola itself doesn't have as much to offer divers. However, there are still some noteworthy destinations. The massive **Brewer's Bay Pinnacles** grow 70 feet high to within 30 feet of the surface; the rock mazes are only for advanced divers because of strong currents and they are not always accessible. Abundant reefs close to shore make **Brewer's Bay** popular with snorkelers, as are **Frenchman's Cay** and **Long Bay Beef Island. Diamond Reef,** between Great Camanoe and Scrub Island, is a small wall about 200 yards long. **Shark Point,** off the northeast coast of Scrub Island, does have resident sharks. Though isolated in open ocean, the wreck of the ***Chikuzen,*** a Japanese refrigerator ship, is a popular site.

THE ISLANDS OF THE SIR FRANCIS DRAKE CHANNEL

Southeast of Tortola lie a string of islands with some of the BVI's finest dive sites, some world famous. The wreck of the royal mail ship ***Rhone*** is between Peter and Salt islands and is, perhaps, the most famous dive site in the BVI. **Wreck Alley,** consisting of three sunken modern ships, is between Salt and Cooper islands. At **Alice in Wonderland,** south of Ginger Island, giant, mushroom-shaped corals shelter reef fish, moray eels, and crustaceans. **Alice's Backside,** off the northwestern tip of Ginger Island, is usually smooth enough for snorkeling and shallow enough so that beginner divers can get a good look at the myriad sealife and sponges.

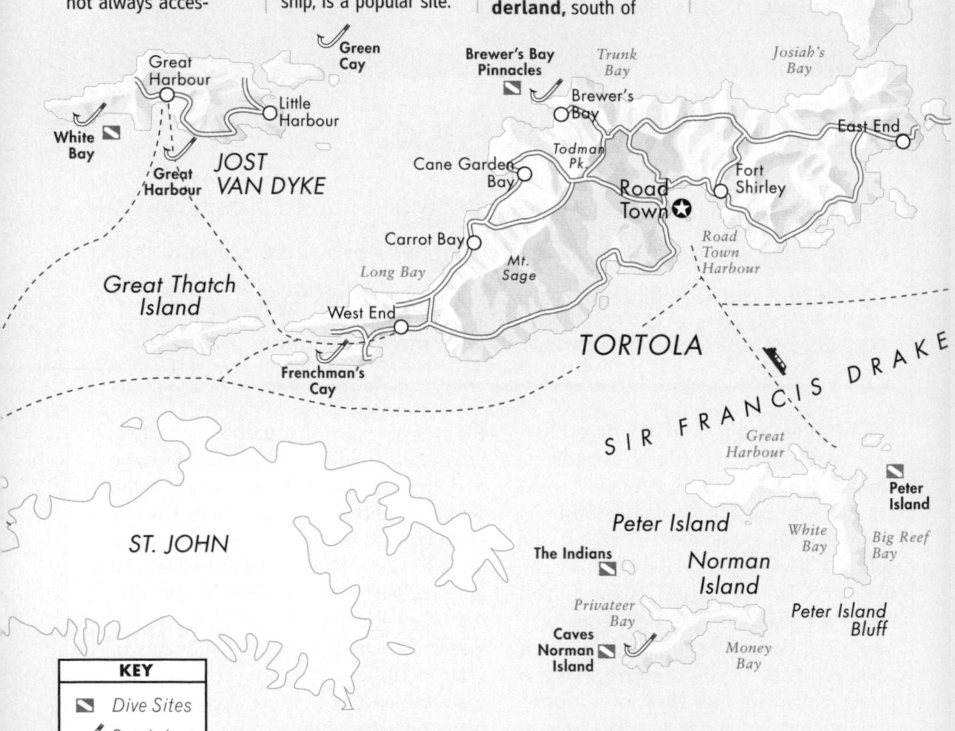

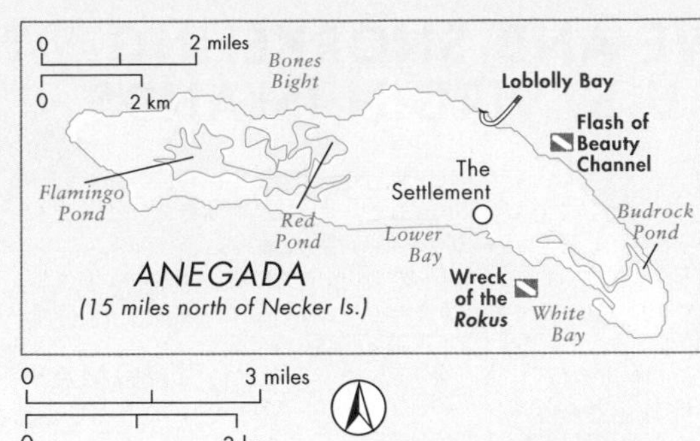

Virgin Gorda

ANEGADA

Surrounded by the third-largest barrier reef in the world, Anegada has great snorkeling from virtually any beach on the island. But there are also some notable dive sites as well. The **Flash of Beauty Channel** on the north shore is a great open-water dive, but only suitable for experienced divers. But even novices can enjoy diving at the **Wreck of the *Rokus*,** a Greek cargo ship off the island's southern shore.

VIRGIN GORDA

The Baths, though busy, offers some of the best snorkeling in the Virgin Islands among giant boulders and the resulting grottoes. Nearby is **Spring Bay,** with fewer visitors and similar terrain. **The Aquarium,** close to Spanish Town and a good novice site, is so called because of the abundance of reef fish that swim around the submerged granite boulders that are similar to those of The Baths. Further west of Virgin Gorda, the Dog Islands have some interesting and popular sites, including **The Chimney,** a natural opening covered by sponges off Great Dog. South of Great Dog, **Coral Gardens** has a large coral reef with a submerged airplane wreck nearby. Fish are drawn to nearby **Cockroach Island.**

DIVE AND SNORKELING SITES IN U.S. VIRGIN ISLANDS

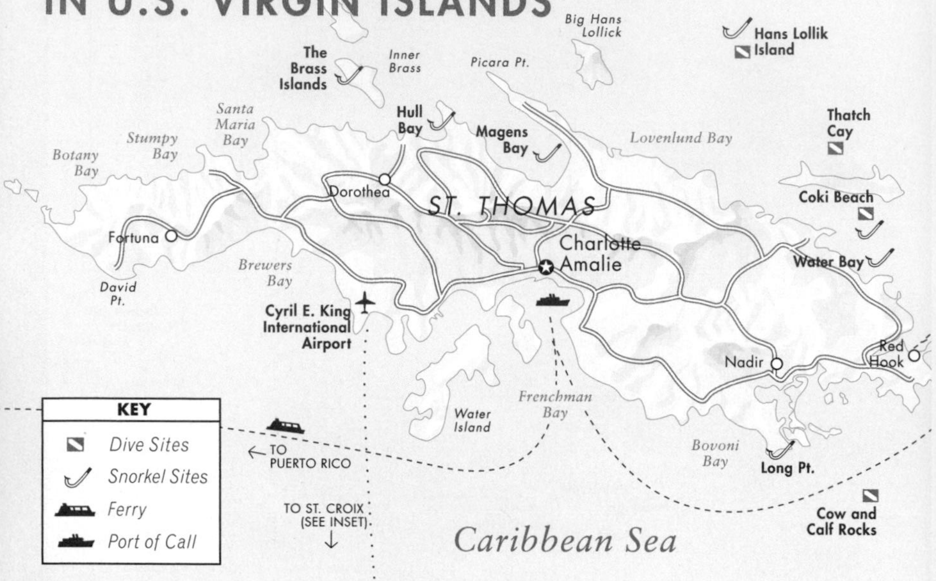

ST. THOMAS

St. Thomas has at least 40 popular dive sites, most shallow. Favorite reef dives off St. Thomas include **Cow and Calf Rocks,** which barely break water off the southeast coast of St. Thomas; the coral-covered pinnacles of **Frenchcap** south of St. Thomas; and tunnels where you can explore undersea from the Caribbean to the Atlantic at **Thatch Cay** (where the Coast Guard cutter *General Rogers* rests at 65 feet). **Grass Cay** and **Mingo Cay** between St. Thomas and St. John are also popular dive sites. **Coki Beach** offers the best off-the-beach snorkeling in St. Thomas. Nearby Coral World offers a dive-helmet walk for the untrained, and Snuba of St. Thomas has tethered shallow dives for non-certified divers. **Magens Bay,** the most popular beach on St. Thomas, provides lovely snorkeling if you head along the edges. You're likely to see some colorful sponges, darting fish, and maybe even a turtle if you're lucky. This is a stop on every island tour.

ST. JOHN

St. John is particularly known for its myriad good snorkeling spots—certainly more than for its diving opportunities, though there are many dive sites within easy reach of Cruz Bay. **Trunk Bay** often receives the most attention because of its underwater snorkeling trail created by the National Park Service; signs let you know what you're seeing in terms of coral and other underwater features. And the beach is easy to reach since taxis leave on demand from Cruz Bay. A patchy reef just offshore means good snorkeling at **Hawksnest Beach.** Additionally, **Cinnamon Bay** and **Leinster Bay** also get their fair share of praise as snorkeling spots. That's not to say that you can't find good dive sites near St. John. **Deaver's Bay** is a short boat ride around the point from Cruz Bay, where you can see angelfish, southern stingrays, and triggerfish feeding at 30 to 50 feet. **The Leaf** is a large coral reef off St. John's southern shore.

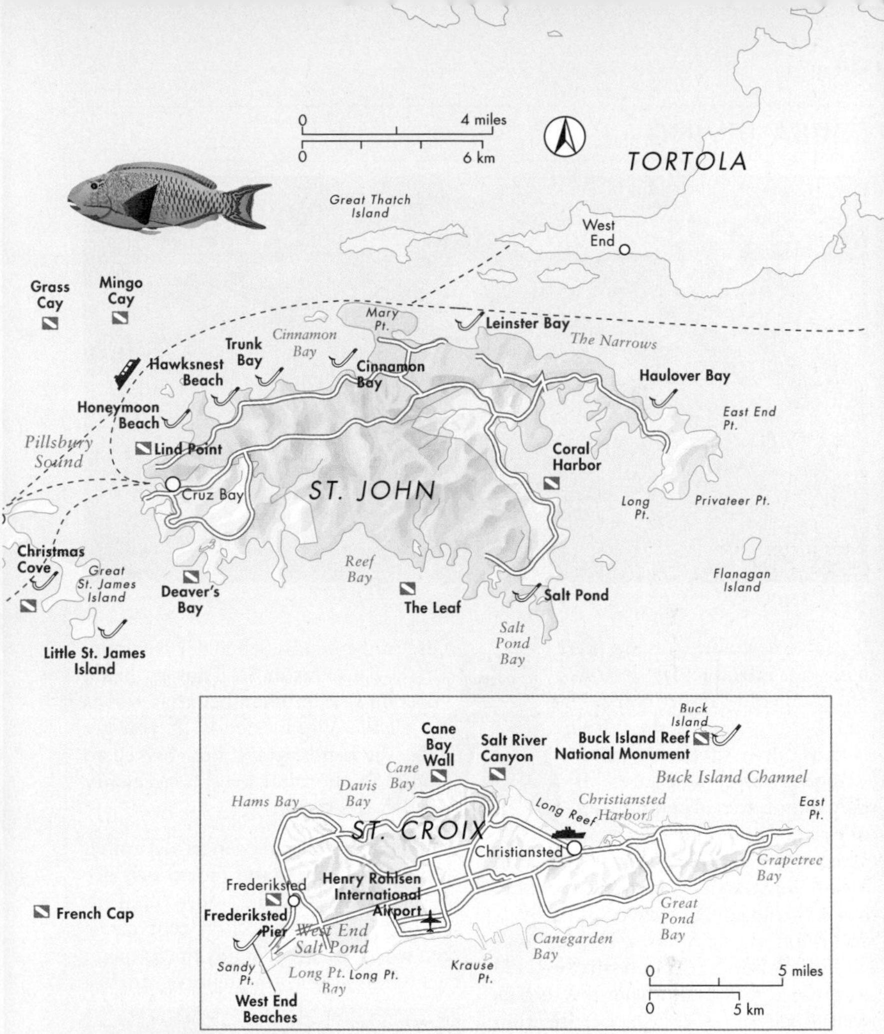

0 4 miles
0 6 km
TORTOLA
Great Thatch Island
West End
Grass Cay
Mingo Cay
Mary Pt.
Leinster Bay
Cinnamon Bay
The Narrows
Trunk Bay
Hawksnest Beach
Cinnamon Bay
Haulover Bay
Honeymoon Beach
East End Pt.
Pillsbury Sound
Lind Point
Coral Harbor
Cruz Bay
ST. JOHN
Long Pt.
Privateer Pt.
Christmas Cove
Great St. James Island
Deaver's Bay
Reef Bay
Flanagan Island
The Leaf
Salt Pond
Salt Pond Bay
Little St. James Island
French Cap

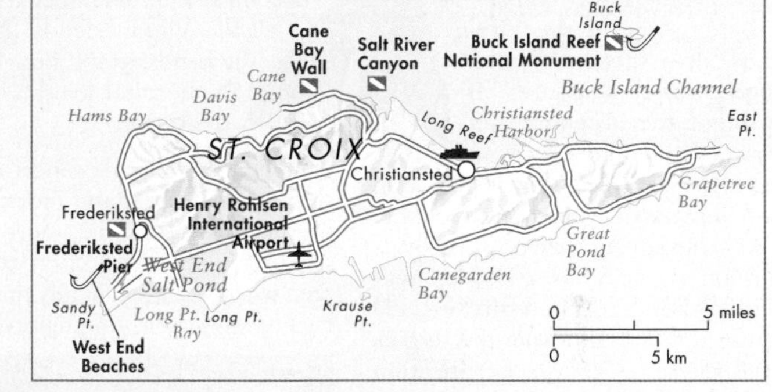

Coral near St. Croix

ST. CROIX

The largest of the U.S. Virgin Islands is a favorite of both divers and snorkelers and offers something for everyone. Snorkelers are often fascinated by the marked snorkeling trail at **Buck Island Reef,** which is a short boat ride from the island's east end; it's a U.S. national monument. Divers are drawn to the north shore, especially the **Cane Bay Wall,** a spectacular drop-off that's reachable from the beach, though usually reached by boat. Another north-shore site is the **Salt River Canyon,** where you can float downward through a canyon filled with colorful fish and coral. On the island's west end, **Frederiksted Pier** is home to a colony of sea horses, creatures seldom seen in the waters of the Virgin Islands. Casual snorkelers would also enjoy snorkeling at the **West End Beaches.**

SCUBA DIVING

St.Croix

If you've never been diving, start with an introductory lesson—often called a "resort course"—run by any one of the Virgin Islands' dive shops. All meet stringent safety standards. If they didn't, they'd soon be out of business. If you're staying at a hotel, you can often find the dive shop on-site; otherwise, your hotel probably has an arrangement with one nearby. If you're on a cruise, cruise-ship companies offer shore excursions that include transportation to and from the ship as well as the resort course. Certification requires much more study and practice, but it is required to rent air tanks, get air refills, and join others on guided dives virtually anywhere in the world.

The number one rule of diving is safety. The basic rules for safe diving are simple, and fools ignore them at their own peril. Serious diving accidents are becoming increasingly rare these days, thanks to the high level of diver training. However, they do still occur occasionally. Surfacing too rapidly without exhaling-–or going too deep for too long—can result in an air embolism or a case of the bends. Schneider Regional Medical Center in St. Thomas has a decompression chamber that serves all the Virgin Islands. If you get the bends, you'll be whisked to the hospital for this necessary treatment.

Fauna is another concern. Though sharks, barracuda, and moray eels are on the most-feared list, more often it's sea urchins and fire coral that cause pain when you accidentally bump them. Part of any scuba-training program is a

Divers learn how to jump in from a boat

St.Croix

review of sea life and the importance of respecting the new world you're exploring. Dive professionals recognize the value of protecting fragile reefs and ecosystems in tropical waters, and instructors emphasize look-don't-touch diving (the unofficial motto is: take only pictures, leave only bubbles). Government control and protection of dive sites is increasing, especially in such heavily used areas as the Virgin Islands.

While you can scuba dive off a beach—and you can find shops renting scuba equipment and providing airfills at the most popular beaches—a trip aboard a dive boat provides a more extensive glimpse into this wonderful undersea world. Since the dive shops can provide all equipment, there's no need to lug heavy weights and a bulky BC in your luggage. For the most comfort, you might want to bring your own regulator if you have one. The dive-boat captains and guides know the best dive locations, can find alternatives when the seas are rough, and will help you deal with heavy tanks and cumbersome equipment. Trips are easy to organize. Dive shops on all islands make frequent excursions to a wide variety of diving spots, and your hotel, villa manager, or cruise-ship staff will help you make arrangements.

If you fly too soon after diving, you're at risk for decompression sickness, which occurs when nitrogen trapped in your bloodstream doesn't escape. This creates a painful and sometimes fatal condition called the bends, not a sickness you want to develop while you're winging your way home after a fun-filled beach vacation. Opinions vary, but as a rule of thumb, wait at least 12 hours after a single dive to fly. However, if you've made multiple dives or dived several days in a row, you should wait at least 18 hours. If you've made dives that required decompression stops, you should also wait at least 24 hours before flying. To be safe, consult with your physician.

The Virgin Islands offer a plethora of dive sites, and you'll be taken to some of the best if you sign on to a dive trip run by one of the many dive operations scattered around the islands.

DIVER TRAINING

(top) Underwater shot of tropical reef, (bottom) Diver silhouette, Cane Bay, St Croix

Good to know: Divers can become certified through PADI *(www.padi.com)*, NAUI *(www.naui.org)*, or SSI *(www.divessi.com)*. The requirements for all three are similar, and if you do the classroom instruction and pool training with a dive shop associated with one organization, the referral for the open water dives will be honored by most dive shops. Note that you should not fly for at least 24 hours after a dive, because residual nitrogen in the body can pose health risks upon decompression. While there are no rigid rules on diving after flying, make sure you're well-hydrated before hitting the water.

SNUBA

Beyond snorkeling or the requirements of scuba, you also have the option of "Snuba." The word is a trademarked portmanteau or combo of snorkel and scuba. Marketed as easy-to-learn family fun, Snuba lets you breathe underwater via tubes from an air-supplied vessel above, with no prior diving or snorkel experience required.

NOT CERTIFIED?

Not sure if you want to commit the time and money to become certified? Not a problem. Most dive shops and many resorts will offer a discover scuba day-long course. In the morning, the instructor will teach you the basics of scuba diving: how to clear your mask, how to come to the surface in the unlikely event you lose your air supply, etc. In the afternoon, instructors will take you out for a dive in relatively shallow water—less than 30 feet. Be sure to ask where the dive will take place. Jumping into the water off a shallow beach may not be as fun as actually going out to the coral. If you decide that diving is something you want to pursue, the open dive may count toward your certification.

■ **TIP→ You can often book discover dives at the last minute. It may not be worth it to go out on a windy day when the currents are stronger. Also the underwater world looks a whole lot brighter on sunny days.**

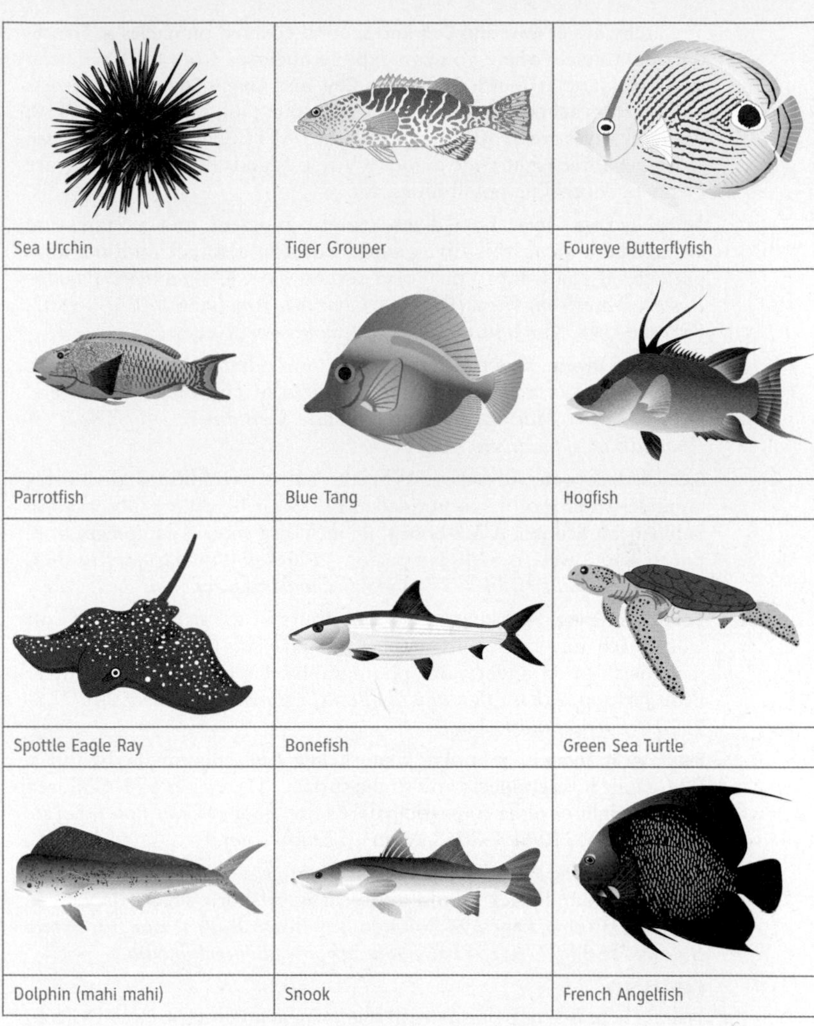

REEF CREATURES IN THE VIRGIN ISLANDS

From the striped sergeant majors to bright blue tangs, the reefs of the Virgin Islands are teeming with life, though not nearly as many as in eons past. Warming waters and pollution have taken their toll on both coral and fish species. But many reefs in the Virgin Islands still thrive; you'll also see sponges, crustaceans, perhaps a sea turtle or two, and bigger game fish like grouper and barracuda; sharks are seen but are rarely a problem for divers. Beware of fire corals, which are not really corals but rather a relative of the jellyfish and have a painful sting; if you brush up against a fire coral, spread vinegar on the wound as soon as possible to minimize the pain.

and archways at **Cow and Calf Rocks,** coral-covered pinnacles at **Frenchcap,** and tunnels where you can explore undersea from the Caribbean to the Atlantic at **Thatch Cay, Grass Cay,** and **Congo Cay.** Many resorts and charter yachts offer dive packages. A one-tank dive starts at $110; two-tank dives are $130 and up. Call the USVI Department of Tourism to obtain a free eight-page guide to Virgin Islands dive sites. There are plenty of snorkeling possibilities, too.

Admiralty Dive Center. Boat dives, rental equipment, and a retail store are available from this dive center. You can also get multiple-tank packages if you want to dive over several days. ✉ *Windward Passage Resort, Waterfront Hwy. (Rte. 30), Charlotte Amalie* ☎ *340/777–9802, 888/900–3483* 🌐 *www.admiraltydive.com.*

Blue Island Divers. This full-service dive shop offers both day and night dives to wrecks and reefs and specializes in custom dive charters. ✉ *Crown Bay Marina, Rte. 304, Estate Contant* ☎ *340/774–2001* 🌐 *www.blueislanddivers.com.*

B.O.S.S. Underwater Adventure. As an alternative to traditional diving, try an underwater motor scooter called BOSS, or Breathing Observation Submersible Scooter. A 3½-hour tour, including snorkel equipment, rum punch, and towels, is $140 per person. ✉ *Crown Bay Marina, Rte. 304, Charlotte Amalie* ☎ *340/777–3549* 🌐 *www.bossusvi.com.*

FAMILY **Coki Dive Center.** Snorkeling and dive tours in the fish-filled reefs off Coki Beach are available from this PADI Five Star outfit, as are classes, including one on underwater photography. It's run by the avid diver Peter Jackson. ✉ *Rte. 388, at Coki Point, Estate Frydendal* ☎ *340/775–4220* 🌐 *www.cokidive.com.*

Snuba of St. Thomas. In Snuba, a snorkeling and scuba-diving hybrid, a 20-foot air hose connects you to the surface. The cost is $74. Children must be eight or older to participate. ✉ *Rte. 388, at Coki Point, Estate Smith Bay* ☎ *340/693–8063* 🌐 *www.visnuba.com.*

St. Thomas Diving Club. This PADI Five Star center offers boat dives to the reefs around Buck Island and nearby offshore wrecks as well as multiday dive packages. ✉ *Bolongo Bay Beach Resort, Rte. 30, Estate Bolongo* ☎ *340/776–2381* 🌐 *www.stthomasdivingclub.com.*

FISHING

Fishing here is synonymous with blue marlin angling—especially from June through October. Four 1,000-pound-plus blues, including three world records, have been caught on the famous North Drop, about 20 miles (32 km) north of St. Thomas. A day charter for marlin with up to six anglers costs $1,800 for the day. If you're not into marlin fishing, try hooking sailfish in winter, dolphinfish (the fish that's also known as mahimahi, not the mammal) in spring, and wahoo in fall. Inshore trips for four hours start at $600. To find the trip that will best suit you, walk down the docks at either American Yacht Harbor or Sapphire Beach Marina in the late afternoon and chat with the captains and crews.

Abigail III. Captain Red Bailey's *Abigail III* specializes in marlin fishing. It operates out of the Sapphire Condominium Resort's marina. ✉ *Estate*

Smith Bay, Rte. 38, 1/4 mile northwest of Red Hook, Sapphire Bay ☎ 340/775–6024 🌐 www.visportfish.com.

Charter Boat Center. This is a major source for sail and powerboat as well as sportfishing charters. Sportfishing charters include full-day trips for marlin as well as full, three-quarter, and half days for offshore and inshore species such as tuna, wahoo, dolphin (mahimahi), snapper, and kingfish. ✉ *American Yacht Harbor, 6300 Smith Bay 16-3, Red Hook ☎ 340/775–7990 🌐 www.charterboat.vi.*

FAMILY **Double Header Sportfishing.** This company offers trips out to the North Drop on its 40-foot sportfisher and half-day reef and bay trips aboard its two speedy 35-foot center consoles. ✉ *Sapphire Bay Marina, Rte. 38, Sapphire Bay ☎ 340/777–7317 🌐 www.doubleheadersportfishing.net.*

Marlin Prince. Captain Eddie Morrison, one of the most experienced charter operators in St. Thomas, specializes in fly-fishing for blue marlin from his 45-foot Viking boat. ✉ *American Yacht Harbor, 6100 Red Hook Quarters No. 2, slip A-16, Red Hook ☎ 340/693–5929 🌐 www.marlinprince.com.*

GOLF

Mahogany Run Golf Course. The Mahogany Run Golf Course is the only course in St. Thomas and it attracts golfers who are drawn by its spectacular view of the British Virgin Islands and the challenging three-hole Devil's Triangle of holes 13–15. This Tom and George Fazio–designed course is not particularly long, but in addition to the scenery, you will experience lots of natural flora and fauna. There's a fully stocked pro shop, snack bar, and open-air clubhouse. Walking is not permitted and the course enforces a dress code. It's open daily, and there are frequently informal weekend tournaments. ✉ *Rte. 42, Estate Lovenlund ☎ 340/777–6006, 800/253–7103 🌐 www.mahoganyrungolf.com 💵 $165 for 18 holes; $115 for 9 holes during peak winter season 🏌 18 holes, 6022 yards, par 70.*

GUIDED TOURS

VI Taxi Association Tropical Paradise St. Thomas Island Tour. Aimed at cruise-ship passengers, this two-hour tour for two people is done in an open-air safari bus or enclosed van. The $29 tour includes stops at Drake's Seat and Mountain Top. Other tours include a three-hour trip to Coki Beach with a shopping stop in downtown Charlotte Amalie for $35 per person, a three-hour trip to the Coral World Ocean Park for $45 per person, and a five-hour beach tour to St. John for $75 per person. For $35 to $40 for two, you can hire a taxi for a customized three-hour drive around the island. Make sure to see Mountain Top, as the view is wonderful. ☎ *340/774–4550 🌐 www.vitaxi.com.*

SEA EXCURSIONS

Landlubbers and seafarers alike can experience wind in their hair and salt spray in the air while exploring the waters surrounding St. Thomas. Several businesses can book you on a snorkel-and-sail to a deserted cay for a half day that starts at $95 per person or a full day (at least $130 per person). An excursion over to the British Virgin Islands starts at $150 per person, not including customs fees. A luxury daylong motor-yacht cruise complete with lunch is $475 or more per person.

Adventure Center. For a soup-to-nuts choice of sea tours including a Stand-Up Paddleboard (SUP) safari, full- and half-day sails, and sunset cruises, contact the Adventure Center. ✉ *Marriott's Frenchman's Reef Hotel, Rte. 315, Estate Bakkeroe* ☎ *340/774–2992, 866/868–7784* 🌐 *www.adventurecenters.net.*

Charter Boat Center. The specialty here is day trips to the British Virgin Islands aboard 42-foot 12-passenger motoryachts *Stormy Petrel* and *Pirate's Penny*. There are also day- or weeklong sailing charters. ✉ *American Yacht Harbor, 6300 Smith Bay 16-3, Red Hook* ☎ *340/775–7990* 🌐 *www.charterboat.vi.*

Treasure Isle Cruises. Jimmy Loveland at Treasure Isle Cruises can set you up with everything from a half-day sail to a seven-day Caribbean cruise. ✉ *Rte. 32, Estate Nadir* ☎ *340/775–9500* 🌐 *www.treasureislecruises.com.*

SEA KAYAKING

Fish dart, birds sing, and iguanas lounge on the limbs of dense mangrove trees deep within a marine sanctuary on St. Thomas's southeast shore.

FAMILY
Fodor's Choice ★

Virgin Islands Ecotours. With Virgin Islands Ecotours you can learn about the islands' natural history in a guided kayak-snorkel tour to Patricia Cay or via an inflatable boat tour to Cas Cay for snorkeling and hiking. Both are 2½ hours long. VI Ecotours also offers three- and five-hour guided kayak tours to St. Thomas's Mangrove Lagoon, Hassel Island, Henley Cay, and St. John's Caneel Bay. All trips include free snorkel instruction with snacks on three-hour trips and lunch on five-hour trips. The historic Hassel Island tour includes a visit to some of the historic forts and military structures on the island, a short hike to a breathtaking vista, and a swim off a deserted beach. ✉ *Mangrove Lagoon, Rte. 32, 2 miles (3 km) east of the intersection of Rtes. 32 and 30, Estate Nadir* ☎ *340/779–2155, 877/845–2925* 🌐 *www.viecotours.com* 🎟 *From $69 per person.*

WINDSURFING

FAMILY

Expect some spills, anticipate the thrills, and try your luck clipping through the seas. Most beachfront resorts rent Windsurfers and offer one-hour lessons for about $120.

Island Sol. If you want to learn to windsurf, try Paul Stoeken's Island Sol. The two-time Olympic athlete charges $85 per hour for a private lesson. There's a free clinic every Tuesday at 9:30 am. There are also private kiteboarding lessons for $385 for 3 hours, and kayak and stand-up paddleboard (SUP) rentals for $25 per hour. ✉ *Ritz-Carlton Destination Club, Rte. 317, on Great Bay, Estate Nazareth* ☎ *340/643–2251* 🌐 *www.islandsol.vi.*

ST. JOHN

Updated by Lynda Lohr

St. John's heart is Virgin Islands National Park, a treasure that takes up a full two-thirds of St. John's 20 square miles (53 square km). The park helps keep the island's interior in its pristine and undisturbed state, but if you go at midday, you'll probably have to share your stretch of beach with others, particularly at Trunk Bay.

The island is booming (its population of 5,000 is joined by more than 800,000 visitors each year), and it can get crowded at the ever-popular Trunk Bay Beach during the busy winter season; parking woes plague the island's main town of Cruz Bay, but you won't find traffic jams or pollution. It's easy to escape from the fray, however: just head off on a hike or go early or late to the beach. The sun won't be as strong, and you may have that perfect crescent of white sand all to yourself.

St. John doesn't have a major agrarian past like her sister island, St. Croix, but if you're hiking in the dry season, you can probably stumble upon the stone ruins of old plantations. The less adventuresome can visit the repaired ruins at the park's Annaberg Plantation and Caneel Bay Resort.

In 1675 Jorgen Iverson claimed the unsettled island for Denmark. By 1733 there were more than 1,000 slaves working more than 100 plantations. In that year the island was hit by a drought, hurricanes, and a plague of insects that destroyed the summer crops. With famine a real threat and the planters keeping them under tight rein, the slaves revolted on November 23, 1733. They captured the fort at Coral Bay, took control of the island, and held it for six months. During this period, about 20% of the island's total population was killed, the tragedy affecting both black and white residents in equal percentages. The rebellion was eventually put down with the help of French troops from Martinique. Slavery continued until 1848, when slaves in St. Croix marched on Frederiksted to demand their freedom from the Danish government. This time it was granted. After emancipation, St. John fell into decline, with its inhabitants eking out a living on small farms. Life continued in much the same way until the national park opened in 1956 and tourism became an industry.

Of the three U.S. Virgin Islands, St. John has the strongest sense of community, which is primarily rooted in a desire to protect the island's natural beauty. Despite the growth, there are still many pockets of tranquility. Here you can truly escape the pressures of modern life for a day, a week—perhaps forever.

EXPLORING

St. John is an easy place to explore. One road runs along the northern shore, another across the center of the mountains. There are a few roads that branch off here and there, but it's hard to get lost. Pick up a map at the visitor center before you start out and you'll have no problems. Few residents remember the route numbers, so have your map in hand if you stop to ask for directions. Bring along a swimsuit for stops at some of the most beautiful beaches in the world. You can spend all day or just a couple of hours exploring, but be advised that the roads are narrow and wind up and down steep hills, so don't expect to get anywhere in a hurry. There are lunch spots at Cinnamon Bay and in Coral Bay, or you can do what the locals do—find a secluded spot for a picnic. The grocery stores in Cruz Bay sell Styrofoam coolers just for this purpose.

Sugar mill ruins at Annaberg Plantation

If you plan to do a lot of touring, renting a car will be cheaper and will give you much more freedom than relying on taxis; on St. John taxis are shared safari vans, and drivers are reluctant to go anywhere until they have a full load of passengers. Although you may be tempted by an open-air Suzuki or Jeep, a conventional car will let you lock up your valuables. You can get just about everywhere on the paved roads without four-wheel drive unless it rains. Then four-wheel drive will help you get up the wet, hilly roads. You may be able to share a van or open-air vehicle (called a safari bus) with other passengers on a tour of scenic mountain trails, secret coves, and eerie bush-covered ruins.

CRUZ BAY

St. John's main town may be compact (it consists of only several blocks), but it's definitely a hub: the ferries from St. Thomas and the British Virgin Islands pull in here, and it's where you can get a taxi or rent a car to travel around the island. There are plenty of shops, a number of watering holes and restaurants, and a grassy square with benches where you can sit back and take everything in. Look for the current edition of the handy, amusing "St. John Map," featuring Max the Mongoose.

WORTH NOTING

Elaine Ione Sprauve Library. On the hill just above Cruz Bay is the Enighed Estate greathouse, built in 1757. *Enighed* is Danish for "concord" (unity or peace). The house and its outbuildings (a sugar factory and horse-driven mill) were destroyed by fire and hurricanes, and the house sat in ruins until 1982. The library offers Internet access for $2 an hour. ✉ *Rte. 104; make a right past St. Ursula's Church* ☎ *340/776–6359* 🎫 *Free* 🕑 *Weekdays 9–5.*

V.I. National Park Visitors Center. To pick up a useful guide to St. John's hiking trails, see various large maps of the island, and find out about current Park Service programs, including guided walks and cultural demonstrations, stop by the park visitor center. ✉ *North Shore Rd., near creek* ☎ *340/776–6201* 🌐 *www.nps.gov/viis* 🕐 *Daily 8–4:30.*

NORTH SHORE

TOP ATTRACTIONS

Fodor's Choice ★ **Annaberg Plantation.** In the 18th century, sugar plantations dotted the steep hills of this island. Slaves and free Danes and Dutchmen toiled to harvest the cane that was used to create sugar, molasses, and rum for export. Built in the 1780s, the partially restored plantation at Leinster Bay was once an important sugar mill. Although there are no official visiting hours, the National Park Service has regular tours, and some well-informed taxi drivers will show you around. Occasionally you may see a living-history demonstration—someone making johnnycakes or weaving baskets. For information on tours and cultural events, contact the V.I. National Park Visitors Center. ✉ *Leinster Bay Rd., Annaberg* ☎ *340/776–6201* 🌐 *www.nps.gov/viis* 🎟 *Free* 🕐 *Daily dawn–dusk.*

WORTH NOTING

Peace Hill. It's worth stopping here, just past the Hawksnest Bay overlook, for great views of St. John, St. Thomas, and the BVI. On the flat promontory is an old sugar mill. ✉ *Off Rte. 20, Denis Bay.*

MID ISLAND

TOP ATTRACTIONS

Fodor's Choice ★ **Reef Bay Trail.** This is one of the most interesting hikes on St. John, but unless you're a rugged individualist who wants a physical challenge (and that describes a lot of people who stay on St. John), you can probably get the most out of the trip if you join a hike led by a park service ranger. A ranger can identify the trees and plants on the hike down, fill you in on the history of the Reef Bay Plantation, and tell you about the petroglyphs on the rocks at the bottom of the trail. A side trail takes you to the plantation's greathouse, a gutted but mostly intact structure with vestiges of its former beauty. Take the safari bus from the park's visitor center. A boat takes you from the beach at Reef Bay back to the visitor center, saving you the uphill climb. It's a good idea to make reservations for this trip, especially during the winter season. They can be made at the Friends of the Park store, in Mongoose Junction. ✉ *Rte. 10, Reef Bay* ☎ *340/779–8700 for reservations* 🌐 *www.nps.gov/viis* 🎟 *$30 includes a safari bus ride to the trailhead, a guided tour, and a boat ride back to the visitor center* 🕐 *Tours at 9:30 am; days change seasonally.*

WORTH NOTING

Catherineberg Ruins. At this fine example of an 18th-century sugar and rum factory, there's a storage vault beneath the windmill. Across the road, look for the round mill, which was later used to hold water. In the 1733 slave revolt Catherineberg served as headquarters for the Amina warriors, a tribe of Africans captured into slavery. ✉ *Catherineberg Rd., off Rte. 10, Catherineberg.*

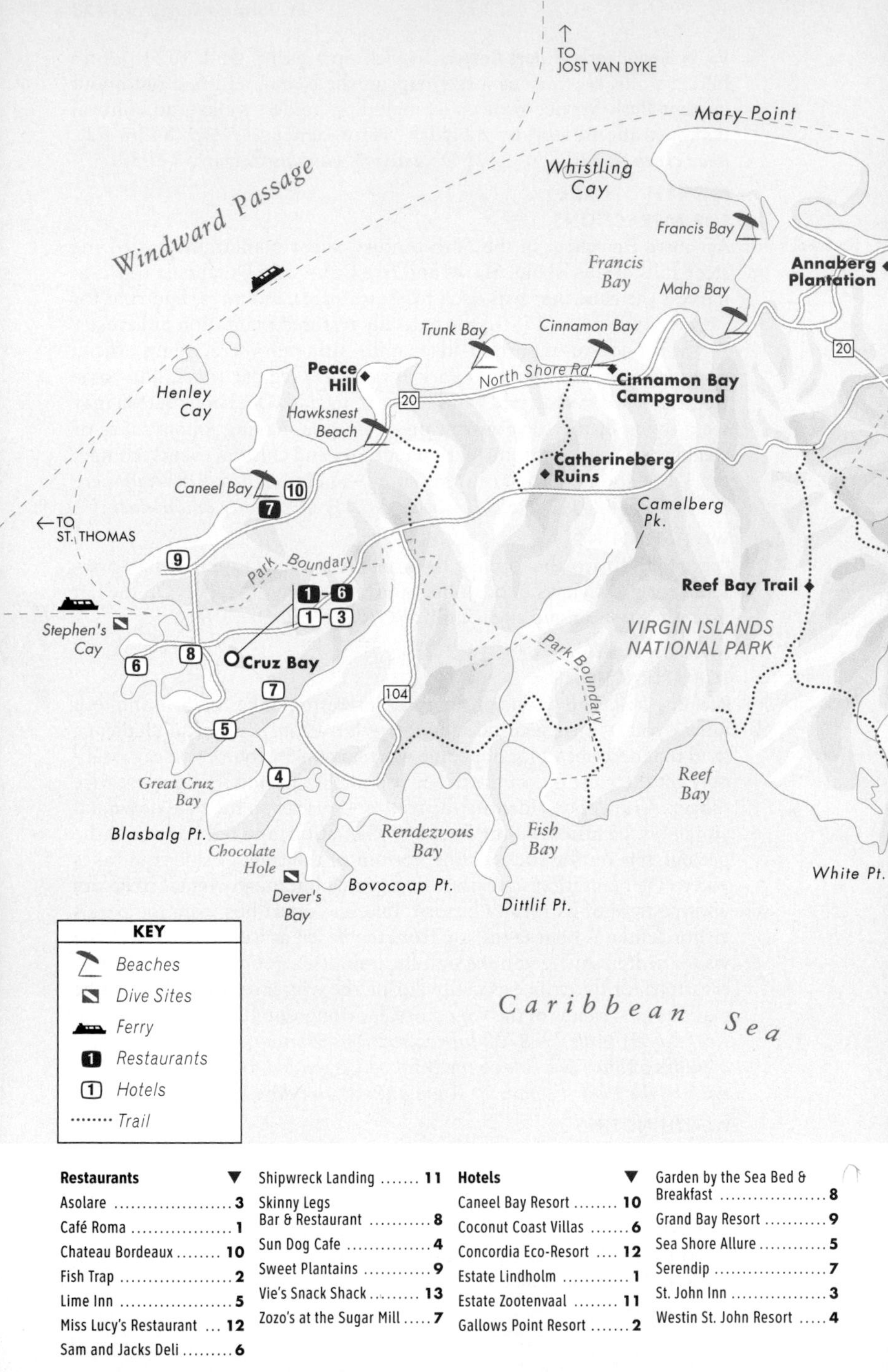

Restaurants ▼

Asolare 3
Café Roma 1
Chateau Bordeaux 10
Fish Trap 2
Lime Inn 5
Miss Lucy's Restaurant ... 12
Sam and Jacks Deli 6
Shipwreck Landing 11
Skinny Legs Bar & Restaurant 8
Sun Dog Cafe 4
Sweet Plantains 9
Vie's Snack Shack 13
Zozo's at the Sugar Mill 7

Hotels ▼

Caneel Bay Resort 10
Coconut Coast Villas 6
Concordia Eco-Resort 12
Estate Lindholm 1
Estate Zootenvaal 11
Gallows Point Resort 2
Garden by the Sea Bed & Breakfast 8
Grand Bay Resort 9
Sea Shore Allure 5
Serendip 7
St. John Inn 3
Westin St. John Resort 4

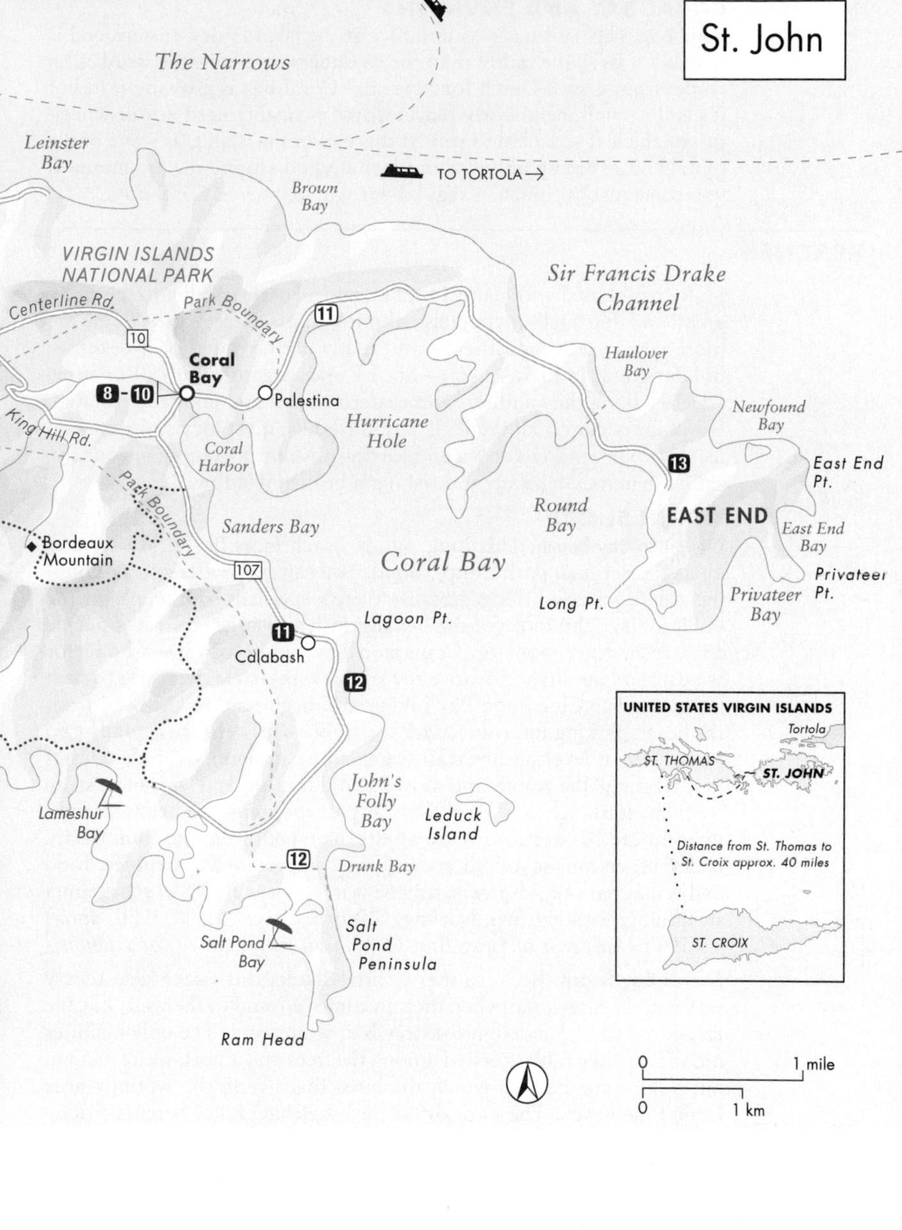
St. John
The Narrows
TO TORTOLA
TO TORTOLA
Leinster Bay
Brown Bay
VIRGIN ISLANDS NATIONAL PARK
Sir Francis Drake Channel
Centerline Rd.
Park Boundary
11
10
Coral Bay
8 - 10
Palestina
Haulover Bay
Newfound Bay
Hurricane Hole
King Hill Rd.
Coral Harbor
13
East End Pt.
Park Boundary
Round Bay
EAST END
Sanders Bay
East End Bay
Bordeaux Mountain
Coral Bay
107
Privateer Pt.
Long Pt.
Privateer Bay
Lagoon Pt.
11
Calabash
12
UNITED STATES VIRGIN ISLANDS
Tortola
ST. THOMAS
ST. JOHN
John's Folly Bay
Lameshur Bay
Leduck Island
Distance from St. Thomas to St. Croix approx. 40 miles
12
Drunk Bay
Salt Pond Bay
Salt Pond Peninsula
ST. CROIX
Ram Head
0
1 mile
0
1 km

CORAL BAY AND ENVIRONS

Coral Bay. This laid-back community at the island's dry, eastern end is named for its shape rather than for its underwater life—the word *coral* comes from *krawl,* Dutch for "corral." Coral Bay is growing fast, but it's still a small, neighborly place. You'll probably need a four-wheel-drive vehicle if you plan to stay at this end of the island, as some of the rental houses are up unpaved roads that wind around the mountain. If you come just for lunch, a regular car will be fine. ✉ *Coral Bay.*

BEACHES

St. John is blessed with many beaches, and all of them fall into the good, great, and don't-tell-anyone-else-about-this-place categories. Some are more developed than others—and many are crowded on weekends, holidays, and in high season—but by and large they're still pristine. Beaches along the southern and eastern shores are quiet and isolated. Break-ins occur on all the U.S. Virgin Islands; most locals recommend leaving your windows down and leaving absolutely nothing in your car, rather than locking it up and risking a broken window.

NORTH SHORE

Cinnamon Bay Beach. This long, sandy beach faces beautiful cays and abuts the national park campground. You can rent water-sports equipment here—a good thing, because there's excellent snorkeling off the point to the right; look for the big angelfish and large schools of purple triggerfish. Afternoons on Cinnamon Bay can be windy—a boon for windsurfers but an annoyance for sunbathers—so arrive early to beat the gusts. The Cinnamon Bay hiking trail begins across the road from the beach parking lot; ruins mark the trailhead. There are actually two paths here: a level nature trail (signs along it identify the flora) that loops through the woods and passes an old Danish cemetery, and a steep trail that starts where the road bends past the ruins and heads straight up to Route 10. Restrooms are on the main path from the commissary to the beach and scattered around the campground. **Amenities:** food and drink; parking; showers; toilets; water sports. **Best for:** snorkeling; swimming; walking; windsurfing. ✉ *North Shore Rd., Rte. 20, about 4 miles (6 km) east of Cruz Bay, Cinnamon Bay* 🌐 *www.nps.gov/viis.*

Francis Bay Beach. Because there's little shade, this beach gets toasty warm in the afternoon when the sun comes around to the west, but the rest of the day it's a delightful stretch of white sand. The only facilities are a few picnic tables tucked among the trees and a portable restroom, but folks come here to watch the birds that live in the swampy area behind the beach. The park offers bird-watching hikes here on Friday morning; sign up at the visitor center in Cruz Bay. To get here, turn left at the Annaberg intersection. **Amenities:** parking; toilets. **Best for:** snorkeling; swimming; walking. ✉ *North Shore Rd., Rte. 20, ¼ mile (½ km) from Annaberg intersection, Francis Bay* 🌐 *www.nps.gov/viis.*

Hawksnest Beach. Sea grapes and waving palm trees line this narrow beach, and there are restrooms, cooking grills, and a covered shed for picnicking. A patchy reef just offshore means snorkeling is an easy swim away, but the best underwater views are reserved for ambitious

CLOSE UP

St. John Archaeology

Archaeologists continue to unravel St. John's past through excavations at Trunk Bay and Cinnamon Bay, both prime tourist destinations within Virgin Islands National Park.

Work began back in the early 1990s, when the park wanted to build new bathhouses at the popular Trunk Bay. In preparation for that project, the archaeologists began to dig, turning up artifacts and the remains of structures that date to AD 900. The site was once a village occupied by the Taíno, a group that lived in the area until AD 1500. A similar but slightly more recent village was discovered at Cinnamon Bay.

By the time the Taíno got to Cinnamon Bay, roughly a century later, their society had developed to include chiefs, commoners, workers, and slaves. The location of the national park's busy Cinnamon Bay campground was once a Taíno temple that belonged to a king or chief. When archaeologists began digging in 1998, they uncovered several dozen *zemis*, which are small clay gods used in ceremonial activities, as well as beads, pots, and many other artifacts.

Near the end of the Cinnamon Bay dig archaeologists turned up another less ancient but still surprising discovery. A burned layer indicated that a plantation slave village had also stood near Cinnamon Bay campground; it was torched during the 1733 revolt because its slave inhabitants had been loyal to the planters. Since the 1970s, bones from slaves buried in the area have been uncovered at the water's edge by beach erosion.

snorkelers who head farther to the east along the bay's fringes. Watch out for boat traffic—a channel guides dinghies to the beach, but the occasional boater strays into the swim area. It's the closest drivable beach to Cruz Bay, so it's often crowded with locals and visitors. **Amenities:** parking; toilets. **Best for:** snorkeling; swimming. ✉ *North Shore Rd., Rte. 20, about 2 miles (3 km) east of Cruz Bay, Hawksnest Bay* 🌐 *www.nps.gov/viis.*

Maho Bay Beach. Maho Bay Beach is a gorgeous strip of sand that sits right along the North Shore Road. It's a popular place, particularly on weekends, when locals come out in droves to party at the picnic tables at the south end of the beach. Snorkeling along the rocky edges is good, but the center is mostly sea grass. If you're lucky, you'll cross paths with turtles. **Amenities:** parking; toilets. **Best for:** snorkeling; swimming. ✉ *North Shore Rd., Rte. 20, Maho Bay* 🌐 *www.nps.gov/viis.*

Fodor's Choice ★ **Trunk Bay Beach.** St. John's most-photographed beach is also the preferred spot for beginning snorkelers because of its underwater trail. (Cruise-ship passengers interested in snorkeling for a day flock here, so if you're looking for seclusion, arrive early or later in the day.) Crowded or not, this stunning beach is one of the island's most beautiful. There are changing rooms with showers, bathrooms, a snack bar, picnic tables, a gift shop, phones, lockers, and snorkeling-equipment rentals. The parking lot often overflows, but you can park along the road as long as the tires are off the pavement. **Amenities:** food and drink; lifeguards;

parking; toilets; water sports. **Best for:** snorkeling; swimming; windsurfing. ✉ *North Shore Rd., Rte. 20, about 2½ miles (4 km) east of Cruz Bay, Trunk Bay* 🌐 *www.nps.gov/viis* 🎫 *$4.*

CORAL BAY AND ENVIRONS

Lameshur Bay Beach. This sea grape–fringed beach is toward the end of a partially paved road on the southeast coast. The reward for your long drive is good snorkeling and a chance to spy on some pelicans. The beach has a couple of picnic tables, rusting barbecue grills, and a portable restroom. The ruins of the old plantation are a five-minute walk down the road past the beach. The area has good hiking trails, including a trek (more than a mile) up Bordeaux Mountain before an easy walk to Yawzi Point. **Amenities:** parking; toilets. **Best for:** snorkeling; swimming; walking. ✉ *Off Rte. 107, about 1½ mile (2½ km) from Salt Pond, Lameshur Bay* 🌐 *www.nps.gov/viis.*

Salt Pond Bay Beach. If you're adventurous, this rocky beach on the scenic southeastern coast—next to rugged Drunk Bay—is worth exploring. It's a short hike down a hill from the parking lot, and the only facilities are an outhouse and a few picnic tables scattered about. Tide pools are filled with all sorts of marine creatures, and the snorkeling is good, particularly along the bay's edges. A short walk takes you to a pond where salt crystals collect around the edges. Hike farther uphill past cactus gardens to Ram Head for see-forever views. Leave nothing valuable in your car, as thefts are common. **Amenities:** parking; toilets. **Best for:** snorkeling; swimming; walking. ✉ *Rte. 107, about 3 miles (5 km) south of Coral Bay, Salt Pond Bay* 🌐 *www.nps.gov/viis.*

WHERE TO EAT

The cuisine on St. John seems to get better every year, with chefs vying to see who can come up with the most imaginative dishes, whether you're at one of the elegant establishments at Caneel Bay Resort (where men may be required to wear a jacket at dinner) or a casual joint near Cruz Bay. For quick lunches, try the West Indian food stands in Cruz Bay Park and across from the post office. The cooks prepare fried chicken legs, pâtés (meat- and fish-filled pastries), and callaloo.

Some restaurants close for vacation in September and even October. If you have your heart set on a special place, call ahead to make sure it's open during these months.

CRUZ BAY AND ENVIRONS

$$$$ ASIAN ✕ **Asolare.** Contemporary Asian cuisine dominates the menu at this elegant open-air eatery in an old St. John house. Come early and relax over drinks while you enjoy the sunset lighting up the harbor. Start with the sesame-crusted goat cheese salad, then move on to entrées such as applewood-smoked tenderloin with wasabi, or pan-roasted cod with a red curry sauce. If you still have room for dessert, try the mimosa-poached pears with honey. 💲 *Average main: $36* ✉ *Rte. 20 on Caneel Hill, Estate Lindholm* ☎ *340/779–4747* 🌐 *www.asolarestjohn.com* ⏲ *No lunch.*

$$$ ITALIAN FAMILY ✕ **Café Roma.** This second-floor restaurant in the heart of Cruz Bay is *the* place for traditional Italian cuisine: lasagna, spaghetti and meatballs, and seafood manicotti. Small pizzas are available at the table, but larger ones are for takeout or at the bar. Tiramisu is a dessert specialty. This casual place can get crowded in winter, so show up early. *Average main: $27 ✉ Vesta Gade ☎ 340/776–6524 ⊕ www.stjohn-caferoma.com ⊙ No lunch.*

$$$$ AMERICAN FAMILY ✕ **Fish Trap Restaurant and Seafood Market.** The main dining room here is open to the breezes and buzzes with a mix of locals and visitors, but the back room has air-conditioning. Start with a tasty appetizer such as conch fritters or fish chowder (a creamy combination of snapper, white wine, paprika, and spices). You can always find steak and chicken dishes, as well as the interesting fish of the day. *Average main: $33 ✉ Bay and Strand Sts., next to Our Lady of Mount Carmel Church ☎ 340/693–9994 ⊕ www.thefishtrap.com ⊙ Closed Mon. No lunch.*

$$$ ECLECTIC ✕ **Lime Inn.** The vacationers and mainland transplants who call St. John home like to flock to this alfresco spot for the congenial hospitality and good food, including all-you-can-eat shrimp on Wednesday night. Fresh lobster is the specialty, and the menu also includes shrimp-and-steak dishes and rotating chicken and pasta specials. *Average main: $30 ✉ Lemon Tree Mall, King St. ☎ 340/776–6425 ⊕ www.limeinn.com ⊙ No lunch Sat. Closed Sun.*

$ DELI Fodor's Choice ★ ✕ **Sam and Jack's Deli.** The sandwiches are scrumptious, but this deli also dishes up wonderful to-go meals that just need heating. If the truffle–wild mushroom ravioli is on the menu, don't hesitate to order it—it's a winner. There are a few seats inside, but most folks opt to eat at the tables in front of the deli. *Average main: $12 ✉ Marketplace Shopping Center, Rte. 104 ☎ 340/714–3354 ⊕ www.samandjacksdeli.com ⊙ Closed Sun. No dinner.*

27

NORTH SHORE

$$ ECLECTIC Fodor's Choice ★ ✕ **Sun Dog Café.** There's an unusual assortment of dishes at this charming alfresco restaurant, which you'll find tucked into a courtyard in the upper reaches of the Mongoose Junction shopping center. Kudos to the white pizza with artichoke hearts, roasted garlic, mozzarella cheese, and capers. The Jamaican jerk chicken salad and the black-bean quesadilla are also good choices. *Average main: $19 ✉ Mongoose Junction Shopping Center, North Shore Rd. ☎ 340/693–8340 ⊕ www.sundogcafe.com ⊙ No dinner Sun.*

$$$$ ITALIAN Fodor's Choice ★ ✕ **Zozo's at the Sugar Mill.** Creative takes on old standards coupled with lovely presentations draw crowds to this restaurant at Caneel Bay Resort. Start with crispy fried calamari served with a pesto mayonnaise. The chef dresses up roasted mahimahi with a pistachio crust and serves it with grilled polenta and a sweet pepper chutney. The slow-simmered osso buco comes with prosciutto-wrapped asparagus and saffron risotto. The sunset views will take your breath away. *Average main: $43 ✉ Caneel Bay Resort, Rte. 20, Caneel Bay ☎ 340/693–9200 ⊕ www.zozos.net ⊙ No lunch.*

MID ISLAND

$$ ECLECTIC **Chateau Bordeaux.** Your hamburgers and sweet potato fries come with a side of fabulous views of Coral Bay and the British Virgin Islands. Located at the popular Bordeaux overlook, this restaurant also serves salads made with local greens, and fish sandwiches. The adjacent ice-cream shop blends up some delicious fruit smoothies, and you can stop by for breakfast, too. *Average main: $18 Rte. 10, Bordeaux 340/776–6611 www.chateaubordeaux.net No dinner Fri.–Mon.*

CORAL BAY AND ENVIRONS

$$$ CARIBBEAN **Miss Lucy's Restaurant.** Sitting seaside at remote Friis Bay, Miss Lucy's dishes up Caribbean food with a contemporary flair. Dishes such as tender conch fritters, a spicy West Indian stew called *callaloo*, and fried fish make up most of the menu, but you also find a generous paella filled with seafood, sausage, and chicken on the menu. Sunday brunches are legendary, and if you're around when the moon is full, stop by for the monthly full-moon party. The handful of small tables near the water is the nicest, but if they're taken or the mosquitoes are swarming, the indoor tables do nicely. *Average main: $25 Rte. 107, Friis Bay 340/693–5244 Closed Mon. No dinner Sun.*

$$$ AMERICAN **Shipwreck Landing.** A favorite with locals and visitors, this alfresco restaurant serves up tasty food in a casual setting. Opt for the tables closest to the road for the best breezes and water views. The menu includes lots of seafood, but the chicken and beef dishes ensure that everyone's satisfied. If it's a day when the chef has prepared homemade soup, try at least a cup. For lunch, the grilled mahimahi sandwich is always a good bet. *Average main: $22 Rte. 107, Freeman's Ground 340/693–5640 www.shipwrecklandingstjohn.com.*

$ AMERICAN **Skinny Legs Bar and Restaurant.** Sailors who live aboard boats anchored offshore and an eclectic coterie of residents and visitors gather for lunch and dinner at this funky spot in the middle of a boatyard and shopping complex. It's a great place for burgers, fish sandwiches, and whatever sports are on the satellite TV. *Average main: $11 Rte. 10 340/779–4982 www.skinnylegs.com.*

$$$ CARIBBEAN FAMILY **Sweet Plaintains.** The food here is a sophisticated take on Caribbean cuisine. The fish of the day—it could be mahimahi or swordfish—is always especially good. Or try one of the curries if you don't want seafood. For a real local taste, start with the saltfish cakes served with shredded cabbage and mango purée. The coconut flan for dessert is another Caribbean favorite. *Average main: $26 Rte. 107 340/777–4653 www.sweetplantains-stjohn.com Closed Sun. and Tues. No lunch.*

$ CARIBBEAN **Vie's Snack Shack.** Stop by Vie's when you're out exploring the island. Although it's just a shack by the side of the road, Vie's serves up some great cooking. The garlic chicken legs are crisp and tasty, and the conch fritters are really something to write home about. Plump and filled with fresh herbs, a plateful will keep you going for the rest of the afternoon. Save room for a wedge of coconut pie—called a tart in this neck of the woods. *Average main: $12 Rte. 10, Hansen Bay 340/693–5033 www.hansenbaycampground.com No credit cards Closed Sun. and Mon. No dinner.*

WHERE TO STAY

St. John doesn't have many beachfront hotels, but that's a small price to pay for all the pristine sand. However, the island's two excellent resorts—Caneel Bay Resort and the Westin St. John Resort & Villas—*are* on the beach. Sandy, white beaches string out along the north coast, which is popular with sunbathers and snorkelers and is where you can find the Caneel Bay Resort and Cinnamon and Maho Bay campgrounds. Most villas are in the residential south-shore area, a 15-minute drive from the north-shore beaches. If you head east, you come to the laid-back community of Coral Bay, where there are growing numbers of villas and cottages. Bands sometimes play at a couple of Coral Bay's nightspots, so if you're renting a villa in the hills above the village, you may hear music later than you'd like. A stay outside Coral Bay will be peaceful and quiet.

If you're looking for West Indian village charm, there are a few inns in Cruz Bay. Keep in mind that when bands play at any of the town's bars (some of which stay open until the wee hours), the noise can be a problem. Your choice of accommodations also includes condominiums and cottages near town; two campgrounds, one at the edge of a beautiful beach (bring bug repellent); ecoresorts; and luxurious villas, often with a pool or a hot tub (sometimes both) and a stunning view.

If your lodging comes with a fully equipped kitchen, you'll be happy to know that St. John's handful of grocery stores sell everything you're likely to need—though the prices will take your breath away. If you're on a budget, consider bringing some staples (pasta, canned goods, paper products) from home. Hotel rates throughout the island are fairly expensive, but they do include endless privacy and access to most water sports.

Many of the island's condos are just minutes from the hustle and bustle of Cruz Bay, but you can find more scattered around the island. St. John also has a handful of camping spots ranging from the basic Cinnamon Bay Campground to the more comfortable Maho Bay Camps. They appeal to those who don't mind bringing their own beach towels from home or busing their own tables at dinner. If you want your piña colada delivered beachside by a smiling waiter, you'd be better off elsewhere—and ready to pay for the privilege.

PRIVATE CONDOS AND VILLAS

Here and there between Cruz Bay and Coral Bay are about 500 private villas and condos (prices range from $ to $$$$). With pools or hot tubs, full kitchens, and living areas, these lodgings provide a fully functional home away from home. They're perfect for couples and extended groups of family or friends. You need a car, since most lodgings are in the hills and very few are at the beach. Villa managers usually pick you up at the dock, arrange for your rental car, and answer questions on arrival as well as during your stay. Prices drop in the summer season, which is generally after April 15. Some companies begin off-season pricing a week or two later, so be sure to ask.

If you want to be close to Cruz Bay's restaurants and boutiques, a villa in the Chocolate Hole and Great Cruz Bay areas will put you a few minutes away. The Coral Bay area has a growing number of villas, but you'll be about 20 minutes from Cruz Bay. Beaches lie out along the North Shore, so you won't be more than 15 minutes from the water no matter where you stay.

RENTAL CONTACTS

Carefree Get-Aways. This company manages vacation villas on the island's southern and western edges. ☎ *340/779–4070, 888/643–6002* 🌐 *www.carefreegetaways.com.*

Caribbean Villas & Resorts. Caribbean Villas handles condo rentals for Cruz Views and Gallow's Point Resort, as well as for many private villas. ☎ *340/776–6152, 800/338–0987* 🌐 *www.caribbeanvilla.com.*

Caribe Havens. Specializing in the budget market, Caribe Havens has properties scattered around the island. ✉ *Box 455, Cruz Bay* ☎ *340/776–6518* 🌐 *www.caribehavens.com.*

Catered to Vacation Homes. Specializing in luxury villas, this company has listings mainly in the middle of the island and on the western edge. ✉ *Marketplace Suite 206, 5206 Enighed, Cruz Bay* ☎ *340/776–6641, 800/424–6641* 🌐 *www.cateredto.com.*

Cloud 9 Villas. Most of the offerings are in the East End, Gifft Hill, and Chocolate Hole areas. ☎ *340/774–9633* 🌐 *www.cloud9villas.com.*

Island Getaways. Options from Island Getaways are mainly villas in the Rendezvous, Chocolate Hole, and Coral Bay areas. ☎ *340/693–7676, 888/693–7676* 🌐 *www.islandgetawaysinc.com.*

On-Line Vacations. On-Line Vacations books villas for most management companies and is based on St. John. ☎ *340/776–6036, 888/842–6632* 🌐 *www.onlinevacations.com.*

Private Homes for Private Vacations. This company handles villa rentals across the island. ✉ *7605 Mamey Peak Rd., Coral Bay* ☎ *340/776–6876* 🌐 *www.privatehomesvi.com.*

Seaview Vacation Homes. As the name implies, this company's specialty are houses with views of the ocean: they are in the Chocolate Hole, Great Cruz Bay, and Fish Bay areas. ☎ *340/776–6805, 888/625–2963* 🌐 *www.seaviewhomes.com.*

Star Villas. Star has cozy villas just outside Cruz Bay. ☎ *340/776–6704* 🌐 *www.starvillas.com.*

St. John Properties. This firm handles villas mainly in the Cruz Bay area but has a couple mid-island properties as well. ✉ *Cruz Bay* ☎ *800/283–1746, 340/693–8485* 🌐 *www.stjohnproperties.com.*

St. John Ultimate Villas ☎ *340/776–4703, 888/851–7588* 🌐 *www.stjohnultimatevillas.com.*

Vacation Vistas. This company's villas are mainly in the Chocolate Hole, Great Cruz Bay, and Rendezvous areas. ☎ *340/776–6462* 🌐 *www.vacationvistas.com.*

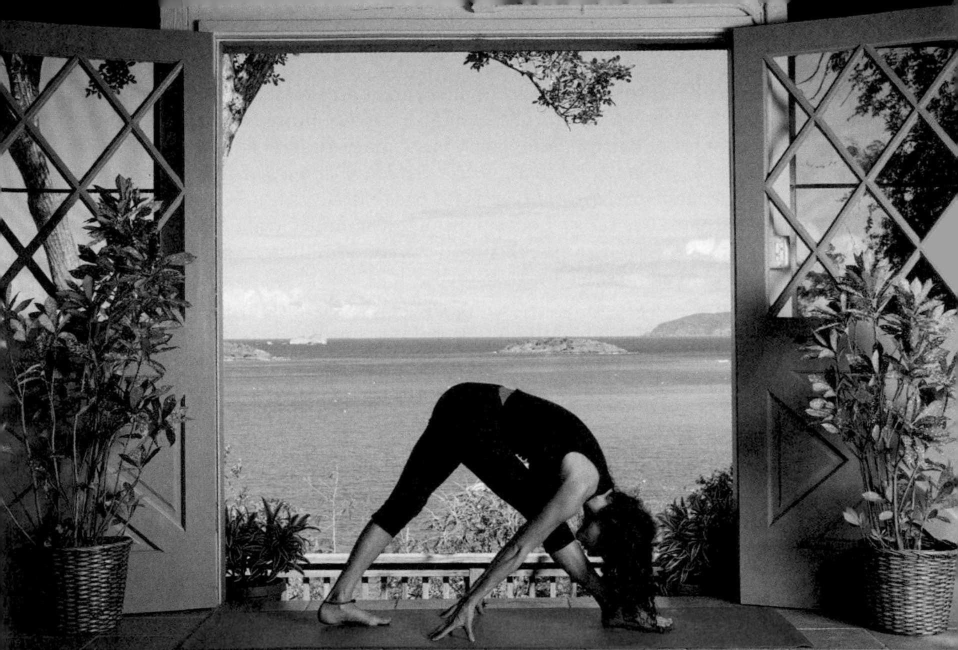

Caneel Bay Resort

Windspree. Windspree's stock is mainly in and around Coral Bay. ✉ *7924 Emmaus, Coral Bay* ☎ *340/693–5423, 888/742–0357* 🌐 *www.windspree.com.*

CRUZ BAY AND ENVIRONS

$$ RENTAL **Coconut Coast Villas.** This small condominium complex with studio, two-, and three-bedroom apartments is a 10-minute walk from Cruz Bay, but is insulated from the town's noise in a sleepy suburban neighborhood. **Pros:** good snorkeling; full kitchens; walk to Cruz Bay. **Cons:** small beach; some uphill walks; nearby utility plant can be noisy. *$ Rooms from: $289* ✉ *Near pond, Turner Bay* ☎ *340/693–9100, 800/858–7989* 🌐 *www.coconutcoast.com* *9 units* *No meals.*

$$ B&B/INN **Estate Lindholm Bed and Breakfast.** Built among old stone ruins on a lushly planted hill overlooking Cruz Bay, Estate Lindholm has an enchanting setting. **Pros:** lush landscaping; gracious host; pleasant decor. **Cons:** can be noisy; some uphill walks; on a busy road. *$ Rooms from: $365* ✉ *Rte. 20, at Caneel Hill, Cruz Bay* ☎ *340/776–6121, 800/322–6335* 🌐 *www.estatelindholm.com* *14 rooms* *Breakfast.*

$$$$ RENTAL **Gallows Point Resort.** You're a short walk from restaurants and shops at this waterfront location just outside Cruz Bay, but once you step into your condo, the hustle and bustle are left behind. **Pros:** walk to shopping; excellent restaurant; comfortably furnished rooms. **Cons:** some rooms can be noisy; mediocre beach; insufficient parking. *$ Rooms from: $495* ✉ *Bay St., Cruz Bay* ☎ *340/776–6434, 800/323–7229* 🌐 *www.gallowspointresort.com* *60 units* *No meals.*

$ B&B/INN **Garden by the Sea Bed and Breakfast.** Located in a middle-class residential neighborhood, this cozy bed-and-breakfast is an easy walk from

Cruz Bay. **Pros:** homey atmosphere; great breakfasts; breathtaking view from deck; near a bird-filled salt pond. **Cons:** noise from nearby power substation; some uphill walks; basic amenities. *Rooms from: $250 Near pond, Enighed 340/779–4731 www.gardenbythesea.com 3 rooms No credit cards Breakfast.*

$$$ RENTAL **Grande Bay Resort.** Located just a few minutes' walk from Cruz Bay's restaurants and shops, this modern condominium complex puts you close to the town's hustle and bustle. **Pros:** close to restaurants and shops; modern decor; walking distance to the ferry. **Cons:** need car or taxi to reach island attractions and the best beaches; beach across the street is minimal. *Rooms from: $405 Bay St., Cruz Bay 340/693–4668 www.grandebayresortusvi.com 64 condos Breakfast.*

$$$$ RENTAL **Sea Shore Allure.** Located at the water's edge in a residential neighborhood, Sea Shore Allure combines attractive and modern decor with an easy, and safe, walk to Cruz Bay's restaurants and shops. **Pros:** lovely decor; waterfront location; close to town. **Cons:** need car or taxi to get to beach; road passes through modest but safe local neighborhood. *Rooms from: $510 Pond Mouth Rd., Turner Bay 340/779–2880, 855/779–2880 www.seashoreallure.com 8 units No meals.*

$ RENTAL **Serendip.** This complex offers modern apartments on lush grounds with lovely views and makes a great pick for a budget stay in a residential locale. **Pros:** comfortable accommodations; good views; nice neighborhood. **Cons:** no beach; need car to get around; nearby construction. *Rooms from: $240 off Rte. 104, Enighed 340/776–6646, 888/800–6445 www.serendipstjohn.com 10 apartments No meals.*

$ B&B/INN **St. John Inn.** A stay here gives you a bit of style at what passes for budget prices in St. John. **Pros:** walk to restaurants and shops; convivial atmosphere; pretty pool. **Cons:** need a car to get around; noisy location; insufficient parking. *Rooms from: $200 off Rte. 104, Cruz Bay 340/693–8688, 800/666–7688 www.stjohninn.com 11 units Breakfast.*

$$$$ RESORT FAMILY **Westin St. John Resort and Villas.** The island's largest resort provides a nice beachfront location and enough activities to keep you busy. **Pros:** entertaining children's programs; pretty pool area; many activities. **Cons:** mediocre beach; long walk to some parts of the resort; need car to get around. *Rooms from: $729 Rte. 104, Great Cruz Bay 340/693–8000, 888/627–7206 www.westinresortstjohn.com 96 rooms, 200 villas No meals.*

NORTH SHORE

$$$ RESORT Fodor's Choice ★ **Caneel Bay Resort.** If you dream of spending your days on gorgeous beaches, paddling kayaks to and fro, and enjoying langorous dinners with your feet in the sand, there's no finer laidback-luxury resort on St. John. **Pros:** seven lovely beaches; gorgeous rooms; lots of amenities. **Cons:** staff can be chilly; isolated location; pricey; no TVs or phones (just a warning for tech-junkies). *Rooms from: $459 Rte. 20, Caneel Bay 340/776–6111, 855/226–3358 www.caneelbay.com 166 rooms Breakfast.*

Yoga is a morning ritual at Concordia Eco-Resort.

CORAL BAY AND ENVIRONS

$ RENTAL Fodor's Choice ★ **Concordia Eco-Resort.** This off-the-beaten-path resort is on the remote Salt Pond peninsula. **Pros:** good views; eco-friendly environment; beach nearby. **Cons:** need car to get around; lots of stairs. *Rooms from: $195* ✉ *Off Rte. 107, Concordia* ☎ *340/693–5855, 800/392–9004* 🌐 *www.concordiaeco-resort.com* *9 condos, 8 studios, 25 tents* *No meals.*

$$ RENTAL **Estate Zootenvaal.** Comfortable and casual, this small cottage colony gives you the perfect place to relax. **Pros:** quiet beach; private; near restaurants. **Cons:** some traffic noise; no air-conditioning in some units. *Rooms from: $290* ✉ *Rte. 10, Hurricane Hole, Zootenvaal* ☎ *340/776–6321* 🌐 *www.estatezootenvaal.com* *4 units* *No meals.*

NIGHTLIFE

St. John isn't the place to go for glitter and all-night partying. Still, after-hours Cruz Bay can be a lively little town in which to dine, drink, dance, chat, or flirt. Notices posted on the bulletin board outside the Connections telephone center—up the street from the ferry dock in Cruz Bay—or listings in *Tradewinds* (🌐 *www.stjohntradewindsnews.com*) will keep you apprised of special events, comedy nights, movies, and the like.

CRUZ BAY

Motu Bar. Drinks made with freshly squeezed juices, frequent theme parties, and stellar views of Cruz Bay create a comfortable ambience for happy hour and beyond. ✉ *1 Bay St., Cruz Bay* ☎ *407/758–6924* 🌐 *www.motubar.com.*

Tap Room. A rotating selection of distinctive brews makes the Tap Room popular with locals and visitors. ✉ *Mongoose Junction Shopping Center, Mongoose Junction, Cruz Bay* ☎ *340/715–7775* 🌐 *www.stjohnbrewers.com.*

Woody's. Folks like to gather here, where the sidewalk tables provide a close-up view of Cruz Bay action. ✉ *Near First Bank, Cruz Bay* ☎ *340/779–4625* 🌐 *www.woodysseafood.com.*

CORAL BAY AND ENVIRONS

Shipwreck Landing. Live rock, bluegrass, and more are on tap several nights a week at this restaurant. ✉ *Rte. 107, Freemans Ground, Coral Bay* ☎ *340/693–5640.*

Skinny Legs Bar and Restaurant. Landlubbers and old salts listen to music and swap stories at this popular casual restaurant and bar on the far side of the island. ✉ *Rte. 10, Coral Bay* ☎ *340/779–4982* 🌐 *www.skinnylegs.com.*

FREE PARKING

Cruz Bay's parking problem is maddening. Your best bet is to rent a car from a company that allows you to park in its lot. Make sure you ask before you sign on the dotted line if you plan to spend time in Cruz Bay.

SHOPPING

CRUZ BAY

Luxury goods and handicrafts can be found on St. John. Most shops carry a little of this and a bit of that, so it pays to poke around. The Cruz Bay shopping district runs from **Wharfside Village,** just around the corner from the ferry dock, to **Mongoose Junction,** an inviting shopping center on North Shore Road. (The name of this upscale shopping mall, by the way, is a holdover from a time when those furry island creatures gathered at a nearby garbage bin.) Out on Route 104, stop in at the **Marketplace** to explore its gift and crafts shops. On St. John, store hours run from 9 or 10 to 5 or 6. Wharfside Village and Mongoose Junction shops in Cruz Bay are often open into the evening.

ART

Fodor'sChoice ★ **Bajo el Sol.** This gallery sells works by owner Livy Hitchcock, plus pieces from a roster of the island's best artists. You can also shop for oils, pastels, watercolors, and turned wood pieces. ✉ *Mongoose Junction Shopping Center, North Shore Rd., Cruz Bay* ☎ *340/693–7070* 🌐 *www.bajoelsolgallery.com.*

Caravan Gallery. Caravan sells affordable jewelry, unique gifts, and artifacts that its owner, Radha Speer, has traveled the world to find. The more you look, the more you see—Caribbean larimar jewelry, unusual sterling pieces, and tribal art cover the walls and tables, making this a great place to browse. ✉ *Mongoose Junction Shopping Center, North Shore Rd., Cruz Bay* ☎ *340/779–4566* 🌐 *www.caravangallery.com.*

Coconut Coast Studios. This waterside shop, a five-minute walk from the center of Cruz Bay, showcases the work of Elaine Estern. She specializes in undersea scenes. ✉ *Frank Bay, Cruz Bay* ☎ *340/776–6944* 🌐 *www.coconutcoaststudios.com.*

BOOKS

National Park Headquarters Bookstore. The bookshop at Virgin Islands National Park Headquarters sells several good histories of St. John, including *St. John Backtime: Eyewitness Accounts from 1718 to 1956*, by Ruth Hull Low and Rafael Lito Valls, and, for intrepid explorers, longtime resident Pam Gaffin's *St. John Feet, Fins and Four-Wheel Drive*, a "complete guide to all of the islands beachs, trails, and roads." ✉ *Rte. 20, Cruz Bay* ☎ *340/776–6201* 🌐 *www.nps.gov/viis.*

CLOTHING

Big Planet Adventure Outfitters. You knew when you arrived that someplace on St. John would cater to the outdoor enthusiasts who hike up and down the island's trails. This store sells flip-flops and Reef footwear, along with colorful and durable cotton clothing and accessories by Billabong. The store also sells children's clothes. ✉ *Mongoose Junction Shopping Center, North Shore Rd., Cruz Bay* ☎ *340/776–6638* 🌐 *www.big-planet.com.*

Bougainvillea Boutique. This store is your destination if you want to look as if you've stepped out of the pages of the resort-wear spread in an upscale travel magazine. Owner Susan Stair carries very chic men's and women's clothes, straw hats, leather handbags, and fine gifts. ✉ *Mongoose Junction Shopping Center, North Shore Rd., Cruz Bay* ☎ *340/693–7190* 🌐 *www.shoppingstjohn.com.*

FOOD

If you're renting a villa, condo, or cottage and doing your own cooking, there are several good places to shop for food; just be aware that prices are much higher than those at home.

Starfish Market. The island's largest store usually has the best selection of meat, fish, and produce. ✉ *The Marketplace, Rte. 104, Cruz Bay* ☎ *340/779–4949* 🌐 *www.starfishmarket.com.*

GIFTS

Bamboula. This multicultural boutique carries unusual housewares, rugs, bedspreads, accessories, and men's and women's clothes and shoes that owner Jo Sterling has found on her world travels. ✉ *Mongoose Junction Shopping Center, North Shore Rd., Cruz Bay* ☎ *340/693–8699* 🌐 *www.bamboulastjohn.com.*

Best of Both Worlds. Pricey metal sculptures and attractive artworks hang from the walls of this gallery; the nicest are small glass decorations shaped like mermaids and sea horses. ✉ *Mongoose Junction Shopping Center, North Shore Rd., Cruz Bay* ☎ *340/693–7005* 🌐 *www.thebestofstjohn.com.*

Donald Schnell Studio. You'll find distinctive clay pieces, unusual handblown glass, wind chimes, kaleidoscopes, fanciful fountains, and pottery bowls here. Your purchases can be shipped worldwide. ✉ *Amore Center, Rte. 104, near roundabout, Cruz Bay* ☎ *340/776–6420* 🌐 *donaldschnell.com/studio.*

Fabric Mill. There's a good selection of women's clothing in tropical brights, as well as lingerie, sandals, and batik wraps here. Or take home several yards of colorful batik fabric to make your own dress.

✉ *Mongoose Junction Shopping Center, North Shore Rd., Cruz Bay* ☎ *340/776–6194* 🌐 *www.fabricmillstj.com.*

Gallows Point Gift and Gourmet. The store at Gallows Point Resort has a bit of this and a bit of that. Shop for Caribbean books and CDs, picture frames decorated with shells, and T-shirts with tropical motifs. Residents and visitors also drop by for a cup of coffee. ✉ *Gallows Point Resort, Bay St., Cruz Bay* ☎ *340/693–7730* 🌐 *www.stjohnadventures.com.*

Nest and Company. This small shop carries perfect take-home gifts in colors that reflect the sea. Shop here for soaps in tropical scents, dinnerware, and much more. ✉ *Mongoose Junction Shopping Center, North Shore Rd., Cruz Bay* ☎ *340/715–2552* 🌐 *www.nestvi.com.*

Pink Papaya. Head to this shop and art gallery for the work of longtime Virgin Islands resident Lisa Etre. There's also huge collection of one-of-a-kind gifts, including bright tableware, trays, and tropical jewelry. ✉ *Lemon Tree Mall, King St., Cruz Bay* ☎ *340/693–8535* 🌐 *www.pinkpapaya.com.*

JEWELRY

Free Bird Creations. This is your on-island destination for special handcrafted jewelry—earrings, bracelets, pendants, chains—as well as a good selection of water-resistant watches. ✉ *Dockside Mall, next to ferry dock, Cruz Bay* ☎ *340/693–8625* 🌐 *www.freebirdcreations.com.*

Little Switzerland. A branch of the St. Thomas store, Little Switzerland carries diamonds and other jewels in attractive yellow- and white-gold settings, as well as strings of creamy pearls, watches, and other designer jewelry. ✉ *Mongoose Junction Shopping Center, North Shore Rd., Cruz Bay* ☎ *340/776–6007* 🌐 *www.littleswitzerland.com.*

R&I Patton goldsmithing. This store is owned by Rudy and Irene Patton, who design most of the lovely silver and gold jewelry on display. The rest comes from various designer friends. Sea fans (those large, lacy plants that sway with the ocean's currents) in filigreed silver, starfish and hibiscus pendants in silver or gold, and gold sand-dollar-shape charms and earrings are choice selections. ✉ *Mongoose Junction Shopping Center, North Shore Rd., Cruz Bay* ☎ *340/776–6548* 🌐 *www.pattongold.com.*

St. Johnimals. Pampered pets are the ultimate consumers for the goods in this cozy store. The shelves are stocked with carriers made of buttery soft leather, leashes and collars made with crystals, hand-painted pet bowls, and toys of all sorts. ✉ *Wharfside Village shopping center, Cruz Bay* ☎ *340/777–9588* 🌐 *www.stjohnimals.com.*

Verace. This store is filled with jewelry from such well-known designers as Toby Pomeroy and Patrick Murphy. Murphy's stunning gold sailboats with gems for hulls will catch your eye. ✉ *Wharfside Village, Strand St., Cruz Bay* ☎ *340/693–7599* 🌐 *www.verace.com.*

CORAL BAY AND ENVIRONS

CLOTHING

Jolly Dog. Head here for the stuff you forgot to pack. Sarongs in cotton and rayon, beach towels with tropical motifs, and hats and T-shirts sporting the "Jolly Dog" logo fill the shelves. ✉ *Skinny Legs Shopping Complex, Rte. 10, Coral Bay* ☎ *340/693–5900.*

Sloop Jones. This store's worth the trip all the way out to the island's East End to shop for made-on-the-premises clothing and pillows, in fabrics splashed with tropical colors. The clothes are made from cotton, gauze, and modal, and are supremely comfortable. Sloop also holds painting workshops. ✉ *Off Rte. 10, East End* ☎ *340/779–4001* 🌐 *www.sloopjones.com.*

FOOD

Love City Mini Mart. The store may not look like much from the road, but it's one of the very few places to shop in Coral Bay and has a surprising selection. ✉ *Off Rte. 107, Coral Bay* ☎ *340/693–5790.*

GIFTS

Mumbo Jumbo. With what may be the best prices in St. John, Mumbo Jumbo carries tropical clothing, stuffed sea creatures, and other gifty items in a cozy little shop. ✉ *Skinny Legs Shopping Complex, Rte. 10, Coral Bay* ☎ *340/779–4277.*

SPORTS AND THE OUTDOORS

BOATING AND SAILING

If you're staying at a hotel or campground, your activities desk will usually be able to help you arrange a sailing excursion aboard a nearby boat. Most day sails leaving Cruz Bay head out along St. John's north coast. Those that depart from Coral Bay might drop anchor at some remote cay off the island's East End or even in the nearby British Virgin Islands. Your trip usually includes lunch, beverages, and at least one snorkeling stop. Keep in mind that inclement weather could interfere with your plans, though most boats will still go out if rain isn't too heavy.

Ocean Runner. For a speedier trip to the cays and remote beaches off St. John, you can rent a powerboat with a captain from Ocean Runner. The company rents two-engine boats for $580 to $710 per day. Gas and oil will run you $100 to $300 a day extra, depending on how far you're going. ✉ *Wharfside Village, waterfront, Cruz Bay* ☎ *340/693–8809* 🌐 *www.oceanrunnerusvi.com.*

Sail Safaris. Even novice sailors can take off in a small sailboat from Cruz Bay Beach to one of the small islands off St. John with Sail Safaris. ✉ *Bay St., Cruz Bay* ☎ *340/626–8181* 🌐 *www.sailsafaris.net* 💵 *From $80.*

St. John Concierge Service. The capable staff can find a charter sail or powerboat that fits your style and budget. The company also books fishing and scuba trips. ✉ *Henry Samuel St., across from post office, Cruz Bay* ☎ *340/514–5262* 🌐 *www.stjohnconciergeservice.com.*

DIVING AND SNORKELING

Although just about every beach has nice snorkeling—Trunk Bay, Cinnamon Bay, and Waterlemon Cay at Leinster Bay get the most praise—you need a boat to head out to the more remote snorkeling locations and the best scuba spots. Sign on with any of the island's water-sports operators to get to spots farther from St. John. If you use the one at your hotel, just stroll down to the dock to hop aboard. Their boats will take you to hot spots between St. John and St. Thomas, including the tunnels at **Thatch Cay,** the ledges at **Congo Cay,** and the wreck of the *General Rogers*. Dive off St. John at **Stephens Cay,** a short boat ride out of Cruz Bay, where fish swim around the reefs as you float downward. At **Devers Bay,** on St. John's south shore, fish dart about in colorful schools. **Carval Rock,** shaped like an old-time ship, has gorgeous rock formations, coral gardens, and lots of fish. It can be too rough here in winter, though. Count on paying $75 for a one-tank dive and $90 for a two-tank dive. Rates include equipment and a tour. If you've never dived before, try an introductory course, called a resort course. Or if certification is in your vacation plans, the island's dive shops can help you get your card.

Cruz Bay Watersports. Cruz Bay Watersports offers regular reef, wreck, and night dives and USVI and BVI snorkel tours. The company holds both PADI Five Star and NAUI-Dream-Resort status. ✉ *Lumberyard Shopping Complex, Boulon Center Rd., Cruz Bay* ☎ *340/776–6234* 🌐 *www.cruzbaywatersports.com* ✉ *Westin St. John, Rte. 104, Great Cruz Bay* ☎ *340/776–6234.*

Low Key Watersports. Low Key Watersports offers two-tank dives and specialty courses. It's a PADI Five Star training facility. ✉ *1 Bay St., Cruz Bay* ☎ *340/693–8999, 800/835–7718* 🌐 *www.divelowkey.com.*

FISHING

Well-kept charter boats—approved by the U.S. Coast Guard—head out to the north and south drops or troll along the inshore reefs, depending on the season and what's biting. The captains usually provide bait, drinks, and lunch, but you need to bring your own hat and sunscreen. Fishing charters run about $1,100 for the full-day trip.

FAMILY **Offshore Adventures.** An excellent choice for fishing charters, Captain Rob Richards is patient with beginners—especially kids—but also enjoys going out with more experienced anglers. He runs the 40-foot center console *Mixed Bag I* and 32-foot *Mixed Bag II*. Although he's based in St. John, he will pick up parties in St. Thomas. ✉ *Westin St. John, 3008 Chocolate Hole Rd., Great Cruz Bay* ☎ *340/513–0389* 🌐 *www.sportfishingstjohn.com.*

GUIDED TOURS

In St. John, taxi drivers provide tours of the island, making stops at various sites, including Trunk Bay and Annaberg Plantation. Prices run around $15 a person. The taxi drivers congregate near the ferry in Cruz Bay. The dispatcher will find you a driver for your tour.

V.I. National Park Visitors Center. Along with providing trail maps and brochures about Virgin Islands National Park, the park service gives several guided tours, both on- and offshore. Some are offered only during particular times of the year, and some require reservations. ✉ *Cruz Bay* ☎ *340/776–6201* 🌐 *www.nps.gov/viis.*

HIKING

Although it's fun to go hiking with a Virgin Islands National Park guide, don't be afraid to head out on your own. To find a hike that suits your ability, stop by the park's visitor center in Cruz Bay and pick up the free trail guide; it details points of interest, trail lengths, and estimated hiking times, as well as any dangers you might encounter. Although the park staff recommends long pants to protect against thorns and insects, most people hike in shorts because it can get very hot. Wear sturdy shoes or hiking boots even if you're hiking to the beach. Don't forget to bring water and insect repellent.

Fodor's Choice ★ **Virgin Islands National Park.** Head to the park for more than 20 trails on the north and south shores, with guided hikes along the most popular routes. A full-day trip to Reef Bay is a must; it's an easy hike through lush and dry forest, past the ruins of an old plantation, and to a sugar factory adjacent to the beach. It can be a bit arduous for young kids, however. The park runs a $30 guided tour to Reef Bay that includes a safari bus ride to the trailhead and a boat ride back to the visitor center. The schedule changes from season to season; call for times and to make reservations, which are essential. ✉ *North Shore Rd., near creek, Cruz Bay* ☎ *340/776–6201* 🌐 *www.nps.gov/viis.*

HORSEBACK RIDING

Carolina Corral. Clip-clop along the island's byways for a slower-pace tour of St. John. Carolina Corral offers horseback trips and wagon rides down scenic roads with owner Dana Barlett. She has a way with horses and calms even the most novice riders. ✉ *Off Rte. 10, Coral Bay* ☎ *340/693–5778* 🌐 *www.carolinacorral.com* 🎫 *$75 for one-hour ride.*

SEA KAYAKING

Poke around the clear bays here and explore undersea life from a sea kayak. Rates run about $70 for a full day in a double kayak. Tours start at $65 for a half day.

Arawak Expeditions. This company uses traditional and sit-on-top kayaks for exploring the waters around St. John on guided tours. ✉ *Mongoose Juction Shopping Center, North Shore Rd., Cruz Bay* ☎ *340/693–8312, 800/238–8687* 🌐 *www.arawakexp.com* 🎫 *From $75 per person.*

Crabby's Watersports. Explore Coral Bay Harbor and Hurricane Hole on the eastern end of the island in a sea kayak or a stand-up paddleboard from Crabby's Watersports. Crabby's also rents snorkel gear, beach chairs, umbrellas, coolers, and floats. ✉ *Rte. 107, next to Cocoloba shopping center, Coral Bay* ☎ *340/714–2415* 🌐 *www.crabbyswatersports.com.*

Hidden Reef EcoTours. Coral reefs, mangroves, and lush sea-grass beds filled with marine life are what you can see on Hidden Reef's two- and three-hour, full-day and full-moon kayak tours through Coral Reef National Monument and its environs. ✉ *Rte. 10, Round Bay* ☎ *340/513–9613, 877/529–2575* 🌐 *www.kayaksj.com.*

WINDSURFING

Cinnamon Bay Campground. Steady breezes and expert instruction make learning to windsurf a snap. Try Cinnamon Bay Campground, where rentals are $40 to $100 per hour. Lessons are available right at the waterfront; just look for the Windsurfers stacked up on the beach. The cost for a one-hour lesson starts at $60, plus the cost of the board rental. You can also rent kayaks, stand-up paddleboards, bodyboards, small sailboats, and surfboards. ✉ *Rte. 20, Cinnamon Bay* ☎ *340/693–5902, 340/626–4769* 🌐 *www.windnsurfingadventures.com.*

ST. CROIX

Updated by Carol Buchanan

History is a big draw in St. Croix: planes are filled with Danish visitors who come mainly to explore the island's colonial history. Of course, like the rest of us, they also make sure to spend some time sunning at the island's powdery beaches, getting pampered at the hotels, and dining at interesting restaurants.

Until 1917 Denmark owned St. Croix and her sister Virgin Islands, a fact reflected in street names in the main towns of Christiansted and Frederiksted as well as the surnames of many island residents. In the 18th and 19th centuries, some of those early Danish settlers, as well as other Europeans, owned plantations, all of them worked by African slaves and white indentured servants lured to St. Croix to pay off their debt to society. Some of the plantation ruins—such as the Christiansted National Historic Site, Whim Plantation, the ruins at St. George Village Botanical Garden, and those at Estate Mount Washington and Judith's Fancy—are open for easy exploration. Others are on private land, but a drive around the island reveals the ruins of 100 plantations here and there on St. Croix's 84 square miles (218 square km). Their windmills, greathouses, and factories are all that's left of the 224 plantations that once grew sugarcane, tobacco, and other crops at the island's height.

The downturn began in 1801, when the British occupied the island. The end of the slave trade in 1803, an additional British occupation (from 1807 to 1815), droughts, the development of the sugar-beet industry in Europe, political upheaval, and an economic depression all sent the island into a downward spiral.

St. Croix never recovered. The end of slavery in 1848, followed by labor riots, fires, hurricanes, and an earthquake during the last half of the 19th century, brought what was left of the island's economy to its knees. In the 1920s, the start of prohibition in the United States ended the island's rum industry, further crippling the economy. The situation remained dire—so bad that President Herbert Hoover called the territory an "effective poorhouse" during a 1931 visit—until the rise of tourism in the late 1950s and 1960s. With tourism came economic improvements coupled with an influx of residents from other Caribbean islands and the mainland. For years Hovensa Oil Refinery was an economic stimulus until it shuttered its doors in 2012. Currently the economy is struggling and a number of businesses have closed.

Today suburban subdivisions fill the fields where sugarcane once waved in the tropical breeze. Condominium complexes line the beaches along the north coast outside Christiansted. Large houses dot the rolling hillsides. Modern strip malls and shopping centers sit along major roads, and it's as easy to find a McDonald's as it is Caribbean fare.

Although St. Croix sits definitely in the 21st century, with only a little effort you can easily step back into the island's past.

EXPLORING

Although there are things to see and do in St. Croix's two towns, Christiansted and Frederiksted (both named after Danish kings), there are lots of interesting spots in between them and to the east of Christiansted. Just be sure you have a map in hand (pick one up at rental-car agencies, or stop by the tourist office for an excellent one that's free). Many secondary roads remain unmarked; if you get confused, ask for help. Locals are always ready to point you in the right direction.

CHRISTIANSTED

In the 1700s and 1800s Christiansted was a trading center for sugar, rum, and molasses. Today law offices, tourist shops, and restaurants occupy many of the same buildings, which start at the harbor and go up the gently sloped hillsides.

Your best bet to see the historic sights in this Danish-style town is in the morning, when it's still cool. Break for lunch at an open-air restaurant before spending as much time as you like exploring the shopping opportunities. You can't get lost, since all streets lead back downhill to the water.

TOP ATTRACTIONS

FAMILY Fodor's Choice ★ **Fort Christiansvaern.** The large yellow fortress dominates the waterfront. Because it's so easy to spot, it makes a good place to begin a walking tour. In 1749 the Danish built the fort to protect the harbor, but the structure was repeatedly damaged by hurricane-force winds and had to be partially rebuilt in 1771. It's now a national historic site, the best preserved of the few remaining Danish-built forts in the Virgin Islands. The park's visitor center is here. Rangers are on hand to answer questions. ■ **TIP→ Your paid admission also includes the Steeple Building.** ✉ *Hospital St.* ☎ *340/773–1460* 🌐 *www.nps.gov/chri* 🎟 *$3* ⏲ *Weekdays 8:30–4:30, weekends 9–4:30.*

Government House. One of the town's most elegant structures was built as a home for a Danish merchant in 1747. Today it houses offices. If you're here weekdays from 8 to 4:30, slip into the peaceful inner courtyard to admire the still pools and gardens. A sweeping staircase leads you to a second-story ballroom, still used for official government functions. ✉ *King St.* ☎ *340/773–1404.*

WORTH NOTING

St. Croix Visitor Center. Friendly advice as well as useful maps and brochures are available from the visitor center. ✉ *Government House, King St.* ☎ *340/773–1404* 🌐 *www.visitusvi.com* ⏲ *Weekdays 8–5.*

St. Croix

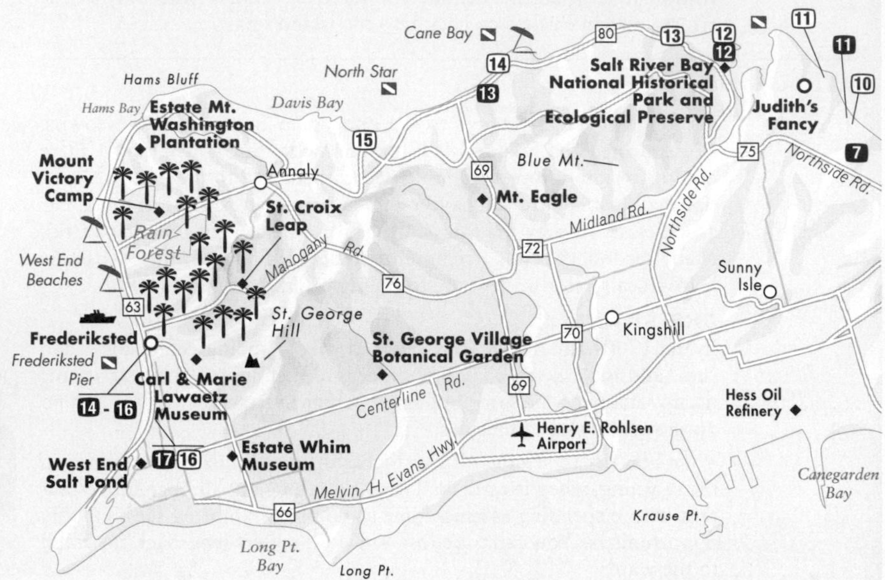

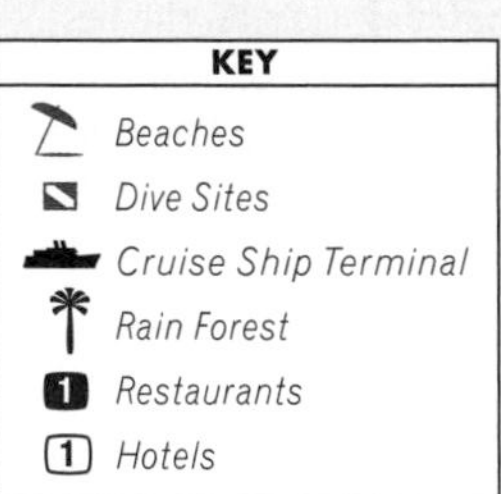

Restaurants ▼

Angry Nates 6
Avocado Pitt 5
Beach Side Café 17
Blue Moon 16
Breezez 11
Café Christine 4
The Deep End 9
Eat @ Cane Bay 12
The Galleon 10
Harvey's 2
Off the Wall 13
Polly's at the Pier 15
Rum Runners 1
Salud Bistro 7
Savant 3
Turtles Deli 14
Tutto Bene 8

Hotels ▼

Arawak Bay 13
The Buccaneer 4
Carringtons Inn 2
Chenay Bay Beach Resort .. 6
Club St. Croix 9
Colony Cove 10

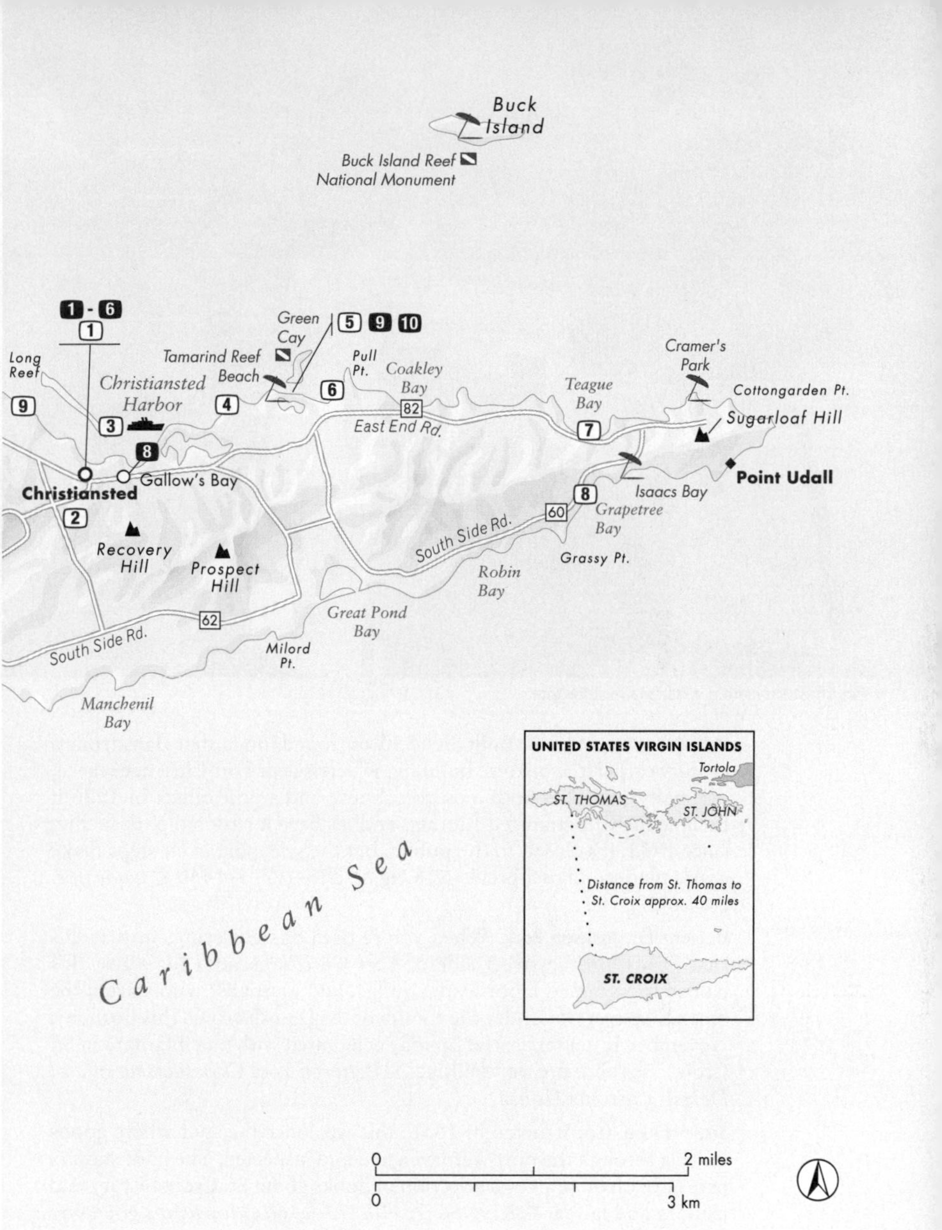

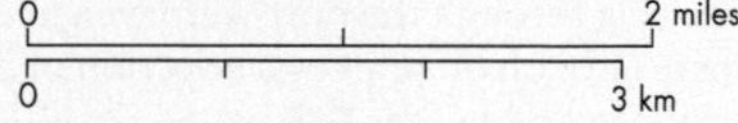

- Divi Carina Bay Resort **8**
- Hotel Caravelle **1**
- Hotel on the Cay **3**
- Palms at Pelican Cove **11**
- Renaissance St. Croix Carambola **15**
- Sandcastle on the Beach **16**
- Tamarind Reef Resort **5**
- Villa Madeleine **7**
- Villa Margarita **12**
- Waves at Cane Bay **14**

Fort Christiansvaern is a National Historic Site.

Danish Customs House. Built in 1830 on foundations that date from a century earlier, the historic building, which is near Fort Christiansvaern, originally served as both a customshouse and a post office. In 1926 it became the Christiansted Library, and it's been a national park facility since 1972. It's closed to the public, but the sweeping front steps make a nice place to take a break. ✉ *King St.* ☎ *340/773–1460* 🌐 *www.nps.gov/chri.*

D. Hamilton Jackson Park. When you're tired of sightseeing, stop at this shady park on the street side of Fort Christiansvaern for a rest. It's named for a famed labor leader, judge, and journalist who started the first newspaper not under the thumb of the Danish crown (his birthday, November 1, is a territorial holiday celebrated with much fanfare in St. Croix). ⚠ **There are no facilities.** ✉ *Between Fort Christiansvaern and Danish Customs House.*

Scale House. Constructed in 1856, this was once the spot where goods passing through the port were weighed and inspected. The park staffers here have on offer a good selection of books about St. Croix history and its flora and fauna. ✉ *King St.* ☎ *340/773–1460* 🌐 *www.nps.gov/chri.*

Steeple Building. The first Danish Lutheran church on the island when it was built in 1753, the Steeple Building is now used as a museum. It's worth the short walk to see the archaeological artifacts and exhibits on plantation life, the architectural development of Christiansted, the island's native inhabitants, and Alexander Hamilton, who grew up in St. Croix. Hours are irregular, so ask at the visitor center. ■ **TIP→ Your paid admission includes Fort Christiansvaern, too.** ✉ *Church St.* ☎ *340/773–1460* 🎫 *$3.*

CLOSE UP

Turtles on St. Croix

Green, leatherback, and hawksbill turtles crawl ashore during their annual April-to-November nesting season to lay their eggs. They return from their life at sea every two to seven years to the beach where they were born. Since turtles can live for up to 100 years, they may return many times to nest in St. Croix.

The leatherbacks like Sandy Point National Wildlife Refuge and other spots on St. Croix's western end, but the hawksbills prefer Buck Island and the East End. Green turtles are also found primarily on the East End.

All are endangered species that face numerous predators, some natural, some the result of the human presence. Particularly in the Frederiksted area, dogs and cats prey on the nests and eat the hatchlings. Occasionally a dog will attack a turtle about to lay its eggs, and cats train their kittens to hunt at turtle nests, creating successive generations of turtle-egg hunters. In addition, turtles have often been hit by fast-moving boats that leave large slices in their shells if they don't kill them outright.

The leatherbacks are the subject of a project by the Earthwatch conservation group. Each summer, teams arrive at Sandy Point National Wildlife Refuge to ensure that poachers, both natural and human, don't attack the turtles as they crawl up the beach. The teams also relocate nests that are laid in areas prone to erosion. When the eggs hatch, teams stand by to make sure the turtles make it safely to the sea, and scientists tag them so they can monitor their return to St. Croix.

EAST END

An easy drive along flat, well-marked roads to St. Croix's eastern end takes you through some choice real estate. Ruins of old sugar estates dot the landscape. You can make the entire loop on the road that circles the island in about an hour, a good way to end the day. If you want to spend a full day exploring, you can find some nice beaches and easy walks with places to stop for lunch.

WORTH NOTING

Buck Island Reef National Monument. Buck Island has pristine beaches that are just right for sunbathing, but there's also some shade for those who don't want to fry. The snorkeling trail set in the reef allows close-up study of coral formations and tropical fish. Overly warm seawater temperatures have led to a condition called coral bleaching that has killed some of the coral. The reefs are starting to recover, but how long it will take is anyone's guess. There's an easy hiking trail to the island's highest point, where you can be rewarded for your efforts by spectacular views of St. John. Charter-boat trips leave daily from the Christiansted waterfront or from Green Cay Marina, about 2 miles (3 km) east of Christiansted. Check with your hotel for recommendations. ✉ *Off North Shore of St. Croix* ☎ *340/773–1460* 🌐 *www.nps.gov/buis.*

Point Udall. This rocky promontory, the easternmost point in the United States, is about a half-hour drive from Christiansted. A paved road takes you to an overlook with glorious views. More adventurous folks can hike down to the pristine beach below. On the way back, look for the Castle Aura, an enormous Moorish-style mansion. It was built by Nadia Farber, the former Contessa de Navarro, who's an extravagant local character. ⚠ **Point Udall is sometimes a popular spot for thieves, so don't leave anything valuable in your car, and leave it unlocked.** ✉ *Rte. 82, Et Stykkeland.*

MID ISLAND

A drive through the countryside between these two towns takes you past ruins of old plantations, many bearing whimsical names (Morningstar, Solitude, Upper Love). The traffic moves quickly—by island standards—on the main roads, but you can pause and poke around if you head down some side lanes. It's easy to find your way west, but driving from north to south requires good navigation. Don't leave your hotel without a map. Allow an entire day for this trip, so you'll have enough time for a swim at a north-shore beach. Although you can find lots of casual eateries on the main roads, pick up a picnic lunch if you plan to head off the beaten path.

TOP ATTRACTIONS

FAMILY Fodor's Choice ★ **Estate Whim Museum.** The restored estate, with a windmill, cookhouse, and other buildings, gives a sense of what life was like on St. Croix's sugar plantations in the 1800s. The oval-shape greathouse has high ceilings and antique furniture and utensils. Notice its fresh, airy atmosphere—the waterless stone moat around the great house was used not for defense but for gathering cooling air. If you have kids, the grounds are the perfect place for them to run around, perhaps while you browse in the museum gift shop. It's just outside Frederiksted. ✉ *Rte. 70, Estate Whim* ☎ *340/772–0598* 🌐 *www.stcroixlandmarks.com* 🎫 *$10* 🕑 *Wed.–Sat. 10–4 and cruise-ship days.*

Fodor's Choice ★ **St. George Village Botanical Garden.** At this 17-acre estate, fragrant flora grows amid the ruins of a 19th-century sugarcane plantation. There are miniature versions of each ecosystem on St. Croix, from a semiarid cactus grove to a verdant rain forest. The small museum is also well worth a visit. ✉ *Rte. 70, turn north at sign, St. George* ☎ *340/692–2874* 🌐 *www.sgvbg.org* 🎫 *$8* 🕑 *Daily 9–5.*

WORTH NOTING

Captain Morgan Distillery. The base for Captain Morgan brand rum is made from molasses at this distillery. The tour includes exhibits on island and rum history; a movie about the process; and a tram tour of the distillery. In keeping with the company's responsible-drinking policy, the drink samples at the end of the tour are limited to two. ✉ *Melvin Evans Hwy. and Rte. 663, Annaberg and Shannon Grove* ☎ *340/713–5654* 🌐 *www.captainmorgan.com* 🎫 *$10* 🕑 *Weekdays 9–5.*

Cruzan Rum Distillery. A tour of the company's factory, which was established in 1760, culminates in a tasting of its products, all sold here at good prices. It's worth a stop to look at the distillery's charming old buildings even if you're not a rum connoisseur. ✉ *West Airport Rd., Estate Diamond* ☎ *340/692–2280* 🌐 *www.cruzanrum.com* 🎫 *$8* 🕑 *Weekdays 9–4.*

FREDERIKSTED AND ENVIRONS

St. Croix's second-largest town, Frederiksted, was founded in 1751. Just as Christiansted is famed for its Danish buildings, Frederiksted is known for its Victorian architecture. A stroll around its historic sights will take you no more than an hour. Allow a little more time if you want to duck into the few small shops. One long cruise-ship pier juts into the sparkling sea. It's the perfect place to start a tour of this quaint city.

WORTH NOTING

Caribbean Museum Center for the Arts. Sitting across from the waterfront in a historic building, this small museum hosts an always-changing roster of exhibits. Many are cutting-edge multimedia efforts that you might be surprised to find in such an out-of-the way location. The openings are popular events. ✉ *10 Strand St.* ☎ *340/772–2622* 🌐 *www.cmcarts.org* 🎫 *Free* ⏲ *Thurs.–Sat. (and any cruise-ship day) 10–5.*

Estate Mount Washington Plantation. Several years ago, while surveying the property, the owners discovered the ruins of a sugar plantation beneath the rain-forest brush. The grounds have since been cleared and opened to the public. You can take a self-guided walking tour of the mill, the rum factory, and other ruins. ✉ *Rte. 63, Mount Washington* ⏲ *Daily dawn–dusk.*

FAMILY **Fort Frederik.** On July 3, 1848, 8,000 slaves marched on this fort to demand their freedom. Danish governor Peter von Scholten, fearing they would burn the town to the ground, stood up in his carriage parked in front of the fort and granted their wish. The fort, completed in 1760, houses an art gallery and a number of interesting historical exhibits, including some focusing on the 1848 Emancipation and the 1917 transfer of the Virgin Islands from Denmark to the United States. It's within earshot of the Frederiksted Visitor Center. ✉ *Waterfront* ☎ *340/772–2021* 🎫 *$3* ⏲ *Weekdays (and any cruise-ship day) 9–4.*

27

Frederiksted Visitor Center. Head here for brochures from numerous St. Croix businesses, as well as a few exhibits about the island. ✉ *Pier* ☎ *340/773–0495* ⏲ *Weekdays 8–5.*

West End Salt Pond. A bird-watcher's delight, this salt pond attracts a large number of winged creatures, including flamingos. ✉ *Veteran's Shore Dr., Hesselberg.*

NORTH SHORE

WORTH NOTING

Judith's Fancy. In this upscale neighborhood are the ruins of an old great-house and tower of the same name, both remnants of a circa-1750 Danish sugar plantation. The "Judith" comes from the first name of a woman buried on the property. From the guardhouse at the neighborhood entrance, follow Hamilton Drive past some of St. Croix's loveliest houses. At the end of Hamilton Drive the road overlooks Salt River Bay, where Christopher Columbus anchored in 1493. On the way back, make a detour left off Hamilton Drive onto Caribe Road for a close look at the ruins. The million-dollar villas are something to behold, too. ✉ *Turn north onto Rte. 751, off Rte. 75, Judith's Fancy.*

Mount Eagle. At 1,165 feet, this is St. Croix's highest peak. Leaving Cane Bay and passing North Star Beach, follow the coastal road that dips briefly into a forest; then turn left on Route 69. Just after you make the turn, the pavement is marked with the words "The Beast" and a set of giant paw prints. The hill you're about to climb is the famous Beast of the St. Croix Half Ironman Triathlon, an annual event during which participants must cycle up this intimidating slope. ✉ *Rte. 69, Davis Bay.*

Salt River Bay National Historical Park and Ecological Preserve. This joint national and local park commemorates the area where Christopher Columbus's men skirmished with the Carib Indians in 1493 on his second visit to the New World. The peninsula on the bay's east side is named for the event: Cabo de las Flechas (Cape of the Arrows). Although the park is still developing, it has several sights with cultural significance. A ball court, used by the Caribs in religious ceremonies, was discovered at the spot where the taxis park. Take a short hike up the dirt road to the ruins of an old earthen fort for great views of Salt River Bay. The area also encompasses a coastal estuary with the region's largest remaining mangrove forest, a submarine canyon, and several endangered species, including the hawksbill turtle and the roseate tern. A visitor center, open in winter only, sits just uphill to the west. The water at the beach can be on the rough side, but it's a nice place for sunning. ✉ *Rte. 75 to Rte. 80, Salt River* ☎ *340/773–1460* 🌐 *www.nps.gov/sari* ⏲ *Nov.–June, Tues.–Thurs. 9–4.*

BEACHES

St. Croix's beaches aren't as spectacular as those on St. John or St. Thomas. But that's not to say you won't find some good places to spread out for a day on the water. The best beach is on nearby Buck Island, a national monument where a marked snorkeling trail leads you through an extensive coral reef while a soft, sandy beach beckons a few yards away. Other great beaches are the unnamed West End beaches both south and north of Frederiksted. You can park yourself at any of the handful of restaurants north of Frederiksted. Some rent loungers, and you can get food and drinks right on the beach. Remember to remove all your valuables from the car and keep them out of sight when you go swimming. Break-ins happen on all three of the U.S. Virgin Islands, and most locals recommend leaving your windows down and leaving nothing in your car.

EAST END

Fodor's Choice ★ **Buck Island.** Part of Buck Island Reef National Monument, this is a must-see for anyone in St. Croix. The beach is beautiful, but its finest treasures are those you can see when you plop off the boat and adjust your mask, snorkel, and fins to swim over colorful coral and darting fish. Don't know how to snorkel? No problem—the boat crew will have you outfitted and in the water in no time. Take care not to step on those black-pointed spiny sea urchins or touch the mustard-color fire coral, which can cause a nasty burn. Most charter-boat trips start with a snorkel over the lovely reef before a stop at the island's beach. An easy 20-minute hike leads uphill to an overlook for a bird's-eye view of the reef below. You'll find restrooms at the beach. **Amenities:** toilets.

Best for: snorkeling; swimming. ✉ *5 miles (8 km) north of St. Croix* ☎ *340/773–1460* 🌐 *www.nps.gov/buis.*

NORTH SHORE

Cane Bay. On the island's breezy North Shore, Cane Bay does not always have gentle waters, but there are seldom many people around, and the scuba diving and snorkeling are wondrous. You can see elkhorn and brain corals, and less than 200 yards out is the drop-off called Cane Bay Wall. Cane Bay can be an all-day destination: you can rent kayaks and snorkeling and scuba gear at water-sports shops across the road, and a couple of casual restaurants beckon when the sun gets too hot. **Amenities:** food and drink; water sports. **Best for:** solitude; snorkeling; swimming. ✉ *Rte. 80, about 4 miles (6 km) west of Salt River, Cane Bay.*

FREDERIKSTED

West End beaches. There are several unnamed beaches along the coast road north of Frederiksted, but it's best if you don't stray too far from civilization. For safety's sake, most vacationers plop down their towel near one of the casual restaurants spread out along Route 63. The beach at the Rainbow Beach Club, a five-minute drive outside Frederiksted, has a bar, a casual restaurant, water sports, and volleyball. If you want to be close to the cruise-ship pier, just stroll on over to the adjacent sandy beach in front of Fort Frederik. On the way south out of Frederiksted, the stretch near Sandcastle on the Beach hotel is also lovely. **Amenities:** food and drink; water sports. **Best for:** snorkeling, swimming, walking. ✉ *Rte. 63, north and south of Frederiksted, Frederiksted.*

WHERE TO EAT

Seven flags have flown over St. Croix, and each has left its legacy in the island's cuisine. Fresh local seafood is plentiful and always good; wahoo, mahimahi, and conch are most popular. Island chefs often add Caribbean twists to familiar dishes. For a true island experience, stop at a local restaurant for goat stew, curried chicken, or fried pork chops. Regardless of where you eat, your meal will be an informal affair. As is the case everywhere in the Caribbean, prices are higher than you'd pay on the mainland. Some restaurants may close for a week or two in September or October, so if you're traveling during these months, it's best to call ahead.

CHRISTIANSTED

$$$ ECLECTIC ✕ **Angry Nates.** Serving breakfast, lunch, and dinner, Angry Nates has something for everyone on its extensive menu. Dinner can be as fancy as tilapia and garlic shrimp with mushrooms, white wine, and garlic butter, or as basic as a burger or chicken sandwich. If your taste buds run to hot, try the shrimp pistolette—a hollowed-out baguette filled with shrimp and laced with really hot sauce. 💲 *Average main: $22* ✉ *King Cross St., at the boardwalk* ☎ *340/692–6283* 🌐 *www.angrynates.com.*

$ ECLECTIC ✕ **Avocado Pitt.** Locals gather at this Christiansted waterfront spot for the breakfast and lunch specials, as well as for a bit of gossip. Breakfast runs to stick-to-the-ribs dishes like oatmeal and pancakes. Lunches include such basics as a crispy chicken-breast sandwich. The yellowfin tuna sandwich is made from fresh fish and gives a new taste to a

Some of St. Croix's best beaches are on the West End of the island around Frederiksted.

standard lunchtime favorite. *Average main: $12* *King Christian Hotel, 59 Kings Wharf* *340/773–9843* *No dinner.*

$$ FRENCH **Café Christine.** At this favorite with the professionals who work in downtown Christiansted, the presentations are as dazzling as the food. The small menu changes daily, but look for dishes such as shrimp-and-asparagus salad drizzled with a lovely vinaigrette or a vegetarian plate with quiche, salad, and lentils. Desserts are perfection. If the pear pie topped with chocolate is on the menu, don't hesitate. This tiny restaurant has tables in both the air-conditioned dining room and on the outside porch that overlooks historic buildings. *Average main: $14* *Apothecary Hall Courtyard, 6 Company St.* *340/713–1500* *No credit cards* *Closed weekends and July–mid-Nov. No dinner.*

$ CARIBBEAN **Harvey's.** The dining room is plain, even dowdy, and plastic lace tablecloths constitute the sole attempt at decor. But who cares?—the food is delicious. Daily specials, such as mouthwatering goat stew and tender conch in butter, served with big helpings of rice and vegetables, are listed on the blackboard. Genial owner Sarah Harvey takes great pride in her kitchen, bustling out from behind the stove to chat and urge you to eat up. *Average main: $11* *11B Company St.* *340/773–3433* *No dinner. Closed Sun.*

$$$ ECLECTIC FAMILY Fodor's Choice ★ **Rum Runners.** The view is as stellar as the food at this highly popular local standby. Sitting right on the Christiansted boardwalk, Rum Runners serves a little bit of everything, including a to-die-for salad of crispy romaine lettuce and tender grilled lobster drizzled with lemongrass vinaigrette. Heartier fare includes baby back ribs cooked with the restaurant's special spice blend and Guinness stout. *Average main:*

$25 ✉ Hotel Caravelle, 44A Queen Cross St. ☎ 340/773–6585 🌐 www.rumrunnersstcroix.com.

$$$ ECLECTIC **Savant.** Savant is one of those small but special spots that locals love. The cuisine is a fusion of Mexican, Thai, and Caribbean—an unusual combination that works surprisingly well. You can find anything from fresh fish to Thai curry with chicken to stuffed fillet with portobello mushrooms and goat cheese. With 20 tables crammed into the indoor dining room and small courtyard, this little place can get crowded. Call early for reservations. *$ Average main: $27 ✉ 4C Hospital St. ☎ 340/713–8666 🌐 www.savantstx.com ⊙ No lunch. Closed Sun.*

$$$ ITALIAN **Tutto Bene.** With murals on the walls, brightly striped cushions, and painted trompe-l'oeil tables, Tutto Bene looks more like a sophisticated Mexican cantina than an Italian *cucina*. One bite of the food, however, will clear up any confusion. The menu includes such specialties as veal saltimbocca and medallions of veal with prosciutto and sage. Among the desserts is a decadent tiramisu. *$ Average main: $24 ✉ Hospital St., Gallows Bay ☎ 340/773–5229 🌐 www.tuttobenerestaurant.com ⊙ Closed Mon. and Tues.*

WEST OF CHRISTIANSTED

$$$ ECLECTIC FAMILY **Breezez.** This aptly named restaurant, *the* place on the island for Sunday brunch, is poolside at the Club St. Croix condominiums. Visitors and locals are drawn by its reasonable prices and good food. Locals also gather for lunch, when the menu includes everything from burgers to blackened prime rib with a horseradish sauce. For dessert, try the Amaretto cheesecake with either chocolate or fruit topping. *$ Average main: $25 ✉ Club St. Croix, 3280 Golden Rock, off Rte. 752, Golden Rock ☎ 340/718–7077.*

$$$ ITALIAN **Salud Bistro.** This eatery's imaginative menu takes its cue from the fresh flavors of the Mediterranean. Start with the savory cheese plate served with homemade bread and crostini before moving on to fresh fish or grilled duck in a hibiscus confit. *$ Average main: $27 ✉ Princess Plaza, Rte. 75, La Grande Princess ☎ 340/718–7900 🌐 www.saludbistro.com ⊙ Closed Sun. No lunch.*

EAST END

$$$ ECLECTIC **The Deep End.** A favorite with locals and vacationers, this poolside restaurant serves up terrific burgers, steak, and seafood, as well as delicious pasta dishes and popular salads. To get here from Christiansted, take Route 82 and turn left at the sign for Green Cay Marina. *$ Average main: $23 ✉ Tamarind Reef Hotel, Rte. 82, Annas Hope ☎ 340/773–4455.*

$$$ ECLECTIC **The Galleon.** This popular dockside restaurant is always busy. Start with the Caesar salad or perhaps a duck-liver pâté with cherry compote and arugula. The chef's signature dish is a beef tenderloin topped with fresh local lobster. Fish lovers should try the pan-seared sea scallops with roasted tomatoes and a kalamata olive risotto. Take Route 82 out of Christiansted, and then turn left at the sign for Green Cay Marina. The Galleon is open daily for dinner and serves Sunday brunch. *$ Average main: $30 ✉ Green Cay Marina, off Rte. 82, Annas Hope ☎ 340/718–9948 🌐 www.galleonrestaurant.com ⊙ No lunch Mon.–Sat.*

NORTH SHORE

$$ AMERICAN Fodor's Choice ★ **Eat @ Cane Bay.** The fabulous food matches the view of Cane Bay at this casual spot in the heart of Cane Bay. The lunch menu includes a build-your-own beef, veggie, or grilled chicken burger that gives you a choice of toppings, dressings, and cheese. If you opt for, say, a roasted turkey club sandwich, the onion rings that come with it are terrific. Dinner offerings include pasta, fish, steak, and sandwiches. *Average main: $18 Rte. 80, Cane Bay 340/718–0360 www.eatatcanebay.com Closed Tues.*

$$ AMERICAN **Off the Wall.** Divers fresh from a plunge at the North Shore's popular Cane Bay Wall gather at this breezy spot on the beach. If you want to sit a spell before you order, a hammock beckons. Deli sandwiches, served with potato chips, make up most of the menu. Pizza and salads are also available. *Average main: $14 Rte. 80, Cane Bay 340/778–4771 www.otwstx.com.*

FREDERIKSTED

$$$ ECLECTIC **Beach Side Café.** Sunday brunch is big, but locals and visitors also flock to this oceanfront bistro at Sandcastle on the Beach resort for lunch and dinner. Both menus include burgers and salads, but at dinner the crispy half duck with berry sauce shines. For lunch, the hummus plate is a good bet. *Average main: $29 Sandcastle on the Beach, 127 Smithfield 340/772–1266 www.beachsidecafestx.com Closed Tues. and Wed.*

$$$ AMERICAN Fodor's Choice ★ **Blue Moon.** This terrific little bistro, which has a loyal local following, offers a changing menu that draws on Cajun and Caribbean flavors. Try the spicy gumbo with andouille sausage or crab cakes with a spicy aioli for your appetizer. The pasta verde with vegetables makes a good entrée, and they serve delicious and decadent desserts. Sunday brunch is served and there's live jazz on Wednesday and Friday. *Average main: $23 7 Strand St. 340/772–2222 www.thebluemoonstcroix.com Closed Mon.*

$$ ECLECTIC **Polly's at the Pier.** With an emphasis on fresh ingredients, this very casual spot right on the waterfront serves delicious fare. The gourmet grilled cheese sandwich comes with your choice of three cheeses as well as delicious additions like basil, fresh Bosc pears, and avocado. Salads are a specialty, and many are made with local Bibb lettuce and organic mixed greens. *Average main: $13 3 Strand St. 340/719–9434 No dinner.*

$ DELI FAMILY **Turtles Deli.** You can eat outside at this tiny spot just as you enter downtown Frederiksted. Lunches are as basic as a corned beef on rye or as imaginative as the Raven (turkey breast with bacon, tomato, and melted cheddar cheese on French bread). Also good is the Beast, named after the grueling hill that challenges bikers in the annual triathlon. It's piled high with hot roast beef, raw onion, and melted Swiss cheese with horseradish and mayonnaise. Early risers stop by for cinnamon buns and espresso. Turtles After Dark, upstairs, is open 5 to 10 pm. *Average main: $12 38 Strand St., at Prince Passage 340/772–3676 www.turtlesdeli.com No credit cards Closed Sun.*

WHERE TO STAY

If you sleep in either the Christiansted or Frederiksted area, you'll be closest to shopping, restaurants, and nightlife. Most of the island's other hotels will put you just steps from the beach. St. Croix has several small but special properties that offer personalized service. If you like all the comforts of home, you may prefer to stay in a condominium or villa. Room rates on St. Croix are competitive with those on other islands, and if you travel off-season, you can find substantially reduced prices. Many properties offer money-saving honeymoon and dive packages. Whether you stay in a hotel, a condominium, or a villa, you'll enjoy up-to-date amenities. Most properties have room TVs, but at some bed-and-breakfasts there might be only one, in the common room.

Although a stay right in historic Christiansted may mean putting up with a little urban noise, you probably won't have trouble sleeping. Christiansted rolls up the sidewalks fairly early, and humming air conditioners drown out any noise. Solitude is guaranteed at hotels and inns outside Christiansted and those on the outskirts of sleepy Frederiksted.

PRIVATE CONDOMINIUMS AND VILLAS

Most of the villas in St. Croix are in the center or on the East End. Renting a villa gives you the convenience of home as well as top-notch amenities. Many have pools, hot tubs, and deluxe furnishings. Most companies meet you at the airport, arrange for a rental car, and provide helpful information about the island.

27

If you want to be close to the island's restaurants and shopping, look for a condominium or villa in the hills above Christiansted or on either side of the town. An East End location gets you out of Christiansted's hustle and bustle, but you're still only 15 minutes from town. North Shore locations are lovely, with gorgeous sea views and lots of peace and quiet.

RENTAL CONTACTS

Vacation St. Croix ✉ *400 La Grande Princess, Christiansted* ☎ *340/718–0361, 877/788–0361* 🌐 *www.vacationstcroix.com.*

CHRISTIANSTED

$ HOTEL **Hotel Caravelle.** A stay at the Caravelle, which is near the harbor, puts you at the waterfront end of a pleasant shopping arcade and steps from shops and restaurants. **Pros:** good restaurant; convenient location; parking. **Cons:** no beach; busy neighborhood. [$] *Rooms from: $150* ✉ *44A Queen Cross St.* ☎ *340/773–0687, 800/524–0410* 🌐 *www.hotelcaravelle.com* *43 rooms, 1 suite* *No meals.*

$ RESORT **Hotel on the Cay.** Hop on the free ferry to reach this peaceful lodging in the middle of Christiansted Harbor. **Pros:** quiet; convenient location; lovely beach. **Cons:** accessible only by ferry; no parking available. [$] *Rooms from: $149* ✉ *Protestant Cay* ☎ *340/773–2035, 855/654–0301* 🌐 *www.hotelonthecay.com* *54 rooms* *No meals.*

WEST OF CHRISTIANSTED

$ B&B/INN Fodor's Choice ★ **Carringtons Inn.** Local flavor, personalized service, and individual style make this intimate inn a welcome respite from the realm of cookie-cutter resorts, with its location in a former private home that offers a lovely pool and unbeatable ocean views. **Pros:** feels like a private home;

welcoming host; tasteful rooms; great breakfasts. **Cons:** no beach; need car to get around. *Rooms from: $150 4001 Estate Hermon Hill, Christiansted 340/713–0508, 877/658–0508 www.carringtonsinn.com 5 rooms Breakfast.*

$ RENTAL FAMILY **Club St. Croix.** Sitting beachfront just outside Christiansted, this modern condominium complex faces a lovely sandy beach. **Pros:** beachfront location; good restaurant; full kitchens. **Cons:** need car to get around; sketchy neighborhood. *Rooms from: $195 Rte. 752, Estate Golden Rock 340/718–9150, 800/524–2025 www.antillesresorts.com 53 apartments No meals.*

$ RENTAL FAMILY **Colony Cove.** In a string of condominium complexes, Colony Cove lets you experience comfortable beachfront living. **Pros:** beachfront location; comfortable units; good views. **Cons:** sketchy neighborhood; need car to get around. *Rooms from: $235 Rte. 752, Estate Golden Rock 340/718–1965, 800/524–2025 www.antillesresorts.com 62 apartments No meals.*

$ RESORT **The Palms at Pelican Cove.** A 10-minute drive from Christiansted's interesting shopping and restaurants, this resort, with its mixed bag of guests, has a gorgeous strand of white sand at its doorstep. **Pros:** nice beach; good dining options; friendly staff. **Cons:** need car to get out and about; neighborhood not the best. *Rooms from: $254 Off Rte. 752, La Grande Princesse 340/718–8920, 800/548–4460 www.palmspelicancove.com 41 rooms No meals.*

EAST END

$$ RESORT FAMILY **The Buccaneer.** Aimed at travelers who want everything at their fingertips, this resort has sandy beaches, swimming pools, and extensive sports facilities. **Pros:** beachfront location; numerous activities; nice golf course. **Cons:** pricey rates; insular environment; need car to get around. *Rooms from: $360 Rte. 82, Box 25200, Shoys 340/712–2100, 800/255–3881 www.thebuccaneer.com 138 rooms, 1 villa Breakfast.*

$ RESORT FAMILY **Chenay Bay Beach Resort.** The seaside setting and complimentary tennis and water-sports equipment make this resort a real find, particularly for families with active kids. **Pros:** beachfront location; pretty grounds; friendly staff **Cons:** need car to get around; lacks pizzazz. *Rooms from: $194 Rte. 82, Green Cay 340/773–2918 50 rooms No meals.*

$$$ ALL-INCLUSIVE **Divi Carina Bay Resort.** An oceanfront location, the island's only casino, and plenty of activities make this resort a good bet. **Pros:** spacious beach; good restaurant; on-site casino. **Cons:** need car to get around; many stairs to climb; staff can seem chilly. *Rooms from: $418 25 Rte. 60, Estate Turner Hole 340/773–9700, 877/773–9700 www.divicarina.com 174 rooms, 2 suites, 20 villas All-inclusive.*

$ HOTEL **Tamarind Reef Resort.** Spread out along a sandy beach, these low-slung buildings offer casual comfort. **Pros:** good snorkeling; tasty restaurant; rooms have kitchenettes. **Cons:** need car to get around; motel-style rooms. *Rooms from: $250 5001 Tamarind Reef, off Rte. 82, Annas Hope 340/718–4455, 800/619–0014 www.tamarindreefresort.com 46 rooms No meals.*

$$ RENTAL **Villa Madeleine.** If you like privacy and your own private pool, you'll like Villa Madeleine. **Pros:** pleasant decor; full kitchens; private pools. **Cons:** lower units sometimes lack views; need car to get around; no beachfront. *Rooms from: $285 Off Rte. 82, Teague Bay 340/718–0361, 877/788–0361 www.vacationstcroix.com 43 villas No meals.*

FREDERIKSTED

$ RESORT **Sandcastle on the Beach.** Right on a gorgeous stretch of white beach, Sandcastle has a tropical charm that harks back to a simpler time in the Caribbean; its nearness to Frederiksted's interesting dining scene is also a plus. **Pros:** lovely beach; close to restaurants; gay-friendly. **Cons:** neighborhood sketchy at night; need car to get around; no children's activities. *Rooms from: $179 127 Smithfield 340/772–1205, 800/524–2018 www.sandcastleonthebeach.com 9 rooms, 10 suites, 3 villas No meals.*

NORTH SHORE

$ B&B/INN **Arawak Bay: The Inn at Salt River.** With stellar views of St. Croix's North Shore and an affable host, this small inn allows you to settle into island life at a price that doesn't break the bank. **Pros:** 20 minutes from Christiansted; good prices. **Cons:** no beach nearby; can be some road noise. *Rooms from: $160 Rte. 80, Salt River 340/772–1684 www.arawakbaysaltriver.co.vi 12 rooms Breakfast.*

$$ RESORT **Renaissance St. Croix Carambola Beach Resort and Spa.** We like this resort's stellar beachfront setting and peaceful ambience. **Pros:** lovely beach; relaxing atmosphere; close to golf. **Cons:** isolated location; need car to get around. *Rooms from: $329 Rte. 80, Davis Bay 340/778–3800, 888/503–8760 www.carambolabeachresort.com 151 rooms No meals.*

$ B&B/INN **Villa Margarita.** This quiet retreat provides a particularly good base if you want to admire the dramatic views of the windswept coast. **Pros:** friendly host; great views; snorkeling nearby. **Cons:** isolated location; need car to get around; limited amenities. *Rooms from: $175 Off Rte. 80, Salt River 340/713–1930 www.villamargarita.com 3 units No meals.*

$ HOTEL **Waves at Cane Bay.** St. Croix's famed Cane Bay Wall is just offshore from this hotel, giving it an enviable location. **Pros:** great diving; restaurants nearby; beaches nearby. **Cons:** need car to get around; on main road; bland decor. *Rooms from: $120 Rte. 80, Cane Bay 340/718–1815 www.thewavescanebay.com 10 rooms No meals.*

NIGHTLIFE AND PERFORMING ARTS

Christiansted has a lively and eminently casual club scene near the waterfront. Frederiksted has a couple of restaurants and clubs offering weekend entertainment. To find out what's happening in St. Croix's ever-changing nightlife and eclectic arts scene, check out the local newspapers—*V.I. Daily News* (*virginislandsdailynews.com*) and *St. Croix Avis*.

CHRISTIANSTED

Fort Christian Brew Pub. Locals and visitors come here to listen to live music several nights a week. ✉ *Boardwalk at end of Kings Alley, Christiansted* ☎ *340/713–9820* 🌐 *www.fortchristianbrewpub.com.*

Hotel on the Cay. This off-shore resort hosts a West Indian buffet on Tuesday night in the winter season, when you can watch a broken-bottle dancer (a dancer who braves a carpet of shattered glass) and mocko jumbie (stilt-dancing) characters. ✉ *Protestant Cay, Christiansted* ☎ *340/773–2035* 🌐 *www.hotelonthecay.com.*

EAST END

Divi Carina Bay Resort. Although you can gamble at the island's only casino, it's really the nightly music that draws big crowds to this resort. ✉ *25 Rte. 60, Estate Turner Hole* ☎ *340/773–7529* 🌐 *www.divicarina.com.*

MID ISLAND

Whim Plantation Museum. The museum outside Frederiksted hosts classical music concerts in winter. ✉ *Rte. 70, Estate Whim* ☎ *340/772–0598* 🌐 *www.stcroixlandmarks.com.*

FREDERIKSTED

Fodor's Choice ★ **Blue Moon.** Blue Moon is a popular waterfront restaurant in Frederiksted, and it's the place to be for live jazz on Wednesday and Friday. It's one of the few nightlife options at this end of the island. ✉ *7 Strand St., Frederiksted* ☎ *340/772–2222* 🌐 *www.bluemoonstcroix.com.*

Fodor's Choice ★ **Sunset Jazz.** This outdoor event is a hot ticket in Frederiksted, drawing crowds of visitors and locals at 5:30 pm on the third Friday of every month to watch the sun go down and listen to good music. ✉ *Waterfront, Frederiksted* ☎ *340/690–1741.*

SHOPPING

Although the shopping on St. Croix isn't as varied or extensive as that on St. Thomas, the island does have several small stores with unusual merchandise. St. Croix shop hours are usually Monday through Saturday 9 to 5, but there are some shops in Christiansted open in the evening. Stores are often closed on Sunday.

CHRISTIANSTED

In Christiansted the best shopping areas are the **Pan Am Pavilion** and **Caravelle Arcade,** off Strand Street, and along **King** and **Company Streets.** These streets give way to arcades filled with boutiques. **Gallows Bay** has a blossoming shopping area in a quiet neighborhood.

BOOKS

Undercover Books. This well-stocked independent bookseller sells Caribbean-themed books as well as the latest good reads. The store is in the Gallows Bay shopping area. ✉ *5030 Anchor Way, across from post office, Gallows Bay* ☎ *340/719–1567* 🌐 *www.undercoverbooksvi.com.*

CLOTHING

From the Gecko. This store sells the hippest island-style clothes on St. Croix, as well as other items. ✉ *55 Company St., Christiansted* ☎ *340/778–9433* 🌐 *www.fromthegecko.com.*

Hot Heads. This small store sells hats, hats, and more hats, which are often perched on top of cotton shifts, comfortable shirts, and trendy tropical wear. If you forgot your bathing suit, this store has a good selection. ✉ *1244 Queen Cross St., Christiansted* ☎ *340/773–7888.*

Island Tribe. Colorful batik dresses, shirts, shifts, and scarves in soft rayon and cotton round out your tropical wardrobe. Sizes range from small to 4X. The clothing, and an interesting array of jewelry, comes from Bali. ✉ *2100 Company St., Christiansted* ☎ *340/719–0936.*

GIFTS

The Blue Mutt. Shop for a good cause at this small store that benefits the St. Croix Animal Welfare Center. The shelves are filled with local art, T-shirts, cards, soaps, candles, and much more. ✉ *5 Company St., Christiansted* ☎ *340/690–4624.*

Cache of the Day. This tiny store sells whatever its sea theme has tossed up. Mermaid dolls recline on shelves next to dishtowels printed with shapes of the sea. There are stuffed animals and jewelry that make perfect gifts. ✉ *55 Company St., Christiansted* ☎ *340/773–3648.*

27

Many Hands. This shop sells pottery in bright colors, paintings of St. Croix and the Caribbean, prints, and maps. They are all made by local artists, and they all make for perfect take-home gifts. ■ **TIP→ The owners ship all over the world.** ✉ *21 Pan Am Pavilion, Strand St., Christiansted* ☎ *340/773–1990.*

Mitchell-Larsen Studio. This glass gallery offers an interesting amalgam of carefully crafted glass plates, sun-catchers, and more. The pieces, all made on-site by a St. Croix glassmaker, are often whimsically adorned with tropical fish, flora, and fauna. ✉ *58 Company St., Christiansted* ☎ *340/719–1000* 🌐 *www.mitchelllarsenstudio.com.*

Fodor's Choice ★ **Royal Poinciana.** The attractive Royal Poinciana is filled with island seasonings and hot sauces, West Indian crafts, bath gels, and herbal teas. Shop here for tablecloths and paper goods in bright tropical colors. ✉ *1113 Strand St., Christiansted* ☎ *340/773–9892.*

Tesoro. Among the colorful and bold merchandise here are metal sculptures made from retired steel pans, mahogany bowls, and hand-painted place mats in bright tropical colors. ✉ *3A Queen Cross St., Christiansted* ☎ *340/773–1212* 🌐 *www.tesorostcroix.com.*

HOUSEWARES

Designworks. This store and gallery carries furniture as well as one of the largest selections of local art, along with Caribbean-inspired bric-a-brac and jewelry in all price ranges. If a mahogany armoire or four-poster bed catches your fancy, the staff can have it shipped to your home at no charge from its mainland warehouse. ✉ *6 Company St., Christiansted* ☎ *340/713–8102* 🌐 *www.islandlivingstore.com.*

JEWELRY

Crucian Gold. St. Croix native Brian Bishop's trademark piece is the Turk's Head ring (a knot of interwoven gold strands). His son, Nathan Bishop, is now creating contemorary sterling and gold pendants, rings, and earrings. ✉ *1112 Strand St., Christiansted* ☎ *340/773–5241* 🌐 *www.cruciangold.com.*

Gold Worker. This shop specializes in handcrafted jewelry in silver and gold that will remind you of the Caribbean. Hummingbirds dangle from silver chains and sand dollars adorn gold necklaces. The sugar mills in silver and gold speak of St. Croix's past. ✉ *3 Company St., Christiansted* ☎ *340/514–6042.*

ib designs. This small shop showcases the handcrafted jewelry of local craftsman Whealan Massicott. Whether in silver or gold, the designs are simply elegant. ✉ *Company St. at Queen Cross St., Christiansted* ☎ *340/773–4322* 🌐 *www.islandboydesigns.com.*

Nelthropp and Low. The jewelers at Nelthropp and Low can create one-of-a-kind pieces to your design. The shop specializes in gold jewelry but also carries diamonds, emeralds, rubies, and sapphires. ✉ *1102 Strand St., Christiansted* ☎ *340/773–0365* 🌐 *www.nelthropp-low.com.*

Sonya's. This store is owned and operated by Sonya Hough, who invented the popular hook bracelet. She has added interesting decoration to these bracelets: the swirling symbol used in weather forecasts to indicate hurricanes. ✉ *1 Company St., Christiansted* ☎ *340/778–8605* 🌐 *www.sonyaltd.com.*

LIQUOR AND TOBACCO

Baci Duty Free. The walk-in humidor here has a good selection of Arturo Fuente, Partagas, and Macanudo cigars. Baci also carries high-end liquor, sleek Swiss-made watches, and fine jewelry. ✉ *1235 Queen Cross St., Christiansted* ☎ *340/773–5040* 🌐 *www.bacidutyfree.com.*

WEST OF CHRISTIANSED

FOOD

Pueblo. This market is similar to those stores back on the mainland. ✉ *Golden Rock Shopping Center, Rte. 75, Christiansted* ☎ *340/773–0118.*

EAST END

FOOD

Sea Side Market and Deli. Although it's on the smallish side, this market has good-quality deli items. ✉ *Rte. 82, Mount Welcome* ☎ *340/719–9393.*

MID ISLAND

FOOD

Cost-U-Less. This warehouse-type store is great for visitors because it doesn't charge a membership fee. It's in the busy Sunny Isle area. ✉ *Rte. 70, Peter's Rest* ☎ *340/719–4442* 🌐 *www.costuless.com.*

Plaza Extra. This supermarket chain has a good selection of Middle Eastern foods in addition to the usual grocery-store items. ✉ *Queen Mary Hwy., Rte. 70, Mount Pleasant* ☎ *340/719–1870* 🌐 *www.plazaextra.com* ✉ *Rte. 70, Sion Farm* ☎ *340/778–6240* 🌐 *www.plazaextra.com.*

Pueblo. This stateside-style market has another branch west of Christiansted. ✉ *Villa La Reine Shopping Center, Rte. 75, La Reine* ☎ *340/778–1272.*

LIQUOR AND TOBACCO

Kmart. The U.S. discount chain has two branches on St. Croix, both of which carry a huge line of deep-discounted, duty-free liquor, among many other items. ✉ *Sunshine Mall, Rte. 70, Frederiksted* ☎ *340/692–5848* ✉ *Sunny Isle Shopping Center, Rte. 70, Sunny Isle* ☎ *340/719–9190.*

FREDERIKSTED

The best shopping in Frederiksted is along **Strand Street** and in the side streets and alleyways that connect it with **King Street.** Most stores close on Sunday, except when a cruise ship is in port. Keep in mind that Frederiksted has a reputation for muggings, so it's best to stick to populated areas of Strand and King Streets, where there are few—if any—problems.

SPORTS AND THE OUTDOORS

BOAT TOURS

Almost everyone takes a day trip to Buck Island aboard a charter boat. Most leave from the Christiansted waterfront or from Green Cay Marina and stop for a snorkel at the island's eastern end before dropping anchor off a gorgeous sandy beach for a swim, a hike, and lunch. Sailboats can often stop right at the beach; a larger boat might have to anchor a bit farther offshore. A full-day sail runs about $100, with lunch included on most trips. A half-day sail costs about $68.

27

Big Beard's Adventure Tours. From catamarans that depart from the Christiansted waterfront you'll head to Buck Island for snorkeling before dropping anchor at a private beach for a barbecue lunch. ✉ *Waterfront, Christiansted* ☎ *340/773–4482* 🌐 *www.bigbeards.com.*

Buck Island Charters. These charters are on two trimarans, *Teroro II* and *Dragonfly,* which leave Green Cay Marina for full- or half-day sails. Bring your own lunch. ✉ *Green Cay Marina, Annas Hope* ☎ *340/773–3161* 🌐 *www.gotostcroix.com.*

Caribbean Sea Adventures. With their crafts leaving from the Christiansted waterfront, Caribbean Sea Adventures has both half- and full-day trips. ✉ *Waterfront, Christiansted* ☎ *340/773–2628* 🌐 *www.caribbeanseaadventures.com.*

DIVING AND SNORKELING

At **Buck Island,** a short boat ride from Christiansted or Green Cay Marina, the reef is so nice that it's been named a national monument. You can dive right off the beach at **Cane Bay,** which has a spectacular drop-off called the Cane Bay Wall. Dive operators also do boat trips along the Wall, usually leaving from Salt River or Christiansted. **Frederiksted Pier** is home to a colony of sea horses, creatures seldom seen in the waters of the Virgin Islands. At **Green Cay,** just outside Green Cay Marina in the East End, you can see colorful fish swimming around the reefs and rocks. Two exceptional North Shore sites are **North Star** and **Salt River**, which you can reach only by boat. At Salt River you can float downward through a canyon filled with colorful fish and coral.

The island's dive shops take you out for one- or two-tank dives. Plan to pay about $65 for a one-tank dive and $100 for a two-tank dive, including equipment and an underwater tour. All companies offer certification and introductory courses called resort dives for novices.

Which dive outfit you pick usually depends on where you're staying. Your hotel may have one on-site. If so, you're just a short stroll away from the dock. If not, other companies are close by. Where the dive boat goes on a particular day depends on the weather, but in any case, all St. Croix dive sites are special. All shops are affiliated with PADI, the Professional Association of Diving Instructors.

Cane Bay Dive Shop. This is the place to go if you want to do a beach dive or boat dive along the North Shore. The famed Cane Bay Wall is 200 yards from the PADI Five Star facility. This company also has shops at Pan Am Pavilion in Christiansted, on Strand Street in Frederiksted, and at the Divi Carina Bay Resort. ✉ *Rte. 80, Cane Bay* ☎ *340/718–9913, 800/338–3843* 🌐 *www.canebayscuba.com.*

Dive Experience. Handy for those staying in Christiansted, Dive Experience runs trips to the North Shore walls and reefs, in addition to offering the usual certification and introductory classes. It's a PADI Five Star facility. ✉ *Boardwalk and Kings Alley, Christiansted* ☎ *340/773–3307, 800/235–9047* 🌐 *www.divexp.com.*

N2 the Blue. N2 takes divers right off the beach near the Frederiksted Pier, on night dives off the Frederiksted Pier, or on boat trips to the Salt River Wall. ✉ *Customs House St., Frederiksted* ☎ *340/772–3483* 🌐 *www.n2theblue.com.*

St. Croix Ultimate Bluewater Adventures. This company can take you to your choice of more than 75 sites; it also offers a variety of packages that include hotel stays. ✉ *Queen Cross St., Christiansted* ☎ *340/773–5994, 877/567–1367* 🌐 *www.stcroixscuba.com.*

FISHING

Since the early 1980s, some 20 world records—many for blue marlin—have been set in these waters. Sailfish, skipjack, bonito, tuna (allison, blackfin, and yellowfin), and wahoo are abundant. A charter runs about $500 for a half day (for up to six people), with most boats going out for four-, six-, or eight-hour trips.

Captain Festus. Captain Festus takes you to spots all around St. Croix on his 55-foot boat *Sea Hunter* and 35-foot *Triton.* ✉ *Kings Wharf, Christiansted* ☎ *340/277–1751.*

Gone Ketchin'. Captain Grizz, a true old salt, heads these trips. ✉ *Salt River Marina, Rte. 80, Salt River* ☎ *340/713–1175* 🌐 *www.goneketchin.com.*

GOLF

Fodor's Choice ★ **Buccaneer Golf Course.** This 18-hole course is close to Christiansted and features views of the Caribbean from 13 of its holes. Golf lessons and club rentals are available. ✉ *Rte. 82, Shoys* ☎ *340/712–2144* 🌐 *www.*

Seaside horseback riding on the shores of St. Croix

thebuccaneer.com ✉ *$110 for 18 holes; $70 for 9 holes; additional $20 for cart rental.* *18 holes, 5688 yards, par 70.*

Carambola Golf Club. Golfers should enjoy the exotic beauty of this difficult course in the rain forest designed by Robert Trent Jones Sr., because they might not enjoy their score. An extra sleeve of balls might also be required. The long water holes never return splash balls and the jungle rough seldom does. Most fairways are forgiving with ample landing area, but the length of many holes makes it challenging. ✉ *Rte. 69, River* ☎ *340/778–5638* 🌐 *www.golfcarambola.com* *$125* *18 holes, 5727, par 72.*

The Links at Divi St. Croix. This attractive minigolf course is just across from the Divi Carina Bay Resort. ✉ *Rte. 60, Turner Hole* ☎ *340/773–9700* 🌐 *www.divicarina.com* *$8* ⏲ *Daily noon–8.*

Reef Golf Course. If you want to enjoy panaromic Caribbean views without paying high costs, the public, nine-hole Reef Golf course on the island's East End is the place to go. The course design is basic, but the views from the hillside are spectacular. Trees on this course very seldom enter into play and sand traps are absent. The seventh hole with its highly elevated tee is the most interesting hole. ✉ *Rte. 82, Teague Bay* ☎ *340/773–8844* *$40* *9 holes, 2395, par 35.*

GUIDED TOURS

St. Croix Transit. Departing from Renaissance Carambola Beach Resort, St. Croix Transit's three-hour van tours start at $65 per person, which includes admission fees to all attractions. ✉ *Renaissance Carambola Beach Resort, Rte. 80, Davis Bay* ☎ *340/772–3333.*

Sweeny's St. Croix Safari Tours. These van tours of St. Croix depart from Christiansted and last about five hours. Costs run from $70 per person, including admission fees to attractions. ✉ *Christiansted* ☎ *340/773–6700* 🌐 *www.gotostcroix.com.*

HIKING

Ay-Ay Eco Hike and Tours. Ras Lumumba Corriette takes hikers up hill and down dale in some of St. Croix's most remote places, including the rain forest and Mount Victory. Some hikes include stops at old ruins. The cost is $60 per person for a three- or four-hour hike. There's a three-person minimum. ☎ *340/772–4079* 🌐 *www.chantvi.org.*

HORSEBACK RIDING

Paul and Jill's Equestrian Stables. From Sprat Hall, just north of Frederiksted, co-owner Jill Hurd will take you through the rain forest, across the pastures, along the beaches, and through valleys—explaining the flora, fauna, and ruins on the way. A 1½-hour ride costs $100. ✉ *Rte. 58, Frederiksted* ☎ *340/772–2880, 340/772–2627* 🌐 *www.paulandjills.com.*

KAYAKING

Caribbean Adventure Tours. These kayak tours take you on trips through Salt River Bay National Historical Park and Ecological Preserve, one of the island's most pristine areas. All tours cost $50. ✉ *Salt River Marina, Rte. 80, Salt River* ☎ *340/778–1522* 🌐 *www.stcroixkayak.com.*

Virgin Kayak Tours. Virgin runs guided kayak trips on the Salt River and rents kayaks so you can tour around the Cane Bay area by yourself. Tours start at $50, and kayak rentals are $40 for the entire day. ✉ *Rte. 80, Cane Bay* ☎ *340/778–0071* 🌐 *www.virginkayaktours.com.*

WATER SPORTS

St. Croix Watersports. St. Croix Watersports rents WaveRunners, stand-up paddleboards, kayaks, windsurfers, and snorkel gear. The half-hour guided WaveRunner tour allows you to zip around Christiansted's harbor in style for $60. ✉ *Hotel on Cay, Protestant Cay, Christiansted* ☎ *340/773–7060* 🌐 *www.stcroixwatersports.com.*

INDEX

A

B

E

F

G

H

M

T

PHOTO CREDITS

Front cover: Lorne Resnick/The Image Bank/Getty Images [Description: Jumby Bay, Antigua] Back cover (from left to right): BlueOrange Studio/Shutterstock; Blacqbook/Shutterstock; Raffles Hotels and Resorts. Spine: Natchapon L./Shutterstock. 1, Timothy O'Keefe / age fotostock. 2, Alvaro Leiva / age fotostock. 5,Carlos Villoch-MagicSea.com / Alamy. Chapter 1 Experience the Caribbean: 10–11, Christian Goupi / age fotostock. 20, Peter Phipp/age fotostock. 21 (left), Philip Coblentz/ Medioimages. 21 (right), TIDCO. 26 and 27 (right), Fabrice RAMBERT/Hostal Nicolas de Ovando. 27 (left), Tatiana Popova/Shutterstock. 28 (left), John A. Anderson/iStockphoto. 28 (top center), John A. Anderson/ iStockphoto. 28 (bottom center), Michael DeFreitas / age fotostock. 28 (top right), Durden-Images/ iStockphoto. 28 (bottom right), MeegsC/wikipedia.org. 29 (top left), The Dominican Republic Ministry of Tourism. 29 (bottom left), St. Vincent & The Grenadines Tourist Office. 29 (center), Alvaro Leiva / age fotostock. 29 (right), Franz Marc Frei / age fotostock. 30, Fyletto | Dreamstime.com. 31, Blue-Orange Studio / Shutterstock. 32, Kmiragaya | Dreamstime.com. 33, Diana DeLucia. 34, Grenada Board of Tourism. 35 (left and right), Casa de Campo. 36, St. Maarten Tourist Bureau. 37 (left), Denis Jr. Tangney/iStockphoto. 37 (right), Dominican Republic Ministry of Tourism. 38, Ramona Settle. 39, Jim Lopes/Shutterstock. 40, Olga Bogatyrenko/Shutterstock. 41, Christian Wheatley/Shutterstock. 44, Aruba Tourism Authority. 45 (left), Brenda S and R Duncan Kirby. 45 (right), Coral World Ocean Park, St. Thomas. 46, Heeb Christian / age fotostock. 47 (top), Nico Tondini / age fotostock. 47 (bottom left and right), Dom/Shutterstock. 48 (top), Kobako/wikipedia.org. 48 (bottom), Rohit Seth/Shutterstock. 49 (top left), Karen Wunderman/Shutterstock. 49 (center left), Mulling it Over/Flickr. 49 (top right), Midori/wikipedia.org. 49 (center right), stu_spivack/Flickr. 49 (bottom), PL.Viel / age fotostock. 50 (top left), Arkady/ Shutterstock. 50 (bottom left), Mlvalentin/wikipedia.org. 50 (top right), ahnhuynh/ Shutterstock. 50 (bottom right), Sakurai Midori/wikipedia.org. 51 (top left), HLPhoto/Shutterstock. 51 (bottom left), Elena Elisseeva/Shutterstock. 51 (bottom right), Only Fabrizio/Shutterstock. 51 (top right), cck/Flickr. 52 (left), Ingolf Pompe / age fotostock. 52, (left center) yosoynuts/Flickr. 52 (right center), Charles Tobias. 52 (right), Knut.C/wikipedia.org. 53 (left), cogdogblog/Flickr. 53 (left center), NorthJoe/Flickr. 53 (top right), Robert S. Donovan/Flickr. 53 (right center), Granstrom/wikipedia.org. 53 (bottom right), pocketwiley/Flickr. 54, Gavin Hellier / age fotostock. Chapter 2 Anguilla: 55, Chris Caldicott / age fotostock. 56 (bottom), aturkus/Flickr. 56 (top), Philip Coblentz/Digital Vision. 58, Ku. 60, Rick Strange / age fotostock. 72, Straw Hat. 74, The Leading Hotels of the World. 78, Viceroy Hotel Group. Chapter 3 Antigua and Barbuda: 83, Philip Coblentz/Medioimages. 84 (top and bottom), Philip Coblentz/Digital Vision. 85, Philip Coblentz/Digital Vision. 86, Geoff Howes/Antigua & Barbuda Tourist Office. 88, Alvaro Leiva / age fotostock. 93, Steve Geer/iStockphoto. 104, nik wheeler / Alamy. Chapter 4 Aruba: 117, Henry George Beeker / Alamy. 118 (bottom), Philip Coblentz/Medioimages. 118 (top), Aruba Tourism Authority. 120, Famke Backx/iStockphoto. 139, Amsterdam Manor Beach Resort Aruba. 149, Aruba Tourism Authority. Chapter 5 Barbados: 153, John Miller / age fotostock. 154, Doug Scott/age fotostock. 156, Barbados Tourism Authority/Andrew Hulsmeier. 166, Walter Bibikow / age fotostock. 171, St. Nicholas Abbey. 185, Fairmont Hotels & Resorts. 187, Coral Reef Club. 189, Roy Riley / Alamy. 195, Christian Goupi / age fotostock. 198 (left), Jose Gil/iStockphoto. 198 (right), Conway Bowman. 199, Nataliya Hora/Shutterstock. Chapter 6 Bonaire: 205, Philip Coblentz/Medioimages. 206 (top), Tourism Corporation Bonaire. 206 (bottom), Suzi Swygert for the Bonaire Tourist Office. 207, Harry Thomas/istock. 208, Harbour Village Beach Club. 221, Harbour Village Beach Club. 226, Kees Opstal/istockphoto. Chapter 7 British Virgin Islands: 231, Alvaro Leiva / age fotostock. 232 (bottom), Joel Blit/Shutterstock. 232 (top), lidian neeleman/iStockphoto. 234, Ramunas Bruzas/Shutterstock. 243, Walter Bibikow / age fotostock. 253, Charles Krallman/Surfsong Villa Resort. 254, Alvaro Leiva / age fotostock. 259, Eric Sanford / age fotostock. 260 (top), Randy Lincks / Alamy. 260 (bottom), iStockphoto. 261 (top), Doug Scott / age fotostock. 261 (bottom), Slavoljub Pantelic/iStockphoto. 262, Doug Scott / age fotostock. 264, Giovanni Rinaldi/iStockphoto. 265, Walter Bibikow / age fotostock. 267, FB-Fischer/imagebroker.net/photolibrary.com. 278, Bitter End Yacht Club International, LLC. 280, Andre Jenny / Alamy. 285, Paul Zizka/Shutterstock. Chapter 8 Cayman Islands: 289, Peter Heiss/iStockphoto. 290 (top and bottom), Cayman Islands Department of Tourism. 291, Kevin Panizza/istockphoto. 292, Cayman Islands Department of Tourism. 297, Cayman Islands Department of Tourism. 320, Don McDougall/Cayman Islands Department of Tourism. 330, Corbis. 337, DurdenImages/iStockphoto. Chapter 9 Curaçao: 349, Philip Coblentz/Digital Vision. 350 (bottom), Fotoconcept Inc./ age fotostock. 350 (top), Curaçao Tourism. 352, Curaçao Tourism. 357, Walter Bibikow / age fotostock. 360, Curacao Tourist Board. 363, Walter Bibikow / age fotostock. Chapter 10 Dominica: 383, Xavier Font/age fotostock. 384, Dominica Tourist Office. 385 (top), John Anderson/istockphoto. 385 (bottom), Dominica Tourist Office. 386, Buddy Mays / Alamy. 387 (left), John Gabriel Stedman/wikipedia.org. 387 (right), J.E. (Julius Eduard) Muller/Tropenmuseum (CC

BY-SA 3.0), via Wikimedia Commons. 388, Winston Davidian/istockphoto. 398, John A. Anderson/ istockphoto. 405, Fort Young Hotel Dominica. 411, Reinhard Dirscherl / age fotostock. Chapter 11 Dominican Republic: 413, Doug Scott/age fotostock. 414 (bottom), Doug Scott/age fotostock. 414 (top), Guy Thouvenin/age fotostock. 416, The Dominican Republic Ministry of Tourism. 423, Harry Pujols/Flickr. 429, The Dominican Republic Ministry of Tourism. 450, tedmurphy/Flickr. 453, Peninsula House. 457 (background photo), Sailorr/Shutterstock. 458 (left), rj lerich/Shutterstock. 458 (top right), Photos 12 / Alamy. 458 (bottom right), Anguilla Tourist Board. 459 (left), Lonely Planet Images / Alamy. 459 (center), Nevis Pirate Festival. 459 (right), unforth/Flickr. 460 (top left), The Print Collector / age fotostock. 460 (top and bottom right), wikipedia.org. 461 (left and center), wikipedia.org. 461 (right), Public domain. Chapter 12 Grenada: 477, Doug Scott/age fotostock. 478 (top and bottom), Grenada Board of Tourism. 480, Grenada Board of Tourism. 491, Haltner Thomas / age fotostock. 513, Grenada Board of Tourism. Chapter 13 Guadeloupe: 515, Bruno Morandi/age fotostock. 516, Bruno Morandi/age fotostock. 518, Susanne Kischnick / Alamy. 519 (left), wikipedia.org. 519 (right), Photocuisine / Alamy. 520, Holger W./shutterstock. 528, TristanDeschamps/F1 Online/age fotostock. 539, Philippe Michel / age fotostock. 550, La Toubana Hotel and Spa. 552, Philippe Giraud. Chapter 14 Jamaica: 565, Ronn Ballantyne / Alamy. 566 (bottom), Torrance Lewis/Jamaica Tourist Board/Fotoseeker.com. 566 (top), Julian Love/Jamaica Tourist Board/Fotoseeker.com. 568, Brian Nejedly. 569 (left), LarenKates/Flickr. 569 (right), Jamaica Inn. 570, Jamaica Tourist Board. 578, Franz Marc Frei / age fotostock. 590, Torrance Lewis/Jamaica Tourist Board/Fotoseeker.com. 607, Nick Hanna / Alamy. 611, Tramonto / age fotostock. 612 (top and center), TimDuncan/wikipedia.org. 612 (bottom), wbrisco.skyrock.com. 613, Dave Saunders / age fotostock. 614, Doug Pearson / age fotostock. 615 (left), NawlinWiki/wikipedia.org. 615 (center), Philippe Jimenez/wikipedia.org. 615 (right), wikipedia.org. 625, Sergio Pitamitz / age fotostock. Chapter 15 Martinique: 627, P. Narayan / age fotostock. 628, Philip Coblentz/Medioimages. 629, Maison de la France/LEJEUNE Nicole. 630, Luc Olivier for the Martinique Tourist Board. 642, GARDEL Bertrand / age fotostock. 646, Walter Bibikow / age fotostock. 648, Luc Olivier for the Martinique Tourist Board. 661, Frameme/wikipedia.org. 668, Luc Olivier for the Martinique Tourist Board. Chapter 16 Montserrat: 671, John Cole. 672 (left), Igor Kravtchenko / KiMAGIC Photo and Design. 672 (right), Wailunip/ wikipedia.org. 674, David Mac Gillivary -Montserrat Tourist Board. Chapter 17 Puerto Rico: 689, Danita Delimont/AWL Images. 690 (bottom), John Rodriguez/iStockphoto. 690 (top), Morales/age fotostock. 692, David R. Frazier Photolibrary, Inc. / Alamy. 693 (left), Steve Manson/ iStockphoto. 693 (right), Christian Sumner/iStockphoto. 694, Lori Froeb/Shutterstock. 702, Katja Kreder / age fotostock. 704, Tomás Fano/Flickr. 705 (left), Franz Marc Frei/age fotostock. 705 (top right), Lawrence Robert/Shutterstock. 705 (bottom right), Franz Marc Frei/age fotostock. 706 (left), iStockphoto. 706 (right), Oquendo/Flickr. 707 (top left), runneralan2004/Flickr. 707 (bottom left), runneralan2004/Flickr. 707 (top center), Franz Marc Frei/age fotostock. 707 (top right), Prknlot/Flickr. 713, Franz Marc Frei / age fotostock. 725, Hotel El Convento. 728, Thomas Hart Shelby. 732, Tres Sirenas Beach Inn. Chapter 18 Saba: 739, Michael S. Nolan/ age fotostock. 740 (top), Simon Wong/wikipedia.org. 740 (bottom), Edwin van Wier/Shutterstock. 742, Rutger Geerling / age fotostock. 747, Rutger Geerling / age fotostock. 752, Rutger Geerling / age fotostock. Chapter 19 St. Barthélemy: 755, Fred Friberg / age fotostock. 756 (bottom), SuperStock / age fotostock. 756 (top), Philip Coblentz/Digital Vision. 758, Hotel Carl Gustaf. 760, Christian Wheatley/ iStockphoto. 769, Restaurant Le Gaiac. 776, Hotel Guanahani and Spa. 778, Eden Rock – St Barths. 782, Tibor Bognar / age fotostock. Chapter 20 St. Eustatius: 786, SuperStock / age fotostock. 788 (left), Hannah Madden/web.me.com/hannah.madden/Site/Welcome.html. 788 (right), Brenda S and R Duncan Kirby. 789 and 790, Hannah Madden/web.me.com/hannah.madden/Site/Welcome.html. 795, Bob Turner / age fotostock. 796, Picture Contact / Alamy. Chapter 21 St. Kitts and Nevis: 803, Peter Phipp/ age fotostock. 804, Doug Scott/age fotostock. 805, Peter Phipp/age fotostock. 806, Lidian Neeleman/ iStockphoto. 814, Roger Brisbane, Brisbane Productions. 817, Winter Park Photography/Ottley's Plantation Inn. 823, Ottley's Plantation Inn. 832, Bob Turner / age fotostock. 839, Peter Peirce. Chapter 22 St. Lucia: 845, Colin Sinclair / age fotostock. 846 (top), Bruno Morandi/age fotostock. 846 (bottom), Angelo Cavalli/age fotostock. 848, Saint Lucia Tourism Board. 856, Helene Rogers/ age fotostock. 860, Ian Cumming / age fotostock. 867, Ladera. 871, Sandals Resorts. 874, Sandals Resorts. 876, JOE MCNALLY/Jade Mountain. 880, Gavin Hellier / age fotostock. Chapter 23 St. Maarten/St. Martin: 889, Angelo Cavalli/age fotostock. 891, St Maarten Tourist Bureau. 892, St Maarten Tourist Bureau. 902, alysta/Shutterstock. 918, Warren Jagger Photography Inc. 920, Le Domaine de Lonvilliers. 921, Chris Floyd. 922, Palm Court Hotel & Caribbean Princess Suites. 925, St Maarten Tourist Bureau. Chapter 24 St. Vincent and the Grenadines: 933, Alvaro Leiva/age fotostock. 934 (bottom), St. Vincent Tourism. 934 (top), SuperStock/ age fotostock. 936, Raffles Hotels and Resorts. 945, Susan E. Degginger / Alamy. 952, Young Island Resort. 961, Christian Goupi / age fotostock. 967, Tamarind Beach

Hotel. 971, The Leading Hotels of the World. Chapter 25 Trinidad and Tobago: 977, Robert Harding Productions / age fotostock. 978 (bottom), Angelo Cavalli/age fotostock. 978 (top), Philip Coblentz/ Digital Vision. 980, dbimages / Alamy. 981 (left), Paul Lowry/Flickr. 981 (right), Trinidad & Tobago Tourism Development Company. 982, Blaine Harrington / age fotostock. 983 (bottom), Blacqbook/ Shutterstock, 983 (top), Peter Adams / age fotostock. 984, Trinidad & Tobago Tourism Development Company. 993, J & C Sohns / age fotostock. 996, Shanel/wikipedia.org. 1010, Bob Turner / age fotostock. Chapter 26 Turks and Caicos Islands: 1023, Takaji Ochi-VWPICS. 1024 (bottom), Angelo Cavalli/age fotostock. 1024 (top), Turks & Caicos Tourism. 1025, Turks & Caicos Tourism. 1026, Ramona Settle. 1044, West Bay Club. 1050, Bill Ross/Flirt Collection/photolibrary.com. 1053, COMO Hotels and Resorts. 1063, Ian Cumming/ age fotostock. Chapter 27 United States Virgin Islands: 1069, Walleyelj | Dreamstime.com. 1070 (bottom), Philip Coblentz/Medioimages. 1070 (top), U.S. Virgin Islands Dept. of Tourism. 1072, U.S. Virgin Islands Department of Tourism. 1080, SuperStock/age fotostock. 1088, Coral World Ocean Park, St. Thomas. 1098, The Ritz-Carlton, St. Thomas. 1109, Carlos Villoch-MagicSea.com / Alamy. 1111, Kendra Nielsam/Shutterstock. 1113, divemasterking2000/Flickr. 1114 (top), Shirley Vanderbilt / age fotostock. 1114 (center), Julie de Leseleuc/iStockphoto. 1114 (bottom), Marjorie McBride / Alamy. 1115, divemasterking2000/Flickr. 1116 (top), David Coleman/iStockphoto. 1116 (bottom), Steve Simonsen. 1122, Walter Bibikow / age fotostock. 1133, Caneel Bay/ Rosewood Hotels & Resorts. 1135, Concordia Eco-Resort. 1146, Walter Bibikow / age fotostock. 1152, Bill Ross/Flirt Collection/photolibrary.com. 1163, Julie Hewitt / Alamy. About Our Writers: All photos are courtesy of the writers except for the following: Roberta Sotonoff, courtesy of Mark Black.

About Our Writers: All photos are courtesy of the writers except for the following: Carol Bareuther, courtesy of Dean Barnes; Carol Buchanan, courtesy of Megan Lee Buchanan; Susan Campbell, courtesy of Aldrich Herelijn; Lynda Lohr, courtesy of Robert Charleston; Ann L. Phelan, courtesy of Seth Dinoi; Eileen Robinson Smith, courtesy of A. Everett.